KU-338-305

Legal Advisors' Library
Department for Culture Media and Sport
2-4 Cockspur Street
London SW1Y 5DH
Tel: 020 7211 6043

ENGLISH PRIVATE LAW

ENGLISH PRIVATE LAW

SECOND EDITION

Edited by

PROFESSOR ANDREW BURROWS
St Hugh's College Oxford

OXFORD

UNIVERSITY PRESS

OXFORD
UNIVERSITY PRESS

Great Clarendon Street, Oxford OX2 6DP

Oxford University Press is a department of the University of Oxford.
It furthers the University's objective of excellence in research, scholarship,
and education by publishing worldwide in

Oxford New York

Auckland Cape Town Dar es Salaam Hong Kong Karachi
Kuala Lumpur Madrid Melbourne Mexico City Nairobi
New Delhi Shanghai Taipei Toronto

With offices in

Athens Auckland Bangkok Bogotá Buenos Aires Calcutta
Cape Town Chennai Dar es Salaam Delhi Florence Hong Kong Istanbul
Karachi Kuala Lumpur Madrid Melbourne Mexico City Mumbai
Nairobi Paris São Paulo Shanghai Singapore Taipei Tokyo Toronto Warsaw
with associated companies in Berlin Ibadan

Oxford is a registered trade mark of Oxford University Press
in the UK and in certain other countries

Published in the United States
by Oxford University Press Inc., New York

First edition published by Oxford University Press 2000
Second edition published by Oxford University Press 2007

© Oxford University Press 2007

The moral rights of the author have been asserted
Database right Oxford University Press (maker)

Crown copyright material is reproduced with the permission of the
Controller of Her Majesty's Stationery Office

All rights reserved. No part of this publication may be reproduced,
stored in a retrieval system, or transmitted, in any form or by any means,
without the prior permission in writing of Oxford University Press,
or as expressly permitted by law, or under terms agreed with the appropriate
reprographics rights organization. Enquiries concerning reproduction
outside the scope of the above should be sent to the Rights Department,
Oxford University Press, at the address above

You must not circulate this book in any other binding or cover
and you must impose this same condition on any acquiror

British Library Cataloguing in Publication Data
Data available

Library of Congress Cataloging in Publication Data
Data available

Typeset by Cepha Imaging Private Ltd, Bangalore, India
Printed in Great Britain
on acid-free paper by
Legoprint S.p.A.

ISBN 978–0–19–922794–5

1 3 5 7 9 10 8 6 4 2

In Memory of Peter Birks 1941–2004

EDITOR

Professor Andrew Burrows QC FBA
St Hugh's College Oxford

CONTRIBUTORS

Mr Neil Andrews
Clare College Cambridge

Professor John Armour
Oriel College Oxford

Professor John Bell QC FBA
Pembroke College Cambridge

Professor Michael Bridge
London School of Economics

Professor Adrian Briggs
St Edmund Hall Oxford

Professor Malcolm Clarke
St John's College Cambridge

Professor William Cornish QC FBA
Magdalene College Cambridge

Dr Stephen Cretney QC FBA
All Souls College Oxford

Mr John Davies
Brasenose College Oxford

Dr James Edelman
Keble College Oxford

Professor Mark Freedland FBA
St John's College Oxford

Professor Richard Hooley
King's College London

Professor Roger Kerridge
University of Bristol

Professor Ewan McKendrick
Lady Margaret Hall Oxford

Professor Charles Mitchell
King's College London

Professor Norman Palmer
King's College London

Professor Francis Reynolds QC FBA
Worcester College Oxford

Professor Lionel Smith
McGill University Montreal

Mr William Swadling
Brasenose College Oxford

Professor Sir Guenter Treitel QC FBA
All Souls College Oxford

CONTENTS—SUMMARY

V LITIGATION

CONTENTS

II THE LAW OF PERSONS

III THE LAW OF PROPERTY

4. Property: General Principles

IV THE LAW OF OBLIGATIONS

8. Contract: In General

V LITIGATION

19. Insolvency

20. Private International Law

PREFACE

The aim of this book is to provide a high-quality overview of the rules and principles that constitute English private law. Along with its companion volume, *English Public Law*, it presents a unique picture of English law that it is hoped will be of great benefit to practitioners, academics, and students alike. Moreover, with the increasing emphasis on globalisation in legal services, it is anticipated that foreign lawyers will find these two volumes of invaluable help in understanding English law, which may otherwise appear to be unstructured and lacking in principle.

To produce a succinct and yet authoritative overview requires mastery of the field in question and it is with that in mind that the team of contributors has been assembled. The authors are acknowledged experts in their respective subject areas and their brief has been to produce as clear, simple and accurate an overview as possible of the relevant rules and principles. What one has here, therefore, is the product of many years of learning in each particular area.

All this was the brainchild of the late Professor Peter Birks, to whom this book is dedicated. Inspired by the example of *Gloag and Henderson's Law of Scotland*, and with the particular encouragement of Lord Rodger of Earlsferry, Birks's goal was for this and *English Public Law* to be on every English lawyer's desk as at least a first point of reference. His mark is indelibly stamped across the whole work not least in the structure which he devised for this book.

It is worth recalling here that, while seeing the enterprise as following in the tradition of Gaius' *Institutes* and Blackstone's *Commentaries*, Birks regarded the need for a well-organized overview, or map, of English private law as responding to two particular challenges in the modern practice of law. He referred to these as 'stovepipe mentality' and 'information overload'. In his words:

> There is a constant complaint of 'stovepipe mentality'. It is an allegation that practitioners—especially young practitioners, since the complaint is usually made by senior people—know their law only in the way that many people know London, as pools of unconnected light into which to emerge from a limited number of friendly tube stations. . .The reason why these 'stovepipe' lawyers cannot move confidently from one area of the law to another is that nobody has shown them the map.[1]

---

[1] Introduction to the First Edition, xxxv–xxxvi.

Later he turned his attention to 'information overload':

> The information explosion makes the need for the structured Blackstonian approach all the more urgent. Information can now be accessed more and more rapidly. The mechanical aspects of the research function are well provided for and constantly being improved. Meanwhile the structure, which is the software which allows the brain to keep the mass of information under intellectual control, is being neglected. While it is becoming ever more essential that lawyers should have a sound grip on the concepts and principles which hold the law together, that need is not being met. . .A high price will be paid if this goes on. Clients will be badly served. The common law will become incoherent, and it will lose respect. That unnecessary disaster is what we hope that *English Private Law*, and its sequel *English Public Law*, will help to prevent, by setting out a coherent, economical account, not only of individual topics, but also of the larger categories of the law and the way that they fit together and, hence, of the law itself.[2]

In addition to a thorough updating—and, in some instances, substantial rewriting—of the chapters, two major changes have been made to this edition. Most importantly of all, it is hoped that publication in a single volume will render this book easier to use. At the same time, some gaps in the coverage of commercial contracts have been filled by new chapters on carriage of goods by air and land, insurance and banking. We welcome Malcolm Clarke and Richard Hooley to the team as authors of those new chapters.

We would like to thank the team at OUP (Roxanne Selby, Benjamin Roberts, and Annabel Moss) for their dedication, skill, and hard work. Annabel Moss was responsible for the early day-to-day overseeing of the project and we are especially grateful to her for being so efficient and patient in dealing with the inevitable complexities of such a multi-authored work. Particular thanks are also due to Richard Walshe for his excellent copy-editing.

Subject to some minor amendments at proof stage, the law is stated as at 30 April 2007.

Andrew Burrows
Oxford
June 30 2007

---

[2]   Introduction to the First Edition, xlviii–xlix.

INTRODUCTION

This introduction explains the structure of this book. It is the scheme pioneered by Professor Peter Birks (inspired most by his beloved Gaius). He was anxious to stress that it is nothing more than 'the best currently available hypothesis as to the structure of our law'.[3]

The scheme is arrived at by first subdividing the whole law into private and public. English public law deals with constitutional law, human rights, administrative law and criminal law. It is the subject-matter of the companion volume in this series and is outside our present concern.

English private law is best viewed as concerned with the rights which, one against another, people are able to realize in courts. There is then a threefold division corresponding to three questions that may be asked about realizable rights. Who can have rights? What are the rights? What are the means by which the rights are realized in court? We therefore arrive at a threefold subdivision between the *law of persons*; the law of rights; and the law of actions for the realization of rights, which in modern parlance can be labelled '*litigation*'. The trichotomy corresponds to, but is not identical to, the Roman proposition to the effect that the concerns of private law are persons, things, and actions.[4]

Two further adjustments are then made in order to arrive at the fivefold division used in this book.

First, one needs a general introduction (applicable to both public and private law) as to what counts as law and that, more specifically and practically, identifies the *sources of law*. This is Part I.

Secondly, the law of rights, which requires the most detailed examination, can be helpfully divided according to who the rights can be enforced against (the question of 'exigibility'). Some rights can be demanded only from the person against whom they first arise or against someone who stands in that person's shoes and thus represents him. Some rights are by contrast, more widely demandable and, of those, some follow things and can be demanded from any person in whose hands the thing is found. When names are added, this makes a division between

---

[3] Introduction to the First Edition, xxxv.
[4] Justinian, *Institutes* 1.1.4: 'there are two aspects of this study, public and private. . .Our business is private law'. And 1.2.12: 'All the law we use concerns persons, things, or actions'.

rights *in rem*—that is, proprietary rights—whose exigibility depends on the location of a thing (in Latin a *res*), and rights *in personam*—that is, personal rights—which are rights exigible only against the person against whom they originally arise or that person's representatives.[5] Rights realizable in court are therefore either proprietary or personal. *The law of property* is the law of proprietary rights;[6] and, as personal rights correlate with obligations, the category of all personal rights is called *the law of obligations*. The law of property and the law of obligations are the two great pillars of private law.

The subdivision of rights between property and obligations brings us to our fivefold division. Private Law is about: I Sources, II Persons, III Property, IV Obligations, V Litigation.

Part IV is itself structured according to the main causative events of personal rights, namely contract, wrongs and unjust enrichment. So Chapter 8 looks at contract in general and Chapters 9–16 examine specific types of contract (agency, sales, carriage, insurance, banking, employment, and bailment). Chapter 17 then deals with torts and equitable wrongs and Chapter 18 is on unjust enrichment.

No such straightforward 'causative events' division of Part III is possible because the focus has to be as much on the different types of proprietary right (which Birks referred to as the 'content question') as on the events by which proprietary rights arise. So a good deal of the general chapter on property (Chapter 4) and the separate chapters on security and intellectual property (Chapters 5 and 6) is concerned with kinds of property right. Chapter 7, on succession, is directed to a causative event, death, and the sub-species of that event, death intestate and death testate.[7]

---

5 It must not be allowed to escape notice that the subdivision of rights between *in rem* and *in personam* is not exhaustive, although, possibly, it might be said to be exhaustive of 'rights realizable in court'. The category which is omitted is the category of rights which are good against all people but do not follow any *res*. All of these are superstructural rights which manifest themselves in the wrongs which infringe them. Thus the right to bodily integrity is protected through the torts which are committed against the body, and the right to reputation is protected by the torts of defamation. Such primary rights are 'superstructural' in that they provide the superstructure over the wrong: every wrong is the infringement of a primary right. Not every primary right is a right *in rem*. A primary right can be *in rem*, *in personam* (say, from contract), or, to give the residue a name, 'purely superstructural'.

6 There is a constant tension between the law of property in the strict sense—the law of proprietary rights—and a loose sense in which 'property' means nothing more than 'assets' or 'items of wealth', hence cars, clothes, money, land, and so on. In this latter sense 'property' engulfs most of the law of obligations, since personal rights can also be regarded as assets. My claims against others are valuable, and many of them can indeed be sold for money—that is, they can be assigned. 'Factoring' or 'debt-factoring' is a business based on buying up, at a discount, the debts owed to others.

7 Chapter 7 (Succession) co-ordinates with that part of the general discussion of property in Chapter 4 concerned with acquisition *inter vivos* but also with the acquisition of security rights (part of Chapter 5) and intellectual property rights (part of Chapter 6).

Birks summarized his explanation of the structure of this book as follows:

> Our business is with the rights which a claimant can if necessary realize through the courts. Part I, with its single chapter on sources of law, is an essential introduction. Part II separates out the study of persons who hold rights. At the other end, Part V deals with the realization of rights. Part III and IV are about the rights themselves. Part III is about property rights. Part IV is about personal rights, called from their negative end, obligations. Property and obligations divide in response to the question which asks against whom rights can be demanded. At lower levels within Part III the treatment of property rights is ordered primarily by two questions, the content question and the causative event question: To what is the right-holder entitled? And, From what events does the right arise? Within Part IV the treatment of obligations is dominated by the latter question: From what events do obligations and their correlative rights arise?[8]

In conclusion, however, it is important to emphasize that Birks was not suggesting, and nor are we, that this structure should be rigidly followed. On the contrary, there are various 'concessions to convenience' as Birks labelled them.

> It does not follow from the need for a structural overview that in its application there can be no concessions to convenience. The important thing is to know what the scheme is, when it is being departed from, and why. Rigorous purity would have brought the whole project to the ground. A more liberal attitude has been adopted. There are a number of places where such concessions have been made, whether to avoid affronting expectations based on longstanding practice or simply because of the extreme inconvenience of separating two consequences of a single causative event. For example, the contract of sale is treated in the law of obligations, where it properly belongs. Obligations arise from contracts and from other events, and sale is a specific contract. A rigid interpretation of the scheme would say that the passing of property under a sale could not be mentioned at this point. The reader should simply be remitted to the law of property. Nevertheless, the chapter on sale does include its own discussion of the proprietary effects. The same is true of the chapter on bailment. Similarly, the chapter on unjust enrichment is considered within the law of obligations, but the effects of unjust enrichment in generating proprietary rights are also considered at some length and are not remitted to the law of property. Again, personal security, though it rests entirely on obligations, is treated alongside mortgages in Chapter 5 within the law of property, and obligations arising from entering into family relationships are considered in Part II on the law of persons and are not postponed to Part IV on obligations. Too many such concessions would dissolve the scheme, but a limited number can be tolerated.[9]

---

[8] Introduction to the First Edition, xliii.
[9] Ibid at xlix–l.

TABLE OF CASES

TABLE OF LEGISLATION, TREATIES AND CONVENTIONS

A. UK STATUTES

C. NATIONAL LEGISLATION IN OTHER JURISDICTIONS

Canada

Germany

Netherlands

E. EC LEGISLATION

Part I

SOURCES OF LAW

1

SOURCES OF LAW

A. Introduction

Under the rule of law decision-makers cannot decide simply on the basis of whatever **1.01**
they personally think is right. They are constrained to offer legal reasons for their
decisions. When judges claim that their decisions are legally right, they need only
claim that the decisions are supported by legal reasons which can be found through
the interpretation of certain sources.[1] In a pluralistic society, personal morality
cannot always be aligned to the moral values which the law enforces. This chapter
presents the kinds of sources from which legal justifications can be drawn in
English law.

The term 'sources of law' is sometimes used to identify the *material* sources— **1.02**
where lawyers look in order to find out what the law is. Thus they might consult
textbooks, encyclopaedias, legal retrieval systems, or increasingly they visit sites
on the Internet. This chapter is concerned not with these material sources of information about the law, but about the sources of legal justifications.

---

[1] R Alexy, *A Theory of Legal Argumentation* (1991), 220 and 289.

3

1.03 When proposing a new law, politicians offer arguments why it would be morally right or economically, politically or socially beneficial. Such reasons are *substantive reasons* for the decision, but are often controversial. To ensure more consistency and stability, society prefers to limit the range of reasons on which a judge or official can rely by identifying a number of acceptable *formal reasons*.[2] For example, a rule of European law, statute or precedent must be treated as an authoritative statement of the law and a judicial decision must be based on one such authoritative source of law. The existence of such sources will either exclude or reduce the weight of the substantive reasons on which the judge might otherwise rely.

B. The Hierarchy of Norms

1.04 Legal rules, principles and guidelines are called collectively legal norms or standards. It is useful to talk of legal norms in terms of a hierarchy—some types of norm prevail over others. The following constitutes the hierarchy of English legal norms: (1) European Union law, (2) the European Convention on Human Rights, (3) the Constitution, (4) the common law (what other legal systems might call 'general principles of law'), (5) statutes, (6) precedents, and (7) customs. Each of these is an authority reason for a legal decision, but there is a clear ranking between them. Statutes and precedents are so substantial that separate sections are devoted to them.

(1) European Union Law

(a) Status of European Union law

1.05 The United Kingdom has been a member of the European Community (now Union) since 1973. The initial accession through the European Communities Act 1972 made the European treaties part of the law of the United Kingdom, authorized the implementation of future European Community legislation by delegated legislation, and established the supremacy of this European law. Treaties signed subsequent to 1973 have been ratified by specific Acts of Parliament, eg the Treaty of Amsterdam was ratified by the European Communities (Amendment) Act 1998. Unlike the laws of some Member States, English law does not provide for a referendum to approve such ratifications.

1.06 A preliminary point of terminology must be dealt with. Since 1993, when the Treaty of Maastricht came into force creating the European Union, it has become quite

---

2 PS Atiyah and RS Summers, *Form and Substance in Anglo-American Law* (1987) 2 and 25.

common for authors to switch from using the terms 'European Communities', 'European Community', 'Community' and 'EC' to using the terms 'European Union' and 'EU' without giving the shift a great deal of thought. All the same, the European Union has three 'pillars'. They are, first, the European Community (EC); second, the Common Foreign and Security Policy (CFSP); and, third, Police and Judicial Co-operation in Criminal Matters (PJCCM). The CFSP and the PJCCM are inter-governmental programmes of co-operation. As far as the hierarchy of norms is concerned, the first pillar (EC) is the only one to produce norms that prevail over national legislation. For this reason, the terms 'EC law' and 'Community Law' continue to be used in relation to the European sources that contribute to English law.

European Union law has several forms. The highest form of legislation is the **1.07** *treaties*, the fundamental framework setting out powers, responsibilities and rights. The treaties recognized in English law are set out in s 1(2) of the European Communities Act 1972 (as amended). Specific policies are then developed through directives and regulations enacted under the provisions of the treaties. *Directives* establish a policy direction towards which all member states have to adapt their national legislation. *Regulations* are rules that apply without adaptation in the same form in all member states.

The priority of European Community law was a principle established well before **1.08** the United Kingdom joined. In a decision of 1964, *Costa v ENEL*,[3] the European Court of Justice (ECJ) ruled that, in creating the European Economic Community (now the European Union), 'Member States have limited their sovereign rights, albeit within limited fields, and have thus created a body of law which binds both their nationals and themselves'. The duty of the courts was then specified in *Amministrazione delle Finanze dello Stato v Simmenthal (No 2)*:[4]

> A national court which is called upon, within the limits of its jurisdiction, to apply provisions of Community law, is under a duty to give effect to those provisions, if necessary by refusing of its own motion to apply any conflicting provisions of national legislation, even if adopted subsequently. . .

A good example of this priority is *R v Secretary of State for Transport, ex p Factortame Ltd*.[5] The criterion for treating ships as of British nationality under s 14 of the Merchant Shipping Act 1988 discriminated against British firms with shareholders from other EU states (here Spain) in breach of the EC Treaty. The ECJ ruled that the Act's provisions were unlawful and the House of Lords then decided to disapply the Act. In a subsequent case, the House of Lords has also given a

---

[3] Case 6/64, [1964] ECR 585.
[4] Case 106/77, [1978] ECR 629.
[5] Case C-213/89, [1990] ECR I-2433; [1991] 1 AC 603, ECJ and HL.

declaration that British legislation on sex discrimination was in breach of EC law, even without a ruling from the ECJ.[6]

(b) Direct effect

1.09   Much EC legislation is said to have 'direct effect' in the sense that it creates rights and duties in domestic law without intermediate national legislation. The treaties are not just agreements between nation states but create a legal order in which individual citizens have rights and duties against those member states.[7] The current test is that the provision of EC law must be (a) clear and unambiguous, (b) unconditional, and (c) not dependent on further action being taken by the Community or national authorities.[8] Direct effect can take two forms. *Vertical direct effect* creates rights only between an individual and a Member State. Directives will not have horizontal direct effect until they are implemented as part of national legislation, but they may have effect between a citizen and the state or its organs. For example, in *Marshall v Southampton & South West Area HA*,[9] Mrs Marshall complained that she was forced to retire at 60 when men need not retire until 65. Directive 76/207 established the principle of equal treatment between the sexes and prohibited all discrimination on grounds of sex in working conditions. The deadline for implementing this Directive had passed, but the UK had not enacted it into domestic law. The ECJ found that it prevailed over the English Sex Discrimination Act 1975 permitting different retirement ages to apply to men and women. Mrs Marshall was able to rely on a directive against an emanation of the state, a health authority.[10] *Horizontal direct effect* creates rights between individual EC residents. Regulations almost invariably fit into this category. Many provisions of the treaties also do. For example, in *Barber v Guardian Royal Exchange Assurance Group*,[11] a man was able to complain successfully against a private pension company that it discriminated unlawfully against him contrary to art 119 EC. Under his pension scheme, women made redundant at the age of 50 qualified for an immediate pension, but men had to wait until they were 55.

---

[6]   *R v Secretary of State for Employment, ex p Equal Opportunities Commission* [1995] 1 AC 1.

[7]   Case 26/ 62, *Van Gend en Loos NV v Nederlandse Administratie der Belastingen* [1963] ECR 1.

[8]   Case 43/75, *Defrenne v SABENA* [1976] ECR 455; Case 41/74, *Van Duyn v Home Office* [1974] ECR 1337.

[9]   Case 152/84, *Marshall v Southampton & SW Hants AHA* [1986] ECR 723; Case C-271/91 *Marshall v Southampton & South West Area HA (No 2)* [1993] ECR I-4367.

[10]   For a body to be treated as 'an emanation of the state', it must be a body (whether a public or private person), which (a) provides a public service; (b) for that purpose has special powers; (c) acts under the decisive or special influence of public authorities: Case C-188/89, *Foster v British Gas* [1990] ECR I-3313.

[11]   Case C-262/88, [1990] ECR I-1889.

Even if an EC legal rule is not directly effective, it may have an impact on national **1.10** law in two ways: either as a principle of interpretation or as a basis for a legal claim for compensation against the State. Where faced with national legislation that is designed to implement a directive, courts should interpret it 'in the light of the wording and the purpose of the Directive'.[12] Even where the member state has failed to implement a directive, the national court is required to interpret existing national law (whether the provisions in question were adopted before or after the directive) 'as far as possible, in the light of the wording and purpose of the directive in order to achieve the result pursued by the latter'.[13] Where a Community obligation has not been implemented, then a national court must be willing to award damages against the state for non-compliance.[14]

(2) The European Convention on Human Rights

The Human Rights Act 1998 gives effect to the European Convention on **1.11** Human Rights. Under s 3(1), 'So far as it is possible to do so, primary legislation and subordinate legislation must be read and given effect in a way which is compatible with the Convention rights'.[15] Although the courts cannot refuse to apply primary legislation that conflicts with the Convention, a declaration of incompatibility authorizes the minister to promote delegated legislation to bring UK law into conformity. There is thus a strong presumption in favour of an interpretation that makes the UK law consistent with the Convention.

In applying s 3(1), there are several stages in reasoning. First, it is necessary to **1.12** examine whether a Convention right (properly understood) is affected by domestic legislation. The clear and constant case law of the European Court of Human Rights will serve as a guide.[16] For example, in *R (on the application of Alconbury Developments Ltd) v Secretary of State for the Environment, Transport and the Regions*,[17] that case law established that judicial review of planning decisions did not require a rehearing of the merits of the application. Secondly, even if a Convention right is affected, the interference may be justified under the terms of the Convention itself. Many Convention rights are not absolute and the

---

12 Case 14/83, *Von Colson v Land Nordrhein-Westfalen* [1984] ECR 1891.

13 Case C-106/89, *Marleasing SA v La Comercial Internacional de Alimentación SA* [1990] ECR I-4135 where provisions of an 1889 Code had to be interpreted so as to implement a 1975 directive.

14 Cases C-6/90 and C-9/90, *Francovich & Bonifaci v Italy* [1991] ECR I-5357; Cases C-46/93 and 48/93 *Brasserie du Pêcheur SA v Germany, R v Secretary of State for Transport, ex p Factortame Ltd* [1996] ECR I-1029, for the damages settlement in this case see [1999] 2 All ER 640.

15 See D Feldman (ed), *English Public Law* (2004), ch 7.

16 See *R (on the application of Alconbury Developments Ltd) v Secretary of State for the Environment, Transport and the Regions* [2001] UKHL 23, [26], *per* Lord Slynn.

17 ibid.

Convention permits interference in certain circumstances to protect other rights or to pursue a public interest goal, provided the interference is proportionate. For example, the privilege against self-incrimination has to be balanced against other Convention rights, and this may justify the requirement that the owner of a vehicle reveal the name of its driver.[18] Thirdly, if a Convention right is affected in an apparently illegitimate way, it is necessary to examine whether the domestic legislation can be construed to be compatible with it. Here the first approach is to see whether ordinary methods of interpretation, as discussed in paras 1.42–1.51, will remove any conflict. If that is insufficient, the more radical approach of s 3(1) of the Human Rights Act 1998 will be invoked under which the domestic legislation is construed as compatible, as far as this is possible, even if the interpretation which has to be adopted to this end is linguistically strained.[19] It may be that, in order to determine either the extent or the justifiability of an interference with a Convention right, this robust approach to interpretation must be adopted.[20] Both the second and the third stages involve interpretation, and it may be that one judge finds no apparent interference with a Convention right, whereas another finds that there is an apparent interference, but no incompatibility between the Convention right and the legislation (properly interpreted).[21] Finally, where it is not possible to interpret the domestic legislation in a way which is compatible with the Convention right, a competent court may make a declaration of incompatibility. An example was *A (FC) and Others v Secretary of State for the Home Department*[22] in which a number of individuals challenged their detention without trial. They were held because they were suspected of being a danger to national security, but they could not be expelled to another country. The House of Lords held that s 23 of the Anti-terrorism, Crime and Security Act 2001 was incompatible with articles 5 and 14 of the European Convention insofar as it is disproportionate and permits detention of suspected international terrorists in a way that discriminates on the ground of nationality or immigration status, and it quashed the Government's derogation from the Convention. It is accepted that where a proposed compatible interpretation departs substantially from a fundamental feature of the Act, it is not a permissible interpretation, but an amendment, which only Parliament can make: for example, in *Ghaidan v Godin-Mendoza*,[23] where the term 'spouse' was interpreted to include a homosexual partner. As Lord Nicholls stated, '[Section 3 allows] a court to read in words which change the

---

[18] *Brown v Stott (Procurator Fiscal, Dunfermline)* [2001] 2 All ER 97.

[19] Lord Steyn in *R v A (No 2)* [2001] UKHL 25; [2002] 1 AC 45 at [44].

[20] See *Poplar Housing and Regeneration Community Association v Donoghue* [2001] EWCA 595; [2002] QB 48 at [75] *per* Lord Woolf CJ; see also *R v Director of Public Prosecutions, ex p Kebilene* [2000] 2 AC 326.

[21] Compare the opinions of Lord Hope and Lord Steyn in *R v A (No 2)* (n 19 above).

[22] [2004] UKHL 56; [2005] 2 AC 68.

[23] [2004] UKHL 30; [2004] 2 AC 557.

meaning of the enacted legislation, so as to make it Convention-compliant. In other words, the intention of Parliament in enacting section 3 was that, to an extent bounded only by what is 'possible', a court can modify the meaning, and hence the effect, of primary and secondary legislation.'[24] By contrast, *Ghaidan* demonstrates that many areas of private law are likely to be affected by the Convention.[25]

Section 6(1) of the Human Rights Act makes it unlawful for a 'public authority'   **1.13** to act in a way that is incompatible with any Convention right.[26] The Convention lists certain inalienable rights: the right to life (art 2), the freedom from torture or inhuman or degrading treatment or punishment (art 3), the freedom from slavery (art 4), the right to liberty and security of the person (art 5), the right to a fair trial (art 6), the right to marry and found a family (art 12), the right to an effective remedy (art 13) and the freedom from discrimination in respect of Convention rights. In addition, some rights can only be subject to such limitations as are necessary in a democratic society, for example in the interests of public safety. These rights are the right to respect for family life, home and correspondence (art 8), the right to freedom of thought, conscience and religion (art 9), the right to freedom of expression (art 10), and the right to freedom of peaceful assembly and association (art 11). The impact of the Convention on private law is more limited. Baroness Hale of Richmond noted, 'The 1998 Act does not create any new cause of action between private persons. But if there is a relevant cause of action applicable, the court as a public authority must act compatibly with both parties' Convention rights.'[27] Consistently with s 3, rules and principles of private law are interpreted in the light of Convention rights. This may lead to the revision of established principles of law, such as the expansion of the tort of breach of confidential information to protect a person's Convention rights to privacy.[28]

Section 8 of the 1998 Act provides for remedies against public authorities where   **1.14** Convention rights have been breached.[29] Nothing in the Human Rights Act prevents a person from making an application under the Convention to the European Court of Human Rights in Strasbourg. The remedies under the Act merely help

---

[24] ibid at [32].

[25] For example, the liability of public authorities in tort for the exercise of their supervisory powers has been the subject of decisions of the European Court of Human Rights in *Osman v United Kingdom* Series A 1998-VIII, 3124; (2000) 29 EHRR 245 and in *Z v United Kingdom*; Application 29392/95, (2002) EHRR 3.

[26] There is no exhaustive definition of a 'public authority' but s 6(3) includes both courts and tribunals and other bodies performing 'functions of a public nature'.

[27] *Campbell v MGN Ltd* [2004] UKHL 22; [2004] 2 AC 457 at [132].

[28] ibid. See paras 17.364–17.366.

[29] See D Feldman (ed), *English Public Law*, ch 19.

to define what counts as the exhaustion of national remedies under the admissibility criteria of art 35 of the Convention.

(3) *The Constitution*

(a) The absence of a single authoritative text[30]

1.15 The highest level of national legal authority lies in the Constitution. Rules laid down in the Constitution define the authority of other sources of law and prevail over them. In some countries, there is a document containing such rules.[31] In Britain, there is no such text. Leading authors such as Dicey and Jennings define the constitution in terms of laws and practices, a mixture of legal and political rules. Dicey argued that political practices and constitutional conventions are only part of the story; they fail to explain the enforcement of the Constitution. For him, 'constitutional law, as the term is used in England, appears to include all rules which directly or indirectly affect the distribution or the exercise of the sovereign power of the state'.[32] Dicey stated that one set of such rules is 'law' in the strictest sense of the word, namely rules that are enforced by the courts (whether they come from statute or the common law). The other set of rules consist of conventions, ie understandings and practices which regulate the conduct of the sovereign power of the state, but which are not enforced directly by the courts.[33] While the precise scope of this distinction is debated, the distinction itself is widely accepted.[34] Thus, while there may not be a 'constitution' in the sense of a single, formally enacted written document, there are actual principles or maxims in terms of which the country ought to be ruled.

1.16 The absence of a written document leads to the criticism, voiced by Jennings, that constitutional law 'is not a system at all but a mass of disconnected rules depending on historical accidents'.[35] It is certainly the case that lawyers often do not see the constitution as a whole with its different kinds of legal norms and their connection to conventions of the constitution.[36] But for some distinguished judges and writers, the solution lies not in producing a written constitution, but in a

---

[30] See ibid, paras 1.09–1.15; D Feldman, 'None, One or Several? Perspectives on the UK's Constitution' [2005] CLJ 329.

[31] For example, the German Basic Law of 1949 lists of fundamental rights is set out which prevail over rules in private law or criminal law.

[32] AV Dicey, *The Law of the Constitution* (10th edn by ECS Wade, 1959), 23: see generally D Feldman (ed), *English Public Law*, paras 1.03–1.08.

[33] ibid 23–4. Conventions may, however, provide a background justification for judicial decisions, eg *A-G v Jonathan Cape Ltd* [1976] QB 752.

[34] See more generally G Marshall, *Constitutional Conventions* (1984), ch 1.

[35] WI Jennings, *The Law and the Constitution* (5th edn, 1959), 71.

[36] See Lord Nolan, and G Wilson in Lord Nolan and Sir S Sedley, *The Making and Remaking of the British Constitution* (1997), chs 1, 6 and esp. ch 7.

clearer appreciation of the role of the common law in establishing constitutional principles and of the role of judges in contributing to the creation of constitutional laws and conventions.

(b) The constitutional texts

Although the United Kingdom does not have a single document called 'the **1.17** Constitution', there are a number of constitutional statutes. To take recent examples, the Scotland Act 1998, the Government of Wales Acts 1998 and 2006, the Northern Ireland Act 1998, the Human Rights Act 1998, the House of Lords Act 1999 and the Constitutional Reform Act 2005 would all rank as constitutional statutes. They create assemblies in Scotland, Wales, and Northern Ireland, and give legal force to the European Convention on Human Rights in the United Kingdom. But, unlike in other legal systems, constitutional statutes cannot be separated from other statutes by virtue of the special procedure required for their enactment.[37] For example, devolution in Scotland and Wales was preceded in September 1997 by consultative referendums on the principle of creating a Scottish Parliament or a Welsh Assembly authorized by the Referendums (Scotland and Wales) Act 1997, but the decisions of the peoples in those countries had no legal force. Rather it created a political mandate for the UK Parliament to vote the detailed constitutional reforms contained in the Scotland Act 1998 and the Government of Wales Act 1998. At best, one can identify certain subject matter as constitutional, and this is the approach adopted in Schedule 5 to the Scotland Act 1998, though the list there is, by its own admission, not exhaustive. The Constitutional Reform Act fits this pattern, as it deals with the independence, appointment and governance of the judiciary and the role of the Lord Chancellor.

The hierarchical priority of certain statutes can be seen in two ways. In the first **1.18** place, their provisions are presumed to apply in relation to subsequent legislation unless there is an irreconcilable conflict. Examples of this are s 28(8) of the Scotland Act 1998 and s 3(1) of the Human Rights Act 1998. In the second place, the statutes may radically reshape the way in which government or Parliament acts so it is virtually impossible to go back to the original arrangement without a further conscious and overt legislative change. Examples are the Act of Settlement 1701 (in relation to succession to the Crown), the Acts of Union 1707 (uniting the English and Scottish Parliaments), the Parliament Acts 1911 and 1949 (determining how Acts of Parliament are voted), the European Communities Act 1972

---

[37] In France, an amendment to the constitution has to be adopted either by referendum or, more normally, by a joint session of both houses of the Parliament: see J Bell, *French Constitutional Law* (1992), 228, 260–1.

and the subsequent Acts amending it, as well as the devolution and human rights legislation mentioned above.

(c) Common law rules

1.19 Common law constitutional rules are more difficult to identify. Again there is no procedural difference in the elaboration of such rules. Unlike many European countries, the UK does not have a constitutional court. The nearest equivalent is the Judicial Committee of the Privy Council which interprets the constitutions of some Commonwealth countries and, most recently, has been given jurisdiction over devolution issues.[38] To identify common law constitutional rules, one needs to consider their subject matter. Common law rules define that an Act of Parliament requires the consent of the Queen, the Lords and the Commons[39] and that the Executive or Parliament alone cannot make laws.[40] The common law also defines the unchallengeability of Acts of Parliament, except where overriding European Community law is involved.[41] The principles for the conduct of the executive are defined through precedents on the judicial review of administrative action.

1.20 It is thus true that constitutional norms are the highest source of domestic law; but it is a difficult exercise to identify which norms count as constitutional. The following subject-matter should be treated as constitutional:

(1) succession to the Crown;

(2) inherent and emergency powers of the Executive;

(3) the powers and procedures of Parliament;

(4) elections to Parliament;

(5) the existence, powers and composition of devolved parliaments and assemblies;

(6) the basic organization of local government;

(7) the definition of fundamental rights and the guarantees essential for their protection;

(8) the independence of the judiciary;

(9) rights to nationality, passports and asylum;

(10) the establishment of religion;

(11) the transfer or acquisition of territory.

---

[38] 'Devolution issues' are defined in para 1 of Schedule 6 to the Scotland Act 1998, para 1 of Schedule 8 to the Government of Wales Act 1998, and para 1 of Schedule 10 to the Northern Ireland Act 1998.

[39] *Prince's Case* (1606) 8 Co Rep 1a.

[40] *Case of Proclamations* (1611) 12 Co Rep 74, *Stockdale v Hansard* (1839) 9 Ad & E 1.

[41] *Edinburgh and Dalkeith Ry v Wauchope* (1842) 8 Cl. & F 710; *Pickin v British Rys Board* [1974] AC 765.

Other countries might include language, culture and the currency as similarly fundamental, but this does not appear to be the case in the United Kingdom.

(4) The Common Law

The common law can be viewed in three ways. First, it is a body of rules and prin- **1.21**
ciples which are judge-made, rather than contained in statutes. Although this distinction is rightly distinguishes different sources of initiative in legal developments, there has been a misconception that statute and common law are distinct bodies of law which do not mix, just as oil does not mix with water.[42] In truth, the task of the lawyer is to integrate rules from these different sources into a coherent whole. Secondly and more specifically, the 'common law' is the body of judge-made rules which has its origins in the common law courts, as opposed to the rules of equity developed by the courts of Chancery. Since the Judicature Act 1873, the courts have tried to integrate these two sets of rules. Thirdly, the most valuable way of looking upon the common law is a source of general principles of law.

The role of the common law as a source of general principles of law is illustrated **1.22**
in cases such as *R v National Insurance Commissioner, ex p Connor*[43] where the provisions of s 24 of the Social Security Act 1975 that '[a] woman who has been widowed shall be entitled to a widow's allowance' were held not to apply where the woman in question had killed her husband. The general principle of law that 'no one can profit from his own wrong' applied, even though it was not expressly mentioned in the statute.

In a more general sense, the term 'common law' is used to describe a legal culture, **1.23**
an attitude towards law and the resolution of legal problems. The cast of mind of the common lawyer is described by Lord Goff:

> the historical fact that common lawyers have been reared on a diet of case law has had a profound effect on our judicial method. Common lawyers tend to proceed by analogy, moving gradually from case to case. We tend to avoid large, abstract, generalisations, preferring limited, temporary, formulations, the principles gradually emerging from concrete cases as they are decided. In other words, we tend to reason *upwards* from the facts of the cases before us, whereas our continental colleagues tend to reason *downwards* from abstract principles embodied in a code. The result is that we tend to think of each case as having a relatively limited effect, a base for future operations as the law develops forwards from case to case—and occasionally backwards if we are modest enough to recognise that perhaps we have gone too far. This method

---

[42] For criticism, see J Beatson, 'Has the Common Law a Future?' [1997] CLJ 291.
[43] [1981] QB 758, DC.

of working can be epitomised in the statement that common lawyers worship at the shrine of the working hypothesis.[44]

At the same time, the common law is seen as a system of principles which cross national boundaries such that American, Irish, Australian and Canadian authorities may all be relevant to an English case. The importance of this culture to legal thinking is that the common law is seen as a set of interlocking principles which should be interpreted as coherently as possible. Yet, at the same time, its formulations are provisional, capable of improvement or change to adapt to new circumstances or situations. This conception suggests that the common law judicial decisions (in law or equity) are provisional statements of fundamental common law principles which have to be reviewed and developed over time. There is no equivalent of the pithy statement in a code or statute that contains an invariable formulation of the basic idea to which the courts add layers of interpretation. On the one hand, this requires the lawyer to build on previous decisions by way of analogy. On the other hand, he is required to offer a constructive reinterpretation of the common law in such a way that a new development fits coherently into it.[45]

(5) Custom

1.24 Custom, as the law understands it, is a usage which has the force of law and binds in relation to a particular place, person or thing.[46] For example, the residents of Windsor had the right to play lawful sports and pastimes on Bachelors' Acre.[47] As there, most customs are local law which supplements the ordinary law of the land. More loosely, there are also practices of particular trades.[48] To count as a custom, it must be reasonable, certain, and be considered by those involved as binding. The law distinguishes between customs that have existed from time immemorial (ie since 3 September 1189), which have equal authority to the common law, and those of more recent date, which do not prevail over the common law.[49]

---

[44] Lord Goff of Chieveley, 'The Future of the Common Law' (1997) 46 ICLQ 745 at 753.

[45] This is the idea contained in RM Dworkin's analogy of the chain novel: *Law's Empire* (1986), 240–5.

[46] *Tanistry Case* (1608) Davis Ir 28 at 31.

[47] *New Windsor Corporation v Mellor* [1974] 2 All ER 510; affd [1975] Ch 580.

[48] Eg *McGowan (Inspector of Taxes) v Brown and Cousins* [1977] 3 All ER 844 at 848 (concerning estate agents).

[49] Scrope CJ, *Plumer v Leicester* (1329) 97 Selden Society 45 at 46.

C. Statutes and Their Interpretation

(1) The Nature of Statutes

(a) Forms of legislation

Statutes and other enactments are the most substantial part of English law. The **1.25** basic principles of many branches of law have been specifically created by statute, eg child law, planning law, company law. Statutes can be either 'public general Acts', or 'local Acts' (applying to a particular locality) or 'private Acts' applying to specific individuals or companies. A public body, such as a local authority or a public corporation, might seek a local Act or a private Act to give it special powers.[50] A typical statute or Act of Parliament is divided into sections, some of which are further divided into sub-sections, and 'schedules', as the annexes are known. Statutes usually contain interpretation sections which define key terms used in the legislation. (Frequently occurring terms are defined in the Interpretation Act 1978.) Among their provisions, Acts of Parliament typically authorize ministers to make delegated legislation in the form of *statutory instruments* or *orders in council*. In addition, local authorities and other bodies may be authorized by statute to pass *by-laws* regulating such things as the use of parks or public spaces, or setting parking restrictions. The principles for interpreting statutes set out in this section apply not only to public and general Acts, but also to these other forms of legislation.

The essential feature of a statute, statutory instrument or by-law is that it is a **1.26** deliberate and systematic attempt to lay down rules of law in a precise, written formulation which tries to anticipate the situations to which it will apply. Case law develops rules in response to specific, concrete situations which present themselves before a court. The rule laid down in a judicial decision will apply to similar future situations, but the court does not have to consider all its implications. By contrast, the legislator is trying to lay down rules in abstract for future situations and is expected to have thought through the consequences of the rule to be adopted.

(b) Problems of interpretation[51]

This abstract character of the words used provides a first problem for the reader, **1.27** since he will have to make them concrete by way of illustration. The second problem is the difficulty for the legislator to foresee how the provision will come to be applied. An example of this is the case of *Royal College of Nursing v Department of*

---

[50] Public general Acts are numbered in a different series from local and private Acts. In terms of rules of interpretation, there is no significant difference between them these days.
[51] See FAR Bennion, *Statute Law* (3rd edn, 1990), part III.

Health and Social Security.[52] The Abortion Act 1967 provided that a lawful abortion had to be 'carried out by a registered medical practitioner'. All the methods of abortion practised in 1967 required the continuous presence of a doctor during the abortion process. By the end of the 1970s, other methods became available which required the presence of a doctor only to start and finish the process. By a majority, the House of Lords ruled that the new medical procedure, though unforeseen in 1967, fell within the purpose of the Act to provide safe abortions and was lawful under the Act.

1.28 A third problem arises where the legislator does foresee a problem, but deliberately leaves it unresolved. For example, s 2(4) European Communities Act 1972 provides that 'any enactment passed or to be passed. . .shall be construed and have effect' subject to the provisions of European Community law. This wording does not clearly state what is to happen when a subsequent statute does not comply with EU law. The courts were left to resolve the issue when it arose in the *Factortame* case[53] when the House of Lords disapplied the Merchant Shipping Act 1988 insofar as it breached EC law.

1.29 Finally, like all human institutions, the legislature makes mistakes. A classic example is *Adler v George*[54] in which s 3 Official Secrets Act 1920 made it an offence for a person to obstruct a member of Her Majesty's forces 'in the vicinity of' a military base. In this case, protesters actually went *inside* an airforce base and obstructed aeroplanes involved in carrying nuclear weapons. When prosecuted, the protesters claimed that they were not 'in the vicinity of' the airbase, since they were actually inside. The Divisional Court upheld their conviction on the ground that it was obvious that the wording intended to prevent obstruction of the armed forces and the wording should be read as making it an offence to obstruct a member of Her Majesty's forces '*in or* in the vicinity of' a military base. The court was effectively altering the wording of the text to deal with the inaccurate use of words by the legislator. This is often described as a 'rectifying interpretation'.

1.30 More commonly, the problem for a reader is not dealing with mistakes or unforeseen situations, but applying the apparently straightforward, general expressions used by the legislature to the complexity of actual situations. For instance, the concept of a 'student' is an everyday notion. In *Chief Adjudication Officer v Webber*,[55] the question was how this notion applied within Reg 61 of the Income

---

52 [1981] AC 800. See also *R v Ireland* [1998] AC 147 where it was held that a telephone call could amount to an assault within the Offences Against the Person Act 1861, even though telephones had not been invented at the time.

53 See para 1.08.

54 [1964] 2 QB 7; see also, *McMonagle v Westminster City Council* [1990] 2 AC 716 where words in s 12(4) of the Greater London Council (General Powers) Act 1986 were ignored as 'surplusage'.

55 [1998] 1 WLR 625, CA.

Support (General) Regulations 1987 which provided that a person is to be treated as a 'student' from the beginning of a full-time course until its last day, including vacations. The Court of Appeal held that this definition did not apply to a person who had failed some of the modules on his full-time course and had to re-sit them as a part-time student.

(2) What are Judges Trying to Find Out?

(a) The 'intention of Parliament'

Statutes express the purposes that legislators are trying to achieve, and judges defer   **1.31** to these. Judges do not try to achieve simply what *they* think would be right or socially desirable, but they try to see how the words of the legislation can be made to achieve the purposes of the legislator. Judges often describe this task as attempting to find 'the intention of Parliament' or 'the intention of the legislature' and then carrying it out. This way of talking gives the impression that there exists somewhere outside the text the expression of 'the intention of Parliament' which judges have to find. But this is a misleading impression. As Lord Reid put it:

> We often say that we are looking for the intention of Parliament, but that is not quite accurate. We are seeking the meaning of the words which Parliament used. We are seeking not what Parliament meant but the true meaning of what they said.[56]

That passage may appear cryptic, but it contains an important point. The courts are not concerned with the subjective opinions of those who made the statute, but are concerned with the objective meaning of the words used read in the context of the materials which the audience for the text is expected to use.

It is obvious that it is actually difficult to identify the appropriate individuals   **1.32** whose opinions might be said to constitute 'the intention of Parliament'.[57] A government bill is typically the product of a long policy-making process that has involved ministers, civil servants, and outside organizations, as well as political parties. Once the policy is formulated, the text is drafted by a professional lawyer, the parliamentary counsel, and approved by the relevant Cabinet committee. Within Parliament, it is examined by the House of Commons and the House of Lords, in debates in the whole House and in a small committee. An Act is not the product of the intention of a single person, but of a legal and political process. When judges talk of 'the intention of Parliament', they are saying that the text of an Act has to be understood as the product of that process.

---

[56] *Black Clawson International Ltd v Papierwerke Waldhof-Aschaffenburg AG* [1975] AC 591 at 613; see now also *R v Secretary of State for the Environment, Transport and the Regions, ex p Spath Holme Ltd* [2001] 2 AC 349, 397 *per* Lord Nicholls.
[57] DN MacCormick and RS Summers, *Interpreting Statutes* (1991), 522–525.

1.33 The reader of the text does not read it in isolation. He will start with some broad understanding of what the legislation was meant to achieve derived from common knowledge. The reader will also be able to fit the text into the pattern of legislation in that field. But even when a court refers to parliamentary debates, this does not make the meaning of the text just depend on what a particular minister said. In *Pepper v Hart*,[58] the House of Lords decided to reverse its previous rule of long-standing and to allow judges to consult *Hansard* in interpreting Acts of Parliament. But Lord Oliver started from the premise that 'a statute is, after all, the formal and complete intimation to the citizen of the particular rule of law which he is enjoined. . .to obey and by which he is both expected and entitled to regulate his conduct'. Thus, the permission to consult *Hansard* 'can only apply where the expression of the legislative intention is genuinely ambiguous or obscure or where a literal or *prima facie* construction leads to a manifest absurdity and where the difficulty can be resolved by a clear statement to the matter in issue'.[59] In such situations, the reader is put on notice by the ambiguity or obscurity of the text or the potential absurdity of a literal interpretation that he needs to look further in order to find an appropriate solution. But where the text is clear, no such enquiry is needed. Furthermore, the reader need bother only with those passages which provide clear solutions.

(b) Purposive construction

1.34 In order to explain their approach, English judges talk not so much about finding the 'intention of Parliament', but rather of the 'purpose of the legislation'. The Law Commission in 1969 suggested in its draft Interpretation of Statutes Bill that 'a construction which could promote the general legislative purpose underlying the provision in question is to be preferred to a construction which would not.'[60] Unlike a literal approach, the courts were to ensure that the words of a provision carried out the objective of the statute, as could be interpreted from the text and other permitted materials. As Lord Griffiths said in *Pepper v Hart*:[61]

> The days have long passed when the courts adopted a strict constructionist view of interpretation which required them to adopt the literal meaning of the language. The courts now adopt a purposive approach which seeks to give effect to the true purpose

---

[58] [1993] AC 593. See paras 1.48–1.50.

[59] ibid at 620; this view, concerning when the permission to consult *Hansard* applies, is confirmed in *R v Secretary of State for the Environment, Transport and the Regions, ex p Spath Holme Ltd* [2001] 2 AC 349, 391, 399 and 413. Lord Hope was alone in suggesting (ibid 407–8) that *Hansard* may be consulted to clarify the meaning of the enacted text, but not the purpose of the legislation.

[60] Law Commission, *The Interpretation of Statutes* (Law Com 21; 1969), clause 2 (a). 'Purposive construction' has replaced earlier approaches to interpretation of a similar kind notably the 'golden rule' and the 'mischief rule': for these see *Cross on Statutory Interpretation*, ch 1.

[61] [1993] AC at 617.

of legislation and are prepared to look at much extraneous material that bears upon the background against which the legislation was enacted.

Similarly, Lord Nicholls has remarked that:

> linguistic arguments. . .should be handled warily. They are a legitimate and useful aid in statutory interpretation, but they are no more than this. . .[B]efore reaching a final decision,. . . one should stand back and view a suggested interpretation in the wider context of the scheme and purpose of the Act.[62]

That said, Laws LJ has doubted whether it is right to suggest that there has been a radical departure from a literal approach by the adoption of the purposive approach. The difference is really one of degree, and a balance has to be struck between the literal meaning of the words used and the purpose of the legislation.[63]

The courts still recognize that there are limits to how far the meaning of words **1.35** used in a text can be strained in order to achieve a satisfactory outcome to a case. *Cutter v Eagle Star Insurance Co Ltd*[64] concerned the liability of insurance companies under s 151 of the Road Traffic Act 1988 to pay for injuries caused to third parties by 'the use of a vehicle on the road'. The question arose whether a car park was a 'road' within s 145 of the Act. Elsewhere in the Act the phrase 'a road or any public place' was used. A car park could not be included within the meaning of the word 'road' in s 145, but elsewhere could be included in the concept of a 'public place'. Consistency of terminology suggested a narrower meaning for 'road', even if this resulted in the absence of compensation for third parties injured by vehicles in a car park.[65] There was an important limit to the acceptable scope for interpretation, even if the outcome did not benefit the accident victim.

(c) European teleological approaches

European influences on interpretation are important. British judges interpret and **1.36** apply European Union law or the European Convention on Human Rights as part of the ordinary law of the land. But some differences of approach are required. First, an emphasis on the literal interpretation of words in, for example, a directive, is inappropriate. Such an enactment is produced in multiple languages and so a precise meaning in English may appear less precise in another authentic language.[66] It is not always appropriate to give weight to the choice of particular vocabulary in such a multi-lingual environment.[67] Secondly, legislative history is

---

[62] *Associated Dairies Ltd v Baines* [1997] AC 524 at 532.
[63] *Ashworth (Oliver)(Holdings) Ltd v Ballard (Kent) Ltd* [1999] 2 All ER 791, 805.
[64] [1998] 1 WLR 1647.
[65] Lord Clyde at [1998] 1 WLR at 1655.
[66] Eg *Customs & Excise Commrs v Bell Concord Educational Trust Ltd* [1990] QB 1040.
[67] See Case C-106/89 *Marleasing SA v La Comercial Internacional de Alimentación SA* [1990] ECR I-4135; Case 283/81 *CILFIT v Minister of Health* [1982] ECR 3415 at 3430, paras 18 and 19.

more complex and less clear. In the European Union, a number of different organs may be involved in the making of legislation—not only the Commission, the Council of Ministers and the Parliament, but possibly also the Economic and Social Committee and the Committee of the Regions. Some of these give reasoned opinions, but the Council of Ministers does not. In the case of the EU Treaties, the preparatory works are incomplete. Thirdly, the complexity of the legislative process in the EU or of the renegotiation of the EU and ECHR treaties, means that it is not possible for a court simply to identify a problem with the existing state of the law and to expect the legislator to correct it. Unlike in the domestic context where the legislator can take prompt action to correct the law, there is more pressure on the courts in the European contexts to adopt a flexible interpretation of the law in order to remedy deficiencies in the drafting of the law. This situation leads to two features of what is known as the *teleological approach* to interpretation.

1.37 The first feature is that the court seeks to define for itself the purpose (*telos*) of the enactment in question. A classic example of this is *Van Gend en Loos*[68] in which the European Court of Justice was faced by an action by a company against a state authority arguing that Dutch customs legislation violated the EEC treaty. The treaty did not expressly provide that it created rights which individuals (as opposed to states) could enforce. The European Court of Justice nevertheless considered that the 'objective of the EEC Treaty' was more than an agreement between states and created rights which were part of an individual's heritage. This purpose was discovered by the Court reading the scheme of the Treaty as a whole, and offering an interpretation of its objective which made sense of what the Court thought the Treaty was trying to achieve, even though this was not identifiable in what had been said by the treaty-makers. The second feature is that the court should seek to interpret the text, as far as possible, to achieve the purpose thus identified. Thus, in *Case C-106/89, Marleasing SA v La Comercial Internacional de Alimentación SA*,[69] the European Court of Justice stated that 'in applying national law, whether the provisions in question were adopted before or after the directive, the national court called upon to interpret it is required to do so, as far as possible, in the light of the wording and purpose of the directive in order to achieve the result pursued by the latter'. In that case, it was held that a Spanish court was required to interpret restrictively long established provisions in the Civil Code of 1889 in order to give effect to a directive which had yet to be implemented in Spanish law, and even though the directive did not have direct effect. But in *Cutter v Eagle Star*,[70]

---

68 Case 26/62, *Van Gend en Loos NV v Nederlandse Tariefkommissie* [1963] ECR 1.
69 [1990] ECR I-4135, [1992] 1 CMLR 305.
70 [1998] 1 WLR at 1656.

Lord Clyde remarked that fidelity to *Marleasing* could not force a construction beyond what is reasonable:

> The adoption of a construction which departs boldly from the ordinary meaning of the language of the statute is. . .particularly appropriate where the validity of legislation has to be tested against the provisions of European law. In that context it is proper to strain to give effect to the design and purpose behind the legislation, and to give weight to the spirit rather than the letter. . . . But even in this context, the exercise must still be one of construction and it should not exceed the limits of what is reasonable.

Similarly, section 3 (1) of the Human Rights Act provides that 'so far as it is possible to do so' primary legislation and subordinate legislation must be interpreted to be compatible with the Convention rights. **1.38**

The role assigned to the court as interpreter by the European teleological approaches is more active than would be acceptable in domestic law. In domestic law, the sources of information about the purpose of legislation are more focused and public, and the legislator is available to reform the law. There is thus a difference in emphasis between the purposive approach to the interpretation of domestic law and the teleological approach to the interpretation of European laws. The rest of this section of the chapter examines the interpretation of domestic law. **1.39**

(3) *Where do Judges Look?*

(a) Basic rules

Cross[71] sets out as the first two rules of statutory interpretation: **1.40**

1. The judge must give effect to the grammatical and ordinary or, where appropriate, the technical meaning of words in the general context of the statute; he must also determine the extent of general words with reference to that context.
2. If the judge considers that the application of the words in their grammatical and ordinary sense would produce a result which is contrary to the purpose of the statute, he may apply them in any secondary meaning they are capable of bearing.

The starting point for interpretation must be that a statute has been drafted by skilled people and that the words have been carefully chosen to convey their intended meaning. The intended reader should thus be able to understand what the text is meant to say from ordinary meaning of words in the context of the statute. Only where the apparent result seems to contradict the apparent purpose of

---

[71] *Cross on Statutory Interpretation*, 49.

the statute is the reader put on alert that he should look for a secondary or less obvious meaning.

(i) Ordinary meaning depends on context

1.41   All words take their meaning from the context in which they are used. The point was clearly stated by Butler-Sloss LJ in *Re C and another(minors) (parent: residence order)*[72] where she noted that even a simple word like 'parent' has different ordinary meanings:

> The term 'parent' must be given its natural and ordinary meaning. It does not follow, however, that that meaning will always include the natural parents. The natural and ordinary meaning of a word is not fixed but changes according to the context in which a word is used. Thus the meaning of 'parent' in a school prospectus will include a person with de facto parental responsibility even if not a natural parent, but exclude a natural parent who has no contact with the child. On the other hand, the meaning of 'parent' in a work on genetics will be the biological parents, including a father who has no more connection than the initial act of fertilisation. The question is therefore whether the natural and ordinary meaning of a 'parent' in the Children Act 1989 can include a natural parent whose child has been freed for adoption.

Her conclusion, and that of the Court of Appeal, was that a natural father did not qualify as a 'parent' under s 10(4)(a) of the Act once a court had ordered that the child be freed for adoption. Therefore he was not entitled to apply to the court for a residence order in respect of the child.

(ii) Identifying the appropriate context

1.42   The context for a provision in a statute is found both within the text itself (eg its title, other provisions, side-notes)[73] and outside the text (eg other statutes on the same subject, general principles of the common law, and policies stated by the courts or the legislature in relation to this area of the law). The reader of any document is expected to read the whole of it and to fit one provision into the scheme of the text as a whole. For example, in *Cutter v Eagle Star*, the exclusion of a car park from the meaning of 'road' in s 145 was strongly influenced by the use of the phrase 'road or other public place' in other sections of the Road Traffic Act 1988.[74]

1.43   In terms of matters outside the text, a reader is expected to be aware of the 'obvious' purpose of the statute to be derived from knowledge of the rest of the law in the area, or as Lord Denning once remarked 'matters generally known to

---

[72] [1994] Fam 1 at 7. On linguistic rules of interpretation, see *Cross on Statutory Interpretation*, 134–41.

[73] On the need to interpret a provision in the context of the text as a whole see *Att-Gen v Prince Ernest Augustus of Hanover* [1957] AC 436 at 461 *per* Viscount Simonds.

[74] [1998] 1 WLR 1647.

well-informed people'.[75] In most cases, the court will look no further to determine the purpose of the statute. For example, *Mandla v Dowell Lee*[76] concerned the interpretation of the word 'ethnic' in the definition of a racial group against whom discrimination was not lawful under s 1(1)(b) of the Race Relations Act 1976. Both the House of Lords and the Court of Appeal relied on general knowledge about the purpose of the Act, but reached different conclusions about its scope and, as a consequence, whether the term 'ethnic' applied to discrimination against Sikhs.

Readers are also expected to be familiar with other statutes on the same subject **1.44** matter. For example, in *Re C*,[77] the Court of Appeal referred to the Adoption Act 1976 in order to support its interpretation of the Children Act 1989. The context of consolidating legislation may include the context in which the original legislation was enacted.[78] In addition, readers are expected to know the common law relevant to the area in question. The legislator cannot be expected to include reference to all the principles of the common law which it expects to be applied, and so they are left unstated.[79] Government announcements or delegated legislation which are contemporaneous with the enactment of the legislation may provide assistance in understanding an Act of Parliament, but this is not always reliable since it reflects the views of the government, not Parliament.[80]

(iii) Technical meaning

In many fields, words have a technical meaning among the specialists who are **1.45** expected to be the principal audience of the legislation. For example, the term 'download' is a technical term in computing and is interpreted according to usage in the field.[81] By contrast, a term such as 'miscarriage of justice' may have a popular meaning, but no technical legal meaning.[82]

---

[75] *Escoigne Properties Ltd v IRC* [1958] AC 549 at 566. Cf Lord Fraser in *Mandla v Dowell Lee* [1983] 2 AC at 562: 'the ordinary experience of those who read newspapers at the present day'.

[76] [1983] 2 AC 548; [1983] QB 1. For an explanation of how parliamentary history might have helped in this case, see St John A Robilliard, [1983] PL 348.

[77] [1994] Fam 1.

[78] See *R v Secretary of State for the Environment, Transport and the Regions, ex p Spath Holme Ltd* [2001] 2 AC 349, 388, but cf Lord Nicholls at 399.

[79] Eg the principle that 'no person can profit from her own wrong': see *R v Chief National Insurance Commr, ex p Connor* [1981] QB 758, see para 1.22.

[80] *Hanlon v Law Society* [1981] AC 124.

[81] See *R v City of London Magistrates' Court, ex p Green* [1997] 3 All ER 551, DC. But words are not always used in a technical sense: cf *Re K (deceased)* [1986] Ch 180, CA.

[82] *R (on the application of Mullen) v Secretary of State for the Home Department* [2005] 1 AC 1; [2004] UKHL 18 at [9] *per* Lord Bingham.

(iv) Secondary meaning

1.46   A secondary meaning is simply a less usual meaning. Such a meaning is adopted
where a simple, ordinary meaning would not achieve the purpose of the legislation. For example, in *Wills v Bowley*,[83] s 28 of the Town Police Clauses Act 1847
provided that a police officer 'shall take into custody, without warrant, and forthwith convey before a justice, any person who within his view *commits*' any of a list
offences. The appellant claimed that, since magistrates had found that she was not
guilty of using obscene language in a street 'to the annoyance of passengers' contrary to s 28, her arrest by police officers under that section was unlawful and so
she could not be convicted of assaulting police officers in the execution of their
duty. At first sight, the lawfulness of an arrest under s 28 appears to be limited to
situations where a person actually 'commits' an offence. Nevertheless, by a majority, the House of Lords held that the wording authorized an arrest where a police
officer honestly believed that a person had been committing an offence within
his view. The Act was one of a family of statutes permitting the arrest of people
caught in the act of committing an offence, and these statutes usually authorized
arrest without warrant upon reasonable suspicion that an offence was being
committed. A secondary, more extended meaning of 'commits' was necessary to
ensure similarly effective police powers under s 28.

(4) Research to Discover the Purpose

1.47   In most situations, it is sufficient for a judge or lawyer to rely on ordinary language
and 'common sense' knowledge in order to determine the purpose and meaning
of a statutory provision. But there are always situations in which some more careful research is needed. English law is much more explicit than most legal systems
in specifying which sources may be used and to what extent. In the past there was
a significant reluctance to enter into wide ranging research into the history of
legislative provisions, especially Parliamentary debates. The three concerns
remain accessibility, reliability and cost. *Accessibility* is important since, as Lord
Diplock expressed it, 'the need for legal certainty demands that the rules by which
the citizen is to be bound should be ascertainable by him (or, more realistically by
a competent lawyer advising him) by reference to identifiable sources that are
publicly accessible'.[84] This still leads to concern about the permissibility of preparatory works for some treaties. *Reliability* is more of a problem. For example,
members of both Houses of Parliament make many statements during the months
in which a bill goes through its various stages. It is often difficult to establish how
far a single statement represents the considered views of either the promoters of a

---

[83] [1983] 1 AC 57.
[84] *Fothergill v Monarch Airlines* [1981] AC 251 at 279.

bill or its supporters. The *cost* of detailed research outside the legislative text has become less of a concern in recent years. But, despite the quality of published commentaries and annotations, a thorough search outside a statute requires time from skilled people and raises the cost of advice or litigation.

In the leading case of *Pepper v Hart*,[85] the House of Lords produced a rule that   **1.48** attempts to meet these concerns while ensuring that the purpose of an enactment is faithfully carried out. Whereas in the past, parliamentary debates published in *Hansard* had been considered inadmissible, the House permitted it, but subject to a number of constraints. Lord Browne-Wilkinson stated that *Hansard* could be referred to where:

(a) Legislation is ambiguous or obscure or leads to an absurdity;
(b) The material relied upon consists of one or more statements by a Minister or other promoter of the Bill together with such other Parliamentary material as is necessary to understand such statements and their effect;
(c) The statements relied upon are clear.[86]

The rule focuses on the necessity to engage in research, the authority of the person making the statement, and the utility of the product of research. Researches into the history of legislation remain exceptional. Even if the lawyers have conducted such researches, they cannot be debated among the lawyers in court unless the researches have produced answers that are authoritative (ie made by the minister or promoter) and are clear in providing an answer to the question of interpretation at issue. Other researches are conducted at the risk of the parties in preparing a case for trial, but need not prolong the hearing. For example, if the material which counsel wishes to present is not clear, then it cannot be used in court.[87] The justification for such a restricted approach remains legal certainty.[88]

Although it is permissible to look at the minister's views as promoter of a bill, it is   **1.49** not permissible to use statements in *Hansard* about the legal meaning of an Act made by a minister after it has been passed.[89] It is permissible to use official guidance or the publication of implementing delegated legislation which are part of the scheme of the Act as a whole and are roughly contemporaneous with the Act.[90]

---

85 [1993] AC 593. See J Steyn, '*Pepper v Hart*: A Re-examination' (2001) 21 *OJLS* 59; S Vogenauer, 'A Retreat from *Pepper v Hart*? A Reply to Lord Steyn' (2005) 25 *OJLS* 624.
86 [1993] AC 593 at 640.
87 *Melluish (Inspector of Taxes) v BMI (No 3)* [1996] AC 454 at 481–2.
88 See the quotation from Lord Oliver, para 1.33; see also *R v Secretary of State for the Environment, Transport and the Regions, ex p Spath Holme Ltd* [2001] 2 AC 349.
89 *Hillsdown Holdings plc v Pensions Ombudsman* [1997] 1 All ER 862 at 898 *per* Knox J.
90 See Lord Lowry, *Hanlon v Law Society* [1981] AC 124 at 193–4; Lord Browne-Wilkinson, *Deposit Protection Board v Dalia* [1994] 2 All ER 577 at 585; Lord Bridge, *Nottinghamshire CC v Secretary of State for the Environment* [1986] AC 240 at 264.

(5) Sources which may be Consulted

1.50 In the light of *Pepper v Hart*, the rules on sources are more liberal than before 1992. That case concerns the intention of the legislator expressed in the legislative process. But in many cases, Parliament is passing legislation to give effect to ideas generated by someone else either when a treaty has been signed, when a committee report makes a recommendation for legislation, or where European legislation is to be implemented.

(a) Treaties

1.51 In English law, a treaty signed by the government does not become law until it is enacted by Parliament. Frequently, the text of the treaty is set out in a schedule to the Act, for example Schedule 1 of the Human Rights Act 1998 contains the text of the European Convention on Human Rights and Fundamental Freedoms of 1950, but this is not essential. In interpreting the English statute, the courts try to ensure that it is construed as far as possible in a way that is consistent with the original treaty.[91] To this end, an English lawyer may have to refer either to the text of the treaty or to the preparatory works (*travaux préparatoires*) which preceded its signature where the words of the statute are ambiguous or unclear.[92] The rule on the use of preparatory works (*travaux préparatoires*) for treaties was laid down by Lord Diplock in *Fothergill v Monarch Airlines Ltd*:[93]

> I think that it would be proper for us. . .to recognise that there may be cases where *travaux préparatoires* can profitably be used. These cases should be rare, and only where two conditions are fulfilled, first that the material involved is public and accessible, and secondly, that the *travaux préparatoires* clearly and indisputably point to a definitive legislative interpretation.

A treaty is negotiated in private and so it is important that the materials which are relied upon in interpreting them are in the public domain.

1.52 The authentic text of a treaty may be in several languages, and so these may need to be compared. For example, *Buchanan & Co Ltd v Babco & Co Ltd*,[94] the House of Lords sought support for its interpretation by reference to the French language text of the Convention on the Contract for the International Carriage of Goods by Road when applying the Carriage of Goods by Road Act 1965.

1.53 A further principle in relation to treaties is that the interpretation given in the United Kingdom should be similar to that in other signatory states. As Lord

---

91 See *A-G v BBC* [1981] AC 303 at 354 *per* Lord Scarman.
92 *Quazi v Quazi* [1980] AC 744 at 808 *per* Lord Diplock.
93 [1981] AC 251, 278.
94 [1978] AC 141. Similarly in *Fothergill v Monarch Airlines Ltd* [1981] AC 251 the French language version of a treaty was used to interpret the Carriage by Air Act 1961 which gave effect to it.

Browne-Wilkinson put it, 'An international convention, expressed in different languages and intended to apply to a wide range of different legal systems, cannot be construed differently in different jurisdictions. The convention must have the same meaning and effect under the laws of all contracting states.'[95] As a result, in that case the term 'acquiescence' used in the treaty enacted by the Child Abduction and Custody Act 1985 was not to be interpreted in accordance with the special rules of English law.

(b) Committee reports

Much legislation is passed as a result of the recommendations of a committee **1.54** independent of government, such as a Royal Commission or the Law Commission. The reports of these bodies are an important and influential guide to the purpose of the legislation and, especially where they produce a draft bill, to the meaning of the Act itself. In *Anderton v Ryan*,[96] the House of Lords had held that a person could not attempt to commit an offence by an action which was objectively innocent, for example by selling a tape recorder thinking (wrongly) that it had been stolen. But in *R v Shivpuri*,[97] the House of Lords overruled this interpretation once it had read the report of the Criminal Law Revision Committee which led to the Criminal Attempts Act 1981.

(c) European legislation

European laws, especially directives, lead to much English legislation. The inter **1.55** pretation of the English law may therefore require analysis of the original European legislation. To interpret the European legislation correctly, it may be necessary to refer to the views of the various EU organs which have been involved in its enactment. For example, in *Three Rivers DC v Bank of England (No 2)*,[98] the Court of Appeal referred to the opinion of the Economic and Social Committee on the Banking Directive which had been implemented through the Banking Act 1979 in order to decide whether the Bank of England was entitled to immunity.

A second feature is that the authentic text of EC legislation exists in several lan **1.56** guages. As with treaties a comparison of the text in the different languages may aid interpretation.[99]

---

[95] *Re H and ors (Minors) (Abduction: Acquiescence)* [1998] AC 72 at 87.

[96] [1985] AC 560.

[97] [1987] AC 1.

[98] [1996] 2 All ER 363 at 366. There was no appeal in relation to this point: see [2003] 2 AC 1; [2001] UKHL 16 at [10].

[99] Eg *Customs & Excise Commrs. v Bell Concord Educational Trust Ltd* [1990] QB 1040 (comparison of English and French language versions of a directive).

(6) Presumptions of Interpretation

1.57 However detailed the text of a statute, there many things that have to be left unsaid. When in doubt, the courts have long resorted to presumptions about what Parliament intended. Some presumptions adopted relate to the way the text is written. For example, it is presumed that a word is used with the same meaning in different parts of the text, unless the contrary is explicitly provided. Other presumptions relate to the values which Parliament is assumed to uphold. Traditionally, these values are said to include:

(1) the strict construction of penal statutes (ie those imposing a penalty)
(2) that Parliament does not intend to interfere with individual liberty (eg in granting powers of arrest or detention)
(3) that Parliament does not intend to deprive people of their property rights
(4) that a tax legislation should be strictly interpreted
(5) that the jurisdiction of the courts should not be ousted.[100]

In broad terms, they are the values of protecting life, liberty and property established by the 1688 Revolution. It has been suggested that these values are no longer predominant, and that the courts simply adopt the solution which public policy requires and which seems to accord most closely with the purpose of the legislation.[101] In any case, wider access to the parliamentary record of proceedings reduces the need to presume what Parliament intended.

1.58 But with the Human Rights Act 1998, discussed in para 1.38, a more modern statement of values has been provided. Section 3(1) of the 1998 Act requires that the courts construe provisions of domestic legislation consistently with the Convention rights and these have thus become the modern test of values which Parliament is presumed to intend, which is more extensive than the list set out in para 1.57. The European Convention is likely to be the more usual point of reference on fundamental values to which judges will refer when interpreting UK legislation.

1.59 There remains a general presumption against unclear changes in the law at least in so far as these affect vested rights.[102] But in most cases, the courts will be able to

---

100 See further *Cross on Statutory Interpretation*, ch 7.

101 For example, for criticism in relation to the presumption in favour of the strict construction of penal statutes, see JC Smith, *Codification of the Criminal Law* (Child & Co Lecture, 1986), 9; G Williams, 'Statutory interpretation, prostitution and the rule of law' in CFH Tapper (ed), *Crime, Proof and Punishment: Essays in Memory of Sir Rupert Cross* (1981), 72; Law Commission, *Criminal Law: A Criminal Code for England and Wales* (Law Com no 177, 1989) para 3.17.

102 *Black Clawson International Ltd v Papierwerke Waldhof-Aschaffenburg AG* [1975] AC 591 at 614 *per* Lord Reid.

resolve the ambiguity by means of a purposive construction without application of the presumption.[103]

The presumption against retrospective application is of greater importance in **1.60** practice and is found in art 7(1) of the European Convention on Human Rights in relation to the specific area of criminal penalties. The current approach of the courts is to ask first whether, in the absence of inescapably clear words to indicate that a provision is to be applied retrospectively, it would be unfair to apply it in this way. Second, if they conclude that it would be unfair, the presumption is applied unless it is rebutted by clear words of necessary implication. The greater the unfairness which would result, the clearer the words of the statute have to be that establish the retrospective effect of the relevant provision.[104]

D. Precedent

Precedent is a method making decisions in individual cases in the light of legal **1.61** principle exemplified in previous cases which is the distinguishing feature of case law as opposed to statute-driven legal development:

> The method of statute requires the use of reason to work out a large plan in advance; the method of precedent applies critical intelligence to reasoning out the best new decision in the light of the prior ones, in the light of what is special about the case in hand, and in the light of the need to maintain a coherent principles body of law.[105]

(1) What is 'Precedent'?

In English law, the concept of 'precedent' covers two ideas that are closely con- **1.62** nected. In the broad sense, precedent involves treating previous judicial decisions as authoritative statements of the law which can serve as good legal reasons for subsequent decisions. In the narrow sense, precedent (often described as *stare decisis*) requires judges in specific courts to treat certain previous decisions, notably of superior courts, as a binding reason. In this sense, the precedent offers a sufficient reason for his decision.

---

[103] See eg *Chief Adjudication Officer v Maguire* [1999] 2 All ER 859, CA; *Oliver Ashworth (Holdings) Ltd v Ballard (Kent) Ltd* [1999] 2 All ER 791; *Cross on Statutory Interpretation*, 167–70.
[104] Staughton LJ, *Secretary of State for Social Security v Tunnicliffe* [1991] 2 All ER 712 at 714, dictum approved in *L'Office Cherifien des Phosphates v Yamashita-Shinnihon Steamship Co Ltd* [1994] 1 AC 486 at 525. For clear examples, see *Plewa v Chief Adjudication Officer* [1995] 1 AC 249; *Bairstow v Queens Moat Houses plc* [1998] 1 All ER 343, CA.
[105] DN MacCormick and RS Summers, *Interpreting Precedent* (1997), 5.

1.63   The broader sense of 'precedent' requires a lawyer to base a legal argument on the available and relevant decisions of previous judges, even when his argument is trying to take the law in a new direction or to depart from its previous direction. In any legal system, as a matter of prudence, lawyers should consult previous decisions to discover possible legal arguments and find out whether they have been successful. But the doctrine of precedent entails that precedent decisions are not merely a source of knowledge about law, but that they are an *authoritative statement of the law*. Where a rule declared in a decision does not accord with principle, judges are likely to distinguish it or otherwise reduce the scope of the rule. To that extent, a single decision will only carry weight if it can be understood to rest upon justifying grounds.[106]

1.64   In a narrow sense, English law equates the doctrine of precedent with the doctrine of *stare decisis*. Cross and Harris define the English doctrine of precedent as follows: 'Every court is bound to follow any case decided by a court about it in the hierarchy, an appellate courts (other than the House of Lords) are bound by their previous decisions.'[107] But they recognize that this formulation is too narrow and does not exclude the broader sense of precedent discussed in para 1.63:

> It does not indicate that only certain aspects of a previous case, called he *ratio decidendi*, are binding, and it does not refer to the existence of important exceptions to the rule of *stare decisis*. . .it must not be forgotten that the rules of precedent are subsidiary to, and far less important than, the obligation of judges to consider case-law.[108]

(2) What does 'Precedent' Involve?

1.65   In most countries, even where precedent is not a formally recognized source of law, lawyers and judges typically cite previous judicial decisions to justify an argument, although this does not always appear from published judgments.[109] Such citation demonstrates that a particular argument fits coherently with the rest of the law. But the English doctrine of precedent goes further and insists that previous decisions are a source to which lawyers *must* refer. Such authoritative statements can have different kinds of weight. A previous case could simply be *persuasive*, ie the previous decision provides an argument in favour of a particular solution by showing it would be consistent with how courts have acted in the past, but the argument can be outweighed by other arguments. The English doctrine of precedent, however, involves treating some judicial decisions not simply as weighty

---

106 MacCormick and Summers, *Interpreting Precedent*, 541.
107 R Cross and JW Harris, *Precedent in English Law* (4th edn, 1991), 6.
108 ibid 6–7.
109 See DN MacCormick and RS Summers, *Interpreting Precedent*. In England, tribunals will commonly cite decisions of other tribunals: J Farmer, *Tribunals and Government* (1974), ch 7.

arguments, but as *binding* statements of the law. In such a case they offer reasons which justify ignoring the countervailing substantive arguments in favour of any alternative decision.[110] For example, in *Smith v Gardner Merchant Ltd*,[111] the Court of Appeal simply applied previous case law of the Court of Appeal and the European Court of Justice that discrimination 'on grounds of sex' did not include discrimination on the ground of sexual orientation.

(3) What Constitutes a 'Precedent'?

The discursive character of English judgments makes it more difficult to identify **1.66** clearly the rule on which a decision is based compared, for example, with a decision of the European Court of Justice. The latter's single judgment lays down in short, numbered paragraphs the formulation of a rule to be applied. By contrast, members of an English appellate court may well give several long judgments which do not clearly identify a single specific passage as central to the decision in the case.

A precedent is a ruling on a point of law that is laid down in a judicial decision as **1.67** the justification for the outcome which is reached in that case. Neil MacCormick offers the following definition:

> A *ratio decidendi* is a ruling expressly or impliedly given by a judge which is sufficient to settle a point of law put in issue by the parties' arguments in a case, being a point on which a ruling was necessary to his justification (or one of his alternative justifications) of the decision in the case.[112]

There are thus four elements that make a precedent: (i) a ruling on a point of law; (ii) expressly or impliedly given by a judge; (iii) related to an issue raised by the arguments of the parties; and (iv) which is necessary as a justification for the decision reached.

(a) A ruling on a point of law

Most of the issues litigated in court are not questions of law, but questions of fact. **1.68** For example, if a pedestrian is injured as a result of being knocked down by a car and sues the driver, several questions of fact might be disputed—was the driver exceeding the speed limit? did the pedestrian look before crossing the road? was the road well lit? Decisions on such points, though important to the parties, are

---

[110] J Raz describes these as 'exclusionary reasons' for decisions: *Practical Reason and Norms* (1975), 35–39.

[111] [1998] 3 All ER 852, following *R v Ministry of Defence, ex p Smith* [1996] QB 517, CA; Case C-249/96 *Grant v South West Trains* [1998] ICR 449, ECJ.

[112] N MacCormick, 'Why Cases have Rationes and What These Are' in L Goldstein (ed), *Precedent in Law* (1987), 170.

not of general application and do not create precedents.[113] By contrast, if the parties dispute whether a driver owes a duty to take care not to knock down a pedestrian, this is a matter of general application and is a question of law. The judge's decision on this point can create a precedent for similar decisions in the future. There may also be issues of classification. The parties may accept that there is a rule of law under which a driver owes a duty to take care not to knock down a pedestrian, but they may dispute the issue of whether exceeding the speed limit constitutes 'careless' driving. The judge's decision on this point is of general significance, but is narrow in scope. It does create a precedent, but only in relation to pedestrians injured by speeding.

(b) Expressly or impliedly given by a judge

1.69 MacCormick rightly points out that the ruling which is derived from the case may not be based on the words used by the judge, particularly when there are several judges. In the first place, the ruling on a point of law may be implicit, not explicit. For example, in *Spencer v Harding*[114] an auctioneer issued a circular stating that they were selling stock by tender to be received on a particular day. The plaintiffs submitted the highest tender, but this was not accepted. Willes J stated:

> If the circular has gone on, 'and we undertake to sell to the highest bidder', the reward cases would have applied, and there would have been a good contract in respect of the persons. But the question is, whether there is here any offer to enter into a contract at all, or whether the circular amounts to anything more than a mere proclamation that the defendants are ready to chaffer for the sale of goods. . . Here there is a total absence of any words to intimate that the highest bidder is to be the purchaser. It is a mere attempt to ascertain whether an offer can be obtained within such a margin as the sellers are willing to adopt.

There is no clear formulation of a rule that, unless there is a specific undertaking to sell to the highest bidder, an invitation to tender is not an offer. Any lawyer reading the judgment has to take account of the issues raised in the case and to reconstruct what the judge said into a ruling that can form the basis of future decisions.

1.70 A case is only authority for the issues raised and those are identified by what Goodhart has described as the 'material facts'.[115] Any case relates to a whole series of facts. For example, in *Donoghue v Stevenson*,[116] one woman bought a drink of ginger beer for a friend in a cafe. The friend alleged that she suffered gastro-enteritis as a result of drinking some of it before she noticed a decomposed snail

---

[113] The judge's decisions on these questions of fact do bind the parties and cannot be contested again except by way of appeal. This is the doctrine of *res judicata*.

[114] (1870) LR 5 CP 561.

[115] A Goodhart, *Essays in Jurisprudence and the Common Law* (1931), ch 1.

[116] [1932] AC 562, HL.

that came out with the contents of the bottom of the bottle. Now, it did not matter that the cafe was in Paisley or that both the purchaser and the consumer of the drink were women. On the other hand, it did matter that the ginger beer bottle was opaque and not clear. As a result, neither the cafe owner, nor the purchaser, nor the ultimate consumer was able to spot the snail before the drink was partly consumed. This was the main reason why the manufacturer was held potentially liable, as is clear from Lord Atkin's formulation of the rule:

> a manufacturer of products, which he sells in such a form as to show that he intends them to reach the ultimate consumer in the form in which they left him with no possibility of intermediate examination, and with the knowledge that the absence of reasonable care in the preparation or putting up the products will result in an injury to the customer's life or property, owes a duty to the consumer to take that reasonable care.[117]

Now Lord Atkin himself is famed for the formulation of a different rule that recasts the facts in a different way:

> the rule that you are to love your neighbour becomes in law, you must not injure your neighbour; and the lawyer's question, Who is my neighbour? receives a restricted reply. You must take reasonable steps to avoid acts or omissions which you can reasonably foresee would be likely to injure your neighbour. Who then is my neighbour? The answer seems to be—persons who are so closely and directly affected by my act that I ought reasonably to have them in contemplation as being so affected when I am directing my mind to the acts or omissions which are called in question.[118]

Mrs Donoghue is here characterized as a 'consumer' or a 'neighbour' and the ginger beer becomes a 'product' or an 'act'. The discursive style of English judgments does not make it clear which of the formulations is the most important.

In one sense, the level of abstraction is set by what is necessary to decide the case. **1.71** MacCormick's formulation clearly points out that the binding legal ruling is related to the issues raised in the case. So, in *Donoghue*, it might be sufficient to say that the plaintiff was a consumer of a negligently manufactured product that was not capable of intermediate inspection or intervention before she suffered her alleged harm. But, any case also becomes re-interpreted over time as subsequent judges see how a particular decision fits into the rest of the law. For example, *Donoghue* was applied in a number of cases in the 1930s which did not fit the narrow formulation of the rule as one applying to manufacturers. In *Brown v Cotterill*[119] it was applied to a case in which a recently erected tombstone fell and injured a child playing in a churchyard, even though there was neither a 'product' nor a 'consumer'. It was then applied to a person injured by the faulty repair

---

[117] [1932] AC 562, 599.
[118] [1932] AC 562, 580.
[119] (1934) 51 TLR 21.

of a lift.[120] These subsequent applications broadened out the case to be closer to the principle encapsulated in the second quotation from Lord Atkin. On the other hand, there are other cases in which this broader formulation has been rejected as too wide. Thus, although it was foreseeable that a prostitute might be killed if the police carelessly failed to apprehend and detain the 'Yorkshire Ripper', the House of Lords held that the police owed no duty of care.[121] Similarly, in *Murphy v Brentwood*,[122] the House of Lords held that a local authority did not owe a duty of care to a subsequent purchaser to ensure builders constructed foundations in accordance with by-laws, even though it could foresee that such a person could suffer as a result.

1.72 MacCormick's quotation is careful not to equate the ruling in a case with what the judge said. A good illustration of this is the case of *Mutual Life v Evatt*.[123] The House of Lords had laid down in *Hedley Byrne v Heller*[124] that a person could commit the tort if they undertook to offer advice in circumstances in which they knew it would be relied upon and, in the words of Lords Reid and Morris, they failed to take 'such care as the circumstances require'. In the subsequent *Mutual Life* case, the majority of the Privy Council took the view that 'this passage should, in their Lordships' view, be understood as restricted to advisers who carry on the business or profession of giving advice of the kind sought'.[125] By contrast, the original authors of the passage under discussion dissented arguing 'We are unable to construe the passages from our speeches cited in the judgment of the majority in the way they are there construed.'[126] The case illustrates that a subsequent judge is not trying to divine the intention of the earlier judge, but simply trying to give the best interpretation of the rule stated by the earlier judge consistent with both the issues argued in the case and the general law of which it is part.

(c) Related to an issue raised by the arguments of the parties

1.73 Case law decision-making takes place in the context of a particular dispute. The judge is faced by the arguments of the parties and does not address issues generally in the same way as the legislator. The ruling that he makes provides an answer in the light of the arguments raised. Future cases may well raise issues that did not occur to the original judge. On the other hand, the judge does not simply justify the decision in relation to the facts of the case. The judge offers a reason that would be applicable in a generalized way to other such situations. But the

---

120 *Haseldine v Daw* [1941] 2 KB 343.
121 *Hill v Chief Constable of West Yorkshire* [1989] AC 53.
122 [1991] 1 AC 398.
123 [1971] AC 793: see J Stone, *Precedent and Law* (1980), ch 9.
124 [1964] AC 465.
125 Lord Diplock, [1971] AC 793 at 807.
126 Lords Reid and Morris, [1971] AC 793 at 813.

authority of a case is limited to the arguments raised.[127] It is this point which Goodhart addressed with his notion of 'material facts'.

(d) Which is necessary as a justification for the decision reached: *ratio* and *obiter*

English lawyers try to identify the ruling on a point of law which is necessary for   **1.74** the decision in the case, since this constitutes the binding part of the precedent. For this they draw a distinction between the *ratio decidendi* and a mere *obiter dictum* in the judgment. The *ratio decidendi* ('the reason for deciding') is that part of a decision which sets out the essential justification for the decision reached. Any other statement is an *obiter dictum* ('a statement made in passing'). All the same, it is important to recognize that there are significant differences in the weight which attaches to *obiter dicta*.

In some cases, there will be specific argument before the court on an issue. Even if   **1.75** a decision on this point is not necessary for the resolution of the case, out of deference to counsel, the court will make observations on the arguments made. Thus, in *Hedley Byrne v Heller*,[128] there was clear argument about the duty of care owed by the bank to the customer of the other bank. In the end, the customer lost because of a disclaimer issued by the bank tendering the advice. All the same, the House of Lords did make clear statements on the issue of the duty of care and these are treated effectively as the *ratio* of the case by subsequent judges. By contrast, where there has been little argument, then the statement is of less weight.

Even though they are only *obiter*, statements made by certain judges of great   **1.76** repute carry particular weight—Lords Reid, Wilberforce and Diplock, and earlier judges such as Lord Atkin and Scrutton LJ.

Long-standing opinions are less frequently overturned, even if they are not for-   **1.77** mally binding on a lower court. For instance, the doctrine of privity of contract was accepted in *Beswick v Beswick*,[129] even though it was not previously laid down by the House of Lords.

---

[127] For example, in *Saif Ali v Sydney Mitchell (a firm)* [1978] AC 198, the House of Lords invited counsel to offer arguments why it should overrule its precedent in *Rondel v Worsley* [1969] 1 AC 191 which established the immunity of a barrister from being sued for the conduct of a case in court. The parties declined and so the House was unable to review the issue. *Rondel v Worsley* [1969] 1 AC 191 was overruled in a later case: see para 1.90.

[128] [1964] AC 465.

[129] [1968] AC 58; but cf *R v R (Marital Rape Exemption)* [1992] 1 AC 599.

(4) Distinguishing

1.78 In interpreting precedents, judges frequently use the technique of 'distinguishing' when they expressly do not wish to follow a precedent. Distinguishing treats the precedent as legally irrelevant to the case at hand. Raz has helpfully identified different forms of distinguishing:[130]

> There is what I shall call 'the tame view' of distinguishing according to which to distinguish a binding precedent is simply to determine that its ratio does not apply to the instant case.... As against this, there is another view of distinguishing according to which one distinguishes a rule by changing it so that a rule which did apply to the present case no longer applies to it in its modified form... Distinguishing...is a very restricted form of law-making. It is subject to two crucial conditions:
>
> (1) The modified rule must be the rule laid down in the precedent restricted by the addition of a further condition for its application.
> (2) The modified rule must be such as to justify the order made in the precedent.

1.79 An illustration is *Blackpool and Fylde Aeroclub Ltd v Blackpool BC*[131] in which an invitation to tender to provide pleasure flights from an airfield was issued by the Council with a deadline of 12 noon. The plaintiff's tender letter was delivered by 11 am, but the postbox was not cleared by Council staff until after 12 noon, and so that tender was not considered by the Council, and the contract was awarded to someone else. In the precedent, *Spencer v Harding*,[132] it had held that there was no liability on the part of an auctioneer for rejecting the lowest tender, since the invitation to tender was merely an invitation to treat. The tender itself was the offer which the auctioneer was free to accept or not. In the *Blackpool* case, that decision was distinguished on the ground that the invitation to tender here amounted at least to an implied promise to consider tenders made in due time, even if not to award the concession to the lowest of them. Now, the rule stated by the Court of Common Pleas was that, in the absence of any words to show that the highest bidder was to be the purchaser, an invitation to tender 'is a mere attempt to ascertain whether an offer can be obtained within such a margin as the sellers are willing to adopt' and does not provide the basis for contractual liability. In *Blackpool*, the Court of Appeal qualifies this rule by adding a further condition that the tender, delivered on time, has been duly considered. Thus the new rule is that, in the absence of an express undertaking to accept such a tender, a person inviting tenders is not liable for refusing to accept the lowest tender, provided he

---

130 J Raz, *The Authority of Law* (1979), 185–6.
131 [1990] 1 WLR 1195.
132 See para 1.69.

has opened and considered the tender in conjunction with all other conforming tenders.[133]

(5) *The Rules of Precedent in Particular Courts*

(a) European Court of Justice

Precedent operates in two significant ways in the law of the European Union.   **1.80**
First, the ECJ itself respects its own previous decisions, though it is not bound by them. Secondly, lower courts ought to respect the judgments of the ECJ and this may justify them refusing to refer a case to the ECJ by application of the *acte clair* doctrine.

On the first point, it is clear that the ECJ does not always follow its previous deci-   **1.81**
sions. In line with many continental European courts, it does not always cite its own precedents nor make it clear when it is departing from them.[134] For example, in *Plaumann*,[135] the Court at first considered that an act of an EC institution had to be annulled before damages could be claimed for the loss caused by that unlawful act. In *Lütticke*,[136] it then held that an action for damages was an independent action and so a prior action for annulment was not required. It then appeared to revert to the *Plaumann* view before confirming *Lütticke* in *Merkur*.[137]

On the other hand, in *Da Costa en Schaake*, where no new arguments had been   **1.82**
presented, the previous judgment of the ECJ on almost identical facts was restated and the parties were referred to it.[138] The Court stated that, although art 177 EEC (now art 234) appeared to create an unreserved obligation on national courts to refer questions of Community law to the ECJ, 'the authority of an interpretation under Article 177 already given by the Court may deprive the obligation of its purpose and thus empty it of its substance. Such is the case especially when the question raised is materially identical with a question which has already been the subject of a preliminary ruling in a similar case'. It developed the point in *CILFIT*[139] in which it commented that national courts need not refer matters to the ECJ 'where previous decisions of the Court have already dealt with the point of law in question, irrespective of the proceedings which led to those decisions, even though the questions at issue are not identical'. The Court thereby in effect

---

[133] Bingham LJ, [1990] 1 WLR 1195 at 1202.
[134] See Brown and Jacobs, *The European Court of Justice* (4th revised edn by LN Brown and T Kennedy, 1994) ch 16.
[135] Case 25/62, [1963] ECR 95.
[136] Case 4/69, [1971] ECR 325.
[137] Case 43/72, *Merkur* [1973] ECR 1055; cf Case 96/71 *Haegman* [1972] ECR 1005.
[138] Cases 28–30/62, *Da Costa en Schaake NV et al v Nederlandse Belastingsadministratie* [1963] ECR 31.
[139] Case 283/81, *Srl CILFIT v Ministry of Health* [1982] ECR 3415.

initiated a system of precedent by declaring that its own decisions should be treated as authoritative. As a result of *CILFIT*, an English court has to treat as a precedent a decision rendered by the ECJ in relation to a case concerning another member state.[140]

(b) House of Lords

(i) *Lower courts are bound*

1.83 Because the House of Lords is the highest court in the English legal system, lower courts must follow its decisions. The House of Lords reiterated this in two decisions in the 1970s, *Cassell v Broome*[141] and *Miliangos v George Frank (Textiles) Ltd*.[142] In the second decision, a precedent[143] had laid down that English courts could not give judgments in foreign currency. The House of Lords agreed with the Court of Appeal that this decision should be overruled as inappropriate in contemporary circumstances. Nevertheless, it stated that the Court of Appeal had no authority to decide that a precedent of the House of Lords was out of date. It should have simply applied the precedent and given leave to appeal to the House of Lords.

1.84 That obligation on lower courts is subject to two exceptions. The first of these is that a decision *per incuriam* is not binding. Lord Donaldson MR explained that:

> the doctrine of per incuriam only applies where. . .[the court] has reached a decision in the absence of knowledge of a decision binding on it or a statute, and that in either case it must be shown that, had the court had this material, it *must* have reached a contrary decision. That is per incuriam. I do not understand the doctrine to extend to a case where, if different arguments had been placed before it, it *might* have reached a different conclusion.[144]

For example, in *IM Properties plc v Cape & Dalgleish (a firm)*,[145] the Court of Appeal refused to follow the House of Lords in *Westdeutsche Landesbank Girozentrale v Islington London BC*.[146] In that case, the House of Lords had awarded interest on a debt owed under s 35A of the Supreme Court Act 1981

---

140 See especially Case 66/80, *International Chemical Corporation v Amministrazione delle Finanze dello Stato* [1981] ECR 1191 on the duty of national courts in respect of the annulment of the acts of Community institutions. The *acte clair* doctrine takes this idea one step further by allowing national courts to refuse to refer a matter to the ECJ where 'the correct application of Community law may be so obvious as to leave no scope for any reasonable doubt as to the manner in which the question raised is to be resolved' (*CILFIT*, n 139 above).
141 [1972] AC 1027.
142 [1976] AC 433, commenting on [1975] QB 487 (CA).
143 *Re United Railways of Havana* [1961] AC 1007.
144 *Duke v Reliance Systems Ltd* [1988] AC 618.
145 [1999] QB 297, CA.
146 [1996] AC 669.

contrary to its precedent in *President of India v La Pintada Cia Navegacion SA*[147] and without argument on the point. The second is where there are two conflicting decisions. For example, in *Moodie v IRC*,[148] the House was faced with two inconsistent precedents of its own. A decision had been reached without argument in the first and a different decision had been reached after argument in the second. In *Moodie*, the House preferred to follow the more reasoned argument in the second case. In an exceptional case, the Court of Appeal in *R v James and Karimi*[149] extended this category by following a more recent decision of the Privy Council rather than a precedent of the House of Lords. But this arose only where the Privy Council was seeking deliberately to clarify English law, its members constituted half the Appellate Committee of the House of Lords, and, as a result, the outcome of an appeal to the House of Lords was a foregone conclusion.

(ii) When will the House of Lords overrule itself?

As regards the House of Lords itself, a rule was established in the course of the nineteenth century that the House was bound by its own previous decisions.[150] But this was altered by the *Practice Statement (Judicial Precedent)*[151] in which the members of the House of Lords declared: **1.85**

> Their Lordships recognise. . .that too rigid adherence to precedent may lead to injustice in a particular case and also unduly restrict the proper development of the law. They propose to modify their present practice and, while treating former decisions. . .as normally binding, to depart from a previous decision when it appears right to do so.
>
> In this connection, they will bear in mind the danger of disturbing retrospectively the basis on which contracts, settlements of property and fiscal arrangements have been entered into and also the especial need for certainty as to the criminal law.

The House of Lords implied here that it would only rarely overrule its previous decisions. Certainly, in the early years after this statement, there were few instances of explicit overruling and in most cases, their Lordships undermined the authority of the precedent by distinguishing.[152]

In an exhaustive study of the House of Lords and the Australian High Court, Harris[153] identified a number of criteria. The principal arguments in favour of overruling can be said to be the necessity to overrule to reach an appropriate **1.86**

---

[147] [1985] AC 104.
[148] [1993] 1 WLR 266, HL.
[149] [2006] EWCA Crim 14, esp. paras 43 and 44.
[150] See *Beamish v Beamish* (1861) 9 HLC 274; *London Street Tramways v London County Council* [1898] AC 735; but compare *Bright v Hutton* (1852) 3 HLC 341.
[151] [1966] 1 WLR 1234.
[152] Eg *Conway v Rimmer* [1968] AC 910.
[153] JW Harris, 'Towards Principles of Overruling—When Should a Final Court of Appeal Second Guess?' (1990) 10 OJLS 135. See also A Paterson, *The Law Lords* (1982), 146–83.

decision in the instant case, the injustice of the precedent, and its incoherence with the rest of the law.

1.87 A major concern is the necessity to overrule a precedent to reach a decision in a case. A good example is provided by the disquiet which the House of Lords felt over *Anns v Merton LBC*[154] for many years. In a number of cases in the mid-1980s, members of the House distanced themselves from the reasoning in *Anns* concerning the scope of the tort of negligence.[155] But they did not try to overrule that case because this was not necessary for the decisions in the cases before them. When, in *Murphy v Brentwood DC*[156] a case presented itself when overruling was necessary for the outcome of the case, then they did overrule *Anns*. In most cases, it will only be necessary to consider overruling where new arguments are raised which were not presented in the previous case.[157]

1.88 The argument about injustice is well flagged in the *Practice Statement* itself. The case of *Miliangos v George Frank*[158] is a clear application of this principle, as injustice to the plaintiff caused by the decline in the value of the currency was the principal reason for the House of Lords decision. This point needs relating to a similar argument that the policy of the legislature has been misinterpreted by a precedent. In *R v Shivpuri*,[159] the speed with which the House of Lords overruled its precedent in *Anderton v Ryan*[160] came from a recognition that this decision had misunderstood the purpose of the legislation in question, as was made clear from the Law Commission report giving rise to the Act, which had not been cited in *Anderton*. Clearly unjust results following from the previous decision will justify the House of Lords overruling itself. In *R v G*,[161] the definition of 'recklessness' set out in *R v Caldwell*[162] led to the conviction for arson of boys of 11 and 12, who had not appreciated the likely consequences of their actions. This unfair result, combined with criticism from academics, judges and practitioners, justified overruling the previous test.

1.89 The *Practice Statement* suggests that criminal law needs especial certainty. To be sure, legal certainty may sometimes justify the House of Lords refusing to overrule

---

154 [1978] AC 728.

155 See *Leigh & Sillavan Ltd v Aliakmon Shipping Co Ltd* [1986] AC 785; *Peabody Donation Foundation (Governors) v Sir Lindsay Parkinson& Co Ltd* [1985] AC 210.

156 [1991] 1 AC 398.

157 See *Fitzleet v Cherry* [1977] 3 All ER 996 and *The Hannah Blumethal* [1983] 1 AC 854.

158 [1976] AC 443. See also *Vestey v IRC* [1980] AC 1148, *R v Howe* [1987] AC 417.

159 [1987] AC 1.

160 [1985] AC 560.

161 [2003] UKHL 50; [2004] 1 AC 1034.

162 [1982] AC 341.

a previous decision which it considers to have been wrongly decided.[163] By contrast, the House of Lords did overrule decisions in *R v Shivpuri* and *R v Howe*.[164] Given that few criminals will plan their lives on the basis of what the courts have decided, the House of Lords will rarely be dissuaded from coming to the decision which it considers most appropriate.

Among the constraints are the attitude of Parliament to law reform in a particular **1.90** area. This is well illustrated by *President of India v La Pintada*.[165] The House of Lords had decided (with regret) that the rule that courts could not award interest on debts was an established feature of the common law. Although the Law Commission had proposed a change in this rule, Parliament had failed to take the opportunity of the Supreme Court Act 1981 in order to change the law, and so the courts should not alter it. On the other hand, inaction by Parliament may simply indicate that it is content for the law to be changed by judicial decision. The House of Lords took this view in *Arthur J S Hall & Co (A Firm) v Simons*[166] in which it abolished the immunity of an advocate from being sued for the conduct of a case in court which was laid down in *Rondel v Worsley*.[167] The House of Lords considered that contemporary public policy no longer justified the immunity.

(c) The Court of Appeal

The Court of Appeal takes different approaches with regard to its Civil and **1.91** Criminal Divisions, and this is based mainly on the different roles they play and the seriousness of the issue of individual liberty in criminal matters.

(i) Civil Division

In broad terms, the Civil Division is bound by its own previous decisions. As was **1.92** stated in *Young v Bristol Aeroplane Ltd*:[168]

> If the Court of Appeal. . .has in a previous case pronounced on a point of law which necessarily covers a later case coming before the Court, the previous decision must be

---

[163] *R v Kansal* [2001] UKHL 62; [2002] 2 AC 69, refusing to overrule *R v Lambert* [2001] UKHL 37; [2002] 2 AC 545.

[164] [1987] AC 1 and [1987] AC 417 respectively. Similarly, the Privy Council overruled recent previous and fully-argued decisions on the implications of fundamental rights for death penalty cases in *Lewis v A-G for Jamaica* [2001] 2 AC 50. Lord Slynn at ibid 75 stated that legal certainty had to be balanced against the importance of saving someone's life.

[165] [1985] AC 104; cf *British Railways Board v Herrington* [1972] AC 877 where Parliament's inaction did not evidence a rejection of the need to change the law.

[166] [2002] 1 AC 615.

[167] [1969] 1 AC 191. Because it considered that *Rondel v Worsley* was correctly decided at the time, the House of Lords did not make use of the *Practice Statement*.

[168] [1944] KB 718; [1946] AC 163 at 169 confirmed by the House of Lords in *Davis v Johnson* [1979] AC 264.

followed (unless, of course, it was given *per incuriam*, or unless the House of Lords has in the meantime decided that the law is otherwise). ...

1.93 The principal justification is that there is always an appeal to the House of Lords and the number of divisions sitting at once is such that there is a real chance of confusion of case law for the lower courts and hence the litigants.

1.94 The rule in *Young* accepts three main exceptions to which a further two can be added. As with the House of Lords, where there are conflicting decisions, then a later court obviously has to choose between them.[169] Where a decision is inconsistent with a decision of a superior court, the House of Lords or the European Court of Justice, then the Court of Appeal must follow the decision of the higher court and not its own precedent.[170] To this might be added that the Court of Appeal may also follow the Privy Council rather than its own inconsistent precedent.[171] The third exception, that the decision was *per incuriam*, has been mentioned in relation to the House of Lords.[172]

1.95 Two further exceptions are worth noting. In the first place, where a decision is interlocutory and will have been decided by a smaller formation of the Court this is not treated as binding on a Court of Appeal hearing a substantive appeal.[173] The second exception is where the kind of case is unlikely to be appealed to the House of Lords, for example because it is a ruling on a committal order or an order to refuse leave. This exception is allowed, provided the previous decision is manifestly wrong.[174] A possible third exception links the Civil Division with the Criminal Division. Where the liberty of the subject is at stake, for example in an application for judicial review concerning a mental patient or in a habeas corpus case, then the arguments which lead the Criminal Division to refuse to follow its own precedents apply with similar force in the Civil Division.[175]

---

169 Eg *Fisher v Ruislip-Northwood UDC* [1945] KB 584.

170 See *Miliangos v George Frank* [1976] AC 43, cf the attitude of the Court of Appeal [1975] QB 487. A good example is *Pickstone v Freemans plc* [1989] AC 66. The potential for confusion arising from the failure of the Court of Appeal to refer to the *Young* principles in *Great Peace Shipping Ltd v Tsavliris Salvage Ltd* [2002] EWCA Civ 1407; [2003] QB 679 at [157] is noted by SB Midwinter, 'The *Great Peace* and Precedent' (2003) 119 LQR 180.

171 See para 98.

172 For example, where one Court of Appeal failed to take account of a section in a statute, then a subsequent Court of Appeal was entitled to refuse to follow that erroneous approach which had led to misapplying the statute: *Dixon v BBC* [1979] QB 546 refusing to follow *BBC v Ioannu* [1975] ICR 276.

173 *Boys v Chaplin* [1968] 2 QB 1.

174 *Williams v Fawcett* [1986] QB 604; *Rickards v Rickards* [1990] Fam 194, CA, (appeal on refusal of extension of time by a County Court judge where the decision involved 'a manifest slip or error').

175 *R v Parole Board, ex p Wilson* [1992] QB 740 at 754–6 *per* Taylor LJ.

(ii) Criminal Division

The Criminal Division is concerned with matters which directly affect the liberty **1.96** of the subject. Given that the state has to justify a person's detention, it would seem strange for a court to argue that the individual should be kept in jail on the basis of a precedent which the court itself thought was wrong. This is especially important since the House of Lords deals with only one or two criminal cases in a typical year. For these reasons, the Court of Appeal in its Criminal Division holds that it will depart from its previous decisions in appropriate cases. Lord Goddard CJ laid down the principle in *R v Taylor*:[176]

> This court has to deal with questions involving the liberty of the subject, and if it finds, on reconsideration that, in the opinion of a full court assembled for the purpose, the law has been either misapplied or misunderstood in a decision which it has previously given, and that, on the strength of that decision, an accused person has been sentenced or imprisoned it is the bounden duty of the court to reconsider the earlier decision with a view to seeing whether that person has been properly convicted.

This statement refers to cases in which the Court of Appeal has laid down an interpretation of the law. It has been made clear that this is only a very limited departure from the basic approach laid down in *Young v Bristol Aeroplane* in order to protect the liberty of the subject.[177] The Criminal Division of the Court of Appeal exercises a degree of discretion to decide whether a previous decision should be treated as a binding precedent in future or not when there are grounds for saying that the decision is wrong. This discretion applies not only when overruling the precedent will benefit the accused, but also when it would deprive the accused of a purely technical defence.[178] It has no application to matters of sentencing, though the 'guidelines' laid down by the Court are to be respected by the lower courts. In individual cases, where a conviction is unsafe, the Court of Appeal may be asked to reconsider a case it has considered before.[179] But this again has nothing to do with precedent.

(d) Divisional Court and High Court

The High Court is a court of first instance in which judges sit on their own. **1.97** It does not seem sensible for one High Court judge to be bound by decisions of predecessors. The position of the Divisional Court used to be different, but in *R v Greater Manchester Coroner, ex p Tal*,[180] it decided that it would apply the same

---

[176] [1950] 2 KB 368.

[177] See May LJ, *R v Spencer* [1985] QB 771 at 778–9. In that the Court of Appeal did refuse to follow its own precedent in *R v Bagshaw* [1984] 1 WLR 477 which conflicted with a previous decision of the same court.

[178] *R v Simpson* [2003] EWCA Crim 1499; [2004] QB 118 *per* Lord Woolf CJ at [38].

[179] Criminal Appeal Act 1968, s 2 (as amended by the Criminal Appeal Act 1995).

[180] [1985] QB 67 at 79–81.

rule as the High Court, namely that it would follow the decision of another judge unless convinced it was wrong.

(e) Privy Council

1.98   The Privy Council is only rarely a court for the United Kingdom, for example in relation to certain professional disciplinary matters, though it has significant constitutional functions under the devolution legislation.[181] Where it is outside the English court hierarchy, its decisions do not bind English courts. All the same, because its members are typically also members of the House of Lords, they are given high regard. Thus the decision of the Privy Council in *The Wagon Mound*[182] justified the Court of Appeal departing from rules on remoteness of damage laid down in its own decision in *Re Polemis*.[183] As noted in para 1.84, the Privy Council may have significant authority when deliberately laying down rules applicable to English law.

1.99   The Privy Council itself is not bound by decisions of English courts, unless it is applying English law. In other cases, it is free to depart from a House of Lords decision.[184] The Privy Council has made it clear that other jurisdictions may quite properly develop the common law on different lines from England.[185] As a result, the authority of Privy Council decisions for English courts will depend on whether it is laying down principles which purport to be drawn from English law or not.

E. Influential Sources of Law

1.100   English law recognizes a number of sources of legal argument which are not formally binding, but help to shape the law.

(1) Treaties

1.101   The courts seek to interpret statutes to be as compatible as possible with the treaty obligations of the United Kingdom.[186] In this way, though not binding sources of law, the treaties are influential in the development of domestic law.[187]

---

181 These functions will pass to the Supreme Court when it is created under the Constitutional Reform Act 2005.

182 [1961] AC 388.

183 *Worcester Works Finance v Gooden Engineering* [1972] 1 QB 210 at 217.

184 Lord Scarman, *Tai Hing Cotton v Liu Chong Bank* [1986] AC 80 at 108: see generally, JW Harris, 'The Privy Council and the Common Law' (1990) 106 LQR 574.

185 *A-G for Hong Kong v Reid* [1994] 1 AC 324 at 338; *Invercargill City Council v Hamlin* [1996] AC 624.

186 *R v Home Secretary, ex p Brind* [1991] AC 696 at 718 and 748.

187 See eg the cases cited at n 14 above.

(2) Doctrinal Legal Writing

Lord Goff explained the judiciary dominates the development of English law on the ground that 'it is important that the dominant element in the development of the law should be professional reaction to individual fact-situation rather than theoretical development of legal principles. Pragmatism must be the watchword.'[188] For him, the judicial role is to decide cases, whereas the jurist's principal role is to formulate legal principle. The danger of principle lies in an over-emphasis on elegance, the fallacy that it offers a complete solution, and that it neglects the historical origins of the law. On the whole, the law is untidy, complex and developed pragmatically in historical circumstances.[189] All the same, Goff notes that 'the work of the judges has become more and more influenced by the teaching and writing of jurists'.[190] In addition, it has to be recognized that judges, such as Lord Goff, are themselves significant legal authors whose academic writings have shaped their subject. Doctrinal legal writing is now a major influence on legal development.

1.102

The reports of the Law Commission constitute a significant source of influence, connected to doctrinal legal writing. These include both scholarly surveys of the existing law and recommendations for change made following consultation among practitioners, the public and academics. The serious process of deliberation gives weight to its proposals and courts frequently refer to them.[191]

1.103

---

[188] R Goff, 'The Search for Principle' (1983) LXIX Proceedings of the British Academy 169, 184–5.

[189] ibid 174–5.

[190] ibid 182; see also P Birks, 'The Academic and the Practitioner' (1998) 18 LS 397.

[191] For example, see *Kleinwort Benson Ltd v Lincoln City Council* [1999] 1 AC 153; *White v Chief Constable of South Yorkshire* [1998] 3 WLR 1509; *Air Jamaica Ltd v Charlton* [1999] 1 WLR 1399; *Yaxley v Gotts* [1999] 3 WLR 1217, 1232.

Part II

THE LAW OF PERSONS

2

FAMILY

A. The Creation of Legal Family Relationships

Legal consequences automatically attach to certain family relationships, notably **2.01** birth, legal adoption, marriage, and civil partnership. In recent years there has developed a tendency to attach similar legal consequences to the relationship (often referred to as 'cohabitation') between a couple who have lived in the same household 'as husband and wife' or 'as civil partners'.[1]

---

[1] See eg Inheritance Provision for Family and Dependants Act 1975, as amended by Civil Partnership Act 2004, sch 4, para 15.

49

(1) Birth

(a) Legal parentage[2]

2.02 English law does not accord legal personality to the unborn child; and the legal consequences of the parent-child relationship do not arise until the child's birth.[3]

2.03 A child's parents were, at common law, the individuals who provided the gametes which resulted in conception and birth. Until comparatively recently there were no reliable means of identifying those persons who had provided the gametes[4] and the law relied heavily on presumptions, but the development of DNA testing and other scientific techniques for ascertaining parentage have made it unusual for reliance now to be placed on presumptions in contested litigation.[5] However, the presumptions remain of some value for everyday purposes when questions of parentage are often settled without any application to the court.

2.04 These presumptions are as follows. First, the common law presumed that a child born or conceived during the parents' marriage was their legitimate child; and this necessarily involves a presumption[6] that the husband of a woman who bears a child during the marriage is the father of that child. Secondly, statute now establishes a presumption that the man whose name is entered as such in the Register of Births is the child's father.[7] Thirdly, a presumption of paternity also follows from findings[8] made in certain legal proceedings.[9] Today the scientific evidence

---

[2] See the analysis of the concepts of natural legal and psychological parentage by Baroness Hale in *Re G (Children)* [2006] UKHL 43; [2006] 1 WLR 2305.

[3] *Paton v British Pregnancy Advisory Service Trustees* [1979] QB 276; compare *A-G's Reference (No 3 of 1994)* [1998] AC 245, HL.

[4] Although it was said that motherhood was a biological fact proved demonstrably by parturition: *The Ampthill Peerage* [1977] AC 457, 577, *per* Lord Simon of Glaisdale.

[5] '. . .the paternity of any child is to be established by science and not by legal presumption': *Re H and A (Children)* [2002] EWCA Civ 383 at [30], *per* Thorpe LJ.

[6] Family Law Reform Act 1969, s 26, provides that this presumption may be rebutted on a balance of probabilities; see *S v McC (orse D) and M (DS intervener)* [1972] AC 24, HL; *W v K (Proof of Paternity)* [1988] 1 FLR 86.

[7] *Brierley v Brierley and Williams* [1918] P 257; Births and Deaths Registration Act 1953, s 34(6). The legislation currently restricts the circumstances in which a father's name can be entered on the register (see Births and Deaths Registration Act 1953, s 10, as amended by Children Act 1989, sch 12, para 6) but in December 2006 the government announced its intention to legislate to require the names of both parents to be registered 'unless it would be unreasonable to do so'. However, 'robust safeguards' are first to be put in place 'to protect the welfare of children and vulnerable children': see *A New System of Child Maintenance* Cm 6979; *Joint Birth Registration* Cm 7160.

[8] See *R v Secretary of State for Social Security, ex p West* [1999] 1 FLR 1223, CA.

[9] Civil Evidence Act 1968, as amended by Courts and Legal Services Act 1990, sch 16, para 2. A declaration of parentage under the Family Law Act 1986, s 58(2) can only be controverted in the most exceptional circumstances: *The Ampthill Peerage* [1977] AC 457, HL.

now available from analysis of blood or other samples will often rebut these presumptions.[10]

The common law drew a sharp distinction between the 'legitimate' child—that is **2.05** to say the child born or conceived at a time when the parents were married—and the 'illegitimate' child, treated in law as *filius nullius*, nobody's child, and often referred to as a 'bastard'. The social stigma of illegitimacy was reinforced by legal disadvantage: the illegitimate child had no legal right to financial support or to succeed as his parents' child to property, whilst statutory references to relationships were deemed to be confined to legitimate relationships. Today, the legal consequences of illegitimacy have been largely removed: statutes culminating in the Family Law Reform Act 1987 have eroded the legal disadvantages[11] flowing from illegitimate birth; and it will now only rarely be necessary to decide whether a child is in law legitimate or not.[12] Perhaps the most significant legal consequence of illegitimacy to survive the 1987 reforms is that, whilst the mother has 'parental responsibility' for her child irrespective of her marital status, the father does not have parental responsibility for the child unless and until he acquires it under procedures laid down by statute (ie where the father has registered the birth jointly with the mother[13] or where he has entered into a parental responsibility agreement[14] or where the court has made a parental responsibility order).[15]

---

[10] See para 2.09. Such evidence will outweigh the presumption that a married woman's husband is the father of her child (see *F v Child Support Agency* [1999] 2 FLR 244) and the presumption that the man registered on the child's birth certificate is the child's father: *Secretary of State for Work and Pensions v Jones* [2003] EWHC 2163.

[11] The 1987 Act does not operate retrospectively so that although a child whose parents were not married may succeed to property as the 'heir': Family Law Reform Act 1987, s 19(2) the right to succeed to a peerage has traditionally been confined to those 'lawfully begotten'. So far as entitlement to British Citizenship is concerned, the Nationality, Immigration and Asylum Act 2002, s 9, redefines the terms 'mother' and 'father' to allow the 'illegitimate' child to derive British citizenship through the father in the same way as if the child were born legitimate; but this change only applies to children born on or after 1 July 2006.

[12] The Family Law Reform Act 1987 seeks to avoid the use of the terms 'legitimate' and 'illegitimate' by referring instead to children whose parents 'were married to each other at the time of the child's birth'. However, this expression is given an extended meaning, and—in an apparent attempt to preserve for the legitimate any advantages still attached to that status,—the Act (s 1) in effect deems: (a) children legitimated by the parents' subsequent marriage; (b) children of a void marriage entitled to be treated as legitimate under the Legitimacy Act 1976; (c) adopted children; and (d) other children entitled by law to be treated as legitimate to be the offspring of parents who were married to each other at the time of the birth, even if they were in fact both unmarried at that time; and, consistently with this approach, the expression 'unmarried father' is often used to describe the father of an illegitimate child. In *Re R (Surname: Using Both Parents)* [2001] EWCA Civ 1344 Hale LJ criticized the use of the term 'illegitimate' in the title of a reported case, but the need for accuracy in legal writing may sometimes make it impossible to avoid use of the traditional legal terminology.

[13] Children Act 1989, s 4(1)(a) as substituted by Adoption and Children Act 2002, s 111.

[14] Children Act 1989, s 4(1)(b); see para 2.162.

[15] Children Act 1989, s 4(1)(a); see para 2.162.

(b) Human assisted reproduction and its implications for the determination of parentage

2.06 Artificial insemination[16] of the infertile by a donor began to be commonly practised in the second half of the twentieth century; and the continued validity of the common law rule (which attributed paternity of a child conceived by such artificial insemination to the sperm donor)[17] was increasingly questioned. The practice of surrogate parenting[18] and the development of scientific techniques permitting the creation of live human embryos outside the human body further complicated the issues. There seemed to be an increasing number of cases in which those who had arranged for the child to be conceived and carried to birth were not those who had provided the gametes used in the embryo's creation; while the development of DNA testing (providing virtually conclusive evidence of a child's genetic parentage) added force to the view that it was desirable to provide greater legal recognition to the position of those who had intended to bring a child into existence and care for it. A Committee of Enquiry chaired by Dame Mary Warnock considered the whole range of issues in detail; and the Human Fertilisation and Embryology Act 1990 was the legislative outcome.

2.07 The Act makes detailed provision about the persons who are to be treated in law as the parents of a child; and in the result:

(1) the woman who bears a child will, at the child's birth, always be regarded as the child's legal mother;[19]

(2) the father of a child is in principle the person who provides the sperm which results in conception.[20]

2.08 The principle that the person providing the sperm is the child's legal father is subject to two important exceptions:

(1) the husband of a woman[21] who is artificially inseminated (or had been implanted with an embryo not created from the husband's sperm) will be treated

---

[16] ie 'manual introduction of sperm into the cervix', *per* Bracewell J, *Re B (Parentage)* [1996] 2 FLR 15, 21.

[17] See para 2.03.

[18] ie the situation in which a woman carries a child under an agreement that she will hand it over to others who will thereafter assume the parental role: see *Re P (Minors)(Wardship: Surrogacy)* [1987] 2 FLR 421, *per* Sir J Arnold P; Surrogacy Arrangements Act 1985, s 1(2).

[19] Human Fertilisation and Embryology Act 1990, s 27, a provision in terms only applicable to cases where a woman carries a child 'as a result of the placing in her of an embryo or of sperm and eggs' (ie to cases where artificial conception techniques have been used); but the application of the common law principle stated in *The Ampthill Peerage* [1977] AC 457, para 2.04, leads to the same outcome in other cases.

[20] *Re Q (Parental Order)* [1996] 1 FLR 369, 370, *per* Johnson J; *Re B (Parentage)* [1996] 2 FLR 15, 21, *per* Bracewell J.

[21] This principle has not been extended to civil partners, but the government has announced its intention of introducing legislation to achieve this result: see *Review of the Human Fertilisation and Embryology Act*, (2006) Cm 6989.

as the father of a child, unless it is proved that he did not consent to the treatment;[22] and

(2) a similar principle applies to an unmarried couple[23] where sperm has been used in the course of 'treatment services'[24] provided for a man and woman together[25] under the licensing regime established by the 1990 Act.[26]

(c) Obtaining scientific evidence of parentage

The development of DNA profiling enables genetic parenthood to be established **2.09** as a matter of virtual certainty provided that the necessary samples of blood (or other bodily fluid or tissue) are available. The Family Law Act 1969[27] empowers the court to give a direction for the use of tests and the taking of the necessary samples in any civil proceedings in which the parentage of a person falls to be determined. Although it is specifically provided that samples are in general not to be taken save with consent,[28] the court may draw such inferences as appear proper in the circumstances from a failure to comply with a test direction; and it has been held[29] that unless a man accused of paternity could give very clear and cogent reasons for his refusal to comply, the inference that he was in truth the father would be virtually inescapable.

(2) Adoption

(a) Nature of adoption in English law

Legal adoption (as distinct from private arrangements which might colloquially **2.10** be described as 'adoption' but which had no direct affect on the child's legal status) was introduced into English law by the Adoption Act 1926, and since then it has

---

[22] Human Fertilisation and Embryology Act 1990, s 28(2). The meaning of 'consent' is discussed in *Leeds Teaching Hospitals NHS v A* [2003] EWHC 259; [2003] 1 FLR 1091 (man who consented to mother being impregnated with his sperm did not consent to her being impregnated with sperm of a third party.

[23] See note 12.
Human Fertilisation and Embryology Act 1990, s 28(2).

[24] The meaning of this expression has been considered in *Re D (a child appearing by her guardian ad litem)* [2005] UKHL 33; [2005] 2 AC 621.

[25] See *R v Human Fertilisation and Embryology Authority, ex p Blood* [1997] 2 FLR 742; *Re D (a child appearing by her guardian ad litem)* [2005] UKHL 33; [2005] 2 AC 621 (necessity for 'joint enterprise'); *Leeds Teaching Hospitals NHS v A* [2003] EWHC 259.

[26] ibid, s 28(3).

[27] s 20.

[28] Family Law Act 1969, s 21. Samples may be taken from a person under 16 if the person with care and control consents: s 21(3); and see *Re R (Blood Test: Constraint)* [1998] 1 FLR 745. In other cases the court may consent on the child's behalf; but will not do so if this would be against the child's interests. It is now generally accepted that it is best for the truth to be established: *Re H and A (Children)*[2002] EWCA 383; *Blunkett v Quinn* [2004] EWCA 2816.

[29] *Re A (A Minor) (Paternity: Refusal of Blood Test)* [1994] 2 FLR 463, 473, CA.

been a fundamental principle—reflecting the importance of the fact that adoption effects a complete and permanent transfer of legal parentage[30]—that only a court can make an adoption order.[31] However, it has increasingly been recognized that decisions about the desirability of adoption should usually depend on skilled social work assessments: in principle only an 'adoption agency'[32]—in practice usually a local authority—may make arrangements for adoption or place a child for adoption.[33] In practice, the decision about matching a child who needs adoption with suitable adoptive parents will be made by the agency and not by the court:[34] and it is adoption agencies who not only take the leading role in making decisions on placing children and assessing what is likely best to serve their welfare but also in dealing with other issues (for example, making arrangements in appropriate cases for an adult who had been adopted to trace his or her birth relatives). Moreover, adoption has increasingly been seen as one of the techniques[35] to be considered in securing the welfare of children in need[36] who for that reason have come to be looked after by the local authority.[37] The Adoption and Children Act 2002 introduced many reforms of the adoption process, comprehensively restates the law, and provides the structure governing the relationship between the courts (which retain their role of ultimate decision taker) and others professionally concerned with adoption.

(b) Eligibility to adopt and to be adopted

2.11 It remains a fundamental principle of English law that adoption is concerned with providing for a child the social and psychological benefits of belonging to a family unit;[38] and (in contrast to some foreign systems) adoption is not to be seen as an institution primarily concerned with regulating or adjusting succession

---

[30] At one time, it was axiomatic that there should be no provision for contact between the child and his birth relatives after an adoption order had been made, but the Adoption and Children Act 2002 recognizes that in some cases continued contact may be desirable: see Adoption and Children Act 2002, s 46(6) (the court must, before making an adoption order, consider whether there should be arrangements for allowing any person contact with the child) and further para 2.22.

[31] A private agreement purporting to transfer parentage to another person would have been void at common law and is now invalid by reason of the provisions of Children Act 1989, s 2(9) debarring a person from surrendering or transferring parental responsibility to another.

[32] Defined by the Adoption and Children Act 2002, s 2(1) as a local authority or a voluntary society registered under the Care Standards Act 2000 (and accordingly subject to the regulatory provisions of the Adoption Agencies Regulations 2005 (SI 389)).

[33] Adoption and Children Act 2002, ss 92–97 Certain family members are excluded from this general prohibition: Adoption and Children Act 2002, s 92(4).

[34] *Re R (Care: Plan for adoption: Best Interests)* [2006] 1 FLR 483.

[35] Adoption and Children Act 2002, s 1(6) specifically provides that a court or adoption agency must always consider the whole range of powers available to it in the child's case. The court's powers include the power to make a residence or other order under the Children Act 1989.

[36] See Children Act 1989, s 17(10).

[37] Children Act 1989, s 22(1).

[38] *Re R (Adoption)* [1967] 1 WLR 34, 41, *per* Buckley J.

rights or other legal incidents of family relationship.[39] Accordingly, an adoption order can only be made in respect of a person who has not attained the age of 19 years[40] and who has never married[41] or contracted a civil partnership.[42]

An adoption order may be made in favour of a couple or a single person.[43] 'Couple' is widely defined[44] to mean spouses, civil partners, and two persons (provided they are living together in 'an enduring family relationship') whether of the same or different sexes. However, there are restrictions[45] on the circumstances in which an adoption order can be made in favour of only one of two spouses or civil partners.   **2.12**

Although the Adoption and Children Act 2002 provides that in reaching any decision relating to an adoption of a child, the paramount consideration for the court and for the agency is the child's welfare,[46] the law continues to recognize that parents have in principle the right to prevent their child from being adopted. But whereas before the coming into force of the 2002 Act the court could only dispense with parental consent in restricted circumstances the court now has power to dispense if the welfare of the child so requires.[47]   **2.13**

(c) The adoption process

Under the Adoption Act 1926 the court would not normally be involved in the adoption process until it had to determine the application for an adoption order;   **2.14**

---

[39] For example, citizenship rights: *Re K (A Minor) (Adoption Order: Nationality)* [1995] Fam 38, CA; *Re B (A Minor) (Adoption Order: Nationality)* [1999] 2 AC 136, HL.

[40] Adoption and Children Act 2002, s 47(9). This provision seems to be intended to allow for cases in which the proceedings are only started shortly before the child's eighteenth birthday (see eg *Re D (A Minor)(Adoption Order: Validity)* [1991] 2 FLR 66) since the application for an order must be made before that date: Adoption and Children Act 2002, s 49(4).

[41] Adoption and Children Act 2002, s 47(8).

[42] Adoption and Children Act 2002, s 47(8A) as inserted by Civil Partnership Act 2004, s 79(3).

[43] Adoption and Children Act 2002, s 49 (1). One or both applicants must be domiciled in part of the British Islands, and all applicants must have been habitually resident in part of the British Islands for a period of not less than a year: Adoption and Children Act 2002, s 49(2), (3). In principle, an adopter must be 21 or over, but this principle is modified where the application is made by a couple: Adoption and Children Act 2002, s 50(2).

[44] Adoption and Children Act 2002, s 144(4) as amended by Civil Partnership Act 2004, s 79.

[45] Adoption and Children Act 2002, s 51(3) as amended. There are also restrictions on the making of an adoption order in favour of the child's mother or father; and the courts are aware of the danger that an adoption order may in some circumstances have the effect of excluding another parent from involvement in the child's upbringing: see *Re B (Adoption: Natural Parent)* [2001] UKHL 70; [2002] 1 WLR 258.

[46] This general principle, laid down in Adoption and Children Act 2002, s 1(2), replaces the requirement found in previous legislation (see Adoption Act 1976, s 6) that the child's welfare should be the 'first consideration'.

[47] Adoption and Children Act 2002, s 52(1). The court may also dispense with parental consent if the parent cannot be found or is incapable of giving consent: see para 2.20.

and little was done to regulate what happened before the hearing. Over the years much greater attention has been given to decisions about placement for adoption, and issues about parental consent will normally be dealt with before the child is placed for adoption. It is intended[48] in this way[49] 'to minimize the uncertainty for prospective adopters (who previously faced the possibility of a contested court hearing at the adoption order stage after the child had been with them for a substantial time) and also to reduce the number of cases in which birth families were effectively faced with a *fait accompli* because their child had been placed for adoption for such a long time that it had become unrealistic for a court committed to securing the child's welfare to refuse an order.

(i) Reports and information

2.15 The Act provides[50] a 'checklist' which must be applied in determining what are the best interests of the child. Courts and agencies must 'have regard to the following matters (among others): the child's ascertainable wishes and feelings (considered in the light of the child's age and understanding), the child's particular needs, the likely effect on the child (throughout his life) of having ceased to be a member of the original family and become an adopted person, the child's age, sex, background and any other relevant characteristics, any harm which he has suffered or is at risk of suffering, and the relationship which the child has with relatives and other relevant persons.[51] The court and agency must always consider the whole range of powers available for dealing with the child.[52] It is specifically provided[53] that in placing a child for adoption, the agency must give due consideration to the child's religious persuasion, racial origin and cultural and linguistic background.

2.16 These factors are especially relevant in structuring the reports about the child, his birth parents and the prospective adopters which the adoption agency is required to produce.[54] In order to assist in the application of the welfare criterion, the agency is required to put these reports before an Adoption Panel (including both

---

48 Department of Health, *Explanatory Notes on the Adoption and Children Act 2002*, para 71.

49 The first step towards having the issue of parental consent dealt with before the hearing of the adoption application was taken by the Children Act 1975 which introduced a procedure whereby the court had power, on the application of an adoption agency, to make an order declaring the child 'free for adoption'. Thereafter the court could (provided, that it was satisfied that to do so would safeguard and promote the child's welfare) make an adoption order without any further investigation into parental agreement.

50 Adoption and Children Act 2002, s 1(4).

51 The Act expands on the factors to be considered: Adoption and Children Act 2002, s 1(4)(f).

52 Including those available under the Children Act 1989.

53 Adoption and Children Act 2002, s 1(5).

54 See generally the Adoption Agencies Regulations 2005, SI 2005/389; and the Suitability of Adopters Regulations 2005, SI 2005/1712.

professional and lay members) which will decide whether to recommend that the child be placed for adoption.

(ii) Placement

The Adoption and Children Act 2002 has greatly increased the importance of the decision on placement in the adoption process; and in principle only an 'adoption agency' (ie a local authority or registered adoption society) is permitted to make arrangements for the adoption of a child or to place a child for adoption.[55] (Exceptionally, the prohibition on so-called 'private placements' does not apply where the proposed adopter is a parent,[56] guardian or relative of the child).[57] 'Placement' is widely defined[58] so as to extend, for example, to the case where foster carers are recognized as the prospective adopters notwithstanding the fact that the 'placement' will involve no change in the physical arrangements for the child. Placement has important legal consequences, not least in effecting a transfer of parental responsibility for the child.[59]

2.17

The initial decision whether to place a child for adoption rests with the adoption agency; but the agency may only place a child for adoption with the consent of the parents or guardians.[60] If that consent is withheld a local authority may apply to the court for a placement order[61] authorizing the local authority to place the child with any prospective adopters it chooses.[62] The court has no power to make a placement order unless the child has no legal parent, is subject to a care order or the 'significant harm' criteria for the making of a care order is satisfied;[63] and the Act provides[64] that the court may only make an order if it is satisfied that the parents have in fact consented to the child being placed with any such person or that

2.18

---

[55] In the past independent placements were sometimes arranged by doctors and others. The Act specifies the steps in arranging an adoption which may only be taken by an adoption agency or a person acting in pursuance of a High Court order: see Adoption and Children Act 2002, s 92; and it is a criminal offence for anyone other than an adoption agency to make arrangements or to place a child for adoption: Adoption and Children Act 2002, s 93. The making or receipt of payments or rewards is also a criminal offence: Adoption and Children Act 2002, s 95.

[56] Or a partner of the child's parent: Adoption and Children Act 2002, s 92(4)(b).

[57] Adoption and Children Act 2002, s 92(4). Moreover, breach of the rules does not prevent the court from making an adoption order where to do otherwise could prejudice the child's welfare *Re A (Placement of a Child in Contravention of Adoption Act 1976, s 11)* [2005] 2 FLR 727.

[58] Adoption and Children Act 2002, s 18(5).

[59] See Adoption and Children Act 2002, ss 25–29.

[60] Adoption and Children Act 2002, s 18(1).

[61] Adoption and Children Act 2002, s 21.

[62] ibid.

[63] See para 2.95. In this way, the Act assimilates the threshold for compulsory intervention in family life by a local authority seeking a care order to cases where the authority has decided that the child should be placed for adoption.

[64] Adoption and Children Act 2002, s 21(3).

it is a case in which it should dispense with parental consent.[65] Once made, a placement order remains in force until an adoption order is made.[66]

(iii) Adoption Order

2.19 It is for the prospective adopters to apply to the court for an adoption order. The court may only make such an order if one of three conditions is satisfied.[67] The first is that each parent consents to the order;[68] the second is that a placement order in favour of the prospective adopters has been made;[69] the third is that the child has been made 'free for adoption' under legislation in force in Scotland or Northern Ireland.[70]

(iv) Dispensing with consent

2.20 The consent of each parent or guardian of the child is in principle a prerequisite to the making of a placement or adoption order. 'Consent' means consent given unconditionally and with full understanding of what is involved.[71] Any consent given by the mother to the making of an adoption order is ineffective if given less than six weeks after the child's birth.[72] The court may dispense with the consent of a parent or guardian to the making of a placement or adoption order but only if it is satisfied that the parent cannot be found[73] or lacks capacity to give consent[74]

---

[65] Applying the test laid down in Adoption and Children Act 2002, s 52.

[66] Or the child marries, enters into a civil partnership, reaches 18, or the order is revoked: Adoption and Children Act 2002, s 21(4).

[67] Adoption and Children Act 2002, s 47(1).

[68] Or that such consent should be dispensed with: Adoption and Children Act 2002, s 47(2). The Act also provides machinery whereby a parent may give consent in advance: Adoption and Children Act 2002, s 20.

[69] And that no parent opposes the making of the order (but a parent requires the court's leave to oppose the making of an adoption order in such circumstances: s 47(4), (5)).

[70] Adoption and Children Act 2002, s 47(6). There are also a number of provisions intended to ensure that the court is in a position to apply the principle that the paramount consideration in reaching a decision is the child's welfare throughout his life: Adoption and Children Act 2002, s 1(2) (a principle reinforced by the provision that the court must not make an adoption order unless it considers that to do so would be better for the child than not doing so: Adoption and Children Act 2002, s 1(6)). Thus, the child must have lived with the adopters for a prescribed period (Adoption and Children Act 2002, s 42), and the Court must have before it a report prepared by the agency which has placed the child: Adoption and Children Act 2002, s 43.

[71] Adoption and Children Act 2002, s 52(5). Regulations lay down formal requirements as to how consent is to be given: Family Procedure (Adoption) Rules 2005, 28(1). Once given, the consent may only be withdrawn in a prescribed form or in writing: Adoption and Children Act 2002, s 47(7).

[72] Adoption and Children Act 2002, s 52(3).

[73] The courts gave a generous interpretation to the corresponding provision of the law previously in force: see *Re A (Adoption of a Russian Child)* [2000] 1 FLR 539.

[74] Within the meaning of the Mental Capacity Act 2005.

or that the welfare of the child requires that the consent be dispensed with.[75] In making that decision, the court must apply the guidelines given in the Act.[76]

(v) Effects of adoption order

The Adoption and Children Act 2002[77] provides that an adoption order is an **2.21** order made by the court giving parental responsibility for a child to the adopters or adopter. Such an order is in principle irrevocable.[78] The order extinguishes the birth parents' parental responsibility and also the parental duty to make maintenance payments.[79] Moreover, the Act provides[80] that an adopted person is the legitimate child of the adopters[81] and in this way, an adoption order destroys, as a matter of law, old family links and creates new family ties.[82] There are, however, some exceptions to this general principle: for example, it is provided that adoption does not affect the descent of any peerage or dignity or title of honour.[83]

For many years, it was axiomatic that an adopted child should have no contact **2.22** with his or her birth parents, and the legislation made it difficult if not impossible for an adopted person to trace the original birth registration details, or for the birth parents to find material which would have enabled them to trace their child: the legislation embodied the principle that the Registrar-General's records (from which the adopted child's original birth registration could be traced) should never be disclosed.[84] But views about the appropriateness of this policy have changed over the years and legislation has given an adopted adult certain rights to seek

---

[75] Adoption and Children Act 2002, s 52(1). Under the provisions of the Adoption Act 1976 there were seven distinct grounds upon which consent could be dispensed with: Adoption Act 1976, s 16. The majority of applications were made on the ground that the parent or guardian concerned was 'withholding. . .consent unreasonably' and the child's welfare was an important (but not the only) factor in deciding whether that was so: the child's welfare was 'relevant in all cases if and to the extent that a reasonable parent would take it into account. It is decisive in those cases where a reasonable parent must so regard it': see *per* Lord Hailsham, *Re W (An Infant)* [1971] AC 682.

[76] Adoption and Children Act 2002, s 1; para 2.15.

[77] s 46(1).

[78] *Re B (Adoption: Jurisdiction to Set Aside)* [1995] Fam 239, CA.

[79] Adoption and Children Act 2002, s 46(2). This does not operate retrospectively: Adoption and Children Act 2002, s 46(3).

[80] Adoption and Children Act 2002, s 67.

[81] The Adoption and Children Act 2002, s 46(3) contains provisions dealing with the situation in which a step-parent adopts his or her partner's child.

[82] However, as the official explanatory notes on the Act put it, these provisions 'are intended only to clarify how an adopted child should be treated in law. They do not touch on the biological or emotional ties of an adopted child and are not intended to do so'. The Act contains provisions dealing with the complex situations which can arise in connection with dispositions of property, especially those which depend on the respective seniority of birth and adoptive children.

[83] Adoption and Children Act 2002, s 71. Section 74 of the Act also excludes various enactments—notably the British Nationality Act 1981 and the Immigration Act 1971, provisions of the criminal law relating to incest, and the prohibited degrees of marriage—from the general principle stated in the text.

[84] Adoption Act 1976, s 50(4).

information from the adoption agency's records and access to the relevant birth registration records.[85] A register now also allows birth relatives to indicate that they wish (or do not wish to have) contact with an adopted person[86] while the courts may in the exercise of their discretionary powers encourage a measure of contact with the birth family.[87]

(vi) Orders available in adoption proceedings

2.23 Adoption applications constitute 'family proceedings' for the purposes of the Children Act 1989[88] and accordingly the court dealing with an adoption application has power (on application or of its own motion)[89] to make a 'section 8' order (such as a residence or contact order)[90] under that Act. Such orders may be made whether or not the application for adoption is successful.

(3) Marriage

2.24 Marriage in English law is founded on the agreement of the parties, but marriage creates a legal status to which the law attaches rights and duties. These rights and duties are determined by law; and according to traditional doctrine the parties have no power to modify them by private agreement. In recent years there has been a move to encourage couples whose relationship has broken down to reach agreement on the financial and other consequences of the breakdown, and the court will certainly take the existence of a fully informed agreement into account in deciding how to exercise its extensive powers to make financial orders in divorce proceedings.[91] But the law has refused to allow ordinary contractual principles to determine the outcome and remains ambivalent about the extent to which domestic arrangements give rise to legally enforceable rights and obligations.[92]

---

[85] Adoption and Children Act 2002, ss 56–65 and Part I, Chapter 5. It should be noted that an adopted person has no absolute right to obtain this information: see *R v Registrar General ex p Smith* [1991] 2 QB 393 and that an adoption agency may in exceptional circumstances obtain a court order prohibiting disclosure: Adoption and Children Act 2002, s 60(2).

[86] See Adoption and Children Act 2002, s 80.

[87] Under the Adoption Act 1976 applications for contact were rarely successful see *Re C (A Minor) (Adoption Order: Conditions)* [1989] AC 1, HL; *Re R (Adoption: Contact)* [2005] EWCA Civ 1128 and compare *Re O (Transracial Adoption: Contact)* [1995] 2 FLR 597.

[88] Section 8(4)(d). The natural mother of an adopted child is no longer a 'parent' for the purposes of the Children Act 1989 s 10(4) and thus is no longer entitled to make an application under that Act for contact etc: *Re C (A Minor) (Adopted Child: Contact)* [1993] Fam 210.

[89] Children Act 1989, s 10(1).

[90] For a striking example of the two procedures being invoked in relation to the same child see *Re AB (Adoption: Joint Residence)* [1996] 1 FLR 27 (adoption order made in favour of one party to a stable unmarried relationship, joint residence order made to him and partner).

[91] *S v S (Divorce: Staying Proceedings)* [1997] 2 FLR 100; and see further para 2.147 ff.

[92] See *Balfour v Balfour* [1919] 2 KB 571, CA; *Jones v Padavatton* [1969] 1 WLR 328, CA; *Xydhias v Xydhias* [1999] 2 All ER 386, CA.

(a) Formation of marriage

If English law is to recognize a couple as married they must each have had **2.25** legal capacity by the law of their domicile to enter into the marriage; and they must have complied with the formalities prescribed by the law of the place of celebration.[93]

(b) Capacity to marry

Legislation[94] provides that a marriage shall be void on certain grounds and **2.26** thus effectively[95] defines the legal capacity required if a person domiciled in this country is to contract a valid marriage.

(i) The prohibited degrees

English law prohibits marriages between certain blood relations (for example, **2.27** father and daughter); and it also prohibits (or permits only in specified circumstances) marriages between certain categories of person whose relationship arises by reason of marriage ('affines').

The prohibited degrees: consanguinity. A person may not marry his or her parent, **2.28** grandparent, child or grandchild, uncle or aunt, nephew or niece.[96] However, English law (in contrast to some foreign systems) does not prohibit marriage between first cousins.

The prohibited degrees: affinity. The Deceased Wife's Sister's Marriage Act **2.29** 1907 marked the beginning of a trend to relax the prohibitions on marriage with affines, and since 1986[97] the law has ceased to impose any absolute bar on such marriages. However, marriage with a stepchild is only permitted if (a) both the intending spouses are 21 or over; and (b) the younger party to the intended marriage has not been a 'child of the family' in relation to the other party at any time before the child attained the age of 18.[98]

---

[93] In certain restricted circumstances English law may recognize the validity of a marriage celebrated abroad but not in accordance with any local law: see eg *Merker v Merker* [1963] P 283.

[94] Marriage Acts 1949 to 1986; Matrimonial Causes Act 1973 s 11(a)–(d).

[95] For the possibility that the law defining the circumstances in which a decree of nullity may be obtained does not necessarily codify all the circumstances in which a person may lack capacity to marry see *S-T (formerly J) v J* [1998] Fam 103, CA.

[96] Marriage Acts 1949 to 1996, sch 1, Part I.

[97] Marriage (Prohibited Degrees of Relationship) Act 1986.

[98] Marriage Acts 1949 to 1986, sch 1, part II. The law formerly prohibited marriage between parents-in-law and sons-in-law or daughters-in-law but these were removed by the Marriage Act 1949 (Remedial) Order 2007 (SI 438) following the decision of the European Court for Human Rights in *B and L v United Kingdom (Application No 36546/02)* [2006] 1 FLR 35. For the meaning of 'child of the family' see para 2.143.

(ii) Minimum age

2.30 Both parties to the intended marriage must have attained the age of 16.[99]

(iii) Bigamy

2.31 Marriage in English law is a monogamous relationship;[100] and accordingly a purported marriage will be void if it is established that at the time of the ceremony either party was validly married to a third party.

(iv) Parties not respectively male and female

2.32 English law is based on the view, deeply embedded in religious and social culture, that marriage is a relationship between two persons of opposite sex; and accordingly it stipulates that parties who are not respectively male and female lack the legal capacity to marry.[101] The application of this principle caused especial difficulty in the case of transsexuals who had received gender reassignment therapy. Eventually, the House of Lords[102] declared the rule that a person correctly classified as a male at birth could never be regarded as a woman for the purpose of determining capacity to marry[103] (notwithstanding the fact that therapy had been successfully carried out) to be incompatible with convention rights. Legislation now allows a transsexual to obtain legal recognition of his or her 'acquired gender'.[104]

---

[99] Marriage Acts 1949 to 1986, s 2. Parental consent is required to the marriage of persons aged 16 or 17, but this requirement is classified as one of form and not capacity.

[100] *Hyde v Hyde* (1866) LR 1 P&D 130; and see *Whiston v Whiston* [1995] Fam 198, CA. It is now provided that a polygamous marriage entered into outside England and Wales by a person domiciled here is void: Matrimonial Causes Act 1973, s 11(d). For this purpose a marriage is only polygamous if it is actually (as distinct from merely potentially) so: Private International Law (Miscellaneous Provisions) Act 1995, sch, para 2(2).

[101] Matrimonial Causes Act 1973, s 11(c); and see *S-T (formerly J) v J* [1998] Fam 103, CA.; *Bellinger v Bellinger (Lord Chancellor Intervening)* [2003] 2 AC 467, 480; *Wilkinson v Kitzinger and HM Attorney-General (The Lord Chancellor Intervening)* [2006] EWHC 835 (Fam). Two persons of the same sex may enter into a civil partnership under the provisions of Civil Partnership Act 2004 (see para 2.45) and that Act contains provisions under which certain 'overseas relationships' (including same-sex marriages valid as such under the local law) will be recognized in English law as civil partnerships: see *Wilkinson v Kitzinger and HM Attorney-General (The Lord Chancellor Intervening)* [2006] EWHC 835 (Fam).

[102] *Bellinger v Bellinger* [2003] UKHL 21.

[103] *S-T (formerly J) v J* [1998] Fam 103, CA.

[104] A gender recognition certificate may be issued to a person who has suffered from gender dysphoria, has lived in the 'acquired gender' throughout the period of two years, and intends to live in that gender until death. The person's birth registration records will then be amended: Gender Recognition Act, 2004.

(c) Formalities for marriage

Until 1753[105] the law of marriage in England and Wales was governed by the com-   **2.33**
mon law, which had in turn left the regulation of marriage to the Church. But
since 1753 statute has laid down rules prescribing the formalities which must be
observed if a valid marriage is to be created in England[106] (although the Church of
England retained its dominant role until 1836, when statute provided for a purely
secular marriage procedure and also gave legal recognition to marriages celebrated
in places of worship other than Anglican churches). These historical facts explain
the complexity of the modern English law, of which only a brief account can
be given.

It is necessary to distinguish between (i) the preliminaries to marriage; (ii) the   **2.34**
marriage ceremony; and (iii) registration requirements.

(i) Preliminaries to marriage

Parental consent. In the case of a person aged 16 or 17[107] the consent of each   **2.35**
parent[108] or guardian is, in principle, required to that marriage; but in cases of
refusal the court may consent, whilst a marriage contracted without consent is not
thereby invalidated.[109]

Banns, certificates, etc. Legislation[110] provides that certain formalities must be   **2.36**
completed prior to the solemnization of a marriage. In the case of marriages
according to the rites of the Church of England,[111] the available procedures are:
the publication of banns, the grant of a special licence by the Archbishop of
Canterbury, the grant of a common licence by the appropriate ecclesiastical

---

[105] The year in which the Clandestine Marriages Act (usually called Lord Hardwicke's Act) was
enacted.

[106] The provisions of the Clandestine Marriages Act did not apply to members of the Royal
Family (a term not defined), or to Quakers and Jews. Quakers and Jews retain the right to solemnize
marriages in accordance with their own rites; but they must comply with statutory requirements as
to preliminaries and registration. It appears that marriages between members of the Royal Family
are not affected by the legislation consolidated in the Marriage Act 1949 (see s 79(5)); but the Royal
Marriages Act 1772 requires descendants of King George II to obtain the consent of the Sovereign
in Council to the proposed marriage.

[107] Marriage Act 1949, s 3, as amended; Church of England Canon B32. The Family Law
Reform Act 1969 (apparently influenced by the belief that to refer to a 17-year-old as an 'infant'
was demeaning) adopted the terminology 'minor' to describe persons under the age of eighteen; but
more recently legislation (for example, the Children Act 1989) has reverted to the practice of using
the term 'child'.

[108] Provided the parent has 'parental responsibility' for the child. The effect is in principle to
exclude the father of an illegitimate child: see para 2.161.

[109] See para 2.39.

[110] Marriage Act 1949, Parts II and III.

[111] Marriage Act 1949, s 5.

authority, and the issue of a certificate by a superintendent registrar.[112] In the case of civil marriages and non-Anglican religious marriages, the most frequently used formality is the superintendent registrar's certificate.[113] The common feature of these procedures is that they are intended (largely by giving a measure of publicity to the intended marriage) to ensure that the parties are legally free to marry, but in recent years adaptations have been made in an attempt to deal with the problem of 'sham' marriages intended to evade the proper application of the immigration rules.[114]

(ii) Solemnization of the marriage

2.37
The law specifically recognizes seven different kinds of marriage ceremony in England and Wales: (1) civil marriage in the office of a superintendent registrar; (2) civil marriage in premises approved for the purpose under the Marriage Act 1994; (3) marriage in the Church of England; (4) marriage in a place of worship registered for the solemnization of marriage; (5) marriage in a naval, military or air force chapel; (6) marriage between two persons professing the Jewish religion; and (7) marriage according to the usages of the Society of Friends. In the case of Anglican, Jewish and Quaker marriages the form of ceremony is determined exclusively by the rules and usages of the religious group concerned; but in other cases, although the parties may in principle use 'such form and ceremony as [they] choose to adopt'[115] statute requires that at some stage they make the prescribed declaration and exchange the prescribed words of contract.[116]

---

112 The superintendent registrar's certificate is the only form of preliminary to marriage equally valid for marriages in the Church of England, other religious marriages, and civil marriages: Marriage Act 1949, s 26. Special considerations apply to the marriages of persons subject to immigration control: Asylum and Immigration (Treatment of Claimants, etc) Act 2004; *R (Balai and Others) v Secretary of State for the Home Department* [2006] EWHC 823.

113 The Immigration and Asylum Act 1999 abolished the Superintendent Registrar's Certificate with Licence, often used to permit marriages to be solemnized at comparatively short notice. But the Marriage (Registrar General's Licence) Act 1970 provides for the Registrar General to license the speedy marriage of a person seriously ill and unable to be moved to a register office or other permitted venue. The Marriage Act 1983 provides that, subject to conditions, a person housebound by reason of illness or disability or detained in prison or under the mental health legislation may be married at the place of residence or detention on the authority of a superintendent registrar's certificate.

114 See Immigration and Asylum Act 1999 Part IX; Asylum and Immigration (Treatment of Claimants, etc.) Act 2004; but note the difficulties exposed by the decision in *R (Balai and Others) v Secretary of State for the Home Department* [2006] EWHC 823; [2006] 3 All ER 608.

115 In the case of civil weddings (whether in the Register Office or on Approved Premises) statute prohibits the use of any religious service: Marriage Act 1949, ss 45, 46B(4) as inserted by Marriage Act 1994, s 1(2). The statutory language has been widely construed by the authorities to prohibit eg any reading from religious texts or hymn singing.

116 Marriage Act 1949, s 44(3); Marriage Ceremony (Prescribed Words) Act 1996.

(iii) Registration requirements

Legislation imposes a duty on the clergyman, registrar, etc to register the **2.38** marriage;[117] and the Registrar General has overall charge of the registration system. Certified copies of entries given in the General Register Office are to be received as evidence of the marriage in question.[118]

(d) Consequence of irregularities

The Marriage Act 1949 provides that if any persons knowingly and wilfully inter- **2.39** marry in breach of a number of specified legislative requirements[119] the marriage shall be void;[120] but it also provides that evidence of other specified defects[121] is not to be given in proceedings touching the validity of the marriage.[122] Statute does not deal with the consequences of irregularities other than those specified— for example, the requirement[123] that the marriage be celebrated between the hours of 8am and 6pm; but it is generally thought that the validity of such marriages is not to be impeached.[124] The courts generally lean in favour of upholding the validity of marriages and may apply a presumption that a couple who have cohabited for a substantial period and held themselves out as husband and wife are indeed validly married, even if there is evidence that the prescribed formalities were not observed.[125]

(e) Legal consequences of marriage

It has already been pointed out[126] that marriage is a legal status from which certain **2.40** legal rights and duties automatically flow; and at one time these rights and duties could be traced to and explained by the doctrine that husband and wife became in law one person, the 'very being or legal existence of the woman [being] suspended

---

[117] Marriage Act 1949, Part IV, as amended; Registration Service Act 1953.

[118] Marriage Act 1949, s 65(3).

[119] For example, the requirements relating to banns, certificate or licence. In *Gereis v Yagoub* [1997] 1 FLR 854 a 'marriage' celebrated in an unregistered Orthodox church was, on proof that the parties had been advised of the need subsequently to go through a civil ceremony, held to be void.

[120] Marriage Act 1949, ss 25, 49.

[121] For example, the requirement of parental consent: s 48(1).

[122] Marriage Act 1949, s 48.

[123] Marriage Act 1949, s 4. It is a criminal offence knowingly and wilfully to infringe this rule: s 75(1).

[124] Note the liberal view taken by the Court of Appeal in *Chief Adjudication Officer v Bath* [2000] 1 FLR 8. It seems that purported marriages by a ceremony not 'in a form known to and recognized by our law as capable of producing. . .a valid marriage'– perhaps, for example, a purported marriage by African customary law in a private house—will be wholly ineffective: see *R v Bham* [1966] 1 QB 159.

[125] See notably *A-M v A-M (Divorce: Jurisdiction: Validity of Marriage)* [2001] 2 FLR 6; *Chief Adjudication Officer v Bath* [2000] 1 FLR 8. But compare *Gandhi v Patel* [2001] 1 FLR 603.

[126] See para 2.24.

during the marriage, or at least. . .incorporated and consolidated into that of the husband. . .'.[127] But this legal fiction (it has been said)[128] has been so eroded by the judges (who created exception after exception to it) and cut down by statute after statute that little of it remains. It may be that in exceptional circumstances[129] some of the consequences recognized at common law of the marital relationship will still be relevant; but for the most part the rights and duties of spouses are now to be found in statute.[130] (In this context it should be noted that a statute referring to a 'husband' or to a 'wife' will apply only to persons who are validly married under the rules set out above; and the fact that the couple have lived together, and may indeed regard themselves as being 'common law' spouses will not suffice.[131])

2.41   In the circumstances, it seems best simply to enumerate some of the more important legal consequences flowing, as a result of statutory provisions, from the relationship of husband and wife and particularly relevant to the ending of that relationship.[132] Of these, the most important (and in many ways the most extensive) relate to *financial matters*. Spouses have the right not to be excluded without court order from property which has been the matrimonial home,[133] and such rights may, by registration, be protected against third parties.[134] One spouse may seek an order for financial provision against the other on the ground that he or she has failed to provide reasonable maintenance for the spouse or children

---

127 Blackstone, *Commentaries on the Laws of England*, Book I, Chapter 15, III.

128 *Midland Bank Trust Co Ltd v Green and Another* [1982] Ch 529, 538, CA, *per* Lord Denning MR.

129 For example, the wife's common law right to be maintained by her husband was for long thought to be relevant in determining the question whether or not he remained in rateable occupation of the former matrimonial home (*Cardiff Corporation v Robinson* [1957] 1 QB 39; cf *Routhan v Arun District Council* [1982] QB 501, CA); whilst the mutual right of spouses to *consortium* (although, since the Administration of Justice Act 1982, no longer sufficient to found an action for tortious interference by a third party) has been held relevant in interpreting statutes referring to spouses 'living together': see eg *Santos v Santos* [1972] Fam 247, CA. Moreover, no statute has interfered with the common law presumption that a wife has her husband's authority to pledge his credit for necessary goods and services. (Compare the wife's so called agency of necessity, abolished by Matrimonial Proceedings and Property Act 1970, s 40.)

130 See eg *Re C (A Minor)(Contribution Notice)* [1994] 1 FLR 111, 116, *per* Ward J. The dictum relates to the common law duty to maintain children, but is of general application.

131 See eg *Rignell v Andrews* (1990) 63 TC 312 (man not entitled to married man's tax allowance in respect of woman with whom he had lived for 11 years).

132 The trend of developments can be seen in the history of compensation for the destruction of a household by death. The Fatal Accidents Act 1846, which gave a surviving spouse a statutory right of action against a person whose wrongful act, neglect or default brought about the other spouse's death and thereby caused financial loss, is probably the first such provision. More than a century later the Administration of Justice Act 1982 conferred a similar right on a cohabitant, but only subject to conditions (for example, as to the duration of the relationship) which do not apply to the married.

133 Under legislation stemming from the Matrimonial Homes Act 1967 husband and wife were entitled to 'matrimonial home rights' but, in consequence of the enactment of the Civil Partnership Act 2004 these rights are now called 'home rights'.

134 Family Law Act 1996, Part III.

of the family;[135] and the court has extensive powers to make financial orders in judicial separation proceedings.[136] Statute provides that (whilst provisions purporting to restrict the right to apply to the court are void) financial arrangements contained in a maintenance agreement are valid (although the court is given wide powers to vary such agreements).[137]

In respect of *property rights*, the most important statutory provision is that con- **2.42** ferring extensive rights on a spouse to succeed on the other's intestacy;[138] whilst if the disposition of a deceased's estate does not make reasonable financial provision for the surviving spouse the court has power[139] to order the making of such provision (not limited to what is required for maintenance). Statute[140] declares that contributions by one spouse to the improvement of real or personal property in which either or both has an interest will entitle the contributor to a share (or enlarged share) in that property. Statute[141] also confers on a wife a beneficial interest in savings from any housekeeping allowance; and created a special summary jurisdiction to resolve issues as to the title to or possession of property.[142]

Statute also lays down certain special rules in respect of the compellability of **2.43** spouses to give evidence, whilst the unity theory lingers on in the provision of the Criminal Law Act 1977 which prevents married couples being convicted of conspiring with one another (although they may now be sued for the tort of conspiracy). There are important *fiscal differences* (especially in relation to Inheritance Tax and Capital Gains Tax) between the position of married and unmarried partners. One spouse does not automatically acquire the other's British citizenship, but the requirements to be satisfied for doing so are less onerous than those applicable in other cases; and the spouse of a person present and settled in the United Kingdom will be granted entry clearance provided that the marriage is genuine.[143]

For many years the question whether a couple were married or not was often of **2.44** greatest significance in relation to their children since a child born or conceived during the parents' marriage will be their legitimate child. However, the legal

---

[135] Under the Domestic Proceedings and Magistrates' Courts Act 1978, and under the Matrimonial Causes Act 1973, s 27.
[136] See para 2.143.
[137] Matrimonial Causes Act 1973, ss 34–36.
[138] Administration of Estates Act 1925, as substantially amended: see paras 7.15–7.26.
[139] Under Inheritance (Provision for Family and Dependants) Act 1975.
[140] Matrimonial Proceedings and Property Act 1970, s 37.
[141] Married Women's Property Act 1964.
[142] Married Women's Property Act 1882, s 17.
[143] British Nationality Act 1981, s 6(2) and sch 1. The complex subject of immigration control is governed by the Immigration Act 1971 and other statutes and by detailed Rules (HC 395, 1994, as subsequently amended) made by the Home Secretary.

disadvantages of illegitimacy have been greatly reduced, and the fact that 'parental responsibility' is now attributed to the father of an illegitimate child (provided his name is recorded as such in the Register of Births) means that there are now few legal disadvantages flowing from the fact that a child's parents have never been married and that accordingly it will rarely be necessary to use the term 'illegitimate'.[144]

(4) *Civil Partnership*

2.45 In 2004, the United Kingdom Parliament enacted the Civil Partnership Act.[145] The Act was intended to create a legal framework for same sex couples comparable to that traditionally provided for heterosexuals by marriage: what had been proscribed and punished[146] was henceforth to be not only countenanced but indeed approved by law.[147] However, the relationship, although intended[148] to mirror as fully as possible' the rights and responsibilities enjoyed by those legally permitted to marry, was not intended to permit *marriage* between same sex couples. Rather, the intention was to create a parallel and equalizing institution designed to redress a perceived inequality of treatment between same-sex and different sex couples.[149] Marriage was to be the template for those rights and responsibilities but it was to remain a legally distinct institution confined to relationships between a man and a woman. The English courts have accepted the validity of that approach and have held that the legislature's decision is not incompatible with the convention rights protected by the Human Rights Act 1998.[150]

---

144 See further n 12 above.

145 The Act is a United Kingdom Act and the definition of civil partnership as a 'a relationship between two people of the same sex' ending only on death, dissolution or annulment' applies throughout the United Kingdom. However, for the most part the Act deals with the law of England and Wales separately from the law of Scotland and the law of Northern Ireland: it is provided that the relationship is formed when the two register under the relevant provisions applicable to England and Wales (Part 2 of the Act) Scotland (Part 3) or Northern Ireland (Part 4). Moreover, separate provision is made for the registration of civil partnerships at British Consulates. and for the registration of civil partnerships by armed forces personnel outside the United Kingdom. The Act also provides that certain 'overseas relationships' are to be treated as having the effect of a civil partnership: see s 1(1) (b) and Part 5 of the Act; and note *Wilkinson v Kitzinger and HM Attorney-General (The Lord Chancellor Intervening)* [2006] EWHC 835 (Fam).

146 Until the enactment of the Sexual Offences Act 1967 sexual acts between males (even consenting) could give rise to prosecution and imprisonment.

147 *Secretary of State for Work and Pensions v M* [2006] UKHL 11; [2006] 2 WLR 637 (Lord Nicholls of Birkenhead).

148 Mrs Jacqui Smith, Official Report (HC) 12 October 2004, vol 425, col 174.

149 *Wilkinson v Kitzinger and HM Attorney-General (The Lord Chancellor Intervening)* [2006] EWHC 835 (Fam) at [50].

150 *Wilkinson v Kitzinger and HM Attorney-General (The Lord Chancellor Intervening)* [2006] EWHC 835 (Fam).

(a) Formation of civil partnership

The Act provides that a 'civil partnership is a relationship between two people of **2.46** the same sex' formed 'when they register as civil partners of each other'; and registration is the only means of creating a civil partnership in the United Kingdom.[151] This provision marks the most obvious distinction between civil partnership and marriage (which may be created in accordance with the rites of the Church of England and other religious groups as well as by a civil procedure carried out in the presence of a Registrar).[152] The relevant rules governing the formation of civil partnerships in England and Wales may be summarized as follows.

(i) Eligibility

The Act (in these respects mirroring the provisions governing capacity to marry) **2.47** provides,[153] in effect, that the two parties to a civil partnership must be of the same sex, aged 16 or over,[154] not lawfully married or already a civil partner, and not within the prohibited degrees (whether of affinity or consanguinity)[155] defined by the Act.[156]

(ii) Preliminaries

The Act[157] stipulates that each intended partner must give notice of the proposed **2.48** civil partnership to a registration authority, and the authority must publicize relevant facts during a 15 day waiting period.[158] In the absence of any valid objection, the registration authority then issues a 'civil partnership schedule'.

---

[151] Civil Partnership Act 2004, s 1: see n 145 above. However, in some cases a person who has been living as 'the civil partner' of another may be entitled to make a claim, eg for provision from the estate of a deceased person: see eg Inheritance (Provision for Family and Dependants) Act 1975, s 1(1B) as inserted by Civil Partnership Act 2004, s 71 and sch 4, para 15(5); and see below on the Fatal Accidents Act 1976, s 1(3)(b)(iii) as amended by Civil Partnership Act 2004, s 83.

[152] See para 2.37.

[153] Civil Partnership Act 2004, s 3.

[154] A person under 18 requires 'parental' consent: Civil Partnership Act 2004, s 4.

[155] Whether there is adequate justification for imposing restrictions in respect of a same sex relationship is a controversial matter.

[156] Civil Partnership Act 2004, s 3 (1)(d). The prohibited degrees of relationship are defined in Civil Partnership Act 2004, sch 1 (but it should be noted that paras 3 and 9 of the Schedule have not been brought into force, thus—consistently with the decision of the European Court of Human Rights in *B and L v United Kingdom* (2005) Application No 36536/02—permitting civil partnerships to be formed between parents and children-in-law without regard to the special conditions imposed by those paragraphs).

[157] ss 8–16. Special procedures are available in cases where a house-bound, detained, or terminally ill person is concerned: Civil Partnership Act 2004, s 5.

[158] The Registrar-General may shorten the period in any particular case for 'compelling reasons' Civil Partnership Act 2004, s 12.

(iii) Registration

2.49 The partnership may then be registered in the place specified in the notice of intended civil partnership.[159] The place must not be in religious premises, nor may any 'religious service'[160] be used whilst the registrar is officiating.[161] Registration is effected by each of the partners signing the civil partnership document[162] in the presence of each other, two witnesses, and the registrar. The civil partnership will then be registered,[163] but it is the signature of the document which creates the legal relationship.[164]

(b) Legal consequences of civil partnership

2.50 The Civil Partnership Act adopts what has been called the 'assimilation principle':[165] it amends the statutory provisions dealing with the legal consequences of marriage and other family relationships[166] so as to replicate their effect for civil partnership save in cases in which there was thought to be some sufficient reason for not doing so.[167] For example, spouses had 'matrimonial home rights' under the Family Law Act 1996;[168] as a result of the Civil Partnership Act civil partners equally have what are now described as 'home rights'.[169] One spouse has statutory rights to seek a financial provision order on the ground that the other spouse has failed to provide 'reasonable maintenance' for him or her; civil partners now have the same right and duty.[170] A surviving civil partner (like a surviving spouse) is entitled to inherit on the other's death intestate.[171] Provisions relating to

---

159 Civil Partnership Act 2004, s 6.

160 This expression has, in the context of the marriage laws, been given a wide interpretation: see para 2.37.

161 Civil Partnership Act 2004, s 6 (1), s 2(5).

162 This will usually be the 'civil partnership schedule', but will be the Registrar-General's Licence in cases in which the 'special procedure' available in cases of terminal illness is used: Civil Partnership Act 2004, ss 7(1) (b), 21–27.

163 Civil Partnership Act 2004, ss 2(4), 28–36.

164 Civil Partnership Act 2004, s 2(1).

165 SM Cretney, *Same Sex Relationships: from 'Odious Crime' to 'Gay Marriage'* (2006) 29.

166 See Civil Partnership Act 2004, sch 27 'Minor and Consequential Amendments: General' (which extends over 30 pages of the Statute Book). Schedules 28 and 29 contain Consequential Amendments dealing with the law of Scotland and of Northern Ireland respectively. A great deal of delegated legislation is also used to amend the law in pursuance of the general policy stated in the text.

167 For example, the Act contains no provision replicating the effect of the Royal Marriages Act 1772 (which requires the consent of the Sovereign to the marriage of a member of the Royal Family). It was presumably thought that the policy of that Act was primarily to control the succession to the throne, and although a same sex couple may, by means of legal adoption, have children of whom both will be the parent, such a child is debarred from succeeding to the throne (or to titles of honour).

168 See para 2.41.

169 Civil Partnership Act 2004, s 82, and sch 9.

170 Civil Partnership Act 2004, s 72 and sch 5, Part 9, sch 6, Part 1.

171 Civil Partnership Act 2004, s 71 and sch 4, Part 2.

landlord and tenant,[172] social security,[173] immigration[174] and nationality,[175] pensions[176] and taxation[177] are applied to civil partners in the same way. In terms of its legal consequences, therefore, civil partnership can be regarded as 'marriage in almost all but name'.[178]

However, there remain differences. First, whilst the Civil Partnership Act deals in **2.51** considerable detail with the relevant *statutory* provisions it does not attempt to deal with the consequences which the common law attaches to the status of marriage.[179] It is true that the common law is today of little practical relevance in this context and that the rights and duties of spouses are for the most part found in statute. But the fact that the common law presumes a husband to be the father of a child born to his wife marriage remains of practical importance. The Civil Partnership Act contains no comparable provision dealing with the parentage of a child born to a civil partner.[180] Secondly, whilst the circumstances in which the court may make dissolution orders and nullity orders in respect of partnerships[181] are similar to those governing the making of divorce and nullity decrees under the Matrimonial Causes Act 1973[182] they are not in all respects identical with them.[183] On one view, these differences are simply consequential on the fact that civil partnership is by definition a relationship between parties of the same sex whereas marriage is by definition a relationship between a man and a woman; but it can also be argued that they reflect a fundamental distinction: that whereas marriage is in principle based on a sexual relationship between the partners the same is not true of civil partnership which (as the Bishops of the Church of England have put it)[184] is not in law 'predicated on the existence of a sexual relationship'. This may be of little practical significance in the interpretation of the Civil Partnership Act by the courts; but it may equally be that uncertainty about the nature of the relationship envisaged by the Civil Partnership Act could be relevant in,

---

172 Civil Partnership Act 2004, s 261 and sch 27.
173 Civil Partnership Act 2004, s 254 and sch 24.
174 Civil Partnership Act 2004, s 249 and sch 23.
175 Civil Partnership Act 2004, s 81 and sch 8.
176 Civil Partnership Act 2004, s 256 and sch 25. Power is taken to amend primary legislation relating to pensions: Civil Partnership Act 2004, s 255.
177 Regulations have been made under statutory powers designed to ensure that civil partnership is, for the purposes of duties and taxes (including Inheritance Tax) 'treated in the same way (or a similar way)' as is marriage: Finance Act 2005, s 103, and see (eg) the Tax and Civil Partnership Regulations 2005, SI 2005 No 3229.
178 Baroness Hale, 'Homosexual Rights' [2004] CFLQ 125, 132.
179 See para 2.40.
180 See para 2.161.
181 The rules are set out at para 2.98.
182 See para 2.76.
183 See para 2.100.
184 *Pastoral Statement from the House of Bishops of the Church of England, Civil Partnerships*, 25 July 2005.

for example, the exercise of the wide discretion to make financial orders. The question of what is 'fair' may in such cases reflect an analysis of the assumptions made by the parties when entering into the partnership about their respective roles and these assumptions may be different from those made by a married couple. But it remains true that the Civil Partnership Act was heavily influenced by the belief, eloquently expressed by Baroness Hale, that there is no relevant distinction between same sex and different sex relationships:

> [H]omosexual relationships can have exactly the same qualities of intimacy, stability and inter-dependence that heterosexual relationships do. . .[M]arried and unmarried couples, both homosexual and heterosexual, may bring up children together . . .Homosexual couples can have exactly the same sort of inter-dependent couple relationship as heterosexuals can. . .Some people, whether heterosexual or homosexual, may be satisfied with casual or transient relationships. But most human beings eventually want more than that. They want love. And with love they often want not only the warmth but also the sense of belonging to one another which is the essence of being a couple. And many couples also come to want the stability and permanence which go with sharing a home and a life together, with or without the children who for many people go to make a family. In this, people of homosexual orientation are no different from people of heterosexual orientation.

On that basis, there would seem to be little justification for drawing distinctions between the two institutions in terms of their legal consequences.

(5) Cohabitation

2.52 Since the First World War (when provision was made for pensions to be paid to the dependants of unmarried service personnel in certain circumstances) the law has increasingly come to accept that hardship may be caused and injustice done if proof of a valid marriage is invariably to be required as a condition for attaching legal consequences to family relationships.[185] The enormous increase recorded in the phenomenon of cohabitation outside marriage—the 2001 census recorded just over two million cohabiting couples in England and Wales (an increase of 67 per cent over the 1991 census figure)[186]—has been accompanied by pressure to

---

[185] Note, for example, the views expressed about the property rights of those sharing a home, *per* Waite LJ in *Midland Bank plc v Cooke* [1995] 4 All ER 562, CA; and *per* Peter Gibson LJ in *Drake v Whipp* [1966] 1 FLR 826, CA.

[186] These figures are taken from the Law Commission's Consultation Paper No 179, *Cohabitation: The Financial Consequences of Relationship Breakdown* (2006) para 205, and Part 2 of that Paper contains a valuable analysis of 'changing social trends'. It appears that a quarter of all unmarried women aged 16 to 49 are in fact cohabiting; whilst 42% of all births are to parents not married to one another (more than three quarters of them jointly registered by parents living at the same address). At the same time, the number of marriages has fallen dramatically; and the average age of those marrying for the first time has sharply increased. However, marriage remains the most common form of domestic partnership for different sex couples: only one in six are cohabiting outside marriage: see paras 2.10–2.13.

assimilate, to a greater or lesser extent, the legal consequences of marriage and of cohabitation. It has been said[187] that the law should recognize the fact that cohabitation (whether heterosexual or homosexual) is widespread; and statute and case law both exemplify the trend towards accepting that marriage is no longer the only form of domestic relationship to which the law should attach consequences. But it is not always easy to detect a consistent policy. For example, whereas in respect of the recognition of a legal relationship between a parent and child, the law has eroded and come close to rejecting altogether the significance of the parent's marital status, in respect of the recognition of the relationship between the partners themselves the initial question must still always be whether they are validly married[188] or not. The extensive rights attached to the status of marriage arise automatically by operation of law whereas some specific statutory or other recognized source must be identified to justify a claim arising out of other relationships. As one judge pointed out[189] in robust language, English law recognizes neither the term 'palimony' (current in some parts of the United States) nor the legal obligation to which it gives effect; and whereas a husband has a legal obligation to support his wife even if they are living apart a man has no legal obligation to support his mistress even if they are living together. Yet in cases in which the availability of a remedy depends on the presumed intention of the parties[190] or the nature of their relationship[191] the courts have become increasingly ready to accept that the legal status of the parties is not primarily relevant.[192] The law certainly remains complex and uncertain, and one judge has compared it to a 'witch's brew, into which various ingredients have been stirred over the years, and in which different ideas—likely to mean nothing to laymen, and often little more to the lawyers who use them—bubble to the surface at different times'.[193]

Statutes increasingly make provision towards assimilating the consequences of **2.53** marriage and cohabitation; and the formula often found defines those affected as 'a man and a woman who, although not married to each other, are living together

---

[187] *Barclays Bank Plc v O'Brien* [1994] 1 AC 180, 198, *per* Lord Browne-Wilkinson.

[188] Or civil partners: see para 2.87.

[189] Millett J, *Windeler v Whitehall* [1990] 2 FLR 505, 506.

[190] This is especially true in relation to property matters: see para 2.107 and *Hammond v Mitchell* [1991] 1 WLR 1127; *Tinsley v Milligan* [1995] 1 AC 340, HL; *Tribe v Tribe* [1996] Ch 107.

[191] See eg *Stephens v Avery* [1988] Ch 449 where the court refused to accept that the protection given by law to an individual's sexual conduct or proclivities (in that case, in the context of a lesbian relationship) was confined to cases in which the person concerned was married; compare *Sutton v Mishcon de Reya* [2003] EWHC 3166.

[192] In *Barclays Bank plc v O'Brien* Lord Browne-Wilkinson noted that 'legal wives' were not the only group now exposed to the 'emotional pressures of cohabitation' and that accordingly a creditor aware of the fact that surety and principal debtor were cohabiting should be on notice of the risk that a transaction might be vitiated in the same way as if the couple concerned were married.

[193] *Stack v Dowden* [2006] 1 FLR 254, at [75].

as husband and wife'.[194] However, this raises a conceptual problem. Marriage is a legally recognized status, and it is not necessary in order to determine whether a couple are married or not to decide which incidents of marital relationship—such as the use of a common name or the existence of a sexual relationship—are essential and which superfluous. But in contrast the question whether or not two people are 'living together as husband and wife' can only be answered by making a value judgment of that kind. This problem[195] has from time to time troubled the courts,[196] although recent case law reflects a more robust approach.

2.54   In the case of many statutes, the only relevant criterion for assimilating the consequences of formal and informal relationships is whether or not those concerned are (or have been) living together 'as husband and wife'[197] (although if the statute confers a discretion on the adjudicator it will often be found that additional matters are required to be taken into account in deciding whether or not and how that discretion is to be exercised).[198] However, some important statutes[199] also impose, as a threshold condition for applicability, a requirement that the relationship should have lasted for a specified period of time (such as two years).

2.55   It is impossible in a work of this kind to give an exhaustive account of the statutory provisions which to a greater or lesser extent assimilate the position of cohabitants to that of spouses (or civil partners); and only examples can be given. 'Unmarried couples'[200] are treated similarly to married couples in respect of

---

[194] See eg the Family Law Act 1996, s 62(1)(a). The Social Security Contributions and Benefits Act 1992, s 137(1) adds the requirement that those concerned be living 'in the same household'.

[195] The same principle has been introduced in the context of civil partnership which amends legislation so as to attach some of the legal consequences of partnership to a situation in which two persons are living together 'as civil partners': see *Secretary of State for Work and Pensions v M* [2006] UKHL 11; [2006] 2 WLR 637.

[196] See eg *Re J (Income Support: Cohabitation)* [1995] 1 FLR 660; *Crake v Supplementary Benefits Commission* [1982] 1 All ER 498, Div Ct. In *Fitzpatrick v Sterling Housing Association* [1999] 3 WLR 1113, the House of Lords held that two persons of the same sex could not be regarded as living together as husband and wife (although in certain circumstances they could, for purposes of succession to social tenancies, be regarded as members of the same family) but compare *Ghaidan v Godin-Mendoza* [2004] UKHL 30, [2004] 2 AC 557, (HL), where the provisions of the European Convention on Human Rights led to a different conclusion.

[197] Or as civil partners.

[198] For example, in exercising its powers to make occupation orders under the Family Law Act 1996, Part III, the court is required to consider the nature of the parties' relationship (and in that context to have regard to the fact that the parties have not given each other the commitment involved in marriage: ss 36(6)(e), 41(2)) the length of time during which they have lived together as husband and wife, and whether there are or have been children.

[199] For example, the right to seek an order that reasonable financial provision be made for the applicant out of the estate of the deceased partner (Inheritance (Provision for Family and Dependants) Act 1975, s 1(6)(a) as inserted by the Law Reform (Succession) Act 1995, s 2) and the right to seek damages for the death of a partner under the Fatal Accidents Act 1976 (as amended by the Administration of Justice Act 1982, s 3(1)).

[200] This convenient description is used in the Social Security Contributions and Benefits Act 1992, s 137(1).

eligibility for and disqualification from income support, succession rights to social housing tenancies, remedies in respect of the occupation of the family home, and claims for reasonable financial provision on death. But there remain many situations in which the 'unmarried spouse' has no standing, not least in seeking orders for financial provision on the breakdown of the relationship. Growing unease about the state of the law led to a reference to the Law Commission, which has included a review of aspects of the law in its Programme of Law Reform.[201]

B. The Termination of Legal Family Relationships

(1) Death

Death terminates both marriage and civil partnership.[202] The deceased's real and personal estate vests in his personal representatives and should be distributed in accordance with the provisions of the law governing testate and intestate succession.[203] The survivor is free to contract another marriage or partnership. **2.56**

Difficulty may be caused where there is insufficient evidence to prove that a spouse or civil partner has died. The court has a common law jurisdiction to presume death and may do so if there is no affirmative evidence that for a continuous period of seven years or more the person concerned was alive, provided (1) that there are persons who would be likely to have heard from him or her during that period; (2) that those persons have not heard from him or her; and (3) that all due inquiries have been made appropriate to the period.[204] **2.57**

The application of this common law presumption did not provide adequate security for persons wishing to remarry on the basis that a marriage had been terminated by death; for if it subsequently transpired that the presumption did not reflect the truth the remarriage would be bigamous[205] and void.[206] For this reason, statutory provision was made under which a person with reasonable grounds for supposing that his or her spouse is dead may petition[207] for a decree of **2.58**

---

[201] See *Ninth Programme of Law Reform* (2005) Law Com No 293; and see the Commission's, *Report*, Law Com No. 307 *Cohabitation: The Financial Consequences of Relationship Breakdown* (2007).

[202] Civil Partnership Act 2004, s 1(3).

[203] See Chapter 7. The Civil Partnership Act 2004, sch 4, amends the enactments relating to wills, administration of estates and family provision so that they apply in relation to civil partnerships as they apply in relation to marriage.

[204] *Chard v Chard* [1956] P 259. There seems no reason to suppose that this principle would not be applied in the case of a civil partnership.

[205] The person concerned would however have a defence to any prosecution under the Offences Against the Person Act 1861: see s 57.

[206] Matrimonial Causes Act 1973, s 11(b).

[207] ibid, s 19(1).

presumption of death and dissolution of marriage. The fact that the other party has been continually absent from the petitioner for a period of seven years or more and the petitioner has no reason to believe that he or she has been alive within that period is evidence that the other party is dead until the contrary is proved.[208] The court now has comparable power to make a presumption of death order which dissolves a civil partnership.[209]

2.59 A decree absolute[210] under this provision terminates the marriage; but if it subsequently is shown that the respondent is in fact still alive he or she may seek financial relief and property adjustment orders.

(2) Adoption

2.60 The Adoption and Children Act 2002[211] lays down the general principle that the making of an adoption order operates to extinguish (i) the parental responsibility which any person had for the child immediately before the making of the order; (ii) any order (for example, a contact order or an order requiring the child's natural father to make financial provision for the child) under the Children Act 1989, and (iii) any duty arising by virtue of an agreement[212] or the order of a court to make payments in respect of the child's maintenance. The Act also provides[213] that an adopted child is to be treated in law as if born the child of the adopters or adopter and their legitimate child; and the general principle is that the adopted child is to be treated as not being the child of any person other than the adopters or adopter.[214]

(3) Divorce and Other 'Matrimonial Causes'

2.61 The High Court, and those county courts designated as divorce county courts, have jurisdiction to hear and determine 'matrimonial causes' (that is, actions for

---

208 ibid, s 19(3).

209 Civil Partnership Act 2004, ss 37, 55.

210 The Civil Partnership Act 2004 uses the terminology of 'conditional order' and 'final order'. A decree nisi (and, presumably, a conditional order) will be rescinded if it is discovered that the respondent is in fact alive: *Manser v Manser* [1940] P 224.

211 Section 46(2). This does not apply to the child's parent where the order is made on the application of that parent's partner as defined in Adoption and Children Act 2002, s 144(4), (7).

212 This provision does not apply to an agreement which constitutes a trust, nor does it apply if the agreement expressly provides to the contrary: Adoption and Children Act 2002, s 46(4).

213 Section 67.

214 Adoption and Children Act 2002, s 67(3)(b). Special provisions apply where the child is adopted by a parent's partner, and by a parent alone: ss 67(3), (4). There are provisions preserving the property interests of an adopted child in certain circumstances: Adoption and Children Act 2002, s 69(4).

nullity of marriage, divorce or judicial separation).[215] The making of decrees of nullity and divorce is in two stages,[216] after a period of time[217] (during which further enquiries may be directed), a decree *nisi*[218] will normally, on the application of a party, be followed by the grant of a decree absolute.

(a) Nullity of marriage

The law governing nullity of marriage was codified by the Nullity of Marriage Act **2.62** 1971 (now consolidated in the Matrimonial Causes Act 1973); and is in a number of respects still based on concepts developed in the canon law administered (until 1857) by the ecclesiastical courts. Nullity petitions are today comparatively rare (no doubt in part because of the wider availability of divorce) yet nullity may still have a significant role (not least in cases in which a person forced into a marriage would, as a divorced woman, suffer a stigma).[219]

The Matrimonial Causes Act 1973 provides that marriages[220] shall be void on **2.63** certain specified grounds, and voidable on others. The main differences between these two categories are, first, that a void marriage has never existed (whereas a voidable marriage is valid until the decree takes effect) and, secondly, that a decree annulling a voidable marriage can only be pronounced during the lifetime of both parties at the instance of one of them (whereas a decree of nullity in respect to a void marriage can be pronounced at any time at the suit of any person with a sufficient interest in the matter). It should however be noted that the court has wide discretionary powers[221] to make orders for financial provision and property adjustment on or after granting a nullity decree on one of the grounds enumerated in the Act, even if the marriage is void. But it appears that that the court may refuse to pronounce a decree of any kind on the ground that there was 'nothing like a marriage' in respect of which it could exercise jurisdiction.[222]

---

[215] Matrimonial and Family Proceedings Act 1984, ss 32–3. Although the making of a decree of judicial separation does not terminate the parties' marriage it does confer on the court wide powers to make financial relief and property adjustment orders: see para 2.84.

[216] Matrimonial Causes Act 1973, ss 1(5), 8, 9, 15.

[217] Now normally six weeks.

[218] 'Unless'—ie unless cause is shown to prevent it being made absolute.

[219] See *P v R (Forced Marriage: Annulment: Procedure* [2003] 1 FLR 661.

[220] Celebrated after 31 July 1971.

[221] For the circumstances in which this discretion may be exercised, see *S-T (formerly J) v J* [1998] Fam 103, CA.

[222] See *A-M v A-M* [2001] 2 FLR 6 (polygamous 'marriage' in London flat in Islamic form); *Gandhi v Patel* [2001] 1 FLR 603 (polygamous 'marriage' in restaurant in Hindu form); compare *Gereis v Yagoub* [1997] 1 FLR 854 (decree granted under Matrimonial Causes 1973, s 11(a) in respect of a 'marriage' solemnized in a Greek Orthodox church not licensed as a place of religious worship: it 'bore the hallmarks of an ordinary Christian wedding and. . .both parties treated it as such'. In some cases the courts have been prepared to presume the existence of a valid marriage where a couple have cohabited for a long period of time and been acknowledged as husband and wife: see *Chief Adjudication Officer v Bath* [2000] 1 FLR 8; *A-M v A-M* [2001] 2 FLR 6.

(i) Grounds on which a marriage is void

2.64 The Matrimonial Causes Act 1973[223] provides that a marriage shall be void on the following six grounds only.[224]

(1) **The parties are within the prohibited degrees of relationship.** These have been set out above.[225]

(2) **Either party was at the time of the marriage under the age of sixteen.** This rule should not be confused with that requiring parental consent to the marriage of a minor. If either party is under sixteen at the date of the ceremony the marriage is void, whether or not either or both parties knew the true facts, and irrespective of whether the parents (or anyone else) agreed to a marriage. In contrast, lack of the requisite parental consent to the marriage of a sixteen- or seventeen-year-old will not invalidate the marriage (although criminal sanctions may be imposed if a false declaration has been made).

(3) **Knowing and wilful disregard of prescribed formalities.** The Marriage Act 1949 provides that a marriage is void if the parties 'knowingly and wilfully' disregard certain prescribed formalities.[226] In contrast, the Act provides that evidence is not to be given of certain irregularities (so that such defects cannot invalidate the marriage); and it seems to be accepted that failure to comply with other prescribed formalities (for example, that the marriage be celebrated with open doors) does not affect the validity of the marriage.

(4) **Bigamy.** A marriage is void if either party was, at the time, already lawfully married (or a party to a civil partnership).[227] The existence of the prior relationship is a matter for proof, and the court will in certain circumstances presume that the person concerned had died in the absence of affirmative evidence that he or she was, over a seven year period, alive.[228]

(5) **Parties not respectively male and female.** It has been said[229] that 'single sex unions' are proscribed as 'fundamentally abhorrent' to the common law's concept of marriage as the voluntary union for life of one man and one woman; and it remains true that a purported marriage between two males or

---

[223] Section 11.

[224] There appears to be one exception to the comprehensive nature of the Act: the Royal Marriages Act 1772, s 1, provides that marriages of members of the royal family shall be void unless the consent of the sovereign has been obtained; and the effect of that provision seems to have been preserved by the Nullity of Marriage Act 1971, s 1(4) and the consolidating Matrimonial Causes Act 1973, sch 1, para 6.

[225] See paras 2.27–2.29.

[226] See para 2.39.

[227] Matrimonial Causes Act 1973, s 11(b) as amended by Civil Partnership Act 2004, sch 27, para 40. Etymologically, bigamy refers to *marriages*, but it seems reasonable to use the same term to describe the incompatibility of having two marriage-like relationships at the same time.

[228] *Chard v Chard* [1956] P 259.

[229] *S-T (formerly J) v J* [1998] Fam 103, 141, CA, *per* Ward LJ.

two females will be void.[230] The law has, however, now[231] come formally to recognize that the rigid demarcation of man and woman does not always adequately reflect modern medical knowledge and practice and that treatment for 'gender dysphoria'[232] may lead to a person properly being assigned to a gender different from that in which he or she was born. The Gender Recognition Act 2004 accordingly provides machinery whereby such persons may obtain recognition of their acquired gender, obtain a new birth certificate, and contract a valid marriage in that gender.[233]

(6) **Polygamous marriage contracted abroad by person domiciled in England and Wales.** For this purpose, the marriage in question must have been actually (as distinct from merely potentially) polygamous.[234]

(ii) Grounds on which a marriage is voidable

The Matrimonial Causes Act 1973[235] provides that a marriage shall be voidable on the following grounds only. **2.65**

(1) **The marriage has not been consummated owing to the incapacity of either party to consummate it.** The question is whether the one party[236] was, at the time of the marriage, permanently and incurably incapable (whether for physiological or psychological reasons)[237] of consummating the marriage.[238] It is immaterial that the party affected may be capable of having sexual relations with other partners. **2.66**

(2) **The marriage has not been consummated owing to the respondent's wilful refusal to do so.** This ground can only be made out if the petitioner satisfies the court that the respondent had, without just excuse, come to a settled and **2.67**

---

[230] Matrimonial Causes Act 1973, 11(c); *S-T (formerly J) v J* [1998] Fam 103, CA; and see *Wilkinson v Kitzinger and HM Attorney-General (The Lord Chancellor Intervening)* [2006] EWHC 835 (Fam) (Sir Mark Potter, P). The Civil Partnership Act 2004 allows two persons of the same sex to contract a civil partnership with many of the legal consequences of marriage.

[231] For many years, the courts insisted that a person's sex was irreversibly fixed at birth: *Corbett v Corbett* [1971] P 83. Eventually, the House of Lords held that this rule was incompatible with the convention rights protected by the Human Rights 1998: *Bellinger v Bellinger* [2003] UKHL 21.

[232] Defined by the Gender Recognition Act 2004, s 25, as 'the disorder variously referred to as gender dysphoria, gender identity disorder and transsexualism'.

[233] In certain circumstances, however, the marriage may be annulled as a voidable marriage: see para 2.70.

[234] Matrimonial Causes Act 1973, s 11(d) as amended by the Private International Law (Miscellaneous Provisions) Act 1995, sch, para 2(2).

[235] Section 12.

[236] The petitioner may rely on his or her own incapacity.

[237] A conscious decision not to permit intercourse is not sufficient: *Singh v Singh* [1971] P 226.

[238] For this purpose, consummation means 'ordinary and complete' sexual intercourse (*D-A v A-G.* (1845) 1 Rob. Eccl. 279 is the classical authority) and this expression is to given its contemporary meaning: *Baxter v Baxter* [1948] AC 274, HL a wilful refusal case in which the House of Lords held that a wife refusing to permit intercourse unless the husband used a condom was not thereby refusing to consummate the marriage.

definite decision not to consummate[239] the marriage. The courts will look at the whole history of the marriage; and the refusal may not be direct: for example, in several cases[240] the courts have held that the husband's failure to arrange religious rites required by the parties' community tradition constitutes a wilful refusal to consummate a marriage contracted in a register office.

2.68 **(3) Lack of consent.** The 1973 Act provides that a marriage is voidable (and not, as remains the case for marriages celebrated before 1 August 1971, void) if either party did not validly consent to it, whether in consequence of duress, mistake, unsoundness of mind,[241] or otherwise. This reflects the fact that the essence of the 'marriage contract' is an agreement between a man and a woman[242] and the crucial element in making out this ground is the lack of consent.[243] In recent years, the phenomenon of 'forced marriages' in some communities[244] has given rise to anxiety, and administrative steps have been taken in an attempt to deal with the problem.[245] But it is important to note that the law does not seek to prevent arranged marriages, which have their part in many societies and communities; and to establish the lack of consent required by the law of nullity there must be evidence that the petitioner's will was overborne by fear.[246] Accordingly, a decree will not be granted where the petitioner has deliberately (albeit reluctantly) entered into the marriage in compliance with a sense of family or

---

[239] See n 238 above.

[240] *Kaur v Singh* [1972] 1 WLR 105; and see *A v J (Nullity Proceedings)* [1989] 1 FLR 110.

[241] It has been held that the contract of marriage is in essence a simple one which does not require a high degree of intelligence to comprehend. and that it can readily be understood by anyone of normal intelligence. In recent years it has been pointed out that setting the test of capacity to marry too high may operate as an unfair, unnecessary and discriminatory bar against the mentally disabled: see *In the Estate of Park* [1954] P 112, CA; *Sheffield CC v E* [2004] EWHC 2808 (Fam), [2005] Fam 326.

[242] See *Sheffield CC v E* [2004] EWHC 2808 (Fam), [2005] Fam 326, in which Munby J accepted that the essence of the marriage contract is an 'agreement to live together, and to love one another as husband and wife, to the exclusion of all others'.

[243] In cases where lack of consent is said to arise from the respondent's mental illness the petitioner must show that this made him or her incapable of understanding the nature of marriage and the duties and responsibilities it creates. In appropriate cases a decree may be granted to a petitioner unable to satisfy the court that the effect of the illness was so severe on the alternative ground (Matrimonial Causes Act 1973, s 12(d)) that the respondent was suffering from mental disorder 'of such a kind or to such an extent as to be unfitted for marriage'.

[244] The difficulties sometimes facing young people brought up to follow the traditional norms of their religious, cultural or ethnic group are highlighted by Singer J in *Re KR (Abduction: Forcible Removal by Parents)* [1999] 2 FLR 542.

[245] A Forced Marriage Unit has been set up by the Home Office and the Foreign and Commonwealth Office: it deals with some 250 cases a year: see *A Choice by Right: the Report of the Working Group on Forced Marriage* (HMSO, 2002); and see *P v R (Forced Marriage: Annulment: Procedure* [2003] 1 FLR 661.

[246] As in *Hirani v Hirani* (1982) 4 FLR 232, CA.

religious obligation.[247] The fact that the marriage has been induced by fraud is not as such[248] a ground upon which it can be annulled; and mistake is only relevant in so far as it negatives consent to marriage (as in cases in which the petitioner believed that the marriage ceremony was a religious conversion rite or a betrothal).[249]

(4) Mental disorder, etc. The narrowness of the traditional grounds for annulment derived from the canon law led to demand for reform, and this was conceded by the Matrimonial Causes Act 1937. It is now provided[250] that a marriage is voidable, first, if either party to the marriage was, at the time, although capable of giving a valid consent, suffering (whether continuously or intermittently) from mental disorder of such a kind or to such an extent as to be unfitted for marriage; secondly, if the respondent was, at the time of the marriage and unknown to the petitioner suffering from venereal disease in a communicable form; and thirdly, if the respondent was at the time of the marriage, unknown to the petitioner, pregnant by some person other than the petitioner. **2.69**

(5) Gender reassignment. The Gender Reassignment Act 2004 creates a situation in which the parties to a valid marriage between a man and a woman may, as a result of gender reassignment, be legally recognized as being of the same sex. The Act accordingly amends the Matrimonial Causes Act 1973 by adding two new grounds upon which a marriage may be held to be voidable. The first[251] is that a Gender Recognition Panel has at some time after the marriage issued to either party an 'interim gender recognition certificate'[252] recognizing the acquisition of a different gender; the second[253] is where the petitioner satisfies the court that at **2.70**

---

[247] See eg *Singh v Singh* [1971] P 226; *NS v MI* [2006] EWHC 1646; and for a full analysis of the legal principles applicable in cases based on duress *Szechter v Szechter* [1971] P 286 (where, however, the decision on the facts that the parties' wills were overborne by fear of action likely to be taken against them by a totalitarian government seems surprising).

[248] *Moss v Moss* [1897] P 273 (man tricked into marriage by woman carrying third party's child). In such cases the marriage might now be annulled under the Matrimonial Causes Act 1973, s 12(f): see para 2.69.

[249] See *Mehta v Mehta* [1945] 2 All ER 690. Mistake as to the legal consequences of marriage is also insufficient to avoid the marriage: *Messina v Smith* [1971] P 322.

[250] See now Matrimonial Causes Act 1973, s 12(d), (e) and (f) as amended.

[251] Matrimonial Causes Act 1973, s 12(g) inserted by Gender Recognition Act 2004, sch 2, para 2. The nullity proceedings must be started within six months from the date of issue of the certificate: Matrimonial Causes Act 1973, s 13(2A) inserted by Gender Recognition Act 2004, sch 2, para 3.

[252] The interim certificate reflects a finding that the statutory conditions for recognition have been established. The court annulling the marriage will then issue a full gender recognition certificate: Gender Recognition Act 2004, s 5(1).

[253] Matrimonial Causes Act 1973, s 12(h) inserted by Gender Recognition Act 2004, sch 4, para 5.

the time of the marriage the respondent's gender had become his or her 'acquired gender' within the meaning of the 2004 Act.[254]

(iii) Bars to relief

2.71 There are no bars to the granting of a decree based on the marriage being void;[255] but it is provided[256] that the court shall not grant a decree of nullity on the ground that a marriage is voidable if the respondent satisfies the court (1) that the petitioner, with knowledge that it was open to him to have the marriage avoided, so conducted himself in relation to the respondent as to lead the respondent reasonably to believe that he would not seek to do so; and (2) that it would be unjust to the respondent to grant the decree. But it should be noted that the fact that annulment would be contrary to public policy is not a statutory bar to the grant of a decree.[257] Moreover, the court cannot grant a decree founded on venereal disease, pregnancy by a third party, or the respondent having an 'acquired gender' at the time of the marriage unless the petitioner was ignorant of the fact at the time of the marriage.[258]

2.72 In the case of petitions founded on lack of consent, mental disability, venereal disease, pregnancy by a third party, or the respondent having an 'acquired gender' at the time of the marriage[259] the court is debarred from granting a decree unless the proceedings were instituted within three years from the date of the marriage.[260]

(iv) Effects of a nullity decree

2.73 Statute has largely negatived the effect of the common law doctrines under which a void marriage had no legal consequences, and a decree annulling a voidable marriage operated retroactively so that the marriage was declared never to have existed. First, a decree relating to a voidable marriage now operates to annul the marriage only as respects any time after the decree has been made absolute, and the

---

254 Gender Recognition Act 2004, ss 24 and 1(2): the acquired gender 'in relation to a person by whom an application [for a gender recognition certificate] has been made means. . .the gender in which the person is living'.

255 Nullity of Marriage Act 1971, s 6(1) (abolishing the bar of collusion). There may, however, be cases in which a party is estopped from putting the validity of a marriage in issue: *Woodland v Woodland* [1928] P 169.

256 Matrimonial Causes Act 1973, s 13(1).

257 See *D v D (Nullity: Statutory Bar)* [1979] Fam 70.

258 Matrimonial Causes Act 1973, s 13(3), as amended.

259 Where the petition is based on the fact that an interim certificate has been issued, the application for a nullity decree must be made within six months: Matrimonial Causes Act 1973, s 13(2A), inserted by Gender Reassignment Act 2004, sch 2, para 3.

260 Matrimonial Causes Act 1973, s 13(2) as amended. Exceptionally, the judge may give leave for proceedings to be instituted after the expiration of the three year period if the petitioner has at some time during that period suffered from mental disorder and in all the circumstances it would be just to do so: Matrimonial Causes Act 1973, s 13(2) and (4), as inserted by the Matrimonial and Family Proceedings Act 1984, s 2(2) and (3).

marriage is treated as if it had existed up to that time notwithstanding the decree.[261] Secondly, the court has power, on or after granting a decree of nullity (and irrespective of whether the marriage was void or voidable) to make financial provision and property adjustment orders for the benefit of either party and any children of the family.[262] (It should however be noted that the power is discretionary; and the court may refuse to exercise it on public policy or other grounds.) Finally, the children of a void marriage are entitled to be treated as the legitimate children[263] of the mother and father provided that at the time of the intercourse resulting in their birth both or either of the parents reasonably believed the marriage to be valid.[264]

(b) Divorce

(i) The background to the legislation

The availability of divorce in English Law is currently governed by provisions **2.74** originating in the Divorce Reform Act 1969 and now consolidated in the Matrimonial Causes Act 1973. The reformed law is much criticized in some quarters, chiefly on the ground that the need to make allegations about, for example, the respondent's behaviour[265] makes the professed objective of removing bitterness distress and humiliation from the divorce process difficult to attain; and the Family Law Act 1996 was enacted in response to such criticism. The provisions of Part II of the 1996 Act would (whilst preserving the principle that irretrievable breakdown of the marriage is the sole ground for divorce) have radically changed the law governing how that ground was to be established. However, it soon became apparent that there were serious grounds for believing that the reforms would not meet all expectations,[266] and in 2001 it was announced that the provisions

---

261 Matrimonial Causes Act 1973, s 16. This reform, intended to remove an anomaly, has operated to the disadvantage of some petitioners: see *Ward v Secretary of State for Social Services* [1990] 1 FLR 119 (entitlement to widow's pension terminated by remarriage notwithstanding annulment granted after one week's cohabitation).

262 Matrimonial Causes Act 1973, ss 23, 24. There are different views about the basis upon which this discretion should be exercised. In *Whiston v Whiston* [1995] Fam 198, CA, the court held that a bigamous wife's claim for financial orders was defeated by the principle of public policy debarring a criminal from profiting from the crime committed; but in *S-T (formerly J) v J* [1998] Fam 103, CA, the majority of the Court of Appeal refused to extend the application of that principle beyond the crime of bigamy. On the facts the application was dismissed in the exercise of the discretion conferred by the Matrimonial Causes Act, but compare *Rampal v Rampal* [2001] EWCA Civ 925 where a claim was allowed to proceed.

263 Children of a voidable marriage will now normally be legitimate because the marriage will be treated as valid until the grant of the decree: see para 2.73.

264 Legitimacy Act 1976, s 1.

265 Matrimonial Causes Act 1973, s 1(2)(b); para 2.76.

266 Two extensive research projects were established to monitor pilot projects concerned with mediation and the giving of information: see J Walker et al., *Information Meetings and Associated Provisions within the Family Law Act 1996, Final Evaluation Report* (Lord Chancellor's Department, 2001).

changing the substantive law were not to be brought into force.[267] In the circumstances, they are not discussed further in this work.

(ii) The ground for divorce: irretrievable breakdown of the marriage

2.75 The Matrimonial Causes Act 1973 provides[268] that a petition for divorce[269] may be presented to the court by either party to a marriage on the ground that the marriage has broken down irretrievably. But no petition is to be presented to the court before the expiration of the period of one year from the date of the marriage.[270]

(iii) How 'irretrievable breakdown' is established: the 'facts' from which breakdown will be inferred

2.76 The effect of the principle that the ground for divorce is the irretrievable breakdown of the marriage is much affected by two provisions governing the circumstances in which that ground will be held to have been made out. First, it is provided that the court hearing a divorce petition is not to hold the marriage to have broken down irretrievably unless the petitioner satisfies the court of one or more of five facts:[271]

(a) that the respondent has committed adultery and the petitioner finds it intolerable to live with the respondent;

(b) that the respondent has behaved in such a way that the petitioner cannot reasonably be expected to live with the respondent;

(c) that the respondent has deserted the petitioner for a continuous period of at least two years immediately preceding the presentation of the petition;

(d) that the parties to the marriage have lived apart for a continuous period of at least two years immediately preceding the presentation of the petition and the respondent consents to a decree being granted;

(e) that the parties to the marriage have lived apart for a continuous period of at least five years immediately preceding the presentation of the petition.

---

[267] Part I of the Act is, however, in force. It states certain 'general principles' (for example that the institution of marriage is to be supported, that the parties should be encouraged to take steps to save the marriage, and that a marriage which has indeed broken down irretrievably should be brought to an end with minimum distress to the parties and children) governing the exercise of functions by the court and others.

[268] s 1 (consolidating provisions originally enacted in the Divorce Reform Act 1969).

[269] Alternatively, a spouse may petition for a decree of judicial separation on the ground that any of the 'facts' specified below exists; but it is expressly provided that the court considering such a petition shall not be concerned to consider whether the marriage has broken down irretrievably: Matrimonial Causes Act 1973, s 17; see para 2.83.

[270] Matrimonial Causes Act 1973, s 3 (as substituted by the Matrimonial and Family Proceedings Act 1984).

[271] Matrimonial Causes Act 1973, s 1(2). There was, before the introduction of the 'special procedure' (see para 2.81) a substantial body of case law on the interpretation to be given to these facts but this will now rarely be relevant in practice.

Secondly, it is provided[272] that if the court is satisfied on the evidence of any such fact,[273] it must grant a divorce, unless it is satisfied on the evidence that the marriage has *not* broken down.[274] In effect, proof of any of the five 'facts' raises a presumption of breakdown and that presumption is difficult to rebut.

(iv) Protection against consequences of divorce

The Matrimonial Causes Act 1973[275] contains three provisions which may be invoked by spouses who seek protection against the adverse consequences of losing the status of a married person. This can be done by preventing (or at least postponing) the legal termination of their marriage notwithstanding the fact that the legal conditions for demonstrating that it has irretrievably broken down are satisfied. **2.77**

Dissolution would cause hardship. The Matrimonial Causes Act 1973[276] provides that the court may dismiss a petition founded solely on the five year living apart fact if two distinct conditions are satisfied: (1) that the legal dissolution of the marriage (as distinct from the fact that it has irretrievably broken down) will result in grave financial or other hardship to the respondent, and (2) that it would be wrong in all the circumstances to dissolve the marriage. But this provision is rarely successfully invoked.[277] It is difficult to establish that the financial hardship[278] often associated with marital breakdown is caused by the legal termination of the marriage (as distinct from the fact that the parties have insufficient funds to sustain two households)[279] and there has been no reported case in which a defence **2.78**

---

272 Matrimonial Causes Act 1973, s 1(4).

273 The Act imposes a duty on the court to inquire, so far as it reasonably can, into the facts alleged by the petitioner and into any facts alleged by the respondent: Matrimonial Causes Act 1973, s 1(3). But the ability of the court to carry out any such inquiry is in practice restricted by the application of the 'special procedure': see para 2.81.

274 In certain restricted circumstances the respondent may oppose the grant of a decree based solely on five years separation on the ground that divorce would cause him 'grave financial or other hardship' and that it would in all the circumstances be wrong to dissolve the marriage: Matrimonial Causes Act 1973, s 5; see para 2.78.

275 As amended by the Divorce (Religious Marriages) Act 2002.

276 s 5.

277 This is not to say that the threat of invoking the defence may not in some cases lead to the petitioner agreeing improved financial or other arrangements: see *K v K (Financial Relief: Widow's Pension)* [1997] 1 FLR 35.

278 Which must, in any event, be 'grave': see *Reiterbund v Reiterbund* [1975] Fam 99, CA (wife's loss of entitlement to widow's pension not grave since welfare benefits would provide similar amount); *Archer v Archer* [1999] 1 FLR 327, CA (loss of widow's pension of £11,000 not grave hardship for wife with capital assets of about half a million pounds).

279 Most of the reported cases in which the s 5 defence has been successfully invoked were concerned with the wife's loss of the pension entitlement which she would have had as her husband's widow (see eg *Parker v Parker* [1972] Fam 116) but the pension-splitting provisions of the Welfare Reform and Pensions Act 1999 will no doubt reduce the number of such cases.

based on 'other' hardship has been successfully raised.[280] Even if a respondent were successful in establishing that dissolution would cause grave financial or other hardship the court is not obliged to withhold a decree but will do so only if it considers it wrong in all the circumstances—including some specified in the legislation—to dissolve the marriage;[281] and the court may feel that achieving the legislative objective of crushing the empty shells of dead marriages[282] outweighs the hardship which that process will cause to the respondent.

2.79 **Protecting respondents in separation cases: postponing decree absolute.** A respondent may apply to the court after decree nisi founded on either of the two 'living apart' facts for consideration of his or her financial position after the divorce; and it is provided[283] that in such circumstances the court must not make the decree absolute unless it is satisfied that the financial arrangements are 'reasonable and fair' or 'the best that can be made in the circumstances'. However, this provision was originally enacted before the court had the wide powers which it now enjoys to make financial orders, and it is comparatively rarely invoked.[284]

2.80 **Protection against spouse's failure to obtain dissolution of religious marriage.** Hardship could be caused if the law of the parties' religion would not recognize the divorce decree as effective to dissolve the marriage. In particular, a wife granted a decree by the court might find that her husband refused to deliver the *get* (or Bill of Divorcement) which alone would be effective according to the parties' personal religious law to free her to remarry. In an attempt to deal with this problem, statute now provides that the court may, on the application of either party, refuse to make the decree absolute until both parties have made a declaration that they have taken such steps as are required to dissolve the marriage in accordance with the appropriate religious usages.[285]

---

   [280] The leading case is *Rukat v Rukat* [1975] Fam 63, CA; and see *Banik v Banik* [1973] 1 WLR 860, CA.
   [281] See *Brickell v Brickell* [1974] Fam 31, CA.
   [282] *Per* Finer J, *Reiterbund v Reiterbund* [1974] 1 WLR 788, 798.
   [283] Matrimonial Causes Act 1973, s 10.
   [284] For a case in which the court held that decree absolute had been properly withheld pending investigation of the parties' financial position see *Garcia v Garcia* [1992] 1 FLR 256, CA but note that the court held that the normal ancillary relief procedure (see para 2.143(5)) would normally provide adequate protection and that accordingly the s 10 procedure should only be used where to do so might prevent complications and bring litigation to an end.
   [285] Matrimonial Causes Act 1973, s 10A(2) as inserted by Divorce (Religious Marriages) Act 2002, s 1(2). The Act applies to cases in which the parties were married in accordance with the usages of the Jews or 'any other prescribed religious usages' but to date no Order has been made prescribing any other religious usage.

(v) The impact of the 'special procedure'

The substantive law, as set out above, suggests that the issue of divorce will be dealt **2.81** with by court hearings of the traditional kind. But in fact a so-called 'special procedure' has, for the past three decades, been applied to all undefended divorce cases. Since very few divorce petitions are defended[286] the effect has been to transform the judicial process whereby marriages were formerly dissolved into what has come to resemble an administrative procedure. The special procedure[287] dispenses with any attendance by the parties at court, and has been authoritatively summarized as follows:

> Following presentation of the petition, the petitioner's solicitor lodges an application for directions for trial together with a standard affidavit. . .In routine cases. . .the [district judge] gives directions for trial by entering the case in the special procedure list and thereafter considers the evidence filed by the petitioner. If he is satisfied that the petitioner has sufficiently proved the contents of the petition and is entitled to the decree sought. . .he will make and file a certificate to that effect. The court then sends notification to the parties of the date, time and place fixed for the pronouncement of the decree nisi. The parties are also told that their attendance at the pronouncement of decree is not necessary. The actual process of pronouncement of the decree has become reduced to a very brief ceremony of a purely formal character in which decrees are listed together in batches for a collective mention in open court before a judge who speaks (or nods) his assent . . . . [T]he sole truly judicial function in the entire process is that of the [district judge] when granting his certificate. Everything that follows is automatic and administrative.[288]

Although the special procedure is only applicable to undefended divorce cases **2.82** (that is to say cases in which the respondent does not oppose the dissolution of the marriage)[289] very few petitions are defended (no doubt in part because public funding is now rarely available for the purpose); whilst changes in the procedural rules have made the requirements of 'proving' a relevant fact a formality in the great majority of cases.[290] It seems that solicitors almost invariably advise clients that divorce is sooner or later (albeit perhaps only after five years' separation) inevitable if one party wishes; and the dissolution of the marriage is seen as largely irrelevant to the financial consequences of divorce and the arrangements to be made for the children. The term 'special procedure' is itself a misnomer since it has

---

[286] See para 2.82.

[287] The procedure is laid down by the Family Proceedings Rules 1991, SI 1991/1247, r 2.24, 2.36.

[288] *Pounds v Pounds* [1994] 1 WLR 1535, 1539, *per* Waite LJ.

[289] It is true that in one case (*Butterworth v Butterworth* [1998] 1 FLR 179) the Court of Appeal criticized judges who gave the impression that it was unreasonable to object to divorce and that the evidence in support of a divorce petition was a formality; but the practical reality seems to support the view stated in the text: see *Bhaji v Chauhan* [2003] 2 FLR 48.

[290] For example, it is no longer necessary to name the third party with whom adultery is alleged to have been committed, and a simple affirmative response to the question on the standard form addressed to the respondent is sufficient proof of the adultery alleged.

become the 'ordinary procedure' in the great majority of cases.[291] Litigation after the formal dissolution of the marriage about the legal and practical consequences of the breakdown[292] has come to provide the forum for ventilating the grievances which at one time would have been at the heart of the divorce suit itself.

(c) Judicial Separation

(i) Grounds for decree

2.83 A petition seeking a decree of judicial separation may be presented at any time after the solemnization of the marriage alleging one or more of the 'facts' on which a divorce petition may be presented[293] (ie adultery, behaviour, desertion, separation); but it is specifically provided[294] that the court shall not be concerned whether the marriage has broken down irretrievably.

(ii) Effect of judicial separation decree

2.84 The court's jurisdiction to grant decrees of judicial separation is derived from the practice of the ecclesiastical courts, and it is presumably because of this that the legislation[295] still provides that 'it shall no longer be obligatory for the petitioner to cohabit with the respondent' after such a decree has been granted. In reality, the 'obligation' to cohabit is no longer legally enforceable, and other procedures are available to protect a spouse against harassment or molestation.[296] But judicial separation still has a part to play in the family justice system. This is because the court has power, on or after granting such a decree, to make financial relief and property adjustment orders;[297] and judicial separation can thus be appropriate where the parties wish to have appropriate financial orders made in consequence of separation,[298] especially where religious considerations point away from divorce

---

[291] See *Pounds v Pounds* [1994] 1 FLR 775. The lack of any searching judicial investigation into the allegations made in the petition makes it possible for the unscrupulous to obtain a decree when no relevant fact exists: see eg *Bhaji v Chauhan, Queen's Proctor Intervening (Divorce: Marriages used for Immigration Purposes)* [2003] 2 FLR 48; but if the truth is discovered the decree may be rescinded (as in *Moynihan v Moynihan* [1997] 1 FLR 52) and those responsible may be prosecuted for perjury or other offences.

[292] However, the court has to consider the arrangements proposed for the children before decree nisi, and applications for protection in the occupation of the family home and for interim financial orders will of course be dealt with before decree. But the main issues about financial matters will usually not be resolved until after the decree nisi and litigation about the children will often continue after decree.

[293] Matrimonial Causes Act 1973, s 17(1).

[294] Matrimonial Causes Act 1973, s 17(2).

[295] Matrimonial Causes Act 1973, s 18.

[296] Notably the provisions of Family Law Act 1996, Part III; see para 2.120.

[297] See para 2.143. For a case demonstrating the utility of this power, see *Le Foe v Le Foe and Woolwich plc* [2001] 2 FLR 970.

[298] Matrimonial Causes Act 1973, s 18(2).

as a remedy.[299] It may also be relevant that the parties will remain husband and wife so that their respective pension entitlements will not be affected (as they would be on divorce).[300] In contrast, if one party to a marriage dies wholly or partially intestate while a judicial separation is in force the property concerned devolves as if the other had been then dead.[301]

(4) 'Civil Partnership Causes'[302]

The Family Division of the High Court[303] and those county courts which have **2.85** been designated as 'civil partnership proceedings county courts'[304] have jurisdiction to deal with applications for the dissolution or annulment of a civil partnership and for the legal separation of civil partners.[305]

(a) Nullity Orders

The Civil Partnership Act provides that the court may make a nullity order[306] **2.86** annulling a civil partnership which is void or voidable.[307]

(i) Grounds upon which partnership void

The Act provides three grounds upon which a civil partnership is void. **2.87**

The parties are not eligible to register as civil partners.[308] In effect, an order **2.88** may be made on this ground if the parties are not of the same sex, if they are within the prohibited degrees, or if either of them is under the age of 16.[309]

---

[299] There is no time restriction on the presentation of judicial separation petitions (cf Matrimonial Causes Act 1973, s 3, as substituted by Matrimonial and Family Proceedings Act 2004) and this may also be a factor in some cases.

[300] See para 2.150. The court's powers to make pension sharing orders are not available in judicial separation proceedings.

[301] Matrimonial Causes Act 1973, s 18(2).

[302] Defined by Matrimonial and Family Proceedings Act 1984, s 32 as inserted by Civil Partnership Act 2004, sch 27, para 91.

[303] See Supreme Court Act 1981, sch 1, para 3(i), inserted by Civil Partnership Act 2004, sch 27, para 70.

[304] See Matrimonial and Family Proceedings Act 1984, ss 32, 36A-D, 37(4), sch 1, para 3(i) (mirroring provisions relating to divorce county courts) as inserted by Civil Partnership Act 2004, sch 27, paras 90–92.

[305] Such an order does not in law terminate the partnership but may suggest that it has broken down: see para 2.84.

[306] The order will in the first instance be a conditional order, and cannot be made final for a period which will normally be six weeks: Civil Partnership Act 2004, ss 37(2), 38. These mirror the provisions under which divorce and nullity decrees are in the first instance decrees *nisi*: see para 2.61.

[307] Civil Partnership Act 2004, s 37(1) (b).

[308] Civil Partnership Act 2004, s 49(a).

[309] Civil Partnership Act 2004, s 3.

2.89 Knowing non-compliance with certain registration procedures.[310]   The Act provides that a civil partnership is void if at the time of registration both parties knew, either (i) that due notice of the proposed partnership had not been given,[311] or (ii) that the 'civil partnership document'[312] had not been duly issued; or (iii) that the document is void because its validity has expired,[313] or (iv) that the place of registration is not that specified in the notice or document,[314] or (v) that no registrar was present.[315]

2.90 Partnership forbidden by person whose consent required.   If a person whose consent is required to the partnership (commonly the parent of a person aged 16 or 17) has caused it to be forbidden, the partnership will be void.[316]

(ii) Grounds upon which civil partnership voidable

2.91   The Act provides that a civil partnership is voidable in the following circumstances.

2.92 Lack of consent.   A civil partnership (like a marriage) is voidable if either party did not validly consent to its formation (whether as a result of duress, mistake, unsoundness of mind or otherwise).[317]

2.93 Mental illness.   A civil partnership (like a marriage)[318] is voidable if either of the parties, albeit capable of giving a valid consent, was at the time suffering from mental disorder such as to render that party unfitted for civil partnership.[319]

2.94 Pregnancy by third party.   A civil partnership (like a marriage) is voidable if at the time of its formation the respondent was pregnant by some person other than the applicant.[320]

2.95 Gender recognition.   A civil partnership (like a marriage) is voidable if the respondent is a person who, at the time of its formation, had acquired a different

---

[310] Civil Partnership Act 2004, s 49 (b).

[311] Civil Partnership Act 2004, s 49(b)(i).

[312] See para 2.48.

[313] Civil Partnership Act 2004, ss 17(3) 27(2) and 49(b) (ii) and (iii).

[314] Civil Partnership Act 2004, s 49(b)(iv).

[315] Civil Partnership Act 2004, s 49(b)(v); and note the provisions of Civil Partnership Act 2004, s 1(2) which make the provisions that a civil partnership is formed when two people of the same sex register as civil partners expressly subject to the provisions of the Act dealing with void partnerships. Note also that the Act confers power on the Lord Chancellor by order to validate a civil partnership which is or may be void under any of the provisions of s 49: Civil Partnership Act 2004, s 53.

[316] Civil Partnership Act 2004, s 49(c).

[317] Civil Partnership Act 2004, s 50(1)(a) mirroring the provisions relating to marriage.

[318] Matrimonial Causes Act 1973, s 12(d).

[319] Civil Partnership Act 2004, s 50(1)(b).

[320] Civil Partnership Act 2004, s 50(1)(c), mirroring the provisions of Matrimonial Causes Act 1973, s 12(f).

gender or if, after the civil partnership had been formed, an interim gender recognition certificate had been issued to either party.[321]

(iii) Bars to relief

2.96 The Civil Partnership Act provides that in circumstances replicating the effect of those governing annulment of marriage[322] the court is debarred from making a nullity order.[323]

(iv) Effects of a nullity order

2.97 The Civil Partnership Act (replicating the effect of the provisions dealing with voidable marriage) provides that an order annulling a voidable civil partnership annuls the partnership only as respects any time after the order has been made final. Again, as with void and voidable marriages,[324] the Act empowers the court to make financial provision and property adjustment orders for the benefit of either party and any children of the family.[325]

(b) Dissolution Orders

2.98 The Civil Partnership Act 2004 mirrors the provisions of the Matrimonial Causes Act 1973[326] relating to divorce: it provides that either civil partner may apply to the court for an order dissolving the partnership on the ground that it has broken down irretrievably.[327] As with divorce, no application can be made before the end of a year from the date of formation.[328] The court is not to hold that the partnership has broken down irretrievably unless satisfied of one or more of certain facts specified in the Act, but if such a 'fact' is proved the court must make a dissolution order unless it is satisfied on all the evidence that the partnership has not broken down irretrievably.[329] The specified facts[330] are identical to those applying to divorce cases,[331] save that the respondent's adultery is not included in the list.[332]

---

[321] Under the provisions of the Gender Recognition Act 2004, see para 2.70. The effect of these provisions is to preserve the principle that civil partnership is a relationship between two persons of the same sex.

[322] See para 2.71.

[323] Civil Partnership Act 2004, s 51.

[324] See para 2.71.

[325] Civil Partnership Act 2004, s 72.

[326] s 1; see para 2.75.

[327] Civil Partnership Act 2004, ss 37(1)(a), 44.

[328] Civil Partnership Act 2004, s 41.

[329] Civil Partnership Act 2004, s 44(2)–(4).

[330] Civil Partnership Act 2004, s 44(5).

[331] Matrimonial Causes Act 1973, s 1(2); see para 2.73.

[332] See further para 2.100. 'Unfaithfulness' may be relied on in support of an allegation that the respondent has behaved in such a way that the applicant cannot reasonably be expected to live with the respondent.

(c) Separation orders

2.99 The Civil Partnership Act 2004 empowers[333] the court to make a separation order providing 'for the separation of the civil partners'. The applicant must establish one or more of the facts—'behaviour', desertion for two or more years, and living apart for five years (or two if the respondent consents to the making of the order)[334] which, in the case of divorce constitute evidence of irretrievable breakdown—and, as in the case of a matrimonial judicial separation decree, the Civil Partnership Act specifically provides[335] that the question whether the partnership has broken down irretrievably is irrelevant: in effect the 'facts' are the real ground for the making of a separation order. As with dissolution and nullity orders, the Civil Partnership Act confers wide powers on the court to make orders for financial relief.[336] The Civil Partnership Act[337] also mirrors the provisions of the Matrimonial Causes Act 1973[338] to the effect that if a civil partner dies intestate while a separation order is in force and the separation is continuing his or her property devolves as if the other were dead. Moreover, the court has extensive powers to make orders for financial relief, in the in the same way as it does in nullity and dissolution cases.[339]

(d) Significance of differences between 'matrimonial causes' and 'civil partnership causes'

2.100 Although the grounds upon which the court may exercise its powers to grant relief in respect of civil partnerships are similar to those applying to marriage, there are (as already noted) certain differences between them which it may be helpful to summarize. First, whether a marriage has been consummated by sexual intercourse is relevant to the question whether it is voidable;[340] but there are no comparable provisions relating to the annulment of a civil partnership.[341] Secondly, whilst the court may annul a marriage on the ground that one spouse was, at the time of the marriage and unknown to the other, suffering from venereal disease in a communicable form,[342] there are no comparable provisions relating to the annulment of a civil partnership. Thirdly, whilst the court may grant a divorce founded on the 'fact' that the respondent has committed adultery and that the petitioner

---

333 s 37(1)(d).
334 Civil Partnership Act 2004, s 56(1).
335 s 56(2).
336 Civil Partnership Act 2004, s 72.
337 s 57.
338 Matrimonial Causes Act 1973, s 18(2).
339 Civil Partnership Act 2004, s 72.
340 Matrimonial Causes Act 1973, s 12; see para 2.67.
341 See para 2.91.
342 Matrimonial Causes Act 1973, s 12 (e); see para 2.69.

finds it intolerable to live with him or her,[343] there is no comparable provision relating to the dissolution of a civil partnership.[344] Finally, it should be noted that whilst the court has power to grant a divorce decree in respect of a marriage and to make a dissolution order in respect of a civil partnership founded on the fact that one party has 'deserted' the other 'desertion' is, in the context of marriage, 'a long-established concept, fully analysed in many judgments of the superior courts; and it can be said with confidence that it involves the separation of the parties coupled with the intention on the part of the respondent to repudiate the obligations of marriage (and specifically the obligation to live together).[345] In contrast, there has been no judicial consideration of the 'obligations' of civil partners; and the statute book might even suggest that civil partners are not obliged to live together.[346] These are among the reasons[347] which have led some to question the coherence of the concept of civil partnership; and also to question whether the factors which guide, for example, the exercise of the court's jurisdiction to make financial orders following the ending of a marriage will be equally applicable to orders following the ending of a civil partnership.

C. The Legal Consequences of Family Relationships

2.101 Family relationships may give rise to legal consequences in respect of entitlement to property, protection in respect of the occupation of the home and protection against violence and harassment, entitlement to financial support, and in respect of issues about children. These are considered in turn.

(1) Rights in Respect of Property

(a) Introduction: the effect of marriage, civil partnership, and other family relationships on entitlement to property

2.102 Until the enactment of the Married Women's Property Acts at the end of the nineteenth century, the doctrine that marriage made the spouses a single entity had far-reaching consequences for the ownership of property. Much of the wife's property vested in the husband (the wife acquiring, in exchange, the right to be

---

343 Matrimonial Causes Act 1973, s 12 (a); see para 2.98.

344 See para 2.98.

345 See eg *Perry v Perry* [1952] P. 203; *Lang v Lang* [1955] AC 402.

346 The Civil Partnership Act 2004 s 57 ('Effects of Separation Order') contains no counterpart of the Matrimonial Causes Act 1973, s 18(1) ('Effects of judicial separation'—the effect of a judicial separation decree is that it shall no longer be obligatory for the petitioner to cohabit with the respondent).

347 See para 2.51.

maintained by him). However, legislation culminating in the Law Reform (Married Women and Tortfeasors) Act 1935 effectively abolished the old law of unity in its application to married women's property: thereafter the starting point was that the rights of the parties to a marriage should be determined on the same principles of law as apply to others.[348] In the years following the end of the Second World War there was increasing pressure for the law to give proper recognition to the contributions in many cases made by married women, in particular to the acquisition of the family home; and more recently attention has focused on the position of those who, whilst not legally married, have lived and contributed as if they were. The courts and the legislature have each responded to these problems; but the result is still not entirely coherent.[349] Finally, the Civil Partnership Act 2004 has applied the substance of statutory provisions dealing with the property rights of married couples to the property rights of civil partners.[350]

(b) Relevance of property law on relationship breakdown

2.103 The Matrimonial Causes Act 1973 and the Civil Partnership Act 2004 give the court extensive powers to make property adjustment orders in divorce, dissolution, nullity and separation proceedings. In exercising its powers under the Matrimonial Causes Act the question of the parties' beneficial interests in their property has rarely been considered relevant to the exercise of the court's discretionary powers: the overall objective is simply to attain an outcome which is as fair as possible in all the circumstances[351] and questions of ownership are made to yield to the demands of relating the means of both to the needs of each, the first consideration being given to the welfare of children.[352]

2.104 In contrast, the question of beneficial ownership remains highly relevant on the breakdown of a relationship between a couple whose relationship has not been

---

[348] *Pettitt v Pettitt* [1970] AC 777, 813, *per* Lord Upjohn. Marriage does create rights of intestate succession: see paras 7.15–7.25.

[349] See the Law Commission's Consultation Paper No 179, *Cohabitation: The Financial Consequences of Relationship Breakdown* which contains a full analysis of the law and provisional proposals for reform; and the discussion in *Stack v Dowden* [2007] UKHL 17, especially *per* Baroness Hale at paras 40–47.

[350] Civil Partnership Act 2004, Part 2, Chapter 3. Relevant minor and consequential amendments are made by Civil Partnership Act 2004, sch 27.

[351] See *White v White* [2001] 1 AC 596, especially *per* Lord Nicholls at 599.

[352] *Hammond v Mitchell* [1991] 1 WLR 1127, 1129, *per* Waite J. It is possible, however, that the decisions of the House of Lords in *Miller v Miller; McFarlane v McFarlane* [2006] UKHL 24 will lead in some cases involving large amounts to a greater emphasis than in the past on the origin of the property (for example, if it is derived from an inheritance) and the way in which it was acquired (especially if business or investment assets have been generated solely or mainly by the efforts of one party): see para 2.154.

formalized in marriage or civil partnership. The courts have neither a statutory[353] nor an inherent jurisdiction to disturb existing property rights on the termination of an unformalized relationship, however long the relationship and however deserving the claimant.[354] In the same way, beneficial entitlement alone will determine the outcome of proceedings between a spouse and a third party claiming an interest—for example under a charge given to secure borrowing for business purposes[355]—in the matrimonial home or other property. Again, identification of the property which vests in an insolvent's trustee in bankruptcy[356] is ascertained by applying the ordinary rules for determining title.

(c) Death and family property

The extent of the property which vests in a deceased's personal representatives is **2.105** also determined by the ordinary rules for determining title; and the personal representatives must distribute that property in accordance with the provisions of the deceased's will or the legislation governing intestate succession.[357] Certain categories of 'dependant' may apply to the court under the Inheritance (Provision for Family and Dependants) Act 1975[358] for an order directing that 'reasonable financial provision' be made for the applicant out of the estate; and in deciding such applications the court has to have regard to all the circumstances, including a number of matters specifically referred to in the Act. In the case of applications by a surviving spouse or civil partner those matters include the provision which the applicant might reasonably have expected to receive if the legal relationship had been dissolved on the day of the deceased's death.[359] These matters are dealt with elsewhere in this book.[360]

---

[353] A limited exception has been created by the Family Law Act 1996, s 53 and sch 7 (power to transfer certain tenancies on separation of cohabitants).

[354] *Windeler v Whitehall* [1990] 2 FLR 505, *per* Millett J. But it may be that the inferences which the court will draw from their conduct (and which may affect the decision about their entitlement) may be different: *Stack v Dowden* [2007] UKHL 17, *per* Baroness Hale at para 40.

[355] The question whether a transaction affected by undue influence or misrepresentation will be ineffective as against a third party will often need to be considered: *Barclays Bank v O'Brien* [1994] 1 AC 180, HL.

[356] As part of the bankrupt's estate, defined by the Insolvency Act 1986, s 306 (and note that that Act has been amended by the Civil Partnership Act 2004, sch 27, paras 112–122 to apply equally to spouses and civil partners). Where the estate includes a concurrent interest in the family home the trustee in bankruptcy may apply to the court for an order for sale; and the court has a discretion in the exercise of its power to make such an order: Insolvency Act 1986, s 336.

[357] See paras 7.07ff.

[358] As amended by Civil Partnership Act 2004, sch 4, paras 15–27.

[359] Inheritance (Provision for Family and Dependants) Act 1975, s 3(2), as amended by Civil Partnership Act 2004, sch 4, paras 17–18.

[360] See paras 7.216ff.

(d) Determining beneficial ownership; the application of the doctrines of implied, resulting and constructive trusts

2.106 In many cases, the application of the ordinary rules for acquisition of title to property to land or other property[361] will leave no room for doubt about the *legal* ownership of the property in question: for example, the Law of Property Act 1925[362] normally requires a deed or other document in writing for the creation or disposition of an interest in land. However, these rules do not affect the creation or operation of resulting, implied or constructive trusts;[363] and it is this exception which has led to many claims to an informally created beneficial interest in the family home being founded on those doctrines[364] and also to claims that the title documents do not accurately reflect the extent of joint owners' respective interests in the property in question. There are two main requirements if such a claim is to succeed.

(i) Intention—actual, presumed, imputed or inferred?

2.107 The threshold question in any case in which a claim is made that the beneficial interest in the property is not accurately reflected in the relevant documents is whether the claimant has discharged the onus of so demonstrating.[365] In some cases, the claimant has no legal title to the property at all; but the courts have been ready to hold that he or she has (notwithstanding the absence of writing or other formality) none the less a beneficial interest in the property arising under a resulting, implied, or constructive trust. Such trusts have been found to exist (1) where the claimant has made a direct contribution to the purchase price[366] (whether at the outset or by subsequent payments of mortgage instalments);[367] (2) where there is clear evidence that prior to the acquisition (or exceptionally at some later date)

---

361 See Chapter 4.

362 Law of Property Act 1925, ss 51–53; and see Law of Property (Miscellaneous Provisions) Act 1989.

363 Law of Property Act 1925, s 53(2). The formal requirements imposed by the Law of Property (Miscellaneous Provisions) Act 1989 respect of contracts for the disposition of land or interests therein are also subject to this exception.

364 There is a mass of reported case law: it is analysed in the most recent decision of the House of Lords, *Stack v Dowden* [2007] UKHL 17.

365 See *Stack v Dowden* [2007] UKHL 17.

366 See *Springette v Defoe* [1996] 2 FLR 388, CA; and *Tinsley v Milligan* [1995] 1 AC 340, HL. In some cases the application of the equitable presumption of advancement in favour of a wife may override the presumption of resulting trust (but see *Ali v Ali* [2002] EWCA 974); whilst the fact that a transfer of property has been carried out for an improper purpose may affect the application of these principles: see *Tinsley v Milligan*; *Tribe v Tribe* [1996] Ch 107, CA. The Civil Partnership Act 2004 does not in terms deal with these equitable principles.

367 *Gissing v Gissing* [1971] AC 886, 908, HL, *per* Lord Diplock; *Lloyds Bank plc v Rosset* [1991] 1 AC 107, HL; *Bernard v Josephs* [1982] 2 Ch 391, CA; *Re Gorman (A Bankrupt)* [1990] 1 WLR 616.

there have been discussions between the parties leading to an agreement,[368] arrangement or understanding[369] between them that the beneficial interests in the property are to be shared; (3) where the parties' dealings[370] have been such that a reasonable person would draw the inference that the parties intended that the property be jointly owned. In 1991 the House of Lords held[371] that, save in cases in which there is evidence of an agreement or understanding, it was 'extremely doubtful' whether anything short of a direct contribution to the purchase price could properly justify the drawing of such an inference; and, whilst the recent House of Lords case of *Stack v Dowden*[372] may have moved the law 'a little more towards a less restrictive view'[373] it appears that, in resolving this threshold question, there has been no fundamental change in the permissible approach.

However, once a claimant has established entitlement to some interest in the property, the court will move to an attempt to determine the parties' intentions regarding the *extent* of that interest; and in making that determination a wide range of factors may be relevant.[374] The court (it seems) is at this stage required to ascertain the parties' shared intentions, actual, inferred or imputed, with respect to the property in the light of their whole course of conduct in relation to it.[375] This is a different test from that towards which the courts seemed at one time to be moving, that is simply to ask what the court would regard as fair, having regard to the whole course of dealing between the parties in relation to the property.[376] The House of Lords, whilst recognizing that the law has 'moved on in response to changing social and economic circumstances',[377] seems to have favoured a return to a more traditional (and perhaps more intellectually sustainable) approach.[378] **2.108**

(ii) Detrimental reliance

Since equity does not assist the volunteer, it is necessary for the court faced with a claim to entitlement under an implied or constructive trust to find evidence that **2.109**

---

[368] See eg *Barclays Bank v Khaira* [1993] 1 FLR 343.

[369] See eg *Hammond v Mitchell* [1991] 1 WLR 1127; *Eves v Eves* [1975] 1 WLR 1338, CA.

[370] See *Le Foe v Le Foe and Woolwich plc* [2001] 2 FLR 97 where the fact that the functioning of the household economy depended on the wife's earnings was held to be sufficient evidence of such an understanding; *The Mortgage Corporation v Shaire* [2001] Ch. 743.

[371] *Lloyds Bank plc v Rosset* [1991] 1 AC 107, HL.

[372] [2007] UKHL 17.

[373] *Stack v Dowden* [2007] UKHL 17, *per* Lord Walker of Gestingthorpe, at para 26.

[374] See *Stack v Dowden* [2007] UKHL 17, especially *per* Baroness Hale at paras 68–70 and *per* Lord Walker of Gestingthorpe, at paras 33–36. For as somewhat different approach see *per* Lord Neuberger of Abbotsbury at paras104–147.

[375] *Stack v Dowden* [2007] UKHL 17, *per* Baroness Hale at para 60.

[376] ibid; and see *Oxley v Hiscock* [2004] EWCA 546, [2005] Fam 211; *Midland Bank plc v Cooke* [1995] 4 All ER 562, CA; *The Mortgage Corporation v Shaire* [2001] Ch. 743; *Le Foe v Le Foe and Woolwich plc* [2001] 2 FLR 97.

[377] *Stack v Dowden* [2007] UKHL 17, *per* Baroness Hale at para 60.

[378] ibid at para 61.

the applicant has suffered a detriment in reliance on the arrangement. Such detriment will often be founded on the contributions (which must, however, be more than trifling)[379] made by the applicant.[380]

(iii) Significance of parties' legal status in determining intention

2.110 Determining the intention of the parties for these purposes is a matter for the trial court; and at one time it was sometimes suggested that clearer evidence of the necessary intention to establish common ownership would be required in the case of the unmarried (who had not necessarily accepted the commitment implicit in marriage)[381] than in the case of husband and wife. But this approach does not seem to have been taken in recent years and was in any case irrelevant to same sex couples denied the opportunity of formal legal recognition. Since what may be in issue depends on drawing inferences from the parties' relationship it would seem that the *content* of that relationship should alone be relevant,[382] and this should be the criterion whether the relationship is same-sex or different sex and whether formalized by marriage or civil partnership or not.

(e) Determining beneficial ownership: claims founded on estoppel

2.111 The doctrine of proprietary estoppel[383] recognizes that if a person incurs expenditure or does some other detrimental act in the belief,[384] encouraged by the legal owner of property, that the claimant already owns or is to be given some

---

[379] The word used in *Lloyds Bank plc v Rosset* [1991] 1 AC 107, 131, HL by Lord Bridge to describe the wife's efforts over seven weeks in trying to make a semi-derelict farmhouse ready for occupation as the family home by Christmas: it was 'the most natural thing in the world for any wife. . .to spend all the time she could spare and to employ any skills she might have. . .in doing all she could to accelerate progress of the work. . .'.

[380] See eg *Lissimore v Downing* [2003] 2 FLR 308 (where the fact that a woman had, with the encouragement of her partner, given up her job as a pharmacist's assistant did not, in the circumstances, constitute a sufficient detriment).

[381] See *Bernard v Josephs* [1982] Ch 391, CA.

[382] Lord Upjohn's statement in *Pettitt v Pettitt* [1970] AC 777, 813 that property rights between husband and wife should be determined as they would be for others 'whilst making full allowance' in view of that relationship supports the view that it is the content of the relationship which is in issue. The courts sometimes showed signs of accepting traditional stereotypes of gender roles (see eg Lord Bridge's remarks in *Lloyds Bank plc v Rosset*, n 379 above) but this is now regarded as unacceptable: there 'is one principle of universal application which can be stated with confidence. In seeking to achieve fair outcome, there is no place for discrimination between husband and wife and their respective roles. . .': *White v White* [2001] 1 AC 596, 599. In the case of same sex relationships the view that findings about contributions should be based on evidence rather than assumptions is even stronger.

[383] For the relationship between estoppel and the doctrines founded on implied resulting or constructive trusts, see *Grant v Edwards* [1986] Ch 836, CA, *per* Sir Nicholas Browne-Wilkinson V-C. However, it has been questioned whether proprietary estoppel and 'common interest' constructive trusts can or should, in this context, be completely assimilated: *Stack v Dowden* [2007] UKHL 17, *per* Lord Walker of Gestingthorpe, at para 37.

[384] See para 2.109, and note the facts of *Lissimore v Downing* [2003] 2 FLR 308.

proprietary interest in a specific asset, an equity arises to have those expectations fulfilled so far as may fairly be done. The underlying and fundamental principle is that equity is concerned to prevent unconscionable conduct[385] and sometimes this doctrine has been invoked in claims to a beneficial interest in the family home.

(f) Determining beneficial interests: claims in contract

The existence of an agreement or arrangement between the parties is, as shown **2.112** above, often central to a successful claim under the doctrines of implied or constructive trust;[386] but in some cases the claim may more straightforwardly be for the enforcement of a contract relating to the ownership or occupation of property. There seems to be no reason why a contract which complies with the appropriate formal requirements, is supported by consideration, and is intended to create a legally enforceable relationship[387] should not take effect.[388] It seems now to be clear that a contract between a cohabiting couple to deal with their financial affairs[389] is not liable to be set aside merely on the ground that it is founded on what was once described as 'an immoral consideration' or is otherwise contrary to public policy.[390] However it must be remembered that statute renders void any contract precluding the court from exercising its powers to make financial relief and property adjustment orders.[391]

(g) Significance of declaration of beneficial interests in conveyance or transfer

The law dealing with claims based on implied resulting or constructive trust **2.113** developed largely in the context of cases in which the conveyance or transfer of the legal estate had been to one of the two partners; but increasingly such documents now vest the legal estate in both. That fact will usually be conclusive in determining that both were intended to have a beneficial interest in the property, but (as *Stack v Dowden*[392] makes clear) it is not of itself conclusive in determining the extent of the beneficial interest (or indeed whether the parties interests are to be

---

[385] *Gillet v Holt* [2000] 2 FLR 266, 232, *per* Robert Walker LJ.

[386] See para 2.106.

[387] *Jones v Padavatton* [1969] 1 WLR 328, CA; and note *Layton v Martin* [1986] 2 FLR 227.

[388] See eg *Tanner v Tanner* [1975] 1 WLR 1346. But it is important not to overlook the ordinary legal requirements for validity: see *Hemmens v Wilson Browne* [1995] Ch 223 (negligence action against solicitor).

[389] As distinct from a contract for sexual relations: *Sutton v Mishcon de Reya* [2003] EWHC 3166.

[390] See *Sutton v Mishcon de Reya* [2003] EWHC 3166, cf *Upfill v Wright* [1911] 1 KB 506 (fact that tenants cohabited outside marriage constituted an immoral user such as to render a lease liable to forfeiture).

[391] Matrimonial Causes Act 1973, s 34(1)(a); Civil Partnership Act 2004, s 72(1) and sch 5, paras 67, 68; and see *Sutton v Sutton* [1984] Ch 184.

[392] [2007] UKHL 17.

treated as a joint tenancy or a tenancy in common).[393] It has been said[394] that conveyancers should, as a matter of invariable standard practice, explain the legal situation, seek instructions, and then record the parties' agreement in an express and explicit declaration of the extent of parties' beneficial interests and whether those interests are held as joint tenants or tenants in common.[395] Such a declaration will (unless and until rectified by the court) be conclusive of the matter.

(h) Occupation and disposal of concurrently owned land

2.114 Where land is vested in more than one person (whether by conveyance of the legal estate or otherwise) it will be subject to a trust of land, and any person interested may apply to the court for an order regulating the occupation of the property or its disposal.[396] In deciding how to exercise those powers the court is required to consider a number of matters, including the purposes for which the property is held, the welfare of children, the circumstances and wishes of the adults concerned, and the interests of any secured creditor.[397] The court may also make orders requiring one owner to make payments to another excluded from the property.[398]

(i) Legislative intervention

(i) The Married Women's Property Act 1964

2.115 This Act reverses a common law presumption by providing that money derived from any allowance made by a husband to his wife for the expenses of the matrimonial home or for similar purposes is, in the absence of contrary agreement, to be treated as belonging to the parties in equal shares. The Civil Partnership

---

[393] The distinction is of great importance on the death of an entitled party.

[394] *Goodman v Carlton* [2002] EWCA 545, *per* Ward LJ.

[395] If title to the land is registered, the Land Registration Rules 1997 require that the parties state whether they are joint tenants, tenants in common in equal shares, or whether the property is held on other trusts, but it appears that the meaning of these concepts is not always understood: *Stack v Dowden* [2005] EWCA 857. In the House of Lords Baroness Hale urged the Land Registry further to review its practice in an attempt to minimize the number of cases in which questions of beneficial ownership were not resolved by the documentation: see paras 49–52.

[396] Trusts of Land and Appointment of Trustees Act 1996, ss 14–15.

[397] Trusts of Land and Appointment of Trustees Act 1996 codifies the law, and decisions taken under the Law of Property Act 1925 should be treated with reserve: *The Mortgage Corporation v Shaire* [2000] EWHC 452; [2001] Ch. 743 *Chan Pui Chun v Leung Kam Ho* [2002] EWCA 1075; [2003] 1 FLR 23; *W v W (Joinder of Trusts of Land and Children Act Applications)*[2004] 2 FLR 321. Where the application is by a trustee in bankruptcy a distinct statutory code applies: Insolvency Act 1986, ss. 335–337; and see *Judd v Brown* [1998] 2 FLR 360; *Barca v Mears* [2004] EWHC 2170. As to applications by creditors generally, see *The Mortgage Corporation v Shaire* [2000] EWHC 452; [2001] Ch. 743; *First National Bank v Achampong* [2003] EWCA 487.

[398] s 13(6)(a); see eg *Stack v Dowden* [2007] UKHL 17, *per* Lord Walker at paras 150–157.

Act 2004 does not seek to replicate these provisions in the context of civil partnership.[399]

(ii) The Matrimonial Proceedings and Property Act 1970

Section 37 of this Act was enacted in order to remove uncertainty about the extent **2.116** to which a spouse who made improvements to the matrimonial home thereby acquired a beneficial interest in it. It declares that where a spouse contributes in money or money's worth to the improvement of real or personal property, that spouse shall (provided the contribution is of a substantial nature and subject to any contrary agreement) be treated as having then acquired such a share (or enlarged share) in the property as may have been agreed or, 'in default of such agreement, as may seem in all the circumstances just' to the court in any proceedings.[400] The Act seems to be rarely invoked;[401] but the Civil Partnership Act 2004[402] applies the same rules to improvements to property made by a civil partner.

(iii) The Law Reform (Miscellaneous Provisions) Act 1970

This Act (introduced in consequence of the decision to abolish the action for **2.117** breach of promise of marriage) created special rules to deal with some of the proprietary consequences arising on the ending of an 'agreement to marry'. The Civil Partnership Act 2004[403] provides that a 'civil partnership agreement' does not have effect as a contract giving rise to legal rights, but the Act contains somewhat similar provisions to those in the 1970 Act so far as property rights and the resolution of disputes about them are concerned.[404]

(iv) 'Home rights' under the Family Law Act 1996, Part IV

The Matrimonial Homes Act 1967[405] gave a spouse who had no beneficial interest **2.118** in the family home rights of occupation and created machinery whereby those rights could by registration be made to bind mortgagees and others subsequently dealing with the property. Over the years, the statutory provisions were extensively revised; and the Civil Partnership Act 2004[406] extended the provisions of

---

[399] It is apparently officially accepted that these provisions require amendment to make them consistent with the European Convention on Human Rights, Protocol 7, Article 5; but no government action has yet been taken to introduce the necessary legislation.

[400] For the exercise of this jurisdiction see *Griffiths v Griffiths* [1974] 1 WLR 1350; *Re Nicholson, dec'd* [1974] 1 WLR 476.

[401] But see *Hosking v Michaelides* [2004] All ER (D) 147.

[402] s 65.

[403] s 73(1), ss 73–74.

[404] ss 73–74. These provisions are worded somewhat differently from the comparable provisions of the Law Reform (Miscellaneous Provisions) Act 1970.

[405] Intended to mitigate the problems arising from the decision of the House of Lords in *National Provincial Bank Ltd v Ainsworth* [1965] AC 1175.

[406] s 82 and sch 9.

Part IV of the Family Law Act 1996 so that they apply equally to civil partners. The result is that the amended 1996 Act now contains a comprehensive codification of the law governing occupation of the family home, and what were formerly described as 'matrimonial home rights' have come to be called simply 'home rights'. In essence 'home rights' consist of the registrable right not to be evicted or excluded from the home or any part of it without leave of the court;[407] and the Act contains provision enabling those rights to be made, by registration, binding on third parties.

(v) Transfer of tenancies: rights conferred by the Family Law Act 1996, Part IV

2.119 The Family Law Act 1996[408] gave the court a discretionary power to order the transfer of certain tenancies of property in which a couple had lived together as husband and wife; and the Civil Partnership Act 2004[409] extends those provisions to two persons who are not civil partners but have 'lived together as if they were civil partners'.

(2) Rights to Protection of the Home and Person

2.120 The Family Law Act 1996 and the Protection from Harassment Act 1997 greatly extended the legal protection available to spouses and others against violence and abuse and seek to secure their occupation of the family home. The legislation was extended by The Civil Partnership Act 2004[410] so as to apply equally to civil partnership families.[411] Part IV of the Family Law Act 1996[412] not only gives the court power to make *occupation orders* relating to the right to occupy a dwelling house[413] but also confers jurisdiction to make *non-molestation orders* prohibiting a person from molesting the applicant or a child. The Protection from Harassment Act 1997 provides that a person must not pursue a course of conduct which amounts to harassment of another and which he knows or ought to know amounts to

---

[407] This is so if the claimant is in occupation. If he or she is not in occupation, the right is a right (with leave of the court) to enter into and occupy the home: Family Law Act 1996, s 30(2) as amended by Civil Partnership Act 2004 s 82 and sch 9, para 1. These rights do not arise in favour of a spouse who is entitled (for example, as joint owner of the legal estate) to occupy the property, it being assumed that such a person is adequately protected both against the other spouse and third parties.

[408] s 53, and sch 7; see *Gay v Sheeran* [1999] 3 All ER 795, CA.

[409] s 82, and sch 9, para 13.

[410] s 82 and sch 9.

[411] The Domestic Violence, Crimes and Victims Act 2004 made amendment to both the 1996 and 1997 Acts. Subsequent references to the 1996 and 1997 Act are, unless otherwise stated, to the relevant provisions as amended by the Civil Partnership Act 2004 and by the Domestic Violence, Crimes and Victims Act 2004.

[412] Rationalizing and expanding the principles first statutorily established by the Matrimonial Homes Act 1967 and the Domestic Violence and Matrimonial Proceedings Act 1976.

[413] See para 2.121. For the meaning of this expression, see the Family Law Act 1996, s 63(1).

harassment of the other. The 1997 Act creates criminal sanctions which are available in certain circumstances against persons breaking this prohibition (or breaking the terms of a so-called restraining order imposed on conviction for an offence under the Act); and it also, in effect, creates a tort of harassment, giving the victim the right to claim damages and injunctions in respect of harassment.

(a) Occupation orders under the Family Law Act 1996, Part IV

The Act provides that persons meeting certain descriptions may apply to the court for an occupation order. However, the terms of the orders which the court has power to make (and the factors relevant to the exercise of the court's discretion) differ depending on the head under which the applicant qualifies. **2.121**

(i) Applications by 'person entitled'

The policy of the 1996 Act appears to be to give the court more extensive powers in respect of applications by persons with some recognized legal, equitable or statutory right in respect of a home than are available to others, whilst still giving the courts adequate powers to protect the legitimate interests of all those with whom the applicant has had a domestic relationship. **2.122**

For the purposes of an application for an occupation order, a 'person entitled' is either a person with 'homes rights'[414] (as described above) or a person 'entitled to occupy a dwelling house by virtue of a beneficial estate or interest' (for example, as joint owner of the fee simple or a tenant) or contract or 'by virtue of any enactment giving him the right to remain in occupation'.[415] The dwelling house in question must either be (or at some time have been or been intended to be) the home of the person entitled and of another person with whom he or she is 'associated'.[416] **2.123**

---

[414] ie the right of a spouse not to be evicted etc: see the Family Law Act 1996, s 30 (replacing the similar provision of the Matrimonial Homes Act 1967).

[415] Family Law Act 1996, s 33(1)(a)(ii) and (i). The Act provides (s 35(11), 36(11)) that a person who has an equitable interest in the property but not the legal fee simple or term of years is to be treated only for the purpose of application as a person not entitled to occupy; but that provision is not to affect the person's right to apply under s 33 (ie as a person entitled). Moreover, it is provided that if application is made (in effect) under any of ss 35 to 38, a court taking the view that it has no power to make the order under the section invoked by the applicant may proceed under the section under which it considers the applicant does qualify, Family Law Act 1996, s 39(3).

[416] This expression is widely defined by the Family Law Act 1996, s 62(3) as amended to include a wide range of domestic relationships—not only a spouse or former spouse civil partner or former civil partner, a cohabitant or former cohabitant, relative (a term itself to be broadly construed: see s 63(1)) certain children, and parties to the same 'family proceedings', but also any person who lives or has lived in the same household, 'otherwise than merely by reason of one of them being the other's employee, tenant, lodger or boarder'.

2.124 On application by such a person the court has power[417] to declare that the applicant is entitled in the manner described (or that the applicant has home rights), and to make orders of various kinds about who is to be entitled to occupy the whole (or parts) of the house and on what terms.[418] In particular the court may make what is often called an 'ouster order' excluding a person from the home,[419] and it has power[420] to exclude the respondent from 'a defined area in which the dwelling house is included'—for example, from the block of flats in which the home is situated—or to prohibit the respondent from coming within a certain distance of the home (a so-called 'perimeter order').[421]

2.125 In deciding whether to exercise its powers to make an ouster order[422] and if so in what manner, the court is required to consider all the circumstances including such matters as the housing needs and housing resources of the family, their financial resources, the likely effect of the court's decision on the family's health, safety or well-being, and the conduct of the parties in relation to each other and otherwise.[423]

2.126 If the court considers that the applicant (or a relevant child)[424] is likely to suffer 'significant harm'[425] attributable to the respondent's conduct[426] it must make an order unless that would be likely to cause the other party (or any relevant child) to suffer 'significant harm' attributable to the other party's conduct as great as or greater than the harm likely to be suffered by the applicant if the order were not made. This is the so-called 'balance of harm' test.[427] In cases in which the applicant fails to satisfy the court that the balance falls in her favour, it still has a discretion as to whether to make an order, and will take into account all the circumstances

---

417 Family Law Act 1996, s 33(4).

418 Family Law Act 1996, s 33(3).

419 ibid, s 33(3)(d)–(f).

420 ibid, s 33(3)(g).

421 An occupation order (other than one made in cases where neither party has any existing right to occupy the property) may also contain ancillary provisions—for example granting either party possession or use of the furniture or other contents of the dwelling house in question—whether the order be made in favour of an entitled or non-entitled person, and imposing obligations in respect of matters such as outgoings and repairs.

422 Or other order under s 33(3): s 33(6).

423 Section 33(6).

424 Defined by the Family Law Act 1996, s 62(2).

425 A term taken from the Children Act 1989 and partially defined in s 63.

426 This qualification appears to have been intended to preserve the effect of the decision of the House of Lords in *Richards v Richards* [1984] 1 AC 174, in which the harm suffered by the child was attributable to the unsatisfactory housing available to her as a result of the local authority's housing policy and the mother's conduct in leaving the husband was held to be unjustified.

427 See eg *B v B (Occupation Order)* [1999] 1 FLR 715, CA: judge wrong to have made occupation order against husband in case in which child living in former matrimonial home with husband likely to suffer more harm if order made than would applicant wife and her baby if order not made.

including those specified in the Act.[428] However, it has been said that occupation orders which override proprietary rights are justified only in exceptional circumstances.[429]

(ii) Applications by the non-entitled

The category of 'non-entitled persons' who may apply for an occupation order is **2.127** limited to cohabitants, former cohabitants, former spouses and former civil partners. The 1996 Act makes fine distinctions in detailing the matters to which the court's attention is directed[430] and the terms (particularly as to duration)[431] of the orders which may be made on applications by different categories of applicant.[432]

(b) Non-molestation orders under the Family Law Act 1996, Part IV

The courts have long had power to grant interlocutory or final injunctions in all **2.128** cases in which it is just and convenient to do so.[433] However, it is a pre-condition to the exercise of what is often described as the 'inherent jurisdiction' that the applicant should have a recognized cause of action, for example in tort;[434] and the fact that English law did not[435] recognize the existence of a tort of harassment[436] meant that it was sometimes difficult for those suffering the consequences of relationship breakdown to obtain appropriate legal protection in the civil courts. The provisions of Part IV of the Family Law Act 1996 were intended to go some way to fill that gap in the law; and the Domestic Violence, Crimes and Victims Act 2004 introduced further measures intended to improve the legal and

---

[428] Section 33(6).

[429] *Chalmers v Johns* [1999] 1 FLR 392, 397, CA.

[430] For example, on applications by a cohabitant, the court is specifically required to consider 'the nature of the parties' relationship' and when considering this it must take into account in particular the level of commitment involved in that relationship: see now Domestic Violence, Crimes and Victims Act 2004, s 2 (replacing the former requirement to have regard to the fact that they had 'not given each other the commitment involved in marriage': Family Law Act 1996, s 41.

[431] The court may renew orders made in favour of former spouses for successive six-month periods, but an order in favour of a non-entitled cohabitant or former cohabitant can be extended only once: cf ss 35(10), 37(5) and ss 36(10), 38(6).

[432] See the Family Law Act 1996, s 35 (former spouse or civil partner with no right to occupy); s 36 (cohabitant or former cohabitant with no right to occupy); s 37 (spouse or former spouse or civil partner—neither applicant nor respondent entitled to occupy); s 38 (cohabitant or former cohabitant—neither applicant nor respondent entitled to occupy).

[433] Supreme Court Act 1981, s 37; County Courts Act 1984, s 38.

[434] See eg *Montgomery v Montgomery* [1965] P 46; *Patel v Patel* [1988] 2 FLR 179, CA.

[435] Prior to the enactment of the Protection from Harassment Act 1997.

[436] See eg *Patel v Patel* [1988] 2 FLR 179, CA. In *Khorosandjian v Bush* [1993] QB 727, CA, it was held that an injunction could be granted to restrain a man who pestered a young woman by making frequent telephone calls to her parents' home since his behaviour constituted the tort of nuisance; but in *Hunter v Canary Wharf Ltd* [1997] AC 655, HL, the orthodox view that the plaintiff in such an action had—unlike Miss Khorosandjian—to have a recognized proprietary interest in the property concerned was reinstated.

other protection available to victims of domestic violence and to provide clarity for the police when called to an incident. This has been done at the cost of considerable legislative complexity.

(i) Persons eligible to apply for non-molestation order: restriction to domestic relationships

2.129 The Family Law Act 1996 gives the court a wide power to make orders[437] prohibiting one person from 'molesting' another. The Act nowhere defines 'molestation',[438] but in effect seeks indirectly to confine the availability of the remedy to interference in family situations by restricting the right of application to those who come within the definition[439] of 'associated person'.[440]

2.130 The Act now[441] provides that a person is 'associated' with another person if:

(a) they are or have been married to each other or they are or have been civil partners of each other;[442]

(b) they are cohabitants or former cohabitants;[443]

(c) they live or have lived in the same household,[444] otherwise than merely by reason of one of them being the other's employee, tenant, lodger or boarder;

(d) they are relatives—a term which is itself widely defined;[445]

---

[437] The court may (and often did) accept an undertaking from any party to the proceedings, but the Domestic Violence, Crimes and Victims Act 2004: imposed restrictions on the power to do so, notably where the respondent has used or threatened violence against the applicant or a relevant child: Family Law Act 1996, ss 46 and 46(3A) as inserted by Domestic Violence, Crimes and Victims Act 2004, sch 10, para 37.

[438] In *C v C (Non-Molestation Order: Jurisdiction)* [1998] Fam 70 the court refused an application for an order against a former wife who had given stories about the husband to a tabloid newspaper.

[439] Family Law Act 1996, s 42(2)(a). The court may also make a non-molestation order in any 'family proceedings' to which the respondent is a party if it considers such an order should be made for the benefit of any other party (or of any relevant child) even though no application has been made: s 42(2)(b).

[440] An associated person who is under the age of 16 may only apply for a non-molestation or occupation order with leave of the court: s 43(1).

[441] As amended by the Domestic Violence, Crimes and Victims Act 2004 and by the Civil Partnership Act 2004.

[442] Family Law Act 1996 s 63(a) and (aa) as inserted by the Civil Partnership Act 2004 sch 9, para 13(2).

[443] Family Law Act 1996, s 62(1)(a) now defines the qualifying relationship as 'two persons who, although neither married to each other nor civil partners of each other. . .are living together as husband and wife or as if they were civil partners': see Civil Partnership Act 2004, sch 9, para 13(2)(a).

[444] This expression is not defined in the Act but it is reasonable to suppose that cases on divorce law (such as *Hopes v Hopes* [1949] P 227) would be followed.

[445] The Act provides that relationships by affinity may for this purpose be created by marriage, civil partnership, or cohabitation: see s 63(1) as amended by Domestic Violence, Crimes and Victims Act 2004 s 41(3) and Civil Partnership Act 2004, sch 9, para 14(4). The complex definition has led to suggestions that any cases of doubt should be resolved in favour of the applicant: *G v F (Non-Molestation Order: Jurisdiction)* [2000] 2 FLR 533.

(e) they have agreed to marry each other or have made a civil partnerships agreement (whether or not the agreement has been terminated);[446]

(f) they have or have had an intimate personal relationship with each other which is or was of significant duration;[447]

(g) they are a child's parents (or connected with a child in other defined[448] ways);

(h) they are parties to the same family proceedings.[449]

The Act[450] also empowers the court to make orders of its own motion in any family proceedings[451] to which the respondent is a party if it considers that the order should be made for the benefit of any other party or any relevant child. In this way the court could, for example, make an order against a person who had obtained leave under the Children Act 1989[452] to seek a contact or other order in respect of a child.[453] **2.131**

(ii) The prohibited conduct

The Family Law Act 1996 provides[454] that an order may prohibit a person from molesting another person who is associated with him or from molesting a relevant child; and that the order may be expressed so as to refer to molestation in general or to particular acts of molestation or to both.[455] The Law Commission[456] stated that the term 'molestation' 'encompassed any form of serious pestering or harassment and applies to any conduct which could properly be regarded as such a degree of harassment as to call for the intervention of the court'. In practice, however, it appears that the term 'molestation' is often misunderstood by respondents (who may think it is restricted to sexual abuse of children) and it seems that some courts prefer to frame orders in general terms prohibiting threatening harassing or pestering but adding any more specific terms (for example, prohibiting the respondent from seeking to contact a child) which are appropriate on the particular facts of the case. **2.132**

---

[446] The Act provides special evidential rules on this matter: s 44(1)(2); the Civil Partnership Act 2004), sch 9, paras 10, 13.

[447] Family Law Act 1996, s 62(1)(ee) as inserted by Domestic Violence, Crimes and Victims Act 2004, s 4. The official 'Explanatory Notes' to the latter Act (prepared by the Home Office to assist the reader) state (para 24) that this definition is intended to 'cover a long-standing relationship which may, or may not, be a sexual relationship, but which is an intimate and personal one. It does not include long term platonic friends or "one night stands".'

[448] See s 62(2)–(6).

[449] As defined in s 63(1), (2), as amended.

[450] s 43(2(b).

[451] As defined in s 63. Any such order ceases to have effect if the family proceedings are withdrawn or dismissed: s 42(8).

[452] See para 2.176.

[453] The court may make a non-molestation or occupation order *ex parte* in certain circumstances: s 45.

[454] s 42(1).

[455] ibid, s 42(6).

[456] *Domestic Violence and Occupation of the Family Home* (Law Com No 207, 1992) para 3.1.

(iii) The discretion to make orders

2.133   The only guidance given to the court about whether to exercise its powers to make a non-molestation order and if so in what manner is that it must have regard to all the circumstances, including the need to secure the health, safety and well-being of the applicant or any relevant child.[457]

(iv) Enforcement of orders

2.134   It is a contempt of court, punishable by imprisonment, to disobey an order made under Part IV of the Family Law Act.[458] That Act also empowered the court to attach a 'power of arrest' to an occupation or non-molestation order (or any term of such orders) empowering a constable to arrest without warrant a person whom he has reasonable cause for suspecting to be in breach of the provisions of the order.[459] The person arrested on the authority of such a power must then be brought before the court.

2.135   The Domestic Violence, Crimes and Victims Act 2004 reflected the view that this remedy was inadequate to deal with cases of domestic violence, and that Act [460] accordingly made it a criminal offence, punishable by imprisonment for up to five years,[461] for a person to do anything he is prohibited from doing by a non-molestation order without reasonable excuse. The police will therefore automatically have power to arrest such a person.

2.136   Perhaps paradoxically, breaking the terms of an *occupation* order is not a criminal offence. For that reason, the procedure for attaching a power of arrest to such orders remains in being to deal with such cases. However, the court now has a duty [462] to consider making a non-molestation order whenever it considers the making of an occupation order; and this is intended to 'ensure that adequate protection is always in place for those persons who need it'.

---

[457]   Or, in the case of an order made by the court of its own motion under s 42(2)(b) the person for whose benefit the order is made: s 42(5).

[458]   And a person who believes that the terms of an order have been broken may apply to the court for the issue of a warrant of arrest.

[459]   s 47(6).

[460]   s 1.

[461]   This provision made the offence 'arrestable' within the definition in the Police and Criminal Evidence Act 1984, s 24). However, the distinction between 'arrestable' and other offences was abolished by the Serious Organised Crime and Police Act, 2004, s 110(1) which substituted a provision that a constable may arrest on reasonable suspicion that an offence has been committed and that he has reasonable grounds to suppose the person concerned is guilty of it, provided that certain criteria (eg that arrest is necessary to protect a child, or to allow the prompt and effective investigation of the person's conduct) are satisfied: s 24(2), (5).

[462]   Family Law Act 1996, s 42(4A), inserted by Domestic Violence, Crimes and Victims Act 2004, sch 10, para 36.

(c) The Protection from Harassment Act 1997

This Act was in part a response to widespread concern about the law's apparent **2.137** inability to deal effectively with the phenomenon of 'stalking'; and it had become clear that not all those with a legitimate claim to protection would necessarily fall within the definition of 'associated person' and thus entitled to seek the remedies against molestation provided by the Family Law Act 1996.[463]

(i) Harassment: the criminal offence

The 1997 Act[464] provides that a person must not[465] pursue a course of conduct[466] **2.138** which amounts to harassment[467] of another and which he knows or ought to know[468] amounts to harassment of the other.[469] A person who does so is guilty of a criminal offence.[470]

The court may, in addition to sentencing the accused, make a 'restraining order' **2.139** against a person convicted (or in certain circumstances acquitted)[471] of this offence;[472] and breach of a restraining order is itself a criminal offence punishable by a maximum of five years' imprisonment.[473]

---

[463] In *Khorosandjian v Bush* [1993] QB 727, CA, for example, the victim was an 18-year-old woman who had met the defendant at a club. Their relationship had not involved cohabitation, nor would the relationship have been of sufficient duration to bring the two within the definition of 'associated persons' for the purposes of the Family Law Act 1996.

[464] s 1.

[465] There are certain defences: for example, the prohibition does not apply if the person concerned can show that his conduct was 'pursued for the purpose of preventing or detecting crime', or (more generally) that in 'the particular circumstances the pursuit of the course of conduct was reasonable': s 1(3).

[466] This requires conduct (which includes speech) on at least two occasions: s 7. It is a question of fact whether this condition is satisfied: *Hipgrave v Jones* [2005] 2 FLR 174; and see *C v C (Non-Molestation Order: Jurisdiction)*[1998] Fam 70; *Lau v DPP* [2000] 1 FLR 799.

[467] This term is not defined, but s 7(1)(a) of the 1997 Act provides that harassing a person includes alarming a person or causing distress. It has been said that the term can cover 'a very wide range of conduct. The actions. . .may be little more than boorishness and insensitive behaviour, so long as it is sufficient to cause distress. . .unwelcome text messages sent, for example, to a woman wrongly perceived to be a girlfriend': *Hipgrave v Jones* [2005] 2 FLR 174.

[468] This requirement is satisfied if a 'reasonable person in possession of the same information would think the course of conduct amounted to harassment of the other's: s 1(2).

[469] And such a person may be arrested: Police and Criminal Evidence Act 1984, s 24(2) as inserted by Serious Organised Crime and Police Act 2004: s 110.

[470] The 1997 Act creates two offences: ss 2 and 4. The more serious (for which a maximum penalty of five years' imprisonment is available) requires proof that the victim was caused on at least two occasions to fear that violence would be used against her: s 4.

[471] In such a case the court must be satisfied that a restraining order is necessary to protect a person from harassment: Protection from Harassment Act 1997, s 7A, as inserted by Domestic Violence, Crimes and Victims Act 2004, s 12(5).

[472] The Domestic Violence, Crimes and Victims Act 2004, s 12, extended the circumstances in which a restraining order is available.

[473] s 5.

(ii) Harassment: the tort

2.140 The Act also provides that a person who is or may be the victim of harassment may bring an action in the High Court or county court. Damages (including damages for any anxiety or financial loss caused by the harassment) may be awarded, and the court may grant an injunction for the purpose of restraining the defendant from pursuing any conduct which amounts to harassment.[474] The claimant may in case of breach of such an injunction apply for a warrant of arrest; and it is a criminal offence punishable by up to five years' imprisonment to do anything prohibited by the injunction without reasonable excuse.[475]

(3) Rights to Financial Support

(a) Introduction: the common law duty to maintain, and the impact of child support legislation on court based statutory remedies

2.141 The common law imposed a duty on a man to maintain his wife,[476] but today this duty is of little or no practical importance and a person seeking financial support on the basis of a family relationship will (in the absence of an enforceable maintenance agreement) do so by making an application under one or more statutory procedures.[477]

2.142 The common law did not impose any clear direct liability on a parent to maintain children;[478] but increasingly statute came to do so. However, the system which depended on the courts determining provision for children on a discretionary case by case basis, proved ineffective and a substantial part of the burden of providing for the children of single parents and parents involved in family breakdown fell on the welfare benefit system. In an attempt to make child support obligations (both in quantifying the liability and in ensuring that it was met) effective, the Child Support Act 1991 created an ambitious scheme under which parental child support obligations would be calculated by reference to a formula and enforced by the Child Support Agency. That system, in an amended form, remains in place; and its existence needs to be kept in mind[479] if only because the Act—founded

---

[474] s 3(2), (3).

[475] s 3(6).

[476] The Civil Partnership Act 2004 made no attempt to create a statutory counterpart to the common law duty of spousal support. The approach the Act adopted was to introduce statutory procedures applying to civil partnerships rules virtually identical to those applicable to the married and the formerly married.

[477] *Re C (A Minor) (Contribution Notice)* [1994] 1 FLR 111, 116, *per* Ward J.

[478] *Manby v Scott* (1663) 1 Mod. 124, 128; compare the views of Baroness Hale (dissenting) in *R (Kehoe) v Secretary of State for Work and Pensions* [2006] 1 AC 42.

[479] In cases where the adults concerned are not themselves on state benefits, they may by submitting to a court consent order effectively take the case out of the Agency's jurisdiction. It seems that many parents do so.

as it was on the assumption that a properly managed and administered system would prove much more effective than the courts—prohibits the courts from 'making varying or reviving any maintenance orders' in relation to the child if the Agency has power to make an assessment.[480] In the event, this assumption has not been confirmed by experience, and indeed the Agency and the system which is administers has been the subject of much criticism from official enquiries and others. In February 2006 the Secretary of State for Work and Pensions announced that the 'current system of child support needed to be 'completely redesigned' and that it could 'never in its current state be made fit for purpose'. In December of that year, the Secretary of State set out an apparently far-reaching proposal to replace the Child Support Agency with a 'tough new organization to deliver a radically different system of child mainte-nance'; and it is intended that this should be in place from 2008.[481] For the time being all that can be said[482] is that the 'system remains in crisis'; and there seems little point in a work of this kind seeking to explore the complexities of the present flawed scheme.

(b) The statutory framework for court ordered financial relief

The judicial procedures primarily relevant to the adjustment of financial matters in the family are as follows: **2.143**

(1) Section 27 of the Matrimonial Causes Act 1973 provides that either party to a marriage may apply to the High Court or a county court for an order on the ground that the other party has failed to provide reasonable maintenance for the applicant, or has failed to provide (or make a proper contribution towards) reasonable maintenance for any child of the family.[483] Similar provision is made in respect of civil partnership.[484]

---

[480] Child Support Act 1991, s 8. The main exceptions are that the courts retain their powers to make property and lump sum orders in favour of children, and to make orders for 'children of the family' who are not the parent's biological or adopted children.

[481] Press Release, Department for Work and Pensions, 13 December 2006, announcing the publication of a White Paper, *A New System of Child Maintenance*, Cm 6979.

[482] N Wikeley, *Child Support, Law and Policy* (2006), vii to which reference should be made for a full examination of the origins and subsequent working of the scheme.

[483] This is subject to the prohibition imposed by Child Support Act 1991, s 8. The term 'child of the family' is defined by Children Act 1989 s 105(1) as amended by Civil Partnership Act 2004 s 75(3) as a child of both the parties to a marriage or civil partnership and any other child, not being a child who is placed with those parties as foster parents by a local authority or voluntary organiza-tion, who has been treated by both of those parties as a child of their family. In practice (although not confined to such cases: see eg *Re A (Child of the Family)* [1998] 1 FLR 347 where the child was held to be a child of its grandparents' marriage) the definition often permits an order to be made against a step-parent in respect of his or her spouse's child. The court has to take account of special guidelines in assessing the order to make against a person who is not the child's parent: see eg Matrimonial Causes Act 1973, ss 27(3) and 25(4).

[484] Civil Partnership Act 2004, s 72(1), sch 5, Part 9.

The questions of what is 'reasonable maintenance' must be resolved by the court in the light of a consideration of all the circumstances of the case, including certain specified matters.[485] The fact that the applicant has committed adultery (or that for some other reason the respondent would be under no common law obligation to maintain) is not conclusive in this respect. If the applicant satisfies the court that there has been such a failure, the court may make an order for periodical payments, secured or unsecured; and it may make a lump sum order.[486]

(2) The applicant may seek a financial order from a magistrates' court[487] on the same 'failure to maintain' ground.[488] However, magistrates exercising this jurisdiction have no power to order that payments (whether periodical or by way of lump sum) be secured; whilst the maximum lump sum which can be ordered in respect of the applicant and each child is £1,000.[489]

(3) Parents,[490] guardians, and persons in whose favour a residence order[491] has been made may[492] apply to the court[493] under the provisions of Schedule 1 to the Children Act 1989 for any of a wide range[494] of financial orders against a child's parent. An adult student or trainee (or other person who can demonstrate special circumstances) may also apply for orders against his or her parent.[495] In practice, the Children Act 1989 is particularly appropriate as

---

485 Matrimonial Causes Act 1973, s 27(3), (3A) referring to the matters enumerated in s 25 of the Act (see para 2.151) with minor variations.

486 The court may order the lump sum to be paid by instalments, and security may be ordered for the payment of instalments: Matrimonial Causes Act 1973, s 27(7)(b).

487 The Civil Partnership Act 2004, s 72(3) and sch 6 make corresponding provision for civil partnerships. Orders made by magistrates' courts are enforceable notwithstanding the fact that the husband and wife or the civil partners are living with each other but cease to have effect if the parties live with each other for a continuous period of six months or more: Domestic Proceedings and Magistrates' Courts Act 1978, s 25.

488 Domestic Proceedings and Magistrates' Courts Act 1978, s 1. The court also has power to make orders for sums agreed by the parties (s 6) and for amounts equal to payments made voluntarily during a period of separation (s 7). Magistrates' courts also have power to make an order on the ground that the respondent has behaved in such a way that the applicant cannot reasonably be expected to live with the respondent (s 1(1)(c)) or that he has deserted the applicant: s 1(1)(d).

489 Domestic Proceedings and Magistrates' Courts Act 1978, s 2.

490 For the purposes of such an application, the word 'parent' includes any party to a marriage or civil partnership in relation to whom the child is a child of the family: Children Act 1989, sch 1, para 16(2).

491 See para 2.179.

492 Subject to the provisions of Child Support Act 1991, s 8; see para 2.142.

493 High Court, county court and magistrates' courts all have jurisdiction, but that of the magistrates is restricted in certain respects: Children Act 1989, sch 1, paras 6, 7, and 9.

494 ie orders for periodical payments (whether secured or unsecured), and lump sum, transfer of property and settlement of property orders: Children Act 1989, sch 1, para 1(2).

495 In this case the definition of parent is not extended beyond the child's legal parent: Children Act 1989, sch 1, para 16(2), as amended by Civil Partnership Act 2004, s 77(4).

the framework for obtaining orders for financial support against the father of an illegitimate child.

In exercising the financial jurisdiction under Schedule 1 the court must consider all the circumstances, including certain specified circumstances. The width of the courts' powers means that orders can be made which will secure that housing is available for the child during his or her dependency,[496] but the courts have adopted the policy that, whilst children are entitled to provision during their dependency and for their education, they are not entitled (in the absence of exceptional circumstances such as disability) to a capital settlement going beyond whatever may be required for those purposes, however rich their parents may be.[497]

(4) Adults may make an agreement to regulate their financial affairs; and any such agreement will, as a contract, have such effect as the law allows.[498] But statute[499] provides that if a maintenance agreement includes a provision purporting to restrict any right to apply to a court for an order containing financial arrangements[500] then (although the other terms are binding on the parties) that provision shall be void. The same Act gives the court power[501] on application by one of the parties[502] to vary or revoke the financial terms (or insert such terms into the agreement).

(5) The Matrimonial Causes Act 1973[503] empowers the court to make orders in divorce, separation and nullity proceedings; and the Civil Partnership Act 2004 gives the court corresponding powers in connection with civil partnerships.[504] This so-called 'ancillary relief' jurisdiction (the term indicating that the making of the financial orders in question is ancillary, or subordinate, to the granting of the principal relief, ie the order dealing with the parties' legal status) is much more extensively used than the other statutory procedures

---

[496] An application under the Children Act 1989, sch 1, has been said to be the appropriate procedure for dealing with the occupation of the family home in cases involving children: see *Pearson v Franklin* [1994] 1 WLR 370, CA.

[497] See *A v A (A Minor: Financial Provision)* [1994] 1 FLR 657; and *J v C (Child: Financial Provision)* [1999] 1 FLR 152 (where an unmarried £1.4 million National Lottery prize-winner was ordered to provide a 4 bedroom house in which his 3-year-old child could live with her mother and two sisters who had a different father, the house to be held on trust for the child until she attained 21 or finished full-time education, the mother having the right then to buy the house at a valuation).

[498] See eg *Amey v Amey* [1992] 2 FLR 89. Where the agreement is to compromise an application for ancillary relief in matrimonial proceedings (see para 2.145) it appears that the agreement (whilst a factor relevant to the exercise of the court's discretion) is not enforceable and that the financial provisions to be made remain a matter for the court: see *Xydhias v Xydhias* [1999] 2 All ER 386, CA.

[499] Matrimonial Causes Act 1973, s 34(1).

[500] A term broadly defined: Matrimonial Causes Act 1973, s 34.

[501] Matrimonial Causes Act 1973, s 35.

[502] An agreement may also be varied after the death of a party: Matrimonial Causes Act 1973, s 36.

[503] Part II.

[504] Civil Partnership Act 2004, s 72(1) and sch 5.

mentioned above and has attracted a substantial body of case law. Subsequent paragraphs are accordingly confined to the exercise of the powers to grant ancillary relief.

(c) Private ordering of the financial consequences of the dissolution of a marriage or civil partnership

2.144   The law encourages the parties to a relationship which had broken down to make their own arrangements for the future—perhaps with the assistance of the court[505] or of third parties such as mediators—rather than having them imposed in hostile litigation.[506] But there remains a public interest in ensuring that such settlements are reasonable and fair;[507] and indeed statute provides that any agreement ousting the jurisdiction of the court to make financial provision is void;[508] and the court has (as noted above) power to vary not only its own orders but agreements made by the parties in relation to financial matters.

2.145   A practice therefore developed whereby any agreement intended to settle the financial arrangements to be made on divorce conclusively and permanently was brought before the court for its approval;[509] and thereafter the parties' rights and duties flowed from the order rather than from the private agreement.[510] Such a court order may only be set aside if the applicant can demonstrate that it contains a vitiating element (such as misrepresentation, mistake, material non-disclosure, or a subsequent fundamental and unforeseen change of circumstances);[511] and the consent order can therefore provide the certainty which parties often seek, particularly where their financial circumstances are such as to justify the approval of a so-called 'clean break' between them.[512] Should the validity of a consent order be put in issue, the court will start from the position that a solemn and freely

---

[505] In 2000 a Financial Dispute Resolution Appointment system was introduced: this was specifically intended to facilitate settlement, not least by examining the case at a so-called 'FDR' conducted by a District Judge. The District Judge (who will not hear the case if it proceeds to trial) may give the parties a carefully prepared and considered 'indication' of the order which the Judge might make if the case came before him: *Rose v Rose* [2002] EWCA 208; [2002] 1 FLR 978.

[506] See eg *X v X (Y and Z intervening)* [2002] 1 FLR 508.

[507] *Hyman v Hyman* [1929] AC 601, HL; and see *Xydhias v Xydhias* [1999] 2 All ER 386, CA.

[508] Matrimonial Causes Act 1973, s 34(1); Civil Partnership Act 2004, sch 5, para 68.

[509] If the parties come to an agreement at the Family Dispute Resolution Appointment its terms will be embodied in a consent order.

[510] *De Lasala v de Lasala* [1980] AC 546, JCPC; *Thwaite v Thwaite* [1982] Fam 1, CA; *Pounds v Pounds* [1994] 1 WLR 1535, CA.

[511] See *per* Thorpe LJ, *Rose v Rose* [2002] EWCA 208; [2002] 1 FLR 978; and note that legislation provides that the court may make an order in the terms the parties have agreed on the basis only of such information as is required to be supplied by Rules of Court: Matrimonial and Family Proceedings Act 1984, s 19; Civil Partnership Act 2004, sch 5, para 66. For non-disclosure and change of circumstances see *Livesey v Jenkins* [1985] AC 424, HL; and *Barder v Caluori* [1988] AC 20, HL.

[512] See para 2.155.

negotiated bargain by which a party with access to competent legal advice defines his own requirements is to be enforced unless some clear and compelling reason to the contrary can be shown.[513] There seems no reason to suppose that any different principle will apply where a consent order has been made in civil partnership proceedings.

The influence of the view that there was a vital public interest in regulating the financial obligations associated with marriage[514] for long made it inconceivable that the court would allow its jurisdiction to make ancillary relief orders to be ousted by an agreement made before, and in contemplation of marriage; and it could confidently be stated that ante-nuptial contracts by which a man and woman sought to regulate their financial liabilities and responsibilities the one towards the other in the event of a divorce were unenforceable in English Law.[515] The fact that such agreements were often enforceable under the provisions of the law of the country in which they were made did, however, mean that the English courts increasingly had to consider how far, if at all, the existence of an agreement should be allowed to influence the terms of the order which the English courts had as a result of matrimonial proceedings having been instituted here. At first, the courts inclined to the view that such agreements had very limited significance;[516] but there seems no doubt that the making of an agreement is one of the 'circumstances' to which the court should have regard in seeking to make a fair resolution of the situation; and increasingly the courts have given significant weight to this factor.[517] There seems no reason to suppose that the courts would adopt any different approach in relation to applications ancillary to the making of a dissolution order in civil partnership proceedings. **2.146**

(d) Ancillary relief in dissolution, nullity and separation proceedings

(i) Interim maintenance

The court may make orders that one party to matrimonial or civil partnership proceedings[518] make periodical maintenance payments[519] pending the outcome **2.147**

---

[513] *Edgar v Edgar* [1980] 1 WLR 1410, CA; and see *Pounds v Pounds* [1994] 2 FLR 775, CA; *Harris v Manahan* [1997] 1 FLR 205; *Xydhias v Xydhias* [1999] 2 All ER 386, CA; *Hall & Co v Simons* [1999] 1 FLR 536.

[514] *Hyman v Hyman* [1929] AC 601, HL.

[515] *Rayden and Jackson on Divorce and Matrimonial Causes*, 17th ed, 1997, para 19.14.

[516] See eg *F v F (Ancillary Relief: Substantial Assets)* [1995] 2 FLR 45 (a case in which a young civil servant had made an ante-nuptial agreement restricting her claims on her husband's £200 million fortune to the modest amount of a German judge's pension).

[517] See *S v S (Divorce: Staying Proceedings)* [1997] 2 FLR 100; *M v M (Prenuptial Agreement)* [2002] 1 FLR 654; and *K v K (Ancillary Relief: Prenuptial Agreement)* [2003] 1 FLR 120.

[518] The Civil Partnership Act 2004, s 72(1) and sch 5, replicates the effect of the provisions applicable in matrimonial proceedings.

[519] There is no power to order payments of capital at this stage: *Wicks v Wicks* [1998] 1 FLR 470.

of those proceedings.[520] In a proper case, such an order may be intended to finance the costs of prosecuting those proceedings.[521]

(ii) Financial provision, property adjustment and pension sharing

2.148 The court's powers in matrimonial and civil partnership cases extend so as to bring virtually all the parties' economically valuable assets within the scope of what has sometimes been called[522] a 'remedy of equitable distribution'. The orders which the court can make are classified as financial provision orders, property adjustment orders, and pension sharing orders.[523]

2.149 *Financial provision orders* consist of orders for *periodical payments, secured periodical payments*[524] and orders to pay a *lump sum*. Such orders can be made in favour of a party to the marriage or civil partnership or a child of the family.[525] A secured order can be made to continue for the lifetime of the applicant (unlike an ordinary periodical payments order which must terminate on the payer's death).[526] Periodical payments orders (secured or unsecured) may also be made for a specified term. All periodical payment orders come automatically to an end if the payee remarries or enters into a civil partnership[527](but not if he or she merely cohabits).[528] The court may order periodical payments to be made by means of standing order or direct debit.[529] A *lump sum* order may require payment by instalments.[530]

2.150 There are four main types of *property adjustment order*.[531] First, a *transfer of property order* by which the court may order the transfer of any property (for example,

---

[520] Civil Partnership Act 2004, s 72(1) and sch 5, para 38; Matrimonial Causes Act 1973, s 22 (which uses the traditional term 'maintenance pending suit').

[521] See *Moses-Taiga v Moses-Taiga* [2005] EWCA Civ 1013; *C v C (Maintenance pending suit: Legal Costs)* [2006] 2 FLR 1207; *Currey v Currey*[2006] EWCA Civ 1338.

[522] See notably *Dart v Dart* [1996] 2 FLR 286, 294, CA, *per* Thorpe LJ. The same expression is commonly used in United States' jurisdictions, where however it appears to have a somewhat broader meaning.

[523] Matrimonial Causes Act 1973, s 21. The court also has power (on making an order for financial relief other than an order for unsecured periodical payments) to order a sale of property; and this power can be exercised notwithstanding the fact that a third party also has a beneficial interest in the property: ibid, s 24A.

[524] Matrimonial Causes Act 1973, s 21(1).

[525] For 'child of the family' see Children Act 1989 s 105(1) as amended by Civil Partnership Act 2004) s 75(3), para 2.143. The power of the court to make such orders has been greatly curtailed by the provisions of the Child Support Act 1991: see para 2.142; and for that reason, the text does not discuss ancillary orders in favour of children.

[526] Matrimonial Causes Act 1973, s 28(1).

[527] Matrimonial Causes Act 1973, s 28(1) as amended by Civil Partnership Act 2004, s 261(1) and sch 27 para 43.

[528] See eg *Clutton v Clutton* [1991] 1 FLR 242, CA.

[529] Maintenance Enforcement Act 1991.

[530] Matrimonial Causes Act 1973, s 23(3)(c).

[531] ibid, s 21(2).

the matrimonial home) to which the one spouse is entitled whether in possession or reversion to the other spouse (or to or for the benefit of a child of the family). Secondly, a *settlement of property order* by which the court directs that property to which one spouse is entitled be settled for the benefit of the other spouse (or children of the family). This power has a particular utility in securing that the former family home continues to be available for occupation as a home for dependent children whilst preserving both spouses' financial interest in it. Thirdly the court may make an order *varying any 'ante-nuptial or post-nuptial' settlement*[532] made on the parties to the marriage for the benefit of the parties or the children of the family. The term 'settlement' has in this context been widely interpreted.[533] Finally, the Welfare Reform and Pensions Act 1999 introduced complex provisions empowering the court to make *pension sharing orders*, based on transferring part or all of the cash equivalent transfer value accrued under the one spouse's pension scheme in order to provide comparable benefits for the other spouse. The court also has power to make a *pension attachment order*, requiring pension fund trustees to pay to one spouse or civil partner sums due under the scheme to the other.[534]

(iii) The exercise of the discretion to make orders in ancillary relief proceedings

The principles to be applied by the court in exercising its wide discretion to make financial orders in divorce and other proceedings are laid down in the Matrimonial Causes Act 1973, as amended by the Matrimonial and Family Proceedings Act 1984.[535] The Civil Partnership Act 2004 contains virtually identical provisions governing the exercise of the court's discretion on the termination of a civil partnership;[536] and case law will in due course no doubt determine whether or not

2.151

---

[532] The term used in relation to civil partnership proceedings is 'relevant settlement': Civil Partnership Act 2004, s 72(1) and sch 5, para 7(3).

[533] It extends to the trusts under which a home was jointly owned: *Brown v Brown* [1959] P 86, CA; and to trusts situated abroad: *C v C (Variation of post-nuptial settlement: Company Shares)* [2003] 2 FLR 493. See also *Brooks v Brooks* [1996] 1 AC 375 (the effect of which has been negatived by Welfare Reform and Pensions Act 1999, sch 3, para 3, in relation to pensions, which can now be dealt with under the pension sharing provisions introduced by that Act); *C v C (Variation of post-nuptial settlement: Company Shares)* [2003] 2 FLR 493. The court also has power to extinguish or reduce the interests of either spouse under a nuptial settlement: Matrimonial Causes Act 1973, s 24(1)(d).

[534] See Matrimonial Causes Act 1973, s 25B–25D as inserted by the Pensions Act 1995.

[535] The Act, gave effect to recommendations by the Law Commission: see *The Financial Consequences of Divorce; the Basic Policy, A Discussion Paper* (Law Com. No 103, 1980) and *The Financial Consequences of Divorce. the Response to the Law Commission's Paper and Recommendations on the policy of the law* (1981) Law Com. No 112: the Act removed the statutory directive obliging the court to seek to place the parties in the financial position in which they would have been had the marriage not broken down, and contained provisions intended to facilitate the making of 'clean break' orders in appropriate cases, to encourage self sufficiency, and to promote the welfare of children affected by parental divorce.

[536] Civil Partnership Act 2004, s 72(1) and sch 5, paras 21–29.

their application will differ to reflect different gender expectations. The scheme of the legislation is as follows:

(a) it is the duty of the court in deciding whether to exercise its powers and, if so, in what manner to have regard to all the circumstances of the case, first consideration being given to the welfare while a minor of any child of the family who has not attained the age of 18;[537]

(b) the court is directed 'in particular' to have regard to certain specified matters;[538]

(c) in dissolution and annulment cases the court has an obligation to consider whether it would be just and reasonable to effect a 'clean break' between the parties to the marriage.[539]

2.152 **First consideration to the welfare of children.** The legislation[540] requires the court, in deciding whether and how to exercise its financial powers in relation to spouses civil partners and children to 'have regard to all the circumstances of the case, first consideration being given to the welfare while a minor of any child of the family who has not attained the age of eighteen'. This justifies what has been described[541] as 'the invariable practice' of the courts in seeking 'to maintain a stable home for the children, and also ensuring that appropriate provision is made for their primary carer.[542] For this reason the courts have made orders transferring the family home to the parent with whom the children are to live[543] or ordered a settlement under which the parent with day to day care and children will occupy the home but each party will retain their financial interest in the eventual sale proceeds.[544] Similarly, the children's welfare may influence the court in favour of making a periodical payments order for the support of the parent with day to day care at least until the children no longer need full-time care.[545] But the court is not required to regard the children's welfare as 'paramount' (as would be the case in relation to a decision about the child's upbringing).[546] Rather it will consider all the circumstances always bearing the children's welfare in mind; and then try to

---

537 Matrimonial Causes Act 1973, s 25(1); Civil Partnership Act 2004, s 72(1) and sch 5, para 20.

538 ibid, s 25(2).; Civil Partnership Act 2004, s 72(1) and sch 5, para 21(2). Matrimonial Causes Act 1973, s 25(3) and Civil Partnership Act 2004, s 72(1) and sch 5, para 22 set out circumstances to which particular regard is to be had in relation to the exercise of the court's powers to make orders in relation to a child of the family.

539 ibid, s 25A; Civil Partnership Act 2004, s 72(1) and sch 5, para 23.

540 ibid, s 25(1); Civil Partnership Act 2004, s 72(1) and sch 5, para 20.

541 By Baroness Hale, *Miller v Miller, McFarlane v Mc Farlane* [2006] UKHL 24 at [128]. Presumably the same would apply to a primary carer in a civil partnership.

542 See *K v K (Ancillary Relief: Prenuptial Agreement)* [2003] 1 FLR 120,133.

543 See *B v B (Financial Provision: Welfare of Child and Conduct)* [2002] 1 FLR 555.

544 *Mesher v Mesher* [1980] 1 All ER 126n but see *B v B(Mesher Order)* [2003] EWHC 3106.

545 *Waterman v Waterman* [1989] 1 FLR 380, CA.

546 Children Act 1989, s 1: see para 2.196ff.

make a financial settlement which is just as between husband and wife.[547] The requirement to give special consideration to the interests of children of the family applies only so long as the child concerned has not attained the age of 18 (even if the child is disabled or still receiving education).

'All the circumstances'. In exercising its powers in relation to a party to the   **2.153** marriage or civil partnership the court is directed in particular to have regard to the following matters:[548]

(a) the income, earning capacity, property and other financial resources which each of the parties has or is likely to have in the foreseeable future, including in the case of earning capacity any increase in that capacity which it would in the opinion of the court be reasonable to expect a party to the marriage or civil partnership to take steps to acquire;

(b) the financial needs, obligations and responsibilities which each of the parties has or is likely to have in the foreseeable future;

(c) the standard of living enjoyed by the family before the breakdown of the marriage;

(d) the age of each party and the duration of the marriage or civil partnership;

(e) any physical or mental disability of either of the parties;

(f) the contributions which each of the parties has made or is likely in the foreseeable future to make to the welfare of the family, including any contribution made by looking after the home or caring for the family;

(g) the conduct of each of the parties if that conduct is such that it would in the opinion of the court be inequitable to disregard it;[549]

(h) in the case of proceedings for divorce, dissolution or nullity, the value to each of the parties of any benefit which by reason of the dissolution or annulment that party will lose the chance of acquiring.[550]

A considerable body of case law has been reported on the application of the   **2.154** statutory guidance in the context of matrimonial proceedings. In particular, the courts have consistently deprecated excessive reliance on what has been decided in the past rather than on the application of the statutory language to the facts of

---

[547] *Suter v Suter and Another* [1987] 2 FLR 232, CA.

[548] Matrimonial Causes Act 1973, s 25(2); Civil Partnership Act 2004, s 72(1) and sch 5, para 21(2).

[549] The legislation had seemed designed to codify the policy adopted by the Court of Appeal in *Wachtel v Wachtel* [1973] Fam 72; whereby one party's conduct was only to be taken into account in exceptional cases where a clear imbalance could be demonstrated (as for example in *Kyte v Kyte* [1988] Fam 145), and see now *Miller v Miller, McFarlane v Mc Farlane* [2006] UKHL 24, especially *per* Lord Nicholls, at para 127). Conduct relating to financial matters may sometimes be a factor: see *Le Foe v Le Foe and Woolwich plc* [2001] 2 FLR 970.

[550] Matrimonial Causes Act 1973, s 25(2); Civil Partnership Act 2004, s 72(1) and sch 5, para 21(2)(h).

each case;[551] and it seems that appellate courts will not interfere with an order which cannot properly be described a 'plainly wrong' provided there has been no evident misdirection, the relevant facts have been found and considered, and the appropriate statutory provisions considered.[552] In particular, reliance on a purely fractional approach—such as the one-third division of assets and income for long traditional in the divorce court—is no longer favoured.[553] In many cases, there are insufficient resources to do more than attempt to meet the parties'[554] basic needs for housing and other essentials.[555] In cases involving more ample resources decisions were often reached by calculating a wife's 'reasonable requirements'[556] and awarding her a lump sum sufficient to provide a stream of net income to meet those needs over her lifetime.[557] But latterly cases increasingly came before the courts in which the assets within the court's jurisdiction were very substantial indeed; and in *White v White*[558] (a case involving assets, mostly invested in the farming partnership in which both husband and wife were actively involved, amounting to some £4.5 million) the House of Lords asserted that the objective implicit in the statutory provisions was (first consideration having been given to the welfare of the children) to achieve a 'fair' outcome, and deprecated reference to concepts such as 'reasonable requirements' rather than the statutory 'needs'. In their Lordships' view, discrimination on the basis of gender was incompatible with fairness, and accordingly if each party had contributed equally (albeit in different spheres) to the family then it was irrelevant that such contribution was made by earning money or in other ways.[559] Subsequently, two cases[560] involving enormous riches came before the House. In contrast to *White* these were not cases involving a working business partnership. Their Lordships' opinions all denounced 'discrimination' based on a perception that only earning and other financial input could be relevant, but there was some difference of opinion as to the

---

551 For a classic example of this approach, see *F v F (Duxbury Calculation: Rate of Return)* [1996] 1 FLR 883.

552 See *White v White* [2001] 1 AC 596, HL; *Miller v Miller, McFarlane v McFarlane* [2006] UKHL 24.

553 Contrast *Wachtel v Wachtel* [1973] Fam 72, CA, with *Dart v Dart* [1996] 2 FLR 286, CA.

554 The fact that both parties need housing has been emphasized: *Cordle v Cordle* [2001] EWCA Civ 1791.

555 Sometimes a settlement was ordered preserving the home for one parent's occupation at least until the youngest child ceases to be dependent, the sale proceeds ultimately being divided between the two parents.

556 See *White v White* [2001] 1 AC 596, HL.

557 The so-called *Duxbury* programme may be used to work out a given level of income allowing for inflation and a number of variables: see generally *F v F (Financial Provision: Reasonable Needs)* [1995] 2 FLR 45. But the Duxbury calculation is a tool, not a rule: *White v White* 1 AC 596, CA, *per* Thorpe LJ.

558 *White v White* [2000] UKHL 54; [2001] 1 AC 596, HL.

559 However, on the facts, the House of Lords refused to interfere with the (unequal) division of assets ordered by the Courts below.

560 *Miller v Miller, McFarlane v Mc Farlane* [2006] UKHL 24.

circumstances in which the source of the assets (for example, from inheritance, or indeed from some kinds of business activity) might be regarded as relevant, especially in cases in which the marriage had been comparatively short. Some of the opinions suggested that the courts should be more ready to compensate one party for the loss of career and other opportunities (although little guidance was given as to the factual basis on which this should be done). It seems inevitable that there will be further litigation (although it should be emphasized that it seems to be only in cases which are literally extraordinary that the basis upon which the court's discretion will be exercised is seriously in doubt).

The 'clean break'. It has been said that the 'clean break' principle originally   **2.155**
referred to an arrangement whereby the wife abandoned her claim for ongoing periodical payments in return for once for all capital provision (often the matrimonial home).[561] This practice was intended to encourage spouses to settle their money and property problems and thereby achieve what Thorpe J described[562] as 'financial as well as emotional independence' and enable them to begin a new life not overshadowed by past bitterness. It has been said that this clean break principle informs the modern legislation;[563] and it seems that some judges[564] take the view that the modern practice is to favour a clean break whenever possible. It is certainly true that the legislation is strongly influenced by the desirability of ending spouses' mutual financial relations; but this must not be done at the expense of the fairness which is the overriding objective.[565] The governing statutory provisions are complex and the relevant provisions require careful analysis in each case.[566]

(iv) The general duty to consider the termination of financial obligations

First, if the court decides to exercise its financial powers in favour of a party to the   **2.156**
marriage,[567] it must consider 'whether it would be appropriate so to exercise those powers that the financial obligations of each party towards the other will be

---

561 *Clutton v Clutton* [1991] 1 FLR 242, 245, CA, *per* Lloyd LJ.
562 *Richardson v Richardson (No 2)* [1994] 2 FLR 1051, 1054.
563 *Minton v Minton* [1979] AC 593, 608, HL, *per* Lord Scarman.
564 See *B v B (Financial Provision)* [1990] 1 FLR 20, 26, *per* Ward J.
565 *White v White* [2000] UKHL 54; [2001] 1 AC 596, HL; *F v F (Clean Break: Balance of Fairness)* [2003] 1 FLR 847.
566 See eg *Richardson v Richardson* [1994] 1 WLR 186 (where the failure to follow the statutory provisions frustrated the parties' intention to terminate the parties' financial obligations).
567 This provision has no application to orders in respect of children. However, if the court is dealing with an application to vary a periodical payments order made in divorce or nullity proceedings the court is required to consider whether in all the circumstances it would be appropriate to terminate the financial relationship between the parties, and it may now require periodical payments to be in effect commuted for a lump sum: Matrimonial Causes Act 1973, s 31(7), 7(A) and 7(B) as inserted by the Family Law Act 1996, sch 8, para 16; Civil Partnership Act 2004, s 72(1) and sch 5, paras 53–4.

terminated as soon after the grant of the decree as the court considers just and reasonable'.[568] This duty arises whenever the court decides to exercise its property adjustment or financial provision powers in favour of a party to the marriage. But it should be noted that the duty is a duty to *consider* whether it would be 'appropriate' to exercise those powers to terminate the reciprocal financial obligations as soon as the court considers would be 'just and reasonable'[569] and there are four other provisions of the 1973 Act which are relevant to the application of this general principle.

(v) Application of the general duty: court to consider potential increase in earning capacity[570]

2.157   The legislation includes amongst the matters to which the court's attention is particularly directed a reference to any increase in earning capacity which it would in the opinion of the court be reasonable to expect a party to the marriage to take steps to acquire; and it seems that this factor will sometimes be particularly relevant to the duty imposed on the court to consider whether any periodical payments order should be made only for a specified term.

(vi) The duty to consider specifying a term for any periodical payments order[571]

2.158   Although the simplest form of 'clean break' involves a capital transfer between the parties and the dismissal[572] of all claims for periodical payments there will be many cases in which this is clearly not appropriate. If the court does decide that an order for periodical payments would be appropriate, the legislation requires that the court in particular 'consider whether it would be appropriate to require those payments to be made or secured only for such term as would in the opinion of the court be sufficient to enable the party in whose favour the order is made to adjust without undue hardship to the termination of his or her financial dependence on the other party'.[573] However, evidence will be required that the person concerned does indeed have a realistic earning capacity;[574] and the fact that he or she may

---

568 Matrimonial Causes Act 1973, s 25A(1); Civil Partnership Act 2004, s 72(1) and sch 5, para 23(2).

569 In *McFarlane v McFarlane* [2006] UKHL 24 the House of Lords upheld an order for periodical payments of £250,000 per annum for the parties' joint lives.

570 Matrimonial Causes Act 1973, s 25(2)(a): see para 2.153.

571 Matrimonial Causes Act 1973, s 25A(2); Civil Partnership Act 2004, s 72(1) and sch 5, para 23(2).

572 For the importance of dismissing all claims for maintenance, see para 2.160.

573 Matrimonial Causes Act 1973, s 25A(2). In some cases an award of periodical payments is not primarily concerned with 'dependency' or with the relief of 'hardship' but is part of a package intended to produce overall fairness in the division of assets; and in such cases the decision to make a fixed term order must reflect that fact: *McFarlane v McFarlane* [2006] UKHL 24.

574 See *M v M (Financial Provision)* [1987] 2 FLR 1; *Waterman v Waterman* [1989] 1 FLR 380, CA; *Flavell v Flavell* [1997] 1 FLR 353; and *G v G (Periodical Payments)* [1998] Fam 1, CA.

have lost employment opportunities by involvement in the relationship is a factor which has to be recognized.[575]

(vii) *Power to direct that no application be made to extend specified term*

The court has power to debar a party in whose favour a periodical payments order **2.159** is made from applying for any extension of the term specified in the order; and unless such a direction is made the court will have jurisdiction to extend the term.[576] Case law in fact establishes that this will rarely be considered appropriate;[577] and accordingly the court will be reluctant to exercise the 'Draconian' power to exclude a party from any possibility of seeking to extend a term especially when there is uncertainty about the future.[578]

(viii) *The power to dismiss a claim for periodical payments*[579]

The Act provides that the court may dismiss any application for periodical pay- **2.160** ments and direct that the applicant be debarred from making any further application for such an order.[580] The court also has power to direct that a party be debarred from seeking provision out of the other's estate under the provisions of the Inheritance (Provision for Family and Dependants) Act 1975; and unless these powers are exercised the other spouse will be at risk that financial issues will be reopened.

(4) *Rights and Duties in Respect of Children*

(a) 'Parental responsibility'

At common law the father alone[581] had 'legal authority' over his legitimate child **2.161** (although some others came under certain duties towards children).[582] But the Children Act 1989 substituted the concept of 'parental responsibility' as the key

---

[575] *Miller v Miller, McFarlane v McFarlane* [2006] UKHL 24.

[576] Matrimonial Causes Act 1973, s 28(1A), Civil Partnership Act 2004, s 72(1) and sch 5, para 47(5).

[577] See *Fleming v Fleming* [2003] EWCA 1841 *McFarlane v Mc Farlane* [2006] UKHL 54.

[578] *Waterman v Waterman* [1989] 1 FLR 380, CA.

[579] Matrimonial Causes Act 1973, s 25A(3).

[580] The court has extensive powers to vary periodical payment orders, even if the order is for a nominal amount: see eg *Jessel v Jessel* [1979] 1 WLR 1148, CA, and accordingly dismissing all claims is the only way in which a 'clean break' can be attained. If a maintenance *agreement* is in force, the court can vary its terms under the provisions of the Matrimonial Causes Act 1973, s 31, see para 2.143(4).

[581] The Guardianship Act 1973 provided that the mother of a child should have the same rights and authority as the law allowed to the father and that the rights and authority of mother and father should be equal. A legal guardian also had authority over the child.

[582] For an analysis of the nature of these rights and duties, see *F v Metropolitan Borough of Wirral DC* [1991] Fam 69, CA.

whereby rights and duties in respect of children were to be allocated; and as explained above[583] it is now 'parental responsibility' which vests in the child's parents[584] at birth.

(i) Who has parental responsibility?

2.162 The following have parental responsibility:

(1) Both parents of the child if they were 'married to each other at the time of the child's birth'.[585]

(2) The father of a child whose parents were not 'married to each other' at the date of the child's birth[586] if he has either been registered as the child's father under the Births Marriages and Deaths registration legislation of England and Wales, Scotland or Northern Ireland;[587] or if the father and the child's mother have made a parental responsibility agreement in the prescribed form;[588] or if the court has (on the basis that such an order will promote the child's welfare) made a parental responsibility order[589] on his application.[590]

(3) The child's mother.[591]

---

[583] See para 2.05.

[584] A father who is not married to the mother does not necessarily acquire parental responsibility: see para 2.162.

[585] Legitimated and adopted children and the children of certain void marriages are, by means of a statutory deeming provision, treated as if their parents were within this definition at the date of birth: Family Law Reform Act 1987, s 1(3): see para 2.05, n 11 above.

[586] Even in the extended meaning of the Family Law Reform Act 1987, s 1(3). The traditional legal description of such a child is 'illegitimate' but continued use of that expression has been the subject of judicial criticism: *Re R (Surname: Using Both Parents')* [2001] EWCA 1344; [2001] 2 FLR 1358.

[587] Children Act 1989, s 4, as substituted by Adoption and Children Act 2002, s 111.

[588] ibid; Parental Responsibility Agreement Regulations 1994, SI 1991/1478 (as amended by Parental Responsibility Agreement (Amendment) Regulations 1994, SI 1994/3157.

[589] Children Act 1989, s 4, as substituted by Adoption and Children Act 2002, s 111. It has been said that the effect of such an order is to give the father the same status as the father of a legitimate child; and accordingly it is not inconsistent to make such an order whilst denying the father any contact with the child: *Re H (A Minor) (Parental Responsibility)* [1993] 1 FLR 484, CA.

[590] The principle that the child's welfare is the paramount consideration has been said to be applicable in deciding whether or not to make an order: *Re H (Parental Responsibility)* [1998] 1 FLR 855, 859, CA, *per* Butler-Sloss LJ. In determining this question, the starting point is a consideration of (i) the degree of commitment shown by the father to the child; (ii) the degree of attachment between them; (iii) the father's reasons for seeking the order: *Re H (Minors) (Local Authority: Parental Rights)* [1991] Fam 151, 158, CA, *per* Balcombe LJ. But those matters are not exhaustive, and if there are other matters adverse to the father which tip the balance the court will decline to make an order: *Re H (A Minor) (Parental Responsibility)* [1993] 1 FLR 484, CA. The court may terminate a parental responsibility order (or agreement) on the application of any person with parental responsibility or on an application made (with leave of the court) by the child: see eg *Re P (Terminating Parental Responsibility)* [1995] 1 FLR 1048.

[591] Children Act 1989, s 2(1), (2).

(4) The child's adoptive parents (and the making of an adoption order operates to end the parental responsibility of the birth parents and others).[592]

(5) The child's step-parent, provided that those concerned have made a parental responsibility agreement[593] or the court has made a parental responsibility order.[594]

(6) The guardian or guardians[595] appointed for a child[596] by will[597] or court order.[598]

(7) A 'special guardian' appointed under the provisions of s 14A of the Children Act 1989.[599]

(8) A person in whose favour a residence order[600] is in force.

(9) The local authority designated by a care order or certain other orders;[601] and any person in whose favour an emergency protection order is in force.[602] The making of a care order does not deprive parents and others of their parental responsibility; but the designated local authority may (provided the authority is satisfied it is necessary to do so in order to safeguard or promote the

---

[592] See para 2.21. The making of a 'parental order' under the Human Fertilisation and Embryology Act 1990, s 30 on the application of spouses one or both of whom have provided the gametes leading to the child's conception also vests in the applicants parental responsibility for a child carried by a surrogate: see *Re Q (Parental Order)* [1996] 1 FLR 369.

[593] In the prescribed form: Parental Responsibility Agreement Regulations 1991, SI 1991/1478; Parental Responsibility Agreement (Amendment) Regulations 2005, SI 2005/2808.

[594] Children Act 1989, s 4A, as substituted by Adoption and Children Act 2002, s 112. For these purposes, a parent with parental responsibility must be either married to, or the civil partner of, the step-parent.

[595] Children Act 1989, s 5(6) but parental responsibility only vests in the guardian when the appointment takes effect (which will not normally happen until the death of others with parental responsibility):ss 5(7) and (8).

[596] The power to appoint by will or other written document can only be exercised by a parent or guardian: Children Act 1989, s 5(3), (4).

[597] A guardian may also be appointed by written instrument complying with statutory formalities: Children Act 1989, s 5(3)–(5).

[598] Children Act 1989, s 5(1). This power is only exercisable if the child has no parent with parental responsibility for him, or if a residence order had been made in favour of a parent subsequently deceased: s 5(1).

[599] As inserted by Adoption and Children Act 2002, s 115. The Court may make such an appointment on the application of (amongst others) a local authority foster parent, or a person in whose favour a residence order has been made. The main effect of the order is to allow the special guardian to exercise parental responsibility which may be exercised to the exclusion of any other person with parental responsibility: Children Act 1989, s 14(c) as inserted by Adoption and Children Act 2002, s 115. According to the official *Explanatory Notes* 'special guardianship orders are intended to meet the needs of children who cannot live with their birth parents, for whom adoption is not appropriate, but who could still benefit from a legally secure placement'.

[600] ie an order settling the arrangements about the person with whom the child is to live: Children Act 1989, s 8(1).

[601] See para 2.193.

[602] See Children Act 1989, s 44.

child's welfare)[603] determine the extent to which a parent or guardian of the child may meet his responsibility for the child.[604]

2.163 The Children Act 1989 reflects the policy that parental responsibility should not be easily lost; and the Act expressly provides[605] that a person does not cease to have that responsibility because someone else acquires parental responsibility for the child (for example, by the making of a residence order or care order).[606] Moreover, a person who has parental responsibility for a child may not surrender or transfer any part of that responsibility to another (although he or she may[607] arrange for it to be met by others—for example, a nanny or school teacher).

2.164 Where more than one person has parental responsibility for the same child that responsibility is in effect enjoyed jointly and severally:[608] the Children Act 1989[609] provides that in that situation each of them may act alone and without the other in meeting that responsibility. But the Act expressly prohibits a person entitled to parental responsibility from acting in a way which would be incompatible with any order—such as a residence or specific issue order—made under the Act with respect to the child.[610] Judicial decisions have emphasized that normally there should be consultation about important steps (such as decisions about education) in the child's life;[611] and it has been said that there is a small group of important decisions made on behalf of a child (for example, sterilization, change of name) which ought not to be made, in the absence of agreement between all those with parental responsibility, without the specific approval of the court.[612]

(ii) Nature of parental responsibility

2.165 The use of the word 'responsibility' to characterize the powers of a parent marks a recognition of the fact that the law now finds the justification for parental decision

---

[603] ibid, s 33(4).

[604] ibid, s 33(3)(b); but this provision does not prevent a parent or guardian who has care of the child from doing what is reasonable in all the circumstances of the case for the purpose of safeguarding or promoting the child's welfare: s 33(5).

[605] Section 2(6).

[606] Special Guardianship Orders are inconsistent with this policy, but the distinctive needs which special guardianship is intended to meet were thought to justify making such an exception.

[607] Section 2(7). Such an arrangement does not affect any liability of the person making it which may arise from failure to meet parental responsibility: s 2(11).

[608] But it has been held that one parent does not have the right to change a child's surname without the consent of all persons with parental responsibility: *Re PC (Change of Surname)* [1997] 2 FLR 730.

[609] Section 2(7).

[610] Section 2(8).

[611] *Re G (Parental Responsibility: Education)* [1994] 2 FLR 964; *Dawson v Wearmouth* [1999] 2 All ER 353, HL.

[612] *Re J (Specific Issue Orders: Child's Religious Upbringing and Circumcision)* [2000] 1 FLR 571, Butler-Sloss P.

taking as being primarily to enable the parents properly 'to raise the child to become a properly developed adult both physically and morally' (as Lord Chancellor Mackay put it).[613] The Children Act 1989 does not, however, give a definition of what it describes as the 'rights, duties, powers, responsibilities and authority which by law a parent of a child has in relation to the child and his property' which are embodied in the concept of parental responsibility.[614] It does expressly provide that parental responsibility 'also includes the rights,[615] powers and duties which a guardian of the child's estate...would have had in relation to the child and his property'[616] but to ascertain what rights and duties a parent had 'by law'[617] requires reference to equity and the common law.[618] It seems to be generally accepted that the following elements are included:[619]

(1) the right to have the child living with the person concerned or otherwise to decide where the child should live; the right to veto the issue of a passport and to decide whether to take the child out of the United Kingdom;

(2) the right to decide on the child's education and to choose his or her religion;

(3) the right to discipline the child;[620]

(4) the right to consent to medical treatment for the child;

(5) the right to withhold consent to a proposed marriage or civil partnership;[621]

(6) the right to administer the child's property and to enter into certain contracts on his behalf;

(7) the right to act for the child in legal proceedings;

(8) the right to the child's domestic services (and possibly the right to receive payment for work which the child does for others);

---

[613] (1989) 139 New LJ 505; and see *Re S (Parental Responsibility)* [1995] 2 FLR 648, 657 *per* Ward LJ.

[614] Children Act 1989, s 3(1).

[615] Including 'in particular, the right of the guardian to receive or recover in his own name, for the benefit of the child, property of whatever description and wherever situated which the child is entitled to receive or recover': Children Act 1989, s 3(3).

[616] Children Act 1989, s 3(2).

[617] In contrast, the Children (Scotland) Act 1995, s 2, does provide a list of the rights which a parent has for the purpose of enabling him or her to fulfil the responsibility which the Act imposes on parents and others concerned.

[618] See *F v Metropolitan Borough of Wirral DC* [1991] Fam 69, CA.

[619] The list includes rights dealt with by statutes modifying the common law.

[620] Children and Young Persons Act 1933, s 1(7) expressly preserved the parental right to administer moderate and reasonable physical chastisement, but after the European Court of Human Rights had, in *A v UK (Human Rights: Punishment of Child)* [1998] 2 FLR 959, held that English law failed to protect a child's convention right not to be subjected to 'inhuman or degrading treatment or punishment' s1(7) was repealed by Children Act 2004, s 58(5). That Act also provided that 'reasonable punishment' should not constitute a defence to charges of cruelty, wounding, or inflicting grievous or actual bodily harm. Corporal punishment is no longer permitted in any school in England and Wales: see generally *R (Williamson) v Secretary of State for Education and Employment* [2005] UKHK 15.

[621] See Civil Partnership Act 2004, s 4.

(9) various miscellaneous[622] and consequential[623] rights such as the right to choose the name by which the child should be known.[624]

2.166 However, it would be misleading to suggest that any such enumeration accurately reflects the reality of the authority which a person with 'parental responsibility' has in respect of a child. First, statute may expressly restrict the exercise of a particular right.[625] Secondly, if the issue comes before a court, the court will apply the principle[626] that the questions which it has to decide about the upbringing of a child[627] are to be resolved by reference to the child's welfare as the paramount consideration.[628] The courts now accept that parental rights (such as the right to consent to medical treatment) 'exist for the performance of the parents' duties and responsibilities to the child and must be exercised in the best interests of the child'; and it follows that, (whilst parental wishes 'command very great respect' and 'may illuminate the quality and value to the child' of the parent child relationship)[629] parental right is 'subordinate to welfare',[630] determined objectively.[631] Thirdly, the Human Rights Act 1998 may be relevant: the Act[632] declares it unlawful for a public authority (for example a local authority exercising its functions in relation to children)[633] to act in a way which is incompatible with a Convention right; and it also requires[634] legislation (both primary and subordinate) to be read and given effect (so far as it is possible to do so) in a way compatible with convention right.[635] Finally (and in some ways of greatest importance)

---

[622] For the position in relation to the disposal of a deceased child's body, see *R v Gwent County Council, ex p B* [1992] 3 All ER 317; *Fessi v Whitmore* [1999] 1 FLR 767.

[623] Such as the right to decide how far to preserve the child's right to confidence in respect of his or her education: *Re Z (A Minor) (Identification: Restrictions on Publication)* [1997] Fam 1, CA.

[624] See generally *Dawson v Wearmouth* [1999] 2 AC 308, HL.

[625] As in the case of the right, clearly recognized by the common law, to administer 'reasonable and moderate' corporal punishment: see n 620 above.

[626] Now embodied in Children Act 1989, s 1.

[627] Or the administration of property or the application of any income arising from it: Children Act 1989, s 1(1).

[628] ibid, s 1(1).

[629] *An NHS Trust v MB (A Child by CAFCASS as Guardian ad Litem)* [2006] EWHC 507.

[630] *Re A (Children)(Conjoined Twins: Surgical Treatment)* [2000] EWCA 254; [2001] Fam 147.

[631] *An NHS Trust v MB (A Child By CAFCASS as Guardian ad Litem)* [2006] EWHC 507.

[632] Human Rights Act 1998, s 6.

[633] See eg *Z v United Kingdom* [2001] 2 FLR 612: *TP and KM v United Kingdom* [2001] 2 FLR 549. In such cases, damages may be awarded: *Re S (Minors)(Care Plan: Implementation of Care Plan)* [2002] UKHL 10; [2002] 2 AC 291.

[634] Human Rights Act 1998, s 3. If a court concludes that it is impossible to construe legislation so as to be compatible with Convention Rights it may make a 'declaration of incompatibility', as in *Bellinger v Bellinger* [2003] UKHL 21; [2003] 2 AC 467.

[635] The following Articles of the European Convention on Human Rights seem particularly relevant in the context of parental authority: Art 3 (degrading treatment), Art 8 (respect for family life), and Art 14 (freedom from discrimination). The 1998 United Nations Convention on the Rights of the Child may also be relevant, particularly in influencing judicial decision-taking: see eg *Re H (Paternity: Blood Test)* [1996] 2 FLR 65, 80, CA, *per* Ward LJ; and cf *Re A (Children: 1959 UN Declaration)* [1998] 1 FLR 354, 358, CA, *per* Thorpe LJ.

the decision of the House of Lords in *Gillick v West Norfolk and Wisbech Area Health Authority* [636] established that parental authority yields to a child's rights to make his own decisions when the child reaches a sufficient understanding and intelligence to be capable of coming to a decision. If there is a conflict between a parent (or anyone else with parental authority) and a 'mature' child, the *Gillick* decision suggests that it is the child's wishes which should prevail.[637]

The result of the interplay between these different principles leads to the conclu- **2.167** sion that the parental authority forming part of parental responsibility remains of importance, primarily because, unless and until a court order is obtained a person who has parental responsibility can in principle lawfully[638] take action—possibly irreversible—in reliance on that authority. The court has power to overrule a 'parental' decision, but unless and until it does so that decision will remain effective. How then will the courts reach decisions in those cases which do come before them? The Children Act 1989[639] provides a legislative framework intended to structure the decision taking process.

(b) Court orders in respect of children's upbringing

The Children Act 1989[640] provides that the court may make orders of the kinds **2.168** specified in section 8 of the Act in 'family proceedings'. Such proceedings fall into

---

[636] [1986] AC 112.

[637] But this may be misleading. First, if the matter comes before a court, the court will apply its own view as to what is in the child's interests, and second, it seems to be the case that a person under 16 has no legal right to reject medical treatment (even though the decision to reject is based on a fully informed awareness of the situation) if any person with 'parental responsibility' does give the required consent or if the court decides that such treatment would be in the child's best interests and should therefore be administered,: see *Re W (A Minor)(Medical Treatment: Court's Jurisdiction)* [1993] Fam 64, CA; *Re C (Detention: Medical Treatment)* [1997] 2 FLR 180; *Re P (Medical Treatment: Best Interests)* [2003] EWHC 2327, and *Re E (A Minor)(Wardship: Medical Treatment)* [1993] 1 FLR 386 (where the court overrode the refusal of a 15-year-old Jehovah's Witness to accept a blood transfusion). It can be argued that these rulings are incompatible with the policy embodied in the provisions of the Children Act 1989 relating to emergency protection orders: here it is specifically provided that a child with 'sufficient understanding to make an informed decision' may refuse to submit to the medical or psychiatric examination or assessment directed by the court: Children Act 1989, s 44(7).

[638] But note that in *Re B (A Minor) (Wardship: Sterilization)* [1988] AC 199, 205, HL, *per* Lord Templeman it was asserted that sterilization of a girl under 18 should never be carried out without leave of the court; and in *Re PC (Change of Surname)* [1997] 2 FLR 730 it was held that a person with parental responsibility should not purport to change a child's surname without the consent of all others with parental responsibility and that schools and other public authorities should not act on a change without evidence that all those consents had been obtained. Note also *Re G (Parental Responsibility: Education)* [1994] 2 FLR 964.

[639] As amended, notably by the Adoption and Children Act 2002, the Children Act 2004, and the Children and Adoption Act 2006.

[640] Although the Children Act 1989 constituted a major codification of the law relating to children, and still remains (as subsequently amended) the central statute, other statutes are also relevant. In particular, there are a number of statutory procedures intended to deal with cases of child abduction. The Child Abduction Act 1984 created criminal offences applicable in cases in which a child

two categories: first, proceedings under the inherent jurisdiction of the High Court in relation to children and, secondly, proceedings under certain statutes specified in the Act.

(i) The inherent jurisdiction of the court: the wardship jurisdiction

2.169 The High Court has a wide inherent jurisdiction to make orders relating to the upbringing of children. This was traditionally invoked by making the child a ward of court; and once this had been done, no important step could be taken in the child's life without the leave of the court. A distinctive feature of the wardship jurisdiction was that a child could be made a ward on the application of any person with a sufficient interest in the issue; and applications were often made by grandparents[641] and others who wished to raise questions about the child's upbringing.[642]

2.170 The Children Act 1989 does not directly restrict the right of private individuals[643] to issue an application that a child be made a ward. But the policy of the legislation was to establish a comprehensive *statutory* code dealing with issues including the standing required of those inviting the court to enquire into a child's upbringing.[644] For this reason, it has been held that the courts will in the exercise of their discretion normally refuse recourse to wardship, and making a child a ward of court is now regarded as an exceptional step. Moreover, it has come to be appreciated that making a child a ward was in fact the *result* of the exercise of the court's inherent jurisdiction: in many cases there would be only one question

---

has been removed from the lawful control of a person with (or entitled to exercise) such control; and the suspicion that such an offence has been committed may suffice to permit pre-emptive action by the police or the immigration authorities. The Child Abduction and Custody Act 1985 gives effect to the Hague Convention on the Civil Aspects of International Child Abduction and to the European Convention on Recognition and Enforcement of Decisions concerning Children and on the Restoration of Custody of Children. The Family Law Act 1986 creates machinery for the recognition, registration and enforcement within the United Kingdom and the Isle of Man of certain orders relating to children. These statutes, and the abundant case law, are analysed in detail in D Hershman and A McFarlane, *Children: Law and Practice* Division E.

641 See eg *B v W (Wardship: Appeal)* [1979] 1 WLR 1041, HL.

642 See for example *Re D (A Minor)(Wardship: Sterilization)* [1976] Fam 185 (application by social worker in respect of child about to be sterilized).

643 In contrast, the Act prohibits a local authority from seeking the exercise of the court's inherent jurisdiction unless the leave of the court has first been obtained; and the court may only grant such leave if satisfied that the result which the authority seeks could not be obtained through the making of other orders and that there is reasonable cause to believe that the child would be likely to suffer significant harm if leave is not granted: Children Act 1989, s 100(4), (5). Even if the inherent jurisdiction is invoked, the court is debarred from exercising it so as to require a child to be cared for by a local authority (s 100(2)). These rules give effect to the policy that state intervention in the upbringing of a child is in principle only justified in the circumstances envisaged in Part IV of the Act; and that in particular children should not be removed from their families simply on the basis that a court considered the state could provide better care: see para 2.194.

644 See para 2.194.

causing difficulty (for example, whether a particular form of medical treatment would be in the child's[645] interests); and in such cases it was unnecessary to vest in the court the extensive powers to regulate the child's life which was the traditional consequence of wardship. Rather, the particular issue could and should be determined 'once and for all' by an order expressed to be made in the exercise of the court's inherent jurisdiction: in such a case the court did not need to, and should not seek to, oversee a treatment plan for a gravely ill child, for example.[646] There may of course be cases where the very flexibility of the wardship jurisdiction (especially where problems requiring the court's intervention are likely to arise in the future, or where the situation is especially complex)[647] makes it desirable for the matter to come before the court without any fresh application, and the fact that the court's powers in the exercise of the wardship jurisdiction are wide[648] and flexible may also be relevant. But generally the court will only allow the inherent jurisdiction to be invoked if a question cannot be resolved under the statutory machinery provided by Part II of the Act in a way which secures the child's best interests, and it will only allow the child to be made a ward of court where the child's 'person is in a state of jeopardy from which he can only be protected' by giving him that status of a ward, or where the court's functions need to be secured from the effects, potentially injurious to the child, of external influences (intrusive publicity for example) and it is decided that conferring on the child the status of a ward will prove a more efficient deterrent than would recourse to proceedings for contempt of court.[649]

If the court does allow the inherent jurisdiction to be invoked, the fact that the Children Act 1989[650] classifies such proceedings as 'family proceedings' will mean not only that the court can couch its orders in the form laid down in the Children Act 1989, but that the other legal incidents of 'family proceedings—for example, the court's statutory powers to seek reports[651]—will be available. **2.171**

---

[645] The inherent jurisdiction (unlike the jurisdiction to make a child a ward of court) can be exercised in relation to vulnerable adults in certain circumstances: see *M v B, A and S (By the Official Solicitor)* [2005] EWHC 1681; [2006] 1 FLR 117.

[646] *Wyatt v Portsmouth NHS* [2005] EWCA Civ 1181.

[647] See eg *Re K (Adoption and Wardship)* [1997] 2 FLR 221.

[648] It was commonly said that the wardship judge had theoretically limitless powers to protect the ward's welfare; but the enactment of the Human Rights Act 1998 will sometimes require the court to balance conflicting Convention rights: see eg *Re S (Identification: Restriction: Restrictions on Publication)* [2004] UKHL 47; [2005] 1 AC 593.

[649] *Re T (A Minor) (Child: Representation)* [1994] Fam 49 *per* Waite LJ.

[650] s 8(3)(a).

[651] Children Act 1989, s 7.

(ii) Proceedings under statute

2.172 The Children Act 1989 classifies proceedings under certain statutes as 'family proceedings'. The relevant statutes are best divided into two groups: first, proceedings under the statutes specified in the Children Act, secondly, what can be described as 'free-standing' applications for orders under that Act itself. The first group is as follows:

(1) the Matrimonial Causes Act 1973 and the comparable provisions of the Civil Partnership Act 2004;[652]
(2) the Adoption and Children Act 2002;[653]
(3) the Domestic Proceedings and Magistrates' Courts Act 1978; and the comparable provisions of the Civil Partnership Act 2004;[654]
(4) the Matrimonial and Family Proceedings Act 1984 Part III;
(5) the Family Law Act 1996;[655]
(6) the Crime and Disorder Act 1998.[656]

2.173 The policy underlying this classification is that the act of starting proceedings (for example, for divorce) is sufficient of itself to justify the court exercising the judicial power of the state if a child's welfare so requires; and the orders the court considers appropriate to deal with a child's upbringing can then be made in the light of all the circumstances. For example, if there are divorce or dissolution proceedings the court may need to regulate the arrangements for contact[657] by making an order under section 8 of the Children Act 1989; and in order to decide whether such an order would best serve the child's interests the court may wish to exercise its powers to ask for a report from an officer of the Child and Family Court Advisory and Support Service ('CAFCASS')[658] Again, there may be circumstances in which the court hearing a divorce or dissolution case forms the view that the case may be one for local authority intervention, in which case it has power[659] to direct the appropriate authority to undertake an investigation of the child's circumstances with a view to deciding whether it should take action. As will be seen,[660] the court may act on its own motion, as well as on the application of a party to the proceedings.

---

[652] Children Act 1989, s 4(ba) as inserted by Civil Partnership Act 2004, sch 27, para 129(2).

[653] Children Act 1989 s 8(4)(d) as substituted by Adoption and Children Act 2002 sch 3, para 55.

[654] Children Act 1989, s 4(ea) as inserted by Civil Partnership Act 2004, sch 27, para 129(3).

[655] Children Act 1989, s 4(h) as inserted by Family Law Act 1996, sch 8, Part III, para 60. These will usually be cases of domestic violence.

[656] ss 11, 12; see Children Act 1989 s (8) (4)(h) as inserted by Crime and Disorder Act 1998, sch 8, para 68.

[657] See para 2.177.

[658] Under the Children Act 1989, s 7; see para 2.183. CAFCASS was established by the Criminal Justice and Court Services Act 2000.

[659] ibid, s 37; see para 2.177.

[660] See para 2.183.

The fact that proceedings under the various statutes are classified as 'family pro- **2.174**
ceedings' does not directly affect the requirements of the particular statute in
question. Thus, in divorce proceedings[661] the Matrimonial Causes Act 1973
obliges the court specifically to consider the arrangements made for the children
of the family;[662] and that procedure must be carried out in accordance with the
terms of the statute. Conversely, an adoption application can only be made under
the Children and Adoption Act 2006, and the requirements of the statute—for
example, as to parental agreement, and as to the qualifications of the applicants—
must be complied with if the court is to have jurisdiction to make a valid adoption
order.[663] The fact that the Children Act 1989 classifies the adoption proceedings
as 'family proceedings' does not affect that principle but it does mean that the
court could for example (provided that to do so would best serve the interests of
the child) make a residence order under the Children Act 1989 rather than the
adoption order sought; whilst it would also be possible for the court making an
adoption order also to make a contact order requiring the adoptive parent to
permit the birth parent or other relatives to have contact with the child[664] (or,
conversely, to make a prohibited steps order prohibiting the birth parent from
attempting to contact the child or the adopters).

This second[665] group—so called 'free-standing' applications—relate to proceed- **2.175**
ings under Part I (Introduction'—including applications for parental responsibility orders),[666] Part II ('Orders with Respect to Children in Family Proceedings')
and Part IV('Care and Supervision')[667] of the Children Act 1989. Their inclusion
in the definition of 'family proceedings' means that once such an application is
before the court it may make 'section 8 orders' and exercise its other powers to
promote the child's welfare. The Act follows the so-called 'open door policy' by
allowing applications to be made by any person who has obtained the court's prior
leave to proceed; but it creates a sophisticated hierarchy seeking to identify those
who should have the right to make applications without any need for prior leave.[668]

---

661 Under the Matrimonial Causes Act 1973: see s 41. Similar provisions apply in civil partnership proceedings.

662 As defined: see para 2.143.

663 See para 2.19.

664 In the past, the courts have considered it to be rarely in the interests of the child to impose a
requirement to allow continued contact: see *Re C (A Minor) (Adoption Order: Conditions)* [1989]
AC 1, HL.

665 See the definition in Children Act 1989, s 8(4)(a).

666 See para 2.20.

667 But the court's power to make orders under s 8 of the Act on the application of a local authority and to make such orders in respect of a child in the care of a local authority is restricted: s 9. This
gives effect to the policy stated in para 2.194.

668 See para 2.184. At this stage it may be helpful to bear in mind one example of how the
Act resolves questions of standing: a concerned friend of the family wishing to question parental decisions about medical procedures on a child would require first to obtain leave to apply for

The question of how the Act deals with the question of standing is best considered after the orders which the court may make in any 'family proceedings' have been identified and explained.

(iii) Orders the court can make in family proceedings: (1) 'section 8 orders'

2.176 The Children Act 1989 classifies four types of orders as 'section 8 orders'.[669]

2.177 *A contact order*[670] is 'an order requiring the person with whom a child lives, or is to live, to allow the child to visit or stay with the person named in the order, or for that person and the child otherwise to have contact with each other'.[671] Such an order may be in general terms (for example, requiring 'reasonable contact' to be afforded); but may be specific and detailed. 'Contact' is not restricted to face-to-face visits and orders for indirect contact (for example, by letter or greetings card) are often made.[672] Serious difficulties have been encountered in respect of contact arrangements; and in particular the enforcement of contact orders in the face of one party's 'implacable hostility'. In 2006 Parliament enacted the Children and Adoption Act[673] which is intended to improve matters, not least by giving the courts powers to make 'contract activity directions', increasing the availability of support to those concerned, and broadening the sanctions available to deter breach of court order.

the appropriate specific issue order (cf. *Re D (A Minor) (Wardship: Sterilization)* [1976] Fam 185) whereas a parent—including the father of an illegitimate child—could make such an application as of right in the absence of any order prohibiting applications by him without prior leave of the court: see eg *Re N (Section 91(14) Order)* [1996] 1 FLR 356, CA.

   [669] The expression extends to orders varying or discharging any of the specified orders: Children Act 1989, s 8(2). It is also provided that a s 8 order may contain directions about how it is to be carried into effect and may impose conditions to be complied with by a parent and by any person in whose favour the order is made: s 11(7). For example, a residence order may contain directions about how the child is to be prepared for a change of home or a condition that the parent with whom the child is to live surrender all passports and travel documents, or that the child be not allowed to come into contact with a named third party. In particular, contact orders may (and often do) contain detailed provisions about the arrangements to be made. On the width of the court's powers see generally *Re O (Contact: Imposition of Conditions)* [1995] 2 FLR 124; but contrast *D v D (County Court: Jurisdiction)* [1993] 2 FLR 802, CA (power could not extend to prohibition on public authority—in that case the police and social service authority—discharging statutory and common law powers).

   [670] Children Act 1989, s 8(1).

   [671] Jurisdiction to make contact (and residence) orders is dependent on the child being habitually resident in England and Wales: see *Re G (Adoption: Ordinary Residence)* [2002] EWHC 1376 [2003] 2 FLR 994.

   [672] See *Re O (Contact: Imposition of Conditions)* [1995] 2 FLR 124, CA, where the court rejected the argument that it had no jurisdiction to order the mother of a two-year-old boy to read his father's letters to him, such a provision being within the court's powers (Children Act 1989, s 11(7)) to impose conditions on s 8 orders.

   [673] See Part I of the Act. (Part II is concerned with adoptions with a foreign element).

A prohibited steps order[674] is 'an order that no step which could be taken by a parent **2.178** in meeting his parental responsibility for a child, and which is of a kind specified in the order, shall be taken by any person without the consent of the court'. Such orders may, for example, prohibit the removal of a child from his home, direct that a child should not be brought into contact with a named person, taken to a particular place or taken out of the country,[675] or forbid the carrying out of medical treatment on the child. The action which is prohibited must be of a kind which could be 'taken by a parent in meeting his parental responsibility'.[676] Accordingly it does not extend to a prohibition against one adult having contact with another for purposes unconnected with the child's upbringing.[677]

A residence order is 'an order settling the arrangements to be made as to the person **2.179** with whom a child is to live'. The Act envisages that an order may be made in favour of two or more persons who do not themselves all live together.[678] However, it has been said[679] that such shared residence orders would normally only be appropriate in cases where the circumstances were somewhat unusual and that it is normally important that the child have a settled home rather than passing to and fro between the parents. The making of a residence order has a number of additional legal consequences. First, where a residence order is in force no person may cause the child to be known by a new surname without the written consent of all those who have parental responsibility for the child or the leave of the court;[680] and no person may remove the child from the United Kingdom (save that the person in whose favour the order has been made may do so for a period of no more than a month).[681] Secondly, the making of a residence order automatically terminates any care order.[682] Thirdly, the making of a residence order confers

---

[674] Children Act 1989, s 8(1).

[675] Such an order may be obtained to prevent a person with a residence order exercising the right which that would otherwise confer to remove the child from the country for a period of no more than a month.

[676] As defined by the Children Act 1989, s 3. See generally *Re Z (A Minor)(Identification: Restrictions on Publication)* [1997] Fam 1, CA, (decision on whether to allow child to appear on television programme was an exercise of parental responsibility, and could accordingly be restrained by prohibited steps order).

[677] *Croydon London Borough Council v A* [1992] Fam 169, CA.

[678] Such an order may specify the periods during which the child is to live in the different households concerned: Children Act 1989, s 11(4).

[679] *A v A (Minors)(Shared Residence Order)* [1994] 1 FLR 669, CA.

[680] Children Act 1989, s 13(1)(a); see generally *Dawson v Wearmouth* [1999] UKHL 18, 2 AC 309; *Re PC (Change of Surname)* [1997] 2 FLR 730.

[681] Children Act 1989, s 13(1)(b), (2). This power may be curtailed or excluded by a specific condition in the order or by a prohibited steps order: see para 2.177. The provisions of the Child Abduction Act 1984, s 1 make it a criminal offence for parents and others 'connected with' a child under 16 to take or send the child out of the United Kingdom without 'the appropriate consent'.

[682] Children Act 1989, s 91(1). Conversely the making of a care order discharges any s 8 order: s 91(2).

'parental responsibility' on the person in whose favour it is made (if that person is not a parent or guardian).[683]

2.180 *A specific issue order* is an 'order giving directions for the purpose of determining a specific question which has arisen, or which may arise, in connection with any aspect of parental responsibility for a child'. Such an order enables the court to make rulings about particular matters (rather than giving a parent or other person a general right to take decisions about the child's upbringing, as is the effect of a residence order or a parental responsibility order). The court may, for example, order that the child be known by a different name[684] or that a child attend a particular school or receive specified medical treatment,[685] or that a child be taken to live permanently abroad.[686] The application must relate to some aspect of parental responsibility for the child, and the Court of Appeal has held that a specific issue order cannot be used to order the ejection of a man from the house of which he is a joint tenant.[687]

(iv) Orders the court can make in family proceedings: (2) court directed investigations

2.181 The traditional adversarial basis upon which civil litigation was conducted is manifestly unsuited for dealing with issues relating to children; and in order to reach a decision the court will often need evidence other than that which the adults in the family concerned choose to put before it. Accordingly, the Children Act 1989[688] provides that a court considering any question with respect to a child

---

683 ibid, s 12(2), but in such a case the person concerned does not have the right to appoint a guardian or give agreement to adoption etc: s 12(3). In *Re G (Residence: Same-Sex Partner)* [2005] EWCA 462;[2005] 2 FLR 957 a shared residence order was made in favour of a lesbian mother and her partner so that both would have parental responsibility for the child (of whom one was the genetic parent). Although the House of Lords allowed an appeal on the basis that on the facts such an order gave insufficient weight to the claims of the genetic parent there seems no question that in an appropriate case such an order may be made: see eg *Re M (Sperm Donor Father)* [2003] Fam Law 94.

684 If a residence order is in force such an application should be made under Children Act 1989, s 13. It appears to be the case that the court is not obliged on a s 13 application to refer expressly to the 'checklist' contained in s 1(3), whereas it is so obliged on an application under s 8; but in either event the court is obliged to consider the application in the light of the impact of the matter on the child's welfare: see *Dawson v Wearmouth* [1999] UKHL 18 [1999] 2 AC 309; *Re B (Change of Surname)* [1996] 1 FLR 791, CA.

685 See eg *Re C (Welfare of Child: Immunisation)* [2003] EWCA 1148; *Re S (Specific Issue Order: Religion: Circumcision)* [2004] EWHC 1282 (where on the facts the application was rejected).

686 The application will be determined by reference to the child's welfare. But the courts accept that the parent with primary care is entitled to select the place and country of residence unless that choice is shown to be plainly incompatible with the child's welfare or otherwise objectionable: see *Re T (Removal from Jurisdiction)* [1996] 2 FLR 352, 355.

687 *Pearson v Franklin* [1994] 1 WLR 370, CA. Such an application should now be made under the Family Law Act 1996, Part IV.

688 Section 7(1).

under the Act may ask a CAFCASS officer[689] or local authority to arrange for a report to be made to the court 'on such matters relating to the welfare of that child as are required to be dealt with in the report'; and such reports are directed in a high proportion of Children Act cases. The primary function of the officer preparing such a report is to assist the court by providing the factual information[690] the court needs to make a decision; but a full report[691] will almost invariably contain a recommendation. The decision on outcome is of course for the court, but it has been held that a court should state its reasons for departing from the recommendation.[692]

There are also cases in which the material before the court suggests that local **2.182** authority intervention in the child's upbringing may be necessary to safeguard the child's welfare;[693] and the Children Act 1989[694] provides that if a question arises in family proceedings with respect to the welfare of a child such as to cause the court to think it might be appropriate for a care or supervision order[695] to be made, the court may direct the local authority to undertake an investigation of the child's circumstances, and to consider whether the authority should apply for a care or supervision order (or provide services or assistance for the child or his family or take other action with respect to the child). An authority which decides not to apply for a care or supervision order must inform the court of the reasons for that decision;[696] but the court is powerless to override the authority's decision.[697]

(v) Standing to apply for section 8 orders

The Children Act combines provisions intended to give the court the flexibility **2.183** necessary to ensure that it always has the powers necessary to protect children whose families are involved in 'family proceedings'[698] with provisions designed to

---

[689] The Criminal Justice and Court Services Act 2000 created the Children and Family Court Advisory and Support Service in an attempt to provide an improved and integrated service to the courts.

[690] The court is given wide powers to take account of material (such as hearsay) which would otherwise be excluded by the rules of evidence: Children Act 1989, s 7(4).

[691] In order to reduce the pressure on the court welfare service, courts will often confine the scope of the inquiry to the matters on which it particularly feels in need of assistance.

[692] *Re CB (Access: Attendance of Court Welfare Officer)* [1995] 1 FLR 622, CA.

[693] The power has been exercised in some case of 'intractable' difficulties over contact which are thought to put the child's emotional welfare at risk: *Re M (Intractable Contact Dispute: Interim Care Order)* [2003] EWHC 1024.

[694] Section 37.

[695] See para 2.193.

[696] Children Act 1989, s 37(3).

[697] *Nottingham CC v P* [1994] Fam 18, 43, *per* Sir Stephen Brown P.

[698] And if it has power to make such an order it may make a 'family assistance order' requiring a CAFCASS officer or local authority social worker to be made available to 'advise assist and (where appropriate) befriend' the child and some others. Such an order can only be made if the court is satisfied that everyone named in the order (other than the child concerned) consents: Children

protect child and family against unwarranted interference.[699] The first of these objectives is attained by giving the court power to make a section 8 order with respect to the child[700] in any 'family proceedings' if it considers that the order should be made even though no application has been made for it.[701] The second is attained by imposing restrictions on the right to make applications for such orders: only people with certain qualifications evidencing an appropriate interest in the matter may make an application as of right. Finally, the Act creates a link between these two provisions by what is called the 'open door' policy: anyone may apply to the court for leave to make an application for a section 8 order, and the Act lays down special guidelines for the court in deciding such applications for leave.[702]

2.184 The structure of the provisions dealing with entitlement to apply for section 8 orders is as follows. First, certain people (enumerated in section 10) of the Act are entitled[703] to apply for any of the orders dealing with matters relating to the exercise of 'parental responsibility' in respect of a child. Secondly, local authority foster parents may, subject to certain conditions, apply for an order relating to the person with whom the child is to live (a 'residence order'). Thirdly, a widely defined class of persons with a link to the child may apply for a residence order or an order requiring the person with whom the child is to live to allow contact by the applicant with the child (a 'contact order'). Fourthly, the Act imposes provisions disqualifying certain local authority foster parents from the entitlement they would otherwise have to apply for residence or contact orders. We consider these in turn; and then consider the special rules governing the granting of leave to persons not entitled under these provisions to make an application for a section 8 order.

Act 1989, s 16(3). The objective of such an order is to enable short term independent help to be provided, for example in re-establishing contact: *Re C (Family Assistance Order)* [1996] 1 FLR 424, 425, Johnson J (where in fact the local authority refused, on grounds of lack of resources, to help the child). The Children and Adoption Act 2006, s 6, removed the restriction that a family assistance order could only be made in 'exceptional' circumstances, and made other amendments designed to improve the effectiveness of such orders.

699 Law Commission, *Family Law: Review of Child Law, Guardianship and Custody* (Law Com No 173, 1988) para 4.41.

700 However, no court may make a s 8 order with respect to a child who has attained the age of 16 (or make an order which is to have effect after the child is 16) unless the circumstances of the case are exceptional: s 9(6), (7).

701 Children Act 1989, s 10(1), (2). In *Gloucestershire CC v P* [1999] 2 FLR 61, CA, the Court held that this power could be exercised to make a residence order in favour of foster-parents who were debarred by Children Act 1989, s 9(3) from seeking such an order or seeking leave to make an application.

702 Where the person seeking leave to make an application is the child concerned, the court may only grant leave if is satisfied that the applicant has sufficient understanding to make the application for the order: Children Act 1989, s 10(8).

703 However, Children Act 1989, s 9, imposes restrictions on the courts power to make section 8 orders where a child has been in the care of a Local Authority: see para 2.188.

Persons entitled to apply for any section 8 order.   The Act[704] provides that any   **2.185**
parent or guardian (including a special guardian)[705] and any person in whose
favour a residence order is in force is entitled to apply for any order.[706] In effect,
these are people with a legitimate interest in seeking the court's intervention, irrespective of the particular circumstances of the case (for example, although an
'unmarried father' may sometimes not have parental responsibility for his child[707]
it was thought that he should be entitled to apply to the court for orders dealing
with the child's upbringing). The reason why anyone in whose favour a residence
order has been made is entitled to apply for any section 8 order is more practical:
such persons have parental responsibility and may need to seek a specific issue
order or a prohibited steps order to enable that responsibility to be properly met,
and may also legitimately need to seek the court's intervention about the details of
residence and contact with others.[708] The entitlement to seek the court's intervention is not absolute. Even parents may make 'unnecessary and disruptive applications';[709] and for this reason the Act contains special provision intended primarily
as a weapon of last resort';[710] the court may, on disposing of any application, make
an order that any named person be debarred from making any application without leave of the court for an order under the Act.[711]

Persons entitled to apply for a residence order, but not for other orders.   The   **2.186**
Adoption and Children Act 2002[712] provides that a local authority foster parent
should be entitled to apply for a residence order in respect of the foster child (thus
terminating any care order)[713] where the child has been in the applicant's care for
at least one year immediately before the application. This provision was inserted

---

[704] Section 10(4)(a), (b).

[705] Children Act 1989, s 10(4)(a) as inserted by Adoption and Children Act 2002, sch 3,
para 56. For the appointment and role of special guardians, see para 2.162.

[706] A civil partner who is not the child's parent will often have parental responsibility by reason of
a parental responsibility agreement, and will thus be entitled to apply for residence or contact orders:
see para 2.162.

[707] For example, if he is not registered as the child's father.

[708] The Law Commission, *Family Law: Review of Child Law, Guardianship and Custody* (Law
Com No 173, 1988) para 4.39, suggested that while in practice such persons would only require
to apply for specific issue or prohibited steps orders (or possibly for contact orders in some circumstances) they should in principle have parental access to the courts so long as they had parental
responsibility under the residence order.

[709] *Re N (Section 91(14) Order)* [1996] 1 FLR 356, CA, *per* Hale J (where the father continued
to make applications about matters such as medication, karate lessons, walking to school, etc).

[710] *per* Butler-Sloss LJ, *Re P(A Minor)(Residence Order: Child's Welfare)* [2000] Fam 15, 37–8.
This case gives guidance on the exercise of the power, and reasons for rejecting the argument that a
prohibition of this kind infringes the provisions of the Human Rights Act 1998, Article 6.

[711] The power to make a s 91(14) order is not confined to cases where there have been 'vexatious' applications: see eg *Re P (Section 91(14) Guidelines)(Residence and Religious Heritage)* [1999]
2 FLR 573, CA.

[712] Children Act 1989, 10(5A) as inserted by Adoption and Children Act 2002, sch 3, para 56.

[713] See para 2.179.

into the Children Act 1989 so that the rules for residence orders should be consistent with those laid down by the 2002 Act for adoption: since a local authority foster parent may apply for an adoption order after a period of one year there seemed to be no ground for refusing to permit an application which would entitle the applicant to have the child continuing to live with the foster-parent but free from the provisions of the care order.

2.187 **Persons entitled to apply for residence or contact orders.**   The Act attempts to define[714] those who may have (or have had) a sufficiently close link with the child to justify their being entitled to apply for contact, or to justify their seeking to have care of the child in their home, without it being appropriate for them to have the right to make applications capable of interfering with the decision-taking powers of others with 'parental responsibility' for the child. The detailed provisions of Children Act 1989, s 10(5) define those entitled to apply for residence or contact orders: in summary, anyone falling into any of the following categories is entitled to make an application:

(a) Anyone to whom the child has ever been a 'child of the family',[715] for example anyone who has at any time been the child's step-parent, or a civil partner who has treated the child of whom he is not the genetic parent as a child of the partners' family;[716]

(b) Anyone with whom the child has lived for three or more years. The period need not necessarily be continuous, but must not[717] have begun more than five years nor ended more than three months before the application;

(c) Anyone who has the consent[718] of either:
  (i)   all those who have the benefit of a residence order;
  (ii) if the child is in care under a care order, anyone who has the consent of the local authority;[719]
  (iii) in other cases, the consent of everyone with parental responsibility for the child.

---

714 Children Act 1989, s 10(5).

715 As defined by the Children Act 1989, s 105(1): see para 2.143.

716 See Children Act 1989, s 105(1) as amended by Civil Partnership Act 2004, s 75.

717 Children Act 1989, s 10(10).

718 The Law Commission (*Family Law: Review of Child Law, Guardianship and Custody* (Law Com No 173, 1988) para 4.48) considered that to impose a requirement to obtain the prior leave of the court could be to impose a 'meaningless formality'. Presumably if those whose consent is required see no reason why the court should not hear a contact or residence application it is difficult to foresee circumstances in which the court should be unwilling to do so.

719 It could also be said that where a child is the subject of a care order the local authority is effectively 'in the driving seat' and will have to act in accordance with the guidelines governing the exercise of its statutory discretions: see Children Act 1989, s 22(5).

Local authority foster-parents: disqualification from applying for residence and   **2.188**
other 'section 8' orders.[720]   The Children Act[721] provides that a person who has
been the child's local authority foster parent within the last six months may not
(save in a number of exceptional cases)[722] seek leave to apply for a residence or
other section 8 order.[723] This rule reflects government policy[724] that the local
authority should have control over the discharge of its responsibilities to children
whom the court has decided should be in the authority's care, and should be
allowed to plan for a child's future (in appropriate cases by removing the child
from foster parents and placing the child for adoption) without the fear that those
plans will be upset by a comparatively short-term foster parent.

Granting leave to persons not entitled under the above rules.   The so-called   **2.189**
'open door' policy: allows the court to make a section 8 order if an application
has been made by a person who has obtained the prior leave of the court to
do so.[725] In effect, therefore, anyone not debarred under the rules already
summarized[726] may bring an issue to the court's notice; but the decision whether
to allow the application to proceed is dependent on the exercise of a judicial
discretion.

---

[720] A local authority is debarred from applying for residence or contact orders, and the court has
no power to make such orders in favour of a local authority: s 9(2) (giving effect to the policy that a
local authority seeking to intervene in a child's upbringing must not merely show that such intervention would be in the child's interests, but must be able to demonstrate that the 'threshold criteria' laid
down by s 31 of the Act (see para 2.193) are met).

[721] Section 9(3).

[722] The prohibition does not apply if the foster parent has the consent of the authority, or is a
relative of the child, or if the child has lived with him for a period or periods totalling three years
preceding (but not starting more than five years before) the application: s 9(3).

[723] Children Act 1989, s 9(3), (4).

[724] It goes considerably further than was proposed by the Law Commission who thought it
illogical to allow people who were not caring for the child to seek leave whilst debarring those who
were doing so from access to the courts. The Commission would only go as far as adding to the criteria applied by the court in dealing with applications by local authority foster parents a consideration
of the plans made by the local authority for the child's future: see *Family Law: Review of Child Law,
Guardianship and Custody* (Law Com No 173, 1988) para 4.43.

[725] Children Act 1989, s 10(1)(a)(ii). The overall objective was to 'enable anyone with a genuine
interest in a child's welfare to make applications to the court' as could previously have been done
by making the child a ward of court: the Law Commission, *Family Law: Review of Child Law,
Guardianship and Custody* (Law Com No 173, 1988) para 4.41. In this way, it was anticipated that
recourse to the wardship jurisdiction would be minimized. The Act contains a power to prescribe
by rules of court categories of persons (perhaps, for example, grandparents and other close relatives
if experience showed that leave applications were so commonly granted that they had become an
unnecessary formality) who would thereby become *entitled* to apply for s 8 orders. This power has
not been exercised.

[726] See para 2.188.

2.190 *If the application is by someone other than the child concerned,*[727] the Act lays down certain criteria for dealing with applications for leave. At one time, the courts tended to ask whether the application showed a 'good arguable case' for making the order in question;[728] but the Court of Appeal has laid down that the courts must rather direct themselves by reference to the statutory provisions requiring the court to have 'particular regard'[729] to:

(a) the nature of the proposed application for the section 8 order;

(b) the applicant's connection with the child;

(c) any risk there might be of that proposed application disrupting the child's life to such an extent that the child would be harmed by it; and

(d) where the child is being looked after by a local authority:

    (i) the authority's plans for the child's future; and

    (ii) the wishes and feelings of the child's parents.

2.191 *If the application is made by the child concerned,* the only statutory guidance in relation to disposing of the application[730] is that the child must have sufficient understanding to make the proposed application. However, to decide this requires the court to analyse the gravity and complexity of the issues[731] and the emotional pressure of the legal process; and the court may take the view that 'understanding' requires a level of insight and imagination on the child's part normally associated with maturity and experience.[732] Children (it has been said)[733] are liable to be 'vulnerable and impressionable, lacking the maturity to weigh the longer term against the shorter, lacking the insight to know how they will react and the imagination to know how others will react in certain situations, lacking the experience to measure the probable against the possible'; and in practice it seems that the courts have been slow to conclude that a child applicant does have the degree of

---

727 A child who seeks an order in relation to another child—for example, for contact with a half-brother—is not 'the child concerned' and accordingly the court's discretion will be exercised in accordance with the more detailed guidance given by the Children Act 1989, s 10(9), rather than by the s 10(8) criterion of sufficient understanding: *Re S (Contact: Application by Sibling)* [1998] 2 FLR 897.

728 *Re G (Child Case: Parental Involvement)* [1996] 1 FLR 857, 866, CA. An application for leave may be made by a person debarred by order under the Children Act 1989, s 91(14) (see para 2.185) but in this case the criterion is simply whether the application demonstrates any need for renewed judicial investigation: *Re A (Application for Leave)* [1998] 1 FLR 1, 4, CA, *per* Thorpe LJ.

729 These displace the principle that the child's welfare is paramount: see *Re A (Minors) (Residence Orders: Leave to Apply)* [1992] Fam 182. The fact that leave has been given (often on the papers) does not mean that there is any presumption in favour of granting the substantive application: *Re A (Section 8 Order: Grandparent Application)* [1995] 2 FLR 153, CA. Conversely, no application should be dismissed without appropriate enquiry: see *Re J (Leave to Issue application for residence order)* [2002] EWCA Civ 1346.

730 Children Act 1989, s 10(8).

731 *Gillick v West Norfolk and Wisbech Area Health Authority* [1986] AC 112, HL.

732 *Re S (A Minor) (Independent Representation)* [1993] Fam 263, 276, *per* Sir Thomas Bingham MR.

733 ibid.

understanding envisaged by the legislation. It is true that to deny a child any involvement in decision making may cause damage to his or her emotional health;[734] but on the other hand the experience of hearing the parents cross-examined[735](for example) may also be damaging. The courts are certainly reluctant to allow 'trivial' family disputes to be ventilated.[736]

(c) Compulsory state intervention in children's upbringing: local authorities and care and supervision orders

Legislation[737] imposes extensive duties on local authorities to provide support for children in need;[738] and gives authorities a wide range of specific duties and powers,[739] including in particular the power to acquire by court order parental responsibility for a child. These are essentially matters of public law; and no attempt at a full exposition can be made in a work concerned with the private law. But a brief outline of the law governing the circumstances in which a local authority may intervene compulsorily in the upbringing of a child must be given, not least because in some circumstances a section 8 order (for example, a residence order in favour of a relative) may be made on an application initiated by a local authority seeking a care or supervision order. Conversely a relative or other person concerned for the child may seek a residence order in respect of a child who has been made subject to a care order because the making of a residence order automatically discharges any care order.[740]

2.192

(i) Conditions for making of care and supervision orders

The court can only make a care order (requiring a local authority to receive a child into its care and keep him in its care[741] while the order is in force)[742] or a

2.193

---

[734] See *Mabon v Mabon* [2005] EWCA Civ 634. (Refusal to grant brothers aged 17, 15 and 13 separate representation overturned).

[735] *Re C (Residence: Child's Application for Leave)* [1995] 1 FLR 927.

[736] *Re C (A Minor) (Leave to Seek Section 8 Orders)* [1994] 1 FLR 26.

[737] The Children Act 1989 Part III is the starting point; but further provision is made by the Care Standards Act 2000, the Children (Leaving Care) Act 2000, the Adoption and Children Act 2002, the Children Act 2004, and the Children and Adoption Act 2006.

[738] See Children Act 1989, s 17.

[739] ibid, s 17(2) and sch 2, Part I.

[740] ibid, s 91(1).

[741] This does not mean that the authority must keep the child physically in its care: children are often cared for by foster parents, and may (subject to a number of precautions imposed by delegated legislation) continue to live with a parent. Moreover, the Children Act 1989, s 34, requires the authority to allow a child in its care 'reasonable contact' with the parents (and some others), and restrictions on contact must be scrutinized closely: see *Re W (Section 34(2) Orders)* [2000] 1 FLR 502.

[742] Children Act 1989, s 33(1).

supervision order (placing the child under the supervision of a designated local authority)[743] if three conditions[744] are satisfied:[745]

(a) a local authority (or 'authorized person')[746] has applied for the order;[747]

(b) the court is satisfied that the 'threshold criteria' set out in section 31 of the Children Act[748] are met; and

(c) the court (having directed itself by reference to the matters to which section 1(3) of the Act requires it to have 'particular regard') is satisfied that the making of an order would promote the child's welfare, (that being, at this second stage[749] of the judicial decision taking process, the paramount consideration) and is also satisfied that making an order would be better for the child than making no order at all.[750]

2.194 These provisions give effect to two policies. First, that the right to initiate proceedings the outcome of which may be to impose considerable responsibility on the community should be confined to those who will bear that responsibility. Secondly (and fundamental to an understanding of the legislative scheme), whereas the child's welfare is properly the overriding consideration when the dispute is between members of the family, the mere fact that the state could do better for the child

---

[743] ibid, s 35, and sch 3, Parts I and II. The court should consider the impact of the two types of order; and a supervision order may be preferred to a care order, particularly where the need is for close monitoring of the child's welfare rather than removal from the home: see *Oxfordshire County Council v L (Care or Supervision Order)* [1996] 2 FLR 693; *Re O (Supervision Order)* [2001] 1 FLR 923, CA.

[744] But it is now also provided (see Children Act 1989, s 31(a) as inserted by Adoption and Children Act 2002, s 121) that the court may not make a care order until it has considered a 'care plan' prepared (in accordance with Regulations) by the Local Authority.

[745] Once an application under s 31 has been made, however, 'family proceedings' are in existence; and the court will have jurisdiction to make a s 8 order whether or not the threshold criteria for the making of a care or supervision order are established.

[746] Under Children Act 1989, s 31(9)(a) the National Society for the Prevention of Cruelty to Children is defined as an 'authorised person' but it is understood that in practice it no longer initiates proceedings. The power conferred on the Secretary of State by s 31(9)(b) to authorize others to bring proceedings has not been exercised.

[747] Children Act 1989, s 31(1) It has been held that, whilst in some cases, the need for an application to the court will be 'readily and immediately a matter of obvious necessity' in other cases it is something not to be 'embarked upon without careful deliberation and professional objectivity'. The need for caution and restraint is reinforced by the provisions of Article 8 of the European Convention on Human Rights: *Lancashire County Council v B* [2000] 2 AC 147, 170; whilst the Children Act 2004 s 53(1) inserted a provision (s 47(5A) into the Children Act 1989 requiring local authorities, so far as is reasonably practicable and consistent with the child's welfare, to ascertain the child's wishes and feelings about what should be done and give them due consideration.

[748] See para 2.195.

[749] ie once the court has satisfied itself at the 'threshold stage' that the condition precedent for intervention has been made out: see *Re M and R (Child Abuse: Evidence)* [1996] 2 FLR 195, 202, CA, *per* Butler Sloss LJ.

[750] Children Act 1989, s 1(5).

than can his family is insufficient to justify compulsory state intervention.[751] It is for these reasons that the court may only make a care or supervision order—however overwhelming the evidence that to do so would promote the child's welfare[752]—if the 'threshold criteria' defined in the Children Act 1989[753] are satisfied.[754]

(ii) The threshold criteria

The court must be satisfied: **2.195**

(a) that the child concerned is suffering,[755] or is likely to suffer[756] significant harm;[757] and

(b) that the harm, or likelihood of harm, is attributable to:

    (i) the care given to the child, or likely to be given to him if the order were not made, not being what it would be reasonable to expect a parent[758] to give to him; or

    (ii) the child is beyond parental control.[759]

---

[751] Lord Mackay of Clashfern LC thought that to adopt a test based solely on the court's view of where the child's best interests lay would pose an all too apparent 'threat to the poor and to minority groups, whose views of what is good for a child may not coincide closely with that of the majority' (1989) 139 New LJ 505, 507.

[752] The Children Act 1989, s 100(1) and (2), repealed the Family Law Reform Act 1969, s 7, under which a court could in wardship proceedings commit a child to the care of a local authority; and the 1989 Act prohibits the court from using the High Court's inherent jurisdiction so as to require a child to be placed in the care, or put under the supervision, of a local authority.

[753] Section 31(2).

[754] For the standard of proof see *Re H (Minors) (Sexual Abuse: Standard of Proof)* [1996] AC 563, HL.

[755] A mere apprehension that the child will suffer harm at some future time is insufficient; but if interim local authority arrangements have been continuously in place from the date at which protective measures (such as the making of an emergency protection order under the provisions of the Children Act 1989, s 44) were first taken down to the time of the hearing the court may look back to that earlier date: *Re M (A Minor) (Care Order: Threshold Conditions)* [1994] 2 AC 424, HL.

[756] The question is whether, on the basis of the facts as admitted or found, there was (at the time when protection procedures were initiated) a 'real possibility'—a possibility that could not sensibly be ignored having regard to the feared harm in the particular case—that the child would suffer significant harm: *Re H (Minors) (Sexual Abuse: Standard of Proof)* [1996] AC 563, HL.

[757] The Children Act 1989 (s 31(9)) defined 'harm' as 'ill-treatment or the impairment of health or development'; and 'development' as 'physical, intellectual, emotional, social or behavioural development'. 'Health' is in turn defined to mean 'physical or mental health'; and 'ill-treatment' includes 'sexual abuse and forms of ill-treatment which are not physical'. The Adoption and Children Act 2002, influenced by the increasing significance of the effect that witnessing domestic violence could have, amended this definition and provided that 'impairment' included 'for example, impairment suffered from seeing or hearing the ill-treatment of another'. The Children Act 1989 also (s 31(10)) provides that where the question of whether harm suffered by a child is significant turns on the child's health or development, his health or development shall be compared with that which could reasonably be expected of a similar child.

[758] The test is objective and does not require culpability on the part of the parent concerned: see *Lancashire County Council v B* [2000] 2 AC 147, HL.

[759] The test is objective and does not require culpability on the part of the parent concerned: *M v Birmingham City Council* [1994] 2 FLR 141.

These provisions have been the subject of extensive judicial exegesis for an account of which reference must be made elsewhere.[760]

(d) The decision whether to make an order in private and public law Children Act proceedings: child's welfare paramount

2.196 The provisions of the Children Act set out above seek to explain the circumstances in which the court will have jurisdiction to make orders about a child's upbringing, whether a 'section 8' order in 'private law' family proceedings or a care or supervision order in 'public law' family proceedings. It is now necessary to outline the criteria which determine whether the court should make an order in such proceedings, and if so what terms that order should contain. Statute[761] requires that wherever a court has to determine any question with respect to the upbringing[762] of a child,[763] that child's welfare should be the court's[764] paramount consideration. This criterion is therefore applied in proceedings under Parts I and II of the Children Act 1989 (ie private law proceedings), in applications in which the exercise of the court's inherent jurisdiction[765] is being considered, and in the 'welfare stage'[766] of care and supervision order proceedings under Part IV of the Children Act 1989. The Act provides guidance on the application of this principle.

(i) Presumption that delay harmful

2.197 The Children Act provides[767] that the court, in any proceedings in which any question with respect to the upbringing of a child arises, is to have regard to the 'general principle' that any delay in determining the question 'is likely to prejudice the welfare of the child'; and various procedural steps have been taken in attempts

---

[760] D Hershman and A McFarlane, *Children: Law and Practice*, a regularly up-dated loose leaf encyclopaedia, gives a full account.

[761] Children Act 1989, s 1(1). This codifies the principles previously applied: see eg *J v C* [1970] AC 668, HL (wishes of 10-year-old child's 'unimpeachable' parents that he return from foster parents living in comfortable surroundings in this country could not prevail over adverse impact of such a move on the child).

[762] The child's welfare is thus not the court's paramount consideration in applications for leave to apply for a s 8 order: *Re A and W (Minors) (Residence Order: Leave to Apply)* [1992] Fam 182, CA or in applications for financial relief for a child: *K v H (Child Maintenance)* [1993] 2 FLR 61, CA. Moreover, the paramountcy principle only applies if the child's upbringing is the central issue for decision: *Richards v Richards* [1984] AC 174.

[763] Or the administration of a child's property or the application of any income arising from it.

[764] For the approach in cases in which children have conflicting interests, see *Birmingham City Council v H (A Minor)* [1994] 2 AC 212, HL.

[765] For example, in cases in which the court is asked to rule on whether medical procedures should be carried out on a child: see eg *Re W (A Minor) (Wardship: Medical Treatment)* [1993] Fam 64, CA.

[766] ie the second stage of the proceedings, the court having found that the relevant criteria have been established in the first 'threshold' stage: *Re M and R (Child Abuse: Evidence)* [1996] 2 FLR 195, 202, *per* Butler Sloss LJ.

[767] Section 1(2).

to minimize harmful delay in dealing with cases. However, in some cases the need to consider evidence fully may be more important than reaching a speedy decision[768] and there is nothing in the Act to prevent the court from deciding that on the particular facts before it there is a case for moving slowly and carefully.[769]

(ii) The 'no order' presumption

The Children Act 1989[770] provides that 'where a court is considering whether or not to make one or more orders under the Act with respect to a child, it shall not make the order or any of the orders unless it considers that doing so would be better for the child than making no order at all'. The Act thus seeks to minimize the risk that the making of an order will polarize the parents' roles, and perhaps alienate the child.[771] Again, it has been said[772] that the courts must not sanction the removal of a child from its family unless satisfied that to do so is both 'necessary and proportionate and that no other less radical form of order would achieve the essential end of promoting' the child's welfare'. But the court will not hesitate to make an order if (having considered all the technical and other implications of the decision)[773] it is satisfied that to do so will benefit the child.

2.198

(iii) Matters to which court to have particular regard

In two situations, the Children Act 1989[774] requires the court to 'have regard in particular' to a 'check-list' of specified factors. These are, first, where any party to the proceedings opposes the making, variation or discharge of any section 8 order which the court is considering; and secondly where the court is considering whether to make, vary or discharge a care or supervision order.[775] These specified factors are as follows:

2.199

(a) the ascertainable wishes and feelings of the child concerned (considered in the light of his age and understanding);

---

[768] *Re K (Non-accidental injuries: Perpetrator, New Evidence)* [2004] EWCA 1181 where excluding the possibility that the child's mother had caused the children's injuries might lead to the family being reunited.

[769] *C v Solihull Metropolitan Borough Council* [1994] 2 FLR 290.

[770] Section 1(5).

[771] See the fears voiced by the Law Commission in its *Report on Guardianship and Custody* (Law Com No 172, 1978, para 3.2).

[772] *Re B (Care: Interference with Family Life)* [2003] EWCA 786.

[773] For example, that the making of a residence order would give a step-parent parental responsibility: *Re H (Shared Residence: Parental Responsibility)* [1995] 2 FLR 883. In any event, an order will usually be appropriate if there is a serious dispute to be resolved between the adults concerned: *Re S (Contact: Grandparents)* [1996] 1 FLR 158, CA.

[774] Section 1(3). The court will often find the 'check-list' useful in other circumstances, but it is only in the two specified circumstances that the court needs expressly to make findings on the matters to which attention is directed: *B v B (Residence Order: Reasons for Decision)* [1997] 2 FLR 602.

[775] Children Act 1989, s 1(4).

(b) his physical, emotional and educational needs;

(c) the likely effect on him of any change in his circumstances;

(d) his age, sex, background and any characteristics of his which the court considers relevant;

(e) any harm which he has suffered or is at risk of suffering;

(f) how capable each of his parents, and any other person in relation to whom the court considers the question to be relevant, is of meeting his needs;

(g) the range of powers available to the court under the Children Act in the proceedings in question.

2.200 There is a considerable volume of case law dealing with the application of the welfare principle, and on the factors specifically referred to in this Children Act 'check-list'.[776] But these are really matters of fact, to be decided on the evidence called by the parties and the reports which the court obtains from the court welfare officer or others. At the end of the day there is a single question and it is unwise to rely on any formula to resolve the problems which will arise in deciding any particular issue.[777] In particular, it must be accepted that concepts of what does indeed represent the best interests of the child change over the years[778] under the influence of social convention and research findings into child development; whilst the dividing line between presumptions of law and a recognition of widely held belief based on practical experience and the workings of nature is often difficult to draw.[779]

---

[776] D Hershman and A McFarlane, *Children: Law and Practice*.

[777] *Pountney v Morris* [1984] FLR 381, 384, CA, *per* Dunn LJ.

[778] See for a striking example *Re Thain* [1926] Ch 676, CA, in which no weight was attached to the view that a child of five would be harmed by removal from the couple who had cared for her since her earliest infancy. The propositions of law stated by the judge in reaching this conclusion were approved by the House of Lords in *J v C* [1970] AC 668 but it seems unlikely that the decision on the facts would be the same if the case had come before the courts in 1976 or 2006.

[779] See *Brixey v Lynas* 1997 SC 1, HL Note also that the weight to be accorded to genetic parentage seems to vary from time to time (and even from judge to judge): in *Re G (Children)* [2006] UKHL 43 the Court of Appeal upheld a residence order made in favour of one party to a lesbian relationship rejecting the claim of the other partner (the child's biological mother) on the ground that blood ties were of little significance where two partners had cared for a child. However, the House of Lords reversed that decision: *per* Lord Nicholls, a child should not be removed from the primary care of his or her biological parents without compelling reason (and the judge should spell that reason out if it was determinative of the outcome); and, *per* Baroness Hale, biological parentage was 'undoubtedly an 'important and significant factor in determining what is best for children' (albeit it raised no presumption in favour of the biological mother).

3

COMPANIES AND OTHER ASSOCIATIONS*

A. Introduction

(1) The Scope of the Chapter

In part A, it will be considered how associations have been generally treated by **3.01** English law, and what is meant when they are said to possess 'artificial personality'; the associations currently recognized by English law will also be categorized into three groups: corporations, quasi-corporations, and unincorporated bodies. In accordance with this threefold classification, various types of association will then be discussed in parts B, C, and D.

---

* This is a revised and updated version of the chapter bearing the same name written for the first edition of *English Private Law* by Professor Charles Mitchell.

(2) Associations in English Law: An Overview

(a) The needs of associates and their impact as social actors

3.02 People often wish to associate with one another, to pool their assets, and to apply their pooled assets to a set of shared objectives.[1] Whatever their common purpose, they are likely to have four basic needs. They are likely to need an efficient means of protecting their collective interests and enforcing their collective rights against outsiders; an efficient means of holding their pooled assets and applying them to their shared purpose; an efficient and fair means of ensuring that their pooled assets are used in the way that they intend, and are not negligently or fraudulently misapplied; and an efficient and fair means of determining their shared objectives and activities, and of resolving any disputes in relation to these matters. When associates act collectively, the successful implementation of their common purpose may have both desirable and detrimental consequences for society at large. Lawmakers therefore have to make choices regarding the extent to which the legal system will facilitate, regulate, or restrict associations.

(b) The treatment generally afforded to associations by English law

3.03 Associations were long regarded by the English Crown as a threat to its political hegemony, and the continuing theoretical debate whether associations derive their legitimacy as legal actors from the state has its roots in the political and religious struggles of the medieval and early modern period. Ecclesiastical bodies and foundations, boroughs, guilds, and trading companies all 'presented the same problem of how to check the tendency of group action...to rival the political power of the state', and as a means of dealing with this problem the 'somewhat vague theory of the later Middle Ages that communal organization not sanctioned by prescription or royal licence was illegal was at least from the fifteenth century on supplemented by the technical doctrine, developed under canonist influences, that there is no capacity to act as a body corporate without positive authorization'.[2] No general right to associate was acknowledged by the Crown during this period, and those who wished to hold meetings were

---

[1] The partitioning of such pools of assets from the personal assets of participants has been said to be the most important function performed by organizational law: H Hansmann and R Kraakman, 'The Essential Role of Organizational Law' (2000) 110 Yale LJ 387.

[2] E Freund, *Standards of American Legislation* (1917) 39, quoted in J Dewey, 'The Historic Background of Corporate Legal Personality' (1926) 35 Yale LJ 655, 667. For an enlightening discussion of the political backdrop to Hobbesian (and later Pluralist) theories of the state, and their links with theories of corporate personality, see J McLean, 'Personality and Public Law Doctrine' (1999) 49 Univ of Toronto LJ 123.

required to obtain a royal charter if they wished to avoid prosecution for conducting an unlawful assembly.[3]

By the late eighteenth century, however, attitudes had changed to the point that **3.04** express legislation was thought necessary to prohibit combinations of workers,[4] suggesting that the common law no longer considered such unauthorized associations to be unlawful *per se*.[5] Thereafter, it became a recurring issue for the English courts, whether to help associates who had joined together without the state's permission, by enabling them to enforce their rights against outsiders or to resolve disputes between themselves. In 1802, Lord Eldon LC thought it 'singular, that this Court should sit upon the concerns of an association, which in law has no existence', and expressed:[6]

> great doubt, whether a voluntary association for the best purpose is to meet without the authority of a corporation, and make laws and statutes, which have no authority, and then call upon the Court to administer all moral justice, that may arise upon the disputes among these, in a sense unauthorised bodies.

Again, in 1812, he maintained that the courts should not intervene to resolve disputes between partners, save where a dissolution had been prayed for, as:[7]

> This Court is not to be required on every occasion to take the Management of every Playhouse and Brewhouse in the Kingdom.

However, as the nineteenth century unfolded, the courts partially abandoned **3.05** this non-interventionist stance in response to pressure from associates. They remained disobliging in their attitude towards trade unions,[8] and their reluctance to interfere in the internal disputes of joint stock companies fed into the rule in *Foss v Harbottle*,[9] that the courts would not ordinarily intervene in a matter at the request of an individual shareholder of a registered company, if the matter was one which can be settled by the company's own internal procedures. But at the same time the courts' attitude towards partnerships underwent a change, and from the 1840s onwards partners were given injunctions and accounts against their fellow partners even where no dissolution had been prayed for.[10]

---

[3] CT Carr, *Select Charters of Trading Companies*, Selden Soc vol 28 (1913) xv, n 1.

[4] Combination Acts 1797, 1799, 1800, and 1817.

[5] Sir JF Stephen, *A History of the Criminal Law of England* (1883) vol 3, 210–11; AV Dicey, 'The Combination Laws as Illustrating the Relation Between Law and Opinion in England During the Nineteenth Century' (1904) 17 Harvard LR 511.

[6] *Lloyd v Loaring* (1802) 6 Ves 773, 778; 31 ER 1302, 1304–5.

[7] *Carlen v Drury* (1812) 1 V & B 154, 158, 35 ER 61, 62. See too *Marshall v Colman* (1820) 2 J & W 266, 37 ER 629; *Richards v Davies* (1831) 2 Russ & M 347, 39 ER 427.

[8] See eg *Hornby v Close* (1867) LR 2 QB 153.

[9] (1843) 2 Hare 461, 67 ER 89; extended in *Mozley v Alston* (1847) 1 Ph 790, 41 ER 833; discussed in para 3.63.

[10] *Fairthorne v Weston* (1844) 3 Hare 387, 391–2; 67 ER 432, 433–4, *per* Wigram V-C; *Watney v Trist* (1876) 45 LJ Ch 412.

Moreover, by 1854, Lord Cranworth LC was to observe of unincorporated joint stock companies and their relationship with outsiders that:[11]

> Lord Eldon frequently said that it would be extremely difficult to enforce the rights of third parties against bodies so numerous, and he therefore. . .doubted whether they were not illegal. But it is idle to speculate on that point; for these companies, being consonant with the wants of a growing and wealthy community, have forced their way into existence, whether fostered by the law or opposed to it.

3.06 During the course of the nineteenth century, Parliament, too, responded to economic and political imperatives, by recognizing various types of commercial and self-help organizations, including trade unions, and by investing some of them with corporate status. Hence, by the start of the twentieth century, many associations had effectively forced Parliament and the courts to acknowledge their status as legal actors, and the attention of English lawmakers had begun to shift to the further question—which became one of their primary concerns during the twentieth century—whether the activities of associates should be regulated by mandatory or default rules governing their relationship with other members of society, and with one another.

(c) Associative forms currently recognized by English law

3.07 English law currently recognizes a range of associative forms by means of which associates are enabled to pursue their collective activities. Seventeen of these will be considered in the following parts of this chapter: statutory and chartered corporations; registered companies; limited liability partnerships (LLPs); open-ended investment companies (OEICs); building societies; industrial and provident societies; community interest companies (CICs); European Economic Interest Groupings (EEIGs); European Public Companies (SEs); trade unions; friendly societies; partnerships and limited partnerships; unincorporated associations; unit trusts; and pension trusts.

3.08 There are several further types of association whose existence is acknowledged by English law, but which will not be discussed here. Housing associations, formed for the purpose of building or improving residential accommodation, can take the legal forms of the trust, the registered company, the industrial and provident society, and the unincorporated association.[12] Employers' associations, whose members are wholly or principally employers, and whose principal function is to regulate the relations between employers and workers or trade unions, can take the forms of the registered company and the unincorporated association;

---

11 *Greenwood's case* (1854) 3 De GM & G 459, 477, 43 ER 180, 187.
12 See the Housing Associations Act 1985, s 1. The activities of housing associations and their relationships with their tenants are regulated by this statute, and also by the Landlord and Tenant Act 1985 and the Housing Acts 1985, 1988, 1996, and 2004.

a registered unincorporated employers' association has capacities similar to those of a registered trade union.[13] Credit unions, co-operative organizations which encourage and educate their members to accumulate savings and lend them money at low rates of interest, can be registered and incorporated as credit unions under the Industrial and Provident Societies Act 1965, in accordance with the Credit Union Act 1979.[14]

Joint ventures, entered into by two or more participants with a view to facilitating **3.09** commercial co-operation, have been argued by some commentators to constitute 'business entit[ies] separate from [their] parents',[15] and are in fact regulated as such by the rules of EC competition law.[16] But although the English courts have developed certain special rules governing the operation and control of joint ventures,[17] they have stopped short of recognizing them as artificial persons, and in practice joint venturers generally use either the registered company or the partnership as the legal form through which to pursue their shared undertaking.[18] Syndicates are often formed by commercial actors, such as Lloyd's underwriting members, for example,[19] but the term 'syndicate' has no precise legal meaning, and the members of a syndicate are no more than an unincorporated association of individuals.[20]

The real estate investment trust (REIT), introduced into English law in January **3.10** 2007, accords certain tax advantages to a registered company engaged in a property rental business and meeting certain restrictions, which are granted in order to facilitate investment in the sector.[21] A REIT is not in fact a trust, but a registered

---

[13] Trade Union and Labour Relations (Consolidation) Act 1992, s 127, considered in *Print v Showmen's Guild of GB* [1999] All ER (D) 1197.

[14] As amended by the Financial Services and Markets Act 2000, Sch 18. For general discussion, see HM Treasury Credit Unions Taskforce, *Report: Credit Unions of the Future* (1999); N Ryder, 'Credit Unions in the United Kingdom: A Critical Analysis of their Legislative Framework and its Impact Upon their Development' [2003] JBL 45.

[15] J Brodley, 'Joint Ventures and Antitrust Policy' (1982) 95 Harvard LR 1523, 1526.

[16] See eg the EC Merger Regulation (139/2004/EC [2004] OJ L24/1).

[17] See eg *Elliott v Wheeldon* [1992] BCC 489, CA; *Dawnay Day & Co Ltd v D'Alphen* [1998] ICR 1068, CA. See too G Bean, *Fiduciary Obligations and Joint Ventures* (1995).

[18] For general discussion, see T Prime, S Gale, and G Scanlan, *The Law and Practice of Joint Ventures* (2nd edn, 1997); I Hewitt, *Joint Ventures* (3rd edn, 2005). A joint venture which does not involve the establishment of a registered company is likely to satisfy the legal definition of a partnership by default, even if that is not what the joint venturers intend, unless they jointly pursue non-profit-making activities such as research or training.

[19] R Merkin (ed), *Colinvaux's Law of Insurance* (8th edn, 2006), para 3–51.

[20] *Barrington-Hume v AA Mutual International Insurance Co Ltd* [1996] Lloyd's Reinsurance LR 19, 22, *per* Clarke J.

[21] Finance Act 2006, s 106. The company must be UK tax resident, be listed on a recognized stock exchange, and must not be an open-ended investment company. In order to maintain a REIT's favourable tax status, no single investor may own more than 10% of its shares, and 90% of its income must be paid out as dividends: Finance Act 2006, ss 107, 114.

company,[22] and not so much a separate form of association as a set of restrictions imposed onto a registered company in order to qualify for a particular tax treatment.

(3) Legal Personality

(a) Natural and artificial persons distinguished

3.11 The word 'person' is now generally used in English to denote a human being, but the word is also used in a technical legal sense, to denote a subject of legal rights and duties.[23] English law recognizes two categories of persons in this legal sense: 'natural persons' and 'artificial persons'. Natural persons are those animate beings which possess a capacity to own legal rights and to owe legal duties; artificial persons are those inanimate entities which possess such a capacity. Artificial persons are sometimes also described as 'legal' or 'juristic' persons, but this usage can be confusing, as the latter terms are also used of both animate beings and inanimate entities, to denote the fact that they have an existence as legal actors, rather than the fact that they exist only in the legal, and not in the biological sphere.[24]

(b) Natural persons

3.12 The only animate beings currently recognized by English law as natural persons are human beings. Other animals have not been thought capable of bearing legal responsibility for their actions since the thirteenth century, although the idea that a non-human animal or indeed an inanimate object should itself be punished for causing the death of a human being underlay the old rule, which was not abolished until 1846, that in such circumstances the animal or object should

---

[22] See HM Treasury, *UK Real Estate Investment Trusts: A Discussion Paper* (2005), 7–10; REITA, *Fact Sheet No 3* (2007), available at <www.reita.org>.

[23] See *Deutsche Genossenschaftsbank v Burnhope* [1995] 1 WLR 1580, 1588, HL, *per* Lord Steyn: 'the ordinary meaning of the word [person] in a contractual stipulation in a commercial contract' is therefore not its everyday meaning ('human being'), but its legal meaning ('natural or artificial entity having rights and duties recognized by the law'). See also Law of Property Act 1925, s 61 (in all contracts and other instruments 'person' includes a corporation unless the context otherwise requires).

[24] For examples of these various usages, see: *Triplex Safety Glass Co Ltd v Lancegaye Safetyglass (1934) Ltd* [1939] 2 KB 395, 409, CA, *per* Du Parcq LJ; *Re Amirteymour, deceased* [1979] 1 WLR 63, 66, HL, *per* Lord Diplock; *De Martell v Merton and Sutton Health Authority* [1992] 3 WLR 637, 644, *per* Phillips J; *Stanhope Pension Trust Ltd v Registrar of Companies* [1994] 1 BCLC 628, 630, CA, *per* Hoffmann LJ; *Winnipeg Child and Family Services (Northwest Area) v G* (1997) 3 BHRC 611, 620, Can SC, *per* McLachlin J, quoted with approval in *St George's Healthcare NHS Trust v S* [1998] 3 WLR 936, 955, CA, *per* Judge LJ.

be forfeit as 'deodand' to the Crown or other franchise-holder.[25] English law has never regarded non-human animals as possessing the capacity to enjoy legal rights, although the argument has been made by some theorists that in principle they should be regarded as possessing this capacity.[26] In the case of human beings, English law assigns them 'status', or standing in law, according to their individual attributes and characteristics, and a human being's legal rights and duties are then determined on a case-by-case basis by reference to relevant aspects of his status.[27] Thus, for example, a human being's capacity to enter a contract can be affected by whether he is a minor or of full age, bankrupt or solvent, mentally capable or incapable. Questions going to the attributes and characteristics of a human being which may or may not have legal significance in different circumstances include: (i) has he been born? (ii) has he acquired full age? (iii) has he died? (iv) what is his gender? (v) is he legitimate, illegitimate, or adopted? (vi) is he single, married, divorced, or in an unmarried cohabiting relationship (heterosexual or homosexual)? (vii) is he a British citizen, a foreign national, a foreign diplomat, or a refugee? (viii) is he bodily capable? (ix) is he mentally capable? (x) is he a prisoner? (xi) is he solvent? (xii) is he a layperson or a cleric? (xiii) is he a member of the armed forces? (xiv) is he a Member of Parliament? (xv) is he a member of the Royal Family?

(c) Artificial persons

Prior to the Supreme Court of Judicature Act 1873, the Admiralty courts sometimes ascribed artificial personality to ships, as a means of circumventing the writs of prohibition issued by the common law courts to restrain the expansion of the Admiralty *in personam* jurisdiction. However, the theory that the ship is the real defendant in an Admiralty action *in rem* fell into decline after 1873,[28] and the only bodies now recognized by English law as artificial persons are 'groups or series of [human] individuals', conceptualized as abstract entities, but possessing 'an essentially animate content'.[29] Thus, English law currently ascribes artificial personality to certain private groups of associates, as discussed in the following

3.13

---

[25] WW Hyde, 'The Prosecution and Punishment of Animals and Lifeless Things in the Middle Ages and Modern Times' (1916) 64 Pennsylvania LR 696; T Sutton, 'The Deodand and Responsibility for Death' (1997) 18(3) Journal of Legal History 44.

[26] S Brooman and D Legge, *The Law Relating to Animals* (1999) chs 2 and 3.

[27] See generally, RH Graveson, *Status and the Common Law* (1953).

[28] For the reasons discussed in *The Indian Endurance (No 2)* [1998] AC 878, 906–9, HL, *per* Lord Steyn, drawing on WR Tetley, *Maritime Liens* (1980) 40–4.

[29] *Bumper Development Corp Ltd v Commissioner of Police of the Metropolis* [1991] 1 WLR 1362, 1371, CA, *per* Purchas LJ.

parts of this chapter, to various public bodies, religious bodies, and their officers, and also to various foreign states and international organizations.[30]

3.14 However, 'formidable conceptual difficulties' would lie in the English courts' way if they wished to recognize a tangible inanimate object as an artificial person, 'something [like a Hindu temple] which on one view is little more than a pile of stones'.[31] They would also find it difficult to permit an action by or against an abstraction such as a fund of money,[32] for as a general rule this is 'a form of proceeding unknown to English law'.[33] Thus, for example, English law does not consider a trust estate to possess the capacity to sue or be sued, and requires trust funds to be vested in trustees with the personal capacity to sue (and to be sued) in their own names in the course of administering the trust business;[34] executors and administrators (collectively termed personal representatives) perform a similar function with respect to a deceased person's estate, as do receivers and liquidators when a company goes into receivership or liquidation.

(d) The nature of personality

3.15 Many legal theorists have written on the nature of personality, and have addressed themselves to such questions as whether personality entails anything more than

---

30 For the ascription of artificial personality to public bodies and their officers, see eg Criminal Justice Act 2003, s 239(1) (Parole Board); Government of Wales Act 2006, s 145 and Sch 8, para 4 (Auditor-General for Wales). See also J McLean 'The Crown in Contract and Administrative Law' (2004) 24 OJLS 129. For the ascription of artificial personality to religious bodies and their officers, see eg Church of Wales Representative Body, Charter of Incorporation Order in Council 1919, SR & O 1919/564 (Church of Wales Representative Body); *Sutton's Hospital Case* (1612) 10 Co Rep 1a, 23a, 29b, and also Dioceses Measure 1978 (No 1), Sch, para 2 (Church of England bishop). But cf *Chapper v Beth Din* (CA, 29 June 1994) *per* Hirst LJ: 'the Beth Din is not a legal personality amenable to being sued in [the English courts]'. On the ascription of personality to states and other international entities and their agents, see I Brownlie, *Principles of public International Law* (6th edn, 2003) ch 3.

31 *Bumper Development* (n 29 above) 1371, *per* Purchas LJ (noting that the position is different under the law of Tamil Nadu). cf *Canea Catholic Church v Greece* (1999) 27 EHRR 521, ECHR (under Greek law, a parish church has personality).

32 Cf *Arab Monetary Fund v Hashim (No 3)* [1991] 2 AC 114, HL (Arab Monetary Fund, endowed with 'independent juridical personality' by an international treaty, recognized as an artificial person by the English courts).

33 *Re Amirteymour, deceased* [1979] 1 WLR 63, 66, HL, *per* Lord Diplock. See also CPR 19.8(2) (proceedings against estates where defendant has died and personal representative not yet appointed).

34 *Re Jordan* [1904] 1 Ch 260, 264. Cf DJ Hayton et al (eds), *Principles of European Trust Law* (1999), 13, Article 1, para (1): 'In a trust, a person called the "trustee" owns assets segregated from his private patrimony and must deal with these assets (the "trust fund") for the benefit of another person called the beneficiary or for the furtherance of a purpose.' This definition deliberately excludes 'those few so-called trusts (eg Ethiopian or Quebec "trusts") arising under special legislation decreeing that an ownerless fund dedicated to the benefit of beneficiaries or for the furtherance of a purpose is a trust': DJ Hayton, 'The Developing European Dimension of Trust Law' (1999) 10 King's College LJ 48, 58.

the possession of a set of duty-owing, right-owning capacities, and whether the possession of such capacities is necessarily a legal construct or can derive from some extra-legal source.[35] Questions of this sort do not often strike the English courts as having a practical bearing on the cases which they must decide, and even when they declare themselves to be 'concerned with abstract jurisprudential concepts [so far as these] assist towards clarity of thought',[36] they generally recoil from discussing them in any detail. In consequence, they have not often expressly considered, still less committed themselves to, any particular jurisprudential theory of personality. However, it has rightly been observed that 'realist theories of the company in which the company is viewed as a real person have had a limited influence on the development of [English company law, by comparison with]. . .Continental Europe, where that theory has been much more significant',[37] and some recent judicial statements confirm that the English courts have no liking for realist theories of artificial personality in general.

In *Bumper Development Corp Ltd v Metropolitan Police Commissioner*,[38] Purchas **3.16** LJ approved the statement in *Salmond on Jurisprudence*, that '[artificial] persons, being the arbitrary creations of the law, may be of as many kinds as the law pleases',[39] and went on to hold that a Hindu temple recognized as an artificial person by the law of Tamil Nadu could therefore be a party to proceedings in the English courts, even though it would not be recognized as a person by English law.[40] In *Meridian Global Funds Management Asia Ltd v Securities Commission*,[41] Lord Hoffmann stated that 'a company exists because there is a [legal] rule. . .which says that a *persona ficta* shall be deemed to exist,' and that although 'a reference to a company "as such" might suggest that there is something out there called the

---

[35] For a clear summary of various standpoints which have been taken on these and other issues, see RWM Dias, *Jurisprudence* (5th edn, 1985) 265–70. There is also a substantial literature on corporate personality, ably discussed in M Stokes, 'Company Law and Legal Theory' in W Twining (ed), *Legal Theory and the Common Law* (1986) 155, which explores the interplay between theoretical concepts of corporate personality and the rules of English company law. The way in which the law conceives of corporate personality varies from jurisdiction to jurisdiction, posing difficulties for the conceptualization of trans-national corporations: see K Iwai, 'The Corporate Personality Controversy and Comparative Corporate Governance' (1999) 47 Am J Comp L 583.

[36] *JH Rayner (Mincing Lane) Ltd v DTI* [1989] 1 Ch 72, 236, CA, *per* Ralph Gibson LJ.

[37] E Ferran, *Company Law and Corporate Finance* (1999) 134.

[38] See n 29 above, 1371–2. Cf *Global Container Lines Ltd v Bonyad Shipping Co* [1999] 1 Lloyd's Rep 287, 305, *per* Rix J: in appropriate circumstances the English courts should 'pay regard to the foreign law which *creates and destroys* the artificial personalities of [foreign] companies' (emphasis added).

[39] PJ Fitzgerald (ed) *Salmond on Jurisprudence* (12th edn, 1966) 306–8.

[40] It does not follow from this, however, that as a matter of English civil procedure a foreign artificial person must necessarily sue or be sued in its own name, rather than in the name of the natural persons who compose it: *Oxnard Financing SA v Rahn* [1998] 1 WLR 1478, CA, discussed in L Collins *et al* (eds), *Dicey and Morris on the Conflict of Laws* (13th edn, 2000) para 7–010.

[41] [1995] 2 AC 500, 506, PC.

company. . .[there] is in fact no such thing as the company as such, no *Ding an sich*, only the applicable rules' which enable the shareholders of the company to conduct their collective activities through the medium of the corporate form.

(e) The use of the terms 'person' and 'personality' in English legal practice

(i) The possession of personality does not entail the possession of a fixed set of legal capacities

3.17 Three broad observations should be made here about the English legal terms 'person' and 'personality'. First, the question whether a human being or abstract entity should be regarded as possessing the capacity to enforce a particular right, or to owe a particular duty, is one that lawmakers can rationally answer by considering the nature of the right or duty in question, by looking at the character of the human being or entity in question, and by assessing in the light of these matters whether it would be consistent with the goals of society at large, and of the legal system in particular, to give a positive answer. But the need to approach the question in this way can be overlooked if the terms 'person' and 'personality' are used carelessly. A human being or entity which has been said by Parliament or the courts to be capable of enforcing a particular right, or of owing a particular duty, can properly be described as a person *with that particular capacity*. But it can be easy to forget the qualifier, and to assume when the question later arises, whether the individual or entity has the further capacity to enforce some other right, or to owe some other duty, that this must be so because he or it has previously been said to be a person *with an unlimited set of capacities*, or to be a person who possesses the 'powers normally attendant on legal personality'.[42] In other words, the careless use of the terms 'person' and 'personality' can create the false impression that a particular human being or entity has been said to possess a larger set of right-owning, duty-owning capacities than is in fact the case.

3.18 Thus, for example, English registered companies are frequently said to possess 'personality', but it would be wrong to infer from this alone that they necessarily possess the capacity to enjoy a privilege against self-incrimination,[43] or the

---

[42] *NUGMW v Gillian* [1946] KB 81, 86, CA, *per* Scott LJ. See too *Clark v University of Lincolnshire and Humberside* [2000] 3 All ER 752, 756, CA, *per* Sedley LJ (describing defendant as 'a statutory corporation with the ordinary attributes of legal personality'); cf *Bonsor v Musicians Union* [1954] Ch 479, 507–8, CA, *per* Lord Denning MR (trade union registered under the Trade Union Act 1871 could not both possess capacity to sue one of its officers for embezzlement and lack capacity to incur tortious liability to others: 'one cannot have the benefits of legal personality without the responsibilities').

[43] Generally, they do, although they are unlikely to be able to rely upon it against state enforcement agencies with statutory powers to gather information: *R v Hertfordshire County Council, ex p Green Environmental Industries Ltd* [2000] 2 AC 412. See also D Feldman, 'Corporate Rights and the Privilege Against Self-Incrimination', in D Feldman and F Meisel (eds), *Corporate and Commercial Law: Modern Developments* (1996) 361.

capacity to perjure themselves,[44] or the capacity to be the subject of defamatory statements,[45] or the capacity to enjoy a right to privacy under Article 8 of the European Convention on Human Rights.[46] Whether they possess these or any other capacities must be considered from first principles when the question arises. To say that a human being or entity possesses the 'powers normally attendant on legal personality' is to suggest that the ascription of personality entails the ascription of a generally agreed and particularized set of capacities, possession of which can be safely assumed of every natural and artificial person. But this is not so. Different human beings and entities may properly be characterized as natural or artificial persons for different purposes even though they possess different capacities from one another.

(ii) The anthropomorphizing quality of the term 'person'

Secondly, problems can also be caused by the insidiously anthropomorphizing quality of the legal term 'person'. Because 'person' is used colloquially to mean 'human being', it is tempting for people to assume that abstract entities described as 'persons' in the technical legal sense must possess the same set of capacities as human beings (and indeed, that human beings described in this way must all possess the same capacities as one another). This can lead people to assume in some situations that an abstract entity possesses a wider set of right-owning, duty-owing capacities than is in fact the case. It can also encourage them to believe that substantive legal rules designed for human beings can meaningfully be applied to abstract entities. This in turn can have unforeseen long-term consequences for the way in which the rules themselves develop,[47] and it can lead to difficulties of 'fit' if the rules are in fact inaptly framed for abstract entities. **3.19**

To give a well-known example of the latter phenomenon,[48] English law specifies that certain types of criminal liability can be incurred only by persons with a **3.20**

---

44 They do: *Sphere Drake Insurance plc v Orion Insurance Co Ltd The Times*, 17 March 2000, CA.

45 They do: *Jameel v Wall Street Journal Europe Sprl* [2006] UKHL 44, [2007] 1 AC 359.

46 *Semble* they do: *Cream Holdings Ltd v Bannerjee* [2003] EWCA Civ 103; [2003] Ch 650 at [80]; see also *Société Colas Est v France* (2002) 23 ECLR 413, ECHR.

47 For example, the theoretical basis of the tort of negligence in English law underwent a shift during the nineteenth and twentieth centuries, from personal moral shortcoming to a failure to achieve societal norms, and one factor contributing to this shift may have been the increasing numbers of corporate defendants fixed with negligence liability, which made 'the link between legal liability and moral delinquency. . .ever more problematic': D Ibbetson, *A Historical Introduction to the Law of Obligations* (1999), 196.

48 For additional 'baffling and sometimes absurdly incongruous' interpretations arrived at by the English courts, who have been 'unable to resist the temptation to draw anthropomorphic parallels [and] mesmerised by the ambiguities latent in the word "person"', see L Sealy, 'Perception and Policy in Company Law Reform', in Feldman and Meisel, n 43 above, 11, 16–20.

particular state of mind, such as intention or knowledge.[49] These rules were developed with a view to mediating relationships between the state and human beings, and they are not couched in terms which admit their application to inanimate entities which physically lack a brain, and so cannot literally be said to possess a state of mind. Nonetheless, the English courts have persisted in treating as apt the question whether a company should be fixed with a liability of this sort, and to answer it they have frequently committed themselves to spurious metaphysical quests for the whereabouts of a company's 'mind'.[50] They could more realistically, and more fruitfully, have approached the question by considering instead whether it lies in the public interest to fix a company with criminal liability for, say, personal injuries or deaths caused by particular types of corporate actions or omissions; on a positive answer being given, they could then have formulated a new set of rules to govern the determination of corporate liability in terms reflecting the reality that a company is an inanimate and hence a literally mindless entity.[51] The Corporate Manslaughter and Corporate Homicide Bill 2007 will, when enacted, introduce a new offence of corporate killing. This will attach criminal responsibility to an organization[52] if 'the way in which its activities are managed' both causes a natural person's death and is a substantial element in a gross breach of a duty of care owed to the deceased.[53] The Bill expressly avoids imposing any new liability on individuals associated with companies.[54] Instead, it directs attention to the entire structure of corporate decision-making, in what has been described as a more apt formula for 'capturing the true nature of corporate fault for the criminal law'.[55]

---

[49] There is a large body of criminological literature on this subject. Recent contributions include: B Fisse and J Braithwaite, *Corporations, Crime, and Accountability* (1993); G Slapper and S Tombs, *Corporate Crime* (1999); C Wells, *Corporations and Criminal Responsibility* (2nd edn, 2001); SS Simpson, *Corporate Crime, Law, and Social Control* (2002); J Gobert and M Punch, *Rethinking Corporate Crime* (2003).

[50] HLA Hart, 'Definition and Theory in Jurisprudence' (1954) 79 LQR 37, 59. See eg *A-G's Reference (No 2 of 1999)* [2000] 3 All ER 182, CA.

[51] Cf *Meridian Global Funds Management Asia Ltd v Securities Commission* [1995] 2 AC 500, 507, PC where Lord Hoffmann acknowledged the need to consider explicitly whether any given rule 'was intended to apply to companies', but considered that the answer to problems of 'fit' lay not in recasting the substantive rule, but in fashioning a 'special rule of attribution for the particular substantive rule'. This is discussed further in paras 3.51–3.52.

[52] The Bill's title is a misnomer: it will apply not only to corporations, but to government departments, partnerships and trade unions or employers' associations: Corporate Manslaughter and Corporate Homicide Bill 2007 cl 1(2).

[53] ibid cl 1. For background, see Law Commission, *Legislating the Criminal Code: Involuntary Manslaughter* (Law Com No 237, 1996) Parts VI–VIII; Home Office, *Consultation Paper: Reforming the Law on Involuntary Manslaughter—The Government's Proposals* (2000) Part 3.

[54] Corporate Manslaughter and Corporate Homicide Bill 2007, cl 18.

[55] J Gobert, 'Corporate Killing at Home and Abroad: Reflections on the Government's Proposals' (2002) 118 LQR 72, 96.

A related point is that people are accustomed to think of human beings as possess- **3.21**
ing separate and mutually exclusive identities: it is a truism that a 'person', in the
sense of a human being, cannot be another 'person' at the same time. This makes
it intuitively hard for people to accept that a bishop of the Church of England, for
example, can simultaneously be a natural person in his private capacity, and an
artificial person in his office-holding capacity, as a corporation sole. But it also
makes it intuitively easy for people to accept that an association endowed with
artificial personality is a separate person from its individual human members. This
in turn can lead them to draw the apparently inescapable conclusions that the
association and its members are not the same, and that for this reason they cannot be fixed with one another's liabilities. Thus, the theory has built up, and
indeed has become a cornerstone of the English courts' conception of artificial
personality, that 'separate legal personality is, in English law, inconsistent with
the members of an association being liable for its debts'.[56]

But other conceptions of artificial personality are possible. For example, the Joint **3.22**
Stock Companies Act 1844, ss 25 and 66 expressly provided that the members of
a joint stock company incorporated by registration under the statute would be
liable for the company's obligations. It may be that these statutory sections
were enacted precisely because incorporation by registration was understood to
create a new artificial person for whose liabilities the members would otherwise
not have been liable.[57] But even if that is right, the point is still made that it
has always been conceptually possible under English law for an association to
exist which possesses artificial personality, but whose individual members are
liable for its debts even though they are regarded as separate persons in other
respects. Indeed, this proposition was regarded by Lord Oliver as 'irrefutable' in
JH Rayner (Mincing Lane) Ltd v DTI,[58] although on the facts of that case he did
not accept that it had been Parliament's intention to create such an entity when
it ascribed artificial personality to the International Tin Council. It follows
that care must be taken not to assume in every case that the members of an association cannot be liable for its obligations, simply because the association has been
said to possess artificial personality.

---

[56] *JH Rayner (Mincing Lane) Ltd v DTI* [1987] BCLC 667, 692, *per* Staughton J. On appeal
[1989] Ch 72, 176, CA, Kerr LJ approved the following passage in LCB Gower, *Principles of Modern
Company Law* (4th edn, 1979) 100: 'It follows from the fact that a corporation is a separate person
that its members are not as such liable for its debts'. See too *Re Sheffield & South Yorkshire PBS* (1889)
22 QBD 470, 476, *per* Cave J; *Von Hellfield v Rechnitzer and Mayers Frères & Co* [1914] 1 Ch 748,
744–5, CA, *per* Phillimore LJ.
[57] *JH Rayner (Mincing Lane) Ltd v DTI* [1990] 2 AC 418, 508, HL, *per* Lord Oliver.
[58] ibid at 507. Cf Partnership Act 1890, s 4(2), which ascribes artificial personality to a Scots firm
whose partners nonetheless remain jointly and severally liable for its debts; Companies Act 2006,
s 3(4), which authorizes the formation of an unlimited company whose members are liable for the
company's debts, in the event that it is wound up and has insufficient assets to meet its liabilities.

(iii) The metaphorical quality of the term 'artificial person'

3.23 Thirdly, as Lord Hoffmann indicated in the passage of his speech in the *Meridian* case which has been quoted above,[59] the English courts have rejected the idea that artificial persons have an extra-legal reality, and it follows that the language of artificial personality which they use to describe certain groups of human associates amounts to nothing more than a convenient metaphorical shorthand. It is shorthand for the conclusion that in certain circumstances it is appropriate to modify or disapply the substantive rules of law which would normally apply to the associates as natural persons.[60]

3.24 From a theoretical perspective, a number of conclusions might be drawn from this insight. First, it might suggest to law-and-economics scholars that the attribution of artificial personality to an association is a potentially misleading heuristic, which distracts attention from the more important functional questions of how different types of business entity partition assets and allocate rights and responsibilities between participants.[61] Secondly, from the standpoint of critical legal theory, the use by the English courts of this metaphorical language might be viewed in a more sinister light, as a means of legitimizing corporate managerial power,[62] or more radically, as a tool for formalizing and legitimizing capitalist social relations and enabling the withdrawal of the capitalist from the production process.[63] Engagement with these critiques lies outside the scope of the present discussion. In the following parts of this chapter it is proposed rather to examine the way in which English law has conceptualized various types of association, in the belief that this helps to explain how the associates are treated as legal actors.

(f) Associations conceptualized as artificial persons

3.25 Some of the associations considered in the following parts of this chapter have never been regarded as artificial persons, while some have been said to possess artificial personality for some purposes and to lack it for others. Whether or not it has been said to possess artificial personality, each association is also currently

---

[59] Text to n 41 above.

[60] See R Grantham, 'Restitution and Insolvent Companies: Honing in on Shareholders' [2000] Company, Financial and Insolvency LR 26, 38.

[61] See R Kraakman et al, *The Anatomy of Corporate Law* (2004) chs 1–2. See also BR Cheffins, *Company Law: Theory, Structure, Operation* (1997), 32–41; MJ Whincop, 'Overcoming Corporate Law: Instrumentalism, Pragmatism and the Separate Legal Entity Concept' (1997) 15 Company and Securities L Jo 411.

[62] M Stokes, 'Company Law and Legal Theory' in W Twining (ed), *Legal Theory and the Common Law* (1986) 155.

[63] P Ireland, I Grigg-Small and D Kelly, 'The Conceptual Foundations of Modern Company Law' (1987) 14 J Law & Soc 149, esp 160–2; C Stanley, 'Corporate Personality and Capitalist Relations: A Critical Analysis of the Artifice of Company Law' (1988) 19 Cambrian Law Review 97.

conceptualized by English law in at least one of the following ways. Either the associates are regarded as having agreed to act for one another as individuals, and to have authorized one another to deal with one another's assets pursuant to their common purpose. Or, secondly, they are regarded as having agreed to the appointment of a selected person to act for them all, to assign their assets to this person, and to authorize this person to deal with their assets. Or, thirdly, they are regarded as having agreed to act as a body, to pool their assets, and to apply them collectively as a body. Under the first and second approaches, each associate is considered to retain his own individual personality, and to act in person, or through an appointed agent; under the third approach, the associates are considered to possess a collective personality when they act *en masse* which is distinct from their individual personalities.

It should be stressed that some of the associations discussed in this chapter **3.26** are conceptualized by English law in one way for some purposes and in another way for other purposes. There are several reasons for this. One is that the way in which some associations have been conceptualized has evolved over time in a piecemeal fashion, with the result that the law's understanding of what they are has altered for some purposes, but for others has remained the same. Thus, for example, many of the rules governing the control and operation of registered companies are now predicated on the view that in exchange for certain rights the shareholders have assigned their assets to a completely separate, reified third party—the company. But for historical reasons which are discussed below,[64] registered companies were originally conceptualized as aggregations of their members—it was thought that the members *were* the company—and this older conception continues to underpin some of the rules by which registered companies are governed.

A second reason is that practical considerations can militate in favour of a group **3.27** of associates being conceptualized as a single unit even though legal orthodoxy states that they should not be thought of in this way. Thus, for example, the legislature and the courts have frequently reiterated that the members of a partnership are a group of individual actors who have no collective personality, and yet this orthodoxy is subverted by the rule of civil procedure which permits partners to sue in the name of their firm.

A third and related reason is that although associates are *prima facie* entitled **3.28** to choose for themselves how their collective undertaking should be conceptualized, it may not always lie in the public interest (as interpreted by Parliament and the courts) to allow their choice to govern the way in which their collective activities are regulated. Thus, for example, the rule that a trade union can be fixed

---

[64] See paras 3.44–3.48.

with certain types of liability as an artificial person was imposed upon trade unions against their members' wishes, and is conceptually difficult to square with trade unions being considered to lack artificial personality in other respects. Again, notwithstanding the current legal orthodoxy that a registered company and its shareholders have separate personalities, and are not liable for one another's debts, the shareholders can nonetheless be sued directly by the company's creditors for the company's debts, if it can be shown that they have sought to take improper advantage of this orthodoxy by 'sheltering behind the corporate veil' for some fraudulent or illegal purpose.[65]

(4) Corporations, Quasi-Corporations, and Unincorporated Bodies

(a) Corporations

3.29 English law recognizes two sorts of corporation: corporations sole, which are essentially governmental, municipal, or religious officers given corporate status for the purposes of administrative convenience, and corporations aggregate, which are made up of several human members. Both sorts of corporation are considered to possess artificial personality, but as has been explained above,[66] the nature of the artificial personality possessed by corporations aggregate can vary according to circumstances, as in some situations they are conceptualized as reified entities and in others they are conceptualized as bodies of associates. As has also been explained,[67] it cannot safely be assumed that all corporations possess the same capacities as each other, that all corporations possess the same capacities as all natural persons, or indeed that all natural persons possess the same capacities as one another. However, it may be said that corporations generally have the capacity to enter contracts with outsiders, subject in some respects to the limitations placed on their capacity to do this by their constitutions.[68] It may also be said that they generally have the capacity to take, hold, and grant property in their own names. Corporations can be incorporated for a limited period, but they are more commonly created with perpetual succession; that is, the ability to continue in existence for an indefinite period notwithstanding the death or departure of their members. Corporations were formerly required to possess a common seal, but this rule was abrogated in 1989.[69]

3.30 Corporations can be created by Crown charter and by statute. Statutory corporations can be created directly by statute, by the order of a Secretary of State

---

65 As in eg *Gilford Motor Co Ltd v Horne* [1933] All ER 109.
66 See paras 3.25–3.28.
67 See paras 3.17–3.24.
68 For discussion see paras 3.37, 3.53–3.58, 3.78, 3.86, 3.89–3.92.
69 See now Companies Act 2006 s 45(1).

pursuant to a statutory power, and by registration in accordance with the terms of a statute which expressly stipulates that the effect of registration is to bring a corporation into being. Most corporations are now created by the latter method, and corporations of this sort include companies registered under the Companies Acts, limited liability partnerships registered under the Limited Liability Partnerships Act 2000 (which are formed by statute as bodies corporate), open-ended investment companies registered under the Open-Ended Investment Companies Regulations 1996 and 2001, building societies registered under the Building Societies Act 1986, industrial and provident societies registered under the Industrial and Provident Societies Act 1965, community interest companies registered under the Companies (Audit, Investigation and Community Enterprise) Act 2004, and friendly societies registered under the Friendly Societies Act 1992. These will all be considered in part B, with the exception of friendly societies for the reasons discussed in paras 3.100–3.101 below.

(b) Quasi-corporations

Certain other types of association are obliged or enabled to enter their names on a **3.31** register, or are regulated in some other way, by statutes which do not expressly confer corporate status on the associations covered by their provisions. During the nineteenth century the English courts considered that associations of this kind could not be presumed to have acquired corporate status by operation of the statute unless this was the 'manifest intent of the legislature'.[70] But from the beginning of the twentieth century, the courts' attitude began to change, following the House of Lords' decision in *Taff Vale Railway Co v ASRS*,[71] that entry on the register of trade unions in accordance with the Trade Union Act 1871 operated to fix trade unions with quasi-corporate status, with the result that they could be sued in tort and their property sequestered to meet their tort liabilities. In some cases thereafter, the courts continued to deny that associations regulated by statute had acquired corporate attributes in the absence of explicit statutory statements to this effect,[72] but in others they held that Parliament had impliedly intended this result, as for example Lord Denning held of friendly societies registered under the Friendly Societies Act 1896, in *Payne v Bradley*.[73] These decisions have been

---

[70] *River Tone Conservators v Ash* (1829) 10 B & C 349, 387, *per* Littledale J. See too *Mayor of Salford v Lancashire CC* (1890) 25 QBD 384, 389, CA, *per* Lindley LJ.

[71] [1901] AC 426, HL.

[72] *Bloom v National Federation of Discharged and Demobilised Sailors and Soldiers* (1918) 35 TLR 50, CA; *Mackenzie-Kennedy v Air Council* [1927] 2 KB 517, 533–4, CA, *per* Atkin LJ.

[73] [1962] AC 343, 356, HL, *per* Lord Denning. See too *IRC v Bew Estates Ltd* [1956] Ch 407 (War Damage Commission a 'quasi-corporation'); *Knight and Searle v Dove* [1964] 2 QB 631 (a trustee savings bank can sue in its own name); *Re Edis' Trusts* [1972] 1 WLR 1135 (volunteer corps a 'quasi-corporation'). And cf *Chaff and Hay Acquisition Committee v JA Hemphill & Sons Pty Ltd* (1947) 74 CLR 375, HCA (committee a corporation 'for some purposes').

criticized as 'veiled manoeuvres which [have effectively made] for changes of social policy' without Parliamentary authority.[74] They also create problems of classification, making it impossible to distinguish cleanly between incorporated and unincorporated bodies recognized by English law.

(c) Corporations, quasi-corporations, and unincorporated bodies: a classification

3.32 The classificatory problems described in the previous paragraph are compounded by the fact that certain other types of unincorporated body have been deemed to possess certain aspects of corporate status, for example the capacity to be sued collectively under a single name, without even being said to possess 'quasi-corporate status'.[75] In the following parts of this chapter, however, an attempt will be made to bring some order to this conceptual chaos by grouping under the heading 'corporations' those associations which are expressly stated to possess corporate status by Crown charter, statute, or statutory order. Associations which are not considered to have acquired full corporate status, but which have acquired some of its incidents by the operation of a statute, are grouped under the heading 'quasi-corporations'. Finally, associations whose status is not considered to have been affected by statute are grouped under the heading 'unincorporated bodies'.

(d) Companies and corporations

3.33 Confusingly, the term 'company' is used by English lawyers in two separate but overlapping senses.[76] It is frequently used to denote a particular sort of corporation, namely a corporation registered in accordance with the Companies Acts. English textbooks and practitioners' works on 'company law' invariably focus upon corporations of this sort, and when used in this sense, the term 'company' is often used in opposition to the term 'unincorporated association', to denote the possession of corporate status.[77] However, the term 'company' is often also used to describe any association of individuals formed for a common purpose, whether incorporated or unincorporated,[78] and references to 'unincorporated companies'

---

[74] KW Wedderburn, 'Corporate Personality and Social Policy: The Problem of the Quasi-Corporation' (1965) 28 MLR 62, 71.

[75] See paras 3.25–3.28.

[76] This has a long history: see eg F Evans, 'What is a Company?' (1910) 26 LQR 259.

[77] See eg *John v Rees* [1970] 1 Ch 345, 387, *per* Megarry J: 'The case I am concerned with...concerns not a company but an unincorporated club or association'; *Enderby Town Football Club Ltd v The Football Association Ltd* [1971] 1 All ER 215, 216, *per* Lord Denning MR: 'The county [football] association is not a limited company, but an unincorporated association of individual clubs.'

[78] For example, partnerships often style themselves as 'companies'. Cf the Companies Act 2006, ss 58–59: the name of an English public registered company must end with the words 'public limited company' or 'plc'; the name of other English registered companies limited by shares

are therefore not uncommon in the statute book[79] and law reports.[80] It is therefore intended to use the term 'registered company' in the body of this chapter to denote corporations registered in accordance with the Companies Acts.

It is also intended to use the term 'statutory corporation' in this chapter to denote **3.34** corporations which are created by the direct effect of a statute or statutory order. This usage is not intended to suggest that corporations created by registration in accordance with the terms of a statute are not also 'statutory corporations' in the sense that they come into being as a result of the statute's operation.

B. Corporations

(1) Statutory and Chartered Corporations

(a) Overview

Some statutes bring corporations into being by the direct operation of their provi- **3.35** sions,[81] while others proceed differently by empowering a Secretary of State to bring corporations into being by order.[82] Chartered corporations are formed in pursuance of letters patent granted by the Crown. There are now very few corporations of either sort by comparison with the number of registered companies in the UK.[83]

Prior to the enactment of the Joint Stock Companies Act 1844, chartered and **3.36** statutory corporations were the only types of corporation recognized by

---

or guarantees must generally end in 'limited' or 'ltd' (subject to the exceptions set out in s 60). The purpose of these rules is to warn outsiders dealing with such registered companies that their members do not owe unlimited liability for their debts. Ironically, however, 'the word "limited", intended to act as a warning, has become a symbol of creditworthiness', as incorporation is widely perceived by small traders to confer prestige and credibility on their undertaking: J Freedman, 'Small Businesses and the Corporate Form: Burden or Privilege?' (1994) 57 MLR 555, 563, n 38.

[79] See eg Taxation of Chargeable Gains Act 1992, s 288; Mental Capacity Act 2005, Sch 2 para 7(3)(b).

[80] See eg *JH Rayner (Mincing Lane) Ltd v DTI* [1987] BCLC 667, 690, *per* Staughton J: 'an unincorporated company has no separate existence'; *Secretary of State for Trade and Industry v Trull* (CA, 20 April 1994), *per* Glidewell LJ: 'such a company is an unincorporated trading association'.

[81] As discussed in GC Thornton, *Legislative Drafting* (4th edn, 1996) 249–73; D Morris, 'Establishing Statutory Corporations: Mere Scissors and Paste?' (1998) 19 Statute Law Review 41.

[82] See eg Housing Act 1988, s 62 and Sch 7; National Health Service Act 2006, s 25 and Sch 4. These respectively authorize the creation of the confusingly named 'housing action trusts' and 'NHS trusts', which in fact are not trusts at all, but corporations: R Bartlett, 'When Is a "Trust" Not a Trust? The National Health Service Trust' (1996) 60 Conv 186.

[83] In March 2006, 50 companies incorporated by special Act of Parliament and 798 companies incorporated by royal charter were listed at Companies House: DTI, *Companies in 2005–6* (2006) Table E3.

English law. This state of affairs was largely dictated by the Bubble Act 1720, which prohibited commercial associates from acting as corporate bodies or raising transferable stock without royal or statutory authority. Consequently many of the corporations in existence during the eighteenth and early nineteenth centuries were governmental, municipal, or ecclesiastical bodies. Whilst some commercial associations were also incorporated by statute during this period,[84] these tended to be formed to undertake activities of a quasi-public nature: for example, the pursuit of a trading monopoly, or the construction of canals or railways.[85] Overwhelming demand for statutory incorporations lead Parliament to repeal the Bubble Act in 1825,[86] and efforts were also made to facilitate the more widespread grant of corporate status by statute or Crown charter. However, the need to do so was then effectively removed by the enactment of the Joint Stock Companies Act 1844, which made it possible to obtain corporate status by registration. In time the registered company came to be preferred by the overwhelming majority of commercial associates seeking corporate status. Statutory and chartered corporations remain in only a relatively small number of situations, involving the pursuit of activities of a public or quasi-public character.

(b) How statutory and chartered corporations are conceptualized

3.37 From the outset, the act of creating a corporation aggregate by statute or Crown charter was understood to create a new legal entity, which could own property and sue (and be sued) in its own name. However, corporations aggregate were initially conceptualized as bodies of associates, and it was only during the course of the nineteenth century that they came to be understood as separate, reified abstract entities, a shift of thinking which also occurred with regard to registered companies, for reasons which are discussed below.[87]

3.38 It is unclear whether the members of statutory and chartered corporations aggregate were ever thought to be generally liable for their debts in the absence of an express statutory provision to that effect. Some early cases suggest that although a corporation's creditors could not recover from the members directly, they could nonetheless reach them via subrogation to the corporation's right to

---

84 See Ron Harris, *Industrializing English Law: Entrepreneurship and Business Organization, 1720–1844* (2000), 132–36, 193–95, 218–22.

85 Some of these, such as the East India Company and the Hudson's Bay Company, were large and powerful organizations: see AM Carlos and S Nicholas, 'Giants of an Earlier Capitalism: The Early Chartered Trading Companies as Modern Multinationals' (1988) 62 Business History Review 398. Once formed, they guarded their monopoly status jealously: see H Hansmann, R Kraakman and R Squire, 'Law and the Rise of the Firm' (2006) 119 Harv LR 1333, 1378–79.

86 Bubble Repeal Act 1825. See Harris, n 84 above 250–68.

87 In paras 3.44–3.48.

make a 'levitation', or call, on the members to meet its liabilities.[88] However, the question whether all corporations had a general power to make calls on their members in this way never seems to have been judicially answered in the seventeenth and eighteenth centuries, and by 1825, it was assumed that in the absence of statutory intervention the Crown lacked the power to bring a chartered corporation aggregate into being whose members would be responsible for the corporation's debts. This is why the Crown was expressly given the power to withhold the privilege of limited liability from the members of a chartered corporation by the Bubble Repeal Act 1825, section 2.[89]

(c) How statutory and chartered corporations act

Like registered companies, statutory and chartered corporations must act through human agents, and the same problems arise in identifying these agents as arise in the context of registered companies.[90] Statutory corporations have such powers as are expressly stated in the statute, or may fairly be regarded as incidental to, or consequential on, these express powers, and in the event that they purport to act in a way that lies outside the scope of their powers, their acts are void because *ultra vires*.[91] In contrast, a chartered corporation has unlimited powers, unless expressly or impliedly limited by statute, and it may therefore validly act in a way that is not expressly authorized by its charter, or indeed, in a way that is expressly prohibited by its charter[92]—although if it does act in such a way, its charter may be revoked by proceedings on a *scire facias*, and for this reason, a member can obtain an injunction restraining the corporation from the commission of an unauthorized or prohibited act.[93]

3.39

---

[88] *Edmunds v Brown* (1668) 1 Lev 237, 83 ER 385; *Salmon v Hamborough Co* (1671) 1 Ch Cas 204, 22 ER 763, HL. The first of these was an unsuccessful action at common law brought by a corporation's creditors who subsequently recovered from the members in a Chancery suit: *Naylor v Brown* (1673) Rep t Finch 83, 23 ER 44.

[89] Parl Debs (series 2) vol 13, col 120 (2 June 1825). Cf *Elve v Boughton* [1891] 1 Ch 501, 507, CA, *per* Lindley LJ, stating that it had never lain in the Crown's power to incorporate a group of persons by charter in such a way as to make them liable for the debts of the corporation, because for that statutory intervention had always been required.

[90] See paras 3.53–3.58.

[91] *Baroness Wenlock v River Dee Co* (1885) 10 App Cas 354, 361, HL, *per* Lord Blackburn; *LCC v A-G* [1902] AC 165, 167, HL, *per* Lord Halsbury LC; *Charles Roberts & Co Ltd v British Railways Board* [1965] 1 WLR 396; *Hazell v Hammersmith and Fulham LBC* [1992] AC 1, HL; *Crédit Suisse v Allerdale BC* [1997] QB 306, 349–50, CA, *per* Hobhouse LJ.

[92] *Sutton's Hospital Case* (1612) 10 Co Rep 1a, 23a, 30b, 77 ER 937, 960, 970; *A-G v Manchester Corp* [1906] 1 Ch 643, 651, *per* Farwell J; *Institution of Mechanical Engineers v Cane* [1961] AC 696, 724–5, HL, *per* Lord Denning; *Hazell v Hammersmith and Fulham LBC* [1990] 2 QB 697, 771, CA, *per* Sir Stephen Brown P, rev'd on another point [1992] AC 1, HL.

[93] *R v Mayor of London* (1692) 1 Show KB 274, 280, 89 ER 569, 573, *per* Holt CJ; *R v Eastern Archipelago Co* (1853) 1 E & B 310, 118 ER 452, aff'd (1853) 2 E & B 857, 118 ER 988; *Jenkin v Pharmaceutical Soc of GB* [1921] 1 Ch 392, 398, *per* Peterson J; *Mechanical Engineers v Cane* ibid 724, *per* Lord Denning.

(2) Registered Companies

(a) Overview

3.40   The overwhelming majority of English corporations are now registered companies,[94] formed in accordance with the procedures set out in the Companies Act 2006[95] or previous companies legislation,[96] and subject to the provisions of the 2006 Act. Most registered companies are companies limited by shares, but there are also a relatively small number of companies limited by guarantee, and an even smaller number of unlimited companies.[97] Almost all registered companies in Great Britain are also private companies, with public companies forming no more than 0.5 per cent of the total.[98] Much of the law governing the activities of English registered companies is contained in the Companies Act 2006, which at 1300 sections is the longest statute passed by the UK Parliament to date.[99] This legislation followed an extensive review and consultation exercise (the 'Company Law Review'), the output from which provides important background to the statute.[100] The Act is being brought into force in stages.[101] The most significant provisions discussed in this chapter, relating to directors' duties[102] and shareholder litigation,[103] came into force on 1 October 2007. However, other provisions, such as those relating to company formation,[104] corporate capacity and related matters,[105] and the corporate constitution,[106] are not due to come into force until

---

[94] In March 2006, there were around 2.2 million of these registered in England and Wales: DTI, *Companies in 2005–6* (2006) Table A1.

[95] A registered company must have a memorandum of association (Companies Act 2006, ss 7 and 8); this, along with certain other documents, must be delivered to the Registrar of Companies (s 9), who then registers the documents delivered to him (s 14) and issues a certificate of incorporation (s 15); on the date stated in the certificate, the company is 'born' (s 16).

[96] Companies Act 2006, s 1(1)(b).

[97] The meaning of these terms is discussed in para 3.76. In March 2006, there were 91,000 registered companies without share capital (0.04% of the total number of registered companies) DTI, *Companies in 2005–6* (2006) Table A7.

[98] ibid Table A2.

[99] It is also the first Companies Act to be accompanied by a comprehensive set of Explanatory Notes: see *Companies Act 2006: Explanatory Notes*.

[100] See generally, DTI, *Modern Company Law for a Competitive Economy* (1998); Company Law Review Steering Group, *The Strategic Framework* (1999); Company Law Review Steering Group, *Final Report* (2001); DTI, *Company Law Reform* (2005). For a valuable overview, see E Ferran, 'Company Law Reform in the United Kingdom: A Progress Report' (2005) 69 RabelsZ 629.

[101] See Companies Act 2006 Implementation Timetable, available at <www.berr.gov.uk/bbf/co-act-2006/index.html>.

[102] See paras 3.59–3.73. However, commencement of the provisions relating to directors' conflicts of interest (Companies Act 2006, ss 175–177; see paras 3.71–3.72) will be delayed until 1 October 2009.

[103] See paras 3.63–3.65 and 3.75.

[104] See n 95 above.

[105] See paras 3.53–3.58.

[106] See para 3.74.

1 October 2009.[107] The Companies Act 2006 is supplemented by other major statues dealing, amongst other things, with insolvency and the regulation of financial services and markets.[108] A good deal of this legislation implements, or provides a framework for the implementation of, European directives harmonizing the legal requirements relating to companies and capital markets.[109] However, the English companies legislation does not constitute a complete statutory code, and many important principles are to be found in the law reports. In addition, for listed companies, the rules produced by the Financial Services Authority (prospectus, listing, disclosure and transparency, and market abuse rules),[110] the Financial Reporting Council (corporate governance and accounting regulation),[111] and the Takeover Panel (takeover bids),[112] are important sources of additional regulation.

The English law governing the operation of registered companies has generally **3.41** been directed towards 'the archetypal middle-sized business company on which all the nineteenth-century thinking was focused', even though companies of this kind 'withered in importance and [became] wholly atypical' during the late nineteenth and twentieth centuries.[113] This trend dates from the onset of the Great Depression in the 1870s, when smaller enterprises first began to use the registered company form in a systematic way, a development whose legal

---

[107] The approach taken in this chapter is to refer to the Companies Act 2006 throughout. For exposition of these matters under the Companies Act 1985, readers are directed to the first edition of this work.

[108] Companies Act 1985, Part XIV; Insolvency Act 1986; Company Directors Disqualification Act 1986; Criminal Justice Act 1993, Part V; Financial Services and Markets Act 2000.

[109] See generally, V Edwards, *EC Company Law* (1999); N Moloney, *EC Securities Regulation* (2002); K Hopt and E Wymeersch, *European Company and Financial Law: Texts and Leading Cases* (2004); B Pettet, 'Company Law and Capital Markets Law: Taking Stock of European Integration' (2004) 57 CLP 393; E Ferran, *Building and EU Securities Market* (2004). The main company law directives which have been adopted into English law are: the First Directive, concerning the protection of third parties dealing with companies and requiring the disclosure of certain information in a public register (Directive 68/151/EEC [1968] OJ Spec Ed (I) 41), now implemented by the Companies Act 2006, ss 39–40, 51, and 1079; the Second Directive, laying down the minimum requirements on the formation of public companies and the maintenance of their share capital (Directive 77/91/EEC [1977] OJ L26/1, as modified by Directive 2006/68/EC [2006] OJ L264/32), now implemented by assorted sections of the Companies Act 2006; the Fourth and Seventh Directives, concerning the preparation and publication of annual accounts (Directives 78/660/EEC [1978] OJ L222/11 and 83/349/EEC [1983] OJ L193/1), now implemented by Parts 15 and 16 of the Companies Act 2006; the Eleventh Directive, imposing minimum and maximum requirements for branches established in one member state by companies formed in another (Directive 89/666/EEC [1989] OJ L395/36), now implemented by the Companies Act 2006, Part 34; and the Thirteenth Directive, on takeover bids (Directive 2004/25/EC [2004] OJ L142/12), now implemented by Part 28 of the Companies Act 2006.

[110] See FSA, *The FSA Handbook*: <fsahandbook.info/FSA/html/handbook/>.

[111] See FRC, *The Combined Code on Corporate Governance* (2006).

[112] See Takeover Panel, *The Takeover Code* (8th edn, 2006).

[113] L Sealy, 'Perception and Policy in Company Law Reform' in D Feldman and F Meisel (eds), *Corporate and Commercial Law: Modern Developments* (1996) 26.

propriety was eventually acknowledged in *Salomon v A Salomon & Co Ltd*.[114] It is said that this direction resulted in a legal regime that paid insufficient attention to the needs of smaller companies.[115]

3.42 The Company Law Review considered and rejected the possibility of introducing a separate form of company specifically directed at the needs of small business, on the grounds that this might impose constraints on firms making the transition from small to large.[116] Instead, the Companies Act 2006 is intended to make English company law more accessible and useful for small companies, through a series of innovations. The first is stylistic: effort has been made to ensure that provisions that are of particular importance to smaller companies (in particular, those relating to company formation, shareholder decision-making, and accounting and audit obligations) have been highlighted in the Act's structure and drafted in a way intended to make them more accessible.[117] Secondly, the content of a number of provisions—including those relating to company formation, shareholder meetings and decision-making, and capital structure, have been streamlined in their application to small companies, in order to avoid the imposition of unnecessary costs.[118] At the same time, a new set of model articles of association will be introduced specifically for private companies, which will be shorter and tailored towards greater shareholder power than the corresponding version for public companies.[119]

3.43 Meanwhile at the other end of the corporate spectrum, mergers and amalgamations of registered companies accelerated during the course of the twentieth century to produce large corporate groups. At the same time the ownership of shares in listed companies became increasingly fragmented,[120] creating a need to render directors accountable to shareholders. For many years, this was met by non-binding codes of best practice developed by the Bank of England, the Stock Exchange, and institutional investors.[121] However, since the mid-1980s, these rules have gradually become juridified, a process which intensified with the enactment of the Financial Services and Markets Act 2000 and concomitant establishment of the Financial Services Authority as UK Listing Authority.

---

114 [1897] AC 22, HL.

115 See DTI Company Law Review Steering Group, *The Strategic Framework* (1999), 56–58; and see too: J Freedman, 'Small Businesses and the Corporate Form: Burden or Privilege?' (1994) 57 MLR 555; A Hicks, 'Corporate Form: Questioning the Unsung Hero' [1997] JBL 306.

116 *The Strategic Framework*, ibid, 62–68.

117 DTI, *Company Law Reform*, Cm 6456 (2005), 29; Companies Act 2006, Parts 2, 13, 15, 16.

118 *Company Law Reform*, ibid 30–36, 40–44, 56–57; Companies Act 2006, Parts 2, 13, 17.

119 See DTI, Companies Act 2006 Implementation Consultative Document February 2007, Annex C: Companies (Model Articles) Draft Regulations .

120 See BR Cheffins, 'Dividends as a Substitute for Corporate Law: The Separation of Ownership and Control in the United Kingdom' (2006) 63 Wash & Lee L Rev 1273.

121 See G Stapledon, *Institutional Shareholders and Corporate Governance* (1996).

In keeping with this trend, the Companies Act 2006 has brought with it additional mechanisms of legal accountability, in the form of a statutory restatement of directors' duties, clarification and expansion of the circumstances under which shareholder litigation may be commenced, and provisions putting certain previously informal mechanisms—most notably, the Takeover Code—onto a statutory footing.

(b) How registered companies are conceptualized

(i) Nineteenth-century developments

To understand how registered companies are now conceptualized in English law, **3.44**
it is necessary to know something of their historical origins and development.[122]
At the start of the nineteenth century, the two forms of commercial association recognized by English law were the partnership and the joint stock company. Because the word 'company' is now used so widely to describe registered companies with corporate status, it is easy to overlook the fact that joint stock companies were not necessarily corporate bodies at that time, and to forget that although some of them were incorporated by statute or Crown charter, the majority were not, for the reasons discussed in the previous section.[123] Thus, in the eyes of contemporaries, joint stock companies were distinguishable from partnerships not because they possessed a different legal status, or were conceptualized in a different way, but because they were economically different: they were larger and a significant proportion of their members played no active management role.

The act of incorporating a joint stock company by statute or Crown charter was **3.45**
understood to create an artificial person, and to confer legal privileges on the members to which neither the members of a partnership nor the members of an unincorporated joint stock company were *prima facie* entitled. However in practice many of the latter contrived to acquire some of the advantages of corporate status by employing a deed of settlement.[124] This was a legal device with marked similarities to the modern-day unit trust,[125] under which the members assigned their assets to trustees, directors were appointed to manage the business, and shares in the company were issued to the members, with such rights to terminate their interest and to transfer their shares as the deed of settlement might provide.[126] For present purposes, however, it is more important to note that

---

[122] The following discussion draws on the work of Paddy Ireland, and in particular, his article 'Capitalism Without the Capitalist: The Joint Stock Company and the Emergence of the Modern Doctrine of Separate Corporate Personality' (1996) 17(1) Journal of Legal History 40.

[123] In para 3.36.

[124] Hansmann et al., n 85 above. Cf Harris, n 84 above.

[125] Described in para 3.114.

[126] Members of unincorporated joint stock companies were jointly and severally liable for the whole debts of the business, and could not escape liability for these on the ground that they were

'the principles of the law of partnership, slightly modified, were thought to be applicable to. . .incorporated, as well as. . .unincorporated [joint stock companies]'.[127]

3.46 Consistently with this, an incorporated joint stock company was not conceptualized as an entity distinct from its individual shareholders, but was understood to *consist of* the shareholders as a body. Thus an incorporated joint stock company was referred to as 'they' rather than 'it',[128] in the view that the shareholders of such a company possessed a direct equitable interest in the company's assets,[129] and that the directors of such a company were the agents of its shareholders, subject to their direct control—a rule which persisted until the end of the nineteenth century.[130]

3.47 During the course of the nineteenth century, however, a shift in thinking took place, and a new conception of the incorporated joint stock company emerged, in accordance with which the company came to be seen as an artificial person which was quite separate from its members, *both individually and collectively*: in Sealy's words, 'the company was ceasing to be an association and was in the process of becoming an institution'.[131] This shift in thinking can be attributed to the fact that from around 1830 there emerged for the first time since the Bubble

---

owed by a separate, legally distinct person. The attempt was made to circumvent this problem by limiting the members' liability in companies' deeds of settlement, but in accordance with privity notions, such terms were effective only against outsiders who were party to them: *Greenwood's Case* (1854) 3 De GM & G 459, 475ff; 43 ER 180, 186ff, *per* Lord Cranworth LC. Also, in some matters relating to the property of a deed of settlement company, the trustees could sue and be sued as legal owners, as in eg *Metcalf v Bruin* (1810) 12 East 400, 104 ER 156. Otherwise, it was necessary to join all the members to lawsuits relating to their shared activities, and to serve them all with copies of the papers, as in eg *Van Sandau v Moore* (1826) 1 Russ 441, 38 ER 171. This requirement could present formidable practical difficulties, and in practice could often be overcome only by going to arbitration, although in the early nineteenth century it was gradually relaxed, and some representative suits were allowed: see the cases cited in M Lobban, 'Corporate Identity and Limited Liability in France and England 1825–67' (1996) 25 Anglo-American L Rev 397, 404, n 20.

[127] P Ireland, 'Company Law and the Myth of Shareholder Ownership' (1999) 62 MLR 32, 39. Cf *Ridley v Plymouth, Stonehouse and Devonport Grinding and Baking Co* (1848) 2 Ex 711, 716, 154 ER 676, 679, *per* Parke B; *Australian Coal and Shale Employees Federation v Smith* (1937) 38 SR (NSW) 48, 53, NSWCA, *per* Jordan CJ.

[128] As in eg *Ex p the Lancaster Canal Co* (1829) 1 Mont Bank Cas 116, 119, *per* Shadwell V-C; *Bligh v Brent* (1837) 2 Y & C 268, 293ff, 160 ER 397, 407ff, *per* Alderson B.

[129] *Sutton's Hospital Case* (1612) 10 Co Rep 1a, 23a, 77 ER 937, 960; *Naylor v Cornish* (1648) 1 Vern 311, 23 ER 489; *Salmon v Hamborough Co* (1671) 1 Ch Cas 204, 22 ER 763; *Child v Hudson's Bay Co* (1723) 2 P Wms 207, 24 ER 702; *Harrison v Pryse* (1740) Barn Ch 324, 27 ER 664. The same was also true of shareholders in a deed of settlement company: *Buckeridge v Ingram* (1795) 2 Ves Jun 652, 30 ER 824; *Howse v Chapman* (1799) 4 Ves Jun 542, 31 ER 278.

[130] Companies Clauses Consolidation Act 1845, s 90; *Isle of Wight Railway Co v Tahourdin* (1883) 25 Ch D 320, 329, CA, *per* Cotton LJ.

[131] L Sealy, 'Perception and Policy in Company Law Reform' in D Feldman and F Meisel (eds), *Corporate and Commercial Law: Modern Developments* (1996) 2.

Act 1720 an active market for company shares,[132] stimulated by the railway booms of 1824–5, 1834–6 and 1845–7.[133] As a result, joint stock company shares became readily realizable liquid assets once again, an economic transformation which was mirrored by a legal reconceptualization, as the courts came around to the view that such shares gave their owners no direct property interest in the assets of the company, and were realizable as money in the share market without liquidating the assets of the company and winding the concern up.[134]

The effect of these developments for the way in which incorporated joint stock **3.48** companies were conceptualized in English law was to externalize the shareholders, and to reify the company as a legal person in its own right, which was capable of existing without reference to them: the company became 'it' rather than 'they'. Thus in 1874, in *Ashbury Railway Carriage Co v Riche*,[135] the House of Lords held that a registered company's shareholders could not evade the operation of the *ultra vires* doctrine by authorizing the company to carry on activities that lay beyond the objects set out in its memorandum of association, even if they purported to do so unanimously;[136] in 1887, in *Trevor v Whitworth*,[137] the same court held that the shareholders could not collectively override the capital maintenance doctrine either, so as to cause the company to repurchase its own shares; in 1897, in *Salomon v A Salomon & Co Ltd*,[138] it rejected the view of the Court of Appeal, that a registered company effectively controlled by a single individual could not be a valid company because the existence of a genuine partnership between

---

[132] M Patterson and D Reiffen, 'The Effect of the Bubble Act on the Market for Joint Stock Shares' (1990) 50 J Econ Hist 163; Harris, n 84 above, 218–223. Apart from the shares in chartered and statutory corporations, the London Stock Exchange dealt primarily in government securities during the century following the Bubble Act: EV Morgan and WA Thomas, *The Stock Exchange: Its History and Functions* (1962) ch 3.

[133] Well-described in RW Kostal, *Law and English Railway Capitalism 1825–1875* (1994) ch 1. There was also a short-lived 'canal mania' between 1791 and 1793, but otherwise shareholdings in canal companies were relatively stable, and dealings in canal company shares were confined to the localities in which the canals were built: JR Ward, *The Finance of Canal Building in Eighteenth Century England* (1974).

[134] The development of the courts' thinking can be traced through: *Bligh v Brent* (1836) 2 Y & C 268, 160 ER 397; *Pinkett v Wright* (1842) 2 Hare 120, 130–4, 67 ER 50, 54–6, *per* Wigram V-C; *Baxter v Brown* (1845) 7 M & G 198, 135 ER 86; *Myers v Perigal* (1852) 2 De GM & G 599, 42 ER 1006; *Watson v Spratley* (1854) 10 Ex 222, 156 ER 424; *Bank of Hindustan v Alison* (1860) LR 6 CP 222; *Entwhistle v Davis* (1867) 4 Eq 272; *Borland's Trustees v Steel Bros & Co Ltd* [1901] 1 Ch 279; *Short v Treasury Commissioners* [1948] 1 KB 116, 122, CA, *per* Evershed LJ (aff'd [1948] AC 534, HL).

[135] (1874) LR 7 HL 653, HL. See too *Rolled Steel Products (Holdings) Ltd v British Steel Corporation* [1986] 1 Ch 246, 296, CA, *per* Slade LJ.

[136] The *ultra vires* doctrine, which has since been abrogated, is discussed in paras 3.53–3.55.

[137] (1887) 12 App Cas 409, HL. See too *Ooregum Gold Mining Co of India v Roper* [1892] AC 125, HL.

[138] [1897] AC 22, HL. The High Court and Court of Appeal decisions in the case are reported *sub nom Broderip v Salomon* [1895] 2 Ch 323.

the members was a prerequisite to incorporation under the Companies Acts; and in 1906, in *Automatic Self-Cleansing Filter Syndicate Co Ltd v Cuninghame,*[139] the Court of Appeal held that the directors were the agents of the company, rather than the shareholders directly.

(ii) Twentieth century developments

3.49 Further developments in the twentieth century reinforcing the disassociation of the registered company from its shareholders included many reaffirmations of the rule in the *Salomon* case,[140] in decisions denying company creditors the right to sue shareholders in respect of a company's liabilities,[141] or enabling the shareholders to enforce rights to which they would not have been entitled, had they been identified with the company.[142] It was held in *R v Phillipou*[143] that the offence of theft may be committed when the sole shareholders of a company take the company's assets with the intention of permanently depriving the company of the assets. And the view was progressively abandoned, that the fiduciary duty owed to a company by its directors, to act in the company's best interests, necessarily equates to a duty to act exclusively for the best interests of the company's present shareholders. This is now reflected in the directors' general duty to promote the success of the company, which requires the directors to take into account, amongst other things, the interests of the company's employees, the need to foster its business relationships with suppliers, customers and others, and the impact of its operations on the community and the environment.[144]

(iii) The legacy of history

3.50 Yet it still cannot be said that English law has consistently conceptualized the registered company as a reified entity separate from its shareholders in every situation. The legislature and the courts continue to refer to a registered company

---

139 [1906] 2 Ch 34, CA. See too *Gramophone & Typewriter Ltd v Stanley* [1908] 2 KB 890, CA, 105–6, *per* Buckley LJ; *Quin & Axtens Ltd v Salmon* [1909] AC 442, HL; *John Shaw & Sons (Salford) Ltd v Shaw* [1935] 2 KB 113, CA; *Breckland Group Holdings Ltd v London & Suffolk Properties Ltd* [1989] BCLC 100; *Mitchell & Hobbs (UK)Ltd v Mill* [1996] 2 BCLC 102. See too Companies Clauses Consolidation Act 1845, s 90; Companies Act 1948, Sch 1, Table A, Art 80; Companies (Tables A-F) Regulations 1985, SI 1985/805, Table A, Art 70; DTI, Companies Act 2006 Implementation Consultative Document February 2007, Annex C: Companies (Model Articles) Draft Regulations, Sch 1, art 2; Sch 3, art 2.

140 See too *Re Noel Tedman Holding Pty Ltd* [1967] Qd R 561, Qd Sup Ct, where it was held that a company could survive the death of all its shareholders.

141 See eg *Adams v Cape Industries plc* [1990] Ch 433, CA.

142 See eg *Lee v Lee's Air Farming Ltd* [1961] AC 12, PC; *Secretary of State for Trade and Industry v Bottrill* [1999] ICR 592, CA; *Butcher Robinson & Staples Ltd v London Regional Transport* [1999] 35 EG 165.

143 [1989] Crim LR 559, CA, affirmed in *DPP v Gomez* [1993] AC 442, HL.

144 Companies Act 2006, s 172.

and its shareholders as interchangeable from time to time.[145] It remains the case that the shareholders have the power to ratify directors' breaches of duty to the company,[146] and that the shareholders have the power to step in and run the company in the event that the board of directors is deadlocked or otherwise incapable of acting.[147] And in certain situations the courts continue to 'lift the corporate veil',[148] so as to fix companies and/or their shareholders with civil or criminal liability for which they would not have been liable,[149] or to enable them to enforce some right to which they would not have been entitled,[150] had their common identity not been affirmed.

(c) How registered companies act

(i) *The rules of attribution*

A registered company can only 'act' by the *attribution* to it of the actions of an individual associated with the company.[151] The circumstances under which the knowledge or actions of an individual will be so attributed are dictated by a combination of the company's own allocation of authority and the policy underlying the substantive rule of liability that it is sought to apply.[152] The starting point is the company's constitution, which delineates, expressly or impliedly, circumstances under which the acts of individuals associated with it should be treated as the acts 'of' the company. These were referred to by Lord Hoffmann in *Meridian Global Funds Management Asia Ltd v Securities Commission* as the company's 'primary' rules of attribution.[153] In addition, the 'general' rules of attribution found in the

3.51

---

145 See eg *HL Bolton (Engineering) Co Ltd v TJ Graham & Co Ltd* [1957] 1 QB 159, 172, CA, *per* Denning LJ: 'this company, through its managers, intend to occupy the premises for their own purposes [*sic*]'; Companies Act 2006, s 16(2) 'The subscribers of the memorandum, together with such other persons as may from time to time become members of the company, are a body corporate by the name stated in the certificate of incorporation.' There is some tension with the implementation of the 12th Council Directive (EEC) 89/667 on Single Member Companies [1989] OJ L395/40 in what is now s 7(1) of the Companies Act 2006, which permits a single person to form a company.

146 Companies Act 2006, s 239.

147 *Barron v Potter* [1914] 1 Ch 895; *Foster v Foster* [1916] 1 Ch 532; *Re Argentum Reductions (UK) Ltd* [1975] 1 WLR 186, 189, *per* Megarry J.

148 Empirical analysis indicates that the courts are likelier both to lift the veil and to keep it in place if asked to do so by a state agency, than they are when asked to do so by a company or its shareholders: C Mitchell, 'Lifting the Corporate Veil in the English Courts: An Empirical Study' [1999] Company, Financial and Insolvency LR 15.

149 As in eg *Creasey v Breachwood Motors Ltd* [1993] BCLC 480; *Re H* [1996] 2 All ER 391, CA; *R v Dimsey* [2000] 2 All ER 142, CA.

150 As in eg *DHN Food Distributors Ltd v Tower Hamlets LBC* [1976] 1 WLR 852, CA; *Al Bassam Trademark* [1994] RPC 315.

151 *Meridian Global Funds Management Asia Ltd v Securities Commission* [1995] 2 AC 500, 506–507, PC.

152 ibid; *Morris v Bank of India* [2005] EWCA Civ 693; [2005] 2 BCLC 328, CA, at [95]–[96].

153 *Meridian*, above n 151.

law of agency and the doctrine of vicarious liability apply equally to companies as they do to natural persons acting as principals.[154]

3.52 However, the attribution of actions to a company for the purposes of establishing liability also depends on the policy behind the substantive rule in question,[155] and this may result in the application of a 'special' rule of attribution that modifies the result reached by reference solely to the primary and general rules of attribution.[156] This approach 'identifies' the company as acting through a human individual for the purpose of the rule in question, with the consequence that his state of mind is deemed to be the company's state of mind, because he 'is' the company at the time of his actions.[157] Whether the attribution of his actions to the company means that they are *not* treated as his own actions also depends on the purpose and context of the substantive rule in question.[158] For example, a statement made in the course of agency will be treated *exclusively* as the company's statement for the purposes of liability for negligent misstatement,[159] but as being made by the agent himself *and* by the company for the purposes of liability in deceit.[160]

(ii) Limitations on their powers to act and the position of third parties

3.53 Ever since joint stock companies were permitted to acquire corporate status by registration under the Joint Stock Companies Act 1844, registered companies have been required to register their constitutional documents for inspection by third parties intending to deal with the company.[161] Until recently, a registered company's memorandum of association was required contain an objects clause, in which the objects of the company were set out,[162] and the company was

---

[154] See eg *Freeman and Lockyer (a firm) v Buckhurst Park Properties Ltd* [1964] 2 QB 480, CA; *British Bank of the Middle East v Sun Life Assurance Co of Canada (UK) Ltd* [1983] 2 Lloyd's Rep 9, HL; *First Energy (UK) Ltd v Hungarian International Bank Ltd* [1993] 2 Lloyd's Rep 194, CA.

[155] Often determined by an exercise in construction of a relevant statutory provision (see eg *Meridian*, above n 151; *Morris*, above n 152) or contract: see eg *KR v Royal & Sun Alliance plc* [2006] EWCA Civ 1454; [2007] 1 All ER (Comm) 161 at [55]; *Jafari-Fini v Skillglass Ltd* [2007] EWCA Civ 261; [2007] All ER (D) 504 at [97].

[156] *Meridian*, above n 151, at 512; *Morris v Bank of India*, above n 152, at [96].

[157] See *Lennard's Carrying Co Ltd v Asiatic Petroleum Co Ltd* [1915] AC 705; *Tesco Supermarkets Ltd v Nattrass* [1972] AC 153.

[158] See N Campbell and J Armour, 'Demystifying Corporate Civil Liability' (2003) 62 CLJ 290.

[159] *Williams v Natural Life Health Foods Ltd* [1998] 1 WLR 830. Because the basis of liability for negligent misstatement is analogous to contract, the contractual attribution rules are used: *Standard Chartered Bank v Pakistan National Shipping Corporation* [2002] UKHL 43; [2003] 1 AC 959 at [21], *per* Lord Hoffmann. See also J Armour, 'Corporate Personality and Assumption of Responsibility' [1999] LMCLQ 246.

[160] *Standard Chartered Bank v Pakistan National Shipping Corporation* at [20]–[22], [39]–[41].

[161] This requirement was abolished by the Companies Act 2006, s 9, which permits companies to register an objects clause if they wish.

[162] See Companies Act 1985, s 2(1)(c).

considered to lack the capacity to enter into transactions for any purpose other than those specified in its objects clause. Although the Companies Act 2006 makes this voluntary, rather than mandatory, for new incorporations, existing companies will of course retain their objects clauses. The articles of association must, in any event, specify which human individuals are authorized to act for the company, and the limitations (if any) on the scope of their authority, and a human individual who purports to act for a company cannot validly do so unless his actions are actually or apparently authorized, or subsequently ratified, by the company.

From 1844 onwards, it was therefore understood to lie in the interests of third **3.54** parties dealing with a registered company to inspect its constitutional documents, to ensure that the company had the capacity to enter the transaction, and to ensure that the individuals purporting to represent the company were in fact authorized to do so. For if the company lacked the necessary capacity the transaction would be void on the ground that it was *ultra vires*, and if the individuals in question were unauthorized the company could deny that their actions should be attributed to it. As the law developed, however, the fact that a company had registered its documents came to work against the interests of third parties, because the courts developed a doctrine of constructive notice under which third parties were deemed to know what was in the documents even if they had never read them.[163] This had the effect that third parties who failed to inspect a company's documents ran the risk that their transactions with the company might later be set aside if it turned out that their validity had been affected by some limitation in the company's constitution.[164]

These risks to third parties were moderated by the development of various rules. **3.55** The doctrine of corporate capacity or *ultra vires* was substantially abrogated by the European Communities Act 1972, section 9; the remaining pieces were abolished by the Companies Act 1989 and now the Companies Act 2006, section 39, which provides that 'the validity of an act done by a company shall not be called into question on the ground of lack of capacity by reason of anything in the company's constitution'.

As regards the risks to third parties arising from lack of authority on the part of **3.56** persons purporting to act on behalf of the company, the courts quickly developed a judicial gloss on the constructive notice rule, which drew most of its teeth. This was the rule established in *Turquand's case*,[165] also known as the 'indoor

---

[163] *Ernest v Nicholls* (1857) 6 HLC 401, 10 ER 351, HL. See too *Irvine v Union Bank of Australia* (1877) 2 App Cas 366, PC (presumption of notice applies to special resolution as well).

[164] See eg *Re Jon Beauforte (London) Ltd* [1955] Ch 131.

[165] *Royal British Bank v Turquand* (1856) 6 El & Bl 327, 119 ER 886; *Mahony v East Holyford Mining Co* (1875) LR 7 HL 869, HL.

management rule', which provides that a party dealing with a company in good faith is entitled to assume that all matters relating to the internal management of the company and procedures required by the articles have been duly complied with.[166] When coupled with the application to companies of agency principles,[167] this means that a third party dealing in good faith will in practice usually be able to rely on a transaction entered into by a corporate agent acting within the scope of their apparent authority; the doctrine of constructive notice, tamed by the *Turquand* rule, does not impede a third party's ability to say that they relied upon the appearance of an agent's authority.[168]

3.57 More extensive protection for third parties is given by the Companies Act 2006, section 40(1), which provides that 'in favour of a person dealing with a company in good faith, the power of the directors to bind the company, or authorise others to do so, shall be deemed to be free of any limitation under the company's constitution'. Under section 40(2)(b)(i), an outsider is not bound to enquire whether there is any limitation on the powers of the directors to bind the company or authorize others to do so; under section 40(2)(b)(ii), an outsider is presumed to have acted in good faith unless the contrary is proved; and under section 40(2)(b)(iii) an outsider shall not be deemed to have acted in bad faith merely because he actually knows that a transaction is beyond the directors' powers under the company's constitution. The cumulative effect of these sub-sections is that an outsider will be protected by section 40 unless the company is able to prove that he had some fraudulent intent. Section 40's predecessor provision, section 35A of the Companies Act 1985, referred to 'limitations on the power of the *board* of directors' (emphasis added). This left some uncertainty over the extent to which an outsider could rely on the section where dealing with an individual director or other employee.[169] Whilst the change from 'power of the board of directors' to 'powers of the directors' will surely raise the

---

[166] Thus, for example, a third party would, by virtue of the doctrine of constructive notice, be deemed to know of the existence of the board of directors' quorum provision in the constitution, but as its satisfaction or otherwise for any particular meeting is not a registrable matter, would be entitled to assume in good faith that it had been met when dealing with the board of directors.

[167] See eg *Freeman and Lockyer (a firm) v Buckhurst Park Properties Ltd* [1964] 2 QB 480, CA; *First Energy (UK) Ltd v Hungarian International Bank Ltd* [1993] 2 Lloyd's Rep 194, CA; *Criterion Properties plc v Stratford UK Properties LLC* [2004] UKHL 28; [2004] 1 WLR 1846, HL; *Hopkins v TL Dallas Group Ltd* [2004] EWHC (Ch) 1379; [2005] 1 BCLC 543 at [87]–[95].

[168] See *Northside Developments Pty Ltd v Registrar General* (1990) 170 CLR 146, noted by DD Prentice 107 (1991) LQR 14. Conversely, the third party cannot rely on the *Turquand* formula to clothe a corporate agent with greater power to bind the company than is comprised in that agent's actual or apparent authority: see *Kreditbank Cassel GmbH v Schenkers Ltd* [1927] 1 KB 826.

[169] The better view is that the 'or authorise others to do so' proviso of the section operated to confer no greater power to bind the company on individual agents than was comprised in their apparent authority at common law, at least in the absence of a specific act of authorization by the board.

question whether the new section extends to cover acts of individual directors, the Explanatory Notes state that the section simply 'restates' the old law.[170] Another difficulty with section 35A of the Companies Act 1985 was that the 'board' was not defined under independently of the company's constitution, leading to circular problems over whether, for example, quorum restrictions constituted a precondition for, or a 'limitation' on, the board's powers to act.[171] These circularity problems appear to be transported to the new section, as the 'powers of the directors' are likewise not defined independently of the company's constitution.

The protection afforded by section 40 of the Companies Act 2006 and its **3.58** predecessors is not intended, however, to allow directors and other corporate insiders to take advantage of the company. Section 41 thus provides that, where a transaction between a company and one of its directors, or a person connected with a director, relies for validity upon section 40, the company may elect to avoid it and/or impose personal liability on the counterparty and directors who authorized it.[172]

(d) Directors' duties and disabilities

(i) Appointment, remuneration, and removal of directors

Under the Companies Act 2006, section 154, private companies must have **3.59** at least one director, and public companies must have at least two. Moreover, at least one director of every company must be a natural person.[173] It is often provided by the articles of association of a registered company that the shareholders in general meeting should have the power to appoint the directors.[174] Executive directors often also enter service contracts with their companies, under which they are entitled to be paid for their services. However, many non-executive directors do not, and in the absence of an extrinsic service contract, problems might arise for a director if the body empowered by the articles to fix his remuneration failed to do so.[175] In these circumstances, he could not bring a contractual claim for payment under the articles, as these are deemed by the Companies

---

[170] *Companies Act 2006: Explanatory Notes*, 18.

[171] *Smith v Henniker-Major (a firm)* [2002] EWCA Civ 762; [2003] Ch 182. See also *EIC Services v Phipps* [2004] EWCA Civ 1069; [2004] 2 BCLC 489.

[172] Cf *Smith v Henniker-Major* at [128]–[129].

[173] Companies Act 2006, s 155.

[174] See DTI, Companies Act 2006 Implementation Consultative Document February 2007, Annex C: Companies (Model Articles) Draft Regulations, Sch 1, art 16; Sch 3, art 19. The board will also be given power to appoint directors (cf Companies (Tables A-F) Regulations 1985, SI 1985/805, Table A, Arts 73–80).

[175] For companies adopting the proposed new model articles, this would be the board: DTI, Companies Act 2006 Implementation Consultative Document February 2007, Annex C: Companies (Model Articles) Draft Regulations, Sch 1, art 18; Sch 3, art 22. Cf Companies (Tables A-F) Regulations 1985, SI 1985/805, Table A, Art 82.

Act 2006, section 33, to constitute a contract between the company and the members alone, and he would therefore be prevented by the rules on privity of contract from enforcing the articles against the company in his capacity as a director—even if he were also a member of the company.[176] Hence, he would have to ask the court instead to imply a contract extrinsic to the articles entitling him to payment,[177] or alternatively to make him a *quantum meruit* award on restitutionary grounds—although a restitutionary award would not be forthcoming if the court considered that he had effectively contracted out of his restitutionary rights.[178]

3.60   The Companies Act 2006, section 168, provides that a director may be removed from office before expiry of his term by an ordinary resolution of the members in general meeting, notwithstanding anything in the company's articles or in an extrinsic contract between the director and the company. If the members invoke section 168 to sack a director with a service contract, however, the company will be liable to pay damages for breach of an implied term of his contract, that the company will do nothing of its own accord to prevent the director from continuing in office.[179] But if the director has no service contract and has been appointed under the articles then he will be unable to recover damages on this basis.[180]

(ii) Directors' duties: an overview

3.61   Sections 170–77 of the Companies Act 2006 impose a range of general duties on directors, all of which are owed to the company.[181] These general duties are based upon, and apply in place of, rules of common law and equity that formerly imposed duties on directors.[182] Their codification was one of the most ambitious innovations in the Companies Act 2006. It is intended to render the law more accessible both to company directors for the purposes of compliance, and to shareholders for the purposes of enforcement.[183] The idea of codification, which

---

[176]   *Hickman v Kent and Romney Marsh Sheep Breeders Assoc* [1915] 1 Ch 881. The Contracts (Rights of Third Parties) Act 1999 does not apply to the statutory contract created by a company's constitution: ibid s 6(2).

[177]   As in eg *Ex p Beckwith* [1898] 1 Ch 324.

[178]   *Re Richmond Gate Property Co Ltd* [1965] 1 WLR 335, distinguishing *Craven-Ellis v Canons Ltd* [1936] 2 KB 403, CA, on this ground.

[179]   *Southern Foundries v Shirlaw* [1940] AC 701, HL; *Shindler v Northern Raincoat Co Ltd* [1960] 1 WLR 1038. On the assessment of the damages payable, see *Clark v B & T plc* [1997] IRLR 348.

[180]   *Read v Astoria Garage (Streatham) Ltd* [1952] Ch 637, CA.

[181]   Companies Act 2006, s 170(1).

[182]   ibid s 170(3).

[183]   On the background to codification, see Law Commission, *Company Directors: Regulating Conflicts of Interest and Formulating a Statement of Duties*, LCCP 153 (1998) and LC261 (1999); Company Law Review, *Final Report* (2001), Ch 3; DTI, *Company Law Reform*, Cm 6456 (2005), 21–24. See also DTI, *Companies Act 2006: Explanatory Notes* (2006), 45–54.

has been debated seriously since the early 1960s, was promoted in the 1990s by the Law Commission after a careful study of the effects of codification in other jurisdictions, and an empirical study of the perceptions of company directors in the UK indicated strong support for a statutory statement of duties.[184] The Law Commission originally proposed only a partial codification, so as to preserve freedom for further judicial development of directors' fiduciary duties; however the Company Law Review, whose thinking was followed by the government, took the view that further significant development of the law relating to directors' duties was unlikely, and preferred the additional accessibility associated with an exhaustive statutory statement of duties.[185] However, in order to preserve some flexibility and the possibility of future development, section 170(4) states that:

> The general duties shall be interpreted and applied in the same way as common law rules or equitable principles, and regard shall be had to the corresponding common law rules and equitable principles in interpreting and applying the general duties.

Thus developments in the law of trusts and fiduciary obligations can be reflected in the interpretation and application of directors' duties.[186]

A range of further, more specific, statutory obligations additionally regulate **3.62** directors in relation to particular circumstances.[187] Directors of quoted companies arealso expected to comply with corporate governance rules found in the UK Listing Rules,[188] the Combined Code on Corporate Governance,[189] and the Takeover Code.[190] If directors have an extrinsic service contract with the company, as is typically the case for executive directors, they will also owe contractual duties—although the Supply of Goods and Services Act 1982, section 13, which

---

[184] Just over 60% of survey respondents considered that it would be useful to have a statement of duties included in the companies legislation. S Deakin and A Hughes, 'Directors' Duties: Empirical Findings—Report to the Law Commissions' (1999), available at <www.lawcom.gov.uk/docs/153study.pdf.>, 31–33.

[185] DTI Company Law Review Steering Group, *Developing the Framework* (2000), 47; DTI, *Company Law Reform*, 20–21.

[186] *Companies Act 2006: Explanatory Notes*, 47.

[187] Companies Act 2006, Part 10, Chapters 3–6.

[188] For example, the requirement that transactions between the company and a related party must be approved by a shareholder vote, excluding any votes held by the related party: Listing Rules, rule 11.

[189] The Combined Code is annexed to the UK Listing Authority's Listing Rules, and listed companies are required to state in their Annual Reports whether they comply with it, and if they do not, to explain why not: Listing Rules, rule 9.8.6(4).

[190] The Takeover Code imposes extensive obligations on directors when their company is or may be in the process of a takeover. It is promulgated by the Panel on Takeovers and Mergers. Formerly a self-regulatory organization, the Panel was given statutory authority to make delegated legislation by the Companies Act 2006, Part 28 and moreover now has the power to request court enforcement of its rulings (*ibid* s 955). See generally, G Morse, 'Implementing the Thirteenth EC Directive—The End of Self-Regulation in Form Only' [2005] JBL 403.

inserts an implied term into contracts for the provision of services, that the supplier will perform the services with reasonable care and skill, does not apply to 'the services rendered to a company by a director in his capacity as such'.[191]

3.63 Breach of a duty owed by a director to a registered company is a civil wrong committed against the company. In a line of cases commencing with *Foss v Harbottle*,[192] the English courts held that the company is therefore the proper person to complain of such a breach of duty, even if the breach causes indirect loss to an individual shareholder by causing the value of his shareholding to diminish.[193] The control of the company's name in litigation is generally vested in the board of directors as part of their management powers.[194] If the nature of the alleged wrongdoing is such that the board is unable to make an independent decision, then the power to commence litigation in the company's name reverted to the shareholders in general meeting,[195] subject to the principle of majority rule.

3.64 The only true exception to this principle arose where a shareholder could show that the wrong committed against the company constituted a 'fraud', that the wrongdoers controlled the company,[196] and that a majority of the independent shareholders favoured litigation against them.[197] And in practice, none of these were easy to prove, albeit that 'fraud' was used in a specialized sense in this context to entail more than the deliberate misappropriation of company property,[198] and to include other breaches of duty in circumstances where the wrongdoer received some benefit from the breach.[199] The effect of the rule has also been to

---

[191] Supply of Services (Exclusion of Implied Terms) Order 1982, SI 1982/1771. At the time when the 1982 Act was passed, it was feared that s 13 would lend statutory weight to the argument that directors should be judged to a minimum objective standard of care and skill, which was not then understood to be the position at common law, although it has since been accepted that they should be judged to such a standard: see para 3.72.

[192] (1843) 2 Hare 461, 67 ER 89; *Mozley v Alston* (1847) 1 Ph 790, 41 ER 833; *Bailey v Birkenhead, Lancashire, and Cheshire Junction Railway Co* (1850) 12 Beav 433, 50 ER 1127; *Anglo-Universal Bank v Baragnon* (1881) 45 LT 362; *Burland v Earle* [1902] AC 83, PC; *Prudential Assurance Co Ltd v Newman Industries Ltd (No 2)* [1982] Ch 204, CA; *Stein v Blake* [1998] 1 All ER 724, CA.

[193] *Prudential Assurance v Newman Industries (No 2)*; *Johnson v Gore Wood & Co (a firm)* [2002] 2 AC 1.

[194] *Breckland Group Holdings Ltd v London & Suffolk Properties Ltd* [1989] BCLC 100.

[195] Consistently with the cases on 'board deadlock' such as *Barron v Potter* [1914] 1 Ch 895 and *Foster v Foster* [1916] 1 Ch 532, and with the result—albeit not the reasoning—in *Marshall's Valve Gear Co Ltd v Manning, Wardle & Co* [1909] 1 Ch 267. See also *Prudential Assurance Co Ltd v Newman Industries Ltd (No 2)* [1982] Ch 204, 221, CA, *per curiam*; *Regentcrest plc v Cohen* [2001] 2 BCLC 80. The issue is discussed in HC Hirt, 'The Company's Decision to Litigate Against its Directors' [2005] JBL 159.

[196] A requirement considered in *Prudential Assurance Co Ltd v Newman Industries Ltd* [1982] Ch 257, CA.

[197] *Smith v Croft (No 2)* [1988] Ch 114.

[198] As in *Menier v Hooper's Telegraph Works* (1874) 9 Ch App 350; *Cook v Deeks* [1916] 1 AC 554, PC.

[199] For example, compare *Pavlides v Jensen* [1956] Ch 565 with *Daniels v Daniels* [1978] Ch 406.

minimize the number of cases brought by registered companies against their directors for breaches of duty, with the result that the law in this area is now effectively moved forward in the rather different contexts of petitions by minority shareholders to remedy unfair prejudice,[200] complaining that their companies have been managed in an unfairly prejudicial manner,[201] and cases brought by the Secretary of State for Trade and Industry under the Company Directors Disqualification Act 1986.[202]

The formidable difficulties placed in the way of minority shareholder litigation **3.65** by the rule in *Foss v Harbottle* have been lessened by the new provisions on derivative actions contained in the Companies Act 2006, Part 11.[203] The new provisions shift responsibility for decision-making on corporate litigation away from the general meeting, and to some extent the board, in favour of the court. The starting point is that a shareholder may now seek permission from the court to pursue a derivative action in respect of any breach of directorial duty.[204] It is no longer necessary to show that the breach was one that constituted 'fraud', or that the perpetrators control the company. Only if the breach has in fact been authorized or ratified by the company is the action automatically barred.[205] Otherwise, the court must consider whether pursuit of the action would be something that a person acting to promote the success of the company would do:[206] if so, then the court has power to grant permission. In deciding whether to do so, the court must take into account the following factors:[207] (i) the good faith or otherwise of the shareholder seeking permission; (ii) the importance of the action from the standpoint of promoting the success of the company; (iii) the likelihood that the action will be ratified,[208] or, if it has yet to occur, authorized; (iv) whether the company has decided not to pursue the claim; (v) whether the

---

[200] Companies Act 2006, ss 994–996.

[201] For example, *Re London School of Electronics* [1986] Ch 211; *Re Purpoint Ltd* [1991] BCLC 491; *Re Macro (Ipswich) Ltd* [1994] 2 BCLC 354.

[202] As in eg *Re Westmid Packing Services Ltd* [1998] 2 All ER 124, CA; *Re Landmark Leasing plc* [1999] 1 BCLC 286; *Re Barings plc (No 5)* [2000] 1 BCLC 523, CA. See A Walters, 'Directors' Duties: The Impact of the Company Directors Disqualification Act 1986' (2000) 21 Co Law 110.

[203] For background, see Law Commission, *Shareholder Remedies* (Law Com No 246, 1997); DTI Company Law Review Steering Group, *Developing the Framework* (2000), 104–109, 123–134; *Completing the Structure* (2000), 98–101; DTI, *Company Law Reform*, Cm 6456 (2005), 24–25. For detailed analysis of the structure and operation of the new provisions, see *Companies Act 2006: Explanatory Notes*, 73–77.

[204] Companies Act 2006, s 260.

[205] ibid ss 263(2)(b), 263(2)(c).

[206] ibid s 263(2)(a).

[207] ibid ss 263(3), 263(4).

[208] Breaches of directors' duties may only be ratified by a majority of members excluding votes attached to shares held by the directors in question and persons connected with them: Companies Act 2006, s 239. See also HC Hirt, 'Ratification of Breaches of Directors' Duties: The Implications of the Reform Proposals Regarding the Availability of Derivative Actions' (2004) 25 Co Law 197.

shareholder seeking permission has an alternative remedy available to him in respect of the wrong complained of; and (vi) in particular, any evidence available as to the views of shareholders without an interest in the matter.

(iii) Fiduciary duties

3.66 At least since the eighteenth century, the directors of chartered and statutory corporations have been understood to occupy a position analogous to that of trustees, as controllers of other people's property,[209] and in the nineteenth century the directors of unincorporated joint stock companies were also held liable for 'breaches of trust' notwithstanding the fact that the company's property was formally vested in trustees under a deed of settlement.[210] Similarly, the directors of a registered company have often been spoken of as 'trustees' of the company's property even though ownership of the property is formally vested in the company,[211] and while the courts have always been aware of the differences between directors and trustees,[212] they have always also been aware of the similarities—and in particular, have always considered directors to owe fiduciary duties of fidelity and loyalty to their companies. The Companies Act 2006 makes clear that most of the codified general duties of directors remain fiduciary in character.[213]

3.67 Section 171 of the Companies Act 2006 provides that directors must act in accordance with the company's constitution,[214] and may only exercise powers for the purposes for which they are conferred.[215] The analogies here are with a trustee's duty to obey the terms of the trust, and (more loosely) with the equitable doctrine of fraud on a power.[216] An important difference from the latter is that

---

209 *Charitable Corp v Sutton* (1742) 2 Atk 400, 26 ER 642. See too *Mayor of Colchester v Lowten* (1813) 1 V & B 226, 35 ER 89; *A-G v Wilson* (1840) Cr & Ph 1, 41 ER 389; *York and North-Midland Railway Co v Hudson* (1845) 16 Beav 485, 51 ER 866.

210 *Benson v Heathorn* (1842) 1 Y & CCC 326, 62 ER 909; *Grimes v Harrison* (1859) 26 Beav 435, 53 ER 966.

211 *Russell v Wakefield Waterworks Co* (1875) LR 20 Eq 474, 479, CA, *per* Jessel MR; *Re Lands Allotment Co* [1894] 1 Ch 616, 638, CA, *per* Lindley LJ; both followed in *Belmont Finance Corp v Williams Furniture Ltd (No 2)* [1980] 1 All ER 393, 405, CA, *per* Buckley LJ. See too *Re Duckwari plc* [1999] Ch 253, 262, CA, *per* Nourse LJ.

212 See eg *Regal (Hastings) Ltd v Gulliver* [1967] 2 AC 134, 147, HL, *per* Lord Russell, following *Re Forest of Dean Coal Mining Co* (1878) 10 Ch D 450, 451–3, CA, *per* Jessel MR. See too LS Sealy, 'The Director as Trustee' [1967] CLJ 83.

213 Companies Act 2006 s 178(2). The exception is the duty of skill and care: see para 3.72. On the distinction between fiduciary and other duties, see *Bristol and West Building Society v Mothew* [1998] Ch 1, 18.

214 *Rolled Steel Ltd v British Steel Corp* [1986] Ch 246, 282–286, 297–298, 303–304; *Clark v Cutland* [2003] EWCA Civ 810; [2003] 2 BCLC 393 at [21]–[31]; *Criterion Properties plc v Stratford UK Properties LLC* [2004] UKHL 28; [2004] 1 WLR 1846.

215 *Howard Smith Ltd v Ampol Petroleum Ltd* [1974] AC 821, 835–837; *Lee Panavision Ltd v Lee Lighting Ltd* [1992] BCLC 22.

216 See R Grantham, 'The Powers of Company Directors and the Proper Purpose Doctrine' (1995) 5 King's College LJ 16; RC Nolan, 'The Proper Purpose Doctrine and Company Directors', in BAK Rider (ed), *The Realm of Company Law* (1998) 1.

courts will give much more leeway to directors than they will to trustees in determining what sorts of purposes are 'proper'. The purposes for which duties are conferred will be determined in the first instance by the company's constitution. Most powers are conferred for the purpose of carrying on the company's business, but where the company has non-commercial objects, this will constrain the purposes for which they may be exercised. Moreover, the exercise of directors' powers in a way so as to interfere with decision-making by the general meeting will be improper.[217]

The centrepiece of the new statutory regime is section 172: directors' duty to **3.68** promote the success of the company for the benefit of its members as a whole. This is a subjective duty, in the sense that it imposes an obligation to act in a way that the directors believe, not what the court believes, will promote the company.[218] Thus it will be breached by actions that are manifestly contrary to members' interests—such that no reasonable director could have believed it would benefit members.[219] However, section 172(1) stipulates a non-exhaustive list of factors to which directors must 'have regard' in so acting: (a) the likely consequences of any decision in the long term; (b) the interests of the company's employees; (c) the need to foster the company's business relationships with suppliers, customers and others; (d) the impact of the company's operations on the community and the environment; (e) the desirability of the company maintaining a reputation for high standards of business conduct; and (f) the need to act fairly as between members of the company. Moreover, in coming to decisions about the exercise of their powers, directors must exercise an independent judgment.[220] The structure of section 172 reflects what the Company Law Review termed an 'enlightened shareholder value' approach:[221] the obligation to consider factors other than the immediate benefit of members is purely *instrumental* to benefiting the members as a whole. This is further reinforced by the fact that only members may appoint and remove directors, and only members may enforce the duty.[222] Whilst section 40 will protect counterparties to transactions where

---

[217] See cases cited above, n 215.

[218] *Re Smith and Fawcett Ltd* [1942] Ch 304, 306; *Regentcrest plc v Cohen* [2001] 2 BCLC 80 at [120]–[123].

[219] *Hutton v West Cork Rly Co* (1883) 23 ChD 654, 671; see also *Extrasure Travel Insurances Ltd v Scattergood* [2003] 1 BCLC 598 at [87]–[91], esp at [90].

[220] Companies Act 2006, s 173.

[221] See JE Parkinson, *Corporate Power and Responsibility* (1993); Company Law Review Steering Group, *The Strategic Framework* (1999), 33–53; *Completing the Structure* (2000), 33–36; A Keay, 'Section 172(1) of the Companies Act 2006: An Interpretation and Assessment' (2007) 28 Co Law 106.

[222] Nevertheless, the mandatory phrasing of the list may raise the possibility of a procedural challenge to directorial decision-making on the basis that they failed to take into account relevant considerations: see *Hunter v Senate Support Services Ltd* [2004] EWHC 1085; [2005] 1 BCLC 175 at [165]–[187].

directors merely exceed their powers under the constitution, this will not extend to circumstances where the counterparty is aware that the directors are *abusing* their powers, in the sense of acting in a way other than what they believe so as to promote the success of the company.[223]

3.69 Should a company be unable to pay its debts, then the interests of creditors must become paramount in the directors' concerns. On the one hand, directors face potential liability for wrongful trading;[224] on the other, the 'success of the company' which they are bound to promote by section 172 will become the interests of its creditors when the company is in financial difficulties.[225]

3.70 As fiduciaries, the directors of a registered company must avoid situations in which there is a reasonable possibility of conflict between their personal interest and the interests of the company.[226] This rule, which applies in particular to the exploitation of any property, information or opportunity,[227] is strictly enforced against directors, even if they have acted in good faith and their actions have enured to the benefit of the company.[228] However, it is open to directors to avoid potential liability by seeking authorization from the other directors (discounting the votes of those interested) or the general meeting.[229] In giving such authorization, the company can be understood as making a determination that there is no *actual* conflict between its interests and those of the director.[230] The purpose of the rule is thus prophylactic:[231] to encourage directors both to avoid putting their own interests ahead of those of the company, and to refer situations in which there is any doubt to the company for resolution.[232]

3.71 Two special cases of conflict of interest are treated separately from the general obligation in section 175. The first is a prohibition on the receipt by directors of

---

223 See Companies Act 2006, s 40(2)(b); see also *International and Agencies Ltd v Marcus* [1982] 3 All ER 551, 559–560; *Rolled Steel Products (Holdings) Ltd v British Steel Corp* [1986] Ch 246, 295, 304; DD Prentice, 'Group Indebtedness' in CM Schmitthoff and F Wooldridge (eds), *Groups of Companies* (1991), 55, 62; see also Nolan, above n 216, 6.

224 Insolvency Act 1986 s 214.

225 Companies Act 2006 s 172(3); *Kinsela v Russell Kinsela Pty Ltd* (1986) 4 NSWLR 722, 730; *West Mercia Safetywear Ltd v Dodd* (1989) 4 BCC 30, 33; *Official Receiver v Stern (No 2)* [2001] EWCA Civ 1787; [2002] 1 BCLC 119 at [32].

226 Companies Act 2006, ss 175(1), 175(4)(a). See also *Bhullar v Bhullar* [2003] EWCA Civ 424; [2003] 2 BCLC 241 at [27]–[30].

227 See eg *Cook v Deeks* [1916] 1 AC 554, PC; *Regal (Hastings) Ltd v Gulliver* (n 212 above); *IDC v Cooley* [1972] 2 All ER 162; *Queensland Mines Ltd v Hudson* (1978) 52 ALJR 399, PC.

228 As in eg *Regal (Hastings) Ltd v Gulliver* (n 212 above).

229 Companies Act 2006, ss 175(4)(b), 175(5), 175(6); s 180(4)(a); *Regal (Hastings) Ltd v Gulliver* (n 212 above).

230 See J Armour and MDC Conaglen, 'Directorial Disclosure' (2005) 64 CLJ 48.

231 See *Lindsley v Woodfull* [2004] EWCA Civ 165; [2004] EWCA Civ 720; [2004] 2 BCLC 131 at [30].

232 See Law Commission, *Company Directors: Regulating Conflicts of Interest and Formulating a Statement of Duties*, LCCP 153 (1998), paras 3.47–3.50.

any benefits from third parties (that is, not mediated through the company) that are linked to his role as director,[233] and which might reasonably be regarded as giving rise to a conflict of interest.[234] The second relates to contracts or transactions with the company, in which a director has a direct or indirect personal interest. For such transactions, the general duty to avoid conflicts of interest does not apply;[235] instead section 177 imposes a duty on the director to disclose the nature and extent of his interest to the board before they consider whether or not to enter into the transaction.[236] The board should then take this information into account in deciding whether, and on what terms, to enter the transaction. This also marks a change from the old law. Prior to the 2006 Act, so-called 'self-dealing' transactions would have fallen within the scope of directors' general duty to avoid conflicts of interest, and so interested directors would have needed to obtain the company's authorization to (their interest in) the transaction to avoid its being liable to be set aside.[237]

(iv) The duty of skill and care

Directors also owe their companies a statutory duty to exercise reasonable care, **3.72** skill and diligence in the performance of the functions entrusted to them in relation to the company.[238] This duty has its origins in analogous duties imposed simultaneously in tort and in equity.[239] Until late in the twentieth century, the standard of care demanded of directors in the discharge of these duties was set at a low level, reflecting the courts' disinclination to double-guess business managers' decisions with the benefit of hindsight,[240] and their view that if shareholders chose to appoint incompetent managers, that was their own look-out.[241] More recently, though, directors have come to be judged to a significantly higher standard, and are now expected to carry out their duties with at least the skill and

---

[233] Companies Act 2006, s 176. Although the company may never approve such payments if made directly, they could be structured, with the company's approval, as payments *from* the company to the director.

[234] See Companies Act 2006 s 176(4).

[235] Companies Act 2006 s 175(3).

[236] Companies Act 2006, s 177. Section 182 imposes an equivalent duty to disclose directors' interests in transactions that have already occurred.

[237] *Aberdeen Railway Co v Blaikie Bros* (1854) 1 Macq 461; *Hely-Hutchinson v Brayhead Ltd* [1968] 1 QB 549, CA. The better view was that this was part of the more general duty to avoid conflicts of interest, as opposed simply to a disability: *Gwembe Valley Development Co Ltd v Koshy (No 3)* [2003] EWCA Civ 1048; [2004] 1 BCLC 131 at [104]–[108], cf *Movitex Ltd v Bulfield* [1988] BCLC 104, 119–121.

[238] Companies Act 2006, s 174; see also Insolvency Act 1986 s 214(5).

[239] *Daniels v Anderson* (1995) 16 ACSR 607, NSWCA. See also *Henderson v Merrett Syndicates Ltd* [1995] AC 145, 205, HL.

[240] *Howard Smith Ltd v Ampol Petroleum Ltd* [1974] AC 821, 835, PC, *per* Lord Wilberforce. Cf *Carlen v Drury* (1812) 1 V & B 154, 158, 35 ER 61, 62, *per* Lord Eldon LC, quoted in para 3.06.

[241] *Turquand v Marshall* (1869) LR 4 Ch App 376; *Daniels v Daniels* [1978] 1 Ch 406.

care that might reasonably be expected of any director occupying a similar position in a similar company, and more is expected of them if their personal qualifications and attainments suggest that they should be capable of more.[242] In particular, it is recognized that whilst directors will in practice need to delegate much decision-making power to employees, they remain responsible for the effective screening of delegates and for maintaining a general oversight of the company's business.

(v) Remedies

3.73 The importance of the origins of directors' duties is most pronounced as regards remedies: the Companies Act 2006 provides that the general statutory duties shall have the same remedial consequences as the corresponding common law rule or equitable principle. Thus the company will ordinarily be able to obtain an account of profits made by a director breaching the duty to avoid conflicts of interest.[243] Although the pre-existing law is modified in relation to corporate transactions in which a director is personally interested, it seems clear that the statutory intention is for remedies that would have applied in relation to such transactions where they gave rise to a potential conflict of interest to apply *mutatis mutandis* to transactions where a director has failed to make a timely disclosure of his interest. Thus the company will be entitled to rescind such a transaction and an account of profits from the director;[244] moreover, it should in principle be entitled to claim equitable compensation in the alternative.[245]

(e) The relationship between the members

3.74 The relationship between the members of a registered company, their right to a say in the formulation of company policy, and their right to a financial return on their investment in the company, are all usually governed by the

---

242 *Dorchester Finance Co Ltd v Stebbing* [1989] BCLC 498 (decided in 1977); *Re Produce Marketing Consortium Ltd (No 2)* [1989] BCLC 520; *Norman v Theodore Goddard* [1992] BCC 14; *Re D'Jan of London Ltd* [1993] BCC 646; *Re Barings plc (No 5)* [2000] 1 BCLC 523, 535–6, CA, *per curiam*, affirming Jonathan Parker J at first instance: [1999] 1 BCLC 433, 483–9. Cf *Daniels v Anderson* (1995) 16 ACSR 607, NSWCA (directors who held themselves out as possessing greater abilities than they actually possessed should be judged to this higher standard).

243 This is, strictly speaking, a personal remedy (see *Ultraframe (UK) Ltd v Fielding* [2005] EWHC 1638 (Ch); [2005] All ER (D) 397 at [1511]–[1517]). However, the company will be entitled to a proprietary claim to the traceable proceeds of property taken from, or improperly diverted from, the company: see *A-G for Hong Kong v Reid* [1994] 1 AC 32.

244 Provided the company has not affirmed the transaction after discovering the director's breach of duty, and that the rights of third parties have not supervened: *Lagunas Nitrate Co v Lagunas Syndicate* [1899] 2 Ch 392, CA; *Transvaal Lands Co v New Belgium (Transvaal) Land & Development Co* [1914] 2 Ch 488, CA. See also R Nolan, 'Directors' Self-Interested Dealings: Liabilities and Remedies' (1999) 3 CFILR 235.

245 *Gwembe v Koshy* at [142]–[147]; see also MDJ Conaglen 'Equitable Compensation for Breach of Fiduciary Dealing Rules' (2003) 119 LQR 246.

company's constitution. Under the Companies Act 2006, section 33, the provisions of the constitution take effect as a contract between the members and the company, and between the members and each other.[246] Under section 21, however, the articles can be unilaterally altered by the company if 75 per cent of the voting members agree to this, and such a 'special majority' of the voting members therefore have the means at their disposal to improve their own position within the company at the expense of the minority. To protect minority shareholders in this situation, the English courts have developed a rule that the majority may only vote to alter the articles if they genuinely believe this to be in the best interests of the company as a whole.[247] Whilst the subjective nature of this test means that it will restrain only the most egregious of abuses, it is open to minority shareholders to bargain for greater protection at the point in time at which they invest in a company. This can be reflected in the constitution through class rights,[248] quorum restrictions,[249] or differential voting rights,[250] so as to limit the ability of the majority to alter the constitution to the detriment of the minority. Greater limitations on the majority's power, in the absence of such express provisions, may be apt to confer an unbargained-for veto power on the minority.[251]

The Companies Act 2006, section 994, also gives minority shareholders the **3.75** right to petition the court in the event that their company is being managed in a fashion which is 'unfairly prejudicial' to themselves, and to ask for an injunction or a buy-out order under section 996. This remedy has proved to be very popular, notwithstanding the costs of mounting an action, as it may be used to enforce understandings or agreements between all the members, even if they are not reflected in the company's constitution. However, in *O'Neill v Phillips*, the House of Lords sought to encourage earlier settlement of such cases by suggesting that refusal of a reasonable offer by the majority to purchase the minority's shares would in most cases be a barrier to relief by the minority.[252]

---

[246] *Hickman v Kent or Romney Marsh Sheepbreeders Association* [1915] 1 Ch 881; *Rayfield v Hands* [1960] 1 Ch 1.

[247] *Allen v Gold Reefs of West Africa Ltd* [1900] 1 Ch 656, 671; *Shuttleworth v Cox Bros & Co (Maidenhead) Ltd* [1927] 2 KB 9, CA; *Greenhalgh v Arderne Cinemas Ltd* [1951] Ch 286, CA; *Rights and Issues Investment Trust Ltd v Stylo Shoes Ltd* [1965] 1 Ch 250.

[248] See Companies Act 2006, ss 629–640.

[249] See *Union Music Ltd v Watson* [2003] 1 BCLC 453.

[250] See *Bushell v Faith* [1970] AC 1099.

[251] It is therefore doubtful whether the Australian case of *Gambotto v WCP Ltd* (1995) 127 ALR 417, HCA, in which a more interventionist approach was adopted, should be followed: see *Citco Banking Corporation NV v Pusser's Ltd* [2007] UKPC 13 at [19]–[20].

[252] [1999] 2 BCLC 1, 16–17, *per* Lord Hoffmann (setting out the characteristics of a reasonable offer).

(f) The extent of the members' liability for the company's debts

3.76 The Companies Act 2006, section 3, distinguishes between three types of registered company: a company limited by shares, a company limited by guarantee, and an unlimited company. The members of an unlimited company are fully liable to its creditors in the event that it is wound up and has insufficient assets to meet its liabilities. However, the Insolvency Act 1986, section 74(2)(d), provides that when a company limited by shares is wound up, no member is liable to make a larger contribution to its assets than the amount (if anything) which remains unpaid on his shares. Correspondingly, section 74(2)(e) provides that when a company limited by guarantee is wound up, no contribution is required from any member exceeding the amount he has undertaken to contribute under the terms of his guarantee.

(3) Limited Liability Partnerships

(a) Historical background

3.77 The limited liability partnership (LLP) form was introduced into English law by the Limited Liability Partnership Act 2000, with effect from 6 April, 2001. The first new generally available form of business entity for over a century, the LLP was in fact a hastily-designed response to lobbying by professional firms (in particular, firms of accountants), whose members were alarmed by the prospect of personal ruin, and by the spiralling costs of professional indemnity insurance,[253] following some well-publicized professional negligence actions brought in respect of auditing work.[254] The resulting form is not, however, restricted to professional firms. It has proved reasonably popular: by 2006, nearly 16,700 LLPs had been registered in England and Wales.[255]

3.78 Quite unlike ordinary partnerships,[256] LLPs are conceptualized as separate legal entities from their members.[257] Whilst in this regard they are correctly classified as aggregate corporations created by statute, they differ from registered companies

---

[253] Professional indemnity insurance premiums increased by a factor of 40 in the UK between 1984 and 1993: R Morris, 'Limiting Auditors' Exposure to Risk' (1996) Palmer's In Company (May issue) 1.

[254] See esp *ADT Ltd v BDO Binder Hamlyn* [1996] BCC 808, which was settled before going to appeal for around £50 million, £20 million more than BDO's insurance cover. See too *Barings plc (in admin) v Coopers & Lybrand (a firm)* [1996] 1 BCLC 427, CA; *BCCI (Overseas) Limited (in liq) v Price Waterhouse (a firm)* [1998] Ch 84. And for discussion, see J Freedman and V Finch, 'Limited Liability Partnerships: Have Accountants Sewn Up the "Deep Pockets" Debate?' [1997] JBL 387.

[255] DTI, *Companies in 2005–6* (2006), Table E4.

[256] See para 3.108.

[257] Limited Liability Partnerships Act 2000, s 1(2) ('A limited liability partnership is a body corporate (with legal personality separate from that of its members)'.)

in that their internal relations between members are governed by default rules modelled on partnership law,[258] and they are for tax purposes treated like partnerships.[259]

(b) Constraints on their power to act, and members' liability

An LLP has unlimited legal capacity, and its members are each agents of the entity.[260] Third parties who deal with members who exceed their actual authority to act are protected by statute so long as they are not aware that the member does not in fact have authority, or do not know that he is a member of the firm.[261] Similarly, the entity is vicariously liable for any liability incurred by a member as a result of any wrongful act or omission.[262] The members of an LLP have limited liability, being required to contribute in its insolvency only to the extent to which they have agreed.[263] There is some uncertainty concerning the extent to which a member acting in the course of the firm's business may be held to be personally liable for negligent misstatement,[264] although this may be capable of resolution by applying an analogy with the position for liability in contract.[265]

3.79

(4) Open-Ended Investment Companies

(a) Background

Towards the end of the twentieth century, participants in the UK collective fund investment industry lobbied for the introduction of a new legal form through which they could undertake their business, arguing that the form which they had used for this purpose since the 1930s, the unit trust,[266] was not readily understood by investors from civil law countries, and that this placed them at a competitive disadvantage in overseas investment retail markets.[267] The maintenance of

3.80

---

258 ibid s 5; Limited Liability Partnerships Regulations 2001, reg 7. This flexibility is reduced somewhat by the need to comply with accounting and audit rules based on those applicable to registered companies, such disclosure being seen as the *quid pro quo* for limited liability: ibid reg 3. See SR Cross, 'Limited Liability Partnerships: Problems Ahead' [2003] JBL 268, 276–7.

259 Limited Liability Partnerships Act 2000, ss 10–13.

260 ibid ss 1(3), 6(1).

261 ibid ss 6(2), 6(3).

262 ibid s 6(4).

263 Limited Liability Partnerships Regulations 2001, reg 5 and Sch 3 (applying modified version of Insolvency Act 1986, s 74, to LLPs).

264 See J Freedman and V Finch, 'The Limited Liability Partnership: Pick and Mix or Mix-up?' [2002] JBL 475, 483–488.

265 See n 159 above and text thereto.

266 Unit trusts are briefly considered in para 3.114.

267 For general discussion, see Securities and Investment Board, *Open Ended Investment Companies*, Consultative Paper 93 (1995); EZ Lomnicka, 'Open-Ended Investment Companies— A New Bottle for Old Wine', in BAK Rider (ed), *The Corporate Dimension* (1998) 47.

share capital provisions of the companies acts made the registered company an unsuitable alternative,[268] and so the open-ended investment company (OEIC) was introduced into English law in 1996,[269] by regulations made under the European Communities Act 1972, section 2(2).[270] These were drafted in accordance with the terms of the UCITS Directive,[271] with the result that OEICs can only have as their sole object 'collective investment in transferable securities of capital raised from the public', and cannot invest in futures, options, deposits, money market instruments, or real property.

(b) How OEICs are conceptualized

3.81 Like registered companies, on which they were modelled, OEICs are conceptualized as reified artificial persons to which the shareholders assign assets in exchange for a set of contractual rights. They are created by registration with the Financial Services Authority, and unlike registered companies they can be brought into being before they have any shareholders or property. Shares in an OEIC are different from shares in a registered company in so far as their issue, redemption, and pricing are not subject to the same constraints, and an OEIC's constitutional structure differs from that of a registered company (and is closer to that of a unit trust) because its property must be vested in a depositary which holds the property on trust for the OEIC, and it must have a single authorized corporate director whose role is similar to that of a unit trust's fund manager. The code governing the activities of OEICs substantially replicates the terms of the Companies Act 2006, ss 39–40, with the result that a third party's dealings with an OEIC may not be set aside on the ground of *ultra vires* or want of directors' authority unless the third party has acted in bad faith.[272]

(5) *Building Societies*

(a) Historical background

3.82 From the end of the eighteenth century, there was a chronic housing shortage in many English towns and cities, as people moved there in search of work.

---

[268] But cf Companies Act 2006, s 833, which permits investment companies registered thereunder to use capital profits as well as revenue profits to repurchase their own shares.

[269] For discussion, see EZ Lomnicka, 'The Single European Passport in Financial Services', in BAK Rider and M Andenas (eds), *Developments in European Company Law, Vol 1/1996* (1997) 181, 191–3. See also FSA, *The Collective Investment Scheme Information Guide* (2006).

[270] See now Financial Services and Markets Act 2000, ss 236, 262; Open-Ended Investment Companies Regulations 2001, SI 2001/1228, as amended by Open-Ended Investment Companies (Amendment) Regulations 2005, SI 2005/923.

[271] Council Directive (EEC) 85/611 on Undertakings for Collective Investment in Transferable Securities [1985] OJ L375/3 (as amended: see Consolidated text: 1985L0611—30/04/2004).

[272] Open-Ended Investment Companies Regulations 2001, regs. 38–39. See also the discussion in Lomnicka (n 267 above) 59–62.

Moreover, workers on low wages often found it difficult to borrow money to build or buy houses for themselves. Building societies were conceived as an answer to these problems. Such societies administer a continuing fund whose primary (and until recently, sole) function is to match up a theoretically unlimited number of borrowers, who wish to raise the money to build or buy a house, with a corresponding number of investors who wish to lend their money against such security.[273] Investors can acquire membership of the society by subscribing for 'shares' upon which interest is paid in accordance with the society's rules, and out of the funds acquired in this way the society can make advances to borrowing members secured on property for their residential use. Building societies can also raise money by borrowing from non-members. They are not required to frame their rules in such a way that borrowing members are characterized as possessing shares in the society (although many do), and they may allow people to become members without holding any shares.

An investing member's shares in a building society differ in several fundamen- **3.83** tal respects from shares in a registered company.[274] Shares in a registered company are transferable rights against the company; ownership of such shares typically brings a proportionate right to vote in the company's general meeting; each share typically gives its owner the right to participate in the profits of the company by payment of dividends; their value is related inter alia to the capital value of the company's assets; and the maintenance of capital rules which apply to registered companies place strict limits on the circumstances in which new shares can be issued and existing shares repurchased by the company. In contrast, shares in a building society are not usually transferred by the investing members to other people; their value does not fluctuate with the success of the business or the size of its capital assets; 'neither borrowing nor shareholding (or investing) members receive a dividend out of profits comparable to the dividends paid by [registered] companies';[275] an investing member may normally withdraw his share by demanding repayment whenever he chooses, as a building society's capital is much more fluid than that of a registered company;[276] and the voting rights bestowed on the members of a building society are not related to the number of shares which they have, since each member entitled to vote is given one vote and one vote only,

---

[273] For descriptions of nineteenth-century permanent building societies, see eg *Grimes v Harrison* (1859) 26 Beav 435, 442, 53 ER 966, 968–9, *per* Romilly MR; *Leeds PBBS v Mallendane* [1897] 2 QB 402, CA. These were distinguished from (now-defunct) 'terminating societies', the existence of which came to an end once their objectives were fulfilled.

[274] Cf *Liquidator of Irvine and Fullarton Property Investment and Building Soc v Cuthbertson* (1905) 8 F 1, 6, Ct of Sess (Inner House) *per* Lord Dunedin.

[275] *Cheltenham and Gloucester BS v BSC* [1995] Ch 185, 191, *per* Nicholls V-C.

[276] The calculations undertaken to determine whether a society meets the statutory capital adequacy requirements do not relate to its share capital in the same way as the maintenance of capital rules affecting registered companies.

regardless of the number of shares he has—indeed, since 1997, it has been possible for borrowing members to vote even though they possess no shares at all.[277] These rules on voting are in accordance with the principle of mutuality which remains the essence of building societies, as does the continuing statutory requirement that the principal purpose of a building society must be the making of loans secured on residential property which are funded substantially by the members.[278]

3.84 At the end of the nineteenth century, there were around 2,200 permanent building societies in the UK; by 2005, there were 63.[279] As late as 1975, the building society sector held 74 per cent of the market in net advances for house purchase; in 2006, building societies' market share had fallen to below 20 per cent.[280] The fall in the number of societies was due in part to merger activity, and in part to a rash of 'demutualizations' in the 1980s and 1990s. These demutualizations occurred when the members of various building societies voted to convert them into registered companies, having been empowered to do so for the first time by the Building Societies Act 1986, sections 97–102.[281] One reason for this was that many societies had taken advantage of the relaxation of the statutory constraints on their activities which was also effected by the 1986 Act, to engage in a wider range of banking activities than had previously been permitted, and their members then wished to avoid the constraints on their activities which remained by converting them into registered companies subject to the less stringent regulatory controls applicable to banks. Another reason was the members' desire to secure for themselves accumulated surpluses within the societies which their managers might otherwise have been unwilling to pay out in the form of loyalty bonuses or other distributions.[282] The prospect of such pay-outs led

---

[277] Building Societies Act 1997, s 43 and Sch 7, para 57(3), inserting Building Societies Act 1986, Sch 2, para 23.

[278] Building Societies Act 1986, s 5(1).

[279] House of Commons Treasury Committee, *Ninth Report for 1998–9: Demutualization* (HC 605, 1999) Appendix 7, para 2; J Cook, S Deakin and A Hughes, 'Mutuality and Corporate Governance: the Evolution of UK Building Societies Following Deregulation' (2002) 2 JCLS 110, 117; FSA, *Building Society Statistics 2006*, Table 1. See too J Vaughan, 'Building Societies', in D Milman, *Regulating Enterprise* (1999) 93; Sir T Lloyd *et al.* (eds), *Wurtzburg and Mills' Building Society Law* (looseleaf edn, August 1999 issue) paras 1.12ff.

[280] Treasury Committee, ibid, paras 5 and 6; Appendix 7, paras 2 and 21; FSA, *Building Society Statistics 2006*, Table 6.

[281] Considered in *Abbey National BS v BSC* (1989) 5 BCC 259; *Cheltenham and Gloucester BS v BSC* [1995] Ch 185; *BSC v Halifax BS* [1997] Ch 255. Ten of the fifteen largest building societies in existence in 1986 had demutualized by the end of 1999: Treasury Committee (n 279 above) para 2.

[282] Entitlement to surplus assets in a society's winding up or dissolution is a matter governed by the rules: see eg *Re West London and General PBS* (1898) 78 LT 393, and see too Building Societies Act 1986, Sch 2, para 3(4), Table, item 14. During the lifetime of a society, however, the application of its funds would normally be a matter for its officers to determine, and 'in

to the widely reported phenomenon of 'carpetbagging' in the 1990s, as many people invested the minimum deposit necessary to acquire membership of numerous societies, and then voted to convert them into registered companies in the hope of a windfall. It is debatable whether these restructurings will prove to have been in the long-term public interest: some have argued that because building societies do not have to generate profits for distribution to shareholders, they can afford to pay higher interest rates to their investors and charge lower rates to their borrowers than banks, and that their conversion into companies has therefore operated to the long-term disadvantage of small borrowers and investors.[283] In any event, changes in the terms of the existing building societies' articles of association, whereby those opening new accounts were required to assign to charity any potential windfall benefits from demutualization, appear to have deterred speculators and prevented the demutualization of any more societies since 2000.[284]

(b) How building societies are conceptualized

Originally, building societies were unincorporated associations, a status which **3.85** the first piece of regulatory legislation to affect them, the Benefit Building Societies Act 1836, did nothing to change. Under the Building Societies Act 1874, however, it was provided that new societies had to be incorporated in accordance with the terms of the statute, and that existing societies had the option of becoming incorporated or not. Under the present regime of the Building Societies Act 1986, authorized building societies are by definition incorporated under the 1986 Act or previous legislation, and unincorporated building societies are now therefore a thing of the past.[285] Since the enactment of the 1874 Act, incorporated societies have been regarded as artificial persons whose capacity to act is derived entirely from the relevant legislation: in Lord Selborne LC's words, an incorporated building society:[286]

> is not a joint stock company; still less is it a common law partnership; but it is a society of a special kind, formed and regulated under particular Acts of Parliament for special purposes.

---

practice,. . .profits are not distributed as such to the members': *Cheltenham and Gloucester BS* ibid 191, *per* Nicholls V-C.

[283] See Cook et al, above n 279; All-Party Parliamentary Group for Building Societies & Financial Mutuals, *Windfalls or Shortfalls? The True Cost of Demutualisation* (2006).

[284] Cook et al, above n 279, 122–123; Building Societies Association, *Building Societies Takeovers and Flotations* (2005) (<www.bsa.org.uk/consumer/factsheets/100010.htm>).

[285] Building Societies Act 1986, ss 5(3) and (4) and 119(1).

[286] *Brownlie v Russell* (1883) 8 App Cas 235, 248, HL.

(c) Constraints on building societies' power to act

3.86 Prior to the 1986 Act, there was only one object which a building society was permitted to pursue, namely raising a fund from members' subscriptions out of which advances could be made to members on security by way of mortgage on real property. Any activities undertaken by a society with some different object in view were *ultra vires* and void,[287] and third parties dealing with a society could be caught out by the fact that they were deemed to be aware of limitations on the society's borrowing powers in its rules.[288] Under the present statutory regime, however, while it remains the case that a building society is a statutory corporation which is constrained as to its principal object,[289] and which must observe a statutory lending limit and a statutory funding limit,[290] a society may also specify in its memorandum whatever further objects and powers it chooses. In this regard, building societies are now therefore much closer to registered companies than was previously the case, and this is also true of the rules governing *ultra vires* acts by building societies, which are contained in Part II of Schedule 2 of the 1986 Act.[291] Paragraph 16(1) of Schedule 2 is substantially similar to the Companies Act 2006, section 39, providing that the validity of an act done by a building society is not to be called into question on the ground of a lack of capacity by reason of anything included in the society's memorandum.

(d) Liability of building society members

3.87 Schedule 2 of the 1986 Act also specifies the extent to which the members of a building society are liable to meet the society's liabilities: it is provided by paragraph 6 that in the event that a society cannot meet its liabilities, investing members shall be liable for them only to the extent that they have already paid, or are liable to pay, the society for their shares,[292] and that borrowing members shall be liable only to the extent of the debt which they owe the society.

(6) Industrial and Provident Societies

(a) Historical background

3.88 Like building societies, industrial and provident societies began as working-class self-help organizations in the late eighteenth century. They emerged out of

---

[287] As in eg *Sinclair v Brougham* [1914] AC 398, HL.

[288] *Chapleo v Brunswick PBS* (1881) 6 QBD 696, 712–3, CA, *per* Bagallay LJ.

[289] Building Societies Act 1986, s 5(1) and (2).

[290] ibid ss 6 and 7.

[291] Paras 16–18, as substituted by the Building Societies Act 1997.

[292] For discussion of the meaning of the statutory precursor to this provision, see *Re Sheffield and South Yorkshire BS* [1889] 22 QBD 470, criticized in *Wurtzburg and Mills* (n 279 above), para 11.26. See too *Sibun v Pearce* (1890) 44 Ch D 354, CA; *Re United Service Share Purchase Soc* [1909] 2 Ch 537.

the workers' co-operative movement, and they are associations whose members engage in commercial and industrial activity for their mutual benefit or for the benefit of the wider community. They too were originally treated as unincorporated associations, but it was then provided by the Industrial and Provident Societies Act 1862, that an industrial and provident society which registered in accordance with the terms of the statute was deemed to acquire corporate personality, and to be entitled to sue and be sued, and to own property in its own name.[293] This continues to be the case under the present legislation, the Industrial and Provident Societies Act 1965, section 3.[294] In 2006, there were 9,456 registered Industrial and Provident Societies.[295]

(b) Constraints on their power to act, and members' liability

Prior to 2003, third parties who entered a transaction with an industrial and **3.89** provident society which lay outside its objects were liable to be caught out, as the transaction could be set aside as *ultra vires* the society.[296] However, a scheme modelled on the third party protection provisions of the Companies Acts was introduced by the Co-operatives and Community Benefit Societies Act 2003, and third parties dealing with an industrial and provident society in good faith are now entitled to rely on the validity of their transactions.[297] The statutory rules governing the liability of members for an industrial and provident society's debts, contained in section 57 of the 1965 Act, are also similar to those which govern the liability of a registered company's members. However, they are complicated by the fact that industrial and provident societies are permitted to let their members withdraw their share capital,[298] something which registered companies may not generally do.[299]

(7) Community Interest Companies

The Community Interest Company (CIC) form was introduced in 2005,[300] **3.90** following concern by the government that there was a lack of appropriately

---

[293] Property vested in a society's trustees prior to its acquisition of corporate status by registration became vested in the society after registration: *Queensbury Industrial Soc v Pickles* (1865) LR 1 Ex 1.

[294] The full history of the legislation affecting industrial and provident societies is helpfully summarized in I Snaith, 'Regulating Industrial and Provident Societies: Co-operation and Community Benefit', in D Milman, *Regulating Enterprise* (1999) 163, 163–7.

[295] DTI, *Companies in 2005–6* (2006), Table E3.

[296] See *Halifax BS v Meridian Housing Association Ltd* [1994] 2 BCLC 540.

[297] Industrial and Provident Societies Act 1965, ss 7A-7F, inserted by Co-operatives and Community Benefit Societies Act 2003.

[298] Industrial and Provident Societies Act 1965, ss 1(1)(b) and 7, and Sch 1, para 9.

[299] For discussion, see Snaith (n 294 above) 174–6.

[300] Companies (Audit, Investigation and Community Enterprise) Act 2004, Part 2 and Schs 3–8; Community Interest Company Regulations 2005, SI 2005/1788.

structured forms for use by organizations intended to serve public, but non-charitable, purposes.[301] By-mid 2007, there were 919 registered CICs.[302] To be registered as a CIC, a company must satisfy the Regulator of Community Interest Companies that it meets the 'community interest test': namely, that a reasonable person would consider its activities are being carried on for the benefit of the community.[303] A CIC must also incorporate provisions in its constitution for an 'asset lock' to ensure that its assets are kept in the furtherance of community interest activities. These prevent the CIC from alienating its assets for less than full value, except (with the consent of the Regulator) to another CIC or charity; moreover, caps are imposed on the payment of dividends or performance-related interest.[304] This limitation, which was in part inspired by the controversies surrounding demutualization in the building society sector, is intended to reassure those advancing funds that they remain employed for the purposes for which they were advanced, and will not at some point in the future be paid out to members. As a CIC is formed as a registered company, with the additional constraints described above. CIC members therefore enjoy limited liability to the same extent as members of a registered company. Moreover, despite the extensive restrictions which must be contained in a CIC's constitution, its basis in the registered company form means that third parties dealing with it in good faith will receive the same protection as they would under the companies legislation.[305]

(8) European Economic Interest Groupings

3.91 The European Economic Interest Grouping (EEIG)[306] is a legal entity given European-wide status by the EC EEIG Regulation.[307] It was introduced into

---

[301] See Cabinet Office Strategy Unit, *Private Action, Public Benefit: A Review of Charities and the Wider Not-For-Profit Sector* (2002), 49–58. However, there is some scepticism as to the reality of this need: see eg S Cross, 'Community Interest Companies: A Tangled Corporate Web' (2003) 19 SLT 157.

[302] Regulator of Community Interest Companies, *List of Community Interest Companies* (2007).

[303] Companies (Audit, Investigation and Community Enterprise) Act 2004, ss 35, 36–39. Companies promoting political or policy-oriented purposes are deemed not to satisfy the test: Community Interest Company Regulations 2005, regs 3, 6.

[304] Companies (Audit, Investigation and Community Enterprise) Act 2004, s 30; Community Interest Company Regulations 2005, Part 6. See generally, Regulator of Community Interest Companies, *Guidance Notes*, Ch 6 (2007).

[305] See paras 3.55-3.57.

[306] For general discussion, see M Anderson, *European Economic Interest Groupings* (1990); D Van Gerven and CAV Aalders, *European Economic Interest Groupings: The EEC Regulation and its Application in the Member States of the European Community* (1990); M O'Neill, 'When European Integration Meets Corporate Harmonisation' (2000) 21 Co Law 173, 177.

[307] Council Regulation (EC) 2137/85 [1985] OJ L199/1.

English law by the EEIG Regulations 1989,[308] and in 2006 there were 185 EEIGs registered in Great Britain.[309] Under English law, EEIGs are essentially joint ventures endowed with artificial personality as bodies corporate,[310] with the result that they have the capacity to enter contracts, own property, and sue and be sued in their own names. Unlike the shareholders of a registered company, however, the members of an EEIG are jointly and severally liable for its debts, and can be sued directly for these, provided that a demand for payment has first been made against the EEIG itself, and the demand not satisfied.[311] The purpose of an EEIG must be to facilitate or develop the economic activities of its members, or to improve or increase the results of those activities, and it may not make profits for itself; furthermore, its activities must be related to the economic activities of its members, and must not be more than ancillary to them.[312] Any actions purportedly taken by an EEIG which go beyond these limitations will be *ultra vires* and void. However, a manager of an EEIG may bind it to a transaction with a third party even though the transaction is *ultra vires*, provided that the third party neither knew nor ought to have known that the transaction fell outside the EEIG's objects.[313] An EEIG may be wound up as though it were an unregistered company under Part V of the Insolvency Act 1986.[314]

(9) European Public Companies

The Societas Europea (SE), or European public company, was introduced in 2004.[315] It is intended to facilitate cross-border mergers and corporate restructuring, and may only be employed following a combination of two or more entities from different member states. Originally conceived as an organizational form to be entirely constituted by European law, political disagreements between member

3.92

---

308 SI 1989/638.

309 DTI, *Companies in 2005–6* (2006), Table E3. At the end of 1997, around 888 EEIGs had been set up across Europe, mostly for co-operative ventures between self-employed professionals: F Blanquet, Chef D'Unité, at DG XV, European Commission, quoted in J Bisacre, 'A European Perspective on Small Business and the Law', in BAK Rider and M Andenas (eds), *Developments in European Company Law, Vol 2/1997* (1999) 87, 91, n 19.

310 EEIG Regs 1989 (n 308 above) reg 3.

311 EC Reg 2137/85, art 24(2).

312 ibid art 3(1).

313 ibid art 20.

314 EEIG Regs 1989 (n 308 above) reg 19.

315 Council Regulation 2157/2001 on the Statute for a European company (SE) [2001] OJ L294/1; Council Directive 2001/86 supplementing the Statute for a European company with regard to the involvement of employees [2001] OJ L294/22, which were implemented in the UK by the European Public Limited-Liability Company Regulations 2004 (SI 2004/2326), in force 8 October 2004. See generally V Edwards, 'The European Company—Essential Tool or Eviscerated Dream?' (2003) 40 CML Rev 443; C Teichmann, 'The European Company—A Challenge to Academics, Legislatures and Practitioners' (2003) 4 German LJ 309.

states lead to many decades of debate.[316] The ultimate resolution was for a very limited skeleton to be enacted in European legislation, and for the detail to be fleshed out by reference to the domestic public company statute of the member state in which the SE has its registered office—meaning, in effect, that there are as many versions of the SE as there are member states.[317] An SE with its registered office in the UK—and by the middle of 2006, only one company had exercised this option[318]—therefore has legal personality, and is subject to the same rules of capacity and attribution, as a domestic registered company. Similarly, its members enjoy limited liability to the same degree as in respect of an ordinary registered company. However, the SE does have two important differences from a domestic public company. A particular innovation was the ability to change the registered office—and hence the relevant governing law—after formation,[319] although recent developments in European corporate mobility make this less unique.[320] Another important feature is that the SE must afford rights to its employees commensurate with the strongest protection they enjoyed under either of the laws of the constituent companies.[321]

C. Quasi-Corporations

(1) Trade Unions

(a) How trade unions are conceptualized

3.93 The extent to which English trade unions can be characterized as artificial persons is a question with a turbulent history which aptly illustrates the point that artificial personality is not always perceived by associates as a desirable benefit, and can instead be seen as a threat to their autonomy as social and political actors. In Wedderburn's words, the question whether a trade union is an artificial person is

---

[316] The idea was first proposed in 1959: see LCB Gower, *Principles of Modern Company Law* (4th edn, 1979), 88–89.

[317] See eg SE Regulation, art 10. There are 84 references to domestic law in the SE Regulation: see M Siems, 'The Impact of the European Company (SE) on Legal Culture' (2005) 30 EL Rev 431, 432.

[318] DTI, *Companies in 2005–6* (2006), Table E3.

[319] SE Regulation, art 8. See L Enriques, 'Silence is Golden: The European Company Statute as a Catalyst for Company Law Arbitrage' (2004) 4 JCLS 77, 79–84.

[320] See Case C-411/03, *SEVIC Systems AG* [2006] OJ C36/5; see also European Parliament and Council Directive 2005/56/EC on cross-border mergers of limited liability companies [2005] OJ L310/1.

[321] SE Directive, arts 3–5. See PL Davies, 'Workers on the Board of the European Company?' (2003) 32 Ind LJ 75.

politically charged, since it relates:[322]

> to the ease with which legal doctrines can be used in the courts, to attack the auton-
> omy of unions via their property, in actions for damages and injunctions, or fines or
> sequestration of property for disobedience to court orders.

At common law, trade unions were regarded as unlawful bodies under the doc- **3.94**
trine of restraint of trade, and for this reason the English courts did not permit
them to bring legal actions, even if they were registered under the friendly societies
legislation and so possessed the capacity to sue.[323] This state of affairs was brought
to an end by the Trade Union Act 1871, section 3, which provided that the purposes of a trade union were not unlawful by reason merely of being in restraint of
trade.[324] Under section 6 of the 1871 Act, an administrative register of trade
unions was also set up, and some minor tax benefits and administrative gains followed from registration. However, this was not made compulsory, and nothing
was said in the section about the legal status of registered unions. Contemporaries
therefore assumed that the 1871 Act did not affect the status of trade unions as
unincorporated associations of human individuals, whose pooled assets were held
by trustees (something which the statute made obligatory), and who possessed no
artificial personality when considered as a group.

Thirty years on, to the surprise and dismay of trade unionists, the House of Lords **3.95**
held in *Taff Vale Railway Co v Amalgamated Society of Railway Servants*,[325] that
entry on the register operated to fix trade unions with artificial personality, with
the result that they could be sued in tort and their property sequestered to meet
their tort liabilities. This decision triggered a wave of industrial agitation which
eventually led to the enactment of the Trade Disputes Act 1906, section 4, which
afforded trade unions statutory protection against civil liability in tort. In
Amalgamated Society of Railway Servants v Osborne,[326] the House of Lords then also
held that the doctrine of *ultra vires* applied to unions as 'quasi-corporate' bodies,
to prohibit their engaging in 'political' activity, a prohibition which was later partially removed by a further piece of legislation, the Trade Union Act 1913.[327]

---

[322] Lord Wedderburn, 'Trade Union Democracy and State Regulation', in Lord Wedderburn,
Labour Law and Freedom (1995) 180, 183. Further discussion of the material considered in this part
can be found in Lord Wedderburn, *The Worker and the Law* (3rd edn, 1986) 521ff and 718ff.

[323] See eg *Hornby v Close* (1867) LR 2 QB 153. The acquisition of the right to sue and be sued
by registration as a friendly society is discussed in para 3.100.

[324] See now the Trade Union and Labour Relations (Consolidation) Act 1992, s 11.

[325] [1901] AC 426, HL. See too *Cotter v National Union of Seamen* [1929] 2 Ch 58, CA.

[326] [1910] AC 87, HL.

[327] This statute was later amended by the Trade Union Act 1984, ss 12–19, now re-enacted as
the Trade Union and Labour Relations (Consolidation) Act 1992, ss 71–86. These sections stipulate
that unions may engage in political activity provided that each member is permitted to contract out
of making political contributions to union funds without disadvantage to his standing and entitlements as a member.

Following these decisions, it was therefore possible to say that trade unions possessed artificial personality to some extent, but it remained 'a somewhat moot point whether [trade unions were] properly to be regarded as legal personalities distinct from their individual members. . .or as having no separate juristic personality, but nevertheless being entitled [by statute] to sue and be sued in their own name'.[328]

3.96 Matters were then brought to a head once more by the enactment of the Industrial Relations Act 1971. Section 74 of the 1971 Act offered full recognition as corporate bodies to those unions which registered on a new register, which was also voluntary, although an incentive to register was provided by making certain liberties to organize and to strike contingent on registered status. However, most TUC-affiliated unions resisted this bait, and following a change of government the 1971 Act was repealed by the Trade Union and Labour Relations Act 1974. Under the relevant sections of the 1974 Act a compromise was struck, and trade unions were accorded some of the incidents of corporate status without full corporate capacity. These sections were subsequently re-enacted by the Trade Union and Labour Relations (Consolidation) Act 1992, and form the basis of the present English law governing the legal status of trade unions. Under section 10(1) of the 1992 Act, a trade union is deemed to be capable of making contracts, of suing and of being sued in its own name in proceedings relating to property, or founded on contract or tort or any other cause of action, and of being a defendant in criminal proceedings. Under section 12, a trade union is also deemed to be capable of being the equitable beneficial owner of property, its property must be held on trust for the union and not for its members, and judgments, awards, and orders may be enforced against any property held in trust for the union.[329] It is further provided by section 10(2), that a trade union 'shall not be treated as if it were a body corporate except to the extent authorized by [these sections]',[330] and it has been held that a union, unlike a company, therefore lacks personality of the sort which can be protected in an action for defamation.[331] Labour organizations which do not fall within the terms of the statutory definition of a 'trade union' contained in section 1 are not affected by the terms of the 1992 Act, and are treated as unincorporated associations.[332]

---

328 *Knight and Searle v Dove* [1964] 2 QB 631, 635, *per* Mocatta J.

329 See too *Hughes v TGWU* [1985] IRLR 382: individual members have neither a severable individual interest nor an interest in common in union property; but cf Trade Union and Labour Relations (Consolidation) Act (TULR(C)A) 1992, s 23(2)(b): an award of damages against a union may not be recovered by enforcement against 'property belonging to any member of the union otherwise than jointly or in common with the other members'.

330 TULR(C)A, s 10(2).

331 *EETPU v Times Newspapers Ltd* [1980] QB 585, 598–601, *per* O'Connor J.

332 As in eg *Boddington v Lawton* [1994] ICR 478.

(b) How trade unions act

As a result of the historical twists and turns described above, the law governing **3.97**
the question how a union may be fixed with liability for the acts and omissions
of its officers is now in a patchy state. Following the House of Lords' decision in
the *Taff Vale* case, the courts developed the rule that unions should be liable for
the torts of all their officials provided that they were acting within the scope
of their actual authority, and that their actions were not *ultra vires* the union.[333]
However, this law was superseded by the enactment of the Trade Disputes Act
1906, section 4, which gave unions a statutory immunity from actions in tort
which lasted until the enactment of the Industrial Relations Act 1971. Those
unions which did not register under the 1971 Act were stated by section 154
to have the capacity to be sued in their own names, subject to the proviso in
section 167(9), that they would be liable only in respect of actions taken by their
'officials' or 'agents' acting in that capacity and within the scope of their authority.
And according to Lord Wilberforce in *Heatons Transport (St Helens) Ltd v TGWU*,
a 'wide range of matters [could] be taken into account in determining scope
of authority' in this context, for:[334]

> [t]he authority may be conferred (1) by the [union] rules expressly or by implica-
> tion (2) under the rules,. . . by express or implied delegation (3) by office held. . .(4)
> 'or otherwise', which must include custom and practice [and] the course of dealing.

The Trade Union and Labour Relations Act 1974, section 14, restored the unions' **3.98**
statutory immunity, but this section was then repealed in turn by the Employment
Act 1982, under section 15 of which it was further provided that a union could be
fixed with tort liability for inducing breach of contract or conspiracy if—but only
if—the acts complained of had been authorized or endorsed by a 'responsible person'. However, the union would not be liable for the actions of such a person if he
was prevented by the rules from authorizing or endorsing the act in question, or if
the act was repudiated by the union. A 'responsible person' was defined to mean
the union's principal executive committee, any other person empowered by the
rules to authorize or endorse the acts in question, the president or general secretary, any other employed official, and any committee of the union to whom an
employed official regularly reports. Section 15 was later re-enacted in a slightly
modified form as the statutory sections which now govern this question, the Trade
Union and Labour Relations (Consolidation) Act 1992, sections 20 and 21.

---

[333] *Giblan v National Amalgamated Labourers' Union of GB and Ireland* [1903] 2 KB 600,
CA; *Denaby and Cadeby Main Collieries Ltd v Yorkshire Miners' Assoc* [1906] AC 384, HL; and
other cases considered in BA Hepple, 'Union Responsibility for Shop Stewards' (1972) 1 ILJ 197,
201–6.
[334] [1973] AC 15, 101, HL.

3.99 Several issues about the operation of these statutory sections and their relationship with the old common law rules remain unresolved, perhaps reflecting the fact that the closing years of the twentieth century saw little industrial action in the UK.[335] It is unclear whether a 'responsible person' must have taken some positive step to affirm strike action before it can relevantly be said that he has authorized or endorsed it, or whether an omission to discipline unofficial strike action by union members should also count as authorization.[336] It is unclear whether a union can ever be liable for an act done by an official which was *ultra vires* the union (although in contrast to the old common law position it clearly can be held liable for its officials' *intra vires* but unauthorized actions). And it is unclear whether the pre-1906 common law rules, or the rules laid down in the *Heatons Transport* case, should apply where it is sought to fix a union with liability for torts other than those mentioned in section 20, for example the tort of nuisance.[337]

(2) Friendly Societies

(a) How friendly societies are conceptualized

3.100 Friendly societies, like building societies and industrial and provident societies, are self-help organizations with a long history. They are mutual insurance associations which first emerged in the late eighteenth century. They provide their members with benefits in the case of sickness, death, or bereavement, funded out of the members' subscriptions. Between 1911 and 1945, they acquired a significant role in the embryonic British welfare state, as deliverers of pensions and medical insurance benefits; since then, their numbers have fallen away, from 2,740 in 1945 to less than 300 in 2007.[338] Like building societies and industrial and provident societies, friendly societies were permitted to register themselves under a series of statutes in the nineteenth century culminating in the Friendly Societies Act 1896. However, the effect of registration on their legal status during this period was less clear cut. They were not expressly stated by the 1896 Act to acquire corporate status by registration, and they were required to vest their property in trustees,[339]

---

335 For further discussion of these questions, see KD Ewing, 'Industrial Action: Another Step in the "Right" Direction' (1982) 11 ILJ 209, 218–23; and for discussion of the means by which a union can be fixed with contractual liability to its members through the actions of its officials, see P Elias and K Ewing, *Trade Union Democracy, Members' Rights and the Law* (1987) 48–51.

336 See *Express & Star Ltd v NGA (1982)* [1985] IRLR 455; *Gate Gourmet Ltd v Transport and General Workers Union* [2005] EWHC 1889 (Ch); [2005] All ER (D) 117, at [19]–[21].

337 Compare eg *Thomas v NUM (South Wales Area)* [1986] 1 Ch 20 with *News Group Newspapers Ltd v SOGAT '82 (No 2)* [1986] IRLR 337.

338 Open University Friendly Societies Research Group, <www.open.ac.uk/socialsciences/friendly-societies-research-group/friendly-societies-for-beginners.php>.

339 Friendly Societies Act 1896, ss 25 and 47.

in whose names all proceedings relating to the property had to be brought,[340] suggesting that they continued to be regarded as unincorporated associations. However, they were permitted by the statute to sue and be sued in their own names, and the courts' findings at the start of the twentieth century with regard to the effect of registration on trade unions[341] suggested by way of analogy that registered friendly societies might also possess some quasi-corporate status. Accordingly, it was later held that a libel action might be brought against a registered friendly society in its own name,[342] and that it could 'own property [in equity],... employ servants,... enter into contracts,... [and] commit wrongs'.[343] The Friendly Societies Act 1974 did nothing to resolve this conceptual uncertainty, and the status of friendly societies registered under this statute therefore remains obscure.

Under the Friendly Societies Act 1992, section 5, however, it was then expressly **3.101** stated that friendly societies which registered in accordance with its provisions should acquire full corporate status. For the purposes of the classificatory scheme adopted in this chapter, friendly societies registered under the 1992 Act therefore properly belong in Part B.[344] However, while the 1992 Act obliged new friendly societies to incorporate themselves by registration in accordance with its provisions, it did not repeal the 1974 Act, and it permitted friendly societies registered under the earlier statute to continue as such.[345]

(b) Constraints on their power to act, and members' liability

Friendly societies registered under the 1974 Act are treated as unincorporated **3.102** associations for the purposes of determining which human individuals are empowered to act for them, and subject to what constraints, and also for the purposes of determining the extent of their members' liability.[346] In contrast, a friendly society incorporated under the 1992 Act is required to specify its purposes in a memorandum of association,[347] but in the event that it enters into an *ultra vires* transaction for value with a third party who has no actual knowledge of the society's lack of capacity, the transaction is deemed to lie within the society's capacity so far as the third party is concerned.[348] The same rule also applies where a third party has dealt with the society's committee of management, and the committee

---

[340] ibid s 94.
[341] See para 3.95.
[342] *Longden-Griffiths v Smith* [1951] 1 KB 295.
[343] *Payne v Bradley* [1962] AC 343, 356, HL, *per* Lord Denning.
[344] See paras 3.29–3.31.
[345] Friendly Societies Act 1992, s 93(2).
[346] Cf discussion at paras 3.112-3.113.
[347] Friendly Societies Act 1992, s 7.
[348] ibid s 8.

has acted beyond its powers as specified in the society's rules.[349] The members of an incorporated friendly society are liable for its debts to no greater extent than the amount of any outstanding subscription they owe to the society.[350]

D. Unincorporated Bodies

(1) Partnerships and Limited Partnerships

(a) Historical background

3.103 As has been discussed above,[351] the principal associative forms employed by English traders in the eighteenth century were the joint stock company and the partnership. Each was conceptualized as an aggregation of individuals, but the joint stock company was larger, and it was presumed in the case of a partnership that 'each partner was an active trader in a joint concern, who had full power to act as the agent of his fellow partners, and who consequently had unlimited liability for the undertakings of the concern'.[352] As an associative form, the partnership was well-adapted to the requirements of commercial life in eighteenth-century England, where 'most manufacturing enterprise was conducted either by single capitalists, or by small partnerships (often centred on the family), which raised their initial capital from family and friends, and then out of the profits they accumulated over a long period of time'.[353] However, as industrial growth accelerated in the nineteenth century, the need grew for commercial concerns to raise money from outside investors, and the law of partnership was slow to adapt to this change. In the late eighteenth century, the defining feature of a partnership had been held to be the sharing of profits by each partner,[354] with the result that lenders to a firm who received a rate of interest in proportion to the profits could be fixed with personal liability for its debts as 'sleeping partners'. This was consistent with the usury laws of the time, as a lender might otherwise have been enabled to lend money to a firm at a higher rate of interest than was legally permitted, but it was unpopular with the mercantile community, since it made investment in a partnership business unattractive to the owners of capital who had no wish to participate in management.

---

[349] ibid s 9.
[350] ibid Sch 3, para 8.
[351] See para 3.44.
[352] M Lobban, 'Corporate Identity and Limited Liability in France and England 1825–67' (1996) 25 Anglo-American LR 397, 399.
[353] ibid 400.
[354] *Grace v Smith* (1775) 2 Wm Bl 997, 96 ER 587; *Waugh v Carver* (1793) 2 H Bl 235, 126 ER 525.

In the mid-nineteenth century, therefore, at the same time that reforms were **3.104** introduced to confer the benefits of limited liability upon the members of registered companies, attempts were made to change the legal definition of a partnership, first by the House of Lords in *Cox v Hickman*,[355] and then by Parliament, with the Partnership Amendment Act 1865. This statute provided that sharing of profits should not be conclusive evidence of partnership, and that lenders, or sellers of goodwill, in consideration of a share of the profits should instead be viewed as deferred creditors. Indeed, when the 1865 Act was enacted, Parliament was thought to have gone even further, and to have legalized a type of limited partnership whose members would be shielded from liability for the firm's debts even if they had actively participated in management. However, the courts soon held that this was not the case,[356] and it also became apparent that the statute had actually worsened the position of sleeping partners by making them deferred creditors on bankruptcy.

English law was also slow to resolve the problems for partners that they could **3.105** not ask the courts to intervene in disputes with their fellow partners without first seeking a dissolution,[357] and that they all had to be joined to a suit against a third party.[358] But even so, the partnership remained the dominant form of business organization in England until the late nineteenth century, when it was overtaken by the registered company, ironically enough at around the time of the Partnership Act 1890, a codifying statute which remains in force, and which rendered the rules of partnership much more certain than they had been hitherto.[359] However, the partnership form has continued to be widely used (intentionally or unintentionally) by small and medium-sized enterprises.[360] From the time of the introduction of the registered company form, large-number partnerships (from 1856, more than 20 partners) were required to incorporate themselves as registered companies, so as to minimize the incidence of the practical problems concerning litigation to which large-number joint stock partnerships gave rise.[361] However, the litigation problems with large partnerships having been solved

---

[355] (1860) 8 HLC 268.

[356] *Syers v Syers* (1876) 1 App Cas 174, HL; *Pooley v Driver* (1876) 5 Ch D 458.

[357] See the cases cited in nn 7 and 10 above.

[358] See the cases cited in Lobban (n 352 above) 404, nn 19 and 20.

[359] The 1890 Act is not a complete code, and s 46 expressly preserves the pre-existing rules of equity and common law in so far as they are not inconsistent with the express provisions of the Act.

[360] At the start of 2005, there were around 520,000 partnerships, as compared to 1,080,000 trading companies (public and private): DTI, *Small and Medium Enterprise Statistics for the United Kingdom 2005* (2005) Table 2.

[361] Law Commission, *Partnership Law: A Joint Consultation Paper* LCCP 159 (2000), 57–59; DTI, *Removing the 20 Partner Limit* URN 01/752 (2001), 9–12.

by innovations in civil procedure,[362] the 20-partner limit became an anachronism, and was finally abolished in 2002.[363]

3.106 Sleeping partners as such were finally given the protection of limited liability by the Limited Partnerships Act 1907, which authorized the formation of a distinct associative form, the limited partnership. By this time, however, the House of Lords had confirmed in *Salomon v A Salomon & Co Ltd*[364] that even a small number of associates were entitled to use the registered company form, and Parliament had begun actively to encourage this by exempting 'one-man' and other 'small private companies' from certain publicity requirements, under the Companies Acts 1900 and 1907. As a result, the limited partnership failed to catch on, and in 2006, there were only 13,426 limited partnerships in Great Britain.[365] As a form, it proved to be unsuited to the needs of a group of commercial associates who all intended to participate in the business, and those associates who wished to invest their money in a business without actively participating in management were far more likely to do so through the medium of a registered company. However, they have developed a niche role as tax-effective means of structuring investment in alternative asset classes, such as venture capital and private equity.[366]

3.107 The law relating to partnership and limited partnerships was recently reviewed by the Law Commission,[367] who proposed a wide-ranging modernization of the law intended to make it more accessible to small business users. However, the government has decided only to implement the proposals for limited partnerships.[368] These proposals, which focus in particular on the needs of private investment funds, who are the principal users of the limited partnership form, will clarify the rights and obligations of limited partners and give those forming limited partnerships the option of either creating an entity with separate legal personality, or of continuing to use the existing unincorporated association framework.[369]

---

362 See n 375 below.
363 Regulatory Reform (Removal of 20 Member Limit in Partnerships etc.) Order 2002, SI 2002/3203.
364 [1897] AC 22, HL.
365 DTI, *Companies in 2005–6* (2006) Table E2.
366 See Law Commission, *Limited Partnerships Act 1907: A Joint Consultation Paper*, LCCP 161 (2001), 2–4; J Armour, 'Law, Finance and Innovation' in JA McCahery and L Renneboog (eds.), *Venture Capital Contracting and the Valuation of Hi-Tech Firms* (2003), 133.
367 See Law Commission, *Partnership Law*, LCCP 159 (2000); Cm 6015 (2003). See also DTI, *Reform of Partnership Law: The Economic Impact* (2004).
368 'Partnership Reform', Statement of Ian McCartney MP, Minister for Trade Investment and Foreign Affairs, 20 July 2006. The responses of consultees to the proposals for partnership were mixed: see DTI, *Summary of Responses to the Consultation on Reform of Partnership Law: The Economic Impact* (2006).
369 See Law Commission, *Partnership Law* Cm 6015 (2003), Parts XV-XIX, esp at 298–302.

(b) How partnerships are conceptualized

The English courts have repeatedly stated that a partnership is nothing more **3.108** than a contractual and fiduciary relationship between two or more persons[370] who have agreed to engage in business together with a view to making a profit, and they have repeatedly denied that the members of a partnership have any collective personality. Thus, for example, Farwell LJ said in *Sadler v Whiteman* that 'in English law a firm as such has no existence; partners carry on business both as principals and as agents for each other within the scope of the partnership business; [and] the firm name is a mere expression, not a legal entity'.[371] In practice, though, it can be easy to lose sight of this legal orthodoxy: partners are commonly referred to as 'a firm';[372] they often trade under a distinctive firm-name which is unrelated to their own names, prepare annual profit-and-loss accounts for the firm as a whole, and maintain a bank account under the firm-name; and firms often continue to trade for a long time under the same name notwithstanding the death or departure of partners and the arrival of new ones.[373] Moreover, 'English law. . .allows certain rights and privileges to the partnership which come near to a recognition of personality':[374] partners should, as respects claims relating to the partnership business, ordinarily sue and be sued in their firm's name;[375] they can sue in respect of a libel on the firm;[376] until recently income-tax assessments were raised on firms rather than their individual partners;[377] and firms can

---

370 Using the word in its legal sense: a registered company can enter a partnership agreement with other persons.

371 [1910] 1 KB 868, 889, CA.

372 Partnership Act 1890, s 4(1).

373 Technically, though, a partnership is dissolved every time a partner retires or dies, and a new partnership brought into existence. The departing partner or his estate will be entitled to withdraw his share of the assets, but disruption to the firm's continuing business is often reduced by clauses in the partnership deed, providing for valuation of his share and deferred payment.

374 *Major (Inspector of Taxes) v Brodie* [1998] STC 491, 502, *arguendo* (opinion of Professor Gretton), contrasting the position under Scots law, which 'begins by recognizing the separate juristic personality of the firm, and then cuts it back somewhat by certain derogations'. Cf *Purdue v Customs and Excise Commissioners* [1994] VATTR 387, 389, London VAT Tribunal, referring to a VAT-registered partnership as a 'quasi-juristic person'.

375 CPR 7.2A, PD7 5A.1-5A.3 (claims by or against partners must be brought in firm name unless it is inappropriate to do so). When used in litigation the firm's name is said to be merely shorthand for the names of all the partners at the date of the accrual of the relevant cause of action, and its use does not affect the substantive legal position that the firm has no personality of its own: *Von Hellfeld v Rechnitzer* [1914] 1 Ch 748, 754, CA, *per* Phillimore LJ; *Meyer & Co v Faber (No 2)* [1923] 2 Ch 421, 435, CA, *per* Lord Sterndale MR; *Mephistopheles Debt Collection Service (a firm) v Lotay* [1994] 1 WLR 1064, 1068, CA, *per* Nourse LJ; *Ernst & Young (a firm) v Butte Mining plc (No 2)* [1997] 2 All ER 471, 477, *per* Lightman J.

376 See the cases cited in RCI'A Banks (ed), *Lindley & Banks on Partnership* (18th edn, 2002) 438, n 12.

377 Income and Corporation Taxes Act 1988, s 111. Cf the amended version of the same section which was substituted by the Finance Act 1994, s 215(1), and which has applied to all firms with effect from the tax year 1997/1998. It has been questioned whether the previous 'separate entity'

be wound up or enter administration as unregistered companies under the regime of the Insolvency Act 1986.[378]

(c) Liability of the members for dealings with third parties

3.109 The Partnership Act 1890, section 5, provides that each partner is an agent of all the others and that they are accordingly bound by those of his acts which are done 'in carrying on in the normal way business of the kind carried on by the firm'. Under ss 5 and 8, they can escape liability in connection with his dealings with a third party on the ground that they were unauthorized only if the third party knows of the limit on his authority. Furthermore, they can limit their liability to a third party in respect of his authorized acts only by entering an express agreement to this effect with the third party,[379] for a provision to this effect written into the partnership agreement will be ineffective even if the third party knows of it.[380]

(2) Unincorporated Associations

(a) How unincorporated associations are conceptualized

3.110 It has been said that unincorporated associations are created under English law whenever two or more people legally bind themselves to one another to pursue a common purpose other than the pursuit of profit, in accordance with a set of agreed rules governing control of the association and the application of its funds.[381] Since the courts have shown themselves willing to imply the existence of such a contract,[382] however, it may be more accurate to say that an unincorporated association comes into being whenever a group of associates creates an organizational system, from the existence of which the courts are prepared to infer that the associates intend to be legally bound to one another.[383] Once this has happened, the members' rights between themselves are governed exclusively by the terms of the association's rules.[384] No formal steps such as registration are needed

---

treatment afforded to firms went to underlying principles of liability rather than forming part of the calculatory 'machinery': *MacKinlay (Inspector of Taxes) v Arthur Young McClelland Moores & Co* [1990] 2 AC 239, 252–3, HL, *per* Lord Oliver, discussed in *Major (Inspector of Taxes) v Brodie* [1998] STC 491, 510, *per* Park J.

[378] Insolvent Partnerships Order 1994, SI 1994/2421, arts 6–7, as amended.
[379] *Hallett v Dowdall* (1852) 18 QB 1, 118 ER 1.
[380] *Greenwood's case* (1854) 3 De GM & G 459, 43 ER 180.
[381] *Conservative and Unionist Central Office v Burrell* [1982] 1 WLR 522, 525, CA, *per* Lawton LJ.
[382] As in eg *Abbott v Sullivan* [1952] 1 KB 189, 194, CA, *per* Evershed MR.
[383] RW Rideout, 'Limited Liability of Unincorporated Associations' (1996) 49 CLP 187, 191–2.
[384] *Re Recher's WT* [1972] Ch 526, 38, *per* Brightman J, followed in *Re Buck's Constabulary Widows' and Orphans Fund Friendly Soc (No 2)* [1979] 1 WLR 936.

to bring an unincorporated association into being, and there is no general restriction upon the associates' power to end the association, to add new members, or to alter their purposes.[385] So long as their common purpose is not illegal, the associates may combine to do anything they wish, be it the pursuit of personal pleasure or advantage, or some outside purpose, charitable or non-charitable.[386] Unincorporated associations are distinguishable from partnerships because partners associate with one another for the shared purpose of acquiring gain, and certain groups who would otherwise be treated as unincorporated associations have been ascribed special status by statute: for example, limited liability partnerships,[387] industrial and provident societies,[388] trade unions,[389] and friendly societies.[390] Unincorporated associations are not considered to be artificial persons under English law, but are seen as amorphous collections of individuals, and the conversion of an unincorporated association into a registered company would therefore be 'no mere formality, but a change of substance'.[391]

The rules of an unincorporated association typically provide that the members **3.111** should contribute to the association's funds by way of subscription, and they may also acquire property from outsiders. Because unincorporated associations lack the capacity to hold property, this must instead be held in one of the following ways. The members can all hold the property as joint tenants, a method which would create practical difficulties for a large group. The property can be held on trust by trustees for the benefit of present and future members, a method which would lead to the absolute vesting of the property in the individual members at the time when the association was wound up, or on the expiry of a relevant perpetuity period, under the Perpetuities and Accumulations Act 1964, section 4(4). The property can be held on trust by trustees for the purposes of the association, provided that these are charitable (if not, such a trust would be void).[392] Or the property can be held by all the members in their capacity as members, with the result that they are contractually bound to apply it in accordance with the rules of the association, and so for the sake of convenience will most likely place it in the hands of the association's officers as custodians. This final 'contract-holding'

---

[385] *Institution of Mechanical Engineers v Cane* [1961] AC 696, 724, HL, *per* Lord Denning.
[386] *Re Recher's WT* [1972] Ch 526, 538, *per* Brightman J.
[387] See para 3.77.
[388] See para 3.88.
[389] See paras 3.93–3.96.
[390] See paras 3.100–3.101.
[391] *Gaiman v National Assoc for Mental Health* [1971] Ch 317, 335, *per* Megarry J.
[392] It is a fairly common practice for unincorporated associations with charitable purposes to vest their funds in a trustee company: Charity Commission, *Incorporation of Charity Trustees*, leaflet CC43 (2002).

method avoids the legal and practical problems of the first three, and for this reason has won favour in the courts.[393]

(b) Members' liability

3.112 'An unincorporated association has certain advantages when litigation is desired against them.'[394] It cannot enter contracts,[395] incur tort liabilities,[396] or commit criminal offences.[397] Its individual members are not liable as such for one another's acts,[398] and are liable only for their own acts, or for the acts of their agents. To establish a member's liability for the acts of his agent, the agency must be proved and will not be implied by the mere fact of the association,[399] and to fix a member with liability for debts incurred by the association's officers, over and above the contributions he has made to the association's funds in the form of subscriptions, it must be proved that he authorized them to pledge his personal credit—and there is a presumption that a member does not intend to do this when he joins an association.[400]

3.113 It follows that a claimant who wishes to sue in respect of matters arising out of an association's activities must proceed carefully, and must be sure to identify an appropriate defendant for his action. One course may be to sue an individual member or officer of the association in respect of obligations for which they are personally liable.[401] It may be noted in this connection that officers who have acted within the authority of an association's rules are likely to be entitled to an indemnity in respect of third party liabilities out of the association's funds, although they will not be so entitled if they have acted in an unauthorized manner, and the funds may be insufficiently large to cover unforeseen tort liabilities. Another course open to a claimant may be to sue all the members of the association, if they have all carried on the activities complained of, or are in overall

---

393 See eg *Neville Estates Ltd v Madden* [1962] 1 Ch 832; *Re Recher's WT* [1972] Ch 526; *Re Lipinski's WT* [1976] Ch 235; *Hunt v McLaren* [2006] EWHC 2386 (Ch); [2006] All ER (D).

394 *Bloom v National Federation of Discharged and Demobilised Sailors and Soldiers* (1918) 35 TLR 50, 51, CA, *per* Scrutton LJ.

395 *Hollman v Pullin* (1884) Cab & Ellis 254; *Currie v Barton The Times*, 12 February 1988, CA, *per* O'Connor LJ.

396 *London Assoc for the Protection of Trade v Greenlands Ltd* [1916] 2 AC 15, HL.

397 *A-G v Able* [1984] 1 QB 795, 810, *per* Woolf J.

398 *Flemyng v Hector* (1836) 2 M & W 172, 150 ER 716.

399 *London Assoc for the Protection of Trade v Greenlands Ltd* [1916] 2 AC 15, 39, HL, *per* Lord Parker.

400 *Wise v Perpetual Trustee Co* [1903] AC 139, HL, where their Lordships surprisingly held that this presumption overrides even the principle that a beneficiary must indemnify his trustee. For critical comment, see TC Williams, Note (1903) 19 LQR 386; R Flannigan, 'Contractual Responsibility in Non-Profit Associations' (1998) 18 OJLS 631, 641–4; Rideout (n 383 above) 198–204.

401 As in eg *Brown v Lewis* (1896) 12 TLR 455, DC; *Bradley Egg Farm Ltd v Clifford* [1943] 2 All ER 378, CA; *Owen v Northampton BC* [1992] LGR 23, 29, CA, *per* Ralph Gibson LJ.

control of them.[402] It is possible to bring a representative action against a member or officer of an association[403] as the representative of all the members under CPR 19.6, provided that the represented members have 'the same interest' in the action.[404]

(3) Unit Trusts[405]

The unit trust was the most commonly used collective investment vehicle in **3.114** England from 1930 until 2002, when its popularity was superseded by the OIEC.[406] At the end of 2006, unit trusts held assets of around £154.4 billion.[407] Unit trusts operating in the UK are subject to the same regulatory regime as OIECs, but their legal structure is quite different.[408] Like any other sort of trust, 'a unit trust is not a separate legal person',[409] and dealings with the investors' pooled assets must therefore be undertaken by a trustee. Unit trusts are brought into being when a trustee, a fund manager, and investors enter into contracts with one another under which they agree that the investors' pooled assets will be held on trust by the trustee, to be invested as the fund manager directs. In exchange for their money, the investors receive a notional share in the pooled assets in the form of 'units', which they can deal with and dispose of as intangible property, and which the manager may undertake either to repurchase or to arrange for the trustee to redeem out of the fund. For this reason, the investors are known as unit-holders. Ownership of units gives a unit-holder no direct property interest in the underlying assets of the trust, but merely a contractual right to be paid a sum of money, being a proportion of the net value of the trust fund, calculated and realizable as the trust deed provides.[410] The fund manager owes both contractual and fiduciary duties to the trustee and to the unit-holders, and the trustee owes fiduciary and contractual duties to the unit-holders.

---

[402] As in eg *Kennaway v Thompson* [1981] QB 88, CA.

[403] A member or officer of an association may be sued in a personal and a representative capacity in the same proceedings: *Hibernian Dance Club v Murray The Times*, 12 August 1996, CA.

[404] The fact that different members may have different defences open to them is not necessarily a bar to a representative action: see eg *University of Oxford v Broughton* [2006] EWHC 2490 (QB), [2006] All ER (D) 157 at [48]–[50].

[405] The best account of the legal doctrines affecting unit trusts is KF Sin, *The Legal Nature of the Unit Trust* (1997).

[406] See Investment Management Association, *Summary of Unit Trusts/OEIC Statistics 1992–2003 Funds Under Management*.

[407] *Financial Statistics* No 459 (July 2000) Table 5.3D.

[408] See Investment Management Association, *Review of the Governance Arrangements of United Kingdom Authorised Collective Investment Schemes* (2005), 15.

[409] *M & G Securities Ltd v IRC* [1999] STC 315, 321, *per* Park J.

[410] The nature of units is discussed in Sin (n 405 above), ch 5. There is normally a difference between the price at which units may be bought and the price at which they may be sold.

(4) Pension Trusts [411]

3.115 Very large sums of money are tied up in British pension schemes—at the end of 2005, around £915 billion.[412] Most of these funds are held on irrevocable trusts, and their application is *prima facie* determined by the terms of the relevant trust deed and rules of the relevant scheme, and by the general rules of trusts law. However, the size and social consequence of many pension schemes are such that special considerations come into play when disputes relating to their administration fall to be resolved by the courts,[413] such as those which recurred throughout the 1980s and 1990s in relation to the proper application of actuarial surpluses.[414] Pension schemes are also subject to the statutory regimes of the Pensions Schemes Act 1993, the Pensions Act 1995 and the Pensions Act 2004.

3.116 Under earnings related pension schemes, an employer and employees typically pay money to the trustees of a trust fund, with a view to keeping these assets safe from the employer's creditors, and available to pay the employees' pensions on retirement. The quantum of the benefits payable is often determined by a formula related to the employees' earnings on retirement and the number of years they have worked, and benefits may be provided for their dependants despite the absence of privity of contract between the dependants and the employer. Under money purchase pension schemes, an employer and employees again typically pay money to the trustees of a trust fund, but the quantum of the employees' contributions is fixed, and the benefit payable depends on the interest and bonuses allocated to each employee each year. These in turn are determined by the performance of the trust fund as a whole.

---

[411] There is a large literature on pensions law. Recent studies include H Arthur, *Pensions and Trusteeship* (1998); M Grant, *The Pensions Ombudsman: Powers, Procedures, and Decisions* (1998); J Marshall, *The Pensions Act 2004: Guide to the New Law* (2005); G Moffat, G Bean and J Dewar, *Trusts Law: Test and Materials* (4th edn, 2005), Ch 13.

[412] Office for National Statistics, *Financial Statistics* (April 2007), Table 5.1B.

[413] See the excellent discussion in D Hayton, 'Pension Trusts and Traditional Trusts: Drastically Different Species' [2005] Conv 229.

[414] See eg *Re Courage Group's Pension Schemes* [1987] 1 All ER 528; *Davis v Richards and Wallington Ltd* [1990] 1 WLR 1511; *Mettoy Pension Trustees Ltd v Evans* [1990] 1 WLR 1587; *Air Jamaica Ltd v Charlton* [1999] 1 WLR 1399, PC.

Part III

THE LAW OF PROPERTY

4

PROPERTY: GENERAL PRINCIPLES

A. Introduction

(1) What is the Law of Property?

4.01 The law of property is that area of the law concerned with certain types of rights between persons with respect to things, those things being either land or goods, and those rights being proprietary rather than personal. This chapter discusses the types of rights which qualify as proprietary, the ways in which such rights can be held, the ways in which they are created and transferred, and, finally, the ways in which they may come to an end. It covers the law of real property (land law), the law of personal property (goods), and the law of trusts. It is unusual in English law to treat these topics together, and some of the headings may therefore appear unfamiliar to a common, though not a civilian, lawyer. The chapter does not deal with proprietary rights as security (for example mortgages and charges) as these are covered in Chapter 5. Moreover, it does not deal in detail with what we might term the 'enforcement/protection' of property rights because, in English law, this is principally, though not wholly, achieved through the law of torts (for example, as regards land, through the torts of trespass to land, nuisance, and negligence and, as regards goods, through the torts of conversion, trespass to goods, and negligence). Enforcement/protection through the law of torts is discussed in Chapter 17 below.

4.02 It must at the outset be noted that the word 'property' is ambiguous. It is sometimes used to refer to the thing itself ('That land is my property'), sometimes to the right a person has in respect of a particular thing ('I have a lease of that land'). The former usage is colloquial, and fails, inter alia, to reflect the fact that more than one type of property right can exist with respect to a particular thing. The correct usage is that which distinguishes between the physical thing and the rights which can exist in respect of that thing.

(2) Property Rights and Personal Rights

4.03 Having made that distinction, the next thing to note is that not all rights in respect of things are property rights. The hallmark of a property right is its ability to bind strangers to its creation. Rights in respect of things which do not have this quality are personal rights.

(a) Personal rights in respect of things

An example of a right in respect of a thing not amounting to a property right can **4.04** be seen in *Hill v Tupper*.[1] A company with a fee simple title (a recognized property right) to a canal and its banks granted a lease (another recognized property right) of premises on its banks to the claimant, a boat proprietor. The claimant was at the same time given 'the sole and exclusive right or liberty to put or use boats on the said canal, and let the same for hire for the purpose of pleasure only'. The defendant, the landlord of an inn adjoining the canal, put his own boats on the canal and the claimant sued him for interfering with his 'exclusive right'. He failed. Pollock CB said that the grant operated merely as a licence or covenant on the part of the grantors, and was binding on them as between themselves and the grantee, but that it gave the latter no right of action against third parties.

(b) Property rights in respect of things

The result would have been different had the right in question been proprietary. **4.05** If, for example, the defendant had interfered with the claimant's right to exclusive possession of the land adjoining the canal, the subject-matter of the lease in his favour, the claimant's action would have been successful despite the fact that the defendant was not party to its creation, for a lease of land is a property right.

However, the result in *Hill v Tupper* would have been no different had the **4.06** defendant landlord been a successor in title of the canal company, the original grantor of the right, for he would have still been a stranger to its creation.[2] In respect of the lease of the bank, however, the position would have again been different. Though not party to that grant, the defendant would have been bound because the lease was a proprietary right. This rule is often expressed in the maxim *nemo dat quod non habet* (no one gives what he does not have). Because the canal company had a fee simple title subject to a lease in favour of the claimant, all it could transfer to anyone else was a fee simple title subject to a lease in favour of the claimant. Thus, and subject to certain rules in favour of good faith purchasers for value,[3] a property right will not be destroyed simply because other rights in respect of the thing over which that property rights exists are transferred to or granted to a third party. In *Farquharson Bros & Co v King & Co*,[4] for example, the

---

[1] (1863) 2 H & C 121, 159 ER 51.
[2] *Keppel v Bailey* (1834) 2 My & K 517, 39 ER 1042. The case is discussed in para 4.10.
[3] See paras 4.479–4.500.
[4] [1902] AC 325, HL.

appellant timber merchants authorized their clerk to make limited sales of timber, over which they had a property right, to their known customers. The clerk, acting under an assumed name, sold some of the timber to the respondents, who were not known customers, but who bought and paid the clerk for the timber in good faith. The House of Lords held that the respondents were nevertheless liable for their wrongful interference with the appellant's superior rights to the timber. Lord Halsbury LC asked:

> [H]ow has the person who has received the goods acquired a right to those goods which . . . originally belonged to the appellants in this case? When has the property been changed, and by what circumstances? It is impossible, I think, to answer that question except in one way. There has been no property changed . . . .[5]

4.07 The fact that property rights bind strangers to their creation is particularly important in the context of an insolvency. Suppose a transfer of title to a car by mistake. If the response of the legal system is to give only a personal right to the transferor for payment of its value, the transferor will rank equally with the ordinary unsecured creditors of the transferee in the event of his insolvency and may well therefore receive only a fraction of what he is owed. If, however, the response is the creation of a property right in the transferor in respect of the car, then the car will not form part of the pool of assets available to satisfy the unsecured creditors. The transferor will therefore stand a much better chance of success if he can establish a proprietary rather than a personal right in such circumstances. Indeed, it is precisely because of the risk of a debtor's insolvency that many creditors insist on being given property rights in respect of their debtor's assets as a condition of the grant of credit.[6] By the same token, it is precisely because property rights are capable of binding third parties that courts are often reluctant to create them merely as a response to some perceived injustice.[7]

4.08 This cuts both ways. A property right is not invariably superior to a personal one. If I lend you a car over which I have a property right and, without any fault on your part, the car is destroyed by fire, I must bear the loss. This is often expressed in the Latin maxim *res perit domino* (the loss falls on the owner). But if at the same time I lend you £100 in cash, and those very notes are destroyed in the same fire, the loss is yours, not mine, for in the latter case my property rights in the banknotes passed to you on delivery and were exchanged for a personal right that you pay me £100. It no defence to my claim in respect of that personal right that the things over which I gave you a property right were destroyed by fire.

---

5 [1902] AC 325, 329, HL.
6 Para 5.001ff.
7 See paras 4.323–4.324.

(c) Distinguishing property rights from personal rights

How is one to tell whether a right in respect of a thing is personal or proprietary? **4.09**
The answer is that there is in English law, as with all developed legal systems,[8] a
numerus clausus (closed number) of property rights. This is again illustrated by
Hill v Tupper, where Pollock CB, in response to the claimant's argument that his
grantor should be at liberty to create a property right consisting of 'the exclusive
right to put pleasure boats on a canal', said:

> The answer is, that the law will not allow it . . . A new species of incorporeal heredita-
> ment cannot be created at the will and pleasure of the owner of property; but he must
> be content to accept the estate and the right to dispose of it subject to the law as set-
> tled by decisions or controlled by Act of Parliament. A grantor may bind himself by
> covenant to allow any right he pleases over his property, but he cannot annex to it a
> new incident, so as to enable the grantee to sue in his own name for an infringement
> of such a limited right as is now claimed.[9]

Thus, as a matter of personal obligation, what the parties had agreed was perfectly **4.10**
valid. But as a matter of property law, it was not. The reason this was so was given
by Martin B, who said that 'to admit the right would lead to the creation of an
infinite variety of interests in land, and an indefinite increase of possible estates'.[10]
Similar sentiments were expressed in the earlier case of *Keppel v Bailey*,[11] where
the defendant's predecessor in title, the lessee of an iron-works, had promised the
claimant that both he and his successors in title would buy all the limestone to be
used in the iron-works from a particular quarry and no other. In holding that the
right given to the claimant did not amount to a property right and could not
therefore bind the defendant, Lord Brougham LC said:

> [I]t must not . . . be supposed that incidents of a novel kind can be devised and
> attached to property at the fancy or caprice of any owner. It is clearly inconvenient
> both to the science of the law and to the public weal that such a latitude should be
> given. There can be no harm in allowing the fullest latitude to men in binding them-
> selves and their representatives, that is, their assets real and personal, to answer in
> damages for breach of their obligations. This tends to no mischief, and is a reasonable
> liberty to bestow; but great detriment would arise and much confusion of rights
> if parties were allowed to invent new modes of holding and enjoying real property,
> and to impress upon their lands and tenements a peculiar character, which should
> follow them into all hands, however remote. Every close, every messuage, might thus

[8] B Rudden, 'Economic Theory v Property Law: The *Numerus Clausus* Problem' in J Eekelaar &
J Bell (eds), *Oxford Essays in Jurisprudence* (3rd edn, 1987) 239; S Bartels & M Milo (eds), *Contents
of Real Rights* (2004).
[9] (1863) 2 H & C 121, 127–8, 159 ER 51, 53. An 'incorporeal hereditament' is a property right
in respect of land which does not give its holder a right to exclusive possession of that land.
[10] (1863) 2 H & C 121, 128, 159 ER 51, 53.
[11] (1834) 2 My & K 517, 39 ER 1042.

be held in a several fashion; and it would hardly be possible to know what rights the acquisition of any parcel conferred or what obligations it imposed.[12]

4.11 The *numerus clausus* principle[13] was affirmed and applied by the House of Lords in *King v David Allen (Billposting) Ltd*,[14] where a contract granting an advertising company the right to affix billposters to the side of a cinema building for a period of four years was held not to bind an assignee of a title to the building itself because it did not amount to an established property right.[15] Importantly, both this case and *Keppel v Bailey* also show that knowledge on the part of the assignee of the existence of the right does not turn an otherwise personal right into a property right, for the fact in each case that the assignee had actual notice of the prior agreement made no difference to the final result.[16] We will see later that knowledge does sometimes play a part in deciding whether a right binds a third party, but only in the negative sense of disqualifying a purchaser from pleading the defence of good faith purchase for value in the limited circumstances in which it is available.[17] Indeed, if knowledge of a personal right did transform it into a property right, the *numerus clausus* would be destroyed. As Lord Brougham LC explained in *Keppel v Bailey*:

> The knowledge by an assignee of an estate that his assignor had assumed to bind others than the law authorises him to affect by his contracts, had attempted to create a real burden upon property which is inconsistent with the nature of that property, and unknown to the principles of the law, cannot bind such assignee by affecting his conscience. If it did, then the illegality would be of no consequence, and, however wild the attempt might be to create new kinds of holding and new species of estate, and however repugnant such devices might be to the rules of law, they would prove perfectly successful in the result . . .[18]

---

12 (1834) 2 My & K 517, 535–6, 39 ER 1042, 1049. This reasoning has not gone unchallenged: see B Rudden, 'Economic Theory v Property Law: The *Numerus Clausus* problem' in J Eekelaar and J Bell (eds), *Oxford Essays in Jurisprudence* (3rd edn, 1987) 238, esp 245–9; T Merrill & H Smith, 'Optimal Standardization in the Law of Property: The Numerus Clausus Principle' (2000) 110 Yale LJ 1; H Hansmann and R Kraakman, 'Property, Contract, and Verification: The Numerus Clausus Problem and the Divisibility of Rights' (2002) Harvard Law School, Public Law Research Paper No 37; Harvard Law and Economics Discussion Paper No 388 (available at SSRN: <ssrn.com/abstract=323301>).

13 Further endorsements, explicit or implicit: *Clore v Theatrical Properties Ltd* [1936] 3 All ER 483, CA; *Ashburn Anstalt v Arnold* [1989] Ch 1, CA; *Rhone v Stephens* [1994] 2 AC 310, HL.

14 [1916] 2 AC 54, HL.

15 It failed to qualify as an easement because it did not benefit any land held by the advertising company. For the substantive requirements of an easement, see paras 4.82–4.95.

16 See also *Clore v Theatrical Properties Ltd* [1936] 3 All ER 483, CA.

17 Paras 4.479–4.500.

18 (1834) 2 My & K 517, 547, 39 ER 1042, 1053.

(d) A different school of thought

There is a competing view on the issue of what rights can constitute property   **4.12**
rights. That school holds that the list is not closed, merely difficult to enter. A good
example is provided by the decision of the House of Lords in *National Provincial
Bank v Ainsworth*.[19] A wife deserted by her husband was left living in the
matrimonial home, to which the husband had a fee simple title. The husband
later mortgaged his title to the bank but defaulted on the loan. The bank sought
to exercise their right to exclusive possession of the house by seeking an order
for possession against the wife. She resisted their claim, arguing that she had
a right *qua* deserted wife to live in the house, which right bound the bank.
The House rejected her claim. Though a husband was under an obligation to
provide a home for his wife, such an obligation was enforceable against him alone.
In other words, the right of the wife was a personal, not proprietary. But the House
did not reject the wife's claim on the ground that the right claimed had not in
the past been recognized as a property right. They did so because it did not
satisfy the criteria for membership of the class of property rights. Lord Wilberforce
said:[20]

> On any division . . . which is to be made between property rights on the one hand,
> and personal rights on the other hand, however broad or penumbral the separating
> band between these two kinds of rights may be, there can be little doubt where
> the wife's rights fall. Before a right or an interest can be admitted into the category
> of property . . . it must be definable, identifiable by third parties, capable in its
> nature of assumption by third parties, and have some degree of permanence or
> stability. The wife's right has none of these qualities; it is characterised by the reverse
> of them.[21]

The essential point here is that, were another right in respect of a thing to seek the
status of a property right, and were it to satisfy Lord Wilberforce's three criteria, it
could, on this view, be admitted to the list. In other words, for Lord Wilberforce
there was no *numerus clausus* but merely a set of exclusive criteria. We should,
however, note that this approach has never been used to admit a right to the list,
and there are many rights which have been rejected even though they satisfy the
criteria.[22]

---

19 [1965] AC 174, HL.
20 [1965] AC 1175, 1247–8, HL.
21 See also [1965] AC 1175, 1233 (*per* Lord Upjohn).
22 An example is the contractual licence to occupy land, held not to be proprietary in *Ashburn
Anstalt v Arnold* [1989] Ch 1, CA.

(3) *Classification*

4.13 A number of divisions have long been made within the law of property. None is particularly useful. However, they remain in use, and it is necessary briefly to explain them.

(a) Real and personal property

4.14 In earlier times, the division between real property (realty) and personal property (personalty) was, because of the rules of succession,[23] crucial: on death, real property rights passed directly to the heir or legatee, whereas personal property rights passed to the deceased's personal representatives for distribution. Nowadays, the distinction is increasingly of only historical significance, although, as we shall see, it is still important in respect of the greater number of interests which can exist in the commonest realty, namely land.

4.15 Real property rights are property rights which, before they were abolished in 1833,[24] were protected by the real actions. A real action was one in which the successful claimant was allowed specific recovery of the thing itself (*res*): hence, 'real' property. These real actions (thing-recovering actions) had their defined area of availability. In all other cases the response was to give the claimant a right to damages against the defendant; whence 'personalty' or 'personal' property. Technically, realty extends beyond interests in respect of land. It also includes chattels within the category of heirlooms and such incorporeal rights as advowsons,[25] tithes, franchises and offices and dignities. On the other hand, the lease of land, though a property right and one giving its holder a right to specific recovery, was never realty. All property rights which are not realty technically fall into the category of personal property.

4.16 This does not mean that personal property rights were unimportant, merely that damages were an adequate and often preferred remedy.[26] The hallmark of a property right is its sphere of enforceability, not the order the court will make in respect of it. It is for this reason that the distinction between real and personal property has nothing to do with the distinction between rights *in rem* and rights

---

[23] The rule that real property could not be left by will, having been evaded by recourse to 'uses', began to be relaxed with the passing of the Statute of Wills 1540. The modern rules of intestate succession are set out from para 7.07. See also the modern restraints on freedom of testation, from para 7.213.

[24] Real Property Limitation Act 1833, s 37.

[25] The perpetual right to present to an ecclesiastical living.

[26] Even in the earliest period the real actions were very slow and only heard in the royal courts, whereas personal actions were relatively quick and heard in the local courts: AWB Simpson, *A History of the Land Law* (2nd edn, 1986) 26–36.

in personam. As was pointed out more than a century ago,[27] these Roman law categories do not match English usage and are a source of confusion.

(b) *In rem* and *in personam*

The question is whether the division between rights *in rem* and rights *in personam*   **4.17** is identical to the division between property rights and personal rights encountered above.[28] Unfortunately, so far as the terms are used in English law, there seems to be no agreement as to the precise point at which the division of rights lies. There is no doubt that a right *in personam* is a right exigible against certain or determinate persons. However there are two views as to the nature of rights *in rem*. The first looks solely to the general *exigibility* of the right: a right *in rem* avails against persons generally or universally. The second is narrower and determines the matter according to the *content* of the right: a right *in rem* is a right in or against a thing, exigible against third parties only by reason of their having or interfering with the defendant's rights in respect of the thing.

The wider of these views means that even one's right not to be assaulted or defamed   **4.18** must be classified as *in rem*. Indeed, the whole superstructure of the law of torts would have to be included here. Yet such rights are not proprietary because they are not rights against other people in relation to things. If rights *in rem* form as large a category as that, they clearly do not coincide with the class of property rights. However, when the criteria of *content* and *exigibility* are combined they produce an exact correspondence with the category of all property rights. Thus, if we say that a right *in rem* is a right in respect of a thing which prevails against persons generally, rights *in rem* coincide exactly with property rights.

(c) Corporeal and incorporeal hereditaments

Hereditament is another word for all types of real property right. They divide   **4.19** between corporeal (those concerned with exclusive possession) and incorporeal (those concerned with rights other than to exclusive possession) hereditaments. The distinction between corporeal and incorporeal rights is of some importance in that modes of alienation differ considerably. It is evident that an incorporeal right does not admit of 'delivery'.[29]

(d) Choses in possession and choses in action

The word 'chose', like *res*, means 'thing'. It is French, rather than Latin. It divides   **4.20** between choses in possession and choses in action. A chose in possession is, as the

---

27 T Cyprian Williams, 'The Terms Real and Personal in English Law' (1888) 4 LQR 394.
28 Paras 4.03–4.04.
29 Paras 4.451–4.460.

name indicates, a right to the possession of a physical thing, while a chose in action is a right to sue in a court of law. Differently to a right to exclusive possession of a thing, which can be enforced by a physical taking of the thing itself, a chose in action can only be enforced by court action. Typical choses in action are debts and company shares. Debts and company shares are not property rights properly-so-called, for, though valuable, and though assignable, they are exigible against only one person, the debtor and company respectively. And though some other choses in action, such as patents, trade marks, and copyrights, are often described as property rights, and are exigible generally, they are not property rights because they are not rights in respect of a physical object, a thing.

(4) The Enforcement of Property Rights

4.21 In the opening paragraph of this chapter, we pointed out that much of the law relating to the enforcement of property rights comprises an examination of various torts: in the context of land, the torts of trespass, nuisance, and negligence and, in the context of goods, the torts of conversion, trespass and negligence. These are dealt with fully in Chapter 17.[30] It should, however, be noted, that, at least as regards land, the picture would be incomplete if attention were only paid to the law of tort, for there is available to a right-holder dispossessed of land an action to recover possession independent of any claim in tort (it is different for chattels, where the court is empowered to order delivery up as a response to the wrong of conversion). We have already seen how the real actions were available in such situations and how their availability gave rise to the category of 'real property'. Those real actions were eventually succeeded by the action of ejectment, a more procedurally convenient remedy, which was in turn replaced by a statutory remedy known as an order for possession. Thus, where a defendant has dispossessed a claimant with a superior right to exclusive possession, the law gives the claimant the ability either to retake the land himself[31] or to obtain an order from the court that possession of the land be given up to him.[32] If the defendant does not comply, the claimant can secure enforcement by an officer of the court.

(5) The Contribution of Equity

4.22 Like the other constituent parts of English private law, the law of property derives from three sources: common law, equity and statute. Although each of

---

30 See paras 17.248–17.254 and 17.316–17.335.

31 Though it is generally a criminal offence to use force in this regard: Criminal Law Act 1977, s 6.

32 CPR Sched 1, R 113 (High Court); Sched 2, C 24 (County Court). A majority of the Court of Appeal (Chadwick LJ dissenting) mistakenly extended this remedy to a claimant with no proprietary right to exclusive possession in *Manchester City Airport plc v Dutton* [2000] QB 133.

these topics will be dealt with in detail below, it is necessary to say something at the outset about the contribution of equity to the law of property, for it is here that the Court of Chancery made its most marked impact. So far as the law of property is concerned, it remains true that equity in general follows the common law. Thus, those rights which have proprietary effect at law likewise have proprietary effect in equity. There are, however, several important differences.

The most important is that the equitable rights which might be seen as 'proprietary' behave in a slightly different fashion to those at common law. At common law, as we have seen, the right is exigible directly against anyone interfering with it. Thus, the holder of a common law easement can sue for damages and an injunction against any third party, be it a successor in title of the original grantor or even a complete stranger, who interferes with his right. This is not generally true for equitable property rights. Take, for example, the case of an option to purchase a fee simple estate in land. As we will see below, such a right will generally bind transferees of the fee simple in question from its grantor, and so is classed as a property right. But it will not bind other third parties, such as squatters. Although a squatter will be bound by easements granted by the person he has dispossessed, he will not be bound by an option to purchase. Indeed, he could not be bound by any such right, for the burden of such a right entails a duty to convey the right contracted to be sold, and the squatter does not have that right. The only exception would seem to be the restrictive covenant, which has been held to bind persons other than a successor in title of the grantor.[33]   **4.23**

The second contribution of equity is the institution of the trust, a device developed for the holding of both personal rights, for example, debts and shares, and property rights. The trust is by far the greatest contribution of equity to the law of property. It is dealt with in detail in part D below.   **4.24**

There are three other significant chancery contributions to the law of property: first, equity has a longer list of property rights than does the common law; second, it sometimes anticipates the grant or transfer of property rights at common law; and third, it is more forgiving than the law of failure to comply with requirements of formality. A brief consideration of each of these three may be found helpful.   **4.25**

(a) A longer list

All rights recognized as property rights at common law are also recognized as such by equity. So, for example, it is possible to have an easement, for example, a right of way over land, both at common law and in equity. But there are also some rights recognized in equity as proprietary which at common law either do not exist at all   **4.26**

---

[33] *Re Nisbet & Pott's Contract* [1906] 1 Ch 386.

or, if they do, are recognized only as personal rights. An example of the latter is the restrictive covenant over land. Others are contracts and options to purchase certain types of legal property rights.[34] The mortgagor's equity of redemption is an example of equity creating a property right where not even a corresponding personal right exists at law.[35]

4.27 A subsidiary issue is whether the equitable list is now closed. Though the *numerus clausus* principle is probably secure at common law, it is possible that this may not be so in equity. We saw that there were two approaches to this question, the closed list approach of *Hill v Tupper* and the 'criteria' approach in the *Ainsworth* case. Might it be argued that this difference of approach can be explained on juris-dictional grounds, that though the common law is past the age of child-bearing, equity is not?

4.28 Given that the equitable list of property rights is longer than the common law list, equity must have a creative capacity. How then does equity give birth to a new species of property right? The last occasion on which it did was in 1848, in the case of *Tulk v Moxhay*,[36] where certain covenants restrictive of the user of land became property rights. In that case Lord Cottenham LC did so purely on the basis of knowledge on the part of the purchaser. He said: 'The question was not whether the covenant runs with the land, but whether a party shall be permitted to use the land in a manner inconsistent with the contract entered into by his vendor, with notice of which he purchased.'[37]

4.29 However, as we have already seen, knowledge of a right does not affect the sub-stance of that right, a fact demonstrated by the later decision of the House of Lords in *King v David Allen*.[38] A right does not cross the personal/property divide merely by the fact that other people are told about it.

4.30 The question then arises whether the fact that a right is one which merits protec-tion in equity, by, for example, the grant of specific performance or an injunction, makes any difference? This was the approach of Denning LJ in *Errington v Errington & Woods*,[39] where the question was whether a contractual right to occupy a home falling short of a recognized property right bound a stranger to its creation. Denning LJ held that it did, at least as far as the courts of equity were concerned, on the basis that until 1948, the only response of the court to a breach of the licence contract on the part of the licensor was the award of common law damages.

---

[34] For example, *London and South Western Rly Co v Gomm* (1882) 20 Ch D 562 (option to purchase fee simple).

[35] Paras 5.06–5.07.

[36] (1848) 2 Ph 774, 41 ER 1143.

[37] (1848) 2 Ph 774, 777–8, 41 ER 1143, 1144.

[38] [1916] 2 AC 54, HL; para 4.11.

[39] [1952] 1 KB 290, CA.

That, however, changed in *Winter Garden Theatre (London) Ltd v Millennium Productions Ltd*,[40] where the House of Lords held that injunctive relief, an equitable response, was also available. The effect of this 'infusion of equity' said Denning LJ, was 'that contractual licences now have a force and validity of their own and cannot be revoked in breach of contract. Neither the licensor nor anyone who claims through him can disregard the contract except a purchaser for value without notice.'[41]

This approach, which effectively says that a right will be a property right, or at least an equitable property right, where equitable relief is available, would also destroy the *numerus clausus*. It was later shown to be wrong in a case already encountered, *National Provincial Bank v Ainsworth*.[42] When the *Ainsworth* case was in the Court of Appeal,[43] Russell LJ delivered a dissenting judgment exposing the fallacy of Lord Denning's reasoning, and that judgment later received the endorsement of the House of Lords. Russell LJ said: **4.31**

> It is to be noted that these rights are rights against her husband . . . They are not proprietary rights or estates or interests, but rights against the husband as such . . . Nor are they made proprietary rights, estates or interests by virtue of the fact that an injunction will be granted against the husband to prevent him interfering with her right *as against him* to occupy . . . The fact that in appropriate cases the courts will grant the equitable relief of an injunction to restrain revocation or breach of a licence is not a ground for asserting that it is other than a licence [personal right].[44]

It would thus seem that the different approaches in both *Tulk v Moxhay* (knowledge) and *Errington v Errington* (availability of equitable relief) to the recognition by equity of novel proprietary rights no longer represent the law. So, despite the denials of one senior judge,[45] it would seem that, at least in this respect, equity may indeed be past the age of child-bearing.

(b) Anticipating the common law

Where there is a specifically enforceable contract for the sale of a common law property right,[46] the court, applying the maxim 'equity looks upon that as done which ought to be done', anticipates the final outcome of the contract and finds that the vendor holds the particular right promised to be sold on a judicially created trust for the purchaser.[47] Thus, in *Lysaght v Edwards*[48] the deceased, who **4.32**

---

[40] [1948] AC 173, HL.
[41] [1952] 1 KB 290, 299, CA.
[42] [1965] AC 1175, HL.
[43] *National Provincial Bank v Hastings Car Mart Ltd* [1964] Ch 665, CA.
[44] ibid 695–6 (emphasis in original).
[45] *Eves v Eves* [1975] 1 WLR 1338, 1341, CA, *per* Lord Denning MR.
[46] For the availability of specific performance in the law of contract, see paras 21.180–21.197.
[47] Para 4.329.
[48] (1876) 2 Ch D 499.

held title to a number of parcels of land, both outright and on trust, had before his death entered into a contract to sell the title of one of the parcels he held outright. He died before the sale was completed. By his will, all titles to land held outright were left to two friends, whereas all titles held on trust went to one of those friends alone. For the purpose of executing the conveyance in favour of the purchaser, the question arose as to who now held the title to the land contracted to be sold. Had it passed via the will to the two friends as the testator's rights held outright, or did it pass to the one alone as a right held on trust? That depended on whether the vendor was a trustee of the title at the moment of his death. It was held that he was a trustee, and that the friend alone should execute the conveyance. As Sir George Jessel MR explained:

> [T]he moment you have a valid contract for sale the vendor becomes in equity a trustee for the purchaser of the estate sold, and the beneficial ownership passes to the purchaser . . .[49]

This doctrine applies not only in the context of succession. Had the testator become insolvent rather than died, the purchaser would have been able to insist on a conveyance of the title itself rather than having to bring a personal claim for damages for breach of contract and sharing equally in the dividend for the unsecured creditors. However, no convincing reason for this preferential treatment of the purchaser in the event of an insolvency yet been formulated.[50]

4.33 There are, however, two limitations to this doctrine. The first is that it does not apply to chattels, for a contract for the sale of chattels is not normally specifically enforceable, most chattels being interchangeable.[51] It does, however, apply to some other rights, for example patents, copyrights and trade marks. The second limitation is that it only applies where the ultimate execution of the contract will lead to the creation or transfer of a common law property right. Many contracts which are specifically enforceable do not involve promises to grant property rights, and the doctrine only operates to give the claimant a property right in equity in circumstances where the eventual performance of the contract would result in property rights at law. Where performance of the obligation would not give rise to a property right at law then the fact that performance can be compelled cannot change the nature of the underlying right. So, for example, the fact that the contracts in *Hill v Tupper*[52] or *King v David Allen (Billposting) Ltd*[53] could have

---

[49] ibid 506.

[50] For criticism, see WJ Swadling, 'The Vendor-Purchaser Constructive Trust' in S Degeling and J Edelman, *Equity in Commercial Law* (2005), 463–488. As the quote from Sir George Jessel MR indicates, the doctrine seems to be based upon a notion of a separate 'beneficial ownership' existing in the vendor before the contract of sale is made. We will see (paras 4.145–4.150) that this notion is fallacious.

[51] Para 21.184ff.

[52] (1863) 2 H & C 121, 159 ER 51.

[53] [1916] 2 AC 54, HL.

been specifically enforced had no bearing on the question whether the rights were personal or proprietary. The rights granted in those cases were not proprietary rights at law and the availability of specific performance could not alter that conclusion. This point is occasionally overlooked.[54]

(c) Forgiving absence of formality

An intended property right may fail to be created at law because of some absence **4.34** of formality, generally the failure to use a deed.[55] The common law does not condone any absence of formality, but in certain circumstances equity will, more particularly where there is present a contract to grant the interest in question, and, by use of the doctrine described immediately above, find an equitable grant of the right.[56] Indeed, one of the most common reasons why a particular property right is equitable rather than legal is because of equity's more relaxed attitude to the issue of formalities.

B. Property Rights in Respect of Land

This part of the chapter considers the various property rights which can exist in **4.35** English law in respect of land. The same question is asked of goods in the next part of the chapter. It is necessary to distinguish between land and goods for two reasons. The first is because the physical nature of land, its permanence, its immovability, its neighbourliness, means that it makes sense to recognize as proprietary rights in respect of land which, were they to exist in respect of goods, might seem inappropriate. The second is historical, for only land was subject to the feudal system.[57]

We have said that there is a *numerus clausus* or closed list of property rights. **4.36** What does this list look like in respect of land? Broadly speaking, it comprises the following:

(1) Fees simple absolute in possession;
(2) Conditional fees;
(3) Determinable fees;
(4) Life estates;

---

[54] For example, in *Bristol Airports plc v Powdrill* [1990] Ch 744, CA.

[55] The modern requirements for a deed are laid down in the Law of Property (Miscellaneous Provisions) Act 1989, s 1.

[56] Para 4.329. Moreover, the court will be prepared to construct a contract out of a failed grant made for consideration: *Parker v Taswell* (1858) 2 De G & J 559.

[57] AWB Simpson, *A History of the Land Law* (2nd edn, 1986) 1–102; EH Burn & J Cartwright, *Cheshire and Burn's Modern Law of Real Property* (17th edn, 2006) 11–35; JH Baker, *An Introduction to Legal History* (4th edn, 2002) 223–247.

   (5) Entails;[58]
   (6) Leases;
   (7) Easements;
   (8) Profits à prendre;
   (9) Rentcharges;
  (10) Restrictive covenants;
  (11) Estate contracts;
  (12) Options to purchase;
  (13) Equities of redemption;
  (14) Legal and equitable charges.

So far as the first five members of this list are concerned, only the first is of any significance today, the rest being part of a now outmoded way of holding land. Accordingly, we will only consider the fee simple absolute in possession before moving on to the lease.

(1) Fees Simple Absolute in Possession

4.37 We will see below that the lease of land is nowadays a recognized property right in English law. Since 1925, such a right has been known as an 'estate' in the land. But this is not strictly correct, for leases were never part of the feudal system, and the word 'estate' is traditionally reserved to describe the length of a feudal relation. In the feudal system, an estate gave a right to exclusive possession. There were various types of estate, among them the life estate, one lasting for the life of the original grantee, and the fee simple absolute in possession, one lasting, for all practical purposes, forever. There were other estates in between, most notably the estate tail or entail (from the French *tallé*, meaning 'cut down'), which passed only to specified descendants of the original grantee and which came to an end when this line died out.[59] For various reasons, primarily of a fiscal nature, but also because of a general trend in treating land as a commercial commodity rather than something which stayed in the family from generation to generation, estates less than the fee simple absolute in possession became unpopular. And though it is still possible to create many of them, albeit since 1925[60] only through the medium of

---

  [58] The entail was abolished by the Trusts of Land and Appointment of Trustees Act 1996.

  [59] The typical words creating such an estate were 'To A and the heirs of his body'. The existence of limited estates provoked a complex set of rules, known as the law of waste, which regulated the use estate holders could make of land to which they had a current right to exclusive possession to the prejudice of those with entitlements in the future.

  [60] Law of Property Act 1925, s 1(1).

a trust, the only estate which is today of significance is the fee simple absolute in possession.[61]

To all intents and purposes, the fee simple absolute in possession gives its holder a **4.38** right to the exclusive possession of land forever. The word 'fee' denotes an estate of inheritance, that the right will descend to the grantee's heirs, the word 'simple' that these heirs are general rather than restricted to a special class (eg, the heirs of the grantee's body male), the word 'absolute' that the estate will not come to an end on the happening of some specified event, and the words 'in possession' signifying that the grantee has a right to immediate possession of the land. Such an estate will not cease to be a fee simple absolute in possession if there is a grant by its holder of a lease, for by statute, 'possession' is defined to include the receipt of rents and profits or the right to receive the same.[62] The only thing which will bring a fee simple absolute in possession to an end is if its current holder were to die intestate and without heirs, an extremely rare occurrence. In such a case, the estate will be escheat to the Crown, by which is meant that the right to exclusive possession will come to an end, so making the Crown's dormant right as feudal superior once again active.

If the time which the holder of a fee simple absolute in possession has is essentially **4.39** forever, the space in which he has that period of time is summed up in the Latin maxim '*Cujus est solum, ejus est usque ad coelum et ad inferos*' (To whomsoever the land belongs, to him also belongs [the space] up to heaven and down to the [deepest] depths).[63] However, the invention of the aeroplane has reduced the space implied in 'up to heaven', so that no tenant in fee simple can complain of trespass by overflying planes.[64]

On the surface of the land every man-made fixture and rooted tree or plant forms **4.40** part of the realty and so 'belongs' to the tenant in fee simple.[65] So far as below the surface is concerned, all mines and minerals also belong to him, except gold and silver, which belong to the Crown. At common law coal thus belonged to the tenant in fee simple. Statutory nationalization of the coal industry changed that, and subsequent privatization has not re-established the original position. Coal is now vested in the Coal Authority, while natural petroleum is vested in the Crown.[66]

---

[61] Detailed treatments of the current status of the doctrine of estates can be found in the standard works on land law. See, eg, EH Burn & J Cartwright, *Cheshire and Burn's Modern Law of Real Property* (17th edn, 2006) 165–181.

[62] Law of Property Act 1925, s 202(1)(xix).

[63] The modern application of this maxim is illustrated by the decision in *Anchor Brewhouse Developments v Berkley House* (1987) 38 Building LR 82 (overhanging cranes).

[64] *Bernstein of Leigh (Baron) v Skyviews Ltd* [1978] QB 479.

[65] Paras 4.463–4.468. In the same context chattels, including treasure, found on and in the land are considered in paras 4.414–4.422.

[66] Coal Industry Act 1994, ss 7 and 8; Petroleum Act 1998, ss 1 and 2.

(2) Leases of Land

4.41 Apart from the fee simple absolute in possession, the other property right giving its holder a right to exclusive possession of land is the lease. The lease, which is more suitable to a 'commercial' rather than a 'family' holding of land, postdates and was therefore never part of the feudal structure. As we shall see, a lease involves a grant of a right to exclusive possession of land. As such, it can only be granted by persons who themselves have a right to the exclusive possession of land.[67] That includes a person with a fee simple estate, but also someone who is themselves a lessee. The person granting the lease is referred to as the landlord or, since the right to exclusive possession will eventually revert to them, the reversioner. Where a lease is granted by a lessee, it is known as a sub-lease. There is no limit on the number of sub-leases which may be created. Both landlord and tenant have, in the absence of any provision to the contrary, an interest which they can assign. Thus, there is no rule in English law that 'sale breaks hire', at least as far as the 'hire' of land is concerned.

4.42 There is much statutory regulation of tenancies in English law which in certain contexts alter the common law rules as to security of tenure and the control of rent.[68] There is no room to deal with these in a work of this nature. Rather our focus is on the general principles of leases.

(a) Substantive requirements of a lease

4.43 The substantive requirements of a lease were said by Lord Templeman in *Street v Mountford*[69] to be as follows:

> To constitute a tenancy the occupier must be granted exclusive possession for a fixed or periodic term certain in consideration of a premium or periodical payments.[70]

(i) Language and intent

4.44 Each of these requirements will be examined in turn. A preliminary question concerns the relevance of the label put on the agreement. Does a contract which would otherwise create a lease cease to do so because the parties say that it does not? The reason this question has been litigated is that tenants have at various

---

[67] In the case where the grantor of a lease has no such right, a tenancy by estoppel will arise, which has effect only between the parties. If the 'landlord' later acquires a right to exclusive possession, then this will 'feed' the estoppel, so giving the tenant by estoppel a right capable of binding third parties. Of course, if the tenant by estoppel is in exclusive possession of the land, that fact alone generates in him a right to exclusive possession as against all bar those with better rights to possession: see paras 4.414–4.420.

[68] For a useful survey, see EH Burn & J Cartwright, *Cheshire & Burn's Modern Law of Real Property* (17th edn, 2006), 336–395.

[69] [1985] AC 809, HL.

[70] ibid 818.

times been given a number of privileges by a series of statutes, colloquially known as the 'Rent Acts'. The most significant of these, now heavily eroded, are the right to pay a 'fair' rather than a 'market' rent, and the right to continue in possession even after the expiry of the agreed term.[71] For this reason, landlords often sought to structure their agreements so as to create only a 'licence' (permission) to occupy.[72] This issue arose in *Street v Mountford* itself.

Mr Street, a solicitor, wanted to hire out two furnished rooms in a house to which he had a fee simple title to Mrs Mountford. Wishing to avoid giving her a Rent Act protected tenancy, he drew up a contract which described itself as a non-assignable licence and which contained the following term: **4.45**

> I [the licensee] understand that a licence in the above form does not and is not intended to give me a tenancy protected under the Rent Acts.

No one else was to share the rooms with Mrs Mountford and the agreed 'licence fee' was £37 per week. After moving in, Mrs Mountford applied to the Rent Tribunal to have it reduced. Mr Street applied to the court for a declaration that the tribunal had no jurisdiction because Mrs Mountford was merely a licensee. The Court of Appeal agreed with him. Slade LJ said Mrs Mountford was only a licensee because 'there is manifested the clear intentions of both parties that the rights granted are to be merely those of a personal right of occupation and not those of a tenant'.[73]

That conclusion was reversed on appeal,[74] where it was held that Mrs Mountford did indeed have a lease. In the House of Lords, Lord Templeman said: **4.46**

> If the agreement satisfied all the requirements of a tenancy, then the agreement produced a tenancy, and the parties cannot alter the effect of the agreement by insisting that they only created a licence. The manufacture of a five-pronged implement for manual digging results in a fork even if the manufacturer, unfamiliar with the English language, insists that he intended to make and has made a spade.[75]

He added: 'the only intention which is relevant is the intention demonstrated by the agreement to grant exclusive possession for a term at a rent.[76] We shall examine each of these substantive requirements in turn.

---

[71] For this erosion see C Harpum (ed), *Megarry and Wade on Real Property* (6th edn, 2000) 1361–1438.

[72] Paras 4.114–4.128.

[73] (1985) 49 P & CR 324, 332, CA.

[74] *Street v Mountford* [1985] AC 809, HL.

[75] ibid 819.

[76] ibid 826. In *Clear Channel UK Ltd v Manchester City Council* [2005] EWCA 1304; [2006] L & TR 7, Jonathan Parker LJ, while saying that he did not intend to cast doubt on the principle laid down in *Street v Mountford*, said that different thinking might apply in the case of two substantial parties of equal bargaining power and with the benefit of full legal advice. For similar thinking, albeit

(ii) The requirements

4.47 **Exclusive possession.** It is clear that any arrangement which falls short of conferring a right to the exclusive possession of land will not qualify as a lease. Thus, the exclusive right to put pleasure boats on the Basingstoke Canal in *Hill v Tupper*[77] could not amount to a lease because it conferred no exclusive right to possession of the canal, merely a franchise of boating rights. Similarly, the agreement in *Clore v Theatrical Properties Ltd*,[78] that the claimant have 'front of house rights'[79] in a theatre, did not amount to a lease of the relevant part of the theatre because those parts had to be shared with the owners of the theatre and their licensees.

4.48 In *Street v Mountford* itself, the landlord admitted that Mrs Mountford had exclusive possession of the rooms; he nevertheless failed in his argument that she was prevented from having a lease because of the lack of intention between them that she have one. In cases since *Street*, however, landlords have attempted to engineer it so that no grant of exclusive possession is actually made. The cases divide between those concerning sole and joint occupiers.

4.49 Attempts have been made to deny exclusive possession to *sole occupiers* in various ways. One is not to give them exclusive possession of any particular room or rooms. This was the case in *Westminster City Council v Clarke*.[80] The claimant city council ran a hostel for homeless single men, including those with personality disorders or physical disabilities. There was a resident warden, who was supported by a team of social workers. The idea was that the accommodation would be temporary and that the residents would move on to more permanent accommodation at a later date. The defendant was housed in the hostel. He paid a weekly accommodation charge and was granted a 'licence to occupy', under which he had no right to the exclusive occupation of any particular room, could be shifted from room to room without notice, could be required to share a room with others, and could not have visitors without the permission of the council. In fact, he occupied one room on his own for six months. The defendant was prone to smashing up furniture and disturbing other tenants, and the claimants sought to evict him. Whether they could do so without taking lengthy court proceedings depended on whether he had a lease or a licence.

4.50 The House of Lords held that he had only a licence. Lord Templeman said that the limitations contained in the licence confirmed the fact that the council

---

in the context of easements, see *IDC Group Ltd v Clark* (1992) 65 P & CR 179. It is, however, difficult to see how such arguments do not undermine *Street v Mountford*.

[77] (1863) 2 H & C 121, 159 ER 51, discussed in paras s 4.04 and 4.06.
[78] [1936] 3 All ER 483, CA.
[79] Essentially, the right to run the bar and the cloakrooms.
[80] [1992] 2 AC 288, HL.

retained possession of all the rooms in the hostel in order to supervise and control the activities of the occupiers. Although the claimant physically occupied the room, he did not enjoy possession exclusively of the council. His Lordship did point out, however, that this was a special case. In *Street v Mountford* itself, the same judge had noted that the courts should be 'astute to detect and frustrate sham devices and artificial transactions whose only object is to disguise the grant of a tenancy and to evade the Rent Acts'.[81] An example of such astuteness is to be found in *Aslan v Murphy (No 1)*.[82] Here, the defendant occupied a small single room (4ft 3in by 12ft 6in) under an agreement which stated that, 'The Licensor is not willing to grant the Licensee exclusive possession of any part of the Room', that the licensee had a licence to use the room between the hours of midnight and 10.30 am and between noon and midnight each day, that the licensor could permit other persons to use the room in connection with the licensee and that the licensor would retain the keys to the room and had an absolute right of entry at all times. Was this a lease or a licence?

The Court of Appeal held that it was a lease. The provisions that the defendant **4.51** was to share and to vacate for 90 minutes each day were both unrealistic and clearly pretences. Provisions as to keys, which the court said were often pretences, did not have any magic in themselves, for the landlord may well need a key so as to effect repairs and do other things which he may be obligated under the lease to perform.

Where *joint occupiers* are involved, the position becomes more complex. **4.52** Essentially, the problem is that because each will have a right to occupy, no one can claim to have a right to exclusive possession of the premises. The only way in which this problem can be resolved in favour of the grant of a lease is to find that there has been a grant to the occupiers together. In other words, it must be possible to say that there is one lease which is 'co-owned'.[83] Anything short of co-ownership means that the occupiers can have only individual licences. The problem of joint occupiers arose in two cases in the House of Lords, *Antoniades v Villiers*[84] and *AG Securities v Vaughan*.[85]

In *Antoniades v Villiers* an unmarried couple entered into two identical licence **4.53** agreements for occupation with a fee simple holder of a one-bedroomed flat. Both agreements recited that the 'licensor' was unwilling to grant exclusive possession of any part of the premises and instead reserved on his own behalf a

---

[81] [1985] AC 809, 825, HL.
[82] [1990] 1 WLR 766, CA. See also *Crancour Ltd v Da Silvesa* (1986) 52 P & CR 204, CA; *Hadjiloucas v Crean* [1988] 1 WLR 1006, CA.
[83] The topic of co-ownership is dealt with in Part E.
[84] [1990] 1 AC 417, HL.
[85] ibid.

right at any time to use the premises in common with the licensee and such other persons as the owner might permit to use the rooms. Although the agreements provided that they were only for 'single occupiers', the 'licensor' provided a double bed at the couple's request. The House of Lords held this to be a lease. The two agreements had an air of total unreality about them when read as separate licences. They were clearly interdependent, because both occupiers would have signed or neither. Consequently they had to be read together so as to constitute a single agreement. The landlord's reservation of a right to share was clearly never intended to be acted upon and inserted solely to avoid the provisions of the Rent Acts. It was not genuine and could be ignored. The combination of these two factors meant that a lease had been granted to the couple under the form of co-ownership known as a joint tenancy.[86] Accordingly, they were entitled to the protection of the Rent Acts.

4.54 A co-ownership solution was not, however, applied in *AG Securities v Vaughan*, which concerned a four-bedroomed flat shared by four single persons. The population was a shifting one, with each occupier entering into separate agreements at separate times for separate amounts of rent with the landlord. A majority of the Court of Appeal held that they were joint tenants of a lease of the flat but the House of Lords disagreed. In the words of Lord Bridge:

> The four respondents acquired their contractual rights to occupy the flat in question and undertook their relevant obligations by separate agreements with the appellants made at different times and on different terms. These rights and obligations having initially been several, I do not understand by what legal alchemy they could ever become joint.

There was nothing in the agreements themselves which was in the nature of a sham and so they had to be given the effect they created in law, namely that they were only licences to occupy the flat.

4.55 A claim to be joint tenants also failed in *Mikeover Ltd v Brady*[87] on facts almost identical to *Antoniades v Villiers*, where the Court of Appeal held that the particular separate arrangements could not amount to a joint tenancy of a lease because they imposed separate obligations on the occupiers in respect of deposits and the payment of rent. The court held that if one occupant did not pay rent for any particular month the landlord would have been unable to sue the other occupier for that amount. There being no joint obligation, there could be no joint tenancy. This difficult point was not fully ventilated in *Antoniades v Villiers*, where the landlord chose to represent himself before their Lordships' House, though arguably it should not have been fatal, for the requirement that in a joint tenancy there

---

[86] Paras 4.355–4.361.
[87] [1989] 3 All ER 618, CA.

be unity of interest means only that the co-owners take the same estate, not that they incur the same liabilities.[88]

In both *AG Securities v Vaughan* and *Mikeover v Brady* the claim of the occupiers **4.56** to be joint tenants of a lease failed because the court found that their obligations were not joint. There are, as we shall see,[89] two forms of co-ownership in English law, the joint tenancy and the tenancy in common. In both decisions, only the former was considered, and there is an argument that had the occupier's case been put forward on the basis of a tenancy in common, where it is certain that no joint obligations are involved, it might well have succeeded.[90]

Certainty of term.[91]   There is no limit on how long the term of a lease might be. **4.57** A lease for 3,000 or even 3,000,000 years will be valid. But there must at least be some limit, and, moreover, that limit must be certain. As Blackstone explained:

> Every estate which must expire at a period certain and prefixed, by whatever words created, is an estate for years. And therefore this estate is frequently called a term, *terminus*, because its duration or continuance is bounded, limited, and determined; for every such estate must have a certain beginning, and certain end.[92]

Thus, it is in the nature of a lease that it has a certain end. So, for example, in *Lace v Chantler*,[93] which concerned a 'lease' of furnished premises at 16s 5d a week, the rent book stated that the premises were taken 'furnished for duration', meaning the duration of the Second World War. A notice to quit was served which was valid to determine a weekly tenancy, but not a lease for the duration of the war, the war not yet being over. The question was whether such a lease could be created, or whether what had in fact been created was a weekly tenancy.

The Court of Appeal held that it was not possible to create a lease for the duration **4.58** of the war. Lord Greene MR said that a term created by a leasehold tenancy agreement must be expressed either with certainty and specifically, or by reference to something which could, at the time the lease took effect, be looked to as a certain ascertainment of what the term was meant to be. Here, at the time the agreement took effect, the term was completely uncertain. Since it was impossible to say how long the tenancy would last, it was void.

---

[88] RJ Smith, *Property Law* (5th edn, 2006) 369.

[89] Paras 4.354–4.363.

[90] S Bright (1992) 142 NLJ 575. It is sometimes said that the reforms made in 1925 to co-ownership (see paras 4.383–4.390) preclude such an argument. But this overlooks the fact that the joint tenancy which arises when a title is attempted to be conveyed to tenants in common is by virtue of s 34(2) of the Law of Property Act 1925 fictitious.

[91] P Sparkes, 'Certainty of Leasehold Terms' (1993) 109 LQR 93; S Bright, 'Uncertainty in Leases–Is it a Vice?' (1993) 13 LS 38.

[92] Blackstone, 2 *Commentaries* 143.

[93] [1944] KB 368, CA.

4.59   This approach was endorsed by the House of Lords in *Prudential Assurance Ltd v London Residuary Body*,[94] where an agreement purported to create a lease of a strip of land to subsist 'until the lessor required the land for road-widening purposes'. No such lease, said the House of Lords, could be created. The rule that a lease must have a certain limit was over 500 years old and too entrenched even for the House of Lords to overturn.

4.60   There are, however, ways round this rule. When it is said that the period of a lease must be certain, what is actually meant is that the *maximum* period of the lease must be certain. It is not fatal to its validity that a lease might come to an end because of the occurrence of some contingency before that date. Thus, in both *Lace v Chantler* and *Prudential Assurance Ltd v London Residuary Body* the lease would have been valid had it been expressed in the following terms:

> to X for 999 years or until [the war ends/land is needed for road-widening purposes] whichever be the sooner.

4.61   A lease may be for a fixed term or may be periodic, for example, from week to week or from year to year. In the latter case the tenancy will continue until one or other party brings it to an end. It is thus uncertain at the outset how long the tenancy will continue. The requirement of certainty of term applies to all tenancies. How then does a periodic tenancy satisfy the test of certainty of term? The answer was given by Lord Templeman in *Prudential Assurance Ltd v London Residuary Body*. He said:

> A tenancy from year to year is saved from being uncertain because each party has power by notice to determine at the end of any year. The term continues until determined as if both parties made a new agreement at the end of each year for a new term for the ensuing year.[95]

4.62   **Premium or periodical payment.**   Lord Templeman's third substantive requirement for a lease in *Street v Mountford* was the payment of a premium[96] or rent. This is dubious. The point arose in *Ashburn Anstalt v Arnold*.[97] In this case the Court of Appeal held that an agreement under which a person could occupy a shop 'rent free' did indeed amount to a lease of the shop. There was no rule, they said, that a tenancy could not exist without a rent. The question of rent arose again in the Court of Appeal in *Skipton Building Society v Clayton*,[98] where the court held that an agreement to purchase a title to a house for one-third of its true value and to guarantee the vendors the right to remain living in it rent-free

---

[94] [1992] 2 AC 386, HL.
[95] [1992] 2 AC 386, 394, HL.
[96] In the case of a long lease it is common to capitalize part of the rent and make it payable in a lump sum at the date the lease is granted. This is known as a fine or a premium.
[97] [1989] Ch 1.
[98] (1993) 66 P & CR 223, CA.

for the remainder of their lives had the effect of granting to the vendors a tenancy of the house which bound mortgagees to whom a mortgage had been granted.

(b) The running of covenants in leases

A lease agreement will normally contain a number of express or implied promises **4.63** or covenants by both parties, including, on the part of the tenant, to pay rent, and, on the part of the landlord, to allow the tenant 'quiet enjoyment' of the land.[99] Other common covenants include the obligation to keep the premises in repair, which may be cast on either party, the obligation to pay rates and taxes, a covenant on the part of the tenant against assignment, underletting, or parting with possession, a covenant to use the premises only as a private dwelling-house, and a covenant to insure. There is no space here to discuss the precise content of these covenants, nor when they will be implied by the courts.[100] The only question we will address is how far such covenants 'run' with assignments of either the lease or the reversion.

We should immediately notice that covenants have two elements, a benefit **4.64** and a burden and, further, that not all covenants contained in a lease place a burden on the tenant. Some, such as a covenant by the landlord to repair, enure to the benefit of the tenant. The question is, if the original landlord assigns the reversion to a third party, whether the original tenant can now enforce the covenant against the assignee. And what of the situation where the original tenant assigns? Can the new tenant claim the benefit of the covenant? The same questions arise where the burden of the covenant is placed on the tenant rather than the landlord.

The law on this topic was radically altered by the Landlord and Tenant (Covenants) **4.65** Act 1995, though not with retrospective effect. There will still be many leases governed, at least in part, by the old law. We will therefore divide our discussion between the law prior to 31st December 1995 and that since 1st January 1996, when the statute came into force. This has the advantage of aiding our understanding of the new law through seeing the problems generated by the old.

---

[99] This does not literally mean that the landlord makes a guarantee against noise: *Jenkins v Jackson* (1888) 40 Ch D 71. A covenant for 'quiet enjoyment' is an undertaking that the tenant will be free from disturbance by the exercise of adverse rights over the land or over other neighbouring land occupied by the lessor or some person for whom he is responsible: *Hudson v Cripps* [1896] 1 Ch 265, 268.

[100] For a detailed treatment, see C Harpum, *Megarry & Wade: The Law of Real Property* (6th edn, 2000), 860–917.

(i) Pre-1996 law[101]

4.66 We will divide our discussion between the position of the original contracting parties and that of assignees. It is as well to notice at the outset that no distinction is drawn between positive and negative covenants, a distinction which is crucial in the running of covenants outside the landlord/tenant relationship, and which explains why there are generally no such things as apartments held under freehold rather than leasehold title. Although there is no theoretical difficulty with blocks of flats being divided on a freehold basis, there is a practical problem in that the burden of positive obligations on either the landlord (to repair outside of building, to maintain common parts etc) or tenants (to contribute to costs of upkeep) cannot run between freeholders. This is not the case with leases where, as we will shortly see, the burden of both positive and negative covenants can run. To counter some of the problems of freehold titles to flats, a new form of landholding, Commonhold, was introduced in 2002.[102]

4.67 **Liability of original contracting parties.** Under the old law, both the original landlord and original tenant were liable to each other on all covenants in the lease, whatever their nature, throughout the continuance of the term. This was so whether or not they had assigned the lease or reversion in question. The reason was the continuing privity of contract between them. It often came as a shock for an original tenant to be sent a bill for rent on a lease which they had assigned many years ago. Yet in a recessionary climate, landlords more and more looked to original tenants when current tenants were unable to perform their obligations.

4.68 **Rights and liabilities of assignees.** Although an assignment of either the lease or the reversion will mean that there is no privity of contract between the current landlord and tenant, there is nevertheless said to be a 'privity of estate'. Broadly speaking, this means that covenants which are integral to the lease can still be enforced by and against such parties. To understand the position of assignees fully, we will consider first the position of the assignees of the reversion, and then the position of assignees of original tenant. It should be stressed that we are still concerned with the position prior to 1996.

---

101 See generally, D Gordan [1987] Conv 103; R Thornton (1991) 11 Legal Studies 47.

102 Briefly, this is a scheme under which an area of land or a building is divided into units. Each unit-holder has a freehold title to his or her unit, but a corporation is formed (the Commonhold Association), in which is vested title to the common parts. All unit-holders are members of the Commonhold Association. Something known as a Commonhold Community Statement determines the rights and obligations of both the Commonhold Association and the individual unit-holders. That Commonhold Community Statement can include both restrictive covenants and positive covenants in the form of obligations to insure, repair, and maintain or to pay sums of money to the Commonhold Association to carry out these tasks. Details should be sought in the standard works on land law, eg, EH Burn and J Cartwright, *Cheshire & Burn's Modern Law of Real Property* (17th edn, 2006), 183–8.

Assignees of the reversion.   The position of assignees of the original landlord **4.69**
was always governed by statute, section 141(1) of the Law of Property Act 1925
providing that:

> Rent reserved by a lease, and the benefit of every covenant or provision therein
> contained, having reference to the subject-matter thereof, and on the lessee's part
> to be observed or performed, and every condition of re-entry and other condition
> therein contained, shall be annexed and incident to and shall go with the reversion-
> ary estate in the land, or in any part thereof . . .

According to this provision, the *benefit* of covenants entered into between landlord and tenant passed automatically with an assignment of the reversion, ie,
without the need for any express assignment of the benefit of the covenants themselves, provided only that they had 'reference to the subject-matter' of the lease.

The passing of the *burden* of the landlord's covenants to an assignee of the reversion   **4.70**
was covered by section 142(1) Law of Property Act 1925, which provided that:

> The obligation under a condition or of a covenant entered into by a lessor with
> reference to the subject-matter of the lease shall . . . be annexed and incident to and
> shall go with the reversionary estate.

Thus, the burden of the landlord's covenants in the lease passed automatically
to an assignee of the reversion, provided again that they had reference to the
subject-matter of the lease.

It is not therefore the case that the benefit and burden of all covenants contained   **4.71**
in the lease run with the reversion. The statute only transmits those 'having
reference to the subject-matter of the lease', which has been held to mean the
same thing as 'touches and concerns the land'.[103] What does this phrase mean?
There may be many covenants contained in a lease and some, such as a covenant
by a landlord of a public house that he would not operate a similar business
with a half mile radius,[104] may have nothing whatsoever to do with the landlord/
tenant relationship. The rule was that only those part of the landlord and tenant
relationship should run with the reversion.

What then is the meaning of 'touching and concerning'? Unfortunately, all   **4.72**
definitions in this area are prone to circularity. The classic is that contained in
Mayor of Congleton v Pattison,[105] where Bayley J said:

> In order to bind the assignee the covenant must either affect the land itself during
> the term, such as those which regard the mode of occupation; or it must be such as

---

[103] *Davis v Town Properties Investment Corpn* [1903] 1 Ch 797. 'Touches and concerns' is the
test used for assignees of the lease, which was governed by common law rather than statute: see
paras 4.72–4.73.
[104] *Thomas v Hayward* (1869) LR 4 Exch 311.
[105] (1808) 10 East 130, 138.

per se, and not merely from collateral circumstances, affects the value of the land at the end of the term.

The·covenant, in other words, must benefit or burden the landlord or tenant in their capacity as landlord or tenant and not because of some extraneous circumstance. The issue arose in *Kumar v Dunning*,[106] where the question was whether a covenant by a surety guaranteeing performance of covenants by a tenant which themselves touched and concerned the land was itself a covenant touching and concerning the land. A number of first instance decisions had held that it was not, on the basis *inter alia* that the covenant should require something to be done which affected the land itself, not merely its value. The Court of Appeal held that it was indeed a covenant which 'touched and concerned' the land. In the course of his judgment, Sir Nicolas Browne-Wilkinson V-C said that the test whether the benefit of a covenant touched and concerned the land was whether it was beneficial to the owner for the time being of the covenantee's land and no one else and, in the case of a covenant to pay a sum of money, whether the existence of the covenant and the right to payment thereunder affected the value of the land in whomsoever it was vested at the time.[107] This definition was subsequently approved by the House of Lords in *P & A Swift Investments v Combined English Stores*.[108]

4.73 The question which covenants do, and which do not, 'touch and concern' the land is best understood by reference to examples.[109] Thus, the following tenants' covenants have been held to touch and concern the land: to pay rent; to repair; not to assign without the consent of the landlord; to insure against fire; to renew the lease; to erect buildings; to act as a surety for the payment of rent. Those which have been held to fall on the other side of the line include covenants: and to pay an annual sum to a third party; to pay rates in respect of other land; and not to employ persons living in other parishes to work in the demised mill. Landlords' covenants which have been held to touch and concern the land include covenants: for quiet enjoyment; to supply the land with water; not to build on certain parts of the adjoining land; not to determine a periodic tenancy during its first three years; and to accept a surrender of the lease from the tenant after a rent review. Landlords' covenants held not to touch and concern the land include: to sell the reversion at a stated price, at the tenant's option; to pay at the end of the lease for chattels not amounting to fixtures; to pay the tenant £500 at the end of the lease

---

106 [1989] QB 193.

107 [1989] QB 193, 204.

108 [1989] AC 632. Doubts have, however, arisen whether the test laid down is applicable outside the context of surety covenants: *Caerns Motor Services Ltd v Texaco Ltd* [1994] 1 WLR 1249.

109 The following are taken from C Harpum, *Megarry & Wade: The Modern Law of Real Property* (6th edn, 2000), 955–6.

unless a new lease is granted; and to allow the tenant to display advertising signs on other premises.

Assignees of the lease.   Although the landlord's position has long been regulated   **4.74**
by statute, the Grantees of Reversion Act 1540 being the forebear of sections 141 and 142 of the 1925 Act, statute made no provision for the passing of the benefit and burden of covenants from the original tenant to his assigns. However, the common law took its lead from statute and held that if the benefit and burden of a landlord's covenants were to pass with the reversion, then the same should apply to assignments of the lease. The starting point is the decision in *Spencer's Case*.[110] Spencer granted a 21-year lease of land to T, who covenanted for himself and his executors to build a brick wall on part of the land. T later assigned the lease to A1, who in turn assigned it to A2. The wall was never built and Spencer brought an action against A2 for breach of covenant. The court, drawing by analogy on the Grantees of Reversion Act 1540, held that the benefit and burden of all covenants in a lease which touched and concerned the land were annexed to the lease itself and passed automatically to assignees of the lease. On the facts, however, the burden of this particular covenant was held not to have passed to A1 and thence to A2, for the reason that the covenant related to a thing not in existence (*in esse*) at the time the covenant was made. Only covenants made in relation to things in existence at the time the covenant was made, for example, a covenant to repair an existing wall, were automatically annexed. Covenants relating to things not in yet existence would only run if they were made between the lessee, his executors *and his assigns*.[111] Thus, *Spencer's Case* did for the transmission of the benefit and burden of leasehold covenants to assignees of the lease what sections 141 and 142 of the Law of Property Act 1925 did for the transmission of the benefit and burden of leasehold covenants to assignees of reversion. In this regard, we should note that once again no distinction was drawn between positive and negative covenants.

Indemnity.   Where the original tenant had assigned his lease, then, as we have   **4.75**
seen, both he and the current tenant were liable on the covenants, the original tenant by virtue of privity of contract, his assignee because of privity of estate.

---

[110] (1583) 5 Co Rep 16a.

[111] As a result, draftsmen would routinely include the words 'and his assigns' to ensure that covenants concerning things not yet in existence would run with assignments of the lease. Since 1925 these words are no longer necessary, for s 79(1) Law of Property Act 1925 provides:

A covenant relating to any land of a covenantor or capable of being bound by him, shall, unless a contrary intention is expressed, be deemed to be made by the covenantor on behalf of himself his successors in title and the persons deriving title under him or them, and . . . shall have effect as if such successors and other persons were expressed.

This subsection extends to a covenant to do some act relating to the land notwithstanding that the subject-matter may not be in existence when the covenant is made.

Where the original tenant is forced to pay in respect of any breach committed by his assignee, he can through the law of unjust enrichment claim to be indemnified by the assignee.[112] This was not, however, a particularly effective remedy for the original tenant, for it depended on the solvency of the current tenant, and the reason why the original tenant was being sued was most likely his insolvency. Moreover, there was no provision for the original tenant to bring the lease to an end. As we shall see, this state of affairs has been radically altered by the new legislation.

(ii) Post-1996 law

4.76 The rule that the original tenant remains liable throughout the currency of the contractual term was considered by many to be harsh and led the Law Commission to recommend that the liability of the original tenant to a lease should not survive its assignment and that because of the inequality of bargaining power between the parties, such a provision should not be capable of being contracted out of. Those proposals were given the force of law in Landlord and Tenant (Covenants) Act 1995.

4.77 The Act does a number of things. First, it provides in section 3(1) that in all tenancies created after the 1st January 1996 the benefit and burden of all covenants in the lease (other than those expressed to be personal to any person (section 3(6)(a)) will pass on any assignment of the lease or reversion to the assignee.[113] What is notable is that the Act, unlike the old law, draws no distinction between covenants which do and do not touch and concern the land: the benefit and burden of all covenants in the lease pass under this provision.

4.78 The second and main provision concerns the continuing liability of the original parties. The position of the tenant is governed by section 5, which provides that an assignment automatically releases the tenant from all liabilities under the covenants in the lease unless, by virtue of section 11, the assignment is in breach of covenant or by operation of law. This extinction of liability applies whether the assigning tenant is the original tenant or a successor in title. In other words, neither the original tenant nor any assignee will be or can be made liable under the lease after parting it. And to ensure that landlords do not exercise their stronger bargaining powers, section 25 contains a no-contracting out provision.

4.79 The reforms in favour of the landlord are not so generous. His position is governed by section 6. If it is the landlord who assigns, then there is no automatic release. Instead, he may apply to the tenant to be released from post-assignment liability under the lease: he will then be released from liability if either the tenant agrees,

---

112 The topic is discussed in detail at paras 18.141–18.148 of this work.
113 Landlord and Tenant (Covenants) Act 1995, s 3(6)(a).

or if he obtains a declaration from the court that it is reasonable for him to be released from liability.

There is only one situation in which the tenant can be liable for post-assignment **4.80** breaches: where the landlord and tenant have entered into an 'authorized guarantee agreement'. Such agreements can only be made where the lease contains a covenant against assignment or a covenant against assignment without the landlord's consent and such guarantee is both required and authorized to be required as a condition of the permission to assign. And though favouring the landlord, this provision does at least have the merit of drawing the issue to the attention of the tenant when he is negotiating the grant of the lease.

(iii) Provisions applicable to all leases

The above reforms only apply to leases created after 1st January 1996. There are, **4.81** however, a number of more general alterations which apply to all tenancies, whenever created. The first is that if the landlord wishes to recover arrears from the original tenant (or a guarantor), then he must within six months of the payment becoming due serve on such person a notice informing him both that the payment is due and that the landlord intends to recover it from the recipient of the notice.[114] Service of such a notice triggers the recipient's right to take what is known as an 'overriding lease' of the premises.[115] This is designed to meet the complaint that the tenant or guarantor who was forced to pay the assignee's rent had neither a power to bring the ongoing liability to an end, nor the ability to take any benefits under the lease he was subsidising. The overriding lease is interposed between the assignee and the landlord, so that the original tenant or guarantor now becomes the landlord of the assignee and can forfeit the lease for non-payment of rent. This then enables him to assign the lease to someone else or to negotiate a surrender with his landlord.

(3) Easements

The value locked up in land does not consist solely of the ability to enjoy its **4.82** exclusive possession. A neighbour, for example, might be willing to pay for the rights of access to his own land across the neighbouring land, or the right to run his drains over neighbouring land to the main sewer. Such rights could of course exist as personal rights of user only, binding on and benefiting the parties to the agreement themselves, but no others. To confine such rights to personal status has the advantage that it does not permanently lower the value of the title to the burdened land passed on to future holders. On the other hand, so long as the right

---

[114] Landlord and Tenant (Covenants) Act 1995, s 17.
[115] Landlord and Tenant (Covenants) Act 1995, s 19.

granted is not too inconsistent with the use to which future titleholders might put the land, the recognition of some property rights beyond those to exclusive possession could be beneficial. After all, the value which a proprietary right of access or drainage over another's land adds to the benefited title will often far outweigh the diminution in value of that which is burdened. It is not surprising, therefore, to find that a limited category of rights of use of land in the exclusive possession of another have been admitted to the status of property rights. They are called easements.

4.83 Common easements are rights of way over land in the exclusive possession of another, rights to run drains under such land, rights of light, rights of storage, and the use of chimney flues. Though it is sometimes said that the list of easements is not closed,[116] this statement must be read in the context of the *numerus clausus* rule outlined above.[117] Although new types of easement can be brought into being, they must at least conform to the standard model. Its requirements are as follows. First, there must be a dominant and a servient tenement. Second, the easement must 'accommodate' the dominant tenement. Third, the rights to possession of the dominant and servient tenements must be in different people. Fourth, the content of the right must be certain.[118] Fifth, no positive obligations may be imposed on the possessor of the servient tenement. And sixth, though subject to limited exceptions, the right must not be negative in nature, but entitle its holder to do something on the servient tenement.

(a) **Dominant and servient tenement**

4.84 An easement is essentially a right of one title-holder over land in the possession of another. For that reason, there must be a both land which is benefited and land which is burdened. This is illustrated by the decision of the House of Lords in *King v David Allen (Billposting) Ltd*.[119] The holder of a fee simple title contracted to allow an advertising company the exclusive right to affix advertisements to the side of an as yet unbuilt cinema for a period of four years. The cinema was built and a lease granted to a third party who, though he knew of the existence of contract when taking his lease, refused to allow the signposting to continue. The advertising company sued the fee simple holder for breach of contract in granting the lease and thereby disabling itself from performing its contract. The fee simple holder argued that the right it had granted was an easement, which therefore bound the

---

116 In *Dyce v Lady Hay* (1852) 1 Macq 305, Lord St Leonards said: 'The category of servitudes and easements must alter and expand with the changes that take place in the circumstances of mankind.'

117 Paras 4.09–4.11.

118 This condition is not, of course, peculiar to easements.

119 [1916] AC 54.

lessee, with the result that he had not acted in breach of contract in letting out the land. The argument was rejected by the House of Lords. The right given to the advertising company was not an easement because it did not relate to any land in the possession of the advertising company. It created mere personal rights, which rights could not bind the lessee. The fee simple holder had therefore acted in breach of contract in letting the land, for it had thereby put it beyond its powers to perform its contract.

It is said to be difficult to justify this rule. Arguably, economically valuable rights **4.85** could be created as easements in gross which are unlikely to make the title to the servient land either unduly difficult to investigate or so encumbered by adverse claims as to deter purchasers.[120]

(b) Benefit to dominant tenement

Not only must there be a dominant tenement, but the dominant tenement must **4.86** be benefited by the easement. The easement, it is said, must 'accommodate the dominant tenement', a requirement also known in civilian systems.[121] The test is whether the right makes the land a better or more convenient property. Thus, a right of way over neighbouring land will generally accommodate the dominant tenement by making access to the dominant tenement more convenient. And a right to run drains under a neighbouring property will clearly have a similar effect. It is not, however, enough that the right granted increases the value of the title to the dominant tenement; it must make the use of the dominant tenement more commodious. Thus, a perpetual right of free entry to Lord's cricket ground might make the title to which it was attached more valuable, but it would not qualify as an easement, for it would not do anything for the land *qua* land.

The cricketing example was given by the Court of Appeal in one of the leading **4.87** cases on easements, *Re Ellenborough Park*.[122] In 1855, the White Cross Estate, which included Ellenborough Park, was being developed for building purposes. The purchasers of titles to several plots surrounding the park were each given in their conveyances certain rights of user over the park, including 'the full enjoyment . . . at all times hereafter in common with the other persons to whom such easements may be granted of the pleasure ground set out in front of the said plot of land . . . in the centre of the square called Ellenborough Park . . .'. The reason for this arrangement was that the houses built on the plots being sold off did not have gardens of their own. During the Second World War, the park was requisitioned by the Crown, and the entitlement of the surrounding titleholders to statutory compensation

---

[120] M Sturley, 'Easements in Gross' (1980) 96 LQR 557.
[121] The so-called 'praedial' rule.
[122] [1956] Ch 131, 174 (Sir Raymond Evershed MR).

depended on whether they had been deprived of a property right. The titleholders claimed that they had, in that they had been deprived of an easement. The Court of Appeal held that the right of enjoyment was indeed an easement appurtenant to the plots bought by the original purchasers and that the plaintiffs were therefore entitled to compensation. Although admitting that the case was borderline, the Court of Appeal held that the use of a garden is closely connected with the use and enjoyment of the land and the right was calculated to afford all the amenities which it was the purpose of the garden of a house to provide.[123] It is difficult, however, to see how it could have made the use of the plot on which the house stood any more commodious. The same problem exists with respect to the grant of rights to park cars. The fact that a titleholder has a right to park his car on neighbouring land can hardly be said to make the use of his own land more commodious. Yet car-parking rights have been held to be capable of amounting to easements in a number of recent cases.[124] It was, however, the failure of the right to accommodate the dominant tenement which prevented it qualifying as an easement in *Hill v Tupper*.[125] Although in that case there was both a dominant and a servient tenement, the 'exclusive right to put pleasure boats on the canal' did not make the occupation of the dominant tenement more convenient. As Sir Raymond Evershed MR pointed out in *Re Ellenborough Park*, it was 'clear that what the plaintiff was trying to do was to set up, under the guise of an easement, a monopoly which had no normal connection with the ordinary use of his land, but which was merely an independent business enterprise. So far from the right claimed sub-serving or accommodating the land, the land was but a convenient incident to the exercise of the right'.[126]

4.88 Somewhat anomalously, it seems to be no objection that the right claimed as an easement benefits only a business being conducted on the land. Thus, in *Moody v Steggles*,[127] the right to affix a sign indicating the existence of a public house was upheld as an easement, Fry J reasoning that 'the house can only be used by an occupant, and . . . the occupant only uses the house for the business which he pursues, and therefore in some manner (direct or indirect) an easement is more or less connected with the mode in which the occupant of the house uses it'.[128] On the other side of the line is of course *Hill v Tupper* itself. Although at first sight it is difficult to see the distinction between them, two possible factors are said to explain the different results.[129] First, the whole point of the easement in

---

[123] [1956] Ch 131, 174–5.
[124] For example, *London & Blenheim Estates Ltd v Ladbroke Retail Parks Ltd* [1992] 1 WLR 1278 (see para 4.91).
[125] (1863) 2 H & C 121, discussed, para 4.04.
[126] [1956] Ch 131, 175.
[127] (1879) 12 Ch D 261.
[128] ibid 266.
[129] KS Gray & SF Gray, *Elements of Land Law* (4th edn, 2005), 625–26.

Hill v Tupper was to set up a business, rather than to benefit an existing business; the right, in other words, was the business. It might be different, for example, in the case of a right granted to a hotel owner to put boats on a canal as part of his hotel business. Second, the right was in effect a commercial monopoly, having no connection with the use of land.

(c) Rights to exclusive possession vested in different people

An easement is a right over land in the exclusive possession of another. It is not **4.89** therefore possible for a right which excludes that other from possession to be classified as an easement, for such a right would be tantamount to the grant of a lease or a freehold estate. It was for this reason that the right claimed in *Copeland v Greenhalf*[130] was held not to amount to an easement. In that case, the plaintiff had a title to an orchard and an adjoining house. Access to the orchard from the road was provided by a strip of land, of varying width, about 150 feet long. The defendant was a wheelwright whose premises were across the road from the plaintiff's land. The defendant proved that for 50 years he and his father before him had, to the plaintiff's knowledge, used one side of the plaintiff's strip of land to store and repair vehicles in connection with his business as a wheelwright, always leaving room for the plaintiff to have access to the orchard. The plaintiff sought an order for possession of the land, but the defendant counter-claimed that he had a prescriptive right to an easement. Upjohn J held that such a right could not be an easement. It went wholly outside any normal head of an easement, and really amounted to a claim of joint user, which could not therefore be acquired by prescription.[131]

What then of an easement of storage? It has been accepted ever since *A-G of* **4.90** *Southern Nigeria v John Holt (Liverpool) Ltd*[132] that there may be an easement to store goods on the servient land. This case was distinguished by Upjohn J in *Copeland v Greenhalf*. A right of storage could be an easement but only so long as it did not allocate a specific area to the sole use of the dominant owner.[133]

Similar difficulties have arisen where claimants have claimed the benefit of **4.91** an easement to park cars. Although not objectionable per se, the courts have held that it is a matter of degree. So, in *London & Blenheim Estates Ltd v Ladbroke Retails Parks Ltd*,[134] it was held that a right to park a car in a large car park did

---

[130] [1952] Ch 488.
[131] Easements (and profits) are unique in English law in that they are the only rights which can be acquired by prescription: detail in C Harpum (ed), *Megarry and Wade on Real Property* (6th edn, 2000), 1118–41. Contrast the operation of lapse of time: see paras 4.469–4.477.
[132] [1915] AC 599, PC.
[133] [1952] Ch 488, 498.
[134] [1992] 1 WLR 1278, Judge Paul Baker QC.

not oust the fee simple holder from possession of the land concerned and so was capable of subsisting as an easement. However, in *Batchelor v Marlow*,[135] the Court of Appeal held that a claim by a car repairer to a prescriptive right to an easement to park six cars on a strip of land during working hours from Mondays to Fridays could not amount to an easement as it left the holder of the dominant tenement without reasonable use of his land either for parking or for any other purpose.

(d) Content of right must be certain

4.92 As with all property rights, indeed all rights whatever, the content of the right must be certain before it can qualify as an easement. It is for this reason that it is said that there can be no easement to a view,[136] to the natural flow of air,[137] or to privacy.[138]

4.93 The reasoning, however, is unconvincing, for, as we will see, it is perfectly possible to obtain a right to a view by the use of a restrictive covenant. The true reason would seem to be that, as we have just seen, easements, unlike restrictive covenants, can be acquired by prescription. The details of prescription are complex,[139] but it essentially allows rights to arise after a continuous period of long-user. The obvious dangers with prescription are twofold. First, the right can be acquired without those who would be burdened by it knowing that time was running against them. And second, even if they did know, it is not always practicable or even possible to take action to, as it were, 'stop the clock'. Evidence for the notion that it is the availability of prescription in fact which lies behind these rules is provided by the fact that a right to the flow of air is capable of forming the subject-matter of an easement when it relates to a defined aperture,[140] and that a right to light can amount to an easement if it exists in relation to a building which receives it through a window.[141] In both these cases, it is at least possible, though inherently wasteful, to stop the right arising. And as we have just seen, more extensive rights can be acquired as restrictive covenants.

---

135 [2003] 1 WLR 764, CA.
136 *William Aldred's Case* (1610) 9 Co Rep 57b, 58b: 'for prospect, which is a matter only of delight, and not of necessity, no action lies for stopping thereof . . . the law does not give an action for such things of delight' (Wray CJ).
137 *Webb v Bird* (1863) 13 CBNS 841.
138 *Browne v Flower* [1911] 1 Ch 219.
139 Details in C Harpum (ed), *Megarry & Wade: The Law of Real Property* (6th edn, 2000), 1118–41.
140 *Bass v Gregory* (1890) 25 QBD 481.
141 *Levet v Gas Light & Coke Co* [1919] 1 Ch 24.

(e) No positive obligation on possessor of servient tenement

A further condition is that the right claimed as an easement must not place any **4.94** positive burden on the possessor of the burdened land.[142] Thus, there can be no easement to maintain a supply of hot water to a house.[143] For the same reason, the possessor of land subject to a right of way in favour of his neighbour comes under no obligation to keep that right of way in good repair.[144] The only thing he must do is allow the right-holder entry to effect his own repairs. This requirement is perfectly orthodox, and is in fact a pre-condition of many modern-day property rights. Anything else would amount to too great an interference with personal liberty.

(f) Right of possessor of dominant tenement must be positive

The final requirement of an easement is that the right conferred on the possessor **4.95** of the dominant land is a right to do something on the servient land rather than one to restrain the possessor of the servient land from doing something on that land. Thus, in *Phipps v Pears*,[145] the Court of Appeal held that there could be no easement to restrain a neighbour from pulling down a building which was giving protection from the weather to a building on land in the possession of the claimant. Two ancient exceptions to this rule are the right to light and the right to support of a building. Such rights are only explicable as having been recognized by the courts before the advent of the restrictive covenant in the middle of the nineteenth century.[146]

(4) Profits à Prendre

A profit is different from an easement in that whereas an easement is a right to do **4.96** something on the land of another, a profit à prendre, as the name implies, is a right to take something from the land of another. And it must be literally 'from' the land. The right must be to take either part of the land itself, for example, minerals or crops, or the wild animals existing on it. Profits are quite ancient rights, and their content reflects an agrarian rather than an industrial economy. Typical profits are the right to graze animals on the land of another (pasture), to fish (piscary), to take game, to cut turf (turbary), to take timber (estovers), or to take minerals. Although they

---

[142] The one exception is the right of a possessor of land that his neighbour fence his own land so as to keep out cattle. It has been described as a 'spurious easement': *Lawrence v Jenkins* (1873) LR 8 QB 274, 279 (Archibald J).

[143] *Regis Property Co Ltd v Redman* [1956] QB 612.

[144] *Jones v Pritchard* [1908] 1 Ch 630.

[145] [1965] 1 QB 76.

[146] I Dawson & A Dunn, 'Negative Easements—A Crumb of Analysis' (1998) 18 LS 510, 517–8.

are generally appurtenant to land, unlike easements, they can exist in gross. There is, in other words, no need for a dominant tenement.

(5) Rentcharges[147]

4.97 A rentcharge is an annual sum of money (rent) issuing and payable out of land, the due payment of which is secured (charged) by a right of distress. A common usage of rentcharges was for the financing of sales of titles to land. However, with the advent of modern secured financing, this need has fallen away, and rentcharges are nowadays something of an anachronism. Rentcharges were also used as part of settlements of land to provide incomes for other members of the family, but with the demise of the settlement they are rarely encountered today. In fact, since 1977 the creation of most types of new rentcharges has been outlawed,[148] and those presently in existence cannot exist beyond the year 2037. They can, however, still be created in limited circumstances, the most important of which is in connection with schemes of development, where they are used to circumvent the rule that easements cannot impose positive burdens on the servient tenement.

(6) Restrictive Covenants

4.98 At common law, the burden of a covenant could not run unless it was a lease, a covenant in a lease where there was privity of estate, an easement, a profit, or a rentcharge. As we saw, it was because the right granted in *Hill v Tupper*[149] did not fall into any of these categories that its burden was held not to bind anyone other than its grantor. The courts of equity, however, took a more relaxed view, and allowed certain limited rights to bind strangers to their creation even though they did not come within the list. One such right is the covenant restrictive of the user of land.

4.99 The genesis of the restrictive covenant is the decision in *Tulk v Moxhay*.[150] In 1808, the plaintiff sold a fee simple title to a plot of land, Leicester Square in London, to one Elms, who covenanted to 'maintain the land as a garden and pleasure ground in an open state uncovered with any buildings and to allow residents, on payment of a reasonable rent, to use the gardens'. Elms sold his title on, and it eventually came into the hands of the defendant, who bought with knowledge of Elms' promise. The defendant proposed to build on the land and

---

[147] Details in C Harpum, *Megarry & Wade: The Law of Real Property* (6th edn, 2000), 1068–77.
[148] Rentcharges Act 1977, s 2.
[149] (1863) 2 H & C 121.
[150] (1848) 2 Ph 774. See generally, DJ Hayton, 'Restrictive Covenants as Property Interests' (1971) 87 LQR 539.

the plaintiff, who still retained titles to several houses in the square, sought an injunction (an equitable remedy) to prevent him from so doing. Despite the fact that the defendant was a stranger to the original covenant, the injunction was granted. Lord Cottenham LC said that if the court had no power to interfere on the plaintiff's behalf to restrain such action, it would be impossible for a title-holder to sell part of it without incurring the risk of what he retained proving worthless. The question was not, said the Lord Chancellor, whether the covenant ran with the land, but whether a party should be permitted to use the land in a manner inconsistent with the contract entered into by his vendor, with notice of which he purchased. The price that the original purchaser paid would, he said, have been reduced because of the covenant, and nothing could be more inequitable than that the original purchaser should be able to sell the property the next day for a greater price because a purchaser from him would not be bound. He said:

> If an equity is attached to property by the owner, no-one purchasing with notice of that equity can stand in a different situation from the party from whom he purchased.[151]

The decision in *Tulk v Moxhay* was given in such wide terms that it potentially **4.100** turned all covenants in respect of land into property rights, at least in equity. This, however, conflicts with the *numerus clausus* principle. It is not surprising, therefore, to find that later cases, while not overruling *Tulk v Moxhay* completely, sought to narrow its impact. They placed three limits on its operation, all borrowed from the law of easements. This has led to restrictive covenants often being described as 'negative easements'.[152] This is not, however, entirely accurate, for, unlike easements, they cannot be acquired by prescription.

The first limit is that the doctrine only applies to negative rather than positive **4.101** covenants. Thus, in *Haywood v Brunswick Permanent Building Society*,[153] a title to a parcel of land was conveyed by Charles Jackson to Edward Jackson, the latter covenanting to keep the buildings on it in repair. Both parties assigned their various rights, and the question arose whether an assignee from Edward, who had bought with knowledge of the covenant, was liable for failure to perform it. The Court of Appeal held that he was not. Brett LJ said that the plaintiff could not rely on *Tulk v Moxhay*. All that that case, and cases which had later followed it, had decided was that covenants which restricted the mode of user could be enforced against purchasers of title to the burdened the land who bought with notice of them. The present case concerned a positive covenant and if the relief

---

[151] (1848) 2 Ph 774, 778.
[152] *London & South Western Rlwy v Gomm* (1882) 20 Ch D 562, 583 (per Jessel MR).
[153] (1881) 8 QBD 403.

contended for was given, the court would be 'making a new equity', which it could not do.[154]

4.102　The second restriction is that there must be both a dominant and servient tenement. In *London County Council v Allen*,[155] a titleholder to a plot of land covenanted with the London County Council (LCC) that neither he nor his successors in title would build on the plot. The reason for this was to afford facilities for the continuation of a street which the LCC proposed to build at a later date. A purchaser of title from the covenantor with notice of the covenant proceeded to build on it and the LCC, relying on *Tulk v Moxhay*, sought an injunction to restrain him. The LCC, however, had no title to any land protected by the covenant in question. The Court of Appeal looked to the justification for the grant of the original injunction in *Tulk v Moxhay*, that otherwise 'it would be impossible for an owner of land to sell part of it without incurring the risk of rendering what he retains worthless'.[156] That justification was not present here, said the court, and they accordingly held that the covenant could not bind the purchaser. According to Buckley LJ, 'The doctrine ceases to be applicable when the person seeking to enforce the covenant against the derivative owner has no land to be protected by the negative covenant.'[157]

4.103　The third restriction is that the covenant must 'accommodate' the dominant tenement. In other words, the covenant must confer a benefit on the covenantee in his capacity of holder of a title to land. But unlike easements, the fact that the benefit to a business carried out on the land rather than the land itself has never been considered problematic.[158]

4.104　A final requirement for the doctrine to apply is that it must be shown that it was the intention of the original parties that the burden of the covenant run with the land concerned. To discover that intention, we look to the words of the conveyance for an indication that the covenant was meant to bind not only the covenantor but persons deriving title through him. A common form of words having this effect will be the recitation that the covenant was made by the covenantor 'for himself, his heirs and assigns'. Since 1925, these words have been supplied by statute.[159]

154　(1881) 8 QBD 403, 408. The rule was reaffirmed by the House of Lords in *Rhone v Stephens* [1994] 2 AC 310, where an argument that it had been abrogated by Law of Property Act 1925, s 79 was rejected.

155　[1914] 3 KB 642.

156　(1848) 2 Ph 774, 777.

157　[1914] 3 KB 642, 659.

158　*Wilkes v Spooner* [1911] 2 KB 473 (covenant not to use the premises as a general butcher); *Newton Abbott Co-operative Society Ltd v Williamson & Treadgold Ltd* [1952] Ch 286 (covenant not to use premises as an ironmonger).

159　Law of Property Act 1925, s 79(1): 'A covenant relating to any land of a covenantor . . . shall, unless a contrary intention is expressed, be deemed to have been made by the covenantor on behalf

As a right only recognized in equity, its holder will have no claim in tort (or **4.105** contract) for damages against third parties who interfere with it: the only claim will be for an injunction. The courts are, however, statutorily empowered to give damages in lieu of an injunction in certain circumstances.[160]

(7) Contracts to Purchase Estates in Land

A contract to purchase an estate in land without more creates in the purchaser **4.106** an equitable, though not a legal (common law), interest in that estate. It is thus another addition which equity has made to the list of property rights in respect of land.

The key to understanding this area of law is to realize that the common law and **4.107** equity take divergent views of the effect of the contract. Put simply, the common law holds that a contract of sale of a title to land creates only personal rights and is not of itself sufficient to pass any property rights from vendor to purchaser. At law, a property right in land will only pass on the execution of a deed (for unregistered land) or alteration of the register (in cases of registered land).[161] But suppose there is a valid contract for the sale of a proprietary right in land, and that the vendor, in breach of contract, refuses to perform (ie, refuses to convey the promised interest). The view taken by the common law is that the purchaser's only right in such a circumstance is to damages for breach of contract. The purchaser will only obtain a property right if and when the vendor does what he has promised and executes a conveyance of the right in favour of the purchaser.

Equity, however, takes a different view of the matter. In equity's eyes, the contract **4.108** of sale has the effect of transferring the promised title vendor to purchaser. The reality being that the title is still in the hands of the vendor, the court says that he holds it on trust for the purchaser. The trust is constructive, for it is created by the court. The reason why a constructive trust is imposed stems from the fact that a contract for the sale of land is one which equity will specifically enforce. Although as a general rule specific performance is an exceptional remedy in contract,[162] it issues as of course where the subject matter of the contract is a title to land, the rationale being that titles to land are unique and damages therefore an inadequate response to any breach of a contract to convey. And the fact that the purchaser will be able to compel the vendor to convey the title as promised has an important

---

of himself his successors in title and the persons deriving title under him or them, and . . . shall have effect as if such successors and other persons were expressed.'

160 Supreme Court Act 1981, s 50. See, eg, *Wrotham Park Estate Co Ltd v Parkside Homes Ltd* [1974] 1 WLR 798, where the measure of damages was such sum of money as might reasonably have been demanded as a quid pro quo for relaxing the covenant.

161 The topic of registration is explained in paras 4.447–4.448, 4.476–4.477, 4.494–4.500.

162 Paras 21.180ff.

consequence, which stems from the rule that 'equity looks upon that as done which ought to be done'. In equity's eyes, the vendor's duty to convey at law is fictionally treated as already performed, even though no conveyance has yet been executed. In equity's eyes, therefore, the purchaser becomes the titleholder on exchange of contracts, even though the title itself will cannot pass until the conveyance is made. It was for this reason that in *Lysaght v Edwards* Sir George Jessel MR said:

> The moment you have a valid contract for sale the vendor becomes in equity a trustee for the purchaser of the estate sold, and the beneficial ownership passes to the purchaser . . .[163]

The existence of this equitable property right in the purchaser even before completion has a number of consequences, the most important of which is that, provided the vendor still has the title in his hands, the purchaser will be able to claim the title itself and, in the event of the vendor's insolvency, will not be relegated to a personal claim for damages. However, why he is given this privileged position has never been satisfactorily explained.[164]

(8) Options to Purchase

4.109 An option to purchase a property right in respect of land, though one stage removed from a contract to purchase the right itself, is also recognized by courts of equity as having proprietary effect. Its recognition as such also turns on the fact that options to purchase, again because property rights in respect of land are unique, are specifically enforceable. Thus, as Sir George Jessel MR explained in *London and South Western Railway v Gomm*:

> [The promisor's] estate or interest is taken away from him without his consent, and the right to take it away being vested in another, the covenant giving the option must give [the promise] an interest in the land.[165]

4.110 On this reasoning, a right of pre-emption or first refusal is, by contrast, not a property right, either at law or in equity,[166] for the grantor of the right of pre-emption still retains control over the direction of the legal estate. The promisee has no right to call for a conveyance of a title to the land whenever he pleases. His only right is to be offered it first should the vendor decide to sell. This means, said Templeman LJ in *Pritchard v Briggs*, that the 'grant of the right of pre-emption creates a mere *spes* which the grantor of the right may either frustrate by choosing

---

[163] (1876) 2 Ch D 499, 506.

[164] For criticism, see WJ Swadling, 'The Vendor-Purchaser Constructive Trust', in S Degeling and J Edelman, *Equity in Commercial Law* (2005), 463–488.

[165] (1882) 20 Ch D 562, 581.

[166] *Pritchard v Briggs* [1980] Ch 338, CA.

not to fulfil the necessary conditions or may convert into an option and thus into an equitable interest by fulfilling the conditions'.[167] The position has, however, been recently altered in the case of registered land, the Land Registration Act 2002 now providing that a right of pre-emption 'has effect from the time of creation as an interest capable of binding successors in title'.[168]

(9) The Equity of Redemption

A mortgage is a device to secure the performance of an obligation on the part of the person who grants it. In its simplest form,[169] a mortgage operates by an out-right conveyance of the borrower's title with a proviso for reconveyance by the lender when the obligation is performed. But though the title is now in the hands of the lender, the borrower is given a new right, and 'equity of redemption' is the name given to the totality of those rights. As the name implies, it is one recognized only in courts of equity, and it is the interest the mortgagor has, no matter whether he has mortgaged a legal or an equitable interest. The equity of redemption is a property right, and so should the lender convey the mortgaged right to a third party, that third party may be bound to redeem the mortgage in favour of the borrower on performance of the secured obligation.   **4.111**

The equity of redemption is not a right peculiar to land, and arises whenever rights, personal or proprietary, are used as security for the performance of an obligation. Because of its complexity, the topic of mortgages (and other security devices) is dealt with in a separate chapter of this work.[170]   **4.112**

(10) Charges

It is also possible to 'charge' property rights in land (and personalty) so as to make them available as security for debts. The difference between a charge and a mortgage is that a charge does not entail a conveyance by the borrower of the right which is the subject matter of the security. Such charges, which are property rights in themselves, are also discussed in that chapter of this work dealing with security.[171]   **4.113**

---

[167] *Pritchard v Briggs* [1980] Ch 338, 418, CA.

[168] Land Registration Act 2002, s 115(1). The statute only affects rights of pre-emption coming into effect on or after 13 October 2004.

[169] Since 1925, it is no longer possible in the case of a mortgage of a title to land to create it by means of an outright conveyance of that title. Instead, a fee simple holder will grant to the mortgagee a long lease (normally for 3,000 years) or a 'charge by deed expressed to be by way of legal mortgage'. A lessee putting forward a lease as security will similarly grant a sub-lease to the mortgagee or a legal charge: Law of Property Act 1925, ss 85–7.

[170] Paras 5.01ff.

[171] Paras 5.04ff.

Originally a creature of equity, they have been introduced to the common law by statute.

(11) Licences: A Doubtful Case

4.114 We have already seen how some covenants, provided certain conditions are met, will constitute proprietary interests in respect of land. But, as decisions such as *Keppel v Bailey*,[172] *Hill v Tupper*[173] and *King v David Allen (Billposting) Ltd*[174] show, not all will have this effect, even in equity, for both the common law and equity operate a *numerus clausus*.

4.115 At times, this closed list comes under pressure to expand, as it did in 1848 with the admission of the restrictive covenant.[175] The question is whether this was the last occasion of expansion. One might have thought the matter settled by the decision of the House of Lords in *King v David Allen (Billposting) Ltd*, but a number of decisions of Lord Denning, all concerning licences to occupy land, have thrown the matter into doubt. And though much of that doubt has been resolved against the proposition that there can be new species of property rights, a little still remains. Its resolution requires first that another development be explained.

(a) Injunctions to keep the licence in being

4.116 At its most basic, a licence is simply a permission to do something on the land of another. In other words, it provides a defence to an action which would otherwise constitute the wrong of trespass to land.[176] That permission may have been given gratuitously, or it may have been bargained for. Suppose, as in *King v David Allen (Billposting) Ltd*, that the permission is to affix posters to the side of a cinema on land in my exclusive possession for the next four years. There is nothing to stop me withdrawing a gratuitous permission at any time, for gratuitous promises, unless contained in a deed, are not enforceable in English law.[177] But if the permission had been bargained for the position would be different. Bargained for promises are actionable.[178] At the time when *King v David Allen (Billposting) Ltd* was decided, it was thought that the only response the law could give to a breach of a contractual licence was the award of a right, at common law, to damages.

---

[172] (1834) 2 My & K 517, 39 ER 1042; para 4.10.
[173] (1863) 2 H & C 121, 159 ER 51; para 4.04.
[174] [1916] 2 AC 54, HL; para 4.11.
[175] *Tulk v Moxhay* (1848) 2 Ph 774, 41 ER 1143; paras 4.98–4.99.
[176] 'A dispensation or licence properly passeth no interest, nor alters or transfers property in any thing, but only makes an action lawful, which without it had been unlawful': *Thomas v Sorrel* (1673) Vaugh 330, 351, 124 ER 1098, 1109, *per* Vaughan CJ.
[177] Paras 8.31–8.32.
[178] Paras 8.33–8.48.

Specific performance or an injunction, both equitable responses, were thought to be available only where the rights infringed were proprietary:

> If a licence is revoked in breach of a contract, the remedy is damages and nothing else, the reason being that the licensee has no estate in the land at all.[179]

That view, which had no logical basis, was exploded in *Winter Garden Theatre* **4.117** *(London) Ltd v Millennium Productions Ltd.*[180] The holder of a title to a theatre (the licensor) had promised Millennium Productions (the licensee) that they could put on plays and other productions in the theatre for a payment of £300 per week. The right, which was not proprietary,[181] was to continue until the giving of six weeks' notice by the licensee. There was no provision for determination by the licensor, who nevertheless purported to determine the licence. The licensee applied for a declaration that the licence could not be revoked in breach of contract.

The trial judge refused to grant the relief sought. He said that even if the contract **4.118** made no provision for determination by the licensor, so that the licensor had no *right* of revocation, it nevertheless had a *power* so to do. In the Court of Appeal, Lord Greene MR disagreed. He said that the licensor had no power to revoke the licence and that an injunction would issue to restrain it from acting in breach of contract. It might once have been correct to say that the licensee's only remedy was an award of damages, but since the Judicature Acts 1873–75 all courts had the power to issue injunctions.[182] Although the House of Lords reversed the decision of the Court of Appeal on different grounds, Lord Greene MR's reasoning on this point was expressly approved.[183]

In theory this improvement in the position of the licensee should have had no **4.119** effect on the analysis of his right as purely personal. A personal right based on contract does not become a proprietary right by the mere fact that it is specifically performable. That is, the right does not thereby become binding on third parties. However, that indubitable proposition has been obscured.

(b) The proprietary licence?

In *Errington v Errington & Woods*[184] a father by contract gave his daughter-in-law **4.120** a right to occupy a house to which he had a fee simple title. The daughter-in-law was a licensee, not a lessee. The father having died, the question was whether that

---

179 *Booker v Palmer* [1942] 2 All ER 674, 677, CA, *per* Lord Greene MR.
180 [1946] 1 All ER 678, CA; r'vsed on other grounds [1948] AC 173, HL.
181 The nearest would have been a lease, but there was no right of exclusive possession.
182 [1946] 1 All ER 678, 685, CA.
183 [1948] AC 173, 202, HL, *per* Lord Uthwatt.
184 [1952] 1 KB 290, CA.

contractual right bound his widow, to whom his fee simple title had been left by will. The Court of Appeal held that it did. Denning LJ, with whom Somervell and Hodson LJJ agreed, reasoned as follows:

> At common law a licence was always revocable at will, notwithstanding a contract to the contrary . . . The remedy for a breach of the contract was only in damages. That was the view generally held until a few years ago . . . The rule has, however, been altered owing to the interposition of equity . . . Law and equity have been fused for nearly 80 years, and since 1948 it has been clear that, as a result of the fusion, a licensor will not be permitted to eject a licensee in breach of a contract to allow him to remain: see *Winter Garden Theatre, London v Millennium Productions Ltd, per* Lord Greene, and in the House of Lords . . . This infusion of equity means that contractual licences now have a force and validity of their own and cannot be revoked in breach of contract. Neither the licensor nor anyone who claims through him can disregard the contract except a purchaser for value without notice.[185]

4.121 Although Denning LJ's discussion of the position as between licensor and licensee is orthodox, the difficulty comes in his last sentence, in which the position of third parties is discussed, and the conclusion drawn, without the citation of authority, that the licence can be enforced not only against the original licensor but against all persons save a bona fide purchaser of a legal estate for value without notice. In other words, the licensee is seen as having a fully fledged equitable proprietary interest in land. Although no reasons are given for this statement, it must have been the availability of equitable relief which led Denning LJ to this result.

4.122 His Lordship's reference to the bona fide purchaser without notice requires it to be emphasized that notice is not, as we have seen, constitutive of a proprietary right[186] but merely negatives a defence which would itself destroy the claimant's proprietary right if indeed he had one. An equitable proprietary right will be lost where the legal right to which it is attached comes into the hands of a bona fide purchaser for value without notice of the equitable right.[187] That the doctrine works only negatively was made clear by Diplock J in *Port Line Ltd v Ben Line Ltd*:

> . . . notice . . . is a shield not a weapon of offence. It protects an already existing equitable interest from being defeated by a purchaser for value without notice. It is not itself the source of an equitable interest.[188]

(c) Recourse to the constructive trust

4.123 In *Binions v Evans* a different approach was taken.[189] The Tredegar Estate gave a retired employee the right to occupy a cottage to which they had a fee simple title

---

185 [1952] 1 KB 290, 298–9, CA.
186 Para 4.11.
187 Para 4.485–4.491.
188 [1958] 2 QB 146, 167–8.
189 [1972] Ch 359, CA.

for the rest of his days. On his death, a similar arrangement was made with his widow, the defendant in this action. She in return undertook to keep the cottage in good repair and to cultivate and manage the garden. The Tredegar Estate later sold their title to the claimants, the sale being expressed to be 'subject to' the widow's rights. Six months later, the claimants sought an order for possession against her. Their action failed before the Court of Appeal.[190] She had an interest binding on them.

Lord Denning MR held that though the widow had no tenancy known to law, **4.124** she occupied the cottage under a contractual licence, which licence bound the purchasers. But instead of relying on his reasoning in the *Errington* case, which had come in for severe criticism,[191] the Master of the Rolls found refuge in the device of the constructive trust,[192] against which, he said, none of the doubts concerning the enforceability of contractual licences against third parties could prevail. Although no such constructive trust arose on the conclusion of the agreement between the widow and the Tredegar Estate:

> . . . she obtained [an equitable interest] afterwards when the Tredegar Estate sold the cottage. They stipulated with the plaintiffs that they were to take the house 'subject to' the defendant's rights under the agreement. They supplied the plaintiffs with a copy of the contract: and the plaintiffs paid less because of her right to stay there. In these circumstances, this court will impose on the plaintiffs a constructive trust for her benefit: for the simple reason that it would be utterly inequitable for the plaintiffs to turn the defendant out contrary to the stipulation subject to which they took the premises. That seems to me clear from the important decision of *Bannister v Bannister* [1948] 2 All ER 133 . . . which I gladly follow.[193]

There are at least three problems with this reasoning. First, *Bannister v Bannister* **4.125** was a case concerned with the question whether oral testimony was admissible to prove a declaration of trust respecting land in the teeth of section 53(1)(b) of the Law of Property Act 1925, whereas the instant case concerned no issue of procedure at all. Secondly, when properly analysed, the *Bannister* case concerned an express, not a constructive, trust. It therefore provides no authority for saying that contractual licences concerning the use of land can be turned into property rights simply by invoking the magic words 'constructive trust'.

---

190 The majority, Megaw and Stephenson LJJ, held that the agreement between the widow and the Tredegar Estate constituted her an equitable life tenant, which interest bound the purchasers because they took with actual notice of it. Their finding that she had a life estate is difficult to support, for that is almost certainly not what the Tredegar Estate intended her to have.

191 'Can it really be so easy to cross the chasm which lies between contract and property?': HWR Wade, 'Licences and Third Parties' (1952) 68 LQR 337, 348.

192 Paras 4.159–4.160, 4.293–4.344.

193 [1972] Ch 359, 368, CA. Note that the widow nowadays might be able to enforce the contractual undertaking of the purchasers by virtue of the Contract (Rights of Third Parties) Act 1999, discussed at paras 8.292–8.314.

4.126   The third is that it is not clear what might be have been the subject-matter of this constructive trust. The subject-matter can hardly have been the title to the cottage for, were that to be so, it would have given the licensee far more than she was ever intended to have. And it could not have been the benefit of the licence either, for that was already vested in her, and it was the purchasers who we are told were the trustees. It might be argued that the subject-matter of the trust was the benefit of the covenant in the conveyance of the fee simple title under which the purchasers promised the vendor that they would respect her rights, and, further, that the purchasers' liability for breach of this covenant could be enforced by the licensee by compelling the vendor to sue on it. But this analysis does not work either, for the benefit of the promise was in the hands of the vendor, not the purchasers.

(d) The present state of play

4.127   The two approaches used by Lord Denning, one based on the availability of equitable relief, the other on the finding of a constructive trust, are flawed. Moreover, there is no authoritative decision from the House of Lords on the subject. The matter has been considered again by the Court of Appeal in *Ashburn Anstalt v Arnold*.[194] There the approach in the *Errington* case was disapproved but the approach in *Binions* endorsed as a 'legitimate application of the doctrine of constructive trusts'.[195]

4.128   The proposition that contractual licences can be proprietary rights therefore rests on insecure foundations. They are certainly not proprietary rights at common law and it is very doubtful they can be so in equity. Yet many commentators now assume the contrary position, especially where the licence arises not under a contract but because of some equitable estoppel.[196] We should regard even this proposition with suspicion, for it is difficult to see how the nature of a right can mutate by reason of a new description of its causative event. If the availability of equitable relief cannot turn a contractual licence into an equitable proprietary right, then the availability of equitable relief for the licensee in the form of estoppel should not do so either. Moreover, a person who bargains for a licence should not be in a worse position than a gratuitous licensee who simply acts to their detriment and

---

194 [1989] Ch 1, CA. See also *DHN Food Distributors v Tower Hamlets LBC* [1976] 1 WLR 852.
195 [1989] Ch 1, 23.
196 Including the Court of Appeal in *Ashburn Anstalt v Arnold* [1989] Ch 1, 17, CA. So far as registered land is concerned, the Land Registration Act 2002, s 116 now 'declares' that an 'equity by estoppel' 'has effect from the time the equity arises as an interest capable of binding successors in title'. No definition of an 'equity by estoppel' is given, and it is to be hoped that the section will be confined to the acquisition of property rights already recognized rather than to what would amount to an abolition of the *numerus clausus* rule. Full discussion in B McFarlane, 'Proprietary Estoppel and Third Parties after the Land Registration Act 2002' [2003] CLJ 661.

thus 'perfects an estoppel'. This topic is dealt with in more detail in the discussion of the acquisition of property rights.[197]

C. Property Rights in Respect of Goods

The list of proprietary rights is closed, or very nearly closed. However, in relation **4.129** to realty the closure leaves a long menu of such rights. This part asks whether the same applies in relation to personalty.

(1) Title

Differently to land, there is no doctrine of estates in personal property. The **4.130** reason is that the doctrine of estates is rooted in feudalism. Besides, at the time when the doctrine was developing there was not the same demand, in relation to things other than land, that the law facilitate dealing in slices of time. Indeed, buying and selling titles to everyday objects would have been disastrously impeded if the law had recognized that they could be invisibly subject to multiple interests of that kind. Finally, so far as there is a demand for such sequential interests in goods, it is met, without adversely affecting commerce, through the law of trusts.

The starting point, therefore, is that the interest which a person can have in respect **4.131** of, say, a car or a coat is single and indivisible, a right to exclusive possession forever. In the case of land, as we have seen, this right carries the name 'fee simple'. Unfortunately, there is no similar compendious term for the equivalent right over goods. Some people use the word 'property', others 'ownership', though we have already seen why neither is appropriate. Better is 'title', derived from 'entitlement', that entitlement being a right to exclusive possession of the thing over which it subsists forever. 'Title', unfortunately, is a much misused word, and is often applied to interests giving their holder rights to things other than exclusive possession. It is even, for example, sometimes applied to debts, which are not property rights at all. To aid clarity of thinking, its use will be confined to rights to exclusive possession of things. And so far as goods are concerned, the only such title there can be is one without limit of time. Thus, it has been said that 'a gift of a chattel for an hour is a gift of it forever'.[198]

---

[197] Paras 4.335–4.336.
[198] Brooke's Abridgement, *Done et Remainder*, pl 157.

(2) Leases of Personalty

4.132 A lease of land is, as we have seen, a property right. The question is whether a lease of goods also creates a property right in the lessee. A lease of goods, at least where it has been performed, is a species of bailment.[199] There are many different types of bailment. The word 'bailee' is derived from the French 'bailler', meaning to deliver up or to hand over. The simplest example of a bailment is a loan of a book from a library. Others include the hire of goods, the placing of goods for repair, for carriage, and so on.[200] Pledges of goods,[201] a security device, are also bailments. Modern usage also speaks of involuntary bailments. A finder is sometimes said to be a bailee, though this is an historical fiction, designed purely to improve the loser's ability to bring claims against the finder when the forms of action prevailed.

4.133 In general, bailments create only personal rights[202] in the parties. One exception is the pledge, which appears to create a right in the bailee which is capable of binding third parties.[203] However, the case of hire, which is not only very common but also most closely resembles the lease of land, probably does not.[204]

(3) Other Bailments

4.134 No other type of bailment seems to amount to a property right save for a pledge, a bailment of a chattel to secure the performance of a personal obligation of the bailor.[205] This is touched on immediately below.

(4) Equities of Redemption

4.135 As we saw in the case of land, the equity of redemption is the name given to the totality of the rights of the mortgagor whilst the mortgage is still on foot. It arises equally where the mortgaged right is one in respect of goods. Like mortgages of land, it is treated elsewhere in this book.[206]

---

199 For a general account, see NE Palmer, *Bailment* (2nd edn, 1991) and ch 16.
200 Chapter 16.
201 Paras 5.66–5.68.
202 The question of the duties owed by the bailee to his bailor in respect of his treatment of the goods is properly a question for the law of obligations and will not be discussed here. See NE Palmer, *Bailment* (2nd edn, 1991) 44–81, and ch 16.
203 Paras 5.66–5.68.
204 For a full discussion, see WJ Swadling, 'The Proprietary Effect of a Hire of Goods' in NE Palmer and E McKendrick, *Interests in Goods* (2nd edn, 1998), 491–526.
205 Paras 5.66–5.68.
206 Paras 5.64–5.108.

(5) Security Devices

Apart from the creation of a mortgage, which involves an outright conveyance **4.136**
of title to the lender, there are other ways in which titles to goods can be used as
security. One option is the pledge or pawn, which involves a physical delivery of
the *res* to the lender (pledgee). The pledgee's rights will bind successors in title
of the bailor and will therefore constitute property rights. In *Franklin v Neate*[207] a
pledgor of a chronometer sold his title to the claimant whilst the chronometer
itself was in the possession of the pledgee. When the pledgee refused to accept
the claimant's tender of the debt and to deliver up the chronometer, he was held
liable in conversion. Rolfe B, giving the judgment of the Court of Exchequer, held
that the pledgor, after pawning the chronometer, had a qualified right of property
to it, namely the right to its return on performance of the secured obligation,
which right had been transferred to the claimant on sale and who was thus able to
redeem the pledge. Implicit in the court's reasoning, is the fact that the purchaser
was nevertheless bound by the rights of the pledgee; if he had simply brought
trover without tendering the amount due, his claim would almost certainly have
failed.

Other forms of security device which give the obligee a property right are fixed and **4.137**
floating charges (both consensual forms of security) and liens (a non-consensual
security). Like mortgages and pledges, they are dealt with in a separate part of this
book.[208]

(6) Other Covenants

A very wide doctrine was enunciated by Knight Bruce LJ in *De Mattos v Gibson*: **4.138**

> . . . where a man, by gift or purchase, acquires property from another with knowledge
> of a previous contract, lawfully and for valuable consideration made by him with a
> third person, to use and employ the property for a particular purpose in a specified
> manner, the acquirer shall not, to the material damage of the third person, in opposi-
> tion to the contract and inconsistently with it, use and employ the property in a
> manner not allowable to the giver or seller.[209]

This doctrine, which bears an obvious resemblence to that laid down by Lord
Cottenham LC a decade earlier in *Tulk v Moxhay*,[210] is no longer, if it ever was, good
law, despite its approval by the Privy Council in *Lord Strathcona Steamship Co v
Dominion Coal Co*.[211] So far as English law is concerned, the true position is that

---

[207] (1844) 13 M & W 481, 153 ER 200.
[208] See paras 5.64–5.108.
[209] (1859) 4 De GF & J 276, 282, 45 ER 108, 112.
[210] (1848) 2 Ph 774, paras 4.98–4.105.
[211] [1926] AC 108, PC.

unless a right relating to goods amounts to a right to exclusive possession, an equity of redemption, a pledge, a charge, or a lien, it will not be a property right.

4.139 It should be immediately noticed that this list is far shorter than is the list for property rights over land. There is, for example, no equivalent of the restrictive covenant over chattels. So, in *Taddy & Co v Sterious & Co*[212] a manufacturer of tobacco sold title to it to a wholesaler on the condition that the title was not to be sold below a certain retail price. A retailer bought the title to the tobacco from the wholesaler with express notice of this condition but proceeded to sell it to the public at a price lower than the minimum retail price. The manufacturer's application for a declaration that the retailer could not do so was refused. Swinfen Eady J said that there was a short answer to the manufacturer's claim: 'Conditions of this kind do not run with goods, and cannot be imposed upon them. Subsequent purchasers, therefore, do not take subject to any conditions which the Court can enforce.'[213] Whether contracts to convey title to goods have, as they do in the case of land, proprietary effect is an open question. Similar doubts surround options to purchase titles to goods.[214]

D. Rights Held on Trust

4.140 Property rights, both real and personal, may be held in one of three ways: outright, on trust, or as security for the performance of an obligation. This section examines what it means to say that a right is held on trust. It is a difficult question whether trusts are properly seen as part of the law of property or as an aspect of the law of obligations. There are a number of reasons for this. First, it is not only property rights which can be held on trust: many personal rights can as well.[215] Second, even where it is a property right which forms the subject-matter of the trust, the trustee, at least in the case of trusts created consensually, will come under a number of duties falling squarely within the law of obligations. Examples are the duty of investment and the duty not to pass the rights held on trust to non-beneficiaries, both of which trigger money remedies enforceable only against the trustee himself. Third, there are a number of instances where third parties can incur

---

212 [1904] 1 Ch 354.

213 ibid 358.

214 Such contracts are governed by the Sale of Goods Act 1979, which has been said to codify the law in this area: *Re Wait* [1927] 1 Ch 606, 630 (Atkin LJ). There is no mention in the Act of contracts to purchase title or options to purchase having proprietary effect. Indeed, somewhat crudely, the Act only talks of 'the property in the goods'. It should also be noted that title can pass by intent alone in the case of a sale of goods, which makes recourse to equity generally unnecessary. For further details of the Sale of Goods, see Chapter 10 of this work.

215 A fact which is obscured by the textbooks, which routinely talk about the trust 'property' without noticing that the rights they describe are more often than not personal.

liabilities in respect of the trust which all agree fall within the law of obligations, most particularly the liability of those who dishonestly assist trustees to commit breaches of trust, undoubtedly part of the law of wrongs, and the liability of those who receive rights dissipated in breach of trust, argued by some to be part of the law of unjust enrichment. And fourth, although beneficiaries of trusts are given in their bundle of rights ones which bind third parties, most notably the right to a reconveyance of rights received in breach of trust, they are not of the same order as the property rights in respect of land and goods so far discussed, for they give no right in respect of the physical thing itself.

(1) The Trust

The institution of the trust is a product of the courts of equity, above all the Court of Chancery. It cannot be understood without some knowledge of the historical origins of that jurisdiction. It is a characteristic feature of English law that it is largely made up of two bodies of law: common law and equity.[216] Equity is more than a mere judicial gloss on the law; it is a separate body of law administered for centuries in separate courts. Although institutional separation is now a thing of the past, the dualism persists. To quote a famous metaphor, 'the two streams of jurisdiction, though they run in the same channel, run side by side and do not mingle their waters'.[217] Opinions differ as to whether more effort should be made to overcome this legacy of the past.[218]   **4.141**

The origins of the duality lie in the first centuries of the common law. The Chancery was initially the department of the royal government charged with the issue of documents and in particular with the issue of the writs which set and kept litigation in motion. As the common law began to settle down, dissatisfied and potentially dissatisfied litigants took to petitioning the Chancellor for special relief. It was as a regularization of the Chancellor's responses to that practice that the Court of Chancery grew up.   **4.142**

A prime example of such special relief was the Chancellor's willingness to enforce 'uses' of titles to land. 'Uses' were the forerunners of trusts. To hold a title for the 'use' of another was to hold it on their behalf.[219] Some reasons why titles to land were frequently conveyed to uses will be discussed immediately below.   **4.143**

---

[216] For a full discussion of the role of equity, see para 4.22–4.34. There are other tributaries, notably admiralty, the law merchant, and ecclesiastical law.

[217] D Browne, *Ashburner's, Principles of Equity* (2nd edn, 1933) 18.

[218] AS Burrows, 'We do this at common law but that in equity' (2002) 22 OJLS 1.

[219] 'Use' here derives from the Latin *'opus'* and old French *'oes'*: to give or receive something 'to the use of another' is to receive it on that other's behalf, to his advantage rather than one's own. 'Feoffment' was a formal conveyance by feoffor to feoffee, and 'feoffment to uses' was a conveyance subject to instructions as to the persons who were to benefit.

A feoffment (conveyance) to uses passed the feoffor's title to the feoffees, the feoffor relying on their honour to respect his wishes. Feoffees, bound in honour but beyond the law, from time to time betrayed their feoffor. The victims of such treachery, having been failed by the *forum internum*, were quick to demand that the machinery of justice intervene. Recurrent petitions to the Chancellor elicited a response. *Ad hoc* relief gradually became regular. In this way, the once extra-legal use became fully protected.

4.144 For various reasons, most notably to facilitate the making of wills of land and to avoid various feudal obligations, most titles to land England were by the sixteenth century held by feoffees to uses, securely protected by the Chancery. The Crown saw this as an abuse, designed to hide the real holding of land, to deprive creditors of their just debts, and the King of his revenue. In 1535, by the Statute of Uses, Henry VIII in effect abolished the use.[220] However, within a century the ingenuity of the lawyers had revived it as the trust.

(2) The Juridical Effect of Placing Rights Behind a Trust

(a) Effect on the right

4.145 It is of the essence of a trust that the placing of a right on trust in no way alters the nature of the right. Thus, personal rights cannot be enforced against third parties, and placing them behind a trust will not alter that fact. Suppose A lends B £10, so creating a personal right in A to the payment to him by B of £10. A might subsequently create a trust of that right in favour of C, using either himself or a third party as trustee. But it is still only B who is obliged to perform the obligation. By the same token, a lease of land, as we have seen, gives its holder rights of enforcement against strangers to its creation, and that effect is not lost when the right is vested in a trustee. In such a case, the trustee will now be able to sue third parties.

4.146 But though the nature of the underlying right is unaltered, the beneficiary of the trust, the person on whose behalf the rights are held, is given rights to control the trustee in the ways in which he exercises those rights. So, for example, if I hold a title to a painting outright and put a match to it, no-one can complain;[221] I am answerable only to myself. But if I hold that title on trust, my setting fire to it will be a breach of trust and open me up to money claims by the persons for whom I held the right, the beneficiaries of the trust. The fact that the right was held on

---

[220] Statute of Uses 1535, 28 Hen 8 c 10. The preamble recites the King's grievances. The way in which the all but complete abolition was achieved was by the 'execution' of the use, which essentially converted every beneficiary's equitable interest into a legal estate.

[221] Save, of course, someone with a better title.

trust means that I am now answerable to the beneficiaries for the way in which I exercised the right to exclusive possession vested in me.

It follows that the rights vested in the beneficiaries cannot be identical to those **4.147** vested in the trustee. So, for example, if a title to land is held by A on trust for B, it will be A, not B, who has a title, a right to the exclusive possession of the land. Similarly, if company shares are held by C on trust for D, it is C, not D, who has the rights shareholding gives, for example, to vote and to receive dividends, not D. For this reason, a beneficiary cannot sue third parties who infringe the rights held by their trustees. Though a trespasser on the land over which A holds a title can be sued by A in trespass, no action can be brought against him by B, for the simple reason that B has no title.[222] Indeed, if it was B who held the title, there would be no trust at all. The only thing B can do in such circumstances is to attempt to sue the trespasser using A's name.[223] The position is different where the beneficiary is himself in physical possession of the land or goods over which the trust right subsists, for that possession will give him a separate and different common law right to possession enforceable against all with no better right to possession.[224]

The fact that the beneficiary has no rights of enforcement of the trust right against **4.148** third parties is often obscured by the language used by judges and commentators in this area. It is, for example, common to talk of a trustee of a title to goods as having a 'legal' title, and his beneficiary having an 'equitable' title. But there is only one 'title', where that word means a right to exclusive possession. Although the beneficiary has rights, has an entitlement, his rights are not of this kind, and therefore not appropriately described in such terms.

This fundamental truth enables us to see the falsity of statements which talk **4.149** in terms of a 'division' or 'separation' of rights when rights are placed in trust,[225] or even worse, of legal and equitable 'titles' existing before the creation of the trust. The best discussion of this issue is to be found in the Australian case of *DKLR Holding Co (No 2) Ltd v Commissioner of Stamp Duties*.[226] A company, 29 Macquarie (No 14) Pty Ltd, was the registered proprietor of a title to certain land. It arranged with another company, DKLR Holding Co (No 2) Ltd, for the latter to hold that title on trust for the former once a change in registration was effected. The question was whether *ad valorem* stamp duty was payable on the document effecting the registration of DKLR as proprietor. DKLR argued that

---

[222] *MCC Proceeds Inc v Lehman Bros International (Europe)* [1998] 4 All ER 675.
[223] For the limited circumstances in which beneficiaries can sue in place of their trustees, see *Hayim v Citibank NA* [1987] AC 730, 747–9.
[224] *Healey v Healey* [1915] 1 KB 938 (goods).
[225] As, eg, did Lord Browne-Wilkinson in *Westdeutsche Landesbank Girozentrale v Islington LBC* [1996] AC 669, 706.
[226] (1982) 149 CLR 431.

only nominal duty was payable, since all that would be received by them would be a bare legal estate, with 29 Macquarie retaining the equitable interest. That argument was rejected in the New South Wales Court of Appeal and in the High Court of Australia. Speaking in the former, Hope JA said:

> [T]he person seised of land for an estate in fee simple has full and direct rights to possession and use of the land and its profits, as well as full rights of disposition. An equitable estate in land, even where its owner is absolutely entitled and the trustee is a bare trustee, is significantly different . . . [A]n absolute owner in fee simple does not hold two estates, a legal estate and an equitable estate. He holds only the legal estate, with all the right and incidents that attach to that estate . . . . [A]lthough the equitable estate is an interest in property, its essential character still bears the stamp which its origin placed upon it. Where the trustee is the owner of the legal fee simple, the right of the beneficiary, although annexed to the land, is a right to compel the legal owner to hold and use the rights which the law gives him in accordance with the obligations which equity has imposed upon him. The trustee, in such a case, has at law all the rights of the absolute owner in fee simple, but he is not free to use those rights for his own benefit in the way he could if no trust existed.[227]

29 Macquarie did not therefore 'retain' an equitable interest; their equitable interest only arose on the transfer and the tax was therefore payable.

4.150 Similar sentiments were expressed when the case reached the High Court. Thus, Brennan J said:

> An equitable interest is not carved out of a legal estate but impressed upon it. It may be convenient to say that DKLR took only the bare legal estate, but that is merely to say elliptically that 29 Macquarie transferred to DKLR the property in respect of which DKLR had declared that it would be a trustee. The charter of 29 Macquarie's interest was DKLR's declaration, not the memorandum of transfer; and DKLR's declaration was moved by the transfer to it of the property to be held on the trust declared.[228]

An equally good metaphor is to see the interest of the beneficiary as being 'engrafted' on to the title. This is the language of McLelland J in the later case of *Re Transphere Pty Ltd*,[229] who said:

> An absolute owner holds only the legal estate, with all the rights and incidents that attach to that estate. Where a legal owner holds property on trust for another, he has at law all the rights of an absolute owner but the beneficiary has the right to compel him to hold and use those rights which the law gives him in accordance with the obligations which equity has imposed on him by virtue of the existence of the trust. Although this right of the beneficiary constitutes an equitable estate in the property, it is engrafted onto, not carved out of, the legal estate.[230]

---

227 [1980] 1 NSWLR 510, 519.
228 (1982) 149 CLR 431, 474.
229 (1986) 5 NSWLR 309.
230 (1986) 5 NSWLR 309, 311.

(b) Effect on third parties

As we have just seen, the beneficiary of a trust has no right to enforce in his own **4.151** name the rights which are held for him on trust. In general, his rights are against the trustee in respect of the trustee's exercise of the right. Where he does have rights against third parties, however, is when the trustee conveys away the rights he is holding in breach of trust. In such circumstances, the beneficiary will have rights against the third party recipient. They are, however, of a limited nature. The recipient of rights dissipated in breach of trust does not automatically step into the trustee's shoes, inheriting the powers and duties of his transferee.[231] All he is liable to do is restore the rights dissipated in breach of trust, either to the former trustee, or, more likely, to other persons nominated by the beneficiaries. This right of the beneficiaries to recover the trust rights is good against all transferees of rights dissipated in breach of trust bar one, the transferee of a common law right who takes in good faith, for value, and without notice, actual or constructive, of the fact of the dissipation being in breach of trust. If the transferee is such a person, compendiously known as 'equity's darling', then the effect of the transfer will be to destroy the beneficiary's right to a reconveyance.

A second situation in which third parties are affected by a trust, albeit indirectly, **4.152** is in the case of the insolvency of the trustee.[232] Broadly speaking, what happens in an insolvency is that the rights held by the insolvent are automatically vested in the trustee in bankruptcy (in the case of an individual insolvency) or company liquidator (in the case of a corporate insolvency). Those rights are then liquidated and the proceeds of sale used to pay the creditors a dividend on the amounts owed. Rights held by an individual or corporation on trust are, however, treated differently. In the case of an individual bankruptcy, section 283(3)(a) of the Insolvency Act 1986 provides that 'property held by the bankrupt on trust for any other person' does not form part of the bankrupt's estate for the purposes of insolvency, with the consequence that such rights do not vest in the trustee in bankruptcy. And though there is no similar provision in the case of corporate insolvencies, it is generally accepted that the same rule applies by analogy. This principle applies however the trust came into existence, and provides the motivation for many claims to court-created trusts in the event of, for example, mistaken payments,[233] payments on bases which have failed,[234] and gain-based responses to wrongdoing.[235]

---

[231] See the account in R Nolan, 'Equitable Property' (2006) 122 LQR 232.
[232] The subject is treated in detail in Chapter 19 of this work.
[233] See, eg, *Chase Manhattan v Israel-British Bank* [1981] Ch 105 (claim to trust successful).
[234] See, eg, *Re Goldcorp Exchange Ltd* [1995] 1 AC 74 (claim to trust unsuccessful).
[235] See, eg, *A-G for Hong Kong v Reid* [1994] 1 AC 324 (claim to trust successful).

4.153 A final way in which third parties may be affected by a trust is by the various personal liabilities, properly part of the law of obligations, which attach to those who, for example, receive trust rights dissipated in breach of trust or who assist trustees to commit breaches of trust. These are dealt with elsewhere in this work.[236]

(3) Why Create a Trust?

4.154 Trusts arise by deliberate act of a settlor or by operation of law. A trust created by an individual is essentially a system for managing wealth in which the manager holds the wealth to be managed. As we have seen, in the past, trusts were used to avoid many of the more unpleasant consequences of feudalism, and it is probably because it was so successful in doing so that feudalism, at least in form, survives to this day. Piecemeal statutory reform has removed the need to use trusts for these purposes, and the trust is nowadays used primarily as an estate planning device, with its purpose often the minimization of the burden of taxation.

4.155 Although one eye is kept constantly on tax, there are other objectives which can be achieved very satisfactorily through a trust, some of them unachievable in any other way. Thus the trust provides a management structure for pension funds and other investment schemes, also for funds donated for the pursuit of charitable purposes.[237] Again, when it comes to providing for the family, the trust allows wealth to be treated as a fund, divisible in many different ways, according to the settlor's wishes. If there are dependants who for one reason or another cannot manage their own affairs, a trust will provide the necessary structure for looking after their material interests.

4.156 If the person whom the settlor wishes to benefit is not legally capable of holding the right concerned, a trust can be set up for him. A minor, for example, cannot hold a title to land in English law.[238] If a settlor wishes to confer a title to land on a minor, the nearest he can get is to set up a trust of that title for the minor. And though there is no prohibition on a minor holding title to goods or the benefit of personal rights at law, prudence sometimes requires that the management of those rights be given to trustees.

(4) Classification of Trusts

4.157 The classification of trusts in English law has not been the most scientific of endeavours. There are a number of different classifications in use, which serve different purposes.

---

236 Paras 17.336–17.342 and 17.381–17.384.
237 Although this could be done by the establishment of a corporation with charitable objects.
238 Law of Property Act 1925, s 1(6).

(a) Express, constructive, and resulting trusts [239]

(i) Express trusts

An express trust, where the word 'express' is used in the sense of 'to press out' or 'to **4.158** represent (a thought, sentiment, state of facts)' is one which arises because of a manifestation of intent on the part of the person wishing to create such a trust. We call such manifestations of intent 'declarations' of trust. Originally, the phrase 'express trust' covered all trusts arising because of such manifestations of consent, howsoever proved, so that an express trust was synonymous with a declared trust.[240] Nowadays, unfortunately, it seems to be reserved for those cases in which the fact of declaration is proved by evidence. Cases in which the declaration is proved by presumption are labelled 'presumed resulting trusts', it coincidentally being the case that the only situations in which declarations can be proved in this way are also ones in which the trust is resulting, by which is meant a trust arising in favour of the transferor of the rights. The label does not, however, assist in any understanding of the subject, and all trusts arising because of a declaration, whether proved by evidence or presumption, should ideally be called express.

(ii) Constructive trusts

The word 'constructive' is related to the verb 'construct', meaning a trust arising **4.159** because it is constructed by the court rather than a response to a manifestation of a right-holder's intent to create a trust.

Two examples will serve to illustrate. In *A-G for Hong Kong v Reid*[241] a highly- **4.160** placed public official took bribes from criminals in order to drop proceedings against them. In so doing, he committed the civil wrong of a breach of the fiduciary duty he owed to the government of Hong Kong. The Privy Council held that as a consequence of his wrongdoing he held those bribes on a constructive trust for his principal. In *Chase Manhattan Bank NA v Israel-British Bank (London) Ltd* [242] the recipient of a mistaken payment was said to hold it on constructive trust for the payor. In neither case, however, was there any manifestation of consent (declaration of trust) to the effect that those rights were to be held on trust.

(iii) Resulting trusts

We touched on these briefly above. They are difficult and controversial, largely **4.161** because of their curious and distracting name. The word 'resulting' comes from the Latin *resilio* and *resulto*, both meaning to jump or leap back. In its widest sense,

---

[239] There was in former times a fourth category of implied trusts. These, however, seem to have fallen into disuse.
[240] *Cook v Fountain* (1676) 3 Swanst 585.
[241] [1994] 1 AC 324, PC.
[242] [1981] Ch 105.

a resulting trust is any trust under which the beneficiary was the person who made the transfer of rights. But because the word 'resulting' describes the identity of the beneficiary rather than the event which brings the trust into existence, it does not align with the other categories. Instead, the natural partner to a 'resulting' (jumping back) trust would be one which jumped forward, though English law does not have a name for such trusts. This problem of misalignment leads to overlap, for a resulting trust can also be express (it is proved by evidence that I conveyed rights to you accompanied by a declaration of trust in my own favour) or constructive (as in *Chase Manhattan Bank NA v Israel-British Bank (London) Ltd*). For this reason, the category is essentially redundant, and we would do better to have only the categories of express and constructive trusts. Unfortunately, that position is still some way off. For the moment, it is enough to notice that the label 'resulting trust' is traditionally confined to two types of trust, one express, the other constructive. Those express trusts labelled resulting are, as we saw above, ones in which a declaration of trust is proved by presumption rather than evidence.[243] Such trusts are traditionally called 'presumed resulting trusts', although that of course fails to reveal the fact thereby proved by presumption. The constructive trusts labelled resulting are those in which a trust arises in favour of a settlor who has conveyed rights to third parties as trustees but which trust has, for one reason or another, failed. Such trusts are commonly known as an 'automatic resulting trust', the word 'automatic' indicating only that the trust arises 'by operation of law',[244] that it is, in other words, constructive.

(b) Other classifications of trusts

4.162 'Express, constructive, and resulting', unsatisfactory as it is, is not the only division between trusts made in English law. Trusts also divide according to whether they are public (charitable) or private (non-charitable), and whether they are fixed or discretionary.[245] We will examine the distinction between public and private trusts below. For the present, it should be noted that under a fixed trust, the beneficiaries' entitlements will be fixed in advance by the settlor and the trustee will have no discretion as to how those rights are allocated. An example of a fixed trust would be a transfer of rights to trustees helot be held on trust 'for my children in equal shares'. By contrast, in a discretionary trust the trustees have the power to choose from a group of potential beneficiaries who shall benefit and in what amounts. The words creating such a trust might read something like 'for such of my children and in such amounts as the trustees in their absolute discretion think fit'.

---

[243] *Westdeutsche Landesbank Girozentrale v Islington LBC* [1996] AC 669.

[244] *Re Vandervell's Trusts (No 2)* [1974] Ch 269, 294 (Megarry J).

[245] Space does not permit the treatment of protective trusts, so-called because they protect beneficiaries in the event of insolvency.

(c) Declared and not-declared trusts

The most useful classification, and the one adopted here, distinguishes trusts   **4.163**
according as they arise because of a declaration of trust (proved by evidence or
presumption), or for reasons other than a declaration of trust. Those which arise
for a reason other than a declaration of trust further divide as to whether the event
triggering the creation of the trust is wrongdoing, unjust enrichment, or some
other event.

(5) Declared (Express) Trusts

When looking at declared trusts, the first question to ask is what a declaration   **4.164**
must contain before it will count as a valid declaration of trust. But it is not enough
that there has been a declaration of trust. When it comes to litigation, the making
of that declaration must be proved. Although this is true of all legally significant
acts, particular attention has to be paid to it in trusts because there are, as we have
seen, situations in which declarations can be proved by presumption rather than
evidence. We need also to notice that where the declaration does need to be proved
by evidence, there are, in certain circumstances, *scil* where the trust is of a title to
land or is testamentary, restrictions on the type of evidence admissible in proof.
Our second question, therefore, concerns the proof of such declarations. And
there is a third question. The rights which are to form the subject-matter of the
trust must be conveyed to the person who is to act as trustee. We call this the
'constitution' of the trust. How is this done? Of course, the settlor himself may
decide to act as the sole trustee, in which case no issues of constitution arise.

(a) Content of a declaration of trust

(i) Preliminaries

There are two preliminary matters to note before we go any further. The first is   **4.165**
that only declarations of trust which have been made manifest, have been
'expressed', will count. As Megarry J said in *Re Vandervell's Trusts (No 2)*, 'the mere
existence of some unexpressed intention in the breast of the owner of the property
does nothing: there must at least be some expression of that intention before it can
effect any result.'[246] The second is that the test of meaning of the words expressed
is objective. As Lord Diplock said in *Gissing v Gissing*:

> As in so many branches of English law in which legal rights and obligations depend
> upon the intentions of the parties to a transaction, the relevant intention of each

---

[246] [1974] Ch 269, 294. Though in *Westdeutsche Landesbank Girozentrale v Islington LBC*
[1996] AC 669, 708, Lord Browne-Wilkinson spoke of a presumption of 'intention' rather than
'declaration', the point was not there in issue.

party is the intention which was reasonably understood by the other party to be manifested by that party's words or conduct notwithstanding that he did not consciously formulate that intention in his own mind or even acted with some different intention which he did not communicate to the other party.[247]

For this reason, a declaration which otherwise satisfies the requirements of a valid declaration will not be rendered ineffective merely because the speaker was telling a deliberate lie.[248]

4.166   The three requirements of a valid declaration, sometimes called the three certainties, are certainty of objects, certainty of subject matter, and certainty of intention. 'Objects' here means beneficiaries. The beneficiaries must be identified with sufficient certainty. The rights—the subject-matter—must likewise be defined with sufficient certainty. And similarly the intention that those rights be held on trust in those shares must be present.

4.167   The discussion of the three certainties easily degenerates into dogma, as though certainty had some mystic value of its own. In fact, the requirements are dictated by practical problems and are set so as to make it possible to operate and administer the trust. For example, if the trustee cannot know who is and who is not a beneficiary, he cannot know whether a distribution to a particular person would be lawful. Hence one requirement has to be that settlors describe their class of beneficiaries in such a way as to make that discrimination possible, both for the trustees and, since they will have to police the arrangement, for the court.

(ii) Certainty of objects

4.168   By the objects of a trust, we mean those who are to benefit under it. The level of certainty required varies according to whether the trust is a fixed trust or a discretionary trust. It is necessary to underline the fact that the key to understanding the various tests is that they reflect the minimum degree of certainty necessary for the trustees, on the one hand, and the court, on the other, to exercise their respective functions. The higher the duty on the trustee, or the more interventionist the role of the court, the stricter the test of certainty of objects will be.

4.169   **Fixed trusts.**   The strictest test for certainty of objects obtains in the case of a fixed trust. A fund cannot, for example, be divided into equal shares unless the person doing the dividing knows how many beneficiaries are to take. Hence, from the information given by the settlor, the trustees must be able to generate a complete list of the objects of the trust, for otherwise they will not be able to perform even their most basic function of distribution. If the settlor directs trustees to distribute his estate equally amongst a certain class, then no share can be distributed to any

---

247   [1971] AC 886, 906.
248   Cf *Eves v Eves* [1975] 1 WLR 1338, discussed in para 4.208.

single member of that class until all its members are ascertained. Because it was not possible to compile such a list, a fixed trust of a capital sum failed in *Inland Revenue Commissioners v Broadway Cottages Trust*.[249]

In that case, the settlor attempted to create a fixed trust of £80,000 capital and a **4.170** discretionary trust in respect of the income it produced. The beneficiaries under the trust of the capital were to take in equal shares. They were expressed to include persons employed in the past or at the date of the settlement or at any time thereafter during the period until 31 December 1980 not only by the settlor and his wife but by his father who died in 1929, by his mother who died in 1940, by another company formed in 1929 and any other limited company which might succeed to the company's business or any other limited company of which the settlor was a director at the date of the settlement, and the wives and widows of all such persons. The Court of Appeal held that it was not possible to draw up a complete list of all the beneficiaries entitled under this provision and that the trust of the capital was therefore void for uncertainty of objects. There could be no division in equal shares amongst a class of persons unless all the members of that class were known.

This does not mean that nothing at all can be done until all the beneficiaries can **4.171** be lined up in front of the trustees. It quite often happens that a beneficiary cannot be found, even that it cannot be known whether he is alive or dead. Such factual problems do not make the trustees' duties impossible. The division can be made, even though one share cannot be paid out.

Discretionary trusts. The starting point here is the decision of the Court of **4.172** Appeal in *IRC v Broadway Cottages*.[250] As we saw, the court held that the fixed trust of capital failed because it was not possible to draw up a complete list of the beneficiaries. The court also said that the discretionary trust failed for the same reason. It would have been valid had it been a power of appointment, an institution in which the 'donee' of the power is given authority by its 'donor' to distribute certain rights of the donor to certain persons, in that while the trustees could never discover all the beneficiaries, they could always tell whether a given individual was or was not a member of the described class. But, for two reasons, that was not sufficient here. First, whereas a power need never be exercised, a trustee under a discretionary trust has a duty to distribute, and that duty could only be performed if he was able to consider the merits of every possible claimant. Second, there was the problem of control by the court. Whereas with a power of appointment no choice need be made at all, if a trustee of a discretionary trust failed or refused to carry out his duty of selection and distribution, the court had to be able to do so.

---

[249] [1955] Ch 20, CA.
[250] ibid.

And, it was said, the court would necessarily distribute equally, on the basis that 'equality is equity'. The reason for this was that it was believed that the discretion to pick and choose must be regarded as personal to the trustee. In the unlikely event of the court having to execute it, the most discretionary trust would be a fixed trust. So the court would need to be able to ascertain the identity of each and every member of the class. For these reasons, said the court, the test of certainty of objects in a discretionary trust had to also be the complete list test.

4.173   The foundation of that reasoning was destroyed by the House of Lords in *McPhail v Doulton*.[251] As to the first reason, a majority of their lordships[252] held that there was no need for trustees under a discretionary trust to survey a complete list of names. Although their duties were more onerous than those of the holder of a power of appointment, they could nevertheless perform their function without the names of all members of the class. As Lord Wilberforce observed:

> A trustee with a duty to distribute, particularly among a potentially very large class, would surely never require the preparation of a complete list of names, which anyhow would tell him little that he needs to know. He would examine the file, by class and category; might indeed make diligent and careful inquiries, depending on how much money he had to give away and the means at his disposal, as to the composition and needs of particular categories and of individuals within them; decide upon certain priorities or proportions, and then select individuals according to their needs or qualifications.[253]

As to the second reason, that in the event of a failure by the trustees to distribute, that task would fall to the court, which could then only proceed by ordering an equal division, the House simply denied that in such an event equal distribution amongst all the possible beneficiaries was the only solution. Equal division was probably the last thing that the settlor wanted (why else did he use a discretionary and not a fixed trust?) and there was no reason why the court could not distribute the rights in some other way, perhaps by authorizing or directing representative persons of the classes of beneficiaries to prepare a scheme of distribution. And in any case, if the original trustees refused to distribute, new trustees could always be appointed, so that it would be very unlikely that the task would ever fall to the court. The appropriate test, said the House of Lords, for certainty of objects in a discretionary trust was the same as for the objects of a power of appointment, namely that it needed to be said with certainty whether a given postulant was or was not a member of the benefited class. It was not necessary for the trustees to be able to generate a complete list of possible objects.

---

251 [1971] AC 424, HL.
252 Lords Hodson and Guest dissented.
253 [1971] AC 424, 449.

The House in *McPhail v Doulton* did not rule on the validity of the trust in the **4.174** case in hand; they merely decided that the courts below had applied the wrong test. This question was remitted to the Chancery Division, and thence to the Court of Appeal. The decision is reported as *Re Baden (No 2)*[254] and illustrates the practical difficulties facing a court applying the 'is or is not' test. The terms of the trust in *McPhail* provided that:

> the trustees shall apply the net income of the fund in making at their absolute discretion grants to or for the benefit of any of the officers and employees or ex-officers or ex-employees of the company or to any relatives or dependants of any such persons in such amounts at such times and on such conditions as they think fit.

Particular difficulty was encountered with the word 'relatives', not because of **4.175** what it meant (someone with whom you share a common ancestor), but because, though it was possible to tell whether a given individual fell *within* the class, ie was a relative of an employee, it was argued that it was impossible to say with certainty whether someone was *outside* the class. It is notoriously difficult to prove a negative, and as Megaw LJ admitted, the most that could be said would often be, 'There is no proof that he is a relative.' The problem was that a strict adherence to the 'is or is not test' would have meant going back to the approach expressly rejected by the House in *McPhail v Doulton*, of drawing up a complete list of potential beneficiaries, for the only sure way of knowing that someone was not a relative would be to compile a complete list of all who were and point to the fact that that person was not on it. The alternative, never discussed, was to accept the fact, on which science and the Book of Genesis agree, that every human being shares a common ancestor with every other.

The members of the Court of Appeal solved this dilemma in various ways. **4.176** Megaw LJ said that too great an emphasis should not be placed on the words 'or is not' and that the test would be satisfied if, as regards a substantial number of objects, it could be said with certainty that they fell within the trust, even though as regards a substantial number of other persons the answer would have to be, not that 'they are outside the trust', but 'it is not proven whether they are in or out'.[255] However, unless a distinction was first taken between conceptual and evidential uncertainty on the lines discussed immediately below, that would amount to accepting classes with no defined boundaries. Stamp LJ thought it necessary to find a core class within the theoretical class, here next of kin, within relatives.[256] That, however, leads back to the fixed list.

---

[254] [1973] Ch 9, CA.
[255] ibid 24.
[256] ibid 29.

4.177 A better approach, true to Lord Wilberforce's own understanding, is that adopted by Sachs LJ. There were two types of uncertainty, he said, conceptual uncertainty and evidential uncertainty, and it was only to the former that the test laid down by the House in *McPhail v Doulton* was directed. As long as the class of persons to be benefited was conceptually certain, eg 'first cousins' (conceptually certain) as opposed to 'someone to whom the settlor was under a moral obligation' (conceptually uncertain), then evidential uncertainty as to whether someone was within or without the conceptually certain class did not matter. 'Once the class of persons to be benefited is conceptually certain it then becomes a question of fact to be determined on evidence whether any postulant has on inquiry been proved to be within it: if he is not so proved, then he is not in it.'[257] 'Relatives of X' is conceptually certain. One knows what question has to be asked in order to put any individual to the test: 'Have you a common ancestor with X?'

4.178 **The problem of administrative unworkability.** This is not strictly an aspect of uncertainty of objects but arises because of the abandonment of the fixed list and the consequent acceptance of the prima facie validity of conceptually certain classes as huge as 'relatives of X' or 'all the inhabitants of Greater London'. The members of such classes cannot be surveyed one by one. It is apparently sufficient if a core class is surveyed. Thus 'relatives of X' is workable because a core class easily identifies itself. All concerned know that the intention was that the survey operate over close relatives. However, 'all the inhabitants of Greater London' is a bad class.[258] Similarly, a discretionary trust in favour of 'any or all or some of the residents of West Yorkshire', even if it were sufficiently certain in terms of intention, subject matter and objects, must fail for administrative unworkability.[259]

4.179 The problem is not one of size. 'Relatives of X', whether or not it is understood as including everyone in the world, is a larger class than 'inhabitants of Greater London'. The problem is solely the identifiability of a core class capable of being surveyed. So, in *Re Manisty's Settlement*[260] Templeman J said that a power of appointment given to a fiduciary in favour of the 'residents of Greater London' was capricious because the terms of the power actively negatived any sensible intention on the part of the settlor as to the core class. If the settlor intended and expected the trustees would have regard to persons with some claim on his bounty he would not have required them to consider only an accidental conglomeration of persons who had no discernible link with the settlor or with any institution. An administratively unworkable class is one in which a core class can only be identified capriciously, with a pin, or on the whim of the trustee. Even 'everyone in the

---

257 ibid 20.
258 *McPhail v Doulton* [1971] AC 424, 457, HL, *per* Lord Wilberforce.
259 *R v District Auditor, ex p West Yorkshire MBC* (1986) 26 RVR 24, Div Ct.
260 [1974] Ch 17.

world other than A, B, and C' leaves open the inference that the settlor intended the core to be those close to him, in the way that the specification of a geographical area does not.[261] 'All persons born on a Sunday' would similarly confuse and contradict routine inferences as to the intended core. It would be unworkable because it could only be worked capriciously.

Continuing tensions.   Some problems persist. One arises from the fact that the   **4.180** law is constantly imposing artificial certainty on words which in ordinary speech lack conceptual certainty. A statute which used the word 'friend' would quickly elicit a definition. It is not clear to what extent it is permissible to engage in that kind of exercise.[262] The assumption seems to be that the words used must be taken in their ordinary lay sense, with whatever sins of uncertainty they carry. Again, the difference between core and periphery suggests that a distribution in the periphery of the class must be capricious and should not be permitted, in which case, however, the core would have to be conceptually certain, which it never is. On the other hand, to permit distribution in the periphery would seem to make a nonsense of the requirement that there be a rationally identifiable core.

(iii) Certainty of subject-matter

Whatever form the subject-matter of the trust takes, it must be specified with   **4.181** reasonable certainty, for it will be otherwise impossible to say which rights are caught by the trust and which are not. For this reason, there could be no trust in *Palmer v Simmonds*,[263] where a testatrix left her residuary estate to one Thomas Harrison, directing him that he must on his death leave its 'bulk' to certain named persons. It was held that Thomas Harrison took absolutely, for, according to Kindersley V-C, given that the word 'bulk' meant 'the greater part of', the testatrix had not designated the subject-matter as to which she had expressed a trust.

Nor was there any trust in *Re London Wine*,[264] where a wine merchant purported   **4.182** to sell his title to bottles of wine to customers which he would then physically store for them. Certificates were issued to the customers stating that they were the 'sole and beneficial owners' of the cases of wine they had bought. But there was never any allocation of any particular cases of wine to any particular customer, simply a warehouse full of wine. When the wine merchant became insolvent, a question arose as to the holding of title to the wine in the warehouse. The purchasers argued,

---

[261] Templeman J in *Re Manisty's Settlement* [1974] Ch 17, 27 held this to be a good class for a fiduciary power of appointment but said *obiter*, and questionably, that it would not support a discretionary trust.

[262] Cf *Re Tuck's Settlement Trusts* [1978] Ch 49, CA.

[263] (1854) 2 Drew 221, 61 ER 704.

[264] [1986] Palmer's Company Cases 121.

inter alia, that a trust of it had been declared in their favour. The argument failed on the ground that there was no certainty of subject-matter.

4.183 The Court of Appeal has relaxed these requirements in the case where the subject-matter of the trust is a chose in action. In *Hunter v Moss*[265] the defendant, Moss, was the registered holder of 950 shares in a company, Moss Electrical Ltd, which had an issued share capital of 1,000. He made an oral voluntary declaration that he held 5 per cent of the issued share capital on trust for the claimant. However, he failed to identify which 50 of his 950 shares were subject to the trust. When the claimant later sought to enforce the trust, Moss, relying on *Re London Wine*, argued that it failed for uncertainty of subject-matter. The judge at first instance distinguished *Re London Wine*, for that case concerned bottles of wine, which could be damaged or corked, whereas here it did not matter that the particular 50 shares had not been identified, for all 950 carried identical rights. The judge said that if immediately after the declaration of the trust the claimant had applied to the court for its execution, there would have been no difficulty ordering the trust to be carried into effect. His decision was upheld by the Court of Appeal.

4.184 A criticism of the decision at first instance had been that it offended the rule in *Milroy v Lord*,[266] discussed below, to the effect that a court of equity will not order the constitution of an imperfectly constituted trust—ie, it will not compel the transfer of rights so as to make good a defective gratuitous transfer made to constitute a trust. Dillon LJ said that that rule was not here offended because 'in the present case there was no question of an imperfect transfer. What is relied on is an oral declaration of trust.'[267] This, however, is to misunderstand the nature of the rule in *Milroy v Lord*. As will be seen, Turner LJ there said that there were essentially three ways of making a gift of rights: by outright transfer; by transfer to trustees on trust for the beneficiary; or by the settlor declaring himself a trustee for the beneficiary. The need to transfer a right is clearly only potentially problematic where the gift is attempted to be made by one of the first two methods. No transfer of rights is necessary where the gift is made by the third method, for there the settlor is merely altering the capacity in which he holds rights already vested in him.

(iv) Certainty of intention

4.185 Although no technical language need be used, a declaration of trust needs to show an intent to impose on oneself or one's transferee a binding obligation to hold the rights identified for another. 'The real question,' said Christian LJ in *McCormick v Grogan*, 'is what did [the settlor] intend to be the *sanction*? Was it to

---

265 [1994] 1 WLR 452, CA; followed in *Re Harvard Securities* [1997] 2 BCLC 369.
266 (1862) 4 De GF & J 264, 45 ER 1185.
267 [1994] 1 WLR 452, 457, CA.

be the authority of a court of justice, or the conscience of the devisee?'[268] On the other side of the line, a wish will do no more than put the transferee under a moral obligation to bear in mind the transferor's wishes.

No trust intention. In *Re Adams and the Kensington Vestry*[269] a husband by will **4.186** left all his real and personal estate to his wife 'in full confidence that she will do what is right as to the disposal thereof between my children, either in her lifetime or by will after her decease'. During her lifetime, the widow attempted to give some of the rights away outside her immediate family. The Court of Appeal held that she was entitled to do so, since no trust had been imposed on her. She had received the rights outright. The words used by the testator were merely precatory. To the argument that the testator would have been very surprised had he known that he had given his widow the power to make dispositions outside the family, Cotton LJ said:

> That is a proposition which I should express in a different way. He would be much surprised if the wife to whom he had left his property absolutely should so act as not to provide for the children, that is to say, not to do what is right. That is a very different thing. He would have said: 'I expected that she would do what was right and therefore I left it to her absolutely. I find that she has not done what I think is right, but I cannot help it, I am very sorry that she has done so.' That would be the surprise, I think, that he would express, and feel, if he could do either, if the wife did what was unreasonable as regards the children.[270]

The same result obtained in *Mussoorie Bank Ltd v Raynor*,[271] where the testator left his entire estate to his widow 'feeling confident that she will act justly to our children in dividing the same when no longer required by her'.[272]

Exactly the same requirement of certainty of intention obtains where what is **4.187** alleged is that the settlor has declared himself a trustee. In such a case it is not enough to show that the settlor desired or intended to benefit another. It must instead be shown that he intended to impose on himself an obligation to hold rights for the benefit that other. In *Jones v Lock*[273] a father handed a cheque for £900 made out to himself to his infant son, saying: 'I give this to baby for himself.' This act was insufficient to transfer the right to sue at law, the right only passing by means of an indorsement.[274] The father soon after died, leaving all his personal

---

[268] (1867) 1 IR Eq 313, 328 (emphasis in original).
[269] (1884) 27 Ch D 394, CA.
[270] (1884) 27 Ch D 394, 409, CA.
[271] (1882) 7 App Cas 321, PC.
[272] Attention has to be paid to the context. Reading the will as a whole, the House of Lords in *Comiskey v Bowring-Hanbury* [1905] AC 84 held, by a majority, that the words 'in full confidence' did create a trust.
[273] (1865) LR 1 Ch App 25.
[274] That is, on its back it must be signed over. Transfer by indorsement and delivery is no longer possible since the enactment of the Cheques Act 1992.

rights to his family by his first marriage. On behalf of the infant, it was argued that the father had declared himself a trustee of the right to sue on the cheque. That argument was rejected. Although there was clearly an intention to make provision for the child, there was no manifestation of intention to create a trust of the right. Lord Cranworth LC said:

> I should have every inclination to sustain this gift, but unfortunately I am unable to do so; the case turns on the very short question whether Jones intended to make a declaration that he held the [right] in trust for the child; and I cannot come to any other conclusion than that he did not. I think it would be of very dangerous example if loose conversations of this sort, in important transactions of this kind, should have the effect of declarations of trust.[275]

4.188 Similarly, in *Richards v Delbridge*[276] an uncle, who held a lease of land used as business premises, wanted to make a gift of it to his nephew. He wrote on the back of the deed by which the lease had been granted to him: 'This deed and all thereto belonging I give to Edward . . . from this time forth.' He then handed the document to the nephew's mother. On his death, the question arose whether the uncle had disposed of the lease during his lifetime, for by his will he left all his real and personal property rights to his wife. There could have been no transfer of the lease at law, for, as we will see, the execution of a fresh deed would have been necessary to effect this.[277] The nephew tried to circumvent this by arguing that the uncle had declared a trust of the lease in his favour. Once again, the argument was rejected. Sir George Jessel MR pointed out that the evidence adduced for this proposition in fact contradicted the nephew's claim:

> [F]or a man to make himself a trustee there must be an expression of intention to become a trustee, whereas words of present gift shew an intention to give over property to another, and not to retain it in the donor's own hands for any purpose, fiduciary or otherwise.[278]

4.189 **Words of trust.** Use of the words 'on trust' will normally do the trick,[279] but even without such words declarations of trusts may still be found, as happened in *Paul v Constance*.[280] Here, a man opened a bank account in his sole name but told the woman with whom he lived that the 'money' in it was as much hers as it was his. It was held that he had declared himself a trustee of the chose in action he had against the bank for himself and the woman. Scarman LJ said that the case could be distinguished from both *Jones v Lock* and *Richards v Delbridge*, because they concerned an intention to make transfer a right, whereas here the intention was

---

275 (1865) LR 1 Ch App 25, 29.
276 (1874) LR 18 Eq 11.
277 Para 4.439.
278 (1874) LR 18 Eq 11, 15.
279 Though not always: *Tito v Waddell (No 2)* [1977] Ch 106.
280 [1977] 1 WLR 527, CA.

not to make a transfer but to hold the right against the bank for the two of them jointly. The words used, 'as much yours as mine', amounted to a declaration of trust and the claimant was accordingly entitled to half the chose in action in equity as the beneficiary of an express, ie declared, trust.

(b) Proving a declaration of trust

Proof of a declaration of trust is complicated by, first, the availability on some facts **4.190** of the device of proof by presumption rather than evidence, and second, in those situations where the presumption does not apply and the declaration must be proved by evidence, statutory restrictions on the type of evidence which courts can admit.

(i) Proof by presumption

In certain limited circumstances a transfer, though there be no evidence adduced **4.191** that it was made with an accompanying declaration of trust, will be seen by the court to have been so made through the operation of a presumption. These situations are twofold. The first is a voluntary (ie gratuitous) transfer of rights made from A to B, which is *inter vivos* rather than *post mortem*, and not made from father to child or someone standing in an equivalent relationship, or from husband to wife. The second is where A *inter vivos* pays C to transfer rights to B and A is not the father or other person standing *in loco parentis* to B, or where A is not the husband of B.

The type of presumption. The presumption is a presumption of law, rather **4.192** than fact, which means that on proof by evidence of the primary facts detailed above, the court *must* find the secondary fact proved. The burden is then on the other party to the litigation to adduce evidence demonstrating the untruth of the fact proved by presumption.[281]

The fact proved by presumption. Although the subject of some dispute, the **4.193** only tenable view is that the fact proved by presumption is that the transferor declared a trust in his own favour. The reason why a declaration of trust is proved by presumption is that, for the historical reasons mentioned above—primarily to make wills of land and to avoid feudal incidents—a declaration of trust in favour of the transferor was the most probable explanation of what was happened when an *inter vivos* gratuitous transfer was made to someone not the wife or child of the transferor.[282]

---

281 *Cook v Fountain* (1676) 3 Swanst 585; *The Venture* [1908] P 218.
282 WJ Swadling, 'A New Role for Resulting Trusts?' (1996) 16 Legal Studies 110, 113–15.

4.194   Although anachronistic and controverted,[283] this reasoning still holds true at the present day.[284] Because the declaration of trust proved by presumption is one which arises in favour of the transferor, the name 'resulting trust' was given to it, and to this day that name has been retained. To aid our understanding, however, the minimum necessary modernization is to describe it at greater length as a 'presumed declaration resulting trust'.

4.195   An example of such a presumed declaration resulting trust is *Re Vinogradoff.*[285] Mrs Vinogradoff gratuitously transferred £800 worth of War Loan stock into the joint names of herself and her four-year-old granddaughter. On Mrs Vinogradoff's death, a question arose as to the holding of the stock. Was it held by the grand-daughter outright as the survivor of joint tenants, or did she hold it as a trustee for Mrs Vinogradoff's estate? Farwell J held that because the initial transfer into joint names was gratuitous, a presumption of declaration arose in favour of Mrs Vinogradoff, which presumption had not been displaced by contrary evidence. The stock was therefore held by the infant on trust for the deceased.[286]

4.196   As we have seen, the second situation in which a declaration of trust will be proved by presumption is where A *inter vivos* pays C to transfer a right to B, and B is not the child or wife of A. In such a case, B will hold the right received on trust for A, in the absence, of course, of any evidence to the contrary. The reason why proof by presumption of declaration occurs here again reflects one of the historical reasons why trusts were created. One reason in the past for the popularity of trusts was that the beneficiary's interest under the trust was immune from dower.[287] Hence, when husbands bought titles to land they often had them conveyed to trustees to hold for them on trust. The practice became so common that whenever titles were paid for by one person but conveyed to another, the best guess was that the avoidance of dower was the reason it was done. This trust is also called a resulting trust, though the use of that language is obviously strained. A variation

---

[283] The counter-argument is that the presumption of declaration of trust is a fiction of the same order as the fiction of implied promise in the earlier law of unjust enrichment: AW Scott, 'Constructive Trusts' (1955) 71 LQR 39, 41. On this view, the presumption has been said to presume only a non-beneficial intent. This competing position is taken by R Chambers, *Resulting Trusts* (1997), throughout. The reason it cannot work, however, is that whatever a 'non-beneficial intent' might be, it is not a fact, and not therefore capable of forming the subject-matter of a presumption. There is in this area an unfortunate tendency to confuse the fundamentally different processes of implication and presumption.

[284] *Westdeutsche Landesbank Girozentrale v Islington LBC* [1996] AC 669, 708, HL *per* Lord Browne-Wilkinson.

[285] [1935] WN 68.

[286] We should ask whether the declaration proved by presumption of trust should not have been rebutted in this case by proof by evidence of the fact that the transfer was made to an infant. This is what happened on similar facts in *Fowkes v Pascoe* (1875) LR 10 Ch App 343, a case unfortunately not cited to Farwell J. It is discussed immediately below.

[287] A one-third share of the husband's land which passed automatically to his widow for her life.

on this theme is where A and B pay C to transfer rights to B. In such a case, B will hold the right on trust for himself and A as co-owners.

A classic example of such a 'purchase money' resulting trust is *Dyer v Dyer*,[288] **4.197** where a father supplied the purchase money in a sale of a title to land, the title being conveyed to himself, his wife and his eldest son. Eyre CB said:

> [T]he trust of a legal estate, whether freehold, copyhold, or leasehold; whether taken in the names of the purchasers and others jointly, or in the names of others without that of the purchaser; whether in one name or several; whether jointly or successive, results to the man who advances the purchase-money.[289]

(ii) Rebutting the presumption

The presumption of declaration of trust in these cases being a legal presumption **4.198** of the fact of declaration, it is consequently possible to rebut the presumption by adducing evidence which proves acts inconsistent with a declaration of trust in favour of the transferor being made. We will also see that in certain circumstances, a so-called counter-presumption, the 'presumption' of 'advancement' (outright transfer) is said to arise.

The clearest situation in which the presumption will be rebutted is where it is **4.199** proved by evidence what words accompanied the transfer of rights. As Lord Wilberforce pointed out in *Vandervell v IRC*,[290] there is no room for the operation of a presumption where all the facts are known. Thus, in *Goodman v Gallant*,[291] a purchase-money resulting trust was held not to arise where the conveyance spelt out that it was a transfer on trust for the transferees. Apart from a declaration of trust proved by evidence, the facts surrounding the transfer might also show that an outright transfer was intended. Thus, in *Fowkes v Pascoe*,[292] on facts very similar to *Re Vinogradoff*,[293] James LJ asked whether it was possible to reconcile with mental sanity the theory that the settlor put money into the names of herself and the grandson as trustee upon trust for herself. What trust, what object could there conceivably be in doing this, he asked.[294] Mellish LJ said that the circumstances showed that it was utterly impossible to come to any other conclusion than that this was intended as a gift rather than a trust.[295]

---

[288] (1788) 2 Cox 92, 30 ER 42.

[289] (1788) 2 Cox 92, 93, 30 ER 42, 43. In fact, the court held that the presumption did not arise on the facts as the transferees were within the 'presumption' of advancement.

[290] [1967] 2 AC 291, 329.

[291] [1986] Fam 106, CA.

[292] (1875) LR 10 Ch App 343, CA.

[293] [1935] WN 68. Unfortunately, *Fowkes v Pascoe* was not cited to Farwell J in *Re Vinogradoff*. If it had been, his decision would arguably have gone the other way.

[294] (1875) LR 10 Ch App 343, 348–9, CA.

[295] ibid 353.

4.200 Proof by evidence of gift apart, there are other situations of transfer in which the facts proved by evidence will be inconsistent with a declaration of trust for the transferor. Take the case of a transfer of rights which the evidence proves to have been mistakenly made to discharge a non-existent debt. Although such a transfer will of necessity be gratuitous, there is no room for any finding of a declaration of trust proved by presumption, for proof by evidence of the mistaken intent to discharge a debt is inconsistent with such a declaration, for it shows that the transferee was intended, albeit mistakenly, to take the rights absolutely, not as a trustee for the transferor.[296] The same is true of a gratuitous transfer of rights proved by evidence to have been caused by the exercise of undue influence on the part of the transferee. If a trust arises in such cases,[297] it cannot be because of proof by presumption that the transferor declared a trust in his own favour. The causative event can only be the unjust enrichment of the transferee.

(iii) The 'presumption' of advancement

4.201 We have said that proof by presumption of a declaration of trust does not occur where the transfer or contribution to purchase involves a father/child or husband/wife scenario. In these situations, a 'presumption' of advancement or outright transfer is said to arise. Thus, in *Dyer v Dyer*[298] itself, proof by presumption of a declaration of trust by the father in his own favour did not arise because the purchaser was instructed to convey to the father, his wife and his eldest son. It is, however, doubtful whether this is a presumption properly-so-called, for no fact is be proved by it. All that seems to be happening is that the court identifies a situation in which a declaration of trust will not be proved by presumption. As Dixon CJ, McTiernan, Fullager, and Windeyer JJ explained in *Martin v Martin*, 'It is called a presumption of advancement but it is rather the absence of any reason for assuming that a trust arose . . .'.[299]

4.202 The presumption of advancement is, however, thought to be rebuttable. In *Warren v Gurney*,[300] a father bought a title to a house in the name of his daughter, and in which he allowed her to live. It was proved by evidence that at all times he retained the title deeds to the property in his possession. On his death, the Court of Appeal held that this proved by evidence fact was inconsistent with him being seen to have made an outright transfer to his daughter, so that in the absence of any other evidence the parties were thrown back on the presumption that there had been a declaration of trust in favour of the father.

---

296 *Westdeutsche Landesbank Girozentrale v Islington LBC* [1996] AC 669, 708, HL.
297 The Court of Appeal was divided on this point in *Allcard v Skinner* (1887) 36 ChD 145.
298 (1788) 2 Cox 92, 30 ER 42, para 4.197.
299 (1959) 110 CLR 297, 303. See also Murphy J in *Calverley v Green* (1984) 56 ALR 483, 498, who described the 'presumption' of advancement as a 'misuse of the term presumption'.
300 [1944] 2 All ER 472, CA.

(iv) Gratuitous conveyances of land

There is an awkward problem which must be addressed in respect of the operation **4.203**
of the presumption. It concerns the case of land. The Law of Property Act 1925,
section 60(3) provides:

> In a voluntary conveyance a resulting trust for the grantor shall not be implied merely
> by reason that the property is not expressed to be conveyed for the use or benefit of
> the grantee.

That sub-section raises the question whether the proof by presumption of a declaration of trust which arises from proof by evidence of a gratuitous transfer, though
not, it should be noted, a contribution to the purchase price, no longer arises
where the subject-matter of the transfer is a title to land. The argument that it still
does is that this section only short-circuits a great deal of legal history having to do
with the words necessary to pass titles. Prior to 1925, an outright gift of a title to
land had to include the words 'unto and to the use of' the transferee. Otherwise,
the right would not pass because of the effect of the Statute of Uses 1535, which
'executed' all uses. The resulting use which would arise in a gratuitous conveyance
would be immediately executed by the statute, thus ensuring that the title was sent
straight back to the transferor, the consequence of which was that the transfer
would be a nullity. Adding the words 'unto and to the use of' in a gratuitous
conveyance had the effect of preventing this happening, because with the words
accompanying the conveyance now known, there was no room for the operation
of the presumption. They thus ensured that the title was not sent back. The Statute
of Uses was abolished by the Law of Property Act 1925, with the result that
such words were no longer needed in order to pass an outright title to land
gratuitously. The same Act introduced a number of word-saving provisions.
Section 60(3) is one of them, though since the 1925 legislation repealed the
Statute of Uses, it is possibly otiose. Arguably, all it does is remind conveyancers
that it is no longer necessary to insert any extra words into gratuitous conveyances
of titles to land.

This is not, however, the present attitude of the courts. They have taken the view **4.204**
on a number of occasions that proof by evidence of a gratuitous transfer of a title
to land no longer attracts the operation of the presumption.[301] The point,
however, has always been *obiter*. Nor has argument been addressed as to why the
legislature would abolish the presumption in such obscure language and then only
in cases of voluntary conveyances of titles to land.

---

[301] *Hodgson v Marks* [1971] Ch 892, CA; *Lohia v Lohia* [2001] EWCA Civ 1691; *Ali v Khan*
[2002] EWCA Civ 974.

(v) Evidence

4.205 There are two situations in which the legislature has required the declaration of trust to be proved by a particular type of evidence: trusts of land and trusts in wills. Only the former will be dealt with here; the latter is a specialized topic within the law of succession. The statutory rule with regard to land is contained in the Law of Property Act 1925, section 53(1)(b):

> A declaration of trust respecting any land or any interest therein must be manifested and proved by some writing signed by some person who is able to declare such trust or by his will.

This is a re-enactment of a similar provision in the Statute of Frauds 1677.[302] The problem it was designed to meet with was the ease with which false allegations could be substantiated before a court in an era when the law of evidence was relatively unsophisticated.[303] The legislature responded, not by a wholesale reform of the law of evidence, but by the enactment of a specific rule for the most problematic case, the claimant who falsely alleged that a landowner had declared himself a trustee of his title to land for him. The thinking was that the incidence of fraud would be reduced by a requirement on the party making such an allegation to produce some written evidence that such a declaration had been made and which bore the signature of the person alleged to have made it.

4.206 The problem with provisions designed to prevent fraud, however, is that they can sometimes be used to perpetrate fraud. A good modern example is *Bannister v Bannister*.[304] A woman agreed to sell to her brother-in-law her freehold title to two cottages, on the oral undertaking by him that he would hold the title to one of the cottages on trust for her for her life. The formal conveyance, however, contained no declaration of trust. The brother-in-law later denied there had been any declaration, on the ground that it could not be proved for lack of written evidence signed by himself.

4.207 The attitude taken by the courts to such cases is that a statute designed to prevent fraud should not be turned on its head and used to engineer a fraud. As Lindley LJ explained in *Rochefoucauld v Boustead*:

> [T]he Statute of Frauds does not prevent proof of a fraud; and . . . it is a fraud on the part of a person to whom land is conveyed as a trustee, and who knows it was so conveyed, to deny the trust and claim the land himself. Consequently, notwithstanding

---

[302] Of which s 7 provided: '. . . all declarations or creations of trusts or confidences of any lands, tenements or hereditaments, shall be manifested and proved by some writing signed by the party who is by law entitled to declare such trust, or by his last will in writing, or else they shall be utterly void and of none effect'.

[303] Details in TG Youdan, 'Formalities for Trusts of Land, and the Doctrine in *Rochefoucauld v Boustead*' [1984] CLJ 306.

[304] [1948] 2 All ER 133, CA.

the statute, it is competent for a person claiming land conveyed to another to prove by parol evidence that it was so conveyed upon trust for the claimant, and that the grantee, knowing the facts, is denying the trust and relying on the term of the conveyance and statute, in order to keep the land for himself.[305]

Thus, where it would be fraudulent for the trustee to shelter behind the statute, he will be disabled from so doing. The declaration of trust will then be proved in the usual way, ie by the admission of what is now perfectly admissible parol evidence, and the express trust[306] thereby arising now given effect.

What amounts to fraud for the purpose of this doctrine?[307] Unfortunately, there **4.208** is no authoritative statement, though the cases indicate that detrimental reliance on the part of the beneficiary is included. In *Eves v Eves*[308] a man bought a fee simple title to a house and orally declared a trust of it in favour of himself and his female cohabitee. Thinking that she now had an interest, the woman acted to her detriment on the faith of his representation by doing a great deal of work on the house. When the man later tried to keep the property for himself, the Court of Appeal held that the initially unprovable declaration of trust could now be proved by parol evidence because of her detrimental reliance.

It should finally be noted that section 53(2) of the Law of Property Act 1925 **4.209** exempts from the section 53(1)(b) the 'creation or operation' of resulting and constructive trusts. This sub-section only states the obvious. As we have seen, constructive trusts arise for reasons other than declarations of trust. A statutory provision regulating the type of evidence admissible to prove a declaration of trust can therefore have no application to such trusts. So too with the 'automatic' resulting trust, which, as we have also seen, is a species of constructive trust. As to the 'presumed' resulting trust, we saw that it arose because on proof by evidence of certain primary facts, the law found proved by presumption a declaration of trust. A provision detailing the type of evidence admissible to discharge a burden of proof can have no application to a litigant in whose favour the fact of declaration is proved by a different method of proof.

---

305 [1897] 1 Ch 196, 206, CA.

306 'The trust which the claimant has established is clearly an express trust . . . The trust is one which both plaintiff and defendant intended to create. This case is not one in which an equitable obligation arises although there may have been no intention to create a trust. The intention to create a trust existed from the first': *Rochefoucauld v Boustead* [1897] 1 Ch 196, 208, CA, *per* Lindley LJ. This is the only case in which the point was argued and decided. There are a number of other cases in which the trust is described as constructive, but in none was the point determinative of the outcome of the case. The most notable are *Bannister v Bannister* [1948] 2 All ER 143, CA; *Gissing v Gissing* [1971] AC 886, HL; *Paragon Finance Ltd v Thakarer* [1999] 1 All ER 400, 409, CA.

307 Another difficulty is that the whole theory is circular, for it is only once the evidence which the statute says is inadmissible is admitted that it will it be known that a 'trustee' is attempting to use the statute as an instrument of fraud.

308 [1975] 1 WLR 1338, CA.

(6) Duties of Trustees of Declared Trusts

4.210 Strictly speaking, the duties of trustees of declared trusts form part of the law of obligations, not the law of property. Breaches of these duties, like the breaches of the primary duties which form the superstructure of the law of tort, are wrongs and create secondary personal rights in the victims of the wrong.[309] Only rarely will a wrong create a property right.[310] However, in order to give a reasonably complete, if outline, picture of the law of trusts, a brief discussion of the duties of trustees is set out below.[311]

4.211 A trustee is accountable to the beneficiaries for his management of the rights he holds for them on trust. That primary obligation of accountability, which is the particular means by which all the management obligations of a trustee are enforced, will be considered after those obligations have been outlined.

(a) The management obligations of the trustee

4.212 Accountability aside, there are three central obligations cast upon a trustee: to promote the interests of the beneficiary; to stay within the terms of the trust; and to act disinterestedly.

(i) The obligation to promote the interests of the beneficiary

4.213 The trustee's principal obligation is to preserve and promote the interests of the beneficiaries. It should be noted that, differently to most other duties found in the law of obligations, it is a positive duty to improve the position of the beneficiaries, not merely one to refrain from causing them harm.[312] The law has to choose the standard to which the trustee must comply, and it has long chosen an objective standard. Until 2000, that standard was to be found exclusively in case-law. So, Sir George Jessel MR said in *Speight v Gaunt*:

> It seems to me that on general principles a trustee ought to conduct the business of the trust in the same manner that an ordinary prudent man of business would conduct his own, and that beyond that there is no liability or obligation on the trustee.[313]

---

309 See the discussion of equitable wrongs in Ch 17.

310 A rare example is *A-G for Hong Kong v Reid* [1994] 1 AC 324: paras 4.297–4.305. This may, however, be the best explanation of what happens where trust rights have been dissipated in breach of trust and the beneficiaries are allowed to 'trace' into any substitute assets, thereby forcing the trustees to hold these substitute assets on trust.

311 For a detailed account, see AJ Oakley, *Parker & Mellows: The Modern Law of Trusts* (8th edn, 2003) 573–623.

312 For a general discussion of such duties of 'altruism', see P Birks, 'The Content of Fiduciary Obligation' (2002) 16 TLI 34.

313 *Speight v Gaunt* (1882) 22 Ch D 727, 739; (1883) 9 App Cas 1, 19, HL, *per* Lord Blackburn. The prudent person of business must also bear in mind that the affairs in question are not his

When Sir George Jessel MR said 'beyond that there is no liability or obligation **4.214** on the trustee', he only meant that there was no stricter standard to be applied to him in his management of the trust affairs. There are certainly other obligations incumbent on a trustee, but the Master of the Rolls was underlining the fact that a trustee is not liable for every loss, for the risk of a loss occurring notwithstanding his having complied with this standard of skill and care lies with the beneficiaries.[314]

The standard in respect of certain acts is now enshrined in legislation. By virtue of **4.215** section 1 of the Trustee Act 2000, a 'duty of care' is laid down, comprising the duty to 'exercise such care and skill as is reasonable in the circumstances, having regard in particular (a) to any special knowledge or experience that he has or holds himself out as having, and (b) if he acts as trustee in the course of a business or profession, to any special knowledge or experience that it is reasonable to expect of a person acting in the course of that kind of business or profession'. This statutory duty, however, applies only where the trustee is exercising one of the functions listed in the Act, which include investment, the appointment and supervision of agents, and effecting insurance.[315] In all other cases, recourse will still have to be had to the standard set by the judiciary.

That standard seems little different from the common standard of care set by the **4.216** reasonable man. That common standard is always fine-tuned to suit the particular facts. And that is what seems to happen here. The duty of the trustee is special in that it requires positive conduct on the beneficiaries' behalf, but in other respects it looks exactly like a liability in negligence.[316] Thus in *Bartlett v Barclay's Bank Trust Co Ltd*[317] the bank was made liable to the beneficiaries for loss caused to the trust portfolio through inert and incompetent management, essentially a straightforward liability for professional negligence.

The same standard appears to apply when it comes to keeping an eye on co-trustees. **4.217** A trustee is not automatically vicariously liable for the acts of other trustees. If the breach in question consists primarily in the act or omission of one trustee, the question will nevertheless arise whether the other or others were at fault in

---

but another's: *Re Whitley* (1886) 33 Ch D 347, 355, CA, *per* Lindley LJ. Most trusts are directed to the financial benefit of the beneficiaries; the trustees must not allow themselves to be distracted by their own political and moral commitments: *Cowan v Scargill* [1985] Ch 270. Charitable trustees have some discretion to avoid investments which would impede or contradict the work of the charity: *Harries v Church Commissioners* [1992] 1 WLR 1241.

[314] *Morley v Morley* (1678) 2 Ch Cas 2, 22 ER 819.

[315] The list is contained in Schedule 1.

[316] The courts have indeed recently said that fiduciary negligence is negligence *simpliciter*: *Henderson v Merrett Syndicates* [1995] 2 AC 145, 205, HL, *per* Lord Browne-Wilkinson; *Bristol and West Building Society v Mothew* [1998] Ch 1, 16, CA, *per* Millett LJ.

[317] [1980] Ch 515, CA.

their monitoring of what that one was doing. The answer is that liability for bad monitoring depends on proof of failure to act as a prudent person of business would act.

(ii) The obligation to keep within the terms of the trust

4.218 There are limits on the way in which a trustee may deploy the rights he holds on trust. Most obviously he must not, except for the purposes of investment, convey them to persons other than the beneficiaries. But he also has limited *vires* in investing and reinvesting. He must not make investments which are not authorized by the trust deed or allowed by the general law.[318] This liability is strict. If a trustee pays the wrong person because of a totally innocent mistake or after taking legal advice, he still has to restore the trust fund.[319] If he makes an unauthorized investment, the beneficiaries can recognize and adopt it or treat it as made out of the trustee's own money and require the authorized investment to be put back in place.[320] The only escape is through the rarely used Trustee Act 1925, section 61, which allows the court to excuse a trustee who has acted honestly and reasonably.[321]

(iii) The obligation to act disinterestedly

4.219 The obligation to act disinterestedly is often described as an obligation not to profit from the trust. When we ask which profits are interdicted, in nearly every case the answer is given by the rule against conflicts of interest. The trustee is under an obligation not to pursue an interest which conflicts or might conflict with his duty to the beneficiaries.[322] The rigour of this obligation is expressed in the hypothetical nature of the inquiry. The question is not whether his pursuit of a given interest did influence him to sacrifice the interests of the beneficiaries or did tempt him to do so but whether it might possibly have tempted the trustee to sacrifice their interests.

---

318 The law as to what investments were authorized used to be exceedingly complex. By virtue of the Trustee Act 2000, s 3(1), at least as regards investments other than land, all are now authorized subject to any contrary term in the trust instrument.

319 *Hilliard v Fulford* (1876) 4 Ch D 389; *National Trustees Company of Australasia Ltd v General Finance Co of Australasia Ltd* [1905] AC 373, HL; *Re Diplock* [1948] Ch 465, CA, affirmed as *Ministry of Health v Simpson* [1951] AC 251, HL.

320 *Shepherd v Mouls* (1845) 4 Hare 500, 67 ER 746; *Knott v Cottee* (1852) 16 Beav 77, 51 ER 705; *Re Lake* [1903] 1 KB 439; *Re Bell's Indenture* [1980] 1 WLR 1217.

321 *Re Evans, Evans v Westcott* [1999] 2 All ER 777 provides a rare example, where a small estate had been distributed by a sister who, until he appeared after many years, honestly believed that her brother was dead. She was excused save so far as she still held assets.

322 *Keech v Sandford* (1726) Sel Cas t King 61, 25 ER 223; *Bray v Ford* [1896] AC 44, 51, HL; cf Lord Cranworth LC in *Aberdeen Rly v Blaikie* (1854) 1 Macq HL 461, 471–2.

The obligation to avoid possible conflicts is thus very rigorous, but, in order to **4.220** count, the possibility of conflict must be real and sensible, not fanciful.[323] The obligation to act disinterestedly thus reduces to the 'no profit' obligation, or more accurately the 'no unauthorized profit' obligation, which is in turn in large measure defined by the 'no conflict' obligation and would be incoherent without it. In a rare case a gain may be interdicted in circumstances in which the bar cannot be explained by the 'no conflict' obligation, as where someone who has ceased to be a trustee exploits information acquired in his capacity as a trustee.

(b) The trustee's accountability

A trustee is under an obligation to render an account of his management. That **4.221** accountability is as a matter of history the matrix of the substantive obligations just described. That is, they are inferences from the way in which the account is worked out. It is still true that account remains the mechanism for realizing those obligations, though they are increasingly discussed as though they had an independent life of their own.

The trustee is debited with all assets received and with some which ought to **4.222** have been received, and he takes credit for proper payments out. The difference between the two gives the actual measure of his liability.

(i) Debits

The trustee is chargeable with all sums and assets received on account of the trust, **4.223** whether from the settlor or in the course of investment and reinvestment. Likewise he is chargeable with sums received in his own name if they are caught by the 'no unauthorized profit' rule discussed immediately above. He is also chargeable for whatever he ought to have received had he not slipped into breach of duty, as for instance where proper management would have raised the investment income or capital growth.

(ii) Credits

On the other hand the trustee must be credited with all lawful payments out, **4.224** whether by way of distribution to beneficiaries or purchase of authorized investments. He also takes credit for lost assets where the loss has happened despite his having kept within his *vires* and maintained the standards of skill and care incumbent on him.[324] By contrast the trustee can take no credit for payments out which are *ultra vires*. If he pays the wrong person or buys an unauthorized investment, he cannot take credit for the disbursement. This is sometimes put by

---

[323] *Boardman v Phipps* [1967] 2 AC 46, 124, HL, *per* Lord Upjohn.
[324] *Morley v Morley* (1678) 2 Ch Cas 2.

saying that he is deemed to have used his own money. It comes to the same thing: the *ultra vires* expenditure is disallowed in account.

4.225 The modern tendency to separate the discussion of a trustee's obligations from their original matrix, a difficult process fraught with hidden traps, is illustrated by *Target Holdings Ltd v Redferns*.[325] There, without discussion, the House of Lords assimilated breach of trust to all other liabilities to pay compensation and never mentioned accountability or the taking of an account. Solicitors were holding a chose in action against a bank worth £1.5m under a bare trust for Target Holdings Ltd. The sum was intended to finance the purchase of certain rights in respect of land, with Target intended to be the mortgagees of those rights when purchased. The solicitors released the monies prior to completion and to a party other than the borrower. In other words, they misdirected the trust fund. In fact, co-operation between the borrower and the payee resulted in completion four days later, and the securities were granted. The outcome was as Target had wanted, though as the story unfolded it turned out that they had lent far more than their security could bear. The question was whether the solicitors' breach of trust obliged them to replace the trust money which they had misdirected. The House of Lords held that though there was an undoubted breach of trust, the liability was confined to the loss which the misdirection had caused. Since Target got what they wanted and suffered only loss which they would have suffered anyhow, the misdirecting solicitors could not be liable simply by reason of the misdirection.[326]

4.226 From an historical perspective, if from no other, this misconceives the nature of the trustee's liability. The solicitors were accountable for the money which they held. They could not take credit for expenditure consisting in a payment to the wrong person. In principle therefore they were liable unless they could take credit in the account for the money which came back from the third party, not to themselves, but to the party whom they were to pay. It has to be assumed that, had the question been put in that accounting framework, the House of Lords would have answered that they were indeed entitled to take that credit.

(7) Powers of Trustees of Declared Trusts

4.227 To understand the institution of the declared trust, it is vital to realise that it is not simply a matter of duties being cast on trustees and rights on beneficiaries. Trustees will usually have an array of powers in relation to their management of the trust fund. Principal among these are the power to appoint agents, to advance income for the maintenance of infant beneficiaries, and to advance capital to

---

[325] [1996] 1 AC 421, HL.
[326] There was another untried issue, whether had the solicitors done all their duty to the lenders, Target would have withdrawn altogether.

infant beneficiaries with contingent interests. A full account of these should be sought in more specialist texts.[327]

(8) Trusts for Purposes

The trusts so far discussed have all been created in favour of persons. The question **4.228** which will now be addressed is whether it is possible to dedicate rights to purposes through the use of a trust. One method of dedicating rights to purposes without the use of a trust would be to give them to a corporation which had as its object the desired purposes.[328] The essential question, however, is whether it can be done without the creation of a new legal person. At common law, the answer is a simple no. The question then narrows to whether it is possible to utilize the device of the trust to achieve such an end. The general answer is that it is possible to create a trust for purposes which are charitable, but for no others. Charitable purposes are sometimes referred to as public purposes, because they are for the public benefit and supervised by public officials. A contrast can thus be made between public and private purposes.

(a) Public purposes

Trusts for charitable purposes are accorded a number of privileges. They are, for **4.229** example, exempt from the beneficiary principle.[329] There is no need for people to enforce them since they are enforced by an officer of the Crown, the Attorney-General. Nor is there a requirement that the objects of the trust be certain,[330] so that a trust simply for 'charitable purposes' will be valid. And charitable trusts may be perpetual. Apart from these benefits, which go to their validity, charitable trusts also have certain fiscal advantages. These tax privileges occasionally come under political debate and scrutiny. Their underlying justification is that they encourage philanthropy. The community as a whole benefits from the pursuit of public purposes with private money.

(i) Definition of charity

In colloquial speech 'charity' brings to mind the relief of destitution. The legal **4.230** concept is much wider. It is clear that an evil or harmful purpose cannot be charitable, but it is broadly true that any purpose which is beneficial to the community and on which, if funds were available, it would not be improper to expend public money will be charitable. Charity can run ahead of public expenditure, because

---

[327] For example, AJ Oakley, *Parker & Mellows: The Modern Law of Trusts* (8th edn, 2003), chs 14, 15, 16, and 18.
[328] Paras 3.35–3.92.
[329] Paras 4.274–4.278.
[330] Paras 4.168–4.177.

charitable giving makes funds available which would otherwise not be. However, the courts have always been reluctant to lay down any precise definition, preferring to deal in lists, examples and categories. One constant problem is that as social values change and the level of material wealth gradually increases, notions of useful and proper public expenditure change too. Hence charity cannot but be a flexible category with a shifting content. It is also worth bearing in mind from the outset that it is a category in which it is easier for the leading edge to move forward than the trailing edge. It would be disruptive in the extreme if long-established charities stood in constant danger of losing their charitable status.

4.231 The traditional starting point is the preamble to the Statute of Charitable Uses 1601, sometimes referred to simply as the 'Statute of Elizabeth'. The preamble, which contains a list of various charitable uses known to the law at the beginning of the seventeenth century, provides as follows:

> Whereas lands, tenements, rents, annuities, profits, hereditaments, goods, chattels, money and stocks of money have been heretofore given, limited, appointed and assigned, as well by the Queen's most excellent majesty, and her most noble progenitors, as by sundry other well disposed persons; some for the relief of aged, impotent and poor People, some for Maintenance of sick and maimed soldiers and Mariners, Schools of Learning, Free Schools and Scholars of Universities, the Repair of Bridges, Ports, Havens, Causeways, Churches, Sea-Banks and Highways, some for Education and Preferment of Orphans, some for or towards Relief, Stock or Maintenance of Houses of Correction, some for Marriages of Poor Maids, some for Supportation, Aid and help of Young Tradesmen, Handicraftsmen and Persons Decayed, some for the Relief or Redemption of Prisoners or Captives, and for Aid or Ease of any poor Inhabitants concerning payments of Fifteens, setting out Soldiers and other Taxes; which Lands, Tenements, Rents, Annuities, Profits, hereditaments, Goods, Chattels, Money and Stocks of Money, nevertheless have not been employed according to the charitable intent of the givers and founders thereof, by reason of frauds, Breaches of trust and Negligence in those that should pay, deliver and employ the same.

4.232 In *Commissioners for Special Purposes of Income Tax v Pemsel*,[331] Lord Macnaghten broke this list down into four categories: trusts for the relief of poverty; for the advancement of education; for the advancement of religion; and for other purposes beneficial to the community. But, as Lord Wilberforce pointed out in *Scottish Burial Reform & Cremation Society v Glasgow Corporation*,[332] the following qualifications of this fourfold classification have to be kept in mind. First, it is a classification of convenience. There may well be charitable purposes which do not fit neatly into one or other heading. Secondly, the terms of the classification must not be construed as though they were part of a statute. Thirdly, the law of charity has evolved since 1891.

---

[331] [1891] AC 531, HL.
[332] [1968] AC 138, 154, HL.

The discussion of the four categories can safely first consider the purposes **4.233** themselves and return later to the question whether the element of public benefit is cancelled out by a restriction in any one case to a particular class of immediate beneficiaries. So, for example, the advancement of education is a charitable purpose, but a trust for the advancement of the education of the settlor's son is clearly not.

By virtue of the Charities Act 2006, this four-fold list has been expanded to twelve: **4.234** (i) the prevention or relief of poverty; (ii) the advancement of education; (iii) the advancement of religion; (iv) the advancement of health or the saving of lives; (v) the advancement of citizenship or community development; (vi) the advancement of the arts, culture, heritage or science; (vii) the advancement of amateur sport; (viii) the advancement of human rights, conflict resolution or reconciliation or the promotion of religious or racial harmony or equality and diversity; (ix) the advancement of environmental protection or improvement; (x) the relief of those in need by reason of youth, age, ill-health, disability, financial hardship or other disadvantage; (xi) the advancement of animal welfare; (xii) other purposes. Under this last head are included purposes recognized as charitable under existing charity law or by virtue of the Recreational Charities Act 1958; purposes that may reasonably be regarded as analogous to, or within the spirit of, any of the purposes listed above; and any purposes that may be reasonably regarded as analogous to, or within the spirit of, any purposes which have been recognized under charity law as falling within the immediately preceding heading. However, since the relevant provisions of the 2006 Act are not yet in force,[333] attention must still focus on the existing law.

(ii) The nominate heads of charitable purpose

Relief of poverty. The word 'poverty' is difficult to define, though it is not to **4.235** be equated with 'destitution'; persons 'in need' will suffice, need being a relative term.[334] For that reason, trusts for 'aged and decayed actors'[335] or 'the permanent aid of distressed gentlefolk'[336] have been upheld under this head.

Advancement of education. The preamble speaks of 'the maintenance of **4.236** schools of learning, free schools and scholars in universities' and 'the education

---

[333] Under s 79(2) of the Act, which is in force, these provisions will be brought into force on such day as the Minister may by order appoint. The 2006 Act also makes changes inter alia to the rules relating to the requirement of public benefit, of *cy près*, and to the administration of charities. These provisions are likewise not yet in force.

[334] *Re Coulthurst* [1951] Ch 661, CA.

[335] *Spiller v Maulde* (1886) 32 Ch D 158n.

[336] *Re Young* [1951] Ch 344.

and preferment of orphans'. Education is not confined to teaching.[337] It includes research and the discovery of knowledge which will be added to the store on which teaching may later draw.[338] It was held in *Re Shaw*[339] that Bernard Shaw's trust for the introduction of a more efficient alphabet was not charitable. Although the judgment in that case would suggest that the mere accumulation of knowledge would not qualify under this head, it has to be read in the context of Bernard Shaw's intention, which was to promote and preach the utility of the reformed alphabet. In short the project was semi-political in nature, rather than an impartial search for truth.[340]

4.237 In *Incorporated Council of Law Reporting v A-G*[341] the question was whether a trust for 'the preparation and publication . . . at a moderate price, and under gratuitous professional control, of judicial decisions of the supreme and appellate courts in England' was charitable. Although no element of instruction was involved, the Court of Appeal held that the Council's purposes were for the advancement of education since the purpose of the law reports was to provide essential material for the study of law, which was a learned profession.

4.238 Although trusts for the promotion of sport are in general not charitable except within the terms of the Recreational Charities Act 1958, a trust for the promotion of sport in an educational setting will be upheld: 'The picture of education when applied to the young . . . is complex and varied . . . It is a picture of a balanced and systematic process of instruction, training and practice containing spiritual, moral, mental and physical elements . . .'.[342]

4.239 **Advancement of religion.** In England the benefit of religion is not so much the cultivation of the relationship between God and mankind but the tendency of religion to produce good citizens in society. A gift to a closed order is thus not charitable, because it does not provide that secular benefit. The members of a

---

337 Indeed, teaching alone will not suffice. A school for pickpockets, for example, would not be charitable: *Re Pinion* [1965] Ch 85, 105, CA, *per* Harman LJ.

338 *Re Hopkins* [1965] Ch 669, 680.

339 [1957] 1 WLR 729.

340 In *Re Hopkins* [1965] 1 Ch 669, 680, Wilberforce J described *Re Shaw* as 'not easy'. It resembles *Re Bushnell* [1975] 1 WLR 1596, where Goulding J found that a trust 'for the advancement and propagation of the teaching of socialised medicine . . . furthering the knowledge of the socialised application of medicine to public and personal health and well-being and to demonstrating that the full advantage of socialist medicine can only be enjoyed in a socialist state' was simply propaganda masquerading as education.

341 [1972] Ch 73, CA.

342 *IRC v McMullen* [1981] AC 1, 425, HL, *per* Lord Hailsham of St Marylebone. That case concerned the provision of football facilities to schools and universities. Cf, taking an earlier line, *Re Mariette* [1915] 2 Ch 284. There the provision of fives courts in a school was held charitable as being subsidiary to education.

closed order do not go out into the world but, on the contrary, cut themselves off from society and devote themselves to intercessory prayer.[343]

Nevertheless, to qualify under this head it is not enough to cultivate the secular benefit through the humanist means. There must be a relationship with the supernatural. This issue arose in *Re South Place Ethical Society*,[344] where the question was whether a trust established for 'the study and dissemination of ethical principles and the cultivation of rational religious sentiment' qualified for charitable status under this head. Dillon J held that these objects were charitable in the fourth category, though not under the head of advancement of religion. 'Religion, as I see it,' he said, 'is concerned with man's relations with God, and ethics are concerned with man's relations with man. The two are not the same, and are not made the same by sincere enquiry into the question: what is God?'[345]

4.240

(iii) Other purposes beneficial to the community

Charities in the first three heads are only charities because they are beneficial to the community. They form convenient nominate categories. The fourth category is residual. Here it must be shown that the selected purposes are beneficial to the community. And not only must the purpose be beneficial, it must be beneficial within the spirit and intendment of the preamble to the Statute of Elizabeth. As Lindley LJ pointed out, 'Not every object of public general utility must necessarily be a charity.'[346] These are no more than elaborate ways of saying that the spectrum of charitable purposes is somewhat shorter than the spectrum of good purposes. It has never been easy to express the difference in plain language.

4.241

Purposes which are evil or equivocal. In this fourth category, the court must find that the purpose in question is beneficial. This is not something encountered under the first three heads of charity. There it is given that advancing religion, education and the relief of poverty are things which are in themselves of public benefit.[347] The requirement of benefit obviously rules out evil purposes. But in English law it also rules out purposes whose beneficial character is equivocal, most obviously political programmes. Political purposes are not charitable. The rule appears to be that an activity whose objective is to change the law is thereby disabled from being a charity. How, it is said, can a trust to change the law be regarded by the law as so beneficial to the community that it deserves the privileges

4.242

---

[343] *Gilmour v Coates* [1949] AC 426, HL.

[344] [1980] 1 WLR 1565.

[345] [1980] 1 WLR 1565, 1571; cf *Bowman v Secular Society* [1917] AC 406, HL: religion implies monotheism.

[346] *Re Macduff* [1896] 2 Ch 451, 456, CA.

[347] Under s 3(2) of the Charities Act 2006 (not yet in force), the so-called 'presumption' of public benefit has been abolished. It is, however, difficult to see how this can operate. Will the Inland Revenue now be able to put the Church of England to proof of the benefit of religion?

of charity? Purposes which many people admire and support have been disqualified on this ground. Although there are hundreds of animal welfare charities, suppression of vivisection is not a charitable purpose, because it both requires campaigning for a change in the law and would require the courts to choose between the competing benefits of animal welfare and advancing medicine.[348] Again the laudable aims of Amnesty International, to press for the release of political prisoners and an end to their mistreatment, are also not charitable because they are political and compete with other goods, such as diplomatic and economic relations with foreign governments.[349]

4.243   The leading case is *Bowman v Secular Society*.[350] There a bequest was made to the Secular Society, an incorporated association. Among the objects of the society was the abolition of religious tests, the disestablishment of the Church, the secularization of education, and the alteration of the law touching religion, marriage, and the observance of the Sabbath. It was argued for the next of kin that because the company could only act for its purposes, a gift to the company was a gift to the company for the purposes of the company and was therefore void as a private purpose trust. Lord Parker said that the argument that there was here a purpose trust was fallacious. There was no trust at all, the company taking outright. Nevertheless, his Lordship went on to consider whether or not the purposes were charitable. He said that they were not. Equity has always refused to regard such objects as charitable. A trust for the attainment of political purposes is always invalid, not because it is illegal, for everyone is at liberty to advocate or promote by any lawful means a change in the law, but because a court has no means of judging whether a proposed change in the law will or will not be for the benefit of the public.[351]

4.244   **The elusive line between 'beneficial' and 'charitable'.**   In *Williams v IRC*,[352] the trust in question was 'to promote Welsh interests in London and to provide means of social intercourse; discuss all questions affecting Welsh interests; foster the study of the Welsh language by lectures on Welsh history, literature, music and art; maintain a library of literature in the Welsh language or relating to Wales; maintain an institute and meeting place for the benefit of the Welsh people in London with a view to creating a centre to promote the moral, social, spiritual and educational welfare of the Welsh people'. This failed to qualify as charitable.

---

[348] *National Anti-Vivisection Society v IRC* [1948] AC 31, HL.

[349] *McGovern v A-G* [1982] Ch 321.

[350] [1917] AC 406, HL.

[351] Similarly, in *National Anti-Vivisection Society v IRC* [1948] AC 31, 50, Lord Wright cited with approval the words of Tyssen, *On Charitable Bequests* (1921), 177: 'The law could not stultify itself by holding that it was for the public benefit that the law itself should be changed . . . . Each court . . . must decide on the principle that the law is right as it stands.'

[352] [1947] AC 447, HL. A similar result was reached in *IRC v Baddeley* [1955] AC 572, HL (social purposes).

The House of Lords held that the undoubted benefit to the Welsh community in London did not in itself satisfy the requirement that the benefit had to be within the spirit and intendment of the preamble. On the other side of the line, in *Scottish Burial Reform and Cremation Society v Glasgow Corporation*[353] the provision of facilities for cremation was held to be for the public benefit and charitable.

There are two ways of finding this elusive line, which might be called 'analogy' **4.245** and 'principle'. The former has long been in use, but the latter offers more hope that the operation will be conducted in an intelligible and rational manner. A third approach, to ask directly whether the purpose deserves the privileges of charity, especially the fiscal privileges, must be rejected. It is reasonable and proper that judges should be asked to decide whether a purpose is charitable. It is for Parliament to decide what privileges charities deserve. Lawyers have no special expertise in that kind of political question.

The analogy approach somewhat resembles the children's game of Chinese **4.246** Whispers. Starting from a foothold in the preamble, a path is marked out through the decided cases leading down to, or almost to, the new candidate. This can be seen in the *Scottish Burial* case itself. There, the provision of crematoria was held to be within the fourth head because the preamble referred specifically to 'the repair of . . . churches',[354] a subsequent decision had held that a trust to repair a parish churchyard was by analogy charitable,[355] another had held that a trust for keeping in good order a burial ground attached to a church was also charitable,[356] and a further case had held that a trust for the maintenance of a cemetery owned and managed by a local authority as a public burial ground was charitable,[357] so that the provision of cremation facilities to the public was only one more step away.

Like most arguments by analogy, this kind of exercise is only saved from arbitrari- **4.247** ness by the fact that it is tacitly controlled by a principle of selection. Analogy is in fact no more than the handmaid of principle, and this has led to calls for it to be kept in its proper place and for 'principle' to take charge.[358] The principled approach would appear to rest on two propositions: first, that, in the absence of specific contaminations discussed immediately below, a beneficial purpose is prima facie charitable in law; and second, that it may nonetheless not be

---

[353] [1968] AC 138, HL.

[354] In fact, the only reference to religion in the whole preamble.

[355] *Re Vaughan, Vaughan v Thomas* (1886) 33 Ch D 187. Warrington J pointed out in *Re Manser, A-G v Lucas* [1905] 1 Ch 68, 74, that there was no difference between a gift to repair God's House and a gift to repair God's acre.

[356] *Re Manser, A-G v Lucas* [1905] 1 Ch 68.

[357] *Re Eighmie, Colbourne v Wilks* [1935] Ch 524.

[358] Russell LJ in *Incorporated Council of Law Reporting for England and Wales v A-G* [1972] Ch 73, 88, CA.

charitable if it falls into the relatively small category of projects which, despite their beneficial character, would, according to the standards and expectations of the time, be a social luxury and as such an improper waste even of money additional to available public resources.

4.248 In post-war England trusts to provide recreational facilities were not charitable. The Recreational Charities Act 1958 changed that, subject to a restraining requirement that the facilities be provided in the interests of social welfare. *Williams v IRC*, obscure as its language is, is best understood on the basis that, according to the standards of the grim post-war years, the facilities which the trust intended to provide were still a social luxury, off the scale of public priorities.

(iv) Contaminating non-charitable elements

4.249 A purpose which is prima facie charitable may be disqualified from being so by the presence in the particular scheme of too great a contaminating element of non-charitable benefit. It is often a difficult question whether the element of private benefit is too great and does therefore negative the charitable character of the project.

4.250 **Non-charitable purposes.**   Where the gift is given on terms which would allow it to be applied to charitable purposes and non-charitable purposes, a distinction has to be drawn according as the non-charitable purposes are ancillary to the charitable purposes or not. If they are, they do not contaminate.[359] If not, the gift is not charitable. Thus, in *Chichester Diocesan Fund v Simpson*[360] a testator, Caleb Diplock, had left the residue of his estate for 'such charitable institution or institutions or other charitable or benevolent object or objects in England' as the trustees might select. The House of Lords held that the word 'or' had to be read disjunctively and that the bequest was therefore capable of being used on non-charitable purposes which were not ancillary to the charitable purposes. The gift therefore fell to be judged by the law applicable to non-charitable trusts and, under those rules, it was void. The courts are not at liberty to sever the non-charitable parts in order to uphold the gift as charitable.[361]

4.251 **Making profits.**   A purpose which is otherwise charitable will always be disqualified if private profit can be taken from it. This is one kind of private benefit which

---

[359] *Re Coxen* [1948] Ch 747 (dinner for the trustees); *London Hospital Medical School v IRC* [1976] 1 WLR 613. On the other side of the line: *IRC v Glasgow Police Athletic Association* [1953] AC 380, HL.

[360] [1944] AC 341, HL. Cf *Morice v Bishop of Durham* (1805) 10 Ves Jr 522, 32 ER 445, where a testamentary trust left property to the Bishop 'for such objects of benevolence and liberality as he in his absolute discretion might choose'.

[361] The Charitable Trusts (Validation) Act 1954 provided that such disposition should be treated as cut down to the charitable objects but only for trusts coming into operation before 16 December 1954 (ie it was a solely retrospective response to the *Chichester* case).

is incompatible with charity: an undertaking pursued for a profit cannot be charitable. Many schools and some hospitals are simply businesses, from which their owners or shareholders take profits. They are not charitable. Thus, in *Re Girls' Public Day School Trust*[362] a company formed for the purpose of establishing in England public day schools for the education of girls was disqualified from charitable status because its articles entitled the preference shareholders, in seeking to enforce their rights in relation to arrears of dividends on the return of their capital, to put the company into liquidation. It was no answer to say that in fact the company had not been conducted on commercial lines for many years past, and it was immaterial that none of the preference shareholders had any intention of enforcing their rights.

Restricted class of immediate beneficiaries.   More difficult questions arise   **4.252** when the class of immediate beneficiaries is cut down in some way, so as to be less than the whole public. One source of restriction frequently arises from the fact that the charity, though it may not distribute profits, charges for its services. Another is the benefactor's express restriction of the benefits of his project to some defined group.

It is no objection that a charity charges for its services. The crematoria in *Scottish*   **4.253** *Burial Reform and Cremation Society v Glasgow Corporation*[363] were not offering free cremations. In the days before the welfare state it would have been barely thinkable that charities should offer their services free of charge. In two areas especially, namely education and health, in which private and public sector compete, it is nowadays highly controversial whether schools and hospitals which are in effect open only to the better off ought to be regarded as charitable. But that is precisely the kind of contentious political decision that only the legislature can make.

Many charitable trusts confine their benefits to a specified class of immediate   **4.254** beneficiary. There is no objection to restrictions to a geographical section of the community, such as the poor of London or the children of the parish of Weston Parva. But some restrictions contaminate, rendering the trust non-charitable. The question arose in *Re Compton*.[364]

The case involved a perpetual trust of income for the education of the children of   **4.255** three families 'to fit them to be servants of God serving the nation'. Lord Greene MR held that the trust was not charitable. As a private trust, it then failed for perpetuity. Because the beneficiaries were defined by reference to a personal relationship, it lacked the quality of being a public trust. The common quality of

---

362 [1951] Ch 400.
363 [1968] AC 138, HL. Cf the private hospital in *Re Resch's Will Trusts* [1968] 1 AC 514, HL.
364 [1945] Ch 123, CA.

the restricted class had to be an impersonal one, neither kinship nor common employment. The *Compton* test was applied in *Oppenheim v Tobacco Securities Ltd* [365] to invalidate a trust to apply income 'in providing for the education of children of employees or former employees' of a British limited company or any of its subsidiary or allied companies. The employees totalled 110,000. It was argued in favour of the trust that this was a trust with a public character. A class of persons defined with reference to their occupation (eg shoemakers) may constitute for this purpose a section of the public and not a collection of private individuals. This is so even though the definition was based on employment by a common employer or employers (eg mineworkers in a nationalized industry). It was a question of fact and degree whether the class should be regarded as constituting a section of the public. The difficulty, it was argued, was that the public was in the end composed of individuals. A majority of the House of Lords rejected this argument. Although the group of persons indicated was numerous, the nexus between them was employment by particular employers, and accordingly the trust did not satisfy the test of public benefit requisite to establish it as charitable. A contract of employment was a personal relationship, which meant that there was no public element and therefore no public benefit. Lord MacDermott dissented. He pointed to the difficulties of formulating a workable test and said that it was always a matter of degree, requiring a general survey of the circumstances. If a trust for the education of those employed in the tobacco industry in Bradford was valid, why not a trust such as this?

4.256 Trusts for the relief of poverty have never had to pass the impersonal nexus test. The Court of Appeal in *Oppenheim* agreed that the trust would have been valid if it had been restricted to poor employees. In *Dingle v Turner* [366] the House of Lords held this to be true. And though trusts for the benefit of the poor seem to form an exception to the rule that there must be a sufficient public element, all five members of the House supported the approach taken by Lord MacDermott. Whether the *Compton* test still stands is therefore a matter of some uncertainty.

4.257 The best answer seems to be to take the 'public' as always being the national community as a whole. The relevant question is whether the restricted class of immediate beneficiaries adds an element of private benefit which cancels out the benefit to the whole community inherent in the project. Is the project, as restricted, still beneficial to the public as a whole? This will depend on whether the restriction itself is one of which the public as a whole would approve. The Recreational Charities Act 1958 provides a model. The facilities must be open to the whole public or, in broad terms, to a needy class. In the former case the whole

---

365 [1951] AC 297, HL.
366 [1972] AC 601, HL.

public benefits directly. In the latter, it benefits indirectly from the relief of the need which defines the class.[367]

If the recreational facilities were confined to the employees of a company, the element of public benefit would not be carried through to the restriction itself: a perk of employment is a contaminating private benefit which it would not be proper for public money to pursue. So too in the case of education, the public takes no benefit from a commercial advantage offered to one company. It is different in the case of poverty. Nobody joins a company to have his poverty relieved. Hence, the public at large still derives some benefit from having poverty relieved, and the degree of competing private benefit can be discounted. In every case, the whole project, the purpose as restricted to the class of immediate beneficiaries, has to be assessed, to see whether the public as a whole derives a benefit of the kind that, according to the standards of the time, public money, or private money running a little ahead of public money, might properly pursue.

4.258

(v) The control of charitable trusts

This is a highly complex topic. Only the barest outline can be given.[368] A problem endemic to purpose trusts is, since there are no human beneficiaries who can complain, how the trustees can be called to account for the exercise of their functions under the trust. In other words, given that the judges do not roam the country looking for breaches of trust, how can any possible breach of trust on the part of the trustees be monitored? The answer is that the state, at the state's expense, has provided machinery to monitor charitable trusts. This is one reason why only those purposes which are beneficial to the public and which have a sufficient public element qualify for charitable status. It may be that a day will come when private purpose trusts will be able to buy into the machinery which links validity and monitoring, as has happened through statutory schemes enacted in some off-shore jurisdictions, though they would of course never expect the fiscal privileges.

4.259

Traditionally, the Attorney-General, an officer of the state, performed a supervisory role: 'It is the province of the Crown as *parens patriae* to enforce the execution of charitable trusts, and it has always been recognised as the duty of the law officers of the Crown to intervene for the purpose of protecting charities and affording advice and assistance to the court in the administration of charitable trusts.'[369] This role is now largely performed by the Charity Commissioners, three persons who, together with their staff, form a department of state responsible to the Home Secretary. The functions of the Commissioners are twofold,

4.260

---

[367] Recreational Charities Act 1958, s 1(2)(b)(i).
[368] Detail in AJ Oakley, *Parker and Mellows: The Modern Law of Trusts* (8th edn, 2003) 493–502.
[369] *Wallis v Solicitor-General for New Zealand* [1903] AC 173, 181, *per* Lord Macnaghten.

the support of charities and their supervision.[370] In performance of these functions, they maintain a register of charities and make decisions on registration. Those decisions are appealable to the High Court.[371]

4.261   Finally the state also makes available the Official Custodian for Charities.[372] The services of the Official Custodian allow charity property to be held on a stable basis and avoid the need for constant transfers every time a charitable trustee is replaced.

(vi) Redirecting charitable funds

4.262   Where a private trust fails, either initially or subsequently,[373] the rights will be held on trust for the settlor or his estate. This rarely happens when charitable gifts fail. The reason is the existence of the *cy près* doctrine. Under this, the fund is generally applied to 'the next best thing', that is, to a project as close as possible to the original one. The circumstances amounting to a failure such as to trigger this kind of redirection of the fund have been considerably liberalized by statute and are now laid down in the Charities Act 1993.[374]

4.263   **Cy près in cases of subsequent failure.**   The rule is that once funds have been validly dedicated to charitable objects, no matter how narrow that dedication may have been, they remain so dedicated, and there will be no room for a trust for the settlor.[375] This applies even where the failure occurs before the funds are ever spent on the charitable purpose, provided only that the gift has taken effect. Thus, in *Re Slevin*[376] the testator gave a 'charitable legacy' to an orphanage which was in existence at his death but which was discontinued shortly afterwards, and before his assets were administered. The Court of Appeal held that the gift took effect on the death of the testator, when the will operated. It did not make any difference that the orphanage might not actually obtain receipt of the money until some time later. For that reason, the funds were not held on trust for the estate but were to be applied *cy près*.

4.264   **Cy près in cases of initial failure.**   An initial failure is a failure which operates to prevent the gift even taking effect. The commonest causes are the demise of the charity to which the gift was intended to go, repudiation of the gift on account of some term attached to it, and impossibility of achieving the project with the

---

370 Charities Act 1993, s 1(3).
371 ibid s 4(3).
372 ibid ss 2, 21, 22.
373 Though query whether there can be anything other than an initial failure in the context of a private trust: paras 4.274–4.278.
374 Charities Act 1993, s 13.
375 *Re Wright* [1954] Ch 347, 362–3, CA, *per* Romer LJ.
376 [1891] 2 Ch 236, CA.

funds made available. There is no automatic *cy près* on initial failure. The property will either never leave the donor or it will be held for him or his estate on trust, unless he can be shown to have had a 'general charitable intent'. If such an intent is found, the funds will be applied *cy près*. Before considering general charitable intent in more detail, it is necessary to say something more on the difficult issue of initial failure.

Has the gift failed? A number of artificial constructions are used to save gifts **4.265** which might at first sight be thought to have failed. If one of these is successfully applied, the *cy près* doctrine will not be invoked or, if it is, it will be invoked on the basis of subsequent failure. These doctrines apply where a gift has on the face of it been made to a charity which, when the gift is to take effect (often on the death of the donor), has ceased to exist. Prima facie such gifts lapse.

In *Re Roberts*[377] money was given to the Sheffield Boys Working Home. It had **4.266** already closed down and passed the balance of its funds to another local charity. It proved possible to hold that, though the specific charity had indeed disappeared, the donor had intended it not for the institution but for its purposes. The name of the institution had merely been used as a shorthand to identify those purposes. Purposes do not disappear. So the gift took effect just as though the donor had spelled out the purposes of the home.

In *Re Finger's WT*[378] a gift was made by will to the National Radium Commission **4.267** (an unincorporated association) and another to the National Council for Maternity and Child Welfare (a body corporate). Both had ceased to exist before the death of the testatrix. Reginald Goff J said that, in the absence of a contrary intention, a construction to the effect that the gift had been intended for the purposes of a named charity applied when the gift was made to an unincorporated association.[379] On the other hand, in the case of a corporation the rule ran the other way. There had to be something positive in the will to indicate a gift to purposes. The gift to the unincorporated Radium Commission had accordingly not failed, for it was a gift to the purposes of that defunct unincorporated association. By contrast, the maternity gift had failed. It was a gift to that specific charity, and that body was no more. This was a case of initial failure. However, Reginald Goff J then saved it for charity by discovering a general charitable intent.[380]

It is sometimes possible to conclude that the charity is still in existence, albeit **4.268** under another name. Though this argument failed in *Re Roberts*, the Sheffield

---

[377] [1963] 1 WLR 406.

[378] [1972] Ch 286.

[379] Applied to non-charitable associations, this would lead to immediate nullity: paras 4.274–4.278.

[380] Paras 4.270 and 4.272.

Boys Working Home case, it had earlier succeeded in *Re Faraker*,[381] where the charity in question had been merged with others. The testatrix, by a will made in 1911, left £200 to 'Mrs Bailey's Charity, Rotherhithe'. There had been at Rotherhithe a charity known as Hannah Bayly's Charity, founded in 1756 for the benefit of poor widows resident in and parishioners of St Mary, Rotherhithe. In 1905, the Charity Commissioners had sealed a scheme in the matter of this and thirteen other charities in Rotherhithe whereby the endowments of all these charities were consolidated, trustees appointed and trusts declared for the benefit of the poor of Rotherhithe. No specific mention was made of widows in the scheme. The residuary legatees under the will argued that the gift had lapsed since the charity had ceased to exist. The Court of Appeal rejected this argument. Cozens-Hardy MR said that Hannah Bayly's charity was not extinct. An endowed charity cannot die. It was important to note that the legacy was not given to Hannah Bayly's charity 'for widows', but was simply a gift to the charity identified by name, ie to the lawful objects of the charity for the time being. Farwell LJ said that the commissioners had no power to kill off the charity.[382]

4.269 **The gift has failed but is saved for the next best thing.** In a situation in which an ordinary gift would have failed, the *cy près* doctrine may yet save a charitable gift if the donor had a 'general charitable intent'. It is evident that in the recurrent competition with the next of kin or residuary legatee the courts lean in favour of charity.

4.270 A general charitable intent is an intent to give to charity which would have survived the particular obstacle which has arisen. Thus, when in *Re Lysaght*[383] the Royal College of Surgeons repudiated a gift for medical studentships on the ground that its terms were unacceptably discriminatory, the court found itself able to conclude that if the testatrix had known of this obstacle she would not have withdrawn her gift but would have given anyhow. Under the *cy près* doctrine the money went to the College without the discriminatory restriction. Again, in *Re Finger*, which was discussed above,[384] the maternity gift, a gift to a defunct body corporate, was applied *cy près*. In that case the will actually recited the testatrix's want of any immediate family and her wish on that account to give her estate to charity.

4.271 *Re Finger* is to a degree exceptional in that, where a gift is construed as being to a specific charitable body once extant, it is difficult to find any wider charitable intent. Thus in *Re Rymer*,[385] a will contained a legacy of £5,000 'to the rector for

---

381 [1912] 2 Ch 488, CA.
382 A different result will obtain where they do have such power: *Re Roberts* [1963] 1 WLR 406.
383 [1966] Ch 191.
384 See para 4.267.
385 [1895] 1 Ch 19, CA.

the time being of St Thomas's Seminary for the education of priests for the diocese of Westminster'. At the date of the testator's death, the seminary had ceased to exist, and the students had been transferred to another seminary in Birmingham. The Court of Appeal held that the gift failed. There was no wider charitable intent than to give to that one seminary. It is different where the body named never existed, since that in itself is some evidence that the paramount intent was to give to a charity in the relevant sector.[386]

A difficulty is encountered in cases in which the gift which fails is non-charitable **4.272** but is embedded in a series of gifts which are, as in *Re Satterthwaite's Will Trusts*,[387] where a misanthropic woman left her estate to various animal charities but included one private animal hospital, defunct when she died. The Court of Appeal held that the character of the will showed an overriding intention to benefit a purpose, namely the welfare of animals, and not to benefit a private individual who was not bound to devote that bequest to a purpose. The gift therefore went *cy près*.[388]

Where funds have been subscribed by donors who can no longer be identified **4.273** and also where donors have executed a written disclaimer, the *cy près* doctrine now operates without further proof of general charitable intent.[389]

(b) Private purposes

Where money is given to campaign for a change in the law, to resist the building **4.274** of a new road, or to fund a prize for a race, the trust will not be charitable. Such a private purpose trust is void, with the effect that there will be an immediate resulting trust. The law has no special animus against such activities. As will be seen, the nullity is dictated by practical problems. Means other than trusts have to be found.

(i) Leading authorities

The most authoritative modern statement on this matter is contained in *Re* **4.275** *Endacott*,[390] where the testator left his residuary estate to the North Tawton Parish Council 'for the purpose of providing some useful memorial to myself'. The Court of Appeal held that the gift failed as a private purpose trust and the rights went on trust to the estate. In the course of his judgment, Lord Evershed MR

---

[386] *Re Harwood* [1936] Ch 285, 288, attacked on other grounds at first instance in *Re Koeppler's Will Trusts* [1984] Ch 243.

[387] [1966] 1 WLR 277, CA.

[388] Contrast, however, *Re Jenkins Will Trusts* [1966] Ch 249, 256, where Buckley J observed that 'If you meet seven men with black hair and one with red hair you are not entitled to say that here are eight men with black hair.'

[389] Charities Act 1993, s 14.

[390] [1960] Ch 232, CA.

said: 'No principle perhaps has greater sanction or authority behind it than the general proposition that a trust by English law, not being a charitable trust, in order to be effective, must have ascertained or ascertainable beneficiaries.'[391] Apart from some anomalies discussed below, there is no escaping this.[392]

4.276   The *locus classicus* is *Morice v Bishop of Durham*.[393] The testatrix left rights to the Bishop of Durham on trust for 'such objects of benevolence and liberality as the Bishop in his own discretion should most approve of'. Sir William Grant MR said that:

> The only question is whether the trust . . . be a trust for charitable purposes. That it is upon some trust, and not for the personal benefit of the bishop is clear . . . That it is a trust, unless it be of a charitable nature, too indefinite to be executed by this Court, has not been, and cannot be, denied. There can be no trust, over the exercise of which this Court will not assume a control; for an uncontrolable power of disposition would be ownership, and not trust. If there be a clear trust, but for uncertain objects, the property, that is the subject of the trust, is undisposed of; and the benefit of such trust must result to those, to whom the law gives the ownership in default of disposition by the former owner. But this doctrine does not hold good with regard to trusts for charity. Every other trust must have a definite object. There must be somebody, in whose favour the Court can decree performance.[394]

(ii)   Rationale

4.277   The objection stated in *Morice v Bishop of Durham* was that the trust did not have a 'definite object'. This has come to be known as the 'beneficiary principle'. A private trust must have a beneficiary, identified with sufficient certainty to allow the trustees to do their job. In the absence of anyone with an interest in the execution of the trust, the trustees could do just as they pleased. This problem is overcome in charitable trusts by the provision of public monitoring machinery. Even the presence of a remainderman behind the primary trust for the purpose will not meet the mischief, since a remainderman will have no interest in ensuring the expenditure of money on the purpose. His interest will obviously favour the conservation of the fund.

4.278   If it were possible to overcome this overwhelming difficulty, others would remain. The trustees could not do their duty unless the purposes were defined with sufficient certainty. And the rules against perpetuities would have to be complied with.

---

[391] [1960] Ch 232, 246, CA.
[392] *Re Wood* [1949] Ch 498 (the BBC good cause of the week); *Re Astor's ST* [1952] Ch 534 ('the maintenance of good relations among nations'; 'the preservation of the independence and the integrity of newspapers'; 'the protection of newspapers from being absorbed or controlled by combines').
[393] (1804) 9 Ves 399, 32 ER 656; (1805) 10 Ves 522, 32 ER 945.
[394] (1804) 9 Ves 399, 405, 32 ER 656, 658.

(iii) Exceptions

There are nonetheless some exceptions.   **4.279**

Deeply rooted anomalies.   These cases all involve trusts for the maintenance of   **4.280**
particular animals[395] or for erection and maintenance of monuments or graves.[396]
They have been admitted to be 'anomalous' exceptions[397] and occasions 'when
Homer has nodded'.[398] Although the Court of Appeal refused to overrule them in
Re Endacott, it held that they were not to be extended, not even to closely analo-
gous situations.[399]

Execution of the purpose enures to the benefit of identifiable persons.   The second   **4.281**
category rests on the decision of Goff J in *Re Denley's Will Trusts*[400] and those cases
which have followed it.[401] In *Re Denley* a company conveyed title to land to trustees to hold for a period determined by lives 'for the purpose of a recreation or
sports ground primarily for the benefit of the employees of the company and
secondarily for the benefit of such other person or persons (if any) as the trustees
may allow'. Goff J admitted that if this was to be construed as a trust for a non-
charitable purpose then it was void. But, he said, it was not a trust for a purpose
but a trust for persons, those persons being the employees of the company. They
were ascertainable and the trust was one which was not so vague as to be beyond
the control of the court. 'The objection [to non-charitable purpose trusts] is not
that the trust is for a purpose or an object per se, but that there is no beneficiary
or *cestui que trust*.'[402] The beneficiary principle was not infringed, he said, where
'the trust, though expressed as a purpose, is directly or indirectly to the benefit of
an individual or individuals'.[403]

The decision is unsound, for it is not at all clear that the beneficiary principle   **4.282**
was satisfied. It certainly cannot be said that there was some person or class of
persons who could be said to be beneficiaries in the usual sense of the word.[404]
Moreover it was clearly not the testator's intention that the employees should have
an unfettered interest even for the designated period. It remains to be seen whether

---

[395] An example is *Re Dean* (1889) 41 Ch D 554 (trust for the maintenance of the testator's
horses and hounds).
[396] *Re Hooper* [1932] Ch 38.
[397] *Re Endacott* [1960] Ch 232, 246, CA, *per* Lord Evershed MR.
[398] ibid 250, *per* Harman LJ.
[399] ibid 246, *per* Lord Evershed MR. Cf the use of analogy in the law of charitable trusts:
paras 4.245–4.247.
[400] [1969] 1 Ch 373.
[401] *Re Lipinski* [1976] Ch 235. A private purpose trust was enforced in *Barclay's Bank Ltd v
Quistclose Investments Ltd* [1970] AC 567, HL, though there the court did not seem to notice that
the trust (if indeed it was a trust) was a purpose trust.
[402] [1969] Ch 373, 383.
[403] ibid 383–4.
[404] For criticism along these lines, see JM Evans (1969) 32 MLR 96.

the underlying problems of unenforceability can really be said to be adequately met on this configuration of facts.

(c) Unincorporated associations

4.283 Where there is a transfer of rights to an unincorporated association, such as a sports or social club, the essential problem is that such a body has no legal personality. Although the members of such an association have legal personality, there is, differently to a corporation, no legal person separate from those members capable of holding rights or bearing duties.[405] Some clubs and societies do incorporate but most do not. A transfer to an unincorporated association seems to make sense, but technically it does not, for it is a conveyance to no-one. Nevertheless, people constantly make such transfers, often by way of gifts in wills.

(i) The dilemma

4.284 Once again it is necessary to underline the fact that the law has no animus against clubs and societies. It simply finds itself in a dilemma. On the one hand, a transfer of rights to an unincorporated association will be perfectly valid as an absolute transfer to its present members jointly, the name of the association being simply shorthand for a full list of its members.[406] But such a construction would give validity at the cost of flying in the face of the donor's true intention. People give to clubs and societies in order to promote their activities, not to make presents to the individual members. On the other hand, respect for the donor's intentions is perfectly reflected in a construction which understands the gift as given on trust for purposes, though at the cost of almost inevitable nullity.[407] Such trusts, as we have seen, almost invariably fail, generating a trust for the donor or his estate.

4.285 This is perfectly illustrated by *Leahy v Attorney-General for New South Wales*,[408] where a testator left his title to a 730 acre farm on discretionary trust 'for such order of nuns or the Christian Brothers as my executors and trustees shall select'. It being admitted that among the orders of nuns were contemplative orders the purposes of which were not regarded as charitable, the question arose as to the validity of the gift. The Judicial Committee of the Privy Council held the gift void. It could not be a charitable gift since the trustees need not select a charitable order, and, since the circumstances showed that the testator did not intend the individuals to take outright, his intention was to be construed as creating a private purpose trust. That trust, in accord with his intentions, was, however, void.

---

405 Paras 3.110–3.113.

406 *Leahy v A-G for New South Wales* [1959] AC 457, PC.

407 The inevitable effect of the 'presumption' used by Reginald Goff J in *Re Finger's Will Trusts* [1972] Ch 286, para 4.267.

408 [1959] AC 457, PC.

(ii) The escape from the dilemma: the contract-holding construction

It has proved possible to escape the dilemma and thus to find a way in which clubs **4.286**
and societies can function and hold property. The escape uses contract, not trusts.
The rights are located in the members jointly, and the purposes are rendered
obligatory because those rights are caught by the contract which binds the
members together—that is, by the rules of the society. Cross J in *Neville Estates v
Madden*[409] identified this middle way:

> [I]t may . . . be a gift to the existing members not as joint tenants, but subject to their
> respective contractual rights and liabilities towards one another as members of the
> association. In such a case a member cannot sever his share. It will accrue to the other
> members on his death or resignation, even though such members include persons
> who became members after the gift took effect.[410]

This construction, though traceable to Cross J, was first applied by Brightman J
in 1972 in *Re Recher*,[411] where it was used to explain how an anti-vivisection
society could and did hold 'its' funds. Despite one or two loose ends, it has
become the orthodox explanation of transfers to and holding by unincorporated
associations.

(iii) The association without rules

At a certain point an unincorporated association becomes a mere movement **4.287**
or group. The campaigners to achieve a local objective might think of themselves
as an association but, if they are one, it is by common purpose, not on the basis
of a set of rules which form the contract between the members. The contract-
holding construction will not work for such a group. It so happens that, except at
local level, the Conservative Party was found to form just such an amorphous
group.[412] A fourth alternative has therefore been contrived, namely that of
'mandate', or agency. This finds the contract—the mandate—between the donor
and the donee. Thus, a donation to the secretary of a campaign will vest in that
person outright but is caught by a contractual obligation to apply it to the purpose
in question. The contract is simply between the donor and the recipient representative of the group or movement. This works where the gift is made *inter vivos*,
but will not work for *post-mortem* gifts, for it is not possible to set up such a
contract to begin after one's death, so to say between one's estate and a legatee.[413]

---

[409] [1962] Ch 832.
[410] ibid 849.
[411] [1972] Ch 526.
[412] *Conservative & Unionist Office v Burrell* [1982] 1 WLR 522, CA.
[413] *Campanari v Woodburn* (1854) 15 CB 400, 139 ER 480; *Pool v Pool* (1889) 58 LJP 67.

(iv) Dissolution of unincorporated associations

4.288   When the members of an association disband it or it is otherwise dissolved, it is necessary to know what happens to the rights which were held by the members *qua* members, or more likely by some of the officers of the association. Nowadays associations sometimes disband precisely because their members think that they will be entitled to divide up the rights between themselves. The cases are in some confusion, partly because, while the consequences of dissolution must reflect the holding as it was before dissolution, it is only relatively recently that the contract-holding explanation has established itself and driven out less satisfactory competitors.

4.289   **The logic of the contract-holding explanation.**   If the rights belong to the members outright but subject to a contract, usually the contract in the rules of the association, it is attractive and seemingly obvious that, if the contract goes, which is what dissolution means, the members simply hold free of the obligations *inter se* by which they were formerly bound. In *Re Buckinghamshire Constabulary Widows and Orphans Fund Friendly Society (No 2)*[414] the society had been dissolved, and Walton J said that the subscriptions of the members were held in trust for the members. Adopting the 'contract-holding' theory of *Re Recher*, he said that all unincorporated associations rest in contract, and when rights were transferred to such an association it was to the members subject to the contractual obligations to apply it to the purposes of the association. But on dissolution, those contractual ties were removed to reveal what had always been the case, that the rights belonged to the members absolutely. Although Walton J had not to decide on funds from any other source, it is clear that legacies in wills, anonymous donations, and the proceeds of entertainments would have been treated in precisely the same way.

4.290   There is a loose end. In the case of money subscribed to a movement or campaign via its secretary,[415] it is tolerably clear that any surplus left when the campaign is abandoned or frustrated must be returned as on a failure of consideration. This is a matter for the law of unjust enrichment.[416] It is by no means clear that the same should not apply to rights transferred on the basis that they be held subject to the contract between the members. Much must depend on the precise construction of the basis on which the donations were given and, in turn, on the rules of the society. The *Buckinghamshire Constabulary* case certainly decides that the rights in such cases belongs to the members, but it does not finally dispose of the question whether in some cases they may not come under an obligation to make restitution of their value to their transferors.

---

414   [1979] 1 WLR 936.
415   The mandate model, in para 4.287.
416   See Chapter 18.

Trust.   Typical of the older case law in this area is the decision of Goff J in *Re West* **4.291**
Sussex Constabulary Widows, Children and Benevolent Fund Trust.[417] The reasoning
in this case may now be impossible to defend. It was not followed by Walton J in
the very similar *Buckinghamshire Constabulary* case.[418]

Here too a fund was set up to pay pensions to the widows and orphans of **4.292**
policemen. When, owing to a reorganization of the police force, the association
was to be dissolved, Goff J had to say how the fund was to be distributed. Besides
members' subscriptions, the fund comprised inter alia donations by street collections and by legacies. As to the latter, he held there were resulting trusts in favour
of the donors. And he would have come to the same conclusion in respect of
the street collections had he not found that anonymous donors had manifested
an intent to abandon their donations in the event of failure of their primary
purpose and that this intent rebutted the presumption of resulting trust. The
rights were therefore ownerless and went *bona vacantia* to the Crown.[419] As for
the members' subscriptions, Goff J again negatived a resulting trust, this time
on the doubtful ground, since repudiated by the Privy Council,[420] that they had
given under a contract and had received all for which they had bargained.

(9)   *Trusts Arising for Reasons Other than Declarations of Trust*

Although the vast majority of trusts arise consensually, ie, because of declarations **4.293**
of trust howsoever proved, it is an oddity of English law that this essentially
consensual institution is sometimes harnessed by the courts to turn defendants
into trustees in situations in which no person has manifested an intent that a trust
be created. This section attempts to give an outline description of the situations
in which a trust will arise though no declaration of trust has occurred. It should
be noted that the trusts here are uniformly bare trusts. The person created a trustee
by the court has no powers or duties in regard to the trust rights, other than to
convey them to the beneficiary on request.

(a) Wrongdoing

In this section a 'wrong' is taken to be an act or omission the consequences of **4.294**
which flow from its characterization as a breach of primary duty.[421] The usual

---

[417] [1971] 1 Ch 1.
[418] [1979] 1 WLR 936.
[419] This reasoning is instrumental in the extreme, designed to achieve a useful end. No *cy près*
doctrine applies to non-charitable trusts, so that anonymous donations (cf for charities para 4.273)
must simply sit in court, indefinitely sterilized (cf *Re Gillingham Bus Disaster Fund* [1959] Ch 62,
CA, affirming [1958] Ch 300).
[420] *Air Jamaica v Charlton* [1999] 1 WLR 1399, PC.
[421] The best exposition is that of Birks, 'The Concept of a Civil Wrong' in D Owen (ed),
Philosophical Foundations of Tort Law (1997), 31–51.

response to wrongdoing is the grant by the court to the victim of the wrong of a right to damages. Such damages can be measured in a variety of ways, usually by reference to the loss suffered by the claimant, but sometimes by reference to the defendant's gain, and sometimes by other measures.[422] The question whether the law will generate a trust in favour of the claimant has only arisen in the case of a profitable breach of duty, in other words, in a claim for restitution for wrongs. One gain-based wrong which has attracted particular attention is breach of fiduciary duty, where opinion is divided. We will also see how unauthorized substitutions, both of rights held outright and on trust, generates trusts of the substituted right. Whether that is as a response to wrongdoing, unjust enrichment, or to some other event, has never been resolved.

(i) Breach of fiduciary duty[423]

4.295   No serious attempt has been made to identify a rationale which would explain why this wrong rather than any others should elicit a trust response. And it is not clear where the line falls between those breaches of fiduciary duty which do and those which do not. The picture is complicated by the fact that the most prominent case, not technically binding in England, is a decision of the Privy Council on appeal from New Zealand.

4.296   **Lister v Stubbs.**   For more than a century, *Lister v Stubbs*[424] stood in the way of turning the fiduciary wrongdoer into a trustee. There the defendant was employed by the claimant company as a buyer. In return for placing the company's orders with certain manufacturers the defendant, so it was alleged, secretly received bribes, £5,000 of which he invested in a title to land and other investments. In interlocutory proceedings the claimant company sought an order restraining the defendant from dealing with those rights. This was long before the modern development of freezing injunctions.[425] As the law then stood the company could only obtain its order if on the facts it put forward the assets were held for it on trust. The Court of Appeal denied the company's claim. Cotton LJ said:

> [T]here is a debt due from the defendant to the plaintiffs in consequence of the corrupt bargain which he entered into; but the money which he has received under that bargain cannot . . . be treated as being money of the plaintiffs . . .[426]

Lindley LJ spoke in similar terms. The defendant was liable to account the moment he received the money. But the relation between the parties was one

---

[422]   See paras 21.142–21.159.
[423]   The wrong of breach of fiduciary duty is discussed at paras 17.346–17.354 of this work.
[424]   (1890) 45 Ch D 1, CA.
[425]   Called until recently 'Mareva injunctions' from *Mareva Compania SA v International Bulkcarriers SA* [1975] 2 Lloyd's Rep 509: paras 22.20–22.27.
[426]   (1890) 45 Ch D 1, 12, CA.

of debtor and creditor, not trustee and *cestui que trust*. Startling consequences would flow if that were the case: if the defendant became bankrupt then the money would be withdrawn from the mass of creditors. The argument of the claimant, said Lindley LJ, confounded ownership with obligation.[427]

A-G for Hong Kong v Reid. In *A-G for Hong Kong v Reid*[428] Reid, a high- **4.297** ranking official in the office of the Hong Kong Director of Public Prosecutions, was convicted of taking $HK12.4 million in bribes to obstruct the prosecution of certain criminals. He was sentenced to eight years' imprisonment. With some of the money he had bought titles to land in New Zealand, and the Hong Kong government sought a declaration that he held them for it on trust. They argued that as a fiduciary agent Reid held each bribe for them on constructive trust from the moment of its receipt, with the result that anything which was the product of the bribe was likewise caught by a trust. The New Zealand Court of Appeal followed *Lister v Stubbs* and held that bribes received by a fiduciary agent were merely owed by the fiduciary to his principal and not held by the agent on constructive trust.[429] The Hong Kong government appealed to the Privy Council.

Lord Templeman gave the opinion of the board. He said that the decision in *Lister v* **4.298** *Stubbs* was unsatisfactory in that it allowed the fraudulent fiduciary to keep for himself any increase in value of the bribe or its product. Moreover, it put the dishonest bribee in a better position than the honest fiduciary in *Boardman v Phipps*,[430] who, said Lord Templeman, was held by the House of Lords to be a constructive trustee of the shares he had bought using information gained while acting as solicitor to the trust fund. He accordingly declined to follow *Lister v Stubbs* and held that the money received was held on constructive trust for the government. He reasoned as follows:

> Equity . . . insists that it is unconscionable for a fiduciary to obtain and retain a benefit in breach of duty . . . The false fiduciary who received the bribe in breach of duty must pay and account for the bribe to the person to whom that duty was owed. In the present case, as soon as [Mr Reid] received a bribe in breach of the duties he owed to the Government of Hong Kong, he became a debtor in equity to the Crown for the amount of the bribe . . . As soon as the bribe was received it should have been paid or transferred instanter to the person who suffered from the breach of duty. Equity considers as done that which ought to have been done. As soon as the bribe was received, whether in cash or in kind, the false fiduciary held the bribe on a constructive trust for the person injured.[431]

---

[427] ibid 15, CA.
[428] [1994] 1 AC 324, PC.
[429] [1992] 2 NZLR 385, NZCA.
[430] [1967] 2 AC 46, HL; discussed in the section on equitable wrongs: paras 17.346–17.354.
[431] [1994] 1 AC 324, 331, PC.

4.299 Although the result was anticipated and indeed no doubt strongly influenced by Lord Millett, writing extra-judicially,[432] the reasoning is open to criticism.[433] The supposed disparity of treatment of the honest fiduciary in *Boardman v Phipps* and the dishonest employee in *Lister v Stubbs*, the former of whom is made a constructive trustee, the latter only an equitable debtor, dissolves unless the premise that *Boardman* was a constructive trustee is secure, which as we shall see it is not.[434] Moreover, the decision involves a misapplication of the rule that 'equity looks upon that as done which ought to be done', which we will encounter when looking at the trust created by a specifically enforceable contract of sale.[435] That which 'ought' to have been done was that the defendant refrain from taking bribes in the first place. Descending from the primary to the secondary level, the argument mistakes the nature of the duty to account. If what ought to have been done was, at that level, an account, the most that can be said is that the duty was to render an account and pay the debt thereby found due. But that debt could be satisfied by the payment of a sum of money from any source. In other words, there is no analogy with an agreement to grant a lease of a particular piece of land, which is an obligation to transfer a particular right. Moreover, the duty to account is not dependent on the bribe money or its traceable proceeds still being in the defendant's hands, for there are cases of liabilities to account arising where the defendant is effectively only paying compensation, and never had any particular funds in his hands.[436] The difficulty is that this personal liability is also described in terms of a liability to account 'as a constructive trustee', so giving the impression that the defendant really is a trustee, albeit a trustee of a constructive rather than an express trust. But this should not lead us to think that there is in fact a trust. The language is borrowed from the liability of trustees of declared trusts, who may themselves incur personal liabilities to make good losses or disgorge gains, and simply means that the defendant is liable to account *as if he were*, which he is not, a trustee.

4.300 A further criticism concerns Lord Templeman's assumption that the only way through to the profits of the bribes was via a trust. There is no logical reason why a personal restitutionary claim should not reach through to such profits. Such a response would both ensure that the fiduciary did not profit from his wrongdoing and, most importantly, equality of treatment amongst creditors.

---

432 Sir Peter Millett, 'Bribes and Secret Commissions' [1993] Restitution LR 7.

433 D Crilley, 'A Case of Proprietary Overkill' [1994] Restitution LR 57. Of special weight are the consequences in criminal law: JC Smith, '*Lister v Stubbs* and the Criminal Law' (1994) 110 LQR 180.

434 See para 4.304. The same assumption was made in *Iran Shipping Lines v Denby* [1987] Lloyd's Rep 367.

435 See para 4.329.

436 An example is *Royal Brunei Airlines v Tan* [1995] 2 AC 378, PC (defendant liable to account as a constructive trustee for losses accruing to the claimant arising through his dishonestly assisting a trustee to commit a breach of trust).

Earlier ambiguity. The leading case favouring a proprietary response is said **4.301** to be *Keech v Sandford*.[437] There a bill prayed that a trustee who had obtained a lease in breach of his fiduciary obligation to his beneficiary held the lease for the beneficiary. The trust aspect of this claim was not questioned by the trustee, the only issue being whether, since he had acted honestly, he should be exonerated. The court held that he should not and ordered him to transfer the lease to the beneficiary with an undertaking that the trustee be indemnified should he become liable on any covenants. Not only is the difference between the a trust and a personal response not discussed in this early case but, in addition, there was in the background a special fact, namely that there was the strongest possible expectation, amounting almost to a right, that this lease would be renewed in favour of the beneficiaries.[438]

Similarly, in *Cook v Deeks*[439] a company with four directors holding 25 per cent **4.302** of the shareholding each was in the business of building railroads. Three directors were dissatisfied with the performance of the fourth and negotiated a contract for a new railway on behalf of a new company set up by themselves. This amounted to a breach of their fiduciary duty to the old company. The Privy Council held that the benefit of the contract was held on trust for the old company. But once again, there was no dispute as to, and so no attention given to, the nature of the response.

The language of trusts was also used in *Williams v Barton*,[440] though the point was **4.303** once again not contested. The defendant, one of two trustees of a will, was employed as a clerk by a firm of stockbrokers on the terms that his salary should consist of half the commission earned by the firm on business introduced by him. On the recommendation of the defendant, the firm was employed to value the testator's securities. The firm's charges were paid out of the testator's estate, and, in accordance with their contract with the defendant, the firm paid to him half the fee so earned. The defendant took no part in making the valuations or in fixing the fees to be charged. His co-trustee claimed that the defendant was bound to treat the fees so paid to him as part of the estate. Russell J held that the defendant had a duty as trustee to give the estate the benefit of his unfettered advice in choosing stockbrokers to act for the estate, but, as the recipient of half the fees earned by the firm on business introduced by him, it was in his interest to choose his own firm to act. The services he rendered to the firm remained unchanged but his remuneration was increased, and increased by virtue of his trusteeship. That increase was a profit which the defendant could not have made but for his position

---

[437] (1726) Sel Ch Cas 61, 25 ER 223.
[438] SM Cretney, 'The Rationale of *Keech v Sandford*' (1969) 33 Conv 161.
[439] [1916] 1 AC 554, PC.
[440] [1927] 2 Ch 9.

as trustee and he was therefore bound to treat it as part of the testator's estate. He was a constructive trustee of any such profit for the benefit of persons entitled under the will.

4.304 The position was unfortunately not made any clearer in the leading case of *Boardman v Phipps*, where, in breach of his fiduciary duty, a solicitor to a trustee made a profit on share-dealings.[441] He had acted honestly and vigorously in the interest of the trust, but he was technically in breach of duty. And though the court appeared to construct a trust of the shares, no argument was addressed as to the correct nature of the response. Since Boardman was anything but insolvent, there was no need for the claimant to explore the difference between a personal response and the creation of a trust.

4.305 There is therefore very little authority in favour of the award of a trust, certainly nothing which could be said to represent the *ratio* of any case, and equally nothing as unequivocally for the proprietary response as *Lister v Stubbs* was against it. One case in the Court of Appeal[442] has already shown a marked lack of enthusiasm for *A-G for Hong Kong v Reid*, though a decision at first instance has, *obiter*, thought it sound.[443] It therefore remains uncertain whether the trust which it recognized as arising from breach of fiduciary duty will survive.

(ii) Unauthorized substitution (tracing)

4.306 Where a conversion takes the form of a substitution—D exchanges a motor-cycle over which C has a better title than D for a car—it may well be the case that C will obtain the benefit of an immediate trust of the substitute right.[444] If so, he is said to be able to 'trace' into the car. So too where the title to the motor-cycle was held on trust for C, and, in breach of trust, the trustee made an unauthorized substitution. But though there is no doubt that trusts arise in such situations, we as yet have no coherent explanation why. The House of Lords in *Foskett v McKeown* told us that it was because the right C had prior to the substitution will 'persists' in respect of the new right.[445] But this clearly does not work, for a right to exclusive possession of a motor-cycle is not the same thing at all as the right of a beneficiary of a trust of a title to a car.[446] Thinking about the question without the use of

---

[441] [1967] AC 46, HL.

[442] *Halifax Building Society v Thomas* [1996] Ch 217, CA.

[443] *Daraydan Holdings Ltd v Solland Int Ltd* [2005] Ch 119.

[444] *Black v S Freeman & Co* (1910) 12 CLR 105; *Foskett v McKeown* [2001] 1 AC 102. Although a pre-existing fiduciary relationship is sometimes said to be a prerequisite of tracing, it is doubtful in the extreme whether this requirement would withstand the scrutiny of the House of Lords. There is certainly no logic behind it.

[445] [2001] 1 AC 102.

[446] See the discussion by P Birks, 'Property, Unjust Enrichment, and Tracing' (2001) 54 CLP 231.

fictions, it may be that the event is some form of wrongdoing, although it is not at this stage of development possible to rule out unjust enrichment and other miscellaneous events.

(iii) Breach of confidence

In Canada, it has been held that breach of confidence can trigger a trust. A company located a goldfield on land to which it had no title. It shared its knowledge in confidence with a prospective partner. The negotiations came to nothing, but the prospective partner went into the market, bought up a title to the land, and developed the goldfield for itself. The Supreme Court of Canada held that it became a constructive trustee of the title.[447] It has since been strongly emphasized that, under the law of Canada, this trust lies in the discretion of the court.[448] **4.307**

In England the notion that there might be a kind of trust—a so-called *remedial* constructive trust—dependent on the discretion of the court, has been firmly rejected.[449] It remains open to argument whether breach of confidence turns the wrongdoer into a trustee. In one case, which concerned acquisitions made by the recipient of information from a surveyor retained by a competing property developer, the Court of Appeal said that no trust would arise in the absence of dishonesty.[450] **4.308**

(b) Unjust enrichment

Just as it is controversial whether wrongs generate trust rights in favour of their victims, so too with unjust enrichments. There is no doubt that personal responses are triggered by unjust enrichments to pay the value by which the defendant was enriched at the claimant's expense. Exceptionally, however, some cases have held that an unjust enrichment gives rise to both a personal right and a trust. This controversial matter is only sketched in here for the sake of completeness. It is considered in more detail in the chapter on unjust enrichment.[451] **4.309**

(i) Spontaneous mistaken payments

The most prominent of these difficult decisions is *Chase Manhattan Bank NA v Israel-British Bank (London) Ltd*,[452] a case of a spontaneously mistaken payment. The claimant, acting under a self-induced mistake, paid US$2 million to the defendant, who, within a matter of days and after being alerted to the mistake, **4.310**

---

[447] *Lac Minerals v Corona Resources Ltd* (1989) 2 SCR 574, 61 DLR (4th) 14, Can Sup Ct.

[448] *Cadbury Schweppes Inc v FBI Foods* (1999) 1 SCC 142, 167 DLR (4th) 577, Can Sup Ct.

[449] *Re Polly Peck (No 2)* [1998] 3 All ER 812, CA.

[450] *Satnam Investments Ltd v Dunlop Heywood* [1999] 3 All ER 652, CA.

[451] Paras 18.173–18.220.

[452] [1981] Ch 105. Another is *Neste Oy v Lloyd's Bank plc* [1983] 2 Lloyd's Rep 658, a case of failure of consideration. It suffers from the same defect of reasoning as in *Chase Manhattan*.

became insolvent. Goulding J held that the claimant had a personal restitutionary right at common law to be paid US$2 million by the defendant. But he also held that an 'equitable title' to the US$2 million mistakenly paid remained in the claimant, who could therefore assert that the traceable product of this sum was held for him on trust. Although the judge answered the question as a matter of American law, he said that this also represented the position in English law. No English authority on the point was, however, cited.

4.311 The reasoning of Goulding J was, however, doubted by Lord Browne-Wilkinson in *Westdeutsche Landesbank Girozentrale v Islington LBC*,[453] who pointed out that it suffered from the defect of assuming a separate legal and equitable title in the claimant prior to the transfer.[454] But further, his lordship said that he could only agree with the result on the basis that the recipient bank's conscience had been affected while it yet held the traceable product of the payment. If it had not discovered the facts before the payment ceased to be traceable, it could not have been turned into a trustee.[455] He said:

> Although the mere receipt of the moneys, in ignorance of the mistake, gives rise to no trust, the retention of the moneys after the recipient bank learned of the mistake may well have given rise to a constructive trust.[456]

4.312 If this is right, it seems to indicate that, subject to traceability, a claimant bringing a claim in unjust enrichment will always have a proprietary claim from the moment the defendant learns of the grounds for reclaiming the property transferred. It is, however, difficult to justify. Not only is it unsupported by authority, it fails to explain why the addition of knowledge on the part of the defendant of the unjust factor should elevate an otherwise personal right to restitution to a proprietary one to the detriment of the defendant's other creditors.

4.313 This might be said to resemble the heresy in *De Mattos v Gibson*,[457] which overlooks the axiomatic truth enunciated by Diplock J in *Port Line Ltd v Ben Line Steamers Ltd*, to the effect that 'notice . . . is a shield not a weapon of offence. It protects an already existing equitable interest from being defeated by a purchaser for value without notice. It is not itself the source of an equitable interest.'[458] Moreover, Lord Browne-Wilkinson's reasoning would seem to support the actual result in *Sinclair v Brougham*,[459] a case which he expressly overruled.[460] In that case

---

[453] [1996] AC 669, 714, 715.
[454] [1996] AC 669, 706.
[455] For criticism, see P Birks, 'Trusts Raised to Reverse Unjust Enrichments' [1996] Restitution LR 3.
[456] *Westdeutsche Landesbank Girozentrale v Islington LBC* [1996] AC 669, 715.
[457] (1859) 4 De G & J 276, 45 ER 108. The point is discussed at paras 4.122, 4.138–4.139.
[458] *Port Line v Ben Line Steamers* [1958] 2 QB 146, 167, 168.
[459] [1914] AC 398, HL.
[460] [1996] AC 669, 713, HL.

customers of an *ultra vires* bank were held to have proprietary claims to recover the traceable proceeds of their deposits. Lord Browne-Wilkinson said that the case was wrongly decided and gave rise to the creation of what he called 'off-balance sheet liabilities'. But in *Sinclair v Brougham* the invalidity of the contract of deposit was discovered while the deposits were still traceably in the defendant's hands. Lord Browne-Wilkinson's doctrine would therefore appear to require cutting down. It may be that it must be understood as meaning that, first, the basic conditions for the generation of a proprietary right must be satisfied, and, secondly, the trust will not be recognized in the absence of supervening unconscientiousness on the part of the recipient. *Sinclair v Brougham* would then have to be understood as a case in which the facts did not satisfy the 'basic conditions', whatever they may precisely be.

(ii) Unauthorized substitutions

It has been said that the trust generated by the unauthorized substitution of rights **4.314** held on trust is a trust generated by unjust enrichment.[461] Although this proposition was denied by the House of Lords in *Foskett v McKeown*,[462] their Lordships' reasoning, in that it refuses to recognize the creation of new rights, is totally unconvincing.[463] However, the arguments of those who say that the explanation for such trusts is the unjust enrichment of the transferee have to overcome the hurdle of the recognition of a novel unjust factor of 'ignorance'.

(iii) Automatic resulting trusts

We saw above that the other type of resulting trust, the 'automatic' variety, where **4.315** automatic is a synonym for 'constructive', arose when rights were transferred on trusts which failed, cases in which rights were transferred accompanied by declaration of trusts which were defective in some respect, most often because of a failure to declare objects of sufficient certainty or as offending the rule against perpetuities. The consequence of such transfers is that the transferee holds the rights on trust for the transferor. The question then is why. In *Vandervell v IRC*[464] the House of Lords held that the answer could not be that a declaration of trust in favour of the transferor had been proved by presumption. As Lord Wilberforce correctly explained, there was no room for presumptions when all the facts were proved by evidence.[465] Unfortunately, the answer their lordships then went on to give, albeit *obiter*, was the discredited one also given in *Chase Manhattan*: there was a trust for the transferor because in failing to declare valid objects or in declaring a trust

---

[461] See also para 4.306.
[462] [2001] 1 AC 102, 108 (Lord Browne-Wilkinson), 127 (Lord Millett).
[463] P Birks, 'Property, Unjust Enrichment, and Tracing' (2001) 54 CLP 231.
[464] [1967] 2 AC 291.
[465] ibid 329.

which tended to perpetuity, the transferor had failed to dispose of his equitable interest.[466]

4.316 Some have argued, though without any attempt to identify the precise 'unjust factor' in play, that the typical 'automatic' resulting trust is in fact a trust responding to the unjust enrichment of the transferee. The unanswered question, however, even if such cases could be described in terms of unjust enrichment (presumably as cases of payments made under mistakes of law), is whether they warrant a response which gives the claimant a better treatment in the event of the transferee's insolvency than a mere personal claim for repayment of the value received.

(c) Other miscellaneous events

4.317 By far the greatest number of non-declared trusts arise for reasons which have nothing to do with either wrongdoing or unjust enrichment. Unfortunately, it is difficult to say anything more informative of their causal event other than it is not declaration of trust (howsoever proved), wrongdoing, or unjust enrichment. What follows, therefore, is an unordered list.

(i) Judicial discretion

4.318 It has sometimes been claimed that judges exercising their equitable jurisdiction have the power to create trusts and thus in effect reallocate rights in situations where the settled rules of law say that the claimant should have no such right. A discretion of this kind can only be based on the notion that the courts can determine when it would be 'unfair' to refuse a reallocation of the rights laid down by law. Such a discretion-based trust is unhelpfully known as a 'remedial constructive trust', as opposed to one arising through the application of rules, which is equally unhelpfully known as an 'institutional constructive trust'.

4.319 Our highest courts have, on a number of occasions, rightly rejected such an approach.[467] One such rejection came as a response to a series of cases in the 1960s in which Lord Denning MR had espoused the notion that in disputes between married partners or those in similar situations, the courts had a general discretion to reallocate property rights in land through the medium of the constructive trust. Typical is *Appleton v Appleton*,[468] where a wife bought a fee simple title to a run-down cottage with money left to her in her mother's will. Her husband did much work on redecoration. The relationship broke down and the wife proposed to sell her title. Because of his work, the husband claimed to be entitled to a share of the

---

[466] [1967] 2 AC 291, 313–4 (Lord Upjohn), 329 (Lord Wilberforce).

[467] For a discussion of perils of such 'discretionary remedialism', see P Birks, 'Rights, Wrongs and Remedies' (2000) 20 OJLS 1 and 'Three Kinds of Objection to Discretionary Remedialism' (2000) 29 U Western Australia L Rev 1.

[468] [1964] 1 All ER 44, CA.

proceeds of sale. The Court of Appeal granted the husband's claim. Lord Denning said that there was no need to try to find any prior agreement that the husband was to have a share. The question was simply what was 'fair and reasonable in the circumstances'. The court held that the husband should have a percentage of the proceeds of sale commensurate with the value by which the title had been increased by his work.

This approach was challenged in the House of Lords in *Pettitt v Pettitt*.[469] A free-hold title to a cottage was bought entirely out of moneys provided by a wife and conveyed to her alone. The husband did decorating work, built a wardrobe, laid the lawn, and constructed an ornamental well and wall in the garden. He later claimed that his labour and expenditure caused the wife to hold her title for the two of them on trust. The House rejected Lord Denning's 'fair and reasonable' approach and overruled *Appleton v Appleton*. The courts had no jurisdiction to create trusts simply on the basis of what was fair and reasonable.

4.320

This conclusion was reinforced in a case which shortly followed, *Gissing v Gissing*, another matrimonial dispute, where once again the notion that courts had a discretion in equity to create trusts was rejected.[470] The only trusts to which the court could give effect were those created by the parties themselves. And to the argument that the courts could find trusts on the basis of some speculative intent, Lord Morris of Borth-y-Gest said:

4.321

> The court does not decide how the parties might have ordered their affairs: it only finds how they did. The court cannot devise arrangements which the parties never made. The court cannot ascribe intentions which the parties in fact never had. Nor can ownership of property be affected by the mere circumstance that harmony has been replaced by discord. Any power in the court to alter ownership must be found in statutory enactment.[471]

Viscount Dilhorne took the view that such a trust could only arise on the basis of consent, and that 'the law does not permit the courts to ascribe to the parties an intention they never had and to hold that property is subject to a trust on the ground that that would be fair in all the circumstances.'[472]

There are at least two reasons for this judicial reluctance to create trusts on an entirely discretionary basis. The first is the consequent uncertainty it would cause, a point well made by Bagnall J in *Cowcher v Cowcher*:[473]

4.322

> In any individual case the application of [the] proposition [that courts must go by settled law and not adjust the law to suit the fairness of the case in hand] may produce

---

[469] [1970] AC 777, HL.
[470] [1971] AC 886, HL.
[471] ibid 898.
[472] ibid 900.
[473] [1972] 1 WLR 425.

a result which appears unfair. So be it; in my view that is not an injustice. I am convinced that in determining rights, particularly property rights, the only justice that can be attained by mortals, who are fallible and are not omniscient, is justice according to law; the justice which flows from the application of sure and settled principles to proved or admitted facts. So in the field of equity the length of the chancellor's foot has been measured or is capable of measurement. This does not mean that equity is past childbearing; simply that its progeny must be legitimate—by precedent out of principle. It is well that this should be so; otherwise no lawyer could safely advise on his client's title and every quarrel would lead to a law suit.[474]

4.323 The second is the effect such trusts would have on third parties. As we have seen, rights held on trust do not vest in the trustee's trustee in bankruptcy in the event of his insolvency. Creating a trust therefore has the effect of diminishing the pool of assets available to pay the unsecured creditors and effectively treating one group of claimants more favourably than another. This is one of the reasons why the Judicial Committee of the Privy Council refused the claim to a trust in *Re Goldcorp Exchange Ltd.*[475] Purchasers had entered into contracts for the sale of title to and storage of gold bullion. These provided that the gold would be stored by the vendor and delivered up on demand. The vendor later became insolvent. The purchasers were one group of claimants in the insolvency. They were held not to have a title to any of the stocks of gold bullion which happened to be in the vendor's hands at the time of the insolvency. The problem for the purchasers was that the vendor had at no time allocated any of the gold to any particular customer, which meant that under orthodox sale of goods rules[476] no title passed to them. Although the vendor was in breach of contract in not undertaking this allocation process, the customers' only right was to damages. To the argument that the court should create a trust in their favour to circumvent these rules based on some perceived unfairness, Lord Mustill said:

> [I]t is argued that the court should declare in favour of the [customers] a . . . trust . . . over the bullion in the company's vaults . . . Such a trust or interest . . . would not arise directly from the transaction between the individual [customers], the company and the bullion, but would be created by the court as a measure of justice after the event . . . [T]he [customers'] argument really comes to this, that because the company broke its contract in a way which had to do with bullion the court should call into existence a proprietary interest in whatever bullion happened to be in the possession and ownership of the company at the time when the competition between the [customers] and the other secured and unsecured creditors first arose. The company's stock of bullion had no connection with the [customers'] purchases, and to enable the claimants to reach out and not only abstract it from the assets available to the body

---

[474] ibid 430.
[475] [1995] 1 AC 74, PC. A similar approach was adopted by the Court of Appeal in *Re Polly Peck (No 2)* [1998] 3 All ER 812, CA.
[476] Paras 10.13–10.21.

of creditors as a whole, but also to afford a priority over a secured creditor, would give them an adventitious benefit devoid of . . . foundation in logic and justice . . .[477]

Goldcorp is a decision of the Privy Council, and therefore not strictly binding **4.324** on English courts. But the same sentiments were expressed by the House of Lords in *Foskett v McKeown*, where Lord Browne-Wilkinson said:

> There is no discretion vested in the court. There is no room for any consideration whether . . . it is in a moral sense 'equitable' for the [claimants] to be so entitled. The rules establishing equitable proprietary interests and their enforceability against certain parties have been developed over the centuries and are an integral part of the property law of England. It is a fundamental error to think that, because certain property rights are equitable rather than legal, such rights are in some way discretionary. This case does not depend on whether it is fair, just and reasonable to give the [claimants] an interest as a result of which the court in its discretion provides a remedy. It is a case of hard-nosed property rights.[478]

The finding of property rights and trusts, in other words, in law as well as in equity, is a matter of the application of established rules to facts, not a question of judicial discretion.

But despite these pronouncements, it cannot be denied that the Court of Appeal **4.325** has of late taken it upon itself to create trusts in precisely the way proscribed by both the House of Lords and the Privy Council.[479] This is through resort to the notion of 'unconscionability', a concept of no certain meaning, and nothing more than a synonym for 'unfair' or 'unjust'. It is therefore doubtful how this line of authority can withstand higher scrutiny.

(ii) Rights dissipated in breach of trust

Where a trustee conveys the rights he holds on trust to a third party in breach of **4.326** trust, then, subject to one exception, that person will hold those rights on trust for the beneficiaries of the trust. This is clearly not the same trust under which the trustee originally held, for the recipient will not be subject to the same duties or possess the same powers as the errant trustee. The recipient's only obligation will be to surrender the rights he holds on request by the beneficiaries, either to them, to the errant trustees, or, more likely, to some new trustees.

---

477 [1995] 1 AC 74, 99, PC.
478 [2001] 1 AC 102, 109, HL.
479 The relevant cases are *Banner Homes Group plc v Luff Developments Ltd* [2000] Ch 372; *Collings v Lee* [2001] 2 All ER 332; *Pennington v Waine* [2002] 1 WLR 2075; *Oxley v Hiscock* [2004] 3 All ER 703.

(iii) Unauthorized substitutions

4.327 As we have seen,[480] the trust arising in cases of unauthorized substitutions may be a response to wrongdoing or unjust enrichment. Either approach is, however, controversial. If it turns out that the trust is not responding to one or other of these causative events, then the only answer is that it responds to some other, as yet unspecified, event.

(iv) Automatic resulting trusts

4.328 As we saw above,[481] automatic resulting trusts have been argued to be a response to unjust enrichment. If that argument is unsound, then the only possibility is that they respond to some as yet unknown event.

(v) Vendor-purchaser trusts

4.329 Probably the most common trust arising for a reason other than a declaration of trust, wrong, or unjust enrichment is that arising in certain cases of contracts of sale. The general rule at common law is that a mere agreement to sell does not pass title to the rights agreed to be sold—something further, for example, the execution of a deed, is required to transfer the right from vendor to purchaser.[482] However, as we saw earlier,[483] in certain cases the effect of the contact alone will be to make the vendor a trustee of the right promised to the vendor. There will not, however, be a trust in every case. The trust arises because of an application of the maxim that 'equity looks upon that as done which ought to be done'. In other words, the trust arises because the court considers the vendor to be under a duty to convey the right contracted to be sold to the purchaser. And this duty must be an equitable duty to convey, not just a legal one. Thus, the doctrine only bites where the contract of sale is one of which a court of equity will order specific performance.[484] Where the purchaser's only remedy for a failure by the vendor to convey is an award of a right to damages, no trust will arise. The clear case in which a trust will arise is that of the contract for the sale of property rights in respect of land.[485] But the rule also applies to specifically enforceable contracts for the sale of choses in action such as shares and copyrights.[486]

---

[480] Paras 4.306 and 4.314.

[481] Paras 4.315–4.316.

[482] The mechanics of passing title are dealt with, in paras 4.439–4.442.

[483] Paras 4.32–4.33.

[484] We are, of course, only talking about contracts which are valid, satisfying the relevant rules of both substance and form. In this respect, it should be noted that contracts for the sale of land are only valid if made in writing and signed by both parties: Law of Property (Miscellaneous Provisions) Act 1989, s 2.

[485] *Lysaght v Edwards* (1876) 2 Ch D 499, 506.

[486] *Poole v Middleton* (1861) 29 Beav 646, 54 ER 778 (shares); *Merchant Adventures Ltd v Grew & Co Ltd* [1972] Ch 242 (copyright).

(vi) Transfer of rights 'subject to' existing personal rights trusts

The use of a 'constructive trust' to hold a third party bound by the grant of a **4.330** personal right to which he was not privy has already been examined in the context of contractual licences to occupy land. It is not, however, confined to that case, and has also been used to hold purchasers of a title to a ship bound by contracts entered into by their predecessors in title in *Lord Strathcona Steamship Co v Dominion Coal Co*,[487] and purchasers from mortgagees exercising a power of sale in *Lyus v Prowsa*.[488] The deficiencies of this doctrine have been noted above.[489]

(vii) Trusts arising on the dissolution of unincorporated associations

These were also dealt with above.[490] As we saw, the modern trend is to distribute **4.331** amongst the members on dissolution of an unincorporated associations. Some older cases, however, have used trusts to return the contributions whence they came. Such trusts are clearly trusts created by the court. Exactly why they are created has never been determined.

(viii) Imperfect gift trusts

The general rule. Sometimes a gift will be imperfect because the law's require- **4.332** ments as to transfer have not been satisfied. Will the failed transaction be treated as having any effect? In general, the answer is no. The leading case is *Milroy v Lord*.[491] A settlor executed a voluntary deed purporting to transfer shares in the Bank of Louisiana to one Samuel Lord to be held on trust for the settlor's niece. However, the purported transfer by deed was ineffective, for a transfer of shares can only be effected by the completion of the appropriate form and registration in the name of the transferee in the company's share register. When the settlor died, the question arose as to the niece's entitlement to the shares. The court held that she had none. Turner LJ said:

> I take the law of this court to be well settled, that, in order to render a voluntary settlement valid and effectual, the settlor must have done everything which, accord-ing to the nature of the property comprised in the settlement, was necessary to be done in order to transfer the property and render the settlement binding upon him. He may of course do this by actually transferring the property to the persons for whom he intends to provide, and the provision will then be effectual, and it will be equally effectual if he transfers the property to a trustee for the purposes of the settlement, or declares that he holds it in trust for those purposes . . . but, in order to

---

[487] [1926] AC 108.
[488] [1982] 1 WLR 1044.
[489] Paras 4.138–4.139.
[490] Paras 4.288–4.292.
[491] (1862) 4 De GF & J 264, 45 ER 1185.

render the settlement binding, one or other of these modes must . . . be resorted to, for there is no equity in this Court to perfect an imperfect gift.[492]

The intention here had been to constitute Lord a trustee of the shares but as they had never vested in him, no trust had been created. It was not for the court in such circumstances to create a trust instead.

4.333 Though this case concerned shares, the principle which it lays down holds good no matter what type of right is alleged to be subject to a trust. Unless it is a case where the settlor declares himself a trustee of the right, there will be no trust unless the rights to be held on trust have been transferred to the trustee. The same thinking applies to failed attempts to make outright transfers. As *Richards v Delbridge*[493] shows, no rights will pass if the requirements of a valid conveyance are not satisfied. But most importantly, both *Milroy v Lord* and *Richards v Delbridge* demonstrate that a failed gift by either method (transfer to trustees on trust or outright) will not be construed as a successful declaration by the settlor of himself as trustee. In *Milroy v Lord* Turner LJ said:

> If [the gift] is intended to take effect by transfer, the Court will not hold the intended transfer to operate as a declaration of trust, for then every imperfect instrument would be made effectual by being converted into a perfect trust.[494]

We have already seen that the reason is that such an assertion of self-declaration of trust is contradicted by the evidence of the failed gift, as Sir George Jessel MR explained in *Richards v Delbridge*.[495]

4.334 **Six exceptions.** Although the general rule is that neither the common law nor equity will perfect an imperfect gift in favour of a donee, some exceptions to this principle have arisen, all of which seem to involve the creation by the court of a trust in favour of the purported donee. There are six exceptions in all: detrimental reliance, the rule in *Strong v Bird*, the rule in *Re Ralli*, the rule in *Re Rose*,[496] *donationes mortis causa*, and appeals to 'unconscionability'. The last is particularly suspect as it infringes the rule against remedial constructive trusts.

4.335 **Detrimental reliance (estoppel).** The first exception occurs where the purported donee acts to his detriment in the mistaken belief that the gift in his favour is valid. It seems that in such circumstances the donor will be compelled by a court of equity to perfect the gift, and in the meantime will hold the rights concerned on trust for the donee. An example is *Pascoe v Turner*.[497]

---

[492] (1862) 4 De GF & J 264, 274, 45 ER 1185, 1189.
[493] (1874) LR 18 Eq 11, CA.
[494] (1862) 4 De GF & J 264, 274, 275, 45 ER 1185, 1189.
[495] (1874) LR 18 Eq 11, 15, CA; para 4.188.
[496] [1952] Ch 499, CA.
[497] [1979] 1 WLR 431, CA. See also *Dillwyn v Llewelyn* (1862) 4 De GF & J 517, 45 ER 1285.

In *Pascoe v Turner*[498] a man walked out on a woman with whom he had been **4.336** cohabiting, telling her that the house in which they lived, and to which he held a title outright, was hers. He also said the same about the house's contents. He later changed his mind and sought to turn her out and reclaim the contents. Although the gift of the contents was held to be perfect,[499] that of the title to the house was not because the man had not executed a deed in the woman's favour. However, in reliance on what she thought was a perfect gift, and with the man's encouragement, the woman had spent money on improvements, repairs and redecoration of the house. The sum involved amounted to £300 out of her total savings of £1,000. The Court of Appeal said that if there had been no expenditure on the land by the woman then there would have been nothing they could do to order the man to perfect the gift. But the court held that her detrimental reliance gave her a right to call on the man to perfect the gift and ordered him to execute a conveyance of the title forthwith.[500] And applying the rule that 'equity looks upon that as done which ought to be done', it would appear that, in the interim, he would have held the title for her on trust.

The rule in *Strong v Bird*.   As the name implies, the rule derives from the case **4.337** of *Strong v Bird*.[501] A creditor wished to forgive her debtor his obligation to repay. She purported to do so by telling him that he need not repay the money he had borrowed from her. But the mere oral forgiveness of a debt is not a sufficient release, for it is only a gratuitous promise not to sue. For a full release of the debt, a deed needs to be executed. But though this was never done, the donor by her will appointed the donee her executor. That, said Sir George Jessel MR, had the effect of perfecting the gift. The common law rule was that the union of benefit and burden of an obligation in the same person destroyed that obligation, even though that person was wearing two different hats, which reasoning was based on the rule that a person could not sue himself. Courts of equity, however, took a different view, and held the debt not to be extinguished. In this case, however, the court said that since it was the testatrix's intention to forgive the debt, the court would not intervene to upset the position at common law. Hence, those entitled under the will could not insist that the executor repay the loan, as they could have done had the debtor not been fortuitously appointed to his office.

The rule has, however, been extended to situations other than the forgiveness of **4.338** debts, situations in which the common law rule of extinction has no application.[502]

---

[498]   [1979] 1 WLR 431, CA.

[499]   The requirements of a valid gift of title to goods are discussed: paras 4.449–4.460.

[500]   For an illuminating discussion: S Moriarty, 'Licences and Land Law: Legal Principles and Public Policies' (1984) 100 LQR 376 and the reply by M Thompson, 'Estoppel and Clean Hands' [1986] Conv 406.

[501]   (1874) LR 18 Eq 315.

[502]   *Re Stewart* [1908] 2 Ch 251.

It has also been held to apply to the donee who takes out letters of administration in the event of the donor dying intestate.[503] One limit to the rule, however, is that the intention to give must continue, or at least not be countermanded, up until the purported donor's death.[504]

4.339   **The rule in *Re Ralli's Will Trusts*.**   This is more controversial than the rule just discussed. In *Re Ralli's WT*, Buckley J held, *obiter*, that an unperformed promise to transfer upon trust after-acquired rights was perfected when the rights in question happened to arrive in the intended transferee, not by transfer from the settlor, but in his capacity as trustee of the settlor's father's will.[505] The decision is, however, inconsistent with *Re Brook's Settlement Trusts*,[506] a decision not cited by Buckley J.

4.340   **The rule in *Re Rose*.**   The rule laid down in *Re Rose* is that where the settlor has done everything *in his power* to transfer the right concerned but the transfer is dependent on the act of a third party then the settlor will in the meantime hold the right on trust for the beneficiary.

4.341   The case itself concerned a settlor who by voluntary deed purported to transfer two parcels of shares in a private company, the first to his wife outright, the second to trustees on trust for his wife and son. Some time later, the transfers were presented for registration by the directors of the company and this was done. When the settlor died it became necessary for tax purposes to ascertain the date on which he ceased the hold the shares outright. Was it at the date of the deed or only later, when the transfer was registered by the directors and the rights passed to the wife and to the trustees? The Crown, relying on *Milroy v Lord*,[507] argued that it was the latter. Until the transfer of rights by registration, there was no trust, so that the settlor held the shares for himself until that point. It was argued for the settlor's estate that by executing the deed purporting to transfer the shares, the settlor thereby constituted himself a trustee of the shares for his wife and son, with the consequence that estate duty was not payable.

4.342   The Court of Appeal, taking a 'common sense' view of the matter,[508] held that the settlor became a trustee [509] of the shares for his wife and son on the day he executed the share transfers so that the estate duty claimed was not payable. *Milroy v Lord* was distinguished on the spurious ground that there the testator had attempted the wrong method of transfer, whereas here he had done all that was required of him.

---

503   *Re James* [1935] Ch 449.
504   *Re Wale* [1952] Ch 110.
505   *Re Ralli's Will Trust* [1964] Ch 288.
506   [1939] 1 Ch 993.
507   (1862) 4 De GF & J 264, 45 ER 1185.
508   [1952] Ch 499, 506, CA.
509   The type of trust is not disclosed, though the only contender is a constructive trust.

Notwithstanding its difficulties, the same approach was more recently applied
to the case of an outright gift of a title to registered land in *Mascall v Mascall.*[510]

Donationes mortis causa. A court of equity will order the perfection of an   **4.343**
imperfect gift which is made conditional upon and in contemplation of death and
where the donor has now died. This doctrine did not arguably start life as an
exception to the rule laid down in *Milroy v Lord*, for it was concerned with cases
of corporeal personalty in which there had been a delivery of the subject-matter
of the gift *inter vivos*. Such conditional gifts were perfected by the condition
occurring and needed no assistance from any court. But the doctrine was later
extended to choses in action,[511] and at that point it truly did become an exception
to the rule. It has recently been held that a gift of a title to land can be so perfected
even though such titles cannot pass by delivery. In *Sen v Headley*[512] it was held to
be sufficient if the donor on his sickbed passed over the key to a box containing
the deeds, the instruments by which unregistered titles are conveyed, relating to
the land.

Unconscionability. An even further dilution of the *Milroy v Lord* principle   **4.344**
occurred in *Pennington v Waine*,[513] where the Court of Appeal said, in the case of
an imperfect gift of shares, that the donor need not even have done everything
necessary to perfect the gift. What mattered instead was whether it would be
'unconscionable' for him to resile from his gift. And, on the facts of this particular
case, it was said to be 'unconscionable' for the donor to resile as she had told the
donee that the gift was perfect. What this 'unconscionable' was unfortunately was
not explained. Moreover, no member of the court seems to have noticed that this
is precisely what happened in *Milroy v Lord*. The court relied on *Choithram v
Pagarani*[514] as authority, though that was a case of an express trust, where it would
of course be 'unconscionable' to resile from a perfectly valid trust. *Pennington*, on
the other hand, was a case of a constructive trust, for whichever way one views it,
the purported donor did not make a self-declaration of trust. It is important to
note that the result cannot be defended through an application of the doctrine in
Re Rose, for the donor had not done all she needed to perfect the gift. Nor can it be
justified on the basis of detrimental reliance on the part of the purported donee.
Although such reliance was arguably present, this was not the basis on which the
case was reasoned.

---

[510] (1985) P & CR 119, CA.
[511] As in *Re Mead* (1880) Ch D 651 (delivery of unendorsed cheque *inter vivos*).
[512] [1991] Ch 425, CA.
[513] [2002] EWCA Civ 227; [2002] 1 WLR 2075.
[514] [2001] 1 WLR 1, PC.

(10) The Coming to an End of Trusts

4.345   Trusts can come to an end in a number of ways, by destruction of the rights held
on trust, by a transfer of those rights to a good faith purchaser for value, by the
exercise by a beneficiary of his right to call for a conveyance of the trust rights to
himself, and by an authorised distribution of the trust rights.

(a) Destruction of rights held on trust

4.346   Where the right held on trust is destroyed, the trust itself must cease to exist, for
the word trust merely describes a way in which rights are held. There are two ways
in which rights may be destroyed, both of which are discussed below under the
heading 'Extinction of Property Rights'.[515] One is where the subject-matter of the
right, the physical thing over which the right exists, is destroyed. An example
would be a painting destroyed by fire. The other is that where the physical thing
over which the right subsists continues to exist, but the right itself is lost by, for
example, the operation of statutes of limitation or the destructive effect of bona
fide purchase.

(b) Conveyance of trust rights to bona fide purchaser for value

4.347   Where the rights which are held on trust are recognized by the common law, not
just equity, and those rights are in breach of trust conveyed to a person who gives
value in exchange and in good faith, the effect of the conveyance will be to destroy
the rights of the beneficiaries of the trust so that the transferee will not be under
the usual duty of a person who receives rights dissipated in breach of trust to
convey them back to the order of the beneficiaries.[516]

4.348   In *Pilcher v Rawlins*,[517] Pilcher held a sum of money on trust for certain
beneficiaries. In 1851 he lent some of the money to Rawlins, a solicitor, who executed a mortgage of a title to land in favour of Pilcher as security for the advance,
the effect of which was to give Pilcher the title, which he then held in trust for
the beneficiaries. Pilcher and Rawlins decided to make some money through a
fraudulent scheme. Rawlins arranged to borrow £10,000 from Stockwell and
Lamb, who were trustees for a second set of beneficiaries. Rawlins agreed to give
Stockwell a legal mortgage of the already mortgaged title as security for the loan
and suppressed the 1851 conveyance so that he appeared to still hold that title.
Pilcher later reconveyed the title to Rawlins, the conveyance being expressed to be

---

[515] Paras 4.462–4.534.

[516] In the case of a purchase for value of a title to registered land, the question will instead be
whether the beneficiary of the trust had a right which overrode the conveyance to the purchaser.
Questions as to the purchaser's state of mind will be irrelevant.

[517] (1872) 7 Ch App 259.

in consideration of the repayment by Rawlins of the money originally lent to him, though this was not in fact done. Later the same day, Rawlins executed a legal mortgage to Stockwell and Lamb who took without knowledge of the 1851 conveyance or reconveyance. One question was whether the interests of the beneficiaries for whom Pilcher was trustee could prevail against the later, but legal, interests of Stockwell and Lamb. The court held that they could not. James LJ said:

> I propose simply to apply myself to the case of a purchaser for valuable consideration, without notice, obtaining, upon the occasion of his purchase, and by means of his purchase deed, some legal estate, some legal right, some legal advantage; and, according to my view of the established law of this Court, such a purchaser's plea of a purchase for valuable consideration without notice is an absolute, unqualified, unanswerable defence and an unanswerable plea to the jurisdiction of this Court. Such a purchaser, when he has once put in that plea, may be interrogated and tested to any extent as to the valuable consideration which he has given in order to show the *bona fides* or *mala fides* of his purchase, and also the presence or absence of notice; but when once he has gone through that ordeal, and has satisfied the terms of the plea of purchase for valuable consideration without notice, then, according to my judgment, this Court has no jurisdiction whatever to do anything more than to let him depart in possession of that legal estate, that legal right, that legal advantage which he has obtained, whatever it may be. In such a case a purchaser is entitled to hold that which, without breach of duty, he has had conveyed to him.[518]

It must be stressed that the right taken by the purchaser must be one recognized by the common law. If, for example, the trustee was holding equitable rights on trust and in breach of trust conveyed them to someone who in good faith and without notice of the breach of trust gave value in exchange, such person would still be liable to reconvey those rights at the suit of the beneficiaries.[519]

(c) Termination by beneficiary

A beneficiary of a trust has a right to call on the trustee to convey the rights he is holding on trust to the beneficiary himself where he is absolutely entitled, an adult, and of sound mind. Where this happens, the trust will cease to exist, for the rights will now be held outright rather than on trust. The right to terminate the trust is illustrated by reference to *Saunders v Vautier*.[520] A testator left his East India stock to trustees on trust to accumulate the dividends until his great-nephew reached the age of 25 and then pay over both the dividends and the stock to him. On reaching the age of 21 (the then age of majority), and being about to marry, the great-nephew sought an order directing the trustees to convey to him both the

4.349

---

[518] ibid 268–9.

[519] *Cave v Cave* (1880) 15 Ch D 639.

[520] (1841) Cr & Ph 240. The right is not recognized in a number of jurisdictions of the United States. For discussion, see P Matthews, 'The Comparative Importance of the Rule in *Saunders v Vautier*' (2006) 122 LQR 266.

stock and accumulated income. Lord Cottenham LC, having held that the great-nephew had a vested interest rather than one contingent on him reaching the age of 25, granted the order sought.

4.350   This right to collapse the trust is also available in the case of a discretionary trust, provided all the objects are of sound mind and full age and are all agreed. Thus, in *Re Smith*,[521] Romer J said that where all those potentially entitled under a discretionary trust were in agreement, they could 'come to Court and say to the trustees: "Hand over the fund to us"'.[522]

(d)   Authorized distribution of trust rights

4.351   Where the trustees make distributions of the trust funds in accordance with the terms of the trust, then those receiving the rights, either the beneficiaries of the trust or those who receive the rights in exchange for value, for example, the vendors of investments, will take the rights received absolutely. In respect of those rights, therefore, the trust will come to an end.

E.   Co-ownership

4.352   Both real and personal property rights, and even personal rights such as a claim in debt or a company share, can be held by two or more persons as co-owners. It is important to realise that the use of the language of co-ownership does not mean that English law is here committing itself to a concept of ownership. Co-ownership describes the holding of a right, not a right in itself. What is co-owned is not ownership but the property rights enumerated above. It would be equally valid to talk of a co-holding instead of a co-ownership.

4.353   Co-ownership is necessary but also troublesome, as co-owned rights are often difficult to buy and sell. It is also necessary where a settlor wishes to set up a trust with two or more trustees. Reforms were introduced in 1925 and modified in 1996. The easiest way into the subject is still through the unmodified common law.

(1)   Types of Co-ownership

4.354   Nowadays, English law knows but two types of co-ownership, the joint tenancy and the tenancy in common. There used to be more, but the others are relics of a past age. The word 'tenancy' does not indicate co-ownership only of leasehold estates. The word 'tenant' here derives from the language of feudalism. It was

---

521   [1928] Ch 915.
522   ibid 918.

extended to co-ownership of titles to goods and leases, neither of which were ever subject to that system.

(a) Joint tenancy

In a joint tenancy no one joint tenant holds any rights on his or her own. Only as **4.355** a group do the tenants hold the right in question. As Lord Browne-Wilkinson explained in *Hammersmith & Fulham LBC v Monk*[523] a transfer of rights to two or more people as joint tenants 'operates so as to make them, *vis à vis* the outside world, one single owner'. The crucial point to note is that no single joint tenant can be said to have anything like a share of the right. A title to a car held jointly by H and W is simply held by them both.

It is for this reason that there is no power in a joint tenant to leave 'his' interest **4.356** to another by will, for as an individual he has no interest to leave. When a joint tenant dies, as he ultimately must,[524] he ceases to be a member of the group holding the right. Since, in the absence of reconveyances to reconstituted groups, the number of joint tenants must thus diminish, the situation will eventually be reached in which only one joint tenant survives, in which case that person will hold the right on his own. This is the 'right of survivorship' or *jus accrescendi*, and it forms the cardinal feature of a joint tenancy. It operates automatically, there being no need for any conveyance from the personal representatives of the deceased to the surviving joint tenants. What happens on the death of a joint tenant is that he drops out of the picture, and it is for this reason that a joint tenant cannot leave his interest by will. If the right is to be conveyed *inter vivos* it must be conveyed by all of the joint tenants acting together.

The four unities

For a joint tenancy to exist there must be present the 'four unities' of possession, **4.357** interest, title and time. If for some reason one of these unities is absent, the most that can have been created is a tenancy in common.

Unity of possession.   Each tenant must be entitled to possession of each and **4.358** every part of the thing over which the co-owned right subsists. If this is not the case, then no joint tenancy will have been created. Indeed, unless there is unity of possession there will be no co-ownership at all, not even a tenancy in common, only separate rights to possession in respect of different physical things.

Unity of interest.   Because they hold but one right between them, the interest of **4.359** each joint tenant must be the same in extent, nature and duration. A joint tenancy

---

[523] [1992] 1 AC 478, 492, HL.
[524] Since a corporation might not die, it could not at common law be a joint tenant, though this rule has been altered by statute: Bodies Corporate (Joint Tenancy) Act 1899.

cannot exist between persons holding interests of a different nature, for example a freeholder and a leaseholder: there is only one title in the case of a joint tenancy. Moreover there is no possibility of unequal shares; indeed, there are no shares at all.

4.360 **Unity of title.** Each joint tenant must claim his title under the same act or document. This requirement is satisfied if all tenants acquired their rights by the same conveyance or if they simultaneously took possession of the thing and thereby acquired title to it by that act of taking possession.

4.361 **Unity of time.** The interest of each joint tenant must vest at the same time. Thus, a conveyance of a title to land to A, remainder to the heirs of B and C, would not create the remaindermen joint tenants because they would acquire their interest at different times.

(b) **Tenancy in common**

4.362 The crucial difference between a tenancy in common and a joint tenancy is that tenants in common have individual interests which they can sell, give away and, most importantly, leave by will. There is no survivorship rule in the case of tenants in common. Each tenant in common has a distinct share, though a share which has not yet been physically carved out of the whole. For that reason, tenants in common are sometimes described as holding in 'undivided shares'.[525]

4.363 Since there is no longer one title, there is no requirement of the unities of interest, title and time. The only unity needed is that of possession, that each have an equal right to possession of the thing, for, as we have seen, without that there would simply be separate titles to physically distinct areas of land or goods. There must at least be a shared holding of the same right. So, for example, a life tenant of land and the remainderman have concurrent interests in respect of the land but are not tenants in common. They hold two separate estates, the former giving a present right to exclusive possession, the latter one in the future.

(2) Choosing Between Types of Co-ownership

4.364 Because the survivorship principle operates so as to deny a joint tenant the ability to leave any interest by will, a joint tenancy is the ideal form of co-ownership for trustees, in that, on death, it ensures that the trust rights never become entangled with those rights which are the trustees' own. The deceased trustee will simply drop out of the picture, leaving the other joint tenant(s) holding the rights; there will be no need for the deceased trustee's personal representatives to execute a conveyance, as there would if the deceased trustee had been a tenant in common.

---

[525] As, for example, in the Law of Property Act 1925, s 1(6).

And because unilateral dealings by a joint tenant cannot take effect, the estate cannot be fragmented. There will only ever be one title, thus making it the ideal form of co-ownership from the point of view of any purchaser.

On the other hand, some co-owners will be averse to the right of survivorship; **4.365** they will want to make their own decisions as to the destination of the right on their death. For instance, if a right is held by two business partners, they might well prefer their 'shares' to go to their own families after death, rather than that the surviving partner take all. Such persons, given the choice, would probably opt for a tenancy in common.

(3) Creation of the Different Tenancies

Common law and equity take different lines. Indeed it is possible on the same **4.366** facts for equity to take a different view from the common law as to whether the co-owners are joint tenants or tenants in common.

(a) At common law

If the four unities are not present, the tenancy cannot be joint. If they are, the **4.367** starting point is always with the words used by the transferor. In the case of titles to land, until 1925 express words needed to be used to stop a joint tenancy coming into being, and this is still the position with titles to goods. The rule at common law is that in the absence of words of 'severance' a joint tenancy will be created. So, for example, a grant simply 'to A and B' creates a joint tenancy at law. A fortiori, a grant 'to A and B jointly' does the same. Where words of severance are used by the transferor, however, a tenancy in common arises. Words of severance are any words in the grant showing that the tenants are each to take distinct shares. Words such as 'to share and share alike', 'to be divided amongst', 'equally', 'between', 'amongst', and 'respectively' have all been held to be words of severance.

(b) In equity

In equity, the rule is that equity 'leans against' a joint tenancy. The reason for this **4.368** lies in the Draconian character of the *jus accrescendi*, which, as was said in *R v Williams*,[526] is looked upon as 'odious' in equity.[527]

This does not, however, mean that a joint tenancy cannot exist in equity. It simply **4.369** means that in cases of doubt, a presumption will apply which leads to a tenancy in common being found. Where the words of the grant expressly state that the parties are joint tenants at law and equity then those words will of course be determinative.

---

[526] (1735) Bunb 342.
[527] ibid 343.

But where there are no words either way, then a presumption in favour of a tenancy in common and against a joint tenancy will arise in three situations: where purchase money is provided in unequal shares; where purchase money is provided by way of mortgage; and in the case of partnership assets.

(i) Where the purchase money is provided in unequal shares

4.370 Where purchase money is provided in unequal shares the purchasers will, in the absence of any words to the contrary regarding the position in equity,[528] take as tenants in common, even though at law they are joint tenants.[529] The size of their respective shares will be determined by the amount of their respective contributions. However, and somewhat illogically, this will not be the case where the purchase money is provided in equal amounts. In that situation the common law position prevails.[530]

(ii) Where money is provided by way of mortgage

4.371 Where money is lent on mortgage by two persons, in whatever shares, then the title the creditors receive as security for the loan will be held by them as tenants in common.[531]

(iii) In the case of partnership assets

4.372 Where partners acquire rights as part of their partnership assets, they will hold those rights in equity as tenants in common. In the words of equity '*Jus accrescendi inter mercatores locum non habet*' (the right of survivorship has no place among commercial people).[532]

(4) Severance of Joint Tenancies

(a) Introduction

4.373 It is possible to turn a joint tenancy into a tenancy in common, a process known as severance. The size of the share then generated is always proportionate to the

---

[528] As in *Goodman v Gallant* [1986] Fam 106, where a joint tenancy arose in equity even though the purchase money had been provided in the ratio of 3:1, because the conveyance had been expressed to be made to the purchasers as 'joint tenants at law and equity'.

[529] *Lake v Gibson* (1729) 1 Eq Cas Abr 290, 21 ER 1052. In *Stack v Dowden* [2007] UKHL 17, a majority of the House of Lords held that this presumption, though it will apply in the case of a conveyance to one of the contributors, does not do so in the case of a conveyance to two, at least in the domestic context. It is difficult, however, to see why different rules should apply in these two cases. The case is discussed in detail in the chapter on Family Law: paras 2.107–2.109, 2.114.

[530] *Aveling v Knipe* (1815) 9 Ves 441, 445, 34 ER 580, 582.

[531] *Morley v Bird* (1798) 3 Ves 628, 631, 30 ER 1192, 1193.

[532] *Hamond v Jethro* (1611) 2 Brownl & Golds 97, 99, 123 ER 836, 837.

number of joint tenants living at the date of severance. So, for example, a severance by a joint tenant while there are four joint tenants living will give the severing party a one-quarter share, though leaving the joint tenancy intact as regards the remaining three-quarters. The act of severance does not require the concurrence of the fellow joint tenants. The price the severing party pays, however, is that he no longer stands to gain the whole right should he survive the others. The availability of severance qualifies the proposition that no joint tenant holds anything in his own right, for each does at least have a potential share equal in size to that of his companions.

It is evident from the nature of the joint tenancy that severance can only be effected **4.374** *inter vivos*. It cannot be effected by will because a will only speaks from death, and by that time the deceased is no longer a joint tenant. The moment, in other words, has passed. The general principle is that severance is effected by destroying one of two of the four unities. Unity of time cannot be destroyed because that relates to the past, and the destruction of the unity of possession is incompatible with any form of co-ownership. The two unities left are unity of title and unity of interest. If either of these is destroyed, a severance happens and a tenancy in common results.

It used to be easier to sever a joint tenancy in personalty than in realty. In the case **4.375** of personalty, severance was essentially a matter of agreement. Thus in *Williams v Hensman*[533] Page-Wood V-C said:

> A joint tenancy [of personalty] may be severed in three ways: in the first place, an act of any one of the persons interested operating upon his own share may create a severance as to that share . . . Secondly, a joint tenancy may be severed by mutual agreement. And, in the third place, there may be a severance by any course of dealing sufficient to intimate that the interests of all were mutually treated as constituting a tenancy in common. When the severance depends on an inference of this kind without any express act of severance, it will not suffice to rely on an intention, with respect to the particular share, declared only behind the backs of the other persons interested.[534]

By the 1925 legislation, these methods were extended to land. Another method, notice in writing, was also introduced.[535] In the review which follows, the three ancient methods of severance, applicable to both realty and personalty, are given first, followed by the methods which were extended or introduced by the Law of Property Act 1925.

---

[533] (1861) 1 J & H 546, 70 ER 862.
[534] (1861) 1 J & H 546, 557–8, 70 ER 862, 866–7.
[535] Law of Property Act 1925, s 36.

(b) Acquisition of another estate

4.376   The subsequent acquisition by one joint tenant of some further estate in respect of the land will destroy the unity of interest since one will now have more than the others. Suppose that a title to land is conveyed to A, B and C for life as joint tenants, remainder to D. If D sells his remainder interest to A then the joint tenancy which exists between A on the one hand, and B and C on the other, will be converted into a tenancy in common. Note, however, that B and C still remain joint tenants *inter se*.

(c) Alienation

4.377   This involves a theoretical puzzle, since a joint tenant cannot alienate his interest. There is nonetheless a form of severance which occurs when one joint tenant alienates his interest *inter vivos*, thus destroying the unity of title since the transferee is no longer able to claim unity of title with the other joint tenants. Such a transaction does not require the assent of the other joint tenants and does not affect the way they will continue to hold the property *inter se*. The theoretical problem is overcome by treating a disposition by one joint tenant as having two natures, both a severance of his interest under the joint tenancy and an alienation of his interest under the tenancy in common to the alienee. Where the tenant merely contracts to sell his interest to another there is no severance at common law. If the contract is specifically enforceable, it will be effective to sever in equity, because of the rule that equity looks upon that as done which ought to be done.[536]

(d) Homicide

4.378   Where one joint tenant murdered another the criminal was treated as having severed his joint tenancy just before the murder so as to ensure that he could not take anything by virtue of the right of survivorship.

(e) Acting upon his own share

4.379   This is the first of the extensions referred to earlier. We have seen that the alienation by a joint tenant of his interest effected a severance whether the right was real or personal. It was doubtful prior to 1925, however, whether some dealing less than complete alienation, such as the granting of a lease, also had this effect.[537] That had always been the case with personalty. Since 1925 the matter has been put beyond doubt. 'Acting upon his own share' essentially means doing something to preclude him from claiming by survivorship. Sufficient for this purpose

---

[536] Para 4.329.
[537] C Sweet, *Challis on Real Property* (3rd edn, 1911) 367.

is alienation, both complete and partial, including the mortgaging of the right. A mere declaration of an intention to sever is not, however, sufficient under this head.

(f) Mutual agreement

Although all joint tenants must agree, no formalities seem to be necessary for this form of severance. The agreement may be specifically to sever, or it may be to deal with the property in a way which necessarily, although not expressly, involves severance. An example is provided by the case of *Burgess v Rawnsley*.[538] There was an agreement between two joint tenants of a title to land, A and B, that A would buy B out. The agreement was never performed and was in any case unenforceable because it did not satisfy the then existing requirements of formality. A died, and B argued that she was solely entitled to the title as the survivor of joint tenants. The Court of Appeal held that although the agreement had never been performed, it was effective to sever the joint tenancy because the destruction of the joint tenancy was necessarily part of the sale of B's interest to A.   **4.380**

(g) Mutual course of dealings

There is no hard and fast rule here; each case will depend on an interpretation of the facts.[539] But the fact that negotiations for severance took place between the parties but terms were never agreed will not normally amount to severance under this head.[540]   **4.381**

(h) Notice in writing

This was introduced by the 1925 legislation. In *Burgess v Rawnsley* Lord Denning suggested that it has always been the law that severance could be effected by written notice to all other joint tenants,[541] but this was later refuted by Deane J in the Australian High Court in *Corin v Patton*.[542]   **4.382**

(5) Rights of Co-owners Inter Se

In both a tenancy in common and a joint tenancy there will be unity of possession: each tenant is as much entitled to the possession of the subject-matter of the right   **4.383**

---

[538] [1975] Ch 429, CA.
[539] A list of examples is provided by KJ Gray and SF Gray, *Elements of Land Law* (4th edn, 2005) 11.90–11.94.
[540] *Burgess v Rawnsley* [1975] Ch 429, 447, CA, *per* Sir John Pennycuick.
[541] [1975] Ch 429, 440, CA.
[542] (1990) 169 CLR 540, 584.

as any of his co-tenants.[543] Accordingly, there is no right for one co-owner to demand payment for the use by the other co-owner of the property concerned. Thus, in *M'Mahon v Burchell* [544] one co-owner occupied a house while the other chose not to. The non-occupying owner claimed 'rent' from the occupying owner. The court held that each co-owner was entitled to live in the house, and if one failed to exercise this right it did not entitle him to claim any rent from the other. Where, however, there has been an ouster of one co-owner by another then the court will order the payment of an occupation 'rent'.

4.384 What happens where the co-owners cannot agree on whether the title be sold or how the thing over which it exists is employed? Whose voice should prevail in the event of dispute? As regards co-owned titles to land, the position is governed by statutory provisions which will be dealt with later. So far as titles to goods are concerned, apart from ships, which are subject to the special Admiralty jurisdiction of the High Court, there seems to be very little law in this area. What there is is contained in the Law of Property Act 1925, section 188(1):

> Where any chattels belong to persons in undivided shares, the persons interested in a moiety or upwards may apply to the court for an order for division of the chattels or any of them, according to a valuation or otherwise, and the court may make such order and give any consequential directions as it thinks fit. It should be noted that the section has no application to joint tenancies, that it only empowers those with a 50% or greater share to apply, and the application can only be for a division.

4.385 As regards titles to ships, English law authorizes the majority in value to employ the ship on any probable design. If the ship is in the possession of a minority co-owner, then the majority can by Admiralty process arrest it. The minority co-owner is protected, however, in that he may disclaim participation in any proposed adventure. He then bears no portion of the expenses but, by way of *quid pro quo*, is unable to share in any profits. The court may also require the majority co-owners to provide the minority co-owner with some security for his share.[545]

(6) Statutory Reforms of Co-owned Titles to Land: 1925

4.386 A number of reforms to co-owned titles to land, though not to co-owned titles to goods, were made by the 1925 legislation, which reforms were themselves the subject of further reform in 1996.

---

543 So much is this so that, in the case of goods, one co-owner could not bring conversion against another co-owner who sold or kept him out. That was changed by the Torts (Interference with Goods) Act 1977, s 10.

544 (1846) 2 Ph 127, 41 ER 889.

545 *The Vanessa Ann* [1985] 1 Lloyd's Rep 549.

(a) Difficulties of dealing with co-owned titles to land

The difficulties of dealing with a co-owned title to land were twofold. In the first **4.387** place it was burdensome and sometimes impossible to collect the consent of every co-owner. Secondly, even where all the co-owners agreed, there was, in the case of tenancy in common, the further burden of investigating the title of each. A purchaser would have to satisfy himself that each tenant in common had not assigned or mortgaged his own share to a third party, and, if he had, the purchaser would have to obtain the consent of that third party to join in the conveyance.

By way of example, Sir Arthur Underhill, an eminent conveyancer of the time, **4.388** wrote that:

> It is by no means uncommon to find the equitable title split up into fifty or sixty individual shares, most of them mortgaged, and some of them settled, and the elusive legal estate so hidden as to be almost beyond the wit of man to discover. Where this is the case, nothing less than an action will suffice to cut the Gordian knot, and when (as frequently happens) the property is small—a few houses or a small farm—the costs of the necessary enquiries leave little to be divided between the unfortunate co-owners.[546]

(b) The trust for sale

An attempt might have been made to outlaw tenancies in common but was not. **4.389** Instead, although tenancies in common were to be permitted, they were to subsist only behind a trust: there could be no tenancies in common at law.[547] The only form of co-ownership which could exist at law was to be the joint tenancy, and even then the maximum number of joint tenants was limited to four.[548] Any attempt to create a tenancy in common at law would henceforth turn the first four persons named in the conveyance into trustees holding the title as joint tenants for all parties named in the conveyance as tenants in common,[549] and the severance of a joint tenancy at law was prohibited.[550]

But to have simply shifted the problem behind a trust would have solved nothing. **4.390** As we have seen, interests under a trust bind all save a bona fide purchaser of the title for value without actual or constructive notice of the disposition being in breach of trust, and so where the purchaser could not claim such a status he would still have to investigate the same number of titles and obtain the same number

---

[546] Sir Arthur Underhill, *A Concise Explanation of Lord Birkenhead's Act (The Law of Property Act 1922)* (1922) 99, 100.

[547] Law of Property Act 1925, s 1(6).

[548] Trustee Act 1925, s 34(2).

[549] Law of Property Act 1925, s 34(2).

[550] ibid s 36(2).

of consents before the title could be dealt with. To overcome this difficulty a special kind of trust was used, a trust for sale.

4.391 A trust for sale is a trust under which rights are given to trustees with a direction that they be sold and the proceeds of sale held on trust for the beneficiaries. From a purchaser's point of view, the beauty of such a trust is that when the trustees sell or mortgage the trust rights, they do so under powers conferred on them by the trust instrument, with the result that the sale or mortgage will not amount to a breach of trust. This means that the beneficiaries can have no recourse against such a purchaser, even if he has actual notice of their interests. If they have any complaint, it is to the holder of the proceeds of sale, the trustee, that the beneficiaries must turn.

4.392 The legislation provided for the imposition of a trust for sale in two circumstances, where title to land was expressed to be conveyed to persons as tenants in common[551] and where it was held in trust for persons as joint tenants.[552] This was, however, problematic, for as regards tenancies in common, it left a number of gaps. A tenancy in common could arise in situations other than where a title was 'expressed to be conveyed to persons in undivided shares'. To take just one example,[553] a tenancy in common would, as we saw above, arise where there was a joint purchase but unequal contributions and no indication in the conveyance as to the position in equity.[554] The trust for sale, where it arose, had a number of distinct consequences, the main one being that the interests of the beneficiaries were overreachable.

4.393 Although the beneficiaries' interests would only be overreached where the purchase money was paid to two or more trustees,[555] they were therefore necessarily less secure than before, for an interest in respect of a fund of money is more easily lost than the same right in respect of land. It also meant that little or no respect was accorded to a beneficiary's interest in the use value of the land; overreaching assumes that the beneficiary has no interest in the nature, as opposed to the value, of the subject-matter of the trust. Although the legislation required some consultation of the beneficiaries by the trustees before any dealings with the title to the land,[556] it was further provided that a purchaser need not concern himself with the question whether such consultation had taken place.[557]

---

[551] ibid s 34(2).

[552] ibid s 36(1).

[553] For a full discussion, see C Harpum (ed), *Megarry and Wade on Real Property* (6th edn, 2000) 502–4.

[554] These gaps were plugged by the Trusts of Land and Appointment of Trustees Act 1996, discussed immediately below.

[555] Law of Property Act 1925, s 2.

[556] ibid s 26(3).

[557] ibid.

(7) *Statutory Reforms of Co-owned Titles to Land: 1996*

The reforms made by the Trusts of Land and Appointment of Trustees Act 1996 **4.394** to co-ownership of titles to land were not radical. They merely tidied up some of the problems left over after 1925. The 1996 Act left unchanged the general scheme for dealing with the problems of co-ownership adopted in 1925.

The most notable omission was any implementation of a key recommendation of **4.395** the Law Commission of England and Wales that occupying co-owners should be given a right of veto over sales or mortgages of the title.[558] Since 1996, it is still the case that a co-owned title to land can be dealt with by the trustees without the consent of the beneficiaries, even if one or more of them use the land as their home. In that respect the assumption is still made that such beneficiaries, even if in occupation of the land, are not interested in the question whether the trust fund comprises a title to land or merely money.

What the legislation did do, however, was to alter very slightly the regime pertain- **4.396** ing to co-owned titles to land. The use of a trust for sale to solve the problems of co-ownership was abandoned, though the use of the device of a trust was not. The difference now is that, while a co-owned title must be held behind a trust, it is not a trust under which the trustees have any *duty* to sell the land, but one in which there is merely a *power* to do so. While retaining the device of overreaching, therefore, the 1996 Act removes the difficulties caused by the application of the doctrine of conversion, by which the duty to sell was fictionally seen to have been performed. This caused problems with regard to the question whether the beneficiaries had 'interests in the land' for the purpose of certain provisions replacing the rules of equity as to good faith purchase. Indeed, the Act goes so far as to abolish the doctrine of conversion in the case of trusts for sale.[559] There was also some doubt as to whether an equitable co-owner had any right to occupy the land. The statute now provides that such a right exists provided that the purpose of the trust is to make the land available for occupation by him or that the land is held by the trustees so as to be so available.[560]

(8) *Disputes Over Co-owned land*

A constant problem with co-ownership arises when the co-owners fall out as **4.397** to whether the right should be sold or its subject-matter put to a particular use.[561]

---

[558] *Transfer of Land-Overreaching: Beneficiaries in Occupation* (Law Com No 188, 1989) para 4.15.
[559] Trusts of Land and Appointment of Trustees Act 1996, s 3.
[560] ibid s 12.
[561] Paras 4.383–4.385.

So far as titles to land are concerned, the imposition by statute of a trust for sale in all cases of co-owned titles had the consequence that, in the event of such a dispute, the court would in general take the view that the duty to sell should prevail.[562] Since 1996, co-owned titles are no longer to be held under a trust for sale. The scheme for resolving disputes is laid down by statute. Section 14 of the 1996 Act gives the court a very wide discretion. There is as yet little guidance on how this new discretion will be exercised.[563]

F. Creation of Property Rights

4.398 This section explains how property rights come into existence. The next section explains how they may be transferred once created. Though logical, this differentiation between creation and transfer is unusual, with the divisions normally being made between original and derivative acquisition, or even simply gift and sale. The latter is clearly deficient, for it excludes very simple transactions such as barter, paying one's tax bill, or even mistaken transfers. The former, though preferable in that it purports to include all relevant transactions, creates duplication, for some instances of derivative acquisition will involve transfers of existing rights, while some will involve the creation of new ones. Accordingly, we will focus in the first instance on how property rights come into being. We have already answered the same question with respect to trusts.[564]

4.399 Property rights arise as a response to events which happen in the world. Just as with personal rights, which correlate with obligations,[565] those causative events generating property rights can be conveniently classified under four headings: consent, wrongs, unjust enrichment, and miscellaneous others. Of these, manifestations of consent are both the most common and the most prominent, though it should be noted that not all manifestations of consent count. A number of requirements are laid down by the law as to the form in which manifestations of consent must be made (for example, a deed is required for the creation of certain property rights in respect of land) before they can have any effect. These will be examined below.

4.400 More rarely, property rights arise independently of consent, upon the happening of an event within one of the other three categories. We have already encountered

---

562 *Re Mayo* [1943] Ch 302. But the court would not always order sale where the land had been bought for a collateral purpose and that purpose still subsisted: *Re Buchanan-Wollaston's Conveyance* [1939] Ch 738, CA.

563 Early indications are that the discretion is not to be seen as embodying the practice under the pre-1996 regime: *Mortgage Corporation v Shaire* [2001] Ch 743.

564 See Part D.

565 See Part A.

this phenomenon in the law of trusts, with trusts sometimes being created in response to wrongs, unjust enrichments and other causative events.[566] The same is true of property rights, though many of those instances of property rights arising by operation of law are, as with trusts, highly controversial.

(1) Consent

Within the category of consent, the way a property right is created depends on the nature of the right itself and not the context in which the act of creation takes place. Thus, if I want to create an easement in favour of my neighbour, the method I need to use is the same whether the context is that of gift, sale, or exchange. **4.401**

(a) Land

So far as concerns the creation of property rights over land, it is generally the case that a deed must be used, at least for those rights capable of taking effect at common law. Thus, if A wishes to grant to B a 21-year lease of land, the grant will be void at common law if not made by deed.[567] The same is true of the express grant of easements.[568] Where the title of the grantor of either a lease or easement is registered, there is in certain cases a further requirement that such 'dispositions' be registered. If not, they will be inoperative at common law.[569] **4.402**

The main exception—the full list of exceptions is given in the Law of Property Act 1925, section 52(2)—concerns short leases of land. By section 54(2), a lease taking effect in possession not exceeding three years may be granted orally. It is important to note that this exception applies only to the creation of such leases; their later assignment still requires the use of a deed.[570] **4.403**

Where the property right in respect of land is equitable rather than legal, no deed will be required, though some form of writing generally will. So, for example, contracts for the sale of interests in land are only valid if made in writing.[571] Options to purchase are also species of such contracts, and their creation too will be void if not written. **4.404**

---

[566] See paras 4.293–4.344.

[567] Law of Property Act 1925, s 52(1).

[568] In certain circumstances, the grant of an easement will be implied in the grant of another right. Details in C Harpum (ed), *Megarry & Wade: The Law of Real Property* (6th edn, 2000), 1105–18.

[569] Land Registration Act 2002, s 27. Leases for less than seven years are, inter alia, exempt from this requirement.

[570] *Crago v Julian* [1992] 1 WLR 372, CA.

[571] Law of Property (Miscellaneous Provisions) Act 1989, s 2.

(b) Goods

4.405 As we have seen, it is doubtful whether rights less than rights to exclusive possession of the goods forever can be created. As a consequence, transactions concerning those goods will involve transfers of pre-existing titles rather than the creation of new rights. However, if such rights can be created, for example, the grant of a lease of goods, then there seem to be no requisite formalities to observe.

(2) Wrongs

4.406 We saw above that a wrong is a breach of duty.[572] The question we will now ask is whether the victim of a wrong ever acquires a proprietary right in respect of things to which a wrongdoer obtains title through the commission of the wrong. We have already seen how for certain wrongs, most notably the wrong of breach of fiduciary duty, some cases, though not all, have said that a trust will arise over rights acquired because of the breach.[573] This section asks whether property rights will ever be so created.

(a) Confiscation and forfeiture

4.407 There are two specialized cases in which wrongs appear to confer proprietary rights but which on closer examination do not. In the criminal law, the court has a jurisdiction to order confiscation of ill-gotten gains.[574] However, in that case the Crown's proprietary rights do not arise immediately from the wrong but from the confiscation order, which the court is not obliged to make. The other case concerns the forfeiture which operates when homicide would bring a benefit to the killer.[575] This forfeiture is now subject to the discretion of the court.[576] Here, though the cases still leave open more than one analysis of what actually happens, it is clear that the wrong does vary the devolution of proprietary rights. However, in that case it is not the victim of the wrong who acquires the right by virtue of that deflection.

(b) Deceit

4.408 The only wrong which might be seen to generate a proprietary right (other than through a trust) is the tort of deceit. The rule is that where a contract of sale is

---

[572] Para 4.294.

[573] Para 4.297.

[574] Criminal Justice Act 1988, s 71; Drug Trafficking Act 1994, s 2; Proceeds of Crime Act 1995; G Jones, 'Stripping a Criminal of the Profits of a Crime' (2000) 1 Theoretical Inquiries in Law 59, 69–78.

[575] *Re Crippen* [1911] P 108; *Gray v Barr* [1971] 2 QB 554; *Re K deceased* [1986] Fam 180, CA, affirming [1985] Ch 85.

[576] Forfeiture Act 1982; *Dunbar v Plant* [1998] Ch 412, CA.

fraudulently induced and the vendor's title to the goods has passed to the fraudulent purchaser, the former has a right to rescind the contract of sale and thereby revest title.[577] An example is provided by *Car & Universal Finance Co Ltd v Caldwell*.[578] Caldwell advertized title to his Jaguar car for sale in a local paper. One evening, he was visited by two men, one of whom called himself Norris, who persuaded Caldwell to part with his title in exchange for a cheque and the possession of a car of lesser value as security. When he tried to cash the cheque the next morning, it was dishonoured. The bank advised Caldwell to go to the police, who told him that there was a warrant out for Norris in the name of Rowley. It was then discovered that the car left as security was stolen. Caldwell told the police to find his car and get it back, and said the same to the Automobile Association. Norris later sold the car to Motobella Ltd, who sold it to G & C Finance Ltd, who sold it to a dealer, who sold it to Car & Universal Finance, which bought it in good faith and for value. In interpleader proceedings, the question for Lord Denning MR, sitting at first instance, and the Court of Appeal was whether Caldwell's act of informing the police and the Automobile Association of his intention to rescind the contract of sale had the effect of revesting title in him. Both held that it did. This meant, said Lord Denning, that:

> . . . the contract of sale to these rogues was avoided and Caldwell then became the owner of the car again. It was only after he avoided it (so that it was once again his property), that these rogues purported to sell it to Motobella and Motobella purported to sell it to G & C Finance. Those sales were ineffective to pass the property because it had already re-vested in Caldwell.[579]

4.409 This right to rescind the contract of sale and revest title is undoubtedly a property right. In *Re Eastgate, ex p Ward*,[580] a debtor fraudulently induced a tradesman to sell him title to furniture on credit. The debtor then committed an act of bankruptcy by absconding, leaving behind the furniture in a rented house. Five days later, and with the consent of the landlord, the tradesman broke in and repossessed the furniture. The debtor was then made bankrupt, the bankruptcy, via the doctrine of relation back, dating back to the date on which he absconded. The trustee in bankruptcy sued the tradesman in conversion, arguing that the exercise of the right of rescission (by the retaking of the goods) was invalid because it had been lost on the commission by the debtor of the act of bankruptcy. Bingham J held that the right to rescind the contract of sale and revest title was exigible not

---

[577] For a general discussion and critique of this right, see WJ Swadling, 'Rescission, Property, and the Common Law' (2005) 121 LQR 123.

[578] [1965] 1 QB 525.

[579] ibid 532. The impact of this decision was almost immediately reversed by *Newtons of Wembley Ltd v Williams* [1965] 1 QB 560.

[580] [1905] 1 KB 465.

only against the debtor but also against his trustee in bankruptcy, with the result that the tradesman had not committed conversion:

> . . . the trustee acquired the interest of the bankrupt in the property subject to the rights of third parties. One of those rights in this case was the right of the vendors of the goods to disaffirm the contract and to retake possession of the goods. I cannot say that I approve of the way in which possession was retaken in this case. But in my opinion [the tradesman] was only taking, though taking in a wrong way, that which was his own. That being so, I think the application of the trustee must be dismissed.[581]

4.410 A similar result obtained in *Tilley v Bowman Ltd*,[582] where a sale of jewellery on credit was induced by fraud. Immediately after delivery, the fraudulent purchaser pledged the goods. He was then declared bankrupt. The defrauded vendor redeemed the pledge and retook possession of the goods. A claim in detinue by the purchaser's trustee in bankruptcy was rejected.

4.411 One unanswered question is whether the same response would be triggered by other fraudulently induced transfers of title. Say, for example, A were to fraudulently represent to B that he owed A £100 in taxes which B paid in cash, or that A were to fraudulently represent to B that he was collecting for charity and that B similarly gave him £100 in cash. On discovering the fraud, would B also have the ability to rescind and revest title? The obvious problem is that there is now no contract to set aside, and the revesting of title described above seems to be the consequence of the rescission of the contract of sale. It is therefore doubtful that any title would return to B in such circumstances.

4.412 It should finally be noted that the right here described is not unequivocally a response to wrongdoing. Since a fraudulently induced transfer will also be a mistaken transfer, it may be that the right arises as a response to unjust enrichment.

(3) Unjust Enrichment

4.413 Just as with wrongdoing, property rights may possibly arise in response to unjust enrichments. This subject is exhaustively treated elsewhere in this work,[583] and so is only touched on here. And as with wrongdoing, one candidate would seem to be the right to rescind a fraudulently induced contract of sale and thereby revest

---

[581] ibid 467. Certain remarks of Lord Mustill, delivering the advice of the Privy Council in *Re Goldcorp* [1995] 1 AC 74, 103, might be seen as throwing doubt on the decision in *Re Eastgate*. However, *Re Eastgate* was there being put forward as authority for the proposition that *any* misrepresentation, fraudulent, negligent, or innocent, gave rise to a right to rescind and revest title. As Lord Mustill rightly said, this was not what *Re Eastgate* decided, and it was only if he was incorrect in that did he think that *Re Eastgate* could not stand.

[582] [1910] 1 KB 745.

[583] Paras 18.173–18.220.

the rights transferred pursuant to it, for, as we saw, it is not clear whether the event triggering this response is wrongdoing or unjust enrichment.[584] There are, however, others which are unequivocally located within this category. Thus, it has been held that one response to the unjust factor of undue influence is the giving to the claimant of a right to rescind any transfer made by them, the exercise of which will turn the recipient into a constructive trustee of the rights transferred.[585] The same is also said to be true, outside the context of the sale of goods, of rights obtained by fraud.[586] Whether other unjust factors such as duress, negligent misrepresentation and innocent misrepresentations generate property rights is less clear.

(4) Other Events

(a) Taking possession

The mere act of taking possession bestows a right to exclusive possession, **4.414** a title good against the whole world save a person with a better title. This is true of all things capable of being physically possessed, viz land and goods. In the leading case of *Armory v Delamirie*[587] a chimney-sweep's boy acquired a right to exclusive possession of a brooch merely by the act of taking possession of it. Pratt CJ said:

> [T]he finder of a jewel, though he does not by such finding acquire an absolute property or ownership, yet he has such a property as will enable him to keep it against all but the rightful owner and consequently may maintain trover.

The words 'against all but the rightful owner' are not perfectly accurate. As **4.415** between the goldsmith who refused to return the brooch and the boy, the boy had the better right to possession, because he had the earlier factual possession. As between the boy and the title-holder of the house where it was found, it is likely that the latter would have had the better title, not because he was 'the rightful owner', but because his possession of his house included possession of the brooch in the chimney and antedated the possession obtained by the boy.

Asher v Whitlock[588] teaches the same lesson in relation to land. The mere act of **4.416** taking possession of a parcel of land gives the actor a right to exclusive possession of that land good against all save those with a superior right to possession.

---

[584] See para 4.412.

[585] *Mitchell v Homfray* (1881) 8 QBD 857, CA; *Allcard v Skinner* (1887) 36 Ch D 145, 186–7 (Lindley LJ), 189–93 (Bowen LJ); Cotton LJ, at 172, held that there was instead an immediate trust.

[586] *Bristol & West BS v Mothew* [1998] 1 Ch 1, CA, 22–23 (Millett LJ).

[587] (1772) Strange 505, 93 ER 664.

[588] (1865) LR 1 QB 1, 6.

4.417 It should be stressed that the interest acquired by the possessor in a case such as *Armory v Delamirie* or *Asher v Whitlock* is legal and not equitable, for both cases involved successful actions in common law courts.

4.418 Finally, we should note that the statement sometimes made that the fact of possession gives rise to a 'presumption' of 'ownership' is a misnomer. Presumptions properly-so-called are methods of proof of facts, and no fact is here in issue, merely a legal inference from facts proved by evidence. Moreover, this 'presumption' cannot be rebutted by adducing evidence showing, as was the case in both *Armory v Delamirie* and *Asher v Whitlock*, that the claimant is not the 'owner'. The 'presumption' is irrebuttable, and an irrebuttable presumption, such as that which provides that a child under the age of 10 cannot commit a crime, is nothing but a rule of substantive law. And the rule of substantive law here is that the mere fact of possession of a physical thing gives its possessor a right at common law to the exclusive possession of that thing against all save those with better rights to exclusive possession.

4.419 The law is, therefore, that a dispute between two claimants as to who has the better right to possession will be resolved in favour of the person whose possession is earlier in time. In cases such as *Armory v Delamirie* or *Asher v Whitlock* this is a relatively straightforward enquiry. It becomes more difficult when the dispute is between a finder of a chattel and a person with a right to exclusive possession of the land on which it was found. As we noticed, if the dispute in *Armory v Delamirie* had been between the chimney-sweep's boy and the person in possession of the house then that person might have claimed that when the jewel was discovered by the boy he was already in possession of the jewel by virtue of his possession of the land. In practice the finder will often lose out to the those with titles to the land on which the thing is found.

4.420 The cases are not easy to reconcile. The dominant position now seems to be that for articles found *in* the land, the better claim is that of the possessor of the land,[589] though for things found *on* the land, the finder has the better claim unless the possessor of the land has manifested an intention to control things found on it.[590] However, no satisfactory explanation is advanced in the case law for this difference of treatment. Often, to get to a thing which is in the land, a finder would have to start digging on the land, which would probably amount to an act of trespass. There are doubtful dicta to the effect that a trespassing finder will be disqualified

---

[589] *Parker v British Airways Board* [1982] QB 1004, CA; *Waverley Borough Council v Fletcher* [1995] QB 344, CA.

[590] ibid *Webb v Ireland and A-G* [1988] IR 353, Supreme Court of Ireland. Compare the position on wrongful mixtures taken by Staughton J in *Indian Oil Corp Ltd v Greenstone Shipping SA Panama (The Ypatianna)* [1988] QB 345, para 4.434.

from all claims.[591] But, given that the object is *ex hypothesi* not already in the possession of the occupier of the land, it is difficult to see why the fact that the finder was a trespasser should destroy the validity of his claim. And in any case, not everyone who digs is a trespasser, as where a workman or gardener digs and finds.

(b) Treasure trove

Special rules apply to articles which qualify as treasure trove, to which the Crown **4.421** will have, by virtue of a prerogative right, a prior right to possession good against all finders. The rules relating to the finding of treasure have recently been reformed by statute. It is still true that treasure trove goes to the Crown. At common law, there were three requirements to be satisfied before an object fell into the category of treasure trove. The first was that it be made of gold or silver. For this reason a hoard of over 7,000 valuable Roman coins made from base metal with only a minimal silver content found on land to which the defendant had a title was not held to be treasure trove.[592] The second was that the object had been concealed by someone who intended to return for it subsequently.[593] So, for example, in *R v Hancock*,[594] a conviction for theft from the Crown in respect of some silver coins found on the site of an ancient temple was quashed because the evidence showed that the coins had probably been buried as a religious offering; there was no evidence that the person burying them ever intended to return for them. The third requirement was that the title to those goods be unknown.

Originally no more than a source of revenue for the Crown, treasure trove became **4.422** in modern times the means by which treasures could be preserved for the nation. The common law proving to be an inadequate means to that end, the law on treasure trove was amended by legislation in 1996.[595] The requirement that the object must have been hidden with a view to being retrieved has been struck out.[596] Objects with only a 10 per cent gold or silver content will be covered. Additionally, a find of over ten coins will be treasure trove, whatever their metal content, provided only that they are more than 300 years old.[597] And so as to encourage the reporting of finds, there are also provisions in the legislation for rewards to be paid to finders.[598]

---

[591] *A-G of the Duchy of Lancaster v Overton Farms* [1982] Ch 277, CA.

[592] *A-G v Trustees of British Museum* [1903] 2 Ch 598.

[593] [1990] 2 QB 242, CA.

[594] Discussed by NE Palmer, 'Treasure Trove and Title to Discovered Antiquities' in N Palmer and E McKendrick (eds), *Interests in Goods* (1993) 305–44.

[595] Treasure Act 1996. C MacMillan (1996) 146 NLJ 1346; J Marston and L Ross, 'Treasure and Portable Antiquities in the 1990s still chained to the Ghosts of the Past: The Treasure Act 1996' [1997] Conv 273.

[596] Treasure Act 1996, s 4(4)(b).

[597] ibid s 1.

[598] ibid s 10.

(c) Wreck

4.423 Modern technology has made this a subject of increasing interest.[599] Wrecks in deep waters can now be found, surveyed, and even raised. There is an obvious commercial interest, and a strong public interest where the wreck or its cargo are of historical interest. As with treasure trove, a prerogative right vests a title to wreck in the Crown. The Crown's entitlement is now laid down by the Merchant Shipping Act 1995, section 241. All wreck brought within the realm has to be reported to the Receiver of Wreck. Since wreck does not destroy the original title-holder's rights, they are then allowed a period of one year to make their claims. The Crown's entitlement bites only on unclaimed wreck. It was held in *The Lusitania*[600] that where the ship sank outside the territorial waters of the United Kingdom but items of wreck were later brought within the realm, the Crown had no prerogative right in respect of unclaimed items. This meant that the salvors had the better possessory title. Though this came as an encouragement to the treasure hunters, it clearly weakened the protection of the public interest.

(d) Bona vacantia

4.424 Another prerogative right of the Crown is that to *bona vacantia* (literally 'vacant goods').[601] The common examples of *bona vacantia* are the estates of persons dying intestate without relatives entitled to succeed, and the rights of dissolved corporations.[602] There has never been a heading in English law to include abandoned things amongst the *bona vacantia* to which the Crown is entitled.[603] Nevertheless, in *Re West Sussex Constabulary Widows, Children and Benevolent Fund*[604] Goff J held that titles to cash given through collection boxes to a trust which subsequently failed had been given with an intention to benefit the trust subject to a secondary intention to abandon it when the trust failed, and that the abandoned contributions fell to the Crown. This was an instrumental finding, designed to avoid the conclusion that the money was held on resulting trust, with the consequence that it would have to be paid into court where it would sit waiting for claims which would never be made. This case is seriously flawed, not least because, even supposing abandonment to be possible, the intent to abandon cannot be found in a vacuum. On similar facts, Harman J had earlier held, quite rightly, that the truth was that the contributors never thought about the event which

---

[599] S Dromgoole and N Gaskell, 'Interests in Wreck' in N Palmer and E McKendrick (eds), *Interests in Goods* (2nd edn, 1998) 141–206.

[600] [1986] QB 384.

[601] ND Ing, *Bona Vacantia* (2nd edn, 1977); A Bell, 'Bona Vacantia' in NE Palmer and E McKendrick, *Interests in Goods* (2nd edn, 1998) 207–26.

[602] Ing (ibid), 113–34.

[603] Differently from Scotland: DL Carey-Miller, *Corporeal Moveables in Scots Law* (1991) 18–20.

[604] [1971] Ch 1.

happened, ie, the failure of the trust, and that there was consequently no reason why a resulting trust should not arise.[605]

(e) New things

New things come into being naturally or by manufacture or by mixture. The latter two cases also involve the destruction of rights to the things used in the manufacturing process or which contributed to the mixture.[606]   **4.425**

(i) Natural reproduction

The young of animals generally fall into the same proprietary condition as their mother: *partus sequitur ventrem*.[607] It follows that a farmer having title to a cow, Buttercup, will also be given title to her calf. The same applies to wool shorn from sheep, or milk taken from a cow. However, where livestock are included in a lease of land or are themselves 'leased' in the sense of being subject to a contract of hire, the lessee/hirer is entitled to the natural increase, not just for the duration of the lease, but forever.[608] Before severance, crops are part of the land and have no separate identity. On severance, a title to them is created in the person with a right to exclusive possession of the land. However, where the land is subject to a limited interest, for example, a lease, those crops which are required to be sown, called 'emblements' (from French '*embler*', to sow), are subject to a special regime designed to reward the labour of the sower. They may be taken by the tenant or his personal representatives, even if still uncut at the termination of the limited interest. Thus the tenant or his representative could take corn still standing after his interest ended, but not apples.   **4.426**

(ii) Manufacture

What happens if you carve a statue out of a block of marble to which I have a better right to possession? Does a right to exclusive possession of the statue vest in me or in you? This is more difficult, because in a certain sense the old thing, the raw material, lives on in the new. There is a competition, therefore, between the titles of the person with the better title to the materials and the manufacturer of the new thing. *Specificatio*[609] is the Roman term. It was the subject of a famous and long-lasting dispute between the two schools of jurists, settled in the   **4.427**

---

[605] *Re Gillingham Bus Disaster Fund* [1958] Ch 300, 314, affirmed [1959] Ch 62, CA.

[606] For the joining of one thing to another (accession), see paras 4.464–4.468.

[607] Blackstone, 2 *Commentaries* 390–1. He notes an exception in the case of cygnets, which in the case in which cob and hen are held by different people are divided between the owners—a rare case, since white swans in open water belong to the Crown.

[608] *Tucker v Farm and General Investment Trust Ltd* [1966] 2 QB 421, CA, where sheep were held on hire purchase and the hirer was entitled to sell the lambs.

[609] From '*novam speciem facere*' (to make a new form).

sixth century by Justinian's middle way. This accorded 'ownership' (a concept used in Roman Law) to the maker, unless the new thing could be reduced to its original materials. The fact that the maker may have been a wrongdoer was considered irrelevant to the question of property, although not to a personal claim for damages for the wrong.

4.428 Bracton[610] and Blackstone[611] give a better right to possession to the maker in English law, and that position is supported in the cases.[612] The matter is not free from controversy. It has been argued that the common law rule is that so long as the substance remains identifiable as the claimant's, the defendant by working on them acquires no better right to them.[613] In most cases the contributor of the materials will anyhow be entitled to a claim for conversion of the materials or for the unjust enrichment of the maker.

(iii) Mixtures[614]

4.429 What happens to property rights when grain to which I have a title is mixed with grain to which you have a title, or wine to which I have a title with wine to which you have a title? There are three possible solutions. The first is that nothing happens: we simply hold the same rights after the mixture as before. But if the contributors' property rights change, then there are two realistic possibilities. First, they might become co-owners of a title to the mass. Alternatively, one alone might acquire a title to the mass.

4.430 **Consensual mixing.** Where the mixing is done on a consensual basis, then the intention of the parties will govern the proprietary consequences,[615] though that intention may be difficult to ascertain.[616] In general the inference will be that they intended co-ownership of a title to the mass, more specifically, a tenancy in common in proportion to their contributions.

4.431 **Non-consensual mixing.** Where the mixing was non-consensual, Roman law distinguished between situations in which there was merely a loss of identifiability (*commixtio*), as with a mixing of sheep, and that where there was not only a loss of identifiability but a loss of physical integrity (*confusio*), such as a mixing of wines. In the former case, the solution of co-ownership of the mass was rejected. So long

---

610 SE Thorne (ed), *Bracton on the Laws and Customs of England, vol II* (1968) 47.

611 Blackstone, 2 *Commentaries* 404.

612 *Re Peachdart* [1984] Ch 131; *Borden (UK) Ltd v Scottish Timber Products Ltd* [1981] Ch 25, CA; cf JH Baker and SFC Milsom, *Sources of English Legal History to 1750* (1986) 533.

613 P Matthews, '*Specificatio* in the Common Law' (1981) 10 Anglo-American LR 121.

614 P Birks, 'Mixtures' in NE Palmer and E McKendrick, *Interests in Goods* (2nd edn, 1998), 227–49.

615 *Barlow Clowes International v Vaughan* [1992] 4 All ER 22, CA; *Re Stapylton Fletcher* [1994] 1 WLR 1181.

616 *Coleman v Harvey* [1989] 1 NZLR 723, NZCA.

as the constituent units retained their physical integrity, ownership remained unaltered. There was, in other words, a situation of 'continuing separate ownership'. But where there was a loss of physical integrity (*confusio*), it was no longer possible to talk of ownership of anything other than the mass itself. Thus the parties were treated as co-owners of the mass.[617]

The position in English law is not so easy to state. One difficulty arises because the English cases often fail to distinguish between fluid and granular mixtures. Instead, they draw a line between wrongdoers and innocent parties. Where there is no wrongdoing by either of the parties, as, for example, where the mixing takes place through the act of a third hand, then the contributors are treated as having a co-owned title to the mass. As Lord Moulton said in *Sandeman v Tyzack*: **4.432**

> [I]f the mixing has taken place by accident or other cause, for which neither of the owners is responsible, a different state of things arises. Neither owner has done anything to forfeit his right to possession of his own property, and if neither party is willing to abandon that right the only equitable solution of the difficulty . . . is that A and B become owners in common of the mixed property.[618]

Thus, in *Buckley v Gross*[619] a fire caused tallow belonging to various persons to run together. A third party took it, and defended his conviction for theft by arguing that all other titles to it had been destroyed. Blackburn J said: **4.433**

> The tallow of the different owners was indeed mixed up into a molten mass, so that it might be difficult to apportion it among them; but I dissent from the doctrine that, because the property of different persons is confused together, that entitles a third party to steal it with impunity. Probably the legal effect of such mixture would be to make the owners tenants in common in equal portions of the mass, but at all events they do not lose their property in it.[620]

But in the case of a wrongful mixture, Lord Moulton said that: **4.434**

> If the mixing has arisen from the fault of B, A can claim the goods. He is guilty of no wrongful act, and therefore the possession by him of his own goods cannot be interfered with, and if by the wrongful act of B that possession necessarily implies the possession of the intruding goods of B, he is entitled to it.[621]

This penal rule, that a wrongdoer forfeits his right to possession, was unknown to Roman law. Although the wrongdoer might be liable in the law of wrongs for any damage he may have caused by his wrongdoing, this did not affect his proprietary rights. The penal rule was consigned to history and a more Roman solution

---

[617] Justinian, *Institutes* 2.1.27, 28.

[618] [1913] AC 680, 695, HL. There is also authority for a continuing separate ownership solution, at least in the case of granular mixtures: *Spence v Union Marine Insurance Co Ltd* (1868) LR 3 CP 427.

[619] (1863) 3 B & S 566, 122 ER 213.

[620] (1863) 3 B & S 566, 574–5, 122 ER 213, 216.

[621] [1913] AC 680, 695, HL.

adopted by Staughton J in *Indian Oil Corpn Ltd v Greenstone Shipping SA (Panama), The Ypatianna*,[622] where it was held that, provided that it could be ascertained how much was contributed by the innocent party, the penal rule had no place. That is, it was really just a rule for resolving an evidential difficulty. Where the contributions were quantifiable, a title to the mixture was held in common, though the innocent party could claim damages from the wrongdoer in respect of any loss he may have suffered in respect of quality or otherwise, by reason of the admixture.

4.435　Thus, the position of English law seems to be that, whether the mixture be innocent or wrongful, or fluid or granular, a co-ownership solution is adopted.[623]

(f) Unauthorized substitutions

4.436　We have already encountered the case of the trustee who, in breach of trust, makes an exchange of rights he holds on trust for other rights. We saw that a trust of the right received in exchange arose in favour of the beneficiary of the trust. A similar thing happens outside the law of trusts. Where someone without my consent exchanges, say, gold plate to which I had a better title than the person making the exchange for a title to a horse, English law gives me the title of the person conveying the title to the person making the exchange, or at least a power to assert that right with regard to the horse. However, the right I have as against the horse cannot rationally be described as the same right as I had in the plate. I have acquired a new right, from a new causative event. Substitution is that event, though often not recognized as such.[624] A mixed substitution will often analyse out as two events: D first mixes some of C's money with some of his own. Next, with the mixed fund, or from it, he buys a title to a cake. There is no very plausible argument that the mixture should be classified as an unjust enrichment, but it is a difficult question whether the second event—substitution without consent—should or should not be regarded as a species of that genus.

(g) Long user (prescription)

4.437　In general, the common law, differently to the civil law, has no doctrine of 'acquisitive prescription', the notion that rights can be acquired by long user.[625]

---

[622] [1988] QB 345.

[623] The rule seems to be different in the case of mixtures of cash: *Jackson v Anderson* (1811) 4 Taunt 24 (the case concerned a mixture of coins, where it was held that one contributor able to sue the other in conversion, an action which would not have been available to him at that time (the rule was changed by s 10 of the Torts (Interference with Goods) Act 1977, s 10) if he and the defendant had been co-owners).

[624] The speeches in *Foskett v McKeown* [2001] 1 AC 102, HL appear to have taken no account of substitution as an event separate from the event from which the right in the first asset arose.

[625] Nor does have it anything equivalent to the idea that rights can be lost through disuse.

The one exception is the case of easements and profits. In certain circumstances, in particular, where the user has been as of right, without force, and without secrecy, long user will generate an easement or profit at common law. The thinking behind this was originally the idea that long user raised a presumption that a grant had been validly made at some point in the past, in accordance with the maxim *omni praesumuntur rite et sollemniter esse acta* (all things are presumed to be correctly and solemnly done), though the idea that there had been a grant soon became a fiction. In general, it is enough nowadays to show a twenty-year user. The topic of prescription is complex, and details must be sought in more specialist works.[626]

G. Transfer of Property Rights

This section considers how property rights, once acquired, can then be transferred **4.438** to others. This may happen in a number of contexts, where they are the subject-matter of a gift,[627] pursuant to a sale,[628] as a transfer on trust, in exchange for other property rights (barter), as a loan for consumption, to meet a liability in tax, as part of a divorce settlement, or even as the subject-matter of a mistaken transfer. As with the creation of property rights, the context in which the transfer is made does not generally affect the rules on how the transfer must be effected. Special rules have, however, been developed in respect of both the sale of goods and testamentary gifts. These are dealt with in the specialist chapters in other parts of this work.[629] We will examine what remains. To do so, we must first distinguish land and goods.

(1) Titles to Land [630]

Originally, titles to land were conveyed purely as a matter between private indi- **4.439** viduals, first by 'feoffment with livery of seisin', a ceremony taking place on the

---

[626] C Harpum (ed), *Megarry & Wade: The Law of Real Property* (6th edn, 2000), 1118–41.

[627] The idea of gift is not peculiar to property rights, for I may make a gift of personal rights, eg, a block of shares, or even of my services, eg, a free hair-cut or free legal advice.

[628] We have, already seen how in certain cases the mere making of a contract to sell turns the vendor into a trustee of the right contracted to be sold: paras 4.32–4.33.

[629] See Chapters 7 (Succession) and 10 (Sale of Goods). Within the context of the carriage of goods by sea, title to goods may be transferred or pledged by a delivery of the bill of lading, which is treated as equivalent to a delivery of the goods themselves: see Chapter 11.

[630] The topic of conveyancing is vast, and the reader is referred to specialist works such as J Farrand, *Contract and Conveyance* (4th edn, 1983); MP Thompson, *Barnsley's Conveyancing Law and Practice* (4th edn, 1996). Shorter accounts can be found in the standard land law textbooks, eg, EH Burn and J Cartwright, *Cheshire & Burn's Modern Law of Real Property* (17th edn, 2006), 853–893; C Harpum (ed), *Megarry & Wade: The Law of Real Property* (6th edn, 2000), 639–726.

land in which the transferor placed a clod of earth into the hands of the transferee, since 1845, by the use of a deed.[631] Since 1925, a deed has to be used, section 52(1) of the Law of Property Act 1925 providing:

> All conveyances of land or of any interest therein are void for the purpose of conveying or creating a legal estate unless made by deed.

4.440 A deed is nothing more than a written document which describes itself as a deed, is signed, and is attested, ie it must be signed in the presence of witnesses and those witnesses must record that fact on the deed. Prior to 1989, a deed needed to be sealed. At common law a signature was not enough, nor even necessary, to signify a person's assent to a document. This could only be done by a person impressing it with his seal. Since 1925, however, a signature has been required by statute, thus rendering the requirement of a seal superfluous. Accordingly, the Law of Property (Miscellaneous Provisions) Act 1989[632] finally removed the requirement of sealing for a valid deed, though adding the new requirement of attestation, something which had never been insisted on at common law. Thus, in the case of land, mere words of transfer will never be enough to pass a title. Nor will it suffice merely to let the grantee into possession. And nor, for that matter, will writing be enough unless that writing takes the form of a deed.

4.441 This is illustrated by the decision of the Court of Appeal in *Richards v Delbridge*.[633] An uncle wished to give his business to his nephew. One asset of the business was a lease of the business premises. On the back of the deed by which the lease had been granted to him, the uncle wrote, 'This deed and all thereto belonging I give to Edward Bennetto Richards from this time forth . . .'. He thereupon handed the deed to the nephew's mother to hold for the nephew. The uncle died, making no specific mention of the lease in his will. The question was whether the lease had passed to the nephew *inter vivos* or whether it now passed under the will as an otherwise undisposed of right to the uncle's residuary legatee. Sir George Jessel MR held that there had been no *inter vivos* conveyance. It was not enough that the uncle both wanted his nephew to have the lease and thought that he had given it to him. Intention, though necessary, is not enough where the law imposes some additional requirement.

4.442 *Richards v Delbridge* concerned an attempted gift of a title to land. Most transfers of title, however, are made pursuant to prior contracts of sale, and a number of special rules apply. The first is that by statute, the Law of Property (Miscellaneous Provisions) Act 1989, such contracts must be made in writing containing all their

---

[631] Real Property Act 1845, s 106. Since 1925, conveyance by deed is the only method allowed.
[632] Section 1.
[633] (1874) LR 18 Eq 11, CA.

terms and bearing the signatures of both parties.[634] If such writing is not executed, there will simply be no contract.[635] As to the content of such contracts, they must contain three elements to be valid: the parties to the contract, the identity of the land and the estate offered in respect of it, and the consideration.

It is common for such contracts to be made according to standard terms, **4.443** including both special conditions, which regulate the details of that particular transaction, such as parties, property, price, the incumbrances to which the title is subject, and so on, and general conditions, those which govern these sorts of transactions generally, such as the payment of deposits, the timetable for the deduction of title, remedies for breach, and so on. Prior to the 'exchange' of contracts, the point at which the contract comes into being, the parties will negotiate under the umbrella of 'subject to contract', the effect of which is to ensure that neither side is inadvertently bound until all details have been agreed. During this period, both parties remain free to withdraw at any time, and it is this fact which can sometimes lead to the unpleasant practice of 'gazumping', where the vendor suddenly insists on a higher price than that agreed, or 'gazundering', where the purchaser insists on a lower one. Once all details have been agreed, the purchaser has satisfied himself as to the physical condition of the property and arranged the necessary finance, then the parties will move to the stage of the exchange of contracts. It is only at this point that they become legally bound to one another. It is then for the vendor to satisfy the purchaser that he has by the date set for completion, the point at which title is conveyed, the title which he purports to sell. How he does so depends on whether the title promised is unregistered or registered. If he fails to do so, then the purchaser is entitled to withdraw from the transaction.

Once there is a valid contract of sale, the vendor, as we have seen,[636] becomes a **4.444** constructive trustee for the purchaser of the title contracted to be sold. This is through an application of the rule that 'equity looks upon that as done which ought to be done'. From that moment on, therefore, the purchaser has an interest which is capable of binding third parties, especially important in the event of the vendor's insolvency. This trust also gives him a claim over the traceable proceeds of sale, as, for example, where the vendor in breach of contract sells the title to a

---

[634] Law of Property (Miscellaneous Provisions) Act 1989, s 2, providing that a 'contract for the sale or other disposition of an interest in land can only be made in writing and only by incorporating all the terms which the parties have expressly agreed in one document or, where contracts are exchanged, in each'. Exceptions are made for contracts for certain short leases, sales by auction, and contracts regulated by the Financial Services and Markets Act 2000 other than a regulated mortgage contract.

[635] In contrast to the position under s 40 of the Law of Property Act 1925, which provided only that such contracts were unenforceable.

[636] See paras 4.32–4.33.

third party.[637] It is, however, a peculiar form of trusteeship,[638] for the vendor will not yet have been paid, and may never be paid. For that reason, he is permitted to occupy the land and take the rents and profits until the day fixed for the conveyance of title (completion).

4.445 However, once the purchase price is paid, the nature of the trust changes, and the vendor will be liable to account for rents and an occupation rent if he stays there himself. Contracts for the sale of land are ones which courts of equity will routinely enforce specifically.[639] Indeed, it is this fact which leads to the constructive trust just mentioned. Thus, where a vendor fails to convey as promised, he can be compelled to do so. If the reason for his failure to convey is that he does not have the title he said he had, then he will be liable to pay damages measured by the purchaser's loss of expectation. If he does have the title but it turns out to be subject to incumbrances not dealt with by the contract, then the purchaser can sue for the difference in value between and encumbered and unencumbered title. Where it is the purchaser who is refusing to complete, even the vendor can obtain specific performance.

(a) Unregistered conveyancing

4.446 As to the conveyance itself, a transferee, especially a transferee for value, will generally only be satisfied with a title which gives him the best right to exclusive possession of the land. A conveyance from one with an inferior title will not be what was wanted. A system of private conveyancing, however, makes it difficult ever to be sure that the title proffered is the best one existing. Purchasers would investigate the title offered by the transferor by examining the deed by which title was conveyed to him, and by examining the deed by which the title was conveyed to his predecessor in title, and so on, but no purchaser could ever be fully certain, even with the operation of the various Limitation Acts from time to time in force,[640] whether the title being transferred was the best possible one. Moreover, the process of investigating the transferor's title every time that title was transferred was a time-consuming, and therefore expensive, because undertaken by professional lawyers, process.

---

[637] *Lake v Bayliss* [1974] 1 WLR 1073.

[638] *Rayner v Preston* (1881) 18 Ch D 1, 6 (Cotton LJ).

[639] Though the position would appear to have changed in Canada, where Sopinka J in the Supreme Court in *Semelhago v Parameadevan* (1996) 136 DLR (4th) 1 thought such an order would not lie where there was nothing unique about the title offered for sale.

[640] Paras 4.470–4.77.

(b) Registered conveyancing

4.447 The solution was the introduction of a state-maintained register of title in 1925,[641] backed up by a system of state insurance. Although the register has been slow to cover the whole country, it is now poised to achieve a complete monopoly, with the whole of the country being since 1ˢᵗ December 1990[642] an area of compulsory registration. But that does not mean that all titles are now registered. Titles become registered either voluntarily or compulsorily. Until recently, compulsory registration only applied in the case of sale, though it now covers most gratuitous dispositions as well. However, in the case of corporations, which of course do not die, there may never even be such a disposition. One incentive which might persuade such bodies to voluntarily register their titles, however, is the more favourable protection the registered system gives against those who dispossess them of land.[643]

4.448 What happens on registration is that the registrar will investigate the title and, in the case of a fee simple title, if satisfied that the title is good, register the applicant with an 'absolute' title. Where he is not fully satisfied, then the title-holder can be registered with a 'qualified' or even a 'possessory' title. In the case of a leasehold title, the title granted may be absolute, good leasehold,[644] or possessory. Once a title is registered, no dealings with it are allowed off the register. Consequently, a transfer of title can only be effected by the Chief Land Registrar altering the centrally-held register in favour of the transferee. This is achieved by the transferor completing a land transfer form asking that the title be transferred, and the registrar complying with that request. Computerized conveyancing will shortly eliminate paper altogether. Although registered conveyancing is now finally taking over, as it did long since in other common law countries, it does not deeply affect the basic principles of the substantive law. It has merely a provided a new and more efficient mode of conveyancing.

(2) Titles to Goods

4.449 Outside sale, titles to goods can be conveyed in one of two ways: deed and delivery.

---

[641] The Land Transfer Act 1897 made title registration compulsory within London. The nation-wide system was introduced by the Land Registration Act 1925, followed by the Land Registration Acts of 1936, 1986, 1997, and 2002.

[642] SI 1989 No 1347.

[643] Para 4.477.

[644] This is where the leaseholder cannot prove the title held by his landlord. As such, it does not affect the enforcement of any estate, right or interest affecting, or in derogation of, the right of the lessor to grant the lease.

(a) Deed

4.450 The requirements of a deed are no different in the case of titles to goods than they are for the conveyance of titles to land.[645] However, if there is a conveyance by deed but no handing over of possession, the transfer will not be binding in the event of the donor's insolvency unless registered as a bill of sale.[646]

(b) Delivery

4.451 Two things are required to perfect a transfer of title by delivery. First, there must be a physical handing over of the thing over which the title subsists to the transferee or some equivalent act. And second, since a physical handing over is an ambiguous act, there must be an intent that the title pass to the deliveree.

(i) The intent to vest the rights in the transferee

4.452 This is never problematic in the case of a deed, but becomes so in the case of delivery here because the mere handing over of a thing is an ambiguous act. The handing over of a book, for example, might be intended as a bailment rather than as a conveyance of a title. The curious case of *Glaister-Carlisle v Glaister-Carlisle*[647] serves to show that a transferor must have an unequivocal intention to transfer his title to the thing. There a husband discovered that a black male poodle to which his wife had a title had mated with a white female poodle to which he had a title. In anger, he threw the female poodle at his wife saying, 'She is your responsibility now.' The husband subsequently left the wife but returned to claim what he said was 'his poodle'. The Court of Appeal held that his words were not sufficiently clear and unequivocal to indicate an intention to transfer his title to the dog.

4.453 The intention must be to make an immediate present transfer of title in respect of the goods. It is not enough that the transferor desired the donee to have the title at some point in the future. This is illustrated by *Re Ridgway*.[648] After the birth of his son Thomas, Colonel Ridgway purchased a title to a quantity of port for Thomas and had the port bottled and laid down in his cellar; from that time on it remained intact in the cellar and was known as 'Thomas's port'. Colonel Ridgway later became bankrupt and the question arose whether the Colonel's title to the port had passed to his son. Cave J held that in order to establish a transfer of this kind, it was necessary to show circumstances from which an intention to make an immediate present transfer could be reasonably inferred. An intention to make a transfer in the future was not enough. Since wine is useless to a child while he

---

645 See paras 4.439–4.440.
646 Bills of Sale Act 1878, s 4(1).
647 (1968) 112 SJ 215, CA.
648 (1885) 15 QBD 447.

remained as such, the circumstances pointed to an intention only to transfer in the future.

(ii) Physical handing over or equivalent

But intention alone will not be enough to pass title. There must also be some **4.454** act of delivery, generally the physical handing over of the thing over which the relevant title exists. The proposition that intention alone is insufficient to transfer a title to goods is illustrated by the decision of the Court of Appeal in *Cochrane v Moore*.[649]

Benzon, who had a title to a racehorse called Kilworth, purported to make an **4.455** immediate present gift of an undivided fourth share of that title to Moore. He did so by notifying Yates, his trainer, who had possession of the animal in Paris, that Moore now had a quarter share. Benzon later mortgaged all his stable to Cochrane who, when Benzon defaulted on the loan, sent the horses to Tattersalls to be sold. Moore claimed an entitlement to one quarter of the proceeds of sale of Kilworth. At first instance, Lopes LJ held that where a gift of a title to a chattel capable of delivery was made *per verba de praesenti* (by words of present gift) to a donee who assents, there is a perfect gift which passes the title without delivery of the thing itself. The Court of Appeal disagreed. There was no effective gift at law because of the absence of any deed or delivery. Moore had argued that delivery served a merely evidentiary function, to show that a gift was intended, and where there was alternative evidence of a gift, it could be dispensed with. Lord Esher MR said that delivery was not merely evidence but essential to the making of the gift, so that, though in this case there was clear evidence of an intention to give, the fact that there was no accompanying delivery meant that the gift was ineffective at law.

In its simplest form, a delivery is a physical handing over of the subject-matter of **4.456** the title from transferor to intended transferee. This will not, however, be necessary where the intended transferee is already in possession of the chattel. Where this is the case it would be futile to insist on any further act of delivery, such as a handing back to the transferor and a return to the intended transferee. Thus, in *Re Stoneham*[650] a testator held a title to a quantity of old furniture, arms and armour, which was kept at one of his two residences. At the testator's request, the claimant and his family lived at the house from 1911 to 1913. In 1913, the testator made a verbal gift of his title to the chattels to the claimant. The testator then died and the question was whether his title to the chattels passed under his will or by virtue of the earlier gift to the claimant. It was argued for those interested under the will, relying on *Cochrane v Moore*,[651] that where there is a parol gift of

---

[649] (1870) 25 QBD 57, CA.
[650] [1919] 1 Ch 149.
[651] (1870) 25 QBD 57, CA.

title to chattels in the possession of the intended donee, the title will not pass until there was some further act of delivery or change of possession. Lawrence J held that *Cochrane v Moore* was not applicable where the subject-matter of a parol gift was already in the possession of the donee. Common sense dictated that it was not necessary for the donee to hand them back to the donor for him then to return them to the donee. The *inter vivos* gift was therefore valid. This exemplifies what the Romans called *traditio brevi manu* (delivery with a short hand).

4.457 It has also been held that there will be a valid transfer where neither the transferor nor the transferee has physical possession but the transferor tells the transferee where the thing is and the transferee subsequently takes physical possession of it. *Thomas v Times Books*[652] concerned the manuscript of Dylan Thomas's 'Under Milk Wood'. He delivered it to a BBC producer called Cleverdon. It was later returned to him but then lost. Thomas was due to fly to America two days later to read from it. He was met at the airport by Cleverdon, who gave him three of the copies which he happened to have made. The grateful Thomas then told Cleverdon that if he could find the original he could keep it and said to him that it might be in any one of half a dozen public houses in Soho or in a taxi. Cleverdon eventually found the manuscript in one of the public houses. Thomas died shortly after arriving in America and his administratrix, his widow, Caitlin, sued the person to whom the producer had sold his title to the manuscript for its return. The success of the action turned on whether there had been a valid *inter vivos* transfer of Thomas's title to the manuscript to Cleverdon. Caitlin Thomas argued that there was not, because there had been no delivery of the subject-matter of the transfer. Plowman J held there to have been an effective transfer. Cleverdon had obtained possession of the manuscript with the consent of Dylan Thomas, from the pub where Dylan Thomas had left it, and that was enough.

4.458 Problems are caused by big things which cannot be literally handed over, in connection with which a question also arises whether it is possible to make a 'symbolic delivery', as, for instance, of a key. In *Rawlinson v Mort*[653] a church needed an organ and one of the churchwardens offered to buy one. He insisted, however, that his title to the organ remain with him and that the thing itself was only on loan. He had the organ erected in the church at his own expense and obtained a confirmatory letter from the vicar that title remained his. The claimant was the church organist. The churchwarden had been so pleased with the claimant's playing that he told him that he should have his title. The claimant accepted, whereupon the warden handed him the vicar's letter and three receipts from the organ builder. Soon afterwards, the claimant was playing the organ at the church

---

[652] [1966] 2 All ER 241.
[653] (1905) 93 LT 555.

and the churchwarden placed his hand on the organ, saying 'I have given this' or 'I give this' to the claimant. Both before and after, the claimant, as organist, had control and use of the organ and held the key. Later, after the claimant ceased to be organist, a dispute arose whether the claimant had the right to remove the organ. The vicar argued that there had been no effective transfer of title. Bray J said that title to the organ had passed to the claimant who was therefore entitled to remove it. He held that the transfer was effected in one of two ways. First, in the case of a chattel which was too bulky to hand over physically, it was possible for delivery to be symbolic. This symbolic delivery was effected by the handing over to the claimant of the vicar's letter and the builder's receipts. Second, even if this was not enough to effect the transfer, it happened when the warden put his hand on the organ and spoke words of gift. In the case of a chattel where manual delivery is impossible, such an act was equivalent to delivery.

This case should, however, be treated with caution with respect to the concept of 'symbolic delivery'. Although there are no decisions on the subject, it would seem to be the case that delivery of, for example, a photograph of an object is not a delivery of the object itself. And delivery of a key probably does not work as symbolic delivery either, though it may do so if the key is in fact the means to possession, as, for example, in the case of a car. *Rawlinson v Mort* is therefore better viewed as a case of actual rather than symbolic delivery, either because the organist did have the key and hence the means of access and control or because of the churchwarden's *traditio longa manu* (delivery with a 'long hand'), which happened when he put his hands on the object and uttered words of gift. Similarly, in *Lock v Heath*[654] a husband successfully gave his wife his title to the furniture in their house by handing over one chair. **4.459**

A severe illustration going the other way is *Re Cole*,[655] where a husband and wife entered their new home and he covered her eyes. Then, removing his hands, he took her round the house and said, 'It's all yours!' When he later became bankrupt, it was held that he had not complied with the requirement of a transfer of title. The gift remained unexecuted: there had been no conveyance. It is fairly clear from the case that had he done something 'symbolic' to make it obvious that he intended a transfer of title to her, as in *Lock v Heath*, title would have passed. **4.460**

(3) Disclaimer of Rights

The transferor's intent to transfer, even when acted upon in accordance with the law's requirements in relation to the particular subject-matter, will not suffice **4.461**

---

[654] (1892) 8 TLR 295.
[655] [1964] Ch 174, CA.

unless the transferee also consents to receive. Rights cannot be forced on unwilling transferees. The transferee's assent will, however, be 'presumed'[656] in the absence of a disclaimer, but the transferee must know of the intended transfer before the right to disclaim can be lost. If the title has passed to him on the basis of 'presumed' assent, an effective disclaimer will then divest him of that right.[657]

H. Extinction of Property Rights

4.462 Much of the law of property is concerned with the acquisition of property rights. An issue usually neglected is their extinction. The most obvious case of extinction is the total destruction of the *res* in question, as where a painting goes up in flames. But there are others: where the right is destroyed by lapse of time; satisfaction of a judgment in conversion; where an inferior title to the subject matter of the right is sold to a good faith purchaser; where titles in respect of which incumbrances exist are sold to third parties; the statutory power to apply for the discharge of outdated restrictive covenants; where, in the case of easements and restrictive covenants, titles to both dominant and servient tenements come into the hands of the same person; and, though this is a doubtful case in English law, abandonment. There are also a number of methods of extinction peculiar to leases of land.

(1) Destruction of the Subject-Matter of the Right

4.463 Destruction of the subject-matter of the right can happen in a number of ways. Although the most obvious is the painting which goes up in flames, others are where the subject-matter is mixed with other physical objects, such as wine with wine, where it is used in some manufacturing process, such as wool turned into a suit, or where it is joined to another physical object, such as a handle affixed to a cup or bricks to land. We have already examined the proprietary effect of mixtures and manufacture,[658] which share the distinction of being events both destructive and creative of rights. There is no need to repeat that examination here. What will be examined is accession, the joining of one physical thing to another.

---

[656] It is not clear that this is a presumption properly-so-called, for it does not seem to be rebutted by proof by evidence that the transferor knew nothing of the transfer.

[657] See, in the context of gifts, *Townson v Tickell* (1819) 3 B & A 31, 38, 106 ER 575, 577; *Hill v Wilson* (1873) LR 8 Ch App 888; *Standing v Bowring* (1886) 31 Ch D 282, CA; N Crago, 'Principles of Disclaimer of Gifts' (1999) 28 UWALR 65; J Hill, 'The Role of the Donee's Consent in the Law of Gift' (2001) 117 LQR 127. It is difficult to see how a disclaimer could work in the case of a registered title to land which has been transferred by the registrar. However, in such cases the transfer will only be effected by the Registrar if both titleholder and transferee have signed the form of transfer. It thus seems in such circumstances that there is no room for a disclaimer to operate.

[658] See 4.427–4.435.

The consequences of accession are that the accessory loses its identity as a separate **4.464**
thing and falls into the proprietary status of that to which it accedes. I mend my
jersey with your wool. The wool accedes to the jersey and is now subject to the
rights to which the jersey is subject. Your rights are destroyed. It is not a question
of me acquiring rights which I did not have before.

A simple case is that of attachments of chattels to land. Suppose bricks to which **4.465**
A has a title are used to build a house on land to which B has a title. The rule is that
if a chattel is annexed to the realty then any title to the chattel itself is extinguished:
the chattel simply becomes part of the realty. In *Hobson v Gorringe*[659] Hobson
hired out a gas engine to the holder of a title to land under a hire purchase
agreement, the agreement providing that no property rights in the engine were
to pass to the hirer until all hire payments were made. To enable it to be used, the
engine had to be affixed to the land by bolts and screws to prevent it from rocking.
The holder of the title to the land later mortgaged that title to Gorringe. When
he defaulted on the mortgage repayments, Gorringe, exercising his rights as
mortgagee, took possession of the land. Hobson sought unsuccessfully to restrain
Gorringe from selling the engine. The Court of Appeal held that despite the words
of the agreement, the engine had become part of the land by virtue of its annexation to it, so that when title to the land was assigned to Gorringe by way of mortgage the engine passed as part of that land.

But when will a chattel be considered annexed to land? The test laid by **4.466**
Blackburn J in *Holland v Hodgson*[660] is that it is a question of fact which depends
on the circumstances of each case, and mainly on two circumstances, as indicating
the intention of the annexor, namely the degree of annexation and the object of
annexation. As a general rule, said Blackburn J:

> [A]rticles not otherwise attached to the land than by their own weight are not to be
> considered as part of the land, unless the circumstances are such as to shew that they
> were intended to be part of the land . . . [but] an article which is affixed to the land
> even slightly is to be considered as part of the land, unless the circumstances are such
> as to shew that it was intended all along to continue a chattel . . .[661]

Blackburn J then went on to suggest that the degree of attachment set up a 'presumption' which could be rebutted by evidence of contrary intent, so that, if the
thing sat on the land by its own weight only, evidence would be needed to show
that it was intended to be a permanent part of the land. The same stones which
would not accede to the land piled in a builder's yard would accede when used to

---

[659] [1897] 1 Ch 182, CA.
[660] (1872) LR 7 CP 328.
[661] ibid 335. Cf AH Hudson, 'Historic Buildings, Listing and Fixtures' (1997) 2 Art, Antiquity
and Law 179–83, discussing a bas relief by Eric Gill made for an *art nouveau* hotel but not difficult
to remove without damage to the building.

make a dry-stone wall. Blackburn J's reasoning was applied in the case of *Elitestone Ltd v Morris*,[662] where a bungalow stood by its own weight on land. Since the bungalow could only be moved by destroying it (unlike a caravan), the House of Lords held it to be a fixture, even though not physically attached.

4.467 What of accessions to chattels? Differently to land, it is not always easy to say which is the major and which the minor component. In *McKeown v Cavalier Yachts*,[663] a yacht hull left in a boatyard title to which had been acquired by the defendants was bit by bit built up into a yacht. The hull itself was worth very little. The materials added to it cost some twelve times as much. Did the hull accede to the materials or the materials to the hull? The materials acceded to the hull, so that the whole belonged to the plaintiff, the holder of a better title to the hull. This shows that value is not decisive. What gave the yacht its identity as such? The hull. It might have been different if the defendants had constructed the deck and superstructure as a unit and had then attached that whole unit to the hull. Compare a car built on a chassis and the body then brought down upon it. The completed chassis would not then accede to the shape-defining body. Note that there is an important question whether the party in the position of the defendant in this case has any claim against the other in respect of the enrichment which the accession brings him.

4.468 It is common for these problems to arise in relation to motor vehicles and other machines, especially in the context of hire purchase, where the hirer retains his title.[664] Suppose the better title to the car is held by X, and Y replaces parts or adds extras, for instance, new tyres or a new engine. An Australian case, *Rendell v Associated Finance Pty Ltd*,[665] proposed a straightforward test:

> The accessories continue to belong to their owner unless it is shown that as a matter of practicality they cannot be identified or, if identified, they have been incorporated to such an extent that they cannot be detached from the vehicle.[666]

This test was applied in New Zealand in *Thomas v Robinson*,[667] which concluded that an engine and carburettor did not accede to the car in which they had been fitted. This last case contains a review of different ways in which the problem has been approached.

---

662 [1997] 1 WLR 687.
663 (1988) 13 NSWLR 303.
664 A Guest, 'Accession and Confusion in the Law of Hire Purchase' (1964) 27 MLR 505.
665 [1957] VR 604.
666 ibid 610.
667 [1977] 1 NZLR 385.

(2) *Lapse of Time* [668]

English law has no doctrine of disuse, no notion that rights are lost if not exercised **4.469** for long periods of time. Lapse of time per se will never destroy a property right. But what English law does have are rules which lay down time limits within which remedies for interferences with rights must be brought. This is not peculiar to the law of property rights. Remedies in respect of personal rights will also be lost if not sought in time. [669] But while my right to physical integrity will not be lost altogether simply because I fail to sue a defendant who punches me on the nose within the relevant period of limitation, it is different with property rights. In certain cases, failure to defend infringements in court will lead to a destruction of the right. To see how property rights might be destroyed in this way, we need to deal separately with the position at common law and that obtaining in equity.

(a) Common law

The basic position taken by the common law is that there is no rule which says **4.470** that I must bring claims to assert my property rights within a certain time. If, for example, you dispossess me of my land, I, or more likely my successors in title, could at common law bring a claim against you to recover possession 100 years later without any objection from the court. But for a number reasons, [670] most importantly the unreliability of witness evidence about incidents taking place many years ago, the legislature has intervened to lay down in statutes of limitation time-limits within which actions must be brought.

It is important to note that the right is not destroyed in every case. The only **4.471** situations in which a property right will be destroyed by not taking court action before a certain time period are those in which the interference amounts to a dispossession of the right-holder of either land or goods. So, for example, if you run a key down the side of a car to which I have a right to exclusive possession, though I will lose my right to sue you for interfering with my right to exclusive possession if I fail to issue proceedings against you within the relevant limitation period, I do not thereby lose my right to exclusive possession, merely the right to sue you for interfering with it.

As to when I will lose the right to exclusive possession itself, section 15(1) of the **4.472** Limitation Act 1980 provides that actions to recover the possession of land may not be brought after the expiration of twelve years from the date on which the right of action accrued, and section 17 further provides that at the expiration of

---

[668] See generally paras 22.15–22.19.
[669] Discussed in paras 22.17–22.18.
[670] M Dockray, 'Why do we need adverse possession?' [1985] Conv 272.

this period the title of the person dispossessed 'shall be extinguished'.[671] In relation to goods, where, as we have seen, there is no claim as of right to recover possession but where rights to possession are protected through the torts of conversion and trespass, section 2 of the same Act provides a general limitation of six years for actions founded on tort. Section 3 makes specific provision in relation to conversion, with sub-section (2) providing that where the time period for bringing a claim in conversion has expired and the recovery of possession of the goods has not in that period been obtained by the claimant, 'the title of that person to the chattel shall be extinguished'.[672]

4.473 Thus, after the expiration of the statutory period, the possessor's title is strengthened because it will be immune from attack by the prior possessor. But it should be stressed, as its wording makes plain, that the statute here works by extinguishing the prior title, not by vesting it in the dispossessor. The title of the current possessor, though now stronger, is still the same title he acquired through his initial act of taking possession. That there is no 'Parliamentary conveyance' is illustrated by *Tichborne v Weir*.[673]

4.474 The claimant granted an 89-year lease of a house to one Baxter, which contained a term that the lessee was to have responsibility for the repair of the building. Baxter was dispossessed thirty-four years later by one Giraud, who forty years after that, assigned his title to the defendant. The defendant delivered the premises up to the claimant at the end of the 89-year term and was promptly sued for failure to observe the repairing covenant. The claimant argued that the effect of the Limitation Act was to convey Baxter's lease to Giraud and thence to the defendant, and with it the obligation to repair.[674] The Court of Appeal rejected this argument. Lord Esher MR said that the effect of the statute was purely negative, that it did not operate so as to convey the right of the

---

[671] It was at one stage thought that time only began to run at the point when the dispossession became 'adverse', and that there would be no 'adverse' dispossession when the person dispossessed had no present use for the land. This rule, which had no foundation in logic but was based on a seeming desire by courts to protect those who were dispossessed, was rightly rejected by the House of Lords in *Pye (J A) (Oxford) Ltd v Graham* [2002] UKHL 30; [2003] 1 AC 419. It was, however, questionably revived by Nicholas Strauss QC, sitting as a Deputy Judge of the High Court, in *Beaulane Properties Ltd v Palmer* [2005] EWHC 1071 (Civ); [2006] Ch 79, so as to reconcile the application of s 17 of the Limitation Act 1980 with the Human Rights Act 1998. However, in *Pye (J A) (Oxford) Ltd v United Kingdom The Times*, October 1 2007, the Grand Chamber of the European Court of Human Rights subsequently held that there was no infringement of the claimant's human rights.

[672] Special provisions apply in the case of theft, such that there is no time-limit in respect of the conversion which is the theft itself or any conversion which falls within the statutory definition of a conversion which is related to the theft: Limitation Act 1980, s 4.

[673] (1892) 67 LT 735, CA.

[674] Had there been a series of assignments from Baxter to Giraud and from Giraud to the defendant, the burden of this covenant would indeed have run with the lease under the doctrine in *Spencer's Case* (1583) 5 Co Rep 16a, 77 ER 72: paras 4.63–4.75.

dispossessed person to the dispossessor, but instead extinguished and destroyed the earlier right, leaving the right of possession gained by the dispossessor now inviolate.

(b) Equity

Claims in respect of the infringement of rights are also barred in equity, and here, **4.475** differently to the position at common law, the effect of barring the remedy seems always to destroy the underlying right. To bar stale claims, equity relied on the doctrines of acquiescence and laches (pronounced 'laitches'). One who knowingly acquiesces in the infringement of his right will be barred from asserting it. Laches, by contrast, will bar a claim if the claimant has been guilty of such delay as to prejudice the other to a degree that that claim ought in justice to be disallowed. The balance has to be struck by the judge.[675] Even where no statutory period has been laid down there is now a marked tendency very readily to apply to equitable causes of action the common law periods by analogy.[676] For this approach to apply, however, it must be the case that the relief sought in equity is essentially the same as that now barred at common. Where it is different, any analogy will be inappropriate.[677]

(c) Registered land

We need finally to note that there are special rules which apply where the title of **4.476** the person dispossessed was one registered in the land registry. The fact that titles can be acquired by the mere taking possession presents a problem for any system of registration of title, for they potentially lead to titles not recorded on the register. One solution would be to abolish altogether the notion of titles arising by possession, but this would be to radically alter the fundamental structure of English land law, and was accordingly not a strategy adopted when the registration of title system was introduced in 1925. The question then was what to do about the operation of statutes of limitation. The decision was taken to make no fundamental alteration in this regard either. Indeed, section 75(1) of the Land Registration Act 1925 laid down the general principle that the Limitation Acts should apply to registered land 'in the same manner and to the same extent' as they did to unregistered land. However, some changes were inevitable. In outline, they were as follows. Where title was registered, the Limitation Acts would not

---

675 *Nelson v Rye* [1996] 2 All ER 186.
676 *Paragon Finance plc v DB Thakerar & Co* [1999] 1 All ER 400, CA; *Coulthard v Disco Mix Club Ltd* [2000] 1 WLR 707.
677 *P & O Nedlloyd BV v Arab Metals Co* [2006] EWCA Civ 1717 (claim for specific performance of a contract as opposed to damages for breach).

cause the extinction of the title of the person dispossessed at the expiry of the relevant period of limitation; that would cause the register to tell a lie. Instead, by section 75(1) of the Land Registration Act 1925, that title would henceforth be held by the dispossessed proprietor on a statutorily imposed trust for the dispossessor. The dispossessor could then apply to the registrar to be registered as proprietor of the estate held for him on trust, in effect exercising his rights under *Saunders v Vautier*,[678] and must have been so registered if the registrar was satisfied of his claim.[679] And in the meantime, the interest of the dipossessor as beneficiary under the trust would be an 'overriding interest', one which, as we shall see,[680] was binding on any person to whom the dispossessed proprietor's title was transferred.[681]

4.477 That regime was radically overhauled by the Land Registration Act 2002. Taking the view that the main purpose of the extinction of title brought about by the Limitation Act 1980 was the facilitation of conveyancing where title to land was unregistered, such provision had no place in registered conveyancing, where transactional security was instead provided by the register. There was no justification, it was thought, for registered title-holders to be deprived of their estates without at least some warning. Accordingly, section 96 of the 2002 Act provides that no period of limitation under section 15 of the Limitation Act 1980 will run against a registered proprietor, and that section 17 will not have the effect of extinguishing any title. Instead, the dispossesor is given a right to apply for registration of the dispossessed's title after 10 years' dispossession. The registrar will then give to the registered proprietor notice of such application. The registered proprietor may then consent to the application, or oppose it by serving a counter-notice. Except in limited circumstances, this will mean that the dispossessor's application will be dismissed. The dispossessor, however, is then given another opportunity to apply for registration. He may make a further application if he is in adverse possession from the date of application for a period of a further two years and the registered proprietor has not commenced proceedings against him to recover possession. In such circumstances, he will be entitled to be registered as proprietor of the relevant estate.

---

[678] (1841) 4 Beav 115, paras 4.349–4.350.

[679] This would indeed seem exceptionally to be a 'Parliamentary conveyance': *Central London Commercial Estates Ltd v Kato Kagaku Ltd* [1998] 4 All ER 948.

[680] Paras 4.496–4.499.

[681] This scheme was held not to violate the claimant's human rights in *Pye (JA) (Oxford) Ltd v United Kingdom, The Times*, October 1 2007, Grand Chamber of the European Court of Human Rights.

(3) Satisfaction of Judgment in Conversion

The measure of damages in a claim for conversion of goods which will awarded **4.478** by the courts is the value of the best title to those goods in the market.[682] Once judgment is satisfied, section 5 of the Torts (Interference with Goods) Act 1977 provides that the claimant's title to the goods will be extinguished. It is important to note that this is indeed an extinguishment of title, not, as is sometimes claimed, a transfer, an acquisition of rights. Although the defendant will now have a title good against the claimant, it is not because of the passing of any title from claimant to defendant, but because the claimant no longer has a title better than the defendant. Consistently with the law on limitation, there is once again no 'Parliamentary conveyance'.

(4) Inferior Title Sold to Good Faith Purchaser for Value

We have seen how a title to land or goods can be obtained by the mere act of taking **4.479** possession.[683] Suppose that title is then conveyed to a third party. What effect will that have on persons higher up the title chain, persons with titles superior to that of the vendor? Are their titles destroyed by the transfer of the inferior one?

(a) The general rule

The general rule is that they are not. This is always the case with titles to land, both **4.480** registered and unregistered. It is also the dominant rule with regard to titles to chattels. We encountered this earlier in *Farquharson Bros & Co v King & Co*,[684] the case of the clerk who made unauthorized sales of timber to which his employer had a superior title, in which the purchasers from the clerk, though completely innocent and giving value to the clerk, were nevertheless liable to the clerk's employer in conversion. As Lord Halsbury LC explained, the act of the clerk had not changed the employer's 'property' in the goods.[685]

(b) Exceptions

However, to this general rule, certain exceptions have developed, all of which **4.481** apply exclusively to those who give value in good faith. But as the *Farquharson* case shows, there is no *general* exception for such persons. In those situations in which an exception is made,[686] the event of good faith purchase for value of an inferior

---

[682] See paras 17.330–17.331.
[683] See para 4.06.
[684] [1902] AC 325, HL.
[685] [1902] AC 325, 329, HL.
[686] For a general account, see WJ Swadling, 'Restitution and Bona Fide Purchase' in WJ Swadling (ed), *The Limits of Restitutionary Claims: A Comparative Analysis* (1997) 603.

title has the effect of destroying a superior one. Such situations are often described as 'exceptions' to the *nemo dat* rule, cases in which an inferior title-holder is said to be able to pass a 'good' title. That description is, however, inaccurate, for the inferior title-holder conveys only what he has—it just so happens that at the same time, the superior title is destroyed. The reason the purchaser then has a 'good' title is not because the holder of the inferior title managed to convey the superior one to him, but because the inferior title, not now being subject to the superior one, is good against the person who formerly held it. In this respect, bona fide purchase is no different to the operation of statutes of limitation and to the satisfaction of a judgment in conversion, for, as we have seen, in both there is no conveyance, merely a strengthening or 'promotion' of pre-existing rights.

4.482　In the ancient doctrine of sale in market overt, there lay the seeds of a general protection of bona fide purchasers. However, those seeds never developed and in the end the doctrine was abolished.[687]

4.483　In the result there is no general doctrine, only a number of specialized concessions to the security of transactions. The most important and the only one approaching generality relates to money in the form of cash. One who takes money in good faith and for value will always defeat someone with a better title. Thus, in *Miller v Race*[688] a stolen banknote was used to pay for hotel accommodation. The hotelier presented the note for payment at a bank, but the bank, realizing that it was stolen, refused both payment or delivery up of the note. The hotelier successfully sued the bank in conversion. The court held that a person taking a banknote bona fide and for value was entitled to retain it against the person from whom it had been stolen. Why was this so? It is often said that the rationale is that money has no 'earmark'. But this is not true. As Best J pointed out in *Wookey v Pole*,[689] even if the superior titleholder had some private mark on his coins, he could not get them back. The true reason for the destructive effect of good faith purchase in the case of money is commercial necessity: 'by the use of money the interchange of all other property is most readily accomplished. To fit it for its purpose the stamp denotes its value, and possession alone[690] must decide to whom it belongs.'[691]

687　Sale of Goods (Amendment) Act 1994. Details in B Davenport and A Ross, 'Market Overt' in NE Palmer & E McKendrick, *Interests in Goods* (2nd edn, 1998), 337–52.

688　(1758) 1 Burr 452, 97 ER 398.

689　(1820) 4 B & Ald 1, 106 ER 839.

690　This is slightly misleading. Possession alone will not suffice to defeat the title of the previous owner. The possessor must have also given value in exchange. A mere donee, for example, will take subject to prior interests.

691　(1820) 4 B & Ald 1, 7, 106 ER 839, 841.

Apart from money, the common law rules on destruction of rights in goods are **4.484**
now embodied in statutes.[692] The two most important are that a seller who remains
in possession of the goods after a sale of his title and who then conveys his inferior
title to an innocent purchaser for value destroys the superior title of his first
purchaser,[693] and that a buyer in possession of the goods with the consent of the
seller but to whom the seller has not yet conveyed his title will likewise destroy his
seller's superior title if he sells his inferior one to an innocent purchaser for value.[694]
It should, however, be noted that the effect of these exceptions to the rule that all
are bound by superior titles is to destroy not all superior titles, but only those of
the sellers or buyers concerned. So, if a car to which A had a title was stolen by B,
and B were to sell his title to C but be allowed by C to remain in possession,
and B were to sell the title he now had to D, though C's title will be destroyed,
A's will not.[695] It is different in the case of money, where good faith purchase seems
to have the effect of destroying all prior titles.

(5) Encumbered Title Sold to Good Faith Purchaser for Value

Suppose now that a title is transferred to a third party, that title being subject to **4.485**
pre-existing encumbrances. To what extent will those encumbrances bind the
transferee? This question is far more complicated than the last, particularly because
of the influence of various systems of registration in the context of land. To understand it, we need to begin with an account of the general position before the
registration systems were introduced, for two reasons. First, the law with relation
to goods is largely still the product of the common law. And second, the statutory
regimes often presuppose the common law as a default position.

(a) The position before statutes intervened

So far as judge-made law is concerned, the basic rule is that encumbrances will **4.486**
bind transferees of the encumbered title. If they did not, then it would not be right
to describe them as species of property rights. And, in line with the attitude taken
to transferees of inferior titles, it generally matters not that the purchaser was

---

692 They are dealt with more fully in the section of this work concerned with the Sale of Goods:
paras 10.22–10.23.

693 Sale of Goods Act 1979, 24. So also a mercantile agent in possession of the goods with the
consent of the 'owner': Factors Act 1889, s 2(1). A special regime is in place for title to cars obtained
on credit: under Part III of the Hire Purchase Act 1964 as re-enacted by the Consumer Credit
Act 1974, the effect is to protect anyone who, being a private as opposed to a trade or finance
purchaser, gives value for the title without notice of the credit contract. Under s 27(2), the bona fide
purchaser takes such title as he would have received if the debtor had actually held the title outstanding in the creditor.

694 Sale of Goods Act 1979, s 25.

695 *National Employers' Mutual General Insurance Assoc Ltd v Jones* [1990] 1 AC 24, HL.

innocent as to the existence of the encumbrance and gave value in good faith in exchange for the title. Thus, at common law, a purchaser for value in good faith of a fee simple title to land was bound by leases and easements granted by his successor in title. The only thing he could do in such circumstances was to sue his vendor for breach of contract, provided, of course, that the sale of an encumbered title amounted to a breach.

4.487 A solitary exception at common law is the rule that a buyer with a title to goods[696] which his seller can avoid because induced by some fraudulent misrepresentation on the buyer's part or possibly duress, can destroy the right to avoid by selling the encumbered title on to a buyer in good faith before any act of avoidance.[697]

4.488 Courts of equity also applied the same general rule that prior encumbrances bound all, even good faith purchasers for value.[698] It did, however, develop one general exception in favour of good faith purchasers for value without notice, actual or constructive, of the encumbrance, though only for those who obtained by their purchase interests recognized by the common law. Such a person is called 'equity's darling'. We have already seen this rule in operation in our discussion of *Pilcher v Rawlins*[699] in the context of the interest of a beneficiary under a trust;[700] all equitable rights operate in the same way.

4.489 Although this doctrine of bona fide purchase applies to the purchase of titles to both land and goods, there is a problem in relation to the latter as to the level of notice which will deprive the bona fide purchaser of his protection. More than a century ago Lindley LJ said: '[I]f we were to extend the doctrine of constructive notice to commercial transactions we should be doing infinite mischief and paralysing the trade of the country.'[701]

4.490 However, rather than say that constructive notice has no place in commercial contexts, it is probably better to let the standard take the strain of differentiating between one context and another. What amounts to reasonable inquiry will vary with the subject-matter of the purchase. The rigorous inquiries which attend the purchase of titles to land are not expected in relation to ordinary commerce.

---

[696] It is unclear whether a concomitant right exists in relation to fraudulently induced transfers of title to land.

[697] Sale of Goods Act 1979, s 23.

[698] *Phillips v Phillips* (1862) 4 De GF & J 208, 215 (Lord Westbury LC); *Cave v Cave* (1880) 15 Ch D 639; *Pilcher v Rawlins* (1872) 7 Ch App 259.

[699] (1872) 7 Ch App 259.

[700] Paras 4.347–4.348.

[701] See, extrajudicially, Sir Peter Millett, 'Equity's Place in the Law of Commerce' (1998) 114 LQR 214, 214–15.

Like good faith purchase for value in the case of inferior titles, the application of **4.491** the rule here operates to destroy the equitable encumbrance. This is illustrated by *Wilkes v Spooner*.[702] Spooner had a leasehold title to two shops, granted by different landlords, 137 and 170 High Street, East Ham, London. At 137, he carried on the business of a pork butcher, and at 170, that of a general butcher. He assigned both the business at 170 and his lease of the premises to the claimant, Wilkes, his former apprentice. He also covenanted with Wilkes on behalf of himself and his successors and assigns, that he would not conduct the business of a general butcher at 137. This amounted to the grant to the claimant of a restrictive covenant over 137, which, as we have seen, is an equitable property right in respect of land.[703] Spooner wanted to give up the business at 137 and pass it on to his son. But he wanted to pass it on free of the restrictive covenant. He therefore devised a scheme. Taking advantage of the rule that equitable property rights are destroyed by an act of good faith purchase of any common law right they encumber, Spooner surrendered the lease of 137 to his landlord, who knew nothing of the restrictive covenant granted by his tenant. The landlord subsequently granted a new lease to the son, who did know of the existence of the covenant. The Court of Appeal held that the son nevertheless took free of the covenant. Vaughan Williams LJ said that because the landlord had no notice of the covenant, he became upon the surrender 'free to deal with the property unencumbered by any equity arising therefrom'.[704]

(b) Unregistered land

As should by now be clear, the currency of the English law of property is titles **4.492** to things, not the things themselves. The phrase 'unregistered land', therefore, means titles to land which have not been registered in the Land Registry. But even with such unregistered titles, there is, somewhat confusingly, a register provided by the state. It is not a register of title, but a register of certain encumbrances over that title, those encumbrances or 'charges' being of a commercial nature. This is the Land Charges Register, and it was brought into force by the Land Charges Act 1925 and re-enacted in the Land Charges Act 1972. Given the prevalence of registered titles, it is now largely redundant, and so will be dealt with only briefly.

The Act provides a list of encumbrances which can be registered. Apart from **4.493** certain security rights, which are dealt with elsewhere in this work,[705] the important

---

[702] [1911] 2 KB 473, CA.
[703] Paras 4.98–4.105.
[704] [1911] 2 KB 473, 484, CA.
[705] Paras 5.109–5.153.

members of the list are estate contracts,[706] restrictive covenants, and equitable easements. If such interests are registered, then the effect is that all persons for all purposes will have actual notice of such rights.[707] It will be recalled that all three rights are equitable, and therefore generally vulnerable to the appearance of equity's darling. The effect of the registration, however, is that no-one can any longer claim that status. Where the encumbrance is not registered, it will be void as against a purchaser for money or money's worth of a legal estate in the land charged with it.[708] And it matters not that such a purchaser had actual notice of the unregistered encumbrance. As Lord Wilberforce said in *Midland Bank Ltd v Green*,[709] what matters is the state of the register, not the state of the purchaser's mind. There are two points to finally note. The first is that failure to register has no deleterious effects with regard to any other persons, including the grantor of the right and donees from him. The second is that where, for whatever reason, the statute does not supply an answer, the fallback position is the case-law position outlined immediately above.

(c) Registered land

4.494 Once again, 'registered land' is a misnomer. What we are here concerned with are titles to land which have been registered. And where that is so, a different system for dealing with encumbrances obtains, though the effect of it is often the same. It is complex, and only a brief outline can be given here.[710] The system was over-hauled by the Land Registration Act 2002, and what follows is a description of the regime under that statute.

(i) Registered dispositions

4.495 To work out whether or not encumbrances will be destroyed on a transfer of the title they encumber, we need to first ask whether they are dispositions which have been registered in their own right. Dispositions which are so registered will bind all transferees or grantees of any rights whatsoever in relation to the land. Those dispositions which are capable of being registered, and indeed by virtue of section 27 of the Land Registration Act 2002 will be void at law for want of registration, include transfers of registered titles, the grant of leases for more than seven years, and the express grant or reservation of easements or profits.

---

706 Including options to purchase.
707 Law of Property Act 1925, s 198(1).
708 Land Charges Act 1972, s 4(6).
709 [1981] AC 513.
710 For a detailed account, see EH Burn and J Cartwright, *Cheshire & Burn's Modern Law of Real Property* (17th edn, 2006), 100–111, 952–987.

(ii) Overriding interests

If the creation of the encumbrance does not amount to a disposition which **4.496** could have been registered but was not, or was not capable of being registered as a disposition at all, then we need to ask whether the encumbrance constitutes an 'overriding' interest. If it does, then, like a registered disposition, it will bind all transferees or grantees of any rights whatsoever in relation to the land. There is no requirement that overriding interests be recorded on the register, and in that sense they provide a trap for transferees. Accordingly, the class of overriding interests is fairly narrow, in fact far more narrow under the 2002 Act than under the 1925 legislation.[711] They are to be found in Schedule 3 of the 2002 Act. The three most important are leases granted for a term not exceeding seven years, the rights of those in actual occupation of the land, and some impliedly granted easements and profits. We shall consider each in turn.

Leases not exceeding seven years. We saw above that the grant of a lease for a **4.497** term exceeding seven years was a disposition which had to be registered in its own right in order to have any effect at law. Leases for lesser periods are dispositions not capable of such registration, the reason being that, if they were, the register would become cluttered with too many temporary interests.[712] A question which arose under the equivalent provision of the 1925 legislation was whether 'equitable' leases, ie, those in which there was no grant of a legal estate, merely a lease in the eyes of equity because of an application of the maxim that equity looks upon that as done which ought to be done, could amount to overriding interests under this provision. In *City Permanent Building Society v Miller*,[713] the Court of Appeal held that the use of the word 'granted' in section 70(1)(k) of the Land Registration Act 1925 meant it applied only to leases actually created, and excluded the case of a mere agreement for a lease. There is no doubt that such reasoning will be carried through to any interpretation of the 2002 Act. Where, however, the lessee is in actual occupation of the land, then they will qualify under the next heading.

Property rights of those in actual occupation of the land. It was made clear by **4.498** the House of Lords in *National Provincial Bank v Ainsworth*,[714] in relation to this provision's predecessor, section 70(1)(g) of the Land Registration Act 1925, that only property rights, including interests under trusts, qualified as overriding interests. This is consistent with the statute introducing only a new method of conveyancing, not destroying the fundamental distinction between property

---

[711] The list of overriding interests under the Land Registration Act 1925 can be found in s 70(1) of that Act.
[712] Under the Land Registration Act 1925, the relevant period was a more cautious 21 years.
[713] [1952] Ch 840.
[714] [1965] AC 1175, discussed in para 4.12.

rights and personal rights. It was also made clear by the House in *Williams & Glyn's Bank Ltd v Boland*[715] that the words 'actual occupation' meant only physical presence on the land, and were not to be construed in the sense of a possession which was adverse to the disponor. Nothing in the 2002 Act suggests that these approaches will not be adopted in any construction of the new provision. Exempted from being overriding interests, however, are those rights which belong to a person of whom enquiry was made before the disposition and who failed to disclose the right when he could reasonably have been expected to do so, and interests of those whose occupation would not have been obvious on a reasonably careful inspection of the land at the time of the disposition and of which the person to whom the disposition was made had no actual knowledge at that time.

4.499 **Impliedly granted easements and profits.**   Under the Land Registration Act 1925, all common law easements and profits were overriding interests. The new legislation, as we have seen, requires the express grant of easements and profits to be registered to take effect at law. If not so registered, they cannot qualify as overriding interests under Schedule 3, for it only covers legal easements and profits. The thinking behind this change is that the fact that the express grant of an easement or profit will generally be an occasion attended with legal advice, and that the legal practitioner can take the opportunity to advise the parties of the need to register the disposition. This will not be so, however, in the case of easements and profits arising other than by express grant, and these rights are accordingly given the status of overriding interests, provided, of course, they take effect at law. It is not, however, every easement and profit arising other than by express grant which is included. A further requirement is that the right must be within the actual knowledge of the transferee, or was obvious on a reasonably careful inspection of the land over which the easement or profit was exercisable, or had been exercised in the period of one year ending with the day of the disposition. It should finally (and again) be noted that the status of overriding interest is only given to those easements and profits taking effect at law, not equity.

(iii) Minor interests

4.500 If the grant of the encumbrance is not by way of a registered disposition and it is not an overriding interest, the basic rule is that it will be destroyed by a transfer of the encumbered title by registered disposition made for valuable consideration unless the encumbrance is protected by the entry of either a notice or restriction on the register. Under the 1925 Act, there was some doubt whether a registered transferee for value who had actual notice of an unprotected encumbrance was bound by it, with some cases adopting the same approach of the House of Lords

---

[715] [1981] AC 487.

towards unregistered land charges in *Midland Bank Ltd v Green*,[716] and holding that the state of the register was everything,[717] and others importing requirements of good faith.[718] And though it does not say so in terms, it is thought that the 2002 Act has removed the possibility of notions of good faith creeping into the equation.

(6) *Obsolete Restrictive Covenants*

Section 84 of the Law of Property Act 1925 provides for the extinction of restric-   **4.501**
tive covenants which have outlived their utility. The Act gives a specialist court, the Lands Tribunal, power to discharge or modify such covenants where they are obsolete, where they are obstructive, where there is agreement between the parties, or where no injury would result to the persons entitled to the benefit of the covenant.[719]

(7) *Extinction of Easements and Restrictive Covenants where Dominant and Servient Tenements Come into the Same Hands*

As we have seen, both easements and restrictive covenants are rights over land   **4.502**
in the possession of another. Accordingly, where the burdened and benefited titles are united in the same person, the easement or restrictive covenant will be extinguished, for a condition of its existence will no longer be present.[720] Thus, where the titles later come into separate hands, the easement or restrictive covenant will not revive. The only exception is in the case of restrictive covenants acquired under a building scheme, which do miraculously revive in such situations.[721]

(8) *Abandonment*[722]

So far as property rights with respect to land are concerned, no argument seems   **4.503**
to have ever been made that it is possible for the holder of such a right to divest himself of it simply by abandonment. The position as regards property rights in respect of goods is less certain. Suppose that, when love cools, a ring is cast away with an appropriately unequivocal adieu. Does the ring become *res nullius*?

---

[716] [1981] AC 513, para 4.493.
[717] For example, *Strand Securities Ltd v Caswell* [1965] Ch 958.
[718] For example, *Peffer v Rigg* [1977] 1 WLR 285.
[719] Full account: C Harpum, *Megarry and Wade on Real Property* (6th edn, 2000) 1040–3.
[720] *Buckby v Coles* (1814) 5 Tunt 311 (easements); *Re Tiltwood, Sussex* [1978] Ch 269 (covenants).
[721] *Texaco Antilles Ltd v Kernochan* [1973] AC 609, PC.
[722] The best discussion is AH Hudson, 'Abandonment' in NE Palmer and E McKendrick (eds), *Interests in Goods* (2nd edn, 1998) 595–619.

4.504 This is a controverted question. The stronger school of thought denies that divesting abandonment of property rights in respect of goods has ever been possible, as the following passage from *Doctor and Student* shows:

> There is no such law in this realm of goods forsaken for though a man waive the possession of his goods and sayeth he forsaketh them yet by the law of the realm the property remaineth still in him and he may seize them after when he will.[723]

This can be backed up by the fact that in England, differently from Scotland, it has never been said that abandoned things belong to the Crown as *bona vacantia*.[724] On the other hand, authority cited in support is weak, in that in many of the supposedly relevant cases there was no intention to abandon.[725]

4.505 By the same token, authority in favour of the view that divesting abandonment is possible is fairly thin on the ground. The only case in which this seems to have occurred is *Pierce v Bemis*,[726] which concerned the sinking by enemy action during the First World War of a British registered passenger liner, *The Lusitania*. Sheen J held that the passengers and crew had abandoned the ship and its contents in order to save their own lives and without any hope or intention of returning to her, and that it was a necessary inference from the facts and the lapse of 67 years before any attempt was made to salve the contents that the owners of the contents abandoned their property. The observations are only *obiter*, for the question arose in the specific and specialized context of the law of wreck. Moreover, there is a great difference between an intent positively to be rid of the thing and a despairing acceptance that it has probably gone for good. The intent of the passengers and crew in any shipwreck is never of the former kind. In short, they never have an intent of the kind which raises the question whether the law knows such a thing as divesting abandonment.

(9) Determination of Leases of Land

4.506 A lease is almost unique among the various property rights in English law in both being temporary and having a large element of on-going positive obligation on

---

[723] Christopher St Germain, *Dialogue between a Doctor of the Civil Law and a Student of the Laws of England* (1523), Bk II, c 51.

[724] Not at least until *Re West Sussex Constabulary Widows, Orphans and Benevolent Fund* [1971] Ch 1. There are dicta in *Westdeutsche Landesbank Girozentrale v Islington LBC* at [1996] AC 669, 708, *per* Lord Browne-Wilkinson, to the effect that abandonment is possible in equity, which no doubt derive from the *West Sussex* case. There are hints to the same effect in *Cunack v Edwards* [1896] 2 Ch 679, 684, CA, *per* AL Smith LJ; *Re Hillier's Trusts* [1956] Ch 622, 633–4, CA, *per* Jenkins LJ.

[725] *Hayne's Case* (1614) 12 Co Rep 113, 77 ER 1389; *R v Edwards and Stacey* (1877) 13 Cox CC 384; *Moorhouse v Angus & Robertson* [1981] 1 NSWLR 700, NSWCA.

[726] [1986] QB 384.

the part of both parties. As a consequence, it can come to an end in ways different to other property rights.[727]

(a) Effluxion of time

Unless some statutory restriction applies, a lease for a fixed period will automatically determine when the fixed period expires. **4.507**

(b) Notice to quit

A lease for a fixed period cannot be determined by a notice to quit unless this is **4.508**
agreed upon in the terms of the lease. In the absence of any such provision, the lease continues for the full period. A periodical lease, however, can be determined by a notice to quit. In the case of a weekly tenancy, a week's notice need be given, in the case of a monthly tenancy a month's notice and so on. In the case of a yearly tenancy, the notice period is six months.

(c) Surrender

If the tenant surrenders his lease to his landlord, and the landlord accepts that **4.509**
surrender, the lease will merge in the landlord's reversion and be extinguished. It should be emphasized that to be effective the landlord must accept the surrender. Mere abandonment by the tenant will not operate as a surrender since the landlord may still wish the tenancy to continue.

(d) Merger

This is the converse of surrender and describes the situation in which the tenant **4.510**
retains the lease and becomes the holder of the reversion, or where a third party buys both lease and reversion.

(e) Forfeiture

(i) *Forfeiture by operation of law or by the terms of the lease*

A landlord may have a right to forfeit the lease, either by operation of law or by **4.511**
the terms of the lease itself. The only example of the former is in the case of a tenant who denies his landlord's title. Such a tenant is automatically made liable to forfeit his lease.[728] As regards forfeiture under the terms of the lease, if the terms

---

[727] Detail in C Harpum (ed), *Megarry and Wade on Real Property* (6th edn, 2000) 810–60.

[728] The explanation for this was based on feudal notions, that the tenant had broken a feudal bond in denying his lord's ability to grant a lease. This was always slightly strange, for the lease was never part of the feudal system. It was rejected by the Court of Appeal in *Abigodun v Frolan Health Care Ltd* [2001] EWCA Civ 1821; [2002] L & TR 16, where the obligation not to deny the landlord's title was said to be simply an implied term of the contract.

are framed as 'conditions', for example, 'upon condition that the tenant shall do X', then any breach of such condition will give the landlord the right to forfeit the lease. If, however, the terms of the lease are framed as 'covenants', then, apart from any covenant to pay rent, an award of a right to damages in favour of the landlord will be the law's only response to a breach unless the lease contains what is known as a forfeiture clause.[729] If there is a forfeiture clause, then the landlord will be able to determine the lease and recover possession of the land. How is forfeiture effected? This is done by the landlord 're-entering' the demised premises, which may comprise either:

(1) a peaceable re-entry on the demised premises;[730] or

(2) the service of a claim form on the tenant seeking possession of the demised premises.

Forfeiture occurs at the moment at which the landlord re-enters.

(ii) Relief against forfeiture

4.512 The effect of forfeiture is to destroy the lease. This may have severe consequences in some cases, particularly where the breach is a trivial one. For example, a landlord may have granted a 99-year residential lease of a flat for a large premium, say £500,000. The lease may contain a covenant on the part of the tenant not to keep pets. In breach of covenant, he keeps a goldfish. That trivial breach, which causes the landlord no loss, may nevertheless, if there is a forfeiture clause, lead to the tenant losing his lease altogether, and with (possibly) no right to recover any part of his premium.[731]

4.513 The common law took an uncompromising approach to this problem, holding the parties to the strict letter of their agreement. The court of equity, however, adopted a more relaxed approach. It took the view that the purpose of the landlord's right of re-entry was merely to provide the landlord with a form of security in case the tenant's covenants were not performed. The view of the court was that provided the tenant was willing to pay for any loss suffered by the landlord by

---

[729] A typical forfeiture clause might take the following form: 'If and whenever any rent hereby reserved shall be in arrear for twenty-one days after becoming due (whether legally demanded or not) or if and whenever any covenant by the Lessees hereinbefore contained (other than the covenant to pay rent) shall not be performed or observed then and in any such case the Lessors may by re-entry determine this demise and thereupon this demise shall absolutely determine but without prejudice to any right of action or remedy of the Lessors in respect of any breach of covenant by the Lessees.'

[730] This is not possible in the case of residential leases, for it will constitute a criminal offence under the Protection from Eviction Act 1977, s 2.

[731] The problem in the past would have been that any unjust enrichment claim would have been limited by the requirement that in a claim based on failure of consideration, the failure must be total. That requirement might still apply where, as here, there would be difficulties valuing the benefits the tenant had already received under the lease: paras 18.11–18.21.

virtue of the tenant's breach of covenant, there was no need for the landlord to re-enter. Accordingly, where the tenant made amends, equity would grant relief against forfeiture.[732]

In the case of non-payment of rent, equity would relieve a tenant against forfeiture **4.514** and revive the lease if the tenant paid the outstanding rent with interest and met any other expenses incurred by the landlord.

However, equity would not normally relieve against forfeiture for the breach of **4.515** other covenants. As a consequence, Parliament enacted section 146 of the Law of Property Act 1925, a re-enactment of section 14 of the Conveyancing Act 1881. Section 146 provides that in the case of covenants other than for the payment of rent:

(1) A right of re-entry or forfeiture under any proviso or stipulation in a lease for a breach of any covenant or condition in the lease shall not be enforceable, by action or otherwise, unless and until the lessor serves on the lessee a notice–

    (a) specifying the particular breach complained of; and

    (b) if the breach is capable of remedy, requiring the lessee to remedy the breach; and

    (c) in any case, requiring the lessee to make compensation in money for the breach; and the lessee fails, within a reasonable time thereafter, to remedy the breach, if it is capable of remedy, and to make reasonable compensation in money, to the satisfaction of the lessor, for the breach.

(2) Where a lessor is proceeding, by action or otherwise, to enforce such a right of re-entry or forfeiture, the lessee may, in the lessor's action, or in any action brought by himself, apply to the court for relief; and the court may grant or refuse relief, as the court, having regard to the proceedings and conduct of the parties under the foregoing provisions of this section, and to all the other circumstances, thinks fit.

Thus, before the landlord can exercise his right to forfeit the lease for breach of any covenant other than one to pay rent, the tenant must first be given written notice of the breach and in certain cases a reasonable opportunity to put the matter right. And even if the landlord does then re-enter, the tenant is still able to apply to the court for relief.

There are a number of points to be made about section 146. First, it was for some **4.516** time thought that it had no application to the case of a denial by the tenant of his landlord's title, also known as a 'disclaimer'. A number of reasons were given, including the fact that forfeiture here arises by operation of law and not under any

---

[732] A similar approach taken in respect of mortgages led to the creation of the equitable interest we now know as the equity of redemption: para 5.07.

stipulation or proviso in a lease, that it would be impossible for a landlord to comply with the notice requirements in section 146, and that it would be strange if a tenant could deny the relationship of landlord and tenant and at the same time seek relief on the footing that the lease still existed.[733] None were particularly convincing, and in *Abidogun v Frolan Health Care Ltd*,[734] the Court of Appeal held that the duty to issue a section 146 notice did indeed apply to the case of a disclaimer by a tenant.

4.517   The second is that the section draws a distinction between breaches which are and are not capable of remedy. In the former, the issue of a section 146 notice is intended to give the tenant one last chance to put things right before throwing himself on the mercy of the court. In the latter, the purpose of the issue of the notice is simply to tell the tenant that he must apply to the court for relief should he wish to keep his lease.

4.518   Which breaches are capable of remedy? The test laid down by the Court of Appeal in *Expert Clothing Service & Sales Ltd v Hillgate House Ltd*[735] turns on 'whether the harm that has been done to the landlord by the relevant breach is for practicable purposes capable of being retrieved'.[736] In other words, what needs to be asked is whether the damage caused by the breach can be put right. The covenant will only be incapable of remedy where the damage is irretrievable. In this regard, a distinction is often drawn between positive and negative covenants.

4.519   **Positive covenants.**   A breach of a positive covenant can generally be remedied by some belated performance of the covenant plus a payment to the landlord of compensation for any loss suffered during the time in which the covenant was unperformed. So, in *Expert Clothing Service & Sales Ltd v Hillgate House Ltd*[737] itself, a covenant that the tenant would reconstruct the premises by a certain date was remediable by the tenant's belated performance and the payment of compensation. Indeed, as a general rule, it seems that any breach of a positive covenant will always be capable of remedy.

4.520   **Negative covenants.**   This is not necessarily the case with negative covenants. At one time, it was thought that breach of a negative covenant, for example, not to use the premises for business purposes, could never be remedied. This was the approach of MacKinnon J in *Rugby School (Governors) v Tannahill*[738] and the Court of Appeal in *Scala House Ltd v Forbes*.[739] Once a breach had occurred, it was

---

733   *Warner v Sampson* [1958] 1 QB 404; *Clark v Dupre Properties Ltd* [1992] Ch 297.
734   [2001] EWCA Civ 1821; [2002] L & TR 16.
735   [1986] Ch 340, CA.
736   ibid 355 *per* Slade LJ.
737   [1986] Ch 340, CA.
738   [1934] 1 KB 965 (not to permit the premises to be used for any illegal or immoral purpose).
739   [1974] QB 575, CA (not to sub-let without the landlord's consent).

too late to put things right. That view has now changed, at least in the case of continuing breaches.[740] The test now is whether future good behaviour and monetary compensation can put the matter right. Sometimes, however, this will not be possible, as *Rugby School (Governors) v Tannahill* [741] itself demonstrates.

In that case, a lease of a house in Great Ormond Street provided that the tenant **4.521** should not use it for any illegal or immoral purpose. The tenant, Ms Tannahill, was running a brothel in the house and was convicted of so doing in the criminal courts. Although she immediately stopped using the premises for this purpose, the landlord issued a section 146 notice which only required her to vacate the premises. She argued that the notice was invalid because it did not request her to remedy the breach. The question then was whether the breach was capable of remedy. The Court of Appeal said that it was not and that the notice was good. Greer LJ, while doubting the view of MacKinnon J at first instance that the breach of any negative covenant was irremediable, said:

> This particular breach, however . . . is one which in my judgment was not remedied by merely stopping this user. I cannot conceive how a breach of this kind can be remedied. The result of committing the breach would be known all over the neighbourhood and seriously affect the value of the premises. Even a money payment together with cessation of the improper use of the house could not be a remedy.[742]

Is relief available once the landlord has peaceably re-entered? It will be recalled **4.522** that the words of section 146(2) confer on the court power to relieve against forfeiture 'where a lessor is proceeding, by action or otherwise, to enforce such a right of re-entry or forfeiture . . .'. Is relief only available where the landlord issues a writ for possession rather than exercises his remedy of self-help? That question arose in *Billson v Residential Apartments Ltd*.[743] In 1989, the appellant company bought for £280,000 the residue of a 33-year lease of some land in South Kensington, the expiry date of which was 1997. The lease contained a covenant by the tenant not to make any alteration in or addition to the demised premises without the landlord's consent. There was also a forfeiture clause for breach of any covenant. In flagrant disregard of this covenant, the new tenant spent over £300,000 on a series of major alterations. The landlord served a section 146 notice but the breach was not remedied within a reasonable time. The premises were not yet occupied and the landlord entered one morning at 6 am and changed the locks. However, by 10 am the same day, the tenant's workman had retaken possession of the property.

---

[740] *Expert Clothing Service and Sales Ltd v Hillgate House Ltd* [1986] Ch 340, CA; *Savva v Houssein* (1996) 73 P & CR 392, CA; *Akici v LR Butlin Ltd* [2006] 1 WLR 201, CA.
[741] [1935] 1 KB 87, CA.
[742] ibid 90–1.
[743] [1992] 1 AC 494, HL.

The landlord then sought an order for possession and the tenant counterclaimed for relief against forfeiture under section 146(2).

4.523   The trial judge and the Court of Appeal both held that the court had no jurisdiction to grant relief. Having already taken possession of the property and thereby determined the lease, the landlord was no longer 'proceeding, by action or otherwise, to enforce' his right of re-entry. The right of re-entry had already been enforced and it was too late to apply for relief. The House of Lords rejected this reasoning. Lord Templeman said that it was historically unsound because the effect of issuing and serving a writ is precisely the same as the effect of a re-entry; in each the lease comes to an end. In both cases the tenant seeks relief because the lease has already been forfeited. In his lordship's view, the words 'where the landlord is proceeding to enforce his right of re-entry' meant 'where the landlord proceeds to enforce his right of re-entry'.[744]

4.524   **Exercise of the judicial discretion to relieve.**   On the assumption that the court has jurisdiction to relieve against forfeiture, the next question is how that jurisdiction is exercised. Would, for example, the tenant in *Billson v Residential Apartments Ltd*[745] have been entitled to relief? The courts have held that relief will only be available where the landlord's position has not been irrevocably damaged by the breach.[746] So, for example, at first instance in the *Billson* case[747] Mummery J would have been prepared to grant relief because of the vast amounts spent by the appellants and the fact that there was no evidence that the value of the landlord's reversion was in any way diminished by the breach.

4.525   Who may apply for relief?[748] The effect of forfeiture is to bring a lease to an end. This will also destroy any interests carved out of that lease, such as sub-leases or mortgages. Since sub-lessees and mortgagees will therefore have an interest in the lease continuing, the question is whether such persons can also apply for relief.

4.526   The position with regard to sub-tenants is governed by section 146(4) of the Law of Property Act 1925. Under this provision, the court is given a broad discretion to vest the forfeited lease or some lesser term in the sub-lessee, except that the maximum duration of the new term is the length of the sub-lease.[749]

---

[744]   ibid 535–6.

[745]   [1992] 1 AC 494, HL.

[746]   *WG Clark (Properties) Ltd v Dupre Properties Ltd* [1992] Ch 297.

[747]   (1990) 60 P & CR 392.

[748]   S Tromans, 'Forfeiture of Leases: Relief for Underlessees and Holders of Other Derivative Interests' [1986] Conv 187.

[749]   Sub-tenants may also claim relief under s 146(2): *Escalus Properties Ltd v Dennis* [1996] QB 231, CA. The advantage is that relief here is retrospective to the time of forfeiture, though available in a more limited range of circumstances.

Mortgagees also fall within section 146(4), as the Court of Appeal confirmed in **4.527** *Abbey National BS v Maybeech Ltd*,[750] on the ground that the definition of lessee in section 146(5) includes persons deriving title under the original lease and mortgagees are such persons. The Court of Appeal also held that the court had an inherent jurisdiction in such cases which went beyond the statute. This pro-position was, however, later doubted by Walton J in *Smith v Metropolitan Properties*,[751] a conclusion preferred by the Court of Appeal in *Billson v Residential Apartments Ltd*.[752]

As for squatters, it is clear that they do not have the right to apply for relief against **4.528** forfeiture, even where they have been in possession long enough to have a title good against the lessee. If the lease is forfeit, the landlord's right to possession will once again arise and he will be able to evict the squatter.[753]

(f) Frustration and repudiatory breach

It should not be forgotten that a lease, as well as being the grant of a property right **4.529** in respect of land, also creates a contractual relationship between landlord and tenant. The question which arises is whether ordinary contractual principles apply so that if, by the rules of contract the contract is determined, this will also have the effect of determining the lease.

(i) Frustration

For many years, the doctrine of frustration[754] was thought to have no application **4.530** to leases. The main argument against it was that a lease is more than a contract: it conveys an estate in land, and a legal estate once granted cannot be divested. In any event, the tenant had what he bargained for, the legal estate. There could therefore be no frustration because the consideration for the tenant's promise was received. That thinking was rejected by the House of Lords in *National Carriers Ltd v Panalpina (Northern) Ltd*,[755] which concerned a ten-year lease of a warehouse. The access road to the premises was closed for 18 months of that period by the local authority because of the dangerous condition of the building opposite, a listed building requiring the Secretary of State's permission for demolition. The House of Lords held that on the facts there was no frustration but did admit the

---

[750] [1985] Ch 190, CA.
[751] (1986) 277 EG 753.
[752] [1992] 1 AC 494, CA. On this point see PF Smith (1986) 136 NLJ 254. There is an inherent jurisdiction nonetheless in the case of an equitable chargee: *Bland v Ingram's Estates Ltd* [2001] Ch 767.
[753] *Tickner v Buzzacott* [1965] Ch 426.
[754] Paras 8.438–8.484.
[755] [1981] AC 675, HL.

possibility of a lease being frustrated. They did say, however, that the circumstances under which the doctrine could apply to a lease of land were exceedingly rare.

(ii) Repudiatory breach

4.531   In *Total Oil Great Britain Ltd v Thompson Garages (Biggin Hill) Ltd*[756] Lord Denning MR said that there could be no such thing as a repudiatory breach of a lease. This was based on the view that a lease cannot be frustrated. The question is whether this finding survives the decision of the House of Lords in the *Panalpina* case. In the Australian case of *Progressive Mailing House v Tabali Pty Ltd*[757] the High Court held that the ordinary rules of contract applied to leases and that a repudiatory breach by the landlord could bring the term to a premature end. And a decision of the county court has also held that a lease can be terminated by a repudiatory breach.

4.532   In *Hussein v Mehlman*[758] the defendant granted the claimants a three-year lease of a dwelling-house subject to the covenant implied on the part of the landlord by statute to keep the premises in good repair. From the commencement of the term, the claimants made several complaints to the defendant about the state of disrepair of the premises and, half-way into the lease, one of the bedrooms was made uninhabitable by the collapse of the ceiling. The defendant refused to carry out these and other repairs and the tenants returned the keys and vacated the premises. They claimed a declaration that the defendant landlord was in repudiatory breach and that by returning the keys and giving up possession they had accepted that repudiatory breach and the lease was therefore at an end.[759] They also claimed damages for breach of covenant.

4.533   The judge held that there had been severe breaches of the implied covenant by the landlord. A lease can come to an end by repudiation. The breaches of the covenant implied by the statute were repudiatory. By vacating the house and returning the keys, the claimants had accepted the repudiatory conduct of the defendant as putting an end to the contract of letting and damages were awarded for breach of contract.[760]

---

756   [1972] 1 QB 318, CA.
757   (1985) 157 CLR 17, HCA.
758   [1992] 2 EGLR 87, Stephen Sedley QC.
759   On repudiatory breach, see paras 8.430ff.
760   Although there is some doubt whether this approach would be endorsed at a higher level, it is arguable that it would, and that the contractual nature of the lease has been acknowledged by a number of cases, first by both the Court of Appeal and the House of Lords in *City of London Corporation v Fell* [1993] QB 589, CA, [1994] 1 AC 458, HL, and in *Friends Provident Life Office v British Railways Board* [1996] 1 All ER 336, CA.

The question whether the doctrine of repudiatory breach applies to leases is **4.534**
important because, if it does, it may allow a landlord to evade the provisions
(discussed above)[761] in section 146 of the Law of Property Act 1925 regulating
the landlord's right to forfeit, and designed to protect the tenant, for now, instead
of applying for forfeiture, a landlord might simply allege a repudiatory breach of
the contract. On the basis that 'what is sauce for the goose, is sauce for the gander',
it is difficult immediately to see how such an argument could be resisted. It has,
however, been said by the Court of Appeal that the usual forfeiture rules apply
to attempts by landlords to terminate leases for repudiatory breach.[762]

---

[761] Paras 4.512–4.528.
[762] *Abidogun v Frolan Health Care Ltd* [2001] EWCA Civ 1821; [2002] L & TR 16 (a decision
on whether relief against forfeiture is available in cases of a tenant's denial of his landlord's title).

5

SECURITY

A. Introduction

A security for an obligation is something that makes it more likely that the **5.01** obligation will eventually be fulfilled. It makes the creditor more secure. Like all developed legal systems, English law recognizes broadly two kinds of security: real security and personal security. The bulk of this chapter is concerned with real security. In real security, the creditor obtains a 'real right' or a proprietary right in one or more assets that belong to the debtor. This gives the creditor security for the obligation owed to him, in several ways. First, if the debtor defaults on the obligation, the creditor has enforcement rights that can be exercised in relation to the assets over which he has security. Depending on the kind of security, he may for example have the right to seize those assets and sell them in order to obtain the money that is owed to him. In most cases, he will be able to exercise these rights without going to court. These possibilities are not available to an ordinary unsecured creditor, whose only recourse is to sue his debtor on the debt. Secondly, if the debtor becomes insolvent or bankrupt, the security rights of a creditor who holds a real security will generally continue to be available. By contrast, the claims of unsecured creditors are reduced *pro rata* when the debtor is insolvent. Finally, the secured creditor's security rights will, in many cases, operate against third party transferees who acquire from the debtor the assets over which the secured creditor holds security. An unsecured creditor can only claim against the debtor.

5.02   Personal security for an obligation arises where one or more persons, other than the debtor, agree that they will also be answerable for the obligation; for example, one person guarantees the obligation of another person. Here the creditor does not have any real rights, but he has security against the default of his primary debtor, because the guarantee means that he has an additional debtor who is liable. It is possible for a creditor to obtain both real security and personal security for the same obligation.

5.03   The structure of this chapter is as follows. The first two main sections discuss real security over land and real security over moveable property. Although there is some conceptual overlap between these two categories, there are a number of important differences due to the way that English law has developed historically. The next main section deals with priorities: that is, the resolution of disputes between the holder of a security interest and the holder of some other interest in the same property. Priority contests arise, for example, where the debtor grants two security interests in the same asset to two different creditors. They can also arise where the debtor has granted a security interest in an asset to a secured creditor, and the debtor then purports to sell the same asset to another party. Whether the secured creditor can continue to enforce his real security rights against the purchaser of the asset is a kind of priority contest. The final main section of the chapter addresses the principles of personal security.

B. Real Security Over Land

(1) Types of Security

5.04   The word 'mortgage' is used throughout this chapter, and it is necessary to say exactly it means. There is a narrow sense of 'mortgage' which distinguishes it from other security interests, such as the 'charge'.[1] This strict sense is not used in this section, 'Real Security Over Land'. Instead, following common legal usage, 'mortgage' refers here to any interest in land held as security for a debt.[2] So, for

---

[1] *Re Bond Worth Ltd* [1980] Ch 228, 250.

[2] This also corresponds to the definition in the Law of Property Act (LPA) 1925, s 205(1)(xvi). Note that this section is concerned with security over land, not over 'real property'; a leasehold

example, this section will include some discussion of the idea of an equitable charge over land; for the purposes of this section, such a charge is merely one kind of mortgage of land. The 'mortgagor' is the debtor who grants this security interest, and the 'mortgagee' is the creditor who acquires it.[3]

Legal mortgages, meaning those in which the mortgagee holds a legal interest in the land, are explained separately from equitable mortgages, in which the mortgagee's interest is purely equitable.[4] They arise according to different principles, and the classification of a security interest as legal or equitable is often crucial when questions of priority arise.

5.05

(a) Legal mortgages

The common law knew no interest in land which was by its nature a security interest. It had no concept of a charge or of a hypothec. It followed that if a creditor was to take a legal interest in land to secure a debt, the interest had to be an estate in the land, pressed into service as a security interest. Different types of estate could be used; the choice was governed partly by prevailing practice, and partly by the estate held by the debtor.[5] If he held the legal fee simple, he could transfer this to the mortgagee; or he could convey (demise) a legal leasehold estate to the mortgagee. If the mortgagor was himself a legal leaseholder, he could either assign his leasehold, or demise a sub-lease to the mortgagee. Historically, the written contract governing the arrangement was always deceptive, in that it did not reveal the true nature of the legal relationship. It provided only for an obligation on the part of the mortgagee to retransfer the mortgaged estate upon payment of all sums due; in the case of a mortgage by demise, it provided for the determination of the lease held by the mortgagee. Moreover, until recently, it generally stipulated that the principal was due after six months, even though the parties had no intention that the loan would be repaid so soon.[6] In appearance, then, the mortgagor retained no property right in the land except in the case of a mortgage

5.06

---

interest in land is personal property, but security over such an interest falls within this section. For 'real property' and 'personal property', see paras 4.15–4.16.

[3] In colloquial language, 'mortgage' is sometimes used to refer to a loan whose repayment is secured by an interest in land, or to the contract governing the relationship between borrower and secured lender. These colloquial senses are avoided here.

[4] See paras 4.22–4.25 for more discussion of the distinction. Note that a mortgage is not classified as legal or equitable based on the kind of interest that the *mortgagor* holds. This is explained below.

[5] AWB Simpson, *A History of the Land Law* (2nd edn, 1986) 242–3. The idea of 'estates' is explained in chapter 4, paras 4.37ff.

[6] Modern forms of mortgage agreement usually stipulate more accurately the obligations of the parties. They may provide for blended payments of interest and principal which, over the term of the loan, will retire the debt; or they may provide for the payment of interest only, the principal to be payable in a lump sum at the end of the term, but with the term reflecting the genuine intention of the parties.

by demise; and even in that case, the mortgagor's interest in the land was subject to the estate demised to the mortgagee. Furthermore, if the mortgagor defaulted, then it appeared that he had no right to recover (or terminate, in the case of a lease) the mortgaged estate, even though that estate might be worth far more than the debt.

5.07 Of course the appearance was inaccurate.[7] The Court of Chancery was concerned to protect the mortgagor, who was assumed always to be in a weaker position than the mortgagee. Moreover, it was willing to look beyond the form of the contract to its substance as a transaction for securing a debt. The most significant aspect of this intervention was that a mortgagor was allowed to 'redeem' the estate transferred to the mortgagee upon payment of the debt, even if the mortgagor had defaulted and so lost his estate under the terms of the contract.[8] No fixed limit of time was imposed upon the right to redeem, but each case was addressed individually. In so protecting the mortgagor, the Court of Chancery created and enforced for him a proprietary interest in the land. This interest became known as the 'equity of redemption'.[9] Its recognition entailed the possibility that at some point, the mortgagee should be able to close off or foreclose the prospect of redemption. This is why 'foreclosure' is the term still used for the process by which a mortgagee takes over the mortgaged estate for his own benefit. Once the equity of redemption was recognized, it was inevitable that parties would attempt to limit it by contractual provision; this was resisted in the strongest possible way.[10] Chancery developed the doctrine that there could be no 'clog on the equity of redemption', and this has important repercussions in the modern law.[11]

5.08 The comprehensive reform of land law which took effect in 1926 has simplified the possibilities for the creation of legal mortgages. Land in England and Wales is held under two systems, registered and unregistered. Most land is now registered. In unregistered land, there are now only two conceptual possibilities for creating legal mortgages: (i) a mortgage by demise and (ii) a legal charge, called in the

---

[7] Lord Macnaghten famously said, 'no one, I am sure, by the light of nature ever understood an English mortgage of real estate': *Samuel v Jarrah Timber & Wood Paving Corp Ltd* [1904] AC 323, 326, HL.

[8] In a mortgage by demise or sub-demise, redemption would entail the determination of the leasehold held by the mortgagee. In a mortgage by conveyance, it would entail a specifically enforceable right of reconveyance.

[9] So it remains colloquial for a person to describe as his 'equity' in his house the difference between the unencumbered value of the estate he holds and the outstanding secured debt. This also appears to be the root of the term 'equity' in corporate finance, where it identifies financing which (unlike debt) carries with it an indirectly beneficial interest in the enterprise.

[10] AWB Simpson, *A History of the Land Law* (2nd edn, 1986) 246: 'in no branch of the law was the sanctity of agreement less regarded'.

[11] Discussed in paras 5.21ff. 'Clog' here does not refer to a blockage but to a restraint; the word 'clog' has a (somewhat archaic) sense of a piece of wood which is attached to an animal to restrain its movement.

legislation a 'charge by way of legal mortgage'.[12] Any transaction which purports to be a conveyance of a legal fee simple by way of mortgage takes effect as a mortgage by demise with a term of 3,000 years.[13] A transaction which purports to be an assignment of a leasehold estate by way of mortgage takes effect as a mortgage by sub-demise, with a term ten days less than the term expressed to be assigned.[14] These provisions operate not only when the transaction's nature as a mortgage is clear from its terms, but also when an apparently absolute transfer is proved by extrinsic evidence to be, in substance, the creation of a mortgage.[15] In registered land, since the coming into force of the Land Registration Act (LRA) 2002, there is only one possibility, and that is the legal charge.[16] A person holding a legal charge over registered land has the power to create a sub-charge over his charge.[17]

The legal charge is a creature of statute. Because it is, in essence, a security interest **5.09** and not an estate in land, it is conceptually different from the mortgage by demise or sub-demise; but its legal incidents are defined 'as if' the mortgagee had taken exactly that kind of mortgage.[18] The legislative intention was to simplify the creation of legal mortgages by dispensing with the creation of the lease, but it was not intended to produce a security interest with different features.[19] There may, however, remain some minor differences between legal charges and mortgages by demise. In particular, if the mortgagor is a leaseholder, the lease will probably stipulate that the creation of a sub-lease requires the consent of the landlord;[20] such a stipulation would not necessarily apply to the creation of a legal charge.[21]

The effect is that when any legal mortgage is given, the mortgagor does not part **5.10** with his legal estate in the land. The concept of the equity of redemption, however, remains just as important as before. If the holder of a legal fee simple estate grants a legal mortgage, he retains the fee simple; but the mortgagee either

---

[12] LPA 1925, ss 85(1), 86(1).

[13] LPA 1925, s 85(2). Second and subsequent mortgages take effect as mortgages by demise of a lease ending one day after the lease demised to the prior mortgagee.

[14] LPA 1925, s 86(2). Again, second and subsequent mortgages take effect as mortgages by subdemise of a lease ending one day after the lease subdemised to the prior mortgagee.

[15] *Grangeside Properties Ltd v Collingwoods Securities Ltd* [1964] 1 WLR 139, CA.

[16] LRA 2002, ss 23(1), 51.

[17] LRA 2002, s 23(2).

[18] LPA 1925, s 87: if the mortgagor holds a fee simple estate, the mortgagee is put in the same position as if a mortgage by demise with a term of 3,000 years had been granted; if the mortgagor holds a leasehold, the mortgagee is treated as though he had been granted a mortgage by sub-demise with a term one day shorter than the term of the mortgaged lease.

[19] *Grand Junction Co Ltd v Bates* [1954] 2 QB 160, 168; approved *Regent Oil Co Ltd v JA Gregory (Hatch End) Ltd* [1966] Ch 402, 431, CA.

[20] Although LPA 1925, s 86(1) provides that permission to create a sub-lease by way of mortgage shall not be unreasonably refused.

[21] *Grand Junction Co Ltd v Bates* [1954] 2 QB 160, 168.

holds a long leasehold interest in the land, or is treated as if he held such an interest. At common law, the mortgagor's fee simple is subject to the leasehold interest. The concept of the equity of redemption still performs its traditional function of ensuring that the mortgagee's interest shall be effective only as a security interest, and that the economic benefits of ownership shall remain in the mortgagor.

(b) Equitable mortgages

5.11 For reasons relating to the effectiveness of the security against third parties, a mortgagee is often best protected if the interest he holds in the land is a legal interest. It is, however, possible to create a mortgage in which the mortgagee's security interest is purely equitable. In some cases an equitable mortgage is entirely satisfactory for the parties' needs; in some cases it is the only kind of mortgage which can be created.

5.12 Before 1926, if a mortgage was created by the conveyance of the mortgagor's legal estate, then the only interest retained by the mortgagor would be the equity of redemption. This could itself be mortgaged to a second mortgagee, but necessarily this second mortgagee (and any subsequent mortgagee) would hold only an equitable mortgage.[22] Similarly, in any case where the mortgagor held only an equitable interest, only an equitable mortgage of that interest could be created; for example, if the mortgagor was the beneficiary of a trust of land. This remains true in the modern law.

5.13 Even where the mortgagor holds a legal interest, an equitable mortgage can be created. An equitable mortgage will arise by operation of law upon the making of an enforceable agreement to create a legal mortgage, once the loan has been advanced. This occurs via the same principle by which an agreement to create a legal lease will create an equitable lease.[23] One implication is that if parties contract, for value given and received, for the creation of a legal mortgage, but they fail to take all the required steps to create one, nonetheless an equitable mortgage will arise.[24] Another implication is that if there is a contract for value to grant a mortgage (whether legal or equitable) over land that the debtor does not yet hold,

---

22 By contrast if a mortgage was created by demise of a lease, second and subsequent mortgages could be created by the creation of further (legal) leases. In the modern law, second and subsequent mortgages can always be legal, since the first mortgage is either a legal charge or a mortgage by demise.

23 See paras 4.32–4.34, 4.106–4.108. In this context the principle only operates once the loan has been advanced, because the contract is not specifically enforceable: EH Burn and J Cartwright, *Cheshire and Burn's Modern Law of Real Property* (17th edn, 2006) 729.

24 It may be that following the agreement and loan, there is some defect in the attempt to create a legal mortgage, such as the failure to execute a deed (in the case of unregistered land) or the failure to register the mortgage (in the case of registered land). Alternatively, it may be that even though there is an agreement to create a legal mortgage, the mortgagee is content to rely on his rights under the equitable mortgage.

an equitable mortgage will arise at the moment the debtor acquires an interest in the land, without any new legal act.[25] This doctrine also used to allow for the creation of equitable mortgages of land without any formal documentation. Until 1989, the physical deposit of the documents of title to land ('title deeds') in the hands of the mortgagee could, without the need for any writing, create an equitable mortgage of the land if the deposit was intended to be by way of security.[26] The parties must have intended the deposit to be by way of security, but this is the inference to which such a deposit usually gives rise.[27] The deposit was also treated as part performance of the agreement to create a mortgage, which obviated the need for the agreement to be evidenced in writing, under the law as it was before 1989. Since 1989, any agreement for the sale or disposition of an interest in land is of no legal effect in the absence of the required writing;[28] and so the mere deposit of title deeds no longer creates an equitable mortgage.[29] It is still possible to create an equitable mortgage via an agreement to create a legal mortgage, but only if the agreement to create the mortgage satisfies the required formalities.[30]

Equity has always recognized the charge as a security interest which can be created **5.14** in any kind of asset. It does not require that the creditor (chargee) take possession of the charged asset, or of title deeds to it. Subject to requirements of writing and registration, discussed below, such a charge may be created over any kind of interest in land. Sometimes equitable charges arise or are imposed without the consent of the holder of the charged asset. Such a charge can be imposed judicially to secure a judgment debt.[31] It can also be obtained under certain

---

[25] Conversely, if the parties wish to create a legal mortgage over that land, the required formal steps will have to be taken.

[26] *Russel v Russel* (1783) 1 Bro CC 269, 28 ER 1121.

[27] See however *Re Alton Corp* [1985] BCLC 27, in which the inference was not drawn, partly because other adequate security had been given for the loan.

[28] Law of Property (Miscellaneous Provisions) Act 1989, s 2 requires a written agreement which is signed by both parties and incorporates all the agreed terms. This is a formal requirement that applies to the agreement to create the mortgage, as opposed to the formalities attached to the creation of a legal mortgage as such. The principles of equitable mortgages can dispense with the latter, but not the former.

[29] *United Bank of Kuwait plc v Sahib* [1997] Ch 107, CA. The decision depends upon the holding that since the 1989 Act denies any legal effect to an agreement which does not comply with its terms, therefore the doctrine of part performance has no longer any role to play. See however *Yaxley v Gotts* [2000] Ch 162, CA, holding that the 1989 does not preclude the operation of proprietary estoppel, and suggesting that it may not preclude the operation of part performance.

[30] Law of Property (Miscellaneous Provisions) Act 1989, s 2. The deposit of title deeds with the mortgagee may still be relevant in unregistered land, as it may affect the registrability of the mortgage (para 5.19), and in any event it provides practical security since it hinders the mortgagor's ability to deal with the land. In registered land, any document is merely evidence of the state of the register and is not a true title deed; possession of such an extract from the register has no effect on registrability of a mortgage, and is not required to make a registered disposition.

[31] Charging Orders Act 1979. See para 22.129. A court can also impose a charge on land to secure unpaid property tax under the Local Government Finance Act 1992, Sch 4, para 11.

statutes, upon the application of a person who has spent money in a way related to the land.[32] One example of a charge that arises by operation of law is the unpaid vendor's lien, which arises upon the making of a contract for the sale of land unless expressly excluded.[33] A charge can also arise where trust property is disposed of without authority. The trust beneficiary who can trace into the proceeds of disposition can treat those proceeds as trust property, or can assert a charge over them to secure his claim for breach of trust.[34] A trustee has a lien over the trust property to secure the recovery of expenses properly incurred in the administration of the trust.[35] There are also charges which arise by operation of law under various statutes.[36]

(2) Creation

(a) Formalities for creation

5.15 In unregistered land, legal mortgages are created either by the grant of a leasehold interest or the creation of a legal charge. A deed is required in each case.[37] A deed involves certain formalities. It must make clear that it is intended by the parties to it to be a deed, and it must be executed by all of them.[38] For an individual this requires a witnessed signature, and delivery as a deed.[39] For a company, authentication

---

32 Examples include charges arising under the Landlord and Tenant Act 1927, s 12 and Sch 1; Agricultural Holdings Act 1986, ss 85–6.

33 *Barclays Bank plc v Estates & Commercial Ltd* [1997] 1 WLR 415, CA. The lien allows the unpaid vendor to remain in possession of the land until fully paid. Even if he gives up possession, he retains an interest in the nature of a charge over the land to secure the full payment of the price. There is also a purchaser's lien over the property to secure the repayment of any deposit paid, where the purchaser lawfully terminates the contract: *Lee-Parker v Izzet* [1971] 1 WLR 1688. On the difference between 'charge' and 'lien', see para 5.14.

34 See paras 18.177–18.182, and 18.212–18.213.

35 *Stott v Milne* (1884) 25 ChD 710, 715, CA. The trustee may secure a declaration of the lien even in respect of contingent or future liabilities, allowing him to retain in trust property which he would otherwise be obliged to distribute, until the extent of liability becomes clear: *X v A* [2000] 1 All ER 490.

36 Examples include a 'limited owner's charge,' which can arise under the Inheritance Tax Act 1984, s 212(2) upon the payment by a life tenant of inheritance tax owing in respect of the land; an 'Inland Revenue charge' which can arise under the same Act, s 237, in respect of unpaid inheritance tax; and some of the miscellaneous 'local land charges' enumerated in Local Land Charges Act 1975, s 1(a). These are not discussed herein, being of a public law character, but they may bind both registered and unregistered land and they are to be registered in registers kept by local government authorities. See EH Burn and J Cartwright, *Cheshire and Burn's Modern Law of Real Property* (17th edn, 2006) 947–8, 977–8.

37 LPA 1925, ss 52, 87.

38 Law of Property (Miscellaneous Provisions) Act 1989, s 1(2).

39 ibid s 1(3). 'Delivery' does not refer to a transfer of possession in this context, but means any unilateral act or statement signifying that the person adopts the deed irrevocably: *Xenos v Wickham* (1867) LR 2 HL 296, 312.

may be by its seal or by signatures; delivery as a deed is also required.[40] In registered land, the only legal mortgage is a registered legal charge.[41] Again, a deed is required;[42] but the charge does not create a legal interest in the mortgagee until it is registered.[43] In the future it will be possible to create a charge on registered land electronically, without any paper documentation; but even in this case, it is provided that a registered charge has the same effects as if it had been made by a deed.[44] This ensures the activation of the mortgagee's powers under LPA 1925, s 101, including the power of sale.[45]

For an equitable mortgage which takes effect by the transfer of an equitable **5.16** interest to the mortgagee, the transfer must be in writing, signed by the transferor or his agent.[46] Where the mortgage takes the form of an equitable charge created consensually by the chargor, the same kind of writing is required.[47] However, equitable interests which arise by operation of law are excluded. This exclusion saves not only charges arising without any element of consent;[48] it also applies to the equitable mortgage which arises upon the making of an enforceable agreement, for value given, to create a legal mortgage. Here a different formality is required, in order to make the *agreement* to create a legal mortgage enforceable. A contract for the sale or disposition of an interest in land can only be made in writing, signed by or on behalf of each party.[49] 'Interest in land' here means any estate, interest or charge in or over land.[50] Hence any agreement for any kind of mortgage must be in this form, or it will have no legal effect as an agreement. This is why the mere deposit of title deeds no longer creates an equitable mortgage.[51]

(b) Defective creation

The transaction by which the mortgage is created may be defective if the mortgagor **5.17** did not properly understand it.[52] More commonly, the mortgagor will argue that the transaction was induced by misrepresentation or undue influence,[53] or that it

---

[40] Companies Act (CA) 1985, ss 36A–36AA; CA 2006, ss 44–6. CA 2006 is expected to be fully in force, replacing CA 1985, by late 2008. For other kinds of corporations, see Law of Property Act 1925, s 74–74A.

[41] LRA 2002, s 23(1)(a).

[42] LPA 1925, s 85(1), 87.

[43] LRA 2002, s 27.

[44] LRA 2002, ss 51, 91(5).

[45] Discussed in paras 5.46ff.

[46] LPA 1925, s 53(1)(c).

[47] ibid s 53(1)(a).

[48] Some examples are given in para 5.14.

[49] Law of Property (Miscellaneous Provisions) Act 1989, s 2.

[50] ibid s 2(6).

[51] See para 5.13.

[52] See para 8.149 (*non est factum*).

[53] For the general law of misrepresentation and undue influence, see paras 8.159–8.206.

resulted from an unconscionable use of bargaining power.[54] Rarely, the problem is said to have originated with the lender.[55] More often, it originates from someone else, usually a spouse or other cohabitant of the mortgagor.[56] Because of the need to protect spouses in such situations, particular principles have been developed which require the mortgagee to take steps to ensure that the mortgage will be valid.[57] As noted above, if there is a valid and enforceable agreement to create a legal mortgage, but there is some defect in the actual creation of that legal mortgage, an equitable mortgage will arise by operation of law.[58] One effect is that in a mortgage of co-owned land, if the consent of one co-owner is ineffective (whether due to misrepresentation, undue influence, forgery or any other reason), the mortgage can be effective as an equitable mortgage of the interest of the other co-owner.[59]

(c) Registration

5.18 Under the registered land system, a legal charge comes into existence when it is registered. Before registration, 'it does not operate at law'.[60] This means that an unregistered charge may take effect as an equitable mortgage. It remains possible to create voluntarily a mortgage which is only equitable;[61] but this is no longer of practical importance.[62] Again, it is possible for a person to hold an equitable mortgage in registered land, where the mortgage arises by operation of law.[63] Since equitable mortgages of registered land are not registered, they cannot benefit from the governmental guarantee that protects all registered interests.[64] They are valid, however, and it is possible to protect them by making a suitable *entry* in the land register. The idea of an entry in the register is distinct from the idea of the registration of an interest. An entry is made in relation to a particular registered interest, but the entry is not itself a registered interest. Entries are either notices or restrictions. A restriction is an entry in the register that regulates dealings with a

---

[54] *Alec Lobb (Garages) Ltd v Total Oil GB Ltd* [1983] 1 WLR 87, 94–95; *Crédit Lyonnais Bank Nederland NV v Burch* [1997] 1 All ER 144, 151, 152–3, CA. Unconscionability can also be used to set aside particular terms of a mortgage agreement, rather than the whole transaction: para 5.28. For discussion of the general law of unconscionable transactions, see paras 8.207, 18.78–18.83.

[55] *Lloyds Bank Ltd v Bundy* [1975] QB 326, CA (transaction set aside); *National Westminster Bank plc v Morgan* [1985] AC 686, HL (transaction upheld).

[56] Often in such cases there is, instead of or in addition to a mortgage, a guarantee.

[57] See paras 8.205–8.206 and 8.209.

[58] See paras 5.13, 5.16.

[59] *First National Bank plc v Achampong* [2003] EWCA Civ 487.

[60] LRA 2002, s 27.

[61] LRA 2002, s 23(2).

[62] The main attraction of equitable mortgages was the possibility of creating them informally; for the reasons discussed in para 5.13, this is no longer possible.

[63] See para 5.14.

[64] Some of them—unregistered legal mortgages—could be registered; but then they would become legal mortgages. Other equitable mortgages cannot be registered.

registered interest, while a notice is an entry in respect of an unregistered interest affecting a registered interest. A notice of an interest does not guarantee that the interest noted has any validity; but, if it is valid, the notice will preserve the priority of the interest noted, in the face of subsequent dispositions of the affected registered interest.[65] Notices may be entered unilaterally. Finally, it can be observed that an equitable mortgage of an equitable interest in registered land is not registrable, nor can it be protected by any entry on the register, because the equitable interest of the mortgagor cannot itself be registered.[66]

If the mortgaged land is unregistered, some mortgages can nonetheless be registered **5.19** in the Land Charges Register.[67] This is a completely separate register from the register of registered land, although it is maintained by the same Land Registrar. It is organized by the name of the proprietor rather than by the location of the land. Registration is not required for validity, but improves the enforceability of the mortgagee's interest against third parties.[68] The holder of a legal mortgage who also has possession of the title deeds to the mortgaged estate cannot register his interest; but he has no need to do so, since the mortgagor is unable to make any further disposition of a legal interest without this mortgagee's consent. A legal mortgage whose holder does not have the title deeds is registrable;[69] so too are equitable charges not secured by deposit of title deeds, including the unpaid vendor's lien,[70] and, it seems, the kind of equitable mortgage which arises when value is given pursuant to an enforceable agreement to grant a legal mortgage.[71] However, an equitable mortgage of an equitable interest in land is not registrable.[72]

---

[65] Priority contests in registered land are discussed at paras 5.131– 5.135.

[66] LRA 2002, s 2. It might be possible to protect the *mortgagor's* equitable interest by restriction or notice, entered in relation to the affected registered legal estate.

[67] Land Charges Act 1972, s 1(1)(a). Note that many dispositions in relation to unregistered land trigger a compulsory registration of the land, including the granting of a first legal mortgage with deposit of title deeds: LRA 2002, ss 4(1)(g), (8). If such a legal mortgage is granted over unregistered land and the mortgaged estate is registered as required, then of course the mortgage has to be registered as discussed in the previous paragraph. If the mortgaged estate is not registered as required, the mortgage will take effect only as an equitable interest (LRA 2002, s 7). The goal is to ensure a continual rise in the proportion of land that is registered.

[68] See paras 5.136– 5.140.

[69] Land Charges Act 1972, s 2(4)(i). Such a mortgage is called a 'puisne mortgage', because in practice it will be a second or subsequent mortgage. 'Puisne' is derived from the French *puis né* but in English it is pronounced the same as 'puny', which indeed is a later evolution of the same word.

[70] ibid s 2(4)(iii).

[71] ibid s 2(4)(iv); see EH Burn and J Cartwright, *Cheshire and Burn's Modern Law of Real Property* (17th edn, 2006) 796. This section does not specifically exclude the case of a mortgage of this type where the mortgagee holds the title deeds, and it has been suggested that such a mortgage may be registrable: C Harpum, *Megarry and Wade: The Law of Real Property* (6th edn, 2000) 1272–3. This would be inconsistent with the scheme of the Act, which appears to be that any mortgage, legal or equitable, which is protected by a deposit of title deeds is not registrable: Burn and Cartwright, 796–7; Harpum ibid.

[72] By the Land Charges Act 1972, s 3 registration is made under the name of the 'estate owner' (mortgagor) and this includes only the holder of a legal estate: ibid s 17(1); LPA 1925, s 205(1)(v).

5.20 Where a company mortgages land, the mortgage agreement and the prescribed details of the mortgage must be submitted to the Registrar under the Companies Act 1985.[73] Failure to register within 21 days of execution makes the mortgage 'void against the liquidator or administrator and any creditor of the company'.[74] It also makes the money secured by the mortgage payable immediately.[75] In general, registration under the Companies Act does not dispense with any requirement to register in the relevant land registry. The exception is the case of unregistered land covered by a company's floating charge; here, the mortgagee is protected by Companies Act registration, without any registration in the Land Charges Registry.[76]

(3) Protection of the Mortgagor

5.21 There is a long tradition in English law of controlling the parties' freedom in relation to the terms of the contract governing the mortgage. The root of much of this intervention was the recognition of the equity of redemption, by which the mortgagor was allowed to redeem the mortgage even if, according to the terms of the contract, he had lost it. By the early seventeenth century, redemption was allowed as a matter of course, without the requirement of showing any particular hardship.[77] This led, by the end of that century, to the recognition of the equity of redemption as a form of property with which the mortgagor could deal like any other. This was carried forward into a far-reaching prohibition against creating any 'clog or fetter' on the equity of redemption. All of these doctrines are said to stem from the fact that regardless of its form or its precise terms, equity looked to the substance of a mortgage transaction as the creation of a security interest only, with the beneficial ownership of the land remaining in the mortgagor.[78] This is said to justify the courts in refusing to enforce any term seen as inconsistent with the nature of the transaction as one that gives the mortgagee security for a debt, but no more than that.[79]

---

[73] CA 1985, ss 395, 396(1)(d); CA 2006, ss 860–1. The word 'charge' in this Chapter of the Act includes a mortgage: CA 1985, s 396(4); CA 2006, s 861(5).

[74] CA 1985, s 395(1); CA 2006, ss 871, 874. See paras 5.142– 5.144.

[75] CA 1985, s 395(2); CA 2006, s 874(3).

[76] Land Charges Act 1972, s 3(7). This is effective even if the company is not the holder of the freehold estate, so that the Companies Act registration is under a different name than the registration that would otherwise need to be made under the Land Charges Act 1972: *Property Discount Corp Ltd v Lyon Group Ltd* [1981] 1 WLR 300, CA, dealing with the situation for mortgages made before 1970, when the Companies Act registration sufficed even if the charge was not floating.

[77] AWB Simpson, *A History of the Land Law* (2nd edn, 1986) 244.

[78] 'Once a mortgage, always a mortgage': *Seton v Slade* (1802) 7 Ves 265, 273, 32 ER 108, 111; '. . .and nothing but a mortgage': *Noakes & Co Ltd v Rice* [1902] AC 24, 33, HL.

[79] *Jones v Morgan* [2001] EWCA Civ 995; [2002] EGLR 125 at [55]. This was cogently criticized in GL Williams, 'The Doctrine of Repugnancy–III: "Clogging the Equity" and Miscellaneous Applications' (1944) 60 LQR 190, 190–3. Williams argued that while the control of mortgage

(a) Excluding or postponing the right to redeem

The starting point is that even though the contract may appear to provide for **5.22** redemption only upon payment within a particular time, this governs only the position at common law; the equitable right to redeem is indefinite in duration. For many years the standard form of mortgage purported to require payment of the full debt within six months, even though such payment was not actually contemplated by either party.[80] The implication was that redemption by the mortgagor could not occur unless the debt was repaid within six months; but this was misleading and it certainly could. This shows that any term that would preclude redemption is void to that extent, no matter how clearly expressed. This principle has been extended even to a term which might have the effect of preventing redemption. In *Samuel v Jarrah Timber & Wood Paving Corp Ltd*,[81] the agreement gave the mortgagee an option to purchase the mortgaged property within one year of the date of the loan.[82] The option was held to be void. The speeches show some reluctance, however, in applying the traditional rules to what was a commercial transaction between two competent parties of equal bargaining power. This is especially clear when it is observed that if the option is part of a separate contract, it will be valid.[83] But it is not enough that the option is created by a separate document. In *Lewis v Frank Love Ltd*[84] the mortgagor had defaulted and the mortgagee had obtained judgment for £6,070. The defendant agreed to lend £6,500 to the mortgagor on the terms that the defendant would have the option to acquire the fee simple in part of the mortgaged land. The defendant paid the debt owing to the original mortgagee and took an assignment of the mortgage, and the mortgagor contemporaneously granted the option.[85] When the defendant tried to exercise the option, the mortgagor successfully brought proceedings

---

contract terms might be justified on the basis that the terms were oppressive, there is no logic in the traditional position, that they are inconsistent with the nature of a mortgage.

[80] Modern forms of mortgage contract usually state more accurately the rights of the parties, including the mortgagee's right to payment and the mortgagor's right to redeem. In this case the mortgagor probably does not need to rely on the equitable right to redeem; this will be coextensive with his legal rights as set out in the contract. The equity of redemption retains its importance, however, in giving proprietary effect to the mortgagor's rights under the contract.

[81] [1904] AC 323, HL.

[82] The property in question here was debenture stock, not land, but the applicable principles are the same.

[83] *Reeve v Lisle* [1902] AC 461, HL, where an agreement which contemplated the possible acquisition by the mortgagee of part of the mortgaged property was made two weeks after the mortgage; it was held to be enforceable.

[84] [1961] 1 WLR 261.

[85] The defendant did not, however, advance the additional £430 which the transaction contemplated.

for a declaration that it was invalid as a clog on the equity of redemption.[86] The question in each case is one of characterization of the substance of the transaction.[87] It is possible that if the House of Lords were faced today with the agreement in *Samuel v Jarrah Timber & Wood Paving Corp Ltd*, it would uphold the validity of the option.[88]

5.23 Terms which delay the mortgagor's ability to redeem are not viewed in so absolute a light as those which could preclude it. The old standard form of mortgage required repayment of the loan after six months. As has been discussed, this was largely illusory and the mortgagor could redeem at any time during the subsistence of the mortgage. But one effect of the six-month term was that the mortgagor could not unilaterally redeem until the end of that period; moreover, if he wished to redeem outside that period, he was required as a rule of equity to give six months' notice to the mortgagee, or to pay six months' interest in lieu of notice.[89] So clearly some postponement of redemption has always been permissible.

5.24 Sometimes the agreement purports to impose a much longer postponement. The leading case is *Knightsbridge Estates Trust Ltd v Byrne*,[90] in which an agreement precluding redemption for a period of 40 years was held to be valid. The court in that case said that a mortgage will not be reformed because it is unreasonable; a delay in the right to redeem would be unenforceable only if it was oppressive or unconscionable,[91] or if it made the right to redeem 'illusory'. This latter concept was used by the court to explain the decision in *Fairclough v Swan Brewery Co Ltd*,[92] which illustrates that the effect of a postponement of redemption can cause more concern where the mortgaged estate is a leasehold, because the postponement may be such that very little of the term of the lease will remain to the mortgagor. In that case the mortgaged estate was a leasehold with over seventeen years to run, but the agreement did not permit redemption until only six weeks of the

---

86 Similar is *Jones v Morgan* [2001] EWCA Civ 995; [2002] EGLR 125, in which the mortgage was created in 1994; the mortgagee acquired a right to part of the mortgaged property in an agreement in 1997; this right was held to be void as a clog, by a majority of the Court.

87 *Warnborough Ltd v Garmite Ltd* [2003] EWCA Civ 1544 at [73].

88 Some academic commentary is hostile to the case: F Pollock (1903) 19 LQR 359; PV Baker (1961) 77 LQR 163; EH Burn and J Cartwright, *Cheshire and Burn's Modern Law of Real Property* (17th edn, 2006) 738. In *Jones v Morgan* [2001] EWCA Civ 995; [2002] EGLR 125, Lord Phillips MR agreed that the impugned term was void as a clog, but said at [86], '. . .the doctrine of a clog on the equity of redemption is, so it seems to me, an appendix to our law which no longer serves a useful purpose and would be better excised.' See also *Warnborough Ltd v Garmite Ltd* [2003] EWCA Civ 1544 at [72].

89 But if the mortgagee demanded payment, he was not entitled to this interest: *Centrax Trustees Ltd v Ross* [1979] 2 All ER 952; nor if he entered into possession of the land: *Bovill v Endle* [1896] 1 Ch 650.

90 [1939] Ch 441, CA; affd on different grounds [1940] AC 613, HL, on which see para 5.25.

91 On which see para 5.28.

92 [1912] AC 565, PC.

lease remained. The Privy Council held that the term postponing redemption was void. The decision is, however, inconsistent with an earlier decision of the Court of Appeal,[93] and is regarded by some commentators as open to review.[94]

The concern expressed in *Samuel v Jarrah Timber & Wood Paving Corp Ltd*,[95] that commercial agreements between equal parties should not be lightly upset, may now have been met by statute. A company may create 'debentures' which are irredeemable, or redeemable only on a contingency (however remote) or after a period of time (however long).[96] On the basis of surrounding legislative provisions, the word 'debenture' might be thought to be confined to investment securities secured on the undertaking of the company; but in *Knightsbridge Estates Trust Ltd v Byrne*,[97] it was held to cover an ordinary mortgage of land.[98] This implies that the rules discussed in this section have no application where the mortgagor is a company. In any event, in modern practice mortgagees more often protect themselves by requiring monetary penalties for early redemption. Such penalties do not interfere with the right to redeem, but they may be challenged on other grounds, as discussed below.

5.25

(b) Collateral advantages

The idea that a mortgage can never be anything but a mortgage generated the doctrine of 'collateral advantages', by which it is meant that the court may invalidate a term of the mortgage agreement under which some advantage accrues to the mortgagee, beyond recovery of the debt with interest. At the turn of the twentieth century the doctrine took on a more modern cast, with the courts refusing to invalidate terms so long as the advantage in question was not expressed to continue in force after redemption.[99] To the extent, however, that an advantage was expressed to survive redemption, it was not enforceable, even by way of damages.[100]

5.26

---

[93] *Santley v Wilde* [1899] 2 Ch 474, CA, upholding a term which required the mortgagor to share with the mortgagee the business profits earned during the ten years remaining in the mortgaged lease. This meant that there could be no redemption during the term of the lease.

[94] EH Burn and J Cartwright, *Cheshire and Burn's Modern Law of Real Property* (17th edn, 2006) 740. *Santley v Wilde* was questioned in *Noakes & Co Ltd v Rice* [1904] AC 24, 31, 34, HL; but there was veiled criticism of the *Fairclough* case in *Kreglinger v New Patagonia Meat and Cold Storage Co Ltd* [1914] AC 25, 53, HL.

[95] [1904] AC 323, HL.

[96] CA 1985, s 193; CA, 2006, s 739.

[97] [1940] AC 613, HL.

[98] Relying on the definition now in the CA 1985, s 744, that the word includes 'debenture stock, bonds and any other securities of a company, whether constituting a charge on the assets of the company or not'. See CA 2006, s 738.

[99] *Biggs v Hoddinott* [1898] 2 Ch 307, CA. This perspective fits with the holding in *Santley v Wilde* [1899] 2 Ch 474, CA, where the advantage in question accrued only during the term of the mortgage.

[100] *Noakes & Co Ltd v Rice* [1902] AC 24, HL; *Bradley v Carritt* [1903] AC 253, HL.

As in the decisions relating to options, the cases show an increasing awareness of the tension between the old protective approach of equity and the recognition that many mortgagors are not particularly in need of paternalistic care. In *Kreglinger v New Patagonia Meat and Cold Storage Co Ltd*,[101] the agreement purported to give the lender a right of first refusal and a right of commission in respect of some assets which the borrower was in the business of selling. The House of Lords upheld the validity of these terms even after the discharge of the security, on the ground that they were effectively terms of a separate agreement.[102] If this can be taken to represent the modern law, then the doctrine of collateral advantages is now of little importance.[103]

(c) Other doctrines

5.27 There are a number of other bases on which terms in mortgage agreements may be invalidated. These, however, derive from more general principles, rather than from the particular approach of equity to mortgage transactions. For this reason they will be dealt with more briefly.

(i) Unconscionability

5.28 In a number of cases, particular terms have been invalidated as unconscionable. Historically, equity has been more willing to intervene on this ground in mortgage transactions than in general; as discussed above, the mortgagor was traditionally seen as being in need of special protection. Unlike rules relating to the equity of redemption, however, the unconscionability jurisdiction does not arise from any particular feature of mortgage transactions.[104] The courts have said repeatedly that it is not sufficient for a term to be unreasonable.[105] In one case, the mortgagor borrowed £2,900 and agreed to repay £4,553 by instalments over six years.[106] The mortgagor's default triggered a clause making the full debt payable immediately,

---

[101] [1914] AC 25, HL.

[102] The security was not a mortgage of land but a floating charge over the assets of the debtor. Their Lordships rejected an argument that different principles applied to such a charge.

[103] The *Kreglinger* case was applied in *Re Petrol Filling Station, Vauxhall Bridge Road, London* (1968) 20 P & CR 1 in upholding a term which required the mortgagor to purchase stock-in-trade only from the mortgagee even after redemption. The conclusion was assisted by the fact that the purchase agreement preceded the mortgage agreement; but the judge said that the purchase agreement would have been enforceable after redemption as a separate agreement from the mortgage, even if the two agreements were properly viewed as parts of a single transaction.

[104] For discussion of the general law of unconscionable transactions, see paras 8.207, 18.78–18.83. It is also possible that the whole mortgage agreement is voidable for unconscionability: see para 5.17.

[105] *Knightsbridge Estates Trust Ltd v Byrne*, [1939] Ch 441, CA; affd on different grounds [1940] AC 613, HL; *Multiservice Bookbinding Ltd v Marden* [1979] Ch 84.

[106] *Cityland & Property (Holdings) Ltd v Dabrah* [1968] Ch 166.

creating an effective interest rate of 38 per cent. The court held that the agreement was not enforceable on its terms, because they destroyed any possibility that there would be any surplus for the mortgagor. It was held that the mortgagee could recover the amount of the advance together with interest at the rate of 7 per cent. The basis of the jurisdiction was clarified in *Multiservice Bookbinding Ltd v Marden*.[107] The mortgagee wanted to be secure against any decline in the value of sterling. The agreement provided for a floating rate of compound interest, and for the sums payable to be indexed to the value of the Swiss franc. At the end of the ten-year term, the effective interest rate was 16 per cent. Browne-Wilkinson J held that although the terms of the agreement were unreasonable, they were enforceable. He said:

> . . .in order to be freed from the necessity to comply with all the terms of the mortgage, the plaintiffs must show that the bargain, or some of its terms, was unfair and unconscionable: it is not enough to show that, in the eyes of the court, it was unreasonable. In my judgment a bargain cannot be unfair and unconscionable unless one of the parties to it has imposed the objectionable terms in a morally reprehensible manner, that is to say, in a way which affects his conscience.

> The classic example of an unconscionable bargain is where advantage has been taken of a young, inexperienced or ignorant person to introduce a term which no sensible well-advised person or party would have accepted. But I do not think the categories of unconscionable bargains are limited; the court can and should intervene where a bargain has been procured by unfair means.

(ii) Restraint of trade

Many cases involve mortgage agreements containing terms by which the mortgagor must deal exclusively with the mortgagee, usually in acquiring stock-in-trade for business. In order to preserve the validity of these 'ties', such agreements commonly postponed the mortgagor's right to redeem; this was to ensure that the restriction was not struck down as a collateral advantage, but it also underpinned the argument that the restriction was more justifiable where the tied party owed money to the other. It was decided in *Esso Petroleum Co Ltd v Harper's Garage (Stourport) Ltd*[108] that the principles of public policy which governed the validity of such ties were the same whether or not there was a mortgage agreement in place.[109] Where the tie is void as contrary to public policy, a postponement of redemption which was inserted to protect the tie is probably also invalid.[110]

5.29

---

[107] [1979] Ch 84. This case also established that it is permissible for a mortgage agreement to make the principal debt variable according to some index.

[108] [1968] AC 269, HL.

[109] For a discussion of the principles see paras 8.237–8.247.

[110] [1968] AC 269, 314, 321, 342, HL.

(iii) Implied terms

5.30 Many mortgage agreements (and many unsecured lending arrangements) have a variable interest rate. It is the lender, of course, that has the power to vary the rate. It has been held that this power is controlled by an implied term of the contract. The implied term is that the power may not be used dishonestly, for an improper purpose, capriciously or arbitrarily; nor may it be used in a way in which no reasonable mortgagee, acting reasonably, would use it.[111]

(iv) Legislative intervention

5.31 Certain legislative interventions are relevant to the control of mortgage terms. In the case of most first residential mortgages, mortgage lenders are subject to regulation under the Financial Markets and Services Act (FSMA) 2000, as are mortgage brokers and mortgage advisors.[112] This means that lenders must be authorized to do business, and there is detailed regulation of advertising and other aspects of seeking and doing business. This is public law regulation, that does not have direct effect on contracts. The Consumer Credit Act (CCA) 1974 provides many protections for consumer debtors, and these often do have direct effect on contracts; but in general, the CCA 1974 will not apply where the FSMA 2000 applies. Many of the provisions of the CCA 1974 apply only to 'regulated agreements'. An agreement is a regulated agreement only if the debtor is an individual.[113] But some agreements are not regulated under the CCA 1974 because they are 'exempt', and these exemptions include any mortgage that is regulated under the FSMA 2000.[114] One exceptional case may be noted. The CCA 1974 provides that if a land mortgage is a regulated agreement, there can be no extrajudicial enforcement;[115] exceptionally, this provision applies even to a mortgage agreement that is otherwise regulated only under the FSMA 2000.[116]

5.32 The CCA 1974, therefore, could apply to a mortgage where the mortgagor is an individual, and either the mortgage is over non-residential property, or it is a second or later mortgage on a residence. The Act allows the debtor in a regulated

---

[111] *Paragon Finance plc v Nash* [2001] EWCA Civ 1466; [2002] 1 WLR 685, CA; *Paragon Finance plc v Pender* [2005] EWCA Civ 760; [2005] 1 WLR 3412, CA.

[112] ss 19, 22(1), and Sch 2, paras 1, 2(1), 3, 7, 10, 23; Financial Services and Markets Act 2000 (Regulated Activities) Order 2001 (SI 2001/544), especially art 61. Basically, the FSMA regime applies in cases where the debtor is an individual, the mortgage is a first mortgage, and the debtor or his family will be living in the mortgaged property.

[113] ss 8, 189(1). In addition, since the Act came into force, agreements have not been regulated if the amount of credit exceeded a certain threshold, currently £25,000 (s 8(2)). Pursuant to amendments made by the CCA 2006, however, which are expected to come into force in 2008, this threshold will be removed.

[114] The exemptions are in ss 16–16B; by s 16(6C), the CCA 1974 does not regulate a mortgage where the lender is regulated under the FSMA 2000.

[115] s 126.

[116] s 16(6D).

agreement to repay the loan at any time regardless of its terms;[117] this would over-ride any term postponing the right to redeem. The Act imposes requirements of form and procedure for the making and enforcement of agreements. The sanction for non-compliance by the lender is generally that the agreement cannot be enforced without a court order.[118] As previously noted, a court order is always required for enforcement of a land mortgage.[119] The Act also includes public law regulation requiring the authorization of commercial lenders, and regulating advertising and other aspects of seeking business.

Under CCA 1974, ss 140A–140D, the court can reopen and revise a credit **5.33** agreement if it determines that the relationship between the debtor and the credi-tor, arising out of the agreement, is unfair to the debtor.[120] These provisions apply even to agreements that are not 'regulated agreements'; but this does not significantly widen their scope in the mortgage context, because they only apply to individual debtors, and they do not apply to mortgage agreements regulated by FSMA 2000.[121] The creditor is required to disprove any allegation that a bar-gain is unfair.[122]

In insolvency, whether of a company or an individual, the court may, on the **5.34** application of the insolvency officer, reopen and revise a credit transaction that is 'extortionate' if it was entered into within three years before the insolvency.[123] This jurisdiction exists to protect other creditors of the insolvent person from the extortionate bargain that one creditor has made. Where the insolvency officer

---

[117] ibid s 94.

[118] eg ss 65(1); 105(7); 111(2). By s 113, any security is only enforceable to the extent of such an order, even if otherwise it would be effective against a third party. Until recently, under ss 127(3)–(4), the court in some situations had no jurisdiction to make an order allowing the enforcement of a defective agreement. Pursuant to amendments made by the CCA 2006, which came into force in 2007, those provisions were repealed and the court now always has the jurisdiction to allow enforcement on such terms as the court approves.

[119] s 126.

[120] These provisions, enacted in 2006, displace ss 137–140, which operated where the agree-ment was 'extortionate'. The new provisions now apply to all new agreements; it is expected that with effect from April 2008, the new provisions will apply to all agreements, even if those made before the 2006 amendments. The new provisions are intended to be easier for the debtor to satisfy than the old ones, which courts rarely found to be satisfied (see eg *Davies v Directloans Ltd* [1986] 1 WLR 823; *Paragon Finance plc v Nash* [2001] EWCA Civ 1466; [2002] 1 WLR 685, CA; *Paragon Finance plc v Pender* [2005] EWCA Civ 760; [2005] 1 WLR 3412, CA). A claim must be brought within 12 years of the making of the agreement: *Rahman v Sterling Credit Ltd* [2001] 1 WLR 496, CA.

[121] CCA 1974, ss 140C(1), 140A(5).

[122] ibid s 140B(9).

[123] Insolvency Act 1986, ss 244, 343. 'Extortionate' is defined as requiring that the transac-tion provides for payments which are 'grossly exorbitant', or that it otherwise 'grossly contravenes ordinary principles of fair trading'. This is the test from CCA 1974, ss 137–140, now being phased out of effect.

alleges that a bargain is extortionate, the creditor is required to disprove the allegation.[124]

5.35 The Unfair Terms in Consumer Contracts Regulations 1999[125] give effect to the Directive on Unfair Terms in Consumer Contracts.[126] These regulations are confined to cases where one party is acting in the course of its business and the other is acting as a consumer.[127] They permit a contract term to be assessed as to whether it is fair; a term which was not individually negotiated is unfair if 'contrary to the requirement of good faith, it causes a significant imbalance in the parties' rights and obligations arising under the contract, to the detriment of the consumer'.[128] If it is unfair, a term is not enforceable against the consumer.[129] There is, however, a further limitation in that a term may not be assessed for fairness if it is a 'core term'; that is, if it defines the main subject matter of the contract, or concerns the adequacy of the price.[130] It has been suggested that this would prevent the assessment for fairness of the interest rate in a mortgage contract. In *Director General of Fair Trading v First National Bank plc*,[131] which was decided under the earlier 1994 regulations,[132] the dispute was over a term that provided that if the creditor obtained a judgment against the debtor, interest should be payable at the contractual rate until the judgment was fully paid. The House of Lords rejected the argument that this was a core term, although the term was held to be fair. The practice of having variable interest rates is, in general, protected from review for fairness by the regulations, so long as there is a 'valid reason' for the variation.[133] The Financial Services Authority has issued some guidance on its views as to fairness of variation clauses.[134]

5.36 The Unfair Contract Terms Act 1977 is wider than the regulations as regards the contracts to which it applies, but it is concerned with exemption clauses and therefore is not likely to have much impact on mortgage contracts.[135]

---

124 Insolvency Act 1986, ss 244(3), 343(3).
125 SI 1999/2083, pursuant to the European Communities Act 1972, s 2(2).
126 Council Directive (EEC) 93/13 [1993] OJ L095/29.
127 SI 1999/2083, regs 3(1), 4(1).
128 ibid reg 5(1).
129 ibid reg 8(1).
130 ibid reg 6(2).
131 [2001] UKHL 52, [2002] 1 AC 481, HL.
132 SI 1994/3159.
133 Sch 2, para 2(b).
134 'Fairness of terms in consumer contracts: Statement of Good Practice', May 2005, <www.fsa.gov.uk>. The FSA is the regulator for contracts governed by the FSMA 2000, which includes most first residential mortgages: see para 5.31. The Office of Fair Trading (OFT) is the regulator of agreements governed by the CCA 1974. This means that FSA is primarily responsible for the application of the Unfair Terms in Consumer Contracts Regulations to consumer mortgages.
135 In *Paragon Finance plc v Nash* [2001] EWCA Civ 1466; [2002] 1 WLR 685, CA, the mortgage agreement had a floating rate of interest. The mortgagors argued that the failure of the

(4) Enforcement

The primary focus here is on the rights arising from the mortgage itself. There will **5.37** of course be a personal obligation created by the transaction, and the mortgagee will have a right to recover the debt owed to it, as stipulated in the mortgage agreement. The personal obligation can generally be cumulated with any other enforcement measure.[136] In other words, if the mortgagee takes steps to enforce the mortgage and there is still a deficiency, so that the mortgagee is still owed money after that enforcement measure, an action may be brought on the personal obligation.[137] A claim to enforce the mortgage which does not also disclose a claim on the personal obligation does not prevent the mortgagee from later making a claim on the personal obligation.[138] Similarly, even if the mortgage as such is effectively unenforceable, the lender may proceed to judgment on the personal claim, which may lead to bankruptcy proceedings and, eventually, realization (on behalf of all creditors) of the mortgagor's interest in the mortgaged land.[139]

(a) Possession

Subject to any contractual stipulation, a legal mortgagee has the right to take **5.38** possession of the land.[140] This does not depend on any default, but is simply an incident of the legal estate which he holds.[141] Equity did not intervene in this

---

mortgagees to lower the rates, as interest rates fell in the general lending market, was a violation of s 3(2)(b) of the Unfair Contract Terms Act 1977, which limits the ability of a party to be excused from performance of its obligations. The court rejected this argument on the basis that the setting of interest rates by the creditor is not a performance by the creditor of its obligation. Note also that some aspects of land mortgage agreements may be outside the Act, since it does not apply to 'any contract so far as it relates to the creation or transfer of an interest in land, or to the termination of such an interest': s 1(2); Sch 1, para 1(b).

[136] *Gordon Grant & Co Ltd v Boos* [1926] AC 781, PC. If the mortgagee has foreclosed the equity of redemption and acquired the mortgaged property beneficially, any claim on the personal obligation requires the mortgagee to allow the mortgagor once again to redeem: ibid 785. Foreclosure followed by sale to a third party, however, precludes any claim on the personal obligation. For more detail, see para 5.53.

[137] The limitation period on the personal obligation is twelve years from the date of breach: Limitation Act 1980, s 20; *West Bromwich BS v Wilkinson* [2005] UKHL 44; [2005] 1 WLR 2303.

[138] In *UCB Bank plc v Chandler* (1999) 79 P & CR 270, CA, an argument that the mortgagee was estopped (see para 22.123) was rejected.

[139] *Alliance and Leicester plc v Slayford* [2001] Bankruptcy and Personal Insolvency Rep 555, CA. In this case the mortgagee could not obtain a possession order against the mortgagor because the mortgage was not effective against mortgagor's wife, who also lived in the house. However the mortgagee could obtain personal judgment against him, leading to bankruptcy and probably the eventual sale of the house.

[140] *Four-Maids Ltd v Dudley Marshall (Properties) Ltd* [1957] Ch 317.

[141] ibid; *Paragon Finance plc v Pender* [2005] EWCA Civ 760; [2005] 1 WLR 3412, CA. Before 1926 he might take a conveyance of the mortgagor's estate, or a lease granted by the mortgagor; either way, at law he had a better right to possession than the mortgagor. After 1925 the mortgagee's rights are, or are treated as, those of a lessee from the mortgagor, with the same effect. In particular,

regard, because the mortgagee's right to possession was not inconsistent with the security nature of his interest in the land. It has been held, however, that the right to take possession may only be exercised *bona fide* and reasonably for the purpose of enforcing the security, and not for an ulterior purpose such as evading legislation governing security of tenure.[142]

5.39 In practice the right to take possession is used only as a means of enforcement. The mortgagee will almost always take possession before exercising the power to sell, because it will be impossible to get the best price unless vacant possession is offered.[143] Possession is less commonly taken for other reasons. For example, the mortgagee might wish to lease the land so that the profits can be applied against the mortgagor's obligations under the mortgage agreement.[144] The drawback of taking possession is that a mortgagee in possession is required to account 'strictly'.[145] This means he must account to the mortgagor for all profits which were, or ought reasonably to have been, realized from the land.[146] If a mortgagee is concerned to preserve the income from a property, it is usually wiser to appoint a receiver.[147]

5.40 Proceedings for possession are usually therefore the first stage in the sale of the property; for this reason, such proceedings often serve as the occasion for determining the validity of a mortgage.[148] In the case of most mortgages granted by individual debtors, an order of the court will be required for the mortgagee to take possession.[149] Otherwise, possession can be taken extrajudicially, but mortgagees usually seek a court order unless the occupier is willing to give up the premises. Forcible entry constitutes an offence if there is an occupier resisting that entry.[150]

---

in providing that the holder of a legal charge has the same protection as if granted a lease, LPA 1925, s 87(1) expressly mentions the mortgagee's right to possession.

142 *Quennell v Maltby* [1979] 1 WLR 318, CA; approved in *Albany Home Loans Ltd v Massey* [1997] 2 All ER 609, CA.

143 See however *Ropaigealach v Barclays Bank plc* [1998] EWCA Civ 1960; [2000] 1 QB 263 (sale by auction without vacant possession).

144 *White v City of London Brewery Co* (1889) 42 ChD 237, CA.

145 The taking of possession by the mortgagee also gives the mortgagor an immediate right to redeem, even if the legal date for redemption has not arrived: *Bovill v Endle* [1896] 1 Ch 648.

146 *White v City of London Brewery Co* (1889) 42 ChD 237, CA.

147 See para 5.54.

148 As for example in *Barclays Bank plc v O'Brien* [1994] 1 AC 180, HL.

149 If the mortgage agreement is a 'regulated agreement' within the CCA 1974 (on which see para 5.31), then an order of the court is required for possession: CCA 1974, s 126; by s 16(6D), s 126 applies even where the mortgage is one that is otherwise regulated by the FSMA 2000 rather than the CCA 1974. The current monetary limitation in the definition of 'regulated agreement' means that most mortgages are not regulated agreements; however, this monetary limitation was removed by amendments made in the CCA 2006, which are expected to come into force in 2008.

150 Criminal Law Act 1977, s 6; by s 6(2), a right to possession of the premises does not excuse this offence.

In the case of residential premises, unlawful eviction is an offence even if it is peaceable.[151]

The mortgagor can be protected from this seemingly Draconian power of the **5.41** mortgagee in various ways. First, the right to take possession can be excluded contractually, and in the case of most modern residential mortgages it is usual to exclude the right to take possession before default. Such an exclusion could be implied, but at least in commercial transactions, the courts will not quickly draw the conclusion that this has been done. For example, the mere fact that the mortgage agreement provides for payments by instalment does not mean that the mortgagee's right to take possession is excluded in the absence of default.[152] Similarly, a mortgage agreement which contemplates no payments of either interest or capital for ten years does not, by that reason alone, exclude the right to possession during the ten-year period.[153]

More significant for the residential mortgagor are the statutory interventions **5.42** which control the right to take possession. The Administration of Justice Act 1970, s 36, applies where the mortgaged premises consist of or include a dwelling-house,[154] and the mortgagee brings an action for possession, not being an action for foreclosure.[155] The section provides that in such a case, the court may adjourn the proceedings, or suspend or postpone the possession order:

> if it appears to the court that in the event of its exercising the power the mortgagor is likely to be able within a reasonable period to pay any sums due under the mortgage or to remedy a default consisting of a breach of any other obligation arising under or by virtue of the mortgage.[156]

It is usual for instalment mortgages to have an 'acceleration clause' by which, in **5.43** the event of a default, the whole of the principal and interest become payable.

---

151 Protection from Eviction Act 1977, s 1. If the eviction is both peaceable and lawful, there is no offence, but a prudent mortgagee will often seek a court order to avoid any doubt.

152 *Esso Petroleum Co Ltd v Alstonbridge Properties Ltd* [1975] 1 WLR 1474, 1484.

153 *Western Bank Ltd v Schindler* [1977] Ch 1, CA.

154 Under the Administration of Justice Act 1970, s 39(1), 'dwelling house' is defined as property 'used' for a dwelling. In *Royal Bank of Scotland v Miller* [2001] EWCA Civ 344; [2002] QB 255, the mortgaged premises included a residential flat; at the time of the granting of the mortgage, this was unoccupied, but at the time that the mortgagee sought possession, it was alleged to be occupied, albeit by someone other than the mortgagor, which would be a breach of a term of the mortgage contract. Nonetheless, it was held that if it was established that the flat was occupied at the time possession was sought, s 36 would apply.

155 On a literal reading s 36 would only apply where there has been a default by the mortgagor, so that if the mortgagee took proceedings for possession in the absence of default, the court would have no discretion to postpone possession. It was held by a majority in *Western Bank Ltd v Schindler* [1977] Ch 1, CA, that the section must be interpreted to apply even if there has been no default under the mortgage agreement.

156 By s 38A, s 36 does not apply to an agreement which is a regulated agreement under the CCA 1974 (on which see para 5.31); but in such a case an order of the court is required for possession: CCA 1974, s 126.

In such a case, for the purposes of s 36, the amount due is to be taken to mean the amount that would be due if there had been no acceleration clause.[157] However, if the debt is payable on demand from the outset, then upon demand being made, the amount due for the purposes of s 36 is the full debt.[158] It was argued by some that the effect of s 36 was impliedly to abrogate the mortgagee's right to take possession extrajudicially, so that possession could be taken only with judicial approval and subject to the statutory discretion. However, it has been held, reading the section literally, that it only applies where there is an *action* for possession. The court cannot interfere if the mortgagee lawfully takes possession extrajudicially.[159]

5.44 Some guidelines have been laid down for the application of s 36. If the mortgagor proposes to pay the arrears in instalments, the court will take into account such factors as the mortgagor's financial means, the prospects for their improvement, and the reasons for the default; the remaining term of the mortgage and its other terms; and the possibilities for paying the arrears, such as different repayment schedules or the capitalization of unpaid interest.[160] If the mortgagor proposes to sell the land, the relevant considerations will include the adequacy of the land as security for the debt, and the time required to effect a sale.[161] If the court is exercising its discretion under s 36, then if the mortgagee is also seeking a judgment on the mortgagor's personal obligation, the court will normally also suspend any such judgment in line with the suspension of the possession order pursuant to s 36.[162]

5.45 The foregoing has been concerned with the case of a legal mortgage. If the mortgagee holds an equitable charge, it seems clear that there is no right to possession except in so far as it may arise by contract or court order;[163] this is because the right to possession arises from the holding of an estate in the land, and the chargee has

---

[157] Administration of Justice Act 1973, s 8(1). This section applies whether the mortgage is a 'repayment mortgage' (which involves blended payments of interest and principal) or an 'endowment mortgage' (in which only interest is payable by instalments and the capital is payable in a lump sum at the end of the term): *Governor and Company of the Bank of Scotland v Grimes* [1985] QB 1179, CA; *Royal Bank of Scotland v Miller* [2001] EWCA Civ 344; [2002] QB 255. It also applies to the older style of mortgage which provided on its face for full payment of principal after six months, but which really had an indefinite term for the repayment of capital: *Centrax Trustees Ltd v Ross* [1979] 2 All ER 952.

[158] *Habib Bank v Tailor* [1982] 1 WLR 1218, CA.

[159] *Ropaigealach v Barclays Bank plc* [1998] EWCA Civ 1960; [2000] 1 QB 263.

[160] *Cheltenham and Gloucester BS v Norgan* [1996] 1 WLR 343, CA.

[161] *Bristol and West BS v Ellis* (1996) 73 P & CR 158, CA; if the security is inadequate, possession will not be postponed: *Cheltenham and Gloucester plc v Krausz* [1997] 1 All ER 21, CA.

[162] *Cheltenham and Gloucester BS v Grattidge* (1993) 25 Housing LR 454, CA.

[163] LPA 1925, s 90 empowers the court to make an order vesting a legal estate in any equitable mortgagee (including a chargee) 'to enable him to carry out the sale', as if the mortgage was a legal one; this would entitle the mortgagee to possession.

no such estate, nor any right to one. It is generally said that the holder of an equitable mortgage (in the narrow sense which excludes a charge) also has no right to possession except by agreement or court order, but the point is arguable.[164]

(b) Sale

(i) Mortgagee's statutory power of sale

In the case of a mortgage made by deed, the mortgagee obtains a power of sale by **5.46** operation of law.[165] This will apply to all legal mortgages of unregistered land, and to any registered legal charge over registered land, since these mortgages must be created by deed.[166] It also applies to any equitable mortgage created by a deed.[167] The power arises 'when the mortgage money has become due'.[168] This refers to the principal, and was apparently drafted with reference to the traditional mortgage, which made the full principal legally due after six months. It is harder to apply to modern forms of mortgage, but they usually provide that for the purposes of this power, the mortgage money is due immediately or after six months, so ensuring that the power of sale has arisen.[169]

The power, having arisen, may not however be properly exercisable. It is properly **5.47** exercisable upon the occurrence of the first of three events:[170]

(1) the mortgagor's failure to pay the mortgage money on three months' notice in writing;[171]
(2) the mortgagor's falling at least two months in arrears on payments of interest;
(3) breach by the mortgagor of an obligation contained in the mortgage agreement or the LPA 1925.

If the power has arisen, but is not properly exercisable, then the purchaser of **5.48** the land will nonetheless take a good title; the mortgagor's remedy is against the mortgagee.[172] In the case of unregistered land, this is qualified in that a sale to a purchaser who has notice of some impropriety in the mortgagee's exercise of the

---

164 HWR Wade, 'An Equitable Mortgagee's Right to Possession' (1955) 71 LQR 204.

165 LPA 1925, s 101(1)(i). A sale by a mortgagee is deemed to be made pursuant to the statutory power unless express provision to the contrary is made: LPA 1925, s 104(3). Because of the safeguards which the statutory power provides for ensuring the effectiveness of the sale, it is usual to rely on it.

166 Para 5.15.

167 This includes an equitable charge made by a deed: C Harpum, *Megarry and Wade: The Law of Real Property* (6th edn, 2000) 1215.

168 LPA 1925, s 101(1)(i).

169 *West Bromwich BS v Wilkinson* [2005] UKHL 44, [2005] 1 WLR 2303 at [25].

170 LPA 1925, s 103.

171 ibid s 196(1) requires that the notice be in writing.

172 ibid s 104(2).

power of sale can be impeached by the mortgagor.[173] In registered land, however, the purchaser always takes an unimpeachable title, unless perhaps he commits some independent wrong such as conspiracy or dishonest assistance in a breach of trust.[174] The power enables the mortgagee to sell the mortgaged property, even though the mortgagee does not (except in an equitable mortgage of an equitable interest) himself hold that property; the purchaser takes free of the interest of the mortgagor, and of any mortgagees subsequent to the one exercising the power of sale.[175] Assuming the power of sale has become exercisable, the mortgagor loses his ability to redeem upon the making of the contract.[176] After conveyance to the purchaser, the mortgagee is a trustee of the purchase money and is required to pay, in this order, the expenses of the sale; the principal, interest and costs due to himself; and then, if there is any surplus, the mortgagor or the next mortgagee if there is one.[177] If there is a deficiency, the mortgagee can normally proceed against the mortgagor as an unsecured creditor.[178] The mortgagor has no grounds for complaint if the first mortgagee pays itself less than it is owed and pays the balance to a subsequent mortgagee, even if the mortgagor takes the view that its position would have been better if the first mortgagee had paid itself all of what it was owed.[179]

5.49 If the mortgagor is not content that the property be sold, or wishes to sell the property himself, the wisest course is to dispute the matter when the mortgagee seeks possession; as discussed above, if the property includes a dwelling-house and

---

[173] *Lord Waring v London & Manchester Assurance Co Ltd* [1935] Ch 310, 318; *Corbett v Halifax BS* [2002] EWCA Civ 1849; [2003] 1 WLR 964. Section 104(2) protects a 'purchaser' and by s 205(1)(xxi), this means a purchaser in good faith.

[174] LRA 2002, s 52.

[175] ibid s 104(1). Similarly, the mortgagee can sell free of the interest held by a purchaser who has contracted to buy the land from the mortgagor: *Duke v Robson* [1973] 1 WLR 267, CA. In the case of an equitable mortgage of a legal estate, it has been said that this section empowers the mortgagee to convey the legal estate (*Re White Rose Cottage* [1965] Ch 940, 951, CA) although some commentators still take the view that the mortgage deed in such a case should contain provisions (such as an irrevocable power of attorney or a declaration of trust) to ensure that the mortgagee will be able to do so (C Harpum, *Megarry and Wade: The Law of Real Property* (6th edn, 2000) 1213). In the case of legal mortgages, the estate held as security by the mortgagee himself is extinguished: ibid ss 88, 89.

[176] *Lord Waring v London & Manchester Assurance Co Ltd* [1935] Ch 310; *National Provincial BS v Ahmed* [1995] 2 EGLR 127, CA.

[177] LPA 1925, s 105. LRA 2002, s 54, provides that for the purposes of LPA 1925, s 105, the mortgagee of registered land is taken to have notice of anything in the register immediately prior to the sale. This bridges the gap between the registration system, which does not generally use the equitable idea of 'notice' of an interest, and the provisions of LPA 1925, s 105, which is drafted in terms of a trust and does not refer to any register. The idea is to create a requirement that a selling mortgagee search the register for other subsequent mortgages, and notices and restrictions, before transferring any surplus proceeds to the mortgagor.

[178] See para 5.37.

[179] *Raja v Lloyds TSB Bank plc* [2001] 19 EG 143, leave to appeal this point denied [2001] EWCA Civ 210.

the mortgagee seeks possession through legal proceedings, the court has a discretion to postpone the taking of possession.[180] In the case of mortgages given by individuals that are 'regulated agreements' under the CCA 1974, a court order is required for sale.[181] Otherwise, the power of sale can be exercised extrajudicially, and it is for the mortgagee to choose the time and the mode of sale, whether private or by public auction.[182] The mortgagee holds the power for his own benefit, and is not a trustee of the power.[183] This means that he has no duty to try to improve the value of the property, or to wait for the most propitious time to sell.[184] In carrying out the sale, however, the mortgagee has certain duties; these are owed to the mortgagor, to any subsequent mortgagees,[185] and anyone else with a financial interest in the equity of redemption;[186] and, to any guarantor of the mortgage debt.[187] Where the mortgagor is a trustee of the land, however, no duty is owed directly to the beneficiary of the trust, even if the mortgagee is aware of the trust; the remedies for improper exercise of the power of sale must be exercised by the trustee mortgagor.[188] The content of the duty may be expressed as follows:

> The mortgagee. . .must show that the sale was in good faith and that the mortgagee took reasonable precautions to obtain the best price reasonably obtainable at the time. The mortgagee is not however bound to postpone the sale in the hope of obtaining a better price or to adopt a piecemeal method of sale which could only be carried out over a substantial period at some risk of loss.[189]

If the mortgagee breaches the duty to act reasonably in selling, the loss caused is to be measured by the difference between the sale price actually obtained and the price which would have been obtained had the mortgagee acted reasonably.[190] A mortgagee who breaches this duty cannot reduce its liability to the mortgagor

---

[180] See paras 5.42–5.44. In *Duke v Robson* [1973] 1 WLR 267, CA, the mortgagee had obtained a possession order but had not sought to enforce it; the mortgagor contracted to sell the land to the claimant; the mortgagee then took possession. It was held that the claimant could not interfere with the mortgagee's power of sale.

[181] CCA 1974, s 126. As noted in para 5.31, this provision applies even to mortgages that are otherwise regulated under FSMA 2000 rather than under CCA 1974. The current monetary limitation in the definition of 'regulated agreement' means that most mortgages are not regulated agreements; however, this monetary limitation was removed by amendments made in the CCA 2006, which are expected to come into force in 2008.

[182] LPA 1925, s 101(1)(i).

[183] *Cuckmere Brick Co Ltd v Mutual Finance Ltd* [1971] Ch 949, 965, CA.

[184] *Silven Properties Ltd v Royal Bank of Scotland plc* [2003] EWCA Civ 1409; [2004] 1 WLR 997.

[185] *Downsview Nominees Ltd v Mutual Finance Corp Ltd* [1993] AC 295, PC.

[186] *Freeguard v Royal Bank of Scotland plc* [2002] EWHC 2509 (Ch).

[187] *Standard Chartered Bank Ltd v Walker* [1982] 1 WLR 1410, CA.

[188] *Parker-Tweedale v Dunbar Bank plc* [1991] Ch 12, CA. The mortgagor's claim will be held for the benefit of the beneficiary, who may, on general principles, require him to exercise it.

[189] *Tse Kwong Lam v Wong Chit Sen* [1983] 1 WLR 1349, PC.

[190] *Skipton BS v Stott* [2001] QB 261, CA. The limitation period for a breach of the duty to act reasonably in selling is six years: *Raja v Lloyds TSB Bank plc* [2001] EWCA Civ 210.

by arguing that if it had realized a higher price, the extra money would in any event have been paid to a subsequent mortgagee.[191] Except via a court-ordered sale, discussed below, it is not possible for the mortgagee to sell to itself, as that is not considered a sale; but there is no absolute bar to selling to a company in which the mortgagee is financially interested. In such a case, however, the sale will be closely examined.[192]

(ii) Court-ordered sale

5.50   In an action for foreclosure, redemption or sale, brought by any interested party, the court has the power to order a sale on the application of the mortgagor or any mortgagee.[193] This means that even if the statutory power of sale does not arise, a sale may be ordered in an action brought by the mortgagee. In this way, the holder of an equitable mortgage which was not created by deed can effect a sale of the mortgaged property.[194] Similarly, a sale may be ordered where the statutory power fails to arise due to the defective drafting of a legal mortgage.[195] Even if the statutory power has arisen, but the mortgagor is impeding its exercise by threatening proceedings against potential purchasers, the court may order a sale to ensure that the purchaser's title will be unimpeachable.[196] On the other hand, the mortgagor may apply for a court-ordered sale, even where the mortgagee wants to retain the property. In *Palk v Mortgage Services Funding plc*,[197] the mortgaged home was worth less than the mortgage debt. The mortgagee wanted to take possession of the mortgaged home and lease it, hoping the value of the home would improve. The court granted the mortgagors' request for an order for sale, because the income from the lease would not cover the interest as it accrued and the debt would increase. In *Cheltenham and Gloucester plc v Krausz*,[198] however, the Court of Appeal made it clear that where a mortgagor is resisting the mortgagee's attempt to gain possession on the ground that the mortgagor wishes to sell the property, the mortgagor should be allowed to retain possession only if it is clear that the sale proceeds will be sufficient to discharge the debt. The court can authorize the mortgagee itself to bid on the property; although this creates an obvious conflict

---

[191] *Adamson v Halifax plc* [2002] EWCA Civ 1134; [2003] 1 WLR 60. However, if there is a serious prospect that the selling mortgagee may be sued by the subsequent mortgagee, the court may order that the money be paid into court against such a possibility.

[192] *Tse Kwong Lam v Wong Chit Sen* [1983] 1 WLR 1349, PC.

[193] LPA 1925, s 91(2).

[194] The court which orders the sale can make various orders to permit the legal estate (held by the mortgagor) to be transferred to the purchaser: ibid s 90(1).

[195] *Twentieth Century Banking Corp Ltd v Wilkinson* [1977] Ch 99, leaving open whether the jurisdiction requires that the mortgagee have a right of foreclosure.

[196] *Arab Bank plc v Mercantile Holdings Ltd* [1994] Ch 71.

[197] [1993] Ch 330, CA.

[198] [1997] 1 All ER 21, CA.

of self-interest and duty, the sale is under the control of the court, which will not approve an inadequate price.[199]

Another situation in which court-ordered sale may be sought is where land is held **5.51** on trust. In English law, any case of joint land ownership usually involves a trust of land.[200] Mortgagees usually wish to take a legal mortgage, and this requires the trustees of the trust to act together. It is possible, however, for a beneficiary, acting alone, to create a mortgage over his beneficial interest alone. This will necessarily be an equitable mortgage.[201] If the mortgagee seeks to enforce, the other beneficiary or beneficiaries are naturally potentially affected. The problem is similar to the case in which joint owners disagree as to whether to sell the land or not. The court has a discretion whether to order the trustees to comply with the wishes of the equitable mortgagee, but the mortgagee's rights will not be ignored.[202]

(c) Foreclosure

As long as the mortgagor has the legal right to redeem under the terms of the **5.52** mortgage agreement, there is no possibility of foreclosure. Once the mortgagor has committed some default, so that he has no right of redemption under the express terms of the agreement, then his only right of redemption is equitable. At this point, it becomes possible for the mortgagee to apply to the court to foreclose this equitable right of redemption.[203] Foreclosure will terminate the mortgage relationship and the equity of redemption, and leave the mortgagee holding beneficially the interest which the mortgagor used to hold in the land.[204]

---

[199] *Gordon Grant & Co Ltd v Boos* [1926] AC 781, 787, PC; *Palk v Mortgage Services Funding plc* [1993] Ch 330, 339–41, CA.

[200] Paras 4.386ff.

[201] The typical story is a couple who live in a jointly owned house. They are legal joint tenants of the fee simple estate, holding it on a trust of land for themselves as equitable joint tenants. The husband fraudulently purports to grant a legal mortgage over the fee simple estate. Acting alone, he is incapable of doing so. The effect is that he succeeds in giving an equitable mortgage over his beneficial share of the house: *First National Bank plc v Achampong* [2003] EWCA Civ 487.

[202] The governing legislation is Trusts of Land and Appointment of Trustees Act 1996, ss 14–15, which require the court to take account of the creditor's interests but also those of any children occupying the land. For discussion, see *Mortgage Corp v Shaire* [2001] Ch 743; *First National Bank plc v Achampong* [2003] EWCA Civ 487; *Edwards v Lloyds TSB Bank plc* [2004] EWHC 1745; [2004] Bankruptcy and Personal Insolvency Rep 1190, [2005] 1 Family Court Rep 139, in which the court made an order for sale but postponed its effect until the children reached the age of 18.

[203] *Twentieth Century Banking Corp Ltd v Wilkinson* [1977] Ch 99. The concept of redemption has never applied to the case of an equitable charge, and so likewise there is no possibility of foreclosure: *Tennant v Trenchard* (1869) 4 Ch App 537, 542, HL.

[204] If a mortgage was created by the conveyance of the mortgagor's estate to the mortgagee, foreclosure simply cuts off the mortgagor's ability to get back the estate he conveyed. (After 1925, in relation to land, this is only possible if the mortgagor's interest is equitable.) If a mortgage was created by demise, or by sub-demise, or by statutory legal charge, the decree of foreclosure effects a transfer to the mortgagee of the mortgagor's estate: LPA 1925, ss 88(2), 89(2). If there is an equitable mortgage of a legal estate, the foreclosure order will direct the conveyance of the legal

For foreclosure to be effective, the interest of any mortgagee subsequent to the foreclosing mortgagee must also be extinguished; any such party must therefore be made a party to the proceeding, and be given the opportunity to redeem the mortgagor's interest.[205]

5.53 It has never been possible to foreclose extrajudicially.[206] For the same reasons that the Court of Chancery controlled the terms of the mortgage agreement, it also controlled the process of foreclosure. The concern was that the mortgagee should not be unjustly enriched by acquiring the benefit of an estate which he was only intended to hold as security. The process therefore proceeds in stages, with the initial 'order nisi' giving the mortgagor six months to pay the debt and redeem the mortgage. Only on the failure of the mortgagor to raise the required funds will the court make the 'order absolute'. Even after that, the mortgagor can apply to open the foreclosure and recover his estate by paying the debt; rarely, this can occur even where the mortgagee has sold the estate to a third party.[207] Furthermore, at the application of the mortgagor or another interested party, the court may order a sale of the property instead.[208] A mortgagee who forecloses is not under any duty to the mortgagor regarding the subsequent sale of the land. Conversely, following such a sale the mortgagee is unable to sue the mortgagor for any sum still owing on the personal obligation which the mortgage secured, since he has put it beyond his power to allow the mortgagor to redeem.[209] For all of these reasons, foreclosure is rarely used today.[210]

---

estate: *Marshall v Shrewsbury* (1875) 10 Ch App 250, 254, DC. If the land is registered then consequent amendments to the register are required: LRA 2002, s 65 and Sch 4; Land Registration Rules 2003, SI 2003/1417, r 112.

[205] In other words, where there are multiple mortgages the principle governing foreclosure is 'foreclose down': not only the mortgagor but all subsequent mortgagees must be foreclosed. Conversely, in redemption the maxim is 'redeem up, foreclose down': if an intermediate mortgagee wishes to preserve its interest against a foreclosure attempt by a superior mortgagee, it must redeem that mortgage (and any others superior to its own), while foreclosing the mortgagor and any inferior mortgagee. See C Harpum, *Megarry and Wade: The Law of Real Property* (6th edn, 2000) 1239–40.

[206] *Re Farnol Eades Irvine & Co Ltd* [1915] 1 Ch 22, 24.

[207] *Campbell v Holyland* (1877) 7 Ch D 166, 172, *per* Jessel MR: 'it is impossible to say a priori what are the terms' on which a foreclosure might be reopened by the court.

[208] LPA 1925, s 91(2). In foreclosure proceedings this order will only be made if the mortgagee's interests can be protected: *Woolley v Colman* (1882) 21 Ch D 169; *Merchant Banking Co of London v London and Hanseatic Bank* (1886) 55 LJ Ch 479.

[209] *Kinnaird v Trollope* (1888) 39 Ch D 636, 642. On the same principle, if the mortgagee has foreclosed but still holds the property, he cannot sue on the personal obligation unless he opens the foreclosure and offers to allow redemption: *Gordon Grant & Co Ltd v Boos* [1926] AC 781, 785, PC.

[210] In *Palk v Mortgage Services Funding plc* [1993] Ch 330, 336, CA, Nicholls V-C said, 'So far as I am aware, foreclosure actions are almost unheard of today and have been so for many years.'

(d) Appointment of a receiver

The mortgagee, whether in or out of possession, may appoint a receiver to take **5.54** control of the mortgaged property and receive the income therefrom.[211] In the case of a mortgage by deed, such a power arises and is exercisable on the same conditions as the statutory power of sale.[212] The receiver is deemed to act as the agent of the mortgagor;[213] this means that if he commits a tort, it is the mortgagor and not the mortgagee who is vicariously liable. This generally makes the appointment of a receiver a more attractive option than taking possession in cases where the mortgagee does not intend to sell. The fact that the receiver is the agent of the mortgagor does not, however, mean that he acts primarily interests of the mortgagor.[214] On the contrary, his primary duty is to the mortgagee, to bring about the payment of the debt; at the same time, the receiver owes certain duties to the mortgagor, and to anyone else with an interest in the equity of redemption.[215] His general duty is to act in good faith; this duty will not be breached in the absence of dishonesty or improper motive.[216] Unlike a mortgagee, a receiver, once appointed, cannot be totally passive if that course would be damaging to the interests of the mortgagor or mortgagee.[217] If the mortgaged property includes a business, the receiver may choose to manage it, but he is not required to do so; if he does, he must act with due diligence, which requires the taking of reasonable steps.[218] If he chooses to sell any part of the mortgaged property, he is subject to the same duties as a mortgagee exercising the power of sale.[219] A receiver appointed under the statutory power is bound to apply money he receives in the order set out by the statute: taxes; payments having priority to the mortgage; his own fee, and insurance; interest on the mortgage debt; and, if directed, principal of the mortgage debt. Any surplus goes to the mortgagor.[220]

---

[211] If the mortgage is a floating charge over all or substantially all of the assets of the mortgagor, the appointment of a receiver has such serious implications for other creditors that it is regulated by the Insolvency Act 1986: see paras 19.18–19.20. Since 2002 the receiver will usually be characterized as an 'administrator' under that Act.

[212] LPA 1925, s 101(1)(iii) (power arises); s 109(1) (power exercisable). For the details see paras 5.46–5.47. By s 109(4), one who pays a receiver need not be concerned whether the power to appoint him was exercisable.

[213] ibid s 109(2).

[214] *Silven Properties Ltd v Royal Bank of Scotland plc* [2003] EWCA Civ 1409; [2004] 1 WLR 997.

[215] *Medforth v Blake* [2000] Ch 86, 102, CA.

[216] ibid.

[217] *Silven Properties Ltd v Royal Bank of Scotland plc* [2003] EWCA Civ 1409; [2004] 1 WLR 997.

[218] *Medforth v Blake* [2000] Ch 86, 102, CA.

[219] *Downsview Nominees Ltd v Mutual Finance Corp Ltd* [1993] AC 295, PC; para 5.49. This means that like a selling mortgagee, the receiver has no duty to try to improve the value of the property, or to wait for the most propitious time to sell: *Silven Properties Ltd v Royal Bank of Scotland plc* [2003] EWCA Civ 1409; [2004] 1 WLR 997.

[220] LPA 1925, s 109(8).

In the case of an equitable mortgage (including a charge) not created by deed, there is no statutory power, but a receiver may be appointed under the terms of the agreement, or by the court.[221]

(5) Miscellaneous Features

5.55 In this section a number of other features of the mortgage relationship are mentioned, although they are not discussed in detail.

(a) Leases

5.56 Subject to the terms of the mortgage agreement, whichever of the mortgagor or the mortgagee is in possession of the mortgaged land is given a statutory power to grant certain leases.[222] The power is constrained in certain ways, in particular as to the length of the lease.[223] A mortgagor in possession may make an unauthorized lease, being either inconsistent with the statutory power, or inconsistent with the terms of the mortgage agreement.[224] It has been held that in such a case, the lease is not enforceable against the mortgagee.[225] He may treat the lessee as a trespasser or accept him as his own tenant; such acceptance may be inferred from conduct.[226]

(b) Other profits

5.57 Subject to the terms of the mortgage agreement, a mortgagee in possession under a mortgage created by deed has a statutory power to cut and sell timber, within certain limits.[227]

---

[221] Supreme Court Act 1981, s 37.

[222] LPA 1925, s 99. By s 100, there is also a power to accept the surrender of a lease in order to grant a new lease. If the mortgagor's power to grant a lease is not excluded by a mortgage agreement, the exercise of the power is usually made conditional on the consent of the mortgagee.

[223] Agricultural or occupation leases may be for up to 50 years; building leases (in which, by ibid s 99(9), the lessee builds or improves buildings on the land) for up to 999 years.

[224] In particular the agreement is likely to require the written consent of the mortgagee to the granting of a lease by the mortgagor.

[225] *Britannia BS v Earl* [1990] 1 WLR 422, CA. Exceptionally in the case of agricultural land, by LPA 1925, s 99(13A), an unauthorized lease is enforceable against the mortgagee, if the lease was granted after 1 March 1948 but before 1 September 1995, and if the other requirements of the LPA 1925, s 99 are satisfied. Of course, if the mortgage is not registered, it may be subordinate to the interest of the lessee. This is effectively a priority contest. For an example decided under the prior land registration statute, see *Barclays Bank plc v Zaroovabli* [1997] Ch 321.

[226] *Chatsworth Properties Ltd v Effiom* [1971] 1 WLR 144, CA; *Nijar v Mann* (CA, 18 December 1998).

[227] LPA 1925, s 101(1)(iv).

(c) Insurance

If the mortgage was created by deed, then the mortgagee has a statutory power to **5.58** insure the property against fire, the costs being chargeable to the mortgagor with the same priority as the sums due under the mortgage agreement.[228] The power is subject to the terms of the mortgage agreement and to a limit as to amount, and does not arise if the mortgagor has insured the property with the consent of the mortgagee.[229]

(d) Possession of title deeds

In the classic legal mortgage by conveyance, the mortgagee would hold the title **5.59** deeds to the mortgagor's estate in the land, having taken a conveyance of that estate. This provided an invaluable safeguard against any unauthorized further dealings by the mortgagor. A mortgage by demise or sub-demise did not, however, give any right at common law to possession of the title deeds, since the estate held by the mortgagee was not the same as that held by the mortgagor; and all legal mortgages are now mortgages by demise or sub-demise, or are treated as such.[230] It is therefore provided by statute that the first legal mortgagee shall have the same right to possession of the title deeds as if his mortgage had been by conveyance of the mortgagor's estate.[231] Upon discharge of the mortgage they must be returned to the mortgagor, or any subsequent mortgagee of which the mortgagee is aware.[232] If an equitable mortgage is protected by deposit of the title deeds, the mortgagee has the right to retain those deeds until the debt is paid.

In registered land, however, the idea of title deeds has become obsolete. The LRA **5.60** 2002 abolishes the 'land certificate' that used to be issued to the holder of a registered title and the 'charge certificate' that used to be issued to the holder of a registered legal charge.[233] The Land Registry will issue 'title information documents', showing the content of the register at a given time. These, however, are not documents of title; they are not needed in order to effect subsequent registered dealings with the land. These changes pave the way for electronic conveyancing, and they make obsolete the mortgagee's right to possession of title deeds.

---

[228] ibid s 101(1)(ii).

[229] ibid s 108.

[230] See para 5.08.

[231] LPA 1925, ss 85(1), 86(1). The mortgagor has the right to inspect and make copies of the title deeds: ibid s 96(1). However, a first legal mortgage of unregistered land with the deposit of title deeds will now trigger compulsory registration of the land: LRA 2002, ss 4(1)(g), (8).

[232] Although registration of a subsequent mortgage of unregistered land is treated as giving notice of it to all parties (LPA 1925, s 198(1)), this rule is overridden in this context (ibid s 96(2)).

[233] Land Registration Act 2002 (Transitional Provisions) Order 2003, SI 2003/1953, art 24.

(e) Consolidation

5.61 Consolidation is an old doctrine by which a mortgagee who holds more than one mortgage, granted by the same mortgagor but on different properties in respect of more than one loan, may resist the redemption of one mortgage until the other debt or debts are also paid. The mortgagee is allowed to consolidate the separate transactions and treat them as one. The matter is complex (and arguably unfair) because the right may be asserted even against a transferee from the original mortgagor, who has no knowledge of the other transaction or transactions. It is only necessary that the right to consolidate be reserved in at least one of the mortgage agreements.[234] Details of the doctrine may be found in specialized texts.[235]

(6) Discharge

5.62 When a mortgage of unregistered land is to be discharged, it is not generally necessary for the mortgagee to reconvey the interest he holds, or in the case of a mortgage by demise or sub-demise, to surrender the leasehold interest he holds. If he signs a receipt on or annexed to the document by which the mortgage was created, then such a reconveyance or surrender will occur by operation of law.[236] It is, however, still possible to discharge the mortgage by a reconveyance or surrender,[237] and this will be necessary if the mortgage is being discharged as to only part of the mortgaged property.

5.63 In the context of registered land, these provisions also apply to equitable mortgages, which are not registered. They do not, however, apply to registered charges on registered land.[238] In that context, the registrar must amend the register to show the discharge of a registered charge upon the request of the charge holder, or upon proof of the satisfaction of the charge.[239]

---

[234] LPA 1925, s 93. In registered land, a right to consolidate can be noted on the register pursuant to LRA 2002, s 57; Land Registration Rules 2003, SI 2003/1417, r 110.

[235] For example C Harpum, *Megarry and Wade: The Law of Real Property* (6th edn, 2000) 1217–1223; EH Burn and J Cartwright, *Cheshire and Burn's Modern Law of Real Property* (17th edn, 2006) 779–82.

[236] LPA 1925, s 115(1). The receipt must state the name of the person who paid the money, and if it is not the person entitled to the equity of redemption, then the receipt generally operates instead as a transfer of the mortgage to the payor: ibid s 115(2). This provision however does not operate in the case of a mortgage held by a building society: see Building Societies Act 1986, Sch 2A, para 1(2).

[237] LPA 1925, s 115(4).

[238] LPA 1925, s 115(10).

[239] LRA 2002, s 65 and Sch 4.

C. Real Security Over Moveables

This section, 'Real Security Over Moveables', will examine in turn each of the **5.64** different kinds of security over moveable property, describing for each one the rules for creation, registration and enforcement. Broadly speaking, the principles discussed in the previous section apply here as well. This is true for principles developed from the case law, such as the prohibition on clogging the equity of redemption, or the principles on unconscionable bargains. As for statutory provisions, consumer protection statutes are generally applicable in both contexts.[240] The statutory protections for residential mortgagors are, however, confined to land mortgages.[241] The statutory powers that are granted by the LPA 1925, where the mortgage is granted by deed and the deed does not otherwise provide, can also apply to security over moveables.[242] In security over moveable property, however, there are many differences related to the formalities for creation and for registration. There is also a difference in terminology between this section and the previous one. In the section on security over land, 'mortgage' was used to include any security interest in land. In this section, it is more important to distinguish between a transfer of title for security and other means of creating a security interest, and so here 'mortgage' is used in the narrower sense of a transfer of title by way of security. Other security interests (such as the charge or the pledge) are always referred to by their precise names. This follows common legal usage in relation to moveables.

(1) Legal Security

Unlike the position in relation to land, the common law (as distinct from equity) **5.65** did recognize certain interests in moveables which were, by their nature, security interests. These security interests depend upon possession by the creditor, which limits their commercial utility. As in the law of land mortgages, there is a long tradition of using legal ownership as a security interest, especially since this makes it possible to leave the debtor in possession.

---

[240] This includes many of the statutory protections discussed in paras 5.31–5.36. The FMSA 2000 will not usually apply to transactions involving security over moveables, but the CCA 1974 may well do (but CCA 1974, s 126 applies only to security over land).

[241] This includes the criminal law protections against eviction (para 5.40) and the judicial discretion to postpone the taking of possession by a mortgagee (paras 5.41–5.43), and CCA 1974, s 126, which forbids any extrajudicial enforcement of a land mortgage within its scope (on which see para 5.31).

[242] These include the power of sale, the power to appoint a receiver, and the power to insure (paras 5.46–5.49, 5.54, 5.58). Regardless of whether there is a deed, the court's power to order sale (para 5.50) is triggered by any mortgage litigation.

(a) Pledge

5.66 Pledge is a transaction in which the debtor (pledgor) transfers possession of a thing to the creditor (pledgee) to hold as security.[243] The focus on possession limits the transaction to tangible assets.[244] In general, no formalities are required beyond the transfer of possession.[245] Upon constitution of the pledge, the pledgee acquires a real right in the pledged thing; the pledgor retains ownership,[246] but does not have a right to possession until the debt secured is paid.[247] The pledgee's interest may be transferred or sub-pledged.[248] It carries with it a power of sale which arises by operation of law upon default by the pledgor;[249] it may, however, amount to a breach of contract for the pledgee to sell the goods without first giving notice to the pledgor.[250] What counts as a default is a matter of agreement between the parties.[251] Subject to agreement, the pledgor may redeem the pledge by paying the full debt with interest, at any time before sale has occurred. The pledgee need not sell the goods but can sue the pledgor on the debt; and if, after sale, there is a deficiency, the pledgee can sue for this.[252] If there is a surplus, it is held on trust for the pledgor; it must be repaid with interest, and if it has been used in business the pledgee will have to account to the pledgor for profits earned.[253]

---

[243] Further discussion from para 16.67. Where the pledgor is an individual the transaction is often called 'pawn' and the pledgee who enters into such transactions in the course of his business is called a 'pawnbroker'. Like anyone whose business involves lending money to consumers, a pawnbroker is required to be licensed under the CCA 1974; failing this, he commits an offence and the transaction is likely to be unenforceable against the debtor: ss 39–40.

[244] This can include documentary intangibles (on which see para 5.75), including securities in bearer form (*Carter v Wake* (1877) 4 Ch D 605); but securities in registered form are considered entirely intangible. A security interest in registered securities can only be taken by way of mortgage or charge: *Harrold v Plenty* [1901] 2 Ch 314; *Stubbs v Slater* [1910] 1 Ch 632, CA.

[245] Again the situation is different in the case of a pawnbroker. He commits an offence if he fails to provide the pledgor with prescribed documentation (CCA 1974, s 115) and the agreement may be unenforceable.

[246] *The Odessa* [1916] 1 AC 145, 158–9, PC. The pledgor may transfer his ownership to another, who will have the same rights against the pledgee as the original pledgor did: *Franklin v Neate* (1844) 13 M & W 481, 153 ER 200.

[247] *Donald v Suckling* (1866) LR 1 QB 585; *Halliday v Holgate* (1868) LR 3 Ex 299, Exch Ch.

[248] Although such a disposition may be a breach of the contract with the pledgor: *Donald v Suckling* (1866) LR 1 QB 585. In the case of a sub-pledge the pledgor will be entitled to recover the goods from the sub-pledgee on tendering the amount due from the pledgor to the original pledgee: ibid.

[249] In the case of pawnbrokers, the CCA 1974, s 120 provides that in the case of debts under £75, a power of sale does not arise but rather the ownership of the pledged goods passes to the pawnee.

[250] *Halliday v Holgate* (1868) LR 3 Ex 299, Exch Ch. In the case of pawnbrokers, the period and form of notice are governed by the statute: CCA 1974, s 121.

[251] If the agreement did not stipulate a date for repayment, the pledgee may demand payment upon reasonable notice: *Ex p Hubbard* (1886) 17 QBD 690, 698, CA; *Deverges v Sandeman, Clark & Co* [1902] 1 Ch 579, 589, CA. In the case of pawnbrokers the pawnor must be given at least six months in which to redeem the pawn: CCA 1974, s 116.

[252] *Jones v Marshall* (1889) 24 QBD 269, DC.

[253] *Mathew v TM Sutton Ltd* [1994] 4 All ER 793.

In order to create the pledge, possession of the goods must be transferred to the **5.67** pledgee.[254] If the goods are held by a third party, the transfer may be by attornment of that party.[255] A formal attornment is not needed if the goods are represented by a document of title. Transfer of possession of a bill of lading, with any necessary endorsement, has always been treated (where the parties so intended it) as equivalent to an attornment to the transferee by the issuer of the bill.[256] Goods may therefore be pledged by the transfer to the pledgee of the bill of lading.[257] At least in the case of a pledgor who is a mercantile agent of the owner, this possibility has been extended by statute to a range of other documents, the transfer of which, at common law, was not apt to transfer a right to possession without an actual attornment from the third party.[258]

Possession by the pledgor himself might be thought to be inconsistent with the **5.68** nature of the transaction. The transfer of possession to the pledgee serves the purpose of removing the asset from the apparent ownership of the pledgor, thereby reducing the potential for problems relating to the deception of third parties. Nonetheless, it has been suggested that a pledge can be created by the pledgor himself attorning to the pledgee, making himself the pledgee's bailee.[259] In any event, once a pledge has been created, it has been held that it is not destroyed by a retransfer of possession to the pledgor, so long as this is done for a limited

---

[254] There is a general equitable principle that if value has been given for a promise to create or transfer a legal interest, a corresponding equitable interest arises immediately: see para 5.13. This principle does not apply to a promise to give a pledge, and so such a promise creates no real rights in the creditor: 'there was no such thing as equitable possession': RM Goode, *Commercial Law* (3rd edn, 2004) 627.

[255] See paras 16.78–16.81. An attornment is a bailee's acknowledgement to a third party, made with the bailor's authority, that the bailee now holds for the third party. It is an exception to the basic principle that possession cannot pass by intention and words alone.

[256] Goode (n 254 above) 886–90.

[257] *Meyerstein v Barber* (1870) LR 4 HL 317. Even if the bill of lading is endorsed to the pledgee, he does not thereby become the owner of the goods, but only has the limited interest of a pledgee: *Sewell v Burdick* (1884) 10 App Cas 363, HL.

[258] The Factors Act 1889, s 2(4), defines 'document of title' to include 'any bill of lading, dock warrant, warehouse-keeper's certificate, and warrant or order for the delivery of goods, and any other document used in the ordinary course of business as proof of the possession or control of goods, or authorizing or purporting to authorize, either by endorsement or by delivery, the possessor of the document to transfer or receive goods thereby represented'; and s 3 provides, 'A pledge of the documents of title to goods shall be deemed to be a pledge of the goods'. In *Inglis v Robertson* [1898] AC 616, HL, it was held under the Scots statute (whose wording was identical) that s 3 only applied to transactions made by a mercantile agent. *Inglis* was apparently approved in *Official Assignee of Madras v Mercantile Bank of India Ltd* [1935] AC 53, 60, PC, although Lord Wright observed that it was 'curious and anomalous' that a mercantile agent should be able to make an effective pledge using one of these documents in the absence of any attornment, while the owner of the goods could not.

[259] *Dublin City Distillery Co Ltd v Doherty* [1914] AC 823, HL; although, if the attornment is effected via a document, it may well be registrable as a bill of sale. See para 5.76.

purpose only.[260] In modern commercial practice it is often necessary for financial institutions, which are pledgees of bills of lading, to release them to the pledgor for the purpose of selling the goods; the debt is paid out of the proceeds of the sale. This is usually done under the terms of a 'trust receipt', by which the pledgor takes possession as trustee for the benefit of the pledgee; because the transfer of possession is for a limited purpose, the pledge is not destroyed.[261]

(b) Lien

5.69 A common law lien is a right to retain possession of a tangible moveable until a debt is paid.[262] Like the pledge, it is a possessory security, but there are several important differences. The lien may arise by agreement, but unlike the pledge it may also arise by operation of law. Another difference is that 'in the case of a pledge the owner delivers possession to the creditor as security, whereas in the case of a lien the creditor retains possession of goods previously delivered to him for some other purpose'.[263] The lien does not give rise to any power of sale but only permits retention.[264] Finally, the interest of the holder of a lien is not transferable; the lien is lost when possession is lost.

5.70 Many liens arise by operation of law, or from recognized usage. A 'common carrier' is who advertises his services to the public, and as a result is obliged by law to accept goods for carriage; as a kind of recompense, such a carrier has a lien on his customers' goods for carriage charges when they become due. A sea carrier also has a lien on cargo for carriage charges, and on passengers' luggage for their fares. The innkeeper, who also follows a common calling, has a lien on the

---

[260] *Reeves v Capper* (1838) 5 Bing NC 136, 132 ER 1057; *Mercantile Bank of India Ltd v Central Bank of India Ltd* [1938] AC 287, PC. This is true even though (as in both of these cases) this situation permits the pledgor to mislead others, by whom the pledgee's legal security interest is undetectable.

[261] *North Western Bank Ltd v John Poynter, Son & Macdonalds* [1895] AC 56, 68; *Re David Allester Ltd* [1922] 1 Ch 211, 216. Because it is said that the pledge continues, the security is not registrable as a bill of sale or charge. Although this will protect the pledgee on the pledgor's insolvency, it may not protect him against a subsequent pledge of the same document of title; the subsequent pledgee may be able to rely on the Factors Act 1889, s 2 (on which see para 10.23): *Lloyds Bank Ltd v Bank of America National Trust and Savings Association* [1938] 2 KB 147, CA.

[262] Excluded from consideration here is the *equitable* lien, a non-possessory security interest in the nature of a charge, the best known example of which is held by the unpaid seller of land: para 5.92.

[263] *Re Cosslett (Contractors) Ltd* [1998] Ch 495, 508, CA.

[264] Note however that in common with anyone who is in possession of another's goods, the holder of a lien may be able to sell uncollected goods under the terms of the Torts (Interference with Goods) Act 1977, ss 12–13. An innkeeper may be authorized to sell goods under the Innkeepers Act 1878, s 1, and an unpaid seller of goods is given the right to resell them by the Sale of Goods Act 1979, s 48.

belongings of guests to secure payment for their food and lodging.[265] The common law also grants a lien to anyone to whom goods are entrusted in order that he can employ his work or skill on them, so long as they are thereby improved.[266] Under maritime law, liens may arise against a ship in respect of work done, or for damage done by it; and against a ship or goods, in respect of salvage; but the principles apply only in tidal waters.[267]

All of these may be classified as 'particular' liens, which allow the goods to be retained only against payment of obligations which are referable to goods in question. Other liens are 'general', meaning that they allow the goods to be retained until all obligations are discharged. In litigation raising the issue whether accountants have a lien over their clients' papers, Lawton LJ summarized the position for many professionals: **5.71**

> The kind of work [accountants] do may be very different from that of a craftsman who is making or repairing a chattel (the kind of work which gave rise to the common law concept of particular liens); but since the beginning of the 19th century arbitrators, architects, conveyancers and parliamentary agents have been adjudged capable of having particular liens. . . Solicitors, bankers, factors, stockbrokers and insurance brokers have long enjoyed the right to general liens.[268]

Liens also arise by statute. The seller of goods has a lien over them until he is paid.[269] An airport has a lien over an aircraft for airport charges and fuel supplied.[270] A garage which, acting as the agent of the police, recovers an abandoned car has a lien over it until it has been paid for its services.[271] **5.72**

Finally, a lien may be created by agreement, or an agreement can modify the lien which would otherwise arise. Carriers commonly stipulate for a general lien,[272] as do warehousemen.[273] Such a lien will not amount to a mortgage or charge **5.73**

---

[265] There is a power of sale under the Innkeepers Act 1878, s 1. By the Hotel Proprietors Act 1956, s 2(2), the lien does not extend (as it did at common law) to the guest's vehicle, nor to any live animal.

[266] *Tappenden v Artus* [1964] 2 QB 185, CA. Because of the requirement of improvement, there is no lien for the maintenance of an animal: *Re Southern Livestock Producers Ltd* [1964] 1 WLR 24.

[267] *The Goring* [1988] 1 AC 831, HL.

[268] *Woodworth v Conroy* [1976] QB 884, 890, CA. It was held that accountants have at least a particular lien, the question whether they have a general one being left open.

[269] Sale of Goods Act 1979, ss 41–3, with a power of sale in s 48.

[270] Civil Aviation Act 1982, s 88, as interpreted in *Bristol Airport plc v Powdrill* [1990] Ch 744, CA.

[271] Road Traffic Regulation Act 1984, s 101, as interpreted in *Service Motor Policies at Lloyds v City Recovery Ltd* [1997] EWCA Civ 2073; *Surrey Breakdown Ltd v Knight* [1999] RTR 84, CA.

[272] *George Barker (Transport) Ltd v Eynon* [1974] 1 WLR 462, CA.

[273] *Chellaram & Sons (London) Ltd v Butlers Warehousing and Distribution Ltd* [1978] 2 Lloyd's Rep 412, CA.

(which would require registration for effectiveness in insolvency), even if it is coupled with a power of sale.[274]

(c) Legal ownership as security

(i) Mortgage

5.74 **General.** As with land, one way to secure a debt is to transfer ownership of moveables to the creditor, with an agreement for retransfer upon payment.[275] Equity will intervene, as in the case of land, to elevate the mortgagor's contractual rights to a proprietary interest or 'equity of redemption'. The advantage of this transaction over a pledge is that the debtor can remain in possession of the asset. However, the common law developed differently in relation to moveables. Since there are generally no documents of title for tangible moveables, a transfer of ownership, with the transferor remaining in possession, creates an appearance of unfettered ownership in the transferor which potentially misleads his other creditors; and such a transaction was almost invariably viewed as a fraud on those creditors, and so void.[276] This left the transferee with no real rights and so no security. For tangible moveables, the mortgage could only succeed if possession were transferred to the mortgagee. The 'chattel mortgage' was therefore not viable in its non-possessory form until the creation of a public registration system for documents by which such mortgages were created.[277] This legislation, the Bills of Sale Acts 1878 and 1882, continues to impose restrictions which limit the commercial utility of the transaction.[278] It does not, however, apply to companies.[279]

---

[274] *Great Eastern Rly Co v Lord's Trustee* [1909] AC 109, HL; *Trident International Ltd v Barlow* [1999] 2 BCLC 506, CA.

[275] As discussed earlier (para 5.06), a legal mortgage of land could be created granting a legal leasehold estate in the land, and the modern 'charge by way of legal mortgage' over land is defined by reference to this transaction (paras 5.08–5.09). A legal mortgage of moveables is always created by the transfer of ownership, since the doctrine of estates is said not to apply to moveables.

[276] Under the Statute of Fraudulent Conveyances 1571, now repealed. The situation was different where there was a register of ownership, as in the case of ships.

[277] Initially the Bills of Sale Act 1854; now, the Bills of Sale Act 1878 and the Bills of Sale Act (1878) Amendment Act 1882, together cited as the Bills of Sale Acts 1878 and 1882. It is a peculiar feature of English law, explicable historically, that the term 'bill of sale' primarily refers not to a document evidencing a sale of goods but rather to one creating a chattel mortgage: see AP Bell, *Modern Law of Personal Property in England and Ireland* (1989) 189.

[278] In particular, the Acts make it impossible to create a transaction which will give the mortgagee even an equitable mortgage in property acquired after the transaction.

[279] Bills of Sale Act (1878) Amendment Act 1882, s 17; *Re Standard Manufacturing Co* [1891] 1 Ch 627, CA. In *NV Slavenburg's Bank v Intercontinental Natural Resources Ltd* [1980] 1 WLR 1076, Lloyd J held that the Bills of Sale Acts do not apply to any corporation. That case concerned a foreign company charging property in England; this situation has been more clearly addressed under CA 2006 but is not discussed here. Lloyd J did not refer to *Re North Wales Produce and Supply Society* [1922] 2 Ch 340 in which it was held that a Welsh industrial and provident society (a co-operative), which is a corporation not formed under the Companies Acts, was subject to the Bills of Sale Acts. It is now provided that if such societies do register charges that they give, the Bills of Sale Acts do not

Companies are subject to a different registration system which allows them to use the chattel mortgage more flexibly.[280]

Intangibles need to be considered in two categories. A 'documentary intangible' is **5.75** a right represented by a document which is apt to transfer the right by delivery, possibly with indorsement.[281] The common law treats it as a tangible, and so it is the proper subject matter of a pledge. It may, however, also be mortgaged. A 'pure intangible' is a right which is not represented by such a document. These could not be assigned at common law, although an attempted assignment would take effect in equity.[282] By statute it is now possible to make a legal assignment of a pure intangible, and in this way a legal mortgage of such an intangible is possible.[283] Some pure intangibles are assigned according to particular statutory rules.[284]

Creation. The creation of a mortgage involves the making of an agreement **5.76** and the conveyance of ownership of the mortgaged moveables. In the case of a mortgage of tangible moveables by an individual or a partnership, the Bills of Sale Acts 1878 and 1882 will generally apply.[285] The document evidencing the agreement will be absolutely void (even against the borrower) unless it is in the

---

apply: Agricultural Credits Act 1928, s 14 (in the case of a charge over farming stock); Industrial and Provident Societies Act 1967, s 1 (in the case of other charges). These registrations, however, appear to be optional, and the Bills of Sale Acts will otherwise apply to charges given by such societies.

280 Para 5.77.

281 RM Goode, *Commercial Law* (3rd edn, 2004) 48–50.

282 The common law did recognize the assignment of debts due to and from the Crown.

283 LPA 1925, s 136(1). The provision applies only to 'an absolute assignment. . .(not purporting to be by way of charge only)' but it has been held that this does not exclude an assignment by way of mortgage: *Tancred v Delagoa Bay and East Africa Rly Co* (1889) 23 QBD 239, approved in *Durham Brothers v Robertson* [1898] 1 QB 765, 772, CA. It may be difficult to distinguish a mortgage of an intangible from a sale: see paras 5.98–5.101.

284 Shares in a company are transferred by amendment of the company's shareholder register (which may or may not require a written form of transfer: CA 1985, s 182(1); CA 1989, s 207; CA 2006, s 544; Stock Transfer Act 1963, s 1; Stock Transfer Act 1982; Uncertificated Securities Regulations 2001, SI 2001/3755). Life assurance policies are assigned under the Policies of Assurance Act 1867; copyright and related rights, under the Copyright, Designs and Patents Act 1988, ss 90, 191B, 222; patents, under the Patents Act 1977, ss 30–3; registered trade marks, under the Trade Marks Act 1994, ss 24–5; registered designs, under the Registered Designs Act 1994, s 19.

285 There are exceptions, including assignments for the benefit of creditors, marriage settlements, ship mortgages, and 'transfers of goods in the ordinary course of business of any trade or calling': Bills of Sale Act 1878, s 4. The 'ordinary course' exemption will cover absolute sales of goods (*Stephenson v Thompson* [1924] 2 KB 240, CA), but it has been interpreted narrowly in the context of transfers by way of security for loans (*Charles Tennant, Sons & Co v Howatson* (1888) 13 App Cas 489, PC; *Re Hall* (1884) 14 QBD 386, 394; *Ian Chisholm Textiles Ltd v Griffiths* [1994] 2 BCLC 291, [1994] BCC 96). The Acts do not apply to an agricultural charge given by a farmer (Agricultural Credits Act 1928, s 8(1); see para 5.102), nor to aircraft mortgages (Mortgaging of Aircraft Order 1972, SI 1972/1268, art 16(1)). There is also an exception for security on imported goods before they are warehoused or reshipped: Bills of Sale Act 1890, s 1; this is probably confined to excepting trust receipts (on which see para 5.68), and does not except a document granting security over future goods: *NV Slavenburg's Bank v Intercontinental Natural Resources Ltd* [1980] 1 WLR 1076.

form required by the Acts.[286] It must be in writing in the prescribed form, attested by at least one witness.[287] The document must also be registered under the Acts within seven days of execution; if this is not done, the security is unenforceable, even against the borrower, although the loan agreement is not affected.[288] The bill must list all of the property covered by it; this means that it is impossible to create a security which will extend to property acquired later.[289] These Acts do not apply to a mortgage of intangibles, which can be created without formality, except in so far as the conveyance of the intangible requires it.[290]

5.77 In the case of a company, there is no prescribed form for the document creating the mortgage. Unlike the situation under the Bills of Sale Acts, a company can create a mortgage that will extend (at least in equity) to after-acquired property as soon as it is acquired.[291] A different registration system applies: certain mortgages must be submitted, along with prescribed particulars, to the Registrar of Companies under the CA 1985.[292] The list of registrable mortgages is such that in practice almost every mortgage is registrable.[293] Failure to register within 21 days of execution makes the mortgage 'void against the liquidator or administrator and any creditor of the company'.[294] It also makes the money secured by the mortgage payable immediately.[295]

---

[286] Money advanced will be recoverable in unjust enrichment: *North Central Wagon Finance Co Ltd v Brailsford* [1962] 1 WLR 1288. The Acts deal in documents and not in transactions; they require documents to be in the correct form and registered, but do not state that a document is essential. It has been suggested that a purely oral mortgage of moveables could therefore be created: RM Goode, *Commercial Law* (3rd edn, 2004) 647 n 1. Given the policies which motivated the Acts, however, it is probably true that unless possession were transferred to the mortgagee, the attempted conveyance would be ineffectual in such a case.

[287] Bills of Sale Act (1878) Amendment Act 1882, ss 9–10. Any bill made in consideration of less than £30 is void in any event: s 12.

[288] ibid s 8. Registration is with a Master of the Queen's Bench Division of the High Court of Justice: Bills of Sale Act 1878, s 13. In addition to the bill of sale and all attachments in duplicate, an affidavit is required: ibid s 10(2).

[289] ibid s 4; it is void (except against the borrower) in respect of property not listed. This means that as against third parties, not even an equitable mortgage could be claimed in such property. Even if the schedule specifies the after-acquired property, it is to this extent void (again, except against the borrower): ibid s 5.

[290] This follows from the definition of 'personal chattels' in the Bills of Sale Act 1878, s 4. There is authority suggesting that if a document grants security over both property that is within the Acts and property that is not, it may be valid as to the property outside the Acts: *Re North Wales Produce and Supply Society* [1922] 2 Ch 340. Note however that by the Insolvency Act 1986, s 344, certain general assignments of 'book debts' (accounts receivable arising in the course of business) are void against a trustee in bankruptcy unless they are registered under the Bills of Sale Act 1878 as if they were absolute assignments (whether the assignment is indeed absolute, or by way of security). In this case a schedule of property is not required. See para 19.85.

[291] Para 5.81.

[292] CA 1985, ss 395, 396(4); CA 2006, ss 860, 861(5).

[293] CA 1985, s 396; CA 2006, s 860. For more detail, see para 5.103.

[294] CA 1985, s 395; CA 2006, s 874(1); para 5.142.

[295] CA 1985, s 395(2); CA 2006, s 874(3).

There are other registers for mortgages of particular kinds of asset. They include **5.78** mortgages of ships[296] and aircraft,[297] and of patents,[298] trade marks,[299] and registered designs.[300] In these systems a failure to register does not invalidate the mortgage, although it will affect its priority. These requirements are, however, cumulative with those of the Companies Acts,[301] and so if the mortgagor is a company the mortgage is subject to avoidance if the Companies Act registration is not made in time.

In any case, the nature of the property mortgaged will dictate what is required **5.79** for the conveyance. In a mortgage transaction, legal title to tangible moveables will pass when the parties so intend, without the need for delivery.[302] The legal assignment of a pure intangible must be in writing, and there must be notice in writing to the debtor.[303] In the case of registered securities, the appropriate steps must be taken to bring about the amendment of the relevant register. Other intangibles may be governed by special rules.[304]

Enforcement. The features of a legal mortgage of moveables are essentially the **5.80** same as those of a mortgage of land. The right to take possession is the same, except in the case of mortgages governed by the Bills of Sale Acts 1878 and 1882, where it is restricted.[305] Unlike in the case of land, a power of sale arises at common law in the case of intangibles,[306] and may also do so for tangible moveables.[307] A power of sale may arise by agreement; if the mortgage was created by deed, then the statutory power which arises under every mortgage so created will generally

---

[296] Merchant Shipping Act 1995, Sch 1, para 7, with requirements as to form. Note however that these provisions do not apply to all ships; the matter turns on how the ship itself is registered. See ibid s 16(2); A Clarke, 'Ship Mortgages' in N Palmer and E McKendrick (eds), *Interests in Goods* (2nd edn, 1998). Because the Bills of Sale Acts 1878 and 1882 do not apply to ship mortgages (Bills of Sale Act 1878, s 4), it follows that if a legal mortgage is given by an individual over an unregistered ship, it is not registrable but it nonetheless binds a good faith purchaser of the ship: *British Credit Trust Ltd v The Owners of the Shizelle (The Shizelle)* [1992] 2 Lloyd's Rep 444.

[297] Mortgaging of Aircraft Order 1972, SI 1972/1268. A floating charge which extends to an aircraft is not registrable under this Order: art 2(2). The Bills of Sale Acts 1878 and 1882 are not applicable to a mortgage of an aircraft by an individual: 1972 Order, art 16(1).

[298] Patents Act 1977, s 33.

[299] Trade Marks Act 1994, s 25.

[300] Registered Designs Act 1949, s 19.

[301] See CA 1985, ss 396(1)(h), (j), (3A); CA 2006, ss 860(7)(h), (i), 861(4).

[302] See AP Bell, *Modern Law of Personal Property in England and Ireland* (1989) 184.

[303] LPA 1925, s 136(1).

[304] See n 284.

[305] The Bills of Sale Act (1878) Amendment Act 1882, s 7, allows seizure only in specified circumstances, such as default, bankruptcy or other events evidencing insolvency, or fraudulent removal of the goods.

[306] *Stubbs v Slater* [1910] 1 Ch 632, CA.

[307] There was disagreement on this point in *Re Morritt* (1886) 18 QBD 222, 233, 235, CA, and it was said to be an open question in *Deverges v Sandeman, Clark & Co* [1902] 1 Ch 579, 589, CA.

be available.[308] The duties of a mortgagee exercising a power of sale are the same as in mortgages of land.[309] Sale can be authorized by the court.[310] If the mortgage was created by deed, there will be a statutory power to appoint a receiver,[311] but again this can also be stipulated in the agreement. The mortgagee can foreclose on application to the court.

5.81 **Limitations of legal mortgages.** In the context of moveables, one deficiency of the legal mortgage relates to after-acquired property. The mortgagor might promise to transfer ownership of property which he will later acquire, but this promise will not convey the legal ownership when the property is acquired. However, a promise, for value given, to create a legal mortgage will create an immediate equitable mortgage if that is consistent with the intention of the parties.[312] In this context, this principle means that as soon as the mortgagor acquires property which is within the scope of the promise given earlier, it will be immediately subject to an *equitable* mortgage, even before the mortgagee transfers legal ownership, or even if he never does. The equitable mortgage will be discussed below, but so long as it is properly registered, an equitable mortgage arising in the circumstances just mentioned will usually differ from a legal one only in respect of priorities.[313]

(ii) Retention of ownership

5.82 A legal mortgage is a *transfer* of ownership by way of security. In some situations, a creditor who is the owner of a moveable thing may instead retain ownership until he is paid in full. This interest is not a security interest by nature; and, unlike a mortgage, the transaction is not a security transaction by its nature. But ownership can function economically as a security interest; and, in the absence of any

---

308 LPA 1925, ss 101(1)(i) (power arises); 103 (power exercisable); 205(1)(xvi), (xx) (showing applicability to moveables). For the distinction between the power's arising and being exercisable, see paras 5.46–5.47. It was held that where the transaction is governed by the Bills of Sale Acts 1878 and 1882, the Bills of Sale Act (1878) Amendment Act 1882, s 7 excluded the statutory power of sale arising under the Conveyancing Act 1881, s 19, which was the predecessor of LPA 1925, s 101: *Re Morritt* (1886) 18 QBD 222, CA. It is not clear whether this holding survives the re-enactment of the power of sale in LPA 1925, s 101: AP Bell, *Modern Law of Personal Property in England and Ireland* (1989) 187. A minority of the judges, however, held that a power of sale impliedly arose under s 7. Note also that by Bills of Sale Act (1878) Amendment Act 1882, s 13, the mortgagee may not sell the goods until they have been held for five days; there is more protection for consumer debtors (see paras 5.31–5.36).

309 *Den Norske Bank ASA v Acemex Management Company Ltd* [2003] EWCA Civ 1559; [2004] 1 All ER (Comm) 904, [2004] 1 Lloyd's Rep 1; para 5.49.

310 LPA 1925, s 91(2).

311 ibid s 101(1)(iii) (power arises); s 109(1) (power exercisable).

312 See para 5.13.

313 Equitable mortgages: para 5.88; priorities: paras 5.126ff. Note, however, that after-acquired property cannot be mortgaged if the Bills of Sale Acts 1878 and 1882 apply: para 5.76.

register of title for moveables, it can raise difficult questions of policy due to problems of apparent ownership.

Forms. There are a number of transactional structures in which ownership of a moveable is separated from possession, while there are obligations owing from the possessor to the owner. In general, such transactions are not treated as security transactions; and this is so whether the parties intend that the owner will ultimately recover possession of the thing (as in an operating lease), or whether they intend the opposite, so that ownership is effectively used as a security interest. The clearest example is a sale of goods in which the buyer takes possession, but ownership is retained by the seller until the price is paid. This is not treated as a security interest; it is merely a postponement of one of the stages involved in any sale, namely the conveyance of the property sold.[314] The same conclusion follows even if the passage of ownership is delayed until the satisfaction of obligations other than the purchase price of the goods.[315] Similarly in a lease of goods, the lessor's ownership is not viewed as a security interest, even in the case of a 'finance lease', where the term of the lease approximates the anticipated useful life of the goods. The same is true in a hire-purchase, which is a lease coupled with an option to purchase, exercisable by the lessee at the end of the lease period.

5.83

Characterization. The situation may be different, however, if the ownership of the goods was originally in the party who later leases them back, or buys them with retention of ownership. Here ownership has been transferred, and not just retained, so that it can be used as security. If the court finds that the substance of the transaction was the creation of a non-possessory security interest, then, looking at the substance over the form, it will so characterize the interest of the creditor.[316] When this will be done is not wholly clear. The courts say that they look for the 'true nature' of the transaction, but do not spell out what this means. They do not look directly to the economic function of the transaction, or else all such transactions would be viewed as secured lending. It appears that if the credit which is effectively advanced is secured by an asset which previously belonged absolutely to the debtor, the form of the transaction is more likely to be ignored.[317] In these cases, there are really only two parties, with the debtor offering the asset

5.84

---

[314] *Clough Mill Ltd v Martin* [1985] 1 WLR 111, CA. By Sale of Goods Act 1979, s 17, ownership passes when the parties intend it to pass.

[315] *Armour v Thyssen Edelstahlwerke AG* [1991] 2 AC 339, HL.

[316] For example, *Re Watson* (1890) 25 QBD 27, CA (bill of sale); *Polsky v S & A Services* [1951] 1 All ER 185, affd [1951] 1 All ER 1062, CA (bill of sale); *Re Curtain Dream plc* [1990] BCLC 925, [1990] BCC 341 (charge). Whether the interest is characterized as a charge or the agreement is characterized as a bill of sale, registration is required.

[317] As in the cases cited ibid. Such a transaction was held valid in *Yorkshire Wagon Co v Maclure* (1882) 21 ChD 309, CA; it might be relevant that in this case, it was legally impossible for the transaction to be structured as a simple loan with security.

as security to the creditor; if a third party is employed, it is for no commercial purpose. On the other hand, if the credit is advanced for the initial acquisition by the debtor of the asset in question, then the transaction is more likely to be effective.[318]

5.85 Proceeds and products.   The effectiveness of the retention of legal ownership has led suppliers of goods to attempt to extend their security further. Often, they authorize the buyer to resell the goods in question, or (depending on the nature of the business) to use them in the manufacture of some other product. In such cases the terms of the contract may stipulate that the supplier shall be the owner (or trust beneficiary) of the proceeds of sale, or of the manufactured products. Considering proceeds first, the approach of the courts is to observe that the interest of the supplier in the proceeds is defeasible upon payment of the price of the original goods; hence, regardless of the contractual language, it is properly characterized as an equitable charge.[319] As to products, the courts are likely to conclude that the parties did not intend the supplier to be the owner of a product whose value has greatly increased due to the processing, so again the interest will be characterized as a charge.[320] Where the processing leads to the creation of a new thing, the conclusion that the supplier's interest is only a charge is even stronger.[321] The cases are not always consistent in their analysis, but in this context the courts look more directly to the economic function of the transaction. They seem driven by a policy of minimizing hidden security interests in proceeds and products.[322]

5.86 Enforcement.   A creditor who holds legal ownership can, in general, take any step that any legal owner can take, including taking possession of the goods and selling them.[323] In some respects, however, courts may be willing to take notice

---

[318] *Staffs Motor Guarantee Ltd v British Wagon Ltd* [1934] 2 KB 305; *Pacific Motor Auctions Pty Ltd v Motor Credits (Hire Finance) Ltd* [1965] AC 867, PC. In such a case, there are genuinely three parties involved (debtor, supplier, and creditor), and it is only some practical difficulty which prevents the adoption of the unchallengeable structure in which the creditor buys the goods from the original supplier and then agrees to sell or lease them to the debtor.

[319] Since it is also seen as consensually created, it is therefore registrable: para 5.102. See *E Pfeiffer Weinkellerei-Weineinkauf GmbH & Co v Arbuthnot Factors Ltd* [1988] 1 WLR 150; *Tatung (UK) Ltd v Galex Telesure Ltd* [1989] BCC 325; *Compaq Computer Ltd v Abercorn Group Ltd* [1993] BCLC 602, [1991] BCC 484. It is unlikely to have been registered; even if it has been, it will almost certainly be subject to a prior registered charge. The proceeds clause was effective in *Aluminium Industrie Vaassen BV v Romalpa Aluminium Ltd* [1976] 1 WLR 676, CA, but no argument was made as to there being a charge, and the result has never been followed.

[320] *Clough Mill Ltd v Martin* [1985] 1 WLR 111, CA; *Re Peachdart Ltd* [1984] 1 Ch 131.

[321] *Modelboard Ltd v Outer Box Ltd* [1992] BCC 945.

[322] See S Worthington, *Proprietary Interests in Commercial Transactions* (1996), 7–42.

[323] If the transaction is regulated under the CCA 1974, enforcement is strictly regulated. See especially ss 90–91.

of the security aspect of the transaction and thereby limit the steps which the creditor may take.[324]

(2) Equitable Security

(a) Equitable lien

There is no such thing as an equitable pledge, but there are equitable liens. They differ from common law liens in that they do not depend on possession by the creditor, and for this reason are not readily distinguishable from equitable charges, discussed below.[325]

5.87

(b) Equitable mortgage

There are several ways to create an equitable mortgage, being a mortgage in which the mortgagee's interest is purely equitable. The first is where the mortgagor's interest is itself purely equitable. This would include the mortgage of a beneficiary's interest under a trust, but also the case where the mortgagor had already granted a legal mortgage and wished to grant a second mortgage; after granting the first mortgage, his only interest is the equity of redemption. Another situation where only an equitable mortgage can be created is where the mortgagor has a legal interest, but is not able to transfer that legal interest. This is illustrated by the case of the mortgage of a pure intangible. At common law this could not be assigned and therefore could not be the subject of a legal mortgage. It was, however, possible to assign a pure intangible in equity, and therefore it could be the subject matter of an equitable mortgage.[326] Furthermore, equitable mortgages can be used even where a legal mortgage is possible. Any asset can be made the subject of an equitable mortgage by the making of an enforceable agreement for

5.88

---

[324] It has been said that a seller who retains title and who recovers the goods on a breach by the buyer must account for the part of the price which has been paid (subject, of course, to any claim for compensation for breach of contract): *Stockloser v Johnson* [1954] 1 QB 476, CA; *Clough Mill Ltd v Martin* [1985] 1 WLR 111, 117–18, 124, 125–6, CA. In hire purchase and finance lease transactions, the courts may recognize that the debtor acquires an interest in the goods, similar to the equity of redemption in mortgages, that is protected by the doctrine of relief against forfeiture: *Transag Haulage Ltd v Leyland Daf Finance plc* [1994] 2 BCLC 88, [1994] BCC 356; *On Demand Information plc v Michael Gerson (Finance) plc* [2002] UKHL 13; [2003] 1 AC 368; L Smith, 'Relief Against Forfeiture: A Restatement' (2001) 60 CLJ 178.

[325] Some say that an equitable lien arises by operation of law (*Re Bond Worth* [1980] 1 Ch 228, 250–1), but the word 'charge' is often used of an equitable security interest so arising; and since a common law lien can arise by agreement, there seems to be no stable terminological difference between 'charge' and 'lien'.

[326] As noted in para 5.75, a legal assignment (and therefore a legal mortgage) of a pure intangible is now possible by statute, but the possibility of an equitable mortgage remains where only an equitable assignment is made (and this includes the case in which the debtor has promised for value to create a legal mortgage). It may be difficult to distinguish a mortgage or charge of an intangible from a sale: see paras 5.98–5.101.

the giving of a legal mortgage.[327] Once the loan has been advanced, an equitable mortgage will arise by operation of law.[328] The mere deposit with the creditor of documentary evidence of an asset may be enough to permit the conclusion that there was an agreement for the creation of a legal mortgage.[329] This principle can apply so as to make property acquired after the date of the agreement subject to the mortgage, at the moment of its acquisition and without any further legal act, if the parties so intended.[330]

5.89 The formalities required for the creation of equitable mortgages are the same as those for legal mortgages.[331] The conveyance to the mortgagee of the property which is the subject of the mortgage may itself require writing, for example in the case of the transfer of an equitable interest.[332]

5.90 The possibilities for the enforcement of an equitable mortgage are much the same as those for a legal mortgage.[333] As with land, it is doubtful whether the equitable mortgagee has a right to take possession by operation of law, but the agreement will generally provide for this on default by the mortgagor. A statutory power of sale, and a power to appoint a receiver, will arise if the mortgage was created by deed.[334] These powers can also be created by agreement, and in any event sale can be authorized by the court.[335]

(c) Equitable charge

5.91 An equitable charge is a security interest in an asset. 'It is of the essence of a charge that a particular asset or class of assets is appropriated to the satisfaction of a debt or other obligation of the chargor or a third party, so that the chargee is entitled to

---

327 See para 5.13. It may be that following the agreement and loan, there is some defect in the attempt to create a legal mortgage; alternatively, it may be that even though there is an agreement to create a legal mortgage, the mortgagee is content to rely on his rights under the equitable mortgage.

328 In this context the principle only operates once the loan has been advanced, because the contract is not specifically enforceable: RM Goode, *Commercial Law* (3rd edn, 2004) 626.

329 *Harrold v Plenty* [1901] 2 Ch 314 and *Stubbs v Slater* [1910] 1 Ch 632, CA show that the deposit of share certificates for registered shares cannot create a pledge; the relevant asset is the share, a pure intangible, and not the certificate, which is mere evidence. The deposit can, however, create an equitable mortgage of the shares, without the need for any amendment to the share register (which would be required for a legal mortgage).

330 However in the case of an individual or partnership, it would be impossible to comply with the requirements of the Bills of Sale Acts 1878 and 1882 in respect of after-acquired property: see para 5.76.

331 See paras 5.76–5.78.

332 LPA 1925, s 53(1)(c).

333 See para 5.80.

334 LPA 1925, ss 101(1)(i), (iii) (power arises); 103 (power exercisable); 205(1)(xvi), (xx) (showing applicability to moveables). For the distinction between the power's arising and being exercisable, see paras 5.46–5.47 above. For the position where the transaction is governed by the Bills of Sale Acts 1878 and 1882, see n 308 above.

335 LPA 1925, s 91(2).

look to the asset and its proceeds for the discharge of the liability.'[336] It may arise by agreement or by operation of law.

(i) Arising by operation of law

As in the case of land, equitable charges can arise without the consent of the holder **5.92**
of the charged asset. A charge can be imposed judicially to secure a judgment debt.[337] Some charges arise by operation of law; these are often called 'equitable liens'. Just as in the case of land, an unpaid vendor's lien arises by operation of law upon the making of a contract for the sale of moveables, other than goods.[338] A charge can also arise where trust property is disposed of without authority. The trust beneficiary who can trace into the proceeds of disposition can treat those proceeds as trust property, or can assert a charge over them to secure his claim for breach of trust.[339] A trustee has a lien over the trust property to secure the recovery of expenses properly incurred in the administration of the trust.[340] Where an insurer indemnifies its insured, and the insured recovers from a wrongdoer in respect of the loss suffered, the insurer has a lien over the funds received to secure its claim against the insured.[341] Charges on moveables arising by operation of law do not need to be registered.

(ii) Arising by consent

Fixed and floating charges.   A fixed charge is one in which the chargor is not **5.93**
authorized to dispose of the charged property without the consent of the chargee.[342] By contrast, a floating charge is one in which the chargor is authorized by the chargee to dispose of the charged asset in the ordinary course of the chargor's business.[343] It has often been said that a characteristic feature of the floating charge

---

[336] *Re Cosslett (Contractors) Ltd* [1998] Ch 495, 508, CA.

[337] Charging Orders Act 1979. See para 22.129.

[338] AP Bell, *Modern Law of Personal Property in England and Ireland* (1989) 180–1. It was suggested in *Re Bond Worth* [1980] Ch 228, 251 that the lien may only arise if the contract was specifically enforceable. In the case of goods, the unpaid vendor has a possessory lien under the Sale of Goods Act 1979, ss 41–3, and this is generally understood to exclude the equitable lien. The purchaser's lien to secure the repayment of any deposit paid also appears to apply to moveables other than goods: Bell 181–2.

[339] See paras 18.177–18.182 and 18.212–18.213. If property subject to a charge were disposed of without authority, the chargee would also be able to assert a charge in the traceable proceeds.

[340] *Stott v Milne* (1884) 25 ChD 710, 715, CA. The trustee may secure a declaration of the lien even in respect of contingent or future liabilities, allowing him to retain in trust property which he would otherwise be obliged to distribute, until the extent of liability becomes clear: *X v A* [2000] 1 All ER 490.

[341] *Lord Napier and Ettrick v Hunter* [1993] AC 713, HL.

[342] This does not mean that the chargor is unable to dispose of the asset clear of the charge, only that it is unlawful to do so.

[343] It is possible to have a floating mortgage if the same kind of authority is provided. In practice there is little distinction between an equitable mortgage and a charge; the theoretical differences are largely as to enforcement, but these differences will usually be removed by agreement.

is that the pool of assets subject to the charge fluctuates and changes.[344] While this is true of almost every floating charge, as the law has developed it is now true of some fixed charges as well: just as in the case of equitable mortgages, property acquired after the date of the agreement can be automatically subjected to the charge at the moment of its acquisition, if the parties so intended.[345] The definitional difference between fixed and floating charges is that a charge is a floating charge if the debtor is authorized to dispose of the charged assets in the ordinary course of its business.[346]

5.94　The distinction between fixed and floating charges is crucial for the resolution of priority disputes and for other issues.[347] In general, the chargee is better protected by holding a fixed charge. It is not always clear, however, where the boundary lies. The label attached to the charge by the parties in their agreement is not determinative.[348] Some restriction on the chargor's liberty to deal with the asset is consistent with the existence of a floating charge.[349] On the other hand, some liberty on the part of the chargor to deal with the charged asset is consistent with the existence of a fixed charge. This is most clearly seen in the cases involving charges over the accounts receivable or 'book debts' of the chargor company. Here the company must have liberty to deal with the charged assets, at least to the extent of collecting the debts in the ordinary course of business, and it was at one time thought that this meant that a charge over book debts must be a floating charge.[350] It has now been held that a fixed charge can be created over a fluctuating body of book debts, so long as the chargor is not free to deal with the proceeds,

---

[344] See eg *Re Yorkshire Woolcombers Assoc Ltd* [1903] 2 Ch 284, 295 CA; affd *sub nom Illingworth v Houldsworth* [1904] 355, HL.

[345] See para 5.88. However in the case of an individual or partnership, it would be impossible to comply with the requirements of the Bills of Sale Acts 1878 and 1882 in respect of after-acquired property: para 5.76.

[346] *Re Cosslett (Contractors) Ltd* [1998] Ch 495, 510, CA; *Agnew v Commissioner of Inland Revenue* [2001] UKPC 28, [2001] 2 AC 710; *Re Spectrum Plus Ltd* [2005] UKHL 41, [2005] 2 AC 680.

[347] For example, some fixed charges need not be registered; see paras 5.102ff. Some other differences: floating charges given near the onset of insolvency may be avoided by Insolvency Act 1986, s 245 (see paras 19.162–19.164); the holder of a floating charge over all (or substantially all) of a company's assets may be able to appoint an administrator of the company, under Insolvency Act 1986, s 8 and Sch B1, paras 14–21(see paras 19.105 ff); and floating (but not fixed) charges are subordinated to preferential creditors (see para 19.105).

[348] *Agnew v Commissioner of Inland Revenue* [2001] UKPC 28, [2001] 2 AC 710; *Re Spectrum Plus Ltd* [2005] UKHL 41, [2005] 2 AC 680.

[349] *Re Brightlife* [1987] Ch 200, 209; *Re Spectrum Plus Ltd* [2005] UKHL 41, [2005] 2 AC 680 at [140]. In particular, it is common for the agreement to restrict the chargor's ability to create any other charge on the same property which ranks prior or equivalent to the charge; although this is regarded as a dealing in the ordinary course of business, this in itself will not make the charge a fixed charge.

[350] *Re Yorkshire Woolcombers Assoc Ltd* [1903] 2 Ch 284, 295 CA; affd *sub nom Illingworth v Houldsworth* [1904] 355, HL.

once collected, in the ordinary course of business.[351] This requires not just a right in the chargee to take control of the proceeds, but an actual ongoing control over the collected proceeds.[352] In most cases, the chargor is free to deal with the proceeds as part of its cash flow, which means that the charge on book debts will be a floating charge.

Crystallization of floating charges.   Upon the happening of certain events, a   **5.95** floating charge 'crystallizes' and becomes a fixed charge. The nature of the chargee's interest before that event is a matter of some academic dispute. On one view, the chargee has no proprietary rights in the charged assets until crystallization.[353] Another view is that the chargee holds some proprietary rights before crystallization, but that these rights are not held in specific assets; they are rights in a 'fund'.[354] A third view is that the chargee's proprietary interest is the same whether it is a fixed charge or an uncrystallized floating charge; the only difference is that in the latter case, there is a licence to deal with the assets, which terminates on crystallization.[355] These and other views continue to be tenable, although the last one seems to be the simplest, since the courts have come to the view that the very essence of the difference between fixed and floating charges is the chargor's ability lawfully to deal with charged assets, not some difference in the interest held by the chargee.

Whether or not crystallization alters the proprietary rights of the chargee, it   **5.96** certainly terminates the authority of the chargor to deal with the charged assets in the ordinary course of business; it converts the floating charge into a fixed charge. Third parties who might have taken free of the charge while it was floating may take subject to the charge once it has crystallized.[356] Crystallization occurs when the management powers of the directors of the chargor company are lost to a receiver or administrator or liquidator, or when the chargor ceases to carry on business.[357] In order to protect the chargee, the agreement may provide for crystallization upon the giving of a notice by the chargee, and also for 'automatic crystallization' upon certain events such as the failure of the chargor to make a payment when due.[358] These provisions cause some concern since they potentially

---

[351] *Agnew v Commissioner of Inland Revenue* [2001] UKPC 28, [2001] 2 AC 710; *Re Spectrum Plus Ltd* [2005] UKHL 41, [2005] 2 AC 680.

[352] *Agnew v Commissioner of Inland Revenue* [2001] UKPC 28, [2001] 2 AC 710 at [48]; *Re Spectrum Plus Ltd* [2005] UKHL 41, [2005] 2 AC 680 at [55]–[58], [116]–[119], [140].

[353] WJ Gough, *Company Charges* (2nd edn, 1996) ch 13.

[354] RM Goode, *Commercial Law* (3rd edn, 2004) 677–80; *Re Spectrum Plus Ltd* [2005] UKHL 41, [2005] 2 AC 680 at [139].

[355] S Worthington, *Proprietary Interests in Commercial Transactions* (1996) 82–100.

[356] See para 5.144.

[357] *Re Woodroffe's Musical Instruments Ltd* [1986] 1 Ch 366; *National Westminster Bank plc v Jones* [2001] EWCA Civ 1541; [2002] 1 BCLC 55; WJ Gough, *Company Charges* (2nd edn, 1996) ch 8.

[358] Crystallization by giving notice is specifically contemplated for floating agricultural charges in the Agricultural Credits Act 1928, s 7(1)(a)(iv).

affect third parties who may be unaware of the crystallization; but in deference to the principle of freedom of contract, it has been held that crystallization by notice is effective, and the reasoning implies that automatic crystallization would be effective as well.[359] One approach which preserves the parties' freedom of contract while yet respecting third party interests is that while the crystallization may be effective to terminate the chargor's actual authority to deal with the charged assets free of the charge, third parties who are unaware of it will be able to rely on the chargor's ostensible authority.[360] Another approach would be to say that the question whether a charge has crystallized is simply the question whether the charge remains floating or has become fixed; and the courts have already held that this issue is determined not by the parties' own labelling, but by whether the chargee actually restricts the chargor's control of the assets.[361]

5.97 Negative pledge. Similar issues arise in the case of the negative pledge clause. The chargor's ability to deal in the ordinary course of business with the assets subject to a floating charge is understood to include an ability to grant fixed charges over those assets which have priority over the floating charge.[362] The negative pledge is a typical term in the charge agreement which excludes this ability; the chargor promises not to create any charge over the charged assets which would rank prior to (or equally with) the floating charge. When such clauses are inserted in agreements governing unsecured lending, they are generally understood to have only personal effects.[363] The matter is not so clear where the clause is inserted in an agreement governing a charge. It has been held that here as well, the clause has only personal and not real effects;[364] but academic commentary is generally opposed to this, suggesting that the clause would have proprietary effect against a third party who had actual notice of it.[365]

---

[359] *Re Brightlife Ltd* [1987] 1 Ch 200. The court rejected an argument that crystallizing events were fixed by law as (1) winding up, (2) appointment of a receiver and (3) ceasing to carry on business, and held instead that it was for the parties to stipulate the crystallizing events.

[360] RM Goode, *Commercial Law* (3rd edn, 2004) 683–4; on ostensible authority, see paras 9.59–9.67. See however WJ Gough, *Company Charges* (2nd edn, 1996) 254–6, casting doubt on this explanation; for example, noting that mere possession of goods by a debtor has never been understood as precluding others from asserting their rights in those goods.

[361] Para 5.94.

[362] *Wheatley v Silkstone and Haigh Moor Coal Co* (1885) 29 Ch D 715.

[363] This is so even if the clause is an 'affirming negative pledge', in which the debtor promises that should it grant security to another creditor, it will provide equal security to the hitherto unsecured creditor. See RM Goode, *Commercial Law* (3rd edn, 2004) 613; J Maxton, 'Negative Pledge and Equitable Principles' [1993] JBL 458. The third party may, if it had knowledge of the clause, be liable in tort for inducing a breach of contract.

[364] *Griffiths v Yorkshire Bank Ltd* [1994] 1 WLR 1427.

[365] RM Goode, *Commercial Law* (3rd edn, 2004) 687; Gough, *Company Charges* (2nd edn, 1996) 225–31. There is however a dispute about whether constructive notice could suffice, and if so what would constitute that. A dictum in *Ian Chisholm Textiles Ltd v Griffiths* [1994] 2 BCLC 291, [1994] BCC 96, drawn from the context of land conveyancing, suggests that notice of the existence

Charge or sale. In most cases there is no difficulty in distinguishing between a **5.98** charge over an asset, granted to secure a loan, and a sale of that asset. In the case of accounts receivable, the distinction may be less clear since the economic effects of the transactions may be very similar and since there is no tangible asset involved. The difference between a mortgage and a sale is obscure because in both transactions the intangible receivable is assigned to the mortgagee or buyer. Of course, a mortgage is associated with a loan and a debt, while a sale is associated with the payment of a price; but in the case of receivables this distinction is not so clear, because in both transactions, it is common that the debtors are not notified, and the seller or mortgagor of the receivables continues to collect them and then to account to the buyer. The distinction is further blurred because while in a sale of tangible assets the price is usually fixed, in a sale of receivables it is common for the agreement to provide for recourse by the buyer against the seller in respect of non-performing receivables. The difference between a sale and a charge might seem clearer, but this is not so because in the case of receivables a mortgage and a charge are also difficult to distinguish except in abstract terms. While in a charge there is no assignment of the receivables, it is typical for the chargor to grant to the chargee not only a power to appoint a receiver, but also an irrevocable power of attorney to effect an assignment of the charged receivables to the chargee.

Although the economic effects are very similar, the legal incidents are quite **5.99** different. A mortgage or charge of receivables by a company must be registered;[366] a sale is not registrable.[367] Conversely, a registrable charge or mortgage which was not registered is void against a subsequent chargee or mortgagee; it is not void against a subsequent purchaser of the mortgaged or charged asset.[368] The accounting treatment may also be different, since, unlike a loan, a sale does not generate a liability, and it removes an asset from the seller's balance sheet.[369] A sale may

---

of the prior floating charge is constructive notice of the negative pledge, but this is inconsistent with the considered holding to the contrary in *Siebe Gorman & Co Ltd v Barclays Bank Ltd* [1979] Lloyd's Rep 142. (*Siebe Gorman* was itself overruled in *Re Spectrum Plus Ltd* [2005] UKHL 41, [2005] 2 AC 680, but only on the question whether the charge agreement created a fixed or a floating charge.) The 'particulars' which must be registered under CA 1985, ss 395, 401, and CA 2006, ss 860, 869, do not include whether or not there is a negative pledge clause, but the registrar will permit it to be noted; the effect is unclear: Goode 663. One commentator has argued that given the prevalence of such clauses, registration of the charge should now be treated as giving notice of the clause to anyone who could reasonably be expected to search the register: JH Farrar 'Floating Charges and Priorities' (1974) 38 Conveyancer and Property Lawyer (New Series) 315, 322, but this is a minority view.

[366] At least if the receivables are 'book debts': CA 1985, ss 396(1)(e), (4); CA 2006, ss 860(7)(f), 861(5). On the meaning of 'book debts', see n 388.

[367] But see, for individuals, Insolvency Act 1986, s 344; see para 19.85.

[368] CA 1985, s 395(1); CA 2006, s 874; *Stroud Architectural Systems Ltd v John Laing Construction Ltd* [1994] 2 BCLC 276, [1994] BCC 18.

[369] But under current accounting standards, a sale of receivables with recourse will leave the receivables on the seller's balance sheet, since in economic terms it is only a loan.

attract value added tax. In some cases a company may be at liberty to sell receivables while it might not be at liberty to charge them, for example under the terms of an earlier loan agreement.

5.100 In deciding whether a transaction is a sale or secured loan, the courts purport to look at the substance and not the form, but this does not mean that they look directly to the economic function.[370] The form of a transaction will be ignored if it is a 'sham', meaning that none of the parties to it intended to conduct themselves in accordance with its terms.[371] It is also possible that the parties have, by their conduct, replaced their formal agreement with another one.[372] Beyond that, the matter is less clear. It has been said that there are some distinguishing factors:[373] in a sale, the seller has no right or obligation to recover the sold asset, while in a secured loan he is obliged to repay the loan and thereby recovers the charged asset. It is, however, acceptable in sales of receivables for the seller to be required to repurchase non-performing receivables;[374] and a seller's option to repurchase does not make a sale into a charge.[375] In a secured loan, the borrower is entitled to any surplus realized from the security, and is liable for any deficiency; while in a sale, the buyer is entitled to the full value of the asset bought, and must bear the risk of its being worth less than the price. But it is acceptable in sales of receivables for the buyer to have recourse against the seller in respect of non-performing receivables, and for there to be adjustments to the sale price after the receivables have been collected, and so these indicia are not determinative.[376]

5.101 English law has historically attached a high importance to the intention of the parties, allowing it to be determinative even where third parties may have been misled. In one case, a company wanted to convert its receivables into cash, without creating a registrable charge in favour of the financier. Under a master agreement with the financier, when the company had agreed a sale of goods with a customer, it actually sold the goods to the financier for cash; it then proceeded to sell the goods to the customer as undisclosed agent of the financier, so that the receivable

---

370 *Lloyds and Scottish Finance Ltd v Cyril Lord Carpets Ltd* (1979) [1992] BCLC 609, HL; *Welsh Development Agency v Export Finance Co Ltd* [1992] BCLC 148; [1992] BCC 270, CA.
371 *Snook v London and West Riding Investments Ltd* [1967] 2 QB 786, 802, CA.
372 *Lloyds and Scottish Finance Ltd v Cyril Lord Carpet Sales Ltd* (1979) [1992] BCLC 609, HL; *Orion Finance Ltd v Crown Financial Management Ltd* [1996] 2 BCLC 78; [1996] BCC 621, CA.
373 *Re George Inglefield Ltd* [1933] Ch 1, CA.
374 *Lloyds and Scottish Finance Ltd v Cyril Lord Carpet Sales Ltd* (1979) [1992] BCLC 609, HL.
375 Even if the repurchase price is calculated by reference to the original sale price plus interest since the date of the original sale: *Orion Finance Ltd v Crown Financial Management Ltd* [1996] 2 BCLC 78, 84; [1996] BCC 621, CA.
376 *Welsh Development Agency v Export Finance Co Ltd* [1992] BCLC 148; [1992] BCC 270, CA; *Orion Finance Ltd v Crown Financial Management Ltd* [1996] 2 BCLC 78; [1996] BCC 621, CA.

owing from the customer vested in the financier. A subsequent secured creditor lent money to the company, taking a charge over its book debts and registering that charge. On the insolvency of the company, this subsequent secured creditor argued that the financier's interest in receivables was by way of a charge, which was unregistered and therefore void against the subsequent creditor. This argument was rejected, and the agency arrangement upheld.[377] This suggests that the language which the parties use in their agreement is more important than its economic effect or its implications for third parties.[378] Recently, however, on the issue of whether a charge is fixed or floating, it has been held that the intention of the parties cannot be determinative where the interests of third parties are affected.[379] In the future it will probably be held, by parity of reasoning, that the question whether a transaction was a sale or a secured loan is not one that is determined by the intentions of the parties.

(iii) Registration

Many, but not all, charges require registration.[380] In the case of a charge created by an individual or a partnership, registration may be required under the Bills of Sale Acts 1878 and 1882. These provisions, which also regulate the form of the document evidencing the agreement, apply only to interests in tangible moveables.[381] The Acts do not apply in the case of an 'agricultural charge', given to a bank by a farmer on all or any of his farming stock.[382] Agricultural charges must be registered in a special register, or else they will be void against anyone except the farmer.[383]

5.102

---

[377] *Welsh Development Agency v Export Finance Co Ltd* [1992] BCLC 148; [1992] BCC 270, CA.

[378] *Lloyds and Scottish Finance Ltd v Cyril Lord Carpet Sales Ltd* (1979) [1992] BCLC 609, HL; *Orion Finance Ltd v Crown Financial Management Ltd* [1996] 2 BCLC 78; [1996] BCC 621, CA.

[379] *Re Spectrum Plus Ltd* [2005] UKHL 41; [2005] 2 AC 680. This case overruled *Re New Bullas Trading Ltd* [1994] 1 BCLC 485; [1994] BCC 36, CA, which had held that the parties' intention could be determinative on the question whether a charge was fixed or floating.

[380] Charges on moveables arising by operation of law are never registrable.

[381] For details, see para 5.76. This legislation requires a listing of the moveables in which the creditor holds a security interest, and this precludes the creation by an individual or partnership of a security interest extending to after-acquired property.

[382] Agricultural Credits Act 1928, s 5(1) permits the charge, and s 5(2) provides that it may be fixed or (unlike security interests registrable under the Bills of Sale Acts 1878 and 1882) floating or both. Agricultural Credits Act 1928, s 5(7) indicates that the farmer must generally be an individual, while the chargee must generally be a bank; it clarifies the permissible subject matter of the charge as being tangible and certain intangible moveables relating to the business of farming. Section 8(1) disapplies the Bills of Sales Acts. By s 14, an industrial and provident society (a co-operative), which is a corporation not formed under the Companies Acts, may also give an agricultural charge, and if it registers it under the Agricultural Credits Act 1928 then the Bills of Sale Acts will not apply.

[383] ibid s 9.

5.103 Where a company creates a charge, registration may be required by the Companies Act 1985.[384] The following charges must be registered:[385]

(1) a charge for the purpose of securing any issue of debentures;

(2) a charge on uncalled share capital of the company;

(3) a charge created or evidenced by an instrument which, if executed by an individual, would require registration as a bill of sale;[386]

(4) a charge on land (wherever situated) or any interest in it, but not including a charge for any rent or other periodical sum issuing out of the land;[387]

(5) a charge on book debts of the company;[388]

(6) a floating charge on the company's undertaking or property;

(7) a charge on calls made but not paid;

(8) a charge on a ship or aircraft, or any share in a ship;[389]

(9) a charge on goodwill, or on any intellectual property.[390]

An example of a charge created by a company that is not registrable is a fixed charge it grants over the shares it holds in a subsidiary company.[391]

---

[384] If an industrial and provident society creates a charge that is not an agricultural charge, then it may optionally register that charge with the FSA, in which case the Bills of Sale Acts will not apply (Industrial and Provident Societies Act 1967, s 1); if it does not, the Bills of Sale Acts will apply: *Re North Wales Produce and Supply Society* [1922] 2 Ch 340.

[385] CA 1985, s 396(1); CA 2006, s 861(7), where the wording is slightly different.

[386] This provision means that all of the law relating to the Bills of Sale Acts 1878 and 1882 is relevant in determining which company charges must be registered.

[387] A charge on land created by a company may need to be registered in the relevant land register as well as in the Companies Act register; although a charge on unregistered land which would otherwise be registrable in the Land Charges Registry need not be registered there if it is a floating charge *and* it is registered in the Companies Act register: Land Charges Act 1972, s 3(7).

[388] A 'book debt' is understood to mean a claim arising in the course of the company's business, and a fixed charge on such debts is registrable even if it is over future book debts: *Independent Automatic Sales Ltd v Knowles & Foster* [1962] 1 WLR 974; but a contingent debt is not a book debt: *Paul and Frank Ltd v Discount Bank (Overseas) Ltd* [1967] Ch 348. The term appears to exclude a bank account: *Re Bank of Credit and Commerce International SA (No 8)* [1998] AC 214, 227, HL. It was held in this case that it is possible for a bank to take a charge over a bank account to secure a loan to the customer even where the bank is itself the debtor on the charged account.

[389] Charges on aircraft and ships may also require another registration, whether or not the chargor is a company: see para 5.78. All of those registers apply to consensually created charges as well as mortgages.

[390] 'Intellectual property' means a patent, trade mark, service mark, registered design, copyright or design right, or any licence thereof: CA 1985, s 396(3A); CA 2006, s 861(4). Charges over patents, trade marks and registered designs will require another registration, whether or not the chargor is a company: see para 5.78.

[391] *Arthur D Little Ltd v Ableco Finance LLC* [2002] EWHC 701; [2003] 1 Ch 217, applying CA 1985 s 410 which applies to Scottish companies. However the same result would follow under s 396, unless the charge secured an issue of debentures. Such a charge would not be registrable as a bill of sale, if granted by an individual, because that legislation does not apply to security in intangible assets.

Registration is also required where a company acquires property which is already **5.104**
subject to a registrable charge.[392] The Companies Act register performs a dual
function, giving notice of security interests but also revealing the financial position
of the company, for example to potential shareholders. This is why each company
is required to keep its own register of charges it has granted, in addition to the
central public register maintained under the Act.[393] It also explains why in many
cases, a registration under the Companies Act is required even though there is
some other system for giving notice of the security interest, which applies whether
or not the debtor is a company.[394] In such cases, the requirements of the Companies
Act are cumulative with the other requirements.[395]

Registration is effected by delivering to the Registrar of Companies a form listing **5.105**
the 'prescribed particulars' of the charge, and the original instrument by which
the charge is created or evidenced.[396] This may be done either by the chargor
or the chargee.[397] It must be done within 21 days of the creation of the charge,
or else the charge will become void as against a liquidator or administrator of the
company, or a secured or execution creditor.[398] If this failure to register occurs, the
debt secured by the charge becomes payable immediately.[399] It is possible to obtain
leave from the court to register outside the permitted time;[400] this will usually be
permitted if other creditors will not be affected.[401] A certificate of registration
from the Registrar is conclusive evidence that the requirements of the Act have

[392] CA 1985, s 400; CA 2006, s 862.

[393] CA 1985, s 407; CA 2006, s 876. This obligation extends to every charge, not just those
that must be publicly registered. The failure to maintain either register is an offence. The company
must also keep a copy of every instrument creating a registrable charge: CA 1985, s 406; CA 2006,
s 875.

[394] Similarly, the requirement of registration applies even to property situated abroad, even
though the validity of the security interest is likely to be governed by the law of that place: CA 1985,
s 398; CA 2006, s 866.

[395] There are some exceptions. A floating charge which extends to an aircraft is not registrable
under the Mortgaging of Aircraft Order 1972, SI 1972/1268: art 2(2); similarly, a charge that
extends to unregistered land, which would otherwise be registrable in the Land Charges Registry,
need not be registered there if it is a floating charge and it is registered under the Companies Acts:
Land Charges Act 1972, s 3(7). A charge on unregistered land may be unregistrable under the Land
Charges Act 1972, because the creditor holds the title deeds: para 5.19; nonetheless, it will probably
need to be registered under the CA 1985, s 396(1)(d); CA 2006, s 860(7)(a).

[396] The particulars include the date the charge was created, the amount secured, the property
charged, and the identity of the chargee. A copy of the document creating the charge is acceptable
in place of the original if (a) the charge is over property situated outside the United Kingdom (CA
1985, s 398(1); CA 2006, s 866(1)) or (b) the charge is over property in Scotland or Northern
Ireland and has been registered there (CA 1985, s 398(4); CA 2006, s 867).

[397] CA 1985, s 399(1); CA 2006, ss 860(1)–(2).

[398] CA 1985, s 395(1); CA 2006, s 874(1); see further para 5.142.

[399] CA 1985, s 395(2); CA 2006, s 874(3); the charge is not void against the chargor company.

[400] CA 1985, s 404; CA 2006, s 873.

[401] RM Goode, *Commercial Law* (3rd edn, 2004) 668–9.

been fulfilled.[402] Although there is no obligation to do so, a company may notify the Registrar when the obligation secured has been satisfied, or when it no longer owns the charged property; and this will be noted on the register.[403]

(iv) Enforcement

5.106 If the charge was created by deed, then a statutory power of sale will generally be available.[404] A power of sale will usually be created by agreement, and in any event sale can be authorized by the court.[405] If the charge was created by deed, there will be a statutory power to appoint a receiver;[406] again, most agreements will provide for such an appointment.[407] The agreement will also generally provide for the taking of possession by the chargee in the event of default. In the case of a charge over receivables, the chargor will commonly grant to the chargee an irrevocable power of attorney to effect an assignment of the charged receivables to the chargee, which will allow them to be collected directly by the chargee if the chargor defaults.

(d) Trust

5.107 A beneficiary's interest under a trust is not considered a security interest; but just as legal ownership can be used to perform the function of a security interest, so too can a trust interest. The creation of trusts, and the rights of beneficiaries, are considered elsewhere.[408] An interest under a trust, as such, is never registrable. Attempts to use the trust to secure obligations are not, however, guaranteed to succeed. It is possible to secure the purchase price of supplied goods by reservation of legal title, allowing the seller to retain a real right which does not require registration.[409] It is not, however, possible to 'reserve' equitable title to achieve a similar effect; any equitable interest held by the seller must have been granted by

---

402 CA 1985, s 401(2); CA 2006, s 885(5).

403 CA 1985, s 403; CA 2006, s 887.

404 LPA 1925, s 101(1)(i) (power arises); s 103 (power exercisable); s 205(1)(xvi), (xx) (showing applicability to moveables). For the distinction between the power's arising and being exercisable, see paras 5.46–5.47. For the position where the transaction is governed by the Bills of Sale Acts 1878 and 1882, see n 308 above. Agricultural charges import a power of sale, which must be by auction unless the agreement provides otherwise, and which cannot be exercised until five days after seizure unless the agreement provides otherwise: Agricultural Credits Act 1928, s 6(1)(b).

405 LPA 1925, s 91(2).

406 ibid s 101(1)(iii) (power arises); s 109(1) (power exercisable).

407 In any event the court has jurisdiction to appoint a receiver: Supreme Court Act 1981, s 37. If a receiver is appointed in respect of a company's property, the Registrar of Companies must be notified and he will note this on the register: CA 1985, s 405; CA 2006, s 871. A creditor whose floating charge relates to all or substantially all of a company's property may appoint an administrator, who will be regulated by the Insolvency Act 1986, s 8 and Sch B1, esp paras 14–21 (see paras 19.19, 19.88.

408 See paras 4.140ff.

409 See paras 5.82–5.86.

the buyer.[410] Moreover, the court will examine the features of the seller's interest; since it is defeasible upon the payment of the relevant debt, it is likely to be characterized as a charge, which is almost certainly registrable.[411] The same line of reasoning would apply where the seller attempts to assert a trust interest in the proceeds of sale of the supplied goods, or in the products made from them.[412] The interest might be upheld as a true trust interest only if the buyer was not allowed to deal with the proceeds or products on its own account, and such an arrangement is not usually commercially practicable.

Where money (or perhaps other property) is advanced for a particular purpose, the *Quistclose* trust lends itself to utilization as a security device.[413] In this transaction, the one who receives the money holds it in trust for the one who advanced it; but the former has the power and authority to apply the money for the agreed purpose.[414] This will allow the money to be recovered in full if the purpose is not fulfilled and the value advanced can be traced. If the money is applied for the agreed purpose, though, the trust interest will be at an end, and another device will be needed if the provider of the money is to have real security. **5.108**

D. Priorities in Real Security

(1) Introduction

The law governing the priority of security interests is not simple.[415] It is a mosaic of general rules of property law, conditioned by principles which respond to fault, modified in many cases by particular statutory provisions. It is usually impossible to solve cases with general principles, as the following example illustrates. A customer C buys a car from a trader, T Ltd, taking possession of the car and giving value in good faith and without any knowledge of prior dealings. If, before the sale, T Ltd had sold the car to someone else, then C will prevail.[416] If, before the sale, T Ltd had given to someone else an equitable charge over the car, then again **5.109**

---

410 *Re Bond Worth Ltd* [1980] Ch 228, 253–6; *Stroud Architectural Services Ltd v John Laing Construction Ltd* [1994] 2 BCLC 276; [1994] BCC 18.

411 *Re Bond Worth Ltd* [1980] Ch 228, 248–9. The charge is unlikely to have been registered; even if it has been, it will probably be subject to a prior registered charge.

412 *Re Peachdart Ltd* [1984] Ch 131; *Compaq Computer Ltd v Abercorn Group Ltd* [1993] BCLC 602; [1991] BCC 484; *Stroud Architectural Services Ltd v John Laing Construction Ltd* [1994] 2 BCLC 276; [1994] BCC 18.

413 *Barclays Bank v Quistclose Investments Ltd* [1970] AC 567, HL; see paras 18.123–18.125.

414 *Twinsectra Ltd v Yardley* [2002] UKHL 12; [2002] 2 AC 164.

415 In this section, as in the earlier text, in the context of land the word 'mortgage' is used to include all interests by way of security: para 5.04. In the context of moveables the word is confined to its technical sense: para 5.64.

416 Factors Act 1889, s 8; Sale of Goods Act 1979, s 24.

C will prevail, even if the charge was properly registered.[417] But an intermediate case would be that T Ltd had earlier granted to someone else a legal mortgage over the car. Here, illogically, it appears that C's interest is subject to the mortgagee's interest, even if the mortgage was not properly registered.[418] The situation is made even more complicated by the fact that there are many registration systems for security interests in English law.[419] A security interest may be registrable in none of them, or one of them, or more than one of them. Whether registration is required, and the effects of registration or failure to register, are not uniform across these systems.

5.110 Priorities may be modified by agreement among secured creditors, and this does not require the consent of the debtor.[420] When a security interest has been discharged, any subordinate security interests are automatically promoted; the debtor cannot keep the prior interest alive for transfer to another creditor.[421]

(2) General Principles

5.111 In general, the first step in solving any priority contest is to characterize the competing interests. Interests may be beneficial or by way of security.[422] If a beneficial

---

417 If the charge was a floating one, then the trader would have been authorized to sell stock in the ordinary course of business so that buyers take free of the charge. Even if the charge was fixed, C would be able to take advantage of the rule that a bona fide purchaser of a legal interest for value takes free of a pre-existing equitable interest of which he did not have notice. The registration of the charge would not be treated as giving C constructive notice. All of these points are developed below.

418 Because the mortgage was legal, C cannot invoke the doctrine of bona fide purchase of a legal interest for value without notice of a pre-existing equitable interest. Because the mortgage was not a sale, C cannot invoke Factors Act 1889, s 8 or Sale of Goods Act 1979, s 24. Moreover, although there is an obligation to register the mortgage under the CA 1985, ss 395–6, failure to do so does not avoid the charge as against a purchaser of the charged asset. The point is illustrated by *British Credit Trust Ltd v The Owners of the Shizelle (The Shizelle)* [1992] 2 Lloyd's Rep 444, where the mortgagor was an individual but the mortgage was not registrable.

419 There are eleven registers that may involve security interests: the Land Register for registered land; the Land Charges Register for mortgages on unregistered land, which is also kept by the Land Registrar; the Companies Act register kept by the Registrar of companies; the register of agricultural charges, kept by the Land Registrar; the register for bills of sale, kept at the High Court; the register for industrial and provident societies, kept by the FSA; the register for ship mortgages; the register for aircraft mortgages; the register for patents; the register for registered trade marks; and the register for registered designs. All of these are discussed in what follows. Furthermore, each local authority keeps a register of 'local land charges'; these are not discussed herein; see note 36.

420 *Cheah Theam Swee v Equiticorp Finance Group Ltd* [1992] 1 AC 472, PC; see P Wood, *The Law of Subordinated Debt* (1990). In relation to registered land, registration may be required if the alteration of priorities is to affect third parties: LRA 2002, s 48(2); Land Registration Rules 2003, SI 2003/1417, r 102.

421 *Grierson v National Provincial Bank of England Ltd* [1913] 2 Ch 18.

422 Retained ownership can be used as a kind of security interest: paras 5.82–5.86; but even so it is a beneficial interest in this context. Ownership transferred by way of mortgage is a security interest.

interest prevails, then the losing interest (whether beneficial or security) will be ineffective; but if a security interest prevails, then the other interest can subsist, merely being postponed to the prior security. Interests can also be legal or equitable, and this may affect the priority contest. The next step is to understand how the general principles of property law will provide a prima facie answer to the contest. These principles are modified in important ways by statute. In particular, they are least likely to be determinative in cases involving land, but they still serve as the starting point. Even for moveables, those principles which involve notice are subject to modification where there is a registration system, since registration may generate constructive notice.

(a) First in time generally prevails

The basic principle is *nemo dat quod non habet;* one cannot give what one does not **5.112** have, which in this context means that interests are ranked in the order of their creation. There are a number of crucial modifications to this basic rule.

(b) Authority to grant later interest

If the holder of the earlier interest consented to the creation of a subsequent interest **5.113** having priority over his earlier interest, this will be effective. For example, if a mechanic repairs a car and then discovers that the party who delivered the car to him is not the owner, the question will arise whether the mechanic can assert his lien against the owner; the crucial question will be whether the owner authorized the repairs.[423] The most important application of this principle in its pure form is the case where the earlier interest is under a floating charge.[424] The essence of this interest is that the chargee grants authority to the chargor to deal with the charged assets in the ordinary course of business. If the chargor takes an asset which he holds, subject to the charge, as stock in trade, and sells it in the ordinary course of business to a customer, then the customer takes free of the charge, without the need for reliance on any principle of good faith purchase. The asset is taken free of the charge because the disposition was authorized by the chargee.

(i) Ostensible authority

Just as actual authority from the holder of an earlier interest can allow a later **5.114** interest to take priority, so too can ostensible or apparent authority.[425] This may

---

[423] *Tappenden v Artus* [1964] 2 QB 185, CA.

[424] The analysis here assumes that the floating charge was still floating when the subsequent interest was created. If, at that time, the floating charge had crystallized, then it was no longer floating but had become fixed: para 5.95. If, however, the crystallization was 'automatic,' then the effectiveness of that crystallization may be overridden by considerations of ostensible authority on the same principles as those discussed here: para 5.96.

[425] See paras 9.59–9.67 and para 10.23.

allow an artificer to maintain his lien against the owner of goods even if the owner did not actually authorize the repair, on the ground that the owner held out another person as having the authority to order repairs.[426] Again, in floating charges, the contract between the chargor and the chargee will determine which dispositions the chargor is actually authorized to make. Even beyond that actual authority, however, the chargor may have ostensible authority to make dispositions that are ordinarily authorized by floating chargees as being in the ordinary course of business, so long as the party taking under that disposition did not have notice of any limitation on the chargor's authority. For example, the granting of subsequent fixed charges having priority over the earlier floating charge is understood to be a disposition in the ordinary course of business.[427] The result is that even if the floating charge agreement prohibits the granting of a fixed charge with priority over the floating charge, the prohibition is generally understood to be ineffective unless the subsequent fixed chargee had notice of it.[428] Similarly, even if, by the terms of the agreement, there has been an automatic crystallization of the floating charge, this crystallization will be ineffective against third parties who lack notice of the terms of the agreement.[429]

5.115   This result is usually understood as based on ostensible authority. That is, the actual terms of the charge delimit the chargor's actual authority; but in allowing the chargor to operate under a floating charge, the chargee is understood to be holding out the chargor as having the authority which the chargor normally has under a floating charge. One difficulty with this analysis is that the ostensible authority appears to be based not on the level of actual authority which chargors normally have now, but on that which they normally had when floating charges were developing, in the late nineteenth and early twentieth centuries. It is not surprising that it was held that a floating chargor generally lacks authority to create a second floating charge ranking in priority to the first;[430] and so it follows that there will be no ostensible authority for such an act. On the other hand, it was held that a floating chargor had actual authority to create a subsequent fixed charge ranking in priority to the floating charge.[431] Today floating charges almost universally

---

[426] *Albemarle Supply Co Ltd v Hind and Co* [1928] 1 KB 307, CA.

[427] *Wheatley v Silkstone and Haigh Moor Coal Co* (1885) 29 Ch D 715.

[428] See para 5.97. Note however that in the case of agricultural charges, by the Agricultural Credits Act 1928, s 8(3), a subsequent bill of sale or fixed agricultural charge is void against an earlier floating agricultural charge.

[429] Para 5.96.

[430] *Re Benjamin Cope & Sons Ltd* [1914] 1 Ch 800. In *Re Automated Bottle Makers Ltd* [1926] Ch 412, CA, it was held that the chargor could effectively create, over a part of the charged assets, a subsequent floating charge which had priority over the earlier charge; but the creation of such a charge was expressly authorized by the earlier charge. The decision must be based on that actual authority, not on the fact that the second charge covered only part of the assets; and such actual authority will be most uncommon.

[431] *Wheatley v Silkstone and Haigh Moor Coal Co* (1885) 29 Ch D 715.

prohibit this as a matter of actual authority, but the law still permits it unless the second chargee has actual knowledge of the prohibition.[432] Basing this result on a theory of ostensible authority derived from 'holding out' may therefore be artificial.[433] Another difficulty with the estoppel theory is the case of the execution creditor. If such a creditor completes his execution before the charge crystallizes, he has priority over the charge. It is hard to understand how an execution creditor can be said to rely on a holding out by the chargee, or indeed how execution on a judgment can be understood as a transaction in the ordinary course of business.[434] It might be more logical to say that the priority of subsequent fixed chargees, or of execution creditors, is an incident of the floating charge that is not subject to freedom of contract.[435]

The principle of ostensible authority can also apply in relation to mortgages of land.[436] **5.116**

(c) Fault

If the priority conflict has arisen due to the fault of the earlier party, who prima facie has priority, he may be postponed to the later party. This principle has primarily been developed in the context of mortgages of land, and in particular in relation to carelessness by the earlier mortgagee regarding the title deeds, which he was entitled to possess.[437] A failure to obtain the deeds might, if it amounted to gross negligence, lead to a legal mortgagee's being postponed to an interest created later.[438] Similarly, if the title deeds had been obtained, then it was possible that gross negligence regarding their custody could lead to the mortgagee's being postponed to a later interest.[439] **5.117**

---

[432] See para 5.97.

[433] See JH Farrar 'Floating Charges and Priorities' (1974) 38 Conveyancer (New Series) 315, 322, effectively arguing that the content of ostensible authority must respond to changing commercial realities.

[434] WJ Gough, *Company Charges* (2nd edn, 1996) 255–6 doubts whether estoppel can apply in favour of such a creditor, but argues (320–1) that the seizure of a debtor's assets in execution of a judgment is within the debtor's ordinary course of business.

[435] In *Re Spectrum Plus Ltd* [2005] UKHL 41; [2005] 2 AC 680, the House of Lords held that the question whether a charge is fixed or floating is determined by the law and is not subject to freedom of contract. This is because it has effects on third parties. The same is true of the priority of the charge as against subsequent interests.

[436] *Brocklesby v Temperance Permanent BS* [1895] AC 173, HL.

[437] Gross negligence by a legal mortgagee might also mean that he would not be allowed to take free of a prior equitable interest, but that principle is not an exception to the *nemo dat* principle; it is discussed in para 5.112.

[438] *Farrand v Yorkshire Banking Co* (1888) 40 Ch D 182; *Grierson v National Provincial Bank of England Ltd* [1913] 2 Ch 18. Fraud is a fortiori.

[439] *Waldron v Sloper* (1852) 1 Drew 193, 61 ER 425; *Northern Counties of England Fire Insurance Co v Whipp* (1884) 26 Ch D 482, CA, holding carelessness is not enough. It is unclear whether the priority of a prior equitable mortgagee was more easily displaced by his carelessness than that

(d) Exceptional assets

5.118   Some kinds of assets are subject to exceptional rules which can displace the normal rule that the earliest interest prevails.

(i) Money and negotiable instruments

5.119   If the asset in question is a form of money, then a party who acquires it as currency, for value, in good faith, and without notice of any earlier interest held by someone other than the transferee, will take free of that earlier interest. This is a defence which the later party must establish. For coins this is a rule of the common law,[440] and it was so for bank notes as well,[441] although bank notes are now dealt with by the Bills of Exchange Act 1882.[442] Under that Act, the defence as applicable to bills of exchange and promissory notes is codified as the status of 'holder in due course'.[443] The uncodified version of the defence is available to holders of a number of other instruments, namely those recognized by the courts (taking notice of commercial usage) as 'negotiable'.[444] Some examples are share warrants, negotiable certificates of deposit, and bearer bonds.[445] For the purposes of this defence, the value which must be given includes any consideration which would support a contract.[446]

(ii) Assignments of trust interests and debts

5.120   If an interest in a trust (whether of land or moveables)[447] is charged or assigned more than once, whether absolutely or by way of security, then priority goes to the

---

of a prior legal mortgagee; see EH Burn and J Cartwright, *Cheshire and Burn's Modern Law of Real Property* (17th edn, 2006) 789.

[440] *Moss v Hancock* [1899] 2 QB 111, DC.

[441] *Miller v Race* (1758) 1 Burr 452, 97 ER 398.

[442] By s 89 the provisions of the Act for bills of exchange also apply, with necessary modifications, to promissory notes. By the Currency and Bank Notes Act 1954, a bank note is a bearer promissory note.

[443] Bills of Exchange Act 1882, s 29(1). The same status can attach to one who has a lien over a bill (ibid s 27(3)). Note that for many bills of exchange (of which cheques are a subset) a transfer requires not only delivery but endorsement. In English law a forged endorsement is a nullity (ibid s 24, codifying the common law rule; although there is special protection for bankers in the case of cheques: ibid ss 60, 80; Cheques Act 1957, s 1). This means that in the case of instruments which require endorsement, the ability to take free of defects in the transferor's title is much more limited than in the case of bearer instruments, where even a thief can give a good title.

[444] This word is sometimes used to designate an instrument transferable by delivery, with any necessary endorsement. In this wider sense it does not connote the possibility that the transferor be able to give a better title than he has. See RM Goode, *Commercial Law* (3rd edn, 2004) 49 n 164.

[445] For a full list, see LS Sealy and RJA Hooley, *Commercial Law* (3rd edn, 2003) 496.

[446] Bills of Exchange Act 1882, s 27(1)(a). At common law and under the statute, this includes an unconditional promise to pay money (*Ex p Richdale* (1882) 19 Ch D 409, 417, CA; *Royal Bank of Scotland v Tottenham* [1894] 2 QB 715, CA).

[447] LPA 1925, s 137(1).

assignee who first gives notice of the charge or assignment to the trustees.[448] This is the rule in *Dearle v Hall*.[449] Notice is not necessary to *constitute* the charge or assignment;[450] but written notice is determinative of priority in the case of multiple dispositions.[451] The later chargee or assignee can take priority over the earlier one by giving the first notice only if, at the time that he gave value for his assignment, the later assignee did not have notice of the earlier disposition.[452]

At common law a debt (not represented by an instrument) could generally be assigned only in equity. In a case of multiple equitable assignments, the rule in *Dearle v Hall* applies. Again, the *validity* of an equitable assignment does not depend on notice to the debtor,[453] but such notice is determinative of priority among multiple assignments; and this is so whether the assigned debts themselves are legal or equitable.[454] The notice must be unequivocal but (unlike in the case of trust interests) it need not be in writing.[455] It is possible by statute to make a legal assignment of a debt; in this case, the assignment must be in writing, and written notice to the debtor is required to constitute the assignment.[456] As in the case of an equitable assignment, that written notice will determine priority in a case of multiple assignments.[457] In both cases, as in assignments of trust interests,

5.121

---

[448] If there are multiple trustees and all are notified, the notice is effective from that date even if some or all of the trustees later leave office (*Re Wasdale* [1899] 1 Ch 163). If not all of the trustees are notified, then the notice is effective only in respect of subsequent notifications made while one of those earlier notified remains in office (*Ward v Duncombe* [1893] AC 369, HL; *Re Phillips' Trusts* [1903] 1 Ch 183). Notice of a trustee who is himself the mortgagor is ineffective (*Lloyds Bank v Pearson* [1901] 1 Ch 865). LPA 1925, s 138 allows a trust settlor, trustees, or the court to nominate a trust corporation as the proper party to receive such notices. Failing this, s 137(2) specifies to whom notice should be given in trusts of or relating to land, although it appears to leave untouched the common law rules regarding multiple trustees. The Act also provides (s 137(4)–(6)) for the giving of notice by endorsement upon the trust instrument, in cases where the giving of notice to trustees is impossible or impracticable; these provisions apply to trusts of land and moveables.

[449] (1823) 3 Russ 1, 38 ER 475, MR; affd (1828) 3 Russ 48, 38 ER 492, LC. The crucial time is that when the notice was received, not sent.

[450] For example, it appears that a consensual chargee who did not give notice takes priority over a subsequent holder of a charging order, who was treated as a chargee not for value and therefore was unable to take advantage of the rule in *Dearle v Hall*: *United Bank of Kuwait plc v Sahib* [1997] Ch 107, 118–120, affd on other grounds [1997] Ch 107, CA.

[451] *Ward v Duncombe* [1893] AC 369, 392, HL. The notice must be written under LPA 1925, s 137(3). The assignment of an equitable interest must itself be in writing under ibid s 53(1)(c).

[452] *Re Holmes* (1885) 29 Ch D 786, CA. An assignee otherwise than for value cannot be promoted over an earlier assignment by being the first to give notice: *United Bank of Kuwait plc v Sahib* [1997] Ch 107, 119–120, affd on other grounds [1997] Ch 107, CA.

[453] For example, it is effective in an insolvency against the liquidator: *Gorringe v Irwell India Rubber and Gutta Percha Works* (1886) 34 Ch D 128, CA (although for individuals, see Insolvency Act 1986, s 344; see para 19.85).

[454] *Compaq Computer Ltd v Abercorn Group Ltd* [1993] BCLC 602; [1991] BCC 484.

[455] *James Talcott Ltd v John Lewis & Co Ltd* [1940] 3 All ER 592, CA.

[456] LPA 1925, s 136(1).

[457] *E Pfeiffer Weinkellerei-Weineinkauf GmbH & Co v Arbuthnot Factors Ltd* [1988] 1 WLR 150; *Compaq Computer Ltd v Abercorn Group Ltd* [1993] BCLC 602; [1991] BCC 484. There is academic

the later assignee cannot acquire priority if, at the time he advanced value for his assignment, he had notice of the earlier assignment.[458]

5.122 It appears that if a trust of a debt is created, this does not attract the rule in *Dearle v Hall* and so the beneficiary of the trust is not required to give notice to the debtor to protect his priority against a later assignee of the debt.[459] Moreover, if a party's interest in a debt is a charge which arose by operation of law, then again the rule probably does not apply. The rule can, however, apply to a consensually created charge, and can subordinate the chargee's interest to that of a later assignee.[460] Furthermore, if a party has an interest in a debt because it had an interest in goods which were sold to generate that debt, the interest in the debt is likely to be characterized as a charge which arose by agreement, and so the rule will apply.[461]

(e) Exceptional transactions

5.123 There is no general principle in English law that a party in good faith is entitled to rely on another party's possession of a thing as indicative that the other party is the owner of that thing. There are, however, a number of situations where particular rules or principles have that effect, and give a later interest priority over an earlier one.[462] These are dealt with in detail elsewhere, but their impact on priorities will be outlined here.

5.124 Where goods are sold and the seller retains ownership to secure the price, the buyer in possession will often be in a position to give to another party whatever title the seller had.[463] Partly for this reason, much secured finance is done by hire purchase. Here the principle is much narrower, although a hirer of a motor

---

argument to the effect that where a statutory assignment has been made, the rule in *Dearle v Hall* should not apply, but rather the rule that a later legal interest, acquired for value and in good faith without notice of an earlier equitable interest, takes priority over that interest: F Oditah, 'Priorities: Equitable versus Legal Assignments of Book Debts' (1989) 9 OJLS 521.

[458] Including constructive notice: *Spencer v Clarke* (1878) 9 Ch D 137. Similarly, a later assignee will be unable to gain priority over an earlier charge on the debt if, at the time he gave value, he had notice of the charge.

[459] *BS Lyle Ltd v Rosher* [1959] 1 WLR 8, 22–3, HL.

[460] The holder of a charge over a debt is not, as such, in a position to secure his priority by giving notice of assignment to the debtor, because the charge is not an assignment and the chargee has no right to payment from the debtor. Registration of the charge may, however, amount to constructive notice of it, preventing a subsequent assignee from taking priority: para 5.143. Also, a consensual charge over a debt is usually combined with a power in the chargee to convert the charge into a mortgage, that is an assignment by way of security: para 5.98. Upon the exercise of that power, the chargee becomes an assignee and can give notice.

[461] On such facts, the court will probably reject attempts to characterize the interest as a trust or as a charge arising by operation of law: *Compaq Computer Ltd v Abercorn Group Ltd* [1993] BCLC 602; [1991] BCC 484; para 5.85.

[462] Factors Act 1889, ss 2, 8, 9; Sale of Goods Act 1979, ss 24, 25; Hire Purchase Act 1964, Part III; see para 10.23.

[463] Factors Act 1889, s 9; Sale of Goods Act 1979, s 25; *National Employers' Mutual General Insurance Assoc Ltd v Jones* [1990] 1 AC 24, HL.

vehicle may be able to give title to a private purchaser.[464] Returning to the case of a sale of goods with retention of ownership, the buyer in possession will also generally be in a position to give a pledge of the goods which will have priority over the seller's ownership.[465] Similarly, if goods are entrusted to a mercantile agent for sale, the agent will be in a position to create a pledge which will have priority over the owner's interest.[466] This provision has also been used to resolve a contest between multiple pledges. A pledgee of a document of title to goods may release it to the pledgor under a 'trust receipt', which allows the pledge to subsist; but where the pledgor created another pledge, the second one had priority.[467]

A party can sometimes enforce a lien against the owner of goods even if they were **5.125** deposited by someone else. This may be because the deposit was with the actual or ostensible authority of the owner.[468] Where the creditor follows a common calling,[469] however, he will be able to assert his lien even if there is no actual or ostensible authority, as where the deposited goods were stolen,[470] or where, to his knowledge, they belong to someone else.[471] This is because such a party is obliged to accept the goods and to provide the relevant services.[472]

(f) Superiority of legal interests

It is important to know whether a party's interest is legal or equitable because **5.126** there is a general principle, albeit modified by statute in many situations, that may permit a later legal interest to prevail over an earlier equitable one. The principle is that if one acquires a legal interest in good faith and for value, and without notice of the prior equitable interest, then one takes free of that interest. In the context of this doctrine of equity, 'value' means money or money's worth, or marriage consideration. It includes the satisfaction of an antecedent debt owed to the purchaser;[473] but it must be executed, and so it excludes a promise made by the purchaser to pay money or transfer property.[474]

---

464 Hire Purchase Act 1964, Part III.

465 Factors Act 1889, s 9; Sale of Goods Act 1979, s 25.

466 Factors Act 1889, s 2. This provision also allows him to sell the goods free of the principal's interest, but the focus here is on contests where at least one of the competing interests is by way of security.

467 *Lloyds Bank Ltd v Bank of America National Trust and Savings Association* [1938] 2 KB 147, CA. Because of the language of s 2, it can generate this result only where the pledgor is a mercantile agent and where the goods or document of title were delivered to him in that capacity.

468 See paras 5.113–5.114 above.

469 For example, a common carrier or an innkeeper.

470 *Marsh v Police Commissioner* [1945] KB 43, CA.

471 *Robins & Co v Gray* [1895] 2 QB 501, CA.

472 Although an innkeeper might not be obliged to accept 'a tiger or a package of dynamite': *Robins & Co v Gray* [1895] 2 QB 501, 504, CA.

473 *Taylor v Blakelock* (1886) 32 Ch D 560, CA.

474 *Story v Windsor* (1743) 2 Atk 630, 26 ER 776.

5.127 The notice may be actual, constructive or imputed. Constructive notice exists where actual notice is absent but would have been present had the purchaser acted reasonably. The scope of constructive notice has always been much broader in transactions involving immoveables, where there are established procedures for investigating title; one who fails to follow them will be said to have constructive notice of that which he would have discovered had he followed them.[475] This context also generated the concept of imputed notice; a party has imputed notice of any interest which was or would have been discovered by his conveyancing solicitor or other agent, had the agent acted competently. This general doctrine regarding notice is now of much less importance for interests in land, because of the statutory priority rules now in place.[476] Constructive notice remains relevant in cases involving moveables, although in the absence of established machinery for searching titles its scope is necessarily narrower.[477]

5.128 The crucial time for determining whether the holder of the legal interest had notice of the equitable interest is not the time at which the legal interest was acquired, but rather the time at which the holder of the legal interest gave value. Assume that the debtor granted equitable mortgages or charges to A and then to B, so that A's interest had priority to B's, but that B lacked notice of A's interest at the time B made his advance. If B were able to acquire a legal interest in the mortgaged asset, for example by exercise of a power to convert his mortgage into a legal mortgage, then B would acquire priority, even if by that time he was aware of A's interest.[478] One aspect of this general doctrine has been abrogated by statute, namely where the legal interest in question is acquired from someone who was himself a mortgagee. If a legal mortgage were given to A, and then equitable mortgages to B and to C, then C's interest ranks last. By the general law, if C had no notice of B's interest at the time C made his advance, C would be able to upgrade his priority by purchasing A's mortgage interest and so acquiring a legal interest in the mortgaged asset, even if, at the time of purchasing A's interest,

---

[475] *Berwick & Co v Price* [1905] 1 Ch 632. For details, see C Harpum, *Megarry and Wade: The Law of Real Property* (6th edn, 2000) 144–50.

[476] See paras 5.131–5.139. There is still some role for constructive and imputed notice, in cases involving unregistrable interests in unregistered land: LPA 1925, s 199(1)(ii); but these doctrines have no role to play for registered land: *Williams & Glyn's Bank Ltd v Boland* [1981] AC 487, HL at 503–4; note 487 below.

[477] *Eagle Trust plc v SBC Securities Ltd* [1993] 1 WLR 484, 504–6. There can, however, be constructive notice by registration: para 5.143.

[478] *Bailey v Barnes* [1894] 1 Ch 25, CA; *McCarthy & Stone Ltd v Julian S Hodge & Co Ltd* [1971] 1 WLR 1547; *MacMillan Inc v Bishopsgate Investment Trust plc (No 3)* [1995] 1 WLR 978, 1003, affd on other grounds [1996] 1 WLR 387, CA. If, to the knowledge of B, the later conveyance of the legal interest is a breach of trust on the part of the debtor, then B cannot prevail (*Mumford v Stohwasser* (1874) LR 18 Eq 556); and the cases suggest that this result will follow even if neither the debtor nor B knew that the conveyance was a breach of trust.

C was aware of B's. This would allow C to recover the amount originally owed to A, and the amount which C had advanced, all in priority to B's interest. This particular application of the general law has been abolished so that the ranking of the three mortgages would be unaffected by C's purchase.[479]

The general doctrine by which a legal interest can prevail over an earlier equitable interest is subject to many of the principles which have been set out above. For example, gross negligence by the holder of a legal interest might mean that he will be postponed to an earlier equitable interest.[480] Where the subject matter of the priority contest is a debt, then there is no room for the doctrine which gives priority to legal interests; even in the case of a legal assignment of a legal debt, the rule in *Dearle v Hall* governs the contest.[481]

5.129

(3) Particular Priority Contests

The application of these general principles to particular situations is modified by statutory interventions.

5.130

(a) Registered land

(i) Where the mortgaged estate is legal

If a mortgagee wishes to have a registered charge on registered land, he must take a charge by way of legal mortgage and register it in the Land Registry.[482] Such registered charges rank according to the order in which they are entered on the register, not the order of the execution of the documents.[483]

5.131

---

[479] LPA 1925, s 94(3), which appears to apply to moveables as well as land (RM Goode, *Commercial Law* (3rd edn, 2004) 656). On facts such as these, C's goal is said to be to 'tack' his own advance on to the prior interest of A, and s 94(3) abolishes all forms of 'tacking' not specifically preserved by ss 94(1),(2) (which are discussed in paras 5.154–5.157); but it did not abolish the general rules regarding the subsequent acquisition of a legal interest: *McCarthy & Stone Ltd v Julian S Hodge & Co Ltd* [1971] 1 WLR 1547, 1556; *MacMillan Inc v Bishopsgate Investment Trust plc (No 3)* [1995] 1 WLR 978, 1002–5, affd on other grounds [1996] 1 WLR 387, CA.

[480] *Oliver v Hinton* [1899] 2 Ch 264, CA. The holder of the legal title made no inquiries about the title deeds; if he had, he would have learned of the earlier equitable mortgage, whose mortgagee held the deeds. The equitable mortgage was given priority. One might have said that the carelessness of the holder of the legal title gave him constructive notice of the equitable interest, so that the basic rule applied, with priority going to the earliest interest: EH Burn and J Cartwright, *Cheshire and Burn's Modern Law of Real Property* (17th edn, 2006) 786 n 464.

[481] See para 5.121.

[482] See para 5.18.

[483] LRA 2002, s 48. An intending mortgagee who obtains a clear search of the register may be concerned that another interest may be registered before the mortgagee completes his own registration. He may protect himself by making an 'official search with priority', which will guarantee priority if the mortgage is registered within 30 days: Land Registration Rules 2003, SI 2003/1417, rr 131, 147–54.

5.132 If a legal mortgagee fails to register his interest, it takes effect only in equity.[484] Similarly, if a mortgagee takes only an equitable mortgage on a legal estate, this cannot be registered as a charge. Equitable mortgages can be protected by entering a notice in the Land Registry.[485]

5.133 A registered charge, or any other registered disposition, which is made for value, will generally take priority over a prior interest that is unregistered, even if the purchaser of the charge is aware of that interest.[486] There are two main exceptions, in which a registered disposition will not take priority over a prior unregistered interest. It will not do so if, at the time of the registration of the disposition, the unregistered interest was protected by a notice. Nor will it do so if the unregistered interest is an 'overriding interest', one that is protected even without registration.[487] As between themselves, unregistered interests rank by the order of their creation, whether or not they are protected;[488] although this is subject to the principle that the earlier mortgagee can be subordinated where fault is attributable to him.[489] In effect, protection of an unregistered interest on the register protects it against later interests, but (unlike full registration) does not improve the interest's priority against existing interests.

5.134 A priority contest may arise between a mortgagee and the beneficiaries of a trust of land; for example, if the trustees (who hold the registered title to the land) grant a registered charge on the land contrary to the terms of the trust. Beneficiaries have always been protected by the principles of equity, including the doctrine of notice; but too much protection of this kind meant that purchasers or mortgagees from trustees had to conduct very extensive inquiries as to the terms of a trust in order to be certain that they would get a clear title. The legislative solution is the principle that a mortgagee or other purchaser of a legal interest takes free of a pre-existing trust interest (even if he is aware of the trust, and even if the trustee is acting in breach of trust) so long as the mortgage advance is paid either to two or more individual trustees, or to a trust corporation.[490] The idea underlying these

---

484 LRA 2002, s 27(1).

485 Para 5.18.

486 LRA 2002, ss 28–30. Actual notice does not affect priorities in respect of registered land.

487 These are listed in LRA 2002, Sch 3. One of the most important (para 2) is an 'interest belonging at the time of the disposition to a person in actual occupation'; this protects, for example, the equitable interest of a person under a trust arising by operation of law, so long as they occupy the land (*Williams & Glyn's Bank Ltd v Boland* [1981] AC 487, HL). The result is that although the old concept of 'notice' does not apply to registered land, a prudent purchaser must not only inspect the register, but must ascertain what rights the occupants may have.

488 LRA 2002, s 28. See, under the LRA 1925, *Barclays Bank Ltd v Taylor* [1974] Ch 137, CA and *Mortgage Corp Ltd v Nationwide Credit Corp* [1994] Ch 49, CA.

489 See, under the LRA 1925, *Freeguard v Royal Bank of Scotland plc* (1998) 79 P & CR 81, CA.

490 LPA 1925, ss 2(1)(ii), 27. Not any corporation qualifies as a trust corporation: LPA 1925, s 205(xxviii). Note that because of the way 'purchaser' is defined (s 205(1)(xxi)), for the purposes of ss 2 and 27, a purchaser need not be in good faith. The consensus is that these provisions of LPA

'overreaching' provisions is that the beneficiaries are sufficiently protected against breach of trust by the requirement of multiple trustees or a trust corporation. If these provisions are complied with, then the mortgagee will have priority over even an overriding beneficial interest.[491] The overreaching provisions are reinforced by requiring that in trusts of land, there should be a restriction on the register that does not allow the trustees to make a disposition except one that will satisfy the overreaching provisions, guaranteeing that the purchaser will take a clear title.[492] In the case of a trust arising by operation of law, for example between married or unmarried cohabitants, this may be impossible since there may be only one individual trustee. In such a case, the statutory overreaching provisions cannot operate.[493] The beneficiary's interest will be protected if he is in actual occupation;[494] or, if it is protected by a restriction on the register; otherwise a subsequent registered charge will take priority under the general rules.[495]

(ii) Where the mortgaged interest is equitable

If the mortgaged interest is equitable, for example an interest under a trust of land, **5.135** then only an equitable mortgage can be created, and it cannot be registered or protected.[496] Priorities among such mortgages are resolved by the rule in *Dearle v Hall*.[497] There are important statutory provisions governing how notice may be given so as to secure priority under this rule.[498]

(b) Unregistered land

(i) Where the mortgaged estate is legal

There may be multiple legal mortgages of a legal estate. Only the holder of the **5.136** first one is entitled to possession of the title deeds; the consequence is that this

---

1925 apply to registered as well as unregistered land; see however N Jackson, 'Overreaching in Registered Land' (2006) 69 MLR 214.

[491] *City of London BS v Flegg* [1988] AC 54, HL. In *State Bank of India v Sood* [1997] Ch 276, CA, it was held that the mortgagee takes priority even where no money was advanced at the time the mortgage was taken, as where it is taken to secure existing and future advances.

[492] LRA 2002, ss 40–47; Land Registration Rules 2003, SI 2003/1417, rr 91–99 and Forms A, B, C.

[493] It is of course possible for a clear title to be conveyed, either with the consent of the beneficiary or by the appointment of a new trustee. The problem discussed in the text arises where the single individual trustee attempts to make a disposition without the consent of a beneficiary. The beneficiary who becomes aware of this possibility in advance can enter a restriction.

[494] LRA 2002, Sch 3, para 2; *Williams & Glyn's Bank Ltd v Boland* [1981] AC 487, HL.

[495] LRA 2002, s 30.

[496] Because the equitable interest of the mortgagor cannot itself be registered: LRA 2002, s 2.

[497] Land Registration Act 1986, s 5(1)(b). The rule is explained in para 5.120. If the mortgaged equitable interest is not an interest in a trust (for example, an estate contract) then it appears that the rule in *Dearle v Hall* does not apply: LPA 1925, s 137(10); *Property Discount Corp Ltd v Lyon Group Ltd* [1981] 1 WLR 300, CA. This means that priority will be determined by order of creation, subject to the rules about fault.

[498] LPA 1925, ss 137, 138; n 448 above.

mortgage is not registrable in the Land Charges Register.[499] Later legal mortgages are registrable, as are equitable mortgages not protected by a deposit of title deeds.[500] Among these registrable mortgages, the general rule is that mortgages rank by the order of their registration.[501] The exception is that a registrable mortgage which was not registered when another interest was subsequently acquired for value is void against the holder of that interest.[502] This means that a subsequent registered mortgage defeats an earlier unregistered one, but it also has a less obvious effect. If A takes a registrable mortgage, and then B takes a registrable mortgage for value, and then A registers, and then B registers, B has priority, since A's interest is void against B.[503] A registrable mortgage which is made void by non-registration against the holder of a subsequent interest is void even if the latter was aware of the earlier interest.[504]

---

[499] Recall, however, that the creation of such a mortgage now triggers compulsory registration of the mortgaged estate, meaning that the land becomes registered land and the mortgage itself will need to be registered: LRA 2002, ss 4(1)(g), (8).

[500] See para 5.19.

[501] LPA 1925, s 97. To the extent that notice may be relevant, by s 198(1) registration constitutes notice to all parties from the date of registration. An intending mortgagee who obtains a clear search of the register may be concerned that another interest may be registered before the mortgagee completes his own registration. If he makes an official search, however, and completes the transaction within 15 days, then he will not be affected by any registration made between search and completion: Land Charges Act 1972, s 11(5). An intending mortgagee may also enter in the register a priority notice at least 15 days before registering his mortgage (ibid s 11(1)–(3)); if he registers within 30 days from entering the priority notice, then the date of creation of the mortgage is treated as the date of registration.

[502] Land Charges Act 1972, s 4(5); the subsequent interest may be a mortgage or a beneficial interest: ibid s 17(1). Section 4(5) covers Class C land charges (other than estate contracts); that includes second and subsequent legal mortgages, and equitable mortgages of legal interests, except equitable mortgages arising from an agreement to give a legal mortgage, which are a type of estate contract. Other types of charges are dealt with by other parts of s 4, and generally the same rule applies, except under s 4(6) which governs estate contracts and Class D land charges (Inland Revenue charges, restrictive covenants, and equitable easements). Here the unregistered interest is only void where the subsequent interest is a legal interest, acquired for money or money's worth (which expression excludes marriage consideration); thus if the second interest is equitable (or a legal interest acquired as a gift) the general law applies, and the earlier unregistered interest will usually prevail (subject to the rules about fault, and the possibility that the holder of the later interest has acquired a legal estate without notice): *McCarthy & Stone Ltd v Julian S Hodge & Co Ltd* [1971] 1 WLR 1547.

[503] The default rule, giving priority to A as the first to register (LPA 1925, s 97), seems inapplicable because A's interest is void against B: EH Burn and J Cartwright, *Cheshire and Burn's Modern Law of Real Property* (17th edn, 2006) 797–8. Depending on the timing, A could avoid the outcome by the use of a priority notice (n 501 above). The interaction of the Land Charges Act 1972, s 4(5) and LPA 1925, s 97 is generally considered unsatisfactory; apart from the result mentioned in the text, the scheme can also produce circular priorities where there are more than two interests. The voidness of A's interest against B also means that if neither interest was registered, B would still prevail even though later in time.

[504] LPA 1925, s 199(1)(i); *Coventry Permanent Economic BS v Jones* [1951] 1 All ER 901; *Midland Bank Trust Co Ltd v Green* [1981] AC 513, HL. If the earlier interest is not made void by non-registration, as where it is an estate contract and the later interest is equitable (see n 502 above), then the non-statutory rules apply: first in time generally prevails, subject to the rule about the

Where a mortgage is protected by deposit of the title deeds, that mortgage is not **5.137** registrable. Priorities are determined by the general principles discussed above; in particular, that interests are generally ranked by the order of their creation, but that this can be displaced by carelessness with title deeds,[505] and by the superiority of legal interests.[506] So if the first interest is protected by the title deeds, it will be important to know whether it is legal or equitable. If it is legal, then the only way the later interest could prevail would be if the first mortgagee was grossly negligent with the title deeds, for example giving up possession of them and so allowing the later mortgagee to be deceived. If the first mortgage, protected by the deeds, is equitable, then a later legal interest not so protected might take priority as the acquisition of a legal interest in good faith, for value and without notice of the earlier equitable interest. The inability of the mortgagor to produce the title deeds, however, might well give the legal mortgagee constructive notice of the earlier interest, so that the basic rule of first in time would govern.[507] If the second mortgage is equitable as well as the first, then again only gross negligence could displace the normal rule ranking the interests by the time of creation.

On the other hand, it might be that the second interest is the one protected by the **5.138** title deeds. This implies that the first interest is registrable, and if it was registered before the second interest was granted, then the second mortgagee is treated as having notice of the first, and so the first takes priority.[508] This would be true even if the first mortgage was equitable and the second was legal, since the legal mortgagee could not claim to have acquired his interest without notice of the other. Only gross negligence could possibly postpone the earlier mortgage. If, on the other hand, the first interest was not registered before the second was granted, the first interest is void against the holder of the second, which therefore takes priority.[509]

As in registered land, a mortgage granted by trustees may come into conflict with **5.139** an earlier beneficial interest under a trust of land. The principles of statutory over-reaching, discussed above, apply also to unregistered land.[510] In unregistered land, the beneficiary's interest is not registrable, nor can it be protected on any register.

---

superiority of a legal estate acquired for value without notice of the earlier equitable interest: ibid s 199(1)(ii); *McCarthy & Stone Ltd v Julian S Hodge & Co Ltd* [1971] 1 WLR 1547.

[505] See para 5.117. LPA 1925, s 13, makes it clear that these principles remain applicable.
[506] See paras 5.126–5.129.
[507] The relevance of constructive and imputed notice in this context is preserved by LPA 1925, s 199(1)(ii). Those doctrines are displaced only when the earlier interest is made void by non-registration: ibid s 199(1)(i).
[508] LPA 1925, s 198.
[509] Land Charges Act 1972, s 4. If, however, the first interest was an equitable mortgage arising from an agreement to grant a legal mortgage, then under s 4(6) it would not be void if the second interest was equitable.
[510] Para 5.134.

A subsequent legal mortgagee can take priority only as a bona fide purchaser for value without notice of the trust. The mortgagee may have actual, constructive or imputed notice of the trust via the beneficiary's occupation of the land.[511] He is relieved, however, from inquiring into whether the trustees have fulfilled all of their trust obligations, unless he has actual notice that they have not.[512]

(ii) Where the mortgaged interest is equitable

5.140 If the mortgaged interest is equitable, for example an interest under a trust of land, then only an equitable mortgage can be created, and it is not registrable.[513] As in registered land, priorities among such mortgages are resolved by the rule in *Dearle v Hall*.[514]

(c) Moveables

5.141 For moveables, the general principles set out above remain of primary importance. For possessory security interests, such as liens and pledges, they are determinative. For non-possessory interests, such as mortgages and charges, statutory registration requirements are usually applicable.[515] The registration systems can modify the general principles in different ways. First, failure to register an interest may make it void; secondly, registration may constitute notice of the registered interest, which has implications for some priority rules; thirdly, priority among registered interests may be determined by the time of registration. But there is no consistent policy or legislative technique across the many registers; in particular, in the crucial case of company charges, the time of registration does not determine priorities.

(i) Company charges and mortgages

5.142 If a charge or mortgage is registrable by a company, and it is not registered within 21 days of its creation, the charge or mortgage will become 'void against the liquidator or administrator and any creditor of the company'.[516] Clearly, as between two registrable charges, a registered charge prevails against an unregistered one; if neither is registered, the later will have priority, as the earlier one will be void

---

[511] LPA 1925, s 199(1)(ii); *Kingsnorth Trust Ltd v Tizard* [1986] 1 WLR 783.

[512] Trusts of Land and Appointment of Trustees Act 1996, s 16.

[513] By Land Charges Act 1972, s 3(1) registration is in the name of the 'estate owner' (mortgagor) and this includes only the holder of a legal estate: ibid s 17(1); LPA 1925, s 205(1)(v).

[514] Para 5.135.

[515] There are however some gaps, such as a mortgage given by an individual over an unregistered ship: *British Credit Trust Ltd v The Owners of the Shizelle (The Shizelle)* [1992] 2 Lloyd's Rep 444.

[516] CA 1985, s 395(1); CA 2006, 874(1). In the remainder of this section, 'Company charges and mortgages', 'charge' should be read to include 'mortgage' (CA 1985, s 396(4); CA 2006, s 861(5)). For the charges which are registrable, manner of registration, and the effect of non-registration between debtor and creditor, see paras 5.103–5.105.

against the later one.[517] Despite the wording of the section, an unregistered charge is not void against an *unsecured* creditor, unless he has completed an execution process.[518] In the absence of a subsequent secured or execution creditor, or a liquidation or administration, there will be no one with standing to prevent the chargee from enforcing an unregistered charge. A registrable but unregistered charge is not void against a purchaser of the asset,[519] although the purchaser might take free of the charge under the general law, for instance if the disposition was authorized under a floating charge, or if he purchased a legal interest for value, in good faith and without notice of the charge. It has also been held that where a charge is void, rights arising out of the contract which created the charge are still enforceable if they are not part of the charge itself; so where a company charged machinery and the charge was void for non-registration in the liquidation of the company, this did not prevent the chargee from exercising its right under the contract to continue to make use of the machinery, as that right was held not to be part of the charge.[520]

If the charge is properly registered, then its priority is governed by the general **5.143** rules, modified by the fact that the registration may constitute notice of the registered interest. There is no principle that the priority of registered charges is determined by the order of registration.[521] Registration does not, as it does in the case of unregistered land, constitute notice to everyone, since acquisitions of interests in moveables cannot always be preceded by registry searches. The legislation does not clarify the point, but the best view appears to be that registration constitutes notice of the charge to any party who could reasonably be expected to conduct a search.[522] This would seem to include a subsequent secured lender or a purchaser of book debts. A registered charge over book debts should therefore have priority over a subsequent assignment of the debts under the rule in *Dearle v Hall*, not because the chargee gives notice to the debtors, but because the later assignee will have constructive notice of the earlier charge.[523] A purchaser of a

---

[517] RM Goode, *Commercial Law* (3rd edn, 2004) 668; for the similar position in unregistered mortgages of unregistered land, see para 5.136.

[518] *Re Ehrmann Bros Ltd* [1906] 2 Ch 697, CA; Goode (ibid) 667.

[519] *Stroud Architectural Services Ltd v John Laing Construction Ltd* [1994] BCC 18.

[520] *Re Cosslett (Contractors) Ltd* [1998] Ch 495, CA. However, in a later round of litigation it was held that the chargee's right under the contract to sell the charged property was part of the charge and was therefore void: *Smith (as Administrator of Cosslett (Contractors) Ltd) v Bridgend County Borough Council* [2001] UKHL 58; [2002] 1 AC 336.

[521] If, however, the charges are registrable under another system, such as ship mortgages, then such a rule may be imposed by that system.

[522] RM Goode, *Commercial Law* (3rd edn, 2004) 663, 666. It appears, however, that those who have actual or constructive notice of the existence of a charge do not have constructive notice of particular terms of the charge, beyond the particulars which are required to be filed: see n 365 above.

[523] On charges over book debts, see para 5.98. On the rule in *Dearle v Hall*, see para 5.121.

single asset in the ordinary course of business would not, however, have constructive notice of a registered charge over the asset. Such a purchaser might therefore be able to rely on the doctrine which allows the good faith purchaser for value of a legal interest to take free of a prior equitable interest if he did not have notice of it.[524]

5.144 A floating charge, even if it be properly registered, will often be subordinate to a later interest. The holder of the later interest can rely on the authority granted to the chargor company to dispose of the charged goods in the ordinary course of business. This reasoning applies even if the holder of the subsequent interest has actual or constructive notice of the earlier charge. Moreover, the relevant authority extends beyond actual authority to ostensible authority, making effective any disposition which is usually authorized under a floating charge, even if the terms of the particular floating charge forbid it.[525] This ostensible authority would extend to the granting of a fixed charge following the floating charge but with priority over it.[526] Similar reasoning makes effective a disposition occurring after the floating charge crystallized, if the crystallization did not occur by one of the events which give notice to the world that the chargor's authority to deal with its assets is at an end.[527]

(ii) Bills of sale

5.145 If a document creating a security interest is registrable as a bill of sale, and it is not properly registered within seven days of execution, the security is unenforceable, even against the debtor.[528] As between the interests of secured creditors under properly registered bills, priority goes to the first to register, displacing the basic rule giving priority to the first interest created.[529] Purchasers may be able to take free of the creditor's security interest even if it is properly registered, since registration does not constitute constructive notice.[530] If the creditor's interest is by way of equitable charge or mortgage, then a purchaser might be able to rely on the

---

[524] This would not, however, be possible if the registered 'charge' was actually a legal mortgage; in that case, both interests are legal.

[525] Constructive notice of the charge does not constitute constructive notice of all of its terms: see n 365 above. It seems that only actual notice of the restriction can prevent the subsequent party from relying on ostensible authority.

[526] Para 5.114.

[527] See para 5.96. Note also that, in insolvency proceedings, a floating charge is subordinated to preferential debts; and, since 2002, some assets that would otherwise fall within a floating charge must be set aside to help meet the claims of unsecured creditors. See paras 19.105–19.112.

[528] Bills of Sale Act (1878) Amendment Act 1882, s 8.

[529] Bills of Sale Act 1878, s 10. This is also true if an 'absolute' bill is granted after a security bill, an absolute bill being a bill of sale conveying an interest which is not by way of security. If, however, a security bill is granted after an absolute bill, then the security bill will be void (except as against the grantor) whether or not the absolute bill was registered: Bills of Sale Act (1878) Amendment Act 1882, s 5. The latter act does not apply to absolute bills: ibid s 3.

[530] *Joseph v Lyons* (1884) 15 QBD 280, 286, CA.

doctrine which allows the good faith purchaser for value of a legal interest to take free of a prior equitable interest if he did not have notice of it.[531]

(iii) Agricultural charges

An agricultural charge is void against everyone except the chargor if not properly **5.146** registered within seven days of creation.[532] As between multiple agricultural charges, priority goes to the earliest registered, again displacing the basic rule giving priority to the first created.[533] Unlike in the case of company charges, a registered floating agricultural charge always takes priority over a later agricultural charge, even if the latter is fixed.[534] Registration of the charge constitutes notice to all persons and for all purposes.[535] However, a purchaser of charged assets can take free of the charge, even if it is a fixed charge, and even if he is aware of it.[536]

(iv) Charges given by industrial and provident societies

An industrial and provident society is a corporation in the nature of a co-operative.[537] **5.147** Such a society may give an agricultural charge, and if it does, it may register it as such.[538] If it gives any other charge, it may register the charge with the FSA which maintains a register of industrial and provident societies.[539] If it makes either one of these registrations, the Bills of Sale Acts will not apply to the transaction; otherwise, they will.[540] Beyond this, it appears that general principles govern.[541]

---

[531] This would not, however, be possible if the secured creditor had taken a legal mortgage; in that case, both interests are legal.

[532] Agricultural Credits Act 1928, s 9(1), providing for extension of time by the court. The register is kept by the Land Registrar, but, unlike the Land Registry of registered land, it is not organized by the location of the land. The register of agricultural charges is organized by the name of the debtor.

[533] ibid s 8(2).

[534] ibid 8(3), also giving the floating charge priority over an interest created under a bill of sale. An agricultural charge can only be given to a bank (ibid s 5(1)), so a charge given by the farmer to any other creditor would probably be registrable as a bill of sale.

[535] ibid s 9(8).

[536] ibid s 6(3), which does not even specify that the sale must be in the ordinary course of business. The ability to take clear of a floating charge is governed by the general law (ibid s 7(1)), which would impose such a limitation.

[537] Paras 3.88–3.89.

[538] Agricultural Credits Act 1928, s 14.

[539] Industrial and Provident Societies Act 1967, ss 1–2.

[540] *Re North Wales Produce and Supply Society* [1922] 2 Ch 340.

[541] For example, a society might grant a charge over intangible property that it holds, and fail to register it, and then grant another charge over the same property, and register the second charge with the FSA. Registration with the FSA is optional, and failure to register does not have any consequence except to bring in the Bills of Sale Acts. Those Acts apply to the first charge, but intangible property is not affected by them so the first charge is valid. It would appear that the unregistered first charge would have priority over the registered second charge.

(v) Other registers

5.148 There are other registers for particular kinds of assets. If the charge or mortgage is given by a company, then the requirements of the Companies Act are generally cumulative.[542] The charge may therefore be avoided by that Act, even if the particular registration system does not avoid it.

5.149 **Ships.** Ship mortgages (including charges) have their own registration system, although it does not apply to every ship mortgage.[543] Where it does apply, it ranks registered mortgages by the time of their registration.[544] An unregistered mortgage is not void, but is subordinate to a registered mortgage, even one created later and with notice of the earlier unregistered mortgage.[545] Outside these cases, it appears that general principles govern.[546]

5.150 **Aircraft.** Aircraft mortgages and charges also have their own registration system.[547] It ranks registered mortgages by the time of registration.[548] As in ship mortgages, an unregistered mortgage is not void, but is subordinate to a registered one, even if created later and with notice.[549] Registration of a mortgage is treated as giving notice of it to all parties.[550] Again, it appears that general principles govern other cases.

5.151 **Patents.** A mortgage or charge on a patent may be registered.[551] Here a registered interest takes priority over an earlier interest only if the earlier interest was unregistered, and the holder of the later interest did not know of the earlier transaction.[552] As between unregistered interests, it appears that the one created first will prevail; and the same principle will govern as between registered interests, there being no provision making priority depend upon order of registration.

5.152 **Registered trade marks.** A mortgage or charge on a registered trade mark may be registered.[553] Under this system, an unregistered interest is ineffective against anyone who acquires a conflicting interest, in ignorance of the earlier interest.[554] This seems to mean that an unregistered interest will be subordinated to a later

---

542 Para 5.104, noting some exceptions.

543 Merchant Shipping Act 1995, Sch 1; as to scope, see n 296 above. Where the system does not apply, general principles are determinative.

544 ibid Sch 1 para 8. There is a system of priority notices (para 8(2)).

545 *Black v Williams* [1895] Ch 408.

546 A Clarke, 'Ship Mortgages' in N Palmer and E McKendrick (eds), *Interests in Goods* (2nd edn, 1998), 684.

547 Mortgaging of Aircraft Order 1972, SI 1972/1268.

548 ibid art 14(2), with a priority notice system.

549 ibid arts 14(1), (4).

550 ibid art 13.

551 Patents Act 1977, s 33(3)(b).

552 ibid ss 33(1),(2).

553 Trade Marks Act 1994, s 25(2)(c).

554 ibid s 25(3).

interest, whether registered or unregistered. But registered interests will take priority by time of creation, there being no provision making priority depend upon order of registration.

Registered designs. A mortgage or charge on a registered design is required to be registered.[555] Until this is done, the document by which it is created is inadmissible in evidence.[556] By this unusual legislative technique, it appears that any registered mortgage will prevail over any unregistered disposition, even if the registered mortgagee is aware of the earlier unregistered disposition, because it will be impossible to prove the unregistered disposition. In a dispute as between unregistered interests, neither party will be able to prove the creation of its interest. On the other hand, registered interests will take priority by time of creation, there being no provision making priority depend upon order of registration.

5.153

(4) Future Advances

The problem of future advances arises where A has a security interest with priority to that of B, and A advances further funds to the debtor. Does the priority of A's security extend to the further advance? An affirmative answer can be given in four cases.[557]

5.154

(a) Arrangement

If, pursuant to an arrangement between them, A shall have priority for the further advance, this is effective.[558]

5.155

(b) Lack of notice

If, at the time he made his further advance, A lacked notice of B's interest, A's priority extends to the further advance.[559] In unregistered land, if B's interest is a

5.156

---

555 Registered Designs Act 1949, s 19(1).

556 ibid s 19(5).

557 The matter is governed by LPA 1925, s 94, which appears to apply to moveables as well as unregistered land (RM Goode, *Commercial Law* (3rd edn, 2004) 656), and LRA 2002, s 49 for registered land. Perhaps by an oversight, the wording of these sections is such that they do not seem to apply to the case where A has not made even his initial advance before B's interest is taken. Here it seems the common law rule, which these provisions otherwise replace, continues to apply: Goode 657–8. That rule says that A's advance cannot have priority if A's mortgage is equitable, and even if it is legal, A loses his priority once he has notice of B's interest; this is the case even if A is contractually obliged to make the advance: *Hopkinson v Rolt* (1861) 9 HL Cas 514, 11 ER 829; *West v Williams* [1899] 1 Ch 132, CA.

558 LPA 1925, s 94(1)(a). LRA 2002, s 48 allows mortgagees of registered land to modify priorities; registration is required for third parties to be affected: ibid ss 48(2), 49(6); Land Registration Rules 2003, SI 2003/1417, r 102.

559 LPA 1925, s 94(1)(b); LRA 2002, ss 48(1).

registered mortgage, then B's registration of his mortgage generally constitutes constructive notice to A, reversing the priorities.[560] If, however, A's security is expressly taken to secure future advances, or to secure a current account, then A will not have constructive notice by B's registration, unless B's registration was in place at the later of the time of A's registration and the time of A's last search of the register.[561] It is therefore general practice for a mortgage agreement to stipulate that the mortgage will secure further advances, while a subsequent mortgagee will be careful to give actual notice to the prior mortgagee. Where A's interest is a registered charge on registered land, the position is slightly different.[562] The basic rule is that A has priority until he has notice of B's registered charge; but A is deemed to receive that notice after a fixed amount of time, depending upon how the notice is sent.[563] In the case of company charges, although there is no express provision regarding the effect of registration, it appears again that B's registration will not constitute constructive notice to A, at least in the case where A is a bank making further advances on a current account, since it would not be reasonable to require the bank to make a search every time a cheque was presented for payment.[564]

(c) Obligation to make further advance

5.157 Even if A has notice of B's interest, nonetheless if A was obliged by his agreement with the debtor to make the further advance, then his priority extends to the further advance.[565]

(d) Advances within registered upper limit

5.158 In registered land only, even if A has notice of B's interest, and even if A was not obliged to make the further advance, A's further advance can still have priority if A's mortgage was taken to secure advances up to a stated maximum amount and that fact is noted in the register.[566]

---

[560] ibid s 198(1).

[561] ibid s 94(2). A similar principle operates for agricultural charges: Agricultural Credits Act 1928, s 9(8).

[562] LPA 1925, s 94 does not apply to any mortgages on registered land (s 94(4)); LRA 2002 s 49 dictates when registered mortgages on registered land have priority for future advances. It would appear that s 49 applies if A's interest is registered but B's is unregistered; if both are unregistered, it would appear that the common law rules govern (above, n 557).

[563] LRA 2002, s 49(2); Land Registration Rules 2003, SI 2003/1417, r 107. For example, if a notice is sent by post, it is deemed to be received on the second day after posting and A will lose priority to B for any advances made after that, even if A never actually receives the notice. When electronic conveyancing is implemented, such a notice will be sent electronically.

[564] RM Goode, *Commercial Law* (3rd edn, 2004) 657 n 77, 666.

[565] LPA 1925, s 94(1)(c); LRA 2002, s 49(3). In registered land, A's obligation must be entered in the register (Land Registration Rules 2003, r 108).

[566] LRA 2002, s 49(4); Land Registration Rules 2003, r 109. Although the LRA does not state this clearly, presumably A's priority extends only to advances up to the registered limit.

(5) After-Acquired Property and Purchase Money Finance

An equitable mortgage or charge can apply to property acquired by the debtor **5.159**
after the date of the agreement, automatically and without any further legal act.[567]
If such a charge has been created in favour of A, the question arises whether a later
creditor B can advance money to allow the debtor to purchase an asset which is
within A's security, in such a way that B will have priority to that asset. Although
in general terms a later security interest is subordinate to an earlier one, in the case
where the later creditor is advancing 'purchase money' finance for an asset, there
are good reasons for allowing priority in relation to that asset. This will remove
what would otherwise be A's credit monopoly; at the same time, it does not
materially harm A, since the loss of priority is only in respect of an asset which
would not have been acquired but for B's advance.

If B is actually the seller of the asset, then he can obtain priority by retaining legal **5.160**
ownership of it. As long as B is the owner, the asset does not belong to the debtor,
and so it cannot be subject to A's security. If, however, B is merely providing the
finance to permit the debtor to acquire the asset, this is not possible; B must
take a security interest, such as a mortgage or charge. On one view, it is logically
necessary for the debtor to acquire the asset before B's interest can be granted to B;
but at the moment the debtor acquires the asset, it will become subject to A's
interest.[568] It has been held, however, that if, before the debtor acquired the asset,
he had agreed with B that it would be charged to B, then B's interest will take
priority.[569] When the purchase of land is being financed, such an agreement will
almost always be found; however, the difficulty with making B's priority turn
on an agreement is that an agreement to give a charge over land is now of no
legal effect unless it is in writing and signed by both parties.[570] If B is to continue
to have priority over A, this result must now be understood to flow from the
status of his interest as a purchase money security interest. The implications for
security in moveables of the reasoning based on agreement has not been fully
worked out.[571]

---

[567] See paras 5.13, 5.88, 5.93.

[568] *Church of England BS v Piskor* [1954] Ch 553, CA.

[569] *Abbey National BS v Cann* [1991] 1 AC 56, 92, 101–102, HL, overruling *Church of England v Piskor*.

[570] Law of Property (Miscellaneous Provisions) Act 1989, s 2(1); RM Goode, *Commercial Law* (3rd edn, 2004) 669–71.

[571] For example, attempts by reservation of title sellers to secure an interest in the proceeds of sub-sales usually fail, because the interest is characterized as a charge created by the company, and is not registered: para 5.85. It is not always practicable for such sellers to make a registration; even where it is, as in a high-value sale, it might be thought to be pointless if the charge would be subordinate to any earlier charge in favour of an institutional creditor. If, however, the reasoning in *Abbey National BS v Cann* [1991] 1 AC 56, HL, applied to such charges over proceeds, the position of such sellers would be materially improved.

E. Personal Security

(1) *Types of Security*

(a) Guarantees and indemnities

5.161 A guarantee is a contract to answer for the default of another. As such, it imposes an obligation which is *secondary* to that of a primary debtor, meaning that the guarantor's liability depends upon default by the primary debtor. The guarantor's obligation is also *accessory* to that of the primary debtor, meaning that it is enforceable only to the extent that the obligation of the primary debtor is enforceable. A guarantee must be distinguished from an indemnity, where one party is obliged to keep another harmless from loss. The obligation assumed in an indemnity is primary and so does not depend on another's default, nor is it affected by any inability to enforce some other obligation. The question whether a particular contract is a guarantee or an indemnity is one of construction of the contract.[572] The court must decide whether the parties did or did not intend that the liability should be secondary and accessory.

5.162 The wide freedom of contract granted by English law means that the boundary between guarantee and indemnity is difficult to draw. For example, an agreement may be a guarantee even though it stipulates that the guarantor is liable as a principal debtor, if the agreement as a whole shows an intention that the obligation be a guarantee.[573] It should also be noted that it is possible to provide real security for another's debt, without incurring any personal liability;[574] even though this is a form of real security, nonetheless if it is provided as a guarantee then the principles governing guarantees will apply.[575]

(b) Other personal securities

5.163 The same freedom of contract permits the creation of agreements which are guarantees in form, but in effect are closer to indemnities. It is common in substantial projects for a party who owes non-monetary obligations to a creditor to

---

[572] *Yeoman Credit Ltd v Latter* [1961] 1 WLR 828, CA; *Marubeni Hong Kong and South China Ltd v Mongolian Government* [2005] EWCA Civ 395; [2005] 1 WLR 2497.

[573] *Heald v O'Connor* [1971] 1 WLR 497, 503. Such a term can however have legal effects. It may mean that the guarantor is not discharged, as he normally is, by a release of the primary debtor: *General Produce Co v United Bank Ltd* [1979] 2 Lloyd's Rep 255; it may mean that the creditor is relieved of the usual requirement that he make a demand on the guarantor before the latter is liable: *MS Fashions Ltd v Bank of Credit and Commerce International SA* [1993] Ch 425, CA.

[574] *Smith v Wood* [1929] 1 Ch 14, CA; *Re Bank of Credit and Commerce International SA (No 8)* [1998] AC 214, HL.

[575] *Smith v Wood*, n 508 above.

procure, for the benefit of that creditor, a performance guarantee from a third party. Such a document may be a true guarantee;[576] but it may instead be a guarantee in form only. In this latter case, the contract is often called a 'first demand guarantee', and the 'guarantor' is usually a bank or other financial institution.[577] Apart from its name, such a contract shares with a true guarantee only the feature that the 'guarantor's' liability is intended to be secondary, so that the guarantee is not to be enforced except in a case of default by the primary debtor. But the 'guarantor's' liability is not accessory, and the default of the primary debtor need not be proved as such; in the usual case, the 'guarantor' is obliged to pay a fixed amount of money upon the presentation by the creditor of a certificate that the primary debtor is in default, or merely upon demand. For this reason, such contracts have more in common with letters of credit than with true guarantees.[578] For example, as in letters of credit, the courts have applied the principle that the bank must pay when the requisite documents are presented unless it has knowledge of fraud; this reflects the parties' intention that the bank's liability is not accessory.[579] On the other hand, as between primary debtor and creditor, it is recognized that the contract is intended to provide a security function, and so it is likely to be construed such that after the creditor is paid under the guarantee, he may recover from the primary debtor any further loss he has suffered, but must also account for any surplus he gained.[580] Still another kind of transaction is a

---

[576] *Trafalgar House Construction (Regions) Ltd v General Security and Guarantee Co Ltd* [1996] AC 199, HL. In this case the guarantee, which may be called a 'performance bond', is usually issued by an insurance company. If the transaction is international, the parties may well incorporate the International Chamber of Commerce's *Uniform Rules for Contract Bonds* (1993).

[577] The terminology is somewhat unstable. The contract may also be called a 'demand' or 'on-demand' guarantee, or the adjectives 'demand', 'first demand' or 'on-demand' may be applied instead to the names 'performance bond' or 'performance guarantee'.

[578] As in letters of credit, there may be two banks and four parties: the primary debtor having secured a bank to issue the guarantee, commonly another bank in the jurisdiction of the creditor will agree with the first bank to make the same promise to the creditor with an arrangement for reimbursement. It may also be noted that if the obligation of the primary debtor is a monetary one, the document may well be styled a 'standby letter of credit', which emphasizes the functional affinity of the first demand guarantee with the letter of credit. The International Chamber of Commerce's *Uniform Customs and Practice for Documentary Credits* (1993) were extended in their most recent revision to cover standby letters of credit, and are often incorporated into such documents, although conceptually these would more suitably be governed by the ICC's *Uniform Rules for Demand Guarantees* (1992). The ICC has also promulgated a set of *Rules on International Standby Practices* (1998). The UK has not acceded to the 1995 UN Convention on Independent Guarantees and Standby Letters of Credit (New York, 11 December 1995).

[579] To maintain its reputation the bank will usually pay unless the primary debtor can obtain an injunction; such an injunction will be granted only if the court considers that the only realistic inference to draw is that of fraud: *Edward Owen Engineering Ltd v Barclays Bank International Ltd* [1978] QB 159, CA. But if a bank resists a claim on a 'demand guarantee' on the basis that the agreement itself is voidable for fraud, and the claimant seeks summary judgment, the test to be applied is whether the bank has shown 'a reasonable or real prospect' that the relevant bond was voidable: *Solo Industries UK Ltd v Canara Bank* [2001] EWCA Civ 1041; [2001] 1 WLR 1800.

[580] *Cargill International SA v Bangladesh Sugar and Food Industries Corp* [1998] 1 WLR 461, CA.

policy of indemnity insurance that a creditor may take out against the risk of a debtor's default.[581]

(2) Creation

5.164 A guarantee is a contract and its formation is governed by the normal rules.[582]

(a) Parties

5.165 The contract may be a tripartite one including the primary debtor, guarantor and creditor, but this is unusual. Most commonly, the parties to the contract are the guarantor and the creditor, although usually the primary debtor has requested the guarantor to enter the contract.[583] If two debtors contract as principal debtors with the creditor, then they may agree between themselves that one shall be primarily liable and the other shall be guarantor; in this case, there is a contract of guarantee only as between the debtors.[584] If, however, the creditor later becomes aware of the understanding between the debtors, then the liability of the guarantor will be subject to the principles governing guarantees; and this is so even if the debtors themselves only came to this understanding after the relevant contracts were formed.[585]

5.166 The parties to a contract of guarantee may change if the creditor or the primary debtor assign their rights to some other party. This has caused particular complications in guarantees of covenants contained in leases of land. If a guarantor guaranteed the obligations of a tenant, and the tenant assigned his leasehold interest to another, then the guarantor might well be liable for the defaults of the assignee. The law has been modified by statute.[586]

---

[581] *Arab Bank plc v John D Wood Commercial Ltd* [2000] 1 WLR 857, CA, noted D Friedmann (2000) 116 LQR 365.

[582] See for example *Capital Bank Cashflow Finance Ltd v Southall* [2004] EWCA Civ 817; [2004] 2 All ER (Comm) 675.

[583] If he has not, this can affect the guarantor's rights against the primary debtor: para 5.182.

[584] *Duncan, Fox & Co v North and South Wales Bank* (1880) 6 App Cas 1, 11–12, HL.

[585] *Rouse v Bradford Banking Co* [1894] AC 586, HL.

[586] Landlord and Tenant (Covenants) Act 1995. The Act also deals with the case in which the landlord assigns his interest, generally ensuring that the assignee will have the benefit of the obligations of the tenant and any guarantor. The most significant changes only apply to leases created after 1995; see C Harpum, *Megarry and Wade: The Law of Real Property* (6th edn, 2000) 975–94.

(b) Formation

(i) Consideration

The agreement is often in the form of a deed.[587] If it is not, then the guarantor's **5.167**
promise must be supported by consideration. As in any contract, this may either
be a promise, or some act or forbearance requested by the guarantor. In this context, there may be a promise to advance funds to the primary debtor, or there may
be the fact of an advance which was requested by the guarantor. If the guarantee is
for an existing debt, then there must either be a promise to forbear from suing on
the debt, or actual forbearance at the request of the guarantor.[588]

(ii) Offer and acceptance: continuing guarantees

It is possible to guarantee future liabilities of the debtor, whether on a particular **5.168**
account or arising generally. In this situation, the guarantor's liability fluctuates
with the balance owing to the creditor, although it may be subject to a limit in the
guarantee. Such contracts are usually understood as unilateral contracts, in which
the guarantor leaves open an offer to guarantee future advances, and the creditor
accepts each time an advance is made. On this analysis, the guarantor can always
terminate the guarantee as to future advances. Such guarantees often provide for
termination of the guarantee after a period of notice. In the absence of a deed, it is
not clear whether the guarantor is bound by the promise to give a period of notice;
if the guarantee is understood as a standing offer, then he is not, since an offer can
always be withdrawn unless it is itself supported by consideration.[589]

Even if the guarantor is bound to give notice, the effect of the notice may be a **5.169**
difficult issue. In *National Westminster Bank plc v Hardman*,[590] the defendant gave
a continuing guarantee to pay on demand, determinable on three months' notice.
The creditor did not make a demand on the guarantor during the three months
after the notice was given, and it was held that there was no liability. The events
were similar in *Bank of Credit and Commerce International SA v Simjee*,[591] but
based on different wording, it was held that the effect of the expiry of the notice
was only to fix the amount of the guarantor's liability. The creditor could still

---

[587] Usually the deed is executed by the guarantor and the creditor. If the parties so intend, even
a deed executed by the primary debtor and the guarantor may create a guarantee enforceable by the
creditor: *Moody v Condor Insurance Ltd* [2006] EWHC 100 (Ch); [2006] 1 WLR 1847.

[588] *Crears v Hunter* (1887) 19 QBD 341, CA.

[589] In some continuing guarantees the creditor will have entered into an irrevocable and indivisible transaction, such as appointing the primary debtor to an office *(Re Crace* [1902] 1 Ch 733); this
can amount to consideration, making enforceable a promise by the guarantor to give notice.

[590] [1988] FLR 302, CA.

[591] CA, 3 July 1996.

make a demand and so make the guarantor liable for the amount owing from the primary debtor at the time that the notice expired.

(iii) Vitiating factors

5.170 The guarantee may be vitiated by any of the factors which affect any contract, such as a fundamental mistake.[592] The guarantor may argue that he did not understand the nature of the transaction.[593] More commonly, the guarantor will argue that the transaction was induced by misrepresentation or undue influence,[594] or that it resulted from an unconscionable use of bargaining power.[595] Rarely, the problem is said to have originated with the creditor.[596] More often it originates from the primary debtor, who is often the spouse or cohabitant of the guarantor. Particularly protective principles have been developed which require the creditor to take steps to ensure that the guarantee will be valid in such a case.[597]

(iv) Duty of disclosure

5.171 In addition to the normal rules of misrepresentation, there is also a limited positive duty of disclosure on the creditor. If there are features of the transaction between the creditor and the primary debtor which make it materially different from what the guarantor would naturally expect, in a way which is potentially disadvantageous to him, then the creditor must disclose these arrangements. This does not extend to background facts about the primary debtor which might be relevant to the credit risk.[598] Breach of the duty permits rescission of the guarantee.

(v) Formalities

5.172 A guarantee is not enforceable unless the agreement, or some memorandum or note thereof, is in writing and signed by the guarantor or his agent.[599] This provision

---

[592] *Associated Japanese Bank (International) Ltd v Crédit du Nord SA* [1989] 1 WLR 255.

[593] In *Lloyds Bank plc v Waterhouse* [1993] 2 FLR 97, CA, one judge (Purchas LJ) would have excused the guarantor on this basis. See para 8.149 (*non est factum*).

[594] For the general law of misrepresentation and undue influence, see paras 8.157–8.206.

[595] *Alec Lobb (Garages) Ltd v Total Oil GB Ltd* [1983] 1 WLR 87, 94–95; *Crédit Lyonnais Bank Nederland NV v Burch* [1997] 1 All ER 144, 151, 152–3, CA. For discussion of the general law of unconscionable transactions, see paras 8.207, 18.78–18.83.

[596] *Lloyds Bank Ltd v Bundy* [1975] QB 326, CA; *Lloyds Bank plc v Waterhouse* [1993] 2 FLR 97, CA; *Barton v County Natwest Ltd* [1999] Lloyd's Rep Bank 408, CA.

[597] See paras 8.206 and 8.209.

[598] *Levett v Barclays Bank plc* [1995] 1 WLR 1260, followed in *Crédit Lyonnais Bank Nederland v Export Credit Guarantee Department* [1996] 1 Lloyd's Rep 200, affd on other grounds [1998] 1 Lloyd's Rep 19, CA, and [1999] 2 WLR 540, HL.

[599] Statute of Frauds 1677, s 4. In *J Pereira Fernandes SA v Mehta* [2006] EWHC 813 (Ch); [2006] 2 All ER 891, it was held that while an email could be sufficient writing, the mere inclusion of the sender's return email address in the header did not constitute a 'signature' within

does not apply to indemnities, and indeed this is the origin of the need to make the distinction between the two transactions. The note or memorandum can be created after the formation of an oral guarantee.[600] All the material terms must be stated, including the identity of the primary debtor and the limit, if any, of the guarantor's liability;[601] but the consideration for which the guarantee was given need not be stated.[602] Failure to comply with this requirement makes the guarantee unenforceable, but not void.[603] If the required writing exists, then extrinsic evidence may be admissible in the interpretation of the contract, according to the normal rules.[604]

Any credit agreement involving an individual debtor may be subject to regulation **5.173** under the CCA 1974.[605] This Act can govern the required form for guarantees and indemnities relating to regulated agreements.[606] It also requires certain information to be made available to guarantors and primary debtors.[607] A guarantee given by an individual may also be subject to the Unfair Terms in Consumer Contracts Regulations 1999.[608]

---

the Statute; a signature must be inserted in a way that shows that it 'governs' the whole document. In *Actionstrength Ltd v International Glass Engineering IN.GL.EN SpA* [2003] UKHL 17, [2003] 2 AC 541 it was held that an argument based on estoppel (on which see paras 8.53–8.57) could not be used to circumvent the requirement of writing.

[600] *Elpis Maritime Co Ltd v Marti Chartering Co Inc (The Maria D)* [1992] 1 AC 21, HL.

[601] *State Bank of India v Kaur* [1996] 5 Banking LR 158, CA.

[602] Mercantile Law Amendment Act 1856, s 3.

[603] *Maddison v Alderson* (1883) 8 App Cas 467, HL; for the significance of this distinction, see para 5.182 and paras 8.72–8.78.

[604] *Perrylease Ltd v Imecar AG* [1988] 1 WLR 463.

[605] On the scope of the CCA 1974, see para 5.31. The Act has provisions that allow the court to reopen credit agreements that are substantively unfair even if they are not otherwise regulated: see para 5.33.

[606] CCA 1974, s 105 and the Consumer Credit (Guarantees and Indemnities) Regulations 1983, SI 1983/1556 thereunder; failure to comply makes the agreement void (s 106). Other violations of the Act may also avoid a guarantee or indemnity (s 113(3)).

[607] ibid ss 107–111.

[608] SI 1999/2083, pursuant to the European Communities Act 1972, s 2(2). On the scope of these regulations, see para 5.35. The regulations apply to a contract between a supplier and a consumer (reg 4(1)); and a supplier is defined to be one acting in the course of his business (reg 3(1)). If the service provided is the guarantee, then it is arguable that the regulations would only apply where the consumer is the creditor and the supplier is giving a guarantee in the course of its business. For discussion, see H Beale (gen ed), *Chitty on Contracts* (29th edn, 2004), para 44–133. The Unfair Contract Terms Act 1977 is wider than the regulations as regards the contracts to which it applies, but it is concerned with exemption clauses and therefore is unlikely to have an impact on guarantees. For discussion of this Act, see paras 8.110–8.118.

(3) Scope of Liability

(a) Co-extensiveness

5.174   The co-extensiveness principle is that the guarantor's obligation is to see to it that the primary debtor performs his own obligation.[609] This means that the guarantor is liable not only for the obligation guaranteed, but also for damages arising from the primary debtor's breach of that obligation.[610] Conversely, it generally means that the guarantor cannot be liable except to the extent that the primary debtor is liable.[611] At common law, if the contract with the primary debtor was void or unenforceable due to the primary debtor's infancy, then so too was the guarantee;[612] this rule has now been changed by statute.[613] The common law principle implies that the same result would follow where the primary debtor is a company, whose contract is void for lack of capacity; but the cases suggest that this may not be so, at least in the case of a guarantor who is a director of that company.[614]

(b) Discharge

5.175   The guarantor's obligations can be discharged in a number of ways. Most obviously, he may pay the creditor what is owed under the guarantee and so be discharged by performance. Other possibilities follow from the normal rules of contract. If the guarantee is limited in time, or can be terminated on notice, then of course the guarantor can be discharged in these ways.[615] If the creditor owes obligations to the guarantor under the contract of guarantee, then the creditor may commit a breach which permits the guarantor to terminate the guarantee.[616]

---

[609]   The obligation of one who gives an indemnity (para 5.161) is not subject to this principle.

[610]   *Moschi v Lep Air Services Ltd* [1973] AC 331, HL.

[611]   In *Hyundai Heavy Industries Co Ltd v Papadopoulos* [1980] 1 WLR 1129, 1137, HL, Viscount Dilhorne suggested that in some cases a guarantor would be liable to pay an instalment even though the primary debtor was not; this is strongly doubted by commentators (see eg G Andrews and R Millett, *Law of Guarantees* (4th edn, 2005) 244).

[612]   *Coutts & Co v Browne-Lecky* [1947] KB 104; but not an indemnity: *Yeoman Credit Ltd v Latter* [1961] 1 WLR 828, CA.

[613]   Minors' Contracts Act 1987, s 2.

[614]   J Steyn, 'Guarantees: The Co-Extensiveness Principle' (1974) 90 LQR 246, 248–51, explaining *Gerrard v James* [1925] 1 Ch 616 and other cases, but noting that if the result follows because the 'guarantor' agreed to be liable regardless of the company's capacity, then the contract is probably better understood as an indemnity. In *Communities Economic Development Fund v Canadian Pickles Corp* [1991] 3 SCR 388, 85 DLR (4th) 88, the incapacity was on the part of the creditor, which lent money to the primary debtor. Although the primary debtor would have been liable in unjust enrichment, it was held that the guarantor was not liable.

[615]   As to the effect of a provision permitting termination of a continuing guarantee by notice, see para 5.169.

[616]   Under normal principles, however, a less serious breach may only give the guarantor a claim in damages for loss suffered: *Bowmaker (Commercial) Ltd v Smith* [1965] 1 WLR 855, CA.

(i) Discharge of primary debtor

It follows from the co-extensiveness principle that the guarantor can be discharged **5.176** through the discharge of the primary debtor's obligation, whether by the primary debtor's performance,[617] or by the lawful termination of the obligations owed by the primary debtor to the creditor,[618] or by frustration of the contract between primary debtor and contractor.[619] If, however, the obligation of the primary debtor is terminated in a situation which generates a secondary obligation to pay damages, then the guarantor is liable for such damages.[620]

If the primary debtor is discharged through a binding agreement with the **5.177** creditor, then the guarantor is also discharged,[621] unless the creditor reserved his rights against the guarantor.[622] Discharge of the primary debtor by bankruptcy does not, however, discharge the guarantor.[623] Similarly, if a debtor company is wound up and ceases to exist, a guarantor of its debts remains liable.[624]

(ii) Discharge by creditor's conduct

Variation of contract between creditor and primary debtor.   There is a strict **5.178** principle that any variation of the contract between the creditor and the primary debtor, which could have the effect of increasing the risk that the guarantor bears, will discharge the guarantor completely. This is so even if later events show that the guarantor was not in fact harmed by the variation.[625] A binding agreement to give the primary debtor further time to pay is a variation which will discharge the guarantor.[626] The same principle will apply to the release by the creditor

---

[617] If there are multiple obligations between the creditor and the primary debtor, the normal rules of appropriation of payments apply to determine whether the primary debtor has paid the guaranteed debt.

[618] *Western Credit Ltd v Alberry* [1964] 1 WLR 945, CA.

[619] Because this is a consequence of the principle of co-extensiveness, the results could be different under an indemnity.

[620] *Moschi v Lep Air Services Ltd* [1973] AC 331, HL. In the English tradition of freedom of contract, Lord Reid left open the possibility of a guarantee which extended to primary obligations only.

[621] *Commercial Bank of Tasmania v Jones* [1893] AC 313, PC.

[622] *Cole v Lynn* [1942] 1 KB 142, CA. The guarantor is also not discharged if the terms of the guarantee preserve his liability in such a case, or if he so agreed at the time the primary debtor was discharged. Like in the situation where a creditor has multiple co-debtors, the guarantor's liability may be preserved where the creditor does not release the primary debtor but merely agrees not to sue him; however, the distinction between a release and an agreement not to sue has recently been questioned in the context of multiple co-debtors: *Johnson v Davies* [1999] Ch 117, CA. If this distinction were abandoned in the context of guarantees, the only question would be whether the creditor had reserved his rights against the guarantor.

[623] Insolvency Act 1986, s 281(7).

[624] *Re Fitzgeorge* [1905] 1 KB 462; *Ali Shipping Corp v Jugobanka DD Beograd* [1997] EWCA Civ 2705.

[625] *Holme v Brunskill* (1878) 3 QBD 495, CA.

[626] *Polak v Everett* (1876) 1 QBD 669, CA.

of a co-guarantor,[627] or the release of real security given by a co-guarantor[628] or by the primary debtor.[629] Upon discharge the guarantor is entitled to recover any real security he provided.[630]

5.179 The principle which discharges the guarantor will not apply if the guarantee excludes it, and commercial guarantees commonly do so.[631] It is also excluded if the guarantor consents to the variation at the time it is made. At least in the case where the variation is an extension of time, it is excluded if, at the time the variation is made, the creditor notifies the primary debtor that he reserves his rights against the guarantor.[632]

5.180 The principle does not rise to the level of a general duty of care owed by the creditor to the guarantor, although particular duties have been recognized.[633] The creditor owes a duty to the guarantor to act reasonably in selling a real security held for the debt, whether it belongs beneficially to the guarantor or to the primary debtor.[634] But a breach of this duty does not discharge the guarantor; it only reduces his liability by the difference between the price actually obtained by the creditor, and the price it would have obtained had it acted reasonably.[635] Also, if the creditor causes loss to the guarantor by carelessly failing to perfect a real security, the guarantor will be discharged to the extent of the resultant loss.[636]

5.181 **Material alteration to the guarantee.** In line with general principles of contract law, a guarantee may be avoided by alteration. If, after the guarantee has been created, the creditor makes a material alteration to the written document in which it is embodied, the guarantor is discharged. An alteration is material if it affects

---

[627] *Mercantile Bank of Sydney v Taylor* [1893] AC 317, PC. This increases the guarantor's risk because there is a right of contribution among co-guarantors: para 5.185. If the co-guarantors are only severally and not jointly liable, it has been held that release of one does not discharge the others fully, but only to the extent that they are harmed by it: *Ward v National Bank of New Zealand Ltd* (1883) 8 App Cas 755, PC.

[628] *Smith v Wood* [1929] 1 Ch 14, CA.

[629] *Re Darwen & Pearce* [1927] 1 Ch 176. It has been suggested the guarantor will not be discharged fully (but only *pro tanto*) by the creditor's releasing securities acquired by the creditor only after the guarantee was given: *Polak v Everett* (1876) 1 QBD 669, 676, CA.

[630] *Bolton v Salomon* [1891] 2 Ch 48; *Smith v Wood* [1929] 1 Ch 14, CA.

[631] A guarantee given by an individual which contained such a term might be subject to review under the Unfair Terms in Consumer Contracts Regulations 1999, SI 1999/2083, pursuant to the European Communities Act 1972, s 2(2); but see n 608 above.

[632] J O'Donovan and J Phillips, *The Modern Contract of Guarantee* (English edn, 2003) 410, suggesting that the primary debtor must agree to the preservation of the guarantor's liability; and that in such a case, the guarantor will not be bound by the extension of time when exercising his rights against the primary debtor.

[633] *China and South Sea Bank Ltd v Tan Soon Gin* [1990] 1 AC 536, PC.

[634] See para 5.49.

[635] *Skipton Building Society v Stott* [2001] QB 261, CA.

[636] *Wulff v Jay* (1872) LR 7 QB 756.

the whole character of the document, but also if it is potentially prejudicial to the guarantor's legal position; actual prejudice need not be shown.[637]

(4) Guarantor's Rights Against Primary Debtor

(a) Indemnity

Upon payment to the creditor, the guarantor has a right of indemnity against the primary debtor.[638] If the guarantor has become liable, but has not yet paid, he may secure a declaration of his right of indemnity, and an order that the primary debtor pay the creditor.[639] The right to indemnity arises even if the guarantee was unenforceable for lack of evidence in writing.[640] There is authority that if the guarantee was not given at the request of the primary debtor, then no right of indemnity arises.[641]   **5.182**

(b) Subrogation

A guarantor who has paid the guaranteed debt is entitled to be subrogated to the rights formerly held by the creditor, irrespective of whether or not the guarantor was aware of them and of whether they were acquired before or after the guarantee was given.[642] This includes not only rights of real security, but also personal rights which the creditor held, which may carry a preferential status.[643] Subrogation operates even in respect of rights which would otherwise have been extinguished when the creditor was paid. To the extent that any right held by the creditor cannot be assigned by operation of law, the guarantor is entitled to demand an express assignment of it;[644] and even if such an assignment has not been taken, he can use the name of the creditor to enforce it for his own benefit.[645]   **5.183**

---

[637] *Raiffeisen Zentralbank Osterreich AG v Crosseas Shipping Ltd* [2000] 1 WLR 1135, CA. Hence if the alteration is beneficial to the guarantor, this doctrine cannot be invoked: *Bank of Scotland v Henry Butcher & Co* [2003] EWCA Civ 67; [2003] 1 BCLC 575 at [72]–[74].

[638] *Re A Debtor (No 627 of 1936)* [1937] Ch 156, CA.

[639] *Ascherson v Tredegar Dry Dock and Wharf Co Ltd* [1909] 2 Ch 401. In *Thomas v Nottingham Incorporated Football Club Ltd* [1972] Ch 596, it was held that the guarantor may obtain this order even though no demand has yet been made upon him as required by the terms of the guarantee. The requirement of the demand is for the benefit of the guarantor and may be waived by him.

[640] *Alexander v Vane* (1836) 1 M & W 511, 150 ER 537; or even if both the guarantee and the primary debtor's obligations were unenforceable: *Re Chetwynd's Estate* [1938] Ch 13, CA, applied in *Argo Caribbean Group Ltd v Lewis* [1976] 2 Lloyd's Rep 289, CA.

[641] *Owen v Tate* [1976] 2 QB 402, CA. The case has been criticized: see para 18.144.

[642] *Forbes v Jackson* (1882) 19 Ch D 615.

[643] *Re Lord Churchill* (1888) 39 Ch D 174; *Re Lamplugh Iron Ore Co Ltd* [1927] 1 Ch 308.

[644] Mercantile Law Amendment Act 1856, s 5.

[645] ibid; *Re M'Myn* (1886) 33 Ch D 575; *Re Lamplugh Iron Ore Co Ltd* [1927] 1 Ch 308.

5.184 Unlike the right of indemnity discussed above, the right of subrogation does not arise until the guarantor pays the full amount of the indebtedness to which his guarantee relates. This raises a point of construction when a guarantee is limited in amount, as is usually the case. If it is a guarantee of the whole debt, but subject to a limit as to the guarantor's liability, then there can be no subrogation until the whole debt is paid, even if it exceeds the guarantor's liability.[646] If, on the other hand, the effect of the limit is to create a guarantee as to only a proportion of the debt, then when the guarantor has paid that proportion, he is entitled to subrogation as to the relevant proportion of any securities.[647]

(5) Guarantor's Rights Against Co-Guarantors

5.185 Subject to a contrary agreement among them, co-guarantors of the same debt bear the burden of their obligations equally. This means that they have rights of contribution against one another.[648] They also have rights of subrogation, if the creditor held real security to secure the obligations of co-guarantors.[649] These rights arise even if a co-guarantor was not aware, at the time he gave his guarantee, of the other co-guarantors. Where the guarantees were of the same debt but had different limits, the guarantors will share the burden in proportion to the limits.[650]

---

[646] This is the normal form for a limited guarantee.

[647] *Re Butler's Wharf Ltd* [1995] 2 BCLC 43, [1995] BCC 717.

[648] Whether they are jointly, severally, or jointly and severally liable, and whether on the same or more than one document, without the need for any agreement: *Dering v Earl of Winchelsea* (1787) 2 B & P 270, 126 ER 1276, 1 Cox Eq 319, 29 ER 1184; *Caledonia North Sea Limited v British Telecommunications Plc (Scotland)* [2002] UKHL 4, [2002] 1 Lloyd's Rep 553 at [12]. If the liability of the claimant co-guarantor arises out of 'damage suffered' by him in paying the creditor, then his claim for contribution must be founded on the Civil Liability (Contribution) Act 1978, s 1. This will be the ordinary construction of most guarantees (see para 5.174), but it leads to a two-year limitation period for the contribution claim (Limitation Act 1980, s 10): *Hampton v Minns* [2002] 1 WLR 1. In that case, however, it was held that the correct construction of some guarantees is that the claimant co-guarantor is liable for a debt, not 'damage'; in that case, the limitation on the contribution claim is six years (Limitation Act 1980, s 5). The distinction is difficult to support.

[649] *Smith v Wood* [1929] 1 Ch 14, 21–2, CA. If the creditor held real security from the primary debtor, and a co-guarantor has acquired it, he must share the benefit in order to claim contribution: *Steel v Dixon* (1881) 17 Ch D 825; *Berridge v Berridge* (1890) 44 Ch D 168.

[650] *Ellesmere Brewery Co v Cooper* [1896] 1 QB 75, DC. In *Hampton v Minns* [2002] 1 WLR 1 the claimant and the defendant were co-guarantors of the debts of a company. The claimant discharged the debt and sought contribution. The defendant argued that he should be liable only as to 20%, since he held 20% of the shares of the debtor company, while the claimant held 80%. The court held that the normal rule of equal contribution applied.

As with indemnity against the primary debtor, a co-guarantor may obtain a **5.186** declaration of another co-guarantor's liability to contribute even before he has paid, so long as he has become liable.[651] A co-guarantor can also be liable to contribute even if his co-guarantor paid the creditor in the absence of a demand which was required to generate liability under the guarantee. Such a requirement being for the guarantor's benefit, it may be waived by him; and contribution will be ordered so long as the payment to the creditor was not officious.[652]

---

[651] *Wolmershausen v Gullick* [1893] 2 Ch 514.
[652] *Stimpson v Smith* [1999] Ch 340, CA.

6

INTELLECTUAL PROPERTY

A. General

(1) Range of the Subject

(a) The generic term

6.01 'Intellectual property' is today used as a broad term, grouping together two distinct types of right. The first type involves forms of legal protection over certain ideas or their expression—patents for inventions, industrial design rights, copyright, database rights, plant variety rights and breach of confidence. The second group is concerned with the protection of distinguishing signs used in marketing and distribution—trade marks, trade names, get-up and the like. This usage of the term has followed from its international adoption (the United Nations organ in the field is the World Intellectual Property Organization (WIPO)) and it now has a place in our statute law.[1]

(b) Intangible property

6.02 The subject matter of intellectual property rights (IPRs) is non-tangible and could be exploited by as many competitors as wish, but for the intervention of the law. The characteristic which brings these rights together is that the rightholder can prevent any other unauthorized person from using the protected subject matter. IPRs are essentially negative in character—no one needs a patent to exploit his own invention or a copyright to publish his own book. They are enforced primarily by civil action for an injunction and damages brought by the rightholder; hence their place in this volume.[2] In large measure they share a territorial character: thus a British patent controls the activities of other users of the invention in the United Kingdom and its adjuncts (oil rigs, ships, aircraft, etc); it is the French patent which has the equivalent effect in France. Where rights require to be granted by an organ of the state, application must be made in or for each country where protection is sought.

(c) Forms distinguished

6.03 Beyond these common foundations, however, each of the schemes of protection has developed its own concepts in order to fit the particular subject matter. That is why each right calls for separate description. As we shall see, some IPRs are

---

[1] See n 18 below. Previously the term signified the protection given to literary and artistic works—a more limited and coherent usage, to be distinguished from 'industrial property'–patents, trade marks, registered designs, etc. For a critical review of the objects and achievements of IP law, see WR Cornish, *Intellectual Property—Omnipresent, Distracting, Irrelevant?* (2004) (Clarendon Lectures, Oxford University, 2002).

[2] Copyright and trade mark infringement also constitutes a nominate crime in many instances. It is therefore possible to call upon the police and also upon administrative agencies, such as trading standards authorities and the customs service, in the battle against piracy and counterfeiting.

effective against those who reach the same conception independently, where others depend upon proof of copying. Some come into existence only upon official grant, while others are informal in nature. Some endure for specified periods, others are in essence indeterminate.

In a commercial situation, more than one form of intellectual property may have **6.04** a bearing. In practice, therefore, specialists have to be conversant with the whole field. The germ for a new product may begin with a technical concept—say, a new heating system for an electric kettle. It may be so novel as to rank as inventive and therefore to lead to a *patent*. As well as this, its effectiveness may depend upon certain ingenuities in the process of production, which can be protected because the know-how has been kept as *confidential information*; this entitlement will, however, only be of value if the ideas cannot be discovered from the marketed product by reverse engineering. Housing the new system may require a special design for the shape of the kettle and other design features may be added which make it appeal to consumers for its appearance. These may qualify for protection by way of *registered design, unregistered design right* and possibly even by *copyright*. Certainly the design plans will bear a *copyright* which will stop them being copied as plans. When it comes to marketing, the choice of *trade marks* and packaging may be more important than any aspect of the product itself. If the product proves a long-lasting success, this last form of right could continue after the time limits on any other form have expired.

(2) Intellectual Property and Monopoly

(a) Market power

Almost all intellectual property confers an exclusive right to stop others behaving **6.05** in specified ways and in that limited sense it confers a legal monopoly. But it does not thereby create a monopoly in the economic sense that the owner will have the power to restrict supply and raise prices to the most profitable level. In the great bulk of cases, the market will contain sufficiently close substitutes outside the range of the right for the rightowner to continue to face the effects of competition. It is only in exceptionally lucky cases (pathbreaking inventions, 'must-have' copyright works), that competition will be displaced. For the most part, other factors need also to be present before such market power can be exerted. This can occur where all the relevant intellectual property is drawn together—as in a pool of patents for a given technology or a copyright collecting society.[3] With these, competition law authorities are necessarily watchful.

---

[3] EC and UK competition laws retain an ultimate power to intervene to prevent an abuse of dominant position: *Radio Telefis Eirann v EC Commission* [1995] ECR I-743 (Cases 241 and 242/91P) (the *Magill* case—copyright in programme listings for TV channels).

(b) Unfair competition

6.06   The various forms of intellectual property give protection against particular types of business competition which are in some sense unfair. Beyond their range, imitation of ideas, information and marketing devices is permitted as a necessary element in the make-up of a liberal economy. Moreover, in contrast with the position in many other countries, no general tort of unfair competition, or unlawful trading has developed in supplementation of the specific forms of intellectual property right, either through case law or statute. Both passing off and breach of confidence can be viewed as examples of unfair competition, but the British choose to treat them as discrete wrongs, thereby keeping competition more open.

(3) Legal Sources

6.07   Not all forms of intellectual property are governed by statute. The basic law of patents, registered and unregistered designs and copyright are all entirely statutory. On the other hand the law of confidential information is judge-made. The law of trade marks and names is a hybrid: in part the protection is a matter of common law, since the torts of passing off and injurious falsehood shield commercial reputation which has been built up by actual trade. But equally trade marks for both goods and services may be protected through registration under the Trade Marks Act 1994. Where a statute governs, it will be applicable to the whole United Kingdom.[4] In theory, case law gains its authority within the particular judicial system where it arises. In practice, there is a strong tendency to consider all judicial precedents in this subject to be applicable throughout the country.

(4) European Union Policies

6.08   Because of the relationship between intellectual property and markets it is appropriate to unify the rights within a political federation, and equally within a unified economic organization such as the European Union. Intellectual property then exists to the same extent across the territory, and can be enforced for the whole area by a single process. In consequence, intellectual property is the field of private law which has moved most rapidly towards 'Europeanization'.

6.09   That movement is nonetheless an extremely complex and cautious one, which has only recently made true progress. For those IPRs which turn upon official grant, the initial plan has in each case been to create a unified Community right as an

---

[4] Ancillary aspects, such as proprietary rights and remedies, vary somewhat, particularly in Scotland.

alternative to the rights available independently in each member state. At the same time, it is necessary to harmonize the national laws at most points, in order to ensure that the alternatives operate to the same extent and in broadly the same way. So far this has been achieved for registered trade marks[5] registered designs[6] and plant variety rights. The plan for the Community patent has long been ready, but remains arrested in waiting.[7] Copyright, as a right which arises informally, is being drawn together at the national level by harmonization directives addressing particular aspects of the right, one by one.[8]

(5) *International Oversight*

While the real basis of IPRs remains within the national, or occasionally the regional, fold, international linkages are becoming more and more important. Since 1883, the Paris Convention on Industrial Property (covering patents, designs, trade marks, and unfair competition) has provided certain mutual bonds between countries around the world.[9] Other important aspects of international collaboration have been worked out in further conventions, such as the Patent Co-operation Treaty of 1970.[10] Since 1886, the Berne Convention on Literary and Artistic Works has provided equivalent protection for the rights of authors, and latterly other conventions have supplemented this—in respect of the rights of performers, sound recording producers and broadcasters.[11] Built upon the principle of national treatment, these conventions secure, first and foremost, that intellectual property rights in one country are not restricted to persons or acts connected with that country alone but are equally applicable when the connection is to another contracting state.

6.10

These earlier international arrangements also moved in varying degrees towards specifying the substantive and procedural content of national laws. The process has been carried much further in the TRIPs Agreement,[12] which forms part of the conspectus of the World Trade Organization established in 1994. The detailed requirements of the TRIPs reflect the standards already observed in a long-established industrial country such as the United Kingdom, but for many developing countries, they are a considerable (and overbearing) novelty. For the least

6.11

---

5 See para 6.107.
6 See para 6.86.
7 See para 6.20, n 22.
8 See para 6.52.
9 See para 6.21.
10 See para 6.20.
11 See para 6.58.
12 Agreement on Trade-Related Aspects of Intellectual Property Rights, including Trade in Counterfeit Goods.

developed the changes represent such a major shift that time for compliance has been allowed for them to introduce new legislation and administrations.[13]

(6) Actions Against Unconnected Infringers

6.12 The prime motivation in giving intellectual property protection is to exclude competition from unconnected third parties—whether they are pirates and counterfeiters who deliberately knock off imitations, or are more respectable traders who claim that their products are different and fall outside the right, or consider that they have an entitlement or licence to do as they wish. If the rights are to be of practical value against the general run of pirates, the law has to provide efficient remedies. Since it is largely left to rightowners to secure their own entitlements by civil action, the courts in England have done a good deal to increase the strength of their armoury, particularly in pre-trial process.

6.13 Interim injunctions have long been the most frequent resort of rightowners, comparatively few cases being fought to an actual trial for final injunction, damages, account of profits or delivery up of infringing articles. Interim injunctions are available, provided that there is a serious case to be tried, largely upon a balance of convenience, taking account of the effect of granting the injunction upon the defendant and, on the other hand, of failure to grant upon the claimant.[14] However, in varying degrees related to the complexity of the issues, courts do also bring into account their first assessment of the actual cause.[15]

6.14 In addition, where it is difficult to find the real source of piracy, an order may be obtained even against an innocent party in the distribution chain requiring revelation of a transshipper's name.[16] Where there is a strong likelihood that evidence of infringement will be destroyed or hidden, the courts allow the surprise tactic of a search order for inspection (*Anton Piller* order).[17] This is granted in a closed hearing sought by the claimant alone and is executed by his solicitor, with supervision by another solicitor to prevent oppressive conduct. The order is likely to contain an interim injunction and also to order revelation of sources and intended recipients.[18] It may well require a freezing injunction

---

[13] Five years for developing countries, ten for the least developed.

[14] *American Cyanamid v Ethicon* [1975] AC 396, HL (an elaborate patent action). See generally paras 22.35–22.37.

[15] *Series 5 Software v Clarke* [1996] 1 All ER 853.

[16] *Norwich Pharmacal v Commissioners of Customs and Excise* [1974] AC 133, HL.

[17] Now governed by the Civil Procedure Rules 1998, Part 25. See generally paras 22.28–22.29.

[18] For the conditional removal of the privilege against incrimination in relation to these demands: Supreme Court Act 1981, s 72 (the first statute to refer to 'intellectual property').

affecting the defendant's assets (*Mareva* injunction) in order to satisfy orders in the cause.[19]

(7) Parallel Importation of Connected Goods

(a) The practice

A second motivation for granting intellectual property may be to allow the right-owner to control its own products, or those of its licensees, after they have been released on the market. Where the right has this added character, it can be used in particular to prevent the activities of the parallel importer. If, as may happen for various reasons, the price of the same products varies between countries, a parallel importer will purchase them in the cheap country and transport them to the expensive country, for competitive sale which will prejudice the rightowner's market position there. Can the rightowner use his intellectual property in that second market to prevent the importation of goods which came from his 'stable' but are no longer connected with him? The matter is at present highly controversial. The case for adding such a power to the right is stronger where the right exists to promote creation and invention (copyright and patents) than where it merely supports an indication of origin (trade marks). **6.15**

(b) EU policies

Within the EU, the basic policy of free movement of goods dictates that intellectual property may not be used in this way to prevent a parallel importer from moving 'legitimate' goods between one member state and another.[20] From outside the European Economic Area (EEA), a 'Fortress Europe' has, for the moment, been sealed off in part by giving intellectual property the opposite effect.[21] **6.16**

---

[19] Civil Procedure Rules 1998, Part 25. See paras 22.20–22.27. For discussion of remedies, see Chapter 21, esp paras 21.72ff (compensation), paras 21.20–21.27 (delivery up), and paras 21.143ff (profits).

[20] EC Treaty (Treaty of Rome, as amended), Arts 28–30, which also affects the rules of competition, Arts 81, 82. The test of what is a parallel import in this context is, have the goods been placed on one member state market by or with the consent of the rightowner in the country of import? See *Centrafarm v Sterling Drug* and *Centrafarm v Winthrop* [1974] ECR 1147, 1183, and the ensuing case law. The rule applies only to the particular goods, not to all goods of the same type: *Sebago v GB-Unic* [1999] European Trade Mark Reports 681.

[21] See para 6.125.

B. Patents for Inventions

(1) Basis of the Law

(a) Nature and objectives

6.17 The patent system offers an incentive to conduct research and investigations which will first of all produce breakthroughs in technical understanding and will then sustain the process of development needed to convert ideas into marketable products or processes. The rightness of rewarding the individual for his inventiveness is one motivating factor, but notions of economic advantage are more important. Patents are not given to all who invent against those who copy from them. They are given to the first to seek protection and they are good even against those who independently discover the same idea. This occurs regularly, since new techniques are there to be worked out by whoever is clever or determined enough to do so. As a corollary of this preference for the first to act, the patentee is required to disclose his invention in his patent specification sufficiently clearly that others can apply it. Thus the whole industry is saved from re-inventing, competitors are put further down the road towards their own improvements, and they are able, once the patent expires, to adopt the invention itself, should it still be in use. Patents therefore go to core features of most production industries and in a few exceptional instances they confer monopoly privileges of immense value.

(b) Development

6.18 The foundations of British patent law stretch back at least to the Statute of Monopolies of 1624. The rights have always turned upon a grant of privilege by the Crown or latterly the state. The governing statute is now the Patents Act 1977 (PA 1977), which is designed to give effect to the European Patent Convention 1973 (EPC), the Patents Co-operation Treaty of 1970 (PCT) and (provisionally) the Community Patent Convention (1975–89) (CPC) or an EU Regulation to replace it. The Patents Act 1977 took effect on 1 June 1978, the date on which the EPC and PCT also came into operation.

(2) The Granting of Patents

(a) British and European granting systems

6.19 Since the beginning of the twentieth century, the United Kingdom has had a system of examining applications for patents before they are granted. Under the modern approach in Europe, that form of control has been considerably strengthened. The process for applying for a patent is accordingly a sophisticated one and most applicants employ a patent agent to draft their patent specification and to negotiate with the relevant patent office or offices. From the outset it will be necessary to consider in which countries around the world it is desirable to achieve patent protection for an invention. Important new technologies are likely to need protection in both developed and developing economies.

So far as the granting process is concerned, British and European alternatives **6.20** exist. As has long been the case, an application may be made to the British Patent Office. But instead, the applicant may now use the European Patent Office (EPO; headquarters in Munich), which offers the opportunity to proceed by a single application all the way to the grant of patents across Europe. If the application is successful, the applicant receives a bundle of national patents for each of those participating countries which he has designated.[22] Almost always the patents will be in common form. Although accused of being cumbersome and slow, the EPO answers international industry's needs and is becoming increasingly popular. Entry into either the EPO or the national route to patents in Europe is assisted by the PCT—a truly international linkage. The PCT permits the initial stages—filing, search and for some countries, preliminary examination—to be undertaken by a single procedure, before files are passed on to local patent offices for completion and grant.[23]

(b) From application to grant

(i) First to file

By and large the procedures of the European and British offices are similar.[24] **6.21** Both are 'first to file' systems, giving the prior right between rival inventors to the first to make an application, not the first to invent.[25] Much therefore turns on the priority date attached to the application, which will be that on which the application is made unless the applicant can take advantage of an earlier application (within the preceding twelve months) which was made in another country belonging to the Paris Industrial Property Convention 1883–1979.[26]

---

[22] He cannot yet opt for a unitary Community patent because the CPC, which would provide for this, remains inoperative. Many member states demand that the Community patent specification be translated into all official languages of the EU; industry resists the exorbitant cost of doing so.

[23] Organized by WIPO, the PCT makes use of a few leading patent offices as International Search Authorities and International Examining Authorities.

[24] For details, see the EPC, Parts III–VII and implementing regulations; PA 1977, ss 7–29 and corresponding rules.

[25] Only the United States retains the luxury of a 'first-to-invent' system—expensive because of the difficulties of resolving the issue.

[26] See the Convention, Art 4, EPC, Arts 87–89, PA 1977, s 5.

(ii) Search

6.22 The first main step in the application procedure is the search for relevant 'prior art'. This is conducted by or on behalf of the patent office concerned and involves a survey of earlier patent specifications and technical literature in order to see if it contains a description of the same invention or one that is very similar. Normal practice is then to publish the patent application—in particular the proposed specification which describes the invention and defines the scope of protection together with the research report eighteen months after the priority date. The applicant then has six months in which to request an examination by the office in the light of the research report.

(iii) Examination

6.23 The examination relates to all the requirements for the validity of a patent and to certain additional matters (concerning in particular the name of the inventor, unity of the invention and the formulation of the claims). During the examination, it is possible to modify the proposed specification in light of the objections or for other reasons, subject to the condition that the original disclosure of the invention is not thereby being added to in any essential feature. A major object of the examination is to guarantee that the invention is sufficiently disclosed by its description in the specification of the patent and that the claims, which define the scope of the monopoly, are justified by that disclosure.

(iv) Grant

6.24 Once the examination is successfully completed, the patent will be granted. Its duration (subject to the payment of progressive renewal fees) will be for a maximum of twenty years, measured from the date of application and not from that of the grant. No action for infringement can be instituted before the patent is granted. However, under certain conditions, damages can be awarded for the period starting at the publication of the application.

(v) Opposition and invalidity proceedings

6.25 Even though an industry will know in detail the content of an application from the time of its early publication, a third party cannot formally intervene (with the right of audience) to object to the application. At most a competitor may draw the attention of the patent office to a publication or other evidence of prior publication or use of the invention or one very similar. After grant, third parties may attack the validity of the patent in a formal opposition procedure.

6.26 Where the European route has been followed, an opposition after grant can be launched within nine months. It may attack the patentability of the invention, the sufficiency of the disclosure in the specification or the permissibility of an amendment to it. Throughout its life the validity of a British patent, whether granted by the EPO or the British office, can be attacked either in the British Patent Office, using a largely written procedure, or more elaborately before a patents court. In England this is the Patents Court of the Chancery Division in the High Court or else the Patents County Court. The question of validity may be raised upon a separate claim or else by way of counterclaim or defence in an infringement action brought by the patentee.[27]

It has long been intended that a Community Patent covering the whole EU would result from an application to the EPO. For over thirty years the project has resisted implementation and its future remains uncertain. The current lack of agreement concerns the languages to be used and the tribunals which would decide patent disputes.

(3) Validity of Patents

(a) Patentable fields

Patents are accorded in order to protect 'inventions' susceptible of industrial application (including in agriculture). A certain number of fields are expressly excluded from what is patentable, such as creations which are purely intellectual or aesthetic, among which are included methods of programming a computer 'as such'.[28] Methods of treating the human or animal body and animal and plant varieties fall outside the scope of the system. But wholly new substances and substances for which a new medical use has been discovered are patentable—indeed patents are more valuable to the pharmaceutical industry than any other.[29] An EU Directive on protection of Biotechnological Inventions was finally accepted in 1998 and now has effect in most member states including the UK.[30] A primary purpose is to specify those objections to patents relating to human and animal genetic identification and alteration that arise on ethical grounds.[31] **6.27**

(b) Prior art: novelty

To be patentable an invention must be both novel and involve an inventive step, when compared with the 'state of the art'. Under the PA 1977 this state of the art, which is assessed at the priority date of the patent, includes any matter made available **6.28**

---

27 EPC, Arts 99–105; PA 1977, ss 72–4.

28 This obscure condition is currently given only limited scope in the UK: *Aerotel Ltd v Telco Holdings Ltd, Macrossan's Application* [2006] EWCA 1371; [2007] RPC 117, [7]–[49].

29 See PA 1977, ss 1, 4, derived from EPC, Arts 52, 53, 54(5), 57. The question whether the exclusion of computer programs can and should be interpreted so as nevertheless to admit computerized business methods is one of the great controversies of the present.

30 Directive 44/98, introduced into the PA 1977 as Appendix A2.

31 Art 6; and for related issues, see also Art 3, 5.

to the public 'by a written or oral description, by use or any other means'.[32] If an inventor has revealed his idea merely to a single person who is free to use it as he wishes, it will enter into the state of the art.[33] Such a revelation, whether it comes from a description or from an observable use, may take place anywhere in the world; the old British system, which took account only of prior art available in the United Kingdom, is now superseded. Accordingly, an inventor who has no interest in obtaining a patent but would not want anyone else to do so, can simply publish it somewhere.

6.29 The test of novelty is essentially a factual investigation to decide whether the very invention claimed in the patent has previously been made available to the public.[34] In the case where an inventor has discovered specific properties of substances or things which previously were known only in general, a selection patent may be available; in it the particular advantages which have been made known determine the right that may be claimed.[35]

(c) Prior art: inventive step

6.30 By contrast, the test for 'inventive step' requires an evaluation which is often difficult to make: given what is already known at the priority date, would the claimed invention have seemed obvious to a skilled worker in the relevant industry who did not possess any capacity to invent? If so the patent to that extent is invalid.[36] This judgment depends very much on the particular circumstances. In many cases, opinions will differ about what is obvious. The testing of inventive step is a major contributing factor to the slowness and expense of obtaining and defending a patent.

(d) Adequate disclosure, acceptable claims

6.31 The patent specification must conform to two main requirements. First, it must contain an apt disclosure of the invention which will suffice for a skilled workman to perform the invention within the claims of the specification. In consequence the claims must not be in broader terms than can be justified by the description.[37] This highly important principle is the chief means by which the monopoly granted is reasonably related to the significance of the invention over the prior art.

---

[32] PA 1977, s 2, derived from EPC, Art 54. The contents of earlier applications, are also brought into account if subsequently published—but only for the assessment of novelty, not inventive step.

[33] *Télémechanique/Power supply unit* [1993] OJ EPO 646.

[34] For example, *Beecham Group's (Amoxycillin) Application* [1980] RPC 261, CA.

[35] *Du Pont's (Wietsiepe) Application* [1982] FSR 303, HL.

[36] English courts have not hesitated to apply this requirement robustly to defeat very broad patents covering laborious but essentially straightforward advances in biotechnology: *Genentech v Wellcome Foundation* [1989] RPC 147, CA.

[37] EPC, Arts 83, 84, 100; PA 1977, ss 14, 72; *Biogen v Medeva* [1997] RPC 1, HL.

Secondly, it is not permissible to introduce amendments to either the description of the invention or the claims if they unfairly amplify the initial description or broaden the monopoly. Thus it is crucial to give all the necessary details at the outset. With important inventions, where continuing research is revealing more as it goes along, the best strategy may be to file a succession of applications, each covering the significant additions to knowledge. But what is relevant is knowledge about how to make something function. It is not possible to patent something simply because more information has been obtained about how it works as it is already known to do.[38]

(4) Infringement

(a) Scope of monopoly

For there to be an infringement of a patent, the defendant must be doing some- **6.32** thing connected with a product, apparatus or process which has every essential characteristic called for in a claim of the specification.[39] The claims accordingly define the scope of the granted monopoly and the meaning of the terms used in them is often the subject of acute controversy. Patents which cover major new advances in a technology give real opportunities to make monopoly profits. Serious competitors will therefore devote considerable energy to discovering alternatives which fall just outside the scope of the patent. The claims fall to be interpreted by reference to the descriptive body of the specification and any accompanying drawings or diagrams. The claims are treated as addressed to skilled workers in the relevant industry, rather than to research scientists or to lawyers.

(b) The protocol to EPC, Article 69

The British approach to claims, which treats them as 'fence posts' rather than **6.33** 'guidelines', leaves little scope for a finding of infringement where one element has been omitted, and British courts are equally wary of treating the defendant's alternative to a claimed element as an equivalent within the scope of the patent.[40] A protocol to Article 69, EPC, seeks to ensure that those member states which formerly had a laxer approach to infringement now adhere to this stricter conception. Its justification is the need to provide industry with clear demarcations between what it can and cannot do; it appears at its harshest when the claims have introduced some limitation which later appears to be unnecessary, thus making it easy for competitors to sidestep the patent. Some variations of approach

---

[38] *Merrell Dow v Norton* [1996] RPC 76, HL.
[39] EPC, Art 69, PA 1977, s 125.
[40] See especially, *Catnic v Hill & Smith* [1982] RPC 183, HL; *Improver v Remington* [1990] FSR 181.

accordingly remain between west European countries, despite a growing acknowl-edgement of the primacy of the claims.[41]

(c) Acts amounting to infringement

6.34 The commercial and industrial activities which constitute infringement in British law are drawn from the CPC, Articles 25–8, though with some variations in lan-guage.[42] It is infringement to make a patented product or to use a patented proc-ess, to dispose of a patented product or a product obtained directly from a patented process, to offer to dispose of such a product, to use it, import it or to keep it for disposal. The acts in question must have been carried out in the United Kingdom. Under the PA 1977, it is also infringement to offer a person a process or to provide him (or offer to provide him) with means relating to an essential element of the invention for putting that invention into effect, knowing that the means are suited to that end and are intended for it. If however the means are a staple commercial product, this form of indirect infringement will occur only if their supply induces the persons supplied to complete the act of infringement.

(d) Exceptions

6.35 There are exceptions relating to uses which are private and non-commercial and to uses which are experimental in the sense of further developing the patented invention,[43] as well as other more specific exceptions. A person who has used an invention before the priority date of the patent can continue to do so despite the grant.[44] This however is a personal right which cannot be transferred to another.

6.36 Traditionally, British patent law recognizes no doctrine of 'exhaustion of rights'. However, as already noted, the principle of free movement of goods applies within the EEA so as in effect to secure an exhaustion of the patent across national bound-aries within the territory.[45] So far as the movement of goods to other parts of the world is concerned, the patent may be used to stop exporting or importing, but only where sufficient notice is given that this is a condition of each and every transfer of ownership of the products.[46]

---

[41] *Kirin-Amgen v Hoechst* [2004] UKHL 46; [2005] RPC 169.

[42] PA 1977, s 60.

[43] For recent changes to the scope of this highly controversial exception, see the EU Directive 27/04. Generic pharmaceutical companies are now permitted to conduct experiments aimed at gaining commercial licences from medicines authorities.

[44] PA 1977, s 64.

[45] See para 6.16 and PA 1977, s 60(4) (not yet in force).

[46] *Betts v Willmott* (1871) LR 6 Ch 239.

(5) Right to a Patent

(a) Initial entitlement

The right to apply for a patent is conferred on the inventor (the person who **6.37** makes the invention), or, in the case where the invention is made in the course of employment, upon the employer. In either case, the right is treated as property and is therefore freely transferable as well as being open to license.[47] Where there are several inventors, they have joint rights. Co-ownership of the patent can result either from joint invention or assignment of interests. Each joint owner is entitled to make or use the invention and perform all other acts within the scope of the patent. But none may assign or mortgage the interest or grant or license to a third party without the consent of the others.[48]

(b) Employees' inventions

The invention of an employee belongs to his employer when he is required to **6.38** use his ability and ingenuity to solve technical problems and also when he occupies a managerial position at such a level as to owe a duty of fidelity to hold inventions for the employer. Otherwise they belong initially to the employee, even if they relate to the employer's business.[49] This rule applies only to an employee and not to a person furnishing services from outside as an independent contractor.

The PA 1977 institutes a special regime giving an employed inventor the right to **6.39** compensation in certain circumstances.[50] No other intellectual property right is treated in this way. If the patent produces an outstanding benefit for the employer, a British employee can claim compensation in two cases: (a) where the invention belongs initially to the employer, and (b) where the invention belongs initially to the employee but it has been transferred to the employer for an inadequate consideration. The amount of compensation and its form (for instance, lump sum or royalty) can be settled in proceedings before the British Patent Office or the High Court. In assessing the amount, all circumstances of the invention, including the costs of its development and subsequent exploitation, must be brought into account. The rules may not be displaced by an individual contract to the contrary, made in advance of the invention, but they may be displaced by the terms of the collective bargain which apply to the employee in question. Since the issue may well not arise until years after the invention, a wise employer keeps careful records of research and its subsequent development for long periods.

---

[47] PA 1977, s 30. For registration of interests, see ss 32, 33.
[48] PA 1977, s 36.
[49] PA 1977, s 39. A contract giving the employer greater rights in advance will be void: s 42(2).
[50] Sections 40–3.

(6) Licences

6.40 In general, English law has treated the licensing of patents and other intellectual property as a matter of free contracting. A patent licence (unlike an assignment) requires no particular form; it may be oral or arise from conduct. Many licences, however, are more than a simple permission to act within the scope of the patent. They are intended to regulate the relations between a technology provider and recipient over a considerable period. Often they cover know-how as well as a patent or patent package. In practice they will be recorded in complex documents, dealing among other things with the rights granted, duration, termination and the payments to be made by the licensee. In all likelihood, there will be provisions relating to the making of improvements by one or other side, to an exclusive licensee's obligation to work the patent effectively and a non-exclusive licensee's right to equal treatment. The main constraints on licences which transfer technology arise from the rules of competition under the EC Treaty[51] and the equivalent rules which are now applied within Britain by the Competition Act 1998.

(7) Compulsory Licences

6.41 Since the end of the nineteenth century, the British patent system has attenuated the exclusive right of the patentee in circumstances where there is deemed to be an abuse of the monopoly. Once three years have elapsed from grant of the patent, the Comptroller-General of Patents has power to grant compulsory licences for the following reasons: the patent is not worked to the fullest extent reasonably practicable in the UK or the EU; the UK demand for a patented product is not being met on reasonable terms or is being met to substantial extent by importation from outside the EU; the UK working is being hindered or prevented by importation from outside the EU; or refusal of licences is preventing an export market from being supplied with UK products or is prejudicing the establishment or development of UK industry.[52] The Comptroller is given considerable discretion in establishing the terms of such licences. In practice very few applications are actually made and pressed to a final result. The provisions are retained in the law as an encouragement towards reasonable exploitation of patents on the basis of voluntary licensing.

---

[51] See in particular the block exemption contained in the Commission Regulation on Technology Transfer 772/2004.

[52] PA 1977, ss 48–50.

(8) Crown Use

A particular form of obligatory licence benefits the Crown. Like individual citizens, the government is in principle subject to patent rights. However acts performed for the services of the Crown may be undertaken without the prior licence of a patentee, subject only to an obligation to pay reasonable compensation for doing so.[53] The acts must be performed for the services of the Crown. Acts of manufacture and use are covered, but not in general trading activities. To this in turn there are exceptions for supplying arms to foreign governments and supplying medicines in the National Health Service. It is for the court to settle the rate of compensation.

6.42

C. Confidential Information

(1) General

Where one person gives another information or causes him to acquire information on terms that it will be held in confidence, the breach of that understanding, either in the form of disclosure or use of the information, is actionable. This form of relief against breach of confidence developed in equity, principally for two reasons: Chancery was the court with power to grant an injunction, the remedy most frequently sought; and the basis of action stemmed from the equitable ideal of good conscience. Liability derives from the moral notion that a person who is given information in secret ought to respect the confidence thus imposed. Today, accordingly, the right is most often characterized as an equitable obligation of good faith distinct from other legal or equitable categories of obligation or property.[54] While it may arise as a result of a contract (and in many cases contract alone is the starting point), equally obligations of confidence can arise in circumstances which are not contractual.[55] Likewise, there is a tendency to treat certain types of confidential information as proprietary in certain traits.[56] Nevertheless the courts hesitate to treat it as such for all purposes. Since the privacy of individuals is now protected under the Human Rights Act 1998, the breach of confidence action has been developed by the courts to give it recognition

6.43

---

[53] Sections 55–9.

[54] See especially, Lord Denning MR, eg in *Fraser v Evans* [1969] 1 QB 349, 361, CA.

[55] *Saltman v Campbell* (1948) 65 RPC 203, CA.

[56] Thus technical know-how is frequently licensed and sometimes transferred, either alongside relevant patents or by itself.

as part of English law. This rapid expansion of liability appears to be generating a new form of tort.[57]

6.44   To be actionable, (1) the subject matter of the confidence must be capable of protection, (2) there must be an undertaking to respect confidence or an equivalent expectation and (3) that obligation must be broken by improper disclosure or use.[58]

(2) Protectable Subject Matter

6.45   The range of subject matter is broad: it may concern technical, commercial, governmental or personal information, unless it is completely trivial.[59] If it is technical in character, it is not necessary to show that it is novel or inventive in the sense of patent law; neither does it have to be expressed in a particular form as would be necessary in copyright law. Useful tricks in industrial production and mere 'ideas' for a television series can both be confidential subject matter.[60] Information which is generally available to the public cannot be protected, but if it is only known to a restricted circle, then it can be.[61] If the information has been given to a defendant in confidence, but it is then made public through disclosure by someone else, it may well cease to be capable of protection.[62] That is also the case, where a product has been put on the market and a purchaser works out its secrets by reverse engineering. However, in circumstances where not all the confidential information can be discovered, the recipient may still be restrained from using it as a springboard to make a head start.[63] Protection may also be refused if there is an overriding public interest in revelation of the information in the manner which the defendant is proposing. This could arise where the information concerns an illegal, improper or dangerous activity, or one

---

[57] The Human Rights Act 1998 gives support to the right to private life of the European Convention on Human Rights, Art 8, which has however to be balanced against the right of free expression in Art 10. See esp. *Peck v UK* [2003] EMLR 15, ECHR; *Von Hannover v Germany* [2004] 40 EHRR 1, ECHR *Campbell v MGN Ltd* [2004] UKHL 22; [2004] 2 AC 457; *McKennitt v Ash* [2007] EMLR 113, CA; *Associated Newspapers Ltd v Prince of Wales* [2006] EWCA Civ 1776; *Douglas v Hello! (No 3)* (appeal conjoined in *OBG v Allen*) [2007] UKHL 21. See generally paras 17.362–17.366.

[58] *Coco v Clark* [1969] RPC 41 at 47 *per* Megarry J.

[59] Private information about newsworthy people is protectable, unless unendurably salacious: *Stephens v Avery* [1988] FSR 510 (relief granted against revealing a lesbian affair).

[60] *Yates Circuit Foil v Electrofoils* [1976] FSR 345; *Fraser v Thames Television* [1983] 1 All ER 101.

[61] *Dunford and Elliott v Johnson & Firth Brown* [1978] FSR 143, CA.

[62] *Mustad v Allcock and Dosen* (1928) [1963] 3 All ER 416n, HL; and see *AG v Guardian Newspapers (No 2) ('Spycatcher')* [1990] AC 109, 285–6; where personal privacy is at stake, the right of action may continue even after substantial, but not complete revelation.

[63] *Terrapin v Builders Supply* [1967] RPC 375, 392, *per* Roxburgh J.

which prejudices the proper administration of justice.[64] Employees may accordingly be left free to act as whistle-blowers.[65]

(3) The Obligation of Confidence

(a) General

If a reasonable person would suppose that information was being supplied under conditions of confidence, an obligation so to treat it will arise.[66] This is equally true where one person requests another to find out information, as where a person is employed or commissioned to do research. There may be an explicit or implied contract to preserve secrecy, but this does not necessarily have to be shown.[67]   **6.46**

(b) Former employees

Where the recipient or discoverer of the information is a former employee,[68] special considerations operate, which reflect a policy of leaving employees reasonable freedom to move jobs or set up their own businesses: **6.47**

(1) in the case of discrete technical information, such as a chemical formula, which an honest person would recognize as belonging solely to the employer, a general obligation in equity exists to preserve the confidence;

(2) where there is incidental information which has been generated by or for the employer, it can be protected provided that there is a contractual stipulation not to divulge it to others or to use it after leaving the employment. That stipulation must not be in unreasonable restraint of trade, particularly in respect of its geographical coverage or duration;

(3) general skill and knowledge which is acquired as a matter of course in the type of employment cannot be protected.[69]

---

64 *Lion Laboratories v Evans* [1985] 1 QB 526, CA (newspaper may reveal that police device for measuring intoxication functions inaccurately; not sufficient just to tell Home Office).

65 For their protection in labour law, see the Public Interest Disclosure Act 1998.

66 *Coco v Clark* [1969] RPC 41.

67 *Saltman v Campbell* (1948) 65 RPC 203, CA (provider of information can sue ultimate recipient, even though no privity between them).

68 While the employment continues, the employee will owe a duty of fidelity. If this is not spelled out expressly, it will arise by implication; but then its scope will be related to the nature of the employment and the degree of responsibility assumed by the employee.

69 Cross J in *Printers & Finishers v Holloway (No 2)* [1965] RPC 269; re-established in *Lancashire Fires v Lyons* [1996] FSR 629, CA; cf *Faccenda Chicken v Fowler* [1987] Ch 117, CA.

(c) Indirect recipients and 'intruders'

6.48 The action for breach of confidence exists not only against the first recipient of the information, but also against third parties to whom it is subsequently transmitted, whether or not they know of the obligation attached to it. This is apparently true even where the indirect recipient acts in good faith and provides valuable consideration.[70] The obligation to conserve secret information exists even when it is procured not as the result of a relationship but because of clandestine surveillance or some equivalent intrusion.[71] Where personal privacy is at stake, this form of behaviour, particularly by the media, has become actionable.[72]

(4) Improper Use

6.49 An obligation of confidence may be violated either by disclosure or by use of the information. A defendant may even be responsible where he has copied subconsciously, having forgotten that he received the information from the claimant.[73] In some circumstances a defendant is only responsible where he has acted to the detriment of the claimant, but it is uncertain whether this is a distinct condition for responsibility.[74]

D. Copyright

(1) General

(a) Nature and objectives

6.50 Copyright confers the right to prevent others without authority from reproducing or performing in substantial measure the whole or part of a protected work. It is a right therefore against copying, not against independent creation, and it concerns the way in which ideas are expressed in a work, rather than the idea or concept which lies behind that expression. Copyright arises not only in the creative activities of writers, composers, artists and film directors, but also by virtue of the investment in 'copyright products'. Accordingly it provides legal shelter against

---

[70] *Stephenson Jordan v McDonald & Evans* (1951) 68 RPC 190; *PSM International v Whitehouse* [1992] FSR 489, CA.

[71] A view apparently favoured in *Francome v Mirror Group* [1984] 2 All ER 408, CA.

[72] See n 57 above.

[73] *Seager v Copydex (No 1)* [1967] 2 All ER 415, CA.

[74] *Coco v Clark* [1969] RPC 41; special public interest considerations arise where the information concerns governmental secrets: *AG v Guardian Newspapers (No 2)* [1990] AC 109.

unjustified misappropriation in a considerable number of industries and its impact upon them varies in numerous ways.

(b) Development

Copyright in a modern sense first emerged with the famous Statute of Anne **6.51** 1710. Before that the London booksellers belonging to the Stationers Company enjoyed rights against piratical interlopers which were aligned to a censorship by the state and church. From 1710, a copyright for authors of books and their assigns existed for a limited term of years and this was gradually extended to engravers, sculptors, other visual artists, playwrights and composers.[75] In 1911 the various copyrights were brought together in a single statute. Today the British law is found in the Copyright, Designs and Patents Act 1988.

The United Kingdom has been a founder member of both the Berne Convention **6.52** on Literary and Artistic Works (originally 1886), the Universal Copyright Convention (1952), the Rome Convention on Performers', Phonogram Producers' and Broadcasters' Rights (1961), the copyright obligations arising under TRIPs (1994),[76] the WIPO Copyright and Performers and Phonograms Treaties of 1996, both concerned with digital communication. By virtue of the Berne Convention, in 1911 the United Kingdom abandoned any requirement of registration as a condition for acquiring copyright; it also adopted the life of the author and a term of years thereafter (now seventy years) as the duration of rights given in literary, dramatic, musical and artistic works. These steps did much to bring British law closer to the authors' rights and neighbouring rights systems of continental Europe, a process which has been strengthened step by step through a recent series of EC directives on harmonization of the national law.[77]

The arrival of digital technology and, above all, the Internet has set a very difficult **6.53** agenda for the future of copyright law. An introduction to this development is given at the end of this Part.[78]

---

[75] The London booksellers claimed that at common law their right was perpetual and that the statute simply gave them enhanced remedies for its limited term—a view which Lord Mansfield and some other judges supported, but others again opposed with equal eloquence. In *Donaldson v Beckett* (1774) 4 Burr 2408, the House of Lords resolved this most intense of all arguments about intellectual property in favour of the limited term prescribed by Parliament.

[76] See n 12 above.

[77] These include Directives on the Legal Protection of the Topographies of Semiconductor Products (87/54); Legal Protection of Computer Programs (91/250); Rental Right, Lending Right and Related Rights (92/100); Copyright and Related Rights applicable to Satellite Broadcasting and Cable Retransmission (93/83); Term of Copyright and Related Rights (93/98); Legal Protection of Databases (96/9); Copyright and Related Rights in the Information Society (01/29); and Resale Rights to Works of Art (01/84).

[78] See para 6.77.

(2) Types of Work Protected

6.54 The 1988 Act confers copyright on *works* which almost always have (or are deemed to have) *authors*.[79] Among these two main types may be distinguished.

(a) The copyright conferred on authors in a traditional sense

6.55 The creators of literary, dramatic, musical and artistic works have long been grouped together as 'authors' in copyright law. Their rights now last for the author's life and seventy years.[80] Their creations are protected if they are 'original' in the very limited sense of not being copied.[81]

6.56 For the most part therefore copyright arises in any of these works which crosses a minimal threshold of content, without there being any test of aesthetic quality. Thus literary works encompass not only novels, poems and scholarly tomes, but also such mundane things as trade catalogues and sporting programmes, and more recently computer programs. Derivative work, such as the writing of a film script from a novel, and ancillary work, such as translation and the preparation of a critical edition, may likewise attract their own copyright.[82] The 'labour, skill and judgment' which leads to the creation of a work can come very largely from an assessment of the commercial value of a particular presentation, such as a compilation.[83] Equivalent approaches are adopted for dramatic and musical works: thus orchestrations and arrangements of compositions attract their own copyright. The writing of a computer program now gives rise to a literary work, though its purpose—the instruction of a machine—is a novel objective.[84]

6.57 The category of artistic works is elaborately defined to include not only (1) graphic works of various kinds and three-dimensional art works, such as sculptures, but also (2) works of architecture and (3) works of artistic craftsmanship. Works in the first of these categories are protected irrespective of artistic quality, but this element must be present in relation to the last two. Indeed a substantial test of quality is applied before artefacts can be treated as being of artistic craftsmanship.[85]

---

[79] Copyright, Designs and Patents Act 1988 (hereafter CDPA 1988), ss 1, 9.

[80] ibid ss 3, 4; for duration, see para 6.61.

[81] *University of London Press v University Tutorial Press* [1916] 2 Ch 601. This has been modified in relation to the copyright in databases, as a first response to an EU campaign to impose a requirement of 'personal intellectual creation' as the test of originality: CDPA 1988, s 3A.

[82] *Sawkins v Hyperion Records Ltd* [2005] EWCA Civ 565; [2005] 1 WLR 3281.

[83] *Ladbroke v William Hill* [1964] 1 WLR 273, HL (form containing a selection of a set of football pool competitions).

[84] CDPA 1988, s 3(1). The work has to be recorded in some permanent form, but it does not matter by whom: s 3(3).

[85] *Hensher v Restawile Upholstery* [1976] AC 64, HL. See further para 6.85.

(b) The copyright conferred directly on investors

Certain investors engaged in cultural productions are also given their own copy- **6.58**
rights and for these purposes are deemed to be 'authors'. Typically these copyrights
run for a period of fifty years from first exploitation of them with the authority of
the right owner.[86] The CDPA 1988 confers such rights on producers of sound
recordings, organizers of broadcasts (a term that includes cablecasts), and publishers in respect of the format of new editions.[87] Such rights are referred to as 'related
rights' or 'neighbouring rights' to copyright.

Thanks to EU intervention, the rights now given in a film are a hybrid between **6.59**
creative copyright and investment copyright. The copyright in a new film is initially
shared between the principal director and the financial producer (though the
former is likely to assign his interest to the latter).[88]

(3) Connecting Factor: Qualification

United Kingdom copyright is conferred (1) where the author qualifies as British **6.60**
and (2) where first publication occurs in the United Kingdom. Thanks primarily
to membership of the Berne Union, British copyright is equally open to authors
with a personal status in another Union state or where first publication occurs in
such a state.[89] In determining whether a work has been published, copies of the
whole work must be made available to the public in sufficient quantity to satisfy
reasonable demand. No account, however, is taken of unauthorized publications.[90]

(4) Duration

By a controversial directive of the EC, most copyright periods were revised so as **6.61**
to bring them up to the highest European factor. As already mentioned, for the
works of true authors the British period was extended on 1 January 1996 to end
seventy years after the author's death. The duration of some of the related rights
was increased to the fifty-year term already mentioned.[91] The directive required

---

[86] CDPA 1988, ss 13A, 14. The term for publisher's format right is 25 years: s 15.

[87] ibid ss 5–8. See, eg, *Newspaper Licensing Agency v Marks & Spencer* [2001] UKHL 38; [2003]
1 AC 551. A separate right (outside copyright) is given for 25 years to the first publisher of a
work which has remained unpublished throughout its copyright: see Copyright and Related Rights
Regulations 1996, SI 1996/2967, rr 16, 17. For performers' rights, see para 6.81.

[88] CDPA 1988, s 9(1). Copyright and Related Rights Regulation 1996, SI 1996/2967, Reg 36.
For measurement of duration in films, see CDPA, s 13B.

[89] See CDPA 1988, ss 154–7 and Orders in Council thereunder.

[90] ibid s 175(1).

[91] See para 6.58.

that these extensions be applied to existing works, including even those which would come back into copyright after a prior expiry.[92]

6.62 Where a work is of joint authorship, because it is made to a common design, the life of the longest living author is taken as the measure.[93] However, in British law works in different categories (for example, the music and the words of a song) are treated as separate works and do not involve joint authorship.[94] There are special rules for works published anonymously or under a pseudonym and more generally, where one or more of the authors is not known. Crown copyright in works produced by its officers or servants lasts for fifty years from publication or 125 years from creation, whichever is the shorter.[95]

(5) Infringement

(a) Substantial taking

6.63 For copyright to be infringed there must be 'copying', ie without the authority of the copyright owner a substantial part of the work has to be taken for reproduction or performance. The general precept must be recalled: it is the expression making up the work, and not the underlying idea, which is protected.[96] In deciding what is substantial taking, the character of the work will be brought into account. Thus the structure and development of a play may be more important than the detailed dialogue; that of a computer program more significant than the line-by-line programming instructions. If the copyright in question concerns selections from, additions to, or comments upon the work of others, it is those elements which must have been taken.[97] The degree of effort, intellectual and commercial, which the creator has put into his production will be significant, as will be the manner in which the defendant has taken advantage of the claimant's work.

(b) Copying

6.64 There will be the separate question whether the defendant copied from the claimant, rather than vice versa, or from a third source or created independently.

---

[92] Such as Kipling's: died 1936; original expiry of copyright: 1986; revival: 1996–2006, subject to exception for those who had already made prior arrangements to exploit in that period: Duration of Copyright and Rights in Performances Regulations 1995, SI 1995/3297, Regs 17–25.

[93] CDPA 1988, s 10.

[94] *Redwood Music v Chappell* [1982] RPC 109, HL. Gilbert's and Sullivan's copyrights expired fifty years after their respective deaths. Many other copyright systems do not follow this approach, with complications for transnational agreements.

[95] CDPA 1988, s 163. There are also special arrangements for certain Parliamentary copyrights and those of international organizations: ss 164–8.

[96] Imprecise the distinction may be, but it is important enough to have found its way into the TRIPs Agreement (n 12 above), Art 9(2).

[97] *Designers Guild v Russell Williams* [2000] 1 WLR 2416, HL.

Once evident similarities are demonstrated, the burden of providing an innocent explanation may pass to the defendant.[98]

(c) Primary and secondary infringement

For primary infringements, ie making copies, issuing copies to the public, renting **6.65** and lending copies, performing in public, communication to the public,[99] and making adaptations, liability arises whether or not the defendant appreciates that infringement is occurring.[100] Secondary infringement occurs in certain forms of commercial activity—importing and trading in copies and organizing public performances. These are wrongful only where the defendant knows that the copies are illicit or the performance unlicensed or has no reasonable grounds for believing that the conduct is legitimate.[101] Primary infringement may occur not only by the commission of one of the proscribed acts, but also from authorizing their commission. This is an extended notion of vicarious liability. Proceedings for infringement by authorizing may thus arise for hiring a band at a dance hall which does not hold the appropriate licence to perform copyright music; or placing a photocopy machine in a library without instructing users not to infringe, through specifying the limits of their freedom to copy.[102]

(d) Parallel importing

Both the primary liability for issuing copies to the public and the secondary liabil- **6.66** ity for importing illicit copies have an effect on the practice of parallel importa- tion. The law is now so formulated that these rights may not be used to stop the movement of copyright works from one EEA state to another; but unauthorized importation of copies from outside the EEA will constitute these types of infringement.[103]

(e) Exceptions

(i) Fair dealing exceptions

British copyright law has no general doctrine of 'fair use' qualifying the opera- **6.67** tion of copyright,[104] although publication and other use may, under narrow

---

[98] *Francis Day v Bron* [1963] Ch 587, CA. A claimant is greatly helped if the same slips or quirks are apparent in the defendant's production.

[99] A response to growth of the Internet: see paras 6.77–6.80.

[100] CDPA 1988, ss 16–21.

[101] ibid ss 22–7.

[102] ibid s 16(2). A person authorizes who 'sanctions, countenances or approves': *Falcon v Famous Players* [1926] 2 KB 474, 491, CA *per* Bankes LJ.

[103] CDPA 1988, ss 18, 27.

[104] Unlike the position in US copyright law.

conditions, be justified as being in the public interest.[105] The CDPA 1988 contains a long list of more or less specific circumstances which amount to complete exceptions to the right or which in some cases permit use but require the payment of compensation.[106] These include three important exceptions for 'fair dealing' for the following purposes:

(1) making single copies of works for non-commercial research or private study;[107]
(2) use of works other than photographs for reporting current events;[108]
(3) use of works for purposes of criticism or review.[109]

In each case what is 'fair' falls to be judged in all the particular circumstances, including the extent to which the taking will interfere with the usual commercial prospects of the copyright owner. The values which these exceptions embody are important and they are accordingly to be liberally interpreted.[110] Unlike other copyright systems, there is no general exception for private copying in general. Many such systems have provided some recompense for this exception which takes the form of a levy on copying equipment or the recording means (tape, CD, etc) used in it, but UK governments have not followed suit.

(ii) Further exceptions

6.68 Among the other exceptions may be noted:

(1) Exceptions designed to encourage collective licensing schemes, for instance, for the recording of broadcasts and cablecasts in educational establishments, the copying of scientific abstracts, reprographic copying by educational establishments, renting sound recordings, films and computer programs;[111]
(2) Exceptions concerning artistic works: representing them when they are situated in a public place; reproducing them in sale catalogues and advertisements; reconstructing buildings, etc;[112]

---

[105] *Hyde Park Properties v Yelland* [2000] RPC 604, CA; *Ashdown v Telegraph Group* [2001] EWCA Civ 1142; [2002] Ch 149. There is also a limit to the range of subject matter in which copyright can exist, so as to exclude what is scandalous and immoral; but it would rarely apply today.

[106] To some extent these have been restricted by the constraints on exceptions and limitations contained in the EU Directive on Copyright in the Information Society (2001/29), Art 5, which confines them by explicit provisions and also by the notorious 'Three-step test' that the cover only special cases, not conflicting with normal exploitation and not unreasonably prejudicing legitimate interests of rightholders. That test has not been spelled out in the UK legislation.

[107] CDPA 1988, s 29, which applies only to copyright in literary works other than databases, dramatic, musical or artistic works and typographical format. In the case of a computer program, special principles apply to decompilation back into a higher level language, which must be in order to secure interoperability of programs: s 50B.

[108] ibid s 30(2),(3). In some instances, there has to be sufficient acknowledgement of source.

[109] ibid s 30(1). There must be sufficient acknowledgement.

[110] *Pro Sieben Media v Carlton UK* [1999] FSR 610, CA.

[111] CDPA 1988, ss 35, 36, 60, 66, 74.

[112] ibid ss 62–5.

(3) Exceptions concerning broadcasts and cablecasts: recabling to areas of poor transmission; free public showings for certain types of work; recording in order to view at a more convenient time;[113]

(4) Exceptions relating to public administration, including use for parliamentary and judicial proceedings, Royal Commissions and statutory inquiries, the making available of public records and other official information.[114]

(6) Moral Rights

(a) Nature in British law

The idea that authors should have 'moral' or 'personality' rights distinct from eco- **6.69** nomic rights in their work is the distinctive feature of civilian systems of authors' rights.[115] In consequence, the right to claim authorship and the right to protect the integrity of a work are acknowledged in the Berne Convention, Article 6 *bis*. In Britain and other common law countries these moral rights have been recognized to a limited degree through the general law, notably in tort (passing off, injurious falsehood and defamation) and through contract, expressed and implied. In the CDPA 1988, moral rights were for the first time put on a statutory basis.[116] They have however been treated with a certain coolness, which is reflected in the conditions and exceptions to them. Most fundamentally, they are open to waiver—by agreement or conduct—which may take place to any extent and at any time, in particular, in advance.[117] They are accordingly in the nature of pre-sumptive rules, rather than exigent guarantees. In this they differ—fundamentally, but not unreasonably—from many foreign laws on authors' rights.

(b) Right to identification

The right to be identified as author of a literary, dramatic, musical or artistic work, **6.70** or as a film director[118]—important to those struggling to get their name estab-lished—comes into effect only if it has been asserted. This will typically be done as part of an assignment of the copyright. There are in any case exceptions: for computer programs, Crown copyright, works made in the course of employment, press publication, the performing of musical works (thus exempting disc jockeys),

---

[113] ibid ss 70–3.

[114] ibid ss 45–50.

[115] There is no agreement among them about the scope and supervailing character of these rights. French law regards them as perpetual, German law as lasting for the term of the eco-nomic rights.

[116] CDPA 1988, Part I, Ch IV; moral rights also extend to the rights of performers: Performances (Moral Rights, etc.) Regs (2006.18).

[117] ibid s 87.

[118] ibid ss 77–9. The right lasts as long as the copyright.

fair reporting of current events on electronic media, some incidental intrusions and industrial design.

(c) Right of integrity

6.71 The right of the same categories of people to object to derogatory treatment of works permits them to object to addition, deletion, alteration or adaptation when it 'amounts to distortion or mutilation of the work or is otherwise prejudicial to the honour or reputation of the author or director'.[119] It is not a right which more generally allows the author to object to placement of a work on a particular site or removal from it, to criticism of it or himself, or to its destruction; nor may he require its withdrawal when he has second thoughts. Related but distinct is a moral right to object to false attribution of work which is not the author's.[120]

(7) Ownership

(a) Initial entitlement

6.72 Since copyright resides in the work as expressed, the author of a traditional copyright work is the person who creates it in this sense. On the other hand, the 'author' of one of the entrepreneurial copyrights is the investor who causes the work to be brought into existence.[121] Copyright vests from the moment of production in the author. To this there is one exception. Where a literary, dramatic, musical or other artistic work is created in the course of employment, then, unless there is a contract to the contrary, it is owned from the outset by the employer.[122] Being a property right, copyright can be dealt with as an owner chooses. If a work is assigned before its creation, as often occurs when works are commissioned, the assignee becomes the owner upon production: at law if the assignment is a signed writing; in equity, if the circumstances demand it.[123]

(b) Co-ownership

6.73 Co-ownership of copyright can arise because there are joint authors or because interests have been assigned. In contrast with patents, one joint owner of copyright

---

[119] CDPA 1988, ss 80–3. This right also lasts for the copyright term.

[120] ibid s 84, deriving from earlier British legislation; it lasts for 20 years from the author's death. There is also a so-called moral right of privacy of the commissioner of a photograph or film for private and domestic purposes to object to its subsequent publication, as where a person in it becomes newsworthy: s 85.

[121] ibid s 9; para 6.57.

[122] ibid s 11. An implication to the contrary may arise out of standard practice (as with academic employment) or from the evident purpose of the transaction.

[123] ibid s 91; *Griggs Group v Evans* [2005] EWCA Civ 11; [2005] FSR 706.

is not entitled to exploit the work without the permission of the others.[124] Equally a licensee needs permission from all the owners. This is one evident reason why, in a complex work such as a film or multi-media package, it becomes vital that all the relevant copyrights are assigned into the hands of the exploiter. Today this will include the rights of performers as well as of authors.[125]

(c) Copyright contracts

Copyright owners exploit their rights through a wide variety of contractual arrangements. Where these are individually negotiated, the parties are largely free to bargain as they see fit. If they have agreed in clear terms that all aspects of copyright, including rights which may evolve with future technology (eg electronic publishing contracts), they will be held to their bargain.[126] However, the terms of management and agency contracts between young pop composers and their publishers and other agents have been treated as void for being in unreasonable restraint of trade, or voidable in equity for undue influence.[127]

6.74

(d) Collecting societies

For many individual copyright owners, the only realistic prospect of a commercial return lies in joining a collecting society. The pioneering case in Britain was the Performing Rights Society, formed to collect royalties on performances of composers' and librettists' copyright music. Record companies, using Phonographic Performance Ltd, follow a similar formula in respect of the sound recording right, and literary authors and their publishers likewise in collecting for photocopying through the Copyright Licensing Agency. Through their links with equivalent societies in other countries, these collecting societies can acquire control over virtually all the available material of interest to users such as broadcasters, dance bands and teachers.

6.75

The societies are accordingly vested with monopoly power in the economic sense and while their necessity is generally acknowledged not all their practices have proved acceptable to competition law authorities. Thus restrictions on membership, rules concerning distribution, and other structural issues may fall to be

6.76

---

124 *Cescinsky v Routledge* [1916] 2 KB 325.

125 When requiring the introduction of a rental right for all relevant copyrights, the EC Directive on Rental Right, Lending Rights and Related Rights (92/100/EEC [1992] OJ L346/61), Arts 2(5), 2(6), 4 provided for a presumption of assignment by creators and performers to the producer, but at the same time guaranteed them a right to equitable remuneration: see CDPA 1988, ss 93A-C, 191F-H.

126 *Campbell Connelly v Noble* [1963] 1 WLR 252.

127 *Schroeder Music v Macaulay* [1974] 1 WLR 1308, HL; *Clifford Davis Management v WEA Records* [1975] 1 All ER 237, CA; *O'Sullivan v Management Agency and Music* [1985] QB 428 and succeeding decisions.

reviewed by the Competition Directorate of the European Commission, or in Britain, by the Competition Commission. So far as concerns the terms which collecting societies offer to users, a separate system of control is in operation. The Copyright Tribunal has power to review the terms offered by a collecting society as part of a general scheme or in a particular case.[128] The root criterion is that the terms must be reasonable in the circumstances. The CDPA 1988 now contains elaborate lists of factors to be taken into account in certain cases. Resort to the Copyright Tribunal is today a regular occurrence.

(8) *Copyright, Digital Format and the Internet*

6.77 The coming of digital technology led to computer programs being treated as literary works for copyright purposes.[129] The expansion of the Internet over recent years to encompass a host of uses, notably on the World Wide Web, provides a medium in which copyright material can be transmitted for viewing, downloading and transferring on to others. Interactive exchanges are commonplace and text and images can be endlessly modified—all with remarkable speed and accuracy. Authors and their entrepreneurs are therefore in danger that there will be widespread taking of copyright material without payment or acknowledgement. This conduct may also be greatly assisted by those who run search engines and the like. Hence the litigation in the United States and elsewhere against Napster, Grokster and KaZaA for their peer-to-peer (P2P) systems and against websites which provide programs for evading protective codes on DVD.

6.78 Already in 1996, the World Intellectual Property Organization (a United Nations organ) fostered the signing of two treaties which were designed to adjust national laws on authors' copyright and related rights laws concerning performers, sound recorders and audio-visual producers, particularly in relation to digitization.[130] In their wake the EU enacted its Directive on Copyright and Related Rights in the Information Society (01/29), a measure leading to adaptations and extensions of copyright protection in the UK.[131] A right of communication to the public was added to the acts constituting infringement, covering not only wireless and wired broadcasting but also Internet and other electronic transmissions sought by individual members of the public.[132]

---

128 CDPA 1988, Part I, Chs VII, VIII. These statutory provisions are elaborate.
129 Para 6.56.
130 Para 6.52.
131 Principally by the Copyright and Related Rights Regs, 2003/2498 which introduced amendments into the CDPA 1988.
132 CDPA 1988, s 20.

Where digital material is placed on the Web or provided in hard copy such as a CD **6.79**
or DVD, electronic measures may be built in by the provider which aim to prevent the making or retransmission of multiple copies.[133] The threat to such technical barriers is that others will devise ways of circumventing them. Under the
Directive, national laws must give the providers rights to attack those who make
these means of circumvention available and powers to do so have been expanded
to meet the requirements of the Directive.[134] If these powers prevent a user from
taking advantage of an exception to copyright in certain limited circumstances it
is possible to pursue a complaint to the responsible government department that
may lead to new legislative protection of this 'access right'. Critics assert that this
solution to a much debated issue is inadequate.

A measure of protection is accorded to Internet Service Providers, (ISPs), where **6.80**
their involvement is only in transient or incidental copying purely in the course
of an Internet transmission from one third party to another (Article 5.1).[135] So
far as concerns ISPs that host websites, arrangements are evolving through the
contracts between them and their content providers under which the ISPs are
entitled to take down material once they are notified that it contains copyright
infringements.

(9) Rights in Performances

Following an EC directive, performers are provided with certain *property* rights **6.81**
in their performances of dramatic, musical or literary material, and also of
variety acts and other similar presentations.[136] To this the CDPA 1988 adds certain
non-property rights belonging to the performer alone, which are outside the
scope of the directive.[137] The CDPA 1988 also gives an investor with an exclusive
contract to exploit the performance a separate, *quasi-proprietary* right.[138] The
rights last for fifty years from the performance, or, if a recording is released within that time, then for fifty years from release.[139] The rights bear a family resemblance to the copyright in sound recordings and the like. The law has become
quite unduly complex. It developed particularly to deal with the illicit recording
of concerts ('bootlegging') where those involved might have no copyright on

---

[133] The Digital Rights Management systems (DRMs) are themselves subject to protection
against copying: CDPA 1988, s 296ZG.
[134] CDPA, ss 296–9.
[135] CDPA 1988, s 28A.
[136] Rental, Lending and Related Rights Directive, n 77 above; CDPA 1988, Part II, ss 180–4,
191A-M. These rights do not extend to the general run of sports, despite the pleas of some promoters.
[137] CDPA 1988, ss 180–4, 192A-B.
[138] ibid ss 185–8.
[139] ibid s 191.

which to rely.[140] The law has been amplified in the hope of enhancing the bargaining position and revenues for performers.[141]

(10) Public Lending

6.82 Under the Public Lending Right Act 1979, the United Kingdom has a special regime for the lending of books by public libraries. The government finances and supports the Public Lending Rights Scheme and distributions are made to British authors and certain others on the basis of a sample of borrowing from selected public libraries. Public borrowing of records is treated in the same way as their rental: the owners of copyright in the works and in the sound recordings are entitled, subject to certain special conditions, to royalties and for these collecting societies exist.

(11) Artists' Resale Right (Droit de Suite)

6.83 The commercial value of a work of visual art frequently attaches to the original, rather than being realised through reproductions. Accordingly, under EU Directive 2001/84, the UK has been obliged to introduce a personal right for artists and their inheritors to a share in the proceeds of resale of the original, where the sale is conducted by an art market professional.[142] The right lasts for the duration of the copyright in the work. Civil proceedings lie to recover payments due, primarily from sellers of the original or their agents. The amount in the UK is set by a sliding scale between 4 per cent of sales up to 50,000 Euros and 0.25 per cent on sales over 500,000 Euros, up to a maximum of 12,500 Euros.

E. Industrial Designs

(1) General

6.84 Industrial designs concern the appearance of mass-produced articles. Design may add noticeably to the attractiveness of one competitor's product, especially when much the same technology is being deployed by various rivals; indeed, with many luxuries today, design elements blend in with other elements of the branding. While it is natural to think of design as a separate element added in an appeal to the eye, the feature carrying the design may also assume its form as part

---

[140] Because they extemporize or use other people's music.

[141] For the moral rights of performers, see n 116.

[142] See Artists' Resale Right Regulations (2006/346), operative for living artists from 2006, but delayed for the inheritors of deceased artists until 2012.

of its function—a specially-shaped handle or socket-connector or whatever. Design protection accordingly strays also into the sphere of the technical. This particularly affects the market in replacement parts for cars and other consumer durables.

It is this consequence, above all others, which makes it difficult to secure an indus- **6.85** trial design law which is politically acceptable to the different interests in industry. Over the last thirty years, Britain has had a particularly turbulent experience of the problems as it has lurched from restricted to over-indulgent protection of designs. Currently, in the Copyright, Designs and Patents Act 1988, it has found some sort of third way, which nonetheless curbs considerably the impact of design rights on spare part supplies.[143] Now EU has taken over part of the field, in the course of creating its own Community Registered Design. This lays down a common plan with registered design systems in the member states, but only to very limited extent standardizes unregistered rights that may exist in national law, whether by way of copyright or unregistered design right. The result in UK law is a curious amalgam, which requires description of (i) registered design laws, at the Community and the UK level, (ii) artistic copyright as it may effect the design of industrial products, and (iii) unregistered design rights, which at the Community level have a strictly limited effect but are more capacious in UK law.

(2) Registered Designs

(a) Scope of the right

In much of Europe, a system of registration for industrial designs has long been **6.86** in existence. In Britain, it has grown from the 1830s, acquiring over time some family resemblance to the patent system. A registered design, now granted under the Registered Designs Act 1949, as substantially amended, first by the CDPA 1988 and then, implementing the EU Directive 1998/71, by the Registered Designs Regulations 2001/3949. In 2003, Community Registered Designs (RDs), granted by the Office for the Harmonisation of the Internal Market (OHIM, Alicante), became available as a unified right throughout the EU.[144] These alternative systems each grant) an exclusive right in the design of a product, which operates even against independent designers who arrive at much the same result. The design has accordingly to be novel and of distinctive character,

---

[143] A decision of the House of Lords provided a prominent signpost for this choice of direction: *British Leyland v Armstrong* [1986] AC 577. Politically acute, it was nonetheless doctrinally obscure: cf *Canon KK v Green Cartridge* [1997] AC 728, PC.

[144] Regulation on Community Designs, 6/2002 (references to equivalent provisions in this Reg. and RDA 1949 will be only to the latter).

when compared with prior art.[145] Before grant, the validity of the design applied for will be the subject of an examination by the office to which application is made, but only if this is requested. If the application succeeds, the right granted will be renewable for a total of twenty-five years (five terms of five years).[146]

(b) Protectable designs

6.87 Community and British RDs consist of 'the appearance of the whole or a part of a product resulting from the features of, in particular, the lines, contours, colours, shape, texture or materials of the product or its ornamentation'.[147] A design cannot therefore be registered for a feature dictated solely by function,[148] or for a design element that 'must fit' onto something else,[149] or for a replacement part of a complex product.[150]

(c) Infringement

6.88 A registered design prevents those without licence from making, importing and trading in articles bearing the design or one that does not produce on the informer users a different overall impression.[151] Striking features in the design will naturally be given most significance.

(3) Artistic Copyright

6.89 During the years 1968–88, it was accepted that a drawing—as a work which, however technical its character, attracts copyright—is infringed by reproduction in three dimensions; and that this can occur by direct or indirect copying. The shapes of a vast range of industrial products and their parts were thus protected against copying, in many cases for very long periods and without any formal registration. The result was extremely inconvenient to many in industry, and the scope of artistic copyright in the industrial sphere was severely curtailed

---

[145] RDA 1949, s 1B. The comparison is not with designs made available to the public world wide, but only with those that could reasonably be known in business in the European Economic Area, designers themselves having a 12-month grace period. A priority right of six months arises under the Paris Industrial Property Convention (para 6.10) Art 4.

[146] Measured from the date of application: ibid s 8.

[147] ibid s 1(1). The element of appearance must be material, as being taken into account by purchasers.

[148] RDA 1949, s 1C. Whether under the European law this exclusion is confined to shapes which alone will allow the function to be carried out, something which occurs very rarely has yet to be settled by an authoritative decision. There is also an exception for methods or principles of construction.

[149] RDA 1949, s 1B(8).

[150] RDA 1949, s 7(5).

[151] RDA 1949, ss 7, 7A. Certain contributory acts are also covered and there are various exceptions.

in 1988, by the substitution of an (unregistered) design right, which is of more limited scope.[152]

Under the 1988 Act, artistic copyright can apply to industrial production only **6.90** where it is for the surface decoration of an article or where the design is for a thing which itself attracts copyright in its own right, most evidently as a 'work of artistic craftsmanship'.[153] Even in these cases, the right is limited to a term of twenty-five years from the first appearance of products legitimately bearing the design.[154] If, however, the design is for features of shape or configuration of an article which itself does not attract copyright, any copyright in the design does not extend to its use in industrial production.[155]

(4) Unregistered Design Right: Community and UK

(a) Community Unregistered Design Right (UDR)

The two varieties of UDR—under Community Law and UK law—are different **6.91** in purpose and effect. Community UDR acts as a preliminary supplement to the Community Registered Design and in general it has the same legal scope.[156] It can be claimed for the first three years after the design has been made available to the public by the designer or other person entitled to it. It can be claimed only against a person who copies the design without permission. The purpose of the right is to provide protection for design products before the registered right can be obtained.

(b) UK Unregistered Design (UDR): Relation to copyright

The CDPA 1988, Part III creates a design right against copying the shape or con- **6.92** figuration of an industrial product, where that product is not itself an artistic work.[157] This is intended in particular as a substitute for the previous artistic copyright in technical designs, but one which is much more limited in scope. It lasts only for a period which in most cases will be ten years from the first market- ing anywhere of products legitimately bearing the design.[158] Being a right only

---

[152] See para 6.87.

[153] For this constricted category of high-art object, see para 6.56. As to surface decoration, see *Lambretta Clothing v Teddy Smith* [2005] RPC 88, CA.

[154] CDPA 1988, ss 51, 52.

[155] The copyright in technical drawings continues to cover their reproduction as drawings.

[156] Reg 6/2002, Art 11.

[157] Where the rights are both available, copyright is preferred: ibid s 236.

[158] CDPA 1988, s 216. During the last five years, it is open to compulsory licences of right; and this may happen even in the first five years, after an adverse reference to the Competition Commission: ss 238, 239.

against copying, it is subject to a test of 'originality', rather than 'novelty'; even so it must not be commonplace in the relevant design field.[159]

(c) Technical design and spare parts

6.93 Because (unregistered) design right is intended in particular to cover purely technical design, there is no need to show that it has any eye appeal. However, again by way of inhibition on claims to right over designs for spare parts, there is no infringement to the extent either that it 'must match' the design for something else (door panel for car) or that its physical embodiment 'must fit' into another thing for functional reasons (light bulb into socket).[160]

(5) The Rights in Comparison

(a) Initial entitlement

6.94 The three categories of rights in industrial designs produce an unduly elaborate system of protection. All at least are property rights and can be dealt with as such. The right inures initially to the designer, or (in all three cases) to an employer when the design is made in the course of employment. A curious complication arises from the fact that commissions to independent designers have the same effect so far as registered designs and design right are concerned; but this does not apply to copyright.

(b) Qualification

6.95 A different variation arises in respect of the qualification to hold the right. While both registered designs (by virtue of the Paris Convention) and artistic copyright (by virtue of the Berne Convention) are open to the nationals of the great majority of states around the world, the UK UDR has been established on a *sui generis* basis, specifically so that its benefits can be restricted to those connected with the few countries which offer reciprocal informal protection. The motivation for this development was the insistence of the United States upon strict reciprocity for the *sui generis* protection of the design of semi-conductor chip circuitry, a form of protection which has now, in the UK, been incorporated into (unregistered) design right, albeit with some special features.[161]

---

[159] CDPA 1988, s 213(1). See *Ocular Sciences v Aspect Vision Care* [1997] RPC 289; *Dyson v Qualtex (UK) Ltd* [2006] EWCA Civ 166; [2006] RPC 769. For what constitutes infringement, see, eg, *Wooley Jewellers v A&A Jewellery (No 2)* [2002] EWCA Civ 1119; [2004] FSR 932.

[160] ibid s 213(3). By special extension this right applies to the design of computer chips: Design Right (Semiconductor Topography) Regs 2006.

[161] See Design Right (Semiconductor Topographies) Regulation 1989, SI 1989/1100; introduced in implementation of EC Directive 87/54 (n 77 above).

F. Trade Marks and Names

(1) General

(a) Rights from trade use

In this separate sphere of intellectual property, the law does not protect ideas or **6.96**
information for their intrinsic value but for their value as a basic commercial tool.
The primary object in protecting trade marks, trade names, get up, packaging,
slogans, logos, etc is to ensure that they are not imitated by others so as to lead
to confusion of customers. That is because they are treated as signs which in a
general sense indicate the origin of the product or services. The starting point
of English law was to protect their actual use in trade. To this end the common
law developed actions against passing off and injurious falsehood. Additionally,
from 1875, a registration system for the protection of trade marks was established,
initially in respect of goods and latterly also for services.

(b) Rights through registration

Trade mark registration has been regarded as a supplementary form of protection, **6.97**
to be conferred only after careful examination. Nonetheless the system is today
in many senses dominant. A Community trade mark system has been created
alongside the national registers of member states.[162] Both are governed in the
main by the same basic principles. They grant rights which can be asserted
more simply and cheaply than by proving trade use. They may in many cases
provide legal protection before any trading has begun. They are available where
previously in Britain it was necessary to rely on the common law action against
passing off. Nevertheless the latter, being firmly based upon an actual reputation
in trade, continues to provide an important substratum of protection. Accordingly
we turn to it first.

(2) Common Law Liability: Passing Off

Liability for passing off is based upon three elements:[163] **6.98**

(1) the claimant must have an reputation with the public, established through
evidence of actual trade or advertising;

---

[162] See para 6.107.
[163] For this classical trinity, see Lord Oliver, *Reckitt & Colman v Borden* [1990] RPC 340, 499,
HL ('Jif' lemon); other formulations, often referred to, are by Lord Diplock and Lord Fraser, *Erven
Warnink v Townend* [1980] RPC 31, 93, 105–6, HL, ('Advocaat').

(2) the defendant must make misrepresentation to the public which is related to this reputation of the claimant; and

(3) the claimant must in consequence suffer damage or be about to do so.

(a) The claimant's reputation

6.99 The claimant's reputation may for instance be founded on a housemark ('British Airways', 'Sainsburys', the Rolls-Royce grille) or on a product mark ('Mini', 'Fiesta'). Where a mark or name has about it some other natural association—as in the case of a geographical name or a descriptive word, or a personal name—the claimant must show a secondary meaning, ie that the public has nevertheless come to associate the mark or name with its goods or services.[164] An enterprise can lose a reputation if it permits an originally distinctive mark to be regularly used as a description of a type of goods (as with 'Formica').[165]

6.100 It is possible for a group of separate traders to enjoy a concurrent reputation in a word or sign and for any one of them to sue to protect it.[166] It is the reputation which gives rise to business goodwill in England that is at stake. Some measure of actual business must therefore be conducted within the jurisdiction.[167] That business reputation must moreover continue: a claimant who has given up business and has no intention of returning to it may not sue in passing off.[168] The reputation attaches to that business and can only be transferred with the business as a whole, not as a separate item of property.

(b) The defendant's misrepresentation

6.101 The claimant must show that the defendant is causing at least a likelihood of confusion among a significant portion of the relevant public. This may be done by imitating a mark, commercial name or get up, or by supplying goods or services in response to an order which uses the mark. The defendant must be responsible for at least some ultimate confusion, as when it places deceptively labelled products in the hands of a knowing distributor; the action may then lie if that distributor intends to export the deceptive products to another country.[169]

---

164 *Reddaway v Banham* [1896] AC 199, HL ('Camel Hair Belting').

165 *Havana Cigar v Oddenino* [1924] 1 Ch 179, CA ('Corona' cigar: limited injunction where some still used the mark in a trade mark sense).

166 *Erven Warnink v Townend* [1980] RPC 31, HL ('Advocaat'); *Taittinger v Allbev* [1993] FSR 641, CA (elderflower champagne); and even *Chocosuisse v Cadbury* [1999] RPC 826, CA ('Swiss chocolate').

167 *Anheuser-Busch v Budejovicky Budvar* [1984] FSR 413, CA ('Budweiser').

168 *Star Industrial v Yap* [1976] FSR 256, JC ('Ace' toothbrush).

169 *Johnston v Orr-Ewing* (1882) 7 App Cas 219, HL.

Passing off retains the flexible character of a common law right. The sudden **6.102** popularity of the Internet has established the domain name as a novel form of desirable commercial symbol. This has induced a new form of unacceptable pre-emption– 'cyber-squatting': an interloper obtains a domain name consisting principally of the name of an internationally famous company or brand, not with a view to trading with it but in order to demand a substantial sum for its transfer. The practice has nonetheless been deemed fraudulent and so to amount to passing off.[170]

(c) Likelihood of damage

When the goods or services offered by both claimant and defendant are the **6.103** same or are very similar, the claimant will almost always suffer damage from the passing off. If, however, the goods or services are not the same, the claimant must show some reason why injury is likely to follow. This can be because the confusion will expose the claimant to useless litigation or to a lowering of reputation in general.[171]

A celebrity can protect his name or image when it is misappropriated to endorse **6.104** or market another's product or service.[172] However, it is difficult to maintain a passing off claim where the misappropriation is of fictitious characters from films and television series whose names or images are being used on lines of goods that have not been the subject of merchandising by the original producer.[173] An action is more likely to succeed where there is a copyright interest deserving protection (as where there are drawings of cartoon characters).[174]

(3) Common Law Liability: Injurious Falsehood

(a) Nature of the tort

Injurious falsehood is a tort distinct from both passing off and defamation. **6.105** It renders actionable false statements, written or oral, which are made with malice and which cause actual damage to the claimant or are likely to cause him damage, in the case where the publication is in writing and is calculated to cause

---

170 *British Telecom v One in a Million* [1999] FSR 1, CA. Alternatively, it may be removed or transferred by the Internet registration body after dispute resolution proceedings provided for by contract.

171 For example, *Annabel's v Shock* [1972] RPC 74 (name of nightclub taken for escort agency); cf *Stringfellow v McCain Foods* [1984] RPC 501, CA (name of nightclub permitted on oven chips).

172 *Irvine v Talksport* [2002] FSR 943.

173 *Wombles v Womble Skips* [1977] RPC 99. Elsewhere in the Commonwealth courts have tended to take a more protective view of personality and character merchandising.

174 *Mirage Studios v Counter-Feat Clothing* [1991] FSR 145.

pecuniary damage in respect of any office, profession, calling, trade or business carried on by the claimant at the time.[175] The requirement of malice continues to restrict the scope of this tort. This requires proof either that the defendant deliberately lied or else acted for some 'by or sinister purpose'.[176]

(b) Comparative advertising

6.106 In relation to marks for goods and services, injurious falsehood has a potential application in the field of comparative advertising.[177] An advertisement in which the advertiser makes untrue statements about a rival's products in order to promote his own will be actionable at common law. But the misstatement has to relate clearly to the other product and it has to involve a real disparagement that a reasonable man would take to be a serious claim.[178] It must, in other words, fall outside the day-to-day exaggerations which are endemic in advertising and which the public mostly recognize as such. In addition, malice will have to be shown, together with a likelihood of damage.

G. Registered Trade Marks

(1) Application Procedures

6.107 The registration of trade marks was the first aspect of intellectual property to be given a thoroughgoing European form. Alongside the national system operating through the Trade Marks Registry of the UK Patent Office,[179] there is an EU system for procuring a Community trade mark through OHIM in Alicante.[180] A Community mark has a unified effect throughout the EU and can therefore be enforced for the whole area in a single set of proceedings. Thanks to a First Directive on harmonization of trade mark law,[181] national law has been made to conform with the substantive principles of this European system. For Britain this is achieved by the Trade Marks Act 1994.

---

175 Defamation Act 1952, s 3.

176 *Serville v Constance* [1954] 1 All ER 662, 665 *per* Harman J.

177 See also para 6.123.

178 *White v Mellin* [1895] AC 154, HL; *De Beers Abrasive v International General Electric* [1975] FSR 45.

179 Set up by the Trade Marks Act 1875.

180 Established by Council Regulation 40/94 on the Community Trade Mark [1994] OJ L11/1; operative from 1996.

181 First Directive (EEC) 89/104 on the Approximation of Member States' Trade Mark Laws [1988] OJ L40/1.

In large measure the procedures for applying to register a mark through the **6.108**
OHIM and the British Registry are equivalent.[182] The OHIM does not of its own
initiative conduct a search in order to see whether there are 'relative' objections,
ie those arising from earlier conflicting rights. It relies on objection by third
party opponents to perform this function. In 2007 the UK registry adopted the
same approach. Standardized Community legislation is one thing; but given
the different traditions in trade mark registration across the countries of the
EU, uniformity of interpretation is another. In consequence the European
Court of Justice and its Court of First Instance have heavy case-loads in trade
mark matters.

(2) Delimitation of Scope and Classification

Trade marks are limited in their scope by the requirement that they be regis- **6.109**
tered for specified goods or services. Infringement of the right is then judged
against this listing;[183] and registrations which cover more than the rightholder's
own trade use may be cut back so as to allow another person to use the same or
a similar mark in the unused areas.[184] Goods and services are grouped according
to an internationally agreed system of classification, and applications to register
have to be made within one of the forty-two classes. But this classification is essentially an aid to searching the register. It has no direct effect on the scope of the
right ultimately granted.

(3) Registered Marks as Property

Registered marks are personal property in English law. This means that they are in **6.110**
principle capable of assignment and licensing. A legal foundation is thus provided, not just for the sale of marks as part of a business, but also for other common business practices, where marks are dealt with as part of a technology licence,
a distribution agreement, the franchising of market outlets, or the merchandising
of personalities, characters and symbols.

There is also a desire to deal in registrations simply as and for themselves for **6.111**
various business and fiscal reasons: an owner may, for instance, lose interest in a
particular mark and dispose of it to an independent buyer. But registration exists

---

[182] Accordingly reference will be made principally to the UK system established by the Trade
Marks Act 1994 (hereafter TMA 1994). A system which allows both British and Community applications to be linked to applications in other countries is provided by the Madrid Arrangement for
the International Registration of Marks, originally of 1891, which the UK has been enabled to
joined by the Madrid Protocol of 1989.

[183] See para 6.124.

[184] See para 6.121.

primarily to ensure that signs and symbols do distinguish the goods or services of one business from that of others. In earlier legislation it was therefore thought necessary to have the Registry oversee transfers and licences of marks, so as to ensure that they did not create any potential for confusion in the market.

6.112 Over time this has come to seem unnecessarily cautious, given that most of those who deal in marks will want them to remain positive symbols of the source of products or services. Accordingly, the present law no longer requires any formalities beyond a written instrument signed by the grantor and entry in the register. Ultimately, if a mark were to be used by its proprietor or a licensee in a way which led to the public being deceived, the registration itself might be rendered invalid. This could arise, for instance, if a well-established mark was allowed to be used by two independent businesses at the same time. Mark-owning enterprises which operate within complex business structures must not, by design or neglect, allow their marks to become 'muddied' in their meaning to the public.

(4) What can be a 'Trade Mark'?

6.113 In the new legislation, 'trade mark' is broadly defined to cover 'any sign capable of being represented graphically[185] which is capable of distinguishing goods or services of one undertaking from those of other undertakings'. This includes 'words (including personal names), designs, letters, numerals or the shape of goods or their packaging'.[186] Only the most unacceptable concepts will be ruled out as not being 'capable' of ever being a mark. The settled description of a thing, such as 'soap', can never be registrable for soap and probably not for a television series,[187] nor can a particular smell be registered for a perfume.

(5) 'Absolute' Grounds of Objection

6.114 Other less categorical objections will be dealt with under the general run of so-called 'absolute' objections to registration, where the word, symbol or get-up has some quality which renders it apparently 'non-distinctive'.[188] It may for instance

---

[185] Smells are very difficult to represent graphically either by simple or technical description: *Sieckmann v Deutsches Markenamt* [2002] ECR I- 11737. Sound marks can be easier to register: *Shield Mark v Kist* [2004] ECR I-14313.

[186] TMA 1994, s 1.

[187] Likewise the established name for a mumps vaccine: *'Jeryl Lynn' Trade Mark* [1999] FSR 491.

[188] TMA 1994, s 3(1). In some instances, it is possible to side-step the objection by disclaiming rights in the unacceptable part of the mark: s 13(1). 'Absolute' objections may also be raised where the mark is contrary to public policy or morality, is liable to deceive, would be contrary to law or is a state, official or royal emblem or the like: ss 3(3)–(5), 4. An application must be in good faith, a ground which may be used against those who seek to pre-empt the famous marks of foreign businesses: s 3(6).

describe a quality of the product or service ('titanium-coated', 'handmade', 'a treat'); it may have a geographical connotation or be recognized as a name ('Granada', 'Elvis');[189] it may be customarily in use or have some other 'non-distinctive' quality about it—for instance, where it is one or more letters, numerals or colours.[190]

There will be an 'absolute' objection where other traders in the same field could legitimately want to use the mark—as for instance with surnames.[191] However, unless the sign is considered quite incapable of ever being a trade mark, the initial objection may be overcome by producing sufficient evidence that the applicant has used the sign as a mark, so that it has become a distinctive indicator of source. The more serious the inherent objection, the stronger the countervailing evidence has to be.[192] In the past, sufficient cases have been made to secure the registration of, for instance, 'BP' for petrol, '999' for cigarettes and 'Smith' for clocks. At OHIM, this type of objection can easily become complicated: words and symbols vary in their linguistic and cultural impact from one country to another, and the position across the EU has to be brought into account.[193]   **6.115**

The registration of shape marks, both for goods and their packaging, introduced in the 1994 legislation, could lead to one competitor getting control over an actual form of the product itself, to the exclusion of others. Accordingly, these 'get-up' marks have not only to satisfy the general tests for distinctiveness but are also excluded if the shape results from the nature of the goods, or has a technical function, or adds substantial value. In consequence, the well-known triangular head of the 'Philishave' electric razor was refused registration: a trade mark could not be allowed to give a monopoly over so basic a feature of product design.[194]   **6.116**

(6) 'Relative' Grounds of Objection

(a) Identity and similarity

In general, the earlier applicant in time—the senior—has the better right to register a mark. Seniority can be established either by actual trade use which is enough to give a right to prevent passing off, or else by prior registration.[195] In the latter   **6.117**

---

[189] In the former case the question is whether the public would later take the name to indicate geographical origin, rather than business source: *Windsurfing Chiemsee v Huber* [1999] ECR I-2779, ECJ.

[190] For colours see *Libertel v BMB* [2003] ECR I-3793.

[191] *Nichols plc v Registrar of Trade Marks* [2005] 1 WLR 1418, ECJ.

[192] See *Windsurfing Chiemsee v Huber*, n 189 above.

[193] *Matratzen Concord v Hukla Germany* [2006] ETMR 771.

[194] *Philips v Remington* [2002] I-ECR 5475, ECJ. TMA 1994, s 3(2).

[195] The Paris Industrial Property Convention, Art 4, gives an international priority of six months.

case, difficulties arise over what is to count as giving priority. If the marks are the same and are to be for the same goods or services, there is an automatic objection. But if either the marks or the goods or services are merely similar, there is an objection only if the public is likely to be confused, judging the issue in the light of all the circumstances of the particular trade: types of display and advertising practices, visual and oral usage, and so on.[196] According to a controversial decision of the European Court of Justice, a mark which has a substantial reputation on the market is likely to lead to confusion with a wider range of similar marks than if it has no reputation.[197]

6.118 Confusion may occur directly, where the two marks are likely to be mistaken for one another; and also more inferentially, where the public can tell them apart but would think that they belonged to one business: as where the senior has a series of marks starting 'Porta-' and the junior wants one starting 'Porto-'.[198] It is not enough to show that the one suggests the other through some loose form of association, if there is not likely to be confusion about trade source.[199]

(b) Dilution

6.119 Exceptionally, an objection arises if the marks are identical or similar, yet the goods or services are not similar. The senior claimant has to show that it has a 'reputation' in the mark—recognition by a substantial portion of the purchasing public in a considerable part of the country[200]—and that use by the junior would be without due cause, taking unfair advantage of, or causing detriment to, that reputation. At least in the UK, it will prove difficult to substantiate such a case.[201] Instances of 'dilution' of marks onto different product lines will not into this category, if the courts also take a strict view of what goods and services are to be treated as 'similar'.[202]

---

[196] Attention is paid to the impression overall; and to the most striking features and the 'idea' of the mark. Again for the Community trade mark, the comparison is complicated by different linguistic and cultural expectations.

[197] *Canon Kabushiki Kaisha v Metro-Goldwyn-Mayer* [1998] ECR I-5507; and see generally *Lloyd Schuhfabrik Meyer v Klijsen* [1999] ECR I-3819, ECJ ('Lloyds'/'Loints' for shoes).

[198] *Portakabin v Powerblast* [1990] RPC 471.

[199] *Sabel v Puma* [1997] ECR I-6191, ECJ (rejecting a broader Benelux notion of 'association'). However, if the mark already has a reputation from trade, it can be brought into account in assessing likelihood of confusion: *Davidoff v Gofkid* [2003] ECR I-389, ECJ; *Adidas-Salomon v Fitnessworld* [2004] ETMR (10) 129, ECJ.

[200] For a Community Trade Mark, a considerable part of the EU.

[201] The inclusion of this third category of objection in the European framework results from pressure from the Benelux countries and elsewhere. Demonstrating that the public are confused about trade source will improve chances of success, but it seems that this is not always a necessary element—as where, for instance, the junior use would 'tarnish' the senior's reputation.

[202] *British Sugar v Robertson* [1996] RPC 261 (in particular circumstances, ice-cream topping and bread spread were treated as not 'similar').

(7) Removal of Marks from the Register

(a) Invalidity

Once a mark has been registered, it remains in effect, provided that the renewal **6.120**
fee is paid at ten-yearly intervals. If it should not have been registered initially,
because either an absolute or relative objection existed, then it may still be invalid
and liable to be expunged. However, if there was an absolute objection to the
distinctiveness of the mark, this may in the interim have been cured by sufficient
evidence of use. If there was a relative objection from a person with senior entitlement, this will cease to have effect where that person has acquiesced without
objection to the junior use in the country for five continuous years.[203]

(b) Revocation

(i) Non-use

A registration may fall prey to attack because of changes which have occurred **6.121**
since it was made.[204] With some frequency, registrations are revoked because
the mark has not been used for an uninterrupted period of five years. This may
be for all the goods or services specified or only for some, depending on what
has (not) happened. The use has to be a genuine effort at trading and not some
colourable attempt to keep a mark stock-piled for future use; or in order to
preclude a competitor from having it; or as a substitute for a mark that is too
descriptive to be registrable (as in the ghost-mark 'Nerit' for 'Merit').[205]

(ii) Mark becoming descriptive

A mark will be revocable if it can be shown to have become the standard descrip- **6.122**
tion of goods or services of a general type. Marks which approach this condition are peculiarly valuable—think of aspirin, shredded wheat, thermos, sellotape,
formica—and those who have built them up under trade mark registrations
need to work hard at promoting a different generic word and at objecting to
generic usage, particularly in dictionary definitions. The test under the present
law is, 'has the mark become a common name for a product or service in the
relevant trade, and not merely among consumers?'[206]

---

203 TMA 1994, s 48.
204 TMA 1994, s 46.
205 *Imperial Group v Philip Morris* [1982] FSR 72, CA; *La Mer Technology v Laboratoires Goemar*
[2004] ETMR 640, ECJ.
206 *Björnekula v Procordia* [2004] ETMR (69) 977, ECJ.

(iii) Mark becoming deceptive

6.123 A mark can also be revoked because it has become liable to mislead the public, particularly as to the nature, quality or geographical origin of the goods or services in question, but only where this follows from the use made of the mark by the proprietor or a person with his consent.[207]

(8) Infringement of a Registered Mark

(a) The types of case

6.124 Upon registration, the proprietor comes to occupy a senior position *vis-à-vis* competitors who wish to use an identical or similar mark. Accordingly, the equivalent tests apply in this obverse sense to those for the relative grounds of objection to an application: (1) if the marks and the goods or services are both identical, there is infringement; (2) if the marks or goods/services (or both) are only similar, then it must be shown that the relevant public is likely to be confused; and (3) additionally, there can be infringement of a mark with a reputation where it is used unfairly for dissimilar goods or services.

6.125 Once more difficulties arise in distinguishing between identity and similarity, similarity and dissimilarity, confusion and non-confusing 'association'. In approaching these issues the European Court of Justice has shown little inclination to accept invitations to view the trade mark right as a radically revised form of protection for any value which can be associated with the investment in the mark. Thus it has refused to hold that there is infringement when a non-authorized car dealer states that he deals and repairs a particular make, or a perfume distributor advertises parallel imports of legitimate products but only in an ordinary, rather than a dressed-up outlet.[208]

(b) In trade and in relation to goods or services

6.126 Whichever of the wide-ranging categories applies, an action infringes only if it is done in trade and in relation to the goods or services. Accordingly, although the Football Association held a registration of the England team logo for cards, a sweetmaker did not infringe by including photocards of the players which showed the logo on their shirts.[209] Moreover, a competitor is allowed to make honest use

---

[207] This could occur if the proprietor granted licences or assignments to unrelated businesses, without retaining any power to control quality, as in *Bowden Wire v Bowden Brake* [1914] 31 RPC 385, HL.

[208] *BMW v Deenik* [1999] ECR I-905, ECJ; *Parfums Christian Dior v Evora* [1997] I-6013, ECJ: only use of the mark in a way which would obviously prejudice the associations with it could amount to infringement.

[209] *Trebor Bassett v Football Association* [1997] FSR 211.

of his own name or address, and of descriptions of the quantity, quality and other characteristics of his goods or services; and he can indicate an intended purpose—for instance, where he says that his film is suitable for a 'Kodak' camera.[210]

(c) Comparative advertising

The broad definition of infringement could be held to prevent all comparative advertising which makes reference to another's goods or services by their trade mark. The TMA 1994 introduces an exception for this, except where the result goes beyond honest practices. English courts allow comparative advertisements under this provision unless there is some material dishonesty which goes beyond the general run of puffing at a rival's expense. It is acceptable to set out the relative advantages of one credit card against others, each of them named, even if other comparisons are omitted.[211] It would not be permissible to make a succession of detailed statements about the functioning of rival computers which are demonstrably false.[212] **6.127**

(d) Parallel importing

The use of trade mark rights to prevent parallel importation from another country is difficult to justify, since the primary purpose of protection is to maintain the mark as an indication of origin and with parallel imports there is no deception about source. Within the EU, trade mark rights may not be used in this way unless special circumstances arise.[213] This principle, initially derived from the EC Treaty, has been confirmed and extended by the Trade Mark Laws Harmonization Directive of 1989.[214] **6.128**

The European Court of Justice has held that it is not open to member states to adopt a principle of 'exhaustion' of the trade mark right, when goods connected with the mark-owner are imported from outside the EEA into some part of it.[215] If the connected goods are sold abroad without any notice that they are not to be exported into the EEA, this does not imply that they may then be taken there for commercial purposes[216] Trade mark law thus lowers a portcullis against the activities of parallel importers from outside 'Castle Europe'. **6.129**

---

[210] TMA 1994, s 11(2).

[211] For example, *Barclays Bank v RBS Advanta* [1996] RPC 307. The EU Directive on Comparative Advertising (97/55) defines what is and is not acceptable: *Pippig Augenoptik v Hartlauer* [2004] ETMR (5) 65.

[212] Cf *Compaq v Dell* [1992] FSR 93.

[213] See para 6.16. The exceptions so far identified in the case law, concern cases where the goods have been repackaged and relabelled with a different national trade mark: *Bristol-Myers Squibb v Paranova* Case C-427/93 [1996] ECR I-3457.

[214] Directive 89/104, Art 7; and see Council Reg 40/94, Art 12.

[215] *Silhouette v Hartlauer* [1998] ECR I-4799.

[216] *Zino Davidoff v A & G Imports* [2002] RPC 403, ECJ.

7

SUCCESSION

A. Introduction

The law of succession is concerned with the transfer or devolution of property on **7.01** death. It can be divided into two principal topics: the law of intestate succession and the law of wills. But there are other ways in which property which belongs to, or which may appear to belong to, an individual during his lifetime may pass on his death *other* than by his will or in accordance with the intestacy rules.

(a) Jointly owned property

7.02 English law provides for two forms of concurrent ownership of real or personal property.[1] Where there is a beneficial tenancy in common, each owner has a separate interest and, on his death, his share passes under his will or under the rules applicable to his intestacy. But where there is a beneficial joint tenancy, there is a single interest and a right of survivorship, the *jus accrescendi*. As each joint owner dies, his rights are extinguished and vest in the surviving joint owner(s). Beneficial joint ownership of real and personal property may be severed with the result that the joint tenancy is converted into a tenancy in common.[2] The creation of, and the failure to sever, a joint tenancy are both acts or omissions which are part of the law of succession in the wider sense;[3] and a will draftsman who fails to give adequate advice to a testator as to the severance of a joint tenancy may be held liable in negligence to an intended beneficiary whose gift is rendered ineffective by such failure.[4]

(b) Property held in trust

7.03 If an individual holds the legal, but not the beneficial, title to property then, on his death, although the legal title will pass under his will or under the intestacy rules applicable to his estate, the beneficial title will remain vested in the person who has beneficial title. This is obvious in the case of an express trust, but it is true also in the case of a resulting or a constructive trust.[5]

(c) Pension fund nominations

7.04 Contributory pension schemes often provide that if an employee, who would have received a pension on retirement, dies before reaching retirement age, the trustees of the pension fund will make a lump sum payment, often called a 'death in service payment'. The rules of the pension scheme will state to whom the payment may be made, and there is usually provision in the rules for the employee to nominate the person(s) he would like to benefit. Whether such a nomination is a testamentary disposition depends on whether the employee, during his lifetime, had an absolute beneficial interest in his share of the fund. If he had such an interest, the disposition of it is a testamentary disposition and the document making the nomination must comply with the formality rules applicable to testamentary

---

[1] See paras 4.354–4.382.

[2] C Harpum, *Megarry & Wade The Law of Real Property* (6th edn, 2000) ch 9, para 9–036. A *beneficial* joint tenancy may be severed, but not a *legal* joint tenancy: ibid para 9–050.

[3] See *Carr-Glynn v Frearsons* [1999] Ch 326, 336A, CA. 'On a proper analysis, the service of a notice of severance was part of the will-making process' (Chadwick LJ).

[4] ibid.

[5] Constructive trusts are most likely to arise where X and Y are cohabiting. For a more detailed discussion of constructive trusts, see Hanbury & Martin, *Modern Equity* (17th edn, 2005) chs 11 and 12. See also paras 2.106–2.110 and 4.159–4.160.

dispositions.[6] But, for tax reasons, the position in England and Wales is that an employee who contributes to a pension fund does not normally have a beneficial interest in the fund;[7] all he has is a power to nominate beneficiaries to receive benefits payable on his death. The nomination is not, in this case, a testamentary disposition and is not, therefore, subject to the Wills Act 1837 formality rules.[8] But the nomination may enable the employee, *de facto*, to control what happens to the money if he dies in service; and pension fund nominations may involve significant sums of money.[9]

(d) Statutory nominations

During the course of the nineteenth century, several statutes were passed which   **7.05** permitted someone entitled to certain forms of investments to dispose of them by a written nomination which became operative on his death. The effect was much like making a will, but the procedure was less formal. Statutory nominations were originally designed to be 'poor men's wills', with no need to involve lawyers. Investments which can, today, be disposed of by statutory nominations include sums not exceeding £5,000[10] payable by friendly societies,[11] by industrial and provident societies,[12] and by trade unions.[13] A statutory nomination, like a will, is ambulatory,[14] ie it has no effect until the nominator dies. But it differs from a will in that the age limit for making a statutory nomination is sixteen, whereas for a will it is normally eighteen; the formalities are different;[15] and whereas a later will generally revokes an earlier will, it does not revoke an earlier statutory nomination.

(e) Donationes mortis causa[16]

A *donatio mortis causa*—described by Buckley J in *Re Beaumont* as a gift 'of an   **7.06** amphibious nature. . .neither entirely *inter vivos* nor testamentary'[17]—has three principal characteristics: it must be made in contemplation of death within the near future;[18] it must be intended to be conditional on death;[19] and the donor

---

6 *Re MacInnes* [1935] 1 DLR 401, Canadian SC.
7 Contrast the position where the fund is held outside the United Kingdom, *Kempe v IRC* [2004] WTLR 955.
8 *Re Danish Bacon Co Ltd Staff Pension Fund Trusts* [1971] 1 WLR 248.
9 *Jessop v Jessop* [1992] 1 FLR 591, CA; *Gold v Hill* [1999] 1 FLR 54.
10 Administration of Estates (Small Payments) Act 1965, ss 2 and 6.
11 Friendly Societies Act 1974, ss 66 and 67.
12 Industrial and Provident Societies Act 1965, ss 23 and 24.
13 Trade Union and Labour Relations (Consolidation) Act 1992 s 17 and Sch 3 para 1(2).
14 See para 7.36.
15 The formalities for statutory nominations vary according to the statute.
16 The Latin expression *donatio mortis causa* means 'gift by cause of death'.
17 [1902] 1 Ch 889, 892.
18 *Re Craven's Estate (No 1)* [1937] Ch 423, 426.
19 ibid.

must part with dominion over the subject matter of the gift before his death. Parting with dominion may consist of actual delivery of the item of property, or a delivery of the means of obtaining a chattel, or the delivery of a document 'which amounts to a transfer'.[20] It seems that almost all forms of personalty, including shares and mortgages,[21] are capable of being the subject matter of a *donatio*, provided that there is delivery of a document which amounts to a transfer.[22] In *Sen v Hedley*[23] the Court of Appeal held that land itself could be the subject-matter of a *donatio*. Nourse LJ thought that *donationes mortis causa* are an anomaly in English law, but that 'anomalies do not justify anomalous exceptions'.[24] A *donatio* is revocable until the donor's death. It is automatically revoked if the donor recovers from the illness from which he contemplated death.[25] If there has been no revocation, it becomes absolute on his death.

B. Intestacy[26]

7.07 Where the deceased does not leave a will, or leaves a will which does not dispose of any beneficial interest in any of his property, he dies totally intestate. Where he leaves a will, but disposes of only part of his property, he dies partially intestate. The principal rules relating to intestacy are contained in the Administration of Estates Act 1925 as amended ('the Act').

(1) Total Intestacy

(a) Administration of assets

7.08 Part III of the Act deals with the administration of assets by the deceased's personal representatives before distribution to the beneficiaries.

(i) Power of sale

7.09 Section 33(1) of the Act provides that:

> On the death of a person intestate as to any real or personal estate, that estate shall be held in trust by his personal representatives with the power to sell it.[27]

---

[20] *Ward v Turner* (1752) 2 Ves Sen 431, 28 ER 275.
[21] *Duffield v Elwes* (1827) 1 Bli NS 497, 4 ER 959.
[22] ibid.
[23] [1991] Ch 425.
[24] [1991] Ch 425, 440, CA.
[25] *Staniland v Willott* (1850) 3 Mac & G 664, 42 ER 416.
[26] See CH Sherrin and RC Bonehill, *The Law and Practice of Intestate Succession* (3rd edn, 2004).
[27] The original section provided for a trust for sale with a power to postpone sale, rather than a power of sale. There appears to be little difference of substance.

(ii) Payment of debts and expenses

The personal representatives must pay the intestate's funeral, testamentary and **7.10** administration expenses, debts and other liabilities out of his ready money and the net money arising from disposing of any other part of his estate.[28]

(iii) The residuary estate

The residue of the money and any investments for the time being representing it, **7.11** and any part of the intestate's estate which remains unsold and is not required for administration purposes[29] is then known as the 'residuary estate' and is distributable among the persons beneficially entitled on intestacy under Part IV of the Act.

(b) Distribution of the residuary estate

The manner in which the residuary estate falls to be distributed depends upon **7.12** which of the deceased's relatives survive him. There are six possibilities.

(i) The deceased is not survived by a spouse or civil partner, but is survived by issue

Where the deceased is not survived by a spouse or civil partner, but is survived by **7.13** issue, ie lineal descendants, the issue take the entire estate on the statutory trusts to the exclusion of any other relative.

What are 'the statutory trusts'?   Under the statutory trusts, such of the intes- **7.14** tate's children as are living[30] at his death are beneficially entitled, if more than one in equal shares, subject to two qualifications:

(a) **subject to representation**, ie subject to the rule that such of the issue of a deceased child as are living at the intestate's death take that child's share, if more than one in equal shares, *per stirpes*.[31] So, if the deceased had three children and one of them died before him, leaving three children of his own surviving him, the deceased child's children would each take a third of their parent's third share.

(b) **subject to the rule that no child or other issue is entitled to a vested interest until he or she attains the age of eighteen years or marries under that age.** If an intestate leaves property worth £300,000 and has three children, two of whom are at least eighteen years of age, or are married, they will receive £100,000 each. If the third is not yet eighteen, he must wait to attain the age of eighteen, or marry, before he receives his share. If he dies before attaining eighteen, or marrying, his prospective share will go equally to his brother(s)

---

28 Administration of Estates Act 1925, s 33(2).
29 ibid s 33(4).
30 References to 'living' include a child (or issue) *en ventre sa mère* at the death: s 55(2).
31 *Per stirpes* means through each stock of descent, from the Latin *stirps* meaning the stock or stem of a plant.

and sister(s). The same rules apply to the deceased's grandchildren who take in place of their parents.

(ii) The deceased is survived both by a spouse, or by a civil partner, and by issue

7.15   The spouse, or civil partner, and issue take the entire estate between them, to the exclusion of any other relative.

7.16   **Civil partners.**   The Civil Partnership Act 2004, which came into force on 5 December 2005, gives same-sex couples who register their partnerships the same succession rights as married couples. To avoid the need for repetition, all references in this chapter to spouses include civil partners, and all references to marriages include civil partnerships.

7.17   **The surviving spouse.**   The deceased's surviving spouse is someone who was legally married to him at the time of his death. It does not matter how long the marriage lasted,[32] but it must have been lawful. A woman who goes through a ceremony of marriage with a man who, unbeknown to her, is married to someone else, is not legally married to him and is not his surviving spouse when he dies.[33] So-called 'common law' spouses have no entitlement on intestacy.[34] A marriage ends with a decree absolute of divorce.[35] If either spouse dies intestate while a separation order is in force and the parties to the marriage remain separated, the surviving spouse is treated as having died before the intestate and takes no beneficial interest.[36] If the intestate dies on or after 1 January 1996, then, in order to take any beneficial interest on his intestacy, the spouse must survive him by 28 days.[37] Other beneficiaries do not need to survive for any particular period and, in the case of other beneficiaries, where the order of deaths is uncertain, the younger is deemed to have survived the elder.[38]

7.18   **The surviving spouse's entitlement where there are issue.**   The spouse first takes *the personal chattels absolutely*. Section 55(1)(x) of the Act defines 'personal chattels' as:

> carriages, horses, stable furniture and effects (not used for business purposes), motor cars and accessories (not used for business purposes), garden effects, domestic animals, plate, plated articles, linen, china, glass, books, pictures, prints, furniture, jewellery,

---

[32]   *Re Park* [1954] P 89.

[33]   *Shaw v Shaw* [1954] 2 QB 429, CA.

[34]   Though they may have entitlements under the Inheritance (Provision for Family and Dependants) Act 1975, see para 7.227.

[35]   A civil partnership ends with a final dissolution order.

[36]   Family Law Act 1996, s 21. The surviving spouse may nevertheless apply to the court for provision under the Inheritance (Provision for Family and Dependants) Act 1975, see para 7.220.

[37]   Section 46 (2A), Administration of Estates Act 1925, inserted by s 1(1), Law Reform (Succession) Act 1995.

[38]   Law of Property Act 1925, s 184. See para 7.186.

articles of household or personal use or ornament, musical and scientific instruments and apparatus, wines, liquors and consumable stores, but do not include any chattels used at the death of the intestate for business purposes nor money or securities for money.

In applying this definition, the first question is whether an article comes within the ordinary meaning of the word used. For example, in *Re Crispin's Will Trusts*[39] 'furniture' included a collection of clocks and it did not matter that the collection was inherited; nor whether the clocks had been used by the intestate, or had been on loan to a museum. But user is sometimes relevant because the article must not be used for business purposes[40] and because articles of household or personal use or ornament fall within the definition.[41]

The spouse then takes the 'fixed net sum', colloquially referred to as *the statutory legacy*, with interest.[42] This sum is adjusted every few years by statutory instrument and was last fixed in 1993. If the intestate dies after 30 November 1993, the spouse's statutory legacy, where the intestate leaves issue, is £125,000.[43] It is payable free of death duties[44] and costs, with interest at the specified rate (6 per cent per annum since October 1983)[45] from the date of death until it is paid.   **7.19**

Lastly, the spouse takes *a life interest in one-half of the balance of the residuary estate*, ie the income from one-half of the balance after withdrawing the personal chattels and providing for the statutory legacy and interest. A surviving spouse who is entitled to a life interest under this head may elect to have it redeemed and to receive its capital value from the personal representatives.[46] The surviving spouse must elect for redemption within twelve months of the date of the grant of representation to the intestate's estate by giving written notice to the personal representatives.[47]   **7.20**

The spouse has a right to *appropriate the matrimonial home*. The personal representatives have a statutory power of appropriation of assets in favour   **7.21**

---

[39] [1975] Ch 245, CA.

[40] *Re Ogilby* [1942] Ch 288, cattle used for farming not personal chattels.

[41] *Re Reynolds' Will Trusts* [1966] 1 WLR 19; *Re Crispin's Will Trusts* [1975] Ch 245, CA.

[42] Administration of Estates Act 1925, s 46(2).

[43] Family Provision (Intestate Succession) Order 1993, SI 1993/2906. In June 2005, the Department for Constitutional Affairs published a Consultation Paper, CP 11/05, reviewing the statutory legacy and suggesting that it be more than doubled, to £350,000 where the deceased leaves issue. This suggestion has not been adopted, but the amount of the statutory legacy is likely to be increased, though not doubled, in the near future.

[44] The term 'death duties' is used in Administration of Estates Act 1925, s 46(1), (2) and now means inheritance tax. Transfers between spouses are normally free of inheritance tax: Inheritance Tax Act 1984, s 18.

[45] Intestate Succession (Interest and Capitalization) Order 1977 (Amendment) Order 1983, SI 1983/1374.

[46] Administration of Estates Act 1925, s 47A.

[47] ibid s 47A(6).

of beneficiaries,[48] but a beneficiary who wishes to take a particular asset of the estate cannot normally require the personal representatives to exercise this power in his favour. The Second Schedule to the Intestates' Estates Act 1952[49] gives the surviving spouse a special right to *require* the personal representatives to appropriate the intestate's interest in a dwelling-house in which the surviving spouse was resident at the intestate's death: the appropriation is to be made in or towards satisfaction of any absolute interest[50] of the surviving spouse in the intestate's estate, or partly in satisfaction of that interest and partly in return for the payment of equality money by the surviving spouse.[51] This special right must be exercised within twelve months of the date of the grant of representation to the intestate's estate by the spouse's giving written notice to the personal representatives.[52] The intestate's interest in the dwelling-house is to be appropriated at its value at the time of the appropriation, not at the time of the intestate's death.[53]

7.22 **Entitlement of the issue where there is a surviving spouse.** Subject to the beneficial interests of the surviving spouse, the residuary estate is held for the issue on the statutory trusts.[54] In practice, the spouse's entitlement to the personal chattels and to the statutory legacy often exhausts the estate. This is particularly likely to be the case if the intestate and the spouse were beneficial joint tenants in the matrimonial home or in other property of value, because such property vests in the surviving spouse, as surviving joint tenant, before the spouse's entitlement to the statutory legacy is calculated.

(iii) The deceased is not survived by issue: but is survived by a spouse, by a parent, by a brother or sister of the whole blood, or by the issue of a brother or sister of the whole blood[55]

7.23 **The surviving spouse's entitlement in this case.** The surviving spouse is entitled to the *personal chattels* and to a *statutory legacy of £200,000.*[56] Interest is again payable.[57] Finally, the surviving spouse is entitled to the *capital of one-half of the balance absolutely.*

---

[48] Administration of Estates Act 1925, s 41.

[49] Intestates' Estates Act 1952, Sch 2, para 5 (2).

[50] This includes the statutory legacy and the capital value of a life interest which the surviving spouse has elected to have redeemed.

[51] *Re Phelps* [1980] Ch 275, CA.

[52] Intestates' Estates Act Sch 2, para 3(1)(c).

[53] *Re Collins* [1975] 1 WLR 309.

[54] Administration of Estates Act 1925, s 46(1) and 47(1).

[55] Brothers and sisters of the *whole* blood have the same father *and* mother; brothers and sisters of the *half* blood have the same father *or* mother.

[56] See n 43. The Department for Constitutional Affairs suggested in the 2005 Consultation Paper that, where the deceased did not leave issue, the statutory legacy should be increased from £200,000 to £650,000.

[57] As under head (ii), para 7.19.

The entitlement of the parents or of the brothers and sisters. Subject to the **7.24**
beneficial interests of the surviving spouse, the residuary estate of the intestate is
held in trust for the intestate's parents. Surviving parents take in equal shares absolutely; if only one survives the intestate, that one parent takes absolutely. If neither
parent survives, the intestate's brothers and sisters of the whole blood take the
share which their parents would have taken. The brothers and sisters take on the
statutory trusts and these correspond to the statutory trusts for the intestate's
issue;[58] so brothers and sisters take only if they attain eighteen or marry, and the
children of a dead brother or sister take in his or her place.[59] It is even more probable in this case that the spouse's entitlement to the personal chattels and to the
statutory legacy will exhaust the estate and that the intestate's parents and brothers
and sisters will obtain no beneficial interest.

*(iv)   The deceased is survived by a spouse but not by issue, or by a parent, or by a
brother or sister of the whole blood, or by issue of such a brother or sister*

The surviving spouse takes the entire residuary estate absolutely,[60] regardless of   **7.25**
its size.

*(v)   The deceased is survived neither by a spouse nor by issue, but is survived by a
specified relative*

A specified relative is a grandparent of the intestate, or someone who is descended   **7.26**
from a grandparent. More distant relatives, such as second cousins, are not
specified relatives. The residuary estate of the intestate is held in trust for the
specified relatives of the intestate in the order set out below.[61] Anyone who takes
a vested interest under a particular paragraph excludes anyone falling under a later
paragraph.

(a) **Parents.** Surviving parents take in equal shares absolutely; if only one survives
     the intestate, he takes absolutely.
(b) **Brothers and sisters of the whole blood on the statutory trusts.** The statu-
     tory trusts applicable here (and under (c), (e) and (f) below) correspond to
     those for the intestate's issue.[62]
(c) **Brothers and sisters of the half blood on the statutory trusts.**
(d) **Grandparents.** Surviving grandparents take in equal shares absolutely; if only
     one survives the intestate, that grandparent takes absolutely.

---

58 Administration of Estates Act 1925, s 47(3).
59 Provided they attain 18 or marry.
60 Administration of Estates Act 1925, ss 46(1)(i) and 47(2)(b) and (4).
61 ibid s 46(1).
62 ibid s 47(3); para 7.14.

(e) **Uncles and aunts of the whole blood, on the statutory trusts.** An uncle or aunt of the whole blood must be a brother or sister of the whole blood of a parent of the intestate—ie an uncle or aunt by birth, not by marriage.

(f) **Uncles and aunts of the half blood, on the statutory trusts.** Such an uncle or aunt must be a brother or sister of the half blood of a parent of the intestate.

(vi) The deceased leaves no surviving spouse, and no issue or other relative of the intestate attains a vested interest under the rules set out under headings (i)–(v) above

7.27 The Crown[63] takes the residuary estate of the intestate as *bona vacantia*.[64] The Crown in its discretion may provide out of the estate for dependants of the intestate, whether or not related to him, and for other persons for whom the intestate might reasonably have been expected to make provision.[65]

(c) Adopted and illegitimate children, children born by artificial insemination

(i) Adopted child

7.28 Under the Adoption Act 1976, an adopted child is treated for purposes of intestacy as the child of the married couple who adopted him (or, in any other case, as the child of his adopter), and not as the child of his natural parents.[66]

(ii) Illegitimate child

7.29 Under section 18 of the Family Law Reform Act 1987, references to any relationship between two persons are to be construed without regard to whether the father and mother of either of them (or of any person through whom the relationship is deduced) were married to each other at any time. This section applies if the intestate dies after 3 April 1988 and reverses the common law rule. A legitimated child, ie one whose parents married one another after he was born, has been entitled since 1976 to take any interest on intestacy as if he had been born legitimate.[67]

(iii) Artificial insemination

7.30 Section 27 of the Family Law Reform Act 1987 states that where a child is born to a married woman as the result of artificial insemination, the child will be treated as the child of the woman and her husband *unless* it is proved that the woman's husband did not consent to the insemination. The Human Fertilization and Embryology Act 1990 covers the case where an embryo, or a sperm and eggs, are placed in a woman who then gives birth to the child. Section 27 of this Act states

---

63 Or Duchy of Lancaster, or Duchy of Cornwall.

64 Administration of Estates Act 1925, s 46(1)(vi). *Bona vacantia* are things which no person can claim as property.

65 ibid s 46(1)(vi).

66 ibid s 39: as to adoption by one of the child's natural parents see s 39(3), and as to protection of personal representatives see s 45.

67 Legitimacy Act 1976, ss 5(1)–(4) and 10(1).

that the woman who carries the child is to be treated as the child's mother and section 28 says that her husband will be treated as the child's father unless it is shown that he did not consent to the placing.[68]

(2) Partial Intestacy

A partial intestacy arises where the deceased effectively disposes of some, but not all, **7.31** of the beneficial interest in his property by will. Most partial intestacies arise because a residuary gift under the will lapses.[69] For example, the testator makes a will leaving legacies to X, Y, and Z and the residue to his wife, who predeceases him. The gifts to X, Y and Z take effect, and the residue passes as it would on intestacy: ie the intestacy rules take effect subject to the provisions contained in the will.[70]

(a) Rules as to administration on a partial intestacy

Both the power of sale and the direction to the personal representatives to pay **7.32** funeral, testamentary and administration expenses, debts and liabilities[71] apply on a partial intestacy. Section 33(2) provides that the personal representatives shall set aside a fund sufficient to provide for any pecuniary legacies bequeathed by the will. Section 33(7) confirms that the section 'has effect subject to the provisions contained in the will'.

(b) Rules as to distribution on a partial intestacy

Where there is a partial intestacy, s 49(1) of the Act states that Part IV of the Act **7.33** (the part which deals with distribution on intestacy) applies to any of the deceased's property not effectively disposed of by his will, subject to the provisions contained in the will. Section 49(1) operates as if the legislature had inserted at the end of every deceased's will an ultimate gift of any undisposed property (or interest in property) in favour of the persons beneficially entitled on intestacy.[72]

(3) Hotchpot[73]

Where the deceased died on or before 31 December 1995, the hotchpot rules **7.34** sometimes applied. Hotchpot applied both on a total and on a partial intestacy where the deceased had, during his lifetime, made advancements, ie significant

---

[68] If the sperm is that of the woman's husband, he will *be* the child's father—see s 28(2)(b).
[69] See para 7.185.
[70] *Re Thornber* [1937] Ch 29, CA; *Re Sullivan* [1930] 1 Ch 84.
[71] Administration of Estates Act 1925, ss 33(1) and (2) respectively.
[72] *Re McKee* [1931] 2 Ch 145, 161, CA.
[73] The word 'hotchpot' comes from the French *hochepot*, a dish shaken up. The principle behind hotchpot is that descendants are entitled to an equal share of their ancestor's property and advances should be accounted for.

gifts, to a child, *or* had made payments on the marriage of a child.[74] Hotchpot also applied on a partial intestacy where the will conferred benefits on a surviving spouse or on issue.[75] In these cases the child, spouse or issue (as the case might be) had to bring into account the advancements or benefits he had received and set them against his entitlement under the deceased's intestacy. The provisions were complicated and were repealed by the Law Reform (Succession) Act 1995 in relation to persons dying on or after 1 January 1996.[76]

C. Wills

(1) The Nature and Contents of Wills

(a) Wills described

7.35 A will is the expression by a person of wishes which he intends to take effect only at his death.

(i) A will is ambulatory and is revocable until death

7.36 A will has no effect until the testator dies.[77] This is the basic characteristic of a will and it is usually expressed by saying that a will, by its very nature, is ambulatory until the testator's death. A will cannot confer benefits whilst the testator is still alive. Another characteristic of a will is that it is, by its very nature, revocable by the testator until his death. A declaration by a testator in his will that it is irrevocable does not prevent him from subsequently revoking it.[78]

(ii) A document intended to take effect only at death is a will

7.37 A document intended by a person to be his will is usually worded so as to describe itself as his 'will'. If the document is intended to be supplementary to a will, it is usually described as a 'codicil'. But it is not necessary for a document which is intended to operate as a will or as a codicil to describe itself as such. Whatever form it takes, any document can be proved as a will or codicil if (1) the person executing it intended it to take effect only at his death and (2) it was duly executed.[79]

---

[74] Administration of Estates Act 1925, s 47(1)(iii).

[75] ibid s 49(1)(aa) and (a).

[76] It might have been better to have reformed, than to have repealed, them, see R Kerridge, 'Reform of the Law of Succession' [2007] Conv 47.

[77] Though revocation of an earlier will by a later will (or codicil) takes effect when the later will is executed; subsequent revocation of the later will does not revive the earlier will; see para 7.123.

[78] *In the Estate of Heys* [1914] P 192, 197.

[79] See para 7.59.

(iii) Ascertaining intention

In deciding whether a document can be proved as a will or codicil, the court ascer- **7.38**
tains the intention of the person who executed it, both from the language of the
document and from extrinsic evidence. If the document appears on its face to be
testamentary, a rebuttable presumption arises that the deceased intended it to take
effect only at his death. An unusual example of the presumption was *Re Berger*,[80]
where a Hebrew manuscript—a 'zavah', which had been duly executed in accordance with the Wills Act 1837—was admitted to probate.

(iv) Comparison with an inter vivos disposition by deed

Unlike a will, an *inter vivos* disposition of property by deed takes effect forthwith; **7.39**
or, if the deed is executed by the grantor conditionally on the occurrence of some
event other than his own death, it takes effect on the occurrence of that event.
If, however, the condition is that the deed shall take effect only at the grantor's
death, it cannot take effect as a disposition *inter vivos*[81] but can operate only as a
will or codicil and must, therefore, be duly executed as a will.

A settlement of property does not become a will merely because it postpones **7.40**
the possession of property by, or even the vesting of property in, a beneficiary until
the death of the settlor. A settlement may be a valid *inter vivos* settlement, if it
settles property on the settlor for life and then on someone else on his death.
Such a settlement takes effect when it is made and is neither ambulatory nor
revocable.[82]

(v) A testator can leave only one will

The word 'will' is often used in the sense of denoting a particular document or a **7.41**
particular expression by a testator of his testamentary intentions—eg 'the deceased
made two wills, one dealing with his house and furniture and the other covering
his business', or 'he made a will and then made three codicils to cover changes
which had taken place in his family circumstances'. But as the Privy Council
pointed out in *Douglas-Menzies v Umphelby*,[83] however many testamentary documents a testator may leave:

> it is the aggregate or the net result that constitutes his will, or, in other words, the
> expression of his testamentary wishes. . . . In this sense it is inaccurate to speak of a
> man leaving two wills; he does leave, and can leave, but one will.[84]

---

80 [1990] Ch 118, CA.
81 *Governors and Guardians of the Foundling Hospital v Crane* [1911] 2 KB 367, CA.
82 A settlement could be revocable *if* the settlor has a power to resettle.
83 [1908] AC 224, 233, PC.
84 Quoted and applied by Sir Denys Buckley in *Re Berger* [1990] Ch 118, CA.

(b) Conditional wills

7.42   A will may be conditional, but such a will must be conditional on its face. So, a testator may state in his will that he intends it to take effect only if some specified condition is satisfied: for example '. . . in case anything should happen to me during the remainder of the voyage. . .'.[85] If the specified condition is not satisfied, the will does not take effect. A testator cannot, by words or conduct outside the terms of his will, impose upon his execution of it a condition which postpones or qualifies its operation. If a testator executes a will which appears on its face to be unconditional, but he intends that it shall become effective only on the fulfilment of an unstated condition, he lacks the necessary *animus testandi*—the intention needed to make a will—and the execution will be invalid. So, where a testatrix executed a will, which was unconditional on its face, but she intended that it should take effect once she had made an *inter vivos* gift, the will was invalid, and remained so even when the condition was fulfilled.[86]

7.43   The next problem is to distinguish between a condition and a reason for making a will. Either may be stated on the face of the will. A testator may refer in his will to the possibility that he may die during the course of a dangerous journey, or while engaged in some hazardous sport. In such a case, he may be imposing a condition, ie he may be saying that the will is to take effect only if he dies in the manner specified; or he may be referring to the danger merely to explain why he has decided to make a will at this time. If he dies otherwise than in the manner specified, a conditional will does not take effect; but an unconditional will, made because the testator thought that there was a particular urgency because of impending danger, does take effect.[87] It is a question of construction whether words used show a conditional will, or simply refer to a possible future event in order to show the testator's reason for making his will.[88] A will draftsman should make it clear whether he is inserting a condition in a will, or merely reciting the reason why the will is being made. Conditional wills are likely to be rare; it is not often that a testator would want his will to take effect if he dies from a particular cause but not to take effect if he dies in some other way.

7.44   A conditional will must be distinguished from a conditional gift in a will. For instance, a gift by will of '£1,000 to X, if he has qualified as a doctor' is a conditional gift: if X does not satisfy the specified condition, the gift to him fails; but the will as a whole is unconditional and still takes effect.

---

[85] *In the Goods of Robinson* (1870) LR 2 P & D 171.

[86] *Corbett v Newey* [1998] Ch 57, CA.

[87] An example of an unconditional will, made because the testator contemplated a dangerous undertaking, is *In the Goods of Dobson* (1866) LR 1 P & D 88.

[88] See *In the Goods of Cawthorn* (1863) 3 Sw & Tr 417, 164 ER 1336.

(c) Solicitor's duty of care in preparation of will

(i) Solicitor's duty to client

If a testator employs a solicitor to prepare a will for him containing a gift to a benefi- **7.45**
ciary and, owing to the solicitor's negligence, the gift to the beneficiary fails to take
effect, the solicitor is liable in damages to the testator both in contract and in tort.[89]
If the testator discovers during his lifetime that the gift to the beneficiary is void,
the damages recoverable by the testator are the costs of making a new and valid will,
or otherwise putting matters right.[90] But if the discovery is made after the testator's
death, it seems that the testator's estate would recover only nominal damages.[91]

(ii) Solicitor's duty to beneficiary under will

In *White v Jones*,[92] the House of Lords held, by a bare majority, that where a client **7.46**
had given instructions to a solicitor for the drawing up of a will for execution, and
where, as a result of the solicitor's negligence, an intended legatee under the will
was reasonably foreseeably deprived of a legacy, the solicitor was liable to the
intended legatee for the loss of the legacy. The result was achieved by extending
the assumption of responsibility principle.[93] In *Esterhuizen v Allied Dunbar
Assurance PLC*,[94] the principle in *White v Jones* was held to apply not only to a
solicitor, but to a company offering a will-making service.[95]

It was held in *Clarke v Bruce Lance & Co*[96] that a solicitor would not be liable to a **7.47**
beneficiary if there were a conflict between the duty owed to the client and the duty
owed to the beneficiary; or if there were a danger of 'double liability' or 'double
recovery', so that the solicitor was liable both to the client's executors and to
the beneficiary.[97] In *Carr-Glynn v Frearsons*,[98] the Court of Appeal held that a
solicitor who failed to advise a client that a notice of severance should be served—to
ensure that the client's interest in property held on a beneficial joint tenancy was

---

[89] *Ross v Caunters* [1980] Ch 297, 306–8; *White v Jones* [1995] 2 AC 207, 262, HL. Whether
a solicitor has a duty to draw his client's attention to the effect of marriage on a will (para 7.110)
depends on the circumstances: *Hall v Meyrick* [1957] 2 QB 455, 475–6 and 482, CA.

[90] *Ross v Caunters* [1980] Ch 297, 303. In some cases, the testator may change his mind and
decide that he does not want to put things right; see *Hemmens v Wilson Browne* [1995] Ch 223.

[91] *Ross v Caunters* [1980] Ch 297, 302; *White v Jones* [1995] 2 AC 207, 262, HL.

[92] [1995] 2 AC 207, HL.

[93] The House of Lords came to the same conclusion as Megarry V-C had come to in *Ross v
Caunters* (see n 89 above), though by adopting different reasoning.

[94] [1998] 2 FLR 668.

[95] But see also *Atkins v Dunn & Baker* [2004] EWCA Civ 263; [2004] WTLR 477, CA, solicitors under no duty to chase client who did not execute will.

[96] [1988] 1 WLR 881, CA.

[97] It is submitted that these principles are clearly correct, though their application to the facts of
Clarke v Bruce Lance causes some problems; see R Kerridge and AHR Brierley, 'Will-Making and
the Avoidance of Negligence Claims' [1999] Conv 399.

[98] [1998] 4 All ER 225, CA.

converted into a tenancy in common and able to pass under the client's will to an intended beneficiary—was liable to the intended beneficiary.

7.48 It is suggested in para 7.96 that a finding of lack of knowledge and approval generally implies misconduct by someone involved in the preparation of the will. Where a will has been prepared by, or its execution has been supervised by, a professional will draftsman, and it is subsequently held that the testator lacked knowledge and approval, it is possible that an action might be brought against the draftsman, seeking the recovery of the costs involved in setting the will aside. There is, as yet, no record of such an action having succeeded in England. Where the will is set aside, then, if an action is to be brought against the draftsman, it should be brought not by those who benefit under an earlier will, or intestacy, as the case may be, but by the personal representatives on behalf of the estate.[99]

(d) Contents of a will

(i) Disposal of property

7.49 The main function of a will is to dispose of the testator's property after his death. By his will the testator may make gifts, either directly to persons beneficially, or to trustees upon trust. These gifts may be legacies or devises.

(ii) Legacies and devises

7.50 Legacies (or bequests) are dispositions by will of personal property (or personalty). Devises are dispositions of real property (or realty). Personal property consists of moveables and leases; real property consists of freehold land and incorporeal hereditaments such as easements. Although leaseholds are personalty, they are akin to realty and are sometimes known as 'chattels real'.

(iii) Specific and general legacies and devises

7.51 Legacies may be specific, general, or demonstrative. Devises may be specific or general. The difference between specific, general and demonstrative legacies and devises is explained in section D below;[100] and the significance of the distinction is explained in section E.[101]

(iv) Appointment of executors

7.52 Apart from disposing of the testator's property, a will may (and should) appoint one or more executors to administer the testator's estate after his death.[102]

---

99 See the English case of *Worby v Rosser* [1999] Lloyd's Rep P N 972, CA; and the New Zealand case of *Knox v Till* [2002] WTLR 1147.

100 See paras 7.160–7.164.

101 See paras 7.176–7.179.

102 See section F.

(v) The testator's body

The law recognizes no property in the dead body of a human being. It follows **7.53**
that a testator cannot by will dispose of his dead body: a direction in a will to executors to deliver the testator's dead body to another person is, therefore, void.[103]
The executors are entitled to the custody and possession of the testator's dead
body until it is buried, and the duty of disposing of the body falls primarily
on them.[104]

If a deceased has expressed wishes during his lifetime as to the disposal of his body, **7.54**
either in his will or otherwise, these wishes are generally not legally enforceable
against his personal representatives, although they may well have effective moral
force. For instance, wishes expressed in favour of, or against, cremation have only
moral force. Certain wishes, however, have some legal effect. Thus, under the
Human Tissue Act 1961, if a person, either in writing at any time or orally in the
presence of two witnesses during his last illness, requests that his body or some
specified part be used after his death for therapeutic purposes or for purposes of
medical education or research, the person lawfully in possession of his body after
his death may authorize this.[105] In the absence of such a request, the person lawfully in possession of the body may authorize this if, having made such reasonable
inquiry as may be practicable, he has no reason to believe that the deceased had
expressed an objection to his body being so dealt with after his death.[106]

A testator needs to ensure that his wishes as to the disposal of his body are quickly **7.55**
brought to the notice of the person in possession of it after his death. The best
course is, in addition to including directions for the disposal of his body in his will,
either to make his wishes known openly in his lifetime, or to express his wishes in
a letter left with his executors and to be opened immediately after his death.

(vi) Appointment of testamentary guardians

The law in relation to guardianship was modified and simplified by the Children **7.56**
Act 1989. A parent who has parental responsibility for his child may appoint
another individual to be the child's guardian in the event of his death;[107] and a
guardian may appoint someone else to take his place in the event of his own
death;[108] *but* the guardian's appointment normally takes effect only when the

---

[103] *Williams v Williams* (1882) 20 Ch D 659.

[104] *Rees v Hughes* [1946] KB 517, CA.

[105] Human Tissue Act 1961, s 1(1).

[106] ibid s 1(2): he must also have no reason to believe that the surviving spouse or any surviving
relative of the deceased objects.

[107] Children Act 1989, s 5(3).

[108] ibid s 5(4).

child no longer has a parent who has parental responsibility for him.[109] The appointment of a guardian may be made by will or in writing, signed and dated.[110] If an appointment is by will, it is revoked by revocation of the will[111] and also by a later written appointment.[112]

(vii) Exercise of testamentary powers of appointment

7.57 By his will the testator may exercise any power of appointment conferred on him and exercisable by will. For instance, he may under a settlement have a life interest in the settled property and a power to appoint the remainder interest by will among his children or remoter issue.

(2) The Making of Wills: Formalities

(a) Formal wills

7.58 The formalities prescribed for making a will are designed to provide a safeguard not only against forgery and undue influence but also against hasty or ill-considered dispositions:[113] the formalities emphasize the importance of the act of making a will. Before s 9 of the Wills Act 1837 came into force on 1 January 1838, there were different formalities for wills relating to different sorts of property. For example, the formalities required for a will intended to devise freeholds were different from the formalities required for a will intended to bequeath leaseholds.[114] The original s 9, first enacted in 1837, was amended by the Wills Act Amendment Act 1852;[115] s 17 of the Administration of Justice Act 1982 then substituted a new s 9; but the change from the original s 9 to the substituted section was more a change of form than of substance.

7.59 If a testator dies after 31 December 1982, the substituted s 9 provides that:

No will shall be valid unless—
(a) it is in writing, and signed by the testator, or by some other person in his presence and by his direction; and
(b) it appears that the testator intended by his signature to give effect to the will; and

---

[109] ibid s 5(8). Before the 1989 Act came into force, the guardian normally acted jointly with the surviving parent.

[110] Children Act 1989, s 5(5). Before 1989 the appointment had to be by *deed* or will.

[111] ibid s 6(4).

[112] ibid s 6(1).

[113] Law Reform Committee's 22nd Report, *The making and revocation of wills* Cmnd 7902 1980, 3.

[114] Holdsworth, *A History of English Law* Vol XV, 172.

[115] Otherwise known as Lord St Leonards' Act. The original s 9, as amended in 1852, applies to any testator who died before 1 January 1983.

(c) the signature is made or acknowledged by the testator in the presence of two or more witnesses present at the same time; and

(d) each witness either—

    (i) attests and signs the will; or

    (ii) acknowledges his signature,

in the presence of the testator (but not necessarily in the presence of any other witness), but no form of attestation shall be necessary.

Section 9 applies to all wills required to be executed in accordance with English internal law, except the wills of privileged testators[116] and 'statutory wills' of mentally disordered persons.[117]

(i) Requirements of section 9

Section 9 has five requirements.

7.60

(1) The will must be in writing. A will must be in writing, but there are no restrictions as to the materials on which, or by which, it may be written, or as to which language[118] may be used. It may be handwritten or typed and a printed form may be used. A will may be made in pencil, or in ink, or in a combination of the two, but there is a presumption that the pencil writing in such a combination is only deliberative and it will be excluded from probate unless the court decides that it represented the testator's definite intention.[119]

7.61

(2) The will must be signed by the testator or in his presence and by his direction. The testator usually signs his own name but he may use an assumed name,[120] and any mark—such as a cross—which is intended by the testator to be his signature will suffice. Initials,[121] a stamped signature,[122] an inked thumb mark,[123] and 'a sort of broken line'[124] have all been held sufficient if intended by the testator as his signature; and it does not matter that the testator's hand was guided by another person.[125] A seal, by itself, is probably not sufficient:[126] although a seal intended as a signature may suffice.[127] If a testator starts to sign his name but

7.62

---

[116] See paras 7.73–7.76.

[117] See paras 7.78 and 7.79.

[118] *Whiting v Turner* (1903) 89 LT 71 (will written in French).

[119] *In the Goods of Adams* (1872) LR 2 P & D 367.

[120] In *In the Estate of Cook* [1960] 1 WLR 353 'Your loving mother' was held to be a valid signature.

[121] *In the Goods of Savory* (1851) 15 Jur 1042.

[122] *In the Goods of Jenkins* (1863) 3 Sw & Tr 93, 164 ER 1208.

[123] *In the Estate of Finn* (1935) 105 LJP 36 ('merely a blot' as his thumb slipped and the mark smudged).

[124] *In the Estate of Holtam* (1913) 108 LT 732.

[125] *Wilson v Beddard* (1841) 12 Sim 28, 59 ER 1041.

[126] *Smith v Evans* (1751) 1 Wils KB 313, 95 ER 636.

[127] *In the Estate of Bulloch* [1968] NI 96, 99.

is too weak to complete the signature, this will be sufficient.[128] The will does not have to be signed by the testator. It may be signed by some other person, provided it is signed in the testator's presence and by his direction. This other person may be one of the attesting witnesses[129] and may sign either the testator's name or his own.[130] If a will is written on more than one page, all the pages should be securely attached—in order to avoid the risk of accidental loss or the risk that the will may be tampered with. It has, however, been held that a will is properly executed if the pages are not attached but are held together by the testator's finger and thumb[131] or pressed together on a table by the testator with his hand.[132]

7.63 **(3) The testator must intend by his signature to give effect to the will.** The original s 9 required that the testator's signature had to be 'at the foot or end' of the will; the substituted s 9[133] does not so require. In *Wood v Smith*[134] the testator made a holograph will[135] which began with the words 'My will by Percy Winterbone. . .' and did not sign the will anywhere else. The Court of Appeal, upholding the trial judge, held that this was the testator's signature, and that there was no problem about its position.[136] Under the substituted s 9, a will is invalid unless 'it appears that the testator intended by his signature to give effect to the will'. *Wood v Smith*[137] establishes that extrinsic evidence[138] may be admitted to show that the testator intended by his signature to give effect to the will and that the testator's signature can give effect to dispositive provisions written after the signature, provided that the signing and the writing of the will are 'all one operation'.[139]

7.64 **(4) The testator's signature must be made or acknowledged in the presence of two or more witnesses present at the same time.**   If the signature is made in the presence of the witnesses, the witnesses do not need to know that the document is a will,[140] but they must see the testator in the act of writing.[141] A testator will not have made his signature in the presence of a witness if the witness leaves

---

128 *In the Goods of Chalcraft* [1948] P 222, but contrast *Re Colling* [1972] 1 WLR 1440.
129 *Smith v Harris* (1845) 1 Rob Ecc 262, 163 ER 1033.
130 *In the Goods of Clark* (1839) 2 Curt 329, 163 ER 428. If someone signs on the testator's behalf, the attestation clause should record this.
131 *Lewis v Lewis* [1908] P 1.
132 *In the Estate of Little* [1960] 1 WLR 495.
133 Applicable on a death on or after 1 January 1983.
134 [1993] Ch 90, CA.
135 A holograph will is one in the testator's handwriting.
136 See also *Weatherhill v Pearce* [1995] 1 WLR 592.
137 [1993] Ch 90, CA.
138 Such as the evidence of the witnesses.
139 See also *Re White* [1991] Ch 1.
140 *In the Estate of Benjamin* (1934) 150 LT 417.
141 *Brown v Skirrow* [1902] P 3.

before the testator has completed his signature.[142] If the testator's signature was not made in the simultaneous presence of two witnesses, it may be acknowledged by him in their simultaneous presence. In this case, the will must already have been signed; the witnesses must see the signature, or have an opportunity of seeing it; and the testator must acknowledge his signature by words or conduct. An express acknowledgement is desirable, but not essential; the testator may acknowledge his signature by gestures.[143] As the signature must be made or acknowledged in the 'presence' of two witnesses, it is necessary for them to be mentally, as well as bodily, present. They will not be present if they are 'asleep, or intoxicated, or of unsound mind'.[144] Section 15 of the Wills Act deprives a witness and his or her spouse of any benefit under the will, but such a witness is permitted to give evidence as to whether or not the will is valid and is, therefore, a good attesting witness. Section 17 specifically states that the executor of a will is a competent witness. A blind person cannot be a witness because a will cannot be signed in his 'presence'.[145]

(5) The witnesses must sign or acknowledge in the presence of the testator.   The   **7.65**
witnesses need not sign in each other's presence, but each witness must sign, or acknowledge his signature, in the presence of the testator. The testator must be mentally, as well as physically, present: if he loses consciousness before both witnesses have signed or acknowledged, the will will be invalid.[146] If a witness signs, the testator must either see him sign, or have the opportunity of seeing him sign if he chose to look.[147]

Attestation clause.   Section 9 provides that no form of attestation is necessary.   **7.66**
Nevertheless an attestation clause[148] is desirable because it facilitates the grant of probate. If there is no attestation clause, the due execution of the will has to be established by affidavit evidence.[149] An attestation clause raises a stronger presumption that the will was duly executed than if no such clause is present; and in *Sherrington v Sherrington*[150] and *Channon v Perkins*[151] the Court of Appeal reversed the trial judges and upheld wills containing attestation clauses, where there was a conflict of evidence as to what exactly happened at the time of execution.

---

142   *Re Colling* [1972] 1 WLR 1440.
143   *In the Goods of Davies* (1850) 2 Rob Ecc 337, 163 ER 1337.
144   *Hudson v Parker* (1844) 1 Rob Ecc 14, 24; 163 ER 948, 952 *per* Dr Lushington.
145   *In the Estate of Gibson* [1949] P 434.
146   *Right v Price* (1779) 1 Doug 241, 99 ER 157; *In the Goods of Chalcraft* [1948] P 222.
147   *Casson v Dade* (1781) 1 Bro CC 99, 28 ER 1010; contrast *Tribe v Tribe* (1849) 1 Rob Ecc 775, 163 ER 1210.
148   An example reads, 'Signed by the said X in our joint presence and then by us in his.'
149   Non-Contentious Probate Rules 1987, r 12.
150   [2005] EWCA Civ 326; [2005] 3 FCR 538, CA.
151   [2005] EWCA Civ 1808; [2006] WTLR 425, CA.

(ii) Interpretation of section 9 of the Wills Act 1837

7.67 Until recently, there was a tendency for judges to interpret s 9 very strictly. This meant that some authentic wills, which unquestionably represented the true intention of the testator, failed for non-compliance with the prescribed formalities.[152] English law knows no doctrine of 'substantial compliance'; so the court has no power to admit to probate an authentic will which is invalid under s 9. Having said this, the courts have recently shown a welcome tendency to be slightly more relaxed about the formalities than was formerly the case. In *Weatherhill v Pearce*[153] there was a doubt as to whether the testatrix had acknowledged her signature in the presence of both witnesses present at the same time; and in *Couser v Couser*[154] there was a question as to whether one of the witnesses had acknowledged her signature. In each case the validity of the will was upheld.[155]

(b) Incorporation by reference

7.68 A testator may incorporate in his will a document which has not been duly executed by him and so make that document part of his will.

(i) Requirements for incorporation

7.69 The doctrine of incorporation by reference applies if three requirements are satisfied. First, the document must already exist when the will is executed.[156] Secondly, the will must refer clearly to the fact that the document exists. In *University College of North Wales v Taylor*[157] a reference to 'any memorandum amongst my papers written or signed by me' was held not to satisfy this requirement. Thirdly, the document must be sufficiently described in the will so as to enable it to be identified.[158]

(ii) Effects of incorporation

7.70 A document incorporated in a duly executed will is admissible to probate as part of the will. This means that the incorporated document, like the will, is open to inspection by the public. If a testator wishes to avoid publicity, he must employ a secret trust.[159] The incorporated document operates as part of the will and is subject to the ordinary rules applicable to wills; for example, the rules as to lapse and

---

[152] *Re Groffman* [1969] 1 WLR 733.
[153] [1995] 1 WLR 592.
[154] [1996] 1 WLR 1301.
[155] See also *Sherrington v Sherrington* [2005] EWCA Civ 326; [2005] 3 FCR 538, CA; and *Channon v Perkins* [2005] EWCA Civ 1808; [2006] WTLR 425, CA.
[156] *Singleton v Tomlinson* (1878) 3 App Cas 404, HL.
[157] [1907] P 228.
[158] *In the Goods of Garnett* [1894] P 90; *In the Estate of Mardon* [1944] P 109.
[159] See para 7.134.

to ademption.[160] An invalidly executed will may be incorporated into a later validly executed will.[161]

(iii) Statutory will forms 1925

Section 179 of the Law of Property Act 1925 authorizes the Lord Chancellor to **7.71** publish these forms which a testator may incorporate into his will. The object is to reduce the length of wills. The forms are, however, seldom used because of the inconvenience of having to refer to the relevant forms in order to understand the will.

(c) Privileged wills

English law followed the pattern set by Roman law in giving a privilege to soldiers **7.72** on military service. The Statute of Frauds[162] enabled soldiers and sailors to make informal wills disposing of their personalty. Section 11 of the Wills Act 1837 confirmed the privilege and provides 'that any soldier being in actual military service, or any mariner or seaman being at sea, may dispose of his personal estate as he might have done before the making of this Act' ie without any formalities. The Wills (Soldiers and Sailors) Act 1918 extended the privilege to realty.

(i) Privileged testators

There are three categories of privileged testators. **7.73**

(1) A soldier in actual military service. Section 11 has been construed liberally **7.74** and the word 'soldier' has been construed to include 'not only the fighting men but also those who serve in the Forces, doctors, nurses, chaplains, WRNS, ATS, and so forth'.[163] The words 'in actual military service' have included a pilot undergoing RAF training in Canada during the Second World War[164] and a soldier employed in internal security operations against terrorists in Northern Ireland.[165]

(2) A mariner or seaman being at sea. These words have also been liberally **7.75** construed and have been held to include a woman typist employed aboard a liner.[166]

---

[160] *In the Goods of Garnett* [1894] P 90; *In the Estate of Mardon* [1944] P 109.
[161] *In the Goods of Almosnino* (1859) 29 LJP 46.
[162] The Statute of Frauds 1677, s 23.
[163] *Re Wingham* [1949] P 187, 196, CA (Denning LJ).
[164] *Re Wingham*, note 163 above.
[165] *Re Jones* [1981] Fam 7.
[166] *In the Goods of Hale* [1915] 2 IR 362 (the *Lusitania*).

7.76 **(3) Any member of Her Majesty's naval or marine Forces so circumstanced that if he were a soldier he would be in actual military service.**[167] Such a person is privileged even though not at sea.[168]

(ii) Extent of the privilege

7.77 A testator who falls within one of the above three categories at the time of making his will can make an informal will even if he is a minor. The will may be written, but need not be signed or witnessed. It may be oral. The testator does not need to know that he is making a will, but he must desire to give expression to wishes which he intends should take effect on his death.[169] An informal will which was made when the testator was privileged remains valid until it is revoked, even if the testator loses his privilege.[170] It has been suggested[171] that this privilege should be abolished. All the arguments in favour of the need for formalities—in particular those which relate to hasty or ill-considered dispositions—apply as strongly to members of the Armed Forces as they do to anyone else. In addition, there can be difficult evidential problems arising from the informality of privileged wills. Members of the Armed Forces should, like everyone else, be strongly recommended to make formal wills.

(d) 'Statutory' wills

7.78 Since 1970 it has been possible for the Court of Protection[172]—the office of the Supreme Court which deals with the property of patients, ie persons suffering from mental disorder—to order the execution of a will for an adult patient whom the Court has reason to believe is incapable of making a valid will for himself. Such a will is commonly referred to as a 'statutory' will. The power to make such a will is now contained in section 96 of the Mental Health Act 1983 and is normally exercised by the Master of the Court of Protection[173] A statutory will may make any provision which the patient could have made if he had not been mentally disordered. The Court, when making a statutory will, will attempt to make for the

---

167 Wills (Soldiers and Sailors) Act 1918, s 2.
168 See *In the Estate of Anderson* [1916] P 49, 52.
169 *In the Estate of Knibbs* [1962] 1 WLR 852.
170 *Re Booth* [1926] P 118.
171 Law Reform Committee's 22nd Report, *The making and revocation of wills* (Cmnd 7902) 1980, 9: cf P Critchley 'Privileged Wills and Testamentary Formalities: A Time to Die?' [1999] CLJ 49.
172 The Court of Protection is an office of the Supreme Court, but Part 2 of the Mental Capacity Act 2005 will, when it comes into force, establish a superior court of record, called the Court of Protection.
173 When the Mental Capacity Act 2005 s 46 comes into force, the Lord Chancellor will nominate judges to exercise the jurisdiction of the newly established court.

patient the will which it supposes he would have made for himself, had he not been incapable.[174]

A statutory will must be executed with the formalities specified in s 97 of the **7.79** Mental Health Act 1983, which requires a statutory will to be:

(a) expressed to be signed by the patient acting by the person authorized by the Court of Protection to execute the will for the patient (such person will usually be the patient's receiver);[175]

(b) signed by the authorized person with the name of the patient, and with his own name, in the presence of two or more witnesses present at the same time;

(c) attested and subscribed by those witnesses in the presence of the authorized person; and

(d) sealed with the official seal of the Court of Protection.

(3) The Making of Wills: Capacity

(a) Age

No will is valid if made by a person under the age of eighteen years[176] unless he is **7.80** a soldier on actual military service or a mariner or seaman at sea.[177]

(b) Testamentary capacity

To be able to make a valid will, a testator needs to understand three things: the **7.81** effect of his will; the extent of his property; and the claims upon him.[178]

(i) The effect of his will

The testator must understand the general effect of his will, ie who benefits under **7.82** it; he does not need to understand the will's legal technicalities.[179]

(ii) The extent of his property

The testator must understand the extent of his property. In *Wood v Smith*,[180] the **7.83** testator told someone (at the time he was making his will) that he had investments worth £17,000, whereas they were actually worth over £100,000. The trial judge

---

[174] *Re D (J)* [1982] Ch 237; *Re C* [1991] 3 All ER 866.

[175] A patient's receiver is the person appointed under s 99, Mental Health Act 1983 and whose main function is to receive the patient's income, but who may be empowered to do all that is necessary in the proper conduct of the patient's affairs.

[176] Wills Act 1837, s 7.

[177] ibid s 11 and Wills (Soldiers and Sailors) Act 1918. For a discussion as to who are soldiers, mariners, etc, see paras 7.73–7.76.

[178] See *Banks v Goodfellow* (1870) LR 5 QB 549, 565 (Cockburn CJ).

[179] *Banks v Goodfellow*, ibid.

[180] [1993] Ch 90, CA.

held that he was 'confused and did not have any sufficient capacity properly to comprehend. . .the real extent of his property'[181] and that his confusion indicated that he lacked mental capacity.[182]

(iii) The claims upon him

7.84 In *Boughton v Knight* Sir James Hannen P said that a testator must have 'a memory to recall the several persons who may be fitting objects of [his] bounty, and an understanding to comprehend their relationship to himself and their claims upon him'.[183] In *Harwood v Baker* a deathbed will was held invalid because the testator was not 'capable of recollecting who [his] relatives were, of understanding their respective claims upon his regard and bounty, and of deliberately forming an intelligent purpose of excluding them from any share of his property'.[184]

(c) Delusions

7.85 A testator suffers from a delusion if he suffers from an irrational belief and is not prepared to be swayed by reasoned argument. Having said this, it is sometimes hard to distinguish between serious misjudgement on the one hand and delusion on the other, particularly where a testator has taken a harsh view of the character of someone who might have expected to benefit under his will.[185] A delusion which has no influence on the provisions of a will does not deprive the testator of testamentary capacity, no matter how absurd the delusion may be.[186]

7.86 A testator normally requires testamentary capacity at the time when he executes his will. It is, however, sufficient if he has capacity when he gives instructions for the preparation of a will, even if he does not have full capacity at the time of execution, provided that the will was prepared in accordance with his instructions and he has sufficient capacity at the time of execution to understand that this is the will for which he earlier gave instructions.[187]

7.87 A will is wholly invalid if executed when the testator lacked testamentary capacity. But if the testator suffered from an insane delusion and that delusion only affects part of the will, the affected part may be deleted and the remainder of the will admitted to probate.[188]

---

181 [1993] Ch 90, 106, CA.
182 Upheld by the Court of Appeal [1993] Ch 90, 114.
183 (1873) LR 3 P&D 64, 65–6.
184 (1840) 3 Moo PC 282, 290, 13 ER 117, 120; see also *Re Loxston* [2006] EWHC 1291; [2006] WTLR 1567.
185 *Dew v Clark* (1826) 3 Add 79, 162 ER 410.
186 *Banks v Goodfellow* (1870) LR 5 QB 549.
187 *Parker v Felgate* (1883) 8 PD 171; *Clancy v Clancy* [2003] EWHC 1885; [2003] WTLR 1097.
188 *In the Estate of Bohrmann* [1938] 1 All ER 271.

(d) Lack of knowledge and approval; cases of mistake

If a testator executes a document as his will, but it is not the document he intended **7.88** to execute, he lacks knowledge and approval of that document and probate of it will not be granted.[189] In the same way, if words are included in a will and the testator did not know that they were there, the will may be admitted to probate but with the words omitted.[190] Having said this, words may be omitted only if the testator did not know that they were in the will; if he knew that they were in the will but misunderstood their legal effect, the will must be admitted to probate with the words included;[191] their interpretation then becomes an issue of construction.[192]

(e) Rectification

When a testator died on or before 31 December 1982, a Court of Probate could **7.89** omit words from his will if he had not known that they were in it, ie if he did not know and approve of them;[193] but it could not add to the will words which had somehow been omitted.[194] But if he dies on or after 1 January 1983, s 20 of the Administration of Justice Act 1982 enables the court to rectify a will if it is satisfied that the will 'is so expressed that it fails to carry out the testator's intentions, in consequence—(a) of a clerical error; or (b) of a failure to understand his instructions'. In *Wordingham v Royal Exchange Trust Co Ltd*[195] the testatrix's solicitor failed to include in her will a clause which had been included in an earlier will. This was the solicitor's error and it was clerical; s 20 of the 1982 Act enabled the court to rectify the will by inserting the clause.

An application for rectification under s 20 must be made no later than six months **7.90** from the date when a grant of representation is first taken out, although the court has a discretion to extend the time limit.[196]

Questions may arise as to the inter-relationship between applications for rectifica- **7.91** tion and actions for negligence. The decisions of the Court of Appeal in *Walker v Medlicott*[197] and *Horsfall v Haywards*[198] appear difficult to reconcile and it is suggested that *Horsfall* is to be preferred.[199]

---

[189] *In the Goods of Hunt* (1875) LR 3 P&D 250.
[190] *Re Phelan* [1972] Fam 33.
[191] *Collins v Elstone* [1893] P 1.
[192] See section D.
[193] *Re Morris* [1971] P 62.
[194] *Harter v Harter* (1873) 3 P & D 11.
[195] [1992] Ch 412.
[196] Administration of Justice Act 1982, s 20(2). For the exercise of the discretion see *Chittock v Stevens* [2000] WTLR 643.
[197] [1999] 1 WLR 727.
[198] [1999] 1 FLR 1182.
[199] See R Kerridge and AHR Brierley, 'Mistakes in Wills: Rectify and be Damned' [2003] 62 CLJ 750–70.

(f) Undue influence and fraud

7.92 In a court of probate, undue influence means coercion:[200] the testator is forced, rather than persuaded, into making a will he does not want to make.[201] Fraud occurs when the testator is deliberately misled, rather than coerced. For example, it would be fraud if someone were to tell the testator, untruthfully, that a prospective beneficiary had done something of which the testator would disapprove, or that a prospective beneficiary had died.[202]

7.93 There has been a tendency in some cases to confuse undue influence and fraud[203] but they are essentially different and should be pleaded separately when a purported will is challenged.[204] A significant difference between a plea of undue influence and a plea of fraud is that, if successful, a plea of undue influence will almost inevitably lead to a decision that the will, or the relevant part of it, will not be granted probate, ie the purported gift will be ineffective so that the relevant property will pass under a residuary provision in the will, or under an earlier will, or under the intestacy provisions. On the other hand, a successful plea of fraud may well lead to a decision that the property should be held on a constructive trust.[205] Having said this, pleas of fraud are extremely rare and appear never to be successful;[206] so there is no direct authority[207] as to what should happen when a plea of fraud succeeds.

(g) Challenging suspicious wills

7.94 Someone who is considering challenging a purported will finds himself in a position of some difficulty. The testator is dead; and it may not be easy to obtain evidence of his mental state [208] and/or evidence as to what happened at the time the will was executed, particularly where the will was not prepared by a solicitor.

7.95 During the nineteenth century, there was a tendency for judges to refer to 'a presumption' which arose where a will had been prepared by a beneficiary, but for them then to leave it unclear as to what was being presumed.[209] The confusion became worse when the plea of lack of knowledge and approval became linked

---

200 *Wingrove v Wingrove* (1885) 11 PD 81, 82 *per* Hannen P.
201 See *Hall v Hall* (1868) LR 1 P&D 481, 482 (Sir JP Wilde).
202 Such lies might be told to persuade the testator to bequeath the property to someone else.
203 See *Barry v Butlin* (1838) 2 Moo PC 480, 12 ER 1089; *Boyse v Rossborough* (1857) 6 HLC 2, 10 ER 1192 and *Low v Guthrie* (1909) AC 278, HL.
204 *White v White & Cato* (1862) 2 Sw & Tr 504, 164 ER 1092.
205 See *Betts v Doughty* (1879) 5 PD 26.
206 The writer has traced no case where a plea of fraud has succeeded.
207 In *Betts v Doughty* (1879) 5 PD 26 the parties came to terms.
208 *Ewing v Bennett* [2001] WTLR 781, CA.
209 *Paske v Ollat* (1815) 2 Phill Ecc 323, 161 ER 1158.

with the 'suspicious circumstances' rule. The leading case is *Wintle v Nye*[210] where a will drawn up by a solicitor, and under which he was a substantial beneficiary, was challenged on the ground that the testatrix had not known and approved of its contents. It was not alleged that the testatrix lacked capacity, or that there was undue influence or fraud. The trial judge warned the jury that the case was one which created a suspicion and that it was the duty of the person propounding the will (the solicitor) to remove it. The jury found in the solicitor's favour. On appeal to the House of Lords, it was held that the trial judge's summing-up to the jury had not sufficiently scrutinized the circumstances in relation to the exceptionally heavy burden of proof which lay on the solicitor. It is not altogether easy to follow this. It raises the issue of 'suspicious circumstances' without making it clear what the 'suspicion' is a suspicion of. The underlying reality is that *Wintle v Nye* was a case about fraud, where fraud was not pleaded.[211] It seems that those who are considering challenging wills are now being encouraged to plead lack of knowledge and approval, rather than fraud or undue influence;[212] but how this fits in with the doctrine of 'suspicious circumstances' is not clear. In *Re Stott*,[213] Slade J followed the approach taken in *Wintle v Nye* and allowed those challenging a will to plead lack of knowledge and approval in a case where there was a thinly disguised allegation of fraud.[214]

If a will is challenged on the grounds of lack of capacity and lack of knowledge and approval, a judge who decides to refuse probate, but who does not wish to suggest misbehaviour by anyone concerned in the preparation of the will, usually finds that the testator lacked capacity, but that there was no lack of knowledge and approval.[215] To find that there was both lack of capacity and lack of knowledge and approval is to hint at misconduct,[216] while a finding of lack of knowledge

7.96

---

[210] [1959] 1 WLR 284, HL. And see R Kerridge, 'Wills Made in Suspicious Circumstances: The Problem of the Vulnerable Testator' [2000] 59 CLJ 310–34.

[211] The solicitor was later struck off.

[212] There are two (apparent) advantages in challenging a will on the ground that there has been lack of knowledge and approval, rather than on the grounds of undue influence or fraud: burden of proof and costs. If a will is challenged on the ground that the testator lacked knowledge and approval, and the claimant fails, costs have *usually* been awarded from the estate, though there is no guarantee that they will be, *Sherrington v Sherrington* [2005] EWCA Civ 326; [2005] 3 FCR 538, CA.

[213] [1980] 1 WLR 246.

[214] This was despite RSC Ord 76, r 9 which dealt with the contents of pleadings in contentious probate and appeared to require that where undue influence or fraud is alleged, they should be separately pleaded. When the new Civil Procedure Rules were introduced in April 1999, RSC Ord 76 r 9 was replaced by CPR Part 49, para 9 and this was again replaced in October 2001 by CPR 57.7, which still appears to require that a plea of lack of knowledge and approval should not be used as a cloak for a plea of undue influence or fraud.

[215] *Re Loxston* [2006] EWHC 1291; [2006] WTLR 1567.

[216] *Richards v Allan* [2001] WTLR 1031.

and approval by itself generally gives a clearer indication.[217] Having said this, challenges based on lack of knowledge and approval rarely succeed,[218] and those minded to challenge suspicious wills should ask themselves whether it might not be better to do so on the grounds of undue influence or fraud and then to call in aid a presumption of undue influence or fraud, based on the 'suspicious circumstances' rule. This approach is based on the speeches of Lord Cairns and Lord Hatherley in *Fulton v Andrew*[219] and is also consistent with the approach taken in relation to lifetime gifts.[220]

(4) Revocation, Alteration, Revival, and Republication of Wills

(a) Revocation

7.97 A will is the expression by a person of wishes he intends to take effect only at his death and is, by its very nature, revocable by the testator until his death.[221] There are four methods by which a will (or codicil) may be revoked: by a later will or codicil; by a duly executed writing declaring an intention to revoke; by destruction; or by marriage. The effect of divorce (or annulment of marriage) on a will is considered later.[222] Other changes in circumstance—such as the birth of children—have no effect on a will.

7.98 Revocation by will or codicil, revocation by duly executed writing and revocation by destruction are all covered by s 20 of the Wills Act 1837; revocation by marriage is covered by s 18.

(i) Revocation by a later will or codicil

7.99 **Express revocation.** A will or codicil, or any part thereof, may be revoked by a later duly executed will or codicil, which will ordinarily contain a revocation clause expressly revoking all earlier 'wills, codicils and other testamentary dispositions'. A revocation clause *may* be much narrower, and a revocation clause in a codicil may revoke a single clause in an earlier will. There is no particular form of words for an express revocation clause, but commencing a will with the standard 'This is the last will and testament of. . .' is not construed as an express revocation clause.[223]

---

217 *D'Eye v Avery* [2001] WTLR 227; *Re Rowinska* [2005] EWHC 2794; [2006] WTLR 487.
218 See *Re Dabbs* [2001] WTLR 527. In both *Fuller v Strum* [2001] EWCA Civ 1879; [2002] 1 WLR 1097, CA and in *Sherrington v Sherrington* [2005] EWCA Civ 326; [2005] 3 FCR 538, CA, the Court of Appeal allowed appeals against findings of lack of knowledge and approval.
219 (1875) LR 7 HL 448 at 463 and 469, HL.
220 *Hammond v Osborn* [2002] EWCA Civ 885; [2002] WTLR 1125, CA.
221 See paras 7.35 and 7.36.
222 See para 7.189.
223 *Simpson v Foxon* [1907] P 54.

A revocation clause will be inoperative, and the clause will not be admitted to pro- **7.100**
bate, if the testator was not aware that it was in his will and so did not know and
approve of it;[224] but the clause will be admitted to probate if the testator knew that
it was in the will but was mistaken as to its legal effect.[225] A revocation clause will
not operate if it is contained in a conditional will which is itself inoperative because
the condition has not been satisfied,[226] or if the clause itself is subject to a condition which is not satisfied.[227]

Implied revocation by will or codicil.   An earlier will or codicil is impliedly   **7.101**
revoked by a later will or codicil in so far as the latter contains provisions which are
inconsistent with the former.

Proof of revocation where later will or codicil is missing.   If an earlier will or   **7.102**
codicil is revoked by a later will or codicil, revocation takes effect when the later
will or codicil is executed and it does not matter that the later will or codicil cannot
be produced.[228] But, in order to establish revocation of an earlier will or codicil by
a later will or codicil which has been lost or destroyed, it must be proved on a reasonable balance of probabilities that the later will or codicil was duly executed and
that it expressly or impliedly revoked the earlier will or codicil.[229]

(ii)   Revocation by duly executed writing

A will or codicil, or any part thereof, may be revoked under s 20 by 'some writing   **7.103**
declaring an intention to revoke the same' and executed in the same manner as a
will.[230] The writing does not need to contain any dispositive dispositions.

(iii)   Revocation by destruction

There are two elements to revocation by destruction: an act of destruction and an   **7.104**
intention to revoke.

Act of destruction.   There must be an act of 'burning, tearing or otherwise   **7.105**
destroying'. It does not suffice that the testator crossed out part of his will, wrote
'All these are revoked' on the back of it and then threw it into a heap of wastepaper;
in such a case the will remains valid.[231] It is not necessary for the testator to destroy
the entire will; it almost certainly suffices if he destroys his signature[232] and probably

---

224 *In the Goods of Oswald* (1874) LR 3 P & D 162.
225 *Collins v Elstone* [1893] P 1.
226 *In the Goods of Hugo* (1877) 2 PD 73.
227 See paras 7.42 and 7.43.
228 *Brown v Brown* (1858) 8 El & Bl 876, 120 ER 327.
229 *Cutto v Gilbert* (1854) 9 Moo PC 131, 14 ER 247, PC; *Re Wipperman* [1955] P 59; *Re Wyatt*
[1952] 1 All ER 1030.
230 *In the Goods of Gosling* (1886) 11 PD 79; *Re Spracklan's Estate* [1938] 2 All ER 345, CA.
231 *Cheese v Lovejoy* (1877) 2 PD 251, CA.
232 *Hobbs v Knight* (1838) 1 Curt 768, 778, 163 ER 267.

suffices if he destroys the witnesses' signatures; but it does not suffice if he changes his mind and stops before completing what he intended to do as an act of destruction.[233]

7.106 If the will is destroyed by someone other than the testator, it must be in his presence and by his direction.[234]

7.107 **Intention to revoke.** The testator must intend to revoke all or part of the will. He must have mental capacity and he must believe that the will is valid; if he destroys a will which he thinks has already been revoked, he does not intend to revoke it.[235]

7.108 If a testator destroys part of his will, the question arises as to whether he intended to revoke the whole will, or only a part of it. If there is no evidence of expressed intention, intention will be inferred: destruction of the testator's signature indicates an intention to revoke the whole will,[236] but cutting out particular legacies does not.[237]

7.109 **Presumptions.** If a will which was last known to be in the testator's possession cannot be found at his death, it is presumed that he destroyed it with the intention of revoking it.[238] But the strength of the presumption varies according to the security of the testator's custody. The safer the security, the stronger the presumption. In *Sugden v Lord St Leonards*[239] the presumption was not applied when Lord St Leonards' will was missing from his deed box at the time of his death. Eight codicils were in the box, but the will was missing. The box had not been kept securely and it was unlikely that a former Lord Chancellor would destroy his will without destroying the codicils and without making another will. Probate was granted of the missing will, as Lord St Leonards' daughter was able to recite its contents.[240]

(iv) Revocation by marriage

7.110 Marriage ordinarily revokes any will made by either party before the marriage, whether or not this is intended.[241]

---

233 *Doe d Perkes v Perkes* (1820) 3 B & Ald 489, 106 ER 740.

234 Solicitor's destruction of his client's will, where instructions had been given to the solicitor on the telephone and the destruction was not carried out in the testator's presence, was a 'considerable professional error': *In the Estate of de Kremer* (1965) 110 SJ 18.

235 *Scott v Scott* (1859) 1 Sw & Tr 258, 164 ER 719.

236 *Hobbs v Knight* (1838) 1 Curt 768, 163 ER 267.

237 *In the Goods of Woodward* (1871) LR 2 P & D 206.

238 *Eckersley v Platt* (1866) LR 1 P & D 281.

239 (1876) 1 PD 154, CA.

240 Nowadays, the contents can usually be proved by a photocopy, see *Re Dickson* [2002] WTLR 1395, CA.

241 Wills Act 1837, s 18. Pension scheme nominations are not testamentary dispositions and will not be covered by s 18. The rules of the particular pension fund may or may not state that marriage will effect a revocation of the nomination: *Baird v Baird* [1990] 2 AC 548, PC.

Void and voidable marriages.   A *void* marriage is treated as never having taken **7.111**
place and does *not* revoke an earlier will.[242] But a *voidable* marriage, ie a marriage
which is valid until it is declared void, *does* revoke an earlier will; and the subsequent annulment of the voidable marriage makes no difference. This creates a
potentially unsatisfactory situation where a marriage is voidable on the grounds of
absence of consent. Before 1971, lack of consent made a marriage void, but since
1971 it makes a marriage voidable.[243] This means that someone who made a valid
will when he had testamentary capacity may revoke it by contracting a voidable
marriage at a time when he no longer has capacity.[244] In *Re Davey* [245] the marriage
of a ninety-two-year-old testatrix, who clearly lacked capacity, revoked a will she
had made when she had capacity; the situation was saved by the execution of a
'statutory will' a week before she died.[246]

Wills made in contemplation of marriage.   Section 18(3) of the Wills Act 1837 **7.112**
states that:

> Where it appears from a will that at the time it was made the testator was expecting
> to be married to a particular person and that he intended that the will should not be
> revoked by the marriage, the will shall not be revoked by his marriage to that
> person.[247]

(v) *Revocation by a privileged testator*

The four methods of revocation outlined above all apply to privileged testators, **7.113**
subject only to the differences which necessarily arise from their ability to make
informal wills.

(b) Conditional revocation

Revocation of the whole or part of a will by another will or codicil, or by duly exe- **7.114**
cuted writing, or by destruction, requires an intention to revoke. The testator's
intention to revoke may be absolute or it may be conditional. If it is absolute, revocation takes place at once; if it is conditional, revocation takes place if and when
the condition is fulfilled. Where revocation is by will or codicil, or by duly executed writing, it is a question of construction whether the testator's intention to

---

[242] *Mette v Mette* (1859) 1 Sw & Tr 416, 164 ER 792.
[243] Nullity of Marriage Act 1971, re-enacted in Matrimonial Causes Act 1973.
[244] *Re Roberts* [1978] 1 WLR 653, CA.
[245] [1981] 1 WLR 164.
[246] For 'statutory wills' see para 7.78.
[247] This sub-section—which was substituted by the Administration of Justice Act 1982 and
applies to wills made on or after 1 January 1983—replaces s 177 of the Law of Property Act 1925,
which still applies to wills made on or before 31 December 1982. Section 177 was more restrictive
in its application and this gave rise to problems, see *Re Coleman* [1976] Ch 1.

revoke is conditional. Where revocation is by destruction, it is a question of fact[248] and evidence as to the testator's declarations of intention are admissible.

(i) Conditional revocation by will

7.115 A revocation clause may be subject to an express condition. For example, a testator may insert in a codicil to his will a revocation clause which is expressed to take effect conditionally on his wife's predeceasing him; the clause does not then operate if she survives. Even if there is no express condition, a revocation clause may be construed as conditional. In *Re Finnemore*[249] a testator made three wills in succession, in each of which C was the principal beneficiary. The two later wills contained standard revocation clauses, but the gifts to C in the second and third wills were void because C's husband was an attesting witness.[250] It was held that the revocation clauses in the two later wills were conditional on the gifts to C in those wills being valid. As the gifts were void, the revocation clauses would not take effect in so far as they purported to revoke the gifts to C in the first will.[251]

(ii) Conditional revocation by destruction

7.116 The testator may intend unconditional revocation of a will by destruction,[252] or he may intend revocation to be conditional upon due execution of a new will, or upon revival of a former will, or upon particular devolution on intestacy. A good example of the last sort of condition is *In the Estate of Southerden*,[253] where the testator burned his will because he thought that his wife would then be entitled to all his property on his death intestate. The condition was not satisfied, and the Court of Appeal held that the testator's will had not been revoked.

(c) Alteration

7.117 Section 28 of the Wills Act 1837 states that:

> No obliteration, interlineation, or other alteration made in any will after the execution thereof shall be valid or have any effect, except so far as the words or effect of the will before such alteration shall not be apparent, unless such alteration shall be executed in like manner as hereinbefore is required for the execution of the will. . .

(i) Alterations made before execution

7.118 If an alteration was made before the will was executed, the alteration forms part of the will. This is subject to the proviso that the alteration was not merely

---

248 *Dixon v Solicitor to the Treasury* [1905] P 42.
249 [1991] 1 WLR 793.
250 See para 7.180.
251 The revocation clause in the last will was effective in revoking the parts of the earlier wills which dealt with the quarter of the residue which did not pass to C; that quarter passed under the provisions of the last will.
252 *Re Jones* [1976] Ch 200, CA.
253 [1925] P 177, CA.

deliberative, but was intended to be final. There is a rebuttable presumption that where a will is written partly in ink and partly in pencil, the pencil writing is merely deliberative.[254] There is also a rebuttable presumption that an unattested alteration was made after the will was executed.[255] This presumption may be rebutted by internal evidence from the will itself,[256] or by extrinsic evidence, such as evidence from the draftsman.[257] If a will is confirmed,[258] its confirmation will validate any alteration made in the will after execution and before republication.[259] But where a will is republished by a codicil, there is a presumption that an unattested alteration to the will was made not only after the will, but also after the codicil;[260] so the alteration will be valid only if this presumption is rebutted.

(ii) Duly attested alterations made after execution of the will

An alteration made after the will was executed is valid if the alteration was executed with the formalities required for the execution of the will. The usual practice is for the testator to sign his initials in the margin of the will, close to the alteration, and the testator should either make or acknowledge this signature in the simultaneous presence of two witnesses who then both sign in his presence by writing their initials in the margin.[261] In *Re White*[262] alterations were made to a will in the testator's presence and at his dictation and were initialled by two witnesses but not by the testator himself: the alterations were held invalid and the original, unaltered, will was admitted to probate. A draftsman should avoid making significant alterations to a will, as they may lead to problems of construction.[263] Any (minor) alterations which are made should be duly executed (ie initialled), even if the alterations were made before the execution of the will, thereby avoiding the need to rebut the presumption that unattested alterations were made after the will was executed. **7.119**

(iii) Unattested alterations which make any part of the will 'not apparent'

Section 21 of the Wills Act 1837 provides that an unattested 'obliteration, interlineation or. . .alteration' of a will shall have no effect 'except so far as the words. . .shall not be apparent. . .'. So, if the testator made an unattested alteration to his will after it was executed, provided he intended by such alteration to revoke **7.120**

---

254 *Hawkes v Hawkes* (1828) 1 Hagg Ecc 321, 162 ER 599.

255 *Cooper v Bockett* (1846) 4 Moo PC 419, 13 ER 419, PC.

256 *Birch v Birch* (1848) 1 Rob Ecc 675, 163 ER 1175; *In the Goods of Cadge* (1868) LR 1 P & D 543.

257 *Keigwin v Keigwin* (1843) 3 Curt 607, 163 ER 841.

258 For confirmation, or 'republication' see para 7.124.

259 Provided the alteration was not merely deliberative.

260 *In the Goods of Sykes* (1873) LR 3 P & D 26.

261 *In the Goods of Blewitt* (1880) 5 PD 116.

262 [1991] Ch 1.

263 Alterations and codicils both have the potential disadvantage that someone who has lost a benefit, or who has had a benefit reduced, will find out that this has happened—admittedly, only after the death of the testator.

that part of his will,[264] and provided the alteration makes that part of the will 'not. . .apparent', that part will be revoked. Probate of the will is then granted with a blank space for the part 'not. . .apparent'.

7.121 **The meaning of 'not. . .apparent'.** Words are 'not. . .apparent' if they are not optically apparent on the face of the will.[265] 'Natural' means may be used to decipher the words, so the paper may be held up to the light[266] and a magnifying glass may be used.[267] But the use of chemicals or infra-red photography[268] is forbidden. Extrinsic evidence cannot be called.[269]

7.122 **Conditional obliteration.** If a testator obliterates part of his will with the intention of revoking it, such intention may be unconditional or conditional. It will be conditional if he intends the revocation to take effect only if, for example, some other provision takes effect. The classic example is where he obliterates a legacy intending to substitute another legacy to the same beneficiary, but the substituted legacy is ineffective because it is not properly attested. If, as in this case, the condition is not fulfilled, the obliterated passage is not revoked, and the obliterated words must be ascertained so that they may be admitted to probate. In this case of conditional obliteration, there is no restriction on the means of proof: the obliterated words may be ascertained by chemicals, or by infra-red photography,[270] and extrinsic evidence may be called. Whether the testator's intention to revoke was or was not conditional is a question of fact, and evidence of the testator's declarations of intention is admissible.[271]

(d) Revival and republication

(i) *Revival of a revoked will*

7.123 A revoked will or codicil may be revived, but only if it is still in existence. A destroyed will cannot be revived. Section 22 of the Wills Act 1837 provides that a will or codicil which has been wholly or partly revoked may be revived either by being re-executed or by the execution of a codicil which shows an intention to revive it. Whether a codicil shows the necessary intention to revive is a question of construction.[272] Under Section 34 of the Wills Act 1837, a revived will is deemed to have been made at the time of its revival. There are no other methods of revival

---

264 *Townley v Watson* (1844) 3 Curt 761, 769, 163 ER 893, 896.
265 *Townley v Watson* (1844) 3 Curt 761, 768, 163 ER 893, 895.
266 *Ffinch v Combe* [1894] P 191.
267 *In the Goods of Brasier* [1899] P 36.
268 *In the Goods of Itter* [1950] P 130.
269 The evidence of the solicitor who drafted the original will is inadmissible; *Townley v Watson* (1844) 3 Curt 761, 768, 163 ER 893, 895.
270 *In the Goods of Itter* [1950] P 130, CA.
271 *In the Goods of McCabe* (1873) LR 3 P & D 94.
272 *In the Goods of Davis* [1952] P 279.

apart from re-execution of a will or execution of a codicil showing an intention to revive. A will which has been revoked by a later will is *not* revived by the subsequent revocation of the later will.[273]

(ii) Confirmation or 'republication'[274]

A will is confirmed or 'republished' if it is re-executed with the proper formalities, **7.124** or if a codicil is executed which contains some reference to the will.[275] Confirmation bears some similarity to revival but, whereas revival revives a revoked will, confirmation endorses an unrevoked will. Confirmation by codicil does not require that the codicil shows an intention to confirm like the intention to revive required by s 22. A will is confirmed by a codicil which merely refers to it;[276] so a codicil which refers to a will has the same effect as if it contained an express confirmation.[277] Confirmation causes a will to operate as if it had been executed at the time of its confirmation. This rule will not be applied so as to defeat the testator's intention by, for example, invalidating a gift which would have been valid if made at the time when the will was made.[278] Confirmation of a will by codicil may also validate a gift in the will which was originally void under s 15 of the Wills Act[279] provided the codicil is attested by witnesses who are not beneficiaries or the spouses of beneficiaries.[280]

(5) Mutual Wills

Where two[281] persons have entered into an arrangement as to the disposal of some **7.125** or all of their property on their respective deaths, and where they have agreed that the survivor of them is to be bound by the arrangement then, when the first of

---

273 *In the Goods of Hodgkinson* [1893] P 339. Note that, in this sort of example, the revocation of the later will might be a conditional revocation (conditional on the earlier will being revived) and, given that the earlier will is not revived, the revocation of the later will may not be effective.

274 Before 1838 some wills had to be 'published' by a declaration by the testator in the presence of witnesses; the term 'republication', though still usual, has been an anachronism since the Wills Act 1837 came into force.

275 *Re Smith* (1890) 45 Ch D 632 (duly executed paper made no reference to previous will: no republication).

276 *Re Taylor* (1880) 57 LJ Ch 430, 434.

277 In a professionally drawn codicil, it is standard practice to include a clause expressly confirming the earlier will except to the extent that the terms of the codicil vary the terms of the will.

278 In *Re Moore* [1907] 1 IR 315 a statutory provision, which would have invalidated a bequest to a charity if the bequest had been contained in a will made within three months of the testator's death, did not invalidate a bequest contained in a will made more than three months before his death where the will had been republished within three months of his death.

279 Gift to witness or spouse of witness.

280 *Anderson v Anderson* (1872) LR 13 Eq 381.

281 In theory, there could be more than two, but there appear to be no reported cases where there have been.

them dies, the survivor will be bound by that arrangement. There are three requirements: the arrangement, the agreement to be bound, and the binding event.

(a) The three requirements

(i) *The arrangement*

7.126 The first requirement is that the parties have made an arrangement as to the disposal of property and have executed wills pursuant to this arrangement. In practice, the parties are almost always husband and wife, but the principle of mutual wills is not so restricted. There are two standard patterns of mutual wills: either each will gives the other party a life interest, followed by a gift of the remainder to the same beneficiary;[282] or each will gives the other party an absolute interest with a similar alternative gift if the other party dies first.[283] In each of these arrangements, the surviving party receives a benefit; but it was held in *Re Dale*[284] that there is no requirement that the other party should receive a benefit. So, if two testators, eg husband and wife, agree that each should leave his or her property to particular beneficiaries, eg their children, the surviving party's property would be subject to a trust for the beneficiaries named in the wills, provided, of course, that the other requirements of mutual wills were present. Similarly, there is no theoretical objection to an arrangement whereby the remainders pass to different, but agreed, beneficiaries. For example, a husband and wife might each agree to leave property to a charity, but on the basis that each was agreeing to leave it to *a* charity and *not* to members of the family.[285]

(ii) *The agreement for the survivor to be bound*

7.127 In order for the doctrine of mutual wills to operate, it is not sufficient (or necessary) that the parties simply agree to make similar, or identical, wills. But it is essential that the parties agree that the survivor shall be bound by the arrangement: and this means that they agree not to revoke the wills which they have made as part of the arrangement once the predeceasing party has died. The fact that two people agree to make, and do simultaneously make, identical wills, does not establish, and does not necessarily indicate, that they have agreed not to revoke them. For example, in *Re Goodchild*[286] a husband and wife executed simultaneous wills in identical form. Each left his residuary estate to the other, and then provided that if the other did not survive him, it should pass to their son. The wife died first and her property passed to her husband under her will. He then remarried and

---

282 *Re Hagger* [1930] 2 Ch 190.
283 *Re Green* [1951] Ch 148.
284 *Re Dale (decd), Proctor v Dale* [1994] Ch 31. See AHR Brierley (1995) 58 MLR 95.
285 The purpose of the mutual wills in this case might be to exclude beneficiaries, rather than to include them.
286 [1997] 1 WLR 1216, CA.

made a new will which departed entirely from the terms of his earlier will. The Court of Appeal affirmed Carnwarth J's decision that the doctrine of mutual wills was not applicable: the parties may have agreed to make identical wills, but there was no indication that they had agreed not to revoke them.[287]

It is, of course, quite usual for people, especially married couples, to agree to make **7.128** identical wills without agreeing not to revoke them. But it is easy to see that misunderstandings may arise where one party assumes that there is some sort of agreement, while the other does not. If there is an agreement between the parties that the survivor shall be bound by the arrangement and shall not be able to revoke his will once the first party has died—and such cases are likely to be rare because of the restrictions which are imposed on the survivor where such an agreement exists—this may be proved by declarations in the wills, or by clear extrinsic evidence.[288] In order to avoid the possibility of arguments and misunderstandings, it is best[289] if any agreement is recorded in the wills, or in some other document a copy of which is given to any intended beneficiary.

(iii) The binding event

Re Dale[290] implies that the binding event must be the death of the first party. **7.129** This means that mutual wills may be altered or revoked by agreement between the parties before the first dies; and may be revoked if one party gives notice to the other while they are both alive.[291] If the first testator dies having revoked, or significantly altered, his mutual will before his death, the binding event does not occur.[292]

(b) Constructive trust

If the three requirements of mutual wills are present, equity enforces the arrange- **7.130** ment against the survivor by treating him as holding the property, the subject of the arrangement, on a constructive trust which obliges him to act in accordance with the terms of the agreement. This constructive trust does not prevent the survivor from revoking his mutual will and making a new will; *but* the executors under the new will, even if different from those under the mutual will, will take

---

287 See also *Re Oldham* [1925] Ch 75.
288 *In the Estate of Heys* [1914] P 192. See also *Re Cleaver* [1981] 1 WLR 939 (proof on balance of probabilities). *Quaere* whether the agreement, if made after 26 September 1989, will be void if it relates to land and is not in writing and signed by each of the parties—see Law Reform (Miscellaneous Provisions) Act 1989, s 2(1).
289 But see para 7.133.
290 [1994] Ch 31.
291 *Dufour v Pereira* (1769) Dick 419, 21 ER 332.
292 *Re Hobley* [2006] WTLR 467.

the property subject to the constructive trust. Equity, while not preventing the unconscionable revocation of the mutual will, nevertheless frustrates it.

(c) Effect of remarriage on mutual wills

7.131 A problem which has never been satisfactorily resolved in relation to mutual wills is what happens if the survivor remarries. The question was not discussed at all in *Re Oldham*;[293] in *Re Goodchild*[294] the issue was discussed obiter at first instance and not mentioned in the Court of Appeal.[295] The obiter view was that remarriage would *not* affect the position of a beneficiary under a constructive trust; but this view is easier to maintain where the parties are relatively old[296] than where they are young and may have children.

(d) The property bound

7.132 The arrangement embodied in the mutual wills determines the extent of the property bound by the constructive trust. It may apply to the whole[297] of each party's estate, or to a part[298] or only to identified property.[299] If the constructive trust applies to the whole, or to a part of each party's estate, the question then arises as to how far the survivor is entitled to dispose, during his lifetime, of property he received from the other party and of property which had been his own property. In the Australian case of *Birmingham v Renfrew*[300] Dixon J suggested that mutual wills might create a form of floating constructive trust which would crystallize on the death of the survivor, but which would not prevent him from disposing of capital during his lifetime, provided any dispositions were not calculated to defeat the intention of the arrangement.

(e) Should testators be advised to make mutual wills?

7.133 Notwithstanding the high incidence of divorce and remarriage—with the consequence that couples may have no children common to both of them, but children by previous relationships—mutual wills are rarely a good idea. They create a

---

293 [1925] Ch 75.
294 [1996] 1 WLR 694.
295 [1997] 1 WLR 1216, CA.
296 They were about eighty years old in *Re Goodchild*.
297 *Re Cleaver* [1981] 1 WLR 939.
298 *Re Green* [1951] Ch 148.
299 In *Healey v Brown* [2002] WTLR 849 the judge followed an approach suggested obiter in the Court of Appeal in *Re Goodchild* and held that the constructive trust to which the survivor was subject applied only to property acquired from the deceased and not to property already owned by the survivor. It is suggested that this is wrong in principle and that the constructive trust should apply according to the terms of the agreement between the parties.
300 (1937) 57 CLR 666 Australian HC.

constructive trust but there may well be a dispute as to what property is covered by the trust and/or as to what is to happen if the survivor wishes to dispose of part of the capital. If two (or more) people wish to be bound by some form of trust it is probably better to create an express trust and to create it while they are both alive; or for them to make clear provision in their wills, eg for life interests; or for them to confer rights of residence in the family home (which may well involve the severance of a beneficial joint tenancy).[301] Later disputes over what was not properly thought through can be upsetting and expensive.

(6) Secret Trusts

(a) Fully secret and half-secret trusts

A secret trust arises when a beneficiary under a will, or someone who would benefit on an intestacy, promises the testator (or would-be intestate) that he will hold the property which he receives under the will or on the intestacy for the benefit of someone else. Traditionally, secret trusts have found favour with testators who do not wish to be seen to be benefiting certain individuals or organizations, eg illegitimate children, or former spouses, or unfashionable organizations. A fully secret trust occurs where the wording of the gift in the will makes no reference at all to the fact that the gift is to be held on trust. A half-secret trust occurs where the will indicates that the gift is to be held on trust, but does not say who the beneficiary is, eg 'I bequeath £10,000 to my solicitor S, to hold on the trusts he knows about'. *Re Snowden*[302] establishes that, in the absence of special circumstances, the standard of proof required to establish a secret trust is the ordinary civil standard of the balance of probabilities; but a secret trust was not established on the facts of that case.

7.134

(b) Enforcement of secret trusts

Secret trusts have been enforced since the seventeenth century[303] but the basis on which they have been enforced has always been in some doubt.[304] The enforcement of secret trusts appears to conflict both with the spirit and the letter of s 9 of the Wills Act 1837. According to one theory, they are enforced because they operate outside, or *'dehors'*, the will.[305] According to another theory they operate to

7.135

---

301 There may also be the need to sever beneficial joint tenancies in matrimonial homes, or other jointly-owned properties, as part of the will-making process.
302 [1979] Ch 528.
303 *Thynn v Thynn* (1684) 1 Vern 296, 23 ER 479.
304 See P Critchley (1999) 115 LQR 631.
305 See *Blackwell v Blackwell* [1929] AC 318, 340 (Viscount Sumner).

prevent fraud,[306] though it is not clear whether the fraud being prevented is fraud on the testator, or fraud on the beneficiaries. Each of these possibilities causes problems.

7.136 The courts have, traditionally, been less enthusiastic about upholding half-secret trusts than fully secret trusts; although there seems to be no logical reason why this should be so. It is possible that there has been a confusion in some cases between the doctrine of secret trusts and the doctrine of incorporation by reference.[307] The cases suggest that there are a number of differences between fully secret trusts and half-secret trusts, one of which is that a fully secret trust may be communicated by the testator to the secret trustee at any time before his death, whereas a half-secret trust must be communicated before the will is executed.[308] It is not agreed whether fully secret or half-secret trusts are express trusts or constructive trusts. The better view is probably that they are both express trusts, although it may be argued that both are constructive or that fully secret trusts are constructive. The point may be relevant if the secret trust concerns land, because of the rules relating to the formalities required for the creation of trusts of land.[309]

7.137 There are a number of other unresolved, or incompletely resolved, problems in relation to fully secret and half-secret trusts. For example, it is not entirely clear what happens if the secret trustee dies before the testator[310] or if the beneficiary under a secret trust dies before the testator. In *Re Gardner (No 2)*[311] Romer J held that the beneficiary's personal representatives took in his place, but this seems contrary to principle, in that it implies that the secret trust comes into existence before the death of the testator. All these problems suggest that secret trusts should, if possible, be avoided. They appear to have few advantages, and an attempt to create a secret trust can easily lead to problems. A matter which appears not to have been discussed in any reported case is what would happen if it were found that an attempt had been made to create a secret trust for the purpose of tax evasion. How would the principle of illegality tie in with the alleged trust? Secret trusts, like mutual wills, should be entered into only with extreme circumspection. If they are entered into, written records should be kept (outside the will) as to exactly what has been agreed, and copies of such records should be supplied to the beneficiaries.

---

306 See *Blackwell v Blackwell* [1929] AC 318, 329 (Lord Buckmaster).
307 See paras 7.68–7.70.
308 Stated obiter in *Re Keen* [1937] 1 Ch 236, CA and in *Blackwell v Blackwell* [1929] AC 318, HL: but contrast *Gold v Hill* [1999] 1 FLR 54, a case involving a nomination.
309 See Law of Property Act 1925, s 53. The point appears to have been overlooked in *Ottaway v Norman* [1972] Ch 698.
310 See dicta in *Re Maddock* [1902] 2 Ch 220, CA.
311 [1923] 2 Ch 230.

D. Construction

(1) The General Principles of the Construction of Wills[312]

(a) Background and history

(i) Two possible approaches

When attempting to construe, or interpret, the words which a testator has used in   **7.138**
his will, there are two possible approaches which a court may adopt: either the
court may focus on what it considers to be the ordinary meaning of the words; or
it may focus on what it thinks was the testator's intention. In most instances, the
two approaches give the same result; and when this happens there is no interpretation problem. But nearly all difficulties in relation to the interpretation of wills
arise because the ordinary meaning of the words used by the testator differs, or
appears to differ, from the meaning he intended to convey. In these cases the court
must choose whether to give to the words their ordinary meaning, or whether to
give to them the meaning the testator intended them to bear. For example, the
testator may leave his residuary estate to be divided amongst 'my nephews and
nieces' and there may be a dispute as to the meaning of the phrase 'nephews
and nieces'. It may be that the court thinks that the ordinary meaning of the
words 'nephews and nieces' is 'children of the testator's brothers and sisters'
(nephews and nieces by blood), but that there is evidence that the testator himself
intended to include also the children of his wife's brothers and sisters (nephews
and nieces by marriage). If the court decides to adopt the ordinary meaning of the
words, it adopts the *literal* (or *grammatical*) approach; whereas, if it decides to
adopt the testator's meaning, it adopts the *intentional* (or *inferential*, or *purposive*)
approach.[313]

The nineteenth century lawyer who did most to champion the literal approach   **7.139**
was Sir James Wigram who brought out the first edition of his book on the construction of wills in 1831.[314] The leading proponent of the intentional approach
was FV Hawkins, who also wrote a book about the construction of wills[315] but
whose views on the general principles of construction were set out in a lecture

---

312 See *Hawkins on the Construction of Wills* (5th edn, 2000) chs 2 and 3.

313 It is not essential that one or other approach is adopted all the time, but some judges appear
not to have understood that there are two approaches; and some seem to have thought that it was
possible to adopt both approaches simultaneously; see, for example, *Re Rowland* [1963] 1 Ch 1,
11–12, CA (Harman LJ).

314 The full title was *An Examination of the Rules of Law Respecting the Admission of Extrinsic
Evidence in Aid of the Interpretation of Wills*. The first edition appeared in 1831, the second in 1834,
the third in 1840, the fourth in 1858 and the fifth in 1914.

315 *Concise Treatise on the Construction of Wills* (1st edn 1863, 5th edn as *Hawkins on the
Construction of Wills*, by R Kerridge, 2000).

which he gave to the Juridical Society in 1860.[316] During the course of the nineteenth century, most judges tended, most of the time, to adopt the literal approach. The House of Lords judge who was its most enthusiastic supporter was Lord Wensleydale,[317] while the judge who most enthusiastically championed the intentional approach was Lord St Leonards.[318] Although the tendency was for Chancery lawyers to adopt a literal approach while Common lawyers tended to be intentionalists, there were a number of exceptions on both sides.[319]

(ii) Perrin v Morgan and Re Rowland

7.140 The difference of approach between the Chancery lawyers and the Common lawyers tended to mean that judgments at first instance and in the Court of Appeal were more likely to follow the literal line than were judgments in the House of Lords.[320]

7.141 In *Perrin v Morgan*[321] the House of Lords had to construe a home-made will which contained the words 'all monies of which I die possessed'. The testatrix had an estate worth more than £30,000 and it consisted almost entirely of stocks and shares. There was extrinsic evidence that she had intended her words to include the whole of her net residuary personalty. The problem was that (literal) case law going back more than two hundred years[322] fixed the word 'monies' as having a relatively narrow meaning, much narrower than that intended by the testatrix. The Court of Appeal considered that it was bound by precedent and, with some reluctance, it followed the case law. The House of Lords unanimously reversed the Court of Appeal and gave the word 'monies' the wider meaning intended by the testatrix. The difficulty with *Perrin v Morgan* is that all five members of the House of Lords reached the same result, but not by the same route. Three of them—Viscount Simon LC, Lord Atkin and Lord Thankerton—took an intentional approach. The others—Lord Russell of Killowen and Lord Romer, both Chancery lawyers—took a semi-literal route: they gave the word 'monies' a wide interpretation but by finding it in the 'context' of the will rather than by saying that 'monies' is a word with many meanings and that they would seek the meaning intended by the testatrix.

---

316 The lecture was published in Vol II of the Papers of the Juridical Society, 298. It was republished as Appendix C to Prof JB Thayer's *Preliminary Treatise on Evidence at the Common Law*, (Boston, 1898).

317 From 1828–34 he was Parke J; from 1834–55 he was Parke B; then he became Lord Wensleydale.

318 The contrast between the two approaches can be seen most clearly in the judgments of these two judges in the case of *Grey v Pearson* (1857) 6 HLC 61, 10 ER 1216, HL.

319 In fact, *both* Lord Wensleydale *and* Lord St Leonards are exceptions.

320 This is illustrated by *Gorringe v Mahlstedt* [1907] AC 225.

321 [1943] AC 399.

322 Starting with *Shelmer's* case (1725) Gilb Rep 200, 25 ER 139.

By contrast, a case which exemplifies the literal approach is the Court of Appeal **7.142** decision in *Re Rowland*,[323] where the court had the task of interpreting a home-made will in which the husband had left all his property to his wife, but had gone on to make provision 'in the event of [her] decease. . .preceding or coinciding with my own decease. . .'. The couple were killed when the boat in which they were travelling sank and the question was whether their deaths had 'coincided'. The Court of Appeal, by a majority,[324] held that their deaths had not 'coincided'. This was a classic example of the literal approach, which purports to look for the 'ordinary meaning' of words, but ends up by construing them as if they had been written by a lawyer. The public reaction to the decision in *Re Rowland* was hostile:[325] non-lawyers did not think that the words had been given their ordinary meaning.

(iii) The Law Reform Committee's nineteenth report

In 1968, the Law Commission asked the Law Reform Committee to examine the **7.143** rules governing the interpretation of wills and later that year the Law Reform Committee began their examination. They produced their nineteenth report in 1973. The report is not an easy document to follow, but its main conclusions were clear. Its recommendation was that the literal approach (in so far as it had survived) should be abandoned and that the intentional position should be adopted.[326] This was, in effect, a reaffirmation of the position taken by the majority in the House of Lords in *Perrin v Morgan*. There was, however, a further problem relating to the admissibility of extrinsic evidence—what sort of extrinsic evidence should be admitted to assist in the construction of a will?

(iv) The admissibility of extrinsic evidence—the three types of evidence

There are three types of extrinsic evidence which could be admitted to assist in the **7.144** interpretation of a will. First of all, there is evidence of circumstances surrounding the testator at the time he made his will; evidence, for example, that he had one child, two stepchildren, no nephews by blood, two nephews by marriage etc. This type of evidence links the words of the will to its subject matter (the property devised and bequeathed) and to its objects (the persons who are to benefit). Secondly, there is evidence as to the testator's use of language; for example, the fact that he habitually referred to his stepchildren as 'my children' or to his nephews by marriage as 'my nephews'. This second sort of evidence is sometimes confused with the first; but it is, essentially, different. Thirdly, there is evidence of the testator's

---

[323] [1963] 1 Ch 1.

[324] The dissenting judge was Lord Denning MR; the judges in the majority were Harman and Russell LJJ, both Chancery lawyers.

[325] The decision was discussed, at length, in the correspondence columns of *The Times*.

[326] Law Reform Committee, Interpretation of Wills (Cmnd 5301, 1973) para 49.

dispositive intention; ie statements made by the testator as to the dispositions in his will. The testator may, for example, have told someone that he had left his residuary estate to his niece by marriage. The first type of evidence must be, and always has been, admissible—whether the approach has been literal or intentional. It is essential to admit evidence to identify a particular person as 'my son' or 'my son John' or to identify a particular ring as 'my engagement ring'. Literalists have always opposed admissibility of the second sort of evidence, (although there has been confusion over this) whereas intentionalists have always wanted to admit it. The third sort of evidence was admissible in England before 1983 only in very limited circumstances.

7.145   The members of the Law Reform Committee were unanimously in favour of moving away from the literal approach and towards the intentional approach and they all wanted to admit the second type of evidence, ie evidence as to the testator's ordinary use of language. But they were divided as to whether to modify the rules in relation to the admissibility of the third sort of evidence—ie evidence of the testator's dispositive intention.

(b) Section 21 of the Administration of Justice Act 1982

7.146   Section 21 of the Administration of Justice Act 1982, which applies where the testator dies on or after 1 January 1983, was based on the recommendations contained in the Law Reform Committee's nineteenth report. It reads as follows:

> 21. (1) This section applies to a will–
> (a) in so far as any part of it is meaningless;
> (b) in so far as the language used in any part of it is ambiguous on the face of it;
> (c) in so far as evidence, other than evidence of the testator's intention, shows that the language used in any part of it is ambiguous in the light of surrounding circumstances.
> (2) In so far as this section applies to a will extrinsic evidence, including evidence of the testator's intention, may be admitted to assist in its interpretation.

The section is not well drafted but its overall pattern is relatively clear. Section 21(1)(a) covers cases—relatively rare—where the testator has used a word or phrase which appears to have no meaning. Section 21(1)(b) covers cases where he has used a word which appears to have several meanings (eg the word 'money'). Section 21(1)(c) covers cases where he has used a word or phrase which has an ordinary meaning or meanings, in circumstances which indicate that he may have intended it to bear not its ordinary meaning, or one of its ordinary meanings, but some other idiosyncratic meaning (eg he has referred to his godson as his nephew). Evidence of the testator's dispositive intention (ie statements made by him) may *not* be called to demonstrate that he has used language idiosyncratically, but evidence as to *his* ordinary use of language may be so called. Once language is shown to be meaningless within s 21(1)(a), or to be ambiguous within s 21(1)(b) or 21(1)(c), evidence of the testator's dispositive intention, as well as evidence of his ordinary use of language, may be called to assist in the interpretation of the ambiguous words or phrases. The result is to adopt the intentional, not the literal, approach and to give the words in a will the meaning intended by the person who drafted it, rather than the meaning which a fictitious reasonable lawyer would give to the same words if he had used them. The application of this approach should be straightforward, and generally has been,[327] though some judges may still be inclined to hold that expressions used by laymen in home-made wills are not ambiguous when, in fact, they are.[328]

(c) Descriptions of persons or things in a will

The enactment of s 21 of the Administration of Justice Act 1982 means that it is **7.147** no longer necessary to distinguish between the first two types of evidence referred to in para 7.133 above: the type which links the words in a will to its subject matter or objects; and evidence as to the testator's use of language. In some pre-1982 cases, judges could escape from the constraints of the literal approach—which would not have admitted the second type of evidence—by confusing the two types. But there were other cases where a failure to understand the distinction led to results which took literalism to extremes which no theory could have justified.[329] Section 21, by admitting evidence of the testator's use of language, avoids a number of problems which were inherent in the literal approach and makes the interpreter's task much easier.

(d) The use of technical terms in a will

Construction cases are heard in the Chancery Division, and before the enactment **7.148** of s 21 of the Administration of Justice Act 1982, most judges at first instance tended to adopt the literal approach, which meant that they tended to interpret words or expressions in a will as though they had been used by a lawyer. They were least inclined to do this when such an approach would result in an intestacy;[330] they were most inclined to do it when the testator had used a technical legal expression—even if the testator was not a lawyer. For example, in *Re Cook*[331]

---

[327] *Re Bowles* [2003] Ch 422.
[328] In *Re Owen* [2002] WTLR 619 it was held that where there was a gift to a wife in a home-made will, followed by a substitutionary gift in the case of her dying 'together with me', and where the wife then pre-deceased the testator, the substitutionary gift did not take effect. There was held to be no ambiguity. But this will was not drafted by a lawyer and should have been interpreted accordingly.
[329] See *National Society for the Prevention of Cruelty to Children v Scottish National Society for the Prevention of Cruelty to Children* [1915] AC 207, HL.
[330] *Perrin v Morgan* [1943] AC 399 (see para 7.141) is an example.
[331] [1948] Ch 212.

a testatrix made a home-made will in which she left 'all my personal estate' to named nephews and nieces. Her estate consisted mainly of realty. Harman J[332] held that the realty did not pass under the will, with the consequence that the testatrix died largely intestate. Even before 1983, not all judges followed this approach. *Re Cook* may be contrasted with *Re Bailey*[333] where Romer J interpreted 'my residuary legatee' to mean 'legatee and devisee'. He did this on the basis of 'context'. In any case, it is submitted that cases like *Re Cook* are no longer good law. It does not matter that a testator has used a technical word or expression. What matters under s 21 of the Administration of Justice Act 1982 is what *he*, the testator, intended by the words he used, not what a lawyer would have meant by them. The object of the exercise is not to punish laymen for drafting their own wills, but to try to understand what they intended by the words they used.

(2) *Specific Rules of Construction*

(a) A general introduction

7.149 Over the years, a number of statutory provisions have been enacted to the effect that particular words or expressions shall be construed in a particular way. There were a number of sections in the Wills Act 1837, as originally enacted, which were concerned with construction. The most important is probably s 24[334] which deals with the date from which a will speaks, but ss 25 to 29 and s 33 are also all concerned with questions of construction. Every one of these sections contains the words 'unless a contrary intention shall appear by the will'.[335] In addition, there are a number of sections in more recent Acts, some of which are referred to in greater detail in paras 7.152–7.158.

7.150 There is one general matter of interest in relation to these sections: what evidence may be called to exclude or override the prima facie rule of construction suggested by the section. This depends on precisely what the section says. The earlier sections, enacted in 1837 when the literal approach was dominant, used the words 'unless a contrary intention shall appear by the will'. Other sections which have been added to the Wills Act,[336] or which have been substituted for sections which were in the original Act,[337] all contain equivalent wording. Similarly, s 61 of the

---

[332] Who later sat in the Court of Appeal in *Re Rowland* [1963] 1 Ch 1 (see para 7.142).

[333] [1945] Ch 191.

[334] See para 7.167.

[335] Another example is s 61, Law of Property Act 1925 which covers 'deeds, contracts, wills. . .and other instruments. . .coming into operation after the commencement of this Act. . .unless the context otherwise requires. . . .'

[336] For example, s 18(A), inserted by the Administration of Justice Act 1982.

[337] Sections 18 and 33, Wills Act 1837, both substituted by the Administration of Justice Act 1982.

Law of Property Act 1925 uses the words 'unless the context otherwise requires'. In all these instances, the statutory provisions are laying down a rule of construction and this can be overridden only by something written in the will. These statutory provisions will prevail over s 21 of the Administration of Justice Act 1982 on the basis that the earlier specific provision prevails over the later general provision.[338] In the case of more recent provisions—such as those in the Family Law Reform Act 1969 and the Adoption Act 1976—there is no requirement that a contrary indication must appear by the will. In other words, extrinsic evidence may be called to show that the testator did not intend his words to mean what the particular section would otherwise assume that they mean. This is the straightforward intentional approach.

In practice, the difference between the two approaches may not be as significant **7.151** as it might in theory appear. At the time when the literal approach prevailed, some judges were astute to discover something which they could call the 'context' so as to enable them to interpret the testator's words as they thought he intended them to be interpreted, rather than in the way that the case law, or the statute, appeared to indicate. It is to be assumed that judges today will be no more literal than these judges were in the past, particularly now that the intentional approach has been enshrined in s 21 of the Administration of Justice Act 1982.

(b) Age of majority

Under the Family Law Reform Act 1969, the expressions 'full age', 'infant', 'infancy', **7.152** 'minor', 'minority', and similar expressions are to be construed by reference to the provision that a person attains full age on attaining the age of eighteen.[339] This construction applies if the will was made on or after 1 January 1970, but if a will was executed before 1970 and confirmed by a codicil made on or after 1 January 1970, it is *not*, for this purpose, treated as made on or after that date.[340] This construction applies 'in the absence of a definition or of any indication of a contrary intention'.[341]

(c) Gifts to children

(i) Adopted children

The Adoption Act 1976 enacts that, 'subject to any contrary indication',[342] an **7.153** adopted child is treated as the legitimate child of the married couple who adopted

---

[338] *Generalia specialibus non derogant*; see FAR Bennion, *Statutory Interpretation* (4th edn, 2002) s 88.
[339] Family Law Reform Act 1969, s 1(1).
[340] ibid s 1(7).
[341] ibid s 1(2).
[342] Adoption Act 1976, s 42(1).

him, or, if not adopted by a married couple, as the legitimate child of the person who adopted him.[343] He is not treated as the child of his natural parents.[344] These principles apply to the construction of the will of any testator who dies on or after 1 January 1976.[345] Where a disposition in a will depends on the date of birth of a child or children, s 42(2) of the Adoption Act 1976 sets out rules of construction which will apply, subject to any contrary intention. The rules apply to gifts such as 'to the children of A living at my death'.[346]

(ii) Legitimated children[347]

7.154 Under the Legitimacy Act 1976, a legitimated person (and any person claiming through him) takes any interest under the will of a testator who dies on or after 1 January 1976 as if he had been born legitimate.[348] This rule of construction is 'subject to any contrary indication'.[349] Where a disposition in a will depends on the date of birth of a child or children, s 5(4) of the Legitimacy Act 1976 sets out rules of construction similar to those applicable to adopted children. Again, the rules are 'subject to any contrary indication'.

(iii) Illegitimate children

7.155 It was a fundamental rule, central to the literal approach to the construction of wills, that a gift by will to children was prima facie construed as referring only to legitimate children. This rule of construction was reversed in part by s 15 of the Family Law Reform Act 1969, which applies to dispositions by will or codicil made on or after 1 January 1970 and before 4 April 1988. Section 19 of the Family Law Reform Act 1987 applies to dispositions made by will or codicil on or after 4 April 1988.[350] A will made before, but confirmed by codicil on or after, 4 April 1988 is not treated as made on or after that date.[351] Under this section, references (whether express or implied) to any relationship between two persons are to be construed without regard to whether the father and mother of either of them, or the father and mother of any person through whom their relationship is deduced, were married to each other at any time. The new rule of construction applies 'unless the contrary intention appears'[352] and does not apply to the

---

343 Adoption Act 1976, s 39(1) and (4).
344 ibid s 39(2); *Re Collins* [1990] Fam 56.
345 ibid s 39(6).
346 For more detailed discussion, see *Hawkins on the Construction of Wills* (5th edn, 2000) 171.
347 A legitimated child is one who was illegitimate at the time of his birth, but who becomes legitimate by his parents' subsequent marriage. Legitimation was introduced into English law by the Legitimacy Act 1926.
348 Legitimacy Act 1976, s 5.
349 ibid s 5(1).
350 *Upton v Nat West Bank* [2004] EWHC 1962; [2004] WTLR 1339.
351 Family Law Reform Act 1987, s 19(7).
352 ibid s 1(1).

devolution of any property which would otherwise devolve along with a dignity or title of honour.[353]

(d) Whether a gift is absolute or for life

Before the Wills Act 1837, a devise without words of limitation passed only a life **7.156** interest, unless there could be found in the will sufficient evidence of an intention to pass the absolute freehold title. So a devise of 'Blackacre to X' gave X only a life interest. Section 28 of the Wills Act 1837 reversed this rule and enacted that a devise of real estate to any person without words of limitation 'shall be construed to pass the fee simple, or other the whole estate or interest which the testator had power to dispose of. . .unless a contrary intention shall appear by the will'. A bequest of personalty 'to X' has always given X an absolute interest, unless a contrary intention can be shown.

Home-made wills can cause problems where testators leave property 'to X' and **7.157** then go on to say that 'on X's death *what remains of the property* [or words to that effect] shall go to Y'. Such a disposition can be construed to give X an absolute interest,[354] or a life interest,[355] or a (hybrid) life interest coupled with a limited power to dispose of capital.[356] The decisions in the cases turn on the construction of the particular wording in the wills in question, construed in such a way as to attempt to discover the testator's meaning.

The problem has arisen most frequently in relation to gifts to spouses. If a testator **7.158** dies on or after 1 January 1983, s 22 of the Administration of Justice Act 1982 specifically provides that such a gift shall be presumed to be absolute provided that: (1) the gift is made to the spouse 'in terms which in themselves would give an absolute interest to the spouse', eg 'my house, Wuthering Heights, to my wife Catherine'; *and* (2) the testator purports by the same instrument to give his issue an interest in the same property, eg 'after her death I give the house to my children'. The purpose of s 22 is to prevent the creation of an unintended life interest for a spouse in a home-made will. But the section applies only where the purported gift over is to the testator's issue. There is no obvious logic in this. The section applies 'except where a contrary intention is shown'.[357]

(e) Rules for ascertaining classes

Wills often contain gifts to classes of beneficiaries. Such gifts may be class gifts in **7.159** the strict sense, eg '£100,000 to the children of A in equal shares absolutely';

---

353 ibid s 19(4).
354 *Perry v Merritt* (1874) LR 18 Eq 152.
355 *Constable v Bull* (1849) 3 De G & Sm 411, 64 ER 539.
356 *Re Stringer's Estate* (1877) 6 Ch D 1, CA.
357 *Harrison v Gibson* [2006] 1 WLR 1212.

or class gifts in the strict sense, but subject to a contingency, eg '£100,000 to the children of B who attain the age of twenty-five years in equal shares absolutely'; or individual gifts to members of the class (not class gifts in the strict sense), eg '£10,000 to each of C's children'. In each case the question may arise as to whether children who come into existence after the testator's death are eligible to take. The provisions of the will may make this clear, but, if they do not, rules of construction known as class-closing rules apply.[358] These rules are discussed in detail in the standard works on the law of succession.[359] They are complicated by the fact that class gifts in the strict sense may be immediate, or may be postponed, and postponed gifts may be accelerated by failure of a preceding interest. The object of the class-closing rules is to make it possible to distribute the estate within a reasonable timescale; but it must be emphasized that, because they are rules of construction, they are not applicable if the testator has shown a contrary intention.

(3) Classification of Legacies and Devises

7.160 It was explained in Section C above that legacies are dispositions by will of personal property, whereas devises are dispositions of real property.[360] It was also explained that legacies may be specific, or general, or (more rarely) demonstrative. Devises may be specific or general.

(a) Specific legacies

7.161 A specific legacy is a gift by will of personalty which is a specified part of the testator's estate, severed or distinguished from the general mass of the estate.[361] A classic example is 'my engagement ring'. The word 'my' indicates a specific legacy, as does any specification which makes it clear that the testator is referring to a specified object which forms part of, but is distinguished from the remainder of, his estate. A specific legacy may be specified so that it is distinguished either at the time the will is executed or at the date of death: 'I give to X the paintings now hanging in my study' or 'I give to X any paintings hanging in my study at the time of my death'.

(b) General legacies

7.162 A general legacy, or general bequest, is a gift of something which is to be provided out of the testator's general estate, but is not a gift of any particular thing. Its subject

---

358 See generally *Hawkins on the Construction of Wills* (5th edn, 2000) ch 14; JHC Morris, 'The Rule against Perpetuities and the Rule in Andrews v Partington' (1954) 70 LQR 61; SJ Bailey, 'Class-Closing, Accumulations and Acceleration' [1958] CLJ 39.

359 See *Hawkins on the Construction of Wills* (5th edn, 2000) ch 14.

360 See para 7.50.

361 *Bothamley v Sherson* (1875) LR 20 Eq 304; *Robertson v Broadbent* (1883) 8 App Cas 812, HL; *Re Rose* [1949] Ch 78.

matter may, but need not, form part of the testator's property at the date of his death. The classic general legacy is a gift of a sum of money 'I give X £10,000'. Sometimes the term 'pecuniary legacy' is used as though it were synonymous with the term 'general legacy' but this is confusing because not all general legacies are pecuniary and not all pecuniary legacies are general. A gift to X of 'all the cash in the safe in my study at the time of my death' would be a specific legacy and a gift of '1,000 shares in Halifax PLC' would be a general legacy.

(c) Demonstrative legacies

A demonstrative legacy is a hybrid, somewhere between a specific legacy and a **7.163** general legacy. It is a legacy which is directed to be satisfied primarily, but not only, out of a specified fund or specified part of the testator's property. A gift to X of '£3,000 to be paid to him out of my partnership share'[362] is a demonstrative legacy. A legacy which can be satisfied only out of a specified part of the testator's property is specific not demonstrative. Demonstrative legacies are rare.

(d) Specific and general devises

A specific devise is a gift by will of realty which is a specified part of the testator's **7.164** estate, severed or distinguished from the general mass of the estate. A classic example is 'my freehold dwelling-house at 10 Cathedral Close, Barchester'. A devise of the residue of the testator's freehold property will be a general devise. It is not possible to have a demonstrative devise.

(e) Significance of classification

The classification of legacies as specific, general and demonstrative, and of devises **7.165** as specific and general, is important because different rules apply to ademption and abatement.[363]

(f) Classification is a question of construction

Whether a legacy is specific, general or demonstrative depends on the construc- **7.166** tion of the particular will. But 'the court leans against specific legacies, and is inclined, if it can, to construe a legacy as general rather than specific; so that if there is any doubt it should, on the whole, be resolved in favour of the view that the legacy is general'.[364] In *Re Willcocks*[365] T by her will gave her father £948 3s 11d Queensland 3½ per cent Inscribed Stock. At the time she made her will,

---

[362] *Re Webster* [1937] 1 All ER 602, CA.
[363] See Section E.
[364] *Re Rose* [1949] Ch 78, 82.
[365] [1921] 2 Ch 327.

T held stock of this description to this exact value. She did not hold it at the time of her death. In the absence of anything to indicate that T intended to give a specific legacy, the court held that this legacy was general.[366]

(4) The Date from which a Will Speaks

(a) Will speaks from death as to property

7.167 Before the Wills Act 1837, it was a rule of law (not construction) that realty acquired after the date of the will could not be devised. Section 3 of the Wills Act 1837 changed this rule of law. Section 24 of the Wills Act 1837 then goes to provide that:

> every will shall be construed, with reference to the real estate and personal estate comprised in it, to speak and take effect as if it had been executed immediately before the death of the testator, unless a contrary intention shall appear by the will.

(i) Pecuniary and general legacies

7.168 If someone leaves a bequest of £10,000, that obviously means £10,000 at the time of death; and a residuary bequest must cover residue at the time of death. So s 24 appears, at first glance, to have no application to general legacies. But it can apply to them. Suppose there is a gift of '1,000 shares' in a named company; s 24 enacts that this means '1,000 shares at the time of death'. If the shares have been divided, or reorganized, between the time when the will was executed and the time of death, the description will apply at death.

(ii) Specific legacies

7.169 Section 24 clearly applies to specific generic legacies and specific generic devises, ie specific gifts worded in such a way that the subject matter is capable of increase or decrease between the date of the will and the date of the testator's death, such as 'all my shares in XYZ plc' or 'all my lands in the County of B'.

(iii) Contrary intention

7.170 Section 24 appears to apply to non-generic specific legacies and devises, such as 'my gold watch' or 'my house', but problems arise in these cases as to whether a 'contrary intention' has appeared from the will. The cases are not easy to reconcile.

7.171 The question as to whether the prima facie rule in s 24 does, or does not, apply may be important for two reasons. If the prima facie rule applies, this may avoid ademption. Ademption occurs where the testator no longer owns property

---

[366] And so the gift was not adeemed—see para 7.176. For an extreme example of the presumption in favour of a legacy's being construed as general, see *Re Gage* [1934] Ch 536.

bequeathed or devised by his will and it leads to failure of the gift.[367] The application of the prima facie rule in s 24 will save some gifts from ademption. For example, if a testator bequeaths 'my gold watch' and then loses the gold watch he had when he made his will and buys another, the straightforward application of s 24 will save the gift. The finding of a 'contrary intention' will lead to failure. The other reason why there may be a dispute as to the application of s 24 is that it may affect the extent of the property. Where there is, for example, a gift of 'my farm' the words may cover more, or less, land at the time of death than at the time the will was executed.

Two elements in the description of property in a will appear to indicate a 'contrary intention' under s 24: a reference to the present time and a detailed description. But the cases follow no very clear pattern and there are exceptions to almost any rule which could be suggested. It seems probable that the identity of the beneficiary has played a part in some borderline cases—the judges have shown sympathy for widows[368]—and in some ademption cases the court appears to have been influenced by the fact that the subject matter of the original gift was worth less than its alleged replacement.[369] Page Wood V-C in *Re Gibson*[370] went so far as to suggest, obiter, that s 24 would never apply to save a non-generic specific legacy from ademption. There are conflicting dicta in the cases of *Castle v Fox*[371] and *Re Evans*[372] as to whether the prima facie rule in s 24 would apply if there were a gift in a will of 'my house in Cavendish Square' and the testator disposed of the house he owned when he made his will and acquired another in the same square. **7.172**

(b) A will speaks from its date as to the object of a gift

Section 24 says nothing about the object of a gift, ie the person who is to benefit. The rule here is that a will speaks from its date as to the object—unless a contrary intention appears. So, a gift to 'Lord Sherborne' means a gift to the person who was Lord Sherborne when the will was made. If he dies before the testator, the property does not pass to the new Lord Sherborne.[373] **7.173**

(c) Effect of republication

A gift which would fail on the basis of the rules set out above may, of course, be saved by confirmation (republication) of the will.[374] **7.174**

---

367 See para 7.176.
368 *Re Willis* [1911] 2 Ch 563.
369 *Re Sikes* [1927] 1 Ch 364.
370 (1866) LR 2 Eq 669.
371 (1871) LR 11 Eq 542.
372 [1909] 1 Ch 784.
373 *Re Whorwood* (1887) 34 Ch D 446, CA.
374 See para 7.124.

E. Failure of Gifts by Will or of Interests on Intestacy

(1) Introduction

7.175 A gift by will may fail for any one of the following reasons:

(a) the gift is adeemed;

(b) the gift abates;

(c) the beneficiary or his spouse is an attesting witness;

(d) the gift fails for uncertainty;

(e) the gift lapses, because the beneficiary predeceases the testator;

(f) the deceased's marriage or civil partnership to the beneficiary is dissolved or annulled;

(g) the beneficiary is convicted of the murder or manslaughter of the deceased;

(h) the beneficiary disclaims.

Heads (a)–(d) apply only to wills, not intestacies. Heads (e) and (f) apply, strictly, to wills but a would-be beneficiary under an intestacy will lose his interest if he predeceases the intestate or if his marriage or civil partnership to the testator is dissolved or annulled. Heads (g) and (h) apply both to beneficiaries under wills and on intestacies.

(2) Ademption

(a) Ademption of specific gifts

7.176 Where the subject matter of a specific legacy or a specific devise is no longer part of the testator's property at the time of his death, the gift is adeemed.[375] Ademption does not depend on the testator's intention.[376] If A leaves 'my gold watch' to B in his will, but has no gold watch at the time of his death, B's gift will fail. The doctrine of ademption does not apply to general legacies. That is one reason why the construction of a legacy as general or specific is important. A demonstrative legacy does not fail by ademption: in so far as it cannot be satisfied out of the specific fund primarily designated for its payment, it is treated as a general legacy.

(b) Change in substance, not in name or form

7.177 Although a change in substance of the subject matter of a specific gift causes ademption, a change in name or form does not. But the dividing line between a change in substance and one of form is not always easy to discern. It was held in *Re Slater*[377]

---

375 *Ashburner v Macguire* (1786) 2 Bro CC 108, 29 ER 62.

376 ibid.

377 [1907] 1 Ch 665, CA.

that there was ademption where a company was taken over and shares in another company were substituted for the original shares. This may be contrasted with *Re Dorman*[378] where a gift of the credit balance in a bank account survived a transfer of the credit balance to a new account. In *Re Viertel*,[379] the Supreme Court of Queensland had to deal with a case similar to *Re Dorman* and came to the same result by a different route. The court held that there would be no ademption where there was a sale by an attorney under an enduring power of attorney.[380] This case implies that, in Queensland, ademption is a question of the testator's intention and not a rule of law; in England, it has been regarded as a rule of law. *Viertel* has not been followed in England.[381] The problem in cases like *Re Slater* can be avoided by an express provision in the will to cover the possibility of ademption in the event of (say) a takeover.

(c) Ademption by contract or option

Ademption occurs not only where the property is sold before the testator's death, **7.178** but also where, after making his will, the testator contracts to sell the property and the sale is completed after his death. The specific legatee may enjoy the property until completion of the sale, but he does not receive the proceeds of sale which pass into residue.[382] The same rule applies where the contract is conditional[383] and (more surprisingly) where there is an option which is exercised after the testator's death.[384] Careful attention needs to be paid to options which may be exercised after the testator's death.[385] Ademption occurs where the contract, conditional contract or option is made after the will; if it is made before the will, the specific legatee will be entitled to the proceeds of sale.[386]

(3) Abatement

Abatement concerns the statutory order of application of assets to the payment **7.179** of expenses, debts and liabilities. Where a deceased's estate is solvent, the burden

---

[378] [1994] 1 WLR 282.

[379] [2003] WTLR 1011.

[380] For enduring powers of attorney in England, see Enduring Powers of Attorney Act 1985. The 1985 Act will be repealed when the relevant sections of the Mental Capacity Act 2005 (ss 9–14) are brought into force, at which point enduring powers of attorney will be replaced by lasting powers of attorney. In the context of property and succession, this will not be a significant change.

[381] *Banks v Nat West Bank* [2005] EWHC 3479; [2006] WTLR 1693.

[382] *Farrar v Earl of Winterton* (1842) 5 Beav 1, 49 ER 478.

[383] *Re Sweeting* [1988] 1 All ER 1016.

[384] This is the rule in *Lawes v Bennett* (1785) 1 Cox 167, 29 ER 1111; and see *Re Carrington* [1932] 1 Ch 1, CA; but contrast *Pennington v Waine (No 2)* [2003] WTLR 1011.

[385] R Kerridge and AHR Brierley 'Will-Making and the Avoidance of Negligence Claims' [1999] Conveyancer 399.

[386] *Re Calow* [1928] Ch 710; *Drant v Vause* (1842) 1 Y & CCC 580, 62 ER 1026.

of his expenses, debts and liabilities as between beneficiaries is regulated by s 34(3) of the Administration of Estates Act 1925 which enacts that, unless the statutory order is varied by his will, the deceased's property will be applied towards the discharge of his expenses, debts and liabilities in the order set out in Part II of the First Schedule. Gifts within the same class abate rateably. General legacies abate before specific legacies or devises. Demonstrative legacies are treated as specific in so far as they can be discharged out of the designated property, which means that, in relation to ademption and abatement, they have the best of both worlds.

(4) Beneficiary or Spouse is an Attesting Witness

(a) General rule

7.180   Section 15 of the Wills Act 1837 enacts that:

> If any person shall attest the execution of any will to whom or to whose wife or husband any beneficial devise, legacy [or] gift. . .shall be. . .given or made, such devise, legacy [or] gift. . .shall. . .be entirely null and void. . .[387]

The section covers gifts[388] to attesting witnesses and to their spouses or civil partners.[389] In either case, although the will is valid, the gift is void. A solicitor who permits a beneficiary, or his spouse or civil partner, to witness a will may be liable in negligence; and the beneficiary may be entitled to recover the value of the lost legacy as damages.[390]

(b) Limits to operation of general rule

7.181   The rule does not apply to an informal will made by a privileged testator.[391] It does not apply if the beneficiary was not the spouse of the witness at the time of the will's execution.[392] It does not apply if the gift is not beneficial but is in trust.[393] It does not apply if the gift is confirmed by a codicil which was not attested by the beneficiary or his spouse.[394] Finally, s 1 of the Wills Act 1968 enacts that an attestation by a beneficiary or his spouse may be disregarded if the attestation is superfluous, so that the will would be duly executed without it.

---

387   See DEC Yale, 'Witnessing Wills and Losing Legacies' (1984) 100 LQR 453.

388   The Trustee Act 2000 s 28(4) reverses the presumption that any payment to which a trustee is entitled in respect of services is to be treated as a gift for the purposes of s 15 of the Wills Act, so a will which contains a charging clause can now be witnessed by the trustee without his losing the benefit of the clause.

389   The Civil Partnership Act 2004 Sch 4, Part 1, para 3, causes s 15 to apply to civil partners as to spouses.

390   *Ross v Caunters* [1980] Ch 297.

391   *Re Limond* [1915] 2 Ch 240.

392   *Thorpe v Bestwick* (1881) 6 QBD 311.

393   *Cresswell v Cresswell* (1868) LR 6 Eq 69.

394   *Anderson v Anderson* (1872) LR 13 Eq 381.

(5) Uncertainty

(a) Scope

A gift by will is void for uncertainty if, after applying the relevant rules of construc- **7.182**
tion, it is not possible to identify either the subject matter or the object of the gift.

(b) Uncertainty of subject matter

In *Anthony v Donges*[395] a gift to a widow of 'such minimal part of my estate. . .as **7.183**
she may be entitled to under English law for maintenance purposes'[396] was held to
be self-contradictory and void for uncertainty.[397]

(c) Uncertainty of object

In *Re Stephenson*,[398] a gift to the children of a cousin, which did not indicate **7.184**
which cousin, failed for uncertainty; though it could be argued that s 21 of the
Administration of Justice Act 1982 would save such a gift today.[399] There is an
exception to this uncertainty rule where a gift is to charity, provided that the gift
is exclusively charitable[400] and provided that there is a general charitable intention. In this case, the gift does not fail for uncertainty of objects merely because
the testator has not indicated which particular charity he wishes to benefit.[401]

(6) Lapse

(a) Beneficiary predeceases the testator

Under this doctrine, which follows from the ambulatory character of a will, a gift **7.185**
by will fails if the beneficiary dies before the testator.[402] The best way of avoiding
the effects of the doctrine is to make a substitutional gift to (say) the children of
the intended beneficiary, if he should predecease the testator. Where there is a gift
to tenants in common in equal shares, one or more shares may lapse. By contrast,
where there is a gift to joint tenants there will be no lapse unless all the beneficiaries die before the testator.[403] Where there is a class gift, it does not matter whether

---

395 [1998] 2 FLR 775.
396 For family provision, see Section G.
397 The testator was a solicitor.
398 [1897] 1 Ch 75, CA.
399 See para 7.146.
400 *Chichester Diocesan Fund and Board of Finance v Simpson* [1944] AC 341, HL. The construction of a gift as exclusively charitable might also be affected by s 21, Administration of Justice
Act 1982; see para 7.146.
401 *Re White* [1893] 2 Ch 41, CA.
402 *Elliott v Davenport* (1705) 1 P Wms 83, 24 ER 304.
403 *Morley v Bird* (1798) 3 Ves 629, 30 ER 1192.

the members of the class take as joint tenants or as tenants in common because the composition of the class is not known until the time arrives for ascertaining it.[404]

(b) Presumption where there is uncertainty as to who survived whom

7.186 In some cases it is impossible to say who died before whom. Before 1926, the onus lay on a beneficiary's personal representatives to prove affirmatively that he had survived the testator. If, for example, two brothers had died in a common accident, and it was uncertain who had survived whom, neither could benefit under the other's will or intestacy.[405] But where the deaths occur on or after 1 January 1926, s 184 of the Law of Property Act 1925 enacts that, for purposes affecting the title to property:

> In all cases where. . .two or more persons have died in circumstances rendering it uncertain which of them survived the other or others. . .the younger shall be deemed to have survived the elder.

It was argued in *Hickman v Peacey*[406] that the section would not apply where a number of people had been killed together by a wartime bomb, because it would then be certain that they had died simultaneously, so the order of deaths would not be uncertain. The House of Lords (by a majority) rejected this argument and held that the section applies to deaths which are (effectively) simultaneous as well as where deaths occurred separately, but the order is not known.

7.187 The statutory presumption under s 184 has not applied as between intestate spouses since 1953.[407] Where an intestate and his spouse die on or after 1 January 1996 then, in order to take any beneficial interest, the spouse must survive by 28 days.[408] When testators make their wills, they should be asked whether they wish to provide that some or all of any legatees or devisees benefit only if they survive by (say) a period of one month.

(c) Exception to lapse doctrine for gifts to children and remoter descendants

7.188 Where a testator dies on or after 1 January 1983, s 33(1) of the Wills Act 1837, as substituted by s 19 of the Administration of Justice Act 1982, applies.

> Where–
> (a) a will contains a devise or bequest to a child or remoter descendant of the testator; and
> (b) the intended beneficiary dies before the testator, leaving issue; and

---

[404] *Doe d Stewart v Sheffield* (1811) 13 East 526, 104 ER 475.
[405] *Wing v Angrave* (1860) 8 HLC 183, 11 ER 397.
[406] [1945] AC 304, HL.
[407] Administration of Estates Act 1925, s 46(3) as amended by the Intestates' Estates Act 1952, s 1(4).
[408] Law Reform (Succession) Act 1995, s 1(1).

(c) issue of the intended beneficiary are living at the testator's death,

then, unless a contrary intention appears by the will, the devise or bequest shall take effect as a devise or bequest to the issue living at the testator's death.

The section applies only to direct lineal descendants of the testator who predecease him; it does not, for example, apply where the testator's nephew has predeceased the testator leaving issue living at the testator's death. The beneficiary's issue living at the testator's death take *per stirpes*, if more than one in equal shares.[409] Section 33(2) covers class gifts to lineal descendants.

(7) Dissolution of Marriage

Before 1983, divorce had no effect on a will. If a testator had made a will leaving property 'to my wife W', had then divorced W and died without remarrying[410] or making a new will, W would have taken under the will. Where a testator died between 1 January 1983 and 31 December 1995 inclusive, s 18A of the Wills Act 1837[411] enacted that a gift to a former spouse should *lapse*. In *Re Sinclair*[412] the Court of Appeal had to consider the effect of this section in a case where the testator had devised and bequeathed all his property to his wife and then provided that, if she predeceased him, it should go to a named charity. The couple were divorced and the testator neither remarried nor made a new will. The Court of Appeal held that the charity did not obtain any benefit under the will. The wife had not predeceased the testator—rather, the gift to her had lapsed—and the property the charity would have received, had the former wife predeceased him, passed on his intestacy. *Re Sinclair* left the law in an unsatisfactory state and s 3 of the Law Reform (Succession) Act 1995 amends s 18A of the Wills Act 1837 so that if the testator dies on or after 1 January 1996 the former spouse is now deemed to have predeceased him unless a contrary intention appears in the will.[413] This means that if the facts of *Re Sinclair* were to recur, the default beneficiary would take rather than the beneficiaries entitled on intestacy.[414] A testator whose marriage is dissolved should be encouraged to make a new will.

7.189

---

[409] (Substituted) s 33(3), Wills Act 1837; this is a stirpital distribution similar to the distribution to issue on an intestacy, see paras 7.13 and 7.14.

[410] If he had remarried, his remarriage would have revoked his will; see para 7.110.

[411] Inserted by s 18(2), Administration of Justice Act 1982.

[412] [1985] Ch 446.

[413] The former spouse is deemed to have predeceased the testator for almost all, but not all, purposes; see R Kerridge, 'The Effect of Divorce on Wills' [1995] Conveyancer 12.

[414] Section 4, Law Reform (Succession) Act 1995 revokes the former spouse's appointment as a testamentary guardian of the testator's infant children, but the revocation will apply only if the former spouse is not the children's parent.

(8) Murder or Manslaughter

(a) Forfeiture rule

7.190 Before 1870, the property of a convicted felon was forfeited to the Crown; murder and manslaughter were both felonies. The Forfeiture Act 1870 abolished forfeiture to the Crown and a judge-made rule, called 'the forfeiture rule',[415] then developed to the effect that someone who commits murder[416] or some forms of manslaughter[417] is debarred from taking any benefit under his victim's will or on his intestacy. Although it is clear that he is debarred, it is not always clear who will take in his place. It had been thought that the killer would hold on a constructive trust and that this would give the court a discretion as to whom to substitute for him, but this approach was not adopted in *Re DWS*[418] and the resulting confusion has led to the suggestion that the law may need to be amended.[419] Another problem with the forfeiture rule is that its ambit is unclear. It applies to murder, but it does not apply to killers found not guilty by reason of insanity.[420] It has never been clear to which forms of manslaughter it applies; nor is it clear whether it applies to causing death by dangerous driving.[421]

(b) Forfeiture Act 1982

7.191 The Forfeiture Act 1982 gives the court the power to modify the effect of the forfeiture rule if it is satisfied that the justice of the case so requires, having regard to the conduct of the offender and of the deceased and of any other material circumstances.[422] There is no power to modify where someone is convicted of murder. The 1982 Act is not well drafted.[423] It is engrafted onto the earlier case law, which was uncertain, so the present position is uncertain too. Suppose that a beneficiary under a will or intestacy is convicted of the testator's or intestate's manslaughter; or of causing his death by dangerous driving. Should he apply for relief from forfeiture? He will need to do this only if his is a case which would have led to forfeiture before the passing of the 1982 Act. But it is not clear which these cases were.

---

[415] Both the *pre*-1870 rule and the *post*-1870 rule are referred to as 'the forfeiture rule'. They are quite different rules so this is potentially confusing.

[416] *In the Estate of Crippen* [1911] P 108.

[417] *In the Estate of Hall* [1914] P 1, CA.

[418] [2001] Ch 568, CA. See 117 LQR (2001) 371.

[419] Law Commission, *The Forfeiture Rule and the Law of Succession*, (Law Com No 295, 2005).

[420] *Re Houghton* [1915] 2 Ch 173.

[421] There appear to be no reported cases where it has been suggested that the rule applies to causing death by dangerous driving. Section 20 of the Road Safety Act 2006 will, when it comes into force, create an additional offence of 'causing death by careless driving'. It is virtually certain that the forfeiture rule will not apply to someone convicted of this new offence.

[422] Forfeiture Act 1982, ss 1, 2, 5, and 7; proceedings for modification must be brought within three months of conviction: s 2(3).

[423] SM Cretney, 'The Forfeiture Act 1982: The Private Member's Bill as an Instrument of Law Reform' (1990) 10 OJLS 289.

In *Re H (dec'd)*[424] Peter Gibson J held that the forfeiture rule did not apply to a case of diminished responsibility, while in *Re K*[425] Vinelott J held that the rule did apply to a case which appears not to have been very different; he then granted full relief under the Act.[426] In *Dunbar v Plant*[427] the Court of Appeal held that the rule applied to aiding and abetting a suicide, but again granted full relief under the Act.[428]

(9) Disclaimer

A beneficiary under a will or intestacy is free to disclaim his gift by deed[429] or by conduct. He cannot disclaim once he has unequivocally accepted the gift.[430] He can accept one gift in a will and disclaim another, which he may wish to do if he thinks one gift, such as a lease, is onerous; but if one single gift includes two or more assets, the beneficiary must take all or none.[431] A voluntary disclaimer of a benefit in a person's estate before that person's death is ineffective because there is nothing to be disclaimed.[432]

7.192

(10) Effect of Failure

In general, a legacy or devise which fails falls into residue; the subject matter passes under any residuary gift contained in the will; if there is no effective residuary gift, it passes on intestacy.[433]

7.193

F. Executors and Administrators

Executors and administrators are known as 'personal representatives', a term which originated when they were concerned only with the deceased's personal property. The term has been a misnomer for more than a hundred years, because, since the

7.194

---

[424] [1990] 1 FLR 441.

[425] [1985] Ch 85; decision affirmed by CA [1986] Ch 180; this is a case where the report does not make it clear of what type of manslaughter the widow had been convicted.

[426] The safest course appears to be to apply for relief under the Act. But the problem is that this may involve unnecessary legal costs and, even if the applicant obtains full relief, he may, by making the application, provoke potential problems in relation to insurance claims and/or state benefits.

[427] [1998] Ch 412.

[428] In *Land v Land* [2006] EWHC 2069 (Ch); [2007] 1 WLR 1009, it was suggested that the forfeiture rule applies to *all* cases of manslaughter, but its effect was then modified by the questionable application of the Inheritance (Provision for Family and Dependants) Act 1975, see Section G. The killer took almost the entire estate.

[429] *Townson v Tickell* (1819) 3 B & Ald 31, 106 ER 575.

[430] *Re Hodge* [1940] Ch 260.

[431] *Re Joel* [1943] Ch 311, CA.

[432] *Re Smith* [2001] 1 WLR 1937.

[433] See generally *Hawkins on the Construction of Wills* (5th edn, 2000) ch 9, and *Leake v Robinson* (1817) 2 Mer 363, 35 ER 979.

Land Transfer Act 1897, they have dealt with realty as well as personalty. An executor is appointed by the testator. An administrator is appointed by the court.

(1) Executors

(a) Appointment of executors

(i) Express appointment by will

7.195 Executors are almost always appointed by the testator in his will. Such appointment may be express or implied. A properly drawn will should contain an express appointment of one or more named persons as executors.[434] An express appointment of an executor may be absolute, or it may be conditional, eg on his attaining a specified age. The appointment may be limited as to time, eg someone may be appointed to act until someone else attains majority. The appointment may be qualified as to subject matter, eg the testator may appoint different persons to be the executors of his business and non-business property. It is prudent to appoint substituted executors who are to act if the person or persons first chosen are unwilling or unable to act.[435]

(ii) Implied appointment by will

7.196 If someone is impliedly appointed as an executor, he is called 'an executor according to the tenor'. In *In the Goods of Adamson*[436] it was held that the words 'I desire GH to pay my all just debts' was an implied appointment.

(iii) Appointment under power conferred in will

7.197 In addition to appointing executors in his will, a testator may authorize another person to appoint executors after his death. For example, he may expressly appoint two executors and then direct that, if one dies, the survivor may appoint a replacement.[437]

(iv) Appointment by court

7.198 The court has a wide power under s 50 of the Administration of Justice Act 1985 to appoint a substituted personal representative in place of any or all of the existing personal representatives. The court may also appoint an additional personal representative to act during the minority of a beneficiary, or during the

---

[434] It is often said that executors are executors of the will; strictly they are executors of the person, the testator's executors; see Williams, Mortimer and Sunnucks, *Executors, Administrators and Probate* (18th edn), 18.

[435] *In the Goods of Foster* (1871) LR 2 P & D 304.

[436] (1875) LR 3 P & D 253.

[437] *In the Goods of Deichman* (1842) 3 Curt 123, 163 ER 676.

subsistence of a life interest if there is only one personal representative (not being a trust corporation).[438]

(b) Transmission of office

The office of executor is one of personal trust[439] and it cannot be assigned. **7.199** Nevertheless, s 7 of the Administration of Estates Act 1925 provides for automatic transmission of the office on death through proving executors.

An executor of a sole or last surviving executor of a testator is the executor of that **7.200** testator[440] as well, provided he has proved the will of his own testator. He is then known as *an executor by representation*. He is not entitled to accept office as executor of the testator who appointed him, and at the same time to renounce office as executor by representation of the original testator.[441] So long as the chain of representation is unbroken, the last executor in the schain is the executor of every preceding testator.[442] The chain is broken by an intestacy, by the failure to appoint an executor, or by the failure to obtain probate.[443]

(c) Number of executors

There is no limit to the number of executors a testator may appoint, but s 114(1) **7.201** of the Supreme Court Act 1981 provides that probate (or administration) shall not be granted to more than four persons in respect of the same part of the estate. There is no minimum number and probate may be granted to one executor.[444]

(d) Who may be appointed executor?

A testator may appoint as his executor a member of his family, a friend, a benefici- **7.202** ary, a professional adviser or a trust corporation. It is advisable not to appoint a minor because a minor cannot obtain probate, or act, until he attains his majority.[445] Similarly, a person who is incapable of managing his affairs by reason of mental or physical incapacity cannot act as executor, or take probate, while his incapacity continues.[446] There is nothing to prevent a testator from appointing as his executors

---

438 Supreme Court Act 1981, s 114(4). For the definition of 'trust corporation' see Supreme Court Act 1981, s 128; a trust corporation includes the Public Trustee and also companies formed to take on the business of acting as trustees or personal representatives. Most trust corporations are subsidiaries of clearing banks.

439 *In the Estate of Skinner* [1958] 1 WLR 1043.

440 Administration of Estates Act 1925, s 7(1).

441 *Brooke v Haymes* (1868) LR 6 Eq 25.

442 Administration of Estates Act 1925, s 7(2).

443 ibid s 7(3).

444 Contrast grants of administration—see para 7.209.

445 Supreme Court Act 1981, s 118.

446 *In the Goods of Galbraith* [1951] P 422.

the persons who will be the partners in a named firm of solicitors or accountants at the date of his death.[447] There is no technical problem with the appointment of a trust corporation,[448] which may obtain probate in its own name.[449]

(e) Passing over

7.203 Under s 116 of the Supreme Court Act 1981, if 'by reason of any special circumstances' it appears to the court to be 'necessary or expedient' to appoint as administrator someone other than the person appointed executor by the will, the court has a discretion to appoint this other person as administrator.[450]

(f) Acceptance and renunciation

7.204 A person appointed executor is free to accept or renounce the office. He accepts by taking probate[451] or by acting as executor and intermeddling in the estate.[452] He renounces in signed writing and his renunciation becomes binding when filed in a probate registry.[453] He cannot renounce in part. If an executor neither accepts nor renounces probate, someone who would be entitled to letters of administration if the executor renounced may apply to the Principal Registry of the Family Division or a district probate registry for the issue of a citation. This calls on the executor to enter an appearance and accept or renounce probate.[454]

(2) *Administrators*

7.205 An administrator is appointed not by the testator, but by the court. There is no transmission of office by administrators.

(a) Order of priority to administration

7.206 The Non-Contentious Probate Rules 1987 set out the classes of persons entitled to letters of administration and the order of priority between them.

(i) *Where the deceased left a will*

7.207 Where the deceased left a will, the order of priority is set out in r 20. If no executor is appointed by the will, or if the executor renounces, the following persons may

---

447 *Re Horgan* [1971] P 50; *Re Rogers* [2006] EWHC 753; [2006] 1 WLR 1577.
448 For the definition of 'trust corporation' see n 438 above. Consideration should, however, be given to the *cost* of employing a trust corporation.
449 Supreme Court Act 1981, s 115(1).
450 *In the Estate of Biggs* [1966] P 118.
451 *In the Goods of Veiga* (1862) 2 Sw & Tr 13, 164 ER 1176.
452 *Re Stevens* [1897] 1 Ch 422.
453 *In the Goods of Morant* (1874) LR 3 P & D 151.
454 Non-Contentious Probate Rules 1987, r 47.

apply for a grant of administration with the will annexed: (1) any residuary legatee or devisee holding in trust; (2) any other residuary legatee or devisee, or any person entitled to residue under the intestacy rules;[455] (3) the personal representatives of a deceased residuary legatee, devisee or person entitled to residue; (4) any other legatee or devisee or creditor of the deceased; (5) the personal representative of any other legatee or devisee or creditor. A person in class (1) has a right to apply for letters of administration before someone in class (2), etc. If someone with a prior right does not apply for letters of administration, he may be 'cleared off' by someone with a subsequent right.[456] Persons in the same class do not need to give notice to one another before they apply for letters of administration.

(ii) *Where the deceased died wholly intestate*

The order of priority begins with the surviving spouse of the deceased and follows the order of priority on intestacy, ie issue, parents, brothers and sisters of the whole blood, etc.[457] A person may apply only if he has a beneficial interest in the estate.[458] If there is nobody with a beneficial interest, the Treasury Solicitor may apply for a grant, if he claims *bona vacantia*.[459] If everyone referred to above has been cleared off, a creditor may apply.[460]

7.208

(b) Number of administrators

Section 114(2) of the Supreme Court Act 1981 states that, if under a will or intestacy any beneficiary is a minor, or if a life interest arises, administration must be granted *either* to a trust corporation *or* to not less than two individuals, *unless* it appears to the court to be expedient in all the circumstances to appoint an individual as sole administrator.

7.209

(c) Capacity of administrators

A minor or a person who is incapable of managing his affairs by reason of mental incapacity cannot take a grant of administration.[461]

7.210

(d) Passing over

Section 116 of the Supreme Court Act 1981 applies to administrators as well as to executors. A person may be passed over for bad character[462] or because he is

7.211

---

[455] This will apply where there is a partial intestacy.
[456] Non-Contentious Probate Rules 1987, r 8(4).
[457] For the order of priority on intestacy see paras 7.12ff.
[458] Non-Contentious Probate Rules 1987, r 22(1).
[459] ibid r 22(2). For explanation of *bona vacantia*, see para 7.27.
[460] Non-Contentious Probate Rules 1987, 22(3).
[461] ibid r 35.
[462] *In the Goods of Ardern* [1898] P 147.

abroad,[463] but in *In the Goods of Edwards-Taylor*[464] the court refused to pass over a twenty-one-year-old residuary beneficiary simply on the ground that she was immature and needed protection from herself.

(e) Acceptance and renunciation

7.212 A person who is entitled to administration may accept or renounce; and he may be cited to accept or to refuse a grant.[465] A person entitled to administration does not accept office by intermeddling in the estate.[466]

G. Family Provision

(1) Introduction

7.213 Until 1938 there was almost total testamentary freedom in England and Wales. The Inheritance (Family Provision) Act 1938 introduced the principle that certain specified 'dependants' of a deceased person could apply to the court for a discretionary order for maintenance out of his estate.[467] The governing statute is now the Inheritance (Provision for Family and Dependants) Act 1975, as amended by the Law Reform (Succession) Act 1995 and the Civil Partnership Act 2004.

7.214 The 1975 Act applies only if the deceased died domiciled in England and Wales,[468] though, where he does die so domiciled, the court is entitled to take account of any property he owned abroad when considering the 'reasonableness' of any provision made by him.[469] An application for family provision may be made either to the Chancery Division or to the Family Division of the High Court or to the county court:[470] it must be made not later than six months from the date on which a valid grant of probate or letters of administration is first taken out.[471] The court has a discretion to extend this time limit and, in *Re Salmon*,[472] Sir Robert Megarry V-C suggested a number of guidelines for the exercise of the discretion.[473]

---

463 *In the Goods of Cholwill* (1866) LR 1 P & D 192.
464 [1951] P 24.
465 Non-Contentious Probate Rules 1987, r 47.
466 *In the Goods of Davis* (1860) 4 Sw & Tr 213, 164 ER 1498.
467 The specified classes of dependants have since been added to.
468 1975 Act, ss 1(1) and 27(2). *Cyganik v Agulian* [2006] 1 FCR 406, CA.
469 *Bheekhun v Williams* [1999] 2 FLR 229, CA.
470 Which now has unlimited jurisdiction under the High Court and County Court Jurisdiction Order 1991, SI 1991/724.
471 Inheritance (Provision for Family and Dependants) Act 1975, s 4.
472 [1981] Ch 167.
473 See also *Stock v Brown* [1994] 1 FLR 840; and *Re W* [1995] 2 FCR 689.

The personal representatives may pay the funeral, testamentary and administra- **7.215**
tion expenses, debts and liabilities before the expiration of the six months' time
limit; and when the six months' period has elapsed, provided no application under
the 1975 Act has been made, they may safely distribute the estate. The personal
representatives are protected; but this does not prejudice an applicant's power to
recover any part of the distributed estate from a beneficiary.[474]

(2) Reasonable Financial Provision

Six classes of applicant may apply for an order under s 2 of the Inheritance **7.216**
(Provision for Family and Dependants) Act 1975.[475]

(a) Two standards of 'reasonable financial provision'

There are two standards of 'reasonable financial provision': the surviving spouse **7.217**
standard, which means 'such financial provision as it would be reasonable in all
the circumstances of the case for a husband or wife. . .[or] civil partner to receive,
whether or not that provision is required for his or her maintenance';[476] and the
maintenance standard, which means 'such financial provision as it would be reasonable in all the circumstances of the case for the applicant to receive for his
maintenance'.[477]

The court does not normally have a discretion as to which standard to apply. **7.218**
There are six categories of applicant. The surviving spouse standard applies automatically to anyone in the first category (deceased's spouse or civil partner) except
where, at the date of death, a separation order under the Family Law Act 1996, or
under the Civil Partnership Act 2004, was in force and the separation was continuing, in which case the separated spouse or civil partner is treated as if he or she
were in the second category. The maintenance standard normally applies to anyone in the second category (a former spouse or civil partner, but not one who has
formed a subsequent marriage or civil partnership) and to any separated spouse or
civil partner who is treated as if he or she were in the second category; but in these
two cases only, the court has a *discretion* to apply the surviving spouse standard,
provided the deceased died within twelve months of the divorce or separation
order and an application for financial provision in connection with the divorce or
separation had been made but not determined.[478] The maintenance standard

---

474 Inheritance (Provision for Family and Dependants) Act 1975, s 20(1).
475 See paras 7.220–7.236.
476 Inheritance (Provision for Family and Dependants) Act 1975, s 1(2)(a) and 1(2)(aa).
477 ibid s 1(2)(b); and see *Re Coventry* [1980] Ch 461, CA; and *Re Dennis* [1981] 2 All ER 140.
478 Inheritance (Provision for Family and Dependants) Act, s 14.

applies to anyone in the third to sixth categories (cohabitants, children, stepchildren and dependants).

(b) Satisfying the court

7.219 The court may make an order under the 1975 Act if it is satisfied that 'the disposition of the deceased's estate effected by his will or the law relating to intestacy. . .is not such as to make reasonable financial provision for the applicant'.[479] The test is objective;[480] and the court takes into account facts known to it at the date of the hearing.[481] The court considers an application in two stages: first it decides whether the disposition of the estate is not such as to make reasonable financial provision for the applicant; then, if it decides that it is not, it exercises its discretion as to whether, and in what manner, it shall exercise its powers.[482] At both stages, section 3 of the 1975 Act requires the court to have regard (1) to general matters which relate to all applicants and (2) to particular matters which vary according to the different categories of applicant.

(3) *Categories of Applicant and Matters to Which Court Must Have Regard*

(a) The deceased's spouse or civil partner

7.220 The Civil Partnership Act 2004, which came into force on 5 December 2005, gives same-sex couples who register their partnerships the same succession rights as married couples. To avoid the need for repetition, all references in this chapter to spouses include civil partners, and all references to marriages include civil partnerships.

7.221 The onus is on the applicant to prove that he was the deceased's spouse at the time of the deceased's death.[483] A party to a voidable marriage which has not been annulled is a spouse for this purpose, as is a party to a void marriage which has not been dissolved or annulled, provided he entered into it in good faith and provided he has not entered into a later marriage.[484]

---

479 Inheritance (Provision for Family and Dependants) Act ss 1(1) and 2(1).

480 'The statutory language is...wholly impersonal.' *Re Goodwin* [1969] 1 Ch 283, 287, *per* Megarry J.

481 Inheritance (Provision for Family and Dependants) Act 1975, s 3(5) and see *Re Coventry* [1980] Ch 461, 491 and 493, CA. But *quaere* whether an applicant whose position changes after death may make a claim *if* he had no grounds for making a claim at the time of death; *Re Hancock (dec'd)* [1998] 2 FLR 346, CA implies that he can, but the point appears not to have been argued.

482 Inheritance (Provision for Family and Dependants) Act 1975, ss 2(1) and 3(1); *Re Rowlands* (1984) 5 FLR 813, CA.

483 *Re Peete* [1952] 2 All ER 599.

484 Inheritance (Provision for Family and Dependants) Act 1975, s 25(4). For void and voidable marriages, see paras 2.62–2.73 and see *Gandhi v Patel* [2002] 1 FLR 603.

(i) The surviving spouse standard

The surviving spouse standard applies and the surviving spouse has at least as **7.222**
good a claim to the family assets as a divorced spouse would have.

(ii) General matters to which the court must have regard

In all cases, whoever the applicant is, the court must have regard to the present and **7.223**
probable future financial resources and needs of the applicant, of any other applicant, and of any beneficiary; to the deceased's obligations and responsibilities; to
the size and nature of the estate; to any physical or mental disability of any applicant or beneficiary; and to any other matter, including the conduct of the applicant or of any other person, which the court may consider relevant.[485]

(iii) Particular matters to which the court must have regard

The court must also have regard to the age of the applicant; the duration of the **7.224**
marriage;[486] the contribution made by the applicant to the welfare of the deceased's
family; and the provision which the applicant might reasonably have been expected
to receive had the marriage been terminated by divorce rather than by death.[487]
The applicant cannot be put in exactly the same position as a divorced spouse,
because in a family provision case the other spouse is dead and so has no future
earning power or future needs. This may mean that the applicant receives more
than he or she would on a divorce.[488] In addition, there is less need for a 'clean
break'; so a life interest may prove to be reasonable provision.[489]

(b) Deceased's former spouse or former civil partner

This heading covers a person whose marriage or civil partnership with the deceased **7.225**
was dissolved or annulled but who has not remarried or formed a subsequent civil
partnership.[490]

The court must have regard to the same matters as in the case of a spouse or civil **7.226**
partner, except that the court does not have to have regard to the provision which
the applicant might reasonably have been expected to receive had the marriage
been terminated by divorce.[491] Successful applications by former spouses will be
rare because the divorce court has wide powers to make appropriate capital and
property adjustments between spouses in matrimonial proceedings; and the

---

485 ibid s 3(1).
486 *Cunliffe v Fielden* [2005] EWCA Civ 1508; [2006] Ch 361, CA.
487 ibid s 3(2); and see *White v White* [2001] 1 AC 596.
488 *Re Bunning* [1984] Ch 480; *P v G, P and P* [2004] EWHC 2944 (Fam); [2006] 1 FLR 431.
489 *Davis v Davis* [1993] 1 FLR 54, CA; see also *Re Besterman* [1984] Ch 458, CA.
490 Inheritance (Provision for Family and Dependants) Act 1975, s 1(1)(b).
491 Except when exercising its discretion–see para 7.218.

object is to arrive at a 'clean break', in appropriate cases, by the time that the matrimonial proceedings have been terminated.[492]

(c) A cohabitant

7.227 If the deceased dies on or after 1 January 1996, an application may be made by a person who is not a spouse or civil partner, former spouse or former civil partner, but who, during the whole of the two years immediately preceding the deceased's death, was living in the same household as the deceased and as the deceased's husband or wife,[493] or civil partner.[494] The expression 'living. . .as. . .husband or wife' is based on the Law Commission's recommendation[495] and follows the wording used in the Fatal Accidents Act 1976. In *Re Watson (dec'd)*[496] Neuberger J dealt with a case where a middle-aged couple lived together and shared expenses but did not share a bedroom or enjoy sexual relations. It was held that, given the multifarious nature of marital relations, the correct approach was to ask whether a reasonable person, with normal perceptions, would think that the couple were living together as husband and wife; he thought that they were. It is easy to understand the court's sympathy for the applicant in the *Watson* case, especially as there was no other claimant to the deceased's estate, except for the Crown claiming *bona vacantia*. But it remains difficult to understand what the expression is intended to mean.[497] If the applicant had been dependent on the deceased, the applicant would have fallen within the sixth category;[498] so applications by persons in the 'living. . .as. . .husband or wife' category cover those who were not dependants.[499] The problem is that situations are likely to arise where the fact that the applicant is a brother or sister of the deceased, rather than a close friend, may be prejudicial to a claim; that seems to be illogical.[500] The phrase 'immediately before the date when the deceased died' will almost certainly be interpreted in exactly the same

---

[492] And see *Re Fullard* [1982] Fam 42, CA.

[493] Inheritance (Provision for Family and Dependants) Act 1975, s 1(1A).

[494] Inheritance (Provision for Family and Dependants) Act 1975, s 1(1B).

[495] Law Commission, *Distribution on Intestacy*, (Law Com No 187, 1989) 15 and 16.

[496] [1999] 1 FLR 878.

[497] In *Southern Housing Group Ltd v Nutting* [2004] EWHC 2982; [2005] 1 FLR 1066, a case concerned with succession to an assured tenancy, Evans-Lombe J thought that the crucial element in 'living together as husband and wife' was a 'commitment to permanence—the relationship must be an emotional one of mutual lifetime commitment, openly and unequivocally displayed to the outside world.'

[498] See para 7.232.

[499] An applicant may, of course, fall into both categories, but if he is a dependant, it will not generally matter whether or not he is a cohabitant; so the real importance of proving cohabitation will be in cases where there is no dependency.

[500] Having said which, had the applicant in the *Watson* case been the deceased's sister, she would have inherited the whole estate on intestacy—but the sister's problem arises where the deceased has left a will giving all his property to (say) charity.

way as 'immediately before the death of the deceased' as it applies to applicants in the sixth category (dependants). That phrase is discussed at para 7.234 below. The matters to which the court must have regard are similar to those which apply to a former spouse.[501]

(d) A child of the deceased

(i) Matters to which the court must have regard

The only particular matter to which the court must have regard is 'the manner in which the applicant was being or in which he might expect to be educated or trained'.[502]   **7.228**

(ii) Applications by adult children

Applications may be made by infant or adult children,[503] but Oliver J said in *Re Coventry* that applications 'by able-bodied and comparatively young men in employment and able to maintain themselves must be relatively rare and need to be approached. . .with a degree of circumspection'.[504] Section 3(1)(d) of the 1975 Act requires the court to have regard to 'any obligations and responsibilities which the deceased had towards any applicant'. In the case of an application by an adult child, he will have to demonstrate special circumstances above and beyond relationship and necessity.[505] Successful applications by adult children may come from those who have not completed their full-time education, or who are in some way handicapped in their earning capacity: but s 3(1)(d) refers to subsisting obligations and responsibilities which the deceased had immediately before his death, not past obligations which he had failed to discharge.[506] 'Special circumstances' may include a moral obligation arising, for example, from unpaid work performed by the child for the deceased over a number of years where the deceased gave the child to understand that he would repay the child by leaving property to him when he died.[507] They may also include a moral obligation arising from the fact that the deceased had inherited property from someone else, for example his spouse (the child's other parent) which that other person expected would pass, eventually, to the child.[508]   **7.229**

---

[501] Inheritance (Provision for Family and Dependants) Act 1975, s 3(2A).
[502] ibid 3(3).
[503] 'Child' includes illegitimate child: ibids 25(1).
[504] [1980] Ch 461, 465, CA; see also *Re Dennis* [1981] 2 All ER 140, 145.
[505] *Re Abram (dec'd)* [1996] 2 FLR 379.
[506] *Re Jennings (dec'd)* [1994] Ch 286, CA.
[507] *Re Abram (dec'd)* [1996] 2 FLR 379; *Re Pearce (dec'd)* [1998] 2 FLR 705, CA.
[508] *Goodchild v Goodchild* [1997] 1 WLR 1216, CA; *Espinosa v Bourke* [1999] 1 FLR 747, CA.

(e) A person (not being a child of the deceased) treated by him as a child of the family in relation to any marriage or civil partnership to which he was at any time a party

7.230   This category covers an infant stepchild but also covers an adult stepchild where there are special circumstances, including a moral obligation.[509]

7.231   The matters to which the court must have regard are the same as for a child of the deceased, but there are three *additional* matters to which the court must have regard:[510]

(a) whether the deceased had assumed any responsibility for the applicant's maintenance and, if so, the extent to which and the basis upon which the deceased had assumed that responsibility and the length of time for which the deceased had discharged it;

(b) whether in assuming and discharging that responsibility the deceased did so knowing that the applicant was not his own child; and

(c) the liability of any other person to maintain the applicant.

(f) A dependant of the deceased

7.232   An applicant who claims that he is in this category must prove that the deceased, immediately before his death, was making a substantial contribution in money or money's worth towards the applicant's needs and that he was doing so otherwise than for full valuable consideration.[511] Some cases which might earlier have caused problems will do so no longer, because applicants will be able to bring themselves within the third category instead of the sixth, and so will not have to prove dependency. The difficult cases now will be those where the applicant cannot show that he lived with the deceased as the deceased's husband or wife for the two-year qualifying period *and* where there are problems demonstrating dependency.

(i) Matters to which the court must have regard

7.233   Section 3(4) requires the court to have regard to 'the extent to which and the basis upon which the deceased assumed responsibility for the maintenance of the applicant and...the length of time for which the deceased discharged that responsibility'. Given that this section refers to 'the basis upon which the deceased *assumed* responsibility...' Megarry V-C held in *Re Beaumont*[512] that the applicant must *prove* this assumption; but the Court of Appeal in *Jelley v Iliffe*[513] decided that,

---

[509] *Re Callaghan* [1985] Fam 1; *Re Leach* [1986] Ch 226, CA. The basis of the moral obligation in these cases is not clearly spelled out, but appears to be linked to the fact that the deceased step-parent inherited a significant amount of property from the child's natural parent.

[510] See Inheritance (Provision for Family and Dependants) Act 1975, s 3(3).

[511] ibid 1(3).

[512] [1980] Ch 444.

[513] [1981] Fam 128, CA.

once it was shown that the deceased had maintained the applicant, there was a presumption that he had assumed the responsibility.

(ii) Immediately before the death of the deceased

The applicant must be maintained by the deceased 'immediately before' his **7.234** death.[514] It has been held that these words refer to the settled basis or arrangement, not to any temporary variation owing, for example, to one of the parties being in hospital.[515]

(iii) Form of dependency

This class of applicant does *not*, of course, include only persons living together. **7.235** In *Re Lankesheer (dec'd)*[516] the court held that it covered someone whom the deceased had allowed to become a tenant of a flat which he owned at a rent which was significantly below the current market rent.

(iv) Weighing contributions

If two people live together and each contributes approximately equally to their **7.236** joint needs, neither is dependent on the other and neither can claim on the other's death. Financial contributions by one may be balanced by work done by the other. The effect of this is that someone who is slothful and uncaring may find it easier to prove dependency than someone who has worked hard and behaved well. To avoid absurdity, the court takes a broad, common-sense view of dependency and will not be inclined to penalize the applicant if, for example, he showed the deceased care and attention, even of an exceptional kind, during the deceased's final illness. Such care and attention cannot be assessed in isolation from the mutual love and support of a couple living together.[517]

(4) Orders the Court May Make

The court may order provision to be made from the deceased's net estate. **7.237**

(a) The net estate

This is widely defined in the Inheritance (Provision for Family and Dependants) **7.238** Act 1975. It always includes all property of which the deceased had power to dispose by his will, less funeral, testamentary and administrative expenses, debts and

---

[514] Inheritance (Provision for Family and Dependants) Act 1975, s 1(1)(e).

[515] *Re Beaumont* [1980] Ch 444, 452–3; *Jelley v Iliffe* [1981] Fam 128, CA; *Re Dix* [2004] EWCA Civ 139; [2004] 1 WLR 1399, CA. The words 'immediately before the date when the deceased died' as applied to applicants in the third category (ie cohabitants) are almost certain to be interpreted in the same way.

[516] [1998] 1 FLR 1041; and see *Re B (dec'd)* [2000] Ch 662.

[517] *Bishop v Plumley* [1991] 1 WLR 582, CA.

liabilities (including tax). It includes property nominated under a statutory nomination[518] and property handed over by the deceased by way of *donatio mortis causa*,[519] but it does *not* include property nominated under a pension fund trust deed,[520] or benefits arising under life assurance policies which are payable direct to a beneficiary and not to the estate.[521] The net estate *may* also include, if the court so orders,[522] the deceased's severable share of any property of which he was a beneficial joint tenant,[523] but only if an application is made to the court within the six months' time limit;[524] and it *may* include, if the court so orders, any sum, or other property, which the court directs to be provided under its anti-evasion powers.[525]

(b) Forms of provision

7.239 The court may, in the exercise of its discretion, make any one or more of the following orders: (1) periodical payments; (2) a lump sum payment; (3) a transfer of property; (4) a settlement of property;[526] (5) acquisition of property for transfer or settlement; (6) variation of a marriage settlement.

(c) Effect of an order

7.240 The order is deemed to take effect from death, and for inheritance tax purposes it is deemed that the deceased disposed of his estate in the way provided by the court.[527]

---

518 See para 7.05.

519 See para 7.06.

520 See para 7.04 and see *Jessop v Jessop* [1992] 1 FLR 591, CA.

521 See para 7.03; *Hanbury v Hanbury* [1999] 2 FLR 255.

522 *Murphy v Murphy* [2003] EWCA Civ 1862; [2004] 1 FCR 1.

523 Inheritance (Provision for Family and Dependants) Act 1975, ss 9 and 25(1). For valuation of deceased's share, see *Dingmar v Dingmar* [2006] EWCA Civ 942; [2007] Ch 109, CA.

524 ibid 9(1). The court has no discretion to permit an extension in this case.

525 ibid ss 10–13 are anti-evasion sections which give the court the power to make orders against donees in whose favour dispositions have been made by the deceased with the intention of defeating applications for family provision.

526 In *Re Abram* [1996] 2 FLR 379 the applicant had entered into an individual voluntary arrangement with his creditors and any capital sum he received would have been paid to them: the court, therefore, ordered that property be settled on the applicant for life on protective trusts.

527 Inheritance (Provision for Family and Dependants) Act 1975, s 19.

Part IV

THE LAW OF OBLIGATIONS

8

CONTRACT: IN GENERAL

A. Introduction

(1) Agreement

8.01   A contract is an agreement which is either enforced by law or recognized by law as affecting the rights and duties of the parties. Usually, but not necessarily,[1] such an agreement arises from an exchange of promises: eg one by a seller to deliver goods and one by a buyer to pay for them. The concept of a contract as an agreement is, however, subject to two significant qualifications.

(a) The objective test

8.02   First, in determining whether an agreement has come into existence, the law normally applies an 'objective' test: if A so conducts himself as to induce B reasonably to believe that A has agreed to terms proposed by B, then A will generally be bound by those terms even though he may not in fact have intended to agree to them.[2] The law adopts this principle because, in the case put, B could be seriously prejudiced if A were allowed to avoid liability by showing that he had no such actual intention. The principle therefore does not apply where B knows that, in spite of the objective appearance, A had no intention of agreeing to B's terms.[3]

(b) Restrictions on freedom of contract

8.03   Secondly, there are many practical and legal restrictions on the principle of 'freedom of contract'. The *practical* restrictions arise where persons (often private consumers) contract with commercial suppliers for goods or services to be supplied on the latter's standard terms.[4] There is obviously room for argument on the question whether, in such cases, the customer has not agreed at all to these terms (of which he may be ignorant) or whether he has agreed to them reluctantly, or has simply taken his chance of them, whatever they may be. Similar questions of degree can arise from *legal* restrictions: for example, where a person is prohibited from refusing to contract with another on specified grounds, such as the other's

---

[1] Not in the case of a unilateral contract (para 8.07).
[2] *Smith v Hughes* (1871) LR 6 QB 597, 607; and see para 8.05.
[3] See paras 8.05, 8.145.
[4] See section D for legal controls of such terms.

race, sex, disability, religion, belief, sexual orientation or age.[5] In such cases, the resulting relationship is generally nevertheless regarded as contractual because its other terms depend on agreement. But some relationships are the result of such a degree of legal compulsion as wholly to lose any consensual nature. There is, for example, no contract where a person's property is compulsorily acquired against his will, even though he receives compensation,[6] or where medicines are supplied to a person under the National Health Service, even though he pays a prescription charge.[7] The borderline between these two types of cases can be hard to draw, especially where a person is employed (usually in the public service) on terms which are in part governed by legislation.[8]

(2) The 'Expectation Interest'

Our concern here will be with the requirements of a legally enforceable agree- **8.04** ment; with factors which, even where these requirements are satisfied, further restrict the legal effectiveness of agreements; with the parties by and against whom contracts can be enforced; and with the legal effects of failure in performance. One such effect is to give rise to certain judicial remedies, discussed in Chapter 21, but one aspect of this topic is of such importance to the nature of contract as a legal and commercial institution that it must be mentioned here. A civil wrong commonly gives the victim the right to compensation for having been made worse off by its commission; but the law of contract goes further in compensating him for the wrongdoer's failure to make him better off. It protects the victim's *expectation interest*: eg by awarding a buyer the difference between the price which he has agreed to pay to the seller and the higher market value of the goods when they should have been, but were not, delivered.[9] The law of tort also sometimes awards damages for 'loss of expectations': eg for loss of expected earnings in personal injury cases. But these expectations exist independently of the wrong which impairs them, while the law of contract protects expectations which owe their very existence to the agreement for breach of which the action is brought. It does so in order to provide a legal framework for, and hence to promote stability in, many

---

[5] See Sex Discrimination Act 1975, Pts II and III and ss 65, 66; Race Relations Act 1976, Pts II and III and ss 56, 57 and 72; Disability Discrimination Act 1995, ss 4, 5, 12 and 19; Employment Equality (Religion or Belief) Regulations 2003 (SI 2003/1660); Employment Equality (Sexual Orientation) Regulations 2003 (SI 2003/1661); Equality Act 2005 Pts 2 and 3; Employment Equality (Age) Regulations 2006 (SI 2006/1031); cf Human Rights Act 1998, s 1 and Sch 1, Pt 1, Art 14.

[6] *Sovmots Investments Ltd v Secretary of State for the Environment* [1977] QB 411, 443, aff'd without reference to this point [1979] AC 144.

[7] See *Pfizer Corp v Ministry of Health* [1965] AC 512.

[8] See *Barber v Manchester Regional Hospital Board* [1958] 1 WLR 181, 196; *Roy v Kensington and Chelsea and Westminster Family Practitioner Committee* [1992] 1 AC 624.

[9] Sale of Goods Act 1979, s 51(3).

spheres of commercial activity; and in this way it serves what is probably its most important purpose in a capitalist society.

B. Constituent Elements

(1) Agreement

(a) Reaching agreement: offer and acceptance

(i) Offer

8.05 **Definition.** The process by which parties reach agreement is usually[10] analysed into the acceptance by one party of an offer made by the other. An offer is an expression of willingness to contract on the terms stated in it as soon as those terms are accepted by the party to whom the statement is made.[11] Under the objective test,[12] a statement by A can be an offer if it induces B reasonably to believe that A intended to be bound by it on acceptance,[13] even though A had no such intention.[14] A will not, however, be so bound if B knew that A had no such intention;[15] nor, probably, if B simply had no view on this question.[16] An offer may be made either expressly or by conduct[17] but probably not by mere inactivity since this, standing alone, is normally equivocal and so unlikely to induce one party to believe that the other intends to be bound.[18]

8.06 **Offer and invitation to treat.** An offer must be distinguished from an invitation to make an offer, known in law as an 'invitation to treat': for example, an owner of property who wishes to sell it may invite offers for it at or about a specified price.[19] In such a case, the offer (if any) will be made to the owner, not by him. In border-line cases, the distinction between an offer and an invitation to treat can be hard to draw (depending as it does on the elusive criterion of intention) and in some

---

[10] There are exceptional cases in which this analysis is hard to apply: eg multipartite agreements, as in *The Satanita* [1895] P 248, affirmed sub nom *Clarke v Dunraven* [1897] AC 59; cf *Gibson v Manchester CC* [1978] 1 WLR 520, 523, reversed [1979] 1 WLR 294.

[11] eg *Storer v Manchester CC* [1974] 1 WLR 1403.

[12] See para 8.02.

[13] See *Centrovincial Estates plc v Merchant Investor Assurance Co Ltd* [1983] Commercial LR 158; *Moran v University of Salford The Times*, 23 November 1993.

[14] *The Splendid Sun* [1981] 1 QB 694.

[15] *Ignazio Messina & Co v Polskie Linie Oceaniczne* [1995] 2 Lloyd's Rep 566, 571.

[16] *The Hannah Blumenthal* [1983] 1 AC 854 as interpreted in *The Leonidas D* [1985] 1 WLR 925; contrast *The Golden Bear* [1987] 1 Lloyd's Rep 330, 341; *The Multitank Holsatia* [1988] 2 Lloyd's Rep 486, 492.

[17] *Hart v Mills* (1846) 15 LJ Ex 200.

[18] *The Splendid Sun* (n 14 above) as explained in *The Hannah Blumenthal* (n 16 above); for a statutory solution of the problem that arose in these cases, see Arbitration Act 1996, s 41(3).

[19] *Gibson v Manchester CC* [1979] 1 WLR 294.

situations of common occurrence the law has reduced this difficulty by laying down prima facie rules on the point. For example, the display of price-marked goods for sale in a shop or an indication on a website of their availability is usually no more than an invitation to treat, the offer coming from the customer when he indicates that he wishes to buy.[20] Similarly, at an auction sale no offer is made by putting the goods up for auction: the offer is made by the bidder and is accepted by the auctioneer, usually on the 'fall of the hammer'.[21] Newspaper advertisements that goods are for sale are likewise not offers;[22] but an advertisement of a reward (eg for the return of lost property) is commonly regarded as an offer,[23] presumably because no further bargaining is expected to result from it. Advertisements relating to the sale or supply of goods can also give rise to contractual liability to buyers who deal as consumers.[24]

(ii) Acceptance

Concept. Assuming that an offer has been made, an agreement comes into existence when the offer is accepted either expressly (by words of acceptance) or by conduct. Usually, the acceptance, as well as the offer, contains a promise and the resulting contract is then bilateral: eg where A has in his offer promised to deliver goods and B in his acceptance to pay for them. There may also be a unilateral contract where A makes a promise but B does not: eg where A promises B to pay him £100 for walking from London to York, and B does so without making any promise.[25]   **8.07**

Correspondence of acceptance with offer. The acceptance must correspond with the offer: for example, an offer to sell something for £1,000 is not accepted by a reply stating that the offeree will pay £800.[26] Such a reply rejects the original offer (so that the offeree can no longer accept it)[27] and it also amounts to a new offer which the original offeror can accept. These rules govern the so-called 'battle of forms' in which each party sends to the other a previously prepared form setting out the terms on which he is prepared to deal. Normally the contract, if any, will be on the terms of the last document in the series which the recipient may accept by conduct (eg by rendering the requested services);[28] but it is also possible for   **8.08**

---

[20] *Pharmaceutical Society of GB v Boots Cash Chemists Ltd* [1952] 2 QB 795; Electronic Commerce (EC Directive) Regulations 2002, SI 2002/2013, reg 12.

[21] Sale of Goods Act 1979, s 57(2); *British Car Auctions Ltd v Wright* [1972] 1 WLR 1519.

[22] *Partridge v Crittenden* [1968] 1 WLR 1204.

[23] Cf *Carlill v Carbolic Smoke Ball Co* [1893] 1 QB 256.

[24] See, eg, Sale of Goods Act 1979, s 14 (2D); Sale and Supply of Goods to Consumers Regulations 2002, SI 2002/3045, reg 15.

[25] See *Great Northern Rly v Witham* (1873) LR 9 CP 16, 19.

[26] Cf *Tinn v Hoffmann & Co* (1873) 29 LT 271.

[27] See para 8.18; *Jones v Daniel* [1894] 2 Ch 332.

[28] *BRS v Arthur V Crutchley Ltd* [1967] 2 All ER 285.

the sender of the last document to indicate his acceptance of terms set out in the other party's earlier document.[29]

8.09 **'Communication' of Acceptance.** The general rule is that an acceptance has no effect unless it is 'communicated' to the offeror[30] or to an agent of his who is authorized to receive it.[31] The rule exists to protect the offeror from the hardship of being bound without knowing that his offer has been accepted. It follows that the rule does not apply where it is the offeror's 'own fault that he did not get it'[32] (the acceptance): eg if the acceptance is typed out on his telex machine during business hours and simply not read by him or any of his staff.[33] It is also possible for the offeror expressly or impliedly to waive the requirement of communication. This is commonly the position in the case of an offer of a unilateral contract since the offeror in such a case does not expect advance notice of the offeree's intention to do the required act.[34]

8.10 **Posted acceptance.** An acceptance contained in a letter sent by post could, in theory, take effect at a variety of points, ranging from the time of posting to that of actual communication to the offeror. What is usually called the general rule of English law is that the acceptance takes effect as soon as it is posted.[35] There may therefore be a contract even though the acceptance is lost in the post;[36] and the contract is made at the time of posting[37] even though the acceptance is delayed in the post.[38] Such loss or delay can prejudice either party who may act on his belief that there is, or is not, a contract; and the posting rule favours the offeree on the not altogether convincing ground that the offeror, by starting negotiations by post, takes the risk of loss or delay in the post.[39] The rule applies only where it is reasonable to use the post as a means of communication[40] and it may be excluded by the terms of the offer.[41] It does not apply to 'instantaneous' communications, eg by telephone, fax, or telex,[42] since where these are used the acceptor will often

---

[29] *Butler Machine Tool Co Ltd v Ex-Cell-O Corp (England) Ltd* [1979] 1 WLR 401.

[30] *Holwell Securities Ltd v Hughes* [1974] 1 WLR 155, 157.

[31] *Henthorn v Fraser* [1892] 2 Ch 27, 33.

[32] *Entores v Miles Far East Corp* [1955] 2 QB 327, 332.

[33] *The Brimnes* [1975] QB 929; for messages received out of business hours, see *The Pamela* [1995] 2 Lloyd's Rep 249, 252.

[34] *Carlill's* case (n 23 above).

[35] *Henthorn v Fraser* (n 31 above); *Adams v Lindsell* (1818) 1 B & Ald 681.

[36] *The Household Fire and Carriage Accident etc Insurance Co Ltd v Grant* (1879) 4 Ex D 216.

[37] *Potter v Sanders* (1846) 6 Hare 1.

[38] *Dunlop v Higgins* (1848) 1 HLC 381.

[39] *Household etc Insurance Co Ltd v Grant* (n 36 above) at 223; the negotiations may in fact have been started by the *offeree*, where he receives a counter-offer.

[40] See *Henthorn v Fraser* (n 31 above).

[41] *Holwell Securities Ltd v Hughes* [1974] 1 WLR 155.

[42] *Entores* case (n 32 above); *Brinkibon Ltd v Stahag Stahl etc* [1983] 2 AC 34; *JSC Zestafoni G Nikoladze Ferroalloy Plant v Ronly Holdings Ltd* [2003] EWHC 245; [2004] 2 Lloyds Rep 335 at [75].

know at once that his attempted communication has failed, and so be able to retrieve the situation. The application of the rule to acceptances by email or in website trading[43] should depend on whether their failure is likewise immediately apparent to the acceptor.

The most important practical consequence of the posting rule is that a posted acceptance prevails over a previously posted but as yet uncommunicated withdrawal of the offer.[44] But the rule, being one of convenience, will not apply where it would lead to 'manifest inconvenience and absurdity'.[45] It would not, for example, apply where the acceptance was lost or delayed as a result, not of an accident in the post, but of the acceptor's carelessness in misdirecting the acceptance.[46] The loss or delay could also be caused by the carelessness of the offeror: eg where he had failed in the offer to give his correct address. In all such cases the resulting loss should fall on the party responsible for the defect in the communication. It is a more open question whether the posting rule should preclude an acceptor who had posted his acceptance from relying on a subsequently posted withdrawal which reached the offeror before or together with the acceptance.[47] The better view is that the posting of the acceptance should curtail the offeree's power to withdraw his acceptance,[48] just as it curtails the offeror's power to withdraw his offer.[49] For if it did not have this effect the offeree could, on a fluctuating market, in practice secure an option at no charge to himself and to the possible prejudice of the offeror.

8.11

Distance contracts.   A consumer who has entered into a 'distance contract' (such as the one made by an exchange of letters or emails) for the supply of goods or services by a commercial supplier has the 'right to cancel' the contract within a specified period.[50] The underlying assumption is that a contract has first come into existence under the rules stated in paragraphs 8.10 and 8.11; the supplier has no corresponding right to cancel.

8.12

---

[43] The Electronic Commerce (EC Directive) Regulations 2002, SI 2002/2013 state that communications in this medium are 'received' when the addressee is 'able to access them' (reg 11(2) (c)); but this does not necessarily answer the question when the contract is made.

[44] *Byrne & Co v Leon van Thienhoven & Co* (1880) 5 CPD 344; see para 8.17.

[45] *Holwell Securities* case (n 41 above) at 161.

[46] *Korbetis v Transgrain Shipping BV* [2005] EWHC 1345 (QB) at [15] (fax message sent to wrong telephone number).

[47] Contrast *Wenckheim v Arndt* (NZ) (1873) 1 Jurists Report 73 with *Morrison v Thoelke* 155 So 2d 889 (1963).

[48] *Korbetis* case (n 46 above).

[49] See *Byrne & Co v Leon van Thienhoven & Co* (n 44 above).

[50] Consumer Protection (Distance Selling) Regulations 2000, SI 2000/2334, reg 10(2); for exceptions, see reg 13.

8.13 **Stipulated mode of acceptance.** The offeror may for his own protection stipulate in the offer that it must be accepted in a specified way: eg by a letter sent by
first class post. The general rule is that an acceptance sent in another way is not
effective[51] and amounts at most to a counter-offer. The rule is subject to an
exception where the method adopted is from the offeror's point of view just as
efficacious as the prescribed method.[52] It also does not apply in the increasingly
common situation in which the terms of the offer are contained in a form drawn
up by the offeree: eg in an application for credit. In such a case the stipulation as
to the mode of acceptance exists for the benefit of the *offeree* and may be waived
by him.[53]

8.14 **Silence.** An offer may specify that it may be accepted simply by failing to reply
to it; but as a general rule such 'silence' does not bind the offeree.[54] The reasons for
this rule are that it would be undesirable to put an offeree who did not wish to
accept the offer to the trouble and expense of rejecting it; and that the offeree's
'silence' is generally equivocal, not giving rise to an inference of intention to accept
'save in the most exceptional circumstances'.[55] Where such circumstances give rise
to an 'obligation to speak',[56] the offeree may be bound by silence: eg where he has
solicited the offer and then failed to reply to it in circumstances leading the offeror
reasonably to believe that it has been accepted.[57] Action by the offeror, to the
knowledge of the offeree, in reliance on the belief that the offer had been accepted
may also estop the offeree from denying that he has accepted the offer.[58] The rule
that 'silence' does not bind the offeree does not mean that his acceptance must be
expressed in words. An offer may be accepted by conduct[59] and the offeror may
waive the normal requirement of communication of such acceptance.[60] 'Conduct'
here refers to some action on the part of the offeree: mere inaction does not suffice,
save in the exceptional situations already described.[61] The general rule that 'silence'
does not amount to an acceptance exists for the protection of the offeree. It is
therefore arguable that the rule should not protect the offeror: ie that he should

---

[51] *Financings Ltd v Stimson* [1962] 1 WLR 1184.

[52] *Manchester Diocesan Council for Education v Commercial & General Investments Ltd* [1970]
1 WLR 241.

[53] See *Robophone Facilities v Blank* [1966] 1 WLR 1423; *Carlyle Finance Ltd v Pallas Industrial
Finance Ltd* [1999] 1 All ER (Comm) 659.

[54] *Felthouse v Bindley* (1862) 11 CBNS 869.

[55] *The Leonidas D* [1985] 1 WLR 925, 927.

[56] *The Agrabele* [1985] 2 Lloyd's Rep 496, 509 (reversed on other grounds [1987] 2 Lloyd's Rep
275); *Re Selectmove* [1995] 1 WLR 474, 478; cf *Vitol SA v Norelf Ltd* [1996] AC 800.

[57] eg *Rust v Abbey Life Insurance Co Ltd* [1979] 2 Lloyd's Rep 334.

[58] Cf *Spiro v Lintern* [1973] 1 WLR 1002, 1011.

[59] See para 8.07; *Roberts v Hayward* (1828) 3 C & P 432.

[60] See para 8.09.

[61] *The Leonidas D* (n 55 above).

be bound where he has by the terms of the offer induced the offeree to believe that the latter's failure to reply would give rise to a contract.[62]

Acceptance in ignorance of offer. A person may, without knowing of an offer, **8.15** do an act apparently amounting to an acceptance of it: eg give information not knowing that a reward has been offered for it. In such a case, there is no agreement and hence no contract.[63] Giving the information with knowledge of the offer can, however, amount to an acceptance even though it was given primarily[64] (though not if it was given exclusively)[65] with some motive other than that of claiming the reward. There is also no contract where two persons make identical cross-offers, neither knowing of the other's when he makes his own.[66] There may be an agreement in such a case, but the rule avoids the uncertainty resulting from the fortuitous nature of the agreement.

Acceptance in case of unilateral contract. In the case of a unilateral contract,[67] **8.16** the offer can be accepted by doing the required act (eg walking to York); there is no need to give advance notice of acceptance to the offeror. It is probable that part performance (eg walking part of the way to York) can also amount to an acceptance and will have this effect where it gives rise to a clear inference of intention to accept.[68] A purported withdrawal of the offer at this stage would then be a breach of contract except where on its true construction the offer reserved a right of withdrawal to the offeror at any time before full performance.[69] Even where the withdrawal was wrongful, the full sum promised would not be due till the offeree had completed performance of the stipulated act[70] (ie walked all the way to York).

(iii) Termination of offer

Withdrawal. Events may happen after an offer has been made which bring it to **8.17** an end, so that it can no longer be accepted. One such event is the withdrawal of the offer, the general rule being that an offer can be withdrawn at any time before acceptance.[71] The offeree must also, in general, have notice of the withdrawal so

---

62 This possibility was doubted in *Fairline Shipping Corp v Adamson* [1975] QB 180, 189 (where, however, the offer did *not* expressly provide for acceptance by silence).

63 *R v Clarke* (1927) 40 CLR 227, 233; *Tracomin SA v Anton C Nielsen* [1984] 2 Lloyd's Rep 195, 203.

64 Cf *Carlill v Carbolic Smoke Ball Co* [1893] 1 QB 256.

65 *R v Clarke* (n 63 above).

66 *Tinn v Hoffmann & Co* (1873) 29 LT 271, 278.

67 See para 8.07.

68 *Errington v Errington* [1952] 1 KB 290, 295.

69 Cf *Luxor (Eastbourne) Ltd v Cooper* [1941] AC 108, 124.

70 See *Daulia Ltd v Four Banks Nominees Ltd* [1978] Ch 231, 238; *Harvela Investments Ltd v Royal Trust of Canada (CI) Ltd* [1986] AC 207, 224.

71 *Routledge v Grant* (1828) 4 Bing 653.

that an offer is not withdrawn merely by the offeror's acting inconsistently[72] with it: eg by disposing of its subject matter to a third party. The notice must actually reach the offeree: mere posting of it does not suffice. Thus if, after a withdrawal has been posted but before it has reached the offeree, the latter posts an acceptance, a contract is concluded even though there was at no stage any agreement between the parties.[73] The rule is based on the consideration of convenience that no offeree could safely act in reliance on his acceptance (eg by selling on the subject matter) if he were subject to the risk that an effective withdrawal might at the time of acceptance have been in the post. The requirement of 'communication' may be displaced by the conduct of the offeree: eg if he simply failed to read a withdrawal sent to his address[74] or if he had moved after receipt of the offer without notifying the offeror. It also does not literally apply to offers made to the public (eg of rewards for information): such an offer can be withdrawn by taking reasonable steps to bring the withdrawal to the attention of the class of persons likely to have seen the offer.[75]

8.18 **Rejection.** Rejection terminates an offer;[76] and a counter-offer amounts to a rejection of the original offer[77] which can then no longer be accepted. A mere enquiry whether the offeror is prepared to vary the terms of the offer (eg by reducing his price) may, however, amount, not to a counter-offer, but to a mere 'request for information'. The distinction between such a request and a counter-offer turns on the intention of the offeree, as reasonably understood by the offeror.[78]

8.19 It seems that a rejection terminates an offer only when communicated: there is no ground of convenience for holding that it should have this effect when posted. Hence it remains open to the offeree after posting a rejection to accept the offer by an overtaking communication. But once the rejection has reached the offeror, he should not be bound[79] by an acceptance which was posted while the rejection was still in the post but reached him only after the rejection had done so.

8.20 **Lapse of time.** An offer which is expressed to last only for a specified time cannot be accepted after the end of that time. If no such time is specified, the offer lapses at the end of a reasonable time.[80] What is a reasonable time depends on such

---

[72] *Stevenson, Jacques & Co v McLean* (1880) 5 QBD 343.

[73] *Byrne & Co v Leon van Thienhoven* (1880) 5 CPD 344.

[74] Cf *Eaglehill Ltd v J Needham (Builders) Ltd* [1973] AC 992, 1011; *The Brimnes* [1975] QB 929.

[75] *Shuey v US* 92 US 73 (1875).

[76] *Tinn v Hoffmann & Co* (1873) 29 LT 271, 278.

[77] *Hyde v Wrench* (1840) 3 Beav 334.

[78] *Stevenson, Jacques & Co v McLean* (n 72 above); *Gibson v Manchester CC* [1979] 1 WLR 294, 302.

[79] ie under the rule stated in para 8.10.

[80] *Ramsgate Victoria Hotel Co Ltd v Montefiore* (1866) LR 1 Ex 109.

facts as the nature of the subject matter and the means used to communicate the offer. On a similar principle, an offer which provides that it is to terminate on the occurrence of some event cannot be accepted after that event has happened. Such a term may be implied so that, for example, an offer to buy goods cannot be accepted after they have been seriously damaged.[81]

Death.   Death of either of the parties makes it impossible for them to reach   **8.21**
agreement, but this should not be an absolute bar to the creation of a contract. To hold that it was such a bar could cause hardship: eg where A made a continuing offer to guarantee loans to be made by B to C and B then made such a loan after, and in ignorance of, A's death.[82] Conversely, where it was the offeree who died, the offeror would not normally be prejudiced if the offer were accepted by the offeree's personal representatives. Death of either party should terminate an offer only if it was one to enter into a contract which, by reason of its 'personal' nature, would be discharged by such death.[83]

Supervening incapacity.   Supervening personal incapacity[84] can arise where   **8.22**
one of the parties becomes mentally ill. That party would not be bound by an acceptance made after his disability had become known to the other party or after his property had become subject to the control of the court; but the other party would be so bound.[85]

(b) Vagueness, uncertainty, and incompleteness

Vagueness.   Even where an agreement has been reached, its terms may be too   **8.23**
vague to give rise to a contract.[86] The courts here must guard against, on the one hand, the danger of imposing on the parties terms to which they have not agreed and, on the other, that of striking down agreements intended to be binding but drafted (perhaps deliberately) in loose terms so as to withstand the stresses of changing economic circumstances. In pursuit of the latter aim, they can resolve apparent vagueness by reference to trade custom or usage[87] or to the standard of reasonableness;[88] or by disregarding meaningless or self-contradictory phrases.[89]

---

[81] *Financings Ltd v Stimson* [1962] 1 WLR 1184.
[82] See *Coulthart v Clementson* (1879) 5 QBD 42.
[83] See para 8.442.
[84] For supervening corporate incapacity, see Chapter 3.
[85] This follows from the rules stated in para 8.277.
[86] *G Scammell & Nephew Ltd v Ouston* [1941] AC 251.
[87] *Shamrock SS Co v Blue Star Line* (1899) 81 LT 413.
[88] *Hillas & Co Ltd v Arcos Ltd* (1932) 147 LT 503. Contrast *Baird Textile Holdings Ltd v Marks & Spencer plc* [2001] EWCA Civ 274; [2002] 1 All ER (Comm) 737, where there were no objective criteria for determining what was 'reasonable'.
[89] *Nicolene Ltd v Simmonds* [1953] QB 543.

They can also impose on the parties, or on one of them the duty to resolve the uncertainty.[90]

8.24 **Failure to specify vital terms.** An agreement may lack certainty because it fails to specify a vital term of the alleged bargain, such as the date on which a lease is to commence[91] or the price to be paid for goods or the remuneration to be paid for services.[92] But if the court is satisfied that the parties nevertheless intended to enter into a binding contract it will, where possible, give effect to that intention so that (for example) a reasonable price or remuneration must be paid.[93] Even where no contract has come into existence, such a remuneration may also be due on restitutionary principles to a person who has rendered services in the belief that there was a contract.[94]

8.25 **Terms to be agreed.** Parties may not wish to bind themselves over the course of a long-term agreement to fixed prices or other terms and may therefore stipulate that such terms are 'to be agreed' from time to time. If the court is satisfied that the parties intended to be bound at once, it will uphold the agreement[95] and require the points left outstanding to be negotiated in good faith;[96] but it will not do so where it concludes that the parties intended to be bound only when the outstanding point was settled.[97] The agreement would then be merely one to negotiate, and even an express agreement to this effect is 'too uncertain to be enforced'.[98] Nor, in a case of this kind, can a term be implied requiring the parties to negotiate 'in good faith' since the requirement of good faith is, in such a case, 'inherently inconsistent with the position of a negotiating party',[99] who must be free to advance his own interests in the negotiations. He can at most undertake to use 'best endeavours' to reach agreement,[100] this phrase referring (presumably) to the *method* of carrying on negotiations rather than to their *substance*.

8.26 **Ways of resolving uncertainty.** An agreement which leaves open matters such as the price is nevertheless binding if it lays down some *standard* (such as 'market

---

[90] *David T Boyd & Co v Louis Louca* [1973] 1 Lloyd's Rep 209; *Scammell v Dicker* [2005] EWCA Civ 405; [2005] 3 ALL ER 838 at [31].

[91] *Harvey v Pratt* [1965] 1 WLR 1025.

[92] *May & Butcher v R* [1934] KB 17n.

[93] Sale of Goods Act 1979, s 8(2); Supply of Goods and Services Act 1982, s 15(1).

[94] *Peter Lind & Co Ltd v Mersey Docks & Harbour Board* [1972] 2 Lloyd's Rep 234.

[95] eg *Foley v Classique Coaches Ltd* [1934] 2 KB 1.

[96] *Petromec Inc v Petroleo Brasileiro SA Petrobas* [2005] EWCA Civ 891; [2006] 1 Lloyd's Rep 121 at [115]–[121].

[97] eg *May & Butcher Ltd v R* [1934] 2 KB 17n.

[98] *Courtney & Fairbairn Ltd v Tolaini* [1975] 1 WLR 297, 301.

[99] *Walford v Miles* [1992] 2 AC 128, 138; and see *Cobbe v Yeomans Row Management Ltd* [2006] EWCA Civ 1139; [2006] 1 WLR 2964 at [4], [51] (where liability was imposed on the basis of proprietary estoppel: paras 8.63, 8.64).

[100] *Walford v Miles*, n 99 above, 138.

value') for resolving the uncertainty;[101] or if it provides some *machinery* for this purpose: eg that the price is to be fixed by the valuation of a third party. If the third party fails to make the valuation, the agreement is avoided;[102] but this result will not follow where the part of the machinery which fails to work is 'subsidiary and incidental':[103] eg where it relates only to the method of appointing the valuer.[104]

Stipulation for execution of formal document.   The parties to an agreement   **8.27** may stipulate for it to be embodied in a formal document. The agreement may then be regarded as incomplete, or as not intended to be legally binding, until the execution of such a document.[105] Alternatively, the document may be intended only as a formal record of an already binding agreement.[106] The distinction between these two categories depends on the purpose of the stipulation in each case.

Agreements for the sale of land by private treaty are usually expressed to be made   **8.28** 'subject to contract'. Such an agreement is incomplete until the terms of the formal contract are agreed;[107] but even after this has been done the agreement is not legally binding until there has been an 'exchange of contracts'.[108] Each party must sign a document containing all the expressly agreed terms;[109] and the requirement of 'exchange' prima facie means that each party must then hand the document signed by him to the other, or send it to him by post.[110] The reason why before 'exchange' there is no contract is not that there is any uncertainty as to the agreed terms: it is that, before then, neither party intends to be legally bound. The law on this point has been criticized[111] as it enables a party to go back on the agreement with impunity; and the criticism has led to mitigations of the requirement: eg by allowing 'exchange' to take place by telephone.[112] A party's freedom to go back on the agreement may also be restricted by the doctrine of a proprietary estoppel;[113] and, as a practical matter, by a collateral contract (known as a 'lock-out' agreement)

---

101 *Brown v Gould* [1972] Ch 53; cf *Hillas & Co Ltd v Arcos Ltd* (1932) 147 LT 503. Contrast *Willis Management (Isle of Man) Ltd v Cable and Wireless plc* [2005] EWCA Civ 806; [2005] 2 Lloyd's Rep 597, where the standard (of fairness) was expressed to be the subject of further negotiations.

102 Sale of Goods Act 1979, s 9(1); *Gillatt v Sky Television Ltd* [2000] 1 All ER (Comm) 461.

103 *Re Malpas* [1985] Ch 42, 50.

104 *Sudbrook Trading Estate Ltd v Eggleton* [1983] 1 AC 444.

105 *BSC v Cleveland Bridge & Engineering Co Ltd* [1984] 1 All ER 504; *Bolton MBC v Torkington* [2003] EWCA Civ 1634; [2004] Ch 66 at [53].

106 *Rossiter v Miller* (1878) 3 App Cas 1184.

107 *Winn v Bull* (1877) 7 Ch D 29.

108 *Chillingworth v Esche* [1924] 1 Ch 97; *Eccles v Bryant & Pollock* [1948] Ch 93.

109 Law of Property (Miscellaneous Provisions) Act 1989, ss 2(1), (3).

110 See *Commission for the New Towns v Cooper (Great Britain) Ltd* [1995] Ch 259, 289, 293, 295.

111 *Cohen v Nessdale Ltd* [1981] 3 All ER 118, 128 (aff'd [1982] 2 All ER 97, Law Commission Paper 65, *Transfer of Land, Report on 'Subject to Contract'* (1975).

112 *Domb v Isoz* [1980] Ch 548.

113 See *A-G of Hong Kong v Humphreys Estate (Quenn's Gardens) Ltd* [1987] AC 114, 124, 127–128 and see para 8.63.

by which he can bind himself for a fixed period not to deal in relation to the land with anyone else.[114]

(c) Conditional agreements

8.29 A conditional agreement is one the operation of which depends on an event which is not certain to occur. The condition is *contingent* where the event is one which neither party undertakes to bring about and *promissory* where it is the performance by one party of his undertaking. A condition is *precedent* (or suspensive) if the obligation subject to it is not to accrue until the event occurs; it is *subsequent* (or resolutive) if on the occurrence of the event an obligation is discharged.

8.30 An agreement subject to a contingent condition precedent may before the event occurs have no binding force at all;[115] but it is also possible for such an agreement, on its true construction, to impose some degree of obligation even before then. One possibility is that, so long as the event can still occur within the specified time, neither party can withdraw;[116] though once it becomes clear that the event can no longer so occur, the obligation is discharged.[117] A second possibility is that before the event occurs neither party must prevent its occurrence,[118] or at least that he must not deliberately[119] or wrongfully[120] do so; though no such duty would normally rest on a party where the condition was his 'satisfaction' with the subject matter or the other party's performance.[121] A third possibility is that one party must make reasonable efforts to bring about the event (eg the grant of an export licence where the contract was 'subject to' such licence).[122] A party who is in breach of one of the *subsidiary* obligations here described is liable in damages for that breach[123] even though, by reason of the non-occurrence of the event, the *principal* obligations (eg to buy and sell) have not accrued.[124]

---

[114] *Pitt v PHH Asset Management Ltd* [1993] 1 WLR 327.

[115] *Pym v Campbell* (1856) 6 E & B 370, 374.

[116] *Smith v Butler* [1900] 1 QB 694.

[117] *Total Gas Marketing Ltd v Arco British Ltd* [1998] 2 Lloyd's Rep 209, 215; *Jameson v CEGB* [2000] 1 AC 455, 478: a condition precedent may then operate as a condition subsequent.

[118] *Mackay v Dick* (1881) 6 App Cas 251.

[119] *Blake & Co v Sohn* [1969] 1 WLR 1412.

[120] See *Thompson v Asda-MFI Group plc* [1988] Ch 241.

[121] *Lee-Parker v Izzet (No 2)* [1972] 1 WLR 775; cf Sale of Goods Act 1979, s 18 r 4; for a possible qualification, contrast *The John S Darbyshire* [1977] 2 Lloyd's Rep 457, 464 ('subject to bona fides') with *Stabilad Ltd v Stephens & Carter Ltd* (No 2) [1999] 2 All ER (Comm) 651, 662 (no 'obligation to act in good faith').

[122] *Re Anglo-Russian Merchant Traders and John Batt (London) Ltd* [1917] 2 KB 679.

[123] eg *Malik v CETA Ltd* [1974] 2 Lloyd's Rep 279.

[124] *Little v Courage Ltd* (1995) 70 P & CR 469, 475 (rejecting the doctrine of fictional fulfilment of the condition in such cases).

(2) *Consideration*

(a) Introduction

(i) *Nature of the doctrine*

Gratuitous and onerous promises. In English law agreements or promises have **8.31** contractual force only if they are either made in a deed or supported by some 'consideration'. The doctrine of consideration is based on the idea of *reciprocity*: in order to be entitled to enforce a promise as a contract, the promisee must have given 'something of value in the eye of the law'[125] in exchange for the promise. An informal gratuitous promise is therefore not binding as a contract.[126] The reasons for this rule are that such promises may be rashly made,[127] that their enforceability might prejudice third parties (such as creditors or dependants of the promisor)[128] and that the claims of a gratuitous promisee are thought to be less compelling than those of one who has given value for the promise. English law does provide a fairly simple mechanism for making gratuitous promises enforceable: an individual can do this by making the promise in a signed and witnessed document which states on its face that it is intended to be a deed.[129] Such formal requirements provide some safeguard against the dangers (listed above) of giving contractual force to *informal* gratuitous promises.

The concept of a gratuitous promise covers not only the simple case of a promise **8.32** by A to make a gift of money or property, but also the case of a promise to provide some other facility to B, such as the loan of a book or to render some service, without reward. In the first of these situations, A would be under no contractual liability if he later refused to make the loan;[130] and in the second he would similarly be under no such liability for simple *non-feasance*, ie for failure to engage in the promised course of action.[131] A might, indeed, be liable in tort for *misfeasance* if he began to render the service and was negligent in performing it and so caused

---

[125] *Thomas v Thomas* (1842) 2 QB 851, 859.

[126] *Re Hudson* (1885) 54 LJ Ch 811.

[127] *Beaton v McDivitt* (1998) 13 NSWLR 162, 170.

[128] *Eastwood v Kenyon* (1840) 11 A & E 438, 451.

[129] Law of Property (Miscellaneous Provisions) Act 1989, s 1; for the rules governing the execution of deeds by companies incorporated under the Companies Acts, see Companies Act 2006, s 46 (not yet in force); Regulatory Reform (Execution of Deeds and Documents) Order 2005, SI 2005/1906; for certain electronic documents as deeds, see Land Registration Act 2002, s 9(5) and (9).

[130] Though the borrower would be liable for failure to perform any promise to return the book in good condition: *Bainbridge v Firmstone* (1838) 8 A & E 743.

[131] *Argy Trading & Development Co Ltd v Lapid Developments Ltd* [1977] 1 WLR 444; *The Zephyr* [1985] 2 Lloyd's Rep 529, 538.

loss to B.[132] Mere *non-feasance* does not generally give rise to such liability in tort.[133] It may exceptionally do so where the circumstances impose on A a 'duty to act';[134] but such a duty will not arise merely because A has made a gratuitous promise. Consideration for A's apparently gratuitous promise may, however, be provided by B's making a counter-promise: eg where a legal relationship (such as that of carrier and passenger) has arisen as a result of A's beginning to perform a promise to give B free rides on A's vehicles, and B has promised A not to sue A for negligence in the performance of the carriage operation.[135]

(ii) Definition

8.33 **Benefit and detriment.**   The notion of reciprocity underlies the often repeated definition of consideration as being *either* a detriment to the promisee (in that he gives value) *or* a benefit to the promisor (in that he receives value).[136] Where the contract is bilateral, each party will make and receive a promise and the requirement of consideration must be satisfied in relation to *each of these promises*. It is wrong to think of the consideration *for the contract*. In a contract of sale, for example, it is a detriment for the seller to part with goods, so that he thereby provides consideration for the buyer's promise to pay the price, even though that price exceeds the value of the goods.

8.34 The twin notions of 'benefit' and 'detriment' have lent themselves to a good deal of judicial manipulation. On the one hand, judges have sometimes regarded any benefit or detriment *which could be detected by the court* as consideration, even though the performance in question was not so regarded by the parties;[137] and in this way they have 'found' or 'invented' consideration for promises which a lay person might regard as gratuitous. Conversely, they have sometimes regarded acts or promises which were benefits or detriments *in fact* as not having this characteristic *in law*: eg because the performance rendered or promised was *already legally due*.[138] In such (and some other) situations, the courts have refused to give contractual force to promises which are not, in any realistic sense, gratuitous; they have done so on many disparate grounds of policy, using the doctrine of consideration as a substitute for other, then imperfectly developed,[139] doctrines.

---

132 *Wilkinson v Coverdale* (1793) 1 Esp 75; cf *Hedley Byrne & Co Ltd v Heller & Partners Ltd* [1964] AC 465.

133 *Customs & Excise Commissioners v Barclays Bank plc* [2006] UKHL 28; [2007] 1 AC 181 at [39].

134 *White v Jones* [1995] AC 207, 261; *Lennon v Metropolitan Police Commissioner* [2004] EWCA Civ 130; [2004] 1 WLR 2954 at [20], [34] (arguably a case of misfeasance).

135 *Gore v Van der Lann* [1967] 2 QB 31.

136 eg *Currie v Misa* (1875) LR 10 Ex 153, 162; the *Argy* case (n 131 above) 455; the *Gore* case, (n 135 above) 42; *Edmonds v Lawson* [2000] QB 501.

137 eg para 8.43 at n 167; *The Alev* [1989] 1 Lloyd's Rep 138, 147; cf *Shadwell v Shadwell* (1860) 9 CBNS 159, 174.

138 eg para 8.47 at n 179; para 8.58.

139 eg the doctrine of duress before the development discussed in para 8.203.

Mutual promises. When *performance* by one of the parties would satisfy the **8.35**
requirement of consideration,[140] a *promise* to render that performance generally has
the same effect: hence a promise by a seller to deliver goods in a month's time given in
exchange for the buyer's promise to pay on delivery is an immediately binding
contract. Difficulty can, however, arise where one of a pair of mutual promises is, for
some reason, not binding in law. Sometimes, such a promise cannot be consideration for a counter-promise: for example, a promise by A to pay B a pension cannot be
enforced if the sole consideration provided for it is B's promise not to compete
with A and that promise is invalid for restraint of trade.[141] But the position is different where the law invalidates B's promise for the protection of a class of which B is a
member: for example, where B is a minor. Then B's promise can constitute consideration for a counter-promise made by A;[142] and the same is true where B's promise has
been procured by A's fraud.[143] The law relating to defective promises as consideration
cannot be logically deduced from the requirement of consideration; it is based rather
on the policy of the rule which, in each case, makes the promise defective.

Mutual promises, though sufficient, are not necessary to satisfy the requirement **8.36**
of consideration. Thus in the case of a unilateral contract performance, and even
part performance, of the required act (such as walking to York)[144] can constitute
consideration.

Effects of promises unsupported by consideration. An informal promise that **8.37**
is not supported by consideration has no contractual force; but it does not follow
that such a promise has no legal effects. In particular, the law may, in circumstances to be discussed later in this chapter, place restrictions on the revocability
of some such promises.[145] It may even protect the promisee's expectation
interest,[146] though only as a matter of discretion and not (as in the case of a promise supported by consideration) as of right.

(b) Adequacy

The requirement of consideration means that *some* value must be given for a **8.38**
promise; but as a general rule the law is not concerned with the question whether
'adequate' value has been given:[147] the doctrine of consideration is not intended as

---

[140] Not if performance would *not* satisfy the requirement: eg if a debtor in the cases discussed in
para 8.58 made a *promise* of part payment of a debt.
[141] *Wyatt v Kreglinger & Fernau* [1933] 1 KB 793.
[142] See para 8.271.
[143] See para 8.176.
[144] See para 8.07.
[145] See paras 8.52, 8.53, 8.60, 8.62.
[146] See para 8.64 at n 262.
[147] *Westlake v Adams* (1858) CBNS 248, 265; *Midland Bank & Trust Co Ltd v Green* [1981]
AC 513.

a price control mechanism. It follows that a promise to pay £1,000 in exchange for a peppercorn or one to convey valuable property for £1 can be binding as a contract. The consideration in such a case is said to be 'nominal' and normally suffices, though there are situations in which a disposition for such a consideration could prejudice third parties and therefore lacks validity.[148] In such cases, a 'nominal' consideration must be distinguished from one which is merely inadequate; and it is submitted that a consideration is, for such purposes, 'nominal' if, as a matter of common sense, it is obviously of no more than token value.[149]

8.39　The general rule stated in paragraph 8.38 is well established; but the law is not insensitive to the problem of unequal bargains, so that the general rule is subject to exceptions to be discussed elsewhere in this chapter.[150] Conversely, a gratuitous promise supported by a nominal consideration may not deserve the same degree of protection as one supported by substantial consideration. For this reason equity will not aid a 'volunteer,' ie a person who has given either no or no substantial consideration.[151] There are also special statutory rules which protect third parties (such as creditors of the promisor) where only nominal or inadequate consideration has been given for the promise.[152]

(c) Past consideration

8.40　The consideration for a promise must be given in exchange for it and this requirement is not satisfied where the consideration consists of something done before the promise was made. Such 'consideration' is said to be 'past' and, in general,[153] bad in law.[154] In applying this rule, the courts, however, apply a functional, rather than a strictly chronological, test. A manufacturer's guarantee may be given shortly after the customer has bought the goods but the consideration provided by the customer is not regarded as past if his purchase and the giving of the guarantee were substantially a single transaction because the customer had been led to believe that he was buying guaranteed goods.[155] A past act can also be good consideration for a promise if it was done at the request of the promisor on the understanding

---

[148] eg Insolvency Act 1986, ss 238, 339, 423.

[149] See *Westminster CC v Duke of Westminster* [1991] 4 All ER 136, 146 (reversed in part on another ground (1992) 24 Housing LR 572); for a different view, see the *Midland Bank* case (n 147 above) 532.

[150] See paras 8.207 and 8.241, and paras 18.80–18.83.

[151] *Jefferys v Jefferys* (1841) Cr & Ph 138. The rule prevents the enforcement of a gratuitous *promise* but does not affect the validity of *a completed gift: Pennington v Waine* [2002] EWCA Civ 227; [2002] 1 WLR 2075.

[152] See n 148 above.

[153] For exceptions, see Bills of Exchange Act 1882, s 27(1)(b); Limitation Act 1980, s 27(5).

[154] *Eastwood v Kenyon* (1840) 11 A & E 438; *Re McArdle* [1951] Ch 669.

[155] A 'consumer guarantee' within Sale and Supply of Goods to Consumers Regulations 2002, SI 2002/3045, reg 15 binds the guarantor by force of the regulation; there is no requirement of consideration.

that payment would be made for it and if such payment would (had it been promised in advance) have been legally recoverable.[156] This rule covers the case in which services are rendered on a commercial basis but the rate of payment is fixed only after they have been rendered. Where, on this principle, a past *act* can constitute consideration, the same is true of a past *promise*.[157]

(d) Consideration must move from promisee

The consideration for a promise must be provided by the promisee[158] who there- **8.41** fore cannot enforce the promise if the whole of the consideration for it was provided by a third party: eg if A promised B to pay him £1,000 if C rendered some service to A and C did so. Consideration need not, however, move to the promisor.[159] Accordingly, the requirement of consideration is satisfied where the promisee at the promisor's request confers a benefit on a third party,[160] or suffers some detriment (such as giving up his job),[161] without thereby conferring any direct benefit on the promisor. By statute a person who is not a party to a contract can sometimes enforce a term in the contract against the promisor even though the claimant has not provided any consideration for the promise;[162] but consideration in such cases still has to be provided *by the promisee*.

(e) The value of consideration

(i) Sentimental motives

Consideration must be of 'value in the eye of the law'.[163] The requirement is not **8.42** satisfied by merely sentimental motives, so that 'natural affection of itself is not a sufficient consideration'.[164]

(ii) Illusory consideration

A promise has no contractual force where the consideration for it is merely illu- **8.43** sory. On this principle, a promisee could not enforce a promise if the alleged consideration for it was a counter-promise from him which was known to be impossible to perform; or if it was one to do an act which he would have done anyway, even if the promise had not been made; or if it was one to refrain 'from a

---

156 *Re Casey's Patents* [1892] 1 Ch 104, 115–16.
157 *Pao On v Lau Yiu Long* [1980] AC 614.
158 *Thomas v Thomas* (1842) 2 QB 851, 859; *Pollway Ltd v Abdullah* [1974] 1 WLR 493, 497.
159 *Re Wyvern Developments Ltd* [1974] 1 WLR 1097.
160 *Bolton v Madden* (1873) LR 9 QB 55.
161 *Jones v Padavatton* [1969] 1 WLR 628.
162 Contracts (Rights of Third Parties) Act 1999, s 1; para 8.303.
163 See para 8.31 at n 125.
164 *Bret v JS* (1600) Cro Eliz 756; *Mansukhani v Sharkey* [1992] 2 EGLR 105.

course of action which it was never intended to pursue';[165] or if his counter-promise left performance entirely to his discretion (ie it was one to do something 'if I feel like it'.)[166] Since, however, consideration need not be adequate, acts or omissions of even trifling value can satisfy the requirement of consideration,[167] at least if they were so regarded by the parties.

(iii) Compromises and forbearances

8.44 Where A has a legal claim against B of uncertain value, and promises to give up that claim in return for B's promise to pay him an agreed sum, there is generally no difficulty with regard to consideration: the consideration for B's promise to make the payment is A's giving up of his claim, while the consideration for A's promise to give up the claim is B's making the payment. The requirement of consideration for B's promise is satisfied even where A makes no *promise* to B but simply forbears in fact from pursuing his claim,[168] so long as it is clear that A's forbearance was induced by B's promise (typically to make a payment to A).[169] The requirement is likewise satisfied if the claim which A gives up, or promises to give up, is one which is *doubtful* in law (since in such a case its relinquishment involves a possibility of detriment to A and of benefit to B);[170] and the same is true where the claim is *clearly bad* in law, so long as A honestly believed it to be a good claim, seriously intended to prosecute it and did not conceal from B any facts which would exonerate B.[171] There may be no detriment to A (or benefit to B) in A's giving up a claim which he was bound to lose, but the law will uphold the agreement in order to encourage reasonable compromises. This reasoning, however, does not apply where the claim is *known* by A (and perhaps by B) to be bad, so that B's promise has no contractual force where the sole[172] consideration provided for it by A is his giving up a 'claim' of this kind.[173]

(f) Existing duties

8.45 A may, before any promise is made to him by B, already be under a legal duty to do an act (or to abstain from doing something). It is arguable that A's merely doing

---

165 *Arrale v Costain Civil Engineering Ltd* [1976] 1 Lloyd's Rep 98, 106.

166 See *Firestone Tyre & Rubber Co Ltd v Vokins & Co Ltd* [1951] 1 Lloyd's Rep 32; *Stabilad Ltd v Stephens & Carter Ltd* [1999] 2 All ER (Comm) 651, 659.

167 *Chappell & Co Ltd v Nestlé Co Ltd* [1960] AC 87; *Well Barn Farming Ltd v Backhouse* [2005] EWHC 1520; [2005] 3 EGLR 109 at [45].

168 *Alliance Bank v Broom* (1864) 2 Dr & Sm 289.

169 *Wigan v English & Scottish Law Life Assurance Association* [1909] Ch 291; and see *Combe v Combe* [1951] 2 KB 215, where the requirement of inducement was not satisfied.

170 *Haigh v Brooks* (1839) 10 A & E 309.

171 *Cook v Wright* (1861) 1 B & S 559; *Callisher v Bischoffsheim* (1870) LR 5 QB 449.

172 Not where there is also other consideration: *The Siboen and The Sibotre* [1976] 1 Lloyd's Rep 293, 334.

173 *Poteliakhoff v Teakle* [1938] 2 KB 816 (gambling debt; such debts are now legally enforceable by virtue of Gambling Act 2005, s 335 (1)).

what he was already legally bound to do cannot *in law* be a detriment to him; and, indeed, that to allow A in such a case to enforce B's promise would lead to the undesirable result of encouraging A to refuse to perform his original duty unless some added inducement were held out to him and so of supporting a form of duress. On the other hand, performance by A in such cases may *in fact* benefit B;[174] and where no element of duress is involved, the law is now moving towards the position that A's performance of (or promise to perform) an existing duty can amount to consideration for B's promise.

(i) 'Public' duty

The above conflict of principles is well illustrated by cases in which A's existing **8.46** duty is a 'public duty', ie one imposed by the general law rather than by contract. Obviously, a person does not provide consideration merely by forbearing to commit a crime;[175] nor should a public officer be able to enforce a promise for doing nothing more than his duty as such.[176] But where there are no such grounds of public policy for refusing enforcement, the prevailing view is that the performance of a 'public' duty can constitute consideration.[177] The same is true where the promisee does more than he is required by the pre-existing duty to do.[178]

(ii) Duty imposed by contract with promisor

The law at one time took the view that the mere performance by A of a duty owed **8.47** by him under a pre-existing contract with B was no consideration for a promise by B to A. Hence a promise to sailors that, if they completed the voyage for which they had signed on, they would be paid higher wages than those specified in their original contract was held not to be enforceable by the sailors.[179] More recently, however, it has been held that the performance of such a duty did constitute consideration, so that a promise by a building contractor to pay a subcontractor more than the originally agreed sum was held binding in the absence of any circumstances amounting to duress on the subcontractor's part. The consideration was said to consist of the *factual benefit* obtained by the contractor from the actual performance of the subcontractor's work.[180] Consideration may also be provided by A's doing *more* than he was obliged to do by his original contact with B.[181]

---

[174] Cf para 8.34.

[175] *Brown v Brine* (1875) 1 Ex D 5.

[176] *Morgan v Palmer* (1824) 2 B & C 729, 736.

[177] *Ward v Byham* [1956] 1 WLR 496, 498.

[178] *Glasbrook Bros Ltd v Glamorgan CC* [1925] AC 270.

[179] *Stilk v Myrick* (1809) 2 Camp 317; cf *The Proodos C* [1980] 2 Lloyd's Rep 390.

[180] *Williams v Roffey Bros & Nicholls (Contractors) Ltd* [1991] 1 QB 1. The reasoning would not apply where A had threatened not to perform the original contract and this threat amounted to duress: see *South Caribbean Trading v Trafigura Beheer BV* [2004] EWHC 2676 (Comm); [2005] 1 Lloyd's Rep 128 at [109].

[181] *Hanson v Royden* (1867) LR 3 CP 47; *The Atlantic Baron* [1979] QB 705.

(iii) *Duty imposed by contract with a third party*

8.48 Performance of a duty owed by A to X under a contract between them can constitute consideration for a promise made by B to A. If, for example, A contracts with
a shipowner X to unload goods belonging to B from the ship, the performance of
that duty can be consideration for B's promise to A not to make any claim against
A in respect of damage done to the goods by A while unloading them;[182] for
although A is already bound by his contract with X to do the work he confers a
factual benefit on B by doing it. On the same principle, a *promise* to perform such
a duty can constitute consideration, eg where A is indebted to the X company and
promises B, a shareholder in that company, to pay the debt, that promise can be
consideration for a counter-promise made by B to A.[183]

(g) Rescission and variation

8.49 Our concern here is with cases in which parties to a contract agree either to release
each other from further performance (rescission) or to alter the terms of the
contract (variation). So far as variation is concerned, the question whether performance from A of his part of the original contract constitutes consideration for
a new promise by B has already been discussed;[184] our present concern is with the
question whether there is consideration for B's promise to be content with some
performance *other* than that originally promised by A.

(i) *Rescission*

8.50 Rescission gives rise to no difficulty with regard to consideration where each party
has, and agrees to give up, outstanding rights against the other. In such cases the
rescission generates its own consideration, but this would not be true where one
party (A) promised to release the other (B) and B made no counter-promise to A;
or if only A had outstanding rights under the contract because B had broken the
contract but A had not done so. Rescission after breach by only one party requires
separate consideration;[185] in technical language there must (in general)[186] be not
only an 'accord' but 'satisfaction': ie a payment, or promise of payment, from the
party in breach.[187]

(ii) *Variation*

8.51 Where a 'variation' amounts to a rescission of the old contract followed by the
making of a new one on different terms, the case is governed by the principles

---

182 *The Eurymedon* [1975] AC 154.
183 *Pao On v Lau Yiu Long* [1980] AC 614.
184 See para 8.47.
185 *Atlantic Shipping Co Ltd v Louis Dreyfus & Co* [1922] 2 AC 250, 262.
186 For an exception, see Bills of Exchange Act 1882, s 62.
187 *British-Russian Gazette Ltd v Associated Newspapers Ltd* [1933] 2 KB 616, 643.

stated in paragraph 8.50. Where the parties agree to vary a contract in a way that is *capable* of benefiting either party (eg where they agree to vary the length of a lease,[188] the time of performance,[189] or the currency of payment[190]) the requirement of consideration is again satisfied, unless the variation is in fact made wholly for the benefit of one.[191] Even where the variation is not supported by a consideration of the kind just described, it may (on proof of the requisite contractual intention) be enforceable as a separate contract, collateral to the main transaction.[192] The cases which give rise to difficulty are those in which the variation can confer a legal benefit on only one of the parties. Sometimes, such a variation has no contractual force unless that party provides some separate consideration for the other's promise: this is, for example, true where a creditor promises to accept part payment of a debt in full settlement.[193] In other cases, however, it is arguable that a variation which can confer a *legal* benefit on only one party is supported by consideration if it *in fact* also confers a benefit on the other.[194]

(iii) Common law waiver

A variation which has no contractual force for want of consideration (or for some **8.52** other reason) may nevertheless have limited legal effects as a 'waiver'. This word is used in many senses[195] and sometimes means no more than 'rescission' or 'variation'. It is also used to describe the legal effects of arrangements which fall short of contractually binding variations and which will here be called 'forbearances'. The party *requesting* such a forbearance cannot refuse to accept performance varied in accordance with it;[196] nor if such performance is rendered and accepted can either party claim damages on the ground that the performance was not in accordance with the original contract.[197] The difficult cases are those in which the party *granting* the forbearance then wants to go back on it and enforce the contract in accordance with its original terms: eg where a buyer who had said that he would accept late delivery then insisted on the originally agreed delivery date. Under the common law doctrine of waiver, he cannot peremptorily take this course;[198] but such a waiver differs from a contractually binding variation in that the party granting it can

---

188 *Fenner v Blake* [1900] 1 QB 426.
189 *South Caribbean* case, n 180 above.
190 *WJ Alan & Co Ltd v El Nasr Export & Import Co* [1972] 2 QB 189.
191 *Vanbergen v St Edmund's Properties Ltd* [1933] 2 KB 233.
192 *Brikom Investments Ltd v Carr* [1979] QB 467.
193 See para 8.58.
194 On the analogy of the *Williams* case, para 8.47.
195 *The Laconia* [1977] AC 850, 871.
196 *Hickman v Haynes* (1875) LR 10 CP 598.
197 *Ogle v Vane* (1868) LR 3 QB 272.
198 *Hartley v Hymans* [1920] 3 KB 475.

generally [199] retract it on giving reasonable notice to the other party.[200] The distinction between such a waiver and a contractually binding variation was said to depend on the elusive criterion of the intention of the parties;[201] and it led to the paradoxical position that the more a party tried to bind himself the less he was likely to succeed; for a binding variation required consideration while a waiver did not.

(iv) Equitable forbearance (or promissory estoppel)

8.53 Equity provided a more satisfactory approach to the problem of variations not supported by consideration in concentrating on the conduct of the party granting the forbearance and its effect on the other party. It developed the principle (sometimes referred to as 'promissory estoppel' because it is in some respects[202] analogous to the doctrine of estoppel by representation, though it more closely resembles[203] the common law doctrine of waiver in the sense of forbearance). The equitable doctrine applies where one party to a contract by words or conduct makes a clear and unequivocal representation which leads the other 'to suppose that the strict rights arising under the contract will not be enforced or will be kept in suspense or held in abeyance'.[204] The party making the representation will then not be allowed to enforce those rights 'where it would be inequitable for him to do so having regard to the dealings which have thus taken place between the parties'.[205] The effects of a promise under this doctrine differ in three respects from those of a variation supported by consideration.

8.54 First, the equitable doctrine normally only *suspends* the rights under the original contract: they can normally be reasserted on giving reasonable notice.[206] This is one respect in which promissory estoppel resembles waiver (in the sense of forbearance).[207] It extinguishes rights only where subsequent events make it

---

199 Not if it would be 'inequitable' to allow him to retract: *The Bunge Saga Lima* [2005] EWHC 244 (Comm); [2005] 2 Lloyd's Rep 1 at [31]; cf para 8.54.

200 *Charles Rickards Ltd v Oppenhaim* [1950] 1 KB 616.

201 *Stead v Dawber* (1839) 10 A & E 57.

202 But not in all: in particular, estoppel by representation was based on a representation of *existing fact*: *Jorden v Money* (1854) 5 HLC 185, while a representation of *intention* or a *promise* suffices for the purpose of the doctrine of 'promissory estoppel'; the former doctrine operates with permanent effect while that of the latter is only suspensive: para 8.54; and the former doctrine prevents a party from denying *facts*, while the latter prevents him from denying the *legal effects* of a promise which is proved or admitted to have been made.

203 In the respects stated in n 202 above.

204 *Hughes v Metropolitan Rly* (1877) 2 App Cas 439, 448.

205 ibid.

206 *Tool Metal Manufacturing Co Ltd v Tungsten Electric Co Ltd* [1955] 1 WLR 761; *The Kanchenjunga* [1990] 1 Lloyd's Rep 391, 399.

207 See para 8.52.

impossible for the promisee to perform the original obligation[208] or make it highly inequitable to require him to do so.[209]

Secondly, the equitable doctrine applies only where it would be 'inequitable' for **8.55** the promisor to go back on his promise. This will normally be the position where the promisee has acted in reliance on the promise so that it is no longer possible to restore him to the position in which he was before he so acted.[210] But even where the promisee has so acted other circumstances may justify the promisor in going back on the promise (even without due notice): for example, a creditor's promise to give his debtor extra time to pay may be revoked on the ground that another creditor is about to levy execution on the debtor's property.[211]

Thirdly, in English law the doctrine merely prevents the enforcement of existing **8.56** rights: it 'does not create new causes of action where none existed before'.[212] It thus does not apply in cases of the kind discussed in paragraph 8.47, in which the effect of a variation is to *increase* the obligations of one party by his promise to make extra payments to the other. This position is sometimes described by saying that the doctrine operates as a shield and not as a sword;[213] but the metaphor is apt to mislead for the doctrine can assist a claimant no less than a defendant: eg where it prevents the defendant from relying on a defence that would have *destroyed the claimant's original cause of action*.[214] What the doctrine cannot do is to prevent a defendant from relying on the point that, apart from the promise, the claimant's original cause of action *never existed at all*.

(v) Distinguished from estoppel by convention

'Estoppel by convention' arises where parties 'act on an assumed state of facts or **8.57** law. . .shared by both or made by one and acquiesced in by the other'.[215] A party then cannot go back on that assumption if it would be 'unconscionable'[216] for him to do so and if the parties have conducted themselves on the basis of the shared assumption.[217] It follows from these requirements that no such estoppel arises where each party spontaneously makes a different mistake and there is no subsequent conduct of the party alleged to be estopped from which his acquiescence in

---

208 *Birmingham & District Land Co v London & North-Western Rly Co* (1888) 40 Ch D 268.
209 *Ogilvy v Hope-Davies* [1976] 1 All ER 683.
210 *Maharaj v Chand* [1986] AC 898.
211 *Williams v Stern* (1879) 5 QBD 409.
212 *Combe v Combe* [1951] 2 KB 215; contrast, in the United States, Restatement 2d, *Contracts*, § 90; and, in Australia, *Waltons Stores (Interstate) Ltd v Maher* (1988) 164 CLR 387.
213 *Combe v Combe* (n 212 above) 224.
214 eg by lapse of time: *The Ion* [1980] 2 Lloyd's Rep 245.
215 *The Indian Endurance (No 2)* [1998] AC 878, 913.
216 *Amalgamated Investment & Property Co Ltd v Texas Commerce Bank International* [1982] QB 84; *The Vistafjord* [1988] 2 Lloyd's Rep 343.
217 *The Captain Gregos (No 2)* [1990] 2 Lloyd's Rep 395, 400.

the other's mistaken assumption could be inferred.[218] Estoppel by convention is distinct[219]from 'promissory estoppel'[220] from which it differs in two ways. The first difference lies in its requirements: it can arise without any 'clear and unequivocal' representation.[221] The second difference lies in its nature or effect: it prevents a person from denying that a promise *has been made*, while 'promissory estoppel' is concerned with *the legal effects* of a promise which is shown or admitted to have been made.[222] Where the assumed promise would, had it been made, have been unsupported by consideration, both doctrines can operate in the same case: estoppel by convention to prevent a party from denying that the promise has been made, and promissory estoppel to determine its legal effects.[223] It seems that estoppel by convention resembles promissory estoppel[224] and estoppel by representation[225] in that it cannot give rise to new rights.[226]

(h) Part payment of a debt

(i) General common law rule

8.58 The general common law rule is that a creditor who promises to accept part payment of a debt in full settlement is not bound by that promise. In *Foakes v Beer*[227] the House of Lords held that a creditor who had made such a promise was nevertheless entitled to recover the balance: there was no consideration for the creditor's promise as the debtor had, in return for it, done no more than he was already bound to do. The rule may once have served the useful purpose of protecting the creditor against the too ruthless exploitation by the debtor of his position as a potential defendant in litigation. But it is also open to the objection that this protective function is now more satisfactorily performed by the concept of duress;[228] and that voluntary part payment may often be a benefit to the creditor. In cases of the kind discussed in paragraph 8.47 a similar factual benefit has been held to satisfy the requirement of consideration; but in the present context such reasoning

---

218 *The August P Leonhardt* [1985] 2 Lloyd's Rep 28.

219 For the distinction between the kinds of estoppel discussed in this Chapter, see *First National Bank plc v Thompson* [1996] Ch 231, 239; *Johnson v Gore Wood* [2002] 2 AC 1, 33, 38–40.

220 See para 8.53.

221 *Troop v Gibson* (1986) 277 EG 1134.

222 Cf para 8.53 n 202. In the cases cited in n 216 above, the promises (if made) would unquestionably have been supported by consideration.

223 eg (apparently) in *Troop v Gibson* (n 221 above).

224 See para 8.56.

225 See para 8.202.

226 *See Johnson v Gore Wood & Co* above, n 219 at 40, *Smithkline Beecham plc v Apotex Europe Ltd* [2006] EWCA Civ 658; [2007] Ch 71 at [109]–[112].

227 (1884) 9 App Cas 605.

228 See para 8.203.

would be inconsistent with *Foakes v Beer*, which is open to challenge only in the House of Lords.[229]

(ii) Common law exceptions

The rigour of the common law rule is mitigated by many exceptions. The rule **8.59** applies only to 'liquidated' claims, ie to claims for a fixed sum such as the agreed price for goods or services. Where the claim is 'unliquidated' so that its value is uncertain, no difficulty with respect to consideration arises out of an agreement fixing its amount.[230] The same is true where the claim is in good faith disputed[231] and where there is some variation (other than in the amount of payment) of the debtor's performance: eg where part payment is made before the due day, or in a different currency, or accompanied by the delivery of a small chattel;[232] or where the debtor confers some benefit (other than the mere fact of voluntary part payment) on the creditor, even though the debtor is already bound by the contract to do this.[233] Consideration may also be provided by the debtor's forbearing to enforce a cross-claim which he has against the creditor.[234] The rule also does not apply where a number of creditors enters into a composition agreement with each other and with the debtor to accept a dividend in full settlement: there is consideration in the benefit which each creditor gets in being assured of some payment and this 'moves' from the debtor in that his co-operation is needed for the operation of the agreement.[235] The rule also does not apply where the part payment is made by a third party to whom the creditor makes a promise not to sue the debtor for the balance.[236] The reason for this rule is that the court will not allow the creditor to break his contract with the third party by suing the debtor for the balance.[237] The debtor may also be entitled to enforce this contract under the Contracts (Rights of Third Parties) Act 1999.[238] An agreement between debtor and creditor to accept part payment in full settlement may finally take effect as a collateral contract, though for this purpose some separate consideration moving from the debtor is required.[239]

---

[229] See *Re Selectmove Ltd* [1995] 1 WLR 474.

[230] *Wilkinson v Byers* (1834) 1 A & E 106.

[231] *Cooper v Parker* (1855) 15 CB 822.

[232] See *Pinnell's* case (1602) 5 Co Rep 117a, and para 8.51.

[233] See the *Anangel Atlas* case [1990] 2 Lloyd's Rep 526.

[234] *Brikom Investments Ltd v Carr* [1979] QB 467.

[235] *Good v Cheesman* (1831) 2 B & Ad 328.

[236] *Hirachand Punamchand v Temple* [1911] 2 KB 330.

[237] The court may even restrain the creditor from doing so: *Snelling v John G Snelling Ltd* [1973] 1 QB 87.

[238] See para 8.303. In the present context it is the debtor who is the 'third party' for the purpose of the 1999 Act.

[239] *Brikom Investments Ltd v Carr* [1979] QB 467.

(iii) Equitable evasion

8.60   The equitable doctrine of 'promissory estoppel' had been established before *Foakes v Beer*[240] but was not in that case thought to be applicable to cases in which a debtor paid part of a debt in reliance on the creditor's promise to accept such payment in full settlement. But in the later *High Trees*[241] case it was said at first instance that the doctrine could apply to such a promise, in that case to one by the lessor of a block of flats to reduce the rent for so long as wartime difficulties of subletting continued. This view is at first sight in direct conflict with *Foakes v Beer*; and the most plausible reconciliation of the two cases is that, under the equitable doctrine, the creditor's promise does not, in general, *extinguish*, but only *suspends*, the creditor's right to the balance, which can therefore be reasserted on giving reasonable notice.[242] So to hold would indeed be appropriate in giving effect to the intention of the parties where the purpose of the arrangement was merely to tide the debtor over what are regarded as temporary financial difficulties.[243] Where the intention was permanently to remit part of the debt, extinctive (as opposed to suspensive) effect could perhaps sometimes be given to the creditor's promise on the analogy of the rule that 'promissory estoppel' can operate extinctively where the promisee can no longer be restored to the position that he was in before he acted in reliance on the promise:[244] eg if in reliance on the promise the debtor had undertaken or fulfilled new commitments in relation to the subject matter of the transaction giving rise to the debt.

8.61   The equitable doctrine applies only where it is 'inequitable' for the promisor to go back on his promise. This requirement would, for example, not be satisfied (so that the creditor would be entitled to go back on his promise) where the debtor had failed to pay the agreed smaller amount.[245] It has been suggested that the court could also take into account the debtor's conduct in procuring the creditor's promise: eg where the debtor had secured the promise by taking undue advantage of the creditor's urgent need for an immediate payment.[246] Such cases are, however, more appropriately dealt with under the now expanded notion of duress,[247] than under some vague notion of promises obtained 'improperly' but in circumstances falling short of duress.[248]

---

[240]   ie in *Hughes v Metropolitan Rly* (1877) 2 App Cas 439; para 8.53.
[241]   [1947] KB 130, *per* Denning J.
[242]   See para 8.54.
[243]   As, for example, in *Ajayi v RT Briscoe (Nig) Ltd* [1964] 1 WLR 1326.
[244]   Cf para 8.54.
[245]   Cf *Re Selectmove* [1995] 1 WLR 474, 481.
[246]   *D & C Builders Ltd v Rees* [1966] 2 QB 617 *per* Lord Denning MR.
[247]   See para 8.203.
[248]   *Pao On v Lau Yiu Long* [1980] AC 614, 643.

(i) Proprietary estoppel

(i) Nature and scope

The doctrine of proprietary estoppel applies to many situations[249] with only one **8.62** of which we are here concerned. This arises where the owner of property (usually land) makes a representation or promise to another person that the latter has, or will be granted, legally enforceable rights in or over the property, and the latter acts to his detriment in reliance on that representation or promise. The landowner may then be estopped from denying the existence of those rights or compelled to grant them even though his promise was not binding as a contract, eg for want of consideration. Illustrations of the doctrine are provided by family arrangements by which a parent (A) promises a child (B) that, if B will build a house on A's land, then A will give the land to B[250] or allow B to stay there for B's life.[251] A may then be precluded from revoking the promise after B has built the house. In such cases, A would be unjustly enriched if he were allowed freely to revoke the promise, but detrimental reliance by B can also give rise to the estoppel even though it does not lead to any improvement of A's land[252] or to any other enrichment of A.[253]

(ii) Requirements

The promise must induce the promisee to believe that legally enforceable rights **8.63** have been or will be created in his favour.[254] It follows that a promise which expressly disclaims an intention to be legally bound (such as one made 'subject to contract' or expressly reserving the promisor's power to revoke) will not normally[255] give rise to a proprietary estoppel.[256] The rights to which the promise refers must, in general, be rights in or over the property of the promisor[257] and it is an open question whether the doctrine can apply in relation to property other than land. The promisee must have relied on the promise to his detriment;[258] and the detriment must be so substantial as to make it unconscionable for the promisor to go

---

[249] So many that the doctrine has been called 'an amalgam of doubtful utility': *Amalgamated Investment & Property Co Ltd v Texas Commerce International Bank Ltd* [1982] QB 84, 103.

[250] *Dillwyn v Llewelyn* (1862) 4 DF & G 517.

[251] *Inwards v Baker* [1965] 2 QB 507.

[252] eg. *Campbell v Griffin* [2001] EWCA Civ 981; [2001] WTLR 98; *Jennings v Rice* [2002] EWCA Civ 159; [2002] WTLR 367 (personal services).

[253] eg *Crabb v Arun DC* [1976] Ch 179.

[254] See *Coombes v Smith* [1986] 1 WLR 808.

[255] ie, unless the promisor has induced the promisee to act on a subsequent promise that the original promise would not be withdrawn: *Cobbe v Yeoman's Row Management Ltd* [2006] EWCA Civ 1139; [2006] 1 WLR 2964 at [57].

[256] *A-G of Hong Kong v Humphrey Estates (Queen's Gardens)* [1987] 1 AC 114.

[257] See *Western Fish Products Ltd v Penwith DC* [1981] 2 All ER 204; for an exception see *Salvation Army Trustee Co v West Yorks Metropolitan CC* (1981) 41 P & CR 179 (promise relating to promisee's land so closely linked with one relating to promisor's land as to form in substance one transaction).

[258] *Greasley v Cooke* [1980] 1 WLR 1306.

back on the promise.[259] Probably the promisee's reliance must relate to some specific property:[260] without such a limitation the doctrine could lead to the enforceability of any gift promise on which the promisee had relied and this would be fundamentally inconsistent with the doctrine of consideration. Before the promisee has acted in reliance on the promise, the promisor can revoke it;[261] and he may be entitled to do so even after such action in reliance if the parties can, in spite of it, be restored to their original positions.

(iii) Effects

8.64   Proprietary estoppel can give rise to a variety of legal effects: it can take the form of ordering the promisor to convey the land to the promisee,[262] or of entitling the promisee to a right of occupation for life,[263] or of giving him a licence for a specified period[264] or one terminable on reasonable notice,[265] or of giving him a charge over the property[266] or of a monetary adjustment in respect of the improvements made by the promisee to the promisor's land.[267] Although the remedy is thus 'extremely flexible,'[268] the courts will, in fashioning it, adopt a 'principled approach'.[269] In particular, they will take into account the terms of the promise, the extent of the promisee's reliance on it and the proportion between that reliance and the promisee's expectation.[270] Where, for example, the remedy is by way of an award of money, the test of proportionality means that the promisee will recover such sum as is reasonable in the light of his reliance, even though the amount may fall short of his expectations.[271] This test may, however, be displaced by the subsequent conduct of the promisor in seeking to go back on the promise.[272] The court

---

259   *Gillett v Holt* [2001] 2 Ch 210, 239; *Jennings v Rice* [2005] EWCA Civ 159; [2002] WTLR 367 at [21], [42].

260   *Layton v Martin* [1986] 2 Financial LR 227; contrast (perhaps) *Re Basham* [1986] 1 WLR 1498, 1508.

261   eg if in the cases cited in nn 250 and 251 above the promise had been revoked before any building work had been done.

262   *Dillwyn v Llewelyn* (n 250 above).

263   *Inwards v Baker* (n 251 above).

264   *Tanner v Tanner* [1975] 1 WLR 1346.

265   *Canadian Pacific Railway v R* [1931] AC 414.

266   *Kinane v Mackie-Conteh* [2005] EWCA Civ 45; [2005] WTLR 345 at [33]; *Cobbe v Yeomans Row Management Ltd* [2006] EWCA Civ 1139; [2006] 1 WLR 2964; leave has been given to appeal to the House of Lords: [2007] 1 WLR 807.

267   *Cobbe v Yeoman's Row Management Ltd* [2006] EWCA Civ 1139; [2006] 1 WLR 2964; *Gillett v Holt* [2001] Ch 210 (combining monetary compensation with an order to convey part of the land).

268   *Roebuck v Mungovin* [1994] 2 AC 224, 235.

269   *Jennings v Rice* (n 259 above), at [43].

270   ibid, at [36], [56]; *Cobbe v Yeoman's Row Management Ltd*, n 267 above at [86], [124]–[126].

271   As in *Jennings v Rice*, n 259 above.

272   *Pascoe v Turner* [1979] 1 WLR 431, 439; *Gillett v Holt* [2001] Ch 210 at 235.

can also order the *promisee* to pay compensation as a condition of his getting title to the land if it is clear to both parties that the promisor did not intend to give up his title gratuitously;[273] and it may deny any remedy at all where, on balance, greater injustice would be caused by enforcing the promise than by allowing the promisor to go back on it.[274]

(j) Irrevocable offers

An offer can be withdrawn at any time before it has been accepted;[275] and this is **8.65** so even though the offeror has promised not to withdraw it for a specified period.[276] In some commercial contexts, this position is well understood and accepted: for example, in the case of share options the grantee expects to provide consideration for the option (unless it is granted by deed). In others, the rule may fail to give effect to the reasonable expectation of the offeree: for example where an offer from a subcontractor to supply materials to a builder is expressed to be 'firm' for a specified period and the builder then on the basis of the offer enters into a commitment with his customer.[277] In such a context, the rule by which such 'firm' offers are freely revocable has been criticized;[278] and the rule is subject (in the interests of commercial convenience) to an exception where payment under a contract (usually for the sale of goods) is to be made by an irrevocable letter of credit to be issued by the buyer's bank. Notification of the credit by that bank normally takes the form of a promise to pay the seller against tender of specified documents; and the commercial understanding is that the bank is bound on such notification, even before the seller can be said to have provided consideration for the bank's promise by performing, or beginning to perform, his part of the contract of sale. The law accepts this position, probably by way of exception to the requirement of consideration.[279]

(3) Contractual Intention

(a) Nature of the requirement

An agreement is not (even if the requirement of consideration is satisfied[280]) bind- **8.66** ing as a contract if it was made without any intention of creating legal relations.

---

[273] *Lim Teng Huan v Ang Swee Chuan* [1992] 1 WLR 113.

[274] *Sledmore v Dalby* (1996) 72 P & CR 196.

[275] See para 8.17.

[276] *Dickinson v Dodds* (1876) 2 Ch D 463.

[277] For a way of avoiding the difficulty, see the Canadian case of *Northern Construction Co Ltd v Gloge Heating & Plumbing* (1984) 6 DLR (4th) 450.

[278] Law Commission Working Paper 60, *Firm Offers* (1975).

[279] See *Hamzeh Malas & Sons v British Imex Industries Ltd* [1958] 2 QB 127; *The American Accord* [1983] 1 AC 168, 183.

[280] See eg *R v Civil Service Appeal Board, ex p Bruce* [1988] ICR 649, 655, 659 (affirmed on other grounds [1989] ICR 171).

(b) Proof of contractual intention

8.67 In deciding whether the present requirement is satisfied, the courts distinguish between implied agreements and express ones. The former are approached on the basis that 'contracts are not lightly to be implied'[281] and that the burden of proof on the issue of contractual intention is on the party alleging the existence of the contract.[282] But where the claim is based on an express agreement made in a commercial context, it is up to the other party to disprove such intention. As 'the onus is a heavy one'[283] and as the courts in such cases apply an objective test,[284] the requirement of contractual intention is (in relation to express agreements) significant only in the somewhat exceptional situations described in paragraphs 8.68 to 8.71.

(c) Illustrations

8.68 Contractual intention is most obviously negatived by an express provision: for example, by an 'honour clause' which states that the agreement is not to be a 'legal agreement',[285] or by the words 'subject to contract' in an agreement for the sale of land,[286] or by the terms of 'letters of intent'.[287] Vagueness in the agreed terms (even if not such as to show that no agreement was ever reached;[288]) may also negative contractual intention.[289] On this ground it has been held that there was no contractual liability for sales talk in promotional literature stating that a manufacturer's product was 'foolproof';[290] though more precise claims (eg that the product would last for seven years) have been held to have contractual force.[291]

8.69 Social and domestic agreements (such as those resulting from acceptance of an invitation to dinner) are not normally contracts;[292] and the same is true of many agreements made within the family circle which relate to the normal running of the household.[293] This may be true even where the parties are living apart, eg

---

281 *Blackpool & Fylde Aero Club v Blackpool BC* [1990] 1 WLR 1195, 1202.

282 *Baird Textile Holdings Ltd v Marks & Spencer plc* [2001] EWCA Civ 274; [2002] 1 All ER (Comm) 737 (burden not discharged); *Modahl v British Athletics Federation* [2001] EWCA Civ 1477; [2002] 1 WLR 1192 (burden discharged).

283 *Edwards v Skyways Ltd* [1964] 1 WLR 349, 355.

284 *Kingswood Estate Co Ltd v Anderson* [1963] QB 169.

285 *Rose & Frank Co v JR Crompton & Bros Ltd* [1925] AC 455.

286 See para 8.28.

287 *Kleinwort Benson Ltd v Malaysian Mining Corp* [1989] 1 WLR 379.

288 See para 8.23.

289 eg *Baird Textile* case, n 282 above.

290 *Lambert v Lewis* [1982] AC 225 (affirmed [1982] AC 268, 271 on other grounds). Such statements are also probably too vague to impose liability to consumers under Sale of Goods Act 1979, s 14 (D) ('specific characteristics' claimed by seller of goods in advertising) or Sale and Supply of Goods to Consumers Regulations 2002, SI 2002/3045, reg 15 (consumer guarantees).

291 Cf *Shanklin Pier Ltd v Detel Products Ltd* [1951] 2 KB 854.

292 *Balfour v Balfour* [1919] 2 KB 571, 578.

293 *Gage v King* [1961] 1 QB 188.

because one party to a marriage is temporarily working abroad.[294] A further reason why such agreements have no legal effect is that they may leave performance largely to the discretion of the promisor;[295] and this factor may negative contractual intention even in a commercial context.[296]

A collective agreement between a trade union and an employer or an association **8.70** of employers is, by statute, 'conclusively presumed not to have been intended by the parties to be a legally enforceable contract' unless it is in writing and expressly provides that it is intended to be legally enforceable.[297]

Contractual intention may be negatived by many other disparate factors. These **8.71** include the nature of the relationship between the parties,[298] the fact that the agreement was a sham,[299] that it was believed simply to give effect to an already existing right (so that there was no intention to make a *new* contract)[300] and that the promissory statement was made in jest or anger.[301] The relevant factors cannot be neatly classified since the question of contractual intention is, in the last resort, one of fact in each case.

(4) Form

(a) General

To say that a contract must be in a certain form means that its conclusion must be **8.72** marked or recorded in a specified manner, typically (in modern legal systems) in writing. The requirement, where it exists, must normally[302] be satisfied in addition to those of agreement, consideration and contractual intention. Formal requirements promote certainty by making it relatively easy to tell when a contract has been made, what type of contract it is and what its terms are. They also act as a safeguard

---

[294] *Balfour v Balfour* (n 292 above).

[295] *Gould v Gould* [1970] 1 QB 275; cf *Vaughan v Vaughan* [1953] 1 QB 762, 765.

[296] *Taylor v Brewer* (1813) 1 M & S 290; *Re Richmond Gate Property Co Ltd* [1965] 1 WLR 335; *Carmichael v National Power plc* [1999] 1 WLR 2042. But such a discretionary promise would have contractual force where the law required the discretion to be exercised 'rationally and in good faith': (see *Horkulak v Cantor Fitzgerald International* [2004] EWCA Civ 1287; [2005] ICR 402 at [48] and *Commerzbank AG v Keen* [2006] EWCA Civ 1536; [2006] 1 WLR 872 at [59] (employee's discretionary bonus)).

[297] Trade Union and Labour Relations (Consolidation) Act 1992, s 179(1) and (2); cf at common law, *Ford Motor Co v AEF* [1969] 2 QB 403.

[298] For example, that between a church and a minister of religion appointed by it: contrast *President of the Methodist Conference v Parfitt* [1984] QB 368 with *Percy v Board of National Mission of the Church of Scotland* [2005] UKHL 73; [2006] 2 AC 28.

[299] *The Ocean Enterprise* [1997] 1 Lloyd's Rep 449, 484.

[300] *The Aramis* [1989] 1 Lloyd's Rep 213; *Judge v Crown Leisure Ltd* [2005] EWCA Civ 571; [2005] IRLR 823.

[301] *Licences Insurance Corporation and Guarantee Fund (Ltd) v Lawson* (1896) 12 TLR 501.

[302] In the case of a deed, the formal requirement can operate as a *substitute* for consideration.

against entering into a contract rashly; and they help to protect the weaker party to a contract by ensuring that he is provided with a written record of its terms. These functions of form are well illustrated by the elaborate formal requirements that protect the debtor under regulated consumer credit agreements.[303] On the other hand, formal requirements may be time-consuming, clumsy and a source of technical pitfalls. Contrary to popular belief, the general rule is that contracts can be made informally, by word of mouth. Exceptions to this general rule now all owe their existence to legislation relating to particular types of contracts. These exceptions cannot be stated in detail here; but two topics of general interest call for discussion.

(b) Types of formal requirements

8.73 Formal requirements vary considerably in their stringency. At one extreme, the requirement is satisfied only by a deed: this is the position with regard to leases of land for more than three years.[304] A second requirement is that the contract must be *made in writing*: this is the position with regard to regulated consumer credit agreements[305] and to most contracts for the sale of interests in land.[306] A third requirement is that there must be a *note or memorandum in writing*: this requirement exists in relation to contracts of guarantee.[307] This requirement can be satisfied by a document coming into existence after the contract was made: for this reason it is said that the contract need not be in writing but only *evidenced in writing*. Such a requirement exists also for policies of marine insurance.[308] A fourth requirement is that one party must supply to the other certain written particulars: for example, an employer must give his employee a document setting out the principal terms of the contract,[309] and under some leases the landlord must give the tenant a rent book setting out specified particulars.[310]

(c) Electronic communications

8.74 The formal requirements described above can generally be satisfied by electronic communications[311] and signatures:[312] eg where a contract is made on a website

---

[303] Consumer Credit Act 1974, ss 55, 60, 61. A consumer credit agreement is a 'regulated agreement' unless it is exempt under s 16 of the 1974 Act (1974 Act, s 8, as amended by Consumer Credit Act 2006, s 2) or by Order made under s 16A (as inserted by s 3 of the 2006 Act).

[304] Law of Property Act 1925, s 52.

[305] Consumer Credit Act 1974, s 61.

[306] Law of Property (Miscellaneous Provisions) Act 1989, s 2(1) and (3).

[307] Statute of Frauds 1677, s 4, repealed so far as it related to certain other contracts by Law Reform (Enforcement of Contracts) Act 1954.

[308] Marine Insurance Act 1906, ss 22.

[309] Employment Rights Act 1996, s 1.

[310] Landlord and Tenant Act 1985, s 4.

[311] The requirement that particulars of a consumer credit agreement must be sent to the debtor by post (Consumer Credit Act 1974 ss 63(3), 64(2)) clearly cannot be satisfied electronically.

[312] Clicking on a website button would not necessarily satisfy the requirement of 'signature'. If it did, the protective function of formal requirements (para 8.72) could be considerably impaired.

or by an exchange of emails.[313] An EC Directive requires member states to ensure that contracts can be made by electronic means,[314] but this requirement does not extend to contracts for the sale of interests in land or to contracts of guarantee.

(d) Effect of non-compliance

Failure to comply with a formal requirement varies according to the nature of the requirement and the terms of the legislation imposing it. **8.75**

One possibility is that the legislation may make the contract 'void'[315] or that the contract simply fails to come into existence. The latter consequence follows from failure to comply with the formal requirements for the making of a contract for the sale of an interest in land;[316] though the hardship that can result from this position (eg to a purchaser who has partly performed or otherwise acted in reliance on the contract) can sometimes be mitigated by the use of such legal devices as constructive trust,[317] proprietary estoppel,[318] rectification[319] or the enforcement of a term omitted from the writing as a collateral contract.[320] **8.76**

A second possibility is that the contract comes into existence but fails to produce all the consequences that it would have produced if the required form had been used. For example, if a lease for over three years were in writing but not made by deed, it would be 'void for the purpose of creating a legal estate'[321] but nevertheless enforceable between the parties as an agreement for a lease.[322] **8.77**

A third possibility is that *one* party's right to enforce the contract may be restricted. For example, an improperly executed regulated consumer credit agreement cannot be enforced against the debtor without an order of the court.[323] In deciding whether to make such an order the court has, in effect, a wide discretion which can prevent the debtor from relying on unmeritorious defences based on technical slips.[324] **8.78**

---

[313] Law Commission paper on *Electronic Commerce: Formal Requirements in Commercial Contracts* (2001).

[314] Directive 2000/31 EC, Art 9. Parts of the Directive (but not Art 9) are implemented by The Electronic Commerce (EC Directive) Regulations 2002, SI 2000/2013.

[315] Bills of Sale Act 1878 (Amendment) Act 1882.

[316] See n 306 above.

[317] See Law of Property (Miscellaneous Provisions) Act 1989, s 2(5); *Yaxley v Gotts* [2000] Ch 162, 193.

[318] *Cobbe v Yeoman's Row Management Ltd* [2006] EWLA Civ 1139; [2006] 1 WLR 2964 at [66]–[68].

[319] Law of Property (Miscellaneous Provisions Act 1989, s 2(4); para 8.153.

[320] eg *Record v Bell* [1991] 1 WLR 853.

[321] Law of Property Act 1925, s 52.

[322] *Walsh v Lonsdale* (1882) 21 Ch D 9.

[323] Consumer Credit Act 1974, s 65.

[324] ibid, s 127, as amended by Consumer Credit Act 2006, s 15.

Where no enforcement order is made, the debtor is not liable to make restitution to the creditor in respect of benefits received under the agreement.[325]

8.79 A fourth possibility is that the contract is valid but cannot be enforced (by action) against the party who has not signed a note or memorandum of it. This is the position with regard to contracts of guarantee.[326] As the contract is not void the party who has not signed it is not entitled to the return of money paid or property transferred by him under it.[327]

8.80 A fifth possibility, laid down for policies of marine insurance, is that the contract is not admissible in evidence unless it complies with the formal requirements.[328]

8.81 A final possibility is that failure to comply with the formal requirement, though amounting to a criminal offence, does not affect the validity of the contract. This is the position where a landlord should have, but has not, provided his tenant with a rent book: the landlord can nevertheless sue for rent.[329]

(e) Formal requirements for rescission and variation

8.82 A contract which is subject to a formal requirement can nevertheless be rescinded informally[330] (unless the rescinding agreement amounts itself to a contract which is subject to a formal requirement). An attempt to vary such a contract may amount to a rescission followed by the making of a new contract. In that case, the rescission is effective but the new contract is subject to the formal requirement.[331] If the attempt is a mere variation (eg by the addition or deletion of a term)[332] it is ineffective and each party can sue (and sue only) on the original contract.[333]

C. Contents

(1) Express Terms

(a) Ascertainment and meaning

8.83 The express terms of a contract are those set out in the words used by the parties. The meaning of these words is determined objectively so that a party cannot

---

325 *Dimond v Lovell* [2002] AC 384, 398.
326 See at n 307 above.
327 *Thomas v Brown* (1876) 1 QBD 714.
328 Marine Insurance Act 1906, s 22.
329 *Shaw v Groom* [1970] 2 QB 504.
330 See *Morris v Baron & Co* [1918] AC 1.
331 ibid.
332 For the distinction between such a variation and a rescission, see *British and Beningtons Ltd v NW Cachar Tea Co* [1923] AC 48, 68.
333 *Goss v Nugent* (1833) 5 B & Ad 58; *McCausland v Duncan Lawrie Ltd* [1997] 1 WLR 38.

enforce the contract in the sense given by him to those words if that sense differed from that which the other party, having regard to the commercial context, has reasonably given to it.[334]

(b) Incorporation by reference

A contractual document may incorporate the terms of another document. Most **8.84** commonly this is done by express reference in the first document to the second (eg by reference in a contract to terms settled by a trade association). Such incorporation may also be effected without express reference if the court is satisfied that the parties intended to incorporate the second document in the first.[335] Since the incorporated document may be one of considerable length and complexity, it is possible for some of its terms to conflict with those of the incorporating document. The court must then resolve the inconsistency and will be inclined to give primacy to the document actually drawn up by the parties, this being likely to express their predominant intention.[336] The requirements for the incorporation of standard terms drawn up *by one of the parties* are discussed below.[337]

(c) The parol evidence rule

This rule states that where a contract has been reduced to writing, then 'parol **8.85** evidence' (ie evidence extrinsic to the document) cannot be used to add to, vary or contradict the written instrument.[338] The purpose of the rule is to promote commercial certainty by holding the parties bound by the writing and by it alone.[339] On the other hand, the rule is capable of leading to injustice where parties have in fact agreed to terms not set out in the document; and the courts have mitigated such injustice by recognizing exceptions to the rule or by limiting its scope.

(d) Qualifications

The rule relates only to evidence as to the *content* of the contract, so that extrinsic **8.86** evidence can be used to challenge its *validity*,[340] eg for lack of consideration; or to establish some vitiating factor such as mistake.[341] On a similar principle, evidence

---

[334] *Eyre v Measday* [1986] 1 All ER 488; *Sirius International Insurance Co (Publ) v FAI General Insurance Ltd* [2004] UKHL 54; [2004] 1 WLR 3251 at [18], [35].

[335] *Jacobs v Batavia & General Plantations Trust Ltd* [1924] 1 Ch 287, affirmed [1924] 2 Ch 329.

[336] See *Adamastos Shipping Co Ltd v Anglo-Saxon Petroleum Co Ltd* [1959] AC 133.

[337] See paras 8.95 to 8.97.

[338] *Jacobs v Batavia & General Plantations Trust Ltd* [1924] 1 Ch 287, 295; *Rabin v Gerson Berger Association Ltd* [1986] 1 WLR 526, 534, 537.

[339] *AIB Group plc v Martin* [2001] UKHL 63; [2002] 1 WLR 94 at [4].

[340] *Kleinwort Benson Ltd v Malaysian Mining Corp* [1989] 1 WLR 379, 392.

[341] *Roe v RA Naylor Ltd* (1918) 87 LJKB 958, 964.

can be admitted to show that the contract is subject to a contingent condition precedent not stated in the written document.[342]

8.87   Extrinsic evidence can be used to elucidate the meaning of the document: eg to explain vague or ambiguous terms[343] or to identify the subject matter[344] or to make it clear which party was buyer and which seller.[345] But where the document names the parties, evidence is not admissible to contradict it to show that one of the named parties was someone else.[346] Evidence is also not admissible for the above purposes of antecedent negotiations[347] (since the object of the document is to supersede these) or of conduct of the parties after the execution of the document;[348] though evidence is admissible to show that the contract has been rescinded or varied by subsequent agreement.[349] Where a contract of sale is in writing, the buyer cannot enforce an oral undertaking as to quality; but he may be entitled to rely on a statement in it as a misrepresentation if it contains a false statement of fact,[350] or as overriding an exemption clause in the written contract.[351]

8.88   The rule excludes evidence of *express* terms but not evidence showing that a term ought to be implied[352] (or evidence negativing a usual implication).[353] Evidence of *custom* may also be used for this purpose,[354] so long as it does not *contradict* the written contract;[355] but this restriction does not apply where custom is used simply to show that words in the contract bore a special (customary) meaning.[356]

8.89   It may be possible to show that parties have made two contracts relating to the same subject matter: one in writing and the other oral. Evidence of the oral contract is then admissible to prove the second (or 'collateral') contract,[357] even (it seems)

---

342   *Pym v Campbell* (1856) 6 E & B 370.
343   *Bank of New Zealand v Simpson* [1900] AC 182.
344   *Macdonald v Longbottom* (1859) 1 E & E 977.
345   *Newell v Redford* (1867) LR 3 CP 52.
346   *Shogun Finance Ltd v Hudson* [2003] UKHL 62; [2004] 1 AC 919 at [49].
347   *Prenn v Simmonds* [1971] 1 WLR 1381, 1384; *Reardon Smith Line Ltd v Hansen-Tangen* [1976] 1 WLR 989, 996; but evidence of a prior *contract* may be admissible: *HIH Casualty & General Insurance Ltd v New Hampshire Insurance* [2001] EWCA Civ 735; [2001] 2 All ER (Comm) 39 at [83].
348   *James Miller & Partners v Whitworth Street Estates (Manchester) Ltd* [1970] AC 586, 603, 606; *Wickman Ltd v Schuler AG* [1974] AC 325.
349   *Morris v Baron & Co* [1918] AC 1.
350   Misrepresentation Act 1967, s 1(a).
351   See para 8.107.
352   *Gillespie Bros & Co v Cheney Eggar & Co* [1896] 2 QB 59.
353   *Burgess v Wickham* (1863) 3 B & S 669.
354   *Hutton v Warren* (1836) 1 M & W 466, 475.
355   *Palgrave Brown & Son v SS Turid (Owners)* [1922] AC 397.
356   *Smith v Wilson* (1832) 3 B & Ad 728.
357   *Mann v Nunn* (1874) 30 LT 526.

if it to some extent contradicts the written contract.[358] Such a collateral contract must, however, satisfy the normal requirements for contract formation such as those of consideration and contractual intention.[359]

The law distinguishes between documents intended only as informal memoranda[360] and those intended to be complete or exhaustive records of what has been agreed. Extrinsic evidence is excluded only where the document is of the latter kind;[361] and if a document appears to a reasonable person to fall into this category, a presumption arises that the document was indeed an exclusive record.[362] Evidence of extrinsic terms (though in fact agreed) will then be excluded unless the party relying on them can show that the other did not regard the document as such a record.

8.90

(2) Implied Terms

(a) Terms implied in fact

A term will be implied in fact if it is one which the parties must have intended to include because it was 'so obvious that it goes without saying' so that, if an 'officious bystander' were to suggest its inclusion as an express term, they would immediately accept the suggestion.[363] It is also often said that the term must be 'necessary to give such business efficacy as the parties must have intended';[364] but this seems to be no more than a practical test for determining what the parties must have intended, under the 'officious bystander' test. This test emphasizes the point that it is not sufficient for the term to satisfy the standard of reasonableness,[365] and that the courts will not 'improve the contract which the parties have made for themselves'.[366] They will also refuse to imply a term where one party simply did not know the facts on which the alleged implication was to be based;[367]

8.91

---

[358] *City & Westminster Properties (1934) Ltd v Mudd* [1959] Ch 129; but see *Angell v Duke* (1875) 32 LT 320; *Henderson v Arthur* [1907] KB 10.

[359] *Heilbut, Symons & Co v Buckleton* [1913] AC 30.

[360] eg *Allen v Pink* (1838) 4 M & W 140.

[361] *Hutton v Watling* [1948] Ch 398.

[362] *Gillespie Bros & Co v Cheney Eggar & Co* [1896] QB 59, 62.

[363] *Shirlaw v Southern Foundries (1926) Ltd* [1939] 2 KB 206, 227 (affirmed [1940] AC 701).

[364] *Luxor (Eastbourne) Ltd v Cooper* [1941] AC 108, 137; *Goshawk Dedicated Ltd v Tyser & Co Ltd* [2006] EWCA Civ 54; [2006] 1 All ER (Comm) 501 at [53]; and see *Concord Trust v The Law Debenture Trust Corporation* [2005] UKHL 27; [2005] 1 WLR 1591 at [37], also discussing other possible tests for implying terms.

[365] *Friends Provident Life & Pensions Ltd v Sirius International Insurance* [2005] EWCA Civ 601; [2005] 2 All ER (Comm) 145 at [32].

[366] *Trollope & Colls Ltd v NW Metropolitan Hospital Board* [1973] 1 WLR 601, 609; *Ultraframe (UK) Ltd v Tailored Roofing Systems Ltd* [2004] EWCA Civ 585; [2004] 2 ALL ER (Comm) 692 at [17], citing earlier cases.

[367] *Spring v NASDS* [1956] 1 WLR 585, 599.

and, generally, where it is not clear that *both* parties would have agreed to the implication.[368] Occasionally, indeed, they may imply a term, even though one party would *not* have agreed to it, on the ground that an intention to incorporate it must be *imputed* to that party; but this power is to be 'sparingly and cautiously used' and only where the implication is 'strictly necessary'.[369]

(b) Terms implied in law

8.92   Many of the obligations arising out of certain types of special contracts are said to be based on 'implied terms': in certain circumstances it is, for example, an 'implied term' of a contract for the sale of goods that the goods are fit for the particular purpose for which the buyer requires them;[370] and an implied term of a contract of employment that the employer will take reasonable care not to endanger the employee's health.[371] Many such terms are implied even though the 'officious bystander' test is not satisfied so that the implication is not based on the court's view as to the common intention of the parties.[372] That intention is relevant only to the extent that it may be open to the parties to exclude the term in question by express contrary agreement.[373] Nor are such terms subject to the 'business efficacy' test as applied to terms alleged to be implied in fact: a contract of sale may well have such efficacy without the implication referred to above.[374] Terms implied in law are 'legal incidents of [particular] kinds of contractual relationships';[375] in deciding whether such terms ought to be implied, the courts are concerned with considerations of 'justice and policy';[376] and to this extent the tests of reasonableness and fairness are relevant to an implication of this kind.[377]

(c) Terms implied by custom or usage

8.93   Where persons deal in a particular market, a custom of that market may be implied into their contract unless the custom is inconsistent with the express terms of the contract or with terms implied otherwise than by custom. In cases of such inconsistency the custom is said to be 'unreasonable'; for example, a custom allowing an

---

[368] eg *Shell UK Ltd v Lostock Garages Ltd* [1976] 1 WLR 1187.

[369] *Equitable Life Assurance Society v Hyman* [2002] 1 AC 408, 459. For criticism (in another context) of the concept of imputed intention, see *Stack v Dowden* [2007] UKHL 17; [2007] 2 WLR 831 at [125]–[127]; contrast at [21].

[370] Sale of Goods Act 1979, s 14(3).

[371] *Johnstone v Bloomsbury Area Health Authority* [1992] 2 QB 333.

[372] *Liverpool City Council v Irwin* [1977] AC 239.

[373] For some legislative restrictions on the right so to exclude certain implied terms, see paras 8.112 and 8.113.

[374] At n 370 above; see the *Liverpool City Council* case (n 372 above) 255.

[375] *Mears v Safecar Securities Ltd* [1983] QB 54, 78.

[376] *The Star Texas* [1993] 2 Lloyd's Rep 445, 452; *Crossley v Faithful & Gould Holdings* [2004] EWCA Civ 293; [2004] 4 All ER 447 at [36].

[377] See *Re Charge Card Services* [1989] Ch 497, 513.

agent to sell his own goods to his principal is unreasonable as it is in conflict with his duty to the principal to buy as cheaply as possible.[378] The question of reasonableness is one of law and where the custom is reasonable it binds both parties whether they knew of it or not.[379] Terms may similarly be implied by usage of the trade in which the contracting parties were engaged.[380]

D. Standard Terms

The terms of many contracts are set out in printed standard forms prepared by or **8.94** for one party and presented to the other. The practice has the advantages of saving time and creating standard patterns of dealing so as to enable parties to know what sorts of risks they will have to bear and cover by insurance. On the other hand, it has also been used by commercial suppliers of goods and services to exploit and abuse superior bargaining power, especially in contracts with consumers. It is this aspect of the subject which has engaged the attention of courts and legislatures, initially in cases involving terms which excluded or limited the supplier's liability, but also in cases in which terms conferred certain unduly advantageous rights on him.

(1) Exemption Clauses at Common Law

(a) Incorporation

(i) Signature

The first method of incorporating an exemption clause in a contract is to get the **8.95** party to be bound by it to sign the document in which it is contained. If that document is one which could reasonably have been expected to contain contractual terms,[381] the signer is then prima facie[382] bound by it even though he did not read it[383] and even though he was incapable of understanding it.[384]

---

378 *Robinson v Mollett* (1875) LR 7 HL 802.
379 *Reynolds v Smith* (1893) 9 TLR 494.
380 *British Crane Hire Corp v Ipswich Plant Hire Ltd* [1975] QB 303.
381 *Grogan v Robin Meredith Plant Hire* The Times, 26 February 1996.
382 Subject to defences such as *non est factum*: see para 8.149.
383 *L'Estrange v F Graucob Ltd* [1934] 2 KB 394; criticized in *McCutcheon v David MacBrayne Ltd* [1964] 1 WLR 125, 133. In the case of a signed document, there is no need to satisfy the requirement of notice (para 8.96): *HIH Casualty & General Insurance v New Hampshire Insurance* [2001] EWCA Civ 735; [2001] 2 All ER (Comm) 39 at [209]; unless, perhaps, the term in question is 'particularly onerous or unusual': *Ocean Chemical Transport Inc v Exnor Craggs Ltd* [2000] 1 Lloyd's Rep 446, 454.
384 *The Luna* [1920] P 22.

(ii) Notice

8.96   The document containing the exemption clause, or incorporating it by reference,[385] may simply be handed to the party to be bound. The clause then becomes part of the contract only if reasonable steps to bring it to the attention of that party have been taken by the other.[386] This depends first on whether the document was intended to have contractual force (so that a term printed on a mere receipt for payment will not be incorporated);[387] and secondly on whether the steps taken to give notice were in all the circumstances sufficient to bring the existence of the term home to the other party.[388] If the clause is an unusual one, the party relying on it must take steps to 'make it conspicuous'.[389] If reasonable steps are taken, the clause is incorporated though not read by the other party.[390] The steps must be taken at or before the time of contracting, not at some later time.[391]

(iii) Course of dealing

8.97   Where parties have entered into a series of contracts on terms incorporating an exemption clause, that clause may be incorporated into a particular contract even though, when making it, the steps required to incorporate it are, by some oversight, not taken.[392] For this purpose there must be a regular course of dealing (not just a small number of transactions within a long time-span);[393] and it must be *consistent*.[394] A term may also be implied by custom or usage[395] even though there is no course of dealing *between the parties.*

(b) Construction

(i) General

8.98   An exemption clause will be construed strictly against the party at whose instigation it was included in the contract and who now seeks to rely on it: for example, a clause stating that 'no warranty. . .*is* given' has been held not to excuse a supplier of goods for breach of a collateral undertaking *previously* given.[396] The rule is less rigorously applied to clauses which merely *limit* liability since it is less 'inherently

---

385   As in *Thompson v London, Midland & Scottish Rly* [1930] 1 KB 41.
386   *Parker v South Eastern Rly* (1877) 2 CPD 416.
387   *Chapelton v Barry UDC* [1940] 1 KB 532.
388   *Parker v SE Rly,* (n 386 above).
389   *Crooks v Allen* (1879) 5 QBD 38, 40; *J Spurling Ltd v Bradshaw* [1956] 1 WLR 461, 466.
390   *Thompson v LM & S Rly,* (n 363 above).; cf *O'Brien v MGN Ltd* [2001] EWCA Civ 1279; [2002] CLC 33 (rules governing newspaper competition).
391   *Olley v Marlborough Court* [1949] 1 KB 532.
392   *Hardwick Game Farm v Suffolk Agricultural, etc Association* [1969] 2 AC 31, 90, 104, 105, 113, 130.
393   *Hollier v Rambler Motors (AMC) Ltd* [1972] 2 QB 71.
394   *McCutcheon v David MacBrayne Ltd* [1964] 1 WLR 125.
395   See para 8.93.
396   *Webster v Higgins* [1948] 2 All ER 127.

improbable'[397] that a party will agree to a limitation than to a total exclusion of the other's liability.

(ii) Negligence

Legislation now restricts a party's power to exclude liability for negligence;[398] and even where it remains possible to do so 'clear words'[399] must be used for this purpose. The most obvious way of satisfying this requirement is to refer expressly to 'negligence'. Such a reference is normally essential where there is a realistic possibility[400] that the party relying on the clause can be made liable without negligence. 'General words' (containing no such reference) are then prima facie construed to cover only his strict liability;[401] though this rule of construction can be displaced by words which clearly show that negligence liability is to be covered.[402] Even the prima facie rule does not apply where the party's *only* liability is for negligence so that then general words *can* cover negligence[403] unless they are construed merely as a warning that the party in question is not liable for loss caused without his negligence.[404]

8.99

(iii) Seriousness of breach

Fundamental breach.   Before exemption clauses were subjected to legislative control,[405] the courts were reluctant to allow a party to rely on an exemption clause where his breach was a particularly serious one; and to this end they developed the so-called doctrine of fundamental breach. According to one view, this made it impossible as a matter of law to exclude liability for such breaches. This 'substantive doctrine' may once have been a useful device for protecting consumers; but it is no longer needed for this purpose now that legislation has intervened, and it was, in any event, not restricted to the consumer context. The House of Lords has accordingly rejected the substantive doctrine and has held that the doctrine of fundamental breach is no more than a rule of construction.[406] As such, the rule amounts to a presumption that general words in an exemption clause will not normally cover certain very serious breaches; but the presumption can be overcome if the words are sufficiently clear.

8.100

---

[397] *Ailsa Craig Fishing Co Ltd v Malvern Fishing Co* [1983] 1 WLR 964, 970.

[398] See para 8.112 and 8.113.

[399] *Gillespie Bros Ltd v Roy Bowles Transport Ltd* [1973] QB 400, 419.

[400] *Smith v South Wales Switchgear Ltd* [1978] 1 WLR 165, 178.

[401] *Canada Steamship Lines Ltd v R* [1952] AC 192, 208.

[402] *Joseph Travers & Sons Ltd v Cooper* [1915] KB 73.

[403] *Alderslade v Hendon Laundry* [1945] KB 189.

[404] *Hollier v Rambler Motors (AMC) Ltd* [1972] 2 QB 71.

[405] See paras 8.109 et seq.

[406] *Suisse Atlantique Société d'Armement Maritime v Rotterdamsche Kolen Centrale NV* [1967] 1 AC 361; *Photo Production Ltd v Securicor Transport Ltd* [1980] AC 827; *George Mitchell (Chesterhall) Ltd v Finney Lock Seeds Ltd* [1983] 2 AC 803.

8.101 **Scope of the rule.**   One group of cases in which the rule applies is that in which there has been a breach of a 'fundamental term', ie of one so central to the purpose of the contract that any breach of it turns the performance rendered into one essentially different from that promised. The example often given is that of a seller who promised to deliver peas and instead delivered beans:[407] exemption clauses have been construed not to cover the breach of such a term.[408] Whether such a breach has been committed depends on the nature of the performance promised and the extent to which that rendered differed from that promised.[409] In contracts for the carriage of goods by sea, the term as to the route to be taken is regarded as fundamental,[410] so that *any*[411] 'deviation' from that route (even if it has not caused the loss) deprives the carrier of the benefit of exemption clauses. This special rule is said to be based on the possibility of the cargo owner's losing his insurance cover in consequence of the deviation[412] and on the consequent need to protect his rights against the carrier.[413] The rule has been extended to land carriage[414] and to storage contracts.[415]

8.102 In a second group of cases, the courts have been concerned with the *manner* of the breach. These cases construe exemption clauses so as not to apply to *deliberate* breaches;[416] they are based on the assumption that 'the parties never contemplated that such a breach should be excused or limited'.[417] This reasoning was, for example, applied to cases of misdelivery of goods by bailees to persons known not to be entitled to them.[418]

8.103 In a third group of cases, the rule of construction applies (irrespective of the nature of the term broken or of the manner of breach) because of the practical *consequences* of the breach. It may, for example, apply to delays in performance which are particularly serious by reason of their extent,[419] or to defects in goods

---

407   *Chanter v Hopkins* (1838) 4 M & W 399, 404.
408   eg *Andrews Bros (Bournemouth) Ltd v Singer & Co Ltd* [1934] 1 KB 17.
409   See the *George Mitchell* case (n 406 above; delivery of defective seed not breach of a fundamental term in a contract for the sale of 'seed').
410   *Joseph Thorley Ltd v Orchis Steamship Co Ltd* [1907] KB 660; *Hain Steamship Co v Tate & Lyle Ltd* (1936) 41 Com Cas 350.
411   *Suisse Atlantique* case (n 406 above) 423.
412   See Marine Insurance Act 1906, s 46.
413   *Hain SS Co* case (n 410 above) 354. For the present status of the rule, see *The Kapitan Petko Voivoda* [2003] EWCA Civ 451; [2003] 1 All ER (Comm) 801 at [10], [14]; paras 11.46–11.50.
414   *London & North-Western Rly v Neilson* [1922] 2 AC 263.
415   *Woolf v Collis Removal Services* [1948] 1 KB 11, 15.
416   *The Cap Palos* [1921] P 458.
417   *Suisse Atlantique* case (n 406 above) 435.
418   *Alexander v Railway Executive* [1951] 2 KB 882; *Sze Hai Tong Bank Ltd v Rambler Cycle Co Ltd* [1959] AC 576.
419   *Suisse Atlantique* case (n 406 above).

which make the goods practically useless to their acquirer[420] even though they do not make the thing delivered *totally* different from that promised.[421]

Nature and the effects of the rule. Breaches of the kinds described in paras 8.101 to 8.103 will be covered by an exemption clause only if the clause 'most clearly and unambiguously'[422] so provides. There is 'a strong, though rebuttable, presumption'[423] that the parties did not intend to cover such breaches. The presumption being rebuttable, it follows that a breach of the most serious kind can be covered, eg by a clause referring expressly to 'fundamental breach'[424] and even by general words if the court is satisfied that they were intended to, and on their true construction did, cover the serious breach that occurred.[425] There may, however, be limits to this approach: the courts may refuse to give effect to a clause which gives so much protection to a supplier as to enable him to supply the specified subject matter or whatever he chooses (eg seeds or sawdust) so as to turn his promise into 'no more than a statement of intent'.[426] The transaction in such a case might not be a contract at all on the ground that the supplier's promise was an illusory one.[427]

8.104

A breach of the kind here under discussion normally gives the injured party a right to damages and a right to rescind the contract.[428] A clause which in terms excludes only the right to damages does not affect that party's right to rescind;[429] but he cannot, by exercising that right, bring the contract to an end retrospectively and so get rid of the clause so far as it relates to loss suffered before rescission.[430] Even liability for prospective loss would continue to be excluded or limited by a clause which on its true construction covered such loss.[431] Conversely, where the injured party elects not to rescind, but to affirm, the contract, he continues to be bound by a clause limiting the damages to which he is entitled by reason of the breach.[432]

8.105

---

[420] eg *Yeoman Credit Ltd v Apps* [1962] 2 QB 508; *Farnsworth Finance Facilities Ltd v Attryde* [1970] 1 WLR 1053.

[421] As in the cases cited in n 420 above.

[422] *Ailsa Craig Fishing Co Ltd v Malvern Fishing Co Ltd* [1983] 1 WLR 964, 966.

[423] *Suisse Atlantique Société d'Armement Maritime v Rotterdamsche Kolen Centrale NV* [1997] 1 AC 361, 432.

[424] See *The Antwerpen* [1994] 1 Lloyd's Rep 213.

[425] As in the cases cited in n 406 above.

[426] *The TFL Prosperity* [1984] 1 WLR 48, 59.

[427] *Firestone Tyre & Rubber Co Ltd v Volins & Co Ltd* [1951] 1 Lloyd's Rep 32, 39. The court may avoid such a conclusion by giving a 'restricted meaning' to apparently wide words: *Mitsubishi Corp v Eastwind Transport Ltd* [2004] EWHC 2924 (Comm); [2005] 1 All ER (Comm) 328 at [29].

[428] See paras 8.358 to 8.383.

[429] See the *Suisse Atlantique* case, (n 423 above).

[430] *Photo Production Ltd v Securicor Transport Ltd* [1980] AC 827. There may be an exception in the deviation cases (regarded as *sui generis* in this case at p 845) to the rule stated in the text above.

[431] This must follow from the rejection (see at n 406 above) of the 'substantive' doctrine of fundamental breach.

[432] *Photo Production* case (n 430 above) 849.

8.106 The rule of construction applies to clauses which limit or exclude liability; but there is less need to apply it to clauses which fix damages in advance[433] since these may benefit either party; and this is true also of arbitration clauses.[434] The rule also does not seem to apply to clauses which specify a party's duty in such a way that his failure to achieve a particular result is not a breach at all.[435]

(c) Other common law limitations

8.107 At common law, a party cannot rely on an exemption clause if he has misrepresented its contents to the other party[436] or if he has at the time of contracting given an express undertaking which is inconsistent with the clause.[437] An exemption clause is also ineffective to the extent that it purports to exclude liability for a party's own fraud[438] or for breach of fiduciary duty[439] or for breach of certain requirements of procedural fairness known as the rules of 'natural justice'.[440] There is also some support for the view that exemption clauses may be invalid (at least in extreme cases) for unreasonableness.[441] But the need for such a development has been reduced by legislation subjecting some exemption clauses to a requirement of reasonableness;[442] and it is also open to the objection that it could extend this requirement to situations from which the legislature had excluded it.

(2) Other Standard Terms at Common Law

8.108 The problems raised by standard terms are not confined to exemption clauses, though these have been the main subject of judicial activity in this field. They can arise also where standard terms confer rights on their proponent: eg the right to unexpectedly high payments to be made by a hirer of goods on failing to return them at the agreed time.[443] There is some support for the view that such terms are subject to a common law requirement of fairness or reasonableness[444] (at least in

---

[433] As in the *Suisse Atlantique* case (n 429 above).

[434] *Woolf v Collis Removal Service* [1948] KB 1.

[435] See *GH Renton & Co v Palmyra Trading Corp* [1957] AC 149.

[436] *Curtis & Chemical Cleaning & Dyeing Co Ltd* [1951] 1 KB 805.

[437] *Couchman v Hill* [1947] KB 554; *Harling v Eddy* [1951] 2 KB 739.

[438] *S Pearson & Son Ltd v Dublin Corp* [1907] AC 351, 353, 362. It is an open question whether a party can exclude liability for the fraud of his own agent; and, even if this can be done, the intention to exclude such liability must be expressed 'in clear and unmistakable terms': *HIH Casualty & General Insurance Ltd v Chase Manhattan Bank* [2003] UKHL 6; [2003] 1 All ER (Comm) 349 at [16]; cf ibid at [24], [82], [92] and [122].

[439] *Gluckstein v Barnes* [1900] AC 240.

[440] *Lee v Showmen's Guild* [1952] 2 QB 329.

[441] *Thompson v London, Midland & Scottish Rly* [1930] 1 KB 41, 56.

[442] See para 8.113.

[443] As in *Interfoto Picture Library Ltd v Stiletto Visual Programmes Ltd* [1989] QB 433.

[444] ibid, 445, *per* Bingham LJ. The point is left open in *Amiri Flight Authority v BAE Systems Ltd* [2003] EWCA Civ 1447; [2003] 2 Lloyd's Rep 767 at [15].

extreme cases);[445] but the more usual restriction on their efficacy is likely to lie in the high degree of notice generally required to incorporate them into the contract.[446] Some such terms are also subject to legislative control.[447]

(3) Legislative Limitations on Effectiveness

Legislative limitations on the effectiveness of standard terms often take the form **8.109** of simply depriving such terms of legal validity; but other techniques will also be considered in paragraphs 8.129 to 8.131.

(a) The Unfair Contract Terms Act 1977

(i) Terminology

The Act generally applies only to terms affecting 'business liability', that is liability **8.110** arising from acts done or to be done by a person (B) in the course of a business, or from the occupation of business premises.[448] It also gives special protection to a person (C) who 'deals as consumer'. A person so deals if he does not make or hold himself out as making the contract in the course of a business[449] (that is, in the *regular* course of his business);[450] in a contract for the supply of goods there is (except where the goods are supplied to an individual)[451] the additional requirement that they must be of a type ordinarily supplied for private use or consumption.[452] Many provisions of the Act strike at terms which 'exclude or restrict liability'. This expression is not defined but is expanded so as to include provisions imposing short time limits or excluding a remedy[453] (but not an arbitration clause).[454] Clauses which do not in so many words exclude or restrict liability may have this effect in substance.[455] The Act generally leaves the parties free to define their *duties*; but it does limit a party's ability to exclude or restrict his duty of care giving rise to

---

[445] *Parker v South Eastern Rly* (1876) 2 CPD 416, 428.

[446] See para 8.96 at n 383; *Interfoto* case (n 443 above) *per* Dillon LJ. The requirement of a high degree of notice probably does not normally apply to a document *signed* by the party alleged to be bound: *HIH Casualty & General Insurance Ltd v New Hampshire Insurance Co* [2001] EWCA Civ 735; [2001] 2 All ER (Comm) 39 at [209].

[447] See para 8.113 at n 473 and para 8.119.

[448] Unfair Contract Terms Act 1977, s 1(3).

[449] ibid, 12(1) (a) and (b).

[450] *R & B Customs Brokers Ltd v United Dominions Trust Ltd* [1988] 1 WLR 321.

[451] Unfair Contract Terms Act 1977, s 12(1A).

[452] ibid, s 12(1)(c). Except in certain cases where the buyer is an individual, sales by auction or competitive tender are excluded by s 12(2).

[453] ibid, s 13(1).

[454] ibid, s 13(2); contrast Unfair Terms in Consumer Contracts Regulations 1999 SI 1999/2083, Sch 2 para 1(q).

[455] eg *Phillips Products Ltd v Hyland* [1987] 1 WLR 659.

liability in negligence[456] and the duties arising out of the statutorily implied terms in contracts for the sale of goods.[457] Even apart from these provisions, the courts will not allow a party to 'emasculate'[458] the Act by drafting what is in substance an exemption clause in terms which purport to define his duty.

(ii) Structure of the Act

8.111 The Act distinguishes between terms which are simply ineffective and those which are ineffective unless the party relying on them shows[459] that they satisfy the requirement of reasonableness.

8.112 **Ineffective terms.** These include terms by which B seeks to exclude or restrict his liability for death or personal injury resulting from negligence;[460] terms excluding or restricting liability for negligence in manufacturers' 'guarantees' of consumer goods;[461] and terms excluding or restricting liability for breach of the statutorily implied terms in contracts for the supply of goods by B to C.[462] There is much other legislation which invalidates exemption clauses in specific contracts.[463]

8.113 **Terms subject to reasonableness requirement.** These include[464] terms by which B seeks to exclude or restrict his liability for negligence giving rise to loss or damage other than death or personal injury;[465] terms purporting to exclude or restrict liability for breach of the statutorily implied terms in contracts for the supply of goods where the acquirer does *not* deal as consumer;[466] other contracts between B and C or on B's written standard terms of business[467] by which B seeks to exclude or restrict liability for his own breach,[468] or claims to be entitled to render a performance substantially different from that reasonably expected of him[469] or no performance at all[470] (though a provision entitling one party to refuse to make a payment because of the other's failure to perform[471] appears not to fall

---

[456] See the references in Unfair Contract Terms Act 1977, s 13(1) to ss 2 and 5.
[457] See the references in ibid, s 13(1) to ss 6 and 7.
[458] *Smith v Eric S Bush* [1990] 1 AC 831, 848.
[459] Unfair Contract Terms Act 1977, s 11(5).
[460] ibid, s 2(1).
[461] ibid, s 5. This section could apply to a 'consumer guarantee' within Sale and Supply of Goods to Consumers Regulations 2002, SI 2002/3045, reg 15.
[462] ibid, ss 6, 7; liability for breach of the implied term as to title is, under these sections, sometimes incapable of being excluded even by a 'private' supplier.
[463] eg Consumer Protection Act 1987, ss 7, 10, 41; Financial Services and Markets Act 2000, s 253; Consumer Protection (Distance Selling) Regulations 2000, SI 2000/2334, regs 7–20, 25.
[464] See also Misrepresentation Act 1967, s 3 and para 8.189.
[465] Unfair Contract Terms Act 1977, s 2(2).
[466] ibid, ss 6(3), 7(3), 7(4).
[467] ibid, s 3(1).
[468] ibid, s 3(2)(a).
[469] ibid, s 3(2)(b)(i).
[470] ibid, s 3(2 (b)(ii).
[471] eg one making an obligation 'entire': see para 8.368.

within this provision); and contracts by which C[472] undertakes to indemnify another person in respect of business liability incurred by the other for negligence or breach of contract.[473]

The Act seeks in two ways to reduce the uncertainty to which a judicially admin- **8.114** istered reasonableness requirement can give rise. First, it provides that the question whether the requirement is satisfied is to be determined by reference to the time of contracting.[474] Secondly it lays down guidelines for determining the reasonableness of terms which limit a party's liability to a specified sum of money[475] and further guidelines where the contract is one for the supply of goods.[476] These statutory guidelines are not an exhaustive list of factors to be taken into consideration for the present purpose.[477] An appellate court will not normally reverse a decision on the issue of reasonableness merely because it disagrees with the decision;[478] but it may do so where the decision was based on a wrong principle of law.[479] Terms incorporated after negotiation between parties 'of equal bargaining power'[480] are unlikely to be struck down for unreasonableness; but even between such parties a term may be unreasonable if it was not the subject of negotiations between them[481] and would (if valid) have affected 'matters which the parties would have regarded as fundamental'.[482]

Partly effective terms. The Act throughout provides that specified liabilities **8.115** cannot be excluded or restricted 'by reference' to certain terms. It follows that if, for example, a contract for the sale of goods contained a term excluding liability for 'any breach', then the term would not protect the seller from liability for breach of his implied undertaking as to title,[483] but it could protect him from liability for

---

[472] ibid, s 4. Where the clause contains a promise by C to B to indemnify B in respect of liability incurred *to C* it is in substance an exemption clause and so subject also to s 2: see *Phillips Products Ltd v Hyland* [1987] 1 WLR 659.

[473] If B1 promises to indemnify B2 in respect of liability to X the case is not within s 4; nor is such a clause an exemption clause: *Thompson v T Lohan (Plant Hire) Ltd* [1987] 1 WLR 649.

[474] Unfair Contract Terms Act 1977, s 11(1); contrast the common law rule under which the efficacy of an exemption clause depends on the *effects* of the breach: see para 8.103.

[475] Unfair Contract Terms Act 1977, s 11(4).

[476] ibid, s 11(2) and Sch 2.

[477] *Smith v Eric S Bush* [1990] 1 AC 831, 838.

[478] *George Mitchell (Chesterhall) Ltd v Finney Lock Seeds Ltd* [1983] 2 AC 803, 810.

[479] *Granville Oil & Chemicals Ltd v Davies Turner & Co Ltd* [2003] EWCA Civ 570; [2003] 1 All ER (Comm) 819.

[480] *Watford Electronics Ltd v Sanderson* [2001] EWCA Civ 317; [2001] 1 All ER (Comm) 696 at [55].

[481] *Balmoral Group Ltd v Borealis (UK) Ltd* [2006] EWHC 1900 (Comm); [2006] 2 Lloyd's Rep 629 at [423].

[482] *Bacardi-Martini Beverages Ltd v Thomas Hardy Packaging Ltd* [2002] EWCA Civ 549; [2002] 2 All ER (Comm) 335 at [26]; *Britvic Soft Drinks Ltd v Messer UK Ltd* [2002] EWCA Civ 548; [2002] 2 All ER (Comm) 321 at [26].

[483] See s 6 (1) (a).

late delivery (subject only to common law restrictions). Similarly, if a single term were severable, the party in breach might be prevented by the Act from relying on one part of it while another might satisfy the requirement of reasonableness or be unaffected by the Act's provisions.[484] But the court will not *modify* the term actually included so as to allow the party in breach to rely, for example, on a reasonable *limitation*, where the term provided for an unreasonable *exclusion*, of liability.[485]

(iii) Restrictions on evasion

8.116 **Secondary contract.**   Section 10 of the Act provides that a person is not bound by a contract depriving him of rights under 'another contract' so far as 'these rights extend to the enforcement of another's liability' which the Act 'prevents' that other from excluding or restricting. The section does not apply where parties to a contract by which an earlier contract containing terms which would be subject to the Act renegotiate those terms or settle disputes under the earlier contract by subsequent agreement.[486] Its purpose is to deal with the situation in which a term in a contract between A and B provides that B is not to exercise rights against C under a separate contract between B and C if such a term, had it been in the contract between B and C, would have been ineffective under the Act.[487]

8.117 **Choice of law clauses.**   The Act[488] prevents a party from evading its provisions by a term 'imposed' mainly for this purpose and providing that the contract is to be governed by the law of a foreign country containing no similar provisions.

(iv) Scope

8.118 Many contract terms fall outside the scope of the 1977 Act because they are not covered by any of its provisions: this would, for example, be true of a term excluding liability for delay in a contract of sale made between two parties neither of whom dealt as consumer and not made on either party's written standard terms of business. A number of other contracts are excepted from specified provisions of the Act. These include contracts of insurance, any contract 'so far as it relates to the creation transfer or termination' of an interest in land,[489] and (to a more limited extent) charterparties and (other) contracts for the carriage of goods by sea.[490]

---

484   *RW Green Ltd v Cade Bros Farms* [1978] 1 Lloyd's Rep 602.
485   *George Mitchell* case, (n 478 above) 816; *Stewart Gill Ltd v Horatio Meyer & Co Ltd* [1992] QB 600.
486   *Tudor Grange Holdings Ltd v Citibank NA* [1992] Ch 53, 65–7; *Re Cape plc* [2006] EWHC 1316 (Ch); [2007] Bus LR 109 at [81]–[89].
487   *Tudor Grange* case, n 486 above, 65–67.
488   Unfair Contract Terms Act 1977, s 27(2); Contracts (Applicable Law) Act 1990, s 1 and Sch 1 art 5 (2) and (4); and see para 8.128.
489   Unfair Contract Terms Act 1977, Sch 1 para 1.
490   ibid, Sch 1 para 2.

The Act does not apply to contracts for the international supply of goods,[491] to contractual provisions authorized or required under other legislation or certain international conventions,[492] or to contract governed by English law by virtue only of a choice of law clause.[493]

(b) The Unfair Terms in Consumer Contract Regulations 1999

(i) General

These Regulations[494] give effect to an EC Council Directive.[495] They apply to **8.119** unfair terms which have not been individually negotiated, in contracts between a commercial seller or supplier and a consumer.[496] Their central provision is that, such an unfair term 'shall not be binding on the consumer'.[497] The Regulations operate side by side with the Unfair Contract Terms Act 1977 so that a party relying on a contract term may fail under either set of rules.[498] In some respects, the scope of the Regulations is narrower than that of the Act: they apply only to terms which have not been individually negotiated[499] and only where one party acts for purposes relating to his business and the other acts as consumer,[500] while the Act is not generally subject to either of these restrictions.[501] On the other hand the Act deals almost exclusively[502] with *exemption* clauses while the scope of the Regulations is not so limited. It is this point which gives the Regulations their potentially wide scope.

(ii) Terminology

The Regulations define[503] '*consumer*' as a natural person who, 'in contracts cov- **8.120** ered by these Regulations' acts for purposes outside his trade, business or profession; and '*seller or supplier*' as a natural or legal person who in such contracts is acting for purposes relating to his trade, business or profession. Hence the Regulations protect only consumers who are *natural* persons; while a corporation can 'deal as consumer' under the 1977 Act.[504]

---

491 ibid, s 26(1).
492 ibid, s 29.
493 ibid, s 27(1).
494 SI 1999/2083.
495 Council Directive (EEC) 93/13 OJL 95/29.
496 See regs 3(1) (definition of unfair terms), 4(1) and 5(1).
497 Unfair Terms in Consumer Contracts Regulations 1999, reg 8(1).
498 For proposals for a unified legislative scheme and other reforms, see the Law Commissions' Report on *Unfair Terms in Contracts*, Law Com No 292, Scot Law Com No 1999 (2005).
499 ibid, reg 5(1).
500 ibid, regs 8(1), 3(1).
501 Only s 3(1) is subject to similar restrictions.
502 The exception is s 4 (which deals with indemnity clauses).
503 Unfair Terms in Consumer Contracts Regulations 1999, reg 3(1).
504 See *R & B Customs Brokers Ltd v United Dominions Trust Ltd* [1988] 1 WLR 321.

8.121   The Regulations apply only[505] to terms which have not been 'individually negotiated'[506] and provide that a term 'shall always be regarded as not having been individually negotiated where it has been drafted in advance[507] *and* the consumer therefore has not been able to influence the substance of the term'.[508] The burden of showing that the term was individually negotiated is on the seller or supplier.[509] Where one or more terms have been individually negotiated, the Regulations may apply to the rest of the contract if, taken as a whole, it is a 'pre-formulated standard contract'.[510]

(iii) Unfairness and good faith

8.122   An unfair term is one which is 'contrary to the requirement of good faith' (ie, of 'fair and open dealing')[511] and 'causes a significant imbalance in the parties' rights and obligations arising under the contract, to the detriment of the consumer'.[512] To reduce the uncertainty resulting from these requirements, account is to be taken[513] of 'the nature of the goods and services for which the contract was concluded' (eg the fact that the goods were second-hand), of 'all the circumstances attending the conclusion of the contract' (eg the fact that the consumer had examined the goods) and 'all the other terms of the contract' (eg the fact that a supplier undertook more extensive duties than were imposed by the general law could justify the imposition of a short time limit). Further guidelines are in effect provided by a long and elaborate list of examples[514] of terms which '*may* be regarded as unfair'.[515] The list is 'indicative and non-exhaustive'[516] so that a term of a kind included in it is only prima facie unfair, and a term may be unfair although it is not included in the list.

8.123   The requirement of fairness, does not apply '(a) to the definition of the main subject matter of the contract, or (b) to the adequacy of the price or remuneration, as against the goods or services supplied in exchange'.[517] The Regulations are not

---

[505] Unfair Terms in Consumer Contracts Regulations, 1999, regs 3 (1), 4 (1) and 5 (1).
[506] ibid, reg 5(1).
[507] ie of the negotiations leading to the contract.
[508] ibid, reg 5(2).
[509] ibid, reg 5(4).
[510] ibid, reg 5(3).
[511] *Director General of Fair Trading v First National Bank* [2001] UKHL 52; [2002] 1 AC 481 at [17], where openness is said to refer to the way in which terms are set out and fairness to their substance.
[512] Unfair Terms in Consumer Contracts Regulations, 1999, reg 5(1). The fact that the term in question was included at the consumer's suggestion may show that there was no such 'imbalance': *Bryen & Langley Ltd v Boston* [2005] EWCA Civ 973; [2005] BLR 508.
[513] Unfair Terms in Consumer Contracts Regulations, 1999, reg 6(1).
[514] ibid, Sch 2.
[515] ibid, reg 5(5).
[516] ibid.
[517] ibid, reg 6(2).

intended as a mechanism of quality or price control:[518] with regard to such *core provisions*, they recognize the parties' freedom of contract. This is, however, true only where terms of this kind are 'in plain intelligible language'.[519] An obscurely worded price term enabling the supplier unexpectedly to increase a price prominently stated elsewhere in the contract could therefore be subject to the requirement of fairness. The courts are also reluctant to give too wide a scope to the concept of a 'core term' since, if they did so, the object of the Regulations would be 'plainly frustrated'.[520] Hence while a term specifying the price payable by the consumer would be a 'core term', one specifying the consequences of his failure to pay that price would be merely 'ancillary'[521] and so subject to the Regulations.

(iv) Excepted terms

The Regulations do not apply to terms which reflect (1) certain 'statutory or regulatory provisions'[522] such as terms which a contract is required under other legislation to contain,[523] or (b) 'the provisions or principles of international conventions to which Member States or the [European] Community are party'.[524]   **8.124**

(v) Excluded contracts

'Contracts relating to employment' are excluded from the Regulations by virtue of the Directive on which they are based.[525] In this respect, the Regulations resemble the 1977 Act;[526] but they differ from it in that they can apply to contracts of insurance,[527] to at least some contracts for the supply of intellectual property (such as contracts to license the use of computer software)[528] and to contracts for the sale of interests in land[529] (though they would not apply to a contract for the sale of a dwelling by one private home-owner to another since neither party to such a sale would act as a commercial seller or supplier).   **8.125**

---

[518] *Director General of Fair Trading v First National Bank*, n 511 above, at [12].

[519] Unfair Terms in Consumer Contracts Regulations, 1999, reg 6(2).

[520] *Director General of Fair Trading v First National Bank* (n 511 above) at [52].

[521] ibid, at [12].

[522] Unfair Terms in Consumer Contracts Regulations, 1999, reg 4(2)(a).

[523] eg see para 8.130.

[524] Unfair Terms in Consumer Contracts Regulations 1999, reg 4(2)(b); for definition of 'Member States' see reg 3(1).

[525] 93/13/EEC (n 495 above), Recital 10.

[526] 1977 Act, Sch 1, para 4 (the exemption is narrower in scope than that of Recital 10, note 525 above).

[527] See 93/13/EEC, note 495 above, Recital 19.

[528] Such a contract could be one for the supply of 'goods or services' within the Directive and the Regulations: cf (in the context of the 1977 Act) *St Albans City and District Council v International Computers Ltd* [1996] 4 All ER 481.

[529] *R (Khatun) v Newham LBC* [2004] EWCA Civ 55; [2005] QB 73 (lease granted by a local authority).

(vi) Drafting and interpretation

8.126 The Regulations require a seller or supplier to ensure that 'any written term of a contract is expressed in plain, intelligible language'.[530] Failure to comply with this requirement is not stated to make the term even prima facie unfair; nor does the requirement extend to oral contracts.[531] If there is doubt about the meaning of a written term (and even 'plain, intelligible language' can have more than one meaning) the interpretation most favourable to the consumer is generally[532] to prevail.[533]

(vii) Effect of unfairness

8.127 An unfair term in a contract to which the Regulations apply is 'not. . .binding on the consumer'.[534] Hence if it is an exemption clause the consumer will be able to enforce rights under the contract as if the term had not been included; if it purports to confer rights on the other party, those rights will not arise; and if effect has been given to them restitution may have to be ordered. The rest of the contract, however, continues to bind *both* parties 'if it is capable of continuing in existence without the unfair term'.[535] Thus the consumer is not relieved from liability for the price merely because the contract contains an unfair exemption clause.

(viii) Choice of law clauses

8.128 The consumer cannot be deprived of the protection of the Regulations by a choice of law clause subjecting the contract to the law of a non-Member State which, but for such a clause, would not apply to it.[536]

(4) Other Legislative Control Techniques

8.129 Simply to deprive standard terms of legal validity might not be an effective way of controlling their abuse, especially in contracts between commercial suppliers and consumers. Legislation therefore makes use of other techniques of control.

8.130 One possibility is to control the contents of a contract by requiring certain terms to be included in it. Extensive use of this technique is made in the consumer credit field where, for example, the debtor must be given a 'cooling off' period[537] and has

---

530 Unfair Terms in Consumer Contracts Regulations, 1999, reg 7(1).
531 These are within the regulations: cf Council Directive (EEC) 93/13, OJ L 95/29, Recital 11.
532 Except in injunction proceedings under, reg 12 of the 1999 Regulations.
533 ibid, reg 7(2).
534 ibid, reg 8(1).
535 ibid, reg 8(2).
536 ibid, reg 9.
537 Consumer Credit Act 1974, ss 67, 68.

the right to earn certain rebates on making early payments.[538] A term inconsistent with such provisions is void.[539] Variants of this technique are to require specified information to be given to be given to a party who deals as consumer[540] and to subject contracts to a kind of supervised bargaining: for example in certain leases covenants by the landlord can be excluded only by a court order made with the consent of both parties.[541]

A second possibility is to invoke the intervention of an outside body, usually but not invariably[542] a public authority, to exercise a form of administrative control. The Enterprise Act 2002 imposes on the Office of Fair Trading (OFT) a duty to promote good consumer practices;[543] and earlier legislation makes it an offence for a commercial seller to use in a consumer sale an exemption clause made void by the Unfair Contract Terms Act 1977.[544] The Unfair Terms in Consumer Contracts Regulations 1999 also impose on the OFT and certain other bodies a duty to consider complaints that any contract term drawn up for general use is unfair and to ask the court to restrain such use by injunction.[545] Such 'pre-emptive challenges'[546] by public authorities may well be more effective than private litigation as a means of controlling standard contract terms which are unfair to consumers.   **8.131**

E. Mistake

The cases on mistake as a vitiating factor fall into two main groups.[547] In the first, the parties make the same mistake: eg both think that the subject matter exists when it does not. Here they reach agreement but the mistake *nullifies* consent, ie deprives their agreement of legal effect. In the second, they make different mistakes: eg one thinks that they are contracting about one thing and the other about another. Here they are at cross-purposes and do not reach agreement so that   **8.132**

---

538   ibid, ss 94, 95, 99, 100.

539   ibid, s 173.

540   eg Consumer Protection (Distance Selling) Regulations 2000, SI 2000/2334 (as to which, see para 8.12) reg 7.

541   Landlord and Tenant Act 1985, ss 11, 12.

542   See Unfair Terms in Consumer Contracts Regulations 1999, Sch 1 Part Two (Consumers' Association).

543   S 8.

544   Consumer Transactions (Restriction on Statements) Order 1976, SI 1976/1813, as amended by SI 1978/127. For terms made void by the 1977 Act, see para 8.112.

545   Regs 10–12; and see Enterprise Act 2002, s 2(3), substituting the OFT for the (former) Director General of Fair Trading.

546   *Director General of Fair Trading v First National Bank* [2001] UKHL 52; [2002] 1 AC 481 at [33].

547   *Bell v Lever Bros Ltd* [1932] AC 161, 217.

the mistake *negatives* consent. The feature which is common to the two situations is that the mistake must be *fundamental* so that a party cannot rely on a 'mistake' which has led him merely to make a bad bargain. The law has to strike a difficult balance between the hardship of holding a mistaken party to his bargain and the uncertainty which could result from too great a readiness to grant relief on the ground of mistake. The common law has stressed the need for certainty; equity has been somewhat more ready to relieve the mistaken party, but recent authority has reduced the scope of such equitable relief.[548]

(1) Mistakes Nullifying Consent

(a) Fundamental mistake at common law

(i) Types of mistake

8.133 **In general.** A mistake will most obviously nullify consent where it relates to the *existence* of the subject matter.[549] It can equally have this effect where it relates to the *identity* of the subject matter,[550] ie, where both parties believe that they are dealing with X when they are actually dealing with Y. The same is again true where the parties mistakenly believe that performance is possible (either physically[551] or legally[552]) when it is not; and perhaps even when it is commercially impossible, in the sense that the commercial object which both parties had in mind cannot be achieved.[553]

8.134 **Mistake as to quality.** If one party *undertakes* that the subject matter has a quality that it lacks, that party is normally in breach (and the other may not be bound to perform).[554] If, however, both parties simply assume that the thing has the quality which it lacks then, in general, the mistake is not regarded as fundamental.[555] It will be so regarded only if it is 'as to the existence of some quality which makes the thing without the quality essentially different from the thing as it was believed to be'.[556] This requirement has been very strictly interpreted. In *Bell v Lever Bros Ltd*[557] a contract was made to pay £50,000 to two employees for

---

[548] See paras 8.139, 8.148.

[549] eg *Galloway v Galloway* (1914) 30 TLR 531; and see para 8.136.

[550] More commonly, this type of confusion will *negative* consent (see para 8.141).

[551] Cf *Sheik Bros Ltd v Ochsner* [1957] AC 136.

[552] *Bell v Lever Bros Ltd* [1932] AC 161, 218; *Norwich Union Fire Insurance Society Ltd v Price* [1934] AC 455, 463; *The Great Peace* [2002] EWCA Civ 1407; [2003] QB 697 at [126]–[128].

[553] *Griffith v Brymer* (1903) 19 TLR 434.

[554] *Gompertz v Bartlett* (1853) 2 E & B 849.

[555] *Scott v Littledale* (1858) 8 E & B 815; *Harrison & Jones v Bunten & Lancaster* [1953] 1 QB 646.

[556] *Bell v Lever Bros Ltd* [1932] AC 161, 218; *Kennedy v Panama Royal Mail Co* (1867) LR 2 QB 580, 588 expresses a somewhat wider view.

[557] [1932] AC 218; cf *The Great Peace*, n 552 above (ship chartered to render salvage services to another under a mistake as to the position of the former ship, making her less useful than expected, but not useless, for rendering the services).

termination of their service agreements and it was held that this contract was not made void for mistake when it was discovered that the service agreements could have been summarily terminated for breach of duty, without compensation. Similarly, if a picture were sold at a high price in the belief that it was an old master when it was a modern copy, then the buyer would have no remedy for mistake.[558] On the other hand, there would be such a remedy if table napkins were bought as relics of Charles I when they were Georgian;[559] and where a policy on the life of X was sold in the belief that X was alive when in fact he was dead so that the policy was worth more than the price paid for it.[560] The various cases and examples given above are not easy to reconcile;[561] but the principle that runs through them is that a mistake as to quality will not generally be regarded as fundamental unless the quality in question is so important to the parties that they use it to *identify* the subject matter. In the example of a modern copy bought and sold as an old master, it is, indeed, hard to accept that the mistake is not fundamental on this principle; but the example is an unrealistic one since such a sale is likely either to contain a warranty or to involve conscious risk-taking, in which case there would be no scope for mistake.[562]

Mistake of law. It used to be thought that the validity of a contract was not **8.135** affected by a mistake of 'law', as opposed to one of 'fact'.[563] But this distinction was hard to draw and even harder to justify. It was first relaxed, at least in equity, by treating as a mistake of 'fact' one as to 'private right' even though it was based on a mistake of law, eg on one as to the construction of a document.[564] It was later rejected in the context of restitution claims[565] and it no longer applies in the present context.[566] The validity of a contract can therefore be challenged on the ground of mistake of law, so long as the mistake is 'fundamental'.[567] But a challenge on this ground will fail where the parties were merely in doubt as to the

---

[558] *Bell v Lever Bros Ltd* [1932] AC 161, 266; cf *Leaf v International Galleries* [1950] 2 KB 86, 89.

[559] See *Nicholson & Venn v Smith-Marriott* (1947) 177 LT 189.

[560] *Scott v Coulson* [1903] 2 Ch 249; cf *Associated Japanese Bank (International) Ltd v Crédit du Nord SA* [1989] 1 WLR 255.

[561] eg *Bell v Lever Bros Ltd* [1932] AC 161 is hard to reconcile with *Scott v Coulson*, (n 560 above).

[562] *Deutsche Morgan Grenfell Group plc v Inland Revenue Commissioners* [2006] UKHL 49; [2007] 1 ALL ER 449 at [27].

[563] *British Homophone Ltd v Kunz* (1935) 152 LT 589, 593; *Solle v Butcher* [1950] 1 KB 671.

[564] *Cooper v Phibbs* (1867) LR 2 HL 1049; cf *Allcard v Walker* [1896] 2 Ch 369 (mistake as to contractual capacity).

[565] *Kleinwort Benson Ltd v Lincoln City Council* [1999] 2 AC 349.

[566] *Brennan v Bolt Burdon* [2004] EWCA Civ 1017; [2005] QB 303 at [10], [17], [26]; cf at [60].

[567] See *Shamil Bank of Bahrain v Beximco Pharmaceuticals* [2004] EWCA Civ 19; [2004] 2 Lloyd's Rep 1 at [59]–[60], where the mistake was not fundamental.

point in question[568] (as opposed to being mistaken about it), or where they took the risk[569] that the law on the point might not be as they had supposed it to be. Such factors may, for example, lead to the rejection of the challenge where the impugned contract was a compromise of a disputed claim.[570]

(ii) Effects of the mistake

8.136 At common law, the starting principle is that a fundamental mistake makes the contract void;[571] but this rule may be displaced if, on its true construction, the contract provides that one party or even both are to be bound in spite of the mistake.[572] In the case of a contract for the sale of goods, for example, the contract will usually be void if the goods without the knowledge of either party had perished when the contract was made;[573] but it is in principle possible for either party to accept the risk of such a mistake: ie, for the seller to *undertake* that the goods are in existence[574] or for the buyer to promise to pay even though they are not. A party may, even in the absence of such an undertaking, be liable on the ground that he was at fault in inducing the other party to make the mistake.[575]

(b) Mistakes for which equity gives relief

(i) Types of mistake

8.137 Developments to be discussed in para 8.139 have curtailed equitable relief for mistake but have left open the availability of at least one such form of relief, to be discussed in para 8.138. For this purpose, the mistake need not be 'fundamental' in the narrow common law sense. In this way, equity to some extent mitigates the hardship to the mistaken party that may result from the narrow common law definition of a fundamental mistake; but in doing so it puts at risk the certainty which that definition is meant to promote. To mitigate this risk, the mistake must be a serious one,[576] so that a mere mistake as to 'the expectations of the parties'[577] (eg as to the development potential of land) will not suffice even in equity.

---

568 *Brennan's* case, n 566 above, at [19], [23], [36].
569 ibid, at [22], [23], [31], [39].
570 ibid, at [12], [51], [63], [64].
571 *Associated Japanese Bank* case (n 560 above), 268.
572 Cf Marine Insurance Act 1906, Sch 1 r 1 ('Lost or not lost' clause).
573 Sale of Goods Act 1979, s 6; cf *Couturier v Hastie* (1856) 5 HLC 673 (where only the liability of the buyer was in issue); *Barrow, Lane & Ballard Ltd v Philips & Co Ltd* [1929] 1 KB 574, 582.
574 *McRae v Commonwealth Disposals Commission* (1951) 84 CLR 377.
575 ibid, 408; *Associated Japanese Bank* case (n 560 above) 268.
576 *William Sindall plc v Cambridgeshire CC* [1994] 1 WLR 1016, 1041.
577 *Amalgamated Investment & Property Co Ltd v John Walker & Sons Ltd* [1977] 1 WLR 164, 172.

(ii) Effects of mistake

Refusal of specific performance.   Even though the contract is valid at law   **8.138**
because the mistake is not fundamental, equity may refuse specific performance,[578]
leaving the claimant to his remedy in damages. It may also order specific performance on terms, eg where land is sold under a mistake as to area, on the
terms that the price is varied.[579] There is no scope for such equitable relief where
the contract is *void* at common law. It can then simply be disregarded by the
parties, though a court order may be necessary to restore them to their original
positions.[580]

No rescission on terms.   At one time, there was considerable support in the   **8.139**
authorities for the view that a contract which was not void because the mistake
was not fundamental in the narrow common law sense[581] could be rescinded in
equity by the mistaken party,[582] on whom terms could in turn be imposed to
ensure that justice was done to the other party.[583] The exercise of this power to
rescind could, no doubt, 'on occasion be the passport to a just result'.[584] But no
satisfactory way was ever found of reconciling it with the common law rule applied
in *Bell v Lever Bros Ltd*[585] or with the interests of certainty which that rule
was intended to promote. To restore doctrinal consistency, the Court of Appeal in
The Great Peace[586] therefore held that there was no longer any power to rescind a
contract for mistake in equity where the contract was valid at law because the mistake was not 'fundamental' in the common law sense.

(2) Mistakes Negativing Consent

A mistake which puts the parties so seriously at cross-purposes as to negative con-   **8.140**
sent will impair the validity of a contract only in a number of somewhat exceptional situations, to be discussed in paragraph 8.146.

(a) Types of mistake

(i) As to subject matter

Consent is negatived where one party intends to deal with one thing and the other   **8.141**
with a different one: eg if a seller intends to sell the cargo on ship A and the buyer

---

578   *Jones v Rimmer* (1880) 14 Ch D 588.
579   *Aspinalls to Powell and Scholefield* (1889) 60 LT 595.
580   As in *Cooper v Phibbs* (1867) LR 2 HL 149.
581   See para 8.134.
582   eg, *Magee v Pennine Insurance Co Ltd* [1969] QB 507.
583   eg, *Solle v Butcher* [1950] 1 KB 671.
584   *West Sussex Properties Ltd v Chichester District Council*, June 28, 2000 at [42].
585   [1932] AC 161, para 8.134.
586   [2002] EWCA Civ 1407; [2003] QB 697.

to buy that on ship B.[587] If the parties are merely at odds as to the quality of the goods intended by both, consent will not normally be negatived since a mistake as to quality is not usually fundamental.[588]

(ii) As to the person

8.142 Consent is negatived if one party (A) to the alleged contract makes a fundamental mistake about the other (B). Usually B is an impecunious rogue who makes some pretence about himself to induce A to give him credit; and between these parties it makes little difference whether the mistake is fundamental so as to make the contract void;[589] for, even if this is not the case, A will be entitled to rescind the contract for fraud.[590] But the point is crucial if B has resold the subject matter to C, a purchaser in good faith: if the mistake was fundamental, no title will pass to B and hence none to C,[591] while if the mistake was not fundamental B will acquire a voidable title and A could not avoid this against C. For this purpose, A's mistake is fundamental if it is one as to the *identity* of B: ie if A deals with B in the belief that B is X;[592] but it is not normally fundamental if A's mistake is merely as to an *attribute* of B: eg if A deals with B in the mistaken belief that B is a person of substance to whom credit can safely be given.[593] A mistake as to an attribute would be fundamental only if it related to *the* attribute by which A had identified B: eg if he had identified B as 'the wife of X'.[594] The distinction between the last two situations may in practice be hard to draw, particularly where A and B are in each other's presence when the contract is made. Prima facie they will then be taken to have identified each other by the ordinary process of sight and hearing;[595] but it may be possible to show that A identified B in some other way, eg as residing in a specified house.[596] Where the contract is in writing, the difficulty of determining whether a mistake is as to an identifying attribute is mitigated in the sense that the question, who the parties to the contract are, then turns on the construction of the contractual document; and prima facie they are the persons described as such in that document.[597]

---

[587] *Raffles v Wichelhaus* (1864) 2 H & C 906, as explained in *Smith v Hughes* (1871) LR 6 QB 597.

[588] See para 8.134.

[589] As B will be aware of the mistake, it is *operative*: see para 8.146.

[590] See paras 8.175, 8.176.

[591] For criticism of this position, see Law Revision Committee, 12th Report (1966) Cmnd 2958, para 15; *Shogun Finance Ltd v Hudson* [2003] UKHL 62; [2004] AC 919 at [5], [60], [84].

[592] *Cundy v Lindsay* (1878) 3 App Cas 459.

[593] *King's Norton Metal Co Ltd v Edridge, Merrett & Co Ltd* (1894) 14 TLR 98.

[594] *Lake v Simmons* [1927] AC 487.

[595] *Phillips v Brooks* [1919] 2 KB 243; *Lewis v Averay* [1972] QB 198.

[596] *Ingram v Little* [1961] 1 QB 31, doubted in the *Shogun* case, n 591 above, at [87], [110], [185].

[597] *Shogun Finance Ltd v Hudson*, n 591 above; alternatively, A had there intended to deal only with X and had made a mistake as to an identifying attribute of the person (B) who had posed as X.

(iii) As to terms

Consent may be negatived by a mistake as to the terms of the contract: eg where a **8.143** seller intended to sell goods at a specified price per *piece* and the buyer to buy for the same price per *pound*.[598] There is some support for the view that a mistake as to terms need not be fundamental, so that, while consent is not negatived by a mistake as to the existence of a non-fundamental quality, it will be negatived by a mistake as to the existence of a *warranty* of that same quality.[599]

(b) Mistake must induce contract

The mistake has no effect on the contract unless it relates to a point of commercial **8.144** significance to the mistaken party and induces him to enter into the contract. If A buys goods from a shop believing it to be owned by B when it had just been sold by B to C, A's mistake is fundamental, but it will in most cases not matter to A so long as he in fact gets the goods he wanted to buy. The mistake will induce the contract only if A had some special reason for wanting to deal with B: eg that B owed him money which A intended to set off against the price of the goods.[600]

(c) Effects of mistake

(i) At common law

Contract generally valid. Where mistake negatives consent, the validity of the **8.145** contract is not affected if, as is generally the case, A has so conducted himself as to induce B reasonably to believe that A was agreeing to B's terms.[601] If, for example, at an auction A bids for one lot when he thinks that he is bidding for another, then it follows from the objective principle[602] that he cannot rely on his mistake even though it is fundamental and has induced the contract.

Contract exceptionally void. A mistake which negatives consent is *operative* (so **8.146** as to make the contract void) only in three exceptional situations to which the objective principle does not apply. These are (1) where there is such *perfect ambiguity* (eg as to the subject matter) that a reasonable person would have no ground for believing that the parties intended to deal with one of two things rather than with the other;[603] (2) where the mistake of one party is *known*

---

[598] *Hartog v Colin & Shields* [1939] 3 All ER 566.
[599] *Smith v Hughes* (1871) LR 6 QB 597; and see n 605.
[600] *Boulton v Jones* (1857) 2 H & N 564; A should then be required to assign to C the debt owed by B to A.
[601] *Centrovincial Estates plc v Merchant Investors Assurance Co Ltd* [1983] Commercial LR 158.
[602] See para 8.02.
[603] *Raffles v Wichelhaus* (1864) 2 H & C 906, as explained in *The Great Peace* [2002] EWCA Civ 1407; [2003] QB 697 at [29].

to the other;[604] and (3) where that mistake is negligently induced by the other party. In the third, and possibly in the second, of these cases, the mistake may operate against the party who negligently induced (or knew of) the other party's mistake, but not against the latter party.[605]

(ii) In equity

8.147 **Bar to specific performance.** Where the contract is not void at law because the mistake is *not fundamental*, equity can refuse specific performance in accordance with the principles already discussed.[606] The contract may also be valid at law under the objective principle where the mistake, though fundamental, is *not operative*: eg where a buyer at an auction by mistake bids for the wrong lot.[607] Specific performance may then be refused (or ordered only on terms)[608] if, but only if, 'hardship amounting to injustice'[609] would result from an unconditional grant of the remedy.[610]

8.148 **No rescission.** Where a mistake has, or is alleged to have, negatived consent, the contract may nevertheless be valid at law for one of two reasons. The first is that the mistake is *not fundamental*; and in cases of this kind the former view, that the contract could be rescinded in equity,[611] can no longer stand after *The Great Peace*.[612] That case was, indeed, concerned with a mistake alleged to have *nullified* consent; but its reasoning (that doctrinal coherence would be destroyed and certainty undermined by allowing contracts which were valid at law to be rescinded in equity for a mistake which was not fundamental)[613] applies as much to mistakes alleged to have negatived consent. The second reason why a mistake alleged to have negatived consent may not affect the validity of the contract is that the mistake, though fundamental, was *not operative*. In such a case, rescission in equity would seriously undermine the objective principle and is therefore not available.[614]

---

604 As in *Cundy v Lindsay* (1878) 3 App Cas 459, para 8.140.

605 Where a seller knew of the buyer's mistaken belief as to the existence of an undertaking as to quality, the seller could (on the objective principle) be treated as if he had given the undertaking and be precluded by his breach of it from enforcing the contract. This is a second possible explanation of *Smith v Hughes* (n 599 above).

606 See para 8.138 at n 578.

607 See para 8.145.

608 *Baskomb v Beckwith* (1869) LR 8 Eq 100.

609 *Tamplin v James* (1879) 15 Ch D 215, 221.

610 As in *Malins v Freeman* (1836) 2 Keen 25.

611 See *Torrance v Bolton* (1872) 8 Ch App 118, perhaps now explicable as a case of misrepresentation.

612 [2002] EWCA Civ 1407; [2003] QB 697.

613 See para 8.139.

614 *Riverlate Properties Ltd v Paul* [1975] Ch 133.

Refusal of specific performance[615] is not open to the same objection since it does not deprive the claimant of his remedy at law.

(3) Documents Mistakenly Signed

(a) Doctrine of 'non est factum'

A person who signs a contractual document is generally bound by it whether he reads it or not; but long ago[616] the law recognized a special defence available to illiterate persons who executed deeds which had been incorrectly read over to them. This was the defence of 'non est factum' (it is not my deed); it was later extended to persons who could read and explained on the ground that 'the mind of the signer did not accompany the signature'.[617] But this extension gave rise to the danger of conflict with the objective principle, particularly where A was by the fraud of B induced to sign a document (such as a guarantee of B's bank overdraft) apparently containing a contract between A and C. To reduce the risk of prejudice to C, the law has restricted the scope of the doctrine in the ways described in paragraphs 8.150 to 8.152.

8.149

(b) Restrictions

The doctrine is not normally available to adults of normal attainments and capacity. It applies only in favour of persons who can have 'no real understanding' of the document 'whether . . . from defective education, illness or innate incapacity';[618] and of those who have been tricked into signing the document.[619]

8.150

The doctrine is restricted by a rule closely analogous to the requirement that a mistake must be 'fundamental'.[620] It applies only where the difference between the document signed and the document as it was believed to be is a 'radical' or 'essential' or 'fundamental' or 'substantial' one.[621]

8.151

The defence is not available to a person who was careless in signing the document.[622] Although the standard of care seems to be subjective,[623] the burden of disproving carelessness lies on the signer and is not easy to discharge.[624]

8.152

---

[615] See para 8.147 at n 610.
[616] *Thoroughgood's* case (1584) 2 Co Rep 9a.
[617] *Foster v Mackinnon* (1869) LR 4 CP 704, 711.
[618] *Saunders v Anglian Building Society Ltd* [1971] AC 1004, 1016.
[619] ibid, 1025.
[620] See paras 8.133, 8.134, 8.141, and 8.142.
[621] *Saunders'* case (n 618 above) 1017, 1019, 1021, 1026, 1034.
[622] *Saunders'* case (n 618 above); *United Dominions Trust v Western* [1976] QB 513 (document containing blanks).
[623] Since a reasonable person cannot normally rely on the defence.
[624] *Saunders'* case (n 618 above), especially at 1023.

(4) Mistakes in Recording Agreements

(a) Remedy of rectification

8.153 The equitable (and hence discretionary) remedy of rectification is available where there has been a mistake, not in the *making*, but in the *recording* of a contract: it brings a document into line with the earlier agreement.[625] A crucial point is that 'Courts of equity do not rectify contracts; they may and do rectify instruments'.[626] A document which accurately records a prior agreement thus cannot be rectified merely because that agreement was made under some mistake:[627] if rectification were available in such a case, the remedy would subvert the rules which limit the kinds of mistake which can invalidate contracts.

(b) Requirements

8.154 The mistake must normally be that of both parties.[628] If, for example, a lease provided for a monthly rent of £1,000, it could not be rectified merely because the landlord intended the rent to be £2,000 since this would impose on the tenant a liability to which he had not agreed or appeared to agree. Rectification could be ordered in such a case only if the tenant was guilty of fraud, or knew of the landlord's mistake or wilfully shut his eyes to it and sought to take advantage of it.[629] Nor, in the absence of such facts, can the tenant be forced to choose between having the lease rectified or rescinded[630] since this course would deprive him of the protection of the objective principle.

8.155 Rectification is available if the document fails accurately to record a prior agreement or (even less stringently) a 'continuing common intention', and 'some outward expression of accord'.[631] Rectification can thus be ordered even though there was no prior binding contract: eg because the prior agreement was not intended to be legally binding before execution of the document. There must, however, be clear evidence of the prior agreement, since the court has to guard against the danger of imposing on a party terms to which he had not agreed.[632]

---

625 *Murray v Parker* (1854) 19 Beav 305; *Allnutt v Wilding* [2006] EWHC 1905; [2006] BTC 8040 at [16].

626 *Mackenzie v Coulson* (1869) LR 9 Eq 369, 375; *The Olympic Pride* [1980] 2 Lloyd's Rep 67, 72.

627 Cf *Frederick E Rose (London) Ltd v William H Pim Jr & Co Ltd* [1953] 2 QB 450.

628 *Faraday v Tamworth Union* (1916) 86 LJ Ch 436.

629 *Garrard v Frankel* (1862) 30 Beav 445, 451; *Blay v Pollard & Morris* [1930] 1 KB 628, 633; *Commission for the New Towns v Cooper* [1995] Ch 259, 277.

630 *Riverlate Properties Ltd v Paul* [1975] Ch 133.

631 *Joscelyne v Nissen* [1970] 2 QB 86, 98.

632 *Fowler v Fowler* (1859) 4 De G & J 250, 265; *The Olympic Pride* [1980] 2 Lloyd's Rep 67, 73.

(c) Restrictions

Rectification may be barred by lapse of time or the intervention of third party rights.[633] The remedy is not barred by impossibility of restoring the pre-contract position;[634] for its purpose is not to undo what has been done but to give effect to the parties' agreement.[635]   **8.156**

Rectification is not available where other machinery is provided by law for correcting mistakes: eg where a mistake has been made in drawing up a settlement which is binding by virtue of a court order.[636]   **8.157**

A claim for rectification of a document may be accompanied by one as to its construction. The claimant should then put forward both claims in the proceedings; for if judgment is given against him on the point of construction his rectification claim will be barred if it could have been, but was not, made in those proceedings.[637]   **8.158**

F. Misrepresentation

A person who has been induced to enter into a contract by certain kinds of misleading statements will, where certain general requirements are satisfied, have remedies by way of damages or rescission or both. Sometimes these remedies (or one of them) are available also for mere non-disclosure.   **8.159**

(1) The Representation

The starting point for this discussion is that the representation must be one of *existing fact*. This requirement is, however, much modified, as the contrast between such and certain other kinds of representation will show.   **8.160**

(a) Statements of opinion or belief

Some kinds of sales talk (such as a description of land as 'fertile and improveable')[638] are so vague as to have no legal effect. Even a more precise statement (such as one that land could support 2,000 sheep)[639] is not a ground for relief if the representor   **8.161**

---

[633] *Bloomer v Spittle* (1872) LR 13 Eq 427; *Beale v Kyte* [1907] 1 Ch 564; *Smith v Jones* [1954] 1 WLR 1089; cf para 8.181.

[634] Contrast para 8.182.

[635] eg *Cook v Fearn* (1878) 48 LJ Ch 63.

[636] *Mills v Fox* (1887) 37 Ch D 153.

[637] *Crane v Hegeman-Harris Co Inc* [1939] 4 All ER 68, (and see [1971] 3 All ER 245).

[638] *Dimmock v Hallett* (1866) LR 2 Ch App 21.

[639] *Bissett v Wilkinson* [1927] AC 177.

had (as the representee knew) no personal knowledge of the relevant facts. A statement of opinion or belief can, however, give rise to liability if the maker professed to have special knowledge or skill with regard to the matter stated;[640] or if the statement by implication contained a representation that the person making it held the belief stated.[641]

(b) Statements as to the future

8.162 A person who promises to do something and then breaks that promise is liable for breach of contract if the promise had contractual force. If it had no such force, he is not liable for misrepresentation unless, when he made the promise, he had no intention of performing it; for in that case he would be misrepresenting his present state of mind, which is 'as much a fact as the state of his digestion'.[642] A person who makes a statement of expectation or belief may similarly by implication state that he holds the belief on reasonable grounds,[643] or at least honestly.[644]

(c) Statements of law

8.163 It was formerly said that a misrepresentation of law (as opposed to one of fact) gave rise to no claim for compensation.[645] But the distinction between the two kinds of misrepresentation has not survived the rejection by the House of Lords of a similar distinction in the context of a restitution claim for the recovery of money paid under a mistake.[646] The reasoning of this decision is regarded as being of general application,[647] so that relief is now available for misrepresentation of law in the same way as it is for misrepresentations of fact.[648]

---

[640] *Esso Petroleum Co Ltd v Mardon* [1976] QB 801; cf *MCI Worldcom International Inc v Primus Communications plc* [2004] EWCA Civ 957; [2004]2 All ER (Comm) 833 at [30].

[641] *Brown v Raphael* [1958] Ch 636, 641; contrast *Harlingdon and Leinster Enterprises v Christopher Hull Fine Art Ltd* [1991] 1 QB 564.

[642] *Edgington v Fitzmaurice* (1885) 29 Ch D 459, 482; cf, in criminal law, Fraud Act 2006, s 2(3).

[643] *The Mihalis Angelos* [1971] 1 QB 164, 194, 205.

[644] *Economides v Commercial Union Assurance Co plc* [1998] QB 587; cf Marine Insurance Act 1906, s 20(5).

[645] *Rashdall v Ford* (1866) LR 2 Eq 750; *Beattie v Ebury* (1872) LR 7 Ch App 693; *André & Cie SA v Ets Michel Blanc* [1979] 2 Lloyd's Rep 427, 434.

[646] *Kleinwort Benson Ltd v Lincoln CC* [1999] 2 AC 349; cf para 8.135; and, in criminal law, Fraud Act 2006, s 2(3).

[647] *Pankhania v Hackney LBC* [2002] EWHC 2441 (Ch) at [68], approved in *Brennan v Bolt Burden* [2004] EWCA Civ 1017; [2005] QB 303 at [11].

[648] If the representee had taken his own legal advice on the point, his claim would fail for want of reliance on the misrepresentation; see para 8.166.

(2) Other Conditions of Liability

(a) Unambiguous

A representation may be capable of bearing two meanings, one true and the other **8.164**
false. There is then no liability in damages for deceit if the representee understood
the representation in the former (true) sense.[649] Even if he understood it in the
latter (false) sense, the representor is so liable only if he intended it to be so understood:[650] ie not if he honestly intended it to bear the true meaning.[651]

(b) Materiality

The representation must, in general, be material, ie it must relate to a matter **8.165**
which would influence a reasonable person in deciding whether, or on what terms,
to enter into the contract.[652] This does not mean that it must, in all the circumstances, be reasonable for the representee to rely on the representation. It might
not be reasonable for him to do this where he had, but did not take, an opportunity of discovering the truth; but this is not of itself a bar to relief.[653] Exceptionally,
there is no requirement of materiality where the representation is fraudulent;[654]
where the requirement is excluded by a term of the contract;[655] or where the claim
is not one for misrepresentation inducing the claimant to enter into a contract
with the defendant but is one for breach of a duty of care arising out of an antecedent contract between these parties.[656]

(c) Reliance

There is no relief for misrepresentation if the representee did not rely on the **8.166**
representation: eg because he knew the truth.[657] The same result follows if the
representation never came to his attention;[658] but a representation made by A to
B can give C a ground for relief against A if A intended the representation to be
(and it was) repeated by B to C, or where this should have been foreseen by A.[659]

---

[649] *Smith v Chadwick* (1884) 9 App Cas 187.
[650] *The Siboen and the Sibotre* [1976] 1 Lloyd's Rep 293, 318.
[651] *Akerhielm v De Mare* [1959] AC 789.
[652] *Mc Dowell v Fraser* (1779) 1 Dougl 260, 261; *Traill v Baring* (1864) 4 DJ & S 318, 326;
Marine Insurance Act 1906, s 20(2).
[653] See para 8.166.
[654] *Smith v Kay* (1859) 7 HLC 750.
[655] *London Assurance v Mansell* (1879) 11 Ch D 363, 368 (basis of contract clauses in insurance
proposal).
[656] See *Bristol & West Building Society v Mothew* [1998] Ch 1, 10–11.
[657] *Eurocopy plc v Teesdale* [1992] BCLC 1067.
[658] *Ex p Biggs* (1859) 28 LJ Ch 50.
[659] *Pilmore v Hood* (1838) 5 Bing NC 97; *Smith v Eric S Bush* [1990] 1 AC 831; cf *Clef Aquitaine
SARL v Laporte Materials (Barrow) Ltd* [2001] QB 488, where B's rights under the contract were
transferred to C.

Reliance is normally negatived where the representee made his own investigations into the matter;[660] but this rule does not apply to cases of fraud[661] since so to apply it would put a premium on skilful deception. The fact that the representee had, but failed to take, an opportunity of discovering the truth is not, of itself, a ground for denying relief;[662] but where it was reasonable for the representee to make use of that opportunity and he failed to do so relief will be denied if the representation was not fraudulent.[663] Relief may be given to a representee who was induced to enter into the contract both by the representation and by other factors,[664] unless these other factors were such decisive inducements that he would have entered into the contract even if he had known the truth.[665]

(3) Damages

(a) Fraud

8.167 A person who suffers loss as a result of being induced by a false statement to enter into a contract can recover damages in tort for deceit if he can show that the person making the statement *either* knew that it was false *or* had no belief in its truth *or* made it recklessly, not caring whether it was true or false.[666] He need not establish an intention to cause loss or other bad motive:[667] an 'intention to deceive' suffices even though there is no 'intention to defraud'.[668]

(b) Negligence at common law

8.168 There is liability in tort where a misrepresentation is made carelessly, in breach of a duty to take reasonable care that the representation is accurate. Such a duty arises when there is a 'special relationship' between the parties;[669] the requirements of

---

660 *Redgrave v Hurd* (1881) 20 Ch D 1, 14; *McInerny v Lloyds Bank Ltd* [1974] 1 Lloyd's Rep 246, 254.

661 *S Pearson & Son Ltd v Dublin Corporation* [1907] AC 351.

662 *Redgrave v Hurd* (n 660 above).

663 *Smith v Eric S Bush* (n 659 above); cf *Peekay Intermark Ltd* [2006] EWCA Civ 386; [2006] 2 Lloyd's Rep 511 (no relief for a misrepresentation corrected by the terms of the contractual document signed, but not read, by the representee). To this extent, the rule in *Redgrave v Hurd* (n 660 above), seems now to be qualified.

664 *Edgington v Fitzmaurice* (1885) 29 Ch D 459; *Standard Chartered Bank v Pakistan National Shipping Corp (No 2)* [2002] UKHL 43; [2003] 1 AC 959 at [14]–[15].

665 *JEB Fasteners Ltd v Mark S Broom & Co* [1983] 1 All ER 583.

666 *Derry v Peek* (1889) 14 App Cas 337; on similar facts see now Financial Services and Markets Act 2000, s 90. For criminal liability, see Fraud Act, 2006.

667 *Polhill v Walter* (1832) 3 B & Ad 114.

668 *Standard Chartered Bank v Pakistan National Shipping Corp* [1995] 2 Lloyd's Rep 365, 375; *Standard Chartered Bank v Pakistan National Shipping Corp (No 2)* [2000] 1 Lloyd's Rep 218, 221, revsd on another ground [2003]1 AC 959.

669 *Hedley Byrne & Co Ltd v Heller & Partners Ltd* [1964] AC 465.

such a relationship are discussed elsewhere in this book.[670] The duty can, and often does, arise where the misrepresentation does not induce the representee to enter into a contract with the representor.[671] But it can arise also where the representation does induce such a contract: eg between prospective lessee and lessor.[672] Such commercial relationships will not be 'special' (so as to give rise to a duty of care at common law) if it is reasonable for the representor to assume that the representee has acted on his own judgment or advice; but even in such a case the representor can be subject to the statutory liability in damages discussed in paragraph 8.169.

(c) Misrepresentation Act 1967, s 2(1)

This subsection creates a statutory liability in damages 'where a person [A] has **8.169** entered into a contract after a misrepresentation has been made to him by another party [B] thereto'. The statutory cause of action is based on negligence[673] but is in two respects more favourable to A than common law liability for negligence: it arises although there is no 'special relationship' between A and B; and the burden is on B to prove that, up to the time the contract was made, he believed on reasonable grounds that the facts represented were true. In deciding whether B had discharged this burden, the court would have regard to the means at his disposal for discovering the truth.[674] The subsection provides that, if B would have been liable had the misrepresentation been made fraudulently, then 'he shall be so liable' even though it was not so made. Opinion is divided as to the extent to which the statutory cause of action is, as a result of this fiction of fraud, governed by special rules applicable at common law in cases of fraud;[675] it would often be inappropriate to apply these rules where there is actual fraud.

(d) Breach of contract

(i) Term of main contract

A pre-contract statement may be a 'mere' representation, inducing the contract, **8.170** or one of its terms. In the latter case, the person making the statement is considered to undertake that it was true and will therefore, if it is untrue, be liable in damages for breach, irrespective of negligence. Where the statement is set out

---

[670] See Chapter 17.
[671] eg in *Hedley Byrne's* case (n 669 above).
[672] *Esso Petroleum Co Ltd v Mardon* [1976] QB 801.
[673] *South Australia Asset Management Corp v York Montague Ltd* [1997] AC 191, 216.
[674] See *Howard Marine & Dredging Co Ltd v A Ogden & Sons (Excavations) Ltd* [1978] QB 574; contrast *William Sindall plc v Cambridgeshire CC* [1994] 1 WLR 1016.
[675] Contrast *Gosling v Anderson* (1972) 223 EG 1743, with *Royscot Trust Ltd v Rogerson* [1991] 2 QB 297; and see *Avon Insurance plc v Swire Fraser* [2000] 1 All ER (Comm) 573.

in the contractual document, it will normally on its true construction[676] be a term, but the intention to guarantee its truth may be negatived by express contrary provision or by other circumstances. Where the statement is not set out in any contractual document, the question whether it has contractual force depends on the intention (objectively ascertained) of its maker.[677] Factors relevant to the ascertainment of this intention include the wording of the statement,[678] its importance to the representee[679] and the relative abilities of the parties to determine its truth: for example a statement as to the age of a car is more likely to be a term when made by a dealer [680] than when made by a private seller.[681]

(ii) Collateral contract

8.171   It may be impossible for a statement to take effect as a term of the contract induced by it: eg because it fails to comply with formal requirements or because of the parol evidence rule.[682] The statement may nevertheless take effect as a collateral contract[683] if the representor had the requisite contractual intention[684] and if consideration was provided by the representee. The latter requirement will usually [685] be satisfied by his entering into the main contract.

(e) Damages in lieu of rescission

8.172   Before 1967, rescission was the only remedy for a wholly innocent misrepresentation and might provide an unduly drastic solution, especially where the misrepresentation related to a relatively minor matter.[686] Section 2(2) of the Misrepresentation Act 1967 therefore gives the court a discretion to uphold the contract[687] and award damages 'in lieu of rescission' where the representee would be entitled to rescind a contract made after a misrepresentation had been made to him otherwise than fraudulently. The subsection gives no *right* to damages, and a claim for damages under it cannot be combined with one for rescission.[688] Its wording also suggests that such a claim cannot be made after the right to

---

[676] *Behn v Burness* (1863) 1 B & S 751, 754.

[677] *Howard Marine* case (n 674 above), 595.

[678] *Hummingbird Motors Ltd v Hobbs* [1986] RTR 276 (statement expressly one of belief only).

[679] *Bannerman v White* (1861) 10 CBNS 855; contrast *Oscar Chess Ltd v Williams* [1957] 1 WLR 370.

[680] Cf *Dick Bentley Productions Ltd v Harold Smith (Motors) Ltd* [1965] 1 WLR 623.

[681] *Oscar Chess* case, (n 679 above).

[682] See paras 8.76 and 8.85.

[683] *De Lassalle v Guildford* [1901] 2 KB 215; *Esso Petroleum Co Ltd v Mardon* [1976] QB 801.

[684] *Heilbut Symons & Co v Buckleton* [1913] 30, 47.

[685] Except, perhaps, where the representee was already bound to enter into the main contract: see para 8.47.

[686] *William Sindall plc v Cambridgeshire CC* [1994] 1 WLR 1016, 1036, 1043.

[687] For refusal to exercise the discretion, see *Highland Insurance Co v Continental Insurance Co* [1987] 1 Lloyd's Rep 109.

[688] Rescission does not bar a claim for damages under s 2(1).

rescind has been lost;[689] but the policy reasons for barring this right scarcely justify this restriction on the discretion to award damages under section 2(2).[690]

(f) Contents of the right to damages

Damages for deceit, for negligence at common law and under section 2(1) of the   **8.173**
Misrepresentation Act 1967[691] are damages in tort and are intended to put the representee into the position in which he would have been if the tort had not been committed; while damages for a misrepresentation having contractual force are damages for breach of contract and are intended to put the representee into the position in which he would have been if the contract had been performed.[692] If, for example, he is induced to buy a thing by a misrepresentation as to a quality which it lacks, his damages in tort will be the difference between the price he paid for the thing and its actual value (assessed prima facie but not invariably[693] at the date of the transaction),[694] while in contract they will be the difference between the thing's actual value and the value that it would have had, if the representation had been true.[695] In addition the representee may be entitled to consequential loss which in contract can include profits which he would have made from the thing if the representation had been true; in tort he can at most recover the profit that an alternative investment would have yielded.[696] Consequential loss is recoverable only if it is not too remote and the test of remoteness is more favourable to the claimant in tort than it is in contract[697] (particularly if the defendant is,[698] or is treated as if he were,[699] guilty of fraud). Damages in lieu of rescission under section 2(2) of the 1967 Act are *sui generis* and may be restricted to the amount by which the value of what the representor received exceeds that of what he gave in return.[700]

---

689 Cf *The Lucy* [1983] 1 Lloyd's Rep 188, 201-2; contrast *Zanzibar v British Aerospace (Lancaster House) Ltd* [2000] 1 WLR 2333.

690 *Thomas Witter Ltd v T B P Industries Ltd* [1996] 2 All ER 573, 591.

691 *F & H Entertainment Ltd v Leisure Enterprises Ltd* (1976) 240 EG 455.

692 *Twycross v Grant* (1877) 2 CPD 496, 504; *South Australia Asset Management Corp v York Montague Ltd* [1997] AC 191, 216.

693 *Smith New Court Securities Ltd v Scrimgeour Vickers (Asset Management) Ltd* [1997] AC 254.

694 *Twycross v Grant* (n 692 above); cf *Clef Aquitaine SARL v Laporte Materials (Barrow) Ltd* [2001] QB 488, where the seller's misrepresentation related to the price at which he sold similar goods to other buyers and the damages in tort were the extra amount which the buyer was thus induced to pay.

695 eg Sale of Goods Act 1979, s 53(3).

696 *East v Maurer* [1991] 1 WLR 461.

697 *The Heron II* [1969] 1 AC 350.

698 *Doyle v Olby Ironmongers Ltd* [1969] 2 QB 158, 167.

699 *Royscot Trust Ltd v Rogerson* [1991] 2 QB 297 as to which see n 675 above.

700 See *William Sindall v Cambridgeshire CC* [1994] 1 WLR 1016, 1038, 1044.

(g) Indemnity

8.174 There is no right to damages for a wholly innocent misrepresentation having no contractual force; nor, where rescission is ordered or upheld, or (arguably) where the right to rescind has been lost, is there any discretion to award damages in lieu.[701] The court may, however, as part of the process of rescission, order the representor to pay an 'indemnity'. Such an order may be made in respect, not only of payments made by the representee to the representor, but also of sums spent by the representee in performing his other obligations under the contract.[702] An indemnity is distinct from damages in that it is not available in respect of loss suffered in consequence of acts which the representee did in reliance on the contract without being required under it to do them.[703]

(4) Rescission

(a) Rescission for misrepresentation

(i) Option to rescind

8.175 Misrepresentation gives the representee the option to avoid the contract.[704] If he exercises the option, the contract is 'wipe(d). . .out altogether'[705] so that each party is released from his obligations under the contract and the representee is entitled to recover what he has given, on terms of restoring what he has received, under it.[706]

(ii) Contract not void

8.176 Unlike mistake, which can make a contract void,[707] misrepresentation makes the contract voidable by the representee. Hence if A is induced by some fraud of B (not inducing a fundamental mistake) to sell and deliver goods to B, then B can transfer a good title to C if C buys the goods from B in good faith before A has rescinded the contract.[708] By contrast, if the fraud does lead to a fundamental mistake B, and hence C, will acquire no title to the goods.[709]

---

701 See para 8.172.

702 *Newbigging v Adam* (1886) 34 Ch D 582; and see (1888) 13 App Cas 308.

703 *Whittington v Seale-Hayne* (1900) 82 LT 49.

704 *Clough v London & North Western Rly* (1871) LR 7 Ex 26, 34; *Redgrave v Hurd* (1881) 20 Ch D 1.

705 *The Kanchenjunga* [1990] 1 Lloyd's Rep 391, 398.

706 See para 8.182.

707 See paras 8.136 and 8.146.

708 *White v Garden* (1851) 10 CB 919; *Lewis v Averay* [1972] 1 QB 198.

709 *Cundy v Lindsay* (1878) 3 App Cas 459, para 8.142.

(iii) Modes of rescission

Under the rule stated in paragraph 8.176 it is crucial to know when the contract **8.177** has been rescinded. This question can give rise to difficulties since rescission can be effected either by taking legal proceedings (which may be needed to work out the consequences of rescission) or extra-judicially: eg by retaking goods obtained by fraud[710] or by giving notice to the representor.[711] Obviously no such steps can be taken where the representor has absconded with goods obtained by fraud. In one such case, giving notice to the police was held to suffice,[712] with the unfortunate result of depriving a good faith purchaser of the goods.[713] This rule seems to be designed to protect victims of fraud and so not to apply where the misrepresentation was negligent or wholly innocent.

(b) Rescission for breach

A breach of contract may entitle the victim to rescind the contract; generally he **8.178** can do so only if the breach is a sufficiently serious one.[714] Since such rescission is based on a defect in the performance, as opposed to one in the formation, of a contract, it does not (like rescission for misrepresentation) retrospectively annul the contract; hence it does not deprive the injured party of his right to damages for the breach.[715] The two processes overlap where a misrepresentation which has induced a contract then becomes one of its terms. The right to rescind for misrepresentation[716] survives such incorporation,[717] though if the matter to which the misrepresentation relates is only slight, then the court may, under section 2(2) of the Misrepresentation Act 1967, uphold the contract and award damages in lieu.[718] If the untruth of the incorporated representation is such as to give rise to a right to rescind for breach, the injured party can rescind either for misrepresentation or for breach. He will usually take the latter course since this can (unlike the former)[719] be combined with a claim for damages for breach and is probably not subject to the court's discretion under section 2(2).

---

[710] *Re Eastgate* [1905] 1 KB 465, doubted on another point in *Re Goldcorp Exchange Ltd* [1995] 1 AC 74, 103.

[711] eg *Reese Silver Mining Co v Smith* (1869) LR 4 HL 64.

[712] *Car & Universal Finance Co Ltd v Caldwell* [1965] 1 QB 525; contrast, in Scotland, *Macleod v Ker* 1965 SC 253.

[713] For criticism, see Law Revision Committee, 12th Report, para 16 (Cmnd 2958, 1966).

[714] For this requirement, and the exceptions to it, see para 8.364 et seq.

[715] See para 8.426.

[716] A mere breach of a promise gives no such right: see para 8.162.

[717] Misrepresentation Act 1967, s 1(a).

[718] See para 8.172.

[719] See para 8.175 at n 705; and cf *The Star Sea* [2001] UKHL 1; [2003] 1 AC 469 at [52] (non-disclosure). Rescission for misrepresentation can, however, be combined with a claim for damages for the misrepresentation under Misrepresentation Act 1967, s 2(1).

(c) Misrepresentation as a defence

8.179 A person who has been induced by a misrepresentation to enter into a contract can, to the extent that he has not performed his part, rely on the misrepresentation as a defence to an action on the contract.[720] This defensive stance is sometimes regarded as a form of rescission but it is not in all respects governed by the same rules as the process of a representee's claiming the return of what he gave under the contract. To make good such a claim, he must restore what he received under the contract;[721] but there is no such requirement where the victim of a fraudulent representation simply relies on it as a defence to a claim by the representor.[722] This somewhat harsh rule is probably meant to deter fraud[723] and there is no authority to support it where the representation is negligent or wholly innocent.

(d) Limits to rescission

8.180 Rescission is a source of potential hardship to (a) third parties and (b) the representor. Of the restrictions on the scope of the remedy (to be discussed below) the first is designed to avoid the former, and the others the latter, type of hardship.

(i) Third party rights

8.181 Once an innocent third party has for value acquired an interest in the subject matter of a contract induced by the misrepresentation, the contract cannot be rescinded so as to deprive him of that interest.[724]

(ii) Restitution impossible

8.182 Except in the situation described in paragraph 8.179, a person seeking to rescind a contract must restore what he has received under it. Where he has received money, restitution need not be in specie: he simply restores an equivalent sum.[725] The difficult cases are those in which some benefit other than money has been received and cannot be fully or literally restored.

8.183 **Changes in subject matter made by representee.**   The right to rescind is barred if the representee has disposed of the subject matter or so diminished its value as

---

[720] *Redgrave v Hurd* (1881) 20 Ch D 1.

[721] See para 8.182.

[722] *Feise v Parkinson* (1812) 4 Taunt 640, 641; Marine Insurance Act 1906, s 84(1) and (3)(a); *Berg v Sadler & Moore* [1937] 2 KB 158. For the position where rescission for *duress* takes the form of simply relying on this factor as a defence, see *Halpern v Halpern* [2007] EWCA Civ 291; [2007] 2 Lloyd's Rep 56, below, para 8.208 n 821.

[723] *South Australia Asset Management Corp v York Montague Ltd* [1997] AC 191, 215.

[724] See para 8.176 and cf para 8.209.

[725] The same may be true of other fungibles: *Smith New Court Securities Ltd v Scrimgeour Vickers (Asset Management) Ltd* [1997] AC 254, 264.

no longer to be able to make substantial restitution.[726] But if he can make substantial, though not precise, restitution, he can rescind on restoring the subject matter with an allowance for the diminution in value[727] and (even if there is no such diminution) for any benefits derived by him from his use of the thing.[728] Diminution in value is not a bar to rescission if it occurs in the course of a reasonable test of the accuracy of the representation.[729]

Changes in subject matter made by representor. Where the misrepresentation **8.184** is that of the buyer, and the seller wishes to rescind, changes made by the buyer do not as a matter of law bar the seller's right to rescind[730] (though they might deprive him of any interest in exercising it). If the seller wishes to rescind, he will have not only to repay the price but also to make an allowance in respect of the buyer's other expenses if incurred in the performance of the contract,[731] though not if they were incurred for some other reason and did not benefit the representee.[732]

Other deterioration or decline in value. Deterioration or decline in value does not **8.185** bar the right to rescind where it is due either to the very defect in the subject matter which it was represented not to have or to some external cause: for example to a fall in the market value of shares[733] or to damage to goods caused by a third party.[734]

(iii) Affirmation

The right to rescind for misrepresentation is lost if, with knowledge of the truth, **8.186** the representee affirms the contract. Affirmation may be express or inferred from conduct, such as retaining goods or shares[735] or remaining in occupation of land.[736] Failure to rescind in ignorance of the truth does not amount to affirmation and will not of itself bar the right to rescind for misrepresentation.[737]

(iv) Lapse of time

The right to rescind for innocent misrepresentation is barred by lapse of time, **8.187** which begins to run when the contract was made or perhaps when the representee

---

[726] *Clarke v Dickson* (1858) EB & E 148; *Lagunas Nitrate Co v Lagunas Syndicate* [1899] 2 Ch 392.
[727] *Erlanger v New Sombrero Phosphate Co* (1878) 3 App Cas 1218.
[728] *Hulton v Hulton* [1917] 1 KB 813, 826; contrast the stricter rule applied in a case of rescission *for breach* in *Hunt v Silk* (1804) 5 East 499.
[729] Cf *Head v Tattersall* (1871) LR 7 Ex 7, 12.
[730] *Spence v Crawford* [1939] 3 All ER 271.
[731] ibid.
[732] Cf *Mackenzie v Royal Bank of Canada* [1934] AC 468.
[733] *Armstrong v Jackson* [1917] 2 KB 822.
[734] *Head v Tattersall* (1871) LR 7 Ex 7.
[735] eg *United Shoe Machinery Co of Canada v Brunet* [1909] AC 330; *Western Bank of Scotland v Addie* (1867) LR 1 Sc & Div 145.
[736] *Kennard v Ashman* (1894) 10 TLR 213.
[737] It may bar the right to rescind for misrepresentation by lapse of time: see para 8.187; or the right to rescind for breach: see para 8.388.

ought, acting reasonably, to have discovered the truth.[738] Where the representation is fraudulent, lapse of time is not itself a bar to rescission though it may, after discovery of the truth,[739] be evidence of affirmation.[740]

(v) Misrepresentation Act 1967, s 2(2)

8.188 This subsection gives the court a discretion to declare the contract subsisting and to award damages in lieu of rescission. The discretion may be exercised even where none of the above bars to rescission has arisen; but if such a bar has arisen the court has no discretion: it *must* refuse to allow rescission.

(5) Excluding Liability for Misrepresentation

8.189 At common law, liability for misrepresentation can be excluded,[741] subject to the restrictions discussed in section D above. But under section 3 of the Misrepresentation Act 1967 the requirement of reasonableness (as stated in the Unfair Contract Terms Act 1977) applies to terms by which one party to a contract purports to exclude or restrict his liability to the other [742] for misrepresentation inducing the contract. The Unfair Terms in Consumer Contracts Regulations 1999 may also apply to such terms, though only in consumer contracts on standard terms. Section 3 of the 1967 Act is not subject to either of these requirements.

(6) Non-disclosure

(a) General rules

8.190 A misrepresentation need not be made in so many words: it may be inferred from conduct (as in the stock case of papering over the cracks)[743] or from stating a misleading half-truth.[744] But where no representation, express or implied, has been made, the general rule is that there is no civil liability either on a seller for failing to disclose facts which reduce,[745] or on a buyer for failing to disclose facts

---

[738] See *Leaf v International Galleries* [1950] 2 KB 86.

[739] *Aaron's Reefs Ltd v Twiss* [1896] AC 273, 287.

[740] *Clough v London & North Western Rly* (1871) LR 7 Ex 26, 35.

[741] *Toomey v Eagle Star Insurance Co Ltd (No 2)* [1995] 2 Lloyd's Rep 88.

[742] Section 3 of the 1967 Act would not apply where the representation induces a contract with a third person, as in *Smith v Eric S Bush* [1990] AC 831. Section 2(2) of the 1977 Act could apply in such a case, but only where the liability in question was 'business liability'; there is no such requirement in s 3 of the 1967 Act.

[743] See *Gordon v Selico Co Ltd* (1986) 278 EG 53.

[744] *Nottingham Patent Brick & Tile Co v Butler* (1886) 16 QBD 778.

[745] *Ward v Hobbs* (1878) 4 App Cas 13.

which increase,[746] the value of the subject matter.[747] The rule is based on the difficulty of specifying which of the many facts known to each party and affecting the
bargain would need to be disclosed.

(b) Exceptional cases

Some duty of disclosure exists in the situations described in paragraphs 8.192 to **8.191**
8.199. In these situations, a person need generally disclose only facts that he (or
his agent)[748] knows at the time of contracting, though the duty in certain cases
ceases before that point.[749] It may also extend after that point, especially where the
contract itself imposes the duty of disclosure.[750]

Change of circumstances. A representation about the subject matter of negoti- **8.192**
ations may be true when made but be wholly falsified by a radical change of
circumstances before the contract is made. That change must then be disclosed,[751]
at least if the interval between the representation and the conclusion of the contract is not so long as to make it unreasonable for the representee still to rely on the
representation.[752] The same rule probably applies where the representation is one
of an intention which is later changed,[753] unless the intention originally stated is
such as is intrinsically likely to be changed.[754]

Utmost good faith. In certain types of contracts (known as contracts *uberrimae* **8.193**
fidei) there is a duty to disclose material facts on the ground that one party is typically
in a much better position than the other to know such facts. The prime example
is the contract of insurance where 'the insurer knows nothing and the. . .[insured]
knows everything'.[755] Hence the latter must, in general,[756] disclose all such facts

---

[746] *Smith v Hughes* (1871) LR 6 QB 587, 604; but there is criminal liability for certain kinds of
'insider dealing' under Criminal Justice Act 1993, Part V. Insider dealing may also amount to 'market abuse' for which the Financial Services Authority can impose penalties: see Financial Services
and Markets Act 2000, s 118(2)(a).

[747] For defects constituting a source of *danger* see para 8.197.

[748] *Blackburn, Low & Co v Vigors* (1887) 12 App Cas 531.

[749] *Cory v Patton* (1872) LR 7 QB 304 (insurance binding before contract as a matter of
business).

[750] *Phillips v Foxall* (1872) LR 7 QB 666 (fidelity bond); *The Star Sea* [2001] UKHL 1; [2003]
AC 469; in such cases, the non-disclosure does not *induce* the contract, but is a *breach* of it: see
para 8.201.

[751] *With v O'Flanagan* [1936] Ch 575; cf *The Kriti Palm* [2006] EWCA Civ 1601; [2007] 1 All
ER (Comm) 667 at [383], [440] (issuer of quality certificate discovering its inaccuracy by carrying
out further tests).

[752] Cf *Argy Trading Development Co Ltd v Lapid Developments Ltd* [1977] 1 WLR 444, 461–2.

[753] *Traill v Baring* (1864) 4 DJ & S 318.

[754] *Wales v Wadham* [1977] 1 WLR 199, disapproved on another ground in *Livesey v Jenkins*
[1985] AC 424 (intention not to remarry).

[755] *Rozanes v Bowen* (1928) 32 Lloyd's List Rep 98, 102.

[756] There are exceptions: eg facts which the insurer knows or which diminish the risk need not
be disclosed: *Carter v Boehm* (1766) 3 Burr 1905, 1910.

as a prudent insurer would take into account in deciding whether or on what terms to accept the risk.[757] The insurer is under a reciprocal duty to disclose facts material to the risk known to him but not to the insured.[758]

8.194 Certain agreements between members of a family for settling disputes as to family property are likewise contracts *uberrimae fidei*.[759]

8.195 **Limited duty of disclosure.** Contracts under which there is a more limited duty of disclosure than that just described include contracts of suretyship, in which the creditor must disclose unusual facts which the surety would not normally expect,[760] and contracts for the sale of land, in which the vendor must disclose unusual defects of title which a prudent purchaser would not be expected to discover.[761] There are also certain requirements of disclosure in relation to compromises of invalid claims and exemption clauses.[762]

8.196 **Relationship of parties.** A duty of disclosure may arise because there is a 'fiduciary' relationship between the parties: eg that of principal and agent.[763] Commonly such a duty is one which arises in the *performance* of a contract; but its breach may also *induce* a further contract[764] and it is with this aspect of the duty that the present discussion is concerned.

8.197 **Latent defects.** A seller is under no duty to disclose latent defects which merely affect the value of the subject matter; but he may be liable in negligence for failing to warn the buyer of a defect which is a source of danger and causes personal injury or damage to other property.[765]

8.198 **Custom.** A duty of disclosure may be imposed by a trade or market custom.[766]

8.199 **Legislation.** Extensive duties of disclosure are imposed by statute in relation to listing of securities and to company prospectuses.[767]

---

[757] *Lambert v Co-operative Insurance Society Ltd* [1975] 2 Lloyd's Rep 485; Marine Insurance Act 1906, s 18(2); *Pan Atlantic Insurance Co Ltd v Pine Top Insurance Co* [1995] AC 501.

[758] *Carter v Boehm* (n 756 above) 1909.

[759] *Greenwood v Greenwood* (1863) 2 DJ & S 28.

[760] *Levett v Barclays Bank plc* [1995] 1 WLR 1260. Typically the contract will be one of suretyship if the surety is selected by the debtor but it may be one of insurance if he is selected by the creditor and so is likely to know less than the creditor about the debtor's creditworthiness: see *Trade Indemnity Co Ltd v Workington Harbour Board* [1937] AC 1.

[761] *Rignall Developments Ltd v Halil* [1988] Ch 190; *William Sindall plc v Cambridgeshire CC* [1994] 1 WLR 1016, 1023.

[762] See para 8.44; *Curtis v Chemical Cleaning and Dyeing Co Ltd* [1951] 1 KB 805, 809.

[763] eg *Armstrong v Jackson* [1917] 2 KB 822; cf *Item Software (UK) Ltd v Fassihi* [2004] EWCA Civ 1653; [2005] ICR 450 (company director); *Conlon v Sims* [2006] EWCA Civ 1749; [2007] 3 All ER 802 at [127]–[128] (prospective partners).

[764] *Sybron Corporation v Rochem Ltd* [1984] Ch 112.

[765] *Hurley v Dyke* [1979] RTR 265, 303.

[766] *Jones v Bowden* (1813) 4 Taunt 847.

[767] Financial Services and Markets Act 2000, ss 80, 86.

(e) Effects of non-disclosure

Cases of 'non-disclosure' can be divided into those of *inferred representation* in **8.200** which a representation is inferred from conduct or from failure to correct a representation falsified by later events; and those of *pure non-disclosure* in which the law provides a remedy though no such inference can be drawn. In cases of inferred representation, the injured parties' remedies by way of damages and rescission are the same as those for express misrepresentation. In cases of pure non-disclosure the remedies are sometimes by way of rescission only: this is the position in contracts of insurance;[768] and sometimes by way of damages only: this is the position where the statutory duty described in paragraph 8.199 is broken.[769] The distinction between the two groups of cases is also relevant for the purposes of the Misrepresentation Act 1967, where the phrase 'misrepresentation made'[770] seems to cover cases of inferred representation but not those of pure non-disclosure.

It is further necessary to distinguish between non-disclosure which *induces* the **8.201** making of a contract and non-disclosure which amounts to a *breach* of a contract after it has been made.[771] In the latter case, the right to rescind is governed by the rules which apply to rescission for breach.[772] Such rescission differs from rescission for an inducing non-disclosure in two ways: it does not retrospectively annul the contract[773] and it is generally available only where the breach is a serious one.[774]

(7) Estoppel by Representation

A person who makes a precise and unambiguous representation of fact may be **8.202** 'estopped' (ie prevented) from denying its truth if the person to whom it was made was intended to act in reliance on it and did so act to his detriment.[775] Such an estoppel does not give rise to a cause of action[776] but only to a defence: eg it could provide a tenant with a defence to an action for breach of covenant to repair without making the landlord liable in damages for disrepair. It could, however, make the landlord liable for wrongfully ejecting the tenant for alleged breach of

---

[768] *Banque Keyser Ullmann SA v Skandia (UK) Insurance Co Ltd* [1990] 1 QB 65, 779–81, aff'd on this point [1991] 2 AC 249, 288.
[769] *Re South of England Natural Gas Co* [1911] 1 Ch 573.
[770] In s 2(1) and (2).
[771] Cf n 750 above.
[772] *The Star Sea* [2001] UKHL 1; [2003] AC 439.
[773] See paras 8.421, 8.423; and cf paras 8.174, 8.177 for an exception in the case of fraudulent insurance claims, see *The Star Sea*, n 772 above, at [62].
[774] See paras 8.364, 8.365.
[775] *Low v Bouverie* [1891] 3 Ch 82; *Woodhouse AC Israel Cocoa Ltd v Nigerian Produce Marketing Co* [1982] AC 741.
[776] *Low v Bouverie* (n 775 above), 101.

covenant to repair, the tenant's cause of action in such a case being based on the lease and not on the representation.[777]

G. Improper Pressure

(1) Duress

8.203 At common law, a contract made under duress is voidable[778] by the victim of the duress. For this purpose 'economic duress'[779] suffices; this can extend to any threat which is illegitimate because either the threat[780] or what is threatened is legally wrongful.[781] Whether the threat actually amounts to duress depends on its coercive effect: the test has been said to be whether the effect of the threat is such that it 'vitiates consent'.[782] Under this test, a threat to break a contract can,[783] but will not necessarily,[784] amount to duress. Mere 'commercial pressure'[785] or a threat to *exercise* contractual rights[786] does not amount to duress.

(2) Undue Influence

(a) **Actual pressure**

8.204 Equity gives relief where, though no threat has been made, undue influence has been exercised by one party over the other. The party claiming relief must show that the influence existed and that its exercise brought about the transaction;[787] he need not show that the transaction was to his manifest disadvantage.[788]

---

[777] Cf in an analogous context, *Coventry, Sheppard & Co v The Great Eastern Rly Co* (1883) 11 QBD 776.

[778] *Pao On v Lau Yiu Long* [1980] AC 614, 634; *The Universe Sentinel* [1983] 1 AC 366, 383, 400. The contract is not *void*.

[779] *The Universe Sentinel* (n 778 above) 383.

[780] *The Universe Sentinel* [1983] 1 AC 366, 401 (blackmail).

[781] ibid, 383.

[782] *Pao On v Lau Yiu Long* [1980] AC 614, 636; for debate as to this rationale, see *The Evia Luck (No 2)* [1992] 2 AC 152, 166; *Huyton SA v Peter Cremer GmbH* [1999] 1 Lloyd's Rep 620, 630.

[783] *B & S Contracts and Designs Ltd v Victor Green Publications Ltd* [1984] ICR 419.

[784] *Pao On v Lau Yiu Long* (n 778 above); *Huyton SA v Peter Cremer GmbH* (n 782 above).

[785] *The Siboen and the Sibotre* [1976] 1 Lloyd's Rep 293, 335; *CNT Cash & Carry Ltd v Gallagher* [1994] 4 All ER 714.

[786] *The Olib* [1991] 2 Lloyd's Rep 108.

[787] *Howes v Bishop* [1909] 2 KB 390.

[788] *CIBC Mortgages v Pitt* [1994] AC 200; *Royal Bank of Scotland v Etridge (No 2)* [2001] UKHL 44; [2002] 2 AC 773 at [12].

(b) Presumed undue influence

Equity also gives relief where the relationship between two persons is such as to **8.205** give rise to a 'presumption of undue influence'.[789] This arises where the party seeking to impugn the transaction establishes[790] that (1) the relationship between A and B is one in which A reposed trust and confidence in B; and (2) the transaction 'calls for explanation': eg because it is a substantial transfer of property (as opposed to a moderate Christmas gift[791]) or a guarantee by A of B's business debts. The effect of establishing these facts is to give rise to 'a rebuttable evidential presumption of undue influence'[792] to the effect that 'in the absence of a satisfactory explanation, the transaction can only have been procured by undue influence'.[793] It will then be up to B to rebut the presumption[794] by introducing evidence which leaves the court in doubt as to whether the transaction was so procured.[795] A common way of rebutting the presumption is to show that A was independently[796] and competently[797] advised; it can also be rebutted by other evidence that A's will was not 'overborne'.[798]

The fact that A reposed trust and confidence in B can be established in one of two **8.206** ways. First, it can be established by showing that the relationship between them belonged to a group in which 'the law presumes irrebuttably'[799] that B had influence over A: eg where the relationship is that of parent and child,[800] trustee and beneficiary[801] or solicitor and client.[802] The effect of this irrebuttable presumption is merely that the influence *exists*. It is not of itself a ground for relief: for example, a moderate Christmas gift from a child to its parent would not be invalid since it would not 'call for explanation'.[803] A second way of establishing that A reposed trust and confidence in B is to show that this was in fact the position. This possibility covers a wide range of situations which 'cannot be

---

[789] *Barclays Bank plc v O'Brien* [1994] 1 AC 180, 189; *Royal Bank of Scotland v Etridge (No 2)* [2001] UKHL 44; [2002] 2 AC 773 (hereafter 'the *Etridge* case') at [16]. The following account is based mainly on the speech of Lord Nicholls (with which Lords Bingham at [3] and Clyde at [91] agreed).

[790] *Etridge* case, n 789 above, at [13], [14].

[791] ibid, at [24], [156].

[792] ibid, at [16], [153], [194].

[793] ibid, at [14]; eg *Randall v Randall* [2004] EWHC 2285; [2005] WTLR 119.

[794] *Allcard v Skinner* (1887) 36 Ch D 145.

[795] *Etridge* case, n 789 above, at [158].

[796] *Inche Noriah v Shaik Allie Bin Omar* [1929] AC 127; for the position between the victim and a third party, see para 8.209.

[797] See *Pesticcio v Hurst* [2004] EWCA Civ 372; [2004] WTLR 699.

[798] *Etridge* case, n 789 above, at [162].

[799] ibid, at [18].

[800] *Bullock v Lloyd's Bank* [1995] Ch 317.

[801] *Ellis v Barker* (1871) LR 7 Ch App 104; *Thomson v Eastwood* (1877) 2 App Cas 215.

[802] *Wright v Carter* [1903] 1 Ch 27.

[803] *Etridge* case, n 789 above, at [14].

listed exhaustively'.[804] It applies to the relationship of husband and wife (or other cohabitants) living together in a successful relationship.[805] Such persons normally repose trust and confidence in each other,[806] but even a substantial gift by A to B, or a guarantee by A of B's business debts will not normally[807] 'call for explanation' since, between such persons, transactions of this kind can plausibly be accounted for by motives of affection or joint interest.[808] The restricted scope of the 'evidential presumption' in such cases reflects the point that the influence often leads to a transaction with a bank which has lent money on the security of the couple's home who then have a common interest in resisting the enforcement of the security. There is, however, a 'minority of cases'[809] in which the husband has taken advantage of the wife's 'vulnerability';[810] the law will then protect the wife against such conduct,[811] though it is not clear whether it will do so on the ground of actual[812] or of presumed[813] undue influence.

(c) Unconscionable bargains

8.207 Even in the absence of actual or presumed undue influence, equity sometimes gave relief against bargains regarded as 'unconscionable' because one party had exploited some weakness of the other.[814] On this ground sales of 'reversions' by 'expectant heirs' could be set aside for simple undervalue, though this is no longer of itself a ground for relief.[815] According to one view, 'inequality of bargaining power' is similarly a ground for giving relief to the weaker party;[816] but the prevailing view is that relief is not *generally* available on this ground alone.[817] There are, however, a number of *specific* instances in which the abuse of superior bargaining power is a ground for relief under legislation[818] or judge-made rules.[819]

---

804 ibid, at [10]; for illustrations, see *Tate v Williamson* (1866) LR 2 Ch App 55 (financial adviser and dissolute client); *O'Sullivan v Management Agency & Music Ltd* [1985] QB 428 (manager and unknown song-writer who later became a celebrity).

805 *Howes v Bishop* [1909] 2 KB 390; *Barclays Bank plc v O'Brien* [1994] 1 AC 180, 198.

806 *Etridge* case, n 789 above, at [45], [159].

807 ibid, at [30].

808 ibid, at [159]; hence in the *Etridge* case two members of the House of Lords rejected or doubted the existence of any presumption in the husband and wife cases.

809 *Etridge* case, n 789 above, at [37].

810 ibid, at [36]; cf at [163].

811 *Barclays Bank v Coleman* [2000] 12 All ER 385, affirmed in the *Etridge* case, n 789 above.

812 ibid, at [130].

813 ibid, at [291].

814 *Evans v Llewellin* (1787) 1 Cox CC 333; *Cresswell v Cresswell* [1978] 1 WLR 255 n.

815 *Aylesford v Morris* (1873) LR 8 Ch App 484; *Nevill v Snelling* (1880) 15 Ch D 679; Law of Property Act 1925, s 174.

816 *Lloyds Bank Ltd v Bundy* [1975] QB 326, 339 *per* Lord Denning MR.

817 *Pao On v Lau Yiu Long* [1980] AC 614, 634; *National Westminster Bank plc v Morgan* [1985] AC 686, 708.

818 See, for example, Consumer Credit Act 1974, ss 140A and 140B (relief for individual debtor under a consumer credit agreement whose relationship with the creditor is 'unfair' to the debtor).

819 For example, para 8.241 (restraint of trade).

(d) Bars to relief

(i) General

Relief on equitable grounds discussed in paragraphs 8.204 to 8.207 is, like **8.208** rescission for misrepresentation,[820] barred by inability to make restitution,[821] affirmation,[822] lapse of time[823] and the intervention of third party rights. Only the last of these bars calls for further discussion.

(ii) Third party rights

Relief for undue influence may be sought against a third party: eg where A is **8.209** induced by such influence exerted by B to mortgage A's house as security for a business debt owed by B to C, or to guarantee such a debt. A can then set the transaction aside against C if C either knew of the undue influence or was 'put on enquiry'.[824] This (not strictly accurate[825]) phrase means that C is under a duty to take reasonable steps[826] to reduce the risk of A's entering into the transaction as a result of undue influence (or other vitiating factor). Whether C is under such a duty depends on two factors. The first is the nature of the transaction. For example, the duty arises where A guarantees B's business debts to C,[827] but not where C makes a joint loan to A and B, since on its face the latter may, while the former does not, benefit A.[828] The second factor is the relationship between A and B. In many of the decided cases, A was B's wife,[829] but the duty can also arise where A is B's husband,[830] where they are unmarried cohabitants (whether hetero- or homo-sexual[831]) or where they are in some other relationship of trust and confidence.[832] The duty may extend to all cases in which A acts as surety for B's debts on a non-commercial basis.[833] Where the duty arises, C must communicate directly[834] with A to the effect that C will require a solicitor acting for A (who may also act

---

820 See paras 8.181 to 8.187.

821 ie substantial restitution: see the *O'Sullivan* case(n 804 above). cf *Halpern v Halpern* [2007] EWCA Civ 291; [2007] 2 Lloyd's Rep 56, a case of alleged duress in which it seems to be assumed that such cases are not governed by the special rule (stated in para 8.179) which applies where rescission for *fraud* takes the form of simply relying on this vitiating factor as a defence.

822 *Mitchell v Homfray* (1882) 8 QBD 587.

823 *Allcard v Skinner* (1887) 36 Ch D 145, 187.

824 *Royal Bank of Scotland v Etridge* (No 2) [2001] UKHL 44; [2002] 2 AC 773 ('the *Etridge* case') at [44].

825 ibid, at [41].

826 ibid, at [54].

827 *Etridge* case, n 824 above, at [48], [47].

828 ibid, at [48].

829 This was the position in the situations under review in the *Etridge* case, n 824 above.

830 ibid, at [47].

831 *Barclays Bank plc v O'Brien* [1994] 1 AC 180 at 196. The rule presumably applies where A and B are civil partners within the Civil Partnership Act 2004.

832 eg *Crédit Lyonnais Bank Nederland NV v Burch* [1997] 1 All ER 144.

833 *Etridge* case, n 824 above, at [87].

834 ibid, at [79].

for B and C[835]) to confirm to C that the solicitor has, at a meeting with A at which B was not present, explained to A the nature and effects of the document embodying the transaction.[836] If C takes these steps, C is normally entitled to rely on the solicitor's confirmation that the transaction has been duly explained to A.[837] Failure to take these steps is not itself a ground for relief: it does not dispense with A's need to make a case of actual or presumed undue influence.

H. Illegality

8.210 The law refuses to give full legal effect to contracts which are illegal (or affected by illegality) because they are contrary either to law or to public policy.

(1) Contracts Contrary to Law

(a) Making of contract forbidden by law

8.211 A contract is illegal if the mere making of it amounts to a criminal offence, such as a criminal conspiracy.[838] A contract to finance another person's litigation in return for a share in the proceeds formerly amounted to the crime of champerty. Such a contract remains illegal even after the abolition of criminal liability for champerty;[839] but legislation now in many cases validates agreements in writing for the payment by a client to a person who provides him with advocacy or litigation services of a 'conditional fee', payable only if the litigation ends in the client's favour.[840]

8.212 Where legislation prohibits the making of a contract without rendering it criminal, the contract is illegal only if in the court's view this was the purpose of the legislation.[841] If the legislation declares the contract to be merely void, it will not be illegal.[842]

---

835 ibid, at [73], [74], [79].

836 ibid, at [66], [76], [79].

837 ibid, at [56].

838 *Scott v Brown* [1892] 2 QB 724.

839 *Re Thomas* [1894] 1 QB 747; Criminal Law Act 1967, ss 13, 14; *Trendtex Trading Corp v Crédit Suisse* [1982] AC 769; *Callery v Gray* [2001] EWCA Civ 117; [2001] 1 WLR 2112, affd [2002] UKHL 28; [2002] 1 WLR 2000.

840 Courts and Legal Services Act 1990, ss 58 and 58A; Conditional Fee Agreements Regulations 2000, SI 2000/692; for an account of the history of legislative changes in this branch of the law see *Callery v Gray* (n 839 above). 'Contingency fee' agreements, by which the legal adviser is remunerated by a share of the proceeds of litigation, remain illegal: ibid, [2001] EWCA Civ at [6].

841 See *Harse v Pearl Life Assurance Co Ltd* [1904] 1 KB 558; cf *Fuji Finance Inc v Aetna Life Insurance Co Ltd* [1997] Ch 173.

842 Marine Insurance Act 1906, s 4(1); *Re London County Commercial Reinsurance Office Ltd* [1922] 2 Ch 67.

(b) Object of contract contrary to law

A contract having as its object the commission of a crime will often be illegal on the ground that it amounts to a criminal conspiracy.[843] It may be illegal even where there is no such conspiracy: eg where the offence is one of strict liability and is committed without guilty intent.[844] On an analogous principle, a contract is illegal if one party to the other's knowledge intended to use the subject matter for an illegal purpose.[845] **8.213**

A contract for the commission of a civil wrong is illegal if both parties share a guilty intent (eg to defraud creditors).[846] But the contract is not illegal if both parties act in good faith;[847] and if only one has a guilty intent, the contract can be enforced by the other.[848] **8.214**

(c) Method of performance contrary to law

An offence may be committed in the method of performing a contract which is lawful in itself: eg where a carrier of goods by sea overloads his ship. In one such case,[849] it was held that this did not make the contract illegal as the purpose of the legislation which had been contravened was to impose a fine for the prohibited *conduct* and not to prohibit the *contract* (as the carrier's consequent loss of freight would far exceed the fine for the offence). **8.215**

A contract subject to a licensing or similar requirement is illegal if it is performed[850] (or intended to be performed)[851] without the requisite licence. This is also true where legislation requires a person to be licensed to carry on a specified kind of business and expressly or impliedly prohibits contracts made in the course of such a business without the licence.[852] The result of holding the contract invalid could, however, be to prejudice persons of the very class which the licensing requirement was meant to protect; and by statute the illegality does not (in certain cases) deprive such persons of their rights under the contract.[853] **8.216**

---

843 See para 8.211.

844 For such cases, see para 8.249.

845 *Langton v Hughes* (1813) 1 M & S 593.

846 *Mallalieu v Hodgson* (1851) 16 QB 689; *Birkett v Acorn Business Machines Ltd* [1999] 2 All ER (Comm) 429.

847 Sale of Goods Act 1979, s 12 makes this assumption.

848 See *Clay v Yates* (1856) 11 H & N 73.

849 *St John Shipping Corp v Joseph Rank Ltd* [1957] 1 QB 267.

850 eg *J Dennis & Co Ltd v Munn* [1949] 2 KB 327.

851 eg *Bigos v Bousted* [1951] 1 All ER 92; *Vakante v Addey & Stanhope School* [2004] EWCA Civ 1065; [2004] ICR 279.

852 *Bedford Insurance Co Ltd v Instituto de Resseguros do Brasil* [1985] 1 QB 966.

853 Financial Services and Markets Act 2000, ss 26(1), 27(1).

(d) Performance contingent on unlawful act

8.217 A promise to pay a person money on his committing an unlawful act is illegal on the principle that a person should not profit from his own wrong; though the application of this rule to a case[854] in which it prevented the estate of an insolvent person from recovering under his life insurance policy on his committing suicide (then a crime) is controversial.[855] The principle is qualified in relation to promises to indemnify a person against criminal liability: the promisee cannot enforce such a promise if he committed the crime with guilty intent,[856] but he probably can enforce it if the offence was one of strict liability and was innocently committed.[857]

8.218 A promise to indemnify a person for civil liability incurred without guilty intent (eg one in an insurance policy against liability for negligence) is valid; indeed a promise of this kind may be implied in law.[858] By contrast, a promise to indemnify a person against liability for an intentional wrong (such as deceit) is illegal.[859] The same is generally true of a promise to indemnify a person against civil liability arising out of his deliberate commission[860] of a crime;[861] but not if the crime was committed without guilty intent.[862] In the case of motor accidents, the *victim* of even deliberate criminal conduct has in certain circumstances rights against the offender's insurer[863] or the Motor Insurers' Bureau.[864]

(2) Contracts Contrary to Public Policy

(a) Introductory

8.219 Contracts are contrary to public policy if they have a clear tendency[865] to bring about a state of affairs which the law regards as harmful. This is an inherently flexible notion, varying in content with changing social and economic conditions. It is therefore a source of uncertainty and of the danger that it could enable courts to invalidate any contracts of which they strongly disapproved. For this reason, the

---

854 *Beresford v Royal Exchange Assurance* [1938] AC 586.

855 Since enforcement would have benefited only the wrongdoer's creditors and not the wrongdoer himself.

856 *Colburn v Patmore* (1834) 1 CM & R 73.

857 eg *Osman v J Ralph Moss Ltd* [1970] 1 Lloyd's Rep 313.

858 *Betts v Gibbin* (1834) 2 A & E 57; *The Nogar Marin* [1988] 1 Lloyd's Rep 412, 417.

859 *Brown Jenkinson & Co Ltd v Percy Dalton (London) Ltd* [1957] 2 QB 621.

860 Not where the deliberate act is that of the defendant's employee, for which the defendant is vicariously liable: *Lancashire CC v Municipal Mutual Insurance Ltd* [1997] QB 897.

861 *Gray v Barr* [1971] QB 554; *Charlton v Fisher* [2002] EWCA Civ 112; [2002] QB 578.

862 *Gardner v Moore* [1984] AC 548, 560.

863 Third Parties (Rights against Insurers) Act 1930.

864 *Hardy v MIB* [1964] 2 QB 743; *Gardner v Moore* [1984] AC 548, 560–1.

865 *Fender v St John Mildmay* [1938] AC 1, 13.

courts have become reluctant to 'invent a new head of public policy',[866] particularly where the allegedly harmful tendency raises issues on which Parliament might be expected to legislate.[867] But they retain a creative role 'where the subject matter is "lawyer's law"':[868] eg in extending existing 'heads'[869] and even in occasionally inventing new ones.[870] They also sometimes invalidate contracts or terms on what are essentially public policy grounds without explicitly mentioning the doctrine.[871]

The following paragraphs will describe most of the types of contracts which are **8.220** contrary to public policy. The law relating to another such type of contracts, those in restraint of trade, is so complex as to call for separate discussion.

(b) Types of contracts contrary to public policy

(i) Sexual immorality

A contract is contrary to public policy if its object is to promote sexual immorality. **8.221** This phrase here refers to extra-marital sexual intercourse so that a contract to procure such intercourse is illegal,[872] as also is a contract which indirectly promotes it, such as one to let a brougham to a prostitute to enable her to attract customers.[873] However, now that extra-marital 'cohabitation, whether heterosexual or homosexual, is widespread'[874] agreements between persons who so cohabit in stable relationships are no longer illegal and can give rise to a variety of legal consequences,[875] including contracts if the requirement of contractual intention[876] is satisfied. This is, a fortiori, true where parties of the same sex have entered into a civil partnership under the Civil Partnership Act 2004.

(ii) Freedom of marriage

A promise not to marry or to pay a sum of money in the event of the promisor's **8.222** marriage is invalid as a restraint of marriage.[877] The rule does not apply where the

---

[866] *Janson v Driefontein Consolidated Mines Ltd* [1902] AC 481, 491.

[867] *D v NSPCC* [1978] AC 171, 235; *McFarlane v Tayside Health Board* [2000] 2 AC 59, 100–1.

[868] *D v NSPCC*, n 867 above, 235.

[869] eg in cases such as *Nagle v Feilden* [1966] 1 QB 633; such extensions might also be made under the influence of the Human Rights Act 1998.

[870] eg *Neville v Dominion of Canada News Ltd* [1915] 3 KB 556; *Johnson v Moreton* [1980] AC 37.

[871] eg in some of the rules of construction applied to exemption clauses: see para 8.100.

[872] *Benyon v Nettlefield* (1850) 3 Mac & G 94; cf *Coral Leisure Group Ltd v Barnett* [1981] ICR 503, 508 (where the allegation failed on the facts); *The Siben* [1996] 1 Lloyd's Rep 35, 62.

[873] *Pearce v Brooks* (1866) LR 1 Ex 213.

[874] *Barclays Bank plc v O'Brien* [1994] 1 AC 180, 198.

[875] eg *Tanner v Tanner* [1975] 1 WLR 1346; *Paul v Constance* [1977] 1 WLR 527; *Ghaidan v Mendoza* [2004] UKHL 30; [2004] 2 AC 557.

[876] See para 8.69.

[877] *Baker v White* (1690) 2 Vern 215.

contract may merely deter a person from marrying without containing a promise not to marry: eg to a contract to pay an allowance until marriage.[878] It may also not apply where the restraint was limited in time or otherwise reasonable.

8.223 To prevent the arranging of marriages from being commercialized, contracts by which one person undertakes for a fee to find a spouse for another (known as marriage brokage contracts) are contrary to public policy,[879] even though their harmful tendencies are far from clear.

(iii) Protecting marriages

8.224 Three rules reflect the principle that an agreement tending to weaken the marriage bond is invalid.

8.225 First, damages in an action for breach of promise of marriage could not generally[880] be recovered by a promisee who knew that, when the promise was made, the promisor was already married.[881] Actions for breach of promise of marriage have been abolished[882] but certain rights in property are available to the parties 'where an agreement [between them] to marry is terminated'.[883] These rights can be enforced by a party to the agreement who was already married when it was made;[884] and it follows a fortiori that they can also be enforced by the other party.

8.226 Secondly an agreement between spouses living together[885] which regulates their rights in the event of their future separation is invalid since it is thought to have a tendency to break up the marriage.[886] But, to encourage reconciliation, such an agreement is valid if it forms part of the terms on which previously separated parties are reconciled.[887]

8.227 Thirdly, agreements tending to facilitate divorce, eg by specifying a wife's right to maintenance, were formerly viewed with suspicion;[888] but such agreements are now (collusion being no longer a bar to divorce) positively encouraged by

---

878 Cf *Gibson v Dickie* (1815) 3 M & S 463; *Thomas v Thomas* (1842) 2 QB 851.

879 *Hermann v Charlesworth* [1905] 2 KB 123.

880 For an exception, see *Fender v St John Mildmay* [1938] AC 1 (promise made after decree nisi of divorce).

881 *Spiers v Hunt* [1908] 1 KB 720.

882 Law Reform (Miscellaneous Provisions) Act 1970, s 1. Agreements to enter into civil partnerships likewise have no contractual force: Civil Partnership Act 2004, s 73.

883 Law Reform (Miscellaneous Provisions) Act 1970, s 2. Similar provisions apply where a civil partnership is terminated: Civil Partnership Act 2004, s 74.

884 *Shaw v Fitzgerald* [1992] 1 FLR 357.

885 Not if they are already separated: *Wilson v Wilson* (1848) 1 HLC 538.

886 See *Brodie v Brodie* [1917] P 271 (agreement made *before* the marriage).

887 *Harrison v Harrison* [1910] 1 KB 35.

888 *Churchward v Churchward* [1895] P 7.

the law.[889] They would now be invalid only if they were corrupt bargains intended to deceive the court.[890]

(iv) Parental responsibility

Parental responsibility for a child cannot be surrendered or transferred[891] but may (in effect) be shared between the parents where (because they were not married when the child was born) it was originally in the mother.[892] **8.228**

(v) Excluding jurisdiction of the courts

A contract purporting to exclude the jurisdiction of the courts is invalid at common law since its enforceability could enable parties to evade peremptory rules of law.[893] Accordingly, the rules of an association cannot validly give its committee exclusive power to construe its rules.[894] Similarly, a wife cannot in a separation agreement bind herself, in return for her husband's promise to pay her an allowance, not to apply to the court for maintenance;[895] though, by statute, she can enforce the husband's written promise to make the payment.[896] **8.229**

Arbitration agreements are valid to the extent that they merely require parties to resort to arbitration before going to court.[897] Such an agreement can,[898] and in some cases must,[899] be enforced, normally[900] by staying an action brought in breach of it. At common law, an arbitration agreement was, however, invalid if it deprived parties of their right to go to court on a completed cause of action or if it excluded (or made nugatory) the court's power to control arbitrators' decisions on points of law.[901] By statute, parties are 'free to agree how their disputes are to be resolved';[902] but this principle is 'subject to such safeguards as are necessary in the public interest'[903] and enforcement or recognition of arbitral awards may be refused on grounds of public policy.[904] An appeal also lies from such awards to the **8.230**

---

889 Matrimonial Causes Act 1973, s 33A.
890 See *Sutton v Sutton* [1984] Ch 184, 194.
891 Children Act 1989, s 2(9); cf at common law *Vansittart v Vansittart* (1858) D & J 249, 259.
892 Children Act 1989, ss 2(1), 4(1)(b) and (3), 1(1).
893 See *Anctil v Manufacturers' Life Insurance Co* [1899] AC 604.
894 *Lee v Showmen's Guild of Great Britain* [1952] 2 QB 392.
895 *Hyman v Hyman* [1929] AC 601; and see para 2.144.
896 Matrimonial Causes Act 1973, s 34.
897 *Scott v Avery* (1855) 5 HLC 811.
898 *Channel Tunnel Group Ltd v Balfour Beatty Construction Ltd* [1993] AC 334; Arbitration Act 1996, s 86(2).
899 Arbitration Act 1996, s 9(4).
900 For an exception, see Arbitration Act 1996, s 91 (consumer arbitration agreements).
901 *Czarnikow v Roth Schmidt & Co* [1922] 2 KB 478; *Home and Overseas Insurance Co Ltd v Mentor Insurance Co (UK) Ltd* [1989] 1 Lloyd's Rep 473, 485.
902 Arbitration Act 1996, s 1(b).
903 ibid.
904 ibid, s 81(1)(c).

court on a point of law,[905] but parties to a written arbitration agreement can, by agreement, exclude such judicial control.[906] An appeal is available only if the parties so agree or with the leave of the court.[907] Such leave is to be given only where the point of law substantially affects the rights of one or more of the parties *and* the decision of the arbitrator is *either* obviously wrong *or* raises a point of 'general public importance' and is 'open to serious doubt'; it must also be 'just and proper' for the court to determine the point.[908]

(vi) Perverting the course of justice

8.231 An agreement to compromise a criminal charge may itself amount to an offence[909] and be illegal on that ground; but even where this is not the case such an agreement is generally[910] illegal since the public has an interest in the enforcement of the criminal law.[911] On a similar principle, corrupt bargains relating to non-criminal proceedings in the outcome of which the public has an interest (such as bankruptcy proceedings)[912] are illegal.

(vii) Deceiving public authorities

8.232 A contract is illegal if its object is to deceive the Revenue or other public authorities in their function as tax-gathering bodies.[913]

(viii) Corrupting the public service

8.233 Contracts for the sale of public offices, commissions in the armed forces or honours are illegal.[914] The same is sometimes, but not necessarily, true of contracts which involve 'lobbying' for government contracts.[915]

---

905 ibid, s 69.

906 ibid ss 5(1), 45(1), 69(1); for a restriction see s 87(1). Neither the arbitration agreement nor the exclusion of judicial control is contrary to Human Rights Act 1991, Sch 1 Pt 1 Art 6, guaranteeing 'a fair and public hearing' in the determination of civil rights and obligations: *Stretford v Football Association Ltd* [2007] EWCA Civ 238; [2007] 2 All ER (Comm) 1; *Sumukan Ltd v Commonwealth Secretariat* [2007] EWCA Civ 243; [2007] 2 All ER (Comm) 23.

907 Arbitration Act 1996, ss 45(2), 69(2).

908 ibid s 69(2) and (3).

909 Criminal Law Act 1967, ss 1, 5(1) (concealing arrestable offence).

910 For an exception, see *Fisher & Co v Apollinaris Co* (1875) LR 10 Ch App 297.

911 eg *R v Panayiotou* [1974] 3 All ER 112.

912 *Elliott v Richardson* (1870) LR 5 CP 744; cf *Kearly v Thomson* (1890) 24 QBD 742.

913 *Alexander v Rayson* [1936] 1 KB 169; *Miller v Karlinski* (1945) 62 TLR 85; contrast *21st Century Logistics Solutions v Madysen Ltd* [2004] EWHC 231 (QB); [2004] 2 Lloyd's Rep 92, where a seller's intention to defraud the Revenue of VAT was said to be 'too remote' from the contract to render it 'unenforceable on the ground of illegality' (at [19]).

914 *Garforth v Fearon* (1787) 1 H Bl 327; *Morris v McCullock* (1763) Amb 432; *Parkinson v College of Ambulance Ltd* [1925] 2 KB 1 (and see Honours (Prevention of Abuses) Act 1925).

915 Contrast *Lemenda Trading Co Ltd v African Middle East Petroleum Co Ltd* [1988] QB 448 with *Tekron Resources Ltd v Guinea Investments Co* [2003] EWHC 2577 (Comm); [2004] 2 Lloyd's Rep 26 at [101].

(ix) Trading with an enemy

It is a statutory offence to trade with an 'enemy' of war;[916] and a contract involving such trading is illegal at common law.[917]   **8.234**

(x) Foreign relations

A contract is illegal if its object is to do an act in a friendly foreign country which is illegal by its law.[918]   **8.235**

(xi) Undue restraints on personal liberty

A contract may, in extreme cases, be illegal because it unduly restricts the personal liberty of a party: eg if a contract of loan imposes such restrictions on the borrower as reduce him to a quasi-servile condition.[919]   **8.236**

(c) Restraint of trade

At common law, contract terms in restraint of trade are prima facie void because of their tendency to cause hardship to the party restrained and injury to the public;[920] but they are valid if reasonable and not contrary to the public interest. They can be divided into the following categories; some of them are also prohibited by legislation governing competition law.[921]   **8.237**

(i) Sale of a business and employment

The validity of a covenant by the seller of a business not to compete with his buyer and of one by a former employee not to compete with his ex-employer depends on the following three factors: **8.238**

A 'proprietary interest'.   The buyer of a business pays for, amongst other things, the goodwill of that business; and his interest in that goodwill is 'proprietary' in the sense of being to some extent protected even in the absence of a covenant.[922] This interest does not extend to other businesses already carried on by him at the time of the contract; or to businesses which he proposes to carry on thereafter.[923] An employer's 'proprietary interest' is more narrowly defined. It does not arise merely because he would suffer from the employee's competitive use of skills   **8.239**

---

916 Trading with the Enemy Act 1939.
917 *Sovfracht (V/O) v Van Udens etc* [1943] AC 203.
918 eg *Foster v Driscoll* [1929] 1 KB 470.
919 *Horwood v Millar's Timber and Trading Co Ltd* [1917] 1 KB 305.
920 *Mitchell v Reynolds* (1711) P Wms 181, 190.
921 See para 8.247.
922 *Trego v Hunt* [1896] AC 7.
923 See *Nordenfelt v Maxim Nordenfelt Guns & Ammunitions Co* [1894] AC 535.

acquired during employment.[924] The employer must normally [925] show *either* that
the employee has come into contact with his customers or clients so as to acquire
influence over them *or* that the employee has learned his 'trade secrets' (such as
secret processes) or certain kinds of highly confidential information.[926] Where the
relationship of the parties is neither that of vendor and purchaser nor that of
employer and employee, the relative bargaining power of the parties is taken into
account in defining the interest. Thus the vendor-purchaser test has been applied
to agreements between professional partners,[927] and the employer-employee test
to one between a comparatively unknown song-writer and his publisher.[928]

8.240 **Reasonableness.** Reasonableness depends primarily on the relation between
the restraint and the 'interest' meriting protection, so that the reasonableness of
the *area* of the restraint depends on the area in which the business to be protected
was carried on;[929] and its reasonableness in point of *time* depends on the period for
which that business was likely to keep its clientele.[930] In employment cases, the
courts are more likely to uphold 'solicitation covenants' (against soliciting the
employer's customers) than 'area covenants' (against working in a designated
area).[931] A lifelong area covenant[932] is now unlikely to be enforced[933] but the same
is not true of a lifelong restraint on the disclosure of confidential information[934]
since this does not prevent the ex-employee from working for others.

8.241 In determining the issue of reasonableness, the court also has regard to the adequacy of the consideration given for the restraint and to its fairness to the weaker
party where there is inequality of bargaining power.[935] These requirements must
be satisfied in addition to those stated in paragraph 8.240.

---

924 *Herbert Morris Ltd v Saxelby* [1916] 1 AC 688.

925 For other possible (non-'proprietary') interests, see *Eastham v Newcastle United Football Club
Ltd* [1964] Ch 413.

926 *Faccenda Chicken Ltd v Fowler* [1987] Ch 117; these interests are 'proprietary' in the sense
that they are to some extent protected even in the absence of a covenant: cf at n 922 above.

927 See *Kerr v Morris* [1987] Ch 90.

928 *Schroeder Music Publishing Co Ltd v Macaulay* [1974] 1 WLR 1308.

929 Contrast the *Nordenfelt* case (n 923 above) with *Mason v Provident Clothing & Supply Co Ltd*
[1913] AC 74.

930 See *M & S Draper Ltd v Reynolds* [1957] 1 WLR 9.

931 See *SW Strange Ltd v Mann* [1965] 1 WLR 629; *Gledhow Autoparts Ltd v Delaney* [1965]
1 WLR 1366; *T Lucas & Co Ltd v Mitchell* [1974] Ch 129; contrast *Hollis & Co v Stocks* [2000]
IRLR 712 (one year covenant operating within 10 mile radius enforced).

932 As in *Fitch v Dewes* [1921] 2 AC 158; contrast *Bridge v Deacons* [1984] AC 705 (fixed term
solicitation covenant).

933 See *Fellowes & Son v Fisher* [1976] QB 122.

934 *A-G v Barker* [1990] 3 All ER 257; *A-G v Blake* [2001] 1 AC 688.

935 *Nordenfelt* case (n 923 above) 565; *A Schroeder Music Publishing Co Ltd v Macaulay* [1974]
1 WLR 1308.

Public interest.　A restraint which satisfies the requirement of reasonableness　**8.242**
is nevertheless invalid if it is contrary to the interests of the public.[936] The two
requirements are not easy to separate; but where the party restrained possessed
some skill for which there was an unsatisfied public need[937] the restraint might be
contrary to the public interest even though it was 'reasonable'.

(ii) Restrictive trading agreements

At common law, such agreements restricting competition between suppliers of　**8.243**
goods and services are subject to the restraint of trade doctrine[938] but differ from
agreements of the kind discussed above in that the interest meriting protection
may be a purely 'commercial', as opposed to a 'proprietary' one.[939] Such agreements were, moreover, not often struck down for unreasonableness,[940] the courts
being generally content to give effect to agreements made between parties bargaining on equal terms.[941] This approach did little to protect third parties who
might be prejudiced by the operation of the agreement. Occasionally such prejudice was taken into account and the agreement struck down at the suit of a party
to it as contrary to the public interest;[942] and to a limited extent the common law
was able to give relief to third parties prejudiced by its operation.[943]

(iii) Exclusive dealing

Exclusive dealing agreements (such as agreements not to buy or sell goods of a cer-　**8.244**
tain description except from or to a specified person, or 'sole agency' agreements)
were only rarely subjected to the restraint of trade doctrine. This approach
was, however, challenged in a line of cases relating to 'solus' agreements by which
garage owners undertook, usually in return for financial help in developing their
premises, to buy petrol only from the oil company providing this help, and to
accept various other restrictions. Such agreements were held to be within the
restraint of trade doctrine,[944] though that doctrine would still not apply to
agreements which 'merely regulate the normal commercial relation between the
parties',[945] such as most sole agency (or distributorship) agreements. Where an

---

[936] *Wyatt v Kreglinger & Fernau* [1933] 1 KB 793; *Bull v Pitney-Bowes Ltd* [1967] 1 WLR 273.
[937] eg *Dranez Anstalt v Hayek* [2002] EWCA Civ 1729; [200] 1 BCC 278 at [25].
[938] *McEllistrims* case [1919] AC 548.
[939] See ibid 564.
[940] ibid.
[941] *English Hop Growers v Dering* [1928] 2 KB 174.
[942] *Kores Manufacturing Co Ltd v Kolok Manufacturing Co Ltd* [1959] Ch 108.
[943] *Eastham v Newcastle United Football Club Ltd* [1964] Ch 413; *Nagle v Feilden* [1966] 2 QB
633; *R v Jockey Club, ex p RAM Racecourses Ltd* [1993] 2 All ER 225; *R v Disciplinary Committee of
the Jockey Club, ex p Aga Khan* [1993] 1 WLR 909.
[944] *Esso Petroleum Co Ltd v Harper's Garage (Stourport) Ltd* [1968] AC 269; undertakings given
by major oil companies now regulate such agreements.
[945] *Esso* case (n 944 above) 327; ibid 328.

exclusive dealing agreement is within the doctrine, the normal requirements for its validity must be satisfied: that is, there must be an 'interest' meriting protection (though a 'commercial' interest suffices);[946] the agreement must be 'reasonable' (a requirement that may lead to an enquiry into its fairness)[947] and it must not be contrary to the public interest.[948]

(iv) Restrictions on land use

8.245 Land may be sold subject to restriction on its use, such as prohibitions against building or trading there. These are not normally subject to the restraint of trade doctrine; and one reason for this position is that the purchaser had 'no previous right to be there' and so he gives up 'no right or freedom which he previously had'.[949] This reasoning, however, ignores the possibility that a restriction imposed on a purchaser may be contrary to the public interest; and legislation makes it possible for such a restriction to be discharged (on payment of compensation) if it 'would impede some reasonable user of the land for public or private purposes'.[950]

(v) Other agreements

8.246 The categories of restraint of trade are not closed[951] and restrictive trading agreements not within any of the groups described above may be invalid by statute[952] or be subject at common law to the restraint of trade doctrine if they have the effect of 'fettering a person's freedom in the future to carry on his trade, business or profession'.[953] Such agreements are not necessarily invalid at common law, but they do require justification under the restraint of trade doctrine.

(vi) Competition law

8.247 Certain agreements affecting trade are prohibited and void under European Community legislation and the Competition Act 1998.[954] These prohibitions can apply to some agreements which are subject to the restraint of trade doctrine at

---

946 ibid.

947 *A Schroeder Music Publishing Co Ltd v Macaulay* [1974] 1 WLR 1308; *Watson v Prager* [1991] 1 WLR 726.

948 *Esso* case (n 944 above), 321, 324, 341.

949 ibid, 298.

950 Law of Property Act 1925, s 84.

951 *Esso* case (n 944 above) 337.

952 Auction (Bidding Agreements) Act 1927.

953 *Shearson Lehman Hutton Inc v MacLaine Watson & Co Ltd* [1989] 2 Lloyd's Rep 570, 615; eg *World Wide Fund for Nature v World Wrestling Foundation* [2002] EWCA Civ 196; [2002] UKCLR 338.

954 European Community Treaty, Art 81 (formerly Art 85); Competition Act 1998, Chapter I; ss 47A and 47B of the Act provide for the payment of compensation to persons who suffer loss or damage as a result of an infringement of its provisions.

common law but they apply only to agreements if their effect on competition is an 'appreciable' as opposed to an 'insignificant' one in percentage terms.[955] They are concerned with the adverse effects of agreements on the economy as a whole, while the common law is at least equally concerned with their effects on the party restrained. An agreement which fails to satisfy the common law tests of validity but satisfies those imposed by Community law cannot be struck down in England for failure to comply with the common law rules.[956]

(3) *Effects of Illegality*

(a) Enforcement

Illegality may prevent the enforcement of a contract (or where, as in the restraint of trade cases, illegality affects only one term of it, the enforcement of that term). A court will never order a party to do the act which is illegal but it may sometimes award damages for failure to do it or enforce the other party's counter-promise.   **8.248**

(i) *Position of guilty party*

A guilty party cannot enforce the contract,[957] even though the other party is equally guilty and so gets the windfall of receiving the former's performance for nothing. The rule has been justified on the ground that 'the courts will not lend their aid to such [ie a guilty] plaintiff',[958] but it can operate harshly[959] where the plaintiff is morally innocent because the offence in question is one of strict liability or he is acting under a mistake of law. Its severity is mitigated in various ways: eg by holding that a person is not a 'guilty' party for this purpose merely because the contemplated[960] or even the actual[961] method of performance is unlawful; by allowing him to sue the other party for a tort independent of the contract;[962] and occasionally by legislation.[963]   **8.249**

---

[955] *Völk v Ets Vervaeke* [1969] CMLR 273; cf *Passmore v Morland plc* [1999] 3 All ER 1005.

[956] *Days Medical Aids Ltd v Pihsiang Machinery Manufacturing Co Ltd* [2004] EWHC 44 (Comm); [2004] 1 All ER (Comm) 991 at [254] to [265].

[957] eg *Pearce v Brooks* (1866) LR 1 Ex 213; *Cowan v Milburn* (1867) LR 2 Ex 230.

[958] *Holman v Johnson* (1775) 1 Cowp 341, 343; and see *Tinsley v Milligan* [1994] 1 AC 340, 358–61, 363–4.

[959] The rule is, however, not affected by Human Rights Act 1998, Sch 1 Pt II: *Shanshal v Al Kishtaini* [2001] EWCA Civ 264; [2001] 2 All ER (Comm) 601.

[960] *Waugh v Morris* (1873) LR 8 QB 202.

[961] *St John Shipping Corp v Joseph Rank Ltd* [1957] 1 QB 267. But the claim would have been barred if the claimant had 'knowingly participated' in the illegal method of performance: *Hall v Woolston Hall Leisure Ltd* [2001] 1 WLR 215, 234.

[962] *Saunders v Edwards* [1987] 1 WLR 1116.

[963] eg Road Traffic Act 1988, ss 65(1), 75(7).

(ii) Position of innocent party

8.250　An illegal contract cannot be enforced by a person who is innocent merely in the sense of being ignorant of or mistaken about the rule of law giving rise to the illegality.[964] When a party is innocent because of his ignorance of relevant facts, some cases have allowed,[965] while others have rejected,[966] his claim. The two groups of cases can perhaps be reconciled on the ground that in the former (but not in the latter) the purpose of the rule of law infringed was merely to impose penalties on the offender, and not to invalidate contracts. An alternative distinction between the two groups may be that the court is more likely to put the innocent party into the position in which he would have been if the contract had *not been made*[967] than into that in which he would have been if it had been *performed*.[968] Where the illegality arises from legislation for the protection of a class its purpose is not promoted by denying a remedy to an innocent member of that class; and in some such cases such a person is by statute given the right to enforce the contract.[969]

8.251　An innocent party may be entitled to restitution in respect of benefits conferred on the other under the illegal contract[970] or to damages in tort where he has been induced to enter into contract by a misrepresentation as to its legality.[971] These remedies differ from enforcement of the contract in that they will not compensate the claimant for loss of his expectation interest.[972] The innocent party may also be entitled to damages for breach of a 'collateral warranty' that the main contract was lawful.[973] These damages are equal to the amount that he could have recovered under the main contract, had it not been illegal. It is not easy to see why, if the public interest bars such recovery, the same amount should be recoverable under the 'collateral warranty'; and, if there is no such public interest bar, it would be better to allow a claim on the main contract.

(b) Severance

(i) Severance of promises

8.252　Where one party's promises are only partly illegal, that part can be severed, and the lawful part enforced, if three conditions are satisfied. First, the illegal promise

---

964　*Nash v Stevenson Transport Ltd* [1936] 2 KB 128.

965　*Bloxsome v Williams* (1824) 3 B & C 232; *Archbolds (Freightage) Ltd v Spanglett Ltd* [1961] 1 QB 374.

966　*Re Mahmoud and Ispahani* [1921] 2 KB 716.

967　This was the nature of the claim in the cases cited in n 965 above.

968　This was the nature of the claim in the case cited in n 966 above.

969　Financial Services and Markets Act 2000, ss 26, 27, 28, 30.

970　See para 8.255 et seq.

971　*Shelley v Paddock* [1980] QB 348.

972　See para 8.04.

973　*Strongman (1945) Ltd v Sincock* [1955] 2 QB 525.

must not be so seriously illegal as to contaminate the whole contract: eg it must not be one for the deliberate commission of a crime.[974] Secondly, under the so-called 'blue pencil' test, it must be possible to sever the illegal part by merely deleting words: the promise cannot be in some other way redrafted so as to make it lawful.[975] Thirdly, severance must not change the nature of the contract so as to turn it into a transaction wholly different from that intended by the parties.[976] Even where parts of an illegal promise cannot be severed, other unrelated parts of the contract may remain enforceable: for example, an employee who has made a wholly void promise in restraint of trade can be restrained from breach of his duty of fidelity.[977] The contract as a whole will be invalid only if its main object was to secure the illegal restraint.[978]

(ii) Severance of consideration

A partly illegal promise may constitute the consideration for a counter-promise, usually to pay for the former promise or its performance. On a claim to enforce the counter-promise, the question then arises whether the illegal part of the consideration for it can be severed. This cannot be done if that part constituted the whole or a substantial part of the consideration for the counter-promise;[979] but if the main part of the consideration was lawful, then that promise can be enforced even though there was also some subsidiary illegal consideration for it[980] (unless that part involved the deliberate commission of a criminal or immoral act).[981] The subsidiary part is not strictly severed (but simply disregarded) since the counter-promise is enforced in full: eg where an employee who has entered into too wide a covenant in restraint of trade recovers his wages.[982]

8.253

(c) Collateral transactions

The illegality of one contract may infect another (itself lawful) contract if the latter helps in the performance of the former, or if its enforcement would amount to indirect enforcement of the illegal one: thus a loan of money is illegal if it is made to enable the borrower to make or to perform an illegal contract.[983] But a contract

8.254

---

[974] See *Bennett v Bennett* [1952] 1 KB 249, 252.

[975] *Mason v Provident Clothing & Supply Co Ltd* [1913] 2 AC 724.

[976] *Attwood v Lamont* [1920] 3 KB 571.

[977] *Commercial Plastics Ltd v Vincent* [1965] 1 QB 623.

[978] *Amoco Australia Pty v Rocca Bros Motor Engineering Pty Ltd* [1975] AC 561; contrast *Alec Lobb (Garages) Ltd v Total Oil (Great Britain) Ltd* [1985] 1 WLR 173.

[979] *Lound v Grimwade* (1888) 39 Ch D 605.

[980] See *Goodinson v Goodinson* [1954] 2 QB 118 (actual decision obsolete since Matrimonial Causes Act 1973, s 34).

[981] *Bennett v Bennett* (n 974 above, 254).

[982] *Carney v Herbert* [1985] AC 301, 311.

[983] *De Begnis v Armistead* (1833) 10 Bing 107; *Spector v Ageda* [1973] Ch 30.

is not illegal merely because one of the parties to it is also a party to a second illegal contract remotely connected with the first.[984]

(d) Restitution

(i) General rule: no recovery of money or property

8.255 A party who cannot enforce an illegal contract cannot as a general rule recover back money paid or property transferred by him under it.[985] The rule is meant to deter the making of illegal contracts, but where the claimant is innocent, it scarcely achieves this result; and where the defendant runs an illegal business, deterrence is more likely to be promoted by allowing than by dismissing restitution claims against him. The rule is therefore subject to many exceptions.

(ii) Exceptions

8.256 **Class-protecting statutes.** Statutes passed for the protection of a class of persons (such as tenants) sometimes expressly provide that members of that class can recover back payments made by them in breach of the statute.[986] Such a right of recovery also exists at common law, even in the absence of such express statutory provisions.[987]

8.257 **Illegal contract made under pressure.** Recovery of money paid or property transferred is sometimes allowed on the ground that the claimant was 'forced' to enter into the contract, either by the other party[988] or by pressure of extraneous circumstances.[989] The pressure must be such as to make it in the court's view excusable for the claimant to enter into the illegal contract.[990]

8.258 **Fraud or mistake inducing the illegal contract.** Money paid or property transferred can be reclaimed by a person who was induced to enter into the contract by a fraudulent misrepresentation as to its legality.[991] This right does not extend to cases in which the misrepresentation was innocent,[992] though if the claimant is entitled to, and does, rescind the contract for misrepresentation,[993] he can then recover back the money or property on that ground. This course would not

---

984 *Euro-Diam Ltd v Bathurst* [1990] QB 1; contrast *Re Trepca Mines Ltd* [1963] Ch 199 (on the illegality of such a contract now, see para 8.211).

985 eg *Scott v Brown* [1892] 2 QB 724.

986 Rent Act 1977, ss 57, 95, 125; *Gray v Southouse* [1949] 2 All ER 1019.

987 *Kiriri Cotton Ltd v Dewani* [1960] AC 192.

988 *Atkinson v Denby* (1862) 7 H & N 934.

989 *Kiriri Cotton* case (n 987 above) 205; *Liebman v Rosenthal* 57 NYS 2d 875 (1945).

990 *Bigos v Bousted* [1951] 1 All ER 92 (where this requirement was not satisfied).

991 *Hughes v Liverpool Victoria Legal Friendly Society* [1916] 2 KB 482.

992 *Harse v Pearl Life Assurance Co* [1904] 1 KB 558.

993 See para 8.175.

normally be open to him where one of the bars to rescission had arisen;[994] but these seem not to apply where the restitution claim is based, not on misrepresentation, but on illegality.[995]

A payment is recoverable by a person who made it under a mistake (shared by both parties) as to the circumstances affecting the legality of the contract.[996] **8.259**

'Repentance'.   The law seeks to encourage a party to give up the 'illegal purpose' **8.260** by allowing him to recover money or property if he 'repent[s] before it is too late'.[997] To bring this rule into operation it is first necessary for the claimant to 'repent': it is not enough for the illegal purpose to be simply frustrated by the defendant's failure or refusal to perform.[998] Secondly, the repentance must come 'before it is too late'; and it will be too late if it comes after the illegal purpose or a substantial part of it has been carried out.[999] But the mere fact that acts have been done in preparation for achieving the illegal purpose is not a bar to the restitution claim.[1000]

No reliance on the contract or its illegality.   Money paid or property transferred **8.261** under an illegal contract can be recovered back if the claimant can establish his right or title to it without relying on the contract or on its illegality.[1001] If, for example, a thing is pledged or let out under an illegal contract, that contract can transfer a special property to the bailee notwithstanding its illegality; and so long as that special property endures, the owner cannot recover back the thing.[1002] But once the special property has come to an end the owner can recover back the thing by simply relying on his title: eg when the term of hire has expired or where the hirer's right to retain the thing has come to an automatic end in consequence of the hirer's breach.[1003] Where, by contrast, goods are *sold* under an illegal contract, the *entire* property in them can pass to the buyer notwithstanding the illegality.[1004] The seller then has no title left on which to rely (eg in the event of the buyer's failure to pay in accordance with agreed credit terms). A payment of money likewise normally vests the entire property in the payee so that the payor cannot recover it back by relying on his title except where the money is not paid out but only deposited with a stakeholder.[1005]

---

[994] See para 8.180–87.

[995] In the fraud cases described at n 991 above.

[996] *Oom v Bruce* (1810) 12 East 225; for the view that mistake of one suffices, see *Edler v Auerbach* [1950] 1 KB 359, 374 (*sed quaere*).

[997] *Harry Parker Ltd v Mason* [1940] 2 KB 590, 609.

[998] *Bigos v Bousted* [1951] 1 All ER 92.

[999] *Kearly v Thomson* (1890) 24 QBD 742.

[1000] *Taylor v Bowers* (1876) 1 QBD 291; *Tribe v Tribe* [1996] Ch 107.

[1001] *Bowmakers Ltd v Barnet Instruments Ltd* [1945] KB 65, 71.

[1002] *Taylor v Chester* (1869) LR 4 QB 309.

[1003] *Bowmakers* case (n 1001 above).

[1004] *Singh v Ali* [1960] AC 167.

[1005] *O'Sullivan v Thomas* [1895] 1 QB 698 (money deposited under a contract then void).

8.262   Where the claim is made by a transferee, he will have to rely on the contract but may nevertheless succeed if he does not have to rely on its illegality. For example, a buyer of goods to whom property has passed under an illegal contract but to whom the goods have not been delivered can recover them from a third party (to whom they have been delivered),[1006] or from a person who takes them away from him,[1007] on the strength of his title.

8.263   The principles stated in paragraphs 8.261 and 8.262 also apply where the title acquired is an equitable one and can be established without relying on the illegality;[1008] though whether it can be so established sometimes depends on highly technical distinctions which determine whether property acquired by (or with means provided by) A in B's name is presumed to be held by B on trust for A or intended as a gift to B.[1009] Such distinctions have little relevance to the policy of the rule of law, the violation of which makes the contract illegal. Even where, under them, there is no right of recovery, there may be one under another of the grounds discussed above: eg on the ground of 'repentance'.[1010]

8.264   The principle of recovery without reliance on the contract or its illegality may not apply where the thing is such that it is unlawful to deal with it at all.[1011]

(iii) Scope of general rule

8.265   The general rule stated in paragraph 8.255 has been held not to apply to marriage brokage contracts,[1012] perhaps reflecting an earlier equitable view[1013] which rejected that rule, and giving rise to the possibility of reviving this view where to do so would promote the policy of the invalidating rule.

I. Lack of Capacity

8.266   This section deals with the contractual capacity of natural persons; corporate contractual capacity is discussed in Chapter 3 of this book.

[1006] *Belvoir Finance Co Ltd v Stapleton* [1971] 1 QB 210.

[1007] *Singh v Ali* [1960] AC 167.

[1008] *Tinsley v Milligan* [1994] 1 AC 340.

[1009] Contrast *Tinsley v Milligan* (n 1008 above) with *Chettiar v Chettiar* [1962] AC 294. In *Tinsley v Milligan* the first of the presumptions referred to in the text was applied when a house occupied by an unmarried cohabiting couple had been conveyed into the names of *one* of them. In *Stack v Dowden* [2007] UKHL 17; [2007] 2 WLR 831 the majority of the House of Lords regarded the presumption as no longer dispositive of the rights of such a couple where the house had been conveyed into the joint names of *both* of them.

[1010] *Tribe v Tribe* [1996] Ch 107.

[1011] *Bowmakers'* case (n 1001 above) 72 (obscene book); see also *The Siben (No 2)* [1996] 1 Lloyd's Rep 35, 62 (consideration for such subject matter; *sed quaere*).

[1012] *Hermann v Charlesworth* [1905] 2 KB 123.

[1013] *Morris v McCullock* (1763) Amb 432.

(1) Minors

Minors are persons below the age of 18. The law limits their contractual capacity **8.267** so as to protect them against bargains which are unfair or improvident; at the same time, it seeks to avoid unnecessary injustice to adults who deal fairly with minors. The practical importance of the subject has been reduced by the lowering of the age of majority[1014] (formerly 21) and by changing social conditions;[1015] but it is far from negligible in relation to (for example) employment contracts and the activities of under-age entertainers or athletes.

(a) Valid contracts

(i) Necessaries

A minor is bound by contracts for necessaries; his liability was said to arise for his **8.268** own good,[1016] on the (not altogether convincing) theory that the supplier would not give credit unless he could enforce liability. Necessaries include goods[1017] and services (such as education and medical or legal services)[1018] supplied to the minor. They are not confined to necessities but extend to goods or services suitable to maintain the minor in 'the state, station and degree. . .in which he is';[1019] but 'mere luxuries'[1020] cannot be necessaries. The supplier must show that the goods or services are not only capable of being, but that they actually are, necessaries at the time at which they are, or are to be,[1021] supplied.[1022] The minor is liable for no more than a reasonable price[1023] where this is less than the contract price. If an adult pays the supplier, the minor must reimburse the payor[1024] (to the extent that the charge was reasonable); and if an adult lends money to the minor to enable him to pay for necessaries the lender can sue on the loan to the extent that it is so used.[1025] Legislation relating to the maintenance of children by absent parents[1026] does not directly affect a minor's liability for necessaries but may indirectly do so if it results in his being adequately supplied with the goods and services in question.

[1014] Family Reform Act 1969, ss 1, 9.

[1015] See *Allen v Bloomsbury Health Authority* [1993] 1 All ER 651, 661.

[1016] *Ryder v Wombwell* (1868) LR 4 Ex 32, 38.

[1017] Sale of Goods Act 1979, s 3(2), as amended by the Mental Capacity Act 2005, s 67(1) and Sch 6, para 14.

[1018] *Helps v Clayton* (1864) 17 CBNS 553; *Roberts v Gray* [1913] 1 KB 250; *Sherdley v Sherdley* [1988] AC 213, 225.

[1019] *Peters v Flemming* (1840) 6 M & W 42, 46.

[1020] *Chapple v Cooper* (1844) 13 M & W 252, 258.

[1021] See *Roberts v Gray* (n 1018 above); *Nash v Inman* [1908] 2 KB 1, 12.

[1022] *Nash v Inman* (n 1021 above).

[1023] Sale of Goods Act 1979, s 3(2), as to which see n 1017 above.

[1024] *Earle v Peale* (1712) 10 Mod 67.

[1025] *Marlow v Pitfeild* (1719) 1 P Wms 558.

[1026] Child Support Act 1991, s 1(1); see also Children Act 1989, s 15 and Sch 5, discussed in Chapter 2.

(ii) Employment and analogous contracts

8.269 A minor is bound by a contract of employment if it is on the whole for his benefit.[1027] So long as this requirement is satisfied, he is bound even though some terms of the contract are disadvantageous to him,[1028] so long as they are not harsh and oppressive.[1029] These principles apply also where the minor is not strictly an employee but enters into a contract by which he makes a living as (for example) an athlete, author or entertainer.[1030] But he is not liable under 'trading contracts': eg where goods are sold by,[1031] or supplied to,[1032] him in the course of his business.

(b) Voidable contracts

8.270 For reasons which are not altogether clear, a minor is in some cases bound by a contract unless he repudiates it. This rule applies where he agrees to buy or sell land[1033] or to take or grant a lease of land;[1034] where he incurs liability for calls on shares in a company;[1035] where he enters into a contract of partnership;[1036] and where he enters into a marriage settlement.[1037] He must repudiate during minority or within a reasonable time of his majority.[1038] Repudiation relieves him from future liabilities[1039] but does not entitle him to recover money paid or property transferred by him under the contract[1040] unless the effect of the repudiation is to bring about a 'total failure of consideration'.

(c) Other contracts

8.271 A contract outside the categories discussed in paragraphs 8.268 to 8.270 does not bind the minor unless he ratifies it after reaching full age;[1041] but it does bind the

---

1027 *Clements v London & North Western Rly* [1894] 2 QB 482; *Mills v IRC* [1975] AC 38, 53; for statutory regulation, see, for example, Employment of Children Act 1973.

1028 As in the *Clements* case (n 1027 above).

1029 *De Francesco v Barnum* (1889) 43 Ch D 165; cf *Goodwin v Uzoigwee* [1993] Fam Law 65.

1030 *Doyle v White City Stadium Ltd* [1935] KB 10; *Chaplin v Leslie Frewin (Publishers) Ltd* [1966] Ch 71.

1031 *Cowern v Nield* [1912] 2 KB 491.

1032 *Mercantile Union Guarantee Corp Ltd v Bell* [1937] 2 KB 498.

1033 *Whittingham v Murdy* (1889) 60 LT 956; *Orakpo v Manson Investments Ltd* [1978] AC 95, 106.

1034 *Davies v Beynon-Harris* (1931) 47 TLR 424.

1035 *North-Western Rly v M'Michael* (1850) 5 Ex 114.

1036 See *Lovell & Christmas v Beauchamp* [1894] AC 607. The Limited Liability Partnership Act 2000 does not refer to minors.

1037 *Edwards v Carter* [1893] AC 360.

1038 ibid.

1039 There are conflicting views on the question whether repudiation also has retrospective effects: see *North-Western Rly v M'Michael* (n 1035 above) 125; *Steinberg v Scala (Leeds) Ltd* [1923] 2 Ch 452, 463.

1040 *Steinberg v Scala (Leeds) Ltd* (n 1039 above).

1041 See *Williams v Moor* (1843) 11 M & W 256.

other party.[1042] Money paid or property transferred by the minor under such a contract cannot be recovered back by him merely on the ground that the contract did not bind him;[1043] while conversely property in goods which are its subject matter can pass to the minor by delivery in pursuance of the contract.[1044] Property can similarly pass *from* him under such a contract.[1045]

(d) Liability in tort

A minor's contractual incapacity cannot be circumvented by suing him in tort **8.272** merely because the act constituting a breach of an invalid contract amounts also to a tort.[1046] He is liable in tort only for doing something wholly outside the scope of the acts envisaged by the parties when they made the contract.[1047]

(e) Liability in restitution

A minor can sometimes be ordered to make restitution in respect of benefits **8.273** obtained by him under a contract which cannot be enforced against him because of his minority.

(i) Minors' Contracts Act 1987, s 3(1)

In the situation just described, this subsection gives the court a discretion 'if it is **8.274** just and equitable to do so' to 'require [the minor] to transfer to the [other party] any property[1048] acquired by the [minor] under the contract, or any property representing it'. Thus if non-necessary goods have been delivered to the minor and not paid for, he can be ordered to restore them; if he has resold them, he can be ordered to restore the money or an object bought with it. But no such order can be made once he has dissipated the thing obtained or its proceeds since in that case there is no longer any 'property obtained' or 'property representing it' on which the order can operate. The order must be one to *restore* property, not to *pay* for it out of the minor's other assets. Where proceeds have been paid into the minor's bank account, the distinction between these two concepts may be hard to draw; and the court will in such cases make the order only if to do so will not amount to indirect enforcement of the invalid contract.

[1042] *Bruce v Warwick* (1815) 6 Taunt 118; but *specific* performance is not available to the minor: *Flight v Bolland* (1828) 4 Russ 298.

[1043] *Wilson v Kearse* (1800) Peake Add Cas 196; *Corpe v Overton* (1833) 10 Bing 252, 259.

[1044] *Stocks v Wilson* [1913] 2 KB 235, 246.

[1045] *Chaplin v Leslie Frewin (Publishers) Ltd* [1966] Ch 71.

[1046] *Fawcett v Smethurst* (1914) 84 LJKB 473.

[1047] *Burnard v Haggis* (1863) 14 CBNS 45; *Ballet v Mingay* [1943] KB 281.

[1048] 'Property' here includes money: see Law of Contract, Minors' Contracts (Law Com No 134, 1984) para 4.21.

(ii) Effects of minor's fraud

8.275 A minor is not liable on a contract merely because he had procured it by a fraudu-lent misrepresentation (typically as to his age);[1049] nor does the misrepresentation make him liable in tort[1050] for the value of what he had obtained.[1051] In equity, such fraud gives rise to liability to restore what has been obtained;[1052] but there is no need to resort to this jurisdiction now that such restitution is available, without proof of fraud, under the Minors' Contracts Act 1987.[1053] The interest of the equity cases lies in their insistence on the nature of the liability as being (like that under the Act) one to *restore* (not to *pay* for) benefits obtained. Hence to the extent that those benefits have been dissipated there is no liability to restore in equity.[1054]

(iii) Restitution at common law

8.276 A minor may be liable to make restitution in respect of a benefit obtained by him under an invalid contract: eg where he has been paid for goods sold by him under a trading contract but not delivered. According to one case,[1055] he is so liable only where he is guilty of fraud; but it would be more appropriate to restrict the remedy to cases where the benefit so obtained, or its proceeds, remained in his hands so that, where the benefit had been dissipated, the liability could not be enforced against his other assets.[1056] In the absence of fraud, the adult could seek restitution under the 1987 Act;[1057] but that remedy is discretionary while the common law remedy, which is preserved by s 3(2) of the Act, lies (where available) as of right.

(2) Mental Patients

(a) General

8.277 A contract with a mental patient[1058] is valid[1059] except in two situations. First, if the other party knows that the patient's disability prevented him from under-standing the transaction,[1060] the contract can be avoided by the patient.[1061]

1049 *Bartlett v Wells* (1862) 1 B & S 836.
1050 See para 8.272.
1051 *R Leslie Ltd v Sheill* [1914] 3 KB 607.
1052 *Clarke v Cobley* (1789) 2 Cox 173.
1053 See para 8.274.
1054 *R Leslie Ltd v Sheill* (n 1051 above) 619, doubting this aspect of *Stocks v Wilson* [1913] 2 KB 235, 247.
1055 *Cowern v Nield* [1912] 2 KB 419.
1056 Cf paras 8.274 and 8.275.
1057 See para 8.274.
1058 A convenient expression to refer to a 'person who lacks capacity because of an impairment of, or a disturbance in the functioning of, the mind or brain' within Mental Capacity Act 2005, s 2.
1059 *Hart v O'Connor* [1985] AC 1000.
1060 See *Re K* [1988] Ch 310.
1061 *Imperial Loan Co v Stone* [1892] 1 QB 599.

Secondly, if the patient's disorder is so serious that his property is subject to the control of the court, then he is not[1062] (though the other party is)[1063] bound by the contract if it purports to dispose of the property or (perhaps) otherwise interferes with the court's control over it. A contract which does not initially bind the patient becomes binding on him by his ratification of it after he is cured.[1064]

(b) Necessaries

Under the rules stated in paragraph 8.277, a mental patient may be bound by a contract for necessaries; but where he is not so bound he must nevertheless pay a reasonable price for them.[1065] There is no such liability where medical treatment is supplied under the National Health Service,[1066] though such cases can give rise to the question whether the treatment is lawful in spite of the patient's lack of capacity to consent to it.[1067] **8.278**

(3) Drink or Drugs

A person cannot escape from liability on a contract merely because, when he made it, his commercial judgment was impaired by drink;[1068] but he can avoid the contract if he was then so drunk that he could not understand the nature of the transaction and the other party knew this.[1069] The right of avoidance is lost by ratification after the effects of drink have worn off.[1070] These rules could, perhaps, be applied by analogy to persons whose judgment was impaired by drugs.[1071] By statute, a drunkard is liable for necessaries supplied to him while suffering from temporary incapacity to contract.[1072] **8.279**

J. Plurality of Parties

Normally, each side of a contract consists of only one party. Our concern here, however, is with contractual promises made by or to two or more persons, so that there is either more than one debtor, or more than one creditor. **8.280**

1062 *Re Walker* [1905] 1 Ch 160.
1063 Cf *Baldwyn v Smith* [1900] 1 Ch 588.
1064 *Manches v Trimborn* (1946) 115 LJ KB 305.
1065 Mental Capacity Act 2005, s 7.
1066 *Re F* [1990] 2 AC 1, 74.
1067 ibid; *Re C* [1994] 1 WLR 290; Mental Capacity Act 2005, ss 24–26.
1068 But *specific* enforcement against him may be refused: *Malins v Freeman* (1836) 2 Keen 25, 34.
1069 *Gore v Gibson* (1845) 13 M & W 623.
1070 *Matthews v Baxter* (1873) LR 8 Ex 132.
1071 *Irvani v Irvani* [2000] 1 Lloyd's Rep 412, 425.
1072 Sale of Goods Act 1979, s 3(2).

(1) Promises by More than One Person

(a) Definitions

8.281 If A and B each *separately* promise to pay C £100, there are two independent contracts under which C is entitled to £100 from A and to a further £100 from B.[1073] But if in the same contract they *together* make the promise, C is entitled to no more than £100 in all and the further effects of the promise depend on whether it is *joint* or *joint and several*. It is joint if it consists of a single promise by both A and B; and joint and several if it consists of such a single promise coupled with a separate promise by each. A promise by two or more persons is deemed to be joint unless it provides the contrary:[1074] eg by saying 'we and each of us promise'.

(b) Similarities

8.282 Each promisor is (whether the promise is joint or joint and several) liable in full but if he pays more than his share he is, unless the contract otherwise provides,[1075] entitled to contribution assessed by dividing the debt by the number of debtors who were solvent when the right to contribution arose.[1076]

8.283 If the creditor releases one of the co-debtors, the others are also released[1077] unless the release on its true construction reserves the creditor's rights against them.[1078]

8.284 A defence available to one debtor is not available to the others if it was personal to him (eg that he was a minor)[1079] but is so available if it goes to the root of the claim (eg if it is that the creditor has not performed his part of the contract).[1080] A guarantor (who usually undertakes joint and several liability with the principal debtor) is similarly not liable if the principal contract is illegal.[1081]

(c) Differences

8.285 At common law the liability of a joint debtor passed on his death to the others;[1082] but this rule was not followed in equity, at least in partnership cases,

---

1073 *Mikeover Ltd v Brady* [1989] 3 All ER 618; cf *Heaton v Axa Equity and Law Life Assurance Society* [2002] UKHL 15; [2002] 2 AC 392.

1074 *Levy v Sale* (1877) 37 LT 709.

1075 As in contracts in which the relationship of the two promisors is that of principal debtor and surety.

1076 *Hitchman v Stewart* (1855) 3 Drew 271.

1077 *Nicholson v Revill* (1836) 4 A & E 675 (joint liability); *Jenkins v Jenkins* [1928] 2 KB 501 (joint and several liability); cf *Jameson v CEGB* [1999] 1 All ER 193 (concurrent tort liability).

1078 *Johnson v Davies* [1999] Ch 117, 127–128. A similar question of construction can arise where the debtors' liability arises under two entirely separate contracts: see the *Heaton* case (n 1073 above).

1079 *Lovell & Christmas v Beauchamp* [1894] AC 607; Minors' Contracts Act 1987, s 2.

1080 *Pirie v Richardson* [1927] 1 KB 448.

1081 *Swan v Bank of Scotland* (1836) 10 Bli NS 627.

1082 *Cabell v Vaughan* (1669) 1 Wms Saund 291 n 4(f).

so that the liability of the deceased was enforceable against his estate.[1083] This rule now probably prevails[1084] and also applies where the liability was joint and several.[1085]

An action on a joint promise must as a general rule be brought against all the **8.286** debtors;[1086] but there are many qualifications of this rule.[1087] If under one of these, or because one joint debtor does not plead non-joinder of the other, judgment is given against one alone (but not satisfied) the creditor can, by statute, sue the others.[1088] An unsatisfied judgment against one of a number of joint and several debtors does not bar the creditor's right to sue the others.[1089]

(2) Promises to More than One Person

(a) Definitions

If A makes separate promises to pay £100 each to X and Y he is cumulatively liable **8.287** for £200; but he may also make a single promise to them both to pay them £100 and no more. Such a promise is *joint* if X and Y are together entitled to the whole of the promised payment (eg if they are the lessors of premises leased to A)[1090] but *several* if each of X and Y is entitled only to a proportionate part (eg if each is owner of part of a cargo insured by A). By statute, certain covenants in deeds made with two or more persons jointly are to be 'construed as being also made with each of them',[1091] so that they are both joint and several.[1092]

(b) Effects of the distinctions

On the death of a *joint* creditor his rights pass to the others by survivorship,[1093] but **8.288** this doctrine does not apply between *several* creditors,[1094] and in equity its effect was mitigated by presuming that a contract for the repayment of money to a number of lenders created a several right in each lender.[1095]

[1083] *Kendall v Hamilton* (1879) 4 App Cas 504, 517; *Thorpe v Jackson* (1837) 2 Y & C Ex 553.

[1084] By virtue of Supreme Court Act 1981, s 49(1).

[1085] *Read v Price* [1909] 1 KB 577.

[1086] *Cabell v Vaughan* (n 1082 above).

[1087] eg *Wilson, Sons & Co Ltd v Balcarres Brook Steamship Co Ltd* [1893] 1 QB 422; Insolvency Act 1986, s 345(4).

[1088] Civil Liability (Contribution) Act 1978, s 3.

[1089] *Blyth v Fladgate* [1891] 1 Ch 337.

[1090] As in *Bradburne v Botfield* (1845) 14 M & W 559.

[1091] Law of Property Act 1925, s 81.

[1092] For recognition of this concept at common law, see *Palmer v Mallett* (1887) 36 Ch D 410, 421.

[1093] *Anderson v Martindale* (1801) 1 East 497.

[1094] *Withers v Bircham* (1824) 3 B & C 254.

[1095] See *Steeds v Steeds* (1889) 22 QBD 537.

8.289　In an action on a *joint* promise all the creditors must (if living) be joined to the action,[1096] but there is no such requirement where the promise is *several*.[1097]

8.290　Payment to or a release granted by one of a number of *joint* creditors prima facie discharges the debt;[1098] but this rule does not apply where the whole is paid to or a release is granted by one of a number of *several* creditors since each is separately entitled to his share.[1099] Similarly, a defence available against one of a number of *joint* creditors is generally[1100] available against the others;[1101] but this rule does not apply where the creditors have *several* rights.[1102]

8.291　A promise made to two persons *jointly* can be enforced by all (or the survivor) even though consideration for it was provided by only one; and where the promise is 'joint and several' a surviving co-promisee can enforce the promise even though the whole consideration was provided by his deceased co-promisee.[1103] Where the promise is *several* consideration must, it seems, be provided by any promisee claiming to enforce it.

K.　Third Parties

(1)　Benefiting Third Parties

8.292　The situation here to be discussed is that in which A contracts with B to confer a benefit on C. This situation must be distinguished from that in which C is mentioned in the contract between A and B only as a person to whom A can pay or deliver what is due to B so as to obtain a good discharge;[1104] and from that in which A enters, in relation to the same subject matter, into both the main contract with B and also into a second collateral contract with C.[1105] In the former case, C is not an intended beneficiary while in the latter he is a party to a separate contract with A.

1096　*Sorsbie v Park* (1843) 12 M & W 146; *Thompson v Hakewill* (1865) 19 CB NS 713.
1097　*Palmer v Mallett* (1887) 36 Ch D 411.
1098　*Powell v Broadhurst* [1901] 2 Ch 160, 164; *Wallace v Kelsall* (1840) 7 M & W 264, 274.
1099　*Steeds v Steeds* (n 1095 above).
1100　Unless it is personal to one of the creditors.
1101　*P Samuel & Co v Dumas* [1924] AC 432, 445.
1102　*Hagedorn v Bazett* (1813) 2 M & S 100.
1103　*McEvoy v Belfast Banking Co* [1935] AC 24 (bank deposit in names of two persons).
1104　See *Coulls v Bagot's Executor and Trustee Co Ltd* [1967] ALR 385; contrast *Thavorn v Bank of Credit & Commerce International SA* [1985] 1 Lloyd's Rep 259.
1105　eg *Shanklin Pier Ltd v Detel Products Ltd* [1951] 2 KB 854; *Charnock v Liverpool Corporation* [1968] 1 WLR 1498; *Re Charge Card Services* [1987] Ch 150, affirmed [1989] Ch 497; *Moody v Condor Insurance Ltd* [2006] EWHC (Ch); [2006] 1 WLR 1487 at [31].

(a) Privity of contract at common law

The general common law rule is that rights arising under a contract can be enforced **8.293** or relied upon only by the parties to the contract.[1106] If, for example, A promised B to pay a sum of money to C, then at common law C could not enforce the promise.[1107] This rule is subject to many exceptions, the most important of which is now contained in the Contracts (Rights of Third Parties) Act 1999[1108] ('the 1999 Act'). This Act subjects the common law rule to a 'wide-ranging exception' but leaves it 'intact for cases not covered by'[1109] the exception because they either fall outside its scope[1110] or are specifically excepted from the Act.[1111] Other exceptions to the common law rule remain in force[1112] and are not subject to the provisions of the 1999 Act. The operation and scope of the rule and the other exceptions to it therefore still call for discussion.

(i) Operation of the contract

Although a contract between A and B for the benefit of C cannot generally be **8.294** enforced by C, it remains binding between A and B; but such a contract does give rise to special problems with regard to B's remedies against A.

Promisee's remedies. Where the contract is specifically enforceable in equity,[1113] **8.295** B can so enforce it against A and C will then obtain the intended benefit.[1114] But where A promises B to pay a sum of money to C and fails to do so, B cannot generally claim that sum for himself;[1115] and though B could claim restitution of his own performance where this remedy was otherwise available,[1116] such a remedy could be wholly inadequate.[1117] Where A's breach has caused loss to B, B can

---

[1106] *Dunlop Pneumatic Tyre Co Ltd v Selfridge & Co Ltd* [1915] AC 847, 853.

[1107] *Tweddle v Atkinson* (1861) 1 B & S 393; *Beswick v Beswick* [1968] AC 58, 72, 81, 83, 92–3, 95.

[1108] See paragraphs 8.303 to 8.311.

[1109] Law Commission, *Privity of Contract: Contracts for the Benefit of Third Parties* (Law Com No 242, 1996) (hereinafter 'Report') paras 5.16, 13.2. The 1999 Act is based on this Report.

[1110] eg because the third party is not 'expressly identified' in the contract, as s 1(3) of the 1999 Act requires: para 8.303.

[1111] 1999 Act, s 6 (para 8.308).

[1112] 1999 Act, s 7(1) (para 8.309).

[1113] A promise by A to B to render personal services to C would not be so enforceable.

[1114] *Beswick v Beswick* [1968] AC 58; for enforcement of promises *not to sue* C (by staying such an action), see *Gore v Van der Lann* [1967] 2 QB 31; *Snelling v John G Snelling Ltd* [1973] 1 QB 87.

[1115] See the *Coulls* case (n 1104 above) 409–11; for an exception, see *Cleaver v Mutual Reserve Fund Life Association* [1892] 1 QB 147, where C had been convicted of murdering B. The sum could also be claimed by B for himself where A's promise to B was to pay it to C *or as B might direct*: see *The Spiros C* [2001] 2 Lloyd's Rep 319, 331. The same reasoning can apply where A promises to render some performance other than to pay money: see *Mitchell v Ede* (1840) 1 Ad & El 888.

[1116] Part performance by A (as in *Beswick v Beswick* (n 1114 above)) may bar this remedy.

[1117] eg where a life insurance policy matures soon after its commencement as a result of the death of the person insured.

recover damages in respect of that loss from A: eg where B has contracted with C for the performance to be rendered by A, or (perhaps) where, on A's breach, B has incurred expense in securing an equivalent benefit for C.[1118] But, as damages in a contractual action are meant to compensate a claimant for his own loss,[1119] B cannot in general recover substantial damages where the only loss resulting from A's breach is suffered by C. This position is, however, 'most unsatisfactory':[1120] as it could give rise to a 'legal black hole'[1121] in allowing A to escape all substantial liability for an established breach. It is therefore subject to exceptions: for example, damages can be recovered by an agent in respect of loss suffered by his undisclosed principal;[1122] by a local authority in respect of a loss suffered ultimately by its inhabitants;[1123] and by a shipper of goods in respect of loss suffered by a consignee to whom the goods have been transferred and who has not acquired any contractual rights of his own against the carrier in respect of the latter's breach.[1124] B can likewise recover damages from A where A's breach of a building contract adversely affects C to whom the site is later transferred[1125] or who already owned it when the contract was made.[1126] The 'narrower ground'[1127] for this conclusion is that it amounts simply to an extension of the earlier carriage cases. The building cases have also been explained on the 'broader ground'[1128] that in them B recovers damages in respect of his *own* loss, ie the cost to B of providing the benefit to C that A should have, but has failed to, provide. On neither view, however, is A liable to B for substantial damages where C has an independent right against A in respect of the loss under a separate contract between A and C.[1129] Any damages recoverable by B under the above exceptions in respect of C's (but not damages in respect of B's own)[1130] loss must be held by B for C.[1131] The need to extend the exceptions further is reduced where C can enforce a term in the contract between A and B

1118 See after n 1128 below.

1119 *The Albazero* [1977] AC 774, 846.

1120 *Woodar Investment Development Ltd v Wimpey Construction Co Ltd* [1980] 1 WLR 277, 291.

1121 *Darlington BC v Wiltshier (Northern) Ltd* [1995] 1 WLR 68, 79.

1122 *Siu Yin Kwan v Eastern Insurance Co Ltd* [1994] 2 AC 199, 207; *Boyter v Thompson* [1995] 2 AC 629, 632.

1123 *St Albans City and District Council v International Computers Ltd* [1996] 4 All ER 481.

1124 *Dunlop v Lambert* (1839) 6 Cl & F 600, 627 as explained and limited in *The Albazero*, (n 1119 above).

1125 *Linden Gardens Trust Ltd v Lenesta Sludge Disposals Ltd* [1994] 1 AC 85.

1126 *Darlington BC v Wiltshier Northern Ltd* [1995] 1 WLR 68, approved in *Alfred McAlpine Construction Ltd v Panatown Ltd* [2001] 1 AC 518, 531, 566 ('the *Panatown* case').

1127 ibid, 575.

1128 *Linden Gardens* case, n 1125 above, at 96–97 (at least if 'the repairs have been or are likely to be carried out': ibid, and see the *Panatown* case, see n 1126 above).

1129 *Panatown* case, n 1126 above, 571; since there is no 'legal black hole' (n 1121 above) in such a case, there is no need to extend the present exception to it.

1130 See above, after n 1128.

1131 *The Albazero* (n 1119 above) 845; *Linden Gardens* case (n 1125 above).

against A under the 1999 Act;[1132] but B's rights against A are preserved by the Act[1133] and continue to be significant: eg where under the Act A has a defence against C which is not available against B.[1134]

Position between promisee and third party. Where A promises B to make a **8.296** payment to C and performs this promise, B is not entitled to recover that payment from C[1135] unless it was made to C as B's nominee. Before performance by A, the contract can be varied by agreement between A and B so as to provide for payment to B, but normally B has no unilateral right to demand payment to himself;[1136] the point is important where it is a matter of concern to A that provision should be made for C.[1137] Where A fails to perform, C cannot normally compel B to bring against A any of the actions described in paragraph 8.295.

(ii) Scope of the doctrine

Under the common law doctrine of privity, C cannot obtain rights *arising under* a **8.297** contract between A and B. But he may benefit from it indirectly[1138] and it may also give rise to the possibility of A's being liable to C in tort.

Liability in negligence. A contract between A and B may give rise to a relation- **8.298** ship between A and C in which A owes a duty of care to C: eg that of carrier and passenger or cargo-owner.[1139] Similarly, where A contracts with B to provide professional services, A may be liable to C for negligence in the performance of the contract.[1140] All such tort liability differs from liability on the contract in that it depends on negligence, while contract liability is often strict;[1141] and in that it does not normally[1142] arise if A simply repudiates the contract with B or takes no steps in its performance. Nor (except in cases of misrepresentation or negligence in providing professional services) is A generally liable in tort to C for purely economic loss.[1143] Nor, even where the damage is physical, is A liable for it to C where it results simply from a defect in the very thing supplied by A (causing it to disintegrate)[1144] or where C has neither the legal ownership of nor a possessory title to

---

[1132] See para 8.303.
[1133] 1999 Act, s 4.
[1134] See ibid, s 3(4).
[1135] See *Beswick v Beswick* [1968] AC 58 (where A had to be compelled to make the payment).
[1136] See para 8.295 at n 1115 above.
[1137] As in *Re Stapleton-Bretherton* [1941] Ch 482.
[1138] eg *Hirachand Punamchand v Temple* [1911] 2 KB 330 (para 8.59).
[1139] *Austin v Great Western Rly Co* (1867) LR 2 QB 442; *The Antonis P Lemos* [1985] AC 711.
[1140] eg *White v Jones* [1995] 2 AC 207; *Henderson v Merrett Syndicates Ltd* [1995] 2 AC 145.
[1141] See para 8.413.
[1142] For an exception, see *White v Jones* (n 1140 above).
[1143] *Simaan General Contracting Co v Pilkington Glass Ltd (No 2)* [1988] QB 758; *Customs & Excise Commissioners v Barclays Bank plc* [2006] UKHL 28; [2007] 1 AC 181.
[1144] *Aswan Engineering Establishment Co v Lupdine Ltd* [1987] 1 WLR 1.

the thing damaged.[1145] Moreover, in a tort action the claimant cannot normally recover damages in respect of his expectation interest[1146] so that where, for example, A's defective performance of a building contract with B causes loss to C, C cannot in a tort action recover from A the cost of making the defects good.[1147]

8.299 Such building contract cases must be distinguished from cases in which A, a solicitor, is engaged by B to draw up a will leaving property to C and A either does nothing to carry out the instructions[1148] or carries them out negligently,[1149] so that C does not get the intended benefit. In some such cases[1150] C has recovered the value of that benefit from A. One ground for upholding such claims has been that, if they were rejected, A would be under no substantial liability for an admitted breach, B's estate having suffered no loss; but they have been upheld even where A's negligent breach did cause loss to B's estate.[1151] The disappointed beneficiary cases can be explained on the ground that in them the benefit intended for C is (unlike that in the building contract cases[1152]) not the product of A's work but existed independently of it and before the conclusion of the contract between A and B. They have been described as 'unusual'[1153] but their principle has nevertheless been extended to closely analogous situations: eg where, as a result of A's negligence in performing a contract with B, C was deprived of benefits under a pension scheme or a trust.[1154]

8.300 **Intimidation.** The tort of intimidation may be committed when A, by threatening to break his contract with B, induces B to act to C's detriment[1155] (eg to stop doing business with C). C's claim against A in such a case is not one to enforce the contract between A and B[1156] but one for compensation for loss suffered by C as a result of A's unlawful threats against B.

1145 *The Aliakmon* [1986] AC 785; *The Starsin* [2003] UKHL 12; [2004] 1 AC 715.
1146 See para 8.04.
1147 *D & F Estates Ltd v Church Commissioners for England* [1989] AC 177; *Department of the Environment v Thomas Bates & Son Ltd* [1991] 1 AC 499.
1148 *White v Jones* (n 1140 above).
1149 *Ross v Caunters* [1980] Ch 287; *Hill v van Erp* (1997) 142 ALR 687.
1150 eg those cited in nn 1148 and 1149 above; contrast *Hemmens v Wilson Browne* [1995] Ch 223; *Walker v Geo H Medlicott & Son* [1999] 1 WLR 727.
1151 *Carr-Glynn v Frearsons* [1999] Ch 326.
1152 At n 1147 above.
1153 *Goodwill v Pregnancy Advisory Service* [1996] 1 WLR 1397, 1403.
1154 *Gorham v British Telecommunications plc* [2000] 1 WLR 2129; *Richards v Hughes* [2004] EWCA Civ 266; [2004] PNLR 35.
1155 *Rookes v Barnard* [1964] AC 1129. Intimidation has been described as 'only one variant of a broader tort usually called. . ."causing loss by unlawful means"': *OBG Ltd v Allan; Douglas v Hello! Ltd; Mainstream Properties Ltd v Young* [2007] UKHL 21; [2007] 2 WLR 920 at [7].
1156 *Rookes v Barnard*, n 1155 above.

(b) Exceptions to the doctrine

(i) Judge-made exceptions

Agency, assignment and land law.   A number of originally judge-made excep-   **8.301**
tions to the doctrine of privity arise under the rules relating to agency, assignment
and covenants affecting land. These are discussed elsewhere in this book.

Trusts of promises.   In equity, a promise by A to B in favour of C can be enforced   **8.302**
against A by C,[1157] joining B as a party to the action,[1158] if B can be regarded as
trustee for C of A's promise. B can be so regarded if three conditions are satisfied:
he must have intended to take the promise for C's benefit (rather than for his
own);[1159] his intention to benefit C must be final and irrevocable;[1160] and it must
be coupled with an intention to *create a trust* to C's favour. This last requirement
is hard to define and is mainly responsible for the restricted scope of the exception.
The courts have become reluctant (where the words 'trust' or 'trustee' are not
used) to infer the existence of a trust, since such an inference will deprive A and B
of their right to rescind or vary the contract by agreement.[1161] The inference is
most likely to be drawn where B obtained A's promise so as to secure the performance of an antecedent legal obligation owed by B to C.[1162] The trust device probably applies only to promises to pay money or transfer property.[1163]

(ii) Contracts (Rights of Third Parties) Act 1999

Third party's right of enforcement.   The main purpose of the 1999 Act is to   **8.303**
enable a third party to acquire rights under a contract if and to the extent that the
parties to the contract so intend. Section 1 accordingly provides that a person (C)
who is not a party to a contract can in his own right enforce a term in a contract
between A (the promisor) and B (the promisee) if (a) the contract expressly provides that he may; or (b) the term purports to confer a benefit on C[1164] unless (in
this latter case) it appears on a proper construction of the contract that A and B
did not intend the term to be enforceable by C.[1165] It is also necessary for C to be
expressly identified in the contract by name, as a member of a class or as answering

---

[1157] *Les Affréteurs Réunis SA v Leopold Walford (London) Ltd* [1919] AC 801; *Nisshin Shipping Co
Ltd v Cleaves & Co Ltd* [2003] EWHC 2606; [2004] 1 All ER (Comm) 481.
[1158] *The Panaghia P* [1983] 2 Lloyd's Rep 653, 655.
[1159] See *West v Houghton* (1879) 4 CPD 197; *Vandepitte v Preferred Accident Insurance Corporation*
[1933] AC 70.
[1160] *Re Sinclair's Life Policy* [1938] Ch 799.
[1161] *Re Schebsman* [1944] Ch 83, 104; contrast *Re Flavell* (1883) 25 Ch D 89.
[1162] See *Re Independent Air Travel Ltd The Times*, 20 May 1961.
[1163] *Southern Water Authority v Carey* [1985] 2 All ER 1077, 1083.
[1164] 1999 Act, s 1(1).
[1165] ibid, s 1(2). The burden under s 1(2) of proving that A and B did not intend the term to
be enforceable by C rests on A: *The Laemthong Glory* [2005] EWCA Civ 519; [2005] 1 Lloyd's
Rep 632.

a particular description (but not for C to have been in existence when the contract was made);[1166] and C will not have a right to enforce a term otherwise than subject to and in accordance with any other relevant terms of the contract[1167] (such as one expressly excluding C's right or specifying time limits for claims under the contract). Where a term 'excludes or limits' liability, references to C's 'enforcing' it are to be 'construed as references to his availing himself of the exclusion or limitation'.[1168] There is no need for C to provide consideration for A's promise.[1169] Under these provisions C would, in many cases previously governed by the doctrine of privity, now have a contractual right against A.[1170] But this would not be true in all such cases: for example in the 'disappointed beneficiary' cases[1171] C would still have no *contractual* rights against the solicitor.

8.304 The 1999 Act does not in general use the fiction of C's having become a party to the contract[1172] but it does provide that for the purpose of enforcing his right C is to have any remedy that would have been available to him if he had been a party to the contract.[1173] He can therefore recover damages in respect of expectation loss,[1174] subject to the usual tests of remoteness, and mitigation, though these might lead to different results where the action was brought by C from those which would follow if it were brought by B.[1175]

8.305 **Right to rescind or vary the contract.** Where C has a right under section 1 to enforce a term of a contract, the right of A and B to rescind or vary the contract by agreement without C's consent is limited but not altogether removed. The general principle, laid down in section 2(1), is that A and B lose this right if C has communicated his assent to the term to A; or if A knows that C has relied on the term; or if A can reasonably foresee that C would rely on the term and C has relied on it. But these conditions may be modified by the terms of the contract;[1176] and the court can in specified circumstances dispense with C's consent: eg where it cannot be obtained because his whereabouts cannot reasonably be ascertained.[1177]

1166 1999 Act, s 1(3).
1167 ibid, s 1(4).
1168 ibid, s 1(6).
1169 Report, para 6.8 n 8.
1170 eg probably in a case such as *Beswick v Beswick* [1968] AC 58, (unless the facts fell within s 1(2)).
1171 See para 8.299.
1172 Cf 1999 Act, s 7(4). For an exception see ibid, s 3(6) (para 8.307 at n 1180 below).
1173 ibid, s 1(5).
1174 See para 8.04.
1175 eg the test of remoteness would be foreseeability of C's (not B's) loss.
1176 1999 Act, s 2(3).
1177 ibid, s 2(4).

The restrictions described in paragraph 8.305 do not normally apply where A **8.306** promises B to perform in favour of C *or as B shall direct*.[1178] If B later directs A to perform in favour of D, the contract is not *varied* but will be performed in accordance with its original terms by A's performing in favour of D.

Promisor's defences against third party.   Section 3 deals with the situation in **8.307** which A seeks, in an action by C to enforce a term of the contract, to rely by way of defence or set-off on matters which would have been available to A if proceedings to enforce the contract had been brought by B. The general principle is that A can so rely on such a matter against C if it 'arises from or in connection with the contract [between A and B] and is relevant to the term' sought to be enforced by C.[1179] A could, for example, rely against C on a valid exemption clause in the contract between A and B or on B's repudiatory breach. Where C's enforcement takes the form of reliance by him on an exemption or limitation clause in the contract between A and B, C likewise cannot rely on it if he could not have done so, had he been a party to the contract:[1180] eg if, on that supposition, it would have been ineffective under the Unfair Contract Terms Act 1977.[1181] The general principle stated above can be modified by agreement between A and B.[1182] The 1999 Act also provides for A to be able to rely against C on defences and counterclaims which would not have been available to A against B but would have been available to A against C if C had been a party to the contract.[1183]

Exceptions to third party's entitlement.   Section 6 lists cases to which C's right **8.308** of enforcement under section 1 does not extend. In some of these excepted cases, the common law rules as to contracts for the benefit of third parties continue to apply, so that C will generally acquire no rights: for example, C cannot enforce 'any term of a contract of employment against an employee'.[1184] In others, C has, or can acquire, rights against A under other rules of law: for example where he is the transferee of a bill of lading issued by A to B, his rights are governed by other legislation[1185] to the exclusion of the 1999 Act.[1186]

Third party's other rights.   C is not deprived by the 1999 Act of any rights **8.309** which he may have apart from its provisions:[1187] eg under other exceptions to the doctrine of privity; in cases which fall outside its scope; or under a direct collateral

---

1178 Cf para 8.295 n 1115.
1179 1999 Act, s 3(2)(a).
1180 ibid, s 3(6).
1181 See para 8.112.
1182 1999 Act, s 3(5).
1183 ibid, s 3(4).
1184 ibid, s 6(3)(a).
1185 Carriage of Goods by Sea Act 1992.
1186 1999 Act, s 6(5).
1187 ibid, s 7(1).

contract between A and C. The point is important not only where C has no right under the 1999 Act and does have one under other rules,[1188] but also where he has rights both under the 1999 Act and apart from it.[1189] By making his claim apart from the 1999 Act, C can avoid the restriction which it imposes on claims made under it.

8.310 **Relation to other legislation.** Section 7(4) provides that C is not to be treated as a party to the contract between A and B for the purpose of other legislation. If, for example, that contract were on A's standard terms of business, the requirement of reasonableness under the Unfair Contract Terms Act 1977[1190] would not apply in favour of C (but only in favour of B). By way of exception or quasi-exception to this principle, where a claim under the 1999 Act is made on behalf of or by C in respect of C's death or personal injury, A cannot rely on an exemption clause in his contract with B which is void under the 1977 Act[1191] because it seeks to exclude or limit liability in respect of death or personal injury resulting from negligence.[1192]

8.311 **Promisee's rights.** The fact that C has acquired rights under the contract 'does not affect any right of the promisee [B] to enforce any term of the contract'.[1193] To avoid the risk of A's being made liable in respect of the same loss to both B and C, the 1999 Act directs the court to reduce any award to C to such extent as it thinks appropriate to take account of the sum recovered by B.[1194]

(iii) Other statutory exceptions

8.312 **Insurance.** The doctrine of privity can be particularly inconvenient in relation to contracts of insurance;[1195] and in this field it is, in addition to being modified by the trust device and by agency, subject to statutory exceptions. These apply where a person insures his or her life for the benefit of his or her spouse, civil partner or children;[1196] where a motor insurance policy covers a person driving a car with the consent of the insured;[1197] where a person who insures property has only a limited interest in it (so as to enable him to insure for the full value, paying over

---

[1188] eg in the 'disappointed beneficiary' cases: see above at n 1171.

[1189] As in *Nisshin Shipping Co Ltd v Cleaves & Co Ltd* [2003] EWHC 2602; [2004] 1 All ER (Comm) 481.

[1190] See para 8.113.

[1191] 1977 Act, s 2(1) (para 8.112).

[1192] 1999 Act, s 7(2) disapplies s 2(2), but not s 2(1), of the 1977 Act.

[1193] 1999 Act, s 4; a restitution claim by B, though not one to 'enforce' the contract, seems likewise to be unaffected by the 1999 Act.

[1194] ibid, s 5.

[1195] In Australia there is some support for not applying the doctrine to such contracts: *Trident General Insurance Co Ltd v McNiece Bros Pty Ltd* (1988) 65 CLR 107; cf, in Canada, *Fraser River Pile and Dredge Ltd v Can-Drive Services Ltd* [2000] 1 Lloyd's Rep 199.

[1196] Married Women's Property Act 1887, s 11; Civil Partnership Act 2004, s 70.

[1197] Road Traffic Act 1988, s 148(7).

any amount in excess of his own interest which he may recover to other persons interested in the property);[1198] and where a house which is insured is destroyed by fire (so as to entitle 'any person. . .interested' to require insurance moneys to be laid out towards reinstating the house).[1199] The scheme established under statute between the Law Society and insurers for the compulsory insurance of solicitors against liability for professional negligence[1200] also gives rise 'by virtue of public law' to rights and duties between solicitors and the insurers.[1201]

Insurance against liability to third parties does not strictly confer any contractual rights on third parties but by statute such third parties have in certain cases the right to enforce the rights of the insured under the policy directly against the insurer.[1202] Where the third party is the victim of a motor accident he has a right against the Motor Insurers' Bureau even though the driver was not insured or cannot be traced.[1203]   **8.313**

Law of Property Act 1925, section 56(1).   This subsection provides that 'A person may take. . .the benefit of any. . .covenant or agreement over or respecting land or other property, although he may not be named as a party to the conveyance or other instrument'. In the 1925 Act 'property' (unless the context indicates the contrary) includes 'any thing in action';[1204] and since a contractual promise falls within these words, it was at one time argued that any written promise by A to B to pay money to C was enforceable by C under section 56(1).[1205] The prevailing view, however, is that the subsection applies only in favour of a person to whom the instrument purports to make a grant or with whom it purports to make a covenant:[1206] in other words, only where C is a party in all but in name.   **8.314**

(2) Binding Third Parties

(a) Third party generally not bound

A contract between A and B cannot impose a positive obligation on C (such as one to pay £100 to B) and this aspect of the doctrine of privity is not affected by the   **8.315**

[1198] Marine Insurance Act 1906, s 14(2).

[1199] Fire Prevention (Metropolis) Act 1774, s 83.

[1200] Under Solicitors Act 1974, s 37.

[1201] *Swain v Law Society* [1983] AC 598, 611.

[1202] Third Parties (Rights Against Insurers) Act 1930, s 1; Road Traffic Act 1988, ss 151–3.

[1203] See *Gardner v Moore* [1984] AC 548, 556; *White v White* [2001] UKHL 29; [2001] 1 WLR 481.

[1204] Law of Property Act 1925, s 205 (1)(xx).

[1205] *Beswick v Beswick* [1966] Ch 538 *per* Lord Denning MR and Danckwerts LJ.

[1206] *Beswick v Beswick* [1968] AC 58, 94, 106; *Amsprop Trading Ltd v Harris Distribution Ltd* [1997] 1 WLR 1025. Exactly why s 56 was said to apply in *OTV Birwelco Ltd v Technical & General Guarantee Co Ltd* [2002] EWHC 2240; [2002] 4 All ER 668 at [12] is not clear from the reported facts.

Contracts (Rights of Third Parties) Act 1999[1207] or by the other exceptions to the doctrine which have been discussed in this section. Under exceptions discussed elsewhere in this book, C may sometimes be so bound: eg under the law of agency or under the law governing covenants relating to land. He may also sometimes be bound by an exemption clause in a contract to which he was not a party.[1208]

(b) Scope of the rule

8.316 C may be adversely affected by a contract between A and B in ways which fall short of requiring him actually to perform terms of that contract. Two possibilities call for discussion.

(i) *Contract creating proprietary or possessory rights*

8.317 If a contract between A and B creates such rights in favour of B, and C later acquires an interest in the subject matter (eg by buying goods hired out by A to B and in B's possession),[1209] then C must respect those antecedent rights.[1210]

(ii) *Inducing breach of contract*

8.318 The principle stated in paragraph 8.317 does not apply where B has no proprietary or possessory right in the subject matter, but only a contractual right relating to it: eg where B is the voyage or time charterer of A's ship.[1211] But if, while the charterparty is in force, A sells the ship to C, the question arises whether B can in any way enforce his rights under the charterparty against C.[1212] Clearly, B cannot require C to *perform* A's obligation to render services under the charter, but an injunction may sometimes be available to restrain C from conduct[1213] inducing a breach of the contract between A and B. One view was that this remedy was based on B's having, by virtue of his contract with A, acquired an equitable interest in the ship.[1214] But this reasoning would have the undesirable result[1215] of applying the doctrine of constructive notice to commercial dealings in chattels; and the preferable view is that C's liability, if any, is based on (or on the analogy of) the tort

---

1207 Report, paras 10.32, 7.6.

1208 See paras 8.322 to 8.326.

1209 See further at n 1219 below.

1210 See *Port Line Ltd v Ben Line Steamers Ltd* [1958] QB 146, 166, where B's claim failed as he had *no* 'proprietary or possessory interest' and for the reason given in n 1218 below.

1211 Such a charter gives B no more than a contractual right to require A to render services by use of the ship: see *The Scaptrade* [1983] AC 694, 702.

1212 This question is distinct from that whether B can enforce the charterparty *against A* by restraining A from dealing with C in a manner inconsistent with it: see *Lauritzencool Ltd v Lady Navigation Inc* [2005] EWCA Civ 579; [2005] 1 WLR 3686 at [16].

1213 Not from mere inaction: *Law Debenture Trust Corp v Ural Caspian Oil Corp Ltd* [1993] 1 WLR 138, 146; for a successful appeal on another point, see [1995] Ch 152.

1214 *Lord Strathcona Steamship Co v Dominion Coal Co* [1926] AC 108.

1215 *Manchester Trust Ltd v Furness Withy* [1895] 2 QB 539, 545.

of inducing A to break his contract with B.[1216] Such liability depends on C's intending to induce the breach,[1217] and hence on his having actual knowledge (and not merely constructive notice) of, not only the contract, but also the term alleged to have been broken.[1218] The same requirement probably has to be satisfied where B's right is one, not *of* actual, but *to* the future, possession of a chattel: eg under a contract of hire, the period of which had not yet begun when C acquired the thing from A.[1219]

(3) Exemption Clauses and Third Parties

(a) Benefiting third parties

(i) Privity and exceptions

Under the doctrine of privity, C could not, in general, take the benefit of an exemp- **8.319**
tion clause[1220] in a contract between A and B. He could do so only if one of the exceptions to the doctrine (such as B's having acted as his or A's agent) operated in his favour;[1221] or where the clause was incorporated into a direct contract between A and C, implied from dealings between them;[1222] or where such dealings gave rise to a bailment relationship between A and C which by implication incorporated the clause.[1223] It followed that such an exemption clause did not protect C merely because he was an employee or agent engaged by B for the purpose of performing B's contract with A.[1224] The 1999 Act now entitles C to 'enforce' an exemption clause in a contract between A and B,[1225] but only if the requirements of the Act

---

[1216] *Lumley v Gye* (1853) 2 E & B 216.

[1217] *OBG Ltd v Allan; Douglas v Hello! Ltd; Mainstream Properties Ltd v Young* [2007] UKHL 21; [2007] 2 WLR 920 at [8],[62]; and see n 1218 below. The requisite intention can be negatived by mistake of law: see [2007] UKHL 21 at [202]; *Meretz Investments NV v ACP Ltd* [2006] EWHC 74 (Ch); [2007] Ch 197 at [370], [372].

[1218] The tort claim failed for want of such knowledge in the *Port Line* case, n 1210 above and in the *Mainstream* case, n 1217 above at [69], [200], [202]; and see ibid at [40], [191], [192], [200]. Deliberately shutting one's eyes would be equivalent to knowledge: ibid at [41] and [192]. A fortiori, there is no liability for this tort where no breach is induced: see the *OBG* case, n 1217 above at [86] and the *Douglas* case, n 1217 above at [129], [248] (where the defendants were held liable on other grounds).

[1219] As in *The Stena Nautica (No 2)* [1982] 2 Lloyd's Rep 336 (where the present point did not strictly arise).

[1220] Including a limitation of liability clause.

[1221] eg *Hall v North-Eastern Rly* (1875) LR 10 QB 437.

[1222] *Elder Dempster & Co v Paterson Zochonis & Co* [1924] 2 AC 522 as explained in *Adler v Dickson* [1955] 1 QB 158, 189.

[1223] *Elder Dempster* case (n 1222 above), as explained in *The Pioneer Container* [1994] 2 AC 324, 339–40.

[1224] *Scruttons Ltd v Midland Silicones Ltd* [1962] AC 446.

[1225] Section 1(6), para 8.303. An exclusive jurisdiction clause would not be covered by s 1(6); cf n 1230 below.

are satisfied; and in some pre-1999 cases they were plainly not satisfied: for example, because C was not 'expressly identified'[1226] in the contract.[1227]

(ii) Himalaya clauses

8.320 The position described in paragraph 8.319 was regarded as inconvenient and avoided by so-called 'Himalaya clauses'[1228] in the contract between A and B. The effect of these elaborate clauses is that, once A begins performance of his contract with B, a separate contract arises between A and C,[1229] giving C the benefit of specified provisions[1230] in the contract between A and B to the extent to which they were valid[1231] in that contract and covered the acts of C giving rise to the loss.[1232] Himalaya clauses were generally upheld by the courts.[1233] Under the 1999 Act, less elaborate clauses will protect C,[1234] but only subject to the provisions of that Act and on a different ground: ie, not because there is a contract between A and C, but because C is entitled to enforce a term in a contract between A and B.[1235]

(iii) Clauses defining duties

8.321 A term in the contract between A and B may be relevant as limiting the duty of care owed by C (eg as building subcontractor) to A and so give C a defence to an action in tort by A.[1236]

(b) Binding third parties

(i) General rule

8.322 The general rule is that C is not bound by an exemption clause in a contract between A and B. Hence if A's breach of that contract amounts to a tort against C, then C will not be adversely affected by such a clause.[1237]

1226 See s 1(3) of the Act.

1227 See eg the *Midland Silicones* case (n 1224 above).

1228 So named after the ship in *Adler v Dickson* (n 1222 above).

1229 *The Eurymedon* [1975] AC 154.

1230 See *The Mahkutai* [1996] AC 650 (exclusive jurisdiction clause not covered).

1231 See *The Starsin* [2003] UKHL; [2004] 1 AC 715, where this requirement was not satisfied.

1232 See *Raymond Burke Motors Ltd v Mersey Docks & Harbour Co* [1986] 1 Lloyd's Rep 155 (acts done by C before beginning of performance of main contract not covered).

1233 *The Eurymedon* (n 1229 above); *The New York Star* [1981] 1 WLR 138; contrast *The Suleyman Stalskiy* [1976] 2 Lloyd's Rep 609.

1234 By virtue of s 1(6).

1235 Cf, in the United States, *Norfolk Southern Railway v James N Kirby Ltd* 125 S Ct 395, 399 (2000).

1236 *Junior Books Ltd v Veitchi Co Ltd* [1983] 1 AC 520, 546; the dictum was doubted in *The Aliakmon* [1986] AC 785, 817 (where the question was whether C was *bound* by the clause) but followed in *Pacific Associates Inc v Baxter* [1990] 1 QB 993.

1237 *The Aliakmon* (n 1236 above).

(ii) Exceptions

C may be bound by an exemption clause in a contract between A and B if B acted **8.323** as C's or A's agent, if only for the limited purpose of restricting C's rights against A by the clause;[1238] or if an implied contract to this effect between A and C could be inferred from their conduct in pursuance of the contract between A and B.[1239] In both these situations C is bound by the clause because there is a contract between him and A; but in the situations described in paragraphs 8.324 to 8.326 C is so bound even though there is no such contract.

Bailment on terms. C may entrust goods to B under a bailment (eg for carriage **8.324** or for cleaning) and authorize B to employ a subcontractor (A). C will then be bound by any terms of the sub-bailment to A to which C has consented,[1240] even though there is no contract between A and C.[1241] This rule has been applied *only* where the relationship between C and A was that of bailor and sub-bailee.[1242] It seems to be based on the fact that the sub-bailment is the sole source of A's duty to C;[1243] and therefore not to apply where C does not need to rely on the bailment to establish A's duty of care to him.[1244]

Clauses defining duties. The terms of A's contract with B may be relevant to the **8.325** scope of any duty of care owed by A to C: eg where the term defines work to be done by A as a subcontractor employed by B for the purpose of the performance of a main contract between B and C.[1245]

Derivative rights. A contract between A and B may contain (1) a promise by A **8.326** to B to render some performance to C and (2) an exemption clause in favour of A. If C sues A to enforce the first of these promises under the 1999 Act, A can rely on the second[1246] since C's right, being derived from B's, is subject to the restrictions which govern B's rights.[1247] This reasoning does not apply where C's claim is not

---

[1238] *The Kite* [1933] P 164, 181; *Norfolk Southern Railway* case, n 1235 above.

[1239] *Pyrene Co Ltd v Scindia Navigation Co Ltd* [1954] 2 QB 402, as explained in the *Midland Silicones* case (n 1224 above).

[1240] *Morris v CW Martin & Sons Ltd* [1966] 1 QB 716, 729; *The Pioneer Container* [1994] 2 AC 324; *East West Corp v DKBS 1912 AF A/S* [2003] EWCA Civ 83; [2003] QB 1509 at [24], [69].

[1241] *Targe Towing Ltd v Marine Blast Ltd* [2004] EWCA Civ 346; [2004] 1 Lloyd's Rep 721 at [28]; alternatively, C's consent to the terms of the bailment may bind C by virtue of an implied contract of the kind described in para 8.323 above: *Sandeman Coprimar SA v Transitos y Transportes Integrales SL* [2003] EWCA Civ 113; [2003] QB 1270 at [63]–[65].

[1242] See *Scruttons Ltd v Midland Silicones Ltd* [1962] AC 446 where the defendants were not bailees. There is perhaps some support in the speech of Lord Goff in *Henderson v Merrett Syndicates Ltd* [1995] AC 145, 196 for the view that C may be bound by the clause even where there is no bailment between C and A.

[1243] *The Pioneer Container* (n 1240 above) 336.

[1244] *The Kapetan Markos NL (No 2)* [1987] 2 Lloyd's Rep 321, 340.

[1245] *Junior Books* case (n 1236 above) 534.

[1246] 1999 Act, s 3(2).

[1247] See Report, para 10.24.

one to enforce a term of the contract between A and B but arises in tort and apart from the 1999 Act: such a claim is not affected by its provisions.[1248]

L. Transfer of Contractual Rights

8.327 A contractual right, such as a debt owed by A to B, can be transferred by B to C by a process called assignment. This is a transaction between B (the creditor or assignor) and C (the assignee).[1249] A (the debtor) is not a party to it and his consent to it is not required.[1250]

(1) Law and Equity

(a) Substantive difference

8.328 Originally, the common law did not generally[1251] give effect to the assignment of a 'chose in action' (that is, of a right such as a contract debt which could be asserted only by bringing an action) since it feared that to do so might lead to maintenance or champerty by encouraging officious intermeddling by C in litigation between A and B. Equity did not share this fear[1252] and gave effect to such assignments[1253] unless they in fact produced such undesirable consequences.[1254] The common law did recognize other methods, such as a tripartite contract known as novation[1255] and acknowledgement by A to C,[1256] by which C could become entitled to enforce B's claim against A, but only (unlike assignment) with A's consent.

(b) Procedure

8.329 In enforcing assignments, equity distinguished between legal choses (such as contract debts, enforceable in common law courts) and equitable choses (rights enforceable only in courts of equity). Assignments of the latter were enforced by allowing the assignee to sue the debtor in the Court of Chancery. But this could not be done where the chose was legal since that Court did not enforce such rights. Effect to an assignment of a legal chose was given by allowing the assignee to sue

---

1248 1999 Act, s 7(1).

1249 Only voluntary assignment of this kind is discussed here. For assignment by operation of law on death, bankruptcy or insolvency of a creditor, see Chapters 7 and 19.

1250 *Mulkerrins v PricewaterhouseCoopers* [2003] UKHL 41; [2003] 1 WLR 1937 at [15].

1251 The most significant exception to the general rule related to negotiable instruments such as bills of exchange and promissory notes: see Chapter 14.

1252 *Wright v Wright* (1750) 1 Ves Sen 409, 411.

1253 *Crouch v Martin* (1707) 2 Vern 595; *Ryall v Rowles* (1750) 1 Ves Sen 348.

1254 See para 8.346.

1255 See *Rasbora Ltd v JCL Marine Ltd* [1977] 1 Lloyd's Rep 645.

1256 *Shamia v Joory* [1958] 1 QB 448.

the debtor in the name of the assignor, who could be compelled by a court of equity to allow his name to be so used in a common law action.[1257]

(2) Statutory Assignment

The Judicature Act 1873 provided for the administration of common law and equity in one unified court system. It thus removed the need for the assignee of a legal chose to sue in the name of the assignor and recognized this state of affairs by making the provision for statutory assignments which is now contained in section 136(1) of the Law of Property Act 1925.[1258] This section provides that the legal right to a 'debt or other legal thing in action' is transferred to the assignee if the assignment is 'absolute' and in writing and if written notice of it has been given to the debtor. An assignment which does not comply with these requirements can remain effective as an equitable one;[1259] but while a statutory assignee can sue the debtor *alone* an equitable assignee must *join the assignor* as a party to the action,[1260] so as to avoid the prejudice which the debtor might suffer if one of these parties were not before the court.[1261]

8.330

(a) 'Absolute' assignment

In accordance with the principle just stated, assignments are not 'absolute' within section 136(1) (and so take effect in equity only) where it is desirable to have the assignor before the court. For example A may be B's tenant and B may assign the accruing rent to C as security for a loan from C to B until the loan is repaid. B's presence before the court is then desirable in an action by C against A since without it the question whether anything remained due from B to C could not be determined so as to bind B. The assignment is therefore not absolute[1262] and B must be joined to the action by C. The assignment would, however, be absolute if it provided for *reassignment* of the debt to B when he had repaid the loan[1263] for in such a case A can safely go on paying C until he gets notice of the reassignment and is not concerned with the state of accounts between B and C. An assignment of part of a debt is likewise not absolute:[1264] here the potential prejudice to A arises

8.331

1257 See *Re Westerton* [1919] 2 Ch 104, 111.

1258 Re-enacting Judicature Act 1873, s 25(6).

1259 *German v Yates* (1915) 32 TLR 52.

1260 See *The Aiolos* [1983] 2 Lloyd's Rep 25, 33; *Weddell v JA Pearce & Major* [1988] Ch 26, 40.

1261 Where there is no such practical need for joinder of the assignor, the courts no longer insist on such joinder: *The Mount I* [2001] EWCA Civ 68; [2001] 1 Lloyd's Rep 597 at [60].

1262 *Durham Bros v Robertson* [1898] QB 765.

1263 *Tancred v Delagoa Bay, etc, Rly Co* (1889) 23 QBD 239.

1264 *Re Steel Wing Co Ltd* [1921] 1 Ch 349.

if he denies the existence of the debt; for he could have to make this denial good many times over if each assignee could sue him alone.[1265]

(b) 'Debt or other legal thing in action'

8.332 A 'debt' in section 136(1) is a sum certain due under contract or otherwise.[1266] 'Other legal thing in action' includes an equitable chose.[1267] Provision for the transfer of certain things in action is governed by special statutory provisions which sometimes must be used instead of s 136(1)[1268] and sometimes provide an alternative mechanism (to that provided by that subsection) for making the transfer.[1269]

(3) *Assignment and Authority to Pay*

8.333 An assignment can take the form either of an agreement between assignor and assignee, or of a direction to the debtor telling him that the debt has been made over to the assignee[1270] (to whom, in such a case, notice of the assignment must be given).[1271] A direction which merely authorizes the debtor to pay a third party is not an assignment.[1272] Where, for example, a person draws a cheque on his bank, payable to a third party, he does not assign part of his balance to the payee.[1273]

(4) *Formalities*

8.334 An assignment can take effect as a statutory one only if it is in writing, but there is, in general, no such or other formal requirement for an equitable assignment. Writing is, however, necessary for the validity of a 'disposition of an equitable interest';[1274] and also where the contract creating the debt imposes such a requirement. For the protection of creditors, certain assignments must be registered.[1275]

  [1265] For the same reason, the creditor must in such a case be joined to an action by an assignee: *Walter and Sullivan Ltd v J Murphy & Son Ltd* [1955] 2 QB 584.

  [1266] eg under statute: *Dawson v Great Northern & City Rly Co* [1905] 1 KB 260.

  [1267] *Re Pain* [1919] 1 Ch 38, 44.

  [1268] eg Companies Act 2006, s 544 (shares in companies); the section is not yet in force.

  [1269] eg Marine Insurance Act 1906, s 50: *The Mount I* [2001] EWCA Civ 68; [2001] 1 Lloyd's Rep 57 at [74] (marine policies); Carriage of Goods by Sea Act 1992, s 2(1)(a) (bills of lading).

  [1270] *William Brandt's Sons & Co v Dunlop Rubber Co* [1905] AC 454, 462.

  [1271] *Re Hamilton* (1921) 124 LT 737.

  [1272] *Timpson's Exors v Yerbury* [1936] 1 KB 645.

  [1273] Bills of Exchange Act 1882, s 53(1); *Deposit Protection Board v Dalia* [1994] 2 AC 367, 400.

  [1274] Law of Property Act 1925, s 53(1)(c), re-enacting Statute of Frauds 1677, s 9.

  [1275] eg Companies Act 2006, s 860, esp subs (7)(f) (not yet in force); Insolvency Act 1986, s 344.

(5) Notice to the Debtor

An equitable assignment is valid even without notice to the debtor, but there are **8.335** three reasons for giving it. First, if written it may turn the assignment into a statutory one.[1276] Secondly, notice (even if oral) perfects the assignee's title against the debtor[1277] who, if he disregards it and pays the assignor, must make a second payment to the assignee.[1278] Thirdly, successive assignees rank in the order in which they give notice to the debtor,[1279] provided that, where the chose assigned is equitable, the notice is in writing.[1280]

(6) Consideration

The question whether an assignment needs to be supported by consideration **8.336** arises where the assignor (or his estate) disputes the validity of the assignment.[1281] The overriding principle is that consideration is not necessary where the assignment is a completed gift; whether it has this character depends on the following factors.

(a) Assignment and promise to assign

A mere promise to assign (as opposed to an actual assignment) is not a completed **8.337** gift and is binding only if it is supported by consideration so as to have contractual force. An attempt to assign a future right (eg the benefit of a contract not yet made) can operate only as a promise to assign;[1282] but this is not true of an assignment of a right to become due under an existing contract[1283] (eg of future rent under an existing lease).

(b) Further acts to be done by assignor

A gift is incomplete if the donor fails to make it in the way (if any) prescribed **8.338** for its subject matter: that is, if something more has to be done by him to transfer the subject matter to the donee.[1284] The donor can be required to do that

---

1276 See para 8.330.

1277 *Warner Bros Records Inc v Rollgreen Ltd* [1976] QB 430.

1278 *Jones v Farrell* (1857) 1 De G & J 208; so far as *contra*, dicta in the *Warner Bros* case (n 1277 above) are with respect open to question in view of the developments described in para 8.330: cf *Three Rivers DC v Bank of England* [1996] QB 292, 315.

1279 *Dearle v Hall* (1828) 3 Russ 1.

1280 Law of Property Act 1925, s 137(3).

1281 For procedure in such a case, see ibid, s 136(1). The point is of no concern to the debtor: *Walker v Bradford Old Bank Ltd* (1884) 12 QBD 511.

1282 *Glegg v Bromley* [1912] 3 KB 474.

1283 eg *Hughes v Pump House Hotel Co Ltd* [1902] 2 KB 190.

1284 *Milroy v Lord* (1862) DF & J 264. For mitigations of the rigour of this rule, see *T Choitram International v Pagarani* [2001] 1 WLR 1 and *Pennington v Waine* [2002] EWCA Civ 227; [2002] 1 WLR 2075.

'something more' only if he has promised to do so and if the donee has provided consideration for that promise.[1285]

(i) Statutory assignment

8.339 It follows from the reasoning in paragraph 8.338 that a statutory assignment need not be supported by consideration, there being nothing more that the assignor need do to transfer the subject matter.[1286]

(ii) Equitable assignment

8.340 The mere fact that a gratuitous assignment is not statutory (and so can take effect only in equity) does not make it an imperfect gift. It will most obviously not make the gift imperfect where the assignment is not statutory for want only of written notice[1287] since such notice can be given by the assignee himself. Where the assignment is not statutory because it is not in writing, the execution of the writing is 'something more' which *could* have been done by the assignor. But as there was no requirement of writing in equity for the assignment of a legal chose,[1288] the assignment can be a completed gift where the intention that it should take effect as such is clear.[1289] Where the assignment is not statutory because it is not absolute it will often be intended to take effect as a contract: eg where it is made as security for a loan (though the assignee's forbearance to sue on the loan will then usually satisfy the requirement of consideration).[1290] If the assignment is not absolute because it is subject to some other condition, the gift will be imperfect if satisfaction of the condition requires some further act of the assignor, such as his approval of work done by the assignee.[1291]

(7) 'Subject to Equities'

8.341 The object of the rule that an assignee takes 'subject to. . .equities'[1292] is to protect the debtor against the risk of being made liable to the assignee for more than he would, if there had been no assignment, have been liable to the assignor.[1293]

1285 In the present context a deed or nominal consideration does not suffice: *Kekewich v Manning* (1851) 1 DM & G 176; *Dillon v Coppin* (1839) 4 My & Cr 647.

1286 *Harding v Harding* (1886) 17 QBD 442.

1287 *Holt v Heatherfield Trust Ltd* [1942] 2 KB 1.

1288 See para 8.334.

1289 *German v Yates* (1915) 32 TLR 52; *Olsson v Dyson* (1969) 120 CLR 365 *contra* seems to be based on the questionable assumption that s 136(1) (para 8.330) *requires* (and does not merely *permit*) the gift to be made by way of statutory assignment.

1290 See para 8.44.

1291 *Re McArdle* [1951] Ch 669.

1292 *Mangles v Dixon* (1852) 3 HLC 702, 732.

1293 *Dawson v Great Northern & City Rly Co* [1905] 1 KB 260; *Offer Hoar v Larkstone Ltd* [2006] EWCA Civ 1079; [2006] 1 WLR 2926.

Hence if nothing is due to the assignor because he has not performed his part of the contract, then the assignee takes nothing.[1294] If the assignor's performance was defective, any damages to which the debtor was entitled in respect of that breach can be set off so as to reduce his liability to the assignee;[1295] though a payment, once made to the assignee, cannot be recovered back *from him* on account of a later breach by the assignor making *the latter* liable to restore it.[1296] If the contract has been induced by the assignor's fraud, the debtor can, by rescinding it, avoid liability to the assignee; and in cases of fraud he should be able to do this even where he can no longer return the subject matter of the contract.[1297]

A claim which the debtor has against the assignor under some transaction *other* **8.342** than the contract assigned can be set up against the assignee only if it arose before the debtor received notice of the assignment.[1298]

The rule that an assignee takes subject to equities does not apply against a holder **8.343** in due course of a negotiable instrument, such as a bill of exchange.[1299]

(8) Rights which are Not Assignable

Rights cannot be assigned if the contract giving rise to them expressly prohibits **8.344** assignment;[1300] though a purported assignment of such rights may make the assignor liable to the assignee.[1301] Assignability is further restricted in the following situations.

(a) Personal contracts

B cannot assign the benefit of his contract with A if the contract is of such a kind **8.345** that it would be unreasonable to expect A to perform in favour of anyone except B. This may be so because the contract was one of personal confidence (so that at common law an employer cannot assign the benefit of his employee's obligation

---

1294 Cf *Tooth v Hallett* (1869) LR 4 Ch App 242.

1295 Cf *Government of Newfoundland v Newfoundland Rly* (1888) 13 App Cas 199.

1296 *The Trident Beauty* [1994] 1 WLR 161.

1297 *Stoddart v Union Trust Ltd* [1912] 1 KB 181, so far as *contra*, overlooks the rule governing rescission for fraud stated in para 8.179 and is viewed with scepticism in *Banco Santander SA v Bayfern Ltd* [2001] 1 All ER (Comm) 776, 778–779.

1298 *Stephens v Venables* (1862) 30 Beav 625; cf *The Raven* [1977] 1 WLR 578 (claim against intermediate assignee).

1299 Bills of Exchange Act 1882, s 38(2).

1300 *Linden Gardens Trust Ltd v Lenesta Sludge Disposals Ltd* [1994] 1 AC 85.

1301 *Re Turcan* (1888) 40 Ch D 5; cf *Don King Productions Inc v Warren* [2000] Ch 291.

to serve);[1302] or because requiring A to perform in favour of C would subject him to duties more onerous than those undertaken, or deprive him of benefits bargained for, under his original contract with B.[1303]

(b) Mere rights of action

8.346 An assignment is invalid if it in fact savours of the wrongs of maintenance or champerty.[1304] For this reason, a right of action in tort cannot generally[1305] be assigned. A liquidated contract claim can be assigned even though the debtor denies liability.[1306] The same is true of a contested contract claim for unliquidated damages if it does not in fact tend to lead to maintenance or champerty; eg where the assignee has a proprietary interest,[1307] or even a 'genuine commercial interest',[1308] in the subject matter. But an assignment of such a claim was held invalid where the assignee took it with a view to reselling it and sharing with his buyer the considerable profits expected from its enforcement.[1309]

(c) Public policy

8.347 On grounds of public policy, a wife cannot assign rights to maintenance and similar payments awarded to her in matrimonial proceedings;[1310] and a public officer (other than one paid out of local funds)[1311] cannot assign his salary.[1312] Other statutory restrictions on assignment are based on similar grounds of public policy.[1313]

(9) Assignment Distinguished from Transfer of Liabilities

8.348 Assignment is the transfer of a right without the consent of the debtor. There is at common law no converse process by which a liability can be transferred without

---

1302 *Nokes v Doncaster Amalgamated Collieries* [1940] AC 1014, 1026; for legislation affecting some such cases, see para 8.350.

1303 *Kemp v Baerselman* [1906] 2 KB 604; contrast *Tolhurst v Associated Portland Cement Co* [1903] AC 414, where there was no such prejudice to A.

1304 See para 8.328.

1305 Exceptionally such rights can be assigned to an insurer who has compensated the victim of the tort who will also on making such compensation be subrogated to the victim's rights: *King v Victoria Insurance Co* [1896] AC 250; *Hobbs v Marlowe* [1978] AC 16, 37.

1306 *County Hotel & Wine Co Ltd v London & North-Western Rly Co* [1918] 2 KB 251, 258; it makes no difference that the assignment is taken with an oblique motive (such as that of making the debtor bankrupt: *Fitzroy v Cave* [1905] 2 KB 364).

1307 *Defries v Milne* [1913] 1 Ch 98; *Ellis v Torrington* [1920] 1 KB 399.

1308 *Trendtex Trading Ltd v Crédit Suisse* [1982] AC 679, 703.

1309 ibid.

1310 *Watkins v Watkins* [1896] P 222.

1311 *Re Mirams* [1891] 1 QB 594.

1312 *Methwold v Walbank* (1750) 2 Ves Sen 238; *Liverpool Corp v Wright* (1859) 28 LJ Ch 868.

1313 eg Social Security Administration Act 1992, s 187; Pensions Act 1995, s 91.

the consent of the creditor[1314] so as to deprive him of his rights against the original debtor. He can be so deprived only with his agreement by a novation extinguishing the original debtor's liability and substituting for it that of a new debtor.[1315] There are, however, situations in which C becomes liable to A for a performance originally undertaken by B; and others in which A cannot object to performance by C of such an obligation.

(a) Benefit and burden

The principle of 'benefit and burden' applies where a benefit transferred by B to C **8.349** is conditional on the discharge by C of an obligation owed by B to A.[1316] This principle has occasionally been extended to cases where discharge of the burden is *not* made a condition of the enjoyment of the benefit; but, to avoid conflict with the general rule that an assignee incurs no liability under the contract assigned,[1317] this extension (known as the 'pure principle of benefit and burden')[1318] is restricted in two ways. First, the burden must be 'relevant to the exercise of the right'[1319] so that the principle did not apply where the right was to occupy one house and the burden to keep the roof of another in repair.[1320] Secondly, B and C must intend to subject C to B's contractual obligation to A; and such an intention will not be inferred merely from the fact that the relationship of B and C is that of assignor and assignee.[1321] Even if C is liable to A, B remains so liable until C performs.

(b) Legislation

The benefit and burden of a contract of employment may be transferred as a result **8.350** of the transfer of the employer's undertaking;[1322] but the employee's 'fundamental right. . .to choose his employer' is preserved in the sense that it is open to him to choose not to enter the employment of the transferee.[1323] A transferee who acquires

---

[1314] *Linden Gardens Trust Ltd v Lenesta Sludge Disposals Ltd* [1994] 1 AC 85, 103.

[1315] eg *Miller's* case (1876) 3 Ch D 391; *Customs & Excise Commissioners v Diners Club Ltd* [1989] 1 WLR 1196.

[1316] eg *Astley v Seddon (No 2)* (1876) 1 Ex D 496.

[1317] *Young v Kitchin* (1878) 3 Ex D 127.

[1318] *Tito v Waddell (No 2)* [1977] Ch 106, 302.

[1319] *Rhone v Stephens* [1994] 2 AC 310, 322.

[1320] ibid.

[1321] *Tito v Waddell (No 2)* [1977] Ch 106, 302.

[1322] Transfer of Undertakings (Protection of Employment) Regulations 2006, SI 2006/246: *Newns v British Airways plc* [1992] IRLR 575, 576.

[1323] *North Wales Training and Enterprise Council v Astley* [2006] UKHL 29; [2006] 1 WLR 2420 at [55].

contractual rights under a bill of lading contract may also incur contractual liabilities under it[1324] but the original shipper remains liable.[1325]

(10) Vicarious Performance

8.351 A's obligation to B may be discharged if C performs it with A's authority,[1326] with B's consent and with the intention of discharging it.[1327] The same result generally follows even where B is unwilling to accept performance from C instead of from A;[1328] but in two situations B can insist on personal performance from A. He can do so first where the contract expressly or impliedly provides that the obligation in question will be performed by A and by no one else;[1329] and secondly where the contract is 'personal' in the sense that it is unreasonable to require B to accept performance from anyone except A (typically because B relied, when making the contract, on A's skill and judgment).[1330]

8.352 Where vicarious performance is permitted, the principle that there can be no 'assignment of liabilities'[1331] is not infringed. No liability is *transferred*, so that A remains liable to B for C's defective performance[1332] (unless A's only undertaking is not to render the performance but to arrange for it to be rendered by C)[1333] and C incurs no liability under the contract between A and B; though C may be liable to B for defective performance in tort[1334] and even for non-performance if B is a third party beneficiary to a sub-contract between A and C.[1335]

M. Performance

8.353 Due performance of a contractual duty discharges the duty and prima facie entitles the party performing it to enforce the other party's undertakings; while failure in performance may give the victim the right to rescind the contract.

1324 Carriage of Goods by Sea Act 1992, s 3(1).

1325 ibid, s 3(3).

1326 See *Crantrave Ltd v Lloyd's Bank plc* [2000] QB 914, where a bank (C) paid a debt of one of its customers (A) without A's authority.

1327 See *Re Rowe* [1904] 2 KB 483, where there was no such intention.

1328 *British Waggon Co v Lea & Co* (1880) 5 QBD 149.

1329 *Davies v Collins* [1945] 1 All ER 247.

1330 eg *Edwards v Newland* [1950] 2 KB 534; *John McCann & Co v Pow* [1974] 1 WLR 1643, 1647.

1331 See para 8.348.

1332 *Stewart v Reavell's Garage* [1952] 2 QB 545; *Wong Mee Wan v Kwan Kim Travel Services Ltd* [1996] 1 WLR 38.

1333 ibid, 41–2 (where the contract was not of this kind).

1334 Cf *British Telecommunications plc v James Thomson & Sons (Engineers) Ltd* [1999] 2 All ER 241.

1335 Contracts (Rights of Third Parties) Act 1999, s 1; para 8.303.

(1) Method of Performance

(a) When performance is due

Performance is due without demand[1336] unless the contract or legislation other- **8.354** wise provides[1337] or unless the party required to perform cannot without demand reasonably be expected to know that performance is due.[1338] Where performance is due on a specified day, there is no default until the end of that day.[1339]

(b) Tender

Tender must be at a reasonable hour.[1340] Tender of money requires actual production **8.355** of (as opposed to a mere offer to produce)[1341] the amount due.[1342] Where a bad tender is rejected and followed within the time fixed for performance by another, good, tender, the latter must generally[1343] be accepted.[1344]

(c) Payment by cheque or credit card

Payment by cheque is (rebuttably)[1345] presumed to be conditional on the cheque's **8.356** being honoured.[1346] By contrast, payment for goods or services by credit card dis- charges the customer; if the issuer of the card fails to pay, the supplier's remedy is against the issuer and not against the customer.[1347]

(d) Alternatives

A contract may call for alternative methods of performance without specifying **8.357** which party has the right to choose between them. The law then has to settle the point: for example where a loan is 'for six or nine months' its period is at the option of the borrower.[1348]

[1336] *Walton v Mascall* (1844) 13 M & W 452.

[1337] *Esso Petroleum Co Ltd v Alstonbridge Properties Ltd* [1975] 1 WLR 1474; Commonhold and Leasehold Reform Act 2002, s 166.

[1338] *British Telecommunications plc v Sun Life Assurance Society plc* [1996] Ch 69, 74.

[1339] *The Lutetian* [1982] 2 Lloyd's Rep 140; *The Afovos* [1983] 1 WLR 195.

[1340] Sale of Goods Act 1979, s 29(5).

[1341] *Farquharson v Pearl Assurance Co Ltd* [1937] 3 All ER 124; cf *Finch v Brook* (1834) 1 Bing NC 253.

[1342] *Betterbee v Davis* (1811) 3 Camp 70.

[1343] ie, unless the first tender is a repudiation or the creditor has acted to his detriment in reliance on it.

[1344] *Tetley v Shand* (1871) 25 LT 658; cf *Borrowman Phillips & Co v Free & Hollis* (1878) 4 QBD 500.

[1345] *Sard v Rhodes* (1836) 1 M & W 153.

[1346] *Sayer v Wagstaff* (1844) 14 LJ Ch 116; *Re Romer & Haslam* [1893] 2 QB 286 treats the condi- tion as precedent; *Jameson v Central Electricity Generating Board* [2000] 1 AC 455, 478 treats it as subsequent. Cf *Esso Petroleum Ltd v Milton* [1997] 1 WLR 938 (payment by direct debit).

[1347] *Re Charge Card Services Ltd* [1989] Ch 497.

[1348] *Reed v Kilburn Co-operative Society* (1875) LR 10 QB 264.

(2) Rescission for Failure to Perform

(a) Introduction

(i) Nature of the remedy

8.358 Failure to perform in accordance with the contract is often a breach, giving the injured party remedies (such as damages) for the *enforcement* of the contract.[1349] It may also (even where it is not a breach) give rise to the remedies here to be discussed, by which a party seeks to *undo* the contract by refusing to perform his part or to accept further performance or by returning the defective performance with a view to reclaiming his own.[1350] Use of the word 'rescission' to refer to these remedies has considerable support in the authorities and in legislation,[1351] though it has not escaped criticism.[1352] Where the failure is due to a supervening event which occurs without default of either party and fundamentally disrupts performance, the contract is automatically discharged under the doctrine of frustration.[1353] Our concern here is with cases in which the failure is not of this kind.

(ii) Practical considerations

8.359 The injured party may prefer rescission to damages since rescission is available even where the failure is not a breach; since mere refusal to perform does not require legal proceedings; and since rescission may enable him to escape from what, for him, is or has become a bad bargain. The other party, by contrast, may wish to resist rescission where he has partly performed or otherwise incurred expenses for the purpose of performance; or where on a falling market the financial prejudice to him of being deprived of the benefit of his bargain exceeds that which the victim would suffer by reason of the defect in performance. The complexity of the subject is due to the need to strike a balance between these conflicting interests.

(b) The order of performance

(i) Conditions precedent, concurrent conditions and independent promises

8.360 A party is entitled to refuse to perform where, under the rules relating to the order of performance, his performance is not yet due. Under these rules, performance

---

1349 See Chapter 21.

1350 *Friends Provident Life & Pensions Ltd v Sirius International Insurance* [2005] EWCA Civ 601; [2005] 2 All ER (Comm) 145 rejects an intermediate possibility described at [31] as 'a new doctrine of partial repudiatory breach'. It followed that the injured party (in that case an insurer) could not, unless the contract expressly so provided (at [33]), rely on the breach as a defence to a particular claim where that breach did not justify rescission of the contract as a whole.

1351 eg *Bunge Corp v Tradax Export SA* [1981] 1 WLR 711, 723, 724; *Gill & Duffus SA v Berger Co Inc* [1984] AC 382, 390, 391. Sale of Goods Act 1979, ss 48, 48A(2)(b)(ii), 48C, 48D(1)(a) and (2)(a).

1352 *Photo Production Ltd v Securicor Transport Ltd* [1980] AC 827, 844, 851.

1353 See section O.

by A may be a promissory[1354] *condition precedent* to the liability of B: eg, where A agrees to work for B at a monthly salary payable in arrear, payment from B is not due until A has done a month's work.[1355] The two performances are *concurrent conditions* where A and B undertake to perform simultaneously: eg in a contract for the sale of goods prima facie the seller cannot claim payment unless he is ready and willing to deliver, nor the buyer delivery unless he is ready and willing to pay.[1356] Where promises are *independent* A can enforce B's promise even though he has not performed his own.[1357]

The courts will, where possible, classify performances as concurrent conditions **8.361** and so reduce the risk of requiring A to perform without any security for B's performance.[1358] But where simultaneous performance is not possible (as in contracts for work to be done over time and paid for on completion) performance by one party is necessarily a condition precedent of the other's liability.[1359] Even where simultaneous performance is possible, a promise may be classified as independent because it is of only trivial importance,[1360] because such was the intention of the parties[1361] or because the commercial setting makes such a classification appropriate.[1362]

(ii) Effects of the distinction

It follows from the nature of an independent promise[1363] that failure to perform **8.362** such a promise does not justify rescission. Failure by A to perform a condition precedent or concurrent condition justifies B's refusal to perform for so long as the refusal continues.[1364] But it does not of itself justify outright rescission in the sense of B's refusal ever to perform (or to accept performance from A).[1365] It has this effect only where A's failure is (in accordance with the principles to be discussed below)[1366] of such a kind as to justify rescission.

[1354] For the distinction between promissory and contingent conditions, see para 8.29.

[1355] *Morton v Lamb* (1797) 7 TR 125; *Miles v Wakefield MDC* [1987] AC 539, 561, 574; cf *Trans Trust SPRL v Danubian Trading Co* [1952] 2 QB 297.

[1356] Sale of Goods Act 1979, s 28.

[1357] *Pordage v Cole* (1669) 1 Wms Saund 619; *Taylor v Webb* [1937] 2 KB 283, 290.

[1358] See *Kingston v Preston* (1773) 2 Doug 689.

[1359] See at n 1355 above.

[1360] *Huntoon Co v Kolynos (Inc)* [1930] Ch 528.

[1361] *The Odenfeld* [1978] 2 Lloyd's Rep 357.

[1362] *Gill & Duffus SA v Berger & Co Inc* [1984] AC 382.

[1363] See para 8.360.

[1364] *Wiluszynski v Tower Hamlets LBC* [1989] ICR 493.

[1365] So that an employee's failure to work does not justify dismissal merely because it justifies withholding of pay.

[1366] In paras 8.364 et seq.

(iii) Wrongful refusal to accept performance

8.363   The rule that B is under no liability if A has failed to perform a condition precedent or concurrent condition may be displaced if, before A's performance was due,
B has, by indicating that he would refuse to accept it, repudiated the contract.
A is then entitled to accept the repudiation by rescinding the contract, and if he
does rescind he is liberated from his duty to perform, so that he can recover damages without showing that he could, but for B's repudiation, have performed that
duty.[1367] This is so not only where B's repudiation induces A's failure[1368] (by causing him to abandon efforts to perform) but also where A could not have performed, even if B had not repudiated.[1369] The purpose of applying the rule to such
cases appears to be to discourage premature repudiation. If A does *not* accept B's
repudiation, A is not liberated from his own duty so that his failure to perform will
make him liable in damages and, if repudiatory, justify rescission by B.[1370]

(c) **General requirement of substantial failure**

8.364   Performance may be in the *order* required by the rules just stated but be deficient
in quantity or quality or be late. The general rule (to which there are important
exceptions)[1371] is that the right to rescind then arises only if the defect in performance deprives the injured party of 'substantially the whole benefit'[1372] which he
was to obtain. It is hard to give precise meaning to such a vague phrase, but a
number of practical factors can be identified as relevant in this context.

8.365   One such factor is the desire to avoid the unjust enrichment which can follow from
allowing the injured party to keep the other's defective performance without paying
for it.[1373] Another is the reluctance to allow rescission where the less drastic remedy
of damages will provide adequate compensation,[1374] particularly where the prejudice that rescission would cause to the party in breach would be wholly out of
proportion to the loss suffered by the injured party as a result of the breach.[1375]
The courts have regard also to the reasonableness of requiring the injured party to
accept further performance: this factor will favour rescission where the failure in

---

1367   *British and Beningtons v North-Western Cachar Tea Co* [1923] AC 48; cf *Braithwaite v Foreign
Hardwood Co* [1905] 2 KB 543, as explained in *The Simona* [1989] AC 788, 805.
1368   eg *Bulk Oil (Zug) AG v Sun International Ltd* [1984] 1 Lloyd's Rep 531, 546.
1369   As in the *British & Beningtons* case (n 1367 above).
1370   *The Simona* (n 1367 above).
1371   See paras 8.366 to 8.385.
1372   *Photo Production Ltd v Securicor Transport Ltd* [1980] AC 827, 849.
1373   See, eg *Boone v Eyre* (1779) 1 Hy Bl 273 n; 2 W Bl 1312.
1374   *Decro-Wall International SA v Practitioners in Marketing Ltd* [1971] 1 WLR 361.
1375   *Friends Provident Life & Pensions Ltd v Sirius International Insurance* [2005] EWCA Civ
601; [2005] 2 All ER (Comm) 145 at [32] (breach causing loss of £50,000 said not be a ground for
rescission in the form of refusing to perform a promise to pay £1 million).

performance gives rise to uncertainty as to future performance[1376] or where the ratio of the failure is high in relation to the performance promised.[1377] Ulterior motives are also taken into account, so that a failure is not readily classified as substantial where the injured party's real reason for rescinding is not to avoid any prejudice resulting from the failure but to escape from a bad bargain.[1378] The list of relevant factors is by no means exhaustive;[1379] but it can help in predicting the operation of the requirement of substantial failure.

(d) Exception to the requirement of substantial failure

Notwithstanding the identification of the factors described in paragraph 8.365, **8.366** the requirement of substantial failure is a source of uncertainty. This is mitigated by a number of exceptions to the requirement, but these have in turn attracted criticism because the certainty which they promote is sometimes achieved only at the expense of justice.

(i) Express provisions

In the interests of certainty, literal effect is as a general rule given to express provisions **8.367** entitling one party (A) to rescind on the other's (B's) failure to perform exactly in accordance with the contract.[1380] The possible hardship to B where the failure is only trivial is mitigated in various ways. The provision will be strictly construed;[1381] and A must act exactly in accordance with it, so that he is not justified in rescinding *before* B's failure in performance even though that failure is at the time of rescission certain to occur.[1382] B may also be entitled to 'relief against forfeiture'[1383] (ie extra time to perform)[1384] where, but only where, rescission would deprive him of a proprietary or possessory right.[1385] Under the Unfair Terms in Consumer

---

[1376] *Bradford v Williams* (1872) LR 7 Ex 259; *Poussard v Spiers* (1876) 1 QBD 410; contrast *Bettini v Gye* (1876) 1 QBD 183 and the *Hong Kong Fir* case [1962] 2 QB 26.

[1377] *Warinco AG v Samor SpA* [1979] 1 Lloyd's Rep 450; contrast the *Maple Flock* case [1934] 1 KB 148.

[1378] *Dakin v Oxley* (1864) 15 CBNS 647, 667–8; *The Hansa Nord* [1976] QB 44, 71.

[1379] *Aerial Advertising Co v Batchelor's Peas Ltd* [1938] 2 All ER 788 (where rescission was allowed) does not fit readily within any of the factors listed here.

[1380] eg *The Laconia* [1977] AC 850; *Union Eagle Ltd v Golden Achievement Ltd* [1997] AC 514.

[1381] *Rice v Great Yarmouth BC* [2001] LGLR 4.

[1382] *The Mihalis Angelos* [1971] 1 QB 164.

[1383] Law of Property Act 1925, s 146; Consumer Credit Act 1974, ss 88, 89. A landlord's right to forfeit certain leases is further restricted by Commonhold and Leasehold Reform Act 2002, ss 167–170. For proposals for more general changes in the law, see Law Com No 303 (2006).

[1384] *Nutting v Baldwin* [1995] 1 WLR 201, 208.

[1385] Not where the right is merely contractual: *The Scaptrade* [1983] 2 AC 694 (time charter); *Sport International Bussum BV v Inter-Footwear Ltd* [1984] 1 WLR 776; contrast *BICC plc v Burndy Corp* [1985] Ch 232, and *The Jotunheim* [2004] EWHC 671 (Comm); [2005] 1 Lloyd's Rep 181 at [47] (demise charter) but relief was refused by reason of the 'commercial character' of the 'freely negotiated' contract (at [67]).

Contracts Regulation 1999, a cancellation clause in a consumer contract may be struck down as unfair;[1386] and if the clause is oppressive it may be open to challenge at common law.[1387] A clause entitling A to refuse to pay in default of exact performance by B may also be invalid as a penalty.[1388]

(ii) Entire and severable obligations

8.368 **Entire obligations.**   An obligation is 'entire' if complete performance of it by B is required before A's counter performance becomes due.[1389] Where, for example, a contract for the carriage of goods by sea provides for payment of freight at the agreed destination, it imposes an entire obligation on the carrier (B) to get the goods there;[1390] and where a building contract provides for payment on completion, it imposes an entire obligation on the builder (B) to complete the work.[1391] A is not liable to make the agreed payment even though B gets the goods nearly to the destination or nearly finishes the work.

8.369 **Severable obligations.**   A contract imposes severable obligations if payment from A falls due on performance of specified parts by B: eg where a contract for the carriage of goods by sea provides for payment of freight of so much *per ton*; or where a building contract provides for part payments as specified stages of the work are completed. If B carries only part of the cargo, or performs only some of the stages of the building contract, he is entitled to corresponding part payments[1392] (though liable in damages for his failure to perform the rest of the contract).[1393]

8.370 **Contract imposing both entire and severable obligations.**   The same contract may impose both entire and severable obligations: eg a contract of carriage may impose an entire obligation to get the cargo to the agreed destination but entitle the carrier to the full freight though as a result of his breach of another term of the contract the goods arrive damaged.[1394] Similarly, a building contract may impose an entire obligation as to the *amount* of work to be done but not as to its quality. Slight defects in the work will then not deprive the builder of his right to be paid.[1395] It is sometimes said that in such cases there has been substantial

---

1386   See paras 8.119 et seq; and see Sch 2 para 1(g) of the Regulations.
1387   *Timeload Ltd v British Telecommunications plc* [1995] Entertainment and Media LR 459, 467.
1388   *Gilbert-Ash (Northern) Ltd v Modern Engineering (Bristol) Ltd* [1974] AC 689.
1389   *Cutter v Powell* (1795) 6 TR 320.
1390   *St Enoch Shipping Co Ltd v Phosphate Mining Co* [1916] 2 KB 624; contrast *The Dominique* [1989] AC 1056 (freight *earned* on loading though not *payable* till discharge).
1391   *Sumpter v Hedges* [1893] 1 QB 673.
1392   *Ritchie v Atkinson* (1808) 10 East 295.
1393   *Atkinson v Ritchie* (1808) 10 East 530.
1394   *Dakin v Oxley* (1864) 15 CB NS 646; *The Brede* [1974] QB 233.
1395   *Hoenig v Isaacs* [1952] 2 All ER 176; though the express terms of the contract can impose an entire obligation as to quality: *Eshelby v Federated European Bank* [1932] 1 KB 423.

performance of an entire contract;[1396] but where one of the *obligations* under the contract is entire, this *means* that it must be completely performed, so that there is no scope for the view that anything less can suffice.

(iii) *Conditions, warranties and intermediate terms*

Statement of the distinction between conditions and warranties. 'Condition' **8.371** is here used in its promissory sense[1397] to refer to a contractual term any breach of which gives the injured party the right to rescind. This usage makes a point, not about the *order* of performance,[1398] but about the *conformity* of the performance rendered with that promised. A seller who tenders goods on the buyer's tender of the price thereby performs a 'concurrent condition'[1399] but will be in breach of condition (in the present sense) if the goods are not up to sample.[1400] Failure to perform a condition in the former sense results *ipso facto* in the buyer's performance not becoming due,[1401] while breach of condition in the latter sense gives the buyer an option to rescind.[1402] A warranty (in modern legal usage)[1403] is a term the breach of which gives the injured party a right to damages but not (at least generally)[1404] a right to rescind.[1405]

Bases of the distinction. One ground for classifying a term as a condition is that **8.372** the parties intended it to take effect as such.[1406] Their use of the word 'condition' with reference to the term is capable of producing this effect;[1407] but it is not decisive and may, particularly where the term can be broken in a way which will cause only trifling loss, be construed simply to refer to a term of the contract.[1408]

Where the intention of the parties is not discoverable from the terms of the con- **8.373** tract, the courts have relied on the requirement of substantial failure so as to classify terms as conditions if their breach caused or was likely to cause serious prejudice to the injured party.[1409] But terms have also been classified by judicial

---

[1396] *Geipel v Smith* (1872) LR 7 QB 404, 411; *Dakin v Lee* [1916] 1 KB 566, 598.

[1397] See para 8.29.

[1398] See para 8.360.

[1399] See para 8.360.

[1400] Sale of Goods Act 1979, s 15.

[1401] *The Good Luck* [1992] 1 AC 233, 262.

[1402] See para 8.419.

[1403] 'Warranty' was formerly used to refer to terms now described as conditions: eg *Behn v Burness* (1863) 3 B & S 751, 755. For survival of a similar usage, see para 8.421.

[1404] See para 8.380.

[1405] Sale of Goods Act 1979, s 61(1) (definition of 'warranty').

[1406] *Glaholm v Hays* (1841) 2 Man & G 257, 266; Sale of Goods Act 1979, s 11(3).

[1407] *Dawsons Ltd v Bonin* [1922] 2 AC 413.

[1408] *Wickman Ltd v Schuler AG* [1974] AC 235.

[1409] *Glaholm v Hays* (n 1406 above) 268; *Bentsen v Taylor* [1893] 2 QB 274, 281; *Couchman v Hill* [1947] KB 554, 559.

decision or by legislation[1410] as conditions even though their breach may not cause such prejudice;[1411] and, once so classified, they will, in the interests of commercial certainty, give rise to a right to rescind 'without regard to the magnitude of the breach'.[1412]

8.374   **Intermediate terms.**   Some applications of the rule just stated have been criticized as 'excessively technical';[1413] for the rule enables a party to rescind even where the breach has not caused him any loss and even where his motive for rescinding is to escape from a bad bargain. The requirements of certainty here conflict with those of justice; and the latter are promoted by recognition of the category of intermediate terms.[1414] These differ from conditions in that their breach gives rise to a right to rescind only[1415] if it amounts, or gives rise, to a substantial failure;[1416] and from warranties in that there is no prima facie rule that the only remedy for breach is in damages.

8.375   Where a term has not been classified as a condition by either express agreement or previous judicial decision or legislation, the judicial tendency is (in the interests of justice) to 'lean in favour'[1417] of classifying it as an intermediate term, so that only a serious breach of it will justify rescission. The interests of certainty, however, give rise to a countervailing tendency to classify clauses in commercial contracts as conditions if they lay down a precise time[1418] by, or interval within, which acts of performance have to be done or notices given.[1419] The reason for this trend is that breaches of such terms are easy to establish and that strict compliance with them is in general of vital commercial importance. It follows that a time clause which is clearly *not* of such importance[1420] (eg because it relates only to an 'ancillary' obligation imposed by the contract)[1421] is unlikely to be classified as a condition. Conversely, a previously unclassified term other than one specifying a precise time

---

[1410] See Sale of Goods Act 1979, ss 12 to 15.

[1411] *Bunge Corp v Tradax Export SA* [1981] 1 WLR 711, 724.

[1412] *Lombard North Central plc v Butterworth* [1987] QB 527, 535.

[1413] *Reardon Smith Line Ltd v Hansen Tangen* [1976] 1 WLR 989, 998.

[1414] *Hong Kong Fir* case [1962] 2 QB 26, 70; *The Hansa Nord* [1976] QB 44.

[1415] See the *Hong Kong Fir* case (n 1417 above).

[1416] As in *Federal Commerce & Navigation v Molena Alpha* [1979] AC 757.

[1417] *Tradax Internacional SA v Goldschmidt SA* [1977] 2 Lloyd's Rep 604, 612; *Bunge Corp v Tradax Export SA* [1981] 1 WLR 714, 715, 727 (where the term in question was classified as a condition).

[1418] If the time is not precise, the term is likely to be classified as intermediate: see the respective treatment of clauses 21 and 22 in *Bremer Handelsgesellschaft mbH v Vanden Avenne-Izegem PVBA* [1978] 2 Lloyd's Rep 109.

[1419] *Bunge Corp v Tradax Export SA* (n 1417 above); *Toepfer v Lenersan-Poortman NV* [1980] 1 Lloyd's Rep 143.

[1420] *State Trading Corporation of India Ltd v M Golodetz Ltd* [1989] 2 Lloyd's Rep 277.

[1421] *Friends Provident Life & Pensions Ltd v Sirius Insurance* [2005] EWCA Civ 601; [2005] 2 All ER (Comm) 145 at [29], [31]. Here the term was classified, not as an intermediate term, but as one for even a serious breach of which the *only* remedy was in damages.

will take effect as a condition if its exact performance is regarded by the parties as vital[1422] or if there is other evidence of their intention to give it this effect.[1423]

Restrictions on the right to rescind for breach of condition. The right to **8.376** rescind a contract for the sale of goods for breach of certain statutorily implied terms cannot, unless the parties otherwise agree, be exercised by a buyer who does not deal as consumer where the breach is 'so slight that it would be unreasonable'[1424] for the injured party to reject the goods. This restriction is intended to prevent abuses of the right to reject (such as its exercise for oblique motives) but it is a regrettable source of uncertainty. It is also one-sided, being inapplicable to the converse case of a breach of condition by a buyer.[1425] A breach which is not 'slight' is not necessarily of the degree of seriousness which would justify rescission for breach of an intermediate term.

A buyer who deals as consumer has under Part 5A of the Sale of Goods Act 1979 **8.377** certain 'additional rights',[1426] including one to require the seller to repair or replace[1427] 'non-conforming' goods (ie goods in respect of which the seller is in breach of certain statutorily implied terms or of an express term[1428]). Where the buyer asks for such repair or replacement, he must not reject the goods until the seller has had a reasonable time to comply with the request.[1429] If by the end of that time the seller has not so complied, the buyer has a right to 'rescind' the contract;[1430] but this right is subject to the discretion of the court, which may instead give effect to another of the buyer's 'additional rights', such as a price reduction.[1431] There is nothing in Part 5A to compel the buyer to ask for repair or replacement and, if he chooses not to do so, his right to reject for breach of condition[1432] remains unimpaired.

The right to rescind for breach of condition can be excluded by an express con- **8.378** tractual term such as a non-cancellation or non-rejection clause, subject to the rules which determine the validity and construction of exemption clauses.[1433]

[1422] *The Post Chaser* [1981] 2 Lloyd's Rep 695, 700.

[1423] eg *Tradax Export SA v European Grain & Shipping Co* [1983] 2 Lloyd's Rep 100.

[1424] Sale of Goods Act 1979, s 15A. Similar restrictions apply where goods are supplied to a person who does not deal as consumer under a contract other than one of sale: see Supply of Goods (Implied Terms) Act 1973, s 11A; Supply of Goods and Services Act 1982, s 5A. Cf also Sale of Goods Act 1979, s 30 (2A) (delivery of wrong quantity).

[1425] As in *Bunge Corp v Tradax Export SA* [1981] 1 WLR 714.

[1426] Heading to Part 5A; for similar rights available to a consumer to whom goods are supplied under a contract other than one of sale: see Supply of Goods and Services Act 1982, Part 1B.

[1427] Sale of Goods Act 1979, s 48A(2)(a), 48B; for restrictions, see s 48B(3) and (4).

[1428] ibid, s 48F.

[1429] ibid, s 48D(1), (2)(a).

[1430] ibid, s 48C(2); the buyer can also rescind where the limitations on the right to ask for repair or replacement set out in s 48B(3) apply.

[1431] ibid, s 48E(3) and (4).

[1432] See paras 8.371–8.373.

[1433] See section D.

8.379 Where a non-fraudulent misrepresentation inducing a contract is incorporated in it as a condition,[1434] the right to rescind for misrepresentation is subject to the discretion of the court,[1435] but this discretion probably does not extend to the right to rescind for breach.[1436]

8.380 **Rescission for breach of warranty.** Where a representation inducing a contract is incorporated in it as a warranty, the right to rescind for misrepresentation survives such incorporation,[1437] subject to the discretion of the court referred to in paragraph 8.379.

8.381 Where a breach of warranty leads or amounts to a substantial failure in performance, there may be a right to rescind on this ground in spite of the classification of the term as a warranty.[1438]

8.382 A buyer who deals as consumer has, in the circumstances specified in Part 5A of the Sale of Goods Act 1979,[1439] a right to 'rescind' the contract in respect of non-conforming goods.[1440] Non-conformity here includes breach of an express term,[1441] which may be a warranty. The buyer's right to 'rescind' is, however, subject to the discretion of the court to award another remedy available under Part 5A, such as a price reduction.[1442]

(iv) Breach of fundamental term

8.383 Breach of a fundamental term[1443] will usually have serious effects; but where a carrier commits such a breach by deviating, the cargo-owner can rescind even though the deviation is 'for practical purposes irrelevant'.[1444]

(v) Deliberate breach

8.384 Rescission is not justified merely because the breach is deliberate, for such a breach may be trivial[1445] or reflect an honest attempt to overcome temporary difficulties in performance. The deliberate nature of the breach will, however, justify rescission

---

[1434] See Misrepresentation Act 1967, s 1(a).

[1435] ibid, s 2(2).

[1436] See para 8.178.

[1437] Misrepresentation Act 1967, s 1(a).

[1438] *The Hansa Nord* [1976] QB 44, 83. Contrast *Friends Provident Life & Pensions Ltd v Sirius Insurance* [2005] EWCA Civ 601; [2005] 2 All ER (Comm) 145 at [31]: no right to reject insurance claim for even a serious breach of an 'ancillary' term (not amounting to a condition) requiring 'immediate' notice of claims.

[1439] See para 8.377; and, where the contract under which the goods are supplied is not one of sale, ibid, n 1426.

[1440] Sale of Goods Act 1979, s 48C.

[1441] ibid, s 48F.

[1442] ibid, s 48E(3) and (4).

[1443] For this concept, see para 8.101.

[1444] *Suisse Atlantique* case [1967] 1 AC 361, 423.

[1445] ibid, 435.

in two situations: where it amounts to fraud[1446] and where it is evidence of an 'intention no longer to be bound by the contract'.[1447] The fact that a party declares that he will perform only in a manner inconsistent with his obligations under the contract may be evidence of such an intention.[1448] But it will not have this effect merely because a party in good faith asserts a view of his duties under the contract which the court later holds to have been mistaken;[1449] in this context, the fact that he relied on legal advice is relevant,[1450] though not decisive.[1451] Where the breach can be cured, refusal to cure it can also be evidence of an 'intention not to be bound' so that its deliberate nature can justify rescission where the breach, apart from this factor, would not have done so.[1452]

(vi) Unilateral contracts and options

Where A promises B £100 if B walks to York, and B makes no counter-promise, **8.385** his accomplishing the walk is a contingent condition[1453] of A's liability to pay the £100, which does not accrue till B has completed the walk.[1454] Even in a bilateral contract, a stipulation (eg as to giving a specified notice) may amount, not to a promise, but to a condition of the other party's liability[1455] which will then not accrue until the stipulation is precisely performed. Contractual provisions which, on their true construction, specify the circumstances in which an option (eg to purchase) becomes exercisable are likewise conditions which must be precisely performed[1456] unless the contract, on its true construction, otherwise provides.[1457]

(e) Limitations on the right to rescind

The right to rescind may be prevented from arising by contractual provisions such **8.386** as non-cancellation clauses.[1458] Our concern here, however, is with cases in which the right, having once arisen, is later lost or limited.

[1446] *Flight v Booth* (1834) 1 Bing NC 370, 376.
[1447] *Freeth v Burr* (1874) LR 9 CP 208, 213; *Bradley v H Newsom Sons & Co* [1919] AC 16, 52.
[1448] *Withers v Reynolds* (1831) 2 B & Ad 882; *Total Oil Great Britain Ltd v Thompson Garages (Biggin Hill) Ltd* [1972] QB 318, 322.
[1449] *Woodar Investment Development Ltd v Wimpey Construction Ltd* [1980] 1 WLR 277.
[1450] *Mersey Steel & Iron Co v Naylor Benzon & Co* (1884) 9 App Cas 434.
[1451] *Vaswani v Italian Motors (Sales and Services) Ltd* [1996] 1 WLR 270, 277.
[1452] *Hong Kong Fir* case [1962] 2 QB 26, 54, 64.
[1453] See para 8.29.
[1454] See para 8.16.
[1455] See *Shires v Brock* (1977) 247 EG 127; *United Dominions Trust Ltd v Eagle Aircraft Ltd* [1968] 1 WLR 74.
[1456] *West Country Cleaners (Falmouth) Ltd v Saly* [1966] 1 WLR 1485.
[1457] *Little v Courage Ltd* (1995) 70 P & CR 469.
[1458] See para 8.378.

(i) Waiver or election

8.387 **Concepts.** Two processes must be distinguished. The first ('waiver in the sense of election') is that by which a party who is entitled to rescind a contract indicates that he will nevertheless perform it: eg if a charterer declares that he will load a cargo in spite of the shipowner's breach of condition.[1459] This election to affirm the contract deprives him of the right to rescind for that breach, though not of his right to damages.[1460] The second ('total waiver') is that by which a party purports *wholly* to give up some or all of his rights in respect of the breach: ie not merely his right to rescind but also his right to performance (or damages).[1461] Our concern here is with the first process, the requirements of which in one respect resemble, and in another differ from, those of the second.

8.388 **Requirement of representation.** The requirement of a 'clear and unequivocal' representation in cases of total waiver is discussed in para 8.53. An 'unequivocal act or statement' is also required for waiver in the sense of election:[1462] there is, for example, no such waiver where the injured party continues to perform or to accept performance while calling for the other's failure to be cured[1463] or reserving his position if this is not done.[1464] Mere failure to rescind is not of itself an election to affirm[1465] but such an election may be inferred from unreasonable delay in rescinding where it is commercially reasonable to expect prompt action.[1466]

8.389 **No requirement of action in reliance.** Total waiver requires the party invoking it to have relied on the representation giving rise to the waiver;[1467] but there is no such requirement for waiver in the sense of election.[1468] This distinction between the two processes is sometimes obscured by the unqualified use of 'waiver' to refer to both of them[1469] and by the fact that some cases raise issues relating to both types of waiver.[1470]

[1459] *Bentsen v Taylor* [1893] 2 QB 274; cf *The Kanchenjunga* [1990] 1 Lloyd's Rep 391; *The Happy Day* [2002] EWCA Civ 1068; [2002] 2 Lloyd's Rep 487 at [64], [65], [68].

[1460] The right to damages may be barred by another term of the contract, as in *The Kanchenjunga* (n 1459 above).

[1461] See paras 8.56 et seq.

[1462] *The Mihalios Xilas* [1979] 1 WLR 1018, 1024.

[1463] *Cobec Brazilian Trading & Warehousing Corp v Alfred C Toepfer* [1983] 2 Lloyd's Rep 386.

[1464] *Bremer Handelsgesellschaft mbH v Deutsche Conti Handelsgesellschaft mbH* [1983] 2 Lloyd's Rep 45.

[1465] ibid; *Allen v Robles* [1969] 1 WLR 1193.

[1466] *The Laconia* [1977] AC 850, 872; *The Balder London* [1980] 2 Lloyd's Rep 489, 491–3.

[1467] See para 8.55.

[1468] See eg *The Athos* [1981] 2 Lloyd's Rep 74, 87–8 (affirmed on this point [1983] 1 Lloyd's Rep 127); *The Kanchenjunga* [1990] 1 Lloyd's Rep 391, 399; *Oliver Ashworth Holdings v Ballard (Kent) Ltd* [2000] Ch 12, 27.

[1469] eg *The Eurometal* [1981] 1 Lloyd's Rep 337, 341.

[1470] eg *Bremer Handelsgesellschaft mbH v C Mackprang Jr* [1979] 1 Lloyd's Rep 221.

Knowledge.   Waiver in the sense of election (being based on affirmation of the   **8.390**
contract)[1471] requires knowledge, not only of the facts giving rise to the right to
rescind, but of the existence of the right itself.[1472] If, however, A so conducts himself
as to give B reasonable grounds for believing that A has (after B's breach) affirmed
the contract, then A may be estopped by his implied representation from denying
that he has affirmed.[1473] For this purpose, there is no requirement of A's knowledge
of the breach; but the estoppel (unlike actual waiver in the sense of election)[1474]
operates only if B has acted in reliance on A's implied representation.

(ii) Voluntary acceptance of a benefit

Partial performance no bar to rescission.   The mere fact that one party has by   **8.391**
part performance conferred a benefit on the other does not bar the latter's right to
rescind. The courts may, indeed, take this factor into account in determining
whether there has been a serious failure in performance;[1475] but they cannot take
this course in cases falling within exceptions to that requirement. If, for example,
there is a failure to complete performance of an entire obligation by a builder's
doing only part of the agreed work,[1476] or by a carrier's carrying goods only part of
the way to the agreed destination,[1477] then the injured party need not pay the agreed
remuneration. It makes no difference that the failure causes no loss to the injured
party[1478] or that his loss is less than the benefit to him of the partial performance.
Unjust enrichment of the victim, as well as hardship to the party in breach, can
result from these rules; these defects are mitigated in ways to be discussed below.

Requirement of 'new contract'.   An injured party who, under the rules just stated,   **8.392**
is not liable for the agreed remuneration may be liable for a reasonable sum. There
is such liability if his acceptance of the partial performance is 'voluntary' so as to
give rise to the inference of a new contract to pay such a sum: eg if the owner of
goods which cannot be carried to the agreed destination asks for their delivery
elsewhere;[1479] or if the owner of the site of an incomplete building makes use of
loose materials left on the site by the defaulting builder.[1480] No such new contract
can, however, be inferred from the owner's merely retaking his own property: he
must, in general, have a real 'option whether he will take the benefit'.[1481]

[1471] *Kwei Tek Chao v British Traders & Shippers Ltd* [1954] 2 QB 459, 477.
[1472] *Peyman v Lanjani* [1985] Ch 457.
[1473] ibid, 501.
[1474] See para 8.389.
[1475] See para 8.365 at n 1373 above.
[1476] *Sumpter v Hedges* [1898] 1 QB 673; *Bolton v Mahadeva* [1972] 1 WLR 1009.
[1477] *Metcalfe v Britannia Ironworks Co* (1877) 2 QBD 423.
[1478] As in *Hopper v Burness* (1876) 1 CPD 137.
[1479] *Christy v Row* (1808) 1 Taunt 300.
[1480] As in *Sumpter v Hedges* [1898] 1 QB 673.
[1481] ibid, 676.

8.393 **Exceptions to requirement of 'new contract'.** A person may be liable to pay a reasonable sum although his acceptance of the benefit was not truly 'voluntary': eg where a cargo-owner simply retakes possession of his own goods after the carrier's unjustified deviation;[1482] and perhaps where an employee commits a repudiatory breach by 'working to rule' and the employer 'of necessity'[1483] accepts the services so rendered.[1484]

8.394 The right to reject goods for breach of condition is barred by 'acceptance';[1485] and although this will not normally take place unless the buyer has had an opportunity of examination,[1486] it need not be truly 'voluntary' as there is no requirement for the buyer to have become aware of the breach. However, where the buyer has the right to reject all the goods, he does not by accepting some lose the right to reject the rest.[1487] Even after acceptance, he may[1488] also be allowed to rescind where a misrepresentation inducing the contract was later incorporated in it as a condition.[1489] The rule that the right to reject for breach of condition is barred by 'acceptance' may not apply where as a result of the breach the performance rendered is 'totally different from that which the contract contemplates':[1490] eg where peas are delivered under a contract for the sale of beans.

8.395 A buyer who 'accepts' delivery of the wrong quantity of goods must pay for that quantity at the contract rate[1491] even though the 'acceptance' is (for the reason stated in paragraph 8.394) not truly 'voluntary.'

8.396 **Part payment.** Failure to complete payments due under a contract may justify rescission.[1492] The question whether the payee must restore the payments received by him is discussed in Chapter 18.[1493]

(iii) Wrongful prevention of performance

8.397 Where A is prevented by B's wrongful repudiation from completing performance of an entire obligation, A can recover a reasonable remuneration for the work that he has done.[1494] A's right in such a case does not depend on the receipt of any benefit by B.

1482 *Hain Steamship Co Ltd v Tate & Lyle Ltd* (1936) 41 Commercial Cases 350, 358, 367.
1483 *Miles v Wakefield MDC* [1987] AC 539, 553.
1484 ibid, 553, 561; the point is left open at 552 and 576.
1485 Sale of Goods Act 1979, s 11(4).
1486 ibid, s 35.
1487 ibid, s 35A.
1488 Subject to Misrepresentation Act 1967, s 2(2) (para 8.172).
1489 Misrepresentation Act 1967, s 1(a).
1490 *Suisse Atlantique* case [1967] 1 AC 361, 393.
1491 Sale of Goods Act 1979, s 30(1).
1492 See *The Blankenstein* [1985] 1 WLR 435, 446.
1493 See paras 18.95–18.103.
1494 *Planché v Colburn* (1831) 8 Bing 14.

(iv) Both parties in breach

It has been suggested that where A's breach consists in failing to avoid the conse- **8.398** quences of B's, then neither party can rescind.[1495] But there is little point in holding parties to a contract which each of them has repudiated and the normal rule is that where both parties have simultaneously committed repudiatory breaches each can rescind.[1496]

(v) Apportionment Act 1870

Under this Act, certain 'periodical payments in the nature of income' (such as **8.399** rents and salaries) are, unless the contract otherwise provides, 'to be considered as accruing from day to day and shall be apportionable in respect of time accordingly'. These words literally apply even in favour of a party in breach: eg an employee who left in breach of contract or was justifiably dismissed during a payment period specified in the contract. Judicial opinion tends, though not conclusively, to support the view that, in such a case, the guilty party can, under the Act, recover a proportionate payment.[1497]

(3) Stipulations as to Time

Failure to perform a stipulation as to time does not differ intrinsically from any **8.400** other failure to perform; but the subject calls for separate discussion because it has acquired its own terminology and because special rules apply to such stipulations in contracts for the sale of land.

(a) Classification

Stipulations as to the time of performance are divided into those which are, and **8.401** those which are not, 'of the essence' of the contract. Where the stipulation is of the essence, any failure (however trivial) to comply with it justifies rescission; where the stipulation is not of the essence, failure to comply with it justifies rescission only if the delay amounts to a serious failure in performance. Time is most obviously of the essence if the contract expressly says so,[1498] or if it says that failure to perform on time is to be a ground for rescission[1499] or that the stipulation

---

1495 *Bremer Vulkan* case [1981] AC 909, 947; *The Hannah Blumenthal* [1983] 1 AC 854.
1496 *State Trading Corporation of India v M Golodetz Ltd* [1989] 2 Lloyd's Rep 277, 286.
1497 There is a conflict of opinion on the point in *Moriarty v Regent's Garage* [1921] 1 KB 432, 434, 448–9 (actual decision reversed on another ground [1921] 2 KB 766); in *Item Software (UK) Ltd v Fassih* [2004] EWCA Civ 1653; [2005] ICR 450 one member of the court at [94], [116]–[121] favoured the view stated in the text above, while the other two did not find it necessary to decide the point.
1498 See para 8.402.
1499 See *Union Eagle Ltd v Golden Achievement Ltd* [1997] AC 514.

is a 'condition'.[1500] In the absence of such express words, some stipulations as to time are prima facie classified by law: for example, in a charterparty a stipulation as to the time of sailing is of the essence,[1501] while one as to the time of loading is not.[1502] The possibly harsh consequences of classifying time stipulations as of the essence may incline the court to reject this classification in cases of first impression,[1503] while the requirements of certainty may, especially in 'mercantile contracts'[1504] favour such a classification.

(b) Sale of land

(i) *Whether time of essence*

8.402   At common law, stipulations as to the time of performance in contracts for the sale of land were of the essence;[1505] but this view was rejected in equity,[1506] which now prevails.[1507] As a general rule, therefore, time is not of the essence in such contracts so that a delay not amounting to a serious breach will not of itself justify rescission.[1508] The general rule, however, does not apply where the contract expressly provides that time is to be of the essence;[1509] or where the subject matter is such as to be likely to fall or to rise rapidly in value.[1510] It has also been said not to apply where the sale is of a 'commercial' nature;[1511] though now that land and houses fluctuate rapidly in value the continuing validity of the distinction between those contracts for the sale of land which are, and those which are not, 'commercial' has rightly been questioned.[1512] A stipulation is also of the essence if it provides for the time of performance of an act by one party which is a condition precedent to the very existence of the contract or to the liability of the other party.[1513]

(ii) *Waiver*

8.403   A party may waive a stipulation which is of the essence by granting the other an extension of time; performance within the extended time is then of the essence.[1514]

1500 In the sense discussed in para 8.371; *The Scaptrade* [1983] 2 AC 694, 703.
1501 *Glaholm v Hays* (1841) 2 Man & G 257.
1502 *Universal Cargo Carriers Corp v Citati* [1957] 2 QB 401.
1503 *United Scientific Holdings Ltd v Burnley BC* [1978] AC 904, 940 ('prima facie not of the essence').
1504 *Bunge Corp v Tradax Export SA* [1981] 1 WLR 711, 716.
1505 *Parkin v Thorold* (1852) 16 Beav 59, 65.
1506 *Parkin v Thorold* (n 1505 above).
1507 Law of Property Act 1925, s 141 (para 8.405).
1508 *United Scientific* case (n 1503 above) 942.
1509 *Union Eagle* case (n 1499 above).
1510 *Hudson v Temple* (1860) 29 Beav 536; *Newman v Rogers* (1793) 4 Bro CC 391.
1511 For example, *Bernard v Williams* (1928) 44 TLR 437; *Lock v Bell* [1931] 1 Ch 35.
1512 *United Scientific* case (n 1503 above) 924; *Union Eagle* case (n 1499 above) 519.
1513 *Re Sandwell Park Colliery Co* [1929] 1 Ch 277; cf *Hare v Nicholl* [1966] 2 QB 130.
1514 *Barclay v Messenger* (1874) 43 LJ Ch 449.

(iii) Notice

Where time is not of the essence of a contract for the sale of land under the rules **8.404** stated in paragraph 8.402, the injured party can make it of the essence by giving notice to the other party, as soon as the latter is in default,[1515] calling on him to complete within the time specified in the notice. This must be the time specified for this purpose in the contract, or, if no time is so specified, a reasonable time.[1516] If *either* party then fails to perform within the time specified in the notice, the other can rescind.[1517]

(iv) Law of Property Act 1925 section 141

This section provides that stipulations as to time which are not of the essence of a **8.405** contract under the rules of equity 'are also construed and have effect at law in accordance with the same rules'. It follows that delay is no longer a ground of rescission merely because it would formerly have been one at common law;[1518] that a party who rescinds when he could not have done so in equity is liable in damages for wrongful repudiation;[1519] and that the party guilty of the delay is in breach and liable in damages for loss resulting from the delay.[1520]

N. Breach

(1) What Amounts to Breach?

A breach of contract is committed when a party, after performance from him **8.406** has become due,[1521] fails or refuses to render it or incapacitates himself from rendering it.

(a) Types of breach

(i) Failure or refusal to perform

Failure or refusal to perform a contractual stipulation is a breach only where an **8.407** obligation to perform has been undertaken. No such obligation is undertaken by the promisee under a unilateral contract,[1522] who therefore commits no breach by failing to do the stipulated act. Similarly, an apparently bilateral contract may

---

[1515] *Behzadi v Shaftsbury Hotels Ltd* [1992] Ch 1.
[1516] ibid.
[1517] *Finkielkraut v Monohan* [1949] 2 All ER 234; *Quadrangle Development and Construction Co Ltd v Jenner* [1974] 1 WLR 68.
[1518] *Raineri v Miles* [1981] AC 1050, 1082-3.
[1519] *Stickney v Keeble* [1915] AC 386, 404; *Rightside Properties Ltd v Gray* [1975] Ch 72.
[1520] *Raineri v Miles* (n 1518 above).
[1521] For refusal *before* performance has become due, see paras 8.430 to 8.437.
[1522] See para 8.07.

be in the nature of a tender by one party, not binding the other unless and to the extent that he accepts it.[1523] Difficulty can also arise in determining the extent of the obligation of a promisor: eg whether an employer promises merely to pay his employee[1524] or to provide him with work.[1525] The answer to this question is likely to depend on whether the employee needs to work to acquire or retain a skill or reputation.[1526]

(ii) Defective performance

8.408 Very seriously defective performance can be regarded as non-performance: eg where peas are delivered instead of beans. But a breach is also committed where performance is of the same kind as that promised and differs from it in point of time, quantity or quality.

(iii) Incapacitating oneself

8.409 A person may break a contract by incapacitating himself from performing it: eg where, having chartered his ship to X, he then sells and delivers her to Y.[1527] Mere insolvency does not incapacitate a person who is under an obligation to pay money:[1528] it has this effect only if no assets are set aside out of his estate for performance of the contract.[1529]

(b) Without lawful excuse

(i) Concept

8.410 After a contractual duty has arisen,[1530] an event may occur excusing performance. The event may so seriously affect performance as to discharge both parties by frustration.[1531] But even where it is less drastic it may excuse one party from performing: eg an employee is not in breach if he is prevented from working by temporary illness.[1532] A party may also have an excuse for non-performance if his rescission is justified by the other's failure to perform.[1533]

[1523] *Churchward v R* (1865) LR 1 QB 173; cf *Firstpost Homes Ltd v Johnson* [1995] 1 WLR 1567.

[1524] *Turner v Sawdon* [1901] 2 KB 653; *Delaney v Staples* [1992] 1 AC 687, 692 ('garden leave').

[1525] *Langston v AUEW* [1974] 1 WLR 185.

[1526] *Herbert Clayton & Jack Waller Ltd v Oliver* [1930] AC 209.

[1527] *Omnium D'Entreprises v Sutherland* [1919] 1 KB 618.

[1528] *Re Agra Bank* (1867) LR 5 Eq 160.

[1529] *Ex p Chalmers* (1873) LR 8 Ch App 289.

[1530] See paras 8.360 to 8.362.

[1531] See section O.

[1532] See *Poussard v Spiers* (1876) 1 QBD 410, 414.

[1533] See paras 8.358 et seq.

Excuses may also be provided by the contract itself: eg by 'exceptions' for delays **8.411**
caused by strikes or weather. Such 'exceptions' are not exemption clauses;[1534] their
purpose is not to exclude liabilities but to define duties.

(ii) Whether excuse must be stated

The party relying on the excuse must show that it existed at the time of his **8.412**
refusal[1535] but need not, in general,[1536] then state the excuse or even have known
of its existence.[1537] A buyer can, for example, justify rejection on account of a
breach of condition of which he did not know (but which existed) at the time of
rejection.[1538] But this rule would not apply where failure to specify the breach
deprived the seller of the chance of curing it[1539] by making a fresh, good tender
within the time allowed for performance.[1540] Even where there is no longer any
such chance of curing the unstated breach, the injured party can also lose his right
to rely on it where his purported rejection was preceded by 'acceptance' of the
defective performance.[1541]

(c) Standard of duty

(i) Strict liability

Many contractual duties are strict.[1542] Lack of fault is, for example, no excuse for **8.413**
inability to pay money brought about by failure of a bank or by exchange
control;[1543] or for inability to deliver generic goods due to difficulties of supply or
transport.[1544] A seller of goods is likewise strictly liable for defects of quality.[1545]

[1534] *The Angelia* [1973] 1 WLR 210 (disapproved on another point in *The Nema* [1982]
AC 724).

[1535] *British & Beningtons v North-Western Cachar Tea Co* [1923] AC 48.

[1536] See at n 1539 below for an exception.

[1537] *Ridgway v Hungerford Market Co* (1835) 3 A & E 171; *Taylor v Oakes, Roncoroni & Co*
(1922) 38 TLR 349, 351 (affirmed ibid 517); *The Azur Gaz* [2005] EWHC 2528 (Comm); [2006]
1 Lloyd's Rep 163 at [54].

[1538] *Arcos Ltd v EA Ronaasen & Sons* [1933] AC 470.

[1539] *Heisler v Anglo-Dal Ltd* [1954] 1 WLR 1273, 1278.

[1540] See para 8.355.

[1541] *Panchaud Frères SA v Etablissement General Grain Co* [1970] 1 Lloyd's Rep 53, as explained
in *BP Exploration Co (Libya) Ltd v Hunt* [1979] 1 WLR 783, 810–11.

[1542] *Raineri v Miles* [1981] AC 1050, 1086.

[1543] *Universal Corp v Five Ways Properties Ltd* [1979] 1 All ER 552; *Congimex SARL (Lisbon) v
Continental Grain Export Corp (New York)* [1979] 2 Lloyd's Rep 346.

[1544] *Barnett v Javeri & Co* [1916] 2 KB 390; *Lewis Emanuel & Son Ltd v Sammut* [1959] 2 Lloyd's
Rep 629.

[1545] *Frost v Aylesbury Dairy Co Ltd* [1905] 1 KB 608; *Daniels & Daniels v White & Sons Ltd
& Tarbard* [1938] 4 All ER 258. Lack of fault can, however, be a defence to a seller's liability
to a consumer in respect of certain public statements relating to goods: Sale of Goods Act 1979,
s 14(2E)(c).

The same is true of a repairer or builder in respect of components supplied by him.[1546]

(ii) Liability based on fault

8.414 Liability for breach of a contract to provide services is often based on fault (ie on negligence):[1547] this is generally[1548] true of contracts to provide professional services.[1549] In a contract to provide services and components, liability for the service aspect is based on fault.[1550]

(iii) Modification of standards

8.415 It is generally possible to vary the standards of liability described above by the contract itself;[1551] and they may also be varied by legislation.[1552]

(iv) Fault and excuses for non-performance

8.416 A party cannot rely on a supervening event which is due to his fault as a ground of frustration[1553] or (generally)[1554] as an excuse for non-performance of the kind described in paragraph 8.410.

(v) Fault and contingent conditions

8.417 A party cannot rely on the non-occurrence of a contingent condition precedent if he has deliberately prevented the occurrence of the event or if he has failed to perform a duty (imposed by the contract) to bring it about.[1555]

(d) Breach and lawful termination

8.418 Where a contract provides for termination by notice, a declaration by the party entitled so to terminate it that he will no longer perform may, if not intended as

---

[1546] *GH Myers & Co v Brent Cross Service Co* [1934] 1 KB 46; *Young & Marten Ltd v McManus Childs Ltd* [1969] 1 AC 454.

[1547] Supply of Goods and Services Act 1982, s 16(3)(a).

[1548] An architect is strictly liable for errors of design: *Greaves & Co (Contractors) Ltd v Baynham Meikle & Partners* [1975] 1 WLR 1095, 1101; *IBA v EMI (Electronics) Ltd* (1980) 14 Building LR 1, 47–8.

[1549] eg *Clark v Kirby-Smith* [1964] Ch 506; *Bagot v Stevens Scanlan & Co Ltd* [1966] 1 QB 197; *Henderson v Merrett Syndicates Ltd* [1995] 2 AC 145.

[1550] *Young v Marten* case (n 1546 above).

[1551] eg by a 'force majeure' clause excusing a seller in the event of difficulty of supply arising from specified causes.

[1552] eg Carriage of Goods by Sea Act 1971, s 3, reducing the common law strict liability of a carrier for unseaworthiness *(Steel v State Line Steamship Co* (1877) 3 App Cas 77, 86) to one of due diligence.

[1553] See para 8.469.

[1554] Except perhaps where illness prevents performance of personal services: cf para 8.471.

[1555] See para 8.30.

an exercise of the power to terminate by notice, amount to a breach:[1556] eg where an employee goes on strike after notice no shorter than that required to terminate the contract.[1557]

(2) Effects of Breach

(a) The option to rescind or affirm

(i) No automatic termination

A breach which justifies rescission[1558] gives the victim the option to rescind **8.419** or affirm.[1559] It does not (in general)[1560] automatically discharge the contract (even if this says that it is to become 'void' on breach);[1561] for if it did have this effect the party in breach would be able to rely on his own wrong to improve his position under the contract[1562] or to deprive the victim of benefits under it.[1563]

(ii) Employment contracts

There is some support for the view that the rule stated in paragraph 8.419 **8.420** does not apply to employment contracts, so that these are automatically terminated when the employee is wrongfully dismissed or leaves in breach of contract.[1564] No doubt the employment *relationship* then comes to an end;[1565] but to hold that this was also true of the *contract* would contravene the principle that the wrongdoer should not be allowed to benefit from his wrong by depriving the victim of benefits under it. The better view therefore is that an employment contract comes to an end in consequence of breach only when the victim rescinds.[1566]

[1556] *Bridge v Campbell Discount Co Ltd* [1962] AC 600 (hire-purchase).

[1557] *Simmons v Hoover Ltd* [1977] QB 284; *Miles v Wakefield MDC* [1987] AC 539, 562.

[1558] On the grounds discussed in section M of this chapter.

[1559] *Howard v Pickford Tool Co* [1951] 1 KB 417, 421; *Heyman v Darwins Ltd* [1942] AC 356, 361, HL; *The Simona* [1989] AC 788, 800.

[1560] For a quasi-exception, see para 8.421.

[1561] *New Zealand Shipping Co v Société des Ateliers etc* [1919] AC 1; *Alghussein Establishment v Eton College* [1988] 1 WLR 587.

[1562] *Alghussein* case (n 1561 above); *Boston Deep Sea Fishing & Ice Co v Ansell* (1888) 39 Ch D 339, 364.

[1563] See *Decro-Wall International v Practitioners in Marketing Ltd* [1971] 1 WLR 361; *Lusograin, etc v Bunge AG* [1986] 2 Lloyd's Rep 654.

[1564] eg *Sanders v Ernest A Neale Ltd* [1974] ICR 565.

[1565] *Wilson v St Helen's BC* [1999] 2 AC 52, 76–7.

[1566] *Gunton v Richmond-upon-Thames LBC* [1981] Ch 448, 474; a fortiori the contract does not come to an end where the employee remains at work after the employer's repudiatory breach: *Rigby v Ferodo Ltd* [1988] ICR 29.

(iii) Insurance contracts

8.421 Breach by the insured of a 'warranty' (such as a promise not to run specified risks) discharges the insurer from the date of the breach without any election on his part.[1567] In this context, there is no risk of the wrongdoer's benefiting from his wrong by the victim's discharge.[1568]

(iv) Qualifications

8.422 The general rule giving the victim the option to rescind or affirm is subject to the practical limitation that damages may be reduced if he fails to take reasonable steps to mitigate his loss. Such steps may put it out of his power to perform the original contract and he will then be taken to have rescinded that contract: eg where a wrongfully dismissed employee takes another job.[1569] Conversely, the mitigation requirement may put pressure on the victim, not exactly to affirm the contract, but to accept performance not strictly in accordance with it: eg they may require a buyer to accept late delivery on a rising market.[1570]

(v) Exercising the option

8.423 The option to rescind is commonly exercised by giving notice of rescission to the party in breach; but any other unequivocal indication of intention to rescind suffices.[1571] The option can be exercised even by 'inactivity': eg by the injured party's failing to take steps which he would have been expected to take, if he had regarded the contract as still in force.[1572] Temporary refusal to perform until the breach is cured or performance resumed does not amount to exercise of the option to rescind.[1573] There is no inconsistency between rescinding for breach and claiming damages for the same breach.[1574]

(b) Effects of rescission

(i) On the obligations of the victim

8.424 The victim is released by rescission from obligations to perform which had not yet accrued at the time of rescission.[1575] He is not released from obligations which had already accrued at that time; and an obligation may have accrued before, though

---

[1567] Marine Insurance Act 1906, s 33(3); *The Good Luck* [1992] 1 AC 233.

[1568] In *The Good Luck* (n 1567 above) a *third party* so benefited, but under a separate contract between that party and the victim.

[1569] *Gunton's* case (n 1566 above) 468; *Dietman v LB of Brent* [1987] ICR 737 (affirmed [1988] ICR 482).

[1570] *The Solholt* [1983] 1 Lloyd's Rep 605.

[1571] *Gunton's* case (n 1566 above) 468.

[1572] *Vitol SA v Norelf Ltd* [1996] AC 800.

[1573] *Wiluszinski v Tower Hamlets LBC* [1989] ICR 493.

[1574] *General Bill Posting Co Ltd v Atkinson* [1909] AC 118.

[1575] *Photo Production Ltd v Securicor Transport Ltd* [1980] AC 827, 849.

it was not to be performed until after, rescission.[1576] He is also not released from certain 'ancillary' obligations.[1577]

On rescission, the victim may be entitled to the return of payments made before **8.425** rescission (eg to the price of rejected goods). Where he has failed to make a payment (due before rescission) to the return of which he would have been so entitled on rescission, he should be relieved from liability to make it, since it makes no sense to hold him liable in one action for what he could recover back in another.[1578]

(ii) On the obligations of the party in breach

The effects of the injured party's election to rescind on the obligations of the guilty **8.426** party depend on a distinction between the latter's primary obligations to perform (eg to make payments specified in the contract) and his secondary obligation to pay damages for the breach.[1579] The general rule is that the election to rescind releases the guilty party from primary obligations not yet due at the time of rescission;[1580] but that it does not release him from primary obligations already then due[1581] (except to the extent that a payment then due could, if it had been duly made, have been recovered back by him)[1582] or from his secondary obligation in damages.[1583] This can extend to loss suffered by reason of the premature termination of the contract: eg where, after rescission of a contract on account of the guilty party's failure to make payments under the contract, the injured party disposes of the subject matter for less than the amount due to him under the original contract, had it run its full course.[1584] Such damages are recoverable as damages for wrongful repudiation, and should not be available where the breach, though justifying rescission, does not amount to repudiation: eg where the breach is objectively trivial but rescission for it is available under an express term of the contract.[1585] The point is sometimes obscured by use of the phrase 'repudiatory

---

[1576] *The Dominique* [1989] AC 1056; cf *Hurst v Bryk* [2001] 1 AC 185.
[1577] See at n 1588 below.
[1578] Cf (for the position of the guilty party in such a situation) at 1582 below.
[1579] *Photo Production* case (n 1575 above) 849.
[1580] ibid. For exceptions, see para 8.427. There is also no such release where the injured party is (exceptionally) discharged without election: *The Good Luck* [1992] AC 233, 263 (insurance: see para 8.421).
[1581] *Brooks v Beirnstein* [1909] 1 KB 98.
[1582] See *McDonald v Denys Lascelles Ltd* (1933) 48 CLR 457, approved in *Johnson v Agnew* [1980] AC 367, 396.
[1583] *Lep Air Services Ltd v Rollowswin Investments Ltd* [1973] AC 331, 350; *The Blankenstein* [1985] 1 WLR 435.
[1584] *Overstone Ltd v Shipway* [1962] 1 WLR 117.
[1585] *Financings Ltd v Baldock* [1963] 2 QB 104, rejecting a claim for damages for repudiation.

breach' to refer to any breach which justifies rescission, whether or not it amounts to a repudiation.[1586]

(iii) Contrary indications

8.427 The above rules as to the effects of rescission can be displaced by contrary agreements or other indications of contrary intention.[1587] For example, rescission does not release a party from an 'ancillary' obligation, such as one to submit disputes under the contract to arbitration.[1588]

(c) Effects of failure to rescind

8.428 If the injured party affirms or simply fails to rescind, the primary obligations of both parties remain in force;[1589] though under the rules relating to the order of performance[1590] the injured party's primary obligation will not have accrued where the breach amounted to a failure to perform a promissory condition precedent.

(d) Change of course

8.429 Election to rescind precludes subsequent affirmation since it releases the guilty party from his primary obligations.[1591] Affirmation, whether in the form of a simple demand for performance or of proceedings for specific performance,[1592] does not of itself preclude rescission for a continuing failure to perform.[1593] It precludes rescission only if it is accompanied by other circumstances from which a waiver of the right to rescind can be inferred.

(3) Repudiation Before Performance is Due

(a) Concept of anticipatory breach

8.430 A party commits an anticipatory breach if, before his performance is due, he either renounces the contract or disables himself by his 'own act or default'[1594] from performing it. Disablement can result not only from an act but also from

---

[1586] See *Lombard North Central plc v Butterworth* [1987] QB 527, awarding such damages with evident reluctance.

[1587] *Yasuda Fire & Marine Insurance Co of Europe v Orion Marine Insurance Underwriting Agency Ltd* [1995] QB 174.

[1588] *Heyman v Darwins Ltd* [1942] AC 536; cf Arbitration Act 1996, s 7.

[1589] *The Simona* [1989] AC 788.

[1590] See para 8.360.

[1591] *Johnson v Agnew* [1980] AC 367, 393.

[1592] As in *Johnson v Agnew* (n 1591 above).

[1593] ibid; cf *Tilcon Ltd v Land and Real Estate Investments Ltd* [1987] 1 All ER 615; *Stocznia Gdanska SA v Latvian Shipping Co* [2002] EWCA Civ 889; [2002] 2 All ER (Comm) 786 at [100].

[1594] *Universal Cargo Carriers Corp v Citati* [1957] 2 QB 401, 441.

an omission such as failing to make an effective supply contract with a third party, but a party who *has* made such a contract will not be in anticipatory breach merely by reason of that third party's default.[1595]

The victim can either 'accept' the anticipatory breach or continue to press for per- **8.431** formance. Acceptance can be by taking legal proceedings, by notice, by conduct and even by omission unequivocally indicating intention to accept.[1596]

(b) Effects of acceptance

(i) Damages

Acceptance of an anticipatory breach entitles the victim to damages at once, before **8.432** the time fixed for performance[1597] and even though his right under the contract is still subject to a contingent condition precedent (eg that of surviving the promisor[1598] or a third party[1599]). Where a person repudiates liability to make future payments, the objection that he will thus have to pay damages before the debt was due is (at least in part) met by allowing 'a discount for accelerated payment'.[1600]

(ii) Rescission

Rescission for anticipatory breach is available where the likely effects of the breach **8.433** satisfy the requirement of 'substantial' failure[1601] and (probably) where one of the exceptions to that requirement[1602] (other than the exception arising from express provisions for termination)[1603] applies.

The question whether the prospective failure justifies rescission depends in cases **8.434** of *renunciation* on whether the victim at the time of rescission *reasonably believed* that the guilty party did not intend to perform.[1604] But in cases of *disablement* it has been said that it must at the time of rescission be *already certain* that the prospective failure would turn out to be sufficiently serious to justify rescission.[1605]

[1595] The *Citati* case (n 1594 above) gives rise to difficulty in this context: see *FC Shepherd & Co Ltd v Jerrom* [1987] QB 301, 323.

[1596] *Vitol SA v Norelf Ltd* [1996] AC 800.

[1597] *Hochster v De la Tour* (1853) 2 E & B 678.

[1598] *Synge v Synge* [1894] 1 QB 466.

[1599] *Frost v Knight* (1872) LR 7 Ex 111 (actual decision obsolete since Law Reform (Miscellaneous Provisions) Act 1970, s 1).

[1600] *Lep Air Services Ltd v Rolloswin Investments Ltd* [1973] AC 331, 356.

[1601] See para 8.364.

[1602] eg breach of condition, as is assumed in the *Citati* case (n 1594 above).

[1603] As in *The Afovos* [1983] 1 WLR 195 (where a dictum at p 203 restricting the right to rescind for anticipatory breaches to those that are 'fundamental' is therefore unnecessary and, it is submitted, too restrictive). And see para 8.367 at n 1382.

[1604] *The Hermosa* [1982] 1 Lloyd's Rep 570, 580.

[1605] *Citati* case (n 1594 above) 449–50.

A's reasonable belief that B would not be able to perform should not be (and is not) a ground for holding B liable in damages;[1606] but it would be more convenient to allow such a belief to justify A's rescission,[1607] as it does where B's breach is in part actual and gives rise to uncertainty as to his future ability to perform.[1608]

8.435 Rescission releases the victim from his duty to perform and entitles him to damages without having to show that he could (but for the anticipatory breach) have performed that duty.[1609]

(c) Effects of not accepting the breach

8.436 If the victim affirms the contract (or simply does not accept the breach) both parties remain bound by the contract and damages cannot be claimed before the time fixed for performance.[1610] The right to damages may, before then, be lost: eg if the guilty party withdraws his repudiation[1611] or lawfully puts an end to the contract under a cancelling clause[1612] or if the contract is frustrated.[1613]

8.437 Affirmation should not bar rescission in the face of a continuing anticipatory breach;[1614] certainly a mere call for performance in response to the breach does not have this effect since it does not of itself amount to affirmation.[1615]

O. Frustration

(1) Introduction

8.438 Under the doctrine of frustration, a contract may be discharged by supervening events which make its performance impossible or illegal or frustrate its purpose. The doctrine was developed in cases of supervening destruction of the subject matter,[1616]

[1606] This was the actual point decided in the *Citati* case (n 1594 above).

[1607] Cf the rule in cases of frustration: stated in para 8.457.

[1608] *Hong Kong Fir* case [1962] 2 QB 26, 57; *Snia v Suzuki & Co* (1924) 29 Commercial Cases 284.

[1609] *British & Beningtons v North-Western Cachar Tea Co Ltd* [1923] AC 48; para 8.363.

[1610] Except perhaps where they are claimed in lieu of specific performance.

[1611] *Harrison v Northwest Holt Group Administration Ltd* [1985] ICR 668.

[1612] *The Simona* [1989] AC 788.

[1613] *Avery v Bowden* (1855) 5 E & B 714.

[1614] For conflicting views on the point, contrast *Stocznia Gdanska SA v Latvian Shipping Co* [1997] 2 Lloyd's Rep 228, 235 (set aside [1998] 1 WLR 574, 594) with *Stocznia Gdanska SA v Latvian Shipping Co* (No 3) [2001] 1 Lloyd's Rep 537 and (on appeal) [2002] EWCA Civ 889; [2002] 2 Lloyd's Rep 436 at [97]–[100], inclining to the view stated in the text above. For the same view in cases of actual breach, see para 8.429.

[1615] *Yukong Line Ltd of Korea v Rendsburg Investments Corp of Liberia* [1996] 2 Lloyd's Rep 604.

[1616] Starting with *Taylor v Caldwell* (1863) 3 B & S 826.

originally as a modification of an earlier view[1617] (traces of which remain)[1618] that contractual duties were generally[1619] not discharged by supervening impossibility.[1620] Its purpose is to allocate or divide the loss resulting from the supervening event by discharging the party who was to render the now impossible performance from his duty to render it and the party who was to receive it from his duty to pay for it.[1621] On the other hand, it should not discharge a party merely because an 'uncontemplated turn of events' has turned the contract, for him, into a bad bargain.[1622] Partly for this reason and partly because parties commonly make express provisions for supervening events, the courts have imposed strict limits on the scope of the doctrine,[1623] particularly where the prevention of performance is only partial or temporary,[1624] and where there is no actual impossibility or illegality.[1625]

(2) Applications

(a) Impossibility

Supervening impossibility of performance is not of itself a ground of discharge. It will not, for example, have this effect where a party's contractual duty is strict,[1626] so that he can be said to have *undertaken* that its performance will be possible. Discharge can occur only where there is no such undertaking but merely an *assumption* by the parties about the continued possibility of performance. **8.439**

(i) Destruction of a particular thing

A contract may be discharged by the destruction of its subject matter: eg of a music-hall to be made available under the contract for a series of concerts.[1627] For this purpose, a thing which is so seriously damaged as to have become 'for business purposes something else'[1628] is taken to have been destroyed; and destruction of part of the subject matter suffices if it is so serious as to defeat the main purpose of the contract.[1629] Destruction of something which is not the subject matter of the **8.440**

[1617] *Paradine v Jane* (1647) Aleyn 26.

[1618] eg *Ashmore & Son v Cox & Co* [1899] 1 QB 436; *Lewis Emanuel & Son Ltd v Sammut* [1959] 2 Lloyd's Rep 629, 642.

[1619] There were exceptions, eg contracts of personal service: see *Taylor v Caldwell* (n 1616 above) 836.

[1620] For discharge by supervening *illegality* see, eg *Atkinson v Ritchie* (1809) 10 East 530, 534–5.

[1621] *Taylor v Caldwell* (n 1616 above) 840 ('*both* parties are excused').

[1622] *British Movietonenews Ltd v London and District Cinemas* [1952] AC 166, 185.

[1623] eg *The Nema* [1982] AC 724, 752.

[1624] See paras 8.440 and 8.444; cf the 'Suez' cases (para 8.449).

[1625] See para 8.450.

[1626] See para 8.413; cf also para 8.441.

[1627] *Taylor v Caldwell* (1863) 3 B & S 826; cf Sale of Goods Act 1979, s 7.

[1628] *Asfar & Co v Blundell* [1896] 1 QB 123, 128 (dates contaminated by sewage).

[1629] As in *Taylor v Caldwell* (n 1627 above).

contract but is essential for its performance can suffice: eg of the factory in which machinery is to be installed.[1630]

8.441   In certain types of contracts, destruction of the subject matter is governed by rules relating to the passing of risk, and these can displace the principle of discharge. For example, where goods are sold and destroyed after the risk has passed to the buyer,[1631] he is not discharged from his duty to pay, while the seller, though discharged from his duty to deliver, is not discharged from certain other duties.[1632]

(ii) Death or disability of a particular person

8.442   Contracts of employment or agency are discharged by the death of either party;[1633] other contracts involving the exercise by one party of personal skill are discharged by the death of that party. The same is true where a party is physically disabled from performing or receiving performance;[1634] and where continued performance would seriously endanger his health.[1635]

(iii) Unavailability

8.443   **In general.**   A contract may be frustrated if its subject matter, though not ceasing to exist, becomes unavailable: eg through requisition[1636] or detention.[1637] A contract for personal services may similarly be frustrated through the conscription[1638] or illness[1639] of the person who was to render them.

8.444   **Temporary unavailability.**   Unavailability at the time fixed for performance will frustrate a contract if that time is of the essence:[1640] eg where the contract is one to play in a concert on a specified day.[1641] Even if time is not of the essence, frustration can result where the delay is so long that performance after its end would no longer serve the originally contemplated purpose of the person who was to have

---

[1630] *Appleby v Myers* (1867) LR 2 CP 651.

[1631] See Sale of Goods Act 1979, s 20(1).

[1632] eg duties to tender documents giving the buyer rights against the carrier or insurer: see *Manbré Saccharine Co Ltd v Corn Products Co Ltd* [1919] 1 KB 198.

[1633] *Campanari v Woodburn* (1854) 15 CB 400; *Whincup v Hughes* (1871) LR 6 CP 78 (apprenticeship).

[1634] *Jackson v Union Marine Insurance Co Ltd* (1874) LR 10 CP 125, 145.

[1635] *Condor v The Barron Knights Ltd* [1966] 1 WLR 87.

[1636] *Re Shipton Anderson & Co* [1915] 3 KB 676; *Bank Line Ltd v Arthur Capel & Co* [1919] AC 435.

[1637] eg *The Evia (No 2)* [1983] 1 AC 736.

[1638] *Morgan v Manser* [1948] 1 KB 184.

[1639] eg *Hart v AR Marshall & Sons (Bulwell) Ltd* [1977] 1 WLR 1067. Dismissal on the ground of illness which is *not* serious enough to frustrate the contract may amount to breach of the employer's duty, under Disability Discrimination Act 1995, s 6, to make reasonable adjustments: *Archibald v Fife Council* [2004] UKHL 32; [2004] ICR 954.

[1640] See para 8.401.

[1641] *Robinson v Davison* (1871) LR 6 Ex 269.

received it;[1642] or if such performance would impose substantially different obligations from those originally undertaken on the party who was to render it. This could be the position because by the end of the delay economic conditions had so changed as either substantially to increase the costs of that party[1643] or to bring the originally agreed remuneration out of line with that then payable for the services.[1644]

Where the amount of performance due is measured by the time taken to render **8.445** it, a claim made after the end of the delay may be merely for any balance then due (eg for the unexpired term of a time charter). Such a claim will fail if the delay lasts or is likely to last for so long that no, or only a relatively insignificant, part of the originally agreed performance then remains possible;[1645] but it will succeed if the part then remaining possible is substantial.[1646] An employee's temporary illness will similarly frustrate the contract of employment only if it is so serious as to put an end 'in a business sense'[1647] to the possibility of further performance.

(iv) Failure of source of supply

Whether contract frustrated. A contract which expressly provides for goods to **8.446** be taken from a specified source may be discharged by failure of that source[1648] (eg where a specified crop fails or a seller is cut off from a specified foreign source by war or natural disaster). The contract will not be frustrated if it contains no reference to a source intended by only one party.[1649] If the unspecified source is contemplated by both parties, the contract will be frustrated by supervening illegality if in time of war that source becomes an enemy source.[1650] The physical failure of a mutually contemplated source may also frustrate the contract[1651] where it would not be reasonable to expect the parties to provide in the contract for such failure.

Partial failure. Where total failure of a source would frustrate a contract,[1652] **8.447** its partial failure excuses the seller to the extent of the deficiency.[1653] He must deliver[1654] (though the buyer need not accept)[1655] the quantity actually produced.

[1642] *Jackson v Union Marine Insurance Co* (1874) LR 10 CP 125.

[1643] eg *Metropolitan Water Board v Dick, Kerr & Co* [1918] AC 119.

[1644] This seems to be the reason why the contract was frustrated in *Bank Line Ltd v Arthur Capel & Co* [1919] AC 435.

[1645] *Countess of Warwick Steamship Co v Le Nickel SA* [1918] 1 KB 372; *The Nema* [1982] AC 724.

[1646] *Tamplin Steamship Co Ltd v Anglo-Mexican Petroleum Co* [1916] 2 AC 397.

[1647] *Jackson's* case (n 1642 above) 145; *Hart's* case, and see n 1639 above.

[1648] *Howell v Coupland* (1876) 1 QBD 258.

[1649] *Blackburn Bobbin Co Ltd v TW Allen & Sons Ltd* [1918] 2 KB 467; cf *Congimex SARL (Lisbon) v Continental Grain Export Corp (New York)* [1979] 2 Lloyd's Rep 346, 353 (source of payment).

[1650] *Re Badische Co* [1921] 2 Ch 331.

[1651] This was conceded in *Lipton Ltd v Ford* [1917] 2 KB 647.

[1652] See para 8.446.

[1653] This was the actual result in *Howell v Coupland* (n 1648 above).

[1654] *HR & S Sainsbury Ltd v Street* [1972] 1 WLR 834.

[1655] Sale of Goods Act 1979, s 30(1) (subject to ibid, s 30(2A)).

8.448   Where a seller has made more than one contract specifying the source, its partial failure may prevent him from fulfilling them all but not from fulfilling one or more. One view is that none of the contracts is frustrated since his choice as to which contracts to fulfil amounts to an 'election', excluding the doctrine;[1656] but there seems to be no true election where partial failure makes it impossible to fulfil all the contracts.[1657] Another view is that he must deliver to such of the buyers as are designated by law (eg by reference to the chronological order in which their contracts were made). Yet a third view (sometimes adopted where the seller relies on express contractual provisions such as force majeure clauses) is that the available supply should be divided *pro rata*;[1658] but where the seller relies on the doctrine of frustration this view gives rise to the difficulty that this doctrine provides only for the discharge, and not for the modification, of contracts.[1659]

(v) Method of performance impossible

8.449   A contract can be frustrated if it provides that it is to be performed *only* by a method that becomes impossible.[1660] Impossibility of a stipulated method that is not intended to be exclusive does not frustrate a contract if performance by another method which remains possible would not be fundamentally different from that specified;[1661] the same is a fortiori true if the method which becomes impossible was merely contemplated by both parties.[1662] No such fundamental difference was held to have arisen when closure of the Suez Canal imposed on one of the parties the extra expense of a longer voyage.[1663]

(b) Impracticability

(i) General rule

8.450   The concept of 'impossibility' is itself a relative one, depending on the current state of technology and on the amount of trouble that one is prepared to take to overcome obstacles. Nevertheless, 'impracticability' goes beyond 'impossibility', covering cases in which performance remains possible but becomes severely more burdensome to the party required to render it. While there are some judicial statements to the effect that impracticability (or 'commercial impossibility') can be a

---

1656 Cf *The Super Servant Two* [1990] 1 Lloyd's Rep 1.
1657 See para 8.472.
1658 See *Tennants (Lancashire) Ltd v CS Wilson & Co Ltd* [1917] AC 495, 511–12; *Bremer Handelsgesellschaft mbH v Vanden Avenne-Izegem PVBA* [1978] 2 Lloyd's Rep 109, 115, 128.
1659 See para 8.474.
1660 *Nickoll & Knight v Ashton Edridge & Co* [1901] 2 KB 126.
1661 eg *The Captain George K* [1970] 2 Lloyd's Rep 21.
1662 *Tsakiroglou & Co Ltd v Noblee Thorl GmbH* [1962] AC 93.
1663 As in the cases cited in nn 1661 and 1662 above.

ground of discharge,[1664] no actual decision supports this view, while others seem to contradict it.[1665] The prevailing view is that impracticability is not, in general, a ground of frustration.[1666]

(ii) Exceptional situations

Increased cost of performance may be a ground of discharge where the super- **8.451**
vening event delays performance[1667] or where the cost is incurred to avoid supervening illegality.[1668] In such cases, however, discharge results not from 'pure'
impracticability, but from impracticability combined with temporary impossibility or prospective illegality. Express provisions for discharge may also sometimes[1669] be brought into operation by severe increases in cost;[1670] but since the
main purpose of such provisions is to *extend* the scope of discharge to situations
not covered by the common law doctrine, such cases give no support to the
view that such increases would discharge the contract under that doctrine. In a
contract of indefinite duration, there is often[1671] a power to terminate by giving
reasonable notice and one motive for so terminating may be that performance
has become more onerous for the party giving the notice.[1672] But there is no
such power to terminate a fixed term contract[1673] so that these cases, too, do not
support any general principle of discharge for impracticability at common law;
indeed if there were such a principle, discharge would be automatic[1674] and not by
notice.

(iii) Inflation and currency fluctuations

Inflation and currency fluctuation are not grounds of discharge at common **8.452**
law.[1675] The possibility that extreme inflation might be so regarded cannot be

---

[1664] eg *Horlock v Beal* [1916] AC 486, 492; *The Furness Bridge* [1977] 2 Lloyd's Rep 367, 377.

[1665] eg *Davis Contractors Ltd v Fareham UDC* [1956] AC 696; and see the 'Suez cases' (para 8.449 above); cf *The Mercedes Envoy* [1995] 2 Lloyd's Rep 559, 563.

[1666] eg *Tennants* case (n 1658 above) 510; *British Movietonenews Ltd v London & District Cinemas* [1952] AC 166, 185; *Thames Valley Power Ltd v Total Gas Power Ltd* [2005] EWHC 2208 (Comm); [2006] 1 Lloyd's Rep 441 at [50].

[1667] See para 8.444 at n 1643.

[1668] *Cory (Wm) & Son v London Corporation* [1951] 1 KB 8 (affirmed [1951] 2 KB 476); special considerations of public interest apply in cases of supervening illegality; see para 8.454.

[1669] Though not generally: see, for example, *Brauer & Co (Great Britain) Ltd v James Clark (Brush Materials) Ltd* [1952] 2 All ER 497; *B & S Contracts and Designs Ltd v Victor Green Publications Ltd* [1984] ICR 419; and the *Thames Valley* case, n 1666 above.

[1670] *Tradax Export SA v André & Cie SA* [1976] 1 Lloyd's Rep 416, 423.

[1671] Not always: see *Watford BC v Watford RDC* (1988) 86 LGR 524.

[1672] As in *Staffordshire Area Health Authority v South Staffordshire Waterworks Co* [1978] 1 WLR 1387.

[1673] See *Kirklees MBC v Yorkshire Woollen District Transport Co Ltd* (1978) 77 LGR 448.

[1674] See para 8.474.

[1675] *British Movietonenews* case (n 1666 above) 185; *Wates Ltd v GLC* (1983) 25 Building LR 1, 34.

ruled out, though legislative regulation is the more likely reaction to such a development.

(c) Frustration of purpose

8.453 Frustration of purpose occurs where the effect of a supervening event is to make one party's performance useless to the other: eg where rooms were hired for the days fixed for King Edward VII's coronation processions for the purpose of enabling the hirer to watch the processions, which because of the illness of the King failed to take place on those days.[1676] The principle applies only if no part of purpose intended by *both* parties can be achieved:[1677] thus where premises were bought, the buyer intending to redevelop them, there was no discharge merely because 'listing' of the building made the redevelopment more difficult or even impossible.[1678] Such restrictions are necessary to avert the danger that the principle might be invoked simply to get out of a very bad bargain.

(d) Illegality

(i) Types of illegality

8.454 The rule that supervening illegality discharges a contract is based not so much on the need to allocate loss between the parties as on the public interest in ensuring compliance with the law. This public interest is particularly strong where in time of war the contract would involve trading with the enemy: the contract is discharged even though its performance might not be impossible.[1679] Other prohibitions can similarly discharge a contract: eg a contract which provides for goods to be exported[1680] can be frustrated by prohibition of export.

(ii) Antecedent and supervening prohibitions

8.455 Our present concern is with supervening prohibitions, as opposed to antecedent ones (which may make a contract void *ab initio*).[1681] This distinction is however blurred where at the time of contracting a law is in force prohibiting performance without the consent of some public body which then refuses to give it. If the refusal is due to a change of government policy with regard to giving

---

[1676] *Krell v Henry* [1903] 2 KB 740; the principle was applied in another context in *Denny, Mott & Dickson v James B Fraser & Co Ltd* [1944] AC 265.

[1677] *Leiston Gas Co v Leiston-cum-Sizewell UDC* [1916] 2 KB 428, esp 433.

[1678] *Amalgamated Investment & Property Co Ltd v John Walker & Son Ltd* [1977] 1 WLR 164.

[1679] eg *Fibrosa Spolka Ackcyjna v Fairbairn Lawson Combe Barbour Ltd* [1943] AC 32.

[1680] Not one in which this is merely the intention of one party: see *D McMaster & Co v Cox McEwen & Co* 1921 SC (HL) 1; *Congimex, etc, v Tradax Export SA* [1983] 1 Lloyd's Rep 250.

[1681] See section H.

such consent, that change can be regarded as a supervening event, leading to frustration.[1682]

(iii) *Partial or temporary illegality*

Supervening partial or temporary illegality frustrates a contract only if it defeats **8.456** the main object of the contract.[1683] If the contract is not frustrated, such illegality nevertheless excuses a party from rendering that part of the performance which has become illegal.[1684]

(e) Prospective frustration

At the time of the supervening event, it may not be certain, but only highly **8.457** likely, that its effects on performance will be such as to frustrate the contract. To prevent rights from being left indefinitely in suspense, the contract can then be frustrated at once, even though a later event unexpectedly restores the possibility of performance.[1685] However, where an event such as a strike causes delays which might be slight or serious, frustration occurs only when the delay has continued for so long as to cause a reasonable person to believe that it would interfere fundamentally with performance.[1686]

(f) Alternatives

A contract imposes an alternative obligation if it requires a person to do X or Y so **8.458** that at the time of contracting it is impossible to tell which is due.[1687] Such a contract is not discharged by supervening impossibility or illegality of only one of the specified performances; the other must then normally[1688] be rendered.[1689] The position is different where a contract requires a person to do X with a liberty to substitute Y. Here X is due until Y is substituted and if, before then, X becomes impossible or illegal the contract is discharged.[1690]

[1682] This was assumed in *Maritime National Fish Ltd v Ocean Trawlers Ltd* [1935] AC 524, where the plea of frustration failed on grounds stated in para 8.472.

[1683] As in the *Denny Mott* case (n 1676 above).

[1684] See *Cricklewood Property & Investment Trust Ltd v Leighton's Investment Trust Ltd* [1945] AC 221, 233, 244; *Sturcke v SW Edwards Ltd* (1971) 23 P & CR 185, 190.

[1685] *Embiricos v Sydney Reid & Co* [1914] 3 KB 45.

[1686] *The Nema* [1982] AC 724, 753.

[1687] In the interests of clarity, such a contract should specify which party is entitled to choose whether X or Y is to be performed: *Mora Shipping Inc v Axa Corporate Solutions Assurance SA* [2005] EWCA Civ 1069; [2005] 2 Lloyd's Rep. 769 at [56].

[1688] ie unless the contract otherwise provides: *Sociedad Iberica de Molturacion SA v Tradax Export SA* [1978] 2 Lloyd's Rep 545.

[1689] *The Furness Bridge* [1977] 2 Lloyd's Rep 367.

[1690] See *The Badagry* [1985] 1 Lloyd's Rep 395; cf *Reardon Smith Line Ltd v Ministry of Agriculture, Fisheries and Food* [1963] AC 691.

(g) Leases of land

8.459 A lease of land can be frustrated.[1691] But supervening events will only rarely have this effect[1692] since in a long lease each party takes the risk that circumstances may change during its currency; since the ratio of the interruption of the intended use of the premises to the length of the lease is likely to be small;[1693] and since the effect on the lease of some potentially frustrating events is likely to be dealt with by its express terms (such as covenants to repair). It has accordingly been held that leases were not frustrated where the premises were destroyed by enemy action[1694] or requisitioned[1695] or where the intended use of the premises was prohibited by wartime legislation.[1696] Even where the lease is not frustrated, supervening events may provide an excuse for non-performance of individual obligations under it.[1697]

(h) Sale of land

8.460 A contract for the sale of land can be frustrated;[1698] but such a contract is not frustrated by the destruction of buildings on the land for the sake of which it was bought. At common law, this followed from the rule that risk passed to the purchaser on contract;[1699] and although this rule is now commonly excluded by agreement,[1700] the contract is likely to contain further express provisions dealing with destruction of or damage to buildings, and such provisions will in turn exclude frustration.

8.461 A contract for the sale of land with buildings to be erected on it can be frustrated, not by destruction of the partly completed buildings, but by delay caused by the supervening event.[1701]

8.462 A contract for the sale of land is not frustrated by the making of a compulsory purchase order relating to the land.[1702] But where actual requisition prevents the vendor from performing his obligation to transfer vacant possession, specific

---

[1691] *National Carriers Ltd v Panalpina (Northern) Ltd* [1981] AC 675.

[1692] ibid, 692, 697.

[1693] Cf para 8.445.

[1694] *Redmond v Dainton* [1920] 2 KB 256.

[1695] *Matthey v Curling* [1922] 2 AC 180 (where the tenant received compensation for the requisition).

[1696] *Cricklewood* case (n 1684 above).

[1697] ibid, 233; *Baily v De Crespigny* (1869) LR 4 QB 180.

[1698] This is assumed in *Amalgamated Investment & Property Co Ltd v John Walker & Son Ltd* [1977] 1 WLR 164.

[1699] *Paine v Meller* (1801) 6 Ves 349.

[1700] Law Society's Standard Conditions of Sale (1992), paras 5.1.1 to 5.1.4.

[1701] *Wong Lai Ying v Chinachem Investment Co Ltd* (1979) 13 Building LR 81.

[1702] *Hillingdon Estates Co v Stonefield Estate Co* [1952] Ch 627.

performance is not available to him[1703] and the purchaser is entitled to the return of his deposit.[1704]

(3) Limitations

(a) Contractual provisions for the event

Contracting parties can expressly provide that the risk of specified supervening **8.463** events is to be borne by one of them[1705] or that on the occurrence of such events their obligations are to be modified[1706] in some way not available under the common law doctrine. A risk-allocating provision may also be implied from the nature of the transaction.[1707] In general, all such provisions exclude frustration.[1708]

On grounds of public policy, the parties cannot exclude discharge by supervening **8.464** illegality where continued performance would involve trading with an enemy in time of war.[1709]

An express provision may literally appear to cover the allegedly frustrating event **8.465** but be held on its true construction to cover only a less serious interference with performance. The provision will then not exclude frustration.[1710] Similarly, a clause may fail to make *complete* provision for the event: eg it may provide an excuse for non-performance for, or give a right to cancel to, one party without excluding frustration.[1711]

Parties commonly provide for modification or discharge of their obligations on **8.466** the occurrence of specified events even though these might not frustrate the contract at common law. Where obligations are thus discharged, this result follows by virtue of the express provisions and not under the common law doctrine.[1712]

(b) Foreseeability

Where a supervening event is or can be foreseen by the parties, the prima facie **8.467** inference is that they have allocated the risk of its occurrence by the contract, so that an event which 'was or might have been anticipated'[1713] is not a ground

---

[1703] *Cook v Taylor* [1942] Ch 349.
[1704] *James Macara Ltd v Barclay* [1945] KB 148.
[1705] *Budgett v Binnington & Co* [1891] 1 QB 35, 41.
[1706] eg by provisions for postponed performance: see *Victorian Seats Agency v Paget* (1902) 19 TLR 16 or for flexible pricing: see *Wates v GLC* (1983) 25 Building LR 1.
[1707] *Larrinaga* case (1923) 92 LJ KB 455.
[1708] *Joseph Constantine Steamship Line v Imperial Smelting Co* [1942] AC 154, 163.
[1709] *Ertel Bieber & Co v Rio Tinto Co Ltd* [1918] AC 260.
[1710] *Metropolitan Water Board v Dick, Kerr & Co* [1918] AC 119.
[1711] *Bank Line Ltd v Arthur Capel & Co* [1919] AC 435.
[1712] So that the Law Reform (Frustrated Contracts) Act 1943 does not apply to such discharge.
[1713] *Krell v Henry* [1903] 2 KB 740, 752.

of discharge.[1714] The question whether such an inference is actually to be drawn depends, however, on the degree and extent of foreseeability. Frustration is not excluded merely because the parties could as a remote contingency have foreseen the event.[1715] The event must have been readily foreseeable: ie be one which persons of ordinary intelligence would regard as likely to occur. The event and its consequences must also have been foreseeable in some detail: to exclude frustration, it is not, for example, enough that *some* interference with performance was or could have been foreseen if the interference which actually occurs is wholly different in extent from the foreseen or foreseeable one.[1716]

8.468 The inference that the risk of foreseen or readily foreseeable events is allocated by the contract may be displaced: eg by evidence that the parties intended, if the event occurred, 'to leave the lawyers to sort it out';[1717] or by the fact that a provision which they made for it is incomplete.[1718] On grounds of public policy a foreseen event can also frustrate a contract if its performance after the event would involve trading with an enemy.[1719]

(c) Self-induced frustration

(i) Discharge generally excluded

8.469 A party cannot rely on 'self-induced frustration',[1720] that is, on an obstacle to performance wholly or partly brought about by his voluntary conduct or by that of those for whom he is responsible. Thus he cannot rely on his own breach of the contract as a ground of frustration,[1721] even where it takes the form of an omission (such as failing to make a ship seaworthy)[1722] and even where the other party's breach also contributes to an allegedly frustrating delay.[1723]

8.470 A party cannot rely as a ground of frustration on his own deliberate act (or its consequences) even where the act is not a breach of the contract;[1724] but the other party may be able to do so. Thus where an employee is prevented from working because he has been imprisoned on conviction for an offence unconnected with

---

1714 *Walton Harvey Ltd v Walker & Homfrays Ltd* [1931] 1 Ch 274.
1715 As they could have done in the Coronation cases (para 8.453).
1716 As in *WJ Tatem Ltd v Gamboa* [1939] 1 KB 132 and *The Eugenia* [1964] 2 QB 226; dicta in these cases on discharge by foreseeable events go further than necessary.
1717 *The Eugenia* (n 1716 above) 234.
1718 As in the *Bank Line* case (n 1711 above).
1719 Cf para 8.464.
1720 *Bank Line* case (n 1711 above) 234.
1721 eg *The Eugenia* (n 1716 above).
1722 *Monarch Steamship Co v A/B Karlshamns Oljefabriker* [1949] AC 196.
1723 *The Hannah Blumenthal* [1983] 1 AC 854.
1724 *Denmark Production Ltd v Boscobel Productions Ltd* [1969] 1 QB 699.

his employment, he cannot, but his employer can, rely on the imprisonment as a ground of frustration.[1725]

(ii) Negligence

A party cannot generally rely as a ground of frustration on an event brought about **8.471** by his negligence; but there may be an exception to this rule where the negligence takes the form of his failing to take care of his health.[1726]

(iii) Choosing between contracts

A person may enter into several contracts with different parties and a supervening **8.472** event may then reduce his capacity to perform, so that he can no longer perform all, but can still perform some, of those contracts. There is judicial support for the view that if he then devotes his now limited capacity to the performance of some of those contracts, he cannot rely on frustration as discharging him from the others as his inability to perform these is due to his 'election' to perform the former ones.[1727] Such reasoning seems, however, to undermine the concept of frustration, since where the reduction in his capacity to perform is due to an event for which he was not responsible, his only choice (to which of the contracts he will devote that reduced capacity) is not a truly voluntary one.[1728]

(iv) Burden of proof

The burden of proving that frustration is self-induced is on the party who so **8.473** alleges.[1729]

(4) Legal Effects of Frustration

(a) In general

Frustration terminates the contract with effect from the time of the frustrating **8.474** event.[1730] It operates automatically (without the need for any election) so that it can usually[1731] be invoked by either party and not only by the party likely to be prejudiced by the frustrating event. It may thus be invoked by the other party with a view to profiting from the event: eg by a shipowner who claims that requisition has frustrated a time charter where the government compensation for requisition

---

[1725] *FC Shepherd & Co Ltd v Jerrom* [1987] QB 301.
[1726] *Joseph Constantine Steamship Line v Imperial Smelting Co* [1942] AC 154, 166–7.
[1727] *Maritime National Fish Ltd v Ocean Trawlers Ltd* [1935] AC 524; *The Super Servant Two* [1990] 1 Loyd's Rep 1.
[1728] Cf para 8.448.
[1729] *Joseph Constantine* case (n 1726 above).
[1730] *Hirji Mulji v Cheong Yue Steamship Co Ltd* [1926] AC 497, 505.
[1731] For an exception, see para 8.470.

exceeds the charterparty hire.[1732] The courts can prevent such misuse of the doctrine only by holding that the interference with performance has not been sufficiently serious to frustrate the contract.[1733]

(b) Problems of adjustment

8.475 Problems of adjustment arise where one party has or should have performed wholly or in part before the frustrating event while the other's counterperformance was not to be rendered until after that event. The common law rules on this subject have been largely superseded by the Law Reform (Frustrated Contracts) Act 1943 ('the 1943 Act') but continue to apply to cases excepted from its provisions.[1734]

(i) *Money paid or payable in advance*

8.476 **Common law.** At common law, money paid before frustration can (unless the contract otherwise provides)[1735] be recovered back by the payor only[1736] if the frustrating event brings about a 'total failure of consideration': eg where it prevents delivery of any of the goods for which an advance payment had been made.[1737] If in such a case money should have been but was not so paid, liability to pay it must be discharged since there is no point in requiring a party to pay money to the return of which he would then immediately be entitled.[1738]

8.477 **Statute.** By section 1(2) of the 1943 Act, money paid before discharge is repayable (without any requirement of 'total failure of consideration') and money which should have been but was not so paid ceases to be payable. But the court has a discretion to allow the party to whom money is so paid (or payable) to retain (or recover) the whole or any part of the sum so paid (or payable) if he has incurred expenses in or for the purpose of the performance of the contract. In exercising this 'broad discretion',[1739] the court can take account of the fact that the payor has also incurred expenses which are wasted as a result of the frustrating event.[1740]

(ii) *Other benefits*

8.478 **Common law.** At common law, a party who has conferred benefits other than money cannot recover anything if the contract is frustrated before the other's

---

[1732] eg *The Isle of Mull* 278 F 131 (1921).

[1733] eg in the *Tamplin* case [1916] 2 AC 397 (see para 8.445); cf also the *Tsakiroglou* case [1962] AC 93 (see para 8.449).

[1734] See paras 8.482 and 8.483.

[1735] *Fibrosa* case [1943] AC 32, 43, 77; and see n 1747 below.

[1736] *Whincup v Hughes* (1871) LR 6 CP 78.

[1737] *Fibrosa* case (n 1735 above).

[1738] *Fibrosa* case (n 1735 above) 53–54. Cf para 8.425 at n 1578; and para 8.426 at n 1582.

[1739] *Gamerco SA v ICM/Fair Warning (Agency) Ltd* [1995] 1 WLR 1226, 1236; insurance moneys received by the claimant must generally be disregarded: 1943 Act, s 1(5).

[1740] *Gamerco* case n 1739 above.

performance became due: for example, under a contract by which a builder agreed to do work on a customer's house for payment due on completion, the builder cannot recover anything in respect of part of the work done before frustration.[1741]

Statute. Section 1(3) of the 1943 Act provides that if one party (A) has, before **8.479** the time of discharge, obtained a 'valuable benefit' by reason of anything done by the other (B) in or for the purpose of the performance of the contract, then the court can allow B to recover such sum (not exceeding the value of the benefit) as it 'considers just'. In identifying the 'valuable benefit', the court has regard, not to the cost to B of his performance, but to the 'end product'[1742] received by A, at least where the nature of the contract is such that its full performance would have left some such 'product' in A's hands.

In deciding how much to award, the court must (under section 1(3)(b)) take **8.480** account of the effect of the frustrating event in relation to the benefit: thus in the building contract example given in paragraph 8.478, the 'just sum' might vary according to whether frustration resulted from supervening illegality[1743] or the destruction of the house. Even in the latter case it seems[1744] that the court could (though it need not) award something since the subsection applies where a valuable benefit is obtained '*before* the time of discharge'. Expenses incurred by A can also be taken into account in assessing the 'just sum'.[1745]

(iii) Severability

Section 2(4) of the 1943 Act provides for severable parts of the contract to be **8.481** treated, for the purposes of the Act, as separate contracts. If, for example, a contract for personal services provided for quarterly payments,[1746] the provisions of the 1943 Act discussed above would apply in respect of the quarter in which the contract was frustrated.

(iv) Contrary agreement

The provisions of section 1 of the 1943 Act can be excluded by agreement: eg **8.482** to the effect that an advance payment should be retained by the payee in any event.[1747]

1741 *Appleby v Myers* (1867) LR 2 CP 651.

1742 *BP (Exploration) Libya Ltd v Hunt* [1979] 1 WLR 783; affirmed [1981] 1 WLR 236, [1983] 2 AC 352.

1743 *Hansard*, HL (series 5) vol 128, col 139 (29 June 1943).

1744 Though the contrary is suggested in *BP (Exploration) Libya v Hunt* (n 1742 above) [1979] 1 WLR 783, 801.

1745 1943 Act, s 1(3)(a).

1746 As in *Stubbs v Holywell Rly* (1867) LR 2 Ex 311.

1747 1943 Act, s 2(3). Such terms are excepted from the Unfair Contract Terms Act 1977 by s 29 of that Act (para 8.118). They may be subject to the Unfair Terms in Consumer Contracts

(v) Excluded contracts

8.483   The 1943 Act does not apply to contracts for the carriage of goods by sea, to insurance contracts, or to contracts for the sale of specific goods where the cause of frustration is the perishing of the goods.[1748] These exceptions are intended to preserve a number of previously established rules, ie the rules that freight payable on delivery could not be claimed,[1749] and that freight paid in advance could not be recovered back,[1750] if frustration prevented the carrier from reaching the agreed destination; the rule that there could be no apportionment of insurance premiums once the risk had begun to run;[1751] and the rules laid down by the Sale of Goods Act 1979 with respect to discharge by the destruction of specific goods.[1752] The 1943 Act does, however, apply to contracts for the sale of goods which are *not* specific, and where contracts for the sale of specific goods are frustrated for some reason *other* than the destruction of the goods. It is hard to find any satisfactory reasons for these distinctions.

(c) Effects of frustration contrasted with those of mistake

8.484   Events of the kind that can frustrate a contract are sometimes compared with circumstances about the existence of which parties are mistaken at the time of contracting, so that their consent is nullified.[1753] Mistake and frustration are, however, 'different juristic concepts',[1754] the former requiring parties affirmatively to believe in the existence of circumstances which do not in fact exist while the latter requires no affirmative belief that the allegedly frustrating event will not occur. Since it is easier to discover existing facts than to foresee the future, the test of mistake is also stricter than that of frustration.[1755] Moreover, while mistake makes a contract void *ab initio*, frustration discharges it only with effect from the frustrating event;[1756] and the 1943 Act does not apply to cases of invalidity for mistake as to antecedent events.[1757]

Regulations 1999 as the 1943 Act is not 'mandatory' within Reg 4(2)(a); this possibility extends also to terms excluding the common law rule (para 8.476 at n 1735 above).

[1748]   1943 Act, s 2(5)(a), (b) and (c).

[1749]   See para 8.368.

[1750]   *Byrne v Schiller* (1871) LR 6 Ex 319.

[1751]   *Tyrie v Fletcher* (1777) 2 Cowp 666, 668.

[1752]   Sale of Goods Act 1979, s 7.

[1753]   See, for example, the citation of frustration cases in the mistake case of *The Great Peace* [2002] EWCA Civ 1407; [2003] QB 679 at [61]–[76] (para 8.134 n 552 above); and see notes 1754 and 1757 below.

[1754]   *Joseph Constantine* case [1942] AC 154, 186; cf *Fibrosa* case [1943] AC 32, 77; cf *The Great Peace*, n 1753 above at [83] (tests of frustration 'may not be adequate in the context of mistake').

[1755]   See examples given in *The Epaphus* [1987] 2 Lloyd's Rep 215, 218, 220.

[1756]   See paras 8.136 and 8.474.

[1757]   *The Great Peace*, n 1753 above, at [161].

9

AGENCY

A. General Considerations

(1) Introduction

An obvious meaning of the word 'agent' is 'someone who acts for or on behalf of **9.01** another'. The law of agency, not surprisingly, deals with situations where one person acts for another. The common law of agency is based on extremely general principles. The paradigm reasoning, on which much of the rest of agency law is based, is that one person, usually called the principal, can give authority to, or authorize, another, the agent, to act on his behalf; and that the giving of authority confers on the agent a power to affect the legal position of the person who gave the authority. The principal may therefore become bound and/or entitled as against

793

persons with whom the agent deals: such persons are usually referred to by the title 'third party'. To distinguish this situation from other applications of agency reasoning,[1] which will be explained below, authority when conferred in the way above described is called 'actual authority'.

(a) Messenger and agent

9.02 In a limited application an appropriate result requires little supporting theory. No special principles are required to accept the notion that if one person sends a messenger to another who simply repeats a message from the person who sent him, a contract may arise (or other legal consequences follow, in property or even in tort) between the sender and the person to whom the message is given. The messenger is in such a case no different from a letter sent by his principal, and no one doubts that legal transactions can normally be accomplished by letter. It does not take much, however, to vary this situation to a point where the person to whom the message is directed is not found, and the agent has to take a decision as to what to do; or where the message is obviously, as the facts turn out, inappropriate, and the messenger varies it. It has to be accepted in general that the agent may himself, within limits, decide what to do. Here we begin to require a fuller law of agency.

(b) Generality of agency reasoning

9.03 Agency reasoning is obviously most commonly employed in commercial situations, but in common law there is no reason of principle whatever why it cannot be used elsewhere. There is in common law no requirement that the agent pursue a recognized type of occupation as a commercial intermediary, or a recognized commercial occupation, or indeed any occupation at all. Many commercial relationships which might not in civil law countries easily be regarded as examples of agency at all can trigger off agency reasoning. Thus agency reasoning is used in connection not only with auctioneers, brokers and the like, but also in regard to some of the functions of solicitors, captains of ships, employees, directors of companies and so forth. It can also be used in completely non-commercial contexts: in connection with parents and children, or husbands and wives and cognate relationships. In all of these one person may act for another. There is (or may be) agency (of a very complicated sort) if one employs a Lloyd's broker; there may be agency if one sends a child to buy a lottery ticket.[2] Agency reasoning is not, however, in general used in common law to deal with official representation of persons lacking capacity such as minors and mental patients.

---

[1] In particular apparent authority: see paras 9.59ff.
[2] A problem of capacity could arise in such a case.

A result of this approach is that the question 'Is he (or she) an agent?', perhaps **9.04** with the addition 'and if so of whom?', which is often asked of lawyers, does not often, at any rate in common law, form the basis for a useful approach to a legal problem. One person may have agency authority for another in some respects and not in other respects. A solicitor, for example, is in some respects merely a person who provides commercial services to clients. But in other respects the solicitor can act for the client, as by signing documents, commissioning the provision of services, or settling claims. Employees have agency powers in some respects but not in others: some can sign receipts, some can place orders, some can receive payment, some can do none of these things. Employment law regulates much of their activities, but not, in general, their agency functions, which are for the law of agency. The fact that someone is called or describes himself as an agent does not mean that there is in law any agency power at all: for example, many distributors of particular goods, such as cars, may describe themselves as agents when in law they are really sellers on their own account—though they may have minor agency functions in respect to manufacturer's warranties and the handling of complaints. Equally, some persons who do not describe themselves as agents— even some who purport to state that they are not agents—may actually be able to act as agents, or at least have some form of authority. In common law an agreed description of a person by some particular title does not of itself establish or exclude agency functions.

(c) Commercial agents

The common law does not in general, therefore, work by identifying types of **9.05** agent, though there are a few which are regulated by statute and hence may require definition in the regulatory legislation.[3] To this there is now one exception, which, significantly, comes from the civil law. An EU directive[4] deals with the relationship between persons called 'commercial agents' and their principals, and confers certain protections on such agents. The category means nothing in common law: to see whether the prescribed incidents of the relationship apply, it is necessary to look carefully at the definition of 'commercial agent' provided in the directive and in the regulations which implement it in the United Kingdom.[5] Before a common law court the situation is therefore not one where special

---

[3] For example, estate agents, regulated by the Estate Agents Act 1979, but even here the regulation is directed at 'estate agency work'.

[4] Council Directive 86/653, [1986] OJ L382/17.

[5] Commercial Agents (Council Directive) Regulations 1993, SI 1993/3053, as amended by SI 1993/3173 and SI 1998/2868, the latter of which deals with conflict of laws implications. On this specialized topic see Christou, *International Distribution, Agency and Licensing Agreements* (4th edn, 2003); Randolph and Davey, *Guide to the Commercial Agents Regulations* (2nd edn, 2003); Saintier and Scholes, *Commercial Agents and the Law* (2005).

incidents have been attributed to the position of a person pursuing a known occupation (which appears to be the intention behind the directive). Rather, it is necessary to see whether a particular person's mode of commercial operation comes within the definition laid down in the regulations. If so, but not otherwise, that person is a commercial agent within them and their special regime applies in accordance with its terms.

9.06   The definition given of a commercial agent is 'a self-employed intermediary who has continuing authority to negotiate the sale and purchase of goods on behalf of another person ("the principal"), or to negotiate and conclude the sale and purchase of goods on behalf of and in the name of that principal'.[6] It will be seen that this excludes employees and persons authorized for one transaction only; however, it includes agents who have no authority to contract (referred to below as 'canvassing agents')[7] as well as those who have. It also uses the civil law terminology of acting 'in the name of' another, a phrase which has no clear meaning for a common lawyer. There is a (rather obscure) exception for those for whom commercial agency is a secondary activity.[8] What is clear however is that an intermediary who purchases for resale is not a commercial agent.[9]

(2)   Internal and External Aspects of Agency

(a)   Basic division

9.07   It is a well-known principle in the civil law that the agency situation can be analysed as having two aspects, the internal and the external, and that these are to be regarded as conceptually separate. The internal aspect is the relationship between principal and agent, starting with, but not confined to, the conferring of authority. The external is the relationship between the principal and a person or persons in the outside world (third parties) which is created by the acts (including words) of the agent. This distinction is frequently useful, but a complete separation of the second relationship from the first depends on finding a basis for the agent's power different from the actual authority above described—for instance, one stemming from powers ascribed to particular sorts of functionaries

---

   6   Reg 2(1). In the United Kingdom the definition is confined to agents for sale and purchase. In some other countries the protection has been extended to persons acting in connection with the provision of services.

   7   See paras 9.15ff.

   8   Reg 2(3), added as a special definition for the UK which was criticized in the *AMB Imballaggi* case (n 9 below). See however *Tamarind International Ltd v Eastern Natural Gas (Retail) Ltd* [2000] EuLR 708. The power to make special provision to this effect is affirmed in *Crane v Sky-in-Home Services Ltd* [2007] EWHC 66; [2007] 1 CLC 389.

   9   *AMB Imballaggi Plastici SRL v Pacflex Ltd* [1999] 2 All ER (Comm) 249, CA; *Mercantile International Group plc v Chuan Soon Huat Industrial Group Ltd* [2002] EWCA Civ 288; [2002] 1 All ER (Comm) 788.

by provisions of a civil code. Such a route is not available in common law because of the generality of the principles used.[10] In common law therefore, as in some civil law systems also, the external relationship actually stems from the internal: it is because the authority has been given, or is to be regarded as having been given, and hence a power conferred, that the external relationship can be created.

(b) External aspect only: apparent authority

Like other legal systems, common law then extends this reasoning to situations **9.08** where the principal has not, even on the most objective interpretation, conferred authority—he may even have forbidden the act in question—but where the third party is reasonable in a belief that he has. All legal systems must accept liability of the principal to the third party on this basis. Here again the agent has a power, but this time it stems from what is called 'apparent' or 'ostensible' authority, as opposed to the 'actual' authority already mentioned. It is dealt with more fully below.[11] It relates initially to the external relationship only, and only imposes liability on the principal: if he has rights also, it is by virtue of other reasoning, especially ratification.

If the internal and external aspects of agency are kept entirely separate, as perhaps **9.09** in some civil law thinking, the justification of the external relationship accounts for the power of the agent not only in this case but also in what common law calls actual authority, and it is possible to concentrate on the theoretical nature of the power conferred in these two cases. For common law, however, actual authority comes within basic principle, but for apparent authority other reasoning must be found. It can ingeniously be explained on the basis that the principal is still manifesting a grant of authority, in such a case not to the agent, but to the outside world, or at least to the third party. This reasoning is not entirely satisfactory and there are difficulties, as in other legal systems, in reconciling the notion of apparent authority, essential though it is, with basic theory.[12]

(c) Features of the internal relationship: fiduciary obligation

It has been said above that agency situations have two aspects, the internal and **9.10** the external. These go together in two senses. The first is that if the internal relationship confers it, the external power exists. The second is that where the power is in fact conferred, the internal relationship, because of the importance of

---

[10] This seems to be the answer to the comment by R Zimmermann, *The Law of Obligations: Roman Foundations of the Civilian Tradition* (1996) 58, who says that common law 'has not put the insight to any systematic use'.

[11] See para 9.59.

[12] See paras 9.59ff.

the external power, attracts special rules. These are due to the fact that a person who holds the authority, or external power, is able to affect his principal's position. He is therefore, even though paid for his services, a contracting party who is bound to act in the interests of his principal. In most commercial contracts the two sides have adverse commercial interests: each hopes to profit from the other. The paradigm example is that of buyer and seller. The internal relationship of principal and agent is however not commercially adverse: even if he is employed on a commercial basis the agent must in general act in the principal's interests. The internal relationship therefore imposes fiduciary duties on the agent which enforce that position and make the relationship in some respects at least not commercially adverse. Such duties apply outside the law of agency also, but agency relationships constitute a prominent example of them. They are discussed below.[13]

(d) Payment by commission

9.11 Another feature of the internal relationship also arises out of the non-adverse nature of the agent's function. The agent is in general not entitled to take his own profit on the 'turn' as would one who bought and resold to another: this would be a secret profit and hence inconsistent with his fiduciary duty. Rather, he charges a fee or commission for his services. There may be difficulty in distinguishing between these situations where the 'commission' includes extra amounts calculated in special ways, but the distinction is clear in principle and commission (in the sense of the type of payment made) is one of the hallmarks of agency.

(e) Duty of care only

9.12 There is another feature of the agent's position which is related to special features of common law reasoning. In common law the starting point as regards many contractual duties is that of strict liability; that is to say, the contracting party does not merely undertake to exercise due care in performance of his functions, but prima facie guarantees a result. This is true, for example, of sellers. It is not of course true of most of those rendering personal services; hence it is not true of agents. Since much agency arises in the context of buying and selling, this test provides a good way of distinguishing an agent from one who buys from or sells to another. The seller owes the strict duties, for example as to quality, associated with sale; the agent simply promises reasonable endeavours to carry out the principal's instructions.[14]

---

[13] See paras 9.137ff.

[14] To the third party, however, he owes a strict duty, to warrant his authority. See para 9.111.

(f) Control

We may then ask whether there are any other features of the internal relationship **9.13** which must be regarded as typical. An obvious candidate is the power to control: the agent acts under the principal's control. The principal relevance of control in law is to justifications for imposing liability in tort for the acts of employees. It can be said that it is the degree of control exercised over an enterprise and those involved in it that makes it appropriate to place the risks arising from the enterprise on the person exercising the control.

Agents are often independent contractors, who will not accept complete control **9.14** over the way in which they do things for their principals; and some will only accept instructions to act in accordance with the usages of their own market. Others may be authorized to do particular things only, as when a stockbroker has specific instructions:[15] no further control is possible. In many such situations the principal's only control lies in his power to revoke the authority, a power which agency law assumes he must (with some exceptions) have at all times.[16] It might seem therefore that control is not a significant feature of the internal relationship. Nevertheless, if a principal gives up all control of his agent, either this amounts to a revocation of authority, or, if this is not so, the relationship was always only doubtfully one of agency. This is one of the problems with some of the arrangements at Lloyd's, which are purportedly based on agency. For these reasons it seems right to retain the principal's control as a feature of agency;[17] but the idea is certainly not used in the same way as in vicarious liability in the law of tort.

(3) The Boundaries of Agency

(a) Internal relationship only: canvassing agents

From these internal features of the agency relationship as expounded above, a **9.15** further problem, certainly of exposition and probably of priority in analysis, now arises. There are a number of commercial and other intermediaries who act for others and hence must owe fiduciary duties, are remunerated on commission, owe duties of care only and are subject to some form of control, but have no authority or power to do things that alter their principal's legal position. A standard example is the real estate agent, who (though practice varies) may be engaged only to introduce customers, with whom the principal then deals direct. He is also remunerated by commission, and undoubtedly owes fiduciary duties, for example not (at any rate without disclosure) to take commission from the other

---

[15] eg *Volkers v Midland Doherty* (1985) 17 DLR (4th) 343.
[16] See para 9.96.
[17] Considerable stress is, however, placed on it by *Restatement, Third, Agency* §1.01 and comment.

side to a transaction or potential transaction, and not to conceal from his principal offers made to him.[18]

9.16 Is such a person to be brought within the law of agency, or are we to say that no external relationship being possible, whatever he calls himself, the person concerned is not an agent, but merely one performing services who owes fiduciary duties and is remunerated on commission? Here again we have a doctrinal choice and the answer to it is not dictated by any legal rule or rules. The problem would not arise if agency was regarded as a branch of law attaching to certain specific occupations: persons such as real estate agents would be governed by their own special rules regardless of whether they came within any definition of agency. The generality of the common law approach, however, creates a problem of how to apply the general principles. Should the external or the internal aspect of agency be regarded as primary for definitional and analytical purposes?

9.17 The current trend has been to say that since such persons call themselves agents, and since their internal relationship with the person on whose account they are acting is so clearly assimilated to those with external powers, it is right to regard them as coming under agency law, and it would indeed be misleading to exclude them. This has the result that it becomes necessary to give the internal aspect of agency analytical priority over the external. The fiduciary nature of the relationship, though it applies to other relationships also, then becomes the key factor. This is the approach taken in the American *Restatement, Agency, Third*[19] and also in some English books. Older writings may confine agency to persons who have the power to alter their principal's legal position.

(b) Indirect representation

9.18 The exposition so far has referred to agents who have the power to alter their principal's legal position, who are involved in both internal and external relationships, and to those who have no such power but are governed by the internal relationship only. Civil law countries may however recognize another institution, that of indirect representation or agency. Such a person is one who acts for another, but on the basis that while internally he is an agent, externally he deals on his own account, with the result that the third party cannot (usually) proceed against the principal, nor can the principal proceed against the third party.[20] This is so even though the

---

18 It may be queried whether a person may validly undertake no more than a commercial duty as 'finder', to locate potential buyers or sellers without attracting any fiduciary duties whatever. It must be possible in principle; but a court might find it difficult to accept that such was really the intention of the parties.

19 §1.01: 'Agency is the fiduciary relationship that exists when one person (a "principal") manifests assent to another person (an "agent") that the agent shall act on the principal's behalf and subject to the principal's control, and the agent manifests assent or otherwise consents so to act.'

20 There are exceptions to this in some jurisdictions.

agent is known to act on this basis, and so is known to be very likely or even certain to have a principal: indeed, the actual name of that principal might be known to the third party. This role is performed by persons conducting certain types of commercial activity (which may vary from country to country), and is often referred to by the French word *commission*, or some parallel to this in another language, the agent being a *commissionnaire* (the word referring to the task undertaken rather than the method of remuneration). If this type of representation is taken into account, it can then be said that there are two types of agency or representation, direct and indirect.[21] To classify this arrangement with other forms of agency again involves giving priority to the internal relationship.

Like the commercial agent, this type of representative does not constitute a category of agent known to English law. Since the law of agency is general, and draws upon general principles, and if it is correct, as has been argued above, that it is the internal aspect that predominates from the analytical point of view, there can be no objection to such an arrangement, nor to the description of a person exercising such functions as an agent. However, although there are dicta of the famous nineteenth-century commercial judge Blackburn J, later Lord Blackburn, recognizing and explaining this mode of operation,[22] there are few decisions going any further. Even where the agent operates in a market (such as the London Stock Exchange as it formerly operated) where agents (in this case brokers) deal with each other on the basis that all transactions are between members only, the courts have often ignored this and assumed that the brokers were ordinary agents known to be acting for unidentified principals; and though they were personally liable on their transactions, their principals were in some cases held liable and entitled also.[23] The only alternative has been seen as that of an intermediary buying for resale.[24] Litigation on the internal relationship, which might have clarified matters or encouraged new analyses, is hard to find. As often, there is probably a pragmatic reason for this. Such agents in the United Kingdom often acted for overseas principals, and litigation between agent and principal

9.19

---

[21] This distinction forms the basis of the Agency section of the *Principles of European Contract Law* (ed. Lando and Beale, 2000); see art 3:102. The UNIDROIT *Principles of International Commercial Contracts* (2004), however, do not employ this distinction and indeed more or less eliminate the significance of the notion of indirect representation (together with the common law doctrine of undisclosed principal).

[22] *Robinson v Mollett* (1875) LR 7 HL 802, 809–10; another famous judgment on this type of function is *Ireland v Livingston* (1872) LR 5 HL 395. It is found also in *Mildred, Goyaneche & Co v Maspons y Hermano* (1882) 9 QBD 530, CA; (1883) 8 App Cas 874.

[23] eg *Hodgkinson v Kelly* (1868) Lr 6 Eq 496; *Scott and Horton v Ernest* (1900) 16 TLR 498.

[24] See the analysis in *Anglo-African Shipping Co of New York Inc v J Mortner Ltd* [1962] 1 Lloyd's Rep 610, CA. *Triffit Nurseries v Salads Etcetera Ltd* [2000] 1 All ER (Comm) 737 appears to concern an agent operating in such a way: this is clearer in the first instance judgment, [1999] 1 All ER (Comm) 110.

(as compared with principal and third party) would be likely to occur, if at all, in overseas jurisdictions.

9.20   Civil law commentators are apt to assume that the undisclosed principal doctrine, to be discussed later,[25] constitutes the English way of dealing with this method of operation, and that (subject to limits) it simply makes the principal of an indirect agent liable and entitled as if the agent were a direct agent—thus rendering this way of operating ineffective to insulate principal from third party. This appears to be an oversimplification of the undisclosed principal doctrine.[26] In any case, this mode of operation becomes confused in the cases with other commercial figures such as del credere agency, *compradors*, confirming houses and later, moving further away, export guarantees and demand guarantees in general.[27]

(c)   Representative terminology

9.21   In this connection, a warning is necessary as to wording which may be used to indicate that one person acts for another (to use about the most neutral phrase possible). There is no stability of terminology in this area. Civil lawyers tend to use wording which usually appears translated into English as 'acts in the name of another'. The phrase 'in the name of' has however no agreed meaning in English law and indeed such wording is not often used. A common lawyer is puzzled in particular as to whether an agent who is known to have a principal but does not give that principal's name should be regarded as 'acting in the name of' that principal. It seems that he usually should, though there may in civil law be specific requirements as to disclosure of the principal's name on demand.[28] Other phrases are 'on behalf of'; another 'for (or 'on') account of', 'for the benefit of', 'in the interest of'. The mere 'for' (as in 'acts for') is completely equivocal. If any such representative formulation is used, it is necessary to examine the facts carefully to see in what legal role the person referred to must be analysed as acting.

(d)   Companies: agent and organ

9.22   This leads finally to special reasoning which may be deployed in the area of company law. Since a company has no real existence it is easy enough to say that it must act by human agents, and that agency law is the key to problems of attribution of rights and liabilities to companies. This can be said to have been the dominant common law approach in the nineteenth century. The direct use of such reasoning did not prove entirely satisfactory, however, and in some areas special company

---

[25] See paras 9.68ff.
[26] And probably of indirect representation see further para 9.70.
[27] See para 9.24.
[28] See para 9.107.

law doctrines have been developed[29] while in others the law has been changed by statute.[30] More recently, a line of reasoning which regards the acts of certain persons as the acts of the company itself (rather than as those of an agent acting under normal principles on behalf of the company) has become more prominent. As often in law the possibility has come to the fore in rather miscellaneous contexts: the shipowner's overall right to limit his liability except where he was seriously at fault,[31] offences under criminal law,[32] the personal liability of directors in tort,[33] and the attribution of knowledge or notice to companies.[34]

(e) Agent and trustee; agent and bailee

There are however in common law other legal roles the attributes of which are **9.23** more clearly worked out, and comparison of these with agency is instructive in showing the overlap between categories, and also the flexible nature of agency reasoning. The most obvious are those of the trustee and the bailee. A *trustee* holds property for another which is regarded as the property of the beneficiary in equity; he is not normally subject to control or revocation of his powers by the beneficiary. A trustee may have agency powers for a beneficiary in certain circumstances; and an agent may hold money received for the principal on trust in certain circumstances.[35] But a trustee may have no agency powers, and an agent may hold no property for his principal at all: he may simply be a debtor to his principal. A *bailee* possesses goods owned by another: he may have agency powers, for example to take steps to preserve them.[36] An agent may hold goods for his principal as bailee (as did the factor), but may hold no goods at all. These various notions are not mutually exclusive.

(f) Lack of significance of types of agent

Since the law of agency does not rely on analysis by means of named types of **9.24** intermediary function, there is in common law no difference of principle between one sort of agent and another, for example between a real estate agent and a shipbroker, though of course they may act in different ways legally. Names of types of agent are not of much significance in common law: what one needs to know is the way in which the agents work. However, a few names should be

---

[29] See eg *Royal British Bank v Turquand* (1856) 6 E & B 327, 119 ER 886; para 9.65.

[30] eg Companies Act 1985, ss 35A, 35B, to be superseded by Companies Act 2006, s 40.

[31] eg *The Lady Gwendolen* [1965] P 294.

[32] eg *Tesco Supermarkets Ltd v Nattrass* [1972] AC 153, HL (regulatory offence). See also *Odyssey Re (London) Ltd v OIC Run-off Ltd* [2001] LRLR1 (perjury), and in general paras 3.17ff, 3.51ff.

[33] See para 9.114.

[34] eg *El Ajou v Dollar Land Holdings plc* [1994] 2 All ER 685, CA; *Meridian Global Funds Management Asia Ltd v Securities Commission* [1995] 2 AC 500, HL.

[35] See para 9.146.

[36] eg *Tappenden v Artus* [1964] 2 QB 185, CA (repairs).

mentioned, if only to dismiss them. The phrases 'general agent' and 'special agent' were used in the nineteenth century and occasionally still are: the difference is (obviously) between one with wide authority and one with more specific authority.[37] It was once toyed with as a basis for what is now called apparent authority, but in common law this reasoning did not prove equal to the task.[38] Nineteenth-century cases often concerned factors and brokers.[39] The factor was a person who held goods, often from overseas, which he might or might not own: he dealt with them without mentioning a principal and raised a problem as to whether he was to be regarded externally as contracting for himself, or as agent for another, and internally whether he acted as agent or bought for resale. His function was obviously similar to that of the *commissionnaire*, and cases on factors are associated with the growth of the undisclosed principal doctrine;[40] but it is dangerous to draw too dogmatic conclusions as to his mode of operation, which is in any case largely a matter of legal history, the use of the word in this sense being largely obsolete. Brokering was a function which developed later: a commodity broker did not hold goods but simply negotiated contracts between others, normally dropping out of the transaction once it was agreed. A number of other types of agent may be mentioned. Del credere agents were agents who guaranteed the liabilities of overseas buyers or sellers to their principals: this function was similar to that of the *comprador*, a functionary found in the Far East. Many of the cases from which early law on agency is derived concerned also masters of ships, auctioneers and solicitors. Other categories of agent have required definition because of statutory regulation placed upon them. As already stated, this is partly true of estate agents[41] and is now true of commercial agents.[42]

(g) Agency law outside its central context

9.25 It is of the nature of law, or at any rate of common law, to extend an established and agreed notion to perform other purposes. Agency reasoning has been particularly prone to this, and the trend continues. Assignment of a right of action achieved by means of appointing an agent to bring suit on one's behalf is ancient; there are of course parallels in the *mandatum* of Roman law. Agency has also been used in what would now be regarded as a restitutionary context, to justify the granting to persons of powers to act for others in situations of emergency, and

---

[37] eg *Smith v M'Guire* (1858) 3 H & N 554, 119 ER 886; *Barrett v Irvine* [1907] 2 IR 462. It occasionally still comes up in specialized contexts even now: eg *Dun & Bradstreet Software Services (England) Ltd v Provident Mutual Life Assurance* [1998] 2 EGLR 175, CA (notices between landlord and tenant).

[38] But see Brown [2004] JBL 391, arguing that it did.

[39] See in general SJ Stoljar, *Law of Agency* (1961) 242–7.

[40] As to which see para 9.68.

[41] See para 9.15.

[42] See para 9.05.

then to deploy the internal rules to entitle the person concerned to some form of indemnity or reimbursement. This institution is called 'agency of necessity'.[43] Attempts have also been made to prolong the effects of a reservation of title on sale into proceeds of resale by seeking to create an agency in the non-paying buyer who resells;[44] and quite recently problems of corporate identity, where the real argument is that the corporate veil ought to be pierced, have been attacked by (mostly unsuccessful) agency arguments.[45] Finally, and rather improbably, a form of the *commission* contract has been used in an attempt to establish a framework of operation achieving favourable tax results. The law of agency, however, now carries baggage with it, largely in the shape of fiduciary duties, (to some extent) powers of control, and certainly powers of revocation. All such invocations of agency law may sometimes therefore carry unexpected and inappropriate consequences.

(h) Agency and tort

The account so far given has confined itself to agency in connection with contract. **9.26** It may then be asked whether the reasoning is equally applicable to tort situations. If so, new and broader basic reasoning would probably be required. On one view it must be so: there must be general principles governing the liability of persons for, and the extent to which they are bound by, the acts of others, whether in a way that triggers off one type of obligation or the other, and also in the law of restitution and in the law of property. For many years agency courses based on this assumption, taking in vicarious liability in tort as well as agency situations in contract, were common and indeed traditional in the United States. There is a choice here as to technique of exposition and as to selection of linking factors, on which views are not right or wrong, but rather, preferable or less preferable.

The view put forward in this chapter is that whereas restitution and (with more **9.27** difficulty) property can be taken in to basic agency law, the assimilation of the law of tort is for the most part unproductive.[46] In contract situations, the idea of conferring authority on others to act represents the general justification for binding and entitling those for whom they then act: and apparent authority is a modification of this approach geared also to the deliberately undertaken

---

[43] See para 9.90.

[44] The '*Romalpa* clause', so called because of the case which first drew attention to the problem, *Aluminium Industrie Vaassen BV v Romalpa Aluminium Ltd* [1976] 1 WLR 676, CA. It has given rise to an extensive jurisprudence of its own: see, eg, RM Goode, *Commercial Law* (3rd edn, 2004), 607ff.

[45] eg *Yukong Lines Ltd v Rendsberg Investments Corp (The Rialto)* [1998] 1 WLR 294 (person 'behind' company not undisclosed principal to its acts); *Williams v Natural Life Health Foods Ltd* [1998] 1 WLR 830, HL (director not liable personally in negligence). See also para 9.107.

[46] But see para 9.128 for a limited exception.

relationships on which contract is based—the third party entering into a transaction is justified in assuming that there has been a conferring of authority on the person with whom he is dealing. The same, though with some reservations[47] can be said of property transfer. Liability for the wrongs of others on the other hand is, at least in common law countries, normally based on different considerations directed to the spreading of loss. Where a person is run down by a truck, the claim against the company owning it and employing its driver is not appropriately based on the idea that its driver was authorized to commit torts. Indeed, a claim against the employer may be justified where the driver was not authorized to drive the truck at all. Also, in tort one speaks only of liabilities: contract involves rights also. The difference is fairly plain in the case law, and though efforts have been made to locate inner principles which would justify rights and liabilities acquired through others across all private law, nothing satisfactory has yet been found. As Lord Wilberforce said:

> It may be that some wider conception of vicarious responsibility other than that of agency, as normally understood, may have to be recognised in order to accommodate some of the more elaborate cases which now arise when there are two persons who become mutually involved or associated in one side of a transaction.[48]

But the gauntlet thus thrown down has not been picked up over a period of 30 years, and acceptable techniques of absorbing the two lines of reasoning have not been found. Marginal situations certainly occur, however, and these will be discussed below.[49]

B. Formation of Agency

(1) Conferring of Authority

(a) Significance of agreement

9.28 The most obvious way of making someone one's agent is by conferring authority on him; and the internal relationship normally requires that there be agreement to the arrangement (in an objective sense) on both sides.[50] The agreement may be a contract, and in a commercial situation normally will be, but it need

---

47 See para 9.119.

48 *Branwhite v Worcester Works Finance Ltd* [1969] 1 AC 552, 587, HL.

49 See para 9.79.

50 'The relationship of principal and agent can only be constituted by the consent of the principal and the agent': *Garnac Grain Co Inc v HMF Faure & Fairclough Ltd* [1968] AC 1130n, 1137, HL *per* Lord Pearson (a case distinguishing between agency and purchase for resale in a string contract).

not be: there can be 'gratuitous agents', operating in situations where at common law no consideration can be found and there is hence no contract.

A minor theoretical difficulty can arise because the pure conferring of authority **9.29** (as opposed to creation of the full internal relationship) appears to be a unilateral act. The principal may confer authority and not require the agent to manifest acceptance of it directly to him (for instance, he may send the agent a power of attorney and go on a journey). Normally, of course, the agent will accept, and agree to the internal relationship, by acting on behalf of the principal; and the principal may have waived notice of acceptance. But it may be asked what happens if the principal sends an agent authority, which the agent does not receive: the agent then acts for the principal (perhaps because he erroneously thinks that his authority covers the act in question, or because he has forgotten that his authority has lapsed, or because he simply decides to take a risk that the principal will ratify). The unilateral model (as opposed to the agreement model) would suggest that in such a situation (admittedly difficult to construct plausibly) the principal has put himself on risk by the conferral of authority and is liable and entitled *vis-à-vis* the third party.[51]

(b) What can be done by an agent

The generality of principle again leads to discussions of what acts can be done **9.30** by an agent. The starting point is that any act can; but there are of course restrictions where a power is conferred on the principal which he must exercise personally, and where statute or other instrument requires acts to be done personally. Proxy signatures are usually admissible.[52]

(c) Formalities not usually necessary

The starting point is that, consistent with the generality of agency principles, **9.31** no formality is needed for the creation of agency. Sometimes however there are specially imposed requirements that authority be conferred in writing, for example in connection with land;[53] and sometimes appointment must be by deed. This is true of powers of attorney, an undefined term covering formal documents conferring (usually) general powers.[54] Such documents are normally used

---

[51] And it was so held in the United States in *Ruggles v American Central Insurance Co of St Louis* 114 NY 415, 76 NY Supp 787 (1889), US. But this case is strongly criticized in *Restatement, Third, Agency*, Reporter's note b.

[52] There is a recent discussion in *General Legal Council v Frankson* [2006] UKPC 42; [2006] 1 WLR 2803, PC.

[53] eg Law of Property Act 1925, ss 53, 54 (certain instruments relating to land).

[54] Powers of Attorney Act 1971, s 1(1) (as amended).

when the circumstances require a clear conferring of authority, with indications of its extent.

(d) Capacity

9.32 The interaction of agency with rules of capacity can be complex, because the rules of capacity can themselves be complex. In general the principal needs to have capacity to do the act to be done on his behalf by the agent, but the agent, who is a mere instrument, does not need formal legal capacity as regards the external function: he merely needs to understand the nature of the acts which he does (though contractual liability on the internal relationship would require capacity). There is no objection of principle to one party to a transaction acting as agent of the other in whole or in part, nor to one agent acting for both parties; but care has to be taken in such situations, as there may be a breach or potential breach of the internal fiduciary obligation.[55]

(2) Ratification

(a) General principle

9.33 Most legal systems accept the convenience of the idea that where a person acts for another without authority, the principal can nevertheless by ratifying the act put himself in the same position as that in which he would have been had he authorized the act in advance. Agents must often act without authority on the basis that their principal, when he learns the facts, is likely to approve. Sometimes this can in fact be dealt with by a generous interpretation of the existing authority, or an assumption that the principal authorizes special acts in unforeseen situations: but not always. The idea of ratification as a solution to cases where there is no antecedent authority is accepted in English law and indeed has even been applied in respect of liability for torts (where its justification is normally in fact quite different).[56] A ratification, like a conferring of authority, appears to be a unilateral juristic act, and as such, though the person ratifying must know, or be attributable with knowledge of, the relevant facts, it seems that the ratification, so long as it can be proved, probably need not be communicated to the person whose act is ratified or to the third party.[57] It may be express or implied from conduct. It is normally said that there can be no ratification in part: either an act is adopted or it is not. This is true at least in the sense that the

---

[55] See paras 9.137ff.

[56] The cases are mostly old and concern matters such as unlawful distress, and the tort of conversion, which moves into property law.

[57] *Pagnan SpA v Feed Products Ltd* [1987] 2 Lloyd's Rep 601, 613; *Shell Co of Australia Ltd v Nat Shipping Bagging Services Ltd (The Kilmun)* [1988] 2 Lloyd's Rep 1, 8, 11, 14.

principal cannot by ratification secure for himself a transaction which is not that which the third party had intended.

Ratification, which is more likely to be invoked against rather than by a principal, **9.34** must be clearly distinguished from other notions such as estoppel, which to be effective would require communication to the third party and some degree of reliance; election, a decisive choice between alternative courses available at law, which would also require communication; and from novation, or substituted contract. There can of course be estoppel as to whether there has been a ratification. But a purported ratification in advance (quite common in certain types of document such as powers of attorney) cannot in principle be a ratification: the starting point is that it can be no more than a promise to ratify.

(b) Void acts

Further discriminations have to be made in the case of acts which can be said to **9.35** be void. It is said that a void act cannot be ratified as there is nothing to ratify; hence there can be no ratification of a forgery in the sense of a counterfeit signature[58] (as opposed to an unauthorized signature, which can also rank as a forgery in criminal law). A person may however be estopped from setting up a forgery in appropriate cases.[59] But as elsewhere in the law the notion of voidness has to be treated with care. Any unauthorized act on behalf of a principal could be said to be void as an act of the principal; but it is precisely such acts to which the doctrine of ratification may apply.[60]

(c) Who may ratify

Obviously, the only person who may ratify is the person on whose behalf the act **9.36** was done. Two problems arise here. The first is whether a person who lacked capacity at that time, or was not born, or was a company that did not yet exist, or was a person or company which existed but was not at the time within the description of the principal given at that time (for example, a subcontractor not yet nominated at the time a liability insurance policy was taken out) can ratify and so take advantage of the doctrine. The answer is fairly clearly that this cannot be done: the purpose of the doctrine is to correct the situation at the time of the act purported to be ratified.[61] A query can however be raised when the contract

---

[58] *Brook v Hook* (1871) LR 6 Ex 89.

[59] eg *Greenwood v Martins Bank Ltd* [1933] AC 51, HL.

[60] eg *Presentaciones Musicales SA v Secunda* [1994] Ch 271 (unauthorized institution of legal proceedings). Such a question can involve consideration of whether the act is void or simply requires cure.

[61] An old leading case concerns a company not yet formed: *Kelner v Baxter* (1866) LR 2 CP 174. The promoter might be held liable, as happened in the case itself: but the question is quite often dealt with by statute. See para 9.111.

appears from the start to contemplate future principals: for example, the insurance contract above might be stated as made on behalf of all present and future subcontractors.[62] It seems likely that clarity of theory should be maintained: rights to sue in such a case could be conferred when appropriate by trust law, which has no objection to future beneficiaries, by rules on insurable interest,[63] and by rules allowing third parties to sue on contracts (in which context in a recent English statute the matter, which might otherwise be arguable, is specifically dealt with so as to allow an action in such a case).[64]

9.37 The second problem relates to unidentified principals. It is clear that an agent can contract on behalf of a principal whom he does not at the time of contracting name or identify, so long as probative material can be adduced in case of dispute to show who that person was.[65] Such a person is called an 'unidentified principal'.[66] This rule obviously creates the possibility in practice of an agent contracting on such a basis and in effect allocating the contract at a later date. This is not permissible as such, but there may in fact be authority from a number of identified principals and it may be difficult to establish that the agent did not act at the time for the one who later ratified. It may then be asked whether there can be ratification of an unauthorized act purportedly performed for an unidentified principal. If there could, the possibility of later adoption by a principal of an unauthorized contract would be increased. It appears that there can in such a case be ratification:[67] the problem of proof as to the person for whom the contract was made is in fact the same in both situations, and if one is allowed, so should the other be. The question of proof of intent can always be raised.[68] It has however long been clear that where the person acting intended to do so on behalf of a particular person, but gave no indication of this to the third party, the person concerned, called an 'undisclosed principal', cannot ratify, even where the person acting was already an agent of the principal.[69]

(d) Retroactivity of ratification

9.38 The whole idea behind ratification is that the later ratifying act supplies the authority not originally existent and makes the act concerned retrospectively valid.

---

[62] As in the Australian case of *Trident General Ins Co Ltd v McNiece Bros Pty Ltd* (1987) 8 NSWLR 270, 276–7, affd without reference to the agency points (1988) 165 CLR 107, Aus.

[63] See *Tomlinson (Hauliers) Ltd v Hepburn* [1966] AC 451.

[64] Contracts (Rights of Third Parties) Act 1999, s 1(3).

[65] Such a person must be distinguished from an undisclosed principal: see para 9.68 ff.

[66] Cf para 9.77.

[67] *National Oilwell (UK) Ltd v Davy Offshore Ltd* [1993] 2 Lloyd's Rep 582, 592–7; see FMB Reynolds, 'Some Agency Problems in Insurance Law' in FD Rose (ed), *Consensus ad Idem: Essays in Honour of Guenter Treitel* (1996) 77ff.

[68] See the *National Oilwell* case (n 67 above).

[69] See para 9.77.

This retroactivity, if accepted as dogma, can however operate prejudicially to the non-ratifying party, and some element of control is needed. Here difficulties are encountered.

A fairly well-established group of cases concerns situations where property rights **9.39** are involved. In the context of landlord and tenant it has been held that where a notice to quit is served without the authority of the landlord, the landlord cannot ratify it after the time for service has expired;[70] and that notice to exercise an option (which creates an equitable property right) cannot be ratified after the time for exercise has expired.[71] An ancient leading case applies the same reasoning to the exercise of an unpaid seller's right to stop in transit.[72] Since these cases involve property reasoning, however, it can also be said more technically that ratification cannot divest a property right.

A second possible line of reasoning is a wider one, that where a time limit is **9.40** involved, ratification after the expiry of the limit is inadmissible.[73] There is some overlap between these types of case, since (for example) an accrued defence under the Limitation Act is sometimes spoken of as a property right of which a party ought not to be deprived. But reasoning based on time limits requires that attention be given to the purposes of particular time limits: thus it has been held fairly recently that ratification of the issue of a writ after the expiry of the relevant period of limitation was effective.[74]

The most recent authority now suggests a much more general test to cover both **9.41** these lines of reasoning, and perhaps others,[75] that ratification is barred where it would cause unfair prejudice to the party against whom it is invoked.[76]

Another well-known difficulty is caused by the application of retroactivity to a **9.42** situation where the third party purports to withdraw from a contract before ratification. If the contract was made expressly subject to ratification, at common law there is normally no transaction from which withdrawal is needed, and any purported ratification would therefore be ineffective.[77] It is in fact in general

---

[70] *Doe d.Mann v Walters* (1830) 10 B & C 626, 109 ER 583.

[71] *Dibbins v Dibbins* [1896] 2 Ch 348.

[72] *Bird v Brown* (1850) 4 Exch 786, 154 ER 1433.

[73] This would apply to the contractual element in the option in *Dibbins v Dibbins* (n 71 above).

[74] *Presentaciones Musicales SA v Secunda* [1994] Ch 271.

[75] For example, that ratification must be effected within a reasonable time: see *Metropolitan Asylums Board v Kingham & Sons* (1890) 6 TLR 217. It is suggested by Tan Cheng-Han that this could be the, or a, main control mechanism against unfair operation of the doctrine: see (2002) 117 LQR 626.

[76] See *Smith v Henniker-Major & Co* [2002] EWCA Civ 762; [2003] Ch 182 at [63]ff; *The Borvigilant* [2003] EWCA 935; [2003] 2 Lloyd's Rep 520 at [59]ff. A special rule for insurance law is that policies of insurance may be ratified after loss, even by one who knows of the loss: *National Oilwell (UK) Ltd v Davy Offshore Ltd* [1993] 2 Lloyd's Rep 582.

[77] See *Watson v Davies* [1931] 1 Ch 455.

difficult to see that at common law the doctrine of ratification can apply at all to a contract made with an agent known to have no authority.[78] But if a contract is made without the agent having authority, and the third party then discovers this, the argument for permitting the third party to withdraw despite subsequent ratification is strong: for a start, the third party is otherwise left in a state of uncertainty. A view that the third party is nevertheless bound by a ratification in such a case is usually derived from the famous, even notorious[79] case of *Bolton Partners v Lambert*.[80] But in that case the third party 'withdrew', not because he had discovered that the agent had not been authorized, but because he alleged that that the contract had not reached the binding stage, and also the contract had been induced by misrepresentations, on both of which points he failed: it would appear that he was not at the time aware of any lack of authority.[81] Hence, however famous, the case is not as clear as is sometimes supposed. The reasoning recently adopted and referred to above would seem helpful for this situation also: the court should similarly ask whether ratification would cause unfair prejudice to the third party.

(e) Internal and external effects

9.43 Obviously, where an act is ratified it ranks as valid when done: that is the purpose of the doctrine. But the difficulties discussed above serve as a warning that such a simple unitary description of the availability and effects of ratification cannot be given. It is necessary to differentiate the internal and external aspects of agency. The discussion above concerns the external consequences of ratification. A further external consequence, which has not been mentioned, is that the ratification protects the agent against the third party. If the act had not been ratified, the agent would have been liable to the third party for loss caused by purporting to have an authority which he did not have, under the contractual doctrine of breach of warranty of authority, which is discussed later.[82] If ratification occurs, there is still a technical breach of contract, but it is likely, though not certain, to cause no loss, as the third party will get what he bargained for. Such loss can occur where, for example, the third party spends money in proceeding against principal or agent before the ratification occurs.

9.44 The internal situation requires, however, more careful analysis in this context. The obvious result of ratification is that the principal confirms that the agent has

---

[78] But the contrary seems to be assumed by the UNIDROIT *Principles of International Commercial Contracts* (2004): see art 2.2.9(3).

[79] It ranks for a specific disavowal in *Restatement, Third, Agency*, §4.05(1).

[80] (1889) 41 Ch D 295.

[81] The account given in H Kötz, *European Contract Law* (1998) is incorrect on this point.

[82] See paras 9.111ff.

acted acceptably in exceeding his authority, and so is liable to the agent for commission, reimbursement of expenses and so forth as if the act had been authorized. The proper explanation of this, where the internal relationship is contractual, is that he has waived the agent's breach of duty, though gratuitous agency may cause more difficulties of analysis. But a principal may ratify reluctantly, to preserve his commercial reputation, or because he has no practical alternative. In such a case he does not necessarily waive the breach of duty on the internal relationship, and in appropriate cases the agent may be liable to him for loss caused by exceeding his authority.[83] In such a case the right to commission would be unlikely to arise, and the right to reimbursement and indemnity would usually be doubtful also.[84]

C. The External Effects of Agency

(1) Express and Implied Authority

Under the central principle of agency law an agent has the authority which he has been given by his principal, which in appropriate cases gives him power to affect his principal's legal position as regards third parties. This sort of authority is called actual authority, to distinguish it from apparent authority, which is discussed below.[85] The agent is regarded as having been actually authorized by the principal. **9.45**

Assuming it exists, the next question is how far this authority extends. It should be remembered however that on the analysis adopted in this chapter there can be agents who have no authority to alter their principal's legal position at all; and to such persons the idea of conferring authority is not really applicable, though they may in some situations have a very limited authority. **9.46**

(a) Express authority

The conferring of authority may be express: even this may be subject to disputes of interpretation. But disputes more often concern the implied conferring of authority. In both cases the law creates (or extends) the authority, and hence the agent's power: but only, in this context, by objectively interpreting the internal relationship between principal and agent—not, as in the case of apparent authority, by looking to the impression received by the third party. **9.47**

---

[83] There may be a difference in the degree of knowledge required of the principal in the two different situations, since in the first there is no need to protect the reasonable interests of the third party: see *Ing Re (UK) Ltd v R&V Versicherung AG* [2006] EWHC 1544 (Comm); [2006] 2 All ER (Comm) 870.

[84] *Suncorp Insurance and Finance v Milano Assicurazioni SpA* [1993] 2 Lloyd's Rep 225, 234–5.

[85] See paras 9.59ff.

9.48   The authority may be conferred in a formal document. Such a document is usually called a power of attorney, and precedents for these are to be found in the Powers of Attorney Act 1971[86] and books of precedents. Such documents do not need to confer powers of a comprehensive nature, though they sometimes do so.[87] Their wording is on the whole strictly construed against the agent. This may seem a breach of the normal practice of construing contract terms *contra proferentem*: but not all such documents are contractual (eg, a power of attorney would not normally be), and in general in this area it may be appropriate to take the view that the transfer of power is a dangerous exercise and should not be presumed to have occurred beyond what is clear. Such construction may plainly be applied to powers of attorney, though precedents of these usually employ very wide wording. An ordinary letter might not attract such hostile construction.

(b) Implied authority

9.49   Beyond this there are numerous examples of implied authority. Terminology here is not universally agreed, but implied authority may for convenience be roughly divided as follows:

(i) Incidental authority

9.50   An agent authorized to do a particular thing is impliedly authorized to do all lesser things required to achieve the principal object. An example is a solicitor acting in the sale of a house.

(ii) Usual authority

9.51   This term tends only to be found in textbooks and may be dangerous to use in that too much significance is sometimes attributed to it, especially in the area of the undisclosed principal. But the general idea which is normally intended to be conveyed is straightforward. Usual authority has two facets. The first is that if one person puts another in a position in which there would usually, in the course of business, be authority to do certain things, that person has implied authority to do those things: for example, a managing director.[88] The second is that if one person uses a person in the course of that person's trade or profession, that person is authorized to do what is normally done in the same context in that trade or profession: for example, a solicitor or auctioneer.

---

[86] s 10 and Sch 1.

[87] Statutory provisions of a detailed nature protect attorneys (agents) who act in good faith, and third parties dealing with them: Powers of Attorney Act 1971, s 5.

[88] See the leading case of *Freeman & Lockyer v Buckhurst Park Properties (Mangal) Ltd* [1964] 2 QB 480, CA.

(iii) Customary authority

An agent authorized to act in a particular market, such as a Stock Exchange or **9.52**
Lloyd's, may be impliedly authorized to do all that is customary in such markets.
This category is limited. Legal customs are difficult to prove: they must be certain
and notorious, and not unreasonable, in the sense that they may not change the
nature of the contract. For example, a custom permitting an agent to assume the
role of seller to his principal would not be effective unless known to the principal,[89] in which case he is accepting the change of status of one who might otherwise appear an agent. But where agents customarily or usually do certain things
(without a legal custom being proved), these may be impliedly authorized under
the categories of incidental authority or usual authority, already referred to.

(iv) Residual category

It is obvious that an agent may be impliedly authorized by virtue of special features **9.53**
of the fact situation which do not fall into any particular category.

All the above types of authority may be negatived, as regards actual authority, by **9.54**
a prohibition or exclusion by the principal.

(c) Other considerations

It is sometimes said that the fact that the agent is acting in fraud of his principal **9.55**
does not negative his authority.[90] This proposition really concerns apparent
authority[91] (or liability in tort); an agent could not easily be regarded as having
actual authority to act in fraud, or contrary to the interests, of his principal, even
if the act was one of a type authorized.[92]

It might be appropriate to add another category of authority, under which an **9.56**
agent is impliedly authorized in situations of necessity to do things which would
not otherwise be authorized.[93] This could be called 'authority of necessity'.
However, such authority could equally well be brought within either (i) or (iii)
above, or within the residual implied authority referred to in (iv). The present status of such reasoning in English law is unfortunately confused by the fact that
there is an ancient set of cases on so-called 'agency of necessity' which has led to a
specialized and dogmatic doctrine developed in the area of maritime commerce

---

[89] *Robinson v Mollett* (1875) LR 7 HL 802.
[90] See *Hambro v Burnand* [1904] 2 KB 10, sometimes treated, probably wrongly, as a case on
actual authority.
[91] As to which see para 9.57.
[92] See *Hopkins v TL Dallas Group Ltd* [2004] EWHC 1379, [2005] 1 BCLC 543; *Criterion
Properties plc v Stratford UK Properties LLC* [2004] UKHL 28; [2004] 1 WLR 1846; *Bowstead and
Reynolds on Agency* (18th edn, 2006) Art 23.
[93] As in *Gokal Chand-Jagan Nath v Nand Ram Das-Atma Ram* [1939] AC 106, PC.

before modern, more general principles of agency were fully worked out. It is also confused by the fact that the internal side of the reasoning was used, also in quite early times, as a means of creating results which would nowadays be looked for in the law of restitution. Further discussion appears below.[94]

(2) Actual and Apparent Authority

(a) Actual authority

9.57 If one asks when persons have power as agents to change the legal positions of their principals, the starting point is that they can do so when they act within the authority actually conferred on them, the actual authority, whether this is express or to be implied from the circumstances (including the interpretation of documents). The paradigm reasoning now to be discussed applies to contract: agency reasoning in connection with property may require different emphasis.[95] Subject to an exception to be mentioned, it only applies to an agent who purports to act as such.

9.58 An agent who so acts may do so in one of two ways: first, where he identifies his principal, and secondly, where he does not do so but indicates at the time of acting that he is acting for a principal—whether expressly (as by writing, in a phrase obviously much used in nineteenth-century commerce 'Bought for our principals'), or impliedly, as where a broker acts in a situation where it is known that, as brokers do, he always, or almost always, acts for others. These situations can be referred to as involving 'named' or 'unnamed' principals, but the words 'identified' and 'unidentified' principal are probably better, as a principal can be clearly identified without his actual name being given.

(b) Apparent authority

9.59 An immense addition to this basic principle is provided by the doctrine of apparent (sometimes called 'ostensible') authority, to which reference has already been made. Under it, a principal may be liable to a third party though the agent is in fact not authorized at all (for example, because internally, as between him and the agent, the principal has never authorized or even forbidden the particular act), but he nevertheless appears to the third party to be so. This doctrine applies even though the agent is acting in fraud of the principal, unless the third party has reason to know this.[96]

---

94 See para 9.90.
95 See para 9.119.
96 *Hambro v Burnand* [1904] 2 KB 10.

(i) *Basis of doctrine*

In determining whether a third party is reasonable in thinking the agent author-   **9.60**
ized, the categories of implied authority come in again, particularly those of incidental and usual authority. The third party is entitled to assume, unless he has
indications to the contrary, that the agent has the authority which someone in his
position would normally have. Indeed, many of the cases on implied authority
actually arise in the context of apparent authority, and in older cases the reasoning
used is often by modern standards confused, in so far as the clear distinction
between the internal and external aspects of agency, between implied and apparent authority, was not clearly established until the twentieth century.

Such reasoning is obviously essential for the fair solution of commercial and   **9.61**
other disputes, but its theoretical basis in common law is not absolutely clear.
It must, for the reasons as to the paradigm of agency given above,[97] come as a supplement to central agency reasoning. General external reasoning, that certain
powers arise from the holding of a particular position whether or not there is
internal authorization, is not deployed (though it might have been had the common law, as at one time seemed likely, made more use of the imprecise notion
of the 'general agent',[98] and as will be seen there are signs of it in connection with
property transfer through agents).[99]

It is clear, first, that the doctrine involves liability only: it does not confer upon   **9.62**
the principal the power to sue, though the principal could usually do so by ratifying, which is permissible up to the last moment of proceedings in court.[100]
Secondly, it has normally hitherto been regarded as based on estoppel arising from
a representation, express or implied, by the principal that the agent is authorized.
A famous passage which requires reproduction in full comes from a judgment
of Diplock LJ, later Lord Diplock, in the leading case on the topic (which actually
concerns company law):

> An 'apparent' or 'ostensible' authority. . .is a legal relationship between the princi-
> pal and the contractor created by a representation, made by the principal to the con-
> tractor, intended to be and in fact acted upon by the contractor, that the agent has
> authority to enter on behalf of the principal into a contract of the kind within the
> scope of the 'apparent' authority, so as to render the principal liable to perform any
> obligations imposed upon him by such contract. To the relationship so created the
> agent is a stranger. He need not be (although he generally is) aware of the existence
> of the representation but he must not purport to make the agreement as princi-
> pal himself. The representation, when acted on by the contractor by entering into

---

[97] See para 9.09.
[98] See para 9.24.
[99] See para 9.119.
[100] See para 9.33. But *Restatement Third Agency* proceeds on the basis that the agent can sue: see
§2.03 and accompanying material.

a contract with the agent, operates as an estoppel, preventing the principal from asserting that he is not bound by the contract. It is irrelevant whether the agent had actual authority to enter into the contract.[101]

This passage clearly bases the doctrine on estoppel. If the classic requirements of estoppel[102] are to apply such reasoning would require evidence of a clear representation by the principal, intended to be acted on, with, in many commercial situations especially those regarding companies, the possibility of consequent problems as to authorization by one agent to another to make such a representation; and reliance by the third party, with consequent problems as to the extent to which he should inquire into the authority of an agent. Some estoppel reasoning has also limited the effect of the estoppel to what is required to satisfy the equity in the particular case, and perhaps in any case to reliance loss.[103]

9.63 None of these requirements is, however, strictly insisted on in the context of apparent authority. In many cases the principal's 'representation'[104] is of a very general nature, for example appointing someone managing director (the subject matter of the case quoted above) and the reliance intended by the principal does not seem to go beyond dealing on the assumption that the agent is authorized. Except where formal documents such as powers of attorney are known to be involved,[105] a duty of inquiry is not imposed, though there are cases where knowledge will be imputed to the third party on an objective basis. And where there is apparent authority, it is clear that the transaction in question is completely valid (as opposed to any form of validation *pro tanto*). An alternative explanation of the doctrine can be put forward, that it is based on an extension to contracts made through an agent of the objective interpretation normally applied to contracts in general.[106] This reasoning however makes it difficult to see why the principal cannot sue on such transactions even without ratifying;[107] and it is in any case contrary to the way in which the doctrine is normally stated in England.[108] It seems better therefore to accept that apparent authority is based on estoppel, but to accept also that the requirements for estoppel are

---

[101] *Freeman & Lockyer v Buckhurst Park Properties (Mangal) Ltd* [1964] 2 QB 480, CA (where a person not properly appointed was permitted to act as managing director). A useful exposition is also to be found in the judgment of Lord Denning MR in another company law case, *Hely-Hutchinson v Brayhead Ltd* [1968] 1 QB 549, CA.

[102] See para 9.67.

[103] See different views expressed in *Commonwealth of Australia v Verwayen* (1990) 170 CLR 394, HCA.

[104] *Restatement, Third Agency* uses the better word 'manifestation', see §§1.03, 3.03.

[105] Here there may be a duty to examine the power: see *Jacobs v Morris* [1902] 1 Ch 816.

[106] This view is taken in *Restatement, Third, Agency*, § 23.03 Comment c.

[107] See ibid 145, accepting that he can.

[108] A recent example is *Ing Re (UK) Ltd v Versicherung AG* [2006] EWHC 1544 (Comm); [2006] 2 All ER (Comm) 870.

different in different contexts;[109] and that the requirements in connection with apparent authority require specific formulation.

Difficult marginal situations can arise where an agent is known not to be author-   **9.64** ized to enter into transactions, but is in general authorized to communicate information relevant to them, for example as to whether a particular transaction has been approved, or to act in connection with it, for example to sign letters of contractual offer which imply such approval. If such reasoning is extensively accepted the doctrine of apparent authority could give greater protection to the third party than might be expected. Thus in a fairly recent English case the branch manager of a bank was known not to have authority to approve a loan application but had authority to sign a letter making an offer of an loan and hence to indicate whether it had been approved. The bank was held liable on such a letter for not making the loan.[110] In some cases however a proper analysis might be that the principal should be liable in tort on the agent's false representation.[111] The guiding principle must be that the manifestation of authority cannot emerge entirely from the agent himself.

(ii) Application to companies

Special problems arise for such reasoning in connection with companies. Its appli-   **9.65** cation is complicated by four factors. The first, already mentioned, is that the initial authorization or representation must normally come from another agent of the company.[112] The second is the doctrine, now largely abolished, that certain acts are ultra vires the company's powers as set out in its constitution and so ineffective: granted its existence, there was also doubt about the scope of this doctrine, particularly in connection with acts of a type authorized but which were done for improper motives.[113] The third was a notion that persons dealing with companies would be taken to have constructive notice of their public documents, and so be unable to plead reliance when inspection of them would have shown that the act in question was outside the company's powers, or that

---

[109] See Handley, *Estoppel by Conduct and Representation* (2006), ch 1, denying the existence of any 'overarching estoppel'.

[110] *First Energy (UK) Ltd v Hungarian International Bank Ltd* [1993] 2 Lloyd's Rep 194, CA; cf an important earlier case, *Armagas Ltd v Mundogas SA (The Ocean Frost)* [1986] AC 717, HL (chartering manager: principal not bound, because agent did no more than say that he had obtained authorization) and *Hirst v Etherington* [1999] Lloyd's Rep PN 938, CA (assurance by partner to third party, that undertaking given by him was in the normal course of business (which alone would confer actual authority), not sufficient to bind his partner).

[111] ie in tort: see para 9.128.

[112] An Australian case on this point, *Crabtree-Vickers Pty Ltd v Australian Direct Mail and Advertising & Addressing Pty Ltd* (1975) 133 CLR 72, HCA, seems to go too far in requiring actual authorization.

[113] Many of the problems were settled in *Rolled Steel Products (Holdings) Ltd v British Steel Corp* [1986] Ch 246, CA.

delegation to the agent in question was not authorized.[114] In contrast, there were rules special to company law protecting third parties where delegation could have been authorized but the third party had no way of knowing whether it had been.[115] The law in England has been much changed by statute, which has abolished most of the doctrine of ultra vires, abolished the constructive notice rule and protects third parties dealing with boards of directors or persons authorized by them.[116] There can however be situations not caught by these protections where some of the previous difficulties of agency law may remain.

(iii) Scope of doctrine

9.66 Apparent authority reasoning applies most frequently to persons who are already agents, where some authority that they might normally be expected to have was never conferred, or was initially excluded. It also applies where a person had authority, but it has, unknown to the third party, been withdrawn.[117] It also applies to the comparatively rare situations where a person who has no agency authority whatever is allowed to act as if he had. A straightforward example is a person permitted to act as managing director who has never been properly appointed;[118] but more picturesque situations can also arise.[119]

(iv) Estoppel as to existence of agency relationship

9.67 What is referred to above as 'classic' estoppel reasoning[120] has however a role to play where true agency reasoning cannot be deployed, but the requirements of estoppel can: for example, where a person himself makes no manifestation of authority but is at fault in not causing or correcting impressions which another is giving or has given in connection with him.[121] The normal requirements of estoppel, in particular the requirement of reliance, would often be more easily satisfied.

(3) Doctrine of the Undisclosed Principal

9.68 The doctrine of apparent authority stresses the external aspect of an agency situation; and any legal system requires some mechanism to achieve the result which

---

[114] *Rama Corp v Proved Tin & General Investments Ltd* [1952] 2 QB 147, 149.

[115] The so-called rule in *Royal British Bank v Turquand* (1856) 6 E & B 327, 119 ER 886.

[116] See especially Companies Act 1985, ss 35, 35A, 35B (substituted by Companies Act 1989; to be superseded by Companies Act 2006, ss 39, 40). See paras 3.40, 3.55ff.

[117] See para 9.99.

[118] As in *Freeman & Lockyer v Buckhurst Park Properties (Mangal) Ltd* [1964] 2 QB 480, CA.

[119] See the remarkable American case of *Hoddesdon v Koos Bros* 135 A 2d 702 (AD NJ 1957), US (impostor 'salesman' in shop: better explained however as a case of estoppel by negligence). A surprising application of the latter reasoning is *Pacific Carriers Ltd v BNP Paribas* (2004) 218 CLR 451, HCA, concerning an illegible signature by a person entrusted with an official rubber stamp.

[120] See para 9.62.

[121] eg *Spiro v Lintern* [1973] 1 WLR 1002. See *Restatement Third, Agency*, §2.05.

that doctrine achieves. There is however another doctrine which is based entirely on the internal aspect of agency and sometimes causes surprise. It is the so-called doctrine of the undisclosed principal. Under this doctrine, where the act of an agent is internally authorized between principal and agent, but the agent in acting does not purport to act for a principal, the principal may, subject to certain limits to be explained, be liable and entitled on the agent's contracts. The agent is also liable and entitled, subject to certain limits.[122] This unusual doctrine makes a third party liable to a person whose connection with the transaction was completely unknown to him, though it also allows him to sue that person. Obviously it can be linked with notions of vicarious liability in tort law, and used as a powerful tool by those who seek to unify agency rules between contract and tort.

(a) Comparison with indirect representation in civil law

Civil lawyers engaged in comparative study not infrequently assume that the situation with which the doctrine deals is that of indirect representation, or the *commissionnaire*, who as between himself and his principal is an agent undertaking only best endeavours and so forth, but deals on his own account with the outside world, though he may be assumed or even known to be acting for a principal.[123] In such cases, the principal is inaccessible to the third party and the third party inaccessible to the principal. Some civil law writers (and systems) take the view that the principal ought to be entitled to intervene in certain circumstances, though perhaps should not be liable: intervention (subject to restrictions) is not unlike assignment, but liability gives the third party a bonus for which he had not bargained.[124] **9.69**

This equation of the doctrine with indirect representation situations seems likely to be too superficial.[125] It is true that the doctrine is said to have originated with property transactions involving the nineteenth-century factor, who, as stated above,[126] held goods for a (usually) overseas principal and sometimes dealt on his own account and sometimes as agent, not always making clear which. It is said that the principal was permitted to intervene in the factor's bankruptcy and claim goods as his; and that somehow this right was developed into a contractual doctrine allowing not only the right to sue in contract but also the liability to be sued.[127] The doctrine is plainly connected with one of the great factual **9.70**

---

[122] See paras 9.108 and 9.109.
[123] See para 9.18.
[124] See eg Zweigert and Kötz, *Introduction to Comparative Law* (3rd edn, 1998) 436–41.
[125] See eg *Hutton v Bulloch* (1874) LR 9 QB 572.
[126] See para 9.24.
[127] See the seminal article of AL Goodhart and CJ Hamson, 'Undisclosed Principals in Contract' (1932) 4 CLJ 320.

puzzles of all agency analysis: the person in commerce who sometimes acts on his own account and sometimes for others, and does not make clear in a particular transaction which he is doing. This doctrine makes both liable, though perhaps in the alternative.[128] 'It has often been doubted' said Blackburn J of it 'whether it was originally right so to hold: but doubts of this sort come now too late'. The result is that when 'the vendor discovers that in reality there is an undisclosed principal behind, he is entitled to take advantage of this unexpected godsend'.[129]

9.71 It seems in fact more likely that the *commissionnaire* would have been dealt with by an old rule called the 'foreign principal' rule, under which a foreign principal was assumed *not* to authorize his agent to bring him into privity with third parties elsewhere (or the converse). This rule was finally rejected in 1968, but at least so long as it applied, it meant that the foreign principal of the *commissionnaire* could not sue *or* be sued.[130] In other situations it seems that the *commissionnaire*, being a functionary not known to English law, might often be treated by an English court as an agent for an *unidentified* principal, who would then become liable and entitled by virtue of simpler reasoning: this in general seems to have happened with stockbrokers in the nineteenth century.[131]

9.72 Despite its original connection with the nineteenth-century factor, who might indeed have been something like a *commissionnaire*, the doctrine of the undisclosed principal seems often to apply to persons discharging no named function, who need not be thought by the third party to act in a representative capacity at all: the discovery that they do so then adds a new dimension to the legal scene. The doctrine is by no means fully worked out, and many cases do not make clear whether they are talking of completely undisclosed or merely unidentified principals. Analogies with assignment and with trusts reasoning (which can be deployed to some extent in many agency situations) prove to be analogies only. It does seem however to be accepted that the straight reasoning that the contract is really that of the principal (though this is sometimes said) is inappropriate. The situation is one of intervention on a contract by one not connected with it.[132]

(b) Limitation and exclusion of the doctrine

9.73 Such a doctrine requires limits. One is obvious: the doctrine does not permit intervention on formal written instruments, where the stated name of a party has

---

[128] See para 9.78.
[129] *Armstrong v Stokes* (1873) LR 7 QB 598, 604.
[130] See para 9.106.
[131] See eg *Hodgkinson v Kelly* (1868) LR 6 Eq 496.
[132] This view was accepted in the Court of Appeal in *Welsh Development Agency v Export Finance Co* [1992] BCLC 148, CA: see 173, 182.

a special significance. This is true of deeds, on which there is special case law; but also of negotiable instruments, and other documents such as bills of lading and waybills, where the right to sue is controlled by a statute which refers to naming or identification of the person entitled to sue (or requires indorsement to such a person or in blank).[133]

9.74 Beyond this, the doctrine is subject to an ill-defined exception to prevent intervention in inappropriate cases. This exception has proved extremely difficult to formulate, for if (for example) one person knows that another will not sell to him he can often avoid this by getting a third person to buy, and then to resell to him,[134] and it is difficult therefore to see why the result should be different if he merely uses an agent.[135]

9.75 For a time it was said that the analogy of assignment should be followed, and that a principal could not intervene where the benefit of the contract was not assignable or its burden could not be vicariously performed.[136] This was denied, however, in a Hong Kong case concerning a contract of insurance: it was held that even if the contract had been expressly made unassignable, intervention was permitted on the ground that the identity of the assured was on the facts a matter of indifference to the principal.[137] This shows that non-assignability is not enough; the mere fact that the benefit of a contract cannot be *transferred* does not necessarily mean that at the formation stage the third party was not in a commercial situation willing to accept the involvement of a principal as well as an agent. But it may be in any case that the decision should be regarded as one concerning an unidentified rather than an undisclosed principal.

9.76 The most recent authority, derived from this case, indicates that the exclusion of the undisclosed principal operates only on the basis that such exclusion is implicit in the interpretation of the contract; but no clear indication is given as to when this should be, and the common law as to implied terms in contract is fairly strict. This is one of the comparatively few areas in common law where a principle of good faith might provide reasoning not otherwise available. At present, in the background is what is described in the case in question as a 'beneficial assumption in commercial cases', that in an ordinary commercial contract it may be assumed that a person is 'willing to treat as a party to the contract anyone on whose behalf the agent may have been authorized to contract', 'unless either [he] manifests his

---

133 See, for example, as to waybills Carriage of Goods by Sea Act 1992, ss 1(3), 2(1)(b); paras 11.107ff, para 11.112; *East West Corp v DKBS AF 1912 A/S* [2003] EWCA Civ 83; [2003] QB 1509 at [16]–[18].

134 As in *Nash v Dix* (1898) 78 LT 445.

135 As in *Dyster v Randall & Sons* [1926] Ch 932.

136 This was the view of Goodhart and Hamson (n 127 above).

137 *Siu Yin Kwan v Eastern Insurance Co Ltd* [1994] 2 AC 199, PC.

unwillingness or there are other circumstances which should lead the agent to realise that [he] was not so willing'.[138] This statement of Diplock LJ is contrary to the spirit of many of the rules on formation of contract *inter partes* but is obviously favourable to a wide undisclosed principal doctrine, as well as to a broad rule concerning unidentified principals.

(c) Other difficulties of the doctrine

9.77 A separate problem concerns the application of the doctrine of ratification. If an *unidentified* principal can ratify when his agent acts without authority,[139] it seems a small step to allow the *undisclosed* principal to ratify; but it was long ago held that this could not be done.[140] Presumably to allow ratification simply on the basis that the unauthorized agent says that he intended at the time of acting to do so for the principal is regarded as one step too far. It would allow too easy intervention by one person on the contract of another.[141] That may be correct if one thinks in terms of an agent who has never been authorized by the principal at all. But if one thinks of the situation (which the case in question in fact concerned) where the agent already has some authority and simply exceeds it, if the undisclosed principal chooses to ratify it is arguable that he should at any rate be liable. The result would certainly be beneficial to the third party.

9.78 A further difficulty is caused by the fact that it was decided in the nineteenth century that the liability is alternative; that is to say, if the third party obtains judgment against the agent he can no longer sue the principal because the cause of action is merged in the judgment, and vice versa.[142] There is further authority that the third party can also lose his right against one simply by manifesting an election, or choice, to sue the other, though this is more doubtful.[143] There seems no real reason why either should be so[144] and these notions of merger and election have not fared well in this context in the United States.[145]

---

[138] *Teheran-Europe Co Ltd v ST Belton (Tractors) Ltd* [1968] 2 QB 545, 555.

[139] See para 9.37.

[140] *Keighley, Maxsted & Co v Durant* [1901] AC 240, HL.

[141] H Kötz, *European Contract Law* (1998), 233 states that for this restriction 'there is no good reason'. This is an oversimplified assessment.

[142] *Priestly v Fernie* (1863) 2 H & C 977, 159 ER 820; *Kendall v Hamilton* (1879) 4 App Cas 504, 513–14.

[143] The most recent leading English cases are *Clarkson Booker Ltd v Andjel* [1964] 2 QB 775, CA and *Chestertons v Barone* [1987] 1 EGLR 15, 17, CA.

[144] For a full discussion see *Bowstead and Reynolds on Agency* (18th edn, 2006) Art 84.

[145] Merger was rejected as regards an undisclosed principal in *Grinder v Bryans Road Building & Supply Co*, 432 A 2d 453 (Md App, 1981), US; see also *Tower Cranes of America Inc v Public Service Co* 702 F Supp 371 (DNH, 1988), US and *Crown Controls Inc v Smiley* 756 P 2d 717 (Wash, 1988), US.

Finally, all common law treatment of the undisclosed principal doctrine involves **9.79** discussion of a famous nineteenth-century case at first instance, *Watteau v Fenwick*.[146] In this case the proprietor of a hotel sold the hotel to another and continued to run it as the buyer's manager. The buyer forbade the manager to buy cigars on credit, but the manager, who had done so when he owned the hotel, continued to do so. Cigars were supplied on credit by a third party who was not aware that the manager no longer owned the hotel. The new owner was held liable. There was therefore no apparent authority, and no actual authority either. On agency reasoning the decision is virtually impossible to justify,[147] but the interesting nature of the fact situation has ensured that it is regularly discussed in connection with the undisclosed principal doctrine, and various justifications have been offered (some of which, of course, run off into wider principles intended to apply to both contract and tort).[148]

The whole undisclosed principal doctrine, despite simplified explanations, **9.80** favourable and unfavourable, from external observers in works on comparative law, remains therefore highly uncertain. Further problems appear in the following paragraphs.[149] It is nevertheless a tool which, used in an imaginative way, is capable of being a useful one for the resolution of disputes.

(4) Defences to Contract Actions

In general the position here is straightforward: the principal is entitled against **9.81** the third party and the third party against the principal. In the case of apparent authority, however, the doctrine only makes the principal liable: he cannot sue without ratifying.

Considerable difficulties, the details of which are beyond the scope of this chapter, **9.82** arise in connection with the pleading of defences in contractual actions. In normal agency situations, that is to say, situations of disclosed principals, whether identified or unidentified, where the principal sues he can be met by contractual defences as if the contract had been made with himself, but not by defences valid against the agent only; and where he is sued he can likewise plead defences arising on the contract, but not defences valid between him and the agent only. The undisclosed principal, however, intervenes on the contract of another. Hence if he sues he can be met by defences personal to the agent which had accrued

---

[146] [1893] 1 QB 346.

[147] As was said by Bingham J in *Rhodian River Shipping Co SA v Holla Maritime Corp (The Rhodian River)* [1984] 1 Lloyd's Rep 373, 379. But see *Restatement Third, Agency*, §2.06 (2) and (surprisingly) UNIDROIT *Principles of International Commercial Contracts* (2004), art 2.2.4(2).

[148] An example is AM Tettenborn 'Agents, Business Owners and Estoppel' [1998] CLJ 274.

[149] And as to damages, see para 9.108.

before the third party learned that there was a principal involved; and if he is sued he can probably plead the agent's defences.

9.83 Well-known problems of principle, largely associated with the undisclosed principal doctrine, arise where third party or principal settles with the agent. In a normal *disclosed* agency situation, again, the third party can only settle with (or, by similar reasoning, set off a debt owed by) the agent if the agent had actual or apparent authority to receive payment. Equally, the principal is only discharged against the third party by paying the agent (or, again by similar reasoning, can only set off a debt owed to him by the agent) if the third party leads him to believe that the agent has paid the third party, or that the third party looks only to the agent for payment.

9.84 Where the principal is *undisclosed*, however, the third party must in principle be, until he learns of the principal, entitled to settle with the agent or exercise a set-off against him; and defences accrued up to the time of such discovery should be available against the principal. This is consistent with the idea of intervention by the principal on another's contract. However, a leading case usually discussed in this connection suggests a basic rule very like that for disclosed principals: that the third party's right to do so is based on the fault of the principal in misleading the third party, as by giving the agent possession of goods, and that if there is no such fault such defences cannot be pleaded. The case in question, *Cooke & Sons v Eshelby*,[150] concerns the perennially difficult situation, to which reference has already been made, of a person who sometimes dealt as principal and sometimes as agent. The third party admitted that at the relevant time he had no particular belief one way or the other, and was held unable to set off against the principal a debt due to him from the agent personally. This is therefore probably a case on a disclosed but unidentified principal, but as has been said, the difficulty in telling such a person from an undisclosed principal is a further problem of the undisclosed principal doctrine.

9.85 Finally comes the case where the undisclosed principal settles with the agent before the third party hears of the principal. Here another famous case, *Armstrong v Stokes*,[151] holds that the principal is no longer liable. The case has been criticized and even doubted.[152] The view put forward in authorities that doubt this conclusion is, reciprocally to that above concerning settlement by third party with agent, that the undisclosed principal should only be discharged if there are acts of the third party that indicate to the principal that the agent has settled the account

---

[150] (1887) 12 App Cas 271.
[151] (1872) LR 7 QB 598.
[152] In *Irvine & Co v Watson & Sons* (1880) 5 QBD 414 and *Davison v Donaldson* (1882) 9 QBD 623.

with the third party, on which the principal relies: ie that the settlement by the principal is attributable to the third party. But as the third party does not know of the principal at the time of the settlement it is difficult to see how his acts *vis-à-vis* the agent can ever be plausibly read in this way. In *Armstrong v Stokes* it was specifically found that the third party had not induced the principal to believe that he (the third party) had settled with the agent,[153] yet the principal was held discharged. The general rule as to the liability of an undisclosed principal was said to be 'subject to an exception, which is not so well established as the rule, and is not very accurately defined, viz, that nothing has occurred to make it unjust that the undisclosed principal should be called upon to make payment to the vendor',[154] and that a 'rigid rule. . .would produce intolerable hardship'.[155] This approach seems better than that suggested in the decisions disapproving the case.

The leading cases appear again actually to concern disclosed but unidentified **9.86** principals, where a rule that the principal is only discharged when he acts in reliance on conduct of the third party is of course not inappropriate. The fact situation in *Armstrong v Stokes*, however, does appear to have concerned a person operating more or less in the manner of a *commissionnaire*,[156] and the issue raised was whether the undisclosed principal doctrine continues the principal's liability when he has settled with his agent before the third party has any knowledge of him. On this two views are possible, and the position in English law has not yet been finally determined. This is another obscurity of the undisclosed principal doctrine.

(5) Delegation of Agency Functions

The confidential nature of his role means that the prima facie rule is that an agent **9.87** may not delegate his function: the principal was relying on his discretion and expertise. The Latin maxim *delegatus non potest delegare* is often cited in this connection. This means that acts done by unauthorized subagents will not be effective, as was held in old cases on service of notice to quit by this means. Mere ministerial acts can however be performed through others, and this principle might save some notices to quit and similar situations.

Delegation may however be expressly or impliedly authorized. An example of **9.88** implied authorization arises in cases of emergency, without recourse to agency of

---

[153] (1872) LR 7 QB 598, 610.
[154] ibid 604.
[155] ibid 610.
[156] See para 9.18.

necessity principles.[157] The principles of apparent authority may also validate an act by an unauthorized subagent; as may those of ratification.[158]

9.89 Where delegation is authorized, the acts of the subagent, done on behalf of the agent, will, in accordance with the principles of authority already described,[159] bind and entitle the principal as being the agent's acts. A question then arises as to whether the subagent has direct contractual privity (where the agency relationship is contractual) with the principal, or not. Obviously the agent may be authorized to create such privity:[160] in such a case he is doing little more than appoint another agent to the principal. The prima facie rule here is however that this has not been done unless there are other indications.[161] The subagent would then have contractual privity with the agent only and the agent would be regarded as performing through another and liable to his principal accordingly if anything went wrong. There is however a strong argument for holding the subagent directly liable to the principal in matters not requiring a contractual action, and this argument has been much developed in the United States.[162] For example, there is no requirement that to be a fiduciary a person has to be an agent of the person to whom he owes fiduciary obligations, and in England it has been held that the subagent is a fiduciary in connection with the taking of a bribe.[163] Fairly recent developments of the law in those fields enable it to be argued that he should be liable to the principal in restitution or tort.[164] The field is as yet incompletely developed.

(6) Agency of Necessity

9.90 Reference has already been made to this topic in connection with the notion of authority,[165] but it is so unusual that it deserves short separate treatment. In English law a long-established and discrete group of decisions confer on an agent the authority in emergency to act in ways which would not otherwise be authorized. The doctrine derives almost entirely from cases about shipmasters,

---

[157] See the leading case of *De Bussche v Alt* (1878) 8 Ch D 286.

[158] See paras 9.33ff.

[159] See paras 9.45ff.

[160] As was the case in *De Bussche v Alt* (n 157 above) itself.

[161] *Calico Printers Assn Ltd v Barclays Bank Ltd* (1931) 145 LT 51.

[162] See Seavey (1955) 68 Harvard L Rev 658.

[163] *Powell & Thomas v Evan Jones & Co* [1905] 1 KB 11.

[164] As in *Henderson v Merrett Syndicates Ltd* [1995] 2 AC 145, HL (managing agent at Lloyd's: but there was a close relationship between the parties). As to the position under the Commercial Agents Regulations (see para 9.05) see *Light v Ty Europe Ltd* [2003] EWCA Civ 1238; [2004] 1 Lloyd's Rep 693, CA.

[165] Para 9.56.

who might have to act in situations of emergency far from home, and, rather quaintly, the acceptor of a bill of exchange for honour of the drawee.[166]

The first of the examples concerns both the internal and external aspects of **9.91** agency, but mostly the external, since the principal is bound by the contract or (often) property disposition, as where the master sells or hypothecates the ship or cargo in a distant port; the second exclusively concerns the internal aspect, since it entitles the acceptor to reimbursement. The doctrine is however supposed to be a single one, and carries specific rules of a rather ancient flavour: there must be impracticability of communication with the principal, the action must be necessary, and the agent must have acted bona fide in the principal's interests. It would seem also that the act must not be prohibited by the principal: this is to be inferred from the fact that communication must be impracticable. The inference must be that if it is practicable, the principal could forbid the act.

If the internal and external aspects are separated, it can be seen that the external **9.92** situation requires no more than the normal rules as to actual and apparent author-ity, with a rider that the actual, and hence apparent, authority of an agent is enlarged in an emergency unless this is forbidden by the principal.[167] Even if the act is forbidden, a third party who has no reason to know of the prohibition should be able to rely on apparent authority,[168] and the same should be the case if he wrongly but reasonably thought that an emergency had arisen or that commu-nication was impracticable. This would not be the case under the ancient rules, which, like the Factors Acts,[169] require specific internal facts, whether or not known to the third party, for their operation. Actual authority would carry with it the normal rights to reimbursement and indemnity as regards authorized acts. This seems to be the position in the United States.[170]

The pure internal situations covered by the doctrine, exemplified by the acceptor **9.93** for honour, raise more general questions of restitution for benefits conferred, and should not in more sophisticated days be connected with agency reasoning at all. Consistently with this, it has been held in *China Pacific SA v Food Corp of India (The Winson)*,[171] concerning the costs of warehousing after salvage, that the strict requirements as to necessity do not apply in purely internal situations.

---

[166] Bills of Exchange Act 1882, ss 65–8.
[167] See para 9.56.
[168] As in *The Unique Mariner* [1978] 1 Lloyd's Rep 438.
[169] See para 9.122. Other examples of this are *Brocklesby v Temperance BS* [1895] AC 173, HL (para 9.121) and *Hambro v Burnand* [1904] 2 KB 10 (para 9.57).
[170] See *Restatement, Third, Agency* 2.02 comment f.
[171] [1982] AC 939, HL.

9.94   As to the external situation, however, in a more recent case, *The Choko Star*,[172] an external relationship case involving the making of a salvage contract, the Court of Appeal simply applied the old requirements, which are really appropriate to days before the evolution of the present rules as to actual and (especially) apparent authority. It seems undesirable that this special doctrine, largely evolved to meet needs of sailing ships in the nineteenth century, should remain in its ancient and undeveloped form; but the matter awaits a case in which the House of Lords can resolve it.

(7) Termination of Authority

9.95   As regards termination of authority, separate treatment of the internal and external aspects of agency is again required.

(a) Internal position

9.96   As regards the internal position it is normally accepted that the principal can withdraw his authority at any time, regardless of whether he promised not to do so. 'The proper conduct of the affairs of life necessitates that this should be so.'[173] Where the agency is contractual, the withdrawal may be a breach of contract making the principal liable to the agent in damages or give rise to other remedies; but the authority itself is regarded as inherently revocable. So actual authority will cease not only when some agreed time limit elapses, or the parties agree that it should, or its purpose is fulfilled, or its purpose is frustrated, but also whenever the principal terminates it, whatever the contractual position with regard to such termination. Such termination would normally require notice to the agent to prevent actual authority continuing.[174] But if notice was given to the third party but not to the agent it seems that not only apparent but also actual authority no longer exists[175]—subject to the agent's internal rights against the principal in such a case.

9.97   To this there is one exception. In some situations agency reasoning is used to reinforce a security: a simple example occurs where a person mortgaging chattels confers authority on the lender to sell them if the debt is not repaid.[176]

---

172 [1990] 1 Lloyd's Rep 516, CA.

173 *Frith v Frith* [1906] AC 254, 259 *per* Lord Atkinson. For a modern American example see *Government Guarantee Fund v Hyatt Corp* 95 F 3d 291 (3rd Cir, 1996), US (agency to manage hotel).

174 As to when this is so see *Bowstead and Reynolds on Agency* (18th edn, 2006) Article 125.

175 But see a Canadian decision to the contrary, *Robert Simpson Co v Godson* [1937] 1 DLR 354, criticized by Wright (1937) 15 Can Bar Rev 196.

176 The leading cases are *Walsh v Whitcomb* (1797) 2 Esp 565, 170 ER 456 and *Smart v Sandars* (1848) 5 CB 895, 136 ER 1132. But they go back to times when presuppositions as to assignment and security where quite different from the present day and historical work is needed on the evolution of this rule.

Obviously a revocation of such authority by the borrower would thwart the whole arrangement, so it is not allowed: the arrangement is referred to as an 'authority coupled with an interest', or in the *Restatement, Third* as 'power given as security'.[177] The agency power is of course not a true one at all: an agent by definition has to act in his principal's interests, but in this case the agent is given the authority in order to protect his own interests.

The result of this is that it is not possible to create irrevocable authority in a normal agency situation merely by promising not to revoke. This view seems correct in principle, but may cause serious problems in practice: the remedy of an agent acting on such a promise not to revoke lies against the principal only. Various devices have been employed to draw the sting of this rule, particularly in connection with underwriting of share issues[178] and with Lloyd's:[179] the first context at least might be regarded as involving the protection of an interest. But it is by no means certain that they will be effective.[180]   **9.98**

(b) External position

The doctrine of apparent authority will operate to protect the third party in many cases; for a principal's representation that an agent has authority may be continuing or need correction.[181] There is sometimes statutory protection in the case of powers of attorney.[182] Estoppel may also operate in some situations. The third party also has the protection of the agent's warranty of authority.[183]   **9.99**

(c) Capacity

Special considerations arise in situations of loss of capacity. The principal may, unknown to the agent, die or become mentally incapable. In such a case the actual authority ceases to exist because there is no longer any competent principal; and this reason can be argued to prevent apparent authority also. One well-known   **9.100**

---

[177] §3.12.

[178] *Re Hannan's Empress Gold Mining and Development Co, Carmichael's Case* [1896] 2 Ch 643. But cf *Schindler v Brie* [2003] EWHC 1804; [2003] WTLR 1361 (authority not drafted so as to be irrevocable).

[179] *Society of Lloyds v Leigh* (QBD), 20 February 1997, affd by CA without reference to this point *sub nom Society of Lloyds v Lyon* [1997] TLR 449, CA.

[180] See FMB Reynolds, 'When is an Agent's Authority Irrevocable?' in RF Cranston (ed), *Making Commercial Law: Essays in Honour of Roy Goode* (1997), ch 10. An injunction against revocation may perhaps sometimes be available: see *Lauritzencool AB v Lady Navigation Ltd* [2005] EWCA Civ 579; [2005] 1 WLR 3686 and material there cited.

[181] *Rockland Industries Ltd v Amerada Minerals Corp of Canada* [1980] 2 SCR 2; (1980) 108 DLR (3d) 513; *AMB Generali Holding A6 v SEB Trygg Liv Holding AB* [2005] EWCA Civ 1237, [2006] 1 Lloyd's Rep 318, CA.

[182] See Powers of Attorney Act 1971, s 5.

[183] See para 9.111.

decision however holds that apparent authority can survive the principal's mental incapacity,[184] though a later decision held the agent liable for breach of warranty of authority in such a case, which is inconsistent.[185] The continuation of apparent authority can be justified in the cases both of death and mental incapacity on the ground of continuing representation, and would certainly be more protective of third parties. Provision was made for some such situations by the Enduring Powers of Attorney Act 1985, which allows the creation of powers of attorney which survive supervening mental incapacity. This is now superseded by the Mental Capacity Act 2005, which creates a wider 'Lasting Power of Attorney'. Permission of the court is however needed to act after that time. There is also statutory protection in the case of powers of attorney.[186] Bankruptcy and insolvency raise specialized questions.

(d) Commercial agents[187]

9.101 The position of a commercial agent under the Commercial Agents (Council Directive) Regulations 1993[188] is however in this context unique in common law, in that he is entitled to special payments on termination of his authority, and his right to these cannot be excluded. These provisions originate from French and (especially) German law and are based on a perception that the agent should be entitled to some form of recompense for work done in building up a clientèle from which the principal benefits. Thus where his authority ends, whether because terminated or in accordance with its terms, or by death or retirement (but not where it is terminated by the agent or by his breach) he is entitled to be 'indemnified. . .or compensated for damage'. Member states were bound to make provision for one or the other, and in the United Kingdom indemnity only applies where agreed by the parties, but the right to compensation cannot be excluded[189] (though it would not apply if the contract is terminated by reason of the agent's default).

9.102 The *indemnity* applies to the extent that new customers have been introduced or business increased, and is calculated on an equitable basis, not to exceed one year's remuneration on a five-year average: the right to damages for breach of contract persists. This is similar to pre-existing German law. The right to damages in addition is specifically preserved.[190] The right to *compensation*, clearly derived from

---

184 *Drew v Nunn* (1879) 4 QBD 661.
185 *Yonge v Toynbee* [1910] 1 KB 215.
186 Powers of Attorney Act 1971, s 5.
187 See *Bowstead and Reynolds on Agency* (18th edn, 2006) ch 11 and the specialized works referred to in n 5 above.
188 See para 9.05.
189 Commercial Agents (Council Directive) Regulations 1993, SI 1993/3053, regs 17, 19.
190 ibid reg 17(5).

existing French law, seems to be based on the idea of causing patrimonial loss in respect of a joint enterprise, whether there is a breach of contract by the principal or not. The House of Lords has recently ruled on the appropriate method of assessment, to the effect that 'what is to be valued is the income stream which the agency would have generated'[191] and that 'compensation should be calculated by reference to the value of the agency on the assumption that it continued'.[192] The right to common law damages is not specifically preserved, but nor is it excluded, and there must be some situations to which it is appropriate.[193]

The only comparison in English law is constituted by the protections against unfair dismissal and redundancy offered by employment law, which have not been thought appropriate for agents in general. Indeed, the assumption of English law, arising once more out of the generality of the notion of agency, is that by reason of the extensive powers accorded to many agents, it is principals who need protection against abuse of position by their agents rather than the reverse.[194]   **9.103**

D. The Agent and Third Parties

(1) Rights and Liabilities on the Main Contract

(a) General principles

Staying in the paradigm field of contract, where an agent who has actual or apparent authority makes a contract for his principal, whether he identifies the principal or not, he may create, as has been already stated, a legal relationship between his principal and the third party. If we turn now to the position of the agent, it might then be assumed that he drops out of the transaction. Such a result can be based on the intentions of the third party, who intends to deal with the principal and not with the agent.   **9.104**

But although there are cases, especially in the nineteenth century, which seem to assume this result by regarding the salient question on a particular set of facts as being one as to whether the contract is with the agent or the principal, it is now clear that such a rule is too simple. Whatever the position in other legal systems, the breadth of common law agency principles does not require that the   **9.105**

---

191 *Lonsdale v Howard & Hallam Ltd* [2007] UKHL 32; [2007] 1 WLR 2055 at [12].

192 ibid at [21], broadly accepting the judgment in the Court of Appeal in the same case, [2004] EWCA Civ 63; [2006] 1 WLR 1281, and not accepting a different approach employed in *King v T Tunnock & Co Ltd* 2000 SC 424.

193 See *Bowstead and Reynolds on Agency* (18th edn, 2006) paras 10–42ff.

194 See paras 9.137ff.

agent drop out of the transaction at all: it is perfectly possible that he may be liable and (less commonly) entitled on it together with his principal.

9.106 On general principles of concurrent liability, his liability may be joint, or joint and several; or be a separate liability as a guarantor of some sort; or arise from a completely separate, probably collateral, contract. The cases indicating liability in the agent come from various contexts. Some relate to situations where the principal is foreign. Here the older view was that the local agent contracted for himself: this was justified, not only on the basis that the local contractor would expect the liability of someone within his own jurisdiction, but also on the more surprising basis that the foreign principal did not authorize the agent to bring him into contractual privity with persons in another country.[195] There is here plainly some connection with indirect representation, ie with the functions of *commissionnaires* in other countries.[196] This so-called 'foreign principal' doctrine has however now been rejected in England. It has instead been said[197] that the fact that the principal is foreign is an indication that the agent intends to undertake liability *together with* him.

9.107 Another case producing such an effect involves a one-man company, holding its effective proprietor liable on the facts as a contracting party together with the company.[198] A long line of cases recognize trade usages and practices under which an agent at certain times and in certain places is liable together with his principal.[199] There are special decisions, some of them rather unusual, on the rights and liabilities of two special types of agent: auctioneers, who of course still exist, and factors, who in the sense of the term used in the old cases do not.[200] *Restatement, Agency, Third*[201] even suggests a prima facie rule that agents for unidentified principals are parties to the contract, though the English Court of Appeal has refused to go so far.[202] Such a rule would be more drastic than those sometimes found in civil law countries, which may make the agent liable only if he does not reveal the name of his principal on demand and within a reasonable time. The latter result could in common law only be achieved by proof of a trade usage

---

195 See *Armstrong v Stokes* (1872) LR 7 QB 598, 605; *Teheran-Europe Co Ltd v ST Belton (Tractors) Ltd* [1968] 2 QB 545, 557–8.

196 Cf *Hutton v Bulloch* (1874) LR 9 QB 572. See also para 9.18ff.

197 In the *Teheran-Europe* case (n 195 above).

198 *The Swan* [1968] 1 Lloyd's Rep 5. This is an example of agency reasoning utilized in connection with problems of the corporate veil. See also para 9.25.

199 A recent example is *Cory Brothers Shipping Ltd v Baldan Ltd* [1997] 2 Lloyd's Rep 58.

200 For details see Murdoch, *Law of Estate Agency and Auctions* (4th edn, 2003); *Bowstead and Reynolds on Agency* (18th edn, 2006), paras 9-014, 9-021.

201 §6.02.

202 *N & J Vlassopoulos Ltd v Ney Shipping Co (The Santa Carina)* [1977] 1 Lloyd's Rep 478 (unwritten contract); see also in Canada *Chartwell Shipping Ltd v QNS Paper Co Ltd* [1989] 2 SCR 683; (1989) 62 DLR (4th) 36, Can (written contract).

or practice, as already mentioned;[203] though of course should the matter proceed to litigation discovery could usually be obtained.

(b) Agent of undisclosed principal

Where the principal is undisclosed, the third party intends to deal with the agent **9.108** and not with the principal. This then provides a separate situation for the agent's personal liability; and indeed not only is the principal's intervention subject, as already mentioned, to any equities between agent and third party accruing before the third party had notice of the principal's existence, but the third party cannot be prevented from insisting on the agent's liability should he so wish.[204] Where in such situation it is the agent that sues, a major problem of theory can arise as to whether one party can recover loss suffered by another. This is one of the early examples of a problem to which attention is now being more generally addressed.[205]

As already stated, this liability of the agent of the undisclosed principal is at least **9.109** in some respects alternative and the third party may be barred from suing the agent by obtaining judgment against the principal, or even perhaps manifesting an election or choice to hold the principal liable. This is itself unsatisfactory.[206] Further difficulty is however caused by the fact that some cases assume that the doctrines of merger and election apply also to cases where both agent and disclosed principal are liable. This seems quite contrary to principle and in any case could not apply where the agent's liability is on a separate contract. As with other problematic situations the difficulties start with cases where it is not clear whether the principal should be regarded as undisclosed or merely as unidentified. They are also confused by straight disputes on formation of contract, turning on the question with which of two possible parties a contract was originally made, and difficulties are made worse by cases where summary judgment is obtained against one party or the other without the facts being argued and analysed, and it is later argued that there has been merger.[207] Though an attempt has recently been made in New Zealand to cut through the difficulties,[208] and there is useful authority in the United States, the problems of merger and election are not yet fully resolved in England.

---

[203] eg *Hutchinson v Tatham* (1873) LR 8 CP 482.

[204] *Montgomerie v UK Mutual SS Assn* [1891] 1 QB 370, 372.

[205] See *Alfred McAlpine Construction Ltd v Panatown Ltd* [2001] 1 AC 518; also *L/M International Construction Ltd v The Circle Ltd Partnership* (1995) 49 Con LR 12, 31–33; Unberath, *Transferred Loss* (2003), ch 7 esp 175ff.

[206] See para 9.78.

[207] See discussion in *Bowstead and Reynolds on Agency* (18th edn, 2006) Article 84.

[208] *LC Fowler & Sons Ltd v St Stephens College Board of Governors* [1991] 3 NZLR 304, NZ.

(c) Oral and written contracts

9.110 In the case of an oral contract the question as to the agent's liability and right to sue will be one of interpretation of the parties' intentions in accordance with the above principles. But where the contract is written, these intentions may well have to yield to, or be derived from, the actual wording used. There are many cases on this topic, though they do not raise great questions of principle.[209] Obviously reliance is placed on signatures; but the body of a document must be taken into account also. Furthermore, account must be taken of the parol evidence rule, which may not permit oral evidence that contradicts the tenor of a document.[210] Where however it simply adds another party to an existing contract, as will often be the case in this context, it can be accepted.[211] As already mentioned, there are special rules for deeds and other formal documents such as bills of exchange and bills of lading.[212]

(2) Liability of the Unauthorized Agent

9.111 Where an agent purports to have authority from a principal and has not, all legal systems seek to make the agent (*falsus procurator*) liable on some basis. Some old English cases succeed in treating him as his own principal,[213] but such reasoning is difficult to sustain. Where his principal did not exist, some early cases on company law succeeded in treating him as undertaking personal liability on the basis that some legal effect to the transaction must have been intended.[214] The problem is dealt with by statute.[215] Liability in tort where the profession of authority was wilfully false has been long accepted; and more recently liability in negligence for misrepresentation causing economic loss has been accepted as actionable in appropriate cases. A broader basis for the agent's liability was however discovered as far back as 1857 and remains as the main technique for imposing such liability.[216] Anyone purporting to act as agent is deemed, in the absence of contrary indication, to warrant, ie promise absolutely, that he has authority. This is called warranty of authority, and is a form of implied collateral contract, perhaps

---

209 A well-known starting point is *Universal SN Co v McKelvie* [1923] AC 492. Many examples appear in *Bowstead and Reynolds on Agency* (18th edn, 2006) Article 101.

210 See *Chitty on Contracts* (29th edn, 2004), paras 12-096 ff.

211 *Higgins v Senior* (1841) 8 M & W 834.

212 See para 9.31.

213 See *Gardiner v Heading* [1928] 2 KB 284; *Rayner v Grote* (1846) 15 M & W 359, 153 ER 888.

214 eg *Kelner v Baxter* (1866) LR 2 CP 174.

215 Companies Act 1985, s 36C(1), held to confer a right of action also in *Braymist Ltd v Wise Finance Co Ltd* [2002] EWCA Civ 127, [2002] Ch 273, CA. See now Companies Act 2006, s 51.

216 The leading case is still *Collen v Wright* (1857) 7 E & B 310, 119 ER 1259, affd (1857) 8 E & B 647, 120 ER 241. Some commentators state a preference for a rule that the agent only undertakes a duty of care: but if one rule is well established, it is that of strict liability in this context.

the oldest example of this genre in English law. The liability is not based on negligence: it is one of guarantee. It can of course be excluded by an agent who makes it clear that he does not promise that he has authority: such an argument was accepted in a case where an agent signed 'by telegraphic authority'.[217]

The damages for breach of this promise ('breach of warranty of authority') will **9.112** normally be such as to put the third party in the position in which he would have been if the agent had had authority: hence if the principal is insolvent, and damages would not have been effectively recoverable against him, the agent's breach may cause no loss.[218] If the principal ratifies, the better view seems to be that the agent is still in breach of contract but causes no loss. In this sort of case damages often include consequential loss, such as the expense of an abortive action against, or at least negotiations with, the principal.

This type of contract is a powerful tool for imposing liability on the agent, and **9.113** it is capable of extension. Thus it may in appropriate cases be held that an agent warrants that he has a principal, and that his principal has authorized the transaction in question (but not that the principal is solvent or has a good cause of action[219] or will perform the contract), thus solving the problems of agents who have no principal or whose principals have no capacity[220] or are non-existent.[221] A warranty may also be regarded as given to someone other than the third party; for example, to a mortgage lender who lent to a purchaser on a representation by the vendor's solicitor.[222] The strict liability is sometimes criticized by comparative lawyers, but the criticism seems largely to rest on assertion.

(3) Agent's Liability in Tort

An agent is liable for his own torts. 'No one can escape liability for his fraud **9.114** by saying "I wish to make it clear that I am committing this fraud on behalf of someone else and I am not to be personally liable"'.[223] Fraud is indeed a good example for this: another is defamation. But in the sphere of negligence there may be scope for argument. A solicitor for one side to a dispute who gives a (non-contractual) undertaking to the other may sometimes be held to have undertaken

---

217 *Lilly, Wilson & Co v Smales, Eeles & Co* [1892] 1 QB 456.
218 *Firbank's Executors v Humphreys* (1886) 18 QBD 54. For a more complex example in connection with a false bill of lading, see *Heskell v Continental Express Ltd* [1950] 1 All ER 1033.
219 See discussion in *AMB Generali Holding, AG v SEB Trygg Liv Holding AB* [2005] EWCA Civ 1237; [2006] 1 Lloyd's Rep 318, CA at [60] ff.
220 *Yonge v Toynbee* [1910] 1 KB 215.
221 See *Delta Construction Co Ltd v Lidstone* (1979) 96 DLR (3d) 457, Can.
222 *Penn v Bristol & West BS* [1997] 1 WLR 1356, CA.
223 *Standard Chartered Bank v Pakistan National Shipping Corp (No 4)* [2002] UKHL 43; [2003] 1 AC 959 at [21] *per* Lord Hoffmann.

a duty of care;[224] and it may be possible to hold the person operating a one-man company personally liable by this route.[225] On the other hand a solicitor for one party to a conveyance who negligently gives wrong answers to inquiries from the other party has been held not liable, though his principal would have been.[226] Whether or not this is correct (it has been said to be based on a rule peculiar to solicitors in conveyancing[227]), there are certainly cases where company directors have been held to undertake no personal duty when acting on behalf of their companies,[228] and it may be that such reasoning, which is still the subject of controversy,[229] could sometimes be extended to others who are not directors. It is said however that an agent may not be liable for the tort of inducement of breach of contract by his principal, for the true liability is that of the principal for the breach of contract.[230] This may be true if the agent is simply acting for his principal in breaking the contract. But if he acts in a way which breaches his own legal duty to his principal and also induces such a breach, he might be liable.[231] A significant line of cases holds an agent not liable in conversion where he deals with property on the instructions of his principal in a purely ministerial way.[232] These can be used to suggest a similar defence (largely) for banks in connection with the receipt of money.

(4) Restitution

9.115 Difficult questions arise where money is paid to an agent which is prima facie recoverable in restitution, as for example where it is paid to him by mistake. If it is paid in pursuance of a transaction entered into by the agent personally, or in connection with a wrong done by the agent, the agent is clearly liable to repay.[233] Beyond this two competing principles are available. One is that money paid to the agent for the principal is paid to the principal and the principal is the person liable to repay it.[234] This is not unlike the tortious defence of ministerial receipt referred to above. The other is that where money is paid to the agent which is not

---

224 *Al Kandari v JR Brown & Co* [1988] QB 665, CA.
225 *Fairline Shipping Corp v Adamson* [1975] QB 180.
226 *Gran Gelato Ltd v Richcliff (Group) Ltd* [1992] Ch 560.
227 *McCullagh v Lane Fox & Partners Ltd* [1996] 1 EGLR 35, 43 *per* Hobhouse LJ; Cane (1992) 108 LQR 539.
228 *Williams v Natural Life Health Foods Ltd* [1998] 1 WLR 830, HL; *Trevor Ivory Ltd v Anderson* [1992] 2 NZLR 517, CA NZ. See paras 17.175ff.
229 See eg Flannigan (2002) 81 Can Bar Rev 247; Campbell and Armour [2003] CLJ 290; Reynolds (2003) 33 HKLJ 51; Stevens [2005] LMCLQ 101.
230 *Said v Butt* [1920] 3 KB 497.
231 See *The Leon* [1991] 2 Lloyd's Rep 611.
232 eg *National Mercantile Bank v Rymill* (1881) 44 LT 767.
233 *Snowdon v Davis* (1808) 1 Taunt 359.
234 *Ellis v Goulton* [1893] 1 QB 350.

due, he is himself liable to repay it unless he has, before notice of any claim for its repayment, in good faith paid it to his principal.[235] This latter defence is not unlike the defence of change of position available in restitution,[236] but is in fact separate and much older.[237] A distinction has been suggested between cases where the duty to repay arises immediately, as in the case of money paid by mistake, where the agent is liable; and those where it arises later, as where the contract on which it is paid later fails for some reason. This distinction has difficulties, and some of the cases cited in this connection do not really concern agents at all, for example where the first receiver is a bank. The matter is one for the law of restitution.[238]

E. The Use of Agency Reasoning in Non-contractual Situations

(1) Agency Reasoning in Connection with Property Issues

The text so far has largely concerned questions of contract made through agents. **9.116** The same reasoning applies, however, in the law of property: a person may transfer property through an agent, or acquire property through an agent.

(a) Land

(i) Conveyance by agent

In the case of land, one would of course expect special rules. Only the owner of **9.117** land can in general convey it, and at common law it requires to be transferred by deed, a formal document signed and witnessed. This can be executed by a mere amanuensis, but otherwise an agent conveying land for his principal would normally require authorization by power of attorney, a formal document conferring the appropriate authority, which must itself be a deed.[239] An agent can of course enter into a *contract* regarding land on his principal's behalf, and this does not need formal authorization in the same way (though the contract itself would be subject to a requirement of writing);[240] it would confer equitable rights on the principal.

---

[235] *Buller v Harrison* (1777) 2 Cowp 565, 98 ER 1243.
[236] See Lord Goff of Chieveley and GH Jones, *Law of Restitution* (7th edn, 2007), ch 40.
[237] See *Portman BS v Hamlin Taylor Neck* [1998] 4 All ER 202, CA.
[238] See Goff and Jones (n 236 above) paras 40-027ff, AS Burrows, *Law of Restitution* (2nd edn, 2002) 597ff; Stevens [2005] LMCLQ 101.
[239] Powers of Attorney Act 1971 as amended, s 1(1).
[240] Law of Property (Miscellaneous Provisions) Act 1989, s 2.

(ii) Conveyance to agent

9.118 If an agent takes a conveyance to himself on his principal's behalf, he holds the land on trust for his principal despite the lack of written evidence required by statute,[241] for to allow insistence on such avoidance would permit the rule (which stems from the Statute of Frauds 1677) to be used as an instrument of fraud.[242]

(b) Chattels

(i) Conveyance by agent

9.119 In the case of chattels there are no such general requirements, and an agent can have actual authority to transfer his principal's property, neither the conferring of authority nor the transfer of the chattel requiring (except in special situations) formality. The doctrine of apparent authority is also applicable here.[243] In this context that doctrine causes special difficulties if, as is normally said, it is based on estoppel, for estoppel is a doctrine operating only between two parties and their privies, a notion considerably developed in connection with land; whereas it has been said by Devlin J, a distinguished authority, that in respect of chattels the effect of a transfer by an agent with apparent authority, at least under a sale, is to confer 'a real title and not merely a metaphysical title by estoppel',[244] ie one which is good against the world.

9.120 Even if apparent authority in contract could be based on the objective interpretation of contracts, a view rejected above,[245] there may be no contract, and even if there is a contract the property transfer is separate. Current English authority suggests that (though genuine estoppel situations are, as in contract, also perfectly possible) the principle invoked is a general one concerning persons held out to the world as authorized to sell goods, and probably also to transfer them in other ways. It is reinforced in the context of sale of goods by section 21 of the Sale of Goods Act 1979, which refers to cases where the 'owner is by his conduct precluded from denying the seller's authority to sell'. The lack in common law of any general provision protecting bona fide purchasers of chattels means that the mere holding of the goods of another does not give rise to apparent authority to dispose of them, for if it did 'no one would be safe in parting with possession of anything'.[246] Something additional is required such as some written authority

---

[241] Law of Property Act 1925, s 53.
[242] *Rochefoucauld v Boustead* [1897] 1 Ch 196, CA.
[243] *Eastern Distributors Ltd v Goldring* [1957] 2 QB 600, CA.
[244] ibid 611.
[245] See para 9.63.
[246] *Weiner v Gill* [1905] 2 KB 172, 182; and see *Farquharson Bros & Co v King & Co* [1902] AC 325, HL.

to dispose of them, or the fact that the holder is a person who normally disposes of the goods of others, such as the nineteenth-century factor.

In this context there are two special variants of the reasoning. The first is the doc- **9.121** trine of apparent ownership, which arises where one person allows another to appear as the owner of goods. Although true estoppel is possible here also, it seems that the general doctrine is no more than a stronger example of that referred to above. However, to trigger it off, it is again not sufficient merely to allow someone else to hold your goods or even documents of title or other documents relating to them, for that person might be a mere bailee: something more is again needed, such as signing a document offering to buy the goods from that person, or permitting registration of the goods in that person's name.[247]

A situation raising greater problems of analysis is the not uncommon one of a **9.122** person given a document, such as the indicia of title to property, and authorized to raise money on the security of the document, who then borrows more than he was authorized. Such a person has no actual authority as regards the sum borrowed, and the mere possession of indicia of title does not confer apparent authority to make a property disposition at all. Nevertheless a well-known but controversial group of cases holds the principal bound on such facts.[248] The principle (if there is one), which has been called the 'arming principle',[249] creates a problem which awaits resolution. The cases seem to involve a confusion with quite different property principles relating to priority of mortgages and it is unlikely that much should be made of them. It is however conceivable that a person exposing himself to such risks could be regarded as conferring actual authority.

Statute here intervenes to protect third parties. The need arose in connection with **9.123** the nineteenth-century factor who, as has been said, was an intermediary holding goods on consignment, often from overseas, who might own them or not and might deal on his own account or on the account of a principal elsewhere. When factors sold goods, the buyer and subsequent buyers were protected by the doctrine of apparent authority as described above, for the factor legitimately held the goods (or the documents of title to them) and his occupation involved the selling of the goods of others. The doctrine of apparent ownership might also apply. Factors however often raised money on the security of goods by pledging them, or when they were in transit by pledging them by means of the documents representing them (which might arrive long before the goods

---

[247] See *Pickering v Busk* (1812) 15 East 38, 104 ER 758; *Central Newbury Car Auctions Ltd v Unity Finance Ltd* [1957] 1 QB 371, CA.
[248] The leading case is *Brocklesby v Temperance BS* [1895] AC 173, HL.
[249] *Macmillan Inc v Bishopsgate Investment Trust plc (No 2)* [1995] 1 WLR 978, 1012, CA.

themselves). It was established that a factor had no apparent authority to *pledge* goods as opposed to selling them. The third party might however have no way of knowing whether the factor owned the goods, or was authorized by the owner, or not.

9.124   To deal with the problem a series of statutes were passed during the nineteenth century to protect third parties in such cases (including that of sale): they are referred to as the Factors Acts. They contain various specialized provisions for achieving some of the same effects as are achieved in some other countries by more general rules. That relevant to basic agency law is section 2 of the Factors Act 1889, which protects third parties buying in good faith from a 'mercantile agent' who is in possession of goods or documents of title to goods (this phrase being interpreted in a wide sense) with the consent of the owner. In many circumstances this legislation can be relied on without the need for establishing apparent authority. The Act is not however entirely a statutory expression of apparent authority as it contains requirements that must exist, yet the existence of which may not be knowable by the third party. This is true in particular of whether the transferor is a 'mercantile agent' (a term defined in a somewhat circular way, but giving rise to considerable case law), whether he holds the goods or documents with the consent of the owner, and in what capacity he holds them

(ii) Conveyance to agent

9.125   Difficulties regarding land apart, property can also be acquired through an agent, though the agent may of course nevertheless retain *possession*. This is made easier by the fact that in the contract of sale property passes by mere intention. Acquisition through *undisclosed* principals raises (as usual) greater problems, since the third party is (often, at least) unaware of the existence of the principal and hence does not intend to transfer property to him. On the basis of pure intention (which controls the transfer of property in sale)[250] property would be transferred to the agent, who then retransfers it (or should) to the principal. On the other hand it is said that the original purpose of the doctrine was to allow intervention by the principal in the agent's bankruptcy, and this would appear to require immediate vesting in the principal. A notoriously obscure, but conceptually significant, provision of the Sale of Goods Act 1979,[251] basing itself on nineteenth-century cases on factors and (perhaps) foreign *commissionnaires*,[252] appears to assume that the property vests first in the agent, as it gives him the rights of an unpaid seller against a buyer in respect of disposal of the goods and stoppage in transit.

---

[250] Sale of Goods Act 1979, s 17.
[251] ibid s 38(2).
[252] eg *Tetley v Shand* (1871) 25 LT 658; *Cassaboglou v Gibb* (1883) 11 QBD 797.

(2) Agency Reasoning Used Against the Principal in Tort Cases

In the United States, traditional agency courses sought to discern general princi- **9.126**
ples of representation applicable in both contract and in tort situations. Such an
exercise is, at least for English law, one of major theoretical creativity, in that the
approach to questions of liability for the acts of others in tort law is for the most
part quite different from that taken in contract and property law. The treatment
adopted in this chapter is to treat agency law as relevant to contract (including
some restitutionary situations) and property; and hence largely to omit discussion
of tort liability. Nevertheless, there is some overlap and brief reference to tort is
necessary.

The normal starting point for liability for torts in English law has been to take a **9.127**
distinction between 'servants' and 'independent contractors'. It is assumed that
for both the liability, when it exists, is vicarious: that is to say the employee (formerly referred to as 'servant') or independent contractor commits a wrong for
which he is responsible, but for which the employer or principal is also responsible. Such vicarious liability is in common law usually treated as a form of strict liability. As to servants or employees, the liability has traditionally been regarded as
covering acts done within the course of their employment, even where they do
something which they have been forbidden to do. However, recently the test has
been reformulated, in response to a need to create vicarious liability where the
employee is guilty of wilful wrongdoing, as requiring that the tort was 'so closely
connected with his employment that it would be fair and just to hold the [employer]
vicariously liable.'[253] This has been taken to replace the traditional test, which
looked at whether the employee's actions were an unauthorized mode of performing an authorized act.

The wrongs of deceit and misrepresentation are frequently committed in con- **9.128**
nection with a contract, by a person who may or may not have authority to make
the statement in question. Hence where these are involved, the terminology of
authority, and the word 'agent' for the employee, may seem more natural and
appropriate than that of employer and employee. It has furthermore been held
in connection with the tort of deceit that where there is no liability on the basis
of authority reasoning (which would include apparent authority reasoning) the
tort 'course of employment' reasoning (as then used) could not be invoked to
make the principal liable on a statement which the agent was known by the third

---

[253] *Lister v Hesley Hall Ltd* [2001] UKHL 22; [2002] 1 AC 215. The problem has been
analysed also in Canada: *Bazley v Currie* [1999] 2 SCR 534: and Australia: *New South Wales v
Lepore* (2004) 212 CLR 511. All these cases concern abuse of children by employees of schools.
The test now adopted comes from the Canadian case, and was rejected in Australia. See in general,
paras 17.385ff.

party to have no authority to make;[254] and the reasoning is capable of being extended to other torts of misrepresentation also. This is the first potential relevance of agency, outside specific authorisation or ratification (which would make the tort that of the authorizer or ratifier) in tort law.

9.129 As to independent contractors, a standard view has been that there was no vicarious liability for them except in the case where they were performing a non-delegable duty. It has however proved difficult to identify and provide a rationale for such duties. It is probably better to regard liability for independent contractors as not vicarious, but as occurring in the course of a primary liability of a principal to secure certain sorts of result. Indeed, a result of the recent reformulation of the applicability of liability for employees, it may be that such an explanation will eventually envelope that also.[255]

9.130 The relevance of agency here is that the duty, however formulated, may sometimes cover the activities of those who can reasonably be called independent contractors, and that agents come frequently in this category. Thus there may be liability for the acts and omissions of estate agents[256] and solicitors;[257] one case makes the principal liable for defamation (of another company) by an independent insurance agent.[258] There can also be liability for the fraud of certain persons who cannot easily be called employees or independent contractors: the most obvious example is a company director.[259] In most of the situations referred to above the agent is liable also, as explained above, though there is doubt in some situations as to a director.

(3) Notification, Notice and Knowledge

9.131 Agency reasoning is also deployed in situations where it is necessary to determine whether a particular person or organization had been notified of, had notice of or knew (or must be taken to have known) certain information. This is an obvious use for such reasoning, particularly in the case of companies, where any knowledge must necessarily be of a human being connected with it. It is however far from clear when such notice can be attributed to a principal through his agent.

---

[254] *Armagas Ltd v Mundogas SA (The Ocean Frost)* [1986] AC 717, HL.

[255] See *Lister v Hensley Hall Ltd* (n 253 above), at [55] *per* Lord Hobhouse of Woodborough.

[256] See *Armstrong v Strain* [1952] 1 KB 232.

[257] *Cemp Properties (UK) Ltd v Dentsply Research and Development Corp* [1989] 2 EGLR 196, CA; see also *Gran Gelato v Richcliff Group Ltd* [1992] Ch 560.

[258] *Colonial Mutual Life Assurance Society Ltd v Producers and Citizens Cooperative Insurance Co of Australia* (1931) 46 CLR 41.

[259] See *Barwick v English Joint Stock Bank* (1867) LR 2 Ex 259; *Lloyd v Grace, Smith & Co* [1912] AC 716, HL.

Where the question concerns formal notification, such as a notice to quit, prob- **9.132**
lems can generally be solved by the usual principles of authority, that is to say, by
asking whether the person giving or receiving the notification had actual or apparent authority to give or receive it.[260]

Where however it concerns actual or constructive notice, as in the doctrine of **9.133**
the bona fide purchaser without notice, or under section 2 of the Factors Act
1889;[261] or knowledge or imputed knowledge, as in the case of accessory liability
to a breach of trust, the question is more difficult. It is certainly true that the
law may impute knowledge to a principal which an agent acquired while acting
as agent, and that in some situations knowledge which the agent already had
when he became agent, or acquired outside his agency function, may also be so
imputed; but a proper analysis of the cases is beyond the scope of this chapter.[262]
Sometimes the matter is one of interpreting what a statutory provision was
intended to cover. It is in this area that leading examples of 'organ' reasoning are
to be found: that is to say, cases where notice or knowledge is sought to be attributed to a company.[263] It is said that for this purpose the knowledge must be of a
person within the organization who has management or control—not necessarily
in general, but in relation to the activity in question.[264]

F. The Internal Relationship Between Principal and Agent

This topic covers not only agents who have power to affect their principal's **9.134**
position externally, but also agents who only have the internal relationship with
their principals, elsewhere referred to as 'canvassing agents', and, if the category
exists at common law, *commissionnaires* or 'indirect agents'.[265] It requires division
into two topics: the duties of the agent towards the principal, and the duties of
the principal towards the agent. The former topic is far more extensive, because
common law has always thought of the principal as being in need of protection
against the agent, rather than the reverse. With the former topic it is also necessary
to distinguish between common law and equity, as the rules of equity are prominent in this area.

---

[260] eg *Tanham v Nicholson* (1872) LR 5 HL 561.
[261] See paras 9.123ff.
[262] See the exposition of Hoffmann LJ in *El Ajou v Dollar Land Holdings Ltd* [1994] 2 All
ER 685, CA: but cf *Permanent Trustee Australia Co Ltd v FAI General Insurance Co Ltd* (2001)
50 NSWLR 679, CA NSW, esp at [76]ff (revsd on other grounds (2003) 214 CLR 514, HCA).
Such imputation may not apply where the agent is defrauding the principal: eg *Rolland v Hart*
(1871) LR 6 Ch App 678. See in general Watts (2001) 117 LQR 300; [2005] NZLRev 367.
[263] See para 9.22.
[264] ibid.
[265] See para 9.22.

(1) Duties of the Agent Towards the Principal

(a) Common law

9.135 Where the agency is contractual, the duties will be based on the express or implied terms of the contract. The first question may be whether the agent has promised to act at all: if not, he is only liable if he does so. This is true, for example, of estate agency arrangements, where the agent need not promise to act in any way.[266] The common law is fairly strict as regards the implication of terms, but there is no great difficulty in holding a person promising services, which is what a contractual agent does, to be under a duty of care to act in the principal's interest, in accordance with normal standards of reasonableness and also, when agent in a trade or profession is involved, the normal standards of that trade or profession. An agent may not act outside his authority, however much it may seem prudent to do so, unless some situation of necessity is involved;[267] and, if he has accepted specific instructions, must carry them out however imprudent he believes them to be.[268] If he acts so as to make the principal liable under the doctrine of apparent authority he is liable, sometimes even if the principal ratifies.[269]

9.136 A contractual agent can also in English law be liable to his principal in tort,[270] and such liability may yield slightly different results, for example in connection with operation of the limitation period. It could not however increase the contractual duty.[271] A gratuitous agent, ie one operating under an arrangement where no consideration can be found, cannot of course be liable in contract, and hence his only liability is in tort. This means that he cannot in principle be held liable for pure non-feasance. But someone who can be called a gratuitous agent can fairly easily be regarded as having undertaken a responsibility which generates a duty to go through with it with due care.[272] The duty undertaken in such a case is not different in principle from that applicable to a non-gratuitous agent, as the common

---

[266] ie in common law terms the contract is unilateral—the agent need not act, but if he does and qualifies for commission he is entitled to it: see *Luxor (Eastbourne) Ltd v Cooper* [1941] AC 108, HL. The appointment of an 'exclusive agent' is normally taken to indicate a bilateral contract with obligations on the agent as well as on the principal.

[267] See para 9.90.

[268] This has arisen in connection with stockbrokers: eg *RH Deacon & Co v Varga* (1972) 30 DLR (3d) 653, affd (1973) 41 DLR (4th) 767n; *Volkers v Midland Doherty* (1985) 17 DLR (4th) 343.

[269] See para 9.44.

[270] *Henderson v Merrett Syndicates Ltd* [1995] 2 AC 145, HL.

[271] *Tai Hing Cotton Mill Ltd v Liu Chong Hing Bank Ltd* [1986] AC 80, PC.

[272] See *Henderson v Merrett Syndicates Ltd* (n 270 above); *London Borough of Bromley v Ellis* [1971] 1 Lloyd's Rep 97; *Norwest Refrigeration Services Pty Ltd v Bain Dawes (WA) Pty Ltd* (1984) 157 CLR 149, HCA. The matter frequently comes up in connection with insurance, especially its renewal: the persons concerned may well be or have been agents in other respects. Sometimes such an agent is in effect 'self-appointed': in such a case he may owe the same sort of duty, and may be liable for going outside it. See *Montrod Ltd v Grundkotter Fleischvertriebs GmbH* [2001] EWCA Civ 1954; [2002] 1 WLR 1975.

law does not accept differences of duty for different types of situation. It has been expressed as 'that which may reasonably be expected of him in all the circumstances'.[273] In practice, of course, there are likely to be differences from contractual agency.

(b) Equity: fiduciary duties [274]

A conspicuous feature of the law of agency, already mentioned, is that all agents are potentially subject to the special controls imposed by equity on fiduciaries generally. It has been said that. 'A fiduciary is someone who has undertaken to act for and on behalf of another in a particular matter in circumstances which give rise to a relationship of trust and confidence.'[275] This definition plainly covers persons exercising agency functions.
9.137

The equitable rules relating to fiduciaries fill gaps which might otherwise be created by the comparative reluctance of common law, at any rate in England, to find implied contract terms; and provide a technique for situations where in other systems notions of good faith might be invoked. But they may go further. 'The essence of a fiduciary obligation is that it creates obligations of a different character from those deriving from the contract itself.'[276] The law on fiduciary duties is rich and flexible, though still in a process of development. The rules are an extension of the duties originally imposed on express trustees, but they are and always have been of a more moderate nature: for example, instead of forbidding certain sorts of act altogether, as in the case of trustees purchasing trust property, they normally only regard such acts as wrong if they are done without full disclosure to the beneficiary of the duty. Older cases made more use of the trust analogy than is common nowadays, when there is more attention to the development of general principles of equity.
9.138

The fiduciary duties are not confined to agency situations but stem from more general principles; hence it can be said that such duties are not a defining feature of the internal agency relationship at all, but simply a set of external rules which can often be applicable in agency situations. This question of the extent to which the fiduciary duties should be regarded as a definitional feature of agency is susceptible of sustained argument, and it has already been said that the answer to it is to some extent a matter of preference in exposition.[277] In *Kelly v Cooper*, a
9.139

---

[273] *Chaudhry v Prabakhar* [1989] 1 WLR 29, 34, 37, CA (person undertaking to inspect car for another).

[274] This is part of a wider topic, on which see *Snell's Equity* (31st edn, 2005), ch 7. See discussion in this book paras 17.346ff.

[275] *Bristol & West BS v Mothew* [1998] Ch 1, 18, CA *per* Millett LJ.

[276] *Re Goldcorp Exchange Ltd* [1995] 1 AC 74, 98, PC *per* Lord Mustill.

[277] See para 9.17.

fairly recent Privy Council decision concerning an estate agent in Bermuda, holding that there was no duty on such an agent to reveal to one client the plans of another even though they affect the first client, there are strong dicta that the relationship between principal and agent turns only on the terms of the contract between them.[278] Assuming the actual decision to be correct, it simply decides that the fiduciary duty does not extend as far as had been argued: any duty lay at common law. Fiduciary duties can however operate in other respects. No one could doubt, for example, that an estate agent should not conceal offers made to him for his client. The agent is in fact a paradigm case for the application of fiduciary duties, and though they can be complied with by disclosure, or modified by agreement or by the circumstances, if they are totally excluded, the supposed agency relationship would no longer rank as such. Even a messenger with a specific message to carry could be under limited duties, for example not to take a bribe or make a secret profit in connection with its delivery.

9.140 It is sometimes argued that the basic fiduciary duties are negative, in that they prohibit conduct rather than impose positive duties; and sometimes also that they are confined to two basic prophylactic duties, not to profit from one's position and not to assume a position in which there could be a conflict of interest.[279] These basic duties then manifest themselves in situations where more specific findings are made and more specific remedies employed. On this approach, other duties relevant to agents may also arise in equity: they can be brought within the scope of a looser term such as 'duties of loyalty', but though related, are not rightly described as fiduciary. They are to be found particularly in connection with company directors, for example a duty to reveal wrongdoing by others,[280] and, according to one case, by the director himself of his own wrongdoing.[281] The question can then arise whether such a duty extends to employees, at any rate senior employees, also.[282] This distinction is not often, if at all, made in the cases where the term 'fiduciary' is often used in a very wide sense; but it can be a useful guide to their analysis.

(i) Scope of the duties

9.141 The applicability of the fiduciary duties and their extent varies very much from one situation to another. There have been numerous warnings in the cases as to

---

278 *Kelly v Cooper* [1993] AC 205, HL, see esp 213–14.

279 See Nolan (1997) 113 LQR 220; Flannigan [2004] JBL 277; Conaglen (2005) 121 LQR 452; Flannigan (2006) 122 LQR 449.

280 *Bell v Lever Bros* [1932] AC 161.

281 *Item Software (UK) Ltd v Fassihi* [2004] EWCA Civ 1244; [2005] ICR 450, CA.

282 See *Helmet Integrated Systems Ltd v Tunnard* [2006] EWCA Civ 1735; [2007] IRLR 126 on intention to leave a post and compete.

the misuse of fiduciary reasoning.[283] It has been said that 'The precise scope of [the obligation] must be moulded according to the nature of the relationship.'[284] The main potentially applicable fiduciary duties may however be listed as follows. The agent must not use his position or his principal's property[285] to secure undisclosed benefits, called 'secret profits', for himself: this rule has been applied very strictly even where the principal would without the agent's intervention have done worse financially, and has sometimes been stated in stern terms which would find a breach of duty because there was no more than a possibility that a conflict of interest *might* arise.[286] He must not without disclosure (which could be satisfied where there was general knowledge and acceptance of a practice) take secret commissions or discounts, often referred to more directly as bribes, from the other party to a transaction, and if he does so is liable whether or not the payment (or promise of it) influenced him.[287] The agent must make full disclosure when he deals with his principal: he must not without disclosure when employed to buy, sell his own property to his principal;[288] nor when employed to sell may he without disclosure buy the property himself.[289] He must not use or make a profit from his principal's confidential information; though this goes outside the scope of fiduciary duties and depends largely on the law as to breach of confidence, which applies in many spheres other than that of agency.[290]

All these situations involve a conflict of interest, or potential conflict, between agent and principal. But the fiduciary duties extend also to situations where there is or may be a conflict of interest between two principals, each of which is entitled to the agent's full loyalty: his loyalty to one may put him in breach of his duty to

9.142

---

[283] A famous example is the dictum of Fletcher Moulton LJ in *Re Coomber* [1911] 1 Ch 723, 728–9, CA.

[284] *New Zealand Netherlands Society 'Oranje' Inc v Kuys* [1973] 1 WLR 1126, 1130, PC *per* Lord Wilberforce.

[285] See the unusual case of *Reid-Newfoundland Co v Anglo-American Telegraph Co Ltd* [1912] AC 555, PC (profit from unauthorized use of telegraph wire).

[286] A leading case on striking facts is *Phipps v Boardman* [1967] 2 AC 46: see, eg, 111. See also, eg, *Aberdeen Rly Co v Blaikie Brothers* (1854) 1 Macq 461, 471 *per* Lord Cranworth LC. The fiduciary and other duties of directors are to be governed by Companies Act 2006, some of which is already in force. See paras 3.40, 3.66 ff.

[287] *Harrington v Victoria Graving Dock Co* (1878) 3 QBD 549. The rules as regards bribery, though raising conceptual difficulties as to remedies, are fairly well worked out. The principle is however wider and probably applies to participation in any breach of fiduciary duty by the agent. The seminal case, *Panama & South Pacific Telegraph Co v India Rubber, Gutta Percha and Telegraph Works Co* (1878) LR 10 Ch App 515, does not concern actual bribery. See further *Petrotrade Inc v Smith* [2000] 1 Lloyd's Rep 486; *Fyffes Group Ltd v Templeman* [2000] 2 Lloyd's Rep 643.

[288] *Regier v Campbell-Stuart* [1939] Ch 766.

[289] *Dunne v English* (1874) LR 18 Eq 524. Even where there is disclosure, there may in both these cases be an additional requirement that he proves the transaction is a fair one.

[290] The different role of confidence principles is well exemplified in the *Prince Jefri Bolkiah* case (n 295 below).

the other, and he must disclose the position to each,[291] even if the matters in respect of which he acts for them are different.[292] The court in *Kelly v Cooper*, cited above,[293] found no such duty in the case of an estate agent; but the conflict could arise in other areas of activity. Even if he discloses to each that he is acting for the other, he 'must not allow the performance of his obligations to one principal to be influenced by his relationship with the other'; nor must he get into a position where 'he cannot fulfil his obligations to one without failing in his obligations to the other'.[294] Problems more specifically based on the law as to breach of confidence may arise also where he has information in respect of a former client which his duty to a present client arguably may require him to disclose. Questions may arise in both the above contexts within firms (for example, of solicitors or accountants), as to whether protection from such conflicts of interest in which different parts of the firm are involved may be secured by 'Chinese walls'. English courts have not so far looked favourably on such devices.[295]

(ii) Exclusion of fiduciary duties

9.143 With the abolition of 'single capacity' rules in financial markets (ie rules that inter alia prevent agents from acting in other capacities), clauses have been increasingly inserted into intermediaries' contracts which seek to establish that the intermediary may, for example, sell his own shares to the principal and in general act in a way inconsistent with the fiduciary duties. Such clauses should only in principle be valid if they constitute the relevant disclosure, or make clear that the person concerned does not act as agent in the legal sense, at least in the relevant respects.[296] Standards are also sometimes laid down by regulatory bodies, and it is argued or assumed that compliance with these cannot contravene the fiduciary duties. It is not clear that this is always correct: a power to override duties imposed by law would need to be clearly conferred. Current practice is based on public regulation of the financial markets,[297] but the fiduciary principles of private law have not yet been superseded.

---

291 *Clark Boyce v Mouat* [1994] 1 AC 428, PC.

292 *Marks & Spencer plc v Freshfields Bruckhaus Deringer* [2004] EWCA Civ 741; [2005] PNLR 4; affirming [2004] EWHC 1337; [2004] 1 WLR 2331.

293 [1993] AC 205, HL: see para 9.139.

294 *Bristol & West BS v Mothew* [1998] Ch 1, 19, CA *per* Millett LJ. For examples see *Moody v Cox & Hatt* [1917] 2 Ch 71 CA; *Hilton v Barker Booth & Eastwood* [2005] UKHL 8, [2005] 1 WLR 567, though both largely concerning the position of solicitors.

295 *Prince Jefri Bolkiah v KPMG* [1999] 2 AC 222, HL (accountants); the *Marks & Spencer* case (n 292 above) (solicitors); Hollander and Salzedo, *Conflicts of Interest and Chinese Walls* (2nd edn, 2004).

296 For a discussion of such a question (relating to trustees) see *Citibank NA v MBIA Assurance SA* [2006] EWHC 3215.

297 Financial Services and Markets Act 2000.

(iii) Remedies[298]

The general remedy of equity is (apart from the decrees of specific performance **9.144** and injunction) the trust; and the basic approach to breach of fiduciary duties is that the law assumes that the agent who makes a secret profit has done so on his principal's account[299] and therefore holds that profit on constructive trust for his principal. Until recently it was assumed that this principle, though applied to other benefits obtained, did not extend to bribes, but it has fairly recently been decided that it does so.[300] The result raises some problems (as do other cases where trusts are found) because of the priority in bankruptcy which it accords. It may also give a more favourable position when limitation of actions is invoked, because the normal rules do not apply to actions to recover trust property from a trustee;[301] and it may give rise to a right to trace property in equity.[302] Hence there has been a trend towards regarding the duty to account as one operating *in personam*.[303] Where agents buy from or sell to their principals, rescission is available;[304] and in the case of bribery the transaction may even be rescinded against the third party (who is also liable in damages).[305] In the case of conflict between the interests of two principals, one of them may obtain an injunction to restrain the agent from acting as he proposes.[306]

The jurisdiction of courts of equity to award damages has long been controversial, **9.145** but there are obviously cases where it can only be said that a breach of duty has caused loss. It is now accepted that there are cases where damages (sometimes referred to as 'equitable compensation') can be awarded in connection with such loss, even though the duty broken only lies in equity.[307] This jurisdiction is

---

[298] Chapter 21, esp paras 21.130–21.134, 21.153–21.155.

[299] See a seminal article by the Hon Sir Peter Millett (now Lord Millett), 'Bribes and Secret Commission' [1993] Restitution L Rev 7.

[300] *A-G for Hong Kong v Reid* [1994] 1 AC 324, PC (but normally regarded as valid for English law also).

[301] Limitation Act 1980, s 21(1); and there are differences in respect of other equitable claims also.

[302] See Lord Goff of Chieveley and GH Jones, *Law of Restitution* (6th edn, 2002), ch 2.

[303] See *Warman International Ltd v Dwyer* (1995) 182 CLR 544, HCA.

[304] The question of profits may require different treatment in the case of agents selling property to their principals. If the agent acquires the property and sells it to his principal, there may be a secret profit, but if he sells property which he already holds the right may be to rescission only.

[305] See *Mahesan v Malaysian Government Officers Cooperative Housing Society Ltd* [1979] AC 374, PC. No credit need be given, in the calculation of damages, for a bribe received: *Logicrose v Southend United FC* [1988] 1 WLR 1256. See n 287 above.

[306] As in the *Prince Jefri Bolkiah* case (n 295) and the *Marks & Spencer* case (n 292).

[307] *Target Holdings Ltd v Redferns* [1996] AC 421, HL. This decision is usually taken as the leading one on the topic for English law; but the true issue can be said to have been the narrower one of restoring the trust estate. See *Youyang Pty Ltd v Minter Ellison Morris Fletcher* (2003) 212 CLR 484, HCA; Elliott and Edelman (2003) 119 LQR 545.

currently developing.[308] It may apply, for example, not only in cases of conflict of duty and interest, but also in cases of conflict of duty and duty: where an injunction is not appropriate, an award of damages for loss caused may be. Often however such awards can be justified on common law principles as based on fraud, or breach of a contractual duty to take care or to place the agent's knowledge at the disposal of the principal. Where this is so the special features of the equitable rules are not to be invoked merely because they might create slightly different results in connection, for example, with damages,[309] or as to limitation periods.[310] Nevertheless, awards made for breach of pure fiduciary duties are not necessarily affected by the same limits as apply to common law damages in respect of remoteness, contributory negligence and so forth, though the courts will be reluctant to compensate for loss which would have occurred in any case.[311] The whole area is one in which decisions from other common law countries, especially Australia, are of considerable significance in England.[312] In Canada[313] and New Zealand,[314] views are held to the effect that the question of remedy is secondary and, when arrived at after the question of breach of duty is determined, should be dealt with entirely flexibly. Such flexibility is found in England in breach of confidence cases, but less elsewhere.

9.146 Without any question of breach of duty, an agent may also hold money which emanates from his principal, or which comes in from outside for his principal. In insolvency situations (and other situations such as limitation) it may be important to know whether such money is held on trust, ie whether in respect of this money the agent is a trustee, or whether he is merely a debtor to his principal. This is one of the situations where trust and agency clearly overlap. It might seem that the agent would always be bound to hold such money on trust, for one of his traditional duties is to keep his principal's money separate. However, by definition that duty only applies where the agent has what can be called 'the principal's money'. Thus it is clear that in many circumstances an agent is put in funds by

---

308 eg *Swindle v Harrison* [1997] 4 All ER 705, CA; *Nationwide BS v Various Solicitors (No 3)* [1999] TLR 141.

309 *Bristol & West BS v Mothew* [1998] Ch 1, CA.

310 *Paragon Finance v DB Thakerar & Co* [1999] 1 All ER 400, CA; see also *Coulthard v Disco Mix Club Ltd* [1999] TLR 220.

311 *Target Holdings Ltd v Redferns* (n 307 above), *Swindle v Harrison* (n 308).

312 Two recent leading Australian decisions on the nature of fiduciary obligation are *Breen v Williams* (1996) 186 CLR 71, HCA and *Paramasivam v Flynn* (1988) 160 ALR 203, FC.

313 *Lac Minerals v International Corona Resources Ltd* [1989] 2 SCR 574; (1989) 61 DLR (4th) 14. Canadian courts go further also as regards the incidence of fiduciary duties: eg, *Norberg v Wynrib* [1992] 2 SCR 226; (1992) 92 DLR (4th) 449 (medical practitioner). But cf the more recent case of *KLB v British Columbia* [2003] 2 SCR 403; (2003) 230 DLR (4th) 513.

314 *Day v Mead* [1987] 2 NZLR 443, NZ; *Aquaculture Corp v New Zealand Green Mussel Co* [1990] 3 NZLR 299, NZ.

his principal on the understanding that he will account overall only on an *in personam* basis, and/or where it is assumed that the agent will maintain a cash flow with respect to money emanating from external sources without holding it on trust.[315] But where the agent is given money by his principal for a specific purpose, or where money is given to him by a third party to hold for his principal, there may be a trust; and a trust is more likely where the agent receives money in connection with a single transaction than when he maintains a general cash flow over several transactions and accounts periodically.[316] The question of how appropriate it is to accord a priority in bankruptcy is one that is or should be taken into account in the determination of such questions as these.

9.147 The liability of an agent to his principal is often referred to as a duty to account, and this phrase is sometimes loosely used. The words hark back to the traditional remedy against the agent, which was to seek an account in equity. Nowadays the phrase tends to be used in a more general sense to refer to remedies for the principal against the agent, whether *in rem* or *in personam*. The Limitation Act 1980[317] itself recognizes that the claims which give rise to the duty to account may differ.

(iv) Commercial agents

9.148 Similar duties are briefly laid down in the Commercial Agents (Council Directive) Regulations 1993. They mostly correspond to the common law duties; but the counterpart to the equitable duties is a broad one to act 'dutifully and in good faith'.[318] It seems likely that courts in common law countries will interpret this duty in a way broadly consistent with the fiduciary duties already existing.

(2) Rights of the Agent Against the Principal

(a) Commission

9.149 The main right of the agent against the principal is to remuneration, which is typically expressed as commission. A gratuitous agent is not of course so entitled; but in most cases, especially of professional agents, it will be assumed that a reasonable commission was impliedly agreed if nothing was said about this when the agent is engaged.[319]

---

[315] eg *Neste Oy v Lloyds Bank plc* [1983] 2 Lloyd's Rep 658.

[316] Two leading cases are *Burdick v Garrick* (1870) LR 5 Ch App 233 and *Kirkham v Peel* (1880) 43 LT 171, affd (1880) 44 LT 195, CA. There is a valuable discussion in *Walker v Corboy* (1990) 19 NSWLR 382, Aust; for a more recent relevant decision, see *Triffit Nurseries v Salads Etcetera Ltd* [2000] 1 All ER Comm 737, CA.

[317] s 23.

[318] Reg 4(1).

[319] eg *Way v Latilla* [1937] 3 All ER 759.

9.150 An enormous number of cases concern the right of the agent to commission. In England, many of them concern real estate agents, but their significance is usually general and they can be cited in connection with any commission dispute. The only principle that emerges is that the right depends entirely on the terms of the particular contract. It can be said that in the case of sale of land, the agent is intended to get his commission from the purchase price,[320] and only if he is an (or perhaps sometimes 'the') effective cause of the sale: on the latter point in particular there is much case law.[321] This may be relevant if no terms are specified, or by way of providing criteria for interpretation of contract terms that are obscure, but is not conclusive. Commission may be due in circumstances far short of this. There is no notion that the principal will not prevent the agent from earning remuneration:[322] in most cases he is free not to deal with persons introduced by the agent, to find customers himself, to revoke the agent's authority or even to close down his business. Occasionally a term may be implied that the principal will not behave in certain ways; in one case there is reference to 'a term which prevents the vendor from acting unreasonably to the possible gain of the vendor and the loss of the agent',[323] which is an example of an implied term creating an effect similar to that of a requirement of good faith. Such an implication would however be fairly rare. The assumption is usually that the agent earns quite a high commission if he succeeds, and until then takes risks. It is also true that some agency contracts do not place any duty on the agent to do anything.[324] The right to remuneration may of course not be exercisable in respect of illegal and other prohibited transactions.

(b) Reimbursement and indemnity

9.151 An agent has the right to be reimbursed expenses and indemnified against liabilities incurred on authorized transactions,[325] including some where he could not himself be sued, as for example barristers' fees,[326] provided again that these are not illegal or otherwise affected by statute. Where the agency is contractual, the duty may be explicable as based on contract; but where it is not the basis must be restitutionary.

---

[320] See *Midgley Estates Ltd v Hand* [1952] 2 QB 432, 435–6, CA *per* Jenkins LJ.

[321] For a dramatic example see *Hodges & Sons v Hackbridge Park Residential Hotel Ltd* [1940] 1 KB 404, where the purchaser introduced acquired the property compulsorily. The agent was not entitled to commission.

[322] See *Luxor (Eastbourne) Ltd v Cooper* [1941] AC 108, HL.

[323] *Alpha Trading Ltd v Dunnshaw-Patten Ltd* [1981] QB 290, CA.

[324] See para 9.135.

[325] For a recent discussion see *Linklaters v HSBC Bank plc* [2005] EWHC 1113 (Comm), [2003] 2 Lloyd's Rep 545.

[326] *Rhodes v Fielder, Jones & Harrison* (1919) 89 LJKB 15.

(c) Lien

The agent may also have a lien, ie a right to retain his principal's property as secu- **9.152** rity for his claims against his principal. This may be confined to property held in connection with the transaction on which money is owed; but certain types of intermediary have by custom a general lien, ie one applying to debts incurred in connection with other transactions also.

(d) Fiduciary duties

It is normally assumed that principals owe no fiduciary duties to their agents. **9.153** In so far as it has arisen, the matter has been considered in connection with franchisors and persons in similar positions. Since they normally sell to their franchisees, or can be said in general to be at arm's length commercially, the view is taken that they owe them no fiduciary duties. This question is not however beyond argument. The fiduciary principles are not confined to agents and are of potential general application. The main obstacle to the franchisor owing fiduciary obligations is that his relationship with the franchisee is primarily the commercially adverse one of seller and buyer.[327]

(e) Commercial agents

The Commercial Agents (Council Directive) Regulations 1993 regulate, for those **9.154** agents to which they refer, the right to commission, in a manner more specific than the general common law rules,[328] though it is not always clear whether or not they are mandatory and to what extent they can be modified by contract terms.[329] They contain a provision requiring the principal to supply information from which commission may be calculated,[330] though how this is intended to operate is again not clear. They also impose on the principal unexcludable duties, which would not necessarily be implied at common law, to act 'dutifully and in good faith',[331] and more specifically concerning the provision of information relating to the operation of the contract,[332] and the provision of a written contract.[333]

---

[327] See extensive discussion, and different views, in *Hospital Products Ltd v US Surgical Corp* (1984) 156 CLR 41, HCA (held no fiduciary duty on buyer). The imposition of fiduciary duties on a seller was rejected in *Jirna Ltd v Mr Donut of Canada Ltd* (1971) 22 DLR (3d) 639, Can.

[328] Commercial Agents (Council Directive) Regulations 1993, SI 1993/3053, regs 6–11.

[329] This is especially true of the remuneration provisions, regs 6–10.

[330] ibid reg 12.

[331] Reg 3 (1).

[332] ibid reg 4(2),(3).

[333] ibid reg 13.

There is in the regulations no provision as to reimbursement or indemnity in the sense just described (though they contain provision for indemnity or compensation on termination of service).[334] The duty to act 'dutifully and in good faith' may well be interpreted as imposing requirements beyond those of common law (and equity), for example, as to the way in which the agency contact is 'operated' by the principal.[335]

334 See para 9.102.
335 *See Simpson v Grant & Bowman Ltd* [2006] EuLR 933.

10

SALE OF GOODS[1]

A. The Statutory Regime

(1) Introduction

For many years the law relating to the sale of goods was governed primarily by the **10.01** Sale of Goods Act 1893. The Act was a codifying statute; the long title stated that it was an 'Act for codifying the Law relating to the Sale of Goods'. After a number of amendments had been made to the 1893 Act it was eventually consolidated in the Sale of Goods Act 1979. The 1979 Act has since been amended on four principal occasions[2] and there is now fresh need for consolidation. A number of interpretative difficulties have been caused by the fact that the original statute was

---

[1] For more detailed consideration of the rules of law see *Benjamin: Sale of Goods* (7th edn, 2006); M Bridge, *The Sale of Goods* (1997); PS Atiyah, *The Sale of Goods* (11th edn, 2005); E McKendrick (ed), *Sale of Goods* (2000).

[2] By the Sale of Goods (Amendment) Act 1994, the Sale and Supply of Goods Act 1994, the Sale of Goods (Amendment) Act 1995 and the Sale and Supply of Goods to Consumers Regulations 2002 (SI 2002, No. 3045, the latter implementing Council Directive (EC) 1999/44 on Certain Aspects of the Sale of Consumer Goods and Associated Guarantees [1999] OJ L171/12).

a codifying statute[3] which was then consolidated[4] and subsequently amended.[5] The patchwork of amendments led one judge to state that 'in terms of the proper construction of its provisions, the Act of 1979 is not to be regarded as more than the sum of its parts',[6] so that a particular phrase might not have the same meaning throughout the Act if the terms were introduced at different stages in the legislative development of what is now the 1979 Act.

10.02 Statements that the 1893 Act is a 'Code'[7] or that the 1979 Act is a 'single code'[8] are apt to mislead. They give the impression that the legislation is the sole repository of the law relating to the sale of goods, when this is far from being the case. The Act is built upon common law foundations[9] and the common law (here used to include equity) has had and continues to have a significant impact upon the development of the law. Thus the Sale of Goods Act has little to say about matters relating to the formation of a contract and to vitiating factors, such as fraud, misrepresentation, duress and mistake.[10] Developments in the general law of contract relating to breach of contract and the classification of terms in a contract have also had an impact on sale of goods law.[11] The impact of judge-made law can also be seen in relation to documentary sales, such as cif and fob contracts, where the

---

3 The proper approach to the interpretation of a codifying statute was set out by Lord Herschell LC in *Bank of England v Vagliano Brothers* [1891] AC 107, 144–5, HL. The essence of this approach was significantly to curtail the ability of the courts to go outside the code to resolve interpretative difficulties. This approach was not, however, literally followed by the courts. Examples can be found of cases in which courts have had regard to pre-1893 case law when interpreting the 1893 Act and, in more recent times, the courts have been more creative or liberal in their interpretation of the legislation and refused to allow it to 'fossilize the law': see, for example, *Ashington Piggeries Ltd v Christopher Hill Ltd* [1972] AC 441, 501, HL.

4 In the case of consolidating statutes the courts have greater liberty to resort to cases decided under the previous legislation because of the operation of the presumption that a consolidating statute does not alter the previous law.

5 The question whether the courts should, when seeking to ascertain the meaning of the amended provision, have regard to cases decided under the legislation prior to its amendment has provoked judicial disagreement. In *Rogers v Parish (Scarborough) Ltd* [1987] QB 933, 942, CA Mustill LJ stated that resort should not be had to the old case law, a view which was not shared by Lloyd LJ in *M/S Aswan Engineering Establishment Co v Lupdine Ltd* [1987] 1 WLR 1, 6, CA.

6 *Stevenson v Rogers* [1999] QB 1028, 1040, CA.

7 See for example *Re Wait* [1927] 1 Ch 606, CA, where there are a number of references to the Sale of Goods Act 1893 as a Code in the judgments of Lord Hanworth MR (616, 617, 620) and Atkin LJ (630–1, 634–7).

8 *Stevenson v Rogers* [1999] QB 1028, 1040, CA.

9 In the sense that the provisions of the 1893 Act reflect, with modifications, the case law on sale of goods as it had developed in the latter part of the nineteenth century.

10 See, for example, s 62(2) of the Sale of Goods Act 1979 which specifically preserves the common law rules except in so far as they are inconsistent with the provisions of the Act. 'Common law' here almost certainly includes the rules of equity: *Benjamin* (n 1 above) paras 1-008 and 1-009.

11 Of particular significance in this context is the development of the innominate or intermediate term in *Hong Kong Fir Shipping Co Ltd v Kawasaki Kisen Kaisha Ltd* [1962] 2 QB 26, CA (see further Chapter 8). The impact of this case on sale of goods law can be seen in *Cehave NV v Bremer Handelsgesellschaft mbH (The Hansa Nord)* [1976] QB 44, CA.

judge-made rules have had a greater impact on the development of the law than the rules formulated in the Sale of Goods Act 1979.[12] The Sale of Goods Act 1979 may be the first port of call for the lawyer seeking to advise on a sale of goods problem but it is not necessarily the last nor the most important.

(a) Application of the Sale of Goods Act 1979

The Sale of Goods Act 1979 applies to consumer sales, the commercial sale of goods (that is to say, a sale which takes place between two businesses) and documentary sales. There is no separate statute which regulates consumer sales, although more recent amendments to the Sale of Goods Act have distinguished between consumer sales and commercial sales.[13] This more recent trend led one judge to comment that the 1979 Act 'transformed the code of the Act of 1893 from that of a corpus of rules which in principle applied to all contracts of sale into one containing a number of variants, dependent on factors such as whether one of the parties is acting in the course of a business. . .or whether a party does or does not deal as a "consumer" '.[14] Yet, while it is true to say that the variants have increased in scope recently, there is still no formal division between the different types of sales contracts. They are all in principle governed by the Sale of Goods Act 1979. In order to be able to accommodate such a wide diversity of sales contracts within its scope, the framework supplied by the Act has had to be a flexible one. Thus many of the provisions of the Act lay down 'default' rules; that is to say, the rule contained in the Act will apply in the absence of an agreement to the contrary by the parties. It is this flexibility which has enabled the legislation to survive for as long as it has; indeed it is noticeable that it is at the points at which the Act lays down compulsory rules that it has attracted the most criticism.[15]

10.03

(b) International sales

Not only does the Sale of Goods Act 1979 apply to a wide range of domestic contracts, it also applies to international sales. English law has not yet followed the

10.04

---

[12] See generally M Bridge, *The International Sale of Goods—Law and Practice* (1999).

[13] See for example s 15A of the Sale of Goods Act 1979, discussed in more detail in para 10.46 and the amendments to the 1979 Act made by the Sale and Supply of Goods to Consumers Regulations 2002 (SI 2002, No. 3045), discussed in more detail at paras 10.67 and 10.68. The 'satisfactory quality' implied term, first introduced in 1994, also appears to have been drafted largely with consumer buyers in mind. The legal regulation of exclusion clauses also distinguishes between consumer sales and commercial sales. The increasingly distinct regulation of consumer sales has led to calls for the separate regulation of consumer sales: see, for example, M Bridge 'What is to be done about Sale of Goods?' (2003) 119 LQR 173.

[14] *Stevenson v Rogers* [1999] QB 1028, 1040, CA.

[15] Thus s 16 of the Sale of Goods Act 1979 which laid down a rule of law that property could not pass in the case of the sale of unascertained goods was heavily criticized in its application to the sale of part of a bulk of goods. Reform has now been introduced in the form of ss 20A and 20B of the Act, see para 10.20.

path taken by many nations in distinguishing formally between domestic and international sales. In the international realm pressure has grown in recent years for the creation of a uniform set of rules that can be applied to sales contracts and the most influential document which has as its aim the promotion of uniformity is the UN Convention on Contracts for the International Sale of Goods (generally referred to as the 'Vienna Convention' or, more commonly, 'CISG').[16] The Convention has now been ratified by 70 states and came into force on 1 January 1988. The United Kingdom is one of the few major trading nations which has not ratified the Convention,[17] although ratification may take place in the not too distant future. When, or if, the Convention is introduced into English law, it will effect a major change to the law relating to the international sale of goods in this country, particularly in remedial terms.[18]

(2) The Scope of the Sale of Goods Act 1979

10.05 The scope of the Sale of Goods Act 1979 (hereafter 'the Act') is obviously confined to contracts for the sale of goods. It is therefore necessary to define a contract for the sale of goods in order to ascertain the limits of the Act. A contract of sale is defined as a 'contract by which the seller transfers or agrees to transfer the property in the goods to the buyer for a money consideration, called the price'.[19] It can be seen from this definition that sale of goods law is essentially an amalgam of contract law and personal property law. The definition can be broken down into a number of distinct components; there must be (a) a contract, (b) goods, (c) price, and (d) transfer of property. Each of these elements is worthy of further elaboration.

(a) A contract

10.06 The existence and validity of the contract is essentially a matter for the general law of contract[20] as is the capacity of the parties to enter into a contract for the sale of goods.[21] A gift of goods, not being a contract, is outside the scope of the Act.[22]

---

[16] On which see generally P Schlechtriem and I Schwenzer (eds) *Commentary on the UN Convention on the International Sale of Goods (CISG),* (Oxford, 2nd (English) edition, 2005).

[17] A valuable outline of the Convention, explaining its potential significance for English lawyers, is provided by B Nicholas, 'The Vienna Convention on International Sales Law' (1989) 105 LQR 201.

[18] On which see FMB Reynolds, 'A Note of Caution' in P Birks (ed), *The Frontiers of Liability* (1994) 18–28.

[19] Sale of Goods Act 1979, s 2(1).

[20] ibid s 62(2). The rules relating to the existence and validity of a contract are discussed in Chapter 8.

[21] ibid s 3(1). Note, however, the obligation to pay a reasonable price for 'necessaries' set out in 3(2) and (3).

[22] The distinction between a gift and a contract is not always easy to draw: *Esso Petroleum Co Ltd v Commissioners of Customs & Excise* [1976] 1 WLR 1, HL (albeit on the facts it was held that the contract between the parties was not one for the sale of the coins).

A sale is, however, more than a contract. It is both a contract and a conveyance. Where there is only a contract to sell but no more, this is defined by the Act as an agreement to sell,[23] rather than a sale. There are no longer any formal requirements which apply to entry into contracts for the sale of goods.[24]

(b) Goods

(i) Distinguished from services or work and materials

The Act only applies to goods. It has no application to contracts for services or for work and materials. This obviously can give rise to difficult questions of demarcation because it is not always easy to distinguish between a contract for the sale of goods and one for services; the different types of contract can, in certain circumstances, shade into each other. The distinction between them has been held to turn essentially on the 'substance' of the contract; if the substance of the contract is the skill and labour then the contract is likely to be one for work and materials but if the substance of the contract is the end product then it is likely that it will be regarded as a contract of sale.[25] The distinction between the two types of contract is not of great practical importance today, largely because the terms implied into contracts for the sale of goods and contracts for work and materials are very similar.[26] **10.07**

(ii) Definition

Goods is defined in s 61(1) of the Act as including 'all personal chattels other than things in action and money' and 'emblements, industrial growing crops, and things attached to or forming part of the land which are agreed to be severed before sale or under the contract of sale' and an 'undivided share in goods'. The scope of the Act is therefore broad. Yet its scope continues to be tested by the infinite variety of transactions entered into in the modern world. Thus, while the sale of computer hardware will constitute a sale of goods, the sale of computer software may not.[27] The status of a contract for the sale of human remains or human tissue, where it is lawful to enter into such a contract, remains uncertain.[28] At the margins **10.08**

---

[23] Sale of Goods Act 1979, s 2(5).

[24] Formal requirements were repealed by the Law Reform (Enforcement of Contracts) Act 1954.

[25] *Robinson v Graves* [1935] 1 KB 579, CA. The problems associated with this test are explored in more detail in *Benjamin* (n 1 above) paras 1-041 to 1-047.

[26] Implied terms are discussed in more detail in paras 10.27–10.38.

[27] In *St Albans City & District Council v International Computers Ltd* [1996] 4 All ER 481, 493, CA Sir Iain Glidewell stated (obiter) that a computer program was not itself 'goods' within the statutory definition. A broader approach has, however, been taken in some other jurisdictions. For more detailed consideration see P Kohler and N Palmer, 'Information as Property' in N Palmer and E McKendrick (eds), *Interests in Goods* (2nd edn, 1998) 1, 17–19.

[28] See generally R Magnusson, 'Proprietary Rights in Human Tissues' in N Palmer and E McKendrick (eds), *Interests in Goods* (2nd edn, 1998) 25, esp 46–8. There is probably no absolute

it has also proved to be difficult to distinguish between the sale of personal chattels (within the Act) and the sale of land (outwith the Act) and between the sale of tangible property (within the Act) and the sale of intangibles (generally outwith the Act). The problems in the former category have been reduced by the extended definition of goods which in general brings the sale of crops and natural products within the scope of the Act.[29] In the latter category the exclusion of things or choses in action means that documentary intangibles do not fall within the scope of the Act: for example, shares, debts, bills of lading and negotiable instruments do not constitute goods.

(iii) Categories of goods

10.09 The Act also distinguishes between different types of goods. Reference is made in the Act to 'existing', 'future', 'specific', 'ascertained', and 'unascertained' goods. To an extent these categories intersect; for example existing goods may be either specific or unascertained. The distinctions assume considerable significance in the context of the passing of property in goods. Existing goods are goods which are owned or possessed by the seller,[30] whereas future goods are goods to be manufactured or acquired by the seller after the making of the contract of sale.[31] Specific goods are goods which are identified and agreed upon at the time a contract of sale is made.[32]

10.10 There is no definition of 'ascertained' or 'unascertained'[33] within the Act itself. The meaning of these phrases has therefore been worked out by the courts.[34]

(c) Price

10.11 The price is the money consideration paid by the buyer. Where the consideration provided by the buyer assumes a form other than the payment of money the

---

rule today which prevents such contracts being regarded as a sale of goods. Evidence of a more relaxed approach by the courts to rights in human remains can be seen in the decision of the Court of Appeal in *Dobson v North Tyneside Health Authority* [1997] 1 WLR 596, CA.

[29] The courts had previously experienced great difficulty in deciding whether or not a sale of crops or natural products was a sale of goods and the cases were not at all easy to reconcile: see *Benjamin* (n 1 above) paras 1-093, 1-094. Provided that there is an obligation to sever, the contract is likely to be one for the sale of goods. Indeed, the definition is so wide that it may overlap with the definition of contracts for the sale of land in other statutory contexts.

[30] Sale of Goods Act 1979, s 5(1). Thus goods may actually exist but nevertheless not constitute existing goods for the purposes of the Act because they are not in the ownership or possession of the seller at the relevant time; such goods are classified by the Act as 'future goods'.

[31] ibid ss 5(1) and 61(1). A sale of future goods can only be an agreement to sell; it cannot be a sale.

[32] ibid s 61(1). The definition also includes 'an undivided share, specified as a fraction or percentage, of goods identified and agreed on as aforesaid'.

[33] The category of unascertained goods must now be subdivided into wholly unascertained goods and, as it has come to be labelled, quasi-specific goods.

[34] Discussed in more detail in paras 10.14–10.20.

contract cannot be one of sale. Thus contracts of exchange or barter do not fall within the scope of the Act.[35] The price payable must generally be fixed by the parties because otherwise a court may conclude that no contract has in fact been made.[36] The price may, however, be fixed in one of three ways: it can be fixed by the terms of the contract itself, it may be left to be fixed in a manner agreed by the contract, or it may be determined by the course of dealing between the parties.[37] Where the price has not been determined in one of these three ways the buyer must pay a reasonable price.[38] What constitutes a reasonable price is a question of fact which depends upon all the facts and circumstances of the case.

(d) Transfer of property

The transfer of property is central to the definition of a sale. Where the contract involves the transfer of possession or the use of goods but not the transfer of property it cannot be a sale. Thus a contract of hire, such as a finance lease, does not fall within the scope of the Act. Equally, a hire-purchase contract is outside the scope of the Act. But the fact that the transfer of property is postponed to a date subsequent to the conclusion of the contract does not in itself take the contract outside the scope of the Act. Thus a conditional sale[39] falls within the scope of the Act.[40] 'Property' is defined in the Act as 'the general property in goods, and not merely a special property'.[41] Thus, the transfer of a limited possessory interest, for example

10.12

---

[35] *Harrison v Luke* (1845) 14 M & W 139, 153 ER 423, Exchequer Division. More difficult is the case where the consideration provided by the buyer consists partly of money and partly of goods (as might be the case where a car is traded in in part-exchange for a new car). Such a transaction is probably a contract of sale (see *Aldridge v Johnson* (1857) 7 E & B 885, 119 ER 1476, Court of Queen's Bench; cf *Flynn v Mackin* [1974] IR 101, Supreme Court). If it is not a sale it will probably fall within the scope of Part I of the Supply of Goods and Services Act 1982. Given the similarity between the two Acts in many cases the classification of the contract will not have practical consequences.

[36] See for example *May and Butcher Ltd v R* [1934] 2 KB 17n, HL.

[37] Sale of Goods Act 1979, s 8(1).

[38] ibid s 8(2). The correct meaning of 'determined' is not entirely clear. Where the contract is silent as to price it is clear that s 8(2) can be invoked. It is less clear whether it can be invoked where there is a mechanism in the 'contract' but it is too uncertain to be enforced. In such a case s 8(2) may be inapplicable.

[39] It can sometimes be difficult to distinguish between a conditional sale agreement and a hire-purchase agreement. For example in *Forthright Finance Ltd v Carlyle Finance Ltd* [1997] 4 All ER 90, CA an agreement which conferred an option to purchase which option was deemed to have been exercised when all the instalments had been paid, unless the hirer elected not to take title to the goods, was held to be a conditional sale and not a hire-purchase.

[40] Of course a conditional sale may also fall within the scope of other legislation, most notably the Consumer Credit Act 1974.

[41] Sale of Goods Act 1979, s 61(1).

by way of bailment[42] or pledge,[43] does not fall within the scope of the Act. This definition of 'property' provides very limited guidance and much academic ink has been spilt on the meaning to be given to 'property' or 'title' as used in the Act.[44] Although the matter is not entirely free from doubt, it would appear that 'property' does not mean the best possible title but that it means any title provided that it is a title to the absolute legal interest in the goods. Thus there can be a sale of goods where the seller has only possessory title to the goods provided that the seller transfers the entirety of such title as he possesses to the buyer.

B. Transfer of Property and Risk

(1) The Passing of Property

10.13   The question whether or not property has passed from the seller to the buyer is obviously one of fundamental importance, particularly in the context of the insolvency of one or other party. But the significance of 'property' is not confined to insolvency. It extends to such matters as the passing of risk[45] and the entitlement of the seller to bring an action for the price of the goods.[46] Indeed, the Act has been criticized because of the 'excessive importance'[47] which it attaches to the concept of property. When deciding whether or not property in the goods has passed in any given case to the buyer, it is important to distinguish between the different types of goods recognized by the Act.

---

[42] Bailment is discussed in greater detail in chapter 13. The relationship between bailment and sale has assumed practical significance in the context of retention of title clauses, discussed at para 10.24.

[43] Pledge is in any event expressly excluded by s 62(4) of the Sale of Goods Act 1979.

[44] In particular, the heading 'transfer of property as between seller and buyer' immediately prior to s 16 has attracted criticism because, of course, the distinguishing feature of the transfer of property is its binding effect on third parties: see, for example, PS Atiyah (n 1 above) 315. For discussion see G Battersby and A Preston, 'The Concepts of "Property", "Title", and "Owner" Used in the Sale of Goods Act 1893' (1972) 35 MLR 268; HL Ho 'Some Reflections on "Property" and "Title" in the Sale of Goods Act' [1997] CLJ 571 and G Battersby, 'A reconsideration of "Property" and "Title" in the Sale of Goods Act' [2001] JBL 1.

[45] Sale of Goods Act 1979, s 20(1) which provides that risk prima facie passes with property, discussed in para 10.24.

[46] ibid s 49(1), discussed in para 10.21.

[47] R Goode, *Commercial Law* (3rd edn, 2004) 216. Further illustrations of the significance of property in English sale of goods law are provided by Professor Goode at 216–9. Professor Goode's criticisms are very much influenced by the functional approach of Professor K Llewellyn (see 'Through Title to Contract and a Bit Beyond' (1938) 15 *New York ULR* 159) but the merits of this functional approach are not universally shared: see, for example, Atiyah (n 1 above) 320.

(a) Specific or ascertained goods

(i) The intention of the parties

The central rule, embodied in s 17 of the Act is that, in the case of the sale of **10.14** specific or ascertained goods, property passes at such time as the parties to the contract intend it to pass.[48] The intention of the parties is to be derived from the terms of the contract, the conduct of the parties and all the circumstances of the case.[49] Thus it is not the delivery of the goods, control over the goods or payment of the price which operate to transfer property; it is the intention of the parties. Delivery, control or payment may be relevant in so far as they can be used to demonstrate the intention of the parties; but they are not conclusive in themselves. Contracting parties frequently make provision in the contract for the passing of property[50] and, in some standard form contracts, it is accepted that property generally passes at a particular point in time, for example the delivery of documents.[51] In an effort to provide the commercial world with some guidance, the Act contains a number of 'rules' which the courts are directed to use when seeking to discern the intention of the parties.[52] These rules are no more than presumptions; they are not conclusive in their effect. The strength of the presumption varies from rule to rule.

(ii) Presumption in respect of goods in a deliverable state

In the case of an unconditional contract[53] for the sale of specific goods[54] in a **10.15** deliverable state[55] property in the goods passes to the buyer when the contract is made.[56] This presumption is applicable even in the case where the date of payment or the time for delivery has been postponed to some later date. However, the presumption has much less force today than in former times: 'in modern times very little is needed to give rise to the inference that the property in specific goods is to

---

48 Sale of Goods Act 1979, s 17(1).

49 ibid s 17(2).

50 The most common example, perhaps, is the retention of title clause, discussed in para 10.21.

51 In the case of a cif contract property normally passes to the buyer when the buyer pays the price in exchange for the relevant documents. But in such a case property passes because this is the intention of the parties, not because the documents themselves contain some particular properties which enable property to pass irrespective of the intention of the parties.

52 Sale of Goods Act 1979, s 18.

53 Although 'unconditional' qualifies 'contract', what is in fact meant is a contract for the unconditional sale of goods.

54 Defined in para 10.09 and n 32 above: see further *Kursell v Timber Operators and Contractors Ltd* [1927] 1 KB 298, CA (where the rule was held to be inapplicable because the goods were not specific).

55 'Deliverable state' is defined in s 61(5) as 'such a state that the buyer would under the contract be bound to take delivery of them'.

56 Sale of Goods Act 1979, s 18, r 1. An example of the application of the rule is provided by *Dennant v Skinner* [1948] 2 KB 164, KBD.

pass only on delivery or payment.'[57] Where the contract is one for the sale of specific goods and the seller[58] is bound to do something to the goods for the purpose of putting them into a deliverable state, property does not pass until the thing is done and the buyer has notice that it has been done.[59] In the case of a contract for the sale of goods in a deliverable state but where the seller[60] is bound to weigh, measure, test or do some other act or thing with reference to the goods for the purpose of ascertaining the price, the property does not pass until the act or thing is done and the buyer has notice that it has been done.[61]

(iii) Delivery on 'on approval' or 'sale or return' terms

10.16   Rather more difficulty arises where goods are delivered to the buyer 'on approval or on sale or return or other similar terms'.[62] In such a case property passes to the buyer when he signifies his approval or acceptance to the seller or does any other act adopting the transaction.[63] Such approval or acceptance may be express or implied.[64] If the buyer does not signify his approval or acceptance to the seller but retains the goods without giving notice of rejection, property may nevertheless pass to the buyer when, if a time has been fixed for the return of the goods, that time has expired, or, if no time has been fixed, on the expiry of a reasonable time.[65] A buyer's notice of rejection need not be in writing and it will generally suffice if it identifies the goods to be returned generically so long as the generic description enables the goods to be identified with certainty.[66]

---

[57] *RV Ward Ltd v Bignall* [1967] 1 QB 534, 545, CA.

[58] Where it is the buyer or a third party who must do the act the rule is inapplicable and resort must be had instead to the general rule in s 17.

[59] Sale of Goods Act 1979, s 18, r 2. An example of the application of the rule is provided by *Underwood Ltd v Burgh Castle Brick and Cement Syndicate* [1922] 1 KB 343, KBD.

[60] Again, the rule is inapplicable where the act is to be done by the buyer or a third party: see, for example, *Nanka Bruce v Commonwealth Trust Ltd* [1926] AC 77, PC.

[61] Sale of Goods Act 1979, s 18, r 3. An example of the application of the rule is provided by *Rugg v Minett* (1809) 11 East 210, 103 ER 985, KBD.

[62] Sale of Goods Act 1979, s 18, r 4. It has been argued that a distinction should in fact be drawn between sales on approval and transactions entered into on a 'sale or return' basis: see J Adams, 'Sales "on Approval" and "Sale or Return"' in J Adams (ed), *Essays for Clive Schmitthoff* (1983) 1.

[63] Sale of Goods Act 1979, s 18, r 4(a). Until property passes, the prospective buyer holds the goods as bailee: *Atari Corporation (UK) Ltd v Electronic Boutique Stores (UK) Ltd* [1998] QB 539, 549, CA. The buyer has an option whether or not to buy, although it would appear that the seller is unable to withdraw his 'offer' to sell the goods. The latter rule has been criticized by I Brown, 'The Sale of Goods and Sale or Return Transactions' (1998) 114 LQR 198.

[64] *Kirkham v Attenborough* [1897] 1 QB 291, CA. In effect this rule can operate as an additional exception to the *nemo dat* rule, on which see paras 10.22 and 10.23.

[65] Sale of Goods Act 1979, s 18, r 4(b).

[66] *Atari Corporation (UK) Ltd v Electronic Boutique Stores (UK) Ltd* [1998] QB 539, CA.

(b) Future or unascertained goods.

In the case of future or unascertained goods the intention of the parties cannot be **10.17** determinative of the time at which property passes because, until such time as the goods which are the subject matter of the contract have been identified with sufficient precision, it is impossible to conclude that property has passed. However, the extent of the identification of the goods which the law requires before property can pass has proved to be a difficult issue. There are two principal ways in which property may pass. The first is by the 'unconditional appropriation' of the goods to the contract.[67] The second is as a result of the operation of section 20A of the Sale of Goods Act 1979.

(i) 'Unconditional appropriation' of the goods

The idea that property in future or unascertained goods can pass as a result of the **10.18** 'unconditional appropriation' of the goods to the contract has a long history but it only operates within very narrow confines.[68] There are a number of elements here. The first is that there must have been an appropriation of the goods to the contract. The exact meaning of appropriation is difficult to pin down. Essentially, it is an overt act of one party,[69] the purpose of which is to identify the goods to be sold.[70] Where the goods are part of a bulk, identification requires that there has been severance of the portion to be sold from the whole.[71] Secondly, that appropriation must have been unconditional, in the sense that it must irrevocably[72] identify certain goods as the goods which are the subject matter of the contract and it must have been assented to by both parties.[73] This is a difficult requirement to satisfy; usually 'it is the last act to be performed by the seller'.[74] The clearest example of an unconditional appropriation is delivery, actual or constructive,[75]

---

[67] The 'rule' can be found in s 18, r 5(1) and (2).

[68] *Carlos Federspiel SA v Charles Twigg* [1957] 1 Lloyd's Rep 240, QBD. A more liberal approach has been taken in other jurisdictions so that the approach adopted in the *Carlos Federspiel* case may yet be open to re-examination in the higher courts (*Re Goldcorp Exchange Ltd* [1995] 1 AC 74, 90, PC).

[69] It is usually the seller but it may be the buyer.

[70] For example, in the case of a cif contract this is often done by issuing a notice of appropriation.

[71] *Healy v Howlett & Sons* [1917] 1 KB 337, KBD; *Laurie & Morewood v Dudin & Sons* [1926] 1 KB 223, CA.

[72] If the seller remains free to change his mind then there can be no unconditional appropriation of the goods: *Carlos Federspiel SA v Charles Twigg* [1957] 1 Lloyd's Rep 240, QBD.

[73] Problems tend to arise where it is alleged that the assent took place prior to the appropriation. Where the assent is subsequent to the appropriation it is rather easier to show that there has been an unconditional appropriation.

[74] *Carlos Federspiel SA v Charles Twigg* [1957] 1 Lloyd's Rep 240, 255, QBD.

[75] Constructive delivery involves the transfer of control over the goods to the buyer, without the transfer of physical possession of the goods, for example by the transfer of a document of title relating to the goods.

of the goods to the buyer or to a carrier.[76] But unconditional appropriation can take place short of delivery provided that it is irrevocable and assented to by both buyer and seller.[77] Thirdly, the contract must be one for the sale of goods by description[78] and the goods must be of the contract description. Finally the goods must be in a deliverable state.[79]

10.19 Where goods have not been unconditionally appropriated to the contract and therefore remain unascertained, s 16 of the Act provides that property in the goods cannot pass until they have been ascertained. This is a rule of law out of which the parties cannot contract. Furthermore, the original s 16 did not distinguish between cases in which the goods were wholly unascertained and cases in which the goods were 'quasi-specific' (that is to say, the bulk in which the goods were contained could be identified but the buyer's share in the goods could not). In both cases s 16 stated that property could not pass. The application of this rule to cases of quasi-specific goods proved to be very controversial.[80] Although there were certain exceptional cases in which a buyer of part of a bulk of goods was able to establish that property had passed[81] these exceptions operated within a very narrow compass.

(ii) Section 20A of the 1979 Act: purchasers of part of a bulk

10.20 Parliament eventually intervened in the form of the Sale of Goods (Amendment) Act 1995 to provide certain purchasers of part of a bulk with proprietary rather than merely contractual rights, by declaring them to be owners in common of the bulk. This new right is, however, rather narrowly drawn. First, a buyer must establish that the goods form part of a bulk of goods.[82] 'Bulk' is rather

---

76 'Appropriation by delivery' is in fact regulated by s 18, r 5(2). Note that there will be no unconditional appropriation where the seller reserves the right of disposal of the goods.

77 *Hendy Lennox (Industrial Engines) Ltd v Graham Puttick Ltd* [1984] 1 WLR 485, 495, QBD.

78 The meaning of which is discussed in para 10.31.

79 As defined in Sale of Goods Act 1979, s 61(5), on which see n 55 above.

80 See, for example, *Re Wait* [1927] 1 Ch 606, CA; *Re London Wine Co (Shippers) Ltd* [1986] Palmer's Company Cases 121, Ch D; *Re Goldcorp Exchange Ltd* [1995] 1 AC 74, PC.

81 Apart from cases where the buyer was able to show that the goods had been unconditionally appropriated to the contract, buyers could show that property had passed to them where the goods had been ascertained by exhaustion (see, for example, *Karlshamns Oljefabriker v Eastport Navigation Corporation (The Elafi)* [1981] 2 Lloyd's Rep 679, QBD and s 18, r 5(3) and (4) of the Sale of Goods Act 1979), where the parties intended to create a co-ownership of the bulk (as in *Re Stayplton Fletcher Ltd* [1994] 1 WLR 1181, Ch D) and, in certain limited circumstances, equity provided the purchaser with some proprietary relief. But the intervention of equity is a vexed issue. The dominant judicial attitude seems to be one of hostility to the intervention of equity in commercial matters (see *Re Goldcorp Exchange Ltd* [1995] 1 AC 74, PC), although occasional examples of the infiltration of equity can be found (see *Hunter v Moss* [1994] 1 WLR 452, CA and *Re Harvard Securities Ltd (in liq)* [1997] 2 BCLC 369, Ch D and, more generally, S Worthington, 'Sorting Out Ownership Interests in a Bulk: Gifts, Sales and Trusts' [1999] JBL 1).

82 If there is no bulk and the goods are wholly unascertained then s 16 of the Sale of Goods Act 1979 continues to apply and property cannot pass.

restrictively defined[83] as a mass or collection of goods which is contained in a defined space or area and is such that any goods in the bulk are interchangeable with any other goods therein of the same number or quantity.[84] Secondly, the buyer must have paid the price for some or all of the goods. A buyer who satisfies these conditions is then declared to be an owner in common of the bulk. The effect of the new provision is, essentially, that the buyer is entitled to recover such share as the quantity of goods paid for and due to him out of the bulk bears to the quantity of the goods in the bulk at that time.[85] In order to protect a buyer in the security of his receipts, it has been provided that one buyer is deemed to have consented to another buyer taking delivery of his share of the goods due to him which form part of the bulk.[86] So, where it is discovered that there is a shortfall in the bulk of the goods, the buyers who do not receive their full entitlement do not have an action against the buyers who have obtained their full entitlement but must content themselves with a claim against the seller for short delivery.[87]

(c) Reservation of right of disposal

A seller of goods is entitled to retain a right of disposal of the goods until certain **10.21** conditions are met.[88] Sellers have endeavoured to exploit this potential to the full by inserting into the contract of sale a clause which seeks to reserve ownership in the goods until payment for them has been made and so provide a substantial measure of protection in the event of the insolvency of the buyer.[89] Initially the courts were receptive to such attempts by sellers and adopted a liberal approach to the interpretation and the validity of these clauses.[90] More recently the courts have had a change of heart and adopted a much more restrictive approach both to issues of interpretation[91] and validity. Where the goods the subject of the retention of title clause have not been mixed by the buyer with any other goods belonging to him, then effect is likely to be given to the clause by the courts. This is so even

---

83 Sale of Goods Act 1979, s 61(1).

84 A particular problem is whether a contractual provision which entitles the seller to supply the goods from outside the defined source prevents there being a bulk. On the facts of both *Re London Wine Co (Shippers) Ltd* [1986] Palmer's Company Cases 121, Ch D and *Re Goldcorp Exchange Ltd* [1995] 1 AC 74, PC it was held that there was no bulk and the same answer would appear to follow under s 20A.

85 Sale of Goods Act 1979, s 20A.

86 ibid s 20B. The provision is rather cumbersome. The point does not appear to have caused practical problems in other jurisdictions.

87 Although it is open to the buyers collectively to adjust the losses between themselves: see Sale of Goods Act 1979, s 20B (3).

88 ibid s 19(1). See, for example, *Transpacific Eternity SA v Kanematsu Corporation (The 'Antares III')* [2002] 1 Lloyd's Rep 233.

89 Retention of title clauses are discussed in more detail in paras 5.82–5.86.

90 *Aluminium Industrie Vaasen BV v Romalpa Aluminium Co Ltd* [1976] 1 WLR 676, CA.

91 See for example *Chaigley Farms Ltd v Crawford, Kaye & Grayshire Ltd* [1996] BCC 957.

where the clause states that property[92] in the goods shall not pass until the buyer has discharged all liabilities which are owed to the seller.[93] But where the goods have been mixed with other goods it is unlikely that the reservation of title clause will be effective to prevent property from passing[94] unless the goods can be easily unmixed.[95] Where the goods have been sub-sold by the buyer and the seller seeks to claim the proceeds of the sale, it is unlikely that the retention of title clause will be effective. Although there is authority which supports the validity of such a clause,[96] the weight of authority supports the conclusion that such a clause will be interpreted as a charge which requires to be registered if it is to be effective.[97]

(2) Transfer of Title by a Non-Owner

(a) Nemo dat quod non habet

10.22 The location of property rights also assumes considerable significance in the case of what are alleged to be unauthorized dealings in goods belonging to another. The general rule, enshrined in s 21 of the Act, is that a seller cannot give a buyer a better title than he, the seller, had; this rule is commonly expressed in the maxim *nemo dat quod non habet*.[98] This rule has been subject to some criticism in its application to contracts for the sale of goods on the ground that it is commercially inconvenient in that it fails to protect third parties who buy in all good faith, unaware of the seller's lack of title.[99] Good faith buyers are said to be particularly worthy of protection because of the need to encourage the free-flow of commerce, which can only be done by creating an environment in which buyers can purchase with confidence. The difficulty here is that the law is essentially seeking to strike a

---

[92] It is not enough for the seller to seek to retain the equitable interest in the goods. A court will view an attempt to retain the equitable interest as a charge which is void for want of registration: see *Re Bond Worth* [1980] Ch 228, Ch D, although the case is not without its critics.

[93] *Armour v Thyssen Edelstahlwerke AG* [1991] 2 AC 339, HL.

[94] *Borden (UK) Ltd v Scottish Timber Products Ltd* [1981] Ch 25, CA; *Re Peachdart Ltd* [1984] Ch 131, Ch D; *Clough Mill Ltd v Martin* [1985] 1 WLR 111, CA.

[95] *Hendy Lennox (Industrial Engines) Ltd v Graham Puttick Ltd* [1984] 1 WLR 485, QBD.

[96] *Aluminium Industrie Vaasen BV v Romalpa Aluminium Co Ltd* [1976] 1 WLR 676, CA.

[97] *E Pfeiffer Weinkellerei-Weineinkauf GmbH v Arbuthnot Factors Ltd* [1988] 1 WLR 150, Ch D; *Re Weldtech Equipment Ltd* [1991] BCC 16, Ch D; *Compaq Computer Ltd v Abercorn Group Ltd* [1991] BCC 484, Ch D.

[98] It is obviously necessary to ascertain the title which the seller has at the outset. Where the seller has a voidable title to the goods and that title has not been set aside at the time at which the seller sold the goods to a buyer who was unaware of the defect in the seller's title then the buyer obtains good title (Sale of Goods Act 1979, s 23. As to the mode of rescission, see *Car & Universal Finance Ltd v Caldwell* [1965] 1 QB 525, CA). Where, however, the title which the seller has is void, the seller has no title which he can transfer to the buyer.

[99] Of course, the buyer will ordinarily have a claim against the person who sold the goods to him for breach of s 12 of the Act (discussed in paras 10.27 and 10.28) but that right of action is of little practical utility when, as is often the case, that party is insolvent.

balance between competing interests: the claim of the original owner of the goods and the claim of the good faith purchaser.[100] English law, unlike some civil law systems, starts from the position that it is the claim of the original owner which has priority, but the exceptions reflect the desire of the courts and the legislature to protect the third party purchaser.

(b) Exceptions to the *nemo dat* rule

Broadly speaking,[101] the law prefers the interest of the third party where the origi- **10.23** nal owner took the risk, or is held to have assumed the risk, that the goods would be sold without his actual authority or was in some way at fault in relation to the sale of goods. Thus a non-owner can pass good title to a buyer if he has actual or apparent authority from the owner to enter into the sale or where, by his conduct, the owner is estopped or prevented from asserting his ownership of the goods.[102] Similarly a mercantile agent[103] who is in possession of the goods or of the documents of title[104] to the goods with the consent[105] of the owner and who sells[106] the goods in the ordinary course of his business as a mercantile agent[107] can pass good title to the buyer provided that the buyer buys in good faith[108] and without notice[109] of the want of authority.[110] A buyer who, having bought the goods from the seller, allows the seller to continue[111] in possession of the goods runs the risk that the seller may sell[112] the goods again and so confer a good title on a

---

[100] See the judgment of Denning LJ in *Bishopsgate Motor Finance Corp v Transport Brakes Ltd* [1949] 1 KB 332, 336–7, CA.

[101] The *nemo dat* rule and its exceptions are discussed in a wide context in paras 4.479ff. The statutory exceptions to *nemo dat* are rather convoluted and are set out here in outline only. For more detailed consideration see *Benjamin* (n 1 above) ch 7.

[102] Estoppel operates within very narrow limits here: see, for example, *Moorgate Mercantile Co v Twitchings* [1977] AC 890, HL; *Lloyds & Scottish Finance Ltd v Williamson* [1965] 1 WLR 404, CA; *Eastern Distributors Ltd v Goldring* [1957] 2 QB 600, CA.

[103] Defined in s 1(1) of the Factors Act 1889.

[104] Defined in s 1(4), ibid.

[105] The consent must relate to possession of the goods in the capacity of a mercantile agent: *Pearson v Rose & Young Ltd* [1951] 1 KB 275, CA.

[106] Or pledges or otherwise disposes of the goods. A contract to sell the goods does not suffice.

[107] *Oppenheimer v Attenborough & Son* [1908] 1 KB 221, CA; *Pearson v Rose & Young Ltd* [1951] 1 KB 275, CA.

[108] By which is meant honesty in fact; see Sale of Goods Act 1979, s 61(3).

[109] Although constructive notice does not generally apply to commercial transactions (*Manchester Trust v Furness* [1895] 2 QB 539, CA), the test of notice probably contains an objective element so that the buyer cannot turn a blind eye to the obvious (*Feuer Leather Corporation v Frank Johnstone & Sons Ltd* [1981] Commercial LR 251, CA).

[110] Factors Act 1889, s 2(1).

[111] While the seller must continue in possession, he need not do so in his capacity as seller. He can do so as a bailee: *Pacific Motor Auctions Pty Ltd v Motor Credits (Hire Finance) Ltd* [1965] AC 867, PC; *Worcester Works Finance Ltd v Cooden Engineering Co Ltd* [1972] 1 QB 210, CA.

[112] Or pledge or otherwise dispose of the goods. There must be a delivery or transfer of the goods or documents of title to the subsequent buyer. It would appear that the delivery need not be actual

subsequent purchaser who buys in good faith and without knowledge of the previous sale.[113] Similarly, a seller who retains title to the goods but nevertheless allows a buyer or person who has agreed to buy[114] them into possession of the goods runs the risk that the buyer may sell[115] the goods to a subsequent buyer and so confer good title on that subsequent purchaser provided that he is in good faith and has no notice of the right of the original seller.[116] Where, however, the goods are stolen from the original owner, he will generally be able to recover them or their value even from a bona fide purchaser for value.[117] In such a case the owner has not entrusted the goods into the custody of another person and so cannot be said to have assumed the risk that they would be sold without his authority. The law has been criticized for its complexity.[118] Proposals were made to extend the scope of protection for innocent purchasers of goods[119] but they were not implemented.

(3) Risk of Loss or Damage[120]

(a) The prima facie rule and its displacement

10.24 The prima facie rule laid down in s 20(1) of the Act is that risk passes with property. So, if the seller is the owner of the goods at the time of loss or damage, then prima facie he is the one who must bear the loss, even if the goods are in the possession or control of the buyer; conversely if it is the buyer who is the owner of

---

but can be constructive: *Michael Gerson (Leasing) Ltd v Wilkinson* [2001] QB 514, CA, noted by Ulph (2001) 64 *MLR* 481.

113 Sale of Goods Act 1979, s 24.

114 A person who has obtained goods on hire-purchase terms has not agreed to buy the goods. It is thus vital in this context to distinguish between a conditional sale agreement and a hire-purchase agreement: see *Forthright Finance Ltd v Carlyle Finance Ltd* [1997] 4 All ER 90, CA.

115 Or pledge or otherwise dispose of the goods. There must be a delivery or transfer of the goods or documents of title to the subsequent buyer. It would appear that the delivery need not be actual but can be constructive: *Forsythe International (UK) Ltd v Silver Shipping Co Ltd* [1994] 1 WLR 1334, QBD.

116 Sale of Goods Act 1979, s 25(1). 'Good faith' is defined in s 61(3) of the Act and the test which the courts apply in relation to notice is an objective one: *Forsythe International (UK) Ltd v Silver Shipping Co Ltd* [1994] 1 WLR 1334, 1349–1351, QBD (see n 109 above).

117 *National Employers Mutual General Insurance Association Ltd v Jones* [1990] 1 AC 24, HL. But the old rule which enabled a buyer in 'market overt' to obtain good title (even against an owner whose goods had been stolen) has been abolished by the Sale of Goods (Amendment) Act 1994. While the 'market overt' rule protected the third party purchaser, and so could be said to have facilitated trade, its abuses, both actual and perceived, led to its abolition.

118 There are other exceptions to the *nemo dat* rule, notably Part III of the Hire-Purchase Act 1965 (re-enacted in Sch 4 to the Consumer Credit Act 1974), which applies to motor vehicles which are subject to a hire-purchase or conditional sale agreement.

119 DTI Consultation Document, Transfer of Title: Sections 21–26 of the Sale of Goods Act 1979 (DTI, January 1994). The DTI proposed that the present law should be replaced by a 'broad principle. . .that where the owner of goods has entrusted those goods to, or acquiesced in their possession by, another person, then an innocent purchaser of those goods should acquire good title'.

120 See generally L Sealy, 'Risk in the Law of Sale' [1972] CLJ 225.

the goods then he must bear the loss. This linkage of property and risk has been criticized as another example of the Act's pre-occupation with the importance of property. Many other legal systems link the passage of risk to possession or control of the goods.[121] However the rule laid down in the Act is only a prima facie one and it can be, and very often is, displaced by the express or implied terms of the contract. The passage of risk and property are most often decoupled in the case of international sales contracts, such as cif and fob contracts.[122] Similarly, a seller may reserve property in the goods until the buyer makes payment, but is unlikely to retain the risk of loss or damage to the goods which will pass to the buyer at an earlier stage.[123] In the case of contracts for the sale of goods from a bulk it is possible for risk to pass to the buyer before property passes provided that there is evidence, such as the transmission to the buyer of a delivery warrant entitling the buyer to take delivery of the goods, from which the court can infer that it was the intention of the parties that risk should pass to the buyer.[124] Where delivery has been delayed through the fault of the seller or the buyer the risk lies with the party at fault as regards any loss which might not have occurred but for such fault.[125]

(b) Goods that have already perished when the contract is made

In the case of a contract for the sale of specific goods,[126] and the goods without the knowledge of the seller have perished[127] at the time when the contract is made, **10.25**

---

121 A tendency which is reflected in Articles 67–9 of the Vienna Convention where the passage of risk is, broadly speaking, linked to control of the goods. Where, under a contract governed by English law, risk passes with possession or control of the goods that will be a product of the intention of the parties and not the default rule enshrined in the Act.

122 In the case of fob contracts risk generally passes on shipment (although the precise time in the shipment process when risk passes to the buyer remains unclear; see *Pyrene Co Ltd v Scindia Navigation Co Ltd* [1954] 2 QB 402, QBD, while property passes when the goods are loaded on board the ship. However it is not uncommon for sellers to take out the bill of lading in their own name with the intention of reserving property in the goods (see, for example, *The Ciudad de Pasto and Ciudad de Neiva* [1988] 2 Lloyd's Rep 208, CA); this practice does not affect the passage of risk. In the case of cif contracts risk passes as from the date of shipment, whereas property generally passes when the buyer makes payment in return for receipt of the relevant documents.

123 A fact which can cause problems for the buyer where the goods are damaged by the negligence of a third party, see *Leigh and Sillivan Ltd v Aliakmon Shipping Ltd* [1986] AC 785, HL. In such a case the buyer is unlikely to have a claim against the third party in tort but may possibly have an action in contract where the contract involves the carriage of goods by sea (see Carriage of Goods by Sea Act 1992, s 2(1)).

124 *Sterns Ltd v Vickers* [1923] 1 KB 78, CA where, it should be noted, that the warehouse-man had attorned to the buyer. The case may have been decided otherwise in the absence of such attornment. *Sterns* should be contrasted with *Healy v Howlett & Sons* [1917] 1 KB 337, KBD.

125 Sale of Goods Act 1979, s 20(2). The operation of this rule is illustrated by *Demby Hamilton & Co Ltd v Barden* [1949] 1 All ER 435, KBD.

126 As to the meaning of which see para 10.09 and n 32 above.

127 Which extends to goods which have been stolen (*Barrow, Lane & Ballard Ltd v Phillip Phillips & Co Ltd* [1929] 1 KB 574, KBD) but not to goods which have never existed (*McRae v Commonwealth Disposals Commission* (1951) 84 CLR, 377, High Court of Australia).

the contract is void.[128] Where the seller has assumed, or is held to have assumed, the risk of the non-existence of the goods, it may be that he can be held liable in damages,[129] although such a proposition does not fit easily with a strict reading of the Act.[130] Where there is an agreement to sell[131] specific goods[132] and subsequently the goods, without any fault[133] on the part of the seller or buyer, perish[134] before the risk passes to the buyer, the agreement is avoided.[135] In the case where only a part of the goods perish the agreement to sell is likely to be avoided in relation to the portion which has perished[136] but the obligation of the seller to deliver the goods which have not perished may still be enforceable.[137]

C. The Contract

(1) The Terms of the Contract

10.26   A contract of sale is likely to consist of a mixture of express and implied terms. Little needs to be said here about express terms. In the event of a dispute a court will interpret them in the usual way.[138] The implied terms are, however, a distinctive feature of the Sale of Goods Act 1979 and, as such, require greater comment. These terms are implied into the contract in an attempt to protect the position of a buyer of goods and substantial restrictions are placed upon the ability of a seller to exclude them.

---

128   Sale of Goods Act 1979, s 6. The section was probably intended to give effect to the decision of the House of Lords in *Couturier v Hastie* (1856) 5 HLC 673, HL, although the word 'mistake' was nowhere used in the judgments of their Lordships.

129   As was the case in *McRae v Commonwealth Disposals Commission* (1951) 84 CLR 377, High Court of Australia.

130   The fact that s 6 states that the contract is void and makes no provision for the parties to agree otherwise may suggest that the draftsman intended the rule to be absolute but this view is not supported by *Benjamin* (n 1 above) 1–132 or PS Atiyah (n 1 above) 103–108.

131   It is otherwise where there is a sale.

132   As to the meaning of which see para 10.09 and n 32 above.

133   Fault is defined in s 61(1) as 'wrongful act or default'.

134   As to the meaning of which see n 127 above.

135   Sale of Goods Act 1979, s 7.

136   See *Howell v Coupland* (1874) LR 9 QB 462; affd (1876) 1 QBD 258, CA. The case is, however, a difficult one, on which see G Treitel, *Frustration and Force Majeure* (2nd edn, 2004) 4–049 ff.

137   *HR and S Sainsbury Ltd v Street* [1972] 1 WLR 834, Assizes. However the buyer is not under an obligation to accept a partial delivery as a result of s 30(1) of the Sale of Goods Act 1979, see para 10.42.

138   The rules of construction adopted by the courts are set out in Chapter 8.

(a) Implied terms about title

(i) Right to sell the goods

10.27 Section 12(1) of the Act provides that there is an implied term that in the case of a sale the seller has 'a right[139] to sell the goods' and, in the case of an agreement to sell, that 'he will have such a right at the time when the property is to pass'.[140] This implied term has a temporal limitation. It applies only at the moment of sale or, in the case of an agreement to sell, at the moment at which property passes to the buyer; it has no future or continuing application.[141] This implied term has the status of a condition[142] so that a breach of it, in principle, gives to the buyer the right to reject the goods and terminate the contract. Section 12 provides evidence of the importance which English law attaches to the concept of property; what the buyer is deemed to have contracted for is title to the goods, not possession of them. Thus a buyer can reject the goods on the ground of the seller's lack of title to sell even where, prior to rejection, he was able to enjoy substantial possession and use of the goods.[143] These decisions have been criticized[144] on the ground that they resulted in the unjust enrichment of the buyers. But it can be argued that any such unjust enrichment was 'at the expense' of the true owner of the goods and not the seller so that there can be no justification for imposing on the buyer an obligation to pay the seller for the use of someone else's goods. A buyer who finds that he is unable to deal in the goods because, for example, he can be restrained by injunction from doing so, may be able to establish a breach of s 12(1).[145]

(ii) Free from undisclosed charge or incumbrance

10.28 Section 12(2) also implies a warranty[146] that the goods are free and will remain free until the time when the property is to pass from any charge or encumbrance

---

[139] The fact that the word used is 'right' not 'power' implies that there is a breach of s 12 even where the buyer obtains good title by virtue of an exception to the *nemo dat* rule. The point is not, however, resolved as a matter of authority. Dicta in *R v Wheeler* (1991) 92 Cr App Rep 279, CA support the view that there is a breach of s 12, whereas dicta in *Niblett v Confectioners' Materials Co* [1921] 3 KB 387, 401–2, CA and *Karlshamns Oljefabriker v Eastport Navigation Corporation (The Elafi)* [1981] 2 Lloyd's Rep 679, 685, QBD suggest the contrary. See generally I Brown, 'The Scope of Section 12 of the Sale of Goods Act' (1992) 108 LQR 221.

[140] Thus the seller under a conditional sale contract need only ensure that he has title to transfer at the moment when property passes to the buyer. But such a seller may be required by the express terms of the contract to be the owner of the goods at the moment of entry into the contract: *Barber v NWS Bank plc* [1996] 1 WLR 641, CA.

[141] *Microbeads AG v Vinhurst Road Markings Ltd* [1975] 1 WLR 218, 221–2, CA.

[142] Sale of Goods Act 1979, s 12(5A).

[143] *Rowland v Divall* [1923] 2 KB 500, CA; *Butterworth v Kingsway Motors Ltd* [1954] 1 WLR 1286, Assizes; *Barber v NWS Bank plc* [1996] 1 WLR 641, CA.

[144] See, for example, M Bridge, 'The Title Obligations of the Seller of Goods' in N Palmer and E McKendrick (eds), *Interests in Goods* (2nd edn, 1998) 303; *Benjamin* (n 1 above) 4–006.

[145] *Niblett v Confectioners' Materials Co* [1921] 3 KB 387, CA.

[146] Sale of Goods Act 1979, s 12(5A).

not disclosed or known to the buyer before the contract is made[147] and that the buyer will enjoy quiet possession of the goods except in so far as it may be disturbed by the owner or other person entitled to the benefit of any charge or encumbrance so disclosed or known.[148] The warranty of quiet possession is of a continuing nature and so can encompass future acts which may interrupt the buyer in his quiet possession of the goods.[149]

(iii) Exclusion clauses

10.29   While a seller cannot exclude liability to a buyer for breach of section 12,[150] he can agree 'to transfer only such title as he or a third person may have'.[151] The line between the sale of a limited title and the attempt to exclude liability is not always an easy one to draw.[152]

(b) Correspondence with description

10.30   Section 13(1) of the Act states that 'Where there is a contract for the sale of goods by description, there is an implied term[153] that the goods will correspond with the description.' This short sentence has proved to be one of the most troublesome in the whole Act. The nub of the problem is that not all descriptive words fall within the scope of the section and the courts have found it extremely difficult to devise a test which can distinguish those descriptive words which fall within its scope from those which do not. Some descriptive words may have no legal force at all.[154] Others may be mere representations which are not incorporated into the contract.[155] Many descriptive words are express, not implied terms of the

---

147   ibid s 12(2)(a). This subsection is of little if any practical significance. Most cases which fall within its scope also fall within s 12(1).

148   ibid s 12(2)(b).

149   *Microbeads AG v Vinhurst Road Markings Ltd* [1975] 1 WLR 218, CA; *Empresa Exportadora de Azucar v Industria Azucarera Nacional SA (The Playa Larga)* [1983] 2 Lloyd's Rep 171, CA. The ambit of the warranty, in terms of its duration, is not entirely clear. But it is not limited to disturbance by the seller himself; it can extend, in certain circumstances, to disturbance by a third party (see the *Microbeads* case at 222–3).

150   Unfair Contract Terms Act 1977, s 6(1)(a).

151   Sale of Goods Act 1979, s 12(3). A seller in such a case must also comply with the requirements laid down in s 12(4) and (5).

152   For example, in the context of exclusion clauses there has been a long debate over whether or not such clauses exist to define the obligations of the parties or whether they operate to provide a defence to a breach of an obligation.

153   The 'term' is stated to be a condition of the contract (s 13(1A)) so that a breach of it, in principle, gives the buyer the right to reject the goods and terminate the contract.

154   As in *Reardon Smith Lines Ltd v Hansen Tangen* [1976] 1 WLR 989, HL (in relation to the yard at which the ship was to be built).

155   *Oscar Chess Ltd v Williams* [1957] 1 WLR 370, CA. In such a case the usual remedies for misrepresentation will be available. The practical difficulty here is that it is often difficult to tell whether a statement is a term or a mere representation. On this distinction see Chapter 8.

contract and it cannot be the case that all express terms fall within the scope of s 13.[156]

(i) Requirement of sale 'by description'

The key to delimiting s 13 lies in the requirement that the sale must be one 'by description'. Some points are tolerably clear. Where the contract is one for the sale of unascertained goods[157] or future goods[158] the sale will generally be by description because the descriptive words will serve to identify the goods. More problematic is the application of s 13 to the sale of specific goods. Where the buyer has not seen the specific goods, the sale will generally be one by description.[159] Where the parties have met and the buyer has seen the goods, the simplest approach to take would have been to conclude that such a sale cannot be by description. However, the courts have refused to take this line and instead concluded that such a sale can, in appropriate circumstances, be by description.[160] To constitute a sale by description the buyer must show that the description was 'influential in the sale. . .so as to become an essential term. . .of the contract',[161] that he relied upon the descriptive words,[162] and that the words used served to identify the goods rather than their attributes.[163] Once it is concluded that the sale is 'by description' the standard applied by the courts is a very strict one[164] so that even minor deviations from specification in principle[165] give the buyer a right to reject the goods and terminate the contract.

10.31

---

156 If they did, s 13 would amount to a statement that there is an *implied* term that the seller must comply with the *express* terms of the contract.

157 Defined in n 33 above.

158 Defined in para 10.09 and n 31 above. Not all sales of future goods are by description. Where the goods have been requested by the buyer and are in the ownership of a third party, the sale may not be one by description.

159 As in *Varley v Whipp* [1900] 1 KB 513, QBD.

160 *Grant v Australian Knitting Mills Ltd* [1936] AC 85, 100, HL. Further s 13(3) of the Act states that a sale is not prevented from being a sale by description by reason only that the goods, having been exposed for sale or hire, are selected by the buyer.

161 *Harlingdon & Leinster Enterprises Ltd v Christopher Hull Fine Art Ltd* [1991] 1 QB 564, 571, CA.

162 ibid 574, CA. The invocation of reliance here has not gone without criticism.

163 The line between identity and attributes is a notoriously difficult one to draw but it has been invoked by the courts in this context: see, for example, *Ashington Piggeries Ltd v Christopher Hill Ltd* [1972] AC 441, 503–4, HL and *Reardon Smith Line Ltd v Yngvar Hansen-Tangen* [1976] 1 WLR 989, 999, HL.

164 See, for example, *Arcos Ltd v EA Ronaasen & Son* [1933] AC 470, HL and *Re Moore & Co and Landauer & Co* [1921] 2 KB 519, CA. These cases might now be decided differently as a result of the enactment of s 15A of the Sale of Goods Act 1979.

165 Subject to the controls enacted in s 15A of the Sale of Goods Act 1979. There had been a suggestion that the courts would themselves reconsider the appropriateness of such a strict approach (*Reardon Smith Line Ltd v Yngvar Hansen-Tangen* [1976] 1 WLR 989, 998, HL) but that reconsideration never took place.

(ii) Exclusion clauses

10.32 Section 13 applies to all contracts of sale; it is not confined to sales which take place in the course of a business.[166] As against a consumer, the implied term cannot be excluded;[167] as against a person dealing otherwise than as a consumer, the term can be excluded if it is reasonable to do so.[168]

(c) Satisfactory quality and fitness for purpose

10.33 Reflecting the influence which the principle of *caveat emptor* has exerted over the development of sale of goods law, there is no implied term 'about the quality or fitness for any particular purpose of goods supplied under a contract of sale'[169] other than those expressly provided for in sections 14 and 15 of the Act. Section 14 contains two such terms, namely that the goods must be of 'satisfactory quality'[170] and they must be reasonably fit for their purpose.[171] These implied terms only apply where the seller[172] sells 'in the course of a business' but these words are to be given a wide construction[173] and do not require that the seller habitually or regularly deal in goods of the type sold.[174] What is excluded from the Act is a 'purely private sale of goods outside the confines of the business (if any) carried on by the seller'.[175]

(i) Of satisfactory quality

10.34 The implied term[176] that the goods supplied under the contract must be of satisfactory quality is of relatively recent origin, having been first introduced in the Sale and Supply of Goods Act 1994. It replaced the implied term which required that the goods be of 'merchantable quality'. As yet there is still relatively little case

---

166 As is the case with the terms implied by s 14 of the Act.

167 Unfair Contract Terms Act 1977, s 6(2).

168 ibid s 6(3).

169 Sale of Goods Act 1979, s 14(1).

170 ibid s 14(2).

171 ibid s 14(3).

172 Where the sale is effected by an agent acting in the course of a business, the principal is caught by these implied terms unless the principal is not selling in the course of a business and either the buyer knows the fact or reasonable steps are taken to bring it to the notice of the buyer before the contract is made: ibid s 14(5). This provision applies to undisclosed principals, in which case both the principal and the agent may incur liability (*Boyter v Thomson* [1995] 2 AC 629, HL).

173 *Stevenson v Rogers* [1999] QB 1028, CA (sale by fisherman of his fishing boat held to take place in the course of his business); cf *Feldarol Foundry plc v Hermes Leasing (London) Ltd* [2004] EWCA Civ 747, CA and *R & B Customers Brokers Co Ltd v United Dominion Trust Ltd* [1988] 1 WLR 321, CA where a much narrower construction was adopted of the words 'in the course of a business' in the context of s 12 of the Unfair Contract Terms Act 1977.

174 'Business' is defined in s 61(1) of the Sale of Goods Act 1979 as including 'a profession and the activities of any government department. . .or local or public authority'.

175 *Stevenson v Rogers* [1999] QB 1028, 1039, CA. The potential anomalies created by this decision are explored by I Brown, 'Sale of Goods in the Course of a Business' (1999) 115 LQR 384.

176 The term is declared to be a condition by s 14(6).

law on the meaning of 'satisfactory quality.'[177] In these circumstances the cases on the meaning of 'merchantable quality' may continue to provide limited assistance,[178] albeit that Parliament did not intend 'satisfactory quality' to be synonymous with 'merchantable quality'. The guidance within the Act itself is very limited. Its central provision is rather vague, if not circular. It states that 'goods are of satisfactory quality if they meet the standard that a reasonable person would regard as satisfactory, taking account of any description of the goods, the price (if relevant) and all the other relevant factors'[179] but does not state what a reasonable person would expect. However the Act does provide an indication of the factors which may be relevant.[180] The quality of the goods includes their state and condition and 'in appropriate cases'[181] the following may be aspects of the quality of goods: (a) fitness for all the purposes for which goods of the kind in question are commonly supplied,[182] (b) appearance and finish, (c) freedom from minor defects, (d) safety,[183] and (e) durability.[184] This indicative list has clearly been drafted principally with consumer contracts in mind and may not apply so well to commercial contracts, although it must be said that, to some extent, the list has simply made explicit what was implicit in the case law on merchantable quality.[185] The satisfactory quality implied term establishes a 'general standard which goods are required to reach',[186] and it is 'primarily directed towards

---

[177] The leading cases include *Balmoral Group Ltd v Borealis (UK) Ltd* [2006] EWHC 1900 (Comm); [2006] 2 Lloyd's Rep 629 [140]–[141]; *Bramhill v Edwards* [2004] EWCA Civ 403; [2004] 2 Lloyd's Rep 653; *Jewson Ltd v Boyhan* [2003] EWCA Civ 1030; [2004] 1 Lloyd's Rep 505 and *Britvic Soft Drinks Ltd v Messer UK Ltd* [2002] 1 Lloyd's Rep 20 (the meaning of 'satisfactory quality' was not considered when the case was appealed to the Court of Appeal).

[178] Some of the leading cases on 'merchantable quality' are briefly summarized in *Benjamin* (n 1 above) 11-044. The influence of these cases is likely to become increasingly muted as time goes by.

[179] Sale of Goods Act 1979, s 14(2A). A relevant circumstance may be the fact that the goods were second-hand (see, for example, *Bartlett v Sidney Marcus Ltd* [1965] 1 WLR 1013, CA; cf *Shine v General Guarantee Corp Ltd* [1988] 1 All ER 911, CA).

[180] Sale of Goods Act 1979, s 14(2B).

[181] What constitutes an 'appropriate case' is a matter of conjecture. It may mean no more than the factors listed are not decisive.

[182] The use of the word 'all' rather than 'some' imposes a higher standard on the seller than was the case under the old 'merchantable quality' standard (where the goods had only to be fit for 'one or more' purposes: *Aswan Engineering Establishment Ltd v Lupdine Ltd* [1987] 1 WLR 1, CA). But note the word 'commonly' which is likely to qualify the seller's obligations.

[183] Where the goods are unsafe a claim may also arise under Part I of the Consumer Protection Act 1987, on which see paras 17.285–17.289.

[184] While durability is undoubtedly a relevant factor, it remains the case that the time at which the goods must be of satisfactory quality is the time of sale.

[185] For example, freedom from minor defects and the appearance and finish of the goods were regarded as relevant factors in *Rogers v Parish (Scarborough) Ltd* [1987] QB 933, 944, CA. The relevance of the durability of the goods was much more uncertain under the old law, although there were some dicta which indicated that it was pertinent (see, for example, *Lambert v Lewis* [1982] AC 225, 276, HL).

[186] *Jewson Ltd v Boyhan* [2003] EWCA Civ 1030; [2004] 1 Lloyd's Rep 505, [46].

substandard goods.'[187] In the case where the buyer deals as a consumer, the factors to be taken into account also include any public statements on the specific characteristics of the goods made about them by the seller, the producer or his representative, particularly in advertising or on labelling. However a public statement is not to be taken into account if the seller shows that (i) at the time the contract was made, he was not, and could not reasonably have been, aware of the statement, (ii) before the contract was made, the statement had been withdrawn in public or, to the extent that it contained anything which was incorrect or misleading, it had been corrected in public, or (iii) the decision to buy the goods could not have been influenced by the statement.[188] Liability is, in principle, strict.[189] Essentially the question whether or not goods are of satisfactory quality is a jury-type issue, involving questions of degree, albeit with the scales weighted in favour of the consumer buyer.

10.35 The implied term does not extend to any matter (a) which is specifically drawn to the buyer's attention before the contract is made, (b) in the case where the buyer examines the goods before the contract is made, which that[190] examination ought to reveal[191] or, (c) in the case of a sale by sample, a matter which would have been apparent on a reasonable examination of the sample.[192]

(ii) Fit for their purpose

10.36 In order to establish a breach of the implied term[193] that the goods must be reasonably fit for their purpose,[194] the buyer must expressly or by implication make known to the seller[195] any particular purpose for which the goods are being bought, whether or not that is a purpose for which such goods are commonly supplied. Thus, where goods are bought for their customary purpose the buyer need not disclose it; the court will imply that that is the purpose for which the goods have

---

[187] *Balmoral Group Ltd v Borealis (UK) Ltd* [2006] EWHC 1900 (Comm); [2006] 2 Lloyd's Rep 629 [140].

[188] Sections 14(2D)–(2F) of the Sale of Goods Act 1979. These provisions were inserted into the 1979 Act by the Sale and Supply of Goods to Consumers Regulations 2002 (SI 2002, No. 3045).

[189] That is to say, there is no requirement that the seller be at fault in any way.

[190] In other words, the examination actually carried out, not one which might have been but was not carried out. This point was overlooked by the Court of Appeal in *Bramhill v Edwards* [2004] EWCA Civ 403; [2004] 2 Lloyd's Rep 653, [51], [54] (on which see C Twigg-Flesner 'Examination prior to purchase: a cautionary note' (2005) 121 LQR 205).

[191] Where the defect is latent it should not be particularly difficult to show that the buyer ought not to have discovered it (see, for example, *Wren v Holt* [1903] 1 KB 610).

[192] Sale of Goods Act 1979, s 14(2C). The onus would appear to be on the seller to show that the implied term is not applicable.

[193] The term is declared to be a condition by s 14(6).

[194] Sale of Goods Act 1979, s 14(3).

[195] Or, where the purchase price or part of it is payable by instalments and the goods were previously sold by a credit-broker to the seller, to that credit-broker.

been bought.[196] A 'particular purpose' means 'a given purpose, known or communicated' and 'is not necessarily a narrow or closely particularised purpose'.[197] The
purpose may therefore be a wide one and extend to the foreseeable range of purposes for which such goods are bought.[198] On the other hand, where goods are
required for a special or unusual purpose, the buyer must generally make that
purpose known to the seller.[199] Where the failure of the goods to meet the intended
purpose arises from an idiosyncrasy, either of the buyer himself or in the circumstances of his use of the goods, which has not been made known to the seller the
seller is not liable, even in the case where the buyer was unaware of the idiosyncrasy.[200] The buyer need not prove that he has relied upon the skill and judgment
of the seller; it is for the seller to prove that he did not so rely[201] or that his reliance
was unreasonable.[202] Liability of the seller is, in principle, strict[203] but the extent
of the obligation is only to sell goods which are *reasonably* fit for their purpose;
they need not be completely or absolutely suitable for their purpose.[204] The
absence or inadequacy of instructions or warnings may render goods not reasonably fit for their purpose.[205]

(iii) Exclusion clauses

As against a consumer, these two implied terms cannot be excluded;[206] as against
a person dealing otherwise than as a consumer, they can be excluded if it is reasonable to do so.[207]

10.37

---

[196] *Priest v Last* [1903] 2 KB 148, CA.

[197] *Henry Kendall & Sons v William Lillico & Sons Ltd* [1969] 2 AC 31, 114, HL.

[198] *Ashington Piggeries Ltd v Christopher Hill Ltd* [1972] AC 441, 477, HL; *Henry Kendall &
Sons (a firm) v William Lillico & Sons Ltd* [1969] 2 AC 31, 114–15, HL; cf *Aswan Engineering
Establishment Ltd v Lupdine Ltd* [1987] 1 WLR 1, 16–17, CA.

[199] *Slater v Finning Ltd* [1997] AC 473, 487, HL. Where the buyer does disclose his purpose in
buying, the specifications laid down by the buyer are likely to limit the range of goods which can
satisfy the purpose: see, for example, *Bristol Tramways etc Carriage Co Ltd v Fiat Motors Ltd* [1910]
2 KB 731, CA.

[200] *Slater v Finning Ltd* [1997] AC 473, HL; *Griffiths v Peter Conway Ltd* [1939] 1 All ER 685,
CA. However a seller may be liable where the goods are likely to cause damage in a wide range of
circumstances, but are particularly dangerous in relation to the use to which the claimant put the
goods: *Ashington Piggeries Ltd v Christopher Hill Ltd* [1972] AC 441, HL.

[201] As, for example, where the buyer relied on his own skill and judgment (see *Tehran-Europe Co
Ltd v ST Belton (Tractors) Ltd* [1968] 2 QB 545, CA). The fact that the buyer has provided specifica-
tions for the goods does not exclude the possibility of reliance by the buyer on the seller (*Cammell
Laird & Co Ltd v Manganese Bronze and Brass Co Ltd* [1934] AC 402, HL).

[202] *Jewson Ltd v Boyhan* [2003] EWCA Civ 1030; [2004] 1 Lloyd's Rep 505 [61].

[203] *Frost v Aylesbury Dairy Co Ltd* [1905] 1 KB 608, CA; *Henry Kendall & Sons v William Lillico &
Sons Ltd* [1969] 2 AC 31, 84, HL.

[204] *Henry Kendall & Sons v William Lillico & Sons Ltd* [1969] 2 AC 31, 115, HL; *Bartlett v Sidney
Marcus Ltd* [1965] 1 WLR 1013, CA.

[205] *Wormell v RHM Agricultural (East) Ltd* [1987] 1 WLR 1091, CA (albeit that on the facts the
goods were found to be reasonably fit for their purpose).

[206] Unfair Contract Terms Act 1977, s 6(2).

[207] ibid s 6(3).

(d) Correspondence with sample

10.38   Section 15 of the Act implies a term[208] that, in the case of a sale by sample,[209] the bulk will correspond with the sample in quality[210] and that the goods will be free from any defect making their quality unsatisfactory which would not be apparent on a reasonable examination of the sample.[211] This implied term applies to all sales, not only to those which take place in the course of a business. As against a consumer, this implied term cannot be excluded;[212] as against a person dealing otherwise than as a consumer, it can be excluded if it is reasonable to do so.[213]

(2) *Performance of the Contract*

10.39   Other than compliance with the implied terms, the principal obligation of the seller is to deliver the goods. The buyer in turn must accept and pay for them in accordance with the terms of the contract of sale.[214] Unless otherwise agreed, delivery and payment are concurrent conditions.[215] Both obligations are frequently regulated by the express terms of the contract. In the absence of an express term, the Act lays down some default rules, particularly in the case of delivery.

(a) Delivery

10.40   Delivery is defined in the Act as 'the voluntary transfer of possession from one person to another'.[216] In most domestic sale transactions delivery will take the form of the transfer of physical possession of the goods to the buyer. But it need not do so. Delivery can be constructive in the sense that what is transferred to the buyer is control of the goods[217] rather than physical possession. Thus in international sale transactions the seller will often perform his delivery obligation by

---

[208]   The term has the status of a condition: Sale of Goods Act 1979, s 15(3).

[209]   A contract for sale by sample is made where there is an express or implied term to that effect in the contract: ibid s 15(1).

[210]   The correspondence must be precise (*E & S Ruben v Faire Bros Ltd* [1949] 1 KB 254, QBD) unless the sample is intended for visual examination only, where material differences may not involve a breach by the seller (*FE Hookway & Co Ltd v Alfred Isaacs & Son* [1954] 1 Lloyd's Rep 491, QBD).

[211]   *James Drummond and Sons v EH Van Ingen & Co Ltd* (1887) 12 App Cas 284, 297, HL.

[212]   Unfair Contract Terms Act 1977, s 6(2).

[213]   ibid s 6(3).

[214]   Sale of Goods Act 1979, s 27.

[215]   ibid s 28. Thus the seller must be ready and willing to give possession of the goods to the buyer in exchange for the price and the buyer must be ready and willing to pay the price in exchange for the possession of the goods. In the case of documentary sales, the obligation of the buyer is generally to pay the price in exchange for the relevant documents.

[216]   ibid s 61(1).

[217]   Another example might be the transfer of some object, such as a key, which gives physical control over the goods themselves. This is sometimes regarded as a form of constructive delivery but it might be more accurate to regard it as a species of physical delivery.

transferring to the buyer a bill of lading which will give the buyer legal control over the goods.[218] Where the goods are in the possession of a third party at the time of entry into the contract of sale, there is no delivery of the goods until the third party attorns to the buyer.[219] Where the seller is authorized or required to send the goods to the buyer, delivery of the goods to a carrier (whether named by the buyer or not) for the purpose of transmission to the buyer is prima facie deemed to be a delivery of goods to the buyer.[220] The seller must, however, enter into a reasonable contract of carriage with the carrier.[221] Where the seller agrees to deliver the goods at his own risk at a place other than where they are sold, the buyer must nevertheless, unless otherwise agreed, take any risk of deterioration in the goods necessarily incident to the course of transit.[222]

(i) Related conditions

Unless otherwise agreed, the place of delivery is the seller's place of business[223] so that it is the duty of the buyer to collect the goods. If no time for delivery is fixed by the contract[224] and the seller is bound to send the goods to the buyer, he must do so within a reasonable time.[225] Delivery must be made or tendered at a reasonable hour.[226] The seller must bear the cost of delivering the goods and of putting the goods into a deliverable state[227] while the buyer must bear the cost of receiving delivery. **10.41**

---

[218] In the case of a cif contract the seller's delivery obligation actually relates to the documents rather than the goods: see *Benjamin* (n 1 above) 19-072. A cif seller must not prevent delivery of the goods from taking place but he is not under an obligation to ensure that actual delivery of the goods takes place.

[219] Sale of Goods Act 1979, s 29(4). A third party attorns to the buyer when he acknowledges to the buyer that he holds the goods on the buyer's behalf.

[220] ibid s 32(1).

[221] ibid s 32(2). A failure to do so may entitle the buyer to reject the goods or to claim damages. Where the goods are sent by a route involving sea transit the seller must give the buyer sufficient notice to enable him to insure the goods. A failure to do so has the consequence that the goods remain at the risk of the seller: Sale of Goods Act 1979, s 32(3). This subsection has been held to apply to fob contracts (*Wimble Sons & Co v Rosenberg & Sons* [1913] 3 KB 743, CA).

[222] Sale of Goods Act 1979, s 33. This provision does not apply to fob and cif contracts where the goods are generally at the buyer's risk after shipment.

[223] ibid s 29(2). However in the case of a contract for the sale of specific goods, which to the knowledge of both parties at the date of entry into the contract are in some other place, the place of delivery is that other place.

[224] Note that contracts may frequently provide that the time of delivery is of the essence of the contract. Breach of such a time stipulation will give the buyer the right to terminate further performance of the contract, on which see para 10.45.

[225] Sale of Goods Act 1979, s 29(3).

[226] ibid s 29(5).

[227] ibid s 29(6).

(ii) Delivery of incorrect quantity

10.42   Where the seller delivers insufficient goods to the buyer, the buyer may reject them or he may accept them;[228] the choice is his. If he does accept them he must pay for them at the contract rate. Where the seller delivers more than he contracted to sell the buyer may reject all of the goods delivered, accept the amount for which he contracted and reject the surplus or accept the entire delivery and pay for the excess at the contract rate.[229] Once again, the choice belongs to the buyer. The buyer's right to reject is however restricted where the buyer does not deal as consumer; in such a case the buyer cannot reject the goods where the shortfall or the excess is so slight that it would be unreasonable for him to reject.[230]

(iii) Delivery in instalments

10.43   Instalment deliveries are rather more complex. A buyer is not bound to accept delivery of goods by instalments unless he agrees to do so.[231] Where the buyer does so agree and the seller makes defective deliveries in respect of one or more instalment the buyer is not necessarily entitled to terminate the whole contract;[232] it depends upon the seriousness of the breach in relation to the delivery obligation as a whole and the likelihood of the breach being repeated.[233]

(b) Payment

10.44   The buyer's obligation to pay the price (in terms of method, place and time of payment) will generally be governed by the terms of the contract. The Act does not purport to regulate the payment obligations of the buyer in any detail. It does however provide that time of payment is not of the essence of the contract unless provision is made in the contract to this effect.[234] Sellers frequently insert such a provision in the contract.[235]

---

228   Sale of Goods Act 1979, s 30(1).

229   ibid s 30(2) and (3).

230   ibid s 30(2A). This provision is 'subject to any usage of trade, special agreement, or course of dealing between the parties' (s 35(5)). It is equivalent to s 15A of the Act and the points made in relation to that section (in para 10.46) are equally applicable here.

231   ibid s 31(1).

232   ibid s 31(2). The same principle applies where the buyer fails to pay the price for one or more instalments which has been delivered.

233   *Maple Flock Co Ltd v Universal Furniture Products (Wembley) Ltd* [1934] 1 KB 148, CA.

234   Sale of Goods Act 1979, s 10(1).

235   The consequences to a buyer of a failure to make payment on time when time is declared to be of the essence can be severe: see *Lombard North Central plc v Butterworth* [1987] QB 527, CA (a case which actually involves a contract of hire but the point also holds good for contracts of sale).

D. Remedies

(1) The Importance of Termination

(a) The pursuit of certainty

In the event of a failure by a seller or a buyer to perform his obligations under the **10.45** contract of sale, the law could adopt one of three different approaches. It could encourage the parties to stay together and seek to sort out their difficulties, it could encourage them to walk away from the deal and seek satisfaction elsewhere or it could adopt some combination of these two approaches. English law has tended to take the second of the three approaches, while the Vienna Convention inclines rather more in the direction of the first.[236] Thus in English law the right of a seller or a buyer to cure his failure to perform in accordance with the terms of the contract operates within narrow confines[237] and there is little emphasis on abatement or reduction of the price as a remedy in the event of breach.[238] The focus is very much on termination of the contract and claims for damages. It is for this reason that the implied terms relating to title to sell, correspondence with description and sample, satisfactory quality and fitness for purpose are all declared to be conditions[239] so that, until recently, any breach, no matter how insignificant, in principle entitled the buyer to reject the goods and terminate the contract. Similarly, sellers often make time of payment of the essence of the contract so that in the event of failure by the buyer to pay on time they can simply terminate the contract. The entitlement to terminate is thus based on the nature of the term broken rather than on the consequences of the breach for the party seeking to terminate.[240]

---

[236] For a very helpful discussion of the remedial provisions of the Vienna Convention from the perspective of an English lawyer see FMB Reynolds, 'A Note of Caution' in P Birks (ed), *The Frontiers of Liability* (1994), 18.

[237] A contracting party may be able to cure his defective performance provided that there is still time for him to tender performance in accordance with the terms of the contract: see generally A Apps, 'The Right to Cure Defective Performance' [1994] *LMCLQ* 525. The right to cure does not, however, extend beyond the contract period, as in s 2-508 of the Uniform Commercial Code and Article 48 of the Vienna Convention.

[238] While price reduction may be a remedy which is used by parties in practice, it was not, until the enactment in 2003 of s 48C of the Sale of Goods Act 1979 (see 10.67—10.68), the subject of much discussion in the books. Contrast, for example, Article 50 of the Vienna Convention.

[239] The meaning and significance of the classification of a term as a 'condition' is discussed in Chapter 8.

[240] This is subject to an important qualification in the case of innominate terms where the courts do focus on the consequences of the breach when deciding whether or not a party is entitled to terminate. See generally *Hong Kong Fir Shipping Co Ltd v Kawasaki Kisen Kaisha Ltd* [1962] 2 QB 26, CA, discussed in more detail in Chapter 8 and, for an application of this type of approach to a contract for the sale of goods, see *Cehave NV v Bremer Handelsgesellschaft mbH (The Hansa Nord)* [1976] QB 44, CA. The Vienna Convention, in Article 25, places greater emphasis on the consequences of the breach.

The advantage of this approach is that it has the appearance of certainty and clarity.[241] It has been applied strictly by the English courts, particularly in relation to compliance with time stipulations.[242] But the price has been a certain harshness in application, especially in the case where a party relies on a 'technical' breach of a condition in order to escape from what has turned out to be a bad bargain.[243] The pursuit of certainty also proved to be something of a double-edged sword for the party seeking to terminate because the courts insisted that the right to terminate be exercised within a very short time: the seller as well as the buyer was entitled to know where he stood.[244]

(b) Restrictions on the right to reject: s 15A of the 1979 Act

10.46 This emphasis on the virtues of certainty has, however, been reduced as a result of the intervention of Parliament which has effected a delicate but important shift in the balance of rights as between seller and buyer. The right of the buyer to reject the goods has been curtailed but, where the right does arise, the buyer may now have a longer period of time in which to exercise it. The restraint on the right of the buyer[245] to reject is to be found in s 15A of the Sale of Goods Act 1979[246] which states that, where the buyer does not deal as a consumer[247] and he has established the existence of a right to reject by virtue of a breach by the seller of one of the implied terms contained in ss 13–15 of the Act[248] but the consequences of the breach are so 'slight' that it would be unreasonable for him to reject the goods, the buyer is confined to a remedy in damages and cannot terminate the contract.

---

[241] In that, once it has been established that the term broken is a condition, the right to terminate is clear. However, outside the statutory implied terms, the appearance of certainty may be deceptive because of the doubt which can exist as to whether or not the term is a condition in the first place: see, for example, *Compagnie Commerciale Sucres et Denrées v C Czarnikow Ltd (The Naxos)* [1990] 1 WLR 1337, HL where the judges had great difficulty in deciding whether or not the term broken was a condition.

[242] See for example *Bowes v Shand* (1877) 2 App Cas 455, HL, *Bunge Corporation v Tradax Export SA* [1981] 1 WLR 711, HL and *Compagnie Commerciale Sucres et Denrées v C Czarnikow Ltd (The Naxos)* [1990] 1 WLR 1337, HL.

[243] See for example *Arcos Ltd v EA Ronaasen & Son* [1933] AC 470, HL.

[244] The most notorious example of the speed with which a buyer was required to exercise his right to reject is *Bernstein v Pamson Motors (Golders Green) Ltd* [1987] 2 All ER 220, QBD. However, in the light of the amendment made to s 35 of the 1979 Act in 1994, *Bernstein* no longer represents the law today: see n 263 below.

[245] There is no equivalent restraint on the right of the seller and, on this basis, the new provision is open to criticism.

[246] Inserted by s 4 of the Sale and Supply of Goods Act 1994.

[247] Defined in s 12 of the Unfair Contract Terms Act 1977. Rejection was thought to be a particularly valuable remedy for the consumer buyer and so no further restrictions were enacted on its exercise.

[248] Thus the restriction on the right to reject does not apply to a breach of s 12(1) of the Sale of Goods Act 1979, nor does it apply to breach of an express term of the contract which has been classified as a condition.

There is, as yet, no case law under s 15A and so it is not clear what constitutes a 'slight' breach for this purpose.[249] It is for the seller to show that the breach is so slight that it would be unreasonable for the buyer to reject the goods.[250] The thrust of the legislation is clear; it aims to prevent buyers from getting out of what is no more than a bad bargain. But in doing so it has introduced uncertainty into commercial transactions.[251] For example, it is not clear what impact the reform will have on the strict approach which the courts have taken towards time stipulations.[252] Section 15A applies 'unless a contrary intention appears in, or is to be implied from, the contract'.[253] But will the courts imply a contrary intention from the commercial context so as to preserve the traditional approach to time stipulations? No clear answer can be given to this question. Much is likely to depend upon the facts of the particular case.[254]

(c) Waiver and acceptance

The prima facie right to terminate the contract may be lost in certain situations, for example, where the buyer or seller is held to have waived the breach in respect of which he now seeks to terminate the contract.[255]   **10.47**

The Act also places limits upon a buyer's right to reject the goods. A buyer cannot reject the goods once he is deemed to have accepted them. Acceptance may occur in one of three ways. First, where the buyer intimates to the seller that he has accepted the goods.[256] Secondly, a buyer will be held to have accepted the goods when the goods have been delivered to him, and he does any act in relation to   **10.48**

---

[249] It cannot be assumed that the effect of the section is to turn the implied terms in ss 13–15 into innominate terms or that it has brought English law into line with Article 25 of the Vienna Convention. A breach may not substantially deprive the buyer of the benefit of the bargain (and so satisfy the test in order to enable the buyer to terminate on the occurrence of a breach of an innominate term) but not be 'slight' either so that the buyer remains free to reject. The section has brought English law closer to the Vienna Convention but it is not identical.

[250] Sale of Goods Act 1979, s 15A(3).

[251] And so has been criticized on that ground: see, for example, G Treitel, *The Law of Contract* (11th edn, 2003) 801–2.

[252] See n 242 above.

[253] Sale of Goods Act 1979, s 15A(2).

[254] The onus of proof of establishing a contrary intent is likely to be upon the seller. In the case of commodity contracts it might not be difficult to lead evidence of a contrary intent, but in other markets it might not be so easy for the seller to adduce such evidence.

[255] Waiver is discussed in more detail in Chapter 8. The application of the doctrines of waiver and estoppel to documentary sales has proved to be particularly problematic. The source of the problem is the decision of the Court of Appeal in *Panchaud Frères SA v Etablissements General Grain Co* [1970] 1 Lloyd's Rep 53, CA, although it has now been held that the case is simply an authority for the application of s 35 of the Act to the case where a cif buyer accepts the documents but rejects or purports to reject the goods (*Glencore Grain Rotterdam BV v Lebanese Organization for International Commerce* [1997] 4 All ER 514, 530–1, CA).

[256] Sale of Goods Act 1979, s 35(1)(a). The intimation may be express or implied.

them which is inconsistent with the ownership of the seller.[257] But, crucially, where goods are delivered to a buyer, and he has not previously examined them, he is not deemed to have accepted them until he has had a reasonable opportunity of examining them for the purpose of ascertaining whether they are in conformity with the contract and, in the case of a contract for sale by sample, of comparing the bulk with the sample.[258] Unless otherwise agreed, a seller must on request give a buyer 'a reasonable opportunity of examining the goods for the purpose of ascertaining whether or not they are in conformity with the contract'.[259] The place of examination is prima facie the place of delivery, although this presumption is frequently displaced in practice.[260] Finally, a buyer will be deemed to have accepted the goods when, after the lapse of a reasonable time, he retains the goods without intimating to the seller that he has rejected them[261] and, in deciding whether or not a reasonable time has elapsed, the court will consider whether the buyer has had a reasonable opportunity of examining the goods.[262] In the interests of finality the courts previously gave buyers a very short period of time in which to examine the goods[263] but, as a consequence of the amendment introduced the courts now adopt a more benevolent approach when determining what constitutes a reasonable time. Whether or not a reasonable time has elapsed is a matter of fact to be considered in the light of all the circumstances of the case.[264]

10.49 A buyer is not deemed to have accepted the goods merely because he asks for, or agrees to, their repair by or under an arrangement with the seller[265] or because the

---

[257] Sale of Goods Act 1979, s 35(1)(b). The exact meaning of this provision is far from clear. It covers the case where the buyer destroys the goods or otherwise deals with them in such a way that they cannot be restored to the seller. See also *Clegg v Andersson* [2003] EWCA Civ 320; [2003] 2 Lloyd's Rep 32 at [57]–[60].

[258] ibid s 35(2). Where the buyer deals as consumer he cannot lose this right by agreement, waiver or otherwise: ibid s 35(3).

[259] ibid s 34.

[260] Particularly in the case of documentary or overseas sales.

[261] Sale of Goods Act 1979, s 35(4).

[262] ibid s 35(5).

[263] *Bernstein v Pamson Motors (Golders Green) Ltd* [1987] 2 All ER 220, QBD. However, the Court of Appeal in *Clegg v Andersson* [2003] EWCA Civ 320; [2003] 2 Lloyd's Rep 32 at [63] concluded that *Bernstein v Pamson Motors (Golders Green) Ltd* no longer represents the law, given the amendments made to the original s 35 of the 1979 Act by the Sale and Supply of Goods Act 1994. Hale LJ stated at [76] that 'if a buyer is seeking information which the seller has agreed to supply which will enable the buyer to make a properly informed choice between acceptance, rejection or cure, and if cure in what way, he cannot have lost his right to reject.' (see FMB Reynolds 'Loss of the right to reject' (2003) 119 LQR 544). There is, however, no absolute rule that a buyer cannot have lost the right to reject while a period of repair is in progress or while a complaint by the buyer and a request for information is being processed by the seller (*Jones v Gallagher (trading as Gallery Kitchens and Bathrooms* [2004] EWCA Civ 10; [2005] 1 Lloyd's Rep 377 (on which see R Bradgate 'Remedying the unfit fitted kitchen' (2004) 120 LQR 558).

[264] Sale of Goods Act 1979, s 59; *Jones v Gallagher (trading as Gallery Kitchens and Bathrooms)* [2004] EWCA Civ 10; [2005] 1 Lloyd's Rep 377.

[265] Sale of Goods Act 1979, s 35(6)(a), on which see *J & H Ritchie Ltd v Lloyd Ltd* [2007] UKHL 9; [2007] 1 WLR 670. In the light of the decision in *Ritchie* it is likely to be necessary to examine the

goods are delivered to another under a sub-sale or other disposition.[266] A buyer also has a right of partial rejection, so that a buyer who has the right to reject goods by reason of a breach on the part of the seller that affects some or all of them may accept some of the goods, including, where there are any goods unaffected by the breach, all such goods.[267]

(d) No obligation to return rejected goods

A buyer who lawfully rejects the goods is not obliged to return them to the seller; **10.50** unless otherwise agreed, the buyer need only intimate to the seller that he refuses to accept the goods.[268]

(2) Remedies of the Seller

The remedies available to the seller in the event of buyer default may be either **10.51** personal or proprietary.

(a) Proprietary remedies

When the buyer is insolvent proprietary remedies obviously assume considerable **10.52** significance. Contracts for the sale of goods often make their own provision for proprietary remedies via the use of retention of title clauses. The limited efficacy of these clauses has already been noted.[269]

The Act itself makes provision for a number of real remedies which the seller can **10.53** exercise against the goods themselves and these can give the seller some protection in the event of buyer insolvency. The rights are, however, hedged round by a number of restrictions which limit their practical utility.[270] These rights are available to an 'unpaid seller' and are applicable notwithstanding the fact that

---

arrangement made between the seller and the buyer in relation to the repair of the goods with some care. A buyer who allows a seller to incur the expense of repairing the goods may be under an implied obligation to accept and pay for the goods once the repair has been completed. But this is not an inevitable inference. In the case where, for example, goods are taken away by the seller for inspection and, if possible, repair, the court may infer that the seller is obliged, upon request, to inform the buyer of the nature of the problem which required to be remedied and a failure by the seller to provide the buyer with such information may entitle the buyer to reject the goods even in the case where the repair has in fact been carried out to a proper standard.

266 ibid s 35(6)(b).
267 ibid s 35A.
268 ibid s 36.
269 See para 10.21 and, more generally, paras 5.82–5.86.
270 They are often unnecessary or unhelpful in international sales because it is the documents relating to the goods which are of greatest practical importance rather than the rights in relation to the goods themselves.

property in the goods may have passed to the buyer.[271] A seller is unpaid when the whole of the price has not been paid or tendered or when a bill of exchange or other negotiable instrument has been received as conditional payment and the condition on which it was received has not been fulfilled by reason of the dishonour of the instrument or otherwise.[272]

(i) The seller's lien[273]

10.54   A lien is a possessory security so that the goods must remain in the possession of the seller for the lien to be exercisable.[274] The lien may be exercisable notwithstanding the fact that the buyer has been allowed into possession of the goods for limited purposes, for example to pack them, provided the goods remain in the seller's general control.[275] Where the goods are in possession of the seller, the seller can retain possession of them[276] until payment or tender of the price in three situations: namely, where the goods have been sold without any stipulation as to credit, where the goods have been sold on credit but the term of credit has expired,[277] and where the buyer becomes insolvent.[278] The lien is lost when the seller delivers the goods to a carrier or other bailee for the purpose of transmission to the buyer without reserving the right of disposal of the goods, when the buyer or his agent lawfully[279] obtains possession of the goods, by waiver of the lien or right of retention.[280]

(ii) Right of stoppage in transit[281]

10.55   This right is more extensive than the lien in that it can be invoked by the unpaid seller after he has parted with possession of the goods but it is more limited in that

---

[271] Where property in the goods has not passed to the buyer, the unpaid seller has a right of withholding delivery similar to and co-extensive with his rights of lien or retention and stoppage in transit where the property has passed to the buyer (Sale of Goods Act 1979, 39(2)). Section 39(2) does not expressly provide for the existence of a right of resale in such a case but it seems that the seller should not be in any worse position in this respect than under s 39(1) (see *RV Ward Ltd v Bignall* [1967] 1 QB 534, CA).

[272] Sale of Goods Act 1979, s 38(1). Note also the extended definition of 'seller' in s 38(2).

[273] ibid s 39(1)(a).

[274] The goods need not remain in his possession as seller; they can be in his possession in his capacity as agent, bailee or custodier for the buyer: ibid s 41(2).

[275] See for example *Goodall v Skelton* (1794) 2 H Bl 316, 126 ER 570, Court of Common Pleas.

[276] Where there has been part delivery of the goods the seller may exercise a lien over the goods yet to be delivered unless the part delivery demonstrates an agreement to waive the lien or right of retention: Sale of Goods Act 1979, s 42.

[277] Thus the lien is deemed to be waived for the period of the credit. The high incidence of credit sales renders the seller's lien of limited practical relevance.

[278] Sale of Goods Act 1979, s 41(1). Insolvency is defined in s 61(4).

[279] Thus the wrongful taking of the goods by the buyer will not suffice.

[280] Sale of Goods Act 1979, s 43.

[281] ibid s 39(1)(b) and s 44.

it only arises upon the insolvency[282] of the buyer. The right of stoppage entitles the seller to retain possession of the goods as long as they are in course of transit and he may retain them until payment or tender of the price. Upon exercising his right the seller essentially resumes possession of the goods and so can assert a lien over them. The right can only be exercised while the goods are in transit.[283] The essential idea is that goods are in transit while they are in the possession of a 'middleman'[284] who is independent of both buyer and seller so that the buyer has not yet taken delivery of the goods. If the carrier attorns to the buyer the transit is at an end.[285] The right of stoppage is exercised by the seller taking actual possession of the goods or by giving notice[286] of his claim to the carrier or other bailee or custodier in whose possession the goods are. Once notice has been given, the carrier must redeliver the goods to, or according to the directions of, the seller and the seller must bear the expenses of such redelivery.[287] The seller's right of lien or retention or stoppage in transit is not affected by any sale or other disposition of the goods which the buyer may have made, unless the seller has assented[288] to it.[289] The seller's rights may also be defeated where he has lawfully transferred a document of title to the buyer and the buyer in turn has transferred that document of title to a third party who has taken in good faith and for valuable consideration.[290]

(iii) The right of re-sale[291]

The exercise by the seller of his right of lien or stoppage in transit does not, of itself, operate to bring the contract to an end nor does it operate to revest property in the seller.[292] A seller who wishes to bring the contract to an end should notify the buyer of his intention to do so. Additionally the seller is given a right[293] to resell the goods. The seller has a right to resell the goods where the original

10.56

---

282 Defined in ibid s 61(4).

283 Rather elaborate rules on the duration of transit are set out in ibid s 45.

284 *Schotsmans v Lancs & Yorks Rly* (1867) LR 2 Ch App 332, 338, CA.

285 Sale of Goods Act 1979, s 45(3).

286 The requirements as to notice are set out in s 46(2) and (3).

287 Sale of Goods Act 1979, s 46(4).

288 Knowledge of the sub-sale is not the same thing as assent to it. See *Mordaunt Brothers v British Oil and Cake Mills Ltd* [1910] 2 KB 502, KBD and contrast *DF Mount Ltd v Jay and Jay (Provisions) Co Ltd* [1960] 1 QB 159, QBD. A seller who attorns to the sub-buyer must also have assented.

289 Sale of Goods Act 1979, s 47(1).

290 ibid s 47(2). See, for example, *DF Mount Ltd v Jay and Jay (Provisions) Co Ltd* [1960] 1 QB 159, QBD.

291 Sale of Goods Act 1979, s 39(1)(c).

292 ibid s 48(1).

293 The seller may also have the power to transfer good title to a second buyer, for example under s 24 or s 48(2) of the Act. Where the seller has power to resell but does not have the right to do so he can confer good title on the third party but will be liable to the buyer in damages. Where the seller also has the right to resell he cannot be liable to the original buyer when he exercises his right to resell.

contract gives him the right to do so[294] and where the buyer has repudiated[295] the contract and the seller has accepted that repudiation, thereby bringing the contract to an end. In addition s 48(3) of the Act provides that where the goods are of a perishable nature, or where the unpaid seller gives notice to the buyer of his intention to resell, and the buyer does not within a reasonable time pay or tender the price, the unpaid seller may resell the goods and recover from the original buyer damages for any loss occasioned by his breach of contract. A seller who exercises his right to resell under s 48(3) thereby terminates the contract so that he cannot sue the buyer for the price but must content himself with a claim for damages.[296]

(b) Personal remedies

10.57 A number of personal remedies are available to the seller in the event of buyer default.

(i) Action for the price

10.58 This is a claim in debt and so is unaffected by doctrines such as mitigation. Perhaps rather curiously, the action for the price is limited to cases where 'property in the goods has passed to the buyer and he wrongfully neglects or refuses to pay for the goods according to the terms of the contract'.[297] When property has not passed to the buyer, the seller's only claim is one for damages. A seller will not be entitled to recover the price where, prior to it being payable, he breached the contract in such a way as to disentitle him to the price.[298] The requirement that property must have passed to the buyer does not apply where the price is payable on a day certain[299] irrespective of delivery.[300] Section 49 may not be exhaustive of the seller's right to sue for the price; the contract of sale itself may give the seller a broader right to sue for the price.[301] The action for the price does not prevent the seller from bringing

---

[294] In such a case the original contract is terminated upon the seller reselling the goods but that termination is without prejudice to any claim which the seller may have for damages: Sale of Goods Act 1979, s 48(4).

[295] The circumstances in which a breach will be held to be repudiatory are discussed in Chapter 8.

[296] *RV Ward Ltd v Bignall* [1967] 1 QB 534, CA. One consequence of this conclusion is that the seller is not liable to account to the buyer for any profit which he makes on the resale.

[297] Sale of Goods Act 1979, s 49(1). Contrast 2-709 of the Uniform Commercial Code, which is favoured by some academic commentators (see, for example, PS Atiyah, (n 1 above) 485–6).

[298] *Wayne's Merthyr Steam Coal and Iron Co v Morewood* (1877) 46 LJQB 746, QBD.

[299] On which see *Shell-Mex Ltd v Elton Cop Dyeing Co Ltd* (1928) 34 Commercial Cases 39, QBD.

[300] Sale of Goods Act 1979, s 49(2).

[301] See *Benjamin* (n 1 above) 16-028 to 16-029, although there are dicta which suggest that s 49 is exhaustive of the seller's right to sue for the price (see, for example, *Colley v Overseas Exporters* [1921] 3 KB 302, 310, KBD).

an action for damages to recover such consequential loss that he has suffered which is recoverable on ordinary principles.[302]

(ii) Damages for non-acceptance

Where property in the goods has not passed to the buyer then the seller will have **10.59** to be content with an action for damages for non-acceptance.[303] The general rule[304] which applies to the assessment of damages is that the seller is entitled to recover 'the estimated loss directly and naturally resulting, in the ordinary course of events, from the buyer's breach of contract'.[305] This is likely to consist of the difference between the contract price and the value of the goods to the seller at the time and place of the breach together with any consequential recoverable losses.[306] The Act also lays down a 'prima facie' rule which is applicable where there is an available market[307] for the goods. In such a case the measure of damages is prima facie to be ascertained by the difference between the contract price and the market or current price at the time or times when the goods ought to have been accepted or, if no time was fixed for acceptance, at the time of the refusal to accept.[308] The merit of this rule is that it is clear or abstract and it is consistent with the requirement that the seller must take steps to mitigate his loss but it is open to criticism on the ground that it can lead to results which are rather arbitrary.[309] Where the buyer commits an anticipatory breach of contract and that breach is accepted prior to the date of delivery it would appear that damages continue to be

---

[302] Sale of Goods Act 1979, s 54. See also s 37 which enables the seller to recover from a buyer who refuses to take delivery a reasonable charge for the care and custody of the goods.

[303] Where property has passed to the buyer the seller has an option either to sue for the price or to sue for damages.

[304] So held in *Dem Dis A Turk Ticaret S/A TR v International Agri Trade Co Ltd (The Selda)* [1999] 1 Lloyd's Rep 729, CA.

[305] Sale of Goods Act 1979, s 50(2). This provision may be thought to be rather odd in so far as it deals, not so much with the measure of damages, as with the rule for remoteness of damages, classically expressed in *Hadley v Baxendale* (1854) 9 Exch 341, Court of Exchequer Chamber (see further Chapter 8).

[306] Sale of Goods Act 1979, s 54.

[307] The meaning of 'available market' is discussed in more detail by *Benjamin* (n 1 above) 16-063 to 16-070.

[308] Sale of Goods Act 1979, s 50(3). Where the seller agrees to a postponement of the date of delivery, the relevant date will be the substituted date.

[309] For example, it may enable a seller to make a profit when he sells the goods for a profit at a later date as a result of a rise in the market price: *Campbell Mostyn (Provisions) Ltd v Barnett Trading Co* [1954] 1 Lloyd's Rep 65, CA. Equally, the fact that the seller made a loss because he retained the goods and the market price then fell is irrelevant. The position may be otherwise where the seller has only one item and resells it *immediately* at a profit: in such a case the court may take account of any profit made by the seller on the resale (see *Benjamin*, n 1 above, 16-075—16-076). The difficulty with any such exception is that it tends to undermine the abstract nature of the rule.

assessed at the date fixed for delivery under the contract[310] unless the seller should have mitigated his loss by re-selling at an earlier date.[311]

(3) *Remedies of the Buyer*

10.60 Here we are concerned largely with the personal remedies available to the buyer. In the event of seller insolvency the buyer will wish to show that property in the goods has passed to him under the contract of sale so that he can obtain priority over the seller's other creditors. The buyer may also be entitled to bring a claim in conversion[312] against any person who wrongfully interferes with the goods. In many ways the primary remedy of the buyer in the event of breach by the seller is the right to reject the goods.[313]

(a) Specific performance

10.61 English law differs from many civil law systems in that it relegates specific performance to a secondary role.[314] The Act gives the court power to make a specific performance order in the case of the breach of a contract to deliver specific[315] or ascertained[316] goods.[317] An order is most likely to be made where the goods are unique[318] and uniqueness may here include commercial uniqueness.[319] Where the goods remain unascertained then the court will not order specific performance,[320] although it is possible that it may do so in an exceptional case.[321]

---

[310] *Millett v Van Heeck* [1921] 2 KB 369, CA.

[311] *Roth & Co v Taysen Townsend & Co* (1895) 73 LT 628, 629–30, QBD.

[312] The principles which govern a claim for conversion are discussed in Chapter 17.

[313] Discussed in paras 10.45–10.49. The buyer may also be able to rescind the contract for misrepresentation in an appropriate case.

[314] The difference between the different systems has resulted in the compromise of Article 28 of the Vienna Convention.

[315] The meaning of which is set out at para 10.08 and n 32 above.

[316] Goods are ascertained if they are identified in accordance with the contract after the contract has been formed: *Re Wait* [1927] 1 Ch 606, 630, CA.

[317] Sale of Goods Act 1979, s 52.

[318] *Falcke v Gray* (1859) 4 Drew 651, 62 ER 250, Vice Chancellor's Court.

[319] *Behnke v Bede Shipping Co Ltd* [1927] 1 KB 649, QBD: cf *Société des Industries Métallurgiques SA v The Bronx Engineering Co Ltd* [1975] 1 Lloyd's Rep 465, CA.

[320] *Re Wait* [1927] 1 Ch 606, CA, where the court emphasized the fact that the 1893 Act was a Code so that it was not possible to go outside its terms in order to find a wider power to order specific performance.

[321] On the basis of *Sky Petroleum Ltd v VIP Petroleum Ltd* [1974] 1 WLR 576, Ch D (the case actually concerned the grant of an interlocutory injunction but it may be applied by analogy to the case of specific performance. The case is, however, a controversial one and it is not easy to reconcile with *Re Wait* [1927] 1 Ch 606, CA.

(b) Recovery of the price

10.62 The buyer may be entitled to recover money paid to the seller where the consideration for the payment has failed.[322] The traditional requirement is that this right is only available where there has been a *total* failure of consideration,[323] although this limitation may not survive further judicial scrutiny.[324]

(c) Damages

10.63 A buyer may bring a claim for damages because the seller has failed to deliver the goods, has delivered them late or has delivered defective goods.

(i) Non-delivery

10.64 Where the seller wrongfully neglects or refuses to deliver the goods to the buyer, the buyer's entitlement to damages corresponds with the seller's entitlement to damages in the event of non-acceptance by the buyer; that is to say the 'available market' test is applied[325] so that the buyer is entitled to recover the difference between the market price of the goods[326] at the time fixed for delivery and the contract price. If there is no available market for the goods, the measure of damages to which the buyer is entitled 'is the estimated loss directly and naturally resulting, in the ordinary course of events, from the seller's breach of contract'.[327]

(ii) Loss suffered by non-delivery

10.65 The Act does not expressly deal with the situation where the seller is late in delivering the goods but the buyer nevertheless accepts delivery and sues for damages for the loss suffered by the late delivery. It would appear that the buyer is prima facie entitled to recover the difference between the market price at the time fixed for delivery and the market price at the time at which delivery was actually made.[328]

---

[322] This right is specifically preserved by s 54 of the Sale of Goods Act 1979. This remedy has assumed particular importance in cases where there has been a breach by the seller of s 12, on which see para 10.27.

[323] See further chapter 18.

[324] Evidence of judicial reluctance to apply the traditional rule can be seen in *Goss v Chilcott* [1996] AC 788, 798, PC.

[325] Sale of Goods Act 1979, s 51(3).

[326] The relevant price is the buying price at which the buyer could obtain the goods: *Williams Bros v Ed T Agius Ltd* [1914] AC 510, HL.

[327] Sale of Goods Act 1979, s 51(2).

[328] Much more difficult is the question of the entitlement of the buyer to recover loss of profits caused by late delivery: see *Victoria Laundry (Windsor) Ltd v Newman Industries Ltd* [1949] 2 KB 528, CA and the discussion of remoteness of damage in Chapter 8.

(iii) Defective goods

10.66 Where the goods delivered are defective in quality the buyer may either set up against the seller the breach of warranty in diminution or extinction of the price or maintain an action against the seller for the breach of warranty.[329] Where the buyer brings a claim for damages the Act provides both that the measure of damages is 'the estimated loss directly and naturally resulting, in the ordinary course of events, from the breach of warranty'[330] and that, in the case of a breach of warranty of quality, the loss is 'prima facie the difference between the value of the goods at the time of delivery to the buyer and the value they would have had if they had fulfilled the warranty'.[331] The relationship between these two provisions is not an easy one. The former has been stated to be the 'starting point'[332] for the court, while the latter is simply a prima facie rule which may be displaced on the facts of a particular case. The courts have in some cases declined to award a buyer damages assessed on the diminution in value measure where this would have given him more than his actual loss.[333]

(d) Additional remedies for consumer buyers

10.67 Consumer buyers have been given additional remedies as a result of the implementation of the EC Directive on Certain Aspects of the Sale of Consumer Goods and Associated Guarantees[334] by the Sale and Supply of Goods to Consumers Regulations 2002.[335] The Regulations have introduced a new Part 5A into the Sale

---

[329] Sale of Goods Act 1979, s 53(1).

[330] ibid s 53(2).

[331] ibid s 53(3).

[332] *Bence Graphics International Ltd v Fasson UK Ltd* [1998] QB 87, 102, CA.

[333] The cases are not entirely easy to reconcile. On the one hand, in cases such as *Slater v Hoyle & Smith Ltd* [1920] 2 KB 11, CA and *Louis Dreyfus Trading Ltd v Reliance Trading Ltd* [2004] EWHC 525 (Comm); [2004] 2 Lloyd's Rep 243, QB the courts took no account of the profit made by the buyer on a sub-sale of the goods. On the other hand, account was taken of the profit made by the buyer in *Bence Graphics International Ltd v Fasson UK Ltd* [1998] QB 87, CA. The majority in *Bence* were clearly reluctant to award the buyers more than what they perceived to be their actual loss. This view is understandable. But there is another side to the story. Assuming that the trial judge was correct to conclude that the goods which the sellers had supplied were 'worthless', why should they be allowed to keep any part of the payment which they had received for delivering worthless goods? The effect of the decision is also to throw upon the buyer the onus of proving that he has in fact suffered a loss where he has sub-sold the defective goods for the price at which he bought the goods and that onus may not be easy to discharge. More importantly, the effect of the majority approach is to replace a rule which is easy to apply with one which requires a careful scrutiny of the facts and which runs contrary to the thrust of sale of goods law which is to favour an abstract approach to the assessment of damages (for criticism of the *Bence* case along these lines see G Treitel, 'Damages for Breach of Warranty of Quality' (1997) 113 LQR 188).

[334] 1999/44/EC; [1999] OJ L171/12, on which see M Bianca and S Grundmann (eds) *EU Sales Directive Commentary* (Intersentia, 2002).

[335] SI 2002, No. 3045, on which see R Bradgate and C Twigg-Flesner *Blackstone's Guide to Consumer Sales and Associated Guarantees* (2003).

of Goods Act 1979 so that the new consumer rights sit, albeit rather awkwardly, within the existing legislative framework. These remedies are only available to a buyer who 'deals as consumer'.[336] The buyer who deals as consumer is given a qualified right to (i) require the seller to repair or replace the goods,[337] (ii) reduce the price,[338] or (iii) rescind the contract.[339] In order to be able to exercise these rights the goods must not conform to the contract of sale at the time of delivery,[340] although here the consumer buyer is given the benefit of a presumption that goods which do not conform to the contract within six months from the date of delivery did not conform at the time of delivery.[341] In other words, the consumer buyer is relieved of the burden of proving that goods did not conform to the contract where the non-conformity occurs within six months of delivery; in such a case it is for the seller to prove that the goods did conform to the contract at the time of delivery.

A number of points should be noted about these new provisions. First, they have **10.68** introduced a more elaborate remedial regime into English law and the consumer buyer[342] is, in principle, given the right to select from this remedial menu. Second, the right of the buyer to choose is not an unqualified one. Thus the buyer cannot require the seller to repair or replace the goods if it would be impossible for the seller to do so or if it would be 'disproportionate' to require the seller to do so.[343] The language of 'proportionality' is new to this area of law in the UK and may be said to introduce a degree of uncertainty into the law. That said, repair and replacement are commonly used in practice in consumer sales and the change may be one that has implications in the realm of legal theory rather than practice. Where the buyer requires the seller to repair to replace the goods the seller must repair or replace them within a reasonable time but without causing significant

---

[336] Sale of Goods Act 1979, s 48A. The phrase 'deals as consumer' is defined in s 61(5A) of the 1979 Act and s 12 of the Unfair Contract Terms Act 1977.

[337] ibid s 48B. 'Repair' is defined in s 61(1) of the Act but 'replacement' is not defined.

[338] ibid s 48C(1)(a).

[339] ibid s 48C(1)(b) and 48C(2).

[340] For this purpose, goods do not conform to the contract if there is, in relation to the goods, 'a breach of an express terms of the contract or a term implied by section 13, 14 or 15' of the Act: s 48F.

[341] ibid s 48A(3) and (4). The presumption only applies for the purpose of the new statutory remedies and is not applicable where the buyer elects to seek a remedy at common law.

[342] In this respect it is important to note that it is the buyer and not the seller who is given the right: contrast Article 48 of the Vienna Convention where the power to remedy the non-conformity is given to the seller.

[343] 'Disproportion' is further defined in s 48B (2) and (3). The test to be applied is one that relates to the 'cost' to the seller of providing the remedy; it does not focus upon the benefit which the buyer will obtain from the remedy. The comparison is to be conducted, first, as between repair and replacement (s 48A(3)(b) and then between the remedies of reduction of the price and rescission (s 48A(3)(c)).

inconvenience to the buyer[344] and must bear any necessary costs incurred in doing so.[345] Third, these provisions accord a higher priority to specific performance (here using the phrase specific performance to encompass the remedies of repair and replacement) than is traditionally to be found in English law. In this respect, the provisions reveal a civilian rather than a common law orientation. Fourth, these provisions introduce into English law the remedy of price reduction. Once again, the consequence may be more apparent at the level of theory than practice given that the remedy of damages frequently reaches results that are very similar to, if not identical with, the result that is reached through reliance on the remedy of price reduction. Finally, the new provisions purport to relegate 'rescission' of the contract to a lowly place in the remedial hierarchy.[346] The meaning of the word 'rescind' in this context is not immediately obvious. It could mean either the prospective or the retrospective setting aside of the contract. Prospective discharge is the consequence which an English lawyer would expect to flow from a breach of contract but it may be that what is meant is 'rejection of defective goods, termination of the contract for breach and recovery of the price if paid'.[347] However the point may not prove to be an important one in practice. The reason for this is that this new remedial regime does not purport to take away the existing common law or other statutory rights of consumer buyers. Given that consumer buyers had a wide to reject non-conforming goods prior to the enactment of Part 5A of the 1979 Act,[348] buyers who wish to reject may be more likely to rely on their existing rights than seek to invoke the additional remedies to be found in Part 5A. The relationship between these new remedies and existing remedies is, however, likely to prove to be an uneasy one.[349] Finally, the courts have been given certain powers in relation to these new remedies[350] and the extent of these powers is likely to give rise to some controversy. A novel feature (from the perspective of English law) is the power given to the court to make a specific performance order which requires the seller to repair the goods. More difficult is likely to be the power given to the court to make an order 'on such terms and conditions as to damages, payment of the price and otherwise as it thinks just'.[351] To the extent that these provisions confer a broad discretionary power on the court it has been

---

[344] S 48B(2)(a). 'Reasonable time' and 'significant inconvenience' are further defined in s 48B(5). A buyer who requires a seller to repair or replace goods cannot reject the goods until he has given the seller a reasonable time in which to repair or replace the goods: s 48D.

[345] S 48B(2)(b).

[346] ibid s 48C(2), on which see Benjamin (n 1 above) 12-106.

[347] Benjamin (n 1 above), 12-095.

[348] See paras 10.45 and 10.46.

[349] Benjamin (n 1 above) 12 -104 and 12-118; Bradgate and Twigg-Flesner (n 335 above) 4.4.1.7.

[350] Sale of Goods Act 1979, s 48E.

[351] ibid s 48E(6) Similar difficulties may arise in relation to the power of the court under s 48E(3)(b) to decide that 'another remedy under section 48B or 48C is appropriate.'

asserted that there is no basis for such a power in the Directive.[352] But it may be that the discretion is more limited than at first sight appears and that, in particular, it does not introduce into the Act the traditional, restrictive approach which English law has taken towards the remedy of specific performance. The court is not directed to consider whether damages at common law would be an adequate remedy; rather, it must exercise its discretion in accordance with the principles which underpin Part 5A and these principles give a higher priority to the remedy of specific performance than has traditionally been the case in English law.[353]

---

[352] R Bradgate and C Twigg-Flesner (n 335 above) 4.4.1.6.
[353] Compare in this respect Benjamin (n 1 above) 12-114 and D Harris 'Specific performance—a regular remedy for consumers?' (2003) 119 LQR 541.

11

CARRIAGE OF GOODS BY SEA

A. Introduction

(1) General

The law of carriage by sea is simply one specialized contract out of many. Its basic **11.01** structure is very similar in most if not all developed countries, largely because of the fairly uniform regime for bill of lading contracts secured by the Hague Rules and their subsequent variants. Valuable short and longer books on it are available.[1]

---

[1] See further Cooke and others, *Voyage Charters* (3rd edn, 2006); Wilford, Coghlin and Kimball, *Time Charters* (5th edn, 2003); Aikens, Lord and Bools, *Bills of Lading* (2006); Treitel and Reynolds, *Carver on Bills of Lading* (2nd edn, 2005).

It may then be asked why it is appropriate to have in this work a special chapter, albeit a brief one, on the subject.

11.02   The reasons are twofold. First, for historical reasons English commercial law generally, and the English law of carriage by sea in particular, was much used and relied on in international commerce in the later part of the nineteenth and the early part of the twentieth century. This had the result that the English law itself became particularly well-developed in this area. That fact led, when traders and carriers became aware of problems of the conflict of laws, to English law being selected for many maritime contracts which had little or no connection with England or the United Kingdom. The overall result is that English law is much used in international shipping and commerce, and London is one of the major centres of maritime dispute resolution, whether by litigation or arbitration,[2] in the world. There are of course several other significant jurisdictions in this context; and within the common law family there are important differences of approach and technique in the United States, another major jurisdiction for the resolution of maritime disputes. But in the result English law is one of the principal systems of private law encountered in the area, and this makes its approach worth setting down.

11.03   The second reason is that much of the general English common law of contract derives in fact from reasoning deployed and developed in shipping cases.[3] In most (but not all) common law countries the law of contract is uncodified and derived from legal decisions. What those legal decisions concern in common law countries depends to some extent on what subject matter happens to be litigated to their highest tribunals, and also on what sort of cases are reported. In England, for the reasons already given, shipping cases have been conspicuous. The result is that a very considerable part of the common law of contract, especially that concerning frustration and discharge of contract by breach, derives from shipping cases, which go well back into the nineteenth century and still continue. For pure common law reasoning, shipping cases have in England at least been a major source of basic contract doctrine, and continue to be so. (Equity has not been prominent in this area.)

11.04   The contract of carriage by sea differs from other contracts of carriage largely in the scale and length of the operation. Ships are large pieces of equipment and have

---

[2] English courts have also exercised considerable control over arbitrators, and this has brought in litigation even on arbitrated disputes. The amount of such control has been much reduced by statutes: the most recent is the Arbitration Act 1996.

[3] Lord Goff of Chieveley has said that for an English lawyer the characteristic commercial contract is one for the carriage of goods by sea: 'The Future of the Common Law' (Wilberforce Lecture, 1997), 46 ICLQ 745, 751. See also Reynolds, *Maritime and Other Influences in the Common Law* [2002] LMCLQ 182.

considerable value in themselves; they can also carry cargo of considerable total size and value. The voyages which they undertake can be very long and take many weeks even now, and of course were much longer in former years. During the transit the ship and its cargo are subjected to many and varied risks, both physical and political (for example, by governmental interference). For this reason sea transport has required more extensive and complex law than other forms of transport.

Sea transport has to be seen, however, also against the background of insurance: **11.05** the risks are so great that all involved are likely to insure. Thus the cargo owner may insure his risks with a cargo underwriter; shipowners insure most of their liability to cargo[4] with a mutual insurance association called a 'P & I Association', or 'P & I Club', or on similar terms elsewhere. They may also insure their ships, and against failure to earn the freight expected on the voyage. This means that much litigation in this area is often technical, designed to clarify points of risk allocation, and supported or brought by insurers on both sides.

The contract has also to be seen against the background of the contracts to which **11.06** the goods carried in the ship are subject. There are of course in-house shipments and coastal shipments; but most shipments are made in pursuance of an export or import sale, or allocated (or 'appropriated') to such a sale during the carriage, and it may often be desired to sell (and resell), or raise money on the security of the goods while they are afloat. This is done largely by the use of a document called a bill of lading, which in English law, and doubtless (with differences of detail) in most legal systems, represents the goods, with the result that dealings in the document may represent dealings in the goods. It is likely therefore that any dispute about damage to or loss of the cargo (obviously the main type of dispute in carriage by sea) may involve analysis of the dealings with the goods, at least in order to ascertain who is the right claimant. There may also be involvement of banks, who finance such sales by holding the shipping documents as security. Meanwhile contractual arrangements relating to the ship itself may require careful analysis to determine who is the correct claimant and (especially) defendant.

Finally, a warning is needed that the English rules as to carriage by sea were princi- **11.07** pally worked out in the late nineteenth century and in the earlier part of the twentieth century, against the background of less sophisticated techniques of ship operation than are usual now. They have of course been the subject of constant development, but not all modern changes have yet been fully addressed in litigation. In particular, there are as yet comparatively few decisions concerning carriage in containers, which raise problems different from those which arose under older methods of packaging and handling. Equally, electronic methods of

---

[4] And for other matters, eg personal injury and oil pollution.

dealing are developing only slowly. The principles worked out under those older methods of dealing are requiring and will require adaptation: but the principles themselves will remain as a guide unless they are found completely inappropriate.

(2) Types of Contract for Carriage by Sea

11.08 Traditionally, there are two types of contract available to a person who wishes to send goods by sea. The first is the charterparty, which is principally intended for those who have a complete cargo, usually of a bulk commodity, which will in effect fill the whole carrying capacity of the ship. Many forms of chartering in this context involve use of the 'tramp ship market', a market of vessels which hold themselves available for such arrangements, and such an arrangement can be called shipping on 'tramping terms'. Charterparties are also used for other purposes, in particular making the ship available for carriage on bill of lading terms (as to which see below). The unusual (and ancient) word charterparty is a contraction of the Latin *carta partita*, or divided document, stemming from a practice of dividing documents in two, one for each party: it appears also in French (*charte partie*). The second type of contract is the bill of lading contract, which is a contract for the carriage of goods in a vessel carrying separate consignments for many consignors; it is usually recorded by the issue of a bill of lading, subject to variants to be explained below. Especially where the goods are shipped in a ship of a regular line running scheduled services, this can be called shipping on 'liner terms'. The phrase 'bill of lading' (regularly shortened to 'B/L') is of course an ancient form of 'bill of loading': the document may be given a different name in other languages (for example, *connaissement, conocimiento de embarque*).

11.09 There is no requirement that either of the above paradigms be adhered to. There can be sub-charters, sub-sub-charters and so forth. There are other variants on chartering. Thus there can be charters of particular holds of a vessel or of space. There is in the container trade a recently developed institution called 'slot chartering', under which the (so-called) charterer contracts for a certain number of container 'slots', ie contracts to use and/or pay for, and the carrier contracts to provide, the space occupied by so many containers on a particular voyage or on several voyages, or for periods otherwise determined. These are only charterparties in a very limited sense.[5] Finally, there can be long-term contracts of affreightment, under which an operator contracts to provide ships to lift cargo within certain periods from certain places, without it being initially settled which

---

[5] The charterer has no control over the ship. However, the Court of Appeal has held a slot charter to be a charterparty for the purposes of Admiralty jurisdiction: *The Tychy* [1999] 2 Lloyd's Rep 11, CA.

ships will be used and when. Such contracts contain provisions for narrowing down to specific vessels at appropriate times, and usually provide for the form of charterparty to be used for the actual voyages.

Conversely, there is no objection in theory to a shipper under a bill of lading contract filling the whole cargo space. And even where a ship is chartered (or any of the above variants are used), a bill or bills of lading will normally be issued as well, to provide a receipt for the shipper, to facilitate delivery at destination and to enable dealings with the cargo while it is afloat. This improtant point is dealt with below.[6] **11.10**

(3) Terminology

Unless the reader is clear on the terminology used in this area, misunderstandings can occur. Also, some words used are by modern usage surprising or old-fashioned and may need explanation. A short glossary is therefore given at this stage. **11.11**

- The owner of the ship may be referred to as the *shipowner* or simply *owner*.
- The captain of the ship is in this context more usually referred to by the older term *master*.
- The person or company who promises by contract to carry the goods is called the *carrier*. The carrier is usually the shipowner. But if the ship is under demise (or 'bareboat') charterparty (see paragraph 11.22 below) the carrier will be the demise (or bareboat) charterer. And sometimes the voyage charterer or time charterer of a ship (see below) is the carrier, ie contracts to carry the goods and performs the contract by using the services of the owner (or demise charterer) as, in effect, a subcontractor.
- The person who sends goods by sea is usually called the *shipper*. If he has chartered the vessel he is also the *charterer*. It may sometimes be necessary to distinguish between the person who contracts for the carriage and the person who actually ships the goods: the latter might merely be a seller to the person contracting for carriage.
- While the goods are afloat their ownership and/or possession may change by reason of dealings with the documents. The person who owns the goods at any one time may be called the *bill of lading holder* or *cargo owner*, though these are not quite the same: the holder of the bill may not at a relevant time own the cargo, and likewise the owner of the cargo may not hold the bill.
- The person who receives them at destination may do so by virtue of being consignee of them under a bill of lading or some other document, or indorsee of the bill of lading. He may be called the *consignee*, or *indorsee* (of the bill of lading),

---

6 See paras 11.74ff.

or again, merely *cargo owner*, but since there are so many possibilities concerning who he is it is often simplest to refer to him as the *receiver* or, if there is a claim, *claimant*.

- *Freight* is the sum payable for the carriage of the goods. It may be paid on delivery of the goods at destination, or in advance (*advance freight*). In time charters (see paragraph 11.17 below) this sum is usually referred to as *hire*.

B. Charterparties

(1) Types of Charterparties

11.12 A charterparty (often shortened to 'charter') is a contract whereby (subject to the reservations made above) the carrying capacity of a ship is by contract placed by the owner[7] at the disposal of another person, referred to as the 'charterer'. Charterparties are of two basic types, the voyage charter and the time charter.

(a) The voyage charterparty

11.13 The voyage charterparty is 'a contract to carry specific goods on a defined voyage or voyages, the remuneration of the shipowner being a freight calculated according to the quantity of cargo loaded or carried, or sometimes a lump sum freight'.[8] This is the older type of charterparty and dates from times when only the shipowner could take the responsibility for estimating the risks and likely duration of the voyage and what he needed to charge for it. The destination of the voyage is specified, though the charterer may have discretion to determine or change it within limits. Voyage charters are made on standard contract forms, but their long history means that there is considerable scope for the application of general principle.

11.14 In substance the voyage is undertaken for a fixed price. The risk of delay affecting the profitability of the carriage contract is therefore on the shipowner, and within that price he normally allows fixed free time for loading and unloading, called 'laytime' (lying time), 'laydays' or other variants. The calculation of this—its starting point, whether it can be interrupted and for how long it runs—gives rise to disputes which, because of the great significance of delay in maritime operations, involve in their resolution technical questions of interpretation of wording, and in their result, large sums of money. If the charterer delays the ship beyond laytime he is in breach of contract and liable in damages, but it is normal to agree these in advance under the title 'demurrage' (French *demeure*, delay money). This is by

---

[7] Or sometimes demise charterer: see paras 11.22 and 11.23.
[8] *Scrutton on Charterparties and Bills of Lading* (20th edn, 1996) 63–4.

modern standards normally classified as liquidated (or agreed) damages for breach of contract by detaining the ship beyond laytime: that is to say, the charterer is not *entitled* to keep the ship on demurrage, but is paying damages for doing so.[9] Demurrage disputes—as to what sorts of losses are covered by demurrage, when demurrage starts, whether on the terms of the contract it can be interrupted and so forth—are likewise technical and involve large sums of money.

Another way in which the charterer may cause the shipowner unjustifiable loss of anticipated profit is, when the freight is calculated by quantity or size of the cargo carried, by not utilizing all the cargo space or not shipping the cargo contracted for. Damages for failure to do the former are equivalent to the freight which would have been earned, and are called 'dead freight'. Here too, complex disputes can arise as to whether indications of cargo carrying capacity in the charterparty (or sometimes elsewhere) are contractual promises by the charterer to load that quantity or fill that space, or simply a general indication of the sort of capacity involved. (The same problem can arise in reverse, where the ship proves unable to carry the anticipated quantity.)   **11.15**

A voyage charterparty is a contract for services (*locatio conductio operarum*), to be rendered by the shipowner, his equipment and employees: it is definitely not a hire of the ship (*locatio conductio rei*).   **11.16**

(b) The time charterparty

Time charterparties are a later invention and date from times when sail had given way to steam and ship movements had become more predictable. 'The shipowner agrees. . .to render services for a named period by his master and crew to carry goods put on board the ship by or on behalf of the time charterer.'[10] The charge payable is usually referred to as 'hire'. The charterer can give commercial (but not navigational)[11] orders to the shipowner within specified geographical limits (which may be anything from very narrow to 'worldwide') during the charter period.   **11.17**

---

[9] In theory a stipulation for demurrage could be a penalty, and relief granted against it accordingly: as to penalties, see paras 21.175ff. But the sum involved is more likely to undercompensate than overcompensate, as high demurrage rates could be a weak selling point. Some standard forms also fix 'dispatch money', a bonus for quick loading or unloading, as a fraction of demurrage; this again discourages high demurrage rates. For a dispute turning on such factors see the famous case of *Suisse Atlantique Cie d'Armement Maritime SA v NV Rotterdamsche Kolen Centrale* [1967] 1 AC 361, HL, which additionally stands as a leading English decision on a much more general issue relating to unfair contract terms.

[10] *Scrutton on Charterparties and Bills of Lading* (20th edn, 1996) 63.

[11] The difference may prove highly controversial, for instance if the charterer specifies a route: see *The Hill Harmony* [2001] 1 AC 638.

11.18   A time charterparty is similar to a voyage charterparty except in the method of calculation of payment and hence the allocation of risk of delay during the carriage. The charterer is paid by time so will usually have no objection to being delayed by the charterer's orders or failure to give them. Hence a counterpart to the laytime and demurrage regime is required, and this is normally seen in the 'off-hire clause' under which no hire is payable while the ship is (in whole or in part, depending on the wording of the clause) in effect not working for the charterer. As with laytime and demurrage, disputes can be complicated and involve large sums of money. The clause simply deals with freight and does not affect liability in damages on either side, which will turn on the contractual allocation of responsibility for the event causing the delay.

11.19   There can also be disputes, again delay-related, regarding the expiry of the charter. Unless a tolerance is specified the ship must be given up within a reasonable period after the end of the charter period: not to do so is a breach of contract, damages for which would take into account any higher freight rate applicable after the end of the charter period.[12] If a tolerance is specified, the ship must be returned within it. If the ship is redelivered early, freight would normally be payable until the end of the charter period, unless a refusal by the shipowner to take it back was totally unreasonable.[13] Here again complicated disputes involving large sums of money are litigated.[14]

11.20   The true nature of a time charter is the subject of some disagreement internationally, but in English law at least it seems clear that, although the charterer can in theory give no orders and simply keep the ship waiting, or use it for storage, it is again a contract of carriage. As such it is a contract for services (*locatio conductio operarum*) rather than a hire of the ship (*locatio rei*), and this despite the use of the term 'hire' for the remuneration payable and other infelicities of terminology (such as 'deliver' and 'redeliver')[15] in most forms of charterparty. The right to the ship's services may be protected in appropriate cases by injunction,[16] although not usually against third parties.[17] The main difference from voyage charters lies in the method of payment and the consequent allocation of delay risks.[18] Time charters

---

[12] See *Hyundai Merchant Marine Co v Geduri Chartering Co Ltd (The Peonia)* [1991] 1 Lloyd's Rep 100.

[13] See *Clea Shipping Corp v Bulk Oil International Ltd (No 2) (The Alaskan Trader)* [1983] 2 Lloyd's Rep 645, applying a limit to the principle of *White & Carter (Councils) Ltd v McGregor* [1962] AC 413, HL that one party cannot force a repudiatory breach of contract on the other.

[14] For a recent example see *Torvald Klaveness A/S v Arni Maritime Corp (The Gregos)* [1994] 1 WLR 1465, HL.

[15] These words are used to mark the charterer's assumption of the right to give orders and the demitting of that right.

[16] See *Lauritzencool AB v Lady Navigation Inc* [2005] EWCA Civ 579; [2005] 1 WLR 3686.

[17] See *Chitty on Contracts* (29th edn, 2004), paras 18–128ff.

[18] Though the charterer's power to give orders can involve disputes as to damage to the ship.

are largely made on standard forms and disputes turn largely on the wording of the form used: there is less scope for general principle than with voyage charters.

There can also be mixed time and voyage charterparties, where the ship is con-   **11.21**
tracted to go to a particular port, but paid on a time basis—perhaps, for example, because the shipowner is uncertain as to the time likely to be required at the destination port. These, often called 'trip charters', are time charters as regards payment; within the voyage route the charterer can give orders[19] and there may be special provisions for delivery and redelivery; but the ship cannot be ordered off the normal route for the voyage.[20]

(c) Demise or 'bareboat' charterparty

This is a totally different arrangement, as the ancient English word 'demise', for-   **11.22**
merly used in a property context, indicates. It is not a contract for services at all but rather a contract for the hire of the ship itself (*locatio conductio rei*). The charterer has possession of the ship, makes contracts of carriage (whether by charterparty or bill of lading) for it, and for most purposes ranks as owner of it during the duration of the charterparty. Such contracts are not contracts for the carriage of goods by sea and are used for different purposes, such as operating ships without capital expenditure, loan financing and various devices connected with the changing of flags. There are nowadays standard forms of demise charter; but there are older cases on the question whether a particular contractual arrangement constituted a demise or a time charter,[21] which would nowadays more usually be clear.

In common law terms a demise charter should be in effect a lease of the ship and   **11.23**
hence create a right *in rem* available against third parties. Since it operates by contract only, it is not clear to what extent it actually does so. If the charterer has possession of the ship he is a bailee, and hence not so reliant on contractual rights. In other situations he may be entitled to an injunction against third parties, but the full legal position is not worked out, and this appears to be true in some other countries also.[22]

(2) The Regime Under Which the Goods are Carried

(a) General common law principles as to carrier's duties

The general principle in this area is that there is complete freedom of contract.   **11.24**
Although international conventions concerning charterparty terms have been

---

[19] *Ocean Tramp Tankers Corp v V/O Sovfracht (The Eugenia)* [1964] 2 QB 226, CA.
[20] See *Temple SS Co Ltd v V/O Sovfracht* (1945) 79 Ll L R 1.
[21] eg *Baumwoll Manufactur von Carl Scheibler v Furness* [1893] AC 8, HL.
[22] See NE Palmer and E McKendrick (eds), *Interests in Goods* (2nd edn, 1998) ch 20.

mooted, they have not yet come to fruition. The perception is that charterers and shipowners are on a more or less equal bargaining footing: indeed, in contrast with the normal situation under bills of lading, some charterers, such as governmental import or export agencies, may be in a stronger position than shipowning companies.

11.25   There are however at common law ancient principles which applied at times when carriage by sea (or by other methods of transport) might be undertaken without written terms. These can still be relevant if no written terms are agreed, and sometimes when the terms of the contract are said to be displaced, as for example by a deviation.[23] They are the principles anciently applicable to common carriers, persons who offered themselves to the public to carry any cargo entrusted to them. Indeed, as a shipowner carrying under charterparty may often carry for one shipper only, it is arguable that such a person may in fact not be a common carrier; but the same principles as those for common carriers are assumed to be applicable.[24] They apply to bill of lading contracts also. The regime is said to be that the carrier promises to deliver the goods at destination in as good condition as that in which they were when entrusted to him, subject to the 'common law' exceptions of act of God, act of Queen's (King's or public) enemies, inherent vice in the goods (which would cover natural and unavoidable deterioration) and defective packing (a refinement of inherent vice).

11.26   This regime was presumably adequate for older navigation conditions, but during the nineteenth century it became inadequate, and shipowners began drafting detailed contracts to protect themselves in respect of various risks (still referred to nowadays by the traditional phrase 'excepted perils'). The basic common law rule then suffered a not very clearly traced metathesis into certain basic common law principles of interpretation of the contract terms used. These remain valid to this day.[25] They are as follows:

(i)   *Duty to furnish a seaworthy vessel.* This as developed covers not only fitness to lie in port with cargo aboard and to go to sea, but also to receive and hold cargo ('cargoworthiness'): in all cases, fitness for the voyage intended and as regards the particular cargo. The notion of seaworthiness is quite wide: it includes efficiency of the crew[26] and possession of appropriate navigational aids and documentation. The ship must be 'cargoworthy' on loading and seaworthy on sailing. That is all: anything which goes wrong subsequently

---

[23] See paras 11.46ff.

[24] See *Scrutton on Charterparties and Bills of Lading* (20th edn, 1996), art 105.

[25] See *Paterson SS Ltd v Canadian Wheat Producers Ltd* [1934] AC 538, 544–5.

[26] See the well-known *Hong Kong Fir* case, at n 52 below; for a recent example see *The Eurasian Dream* [2002] EWHC 118; [2002] 1 Lloyd's Rep 719 (crew inadequately trained and equipped for carriage of motor cars).

in this respect ranks for consideration under the rules relating to the prosecution of the voyage, to which the next heading, (ii), may be relevant.

(ii) *Duty to exercise due care (ie, not to be negligent in respect) of the cargo loaded.* These duties would of course apply even if the ship never moved. They are really warehousing duties, and a ship is in a sense a floating warehouse.

Two further duties apply to the voyage:

(iii) *Duty to proceed with reasonable dispatch.* The meaning of this is obvious.[27]

(iv) *Duty not to deviate from the contract route.* This attracts special considerations explained below.[28]

It is often said that there is a further implied duty: that to contribute in general **11.27** average. This refers to a specialized maritime institution whereby the cost of extraordinary sacrifice (eg, burning cargo for fuel) or expenditure (salvage contracts with tug operators) is shared among those participating in the adventure (another old term).[29]

Contract terms in charterparties and bills of lading are interpreted against the **11.28** background that these principles are assumed not to have been excluded unless clearly, and there are many dramatic examples of this.[30] But if they are clearly excluded, freedom of contract applies in both types of contract and the term is valid: unlike the position in some countries, there is no rule of law making terms excluding these duties (for example, excluding liability for negligence) ineffective on grounds of public policy. Indeed, this was one of the factors leading to the adoption of the Hague Rules, which regulate the liability of the carrier under bill of lading contracts.[31] The Unfair Terms in Consumer Contracts Directive[32] is obviously not relevant, as these are not consumer contracts; and the only general law in the United Kingdom on unfair contract terms, the Unfair Contract Terms Act 1977,[33] is specifically excluded from the vast majority of maritime contracts,[34] as from international supply contracts.[35]

---

[27] Most cases in fact concern delay on the approach voyage, as to which see para 11.36. Delay problems are often caused by the need to complete a previous charter: see, eg *Evera SA v North Shipping Co* [1956] 2 Lloyd's Rep 367.

[28] See paras 11.46ff.

[29] See *Scrutton on Charterparties and Bills of Lading* (20th edn, 1996) art 134. However, it is not clear that this duty is really contractual: see a book review by Sir Christopher Staughton (1998) 114 LQR 677.

[30] eg *Tattersall v National SS Co* (1884) 12 QBD 297.

[31] See paras 11.56ff.

[32] Operative under the Unfair Terms in Consumer Contracts Regulations 1999, SI 1999/ 2083.

[33] See paras 8.110ff.

[34] Unfair Contract Terms Act 1977, sch 1 excludes from the Act contracts for the carriage of goods by sea except (i) in respect of exclusion or restriction of liability for death or personal injury resulting from negligence or (ii) in favour of a person dealing as consumer.

[35] ibid s 26.

(b) Duties of charterer

11.29 Implied duties are here less prominent, but in general a charterer must have cargo ready (a separate duty, but usually subsumed into the laytime and demurrage obligations); load a full[36] cargo of the merchandise specified; and not without agreement of the owner ship dangerous goods (a topic the subject of much case law, in particular on who takes the risk as to goods not known to either side to be dangerous).[37] These duties are strict, in the absence of other indication.

(c) Loading and unloading

11.30 The questions of who pays for and who takes the risks involved in[38] loading or unloading operations turn on the individual contract. The starting point is often said to be that the charterer lifts the goods to the ship's rail and the shipowner takes them from that point, though it is also said that the duty prima facie rests with the owner.[39] In any case, this is, however, virtually always modified by contract terms, usage or custom of the port.[40] The time at which the risk passes under a contract of sale regarding the goods need not be the same as the time when the shipowner assumes responsibility for the goods: the former is more likely to be the moment of crossing the ship's rail,[41] which is thought to be a notion still familiar to merchants.[42]

(3) Remedies for Breach of the Contract Duties

(a) General common law approach

11.31 The English law as to the remedies for breach of the duties in a contract for carriage by sea is well developed, and forms the origin of much of the general law on the topic.

11.32 Any term infringed will normally be an express one in the charterparty, for even the implied duties referred to above are usually reproduced in some form,

---

36 See para 11.15.

37 See *The Giannis NK* [1998] AC 605 (a case on the Hague Rules, but a leading case on this topic in general).

38 These are not necessarily the same: the burdens could lie on different parties. The standard term 'FIO' ('free in and out') indicates that the freight agreed does not cover the cost of loading or unloading. But the question who takes the responsibility for these functions (as opposed to pays for them) requires further study of the contract terms. See *The Jordan II* [2004] UKHL 49; [2005] 1 WLR 1363.

39 See *The Jordan II*, (n 38 above), at [11].

40 *Pyrene Co Ltd v Scindia Navigation Co Ltd* [1954] 2 QB 402.

41 Which seems to have been the case in the *Pyrene* case (ibid).

42 It is still used in the International Chamber of Commerce's INCOTERMS for cif and fob sales.

even though limited,[43] in the charterparty itself. For breach of such a term, express or implied, an action for damages will lie for loss caused by that breach (but not for loss not so caused).[44]

However, in many cases the person affected (usually the charterer) may wish to **11.33** terminate the contract: in common law terms, treat it as discharged for breach.[45] This right is of great importance in common law, and does not exclude an additional right to damages. It cannot be exercised if it is waived, ie the person entitled to it clearly indicates that he will not exercise it (so-called 'election').[46] If this occurs, the right to damages remains. That can be waived also, but such a waiver is more difficult to establish, since it amounts to giving up all rights on the contract. As such it would normally require consideration to be binding.[47]

(b) Termination of the contract

To determine when the breach is sufficiently serious to entitle the innocent **11.34** party to treat the contract as discharged, it can be said that three techniques are available, two of them at least stemming from maritime law.

(i) Condition or warranty

The first technique looks to the term (or promise) of the contract broken and asks **11.35** whether it is a term in respect of which the parties are to be regarded as having agreed that there should be exact compliance.[48] If so, where there has been no such compliance the innocent party may terminate the contract, at least unless the other party can put the matter right within any express or implied time limit, and sue for damages also. Such a term is called a 'condition'; a term not giving rise to this right, but only to a right in damages, is called a 'warranty'. This is an established but curious use of the term 'condition': the term is really a promise rather than a condition. What is the condition is in fact the making good of the promise, which is a condition precedent to the other party's duty to proceed.

The origin of this use of the term 'condition' actually stems from the law of **11.36** carriage of goods by sea. A ship when chartered is often not at the place where it is

---

[43] If the duty imposed by the contract term is interpreted as more limited than the common law duty, eg as to the time at which the ship must be seaworthy (which could be the time of making the contract), the common law duty will normally apply also, unless the wording of the clause is interpreted as limiting the common law duty.

[44] For an instructive example see *The Europa* [1908] P 84, where part of the loss was caused by unseaworthiness and part by negligence in navigation (an excepted peril).

[45] See *Chitty on Contracts* (29th edn, 2004) ch 24.

[46] ibid ss 24–002ff.

[47] See paras 8.49ff; *Chitty on Contracts* (29th edn, 2004) paras 3–085ff.

[48] See *Photo Production Ltd v Securicor Transport Ltd* [1980] AC 827, 849, HL *per* Lord Diplock, who was largely responsible for the development of this branch of the law.

required to load: it must first proceed there (the voyage to the place of loading often being called the 'approach voyage'). The charterer's duty to load the ship is conditional upon its having been in the place at which it was said to be at the time of the charter. Thus, in the context of nineteenth-century slowness of communication, where a ship was described in the charterparty as 'now in the port of Amsterdam' but at that time had not yet even arrived at Amsterdam, the charterer was held entitled to refuse to load it when it arrived in England, and hence to terminate the contract and sue for damages.[49] The position of the ship at the time of chartering was crucial for the charterer's calculations as to the timescale.

11.37 There is no need for the word 'condition' to be used in the contract; and even if it is, the court may say that the term in question was not a condition in the technical sense. Most of the statements of fact in charterparties relating to the ship, its flag, carrying capacity and expected readiness to load would rank as conditions, depending always on the interpretation of the particular contract. This technique is still extensively used in this area of the law,[50] and in general of 'time clauses in mercantile contracts'.[51]

(ii) Innocent party deprived of 'substantially the whole benefit' of the contract

11.38 The second technique looks at the nature and consequences of the breach. Its classic formulation, derived from the judgment of Diplock LJ in *Hong Kong Fir Shipping Co Ltd v Kawasaki Kisen Kaisha Ltd*,[52] a seminal case for the general law, but actually on the seaworthiness term, asks whether the effect of the breach is to deprive the innocent party of 'substantially the whole benefit' of the contract.[53] This is more adverse to termination than the 'condition' technique: 'deprive of substantially the whole benefit' is not the same as 'substantially deprive of the benefit'. Its most common application is to cases of delay, where it is asked whether (for example) to make the charterer load in the circumstances created by the breach would be to hold him to a different contract from that which he had made.[54] Such a delay is often called a 'frustrating delay', and the test is the same as that in the doctrine of frustration, which releases both parties by a change of

---

49 *Behn v Burness* (1863) 3 B & S 751, 122 ER 281.

50 As to expected readiness to load see *Maredelanto Cia Naviera v Bergbau-Handel GmbH (The Mihalis Angelos)* [1971] 1 QB 164, CA (a leading case on the condition technique). An instructive consideration of various terms in an affreightment contract, and which of them were to be regarded as conditions, is to be found in *The Mavro Vetranic* [1985] 1 Lloyds Rep 580.

51 See an international sale of goods case, *Bunge Corp v Tradax International SA* [1971] 1 WLR 711, 715–16, HL *per* Lord Wilberforce.

52 [1962] 2 QB 26.

53 See ibid 70–1. In the *Photo Production* case (n 48 above) he called this a 'fundamental breach' (see p 849), which invites confusion with older cases using this notion in connection with unfair exclusion clauses: the *Suisse Atlantique* case [1967] 1 AC 361 concerns this usage.

54 *Freeman v Taylor* (1831) 8 Bing 124, 131 ER 348.

circumstances attributable to neither.[55] Indeed, the latter doctrine in its modern form originates in maritime law also, and a party is again released on the same basis, that to make him go ahead would be to hold him to an obligation into which he had not entered.[56] In this case however there is no breach by the other party.

The origin of this doctrine for the whole common law lies in cases where by virtue **11.39** of breach of contract the ship arrives from the approach voyage very late for loading: the charterer is not bound to load it.[57] If the lateness is a breach of contract, the situation is one for discharge by breach (and damages); if it is excused, there may be frustration and both parties are released.[58]

(iii) Repudiation or renunciation

The third technique, quite close to the second, asks whether one party has behaved **11.40** towards the other in such a way as to indicate repudiation or renunciation of his obligations under the contract.[59] Here the breach need not be of condition, nor its consequences in themselves so drastic as are required by the *Hong Kong Fir* test referred to in paragraph 11.38 above, but the situation must be sufficient to raise grave doubts in the innocent party as to the likelihood of the contract being properly performed over a period. Such reasoning is found in maritime cases, but more often in cases of instalment sales.[60] There are some difficulties in applying this to situations of anticipatory breach of contract, ie where no breach has yet occurred but it reasonably appears that it will occur.[61] Orthodox doctrine, derived from this area of the law, indicates that there is no anticipatory breach merely because a reasonable person would think that the contract would not or could not be performed when the time came: it would be necessary to establish an express or implied refusal to perform, or that it will certainly be impossible to perform at that time.[62] Where there is an actual (as opposed to an anticipatory) breach,[63] however, uncertainty as to what may happen may justify termination of the contract under the third technique.[64]

---

[55] See paras 18.438ff.

[56] See *Jackson v Union Marine Insurance Co* (1874) LR 10 CP 125.

[57] See *Freeman v Taylor* (n 54 above); *Jackson v Union Marine Insurance Co Ltd* (ibid). Compare *Behn v Burness* (n 49 above) where there was breach of a term as to position of the ship and 'condition' reasoning could be used.

[58] See *Jackson v Union Marine Insurance Co* (n 56 above). The monetary consequences are regulated by statute: Law Reform (Frustrated Contracts) Act 1943 but not in this actual context.

[59] See *Withers v Reynolds* (1831) 2 B & Ad 882, 109 ER 1370 (a case on sale of goods).

[60] See Sale of Goods Act 1979, s 31.

[61] See paras 18.430ff; *Chitty on Contracts* (29th edn, 2004) paras 24–018ff.

[62] *Universal Cargo Carriers Corp v Citati* [1957] 2 QB 401, CA where a chartered ship sailed away because the master formed the view that no cargo would be forthcoming.

[63] ie occurring at the time at which performance was due, as opposed to earlier.

[64] See *Maple Flock Co Ltd v Universal Furniture Products (Wembley) Co Ltd* [1934] 1 KB 148 (instalment sale).

(c) Specific contract clauses

11.41   The inevitable uncertainties of invoking the general law on termination (except where there is no doubt that the term concerned ranks as a condition) lead to the presence in charterparties of clauses designed to enable one party to avoid uncertainty and terminate regardless of whether the general law permits. Of these, two, one in favour of the charterer and one in favour of the shipowner, deserve explanation here, since they impinge on and interact with general contractual principles.

(i) The cancelling clause

11.42   This can be found in voyage and in time charterparties, and in general permits the charterer to cancel the contract if the ship does not arrive for loading by a certain time. The same objective could be partially achieved by stipulating that the time of sailing on the approach voyage, or of tender for loading, is a condition of the contract.[65] The cancelling clause is however wider in several respects and cannot be regarded simply as a condition expressed in other wording (against which there is no objection in principle). First, it applies even where the late arrival is excused by an excepted peril, ie is not a breach of contract at all: in this sense it may enable the charterer to act without reference to the doctrine of frustration.[66] Secondly, however, it does not displace the general law as to discharge by breach[67] and frustration,[68] with the result that even if the clause is not exercised, a later frustrating delay would entitle the innocent party to terminate the contract if there was a breach, or if there was not, the contract could be frustrated. Finally, it can be exercised exactly according to its terms; under many forms of the clause the charterer may and even must wait until the ship arrives, even if it is certain to be late, before deciding whether to cancel. By the same token, however, a cancellation outside the terms of the clause, for example, too soon,[69] may be ineffective, even if late arrival is at that point inevitable. It will be seen therefore that as elsewhere in English shipping law, the parties are held strictly to the terms of their contract, and in general no argument is possible that the right was exercised from what may be argued to have been inappropriate motives.

(ii) The withdrawal clause

11.43   This is peculiar to the circumstances of time charterparties. It provides (with many variants of detail) that if the hire is not paid by or before a certain time, the shipowner may withdraw the vessel, ie terminate the charter. This again protects the

---

65   eg *Glaholm v Hays* (1841) 2 Man & G 257, 133 ER 743.
66   *Smith v Dart & Son* (1884) 14 QBD 105.
67   *Hong Kong Fir Shipping Co Ltd v Kawasaki Kisen Kaisha Ltd* [1962] 2 QB 26, CA.
68   *Bank Line Ltd v Arthur Capel & Co* [1919] AC 435.
69   *The Madeleine* [1967] 2 Lloyd's Rep 224.

shipowner from the general law as to discharge by breach, which does not easily apply to late payment. For example, in land transactions it is often said that time of payment is not 'of the essence'.[70] Again, the power can only be exercised in exact accordance with its terms, but again the motive for doing so is not relevant. So it can sometimes, depending on its formulation, be exercised by a shipowner who has already received late payment (unless this constitutes a waiver, which it is unlikely to do since banks, to whom such payment is made, may have no authority to waive contract terms).[71] On the other hand it cannot be exercised before the time stipulated for its exercise, even if it is clear that timely payment can no longer be made.[72]

Unlike late arrival, late payment will rarely be excused by any contract term, and **11.44** the withdrawal clause is therefore almost bound to be exercised in respect of a breach of contract. It is arguable, therefore, that unlike the cancelling clause it is to be regarded as a condition of the contract expressed in other words: interpretation is a matter for the court, and there is no objection to a condition not specifically expressed as such. It seems clear however that this is not so, though a small addition to the wording could give it this effect.[73] The difference in practice is this. If the withdrawal clause is a condition, the shipowner who withdraws the vessel is exercising his right to treat the contract as discharged under the general law and can sue, not only for accrued unpaid instalments, but also for loss of the profit contemplated from the rest of the charterparty, as arising from breach of contract, damages being available at common law in addition to termination. If it is not, no such damages are recoverable, the shipowner having himself chosen to cause the ending of the contract: all that is recoverable is the instalments already due but unpaid.[74] It seems clear that the latter represents the present position in English law. The result is that the shipowner can only sue for full damages for loss of the remainder of the contract if the late payment constituted a repudiatory breach on general principles.[75] Some doubt has however been cast on this result in Australia in connection with similar clauses in hire-purchase and other financing contracts, which are of course analogous.[76]

---

[70] See also Sale of Goods Act 1979, s 10. Cf however the words of Lord Wilberforce as to time clauses in mercantile contracts, quoted above, text to n 51.

[71] See on both points *Mardorf Peach & Co v Attica Sea Carriers Corp (The Laconia)* [1977] AC 850, HL.

[72] *Afovos Shipping Co SA v Pagnan & F.lli (The Afovos)* [1983] 1 WLR 195, though the speech of Lord Diplock seeks to solve the case on the wider and more doubtful ground that the clause constitutes a condition, and there can be no anticipatory breach of condition. 'Anticipatory breach is but a species of the genus repudiation and applies only to fundamental breach' (at 203).

[73] As, in the context of hire purchase, in *Lombard North Central plc v Butterworth* [1987] QB 527, CA ('punctual payment [of] which shall be of the essence').

[74] *Financings Ltd v Baldock* [1963] 2 QB 104.

[75] As in *Leslie Shipping Co v Welstead* [1921] 3 KB 420.

[76] *Esanda Finance Corp Ltd v Plessnig* (1989) 166 CLR 131 esp *per* Brennan J.

11.45   Finally, it will be seen again that the right to withdraw the vessel can, depending on the drafting of the clause, be exercised in a manner onerous to the charterer, who (or whose bank) may have done no more than make a mistake in telex addresses or time zones. In the context of landlord and tenant similar clauses appear in leases in favour of landlords, but the courts have long exercised a jurisdiction to relieve against forfeiture of the lease by granting more time to pay. It might be arguable that a similar jurisdiction should be exercised in connection with charterparties. The principal difference is that in English law a lease creates a property right, protected in appropriate cases by a decree of specific performance, and it is this right that is protected from being forfeited. The right under a time charter is purely contractual, and a decree of specific performance would rarely be appropriate. For such reasons the House of Lords has rejected any such jurisdiction in the case of the withdrawal clause,[77] citing the firm judgment of Robert Goff LJ in the Court of Appeal below.[78] This is consistent with the absence of any doctrine of good faith in English law, at least in this part of it. It is possible that other common law jurisdictions, particularly those inclined to make more use of equitable doctrines in commercial law, might take a different view.[79]

(4) Deviation[80]

11.46   A somewhat unusual doctrine operates in English law in connection with deviation from the contract route. It applies both to voyage charterparties and to bills of lading, including bills of lading governed by the Hague Rules.[81] This route must first be ascertained from the terms of the contract and commercial and navigational practice. It need not be a direct geographical route; and in bill of lading contracts especially, which are likely to involve a ship which calls at several ports, it is unlikely to be so. Most contracts will in fact contain a clause purporting to permit what would otherwise be a deviation in very wide terms, frequently ending with wording such as 'and all of the above shall be deemed to be part of the contract voyage'. Even with such wording these clauses, called 'liberty clauses', have been subjected to very extreme techniques of interpretation *contra*

---

[77] *Scandinavian Trading Tanker Co v Flota Petrolera Ecuatoriana (The Scaptrade)* [1983] 2 AC 694, HL; but cf *Lauritzencool AB v Lady Navigation Inc* [2005] EWCA Civ 579; [2005] 1 WLR 3686 (n 16 above).

[78] [1983] QB 529.

[79] See *Esanda Finance Corp Ltd v Plessnig* (n 76 above).

[80] See in general FMB Reynolds, 'The Implementation of Private Law Conventions in English Law' in *The Butterworth Lectures 1990–91* (1992).

[81] *Stag Line Ltd v Foscolo Mango & Co Ltd* [1932] AC 328, HL. As to the Hague and Hague-Visby Rules see paras 11.56ff. There seems no reason why the doctrine should not apply under the Hague-Visby Rules also: even though these have by virtue of their enacting statute the 'force of law', they only apply to contracts, and if the contract is displaced they would be displaced also. This is one of the matters that a reform of the Rules could cover. See para 11.69.

proferentem: they have been read to be consistent with the contract voyage and not as justifying a ship departing from the normal route.[82]

The contract route being ascertained, a deliberate[83] going off it is a deviation unless specially justified by the requirements of preserving the safety of the adventure, or saving life.[84] The accepted result of this in English law at present appears to be that the shipowner, from the moment of the deviation,[85] loses the benefit of all excepted perils and is remitted to the common law position of a common carrier,[86] the common law exceptions also being displaced, with the result that he is liable unless he can establish that the loss would necessarily have occurred even though he had not deviated.[87] Further than this, it appears, though from less strong authority, that he is equally unable to rely on other contract terms to his benefit, for example demurrage clauses operative on discharge,[88] the duty to pay general average contribution in respect of an event occurring after the deviation,[89] and the contract provision for the payment of freight[90] (other than advance freight)[91] though in the first case it is assumed that he can have damages at large for delay beyond laytime, and in the third it has been said that though not entitled to the contract freight he is entitled to reasonable freight,[92] presumably on a restitutionary basis.[93]

11.47

The doctrine is said to be a reaction to the insurance position, under which when a ship went off the normal route it and its cargo were uninsured: hence the carrier, by doing this took on the insurer's liability[94] and became absolutely liable—but subject to the exception regarding events which would have occurred anyway.

11.48

---

[82] eg *Glynn v Margetson & Co* [1893] AC 351, HL (starting off in wrong direction).

[83] A negligent departure from the route could be negligence in navigation, an excepted peril in most contracts.

[84] A deviation to save the property of others, eg for the purpose of earning a salvage award, would not be justified unless permitted by the terms of the contract—which it often is, and is in most bill of lading contracts by virtue of the Hague Rules and their variants: see Article IV.4.

[85] For a different approach, that the contract is displaced from the beginning, see the authoritative but in this case extremely doubtful view of *Scrutton on Charterparties and Bills of Lading* (20th edn, 1996) 259, n 84. (In an authoritative work of this sort, pregnant footnotes such as this can be of great forensic importance.)

[86] See para 11.25.

[87] *Davis v Garrett* (1830) 6 Bing 716, 130 ER 1456. This in effect limits the operative perils to inherent vice.

[88] *US Shipping Board v Bunge y Born* (1925) 23 Ll L Rep 257, though the point was assumed, not argued or decided.

[89] *Hain SS Co Ltd v Tate & Lyle Ltd* (1936) 41 Com Cas 350, HL.

[90] See *Hain SS Co Ltd v Tate & Lyle Ltd* in the Court of Appeal, (1934) 39 Com Cas 259.

[91] Liability for which would accrue on loading and so before deviation: see para 11.88.

[92] *Hain SS Co Ltd v Tate & Lyle Ltd* in the House of Lords, (1936) 41 Com Cas 350.

[93] See Lord Goff of Chieveley and GH Jones, *Law of Restitution* (6th edn, 2002) paras 20-053, 20-054.

[94] He was even sometimes called an insurer, though this was to use the word in a different sense from its modern meaning.

This could explain the displacement of excepted perils, but not of demurrage, general average and freight provisions.

11.49   The doctrine seems historically to be an amalgamation of rules of proof regarding bailment (a bailee who stores goods in an unauthorized place is liable unless he can establish that the loss must have occurred anyway);[95] interpretation (excepted perils are not intended to apply where the goods are subjected to risks totally different from those contemplated);[96] insurance (an insurance policy is avoided if the ship deviates);[97] and discharge of contract by breach. This last explanation was accepted in the most authoritative case on the doctrine, the decision of the House of Lords in *Hain SS Co Ltd v Tate & Lyle Ltd.*[98] The main issue in this case was however whether a deviation could be waived: on the basis that it was a breach of condition[99] it was held that it could. But the doctrine of discharge by breach has been further developed since that case, and it is now accepted that where the innocent party chooses to terminate the contract, it comes to an end at that moment only and not *ab initio*, nor from the time of breach.[100] Since few cargo owners are aware of the deviation when it occurred,[101] this means that the discharge by breach explanation does not account for substantial features of the doctrine, in particular the displacement of the contract from the moment of deviation, which would in most cases have to be retrospective.

11.50   The English doctrine is a tight one, based on a small number of leading cases. It may be possible to limit it to geographical deviation only, but there are quite strong arguments for extending it to wrongful stowage on deck, since this, like geographical deviation, may subject the goods to different risks from those contemplated. However, in a fairly recent decision (concerning the time bar under the Hague-Visby Rules) the doctrine was not applied in a case where there had been wrongful deck stowage, and Lloyd LJ expressed doubt as to the continued validity of the special doctrine altogether.[102] And it has now been specifically decided that wrongful deck stowage does not displace the package or unit limitation of

---

[95] *Lilley v Doubleday* (1881) 7 QBD 510.

[96] *Gibaud v Great Eastern Rly Co* [1921] 2 KB 426.

[97] The leading case on this point, *Joseph Thorley Ltd v Orchis SS Co Ltd* [1907] 1 KB 660, invokes, however, the rules on displacement of insurance by unseaworthiness, which, since the seaworthiness duty applies at the time of sailing, applies from that point. This has been a source of confusion. In the case itself the difference does not appear to have mattered, since the ship took a wrong route immediately on leaving port.

[98] n 89 above.

[99] See para 11.33.

[100] See *Photo Production Ltd v Securicor Transport Ltd* [1980] AC 827, HL.

[101] Though it was so in *Hain v Tate & Lyle*: indeed this is what gave rise to the principal issue, which concerned waiver.

[102] *The Antares (Nos 1 & 2)* [1987] 1 Lloyd's Rep 424. But for a different explanation see Kerr LJ in *State Trading Corp of India Ltd v M Golodetz Ltd* [1989] 2 Lloyd's Rep 277, 287, CA; cf however Lloyd LJ at 289.

the Hague Rules.[103] Although the decision is influenced by the wording of the Rules themselves, it may be assumed that the deviation doctrine, even if valid, should not be extended to wrongful carriage on deck. In the United States it would appear that the doctrine is somewhat wider as to what can be a deviation, but narrower in its consequences. Although it has been suggested that the doctrine is to be justified as a special one of maritime law,[104] its insurance justification seems now to be inapplicable[105] and it is not unlikely that should the question come before the House of Lords at the present day the whole doctrine would be at the very least, much reduced in effect, even as to geographical deviation. Until it obtains such a review, however, the position remains uncertain.

C. Carriage Under a Bill of Lading

(1) The Nature of the Contract and How it is Made

The nature of a bill of lading contract has already been explained. It is a contract for the carriage of goods by sea under which the carrier accepts goods for carriage in a ship carrying many such consignments, very often running to a schedule and calling at many ports, and issues a bill or bills of lading. It is again, and here obviously, a contract for services (*locatio conductio operarum*). **11.51**

It is important to know in a general way how the bill comes to be issued. Plainly practices must vary enormously over the world. But one may start with the proposition that a shipper or his agent may make a reservation for goods to be carried. If so, an issue may arise as to whether this is contractual, ie binds the carrier to carry, and (though not necessarily) the shipper to ship.[106] It may or may not be. Depending on the facts, the goods may then be sent down, and at the latest a contract of carriage is (normally) formed when they are loaded on the ship. After they have been loaded (and often after the ship has sailed) the carrier gives or returns a bill of lading[107] to the shipper, usually signed by or on behalf of the master, who is an employee of the owner. The bill of lading being issued after the goods are loaded, it is in theory a record of a contract previously made; hence if it is not in accord with prior contractual arrangements, they and not the bill in **11.52**

---

[103] *The Kapitan Petko Voivoda* [2003] EWCA Civ 451; [2003] 2 Lloyd's Rep 1.

[104] *Photo Production Ltd v Securicor Transport Ltd* [1980] AC 827, 845, HL *per* Lord Wilberforce.

[105] Because of clauses in insurance policies providing for deviation (so-called 'held covered' clauses): for an example see *Vincentelli v Rowlett* (1911) 16 Com Cas 310.

[106] See *Scancarriers A/S v Aotearoa International Ltd (The Barranduna and the Tarago)* [1985] 2 Lloyd's Rep 419, PC.

[107] Actually more than one: see para 11.91.

theory prevail.[108] But for most practical purposes the bill of lading is the contract; and it certainly is when in the hands of a third party transferee.[109]

(2) The Common Law Regime

11.53   The regime under which the goods are carried is basically the same as that for voyage charters, with appropriate differences arising from the fact that the whole carrying capacity of the vessel is not being used. The basic common law regime is the same: the principles of interpretation are the same and the deviation rules are likewise applicable, though obviously a ship carrying on bill of lading terms is likely to call at more ports than a ship performing a voyage for a charterer. Dangerous goods raise the same problems. The terms of the contract will not contain the sort of statements about the ship, its position and carrying capacity that are found in charterparties; there will be no provisions (other than incidental ones referring to other contracts) for laytime and demurrage; nor will there be a cancelling clause. The principles as to loading and unloading are the same, though in bill of lading contracts the carrier is likely to undertake these functions: this indeed is a meaning of the phrase 'liner terms'.

11.54   The most conspicuous result of this is that excepted perils favouring the carrier are subject in English law to no more than principles of interpretation, that they do not exclude the basic duties of a carrier unless clearly. On some views such terms could be unfair to cargo interests, as being imposed by carrier monopolies on weaker individual shippers. In the United States wide exclusions could be held void as contrary to public policy.[110] By the end of the nineteenth century the American merchant marine had become less strong than previously, and some American shippers and cargo owners regarded themselves as being at a disadvantage as against European carriers, on whom they depended. This was perhaps the beginning of a division within the shipping industry between those who are perceived as viewing matters from the point of view of cargo shippers and those who are perceived as taking the carrier's position. There is much to be said on both sides.

11.55   An important change was effected by the United States Harter Act of 1893, which established (largely in the interests of cargo) certain basic unexcludable duties of the carrier. The carrier was not permitted to exclude his liability in respect of the two basic duties mentioned above: to provide a seaworthy (including 'cargoworthy') ship, and to exercise due care of the cargo. But there was a *quid pro quo* for the

---

108   *The Ardennes* [1951] 1 KB 55.
109   See paras 11.107ff.
110   See for example *Re Missouri SS Co* (1888) 42 Ch D 321, referring to *The Brantford City* 29 F 373 (1886). The court held that the contract was governed by English law because the carrier could not have intended that his terms be void under American law.

carrier: he was not liable for negligence in navigation or management of the ship (the phrase can be made neater in some other languages, for example, *faute nautique*). The reasons for this protection, which may seem odd to someone unfamiliar with this area of law, were perhaps first, that in early times when sea carriage was genuinely an 'adventure' it might be difficult to establish negligence in a carrier, or even to establish what happened at all; secondly, the fact that once the ship had sailed the master was out of the owner's control; and thirdly some element of assumption (not always justified in modern times at least) that carriers would in their own interests take care in navigation, in order to preserve their ship and indeed the lives of those involved.

(3) The Hague Rules Regime

(a) Emergence of the Hague Rules

Further work on control of bill of lading terms went on in various ways in the late nineteenth century, and after the First World War it was resumed in earnest at meetings of the International Law Association at The Hague in 1921, to a considerable extent under American leadership. A new argument for the work then became prominent: the value of uniformity of the documentation which was used in connection with sea carriage—documentation which can be used to transfer the cargo and with it the contract, and which for the same reason passed and passes through banks financing sales. These came to finance many international sales on the security of the goods as represented by the documents, and had an interest in similarity of regime between one bill of lading and another. It was also true that quite a lot of international uniformity could be secured through the great colonial empires of the time. All this gave an impetus to the idea of an agreed international regime. **11.56**

The meetings produced draft rules which were the result of compromise between cargo and shipowning interests. They were drafted in English and translated into French (the main diplomatic language of the time) and adopted at a Diplomatic Conference in Brussels in 1924. They were then translated back into English. This explains some oddities of phraseology; and in some countries the French text prevails, in some the English (or sometimes the text in some other language). The Rules are normally called the Hague Rules, though they were in fact adopted in Brussels in 1924. Information about them is available the world over. They are not of course a feature specific to English law. Hence, only a very brief account is given here for completeness. **11.57**

They apply to contracts covered by a bill of lading 'or any similar document of title'.[111] **11.58**

---

[111] Article I. (b). See para 11.110.

(b) Non-excludable duties of the carrier

11.59   The key feature of the Hague Rules was a division of the risks which was in effect the same as that under the Harter Act (which, though largely superseded, still applies in limited circumstances in the United States). The carrier owes non-excludable[112] duties of:

(i)   'due diligence' in the furnishing of a seaworthy (including cargoworthy) ship (Article III.1);

(ii)   and in the care of cargo (Article III.2)—the two basic principles already mentioned above,[113] but in English law the subject of principles of interpretation only.

(c) The excepted perils

11.60   In return, the carrier:

(iii)   is not liable in respect of seventeen listed exclusions, traditionally again called 'excepted perils', of which the most significant are 'act, neglect or default [ie negligence] in the navigation or management of the ship' (which may be more concisely referred to as 'nautical fault'), and 'fire unless caused by the actual fault or privity of the carrier' (Article IV.1, 2).

11.61   It will be seen that this compromise between the interests of cargo and ship places some risks on one party, some on the other. To make it work it is necessary first to know the facts, in order to determine into which sphere of risk the event which occurred came. This, at least in the negotiating stages of a dispute, may result in the burden of proof rules becoming of considerable importance. Even where the facts are known, it may be arguable to the highest tribunal into which sphere of risk those facts came: for example, they might arguably constitute negligence in care of cargo, for which the carrier is liable, or negligence in management of the ship, for which he is not.[114] Equally, a ship may be navigated negligently; but the cause of an event may be held to be an inadequate crew making the ship unseaworthy.[115] It is argued that this creates inefficiency, and that a single rule based on fault

---

[112] Article III.8.

[113] See para 11.26. The common law seaworthiness duty was however a strict one, not merely one of due diligence.

[114] For an example of this sort of dispute see an early case on the Rules, *Gosse Millerd Ltd v Canadian Government Merchant Marine Ltd* [1929] AC 223, PC (unseaworthiness or negligence in management). For a more recent example see *The Aquacharm* [1982] 1 Lloyds Rep 7 (unseaworthiness or negligent stowage).

[115] The shipper is under a strict duty not to ship dangerous goods. This, where neither shipper knows or should know of the danger, is a rule of risk allocation.

liability (as can be found, in slightly different forms, in Conventions on road, rail and air transport) would be preferable.

(d) Limitation of liability

11.62 There was however a new feature introduced. Unless a higher value is stated (which is rare) the carrier's liability in respect of the goods was (and is) limited to a specific sum per 'package or unit'. Reasons for this limitation were, first (perhaps), that carriers had been able previously by wide exclusions effective in many countries to exclude their liability almost completely; and (a more obvious argument) that carriers do not easily know what purpose goods they carry are intended to serve, or even sometimes what they are: like burglar-alarm suppliers, they cannot undertake unlimited liability. But the sum set was at the time quite high: £100 sterling in the English version, and the same or roughly equivalent sums elsewhere.

(e) Insurance

11.63 Shipping is dominated by insurance. Therefore within this regime the *cargo owner* may, though he need not, carry general insurance in respect of all or particular risks relating to the goods. This will protect him also against matters in respect of which the carrier is not liable (negligence in navigation or management, etc) and loss above the package/unit limitation. This is insurance of goods. The *carrier* usually insures most of his *liabilities* through a mutual insurance association (P & I Club), or on similar terms in the market, by way of liability insurance. Cargo insurers may prosecute claims against carriers by way of subrogation, with the result that, as already stated, litigated disputes in connection with carriage by sea are often really between insurers.

(f) Time bar

11.64 Another new feature was that actions against (but not by) the carrier were made subject to a one-year time bar. This is still a trap for non-specialist lawyers: it is justified on the basis that the carrier cannot be expected to keep records indefinitely and must be able to close his books on particular voyages fairly quickly.

(4) The Hague-Visby Rules

11.65 The Hague-Visby (or Visby) Rules are the same as the Hague Rules, with the addition of certain fairly minor changes, mostly perceived (rightly or wrongly) by cargo interests as being for the convenience of carriers, originating from a conference of the CMI (Comité Maritime International) in Stockholm in 1963.

A proposed draft was signed at the ancient Baltic City of Visby, and a modified version was finally adopted at Brussels in 1968 as a Protocol to the 1924 Convention.[116] The most conspicuous changes dealt with:

(i) 'inflation-proofing' the package or unit limitation (which had been adopted in most countries as a fixed sum thought appropriate in the 1920s or at some other later time, but in any case had been over the years subjected to the ravages of inflation)[117] by linking it to gold value by the Poincaré franc, a monetary unit defined by reference to gold value;[118]

(ii) adding a weight limitation (for bulk cargo and heavy packages): a certain sum per kilo of gross weight whichever (of this and the package or unit limitation) is higher;[119]

(iii) the application of the package or unit limitation in respect of containers, a point to which the Rules of 1924 were not of course directed: whether or not the container is a 'package' depends on whether the bill of lading is filled in so as to 'enumerate' its contents;[120]

(iv) the application of the Rules to tort actions,[121] especially against stevedores, who were intended by carriers to be entitled to the same protections as themselves. The strong English rule as to privity of contract prevented this being achieved unless a special clause was used, the so-called 'Himalaya' clause,[122] which was held to create a separate contract between claimant and stevedore incorporating the limit.[123] A new Article IV.*bis* was intended to deal with this problem, referred to in the negotiations as the 'Himalaya problem', but in fact it does not appear on its wording to protect stevedores, because it

---

[116] For an authoritative and comprehensive account of the Hague-Visby Rules, containing much information as to their genesis and as to the Hague Rules also, see AEJ Diamond 'The Hague-Visby Rules' [1978] LMCLQ 225. See further books listed in n 1 above.

[117] In *The Rosa S* [1989] QB 419 it was said that the modern equivalent of £100 in 1924 was, converted by the relative values of gold between one time and the other, at the later time £6,630.50.

[118] Article IV.5(a).

[119] ibid.

[120] Article IV.5(c). The interpretation of the 1924 Rules is, at any rate in England, different and more favourable to the cargo owner: see *The River Gurara* [1998] QB 610. There had meanwhile been a number of cases on the application of the Rules to containers in the United States, and a smaller number in Canada and Australia. For a recent Australian case on the limitation containing most elaborate discussion, see *El Greco (Australia) Pty Ltd v Mediterranean Shipping Co SA* [2004] 2 Lloyd's Rep 537.

[121] Article IV.*bis*.

[122] The reason for this is that the possibility of evading contract terms by suing in tort was first exposed in a case on carriage of passengers involving the P & O liner 'Himalaya': *Adler v Dickson* [1955] 1 QB 158. A clause to deal with the problem was then drafted for insertion into bills of lading, which was (and is) colloquially referred to as the 'Himalaya' clause.

[123] *New Zealand Shipping Co Ltd v AM Satterthwaite & Co Ltd (The Eurymedon)* [1975] AC 154, PC.

specifically excludes independent contractors.[124] Not all countries favour the extension of the carrier's protections to stevedoring companies;[125]

(v) making the Rules more effective internationally under conflict of laws rules (closing the so-called '*Vita Food* gap').[126]

Words were also inserted dealing with the probative effect of statements in bills of lading.[127] These changes have been in effect in the United Kingdom since 1977.[128]

(a) The SDR protocol

Problems with the gold standard applied by the Poincaré franc have led to the later adoption of another Protocol which states the package or unit and per kilo limitation in terms of special drawing rights on the International Monetary Fund. It is now, under this method, approximately at present US $1,000 per package or unit (which, bearing in mind that a container need not, and will not usually, be a package, is said (by some at least) to be adequate in most situations). This Protocol is effective in the United Kingdom.[129] **11.66**

(b) International variations

Over the years since 1924 many countries have adhered to the Hague Rules, with the results that bills of lading governed by the laws of those countries are usually compulsorily governed by those Rules, at least in respect of outward shipments and before the courts of a contracting state of shipment. **11.67**

Of these some have moved to the Hague-Visby Rules; and of those that did, some have adopted the SDR Protocol and some not—which gives three types of state. Others did not adhere to the Convention at all, but enacted something very **11.68**

---

[124] Article IV.*bis* 2.

[125] This seems particularly so in Australia.

[126] The problem was first exposed in an appeal to the Privy Council in London from Nova Scotia, *Vita Food Products Inc v Unus Shipping Co Ltd* [1939] AC 277, PC. A bill of lading might contain a clause choosing the law of a country which either did not apply the Rules at all or did not apply them to the voyage in question. This is a manifestation of the problem of the international operation of mandatory rules, towards which Article 7 of the Rome Convention on the Law Applicable to Contractual Obligations is now directed. Article 7(1), highly relevant to this form of the problem, is not however adopted in all states. The solution adopted in England was to give the Rules the 'force of law': since they provide that they apply on (in general) shipment out of contracting states, this binds an English court to apply them to shipment out of any other contracting state whichever law is applicable to the bill of lading in general. The technique was held effective (in respect of a shipment out of Scotland governed by Dutch law and jurisdiction) in *The Hollandia* [1983] AC 565, HL.

[127] Article III.4, second sentence. These had a useful effect in England because of the old case of *Grant v Norway* (1851) 10 CB 665, 138 ER 263, as to which see para 11.97.

[128] Carriage of Goods by Sea Act 1971, effective 1977.

[129] Merchant Shipping Act 1981, s 2(4). The amounts are 666.67 units of account per package or unit or 2 units of account per kilogramme weight of the goods lost or damaged.

similar in their local law (eg until comparatively recently, Greece—raising problems in the conflict of laws).[130] Others again did none of these things; but of these
most if not all would recognize a specific incorporation of the Rules into a bill of
lading, which is a very common type of clause.

11.69　It will be seen that considerable diversity between regimes has developed. It is also
undoubtedly true that the Rules have been interpreted differently from one country to another.[131] But on the whole there has been still a reasonable measure of
uniformity worldwide, if differences in detail.

(5)　The Hamburg Rules of 1978

11.70　There is now however a further possible regime for carriage by sea, that of the
Hamburg Rules. These originate from work by first UNCTAD and then
UNCITRAL in the 1970s and were adopted at a Diplomatic Conference at
Hamburg in 1978. They constitute a completely different regime. They were
intended further to redress an imbalance said to exist in favour of the carrier under
the existing regimes, and said to be prejudicial to developing countries. The main
criticism related to the split of risks achieved in 1924, the problems of which have
already been mentioned: the Hamburg Rules replace this with what is intended to
be a more or less unitary regime (similar to but not the same as those applicable in
carriage by air and road), that the carrier is liable unless he proves that he was not
at fault.

11.71　The Hamburg Rules have so far been ratified by about 23 countries, several of
which are land-locked and few of which are conspicuously involved in maritime
commerce; and of these it does not at present appear that many have actually
brought the Rules into force.

(6)　The Present Situation

11.72　There is at present some danger of international fragmentation of a more or less
international regime. There is dissatisfaction in some quarters with the Hague
Rules and their variants, but the Hamburg Rules are in many quarters not found
attractive either. Work is being conducted under the auspices of UNCITRAL

130　See *The Komninos S* [1991] 1 Lloyd's Rep 370.

131　A well-known example is the so-called 'before and after' problem, concerned with which
operations of loading and unloading are covered by the Rules. The English view is that the contract can determine the limits of operation of the Rules in this respect: see *Pyrene Co Ltd v Scindia
Navigation Ltd* [1954] 2 QB 402, the reasoning of which is affirmed in *The Jordan II* [2004] UKHL
49; [2005] 1 WLR 1363, HL (n 38 above). In other countries this might be regarded as an exclusion of the Rules: an example appears in *The Saudi Prince (No 2)* [1988] 1 Lloyd's Rep 1. Similar
problems occur in connection with the demise clause: see n 149 below.

with a view to revising the Hague Rules to incorporate what are regarded as the best features of the Hamburg Rules. At the same time other countries[132] have revised their domestic law to take in some features of the Hamburg Rules and some special features of their own; and in the United States there have been proposals for changing the law in a way that would destroy uniformity even further.

(7) Global Limitation of Carrier's Liability

It should be remembered that in most countries shipowners operate *also* under a **11.73** global limitation of all liability in respect of any single incident, usually related to the tonnage of the ship.[133] This is an ancient privilege, not applicable to other forms of transport.[134]

D. Bill of Lading for Goods in a Chartered Ship

It was stated early in this chapter that even though a shipper had a full cargo and **11.74** hence was chartering a vessel, a bill or bills of lading would normally be issued to provide evidence of shipment and facilitate transfer of the cargo during transit. This point now needs further elaboration.

Bills of lading for goods in a chartered ship are in fact issued in two different **11.75** types of situation. They may first be issued to a charterer who requires a receipt, wishes thereby to facilitate delivery, and may wish to be able to transfer the goods after shipment. That is the situation referred to at the beginning of this chapter. But there is a second situation, that arising where the ship is under charter, but is used to carry shipments under bills of lading exactly as an owner carrying on liner terms might use it. An obvious background to this situation is that where the charterer is in fact a line operator who has chartered extra tonnage,[135] but there are many other possibilities. For example, a ship operator may enter into contracts of carriage with shippers without owning any ships, but simply chartering them.[136]

---

132 Notably the Nordic countries, China and Japan.
133 The relevant United Kingdom legislation is the Merchant Shipping Act 1995, which implements the Convention on Limitation of Liability for Maritime Claims of 1976.
134 See the Rt Hon Lord Mustill, 'Ships Are Different Or Are They?' [1993] LMCLQ 403.
135 As in the famous case of *Elder Dempster & Co Ltd v Paterson, Zochonis & Co Ltd* [1924] AC 522, HL.
136 In some contexts the acronym 'NVOCC' ('Non-vessel owning contracting carrier') or something similar may be used.

(1) Bill of Lading Given to Charterer

11.76 Here there are potentially two contracts of carriage, and they are likely to have different terms: apart from anything else, the Hague Rules or a variant are likely to apply to the bill of lading but not to the charterparty.[137] In this case, as a matter of interpretation, the contract with the charterer is in English law the charterparty, and the bill of lading is merely a receipt: in case of a clash of terms the charterparty prevails.[138] This is so even if, as is common in fob sales, the bill of lading is first issued to a shipper other than the charterer (who may for example need it as security against his purchaser), and then indorsed to the charterer.[139] In such a case the bill has already had a contractual operation as such, but loses it.

11.77 When however such a bill of lading is then indorsed to a third party, a contract springs up between that party and the carrier on bill of lading terms,[140] including normally the Hague Rules. The charterer remains liable and entitled on the charterparty,[141] though particular forms of contract clause can be used to seek to limit this effect.[142] Potentially, however, the carrier has contracts with two parties on different terms, though the problem may be met in part by incorporation of charterparty terms into the bill of lading.[143]

(2) Bills of Lading Given to Other Shippers

11.78 This occurs where a ship which is chartered is made available for the carriage of goods on bill of lading terms. There are here two main problems: the 'identity of carrier' problem and the 'actual carrier' problem.

(a) The 'identity of carrier' problem

11.79 The difficulty here is to ascertain who is the carrier, ie the party who contracts to carry the goods. It is unfortunately true that the bill of lading often does not make this clear, and unless a requirement that the name of the carrier be stated in a certain way can be identified by international convention, which is sometimes

---

137 The Hague Rules are however in such situations sometimes incorporated into the charterparty. Since their wording is in many ways inappropriate to charterparties, this may raise difficult problems of interpretation. A leading case is *Adamastos Shipping Co Ltd v Anglo-Saxon Petroleum Co Ltd* [1959] AC 133.

138 *Rodocanachi Sons & Co v Milburn Brothers* (1886) 17 QBD 316.

139 *President of India v Metcalfe Shipping Co Ltd (The Dunelmia)* [1970] 1 QB 289.

140 *Hain SS Co v Tate & Lyle Ltd* (1936) 41 Com Cas 350, 357, 364, HL.

141 See *The Albazero* [1977] AC 774.

142 Notably the 'cesser' clause, which removes the charterer's liability for matters covered by the carrier's lien. It gives rise to complex problems of interpretation.

143 From a receiver's point of view the most dangerous clauses which might be incorporated are probably arbitration clauses and liens.

suggested, the problem will remain. A particular difficulty for a cargo claimant is that the correct defendant must be established within the Hague Rules time bar.[144] There are two main indications on the face of the bill: the logo or heading at the top, and the attesting signature at the bottom. The former may well indicate the name of the commercial operator of the vessel—in a simple situation, that of the charterer. The latter is often preceded by printed wording such as 'for the master'. Since the master is normally employed by the shipowner,[145] that would indicate a contract with the shipowner. On the whole English courts tend to give preference to the signature and in the absence of other indications hold the shipowner to be the carrier.[146] This may have the advantage of facilitating arrest of the ship on a cargo claim; but courts from one country to another may differ on the resolution of this question.[147]

If the issue arises in connection with the original shipper, there is the further complication that the form of the bill of lading is not conclusive, since in theory at least it only evidences a contract made earlier,[148] and the initial dealings between the relevant parties may have to be taken into account.   **11.80**

Finally, clauses may appear on the reverse of a bill of lading which purport to create the result that the contract is with the owner, notwithstanding anything that appears (on the face or elsewhere) to the contrary. They appear in various forms and are often called 'demise' or 'identity of carrier' clauses.[149] If effective, they are, again, in some respects advantageous to a cargo claimant. They raise considerable problems if the court seeks, as it often does in other parts of law, to interpret the document as a whole. It has recently been held, however, that where the front is absolutely clear as to who is the carrier, this may prevail over such clauses on the reverse.[150]   **11.81**

---

[144] See para 11.64.

[145] Or, as always, the demise charterer.

[146] The leading case is *The Rewia* [1991] 2 Lloyd's Rep 325.

[147] This was so in *The Rewia* (ibid), itself, where German law was apparently different.

[148] See para 11.93.

[149] For the origin of such clauses, which is not what might have been expected, see Lord Roskill (1990) 106 LQR 403. The clause can be said to have a beneficial effect in facilitating arrest of the ship on a cargo claim; but a problem is that such a clause often appears only in very small print on the reverse of the document, and hence can be overlooked until it is (by virtue of the time bar) too late. It is sometimes argued that they are contrary to the Hague Rules in removing the liability of the party who is in truth the carrier. The English view is, rather, that they identify the carrier: see *The Berkshire* [1974] 1 Lloyd's Rep 185.

[150] *The Starsin* [2003] UKHL 12; [2004] 1 AC 715. Some reliance is placed on the Uniform Customs and Practice on Documentary Credits, under which banks to no accept responsibility to look on the reverse of bills of lading: see [126].

(b) The 'actual carrier' problem

11.82 Where the contract of carriage is established as made with a *charterer* (which, as has been said above, is in English law the minority rather than the majority interpretation) a further difficulty arises. If there is a cargo claim, it may be sought to sue the shipowner who actually carried the goods, who can be called the 'actual carrier' in distinction to the charterer, who may be called the 'contracting carrier'.

11.83 The reasons for seeking to do this may vary. It is the shipowner whose operations actually caused the loss or damage. The ship may be in port and amenable to arrest. It may not be clear who is legally the carrier until a late stage, when proceedings against the shipowner are under way. Finally, it may be to a claimant's advantage to use the argument that the shipowner, being not a party to the contract of carriage, cannot rely on the exclusions and limitations in it, and in particular package or unit limitation and time bar of the Hague Rules or a variant.[151]

11.84 The action against the shipowner would be in tort, and in general could only be brought by a party who owned, or had a possessory interest in,[152] the goods at the time they were lost or damaged.[153] A claim on any other basis would be a claim for pure economic loss and in general could not be easily brought in English law.[154] This restriction would in practice make claims much more difficult to establish where (as is common) the ownership of the goods had changed several times while they were in transit. Beyond this however the doctrine of privity of contract in English law has made it difficult to avoid the conclusion that the shipowner is unprotected by the Rules. He may be protected if the problem has been foreseen and a 'Himalaya' clause[155] is present in the contract, though the wording of these is not always appropriate to this situation because they were originally designed to protect stevedores and employees rather than actual carriers. A standard form starts by giving the subcontractor (or other relevant party) complete immunity, but in a second paragraph simply purports to confer the benefits of the contract defences (which usually means the Hague or Hague-Visby Rules). The first is appropriate to stevedores, but not to actual carriers, who however might justifiably rely on the second part. An important recent decision of the House of Lords[156] holds the first part of the clause void as contrary to Article III.8 of the Hague and Hague-Visby Rules, which in effect prohibit the carrier from contracting out of

---

151 See paras 11.62 and 11.64.
152 Such as a bank holding the documents as pledgee.
153 *Leigh & Sillavan Ltd v Aliakmon Shipping Co Ltd (The Aliakmon)* [1986] AC 785, HL.
154 *Candlewood Navigation Corp Ltd v Mitsui OSK Lines Ltd (The Mineral Transporter)* [1986] AC 1, HL.
155 See para 11.65.
156 *The Starsin* [2003] UKHL 12; [2004] 1 AC 715.

his responsibilities thereunder,[157] though the reasoning is not completely unanimous. This leaves the second part of the clause to apply to actual carriers. Another clause that may be used is a 'circular indemnity' clause.[158] There is a mysterious provision inserted in the Hague-Visby Rules, Article IV. *bis*1, which might cover this situation, but it is far from clear that it does, and the Court of Appeal has held[159] that it does not.[160] Where these devices are not effective, English courts have experimented with reasoning arising out of the common law concept of bailment (which could assist here, though not in the stevedore situation since stevedores as such are not bailees).[161] The reasoning is that the actual carrier, as bailee or sub-bailee, takes the goods on the terms which he agreed with the contracting carrier, to which the latter has been authorized to subject them.[162] This has not yet been fully worked out, though as in other areas discussion in maritime law may yield reasoning applicable elsewhere, for example in warehousing. The Supreme Court of Canada has in the context of warehousing suggested even wider, largely tort-based reasoning, the application of which has been commended by Lord Goff of Chieveley.[163] In any case it seems now that statutory reform of the law of privity of contract in England may solve the problem, at least where the bill of lading is clear as to such beneficiaries.[164]

E. Freight

The rules regarding accrual of freight liability can appear very technical, and, as elsewhere in this part of the law, turn very specifically on the contract wording used. All that can be done here is to draw attention to certain salient points. The normal understanding as to freight (other than time charter hire) is that, as with many contracts for services, it is payable on delivery of the goods at destination;[165]   **11.85**

---

[157] See para 11.59.

[158] ie a clause under which the shipper promises not to sue the carrier's employees and subcontractors, and to indemnify the carrier for any loss it may cause the carrier in doing so. These clauses are much in use by freight forwarders.

[159] *The Captain Gregos* [1990] 1 Lloyd's Rep 310, though not after very full argument.

[160] The Hamburg Rules (paras 11.70ff) contain provisions intended to deal with the problem, but they are not at all clear: see Articles 10, 11.

[161] *The Pioneer Container* [1994] 2 AC 324, PC; *The Mahkutai* [1996] AC 650, PC. The facts in the first case are particularly instructive as to the complexities which can arise in practice.

[162] This is a possible solution to *The Starsin*, above: see at [132]ff. The case was resolved in the basis of the Himalaya clause.

[163] See *London Drugs v Kuehne & Nagel International Ltd* [1992] 3 SCR 299; (1992) 97 DLR (4th) 261, referred to in *The Mahkutai* (n 161 above) at 665. The *London Drugs* case actually offers three different lines of reasoning, and in respect of a clause that did not even refer to third parties.

[164] See Contracts (Rights of Third Parties) Act 1999, ss 1(5), 6(2)(a).

[165] But not at a different place, unless the goods were voluntarily accepted there: *Hopper v Burness* (1876) 1 CPD 137.

and a carrier normally has a lien for it.[166] If the goods arrive damaged or short and the cause of this is within the carrier's responsibility, he is entitled to freight but liable in damages.[167] But if they do not arrive at all, and the cause is an excepted peril, the carrier is not liable, yet earns no freight or, in the case of part delivery, only a reduced freight.[168] It may then be said that the 'risk of freight' is on the carrier, and he may seek to insure this risk.

11.86 As to the amount of freight payable, a distinction is drawn between contracts where the freight is a lump sum not conditioned to the dimensions or weight of the cargo, and those where it is so calculated. In the former case the full freight is payable if there is sufficient cargo delivered to rank as a delivery:[169] shortages or damage are compensated in damages where the cause of loss is the carrier's responsibility, but the freight itself is earned.

11.87 If however the freight is calculated by the dimensions or weight of the cargo it is only earned on cargo delivered. But the mere fact that the cargo delivered is damaged does not prevent liability for freight from accruing:[170] freight is again payable, but the damage can be claimed for if it was within the carrier's responsibility, unless the damage is so serious that the goods have in effect become something else, so that it cannot be said that there has been delivery of the goods shipped at all.[171]

11.88 An unusual arrangement, perhaps unique to common law, is constituted by the notion of advance freight. This refers to an arrangement whereby the freight is stipulated as earned on shipment: if the goods are taken on board,[172] the freight becomes due irrespective of delivery at destination, though of course if non-delivery or damage is within the carrier's responsibility he is liable in damages. Where it is not, however, the freight is still due, and if paid cannot be recovered: hence this arrangement reverses the 'risk of freight'. The origin of advance freight lies in methods of financing and insuring the long voyages between Europe and the Far East in the nineteenth century.[173]

---

[166] The carrier's lien may cover other matters as well such as advance freight and demurrage, even sometimes at the port of loading. The law is complex and often involves incorporation of charterparty terms in the bill of lading. See *Scrutton on Charterparties and Bills of Lading* (20th edn, 1996) ch XVIII.

[167] Subject in the case of most bills of lading to the Hague Rules time bar.

[168] But see paras 11.86 and 11.87.

[169] *William Thomas & Sons v Harrowing SS Co* [1915] AC 58, HL.

[170] *Dakin v Oxley* (1864) 15 CB (NS) 646, 143 ER 938.

[171] *Asfar & Co v Blundell* [1896] 1 QB 123 (dates saturated by sewage).

[172] And, perhaps, the ship sails.

[173] See *Allison v Bristol Marine Insurance Co* (1876) 1 App Cas 209, 223, 225.

In neither case can a claim against the carrier be enforced by a simple deduction **11.89** from freight, even though this is normal in construction contracts.[174] The freight remains due, and the claim against the carrier must be maintained separately.[175] This can obviously give rise to procedural technicalities and arguments. It is not true in other contracts such as those for construction, and is a special maritime rule concerned with the desirability of speedy settlement of liquidated claims.

F. The Functions of the Bill of Lading and Other Documents

(1) The Bill of Lading

The bill of lading has long been a key document in the performance of inter- **11.90** national sale transactions, though it is now to some extent being superseded by documents which are simpler at least on their face; and present day paper documentation may in due course itself be superseded by electronic methods. For the present however there is no doubt that an understanding of traditional bills of lading is required for a proper comprehension of international transactions involving carriage by sea. As in the case of contracts of carriage, international sale contracts are frequently governed by English law. The United Kingdom has not adopted the Vienna Convention on International Sales, and the majority of sale disputes litigated in superior tribunals in the United Kingdom involve large scale transactions, often concerning bulk commodities, governed by standard terms which exclude the Convention specifically, and as 'international supply contracts' are not subject to the Unfair Contract Terms Act 1977.[176]

The bill of lading is a document which states that described goods have been **11.91** shipped by a named party, in 'apparent good order and condition' unless otherwise stated, for carriage to a designated port on a named ship, and delivery there to a named consignee or in accordance with other instructions. The principal indications are given in boxes on the face of the document. On the reverse of the traditional bill[177] appear terms of the contract, usually in extremely small type, though these are in most situations subject to the Hague Rules or their variants.[178] As previously explained, it is not normally issued till the goods are on board. In principle it ought to be tendered at destination by the person claiming

---

[174] *Aries Tanker Corp v Total Transport Ltd (The Aries)* [1977] 1 WLR 185, HL; *Bank of Boston v European Grain and Shipping Ltd (The Dominique)* [1989] AC 1056, HL.

[175] Though how this is done is a matter of procedural law.

[176] s 26. The Convention is not well suited to such contracts.

[177] There can be 'short form bills' with a blank reverse, where the terms are incorporated by reference.

[178] See paras 11.56ff.

the goods.[179] By ancient custom it is normal in international carriage to have several bills of lading, each of which ranks as 'the bill of lading', originally in order that different bills might be sent to the destination by different routes, on the basis that at least one might arrive in time to enable the goods to be claimed. The carrier is entitled to deliver against one of these only.[180] This practice obviously gives rise to possibilities of fraud,[181] and buyers, and banks financing sales on letters of credit, will normally stipulate for all the bills (a 'full set'), as may buyers. It is not clear what beyond tradition maintains this practice of having several bills of lading at the present day.

(2) Functions of the Bill of Lading

11.92 A bill of lading is normally said to be evidence of the contract of carriage, a receipt for the goods and a document of title. To this should be added that it constitutes, by statute in United Kingdom law, a transferable contract.

(a) Evidence of the Contract of Carriage

11.93 This point has been mentioned already.[182] The way in which the contract is made means that the bill of lading, which acknowledges shipment, will in the normal course of things only be issued when the goods are on board. Receipt on board is likely to be the latest moment at which the contract of carriage is made: if the booking of space creates on the facts a contractual obligation, it can be made earlier. Hence it can be said that as regards the original contracting party the bill of lading is no more than evidence of a contract made earlier, and that in case of difference the contract made earlier prevails.[183]

11.94 This point is however a small one: for most practical purposes the terms on the bill constitute the contract terms, whether by course of dealing, because the shipper is regarded as having accepted the carrier's terms whatever they are, or because

---

[179] This was recently reaffirmed in *The Sormovskiy 3068* [1994] 2 Lloyd's Rep 266 and *The Houda* [1994] 2 Lloyd's Rep 541. It has been held that the carrier does not perform by delivery against a forged bill of lading: *Motis Exports Ltd v Dampskibsselkabet AF 1912* [2000] 1 Lloyd's Rep 211, CA. But where bills of lading are extensively traded, they may arrive long after the goods. It is common therefore for charterparties to contain contractual provisions obliging the carrier to deliver without a bill of lading, in return for the promise of an indemnity against any liability incurred as a consequence of so doing (eg, because delivery is made to a person not entitled). Since the carrier may not be covered by his P & I insurance, he should be guaranteed by a bank.

[180] This is usually secured by traditional wording on the bill such as 'In witness whereof the master has signed three bills of lading, all of this tenor and date, *one of which being accomplished, the others shall stand void*'. Such bills are called 'originals'. There may also be file copies.

[181] As occurred in *Glyn Mills, Currie & Co v East & West India Dock Co* (1882) 7 App Cas 591.

[182] See para 11.79.

[183] See para 11.52.

the oral contract can be said to be reduced to writing by the bill. And, bills of lading being transferable, there is no doubt that in the hands of the third party the bill of lading constitutes the contract, for the third party has (except in unusual circumstances) no knowledge of the original dealings and has a contract based only on what appears on the face and reverse of the document. Thus a permission given by the original shipper to make what would otherwise be a deviation does not affect the transferee.[184]

It may be noted that the bill is not conclusive as to who are the parties to the contract of carriage. It is likely that the party named in the 'shipper' box is such a party, but this need not be so: the party named may be an agent (and in common law there can be agency for completely undisclosed principals)[185] or simply a person who delivered the goods to the ship, perhaps as an fob seller to the person contracting for carriage. In the latter situation, the seller may by virtue of the bill of lading have an initial contract, probably of carriage, with the carrier while he holds the bill as a security against payment, even though the fob buyer has chartered the vessel. And as has been explained, the question of who is the carrier may not be clearly answered by the bill and require solution by techniques of contract interpretation.[186]   **11.95**

(b) Receipt for the Goods

A bill of lading normally contains printed words such as 'Shipped in apparent good order and condition unless otherwise stated' and is signed on behalf of the carrier. This constitutes an acknowledgment by the carrier that the goods have been received as described: if the goods do not arrive as described or at all, the acknowledgement is obviously of great importance in the maintenance of a claim against the carrier, who may otherwise wish to argue that the goods were never shipped, or short shipped, or were in bad condition on shipment. The words concerned are in the form of a statement not a promise, and hence carry the legal consequences of statements. They therefore constitute prima facie evidence against the carrier: but this can be disproved.   **11.96**

It might be thought further that under the general common law doctrine of estoppel the carrier would be estopped by such a statement from proving the contrary. In accordance with the normal rules, there is a statement of fact which may be relied on by the holder of the bill.[187] There may be difficulty in proving reliance if the claimant is the original shipper, for as such he should be aware,   **11.97**

---

[184] See *Leduc & Co v Ward* (1888) 20 QBD 475.
[185] See paras 9.68 ff.
[186] The 'identity of carrier' problem: see para 11.79.
[187] On different kinds of estoppel, all of which bind a person to some statement, state of affairs, assumption, or promise, see paras 8.52ff, 8.60ff, 8.202.

whether directly or through others, of what was shipped and the condition in which it was at the time. A transferee of the bill of lading, however, will not find it difficult to prove such reliance, simply by 'taking up' the bill, ie buying it or lending money on its security.[188] Difficulties have however been encountered where the complaint is of non-delivery or short delivery and the carrier seeks to prove that, contrary to what is on the bill, the goods were never shipped, or that fewer goods were shipped than what is stated. In the famous nineteenth-century case of *Grant v Norway*[189] it was held that the carrier could rely on the argument that the master had and was generally known to have no authority to sign for goods not on board, with the result that a statement as to quantity shipped did not bind the carrier. This is obsolete reasoning by modern standards: the master may have no actual authority to sign in such a case, but he surely has apparent authority to do so, or at least to state whether the goods are on board or not.[190] The case has never come before the House of Lords, which alone could probably now overrule it.[191] In the absence of judicial decision the matter has now been dealt with by statute;[192] but it is important to understand what it was that gave rise to the statutory reform.[193]

11.98 Estoppels on the statements as to apparent good order and condition were never subjected to these difficulties, perhaps because the leading decisions came later, and the carrier can be estopped by such statements.[194] There are, however, some statements, usually inserted by the shipper for reasons of his own documentary requirements, to which the carrier is not in any case as a matter of interpretation usually regarded as attesting despite his signature, for example quality indications.[195]

---

[188] See *Silver v Ocean SS Co* [1930] 1 KB 416.

[189] (1851) 10 CB 665, 138 ER 263.

[190] The leading case rejecting such reasoning, but in a tort claim, is *Lloyd v Grace, Smith & Co* [1912] AC 716, HL. As to apparent authority see paras 9.59 ff.

[191] In *The Nea Tyhi* [1982] 1 Lloyd's Rep 606 and *The Saudi Crown* [1986] 1 Lloyds Rep 261, it was found that there was too much related authority for a judge of first instance to reject the reasoning, though the case could be distinguished.

[192] Carriage of Goods by Sea Act 1992, s 4; see also Hague-Visby Rules, Art III.2 (para 11.65), a less clearly effective provision which in any case was not specifically directed at this problem.

[193] For an example of the complexities generated see *Heskell v Continental Express Ltd* [1950] 1 All ER 1033, where the claim was by the original shipper, and was also complicated by the fact that no goods had ever been shipped, thus generating the argument that, the contract of carriage being in this case only made by actual taking on board, there was no contract of carriage on which to sue. The case was however decided before an action in negligence for economic loss caused by statements became available, which occurred in 1964: *Hedley Byrne & Co Ltd v Heller & Partners Ltd* [1964] AC 465, HL.

[194] *Compania Naviera Vasconzada v Churchill & Sim* [1906] 1 KB 237.

[195] *Cox, Patterson & Co v Bruce & Co* (1886) 18 QBD 147.

In this connection two further problems require discussion. The first arises from **11.99**
the fact that carriers frequently print on their bills of lading 'blanket' clauses indicating that they do not in fact attest to the statements made (which are in general
inserted by the shipper in a box on the document). An example is 'All particulars
as furnished by the shipper but not checked by the carrier on loading'. Plainly
such clauses on their face take away the probative effect of the wording inserted in
the boxes. This is unobjectionable where the carrier has in fact no way of checking
whether the cargo particulars (which are often required by the associated sale and
letter of credit arrangements) are correct. This is true for crates, and containers not
'stuffed' by or for the carrier, and such disclaimers are regular in respect of containerized goods. In other situations they are more objectionable. The Hague Rules
and their variants[196] provide that carriers must on demand issue bills of lading
making certain statements as to what was shipped and its apparent order and condition,[197] which buyers will obviously want and which also assist in the event of
cargo claims. It is difficult to see however what remedy is intended where the carrier inserts disclaimers of the sort mentioned. To hold them invalid as inconsistent
with the carrier's liability under the Rules[198] would require robust construction,
since in part such provisions are undoubtedly unexceptionable. It is their breadth
that causes the problem. It has recently been held in England that the only
remedy is for the shipper to refuse the bill of lading;[199] but since the ship has often
sailed when the bill is returned to him, this may be impracticable.[200] A gap in the
protection of the Rules seems to exist here.

The second problem concerns specific reservations as to the apparent condition of **11.100**
the goods on loading. Carriers who wish to protect themselves against the evidentiary effect of such statements may insert reservations in the margin of the bill of
lading: an example is 'Bags torn and stained'.[201] A master wishing to protect his
owner may be zealous to do this,[202] but a bill so marked is called 'claused' and
may not be acceptable under the sale contract and/or letter of credit in pursuance
of which the goods are being shipped, which usually call for a 'clean' (ie not
claused) bill. Hence shippers may request the issue of a 'clean' bill and promise to

---

196 See para 11.56ff.
197 Article III.3.
198 Article III.8.
199 *The Mata K* [1998] 2 Lloyd's Rep 614; see also *The Atlas* [1996] 1 Lloyd's Rep 642.
200 And, presumably, for a buyer to whom such a bill of lading is tendered to refuse it; but this
again may be impracticable and conceivably not even justifiable legally, if the bill can be regarded as
of a type current in commerce.
201 There are numerous technical variants, eg, 'FCL' ('Full Container Load').
202 An unresolved question arises as to whether the carrier, through the master, owes a duty to the
shipper not to add reservations unnecessarily: even if he does, it is far from clear how the duty should
be formulated. See discussion of the master's duty in *The David Agmashenebeli* [2002] EWHC 104
(Admlty); [2003] 1 Lloyd's Rep, 92, esp at 105.

indemnify the carrier against any liability he suffers in a cargo claim because it was not appropriately claused to protect him. Such contracts, though in general quite reasonable in their objectives, are often unenforceable as contrary to public policy, for they may constitute a promise to indemnify against the consequences of what is technically a wilful false statement, ie a fraud.[203]

11.101 It should finally be noted that the person signing the bill as agent may be liable in tort for wilful or negligent false statements in it. He may also be liable for breach of warranty of authority, for agents warrant (in the absence of other indications) that they have authority to sign,[204] and if the goods are not as described he has no such authority. If the signature is that of a ship's agent or the like on behalf of the master, any of these remedies may be worth pursuing.[205]

(c) Document of Title

11.102 In addition to the above features, the bill of lading has a third and important characteristic, that by the custom of merchants such documents are transferred from one person to another while the goods are in transit[206] for the purpose of transferring (or pledging) the goods to which they relate.[207] This effect is reinforced by, or even partly based on, the fact that the goods should not be delivered up except against surrender of one bill.

11.103 The descriptive term used for such a document in English law is 'document of title'. The words are somewhat misleading, as they could be taken to suggest that only by this means can title to the goods be transferred. The transfer of a document of title certainly can have this effect, but in English law property can be transferred in the contract of sale by mere intention[208] and it is therefore not

---

203 *Brown Jenkinson & Co Ltd v Percy Dalton (London) Ltd* [1957] 2 QB 621; compare *Malayan Motor & General Underwriters (Pte) Ltd v Abdul Karim* [1982] 1 Malayan LJ 51, where this was not so and the contract of indemnity was enforceable. A good example of how problems arise is the Australian case *Hunter Grain Pty Ltd v Hyundai Merchant Marine Ltd (The Bunga Kenanga)* (1993) 117 ALR 507.

204 See paras 9.111ff.

205 As in *V/O Rasnoimport v Guthrie & Co Ltd* [1966] 1 Lloyds' Rep 1. But as with all such actions there may be complexities as regards damages: the lack of authority may cause no loss as in *Heskell v Continental Express Ltd* (n 193 above).

206 At some point the document must cease to be a document of title. The obvious time for this is when the goods have been delivered at destination against surrender of the bill to a person entitled to them. More complex situations can give rise to difficulties: see *The Future Express* [1992] 2 Lloyd's Rep 79, 96–100 (affd without reference to this point [1993] 2 Lloyds Rep 542). The Carriage of Goods by Sea Act 1992 (para 11.109) assumes that a bill of lading may cease to have effect as such, but relies on the (uncertain) general law to determine when this is: see s 2(2), discussed in *The Ythan* [2005] EWHC 2399 (Comm); [2006] 1 Lloyd's Rep 457.

207 *Lickbarrow v Mason* (1787) 2 TR 63, 100 ER 35.

208 Sale of Goods Act 1979, s 17: subject to special difficulties as to bulk goods, as to which see paras 10.20ff.

necessary to use such a document at all. The true significance of the phrase for English law appears to be that by its transfer the *constructive possession* of the goods can be transferred,[209] and the principal consequence of this is that the cargo can be pledged to a bank while it is afloat: the transferee is also entitled to possessory remedies.

It is possible for a legal system to give the bill of lading the status of something like **11.104** a negotiable instrument, in the sense that transfer to a third party acting in good faith may override prior proprietary interests in the goods represented. A bill of lading does not have this feature in English law, and hence though it is often said to be 'negotiable' (or at least, pure copies are described as 'non-negotiable'), the word 'transferable' might be better. The document is in general treated as if it was the goods: hence a holder may pass a better title than he has only where he could do so under the general law as the holder of chattels.[210]

For a bill to be transferable, and hence a bill of lading in the true sense, the **11.105** 'consignee' box on the face should contain the words 'or order' or 'or assigns' to indicate that transfer is contemplated. Otherwise, the document may be no more than a 'straight' bill of lading or a waybill. The transfer of the bill is effected, where a person is named as consignee, by mere handing over to that person; where the bill is transferred by a shipper who took it to 'order' (ie his own order), by indorsement and delivery; where it is transferred by a consignee or indorsee, by indorsement and delivery. These last two situations can involve indorsement to a named person ('special endorsement'). A bill indorsed in blank, however, like a cheque, becomes a bearer bill and only requires delivery. However it can be converted by a further special endorsement.[211]

It should be borne in mind that not every transfer, with the requisite indorsement **11.106** if required, transfers property and constructive possession of the goods, or even constructive possession only. As in the case of the transfer of chattels, of which the bill is a symbol, everything turns on the intention of the parties. A bill may be transferred in order to transfer ownership and possession: this is usually true of sellers transferring against payment. It may be transferred, usually to a bank,

---

[209] See the *locus classicus* for discussion of this topic, *Benjamin's Sale of Goods* (7th edn, 2006) paras 18-006ff.

[210] The relevant provisions are ss 21, 24 and 25 of the Sale of Goods Act 1979 and s 2 of the Factors Act 1889. See in general M Bools, *The Bill of Lading* (1997) chs 2, 3. There are differences on this point in the law of the United States.

[211] A bill that has been specially indorsed must be reindorsed if a transferee is to sue on it: it is not enough merely to hand it over, as by giving it back: *Keppel Tatlee Bank Ltd v Bandung Shipping Pte Ltd* [2003] 1 Singapore LR 295; [2003] 1 Lloyd's Rep 619, CA Sin.

to create a pledge only.[212] But it may also be transferred merely to permit the holder to collect the goods, perhaps as agent of the transferor.[213]

(d) Transfer of the contract

11.107   The final receiver of the goods may wish to exercise a cargo claim against the carrier. However, on principle since he is not a party to the contract of carriage he cannot do so. Early cases were sometimes able to solve this by holding that the seller shipped as agent for the distant buyer, but this is obviously an unreliable device. The law in England was therefore altered by statute a considerable time ago, by the Bills of Lading Act 1855, which in some form is still operative in very many common law territories.[214] This used the mechanism of transferring not only the benefit but also the burden of the contract (for example as to payment of freight or dangerous goods) on transfer of the property in the goods by means of the bill of lading. This worked well for more than 100 years, but in the 1970s difficulties began to develop because of the greater size of ships, especially bulk carriers. The rule of English law then operative that property cannot pass in unascertained goods[215] led to the result that property in goods carried in such ships would often only pass when the cargo was measured out to different buyers at destination. There were also other complications.

11.108   There were (and still are) two other possibilities for cargo claimants. The first is to sue in tort for loss or destruction of the goods: but this has been held to require that the claimant prove property or a possessory interest in the goods at the time they were lost or damaged, which might not be easy to establish.[216] The second was to sue on a contract which might be implied where a receiver took delivery of goods in return for payment of outstanding charges (or other consideration for the contract): it might be held that the carrier could be interpreted as agreeing to deliver on bill of lading terms. Such a contract is referred to as a '*Brandt v Liverpool* contract'.[217] The value of this device was much reduced when the Court of Appeal interpreted it strictly in 1989,[218] but it remains a weapon in the armoury which it

---

[212] Where a sale is financed by a bank, transfer of the bill to the bank would normally pass possession (pledge interest) to the bank and property to the buyer.

[213] As in the famous case of *Leigh & Sillavan Ltd v Aliakmon Shipping Co Ltd (The Aliakmon)* [1986] AC 785, HL.

[214] The United States legislation however was, and is, quite different. All common law countries have however found some form of statute to be necessary.

[215] Sale of Goods Act 1979, s 16; now much modified by the Sale of Goods (Amendment) Act 1995, inserting ss 20A and 20B into the 1979 Act.

[216] *Leigh & Sillavan Ltd v Aliakmon Shipping Co Ltd (The Aliakmon)* (n 153 above). See also *The Starsin* (n 156 above) at [87] ff.

[217] An allusion to the leading (but by no means first) decision on it, *Brandt v Liverpool, Brazil and River Plate Steam Navigation Co* [1924] 1 KB 575.

[218] *The Aramis* [1989] 1 Lloyd's Rep 213.

may occasionally be necessary to invoke in irregular situations even after the legislation of 1992 next referred to.

The law in England was therefore altered by statute in the Carriage of Goods by **11.109** Sea Act 1992,[219] which contains separate provisions as regards benefit and burden of the contract. Similar legislation has been enacted in certain other common law territories. Ability to sue depends on being 'lawful holder' of the bill of lading, regardless of the incidence of property:[220] there is a provision to permit the lawful holder to recover loss on behalf of the party really at risk, if that is someone different.[221] It was not practicable to make lawful holders liable on the contract also, for banks holding bills of lading as security, thus ranking as lawful holders, would then have become liable, something that was not the case before[222] and not an intended incident of a letter of credit transaction. Instead, the lawful holder is liable if he also takes or seeks delivery or claims on the contract.[223] A bank realizing its security and doing this would expect to incur liability: indeed this is the basis of the *Brandt v Liverpool* contract. The Act is a complex piece of draftsmanship and some of the first cases on it are controversial.[224] Its conflict of laws status (whether procedural or substantive) is not clear.[225]

(3) 'Straight' Bills of Lading

A bill of lading naming a consignee but not containing a reference to 'order' (or **11.110** 'assigns'), or from which these words have been deleted, may be called a 'straight' bill of lading. Such a document is not transferable (though it often nevertheless contains wording appropriate to an ordinary bill of lading)[226] and its status has been doubtful. It has been held that it is a 'bill of lading or any similar document of title' for the purpose of making the Hague-Visby (or Hague) Rules applicable,[227] and the House of Lords, in deciding this, approved a decision of the Court of Appeal

---

219 See *Carver on Bills of Lading* (2nd edn, 2005) Ch 5.

220 Carriage of Goods by Sea Act 1992, s 2(1)(a). But a shipper who has indorsed the bill to a lawful holder may nevertheless be able in some situations to claim against the carrier in bailment: see *East West Corp v DKBS AF* [2003] EWCA Civ 83; [2005] QB 1509.

221 ibid s 2(4).

222 See *Sewell v Burdick* (1884) 10 App Cas 74.

223 s 3(1). But if he then endorses the bill away he may cease to be liable: see *The Berge Sisar* [2001] UKHL 17; [2002] 2 AC 205, HL.

224 There is a valuable discussion of its history and operation in *The Berge Sisar*, above.

225 See KS Toh 'Conflict of Laws Implications of the Carriage of 'Goods by Sea Act 1992' [1994] LMCLQ 280. In general the Contract (Rights of Third Parties) Act 1999 is excluded when the 1992 Act applies: s 6(5). But see Treitel, *Lex Mercatoria*, ed Rose (2000), ch 17.

226 Such as a requirement for surrender of a negotiable bill of lading. This is because such documents often contain words such as 'Not negotiable unless consigned to order', which enables them to be used either way.

227 *The Rafaela S* [2005] UKHL 11; [2005] 2 AC 423.

of Singapore[228] to the effect that a carrier must only deliver the goods against surrender of such a document (which would not be true of a non-negotiable sea waybill[229]). It can be transferred once, by physical handing over to the named consignee, who can then sue on it, though the reason in English law for the right to sue is that the document, whatever it is called, must rank as a non-negotiable sea waybill under the purposes of the Act of 1992 by reason of the drafting of that Act. It is not clear whether such a document should really be called a document of title in the general common law sense. Only if it is would the consignee with possession of the document rank as having constructive possession of the goods, wherever they are, through the document alone. The law in the United States is not the same as that stated above.

(4) Other Documents Used in Connection with Sea Carriage

11.111 Other documents are sometimes used, which may replace the bill of lading or operate together with it. The legal analysis of situations arising out of the use of such documents can be very complex, and in general, where disputes may occur, the bill of lading is much preferable.

(a) Non-negotiable sea waybills[230]

11.112 These, a fairly recent invention, are used for short or quick sea transit where the parties do not need to trade in the goods or use them as security while they are in transit, and the safeguard that the goods should only be surrendered against a bill of lading is not desired.[231] They simply constitute a memorandum of the contract of carriage or, depending on the circumstances, the contract itself, and a receipt for the goods.[232] The goods are claimed by the consignee identifying himself at destination.

11.113 Thus retention of such a document is not likely to give the unpaid seller security: the goods can be delivered without it. Equally, a buyer who pays on the issue of such a document takes a risk, for the seller may, depending on the terms of the contract of carriage and/or the agreement of the carrier, be able to redirect the goods to another receiver.[233] Waybills (unlike straight bills of lading) are not bills of lading and do not attract the Hague Rules or variants, though these can be specifically incorporated. The receiver formerly had no rights on the contract,

---

228 *APL Co Pte Ltd v Voss Peer* [2002] 2 Lloyd's Rep 707; [2002] 4 SLR 481, CA Sin.
229 See para 11.112.
230 See *Carver on Bills of Lading* (2nd edn, 2005) paras 8–001ff.
231 Bills of lading frequently arrive long after the goods, especially in certain trades.
232 See the definition in s 1(3) of the Carriage of Goods by Sea Act 1992.
233 An attempt is made to deal with this in the CMI Uniform Rules for Sea Waybills.

save perhaps under a *Brandt v Liverpool* contract or in tort;[234] but the Carriage of Goods by Sea Act 1992, which altered the law as to actions on bills of lading, now gives rights and (in accordance with its terms) liabilities under the contract of carriage to the person to whom delivery is to be made in accordance with the contract.[235]

(b) Ship's delivery orders[236]

These are used for splitting bulk cargoes. When large bulk carriers set off, it may not be clear in what proportions the cargo is to be sold, and hence for what quantities bills of lading (even should so many be obtainable) are required. At a later stage therefore a bill of lading holder may obtain delivery orders for specified quantities against surrender of the bill or bills of lading. A ship's delivery order ('ship's D/O') contains an acknowledgement by the carrier, usually against surrender of the bill of lading, that he holds a specific quantity of goods in or from a certain ship, to the order of a certain person.[237] These documents tend to be transferred and indorsed just like bills of lading. **11.114**

The main difference with bills of lading is that like waybills they are not documents of title, and hence transfer of them does not transfer constructive possession of the goods. For a transferee from the original person to whom the document is issued to gain constructive possession, the order must be returned to the carrier, who must attorn to the new holder. Since these documents are used in connections with parts of a bulk, they also attract the complexities of recent legislation on ownership of part of a bulk.[238] They can also raise many other complexities. As with waybills, the holder formerly had no rights on the contract of carriage, save possibly under a *Brandt v Liverpool* contract[239] or in tort. But now the person to whom delivery of the goods is to be made can sue on the underlying contract of carriage by virtue of the 1992 Act.[240] **11.115**

Ship's delivery orders must be carefully distinguished from similar documents issued not by ships but by land-based warehouse operators, sometimes called 'merchant's delivery orders'. These raise similar problems, but they operate after the contract of carriage has ended, are not connected with the contract of carriage by sea and not affected by the Act of 1992. **11.116**

---

[234] See para 11.108.
[235] s 2(1)(b).
[236] See *Carver on Bills of Lading* (2nd edn, 2005), paras 8—027ff.
[237] See the definition in s 1(4) of the Carriage of Goods by Sea Act 1992.
[238] Sale of Goods Act 1979, ss 20A and 20B, inserted by Sale of Goods (Amendment) Act 1995.
[239] As in *Cremer v General Carriers SA* [1974] 1 WLR 341.
[240] s 2(1)(c).

(c) Freight forwarder's documents

11.117   Freight forwarders sometimes act as carriers, and as such may issue bills of lading in the normal way even if they perform the contract of carriage entirely by means of subcontractors. More often however they act as agents and make contracts of carriage on behalf of shippers, who may be disclosed or undisclosed principals to the contracts in question. In some cases of this sort they may issue a document indicating receipt of the goods for carriage, which may on a superficial glance look in its format quite like a bill of lading. They themselves may then obtain a bill of lading. Complex questions may arise as to the effect of the first document and the interrelation between the two, and the documentation used is likely to require careful analysis.[241]

(d) Mate's receipts

11.118   Mate's receipts are preliminary documents used in some circumstances as a preliminary to the issue of a bill of lading. The shipper obtains one on loading, and later exchanges it for a signed bill of lading. In theory a mate's receipt is signed by or for the mate (first officer) but such documents are sometimes signed by masters. As would be expected, they are inferior to bills of lading. They are evidence that *some* contract has been made, and there seems in principle no reason why some forms of estoppel should not arise on them; but they are not documents of title (unless so proved) and their effectiveness when retained by way of security is very limited.[242] In one case however the usage of merchants that mate's receipts were used instead of bills of lading was accepted in respect of a local trade,[243] but finally it was rejected on the ground that the document itself was marked 'non-negotiable'.[244]

(e) Combined transport documents

11.119   Combined, or multimodal, transport documents are issued by operators of such transport undertaking to carry goods, usually containerized, from one destination to another: neither place need be a port, and different means of transportation may be used. Such documents are to be distinguished from ordinary bills of lading containing provisions under which the carrier agrees to forward the goods on after the principal voyage, usually as agent only (sometimes called 'through bills of

---

[241] For examples see *Carrington Slipways Pty Ltd v patrick Operations Pty Ltd (The Cape Comorin)* (1991) 24 NSWLR 745; *Norfolk Southern Rly Co v James Kirby Pty Ltd* 125 S Ct 385 (2004), US Sup Ct.

[242] See *Nippon Yusen Kaisha v Ramjiban Serowgee* [1938] AC 429, PC.

[243] That between Sarawak and Singapore.

[244] *Chan Cheng Kum v Wah Tat Bank Ltd* [1971] 1 Lloyd's Rep 439, PC. But the bank was held to have security by way of possession without the aid of the document.

lading'). Some combined transport documents purport only to be waybills, and have legal consequences as such. Others are headed as, and are intended to be, bills of lading. They are plainly different from the bills of lading which the main authorities concern, for they envisage carriage in various modes of transport and do not indicate that the goods are on a ship, but merely that they have been received: a purported bill of lading to that effect would only doubtfully be a bill of lading at all.[245] The regime or regimes under which such goods are carried may be uncertain, as despite the overall undertaking by the operator the goods may, as they pass through different countries, be subject to various mandatory regimes for the type of transport involved (for example the Hague Rules), and if the goods do not arrive, or arrive short or damaged, it may also be difficult to know on which leg of the carriage the damage occurred. Although some bills of lading and waybills contain extensive provision to meet such problems, the present status of such documents is therefore in doubt—as to whether they rank as bills of lading and all that that entails, particularly as to whether they constitute documents of title. They are accepted by banks under letters of credit, and it seems likely that they would be accepted as documents of title if the question arises before new electronic methods take over; but at present the situation is uncertain and there is much to be worked out.

---

[245] See *Diamon Alkali Export Corp v Fl Bourgeois* [1921] 3 KB 443. This fact alone would not prevent it being a bill of lading for the purposes of the Carriage of Goods by Sea Act 1992, which transfers the contract: s 1(2)(b).

12

CARRIAGE OF GOODS BY AIR AND LAND[1]

A. Internal Carriage

(1) The Contract

(a) Applicable law

Contracts to carry goods by rail or road within the United Kingdom are governed **12.01**
by common law. Carriage by air is governed by statutory instrument[2] closely based
on the rules for international carriage. However, if there are gaps in the regime,
common law usually applies. Otherwise common law is distinct from the law
governing international carriage which, therefore, is discussed separately in this
chapter: 12.49ff. In practice all the contracts are supplemented importantly by
standard terms. Absent any contract, unusual today, internal carriers may have the
duties of common carriers at common law.

---

[1] Books referred to in this chapter: Kahn-Freund: O Kahn-Freund, *The Law of Carriage by Inland Transport* (1965); Clarke, Air: MA Clarke, *Contracts of Carriage by Air* (2002); Clarke, CMR: MA Clarke, *International Carriage of Goods by Road: CMR* (4th edn, 2003).

[2] SI 1999/1737.

(b) Contract Formation

12.02   Carriage contracts are concluded like other types of contract.[3] Commonly customers, either consignors or consignees of goods, obtain a copy of the carrier's consignment note or air waybill, and send it with details of the service required to the carrier. Sending the note usually amounts to an offer to contract, an offer which the carrier may accept or reject. Carriers may accept customers' offers expressly or by conduct,[4] such as loading the goods on a trailer going to the destination.

12.03   Parties must agree essential terms such as the destination. Certain terms may be settled implicitly, for example, freight by reference to standard rates.[5] Parties may also refer to carriers' standard terms, such as the Road Haulage Association Conditions of Carriage, 1998; and for rail the Freightliner Conditions 2002 or the EWS General Conditions of Carriage, 2004.[6] Moreover, carriers advertise their services and, expressly or implicitly, offers by customers may incorporate some of the statements in advertisements.

12.04   Whether terms are indeed part of the contract depends, as with other kinds of contract, on whether customers have signed them[7] or been given sufficient notice that they are to be part of the contract.[8] Even then terms are not binding if they are not accessible to customers (available on request or perhaps on the internet) as well as being comprehensible.[9] Nor will they bind customers, if they are onerous and unusual, unless specifically drawn to their attention.[10]

12.05   If advertisements by carriers contain actionable misrepresentations, a carriage contract may be rescinded. Apart from misrepresentation, equitable relief, including rescission, may be granted for economic duress amounting to illegitimate commercial pressure. In one case,[11] a carrier, knowing that the commercial survival of the customer depended on delivery, informed it that there would be no more deliveries unless it paid twice the agreed freight rate. Being unable to find another carrier in time, the customer agreed 'unwillingly and under compulsion'.[12]

---

   [3]   See paras 8.05ff.
   [4]   *Brogden v Metropolitan Ry Co* (1877) 2 App Cas. 666.
   [5]   *Foley v Classique Coaches Ltd* [1934] 2 KB 1, CA.
   [6]   See annotated copy in MA Clarke and D Yates, *Contracts of Carriage by Land and Air* (2004).
   [7]   *Harris v GWR Co* (1876) 1 QBD 515.
   [8]   *Circle Freight International Ltd v Medeast Gulf Exports Ltd* [1988] 2 Lloyd's Rep 427, CA. See paras 8.83ff.
   [9]   Generally carriers are entitled to assume that customers understand English: *Geier v Kujawa* [1970] 1 Lloyd's Rep 364.
   [10]   *Lacey's Footwear (Wholesale) Ltd v Bowler Int Freight Ltd* [1997] 2 Lloyd's Rep 369, 384–5, CA.
   [11]   *Atlas Express Ltd v Kafco (Importers and Distributors) Ltd* [1989] QB 833, 839. See generally paras 8.203.
   [12]   ibid 838.

The carrier's enforcement action failed. The customer's consent had been induced by illegitimate pressure.

(2) Transit

(a) Duration

Transit begins not when the aircraft or motor vehicle moves off but earlier when **12.06** carriers get (custody and control of) the goods.[13] That is when, as insurers see it, the carriage risk really begins,[14] a matter often regulated by a 'transit clause'.[15] Storage by a carrier in the wrong place would be a serious contract breach, a 'quasi-deviation'.[16] Moreover, to send goods to the wrong destination[17] or on the wrong kind of vehicle[18] is fundamentally different from what has been promised and the contract transit as such has not commenced. Transit ends on delivery, when custody and control pass from the carrier: 12.12.

(b) Means

Although contracts may require consignors to provide equipment for loading and **12.07** unloading, prima facie it is for carriers to choose the appropriate wagon,[19] vehicle or aircraft. The choice is influenced, however, by the needs of the particular goods, something usually better known to consignors than carriers, although rarely to a degree that relieves carriers of all responsibility. Sensible parties get together beforehand and agree what is required.

Absent agreement, courts ask whether there is any express or implied[20] term of the **12.08** contract of carriage governing the type of vehicle or special equipment to be used. The implied warranty, that ships be fit to receive and carry the cargo,[21] is also applied to road vehicles except that the duty is not absolute but one of reasonable care.[22] Hence courts take account of what a carrier knew and should have known

---

[13] *Crow's Transport Ltd v Phoenix Assurance Co Ltd* [1965] 1 Lloyd's Rep 139, 143, CA; *SCA (Freight) Ltd v Gibson* [1974] 2 Lloyd's Rep 533, 534.

[14] *Re Traders & General Ins Assoc Ltd* (1924) 18 Ll LRep 450, 451.

[15] *Symington & Co v Union Ins Sy of Canton Ltd* (1928) 30 Ll L Rep 280, 283; (1928) 31 Ll L Rep 179, 181, CA. Also storage pending delivery to the consignee: *Crow's Transport Ltd v Phoenix Assurance Co Ltd* [1965] 1 Lloyd's Rep 139, 144, CA.

[16] *Gibaud v GE Ry* [1921] 2 KB 426.

[17] *Israel & Co v Sedgwick* [1893] 1 QB 303, CA.; *Nima v Deves* [2002] EWCA Civ 1132; [2003] 2 Lloyd's Rep 327, [54].

[18] *Kallis (Manufacturers) Ltd v Success Ins Ltd* [1985] 2 Lloyd's Rep 8, PC.

[19] Eg *Gunyan v SE and Chatham Ry* [1915] 2 KB 370.

[20] *Liverpool CC v Irwin* [1977] AC 239; *Scally v Southern Health and Social Security Board* [1992] 1 AC 294.

[21] *Trickett v Queensland Insurance Co* [1936] AC 159, 165.

[22] *John Carter (Fine Worsteds) v Hanson Haulage (Leeds)* [1965] 2 QB 495, 517, 528–529, and 534–535, CA. Kahn-Freund, 268–269.

about the transit and, in particular, the goods. Arguably the same is true of carriage by rail and by air.

12.09 Sub-contracting is usually permitted, expressly[23] or by implication, and is common in carriage by road and by air. Exceptions arise when the personal care, skill or integrity of the contracting carrier is particularly important, for example, in the case of valuables.[24] The Supply of Goods and Services Act 1982, section 13, requires reasonable care in the selection of competent and trustworthy sub-contractors.[25] Moreover, arguably, it requires care in the work itself so that, if sub-contractors are negligent, carriers are liable: carriers can delegate performance but not responsibility.[26]

(c) Route

12.10 If not agreed expressly, it is implied that carriers will take the usual route, if there is one. This is assumed to be the shortest route or that which, to customers' knowledge, carriers normally take.[27] Courts imply a duty of 'reasonable dispatch'.[28] Nonetheless, road transit includes ordinary incidents of transit such as convenience breaks for drivers,[29] and minor detours to avoid obstacles.[30] Moreover, transit may 'be interrupted for efficient and economical loading, transhipment, discharge and storage to await the most convenient carrier. . .but not merely for the commercial convenience of one of the parties'.[31] The degree of interruption allowed depends on the circumstances.[32]

12.11 Unjustified departure from the route is 'quasi-deviation'.[33] If carriage becomes more difficult or more expensive than expected, carriers are obliged nonetheless to perform the contract and to bear the cost: difficulties en route are at carriers' risk.[34]

---

[23] Eg Condition 4 of the Freightliner Conditions 2002; Condition 2.2. of the EWS Conditions 2004.

[24] *Garnham, Harris & Elton v Alfred Ellis (Transport)* [1967] 2 All ER 940. See also *Edwards v Newland & Co* [1950] 2 KB 534, CA.

[25] *John Carter (Fine Worsteds) v Hanson Haulage (Leeds)* [1965] 2 QB 495, CA; see also *Gillette Industries Ltd v W.H. Martin Ltd* [1966] 1 Lloyd's Rep 57, CA; and *Metaalhandel JA Magnus BV v Ardfields Transport Ltd* [1988] 1 Lloyd's Rep 197.

[26] *Metaalhandel* (ibid).

[27] *Hales v LNW Ry Co* (1863) 4 B & S 66, 72.

[28] Clarke, CMR, 210b.

[29] *Sadler Bros Co v Meredith* [1963] 2 Lloyd's Rep 293, 307.

[30] Or similar obstructions: *Taylor v GNR Ry* (1866) LR 1 CP 385, 388.

[31] *Verna Trading Pty Ltd v New India Assurance Co Ltd* [1991] 1 VLR 129, 168 (Vict Sup Ct), a case of carriage by sea.

[32] *Commercial Union Assurance Co v Niger Co Ltd* (1922) 13 Ll L Rep 75, 81–82, HL.

[33] *LNW Ry Co v Neilson* [1922] AC 263; 'fundamental breach' in carriage by sea: *The Berkshire* [1974] 1 Lloyd's Rep 185, 191.

[34] Eg *Tsaskiroglou & Co v Noblee & Thorl GmbH* [1962] AC 93 (carriage by sea).

If, however, the only route is blocked, subject to contract terms, the agreed performance has become impossible and the contract is discharged.[35]

(3) Delivery

Carriers are obliged to deliver goods at the destination agreed. If the precise point **12.12** of delivery there has not been agreed, a duty is implied to deliver at consignees' place of business,[36] and to notify them.[37] If, however, carriers receive a reasonable request to deliver at a point en route short of destination, they are not only entitled[38] but also obliged to comply, at consignee's expense.

If carriers have agreed to reach a place and wait until contacted, they hold goods **12.13** as carriers until the consignee takes them over or until a reasonable time has elapsed, whereafter they hold as bailees for reward,[39] subject commonly to contract terms.[40] If, however, goods reach destination but carriers find that access or unloading facilities there are inadequate or unsafe, carriers are justified in declining to make actual delivery. Transit ends[41] nonetheless when goods have been properly tendered to the consignee;[42] subject commonly to contract terms,[43] which may provide for eventual sale of the goods by the carrier.[44]

Consignees of goods usually lack transport documents, like bills of lading, which **12.14** demonstrate their right to the goods; but it suffices that they can identify themselves in other ways as entitled to receive the goods. Carriers, for their part, are obliged to exercise reasonable care[45] to deliver to persons with apparent authority to receive the goods. If goods are delivered in circumstances which should arouse suspicion, and it turns out that the recipient had no right to the goods, the carrier is liable.[46] Moreover, if a carrier is aware that it was the wrong person, delivery is a

---

[35] *Fibrosa SA v Fairburn Lawson Combe Barbour* [1942] 1 KB 12, CA, reversed on different grounds: [1943] AC 32.

[36] Kahn-Freund, 301.

[37] Kahn-Freund, 303, with some support from *Mitchell v Lancashire & Yorkshire Ry Co* (1875) LR 10 QB 256, 260.

[38] *L & NW Ry v Bartlett* (1861) 7 H & N 400, 408; *Cork Distilleries Ltd v GS & W Ry* (1874) LR 7 HL 269.

[39] See *Chapman v GW Ry Co* (1880) 5 QBD 278, 281–282.

[40] See eg EWS Condition 12, RHA Condition 6(2) and Condition 9(3) and *Mitchell v Lancashire & Yorkshire Ry Co* (1875) LR 10 QB 256.

[41] *SCA (Freight) Ltd v Gibson* [1974] 2 Lloyd's Rep 533, 535.

[42] *Heugh v LNW Ry* (1870) LR 5 Ex 51; *Startup v Macdonald* (1843) 6 Man & G 593.

[43] See eg RHA Condition 6.

[44] Eg RHA Condition 7.

[45] *M'Kean v M'Ivor* (1870) LR 6 Ex 30, 41.

[46] *Stephenson v Hart* (1828) 4 Bing 576.

fundamental breach of contract, which deprives the carrier of contractual defences.[47]

12.15 Delivery, legally distinct from unloading,[48] is the point when custody and control of the goods pass from carrier to consignee or third party.[49] On the one hand, goods on consignees' premises but still on the carrier's vehicle have not been delivered, even if the premises are locked and the vehicle is not.[50] On the other hand, goods handed over to customs authorities, port authorities or warehousemen, have been delivered, unless the latter are agents of the carrier.[51] Moreover, handing goods over to a third party in mistake for the consignee is also delivery, if done in the reasonable belief that it was the proper consignee.[52] Transit has ended.

(4) Claims: Title to Sue

(a) Agency

12.16 Claimants in tort, most likely negligence, must be persons to whom carriers owe a duty of care, usually goods owners. Prima facie consignees are owners, because in sales of goods ex warehouse, ex factory, and free on board (FOB), ownership passes from consignor to consignee when 'the seller delivers the goods. . .to a carrier. . .for the purpose of transmission to the buyer, and does not reserve the right of disposal'.[53]

12.17 Claimants in contract must be party to a contract with the carrier concerned. Early cases support a presumption that the carrier's contract is with the consignee.[54] Prima facie consignees are third parties to carriage contracts negotiated by consignors, but courts have presumed that consignors act as agents of consignees. Hence consignees are bound by contract terms agreed by consignors

---

[47] *Sze Hai Tong Bank v Rambler Cycle Co* [1959] AC 576, PC. Clarke, CMR, para 240.

[48] Standard contracts regulate loading and unloading without identifying who must do it. Parties must agree that.

[49] *Bartlett & Partners Ltd v Meller* [1961] 1 Lloyd's Rep 487, 489.

[50] *A Tomlinson (Hauliers) Ltd v Hepburn* [1964] 1 Lloyd's Rep 416 appeals on other grounds dismissed: [1966] 1 QB 21, CA; [1966] AC 451.

[51] See *Marten v Nippon Sea & Land Ins Co Ltd* (1898) 3 Com Cas 164; and *A Gagniere & Co v The Eastern Co Ltd* (1921) 7 Ll LRep 188, CA.

[52] *Scothorn v South Staffordshire Ry Co* (1853) 8 Exch 341, 344.

[53] Sale of Goods Act 1979 s 18, rules 5(1) and (2).

[54] *Stephenson v Hart* (1828) 4 Bing 476, 487; *Heugh v LNW Ry* (1870) LR 5 Ex 51, 57–58; *The Albazero* [1977] AC 774, 785–786, and cases cited, a review approved in the House of Lords: [1977] AC 774, 842; *Texas Instruments Ltd v Nasan (Europe) Ltd* [1991] 1 Lloyd's Rep 146, 148–149. Kahn-Freund, 210.

with carriers,[55] unless they differ from those that a consignee was led reasonably to expect;[56] and can enforce the contract against the carrier concerned. Otherwise contractual rights are enforceable by whoever owns the goods at the time of loss, damage or delay (LDD).[57]

(b) Statute

The Contracts (Rights of Third Parties) Act 1999 confers a right of enforcement on third parties, if they are 'expressly identified in the contract by name, as a member of a class or as answering to a particular description': section 1(3). The right of enforcement is conferred by section 1(1) where (a) 'the contract expressly provides' that a person may enforce it; and (b) when a contract term 'purports to confer a benefit on him'. That establishes a presumption, rebuttable, however, 'if on a proper construction of the contract it appears that the parties did not intend the term to be enforceable by the third party': section 1(2).[58]   **12.18**

The Law Commission Report which led to the Act gave illustrations, which included the right under the Sale of Goods Act of donees, to whom goods were delivered, against suppliers of the goods.[59] Another concerned the rights of a performing sub-carrier of goods to benefit from defences in the contract concluded by the principal carrier.[60] A similar presumption appears to arise in favour of designated consignees of goods.   **12.19**

The right of enforcement is given directly to the third party but by section 1(4), enforcement is 'subject to and in accordance with any other relevant terms of the contract',[61] such as notice of the route agreed between consignor and carrier. Moreover, under section 2(1) the contracting parties are free to vary or cancel a term conferring a right of enforcement, unless inter alia[62] the carrier is aware that the consignee has relied on the term, or the carrier can reasonably be expected to have foreseen that the consignee would rely on the term and the consignee has in fact relied on it. Reliance might well include the case in which the consignee has agreed to sell the goods to another person.   **12.20**

---

[55] *Morris v Martin & Sons* [1966] 1 QB 716, 729–730, CA; *The Pioneer Container* [1994] 2 AC 324; *The Mahkutai* [1996] AC 650; *Spectra Int plc v Hayesoak Ltd* [1997] 1 Lloyd's Rep 153: appeal allowed on a different point: [1998] 1 Lloyd's Rep 162, CA.

[56] Eg an unexpected contract route: *Leduc v Ward* (1888) 20 QBD 475, CA, approved by Lord Wright in *Tate & Lyle v Hain SS Co* (1936) 55 Ll L Rep 159, 178, HL.

[57] *The Albazero* [1977] AC 774, 847; *The Kapetan Markos NL (No 2)* [1987] 2 Lloyd's Rep 321, 329, CA.

[58] See *The Laemthong Glory (No 2)* [2005] EWCA Civ 519; [2004] 1 Lloyd's Rep 688, [49].

[59] Law Com No 242 (1996, Cm 3329), para 7.41.

[60] Para 7.44.

[61] See also s 1(5).

[62] Other cases of restriction are found in s 2(3).

(5) Carriers' Liability

12.21 Carriers are strictly liable to claimants for loss of or damage to goods, as well as delay (LDD), while goods are in their charge (custody and control).[63] Failure to deliver goods in the state in which they were received, or at all, is a breach of the contract of carriage.[64] Concurrent liability in tort, usually negligence, might be established too, but claimants must prove negligence in addition to LDD, and the extent of a carrier's liability in tort is unlikely to be greater than in contract.[65] The advantage of tort actions lies in the Limitation Act 1980 section 14A.[66] In practice most contracts seek to modify the basic liability just described.

12.22 Carriers' first line of defence is proof that LDD was due to some cause for which the carrier is excused by contract. Failing this, a second line of defence is that the action is out of time[67] or that the monetary amount of liability is limited. These defences can be defeated, however, if claimants can establish that the relevant term is unreasonable under the Unfair Contract Terms Act 1977.

(6) Breach of Contract

(a) Loss, Damage and Delay (LDD)

12.23 Loss, partial or total, occurs when goods become less in volume or quantity than they were before transit. Loss also includes misdelivery,[68] whether to the wrong person[69] or in the wrong place, because the goods are unavailable to the consignee. One should distinguish financial loss which is caused by breach and must be established, if claimants are to recover compensation.

12.24 Damage means 'mischief done to property',[70] a change in the physical condition of goods which impairs their value.[71] The precise definition depends on context.[72] For example, fish which is perfectly fit for immediate consumption on delivery, but which has a shortened shelf life because the vehicle was too warm, is damaged goods to consignees who want it not for immediate consumption but for sale later.

---

[63] *Peek v North Staffs Ry* (1863) 10 HL Cas 472, 560.
[64] Common law liability as 'common carrier' is superseded by the contract. In the author's view the same is true of their liability as bailee: Clarke, CMR, para 222.
[65] See para 12.31.
[66] See para 22.18.
[67] Clarke, CMR, para 218.
[68] *Shipworth v GW Ry* (1888) 59 LT 520.
[69] *Hearn v LSW Ry Co* (1855) 10 Ex 801. See also *Skipworth v GW Ry Co* (1888) 59 LT 520.
[70] *Smith v Brown* (1871) 40 LJQB 214, 218.
[71] *Promet Engineering (Singapore) Pte Ltd v Sturge* [1997] CLC 966, 971, CA.
[72] *Swansea Corp v Harpur* [1912] 3 KB 493, 505, CA.

Carriers are liable for delay, if they deliver later than promised. If not express, **12.25**
'there is an implied contract to deliver within a reasonable time. . .using all reasonable exertions'[73] in the circumstances, breach of which implies negligence.[74] Early
cases support the implication,[75] although generally in contract law time promises
are strictly construed. In practice the point is regulated by contract terms and, for
example, carriers may be excused by *force majeure*.[76]

(b) Proof

Delay is proved by reference to the contract and the time of actual delivery. Loss **12.26**
or damage is proved by documentation of two kinds. One proves the state or
quantity of goods on delivery. The other proves that goods were greater in volume
or quantity or in better condition when first taken over. Carriers are obliged not
to deliver goods in a state of perfection but in the same state, whatever that was, in
which they were taken over.

As to their state on delivery, commonly claimants obtain the report of reliable **12.27**
third parties as soon as possible, to avoid the riposte that the damage or loss
(eg vandalism or pilfering) occurred between the time of delivery and report. As
to their state on being taken over, proof depends on the efficacy of the consignment note or air waybill, in its role as receipt. Unless carriers have no reasonable
means of checking the accuracy of what is stated, such documents are prima facie
evidence of statements therein. In practice, however, their evidentiary value is
commonly reduced by contract terms. Thus claimants may have to resort to proof
of events en route, such as an accident which appears to explain the loss or damage
established later. If claimants allege non-delivery of the entire consignment,
ex hypothesi, there are no goods at destination to be checked, and attention
focuses more closely then ever on the transport document and what, if anything,
can be proved to have occurred during transit.

(c) Causation[77]

To recover compensation claimants must establish that they have suffered finan- **12.28**
cial loss, of which the carrier's breach of contract was the 'effective or dominant'
cause.[78] Causation was once regarded largely as an aspect of remoteness of loss

---

[73] *Taylor v GN Ry Co* (1866) LR 1 CP 385, 387. See also *Raphael v Pickford* (1843) 5 Man &
G 551; *Postlethwaite v Freeland* (1880) 5 App Cas 599. Kahn-Freund, pp 277 *et seq*.
[74] See the Supply of Goods and Services Act 1982, s 4(1).
[75] Eg *Taylor v GN Ry* (1866) LR 1 CP 385.
[76] Eg EWS Condition 9.
[77] See paras 21.38ff.
[78] *Heskell v Continental Express Ltd* [1950] 1 All ER 1033.

or damage[79] but today courts tend to treat it as a separate issue. In most cases claimants must simply establish that *but for* the breach the loss would not have occurred.[80] The main limit on recovery lies in the rule of remoteness together, in some cases, with a limit on the scope of the carrier's duty.[81] Even so, as regards causation, some cases are not simple.

12.29   First, if a breach is the first of two or more consecutive causes, the breach remains the effective and dominant cause if the intervention of a later cause consisted of 'the very kind of events the terms of engagement were designed to forestall'.[82] These would be events which a carrier had assumed responsibility to guard against, such as theft. Careless carriers are liable for theft, whether the intervention of a thief was probable or not.[83] Second, Devlin J once stated that, if the carrier's breach is one of two concurrent causes, 'both co-operating and both of equal efficacy', the breach is nonetheless 'sufficient to carry a judgment for damages',[84] but not necessarily a judgment for the full amount. If one of those causes is the claimant's fault, the court may apportion liability.[85] In any event, in all cases general contract law imposes a 'duty' to mitigate loss or damage. Thus, for example, claimant consignees whose goods have been damaged must seek alternative goods.[86]

(7) Liability in Tort

(a) Duty of Care

12.30   To establish the tort of negligence, claimants must prove breach of a duty of care. In *Customs and Excise Commissioners v Barclays Bank plc*[87] the House of Lords reconsidered the tests for such a duty. It preferred that which asked, 'whether the defendant assumed responsibility for what he said and did', but warned that this test should be applied objectively 'as a sufficient but not a necessary condition of liability', which, 'if answered positively, may obviate the need for further inquiry'.[88] If further inquiry were needed, consideration should be given to 'the particular relationship between the parties in the context of their legal and factual situation

---

[79] Eg *Monarch SS Co v Karlhmans Oljefabriker* [1949] AC 196, 227–228. As regards remoteness, see para 12.39.

[80] ibid.

[81] See para 12.39.

[82] *County Ltd v Girozentrale Securities* [1996] 3 All ER 834, 847, CA.

[83] *Stansbie v Troman* [1948] 2 KB 48; *Lambert v Lewis* [1982] AC 225, 276–277.

[84] *Heskell v Continental Express Ltd* [1950] 1 All ER 1033, 1048, *per* Devlin J.

[85] *Caledonian Ry v Hunter* (1858) 20 Sess Cas 2nd Ser 1097; Law Reform (Contributory Negligence) Act 1945.

[86] *Stroms Bruks A/B v Hutchison* [1905] AC 515.

[87] [2006] UKHL 28; [2007] 1 AC 181. See 17.179.

[88] At [4].

as a whole'.[89] In the carriage context one should ask whether carriers were or should have been in control of the operation (affirmative); and whether carriers rather than goods interests are best placed to cover the loss in question by insurance (also affirmative). Indeed, the liability of carriers as such is a traditional 'duty situation', and this is unlikely to be contested.

(b) The Context of Contract

The emphasis on assumption of responsibility complements the current approach **12.31** to the extent of liability in contract.[90] Moreover, when parties to an alleged tort 'have come together against a contractual structure which provides for compensation in the event of a failure of one of the parties involved, the court will be slow to superimpose an added duty of care beyond that which was in the contemplation of the parties at the time that they came together'.[91] So, even when claimant consignees do not contract with a carrier, the contract of carriage between carrier and consignor is the 'contractual structure' in which the court assesses the existence and extent of any duty of care owed by a carrier to claimant consignees. The latter are taken to know that the carriage contract is subject to terms,[92] notably terms limiting carriers' liability; and carriers' duty of care to consignees is modified accordingly. Thus, except in certain cases where the limitation period may be longer,[93] claimants have little to gain by proving negligence for a claim in tort rather than claiming in contract.

(8) Counterclaim and Set-off

In 1995 a road carrier brought a claim for freight charges, and the customer cross- **12.32** claimed for breach of contract.[94] Cross-claims are usually admitted, but this time the carrier argued for the application of a maritime exception regarding cross-claims.[95] This, said the court, has 'little if any intrinsic justification but applies to carriage of goods by sea because it is a rule of considerable antiquity'.[96] Nonetheless, finding that the exception had been consistently applied to international carriage

---

[89] At [8]. See also at [35] and [53].
[90] See para 12.28.
[91] *Pacific Associates Inc v Baxter* [1989] 2 All ER 159, 170, CA; see also *The Nicholas H* [1996] 1 AC 211, 239–240. As regards land carriage similar decisions have been reached, albeit on different reasoning: *Hall v North Eastern Ry Co* (1875) LR 10 QB 437, 442; *Mayfair Photographic Supplies (London) v Baxter Hoare & Co* [1972] 1 Lloyd's Rep 410.
[92] *Circle Freight International Ltd v Medeast Gulf Exports Ltd* [1988] 2 Lloyd's Rep 427, CA.
[93] See the Limitation Act 1980 s 14A.
[94] *United Carriers Ltd v Heritage Food Group (UK) Ltd* [1995] 4 All ER 95.
[95] *Aries Tanker Corp v Total Transport* [1977] 1 All ER 398, HL. The former rationale, the liquidity needed to finance carriage by sea, was rejected altogether in *Gilbert-Ash (Northern) v Modern Engineering (Bristol)* [1974] AC 689, 707 (building contracts).
[96] [1995] 4 All ER 95, 102.

by road, it held with 'unconcealed reluctance' that the exception also applied to road carriage in the United Kingdom.[97]

12.33 An enduring point in favour of the maritime exception is the desirability of 'speedy settlement of freight and other liquidated demands'.[98] To allow cross-claims or set-off 'would enable unscrupulous persons to make all sorts of unfounded allegations—so as to avoid payment', and that 'even with the most scrupulous, it would lead to undesirable delay'.[99] That is no less true of carriage by road, in which (unlike carriage by rail) carriers are often in the weaker bargaining position.[100] Moreover, in *Overland Shoes Ltd v Schenkers Ltd*,[101] a challenge to a 'no set-off' clause in a road contract, on the ground that it was unreasonable and without effect under the Unfair Contract Terms Act 1977, failed.

(9) *Contract Defences*

(a) Causation

12.34 With one reservation, carriers that establish contract defences are exonerated, provided that the exonerating event caused the LDD. Such clauses are strictly construed. Indeed, arguably the event must be the proximate cause:[102] it must have led more or less inevitably to the LDD.[103] The reservation is that claimants can counter defences by establishing that the real cause, or one of them, was breach of carriers' residual and 'overriding' duty of care. If a carrier's 'negligence has brought on the peril, the damage is attributable to his breach of duty, and the exception does not aid him'.[104] For example, a carrier does nothing about patently inadequate packing but nonetheless pleads the packing as a defence to a damage claim.[105] The defence fails.

(b) External events

12.35 (i) Act of God, a common law defence found in older standard contracts,[106] means some elemental force of nature which could not have been foreseen or, if foreseen, could not have been guarded against by any ordinary or

---

[97] ibid.

[98] *Dakin v Oxley* (1864) 15 CB NS 646, 667.

[99] *The Brede* [1974] QB 233, 249–250, 254.

[100] No such case on rail carriage has been reported.

[101] [1998] 1 Lloyd's Rep 498, CA.

[102] See *Reardon Smith Line v Ministry of Agriculture, Fisheries and Food* [1960] 1 QB 439, 492; affirmed [1962] 1 QB 42, CA; affirmed on other grounds [1963] AC 691.

[103] The *causa proxima* of insurance law: see para 13.89.

[104] *Gill v Manchester, Sheffield & Lincolnshire Ry Co* (1873) LR 8 QB 186, 196; *LNW Ry Co v Hudson* [1920] AC 324, 340.

[105] *LNW Ry Co v Hudson.*

[106] Eg RHA Conditions 9(2)(b)(i).

reasonable precaution.[107] Examples include injury to animals in transit when snow blocked the road.

(ii) 'Strikes' are sometime specifically excluded,[108] as are 'seizure or forfeiture under legal process',[109] which includes events such as detention of debtors' goods.[110]

(iii) Public violence is commonly excluded, notably the 'consequences of war',[111] and 'civil war': war internal to states[112] rather than war between states. Also excluded are 'rebellion' and 'insurrection', which are closely related.[113] Each connotes an organized attempt to overthrow government,[114] whereas another exclusion, 'civil commotion', does not.[115] Lower on the scale of disorder is 'riot', which requires only twelve people,[116] as long as they have a common purpose and use or threaten to use unlawful violence. Controversially, the definition lacks any element of tumult.[117]

(iv) An important defence relating to external events is wording such as 'any cause or event which the Company is unable to avoid and the consequences whereof the Company is unable to prevent by the exercise of reasonable diligence'. This can replace many of the specific defences listed above and reflects the overriding duty of care.[118] The same is largely true of 'force majeure'.[119] However, if carriers are unable to perform the contract through causes entirely beyond their control they can rely on the common law defence of 'frustration'.[120]

(c) State of the goods

(i) 'Inherent vice' is a defect in goods which, through internal development, tends to their injury or destruction, so that they are unfit for their normal commercial use or purpose for a reasonable time after delivery.[121] Goods are

12.36

---

107 *Nugent v Smith* (1876) 1 CPD 423, 437 (carriage by sea).

108 Eg *Seeburg v Russian Wood Agency Ltd* (1934) 50 Ll LRep 146.

109 Eg RHA Condition 9(2)(b)(iii).

110 Cf *The Wondrous* [1991] 1 Lloyd's Rep 400, affd [1992] 2 Lloyd's Rep 566, CA.

111 *Kawasaki Kisen Kabushiki Kaisha v Bantham SS Co (No 2)* [1939] 2 KB 544, CA; *Pesquerias y Secaderos de Bacalao de Espana SA v Beer* (1949) 82 Ll L Rep 501, HL.

112 *Spinney's (1948) Ltd v Royal Ins Co Ltd* [1980] 1 Lloyd's Rep 406, 429.

113 *National Oil Co of Zimbabwe (Pte) v Sturge* [1991] 2 Lloyd's Rep 281.

114 *Spinney's* (n 112 above) p 437.

115 See *London & Manchester Plate Glass Co Ltd v Heath* [1913] 3 KB 411, 416, CA; *Levy v Assicurazioni Generali* [1940] AC 791, 800, PC.; and *Spinney's* (n 112 above) 438.

116 Public Order Act 1986 s 1(1).

117 See *The Andreas Lemos* [1982] 2 Lloyd's Rep 483, 492.

118 See para12.34.

119 Eg EWS Condition 9.

120 See paras 8.438ff.

121 *Blower v GW Ry* (1872) LR 7 CP 655, 662. See also leading maritime cases: *Albacora SRL v Westtcott & Laurance Line Ltd* [1966] 2 Lloyd's Rep 53, HL; and *Noten BV v Harding* [1990] 2 Lloyd's Rep 283, CA.

expected to be fit to withstand the ordinary incidents of the transit,[122] assuming they receive the degree of care required either by current practice or by the contract of carriage. 'Insufficient packing', may be excluded expressly but, anyway, is an instance of inherent vice.[123] Sufficiency turns in part on the handling to be expected of the carrier[124] which, in turn, depends on what the carrier can be taken to know about the contents and what it has promised.[125]

(ii) 'Latent defect' in goods is one not discoverable by the exercise of reasonable care and attention at the time of consignment.[126] Distinguish 'inherent vice' (above), which does not have to be latent. However, carriers' general duty of care[127] is such that 'inherent vice' is unlikely to be an effective defence, unless the vice is 'latent' and thus unknown to the carrier or, if not, there was nothing that the carrier could reasonably be expected to do anyway.

(iii) 'Dangerous goods' are commonly the subject of special contract terms, the effect of which is qualified exclusion of liability. For example, carriers exclude liability in respect of such goods, unless, prior to loading, the carrier has 'received in writing precise and correct identification of the Goods and has further agreed in writing to accept the same for carriage'.[128] If so, carriers are liable in the normal way. If unbeknown to either party the goods are dangerous, this is an instance of 'inherent vice' (above).

(10) Interpretation Contra Proferentem

12.37 Ambiguous exoneration clauses are construed *contra proferentem*, ie restrictively against carriers,[129] albeit less strictly between commercial entities of roughly equal bargaining strength than between carriers and consumers;[130] and less strictly as regards clauses limiting the amount of liability rather than excluding liability

---

[122] *Albacora* (ibid) 59 and 62.

[123] *LNW Ry Co v Hudson* [1920] AC 324, 333.

[124] *Decca Radar Ltd v Caserite* [1961] 2 Lloyd's Rep 301, 308.

[125] *Hudson* (n 123 above) p 340; *Lister v Lancs & Yorks Ry Co* [1903] 1 KB 878, 880.

[126] *The Amstelslot* [1963] 2 Lloyd's Rep 223, HL (sea).

[127] See para 12.34.

[128] EWS Condition 5.

[129] Eg *Alexander v Railway Executive* [1951] 2 KB 882. English courts have construed clauses narrowly also when perfectly clear but contrary to commercial common sense, ie when 'drawn in extravagantly wide terms, which would produce absurd results if applied literally': *UGS Finance Ltd v National Mortgage Bank of Greece* [1964] 1 Lloyd's Rep 446, 453, CA. However, domestic carriage disputes are subject to the Unfair Contract Terms Act 1977: 12.42. It is hard to imagine that, having found a clause reasonable under the Act, the court would then find that it 'would produce absurd results'.

[130] *Photo Production Ltd v Securicor Transport Ltd* [1980] AC 827.

altogether.[131] Ambiguity is assessed objectively by the court,[132] ie as understood by lawyers rather than lay persons. Today, however, there is some evidence of a 'softer' approach.[133]

An important application of this rule concerns clauses, whereby carriers seek to   **12.38**
exclude liability for negligent breach.[134] If, first, the clause expressly exempts carriers from the consequences of negligence, the clause must be literally applied.[135] Second, if not, courts ask whether the words used are wide enough, in their ordinary meaning, to cover negligence. Third, if so,[136] courts restrict the clause to the underlying strict liability of carriers at common law and construe it restrictively as inapplicable to negligence.[137]

(11) Remedies

(a) Compensation

Compensation is recoverable from carriers in accordance with general principles   **12.39**
of law.[138] The loss claimed must not be too remote. Claimants may recover loss of profit (expectation loss) only if, at the time of contracting, loss of that kind should have been within the reasonable contemplation of the carrier as not unlikely to result from the breach.[139] This rule will be applied subject, however, to any issues of assumption of responsibility, sometimes raised by what has been called a 'tort' approach.[140] For example, courts ask not only whether the loss was within the contemplation of the carrier as a likely consequence of the delay (remoteness) but also whether and to what extent the carrier has agreed to bear all the consequences.[141] A carrier may be well aware that, if the computer is not delivered on time, the consignee's business will grind to a halt with great loss; but it does not follow that the carrier has undertaken such a degree of responsibility that it must

---

[131] *Ailsa Craig Fishing Co v Malvern Fishing Co* [1983] 1 All ER 101, HL; *George Mitchell (Chesterhall) v Finney Lock Seeds* [1983] 2 AC 803, 814.

[132] *Higgins v Dawson* [1902] AC 1.

[133] Eg *Lancashire County Council v Municipal Mutual Ins Co Ltd* [1997] QB 897, 904, CA.

[134] *Canada SS Lines Ltd v R* [1952] AC 192, 208, PC; *The Raphael* [1982] 2 Lloyd's Rep 42, CA.

[135] *Smith v South Wales Switchgear Ltd* [1978] 1 All ER 18, 26, HL.

[136] Eg 'any act or omission': *The Raphael* (n 134 above) at 45.

[137] *Mitchell v Lancs & Yorks Ry Co* (1875) LR 10 QB 256; *Alderslade v Hendon Laundry Ltd* [1945] 1 KB 189, 192, CA.

[138] *Ruxley Electronics and Construction Ltd v Forsyth* [1996] AC 344, 365.

[139] *Hadley v Baxendale* (1859) 9 Ex 341, as interpreted in *The Heron II* [1969] 1 AC 350.

[140] See *South Australia Asset Management Corp v York Montagu Ltd* [1997] AC 191, 214.

[141] R Halson, 'Indemnity Clauses: Remoteness and Causation' [1996] LMCLQ 438–441, 441. *Aneco Reinsurance Underwriting Ltd v Johnson & Higgins Ltd* [2001] UKHL 51; [2002] 1 Lloyd's Rep 157, [2], [17] and [40].

compensate the consignee in full.[142] Generally, however, if late delivery causes goods to miss a market,[143] carriers are liable for customers' loss of profit there.

(b) Other remedies

12.40   In the event of a serious breach of a contract of carriage, the innocent party may terminate the contract in accordance with general principle.[144] Carriers in possession of goods, but facing customer refusal to pay charges, may be entitled to perform the contract in order to retain a lien on the goods as security for payment.[145] A lien 'consists of the right to retain possession of goods of another until his claims are satisfied'.[146] Goods susceptible to possession include documents, however, possession of documents does not give a lien on goods to which the documents relate. Liens are effective only as long as the lienor retains possession.[147] However, carriers that hand the goods over to sub-carriers nonetheless retain possession of the goods for the purposes of a lien.[148] Rights are lost not only by loss of possession but also by the assertion of entitlement to the goods on grounds incompatible with the exercise of a lien,[149] as well as use of the goods in a manner inconsistent with proper exercise of a lien.[150]

12.41   Liens 'may be particular or general'.[151] Carriers have a particular lien for freight and charges payable on delivery of the goods in question. The lien also extends to the recovery of expenses reasonably incurred to protect and preserve the goods en route[152] unless, of course, the necessity was brought about by the carrier in breach of duty. In contrast, at common law carriers have no general lien on goods in their possession, ie no lien on the goods in respect of debts due by the particular customer in respect of other goods and other contracts of carriage. However, carriers have no right to sell the goods,[153] unless there is a commercial necessity to

---

[142]   Cf *Hadley v Baxendale* (1859) 9 Ex 341.

[143]   Christmas market: *Panalpina Int Transport Ltd v Densil Underwear Ltd* [1981] 1 Lloyd's Rep 187; *The Heron II* (n 139 above). Regular cattle market: *Simpson v LNW Ry Co* (1876) 1 QBD 274; cf *Horne v Midland Ry Co* (1873) LR 8 CP 131.

[144]   *Vitol SA Ltd v Norelf Ltd* [1996] AC 800. See 8.416–8.433.

[145]   *White & Carter (Councils) Ltd v McGregor* [1962] AC 413, as applied in *George Barker (Transport) Ltd v Eynon* [1974] 1 Lloyd's Rep 65.

[146]   *Hewitt v Court* (1982) 149 CLR 639, 653. Generally see Jackson *Enforcement of Maritime Claims* (2nd edn, 1996), ch 20.

[147]   Jackson ibid 443.

[148]   Scrutton, *Charterparties and Bills of Lading* (20th edn, 1996) 373.

[149]   *Weeks v Goode* (1859) 6 CB (NS) 367.

[150]   *Gurr v Cuthbert* (1843) 12 LJ Ex 309. While exercising the lien, quite apart from their duties as carriers, carriers are bound to treat the goods with reasonable care: *Crouch v GW Ry* (1858) 27 LJ Ex 345, 349 *per* Willes J.

[151]   *Hewitt v Court* (1982) 149 CLR 639, 653.

[152]   Scrutton (n 148 above) 266ff. The lien does not, however, extend to expenses incurred in retaining and maintaining goods in possession in order to exercise the lien: see Jackson 440 and cases cited.

[153]   *Mulliner v Florence* (1878) 3 QBD 484.

sell eg perishable goods,[154] or the goods have been abandoned by the person otherwise entitled to the goods.[155] Today in practice such details are clarified by the widespread use of contractual liens.[156]

Carriers have an action in debt for carriage charges but only for charges due. Thus **12.42** for charges due on delivery, carriers must have properly delivered the goods or, at least, been ready and willing to deliver them. Unless the contract stipulates for advance freight or freight pro rata itineris,[157] freight is presumed to be payable by the consignee on delivery.[158]

(12) Public Policy

(a) Unfair terms

The Unfair Contract Terms Act, 1977,[159] nullifies terms altering or reducing busi- **12.43** ness liability when their effect is unreasonable. It applies to internal carriage contracts,[160] the terms of which are contained in written standard terms of business such as consignment notes.[161] Reasonableness is a matter of impression formed by reference to certain factors[162] listed below. Contracts of carriage are most affected by factors (i) to (v) and (ix).

(i) The relative bargaining strength of the parties[163] by reference to whether customers:
  (a) knew or should have known that it was possible to enter such a contract with another carrier without having to agree to a such clauses;[164]
  (b) were experienced in transactions of that kind; or
  (c) had relied on the advice of the carrier.

---

[154] *Prager v Blatspiel Stamp and Heacock Ltd* [1924] 1 KB 566, 573 *per* McCardie J; *Sachs v Miklos* [1948] 2 KB 23, 35–36 *per* Lord Goddard CJ, CA.

[155] Scrutton (n 148 above) 382.

[156] Eg *K Chellaram & Sons (London) v Butlers Warehousing and Distribution Ltd* [1978] 2 Lloyd's Rep 412, CA, in which it was held that a contractual lien might be effective even against non-contracting goods owners provided that they were aware that such terms might apply. Also *Young (W) & Son (Wholesale Fish Merchants) v BTC* [1955] 2 QB 177. See further Kahn-Freund, 402 *et seq*.

[157] *Appleby v Myers* (1867) LR 2 CP 651, 661, *per* Blackburn J.

[158] *Dickenson v Lano* (1860) 2 F & F 188, 190 *per* Blackburn J. See also *Barnes v Marshall* (1852) 21 LJQB 388; 118 ER 296; *Metcalfe v Britannia Ironworks* (1877) 2 QBD 423. Cf *Christy v Row* (1808) 1 Taunt. 300, where there was subsequent agreement for delivery short of destination.

[159] Generally, see paras 8.110–8.118.

[160] The Act is inapplicable to 'international supply contracts': s 26.

[161] *The Flamar Pride* [1990] 1 Lloyd's Rep 434, 438.

[162] *Smith v Bush* [1990] 1 AC 831, 858.

[163] This factor like the others are applied by analogy with those listed in Sched 2(a) the direct application of which is restricted to contracts other than contracts of carriage.

[164] *Overseas Medical Supplies Ltd v Orient Transport Services Ltd* [1999] 2 Lloyd's Rep 273, at [21], CA.

(ii) The party best able to insure against the risk.[165] In the risks associated with carriage indemnity insurance is regarded as more efficient than liability insurance.[166] In practice carriers usually obtain first party insurance on goods for the benefit of goods owners.[167]

(iii) The party best able to avoid LDD[168]—usually the carrier.

(iv) Any inducement offered by carriers, such as reduced charges, in return for the reduced liability sought by the exclusion.[169]

(v) Whether the term is in established and widespread use in the trade context.[170] Standard terms of the Road Haulage Association Conditions of Carriage, 1988 (RHA) or English Welsh & Scottish Railway Ltd General Conditions of Carriage 2004 (EWS) are likely to be respected.[171]

(vi) Whether and to what extent customers had actual notice of terms.[172]

(vii) Proportionality:[173] if the loss claimed is large in relation to the carriage charges the term will receive favourable consideration.

(viii) Any special difficulty or danger in performing the work in respect of which liability is excluded or limited.[174]

(ix) In the case of limits on the amount of liability, courts consider '(a) the resources he could expect to be available to him for the purpose of meeting the liability that should arise and (b) how far it was open to him to cover himself by insurance': s 11(4).[175]

(b) Unlawful Carriage: Non-Enforcement

12.44 Contracts of carriage may be void or unenforceable[176] because of how they are formed or performed, or in view of their purpose. Usually it is because they are contrary to statute containing an express prohibition of some aspect of carriage, which may also prescribe non-enforcement of the contract of carriage. Absent any such prescription, courts have sometimes implied the same consequence.[177] This may be

---

[165] s 11(4). *Monarch Airlines Ltd v London Luton Airport Ltd* [1998] 1 Lloyd's Rep 403, 413.

[166] *Rutter v Palmer* [1922] 2 KB 87, 90, CA.

[167] *Tomlinson (Hauliers) Ltd v Hepburn* [1966] AC 451. Insurance is enforceable by goods owners under the Contracts (Rights of Third Parties) Act, 1999.

[168] *Phillips Products Ltd v Hyland* [1987] 2 All ER 620, 629–630, CA.

[169] Sched 2(b).

[170] Sched 2(c). *Monarch* (n 165 above).

[171] *Schenkers Ltd v Overland Shoes Ltd* [1998] 1 Lloyd's Rep 498, CA. Cf *Overseas Medical* (n 164 above).

[172] Sched 2(c).

[173] *Smith v Bush* [1990] 1 AC 831, 859.

[174] ibid.

[175] ibid.

[176] A point of doctrinal disagreement but of no immediate importance.

[177] Eg *Phoenix General Insurance Co of Greece SA v ADAS* [1988] QB 216, 271–272, CA, citing *Archbolds (Freightage) Ltd v S Spanglett Ltd* [1961] 1 QB 374, CA Cf *St John Shipping Corp v Joseph Rank Ltd* [1957] 1 QB 267, CA; and *Howard v Shirlstar Container Transport* [1990] 3 All ER 366, CA. See generally paras 8.210ff.

controversial because public policy 'may at times be better served by refusing to nullify a bargain save on serious and sufficient grounds'.[178]

In one case[179] carriers defended on the ground that the contract was unenforceable because the vehicle was not properly licensed, as required by statute. Pearce LJ pointed out[180] that the contract was not expressly forbidden by the statute, and asked if it was forbidden by implication. The object of the statute, he said, was not 'to interfere with the owner of goods or his facilities for transport, but to control those who provided the transport, with a view to promoting its efficiency'. The carriers' argument failed. In another contrasting case[181] carriers used a vehicle loaded in excess of the permitted statutory weight, which overturned en route. The goods were damaged. The carriers' plea that the contract was illegal and unenforceable was upheld.   **12.45**

The difference is that in the second case, not only was there a concern about public safety, but the consignors knew or should have known about the overloading, and failed to protest; use of a more suitable vehicle would have cost more. A different decision in the first case would have permitted culpable carriers to defend an action simply by pointing to their own breach of regulation.[182]   **12.46**

When contracts of carriage are unlawful in their purpose, for example, smuggling or the distribution of illegal substances, enforcement has also been refused on grounds of public policy. If the smuggling is by the carrier or its employees, a breach of contract remains actionable by customers. If by customers, they cannot enforce the contract of carriage against the carrier,[183] and carriers, if implicated in the illegal venture, will be unable to enforce the contract against customers. Carriers are implicated if they knew or should have known about customers smuggling.[184]   **12.47**

The main consequence in these situations is non-enforcement of the contract, wholly or in pArt[185] Carriers cannot recover carriage charges. Customers cannot recover damages from carriers for LDD. Moreover, they cannot recover the goods or damages for their detention, if they have to rely on the terms of the contract or   **12.48**

---

178 *Vita Food Products Inc v Unus Shipping Co Ltd* [1939] AC 277, 293, PC. The imposition of a fine may suffice; see *St John Shipping* (ibid).

179 *Archbolds (Freightage)* (n 177 above).

180 [1961] 1 QB 374, 385–386.

181 *Ashmore, Benson, Pease & Co v AV Dawson* [1973] 1 WLR 828, CA.

182 [1961] 1 QB 374, 385–386.

183 *Foster v Driscoll* [1929] 1 KB 470, CA; *Regazzoni v KC Sethia (1944) Ltd* [1958] AC 301; *Mackender v Feldia AG* [1967] 2 QB 590, CA.

184 *Pearce v Brooks* (1866) LR 1 Exch 213.

185 *Holman v Johnson* (1775) 1 Cowp 341, 343; *Tinsley v Milligan* [1994] 1 AC 340, 355. Occasionally the unlawfulness concerns just part of the contract, and the rest may be enforced: *Fielding & Platt Ltd v Najjar* [1969] 1 WLR 357, 362, CA.

on the fact that it is illegal. Although the contract is illegal, carriers can still defend by reference to contract terms or the fact that the contract is unenforceable,[186] or assert property rights obtained under the illegal contract.[187]

B. International Carriage

(1) International Conventions

12.49 International contracts of carriage are based largely, albeit not entirely, on international agreement found in diplomatic conventions, supplemented where necessary by rules of common law.

12.50 The oldest convention is CIM for carriage by rail,[188] appended to a framework convention called COTIF.[189] The current version of CIM came into force in the UK in June 2006.[190] For carriage by road, CMR[191] was signed at Geneva in 1956 and came into force in the UK in October 1967.[192] Carriage by air in recent times has been subject mainly to the Warsaw Convention 1929 (WSC), as amended by the Hague Protocol 1955 and supplemented by the Guadalajara Convention 1961.[193] However, in 2006 an updated and consolidated version came into force: the Montreal Convention 1999 (MC).

(2) Scope of Application

(a) Conflicts of Law

12.51 Courts characterize a case not as 'contract' but 'international contract of carriage' and apply a unilateral conflicts rule in favour of the appropriate convention as *lex fori*.[194] What makes a case international is not the nationality of the parties but movement of goods from one country to another.[195] Were it nationality, a large

---

[186] *Bowmakers Ltd v Barnet Instruments Ltd* [1945] KB 65, CA.

[187] *Taylor v Chester* (1869) LR 4 QB 309.

[188] Règles uniformes concernant le transport international ferroviaire des marchandises, referred to in France as RUCIM but elsewhere more commonly as CIM. Annexes to CIM deal eg with the carriage of dangerous goods.

[189] Convention relative aux transports internationaux ferroviaires. See <www.otif.org>.

[190] SI 1996/2092.

[191] La Convention relative au Contrat de Transport International de Marchandises par Route.

[192] Schedule to the Carriage of Goods by Road Act 1965 (amended by the Carriage by Road and Air Act 1979) came into force in the UK on 19 October 1967.

[193] See the Carriage by Air Act 1961 and Carriage by Air (Convention) Order 1967: SI 1967 No. 479.

[194] MA Clarke, *Aspects of the Hague Rules* (1976) 11 ff.

[195] As the destination might be changed post contract, what counts is the destination originally agreed: *Grein v Imperial Airways Ltd* [1937] 1 KB 50, 77.

cargo aircraft, stopping at different airports in different countries with goods belonging to persons of different nationalities, might well contain goods subject to different air regimes. The territorial factor makes this less likely, and goods can be grouped according to the order of loading and unloading and hence according to the relevant legal regime.

For CMR it suffices that just one of the states is a Contracting State: Art 1.1. Thus, **12.52** in practice, CMR extends to Eastern Europe and the Middle East. However, the air regimes are more restricted: both place of departure and place of destination must be in Contracting States: Article 1.2. Most States own airlines and take a more than merely regulatory interest in their airspace. All the regimes can be extended by national legislation to internal movements, in the UK the case of the air regimes, and by voluntary adoption by contracting parties.

None of the regimes cover all matters relating to the contracts in question but, in **12.53** the case of carriage by air, they are exclusive on what they do cover.[196] CIM and CMR do not prohibit alternative suit in tort but such actions do not extend carrier liability.[197] However courts may seek the meaning of concepts in the substratum of national law, for example, even key concepts such as inherent vice and causation.

(b) Factual Delimitation

Each regime defines the activity concerned: the carriage of goods. CIM is for **12.54** carriage 'by rail' (title). CMR applies to carriage 'by road in vehicles': Art 1.1. WSC and MC apply to carriage 'performed by aircraft': Art 1.1. Although the regimes apply to contracts of carriage, the liability rules are confined to the period of transit. If carriers fail to take over goods at all, the case is governed by national law.[198] The key feature of transit is not movement but custody and control.[199]

Goods comprise every transportable object, unless the regime is considered **12.55** inappropriate. Thus 'funeral consignments' and household goods are excluded from CMR: Art 1.4, although corpses are commonly repatriated by air subject to WSC or MC. Also a more specific regime may be preferred, for example for postal packets.[200]

Documents, consignment note or waybill, were once a condition of the applica- **12.56** tion of regimes such as WSC. Today, however, a transport document is required in all cases but, if none is issued, the regime applies nonetheless.

---

196 *Sidhu v BA* [1997] AC 430, 453; also *Fellowes v Clyde Helicopters* [1997] 1 All ER 775, HL.
197 CIM Art 41; CMR Art 28.
198 Clarke, CMR, para 65.
199 *Westminster Bank v Imperial Airways Ltd* [1936] 2 All ER 890.
200 CMR Art 1.4.

(3) Claims

(a) Forum

12.57 Jurisdiction is in the usual places: carriers' domicile, habitual residence or principal place of business, as well as the place of destination and the 'court or tribunal of a contracting country designated by agreement between the parties.[201] A further possibility, an important reflection of worldwide air freight and electronic trading, is the branch or agency through which the contract of carriage was made.[202] The *lex fori* regulates questions of procedure.[203]

(b) Time

12.58 A limitation period of one year is prescribed by CIM Art 47 and CMR Art 32,[204] extended in cases of serous breach to two years in CIM and three years in CMR. The air regimes speak of 'extinction',[205] whereby rights of action cease to exist,[206] after two years from when aircraft arrived or should have arrived. The absence of extension for serious breach reflects considerations concerning actions for death and injury to passengers, which are also regulated. Residual aspects such as suspension are governed by the *lex fori*.

(c) Proof of loss

12.59 Partial loss or damage to goods is established, first, by proof of the quantity or state of the goods on delivery; and, second, by way of contrast, proof of the (greater) quantity or (better) state of the goods when they were taken over, as evidenced by the transport document. As to the first, under CIM Art 42 claimants have only to allege partial loss or damage for carriers to be obliged to arrange an examination of the goods and draw up a report. If its findings are not accepted by claimants, they are entitled to further investigation by an expert appointed by the parties or by the court. CIM reflects the public service role of railways. Compare CMR, Art 30.2, whereby, if consignees check the goods with the carrier, whatever they agree is conclusive, except as regards matters not then apparent.[207] Compare too the air regimes, in many ways the most modern, which do not regulate the process but leave it to the *lex fori*.

---

[201] CIM Art 46 and CMR Art 31.

[202] *Rothman's of Pall Mall v Saudi Arabian Airlines Corp* [1981] QB 368, CA.

[203] Issues of *lis pendens* are resolved by reference to the Brussels Convention 1968: eg *Andrea Merzario Ltd v Spedition Leitner GmbH* [2001] EWCA Civ 61; [2001] 1 Lloyd's Rep 490, CA.

[204] Resulting in litigation: *ICI Fibres v MAT Transport* [1987] 1 Lloyd's Rep 354.

[205] WSC Art 29.1; MC Art 35.

[206] Eg *Proctor v Jetway* [1982] 2 NSWLR 264, 271.

[207] This shadows the French *constatation aimable*.

As for total loss, if the allegation is non-delivery of the entire consignment, *ex* **12.60**
hypothesi there are no goods to be examined. However, if goods can be proved to
have been taken over and not delivered within the stated number of days after the
expiry of the transit period, total loss is presumed: eg CMR Art 20. Much turns
on the evidential role of transport documents, which are prima facie evidence of
what should have been apparent to carriers when goods are taken over.[208]

The issue of transport documents containing specified information is required **12.61**
by each regime. The information varies, the main items being the nature and
quantity of goods, the number of packages, the consignment weight, marks and
(WSC only) dimensions. What is stated about the apparent order and condition
of the goods carries with it an implication about the state or sufficiency of packing.
Under CIM and CMR carriers may enter reservations on matters which they have
no reasonable means of checking, the same being true[209] of the condition of goods
or the contents of a package, if it has been actually checked.

(4) Liability

The regimes apply as terms of the contracts of carriage. This format provides a **12.62**
perspective from which the underlying liability regime is best interpreted.
Claimants must prove breach of contract, breach of the strict obligation to deliver
goods at destination in the same quantity and condition received, and without
delay. Carriers are strictly liable for loss of or damage to the goods occurring while
the goods are in their charge qua carrier. Carriers are presumed to have performed
as promised until the contrary is proved.[210]

On proof of breach carriers' first line of defence is to dispute the evidence of loss, **12.63**
damage or delay (LDD) brought by the claimant. The second is that the LDD was
caused by claimant fault, inherent vice in the goods or by some other cause which,
to a degree that may vary according to the regime, was beyond the carrier's control
and for which the carrier has not assumed responsibility. Failing this, the third line
of defence is that the claim is out of time, has been brought in the wrong court, or
that the monetary amount of liability is limited. Under the land regimes defences
in the third line are defeated, if the claimant can establish serious fault on the part
of the carrier.

---

[208] Rail: apparent condition of goods and packaging, number of packages, marks, gross mass
or quantity otherwise expressed, when loading is performed by carriers: CIM 1999 Art 12.2.
Road: apparent condition of goods and packaging, number of packages, marks: Art 9.2. Air:
weight, dimensions, packing, number of packages: WSC Art 11 (2); and MC Art 11.2. Cf CIM
1980 Art 21.

[209] Likewise MC Art 11.2.

[210] CMR Art 30.1; WSC Art 26.1, MC Art 31.1. Cf however, CIM 1999 Art 42.

(5) Defences

(a) Patterns

12.64 Carriers' second line of defence lies in one or more of the grounds of exoneration stated in the relevant regime. The long list in CIM compares with the short list of five in MC. Categories of defence are (1) matters in the risk sphere of cargo (eg inherent vice in goods and insufficient packing), (2) third party intervention (eg war), and (3) the impact of nature. The last of these are not specified in the regimes but in more venerable standard contracts are referred to as Act of God. However, category (3) survives in the regimes as an instance of the wider defence of 'unavoidable circumstances'. In addition, in the land regimes carriers may defend by reference to 'special risks': defences by reference to the risk sphere of cargo but with a different and, from the common law perspective, unusual allocation of the onus of proof.[211] Note that the Unfair Contract Terms Act 1977 does not apply to contracts governed by CIM, CMR or the corresponding air conventions.[212]

(b) Inherent vice

12.65 This is one of the defences: CIM Art 23.2, CMR Art17.2, WSC Art 18.3(a), and MC Art 17.2(a). It has the same meaning in each.[213] In *Ulster-Swift v Taunton Meat Haulage*,[214] a typical CMR case, pig carcasses in a refrigerated trailer were decaying on arrival in Basle. The carriers pleaded inherent vice because the carcasses were at too high a temperature, when taken over. The defence would have succeeded, if the trailer itself had been as cool as it should have been; but it was not and the defence failed. At common law goods inadequately packed also suffer from inherent vice, however, in the regimes this is a specific defence. The defence is well known to English shipping and insurance law, to which courts refer.

12.66 Inherent vice may also be an instance of 'unavoidable circumstances'[215] or, under the land regimes, a case of 'sensitivity of goods'.[216] However, sensitivity differs, being a permanent feature of all goods of that kind, whereas inherent vice, eg in *Ulster-Swift*, is found only in some.

---

[211] See paras 12.73ff.
[212] s 6(5)(b). Also most non-domestic carriage contracts are 'international supply contacts' and thus excluded from the Act: s 26.
[213] *Soya v White* [1983] 1 Lloyd's Rep 122, 126, HL.
[214] [1975] 2 Lloyd's Rep 502, affirmed [1977] 1 Lloyd's Rep 346.
[215] Eg *Centrocoop Export-Import SA v Brit European Transport* [1984] 2 Lloyd's Rep 618, 625.
[216] See para 12.74.

(c) Claimant fault

Under the land regimes defences include contributory negligence and claimants' **12.67**
fault, whether of consignors or consignees. Indeed carriers can plead the fault of
consignors even to claims by consignees. Commonly they allege defective loading
or defective packing. The point is controversial but English courts would probably prefer the Austrian view,[217] that the defence is effective only if the claimant was
literally at fault. Delay where consignees refuse to accept goods, for example, is not
necessarily their fault. Anyway, LDD caused by 'the instructions of the claimant
given otherwise than as the result of a wrongful act or neglect on the part of the
carrier' is a also a specific defence.[218] Fault is not required. An example is instructions about care of goods during transit[219] from a source normally reliable but
erroneous on that occasion. However, the defence fails when the instructions were
given 'as the result of a wrongful act or neglect on the part of the carrier'. If goods
are damaged in transit, carriers at fault and obliged to seek instructions cannot
plead the instructions to excuse any extra damage that results.

(d) Third party intervention

An 'act of war or an armed conflict' and 'an act of public authority carried out in **12.68**
connection with the entry, exist or transit of the cargo'[220] are specified defences in
MC but not CIM, CMR or WSC, where, however, they may well be instances of
'unavoidable circumstances'.[221]

(e) Unavoidable circumstances

An important defence is 'circumstances which the carrier could not avoid'.[222] Air **12.69**
carriers are not liable under WSC if they took 'all necessary measures to avoid the
damage or. . .it was impossible. . .to take such measures', MC likewise but only for
delay.

This defence is the key to carriers' general duty[223] because the corollary is the **12.70**
benchmark of the degree of care and skill required of them. With two exceptions,
circumstances are unavoidable only if carriers have exercised the 'utmost care'.
That is a standard 'somewhere between, on the one hand, a requirement to take
every conceivable precaution, however extreme, within the limits of the law and,
on the other hand, a duty to do no more than act reasonably in accordance with

---

[217] Loewe (1976) 11 ETL 311, para 151.
[218] CMR Art 17.2.
[219] Eg temperature for fruit: *Cass. 23.2.82* (1983) 18 ETL 13 (France).
[220] Art 18.2 (c) and (d) respectively.
[221] For likely interpretation see para 12.35(iv).
[222] See Clarke, CMR, para 74.
[223] See Haenni, *International Encyclopedia of Comparative Law*, vol. XII, ch 2, para 243.

current practice'.[224] This view was reached by distinguishing *force majeure*, 'due diligence' and 'reasonable care': if such had been intended those well known words would have been used.[225] Nonetheless to apply the defence courts consider the knowledge and information available to carriers and drivers at the time (for example, of security measures available), the likelihood of LDD (certain goods are more attractive to thieves than others), and legal regulations (notably permitted driving hours).[226] The duty extends not only to avoiding incidents which cause LDD but also to mitigating effects of LDD.

12.71   One exception concerns circumstances in the claimant's area of risk. When responding to a threat to the goods arising from defective packing, for example, by consignors, the standard is merely that of reasonable care in the light of current haulage practice.[227] However, a further and tougher CMR exception concerns vehicle defects, carriers' area of risk. The unavoidable circumstances must be *external* to the vehicle.[228] Thus, unless caused by something like vandalism rather than defective manufacture or mounting, carriers are strictly liable for bursting tyres.

12.72   In WSC the words 'all necessary measures' were initially construed to mean 'all reasonable measures', while still imposing a somewhat higher duty on carriers than an ordinary duty of care.[229] Over time, however, the words have been construed more strictly to mean something close to the 'utmost care' of CIM and CMR.[230] This can be seen in the second of two lines of approach to what carriers must prove. The first is an *a priori* approach, whereby, without regard to what actually occurred, carriers must show that all the general measures that could be expected were taken, notably providing airworthy aircraft and competent personnel. The second approach, more likely in the UK, is an *a posteriori* approach whereby courts focus on what actually occurred and ask what could or should have been done about that. This is stricter in that, when causes are unknown carriers are unlikely to be excused.[231] Subject to that, courts reach decisions by consideration of factors similar to those considered in CMR cases.[232]

---

224 *Silber v Islander Trucking* [1985] 2 Lloyd's Rep 243, 247. Also *Cicatiello v Anglo-European Ltd* [1994] 1 Lloyd's Rep 678. Clarke, CMR, para 74e.
225 Kahn-Freund 433; also *Silber* (ibid).
226 *Silber* (n 224 above).
227 See para 12.76.
228 Art 17.3. cf *Walek v Chapman & Ball* [1980] 2 Lloyd's Rep 279.
229 *Swiss Bank Corp v Brinks-MAT Ltd* [1986] 2 Lloyd's Rep 79, 96–97.
230 Clarke, Air, 135.
231 *Panalpina International Transport v Densil Underwear* [1981] 1 Lloyd's Rep 187.
232 See *Thomas Cook Group Ltd v Air Malta Co Ltd* [1997] 2 Lloyd's Rep 399.

(6) Special Risks

When land carriers prove special risks, it is presumed in cases of loss or damage **12.73** (but not delay), that they were not in breach of contract. When goods are loaded by consignors, for example, carriers prove, not that the loading did cause the loss or damage, but that it *could* have caused it: no more than a plausible hypothesis.[233] The presumption resembles one found in the common law of bailment.[234]

The special risks, listed in CIM Art 23.3 and CMR Art 17.4, are (a) uncovered **12.74** vehicles; (b) lack of or defective packing of goods which, for the kind of transit agreed, usually need packing;[235] (c) loading or unloading by consignors or consignees; and (d) carriage of sensitive goods, such as fruit or meat.[236] However, if the vehicle 'is specially equipped to protect goods', notably refrigerated vehicles, road carriers must also prove that the equipment was appropriate and in good order.[237] The other special risks are (e) insufficiency of marks or description; (f) carriage of livestock; and (g) under CIM only, risks against which the contract requires an attendant to accompany the goods.

Where carriers establish a special risk, it is for claimants to prove that 'the loss or **12.75** damage was not, in fact, attributable either wholly or partly to one of these risks'.[238] Usually they try to prove the actual cause but they are not obliged to: it suffices to provide evidence of another hypothesis sufficiently plausible to suggest that the cause of loss or damage may not have been the special risk after all. Other issues of proof are for the *lex fori*.[239]

Attribution may be partial and responsibility apportioned. For example, rolls of **12.76** lead worked loose and were damaged during road carriage, due partly to improper loading by the consignor and partly carrier negligence in response to the danger.[240] Carriers' employees cannot simply ignore the fate of goods, especially when third parties are at risk. They have a residual duty of care, firstly, as the corollary of the defence of unavoidable circumstances and the duty to exercise the 'utmost care'.[241] However, secondly, when dealing with special risks, especially defective

---

[233] See *Ulster-Swift v Taunton Meat Haulage* [1975] 2 Lloyd's Rep 502; affirmed [1977] 1 Lloyd's Rep 346, CA.

[234] *Levison v Patent Steam Carpet Cleaning Co Ltd* [1978] QB 69, CA; apparently overlooked in *Datec Electronic Holdings Ltd v UPS Ltd* [2007] UKHL 23; [2007] 1 WLR 1325.

[235] *Tetroc v Cross-Con (International)* [1981] 1 Lloyd's Rep 192.

[236] *Donald & Son (Wholesale Meat Contractors) Ltd v Continental Freeze Ltd* 1984 SLT 182. Cf inherent vice: para 12.65.

[237] CMR Art 18.4; *Ulster-Swift* (n 233 above).

[238] CMR Art 18.2. Likewise CIM Art 25.2.

[239] *Ulster-Swift* 352.

[240] *OLG Saarbrücken 21.11.74* (1976) 11 ETL 261.

[241] Para 12.70.

packing or loading by consignors,[242] their residual duty to respond is pitched at the lower level of reasonable care. Case law across Europe is copious, but uncertainty remains. The concept of special risks is not found in other transport regimes.

(7) Remedies

12.77 Termination of contract, liens on goods, and recovery of carriage charges are matters for national law; compensation too under WSC and MC but CIM and CMR have rules, including unusual provisions for the possibility that, if lost goods are recovered, claimants may repay the compensation and recover the goods.[243]

12.78 For damaged goods carriers under CIM and CMR are liable not for cost of repair but for diminution in value[244] by reference to the value of goods not at destination but 'at the place and time at which they were accepted for carriage'.[245] The reason for the latter lies in the intention not to allow compensation for consequential loss, unless there is a declaration of special interest[246] or an especially serious breach of contract. The amount must not exceed that payable on a total loss,[247] to which with partial loss the same measure applies.[248]

12.79 In addition to compensation, in case of loss of goods under CMR and CIM 'the carriage charges, Customs duties and other charges incurred in respect of the carriage of the goods shall be refunded'.[249] Narrowly interpreted these are charges, such as the cost of packing and insurance, incurred *for the purpose* of carriage.[250] The broad interpretation preferred by the House of Lords in *Buchanan & Co v Babco Forwarding & Shipping (UK)*[251] extends to expenses *consequential* on how the carriage was actually carried out in breach of contract, such as the cost of surveying damaged goods,[252] or of extra duty payable,[253] as well as return carriage charges.[254] In 2003, however, the Court of Appeal distinguished *Buchanan*,[255]

---

242 Clarke, CMR, paras 84 and 87ff.

243 CMR Art 20; CIM Art 29.

244 CMR Art 25.1; CIM Art 32.1.

245 CMR Art 23.1 Idem: CIM Art 30.1. *Buchanan & Co v Babco Forwarding & Shipping (UK)* [1978] AC 141, 151.

246 CMR Art 26; CIM Art 35.

247 CMR Art 25.2; CIM Art 32.2.

248 CMR Art 23.1; CIM Art 30.1.

249 CMR Art 23.4; CIM Art 30.4.

250 The minority view in *Buchanan & Co v Babco Forwarding & Shipping (UK)* [1978] AC 141.

251 ibid.

252 *ICI Fibres v MAT Transport* [1987] 1 Lloyd's Rep 354.

253 *Buchanan* (n 250 above).

254 *Thermo Engineers Ltd v Ferrymasters Ltd* [1981] 1 All ER 1142, 1150.

255 *Sandeman Coprimar SA v Transitos y Transportes Integrales SL* [2003] EWCA Civ 113; [2003] QB 1270.

acknowledging 'the need to restrict the scope of *Buchanan*', because it inappropriately imports English rules of remoteness to the scheme of the CMR which 'contemplates an identical liability imposed on a succession of carriers'.[256] The narrow interpretation is also that of most courts in other CMR states.[257]

(8) Maximum Liability

Carriers should have a viable limit on their exposure. Firstly, the amount must be **12.80** ascertainable so that carriers can estimate their exposure without having to open packages. So, the limit is usually an amount per unit of weight, including packing. Secondly, the limit must be not so high that liability is uninsurable but not so low that carriers have insufficient incentive to take care.

The limit varies. CMR has lower limits than CIM. Moves on environmental **12.81** grounds to reverse the position and make railways more competitive have yet to be realized. The limit for carriage by air, the highest, reflects the value of goods carried by air and high freight charges. A significant feature of MC is a provision for reviewing the limits every five years without resort to the full diplomatic process.[258]

(9) Serious Breach

(a) Wilful Misconduct

Carriers lose their liability limits[259] when they are guilty of serious breach of **12.82** contract. This is the 'wilful misconduct' of CMR, Art 29.1, taken from the 1929 text of WSC, Art 25, even though the conference knew that in WSC Art 25 the rule had produced an unacceptable divergence between the decisions in civil law countries and decisions in countries of common law,[260] and that it was likely to be changed.[261]

In England the 'starting point' for enquiry about wilful misconduct 'is an enquiry **12.83** about the conduct ordinarily to be expected in the particular circumstances,' and next to ask whether the acts of omissions 'were so far outside the range of such conduct as to be properly regarded as 'misconduct'.[262] Only then will the court

---

[256] ibid [42].

[257] Notably Austria, Germany and Holland although not France. It is also the inference from the *travaux préparatoires*: Clarke, CMR para 98.

[258] Art 24.

[259] Under CMR Art 32.1 the time limit also.

[260] R Rodière 'La faute inexcusable du transporteur aérien' (1978) 13 ETL 24, 25.

[261] See the travaux préparatoires: TRANS/WP/9/35 No 73, 19–20.

[262] *Thomas Cook Group Ltd v Air Malta Co Ltd* [1997] 2 Lloyd's Rep 399, 407, with reference to *Lacey's Footwear (Wholesale) Ltd v Bowler International Freight Ltd* [1997] 2 Lloyd's Rep 369, CA, on CMR.

consider 'whether the misconduct is wilful',[263] a search to establish the actor's state of mind. Typically, in *Jones v Bencher*,[264] a CMR case of 1984, the court turned back to nineteenth-century railway cases[265] and cases on the unamended WSC, which put a subjective interpretation on 'wilful misconduct'. Nonetheless the CMR rule is said to be substantially the same as the amended WSC and CIM,[266] in which the key elements of the wording are intent to cause damage, recklessness, and knowledge that damage would probably result.

(b) Intent and recklessness

12.84 Intent to cause damage is obvious and rarely an issue in litigation. Motive is irrelevant. A pilot who allows perishable cargo to perish while deviating to get a passenger to hospital, has the best of motives but the damage is intentional nonetheless.

12.85 A continuum 'runs from simple negligence through gross negligence to intentional misconduct', and recklessness 'lies between gross negligence and intentional harm'.[267] Recklessness is a concept well known at common law. In carriage regimes, however, recklessness must be read in context and in close collocation with the phrase 'with knowledge that damage would probably result'.[268] So English courts require evidence of actual awareness on the part of the actor.

(c) Knowledge and awareness

12.86 A person 'must appreciate that he is acting wrongfully, or is wrongfully omitting to act, and yet persists in so acting or omitting to act regardless of the consequences'.[269] This is not easily established when driver or pilot is dead. Thus a more objective approach is found in other countries, notably in air cases in the USA, where the misconduct is 'the wilful performance of an act that is likely to result in damage or wilful action with a reckless disregard of the *probable consequences*'.[270] Courts there have been more ready than courts in England to infer a state of mind from the evidence. Otherwise, they say, claimants would be 'at the mercy

---

263 *Air Malta* (n 262 above) p 407.

264 [1986] 1 Lloyd's Rep 54; approved in *TNT Global v Denfleet* [2007] EWCA Civ 405. See also *Texas Instruments Ltd v Nasan (Europe) Ltd* [1991] 1 Lloyd's Rep 146, 154; and *Lacey's Footwear* (n 262 above) p 374.

265 Notably *Lewis v GWR* (1877) 3 QBD. 195, 206, CA, and *Forder v GWR*. [1905] 2 KB 532, 535.

266 Respectively Art 25 and Art 36.

267 *Saba v Air France*, 78 F 3d 664, 667 (DC Cir, 1996).

268 *Cortes v American*, 177 F 3d 1272, 1284ff (11 Cir, 1999).

269 *Horabin v BOAC* [1952] 2 All ER 1016, 1022. See also *Rustenburg Platinum Mines v SAA* [1977] I Lloyd's Rep 564, 569; affd [1979] 1 Lloyd's Rep 19 (CA); *Goldman v Thai Airways International* [1983] 1 WLR 1186, CA; and *Lacey's Footwear* (n 262 above).

270 *Wing Hang Bk Ltd v JAL Co* (1973) 357 F. Supp. 94, 96–97 (SD NY), with emphasis added. See also *Republic National Bank v Eastern Airlines* (1987) 815 F 2d 232, 239 (2 Cir).

of those capable of the most invincible self-deception'.[271] The point is perhaps less compelling in England, where there is no jury in such cases and where states of mind, associated for example with fraud, are regularly assessed by the court.

Wilful misconduct may lie in series of acts or a single act and what 'may amount on one occasion to mere negligence' may amount 'on another to wilful misconduct'.[272] A driver may cross a red light absentmindedly, or quite deliberately because he reckons that the roads are deserted and nothing will cross his path—that is wilful misconduct.[273] The difference is between a risk and a calculated risk.

12.87

The rule now found in MC and CIM but not CMR requires conduct 'with intent to cause damage or recklessly and with knowledge that damage would *probably* result'.[274] However, in *Nugent v Goss Aviation Ltd* the Court of Appeal rejected the argument that such knowledge could be imputed.[275] There must still be 'actual knowledge, in the sense of appreciation or awareness at the time of the conduct in question, that it will probably result in the type of damage caused. Nothing less will do'.[276] It is 'not sufficient to show that, by reason of his training and experience, the pilot ought to have known that damage would probably result from his act or omission. The test is subjective'.[277]

12.88

Nonetheless, as to evidence of awareness, English courts today are moving towards the more objective approach taken in the USA. In particular, in *Nugent* Auld LJ conceded that the 'greater the obviousness of the risk the more likely the tribunal is to infer recklessness and that, the defendant, in so doing, knew that he would probably cause damage'.[278] He also referred to an air cargo case, in which vulnerable goods were left out on the tarmac in a thunderstorm,[279] and where the

12.89

---

[271] *Re Air Crash near Cali, Columbia*, 985 F Supp 1106, 1129 (SD Fla, 1997). Also *Saba v Air France* 78 F 3d 664, 667 (DC Cir, 1996).

[272] *Horabin v BOAC* (note 269 above).

[273] The illustration is based on a much quoted passage in *Horabin* (note 269 above) eg *Rustenburg Platinum Mines v SAA* [1977] 1 Lloyd's Rep 564, 569.

[274] Emphasis added but the point was underlined by Auld LJ in *Nugent v Goss Aviation Ltd* [2000] 2 Lloyd's Rep 222, 223, CA.

[275] ibid. The argument of Pill LJ at 231, that the probability of damage was 'within his knowledge' even if not present in his mind at the material time; and that, for example, a 'pilot does not escape liability merely because, by reason of, for example, drink or tiredness, he forgets for a moment his training and the general knowledge his experience of flying brings him' was rejected by the other members of the Court.

[276] ibid 228. See also *TNT Global* (note 264 above).

[277] ibid 232.

[278] ibid 227.

[279] *SS Pharmaceutical Co Ltd v Qantas Airways Ltd* [1991] 1 Lloyd's Rep 288, CA NSW.

combination of 'deplorably bad handling' and a failure to call evidence that might excuse it enabled the court to infer recklessness.[280]

(d) Probable results

12.90 Probable results are results that are likely to happen,[281] and thus more than merely foreseeable. Hence, if carriers have an unsafe system for handling cargo, without more, damage to cargo is (reasonably) foreseeable but it is not probable; there may be breach but not serious breach.[282] If, however, some loss or damage is probable, claimants do not have to establish the degree of loss that is probable.[283] Compensation is recoverable for the entire damage.

12.91 Allegedly courts must consider whether 'the wilful misconduct (if established) *caused* the loss or damage to the goods'.[284] Certainly carrier misconduct must be a 'but for' cause of the deleterious results, but that alone is not sufficient. In the USA it is not required to be the sole cause.[285] English courts are likely to agree. However, for the rest American courts have turned to domestic law, in particular, to tort law.[286] The trouble is that 'tort law' or equivalent differs from country to country, especially on causation. Moreover, the American courts were mostly applying the Warsaw text of 1929 and not the amended text of 1955, in which, it is submitted, there is guidance enough. What matters is simply that the results were *probable* results.

---

[280] Similar inferences have been drawn by the French *Cour de Cassation* when valuable cargo was exposed to theft: *British Airways v UAP* (1992) 27 ETL 141.

[281] *Goldman v Thai Airways International* [1983] 1 WLR 1186, CA.

[282] *Rolls Royce Plc v Heavylift-Volga DNEPR Ltd* [2000] 1 Lloyd's Rep 653.

[283] The inference from *Husain v Olympic*, 116 F Supp 2d 1121, 1140 (ND Cal, 2000).

[284] *Thomas Cook Group Ltd v Air Malta Co Ltd* [1997] 2 Lloyd's Rep 399, 408 (emphasis added).

[285] *Korean Air Lines v Alaska*, 22 Avi 17, 388 (Alaska, 1989).

[286] *Re Air Crash near Cali, Columbia*, 985 F Supp 1106, 1146 (SD Fla, 1997).

13

INSURANCE[1]

---

[1] Books referred to in this chapter: MacGillivray: *MacGillivray on Insurance Law* (10th edn, 2003); Rose: FD Rose, *Marine Insurance: Law and Practice* (2004); Clarke 2006: Clarke, *The Law of Insurance Contracts* (5th edn, 2006); Clarke 2007: *Policies and Perceptions of Insurance in the Twenty-first Century* (revised edn, 2007).

A. Introduction

(1) Insurance and the Law

13.01 Generally, contracts of insurance are governed by the same rules of law and interpretation as other kinds of contract.[2] For that reason this chapter starts by presenting the law in a way familiar to readers of general works on contract law. It looks first at the formation of insurance contracts on the basis of mutual consent, next the effect of flaws in consent brought about by mistake, misrepresentation and, a possibility that distinguishes insurance contracts from other contracts, non-disclosure. Once a contract has been validly formed, then next comes its content, necessarily preceded by an outline of the relevant rules of interpretation. After that the law presented is particular to insurance: insuring clauses, which express cover in positive terms, exclusions delimiting cover in negative terms and giving cover its final shape, and warranties which underlie the contract of insurance as conditions precedent to cover. Finally, the chapter deals with policyholder claims against insurers for the sum insured. The rules apply to both marine and non-marine contracts, unless otherwise indicated.

(2) Insurance Contracts

13.02 All-embracing 'definitions' of insurance, found in some common law countries, are regarded in England as too bland to be useful.[3] There is an element of insurance in any binding promise by one person to another in which the law recognizes an assumption of risk. Clearly, not all such arrangements can be regarded as insurance contracts.[4] The attitude of English courts remains that of Templeman J: 'no difficulty has ever arisen in practice, and therefore there has been no all-embracing definition'. He went on to explain that definitions are undesirable because they 'tend sometimes to obscure and occasionally to exclude that which ought to be included'.[5] Mostly it is clear whether there is insurance or not, but there is a marginal penumbra of obscurity where traditional insurance products meet the ingenuity of innovative financial markets. From this perspective the Financial Services Authority (FSA) has observed that there are nonetheless some 'generally accepted'

---

[2] See paras 8.05 ff.

[3] Clarke, 2006, 1-1.

[4] Assumption of risk is insufficient to draw the (difficult) distinction between insurance and any other 'normal' contract, in which there is a secondary promise by a contractor to pay damages for its breach of primary promises. One answer in the USA is the 'principal object' test. For example, a product guarantee is ancillary to the sale of the product which is what characterizes the transaction and distinguishes it from insurance: Williams, 98 Col L Rev 1996, 2019 ff (1998). Test rejected: *Fuji Finance Inc v Aetna Life Ins Co Ltd* [1997] Ch 173, CA.

[5] *DTI v St Christopher Motorists Assn* [1974] 1 Lloyd's Rep 17, 18 ff.

features of archetypical insurance,[6] as described by Channell J in the *Prudential case*,[7] and that contracts lacking those elements are unlikely to be classified as insurance.

First, the business must be insurance business.[8] The insurer may be a charity and insurance may be just one part of its business, but that is insurance business nonetheless. Second, there must be a legally binding promise[9] to pay—in money or in kind.[10] Usually it is money, but sometimes insurers provide something other than or in addition to money: services such as reinstatement of damaged buildings in property insurance and, in travel insurance, transport home and medical treatment. Third, the promise to pay must be contingent on the occurrence of a specified event, such as fire or death. Fourth, at the time of contract the event must be uncertain,[11] uncertain as to whether it will occur (eg fire), as to when it will occur (eg death), or as to how often it will occur (eg damage to taxis). Moreover, fifth, the event must be one that is adverse to policyholders.

13.03

Adversity is obvious in cases such as fire or burglary. Doubt has been expressed about financial vehicles such as life polices maturing at a stated age, such as 65.[12] In England this is valid insurance. As was said in Australia, a whole life policy is an insurance against dying too soon, an endowment policy maturing before death is insurance against living too long.[13] For some the passage of the years is unkind and uncomfortable. Money may be spent to ease the discomfort. Courts approach issues of this kind with a mixture of principle and pragmatism.

13.04

B. Contracting

(1) The Process

Contracts of insurance like other contracts are made when the offer of one party is accepted by the other party, usually the insurer. Insurance applicants, especially applicants for standard consumer cover, may deal directly with insurers. In other cases they deal through insurance intermediaries, such as brokers. Relations with

13.05

---

   6 <www.fsa.gov.uk/pubs/policy/ps04_19.pdf>, para 6.3.4.
   7 *Prudential Ins Co v IRC* [1904] 2 KB 658, 663.
   8 *Hall d'Ath v British Provident Assn* (1932) 48 TLR 240.
   9 *Medical Defence Union Ltd v Dept of Trade* [1980] Ch 82.
   10 *Hampton v Toxteth Co-operative Provident Sy Ltd* [1915] 1 Ch 721, CA.
   11 *Medical Defence* (n 9 above) at 89.
   12 *Medical Defence* (n 9 above) at p 93 *per* Megarry V-C: a 'feat of survival can hardly be called an event that is adverse to his interests'.
   13 *National Mutual Life Assn v FCT* (1959) 102 CLR 29, 45 (HCA).

intermediaries are governed by the law of agency, as well as regulations made under the FSMA.[14]

13.06 Whether through intermediaries or not, applicants commonly obtain a quotation from an insurer. In the language of contract law the quotation is an 'invitation to treat'. Applicants who 'accept' the quotation by completing the insurer's proposal form, submit what the law sees as an offer—to be accepted (or not) by the insurer. If insurers are not willing to accept offers, they may respond with a counter-offer,[15] which may (or may not) be accepted by the applicant. Applicants may respond with a further (counter) offer of their own for acceptance (or rejection) by the insurer. This process continues until a final counter-offer from one of them is accepted or rejected. The template of offer and acceptance, although useful,[16] is not a rigid or exclusive format for concluding insurance contracts; it is just a guide.[17]

13.07 Contracts are concluded when offers are accepted unless, important in this context, parties agree otherwise. Acceptance of an offer, provided that the offeror accepts a new term, is not acceptance at all: no contract results.[18] Agreement on terms, however, *may* still be no contract if subject to satisfaction of specified conditions. Such 'conditions precedent' are found in life or health insurance, where insurers require payment of premium or satisfactory medical reports before becoming bound.

13.08 Here the first possibility is that there is not a binding contract of insurance at the time of agreement until the condition is satisfied.[19] The second is that there is a contract from the time of agreement (acceptance) but no cover until the condition is satisfied.[20] Alternatively, the same situation may be seen as a contract of insurance with cover from the time of agreement but cover that may be defeated later by, for example, an unfavourable medical report; the contract is subject to a 'condition subsequent'.[21] A further alternative is that there is not one contract but two: a preliminary contract with interim cover and, if the condition is satisfied (the report is favourable) a main contract for the full period of cover.[22]

---

[14] See para 13.50.

[15] Eg *Canning v Farquhar* (1886) 16 QBD 727, CA.

[16] *The Zephyr* [1984] 1 Lloyd's Rep 58, 72.

[17] *CTI Inc v Oceanus Mutual Underwriting Assn (Bermuda) Ltd* [1984] 1 Lloyd's Rep 476, 505, CA.

[18] *Canning* (n 15 above).

[19] ibid 731.

[20] ibid.

[21] The Canadian view: *Zurich Life Ins Co v Davies* (1981) 130 DLR (3d) 748, 751, Can SC.

[22] The Scots view in *Sickness & Accident Assurance Assn Ltd v General Accident Assurance Corp Ltd* (1892) 19 R 977, 985.

(2) Certainty of Terms

Unless contracting parties appear to be certain about the essentials of what they are binding themselves to, courts are slow to infer intention to contract. Uncertainty may appear both in what parties have said (ambiguity), and in what parties have not said (incompleteness). Terms essential to insurance contracts are terms which identify the parties, the kind of risk covered (eg fire), the subject-matter (eg St. John's College), the duration of cover (commonly one year), and the premium to be paid by the policyholder. In some instances, notably life insurance, parties must agree the amount of money payable under the policy: they alone can put a value on the life insured. In other instances, such as property insurance, the amount payable is the amount of actual loss but insurers often stipulate a ceiling on this amount. Such terms have to be expressed but other terms (eg duration and premium)[23] can be implied.

13.09

Implied terms are categorized according to their source. First, terms may be implied by law, ie from statute[24] or, when necessary to give business efficacy to the contract,[25] from precedent. Second, terms may be implied from previous dealings between the particular parties.[26] Third, terms may be implied from customs of the insurance market. An important instance is the presumption that applications for insurance are on the basis of insurers' standard terms (if any) for the kind of risk in question.[27]

13.10

Marine insurance merits special mention. The law differs in certain respects mentioned in this chapter. Marine cover is identified by subject-matter: ships (hull), cargo, and freight which can be separately insured.[28] Reinsurance of such subject-matter is also regarded as marine. Further, whereas, unless otherwise specified, the insurance period for non-marine insurance is customarily one year, marine insurance differs in two respects that should be noted. First, cargo may be insured for the transit in question. Alternatively, regular exporters insure all cargo of the type they deal with for a period (often one year) under 'floating' or 'open' covers.[29] Second, ships are under voyage policies or time policies.[30]

13.11

---

[23] *American Airlines Inc v Hope* [1973] 1 Lloyd's Rep 233, CA affirmed on other points [1974] 2 Lloyd's Rep 301; *Baker v Black Sea & Baltic General Ins Co* [1998] 1 WLR 974, 983, HL.

[24] None at all in the case of non-marine insurance; cf Marine Insurance Act 1906 s 36ff.

[25] *Scally v Southern Health & Services Board* [1992] 1 AC 294.

[26] *Hope* (n 23 above) 253.

[27] *General Accident Ins Corp v Cronk* (1901) 17 TLR 233; *Rust v Abbey Life Assurance Co Ltd* [1979] 2 Lloyd's Rep 334, 339, CA. Marine insurance is commonly contracted on one of the standard forms of Institute Clauses developed by the London Underwriters: Rose, 6.28 ff and Appendices 7–19.

[28] Marine Insurance Act s 90.

[29] ibid s 29. Rose 6.65 ff.

[30] ibid s 25. Rose ch 10.

(3) Certainty of Intention

13.12 Offers must indicate a definite willingness to be bound on the part of the offeror. This is a matter of construction of the offer. Documents that appear to contain firm offers, such as insurance application forms, are presumed to do so. No such presumption arises, if there is reason to infer otherwise from context. That is usually the case of documents issued by insurers inviting applications; it makes little sense for insurers to be bound without first assessing the particular risk.

13.13 Definite offers may come to an end before being accepted. First, unaccepted offers end after any period of time stipulated for acceptance or, in the absence of stipulation, a reasonable time.[31] Second, offers end on the failure of a condition subject to which an offer was made.[32] Offers by insurers are implicitly conditional on there being no material change in the risk proposed between offer and acceptance.[33] Third, offers end on rejection. Counter-offers are regarded as rejections;[34] but a response by the offeree is a counter-offer only if it is inconsistent with the offer.[35] Fourth, offers end by revocation[36] communicated to the offeree.[37]

(4) Unequivocal Acceptance

13.14 Acceptance of an offer must be unequivocal, unconditional, and communicated to the offeror, whether by speech or conduct.[38] Payment of premium, and policy delivery are examples of such conduct, although not essential to conclude contracts unless required by the terms of the offer.[39] Silence is equivocal and not normally sufficient evidence of acceptance,[40] unless that can be inferred from the circumstances of the case.[41]

13.15 If the terms purportedly accepted differ from the terms of the offer, there is no acceptance. However, the difference must be definitive. Sometimes insurers respond to applications with a policy in general terms which are not tailored to the application but can be reconciled with it; that may well be valid acceptance.

---

[31] *Ramsgate Victoria Hotel Co v Montefiore* (1866) LR 1 Ex 109.

[32] *Financings Ltd v Stimson* [1962] 1 WLR 1184, CA.

[33] *Canning v Farquhar* (1886) 16 QBD 727, 733, CA.

[34] *Lark v Outhwaite* [1991] 2 Lloyd's Rep 132, 139.

[35] *Jones v Daniel* [1894] 2 Ch 332, 335.

[36] *Canning* (n 33 above) 731.

[37] *Byrne & Co v Van Tienhoven & Co* (1880) 5 CPD 344; *General Re Corp v Forsak Fennia Patria* [1982] QB 1022; reversed on other grounds [1983] QB 856, CA.

[38] See paras 8.07ff.

[39] *Xenos v Wickham* (1866) LR 2 HL 296; *Wooding v Monmouthshire Mutual Indemnity Sy Ltd* [1939] 4 All ER 570, HL.

[40] *The Anticlizo* [1987] 2 Lloyd's Rep 130, CA.

[41] *New Hampshire Ins Co v MGN Ltd* [1997] LRLR 24, 54, CA.

Sometimes a response with different terms is a tentative move to see if the other will agree to them. Such moves are not acceptance but nor are they rejection of the other's position, which remains on the table to be taken up. If, however, a response with different terms is not tentative but firm, it is a counter-offer which rejects and extinguishes the last offer.[42] The legal nature of all such moves depends on the interpretation of reasonable persons in receipt of such.[43]

In addition, however clear the apparent intention of parties, their consent must   **13.16**
be genuine. If either or both are sufficiently mistaken about the terms of the contract or the nature of the subject-matter, what appears to be a contract of insurance may have been vitiated by the mistake. Cases of this kind concerning insurance contracts have rarely been reported.[44] In the unlikely event of a mistake about the identity of one of the parties, the issue will be resolved by reference to the policy.[45]

(5) Communicated Acceptance

Acceptance does not conclude a contract until the fact of acceptance has been   **13.17**
communicated to the offeror[46] Buyers of insurance through intermediaries may think they have cover by communicating with the intermediary. However, in the case of brokers, acceptance is generally ineffective until the broker communicates it to the chosen insurer.[47]

Acceptance has been communicated when received but, in a world of global   **13.18**
business and communication, when is that? To answer that courts today proceed 'by reference to the intentions of the parties, by sound business practice, and in some cases by a judgment where the risks should lie'.[48] Generally the answer is the point of receipt. First, anyone who gives out a telephone[49] or telex number,[50] or an email or postal address,[51] represents that any message properly sent there during business hours will be dealt with.[52] Second, people who give out mailboxes, phone or telex numbers are usually the better risk avoider, as regards what happens to information that has reached the address or number, especially in large firms

---

[42] *Allis-Chalmers Co v Maryland Fidelity Co* (1916) 114 LT 433, HL.
[43] *Lark v Outhwaite* [1991] 2 Lloyd's Rep 132, 139.
[44] See Clarke, 2006, ch 21.
[45] *Shogun Finance Ltd v Hudson* [2003] UKHL 62; [2004] 1 AC 919.
[46] *Brinkibon Ltd v Stahag Stahl mbH* [1982] 1 All ER 293, HL.
[47] *Manufacturers' Mutual Ins Ltd v John Boardman Ins Brokers Pty Ltd* (1993–1994) 179 CLR 650, HCA.
[48] *Brinkibon* (n 46 above), 296.
[49] *Hadenfayre Ltd v British National Ins Sy Ltd* [1984] 2 Lloyd's Rep 393.
[50] *The Brimnes* [1975] QB 929, 945, CA.
[51] *Holwell Securities Ltd v Hughes* [1974] 1 All ER 161, 164, CA.
[52] *The Brimnes* (n 50 above).

like insurance companies.[53] Third, a receipt rule of this kind best meets the need for certainty. In the case of email, however, those who give out their address have chosen the server but do not control it. Hence messages are deemed to be received when the addressee is able to access them.[54]

13.19 Receipt of acceptance is a requirement that may be waived by the offeror.[55] Offerors who send offers by post impliedly authorize the offeree to use the same medium, although in law postal acceptance is effective when sent. They assume the risks of the authorized medium, unless acceptance is lost or delayed by the fault of the offeree: that is not a risk offerors are taken to have assumed. People keen to accept an offer of cover can cut the corner and the risk with acceptance by any other mode which satisfies the apparent concerns of the sender as to speed, proof or confidentiality. Only if a mode of acceptance is exclusive, must it be followed in any event.

13.20 Finally, offerors may waive the requirement of communication altogether: in that case, once there is evidence that an offeree's intention is to accept, there is a contract, whether the offeror is aware of it or not. Waiver may be inferred from the practice of the insurance market.[56] An established instance is that, if insurers sign and seal a policy, acceptance is effective at that time, whether the applicant is aware of it or not.[57]

(6) Lloyd's[58]

13.21 Applicants instruct a Lloyd's broker, who prepares a standard 'MR slip' stating the essentials of the risk proposed and takes it around Lloyd's seeking subscriptions to the risk.[59] Subscription by initialling the slip ('scratching') signifies acceptance of (usually a small part of) the risk offered. The broker continues around the market until the amount sought has been fully subscribed.[60] In the case of specialized risks, underwriters may subscribe as 'following' underwriters through the agency of a 'leading' underwriter, the contracts of all underwriters concerned

---

[53] *Hadenfayre* (n 49 above); *Nissho Iwai Petroleum Co Inc v Cargill International SA* [1993] 1 Lloyd's Rep 80, 84.

[54] See the Electronic Commerce (EC Directive) Regulations 2002 (SI 2002 No 2013), which also provide that where orders are placed using electronic means, the insurer must acknowledge receipt of the order without undue delay.

[55] See paras 8.09ff.

[56] Eg interim motor cover: *Taylor v Allon* [1966] 1 QB 304.

[57] *Xenos v Wickham* (1866) LR 2 HL 296.

[58] Generally: Clarke, 2006, 11-3; MacGillivray 35–7 ff.

[59] *American Airlines Inc v Hope* [1974] 2 Lloyd's Rep 301, 304, HL.

[60] Concerning over-subscription and the practice of signing-down, see *The Zephyr* [1984] 1 Lloyd's Rep 58, 72.

being nonetheless separate. Full disclosure is made by brokers only to the leader and by market practice that is sufficient for all of them.[61]

Market practice at Lloyd's creates difficulties in law. First, if the broker fails **13.22** to obtain subscriptions the broker's client, who is seeking cover may well look elsewhere for insurance. Can the contracts of insurance already concluded, the subscriptions, be cancelled? Second, the broker can obtain contracts for all of the risk but only by agreeing different terms with different underwriters. However, 'market practice abhors a slip on different terms; it is possible but daft',[62] from the point of view of administering the cover and the associated transaction costs. These difficulties have been solved by market practice—to the satisfaction of the market although not their legal advisers.[63]

Except in practice for reinsurance, a policy on the terms of the slip is issued later **13.23** although, apart from marine insurance, insurance policies are not required by law.[64] Lloyd's polices, once issued, are evidence of the series of separate contracts between the insured and each member of each syndicate whose underwriter has scratched the slip.[65] Since 1992 all this can be done electronically. In the interests of certainty, use of the standard 'MR' contract was compulsory from November 2007.

(7) Renewal

Renewal of cover for a further period and on broadly the same terms as before but, **13.24** perhaps, with slight changes such as the amount of premium, is regarded as the conclusion of a new contract.[66] When insurers send renewal notices to policy-holders, this is an offer of cover for the further period for acceptance (or rejection) by policyholders. However, insurers are not obliged to renew and, therefore, are not obliged to send out renewal notices.[67] Exceptionally, a contract term requiring notice has been implied from previous dealings in the USA[68] and, in principle, the same could be held in the United Kingdom.

As renewal of insurance is a new contract, some of the terms may be new and **13.25** terms, therefore, of which the policyholder may be unaware. However, although

---

[61] *Aneco Re Underwriting Ltd v Johnson & Higgins* [1998] 1 Lloyd's Rep 565. Also *International Management Group v Simmonds* [2003] EWHC 177 (Comm); [2004] Lloyd's Rep IR 247.

[62] *General Reinsurance Corp v Forsak Fennia Patria* [1982] 2 QB 1022, 1039.

[63] See this case on appeal: [1983] 1 QB 856 (CA).

[64] *Thompson v Adams* (1889) 23 QBD 361.

[65] *General Reinsurance* (n 62 above) 864.

[66] Cf variation or extension of cover during the current period which is not an entirely new contract: *Jones Construction Co v Alliance Assurance Co Ltd* [1961] 1 Lloyd's Rep 121, CA. The difference is a matter of intention and degree.

[67] *Windus v Lord Tredegar* (1866) 15 LT 108, HL.

[68] Eg *Palomar v Guthrie* 583 So 2d 1304 (Ala, 1991).

policyholders are expected to read the policy when they first contract, they are entitled to presume that, apart from the level of premium and the dates, renewal is on broadly the same terms as before. If the insurer intends otherwise, it must give clear notice of the new terms.[69] Moreover, insurers have statutory duties about 'product disclosure' which lead to the same result.[70]

C. Validity

(1) Contracts Enforced

13.26 A duly concluded contract will be enforced. Exceptions occur when a 'contract' is void for mistake, which is very rare in insurance, or void (or unenforceable) because it is unlawful.[71] If the insurance contracted for is unlawful in a sense which is or should be obvious to the party who seeks to enforce the contract, it will not be enforced. If the unlawfulness is not obvious, the position is the same[72] but the unlawfulness must be established by the insurer as if it were an express exception to cover. The unlawfulness may be that the 'insured' lacks insurable interest and, therefore, that the insurance is contrary to public policy. Alternatively, it may be that the insurance is the vehicle for promotion of an unlawful object or because, although that was not the intention, enforcement in the particular case would have that effect. Liability insurance, for example, is lawful unless it would relieve policyholders of the burden of penalties for crime or awards of damages that public policy requires them to bear themselves.

(2) Insurable Interest: Property [73]

13.27 Contracts of insurance are unlawful, if policyholders lack insurable interest. They must have, first, a relation in fact to the subject-matter insured giving rise to an economic interest such that, if it is lost or damaged they will be worse off. Second, they must have a 'legal or equitable relation' to the subject-matter.[74]

13.28 In most common law countries the second requirement has been abandoned as pointless in modern society,[75] and unnecessary. Nonetheless English law persists with a rule which Waller LJ has demonstrated is difficult to define in words

---

[69] *Burnett v Westminster Bank* [1966] 1 QB 742, CA.

[70] See Insurance Conduct of Business Rules 5 <fsahandbook.info/FSA/handbook.jsp?doc=/handbook/ICOB>.

[71] Generally, see Clarke, 2006, ch 24.

[72] *Harse v Pearl Life Assurance Co* [1904] 1 KB 558, CA.

[73] See Clarke, 2006, ch 3 (life insurance) and ch 4 (property insurance).

[74] *Macaura v Northern Assurance Co* [1925] AC 619.

[75] See eg *Kosmopoulos v Constitution Ins Co* [1987] 1 SCR 2, Can SC.

applicable to all situations.[76] Much depends on the context and the terms of the policy. In particular, he pointed out that there is 'no hard and fast rule that because the nature of an insurable interest relates to a liability to compensate for loss, that insurable interest could only be covered by a liability policy rather than a policy insuring property or life or indeed properties or lives. [It] is a question of construction'.[77]

In the case of liability insurance, it is sometimes said that the subject-matter is **13.29** the insured's liability. However, it makes more sense to say that what is covered is the assets of the insured against loss in the event of policyholder liability to third parties. It also chimes with the classic description of insurable interest by Lord Eldon as 'a right in the *property*, or a right derivable out of some contract about the *property*, which in either case may be lost upon some contingency affecting the possession or enjoyment of the party'.[78]

Reinsurance was once thought to be liability insurance: that reinsurers cover **13.30** the liability of primary insurers to meet their obligations to pay policyholders. Reinsurers are not liable to pay 'until the amount of the reinsured's liability has been ascertained by judgment, award or settlement',[79] and this remains true. Today, however, the established view is that reinsurance is not insurance of 'the primary insurer's potential liability or disbursement' but 'an independent contract between reinsured and reinsurer in which the subject-matter of the insurance is the same as that of the primary insurance, that is to say, the risk to the ship or goods or whatever might be insured'.[80] Reinsurance claimants prove not what they paid to primary policyholders but the loss suffered by the latter.

Other instances are less problematic. Section 1 of the Life Assurance Act 1774 **13.31** prohibits life insurance without interest. Section 2 requires the life to be named in policy: the policyholder or in a limited range of cases, a third person; see 13.34. In the case of indemnity insurance, such as fire insurance, the subject-matter is the property insured against loss by fire. The Marine Insurance Act 1906 (MIA) s 4 expresses the common law rule by prohibiting 'wager' policies. In all apparently bona fide cases, however, courts lean in favour of finding an insurable interest in commercial transactions.[81]

---

[76] *Feasey v Sun Life Assurance Co of Canada* [2003] EWCA Civ 885; [2003] Lloyd's Rep IR 637, CA.

[77] [97]. See also [119]–[120] and [123]. *Ramco (UK) Ltd v International Insurance Co of Hannover Ltd* [2004] EWCA Civ 675; [2004] 2 Lloyd's Rep 595, CA.

[78] *Lucena v Craufurd* (1806) 2 Bos & Pul 269, 321.

[79] *CGU Int Ins plc v Astrazeneca Ins Co Ltd* [2005] EWHC 2755 (Comm); [2006] Lloyd's Rep IR 409, [126].

[80] *Charter Reinsurance Co Ltd v Fagan* [1997] AC 313, 392, and 387.

[81] *CGU* (n 79 above), [71].

13.32   The marine market, in particular, has dealt with difficult cases by 'honour' policies: unenforceable in law but rarely challenged in practice. Otherwise known as PPI (policy proof of interest) insurances, they include, for example, insurance of anticipated profits and policies on goods in transit, insured on shipment, but which later increase in value to an extent that is hard to pre-estimate.[82] In view of the personal character of most risks, the 'moral hazard', most insurances cannot be assigned.[83] However, marine insurance, notably cargo insurance would be largely ineffective, if assignment were not possible and, indeed, facilitated.[84]

13.33   English law requires that the insured have an insurable interest at the time of loss: MIA 1906 s 6(1) states the common law rule for all indemnity insurance. Although they often do, the law does not require policyholders to have an insurable interest at the time of contract, except in the case of life insurance, which differs in this,[85] and other respects.

(3) Insurable Interest: Life

13.34   People's affection for themselves is presumed to be such that they will not kill themselves, and that gives them an insurable interest in their own life.[86] Similarly people are allowed to insure their very nearest and dearest. Thus in England husbands may insure their wives[87] and wives their husbands[88] but, curiously, not their children.[89] Nor is insurance allowed between co-habitees—in theory, however, practice stretches theory. An important instance is 'keyman' insurance, whereby firms insure personnel whose continued life and health is crucial to the prosperity of the firm. Firms cannot insure the life of the Queen, but they can contract 'business interruption' or 'consequential loss' insurances, ie insurance against loss of profits, against the impact of national mourning. However, these are indemnity insurances, so firms face the difficulty of proving actual loss. That is why nobody has disputed keyman life insurance of 'star' racing drivers, footballers or fashion models, as well as less prominent back room boffins. Nobody doubts that the death of a star may cause loss but the amount is likely to be hard to prove. Keyman life insurance is non-indemnity (contingency) insurance; and the policy pays the amount insured, without proof of loss.

---

82   Marine Insurance Act 1906 s 4(2)(b). Rose, 3.1 ff.
83   See Clarke, 2006, ch 6.
84   See Rose, ch 7.
85   *Barnes v London, Edinburgh & Glasgow Life Assurance Co* [1891] 1 QB 864, CA.
86   *Griffiths v Fleming* [1909] 1 KB 805, CA.
87   ibid.
88   ibid.
89   *Harse v Pearl Life Assurance Co* [1904] 1 KB 558, CA.

The 'keyman' case shows that, although theoretically grounded originally on **13.35**
affection,[90] the real basis is financial dependence. Wives, for example, need financial support when husbands die, no less today when the income of both is needed
to discharge a mortgage. But the law still lacks consistency.[91] One of the earliest
instances of enforceable life insurance was that of creditors on the life of their
debtors,[92] but children cannot contract insurance on the life the parents that
support them, for example, through college, unless they make parents their
legal debtors. Employers can insure the lives of key employees but the right of
employees to insure the life of their employer, even in the case of the 'one man'
company, is severely circumscribed.[93]

(4) Unlawful Insurance

Insurance purporting to cover property (cargo) in the course of committing **13.36**
a crime (an unlawful voyage) will not be enforced.[94] Moreover, courts will not
enforce an indemnity in respect of a penalty paid by policyholders in respect of
offences involving intent[95] or culpable negligence.[96] The court must have regard
'to the necessity of deterring him and others from doing the same thing again'.[97]
However, distinguish punitive damages: punishment and deterrence are not the
only purposes of such damages, which also serve, for example, to appease victims.
So, prevailing public policy allows insurance against payment,[98] although in practice many liability policies exclude such cover.

Liability to a passer-by for injury caused by dangerous driving getting away from **13.37**
the scene of the crime will be covered[99] but, curiously, a similar injury inflicted
with firearms will not.[100] In *Gardner v Moore*[101] the House of Lords accepted the
view of Diplock LJ that the 'court has to weigh the gravity of the anti-social act
and the extent to which it will be encouraged by enforcing the right sought to be

---

[90] *Griffiths* (n 86 above), 821.
[91] The law in other common law countries is more accommodating: Clarke, 2006, 3–7.
[92] *Godsall v Boldero* (1807) 9 East 72.
[93] To the pecuniary of rights of continued employment: *Hebdon v West* (1863) 3 B & S 579.
[94] *Lubbock v Potts* (1806) 7 East 449.
[95] *Smith (WH) & Sons v Clinton* (1909) 99 LT 840: a promise to indemnify a publisher against
criminal libel damages.
[96] *Askey v Golden Wine Co Ltd* (1948) 64 TLR 379.
[97] *Askey*, 380: there was 'culpable negligence': selling liquor unfit for consumption. In *Osman
v Moss* [1970] 1 Lloyd's Rep 313, CA, however, a convicted motorist had reason to believe that
his insurance was valid, and the indemnity was enforced.
[98] *Lancashire CC v Municipal Mutual Ins Ltd* [1995] LRLR 293; affirmed [1996] 3 All ER
545, CA.
[99] *Gardner v Moore* [1984] AC 548.
[100] *Gray v Barr* [1971] 2 QB 554 at 587, CA.
[101] [1984] AC 548 The motorist drove his van at a pedestrian in anger and severely injured him.

enforced against the social harm which will be caused if the right is not enforced' and that social policy favoured compensation for road victims.[102] From such statements it seems that enforcement is less likely when there is no third party in need of compensation.[103] They might also suggest that similar 'balancing up' should be applied to all other kinds of liability insurance, however, it now seems not.

13.38   More recently courts have declined the task of 'balancing', partly because they consider that social engineering is not their job, in the absence of clear instructions from Parliament;[104] and partly because the requisite information may be lacking.[105] The position now is that victims of crime will get liability insurance money compensation only if they have 'an independent cause of action', only when the liability insurance is compulsory.[106] This position would be easier to understand and thus to support, if a principled line were apparent between where liability insurance is compulsory and where it is not. For running cars, aircraft or riding stables it has been compulsory but for trains, boats and jet skis it has not.[107]

D. Misrepresentation

(1) Flawed Consent

13.39   Contracts are void or voidable if the consent of either party is sufficiently flawed. Consent is flawed if one party is mistaken about a fundamental feature of the contract (mistake), or is induced to contract on the basis of wrong information (misrepresentation) or insufficient information (non-disclosure).[108] Operative mistake is rare.[109]

13.40   Either party's consent may be flawed but, in practice, the question usually arises when claims are brought and insurers defend on that ground: that their consent was flawed by the way the risk was presented at the time of contract, be it by misrepresentation, non-disclosure or both. Often clear lines cannot be drawn between them. If an applicant states that in the past five years one burglary has occurred at the premises whereas in truth there were two, is that misrepresentation of the number of burglaries or non-disclosure of the second? Legally the

---

[102]   *Hardy v MIB* [1964] 2 QB 745 at 767–768, CA.

[103]   *Haseldine v Hosken* [1933] 1 KB 822, 833, CA.

[104]   Eg Devlin, *The Enforcement of Morals* (1965) 56.

[105]   Clarke, 2007, 275 ff.

[106]   *Charlton v Fisher* [2001] EWCA Civ 112; [2001] Lloyd's Rep IR 287, [83] Notably under the Road Traffic Act 1988, s 151.

[107]   RK Lewis (2004) 154 NLJ 1474.

[108]   Clarke, 2006, 21–23; MacGillivray, 15–18.

[109]   *Pritchard v Merchants' & Tradesmen's Mutual Life Assurance Sy* (1858) 3 CB (NS) 622: parties contracting life reinsurance, were unaware that the life had dropped (died).

defences are distinct but the law has important features in common and developments in the law in the last decade of the twentieth century have been in the direction of convergence. Moreover, for 'retail' customers of insurers,[110] there have been significant changes in the law made under section 138 of the Financial Services and Markets Act 2000 (FSMA), in the form of 'rules' and 'guidance', by the Financial Services Authority (FSA).[111] In 2007 the FSA promised a revised version with less detail.

(2) Truth

An operative misrepresentation is an untrue statement of fact (or law) by an applicant which induces[112] the insurer to make the contract of insurance. A statement is untrue if it is substantially untrue in the context in which it was made, objectively viewed,[113] ie if the degree of inaccuracy would be material to prudent insurers of that kind.[114] Such a misrepresentation is nonetheless a misrepresentation, and actionable as such, if it is made innocently and in good faith. Truth does not mean true to the best of the knowledge and belief of the applicant unless, as is common for consumers, that is what is stated in the application form.[115]   **13.41**

(3) Fact and Opinion

To be factual, statements must be statements about the present or past. Statements about security precautions the applicant plans to take next month against theft are not present facts.[116] However, if the applicant has no intention to carry out those plans, the statement is an untrue statement of fact about current management intention.[117] Further, to be fact statements must be statements that the applicant appears (to the insurers) to have the knowledge, information or experience to make. Otherwise they are mere statements of opinion which the law does not regard as actionable representations of fact,[118] and which reasonable insurers should realize cannot be relied on. That is the key to the distinction. Thus, for example, confident assertions by   **13.42**

---

[110] These are natural persons acting for purposes outside their trade, business or profession.

[111] See <fsahandbook.info/FSA/handbook.jsp?doc=/handbook/ICOB>.

[112] Generally, see paras 8.159ff. As to inducement, see para 13.53.

[113] *McInerny v Lloyds Bank Ltd* [1974] 1 Lloyd's Rep 246, 254, CA.

[114] *Yorke v Yorkshire Ins Co* [1918] 1 KB 662, 669. Concerning what is material, see 13.45.

[115] *Economides v Commercial Union Assurance Co plc* [1998] QB 587, CA.

[116] *Benham v United Guarantie and Life Assurance Co* (1852) 7 Exch 744.

[117] *Hill v Citadel Ins Co Ltd* [1995] LRLR 218, 227, affirmed [1997] LRLR 167, CA. See also promissory warranties: para 13.71.

[118] *Bisset v Wilkinson* [1927] AC 177, PC.

overweight applicants of 60 that they are in the best of health are opinions; but medical 'opinion', that their blood pressure is too high,[119] is fact.

13.43 Controversy continues over opinions of probity, and associated moral hazard. If the applicant's CEO has been charged with fraudulent accounting, that, it might be said, states no more than the prosecutor's opinion, which has yet to be established as fact by a court of law. However, imminent prosecution is a fact that must be disclosed.[120] What counts is less whether prosecution is factual than whether it is material. Indeed applicants must disclose any 'rumours which materially affect the risk, even when these subsequently turn out to have been unfounded',[121] including rumours circulating in the press. Insurance law backs insurers and their suspicion that there may be no smoke without fire in the face of the righteous indignation of applicants.[122] However, the law is subject to two qualifications.

13.44 First, the materiality of a rumour must be judged subject to the possibility raised by Mance LJ that, if there had been full disclosure, 'it would have embraced *all* aspects of the insured's knowledge, including his own statement of his innocence and such independent evidence as he had to support that by the time of placing'.[123] This might well 'throw a different light' on whether rumours are material. Materiality must be judged by reference to all of the evidence available at the time of placing, whether disclosed or not. Subsequently this view was accepted, with a second qualification. The test is 'an objective test, and the characteristics to be imputed to a prudent insurer are in substance a matter for the courts to decide'. A robust court thus has room to manoeuvre, including 'room for a test of proportionality, having regard to the nature of the risk and the moral hazard under consideration'. On that basis there may be disclosable matters which, in the view of the court, are 'too old, or insufficiently serious to require disclosure'.[124]

(4) Materiality and Inducement

13.45 To be material, misrepresentation does not have to influence the judgment of insurers decisively; it is enough, it has been said, that the representation was

---

[119] *British Equitable Ins Co v Great Western Ry* (1869) 20 LT 422.
[120] *March Cabaret & Casino Club Ltd v London Assurance* [1975] 1 Lloyd's Rep 169, 177; *The Dora* [1989] 1 Lloyd's Rep 69, 93.
[121] *CTI Inc v Oceanus Mutual Underwriting Assn (Bermuda) Ltd* [1984] 1 Lloyd's Rep 475, 506, CA; *Brotherton v Aseguradora Colseguros (No 2)* [2003] EWCA Civ 705; [2003] Lloyd's Rep IR 746, CA; *North Star Shipping Ltd v Sphere Drake Ins plc* [2006] EWCA Civ 378; [2006] 2 Lloyd's Rep 183.
[122] *North Star* (ibid), [17] ff.
[123] *Brotherton (No 2)* (n 121 above), at [22].
[124] *Norwich Union Ins Ltd v Meisels* [2006] EWHC 2811; [2007] Lloyd's Rep IR 69, [25].

'actively present' in the mind of the person assessing the risk.[125] That was said in the context of fraud. Be that as it may,[126] the law also requires inducement in the senses of causation: that the actual underwriter was decisively influenced by the misrepresentation. The same requirement is found in respect of the hypothetical influence of material facts undisclosed: see 13.52 and 13.53.

In general contract law received doctrine is that it is irrelevant that the representee **13.46** was careless in not discovering that the representation was untrue. In other words, the representee was nonetheless induced by the misrepresentation rather than his own carelessness. The usual citation in support is *Redgrave v Hurd*.[127] That decision can be explained, however, on the basis that the representor should himself have been much better informed than the misrepresentee about relevant documents in his own possession. A wider review of precedent indicates that courts 'balance the equities',[128] case by case; and that each time they ask whether the risk should be allocated to the representor or the representee, as appropriate, applicant or insurer. In particular, they ask which party was better informed or best placed to be better informed. In the insurance world today that person will often be the representee, the insurer.[129]

E. Non-disclosure

(1) Disclosure

The duty of disclosure is sometimes described as a duty of insurance good faith,[130] **13.47** or utmost good faith; but it is an information duty quite distinct from general duties of good faith recognized in civil law countries such as France and Germany. In the insurance context the issue of disclosure usually arises as a defence to a claim, so it is insurers who seek to prove breach of the duty, *non*-disclosure. Note also that, if an insurer proves breach, the defence will still fail, if the insured proves that the undisclosed fact was already known to the insurer[131] or that its disclosure was waived by the insurer.[132]

---

[125] *Edgington v Fitzmaurice* (1885) 29 Ch D 459, 483, CA.

[126] In actions for damages for deceit, however, the general law requires causation: *Smith v Chadwick* (1884) 9 App Cas 187, 195–196.

[127] (1881) 20 Ch D 1, CA.

[128] See eg *Peekay v ANZ Banking Group Ltd* [2006] EWCA Civ 386; [2006] 2 Lloyd's Rep 511.

[129] With careless insurers, courts may reach a similar result by finding that the insurer has waived the matter.

[130] Clarke, 2006, chs 23 and 27; MacGillivray, ch 17; MacDonald Eggers and Foss, *Good Faith and Insurance Contracts* (2nd edn, 2004) ch 7ff.

[131] See para 13.57.

[132] See para 13.58.

13.48 Disclosure means communication of material facts to the right persons,[133] persons in the company underwriting such risks. This may be done directly, for example at Lloyd's, or, in the case of mass risks, through an agent of the insurer who can be expected to pass the information to the underwriters. The information comprises all facts known to the applicant at the time of contracting that are material to the risk.

(2) Facts Material to the Risk

13.49 Material facts comprise every 'circumstance which would influence the judgment of a prudent insurer in fixing the premium, or determining whether he will take the risk': MIA, section 18(2), which states the common law rule applicable to both marine and non-marine insurance. The 'prudent insurer' is not the particular insurer[134] but a stereotype in the relevant sector of the market[135] at the time of the contract.[136] The stereotype is controversial. In Scotland and many other common law countries the point of reference is the 'reasonable insured'.[137]

13.50 For natural persons acting for purposes outside their trade, business or profession ('retail customers') the law changed with effect from 14 January 2005 on the entry into force of rules made under section 138 of the Financial Services and Markets Act 2000 (FSMA).[138] These included rules for general insurance, the Insurance Conduct of Business Rules (ICOB),[139] which apply to all 'non-investment insurance contracts' other than reinsurance contracts and 'contracts of large risks' (marine, aviation and transport, credit and surety and other commercial risks) where the risk is situated outside the EEA.[140]

13.51 ICOB Rule 7.3.6 provides that 'except where there is evidence of fraud', insurers must not 'refuse to meet a claim made by a retail customer on the grounds of non-disclosure of a fact material to the risk that the retail customer *could not reasonably be expected to have disclosed*', thus basing the test of materiality not on the perspective of prudent insurers but on the view of reasonable applicants. However, insurers prohibited from rejecting a claim by Rule 7.3.6 are still free to

---

[133] *Hadenfayre Ltd v British National Ins Sy Ltd* [1984] 2 Lloyd's Rep 393.

[134] Cf the requirement of inducement: para 13.53.

[135] *Zurich General Accident & Liability Ins Co Ltd v Morrison* [1942] 2 KB 53, 58, CA; *CTI Inc v Oceanus Mutual Underwriting Assn (Bermuda) Ltd* [1984] 1 Lloyd's Rep 476, 511.

[136] *Associated Oil Carriers Ltd v Union Ins Sy of Canton Ltd* [1917] 2 KB 184.

[137] *Cuthbertson v Friends' Provident Life Office* 2006 SLT 597.

[138] Clarke 2006, 7–1.

[139] <fsahandbook.info/FSA/handbook.jsp?doc=/handbook/ICOB>. A less detailed version is likely in 2008.

[140] ICOB 1.2.1.15. Controversial is the exclusion too of extended warranties on goods (other than motor vehicles) and travel insurance linked to travel arrangements.

decide that they want a claimant off their books and rescind the contract on the basis of the common law and the stricter prudent insurer test.

(3) Influence

As with actionable misrepresentation,[141] material facts must be such as would **13.52** 'influence' the judgment of prudent insurers: MIA section 18(2)—applicable to both marine and non-marine insurance. Influence does not have to be decisive in the sense that, if a fact had been disclosed, the insurer would have declined the risk or offered different terms. It is enough that prudent insurers would have considered it relevant;[142] there are nonetheless degrees of relevance. 'The difference is whether the relevance of the hypothetical facts, assuming that they had been disclosed, is judged at the moment the underwriter is deciding whether or not to accept the risk or at the moment when he undertakes an investigation of the risk'.[143] The former is the Australian view and probably the UK position also.[144] Exception is made for information which evidently diminishes rather than increases the risk: that might well influence judgment but does not have to be disclosed.[145] Note also that, except in cases of fraud, when materiality is not required,[146] there is a similar 'influence' rule for operative misrepresentation.[147]

(4) Inducement

The mildness of the requirement of influence on prudent insurers matters little **13.53** because, whether misrepresented or undisclosed, the facts must also have induced the *actual* insurer to contract the insurance—decisively. The facts must have been such that, if they had been disclosed, the insurer would have declined the risk or offered less favourable terms.[148] However, this stricter requirement is easily met: where there 'is a material representation *calculated to induce* him to enter into the contract, it is an inference "of fact" that he was induced by the representation to enter into it'.[149] This is a presumption of general contract law applicable to

---

141 See para 13.45.

142 *Pan Atlantic Ins Co Ltd v Pine Top Ins Co Ltd* [1995] 1 AC 501.

143 *Barclay Holdings (Australia) Pty Ltd v British National Ins Co Ltd* (1987) 8 NSWLR 514, 523.

144 *CTI* (n 135 above).

145 See *The Dora* [1989] 1 Lloyd's Rep 69, 90.

146 *Smith v Kay* (1859) 4 HLC 750.

147 See para 13.45.

148 *Pan Atlantic Ins Co Ltd v Pine Top Ins Co Ltd* [1995] 1 AC 501.

149 *Redgrave v Hurd* (1881) 20 Ch D 1, 21, CA, emphasis supplied. Also in this sense: *Smith v Chadwick* (1884) 9 App Cas 187 at 196. See also *Halsbury's Laws of England* (4th ed), Vol. 31, para 1067, which was applied to a case of non-disclosure in *St Paul Fire & Marine Ins Co (UK) v McConnell Dowell Constructors* [1995] 2 Lloyd's Rep 116, 127, CA.

misrepresentations that applies also to insurance contracts for both misrepresentation and non-disclosure.[150] Examples in property insurance are past fires or theft at the premises insured.

13.54   Except in such cases of presumed inducement, inducement must be proved by insurers.[151] Proof might take the form of evidence from the practice of the actual underwriter, if available.[152] If not, insurers might show that the market (of prudent underwriters) would have been induced thereby and therefore, it probably had that effect on the actual underwriter.[153] A plea of misrepresentation is open to the objection that it was not relied upon by the insurer and thus did not induce the contract.[154] Likewise, claimants may argue that undisclosed information would have had no effect if disclosed because the insurer relied on its own sources or investigation. Insurers often send assessors to survey the risk, for example of fire and burglary. The reply may well be, of course, that reliance was placed on the application as well as the assessors' report. However, if the claimant's argument succeeds, the insurer's plea fails for want of inducement.

(5) Facts Known to Applicants

13.55   A misrepresentation is actionable nonetheless because what made it untrue was some fact quite unknown to the applicant. Non-disclosure, however, is not actionable at all if the information is not something that applicants knew or could reasonably be expected to know.[155] Applicants in business are expected to know, first, information they can be expected to acquire 'in the ordinary course of business'.[156] Second, they, like consumers, are treated as knowing what is known or should be known to their agents.[157] The agents include not only agents they employ to contract the insurance[158] but also those employed for some other purpose but whose work includes the receipt or collation of relevant information.[159] Applicants

---

[150] *Assicurazioni Generali SpA v ARIG* [2002] EWCA Civ 1642; [2003] 1 WLR 577, [61], CA. That is what Lord Mustill referred to as a 'presumption of inducement': *Pan Atlantic* (n 148 above) 551. The presumption was applied, for example, in *Aneco Reinsurance Underwriting Ltd v Johnson & Higgins Ltd* [1998] 1 Lloyd's Rep 565.

[151] *Assicurazioni Generali* (n 150 above) at [61], CA, *per* Clarke LJ.

[152] See eg *GE Capital Corporate Finance Group v Bankers Trust Co* [1995] 1 WLR 172, CA, concerning the disclosure of past transactions that might bear on investment strategy.

[153] See eg *St Paul Fire* (n 149 above).

[154] *Smith* v *Land & House Property Corp* (1884) 28 Ch D 7 at 15, CA.

[155] *Joel v Law Union & Crown Ins Co* [1908] 2 KB 863, CA.

[156] *Proudfoot v Montefiore* (1867) LR 2 QB 511, 521–522. Cf *PCW Syndicates v PCW Reinsurers* [1996] 1 All ER 774, CA.

[157] *Blackburn v Vigors* (1887) 12 App Cas 531, 536–537. Marine Insurance Act s 19.

[158] *ANZ Ltd v Colonial & Eagle Wharves Ltd* [1960] 2 Lloyd's Rep 241; *Group Josi Re v Walbrook Ins Co Ltd* [1996] 1 WLR 1152, CA. It matters not that the material information was acquired while working for another client: *PCW* (n 156 above) 149, and 157.

[159] *Blackburn v Vigors* (1887) 12 App Cas 531, 541.

should check with such persons before contracting insurance. Third, the knowledge of a firm may be composite. A chief executive officer, who may well be the person contracting the insurance, may be taken to know something known only to the chairman,[160] including knowledge acquired by the latter before becoming chairman.[161]

Composite knowledge has become problematic as firms, not least partnerships, **13.56** have become larger. *Prima facie* professionals in partnership are insured against partnership liability jointly. In England the received rule is that when two or more persons 'are jointly insured and their interests are inseparably connected so that loss or gain necessarily affects them [all] the misconduct of one is sufficient to contaminate the whole insurance'.[162] The skeleton in the cupboard may bring the whole house down. The past peculations of one partner may leave the rest without cover. Although the 'contamination' rule does not apply to insurance that is not joint but composite,[163] it still applies to joint insurance. In Canada, which received the same rule from England, the Supreme Court has based the 'contamination' rule on contract interpretation rather than public policy,[164] and has thus left the liability cover of large firms of lawyers intact.[165] Courts in England may well follow that line today. Meanwhile groups contracting insurance can contract out of the 'contamination' rule with clauses, described as 'anti-avoidance clauses' or 'incontestable clauses'.[166]

(6) Facts Known to Insurers

Applicants are not obliged to disclose material facts already known to the insurer.[167] **13.57** For example, every insurer 'is presumed to be acquainted with the practice of the trade he insures'.[168] Moreover, insurers are expected to keep up with current affairs and to make a connection between reported events and the kind of risks they cover. However, insurers are not expected to recall facts peculiar to a particular applicant, unless referred to the relevant sources by the applicant, even if the facts have been widely reported in the media. This is especially true of

---

160 *Regina Fur Co v Bossom* [1957] 2 Lloyd's Rep 466.

161 *ERC Frankona Re v American Nat Ins* Co [2005] EWHC 1381; [2006] Lloyd's Rep IR 157.

162 *Samuel v Dumas* [1924] AC 431, 445.

163 *New Hampshire Ins Co v MGN Ltd* [1997] LRLR 24, CA.

164 Apparently the view taken in *Samuel v Dumas* (n 162 above). Cf the more recent *State of The Netherlands v Youell* [1998] 1 Lloyd's Rep 236, CA.

165 *Scott v Wawanesa Mutual Ins Co* (1989) 59 DLR (4th) 660, 667, SCC; and *Fisher v Guardian Ins Co Ltd* (1995) 123 DLR (4th) 336, 350.

166 *Anstey v British Natural Premium Life Assn Ltd* (1908) 24 TLR 871, CA; and *Toomey v Eagle Star Ins Co Ltd (No 2)* [1995] 2 Lloyd's Rep 88.

167 *Carter v Boehm* (1766) 3 Burr 1905, 1911. Marine Insurance Act, s.18(3)(b). Cf *HIH Casualty & General Ins Ltd v Chase Manhattan Bank* [2003] Lloyd's Rep IR 230, [86–87], HL.

168 *Noble v Kennaway* (1780) 2 Doug 511, 513.

past events, however prominently reported at the time, and which appeared then to have no bearing on the insurer's business but which turn out to be relevant to a risk written later.[169] Moreover, even if relevant information is on file, English precedent does not expect insurers to retrieve it and check it before writing new risks. However, the precedents concerned paper records[170] and, in the light of decisions in other common law countries,[171] it may well be that the use of computers and the availability of powerful search engines will lead to different decisions in future.

(7) Waiver

13.58 Insurers cannot plead non-disclosure of information, the disclosure of which they have waived. The possibility of waiver arises at three points in the relationship. First, insurers may waive disclosure altogether from the beginning. Marine cargo insurers commonly contract 'seaworthiness admitted': consignors are not expected to know material information about the vessel in question.[172] Second, where material information has been disclosed but not in sufficient detail to enable prudent insurers to assess its full significance, insurers may press for further particulars. If they do not, the result is that they have waived (further) performance of the duty, as regards those particulars. This type of waiver sometimes shades into the first type. Third, sometimes when a claim comes in, insurers discover non-disclosure, but nonetheless wish to affirm the contract and keep the customer. That is waiver not of disclosure but of the right of rescission. In the third instance, in particular, the waiver argument is sometimes framed as estoppel.[173]

13.59 Omission to any questions at all about the risk at the beginning is not waiver.[174] That is not the positive conduct required by the law for waiver. However, if insurers ask questions about some things but not about other related things, that may amount to waiver of disclosure of the latter.[175] For example, to ask about

---

[169] *Bates v Hewitt* (1867) LR 2 QB 595; *Greenhill v Federal Ins Co* [1927] 1 KB 65, CA; *Malhi v Abbey Life Assurance Co Ltd* [1996] LRLR 237, CA. The point is controversial; cf *Carter v Boehm* (1766) 3 Burr 1905; *Glencore Int v Alpina Ins Co Ltd* [2003] EWHC 2792 (Comm); [2004] 1 Lloyd's Rep 111. Clarke, 2006, 23-9B.

[170] *Malhi* (n 169 above). Cf *Columbia National Life Ins Co v Rodgers*, 116 F 2d 705 (10 Cir, 1940), cert den 313 US 561.

[171] Eg *Coronation Ins Co v Taku Air Transport Ltd* (1991) 85 DLR (4th) 609, Can SC.

[172] Concerning non-marine insurance, see *HIH Casualty & General Ins Ltd v Chase Manhattan Bank* [2001] 1 Lloyd's Rep 30, [23].

[173] There are differences between waiver and estoppel but the differences are usually of no consequence in context: Clarke, 2006, 23-11 and 26–4; MacGillivray, 17–78 ff.

[174] *McCormick v National Motor & Accident Ins Union* (1934) 49 Ll L Rep 361, 363; *Schoolman v Hall* [1951] 1 Lloyd's Rep 139, CA.

[175] *Schoolman* (ibid) 143; *Roberts v Plaisted* [1989] 2 Lloyd's Rep 341, CA; *Wise (Underwriting Agency) Ltd v Grupo Nacional Provincial SA* [2004] EWCA Civ 962; [2004] 2 Lloyd's Rep 483, [118] CA.

burglaries on the premises over the last five years is waiver (of the second kind) about information about any burglaries before that. An instance of a similar kind arises where applicants have disclosed information which puts insurers on enquiry but insurers do not pursue the matter. That is waiver of what enquiry would have disclosed.[176] In the landmark case of *Carter v Boehm*,[177] insurance was taken out on 'Fort Marlborough' which was located, as the insurer knew, in a potential theatre of war. Lord Mansfield held that, given the insurer's knowledge, it was for the insurer to enquire about the defences and the likelihood of successful attack. A more mundane instance of this kind of waiver occurs where applicants give the insurer the opportunity to consult documents,[178] such as the proposer's records. The applicant is considered to have disclosed the contents of all the documents concerned.

F. Remedies

(1) Rescission[179]

The effect of operative misrepresentation or non-disclosure is that the insurer's **13.60** consent to the insurance contract is flawed. Accordingly, the purpose of any remedy at law is to negate the effect. To achieve this an award of damages would be neither inappropriate nor without precedent.[180] However, no award of such damages in favour of insurers has been reported. Moreover, a right to damages for breach of the insurance duty of good faith, as such, has been rejected.[181] In practice the insurer's remedy lies in avoidance of the contract, rescission.[182] Rescission is not automatic. Insurers have a right of election: they can either rescind the contract or affirm the contract,[183] and if the choice is rescission, that requires not court intervention but simply notice to the insured. Rescission dates from the time of notice.[184] The effect is that it 'terminates the contract, puts the parties *in statu quo ante* and restores things, as between them, to the position

---

[176] *Asfar & Co v Blundell* [1896] 1 QB 123 at 129, CA.

[177] (1766) 3 Burr 1905. Cf *Greenhill v Federal Ins Co* [1927] 1 KB 65, CA.

[178] *Pan Atlantic Ins Co Ltd v Pine Top Ins Co Ltd* [1993] 1 Lloyd's Rep 496, CA, affirmed on other grounds: [1995] 1 AC 501.

[179] See paras 8.175ff.

[180] Eg under section 2(1) of the Misrepresentation Act 1967 or, in the case of fraud, for the tort of deceit: *London Assurance Co v Clare* (1937) 57 Ll L Rep 254, 270.

[181] *Banque Financière de la Cité SA v Westgate Ins Co Ltd* [1990] QB 665, CA, affirmed on different grounds: [1991] 2 AC 249. Cf *HIH Casualty & General Ins Ltd v Chase Manhattan Bank* [2001] EWCA Civ 1250; [2001] 2 Lloyd's Rep 483, [163] and [169].

[182] The words are used 'more or less interchangeably': *HIH* (ibid), [174].

[183] *Mackender v Feldia AG* [1966] 2 Lloyd's Rep 449, 455, CA.

[184] *Reese River Silver Mining Co Ltd v Smith* (1869) LR 4 HL 64.

in which they stood before the contract was entered into'.[185] Rescission, therefore, is retroactive and must be total.[186] Thus, insurers are not liable for claims arising prior to the date of rescission. Moreover, as a matter of general principle of restitution, insurers must return the premium,[187] unless the contract provides otherwise.[188]

13.61 As regards retroactive effect, exception is made, first, for extensions of cover, which are treated as severable parts of the main contract so that what happens to the extension does not necessarily affect the rest of the contract.[189] Second, exception is made for arbitration clauses,[190] which are regarded as distinct from or collateral to the main contract. When that is rescinded the clauses survive. Third, by analogy, the same applies to jurisdiction clauses.[191] Fourth, if a single policy covers two distinct classes of property, each being a distinct subject of insurance, rescission as regards one class may not affect the other.[192] Similarly, in the case of a single policy covering jointly the liability of a number of members of a firm, the current tendency is to see the policy as one recording as many contracts as there are members insured, so that avoidance of one does not affect the others.[193] Finally, since ICOB came into force in January 2005,[194] insurers entitled to rescind insurance on account of non-disclosure or misrepresentation may nonetheless be bound to pay the claim, as long as the claimant was not in business or fraudulent.[195] This rule applies, it seems, whether in a particular case insurers elect to rescind the contract or not.

(2) Limits on Rescission

13.62 In the case of misrepresentations made 'otherwise than fraudulently', ie those made negligently or innocently, the Misrepresentation Act 1967, s 2(2) gives courts a discretion to refuse rescission and to award damages instead. Section 2(2) affects any person who 'has entered into a contract after a misrepresentation has

---

[185] *Abram Steamship Co Ltd v Westville Shipping Co Ltd* [1923] AC 773, 781; see also *Johnson v Agnew* [1980] AC 367.

[186] *Urquhart v Macpherson* (1878) 3 App Cas 831, PC; *West v National Motor & Accident Union* [1955] 1 Lloyd's Rep 207, CA. For exceptions, see Clarke, 2006, 23–17C.

[187] *Cornhill Ins Co Ltd v L & B Assenheim* (1937) 58 Ll L Rep 27, 31.

[188] *Sun Fire Office v Hart* (1889) 14 App Cas 98, PC.

[189] *The Star Sea* [1997] 1 Lloyd's Rep 360, 370, CA.

[190] *Harbour Ins Co (UK) Ltd v Kansa General International Ins Co Ltd* [1992] 1 Lloyd's Rep 81, 91.

[191] *Pan Atlantic Ins Co Ltd v Pine Top Ins Co Ltd* [1993] 1 Lloyd's Rep 496, 502, CA.

[192] By analogy with breach of insurance warranty, and *Printpak v AGF Ins Ltd* [1999] Lloyd's Rep IR 542, CA.

[193] See para 13.55.

[194] See para 13.50.

[195] Rule 7.3.6 (2).

been *made* to him'.[196] Hence, it seems, whereas it applies to half truths—statements literally true but rendered false by related omission, it does not apply to 'pure' non-disclosure. Insurance cases are likely to be few and far between.[197]

A second limit is affirmation of the contract, sometimes called waiver of the **13.63** right to rescind, by misrepresentee insurers. It must 'be an informed choice made with knowledge of the facts giving rise to the right'.[198] If insurers know the true facts about the risk, knowledge of the right to rescind will be presumed;[199] and if then they affirm the cover unequivocally, they lose the right to rescind on this occasion and the cover continues. That is the rule, whether policyholders rely on the affirmation or not.[200] However, reliance has the lesser function that, if present, it will clinch the matter, for example, in cases in which insurers remain silent and the insurer's intention, to affirm or not, is unclear. In *Clough*,[201] Mellor J said that 'as long as he has made no election, he retains the right to determine it either way, subject to this, that if, in the interval whilst he is deliberating,. . .in consequence of his delay, the position even of the wrongdoer is affected, it will preclude him from exercising his right to rescind'. Delay in reaching a decision is sometimes stated to be a distinct bar to rescission. The better view of the insurance cases, however, is probably that it is not a distinct bar but a kind of affirmation.[202]

A third limit may be unconscionability: that to allow rescission would be unfair to **13.64** the policyholder. The issue is seen in cases where, by the time the insurer purports to rescind, it has become clear that the misrepresentation or non-disclosure was such that, had the insurer been aware of the true or full picture at the time of contracting, the insurer would have issued exactly the same policy anyway. The short answer originally given obiter in *Brotherton*[203] appears to be that insurers can rescind nonetheless. Insurers can rescind simply by notice[204] and thus without court control or supervision. Further, issues of materiality and inducement should be judged at the time of contract only and not later when the contract is rescinded.[205]

---

[196] Emphasis added.
[197] See para 13.60 and *Highlands Ins Co v Continental Ins Co* [1987] 1 Lloyd's Rep 109, 118.
[198] *The Kanchenjunga* [1990] 1 Lloyd's Rep 391, 399, HL; *Eagle Star Ins Co Ltd v National Westminster Finance Australia Ltd* (1985) 58 ALR 165, 174, PC; *Hill v Citadel Ins Co Ltd* [1997] LRLR 167, CA.
[199] *Eagle Star* (n 198 above) 174.
[200] *The Kanchenjunga* (n 198 above).
[201] *Clough v LNWR* (1871) LR 7 Ex 26, 35; see also *Morrison v Universal Marine Ins Co* (1873) LR 8 Ex 197, Ex Ch; *Simon Haynes, Barlas & Ireland v Beer* (1945) 78 Ll L Rep 337, 369.
[202] See eg *Allen v Robles*, [1969] 2 Lloyd's Rep 61, 64, CA.
[203] *Brotherton v Asegurado Colseguros SA (No 2)* [2003] EWCA Civ 704; [2003] Lloyd's Rep IR 746, CA.
[204] See para 13.60.
[205] [27] ff *per* Mance LJ.

The question was more directly in point subsequently in *Drake*[206] in which the Court of Appeal majority confirmed that insurers' rights to rescind depended not on what was disclosed at the time of contract but on the true facts at that time, as they appeared later. On the broader question whether, if an insurer had a right to avoid for non disclosure, that right was constrained by the doctrine of good faith, Rix LJ, in particular, gave a cautious and qualified but affirmative answer.[207] His answer appears to be in accord with general contract law,[208] as well as judicial statements about rescission. Lord Lloyd once reminded us that, as 'Lord Mansfield warned in *Carter v Boehm*,. . . there may be circumstances in which an insurer, by asserting a right to avoid for non-disclosure, would himself be guilty of want of utmost good faith'.[209] This reminder was accepted by Rix LJ in *Drake*,[210] who concluded inter alia that 'the doctrine of good faith should be capable of limiting the insurer's right to avoid in circumstances where that remedy, which has been described in recent years as draconian, would operate unfairly'.[211]

(3) Clauses Affecting Rescission

13.65 The right to rescind for non-disclosure is commonly modified by policy terms, whereby, for example, the insurer undertakes not to 'exercise its rights to avoid this Policy where it is alleged that there has been non-disclosure or misrepresentation of facts' by the insured, provided that the insured shall establish to the satisfaction of the insurer that the insured in this regard was 'free of any fraudulent conduct or intent to deceive'.

(a) Validity

13.66 One issue arising out of these clauses is the 'bootstrap' point. In *Toomey (No 2)*,[212] a reinsurer pleaded misrepresentation and the claimant insurer countered by reliance on a clause which stated that the reinsurance was 'neither cancellable nor avoidable by either party'. However, the reinsurer argued that the defence was circular: the clause could only be effective if contained in a valid contract not

---

206 *Drake Ins plc v Provident Ins plc* [2003] EWCA Civ 1834; [2004] QB 601, CA.
207 [88] ff.
208 Clarke, 2006, 23–18I.
209 *Pan Atlantic Ins Co Ltd v Pine Top Ins Co Ltd* [1995] 1 AC 501, 555. *Carter v Boehm* (1766) 3 Burr 1906, 1918.
210 At [85] to [86], together with a similar statement by Lord Hobhouse in *The Star Sea, Manifest Shipping Co Ltd v Uni-Polaris Shipping Co Ltd* [2001] UKHL 1; [2003] 1 AC 469 at [57]. See also *Spence v Crawford* [1939] 3 All ER 271, 278.
211 At [87]. On the facts of *Drake*, however, he concluded at [90] that it was not 'open to this court to go behind the finding of the judge that Provident acted in perfectly good faith in avoiding the contract'.
212 *Toomey v Eagle Star Ins Co Ltd (No 2)* [1995] 2 Lloyd's Rep 88.

subject to avoidance; but contracts like that *in casu* were valid only if the clause was effective. The logic of this objection appealed to Colman J but he felt bound by precedent²¹³ and analogy with jurisdiction and arbitration clauses, which survive avoidance or termination of the contract. However, the analogy is rough. A clause about forum or dispute procedure is more easily detached from the core of the contract than one concerning the very validity of the contract itself.

13.67 Could the same result be achieved without resorting to the dubious logic of bootstraps? Colman J started from the premise that the clause was an exclusion of liability in favour of a party in breach of duty imposed by the contract or by the law. Subsequently Aikens J started from a different premise.²¹⁴ Given that the scope of the duty of disclosure can be limited by what is (or is not) required of applicants when they complete the application, 'it is conceptually possible to draft a clause in a contract of insurance whereby the parties agree that the *duty of disclosure* of the assured (or his agent) is excluded'. In other words, if applicants are not obliged to disclose something, the contract cannot be breached on that account, the contract is valid and the clause also.²¹⁵ For misrepresentation the Aikens approach is more difficult. English law does not normally speak of a 'duty' not to misrepresent facts, a duty to be excluded by contract, as the judge suggested. Given, however, the context—utmost good faith, the law might well countenance waiver on certain points of duty to make an accurate presentation of the risk. Courts are likely to be receptive to argument for enforcing clauses modifying the sometimes exorbitant effects of misrepresentation and non-disclosure, if that is what parties have intended.

(b) The satisfied insurer

13.68 Another issue is the meaning of 'the satisfaction of the insurer'. How demanding are insurers entitled to be? In other insurance contexts the meaning has been limited to particulars 'with which reasonable men would be satisfied'.²¹⁶ More recently, in such a case,²¹⁷ insurers argued that it was sufficient that their decision (not to pay) was made in (subjective) good faith. The effect of the argument would have been that insurers would be judge in their own cause, unless claimants could successfully challenge their good faith in court. Against that argument, the

---

²¹³ See *Pan Atlantic Ins Co Ltd v Pine Top Ins Co Ltd* [1993] 1 Lloyd's Rep 496, 502, CA.

²¹⁴ *HIH Casualty & General Ins Ltd v Chase Manhattan Bank* [2001] 1 Lloyd's Rep 30.

²¹⁵ [2001] 1 Lloyd's Rep 30, [24]; see also [64]. This point, not central to the appeal, was apparently accepted: [2001] 2 Lloyd's Rep 483, [128] and [141]. Likewise: [2003] UKHL 6; [2003] 2 Lloyd's Rep 61, HL, [6] and [59].

²¹⁶ *Moore v Woolsey* (1854) 4 El & Bl 243, 256. See also in his sense: *London Guarantie Co v Fearnley* (1880) 5 App Cas 911, 916 *per* Lord Blackburn. Idem re party discretion in other commercial contexts; eg *Niarchos (London) Ltd v Shell Tankers Ltd* [1961] 2 Lloyd's Rep 496.

²¹⁷ *Napier v UNUM* [1996] 2 Lloyd's Rep 550.

claimant contended that the insurers were under an implied obligation to act reasonably. Tuckey J drew a distinction between the evidence insurers can call for ('vouching'), and their evaluation of that evidence; and held that the 'proof satisfactory' clause was confined to 'vouching' and, moreover, that their evidential demands must be reasonable. As to evaluation, in the absence of precedent, the judge was less sure. To reach a result that 'the insurer's decision to reject an adequately vouched claim cannot be disputed in the courts on grounds other than lack of good faith', as contended by the insurers, 'very clear words would be required'. However, to say that the insurers' evaluation must always be reasonable, as contended by the claimant, was not 'necessary'. Moreover, if so 'the Court's role is restricted. I feel instinctively unhappy about such a restriction'.[218] Quaere whether in practice insurers' evidential demands ('vouching') and evaluation of the evidence can be easily separated.

G. Cover

(1) Insuring Clauses

13.69 Insurance buyers pay for cover: usually the right to a sum of money on the occurrence of the insured event. In the case of contingency (non-indemnity) insurance, notably life insurance, the sum depends on how much they pay (premium) for the cover. In the case of indemnity insurance, the insurance money payable depends principally on the amount of loss suffered. Consequential loss is not covered unless specifically insured.[219] Constructive total loss is recoverable in marine insurance only.[220] Cover, notably the insured event, is defined in the insuring clauses of the policy.

(i) In property insurance, the event is usually damage to identified property caused by stated perils. Damage to tangible property usually means a change in the physical state of the property.[221] Damage has also been described as 'mischief done to property',[222] but the precise meaning depends on the context.[223]

---

[218] ibid 553–554.
[219] *Theobald v Railway Passengers Assurance Co* (1854) 10 Exch 45.
[220] *Moore v Evans* [1918] AC 185. MIA s 60.
[221] *Bolton MBC v Municipal Mutual Ins Ltd* [2006] EWCA Civ 50; [2006] 1 WLR 1492, CA. See also *Pilkington (UK) Ltd v CGU Ins plc* [2004] EWCA Civ 23; [2004] Lloyd's Rep IR 891, CA.
[222] *Smith v Brown* (1871) 40 LJQB 214, 218.
[223] *Swansea Corp v Harpur* [1912] 3 KB 493, CA.

(ii) Personal accident insurance covers accidental 'bodily injury', ie any localized abnormal condition of the living body, trauma both outside and inside the body,[224] but not disease.[225]

(iii) All risks insurance covers any loss or damage to property which was not a certainty at the time of contract.[226] Excluded, therefore, are the effects of inherent vice,[227] and ordinary wear and tear.[228] Also excluded, as it is in all kinds of insurance, is that caused by policyholders' 'wilful misconduct'.[229]

(iv) People sometimes say that there is no smoke without fire, but for fire insurance, there must be ignition.[230] If so, there is fire regardless of cause, be it lightning,[231] spontaneous ignition[232] or arson by a third party.[233] Explosions caused by fire are covered[234] but not fires caused by explosion,[235] although they are often included expressly in fire insurance. Fire caused by policyholder negligence is covered[236] but not fire started deliberately (wilful misconduct) unless for some greater good, for example, lest shipping fall into enemy hands.[237] Fire cover includes the immediate consequences of fire: damage by water to extinguish fire,[238] by smoke[239] and by falling masonry,[240] but not loss caused by theft or looting.[241]

(v) Liability insurance covers the monetary impact of legal claims[242] against policyholders and, crucially, the cost of defending claims.[243] 'Claims made' insurance covers claims made against policyholders during the period of cover. However, policies often cover claims brought after the period, provided

---

[224] Eg *Dhak v INA (UK) Ltd* [1996] 1 Lloyd's Rep 632, CA.

[225] *De Souza v Home & Overseas Ins Co Ltd* [1995] LRLR 453, CA.

[226] *British & Foreign Marine Ins Co Ltd v Gaunt* [1921] 2 AC 41.

[227] *Mayban General Assurance BHD v Alstom Power Plants Ltd* [2004] EWHC 1038 (Comm); [2004] 2 Lloyd's Rep 609.

[228] *Gaunt* (n 226 above), p 46.

[229] *Gaunt* (n 226 above), p 57.

[230] *Everett v London Assurance Co* (1865) 19 CB (NS) 126.

[231] *Gordon v Rimmington* (1807) 1 Camp 123.

[232] *Tempus Shipping Co Ltd v Dreyfus & Co Ltd* [1930] 1 KB 699, 708.

[233] *Upjohn v Hitchens* [1918] 2 KB 48, CA.

[234] *Curtis & Harvey (Canada) Ltd v North British & Mercantile Ins Co Ltd* [1921] 1 AC 303, PC.

[235] *Boiler Inspection & Ins Co of Canada v Sherman-Williams Co of Canada Ltd* [1951] AC 319, PC.

[236] *Shaw v Robberds* (1837) 6 Ad & E 75; *Harris v Poland* [1941] 1 KB 462.

[237] *Gordon v Rimmington* (1807) 1 Camp 123.

[238] *Symington & Co v Union Ins Sy of Canton Ltd* (1928) 34 Com Cas 23, CA.

[239] *The Diamond* [1906] P 282.

[240] *Re Hooley Hill Rubber & Chemical Co Ltd v Royal Insurance Co Ltd* [1920] 1 KB 257, 271–272, CA.

[241] *Marsden v City & County Assurance Co* (1865) LR 1 CP 232.

[242] *Thorman v NHIC (UK) Ltd* [1988] 1 Lloyd's Rep 7, CA.

[243] Eg *Callery v Gray (No 1)* [2002] UKHL 28; [2002] 1 WLR 2000; but not automatically: *Brice v JH Wackerbarth (Australasia) Pty Ltd* [1974] 2 Lloyd's Rep 274 CA; and not the cost of mitigating the state of property to avoid liability: *Yorkshire Water Services Ltd v Sun Alliance & London Ins Plc (No 1)* [1997] 2 Lloyd's Rep 21, CA.

that the insurer has been notified during the insurance period of circumstances suggesting that such a claim might be brought.[244] As insurance generally does not cover loss deliberately or wilfully caused by the insured, liability does not cover deliberate breach of contract, lest policyholders be tempted to transfer to their insurer their liability loss on a bad deal.

Insurance cover comes at a cost: premium, essentially monetary payment like any other. Time is not of the essence.[245] However, there are some harsh rules. In life insurance, if payment is later than the 'days of grace' allowed by the policy, cover ends and many years of 'investment' are lost. No property interest is involved so, even for aged and forgetful policyholders, there can be no relief against forfeiture.[246] Moreover, if indemnity cover 'has once commenced, there shall be no apportionment or return of premium afterwards'.[247]

(2) Interpretation

13.70   When reading contracts, the overriding aim has sometimes been said to be to find the intention of the parties.[248] However, today the trend is to the 'objective theory' of interpretation; although the aim is still 'to give effect to the intention of the parties', the methodology 'is not to probe the real intentions of the parties but to ascertain the contextual meaning of the relevant contractual language. Intention is determined by reference to expressed rather than actual intention'.[249]

13.71   Insurance contracts have been described in the USA as the archetype of 'contracts of adhesion', tantamount to private or delegated legislation.[250] Legislation they are not: unlike that of some countries, English law does not prescribe the standard forms, these products are the proud work of insurers; there are many forms vying with each other in the market place. They are subject nonetheless to the same rules of interpretation as other commercial contracts,[251] an outline of which follows.

(i)   Words are to be understood in their ordinary sense as they would be understood by ordinary people.[252] Ordinary people use a dictionary and are

---

[244] *J Rothschild Ins Plc v Collyear* [1999] Lloyd's Rep IR 6; *Layher Ltd v Lowe* [2000] Lloyd's Rep IR 510, CA.

[245] *Figre Ltd v Mander* [1999] Lloyd's Rep IR 193. Clarke, 2006, ch 13.

[246] *The Scaptrade* [1983] 2 AC 694.

[247] *Tyrie v Fletcher* (1777) 2 Cowp 666, 668.

[248] Clarke, 2006, ch 15; MacGillivray, ch 11.

[249] *Deutsche Genossenschaftsbank v Burnhope* [1996] 1 Lloyd's Rep 113, 122, HL. See 8.05 ff.

[250] V P Goldberg, 'Institutional Change and the Quasi-Invisible Hand', 17 J L & Econ 461, 484 (1974).

[251] *Cementation Piling & Foundations Ltd v Aegon Ins Ltd* [1995] 1 Lloyd's Rep 97 at 101, CA.

[252] For example, 'actually paid' means 'really paid' and not 'notionally paid' or 'prospectively paid': *Charter Re Co Ltd v Fagan* [1996] 2 Lloyd's Rep 113, 116, HL. See also *Hayward v Norwich Union Ins Ltd* [2001] Lloyd's Rep IR 410, [10] CA. Clarke, 2006, 15-2.

assumed to know what is going on in the world immediately around them.[253] Moreover, the ordinary person is a useful ally who can be summoned to the aid of a court that might have reason to eschew the pursuit of precision and construe words as a matter of impression.[254] Be that as it may, words are to be understood not in isolation but in context. The immediate context is a series of circles: the phrase, then the sentence, the paragraph and the policy section. In that context words are read with the aid of certain traditional canons of interpretation. The chief canons of interpretation are, first, that, if particular words have a generic character, more general following words are construed as having the same character *(eiusdem generis)*. Thus 'flood' in 'storm, tempest or flood' means a sudden flood on a large scale.[255] Second, the express mention of one thing may imply the exclusion of another related thing *(expressio unius est exclusio alterius)*. Thus if policy term A is expressed to be a 'condition precedent' to cover but policy term B is not, the inference is that indeed term B is not.[256]

(ii) In the event of inconsistency in the ordinary meaning of words in different parts of the contract, courts adopt the meaning that best reflects the intention of the parties.[257] In particular, preference is given to non-standard parts of a policy, such as the Schedule, to which the parties gave actual attention[258] or which appear to better reflect their final intention.[259] In the important instance of inconsistency between a master policy and a certificate issued to a beneficiary of the policy, priority is accorded to the certificate.[260]

(iii) If it appears that the words have been used in a special sense, either, first, as previously defined by the courts, for example 'theft',[261] or, second, the sense used in a particular commercial context, such as 'motor racing',[262] the words will be interpreted in that special sense. The same is true of the sense used in a particular commercial context with which both parties are familiar.[263] This rule is justified as promoting the interests of certainty in commercial transactions.

---

253 *Investors Compensation Scheme Ltd v West Bromwich BS* [1998] 1 WLR 896, 912 (HL).
254 *Lewis Emanuel & Son Ltd v Hepburn* [1960] 1 Lloyd's Rep 304, 308.
255 *Young v Sun Alliance & London Ins Ltd* [1976] 2 Lloyds Rep 189, 191 (CA).
256 *Home Ins Co v Victoria-Montreal Fire Ins Co* [1907] AC 59, 64.
257 *Woolfall & Rimmer Ltd v Moyle* [1942] 1 KB 66, 73 ff. (CA).
258 *Farmers Coop Ltd v National Benefit Assurance Co Ltd* (1922) 13 Ll L Rep 417, 530, 533, CA.
259 *Izzard v Universal Ins Co Ltd* [1937] AC 773.
260 *D & J Koskas v Standard Marine Ins Co Ltd* (1927) 32 Com Cas 160, CA; *De Monchy v Phoenix Ins Co of Hartford* (1928) 33 Com Cas 197, CA.
261 *Hayward* (n 252 above); *Deutsche Genossenschaftsbank v Burnhope* [1996] 1 Lloyd's Rep 113, HL. See also *The Starsin* [2004] 1 AC 75, [7]. Cf policies for cover in other jurisdictions: *Canelhas Comercio Importacao e Exportacao Ltd v Wooldridge* [2004] EWCA Civ 984; [2004] Lloyd's Rep IR 914.
262 *Scragg v UK Temperance & General Provident Institution* [1976] 2 Lloyd's Rep 227, 233.
263 *The Kleovoulos of Rhodes* [2003] EWCA Civ 12; [2003] 1 Lloyd's Rep 138, [26].

(iv) If after the application of rules (i) and (ii), the meaning remains unclear and rule (iii) does not assist, courts are faced with ambiguity. In this situation the words will be read with reference to any evidence of the immediate purpose of the wording;[264] and the words will be construed *contra proferentem*, that is, against the insurer and liberally in favour of policyholders.[265] Ambiguity is a relative matter. At common law words are not ambiguous or unclear just because they are complex; if lawyers can find the meaning of words, the words are not ambiguous.[266] Consumers,[267] however, benefit from the Unfair Terms in Consumer Contracts Regulations 1999.[268] Written contract terms must be 'expressed in plain and intelligible language',[269] plain and intelligible not only to lawyers but to non-lawyers.[270] To pronounce on particular wordings is the responsibility of the Office of Fair Trading (OFT). The OFT has condemned 'legal jargon' such as 'indemnify', 'consequential loss', and 'events beyond your control'.[271]

(v) Rule (v) is the rule against absurdity.[272] The meaning of words must be intelligible but it does not have to be reasonable, however much courts dislike it, unless the result can be described as absurd. So, if application of the other rules produces a result that is so very unreasonable or inconvenient as to be absurd, that result will be ignored.[273] For example, the contention of an insurer that literal effect should be given to an exclusion of injury caused by degenerative conditions was rejected, because that would include the normal ageing process and the effect would be substantially to deprive the policyholder of the protection that the insurance was designed to provide.[274] To find a sensible meaning, courts looks to the external context,[275] in particular the commercial purpose of the policy broadly conceived.

13.72 Contracts generally are interpreted in a broader context than before. In the past interpretation was conducted largely within the boundaries of the policy itself,

---

[264] *Cornish v Accident Ins Co* (1889) 23 QBD 452, 456, CA.

[265] Eg *English v Western Ins Co* (1940) 67 Ll L Rep 45, CA.

[266] *Higgins v Dawson* [1902] AC 1.

[267] A natural person contracting insurance for a purpose 'outside his trade, business or profession': SI 1999/2083, reg. 3(1).

[268] SI 1999/2083.

[269] ibid reg. 7.

[270] *Unfair Contract Terms*, OFT Bulletin No. 4, December 1997, p 16.

[271] Respectively OFT Bulletin No 25 (p 8), No 5 (p 72) and No 25 (p 8). Bulletins can be read at <www.oft.gov.uk>.

[272] *Smit Tak Offshore Services Ltd v Youell* [1992] 1 Lloyds Rep 154, 159 (CA).

[273] *Prenn v Simmonds* [1971] 1 WLR 1381, 1385, HL.

[274] *Blackburn Rovers Football & Athletic Club plc v Avon* [2006] EWHC 840; [2005] Lloyd's Rep IR 239, reversed on different grounds: [2005] EWCA Civ 423; [2005] Lloyd's Rep IR 239, CA. See also *Charter Reinsurance Ltd v Fagan* [1996] 2 Lloyds Rep 113, 118, HL.

[275] *Toomey v Eagle Star Ins Co Ltd (No 1)* [1994] 1 Lloyd's Rep 516, 519–520, CA.

in accordance with parole evidence rule. Exceptions have been confined to rule (iii) (ambiguity) and rule (v) (absurdity) where courts look beyond the policy to ascertain, for example, the purpose of the insurance. But in the *ICS* case[276] Lord Hoffmann said that the meaning of a document, 'is what the parties using those words against the relevant background would reasonably have been understood to mean'; and the background is 'absolutely anything which would have affected the way in which the language of the document would have been understood by a reasonable man', and which a reasonable man would have regarded as relevant,[277] except evidence of previous negotiations.[278] This statement opened the stable door once formed by the parole evidence rule.

Decisions reported since 1998 suggest that the impact of Lord Hoffmann's state-   **13.73** ment on insurance cases has been slight. In *MDIS Ltd v Swinbank*, for example, the Court of Appeal followed his approach but the background it looked at was something 'well known amongst insurance lawyers and indeed brokers for many years'.[279] Certain judges with experience of the Commercial Court have been critical. It is 'hard to imagine a ruling more calculated to perpetuate the vast cost of commercial litigation'.[280] That was also the view of Saville LJ,[281] who raised the further objection that third parties 'are unlikely in the nature of things to be aware of the surrounding circumstances' in which the contract was concluded and are entitled to take the wording at face value. This point affects cargo and transit insurance, where buyers usually get an insurance document from their seller who contracted the cover, as well as employees insured under a group scheme arranged for them by their employer. Indeed, Lord Hoffmann did qualify his statement with the requirement that the background information must have been 'reasonably available to the parties'; and accessibility, surely, must take account of the parties' resources, both financial and otherwise. Lord Bingham approved the Hoffmann statement but continued: 'the court reads the terms of the contract as a whole, giving the words used their natural and ordinary meaning in the context of the agreement, the parties' relationship and all the relevant facts surrounding the transaction *so far as known to the parties*'.[282]

---

[276] *Investors Compensation Scheme Ltd v West Bromwich BS* [1998] 1 WLR 896, 912–913 HL.

[277] *BCCI SA v Ali (No 1)* [2002] UKHL 8; [2002] 1 AC 251, [39].

[278] *Prenn v Simmonds* [1971] 1 WLR 1381, 1384, HL. See also *Absolom v TCRU* [2005] EWCA Civ 1586; [2006] 1 All ER (Comm) 375, [7] (CA); however cf *Proforce Recruit Ltd v Rugby Group Ltd* [2006] EWCA Civ 69.

[279] *MDIS Ltd v Swinbank* [1999] Lloyd's Rep IR 516, 522, CA. Idem *King v Brandywine Reinsurance Co (UK) Ltd* [2005] EWCA Civ 235; [2005] 1 Lloyd's Rep 655, in which insurers were taken to be aware of what was available to them in the reinsurance market.

[280] C Staughton, 'Interpretation of Contracts' [1999] CLJ 303, 307. The Civil Procedure Rules, whereby judges assume responsibility for case management, state in Part 1.1 (2) (C) that the handling of a case is to be proportionate to the financial position of the parties.

[281] *Nat Bank of Sharjah v Dellborg*, CA, 9 July 1997; Thorpe and Judge LJJ concurred.

[282] *BCCI* (n 277 above), [8], emphasis added.

(3) Policy Terms

13.74 Policy terms can be grouped according to their function. Suppose motor insurance covering (a) private saloon car SI23 JEB against inter alia theft, provided that (b) it is locked, and that (c) reasonable steps are taken to maintain the vehicle in efficient condition; and requiring also (d) that any theft be notified to the police and to the insurer within 48 hours.

   (i) Term (a) defines cover in positive terms of the subject-matter of the insurance, the car, and the peril covered, theft. Term (b) is called an exception (also an exclusion, restriction, or limit); this also defines cover but in negative terms, qualifying term (a). Term (c) also qualifies cover, but in a different way, and is called a warranty. Term (d) has nothing to do with the scope of cover, but is designed, in part at least, to make the contract less burdensome to the insurer; these are called procedural conditions and are considered later.[283]

   (ii) Term (a) is case-specific as regards the car. If the seat covers are changed, the subject-matter remains the same and cover continues. If, however, the vehicle is modified, for example for rallying, or the policyholder replaces it, for the purpose of insurance the car insured no longer exists—just as if it had been destroyed. Cover ends. Theft, on the other hand, is a peril defined by law.

   (iii) Term (b) in common with term (c) may be called a condition and operate to defeat a claim. However, they differ importantly in that breach of (b) must be a cause of the loss claimed, whereas breach of (c) defeats a claim regardless. Moreover, if the policyholder is in breach of (b), the effect on cover is not permanent but only suspensive. But if the brakes are out of order, unless repaired as soon as reasonably possible, their condition is a breach of warranty, term (c), and the effect is that the cover ends immediately and automatically. Breach of term (d), unlike the others, gives insurers a right, albeit one they never exercise, to damages, but generally does not end cover.

(4) Conditions Precedent: Warranties

13.75 Warranties are said to be 'conditions precedent' to cover, and breach terminates cover,[284] even though there may be no causal connection at all between the breach

---

[283] See para 13.81.
[284] *The Good Luck* [1992] 1 AC 233.

of warranty and either the loss or the risk of such loss.[285] In marine insurance cover two important warranties, seaworthiness and legality, are implied by statute.[286]

To identify warranties, generally, the first step is to see whether the contract itself **13.76** classifies terms as such. What policies describe as 'conditions' are not necessarily warranties. On the one hand, the consequences of breach of warranty are so severe for policyholders that if 'there is any ambiguity, it must be construed most strongly against' the insurer[287] and, therefore, as something less draconian than a warranty. On the other hand, it is not necessary that the word 'warranty' be used.[288] Currently one way of creating warranties is to write a 'basis' clause, that the proposal 'shall be the basis of this contract', in the proposal. Courts, which regard them as a trap for most policyholders, are hostile to these clauses,[289] but they have yet to be banned. Where polices do not settle the issue, courts seek the essential nature of the term by asking whether it is aimed at circumstances which give rise to an increase of risk that is more than *temporary*: if temporary, terms are likely to be construed not as warranties but as exceptions.

Increase in the risk may be addressed more directly by clauses requiring policy- **13.77** holders to notify the insurers of any risk. More draconian clauses purport to suspend cover until the insurer has agreed to continue it. Courts have refused to apply these literally.[290] However, to counter judicial construction like that insurers may include cancellation clauses on, for example, 30 days' notice, so that they can escape bad risks. These clauses have been enforced regardless of the motives of the insurer.[291]

(5) Exceptions

Like insuring clauses exceptions define the scope of the cover, however, in nega- **13.78** tive terms. Exceptions qualify insuring clauses, and limit the extent of the cover provided by the latter. Some policies, such as professional indemnity (PI) policies, usually contain a separate section headed 'Exclusions'. This is usually sufficient to distinguish them from the warranties[292] which are usually found in PI policies' 'Conditions'. In case of doubt courts seek the essential nature of the term.

---

285 *Dawsons Ltd v Bonnin* [1922] 2 AC 413.
286 Respectively Marine Insurance Act s 39 and s 40. See Rose, 9.40 ff.
287 *Thomson v Weems* (1884) 9 App Cas 671, 682.
288 *Dawsons* (n 285 above).
289 *Zurich General Accident & Liability Insurance Co Ltd v Morrison* [1942] 2 KB 53, CA.
290 *Kausar v Eagle Star Ins Co Ltd* [2000] Lloyd's Rep IR 52, CA. See also *Hussain v Brown* [1996] 1 Lloyd's Rep 627, CA.
291 *Sun Fire Office v Hart* (1889) 14 App Cas 98, PC. Cf *Kazakhstan Wool Processors (Europe) Ltd v NCM* [2000] Lloyd's Rep IR 371, CA.
292 See para 13.71.

If the circumstances envisaged by a condition give rise to an increase of risk that is no more than *temporary*, terms are likely to be construed not as warranties but as exceptions.

13.79 Exceptions can be classified as follows. First, descriptive exceptions concern subject-matter, for example, claims for bodily injury are commonly excluded from PI polices. Regions of the world may be excluded from travel policies unless an additional premium (AP) is paid. Second, circumstantial exceptions state situations in which loss tends to occur but which insurers do not cover in standard policies. Thus travel policies may exclude loss caused by disease or medical expenses incurred in the USA. Third, 'temporal' exceptions, found for example in travel or accident policies, exclude injury sustained 'while intoxicated'. To establish a descriptive exception, usually insurers must prove no more than the circumstance envisaged, for example, that the claim against the policyholder is based on bodily injury. To establish circumstantial exceptions, insurers must also establish causation,[293] for example, that the hospital expense was incurred as a result of disease rather than accident, for example, sunstroke rather than breaking a leg. To establish temporal exceptions, insurers must establish only that the circumstance prevailed at the time, in the example given, that the policy-holder was intoxicated.[294]

13.80 The Unfair Contract Terms Act 1977 does not apply to insurance contracts,[295] although the spirit of the Act has been applied by the Insurance Ombudsman, in particular, to policy provisions producing an unexpected loss of cover.[296] The Unfair Terms in Consumer Contracts Regulations 1999,[297] from which insurance contracts are not specifically excluded, has two main thrusts. One, applicable to insurance contracts, requires that terms be 'expressed in plain and intelligible language', and, in case of doubt, 'the interpretation which is most favourable to the consumer shall prevail'.[298] The other, that certain terms must not be unfair, does not apply to core provisions. Regulation 6(2) provides that 'the assessment of fairness of a term shall not relate—(a) to the definition of the main subject matter of the contract, or (b) to the adequacy of the price or remuneration, as against the goods or services supplied in exchange'. Like the common law the Regulations do not question the adequacy of consideration.

---

[293] *Munro Brice v War Risk Association* [1918] 2 KB 78; *Fraser v Furman (Productions) Ltd* [1967] 1 WLR 898, 905, CA.
[294] *Kennedy v Smith* 1976 SLT 110.
[295] Sched 1, para 1(a).
[296] *Annual Report 1990*, para 2.4.
[297] SI 1999 No 2083.
[298] Reg 7.

Thus, insofar as insurance exceptions define the scope of cover, they are core terms outside the Regulations.[299]

(6) Procedural Conditions

Many policy conditions are merely procedural, ie designed to make the policy **13.81** 'work' in a way which is least costly to the insurer. A leading example is the condition requiring notice of loss to the insurer.[300] Others concern jurisdiction and arbitration. An associated underlying rule of law is that which establishes policyholders' duty of co-operation.[301] An instance of that is the duty of policyholders to assist the insurer to exercise rights in subrogation against any other person responsible for the loss insured.

H. Claims

(1) Claimants

Persons primarily entitled to claim under insurance contracts are the policy- **13.82** holders, who contract the insurance, and sometimes others who are insured under the policy in question. The latter, however, are barred from enforcing claims by the rule of privity of contract, unless entitled by statute.[302] The earliest surviving statute is the Married Women's Property Act 1882. Section 11 provides that a 'policy of assurance effected by any man on his own life, and expressed to be for the benefit of his wife, or of his children, or of his wife and children, or any of them, or by any woman on her own life, and expressed to be for the benefit of her husband, or of her children, or of her husband and children, or any of them, shall create a trust in favour of the objects therein named' and be enforceable as such.

More recently and more importantly, the Contracts (Rights of Third Parties) **13.83** Act 1999, section 1(1), confers a right of enforcement on third parties in general, provided that the intention of contracting parties to that effect is clear and the third parties are sufficiently identified. By section 1(3), third parties must be 'expressly identified in the contract by name, as a member of a class or as answering to a particular description'. This means, notably, that liability insurance can be extended to persons such as subcontractors, that the benefit of life insurance can be extended beyond spouses, and that employers can contract

---

[299] Generally see *Director General of Fair Trading v First National Bank* [2001] UKHL 52; [2002] 1 AC 481.
[300] See para 13.85.
[301] *Mackay v Dick* (1881) 6 App Cas 251.
[302] Clarke, 2006, ch 5.

accident and medical insurance for employees, which the latter can enforce themselves.

13.84 Important in the area of liability insurance is the Third Parties (Rights Against Insurers) Act 1930: claimants have a direct right of action against liability insurers of debtors who are bankrupt. The conception behind the Act led to direct actions against debtors, whether bankrupt or not, in the case of motor insurance: Road Traffic Act 1988, section 151. For cases that elude section 151, there are the Uninsured Drivers Agreement 1999 and the Untraced Drivers Agreement 2003. The Agreements are between the Motor Insurers' Bureau (MIB) and the government. Arguably victims can enforce the Agreements under the Contracts (Rights of Third Parties) Act 1999.

(2) Notice of Loss

13.85 A common 'procedural' condition requires notice of loss to the insurer within a certain time. If not, as common sense as well as common law, there will be implied a term requiring reasonable notice of loss. Express terms requiring 'immediate' notice are not construed literally but as meaning the same. What is reasonable depends on striking a balance between the interests of the parties. Claimants may need time to discover that the loss has occurred at all, or that relevant insurance exists.[303] Insurers want notice as soon as possible to test claims before the evidence disappears, and to mitigate the extent of loss. If notice is required within a specified period, for example 14 days, courts' hands are tied, however, subject to the effect of legislation.[304]

13.86 Notice is not effective until received by the right person,[305] usually the person apparently authorized to handle claims. Insurers' local agents[306] are usually authorized channels of communication to that person, and notice to brokers is effective, provided it is in time to reach the handler in the normal course of business within the time required. Insurers bear the risk of flaws in their information channels.[307] Notice in time is commonly expressed to be and enforced as a condition precedent to the claim. Otherwise the effect of late notice on claims is controversial.[308]

---

[303] *Verelst's Administratrix v Motor Union Ins Co* [1925] 2 KB 137.
[304] See para 13.80. *Bankers Ins. Co. Ltd v South* [2004] Lloyd's Rep IR 1.
[305] *Holwell Securities Ltd v Hughes* [1974] 1 All ER 161, CA.
[306] *Roche v Roberts* (1921) 9 Ll L Rep 59.
[307] *A/S Rendal v Arcos Ltd* (1937) 58 Ll L Rep 287, HL.
[308] See Clarke, 2006, 26-2G.

(3) Proof of Loss

Claimants must not only give notice of loss but also prove what is alleged in the **13.87**
notice. Under indemnity insurance, claimants must prove the amount of loss
suffered; and in all cases that the loss was caused by an event (peril) covered by the
policy.[309] As to the distribution of the onus of proof,[310] if, for example, a claimant
shows that cargo was damaged by fire, it is for the insurer to show that the fire
was caused by an exception, such as inherent vice.[311] The scope of the exception
(fire caused by inherent vice) is narrower than the scope of the cover (fire from
whatever cause). Compare general exceptions, such as an excess of £100 in a
motor policy; these operate in all cases, the claimants must show damage in excess
of £100 to establish a claim in the first place.[312]

Proof is on the balance of probabilities, unless the defence alleges fraud or **13.88**
wilful misconduct, such as arson, by the policyholder. Then the onus will be heavi-
er: on a sliding scale in the direction of the criminal law rule, that requires
proof beyond reasonable doubt, according to the gravity of the allegation.[313]
Policies sometimes require 'proof satisfactory to the insurer', but this has been
held to mean such proof as the insurer might *reasonably* require.[314]

(4) Causation

Claimants must show that the loss was caused by an insured peril. The law **13.89**
sees causation as a matter of policy construction; and only perils (or excepted
causes) actually mentioned as such in the policy are to be considered as
possible causes.[315] However, given the purpose of most insurance, there is strong
presumption that policyholder negligence is covered.[316] Effective risk assessment
requires prediction on the basis of a close connection between the peril and the
loss, and thus the intention of insurers is that the cause, whether peril or exception, must be a 'proximate' cause of the loss claimed. Accordingly the proximate cause is that which led (more or less) inevitably to the kind of loss in
question.[317] Further, however, if the proximate cause is a peril insured, insurers are

---

309 *British & Foreign Marine Ins Co Ltd v Gaunt* [1921] 2 AC 43.
310 *Munro Brice & Co v War Risk Association* [1918] 2 KB 78; and *Fraser v BN Furman (Productions) Ltd* [1967] 1 WLR 898, 905, CA.
311 *The Galatia* [1979] 2 All ER 726.
312 *Munro Brice* (n 310 above).
313 *Hornal v Neuberger Products* [1957] 1 QB 247, CA; *Re H* [1996] AC 563.
314 See para 13.66.
315 *The Miss Jay Jay* [1987] 1 Lloyds Rep 32, CA.
316 *Canada Rice Mills Ltd v Union Marine & General Ins Co Ltd* [1941] AC 55, PC.
317 *Leyland Shipping Co Ltd v Norwich Union Fire Ins Society Ltd* [1918] AC 350.

liable for the entire loss, even though its extent was not inevitable, as long as its extent was not too remote.[318]

13.90 If, as may be,[319] there is more than one proximate cause, and an insured peril leads (more or less inevitably) to an excepted and proximate cause of loss, the loss is covered.[320] If, however, an excepted cause leads to an insured peril, and to loss, the loss is not covered.[321] If two such causes, one covered and one excepted, are construed to be not consecutive but to operate concurrently, the loss is not covered.[322]

13.91 'Rules' of interpretation like these may be changed by clear policy language. However, 'originating from', 'in consequence of', 'arising from', 'effectively caused by', and 'directly caused by' have all been construed as requiring a 'proximate cause'.[323] On the other hand, phrases like 'directly or indirectly' indicate a looser connection.[324] Alternatively, some judges, led at one time by Lord Denning,[325] dismiss 'rules' of causation as intellectual abstraction, and argue that proximate causes can be identified simply and solely by common sense. This position is attractive in its simplicity; however, as Lord Mustill once observed: 'Common sense for one person may be uncommon sense for another.'[326] Arguably this approach is a fiat for judicial intuition and, consequently, policyholder suspicion.

(5) Good Faith

13.92 Whenever policyholders supply information to enable insurers to make a decision about cover, they must observe a legal duty of good faith, a duty which continues throughout the insurance period at a level appropriate to the decision. The duty ends as regards a particular claim when the claim has been paid, or rejected and the policyholder must accept the rejection or commence proceedings.[327] Evidently a fraudulent claim is not in good faith.

---

318 *Reischer v Borwick* [1894] 2 QB 548, CA.
319 *Midland Mainline Ltd v Eagle Star Ins Co Ltd* [2004] EWCA Civ 1042; [2004] 2 Lloyd's Rep 604, CA.
320 *Re Etherington and Lancashire & Yorkshire Accident Insurance Co's Arbitration* [1909] 1 KB 591, CA.
321 *The Salem* [1983] 1 Lloyd's Rep 342, HL.
322 *Wayne Tank & Pump Co Ltd v Employers' Liability Corp* [1973] 2 Lloyd's Rep 237, CA.
323 *Oei v Foster* [1982] 2 Lloyd's Rep 170, 174–175.
324 ibid.
325 *Wayne Tank* (n 322 above), 240.
326 'Humpty Dumpty and Risk Management' [1997] LMCLQ 488–501, 500. See also Clarke, 2006, 25-1.
327 *The Star Sea* (n 210 above).

(a) The meaning of fraud

To defeat claims on grounds of fraud, insurers must show them to be 'wilfully **13.93** false' in a 'substantial respect'.[328] A claim is wilfully false if the claimant knows that it is false, does not believe it to be true or makes it recklessly, not caring whether it is true or false,[329] ie a case of common law fraud.[330] Prima facie deliberate exaggeration is fraud, but some cases suggest that exaggeration is not fraud but merely a bargaining position[331] but the balance of precedent confirms that it is fraud.[332] Nonetheless, claimants usually get the benefit of any reasonable doubt. After all, claimants are human, 'different views of values are common; memory is faulty'.[333]

Whether a falsehood is substantial depends on the *de minimis* rule. More signifi- **13.94** cant is the associated requirement that the falsehood be material. Until 2002 falsehood was not material unless it had a decisive effect on the readiness of the insurer to pay—whether to pay and to whom, or the amount to be paid.[334] Thus, false evidence submitted to bolster an otherwise valid claim was not material.[335] However, in *The Aegeon*[336] fraud extended to 'fraudulent devices' employed by claimants, who believe that that they have indeed suffered the loss claimed, but seek to improve or embellish the facts by telling lies. Such claimants nonetheless seek to gain by the device, albeit not from insurers. Fraud, said Roche J., includes deceit used to secure 'quicker payment of the money than would have been obtained if the truth had been told'.[337] Indeed, if 'time is money' a claimant is significantly better off, and it not a lie which necessarily damages the insurer—the fraud may save insurers the cost of prolonged investigation of a claim. Only irrelevant falsehood such as concealment to avoid embarrassment, will be excluded from this broad notion of fraud. Morally, the device rule can be supported, but doubts stem from the severe consequences that follow a finding of fraud.

(b) The consequences of fraud

If fraud is discovered after a claim has been paid, insurers may recover the money **13.95** as money paid by mistake. If fraud is established before any or all of the insurance money has been paid, insurers are not obliged to pay any of the amount claimed,

---

[328] *Britton v Royal Ins Co* (1866) 4 F & F 905.
[329] *Lek v Mathews* (1927) 29 Ll L Rep 141, 145, HL.
[330] *Twinsectra Ltd v Yardley* [2002] UKHL 12; [2002] 2 AC 164.
[331] *Nsubuga v Commercial Union Assurance Co plc* [1998] 2 Lloyd's Rep 682.
[332] *Orakpo v Barclays Insurance Services* [1995] LRLR 443, CA.
[333] *Soler v United Firemen's Ins Co*, 299 US 45, 50 (1936).
[334] Cf material misrepresentations: para 13.45.
[335] *The Mercandian Continent* [2001] EWCA Civ 1275; [2001] 2 Lloyd's Rep 563, [35].
[336] *Agapitos v Agnew (No 1)* [2002] EWCA Civ 247; [2003] QB 556, CA.
[337] *Wisenthal v World Auxiliary Ins Corp Ltd* (1930) 38 Ll L Rep 54, 61.

even a genuine but exaggerated claim: courts apply the maxim *fraus omnia corrumpit* to discourage dishonesty.[338] Further, insurers are usually entitled to terminate insurance contracts under a policy provision. Anyway, fraud being a breach of the duty of good faith, insurers are entitled to terminate by law.[339] Some feel that, as with contracts under the general law,[340] termination should be allowed only if policyholder breach is 'substantial'. However, the contrary view, also in harmony with contract law at large, is that fraud is a factor that pumps up the perceived gravity of breach. Certain contractual relationships, among them the insurance relationship, can only work properly if trust and confidence are maintained.[341] Any fraud puts a new and darker light on a policyholder and, therefore, insurers are entitled to reconsider and, if so minded, terminate their contract.[342] Precedent[343] exists for the more drastic consequence of 'forfeiture', which would be retroactive and require claimants to reimburse any insurance money received during the insurance period. However, in the words of Lord Hobhouse, termination 'only applies prospectively and does not affect accrued rights'. The idea of forfeiture, that a failure of good faith at the end of the insurance period should entitle the insurer to recover the amount of a good faith claim paid earlier in the period 'cannot be reconciled with principle'.[344]

I. Indemnity

(1) Amount

13.96 Under life or other non-indemnity (contingency) policies successful claimants recover the amount stipulated in the policy. Under indemnity policies the object of payment is to put claimants in the position they would have been in, if the insured loss had not occurred. Claimants recover their actual provable loss subject, however, to certain limits. One is that the amount recoverable is reduced by any indemnity for the same loss already obtained from a third party. Commonly other limits on the amount recoverable are expressed in or implied from the policy.

---

[338] *Galloway v Guardian Royal Exchange (UK) Ltd* [1999] Lloyd's Rep IR 209, CA.

[339] *Orakpo* (n 332 above).

[340] *Hongkong Fir Shipping Co Ltd v Kawasaki Kisen Kaisha Ltd* [1962] 2 QB 26, CA.

[341] Generally: *Malik v Bank of Credit and Commerce International SA* [1998] AC 20.

[342] Concerning the fraud problems posed by joint insurance contracted by associations, see para 13.56.

[343] Surveyed by Rix J in *Royal Boskalis Westminster NV v Mountain* [1997] LRLR 523, 593.

[344] *The Star Sea* [2003] 1 AC 469, [50].

(i) Limits are implied from the nature of the cover. A fire policy covers loss or damage caused by fire but not cost incurred, however reasonably, to prevent fire.[345]

(ii) Policies commonly limit the amount of recoverable loss to specified sums. Unless otherwise stipulated, insurers are liable for any number of successive losses caused by insured perils during the insurance period, whether individually subject to such limits or not, even though the aggregate of amounts payable exceeds the ceiling; there is a presumption in favour of full indemnity. Commonly, however, the overall amount recoverable is limited by means of aggregation clauses.[346]

(iii) If property has been insured but undervalued, the amount of any insurance money payable on a claim is 'subject to average': the amount is limited to the proportion of actual loss, which the sum insured bears to the actual value of the property insured at the time of the loss. If, for example, property insured for 10x is actually worth 12x, actual loss of 6x is subject to average (10:12) and the amount payable is limited to 5x (10 x 6/12).

(iv) Policies usually contain an 'excess clause' (deductible), whereby the insured bear the first part of any loss, expressed as an amount of money or as a percentage of loss. The purpose is to encourage policyholders to be risk averse, and to reduce transaction costs incurred by insurers by ruling out small claims.

(v) Policies may exclude, for example, any loss 'in respect of which the insured is entitled to indemnity under any other insurance except in respect of any excess beyond the amount which would have been payable under such insurance, if this policy had not been effected'. Such clauses are troublesome. The effect is to convert the insurance into 'excess of loss' insurance: a contract on a different layer of risk from any other covering the same risk and, therefore, one designed to exclude contribution between insurers. If two policies on the same risk contain such clauses, *prima facie* neither insurance pays, a result described as absurd and unjust.[347] In England that has been avoided by a robust rule of construction that looks 'at each policy independently and if each would be liable but for the existence of the other, then the exclusions would be treated as cancelling each other out, both insurers are then liable', and the one who pays can claim contribution from the other.[348]

In contrast, claimants may recover more or less than their actual loss in the case of 'honour policies'.[349] An honour policy is one which stipulates that, in

13.97

---

[345] *Yorkshire Water Services Ltd v Sun Alliance & London Ins plc* [1997] 2 Lloyd's Rep 21, CA. Clarke, 2006, 28-8G.

[346] See Simpson (ed) *Professional Negligence and Liability* (2006) 5–162 ff.

[347] *National Employers' Mutual General Ins Assn Ltd v Haydon* [1980] 2 Lloyd's Rep 149, 152.

[348] ibid.

[349] See para 13.32.

the event of a claim, the property insured shall be assumed to have the value stated therein.

(2) The Measure of Indemnity

13.98 Recoverable loss is assessed at the time it occurred.[350] Insurers undertake to hold their policyholders harmless—as if the loss had not occurred at all, and the measure of loss is analogous to that found in the law of tort. It involves 'two quite different measures of damage, or, occasionally a combination of the two. The first is to take the capital value of the property in an undamaged state and to compare it with its value in a damaged state. The second is to take the cost of repair or reinstatement. Which is appropriate will depend on a number of factors, such as the plaintiff's future intentions as to the use of the property and the reasonableness of those intentions'.[351]

13.99 In the case of real property, if policyholders intended to sell the property, the basis of assessment is the market value of the property.[352] If that was not their intention but becomes their intention as an immediate consequence of the loss, the measure is likely to be the cost of finding alternative property.[353] If their intention was to retain and use the property, the measure of indemnity is the cost of reinstatement, whether they intend to use the insurance money to reinstate the property or not.[354] As regards claimants under the insurance with a security interest in property, their loss is the amount of their debt outstanding.[355]

13.100 What is true of real property is broadly true also of other kinds of corporeal property. If the property was for sale at the time of loss, reference is made to the market. If the thing is such that there is a second-hand market, that is the relevant market; but, if there is no such market, the only way to indemnify the claimant may be to repair it (even at unreasonable cost) or to replace it with a new one.[356] When the property is fine art, and there are two markets (the auction market and the private dealers' market) it is the market where it is likely to fetch the higher price.[357] When the property is commercial, the measure of value is the value of the property as part of a going concern and not that obtainable upon a 'break-up sale' of the insured's business. Similarly, the value of components may be their value as part of a greater manufactured product.

---

[350] *Castellain v Preston* (1883) 11 QBD 380, CA.
[351] *Dodd Properties (Kent) Ltd v Canterbury CC* [1980] 1 All ER 928, 938, CA.
[352] *Leppard v Excess Insurance Co Ltd* [1979] 2 Lloyd's Rep 91, 96, CA.
[353] *Dominion Mosaics & Tile Co Ltd v Trafalgar Trucking Co Ltd* [1990] 2 All ER 246, CA.
[354] *Keystone Properties Ltd v Sun Alliance& London Ins*, 1993 SC 494.
[355] *Westminster Fire Office v Glasgow Provident Investment Sy* (1888) 13 App Cas 699.
[356] *Dominion Mosaics* (n 353 above) 255.
[357] *Quorum A/S v Schramm* [2002] 1 Lloyd's Rep 249.

When property is replaced or reinstated, the amount recoverable, it has been **13.101** said,[358] should be subject to a discount for depreciation—an allowance or deduction for the 'betterment' of the thing reinstated. On the other hand, deduction 'would be the equivalent of forcing the plaintiffs to invest money in the modernizing of their plant which might be highly inconvenient for them'.[359] Whether the doctrine of betterment still applies to insurance cases is not entirely clear, but the safer view is that it does.[360] In practice the issue is often settled by the policy, for example 'replacement cost basis' cover, or cover 'new for old'.

(3) Reinstatement

Insurers are entitled to reinstate property rather than pay insurance money under **13.102** a policy term to that effect, if any, or, if they suspect fraud or arson, under the Fires Prevention (Metropolis) Act 1774, section 83. Section 83 also obliges insurers to reinstate, if requested to reinstate by persons other than the insured but with an interest in premises damaged by fire, such as tenants[361] and mortgagees.[362] If insurers elect for reinstatement, the effect is that the insurer 'is in the same position as if he had originally contracted to do the act which he has elected to do'.[363] If, however, reinstatement becomes physically or legally impossible, the better view is that the insurer is not discharged but that the obligation to pay the loss as insurance money revives.[364] If reinstatement work is undertaken, like builders or repairers, insurers are liable, if the work is poor under legislation such as the Supply of Goods and Services Act 1982, and the Sale of Goods Act 1979. To appoint competent contractors to reinstate is not enough: insurers are responsible for the quality of the work.[365] Moreover, reinstatement must be completed within a reasonable time, otherwise the insurer is liable to pay damages to the insured for loss of use.[366]

(4) Payment

Payment must be to policyholders, or in joint insurance, to any one of them,[367] or **13.103** to any other designated persons (loss payees) such as mortgagees. If payment is

---

358 *Reynolds v Phoenix Assurance Co Ltd* [1978] 2 Lloyd's Rep 440, 450 ff.
359 *Harbutts Plasticine Ltd v Wayne Tank & Pump Co Ltd* [1970] 1 QB 447, CA.
360 See *Dominion Mosaics* (n 353 above) loc cit.
361 *Wimbledon Golf Club v Imperial Ins Co* (1902) 18 TLR 815.
362 *Sinnott v Bowden* [1912] 2 Ch 414.
363 *Brown v Royal Ins Co* (1859) 1 El & El 853, 858–859.
364 Clarke, 2006, 29-2C.
365 *Anderson v Commercial Union Assurance Co* (1885) 55 LJQB 146; *Argy Trading Development Co Ltd v Lapid Developments Ltd* [1977] 1 Lloyd's Rep 67.
366 *Davidson v Guardian Royal Exchange Assurance* [1979] 1 Lloyd's Rep 406.
367 *General Accident Fire & Life Assurance Corp Ltd v Midland Bk Ltd* [1940] 2 KB 388, CA. Cf composite insurance: *New Hampshire Ins Co v MGN Ltd* [1997] LRLR 24, CA.

made by mistake as to amount or entitlement, recovery is governed by the law of restitution.[368] Dispute settlements are stand alone contracts subject to the usual rules of contract validity and, in particular, subject to certain assumptions of risk. On the one hand, courts are 'very slow to infer that a party intended to surrender rights and claims of which he was unaware and could not have been aware'.[369] On the other, courts readily infer that insurers might well accept short-term losses for long-term gains from continued contractual relations with a particular customer or to maintain market reputation for prompt settlement. The inference is reinforced by the principle of finality and public policy to avoid unnecessary litigation.[370]

(5) Recovery by Insurers from Third Parties

13.104 Having paid claimants, insurers may wish to seek recovery from third parties. In the case of accident policies, they may seek recovery in the shoes of the claimant against persons liable to the claimant for the accident: an action in subrogation. If there is more than one insurer on risk, the one who has paid may seek contribution from any of the others.

(6) Non-payment

13.105 Express terms apart, insurance is an agreement to pay a sum on the occurrence of the insured event. In the case of contingency (non-indemnity) insurance, actions against insurers are regarded as actions for debt. Although the court has a discretion to award interest against debtors who pay late, potentially two kinds of loss are left uncompensated. First, the court has no power to award interest if the debtor pays late but before proceedings for recovery have been begun; and, secondly, interest as such does not compensate special damage over and beyond loss of the normal use of the money. However, the better view is that usual rules of remoteness of damage apply.[371]

13.106 In the case of indemnity insurance, insurance contract law differs from general contract law. The insurers' obligation to pay is regarded as an obligation to pay damages[372] for breach of contract for failure to prevent the insured suffering loss,[373] although the duty actually to pay the policyholder may be postponed, both in reality

---

[368] *Kelly v Solari* (1841) 9 M & W 54; *Lipkin Gorman v Karpnale Ltd* [1991] 2 AC 548.

[369] *Bank of Credit and Commerce International SA v Ali (No 1)* [2001] UKHL 8; [2002] 1 AC 251, [10].

[370] Eg *Barclays plc v Villers* [2001] Lloyd's Rep IR 162.

[371] See paras 21.27–21.37, 21.56–21.59.

[372] *Sprung v Royal Ins Co* [1997] CLC 70, CA.

[373] *The Italia Express* [1992] 2 Lloyd's Rep 281.

and in law, until loss has been quantified.[374] It 'is not a condition precedent. . .that the plaintiff has quantified the amount of his claim'; and 'the insurer may technically be in breach of his contract before any demand is made on him'.[375] This is not what most people might expect. If a roof is damaged by fire and the insurer elects to have it repaired but the work is done badly, that insurer, like any repairer, is liable for consequent rain damage to contents to the policyholder. If insurers elect to pay insurance money instead, but pay late with the same result, because the policyholder cannot afford to have the roof repaired, people might reasonably expect insurers to be liable for the damage. That is the law in other common law jurisdictions,[376] as well as Scotland.[377] In England that is the view of the FOS—but not the courts. A more sensible view of indemnity insurance can be based on policy terms, as well as the nature of contracts of insurance: simply that payment is not due at all until after the procedural conditions, such as notice and proof, have been satisfied. On that basis late payment puts insurers in breach of contract like any other. However, good sense has not prevailed. Although criticized,[378] the reasoning and the rule stand.

In general contract law damages are now recoverable for distress in cases of **13.107** breach of promise to ensure peace of mind or freedom from distress,[379] benefits often promised by advertisements on television promoting the sale of insurance. Such damages in insurance cases have been awarded by the FOS[380] and by courts in other countries of common law, but the limited precedent to date in England is to the contrary.[381]

In the relatively rare case of an insolvent insurer, claimants once obtained recovery **13.108** from the Policyholders Protection Board under the Policyholders Protection Act 1975, as amended in 1997. With effect from 30 November 2001 that scheme was replaced by the Financial Services Compensation Scheme (FSCS), established under Part XV of the Financial Services and Markets Act 2000. The amount recoverable varies according to the kind of policy in question.[382]

---

[374] *Virk v Gan Life Holdings plc* [2000] Lloyd's Rep IR 159, CA.
[375] *Chandris v Argo Ins Co Ltd* [1963] 2 Lloyd's Rep 65, 74. Cf *Jabbour v The Custodian of Absentee Israeli Property* [1954] 1 WLR 139, 144.
[376] Clarke, 2006, 30-9B1.
[377] *Scott Lithgow Ltd v Sec of State for Defence* (1989) 45 BLR 1, HL.
[378] See Clarke (n 376 above).
[379] See paras 21.48ff.
[380] *Ombudsman News*, January 2002.
[381] Clarke, 2006, 30-9C.
[382] See Clarke, 2006, 30-11.

14

BANKING

This chapter is concerned with private law aspects of the bank-customer relation- **14.01**
ship, together with the law relating to the main methods of payment effected
through the banking system.

A. The Bank-Customer Relationship

(1) Definition of a Bank

The terms 'bank', 'banker' and 'banking' cannot be uniformly defined for all **14.02**
purposes. It is now common for most statutes, especially those dealing with regulatory matters, to define a bank in terms of a domestic institution granted permission by the Financial Services Authority to accept deposits or an 'EEA firm'
authorized in another European Economic Area state to accept deposits and, relying on its 'single European passport', doing so in the UK.[1] Relatively few statutes
use the terms 'bank', 'banker' and 'banking' without further or proper definition.
The most important statutes that fall into this category are the Bills of Exchange
Act 1882 and the Cheques Act 1957, where a 'banker' is defined to include 'a body

---

[1] See the Financial Services and Markets Act 2000, Part IV and Sch 3.

of persons whether incorporated or not who carry on the business of banking'.[2] In such cases, it is necessary to turn to the common law for a definition of the 'business of banking'. The common law definition is also important because under the general law certain rights and duties are only conferred on a 'bank' or 'banker', eg the banker's lien,[3] the banker's right to combine accounts,[4] and the banker's duty of confidentiality.[5] The common law definition of a 'bank' is based on treating it as an institution engaged in banking business. The leading case is *United Dominion Trust v Kirkwood*,[6] where Lord Denning MR described the main facets of banking business as the conduct of current accounts, the payment of cheques and the collection of cheques for customers.[7] Diplock and Harman LJJ agreed.[8] However, their Lordships took different views to as to the importance of reputation for determining whether or not a given institution was a bank. Lord Denning was prepared to hold an institution to be a bank merely because it was so regarded in the business community,[9] Diplock LJ considered the question of reputation to be of marginal importance,[10] and Harman LJ, dissenting in the actual decision in the case, thought it irrelevant.[11] It is submitted that, in the interests of certainty, the test of whether an institution is or is not a bank should be entirely objective and should not based on subjective criteria such as reputation.

14.03 The courts have consistently held that banking business may change over time.[12] In recent years the use of cheques has declined and money is frequently transferred into and out of bank accounts using electronic means. In the light of this modern practice, it is submitted that the common law definition of the terms 'bank', 'banking' and 'banking business' should not turn on the precise mechanism by which money is paid into and out of bank accounts.[13]

14.04 An institution may be held to be a bank even though its activities are not confined to the carrying on of banking business.[14] The issue turns on whether the institution's banking business is real in terms of its entire business. It is immaterial that

---

2 Bills of Exchange Act 1882, s 2; Cheques Act 1957, s 6(1).

3 Para 14.48.

4 Paras 14.46–14.47.

5 Paras 14.40–14.45. It should be noted that a duty of confidentiality can also arise between a bank and someone who is not its customer.

6 [1966] 2 QB 431, CA.

7 At 447.

8 Diplock LJ, at 466, held them to be 'essential' characteristics.

9 At 454.

10 At 475–476.

11 At 460–461.

12 *Woods v Martins Bank Ltd* [1959] 1 QB 55, 70; *United Dominion Trust Ltd v Kirkwood*, n 6 above, 446.

13 See *Commissioners of the State Savings Bank of Victoria v Permewan, Wright & Co Ltd* (1915) 19 CLR 457, 470–471, Aust HC.

14 *Re Roe's Legal Charge* [1982] 2 Lloyd's Rep 370, CA.

the size of the institution's banking business is negligible in comparison with that of a clearing bank. It is also irrelevant that the institution does not carry on all facets of banking business and that its main activities are in different fields.

(2) Definition of a Customer

There are occasions when it is important to ascertain whether a person is or is not **14.05** a customer of a bank. First, there are particular incidents that attach to the bank-*customer* relationship, eg the bank's duty to obey its customer's mandate,[15] to exercise reasonable care and skill,[16] and the duty of confidentiality.[17] Secondly, some statutes use the term 'customer' without further definition, as is the case with s 4 of the Cheques Act 1957.[18]

A person becomes a customer of a bank either when the bank opens an account in **14.06** his name[19] or when the bank agrees to open the account in question.[20] Where a bank performs a casual service for a person, such as, for example, cashing a cheque for someone introduced by one of its customers, that person does not become a customer even if the service is performed on a regular basis.[21] The bank-customer relationship turns on the flow of funds into and out of the customer's account and the mechanisms that bring about those movements. But modern banks also offer a wide variety of other services to account and non-account holders alike, eg, financial advice, fund management, bank finance. In the broadest sense, those who receive these other services are also 'customers' of the bank. However, for the purposes of the bank-customer relationship it is the holding of an account which is critical. Both the *Banking Code* and the *Business Banking Code*, voluntary codes of best practice for banks when dealing with their personal and business customers in the UK, are primarily concerned with the account relationship.[22]

A person does not become a customer of a bank just because an account is **14.07** opened in that person's name.[23] The account must be opened with the customer's

---

[15] Paras 14.12–14.33.

[16] Paras 14.34–14.36.

[17] Paras 14.40–14.45.

[18] Para 14.67.

[19] *Lacave & Co v Crédit Lyonnais* [1887] 1 QB 148.

[20] *Ladbroke & Co v Todd* (1914) 30 TLR 433; *Woods v Martins Bank Ltd* [1959] 1 QB 55.

[21] *Great Western Railway Co v London and County Banking Co Ltd* [1901] AC 414, HL; *Taxation Comrs v English, Scottish and Australian Bank Ltd* [1920] AC 683, PC.

[22] The *Banking Code* (2005 edn) defines a 'personal customer' as 'any person who is acting for purposes which are not linked to their trade, business or profession'. The *Business Banking Code* (2005 edn) defines a 'business customer' as 'a customer who runs a non-personal account and who has a yearly trading turnover of under £1 million (or an income of under £1 million in the case of charities and clubs)'.

[23] *Stoney Stanton Supplies (Coventry) Ltd v Midland Bank Ltd* [1966] 2 Lloyd's Rep 373, CA.

authority or, if not, he must have subsequently ratified the opening of the account.[24] A person may open an account in the name of a nominee and remain the bank's customer.[25] In all cases it is important for a bank to know the identity of its customer. If the bank fails to have appropriate identification procedures in place, it risks committing an offence under legislation designed to combat money laundering. The Money Laundering Regulations 2003 require the bank to maintain identification procedures which ensure that prospective customers produce satisfactory evidence of their identity before an account is opened or other banking service provided to them.[26] There are only a limited number of exceptions to this rule, eg where the customer is another regulated bank.[27]

(3) Nature of the Bank-Customer Relationship

14.08 The relationship between bank and customer is contractual and includes the relationship of creditor and debtor with regard to the balance in the customer's bank account. The classic formulation comes from Lord Cottenham in *Foley v Hill*:[28]

> Money, when paid into a bank account, ceases altogether to be the money of the principal. . .it is then the money of the banker, who is bound to return an equivalent by paying a similar sum to that deposited with him when he is asked for it. . .The money placed in the custody of a banker is, to all intents and purposes, the money of the banker, to do with as he pleases . . .

When the account is in credit, the customer is the creditor and the bank the debtor; when the account is overdrawn, the roles are reversed.[29]

14.09 The nature of the bank-customer relationship was further analysed by the Court of Appeal in *Joachimson v Swiss Bank Corporation*.[30] Atkin LJ, giving the leading

---

[24] *Rowlandson v National Westminster Bank Ltd* [1978] 1 WLR 798.

[25] *Thavorn v Bank of Credit and Commerce International SA* [1985] 1 Lloyd's Rep 259. But where an account is opened in the name of a company, it is the company and not its sole owner that is the bank's customer: *Diamantides v JP Morgan Chase Bank* [2005] EWHC 263 (Comm), upheld on different grounds [2005] EWCA Civ 1612.

[26] SI 2003/3075, art 4(3). As from 15 December 2007, see the Money Laundering Regulations 2007, SI 2007/2157.

[27] ibid art 5.

[28] (1848) 2 HLC 28, 36.

[29] The bank is entitled to repayment of an overdraft on demand unless otherwise agreed (*Williams and Glyn's Bank v Barnes* [1981] Com LR 205). It is important to construe the terms of the facility letter under which the overdraft is granted. Facility letters are usually expressed in such a way that the bank will be held to have reserved the right to call for repayment on demand even though a fixed time period for the facility may have been indicated (*Lloyds Bank plc v Lampert* [1999] 1 All ER (Comm) 161, CA; *Bank of Ireland v AMCD (Property Holdings) Ltd* [2001] 2 All ER (Comm) 894). In exceptional circumstances, a reservation of the right to repayment on demand may be held repugnant to the agreement as a whole and be read subject to the overriding provision that the debt should be repayable at a fixed future date (*Titford Property Co Ltd v Cannon Street Acceptances Ltd*, unreported, 22 May 1975).

[30] [1921] 3 KB 110, CA.

judgment,[31] stated that there was only one contract between a bank and its customer, the implied terms of which included the following: the bank undertakes to receive money and to collect cheques for its customer's account; the proceeds so received are not held in trust by the bank but represent a loan from the customer which the bank undertakes to repay; the bank undertakes to repay on the customer's demand at the branch were the account is kept during banking hours;[32] the customer undertakes to exercise reasonable care in executing his written orders so as not to mislead the bank or to facilitate forgery. His Lordship concluded that the bank was not liable to pay its customer until he had demanded payment.

The requirement that the customer must make a demand for payment before the **14.10** bank is liable to repay sums deposited to the credit of the account is central to the operation of a current account or of a savings account which provides for payment at call.[33] The limitation period will only start to run from the day on which the amount is payable, which means that it commences on the day on which the demand is made and refused.[34] The fact that modern banks allow their customers to access their accounts at distance, for example, through the use of telephone and internet banking services, or through the use of debit cards, illustrates that the requirement to make demand at the branch where the account is keep is frequently waived.[35]

The general rule is that the contract between a bank and its customer is governed **14.11** by the law of the place where it is kept, unless there is an agreement to the contrary.[36] In the absence of contrary agreement, where the customer has accounts held at branches of the same bank located in different countries, each

---

[31] At 127.

[32] Atkin LJ left open the question whether the customer's demand for repayment must be in writing. But even a customer's irrevocable authority to a bank to accept the written demand of a particular person may be overridden by the oral instructions of the customer himself: *Morrell v Workers Savings & Loan Bank* [2007] UKPC 3 at [10].

[33] In the case of a fixed deposit, maturing at a predetermined time, the amount involved becomes payable on a designated day.

[34] *National Bank of Commerce v National Westminster Bank* [1990] 2 Lloyd's Rep 514; *Bank of Baroda v ASAA Mahomed* [1999] Lloyd's Rep (Bank) 14, CA.

[35] In Singapore it has even been tentatively suggested that, in the light of modern technological and business developments, the requirement for a demand to be made at the branch where the account is kept may no longer represent good law: *Damayanti Kantilal Doshi v Indian Bank* [1999] 4 SLR 1, 11, Sing CA.

[36] *Libyan Arab Foreign Bank v Manufacturers Hanover Trust Co* [1988] 2 Lloyd's Rep 494; *Attock Cement Co Ltd v Romanian Bank for Foreign Trade* [1989] 1 WLR 1147, CA; *Libyan Arab Foreign Bank v Manufacturers Hanover Trust Co (No 2)* [1989] 1 Lloyd's Rep 608. The Contracts (Applicable Law) Act 1990 does not alter this general rule (*Sierra Leone Telecommunications Co Ltd v Barclays Bank plc* [1998] 2 All ER 821, 827).

account will be governed by law of the country where the account-holding branch is located.[37]

(4) Bank's Duty to Honour the Customer's Mandate

(a) The duty

14.12 The bank is under an obligation to honour cheques drawn by the customer provided there are sufficient funds in the customer's account to meet the cheque or the bank has agreed to provide the customer with overdraft facilities sufficient to meet the cheque.[38] The bank may also agree to honour payment instructions delivered by other means, eg, by use of a debit card or by use of a password communicated to the bank over a telephone or internet link. The bank is probably not obliged to provide these services to its customer without special agreement, whereas it is obliged to honour cheques drawn by its customer under the express or implied terms of the bank-customer contract.[39] Where the bank honours its customer's cheque or other payment instruction it acts within its mandate and is entitled to debit the customer's account with the amount of the cheque or other instruction.[40]

(b) Limits on the duty

14.13 There are several limitations to the bank's duty to honour its customer's payment instructions.

(i) Lack of funds

14.14 The bank is obliged to honour its customer's payment instruction only if there are sufficient cleared funds in the customer account or available by way of an agreed overdraft facility.[41] Where there are insufficient funds available to cover the full amount of the customer's payment instruction, the bank may ignore it completely. The customer's payment instruction then stands as an offer to the bank to extend credit to him on the bank's standard terms as to interest and other charges, unless other terms have been agreed between them.[42] The bank may accept or reject this offer.[43]

---

[37] *Libyan Arab Foreign Bank v Bankers Trust Co* [1989] QB 728, 747, where Staughton J stressed that there was still only one contract between the bank and its customer.

[38] *Joachimson v Swiss Bank Corp*, n 30 above; *Bank of New South Wales v Laing* [1954] AC 135, 154.

[39] *Libyan Arab Foreign Bank v Bankers Trust Co*, n 37 above, 749.

[40] *Sierra Leone Telecommunication Co Ltd v Barclays Bank plc*, n 36 above, 827.

[41] n 38 above.

[42] *Emerald Meats (London) Ltd v AIB Group (UK) Ltd* [2002] EWCA Civ 460 at [12], CA; *Lloyds Bank plc v Voller* [2000] 2 All ER (Comm) 978, 982, CA; *Barclays Bank Ltd v WJ Sims, Son & Cooke (Southern) Ltd* [1980] QB 677, 699.

[43] ibid.

(ii) Unclear or irregular instructions

The customer's payment instructions must be unambiguous in form otherwise **14.15**
the bank may refuse payment.[44] Where the instructions are given by cheque, the
bank may refuse to pay if the cheque is not properly drawn.[45] In the absence of
special instructions to the contrary from their customers, it is the practice of banks
not to pay a 'stale' cheque, ie one presented for payment six months or more after
the date written on it. The practice is so widespread that there is probably a term
implied into the bank—customer contract that the bank may refuse to honour a
cheque if not presented until an unreasonable time after its date.

(iii) Unauthorized instructions

Where a bank has reasonable grounds for believing that there is a serious or real **14.16**
possibility that a payment instruction has been given without the proper authority of its customer, although it is regular and in accordance with the mandate, the
bank is justified in refusing to honour the instruction—the bank would be in
breach of duty to its customer if, without inquiry, it did otherwise.[46] Similarly,
where a bank has serious grounds for doubting the continuing authority of those
operating the account on behalf of the customer, the bank is entitled, and indeed
bound, to refuse to honour their payment instructions, at least until the court
determines the identity of the authorized signatories or the signatories are able to
provide the bank with adequate evidence of continuing authority.[47]

(iv) Renders the bank liable to a third party

A bank is entitled, and indeed bound, to refuse to pay a payment instruction **14.17**
where to do so would render it liable as an accessory to misfeasance or breach of
trust.[48] The bank must have positive evidence of misfeasance or breach of trust:
mere suspicion is not enough to refuse its customer's instructions.[49]

(v) Renders the bank criminally liable

A bank must freeze an account where it knows or suspects that the account **14.18**
contains the proceeds of crime.[50] The bank does not act in breach of contract by

---

[44] *London Joint Stock Bank Ltd v Macmillan* [1918] AC 777, 815, HL.

[45] *Cunliffe Brooks & Co v Blackburn and District Benefit Building Society* (1884) 9 App Cas 857,
864, HL.

[46] *Barclays Bank plc v Quincecare Ltd* [1992] 4 All ER 363, 375–376; *Lipkin Gorman (a firm) v
Karpnale Ltd* [1992] 4 All ER 409, 439, 441, CA. See para 14.36.

[47] *Sierra Leone Telecommunications Co Ltd v Barclays Bank plc*, n 36 above.

[48] *Royal Brunei Airlines Sdn Bhd v Tan* [1995] 2 AC 378, PC.

[49] *TTS International v Cantrade Private Bank* (1995), unreported decision of the Royal Court of
Jersey.

[50] *Squirrell Ltd v National Westminster Bank plc* [2005] EWHC 664 (Ch); [2006] 1 WLR 637,
considering s 328 of the Proceeds of Crime Act 2002 (facilitation offence).

refusing to honour its customer's payment instructions where it is suspicious that the money in the account is criminal property.[51]

(vi) Third party debt orders

14.19 A third party debt order, formerly called a 'garnishee order', is an order of the court granted to a judgment creditor, which attaches to funds held by a third party (eg a bank) who owes money to the judgment debtor (eg the bank's customer).[52] Once an interim order is served on the bank, it must not make any payment from its customer's account that reduces the balance below the amount specified in the order. Should the court make the order final,[53] the bank will be ordered to pay over the amount specified in the order to the judgment creditor. Compliance with the final order discharges the bank's indebtedness to its own customer.[54]

(vii) Freezing injunctions

14.20 Where a bank has notice of a freezing injunction directed to its customer, the bank's duty to honour the customer's mandate is suspended.[55] However, the terms of the injunction may allow payment of trade creditors in the ordinary course of business.[56] Further, cheques supported by cheque guarantee cards, and drawn prior to the date the order is served on the bank, fall outside the ambit of the injunction. As the bank is entitled and bound to honour its own collateral obligation to the third party (made via the cheque guarantee card) to pay the cheque, it may debit its customer's account accordingly.[57] Similarly, freezing injunctions have been held not to affect a bank's duty to make payment under letters of credit, negotiable instruments and documentary collections, save in very exceptional circumstances.[58] The courts are most reluctant to grant a freezing injunction

---

[51] *K Ltd v National Westminster Bank plc* [2006] EWCA Civ 1039; [2007] 1 WLR 311, where it was held that the bank does not have to adduce evidence to support any such suspicion or show that there were reasonable grounds for the suspicion.

[52] Part 72 of the Civil Procedure Rules 1998. See also *Alawiye v Mahamood* [2005] EWHC 277 (Ch); [2006] 3 All ER 668 (on evidence relating to state of judgment debtor's account).

[53] A court will not make the order final where there is a prior equitable charge or flawed asset arrangement over the account: *Fraser v Oystertec plc* [2004] EWHC 1582 (Ch); [2005] BPIR 381; nor will it do so where the account in question is held at an overseas branch or bank: *Société Eram Shipping Co Ltd v Compagnie Internationale de Navigation* [2003] UKHL 30; [2004] 1 AC 260; *Kuwait Oil Tanker Co SAK v Qabazard* [2003] UKHL 31; [2004] 1 AC 300.

[54] But there is no discharge if the bank pays in reliance on only an interim order: *Crantrave Ltd v Lloyds TSB Bank plc* [2000] QB 917, CA.

[55] *Z Ltd v A-Z and AA-LL* [1982] QB 558, CA. But a bank given notice of the grant of a freezing injunction does not owe the successful applicant a duty to take reasonable care to comply with its terms: *Customs and Excise Commissioners v Barclays Bank plc* [2006] UKHL 28; [2007] 1 AC 181.

[56] *Iraqi Ministry of Defence v Arcepey Shipping Co SA* [1981] QB 65.

[57] *Z Ltd v A-Z and AA-LL*, n 55 above, at 592–593.

[58] ibid; *Lewis & Peat (Produce) Ltd v Almatu Properties Ltd* [1993] 2 Bank LR 45, CA.

against a bank itself as this would affect the bank's ability to pay its creditors their due debts.[59]

(viii) Customer's death or insanity

Under s 75(2) of the Bills of Exchange Act 1882, the bank's duty and authority **14.21** to pay cheques is terminated when it obtains notice of the customer's death. This section overrides the general rule that an agent's authority is automatically determined by the principal's death. As the bank-customer relationship is not purely one of principal and agent, it is submitted that notice of the customer's insanity, and not merely the insanity itself, terminates the bank's authority to pay.[60]

(ix) Winding up or bankruptcy of customer

By s 127 of the Insolvency Act 1986, in a winding up of a company by the court, **14.22** any disposition of the company's property made after the commencement of the winding-up is, unless the court otherwise orders, void. Payments into an account in credit have been held not to constitute dispositions of the company's property as the amount standing to the credit of the customer's account is increased.[61] Payments into an overdrawn account do constitute dispositions of the company's property and are void under s 127 unless validated by the court.[62] Payments made out of a company's bank account, whether the account is in credit or overdrawn, have been held not to constitute a disposition of the company's property to the bank, which merely acts as the company's agent in making a disposition in favour of the third party.[63] In any event, a bank is well advised to ask the company for a validation order under s 127 before allowing it to continue to operate the account. If a disposition is made in good faith in the ordinary course of business when the parties are unaware of the presentation of the petition, and it is completed before the winding up order is made, the court is likely to validate it.[64] Similar principles apply in the case of the bankruptcy of a customer.[65]

---

[59] *Polly Peck International plc v Nadir (No 2)* [1992] 4 All ER 769, CA; *Camdex International Ltd v Bank of Zambia (No 2)* [1997] 1 All ER 728, CA.

[60] But the position may be different were an order has been made under the Mental Capacity Act 2005: see AG Guest, *Chalmers and Guest on Bills of Exchange and Cheques* (16th edn, 2005), para 13–047.

[61] *Re Barn Crown Ltd* [1994] 4 All ER 42.

[62] *Re Gray's Inn Construction Ltd* [1980] 1 WLR 711, CA.

[63] *Hollicourt (Contracts) Ltd v Bank of Ireland* [2001] Ch 555, CA, endorsing the ruling of Lightman J in *Coutts & Co v Stock* [2000] 1 WLR 906.

[64] Unless it can be challenged as a preference: *Re Tain Construction Ltd* [2003] BPIR 1188.

[65] Insolvency Act 1986, s 284.

(x) Countermand

14.23 Under s 75(1) of the Bills of Exchange Act 1882, the bank's authority or mandate to pay a cheque drawn on it by its customer is determined by countermand of payment. Notice of countermand must be clear and unambiguous,[66] and it must be brought to the actual (not merely constructive) notice of the bank.[67] Unless otherwise agreed, notice of countermand must be given to the branch of the bank were the account is kept.[68] Where a customer is given access to his account by other means, eg, by debit card or through telephone or internet banking services, the specific contract allowing such access will usually contain express provision dealing with countermand. The terms of issue of a cheque guarantee card will usually prohibit countermand of a cheque supported by the card.

(c) Remedies for wrongful dishonour of customer's mandate

14.24 Wrongful dishonour of the customer's cheque or other payment instruction will render the bank liable in damages for breach of contract. For many years the amount of damages recoverable by the customer differed according to whether he was a trader or a non-trader. Where the customer was a trader he could recover substantial damages for injury to his credit and reputation without proof of actual loss,[69] but where he was a non-trader he could only recover nominal damages for breach of contract, unless he proved actual loss.[70] However, the distinction between traders and non-traders was swept away in *Kpohraror v Woolwich Building Society*,[71] where the Court of Appeal held that in every case—trader and non-trader alike—there is a presumption of fact that the customer suffers some injury to his credit and reputation when his cheque is wrongfully dishonoured.

14.25 A bank which wrongfully dishonours its customer's cheque may also be liable to its customer, the drawer, in defamation. It is standard banking practice for the drawer's bank to note the reason for dishonour on the cheque, and this statement will be passed back to the collecting bank and the holder of the cheque. Where the drawer's bank implies that the cheque was dishonoured for supposed lack of funds (eg, by using the now notorious phrase 'refer to drawer'—held to be potentially defamatory by the jury in *Jayson v Midland Bank Ltd*),[72] the drawer will have an action for defamation against his bank should it turn out that the cheque was

---

66 *Westminster Bank v Hilton* (1926) 43 TLR 124, HL.
67 *Curtice v London City and Midland Bank Ltd* [1908] 1 KB 293, CA.
68 *London, Provincial and South Western Bank Ltd v Buszard* (1918) 35 TLR 142.
69 *Wilson v United Counties Bank Ltd* [1920] AC 102, 112, HL.
70 *Gibbons v Westminster Bank* [1939] 2 KB 882; *Rae v Yorkshire Bank plc* [1988] FLR 1, CA.
71 [1996] 4 All ER 119, CA.
72 [1968] 1 Lloyd's Rep 409.

wrongfully dishonoured. Dishonour of a cheque without stating a reason is probably not defamatory.[73]

(d) Defences

Common law and equity confer certain defences on a bank charged with having **14.26** breached its duty to honour its customer's mandate. Those statutory defences available to a bank upon which a cheque is drawn are considered later in this chapter.[74]

(i) Breach of duty

The customer owes a duty to his bank to exercise reasonably care when drawing a **14.27** cheque (or other payment order) so as not to facilitate fraud or forgery.[75] The customer will be held responsible for any loss sustained by the bank as a result of his breach of duty. The test is whether the customer was careless, and this must be assessed in the light of all the circumstances.[76] The duty is of narrow scope. Negligence which is not connected with the actual drawing of the cheque or other payment order does not usually afford a defence to the bank.[77]

(ii) Estoppel

The customer may be precluded (estopped) by his conduct from denying that a **14.28** payment was authorized. The customer may have made an explicit representation to the bank to that effect.[78] Alternatively, the customer may have failed to inform the bank of forgeries or other fraudulent use of his account as soon as he became aware of it.[79] The customer must have actual knowledge of the fraud or forgery, constructive knowledge, in the sense of merely having the means of knowledge, is not enough.[80]

(iii) Wider duty?

In *Tai Hing Cotton Mill Ltd v Liu Chong Hing Bank Ltd*,[81] the Privy Council **14.29** rejected the idea that a customer owes his bank a wider duty to run his business

---

73 *Frost v London Joint Stock Bank Ltd* (1906) 22 TLR 760, CA.

74 Paras 14.62–14.63.

75 *London Joint Stock Bank Ltd v Macmillan* [1918] AC 777, HL. See also the *Banking Code* and the *Business Banking Code* (2005 edns), para 12.6.

76 *Slingsby v District Bank Ltd* [1931] 2 KB 588, affd [1932] 1 KB 544; cf *Lumsden & Co v London Trustee Savings Bank* [1971] 1 Lloyd's Rep 114, 121.

77 *Bank of Ireland v Evans' Trustees* (1855) 5 HLC 389.

78 *Brown v Westminster Bank Ltd* [1964] 2 Lloyd's Rep 187.

79 *Greenwood v Martins Bank Ltd* [1933] AC 51, HL.

80 *Price Meats Ltd v Barclays Bank plc* [2002] 2 All ER (Comm) 346; *Patel v Standard Charetered Bank* [2001] 1 Lloyd's Rep 229.

81 [1986] AC 80. See also *Lewes Sanitary Steam Co Ltd v Barclay & Co Ltd* (1906) 95 LT 444; *Kepitigalla Rubber Estates Ltd v National Bank of India Ltd* [1909] 2 KB 1010.

in such a way as to make it difficult for fraud to occur,[82] or that he owes a duty to check his periodic bank statements to identify the fraudulent use of his account at an early stage and thereby prevent further fraud.[83] These duties were not to be implied into the bank-customer contract and did not arise in tort. Lord Scarman, delivering the advice of the Privy Council, said that the solution was for banks to increase the severity of their terms of business,[84] eg, through the use of 'verification clauses' which require the customer to notify the bank within a specific time of any errors in his bank statement, which would otherwise be deemed correct.[85]

14.30   Where banks give customers access to their accounts by remote means, eg through the use of debit cards or through the operation of telephone and internet banking services, the terms and conditions of the specific contracts under which those services are provided usually impose obligations on the customer to look after their personal identification numbers, passwords and other security information, or risk being held liable for loss caused by unauthorized use of the remote access system.[86]

(iv) Ratification

14.31   Ratification may occur where a bank pays a cheque drawn in breach of mandate but the customer nevertheless approves the transaction or the breach of mandate, or elects to treat the transaction as valid.[87]

(v) Liggett defence

14.32   A bank may be able to raise a defence to the customer's claim that his account was wrongly debited by pleading that the payment was made for the benefit of the customer in payment of his debts. This is known as the *Liggett* defence, taking its

---

82   The extent to which a bank could claim that the customer is to be held vicariously liable for his employee's fraud remains uncertain: the defence was pleaded but not pursued in *Tai Hing*. The defence gains support from dicta of Richmond J in *National Bank of New Zealand Ltd v Walpole and Paterson Ltd* [1975] 2 NZLR 7, 14, and that of La Forest J, dissenting, in *Boma Manufacturing Ltd v Canadian Imperial Bank of Commerce* (1996) 140 DLR (4th) 463, 499. See *Crédit Lyonnais Bank Nederland NV v Export Credit Guarantee Department* [2000] AC 486, HL.

83   See also *Wealdon Woodlands (Kent) Ltd v National Westminster Bank Ltd* (1983) 133 NLJ 719; *Canadian Pacific Hotels Ltd v Bank of Montreal* (1987) 40 DLR (4th) 385, Sup Ct; cf Uniform Commercial Code, s 4–406(f).

84   At 106.

85   But note that the verification clauses in *Tai Hing* were held to be ineffective on grounds of construction (see also *Financial Institutions Services Ltd v Negril Negril Holdings Ltd* [2004] UKPC 40). There could also be problems with the Unfair Contract Terms Act 1977, s 13(1)(c), and the Unfair Terms in Consumer Contracts Regulations 1999, SI 1999/2083, Sch 2, para 1(q).

86   See the *Banking Code* and the *Business Banking Code* (2005 edns), paras 12.5 and 12.11.

87   *London Intercontinental Trust Ltd v Barclays Bank Ltd* [1980] 1 Lloyd's Rep 241; *HJ Symons & Co v Barclays Bank plc* [2003] EWHC 1249 (Comm); cf *Limpgrange Ltd v BCCI SA* [1986] Fin LR 36. A forged signature cannot be ratified (*Brook v Hook* (1871) LR 6 Ex 89), but it may be 'adopted' by the customer (*Greenwood v Martins Bank Ltd* [1932] 1 KB 371, 379, *per* Scrutton LJ).

name from *Liggett (Liverpool) Ltd v Barclays Bank Ltd*.[88] In that case the bank was in breach of mandate because it honoured cheques signed by only one director of its corporate customer when signatures of two directors were required. The cheques were drawn in favour of the customer's creditors. Wright J held that the bank was entitled to debit the customer's account because the payments discharged the customer's debts and the bank was entitled to take over (ie to be subrogated to) the creditors' remedies against the customer. *Liggett* can be explained as reversing the unjust enrichment of the customer at the expense of the bank, the unjust factor being the bank's mistake.[89]

The *Liggett* defence rarely succeeds. It is a well established rule that the payment **14.33** of another's debt does not discharge that debt unless the payment is authorized, ratified or made under legal compulsion or by necessity.[90] In *Re Cleadon Trust Ltd*,[91] a majority of the Court of Appeal considered that the decision in *Liggett* could be upheld only on the basis that the bank had been expressly authorized to pay by one of the company's directors, and that the director himself had the company's authority to do this, even though the director was not authorized to draw a cheque on the company's account for that purpose on his signature alone.[92] The majority's reasoning has since been applied by the Court of Appeal in *Crantrave Ltd v Lloyds TSB Bank* plc,[93] where it was held that the *Liggett* defence arises only where the payment from the account is applied to reduce the customer's debt with the customer's authority, or if the customer has ratified the payment.[94] This means that the *Liggett* defence would not be available where the bank ignored the customer's earlier, effective countermand of a payment instruction, there being no authority to discharge the customer's debt.[95]

(5) Bank's Duty of Care

It is an implied term of the bank-customer contract that the bank will exercise rea- **14.34** sonable care and skill when carrying out operations that fall within that contract.[96]

---

88 [1928] 1 KB 48.
89 See generally para 18.216.
90 See, eg, *Belshaw v Bush* (1851) 11 CB 191.
91 [1939] Ch 286.
92 Reasoning which is itself open to challenge: see C Mitchell, *The Law of Subrogation* (1994), 128–129.
93 [2000] QB 917.
94 It should be noted, however, that Pill and May LJJ also considered that the bank might have a defence to a claim for breach of mandate where it could be established on the evidence that the customer had been 'unjustly enriched' by the unauthorized payment (ibid 924 and 925). See also *Majesty Restaurant Pty Ltd v Commonwealth Bank of Australia Ltd* (1999) 47 NSWLR 593.
95 *Liggett* can be distinguished from *Barclays Bank Ltd v WJ Simms Son & Cooke (Southern) Ltd* [1980] QB 677, 700, on this reasoning.
96 Supply of Goods and Services Act 1982, s 13.

The standard of reasonable care and skill is an objective standard applicable to banks.[97] The duty may also arise concurrently in tort.[98] But where the bank provides specialist banking services to financially sophisticated customers under the terms of contractual documentation drafted by specialist lawyers, the court will be slow to find a duty of care in tort going beyond the rights and obligations carefully set out in the documents.[99] In those exceptional cases where a bank and its customer are in a fiduciary relationship, a duty of care may be imposed as a matter of fiduciary law.[100]

14.35 The bank's duty to exercise reasonable care and skill may also arise when services are provided outside a contractual relationship. Thus, a bank may be held liable in tort for negligent advice/misstatements made to customers,[101] and to non-customers, under the *Hedley Byrne* principle.[102] The House of Lords has held that the *Hedley Byrne* principle extends beyond negligent advice/misstatements so that it can apply to economic loss caused by negligent provision of services, and that the basis of a *Hedley Byrne* claim is an assumption of responsibility by the defendant to the claimant.[103] The fact that the bank accepts a request for advice is strong evidence of an assumption of responsibility, although an antecedent request for advice is not necessary where the advice is given within the scope of the bank's business.[104] Where a bank assumes a duty to exercise reasonable care in giving advice and complies with that duty, it does not assume a further continuing obligation to keep the advice under review and, if necessary, correct it in the light of supervening events.[105] Furthermore, a bank will not be liable where information or advice supplied by it to a customer is passed on without the bank's knowledge to third parties who rely on it.[106]

---

97 *Selangor United Rubber Estates Ltd v Cradock (a bankrupt) (No 3)* [1968] 1 WLR 1555.

98 *Henderson v Merrett Syndicates Ltd* [1995] 2 AC 145, HL.

99 *IFE Fund SA v Goldman Sachs International* [2006] EWHC 2887 (Comm); [2007] 1 Lloyd's Rep 264 at [63] affd [2007] EWCA Civ 811. But see also *Sumitomo Bank Ltd v Banque Bruxelles Lambert SA* [1997] 1 Lloyd's Rep 487, 513.

100 See para 14.38.

101 *Box v Midland Bank Ltd* [1979] 2 Lloyd's Rep 391.

102 *Hedley Byrne & Co Ltd v Heller & Partners Ltd* [1964] AC 465, HL, where a bank only avoided liability for negligent advice given about a customer's credit-worthiness in a bank reference provided to a third party because of its disclaimer. See generally paras 17.171–17.181.

103 *Henderson v Merrett Syndicates Ltd*, n 98 above; *Williams v Natural Life Health Foods Ltd* [1998] 1 WLR 830, HL. But in *Customs & Excise Commissioners v Barclays Bank plc* [2006] UKHL 28; [2007] 1 AC 181, the House of Lords held that, in cases of pure economic loss, an 'assumption of responsibility' was a sufficient, but not a necessary, condition for the imposition of a duty of care: whether there was a duty of care could also turn on the threefold test of foreseeability, proximity and whether it was fair, just and reasonable to impose the duty.

104 *Morgan v Lloyds Bank plc* [1998] Lloyd's Rep (Bank) 73, 80, CA.

105 *Fennoscandia Ltd v Clarke* [1999] 1 All ER (Comm) 365, CA.

106 *Mann v Coutts & Co* [2003] EWHC 2138 (Comm); [2004] 1 All ER (Comm) 1, applying *Caparo Industries plc v Dickman* [1990] 2 AC 605, HL, the leading case on auditors' negligence. Contrast *Riyad Bank v Ahli United Bank (UK) plc* [2006] EWCA Civ 780; [2006] 2 Lloyd's Rep 292,

The bank's duty to honour its customer's mandate and its duty to exercise reason- **14.36**
able care and skill in the execution of its customer's order to transfer money may
sometimes conflict. The problem could arise, for example, where the director of a
company is authorized to draw cheques on the company's account, but does so to
defraud the company. Where the account is in credit, the bank's primary obligation is to honour cheques drawn within the bank's mandate, but the bank would
act in breach of its duty of care owed to its customer if it honoured a cheque knowing the authorized signatory was defrauding that customer, or if it turned a blind
eye to the obvious.[107] In other cases, the bank would be in breach of its duty of
care, and so should refrain from executing an order, where it has reasonable
grounds (although not necessarily proof) for believing that the order was an
attempt to misappropriate funds.[108] Whether the bank has such reasonable
grounds for belief is to be assessed on an objective basis according to the standards
of the ordinary prudent banker.[109] It has been held that where the signatory of a
cheque is not necessarily the account holder,[110] or the signatory of the cheque is
not the only person who is liable on it,[111] then 'the possibility of fraud is always
more likely to be present'.[112] By contrast, where the apparent signatory of the
cheque is himself the account holder, then 'if the bank has no reason not to believe
the signatory to be genuine, no question on the face of it can arise of some fraud
being committed on the signatory'.[113] Similarly, if one joint account holder was
entitled under the mandate to draw on the account in his name alone, and he did
so in breach of a private agreement with the other account holders, it is unlikely
that the bank would be held to be in breach of a duty of care owed to the other
account holders unless the bank had some reason for supposing that the mandate
was being abused by the joint account holder.[114]

---

where it was held to have been obvious that advice given by the bank would be passed on to a third
party who would be likely to act on it.

[107] *Lipkin Gorman (a firm) v Karpnale Ltd* [1989] 1 WLR 1340, 1356, 1372, 1377, CA; *Barclays
Bank plc v Quincecare* [1992] 4 All ER 363, 376.

[108] ibid.

[109] ibid.

[110] As in *Barclays Bank plc v Quincecare*, n 107 above.

[111] As in *Lipkin Gorman (a firm) v Karpnale Ltd*, n 107 above.

[112] *Verjee v CIBC Bank & Trust Co (Channel Islands) Ltd* [2001] Lloyd's Rep (Bank) 279, 282.
But full weight must also be given to the principle 'that trust, not distrust, is. . .the basis of a bank's
dealings with its customers' (*Quincecare*, n 107 above, 376; applied in *Izodia v Royal Bank of Scotland
International Ltd*, unreported, 1 August 2006, Royal Court of Jersey: noted (2007) 3 JIBFL 143).

[113] ibid.

[114] *Royal Bank of Scotland plc v Fielding* [2004] EWCA Civ 64 at [107]–[108].

(6) Bank's Fiduciary Duties

14.37 The core banking activities of deposit-taking and lending are not fiduciary in character.[115] It is well-established that 'on the face of it the relationship between a bank and its customer is not a fiduciary relationship'.[116] A fiduciary is expected to act selflessly, whereas a bank can usually be expected to further its own commercial interests ahead of those of its customer.[117] Some other activities that modern multifunctional banks engage in are more obviously fiduciary in character, eg, where a bank acts as a trustee of an investment fund, or where a bank has power to manage its customer's investments under the terms of a discretionary management agreement. But even then, it always remains open to the bank to exclude or modify the fiduciary obligations that it would otherwise owe through the terms of the underlying contract under which the services are provided.[118]

14.38 In an exceptional case a bank might be held to owe fiduciary obligations to its customer where it knows that the customer is placing his trust and confidence in the bank and is relying on it. This was the explanation given by Salmon J in *Woods v Martins Bank Ltd*[119] when holding that the defendant bank was liable for advice given to the financially naïve claimant to invest in a company that had a substantial overdraft with the bank. Liability would be much more likely to be imposed today under the *Hedley Byrne* principle[120] without reference to fiduciary concepts.[121] Nevertheless, the possibility remains that a fiduciary relationship might arise in those rare cases where the customer has placed trust and confidence in the bank so as to give it influence over him.[122]

---

[115] *Foley v Hill*, n 28 above.

[116] *Governor and Company of the Bank of Scotland v A Ltd* [2001] EWCA Civ 52; [2001] Lloyd's Rep (Bank) 73 at [25], *per* Lord Woolf CJ.

[117] In *National Westminster Bank plc v Morgan* [1983] 3 All ER 85, 91, Dunn LJ famously observed that banks 'are not charitable institutions'.

[118] *Kelly v Cooper* [1993] AC 205, 214–215, PC; *Henderson v Merrett Syndicates Ltd* [1995] 2 AC 145, 206, HL. The technique is subject to the usual statutory controls as found in the Unfair Contract Terms Act 1977 and the Unfair Terms in Consumer Contract Regulations 1999 (the legislation does not apply to trust instruments because a trust instrument is not a 'contract': *Baker v JE Baker & Co (Transport) Ltd* [2006] EWCA Civ 464). Provisional recommendations by the Law Commission to prohibit professional trustees from relying on clauses to exclude or limit liability for breach of trust arising from negligence were abandoned in its final report: *Trustee Exemption Clauses* (Law Com 301, 2006), para 6.53.

[119] [1959] 1 QB 55. *Woods* pre-dates *Hedley Byrne*.

[120] *Hedley Byrne & Co Ltd v Heller & Partners Ltd*, n 102 above.

[121] As it was in *Verity & Spindler v Lloyds Bank plc* [1995] CLC 1557, in many ways a similar case to *Woods*.

[122] See *Lloyds Bank Ltd v Bundy* [1975] QB 326, CA, where the unusual circumstances of the case were expressly recognized by the court itself (at 340 and 347). Contrast, *National Westminster Bank plc v Morgan* [1985] AC 686, HL, resg [1983] 3 All ER 85.

It is important to distinguish between those situations where a bank is held **14.39**
liable for breach of fiduciary duty and where a bank becomes liable 'as a constructive trustee'. The bank can be held liable as a constructive trustee either
because it has beneficially received misapplied trust property,[123] or because it
has assisted or otherwise been an accessory to another's breach of trust, when
it might not have received any property at all.[124] The bank is liable for receipt
only if the state of its knowledge is such as to make it unconscionable for the bank
to retain the benefit of the receipt;[125] it is liable as an accessory only where it has
acted dishonestly.[126]

(7) Bank's Duty of Confidentiality

(a) The duty

It was established in *Tournier v National Provincial and Union Bank of England* **14.40**
that a bank is under a common law duty of confidentiality, arising out of an
implied term of the bank-customer contract, in relation to information concerning its customer and his affairs which it acquired in the character of his
banker.[127] The duty extends to all information gained by virtue of the banking

---

[123] See *Agip (Africa) Ltd v Jackson* [1990] Ch 265, 292, where Millett J (obiter) stressed that
paying and collecting banks would not normally be brought within the receipt category because
they do not generally receive money for their own benefit, acting only as their customer's agent,
but that the position would be otherwise if the collecting bank used the money to reduce or discharge
the customer's overdraft (and there must also be a conscious appropriation of the sum paid into
the account in reduction of the overdraft: PJ Millett, 'Tracing the Proceeds of Fraud' (1991) 107
LQR 71, 83, n 46). See generally para 18.247.

[124] Hence why it is misleading to describe the bank as a 'constructive trustee': see, eg, *Dubai
Aluminium Co Ltd v Salaam* [2002] UKHL 48; [2003] 2 AC 366 at [141], *per* Lord Millett.

[125] *Bank of Credit and Commerce International (Overseas) Ltd v Akindele* [2001] Ch 437, 455,
CA. See also *Criterion Properties plc v Stratford UK Properties LLC* [2003] EWCA Civ 1883; [2003]
1 WLR 2108 at [38], affd on different grds [2004] UKHL 28; [2004] 1 WLR 1846; *Crown Dilmun v
Sutton* [2004] EWHC 52 (Ch); [2004] 1 BCLC 468 at [200]; cf *Papamichael v National Westminster
Bank plc* [203] EWHC 164 (Comm); [2003] 1 Lloyd's Rep 341 at [247]. See paras 18.50–18.51.

[126] *Royal Brunei Airlines v Tan* [1995] 2 AC 378, 389, 392, PC. Dishonesty in this context means
that the defendant knew of the elements of the transaction which made it dishonest according to
normally accepted standards of behaviour even though he may not himself have been conscious that
the transaction was dishonest: *Twinsectra Ltd v Yardley* [2002] UKHL 12; [2002] 2 AC 164, HL, as
explained in *Barlow Clowes International Ltd v Eurotrust International Ltd* [2005] UKPC 27, [2006]
1 All ER (Com) 478, and in *Abou-Rahmah v Abacha* [2006] EWCA Civ 1492; [2007] 1 Lloyd's
Rep 115. See paras 17.381–17.384.

[127] [1924] 1 KB 461, CA. Cf R Cranston, *Principles of Banking Law* (2nd edn, 2002) 171–174,
where the bank's duty of confidentiality is located within the general principles governing breach
of confidence rather than treated as a discrete area of law. In any event, those general principles, set
out by Lord Goff in *A-G v Guardian Newspapers Ltd (No 2)* [1990] 1 AC 109, 281–282, can be
used to protect confidential information revealed to a bank by a customer in a non-banking context
(eg when the bank provides investment advice or asset management services) or by a non-customer
(eg when presenting a business plan to secure bank finance). The bank may also give an express
undertaking to keep such information confidential.

relationship and is not limited to information from or about the account itself.[128] The bank remains subject to the duty even after the termination of the bank-customer relationship in respect of information acquired by the bank during the currency of that relationship. The courts take a common sense approach when deciding which information is caught by the duty. It has been held, for example, that a bank did not breach the duty by revealing information to someone who had already obtained it from another source, in this case, under the statutory scheme for the registration and cancellations of cautions over land.[129]

(b) Qualifications

14.41 The bank's duty of confidentiality is not absolute but is a qualified one. It does not exist in the four exceptional circumstances identified by Bankes LJ in *Tournier*.[130]

(i) Where disclosure is under compulsion of law

14.42 There are now over 20 statutes under which disclosure can be compelled. The list includes the Banker's Book Evidence Act 1879, s 7 (orders for inspection may be made in civil or criminal proceedings); the Police and Criminal Evidence Act 1984, s 9 (a bank may be ordered to produce documents for the purposes of a criminal investigation);[131] the Insolvency Act 1986, ss 236 and 366 (a bank can be compelled to disclose information about the affairs of insolvent customers); the Financial Services and Markets Act 2000, Part XI (powers to order disclosure of information in connection with the exercise of the Financial Services Authority's functions and to aid investigations).[132] Legislation to combat money laundering and the financing of terrorist activities is particularly draconian. A bank commits an offence if it fails to disclose to the police its knowledge or suspicion, or that it has reasonable grounds for knowledge or suspicion, that a customer is engaged in money laundering or terrorist offences.[133] Such disclosure is a 'protected

---

[128] The judgments of Bankes LJ (at 473) and Atkin LJ (at 485) being preferred to that of Scrutton LJ (at 481) on this point. See also Lord Donaldson MR in *Barclays Bank plc v Taylor* [1989] 3 All ER 563, 565.

[129] *Christofi v Barclays Bank plc* [1999] 2 All ER (Comm) 417, CA: the Court of Appeal added that the situation would be otherwise where the bank had expressly undertaken not to reveal the information.

[130] n 127 above, at 472–473. The general duty and its qualifications are also set out in the *Banking Code* and the *Business Banking Code* (2005 edns), para 11. Personal data relating to customers who are natural persons is held by a bank subject to the Data Protection Act 1998.

[131] *Barclays Bank plc v Taylor*, n 128 above, CA: bank owes no duty to customer to oppose application for disclosure or to inform him that application has been made. Cf *Robertson v Canadian Imperial Bank of Commerce* [1994] 1 WLR 1493, PC: bank might be under a duty to use best endeavours to inform customer of service of witness summons.

[132] Section 175(5) provides specific grounds upon which banks can object to disclosure: in practice they are unlikely to enable a bank to refuse disclosure although they ensure such disclosure does not constitute a breach of the duty of confidentiality.

[133] Proceeds of Crime Act 2002, s 330; Terrorism Act 2000, s 21A, as inserted by the Anti-terrorism, Crime and Security Act 2001, Sch 2, Pt 3.

disclosure', ie it 'is not to be taken to breach any restriction on the disclosure of information (however arising)'.[134] Banks may also be the subject of *Norwich Pharmacal* orders,[135] *Bankers Trust* orders[136] and disclosure orders made in aid of a tracing claim.[137]

(ii) Where there is a duty to the public to disclose

Whereas the first qualification *requires* information to be disclosed by the bank, this qualification *permits* disclosure by the bank. However, given the number of statutes which require or permit disclosure by a bank, this second qualification is of only limited value. There are few cases where the courts have had to adjudicate on the propriety of disclosure by a bank under this qualification. In *Libyan Arab Foreign Bank v Bankers Trust Co*,[138] Staughton J was of the tentative opinion that the qualification justified disclosure of customer information by the bank in New York to the US regulatory authorities. In *Pharaon v Bank of Credit and Commerce International SA (in liquidation)*,[139] Rattee J held that the public interest in upholding the bank's duty of confidentiality was subject to being overridden by the greater public interest in making confidential documents relating to the alleged fraud of an international bank available to the parties to private foreign proceedings for the purpose of uncovering that fraud.

14.43

(iii) Where the interests of the bank require disclosure

In *Tournier*,[140] Bankes LJ said the qualification would apply, for example, when, in order to claim repayment of an overdraft, the bank disclosed that the customer's account was overdrawn. But the self-serving nature of this qualification makes it the most controversial.[141] In *Sutherland v Barclays Bank Ltd*[142] it was held that the qualification justified disclosure of information by the bank to the customer's husband when the bank's reputation was questioned by him. This qualification cannot be used to justify the transfer of customer information to other companies for marketing purposes.[143]

14.44

---

[134] Proceeds of Crime Act 2002, 337(1); Terrorism Act 2000, s 21B(1), as inserted.
[135] Para 22.55.
[136] *Bankers Trust Co v Shapira* [1980] 1 WLR 1277, CA.
[137] See *AJ Bekhor & Co Ltd v Bilton* [1981] QB 923, 953–955, CA.
[138] [1988] 1 Lloyd's Rep 259.
[139] [1998] 4 All ER 455.
[140] n 127 above, 473.
[141] See Cranston, n 127 above, 174–176.
[142] (1938) 5 LDAB 163, CA, where it was also said that the disclosure was justified on grounds of implied consent (wife allowed husband to join telephone conversation with bank).
[143] *Banking Code* and *Business Banking Code* (2005 edns), paras 8.3 and 11.1. See also the Data Protection Act 1998, s 11(1) and the Privacy Electronic Communications (EC Directive) Regulations 2003, SI 2003/2426.

(iv) Where the disclosure is made by the express or implied consent of the customer

14.45 For many years banks have provided each other with credit references relating to their customers. In *Turner v Royal Bank of Scotland plc*,[144] the bank tried to justify the practice on the ground that their customers gave their implied consent to it when they opened their accounts. The Court of Appeal held that the bank had breached its duty of confidentiality as the practice was not sufficiently well known to the bank's customers to make it an implied term of the bank-customer contract. The *Banking Code* and the *Business Banking Code* now provide that a credit reference should only be given by a bank when it has the customer's written consent.[145]

(8) Bank's Right of Combination

14.46 In certain circumstances a bank may combine a customer's bank accounts by setting the credit balance on one account off against the debit balance on another to determine the total state of indebtedness between that customer and the bank. This is known as the banker's right of combination. It may allow the bank to refuse to honour a payment instruction received from the customer unless the overall credit balance on the customer's accounts taken together is sufficient to meet the payment. Of course, the bank would only seek to do this where it was doubtful about the customer's solvency. A customer has no right to insist that the bank excise its right of combination so that a cheque is honoured when there are insufficient funds in the particular account on which it is drawn.[146] However, in practice, the bank will usually honour the customer's cheque and hold the credit balances on other accounts as security for the overdraft, combining the accounts if necessary.

14.47 The banker's right of combination should not be confused with the exercise of a banker's lien. A lien is a right to retain possession of property that belongs to someone else, and the bank has no lien over funds which, when deposited by the customer, becomes its own property.[147] The right of combination is a particular form of contractual set-off.[148] It may be excluded by express or implied agreement of the bank and customer, however, it is more common for the bank to reinforce or even

---

144 [1999] 2 All ER (Comm) 64.

145 2005 edns, para 11.2.

146 *Garnett v McKewan* (1872) LR 8 Exch 10, 14.

147 *In re Spectrum Plus Ltd* [2005] UKHL 41; [2005] 2 AC 680 at [60], *per* Lord Hope. See also *Halesowen Presswork and Assemblies Ltd v National Westminster Bank Ltd* [1971] 1 QB 1, 46, *per* Buckley LJ. But a credit balance on the account can be charged to the bank: *Re Bank of Credit and Commerce International SA (No 8)* [1998] AC 214.

148 PR Wood, *English and International Set-Off* (1989), 92–94; RM Goode, *Legal Problems of Credit and Security* (3rd ed, 2003), paras 7.32 *et seq*; cf S McCracken, *The Banker's Remedy of Set-Off* (2nd ed, 1998), ch 1; R Derham, *The Law of Set-Off* (3rd edn, 2003), ch 15.

increase the ambit of its right of combination through express provision in the bank-customer contract. The bank may exercise its right of combination without notice to its customer, unless the bank has previously agreed not to combine accounts; if it were otherwise the bank would run the risk that a customer placed on notice of combination would empty the account in credit and render the right of combination useless. The banker's right of combination is lost if the bank and customer have agreed to keep accounts separate.[149] Such an agreement may be implied, as is usually the case when a customer opens a loan account,[150] or where a deposit account has a fixed maturity date as opposed to being repayable on demand. Combination is also inapplicable where a fund is deposited with the bank for a special purpose of which it has knowledge.[151] There is some controversy as to whether the mere fact of maintaining accounts in different currencies or different jurisdictions should itself give rise to an implied agreement not to combine.[152] Further, an account opened by a customer as trustee, agent or nominee of another person, may not be combined with the customer's private account.[153] However, unless the bank-customer contract provides otherwise, the bank may be able to exercise an equitable right of set-off between a personal account and a 'nominee' account, if there is clear and undisputed evidence that the customer entitled to the funds in both accounts is one and the same person.[154] There is some uncertainty as to the availability of combination between a customer's personal account and a joint account. Dicta in some cases suggests that combination can only occur when the customer is entitled to the entire interest in the joint account,[155] however, it is submitted that combination should be allowed where it can be clearly established that the debtor is solely entitled to a discrete part of the joint account.[156]

(9) Banker's Lien

By mercantile custom, a bank has a lien over commercial paper deposited by the customer in the ordinary course of its banking business.[157] The lien extends to all

14.48

---

[149] *Barclays Bank Ltd v Okenarhe* [1966] 2 Lloyd's Rep 87, 95; cf the statutory right of set-off on insolvency under s 323 of the Insolvency Act 1986, applied to companies under r 4.90 of the Insolvency Rules 1986, which cannot be overridden by contract: *Halesowen Presswork and Assemblies Ltd v National Westminster Bank Ltd* [1972] AC 785 at 805, 809, 824, HL.

[150] *Bradford Old Bank Ltd v Sutcliffe* [1918] 2 KB 833.

[151] *Barclays Bank Ltd v Quistclose Investments Ltd* [1970] AC 567, HL.

[152] McCracken, n 148 above, 32.

[153] *Union Bank of Australia v Murray-Aynsley* [1898] AC 693.

[154] *SAMA v Dresdner Bank AG* [2004] EWCA Civ 1074; [2005] 1 Lloyd's Rep 12, CA; *Uttamchandami v Central Bank of India* (1989) 133 Sol Jo 262, CA; *Bhogal v Punjab National Bank* [1988] 2 All ER 296, CA.

[155] *Ex p Morier* (1879) 12 Ch D 491, 496, CA; *Bhogal v Punjab National Bank*, ibid, 301.

[156] See *Abbey National plc v McCann* [1997] NIJB 158, 172, NICA.

[157] *Brandao v Barnett* (1846) 12 Cl & F 787.

classes of negotiable and semi-negotiable paper deposited by the customer and belonging to him, including bills of exchange, cheques and promissory notes, as well as share certificates[158] and money transfer orders.[159] But the lien does not extend to securities delivered to the bank for mere safe custody as they are retained by the bank as a bailee and not in the ordinary course of its banking business.[160] Usually the lien attaches to secure the customer's total indebtedness to the bank at any one time. A special feature of the banker's lien, which is not found in other types of common law lien, is that the lien carries with it the right to sell the security.[161] But the extent of the lien can be limited by express or implied agreement.[162]

(10) Termination of the Bank-Customer Relationship

14.49 The banker-customer relationship will continue until terminated by the customer, by the bank or by operation of law. Usually the courts deal with termination of the banker-customer relationship in the context of closure of the customer's account, although it is important to note that some aspects of the relationship may continue beyond then, eg, the banker's duty of confidentiality in respect of the customer's account extends beyond the point when the account is closed,[163] and the customer's claims in respect of unauthorized transactions will, in the absence of an agreement to the contrary, continue to be valid.[164]

14.50 Fixed term deposit accounts will mature at the agreed time so that neither bank nor customer may unilaterally terminate their relationship before then, although in practice the bank will usually allow the customer to close the account prematurely on sufferance of an interest penalty. Customers with current accounts or ordinary deposit accounts may unilaterally terminate the relationship at any time by drawing out the remaining funds *and* asking for the account to be closed.[165]

14.51 It is an implied term of the banker-customer contract that the bank must give reasonable notice before closing a customer's account and terminating their relationship.[166] Reasonable notice must be long enough in the circumstances to

---

158 *Re United Service Co, Johnson's Claim* (1870) 6 Ch App 212, 217.
159 *Misa v Currie* (1876) 1 App Cas 554, 567, 573.
160 *Leese v Martin* (1873) LR 17 Eq 24, 235.
161 *Rosenberg v International Banking Corporation* (1923) 14 Ll LR 344, 347.
162 See, eg, *Re Bowes* (1886) 33 Ch D 586.
163 *Tournier v National Provincial and Union Bank of England*, n 127 above, 473, CA.
164 *Limpgrange Ltd v Bank of Credit and Commerce International SA*, n 87 above.
165 *Bank of Baroda v ASAA Mahomed* [1999] Bank LR 14, CA.
166 *Joachimson v Swiss Bank Corpn*, n 30 above, 125, 127.

enable the customer to make alternative banking arrangements.[167] The bank does not terminate the banker-customer relationship by simply demanding repayment of the sum outstanding on the customer's account.[168]

The bank-customer relationship, being of a personal nature, terminates automati- **14.52** cally by operation of law on the customer's death, bankruptcy, dissolution (if a partnership) or liquidation (if a company).[169] The balance held by the bank becomes payable to the customer, to his estate, or to the liquidator, as the case may be. On liquidation of the bank the relationship terminates and the balance standing to the customer's account becomes payable at once without the need for a demand.[170]

B. Payment Methods

(1) Cheques

(a) Definition

Section 73 of the Bills of Exchange Act 1882 ('BEA') defines a cheque as a bill **14.53** of exchange drawn on a banker payable on demand, and, except as otherwise provided in Part III of the BEA, the provisions of that Act applicable to a bill of exchange payable on demand apply to cheques. A bill of exchange is an unconditional order in writing, addressed by one person to another, signed by the person giving it, requiring the person to whom it is addressed to pay a sum certain in money on demand or at a fixed or determinable future time to or to the order of a specified person, or to bearer.[171]

(b) Functions

A cheque is capable of performing two different functions. The first is a payment **14.54** function enabling the drawer of the cheque to instruct his bank to make payment to himself or a third party, and the holder to obtain payment from the drawer.

---

[167] *Prosperity Ltd v Lloyds Bank Ltd* (1923) 39 TLR 372. The 2005 editions of both the *Banking Code* (para 7.5) and the *Business Banking Code* (para 7.7) state that, under normal circumstances, the bank will not close an account without giving the customer at least 30 days' notice.

[168] *National Bank of Greece SA v Pinios Shipping Co, The Maira* [1990] 1 AC 637, HL.

[169] S 75(2) of the Bills of Exchange Act 1882 provides that it is notice of the customer's death that determines the duty and authority of a banker to pay a cheque drawn on him by his customer, and the same rule probably applies in the case of the customer's insanity (see para 14.21).

[170] *Re Russian Commercial & Industrial Bank* [1955] Ch 148; cf *Bank of Credit and Commerce International SA v Malik* [1996] BCC 15.

[171] BEA, s 3. A cheque is not invalid by reason of the fact it is ante-dated or post-dated (BEA, s 13(2)) or even not dated at all (BEA, s 3(4); *Aspinall's Club Ltd v Fouad Al-Zayat* [2007] EWHC 362 (Comm) at [8], [10]).

The second is a transfer and negotiation function enabling title to the cheque to be passed by transfer from person to person and for the transferee to enforce his rights under the cheque free from any defects in title of the transferor.

14.55 The payment function is the most important function of a cheque.[172] Modern banking law and practice means that virtually all cheques issued in the UK since 1992 are crossed cheques marked 'account payee' or 'account payee only' which makes the cheque non-transferable and, therefore, non-negotiable.[173] Most of the law relating to negotiability and indorsement is irrelevant to the typical modern cheque and is not considered in this chapter.[174]

(c) Cheques as payment instructions

(i) Basic rules

14.56 A cheque constitutes the customer's mandate to his bank to make payment from his account. The rules relating to honouring the customer's mandate are considered in paras 14.12–14.33 above and are relevant in this context. Three rules merit repetition. First, the bank is only obliged to honour a cheque drawn on its customer's account where there are sufficient funds in the account to meet the whole of the amount of the cheque or where the cheque is within an agreed overdraft facility.[175] Secondly, the cheque must be signed by the customer or other mandated signatory. A forged or unauthorized signature is 'wholly inoperative',[176] which means that where the drawer's signature is forged or unauthorized the bank cannot debit the account. In some cases the customer may be estopped from raising the fraud against the bank,[177] in other cases the bank may be able to rely on the fact that the customer's negligence allowed the fraud to take place.[178] Thirdly, a cheque can be countermanded under s 75 of the BEA,[179] but not if it is supported

---

[172] Unless the facts indicate otherwise, payment by cheque operates as conditional payment only (*Re Charge Card Services* [1989] Ch 497, 511, CA; *Crockfords Club Ltd v Mehta* [1992] 1 WLR 355, 366, CA; *Homes v Smith* [2000] Lloyd's Rep (Bank) 139 at [35], CA). It is likely that the use of a cheque guarantee card to support the cheque does not alter this presumption (*Re Charge Card Services* [1987] Ch 150, 166, *per* Millett J, obiter; the Court of Appeal left the issue open). Cross claims for unliquidated damages cannot be set up in answer to a claim on a cheque (*Nova (Jersey) Knit Ltd v Kammgarn Spinnerei GmbH* [1977] 1 WLR 713, HL) but one for total (or quantified partial) failure of consideration can offer a defence against the payee, as can a defence which calls the validity of the cheque into question, eg that its issue was induced by fraud or conspiracy (*Solo Industries UK Ltd v Canara Bank* [2001] EWCA Civ 1059; [2001] 2 All ER (Comm) 217).

[173] Bills of Exchange Act 1882, s 81A(1), inserted by the Cheques Act 1992.

[174] The law can be found in AG Guest, *Chalmers and Guest on Bills of Exchange and Cheques* (16th edn, 2005); N Elliott, J Odgers and JM Phillips, *Byles on Bills of Exchange and Cheques* (27th edn, 2002).

[175] Para 14.14.

[176] BEA, s 24.

[177] Para 14.28.

[178] Para 14.27.

[179] Para 14.23.

by a cheque guarantee card.[180] The bank must receive the countermand in time for it to refuse payment of the cheque.[181]

(ii) Crossed cheques

A cheque is crossed when two parallel transverse lines are drawn across its face. **14.57** This is a general crossing and means that the cheque must be presented for payment through a bank account.[182] The holder of the cheque cannot present it in person for cash. Sometimes the name of a bank will be written on the face of the cheque. This is a special crossing and means that the cheque must be presented for payment through the named bank.[183] A transferee of a crossed cheque which is also marked 'not negotiable' cannot acquire a better title than his transferor had, although the cheque remains transferable.[184] An uncrossed cheque marked 'not negotiable' is probably non-transferable.[185] Crossed cheques marked 'not negotiable' and uncrossed cheques are hardly ever seen today.

In 1992, following the enactment of the Cheques Act 1992, which introduced **14.58** s 81A(1) into the BEA, where a cheque is crossed and bears across its face the words 'account payee' or 'a/c payee', either with or without the word 'only', the cheque is non-transferable and is only valid as between the parties to it, ie the drawer and the payee. Today virtually all cheque forms supplied by UK banks to their customers are crossed and pre-printed 'account payee'. Only the named payee can be the holder of such a cheque.

In general, only the drawer and holder may cross a cheque.[186] Where a cheque **14.59** is crossed specially, the bank to whom it is crossed may again cross it specially to another bank for collection.[187] The bank on whom the cheque is drawn (the drawer's bank) must be careful to pay in accordance with the crossing. The crossing is part of the mandate and failure to adhere to it prevents the bank from debiting the drawer's account.[188] Moreover, s 79(2) of the BEA provides that the bank will be liable to the 'true owner' of the cheque for any loss incurred owing to the cheque having been paid contrary to the crossing, eg, where a thief steals a crossed cheque from the payee and the bank allows the thief to present it for payment over the counter. If the true owner is the drawer he will have no claim since he can

---

180 Para 14.23

181 See further *Chalmers and Guest*, n 174 above, para 13–039.

182 BEA, s 76(1), sometimes the words 'and company' are inserted between the parallel lines but this adds nothing.

183 BEA, s 76(2).

184 BEA, s 81.

185 *Hibernian Bank Ltd v Gysin and Hanson* [1939] 1 KB 483, CA.

186 BEA, s 77(1)-(4).

187 BEA, s 77(5). Where a bank receives an uncrossed cheque, or a cheque crossed generally, for collection, it may cross it specially to itself (s 77(6)). This sub-section adds little.

188 *Bellamy v Majoribanks* (1852) 7 Exch 389, 404; *Bobbett v Pinkett* (1876) 1 Ex D 368, 372.

require the bank to reinstate his account.[189] Section 79(2) goes on to protect the drawer's bank against a claim by the true owner, and allows the bank to debit the drawer's account, where the cheque does not appear (i) to be crossed, or (ii) to have had a crossing which has been obliterated, or (iii) to have a crossing which has been added to or amended in an unauthorized manner, provided that the bank acted in good faith and without negligence.

(iii) Collection of cheques

14.60   A cheque is a debit instrument. On receipt of a cheque, the payee will give it to his bank (the collecting bank) which will then present it for payment to the drawer's bank (the paying bank). This process is known as collecting the cheque. The cheque clearing system facilitates the process by enabling the bulk presentation of cheques from collecting banks to paying banks in order that they may be paid or dishonoured.[190] Not all cheques are presented for payment through the clearing system. Sometimes the payee will request his bank to make a special presentation of the cheque directly to the branch of the paying bank upon which it is drawn thereby speeding up the process. Cheques drawn on the same or different branches of the payee's bank do not go through the clearing.

14.61   It used to be the case that a cheque had to be physically presented for payment at the branch of the bank on which it was drawn.[191] This is no longer required. The electronic transmission of the essential details or an image of the cheque by collecting bank to paying bank is sufficient. This is known as cheque truncation.[192]

(d) The paying bank

14.62   We have already considered the common law defences that may be available to the drawer's (paying) bank when it pays a cheque in breach of mandate.[193] There are also a number of statutory defences available to the paying bank. Section 60 of the BEA protects a bank that pays a cheque payable to order that bears an indorsement that is forged or which was made without authority. Section 1 of the Cheques Act 1957 protects a bank that pays a cheque that lacks a proper indorsement. In both cases the bank must show that it acted in good faith and in the ordinary course of business.[194] However, the modern practice of banks providing their

---

[189] *Channon v English, Scottish & Australian Bank* (1918) 18 SR (NSW) 30, 38.

[190] For details of how the cheque clearing system works, see EP Ellinger, E Lomnicka and R Hooley, *Ellinger's Modern Banking Law* (4th edn, 2006), 355–364.

[191] *Barclays Bank plc v Bank of England* [1985] 1 All ER 385, 386.

[192] Deregulation (Bills of Exchange) Order 1996, SI 1996/2993, inserting ss 74A–74C into the BEA.

[193] Paras 14.26–14.33.

[194] *Carpenters' Co v British Mutual Banking Co Ltd* [1938] 1 KB 511, CA.

customers with pre-printed 'account payee' (non-transferable) cheque forms has rendered both defences of marginal relevance as such cheques are not payable to order and do not require indorsement.

Section 80 of the BEA protects a bank that pays a crossed cheque to a bank that **14.63** collects the cheque on behalf of someone who is not the true owner.[195] The bank must show that it made the payment in good faith and without negligence. Where the bank falls within the protection of the section it may debit its customer's account and it is given a defence against any action in conversion brought against it by the true owner. Section 80 affords protection where the cheque bears a forged or unauthorized indorsement, but it will not protect the paying bank where the drawer's signature has been forged or made without his authority as the instrument is not then a cheque at all, for the signature is wholly inoperative.[196] Neither will the section protect the paying bank where the cheque has been materially altered so as to be caught by s 64(1) of the BEA. The effect of the material alteration is to render the instrument void with the result that it is no longer a cheque but a 'worthless piece of paper'.[197] However, the paying bank can normally ignore any purported indorsement on an 'account payee' cheque, as it is the responsibility of the collecting bank to ensure that a non-transferable cheque is collected only for the account of the named payee.[198]

(e) The collecting bank

The collecting bank owes its customer a duty to collect a cheque promptly and, **14.64** once collected, to credit the customer's account with the amount. In the absence of an express provision in the bank-customer contract, it is likely that a term will be implied to the effect that cheques are to be collected within a reasonable time, which will be fixed according to the custom and practice of bankers.[199] The fact that the vast majority of cheques drawn on one bank and collected by another are presented for payment through the cheque clearing system means that a court would have regard to all reasonable rules of practice of the clearing system when deciding what is a reasonable time.

---

[195] The true owner is the person with an immediate right to possession of the cheque: *Marquess of Bute v Barclays Bank Ltd* [1955] 1 QB 202. In cases of misappropriation, the identity of the true owner depends on whether the cheque has been delivered by the drawer to the payee. If it is uncertain whether a cheque was misappropriated whilst in the hands of the drawer or the payee, by s 21(3) of the BEA the payee will be deemed to have received a valid and unconditional delivery of the cheque, and hence be the true owner, until the contrary is proved: *Surrey Asset Finance Ltd v National Westminster Bank plc* (2000) Times, 30 November; permission to appeal refused [2001] EWCA Civ 60.

[196] BEA, s 24.

[197] *Smith v Lloyds TSB Bank plc* [2000] 2 All ER 693, 703, CA.

[198] BEA, s 81A(2).

[199] BEA, s 45(2) and s 74(2).

14.65 The collecting bank receives the cheque as agent for its customer for the purposes of collecting it on the customer's behalf.[200] For these purposes, the collecting bank's customer may be another domestic or foreign bank using the collecting bank as its agent to gain access to the cheque clearing system.[201] In theory, the collecting bank could give the customer value for the cheque and collect the cheque, to the extent that value was given, on its own behalf as a holder for value, but the fact that banks now invariably issue cheque forms to their customers crossed 'account payee', thereby making the cheque non-transferable, means that this is very rare indeed, for a collecting bank cannot become the holder of a non-transferable cheque.[202]

14.66 Where the collecting bank collects a cheque for anyone other than the true owner,[203] the bank may be liable to the true owner for conversion of the cheque. For the purposes of an action in conversion, the cheque is deemed to have a value equal to the amount for which it is drawn.[204] The rule does not apply where the cheque has been materially altered by an unauthorized person for then it is deemed to be a 'worthless piece of paper'.[205] Alternatively, the amount received for the cheque may be recovered from the bank by the true owner as money had and received. In theory, the collecting bank may have a right of indemnity or recourse against its customer, but in practice this may prove worthless.[206] As the collecting bank will have a defence to the restitutionary claim for money had and received if it has already paid the proceeds of the cheque over to its customer in good faith and in ignorance of the claim, the most common form of action brought by the true owner against the bank is an action in conversion.

14.67 The main statutory defence that a collecting bank can raise to a claim in conversion is to be found in s 4(1) of the Cheques Act 1957.[207] The section provides as follows:

> Where a banker, in good faith and without negligence –
> (a) receives payment for a customer of an instrument to which this section applies; or

---

[200] But the proceeds of the cheque are not held on trust for the customer: *Emerald Meats (London) Ltd v AIB Group (UK) Ltd*, n 42 above.

[201] *Hon Soc of the Middle Temple v Lloyds Bank plc* [1999] 1 All ER (Comm) 193; *Linklaters (a firm) v HSBC Bank plc* [2003] EWHC 1113 (Comm); [2003] 2 Lloyd's Rep 545.

[202] Hence why the collecting bank's defence of holder in due course is not considered in this chapter.

[203] See n 195 above.

[204] *Morison v London County and Westminster Bank Ltd* [1914] 3 KB 356, 365, CA.

[205] *Smith v Lloyds TSB Group plc*, n 197 above, applying BEA, s 64(1).

[206] Unless the customer is a bank itself: *Hon Soc of the Middle Temple v Lloyds Bank plc*, n 201 above; *Linklaters (a firm) v HSBC Bank plc*, n 201 above.

[207] There is also a statutory defence of contributory negligence in s 47 of the Banking Act 1979. Common law defences of ratification, illegality and even the *Liggett* defence (para 14.32) may also apply.

(b) having credited a customer's account with the amount of such an instrument, receives payment thereof for himself;

and the customer has no title, or a defective title, to the instrument, the banker does not incur any liability to the true owner of the instrument by reason only of having received payment thereof.

The section applies to a cheque and protects the collecting bank from claims for conversion and also for money had and received.[208]

To avail itself of the protection afforded by s 4, the collecting bank must be able to prove that it acted in good faith and without negligence. Often good faith is presumed and negligence is in issue. Negligence is judged against the objective standard of the reasonable banker.[209] A failure by the bank properly to identify its customer when opening the account is likely to be held to be negligent.[210] Similarly, there may be negligence in the collecting of the cheque itself, eg, in the absence of special circumstances, it would generally be negligent to collect payment of an 'account payee' cheque for someone other than the named payee without further inquiry.[211] But in each case the enquiry is fact sensitive and current banking practice is highly relevant to the issue of negligence.[212] There are differing views as to whether the bank's negligence should be disregarded where it can be shown that it had no causative effect on the true owner's loss.[213]

14.68

---

[208] *Capital and Counties Bank Ltd v Gordon* [1903] AC 240, HL.

[209] *Marfani & Co Ltd v Midland Bank Ltd* [1968] 1 WLR 956, 973, CA; *Linklaters (a firm) v HSBC Bank plc*, n 201 above, at [106].

[210] *Marfani & Co Ltd v Midland Bank Ltd*, ibid. Banks must also have proper procedures for identifying their customers so as to comply with the Money Laundering Regulations 2003, SI 2003/3075; to be replaced, as from 15 December 2007, by the Money Laundering Regulations 2007, SI 2007/2157. See also the *Banking Code* and the *Business Banking Code* (2005 edns), para 3.1.

[211] When acting as agent for a domestic collecting bank it would generally be reasonable for the collecting agent to assume its principal was aware of its responsibilities under the Cheques Act 1992 and that the principal would ensure that the cheque was collected for the named payee: *Hon Soc of the Middle Temple v Lloyds Bank plc*, n 201 above (held collecting agent not entitled to assume foreign bank aware of responsibilities under the 1992 Act).

[212] *Architects of Wine Ltd v Barclays Bank plc* [2007] EWCA Civ 239; [2007] 2 All ER (Comm) 285 at [12], *per* Rix LJ, who added that '[a] bank's evidence about its practice is, especially if unchallenged, relevant evidence of the current practice of bankers'.

[213] Contrast M Hapgood (ed), *Paget's Law of Banking* (13th edn, 2007), para 24.42, citing, *inter alia, Marfani & Co Ltd v Midland Bank Ltd*, n 209 above, 976, CA, *Hon Soc of the Middle Temple v Lloyds Bank plc*, n 201 above, 226, with M Brindle & R Cox (eds), *Law of Bank Payments* (3rd edn, 2004), para 7–167, citing, *inter alia, Thackwell v Barclays Bank plc* [1986] 1 All ER 676, 684.

(2) Payment Cards

(a) Cheque cards

14.69 A cheque card is issued by a bank for use with its customer's cheques. Through the card the bank undertakes to the payee of the cheque that payment will be made (up to the limit indicated on the card itself) regardless of the state of the customer's account, provided that certain conditions are met.[214] In *Re Charge Card Services*,[215] Millett J described the obligation undertaken by the bank to the payee as being not to dishonour the cheque on presentation for lack of funds in the account, so that the bank is obliged, if necessary, to advance moneys to the customer to meet it. The description 'cheque guarantee card' is strictly a misnomer because the obligation assumed by the bank is not a secondary obligation dependent on default by the card-holder, but a separate independent obligation.[216]

14.70 The contract between the card issuing bank and the payee of the cheque is created by the payee's acceptance of the offer contained in the card. It is an offer of a unilateral contract. The offer is conveyed to the payee by the person in possession of the card and so that person must have the bank's actual or apparent authority to convey that offer. The authorized signatory has actual authority to convey the offer and, even if that authority has for some reason terminated, he will continue to have apparent authority. Someone who is not the authorized signatory, eg, a thief, cannot have actual authority to convey the offer but he may, depending on the conditions governing use of the card, have apparent authority.[217]

(b) Credit cards and charge cards

14.71 A credit card gives the card-holder a revolving credit facility with a monthly credit limit. The card-holder does not have to settle his account in full at the end of the each month but has the option to take extended credit, subject to an obligation to make a specified minimum payment each month. Amounts outstanding at the end of a set period commencing with the date of the monthly statement attract interest charged on a daily basis. Unlike a credit card, the main function of a charge card is to facilitate payment, rather than to provide a credit facility. The holder of a charge card must normally settle his account in full within a specified period after the date of a monthly statement. Overdue accounts may be charged a sum equal to interest but this is described by the card-issuer as 'liquidated

---

[214] Standard conditions for use of cheque cards have been agreed by all major cheque card issuers and are set out on the Card Watch website <www.cardwatch.org.uk>.

[215] [1987] Ch 150, 166 (affd [1989] Ch 497).

[216] *First Sport Ltd v Barclays Bank plc* [1993] 1 WLR 1229, 1236, CA.

[217] ibid. The standard conditions of use of cheque cards have since been tightened up and now provide that the cheque must be signed 'by the account holder' (see n 214 above).

damages'. In the case of both credit cards and charge cards, a separate card account is usually maintained for the card-holder and payments are made into the account from a current account with a bank by cheque, by direct debit or sometimes even by standing order. In fact, there are more similarities than differences between credit cards and charge cards. One important difference is that credit cards are subject to regulation under the Consumer Credit Act 1974, whereas charge cards are exempt by virtue of s 16(5)(a) of that Act and art 3(1)(a)(ii) of the Consumer Credit (Exempt Agreements) Order 1989.[218]

The contractual relations involved in credit or charge card transactions were **14.72** identified by the Court of Appeal in *Re Charge Card Services Ltd* as follows:[219] (i) between card-holder and supplier, ie contract of sale or supply; (ii) between card-issuing bank and card-holder; and (iii) between card-issuing bank and supplier. *Re Charge Card Services Ltd* involved a simplified 'three-party' card scheme, ie a single card-issuer, a card-holder and a supplier. In fact there are often four parties involved in any particular transaction.[220] The fourth party is known as a 'merchant acquirer'. The merchant acquirer (often the supplier's own bank) gives the supplier admission to the scheme. The merchant acquirer arranges to receive credit card and transaction details from the supplier and makes the appropriate payments to the supplier less a handling charge. Under the terms of a master agreement between the banks, the merchant acquirer obtains reimbursement from the card-issuer.

Payment by credit card or charge card is presumed to be intended by the parties to **14.73** constitute absolute payment, as the supplier accepts the card-issuer's payment undertaking, or that of the merchant acquirer who admitted him to the scheme, in place of the card-holder's liability.[221]

(c) Debit cards

A debit card can be used to obtain cash or make a payment at point of sale or at **14.74** distance, eg, over the telephone or internet. The card-holder's current account is debited for such a transaction without deferment of payment. Some debit card transactions are manual using paper vouchers, but most are now electronic and use an EFTPOS system.[222] EFTPOS allows payment to be made for goods and services by the electronic transfer of funds from the customer's account to the

---

[218] SI 1989/869.

[219] [1989] Ch 497, 509.

[220] Alternatively, the arrangement may be only 'two-party' as where the card is issued by a shop or store for purchase of their own goods or services.

[221] *Re Charge Card Services Ltd* [1989] Ch 497, CA.

[222] EFTPOS stands for Electronic Funds Transfer at Point of Sale. Since 14 February 2006, card-holders have been required to know their personal identification numbers, but some of the voucher-type card readers remain in circulation.

supplier's account. Where the system is entirely on-line, this could be virtually instantaneous.

14.75 Debit card transactions involve four discrete contractual relationships: (i) between card-holder and supplier, ie the contract of sale or supply;[223] (ii) between card-issuing bank and card-holder, giving the card-holder authority to use the card and the card-issuing bank authority to debit the card-holder's account with the amount of any transaction entered into; (iii) between supplier and merchant acquirer, obliging the supplier to accept all cards issued under the scheme in payment for goods or services and containing the merchant acquirer's undertaking to pay the supplier for the value of goods and services supplied; and (iv) between the participating banks and financial institutions, covering various matters including the means of transfer of funds from one institution to another. By analogy with payment by credit card,[224] payment by debit card probably constitutes absolute payment.[225]

(d) ATM cards

14.76 Automated teller machines (ATMs) are not a method of payment but a means of providing customers with cash, so as to pay for goods and services. The ATM or cash card can be used only in the ATMs of the card-issuing bank and those of other banks with whom the issuing bank has reached an agreement.[226] There is some dispute as to whether these other banks act as agents of the card-issuing bank when dispensing cash to the card-holder, or whether they act as principals. An ATM function is usually incorporated into credit cards and debit cards.

(e) Digital cash cards

14.77 EC Directive 2000/46 on the taking up, pursuit of and prudential supervision of the business of electronic money institutions describes electronic money as 'an electronic surrogate for coins and bank notes, which is stored on an electronic device such as a chip card or computer memory and which is generally intended for the purpose of effecting electronic payments of limited amounts'.[227] Electronic money, or 'digital cash', systems are either smart card systems, where electronic value is stored in a microchip on a smart card, or software based systems where tokens or coins are stored in the memory of a computer. The 'value', 'tokens' or 'coins' take the form of digital information. Digital cash allows payment to be

---

[223] *Debenhams Retail plc v Customs & Excise Commissioners* [2005] EWCA Civ 892; [2005] STC 1155.
[224] n 221 above.
[225] *Paget's Law of Banking*, n 213 above, para 17.220.
[226] See *Royal Bank of Scotland Group plc v Commissioner of Customs and Excise* [2002] STC 575.
[227] Recital 3. See [2000] OJ L275, p 39.

made simply by transferring digital information directly between debtor and creditor so that value is transferred immediately upon delivery. In some systems the recipient of digital cash can immediately use it to pay for other goods or services. Other systems require the token to be deposited in a bank account or with the issuer who will then issue a token of equivalent value or credit the value to an account.

Digital cash systems depend on various contractual relationships for legal effect. **14.78** Digital cash is issued by an 'originator' (a private company) to banks participating in the scheme that pay for it in real funds. Participating banks re-issue digital cash to customers by charging their digital cash card, or the memory of their computer in a software system, with digital information representing the value purchased from the bank by the customer (usually through a debit to their account). There is a clear contractual relationship between the originator and the participating banks and between those banks and their own customers. However, for a digital cash scheme to operate, holders of digital cash must have confidence that the originator will ultimately be liable to redeem the digital cash for real value. This can be achieved by treating digital cash systems as giving rise to a series of standing offers of unilateral contracts,[228] or through reliance on the Contracts (Rights of Third Parties) Act 1999, so long as the originator and participating banks have not contracted out of that Act.[229]

Digital cash does not constitute legal tender.[230] By analogy with payment by credit **14.79** card,[231] payment by digital cash card probably constitutes absolute payment.[232]

(f) Liability for unauthorized transactions

(i) *Terms of the contract*

Resolution of any dispute between card-holder and card-issuer, card-holder and **14.80** supplier, supplier and card-issuer (or other financial institution that admitted the supplier to the scheme), and between the financial institutions that are members of the particular payment card scheme, will normally depend on the terms of the contract governing the relevant contractual relationship in issue. The card-issuing contract and the merchant agreement by which a supplier becomes a member of a particular scheme will generally be on the bank's or other financial institution's written standard terms of business and be caught by the Unfair Contract Terms Act 1977. But the 1977 Act only catches terms which can broadly be described as

---

228 See R Hooley, 'Payment in a Cashless Society' in BAK Rider (ed), *The Realm of Company Law— A Collection of Papers in Honour of Professor Leonard Sealy* (1998) 245.
229 S 1(2).
230 Hooley, n 228, 253–259.
231 n 221 above.
232 *Paget's Law of Banking*, n 213 above, para 17.225.

'exclusion' or 'limitation' clauses.[233] The Unfair Terms in Consumer Contracts Regulations 1999 are much broader in scope catching virtually all terms in a consumer contract where that term has not been individually negotiated.[234] The Regulations apply to the card-issuing contract where the contracting card-holder is a consumer (defined in such as way as to exclude companies), but not where the card-holder is acting in a business capacity. The Regulations do not apply to a merchant agreement between a supplier and the bank or other financial institution that admitted the supplier to the scheme.

(ii) Consumer Credit Act 1974

14.81 In certain circumstances the card-holder may be able to argue that his payment card is a 'credit-token',[235] issued to him under a 'credit-token agreement',[236] and that his liability for unauthorized use should be limited under ss 83 and 84 of the Consumer Credit Act 1974 ('CCA'), in effect, to a maximum of £50 prior to notification to the bank that the card is lost, stolen or otherwise liable to misuse. On the other hand, the card-holder can be held liable for all loss occasioned through use of the card by a person who acquired possession of it with his consent.[237] However, after the card-issuer has been so notified in accordance with the provisions of s 84, the card-holder will not be liable for further loss arising from use of the card.[238] Moreover, where the Act applies and the card-holder claims that the use of his card was unauthorized, then under s 171(4)(b) of the CCA it is for the bank to prove either that the use was authorized, or that the use occurred before the bank had been given notice as stated above.

14.82 The protection offered by ss 83 and 84 of the CCA only applies to payment cards issued under credit-token agreements. A credit card is issued under a credit-token agreement when issued to an individual (including a sole trader or small partnership).[239] But there is some controversy as to whether debit cards and ATM cards are protected by these provisions.[240] It seems reasonably certain that cheque cards, charge cards used to acquire goods or services, and digital cash cards are not covered by the protection offered by ss 83-84.[241]

---

[233] Paras 8.110–8.118.
[234] SI 1999/2083. See paras 8.119–8.128.
[235] Consumer Credit Act 1974 ('CCA'), s 14(1).
[236] CCA, s 14(2).
[237] CCA, s 83(3).
[238] CCA, s 84(3).
[239] A previous financial limit of £25,000 was removed by the Consumer Credit Act 2006, although the Act introduced exemptions relating to agreements exceeding £25,000 which relate to the debtor's business and to 'high net worth' debtors. 'Individual' is defined in s 189(1) of the CCA 1974.
[240] Ellinger, Lomnicka and Hooley, n 190 above, 598–603.
[241] ibid. For charge cards, see also para 14.71.

(iii) Banking Codes

By contrast, the *Banking Code* and the *Business Banking Code* take a much more **14.83**
consistent approach to the different types of payment cards so far as personal and
(small) business customers are concerned. Save for digital cash cards,[242] the Codes
do not distinguish between different types of payment card. Both Codes contain
provisions that limit the card-holder's liability for misuse of his card in similar, but
not identical, terms to those in ss 83 and 84 of the CCA. The relevant terms of
the Codes are usually expressly incorporated into the contract under which the
payment card is issued.

Both Codes provide that, unless the card issuer can establish that the customer **14.84**
acted fraudulently or without reasonable care, the customer's liability for misuse
of the card is to be limited.[243] First, where someone else uses the card before
the customer informs the card issuer that it has been lost or stolen or that someone
else knows the PIN (personal identification number), the customer's liability
is capped at £50. Secondly, where someone else uses card details without the
customer's permission, and the card has not been lost or stolen, the customer is
not liable at all. Thirdly, the customer is not liable where the card is used before
he receives it.

Both Codes treat 'electronic purses' (digital cash cards) differently. An electronic **14.85**
purse is treated like cash so that if the purse is lost or stolen the card-holder loses
the electronic money loaded onto it.[244] However, the Codes recognize that a card-
holder requires protection where value can be loaded on to his electronic purse
through direct access to his bank account. Both Codes provides that, unless the
card-issuer can establish that the card-holder acted fraudulently or without reasonable care, the latter's liability for misuse of his electronic purse will be capped
at £50 if the electronic purse is credited by unauthorized withdrawals from his
account before he informs the card-issuer that the electronic purse has been lost,
stolen or misused.[245] On the other hand, the card-holder will not be liable for any
sum transferred from his account to his electronic purse after he has informed the
card-issuer that the electronic purse has been lost, stolen or that someone else
knows the PIN.[246]

---

[242] See para 14.85.
[243] 2005 edns, para 12.12. Failure to follow the guidance in para 12.5 may show lack of reasonable care: both Codes, para 12.11.
[244] ibid para 12.14.
[245] ibid para 12.15.
[246] ibid para 12.16.

(iv) Distance contracts

14.86 The Consumer Protection (Distance Selling) Regulations 2000[247] apply to contracts for goods or non-financial services to be supplied to a consumer where the contract is made exclusively by means of distance communication, eg, by telephone, by e-mail or over the internet, as a result of an organized marketing campaign. Regulation 21 provides that a consumer is entitled to cancel payment where fraudulent use has been made of his payment card in connection with distance contracts covered by the Regulations, and that in the event of fraudulent use, the consumer is entitled to be recredited with the sums paid or have them repaid by the card issuer. The term 'payment card' is broadly defined in the Regulation and 'includes credit cards, charge cards, debit cards and store cards'.[248] Digital cash cards probably fall outside this definition. Regulation 14 of the Financial Services (Distance Marketing) Regulations 2004[249] makes similar provision with respect to the fraudulent use of a consumer's payment card in connection with a distance contract for the provision of financial services. Neither regulation 21, nor regulation 14, apply were the card is a 'credit-token' protected by the CCA.[250] In such a case s 83(1) of the CCA provides that the debtor is not to be liable for loss arising from use of the credit facility. It is not possible to impose any liability on the card-holder.[251]

(g) Connected lender liability

14.87 Section 75(1) of the Consumer Credit Act 1974 ('CCA') provides that 'if a debtor under a debtor-credit-supplier agreement falling within s 12(b) or (c) of the Act has, in relation to a transaction financed by the agreement, any claim against the supplier in respect of a misrepresentation or breach of contract, he shall have a like claim against the creditor, who, with the supplier, shall accordingly be jointly and severally liable to the debtor'.[252] In the context of payment cards, this important provision only applies to purchases made using 'three-party' credit cards (being debtor-creditor-supplier agreements), although it has been recently been held that 'four-party' credit card transactions (supplier recruited by merchant acquirer who is not the card issuer) also fall within s 75(1).[253] It does not apply to purchases made using a 'two-party' credit card (which fall under s 12(a), not s 12(b) or (c),

---

[247] SI 2000/2334, as amended by SI 2005/689.
[248] Reg 21(6).
[249] SI 2004/2095.
[250] SI 2001/2334, reg 21(4); SI 2004/2095, reg 14(3).
[251] CCA s 84(3A)-(3D).
[252] See also CCA, s 56(1)(c), (2), which provides that negotiations by the supplier with the debtor are deemed to be conducted by him as agent of the creditor. This means that a card-issuer may be held liable for any misrepresentations made by the supplier.
[253] *Office of Fair Trading v Lloyds TSB Bank plc* [2006] EWCA Civ 268; [2007] QB 1.

of the CCA), or a charge card (which are 'exempt' if the card can only be used to acquire goods or services, and are debtor-creditor agreements, not debtor-creditor-supplier agreements, if the card can be used to acquire cash on credit), or an EFTPOS debit card (which is expressly excluded from the operation of s 75 by s 187(3A) of the CCA), or a cheque card (which are not debtor-creditor-supplier agreements), or an ATM card (again, not debtor-creditor-supplier agreements), or a digital cash card (again, not debtor-creditor-supplier agreements). Where s 75 applies, so as to make the credit card-issuer liable to the card-holder who has contracted with the issuer (where an additional non-contracting card-holder uses the card s 75 does not apply), then the card-issuer is entitled to be indemnified by the supplier, subject to any agreement between them.[254] The card-holder has a claim against the issuer even if, in entering the transaction with the supplier, he has exceeded his credit limit or otherwise contravened the credit agreement.[255]

There is an important limitation to the availability of a s 75 claim against a card-issuer. By virtue of s 75(3), s 75(1) does not apply to a claim 'so far as the claim relates to any single item to which the supplier has attached a cash price not exceeding £100 or more than £30,000'. However, it should be noted that a claim may be made where a credit card is used to make part payment of less than £100 in respect of an item priced over £100. It has been unclear for some time as to whether s 75 extends to a claim by a card-holder in respect of a transaction made abroad with a foreign supplier and which may be subject to foreign law. In *Office of Fair Trading v Lloyds TSB Bank plc*,[256] the Court of Appeal recently held that s 75(1) does indeed apply to foreign transactions. **14.88**

(3) Funds Transfers

(a) Nature of a funds transfer

Funds transfers involve the movement of credit balances from one bank account to another. A funds transfer system can be paper-based, eg, as with bank giro credit transfers, but modern banking relies much more heavily on electronic funds transfer ('EFT') systems where the messages that pass between the banks involved in the funds transfer process are in electronic form. In all funds transfer operations, whether paper-based or electronic, the movement of a credit balance from one account to another is brought about through adjustment of the balances of the payer's and the payee's accounts. There is no transfer of property by this **14.89**

---

[254] CCA, s 75(2).
[255] CCA, s 75(4).
[256] n 253 above.

process, simply the adjustment of separate property rights of the payer and the payee against their own banks.[257]

(b) Payment by funds transfer

14.90 Payment through the use of a funds transfer system is not payment by legal tender. Unless he has expressly or impliedly agreed to accept payment by some other means, a creditor is entitled to demand, and is only obliged to accept, payment in legal tender.[258] The mere fact that the creditor has a bank account is not in itself to be construed as evidencing implied consent to accept payment into that account.[259] But the courts have been willing to construe the terms of commercial contracts to allow for payment through the transfer of funds between bank accounts.[260]

(c) Credit and debit transfers

14.91 A credit transfer involves the payer giving instructions to his own bank to cause the account of the payee, at the same or another bank, to be credited. The payer's instructions can be for an individual credit transfer, eg, through a CHAPS payment, or for a recurring transfer of funds under a standing order.[261] In the case of a debit transfer, it is the payee who conveys instructions to his own bank to collect funds from the payer's bank. These instructions may be initiated by the payer himself and passed on to the payee, eg, as happens with the collection of cheques; alternatively, they may be initiated by the payee himself pursuant to the originator's authority, as happens with direct debits.[262]

14.92 A payer's order to his bank to make a credit transfer to the payee is not a negotiable instrument.[263] The same applies in the case of debit transfer orders, save where

---

[257] *R v Preddy* [1996] AC 815, 834, HL. The debt owed to the payer by his bank, assuming his account is in credit, is not assigned to the payee: *Libyan Arab Foreign Bank v Bankers Trust Co* [1989] QB 728, 750; *Customs & Excise Comrs v FDR Ltd* [2000] STC 672 at [36]–[37], CA; *Foskett v McKeown* [2001] 1 AC 102, 128, HL.

[258] See, eg, *Libyan Arab Foreign Bank v Bankers Trust Co*, n 37 above.

[259] *Customs & Excise Comrs v National Westminster Bank plc* [2002] EWHC 2204 (Ch); [2003] 1 All ER (Comm) 327, applying *TSB Bank of Scotland plc v Welwyn Hatfield DC* [1993] 2 Bank LR 267.

[260] See, eg, *Tenax Steamship Co Ltd v The Brimnes (Owners), The Brimnes* [1975] QB 929, CA.

[261] But a bank is under no duty to make a standing order payment if there are insufficient funds to the credit of the account, or overdraft facility available, when the payment is to be made, and is under no duty subsequently to monitor the account to establish whether sufficient funds have been paid into the account to meet the payment: *Whitehead v National Westminster Bank Ltd*, The Times, 9 June 1982.

[262] The payee's failure properly to implement a correctly completed direct debit mandate might constitute a breach of an implied term of the underlying contract between them, or even a breach of a duty of care in tort owed by the payee to the payer: *Weldon v GRE Linked Life Assurance Ltd* [2000] All ER (Comm) 914.

[263] *The Brimnes*, n 260 above, 949, 969. There are good reasons for distinguishing cheques from funds transfer systems: see M Brindle & R Cox (eds), *Law of Bank Payments* (3rd edn, 2004), para

the debit transfer is effected by cheque, which may be a negotiable instrument.[264] However, it has been held that payment arrangements of the parties by direct debit are to be treated as assimilated to those of payment by cheque so that there can be no set-off or counterclaim arising from the underlying contract unless there is fraud or failure of consideration.[265]

(d) Clearing and settlement

Where the payer and the payee have accounts at the same bank, the transfer of **14.93** funds between the two accounts will usually involve a simple internal accounting exercise at the bank (known as an 'in-house' transfer). The payer's account is debited and the payee's account is credited. Where they hold accounts at different banks (known as an 'inter-bank' transfer), payment instructions will pass from bank to bank, sometimes via intermediary banks. The process of exchanging payment instructions between participating banks is known as clearing. Each inter-bank payment instruction must be paid by the bank sending the instruction to the bank receiving it. It is this process, whereby payment is made between the banks themselves of their obligations *inter se*, which is known as settlement.

Settlement can occur either on a bilateral or a multilateral basis. Bilateral **14.94** settlement occurs where the bank sending the payment instruction and the bank receiving it are correspondents, meaning that each holds an account with the other. Multilateral settlement involves the settlement of accounts of the sending bank and the receiving bank held at a third bank. The banks that participate in the main paper-based and electronic funds transfer systems that operate in the UK settle across accounts held at the Bank of England.

Settlement can also be either gross or net. With gross settlement, the sending **14.95** and receiving banks settle each payment order separately without regard to any other payment obligations arising between them. This is usually done on a real-time basis, with settlement across the accounts of participating banks held at the Bank of England as each payment is processed. With net settlement, the mutual payment obligations of the parties are set off against each other and only the net balances paid. Net balances are usually settled either at the end of the day or the next day.

3–005.

[264] But not if it is crossed 'account payee': see para 14.55.
[265] *Esso Petroleum Co Ltd v Milton* [1997] 1 WLR 938, CA (criticized by R Hooley [1997] CLJ 500 and A Tettenborn (1997) 113 LQR 374).

(e) Clearing systems

14.96 There are four major clearing systems in the United Kingdom:[266]

   (i) the cheque clearing system, which is used for the physical exchange of cheques (cheque truncation has only been partially adopted in the UK);[267]

  (ii) the credit clearing system, which is a paper-based credit transfer system used for the physical exchange of high-volume, low-value, credit collections such as bank giro credits;

 (iii) BACS, which provides high-volume, low-value, bulk electronic clearing services for credit and debit transfers, including standing orders, direct debits, wages and salaries, pensions and other government benefits;

 (iv) CHAPS, which is a dual currency, real-time gross settlement ('RTGS') system. It is made up of an electronic sterling credit transfer clearing, normally used for high-value transfers, called CHAPS sterling, and an electronic euro credit transfer clearing, called CHAPS euro, that enables euro payments to be made domestically between member banks in the UK and also between those members and members of other RTGS systems elsewhere in the European Union through TARGET, which is the interlinking network connecting the various RTGS systems operating in individual EU member states.

14.97 Each clearing system has its own rules. These rules are binding on the members of the system *inter se*. A customer of a member bank may be bound by, and able to rely on, the system rules against his own bank through an implied term of the bank-customer contract.[268] The customer is taken to have contracted with reference to the reasonable usage of bankers, including those system rules which represent such reasonable usage.[269] However, where system rules derogate from the customer's existing rights, the usage codified in the rules will be deemed unreasonable and will not bind the customer without his full knowledge and consent.[270]

---

[266] Each system is run by separate companies under the umbrella of the Association for Payment Clearing Services ('APACS'). A number of payment networks operate outside APACS, such as the Visa and MasterCard networks, which handle various types of payment cards.

[267] See para 14.60.

[268] System rules usually expressly exclude the operation of the Contract (Rights of Third Parties) Act 1999.

[269] *Hare v Henty* (1861) 10 CBNS 65; *Tayeb v HSBC Bank plc* [2004] EWHC 1529; [2004] 4 All ER 1024 at [57].

[270] *Barclays Bank plc v Bank of England* [1985] 1 All ER 385, 394; *Turner v Royal Bank of Scotland plc* [1999] 2 All ER (Comm) 664, CA.

(f) Duties of the banks involved in a funds transfer

(i) Payer's bank

The payment order given by the payer to his bank is a mandate. In the leading case **14.98** of *Royal Products Ltd v Midland Bank Ltd*,[271] Webster J described the customer's instructions to make an inter-bank transfer as 'simply an authority and instruction from a customer to his bank to transfer an amount standing to the credit of that customer with that bank to the credit of [the payee] with another bank'. In carrying out the payment order, the payer's bank acts as the payer's agent and, as such, owes the payer a duty to use reasonable care and skill.[272] The doctrine of strict compliance, which applies to a documentary credit transaction,[273] does not apply to a customer's instruction to his bank to transfer funds.[274] In cases where a payment is not made at all, delayed or misdirected, the payer's bank is only liable to the payee for damages arising from breach of the duty to exercise reasonable care and skill.

The payer's bank is vicariously liable for the negligence or default of its employees **14.99** and agents.[275] This means it will be liable for the negligence of any intermediary bank it uses as its agent. It is common practice, however, for the payer's bank to disclaim liability for the negligence and default of the intermediary in the terms of the standard payment instruction form supplied by the bank for the payer's use. Such terms may be subject to review under the provisions of the Unfair Contract Terms Act 1977 and the Unfair Terms in Consumer Contracts Regulations 1999.[276]

In some cases the position of the payer's bank must be assessed against the **14.100** standards imposed by the Cross-Border Credit Transfer Regulations 1999.[277] These regulations apply to 'cross-border credit transfers' which do not exceed €50,000 or its equivalent in another European Economic Area ('EEA') currency. A cross-border credit transfer is defined in reg 2(1) as 'a transaction or series of transactions carried out as a result of instructions given directly by an originator to an institution in one EEA state, the purpose of which is to make funds in an EEA currency available to a beneficiary in another EEA state'. For these purposes, the originator's institution and the beneficiary's institution may be two branches

---

[271] [1981] 2 Lloyd's Rep 194, 198.
[272] ibid.
[273] See paras 14.116–14.119.
[274] ibid 199. But Geva rightly submits that strict compliance ought to be the standard when the payer's bank issues onward a corresponding payment order matching that of the payer: B Geva, *Bank Collections and Payment Transactions* (2001), 292.
[275] *Royal Products*, n 271 above, 198.
[276] See paras 8.110–8.118 and 8.119–8.128 above.
[277] SI 1999/1879, implementing EC Directive 97/5.

of the same bank located in different EEA states, and the originator (payer) and the beneficiary (payee) may be one and the same person.

14.101 Reg 6 provides for the payment of interest to the originator by the originator's bank where a transfer is not made within the relevant time, unless the delay is attributable to the fault of the originator. This gives rise to strict liability on the part of the originator's bank. In the absence of agreement to the contrary, the time limit for the originator's bank to ensure money is credited to the beneficiary's bank is the end of the fifth banking day following acceptance of the cross-border credit transfer order by the originator's bank, so long as the necessary funds were also available to it at that time. Reg 9 also provides for a 'money back guarantee' in the event of a failed transfer. Where funds do not reach the beneficiary's bank, the originator's bank must provide the originator with a refund of the amount of the failed transfer (capped at €12,500 or its equivalent in another EEA currency), plus interest and charges. Again, liability is strict. But the originator's bank is not liable where its failure to perform its part of the transfer was due to its compliance with relevant money laundering legislation or was due to reasons of *force majeure*.[278]

14.102 The contractual duty of care and skill owed by the payer's bank to the payer, does not extend to the payee. There is no contractual link between them, although where the payee is also a customer of the payer's bank, the bank will owe him a contractual duty of care and skill in its capacity as the payee's bank. It seems unlikely that within the context of a funds transfer operation taken as a whole, the payer and his bank intend to confer an enforceable benefit on the payee so as to allow him to take advantage of the Contracts (Rights of Third Parties) Act 1999.[279] In any event, it is common practice for banks to exclude the operation of the Act in this context. In the normal course of events, the payer's bank will not owe the payee a duty of care in tort,[280] although direct communication between the bank and the payee, eg where the bank responds to an enquiry made by the payee, might give rise to such a duty.[281]

(ii) Intermediary banks

14.103 Intermediary banks may be employed in domestic transfers, eg, to give the payer's bank, the payee's bank or both banks, access to a funds transfer system when not

---

[278] Reg 12(1).

[279] Ss 1(1)(b) and 1(2). The payee would be suing the payer's bank for breach of its duty to exercise reasonable care and skill: the bank does not guarantee the payment. On the operation of ss 1(1)(b) and 1(2), see *Nisshin Shipping Co Ltd v Cleaves & Co Ltd* [2003] EWHC 2602 (Comm); [2004] 1 All ER (Comm) 481; *Laemthong International Lines Co Ltd v Artis* [2005] EWCA Civ 519; [2005] 2 All ER (Comm) 167.

[280] *Wells v First National Commercial Bank* [1998] PNLR 552, CA.

[281] ibid 563 (dicta of Evans LJ).

members of that system. Intermediary banks are more commonly used in international funds transfers. It has been held that the payer's bank is deemed to have the payer's authority to employ the services of an intermediary bank to effect the transfer where it would be normal banking practice to use an intermediary.[282] The intermediary bank will act as the payer's sub-agent, but there will usually be no privity of contract between them.[283]

An intermediary bank appointed by another bank owes that other bank an implied **14.104** contractual duty of care and skill.[284] Where an intermediary bank incurs liability as a result of carrying out the instructions of the payer's bank, it will usually be entitled to an indemnity or contribution from that bank.[285] On the other hand, where the Cross-Border Credit Transfer Regulations 1999 apply, the intermediary bank is liable to reimburse the originator's bank for compensation paid to the originator as a result of a late transfer where the intermediary bank was responsible for the delay.[286] Similarly, where the originator's bank is liable to refund the originator for a failed transfer, it may pass on that loss (capped at €12,500) to any intermediary bank it instructed, and then the loss will pass down the chain until it reaches the bank responsible for the failed transfer.[287]

(iii) Payee's bank

The payee's bank receives a payment instruction from the payer's bank, or via its **14.105** intermediary, as the agent of the payer's bank, but once the payee's bank executes the instruction, or otherwise accepts it, the bank does so as the payee's agent, provided it has the payee's actual or ostensible authority to do so.[288] In the case of a credit transfer, where the payee has supplied the payer with details of his bank account, the payee's bank is deemed to have his authority to accept funds into the account.[289] In direct debits the bank nominated by the payee to accept

---

282 *Royal Products Ltd v Midland Bank Ltd*, n 271 above, 197–198. It is submitted the same principle should apply to the payee's bank.

283 *Calico Printers' Association Ltd v Barclays Bank Ltd* (1931) 145 LT 51, affd at 58; *Royal Products*, n 271 above, 198; cf *Bastone & Firminger Ltd v Nasima Enterprises (Nigeria) Ltd* [1996] CLC 1902. See also *Grosvenor Casinos Ltd v National Bank of Abu Dhabi* [2006] EWHC 784 (Comm) at [39]–[42].

284 A concurrent duty of care will arise in tort.

285 *Honourable Society of the Middle Temple v Lloyd's Bank plc*, n 201 above; *Linklaters (a firm) v HSBC Bank plc*, n 201 above.

286 Reg 6(6), (7). But subject to the *force majeure* provision in reg 12(1).

287 Reg 10(1),(2). But see also the exceptions to liability set out in reg 10(3),(5) and the *force majeure* provision in reg 12(1).

288 The agency is momentary as the payee's bank immediately borrows the money representing the transferred funds back from the payee and the underlying debtor-creditor relationship of bank and customer is restored.

289 *Royal Products Ltd v Midland Bank Ltd*, n 271 above, 198. See also *Dovey v Bank of New Zealand* [2000] 2 NZLR 641, 649–650, NZCA (payee nominated bank to which funds to be transferred and so gave it authority to accept funds on his behalf). Cf *Customs & Excise Comrs v National Westminster Bank plc*, n 259 above (bank not authorized to receive payment simply because customer had account with bank).

payment from the payer's bank does so as the payee's agent. In some case, however, where the payer makes payment contrary to the terms of his underlying contract with the payee, eg, late payment of hire under a charterparty, the payee's bank will be deemed to receive the payment purely in a ministerial capacity and not to have accepted it on the payee's behalf.[290] The payee may then accept or reject the payment, so long as he has not waived his right of rejection, eg, by representing to the payer that the payee's bank has his authority to accept the payment.

14.106 The payee's bank owes the payee a contractual duty of care and skill. Where the Cross-Border Credit Transfer Regulations 1999 apply, they provide that, in the absence of any contrary agreement, the beneficiary's bank must make funds available to the beneficiary by the end of the next banking day following their receipt.[291] The liability of the payee's bank to the payee for refusing to accept a transfer of funds into his account turns on the terms of the contract between them. In *Tayeb v HSBC Bank plc*,[292] Colman J took account of the CHAPS clearing rules and held that a CHAPS transfer was ordinarily irreversible once authenticated, acknowledged and credited to the payee's account, although a bank with cogent evidence of fraud or, probably, illegality could decline to make payment to the payee.[293]

14.107 The payee's bank does not owe a duty of care to a non-customer payer of a funds transfer to pay money received only to the payee identified by the payer's instructions, or to clarify any discrepancies in those instructions as to the payee's identity with the payer.[294]

(4) Documentary Credits

(a) Function

14.108 A documentary credit represents a bank's assurance of payment against presentation of specified documents.[295] It is the most common method of payment in

---

[290] *Mardorf Peach & Co Ltd v Attica Sea Carriers Corpn of Liberia, The Laconia* [1977] AC 850, 871–872, HL. Cf R King, 'The Receiving Bank's Role in Credit Transfer Transactions' (1982) 45 MLR 369.

[291] Reg 7(1), (2). But note the *force majeure* provision in reg 12(1).

[292] [2004] EWHC 1529 (Comm); [2004] 4 All ER 1024.

[293] ibid at [85].

[294] *Abu-Rahman v Abacha* [2005] EWHC 2662 (QB); [2006] 1 All ER (Comm) 247, affd [2006] EWCA Civ 1492; [2007] 1 Lloyd's Rep 115 (but with no appeal on this issue).

[295] The terms 'documentary credit', 'banker's commercial credit' and 'commercial letter of credit' are synonymous. Standby credits, performance bonds and demand guarantees have a different function to that of documentary credits. Whereas the function of documentary credits is to provide payment for goods and services against documents, the function of standby credits, performance bonds and demand guarantees is to provide security against default in performance of the underlying contract. See para 5.163 above.

international sales. The seller stipulates in the contract of sale that payment is to be by documentary credit. The buyer (the 'applicant' for the credit) then gets his bank (the 'issuing bank') to issue a credit in favour of the seller (the 'beneficiary' of the credit), so that the seller has the bank's independent payment undertaking. The issuing bank may get another bank (the 'confirming bank') in the buyer's country to add its own payment undertaking to the credit if this is required under the terms of the underlying contract of sale. Sometimes the bank (the 'advising bank') in the buyer's country will merely advise the buyer that the credit has been opened without adding its own payment undertaking. Subject to the solvency of the bank,[296] the seller is certain of payment under the credit provided he can present conforming documents to the 'nominated bank' (often the confirming bank) and comply with the other terms of the credit.

(b) Uniform Customs and Practice

The Uniform Customs and Practice for Documentary Credits (the 'UCP) is a set **14.109** of rules governing the use of documentary credits. It was first published by the International Chamber of Commerce ('ICC') in 1933 and has been revised six times since then. UCP 600, the most recent revision, came into effect on 1 July 2007.[297] A supplement to the UCP, called the eUCP, deals with the electronic presentation of documents.

The UCP applies to any documentary credit 'when the text of the credit expressly **14.110** indicates that it is subject to these rules'.[298] It has been argued that, even in the absence of express incorporation, the UCP may be incorporated as a matter of business practice because it is so widely used by banks all over the world.[299] However, given the (new) wording of UCP 600, express incorporation is advised. The eUCP must be expressly incorporated into the credit if it is to apply.[300] Incorporation of the eUCP has the effect of incorporating the UCP into the credit without express incorporation of the UCP.[301]

The UCP may be expressly excluded by the terms of the credit.[302] Unless there has **14.111** been express exclusion of the UCP, the courts will endeavour to construe the

---

[296] Unless otherwise agreed, payment by documentary credit constitutes conditional payment of the price so that if it is not honoured, the debt is not discharged and the seller has a remedy in damages against both bank and buyer: *WJ Alan & Co Ltd v El Nasr Export and Import Co* [1972] 2 QB 189, 212, CA.

[297] Unless otherwise stated, all references in this chapter are to this revision.

[298] UCP 600, art 1.

[299] R Goode, *Commercial Law* (3rd edn, 2004), 969, relying on analogous case of *Harlow and Jones Ltd v American Express Bank Ltd* [1990] 2 Lloyd's Rep 343.

[300] eUCP, art e1(b).

[301] eUCP, art e2(a).

[302] UCP 600, art 1.

express terms of the credit so as to avoid conflict with the rules of the UCP.[303] If there is conflict, then the express terms of the credit prevail over the UCP.[304] The UCP will usually be construed in a purposive way.[305]

(c) Types of credit

14.112 UCP 600 defines a documentary credit as 'any arrangement, however named or described, that is irrevocable and thereby constitutes a definite undertaking of the issuing bank to honour a complying presentation'.[306] The bank may undertake to pay on sight of the specified documents, or to incur a deferred payment undertaking and pay at maturity,[307] or to accept a bill of exchange drawn by the beneficiary and pay at maturity.[308] A complying presentation is one which is in accordance with the terms and conditions of the credit, the UCP and international standard banking practice.[309]

14.113 A credit may be either *revocable* or *irrevocable*. But UCP 600 does not apply to revocable credits, ie where the issuing bank is free to modify or cancel the credit at any time without notice to the beneficiary.[310] Except as otherwise provided by UCP 600, art 38 (transferable credits), an irrevocable credit cannot be modified or cancelled after it has been communicated to the beneficiary without the consent of the issuing bank, confirming bank, if any, and the beneficiary.[311] A credit which does not indicate whether it is revocable or irrevocable will be deemed irrevocable.[312]

14.114 A credit may be either *confirmed* or *unconfirmed*. A confirmed credit is one to which the advising bank has added its own definite undertaking to honour or negotiate the credit, provided there is a complying presentation.[313] This is done in

---

[303] *Forestal Mimosa Ltd v Oriental Credit Ltd* [1986] 1 WLR 631, 639, CA.

[304] *Royal Bank of Scotland plc v Cassa di Risparmio Delle Provincie Lombard* [1992] 1 Bank LR 251, 256, CA.

[305] *Glencore International AG v Bank of China* [1996] 1 Lloyd's Rep 135, CA.

[306] UCP 600, art 2.

[307] A deferred payment credit can be discounted before its maturity date by the discounting bank taking an assignment of the beneficiary's rights under the credit. UCP 600, art 12(b), extends the mandate of a nominated bank to discounting a deferred payment undertaking so that the risk of fraud is placed on the issuing bank (which can recover from the applicant) and not the discounting bank (thereby reversing the outcome of *Banco Santander SA v Bayfern Ltd* [2000] 1 All ER (Comm) 776, CA). See also UCP 600, arts 7(c), 8(c).

[308] UCP 600, art 2.

[309] ibid.

[310] Revocable credits are rare, but if the parties to the underlying contract want to use one, they should make the credit subject to UCP 500, an earlier version of the UCP, which extends to revocable credits.

[311] UCP 600, art 10.

[312] ibid art 3.

[313] ibid art 2.

response to a request from the issuing bank. The credit is unconfirmed when the advising bank has not provided such an undertaking. In practice, an advising bank will only confirm an irrevocable credit. Sometimes the advising bank will confirm the credit at the request of the beneficiary. This is called a 'silent confirmation'.

A credit may be either a *straight* credit or a *negotiation* credit. With a straight credit **14.115** the issuing bank's payment undertaking is directed solely to the beneficiary. With a negotiation credit, the issuing bank's payment undertaking is not confined to the beneficiary but extends to the bank authorized to negotiate (ie purchase) bills of exchange ('drafts') drawn by the beneficiary on another party (often, but not always, the issuing bank) and/or documents which strictly comply with the terms and conditions of the credit.[314]

(d) Fundamental principles

(i) Strict compliance

The principle of strict compliance requires that tendered documents must strictly **14.116** comply with the terms of the credit. In the words of Viscount Sumner in *Equitable Trust Co of New York v Dawson Partners Ltd*: '[t]here is no room for documents which are almost the same, or which will do just as well'.[315] The principle applies to all contracts arising out of a documentary credit transaction.[316]

The wording of the credit is of paramount importance when determining whether **14.117** there has been compliance with its terms. Even an apparently trivial discrepancy will justify rejection of the documents if the credit is specific as to that requirement.[317] On the other hand, the courts are willing to overlook a trivial defect in the tendered documents where there is a patent typographical error or other obvious slip or omission.[318] But where it is not clear whether the departure from the detail set out in the credit was a draftsman's error or not, the discrepancy justifies the rejection of the documents.[319] It is sometimes difficult to draw a clear line between the two types of cases.[320]

---

[314] ibid.

[315] (1927) 27 Ll L Rep 49, 52 (a bank v applicant case).

[316] *JH Rayner & Co Ltd v Hambro's Bank Ltd* [1943] KB 37, CA (a beneficiary v bank case); *Bank Meli Iran v Barclays Bank DCO* [1951] 2 Lloyd's Rep 367 (a bank v bank case); cf *Bunge Corpn v Vegetable Vitamin Foods (Pte) Ltd* [1985] 1 Lloyd's Rep 613 (where 'substantial compliance' test used in underlying contract).

[317] *Seaconsar Far East Ltd v Bank Markasi Jomhouri Islami Iran* [1993] 1 Lloyd's Rep, CA (revsd on other grounds, [1994] 1 AC 438) and [1999] 1 Lloyd's Rep 36, 38, CA.

[318] See, eg, *Hing Yip Hing Fat Co Ltd v Daiwa Bank Ltd* [1991] 2 HKLR 35, HKSC.

[319] See, eg, *Beyene v Irving Trust Co Ltd* (1985) 762 Fed Rep 2d 4, USCA.

[320] *Kredietbank Antwerp v Midland Bank plc* [1999] 1 All ER (Comm) 801, 806, CA. But UCP 600, art 14(j) does clarify the position where the addresses and contact details (phone, fax, e-mail etc) of the beneficiary and the applicant do not correspond.

14.118 A 'mirror image' interpretation of the strict compliance rule is unworkable in practice. Rejection of tendered documents becomes the norm. Bankers have recognized this for some time. This has led the ICC to promote a more flexible approach to documentary compliance. Article 14(a) of UCP 600 calls on the banks 'to examine a presentation to determine, on the basis of the documents alone, whether or not the documents appear on their face to constitute a complying presentation'. It will be recalled that a complying presentation is one in accordance with, *inter alia*, international standard banking practices.[321] The ICC has detailed relevant practices in a publication called *International Standard Banking Practices for the Examination of Documents under Documentary Letters of Credit*.[322] In addition, the latest revision of the UCP contains a number of new provisions which are designed to ensure that tendered documents are not rejected for overly technical reasons, eg, that documents need not be mirror images of each other, merely that they must not be inconsistent,[323] that non-documentary conditions are to be ignored unless they can be clearly linked to a document stipulated in the credit.[324]

14.119 The basic rule is that original documents must be tendered to the bank, unless the credit calls for copy documents. But, in a world dominated by the word-processor and the photocopier, there has been uncertainty as to what constitutes an original document, uncertainty that has been reflected in the case law.[325] Article 17 of UCP 600 clears up the uncertainty. It states that at least one original of each stipulated document must be tendered,[326] and provides that a bank must treat as original any document bearing an apparently original signature, mark, stamp or label of the issuer of the document, unless the document itself indicates that it is not original.[327] Unless a document indicates otherwise, a bank is also to accept a document as original (i) if it appears to be written, typed, perforated or stamped by the document issuer's hand; or (ii) appears to be on the document issuer's original stationery; or (iii) states that it is an original, unless the statement appears not to apply to the document presented.[328]

---

[321] Para 14.112.

[322] 2007 revision, ICC Publication No 681.

[323] UCP 600, art 14(d).

[324] ibid art 14(h). Note also the following provisions of UCP 600, which also appeared in UCP 500, namely, art 14(e) (for documents other than the commercial invoice) and art 30 (tolerances).

[325] See *Glencore International AG v Bank of China*, n 305 above; *Kredietbank Antwerp v Midland Bank plc*, n 320 above, *Crédit Industriel et Commercial v China Merchants Bank* [2002] EWHC 973 (Comm); [2002] 2 All ER (Comm) 427.

[326] UCP 600, art 17(a).

[327] ibid art 17(b).

[328] ibid art 17(c).

(ii) Autonomy of the credit

A documentary credit is separate from, and independent of, the underlying con-   **14.120**
tract between the applicant and the beneficiary, and from the relationship between
the issuing bank and the applicant or between the banks themselves. In general,
therefore, the beneficiary's breach of the underlying contract is no defence to the
issuing bank or to the confirming bank. By the same token, the issuing bank
cannot refuse to honour its undertaking just because of the applicant's failure to
put it in funds.

The principle of autonomy of the credit is enshrined in the UCP. Article 4 of UCP   **14.121**
600 provides that 'a credit by its nature is a separate transaction from the sale or
other contract on which it may be based. Banks are in no way concerned with or
bound by such contract, even if any reference whatsoever to it is included in the
credit'. The autonomy rule is also linked to the principle, to be found in art 5, that
in credit operations '[b]anks deal with documents and not with goods, services or
performance to which the documents may relate'. Similarly, art 34 makes clear
that in credit operations banks have no responsibility for anything other than
conformity of the documents to the credit. The English courts have applied the
principle of autonomy of the credit on numerous occasions.[329]

(iii) Autonomy and the fraud exception

The autonomy principle is not absolute. The most important exception to the   **14.122**
rule is where there is a fraud on the part of the beneficiary or his agent in relation
to the presentation of documents to the bank.[330] The classic formulation of the
fraud exception to the autonomy principle is to be found in the speech of Lord
Diplock in *United City Merchants (Investments) Ltd v Royal Bank of Canada*.[331]
Lord Diplock began by affirming the principle that with credits the parties deal in
documents, and not in goods, and continued:[332]

> To this general statement of principle as to the contractual obligations of the con-
> firming bank to the seller, there is one established exception: that is where the seller,
> for the purposes of drawing on the credit, fraudulently presents to the confirming

---

[329] See, eg, *United City Merchants (Investments) Ltd v Royal Bank of Canada, The American Accord*
[1983] 1 AC 168, 182–183, HL; *Tukan Timber Ltd v Barclays Bank plc* [1987] 1 Lloyd's Rep 171,
174; *Themehelp Ltd v West* [1996] QB 84, 89, CA.

[330] One other exception is where illegality taints the credit itself; but it is uncertain whether
the English courts will enforce a credit, not itself tainted with illegality, where the credit has been
entered into pursuant to an underlying contract that is itself illegal: see *Mahonia v JP Morgan Chase
Bank* [2003] 2 Lloyd's Rep 911 at [68]; *Group Josi Re v Walbrook Insurance* [1996] 1 WLR 1152,
1164, CA. A further exception is that a bank may be able to invoke a limited right of set-off based
on a debt owed by the beneficiary to the bank: *Hong Kong and Shanghai Banking Corporation v
Kloeckner & Co AG* [1990] 2 QB 514.

[331] n 329 above.

[332] ibid 183.

bank documents that contain, expressly or by implication, material representations of fact that to his knowledge are untrue.

If the fraud is a fraud by an independent third party, as it was in *United City Merchants*, where the fraud was that of loading brokers, who were the carrier's agents, then the beneficiary can still enforce the credit. Moreover, there is no separate exception to the autonomy principle that applies simply because the tendered document is a 'nullity' in the sense that it is forgery or executed without the authority of the person by whom it purports to be issued.[333]

14.123 A bank is not justified in refusing to honour the credit unless fraud is clearly established.[334] Mere suspicion is not enough.[335] By contrast, if the bank is unaware of the fraud, and accepts the documents and pays the beneficiary, it may claim reimbursement from the applicant or the issuing bank, as the case may be, despite the fact that evidence of fraud has since come to light.[336] The applicant for the credit who alleges fraud on the part of the beneficiary may apply to the court for an interlocutory injunction to restrain the bank from honouring the credit. In practice, such injunctions are rarely granted. There are three hurdles that face the applicant. First, there may be difficulty in establishing a cause of action against a bank other than the issuing bank.[337] If the applicant is enjoining the issuing bank it can rely on an implied term of the contract between them to the effect that the bank must not pay out on a fraudulent claim.[338] In cases where the beneficiary has agreed not to draw on the credit unless certain conditions are fulfilled, the applicant may find it easier to enjoin the beneficiary.[339] Secondly, the burden of proof is high. At the interlocutory stage what has to be established is a good arguable case that the only realistic inference is fraud.[340] Thirdly, the balance of convenience will almost always be against the grant of an injunction.[341] The applicant may do better to seek a freezing order against the beneficiary, freezing the proceeds of the credit in his hands.

---

[333] *Montrod Ltd v Grundkotter Fleischvertriebs GmbH* [2001] EWCA Civ 1954; [2002] 1 All ER (Comm) 257, CA; cf *Beam Technology (MFG) PTE Ltd v Standard Chartered Bank* [2003] 1 SLR 597, Sing CA.

[334] *Edward Owen (Engineering) Ltd v Barclays Bank International Ltd* [1978] QB 159, 169, 173, 175, CA.

[335] *Society of Lloyd's v Canadian Imperial Bank of Commerce* [1993] 2 Lloyd's Rep 579.

[336] *Gian Singh & Co Ltd v Banque de l'Indochine* [1974] 2 All ER 754, PC.

[337] Cf *Group Josi Re v Walbrook Insurance*, n 330 above, 1160.

[338] *Czarnikow-Rionda Sugar Trading Inc v Standard Bank London Ltd* [1999] 2 Lloyd's Rep 187.

[339] *Sirius International Insurance Corp (Publ) v FAI General Insurance Co Ltd* [2003] EWCA Civ 470; [2003] 1 WLR 2214 (revsd on other grounds, [2004] 1 WLR 3251).

[340] *United Trading Corpn SA v Allied Arab Bank Ltd* [1985] 2 Lloyd's Rep 554n, 561, 565, CA.

[341] *Czarnikow-Rionda*, n 338 above.

(e) Examination and rejection of documents

UCP 600 states that a bank must examine tendered documents to determine **14.124** whether they appear on their face to constitute a complying presentation. Unlike UCP 500,[342] the version of the UCP that immediately preceded it, UCP 600 does not expressly state that the bank must conduct its examination with reasonable care. But English common law is likely to maintain the requirement.[343] Each bank has a maximum of five banking days following the day of presentation to determine if the presentation is complying.[344]

UCP 600 provides that where a bank decides to refuse to honour or negotiate the **14.125** credit, it must give a single notice to that effect to the presenter.[345] The notice must state each discrepancy in respect of which the bank refuses to honour or negotiate.[346] The notice must be given by telecommunication or, if that is not possible, by other expeditious means no later than the close of the fifth banking day following the day of presentation.[347] If an issuing bank or a confirming bank fails to act in accordance with these rules, the bank is precluded from claiming that the documents do not constitute a complying presentation.[348]

---

[342] UCP 500, art 13(a).

[343] *Gian Singh & Co Ltd v Banque de l'Indochine*, n 336, 757–758, *per* Lord Diplock.

[344] UCP 600, art 14(b) (a 'banking day' is defined in art 2). Cf UCP 500, art 13(b), which gave the bank a reasonable time, not to exceed seven banking days, to examine the documents and make the determination.

[345] UCP 600, art 16(c).

[346] ibid. Cf *Kydon Compania Naviera SA v National Westminster Bank Ltd, The Lena* [1981] 1 Lloyd's Rep 68, 79, for the position at common law.

[347] ibid art 16(d).

[348] ibid art 16(f).

15

EMPLOYMENT

A. Definition, Sources,[1] and Scope of the English Private Law of Employment

(1) Definition

(a) The general definition of the English private law of employment

15.01 This discussion is confined to the private law of employment.[2] A somewhat complex working definition is indispensable. For present purposes therefore it is taken that we are concerned with the body of common-law based legal principles and rules governing personal work relationships between individual workers and their employers, viewed as private persons whose relations are governed by English private law. Some explanation is necessary.

15.02 The definition confines discussion to personal work relationships between individual workers and their employers. This chiefly cuts out purely commercial or business relationships. It is not always easy to draw this line.[3]

15.03 The definition confines itself to legal principles and rules. This excludes extra-legal or para-legal sources such as collective agreements, or governmental statements of policy or guidance.[4]

15.04 Deakin and Morris speak of labour law as having 'diverse origins in the law of obligations and in the regulatory intervention of the state'.[5] Our definition deliberately emphasizes the aspects of employment law which rest on the law of obligations rather than the aspects attributable to the regulatory intervention of the state.

15.05 It would be very unsatisfactory from many points of view to attempt a complete separation between common law and statute law in the field of employment law. Nevertheless, by focusing on the principles of employment law which derive from, or are strongly connected to, the common law of contract and tort, we can hope to pinpoint the authentically private law part or aspect of employment law.

15.06 The definition speaks in terms of relations between individual workers and their employers, viewed as private persons whose relations are governed by English

---

[1] The statute law of employment has been largely (though by no means entirely) consolidated into two statutes, the Trade Union and Labour Relations (Consolidation) Act 1992 ('TULRCA 1992'), and the Employment Rights Act 1996 ('ERA 1996'). Employment legislation often takes the form of amendment of those and other statutes. All statutory references in this chapter are to the legislation in question as amended down to the reference date for this work unless it is stated to the contrary.

[2] See para 15.06.

[3] See paras 15.15–15.18.

[4] See paras 15.08–15.14.

[5] S Deakin and GS Morris, *Labour Law* (4th edn, 2005) 1.

private law. This separates that part of employment law in which employers are viewed as public bodies, and/or in which workers are viewed as public functionaries, and in which their relations are governed by public law. Again the separation cannot be rigid or complete. The impact of public law upon employment law in recent decades has been too wide-ranging, and yet too fragmentary, to permit of such a strong dichotomy.[6]

Narrower in these respects than employment law as a whole, the definition is in one way broader. For employment law has tended to be overwhelmingly concentrated on a certain limited set of work relationships, namely contracts of employment strictly so called, or contracts of service,[7] in contrast with contracts between employers and independent contractors or contracts for services. Our working definition extends across the full range of personal work relationships.[8]   **15.07**

(2) Sources

(a) Common law and equity

Many parts or aspects of the common law and of the law of equity have a bearing upon or a contribution to make to the law of work relationships. Kahn-Freund reminds us that the 'law of master and servant' finds its historical origins in the common law of domestic relations.[9] The modern law concerning occupational pensions is constructed upon the basis of the law of private trusts.[10] The legal regulation of the governance of trade unions is, in origin at least, part of the common law of voluntary associations.[11] The law of restitution is occasionally involved, for example when the notion of economic duress is invoked against trade union industrial action,[12] or in order to recover an overpayment of wages which has resulted from a mistake of fact.[13] The law of equitable remedies often has a crucial role, for example in determining when interim injunctions are available against industrial action.[14] However, contract and tort unquestionably dominate.   **15.08**

---

[6] See PL Davies and MR Freedland, 'The Impact of Public Law on Labour Law 1972–1997' (1997) 26 ILJ 311–35.

[7] Compare, for instance, O Kahn-Freund, 'Blackstone's Neglected Child: the Contract of Employment' (1978) 93 LQR 508–28.

[8] See para15.15.

[9] Kahn-Freund (n 7 above) at 508–12, showing how Blackstone expounded the law of master and servant as part, in effect, of family law.

[10] See generally, R Nobles, *Pensions, Employment and the Law* (1993).

[11] See C Grunfeld, *Modern Trade Union Law* (1965) ch 1.

[12] Compare *Universe Tankships Inc of Monrovia v International Transport Workers Federation* [1982] ICR 262, HL.

[13] Compare *Avon County Council v Howlett* [1983] IRLR 171, CA.

[14] See S Deakin and GS Morris, *Labour Law* (4th edn, 2005), 11.48—11.51.

(i) The common law of contract

15.09   It has been said that the contract of employment forms the cornerstone of our system of labour law.[15] This chapter therefore inevitably consists, at a number of points, of exposition of the main principles of the common law of the contract of employment, itself an integral part of the law of contract as a whole. There is a further set of issues, less actively discussed now than in the past, about the distinctiveness of the common law of contract in its application to collective agreements between employers and trade unions. That set of issues has been largely resolved by the enactment of a conclusive presumption that a collective agreement was not intended to be a legally enforceable contract unless it is in writing and contains an express provision that it was so intended.[16]

(ii) The common law of tort

15.10   The importance of tort can be seen chiefly in two contexts. First, the evolution of economic torts, such as interference with the performance of contracts, and of an economic aspect to torts such as nuisance, has provided the basis for the legal regulation of industrial action. Despite extensive statutory interventions, industrial action is still one of the primary areas for the development of the economic torts themselves, and of the economic aspect of other torts. Secondly, the tort of negligence imposes very significant obligations upon employers towards workers, particularly in the area of the health, safety, and welfare of workers. Here again the common law, much modified by statute, continues to provide a dynamic body of principles for application to emerging issues of this kind, and as such it interacts in significant ways with the common law of contract, above all when the latter generates implied terms of work contracts which result in tort-like liabilities.[17]

(b) English statute law

15.11   Our working definition requires that particular attention be paid to statute law where it modifies and contributes to the common-law principles of employment law. A path has to be found between two extremes. At one extreme, it could be said that in a loose sense, all of the statute law of employment operates to modify the common law of employment. At the other, it could be insisted that the statute law of employment can be regarded as modifying the common law of employment only when it is formally expressed as doing so—as, for example, where a statute expressly implies a term into the contract of employment, or changes the conditions of application of a common law tort.

---

15   O Kahn-Freund, 'Legal Framework' in A Flanders and H Clegg (eds), *The System of Industrial Relations in Britain* (1954) 45.

16   See TULRCA 1992, s 179.

17   See paras 15.45–15.52.

A sensible compromise will accept legislation as generally a potential source of the **15.12** private law of employment, which becomes an actual source only where one can identify its particular contribution to the body of basic (and common-law based) principles of the private law of employment. Viewed in this way, the statute law of employment discrimination, for instance, ranks as a source of the private law of employment. To take a major example, among the Articles of the European Convention of Human Rights which are incorporated into English law by the Human Rights Act 1998, are Article 8 which protects the right to private life and family life and Article 11 which protects freedom of association, including the right to form and join trade unions; they have an obvious bearing on the private law of employment.

(c) European Community law

Similar arguments arise in respect of Community law. Here again, it seems coher- **15.13** ent to envisage a middle way, treating European Community employment law as a potential source; but this time the conditions for regarding it as an actual source should be more stringent. That is for two reasons. First, European Community employment measures are more apt than English statute law to have the character of general regulatory intervention which does not have any significant impact on the law of obligations. Secondly, many significant European Community employment law measures, particularly those embodied in directives, require or are the subject of English primary or secondary legislation for their implementation, and to that extent only operate indirectly upon the English private law of employment.

Nevertheless, there are significant areas in which European Community employ- **15.14** ment law does shape the development of the common-law based principles of the English private law of employment. This is true of the European Community measures concerning equal pay and equal opportunity as between women and men at work, and also those concerning discrimination on the grounds of race, religion or belief, sexual orientation, disability, and age.[18] It is also true in the area of transfer of employment, where the Acquired Rights Directive of 1977[19] effected or required a fundamental modification of the common-law principle against the transferability of employment which was associated with the leading case of *Nokes v Doncaster Amalgamated Collieries Ltd.*[20]

---

[18] See paras 15.39–15.44.
[19] Council Directive (EEC) 77/187, since amended and consolidated into (EC) 2001/23; see further paras 15.102–15.110.
[20] [1940] AC 1014, HL.

(3) The Range and Classification of Work Relationships Falling within the English Private Law of Employment

(a) The contract of employment and other personal work contracts

15.15 As was indicated earlier, the private law of employment as envisaged in this chapter extends to at least some contracts for services as well as to contracts of employment. More particularly, it extends to those contracts for services which embody personal work relationships.

15.16 There are a number of reasons for taking this view. First, as we shall see at various points, the statute law of employment extends in varying degrees beyond contracts which are not contracts of employment in the strict sense. Secondly, and more important, the common-law based principles of the private law of employment also apply at least in part to other personal work contracts. In any case, though the line has to be drawn for some purposes, the practice of the labour market makes it increasingly difficult to distinguish between contracts of employment and other personal work contracts.

15.17 There are good reasons for confining the purview of the private law of employment to personal work relationships which are personal ones in the sense that the work in question is to be performed by the worker personally. Again, this follows the pattern of the statute law of employment, which, even in its most inclusive forms (subject to a minor exception in respect of homeworkers)[21] does so confine itself. Moreover, the common law itself differentiates between personal work relationships and purely commercial relationships. The best, though not the only, example is the equitable principle against the specific enforcement of personal work obligations.[22]

(b) The meaning of 'personal' in the context of work relationships

15.18 'Personal' indicates that individuals provide their own services rather than arranging to provide the services of others. A contract for the provision of the services of others is archetypally a commercial contract rather than a contract for personal work or employment. That seems to be the distinction intended by the statutory provisions relating to the various forms of unlawful discrimination in employment, as in the Equal Pay Act 1970,[23] the Sex Discrimination Act 1975,[24]

---

[21] Some employment legislation is applied to homeworkers even though they may themselves employ assistants to carry out the work. Compare for example s 35(1) of the National Minimum Wage Act 1998 which provides that 'In determining for the purposes of this Act whether a home worker is or is not a worker [the definition of 'worker'] shall have effect as if for the word "personally" there were substituted "(whether personally or otherwise)"'.

[22] See paras 15.98–15.100.

[23] Section 1(6)(a).

[24] Section 82.

and the Race Relations Act 1976,[25] or by the variant used in the Disability Discrimination Act 1995.[26] However, many contracts or arrangements for work permit a party, who contracts to provide his own services, to make some use of the services of others, or they leave that matter open. In the leading case of *Mirror Group Newspapers Ltd v Gunning*,[27] the Court of Appeal's test was whether the personal execution of services was the 'dominant purpose' of the contract in question, rather than merely an incidental aspect of it.

(4) The Distinctions between the Different Types of Personal Employment Contracts

It is a complex question how far the private law of employment can be said to apply uniformly to the different work relationships. It is quite clear, moreover, that the statute law creates a number of sub-categories of such relationships. For example, recent legislation applies to 'workers', defined so as to include individuals who have personal work contracts which are not contracts of employment unless the status of the other party to the contract is 'that of a client or customer of any profession or business undertaking carried on by the individual'.[28] However, unquestionably the most important distinction is still that between contracts of employment strictly so-called and other personal work contracts, or personal contracts for services, and that distinction is accordingly examined further in the following paragraphs.   **15.19**

(a) The contract of employment distinguished from other personal work contracts

The very extensive case law[29] leaves continuing uncertainty as to what tests are to be applied, as to how far the drawing of the distinction is an issue of law or of fact, and as to whether the treatment of the issue should be uniform throughout the different contexts in which it arises. Those issues are addressed in summary form in the succeeding paragraphs.   **15.20**

The most authoritative general recent statement as to what test or tests are to be applied is to be found in the case of *Hall v Lorimer*,[30] which concerned the income tax status of a freelance worker who entered into short-term work contracts with a number of different employers. It emerges from the judgments given in that case   **15.21**

---

25 Section 78.
26 Section 68(1).
27 [1986] ICR 145.
28 For example the National Minimum Wage Act 1998, s 54(3)(b).
29 A full treatment of it is to be found in *Chitty on Contracts* (29th edn, 2004) 39–010 to 39–028.
30 [1994] ICR 218, CA.

that there is a modern consensus against there being any one decisive test for the presence of a contract of employment, but rather in favour of there being an obligation upon those adjudicating that issue to consider a multiplicity of indications for or against an employment relationship in the narrow strict sense. There is quite a general acceptance that a highly significant indicator, almost amounting to a prevailing test, is to be found in the formulation of Cooke J that:

> The fundamental test to be applied is this, 'Is the person who has engaged himself to perform those services performing them as a person in business on his own account?'[31]

15.22 If there is a measure of agreement about the main indicators which are to be used to test whether a work relationship takes place under a contract of employment, there is nevertheless still great scope for argument about the outcome of that adjudication in any given fact situation; and the result has been considerable debate as to how far the issue is one of law, and hence the subject of an appeal on a point of law. Again, *Hall v Lorimer*[32] seems to reflect a modern consensus on this point also, to the effect that the issue is one of mixed fact and law, so that an adjudication upon the issue is appealable to the extent, but only to the extent, that there can be shown to be a particular error of law in the way that it was arrived at.

15.23 There is, moreover, even less agreement as to whether the distinction between the contract of employment and other personal work contracts, or the distinction between 'employees' and other workers, is to be uniformly drawn as between the different statutory and regulatory contexts in which it falls to be applied. There seems to be a general preference for maintaining the distinction as a fairly uniform one for whatever purpose it is being drawn; the main exception seems to be a tendency to lean in favour of finding a contract of employment where that places a worker within the scope of legislation designed to protect health and safety in the workplace.[33] In some degree of contrast to the approach in that context, there is some insistence, in the context of legislation protecting the security of employment of 'employees'—notably the legislation providing remedies for unfair dismissal—that work relationships must evince a high degree of 'mutuality of obligation' before the workers concerned can be regarded as 'employees'.[34]

(b) Intermittent work relationships

15.24 The classificatory and analytical role which the private law of employment has to perform with regard to work relationships in general becomes even more complex with regard to the large and growing number of types of work relationships

---

[31] *Market Investigations Ltd v Minister of Social Security* [1969] 2 QB 173, 184.
[32] [1994] ICR 218, CA.
[33] Compare *Lane v Shire Roofing Co (Oxford) Ltd* [1995] IRLR 493, CA.
[34] See for instance *Express & Echo Publications Ltd v Tanton* [1999] ICR 693, CA.

which are in some sense intermittent—that being the quality which, for example, casual, seasonal, and temporary work generally have in common. This added complexity is due to the fact that, with regard to such work relationships, it is often necessary not only to draw the distinction between the contract of employment and the contract for services, but also to decide (for the purposes of a number of statutory rights) whether the contractual relationship is a continuous one, constituted by a single continuing contract or, if by more than one contract, by temporally contiguous contracts.

For a time, the courts seemed to prefer to address this set of issues by asking, in relation to intermittent work arrangements, whether they could discern on the facts the presence of a 'global' or 'umbrella' contract which could be viewed as subsisting both during and between intermittent periods of work; if so, they were ready to characterize that contract as a contract of employment.[35] The current method of analysing intermittent work arrangements seems to be to ask whether there is sufficient continuing mutuality of obligation to identify the whole relationship as taking place in the form of a contract of employment. It will often be debatable in the case of casual employment whether there is a reciprocal obligation to offer and accept work;[36] but in the absence of any such reciprocal obligation, the worker cannot be counted as an employee with a contract of employment.[37]

15.25

(c) Work relationships involving intermediaries

Problems of analysis and classification present themselves with regard to work relationships involving intermediaries in at least as severe a way as they do with regard to intermittent work relationships; moreover, a large and growing number of work relationships combine both those features. The most significant, though not the sole, form of work relationship involving an intermediary is that which arises where the worker is not merely introduced, but in some sense continuingly employed, via an employment agency or employment business—the latter terminology being now regarded as appropriate to denote the continuing intermediary role in relation to so-called 'agency workers'. With regard to work relationships in that form, there are serious difficulties in deciding whether the worker has a personal contract either with the intermediary agency or with the actual user of his services, or with both, and furthermore in deciding whether that contract or those contracts is or are a contract or contracts of employment or not.

15.26

In response to the question, 'does the worker in such situations have a contract with the intermediary, or with the user of his services, or with both?', the courts

15.27

---

[35] *Airfix Footwear Ltd v Cope* [1978] ICR 1210, EAT; and compare *Nethermere (St Neots) Ltd v Taverna and Gardiner* [1984] ICR 612, CA.

[36] Compare *Carmichael v National Power plc* [1999] ICR 1226, HL.

[37] *Clark v Oxfordshire Health Authority* [1998] IRLR 125, CA.

have tended to view the worker as having a contract with the intermediary rather than with the user of his services; it has generally required statutory intervention to apply parts of employment law, notably the laws about employment discrimination, to the relationship between the worker and the user of his services, in the shape of provisions about 'contract workers' who are employed by an intermediary and supplied to work for a principal under a contract made between the intermediary and the principal.[38]

15.28 In response to the further question, what kind of contract does the worker have with the user of his services, or, more typically as we have seen, with the intermediary, in the important case of *McMeechan v Secretary of State for Employment*,[39] the Court of Appeal seemed readier than formerly to accept that the worker might be regarded as having either a general engagement with the agency which takes the form of a contract of employment, or a series of contracts of employment with the agency in respect of the specific engagements which are made by the agency for that worker. Subsequent case law shows that this is still a highly contested area.[40]

(d) Conclusion

15.29 It will have become apparent that the private law of employment, as defined and envisaged for the purpose of this chapter, is concerned with a wide and multifarious range of work relationships, to which it is often difficult to apply the traditional categories of contracts of service and for services. In describing the general principles of the private law of employment, we shall generally be describing the law as it applies to work relationships which take place under contracts of employment in the strict sense; but we shall where appropriate consider how those principles apply to work relationships which take place under personal work contracts which are not contracts of employment as such.

15.30 The private law of employment has been defined and described in such a way as to make it clear that it includes the law regarding collective relationships between employers and trade unions (as well as other structures for workplace representation, such as works councils). However, it is appropriate, in view of the exigencies of space, to concentrate, in the remainder of this chapter, on those aspects of the private law of employment which are closely focused upon personal work relationships expressed through the legal medium of personal work contracts. Accordingly, it will not be attempted in this chapter further to describe the common law and statute law relating to the tort-based liabilities in respect of industrial

---

[38] See s 9 of the Sex Discrimination Act 1975; s 7 of the Race Relations Act 1976; and s 12 of the Disability Discrimination Act 1995. Compare *Harrods Ltd v Remick* [1998] ICR 156, CA.

[39] [1997] ICR 549, CA.

[40] Compare *Dacas v Brook Street Bureau (UK) Ltd* [2004] ICR 1437, CA, *Muscat v Cable & Wireless plc* [2006] ICR 975, CA.

action and the immunities from those liabilities,[41] nor the equally important body of common and statute law concerning the governance of trade unions and their relations with their members and other workers,[42] nor, finally, the provisions relating to the recognition of trade unions for the purposes of collective bargaining.[43] This necessary set of omissions from the present chapter should not be allowed to cast doubt upon the integrality of those topics to a full understanding of the structure and working of the law of employment as a whole.

B. The Formation and Content of Work Relationships

(1) The General Basis and Method of Regulation at Common Law and under Statute Law

(a) Personal work contracts as standard contracts

Many treatises on employment law, when expounding the law about the forma- **15.31** tion and content of personal work relationships or contracts, concentrate largely or exclusively upon the contract of employment, and treat the formation and the content of those contracts as two distinct areas of discussion. This present exposition proceeds on the assumption that the general position of private employment law may be more clearly understood if personal work contracts are considered as a whole, and if the formation and content of those contracts are regarded as presenting a single continuous set of issues. In fact that set of issues can usefully be condensed into a single central question, which is that of how far the private law of employment imposes standard regulatory types of personal work contracts, and, to that extent, what are the standard types and how exacting are they? (This is distinct from the question of whether the terms of a contract of employment may amount to the employer's 'standard terms of business' within the meaning of section 3 of the Unfair Contract Terms Act 1977, as to which a negative conclusion was reached by the Court of Appeal in *Commerzbank AG v Keen*.[44])

This is a question which employment lawyers have often considered in the form **15.32** of a discussion whether the employment relationship should be regarded as a contract or as a status.[45] At one extreme lies the view that the formation and the establishing of the content of work relationships can be regarded as the exercise of a substantial freedom of contract, not necessarily in the sense that meaningful

---

41 See TULRCA 1992, ss 219–35C; *Clerk & Lindsell on Torts* (19th edn, 2005) ch 25.
42 See ss 1–121 of TULRCA 1992; S Deakin and GS Morris, *Labour Law* (4th edn, 2005) ch 10.
43 See Sch A1 to TULRCA 1992 as inserted by the Employment Relations Act 1999, s 1 and Sch 1.
44 [2006] EWCA Civ 1536.
45 See especially O Kahn-Freund, 'A Note on Status and Contract in Modern Labour Law' (1967) 30 MLR 635–44.

bargaining takes place between the parties, for the substance of the matter may well be controlled entirely by the employer, making it a contract of adhesion, but in the sense that there is a wide or open set of possibilities as to the shape and terms that the contract may take and contain. At the other extreme lies a contrary view that the employment relationship has been so tightly regulated especially by statute law that the formation of employment relationships is not in a meaningful sense a contractual process at all, but rather a process of allocation of one of a small number of highly standardized employment statuses.

15.33   A coherent view can be found between those two extremes, in which it is accepted that employment relationships are indeed standardized in varying degrees by many different parts or aspects of employment law, so that a full understanding of the function and operation of the private law of employment depends on an analysis of how far its different elements operate as, on the one hand, *jus cogens*, or mandatory law or, on the other hand, as *jus dispositivum*, or optional law at the disposal of the parties.[46] It is far from being the case, in the present context at least, that the statute law of employment always represents the mandatory element and that the common law of employment always represents the optional element in the determination of the form and content of work relationships. There are many important instances where the statute law of employment is derogable by agreement between the parties; on the other hand, we shall find that the terms which are implied by law into contracts of employment, and possibly other personal work contracts too, sometimes have a mandatory or non-displaceable character.

(2) Incapacity and Illegality in the Making of Personal Work Contracts

15.34   One possible way in which the private law of employment may control the formation and content of employment relationships is by treating as void or unenforceable, on the basis of incapacity or illegality, either personal work contracts as a whole or particular provisions of personal work contracts. It might in theory be possible for many kinds of legal restrictions or propositions of public policy to be implemented in this way. We should certainly regard it as an underlying principle of the private law of employment that:

> The courts will not enforce a contract of employment the terms of which are so stringent that the employee is virtually treated as his employer's 'slave or chattel', without any freedom in his private life.[47]

---

[46]   See O Kahn-Freund (ibid) 640; MR Freedland 'Jus cogens, Jus Dispositivum and the Law of Personal Work Contracts', chapter 12 of P Birks and A Pretto (eds) *Themes in Comparative Law—In Honour of Bernard Rudden* (2002).

[47]   *Chitty on Contracts* (29th edn, 2004), para 39-032.

In general, however, this is not a very prominent mode of intervention within the sphere of private employment law. Thus, the controls which exist upon the employment of children and young persons do not generally take the form of restrictions upon their capacity to enter into personal work contracts.[48] Nor do the very stringent controls upon employment of immigrants who do not have permission to work; those controls are primarily enforced by making it a criminal offence to employ persons who are in that position.[49] There are, however, two areas of intervention on the basis of illegality, or conflict with public policy, which constitute significant exceptions; these are described in the following paragraphs.

(a) Personal work contracts involving tax or social security fraud

An important application of the principle that the courts will not enforce illegal contracts has occurred where employers have resisted assertions, by employees, of statutory rights which depend upon their having contracts of employment, by alleging fraud upon the Revenue or social security fraud in the way that the contract is formulated or implemented. Such arguments have had some success; as Bristow J quoted in 1977, '…"the dirty dog gets no dinner here". We take it to be clear law that someone who tries to assert in the courts a right contained in an illegal contract will not succeed.'[50] However, it has been held that the employee is not prevented from asserting statutory rights, such as the right to remedies for unfair dismissal, where he has not benefited from and is not an essential party to the fraud.[51] It has even been held, in *Leighton v Michael*[52] that an employee whose remuneration arrangements involved a fraud upon the Revenue could nevertheless bring a complaint of unlawful sex discrimination without having to 'enforce, rely upon, or found a claim upon' her contract of employment in such a way as to confront the principle of illegality of contracts.

15.35

(b) Restraint of trade

We could regard the doctrine of restraint of trade as one which permeates the private law of employment; it is an extremely important general common law proposition that the courts will not enforce a contract or contractual undertaking where to do so would unreasonably restrain a person's freedom to work or to

15.36

---

48 They consist of very severe restrictions on the employment of children under 16, contained in the Children and Young Persons Acts 1933 and 1963, as now modified by the Children (Protection at Work) Regulations 1998, SI 1998/276.

49 Asylum and Immigration Act 1996, s 8.

50 *Tomlinson v Dick Evans 'U' Drive Ltd* [1977] ICR 639, 642, EAT.

51 *Hewcastle Catering v Ahmed* [1992] ICR 626, CA.

52 [1995] ICR 1091, EAT; compare also *Hall v Woolston Hall Leisure Ltd* [2000] ICR 99, CA, now the leading authority on this point.

engage in the occupation of his choice.[53] This has even been envisaged as amounting to a 'right to work' at common law, so that Salmon LJ could say, in *Nagle v Fielden*,[54] that:

> The principle that the courts will protect a man's right to work is well recognized in the stream of authority relating to contracts in restraint of trade.

That way of conceptualizing the role of the restraint of trade doctrine in employment law has since been disfavoured;[55] but that role has nevertheless remained highly significant, most prominently as a control upon restrictive covenants whereby workers are limited from competitive activity after the termination of their employment.[56] Within the wider sphere of personal work contracts which are not contracts of employment as such, the doctrine of restraint of trade also has an important function in relation to undertakings against competitive activity during the continuance of the contracts, for example in the case of sportspersons, or entertainers.[57]

(3) Form and Formality in the Making of Personal Work Contracts; Statutory Particulars of the Terms of Contracts of Employment

15.37 The form of personal work contracts is not directly controlled or constrained by the private law of employment, either by the common law or by statute law, nor are any formalities directly required for the valid making of such contracts. However, so far as contracts of employment strictly so-called are concerned, the employer is subject to statutory obligations to provide written particulars of certain terms of employment and certain information about the employment, such as the names of the parties, the date of commencement of employment, the details of remuneration, of hours of work, of holidays, of the place of work, and the job title.[58] The employer is also required to give written particulars of changes in those terms and conditions;[59] and the employee has the right to apply to an Employment Tribunal for rectification of failure to supply particulars or the supply of inaccurate particulars.[60] Further important requirements of particularization are made in relation to itemized pay statements.[61]

---

[53] See in general DJ Heydon, *The Restraint of Trade Doctrine* (2nd edn, 1999).
[54] [1966] 2 QB 633, 654, CA.
[55] See for instance Megarry J in *McInnes v Onslow Fane* [1978] 3 All ER 211, 217.
[56] See para 15.99.
[57] Compare, for instance, *Watson v Prager* [1991] ICR 603; *Instone v A Schroeder Music Publishing Co Ltd* [1974] 1 WLR 1308, HL.
[58] ERA 1996, s 1 (as amended by ss 35—38 of the Employment Act 2002).
[59] ibid s 4.
[60] See ss 11, 12 of the ERA 1996.
[61] ibid ss 8–10.

Indirectly, these requirements do have an influence on the form and shape of contracts of employment in certain ways. Thus, the written particulars will readily be accepted as the best evidence of the terms of the contract of employment itself, and may even, as the important case of *Gascol Conversions Ltd v Mercer*[62] established and showed, be held, on the appropriate facts, to amount to the written contract in and of themselves. Moreover, some of those requirements have the effect that the employer has to make provisions which might otherwise not have been made, in order to be able to provide the particulars in question. This is true, for instance, of the requirement that the statement of particulars shall include a note specifying, among other things, a person to whom the employee can apply if dissatisfied with a disciplinary decision relating to him, or for the purpose of seeking redress for any employment grievance.[63]

15.38

(4) Control of Discrimination in the Formation and Content of Personal Work Contracts

Employment discrimination law can be seen as affecting both formation and content of personal work contracts. The term 'employment discrimination law' is used in this chapter to refer to the body of law which relates, first, to equal pay and treatment as between men and women in employment, and secondly to various other kinds of discrimination in employment, that is to say those relating to race, disability, religion or belief, sexual orientation, and age. (The law of equal treatment as between men and women in employment has been construed so as to control discrimination against women on the ground of pregnancy;[64] there is, however, a distinct body of law which protects pregnant women in employment[65] and confers a variety of rights in connection with parenthood and the discharge of parental and other caring responsibilities.)[66] There are other aspects of employment law which could be regarded as being concerned with the control of other types of discrimination in employment, for example the law relating to freedom of association in employment,[67] the law about public interest disclosures, which

15.39

---

[62] [1974] ICR 420, CA.

[63] See ERA 1996, s 3(1)(b).

[64] Case 177/88 *Dekker v VJV Centrum* [1992] ICR 325, ECJ; compare *Webb v EMO Air Cargo Ltd* [1995] ICR 175, HL; and see now the Employment Equality (Sex Discrimination) Regulations 2005 SI 2005/2467 reg 4.

[65] See, particularly, ERA 1996, s 99 (protection from unfair dismissal with regard to pregnancy and childbirth, giving effect to Council Directive (EEC) 92/85 on pregnant workers); and 2005 SI 2005/2467 reg 4 (ibid).

[66] The provisions of ERA 1996, ss 71-80I as inserted or amended by the Employment Relations Act 1999, the Employment Act 2002, the Work and Families Act 2006 and various statutory instruments, provide for maternity leave, adoption leave, parental leave, paternity leave and a right to flexible working in connection with parenthood and other caring responsibilities.

[67] See the very important provisions of TULRCA 1992, ss 137–43 on refusal of employment on grounds related to trade union membership, and of ss 146–51 on action short of dismissal on

serves to protect 'whistleblowers' in employment,[68] the law about freedom of movement of workers within the European Union,[69] and also the law about the treatment of part-time workers by comparison with full-time workers[70] and the treatment of fixed-term workers by comparison with workers employed on an open-ended or permanent basis.[71]

15.40 Here we develop in slightly greater detail the law concerning the main heads of discrimination as identified above. The law of equal pay and treatment as between men and women in employment is contained, as was indicated earlier, partly in domestic legislation—the Equal Pay Act 1970 and the Sex Discrimination Acts 1975 and 1986, and partly in European Community measures, especially Article 119 of the Treaty of Rome,[72] and the directives on equal pay[73] and on equal treatment.[74] There was a partial re-definition of sex discrimination under s1 of the Sex Discrimination Act 1975 by the Sex Discrimination (Indirect Discrimination and Burden of Proof Regulations) Regulations 2001,[75] and an extension of the Act to include gender re-assignment by the Sex Discrimination (Gender Reassignment) Regulations 1999.[76]

15.41 The law relating to racial discrimination was originally introduced by the Race Relations Act 1976, and that relating to disability discrimination by the Disability Discrimination Act 1995. The latter Act was amended and extended in various respects by the Disability Discrimination Act 2005. As previously explained, all this legislation regarding employment discrimination applies to the whole range of personal work contracts.[77]

15.42 Moreover, the European Community acquired a new capacity to legislate about a wide range of types of discrimination, in relation to employment as well as to various other areas of activity, under the 1997 Treaty of Amsterdam which introduced what is now numbered Article 13 of the Treaty establishing the European

---

grounds related to trade union membership and activities; and compare those of ss 168–73 on time off for trade union duties and activities.

[68] See para 15.108.

[69] This derives from Art 48 of the Treaty of Rome.

[70] See the Part-time Workers (Prevention of Less Favourable Treatment) Regulations 2000 SI 2000/1551.

[71] See the Fixed-term Employees (Prevention of Less Favourable Treatment) Regulations 2000 SI 2002/ 2034. See also para 15.82.

[72] Article 141 of the Treaty establishing the European Community as renumbered under the provisions of Art 11 of the Treaty of Amsterdam.

[73] Council Directive (EC) 75/117 on equal pay for men and women [1975] OJ L45/19.

[74] Council Directive (EC) 76/207 on equal treatment for men and women [1976] OJ L139/40.

[75] SI 2001/2660.

[76] SI 1999//1102.

[77] See para 15.18.

Community. That power was used to enact what have become known as the Race Directive[78] which concerned discrimination on the grounds of race or ethnic origin, and the Employment Framework Directive[79] which concerned discrimination in employment on the grounds of religion or belief, disability, sexual orientation or age.

Measures to implement these Directives in English law and generally to revise the existing legislation concerned with discrimination have since been enacted and came into effect from 2003 onwards. These measures were the Race Relations Act (Amendment) Regulations 2003,[80] the Sex Discrimination Act 1975 (Amendment) Regulations 2003,[81] the Employment Equality (Religion or Belief) Regulations 2003,[82] the Employment Equality (Sexual Orientation) Regulations 2003,[83] the Disability Discrimination Act 1995 (Amendment) Regulations 2003,[84] and the Employment Equality (Sex Discrimination) Regulations 2005.[85]   **15.43**

Finally, a new code of controls upon age discrimination was enacted by the Employment Equality (Age) Regulations 2006,[86] and took effect in October 2006; it involved among other things an elaborate re-working of the way in which retirement is defined and regulated in English employment law.[87]   **15.44**

(5) The Construction and Implied Terms of Personal Work Contracts in General

(a) Construction as regulation in the common law of personal work contracts

Whether it does so by way of application of the general principles of contract law, or whether it creates a distinct body of law, the common law concerning the construction of personal work contracts has a major regulatory impact upon the formation and content of personal work relationships. In making that assertion, and in expounding it in greater detail in the ensuing paragraphs, we include, within the notion of the 'construction' of personal work contracts, not only the rules for determining the meaning and effect of the express terms of those contracts, but also the principles which govern the implying of terms into them, whether as a matter of 'fact' or of 'law'. We should also include, within this notion   **15.45**

---

78 Council Directive (EC) 2000/43 [2000] OJ L199/86.
79 Council Directive (EC) 2000/78 [2001] OJ L002/42.
80 SI 2003/1626.
81 SI 2003/1657.
82 SI 2003/1660.
83 SI 2003/1661.
84 SI 2003/1673.
85 SI 2005/2467.
86 SI 2006/1031.
87 Introducing new ss 98ZA to 98ZH into the Employment Rights Act 1996.

of construction, the ascribing of legal effect to the actions of the parties during the continuance of those contracts.[88]

(b) The construction of the terms of personal work contracts

15.46 We can say of personal work contracts at large, and not least of contracts of employment in particular, that they tend, to an extent which is singular, without being unique, among contracts generally, to be incompletely specified at the time of their initial formation, and very often to remain incompletely specified (despite the employer's statutory obligation to provide written particulars of the certain major terms of contracts of employment in the strict sense).[89] The contractual status of these norms of work is often far from clear, and competition or conflict between them has to be resolved. Such competition or conflict has tended to centre upon the relationship between (1) employers' rules of work, or normative exercise of 'managerial prerogative', (2) collective agreements between employers and trade unions or other representative groupings, and (3) other custom and practice alleged to have normative force.

15.47 We could think of the private law of employment as drawing upon principles of construction derived directly from the general common law of contract. A good example is the principle that a custom may be incorporated into a contract if it is 'reasonable, certain, and notorious', which has been invoked in some important employment cases.[90] Indeed, one of the key developments of the common law of the contract of employment in the modern period was the suggestion that the results of collective bargaining could satisfactorily be construed as informing individual contracts of employment on the footing that collective agreements might represent the 'crystallized custom' of the workplace.[91] However, the current patterns of work relationships are so rapidly changing, and so highly localized or even individualized, that there seems little prospect of recognition of customary terms at the present day, or of the terms of collective agreements qualifying as such.[92]

15.48 Alternatively, we might regard the body of employment case law which concerns the implication of terms from extraneous sources such as collective agreements as an application of general common-law construction principles

---

[88] For instance, the fundamentally important analysis of strike notice as notice of *breach* rather than of *termination*, in the leading cases of *Rookes v Barnard* [1964] AC 1129, HL, and *Stratford Ltd v Lindley* [1965] AC 269, HL.

[89] See para 15.37.

[90] See *Devonald v Rosser & Sons* [1906] 2 KB 728; *Sagar v Ridehalgh & Sons Ltd* [1931] 1 Ch 310, CA.

[91] See O Kahn-Freund in Flanders and Clegg (eds), *The System of Industrial Relations in Great Britain* (1954) 58.

[92] For an exception which proves the rule, compare *Henry v London General Transport Services Ltd* [2002] ICR 910.

about incorporation of documents and the parol evidence rule. However, there would still have to be said to be grave doubt as to whether the employment case law could satisfactorily be so regarded. The discussion about the incorporation of terms from collective agreements has become highly specialized, not least because it often in practice turns on the statutory written particulars of terms of employment, in which, since 1993, employers have been obliged to include particulars of any collective agreements 'directly affecting the terms and conditions of the employment'.[93]

(c) Implied terms in personal work contracts

If the highly specific evaluations, which the employment case law about incorporation of terms involves, cast doubt on the status of that case law as falling within the general principles of construction of the common law of contract, they also make the decisions in question very difficult. We may conclude that the courts feel conscious of these difficulties, since they show a marked tendency to resolve issues of this kind by fashioning different conceptual tools which seem to serve their purpose better. In particular, there has been a strong tendency to address these issues by the use of reasoning about the implied terms of personal work contracts, and more especially about the general or over-arching implied terms. An example is provided by the leading case of *Secretary of State for Employment v ASLEF (No 2)*,[94] where the issue was whether railway workers were in breach of their contracts of employment when, by way of industrial action, they deliberately applied some provisions of the employer's rule-book with excessive zeal so as to disrupt the working of the railway. It was held, regardless of the contractual status of the works rules, that these workers had acted in breach of an implied obligation of co-operation, or, more precisely, an obligation to refrain from wilful disruption of the working of the enterprise.[95]

15.49

Where terms of that kind are implied, various juridical analyses are suggested to explain what has occurred. There is a lack of consensus as to whether such terms are implied as a matter of 'fact' or of 'law'.[96] The process may be regarded as an application or an analogy of the process of ensuring that contracts are so construed as to satisfy the notion of 'business efficacy'[97] or so as to reproduce that which the

15.50

---

[93] See now ERA 1996, s 1(4)(j). See the discussion of the 'bridge term' in S Deakin and GS Morris, *Labour Law* (4th edn, 2005) 265–6.

[94] [1972] ICR 19, CA.

[95] This kind of construction of contracts of employment has, since that time, continued to play an important role in determining the effects of industrial action short of strike action, and in particular the extent to which remuneration may be withheld in response to such action; see, for instance, *Sim v Rotherham Metropolitan Borough Council* [1986] ICR 897; *Miles v Wakefield Metropolitan District Council* [1987] ICR 368, HL.

[96] Compare *Chitty on Contracts* (29th edn, 2004) 13-003–010.

[97] See *Shirlaw v Southern Foundries (1926) Ltd* [1939] 2 KB 206.

'officious bystander'[98] (or impartial observer) would regard as their obvious content. Alternatively, various dicta in the leading case of *Liverpool City Council v Irwin*[99] suggest that the courts may be engaged in establishing what are the 'necessary incidents' of a contract which establishes a certain kind of relationship, such as that of employment.[100]

(d) The implied term as to mutual trust and confidence

15.51 In the common law of the contract of employment, there is a long tradition of expounding the 'necessary incidents' of the 'master and servant' relationship, in the form, particularly, of implied which assert the employee's basic obligations of obedience, care and competence, and fidelity.[101] In more recent years, there has been extensive development of a general implied term requiring the parties to the contract of employment so to conduct themselves as to deserve and retain the trust and confidence of the other party. Although reciprocally applicable to both parties, it has been developed especially as a control upon the conduct of employers; as such, it received the recognition of the House of Lords in the landmark, case of *Malik v Bank of Credit and Commerce International SA*,[102] where the employing bank was held to have breached that obligation to its managerial staff in that the conduct of the enterprise was so disreputable as to damage the subsequent employment prospects even of employees who were not personally implicated in that misconduct. However, in the subsequent leading case of *Johnson v Unisys Ltd*,[103] the House of Lords identified or imposed a significant restriction upon the scope of application of the implied term as to mutual trust and confidence, holding that it did not apply so as to give a remedy in damages in respect of the employer's way of exercising a contractual power or right of dismissal.[104]

15.52 The implied term as to mutual trust and confidence functions so as, in effect, to impose a duty on the employer and upon the worker to behave responsibly with regard to the interests and concerns of the other. It appears, from decisions in cases such as that of *Imperial Group Pension Trust Ltd v Imperial Tobacco Ltd*[105] that this duty may operate so as to control the way in which employers use their

---

[98] See *The Moorcock* (1889) 14 PD 64.

[99] [1977] AC 39, HL.

[100] See Stephenson LJ in the employment case of *Mears v Safecar Security Ltd* [1982] ICR 626, 650, CA.

[101] See further paras 15.74–15.78.

[102] [1997] ICR 606, HL; alternatively cited by the name of the other appellant as *Mahmud* etc.

[103] [2001] ICR 480.

[104] Determining how far the restriction applies to *constructive* dismissal has proved difficult; see *Eastwood v Magnox Electric Plc* [2005] 1 AC 503, HL.

[105] [1991] ICR 524. There are also a number of decisions concerning the awarding of discretionary bonuses, see especially *Horkulak v Cantor Fitzgerald International* [2005] ICR 402 (distinguishing

contractual or other powers—in that particular instance, the employer's powers conferred by its pension scheme trust deed. It is much less clear whether and how far this implied obligation may override other terms of contracts of employment, or, to put it the other way round, whether and how far the implied obligation may be excluded by terms which are directly or indirectly inconsistent with it.[106] It is also unclear how far the implied term is confined to contracts of employment as such, or how far, on the other hand, it may extend to other personal work contracts. The Court of Appeal in *Express & Echo Publication Ltd v Tanton*[107] seemed to regard the implied term as an integral, non-displaceable, identifying feature of contracts of employment strictly so-called, closely associated with the idea that contracts of employment must display continuing mutuality of obligation.[108]

(6) The Legal Regulation of Remuneration for Employment

It should not occasion surprise to state that the common law of personal work contracts is not closely concerned with the regulation of remuneration for employment; the area of remuneration is one in which the common law basic leaning in favour of the freedom of contract provides the dominant impulse. Nevertheless, the common law has had a role in regulating the security of income, and the law of equity and trusts has provided the basis for the legal regulation of occupational pension schemes. Equally, it should occasion no greater surprise to point out that the statute law of employment has been and remains concerned with the regulation of remuneration and pensions to quite a significant extent.   **15.53**

(a) Minimum rates of pay

We may observe this underlying contrast between the way in which common law principles are brought to bear upon questions of remuneration for work, and the way in which legislation does so, that whereas statutory intervention may be precisely specified, if needs be in pecuniary terms, common law implied terms are confined to more general and qualitative prescriptions. Thus, while there may have been occasional reference as a matter of common law to the notion of 'a fair day's work for a fair day's pay', the common law courts have not presumed to be able to quantify that notion in money terms. The legislature, for its part, does not seek to enact a notion of equitable wages; but it has instituted, in the National Minimum Wage Act 1998, a method of identifying and enforcing a statutory   **15.54**

Lavarack v Woods of Colchester Ltd [1967 1 QB 78, CA) and *Commerzbank AG v Keen* [2006] EWCA Civ 1536.

[106] Compare Lord Steyn in *Malik v BCCI* [1997] ICR 606, 621–2; D Brodie, 'The Heart of the Matter–Mutual Trust and Confidence' (1996) 25 ILJ 121, 126–8.

[107] [1999] ICR 693.

[108] See para 15.23.

minimum hourly rate of pay for workers over the age of 26[109]—which may be, and in fact has been, reduced in relation to some younger workers.[110]

(b) Unlawful deduction from wages

15.55 The regulation of deductions from wages has formed and continues to form an important aspect of the statutory regulation of workers' remuneration. The common law of the contract of employment, and a fortiori that of other personal work contracts, has not posed any systematic obstacles to arrangements which employers make for deductions from wages in respect, for example, of benefits paid in kind, or of defective work, or for the purpose of payment of subscriptions or contributions of any kind—though the principles of construction which determine whether such arrangements form part of the contract may, as we have seen earlier, require a consideration of whether practices of deduction are too arbitrary to give rise to contractual terms derived from custom.[111] The statute law of employment, by contrast, exerted extensive, if rather complex and poorly co-ordinated, controls over deductions from wages in the form of the Truck Acts, which were replaced by a less exacting but better organized set of controls originally enacted in the Wages Act 1986 and now contained in the part of the Employment Rights Act 1996 which deals with the protection of wages.[112]

15.56 With the exception of some provisions concerning deductions for cash shortages and stock deficiencies in retail employment,[113] the legislation on the protection of wages consists not of outright limits or prohibitions upon deductions from wages, but rather of the conferment upon workers of rights not to suffer deductions from wages, nor to have to make payments to their employer, unless those deductions or payments are authorized by statute or by the worker's contract, or the worker has agreed in writing to the making of the deduction or payment.[114] This might have been expected to reduce the provisions on the protection of wages to the level merely of a set of requirements of written formalities; they have, however, acquired a much greater significance by reason of the construction which has been accorded to the concept of 'deduction from wages', as described in the following paragraph.

---

[109] National Minimum Wage Act 1998, ss 1–8.

[110] See ibid s 3 and regulations made thereunder.

[111] See para 15.47.

[112] ERA 1996, Part II.

[113] See ibid ss 17–22.

[114] See ibid ss 13, 15. In an interesting example of a statutory recognition of a restitutionary right, exceptions are made for deductions or payments by way of recovery by the employer of over-payments of wages or in respect of expenses: see ss 14, 16.

A conflict of judicial opinion arose, which was resolved in the leading case of **15.57**
Delaney v Staples;[115] there was a narrow view of the concept of 'deduction from
wages' which, essentially, insisted that deduction was limited to the taking back of
sums of money by the employer from wages which had been otherwise allocated
to the worker. A contrastingly wide view asserted that there was no such limitation
upon the concept of deduction, and that it extended to simple failure to pay that
which was due. The fact that the Court of Appeal took the latter view in the
Delaney case (in a decision upheld by the House of Lords, though not appealed on
this point) had the major consequence that the right to complain of unauthorized
deductions from wages would henceforth offer a convenient process whereby
workers could secure an adjudication upon all kind of disputes about what
remuneration was 'properly payable' to them.[116]

(c) Stability of income and the laying-off of workers by employers

One of the principal issues which arises, as part of the question of legal protection **15.58**
of stability of income, is that of whether and how far the private law of employment
limits the employer's freedom to contract for work on the basis that the worker may
be suspended from working and earning remuneration (though retained in employment), or 'laid off', when the employer sees fit to do so. Both the common law and
the statute law of the contract of employment exert some controls; they approach
the issue in distinctly different ways. At common law, the decision of the Court of
Appeal in *Devonald v Rosser & Sons*[117] has come to stand for the proposition that
the employer cannot assert an unlimited power to lay off workers, merely by pointing to a lack of demand for their work for the period in question; the power to lay
off is qualified by an obligation to provide a reasonable amount of work during the
subsistence of the employment contract in question.[118]

The protection thus afforded by the common law was, however, always regarded **15.59**
as vulnerable to being displaced by express, or even implied, positive provision for
employers to lay off their workers, and from 1975 onwards there has been statutory provision of a right to guarantee payment.[119] This is essentially the right to be
paid at the worker's average daily rate of pay in respect of days without work for
up to a specified number of days, currently set at five days, within any specified
period, currently set at three months;[120] it is subject to a daily maximum amount[121]
currently equivalent to about the statutory minimum wage rate for approximately

---

[115] [1991] ICR 331, CA, [1992] ICR 483, HL.
[116] The wording is that of s 13(3), ERA 1996.
[117] [1906] 2 KB 729.
[118] Compare the application of that decision in *Johnson v Cross* [1977] ICR 872, EAT.
[119] The provisions are now contained in Part III of the ERA 1996, ss 28–35.
[120] See ibid ss 30–1.
[121] See ibid s 31(1) as varied from time to time by statutory order.

four hours' work. Even that degree of statutory protection is applicable only to 'employees' with contracts of employment, and not to workers with personal work contracts which do not so qualify, and does not extend to those employees who do not have 'normal working hours'.[122]

15.60 These are significant qualifications, given the number of workers who are employed on a casual basis, sometimes under so-called 'zero-hours contracts' which purport to guarantee them no minimum amount of employment at all. It is arguable that such arrangements might, by reference to the notion of mutuality of obligation, be deemed to be contracts of employment which were subject to a non-derogable obligation of the kind recognized in *Devonald v Rosser*.[123] Some current case law suggests that the courts may veer in the opposite direction, simply treating the expressed absence of a minimum amount of employment as a reason for regarding the worker in question as not having a continuous contract of employment;[124] we may regard the decision of the House of Lords in *Carmichael v National Power Plc*[125] as giving some support to the latter line of argument.

(d) Stability of income during absence due to sickness

15.61 The legal regulation of continuity of income during sickness takes the form of a combination of common law principles of construction with a statutory regime, rather comparable to the regulation of the employer's power to suspend employment by 'laying off' workers, as considered in the foregoing paragraphs. The courts, in construing contracts of employment, at one stage came surprisingly close to adopting a presumption in favour of the indefinite continuity of pay during absence due to sickness in the absence of an express term to the contrary.[126] But the Court of Appeal showed itself unwilling in *Mears v Safecar Security Ltd*[127] to allow anything more than a leaning in favour of the employee if there was no other way of deciding whether sick pay was payable or not, and has since emphasized that employment tribunals, at least, should not impose non-mandatory terms such as those relating to sick pay or holiday pay.[128] (The separate question of holiday pay is considered further under another heading).[129]

---

[122] See Part III of the ERA 1996, s 30 and compare *Mailway (Southern) Ltd v Willsher* [1978] ICR 511, EAT.

[123] See n 118 above; and compare para 15.25.

[124] Compare, for instance, the nurses belonging to a 'nurse bank' whose employment status was under consideration in the recent case of *Clark v Oxfordshire Health Authority* [1998] IRLR 125, CA.

[125] [1999] ICR 1226, HL.

[126] Compare *Orman v Saville Sportswear Ltd* [1960] 1 WLR 1055.

[127] [1982] ICR 626.

[128] In *Eagland v British Telecommunications plc* [1993] ICR 644, 652, 654. That decision leaves little or no scope for the importation of a 'reasonable term having regard to the normal practice in the industry' which had been sanctioned by the decision in *Howman v Blyth* [1983] ICR 416, EAT. Sick pay is one of the matters of which the employer is required to give employees written particulars: see para 15.37.

[129] See para 15.71.

Since 1982, the common law relating to sick pay has been supplemented, and in **15.62** practice largely superseded, by a statutory regime the provisions of which are now contained in the legislation which consolidates the statute law relating to social security contributions and benefits.[130] This indicates the provenance of statutory sick pay; it represents the transfer of responsibility for maintenance of employment income during short-term sickness from the social security system to employers. Originally, this was on the footing that statutory sick pay was reimbursed to employers from the National Insurance Fund; but since 1994, such reimbursement has been confined to small employers, and to a small proportion of the payments which they make.[131] The statutory sick pay provisions apply only to 'employees',[132] and it may be assumed that the courts would not be at all willing to imply any sick pay obligations into personal work contracts which were not contracts of employment. The relationship between provision for employees and for those with other personal work contracts is similarly divergent in relation to the legal regulation of retirement pensions, which is considered in the ensuing paragraphs.

(e) The legal regulation of occupational pensions

As financial provision for retirement has become a more and more important **15.63** aspect of the expectations which are based upon personal work relationships, so the legal regulation of occupational pensions has become a more and more prominent issue. One might have imagined that such regulation would be fully integrated into the general legal regulation of personal work contracts. There are, however, a number of factors which have brought about a state of affairs in which occupational pension schemes are actually regulated quite separately from personal work contracts. Historically the first, and still the most important, such factor has been the long-term fiscal policy of allowing pension provision to take place within a specially favourable taxation regime as compared with the tax regime for other forms of income for employment. The main concern of the fiscal authorities has been to insist, because of that, upon a strict separation between the financing of pension provision, and the general finances of employing enterprises. The means of achieving that separation has been the embodiment of occupational pension provision in trust funds held and administered by, or under the supervision of, trustees. Hence it is trusts law rather than the law of personal work contracts which has provided the framework of regulation.[133]

---

[130] Social Security Contributions and Benefits Act 1992, Part XI.

[131] See Statutory Sick Pay Act 1994, and regulations made under that Act.

[132] See s 151 of the Social Security Contributions and Benefits Act 1992.

[133] See, for an excellent account of this development, R Nobles, *Pensions, Employment and the Law* (1993) 1–31.

15.64 The separation between the private law of employment and the legal regulation of occupational schemes has, from that set of starting points, been enhanced by recent legislation. The Social Security Act 1986 contained measures to enable workers to invest in personal pension schemes provided by private financial institutions, so that their pension arrangements could if they wished be quite independent of their contracts of employment or other personal work contracts; hence the provision, now contained in the 1993 consolidation of legislation about the regulation of pension schemes, rendering void any term of a contract of service, or any rule of a personal or occupational pension scheme, restricting the choice of an employed earner by making requirements as to his membership of personal or occupational pension schemes in general or of particular schemes, or as to payment of contributions to such schemes.[134] When the law about occupational pensions was reformed in 1995 to improve the safeguards of the interests of individual workers and pensioners, those safeguards were constructed around the relationships between the trustees and managements of pension schemes and the pension scheme members, rather than around the personal work contracts of those members. There were, for instance, new rights for pension scheme members to nominate trustees and directors of corporate trustees of their pension schemes.[135] A further significant regulatory reform has since been made by and under the Pensions Act 2004.

15.65 In that situation, in which the legal regulation of the management of occupational pension schemes was drawing away from the private law of employment, it was of great significance that, from the starting point of the landmark decision in the *Imperial Tobacco* case,[136] which was considered in an earlier section,[137] the obligations of the employer in relation to the occupational pension scheme have been aligned with the employer's obligations under the contract of employment, linked by the common notion of a duty to maintain mutual trust and confidence. This link was reinforced by the equally important decision of the House of Lords in *Scally v Southern Health and Social Services Board*[138] to the effect that the employer, a public health authority, was under a duty to keep its employees informed of advantageous options open to them under the statutory occupational pension scheme which was associated with their employment. In these ways, the contract of employment is again becoming one of the focal points for the legal regulation of occupational pension provision. We shall observe this partial re-emergence of common law (and, to a lesser extent, the law of equity) as a basis of regulation of

---

[134] See Pension Schemes Act 1993, s 160.
[135] See Pensions Act 1995, ss 16–21.
[136] *Imperial Group Pension Trust Ltd v Imperial Tobacco Ltd* [1991] ICR 524.
[137] See para 15.52.
[138] [1991] ICR 771, HL on appeal from the Court of Appeal in Northern Ireland.

various aspects of personal work relationships, for example with regard to health, safety, and welfare at work, which we consider in the ensuing paragraphs.

(7) The Legal Regulation of Health, Safety, and Welfare at Work

The legal regulation of the health, safety and welfare of workers, obviously one of **15.66** the central concerns of the private law of employment, takes the form of a complex interaction between contract law, the law of tort, and statutory regulation, in which each of those components operates to modify the others. Historically, the common law of contract and tort took an approach to the regulation of health and safety which was restricted in certain crucial respects, especially by the doctrine of 'common employment' whereby workers were deemed to accept the risk of injury from those in the same employment as themselves.[139] These restricted protections were supplemented by various specific health and safety measures in the Factories Acts 1844–1961, and the doctrine of common employment was abolished by statute in 1948;[140] from 1974 onwards the common law of contract and tort were systematically overlaid with a general statutory framework of protection, but they continue to constitute a significant interstitial source of protection and liability. They do so in a composite form, since, in an approach endorsed by the House of Lords in the leading case of *Lister v Romford Ice & Cold Storage Co Ltd*,[141] the employer's common law health and safety obligations can be alternatively regarded either as the product of tort law—especially of the tort of negligence—or as mandatory implied terms of the personal work contract.

The basic legislative code for health and safety at work which was enacted in **15.67** 1974[142] imposed, among others, three core sets of duties upon employers or those in control of workplaces, that is to say the general duties of employers to their employees, the general duties of employers and the self-employed to persons other than their employees, and the general duties of persons concerned with premises to persons other than their employees.[143] These duties, the failure to discharge which is constituted a criminal offence by the legislation,[144] operate, as construed by the courts in cases such as *R v Associated Octel Co Ltd*,[145] to provide a reasonably systematic framework of obligations and protections which are not limited by the facts that the worker is employed other than as an employee with a contract of

---

[139] *Priestley v Fowler* (1837) 3 M & W 1, 150 ER 1030.
[140] Law Reform (Personal Injuries) Act 1948, s 1.
[141] [1957] AC 555.
[142] The Health and Safety at Work etc Act 1974. (The word 'etc' is part of the formal title and expresses the fact that the Act is not entirely confined to work situations.)
[143] Respectively ibid s 2, s 3, and s 4.
[144] See s 33 of the 1974 Act.
[145] [1996] ICR 972, HL.

employment in the strict sense, or that he or she is separated from the user of his work by intermediaries such as sub-contractors.

15.68 The level of legal protection or regulation of health, safety and welfare at work has been further heightened as the result of European Community measures in this field, the most generally significant of which is the so-called Framework Directive on Health and Safety of 1989,[146] which, as implemented in the United Kingdom, has imposed new requirements such as the undertaking of risk assessments as to risks to health and safety in the working environment,[147] and has required enhanced arrangements for consultation with employee safety representatives.[148] Nevertheless, the common law, in the shape of negligence liability or mandatorily implied terms in personal work contracts, is still operating so as to reinforce those protections, as most notably as the result of the decision in *Walker v Northumberland County Council*,[149] in which the employer was held liable on these alternative bases where the employee suffered psychiatric illness as the result of having been placed or left in a situation of extreme stress at work. The principles governing this common law obligation have been clarified by the Court of Appeal in *Hatton v Sutherland*.[150]

(a) Welfare, harassment, and privacy

15.69 Although the common law thus demonstrated a capacity to develop protections for the general welfare of workers in their work relationships—a capacity enhanced by the implied term as to mutual trust and confidence[151]—there are nevertheless aspects of welfare at work which it scarcely touches, and in relation to which the evolution of legal regulation depends upon the presence of statutory starting points. This seems to be true of the area of harassment, where the capacity for legal intervention is effectively dependent upon the possibility of treating harassment as one of the kinds of discrimination which is specifically made unlawful, in the way that sexual harassment has been brought within the scope of sex discrimination from the time of the leading case of *Porcelli v Strathclyde Regional Council*.[152] So far as the protection of workers' privacy is concerned, this too has been effectively dependent upon its coming within a specific area of statute law, that of data

---

[146] Council Directive (EEC) 89/391 on improvements in the safety and health of workers at work [1989] OJ L183/9.

[147] See the Management of Health and Safety at Work Regulations 1992, SI 1992/2051, reg 3.

[148] See the Health and Safety (Consultation with Employees) Regulations 1996, SI 1996/1513.

[149] [1995] IRLR 323.

[150] [2002] ICR; see also *Intel Incorporation (UK) Limited v Daw* [2007] EWCA Civ 70.

[151] See para 15.51.

[152] [1986] ICR 564, Ct of Sess; and see now the specific legislative provision of the Employment Equality (Sex Discrimination) Regulations 2005 SI 2005/2467 reg 5 inserting new s 4A into the Sex Discrimination Act 1975.

protection, now covered by the Data Protection Act 1998.[153] However, it seems, following the decision of the European Court of Human Rights in the *Halford*[154] case, that workers might be afforded significant protection against certain forms of surveillance by employers by Article 8 of the European Convention on Human Rights, which deals with the right to respect for private and family life, and is among those articles incorporated into English law under the provisions of the Human Rights Act 1998.[155]

(8) *The Legal Regulation of Working Time*

The regulation of working time by the private law of employment has been almost   **15.70**
entirely the province of statute law; the common law of contract and tort have in practice placed few if any restrictions upon the freedom of employers to propose, and upon the freedom of workers to agree to, any arrangements about hours of work, rest periods, and holidays, which they may see fit to make. The most significant exception to that general proposition is suggested by the decision concerning the working hours of junior hospital doctors in *Johnstone v Bloomsbury Health Authority*,[156] where it was held by a majority in the Court of Appeal that, by reason of their implied obligation to take reasonable care of the employee doctor's health and safety, the health authority employer could not require him to work a large number of hours in excess of his standard working week of 40 hours, although one of the express terms of the contract of employment appeared to confer that power upon them.

Nevertheless, the main burden of regulation of working time has been borne by   **15.71**
the legislature. Until relatively recently, that statutory regulation was 'selective and partial', and was itself significantly alleviated during the 1980s and early 1990s,[157] a process which included the replacing of the restrictions of working hours in shops, both on Sundays and weekdays, by a much more permissive regime.[158] This state of affairs was significantly altered by the enactment, at European Community level, of the Working Time Directive in 1993[159] and the Young Workers Directive

---

[153] Which was introduced in order to implement Directive (EC) 95/46 on data protection [1995] OJ L 281/31–50.

[154] *Halford v United Kingdom* [1997] IRLR 471.

[155] Such protection may, however, be to some extent offset by the Telecommunications (Lawful Business Practice) (Interception of Communications) Regulations 2000 SI 2000/2699.

[156] [1991] ICR 269.

[157] S Deakin and GS Morris, *Labour Law* (4th edn, 2005) 309 where details are given.

[158] See now the Sunday Trading Act 1994, which replaced the Sunday trading restrictions of the Shops Act 1950; the weekday restrictions were repealed by the Deregulation and Contracting Out Act 1994.

[159] Council Directive (EC) 93/104 concerning certain aspects of the organization of working time [1993] OJ L307/18.

in 1994,[160] and the implementation of the former and the working time aspects of the latter in the United Kingdom by the Working Time Regulations 1998.[161] Those regulations impose, subject to various derogations, the following requirements or standards as to working time: first, an upper limit of 48 hours upon the length of the working week; secondly, an upper limit of 8 hours per day on night work; thirdly, requirements of one day off each week, 11 hours consecutive rest each day, and a minimum rest break of 20 minutes where the working day exceeds 6 hours; and fourthly, a minimum of four weeks' annual paid leave.[162]

15.72   These requirements are, however, subject to very significant derogations which both limit their scope in some ways and make them wholly or partly non-mandatory in other ways. While the regulations generally extend to a broadly defined category of 'workers',[163] a number of sectors or occupations, such as hospital doctors and transport workers, are excluded from the scope of some or all of the requirements;[164] and, moreover, the provisions relating to weekly working time and night work do not apply to workers with 'unmeasured working time'.[165]

15.73   No less important is the other kind of permitted derogation, whereby various of the working time requirements may be disapplied by agreement of certain specified kinds. Thus individual workers can voluntarily agree to disapply the weekly working hours limits;[166] while most of the requirements can be disapplied as the result either of collective agreements with independent trade unions, or of 'workforce agreements' where there is no recognized trade union, which are either to be signed by individual workers where a firm employs 20 or fewer workers, or to be made by representatives elected by the workforce to negotiate on its behalf.[167] Permissive derogations of this kind tend to transform the statutory requirements, to which they apply, into 'default terms' of personal work contracts, that is to say into terms which apply in the absence of express provision about the matter in question. This serves to reduce the difference in character and effect between statutory requirements and terms implied by common law, some further aspects of which are considered in the ensuing paragraphs.

(9)   The Implied Obligations of Workers under Personal Work Contracts

15.74   When we turn our attention from those aspects of the legal regulation of the content of personal work relationships which consist of obligations upon employers

---

160   Council Directive (EC) 94/33 on the protection of young people at work [1994] OJ 216/12.
161   SI 1998/1833.
162   See, respectively, regs 4, 6, 10–12, 13.
163   See reg 2(1); there is an extension, in reg 36, to 'agency workers not otherwise "workers"'.
164   See reg 18, 'excluded sectors'.
165   See reg 20.
166   See reg 5.
167   See reg 23.

to those aspects which consist of obligations upon workers (that distinction being admittedly an imperfect one), we find that the common law, especially the common law of the contract of employment, has a greater role by comparison with that of statute law—no doubt because the demand for statutory regulation has been concentrated upon the conduct of employers rather than that of their workers (except in the context of industrial action).[168] Thus, we find that the obligations of workers, at least those with contracts of employment as such, tend very much to continue to be formulated as implied terms of their personal work contracts.

(a) Implied terms as to obedience, care and skill, and fidelity

As was indicated in the previous paragraph, historically the disciplinary powers of the 'master' in the 'master and servant relationship'—including the power of summary dismissal—were constructed around what came to be regarded as the three core implied obligations of the 'servant', those of obedience to all lawful and reasonable orders,[169] the exercise of care and skill in the carrying out of work,[170] and service to the employer with fidelity and in good faith.[171] These three implied obligations would seem to remain applicable to present-day contracts of employment. Thus, we might find the first of them invoked in order to test out what it is 'lawful and reasonable' for the employer to instruct the employee to do.[172] The second may be important in enabling an employer, typically at the insistence of the insurer, to refer back to the employee a vicarious liability to a third party which the employer incurs as the result of the employee's negligence in the course of employment.[173] The third is important as indicating the strictness of the employee's obligation not to work for or serve the interests of a rival employer during the continuance of the employment relationship.[174] However, it is more frequently the case today that disputes about the content and extent of the employee's obligations to the employer are resolved by reference to a different set of emerging implied terms, which are described in the ensuing paragraphs.

15.75

(b) Implied terms as to co-operation, flexibility, and loyalty

Thus, to develop the suggestion made at the conclusion of the previous paragraph, we find that issues which used to be addressed in terms of the worker's

15.76

---

[168] See paras 15.30 and 15.49.

[169] Compare *Turner v Mason* (1845) 14 M & W 112, 153 ER 411.

[170] Compare *Harmer v Cornelius* (1856) 5 CBNS 236, 141 ER 94.

[171] Compare *Robb v Green* [1895] 2 QB 315.

[172] As in *Bouzourou v Ottoman Bank* [1930] AC 271, HL.

[173] As was held to be possible in *Lister v Romford Ice & Cold Storage Co Ltd* [1957] AC 555, HL.

[174] As in *Hivac Ltd v Park Royal Scientific Instruments Ltd* [1946] Ch 169, CA, where it was the basis of an injunction to restrain the rival employer from engaging the spare-time services of an employee who was expert in the high-technology activities of his employer.

'obedience' or (to a lesser extent) 'care and skill' will now more commonly be considered as issues of 'co-operation' or 'flexibility'. We have seen in an earlier paragraph[175] how the employee's duty of co-operation was articulated in the *ASLEF* case,[176] in the form of an obligation not to disrupt the functioning of the employing enterprise; it has since been used, as it was in that very case, to determine, in particular, the extent of employees' contractual duties in the context of industrial action, falling short of outright strike action, taken by those employees.[177] In similar vein, in the leading case of *Cresswell v Board of Inland Revenue*,[178] the central issue was whether clerical workers for the Inland Revenue were in breach of their contracts of employment or terms of service[179] in refusing to operate the new computer system which the Inland Revenue was introducing with regard to the work they were employed to do. It was held that the workers concerned were in breach of an implied obligation to adapt to such changes in their system of work, as long as the changes were not such as to mean that the work they were now asked to do was quite different from the work they had been employed to do.

15.77 Equally, while it is still possible meaningfully to speak of the employee's implied obligation of fidelity, it is probably now preferable to envisage a rather broader discussion about the duties of loyalty which the employee owes to the employer as a consequence, or set of consequences, of the existence of his contract of employment. That discussion covers a range of issues, some of which are wholly or partly the subject of statutory regulation. Thus, the employee has a duty to safeguard the employer's specifically confidential information or 'trade secrets' which extends into the period after the end of the employment relationship.[180] (It should be noted, on the other hand, that the worker is now the subject of specific statutory protection[181] when, in specified circumstances, engaging in what is known as 'whistleblowing', that is to say making disclosure in the public interest of malpractice of various kinds within the employing enterprise.) Thus, again, while the courts seem unwilling, mainly as the result of the decision in *Bell v Lever Bros Ltd*,[182] to treat employees as under a general duty to disclose their own misconduct, they are prepared to treat at least managerial employers as under a

---

[175] See para 15.49.

[176] *Secretary of State for Employment v ASLEF (No 2)* [1972] ICR 19, CA.

[177] Compare *Sim v Rotherham Metropolitan Borough Council* [1986] ICR 897; *British Telecommunications plc v Ticehurst* [1992] ICR 383, CA.

[178] [1984] ICR 408.

[179] It was unclear at that time whether workers for a Department of the Crown had contracts of employment as such; the case proceeded exactly as if it was clear that they did have such contracts, which would clearly now be the preferred view; compare *R v Lord Chancellor's Department, ex p Nangle* [1991] ICR 743, Div Ct.

[180] As, for instance, in *Roger Bullivant Ltd v Ellis* [1987] ICR 464, CA.

[181] Under the Public Interest (Disclosure) Act 1998.

[182] [1932] AC 161, HL.

duty to disclose the fraudulent misconduct of fellow employees, as in the important case of *Sybron Corporation v Rochem Ltd.*[183] There is a further, associated, set of issues about the ownership, as between the employer and the employee, of the intellectual property in the literary, scientific, or other intangible products of the employee's work and mental activity in the course of employment. Those questions are now largely regulated by statute, in the shape of the employment provisions of the legislation relating to copyright[184] and to patents.[185]

Hence, apart from such areas of specific statutory regulation, there is a general **15.78** tendency to conceive of the implied obligations of employees in terms of co-operation, flexibility, and loyalty. It is probably appropriate to see that development as part of a still larger trend, which we encountered earlier in relation to the implied obligations of the employer,[186] to re-formulate the whole of the common law shaping of the formation and content of the contract of employment by reference to the notion of an underlying set of reciprocal duties to maintain mutual trust and confidence. If that is the case, it becomes especially important to know how far that kind of reasoning may extend beyond the scope of the contract of employment strictly so-called to other personal work contracts. There is some reason for thinking that it might, where appropriate, do so. For instance, in the leading case of *Spring v Guardian Assurance plc,*[187] the House of Lords expounded the duty of care of the employer to the worker in respect of the giving of a reference to a potential subsequent employer. They did so in terms very close indeed to the language of the implied obligation of mutual trust and confidence, while at the same time acknowledging that it was unclear whether the worker in question was employed under a contract of employment or under some other form of personal work contract.[188]

(10) The Evolutionary Nature of Personal Work Contracts

The foregoing discussion places us in a position to draw some conclusions to this **15.79** section, and moreover to identify some links between it and the preceding and succeeding sections of this chapter. Essentially, in the first section we considered the range and scope of personal work relationships, and the ways in which the private law of employment creates and applies different categories of personal work contracts as frameworks for the legal regulation of those relationships. In the present section, we have seen how the formation and content of those

---

183 [1983] ICR 801, CA; compare also *Item Software (UK) Ltd v Fassihi* [2005] ICR 450, CA.
184 See Copyright, Designs and Patents Act 1988, s 11.
185 See Patents Act 1977, ss 39–43.
186 See paras 15.51 and 15.52.
187 [1993] ICR 412. See also *Cox v Sun Alliance Life Ltd* [2001] IRLR 448, CA.
188 Compare, for instance, Lord Slynn at 630–1.

personal work contracts is governed by legal principles which, admittedly in varying degrees, recognize and respond to the evolutionary nature of personal work contracts. That is to say, the legal principles come to embody the realization that the shape, and therefore the classification and the obligations, of personal work contracts, resolve themselves over periods of time and within the context of continuing work relationships.

15.80   It is a major feature of the private law of employment that many of the issues and problems, of that essentially evolutionary system, present themselves, as it were, retrospectively when disputes arise when employment relationships come to an end or when major transformations of situation occur with regard to them, such as a change in the identity of the employing enterprise. Hence much of the law of and around personal work contracts, which has been under consideration in the first two sections of this chapter, is actually formed, or at least crucially influenced, by legal regulation which is ostensibly directed at the termination and transfer of employment relationships. That will turn out to create an underlying functional continuity between the matters which have been discussed in the first two sections and those which are discussed in the next one.

C. The Termination and Transfer of Work Relationships

(1) The Duration and Variation of Personal Work Contracts

15.81   We shall find, in the context of the termination and transfer of personal work contracts, that, even more obviously than in the contexts hitherto considered, the private law of employment combines the two functions of, on the one hand, defining the shapes and outcomes of personal work contracts, and, on the other hand, regulating those shapes and those outcomes. A good illustration of this combination is to be found in the body of law which deals with, and inter-relates, the termination, duration and variation of those contracts. However, before considering the details of that body of law, we should acknowledge that, in common with most of the law discussed in the present section of the chapter, it has been developed and expounded almost entirely in relation to those personal work contracts which are contracts of employment in the strict sense. Due effort will be made to establish how far and in what terms this body of law might be applied to other personal work contracts, but that is to a considerable extent a matter of speculation rather than of established law.

(a) Duration, and terminability by notice, or by payment in lieu of notice

15.82   The common law of the contract of employment allows employers and employees almost unlimited freedom of choice in the arrangements they may see fit to make for the duration of the contract and/or its terminability by notice, but also presumes in favour of certain standard patterns of duration and terminability which are themselves shaped by case law and to some extent regulated by statute. That is to say, the common law allows a contract of employment to be made for as long a duration as may be wished, subject only to the public policy objection to contracts of employment so constraining of the liberty of the employee as to amount to enslavement.[189] The contract may, equally, be for as short a duration as may be wished; and it may either be for a fixed term, or it may be, as it has tended to be expressed, either for 'permanent' employment or of indefinite duration. If the contract is for 'permanent' employment, that will usually be expressed to mean, and otherwise will be deemed to mean, that it is for employment until the applicable age of retirement, and terminable by the employer, before that, only 'for good cause' in the sense of serious misconduct or other failing on the part of the employee.[190] Under the Fixed-term Employees (Prevention of Less Favourable Treatment) Regulations 2002, employees under successive fixed-term contracts of employment are converted into 'permanent employees' where they have been continuously employed for four years or more, and where the employment for a fixed term was not justified on objective grounds at the specified time.[191]

If, however, the contract is 'of indefinite duration', in the sense that it does not expressly provide for its duration or terminability, it will be presumed to be an enduring contract (by contrast with the approach in many states of the USA, where this is generally presumed to amount to 'employment at will', that is to say terminable at the will of either party) but a contract which is nevertheless terminable by 'reasonable notice'; a (now rather antiquated) body of case law indicates what the courts have regarded as a reasonable length of notice for various different occupations and types of employment.[192] That case law is not much invoked, partly because the length of notice is usually expressly specified, but partly also because the minimum periods of notice now required by statute would generally be treated as the applicable period of notice in the absence of express stipulation. Those minimum periods are set by the legislation as one week on the part of the employee, and, on the part of the employer, one week for an employee of no more than two years' standing (that is, who has been continuously employed for that

15.83

---

[189] See para 15.36.
[190] Compare *McClelland v Northern Ireland General Health Service Board* [1957] 1 WLR 594, HL (NI) (which can be regarded as a private law case for the present purpose).
[191] SI 2002/2034 reg 8.
[192] See *Chitty on Contracts* (29th edn, 2004) paras 39–154-5.

period by the employer in question or an associated employer),[193] and thereafter one week for each year of continuous employment up to twelve years.[194]

15.84 Often, where contracts of employment are terminable by notice, employers in fact purport to terminate them, not by giving notice which the employee duly works out, but rather by making a 'payment in lieu of notice', which is accompanied by an immediate cessation of work and remuneration. There has been a good deal of debate and uncertainty as to the effect of such 'payments in lieu of notice', but Lord Browne-Wilkinson has provided an analysis of the main alternatives[195] which has become accepted as fully authoritative.[196] The four main alternatives are, essentially, (1) notice, plus waiver by the employer of the right to the employee's services during the notice period, plus payment of wages for the notice period; (2) the exercise of an expressly conferred right to terminate by payment of a sum in lieu of notice; (3) ad hoc agreement between the employer and the employment for the employment to be ended by payment in lieu of notice; or (4) summary dismissal, accompanied by a payment in lieu of notice. In the fourth case, which was said to be the most common one of the four, the payment in lieu of notice is in the nature of liquidated damages and, it was held in the case concerned, could therefore not count as 'wages' so as to fall within the statutory protection from deductions from wages.[197]

(b) Termination, and variation of terms

15.85 The issue of how far and how the terms of the contract of employment may lawfully be varied (that is to say, without involving breach of contract) presents the first of the major inter-connections which we shall encounter between the law concerning termination of personal work contracts and the law concerning the content of those contracts. For the capacity lawfully to vary the terms of a contract of employment is essentially derived from the capacity lawfully to terminate the contract. It will often not be necessary to draw upon that capacity in order to vary the conditions of work, for the employer in particular will often have stipulated for, or be deemed to have stipulated for, terms of employment with an in-built flexibility. For example, there may be an express or implied 'mobility clause' whereby the employer may vary the location of work within reasonable limits.[198] Moreover, the employer may invoke a general obligation of reasonable flexibility

---

[193] See ERA 1996, ss 210–219 for the details of the concept of 'continuous employment'.
[194] See ibid s 86 and ss 87–90 for the rights of the employee to be paid during the statutory minimum period of notice.
[195] In *Delaney v Staples* [1992] ICR 483, 488–9, HL.
[196] As, for instance, in *Abrahams v Performing Right Society Ltd* [1995] ICR 1028, CA.
[197] See paras 15.55–15.57.
[198] Compare *United Bank Ltd v Akhtar* [1989] IRLR 507, EAT; *White v Reflecting Roadstuds Ltd* [1991] ICR 733, EAT.

on the employee's part to require acceptance, for instance, of some degree of technical innovation, as was explained in an earlier paragraph.[199]

However, where there is no such scope to effect change in working conditions **15.86** within the existing terms of the contract, or no express power to vary the terms, the contractual lawfulness, of a claim to have varied the terms, will depend upon whether the purported variation complies with the conditions for a lawful termination of the contract; in particular, whether it has been preceded by notice of the length required in order lawfully to terminate the contract.[200] There is some scope for debate whether special considerations apply to the case where the purported variation consists of the employer's abrogating or resiling from a collective agreement,[201] but the best view would seem to be that those transactions are to be judged in accordance with the general law about the incorporation and variation of contractual terms.[202]

(c) Application to personal work contracts other than contracts of employment

The principles and rules discussed in the immediately foregoing paragraphs have **15.87** been formulated in the context of contracts of employment, and, in the case of the statutory requirements for minimum periods of notice, are certainly confined to contracts of employment. It is debatable how far the common law implications of terminability by reasonable notice (and probably therefore of variability by reasonable notice) extend to other personal work contracts. It has been authoritatively argued that contracts may generally be presumed to be terminable by reasonable notice where they are of such a nature as to require trust and confidence between the parties, and that this presumption probably extends to retainers for professional service.[203] No doubt most personal work contracts other than contracts of employment will in practice be of specified duration, if only in the sense that they are tied to the completion of a specific task for which a maximum time limit is stated. In the succeeding paragraphs, we consider another aspect of the law relating to the termination of personal work contracts, which is highly specific to contracts of employment as such, namely that concerning the concept of dismissal.

(2) Dismissal and Its Alternatives

(a) The concept of dismissal

That part of the private law of employment which concerns the termination of **15.88** employment—which itself, as we have indicated, also bears upon the legal content

---

199 See para 15.76.
200 See MR Freedland, *The Personal Employment Contract* (2003), 275–8.
201 See S Deakin and GS Morris, *Labour Law* (4th edn, 2005) 275–8.
202 Compare *Robertson v British Gas Corporation* [1983] ICR 351, CA.
203 See R Carnegie, 'Terminability of Contracts of Unspecified Duration' (1969) 85 LQR 392.

of employment relationships—is to a very great extent constructed around the concept of dismissal. That is to some extent because the common law of the contract of employment has been considerably focused upon the action for wrongful dismissal. However, it is really the statutory regulation of the termination of employment, and above all the legislation concerning unfair dismissal, which has turned the concept of dismissal into one of the central organizing features of the private law of employment. The ensuing paragraphs therefore describe the statutory concept of dismissal, although, as will become apparent, that concept is built upon a common law base. The main statutory definition of dismissal is found within the unfair dismissal legislation.[204] There are some variants upon that definition; the most important of those occurs in the context of the legislation relating to redundancy payments.[205]

15.89 At the core of the statutory concept of dismissal is the idea of termination of the contract of employment by the employer, whether with or without notice.[206] That core concept is extended in two crucial respects; first, it is extended to include the case where the term of a fixed-term contract of employment expires without being renewed.[207] This has the major consequence that, for the purposes of the statutory regulation of the termination of employment, fixed-term contracts of employment are treated, in effect, as if they were contracts of indefinite duration. Secondly, it is extended to include the case where the employee terminates the contract (with or without notice) 'in circumstances in which he is entitled to terminate it without notice by reason of the employer's conduct' (which is known as 'constructive dismissal').[208] This has the equally major consequence that the legal regulation of the termination of employment extends to the regulation of the employer's actions and conduct during the continuance of employment, where those actions or that conduct give the employee grounds for ending the employment.

15.90 This statutory definition of 'dismissal' is interpreted by reference, sometimes direct and sometimes indirect, to the common law of the contract of employment, not only to determine the 'effective date of termination' of the employment,[209] but also to elaborate the meaning of dismissal itself. This is true in at least two senses. First, in the leading case of *Western Excavating (ECC) Ltd v Sharp*,[210] it was

---

[204] See ERA 1996, ss 95–7.
[205] See ibid ss 136–8.
[206] ibid s 95(1)(a).
[207] ibid s 95(1)(b). The Fixed-term Employees Regulations SI 2002/2034 (see para 15.82) have substituted the new terminology of 'limited term contracts terminated by virtue of the limiting event'.
[208] ibid s 95(1)(c).
[209] See ibid s 97.
[210] [1978] ICR 221, CA.

held that the test for 'constructive dismissal' was whether the employer's actions or conduct amounted to a repudiatory breach of the contract of employment. This decision produced extensive development of the law concerning the implied obligations of the employer under the contract of employment.[211] Secondly, the concept of dismissal is limited by reference to the alternative ways in which the common law of the contract of employment envisages the contract as having been terminated, as, for example, where it is held that there has not been a dismissal because the contract has been terminated by the operation of the doctrine of frustration of contracts. These alternatives are detailed in the ensuing paragraphs.

The first, and most obvious, alternative to termination by dismissal is simply that **15.91** the employee is viewed as having terminated the employment of his own volition, by resigning, retiring, or simply leaving the employment. It may, however, be unclear whether it is more appropriate to view an ending of employment as a termination by the employee or as a dismissal, especially where it is left to the employer to take the formal step which asserts or declares that the employment is at an end. At one time, the courts seemed disposed to develop a notion of 'self-dismissal' which would, despite that, attribute the termination of employment to the employee in appropriate cases;[212] but later decisions have been against a distinct category of that kind.[213]

Another important alternative is to hold that employment has been terminated, **15.92** not by dismissal, but rather by the agreement of both parties. Since it is frequently the case that a mutually agreed arrangement for termination will have resulted from an initiative taken by the employer, as where an employer seeks 'volunteers for early retirement', there has been a major issue as to whether and how far such employer-initiated arrangements can count as termination by agreement rather than by dismissal. It seems to have been resolved that such arrangements can be treated as termination by agreement provided that the apparent consent of the employee is scrutinized to make sure that it was not procured by pressure,[214] and that the presence or absence of such genuine consent is a question of fact for the tribunal of first instance.[215]

A further alternative, as indicated earlier, is to hold that the contract has been **15.93** terminated, not by dismissal, but by the automatic operation of the doctrine of frustration. In one of the leading commentaries, it is argued that to allow scope for

---

[211] Compare paras 15.49–15.52.

[212] As in *Gannon v JC Firth Ltd* [1976] IRLR 415, EAT.

[213] Compare *Rasool v Hepworth Pipe Co Ltd* [1980] ICR 494, EAT; *London Transport Executive v Clarke* [1980] ICR 532, CA.

[214] See *Birch v University of Liverpool* [1985] ICR 470, CA.

[215] *Scott v Coalite Fuels & Chemicals Ltd* [1988] ICR 355, EAT.

the operation of this doctrine in the present context is to enable employers to take unwarranted opportunities to avoid submitting their terminations of employment to scrutiny as to whether they amount to unfair dismissal.[216] Nevertheless, there is still a significant possibility that the analysis in terms of frustration of the contract, rather than in terms of dismissal, may be held to be applicable where it becomes clear that the employee will be rendered unfit for work on a long-term basis by reason of illness,[217] or where the employee receives a custodial sentence of significant length in relation to the employment in question.[218] There are yet further alternatives; the most important of them, considered later in this section,[219] is that an event, which would otherwise have been regarded as a dismissal, is treated as resulting in a transfer of employment to a different employer.

(3) Wrongful Dismissal, and Other Common Law Regulation Based Upon Termination of the Contract of Employment

(a) The modern role of the law of wrongful dismissal

15.94 It is possible to view the common law regulation of the termination of the contract of employment as consisting largely or entirely of the 'law of wrongful dismissal'. On that view, wrongful dismissal can be seen as the counterpart of the employer's express or implied rights either to terminate the contract of employment by notice, or to rely upon the expiry of a fixed term as terminating the contract, or summarily to dismiss the employee for 'misconduct, incompetence, or neglect'[220] or for specified good cause. There has, however, been a general tendency to consider the law of wrongful dismissal and the law of summary dismissal simply as specific applications, in the employment context, of the common law of contract relating to termination by repudiatory breach or wrongful repudiation, or by rescission in response to them.[221]

15.95 That is not to say that the common law regulation of the termination of the contract of employment should be understood simply as the direct operation of the general principles of the common law of contracts as a whole. There is, for instance, a major and still far from resolved debate about whether the wrongful repudiation of a contract of employment has the effect ascribed to it in the general law of contract, namely to give the injured party an election whether to accept the repudiation as a

---

[216] S Deakin and GS Morris, *Labour Law* (4th edn, 2005) 463.
[217] See *Notcutt v Universal Equipment Co (London) Ltd* [1986] ICR 414, CA.
[218] Compare *Shepherd & Co Ltd v Jerrom* [1986] ICR 802, CA.
[219] See paras 15.113–15.115.
[220] For details of the employer's implied powers of summary dismissal, see *Chitty on Contracts* (29th edn, 2004) paras 39–175 to 39–180.
[221] Compare, for example, *Laws v London Chronicle (Indicator Newspapers) Ltd* [1959] 1 WLR 698, 700, CA, where Lord Evershed MR analyses the law of summary dismissal in those terms.

termination of the contract, or whether on the other hand it operates automatically to terminate the contract. The elective theory is on the whole preferred,[222] but with a growing judicial reluctance.[223] However, that kind of theoretical argument only really becomes meaningful in the context of the actual remedial processes by which the common law regulation and the statutory regulation of termination of employment take place, so it is to those that we turn our attention.

(b) Damages

The remedy of damages for breach of contract in connection with the termination of employment has generally been regarded as crucially limited by the principle that, so far as damages are intended to compensate for loss of prospective employment, only that period of employment will be taken into account within which the contract of employment could have been lawfully terminated, for example by the employer giving notice.[224] Moreover, the claimant is under a duty to mitigate his loss even in respect of that period of notional loss of employment.[225] The decision of the House of Lords in *Addis v Gramophone Co*[226] has also been viewed as giving rise to a principle, which reinforces those limitations, to the effect that damages for wrongful dismissal could not include damages for loss of reputation or in respect of the injurious manner of dismissal. That view is reinforced by the decision of the House of Lords in the case of *Johnson v Unisys Ltd*.[227] **15.96**

However, some recent developments may serve to lift those restrictions to a certain extent. Thus in the *Gunton*[228] and *Boyo*[229] cases, the elective approach to termination was combined with the decision, that in each case the employer was contractually bound to follow a dismissal procedure before giving notice to terminate the employment on the ground of misconduct, to produce the result, not, as the employee claimants sought, that the restriction of damages to the notice period did not apply at all, but that the damages could take account of the further time which it would have taken to follow the dismissal procedure. **15.97**

(c) Injunctions and specific enforcement

In a pattern not dissimilar to that which we found in relation to damages, the availability of injunctions in relation to, and remedies in the nature of specific **15.98**

---

222   See *Gunton v Richmond-upon Thames London Borough Council* [1980] ICR 755, CA.
223   See *Boyo v Lambeth London Borough Council* [1994] ICR 727, CA.
224   Compare, for instance, *Lavarack v Woods of Colchester Ltd* [1967] 1 QB 278, CA.
225   Compare, for instance, *Yetton v Eastwoods Froy Ltd* [1967] 1 WLR 104.
226   [1909] AC 488.
227   [2001] ICR 480, see para 15.51. The extent of this exclusionary rule was further defined in *Eastwood v Magnox Electric Plc* [2005] 1 AC 503, HL.
228   See n 222.
229   See n 223.

enforcement of, the contract of employment appears to be extremely limited, but there turn out to be some significant exceptions to those limitations. Thus, the starting position is that there is a general principle against the specific performance of contracts for personal service;[230] that principle has been accorded statutory force to the extent that no court may issue an order for specific performance or an injunction which would amount to a compulsion upon an employee to work.[231]

15.99   However, there have for long been these partial exceptions, that an injunction will lie to enforce those covenants by employees, against competition with the employer after the end of the employment, which are not in unreasonable restraint of trade,[232] and that an injunction will also lie to restrain an employee from competition with the employer during the continuance of the contract of employment, unless that would amount to a compulsion upon the employee to work for the original employer because it would amount to an order to 'work or starve'.[233] This has sometimes enabled employers to keep employees from working for rival firms on the basis that they are still serving out a long period of notice with the original employer, albeit no longer required actually to work for that employer—a practice known as that of 'garden leave', and a further instance of the operation of the elective theory of termination in response to repudiatory breach.[234]

15.100   There now, moreover, seems to be a new genre of exceptions to the rule against injunctions enforcing contracts of employment, this time in favour of employees. For employee claimants have in various instances succeeded in obtaining injunctions to restrain employers from dismissing them in breach of terms of their contracts of employment which specifically protect their security of employment, especially by imposing procedural requirements upon dismissal.[235] Employees may similarly secure injunctive relief against unilateral variation of the terms of their contracts of employment;[236] and, although the defendant employer may allege that such a remedy is not permissible where the employer has 'lost trust and confidence' in the employee, the courts seem more willing than once they were to override objections of that kind.[237]

---

[230] Compare, for a modern affirmation of the general principle, *Chappell v Times Newspapers Ltd* [1975] ICR 145, CA.

[231] A provision now contained in TULRCA 1992, s 236.

[232] See, for a useful succinct survey of the case law, S Deakin and GS Morris, *Labour Law* (4th edn, 2005) 345–7.

[233] Compare *Warner Bros Pictures Inc v Nelson* [1937] 1 KB 209.

[234] Compare, for instance, *Evening Standard Co Ltd v Henderson* [1987] ICR 588, CA.

[235] Compare *Irani v Southampton and South West Hampshire Health Authority* [1985] ICR 590.

[236] As in *Hughes v Southwark London Borough Council* [1988] IRLR 55.

[237] The decision of the Court of Appeal in *Hill v Parsons & Co Ltd* [1972] Ch 305, CA, gave a significant lead in that direction.

(d) The position with regard to other personal work contracts

As has been indicated earlier, much of the foregoing account of the common law **15.101** regulation of termination of employment relates to principles evolved and applied in the context of contracts of employment in the strict sense. The degree to which it is applicable to other personal work contracts is uncertain. In general, we might expect that the objections to anything in the nature of specific enforcement of personal obligations would apply with rather less force to other personal work contracts, where the work relationships involved are less fully dependent ones. At all events, we turn to consider the area of statutory regulation of termination of employment, the main aspect of which, namely the law of unfair dismissal, is strictly confined to contracts of employment as such.

(4) Unfair Dismissal, and Other Statutory Regulation Constructed on the Basis of It

(a) The concept of unfair dismissal

From 1971 onwards,[238] unfair dismissal legislation[239] has effected a significant **15.102** reorientation of the private law of employment, by superimposing a set of statutory concepts upon the common law relating to the termination of contracts of employment. Some of those statutory concepts relate back to the common law of the contract of employment; we have seen in earlier paragraphs that this is significantly the case with the concept of dismissal.[240] At least in the design of the framers of the legislation, the basic concept of 'unfairness'[241] is fully independent of the common law.

The concept is articulated as an evaluation of an employer's (actual or construc- **15.103** tive) dismissal of an employee which proceeds in two stages. At the first of those stages, it is for the employer to show the reason for the dismissal, and to show that it falls within a specified category of reasons.[242] That category is specified so that it includes, in effect, (1) want of capability of the employee, (2) misconduct of the employee, (3) redundancy of the employee, and (4) need to comply with a statutory duty or restriction,[243] and so that it also, in effect, may include any other substantial justificatory reason.[244] The interpretation of the notion of 'some other

---

[238] When it was introduced by the Industrial Relations Act 1971.
[239] Now contained in the ERA 1996 ss 94–134.
[240] See paras 15.88–15.93.
[241] As set out in the ERA 1996, s 98.
[242] ibid s 98(1).
[243] ibid s 98(2).
[244] ibid s 98(1)(b).

substantial reason', in the leading case of *Hollister v National Farmers Union*,[245] as including the employer's need to reorganize the work of the enterprise in the interests of efficiency, has ensured that the whole category is applied in a broad and inclusive way. (There is a statutory obligation upon the employer to provide the dismissed employee, upon request, with a written statement of the reasons for dismissal.)[246]

15.104 As a result, much of the weight of the adjudication of unfairness falls upon the second stage of the process, at which, if the employer has proved what is required at the first stage, it is determined (without a burden of proof on either side) whether the employer acted 'reasonably or unreasonably' in treating the reason as a sufficient one for dismissing the employee.[247] One of the most important questions to arise in the application of this notion of reasonableness has been whether and how far it (unlike the common law of wrongful dismissal) imports procedural requirements. As the result of the decision of the House of Lords in the leading case of *Polkey v Dayton Services Ltd*,[248] it was established that the employer may be judged to have acted unreasonably by reference to procedural defects in the dismissal process, unless it can be shown that it was quite manifest that the following of non-defective procedure would not have altered the outcome. In any event, the overall question is held to be the inclusive one of whether the employer's decision to dismiss 'fell within the band of reasonable responses which a reasonable employer might have adopted'.[249] The position has been modified by Part 3 of the Employment Act 2002, which provided for a new framework of statutory dispute resolution procedures and amended the law of unfair dismissal in significant respects so as to reflect the failure of employers or employees to follow the procedural requirements respectively placed on them but also so as partly to reverse the rule in *Polkey v Dayton* itself.[250]

(b) The right to remedies for unfair dismissal, and procedure

15.105 The unfair dismissal legislation confers a general right not to be unfairly dismissed[251] (subject to a qualifying period[252]) and provides for complaint to employment tribunals and the awarding of remedies by employment tribunals in

---

[245] [1979] ICR 542, CA.

[246] See ERA 1996, ss 92–3.

[247] See ibid s 98(4).

[248] [1988] ICR 142.

[249] Browne-Wilkinson J in *Iceland Frozen Foods Ltd v Jones* [1983] ICR 17, 25, EAT. Cf *Foley v Post Office* [2000] ICR 1283, CA.

[250] See new ERA 1996, s 98A(2) as added by s 34 of the 2002 Act.

[251] See ERA 1996, s 94.

[252] Set at two years of continuous employment before 1 June 1999 or one year thereafter: see s 108 as amended by the Unfair Dismissal and Statement of Reasons for Dismissal (Variation of Qualifying Period) Order 1999, SI 1999/1436.

respect of unfair dismissal.[253] As with the concept of unfairness, the statutory framing of the remedies for unfair dismissal is clearly intended to represent a discarding of some of the restrictions upon remedies which are imposed by the common law of wrongful dismissal; it is, however, questionable how far that aim has been achieved. Thus, it was wished to override the common law/equity objection to positive enforcement of the contract of employment, and accordingly provision is made for orders of reinstatement or re-engagement,[254] and indeed it is required that the successful applicant be asked by the adjudicating tribunal whether he wishes for that remedy.[255] However, the tribunals have in practice made such orders only in a very small proportion of all the cases in which remedies have been given, and both at first instance and on appeal, full weight has been given to the requirement that consideration be given to the question whether it is reasonably practicable for the employer to comply with such an order.[256]

Equally, it was intended that awards of compensation for unfair dismissal should **15.106** not be confined by the common law rule which in effect limits damages for wrongful dismissal to loss of employment to the period of notice required to terminate the contract of employment in question.[257] Provision is therefore made for compensation for unfair dismissal generally to consist of two elements, namely a basic award which is, essentially, the equivalent of the statutory redundancy payment to which the employee was or would be entitled upon dismissal for redundancy,[258] and a compensatory award assessed as such amount as the adjudicating tribunal considers just and equitable having regard to the loss sustained and its attributability to the employer's action.[259] The significance of these awards had itself been considerably curtailed by the placing of a maximum upon the amount of the compensatory award, which had been in the region of £12,000[260] until it was subsequently raised to more than £50,000.[261] This considerable raising of the limit increased the use which is made of this jurisdiction, especially by higher paid employees. However, in *Dunnachie v Kingston upon Hull City Council*,[262] the House of Lords confirmed an earlier determination[263] that the power to award compensation did not extend to non-economic loss.

---

[253] See ERA 1996, ss 111–32.

[254] ibid ss 113–17.

[255] See ibid s 112.

[256] ibid s 116(1)(a); compare, for instance, *O'Laoire v Jackel International Ltd* [1990] ICR 197, CA.

[257] See para 15.83.

[258] See ERA 1996, ss 119–22.

[259] See ibid s 123(1).

[260] ibid s 124, as amended by statutory instrument.

[261] Employment Relations Act 1999, s 34(4) and subsequent statutory instruments—this limit is usually increased on an annual basis.

[262] [2005] 1 AC 226.

[263] By the then existing National Industrial Relations Court in *Norton Tool Co Ltd v Tewson* [1973] 1 WLR 45.

15.107   A further way in which the framers of the legislation have sought to ensure that the unfair dismissal jurisdiction would be free of some of the constraints and limitations of the common law of wrongful dismissal has been by aiming to provide a relatively informal forum of adjudication, namely the industrial tribunals as they were, until recently, styled, and a correspondingly informal appellate body, namely the Employment Appeal Tribunal, in both of which the members of the adjudicatory panel would consist of suitably qualified lay persons sitting with a legally qualified chairman (who, in the case of the Appeal Tribunal, is in practice a High Court Judge).[264] Despite these efforts, the tribunals have not avoided the growth of legalism, and the Employment Appeal Tribunal has had to become the crucible in which the private law of employment is distilled. The Employment Rights (Dispute Resolution) Act 1998 sought to reconstitute the tribunal system to make it conform more nearly to its original aims. It renamed the industrial tribunals as 'employment tribunals';[265] it in various ways simplified and expedited some at least of the hearings of the tribunals;[266] and it sought to promote the use of other methods of dispute resolution, especially arbitration,[267] and the making of compromise agreements.[268] Reference has been made above[269] to the further endeavours which were made in this direction by Part 3 of the Employment Act 2002.

(c)   Extensions and modifications of unfair dismissal law

15.108   There are three important senses in which unfair dismissal law has become the focal point for a larger system of statutory regulation of the termination of employment. The first of these consists in the fact that it has been seen as appropriate to use unfair dismissal law to reinforce a large number of statutory rights of employees by treating dismissals as automatically unfair when they violate or encroach upon those rights. The first statutory right to be so protected was that of freedom of association, so that it is automatically unfair to dismiss on grounds related to union membership or activities (in the particular circumstances specified by statute, which include refusal to belong to a trade union, hence prohibiting the 'closed shop').[270] Among the other instances of dismissals automatically deemed unfair are those for reasons connected with pregnancy or childbirth;[271] those connected with the protection of health and safety at work,[272] those which are for refusal of Sunday work by shop workers or betting workers,[273] or those which are for

---

[264]   See generally the Industrial Tribunals Act 1996.
[265]   Employment Rights (Dispute Resolution) Act 1998, s 1.
[266]   See ibid ss 2–4.
[267]   See ibid ss 7–8.
[268]   See ibid ss 9–10.
[269]   Para 15.104.
[270]   See TULRCA 1992, s 152.
[271]   See ERA 1996, s 99.
[272]   See ibid s 100.
[273]   See ibid s 101.

making a protected public interest disclosure.[274] Indeed, the legislation now protects in this way a whole category of assertions of a statutory right,[275] so that as new statutory rights are created, the category of protected dismissals can be increased accordingly. Dismissals which amount to unlawful discrimination are not automatically deemed unfair as such, but, as well as being proscribed by the respective discrimination statutes,[276] may also be held to amount to unfair dismissal.

The second kind of extension of unfair dismissal law is itself associated with the first. There are several instances of recent employment legislation where new statutory rights are created, and where dismissal in violation of those rights is rendered automatically unfair, as described in the previous paragraph, but where the statutory rights apply not just to employees with contracts of employment, but also to a wider category of workers.[277] As the unfair dismissal legislation applies only to employees with contracts of employment, those other workers lie outside the scope of that kind of protection. Accordingly, it is becoming customary in such instances for the legislation to accord a parallel protection to that wider category of workers by creating a general 'right not to suffer detriment from actions of the employer taken for the reason in question'. Provision of this kind was made, for instance, by the Public Interest Disclosure Act 1998,[278] by the National Minimum Wage Act 1998,[279] and by the Working Time Regulations 1998.[280] **15.109**

The third and final sense in which unfair dismissal law has become the focus or starting point for a larger system of statutory regulation of the termination of employment consists in the fact that it has come to play an important part in the legal regulation of industrial action. That is because there is a set of provisions which result in the loss of unfair dismissal protection, in certain specified circumstances, for workers taking part in a strike or other industrial action or who are the subject of a lock-out by their employer.[281] As modified by the Employment Relations Act 1999, these provisions differentiate not only between trade union or 'official' industrial action and 'unofficial' industrial action but also, within the category of 'official' industrial action, between 'protected' or lawful industrial action and other official industrial action.[282] **15.110**

---

274 See ibid s 103A as inserted by s 5 of the Public Interest Disclosure Act 1998.
275 See ERA 1996, s 104.
276 Sex Discrimination Act 1975, s 6(2)(b); Race Relations Act 1976, s 4(2)(c); Disability Discrimination Act 1995, s 4(2)(d).
277 Compare para 15.19.
278 Section 2, inserting s 47A into the ERA 1996.
279 Section 23.
280 See SI 1998/1833 reg 31.
281 See TULRCA 1992, ss 237–39.
282 Compare ss 237, 238, and 238A as inserted by s 16 of, and Sch 5 to the Employment Relations Act 1999.

(5) *Redundancy and Transfer of Employment*

(a) Redundancy

15.111 An account of the ways in which the termination of employment is regulated by the private law of employment would not be complete without a description of the statutory interventions which are based upon the concept of redundancy, or which involve the transfer of employment. Since 1965, there has been a set of provisions for statutory severance payments[283] for employees dismissed by reason of redundancy,[284] provided that the employee has not unreasonably refused the employer's offer of the employment on the same terms as before, or of different but suitable employment,[285] and provided that the employee has been continuously in the employment of the employer in question, or an associated employer, for two years or more.[286]

15.112 The legislation defines 'redundancy' in terms either of the employer's ceasing to carry on the business in question, whether entirely or 'in the place where the employee was employed', or of the requirements for employees to carry out work of a particular kind, whether generally or in the particular place of employment, having ceased or diminished or being expected to do so.[287] Further legislation is constructed around that concept of redundancy; thus, as was remarked earlier, it forms one of the grounds on which a dismissal may be judged to be fair rather than unfair.[288] Moreover, important requirements, including those of consultation with the representatives of recognized trade unions, or other representatives elected by the relevant workforce, apply where an employer is proposing to dismiss more than certain specified numbers of employees as redundant within specified periods of time.[289]

(b) Transfer of employment

15.113 The legal regulation of the termination of employment involves the necessity to ascribe appropriate effects to various events which are in the nature of changes in ownership or in structure of the employing enterprise. As was indicated earlier, the concern of the common law was primarily to ensure that employees were not subjected to an assignment or novation of the contract of employment without their agreement.[290] A different approach, more concerned with ensuring that the

---

[283] The provisions as to the amount of such payments are contained in ERA 1996, s 162.
[284] See now ERA 1996, s 135 (as modified or qualified by ss 136–8).
[285] See ibid s 141.
[286] See ibid s 155.
[287] See ibid s 139.
[288] See para 15.103.
[289] See TULRCA 1992, ss 188–98 ('Procedure for Handling Redundancies').
[290] *Nokes v Doncaster Amalgamated Collieries Ltd* [1940] AC 1014, HL; see para 15.14.

employee's rights derived from the employment contract or relationship survived the change in ownership or legal structure of the employer, came to be required by European Community law[291] and was implemented by the Transfer of Undertakings (Protection of Employment) Regulations 1981.[292] These regulations, as subsequently amended,[293] involve three main kinds of intervention or regulation.

First, a new general principle is enunciated by regulation 5 that, in effect, upon the **15.114** transfer of an undertaking to which the regulations apply, the contract of employment, of any person employed by the transferor, at or immediately before the time of transfer,[294] in the undertaking or part thereof which is transferred, shall not be terminated by the transfer but shall have effect as if originally made between the employee and the transferee. Second, regulation 8 provides, essentially, that where an employee is, before or after the transfer, dismissed by reason of the transfer or for a reason connected with the transfer, that is automatically an unfair dismissal;[295] where, on the other hand, a dismissal, before or after a transfer, is for an economic, technical or organizational reason entailing changes in the workforce of either the transferor or the transferee, it is to be treated as having been for a substantial reason of the kind justifying dismissal[296] so that it then has to be decided whether the employer (ie the transferor or the transferee as the case may be) acted reasonably in dismissing.[297] Finally, regulation 10 imposes a duty to inform and consult with trade union or workforce representatives about a proposed transfer, which is similar to the duty of consultation in connection with proposed dismissal for redundancy which was considered earlier.[298]

There is a large and intricate body of case law, both in the British courts and in **15.115** the European Court of Justice, both about what counts as the transfer of an undertaking for this purpose,[299] and about the effects of a transfer under the 1977

---

[291] Specifically, Council Directive (EC) 77/187 on the safeguarding of employees' rights in the event of transfers of undertakings, businesses or parts of businesses [1977] OJ L161/23, as since amended and consolidated into Council Directive (EC) 2001/23 [2001] OJ L082/16.

[292] SI 1981/1794.

[293] By the Trade Union Reform and Employment Rights Act 1993, the Collective Redundancies and Transfer of Undertakings (Protection of Employment) (Amendment) Regulations 1995 and 1999, SI 1995/2587 and SI 1999/1925, and the Transfer of Undertakings (Protection of Employment) Regulations 2006, SI 2006/246.

[294] See reg 5(3); the scope of application of the Regulations has been increased by reg 3 of SI 2006/246 which extends the definition of a 'relevant transfer' to include a 'service provision change'.

[295] Compare para 15.108.

[296] See reg 8(2).

[297] See para 15.104.

[298] See para 15.112.

[299] Compare, for instance, the leading case, Case C-13/95 *Süzen v Zehnacker GmbH* [1997] ICR 662, ECJ. However, note should be taken of the extension of the UK TUPE legislation by the

Directive and the 1981 Regulations. As to the latter, two crucial decisions may be singled out. In *Litster v Forth Dry Dock Ltd*,[300] the House of Lords held that the effects of regulations 5 and 8 should be combined so that the transfer of employment should extend to workers who would have been in the employment of the transferor immediately before the transfer had they not been unfairly dismissed by reason of the transfer. In *Wilson v St Helen's Borough Council, Meade v British Fuels Ltd*[301] on the other hand, the House of Lords ruled against claims that, in the circumstances concerned, employees remained entitled, as against the transferee, to the terms and conditions which had existed between them and the transferor prior to the transfer, in such a way as to override their agreement to less favourable terms and conditions with the transferee—though this issue is not resolved beyond doubt in all circumstances. This is a fitting point at which to conclude the discussion of legal regulation of the termination and transfer of personal work contracts, and indeed to conclude the chapter as a whole, because it illustrates very well the inter-activeness between the common law and statute law, and between the law about formation, variation, and termination of personal work contracts or relationships, which has been put forward throughout this chapter as the main key to the understanding of the English private law of employment.

---

inclusion of 'service provision changes', to which reference was made at n 294 above.
300 [1989] ICR 341.
301 [1998] ICR 387.

16

BAILMENT

A. Definition and General Character

(1) Introduction

(a) Bailment as voluntary possession

Bailment is a legal relationship distinct from both contract and tort.[1] It exists **16.01**
whenever one person (the bailee) is voluntarily in possession of goods which

---

[1] *Building and Civil Engineering Holidays Scheme Management Ltd v Post Office* [1966] 1 QB 247, 261, CA *per* Lord Denning MR; *The Pioneer Container* [1994] 2 AC 324, 341–2, PC, *per* Lord Goff of Chieveley; *Sutcliffe v Chief Constable of West Yorkshire* [1996] RTR 86, 90, CA *per* Otton LJ.

belong to another (the bailor).[2] The bailee gets a special property while the bailor retains the general property.[3] Common forms of bailment are carriage of goods, delivery for custody or repair, hire, pledge and loan. The concept of bailment underlies many modern commercial transactions such as title retention,[4] marine salvage[5] and finance leasing.[6]

(b) Basic obligations common to all bailments

16.02 Bailment imposes certain basic obligations on every bailee. The bailee must take reasonable care of the goods and abstain from converting them.[7] He must not deviate from the terms of the bailment and becomes an insurer of the goods if he does so.[8] In most cases he must also refrain from denying the bailor's title.[9] These obligations can normally be varied by special agreement,[10] and in some cases they are superseded by statute.[11] Where goods are lost or damaged while in the bailee's possession the bailee is liable unless he can show that the misadventure occurred independently of his fault.[12] In this and other respects[13] bailment is

---

[2] *The Pioneer Container* [1994] 2 AC 324, PC; *East West Corp v DKBS 1912* [2003] EWCA Civ 83; [2003] QB 1509; *Sandeman Coprimar SA v Transitos y Transportes Integrales SL* [2003] EWCA Civ 113; [2003] QB 1270; *Marcq v Christie Manson & Woods Ltd (t/a Christie's)* [2003] EWCA Civ 731; [2004] QB 286. In *East West Corp v DKBS 1912* at 1530 Mance LJ approved the statement in NE Palmer, *Bailment* (2nd edn, 1991) 1285, 3rd edition pending, that: 'The important question is not the literal meaning of bailment but the circle of relationships within which its characteristic duties will apply. For most practical purposes, any person who comes knowingly into the possession of another's goods is, prima facie, a bailee.'

[3] Thus, 'it is of the essence of a bailment that the general property in the goods concerned remains in the bailor, while only a special property passes to the bailee': *Re Bond Worth Ltd* [1980] Ch 228, 247 *per* Slade LJ.

[4] *Clough Mill Ltd v Martin* [1985] 1 WLR 111, CA.

[5] *China Pacific SA v Food Corp of India, (The Winson)* [1982] AC 939, HL.

[6] *On-Demand Information plc v Michael Gerson (Finance) plc* [2002] UKHL 12; [2003] 1 AC 368.

[7] *Morris v CW Martin & Sons Ltd* [1966] 1 QB 716, 738, CA *per* Salmon LJ. See now also *East West Corp v DKBS 1912* [2003] EWCA Civ 83; [2003] QB 1509.

[8] *Lilley v Doubleday* (1881) 7 QBD 510; *Shaw & Co v Symmons & Sons Ltd* [1917] 1 KB 799; *Mitchell v Ealing London Borough Council* [1979] QB 1.

[9] *Biddle v Bond* (1865) 6 B & S 225, 122 ER 1179; *Ross v Edwards & Co* (1895) 73 LT 100. The prohibition on denying title can be avoided by procedural machinery established under statute; see Torts (Interference with Goods) Act 1977, s 8; para 16.24.

[10] Subject to the Unfair Contract Terms Act 1977, and the Unfair Terms in Consumer Contracts Regulations 1999, SI 1999/2083.

[11] The most notable examples are bailments by way of international carriage of goods: see Chapters 11, 12.

[12] *Travers & Sons v Cooper* [1915] 1 KB 73; *Port Swettenham Authority v TW Wu & Co (M) Sdn Bhd* [1979] AC 580, PC; *Frans Maas (UK) Ltd v Samsung Electronics* [2004] EWHC 1502; [2004] 2 Lloyd's Rep 251; *Coopers Payen Ltd v Southampton Container Terminal Ltd* [2003] EWCA Civ 1223; [2003] 1 Lloyd's Rep 331.

[13] For example, the binding effect of a promise given by an unrewarded bailee in relation to the goods, and the liability of such a bailee for a deviation from the terms of the bailment, despite in each case the absence of any underlying contractual relationship: see para 16.38.

an independent legal relation[14] having qualities not complemented by the normal law of contract or tort.[15]

(c) Bailment and delivery, contract, agreement

A bailment can arise without any physical delivery of goods from the bailor to the **16.03** bailee.[16] A seller of goods who remains in possession after property has passed to the buyer holds as a bailee.[17] A bailee of goods whose bailor sells them during the bailment becomes the bailee of the new owner once he attorns to the new owner.[18] Bailment can also arise without any contract or agreement between the parties and without the bailor's consent.[19] A gratuitous loan of goods is not a contract[20] but is still a bailment.[21] Where a bailee sub-bails,[22] three bailments are likely to arise: between bailor and head bailee,[23] between head bailee and sub-bailee,[24] and between bailor and sub-bailee.[25] A finder of goods is treated as a bailee,[26] as is a person who assumes possession without the owner's express or implied consent.[27] But an involuntary bailee (ie, someone in possession without consent)[28] is not strictly a bailee because he is not voluntarily in possession.[29] The same can be said

---

14 *Sutcliffe v Chief Constable of West Yorkshire* [1996] RTR 86, 90, CA *per* Otton LJ.

15 See generally NE Palmer, *Bailment* (2nd edn, 1991) ch 1.

16 ibid 15–18.

17 *Union Transport Finance v Ballardie* [1937] 1 KB 510; *Worcester Works Finance Ltd v Cooden Engineering Co Ltd* [1972] 1 QB 210.

18 F Pollock, and RS Wright, *An Essay on Possession in the Common Law* (1888) 134; para 16.78 et seq. See now also *East West Corp v DKBS 1912* [2003] EWCA Civ 83; [2003] QB 1509.

19 *The Pioneer Container* [1994] 2 AC 324, PC; NE Palmer, *Bailment* (2nd edn, 1991), 19–40; *East West Corp v DKBS 1912* ibid.

20 *Walker v Watson* [1974] 2 NZLR 175; cf *Blakemore v Bristol & Exeter Rly* (1858) 8 E & B 1035, 1051–2, 120 ER 385, 391 *per* Coleridge J.

21 See further para 16.45.

22 *The Pioneer Container* [1994] 2 AC 324, PC (the leading modern authority). See now also *East West Corp v DKBS 1912* (n 18 above); *Sandeman Coprimar SA v Transitos y Transportes Integrales SL* [2003] QB 1270.

23 *Morris v CW Martin & Sons Ltd* [1966] 1 QB 716, CA; cf *Metaalhandel JA Magnus BV v Ardfields Transport Ltd* [1988] 1 Lloyd's Rep 197 (quasi-bailment).

24 *The Hamburg Star* [1994] 1 Lloyd's Rep 399.

25 *The Pioneer Container* [1994] 2 AC 324, PC; and see for earlier authority *Morris v CW Martin & Sons Ltd* [1966] 1 QB 716, CA; *Gilchrist, Watt and Sanderson Pty Ltd v York Products Pty Ltd* [1970] 1 WLR 1262, PC; *James Buchanan & Co Ltd v Hay's Transport Services Ltd* [1972] 2 Lloyd's Rep 535.

26 *The Pioneer Container* [1994] 2 AC 324, 336–8, PC *per* Lord Goff; *Southland Hospital Board v Perkins Estate* [1986] 1 NZLR 373, 375–6 *per* Cook J; cf *Parker v British Airways Board* [1982] QB 1004, 1017, CA *per* Donaldson LJ; and see generally NE Palmer, *Bailment* (2nd edn, 1991) ch 23.

27 *Burns v Roffey* (HC, 16 March 1982).

28 See generally para 16.86 et seq.

29 *Lethbridge v Phillips* (1819) 2 Stark 544, 171 ER 731; *Howard v Harris* (1884) Cab & Ellis 253; *Neuwith v Over Darwen Co-operative Society Ltd* (1894) 63 LJQB 290 (possessor owes no general duty of care).

of an 'unconscious bailee' who is unaware of his possession of goods, or of the fact that goods in his possession belong to another.[30]

(d) Bailment and prior possession and ownership

16.04   A bailment can arise without any previous possession on the part of the bailor.[31] A bailment exists where goods are sold to one person but delivered directly on his instructions to another, who has agreed to hold them as his bailee.[32] From the moment that he receives possession the recipient is the bailee of the new owner.[33]

16.05   Bailments can arise where the bailor is not the owner.[34] All that is necessary is that the bailor should have some superior right to the possession of the goods.[35] Subject to that requirement, a bailment can arise between a head bailee and a sub-bailee,[36] or between an original bailor and bailee where the bailee bails the goods back to the bailor for a period shorter than the original bailment.[37] A bailor is a person who has a reversionary interest in goods.[38] But bailment is a common law relation[39] and the bailor must have a legal interest in the goods;[40] a mere

---

[30] *AVX Ltd v EGM Solders Ltd The Times*, 7 July 1982; *Consentino v Dominion Express Co* (1906) 4 WLR 48; para 16.91 et seq; *Marcq v Christie Manson & Woods Ltd (t/a Christie's)* [2003] EWCA Civ 731; [2004] QB 286.

[31]   See NE Palmer, *Bailment* (2nd edn, 1991) 113.

[32]   *Belvoir Finance Co Ltd v Stapleton* [1971] 1 QB 210, CA; *Johnson Matthey & Co Ltd v Constantine Terminals Ltd* [1976] 2 Lloyd's Rep 215 (not followed in *The Pioneer Container* [1994] 2 AC 324, PC, but not on this point).

[33]   For cases where liability akin to that of a bailee can arise even before the reception of possession, see para 16.85 et seq.

[34]   NE Palmer (n 31 above) 112–22; N Palmer, 'Possessory Title' in N Palmer and E McKendrick, *Interests in Goods* (2nd edn, 1998).

[35]   *Leigh and Sillivan Ltd v Aliakmon Shipping Co Ltd (The Aliakmon)* [1986] 1 AC 785, 809, HL *per* Lord Brandon; *Green v Stevens* (1857) 2 H & N 146; *The Hamburg Star* [1994] 1 Lloyd's Rep 399; *Mayflower Foods Ltd v Barnard Bros Ltd* (HC, 9 August 1996); *MCC Proceeds Inc v Lehmann Bros International (Europe)* [1998] 4 All ER 675, CA; *East West Corp v DKBS 1912* [2003] EWCA Civ 83; [2003] QB 1509; *The Homburg Houtimport BV v Agrosin Private Ltd (The Starsin)* [2003] UKHL 12; [2004] 1 AC 705; cf *China Pacific SA v Food Corp of India (The Winson)* [1982] AC 939, HL.

[36]   *Morris v CW Martin & Sons Ltd* [1966] 1 QB 716, 729, CA *per* Lord Denning MR; *The Hamburg Star* [1994] 1 Lloyd's Rep 399; *The Pioneer Container* [1994] 2 AC 324, PC.

[37]   *Roberts v Wyatt* (1810) 2 Taunt 268, 127 ER 1080; *Brierly v Kendall* (1852) 17 QB 937, 117 ER 1540.

[38]   For cases using the word 'reversion' in this context, see *Kwei Tek Chao (t/a Zung Fu Co) v British Traders & Shippers Ltd* [1954] 2 QB 459, 487 *per* Devlin J; *Empressa Exportadora De Azucar v Industria Azucarera Nacional SA (The Playa Larga and Marble Islands)* [1983] 2 Lloyd's Rep 171, 179, CA *per* Ackner LJ; *Candlewood Navigation Corp Ltd v Mitsui OSK Lines Ltd (The Mineral Transporter)* [1986] AC 1, 18, PC *per* Lord Fraser; and see *HSBC Rail (UK) Ltd v Network Rail Infrastructure Ltd* [2005] EWCA Civ 1437; [2006] 1 WLR 643.

[39]   *MCC Proceeds Inc v Lehmann Bros International (Europe)* [1998] 4 All ER 675, 702, CA *per* Hobhouse LJ.

[40]   *MCC Proceeds Inc v Lehmann Bros International (Europe)* [1998] 4 All ER 675, CA; and see *Leigh and Sillivan Ltd v Aliakmon Shipping Co Ltd (The Aliakmon)* [1986] 1 AC 785, HL.

equitable interest (such as that of a beneficiary under a trust)[41] will not suffice,[42] unless that interest draws with it a right to the immediate possession of the subject goods.[43]

(2) The Essential Role of Possession

(a) Bailment obligations and possession

Possession is central to bailment.[44] Unless one person is in possession of goods **16.06** to which another has a superior right of possession there can be no bailment.[45] Obligations akin to those on a bailment can arise, however, without possession of another's goods. A person who agrees to take possession of goods at a particular time and fails to do so may owe duties similar to those of a normal bailee,[46] as may a person who, having the option of taking possession of goods or delegating the task to another, chooses to delegate; that person may then be liable for the defaults of the delegate,[47] as he would if he were bailing the goods under a conventional sub-bailment, having first got possession in person.[48] It is said that a bailment by way of hire[49] can arise though the hirer gets no possession because the chattel is supplied with an operator who continues to be employed by the lessor and to retain possession on his behalf,[50] but that is doubtful.[51]

(b) Bailment and employment

The requirement of possession may mean that no bailment arises between **16.07** employer and employee.[52] Traditionally, employees who have charge of their

---

41 See generally *Halsbury's Laws of England* (4th edn Re-issue) Trusts.

42 *MCC Proceeds Inc v Lehmann Bros International (Europe)* [1998] 4 All ER 675, CA, explaining *Healey v Healey* [1915] 1 KB 938 and *International Factors Ltd v Rodriguez* [1979] 1 QB 351, CA.

43 As in *International Factors Ltd v Rodriguez* [1979] 1 QB 351, CA, as explained by *MCC Proceeds Inc v Lehmann Bros International (Europe)* [1998] 4 All ER 675. As to the sufficiency of a right of possession to cast the party thus entitled in the position of a bailor of the possessor, and so to ground a bailment between those parties, see *East West Corp v DKBS 1912* [2003] EWCA Civ 83; [2003] 1 Lloyd's Rep 239.

44 See generally NE Palmer, *Bailment* (2nd edn, 1991) 99–112, chs 5, 6 and 7.

45 Hence at common law a person cannot bail goods to himself: *Harding v Comr of Inland Revenue* [1977] 1 NZLR 337 (decided under New Zealand property legislation).

46 *Quiggin v Duff* (1836) 1 M & W 174, 150 ER 394; *Edwards v Newland & Co* [1950] 2 KB 534, CA.

47 *Metaalhandel JA Magnus BV v Ardfields Transport Ltd* [1988] 1 Lloyd's Rep 197; and see *The Pioneer Container* [1994] 2 AC 324, 345, PC *per* Lord Goff; Palmer (n 44 above) 1291–5.

48 See *Morris v CW Martin & Sons Ltd* [1966] 1 QB 716, CA; and Palmer (n 44 above) 1298–301.

49 See generally as to hire para 16.61 et seq.

50 *Fowler v Lock* (1872) LR 7 CP 272, 282 *per* Byles J.

51 NE Palmer, (n 44 above) 470.

52 ibid ch 7.

employer's property in the course of employment have mere custody and no independent possession.[53] They cannot therefore sue third parties in trespass or conversion[54] and they cannot be liable as bailees.[55] The rule is antiquated and may in any event not apply where there is a substantial distance and lack of control between the employer and the employee,[56] or where the employee receives from a third party goods intended for the employer; in that case, the employee may get an independent possession (and may therefore be a bailee) until he appropriates the goods to the employer.[57] An employee who loses or damages the employer's goods during the course of employment can be sued in tort for negligence[58] and for breach of an implied term of the contract of employment.[59] An employee to whom a chattel is loaned by the employer for a purpose unconnected with employment can of course be a bailee.[60]

16.08   Employers can be bailees of their employees' chattels, as where employees' work tools are left on the employer's premises overnight,[61] or coats are deposited during working hours.[62] A statutory obligation of care[63] may also apply in respect of clothing.[64] In the absence of bailment or statutory obligation, an employer does not normally owe a duty to protect his employees from theft.[65] No such duty arises under the law of occupier's liability,[66] or any implied term of the contract of employment,[67] or the general law of tort.[68]

---

[53] *Lotus Cars Ltd v Southampton Cargo Handling plc (The Rigoletto); Southampton Cargo Handling plc v Associated British Ports* [2000] 2 Lloyd's Rep 532 at 539; *Alexander v Southey* (1821) 5 B & Ald 247, 106 ER 1183; *Associated Portland Cement Manufacturers (1910) Ltd v Ashton* [1915] 2 KB 1, CA; *R v Harding* (1929) 46 TLR 105. The non-possession rule does not apply to agents and independent contractors, who may get possession and be answerable as bailees: *Lotus Cars Ltd v Southampton Cargo Handling plc (The Rigoletto); Southampton Cargo Handling plc v Associated British Ports* above. And see para 16.20.

[54] *Hopkinson v Gibson* (1805) 2 Smith 2021 (trover).

[55] *Wiebe v Lepp* (1974) 46 DLR (3d) 441. But a general duty of care may be owed, unaccompanied by the peculiar bailee's burden of proof: See para 16.33.

[56] *The Jupiter III* [1927] P 122, 131 *per* Hill J, affd [1927] P 250; *Boson v Sandford* (1690) 1 Shower 101, 89 ER 477; *Moore v Robinson* (1831) 2 B & Ad 817, 109 ER 1346.

[57] *Marshall v Dibble* [1920] NZLR 497; F Pollock and RS Wright, *An Essay on Possession in the Common Law* (1888) 60.

[58] *Superlux v Plaisted* [1958] Current Law Year Book 195.

[59] *Rowell v Alexander Mackie CAE* (1988) Aust Torts Rep 67, 727, NSWCA.

[60] *Haira v Attorney-General* [1962] NZLR 549.

[61] *MacDonald v Whittaker Textiles (Marysville) Ltd* (1976) 64 DLR (3d) 317.

[62] *Tremear v Park Town Motor Hotels Ltd* [1982] 4 Western Weekly Reports 444.

[63] Offices, Shops and Railway Premises Act 1963, s 12(1)(9); Factories Act 1961, s 59. Preceding legislation was held to render employers responsible for taking reasonable steps to ensure that the accommodation provided was reasonably secure against the risk of theft: *McCarthy v Daily Mirror Newspapers Ltd* [1949] 1 All ER 801.

[64] *McCarthy v Daily Mirror Newspapers Ltd* [1949] 1 All ER 801.

[65] *Deyong v Shenburn* [1946] 1 KB 227, CA.

[66] *Edwards v West Herts Group Hospital Management Committee* [1957] 1 WLR 415, CA.

[67] ibid.

[68] *Deyong v Shenburn* [1946] (n 66 above).

(c) Machines supplied with operators

Where a machine is supplied along with an operator, the existence of a bailment **16.09** between the owner and the client depends on such factors as the identity of the employer for the period of use, the location and nature of the work, the arrangements for safekeeping while the machine is not in use and the degree of control exercised by the party for whose use the machine is engaged.[69] The fact that the operator continues throughout in the general employment of the owner[70] does not count decisively against the creation of a bailment but it is a strong factor in favour of that conclusion.[71] The charterer under a time or voyage charterparty is not a bailee of the vessel but the charterer under a bareboat charter is.[72] Most cases turn on their facts.[73]

(d) Bailments and licences

The requirement of possession may also prevent a bailment from arising where **16.10** goods are left on land or premises with the occupier's permission.[74] This question commonly arises under car-parking arrangements,[75] or where patrons deposit garments in cloakrooms at restaurants or other places of public resort.[76] If there is no transfer of possession to the occupier, the relationship is that of licensor and licensee, and the occupier owes no duty to protect the goods against theft.[77] Factors relevant to this distinction include the physical layout of the land,[78] the procedures for reclaiming goods,[79] the presence and function of attendants,[80] the distance between the owner and the goods,[81] the value of the goods,[82] the scale

---

[69] These factors are discussed at length in NE Palmer, *Bailment* (2nd edn, 1991) 470–93.

[70] See generally as to the test for establishing this: *Mersey Docks and Harbour Board v Coggins and Griffiths (Liverpool) Ltd* [1947] 1 AC 1, HL.

[71] See, eg, *British Crane Hire Corp Ltd v Ipswich Plant Hire Ltd* [1975] 1 QB 303, CA; cf *Deane v Hogg* (1834) 10 Bing 345, 131 ER 937.

[72] *Deane v Hogg* (1834) 10 Bing 345, 131 ER 937; *The Lancaster* [1980] 2 Lloyd's Rep 497.

[73] NE Palmer, *Bailment* (2nd edn, 1991) 471 et seq.

[74] ibid ch 5. The leading authority is *Lotus Cars Ltd v Southampton Cargo Handling plc (The Rigoletto); Southampton Cargo Handling plc v Associated British Ports* (n 53 above).

[75] *Ashby v Tolhurst* [1937] 2 KB 242, CA; *Tinsley v Dudley* [1951] 2 KB 18, CA.

[76] *Samuel v Westminster Wine Co The Times*, 16 May 1959; *Davis v Educated Fish Parlours Ltd* [1966] Current Law Yearbook 539.

[77] *Ashby v Tolhurst* [1937] 2 KB 242, CA.

[78] ibid; *Tinsley v Dudley* [1951] 2 KB 18, CA; *BRS (Contracts) Ltd v Colney Motor Engineering Co Ltd The Times*, 27 November 1958, CA; *BG Transport Service Ltd v Marston Motor Co Ltd* [1970] I Lloyd's Rep 371; *Fred Chappell Ltd v National Car Parks Ltd The Times*, 22 May 1987; *Halbauer v Brighton Corp* [1954] 1 WLR 1161, CA; *Hinks v Fleet The Times*, 7 October 1986, CA.

[79] *Ashby v Tolhurst* [1937] 2 KB 242, CA; *Sydney City Council v West* (1965) 114 CLR 481; *Walton's Stores v Sydney City Council* [1968] 2 NSWR 109.

[80] *Ashby v Tolhurst* [1937] 2 KB 242, CA.

[81] *Halbauer v Brighton Corp* [1954] 1 WLR 1161, CA; *Ultzen v Nichols* [1894] 1 QB 92.

[82] *James Buchanan Ltd v Hay's Transport Services Ltd* [1972] 2 Lloyd's Rep 535.

and means of exaction of any fee for the facility,[83] the terms of any documentation issued by the occupier,[84] the commercial expectations of the parties[85] and any other circumstances which indicate whether a duty of care was being assumed.[86]

(3) Consent to Possession

(a) Burden of proof

16.11 Just as it is for the person asserting a bailment to prove the necessary possession,[87] so that person must also prove that the putative bailee consented to possession.[88]

(b) Implying consent to possession

16.12 Consent may be express or implied.[89] It may be inferred from the nature of a containing chattel,[90] or from a warning given at the time of deposit,[91] or from the location in which the goods are bailed,[92] or from the character of bailor or bailee.[93] The mere fact that the bailee is unaware of the presence or specific nature of goods in his possession does not preclude a bailment of them.[94] Such a person may still

---

[83] *Ashby v Tolhurst* [1937] 2 KB 242, CA; *Fred Chappell Ltd v National Car Parks Ltd The Times*, 22 May 1987.

[84] *Ashby v Tolhurst* ibid; *Fred Chappell Ltd v National Car Parks Ltd* ibid; *Sydney City Council v West* (1965) 114 CLR 481; *Walton's Stores v Sydney City Council* [1968] 2 NSWR 109.

[85] *Lotus Cars Ltd v Southampton Cargo Handling plc (The Rigoletto); Southampton Cargo Handling plc v Associated British Ports* (n 53 above).

[86] See further *WD & HO Wills (Australia) Ltd v State Rail Authority of New South Wales* (1998) 43 NSWLR 338; see now also *Lotus Cars Ltd v Southampton Cargo Handling plc (The Rigoletto); Southampton Cargo Handling plc v Associated British Ports* (n 53 above).

[87] ibid; *G Merel & Co Ltd v Chessher* [1961] 1 Lloyd's Rep 534.

[88] *WD & HO Wills (Australia) Ltd v State Rail Authority of New South Wales* (n 86 above). In general terms, the alleged bailee must also consent to hold as bailee of the particular party interested in the goods, though such consent can be implied: See *KH Enterprise v Pioneer Container, The Pioneer Container* [1994] AC 324, PC; *Marcq v Christie Manson & Woods Ltd (t/a Christie's)* [2003] EWCA Civ 731; [2004] QB 286, and paras 16.82, 16.83.

[89] *Martin v London County Council* [1947] KB 628.

[90] *Moukataff v BOAC* [1967] 1 Lloyd's Rep 396.

[91] *Mendelssohn v Normand Ltd* [1970] 1 QB 177, CA; *Minichiello v Devonshire Hotel (1967) Ltd* (1977) 79 DLR (3d) 619.

[92] *Brown v Toronto Autoparks Ltd* [1955] 2 DLR 525; *Heffron v Imperial Parking Co Ltd* (1976) 46 DLR (3d) 642.

[93] There is no decision exactly in point, but the character of the bailee (and the nature of the bailee's operations) is generally taken to be a factor in gauging the quality of service to which the bailor can reasonably believe himself to be entitled.

[94] See generally NE Palmer, *Bailment* (2nd edn, 1991) ch 6; cf *AVX Ltd v EGM Solders Ltd The Times*, 7 July 1982.

be a bailee where the goods are of a class that could reasonably be expected to be in his possession.[95]

(4) Redelivery

(a) In general

A bailment can arise though the possessor is not obliged to return the goods to **16.13** the person from whom he received them.[96] Such a bailment may occur where the possessor is instructed to deliver the goods to a third party after an agreed period of possession,[97] or to sell them on the owner's behalf.[98] The delivery of goods to a lessee on hire-purchase[99] or to a buyer on title retention terms[100] is a bailment though the parties contemplate the ultimate transmission of property to the bailee.[101] The sub-bailment is a common example of a bailment where the bailee delivers the goods to a third party yet retains the character of bailee during the subsidiary possession.[102] Similarly, a bailment can arise though it is contemplated by the terms of delivery that the goods will eventually be consumed by the bailee or that their identity will change by reason of amalgamation or other treatment on the part of the bailee.[103] None of these considerations prevents the recipient from becoming a bailee during the interval between his receiving possession and the occurrence of the obliterating event. In this context, however, the bailor must retain some realistic right of possession over the goods for the period before consumption or transformation if the relation during that period is to be classed as a bailment.[104]

---

[95] eg *Mendelssohn v Normand Ltd* [1970] 1 QB 177, CA (suitcase of silver left in Rolls-Royce parked in underground car park by diner at expensive hotel; but here a warning about the presence of valuables was given to an attendant).

[96] *Gamer's Motor Centre (Newcastle) Pty Ltd v Natwest Wholesale Australia Pty Ltd* (1987) 163 CLR 236, (1987) 61 ALJR 415, 426 *per* Dawson J.

[97] *Brambles Security Services Ltd v Bi-Lo Pty Ltd* (1992) Aust Torts Reps 81–161; cf *Wincanton Ltd v P & O Trans European Ltd* [2001] EWCA Civ 227.

[98] eg *Gutter v Tait* (1947) 177 LT 1.

[99] *Motor Mart Ltd v Webb* [1958] NZLR 773.

[100] *Aluminium Industrie Vaassen BV v Romalpa Aluminium Ltd* [1976] 1 WLR 676, CA.

[101] Otherwise where the circumstances indicate no intention to retain any residual property in the deliveror following delivery to the alleged bailee: *Wincanton Ltd v P & O Trans European Ltd* [2001] EWCA Civ 227.

[102] *The Pioneer Container* [1994] 2 AC 324, PC.

[103] *Clough Mill Ltd v Martin* [1985] 1 WLR 111, 116, CA *per* Robert Goff LJ.

[104] *Borden (UK) Ltd v Scottish Timber Products Ltd* [1981] Ch 25, 35, CA *per* Bridge LJ; *Wincanton Ltd v P & O Trans European Ltd* [2001] EWCA Civ 227.

(b) Mixtures and fungible goods

16.14   Where fungible goods are delivered by several depositors to a common depository, and are commingled so that the original deposits are unidentifiable, the inability of each depositor to demand redelivery of the specific goods which he has delivered will normally inhibit the creation of a bailment.[105] Such depositors, being unable to identify the subject matter of the alleged bailment, cannot be bailors, cannot enforce the obligations of a bailee against the recipient, and cannot assert a proprietary interest against third parties.[106] That conclusion was reached in several cases where wheat was deposited by numerous depositors in a 'wheat bank' on terms that equivalent quantities could be withdrawn on demand; the court held that no bailment arose.[107] Similar reasoning will normally preclude a bailment where money is delivered on terms that it shall be repaid.[108] It makes no difference in such cases that the recipient undertakes to deliver up equivalent goods or cash on demand, because the line of heredity between what is deposited and what is returned is broken. Similar disabilities affect at common law the buyer of generic goods who is falsely assured by the seller that the seller will segregate goods answering the contract description and retain possession of them as the buyer's bailee.[109] Such a buyer cannot assert a bailment (or any proprietary interest akin to that of bailor and sustainable against third parties) because he cannot point to any specific goods which are the subject of that bailment;[110] and neither the doctrine of the bailee's estoppel,[111] nor that of attornment,[112] will fortify his rights against a third party creditor of the seller. But a tenancy in common may arise by agreement among individual contributors to a communal pool where an intention to that effect is clearly evinced by the underlying contract,[113] or by

---

[105] *South Australian Insurance Co Ltd v Randell* (1869) LR 3 PC 101, PC; *Chapman Bros Ltd v Verco Bros Ltd* (1933) 49 CLR 306; cf *Mercer v Craven Grain Storage Ltd* [1994] CLC 328, HL; see also *Coleman v Harvey* [1989] 1 NZLR 723.

[106] *Re Goldcorp Exchange Ltd* [1995] 1 AC 74, PC.

[107] *South Australian Insurance Co Ltd v Randell* (1869) LR 3 PC 101, PC; *Chapman Bros Ltd v Verco Bros Ltd* (1933) 49 CLR 306; *Mercer v Craven Grain Storage Ltd* [1994] CLC 328, HL; *Coleman v Harvey* [1989] 1 NZLR 723.

[108] *Walker v British Guarantee Assoc* (1852) 18 QB 277, 118 ER 104; *R v Hassall* (1861) Le & Ca 58, 169 ER 1302; *Brambles Security Services Ltd v Bi-Lo Pty Ltd* (1992) Aust Torts Reps 81–161; *Ferguson v Eakin* (NSWCA, 27 August 1997). And see *Parastatidis v Kotarides* [1978] Victoria Reports 449 (*mutuum*, or loan of money, is not a true bailment). See further as to *mutuum*, *Wincanton Ltd v P & O Trans European Ltd* [2001] EWCA Civ 227; [2001] CLC 962.

[109] *Re Goldcorp Exchange Ltd* [1995] 1 AC 74, PC; *Re London Wine Co (Shippers) Ltd* [1986] Palmer's Company Cases 121.

[110] *Re Goldcorp Exchange Ltd* [1995] 1 AC 74, PC; and see *Re London Wine Co (Shippers) Ltd* ibid; cf *Re Stapylton Fletcher Ltd* [1994] 1 WLR 1181.

[111] See para 16.21 et seq.

[112] See para 16.78 et seq.

[113] *Mercer v Craven Grain Storage Ltd* [1994] CLC 328, HL (deposits of grain); *Re Stapylton Fletcher Ltd* [1994] 1 WLR 1181 (sale of wine); cf *Gill and Duffus (Liverpool) Ltd v Scruttons Ltd* [1953] 1 WLR 1407 (where bags of chestnuts consigned to different consignees burst and intermingled in

statute under certain sales of goods.[114] Such tenancy in common, which confers a legal interest in goods,[115] can extend to the recipient or seller of the goods where he has contributed to the mixed pool upon which the tenancy in common fastens. Its existence enables the depositor or buyer to sue the recipient or seller as a bailee of the recipient or buyer,[116] and to assert a proprietary interest against third parties.[117] That entitlement is, of course, especially important where the recipient or seller is insolvent.

(5) Subject Matter of Bailment

Bailment is limited to tangible chattels. It does not apply to intangible property **16.15** such as a debt or copyright.[118] Obligations akin to those on a bailment may arise, however, from an entrustment of confidential information.[119] It is argued that principles akin to those of bailment should govern the 'global custody' of electronically stored securities which have no material existence.[120] Bailment does not apply to live human beings such as children entrusted for custody.[121] Human remains, and human body parts and products are not normally capable of being the subject of proprietary or possessory rights and cannot therefore be bailed.[122]

---

the hold of the vessel, and the master porter rebagged them proportionally to the amounts in the bills of lading, it was held that a tenancy in common arose among the original consignees). See also *Glencore International AG v Metro Trading International Inc* [2001] 1 Lloyd's Rep 2000.

[114] Sale of Goods Act 1979, s 20A, added by the Sale of Goods (Amendment) Act 1995; see para 10.20. L Gullifer, 'Constructive possession after the Sale of Goods (Amendment) Act 1995' (1999) LMCLQ 93.

[115] Cf *MCC Proceeds Inc v Lehman Bros International (Europe)* [1998] 4 All ER 675, CA (bailment requires legal interest in bailor).

[116] See *Mercer v Craven Grain Storage Ltd* [1994] CLC 328, HL, *per* Lord Templeman (defendant farmers' co-operative, as recipient of deposits of grain from claimant growers, committed conversion 'if it allowed the mix to be so depleted by withdrawals that the balance remaining was not sufficient to satisfy the demands of the [claimants]'). Cf *Wincanton Ltd v P & O Trans European Ltd* [2001] EWCA Civ 227 (no bailment where pallets mixed with others of indistinguishable nature supplied from other sources).

[117] *Mercer v Craven Grain Storage Ltd* [1994] CLC 328, HL; *Re Stapylton Fletcher Ltd* [1994] 1 WLR 1181.

[118] *OBG Ltd v Allan* [2007] UKHL 21; [2007] 2 WLR 920.

[119] See *Hospital Products Ltd v United States Surgical Corporation* (1984) 156 CLR 41, 105–6 *per* Mason J; *Watson v Dolmark Industries Ltd* [1992] 3 NZLR 311, 315 *per* Cooke J; *Reading v R* [1949] 2 KB 232, 236 *per* Asquith J. As to whether information can count as property in English private law, see generally N Palmer and P Kohler, 'Information as Property' in N Palmer and E McKendrick (eds), *Interests in Goods* (2nd edn, 1998); 8(1) *Halsbury's Laws of England* (4th edn Re-issue) paras 407, 408.

[120] See AW Beaves, 'Global Custody—A Tentative Analysis of Property and Contract' in Palmer and McKendrick ibid.

[121] Cf *ST v North Yorkshire County Council* [1999] IRLR 98; *Lister v Hesley Hall Ltd* [2002] 1 AC 22.

[122] *Dobson v North Tyneside Health Authority and Newcastle Health Authority* [1997] 1 WLR 596, CA; *R v Kelly* [1998] 3 All ER 741, CA.

But the position may be otherwise where bodily material is subjected to treatment rendering it something different from a mere corpse awaiting burial;[123] and modern law may eventually admit other exceptions to the general rule.[124] Money can be bailed, but a bailment of money will arise only where the specific coins or notes are to be returned to the deliveror or applied in accordance with his instructions, as where a bank note is pledged,[125] or shop takings are to be collected by a security company and delivered to the proprietor's bank.[126] Where cash is loaned or deposited in a bank, and the recipient's obligation is merely to repay to the lender or depositor an equivalent amount, the relationship between lender and borrower is one of debtor and creditor not bailor and bailee.[127]

(6) Bailment Distinguished from Other Transactions

(a) Bailment and trust

16.16   Bailment and trust are distinct and, for the most part, mutually exclusive.[128] Their main difference lies in the identity of the person who has the legal property and can confer it on others. In bailments, it is the bailor who has the legal property and can transmit it to third parties, while in trusts it is the trustee who has the legal property and can transmit it to third parties, the beneficiary having only an equitable title.[129] Since bailment is a legal relationship capable of generating legal remedies, only a person with a legal interest can be a bailor.[130] Because there is no bailment between trustee and beneficiary, a beneficiary cannot invoke that line of authority[131] which gives the bailor an immediate right of possession when the bailee commits an act repugnant to the bailment.[132] Certain bailees do, however, occupy a fiduciary position toward their bailors. For example, a pledgee who exercises his power of sale on default by the pledgor holds the surplus proceeds on trust for the pledgor,[133] and a custodian for reward who charges his bailors for the cost

---

[123] *Doodeward v Spence* (1908) 6 CLR 406, 414 *per* Griffith CJ; *Dobson v North Tyneside Health Authority and Newcastle Health Authority* [1997] 1 WLR 596, CA; *R v Kelly* [1998] 3 All ER 741, CA.

[124] *R v Kelly* [1998] 3 All ER 741, 750, CA *per* Rose LJ.

[125] Cf *Taylor v Chester* (1869) LR 4 QB 309.

[126] *Brambles Security Services Ltd v Bi-Lo Pty Ltd* (1992) Aust Torts Reps 81–161; cf *Lipkin Gorman v Karpnale Ltd* [1991] 2 AC 548, HL.

[127] *Ferguson v Eakins* (unreported, NSWCA, 27 August 1997).

[128] *MCC Proceeds Inc v Lehmann Bros International (Europe)* [1998] 4 All ER 675, CA.

[129] ibid.

[130] ibid, 701–3, CA *per* Hobhouse LJ.

[131] *Union Transport Finance Ltd v British Car Auctions Ltd* [1978] 2 All ER 385, CA.

[132] *MCC Proceeds Inc v Lehmann Bros International (Europe)* (n 128 above).

[133] *Mathew v TM Sutton Ltd* [1994] 4 All ER 793.

of insurance may hold the policy monies on a fiduciary obligation for them.[134] According to circumstances, obligations owed by a holder of goods toward another person who has a reversionary interest in them might alternatively be rationalized in terms of bailment or trust.[135]

(b) Bailment and sale of goods

A bailment, unlike a sale, passes no general property to the recipient party, but merely a special property in the form of possession.[136] Bailment involves the retention of general property by the bailor and does not attract the special legislation applicable to sale.[137] But sale and bailment can co-exist in relation to a single chattel, as where goods are supplied to a person who has agreed to buy them subject to a title retention clause,[138] or on hire-purchase,[139] or where containers are supplied on refundable deposit along with their contents.[140] A bailment of goods on a finance lease closely resembles a sale and has been held in New Zealand[141] to attract at least one of the legal incidents of hire-purchase, namely the special measure of damages applicable in a claim between bailor and bailee, or bailor and third party, respectively.

16.17

Although some judges appear to treat bailment and sale as mutually exclusive in the context of title retention,[142] the mere fact that a person who has voluntary possession of another's goods is given extensive liberties in relation to them (such

16.18

---

[134] *Re E Dibbens & Sons Ltd* [1990] BCLC 577.

[135] *Re Swan, Witham v Swan* [1915] 1 Ch 829.

[136] *Re Bond Worth Ltd* [1980] Ch 228, 247 *per* Slade J.

[137] Differentiating the two transactions may require detailed examination of the contract: see, eg, *Stellar Chartering & Brokerage Inc v Efibanca-Ente Finanziario Interbancario SpA (The Span Terza) (No 2)* [1984] 1 WLR 27, HL.

[138] See eg *Aluminium Industrie Vaassen BV v Romalpa Aluminium Ltd* [1976] 1 WLR 676, CA; *Armour v Thyssen Edelstahlwerke AG* [1991] 2 AC 339, HL; *Clough Mill v Martin* [1985] 1 WLR 111, CA; *Hendy Lennox (Industrial Engines) Ltd v Grahame Puttick Ltd* [1984] 1 WLR 485; *Re Andrabell Ltd (in liq); Airborne Accessories Ltd v Goodman* [1984] 3 All ER 407; *Re Peachdart Ltd* [1984] Ch 131; *Borden (UK) Ltd v Scottish Timber Products Ltd* [1981] Ch 25, CA; *Re Bond Worth Ltd* [1980] Ch 228; *E Pfeiffer Weinkellerei-Weineinkauf GmbH & Co v Arbuthnot Factors Ltd* [1988] 1 WLR 150; *Compaq Computer Ltd v Abercorn Group Ltd* [1991] BCC 484; *Tatung (UK) Ltd v Galex Telesure Ltd* (1989) 5 BCC 325; *Forsythe International (UK) Ltd v Silver Shipping Co Ltd (The Saetta)* [1993] 2 Lloyd's Rep 268.

[139] See eg *Shogun Finance Ltd v Hudson* [2004] 1 AC 919, [2004] 1 All ER 215, [2004] 1 Lloyd's Rep. 532; *Motor Mart Ltd v Webb* [1958] NZLR 773; *Gamer's Motor Centre (Newcastle) Pty Ltd v Natwest Wholesale Australia Pty Ltd* (1987) 163 CLR 236.

[140] See eg *Geddling v Marsh* [1920] 1 KB 66; *Leitch & Co Ltd v Leydon* 1930 SC 41, 52–3 *per* Lord Clyde; *Doble v David Greig Ltd* [1972] 1 WLR 703; cf *Beecham Foods Ltd v North Supplies (Edmonton) Ltd* [1959] 1 WLR 643. These authorities are discussed in Palmer (n 94 above) 137–43.

[141] *NZ Securities & Finance Ltd v Wrightcars Ltd* [1976] 1 NZLR 77.

[142] See eg *Re Peachdart Ltd* [1984] Ch 131, 142 *per* Vinelott J; *Hendy-Lennox (Industrial Engines) Ltd v Grahame Puttick Ltd* [1984] 1 WLR 485, 499 *per* Staughton J; *Re Andrabell Ltd (in liq); Airborne Accessories Ltd v Goodman* [1984] 3 All ER 407, 414 *per* Peter Gibson J; *E Pfeiffer*

as the right to consume or alter them, or to dispose of them as a third party) does not confute the existence of a bailment so long as the goods exist and the possessor has possession.[143] If, however, the terms of the agreement give the supplier no realistic prospect of resuming possession of the identical goods before their consumption or disposal, there is probably no bailment.[144] Similarly, a bailment is unlikely to arise where an owner of fungible commodities (such as wheat,[145] flour,[146] fuel[147] or money)[148] deposits them in a general store operated by the recipient, agreeing that they are to be mingled with similar goods belonging to the recipient or to other depositors, and that an equivalent quantity will be redelivered to the depositor. Such an arrangement will normally be construed as a relinquishment of property in the deposited commodities in return for a substituted property in the redelivered commodities, and not as a bailment.[149] But a bailment may arise by agreement (as where all the depositors and the recipient agree that the depositors shall be tenants in common of the overall quantity deposited)[150] or by custom or statute,[151] and may even be imposed by the court in the interests of justice.[152]

(c) Bailment and work and labour

16.19 Occasionally it is unclear whether the delivery of one person's chattel to another, to enable the other to perform work on the chattel and redeliver it to the original owner, is a bailment of the chattel or a contract by which property passes to the recipient and is transferred back to the original deliveror. In each case the solution depends on the intention of the parties as objectively inferred from the terms and circumstances of the contract.[153] According to circumstances, the answer

Weinkellerei-Weineinkauf GmbH & Co v Arbuthnot Factors Ltd [1988] 1 WLR 150, 159 *per* Phillips J.

143 *Clough Mill Ltd v Martin* [1985] 1 WLR 111, 116 *per* Robert Goff J.
144 *Borden (UK) Ltd v Scottish Timber Products Ltd* [1981] Ch 25, 35, CA *per* Bridge LJ (cf 45 *per* Buckley LJ); *Wincanton Ltd v P & O Trans European Ltd* [2001] EWCA Civ 227.
145 *South Australian Insurance Co Ltd v Randell* (1869) LR 3 PC 101, PC; *Chapman Bros v Verco Bros & Co Ltd* (1933) 49 CLR 306; *Mercer v Craven Grain Storage Ltd* [1994] CLC 328, HL.
146 *South Australian Insurance Co Ltd v Randell* (1869) LR 3 PC 101, PC.
147 *Stellar Chartering & Brokerage Inc v Efibanca-Ente Finanziario Interbancario SpA (The Span Terza) (No 2)* [1984] 1 WLR 27, HL (coal); *Indian Oil Corp Ltd v Greenstone Shipping SA (Panama) (The Ypatianna)* [1988] QB 345 (oil).
148 *R v Hassall* (1861) Le & Ca 58, 169 ER 1302; *Coleman v Harvey* [1989] 1 NZLR 723.
149 *Wincanton Ltd v P & O Trans European Ltd* [2001] EWCA Civ 227; cf *Mercer v Craven Grain Storage Ltd* [1994] CLC 328, HL; *South Australian Insurance Co Ltd v Randell* (1869) LR 3 PC 101, PC.
150 *Mercer v Craven Grain Storage Ltd* [1994] CLC 328, HL.
151 Sale of Goods (Amendment) Act 1995, amending Sale of Goods Act 1979.
152 *Gill and Duffus (Liverpool) Ltd v Scruttons Ltd* [1953] 1 WLR 1407; cf *Coleman v Harvey* [1989] 1 NZLR 723.
153 *Dixon v London Small Arms Co Ltd* (1876) 1 App Cas 632.

may turn on the terms of the agreement,[154] or trade practice,[155] or the requirements of justice.[156]

(d) Bailment and agency

Bailment and agency often coincide. A bailee may be the agent of the bailor,[157] **16.20** and an agent may be the bailee of the principal.[158] Both are transactions where one person may be in the service of the other.[159] But agency and bailment are distinct relations and each can exist without the other. There are parallels however, between the liability of agents and bailees,[160] and the coincidence of the two relations has been seen as justifying convergent results in particular cases.[161]

B. Principles Common to All Bailments

(1) The Bailee's Estoppel

(a) General

At common law, a bailee is estopped from denying his bailor's title.[162] He cannot **16.21** invoke the bailor's lack of title to the goods as a ground for resisting liability to him. The prohibition applies both where the lack of title is relied on as showing a lack of qualification to sue in the bailor, and where it is invoked to show that the

---

154 *Moorhouse v Angus and Robertson (No 1) Pty Ltd* [1981] 1 NSWLR 700.

155 *Best Plastics Ltd v Burnett Jones Ltd* (1984) 10 NZ Recent Law 3.

156 *Coleman v Harvey* [1989] 1 NZLR 723.

157 eg a bailee to whom goods are entrusted for sale (*Gutter v Tait* (1947) 177 LT 1) or the bailee of goods under a title retention clause (*Aluminium Industrie Vaassen BV v Romalpa Aluminium Ltd* [1976] 1 WLR 676, CA).

158 The agent gets a possession independent of the principal: *Lotus Cars Ltd v Southampton Cargo Handling plc (The Rigoletto); Southampton Cargo Handling plc v Associated British Ports* [2000] 2 Lloyd's Rep 532, at 539 *per* Rix LJ, CA; *Transcontainer Express Ltd v Custodian Security Ltd* [1988] 1 Lloyd's Rep 128, 135, CA *per* Slade LJ.

159 This observation, while universally true of agents, is not necessarily true of bailees; for example, the bailee by way of hire is in the relation of bailee for his own advantage, and the same may be said of the bailee under a title retention clause: *Hendy Lennox (Industrial Engines) Ltd v Grahame Puttick Ltd* [1984] 1 WLR 485; *Re Andrabell Ltd (in liq); Airborne Accessories Ltd v Goodman* [1984] 3 All ER 407.

160 For example, both may generate fiduciary obligations.

161 For example, those on title retention; see paras 5.74–5.78 and 10.21.

162 *Cheesman v Exall* (1851) 6 Exch 341, 155 ER 574; *Biddle v Bond* (1865) 6 B & S 225, 122 ER 1179; *Rogers Sons & Co v Lambert & Co* [1891] 1 QB 318; *Ross v Edwards & Co* (1895) 73 LT 100, PC; *The Albazero* [1977] AC 774, HL; *China Pacific SA v Food Corp of India (The Winson)* [1982] AC 939, HL; *Mayflower Foods Ltd v Barnard Bros Ltd* (HC, 9 August 1996); *East West Corp v DKBS 1912* [2003] EWCA Civ 83; [2003] 1 Lloyd's Rep 239; cf *Sandeman Coprimar SA v Transitos y Transportes Integrales SL* [2003] EWCA Civ 113; [2003] QB 1270.

bailor has suffered no loss.[163] Martin B said that it would be impossible to transact business on any other basis.[164]

(b) Basis of estoppel

16.22 In cases of consensual bailment the prohibition can be analysed as one of the bailee's implied undertakings, in return for which possession is conferred.[165] But the estoppel may also apply between a head bailor and a sub-bailee, who have no direct communication.[166] The estoppel appears to apply to all bailments, with the exception of those which arise by finding[167] or wrongful taking,[168] and of those purporting to confer either an ultimate title, or the present use and enjoyment of goods on the bailee: for example, hire-purchase, hire, and the delivery of goods under a conditional sale,[169] where, statute grants the possessor specific rights of security of title and/or possession enabling him to challenge any lack of ownership or right to bail the goods on the part of the bailor.[170] It is highly unlikely that a similar right would operate in favour of the borrower of goods.

(c) Exceptions to the estoppel: common law

16.23 There are two sets of exceptions to the general rule, common law and statutory. At common law, the bailee's estoppel is displaced where he defends the bailor's claim with the authority of the true owner,[171] or where he is evicted from the goods by title paramount;[172] the latter exception does not require physical eviction, but merely the making of an adverse demand by the true owner against the bailee.[173] In cases of doubt as to the true location of title the bailee should interplead,[174] though this resource is not available unless there are two or more adverse claims; mere suspicion of a third party claim is not enough.[175] A bailee who elects to deliver the goods to someone other than the party entitled to them

---

[163] *The Albazero* [1977] AC 774, 841, 846, HL *per* Lord Diplock; *China Pacific SA v Food Corp of India (The Winson)* [1982] AC 939, 958–60, HL.

[164] *Cheesman v Exall* (1851) 6 Ex 341, 155 ER 574, 346.

[165] *Ross v Edwards & Co* (1895) 73 LT 100, PC.

[166] *The Hamburg Star* [1994] 1 Lloyd's Rep 399 (point arguable).

[167] See NE Palmer, *Bailment* (2nd edn, 1991) 279–80, 1424–5.

[168] ibid 282.

[169] ibid 276.

[170] See Supply of Goods and Services Act 1982, s 7 (hire of goods); Supply of Goods (Implied Terms) Act 1973, s 8(1)(a), as amended by the Consumer Credit Act 1974, Sch 4, para 35 (hire purchase).

[171] *Biddle v Bond* (1865) 6 B & S 225, 122 ER 1179; *Rogers Sons & Co v Lambert & Co* [1891] 1 QB 318.

[172] *Biddle v Bond* (1865) 6 B & S 225, 122 ER 1179.

[173] ibid.

[174] CPR Part 50; Sch 1, modifying in part RSC Ord 17, Interpleader.

[175] *Redler Grain Silos Ltd v BICC Ltd* [1982] 1 Lloyd's Rep 435, 438–9 *per* Kerr LJ, 440 *per* Stephenson LJ, CA.

is liable to that other party in conversion.[176] A bailee who refuses to deliver the goods to the person entitled may be liable to that person in conversion.[177]

(d) Exceptions to the estoppel: statute

By statute, a person sued for wrongful interference with goods is entitled to show **16.24** in accordance with rules of court[178] that someone other than the claimant has a better right to the goods or in right of which he sues, and any rule of law to the contrary (sometimes called *jus tertii*) is abolished.[179] It is unclear whether it has abolished the common law grounds on which the bailee might plead the better right of a third party; the only case to consider the point left it open.[180] It is arguable that the statutory exception can be averted by a bailor in one of two ways: either by casting the claim in bailment or contract rather than in tort,[181] or by arguing that the estoppel between bailor and bailee is not a 'rule of law' imposed externally on the parties but an implied term of the bailment, and as such beyond the statute.[182] The defendant in an action for wrongful interference with goods can plead the right of a third party where, at the date of the application or hearing, the third party no longer has that right, provided the right existed at the time of the wrong.[183]

(2) Possession as Title

(a) Common law; possession counts as title

At common law, as against a wrongdoer, the possession of goods counts as title.[184] **16.25** In the absence of the true owner, the possessor of goods can sue any third person who inflicts a wrong on those goods, and can recover damages calculated as if the possessor were the owner.[185] If the goods are lost or destroyed and the owner brings no claim, the possessor can, in a claim for conversion, trespass, negligence or other tort, recover their full value. If the goods are damaged the possessor can

---

176 NE Palmer, *Bailment* (2nd edn, 1991) 275–6.

177 *Batuit v Hartley* (1872) 26 LT 968.

178 CPR 19.5A.

179 Torts (Interference with Goods) Act 1977, s 8(1).

180 *De Franco v Comr of Police of the Metropolis The Times*, 8 May 1987, CA.

181 Cf *Sutcliffe v Chief Constable of West Yorkshire* [1996] RTR 86, 90, CA *per* Otton LJ; Palmer (n 176 above) 285–6.

182 Palmer (n 176 above) 285–6. These points have never been tested.

183 *De Franco v Comr of Police of the Metropolis The Times*, 8 May 1987, CA.

184 *The Winkfield* [1902] P 42; *The Jag Shakti* [1986] AC 337, PC; *O'Sullivan v Williams* [1992] 3 All ER 385, CA; *HSBC Rail (UK) Ltd v Network Rail Infrastucture Ltd* [2005] EWCA Civ 1437; [2006] 1 WLR 643. For a full discussion see Palmer (n 176 above) ch 4; N Palmer, 'Possessory Title' in N Palmer and E McKendrick (eds), *Interests in Goods* (2nd edn, 1998) 66–71.

185 As to the categories of loss recoverable, see Palmer (n 176 above) 318–40.

recover, according to circumstances, the diminution in value or the cost of reinstatement.[186] The bailee's right to claim does not depend on being personally liable to the bailor for the wrong[187] or on their having the bailor's authority to sue the wrongdoer,[188] or on their having suffered personal loss equivalent to the value of the goods.[189] This principle has been described[190] as an exception to the normal rule that damages are compensatory,[191] for the bailee recovers more than his personal loss.[192]

(b) Destination of damages

16.26   The bailee who recovers full damages under this principle must account for them to the bailor, though he may subtract the value of his own interest and any other personal losses suffered in consequence of the wrong.[193] Shares are abated rateably where the bailee recovers less than full value in a claim which relieves the wrongdoer of further liability.[194] It is uncertain whether the relationship in regard to these surplus proceeds is one of trust but that analysis seems likely.[195]

16.27   The recovery by either bailor[196] or bailee[197] of full damages from the wrongdoer precludes any further claim against that wrongdoer by the other party to the bailment. The third party wrongdoer is not relieved of further liability, however, where the person to whom he pays full damages was himself a wrongdoer in possession at the time of the wrong.[198]

---

[186] Cf *HL Motorworks (Willesden) Ltd v Alwahbi* [1977] RTR 276; see NE Palmer, *Bailment* (2nd edn, 1991) 331–3.

[187] *The Winkfield* [1902] P 42, CA.

[188] *The Winkfield* [1902] P 42, CA; *The Albazero* [1977] AC 774, HL; *Glenwood Lumber Co Ltd v Phillips* [1904] AC 405, PC; *Eastern Construction Co Ltd v National Trust Co Ltd* [1914] AC 197, PC; *China Pacific SA v Food Corp of India (The Winson)* [1982] AC 939, HL; and see G McMeel, 'Complex entitlements: the *Albazero* principle and restitution' [1999] Restitution L Rev 22.

[189] *The Winkfield* [1902] P 42, CA.

[190] *The Albazero* [1977] AC 774, 841, HL *per* Lord Diplock.

[191] See paras 21.14ff.

[192] Cf *The Sanix Ace* [1987] 1 Lloyd's Rep 465, *The Aramis* [1989] 1 Lloyd's Rep 213, CA.

[193] *The Winkfield* [1902] P 42, CA. See further NE Palmer, *Bailment* (2nd edn, 1991) 335–40.

[194] *The Johannis Vatis* [1922] P 92, CA.

[195] No such terminology is employed in *The Winkfield* [1902] P 42, CA or in *O'Sullivan v Williams* [1992] 3 All ER 385, CA; cf *Re E Dibbens & Sons Ltd* [1980] BCLC 577; *Mathew v TM Sutton Ltd* [1994] 4 All ER 793.

[196] *O'Sullivan v Williams* [1992] 3 All ER 385, CA.

[197] *The Winkfield* [1902] P 42, CA.

[198] *Attenborough v London and St Katharine's Dock Co* (1878) 3 CPD 450; cf Torts (Interference with Goods) Act 1977, s 7, s 8.

(c) Mere right of possession

The general principle applies not only to persons who are in possession of goods **16.28**
at the time of a wrong but also to those who have an immediate right to possession, unaccompanied by possession itself, at that time.[199]

(d) Exceptions: common law [200]

The general principle does not apply where the wrongdoer has, since the time **16.29**
of the wrong, become the owner of the goods,[201] or where the wrongdoer defends
the claim with the owner's authority,[202] or where the act itself was performed
under the owner's authority,[203] or where the wrongdoer has an enforceable cross-
claim or right of set-off against the bailee,[204] or where an award of full damages
would lead to circuity of actions.[205] Nor does it apply where the wrongdoer is
the owner or bailor or some other person having an interest in the goods,[206] or
where the owner has already recovered full damages from the wrongdoer before
the bailee makes a claim against the same person.[207] Of course these exceptions
overlap. In all such cases the bailee can recover at most for his personal loss.

(e) Exceptions: statute

By statute, a defendant in an action for wrongful interference with goods is **16.30**
entitled to show, in accordance with rules of court,[208] that a third person has a
better right than the claimant as respects all or any part of the interest claimed by
the claimant, or in right of which the claimant claims.[209] The restriction of these

---

[199] *The Jag Shakti* [1986] AC 337, PC; *East West Corp v DKBS 1912* [2003] EWCA Civ 83;
[2003] 1 Lloyd's Rep 239; *HSBC Rail (UK) Ltd v Network Rail Infrastructure Ltd* [2005] EWCA Civ
1437; [2006] 1 WLR 643 (obiter).

[200] See generally *Chartered Trust v King* [2001] All ER (D) 310, CA, approving Palmer, *Bailment*
(2nd edn, 1991) 316.

[201] *Eastern Construction Co Ltd v National Trust Co and Schmidt* [1914] AC 197, PC; *Webb v
Ireland and A-G* [1988] Irish R 353.

[202] *The Winkfield* [1902] P 42, CA.

[203] ibid.

[204] *The Jag Shakti* [1986] AC 337, 345–6, 348, PC *per* Lord Brandon, who described this as 'the
only exception' to the rule in *The Winkfield* [1902] P 42, CA.

[205] *Maynegrain Pty Ltd v Compafina Bank* [1982] 2 NSWLR 141, 156–7 *per* Hutley JA; revsd
without reference to this point [1984] 1 NSWLR 258, PC.

[206] *Brierley v Kendall* (1852) 17 QB 937, 117 ER 1540; and see further *Standard Electronic
Apparatus Laboratories Pty Ltd v Stenner* [1960] NSWLR 447; *Maynegrain Pty Ltd v Compafina
Bank* [1982] 2 NSWLR 141, 156–7 *per* Hutley JA; revsd without reference to this point [1984]
1 NSWLR 258, PC.

[207] *O'Sullivan v Williams* [1992] 3 All ER 385, CA.

[208] Power to make rules of court is conferred by the Torts (Interference with Goods) Act 1977,
s 8(2), without prejudice to any other power of making rules of court: Torts (Interference with
Goods) Act 1977, s 8(3). See CPR 19.5A.

[209] Torts (Interference with Goods) Act 1977, s 8(1), which also states that any rule of law to the
contrary (sometimes called *jus tertii*) is abolished.

provisions to cases of wrongful interference with goods (which are exclusively wrongs in tort)[210] appears to debar their application to claims by bailees against third parties for breach of contract.[211] The provisions apply where the third party had an interest in the goods at the time of the wrong but has since ceased to have that or any other interest.[212] It is uncertain whether the provisions have extinguished the former common law exceptions to the general prohibition on a wrongdoer's pleading the right of a third party in response to claims by a possessor,[213] but it is submitted that they have not.[214]

(3) Insurance

16.31   Under a normal custodial bailment the bailee owes no obligation to the bailor to insure the goods.[215] But a bailee has an insurable interest in the goods[216] and can, under a suitably worded policy,[217] insure them for their full value, even though this may exceed the value of his personal interest in them, or the amount of his likely loss in the event of misadventure.[218] Having recovered the insurance proceeds the bailee must account for the excess to the bailor, and he may hold those excess proceeds subject to an equitable proprietary interest in the bailor, at least where the bailor has paid him separately to insure the goods.[219] The bailor also has an insurable interest and where the bailee is a co-insured the bailee may resist a subrogation claim by the bailor's insurer by reference to the principle that an insurer cannot sue one co-insured in the name of another.[220]

---

[210]   Torts (Interference with Goods) Act 1977, s 1.

[211]   See NE Palmer, *Bailment* (2nd edn, 1991) 285–6.

[212]   *De Franco v Comr of Police of the Metropolis The Times*, 8 May 1987, CA.

[213]   See NE Palmer, *Bailment* (2nd edn, 1991) 246–8.

[214]   NE Palmer, *Bailment* (2nd edn, 1991) 284–6; *De Franco v Comr of Police of the Metropolis The Times*, 8 May 1987, CA.

[215]   See para 13.51, n 305 below. For more detailed discussion, see Palmer (n 214 above) 788–90, 1677.

[216]   *Hepburn v A Tomlinson (Hauliers) Ltd* [1966] AC 451, HL; *Waters and Steel v Monarch Fire and Life Assurance Co* (1856) 5 E & B 870, 119 ER 705; *Castellain v Preston* (1883) 11 QBD 380; *The Albazero* [1977] AC 774, HL; *Feasy v Sun Life Assurance Co of Canada* [2003] EWCA Civ 885; *Ramco (UK) Ltd & Ors v International Insurance Company of Hannover Ltd & Anor* [2003] EWHC 2360 (Comm) (which holds that whether an insurance policy taken out by a bailee covers property or the bailee's liability for it depends on the wording of the particular transaction).

[217]   The usual reference is to goods held in trust or on commission. Cf the *Ramco* decision.

[218]   *Hepburn v A Tomlinson (Hauliers) Ltd* [1966] AC 451, HL; *Waters and Steel v Monarch Fire and Life Assurance Co* (1856) 5 E & B 870, 119 ER 705; *Castellain v Preston* (1883) 11 QBD 380.

[219]   *Re E Dibbens & Sons Ltd* [1990] BCLC 577; *DG Finance Ltd v Andrew Scott and Eagle Star Insurance Co Ltd* (CA, 15 June 1995). As to the obligation of the bailee to account to the bailor for an excess of any insurance proceeds see *Ramco (UK) Ltd & Ors v International Insurance Company of Hannover Ltd & Anor* [2003] EWHC 2360 (Comm) (15 October 2003).

[220]   *Petrofina (UK) Ltd v Magnaload Ltd* [1984] 1 QB 127, 137 *per* Lloyd J, following *Simpson v Thomson* (1877) 3 App Cas 279.

C. Gratuitous Bailments and Bailments for Reciprocal Advantage

(a) Reasons for making the distinction

Older authorities drew a distinction between those bailments under which one **16.32** party receives no benefit (such as gratuitous deposit or loan) and those that benefit both parties (such as custody for reward, or pledge, or hire). Such a distinction was justifiable when the obligations of a bailor and bailee varied along a sliding scale[221] according to the location of benefit. Nowadays, the conceptual differences among different bailments are slight and there is little need to determine whether a bailment is gratuitous or reciprocally beneficial. Our adoption of the distinction is purely for purposes of exposition.

The duty of care required of any bailee, for example, is that of reasonable care in **16.33** all the circumstances; modern cases reject the older standard of gross negligence as determining the liability of the unrewarded bailee.[222] At least one senior judge has said that the line separating the standards of care demanded of each class of bailee is a very fine one, difficult to discern and impossible to define.[223] On one view, the ability of a bailee to bind himself by promises greater than the duty which he would owe at common law varies according to whether the bailment is contractual.[224] There is some authority for the view that an unrewarded bailee's liability for the unauthorized wrongs of his employees is confined to cases where the bailor is personally negligent in employing or supervising the malefactor.[225]

(b) Making the distinction[226]

A bailment for reward (or mutual advantage) is one which either confers or can **16.34** reasonably be expected to confer a benefit on both parties. Normally in a bailment for reward one party gets a monetary payment while the other gets the benefit of some service to the goods. The service is usually provided by the bailee to the

---

[221] Ranging from gross negligence, through ordinary negligence, to slight neglect: see generally *Coggs v Bernard* (1703) 2 Ld Raym 909, 92 ER 107.

[222] *Houghland v RR Low (Luxury Coaches) Ltd* [1962] 1 QB 694, CA; *Griffiths v Arch Engineering Co (Newport) Ltd* [1968] 3 All ER 217; and see *AVX Ltd v EGM Solders Ltd The Times*, 7 July 1982.

[223] *Port Swettenham Authority v TW Wu & Co (M) Sdn Bhd* [1979] AC 580, 589, PC *per* Lord Salmon, and see *Sutcliffe v Chief Constable of West Yorkshire* [1996] RTR 86, 90, CA *per* Otton LJ. See now also *G Bosman (Transport) Ltd v LKW Walter International Transportorganisation AG* [2002] All ER (D) 13 (May), CA; cf *Khan v Grocutt* [2002] All ER (D) 154 (Dec), CA.

[224] *Parastatidis v Kotarides* [1978] Victoria Reports 449 and see para 16.38.

[225] *Morris v CW Martin & Sons Ltd* [1966] 1 QB 716, 725, CA *per* Lord Denning MR (obiter); but this is believed to be wrong. The point was left open by Mance LJ in *East West*; see also *Lister v Hesley Hall* and cf para 16.36.

[226] See generally, NE Palmer, *Bailment* (2nd edn, 1991) ch 8. See now also *Wincanton Ltd v P & O Trans European Ltd* [2001] EWCA Civ 227; [2001] CLC 962.

bailor, as where a bailor bails goods for storage[227] or to be worked on for payment,[228] but it may be provided by the bailor to the bailee, as where the goods are bailed on hire.[229] A bailee who takes custody without specific reward, but expecting remuneration if the owner later engages his services, takes from the beginning as a bailee for reward.[230] But a decision of the House of Lords appears to hold that an original bailee for reward (in this case, a salvor) who retains possession when the contract ceases to exist becomes a gratuitous bailee.[231] A bailment for mutual advantage may arise though reward does not pass directly between the bailor and bailee.[232]

D. Gratuitous Bailments

(1) Gratuitous Custody

(a) Identity and character

16.35 Where one person agrees to take possession of and care for goods belonging to another on terms that the custody is to be unrewarded, the bailment which arises is the type classified by Holt CJ as *depositum*, or gratuitous safekeeping.[233] A bailment of this character can arise as an independent service in itself or incidentally to some other relationship between bailor and bailee.[234] It is not a contract because the bailor supplies no consideration, but the bailee appears to be bound by promises he makes in relation to the goods, from the moment he takes possession.[235]

---

227 See para 16.48.

228 See para 16.55 et seq.

229 See para 16.61 et seq.

230 *Port Swettenham Authority v TW Wu & Co (M) Sdn Bhd* [1979] AC 580, PC; *G Bosman (Transport) Ltd v LKW Walter International Transportorganisation AG* [2002] All ER (D) 13 (May), CA.

231 *China Pacific SA v Food Corp of India (The Winson)* [1982] AC 939, HL; cf *City Television v Conference and Training Office Ltd* (CA, 29 November 2001) (the recipient of goods that had been ordered by a third party pursuant to a deception practised on both owner and recipient-possessor was treated, apparently without argument, as a gratuitous bailee).

232 *Andrews v Home Flats Ltd* [1945] 2 All ER 698; *The Pioneer Container* [1994] 2 AC 324, 338, PC *per* Lord Goff, citing *Morris v CW Martin & Sons Ltd* [1966] 1 QB 716, CA.

233 *Coggs v Bernard* (1703) 2 Ld Raym 909, 912–13, 92 ER 107, 110.

234 See for example *Phipps v New Claridges Hotel* (1905) 22 TLR 49 (hotel and guest); *China Pacific SA v Food Corp of India (The Winson)* [1982] AC 939, HL (salvor and cargo owner).

235 *Kettle v Bromsall* (1738) Willes 118, 125 ER 1087; *Chapman v Morley* (1891) 7 TLR 257; *The Oriental Bank Corporation v The Queen* (1867) 6 SCR (NSW) 122; *Roufos v Brewster* [1971] 2 South Australian State Reports 218, 223–4 *per* Bray CJ (obiter); *Mitchell v Ealing London Borough Council* [1978] 2 WLR 999.

(b) Obligations of gratuitous custodian

The bailee must take reasonable care of the goods, this standard being gauged **16.36** according to all the circumstances of the deposit.[236] Those circumstances will include the value, portability, sensitivity and disposability of the goods, their attractiveness to thieves or vandals, their general vulnerability to crime, the environment where they are kept and in special cases the bailor's knowledge of defects in the bailee's facilities.[237] A further relevant circumstance may be the gratuitous nature of the service,[238] though in cases of gratuitous custody by professional custodians this factor may be subordinate to others, such as the expectation generated in the bailor as to level of service.[239] The duty of care extends to the taking of reasonable measures to protect the goods against the foreseeable acts of vandals.[240] The burden of showing that he has taken reasonable care rests on the bailee.[241] If this burden cannot be discharged, the bailee has the alternative possibility of showing that any lack of reasonable care on his part did not cause or contribute to the loss,[242] but courts are reluctant to allow this defence to succeed where bailees, whose premises are burgled via a security flaw attributable to them, contend that, even without the flaw, the burglars would have succeeded in penetrating the building anyway.[243] Though contrary statements can be cited,[244] the better view is that the depositary is answerable for any theft or collusion in theft on the part of any employee or independent contractor to whom he has delegated any part of his duty of care in relation to the goods, regardless of whether the bailee has been negligent in his employment, training or supervision of the malefactor.[245] A similar principle should apply to acts of deliberate damage.

---

[236] *Port Swettenham Authority v TW Wu & Co (M) Sdn Bhd* [1979] AC 580, 589, PC *per* Lord Salmon; *China Pacific SA v Food Corp of India (The Winson)* [1982] AC 939, 960, HL *per* Lord Diplock; *Mitchell v Ealing London Borough Council* [1979] QB 1; *James Buchanan Ltd v Hay's Transport Services Ltd* [1972] 2 Lloyd's Rep 535; *Garlick v W & H Rycroft Ltd* [1982] CAT 277, CA; *Houghland v RR Low (Luxury Coaches) Ltd* [1962] 1 QB 694, CA; *Blount v The War Office* [1953] 1 WLR 736; *City Television v Conference and Training Office Ltd* (CA, 29 November 2001); *Khan v Grocutt* [2002] All ER (D) 154 (Dec), CA (bailment of insurance documents); cf *G Bosman (Transport) Ltd v LKW Walter International Transportorganisation AG* [2002] All ER (D) 13 (May), CA.

[237] *Houghland v RR Low (Luxury Coaches) Ltd* [1962] 1 QB 694, CA. See para 16.49.

[238] *Garlick v W & H Rycroft Ltd* [1982] CAT 277, CA.

[239] *James Buchanan Ltd v Hay's Transport Services Ltd* [1972] 2 Lloyd's Rep 535; *Port Swettenham Authority v TW Wu & Co (M) Sdn Bhd* [1979] AC 580, PC.

[240] *Mitchell v Ealing London Borough Council* [1979] QB 1; *Garlick v W & H Rycroft Ltd* [1982] CAT 277, CA.

[241] *Port Swettenham Authority v TW Wu & Co (M) Sdn Bhd* [1979] AC 580, PC; *Mitchell v Ealing London Borough Council* [1979] QB 1; *Houghland v RR Low (Luxury Coaches) Ltd* [1962] 1 QB 694, CA.

[242] This proposition is based on analogy with the burden of proof applicable to bailees for reward: see para 16.50.

[243] *Fletcher Construction Co Ltd v Webster* [1948] NZLR 514, 519 *per* Callan J.

[244] eg *Morris v CW Martin & Sons Ltd* [1966] 1 QB 716, 725, CA *per* Lord Denning MR.

[245] NE Palmer, *Bailment* (2nd edn, 1991) 554–60; para 16.50.

If that is correct, the bailee should also carry the burden of showing, in the event of loss or damage while the goods are in his custody, that the loss or damage was not inflicted by any employee or independent contractor to whom he entrusted the goods.

(c) Bailee's duty to return goods

16.37 The bailee must return the goods at the end of the bailment[246] unless he has undertaken to deal with them in some other way, in which case that undertaking must be kept.[247] The bailee need not, however, take the goods to the bailor's premises; it is sufficient if he makes them available for the bailor to collect, unless some other arrangement has been made.[248]

(d) Promises on gratuitous bailments; deviation

16.38 If the bailee promises a greater responsibility than that imposed by common law (for example, to be strictly liable for the safety of the goods,[249] or to return them in the same condition as bailed not excepting reasonable wear and tear,[250] or to keep them in a particular place,[251] or return them at a particular time)[252] he appears to be bound by that promise once possession is assumed.[253] That is so notwithstanding the absence of contract through want of consideration from the bailor. Moreover, a gratuitous bailee can be liable for a deviation, in much the same way as a rewarded bailee, so that if he departs from one of the fundamental terms of the bailment he forfeits his status as a bailee and becomes strictly liable for the goods as an insurer.[254] This may occur where the bailee delegates custody to a third person without the bailor's consent,[255] for it is a normal obligation of gratuitous custody that the bailee will exercise the custodial function personally and not vicariously.[256] A deviation may also occur where the bailee retains possession of

---

[246] *Cranch v White* (1835) 1 Bing NC 414, 420, 131 ER 1176, 1179; *Wetherman v London and Liverpool Bank of Commerce Ltd* (1914) 31 TLR 20; *United States of America and Republic of France v Dollfus Mieg et Cie SA and Bank of England* [1952] AC 582, 611, HL; *Jones v Dowle* (1841) 9 M&W 19, 152 ER 9; *Houghland v RR Low (Luxury Coaches) Ltd* [1962] 1 QB 694; *Capital Finance Co Ltd v Bray* [1964] 1 WLR 323.

[247] *Anon* (1642) March 202, 82 ER 475; *Wilkinson v Verity* (1871) LR 6 CP 206.

[248] *Capital Finance Co Ltd v Bray* [1964] 1 WLR 323, CA; Palmer (n 245 above) 565.

[249] *Kettle v Bromsall* (1728) Willes 118, 125 ER 1087.

[250] *Coggs v Bernard* (1703) 2 Ld Raym 909, 92 ER 107, 109 *per* Powell J.

[251] *Edwards v Newland* [1950] 2 KB 534, CA.

[252] *Mitchell v Ealing London Borough Council* [1979] QB 1.

[253] Para 16.35 and *Trefitz & Sons Ltd v Canelli* (1872) LR 4 PC 277.

[254] *Mitchell v Ealing London Borough Council* (n 252 above).

[255] *Bringloe v Morrice* (1676) 1 Mod Rep 210, 86 ER 834; see also *Chapman v Robinson* (1969) 71 Western Weekly Reports 515 (obiter) (case of loan).

[256] *Edwards v Newland & Co* [1950] 2 KB 534, CA; *Mitchell v Ealing London Borough Council* [1979] QB 1.

the goods after the bailor has lawfully demanded their return.[257] When deviation occurs, the bailee is answerable for all ensuing damage or loss, whether caused by his negligence or not, unless the misadventure would have occurred in any event, or can be attributed to the conduct of the bailor.[258] The burden of proving these exonerating events is on the bailee.[259] If the bailee deviates and it later emerges that the goods have been damaged or lost at some unidentified point while in his possession, it is for the bailee to prove that the damage or loss occurred outside the deviation period, at a time when his duty was one of reasonable care.[260]

(e) Duties of bailor

The bailor owes a duty of reasonable care towards the bailee.[261] He is therefore **16.39** answerable if the bailee is injured or suffers damage to his real or personal property by reason of some defect in the goods, where the bailor should reasonably have identified and corrected the defect or have warned of it.[262] Since the bailment is not a contract, the bailor is probably not bound by any agreement to leave the goods in the bailee's custody for a fixed period, though symmetry with decisions on the liability of the bailee for superadded promises might suggest otherwise.[263]

Where the bailee is put to expense in safeguarding the goods against some extra-**16.40** ordinary hazard, and the acts which he performs are compelled by his duty of care, he is entitled to recover his expense from the bailor, at least where the bailor knew that it was being incurred and raised no objection.[264] Such recovery accords with general principles of unjust enrichment.[265] It is an open question whether the bailee can alternatively rely on the doctrine of agency of necessity as a means of recovering such outlay.[266]

---

[257] *Mitchell v Ealing London Borough Council* [1979] QB 1.

[258] ibid.

[259] *Port Swettenham Authority v TW Wu & Co (M) Sdn Bhd* [1979] AC 580, PC. See further NE Palmer, *Bailment* (2nd edn, 1991) 581.

[260] *Mitchell v Ealing London Borough Council* (n 257 above); cf *JJD SA (a company) v Avon Tyres Ltd* (HC, 19 January 1999); revsd on other grounds (CA, 23 January 2000).

[261] NE Palmer, *Bailment* (2nd edn, 1991) 583. The point is not covered by authority.

[262] There is no authority favouring a strict warranty of safety or fitness to be bailed, either in this context or in that of general bailments for reward. See Palmer (n 261 above) 583–4.

[263] See para 16.38.

[264] *China Pacific SA v Food Corp of India (The Winson)* [1982] AC 939, HL.

[265] See Chapter 18.

[266] *China Pacific SA v Food Corp of India (The Winson)* [1982] AC 939, HL, 958 *per* Lord Diplock and 965 *per* Lord Simon of Glaisdale. See Palmer (n 261 above) 589–90.

(2) Gratuitous Work and Labour

(a) Comparison with gratuitous deposit

16.41 Bailment for gratuitous work and labour (traditionally known as *mandatum*) resembles gratuitous deposit, but with two main differences. First, the mandatary's custody of the goods is incidental to his performance of some personal service in relation to them, in relation to which separate obligations are owed. Secondly, the burden of proof in an action for breach of the bailee's promise to perform the gratuitous service differs from that applicable to claims for breach of the bailee's duty of care. In common with the case of contractual promises, it is for the bailor to establish not only the promise itself but three further matters: breach of the promise, the occurrence of the loss for which the bailor claims, and the causal relation of the breach to the loss.[267]

(b) Duties of the bailee[268]

16.42 Beyond that, the incidents of *mandatum* correspond largely with those of *depositum*: the bailee gets possession which at common law counts as title and enables him to sue third party wrongdoers, his duty is one of reasonable care unless varied by agreement, the duty of care includes a duty to answer for the deliberate wrong-doing of those to whom he lawfully entrusts the goods, he carries the burden of proving either reasonable care or its irrelevance to any loss, and of negativing deliberate misdeeds by employees, the bailee must perform the service and retain custody in person, becoming strictly liable if he departs from this or any other essential term of the bailment, and the mandatary is bound by promises which he has made in relation to the goods (including performance of the personal service for purposes of which possession is given to him) once he takes possession.[269]

(c) Duties of the bailor[270]

16.43 Since *mandatum* is by definition a gratuitous transaction, the mandatary cannot charge for the services once performed and has no lien on the goods. As in the case of *depositum*, however, a mandatary who in discharge of his duty of care and to the knowledge of the mandator expends money to safeguard the goods against extra-ordinary hazards may recover that cost from the mandator under principles of unjust enrichment.[271] Even in that event, however, it seems that he has no lien.

---

[267] *Lenkeit v Ebert* [1947] St R Qd 126 (semble); cf *Houghland v RR Low (Luxury Coaches) Ltd* [1962] 1 QB 694, CA.
[268] Palmer (n 261 above) 594–628.
[269] *Oriental Bank Corp v R* (1867) 6 SCR (NSW) 122, 155 *per* Faucett J.
[270] Palmer (n 261 above), 628–9.
[271] See para 16.40.

The mandator owes a duty of reasonable care to ensure that the mandatary is not **16.44** injured, or his property damaged, by the unsafe condition of the chattel.[272] It is uncertain whether this liability extends to economic loss suffered by the mandatary through the unsuitable nature of the chattel for the task entrusted to him.

(3) Loan for Use

(a) Definition and character

Gratuitous loan is a form of bailment under which the bailee is allowed the use **16.45** and enjoyment of the goods without any advantage to the bailor.[273] It is not a contract because the borrower provides no consideration in return for the use of the goods.[274] The borrower gets possession and can exercise the normal possessory remedies against third parties who invade that possession.[275]

(b) Duties of the borrower

The borrower must take reasonable care of the goods.[276] He must return the goods **16.46** in a condition no worse than that in which they were delivered to him (fair wear and tear excepted) and compensate the bailor for any damage caused by his negligence or misuse.[277] The borrower is bound, in the event of any loss or impairment of the goods, to show either that he took due care or that his failure to do so played no part in the misadventure; in the absence of such proof he is liable to the lender[278] though the true cause of the loss or impairment remains unknown. His liability extends to any misappropriation or complicity in misappropriation on the part of any employee or independent contractor to whom he has entrusted the goods for the purpose of discharging any part of his duty of care.[279] The burden of proof conforms to that applying where the lender alleges a want of due care. If the

---

[272] There is no common law authority on this point: Palmer (n 261 above) 628. Cf *Flack v Hudson* [2001] 2 WLR 982, CA, the decision under the Animals Act 1970.

[273] *Coggs v Bernard* (1703) 2 Ld Raym 909, 918, 92 ER 107, 113 *per* Holt CJ. See now also *Wincanton Ltd v P & O Trans European Ltd* [2001] EWCA Civ 227; [2001] CLC 962 (reciprocally beneficial bailment of pallets not a gratuitous load).

[274] *Walker v Watson* [1974] 2 NZLR 175; *National Bank of New Zealand Ltd v Waitaki International Processing (NI) Ltd* [1997] 1 NZLR 724; Cf *Cottee v Franklin Self-Serve Pty Ltd* (1995) Aust Contract Reports 90–060.

[275] See para 16.25 et seq.

[276] *Swann v Seal* (CA, 19 March 1999); *Walker v Watson* [1974] 2 NZLR 175; *Fairley and Stevens (1966) Ltd v Goldsworthy* (1973) 34 DLR (3d) 554. Cf *Wincanton Ltd v P & O Trans European Ltd* [2001] EWCA Civ 227; [2001] CLC 962 (question whether borrower liable for even 'slight neglect' left open as not material to decision).

[277] *Swann v Seal* (CA, 19 March 1999) *per* Chadwick LJ.

[278] *Houghland v RR Low (Luxury Coaches) Ltd* [1962] 1 QB 694, CA; *Port Swettenham Authority v TW Wu & Co (M) Sdn Bhd* [1979] AC 580, PC (burden of proof on gratuitous bailee generally).

[279] The rules here are precisely analogous to those which govern the depositary: See para 16.36.

borrower deviates from the essential or fundamental terms on which his possession was granted he becomes strictly liable for the goods and must answer for
them regardless of whether he is negligent.[280] Deviation may occur by keeping the
goods beyond an agreed return date, or moving them to a place other than that
agreed, or allowing someone other than the borrower or his authorized personnel
to use them.[281] The borrower must return the goods to the bailor, or otherwise
deal with them as he instructs, at the end of the bailment.[282] The borrower is
not generally bound to deliver the goods to the lender's residence or place of
business at the end of the bailment,[283] but must make them available for collection
by the lender at the place where the goods are situated.[284] Where borrowed goods
have been dismantled, the borrower must normally reassemble them before
redelivery.[285] Subject to statutory procedures which enable the joining of third
parties in claims for wrongful interference with goods, the borrower is normally
estopped from denying the bailor's title.[286]

(c) Duties of the lender

16.47   The lender must exercise reasonable care in ensuring that the goods are safe and
fit for their purpose.[287] It is uncertain whether the negligent lender is liable for
pure economic loss caused by the failure of a loaned chattel to fulfil its intended
function:[288] much may depend on whether the claim is characterized as contractual, tortious or in bailment.[289] Similar uncertainty surrounds the bailor's ability
to withdraw the goods from the bailee before the expiry of an agreed period of use.
A contractual analysis suggests that the lender can do this with impunity because
the borrower has given no consideration for the promise.[290] But some authorities,
relying on the peculiar nature of bailment, argue that he should be bound by

---

[280]   *Bringloe v Morrice* (1676) 1 Mod Rep 210, 86 ER 834; *Chapman v Robinson and Ferguson*
(1969) 71 Western Weekly Reports 515. The rules here are precisely analogous to those which
govern the depositary: see para 16.38.

[281]   See generally NE Palmer, *Bailment* (2nd edn, 1991) 665–76.

[282]   ibid; *Swann v Seal* (CA, 19 March 1999).

[283]   *Capital Finance Co Ltd v Bray* [1964] 1 WLR 323, CA.

[284]   *Mitchell v Ealing London Borough Council* [1979] QB 1.

[285]   See NE Palmer, *Bailment* (2nd edn, 1991) 676. But the borrower will not normally be liable
for ordinary wear and tear: *Swann v Seal* (CA, 19 March 1999); cf *Moorhouse v Angus and Robertson
(No 1) Pty Ltd* [1981] NSWLR 700, 708 (apparently a case of bailment for mutual advantage).

[286]   See para 16.21 et seq.

[287]   *Griffiths v Arch Engineering Ltd* [1968] 3 All ER 217; *Wheeler v Copas* [1981] 3 All ER 405
(semble); cf *Flack v Hudson* [2001] 2 WLR 982, CA; *Blakemore v Bristol and Exeter Rly Co* (1858)
8 E & B 1035, 120 ER 385; *Coughlin v Gillison* [1899] 1 QB 145, CA. See further NE Palmer,
Bailment (2nd edn, 1991) 638 et seq.

[288]   Cf *Blakemore v Bristol and Exeter Rly Co* (1858) 8 E & B 1035, 1050–1, 120 ER 385, 391 *per*
Coleridge J.

[289]   NE Palmer, *Bailment* (2nd edn, 1991) 628.

[290]   ibid 658 et seq; cf *Parastatidis v Kotaridis* [1978] Victoria Reports 449 (*mutuum*).

his promise.[291] The doctrine of promissory estoppel may also safeguard the borrower's position.

E. Bailments for Reward or Reciprocal Advantage

(1) Custody for Reward

(a) Definition and character

Bailment by way of custody for reward arises where one person has possession **16.48** of another's goods on terms that he will store or safeguard those goods in return for an advantage. This form of bailment ranges from direct custody (the entrustment of goods to a warehouse or luggage office)[292] to the many types of incidental custody which arise from the provision of other services; for example, the safekeeping of a client's coat in a restaurant cloakroom,[293] or the custody of an animal by a vet to whom it is bailed for treatment. Most direct forms of custody for reward (and many indirect forms) are governed by special contract terms, beyond the scope of this title. What follows is a short account of the underlying rules of bailment that apply where no special terms obtain.

(b) Duties of the custodian for reward

Like most bailees the custodian for reward must take reasonable care of the **16.49** goods.[294] He must exercise the precautions that can reasonably be expected of a reasonably conscientious and competent member of his trade[295] to guard the

---

291 NE Palmer, *Bailment* (2nd edn, 1991) 658 et seq. See the cases on depositum and mandatum, paras 16.42–16.43.

292 *Stallard v GW Rly Co* (1862) 2 B & S 419, 121 ER 1129; *Alexander v Railway Executive* [1951] 2 KB 882.

293 *Ultzen v Nichols* (1894) 1 QB 92; *Murphy v Hart* (1919) 46 DLR 36.

294 *Port Swettenham Authority v TW Wu & Co (M) Sdn Bhd* [1979] AC 580, PC; *Coldman v Hill* [1919] 1 KB 443, CA; *Brook's Wharf and Bull Wharf Ltd v Goodman Bros* [1937] 1 KB 534, CA; *Glebe Island Transport Pty Ltd v Continental Seagram Pty Ltd (The Antwerpen)* [1994] 1 Lloyd's Rep 213 (NSWSC). Where a bailee lawfully and with the express or implied consent of the bailor entrusts to a third party the discharge of any part of his duty of care in respect of the goods (as, for example, where he engages a firm of security contractors to patrol the place where the goods are kept, or to install protective devices) he remains responsible for the manner in which the delegated task is performed, and is accordingly liable for the delegate's defaults: *G Bosman (Transport) Ltd v LKW Walter International Transportorganisation AG* [2002] All ER (D) 13 (May), CA, following *British Road Services v Arthur V Crutchley* [1968] 1 All ER 811, CA; cf *East West v DKBS* above. And see further paras 16.52 (bailee committing deviation where delegation of possession unlawful), 16.83 (sub-bailment).

295 *Port Swettenham Authority v TW Wu & Co (M) Sdn Bhd* [1979] AC 580, PC; *Houghland v RR Low (Luxury Coaches) Ltd* [1962] 1 QB 694, CA.

goods against foreseeable hazards.[296] These include theft,[297] fire,[298] vandalism,[299] weather,[300] flood,[301] natural deterioration[302] and legal challenges to the bailor's title.[303] The bailee is also liable for any deliberate wrongdoing (or complicity in such wrongdoing) on the part of any employee or independent contractor to whom he has entrusted any part of his duty of care.[304]

(c) Burdens of proof

16.50 In any claim for breach of the custodian's duty of care, the bailor must prove both the fact and the breach of the bailment. He must show that the defendant was voluntarily in possession of the goods[305] and that during his possession they were lost, stolen, destroyed, damaged or otherwise impaired.[306] The bailor who alleges damage will therefore fail if he cannot show that the condition of the goods on their return to him was worse than their condition when the bailee got possession. If such matters are proved, the burden shifts to the bailee to show either that he took reasonable care of the goods[307] or that any failure on his part to exercise such care did not cause or contribute to the misadventure.[308] He must also show that the misadventure did not result from the misconduct of any employee or independent contractor to whom he entrusted any part of his duty towards the goods.[309] A bailee who shows that an original threat to the

---

296 *Pitt, Son & Badgery v Proulefco SA* (1984) 52 ALR 389.

297 *Coldman v Hill* [1919] 1 KB 443, CA.

298 *Smith v Taylor* [1966] 2 Lloyd's Rep 231; *Pitt, Son & Badgery v Proulefco SA* (1984) 52 ALR 389.

299 *Pitt, Son & Badgery v Proulefco SA* (1984) 52 ALR 389; *Garlick v W & H Rycroft Ltd* [1982] CAT 277, CA.

300 *Edwards v Newland & Co* [1950] 2 KB 534, CA.

301 *Harper v Jones* (1879) 4 VLR (L) 536.

302 *Sharp v Batt* (1930) 25 Tasmanian LR 33 (protection of apples from deterioration).

303 *Ranson v Platt* [1911] 2 KB 291, CA.

304 *Morris v CW Martin & Sons Ltd* [1966] 1 QB 716, CA; *Port Swettenham Authority v TW Wu & Co (M) Sdn Bhd* [1979] AC 580, PC; *Frans Maas (UK) Ltd v Samsung Electronics (UK) Ltd* [2004] 2 Lloyd's Rep 282 (bailees liability extended to defaults of employees entrusted with security of buildings where goods kept). And see generally *Lister v Hesley Hall Ltd* [2002] 1 AC 22, HL.

305 *The Ruapehu* (1925) 21 Ll L Rep 310, CA.

306 *G Merel & Co Ltd v Chessher* [1961] 1 Lloyd's Rep 534; *WD & HO Wills (Australia) Ltd v State Rail Authority of New South Wales* (1998) 43 NSWLR 338, 353–4 per Mason P.

307 *Port Swettenham Authority v TW Wu & Co (M) Sdn Bhd* [1979] AC 580, PC; *The Antwerpen* [1994] 1 Lloyd's Rep 213, 238, NSWCA per Sheller JA.

308 *Joseph Travers and Sons Ltd v Cooper* [1913] 1 KB 73, CA. See now also *AP(2)T v PS* [2004] EWHC 32, QB.

309 *Port Swettenham Authority v TW Wu & Co (M) Sdn Bhd* [1979] AC 580, PC; *Morris v CW Martin & Sons Ltd* [1966] 1 QB 716, CA; *G Bosman (Transport) Ltd v LKW Walter International Transportorganisation AG* [2002] All ER (D) 13 (May), CA.

goods occurred without his fault may nevertheless be liable if he failed to take reasonable steps to counter that threat.[310]

(d) Specific instances of bailee's duty of care

The exercise of reasonable care depends on all the circumstances. It can take many **16.51** forms. It may require the bailee to exercise care in the appointment,[311] training,[312] and supervision of staff,[313] to check or move goods periodically,[314] to monitor the proximity of other potentially noxious goods,[315] to notify the bailor of adverse events,[316] to install alarms[317] or engage security staff,[318] or to develop satisfactory warning routines in general. The bailee must take into account the size, value, rarity, mobility, marketability anonymity, fragility, sensitivity and liquidity of the goods,[319] the human and physical environment within which they are kept,[320] the standards of other reasonable members of his occupation,[321] and any expectations which the bailor can reasonably be expected to hold as to the quality of safekeeping.[322] There is no general obligation to insure[323] but such a duty may arise from agreement,[324] trade custom,[325] or other special circumstance.[326] In many cases the question of insurance can be decided by reference to the normal test for implying terms into contracts, and it is submitted that a similar test should

---

[310] eg *Coldman v Hill* [1919] 1 KB 443, CA (cows; disappearance from bailee's field; failure to tell police or bailor); *Ranson v Platt* [1950] 2 KB 534, CA (third party title claim; inadequate response by bailee who failed to notify bailor); *Edwards v Newland & Co* [1911] 2 KB 291, CA (bomb damage and exposure to weather).

[311] *Mintz v Silverton* (1920) 36 TLR 399; *Nahhas v Pier House (Cheyne Walk) Management* (1984) 270 EG 328.

[312] *Global Dress Co Ltd v WH Boase & Co Ltd* [1966] 2 Lloyd's Rep 72, CA.

[313] *Morris v CW Martin & Sons Ltd* [1966] 1 QB 716, 726, CA *per* Lord Denning MR.

[314] *Cowper and Cowper v J & G Goldner Pty Ltd* (1986) 40 South Australian State R 457 (failure to carry out regular checks of animals in transit).

[315] *Pipicella v Stagg* (1983) 32 South Australian State R 464.

[316] *Ranson v Platt* [1911] 2 KB 291, CA; *Coldman v Hill* [1919] 1 KB 443, CA.

[317] *Johnson Matthey & Co Ltd v Constantine Terminals Ltd* [1976] 2 Lloyd's Rep 215, 218 (bailees negligent in omitting to install alarm on roller shuttered doors).

[318] *British Road Services Ltd v Arthur V Crutchley & Co Ltd* [1968] 1 All ER 811, CA.

[319] *Spriggs v Sotheby Parke Bernet & Co* [1986] 1 Lloyd's Rep 487, CA; *Garnham, Harris and Elton Ltd v Alfred W Ellis (Transport) Ltd* [1967] 1 WLR 940.

[320] *British Road Services Ltd v Arthur V Crutchley & Co Ltd* [1968] 1 All ER 811, CA; cf *Brabant & Co v R* [1895] AC 632, PC.

[321] *British Road Services Ltd v Arthur V Crutchley & Co Ltd* [1968] 1 All ER 811, CA.

[322] Cf *James Buchanan Ltd v Hay's Transport Services (London) Ltd* [1972] 2 Lloyd's Rep 535.

[323] *Lockspeiser Aircraft Ltd v Brooklands Aircraft Ltd The Times*, 7 March 1990; *Mason v Morrow's Moving & Storage Ltd* [1978] 4 Western Weekly R 534; NE Palmer, *Bailment* (2nd edn, 1991) 788–90.

[324] *Lockspeiser Aircraft Ltd v Brooklands Aircraft Ltd The Times*, 7 March 1990.

[325] *Kay v Shuman The Times*, 22 June 1954.

[326] *Eastman Chemical International AG v NMT Trading and Eagle Transport Ltd* [1972] 2 Lloyd's Rep 25; *Punch v Savoy's Jewellers Ltd* (1986) 26 DLR (4th) 546. Cf *Von Traubenberg v Davies, Turner & Co Ltd* [1951] 2 Lloyd's Rep 152, CA (forwarding agent).

apply within gratuitous bailments or sub-bailments. Small goods of exceptional value are more likely to attract an exceptional duty to insure than bulky or every-day goods.[327] The bailor's knowledge of the circumstances in which the goods are kept, or of the character of the bailee, does not generally relieve the bailee from precautions which it would otherwise have been reasonable to exact from him,[328] but it may relieve him where it affords evidence that the bailor agreed to accept a lower standard of care.[329] It is insufficient for the bailee to show that he had a sophisticated system of safekeeping if he cannot show that he administered that system diligently on the particular occasion.[330]

(e) Deviation

16.52 Even without negligence, the custodian is liable if he departs from one or more of the essential terms of the bailment and the goods are then lost or damaged.[331] In the event of such deviation, and subject to the terms of the agreement, the bailee loses any right to the continued possession of the goods[332] and becomes an insurer of the goods,[333] being liable regardless of any want of reasonable care for all later misadventures except those which he can show would have occurred irrespective of the deviation, or were attributable to the conduct of the bailor.[334] He may also forfeit the protection of any exclusion or limitation clause in the bailment agreement.[335]

(f) Lien and rights against third parties

16.53 The custodian has no common law particular lien because he does not improve the goods.[336] Any lien must be stipulated in the contract. A general lien may arise in relation to a particular location or occupation, but such liens are rare

---

[327] *Punch v Savoy's Jewellers Ltd* (1986) 26 DLR (4th) 546.

[328] *Brabant & Co v R* [1895] AC 632, PC; *Edwards v Newland & Co* [1950] 2 KB 534, CA; see generally Palmer (n 323 above) 818–23.

[329] *Skyway Service Station Ltd v McDonald* [1986] 1 NZLR 366.

[330] *Port Swettenham Authority v TW Wu & Co (M) Sdn Bhd* [1979] AC 580, 591, PC *per* Lord Salmon; *Spriggs v Sotheby Parke Bernet & Co* [1986] 1 Lloyd's Rep 487, 492, CA *per* Neill LJ.

[331] *Lilley v Doubleday* (1881) 7 QBD 510; *Edwards v Newland & Co* [1950] 2 KB 534, CA.

[332] In this event, the immediate right to possession of the goods will ordinarily revert to the bailor, if it did not already reside with him: see *MCC Proceeds Inc v Lehmann Bros International (Europe)* [1998] 4 All ER 675, 686, CA *per* Mummery LJ.

[333] *Lilley v Doubleday* (1881) 7 QBD 510; *Hain Steamship Co Ltd v Tate & Lyle Ltd* [1936] 2 All ER 597, HL.

[334] *Hain Steamship Co Ltd v Tate & Lyle Ltd* [1936] 2 All ER 597, HL.

[335] As to whether this consequence follows automatically or only on the construction of the particular agreement, see NE Palmer, *Bailment* (2nd edn, 1991) 59–61; *Daewoo Heavy Industries Limited v Klipriver Shipping Limited, The Kapitan Petko Voivoda* [2002] EWHC 1306, [2002] 2 All ER (Comm) 560.

[336] As to common law particular liens, see para 16.57.

and courts do not generally favour them.[337] Being in possession, the custodian can exercise the normal rights of action against third parties who take or injure the goods.[338]

(g) Duties of the bailor

The bailor must pay the agreed charge or, where none is agreed, a reasonable charge.[339] No charge is payable where it is clear from the circumstances that none was intended, for example where the bailment arises incidentally to the bailee's performance of some other service, in respect of which he receives payment or some other advantage. The bailor is liable for injury or damage if he fails to take reasonable care to ensure that the goods are safe and suitable for storage or to warn the custodian that they are not,[340] but, subject to the particular contract, he does not strictly warrant that they are safe or suitable.[341]

16.54

(2) Work and Labour for Reward

(a) Comparison with custody for reward

This form of bailment resembles custody for reward, but with the further ingredient that the bailee undertakes to perform some service (other than mere storage or safekeeping) in relation to the goods.[342] Examples are the delivery of an animal to a veterinary surgeon for treatment, or of a garment to a dry cleaner, or of a picture to a restorer, or of shoes to a repairer, or of a car to a garage for servicing. The duties which flow from this form of bailment (in particular the bailee's duty of care and its attendant burden of proof, and the obligations of the bailor as to payment and fitness of the goods) are substantially the same as those which flow from mere custodial bailments.[343] The bailee is treated as a bailee for reward in regard to the custody of the goods even though there is no separate charge for safekeeping.[344] Several differences nevertheless exist.

16.55

---

[337] *Rushforth v Hadfield* (1806) 7 East 224, 103 ER 86; *Majeau Carrying Co Pty Ltd v Coastal Rutile Ltd* (1973) 129 CLR 48.

[338] *The Winkfield* [1902] P 42, CA; and see para 16.25.

[339] Supply of Goods and Services Act 1982, s 15(1), which reflects the common law. What is reasonable is a question of fact: ibid s 15(2).

[340] Palmer (n 335 above) 777. There is no authority in point.

[341] Cf the consignor of goods to be carried: *The Giannis NK* [1998] 2 Lloyd's Rep 337, HL.

[342] See Palmer (n 335 above) ch 14.

[343] See paras 16.49 and 16.54.

[344] *Sinclair v Juner* 1952 SC 35, 43 *per* the Lord President.

(b) Bailee's obligations as to quality and result of work

16.56 In addition to his basic duty to take reasonable care in keeping the goods,[345] the bailee owes distinct obligations in regard to the work to be performed. He must carry out the work with reasonable care and skill[346] and (where no time for performance is agreed) within a reasonable time.[347] If the bailor relies on the bailee to produce goods that are fit for a particular purpose, a strict obligation to that effect may be implied,[348] similar to that affecting sales of goods.[349] Where the bailee, acting in the course of a business, supplies goods or materials in addition to his work (for example, where spare parts are fitted to a car, or an animal is injected with drugs) strict statutory obligations are implied into the agreement that the goods or materials are of satisfactory quality,[350] are reasonably fit for their purpose[351] and correspond with any sample by reference to which they are supplied.[352] Further strict statutory terms are implied (irrespective of the status of the bailee) to the effect that the bailee has the right to supply such goods or materials,[353] that the bailor will have quiet possession of them,[354] that they are free from any charge or encumbrance not disclosed or known to the bailor,[355] and that they comply with any description by which they are supplied.[356] These statutory terms as to goods and materials resemble closely those implied into contracts for the sale of goods. In contrast to the normal burden of proof in bailment,[357] and in common with that applying in contract, it is ordinarily for the bailor to show that the bailee has broken a particular obligation with regard to the work to be performed, rather than for the bailee to negative breach.[358]

---

[345] See para 16.49.

[346] Supply of Goods and Services Act 1982, s 13 (which applies to services supplied in the course of a business, but is reflected by a general common law rule applicable to all contracts for services: see *Smith v Eric S Bush* [1989] 2 All ER 514, 519–20, HL *per* Lord Templeman; *Harmer v Cornelius* (1858) CB (NS) 236, 141 ER 94; *Metaalhandel JA Manus BV v Ardfields Transport Ltd* [1988] 1 Lloyd's Rep 197).

[347] Supply of Goods and Services Act 1982, s 14(1) (which applies to services supplied in the course of a business). A 'reasonable time' is a question of fact: ibid s 14(2).

[348] Cf *Greaves & Co (Contractors) Ltd v Baynham Meikle & Partners* [1975] 1 WLR 1095, CA (design of building).

[349] Sale of Goods Act 1982, s 14.

[350] Supply of Goods and Services Act 1982, s 4, as amended by the Sale and Supply of Goods Act 1994, s 7, Sch 2, para 6(3).

[351] ibid.

[352] Supply of Goods and Services Act 1982, s 5 (as amended).

[353] ibid s 2(1) (as amended).

[354] ibid s 2(2)(b) (as amended).

[355] ibid s 2(2)(a) (as amended).

[356] ibid s 3 (as amended).

[357] See para 13.50.

[358] *Fankhauser v Mark Dykes Pty Ltd* [1960] Victoria Reports 376.

(c) Bailee's lien

(i) Particular lien

The artificer bailee may have a common law particular lien over the goods if he **16.57** improves them.[359] Examples of such improvement are the repair[360] or restoration (but not the mere washing or servicing)[361] of a car, the treatment[362] or training of an animal, or the printing of a book on paper supplied by the bailor.[363] The lien applies only to goods on which work is performed and not to goods with which work is to be performed.[364] Where goods are entrusted to an artificer by someone other than their owner, the artificer acquires a lien[365] only where the person entrusting them had the owner's actual or ostensible authority to create a lien.[366]

The particular lien is a common law 'self-help' remedy arising independently of **16.58** contract.[367] It entitles the bailee to retain possession of the goods as security for payment, but not to sell them, which would be conversion.[368] Nor does it generally entitle the artificer to charge for storage during the exercise of the lien,[369] though the position may differ where his keeping of the goods is substantially for the bailor's benefit.[370] While detaining the goods in exercise of his lien, the artificer must take reasonable care of them.[371] Where the bailor countermands the work before the bailee completes it, the bailee may at least have a lien for his fees

---

[359] *Judson v Etheridge* (1833) 1 Cr & M 743, 149 ER 598; *Scarfe v Morgan* (1838) 4 M & W 270, 150 ER 1430; *Re Southern Livestock Producers Ltd* [1963] 3 All ER 801; *Re Witt, ex p Shubrook* (1876) 2 Ch D 489, CA; and see NE Palmer, *Bailment* (2nd edn, 1991) 944–55.

[360] *Tappenden v Artus* [1964] 2 QB 185, CA.

[361] *Hatton v Car Maintenance Co* [1915] 1 Ch 621; see also *Graham v Voight* (1989) 95 FLR 146, 153 *per* Kelly J.

[362] *Scarfe v Morgan* (1838) 4 M & W 270, 150 ER 1430, 1436.

[363] *Brown v Sommerville* (1844) 6 Dun 1 (Ct of Sess) 1267.

[364] *Welsh Development Agency (Holdings) Ltd v Modern Injection Mouldings Ltd* (HC, 6 March 1986).

[365] See Halsbury's Laws of England (4th edn, Reissue) Vol 28, para 723. Cf *Johnson Matthey & Co Ltd v Constantine Terminals Ltd* [1976] 2 Lloyd's Rep 215; not followed in *The Pioneer Container* [1994] 2 AC 324, PC.

[366] *Tappenden v Artus* [1904] 2 QB 185, CA; *Albemarle Supply Co Ltd v Hind & Co* [1928] 1 KB 307, CA.

[367] *Tappenden v Artus* [1964] 2 QB 185, 195, CA *per* Diplock LJ.

[368] *Bolwell Fibreglass Pty Ltd v Foley* [1984] Victoria R 97. In this respect a lien is distinguishable from a pledge. As to the differences between lien and pledge, see *Re Cosslett (Contractors) Ltd* [1997] 4 All ER 115, 126, CA *per* Millett LJ; cf *Marcq v Christie Manson & Woods Ltd* [2003] EWCA Civ 731; [2004] QB 286.

[369] *Somes v Directors of the British Empire Shipping Co* (1860) 8 HL Cas 388, 11 ER 459. Applied in *Morris v Beaconsfield Motors* (2001) unreported 24 June, CA.

[370] *China Pacific SA v Food Corp of India (The Winson)* [1982] AC 939, HL. Cf *Morris v Beaconsfield Motors* (2001) unreported 24 June, CA.

[371] *Irving v Keen* (1995) unreported 3 March, CA, *per* Stuart-Smith LJ (obiter); *Nightingale v Tildsley* [1980] Current Law Year Book 134; *Angus v McLachlan* (1883) 23 Ch D 330.

in relation to the completed part of the work,[372] and may also be entitled to complete the work and exercise the lien for the full fee,[373] provided such completion does not require the bailor's co-operation and the bailee has a legitimate reason for completing.[374] The bailee acquires no lien if some other aspect of the agreement is inconsistent with such security, for example a term providing for a periodic account,[375] or entitling the bailor to repossess the goods at will for his own purposes.[376] Both in their creation and in their continuation, particular common law liens depend on possession,[377] so none will arise where the artificer does not get possession, and an existing lien may expire where the bailee surrenders or loses possession.[378] In the latter event the later recovery of possession does not ordinarily revive the lien.[379] But a lien may be a transmissible security, assignable with the debt which it secures,[380] and it may also survive a sale of the goods by the bailor after the lien was created.[381] The common law lien also expires on payment or tender of the sum due.[382] All these characteristics can be varied by agreement.

(ii) General lien

16.59 A common law general lien may exist in regard to particular areas or trades.[383] Common law general liens are, as noted,[384] judicially unpopular and rarely discovered, but they are a common subject of express contractual provision.

(iii) Registration of lien

16.60 A possessory lien need not be registered.[385]

---

372 *Lilley v Barnsley* (1844) 1 Car & Kir 344, 174 ER 839.

373 *Bolwell Fibreglass Pty Ltd v Foley* [1984] Victoria R 97.

374 See *White & Carter (Councils) Ltd v McGregor* [1962] AC 413, HL, applied in *Bolwell Fibreglass Pty Ltd v Foley* [1984] Victoria R 97.

375 *Wilson v Lombank Ltd* [1963] 1 WLR 1294.

376 *Ward v Fielden* [1985] Current Law Yearbook 2000.

377 *Protean Enterprises (Newmarket) Pty Ltd v Randall* [1975] Victoria Reports 327.

378 *The Freightline One* [1986] 1 Lloyd's Rep 266, 270 (obiter); *Lickbarrow v Mason* (1973) 6 East 20n; *Krager v Wilcox* (1755) Amb 252, 27 ER 168; *Hathersing v Laing* (1873) LR Eq 92.

379 *Jones v Pearl* (1723) 1 Stra 557; *Sweet v Pym* (1800) 1 East 4. Cf *Euro Commercial Leasing Ltd v Cartwright & Lewis* [1995] 2 BCLC 618.

380 *Bull v Faulkner* (1848) 2 De G & Sm 772, 64 ER 346; see now *Vered v Inscorp Holdings Ltd* (1993) 31 NSWLR 290.

381 *The Freightline One* [1986] 1 Lloyd's Rep 266, 272 *per* Sheen J (obiter).

382 *Caunce v Spanton* (1844) 1 C & P 575, 171 ER 1323.

383 NE Palmer, *Bailment* (2nd edn, 1991) 955–8.

384 See para 16.53.

385 *Trident International Ltd v Barlow* (1999) 2 BCLC 506; *Re Cosslett (Contractors) Ltd* [1997] 4 All ER 115, CA.

(3) Hire[386]

(a) Definition and character

Hire is a form of bailment under which the bailor (the 'lessor') permits the bailee **16.61**
(the 'lessee' or 'hirer') to use the goods for his own benefit in return for some
advantage accruing to the lessor, and confers possession on the bailee for that
purpose.[387] Both at common law and by statute the bailor's benefit may be either
money or some other valuable advantage,[388] such as work performed for him by
the bailee (whether with or without the bailed goods)[389] or some form of 'exchange
bailment' by which the bailee counterbails (ie, creates a reciprocal bailment of his
own goods) to the bailor.[390] The hirer gets a possessory interest defensible on
normal principles against third parties who interfere with the goods without
the authority of either the lessor or the hirer.[391] In cases, at least, where the hirer
goes into possession of the goods, he may also be protected against eviction from
the goods by a purchaser or other alienee of the lessor, where that alienee knew
of the pre-existing hire and its terms.[392] These and other features of the hirer's
position[393] have led commentators to speculate that the hirer has a proprietary
interest.[394]

(b) Duties of the hirer

The hirer's duties, and the related burdens of proof, correspond substantially to **16.62**
those affecting any other bailee for mutual advantage. The hirer must take reasonable care of the goods,[395] refrain from converting them, answer for the deliberate
misconduct of those to whom he delegates possession and avoid deviating from

---

[386] See generally Palmer (n 383 above) ch 19.
[387] See ibid 1208.
[388] Supply of Goods and Services Act 1982, s 6.
[389] *Derbyshire Building Co Pty Ltd v Becker* (1962) 107 CLR 633.
[390] *Bryce v Hornby* (1938) 82 Sol Jo 216; *Queen Sales and Service Ltd v Smith* (1963) 28 Maritime
Provinces R 364; *Swann v Seal* (CA, 19 March 1999).
[391] See para 16.25.
[392] This may be collected from *Port Line Ltd v Ben Line Steamers Ltd* [1958] 2 QB 146, 151 *per*
Diplock J.
[393] eg *Wickham Holdings Ltd v Brookhouse Motors Ltd* [1967] 1 WLR 295, CA, applied in New
Zealand to a simple lease: *NZ Securities & Finance Ltd v Wrightcars Ltd* [1976] 1 NZLR 77.
[394] NE Palmer, *Bailment* (2nd edn, 1991) 81–2, 86–7, 1666; *Bristol Airport v Powdrill* [1990]
2 WLR 1362 at 1372 *per* Browne-Wilkinson V-C; *AL Hamblin Equipment Pty Ltd v Federal
Commissioner of Taxation* [1974] ATC 4310, 4318 *per* Mason J; cf W Swadling, 'The Proprietary
Effect of a Hire of Goods' in N Palmer and E McKendrick (eds), *Interests in Goods* (2nd edn,
1998).
[395] *Blackpool Ladder Centre v BWB Partnership* (2000) unreported, 13th November, CA; *Ludgate v
Lovett* [1969] 1 WLR 1016, CA; *British Crane Hire Corp Ltd v Ipswich Plant Hire Ltd* [1975] 1 QB
303, 311–12, CA; cf *Coggs v Bernard* (1703) 2 Ld Raym 909, 92 ER 107, 111.

the bailment.[396] The consequences of a breach of these obligations are essentially the same as for other bailments. In addition, and subject to the particular terms of the contract,[397] the hirer must make the goods available to the lessor at the end of the hiring period and bear the cost of retrieving them from any place in which they have become stranded through adverse events.[398] This obligation exists though the events in question were unforeseen and occurred irrespective of any lack of reasonable care on the hirer's part, though it may be displaced where the immobilization occurred through the fault of the lessor, or where the relevant events were sufficiently severe to frustrate the contract.[399]

(c) Right to hire and quiet possession

16.63 In other respects the position of the hirer (whose possession is for personal advantage) differs from that of a normal bailee (whose possession is to enable him to act in the service of his bailor). To take an obvious example, the hirer is under no duty to account to the lessor for profits made from the hiring, unless the hirer makes these through a breach of the bailment.[400] Moreover, and because the object of the transaction is to give the hirer the use and enjoyment of the goods, the normal bailee's estoppel against pleading the right of a third party gives way in favour of statutory implied terms that the bailor has the right to hire out the goods[401] and that the hirer will enjoy quiet possession of them.[402] It appears that similar terms existed at common law.[403]

(d) Quality and fitness of hired goods

16.64 The lessor is also bound by statutory implied terms as to the quality and fitness of the goods. In general, the goods must correspond with their description[404] and with any sample provided,[405] and must be reasonably fit for their purpose[406] and of satisfactory quality.[407] The term as to correspondence with description

---

[396] *Roberts v McDougall* (1887) 3 TLR 666. But the hirer may, according to circumstances, be entitled to conclude a sub-hiring agreement with a third party, or to depute another to operate or take care of a hired machine.

[397] See generally *British Crane Hire Corp Ltd v Ipswich Plant Hire Ltd* [1975] 1 QB 303, CA.

[398] *Roberts v McDougall* (n 396 above).

[399] *British Crane Hire Corp Ltd v Ipswich Plant Hire Ltd* [1975] 1 QB 303.

[400] *Brambles Security Services Ltd v Bi-lo Pty Ltd* (1992) Aust Torts Reports 81–161, NSWCA *per* Clarke JA.

[401] Supply of Goods and Services Act 1982, s 7(1).

[402] ibid s 7(2).

[403] *Lee v Atkinson and Brooks* (1609) Cro Jac 236, 79 ER 204; *Warman v Southern Counties Motors Ltd* [1949] 2 KB 576; *Australian Guarantee Corp Ltd v Ross* [1983] 2 Victoria Reports 319.

[404] Supply of Goods and Services Act 1982, s 8.

[405] ibid s 10.

[406] ibid s 9(5) as amended by the Sale and Supply of Goods Act 1994, s 7, Sch 2, para 6(7).

[407] ibid s 9(2) as amended by the Sale and Supply of Goods Act 1994, s 7, Sch 2, para 6(7).

applies to both private and trade hiring, but the other terms are confined to cases where the lessor leases in the course of a business.[408] These terms (and the circumstances in which liability for breach of them can be excluded or restricted) are closely akin to the equivalent terms implied into contracts of sale of goods. Similar, but more vaguely formulated, terms were implied at common law.[409]

(e) Payment of hire charges

The hirer must pay the agreed hire at the agreed times.[410] Failure to pay may **16.65** entitle the lessor to evict him from the goods and to resume possession.[411] This will occur where the breach is repudiatory according to general contractual principles (ie, where the hirer evinces by his non-payment an intention to be no longer bound by the contract)[412] or where the contract otherwise entitles the lessor to possession in the event occurring. A term of the contract which makes punctual payment of the essence of the contract is likely to be construed as a condition, in which case the non-payment of any instalment will be a repudiatory breach, enabling the lessor to set aside the contract and recover 'loss of bargain' damages, consisting of all future instalments both due and to become due, minus a rebate for accelerated performance.[413] Where, on the other hand, the hirer's non-payment is not a repudiation and the lessor relies on a term which does not make punctual payment a condition of the contract, but merely entitles him to terminate the contract in the event which has occurred, damages are limited to the sums outstanding at the time of termination, plus any loss the lessor has suffered through delayed payment.[414]

(f) Relief for defaulting hirer

Statute affords a measure of relief to certain classes of defaulting hirers.[415] The **16.66** doctrine of equitable relief against forfeiture can also apply to hirers of goods[416]

---

[408] Supply of Goods and Services Act 1982, s 9.

[409] See NE Palmer, *Bailment* (2nd edn, 1991) 1215–16.

[410] See 2 *Halsbury's Laws of England* (4th edn Re-issue) para 1858; Palmer ibid 1250–63.

[411] The remedies available to the lessor in the event of non-payment, and the quantification of damages payable by the hirer, depend on the terms of the contract and the general law: *Bowmakers Ltd v Barnet Instruments Ltd* [1945] KB 65; and see Palmer (n 409 above) 1250–63.

[412] eg where the failure to pay is persistent: *Interoffice Telephones Ltd v Robert Freeman Co Ltd* [1958] 1 QB 190; *Bowmakers Ltd v Barnet Instruments Ltd* [1945] KB 65.

[413] *Lombard North Central plc v Butterworth* [1987] QB 527, CA; cf *Financings Ltd v Baldock* [1963] 2 QB 104, CA.

[414] *Financings Ltd v Baldock* [1963] 2 QB 104, CA.

[415] Consumer Credit Act 1974, ss 87–93.

[416] *Transag Haulage Ltd v Leyland DAF Finance plc* [1994] Consumer Credit LR 111. *On Demand Information v Michael Gerson (Finance) Plc* [2002] UKHL 13; [2003] 1 AC 368, HL. *As* to chattel leasing generally see *Bristol Airport v Powdrill* [1990] 2 WLR 1362.

as to other holders of rights in personal property.[417] The rule against penalties[418] can also relieve hirers from contractual terms which purport to impose on them excessive liabilities in consequence of breach.[419] But the rule against penalties does not protect the hirer against a term which makes particular provisions (such as those requiring punctual payment) of the essence of the contract, and therefore conditions of the contract.[420]

(4) Pledge

(a) Definition and character

16.67 Pledge is one of the four types of consensual security known to English law.[421] It arises where one person (the pledgor) confers possession of goods on another (the pledgee) as security for the payment of a debt,[422] or for the performance of some other obligation,[423] owed by the former to the latter. The pledgee's possession acts both as evidence of the debt between the parties and as an advertisement of it to third parties. Partly for this reason, a true pledge does not require registration under the Bills of Sale Acts or the Companies legislation.[424]

(b) Distinction from lien and mortgage

16.68 Pledge differs from lien in that the pledgee has an inherent power of sale to enforce the secured obligation. Both pledge and lien are, however, possessory securities and a lien (like a pledge) need not be registered.[425] Moreover, it may be that a lien like a pledge can be assigned to a third person.[426] Pledge differs from mortgage in

---

[417] *Sport International Bussum BV v Inter-Footwear Ltd* [1984] 1 WLR 776; *BICC plc v Burndy Corp* [1985] Ch 232, CA.

[418] See paras 18.163–18.167.

[419] *Ariston SRL v Charly Records Ltd* The Independent, 13 April 1990, CA; and see *Interfoto Picture Library Ltd v Stiletto Visual Programmes Ltd* [1989] QB 433.

[420] *Lombard North Central plc v Butterworth* [1987] QB 527, CA.

[421] *Re Cosslett (Contractors) Ltd* [1997] 4 All ER 115, 126, CA *per* Millett LJ.

[422] *Halliday v Holgate* (1868) LR 3 Ex 299, 302 *per* Willes J.

[423] *Australia and New Zealand Banking Group Ltd v Curlett, Cannon and Galbell Pty Ltd* (1992) 10 Australian Company Law Cases 1292. But cf *Marq v Christie, Manson & Woods Ltd* [2003] EWCA Civ 731; [2004] QB 286, CA (delivery of a chattel to auction house for sale, and acceptance by auction house under contract giving auction house extensive powers of retention and sale designed to enforce obligations undertaken by the party delivering the chattel, held not to constitute a pledge of the chattel for purposes of the Torts (Interference with Goods) Act 1977, s 11(2)).

[424] *Waight v Waight and Walker* [1952] 2 All ER 290; and see n 425 below.

[425] *Re Hamlet International plc (in administration), Trident International Ltd v Barlow* (1999) 2 BCLC 506; *Re Cosslett (Contractors) Ltd* [1997] 4 All ER 115, CA.

[426] *Bull v Faulkner* (1848) 2 De G & Sm 772, 64 ER 346; see now *Vered v Inscorp Holdings Ltd* (1993) 31 NSWLR 290.

that the secured party must get possession while the indebted party retains the general property in the goods. A further difference is that pledgees have no power of foreclosure.

The securing of an obligation need not have been the original purpose of the   **16.69**
bailment. A pledge can arise where parties to some other form of bailment (such as custody for reward) agree that their relationship shall henceforth be one of pledgor and pledgee.[427] But an agreement that one party shall be entitled to take possession of another's goods on default of some obligation is not a pledge.[428] The essence of pledge is the delivery of goods as security against the non-performance of some future obligation. The conferment of possession must precede the crystallization of the right to possess.[429]

The pledgor can be any person who has an interest in the goods superior to that   **16.70**
of the pledgee, and need not be the owner. Indeed, there may be a repledge of goods by an original pledgee to a third person, provided that the amount secured by the repledge does not exceed that secured by the original pledge;[430] where it does, the pledgee must yield up the goods to the original pledgor on tender of the sum secured by the original pledge.[431]

Pledge creates a proprietary interest (or 'special property')[432] in the pledgee and   **16.71**
the security to which it gives rise is assignable. It survives a sale of the goods by the pledgor, so that the pledgee can resist the buyer's claim to possession of the goods and retain them until the debt is discharged;[433] the buyer, on the other hand, has the right to redeem the goods on payment of the sum originally secured.[434] In common with other bailees, the pledgee can sue third parties who maltreat or misappropriate the goods during his possession, and can at common law recover damages assessed according to the full value of the goods.[435] The pledgee has an insurable interest in the goods and can, under an appropriately worded policy, recover their full value in cases of loss, or the full depreciation in cases of damage.[436] This right, together with the pledgeor's general right to sue in

---

[427] *RA Barrett & Co Ltd v Livesey* (CA, 6 November 1980).
[428] *Re Cosslett (Contractors) Ltd* [1997] 4 All ER 115, 126, CA *per* Millett LJ.
[429] ibid.
[430] *Donald v Suckling* (1866) LR 1 QB 585.
[431] ibid 610 *per* Mellor J.
[432] ibid 609 *per* Mellor J, 617 *per* Blackburn J.
[433] *Franklin v Neate* (1844) 13 M & W 481, 153 ER 200; *Halliday v Holgate* (1868) LR 3 Ex 299, 302 *per* Willes J.
[434] *Franklin v Neate* (1844) 13 M & W 481, 153 ER 200; *Rich v Aldred* (1705) 6 Mod 46, 87 ER 968.
[435] *The Winkfield* [1902] P 42, CA; and see para 16.25.
[436] See para 16.31.

tort for acts of negligence or conversion inflicted on the goods, applies even though his exposure under the pledge is less than the full value of the goods or the cost of depreciation, and even though he is not answerable to the pledgor for the misadventure.[437]

(c) General duties of the pledgee

16.72   The pledgee must take reasonable care of the goods[438] and must answer for any deliberate wrongdoing on the part of anyone to whom he has entrusted them. The burden of negativing these forms of fault is on him.[439] If he deviates from the terms of the entrustment to him (for example, by keeping the pledged goods somewhere other than agreed, or by retaining them longer than agreed, or by delegating custody to a third party) he is strictly answerable for all ensuing loss or damage.[440]

(d) Pledgee's power of sale

16.73   On default of the secured obligation, the pledgee has a right of sale, which is inherent in pledge and need not be expressly agreed in order to create a pledge.[441] In exercising the right, the pledgee must take reasonable care,[442] and it appears that he owes a similar duty to a guarantor of the debt.[443] The debt survives the sale and the pledgor remains liable for any shortfall.[444] Where the proceeds of sale exceed the debt, the pledgee holds the surplus on trust for the pledgor and must pay interest,[445] though he can set off from the surplus any other debts owed to him by the pledgor.[446] The pledgor has the right to redeem the goods at any time before the pledgee sells them.[447]

---

[437]   *The Jag Shakti* [1986] AC 337, PC. Otherwise, where the bailor has a mere reversionary interest in the goods and no immediate right to possession sufficient to enable him to sue for negligence or conversion. In that event he must prove enduring damage to his reversionary interest and will recover only to the extent of that permanent deprivation or impairment: *East West Corp v DKBS 1912* [2003] EWCA Civ 83; [2003] QB 1509 at 1532–1534 *per* Mance LJ; *HSBC Rail (UK) Ltd v Network Rail Infrastructure Ltd* [2005] EWCA Civ 1437; [2006] 1 All ER 343 at 349–351 *per* Longmore LJ.

[438]   *Giles v Carter* (1965) 109 SJ 452; *Coggs v Bernard* (1703) 2 Ld Raym 909, 917, 92 ER 107, 112 *per* Holt CJ.

[439]   *Giles v Carter* (1965) 109 SJ 452; see para 16.50.

[440]   *Coggs v Bernard* (1703) 2 Ld Raym 909, 916, 92 ER 107, 111 *per* Holt CJ; *The Odessa* [1916] AC 145, 149, HL *per* Lord Mersey (semble).

[441]   *The Odessa* [1916] AC 145, 149, HL *per* Lord Mersey (semble).

[442]   ibid.

[443]   *BCCI SA v Aboody* (HC, 30 September 1987), affd on a different point [1989] 2 WLR 759, CA.

[444]   *South Sea Co v Duncomb* (1731) 2 Stra 919, 93 ER 942.

[445]   *Mathew v TM Sutton Ltd* [1994] 4 All ER 793.

[446]   *Young v Bank of Bengal* (1836) 1 Moo 150, 12 ER 771, PC.

[447]   *Singer Manufacturing Co Ltd v Clark* (1879) 5 Ex D 37.

(e) Pledgor's duties: warranty as to title, duty of care

The pledgor warrants that he has title to the goods.[448] Where the pledgor is not the **16.74** owner, the undertaking is satisfied by showing that he had the right to pledge them to the pledgee.[449] An original pledgee who repledges to a third person is deemed to satisfy this obligation if repledge was not expressly or impliedly prohibited by the terms of the first pledge.[450] Ordinarily, no such prohibition will be discovered. The pledgor owes the pledgee a duty of care in respect of the goods and is answerable to the pledgee if he could by taking reasonable care have discovered and guarded against any unsafe condition in the goods which injures the pledgee or damages his property.[451] There is no case law suggesting any stricter liability, and statutes imposing strict liability on suppliers of goods exempt pledge from its provisions.[452]

(f) The role of possession

Possession is essential to pledge.[453] It must be received by the pledgee in order to **16.75** create a pledge and must remain with the pledgee in order to sustain a pledge. There are at least four exceptional cases, however, where a pledge can arise in favour of a person who does not receive or keep possession. These are: where the pledge arises by attornment,[454] where the pledgor obtains redelivery of the goods by fraud,[455] where the pledgee repledges to a third person,[456] and where the pledgee redelivers the goods to the pledgor for a limited period or purpose not inconsistent with the continuation of the pledge.[457] It is on the last of these exceptions that the trust receipt is founded.[458]

The mere failure of the payment method used by the pledgor to redeem the goods **16.76** does not, in the absence of clear words to the contrary, revive the pledge and entitle the pledgee to resume possession of the goods as continuing security. In Australia, where a cheque delivered in purported discharge of a debt was not met

---

[448] *Cheesman v Exall* (1851) 6 Ex 341, 155 ER 574.

[449] This proposition follows from general principle and by analogy with the obligation owed by a seller of goods.

[450] *Donald v Suckling* (1866) LR 1 QB 585.

[451] This proposition follows from general principle; there is no specific authority on point. See generally para 16.54.

[452] Sale of Goods Act 1979, s 62(4); Supply of Goods and Services Act 1982, s 1(2)(e).

[453] *Dublin City Distillery Ltd v Doherty* [1914] AC 823.

[454] *Askrigg Pty Ltd v Student Guild of Curtin University of Technology* (1989) 18 NSWLR 738.

[455] *Mocatta v Bell* (1857) 24 Beav 585, 53 ER 483; *TEA (1983) v Uniting Church (NSW) Trust Association* [1985] Victorian Reports 139, 141 *per* Brooking J.

[456] *Donald v Suckling* (1866) LR 1 QB 585.

[457] *Reeves v Capper* (1838) 5 Bing NC 136, 132 ER 1057, distinguished in *Dublin City Distillery Ltd v Doherty* [1914] AC 823, 845, HL *per* Lord Atkinson; *Martin v Reid* (1862) 11 CB (NS) 730, 142 ER 982.

[458] *Re David Allester Ltd* [1922] 2 Ch 211.

for insufficient funds, and certain bills previously delivered as security for the original debt had already been returned to the pledgor on delivery of the cheque, the pledgee was not entitled to recover possession of the bills in order to revive the pledge.[459] It has also been held in Australia that a pledge survived the delivery of the goods by the pledgee to his own bailee for some special purpose, and that this continuing pledge was not displaced by the purported creation of a direct and inconsistent security between the pledgor and the pledgee's bailee.[460]

16.77 A pledge may arise by delivery of a bill of lading, in which event the recipient of the bill may acquire an immediate right to the possession of the cargo and be treated as a pledgee of it. Where a third person converts the cargo, the pledgee with an immediate right of possession can at common law recover damages calculated by reference to the full market value of the goods and not merely (where this is less) the amount secured by the pledge.[461] It is a matter of intention and construction as to whether the pledge has become effective at the material time and whether any liminal condition to which the pledge is subject has been satisfied.[462] A claimant who knew, when the pledge to him was purportedly created, that the goods had already been dispersed on discharge from the vessel, cannot normally show the necessary possession of the goods or the necessary intention that the relevant bills of lading should confer constructive possession of the goods.[463]

F. Attornment, Sub-bailment, and Other Ambulatory Bailments

(1) Attornment

16.78 We have seen that a bailment can arise by attornment.[464] An attornment, for this purpose, is any overt and unequivocal demonstration by one person (the attornor) to another (the attornee) that the first person now holds goods in his possession as bailee of the second.[465] Attornment can have two effects: it may bring about the passing of a general or special property to the attornee, according to the nature of the transaction (sale or pledge) giving rise to the attornment;[466]

---

[459] *TEA (1983) v Uniting Church (NSW) Trust Association* [1985] Victorian Reports 139.

[460] *Gunnedah Municipal Council v New Zealand Loan and Mercantile Agency Ltd* [1963] NSWR 1229.

[461] *The Jag Shakti* [1986] AC 337, PC, subject to the Torts (Interference with Goods) Act 1977, s 8.

[462] *The Future Express* [1993] 2 Lloyd's Rep 542.

[463] ibid.

[464] See para 16.03.

[465] See eg *Askrigg Pty Ltd v Student Guild of the Curtain University of Technology* (1989) 18 NSWLR 738; *Re London Wine Co (Shippers) Ltd* [1986] Palmer's Company Cases 121.

[466] *Maynegrain Pty Ltd v Compafina Bank* [1982] 2 NSWLR 141; revsd without reference to this point [1984] NSWLR 258, PC.

and it may estop the attornor from denying the truth of the facts represented in the attornment.[467]

Very little may be needed to constitute an attornment, which may occur either orally or in correspondence, but attornment requires something more than the mere receipt of delivery orders without objection,[468] or the alteration of the bailee's own records.[469] Once attornment occurs, the attornor owes the normal obligation of a bailee to the attornee, though any clauses qualifying his liability in the original bailment appear to be carried over into the new bailment.[470] At the same time, the attornor ceases to owe the obligation of a bailee to the original bailor. Attornments commonly occur where a seller of goods indicates to his buyer, to whom property but not possession have passed, that he now holds the goods on the buyer's behalf;[471] or where an owner of goods pledges them but retains possession and indicates to the pledgee that he now holds them as that person's bailee;[472] or where the bailees of either sellers[473] or pledgors[474] tell the buyers or pledgees that they now hold the goods as their bailees. **16.79**

Where the goods comprised in the attornment are specific or ascertained, and the attornment arises on a sale, the attornment may pass property to the attornee, for example by constituting the necessary unconditional appropriation.[475] Where the goods are unascertained, and the bailee of a larger bulk merely attorns in respect of an undivided part of that bulk, the attornment will not normally pass property in any particular goods to the attornee, for the bulk remains undivided and the goods unascertained.[476] The bailee will, however, be estopped from denying that such a division and passing of property has occurred and may be answerable in damages for the loss suffered by the inaccuracy of the attornment;[477] it appears **16.80**

---

[467] ibid 148 *per* Hope JA. For comparison of the proprietary effects of an attornment and the Sale of Goods Act 1979, s 20A, see L Gullifer, 'Constructive Possession after the Sale of Goods (Amendment) Act 1995' (1999) LMCLQ 93.

[468] *Laurie and Morewood v John Dudin & Sons* [1926] 1 KB 223, CA.

[469] ibid.

[470] *HMF Humphrey Ltd v Baxter Hoare & Co Ltd* (1933) 149 LT 603; *Leigh and Sillivan Ltd v Aliakmon Shipping Co Ltd (The Aliakmon)* [1986] AC 785, 818, HL *per* Lord Brandon; *The Captain Gregos (No 2)* [1990] 2 Lloyd's Rep 395, 405, CA *per* Bingham LJ; and see *East West Corp v DKBS 1912* [2003] EWCA Civ 83; [2003] 1 Lloyd's Rep 239.

[471] *Gamer's Motor Centre (Newcastle) Pty Ltd v Natwest Wholesale Australia Pty Ltd* (1987) 163 CLR 236.

[472] *Askrigg Pty Ltd v Student Guild of Curtin University of Technology* (1989) 18 NSWLR 738.

[473] *Dublin City Distillery Ltd v Doherty* [1914] AC 823, HL.

[474] *Madras Official Assignee v Mercantile Bank of India Ltd* [1935] AC 58, PC; *Maynegrain Pty Ltd v Compafina Bank* [1982] 2 NSWLR 141.

[475] Sale of Goods Act 1979, s 18, r 5(1); *Maynegrain Pty Ltd v Compafina Bank* [1982] 2 NSWLR 141; revsd without reference to this point [1984] NSWLR 258, PC.

[476] Sale of Goods Act 1979, s 16; *Re London Wine Co (Shippers) Ltd* [1986] PCC 121; *Re Goldcorp Exchange Ltd* [1995] 1 AC 74, PC.

[477] *Maynegrain Pty Ltd v Compafina Bank* [1982] 2 NSWLR 141.

that this estoppel does not require acts of reliance by the attornee.[478] The obligation to which the estoppel gives rise is, however, personal to the parties to the
attornment, and does not entitle the attornee to assert any general property in the
goods exigible against third parties.[479] By statute, however, buyers of specified
quantities of unascertained goods which form part of a bulk may gain property in
an undivided share in the bulk and become owners in common with other persons
whose interests are comprised in the bulk. For this purpose, the appropriate shares
will be rated or abated proportionally according to the ratio which the quantity
of goods paid for and due to the buyer out of the bulk bears to the quantity of
goods in the bulk at any relevant time.[480] Further, buyers of specified quantities
of unascertained goods which form part of a bulk may in certain circumstances
gain property in the residue of that bulk once it is reduced to the specified quantity
or to less than that quantity.[481] Moreover, where several depositors deliver generic
fungible goods into a common store, on terms that they may later withdraw
equivalent amounts, the depositors may (if that accords with their intention) be
tenants in common, and thus bailors, of the overall amount in store.[482]

16.81 Where the attornment is made to an agent who acts for an undisclosed principal,
the relevant passing of property and estoppel may operate in favour of either the
agent or the principal, according to their election.[483]

(2) Sub-bailment

16.82 Sub-bailment arises where an original bailee of goods grants possession of them
to a third person while retaining a right of possession against that person.[484]

---

478 ibid.

479 *Re Goldcorp Exchange Ltd* [1995] 1 AC 74, 93, PC *per* Lord Mustill; *Re London Wine Co
(Shippers) Ltd* [1986] PCC 121; *Simms v Anglo-American Telegraph Co* (1879) 5 QBD 188.

480 Sale of Goods Act 1979, ss 20A, 20B as inserted by the Sales of Goods (Amendment) Act 1995,
s 1(3). See L Gullifer, 'Constructive Possession after the Sale of Goods (Amendment) Act 1995'
(1999) LMCLQ 93.

481 Sale of Goods Act 1979, s 18, r 5(3) as amended by the Sales of Goods (Amendment) Act
1995, s 1(2).

482 See eg *Mercer v Craven Grain Storage Ltd* [1994] CLC 328, HL.

483 *Maynegrain Pty Ltd v Compafina Bank* (n 477 above); revsd without reference to this point
[1984] NSWLR 258, PC.

484 *China Pacific SA v Food Corp of India (The Winson)* [1982] AC 939, 959, HL *per* Lord
Diplock. see now also *Lotus Cars Ltd v Southampton Cargo Handling plc and Associated British Ports
(The Rigoletto)* [2000] 2 Lloyd's Rep 532, CA; *Wincanton Ltd v P & O Trans European Ltd* [2001]
EWCA Civ 227 *per* Dyson LJ (no sub-bailment, but rather substitutional bailment as to which see
Main Work para 13.84). See also *Marcq v Christie Manson & Woods Ltd (t/a Christie's)* [2003] EWCA
Civ 731; [2003] 3 WLR 980; *East West Corp v DKBS 1912* [2003] EWCA Civ 83; [2003] 1 Lloyd's
Rep 239; *Sandeman Coprimar SA v Transitos y Transportes Integrales SL* [2003] EWCA Civ 113;
[2003] QB 1270; *G Bosman (Transport) Ltd v LKW Walter International Transport-organisation AG*
[2002] All ER (D) 13 (May), CA; *Jarl Tra AB v Convoys Ltd* [2003] EWHC 1488 (Comm).

The third person becomes both a sub-bailee of the original bailor and a bailee of the original bailee.[485] It is said that, for this consequence to follow, the original bailee must continue to have a right of possession to the goods against the original bailor.[486] But in principle a sub-bailment should be capable of arising even where the grant of possession by the original bailee occurs without the original bailor's consent and thus involves a forfeiture of his right of possession against the original bailor.[487] The critical questions which depend on the existence of a sub-bailment are the liability of the bailee to the head bailor and the rights of the middle bailee against the ultimate bailee; in neither case is the legitimacy of the original bailee's right of possession against the original bailor decisive. It appears that the subsidiary bailee's lack of knowledge as to the identity of the original bailor does not normally prevent him from owing the original bailor the duties of a sub-bailee,[488] though the position may differ where the existence or identity of an original bailor is crucial to the subsidiary bailee's decision to accept possession, for such a misapprehension may mean that he is not voluntarily in possession with regard to the original bailor.[489]

A sub-bailee owes the normal common law duties of a bailee both to the original **16.83** bailor and to the original bailee.[490] In particular, he must take reasonable care of the goods[491] and answer to each of his bailors for any breach of this obligation.[492] He must also answer to both bailors for the deliberate wrongs of employees or

---

[485] See para 16.83. As to the principles of sub-bailment generally, see the important decision in *East West Corp v DKBS 1912* [2003] EWCA Civ 83; [2003] QB 1509, which confirms many of the propositions stated in the text of both this and the following paragraph, and indeed of the law of bailment generally. See also *Sandeman Coprimar SA v Transitos y Transportes Integrales SL* [2003] EWCA Civ 113; [2003] QB 1270; *G Bosman (Transport) Ltd v LKW Walter International Transportorganisation AG* [2002] All ER (D) 13 (May), CA; *Jarl Tra AB v Convoys Ltd* [2003] EWHC 1488 (Comm).

[486] *China Pacific SA v Food Corp of India (The Winson)* [1982] AC 939, 959, HL *per* Lord Diplock; *Chapman v Robinson and Ferguson* (1969) 71 Western Weekly R 515. See now also *Marcq v Christie Manson & Woods Ltd (t/a Christie's)* [2003] EWCA Civ 731; [2003] 3 WLR 980.

[487] NE Palmer, *Bailment* (2nd edn, 1991) 1282–3; cf *Trancontainer Express Ltd v Custodian Security Ltd* [1998] 1 Lloyd's Rep 128, where the intermediate carriers brought no evidence of any right on their part to resume possession of the goods from the sub-carriers. See also *RM Campbell (Vehicle Sales) Pty Ltd v Machnig* (SC NSW, 22 May 1981); *The Anderson Group Pty Ltd v Tynan Motors Pty Ltd* [2006] NSWCA 22.

[488] *Balsamo v Medici* [1984] 1 WLR 951, 959 *per* Walton J.

[489] *The Pioneer Container* [1994] 2 AC 324, 342, PC *per* Lord Goff. Cf *Marcq v Christie Manson & Woods Ltd (t/a Christie's)* [2003] EWCA Civ 731; [2003] 3 WLR 980 (auctioneer who accepts stolen painting for sale is not a bailee of the true owner where he has no notice (or, it appears, no means of acquiring notice) of the existence of the owner's interest. In this case the theft of the work was registered on a professional register on stolen art).

[490] ibid 338–42, PC *per* Lord Goff; *Morris v CW Martin & Sons Ltd* [1966] 1 QB 716, CA; *China Pacific SA v Food Corp of India (The Winson)* [1982] AC 939, 957–9, HL *per* Lord Diplock.

[491] *The Pioneer Container* [1994] 2 AC 324, PC; *Morris v CW Martin & Sons Ltd* [1966] 1 QB 716, CA; *China Pacific SA v Food Corp of India (The Winson)* [1982] AC 939, HL.

[492] Cf *The Hamburg Star* [1994] 1 Lloyd's Rep 399.

independent contractors to whom he has entrusted the goods.[493] The burden of proof in each case corresponds with that applicable to a normal bailee by direct delivery.[494] In addition, the sub-bailee may be bound by the normal common law estoppel against contesting the title of both of his bailors,[495] and may claim against both of them for extraordinary expense incurred in discharging his duty of care, at least where the bailments are gratuitous.[496] But these obligations may be modified by agreement or by statute. The direct relations between original bailee and sub-bailee clearly enable the sub-bailee to impose exclusions or limitations of his normal responsibility to the original bailee, or to enlarge his commitments; these variations are normally but not necessarily contractual and may attract legislative control. The absence of direct relations between the normal head bailor and sub-bailee does not prevent the sub-bailee from positively undertaking to the head bailor some larger obligation than would otherwise obtain at common law, by means of some direct promise (whether contractual or otherwise) given to the head bailor as to the conduct of the sub-bailment.[497] Nor does this absence of direct relations necessarily prevent the sub-bailee from invoking the terms of the sub-bailment agreement between the original bailee and himself in defence to an action by the original bailor. In such an action, the sub-bailee can rely on any protective term contained in the sub-bailment agreement if the head bailor has expressly or impliedly consented to the sub-bailment on those terms,[498] or

---

[493] See paras 16.42 and 16.49. See now also *G Bosman (Transport) Ltd v LKW Walter International Transportorganisation AG* [2002] All ER (D) 13 (May), CA.

[494] *The Pioneer Container* [1994] 2 AC 324, 338–42, PC *per* Lord Goff; *Morris v CW Martin & Sons Ltd* [1966] 1 QB 716, CA.

[495] *The Hamburg Star* [1994] 1 Lloyd's Rep 399, 405 *per* Clarke J (proposition at least arguable).

[496] *China Pacific SA v Food Corp of India (The Winson)* [1982] AC 939, HL.

[497] *Brambles Security Services Ltd v Bi-Lo Pty Ltd* (1992) Aust Torts Rep 81–161 and see also *City Television v Conference and Training Office Ltd* (CA, 29 November 2001) *per* Sedley LJ.

[498] *The Pioneer Container* [1994] 2 AC 324, 339–40, PC *per* Lord Goff, following *Morris v CW Martin & Sons Ltd* [1966] 1 QB 716, 719–30, CA *per* Lord Denning MR. See further *Lotus Cars Ltd v Southampton Cargo Handling plc (The Rigoletto); Southampton Cargo Handling plc v Associated British Ports* [2001] 2 Lloyd's Rep 532, CA. In exceptional cases the head bailor and the sub-bailee may occupy a direct contractual relationship, in which event the particular immunities and obligations arising under the terms of the sub-bailment might be directly enforced between those two parties: *Sandeman Coprimar SA v Transitos y Transportes Integrales SL* [2003] EWCA Civ 113; [2003] QB 1270; and cf *The Homburg Houtimport BV v Agrosin Private Ltd (The Starsin)* [2003] UKHL 12; [2004] 1 AC 705. But the head bailor's actual or ostensible consent to the terms of the sub-bailment can also (it appears) justify the direct enforcement of positive obligations between head bailor and sub-bailee, irrespective of whether they are contractually related: *Sandeman Coprimar SA v Transitos y Transportes Integrales SL* [2003] EWCA Civ 113; [2003] QB 1270; *Targe Towing Ltd v Marine Blast Ltd* [2004] EWCA Civ 346; [2004] 1 Lloyd's Rep 721 (consensual sub-bailment and contractual relationship between head bailor and sub-bailee are 'conceptually different').

(probably) if the intermediate bailee had ostensible authority to sub-bail on those terms,[499] but not otherwise.[500]

(3) Substitutional Bailment

Sub-bailment differs from substitutional bailment, which is in the relationship arising where an original bailee vacates possession in favour of a successor bailee and (if the successor is authorized and chosen with reasonable care) withdraws henceforth from the scheme of obligation.[501] In that event, the incoming bailee becomes the direct bailee of the bailor and owes his normal common law obligations as bailee exclusively to him.[502] This direct relationship may or may not be contractual and may be modified by agreement. The bailment by attornment which arises between a buyer and the seller's bailee is a typical substitutional bailment.[503]

16.84

(4) Quasi-bailment

This anomalous form of bailment arises where a person who is entitled to take possession of another's goods chooses instead to delegate the assumption of possession to a third person without taking possession personally.[504] If the delegation is unauthorized the person making the delegation owes to the bailor a strict liability similar to that of a deviating bailee.[505] If it is authorized, the person making the delegation remains answerable for the defaults of the third person, in

16.85

---

[499] *The Pioneer Container* [1994] 2 AC 324, 341, 342, PC *per* Lord Goff (obiter); *Westpac Banking Corp v Royal Tongan Airlines* (SC NSW, 5 September 1996).

[500] The decision in *Johnson Matthey & Co Ltd v Constantine Terminals Ltd* [1976] 2 Lloyd's Rep 215 that a sub-bailee could also rely on essential exculpatory terms in the sub-bailment to which the principal bailor had not consented, at least where the duty on which the principal bailor was suing would not have arisen but for the fact of the sub-bailment, was not followed in *The Pioneer Container* [1994] 2 AC 324, 340–2, PC.

[501] The leading modern authorities are *China Pacific SA v Food Corp of India (The Winson)* [1982] AC 939, HL and *Wincanton Ltd v P & O Trans European Ltd* [2001] EWCA Civ 227 *per* Dyson LJ see also *Mayflower Foods Ltd v Barnard Bros Ltd* (HC, 9 August 1996).

[502] Cf the new bailment which arose from the dealer's constructive delivery of goods held on title retention terms to a bona fide purchaser in *Gamer's Motor Centre (Newcastle) Pty Ltd v Natwest Wholesale Australia Pty Ltd* (1987) 163 CLR 236. See generally *East West Corp v DKBS 1912* [2003] 1 Lloyd's Rep 239; *Sandeman Coprimar SA v Transitos y Transportes Integrales SL* [2003] EWCA Civ 113; [2003] 3 All ER 108, [2003] 2 Lloyd's Rep 172, CA; *G Bosman (Transport) Ltd v LKW Walter International Transportorganisation AG* [2002] All ER (D) 13 (May), CA.

[503] See para 16.79.

[504] NE Palmer, *Bailment* (2nd edn, 1991) 34, 1291. The term 'quasi-bailment' is used in *The Pioneer Container* [1994] 2 AC 324, 344–5, PC *per* Lord Goff; *Metaalhandel JA Magnus BV v Ardfields Transport Ltd* [1988] 1 Lloyd's Rep 197, 202–3 *per* Gatehouse J.

[505] *Edwards v Newland & Co* [1950] 2 KB 534, CA.

much the same way as a normal bailee who sub-bails with authority.[506] He is also liable for any resulting loss or damage resulting if he appointed the possessor negligently or contrary to instructions.[507] He probably does not, however, carry the same burden of proof as a normal bailee, so that fault must be positively proved;[508] the lack of possession makes this aspect of the bailee's liability inapposite.[509] The third person who gets possession ('the quasi-bailee') owes the normal common law duties of a bailee to the original bailor unless the original bailor has consented to the quasi-bailment on exculpatory terms[510] (in which case those terms can probably be raised against the original bailor)[511] or unless perhaps the quasi-bailee was unaware of the identity of the original bailor and would not have consented to hold goods on his behalf[512] (in which case he may enjoy an immunity from duty of care similar to that of the involuntary bailee).[513]

G. Involuntary and Undisclosed Bailment

(1) Involuntary Bailment

16.86 An involuntary bailment can take one of two forms. An originally involuntary bailment arises where a person is put in possession of goods without his initial consent.[514] A typical example is the relationship between sender and recipient of unsolicited goods.[515] Such a relationship cannot strictly be called a bailment at all, because the possessor's consent is vital to bailment.[516] A subsequently

---

[506] *Metaalhandel JA Magnus BV v Ardfields Transport Ltd* [1988] 1 Lloyd's Rep 197; *Hobbs v Petersham Transport Co Pty Ltd* (1971) 124 CLR 220.

[507] *Metaalhandel JA Magnus BV v Ardfields Transport Ltd* ibid.

[508] ibid 203 *per* Gatehouse J; Palmer (n 504 above) 1359–61.

[509] *Metaalhandel JA Magnus BV v Ardfields Transport Ltd* (n 506 above), 203 *per* Gatehouse J; *Hobbs v Petersham Transport Co Pty Ltd* (1971) 124 CLR 220, 232 *per* Barwick CJ, 242–3 *per* Windeyer J.

[510] *The Pioneer Container* [1994] 2 AC 324, 338, 342, PC *per* Lord Goff. But Lord Goff ultimately left the point open as not needing decision. See further Palmer (n 504 above) 1293–5. Where a quasi-bailor retains a possessory right to the goods, the quasi-bailee may owe the duties of a bailee to him as well as to the head bailor: *Edwards v Newland & Co* [1950] 2 KB 534, CA; cf *Transcontainer Express Ltd v Custodian Security Ltd* [1988] 1 Lloyd's Rep 128, CA (no possessory title shown); *The Hamburg Star* [1994] 1 Lloyd's Rep 399.

[511] *The Pioneer Container* [1994] 2 AC 324, 345, PC, (point formally left open); *Lukoil-Kalingradmorneft plc v Tata Ltd* [1999] 1 Lloyd's Rep 365 at 374 *per* Toulson J.

[512] Cf *The Pioneer Container* [1994] 2 AC 324, 338, 342, PC *per* Lord Goff; *Marcq v Christie, Manson & Woods Ltd* [2003] EWCA Civ 731; [2004] QB 286 at [50]–[51], *per* Tuckey LJ.

[513] See para 16.87.

[514] Cf the bailment by concealment, where the person in possession is unaware of the fact of his possession, or may be aware of his possession but unaware the goods belong to someone else. See para 16.87.

[515] This is now governed by legislation: see the Unsolicited Goods and Services Act 1971.

[516] *The Pioneer Container* [1994] 2 AC 324, PC; and see para 16.01.

involuntary bailment arises where a person who was originally a voluntary possessor of goods becomes an involuntary possessor by reason of passage of time, conduct of the bailor, or some other cause. This situation can arise where bailors of goods for repair, cleaning or some other service fail to collect them.[517] In cases of this type, courts are reluctant to find that the bailee has ceased to owe all responsibility for the goods, though they may well find that the duty of care has abated.[518]

Where possession is involuntary from its inception, the possessor owes no duty **16.87** of care to protect the goods against loss or damage.[519] He must abstain from deliberate and (probably) reckless damage but beyond that he is not liable for the physical security of the goods.[520] He will be answerable to the owner in conversion if, without authority[521] and knowing that the goods are not his, he deliberately consumes them or otherwise deals with them in a manner contrary to the owner's right.[522] If he commits an innocent conversion of the goods (for example, by delivering them to someone whom he erroneously believes to be the owner) and the goods are lost to the owner in consequence, the possessor is liable only if, in doing the act, he acted without reasonable care.[523] The involuntary bailee is probably entitled to do whatever is reasonable to rid himself of the goods[524] and to recover the reasonable costs of doing so, though the precise extent and rationale of these rights are uncertain.[525]

Where a bailee is left in possession of goods for a period longer than that con- **16.88** templated, various doctrines may enable him to lessen his responsibility.[526] At one extreme, the court may find that he has become an involuntary bailee and no longer owes any duty to take care to safeguard the goods from theft or other

---

[517] See para 16.88.

[518] See eg *Mitchell v Davis* (1920) 37 TLR 68.

[519] *Lethbridge v Phillips* (1819) 2 Starke 544, 171 ER 731; *Howard v Harris* (1884) Cab & Ellis 258; *Neuwith v Over Darwen Co-operative Society Ltd* (1894) 63 LJ QB 290.

[520] ibid. Cf *Scotland v Solomon* [2002] EWHC 1886 (Ch), Deputy Judge David Kitchin QC at [23]; 'if persons are involuntary bailees and have done everything reasonable they are not liable to pay damages if something which they do results in the loss of the property. There is an obligation on the part of involuntary bailees to do what is right and reasonable'.

[521] eg under the Torts (Interference with Goods) Act 1977, ss 12 and 13.

[522] *Foster v Juniata Bridge Co* 16 P St 393 (1851).

[523] *Elvin and Powell Ltd v Plummer Roddis Ltd* (1933) 50 TLR 158; *Motis Exports Ltd v Dampskibsselskabet AF 1912* [1999] 1 All ER (Comm) 571, 582–3 *per* Rix J; on appeal without reference to this point [2000] 1 Lloyd's Rep 211; *Scotland v Solomon*. Cf *City Television v Conference and Training Office Ltd* (CA, 29 November 2001); *Marcq v Christie Manson & Woods Ltd (t/a Christie's)* [2003] EWCA Civ 731; [2004] QB 286.

[524] *Pedrick v Morning Star Motors Ltd* (CA, 14 February 1979); *Haniotis v Dimitriou* [1983] 1 Victoria Reports 498; *Bowden v Lo* (1998) 9 BPR 16, 317, (1998) NSW Conv R 56, 807.

[525] Contrast *Nicholson v Chapman* (1793) 2 H Bl 254, 126 ER 536 *per* Eyre CJ with *Kolfor Plant Ltd v Tilbury Plant Ltd* (1977) 121 SJ 390.

[526] NE Palmer, *Bailment* (2nd edn, 1991) 705–19.

physical hazard.[527] This conclusion will be easier to reach where the bailment was for a fixed period, though even in that event the court may imply a period of grace before the duties of the bailee determine. Where the period of the bailment was not fixed, the court may hold that possession was to be for a reasonable time and that the bailor's consent to possession has expired once such time has passed, relieving him of further responsibility.[528] Alternatively, it may conclude that the bailor has abandoned the property in the goods and can therefore no longer stand as bailor, in which case he cannot sue for any loss or damage occurring after that date.[529] But a defence of abandonment requires, at the least, proof of conduct from which one can infer an intention by the bailor to relinquish his property in the goods.[530] A period of inaction may be insufficient for this purpose.[531] In other cases, the appropriate conclusion may be that the bailment has changed from a bailment for mutual advantage to a gratuitous bailment, with the bailee as the party deriving no benefit.[532] But modern decisions suggest that there is no difference in principle between the duties owed by a bailee for reward and those owed by a gratuitous bailee.[533]

16.89 Where no time is fixed for termination of the bailment, the courts will probably imply into the bailment an obligation on the part of the bailor to collect the goods within a reasonable time.[534] Hitherto this approach has been confined to contractual bailments. Where the obligation is a condition of the contract,[535] the bailor's failure to collect the goods may entitle the bailee to contend that both contract and bailment are at an end and that his duty of care towards the goods has ceased.[536]

---

[527] *Maritime Coastal Containers Ltd v Shelburne Marine Ltd* (1982) 52 NSR (2d) 51.

[528] ibid.

[529] It is submitted that a chattel owner can divest himself of ownership by a means of abandonment though the position is uncertain: see A Hudson, 'Abandonment' in N Palmer and E McKendrick, *Interests in Goods* (2nd edn, 1991); cf *Moorhouse v Angus and Robertson (No 1) Ltd* (1981) 1 NSWLR 700.

[530] *Moorhouse v Angus and Robertson (No 1) Ltd* (1981) 1 NSWLR 700.

[531] ibid.

[532] Cf *Davis v Henry Birk & Sons Ltd* [1981] 5 Western Weekly R 559, on appeal (1983) 142 DLR (3d) 356.

[533] *Graham v Voight* (1989) 95 Federal LR 146; *Mitchell v Ealing London Borough Council* [1979] QB 1; *Port Swettenham Authority v TW Wu & Co (M) Sdn Bhd* [1979] AC 580, PC; *Bowden v Lo* (1998) 9 BPR 16,317, (1998) NSW Conv R 56,807.

[534] *Pedrick v Morning Star Motors Ltd* (CA, 14 February 1979); *Ridyard v Roberts* (CA, 14 February 1979); *Davis v Henry Birk & Sons Ltd* [1981] 5 Western Weekly R 559, on appeal (1983) 142 DLR (3d) 356; *JJD SA (a company) v Avon Tyres Ltd* (HC, 19 January 1999); revsd on other grounds (CA, 23 February 2000).

[535] Or an innominate term whose breach deprives the bailee of substantially the whole of the expected contractual benefit.

[536] *Pedrick v Morning Star Motors Ltd* (CA, 14 February 1979); *Ridyard v Roberts* (CA, 14 February 1979); *Davis v Henry Birk & Sons Ltd* [1981] 5 Western Weekly R 559, on appeal (1983) 142 DLR (3d) 356; *JJD SA (a company) v Avon Tyres Ltd* (HC, 19 January 1999); reversed on other grounds (CA, 23 February 2000).

Breach of such a term may also entitle the bailee to argue that remedial steps taken by him to relieve himself of the burden of the goods, such as removing an unwanted car to a public car park,[537] were a reasonable attempt to mitigate the loss which he would otherwise have suffered through the breach,[538] and not therefore wrongful.[539]

The bailee may be able to invoke statutory machinery for the disposal of uncollected goods. The Torts (Interference with Goods) Act 1977, s 12(3) gives a general power of sale over goods bailed after commencement of the Act, but the bailee must give notice to the bailor of his intention to sell the goods.[540] Such a sale gives the buyer of the goods a good title as against the bailor alone.[541] Alternatively, the court may authorize the sale under the Torts (Interference with Goods) Act 1977, s 13. A decision of the court authorizing a sale under the Torts (Interference with Goods) Act 1977, s 13 is conclusive,[542] as against the bailor, of the bailee's entitlement to sell the goods, and gives a good title to the purchaser as against the bailor.[543]

16.90

(2) Undisclosed or Unconscious Bailment

A person who has possession of another person's goods but is unaware of the fact of his possession is not a bailee because he has not consented to possession.[544] Such a person is sometimes known as an unconscious bailee, his relationship with the owner being identified as one of undisclosed bailment. A further example of such a relation may arise where a person is aware of his possession of goods but mistakenly believes that they belong to him.[545] An undisclosed bailment of

16.91

---

[537] *Pedrick v Morning Star Motors Ltd* (CA, 14 February 1979). See generally NE Palmer, *Bailment* (2nd edn, 1991) ch 6, 447–53.

[538] eg in the form of storage costs, or lost business caused by the presence of the goods cluttering a workshop: see *Pedrick v Morning Star Motors Ltd* (CA, 14 February 1979); *Jeffersen Ltd v Burton Group Ltd* (HC, 13 April 1984).

[539] *Pedrick v Morning Star Motors Ltd* (CA, 14 February 1979).

[540] Torts (Interference with Goods) Act 1977, s 12(3), Sch 1 Pt II. Cf *Irving v Keen* (1995) unreported 3 March, CA (letters by bailee to owner ineffective as, even if received, they did not comply with the Act).

[541] ibid s 12(6).

[542] Subject to any right of appeal.

[543] Torts (Interference with Goods) Act 1977, s 13(2).

[544] *Consentino v Dominion Express Co* (1906) 4 WLR 498; and see *The Pioneer Container* [1994] 2 AC 324, 341–2, PC *per* Lord Goff.

[545] *AVX Ltd v EGM Solders Ltd* (HC, 7 July 1982). A further category of undisclosed bailment might arise where the possessor mistakenly believes that the party delivering the goods to him is the owner, whereas the goods are stolen and the true owner is someone other than the party making the delivery: cf *Marcq v Christie Manson & Woods Ltd (t/a Christie's)* [2003] EWCA Civ 731; [2004] QB 286 (no duty of care to verify title).

this sort may occur where the innocent purchaser of a stolen chattel takes possession without realizing that it still belongs to the person from whom it was stolen.

16.92   Like involuntary bailments[546] (where the possessor knows that he has possession but has not agreed to it) undisclosed bailments are not true bailments. The possessor does not ordinarily owe a duty of care in relation to the goods.[547] If, however, the unconscious bailee proposes to damage or destroy the goods, he owes a duty to take reasonable care to establish the fact of his ownership before doing so. If he fails to make this check he is answerable to the owner.[548] It may be assumed that a similar duty binds an unconscious bailee who proposes to dispose of the goods by sale or otherwise. A bailee who fails to perform this precaution, and who would have discovered the existence or ownership of the goods had he done so, may be deemed to be constructively aware of his possession of another person's goods, and thenceforth answerable for those goods in much the same way as an involuntary bailee.[549]

16.93   A person who finds goods on his land owes a duty to take them into his possession, to take reasonable steps to reunite them with their owner, and to take reasonable care of them meanwhile.[550]

---

[546]   See para 16.86.

[547]   *Consentino v Dominion Express Co* (1906) 4 WLR 498; but cf *Awad v Pillai* [1982] RTR 266, CA.

[548]   *AVX Ltd v EGM Solders Ltd* (HC, 7 July 1982) distinguished in *Marcq v Christie Manson & Woods Ltd (t/a Christie's)* [2003] EWCA Civ 731; [2004] QB 286 (auctioneer not liable for redelivering unsold chattel to party who had delivered it for sale, where that party was believed to be the owner; auctioneer owed no duty of care to verify that party's ownership either on taking original delivery from him or on making redelivery to him).

[549]   NE Palmer, *Bailment* (2nd edn, 1991), 447–9.

[550]   *Parker v British Airways Board* [1982] QB 1004, 1017, 1018, CA *per* Donaldson LJ.

17

TORTS AND EQUITABLE WRONGS

A. Introduction

17.01 The French word 'torts' is used by English law to denote many of its civil wrongs. Scots law uses 'delict'.[1] However, for historical reasons, the law of torts is only a subset of the law of civil wrongs. A tort is defined in formal terms as a civil wrong which gives rise to an action for damages, other than one which is exclusively a breach of contract or breach of trust or other equitable obligation. In the words of Sir Percy Winfield:

> Tortious liability arises from the breach of a duty primarily fixed by the law: such duty is towards persons generally and its breach is redressible by an action for unliquidated damages.[2]

17.02 This definition is not adequate.[3] The requirement that the primary duty be fixed by law and good against persons generally excludes tortious liability based upon a responsibility which is genuinely and voluntarily assumed.[4] Even less defensible to modern eyes is the specific exclusion which Winfield made of those breaches of duties which were originally recognized by the courts of Chancery rather than the courts of common law.[5] Historically, the consequence has been the exclusion of equitable wrongs from consideration alongside torts even when the equitable wrongs are materially identical to torts, such as deceit and negligence. Other casualties are breach of trust and fiduciary duty, dishonest assistance in a breach of trust or fiduciary duty, and breach of confidence. The last mentioned of these has been heavily influential in pushing open the door.[6] Especially with the multiplication of litigation based on breach of fiduciary duties, the traditional definition creates an evident danger of needlessly developing two parallel, and overlapping, laws of civil wrongs; a law of torts at common law and a law of meta-torts in equity. Some judges have resisted this tendency.[7] The leading text, *Clerk and*

---

[1] Many of the leading cases in tort happen to be Scottish: *Donoghue v Stevenson* [1932] AC 562, HL; *Bourhill v Young* [1943] AC 92, HL; *Hughes v Lord Advocate* [1963] AC 837, HL; *Junior Books Ltd v Veitchi Co Ltd* [1983] 1 AC 520, HL.

[2] PH Winfield, *The Province of the Law of Tort* (1931) 32.

[3] WVF Rogers (ed), *Winfield and Jolowicz on Tort* (17th edn 2006) 5–19; A Dugdale and M Jones (eds), *Clerk and Lindsell on Torts* (19th edn, 2006) 4–5.

[4] See paras 17.175–17.181.

[5] Winfield, *Province* (n 2 above) 113–15.

[6] P North, 'Breach of Confidence: Is There a New Tort?' (1972) 12 J Society of Public Teachers of Law 149. In *Campbell v Mirror Group Newspapers Ltd* [2004] UKHL 22; [2004] 2 AC 457, 465 [14], Lord Nicholls described breach of confidence as a tort and said that 'the essence of the tort is better encapsulated now as misuse of private information'.

[7] For instance, Millett LJ in *Bristol and West Building Society v Mothew* [1998] Ch 1, CA and in *Paragon Finance plc v DB Thakerar & Co* [1999] 1 All ER 400, CA approved by Lord Walker in *Hilton v Barker Booth & Eastwood* [2005] UKHL 8; [2005] 1 WLR 567, HL. See also Lord Browne-Wilkinson in *Henderson v Merrett Syndicates Ltd* [1995] 2 AC 145, 205, HL; discussion in S Elliott, 'Fiduciary Liability for Client Mortgage Frauds' (1999) 13 Trust Law International 74, esp 81.

Lindsell on Torts, now includes extended treatment of the equitable wrongs of breach of confidence and breach of fiduciary duty although it has not opened the door to other equitable wrongs.[8] A rational account of the law of civil wrongs cannot confine itself to torts.[9]

In order to present a more coherent picture here of the operation of civil wrongs **17.03** we therefore consider, alongside torts, those equitable wrongs that are motivated by identical concerns (such as deceit and negligence) as well as other breaches of duty in equity, namely breach of trust and fiduciary duty, dishonest assistance in a breach of trust or fiduciary duty, and breach of confidence.[10] In order to appreciate the operation of these civil wrongs, it is necessary to look to the structure and then to the scope of wrongdoing at both common law and equity together, although the emphasis will inevitably be on torts, which are the main corpus of English civil wrongs.

(1) Structure

(a) The legacy of history

At common law, the law of torts grew up without a unified structure.[11] The devel- **17.04** opment of the law of torts from the writ of trespass and the originally supplementary actions on the case created a list of wrongs. The list, alphabetic since no other classification was available, survived into the nineteenth century and continues to have a ghost life long after the abolition of the forms of action.[12] The forms of action, essentially set forms of winning propositions, were replaced by causes of action, essentially configurations of facts disclosing a right realizable in court. However, the names of the old forms of action continued to be used to describe the causes of action.

The English law of torts still appears to consist of a list of over seventy wrongs, **17.05** distinct though sometimes overlapping, each with its own name and conditions of liability.[13] The persistence of named torts is to some extent a matter of habit

---

Arguing for a single law of civil wrongs: P Birks, 'Civil Wrongs: A New World' *Butterworth Lectures 1990–91* (1992) 55; J Edelman *Gain-based Damages* (2002) ch 2.

[8] A Dugdale and M Jones (eds), *Clerk and Lindsell on Tort* (19th edn, 2006) ch 28 (breach of confidence), 577–582 (breach of fiduciary duty).

[9] A Burrows, 'We Do This At Common Law But That in Equity' (2002) 22 OJLS 1, 9.

[10] Claims for damages for breach of the Human Rights Act 1998 are considered in D Feldman (ed), *English Public Law* (2004) ch 19.

[11] JH Baker, *An Introduction to English Legal History* (4th edn, 2002) 401–465; D Ibbetson, *A Historical Introduction to the Law of Obligations* (1999) 39–70, 97–125, 153–87.

[12] The abolition of the forms of action was a three-stage process, in which the second stage, Common Law Procedure Act 1852, was decisive. JH Baker (n 11 above) 53–70, esp 67–69.

[13] BA Rudden, 'Torticles' (1991–92) 6/7 Tulane Civil Law Forum 105.

and convenience rather than substance. As Diplock LJ said in *Letang v Cooper*, 'when, since 1873, the name of a form of action is used to identify a cause of action, it is used as a convenient and succinct description of a particular category of factual situation which entitles one person to obtain from the court a remedy from another person'.[14]

17.06 However, the difference between one tort and another can still be a significant issue. The distinction between trespass and negligence survives for limitation of action purposes through a muddled legislative history; recent decisions of the House of Lords have discussed the limits of liability for torts in terms of the historical origins of particular torts and the appropriateness of using one tort rather than another.[15] In this sense, it is still true to say that at common law we have a law of torts rather than a law of tort.

17.07 In the years following the abolition of the forms of action, debate raged about the structure of the law of torts. Two prominent views emerged in the United States in the late nineteenth century. One view was that the law of torts should be structured around the invasion of particular rights such as rights to personal security (assault, battery, false imprisonment) or to real property (trespass to land and waste).[16] In contrast, a completely different approach was that the structure of the law of torts ought to be more general and focus upon the fault of the defendant. On this view, torts should be divided according to whether they are based on intentional acts, negligent acts or acts without any requirement of fault (strict liability).[17] The same debate occurred later in England with one group of leading torts scholars adopting the traditional, Blackstonian, view that the law of torts should be structured around the particular rights protected[18] and another arguing for a general principle of liability for fault.[19] Underlying these

---

[14] [1965] 1 QB 232, 243, CA.

[15] *Stubbings v Webb* [1993] AC 498, HL; *Hunter v Canary Wharf Ltd* [1997] AC 655, HL; *Cambridge Water Co Ltd v Eastern Counties Leather plc* [1994] 2 AC 264, HL; *Spring v Guardian Assurance plc* [1995] 2 AC 296, HL; *Gregory v Portsmouth City Council* [2000] 1 AC 419, HL.

[16] T Cooley *A Treatise on the Law of Torts or the Wrongs which arise Independent of Contract* (1880) chs 6, 10. Cooley was the Chief Justice of the Michigan Supreme Court.

[17] Anon, 'The Theory of Torts' (1872) 7 Am L Rev 652. Although the article is not signed, as Vandevelde has observed much of the language in the article appears in OW Holmes *The Common Law* (1889); K Vandevelde 'A History of the Prima Facie Tort: The Origins of a General Theory of Intentional Tort (1990) 19 Hoftstra L Rev 447. Holmes' biographer also attributes the article to Holmes: M Howe *Justice Oliver Wendell Holmes The Proving Years 1870–1882* (1963), 184.

[18] W Blackstone *Commentaries on the Laws of England* (1765), Book III. See J Salmond, *Torts* (2nd edn, 1910), 8–9; A Goodhart, 'The Foundations of Tortious Liability' (1938) 2 MLR 1.

[19] F Pollock, *The Law of Torts* (1887); P Winfield, *The Province of the Law of Tort* (1931), 32–39. One initial review of Pollock complained that 'the full extent of the fundamental [scientific] principle that a man is liable for all the consequences of his acts which as a reasonable man he ought to have foreseen...has not yet been thoroughly worked out by the courts': Anon (1886–1887) 12 Law Mag & L Rev 5th Ser 270, 275, 277.

two theories were deep questions about the nature of liability for civil wrongs. As we will see, English common law did not exclusively adopt either position but adopted a bi-focal structure with one group in which the torts focused upon the particular right which is infringed and another group in which the torts focused generally upon the fault of a defendant, irrespective of any infringement of a particular right.[20] As we will also see, concurrently with this common law development of the law of torts, the courts of Chancery independently developed the same structure for equitable wrongs.

(b) The place of negligence in the law of torts

The traditional Blackstonian structure of the law of torts was a common law picture of liability as based on a list of distinct nominate torts, reflecting infringements of particular rights. But that conceals the structure of modern tort law and especially the relationship between the tort of negligence and most of the other torts. Negligence, although correctly described as a tort, is 'innominate'. It does not, even obliquely, identify any particular right, or protected interest, because negligence describes a standard of liability. A secondary right to compensation arises where loss has been caused by the fault of the defendant. The general primary right is however cut back in particular circumstances. The same is true of deceit and other torts which focus on fraudulent intention of the defendant.[21] The focus of the general right to be treated without fault in negligence and deceit is on the blameworthy conduct of the defendant in causing harm. In other torts, the focus is on the particular right protected. Indeed most nominate torts are identified precisely as protecting a particular right, and the degree of desired protection thus dictates the rules of liability within the particular tort. **17.08**

Defamation protects reputation. Private nuisance protects the enjoyment of land. Conversion protects property rights in goods. Trespass to land protects property rights in land. In effect, therefore, the list of torts is a mixed list, with some wrongs defined in terms of protected rights and torts such as negligence or deceit potentially cutting across all protected nominate rights and belonging in a series in which the liability focuses upon principles of fault rather than particular rights. This is why the liability for the fault of a manufacturer who causes illness by carelessly leaving a snail in a bottle of ginger beer is naturally extended to the manufacturer that did so deliberately (*dolus*).[22] **17.09**

---

[20] Although one commentator has issued a cry for a return to a structure based solely on particular or nominate rights. See R Stevens *Torts and Rights* (2007).

[21] See paras 17.372–17.373.

[22] C Gearty, 'The Place of Nuisance in the Modern Law of Torts' [1989] CLJ 214, 223; Cane, *The Anatomy of Tort Law* (1997) 100. Deceit is considered in more detail at para 17.372.

17.10   All the nominate rights-based torts resist generalization. Negligence, by contrast, is capable of generalization and was the chief engine of the huge expansion of tort liability throughout most of the twentieth century. Negligence became the most wide-ranging of all forms of tort liability.[23] But the growth of negligence liability did more than expand the scope of that tort; it also had important effects on the rest of the law of torts, and indirectly on the law of contract. In some instances negligence has replaced older forms of liability: *Donoghue v Stevenson*[24] made the older category of chattels dangerous *per se* redundant.[25] More commonly, nominate torts were infiltrated by aspects of negligence. The *Wagon Mound*[26] test of remoteness of damage propounded as particularly appropriate for negligence is now applied to nominate torts once thought to turn on rules of strict liability.[27] Nuisance, though not absorbed by negligence, is now categorized as a form of fault-based liability.[28]

17.11   English law's tolerance of concurrent liability increases the difficulty of coherent classification.[29] A negligent defamatory statement in a reference causing economic loss may now be actionable as negligence or defamation;[30] a malicious defamatory statement may be actionable as defamation or malicious falsehood;[31] and an intentional deprivation of liberty may be actionable as false imprisonment or misfeasance in public office.[32] There may be very strong reasons why an action based on negligence might be preferred to one based upon a particular nominate right. In *Spring v Guardian Assurance plc*[33] an employer had written a reference which negligently proceeded on incorrect facts, thus prejudicing the employee's employment prospects. Within the tort of defamation this reference was clearly the subject of qualified privilege. Hence the employer could not

---

[23]   T Weir, 'The Staggering March of Negligence' in P Cane and J Stapleton (eds), *The Law of Obligations: Essays in Celebration of John Fleming* (1998) 97. A claim in negligence has become an almost invariable long stop behind other claims: 'Since *Anns v Merton London Borough Council* [1978] AC 728 put the floodgates on the jar, a fashionable plaintiff alleges negligence': *CBS Songs Ltd v Amstrad Consumer Electronics plc* [1988] AC 1013, 1059, HL, *per* Lord Templeman.

[24]   [1932] AC 562, HL.

[25]   *Griffiths v Arch Engineering Ltd* [1968] 3 All ER 217.

[26]   *Overseas Tankship (UK) Ltd v Morts Dock and Engineering Co Ltd (The Wagon Mound)* [1961] AC 388, PC.

[27]   *Overseas Tankship (UK) Ltd v Miller Steamship Co Pty Ltd (The Wagon Mound) (No 2)* [1967] 1 AC 617, PC; *Cambridge Water Co Ltd v Eastern Counties Leather plc* [1994] 2 AC 264, HL.

[28]   *Leakey v National Trust* [1980] QB 485, CA; *Overseas Tankship (UK) Ltd v Miller Steamship Co Pty Ltd (The Wagon Mound) (No 2)* [1967] 1 AC 617, PC.

[29]   *Henderson v Merrett Syndicates Ltd* [1985] 2 AC 145, HL, discussed in AS Burrows, *Understanding the Law of Obligations* (1998) 16–34.

[30]   *Spring v Guardian Assurance* [1995] 2 AC 296, HL.

[31]   *Joyce v Sengupta* [1993] 1 WLR 337, CA, but see also *Lonrho v Fayed (No 5)* [1993] 1 WLR 1489, CA.

[32]   *Karagozlu v Commissioner of Police of the Metropolis* [2006] EWCA Civ 1691; [2007] 2 All ER 1055, CA.

[33]   [1995] 2 AC 296, HL.

be liable in the absence of proof of malice.[34] However, the House of Lords held that this was a case in which, in the tort of negligence, the employer could be liable for the claimant's pure economic loss.

The overlap between liability for the infringement of particular protected rights **17.12** and liability for negligence has been extremely controversial. For instance, there is a dictum of Lord Phillips in the Court of Appeal in *D v East Berkshire NHS Trust*[35] which is flatly against what was allowed in *Spring v Guardian Assurance*. He said that there is no question of sidestepping the defence of qualified privilege by advancing a claim for defamation in the guise of a claim in negligence.[36] Concurrent liability in tort and contract, accepted and largely unproblematic in cases of negligence causing physical injury, has provoked controversy about the proper function of the law of torts where the loss is economic.[37] In these cases the extension of negligence appears to achieve results which the law of contract could not reach. In some views 'could not reach' means 'ought not to be reached', so that the new position in the law of tort directly negatives a considered position. There are, all in all, very few aspects of the law of obligations which have remained wholly unaffected by the principles of negligence, and not infrequently the cross-cutting intrusion of the tort of negligence has proved disruptive.

(2) Scope

(a) The scope of each group of civil wrongs

As Professor Lawson explained in 1951, and as we have seen, civil wrongs in **17.13** England historically divide into two groups. One group of civil wrongs consists of liability for harm caused by fault and another focuses upon infringements of particular rights.[38] In this respect English law is bifocal, like German law.[39] The largest, and most dominant, member of the first group of civil wrongs is the tort of negligence, although we have already seen that other prominent members are torts involving fraudulent intention, like deceit. The potentially broad scope of

---

[34] ibid 346.

[35] [2003] EWCA Civ 1151; [2004] QB 558, 594 [102], CA. There was no comment on this point on appeal to the House of Lords: *JD v East Berkshire Community Health NHS Trust* [2005] UKHL 23; [2005] 2 AC 373, HL.

[36] The claims in *D v East Berkshire NHS Trust* were for psychiatric harm resulting from false accusations of child abuse which, as Lord Phillips remarked, have the elements of defamation. Perhaps the extreme sensitivity of investigations into child abuse suffices to distinguish this case from the commercial world of the *Spring* case.

[37] *Henderson v Merrett Syndicates* [1995] 2 AC 145, HL; *Junior Books v Veitchi Co Ltd* [1983] 1 AC 520, HL; *White v Jones* [1995] 2 AC 207, HL.

[38] FH Lawson *The Rational Strength of English Law* (1951) 122–3.

[39] §823 of the *Bürgerliches Gesetzbuch* provides for delictual liability consequent upon infringement of protected interests whereas §826 focuses upon acts *contra bonos mores*.

the tort of negligence, and the underlying innominate (and general) right not to be subjected to loss by the carelessness of another, is constrained by a concept described as 'duty of care'.[40] Although negligence was also historically actionable in courts of Chancery, these duty of care rules were developed in more detail at common law.

17.14   The second group of wrongs, namely those concerned with particular rights, are a collection of causes of action, each made up of three main components: a particular right protected by the law, conduct affecting that right which the law sanctions, and a remedy by which the right is protected and the conduct sanctioned.[41] It is necessary to ask both whether a particular recognized right has been infringed, and also against what forms of infringing conduct protection is given. This second group of civil wrongs is therefore constrained by the need for a protected right and the required conduct which will suffice to amount to an infringement of the particular recognized right.

(b) Acts and omissions

17.15   In either group of cases, whether liability is based upon fault causing harm or upon the infringement of a particular right, the wrongful conduct may be either an act, a statement, or a failure to act. Liability for acts which cause damage to others is more general than liability for failure to take steps to prevent harm to others. Liability for failure to act is imposed only in particular circumstances or where there is a special relationship between the parties: 'There must be some special justification for imposing an obligation of this character. Compulsory altruism needs more justification than an obligation not to create dangers to others when acting for one's own purposes.'[42] Special considerations also limit liability for words, both in the general tort of negligence and in the torts of defamation, deceit, and malicious falsehood.

(c) Protected nominate rights

17.16   The list of protected nominate rights is not closed, but some rights are only given partial protection and others are not protected at all. English law has been criticized, for example, for its reluctance to recognize the invasion of privacy as an independent tort.[43] At the centre of the law of torts is the protection of persons

---

[40]   *Dorset Yacht Co Ltd v Home Office* [1969] 2 QB 412, 426, CA *per* Lord Denning MR.

[41]   P Cane, *The Anatomy of Tort Law* (1998) 1. The author examines each of the three components in chapters 2, 3, and 4, although he speaks of 'interests' rather than rights.

[42]   *Stovin v Wise* [1996] AC 923, 930, HL, *per* Lord Nicholls.

[43]   BS Markesinis, 'Subtle Ways of Legal Borrowing: Some Reflections on the Report of the Calcutt Committee "On Privacy and Related Matters"' in B Pfister and MR Will (eds), *Festschrift für Werner Lorenz zum Siebzigsten Geburtstag* (1991) 717–37, and 'Our Patchy Law of Privacy: Time To Do Something About It' (1990) 53 MLR 802. Cf BS Markesinis and SF Deakin, *Tort Law* (5th edn, 2003) 696–7. See further at paras 17.362–17.366.

from physical injury and, to a limited extent, from psychological harm, but other rights, such as civil liberty and reputation, are also protected. Torts are also the main source of civil remedies for physical damage to property and infringements of rights to possess or enjoy land or goods. Other rights, such as the right to confidential information, are protected by equity.

Both torts and equitable wrongs have a part in the protection of intellectual property and other commercial rights. Thus, a party to a contract has rights which are protected, not only in the law of contract, but also by the tort of inducing breach of contract.[44]   **17.17**

(d) Conduct amounting to infringement of nominate rights

Liability in modern English law for infringement of particular nominate rights can be based on fault but in some cases the liability for the infringement of a particular right is strict. Although there is usually reference to a requirement of 'intention', if the tort is protecting rights to the person, to property, liberty or reputation, 'intention' usually means no more than that the act is willed; trespass to goods, to land and to the person, defamation, conversion, detinue, assault and battery are all examples of strict liability torts where fault is irrelevant.[45] In equity, liability for breach of fiduciary duty is also strict. Vicarious liability, the liability of an employer for torts committed by his employees in the course of their employment although the employer is personally blameless, is a form of strict liability but the dominant view is that it is not a type of wrongdoing, for the employer is not conceived to have been in any breach of duty.   **17.18**

On the other hand, other particular rights such as the right to free enjoyment of land at common law or the right to confidential information in equity are only infringed when the defendant is at fault. Fault may be negligence or unreasonableness, which nowadays are both essentially the failure to observe community standards of behaviour, or it may arise from a culpable state of mind. Negligence is the general standard of fault liability in tort, corresponding to the French *faute* or Roman *culpa*.   **17.19**

---

[44] Running back to *Lumley v Gye* (1853) 2 E & B 216, 118 ER 749.

[45] See para 17.355 for discussion of 'intention'. Civilians on the whole prefer to avoid the term 'wrong' or any equivalent in order to admit the possibility of strict liability: C von Bar, *The Common European Law of Torts* (1998) 3. English law has had no difficulty in treating as a wrong any conduct which takes its consequences by virtue of its characterization as a breach of duty, even when that duty is so designed as to be broken even without fault: P Birks, 'The Concept of a Civil Wrong' in D Owen (ed), *Philosophical Foundations of Tort Law* (1997) 31; T Honoré, 'The Morality of Tort Law' ibid 73, 88–94.

(e) Remedies[46]

17.20   The routine consequence of a tort is that the victim acquires a right to a money award, which is in general called damages and is usually a right to compensation.[47] However, a further aim of torts is to prevent, or to prevent repetition of, an injury. In some torts therefore, damages take second place to the remedy of an injunction, if damages are sought at all.[48] Torts can also be used to determine title to, or to obtain restitution of, chattels or land.[49] Other remedies of a self-help kind are available in some torts but not encouraged.

17.21   The principal remedy for torts is an award of damages. Some torts are actionable only if harm is caused, others are actionable without proof of damage (*per se*).[50] The distinction is an accident of history but can be rationalized. Torts actionable without proof of damage are either torts where damage can be presumed, or they are torts whose function is to protect particular rights from any invasion, whether or not damage has resulted. Nominal damages may be given to signify that a right has been invaded although no harm has been done.

17.22   The main measure and purpose of damages, and one of the principal aims of the law of torts, is to compensate for harm. Damages to punish and deter wrongdoing are currently exceptional. However, English law has never unequivocally embraced the dogma that the law of civil wrongs must concern itself solely with compensation for losses.[51] It will be very difficult, without distortion, to accommodate English law to Professor von Bar's vision of this area of law as pursuing the single goal of compensation for loss.[52]

17.23   The American, and indeed the Roman, experience shows that a purely compensatory law of civil wrongs is not a jurisprudential necessity but simply a choice made by particular systems at particular times. Professor Cane correctly says

---

[46] For a full account of remedies see Chapter 21.

[47] It is not usual to refer to gain-based awards in equity as 'damages': *Watson v Holliday* (1882) 20 Ch D 780, affirmed (1883) 52 LJ Ch 543, CA although the phrase 'gain-based damages' is sometimes used to describe these awards, particularly when they are made at common law: see J Edelman *Gain-based Damages* (2002).

[48] *Regan v Paul Properties Ltd* [2006] EWCA Civ 1319, CA. See also paras 21.207–21.211.

[49] See para 17.318–17.320.

[50] The interplay between 'damage', which is harm done, and 'damages', which is the award made, is inescapable.

[51] It is undeniable that gain-based awards are regularly made for wrongs: see J Edelman *Gain-based Damages* (2002) and paras 21.142–21.160. However, the House of Lords has twice endeavoured to commit the law to the proposition that all measures of recovery other than compensation for loss are anomalous: *Rookes v Barnard* [1964] AC 1129, HL; *Cassell & Co v Broome* [1972] AC 1027, HL. But the speech of Lord Wilberforce in the latter case rightly shows that English law has been more pragmatic. See also Law Commission, *Aggravated, Exemplary and Restitutionary Damages* (Law Com No 247, 1997).

[52] C von Bar, *The Common European Law of Torts* (1998) 2.

that, in the common law, the law of torts is to be regarded as 'a system of ethical rules and principles of personal responsibility'.[53] Where the compensatory aim achieves an exclusive hegemony, the welfare role of tort squeezes out this normative role. The normativity of tort is represented, at the level of damages, by exemplary and gain-based damages. Indeed, for equitable wrongdoing the right to compensation– which is rarely called damages although it amounts to the same thing[54]– has historically been regarded as more exceptional than gain-based awards such as an account of profits.

B. Negligence: Basic Concepts

In an analysis of states of mind, negligence contrasts with intention. Negligence **17.24** means blameworthy inadvertence. At common law and in equity, however, negligence is usually a description of conduct rather than of a mental state. It is conduct which fails to conform to a required standard of care. However, not all negligent conduct gives rise to liability, nor is liability, where it exists, unlimited. The common law tort of negligence has been subject to considerably more development and scrutiny than its equitable counterpart. For this reason, the focus on negligence in this chapter is upon the tort of negligence, although we will see that the negligence can also be actionable in equity.[55]

The boundaries of liability for the tort of negligence are drawn by the three prin- **17.25** cipal elements of the tort, a duty of care, breach of that duty, and damage caused by that breach. The defences to actions for negligence then impose further limits. Negligence is tortious, and liability will follow, if it is a breach of a duty of care owed to the claimant which has caused damage of an actionable kind, subject to defences. This reasonably straightforward sentence provides the programme for the exposition which follows.

---

[53] P Cane, *The Anatomy of Tort Law* (1998) 1. Compare also JM Kelly, 'The Inner Nature of the Tort Action' (1967) 2 Ir Jur (NS) 279 and the judgment of Windeyer J in *Uren v John Fairfax & Sons Pty Ltd* (1967) 117 CLR 118, 148, both of which maintain that the law of tort has to do much more than distribute compensation for losses.

[54] *Bartlett v Barclays Bank Trust Co Ltd (No 2)* [1980] Ch 515, CA (Brightman LJ)'not readily distinguishable from damages except with the aid of a powerful judicial microscope'. See also P Birks, 'Civil Wrongs: A New World' *Butterworth Lectures 1990–91* (1992). This view is defended in J Edelman 'Gain-based Damages and Compensation' in A Burrows and A Rodger (ed) *Mapping the Law: Essays in Honour of Peter Birks* (2006) ch 8.

[55] *Henderson v Merrett Syndicates Ltd* [1995] 2 AC 145, 205, HL, *per* Lord Browne-Wilkinson; *Bristol and West Building Society v Mothew* [1998] Ch 1, 16–18, CA, *per* Millett LJ; *Hilton v Barker Booth Eastwood* [2005] UKHL 8, [29], HL, *per* Lord Walker.

(1) Duty of Care

17.26 The duty of care is the main conceptual device for expressing the limits on liability for negligence. The inquiry into the duty of care operates at two levels. First, it answers the general question whether there can in principle be a right not to be subjected to loss by carelessness in the kind of situation to which the particular facts belong. Secondly, it addresses the question whether on the particular facts the defendant did indeed owe a duty to the claimant. If he did, the first element of liability slots immediately into place. The existence of a duty of care is a question of law. Much of the historical importance of the duty concept lies in its use to control the growth of the tort and determine its frontiers at a time when issues of fact were tried by juries.[56]

17.27 By way of example, a question can be formulated whether there is any duty of care in respect of words spoken or written (a) if the words cause physical damage (as by causing the person addressed to fall over a cliff) and (b) if they cause the person addressed to lose some money (as by investing badly). That question is probing the frontiers of the tort of negligence. We might instead ask, very bluntly, 'Can a person be liable for negligent statements?' The way in which an inquiry of that kind is put in the law of negligence is always to ask whether there is, in the given circumstances, a duty of care.

(a) The neighbour principle

17.28 The modern approach has roots running back to the seventeenth century,[57] but nowadays it may for all practical purposes be regarded as founded on Lord Atkin's formulation of the neighbour principle in *Donoghue v Stevenson*.[58] The question in that case was whether, if a person became ill through consuming contaminated food (here ginger beer contaminated by the remains of a snail), an action in negligence could lie against the manufacturer. By a majority the House of Lords held that it could. Lord Atkin's approach was to assemble the fragments of the nineteenth century law of negligence under one principle:

> [I]n English law there must be, and is, some general conception of relations giving rise to a duty of care, of which the particular cases found in the books are but instances.

---

[56] D Ibbetson, *A Historical Introduction to the Law of Obligations* (1999) 170–4.

[57] JH Baker, *Introduction to English Legal History* (4th edn, 2002) 410–11; D Ibbetson, *A Historical Introduction to the Law of Obligations* (1999) 164–74, 178–81, 188–93. Of particular interest and importance: (1) Buller's *Nisi Prius* (1767/1772) 36; (2) Sir William Jones, *Essay on the Law of Bailments* (1781) esp 6–8, 42–4, 66–8; (3) Chancery formulations of the duty of trustees from *Charitable Corporation v Sutton* (1742) 2 Atk 400, 406, 26 ER 642, 645 *per* Lord Hardwicke LC, to *Clough v Bond* (1838) 3 M & C 490, 496, 40 ER 1016, 1018 *per* Lord Cottenham LC; (4) Brett MR in *Heaven v Pender* (1883) 11 QBD 503, 509, CA.

[58] [1932] AC 562, HL. For the background, see A Rodger (Lord Rodger of Earlsferry), 'Mrs Donoghue and Alfenus Varus' (1988) 41 Current Legal Problems 1, and 'Lord Macmillan's Speech in *Donoghue v Stevenson*' (1992) 108 LQR 236.

The liability for negligence, whether you style it such or treat it as in other systems as a species of 'culpa', is no doubt based upon a general public sentiment of moral wrongdoing for which the offender must pay. But acts or omissions which any moral code would censure cannot in a practical world be treated so as to give a right to every person injured by them to demand relief. In this way rules of law arise which limit the range of complainants and the extent of their remedy. The rule that you are to love your neighbour becomes in law, you must not injure your neighbour; and the lawyer's question, Who is my neighbour? receives a restricted reply. You must take reasonable care to avoid acts or omissions which you can reasonably foresee would be likely to injure your neighbour. Who, then, in law is my neighbour? The answer seems to be—persons who are so closely and directly affected by my act that I ought reasonably to have them in contemplation as being so affected when I am directing my mind to the acts or omissions which are called in question.[59]

17.29 It is as well to say at once, though we shall have to return to the matter in greater detail below, that Lord Atkin knew very well that foreseeability could not itself be the single key to finding a duty of care. The whole structure of his speech shows that he regarded the passage quoted above as an open-textured principle formulated to hold together all the known islands of liability, and, further, that he never intended the general principle to be more than a guide to the interpretation and development of the specific rules of liability instantiated in the decided cases.[60] Lord Atkin would certainly have agreed with Professor Baker when he says:

> The definition in advance of all the situations in which a duty of care is owed to one's neighbour is impossible; and despite attempts to formulate a general rule, a policy decision has to be made whenever new cases arise. Indeed, over the course of time very different outer limits have been set to the notion of actionable wrong in the context of negligence. Although the 'neighbour' principle was voiced three centuries ago in words which might still be accepted today, in practice far fewer kinds of injury were then under its ambit.[61]

17.30 In this passage Baker encapsulates the notion, still essential to the understanding of the law of negligence, that a general principle can have a constant validity and utility even though, under varying social circumstances, it is likely to be realized in different ranges of liability. It is easy to suppose that, under the open-textured principle, the frontiers of liability constantly expand, but they can also contract.

---

[59] [1932] AC 562, 580, HL. The Biblical background will be apparent. In the Book of Leviticus it is laid down that we should love our neighbour as ourselves, and 'neighbour' is explicitly extended to 'alien': Lev 19.18, 33. Compare in the New Testament: Mt 22.38, 39; Mt 19.19; Rom 13.9; Gal 5.14; Jas 2.8. Lord Atkin's immediate reference is to the lawyer's question at Lk 10.29 and the answering parable of the Good Samaritan, Lk 10.30–37.

[60] Lord Atkin's understanding of the interpretative relationship between the general and the particular, essential to common law method, is brilliantly explained by Lord Devlin in *Hedley Byrne & Co Ltd v Heller & Partners Ltd* [1964] AC 465, 524, HL.

[61] Baker (n 11 above) 415.

(b) The onset of caution

17.31 Expansionist resort to the neighbour principle reached its apogee in the 1970s, at which time a lay observer might have been forgiven for thinking that the general principle had become an immediate rule of liability. In *Anns v Merton London BC*[62] Lord Wilberforce allowed himself to say:

> The position has now been reached that in order to establish that a duty of care arises in a particular situation, it is not necessary to bring the facts of that situation within those of previous situations in which a duty of care has been held to exist. Rather the question has to be approached in two stages. First one has to ask whether, as between the alleged wrongdoer and the person who has suffered damage there is a sufficient relationship of proximity or neighbourhood such that, in the reasonable contemplation of the former, carelessness on his part may be likely to cause damage to the latter—in which case a prima facie duty of care arises. Secondly, if the first question is answered affirmatively, it is necessary to consider whether there are any considerations which ought to negative, or to reduce or limit the scope of the duty or the class of person to whom it is owed or the damages to which a breach of it may give rise.[63]

17.32 That was the position to which earlier cases seemed to have arrived.[64] Nor could Lord Wilberforce's statement be faulted, since the second stage of his inquiry made evident room for eliminating any overkill implicit in the first. However, the prima facie liability established by the first inquiry seemed to give the law a dynamic in favour of constantly expanding the frontiers of liability. In consequence, in England, though not in other Commonwealth countries such as Canada and New Zealand, a reaction set in, which favours something approaching a return to the traditional approach in which the one tort of negligence is seen, less as a federation united by the neighbour principle, and more as a confederation of islands of liability, each with its own semi-independent regime.[65] This shift of emphasis was achieved in *Caparo Industries plc v Dickman*[66] and by a seven-judge decision of the House of Lords in *Murphy v Brentwood District Council*.[67] In the latter the *Anns* case was formally overruled, and the approach which it had adopted was repudiated.

---

62 [1978] AC 728, HL.

63 ibid 751–2.

64 Especially *Dorset Yacht Co v Home Office* [1970] AC 1004, 1027, HL *per* Lord Reid.

65 The two-stage *Anns* test was subsequently refined by the Supreme Court of Canada so that policy considerations relevant to the proximity between claimant and defendant could be recognized at the first stage: *Cooper v Hobart* [2001] SCC 79; [2001] 3 SCR 537, SCC.

66 [1990] 2 AC 605, HL.

67 [1991] 1 AC 398, HL; *Junior Books Co Ltd v Veitchi Co Ltd* [1983] 1 AC 520, HL, decided almost exactly 50 years after *Donoghue v Stevenson* [1932] AC 562, HL is widely thought to mark the limit of expansionism and to have been the trigger for the new caution.

Experience shows that the effect of this change of emphasis should not be exaggerated. It bears chiefly on the special areas which are discussed below,[68] and it chiefly means that the court is supposed to start on the other foot, assuming that there is no duty of care until a careful three-pronged inquiry has been made. The second and third of these inquiries are linguistically less than satisfactory since they do little more than encode, and obscure, the policy decision referred to by Professor Baker in the passage quoted above.[69]

17.33

(c) The three-pronged inquiry

The questions which the cases now ask are, first, whether the defendant should have foreseen harm to the claimant; secondly, whether there was a relationship of proximity between the claimant and the defendant; and, thirdly, whether it is fair, just, and reasonable that the defendant should owe a duty of care to the claimant.

17.34

(i) Foreseeability

The first condition for the existence of a duty of care remains that the defendant should be able to foresee that his conduct may cause injury, in the widest sense of that word, to the claimant. If no injury of any kind should be anticipated to the claimant, then no duty is owed to him. It is irrelevant that the defendant should have foreseen injury to a person other than the claimant. No one can found a claim on a duty of care owed to another person.[70]

17.35

Although a duty of care can arise towards a particular person by virtue of an assumption of responsibility for the interests of that person, in general there is no requirement that the defendant must have foreseen injury to the claimant as an individual person. Many duties of care arise in standard relationships, in which the beneficiaries of the duty form a class and the class happens to include the claimant. So, all users of the highway owe a duty of care to all other users, and all employers owe a duty of care to their employees. Where duties are owed to a certain class, there is no assumption that every member is a stereotypical representative of the community. So for example duties are owed to disabled people in situations in which it is likely that disabled people may be present.[71] Actual or

17.36

---

[68] Paras 17.87–17.196.

[69] Para 17.29.

[70] *Palsgraf v Long Island Railroad Co* 248 NY 339, 162 NE 99 (1928): a passenger tried to board a train as it was leaving the station, railwaymen assisting him caused him to drop a packet, which happened to contain fireworks. The fireworks exploded and caused a weighing machine to fall on P, who had innocently been waiting for her train to pull in on the next platform. It was not foreseeable to the railwaymen that what they were doing could injure P and they owed no duty to her. Cf *Bourhill v Young* [1943] AC 92, HL.

[71] *Haley v London Electricity Board* [1965] AC 778, HL.

imputed knowledge of a specific disability, such as an employer might be expected to have in relation to his employee, may extend the scope of the duty to that person.[72]

17.37 In situations in which negligent conduct is likely to cause physical injury or damage, to persons or property, foreseeability is almost invariably conclusive as to the existence of a duty of care. It should not be overlooked that in practice that one sentence covers the majority of cases that arise. The complexities which so trouble the courts arise on the periphery of that large area in which there is no doubt as to the existence of the duty of care.

17.38 This is why Roman law never needed the concept of a duty of care: its delict of wrongful loss (*damnum iniuria datum*) contemplated liability only for loss arising from physical damage. It is also, in part, the reason why, writing shortly after *Donoghue v Stevenson*, the great Romanist, WW Buckland, could describe the English requirement of a duty of care as 'the fifth wheel on the coach'.[73] In fact, however, it turns out that, even in the case of physical injuries, there are some cases in which foreseeability is not conclusive of duty.[74] The most obvious case is that in general there is, as it is always said, no duty to intervene to rescue a child drowning in one foot of water.[75]

(ii) Proximity

17.39 Lord Atkin himself said, in *Donoghue v Stevenson*, that liability for foreseeable injury was limited by the requirement of proximity.[76] Proximity was a requirement superadded to neighbourhood and, like neighbourhood, it was to be understood abstractly or metaphysically, not simply in terms of geographical propinquity. There must be some close connection between the parties. However, the impalpable nature of closeness when it is not confined to physical facts means that this requirement has become a perfect tool for hiding policy decisions in situations in which there is reason to be apprehensive about escalating and perhaps uninsurable liabilities. Physical damage, physically caused, sets its own limits. Once the law contemplates allowing liability to extend to loss which does not arise from physical injury or damage, these fears become real, and artificial restrictions are then understandably invoked.

---

[72] *Paris v Stepney Borough Council* [1951] AC 367, HL.
[73] WW Buckland, 'Duty to Take Care' (1935) 51 LQR 637, 639.
[74] Para 17.111 (psychiatric injury) and para 17.44 (wrongful life).
[75] *Stovin v Wise* [1996] AC 923, 930–1, HL, *per* Lord Nicholls. See para 17.89. Confidence in this proposition is waning, rightly. In WVH Rogers (ed), *Winfield and Jolowicz on Tort* (12th edn, 1984) 80, the child was left to drown. But in WVH Rogers (ed), *Winfield and Jolowicz on Tort* (17th edn, 2006) 170–182, the drowning child has gone, replaced by a much more subtle analysis.
[76] [1932] AC 562, 580–2, HL.

It is not surprising, therefore, to find that judges can themselves be puzzled by the **17.40** requirement of proximity and are occasionally willing to admit that it is indeed code for the pragmatic restriction of a worrying liability. In *Caparo Industries plc v Dickman*, Lord Bridge said that 'proximity' was one of those terms which:

> are not susceptible of any such precise definition as would be necessary to give them utility as practical tests, but amount in effect to little more than convenient labels to attach to the features of different specific situations which, on a detailed examination of all the circumstances, the law recognizes pragmatically as giving rise to a duty of care of a given scope.[77]

Psychiatric injury lies on the boundary of the physical. If, as is probably correct, **17.41** we count it as falling just inside that boundary, it is a species of physical injury which already awakens the kinds of anxiety associated with liability for non-physical losses. It is all too foreseeable that every crash will bring with it a wave of psychiatric harm. However, the policy of the common law is generally opposed to granting remedies to third parties for the effects of injuries to other people.[78] Television illustrates the possibility of the breadth of liability that would otherwise result. Millions may be traumatized by witnessing disaster. Hence, in such cases reliance is placed on the restrictive potential of the requirement of proximity. A relative of an accident victim can only recover for psychiatric injury if present at the scene of the accident or its immediate aftermath and, in addition, is one bound by ties of love and affection to the victim.[79]

Again, where loss is suffered through reliance on statements which turn out to be **17.42** untrue, there is the same danger of an escalating and disproportionate liability. Here the requirement of proximity is again invoked. Usually this is only satisfied where there is a voluntary assumption of responsibility to the party relying upon the statement.[80] There will be no proximity when the defendant has no direct control over a situation.[81] Nor is the relationship between the police and the class of all potential victims of a murderer or rapist proximate, with the effect that those who suffer at his hands cannot complain of his not having been caught earlier.[82]

---

[77] [1990] 2 AC 605, 618, HL, cf 633 *per* Lord Oliver. For defences of proximity see A Kramer, 'Proximity as principles: Directness, community norms and the tort of negligence' (2003) 11 Tort L Rev 70, C Witting (2005) 25 OJLS 33.

[78] *JD v East Berkshire Community Health NHS Trust* [2005] UKHL 23; [2005] 2 AC 373, 410–12 [100]–[105], HL *per* Lord Rodger.

[79] See paras 17.111ff.

[80] A requirement first recognized in *Hedley Byrne & Co Ltd v Heller & Partners Ltd* [1964] AC 465, HL. See further paras 17.171–17.181.

[81] *Sutradhar v Natural Environment Research Council* [2006] UKHL 33; [2006] 4 All ER 490, [38], HL. See also para 17.152.

[82] *Hill v Chief Constable of West Yorkshire* [1989] AC 53, HL; *Brooks v Commissioner of Police for the Metropolis* [2005] UKHL 24; [2005] 1 WLR 1495, HL.

(iii) Fair, just and reasonable

17.43   Given the all-embracing and manipulable nature of 'proximity', there seems little room for any further requirement, and some judges have clearly regarded the third inquiry as superfluous.[83] There are, however, cases in which even foreseeability and proximity would not suffice to impose a duty of care. Such cases have usually concerned arguments for limiting the duties of public authorities,[84] but they can turn on commercial considerations[85] or, again, on considerations of distributive justice.[86]

17.44   The law relating to wrongful life is also probably best explained under this sub-head. At common law, there is a recognized duty to the child *in utero* to take care not to harm it.[87] However, the child can bring no action for failure to terminate the pregnancy—that is, no action for wrongful life.[88] The duty is not negatived for want of foreseeability or proximity but first, difficult quantification problems aside, because to allow the action would be inconsistent with the sanctity of life and, secondly, because it was beyond the power of reason to conceive of a duty owed to a person to terminate that person's existence, so that the duty of care could not include a duty to terminate. To these reasons must be added the intolerable burden upon doctors and others in giving abortion advice under the threat of civil liability.[89] These reasons operated at common law, but the Congenital Disabilities

---

[83] *Caparo Industries plc v Dickman* [1990] 2 AC 605, 633, HL, *per* Lord Oliver; *Stovin v Wise* [1996] AC 923, 931–3, HL, *per* Lord Nicholls.

[84] *Hill v Chief Constable of West Yorkshire* [1989] AC 53, HL; *X (Minors) v Bedfordshire CC* [1995] 2 AC 633, HL. Loose use of 'fair, just and reasonable' to deny any duty of care towards parents and children on the part of child protection authorities has had to be revised in the aftermath of *Osman v UK* (1998) 5 BHRC 293, ECHR and in the light of the incorporation of the Convention by the Human Rights Act 1998, so that it is now accepted that a common law duty of care is owed to the children. However, one reason why it is not owed to the parents, whose lives stand in equal danger of being ruined when such interventions go wrong, is that it would create a conflict of interest incompatible with the paramountcy of the interests of the children: *JD v East Berkshire Community Health NHS Trust* [2005] UKHL 23; [2005] 2 AC 373, HL. See also *B v Attorney General of New Zealand* [2003] UKPC 61; [2003] 4 All ER 833, PC.

[85] *Marc Rich & Co AG v Bishop Rock Marine Co Ltd (The Nicholas H)* [1996] 1 AC 211, HL.

[86] *Frost v Chief Constable of South Yorkshire* [1999] 2 AC 455, HL. The immunity of advocates from suits in professional negligence provided another example of the exclusion of a duty of care on the grounds of public policy. A duty of care was thought to be inimical to the public interest in eliminating impediments to the smooth and reliable running of the process of litigation and adjudication. However, the House of Lords held that in modern conditions the exclusion of a duty of care can no longer be justified: *Arthur JS Hall & Co v Simons* [2002] 1 AC 615, HL. Three years later, the High Court of Australia, by a majority of 6 to 1, reached the opposite conclusion: *D'Orta-Ekenaike v Victoria Legal Aid* [2005] HCA 12, (2005) 223 CLR 1, HCA. New Zealand followed England in preference to Australia: *Chamberlains v Lai* [2006] NZSC 70, NZSC.

[87] *Burton v Islington Health Authority* [1993] QB 204, CA.

[88] *McKay v Essex Area Health Authority* [1982] QB 1166, CA: the court held that a duty to terminate could not be owed to a child deformed because its mother had rubella. See also *Harriton v Stephens* [2006] HCA 15, HCA.

[89] Law Commission, *Injuries to Unborn Children* (Law Com No 60, 1974) para 89.

(Civil Liability) Act 1976 comes to the same conclusion:[90] the Act requires the court to assume that the child would have been born healthy, not that it would not have been born at all.[91] Similar considerations of fairness, justice and reasonableness also explain why, although a duty to terminate can be owed to a parent,[92] no such duty is imposed on doctors, who undertake the sterilization of adults, in respect of the expenses involved in the subsequent arrival of a healthy child.[93] A doctor's liability for a failed sterilization is limited to an award for the pain and suffering of the birth as well as a fixed conventional award of £15,000 to reflect the injury to the sexual and developmental autonomy of the parents.[94]

(iv) Summary

Most cases involve straightforward physical injury to persons or damage to property caused by the defendant's activity. In such cases the neighbour principle applies and a duty of care results. On the periphery of that core, where there is physical harm but not of a straightforward kind or where the harm consists in pure economic loss without physical injury or damage, the second and third phases of the inquiry become prominent. And, in addition, some weight is given to the desire not to extend the law beyond the liabilities recognized in the past. There is not and there cannot be a single test for the existence of a duty of care. Professor Stapleton has identified a menu of duty factors.[95] In broad terms it can be said that, in the awkward periphery, the existence and the scope of a duty require consideration of the parties by whom and to whom the duty may be owed, the conduct in respect of which the duty is to be owed, and the kind of harm in

17.45

---

[90] A disabled child born after the Act's commencement may rely on this Act to sue the person responsible, though not the mother unless the cause arose from her driving a motor vehicle—an exception created to give the child the benefit of the compulsory motor insurance regime. It has been recommended that a general rule be applied to both parents restricting claims against them to those in respect of which there is compulsory insurance: *Royal Commission on Civil Liability and Compensation for Personal Injury* (1978) Cmnd 7054–1 vol 1, paras 1471, 1472.

[91] Congenital Disabilities (Civil Liability) Act 1976, s 1(1), (2).

[92] *Rance v Mid-Downs Health Authority* [1991] QB 587.

[93] *McFarlane v Tayside Health Board* [2000] 2 AC 59, HL. This exclusion of a duty of care extends to lost earnings on the part of the mother (*Greenfield v Irwin* [2001] EWCA Civ 113; [2001] 1 WLR 1279, CA). The exclusion probably does not extend to expenses of caring for a disabled child which arise because of the disability (*Parkinson v St James and Seacroft University Darlington Memorial Hospital NHS Trust* [2001] EWCA Civ 530; [2002] QB 266, CA: the correctness of which was doubted by Lords Bingham and Scott but affirmed by Lords Nicholls, Hope and Hutton in *Rees v Darlington Memorial Hospital NHS Trust* [2003] UKHL 52; [2004] 1 AC 309 [9], [147], [35], [57], [91], HL).

[94] *Rees v Darlington Memorial Hospital NHS Trust* [2003] UKHL 52; [2004] 1 AC 309, HL. The High Court of Australia, by a majority of 4:3 took the opposite view that the parents could recover the whole cost of the upbringing of the unwanted child: *Cattanach v Melchior* (2003) 215 CLR 1. Most Australian States passed legislation shortly thereafter to reverse this decision.

[95] J Stapleton, 'Duty of Care Factors: A Selection from the Judicial Menus' in P Cane and J Stapleton (eds), *The Law of Obligations, Essays in Celebration of John Fleming* (1999) 59.

respect of which it is to be owed. But this is hardly more helpful than saying that all relevant matters and arguments must be considered. The function of the three-pronged test is to provide a framework for the discussion and thus to group the arguments which may be deployed.

(2) Breach

(a) The traditional standard at common law

17.46 The standard by which negligence is judged at common law has traditionally been regarded as an objective one. It was negligent to fail to take the care expected by the community for the activity in question. The personification of community standards was simply the reasonable man, the man on the Clapham omnibus, more recently the commuter in the underground.[96]

17.47 What a reasonable person would do in the circumstances was, to some extent, a question of fact on which evidence could be given. Expert evidence, evidence of trade or professional practice, and regulations such as the highway code, could all give factual content to the standard of care, but in the last resort it was the court that decided what was reasonable in the circumstances.

17.48 *Nettleship v Weston* demonstrates the traditional approach.[97] The court there held that a learner driver on her third lesson was negligent if she failed to display the competence of an experienced driver. The whole court agreed that this was the standard required with regard to other highway users. Lord Denning's view was that the application of the objective standard to learners was simply an allocation of risk in an activity covered by compulsory insurance. Megaw LJ preferred to say that varying standards would make the law too complicated.

17.49 The reasonable person was intended to represent the average citizen but, since he was the judicial idea of the average citizen, there was undoubtedly a tendency to think that the reasonable person has rather high standards of care. Moreover, the more the law of tort moved towards becoming an insurance-based compensation system, the more prudent and far-sighted the reasonable person became.

(b) Tailoring the standard to the circumstances of the defendant

17.50 The reasonable person at common law was not always entirely divorced from the circumstances of the defendant. Consideration of the defendant's circumstances was permitted in cases of those who, from mental illness, had no understanding

---

[96] *McFarlane v Tayside Health Board* [2000] 2 AC 59, 82, HL, *per* Lord Steyn. An early formulation of negligence as guided by the conduct of the reasonable man is *Blyth v Birmingham Waterworks Co* (1856) 11 Ex 781, 784, 156 ER 1047, 1049, *per* Alderson B.
[97] [1971] 2 QB 691, CA.

of what they were doing,[98] and for children, from whom it was required only that such care be taken as could reasonably be expected of a child of that age.[99] But these exceptions were traditionally narrow. In most cases it was thought that a defendant could not hope to plead his personal failings of knowledge or skill to avoid paying compensation for damage he has caused. It was no defence that he was doing his incompetent best. The defendant was measured against the external standard of the reasonable person and no account was taken of the fact that he might be incapable of reaching it. The conflict between a standard of care focusing purely on the reasonable person and a standard focussed on the reasonable person with the attributes of the defendant, was first recognized by the Romans who labelled the first *culpa levis in abstracto* and the second *culpa levis in concreto*. The contrast is not between different levels of duty. The concrete duty might be higher or lower than the abstract one depending upon the ability of the defendant. Rather, the contrast is between different ways of proving fault.

In the case of equitable wrongs there were more significant departures from the abstract standard than the traditional position at common law. A company director was expected by courts of equity to exercise the standard of care of a reasonable person with his or her level of skill and experience.[100] On the other hand, trustees were expected to live up to the standard that an ordinary person would exercise in making an investment for a person for whom he felt morally obliged to provide. No provision was made for the trustee who had a lower level of experience or skill than was ordinary.[101] **17.51**

More recently common law cases have also begun to depart from the purely abstract notion of the reasonable man. In *Wilsher v Essex Area Health Authority*[102] a junior doctor was held not to be negligent for mistakenly inserting an umbilical catheter into a baby's vein, although a senior doctor was negligent for failing to **17.52**

---

[98] *Morriss v Marsden* [1952] 1 All ER 925, a claim for battery, but Stable J took the rule to be of general application. See also *Mansfield v Weetabix Ltd* [1998] 1 WLR 1263, CA.

[99] *Mullin v Richards* [1998] 1 WLR 1304, CA.

[100] *Lagunas Nitrate Co v Lagunas Syndicate* [1899] 2 Ch 392, 435, CA *per* Lindley MR; *Re City Equitable Fire Insurance Co* [1925] 1 Ch 407, 428–9; an appeal to the Court of Appeal was dismissed and this point was not addressed: [1925] 1 Ch 501, CA. In *Re D'Jan of London Ltd* [1993] BCC 646, CA, Hoffmann LJ held that the standard should mirror that in the *Insolvency Act* 1986 s 214(4) and should require satisfaction of both the concrete and abstract standards.

[101] *Speight v Gaunt* (1883) LR 9 App Cas 1, 4 *per* Selborne LC, 19 *per* Lord Blackburn, 33 *per* Lord Fitzgerald, HL; *Re Whiteley* (1886) 33 ChD 347, CA; *Nestle v National Westminster Bank plc* [1993] 1 WLR 1260, 1267, CA. It is unlikely that the duty enshrined in the *Trustee Act* 2000 s1(1), namely 'such care and skill as is reasonable in the circumstances' has changed this position since the circumstances include 'special knowledge or experience that it is reasonable to expect of a person acting in the course of that kind of business' (s1(1)(b)).

[102] [1987] 2 WLR 425, CA. Reversed on other grounds [1988] AC 1074, HL.

notice this error. Only Glidewell LJ thought that the junior doctor should be judged by a purely objective standard for the profession.[103] In contrast, Mustill LJ considered that the duty of care should be confined to the post assumed by the doctor. Browne-Wilkinson V-C posed a test which was tailored most closely to the circumstances of the defendant. His Lordship said that a court should consider the experience and knowledge of the particular doctor, explaining that doctors at the beginning of a post have less experience than those at the end; they cannot be held at fault for failing to meet a standard attainable only by experience. There was no suggestion by either Browne-Wilkinson V-C or Mustill LJ, or any factual basis to conclude, that the junior doctor had held himself out to the baby's parents as having only limited medical experience.[104]

17.53 There are signs that the more concrete approach of Browne-Wilkinson VC will prevail. In a recent decision of the House of Lords, concerning whether an advocate was negligent, two Law Lords (with whom another two agreed) held that advice given by the advocate was 'within the range of that to be expected of reasonably competent counsel of the appellant's seniority and purported experience.'[105] There could be no justification for a different approach to the standard of care expected of a plumber or a builder. Indeed, some cases have gone even further and considered not merely the reasonable person with the defendant's skill and experience but even the financial means of the defendant. In *Goldman v Hargrave*, the defendant occupier was liable for failure to protect his neighbour from natural disasters emanating from his land, although the physical and material resources of the defendant were relevant to a finding of negligence, since 'the law must take account of the fact that the occupier on whom the duty is cast has, ex hypothesi, had this hazard thrust upon him through no seeking or fault of his own.'[106] The Court of Appeal took the same view in another natural disaster case:

> The criteria of reasonableness include, in respect of a duty of this nature, the factor of what the particular man—not the average man—can be expected to do, having regard, amongst other things, where a serious expenditure of money is required to eliminate or reduce the danger, to his means.[107]

---

[103] Even this abstract approach could involve very difficult questions. What is the standard of care for the practitioner of traditional Chinese medicine? *Shakoor v Situ* [2001] 1 WLR 410.

[104] Cf *Herrington v British Railways Board* [1972] AC 877, 899, HL.

[105] *Moy v Pettmann Smith (a firm)* [2005] UKHL 7; [2005] 1 WLR 581, 601 [62], HL, *per* Lord Carswell. See also at 588 [22], *per* Lord Hope; *Contra* Baroness Hale at 589 [25]. See also *Vowles v Evans* [2003] EWCA Civ 318; [2003] 1 WLR 1607, 1618 [28], CA (volunteer referee cannot reasonably be expected to show the same level of skill as expert referee).

[106] [1967] 1 AC 645, 663–4, PC, *per* Lord Wilberforce.

[107] *Leakey v National Trust* [1980] 1 QB 485, 526, CA, *per* Megaw LJ.

There is also further indication that the defendant's resources should be consid- **17.54** ered in other situations where the law imposes a duty to take positive action to protect others.[108]

(c) A higher standard where special skills are professed

If the defendant professes to have particular skills, at both common law and equity **17.55** he is judged by the standard which would have been exercised by a reasonable person with the knowledge and skills professed, regardless of his actual expertise or experience.[109] There is much detailed law on these matters to be found in the relevant specialist work, be it medical law or construction law. There may be an initial question as to which trade or professional standard is the one professed. A prison hospital, for instance, is a subsidiary part of an institution with other functions, and cannot be expected to have the same resources as a hospital whose specialized function is the treatment of mental illness.[110] Similarly, and a matter not considered in *Wilsher*, a difficult question is whether an inexperienced defend-ant who remains silent about his experience, holds himself out as having the level of skill of the ordinary person in that profession or trade.

An exclusionary test which demonstrates attainment of the standard of care **17.56** required of the medical profession, or any other person professing some skill or competence, is the *Bolam* test.[111] In the *Bolam* case McNair J laid down that a doctor:

> is not guilty of negligence if he has acted in accordance with a practice accepted as proper by a responsible body of medical men skilled in that particular art. . .merely because there is a body of opinion who would take a contrary view.[112]

Recent reformulations have emphasized that the body of professional opinion **17.57** must be respectable and reasonable as well as responsible.[113] The court must be satisfied that the body of opinion relied on has a logical basis and that, in forming their views, the experts have weighed the comparative risks and benefits and reached a defensible conclusion on the matter. Legal professional opinions can

---

[108] *Smith v Littlewoods* [1987] AC 241, 269, HL, *per* Lord McKay; *Stovin v Wise* [1996] AC 923, 933, HL, *per* Lord Nicholls.

[109] The classic statement in equity is of Brightman J in *Bartlett v Barclays Bank Trust Co Ltd (No 1)* [1980] Ch 515, 534. See now *Trustee Act* 2000 s1(1). At common law see *Chaudhry v Prabhakar* [1989] 1 WLR 28, CA.

[110] *Knight v Home Office* [1990] 3 All ER 237.

[111] *Bolam v Friern Hospital Management Committee* [1957] 1 WLR 582, 587.

[112] ibid.

[113] *Bolitho v City & Hackney Health Authority* [1998] AC 232, 241–2, HL.

also be held to be wrong although judges must be careful not to decide the case on the basis of what they would have done.[114]

17.58 Particularly in medical cases, the state of knowledge at the time may be important. The question is whether the defendant acted reasonably in the light of what was known then, not what is known now.[115] A doctor's duties include warning the patient of the inevitable risks of treatment. In England the extent of the duty to warn is also a matter of professional judgment, subject to the overall control of the court.[116]

(d) Costs and risks

17.59 What reasonable care requires in a given situation is often to be ascertained by weighing in the balance four considerations: the likelihood that the activity in question will cause damage, the likely severity of the damage if it occurs, the difficulty and expense of averting the danger and, in appropriate cases, the value to society of the activity undertaken.[117] If, therefore, damage although foreseeable is very unlikely to happen, it may well not be negligent to fail to take steps to avoid it.[118] But if even an unlikely risk can be eliminated without difficulty or expense, and particularly if the damage is likely to be severe if it does occur, the reasonable man would take the necessary steps.[119]

17.60 When considering the severity of the likely damage, it is relevant that the defendant knows or ought to know that the damage will be particularly severe to a particular person; for example, to an employee known to have only one eye.[120] The reasonable man also takes into account the likely presence of persons with reasonably common disabilities.[121] The importance of the object to be attained may be an important factor. It is justifiable to perform a highly dangerous operation if it

---

[114] *Edward Wong Finance Co Ltd v Johnson, Stokes and Master* [1984] AC 296, PC. For the warning about judges deciding cases see *Moy v Pettmann Smith (a firm)* [2005] UKHL 7; [2005] 1 WLR 581, 587–8 [19], HL, *per* Lord Hope.

[115] *Roe v Minister of Health* [1954] 2 QB 66, CA.

[116] *Sidaway v Royal Bethlem Hospital* [1985] AC 871, HL. Contrast the position in Australia: *Rogers v Whittaker* (1992) 175 CLR 479, HCA.

[117] The first three considerations constitute the 'Learned Hand formula'. Justice Learned Hand said that a breach of duty would occur when 'B<PL', ie where the Burden of taking care was less than the Probability multiplied by the gravity of the Loss: *US v Carroll Towing Co* 159 F 2d 169, 173 (2d Cir 1947). In *Conway v O'Brien* 111 F 2d 611, 612 (2d Cir 1940) he admitted that this formula could not really be reduced to anything like mathematical precision. The Learned Hand calculus is not expressly adopted in England but there is little difference in approach.

[118] *Bolton v Stone* [1951] AC 850, HL.

[119] *Wagon Mound (No 2)* [1967] 1 AC 617, PC. Cf *Tomlinson v Congleton BC* [2003] UKHL 47; [2004] 1 AC 46, HL, discussed at para 17.191.

[120] *Paris v Stepney BC* [1951] AC 367, HL.

[121] *Haley v London Electricity Board* [1965] AC 778, HL.

is the only chance of saving life,[122] provided that other lives are not thereby threatened.[123]

(e) Proof of negligence

As in all civil cases, the burden of proving negligence, and of proving that the neg- **17.61** ligence caused or contributed to damage, lies on the claimant. The standard of proof required in civil cases is the balance of probabilities. The claimant has to show that it is more probable than not that the defendant was negligent and caused or contributed to the damage.

The general rules of evidence in civil cases apply. Two aspects of the law of evi- **17.62** dence particularly concern the law of tort. The first is the Civil Evidence Act 1968, section 11, which permits evidence of a criminal conviction to be admitted in civil proceedings to show that the person committed the offence, unless the contrary is proved. The section, therefore, creates only a presumption which can be rebutted by, for example, new evidence which shows that the conviction was wrong.

The second presumption is a presumption of negligence arising from the cir- **17.63** cumstances: *res ipsa loquitur* (the matter speaks for itself). If the accident which injured the claimant is one which does not usually happen unless someone has been negligent, and the claimant can show that the event causing damage was under the control of the defendant or his employees, then, in the absence of an explanation, the court may presume that the defendant was negligent. Both the leading authorities concerned claimants who were injured while walking in Victorian London by objects falling from premises occupied by the defendant.[124] The presumption arises only where the cause of the accident is not known. Whether the accident is one which does not normally happen without negligence is a matter for the judge.

There has been controversy about the level of explanation by the defendant **17.64** required to rebut the presumption. It is obviously sufficient for the defendant to prove how the accident happened or, if that is unknown, to prove that he was not negligent. If the defendant cannot prove either the cause or the absence of negli- gence, there is some suggestion that the claimant should win; that is, that the pre- sumption operates to shift the burden of proof. But that would put claimants with no evidence in a better position than those with some evidence. The orthodox view is that it is sufficient for the defendant to produce a reasonable alternative

---

[122] *Baker v TE Hopkins & Sons Ltd* [1959] 1 WLR 966, CA. See also Compensation Act 2006, s 1.

[123] *Ward v LCC* [1938] 2 All ER 341.

[124] *Byrne v Boadle* (1863) 2 H & C 722, 159 ER 299; *Scott v London & St Katherine Docks Co* (1865) 3 H & C 596, 159 ER 665.

explanation of the accident: that the accident could have happened without his negligence. This is probably the current position.[125]

17.65 It is in the nature of the presumption that it applies only in commonplace situations where evidence of negligence is hardly required. It might therefore be said to be no presumption at all, evidence of facts being in itself evidence of the negligence. The Supreme Court of Canada has indeed decided that the presumption serves no useful purpose in modern law.[126]

(3) Damage

17.66 Once it is established that a defendant was under a duty of care and was in breach of that duty, it remains for the claimant to establish that he has suffered relevant damage. Relevant damage is damage caused by the breach of duty. However, since there is no end to the causes of causes, there has to be some cut-off. Hence, damage which is caused by the breach may yet be too remote. Causation and remoteness are therefore the principal matters to be considered under this head.

(a) Causation

17.67 Negligence is only actionable if it causes damage. Duties of care are duties to avoid causing damage. Sometimes the duty is cut down, so as to be a duty to avoid causing only a particular kind of damage. It is for the claimant to prove that the defendant's breach of duty caused the damage of which he complains. It is not necessary to show that the defendant was the sole, or even the major, cause so long as he proves that but for the defendant's negligence the damage would not have happened. Difficult problems arise where there are multiple possible causes.

(i) The 'but for' test

17.68 The general test of causation is the 'but for' test. If the injury to the claimant would not have occurred but for the negligence of the defendant, that negligence is an operative cause.[127] The 'but for' rule is adequate for simple cases. More difficult causation problems require more elaborate solutions. For instance, recovery

---

[125] *Ng Chun Pui v Lee Chuen Tat* [1988] RTR 298, PC.

[126] *Fontaine v Loewen Estate* [1998] 1 SCR 424; (1997) 156 DLR, 4th, 181, SCC, on which see M McInnes, 'The Death of *Res Ipsa Loquitur* in Canada' (1998) 114 LQR 547.

[127] *Barnett v Chelsea and Kensington Hospital Management Committee* [1969] 1 QB 428; *Performance Cars Ltd v Abraham* [1962] 1 QB 33, CA. Reforming causation to recognize that 'but for' is simply one way of proving the test for causation, namely where the breach of duty is 'historically involved' as a factor in the damage suffered, is powerfully advocated by Professor Stapleton: J Stapleton 'Cause-in-Fact and the Scope of Liability for Consequences' (2003) 119 LQR 388.

will be denied although the 'but for' test is apparently satisfied, in cases where the injury arises by coincidence. Examples include a taxi that is hit by a falling tree injuring the passenger which would not have occurred if the taxi had not been speeding,[128] or allegedly careless advice that leads a claimant to take over a business which collapses years later.[129] The line separating coincidental events from applicable 'but for' causes can be a fine one. In *Chester v Afshar*[130] the claimant agreed to a back operation but the doctor had negligently failed to advise her of an unavoidable 1–2 per cent risk of permanent injury. When the unwarned injury resulted she claimed that but for the doctor's negligence she would not have had the operation on that day, but would have deferred it. A bare majority of the House of Lords concluded that even though the same risk would exist whenever the operation took place, the injury suffered on that day was not simply a coincidence and causation was satisfied because the claimant's right to choose had been violated. The paragraphs which follow identify four situations which are generally thought to cause difficulties for a straightforward application of the 'but for' test.

(ii) Increased risk of damage which results

The traditional rule is that it is not sufficient to show that the defendant's negligence increased the risk of injury. Evidence is required to show that out of several possible causes the defendant's negligence was a 'but for' cause on the balance of probabilities. In *Wilsher v Essex AHA*[131] a premature baby became blind. Expert evidence adduced five possible causes of this outcome. One of these was that the health authority, through the doctors, had negligently administered too much oxygen. But there was no evidence to justify the conclusion that on the balance of probabilities that cause had operated. Hence the claim failed. This rule has the potential to produce harsh results in cases where medical knowledge is not able to establish but-for causation on a balance of probabilities. A claimant who can show a 51 per cent degree of probability that the defendant's negligence injured him gets full compensation. Another claimant, who can show only a 49 per cent degree of probability, gets nothing.

17.69

An apparent erosion of this rule occurred in *Fairchild v Glenhaven Funeral Services Ltd*.[132] A worker who had contracted mesothelioma after multiple exposures to asbestos arising from the negligence of successive employers. The question was whether he could recover against his employers. Medical evidence showed

17.70

---

[128] The example given by Lord Walker in *Chester v Afshar* [2004] UKHL 41; [2005] 1 AC 134, 164 [94], HL.

[129] *Galoo Ltd v Bright Grahame Murray* [1994] 1 WLR 1360, CA.

[130] [2004] UKHL 41; [2005] 1 AC 134, HL. See Stapleton (2006) 122 LQR 426.

[131] [1988] AC 1074, HL; cf *Pickford v Imperial Chemical Industries plc* [1998] 1 WLR 1189, HL.

[132] [2002] UKHL 22; [2003] 1 AC 32, HL.

that a single fibre of asbestos was just as likely to cause mesothelioma as multiple exposures so it was impossible on the state of scientific knowledge to prove on the balance of probabilities which employer caused the mesothelioma. The House of Lords held that it was in the interests of justice that the claimant could recover from either of the negligent employers. It was enough that an employer had increased the likelihood of the claimant's injury. An attempt to extend this principle to the whole of medical negligence was narrowly rejected by the House of Lords in *Gregg v Scott*.[133] In that case, negligent medical advice caused a nine-month delay in the treatment of the claimant's cancer, reducing his chance of survival from 42 per cent to 25 per cent. A majority of the House of Lords refused to award damages for the reduction in his chance of survival, seeing *Wilsher* as an impermeable obstacle.[134]

17.71 After *Gregg*, it might have been thought that *Fairchild* represented only a very narrow exception to the traditional rule. But just one year later the House of Lords squarely confronted the limits of *Fairchild* and confined *Wilsher* and *Gregg*. In *Barker v Corus plc*[135] the House heard three joint appeals involving claimants who suffered mesothelioma after successive periods of exposure to asbestos by different employers including, in one case, a period of self-employment. A majority of the House of Lords held that the *Fairchild* principle applied whenever a defendant materially increased the risk that the claimant will suffer damage even if the defendant could not be proved to have caused the damage because it was impossible to show, on a balance of probability, that it was not caused by some other exposure to the same risk.[136] The principle applied irrespective of whether the other possible causes were tortious or non-tortious. Lord Hoffmann explained that since liability in these cases was based upon the negligent increase in a risk of the injury which the claimant suffered, it followed that the damage was the creation of that risk. The cases are therefore not anomalous at all: but for the defendant's negligence the risk would not have been increased.[137] An employer should only be liable for the proportion of damages corresponding to the extent to which it increased the risk.[138] The employee therefore bears the risk of

---

[133] [2005] UKHL 2; [2005] 2 AC 176, HL.

[134] Contrast cases where the chance lost is a *financial* chance: *Allied Maples Group Ltd v Simmons & Simmons* [1995] 1 WLR 1602, CA; *Kitchen v Royal Air Force Association* [1958] 1 WLR 563, CA and the contract case of *Chaplin v Hicks* [1911] 2 KB 786, CA.

[135] [2006] UKHL 20; [2006] 2 AC 572, HL, noted A Kramer (2006) 122 LQR 547.

[136] [2006] UKHL 20; [2006] 2 AC 572, 584–5 [17], Lord Hoffmann (Lords Walker and Scott and Baroness Hale agreeing).

[137] Lord Rodger, in a strong dissent on this issue, considered that the damage was the injury that resulted and that *Barker*, like the cases before it, were exceptions to the but-for test: [2006] UKHL 20; [2006] 2 AC 572, 601 [72], [90], HL.

[138] [2006] UKHL 20; [2006] 2 AC 572, 589–90, 592 [35], [43], HL. Not yet resolved are cases where the defendant is proved to have materially contributed to the disease rather than just

under-compensation if one or more employers become insolvent. Although this proportionate liability approach strains the language of the Fatal Accidents Act 1976,[139] and has been reversed by Parliament in mesothelioma cases,[140] it now applies to all other cases apart from mesothelioma.

Two qualifications to this principle were introduced in *Barker*. The first qualifica- **17.72** tion was that there must be a single 'causative agent'. All the possible causes must operate in the same way.[141] *Wilsher* was therefore distinguished because the five possible causes of blindness were all different. This introduces a very fine distinction between causes which operate in the same way and those which do not. For instance, *McGhee v National Coal Board*[142] was described as an instance of causes operating in the same way: the claimant suffered dermatitis which could have been caused by the negligent failure of his employer to provide showers to wash off brick dust or the non-tortious effect of cycling home with brick dust on his skin. It is difficult to see why a failure to provide showers is a cause operating in the same way as exposure of the dust to the air while cycling but, unless *Hotson v East Berkshire AHA*[143] is to be overruled, falling out of a tree and delay in treatment leading to a 25 per cent reduction in chance of avoiding permanent disability, are causes operating in different ways.

A second qualification introduced by Lord Hoffmann in *Barker v Corus* was that **17.73** actual damage must still be suffered: a person cannot claim for a risk unless it has materialized.[144] The denial of liability in *Gregg v Scott* was re-explained as based

---

increased the risk, although not necessarily being but-for cause: *Bonnington Castings Ltd v Wardlaw* [1956] AC 613, HL is probably now best understood as requiring liability only for the extent of the material contribution. Compare *Holtby v Brigham & Cowan (Hull) Ltd* [2000] 3 All ER 421, CA and *Mountford v Newlands School* [2007] EWCA Civ 21, [18]–[20], CA where liability was imposed for the full extent of the injury. See also J Stapleton 'Cause in Fact and Scope of Liability for Consequences' (2003) 119 LQR 388 who supports a test for causation of 'historical involvement' limited by policy concerns at a remoteness stage.

[139] Section 1 of the Fatal Accidents Act 1976 which was the basis of the claim in *Barker* provides for liability to dependents where 'death is caused by any wrongful act, neglect or default' not where there is a material increase in the risk of the death which results. On the approach in *Barker* it appears that s 1 would be satisfied even where the predominant 'cause' of death was non-tortious despite the literal wording of the Act.

[140] The Compensation Act 2006, s 3.

[141] The notion of a cause of a different nature might justify the result, although not the reasoning, of the Court of Appeal decision shortly before *Barker* in *Clough v First Choice Holidays and Flights Ltd* [2006] EWCA Civ 15, CA. The Court of Appeal dismissed a case of a drunk tourist who broke his neck after slipping on the wall of a swimming pool which had not been coated with non-slip paint. The failure to coat the wall with paint increased the risk of his injury but the result might now be explained on the basis that his drunken state was a cause of a different nature.

[142] [1973] 1 WLR 1, HL.

[143] [1987] AC 750, HL.

[144] A simple, fictitious example was given by Latham LJ in *Gregg v Scott* [2002] EWCA Civ 1471, [39], CA of persons exposed to asbestos dust near a factory who suffer no injuries save the

on the fact that the claimant had not died.[145] One is left to wonder what the result would be if a future claimant like Mr Gregg were to die the night before judgment.

(iii) Successive unrelated events

17.74   Suppose that C's leg is injured due to the negligence of D and that, on the balance of probabilities, it is in an irremediable condition: he will never be able to use the leg again. In that condition he is attacked by robbers and, having been shot, suffers an amputation of his already injured leg. It is clear that the second wrongdoer's liability will be reduced by the disablement which happened before they shot, for the quality of life and earning capacity of the victim are already seriously impaired,[146] but the question arises whether D's liability for the injured leg is affected by the amputation, on the ground that with hindsight we can say that in fact C was all along destined to be disabled. In *Baker v Willoughby*, the House of Lords held it was not.[147]

17.75   The same result would seem at first sight to follow when, after the first injury, C contracts an illness which, as effectively as a second tort, deprives him of his earning capacity. In fact the opposite result is reached. In *Jobling v Associated Dairies Ltd* an employee was wrongfully injured and later found to be seriously and irremediably ill.[148] His damages for loss of earnings were reduced. The distinction drawn by Lords Keith and Russell was that the tortious event in *Baker* involved a subsequent injury which could not be characterized as a vicissitude of life which should be taken into account as a possibility at the time of the initial injury. This is not to say that injury from subsequent torts can never be a vicissitude of life. The Court of Appeal has held that if a claimant's career in the police force made it likely that he might be the later victim of tortious incidents which would shorten that career, that must be taken into account in assessing damages for future earnings.[149] Further, in another decision, faced with successive torts albeit where the first tort (an eye injury from an attack) was a cause of the second (negligent treatment), the Court of Appeal saw no inconsistency between the *Baker* and *Jobling* and followed the former, making no reduction in the award.[150]

---

statistical possibility of future harm.

  [145] [2006] UKHL 20; [2006] 2 AC 572, 593–4 [48], HL, cf [38].

  [146] *Murrell v Healy* [2001] EWCA Civ 486; [2001] 4 All ER 345, CA.

  [147] [1970] AC 467, HL.

  [148] [1982] AC 794, HL.

  [149] *Heil v Rankin* [2000] TLR 475, CA: 'The effect of supervening events upon compensation was to be approached in general terms to provide just and sufficient but not excessive compensation, rather than on the basis of general logical or universally fair rules.'

  [150] *Rahman v Arearose Ltd* [2001] QB 351, CA.

(iv) Aggravations by the claimant's own conduct

If C's own careless conduct increases the damage caused by D, that will usually **17.76** operate as contributory negligence, leading to a reduction in C's damages.[151] The court may, however, regard C's conduct as so unreasonable as to break the causal chain of responsibility. In *McKew v Holland Hannen & Cubitts (Scotland) Ltd*[152] the claimant was injured by the defendant and later broke his ankle. He argued that the second injury was a simple sequel to the first, caused by the tort. But the House of Lords held that he had brought it entirely on himself by rashly insisting on descending stairs in his injured condition without assistance. An easier explanation of this result, as we will see with aggravations caused by the conduct of a third party, may be to say that it is not a qualification of the but for test but an application of principles of remoteness of loss. It is then easy to see why unreasonable actions of the claimant himself, but which the defendant had a duty to prevent, such as suicide whilst in police custody, will not prevent the imposition of liability.[153]

(v) Aggravations by the conduct of a third party

If by negligent behaviour D knocks C unconscious, thus giving X a chance to steal **17.77** C's wallet from him, there are two ways in which it might be said that D is not liable for the theft by X. The intervention by X might be said to break the chain of causation, so that D did not cause the loss of C's wallet. Alternatively, it might be said that D did cause that loss but that the loss is nevertheless too remote to be recoverable. On the whole the latter is the more easily intelligible technique which, as we have seen, explains why liability will still be imposed in a case in which it is found that D was under a duty to prevent any X from doing the very thing that happened. So, if a decorator who is working for a householder goes out to buy some new supplies and leaves the door open, so that a thief enters and steals, the decorator will be held to have been under a duty to keep the house safe and will be liable for the loss caused by the theft.[154]

The general rule is that D is not liable for damage caused by an independent **17.78** third party solely by virtue of the fact that his negligence facilitated the tort. Thus in *Lamb v Camden London BC*[155] the local authority negligently damaged a water main. The escaping water undermined the claimant's house. The house had to be vacated because of subsidence. Squatters then moved in and did a good

---

[151] Paras 17.198–17.211.
[152] [1969] 3 All ER 1621, HL. Contrast *Wieland v Cyril Lord Carpets Ltd* [1969] 3 All ER 1006.
[153] *Reeves v Commissioner of Police of the Metropolis* [2000] 1 AC 360, HL; *Corr v IBC Vehicles Ltd* [2006] EWCA Civ 331; [2007] QB 46, CA.
[154] *Stansbie v Troman* [1948] 2 KB 48, CA. Cf paras 17.96–17.98.
[155] [1981] QB 625, CA.

deal of damage. It could have been held that the squatters were an entirely new event, breaking the chain of causation: the negligent authority did not cause the damage which the squatters caused. Such a strained analysis used to be called *novus actus interveniens*, the intervention of a new act, restarting the chain of causation. In fact the court negatived the liability of the authority for the squatter damage by using the language of remoteness. It was clearly easier to take it that the negligent digging did cause the loss arising at the end of the chain of causes, while invoking the cut-off principle in order to deny recovery of that particular loss.

(b) Remoteness

17.79 Despite proving that the defendant caused or substantially contributed to the damage, the claimant may not recover all the loss so caused. The consequences of the tort (or some of them) may be so unusual or extreme that they cannot fairly be attributed to the defendant.[156] We have noted that some items may be excluded as not having been caused by the defendant. Leaving those aside, a loss which was caused by the defendant may be excluded on the ground that he owed no duty in respect of loss of that kind. A number of modern negligence cases have used the duty argument rather than remoteness to limit the extent of liability for economic loss.[157] However, exclusions are usually put down to remoteness: although the defendant did owe a relevant duty of care and its breach caused loss, some of that loss was too remote. The ever-enlarging cone of causation simply has to be cut off at some point.

(i) Direct consequences

17.80 There have been two lines of authority on the test for remoteness. The first was that the risk of unforeseeable consequences should be borne by the person whose negligence caused them. On this view, represented by *Re Polemis and Furness, Withy & Co Ltd*,[158] the defendant was liable for all direct consequences of his negligence. Foreseeability was considered to go to culpability, not to compensation. To determine culpability, you needed to know that a defendant had failed to take precautions against foreseeable harm. Once he was culpable, he must

---

[156] J Cartwright, 'Remoteness of Damage in Contract and Tort: A Reconsideration' [1996] CLJ 488.

[157] *Banque Bruxelles Lambert SA v Eagle Star Insurance Co Ltd* [1997] AC 191, HL. Public policy is as much an issue in remoteness of damage questions as it is in the duty of care: *Pritchard v JH Cobden Ltd* [1988] Fam 22, CA; *Meah v McCreamer (No 2)* [1986] 1 All ER 943. In so far as modern formulations of duty are often expressed as duties to take care in respect of particular kinds of damage, duty and remoteness issues become indistinguishable.

[158] [1921] 3 KB 560, CA.

compensate for all the direct consequences.[159] 'Directness' of causation was on this view the arbiter of recoverability.

In the *Polemis* case itself the defendant stevedores negligently dropped a plank **17.81** into the hold of a ship. Some damage was foreseeable from such an event. A falling plank is likely to do damage on impact. In fact, however, the ship was utterly destroyed. There was petrol vapour in the hold, and the fall caused a spark, and thence an explosion and a fire. The extreme consequence was directly caused but not foreseeable. The defendants were held liable.

(ii) Foreseeable consequences

The other view, introduced by the first of the celebrated *Wagon Mound* cases[160] **17.82** and now dominant,[161] is that the defendant should only be liable for foreseeable damage. In that case a ship negligently spilled oil into the waters of Sydney Harbour and sailed off. Three days later and some hundreds of yards away the oil ignited and burned down a wharf. The fire was caused because a spark from welding operations fell on a piece of rag, which caught fire and in turn set off the floating oil. On the expert evidence in that case, nobody thought it possible for the oil to ignite, though pollution damage was certainly foreseeable, hence the damage was too remote.[162]

(iii) Narrowing the distance between the two views

The seeming difference between the two tests of remoteness is much reduced **17.83** by the fact that, even under the foreseeability test of the *Wagon Mound* case a distinction is taken between the foreseeability of the general kind of damage and foreseeability of the damage which actually happened. It is not necessary that the defendant ought to have foreseen the damage which actually happened, so long as he should have foreseen damage of that general kind. Hence actual damage which counts as foreseeable may not have been foreseeable at all, in the sense that it may be a hundred times worse than what could be foreseen.

---

159 [1921] 3 KB 560, 570–2, CA, *per* Bankes LJ.

160 *Overseas Tankship (UK) Ltd v Morts Dock and Engineering Co Ltd (The Wagon Mound)* [1961] AC 388, PC.

161 Cartwright (n 156 above) 513. The foreseeability test of remoteness has been extended to other torts: *The Wagon Mound (No 2)* [1967] 1 AC 617, PC; *Cambridge Water Co v Eastern Counties Leather plc* [1994] 2 AC 264, 306, HL, Cartwright (n 156 above) 510–11. But there are exceptions: a defendant in the tort of deceit cannot plead that the losses caused were unforeseeable: *Smith New Court Securities Ltd v Scrimgeour Vickers (Asset Management) Ltd* [1997] AC 254, 265–7, HL.

162 Different expert evidence led to a different factual conclusion in *The Wagon Mound (No 2)* [1967] 1 AC 617, PC.

17.84 Thus in *Hughes v Lord Advocate*[163] a hole in the road was lit by paraffin lamps during roadworks. It was foreseeable that young boys might play with the lamps, might fall in the hole and might get burned. But when boys started messing with the lamps what actually happened was once again a major explosion. Yet such an escalation is taken to be within the foreseeable risk, because it was of the same generic type as what could be foreseen. Even the fire in the *Polemis* case itself might at a stretch be said to be foreseeable on this basis. In contrast with the decision in *Hughes*, in *Doughty v Turner Manufacturing Ltd*[164] burns from an explosion of molten metal were held to be different from foreseeable burns from a splash of the same molten metal. Although *Doughty* has now been doubted by the Privy Council,[165] the decisions as to whether damage is within the foreseeable type remain erratic.[166]

(iv) The 'eggshell skull' rule

17.85 This is another manifestation of the same phenomenon. The rule that the tortfeasor must take his victim as he finds him has remained constant during varying formulations of the remoteness test. A tortfeasor cannot complain if his victim's injuries turn out to be unexpectedly serious because of some pre-existing weakness.[167] This 'eggshell skull' rule is particularly significant in personal injury cases.

17.86 For many years this rule did not carry over to claims for economic loss. In *Liesbosch (Dredger) v SS Edison*[168] the House of Lords had to decide whether defendants who had sunk the claimants' dredger had to make good the extortionately high costs incurred by the claimants in hiring another to finish their contract. This outlay was disallowed because it was attributable to the fact that the claimants could not buy a replacement owing to their own impecuniosity. In *Lagden v O'Connor*[169] the House of Lords confronted this apparent contradiction.

---

[163] [1963] AC 837, HL.

[164] [1964] 1 QB 518, CA.

[165] *Attorney General for the British Virgin Islands v Hartwell* [2004] UKPC 12, [2004] 1 WLR 1273, 1281[27]–[30], PC.

[166] In *Bradford v Robinson Rentals Ltd* [1967] 1 WLR 337 frostbite was the same kind of damage as a cold, but in *Tremain v Pike* [1969] 1 WLR 1556 Weill's disease, carried in rat urine, was different from other rat contaminations and infections; physical injury and psychological harm are the same kind of damage: *Page v Smith* [1996] AC 155, HL. In *Jolley v Sutton LBC* [1998] 1 WLR 1546, CA the court thought foreseeable injuries to 13-year-olds from playing with a boat were not the same as injuries which happened trying to repair it, but the House of Lords disagreed: [2000] 1 WLR 1082, HL, restoring the first instance finding and observing that these are decisions of fact, not reducible to propositions of law: comparing one outcome with another was 'a sterile exercise': [2000] 1 WLR 1082, 1089, HL *per* Lord Steyn.

[167] *Smith v Leech Brain & Co Ltd* [1962] 2 QB 405: small burn became fatal through cancer, because of undetected pre-cancerous condition.

[168] [1933] AC 449, HL.

[169] [2003] UKHL 64; [2004] 1 AC 1067, HL.

Mr Lagden's car was damaged as a result of Ms O'Connor's negligence. He could not afford to hire a replacement while his car was being repaired without the extension of credit from a credit hire company. The House of Lords unanimously departed from *Liesbosch* and accepted that impecuniosity is an economic characteristic of a victim that must be taken as he is found in the same way as the law treats his physical characteristics.[170]

C. Negligence: Particular Cases

This section gathers together four troublesome applications of the tort of negligence, the two most common of which—psychiatric injury and economic loss—are concerned with the special regimes necessitated by the type of harm suffered by the claimant, in particular with the restricted recognition of any duty of care in respect of those kinds of loss. However, the section begins with a restriction which arises, not from the type of harm, but from the line between doing and not doing. **17.87**

(1) Omissions

Lord Atkin's neighbour principle began by pointing out that there are limits to the law's enforcement of morals: 'The rule that you are to love your neighbour becomes in law, you must not injure your neighbour, and the lawyer's question, Who is my neighbour? receives a restricted reply.'[171] One important element in this gap between law and morals concerns omissions to act. It is often readily foreseeable that, if we do not take action, another will suffer harm, but the law has difficulty in imposing liability for omissions, for harm which the defendant has not actively done but has allowed to come about. **17.88**

(a) The general nature of the problem

Every legal system has to face this problem. The main arguments for not in general requiring positive action were elegantly summarized by Lord Hoffmann in *Stovin v Wise*.[172] He distinguished three strands, political, moral, and economic: **17.89**

> In political terms it is less of an invasion of an individual's freedom for the law to require him to consider the safety of others in his actions than to impose upon him a duty to rescue or protect. A moral version of this point may be called the 'why pick

---

[170] ibid 1072 [6] (Lord Nicholls), 1088 [61] (Lord Hope) approving B Coote, '*The Liesbosch* and Impecuniosity' (2001) 60 CLJ 511. The House divided only on the issue of whether the full hire charges could be recovered without deduction for additional benefits received by Mr Lagden.

[171] Para 17.28.

[172] [1996] AC 923, HL.

on me?' argument. A duty to prevent harm to others or to render assistance to a person in danger or distress may apply to a large and indeterminate class of people who happen to be able to do something. Why should one be held liable rather than another? In economic terms, the efficient allocation of resources usually requires an activity should bear its own costs. If it benefits from being able to impose some of its costs on other people. . .the market is distorted because the activity appears cheaper than it really is.[173]

17.90 The distinction between acts and omissions might sometimes seem be only a matter of verbal formulation. Omitting to give a signal is negligent driving. Almost every negligent act entails the omission of precautions. However, the broad distinction between causing harm and failing to prevent it is usually clear. An omission is a failure to intervene to prevent the consequences of acts other than one's own or of events not of one's own creation. In such cases of failure to intervene, in the absence of a duty to take action there is arguably no causal link between the inert defendant and the harm which occurs.

17.91 The legal duty cannot but be restricted. Even when the damage in question is physical, foreseeability that it will occur unless the intervention is made will not itself establish a legal duty to act. Hence the law must, rather cautiously, identify the factors which put a person under a responsibility to take action in the interest of another. There is no exhaustive list and no generally applicable test.

(b) Responsibility for other persons

17.92 One basis for a positive duty to act is a relationship such that one person is responsible for the welfare of the other or responsible for preventing the other from doing harm to third parties. The routine example supposes a child drowning in shallow water and affirms that there is no obligation on a nearby adult to rescue it.[174] That will certainly not be true in cases in which the defendant genuinely assumes responsibility for another or undertakes to look after the other person. A callous adult *in loco parentis* will not escape liability for a child left to drown in shallow water. Schools, for instance, may also be under an obligation to prevent injury to the children, and to prevent the children getting out and causing accidents.[175] But the burden is not unlimited; it depends on the nature of the undertaking. It is reasonable to expect a school to take responsibility for training its pupils in sports and for supervising them, but the duty does not extend to

---

[173] ibid 943–4. Further discussion: Ernest Weinrib, 'The Case for a Duty to Rescue' 90 Yale LJ 247 (1980); Richard Wright, 'Standards of Care in Negligence Law' in David G Owen (ed), *Philosophical Foundations of Tort Law* (1997) 272–4; The Hon Justice Izhak England, 'The Duty to Control Conduct of Other Persons: The Prevention of Crime', ch 13 in his *The Philosophy of Tort Law* (1993).

[174] Paras 17.38 and 17.88–17.110.

[175] *Camarthenshire CC v Lewis* [1955] AC 549, HL.

insuring them against sporting accidents.[176] In contrast, in *Watson v British Boxing Board of Control*[177] the Boxing Board was held liable for negligence when Watson, a boxer, suffered serious brain damage from a cerebral haemorrhage and could not be treated expeditiously at the ringside. The Board had not organized the fight but controlled the sport, the object of which was physical injury, and assumed responsibility for keeping the degree of that injury within reasonable bounds. Further, the boxing community was not so large as to open up the prospect of indeterminate liability and comprised individuals whose character and disposition rendered protection from excesses especially necessary. The Board's counter-argument that it should be spared liability because it operated on a not-for-profit basis was rejected.

These common law positive duties to act so as to protect another may arise in a **17.93** number of relationships recognized in tort law as well as by contract. The commonest is the employer's duty to provide employees with a safe system of work. That duty arises in both tort and contract.[178] Again a host may be or in some circumstances become responsible for the welfare of his guests, and one who engages in a rescue attempt may be under a duty to carry it through carefully to the extent that his resources permit.[179] However, the host's duty will rarely extend to third parties as, for instance, where a drunken guest leaves the host's party and injures a third party by negligent driving.[180]

There are some relationships in which an even higher positive duty is imposed. **17.94** These relationships involve persons such as trustees, directors or solicitors, commonly called 'fiduciaries'. They are required to act positively to protect the interests of their beneficiaries with reasonable care, but are also expected to show loyalty. Unless authorized, they must abstain from any interest of their own which might tempt them to sacrifice the beneficiaries' interests.[181]

---

176 *Van Oppen v Clerk to the Bedford Charity Trustees* [1990] 1 WLR 235; cf *Reid v Rush & Tompkins Group plc* [1990] 1 WLR 212, CA—no duty on employer to insure employee working overseas. See also *Hamilton and others (Appellants) v Allied Domecq plc (Respondents) (Scotland)* [2007] UKHL 33, HL: no duty to disclose information in commercial negotiations in the absence of an assumption of responsibility.

177 [2001] QB 1134, CA.

178 *Johnstone v Bloomsbury HA* [1992] 1 QB 333, CA. Professional duties may include the duty to protect people from financial loss: *Henderson v Merrett Syndicates Ltd* [1995] 2 AC 145, HL; *White v Jones* [1995] 2 AC 207, HL.

179 Both propositions are supported by a Canadian case in which a host running a party on a boat was held to be under a duty to attempt to rescue a guest and, having begun the attempt, to carry it through without serious errors of judgment: *Horsley v MacLaren (The Ogopogo)* [1971] 2 Lloyd's Rep 410, SCC. In the end, on the facts the host was held not to be liable.

180 *Childs v Desormeaux* [2006] SCC 18; [2006] 1 SCR 643, SCC.

181 See paras 17.350–17.354.

(c) Responsibility for dangers on property

17.95 The liability of an occupier of premises for the safety of his visitors is a positive duty to take steps to see that the visitors are reasonably safe.[182] The occupation of land and buildings also imposes duties to protect neighbours' property from damage arising from its condition.[183] However, if the danger arises from the natural condition of the land, the personal resources of the occupier may be taken into account in determining precisely what it is reasonable for the occupier to do for the protection of his neighbour.[184]

(d) Responsibility for the torts of others

17.96 Duties to prevent wrongful conduct by others are exceptional. If the miscreant is in the custody of the police or some other public authority, the authority may be under a such a duty. Prison authorities for instance are under a duty to prevent prisoners from attacking other inmates, and they may exceptionally be liable to persons whose property is damaged by prisoners who escape.[185] However, special considerations apply to public authorities. These are considered immediately below.

17.97 The leading authority on the possible liability of private citizens is *Smith v Littlewoods Organization Ltd*.[186] There the claimants sought to make the owners of a mothballed building liable for not preventing vandals from getting into it and setting it on fire, to the ultimate damage of the claimants' neighbouring property. It was conclusive against their having been under any duty that they did not know and had not been informed that strangers were obtaining entry. There was a marked difference of emphasis as to the approach their Lordships would have taken had the defendants had that knowledge.

17.98 Lord Mackay thought that if the knowledge made the dangerous acts of the intruding vandals foreseeable and probable, then there would have been a duty to intervene to keep them out. Lord Goff thought it would require something more exceptional. There might be a duty in such circumstances if there were some known source of danger in the building and it was known that intruding trespassers might spark it off. Lord Goff's speech emphasizes that it is only very rarely indeed that one person can incur a personal liability for the wrongful conduct of another.[187]

---

[182] Occupiers' Liability Act 1957, paras 17.183–17.186.

[183] *Goldman v Hargrave* [1967] 1 AC 645, PC; *Leakey v National Trust* [1980] QB 485, CA.

[184] Cases in n 106, 107 above. See also para 17.184.

[185] *Dorset Yacht Co v Home Office* [1970] AC 1004, HL.

[186] [1987] AC 241, HL, discussed in BS Markesinis, 'Negligence, Nuisance, and Affirmative Duties of Action' (1989) 105 LQR 104.

[187] See also paras 17.385–17.393, distinguishing such personal liability from vicarious liability.

(e) Liability of public bodies for failure to prevent damage

This is an important and controversial area of the law about which a great deal has been written, especially from the perspective of public law.[188] Only a brief outline can be given here. The necessary background is that, in English law, a public authority has no immunity from actions in tort, unless and so far as the body is able to invoke the defence of statutory authority for the acts in question. In principle, therefore, a public authority can be liable for breach of statutory duty to prevent damage, if the statute is construed as so intending. The difficult questions arise when it merely has a power to prevent harm. It was for a long time clear that there was no duty to exercise a power to prevent harm. Hence an authority could not be made liable in negligence in its chosen exercise of the power unless it made things worse than they would have been if it had done nothing at all. For doing nothing at all it would incur no liability.[189] **17.99**

(i) The Anns case

That assumption was thrown into doubt by the decision of the House of Lords in *Anns v Merton London BC*.[190] In that case it was accepted that a local authority with power to inspect the foundations of new buildings before the building went ahead could be liable in negligence for the manner in which it exercised that power, notwithstanding the fact that bad inspection could not make matters worse than no inspection at all. Thirteen years later the *Anns* case was overruled in *Murphy v Brentford DC*.[191] **17.100**

(ii) Return to the pre-Anns position?

There is no doubt of the effect of *Murphy v Brentwood DC* on the law as to the inspection by local authorities of foundations, but the wider question, whether statutory powers can be the basis for a common law duty of care, remains, after extensive litigation, controversial. The doctrine of the *Anns* case was also rejected in Australia,[192] but it was accepted in Canada,[193] and in New Zealand.[194] Revisiting the matter in *Stovin v Wise*,[195] the House of Lords showed itself divided. **17.101**

---

[188] P Craig, *Administrative Law* (5th edn, 2003) 888–908; P Cane, 'Suing Public Authorities in Tort' (1996) 112 LQR 13; D Brodie, 'Public authorities–negligence actions–control devices' (1998) 18 Legal Studies 1; R Bagshaw, 'The duties of care of emergency service providers' [1999] Lloyd's Maritime and Commercial LQ 71; BS Markesinis et al, *Tortious Liability of Statutory Bodies* (1999); D Fairgrieve, 'State Liability in Tort' (2003).

[189] *East Suffolk Rivers Catchment Board v Kent* [1941] AC 74, HL.

[190] [1978] AC 728, HL.

[191] [1991] 1 AC 398, HL.

[192] *Sutherland Shire Council v Heyman* [1985] 157 CLR 424, HCA.

[193] *City of Kamloops v Nielsen* [1984] 2 SCR 2, 10 DLR (4th) 641, SCC.

[194] *Invercargill City Council v Hamlin* [1996] AC 624, PC.

[195] [1996] AC 923, HL.

17.102 Lord Nicholls and Lord Slynn, dissenting, thought that the *Anns* decision had liberated the law from the 'unacceptable yoke' of immunity from liability from negligence in the exercise of statutory powers, but Lord Hoffmann, speaking for the majority, was prepared to go no further than to leave open the question whether there could be any exceptions at all to the negative in *East Suffolk Rivers Catchment Board v Kent*.

17.103 On the facts of *Stovin v Wise* itself there was no liability. An accident had occurred on a stretch of road which the local council knew to be dangerous because visibility was impaired by a bank of earth on neighbouring British Rail land. The council had been in dilatory negotiation with British Rail for months, until the matter had gone cold. The council had not availed itself of its power to order British Rail to remove the obstruction. Nevertheless it was for the council to order its priorities. Mere foreseeability of injury did not put it under any duty to put roads and, in particular, this black spot at the top of its list. Lord Hoffmann thought that, if there were to be any exceptions, it could only be where it would be irrational not to exercise the power and, even then, there would have to be a discoverable policy in the relevant statute in favour of compensating those who suffered from failure to do so.

17.104 In *Gorringe v Calderdale MBC*[196] the claimant skidded and collided with a bus on a sharp bend in the road. The question for the House of Lords was whether the highway authority should be liable for failing to maintain a sign on the road-way which warned motorists to slow down. Lord Hoffmann's general approach was applied and the authority was held not to be liable for its pure omission. Lord Hoffmann described as 'ill advised' speculation, his earlier comments on irrationality and said that he could not imagine a case in which a common law duty could be founded simply upon the failure (however irrational) to provide some benefit which a public authority has power to provide.[197]

17.105 The line between a failure to act and a careless act can sometimes be very fine. An example is the decision of the Court of Appeal in *Kane v New Forest DC*.[198] There the claimant was seriously injured as he emerged from a New Forest footpath on to a road. The defendant planning authority had required the con-struction of the path as part of a development to which it had consented. It had been warned more than once that the path could not safely give on to the inside of a bend, but it had not ensured that plans to open up the blind spot were carried through. The claimant's action was summarily dismissed on the basis of *Stovin v Wise*, but the Court of Appeal allowed it to proceed, distinguishing

---

[196] [2004] UKHL 15; [2004] 1 WLR 1057, HL.
[197] ibid 1067 [32] (Lord Hoffmann). See also 1060–1 [4]–[5] (Lord Steyn).
[198] [2001] EWCA Civ 878; [2002] 1 WLR 312, CA.

Stovin v Wise on the basis that the instant case was not a pure omission because the danger had been created by the defendant's act in requiring the construction of the footpath and its knowledge that it had been constructed in a dangerous way. It is a fine line between this decision and the later decision in *Gorringe*, where it was the earlier roadworks of the highway authority that had removed the 'go slow' sign.

In *Stovin v Wise*, Lord Hoffmann also considered an alternative argument in **17.106** favour of liability, based on general reliance by the public on measures being taken against a given harm. Mason J suggested in *Sutherland Shire Council v Heyman* that a duty of care would attach in a case in which powers were designed to prevent or minimize a risk of personal injury of such magnitude or complexity that individuals could not or probably would not take adequate steps to protect themselves.[199] Lord Hoffmann did not reject this approach but thought that it would require careful and difficult analysis in practice. For instance did it apply to the public's relationship with the fire brigades? Did the public rely on the brigades or on their insurance?

The answer to this question was given in the conjoined appeals in *Capital and* **17.107** *Counties plc v Hampshire County Council*.[200] The Court of Appeal held that the traditional rule applied: fire brigades could only be sued if their intervention actually made things worse: 'If therefore they fail to turn up or fail to turn up in time because they have carelessly misunderstood the message, got lost on the way or run into a tree, they are not liable.'[201] Here the Court of Appeal showed no enthusiasm for any exceptions. It rejected any liability based on a specific assumption of responsibility to put out a particular fire arising from the acceptance of a call; liability was imposed only in the two cases where the intervention of the fire brigade made matters worse by turning off the sprinkler system. The general principle must reflect the court's view that fire brigades have difficult decisions to make between the conflicting interests of different property owners. In *Kent v Griffiths* where there was no such conflict, the Court of Appeal held that an ambulance service did incur a duty of care to attend once it accepted a call and undertook promptly to attend.[202]

---

[199] [1985] 157 CLR 424, 464, HCA. A possible example of this approach in England is *Perrett v Collins* [1998] 2 Lloyd's Rep 255, CA, where the relevant defendant was the Popular Flying Association, exercising statutory powers under the Civil Aviation Act 1992 in relation to the airworthiness of small planes. See D Brodie, 'The Negligence of Public Authorities: A Traditional Solution' [1999] Lloyd's Maritime and Commercial LQ 16.

[200] [1997] QB 1004, CA. The opposite result was reached in the High Court of Australia in *Pyrenees Shire Council v Day* (1998) 192 CLR 330, HCA.

[201] ibid 1030, *per* Stuart Smith LJ; cf *OLL Ltd v Secretary of State for Transport* [1997] 3 All ER 897 where May J held that the coastguard could not be liable for misdirecting rescue services.

[202] [2000] 2 WLR 1158, CA.

(iii) Public law and human rights

17.108   Many of the issues in this difficult area derive from its straddling the fault-line between private and public law. However, Lord Hoffmann's approach in *Gorringe* suggested that the problems can be solved using the ordinary methods and patterns of thought familiar within private law.

17.109   In *Osman v Ferguson*[203] an unsuccessful claim had been brought against the police for failing to protect a boy and his family from the obsessive attentions of a teacher, which led in the end to the boy's father being shot dead and the boy himself being wounded. The English courts had taken the view that any action was unarguably precluded by the principles discussed above and, in particular, by *Hill v Chief Constable of West Yorkshire*.[204] In the decision of the European Court of Human Rights in *Osman v United Kingdom*,[205] it was held that the denial of any duty of care created in effect a blanket immunity for the police which led to a breach of the right to a fair hearing (Article 6). The European Court of Human Rights subsequently moderated its position and held that the exclusion of a duty of care did not amount to the breach of a right to a fair hearing under Article 6.[206] The shift was facilitated by the House of Lords insisting that denial of a duty of care as not being 'fair, just and reasonable' was not and was not to appear to be a dogmatic assertion of a blanket immunity but reflected a careful balancing of competing interests.[207]

17.110   The most recent decision of the House of Lords signifies the model for future cases in this area. In *JD v East Berkshire Community Health NHS Trust*,[208] claims were brought by parents against healthcare and local authorities for damages for psychiatric harm suffered as a result of negligent diagnosis of child abuse. The House of Lords gave summary judgment in favour of the healthcare and local authorities but did not rest the decision merely on the ground that the responsibility had been assumed to the children, not the parents. The careful decision of the majority explained that a duty to the parents would not be fair, just or reasonable

---

203   [1993] 4 All ER 344, CA.

204   [1989] AC 53, HL. See now *Brooks v Commissioner of Police for the Metropolis* [2005] UKHL 24; [2005] 1 WLR 1495, HL.

205   [1999] 1 FLR 193, ECHR.

206   *Z v United Kingdom* [2001] ECHR 333, (2001) 34 EHRR 97, ECHR esp [99] and [100]; *TP and KM v United Kingdom* [2001] ECHR 332, (2001) 34 EHRR 42, ECHR. For a lucid and balanced exposition: E McKendrick, 'Negligence and Human Rights: Reconsidering *Osman*' in D Friedmann and D Barak (eds), *Human Rights and Private Law* (2002) 332.

207   *Barrett v Enfield LBC* [2001] 2 AC 550, HL; *W v Essex CC* [2001] 2 AC 592, HL. See also the liability imposed on local education authorities that had undertaken to exercise professional skill in diagnosis of learning disorders and failed to do so: *Phelps v Hillingdon LBC* [2001] 2 AC 619, HL.

208   [2005] UKHL 23; [2005] 2 AC 373, HL.

particularly because of the seriousness of child abuse as a social problem and the danger of subjecting health care professionals to conflicting duties.[209]

(2) Psychiatric Injury

Mental suffering in the form of pain, fear, emotional distress or shock is clearly actionable so far as it is an aspect of physical injury. Most personal injury actions will include claims for pain and suffering and loss of the amenities of life. Emotional and psychiatric damage which is not an aspect of the claimant's own physical injury is treated as a special case.[210] It is subjected to restrictive rules which, precisely because restriction of liability is their function, can seem arbitrary and unjust. One reason for this special treatment is that knowledge of psychiatric illness is relatively recent and has been regarded as presenting difficulties of proof. Another is certainly a fear of an excessive number of claims, of opening the floodgates of litigation and raising insurance premiums to unacceptable levels. **17.111**

In modern times this fear has been fuelled by the relatively few occasions on which horrific events, such as the Hillsborough stadium disaster, have been caught on television, witnessed by millions of people, all of them potentially traumatized. We are still some way from understanding the true scale of the possible escalation of liability. Whether the fear is justified or not, it has caused claims for psychiatric damage to be surrounded by increasingly complicated restrictions on recovery. **17.112**

(a) The earliest instances of liability

The law on recovery for psychiatric damage developed slowly. Liability for intentional conduct causing shock and illness was imposed in *Wilkinson v Downton*.[211] The first successful action for negligently causing shock resulting in a miscarriage was *Dulieu v White & Sons* in 1901, where the defendant negligently drove his van into the public house where the claimant was serving behind the bar.[212] Kennedy J emphasized, however, that she recovered because she was in fear for her own personal safety. **17.113**

---

[209] It has subsequently been held that it matters not whether the decision to be made is an evaluative one or merely a careless operational decision and also that the principle applies even after an evaluative care order is made: *AD v Bury Metropolitan Borough Council* [2006] EWCA Civ 1, CA; *L v Reading Borough Council* [2006] EWHC 2449.

[210] It is comprehensively treated in PR Handford (ed) *Mullany and Handford's Tort Liability for Psychiatric Damage* (2nd edn, 2006).

[211] [1897] 2 QB 57; PR Glazebrook, '*Wilkinson v Downton*: A Centenary Postscript' (1997) 32 Irish Jurist (New Series) 46. See paras 17.358–17.361.

[212] [1901] 2 KB 669.

17.114   Psychiatric damage caused by fear for others was not admitted until *Hambrook v Stokes Bros* in 1925, where a mother suffered shock through fear that her children would have been run over by a runaway lorry which she saw gathering speed downhill towards the place where she had just left them.[213] The Court of Appeal could not accept that only those who feared for themselves could sue: a mother whose first thought was for her children must be allowed to recover.

17.115   *Hambrook v Stokes* set the pattern in which the law would develop for the rest of the century. It opened the door to relational or secondary victims who had suffered shock. But it also introduced a limiting requirement, that the shock must result from what the mother had heard or seen with her own unaided senses, not from what she had been told by a third party. Both aspects of the innovation have been productive of much litigation. The only one of the early cases to reach the House of Lords was *Bourhill v Young*.[214] There *Hambrook v Stokes* was approved, but the pursuer failed to recover. She had been an immediate witness of a highway collision in Edinburgh. The shock caused her to miscarry. However, the crash was between strangers. It did not involve anyone near and dear to herself, and she herself was not at risk of any physical impact.

17.116   It is probably now unnecessary to go back to the older decisions. The extensive litigation of the last twenty years, in particular the four leading decisions of the House of Lords since 1982, has given detailed consideration to the modern law. Lord Hoffman has indeed warned that after these developments, older decisions are not reliable statements of the law.

(b) Four leading cases in outline

17.117   Two of the four major decisions are closely connected. They both arose from the Hillsborough football stadium disaster. Due to police mismanagement, a large number of people were crowded into one part of the ground. In the resulting crush ninety five people were killed and over four hundred were injured. *Alcock v Chief Constable of South Yorkshire* was an action brought by relatives and friends of the victims for compensation for the psychiatric damage caused by the event.[215] All their claims failed. *Frost v Chief Constable of South Yorkshire* was an action brought by the police officers on duty at Hillsborough for the psychiatric damage they had suffered.[216] Their actions also failed. The other two decisions arose from highway accidents.

---

[213] [1925] 1 KB 141, CA.
[214] [1943] AC 92, HL.
[215] [1992] 1 AC 310, HL.
[216] [1999] 2 AC 455, HL.

In *McLoughlin v O'Brian* a mother suffered serious illness in the immediate after-   **17.118**
math of a catastrophic road accident which injured her husband and two of her
children and caused the death of her third child.[217] She was told of the accident
some two hours after it happened and, driven to the hospital, saw the injuries and
heard of the death. Her claim succeeded. In *Page v Smith* the claimant himself was
involved in a motor accident of a relatively minor kind, in that nobody suffered
physical injury.[218] He almost immediately suffered a relapse into chronic fatigue
syndrome, from which he had suffered earlier in his life. He was held to have a
good claim.

It is notable that in the mass disaster cases the House of Lords insists on the need   **17.119**
to maintain, and even to raise, the barriers against excessive liability. In both the
highway cases, a more relaxed view was taken. In *McLoughlin v O'Brian* Lord
Bridge went so far as to say that knowledge of psychiatric problems had advanced
to the stage where it was no longer necessary to have special rules. Lord Wilberforce
was more cautious, preferring to mark out special rules for sufficient proximity,
and in the *Alcock* case a unanimous House of Lords preferred Lord Wilberforce's
three-pronged test of sufficient proximity.

The present law on psychiatric damage can only be stated in terms of special rules.   **17.120**
To start with there is a general exclusion of recovery for mere misery, as distinct
from illness arising from shock. Thereafter it is necessary to distinguish between
primary and secondary victims.

(c) The requirement of psychiatric illness

Leaving aside the suffering which is an aspect of physical injury, compensation   **17.121**
is given only for a recognized psychiatric illness, hence not for such ordinary
human emotions as grief or unhappiness, however foreseeable. The line may
be hard to draw, since grief may in extreme cases develop into a psychiatric disorder, which is then actionable.[219] There is one statutory exception to the exclusion
of damages for grief: a fixed award for bereavement, currently £10,000, is payable to the spouse of a person or the parents of an unmarried minor tortiously
killed under the Fatal Accidents Act 1976, as amended by the Administration
of Justice Act 1982.[220]

---

[217] [1983] 1 AC 410, HL.
[218] [1996] AC 155, HL.
[219] *Vernon v Bosley (No 1)* [1997] 1 All ER 577, CA: father witnessed unsuccessful attempts to
save his children from a car in a river, later suffered pathological grief syndrome, for which damages
were awarded. Note, however, *Vernon v Bosley (No 2)* [1999] QB 18, CA.
[220] The amount of £10,000 was fixed by the Bereavement (Variation of Sum) (England and
Wales) Order 2002 SI 2002/644.

17.122   The name used in the early cases, which at first required shock producing physical consequences, is nervous shock. Some judges have criticized the term as pre-scientific.[221] With the advance of science the unprovable requirement of physical lesion has mutated to psychiatric illness, but one of the most significant aspects of the first Hillsborough case, *Alcock v Chief Constable of South Yorkshire Police*, is that it emphasized the requirement of shock. The psychiatric illness must have been brought on by a shock. Lord Keith said that the illness must be caused by 'a sudden assault on the nervous system'[222] or, in Lord Ackner's words, 'the sudden appreciation by sight or sound of a horrifying event which violently agitates the mind'.[223] It is not argued that psychiatric illness is more likely, or more likely to be serious, if produced by a single, sudden event. It is hard to see the rule as anything other than an arbitrary device for limiting the number of claimants. It has produced harsh decisions, in which parents who have watched a child's lingering death in hospital have been denied compensation because their psychiatric illness was not the result of a single sudden event.[224] However, recent decisions have shown flexibility as to what counts as a single 'event'. In *North Glamorgan NHS Trust v Walters*[225] a period of 36 hours during which a mother saw her baby die was held to be a single, horrifying event. It is not completely clear whether this restrictive requirement also applies to primary, as opposed to secondary, victims.[226]

(d) Primary victims

17.123   The distinction between primary and secondary victims is central to the modern law. A primary victim is one who is, or reasonably believes himself to be, within the area of physical danger.[227] A secondary victim is one who is not in the danger area but suffers shock because of a relationship with the primary victim.

17.124   A primary victim can recover for psychiatric illness on the foundation of the duty of care owed by the defendant not to cause physical injury. If there is a danger of physical injury, the claimant can recover for psychiatric injury whether or not physical injury occurs, and whether or not psychiatric injury was foreseeable. In *Page v Smith* a man recovered for the recurrence of a long history of chronic fatigue syndrome when involved in a minor collision between two cars which

---

[221] *McLoughlin v O'Brian* [1983] 1 AC 4 10, 432, HL, *per* Lord Bridge; *Attia v British Gas plc* [1988] QB 304, 317, CA, *per* Bingham LJ.

[222] [1992] 1 AC 310, 398, HL.

[223] ibid 401.

[224] *Sion v Hampstead Health Authority* [1994] 5 Med LR 170. The Law Commission has recommended the abolition of the shock requirement: Law Commission, *Liability for Psychiatric Illness* (Law Com No 249,1998) para 5.33.

[225] [2003] EWCA Civ 1792; [2003] PIQR P16.

[226] Para 17.128.

[227] *Page v Smith* [1996] AC 155, HL; *McFarlane v EE Caledonia Ltd* [1994] 2 All ER 1, CA.

would not have been likely to cause shock to the average person, because he was in the area of physical danger. Prior to this case, it had been settled law that foreseeability of shock was an essential element in all shock cases. However, the House of Lords held in *Page* that, since persons put in physical danger might suffer either physical or psychiatric harm, primary victims need only show that some form of personal injury, physical or psychiatric, was forseeable. Lord Lloyd explained that a secondary victim is required to prove the forseeability of psychiatric harm because, not being in the area of physical danger, psychiatric harm is the only form of personal injury a secondary victim can sustain.[228]

This sharp distinction between the rules applicable to primary and secondary victims has proved controversial.[229] Lord Lloyd's justification for drawing it was that the restrictions on recovery by secondary victims, being control mechanisms imposed for reasons of policy, were not necessary in claims by primary victims. A similar point was made by Lord Oliver in the *Alcock* case.[230]   **17.125**

Lord Oliver, however, drew the line in a different place. His distinction was between those directly involved in an accident as participants and those who merely witness injury to others. As his examples showed, not all participants were persons in physical danger. Direct participation seemed to be a more flexible test of proximity than physical danger.   **17.126**

Subsequent litigation has followed the *Page v Smith* classification but a recent decision of the House of Lords suggests that some flexibility remains. In *W v Essex CC*[231] the House of Lords refused to strike out an action by parents who had not witnessed the sexual abuse of their children and had been in no danger themselves, but felt responsible for unwittingly allowing the child abuser into their home. On the other hand, in *Rothwell v Chemical and Insulating Co Ltd*[232] the Court of Appeal considered cases in which clinical depression had been developed as a result of the presence of the development of pleural plaques, which signified a more than normal possibility of an asbestos related injury, to which the appellants had been exposed by their employer. The Court of Appeal held that the mere risk of exposure to the injury was not sufficient to bring the appellants within the class of primary victims.   **17.127**

---

228 [1996] AC 155, 187, HL, *per* Lord Lloyd of Berwick; cf *Hughes v Lord Advocate* [1963] AC 837, HL (n 163 above).

229 *Frost v Chief Constable of South Yorkshire* [1999] 2 AC 455, HL, para 17.139; cf *Liability for Psychiatric Illness* Law Commission 249, paras 5.45–5.54.

230 [1992] 1 AC 310, 407–8, HL.

231 [2001] 2 AC 592, HL; *Dooley v Cammell Laird & Co Ltd* [1951] 1 Lloyd's Rep 271.

232 [2006] EWCA Civ 27; [2006] 4 All ER 1161, CA. Currently on appeal to the House of Lords.

17.128   The distinction between primary and secondary victims, derived from the model of traumatic catastrophes, does not comfortably cover situations in which there is no single event. In *Barber v Somerset County Council*[233] employees, including school teachers, had suffered breakdowns and continuing psychiatric injury because of years of overwork, exacerbated by innovations and efficiency gains such as are now commonplace. Such claimants count as primary victims. There are no artificial inhibitions of their right to recover damages from their employer, as there are for secondary victims and an employee suffering psychiatric injury at work is now treated no differently in principle from an employee suffering physical injury.[234]

17.129   However, in such cases, an instrument of restraint is old-fashioned insistence on the standard of the reasonable person in the employer's position, endowed with neither special prescience nor limitless resources. The early signs of mental illness are often not visible and, if they are picked up, there is often not much that can be done. It is rarely reasonable to sack someone for his own good. However, if a victim has asked for assistance, or has been treated in an exploitative and unsympathetic manner, psychiatric harm will be reasonably foreseeable.[235] Further, psychiatric injury will also be reasonably foreseeable if the employer knows that particular stresses carry with them the risk of psychiatric injury, even if the vulnerability of the particular employee is not known.[236]

(e) Secondary victims

17.130   The conditions governing the recovery of compensation by secondary victims received their present form in *Alcock v Chief Constable of Yorkshire*,[237] in which the House of Lords unanimously adopted the triple test of proximity proposed by Lord Wilberforce in *McLoughlin v O'Brian*.[238] It was necessary to show proximity of relationship, proximity in time and space, and hearing or seeing the event or its immediate aftermath with one's own unaided senses, rather than being told by a third party. Lord Wilberforce had speculated on the answer to be given to a claimant who had watched an accident on television.

---

[233] [2002] EWCA Civ 76; [2002] 2 All ER 1, CA. The principles were affirmed by the House of Lords: [2004] UKHL 13; [2004] 1 WLR 1089, HL.

[234] *Hartman v South Essex Mental Health and Community Care NHS Trust* [2005] EWCA Civ 6; [2005] ICR 782, CA.

[235] This was the case of Mrs Jones in the conjoined appeals in the Court of Appeal [2002] EWCA Civ 76; [2002] 2 All ER 1, CA. No appeal was brought to the House of Lords by the employer in her case. 'Close to the borderline' but allowing recovery, was Mr Barker's case where the only known information was that the employee had taken three weeks' leave for reasons explained by his doctor as stress-related: *Barber v Somerset County Council* [2004] UKHL 13; [2004] 1 WLR 1089, HL.

[236] *Melville v Home Office* [2005] EWCA Civ 6; [2005] ICR 782, CA.

[237] [1992] 1 AC 310, HL.

[238] [1983] 1 AC 410, HL.

The purpose of the appeals in the *Alcock* case was to test these criteria against the **17.131**
claims of various relatives and friends of the primary victims, who had been
affected by the disaster in different ways: being present in another part of the stadium, watching the disaster on live television, seeing later recordings, or identifying bodies some hours later. There was a high degree of agreement both as to result
and as to reasoning. None of the claims succeeded. They failed to satisfy every element in Lord Wilberforce's profile of close proximity.

(i) Proximity of relationship

Recovery is not limited to parents and spouses, or indeed to any specific relation- **17.132**
ship. Proximity of relationship requires a close tie of love and affection, which is a
question of fact to be established by evidence. In some relationships, such as parents or spouses, the closeness of the tie can be presumed, unless there is evidence
to the contrary. No firm guidance was given as to which relationships benefited
from the presumption of affection. Lord Keith was willing to include fiancées but
not grandchildren, Lord Ackner was not willing to include brothers, much less
brothers-in-law.

(ii) Proximity in time and space

It was not enough to have witnessed the disaster on live television, because pic- **17.133**
tures of the suffering of identifiable individuals were not shown and, since such
pictures would be contrary to the broadcasting code of ethics, it was not foreseeable that they would be. Nor was it enough to have witnessed the accident from
another part of the stadium, since individual relatives were not identifiable; nor to
have identified the body nine hours later. That was not part of the immediate
aftermath.[239]

(iii) Hearing and seeing

Watching live television was not sufficient proximity in the circumstances of **17.134**
the code of ethics. If pictures of individuals had been shown, the fact that they
should not have been shown would justify a conclusion that the chain of causation had been broken. There was, however, some support for the idea that an
unexpected disaster on television, such as an exploding balloon, might cause
actionable psychiatric damage to the relatives of those known to be aboard.
It has since been held that if the accident is not actually seen at any stage, there

---

[239] Compare three hours in eg *McLoughlin v O'Brian* [1983] 1 AC 410, HL. Recovery was also
allowed in *Galli-Atkinson v Seghal* [2003] EWCA Civ 697, CA where the interval between the
accident and seeing the victim's body in the mortuary was 2 hours and the purpose of the visit to the
mortuary was not merely formal identification.

can be no recovery for 'survivor's guilt' by one who thinks himself unwittingly responsible for it.[240]

17.135 Suppose that the traumatized person has witnessed the event but that it was brought about by the victim himself, negligently or deliberately seeking to injure himself. Can the victim be sued in the same way as rescuers have succeeded in recovery for physical injury from those who put themselves in danger?[241] It has been held in *Greatorex v Greatorex*,[242] following dicta in a number of cases,[243] that the witness has no action. A father who as a fireman was a rescuer of his own son from a car crash caused by the son's drunken and careless driving could not claim to be a primary victim, not having faced any physical danger himself. On the other hand he did satisfy the restrictive conditions which normally allow secondary victims to recover—relationship of affection, direct perception, immediate aftermath. However, he could not recover in respect of his post-traumatic stress disorder because on the facts it was not proper to recognize a duty of care. One reason given was that such actions would be potentially productive of family strife. Perhaps more convincing was the argument that liability would curtail an individual's right of self-determination. There are issues of individual autonomy here which, in the Law Commission's view, should be dealt with in legislation.[244]

(iv) Other possible cases

17.136 From the whole class of those who suffer foreseeable psychiatric injury, the *Alcock* guidelines, with their combination of the distinction between primary and secondary victims and the profile of special proximity, effectively eliminated the majority of potential claimants. There nevertheless remained some doubtful cases.

17.137 **The unrelated spectator.** Both Lord Ackner and Lord Keith thought that there might be accidents so dreadful that psychiatric illness would be foreseeable even to unrelated bystanders. However, as the Law Commission commented, if Hillsborough were not such a disaster, it was difficult to imagine what would be. The possibility of such a claim by unrelated bystanders appears to have been ruled out in subsequent decisions.[245]

17.138 **The rescuer.** It was argued in *Frost v Chief Constable of South Yorkshire*[246] that the common law's policy of encouraging rescuers would entitle them to recovery

---

[240] *Hunter v British Coal Corporation* [1999] QB 140, CA.
[241] *Harrison v British Railways Board* [1981] 3 All ER 679.
[242] [2000] 1 WLR 1970.
[243] *Alcock v Chief Constable of South Yorkshire* [1992] 1 AC 310, 418, HL, citing the judgment of Deane J in *Jaensch v Coffey* [1984] 155 CLR 549, HCA.
[244] Law Com No 249, paras 5.43 and 6.49.
[245] *MacFarlane v EE Caledonia Ltd* [1994] 2 All ER 1, CA.
[246] [1999] 2 AC 455, HL.

as participants in, or primary victims of, an accident.[247] However, the court held that, while the status of rescuer precluded the defences of *volenti non fit injuria* (no wrong to one who consents) or *novus actus interveniens* (new event interrupts the chain of causation),[248] a rescuer could only recover for psychiatric injury on the same basis as other claimants, as a primary victim in the area of physical danger, or as a secondary victim related to the primary victim and otherwise within the required profile of close proximity.

The employee.   It was also argued in the *Frost* case that, as part of the duty to provide a safe system of work, an employer owed a duty to employees to take reasonable care not to expose them to psychiatric injury. The answer was again negative: that the duty owed to employees does not exempt them from satisfying the other conditions of recovery for psychiatric injury.[249] This encounters some contradictory matter. It is clear in modern employment law that an employer's responsibilities can extend further than physical safety.[250] In *Walker v Northumberland CC*, without reference to the psychiatric injury cases, it had been held that the defendants were liable for subjecting one of their employees to excessive stress in dealing, without proper support, with child abuse cases.[251] In the *Frost* case, Lord Hoffmann said that Walker was in no sense a secondary victim,[252] but it is not clear in what sense he could be regarded as a primary victim which would not also include the police claimants in *Frost* itself. There was one special feature in the *Walker* case. Walker had been persuaded to return to work after a first breakdown by a promise to provide additional support. In the House of Lords in *Barber v Somerset County Council*,[253] Lord Rodger observed that the corollary to this was that the contract of employment should be scrutinized carefully to see whether such an undertaking is contractually limited in any way. The undertaking or assumption of particular responsibility also explains the decision of the Court of Appeal in *Butchart v Home Office*[254] to wave aside the restrictions in *Frost* in a case in which a psychologically vulnerable prisoner suffered psychological harm after being left with an at risk prisoner who committed suicide.[255]

17.139

---

[247] *Chadwick v British Railway Board* [1967] 1 WLR 912.

[248] Paras 17.212 and 17.78.

[249] [1999] 2 AC 455, 464 (Lord Griffiths), 497–8 (Lord Steyn), 506–7 (Lord Hoffmann), HL.

[250] *Johnstone v Bloomsbury HA* [1992] QB 333, CA; *Malik v BCCI* [1998] AC 20, HL.

[251] [1995] 1 All ER 737.

[252] [1999] 2 AC 455, 506.

[253] [2004] UKHL 13; [2004] 1 WLR 1089, 1100–1 [31]–[35], HL.

[254] [2006] EWCA Civ 239; [2006] 1 WLR 1155, CA.

[255] It also explains treatment as secondary victims and dismissal of psychiatric injury claims by police officers arising from a chain of events which commenced with an untoward shooting by a fellow officer during a raid: *French v Chief Constable of Sussex Police* [2006] EWCA Civ 312, CA.

17.140 **Shooting the messenger.** It is unclear whether an action lies against one who negligently communicates distressing information which causes psychiatric injury. The only modern authority, *AB v Tameside and Glossop HA*, decided that the authority had not in fact been negligent but did not decide the issue of principle.[256] It could be argued that a distinction should be made between true and false information in the interests of free speech.[257] In *Leach v Chief Constable of Gloucestershire*[258] the court refused to strike out a claim for compensation for failure to provide counselling for the task of listening to distressing information.

17.141 **The immediate aftermath.** The immediate aftermath rule is still largely undefined. In the *Alcock* case, Lord Keith, following the High Court of Australia,[259] thought that the aftermath remains 'immediate' as long as the victim is in the distressing untreated condition produced by the accident.[260] Lord Ackner and Lord Jauncey emphasized the relevance of lapse of time. However, in *W v Essex County Council*[261] Lord Slynn did not strike out the action of parents who only discovered their children had been sexually abused after several weeks.

17.142 **Damage to property.** In *Attia v British Gas* the Court of Appeal refused to strike out a claim for psychiatric damage caused by the claimant's witnessing the destruction of her house by fire.[262] The case may be explained as turning on remoteness of damage consequent on an admitted breach of duty. If damage to property is capable of supporting a claim for psychiatric injury, it must be expected that appropriate rules of proximity will be developed.

(f) Reform

17.143 It goes almost without saying that this accretion of rules is not capable of logical or scientific explanation. Nor has the House of Lords sought to provide one. Lord Oliver thought that they represented the current judicial view of what was acceptable, and that the whole matter would ultimately be better dealt with by legislation.[263]

---

[256] (1997) 8 Med LR 91, CA: communicating HIV exposure. The health authority made concessions which eliminated the point of principle.

[257] Law Com No 249, paras 7.32–7.33.

[258] [1999] 1 WLR 1421, CA.

[259] [1992] 1 AC 310, 397–8, HL following *Jaensch v Coffey* [1984] 155 CLR 549, HCA.

[260] eg *McLoughlin v O'Brian* [1983] 1 AC 410, HL: visit to hospital where injured members of the family were being treated, one having died.

[261] [2000] 2 WLR 601, HL.

[262] [1988] QB 304, CA.

[263] *Alcock v Chief Constable of South Yorkshire* [1992] 1 AC 310, 418–19, HL. This opinion was echoed in *Frost v Chief Constable of South Yorkshire* [1999] 2 AC 455, 500, HL *per* Lord Goff.

The shape of the problem is clear. First, the complexity of the present law is not **17.144** redeemed by clarity in the resolution of individual cases. There is no clearer evidence of this than the need for repeated appeals to the House of Lords. Secondly, there is the evident arbitrariness of the distinctions made, which are little more than elaborations of the lines which were drawn on an ad hoc basis in the decisions of the first half of the twentieth century. Thirdly, there are persistent uncertainties, not only about the borderlines between the rules, but also about the relationships between the nervous shock cases and the other emerging heads of liability for non-physical damage.[264] It is not so clear how these problems might be solved. Indeed the state of the law reflects the difficulty of coming up with solutions which are principled and practical.

There are two radical solutions, and several compromises. The choice between **17.145** them will depend on how well, on reflection, each meets the criticisms of the present state of the law and the anomalies which it creates, while retaining public confidence. There can be no question of the anomalies. As Lord Goff said in the *Frost* case, if there are two rescuers equally affected by the horrors of the spectacle before them, neither thinking of his own personal safety, both suffering long-term psychiatric consequences, they are all too likely to face wholly different outcomes. The one who happened to be working under a collapsing roof will recover, the other will not.[265]

The *Frost* case itself reflects the necessity of public acceptability. Lord Hoffmann **17.146** frankly acknowledged that the reason for his decision was that it would not be publicly acceptable for police officers at Hillsborough to be compensated when the relatives of the victims were not.[266] Again, applicability speaks for itself. Repeated judgments of the House of Lords have failed to clarify the criteria upon which cases should be settled.

The first radical solution is powerfully argued by the leading authority on liabi- **17.147** lity for psychiatric illness, Professor Handford.[267] His solution is to stop treating psychiatric illness as a special category of tortious liability and to apply instead the general rules and tests for establishing liability in negligence. However attractive this strategy might appear to be—it received the support of Lord Bridge in

---

[264] As for instance under the Protection from Harassment Act 1997, which may later be seen as protecting an interest in personal dignity formerly protected only parasitically through awards of enhanced damages in cases of outrageous conduct falling within the definitions of other torts: P Birks, 'Harassment and Hubris: The Right to an Equality of Respect'(1997) 32 Irish Jurist 1, esp 18–32; paras 17.358–17.361.

[265] [1999] 2 AC 455, 487, HL.

[266] ibid 510.

[267] PR Handford (ed) *Mullany and Handford's Tort Liability for Psychiatric Damage* (2nd edn, 2006) ch 15.

McLoughlin v O'Brian[268] and was adopted in Australia[269]– it is unlikely that is open to the English courts in the absence of legislation. It assumes that the flood-gates anxieties are unreal and the fear of hugely increased insurance premiums correspondingly illusory. Moreover, in the absence of jury trial such a solution might merely transfer the problem from the appellate courts to the courts of first instance. It is not clear that anomalies which emerge from the finding of the facts will ever be more acceptable to the public than the anomalies which currently lie open in the statement of the law.

17.148 The alternative radical solution is proposed by Professor Stapleton. She would be prepared to abolish all claims for psychiatric injury, thus in effect transferring the burden of insurance to the individual.[270] This solution is equally unavailable to English courts in the absence of legislation. In other respects, it may have much to commend it in discouraging show trials designed to pinpoint blame rather than to compensate for loss. But perhaps for this very reason it is unlikely to be publicly acceptable.

17.149 The Law Commission's investigation of this area has not resulted in support for either of the radical solutions, certainly not for any hasty repudiation of the floodgates argument.[271] The Commission's judgment is that some improvements could be achieved and that legislation is desirable to that end. It proposes no more than modification of the regime worked out in the cases, tending towards a slight expansion of liability. The proposals would remove the requirement of shock[272] and, for close relationships, the requirement of witnessing the event or its aftermath.[273] It would also introduce a statutory list of the relationships in which a close tie is deemed to exist,[274] though without restraining judicial development of protection for unrelated bystanders.[275]

(3) Economic Loss

17.150 In a loose sense the great majority of actions in tort are concerned to make good economic loss. However, serious problems are encountered wherever the loss in question has arisen independently of physical damage. Separate nominate torts

---

[268] [1983] 1 AC 410, HL; para 17.118.

[269] *Tame v New South Wales* (2002) 211 CLR 317, HCA; *Annetts v Australian Stations Pty Ltd* (2002) 211 CLR 317, HCA.

[270] J Stapleton, 'In Restraint of Tort' in P Birks (ed), *Frontiers of Liability* (vol 2, 1994) 95–6; PS Atiyah, *The Damages Lottery* (1997) 56–62.

[271] Law Commission, *Liability for Psychiatric Illness* (Law Com No 249 1998) paras 6.8–6.10.

[272] ibid para 5.33.

[273] ibid para 6.16.

[274] ibid para 6.26.

[275] ibid para 7.15.

provide for the recovery of such pure economic loss in certain situations in which it is intentionally caused.[276] In actions for negligence, economic loss can be recovered if it is the direct result of physical damage to the claimant's person or property. Thus an action for damages for personal injuries will usually include a claim for loss of earnings caused by the injury and for medical expenses incurred. But the general rule is that there is otherwise no duty of care in respect of economic loss. There has been constant pressure to break down this barrier.

(a) The exclusion of liability for foreseeable pure economic loss

The difficult area is 'pure' economic loss, financial losses suffered other than as a result of physical damage to the claimant's person or property. There is on some facts a fine line between economic loss arising from physical damage and pure economic loss,[277] but, once the loss is classified as 'pure' economic loss, the general rule is that it is not recoverable in an action for negligence. A number of reasons are commonly put forward for this position. **17.151**

The exclusion of liability is most frequently justified by the floodgates argument, the fear that claims for pure economic loss would lead to indeterminate, unmanageable liability. Convincing examples of the danger are easily found. Releasing the foot-and-mouth disease virus will entail physical damage to some but may bring financial disaster to a whole interdependent agricultural community.[278] Carelessly cutting a power cable in an industrial area may cause a wholly unpredictable amount of financial loss to an unpredictable number of businesses dependent on it, and these financial losses may spread in an ever-widening circle.[279] In such cases the floodgates danger is a real one. In others it is less convincing. **17.152**

There are other arguments to justify the denial of any duty of care to protect people from pure economic loss. Such further objections can include the undesirability of the interference of tort law with market principles of competition and distortion of market principles of risk (against which it is often said that an efficient activity should bear its own costs). It is said to be easier, and more efficient, to insure against one's own losses than the losses of others and that protection of financial and commercial rights is properly a matter for the law of contract. A secondary argument allied to the floodgates argument is that the **17.153**

---

[276] Paras 17.374–17.380.

[277] Hence the dissent in *Spartan Steel and Alloys Ltd v Martin & Co Ltd* [1973] QB 27, 39–46, CA. Cf para 17.155; Edmund Davies LJ argued that, provided economic loss was foreseeable and direct, the occurrence of physical damage was irrelevant.

[278] *Weller & Co v Foot & Mouth Disease Research Institute* [1969] 1 QB 569. See also *Sutradhar v Natural Environment Research Council* [2006] UKHL 33; [2006] 4 All ER 490, [38], HL.

[279] *Spartan Steel and Alloys Ltd v Martin & Co Ltd* [1973] QB 27, 38–9, CA, *per* Lord Denning MR.

indeterminacy of these claims undermines commercial certainty. Finally, in the public law context, there are often implications for the resources and budgets of local authorities.[280]

(b) Economic loss arising from damage to another's person or property

17.154   The longest and most consistently negative line of English authority is the succession of cases which have rejected claims for economic loss resulting from damage to someone else's person or property. The traditional position of the common law is clear: only the person injured in a personal injury case, or a person with a possessory or proprietary right to property which is damaged can sue for resulting economic loss.[281] In personal injury cases this position has been modified to some degree by statute, as by the Fatal Accidents Acts 1846–1976, and also by some still imperfectly understood developments in the law of damages.[282] These developments are confined to family relationships and others very similar.

17.155   The exclusion of liability is rigorously maintained in other contexts. Thus in *Spartan Steel and Alloys Ltd v Martin & Co Ltd*[283] the defendants' negligence damaged a cable belonging to the electricity board, causing a power failure. The claimants, whose factory was brought to a standstill, obtained damages for the physical damage to metal in their machines at the time of the failure and for the financial loss resulting from that physical damage, but not for the general financial loss of business incurred during the period before power was restored. A majority of the Court of Appeal held that the last item was pure economic loss and irrecoverable. It not infrequently happens that such an interruption of the power supply forces shops and offices to close. There is no liability in negligence for the lost business.

17.156   Since the principal argument used to deny recovery in these cases is the floodgates argument, a question arises whether an exception to the general rule should be admitted on facts in which the floodgates danger does not exist, because the class of persons likely to be affected is known to be limited. In Australia this exception has been made.[284] Thus in *Caltex Oil (Australia) Ltd v The Dredge Willemstad*,[285]

---

[280]   *Yuen Kun Yeu v AG of Hong Kong* [1988] AC 175, PC; *Murphy v Brentwood DC* [1991] 1 AC 398, HL.

[281]   *Cattle v Stockton Waterworks* (1875) LR 10 QB 453.

[282]   *Hunt v Severs* [1994] 2 AC 350, HL. The underlying proposition is that damages will be awarded to a disabled victim on trust for a relative or other loved one who has incurred economic loss in providing care. To the contrary: *Kars v Kars* (1996) 187 CLR 354, HCA. S Degeling, 'Trusts of Damages' (1999) Trust Law International 1; P Matthews and M Lunney, 'A Tortfeasor's Lot is not a Happy One' (1995) 58 MLR 395.

[283]   [1973] QB 27, CA.

[284]   *Caltex Oil (Australia) Ltd v The Dredge Willemstad* (1976) 136 CLR 529, HCA; *Perre v Apand Pty Ltd* (1999) 198 CLR 180, HCA.

[285]   (1976) 136 CLR 529, HCA.

the defendants had damaged an undersea oil pipeline and put the claimants to the expense of transporting oil by different means. The High Court allowed recovery of this economic loss because the claimants belonged to a limited class of identifiable persons who would suffer from such negligence.

In England, however, the rule has been strictly adhered to even where the danger **17.157** of indeterminate liability is remote. In *Candlewood Navigation Corporation Ltd v Mitsui OSK Lines (The Mineral Transporter)*,[286] a time charterer of a damaged ship was refused recovery in tort for want of the relevant proprietary right to the ship. There the Privy Council expressly rejected the High Court of Australia's *Willemstad* exception. The main reason given was that the rule against recovery of relational loss was clear, well-known and internationally accepted. Admitting exceptions would detract from the clarity and certainty of the rule.

In *Leigh and Sillavan Ltd v Aliakmon Shipping Co Ltd (The Aliakmon)*,[287] buyers **17.158** of steel coils shipped to them from Korea sued the carriers for negligently damaging them en route. They lost. Even though risk had passed to them, so that they still had to pay, the property had not passed to them. Hence, at the relevant time, they had no proprietary right to the damaged goods. They had no rights against the negligent carrier with whom they had no contract.[288] In the Court of Appeal Robert Goff LJ argued for an exception to be made in such a case of 'transferred loss',[289] but this was robustly rejected in the House of Lords. The transferred loss argument was received with more sympathy in *White v Jones* but was not thought applicable on the facts.[290] For the moment, therefore, no breach has been made in this restrictive rule.[291]

---

[286] [1986] AC 1, PC.

[287] [1986] AC 785, HL. But see now the Carriage of Goods by Sea Act 1992 which changed the law applicable to this case without altering the general rule.

[288] Under the Carriage of Goods by Sea Act 1992, s 2 such a claimant would now take the shipper's rights under the contract. Further discussion: *Benjamin on the Sale of Goods* (6th edn, 2006) 18–138.

[289] [1985] QB 350, 399, CA.

[290] [1995] 2 AC 207, 265 (Lord Goff), 281–2 (Lord Mustill), HL.

[291] There is one apparently exceptional case, in which a majority of the House of Lords allowed a cargo owner, required to contribute to the cost of a collision at sea, to recover his contributions from the negligent defendant although his cargo was undamaged, *Morrison Steamship Co Ltd v Steamship Greystoke Castle* [1947] AC 265, HL. It is usually explained as a peculiarity of maritime law and has not been followed elsewhere: *Candlewood Navigation Corporation Ltd v Mitsui OSK Lines (The Mineral Transporter)* [1986] AC 1, 24, PC; *Leigh and Sillavan Ltd v Aliakmon Shipping Co Ltd* [1986] AC 785, HL (where it had been eliminated in the Court of Appeal: [1985] 1 QB 350, 394, CA, *per* Goff LJ, referring to PA Atiyah 'Negligence and Economic Loss' (1967) 83 LQR 248, 354). An alternative explanation of the result today might be as restitutionary recovery based on unjust enrichment by the compulsory discharge of the defendant's liability, although Lord Roche's lorry driver example shows that he was comprehending a principle of negligence. He spoke of a lorry driver being liable to a claimant for damaging a truck carrying the undamaged goods of the claimant.

(c) Disappointingly defective goods and houses

17.159 If I buy a disappointingly defective thing, my first hope of redress will be the contract. The seller may be in breach of an express or implied term as to its quality. If he is, he will have to make good my economic loss, the difference between the value of what he was contractually liable to supply and what he did supply. The question is whether there can also be a liability in tort.

(i) The starting point

17.160 The starting point is that there will be no liability outside contract in the absence of physical damage. If the defect is such as to make me ill or inflict some other kind of actual damage, I may turn to tort. One advantage of doing so will be that tortious redress will not be confined by privity of contract. In tort, but not in contract, a manufacturer who sold to my seller or a sub-contractor who worked for my seller can be reached. However, *Donoghue v Stevenson*,[292] which established the liability of manufacturers to consumers for defective goods in negligence, did not go beyond negligent defects which caused physical injury or damage; it offered no redress for the economic loss inherent in having paid for a useless thing. Statutory reform of the law, strengthening the position of consumers in relation to liability for defective goods in tort, has continued to be confined to goods which cause personal injury or damage to property.[293]

17.161 In the case of defective buildings, the law's starting point is the same. However, larger sums are at stake, and, often, more distress too. As a consequence there has been stronger pressure on the law of tort to provide redress outside and beyond contract in respect of the loss implicit in a badly built house.

17.162 A statutory solution has been enacted, but for a number of reasons, some of which are no longer operative, it appears not to meet the need. The Defective Premises Act 1972 works within a limitation period of six years which runs from the completion of the dwelling. Many defects take longer to emerge. The Act would be more useful if it had run the period from 'discoverability' as does the Latent Damage Act 1986.[294] Subject to this fatal shortcoming, the Defective Premises Act 1972 imposes on those who take on work for the provision of a dwelling a duty to ensure that it is constructed in a workmanlike manner so that the dwelling is fit for habitation. And this duty extends beyond contract to all who acquire an

---

[292] [1932] AC 562, HL.

[293] Consumer Protection Act 1987 Part 1; paras 17.282–17.289.

[294] Inserting sections 14A and 14B into the Limitation Act 1980. This regime allows three years after discoverability, subject to a 15 year long stop.

interest in the building.[295] The Act makes clear in effect that, as a matter of law, there is an assumption of responsibility for habitability.

At common law, complex case law at first yielded to the pressure for redress **17.163** outside contract, but, at least in England, the courts later recanted. The complexities ramify, reaching into, inter alia, the identity of the defendants, the limitation of actions, and the nature of the loss. Our primary concern at this point is with the nature of the loss, though that issue cannot be entirely separated from the other questions.

(ii) Two expansionist cases

Two cases seemed to accept the possibility of suing in negligence for this kind of **17.164** purely economic disappointment. Fifty years after the decision in *Donoghue v Stevenson* another Scottish case allowed recovery for defects in a building which had not caused physical damage and was not alleged to be dangerous. *Junior Books Co Ltd v Veitchi Co Ltd*[296] was the high point of builders' liability. A subcontractor had constructed the floor of a factory. Its surface developed many small cracks but it caused no damage to anything else, nor any injury to any person. It was simply a disappointingly defective floor, bad value for money. The customer leap-frogged the contractor and was able to recover in negligence against the sub-contractor. It is a curious fact that, in the retrenchment described immediately below, the *Junior Books* case has never been overruled. It stands in precarious isolation, not condemned but never followed. It has to be regarded as turning on its own particular facts,[297] but it is not clear quite what the peculiarity of those facts should be said to be.[298]

The other expansionist case was the ill-fated decision of the House of Lords in **17.165** *Anns v Merton London BC* which had been decided five years earlier.[299] It had several aspects. First, so far as there had been any doubt, it made clear that *Donoghue v Stevenson* did apply to buildings: those responsible for constructing a building which causes physical damage to persons or other property are liable on ordinary negligence principles. Secondly, it held that local authorities were liable in tort if

---

295 Defective Premises Act 1972, s1(1) and s 3.
296 [1983] 1 AC 520, HL.
297 [It] cannot be regarded as laying down any principle of general application in the law of tort or delict': *D & F Estates Ltd v Church Commissioners* [1989] AC 177, 202, HL, *per* Lord Bridge.
298 *Tate & Lyle Industries v GLC* [1983] 2 AC 509, HL; *Simaan General Contracting Co v Pilkington Glass Ltd (No 2)* [1988] QB 758, CA; *Greater Nottingham Co-operative Society Ltd v Cementation & Piling & Foundations Ltd* [1989] QB 71, CA. In Scotland it is applied but only where pursuer and defender are connected by a chain of contracts: JM Thomson, 'A Prophet not Rejected in its own Land' (1994) 110 LQR 361.
299 [1978] AC 728, HL.

they negligently exercised their statutory powers to control house construction. Thirdly, it expanded the definition of physical damage.

(iii) Retrenchment

17.166   The second and third of these *Anns'* propositions have been swept away. The former, for a time of great importance, was overruled by *Murphy v Brentwood DC*.[300] As for the latter, it was underpinned by a crucial extension of the notion of physical damage. Physical damage was to include the costs of repairing dangerous defects in the structure, even though the building had not yet caused injury to persons or other property.[301] The seductive argument was that no distinction could be taken between physical damage which was actually brought about and the cost of preventing it coming about. How, for example, could the law distinguish between the costs of an accident caused by a lorry with defective brakes and the cost of putting the brakes right before the accident happened? Nevertheless, this transgression of the line between contract and tort was questioned in *D & F Estates v Church Commissioners for England & Wales*,[302] and overruled in *Murphy v Brentwood* itself.[303]

17.167   *Murphy v Brentwood* was a variation on *Anns v Merton London BC*. The facts were that the house which the claimant had bought from a developer had been constructed over a filled-in site and supposedly stabilized by means of a huge concrete raft which was put in beneath the foundations. A decade later the house began to crack as subsidence set in. The cause proved to be the inadequacy of the concrete raft. The claimant had to take a £35,000 reduction in the selling price. To have done the necessary repairs would have cost somewhat more. An action to recover the reduction in value was brought against the local authority for negligently inspecting the foundations, relying on the *Anns* decision, but it was thrown out and with it the law as developed in that case.

17.168   An unfortunate side effect of *Murphy v Brentwood* is its impact on duties of manufacturers to warn consumers of defects in their products which come to the manufacturers' knowledge after the product has been in circulation. It has been held that the exclusion of liability for potentially dangerous products

---

[300] [1991] 1 AC 398, HL. The overruling left open just one possibility, namely that an authority might be liable if its negligence failed to prevent the house causing personal injury to an occupier.

[301] *Anns v Merton London BC* [1978] AC 728, 759–60, HL, approving *Dutton v Bognor Regis UDC* [1972] 1 QB 373, CA and Laskin J in *Rivtow Marine Ltd v Washington Ironworks* [1974] SCR 1189, 1223; 40 DLR (3d) 530, 533 (1974) SCC.

[302] [1989] AC 177, HL.

[303] [1991] 1 AC 398, 471, 475, 489, HL. Lord Bridge would have allowed the cost of repairing a defective building so near the boundary of the land as to constitute a danger to neighbouring property or the highway: ibid 475. Lord Oliver reserved his opinion on this point: ibid 488–90.

causing only economic disappointment relieves manufacturers of any general duty to warn consumers of such defects discovered in their products. Hence such a duty will now only be found where there is a special relationship between the parties.[304] This can only encourage manufacturers to keep quiet about defects in their products. This is, however, only one among many criticisms which have been made of a retrenchment which has found few friends.

(iv) Rejection in other jurisdictions

Murphy v Brentwood has not been followed in other Commonwealth countries.[305] **17.169** In Canada, the Supreme Court has approved *Anns v Merton LBC* both as regards the tort liability of housing authorities[306] and liability for the cost of repairing dangerous defects.[307] The High Court of Australia did not adopt the *Anns* liability of housing authorities for failure to prevent defects[308] but has held builders liable to subsequent owners for the cost of repairing defective houses, even though they are not dangerous.[309] The High Court of Australia has, however, held that this principle does not apply to a subsequent owner of commercial premises which might have been able to protect itself from the economic consequences of the negligence.[310] As for New Zealand, even an appeal to the Privy Council did not result in the imposition of the *Murphy* restrictions on that country.[311]

The justification for the Commonwealth position may rest on the fact that **17.170** houses are different from other products: they are the most expensive thing most people ever buy, they are intended to have an extended life and are likely to have a succession of owners who will not be able to abandon or replace a defective house as easily as other products.

(d) The *Hedley Byrne* principle

So far we have established that in England there is almost no possibility of recover- **17.171** ing pure economic loss in any action in tort. There is one exceptional line of cases. Expressed at a very general level, pure economic loss is recoverable in

---

304 *Hamble Fisheries v Gardner & Sons Ltd* [1999] 2 Lloyd's Rep 1.
305 IN Duncan Wallace, 'No Surprises in the Privy Council' (1996) 112 LQR 369. For a comparison between English and Commonwealth approaches to problems of economic loss see J Stapleton, 'Comparative Economic Loss: Lessons from Case-law-focused "Middle Theory"' (2002) 50 UCLAL Rev 531.
306 *City of Kamloops v Nielsen* [1984] 2 SCR 2, 10 DLR (4th) 641 (1984) SCC.
307 *Winnipeg Condominium v Bird Construction Co* [1995] 1 SCR 85, 121 DLR (4th) 193, SCC.
308 *Sutherland Shire Council v Heyman* [1985] 157 CLR 424, HCA.
309 *Bryan v Maloney* (1995) 182 CLR 609, HCA.
310 *Woolcock Street Investments v CDG Pty Ltd* (2004) 216 CLR 515, HCA.
311 *Invercargill CC v Hamlin* [1994] 3 NZLR 513, NZCA, [1996] AC 624, PC; Sir Robin Cooke, 'An Impossible Distinction' (1991) 107 LQR 46.

negligence if there is a special relationship between the parties which raises a duty of care specifically in relation to that particular kind of loss.

17.172 In *Hedley Byrne & Co Ltd v Heller & Partners Ltd*[312] a bank's credit reference was alleged to have caused financial loss to a firm that relied on it by giving credit to a client who turned out to be unsatisfactory. The reference had been given 'without responsibility' and this disclaimer was held to be effective to protect the defendants, but the House of Lords went on to consider the question of liability in principle. It was held, reversing *Candler v Crane Christmas & Co*,[313] that, if there was a special relationship between the parties, there could be liability for negligent misstatements causing economic loss. The *Hedley Byrne* principle is the major exception to the general rule that pure economic loss is not recoverable in negligence. It has been greatly expanded and its scope is still at some points uncertain.

(i) Words, acts, omissions

17.173 The speeches in *Hedley Byrne* were mainly concerned with the need to place restrictions on liability for words which, it was argued, carry particular danger of indeterminate liability. Very little attention was given in the case itself to the fact that the loss was economic loss. Lord Devlin thought the distinction irrelevant. It has since become clear that the nature of the loss is the heart of the problem: relatively little difficulty has been experienced with cases of negligent misstatements causing physical injury.[314] But it was argued and for a long time accepted that the *Hedley Byrne* principle was limited to negligent misstatements causing economic loss.[315]

17.174 The line between negligent statements and negligent acts proved hard to draw, particularly with respect to professional services which are often a combination of the two, a survey, examination or service resulting in a certificate or advice. The distinction also served to conceal, and sometimes to create, anomalies between the liability of different persons involved in the manufacture and distribution of products.[316] Subsequent House of Lords decisions extended the *Hedley Byrne* principle to include negligence in the provision of services, whether by words, acts or omissions, within a special relationship.[317] The category of negligent misrepresentations will continue to be significant because of its links with contract rules

---

[312] [1964] AC 465, HL.
[313] [1951] 2 KB 164 CA.
[314] *Clay v AJ Crump & Sons Ltd* [1964] 1 QB 533, CA.
[315] PS Atiyah, 'Negligence and Economic Loss' (1967) 83 LQR 248.
[316] J Stapleton, 'Duty of Care and Economic Loss: A Wider Agenda' (1991) 107 LQR 249.
[317] *Henderson v Merrett Syndicates* [1995] 2 AC 145, HL; *White v Jones* [1995] 2 AC 207, HL.

concerning remedies for misrepresentation, but it no longer marks the limits of *Hedley Byrne* liability. That depends on the relationship between the parties.[318]

(ii) Special relationships, assumption of responsibility and reliance

The speeches in *Hedley Byrne & Co Ltd v Heller & Partners Ltd* did require a special   **17.175**
relationship between the parties, but the nature of the special relationship required
for liability was discussed only in general terms. Statements made informally in
the course of a social relationship were excluded.[319] Their Lordships emphasized
as pointing to a duty: the possession of special knowledge or special skill, a
voluntary assumption of responsibility, reasonable reliance on the maker of the
statement, and the relationship's resemblance to contract. A general business relationship, such as that of banker and customer, would suffice, but a relationship in
a particular transaction was not excluded.

The principal importance of the *Hedley Byrne* decision was in extending the   **17.176**
non-contractual liability of professional advisers, particularly in the financial
services. The leading decisions concern such professional liability, but an early
attempt to limit the operation of the principle to persons in the business of giving
financial advice, or claiming the skill of a professional adviser, has not been
followed in England.[320] Most cases have required a special relationship equivalent
to contract, in which there has been an assumption of responsibility by one party
and reasonable reliance by the other. It is said that an assumption of responsibility and reasonable reliance on it establish proximity and make it fair, just,
and reasonable to impose liability for financial loss.[321]

The assumption of responsibility test has been criticized for its ambiguity.[322]   **17.177**
The test has been described judicially as being neither helpful nor realistic.[323]

---

[318] On misrepresentation in contract and tort, see J Cartwright, *Misrepresentation, Mistake and Non-Disclosure* (2006).

[319] *Chaudhury v Prabhakar* [1989] 1 WLR 29 is a borderline case. The decision may depend on an unwise concession in the court below.

[320] *Mutual Life and Citizens Assurance Co Ltd v Evatt* [1971] AC 793, PC; *Esso Petroleum Ltd v Mardon* [1976] QB 801, CA.

[321] *Henderson v Merrett Syndicates* [1995] 2 AC 145, HL; *Williams v Natural Life Health Foods* [1998] 1 WLR 830, HL.

[322] Stapleton condemns it for both want of clarity and a certain degree of dishonesty, in that it suggests that the courts are looking for a fact identifiable as an assumption of responsibility when in truth they seem to be looking for unnamed facts which justify the conclusion that the defend-ant should be taken to have assumed responsibility. In other words assumption of responsibility is a restatement of the problem masquerading as a solution: J Stapleton, 'Duty of Care Factors' in P Cane and J Stapleton, *The Law of Obligations, Essays in Celebration of John Fleming* (1998) 59, 64–5. See also S Whittaker, 'The application of the broad principle of *Hedley Byrne*' (1997) 17 Legal Studies 169 and K Barker, 'Wielding Occam's Razor: Pruning Strategies for Economic Loss' (2006) 26 OJLS 29.

[323] *Smith v Eric S Bush* [1990] 1 AC 831, 862, HL, *per* Lord Griffiths.

It is capable of both a broad and a narrow interpretation. The narrow interpretation emphasizes the contractual analogy, first drawn by Lord Devlin in the *Hedley Byrne* case.[324] The tacit premise is that, since a person can by contract make himself responsible for pure economic loss, the only problem is the technical one that under English law there is no parol contract, properly so-called, in the absence of consideration. The 'relationship equivalent to contract' approach thus requires that the *Hedley Byrne* principle be confined to bilateral relationships, of which the essence is mutuality.[325] It also explains why liability will depend upon whether the parties arranged their relationship, perhaps through intermediaries, in a manner designed to avoid an assumption of contractual liability.[326]

17.178 This narrow approach, which relies on the contractual analogy, runs into difficulty with the decision of the House of Lords in *White v Jones*.[327] There a majority of the House of Lords held that a solicitor could be liable to disappointed beneficiaries for negligently drawing up or in failing to draw up a will. In the particular case, the intended beneficiaries knew of the testator's intentions, but the whole House agreed that this was not a significant factor. There was no assumption of responsibility, in any natural sense, to the potential beneficiaries. *White v Jones* was subsequently applied[328] and extended beyond the legal profession.[329]

17.179 In *Customs and Excise Commissioners v Barclays Bank Plc*[330] the House of Lords accepted that the contractual analogy cannot strictly be insisted upon in pure economic loss cases. In that case, the Commissioners sought to hold Barclays Bank liable for loss suffered when the bank carelessly released money from frozen accounts. The Commissioners argued that Barclays Bank had assumed responsibility to ensure that there were no payments from the accounts which had been frozen after a legal order obtained by the Commissioners had been served on the bank. The House of Lords unanimously held that the bank owed no duty of

---

[324] [1964] AC 465, 528–9, HL. See eg *Commissioner of Police of the Metropolis v Lennon* [2004] EWCA Civ 130; [2004] 1 WLR 2594, CA.

[325] Hence in *White v Jones* [1995] 2 AC 207, HL, Lord Mustill's dissent. Cf Lord Steyn in *Williams v Natural Life Health Foods* [1998] 1 WLR 830, 834–8, HL.

[326] A recent decision has insisted that a second stage of analysis must be whether the recognition of a duty of care would interfere with any contractual structure or regime chosen by the parties: *Riyad Bank v Ahli United Bank (UK) Plc* [2006] EWCA Civ 780, CA. See also *West Bromwich Albion Football Club Ltd v El Safty* [2006] EWCA Civ 1299, CA.

[327] [1995] 2 AC 207, HL.

[328] *Carr-Glyn v Frearsons* [1999] Ch 326, CA; *Esterhuizen v Allied Dunbar Assurance plc* [1998] 2 FLR 668; *Horsfall v Haywards* [1999] 1 FLR 1182. The last of these appears to limit the Court of Appeal's decision in *Walker v Geo Medlicott & Son* [1999] 1 WLR 727 to the effect that a right to rectify the will, where available, would displace the action against the draftsman.

[329] *Gorham v British Telecommunications Plc* [2000] 1 WLR 2129, CA, holding an insurance company liable for negligent pensions advice and applying the principle to recognize a duty of care towards the dependents of a man who made it clear that his aim was to benefit his family.

[330] [2006] UKHL 28; [2006] 3 WLR 1, HL.

care to the Commissioners. Responsibility had not been voluntarily assumed: it had been thrust upon the bank.[331] All their Lordships observed that the further the concept of assumption of responsibility departs from the contractual analogy and the less it focuses on the actual actions and manifested intentions of the defendant, the less useful it will become.[332] The way forward signalled by the House of Lords is to regard genuine assumption of responsibility as sufficient for liability but not necessary.[333] Other cases may fall within the usual three-fold test, developed incrementally.

However, conflicts immediately emerge when the three-fold test is used as a general approach for cases of pure economic loss. In *Smith v Eric S Bush* a purchaser was allowed to recover from the mortgagee's negligent surveyor whom the purchaser had relied upon.[334] The contrast with *Caparo Industries plc v Dickman* is striking.[335] In that case an action was brought against accountants for alleged negligence in auditing the accounts of a company. The claimants had not themselves commissioned the accountants but had relied on them first in buying shares in the company and then in taking it over. The House of Lords held that the defendants owed no duty of care to the claimants, either as prospective investors or as shareholders who had taken over the company because there was no special relationship between them. The general principle of proximity seems to be that commercial parties can generally be expected to rely on their own advisers[336] but if it can be shown that a statement, though nominally addressed to others was actually intended to influence the claimant, that may be enough to establish responsibility.[337]

17.180

---

[331] The line between this decision and *Spring v Guardian Assurance plc* [1995] 2 AC 296, HL is a fine one. In *Spring*, an investment company was held to have voluntarily assumed responsibility for an ex-employee's reference, even though the regulatory body required the employer to supply a reference. However, it might be said that the company assumed this responsibility by voluntarily entering into the employment contract with the employee.

[332] ibid [5] (Lord Bingham), [38] (Lord Hoffmann), [52] (Lord Rodger), [73] (Lord Walker), [93] (Lord Mance). See also *Martin v Commissioners of Her Majesty's Revenue and Customs* [2006] EWHC 2425.

[333] ibid [4] *per* Lord Bingham, [52] *per* Lord Rodger, [33] *per* Lord Mance. See also *Ministry of Housing and Local Government v Sharp* [1970] 2 QB 223, CA which was approved by the House of Lords in *Customs and Excise Commissioners* and in which Lord Denning, at 268, had emphasized that the recovery of pure economic loss in that case could not be based on a voluntary assumption of responsibility by a clerk performing his statutory duty.

[334] [1990] 1 AC 831, HL: undeterred by a disclaimer of responsibility by the surveyor, which was also held to be unreasonable and therefore ineffective against the purchaser under the Unfair Contract Terms Act 1977, for houses at this lower end of the market.

[335] *Caparo Industries plc v Dickman* [1990] 2 AC 605, HL.

[336] *James McNaughton Paper Group Ltd v Hicks, Anderson & Co* [1991] 2 QB 113, CA.

[337] *Morgan Crucible Co Ltd v Hill Samuel Bank Ltd* [1991] Ch 295, CA.

17.181 This approach to proximity was restated in similar terms recently in *Sutradhar v Natural Environment Research Council*.[338] The absence of a reference to possible arsenic contamination in a geological report in Bangladesh induced the health authorities to take no action to prevent arsenic contamination. But no duty was owed because 'there must be proximity in the sense of a measure of control over and responsibility for the potentially dangerous situation'.[339]

(4) Statutory Negligence

17.182 This section discusses two areas where statutes have replaced the common law of negligence.[340] Statutory negligence in this sense should not be confused with two quite different relationships between statute and the common law. The first, the circumstances in which there may be liability for common law negligence in the exercise of a statutory power, has already been discussed.[341] The power is statutory, but the liability is for breach of a common law duty. The second possible source of confusion is the separate tort of breach of statutory duty. Statutes not directed to the law of tort but imposing duties or regulating standards, for breach of which a criminal penalty is usually imposed, sometimes specify whether breach of the statute is also to give rise to civil liability. Many do not. If they do not, the approach of English courts to these statutes has been to ask whether Parliament intended to confer a private right of action.[342] Discerning an unexpressed intention is a task of some difficulty; Lord Denning described it as a 'game of chance'.[343] Where this intention is found, however, the action for breach of statutory duty is regarded as a distinct tort, which can and often does operate concurrently with negligence liability. The standard of liability in an action for breach of statutory duty depends on the wording of the statute in question. Liability is generally stricter than negligence, but there are instances where the common law duty of care is more demanding than the statutory duty.[344] Many actions for negligence and breach of statutory duty relate to safety in employment.

---

[338] [2006] UKHL 33; [2006] 4 All ER 490, HL.

[339] [2006] UKHL 33; [2006] 4 All ER 490, [38], HL.

[340] On statutes in the law of tort generally see Stanton, Skidmore, Harris and Wright, *Statutory Torts* (2003).

[341] Paras 17.99–17.107.

[342] KM Stanton, *Breach of Statutory Duty in Tort* (1986), RA Buckley, 'Liability in Tort for Breach of Statutory Duty' (1984) 100 LQR 204; Glanville Williams, 'The Effect of Penal Legislation in the Law of Tort' (1960) 23 MLR 233. For the American and Canadian approaches, see JG Fleming, *The Law of Torts* (9th edn, 1998) 137–9.

[343] *Ex p Island Records* [1978] 1 Ch 122, 135.

[344] *Bux v Slough Metals Ltd* [1973] 1 WLR 1358.

(a) The Occupiers' Liability Acts 1957 and 1984

Replacing excessively complicated common law, these Acts are a Code governing **17.183** the liability of an occupier of premises to persons injured there.[345] The 1957 Act provides for an occupier's duty to his visitors and the 1984 Act provides for people other than visitors. It is not necessary that the occupier have entire or exclusive control; there can be more than one occupier.[346]

(i) The duty to visitors

Section 2(2) of the 1957 Act says that an occupier owes to his visitors the duty 'to **17.184** take such care as in all the circumstances of the case is reasonable to see that the visitor will be reasonably safe in using the premises for the purposes for which he is invited or permitted to be there'. The duty imposed on the occupier is a duty of positive action, to see that visitors are reasonably safe. Under section 1(1) the duty is in respect of dangers arising from the state of the premises or from things done or omitted to be done on them. By section 1(3)(a) premises include any fixed or moveable structure, vessel, vehicle or aircraft. Visitors are persons who enter with the occupier's express or implied invitation or permission: 'persons who would at common law be treated as his invitees or licensees' (section 1(2)).[347] Special provisions govern the position of those who enter the premises in exercise of some public or private right (section 1(4) and 1(6)).[348]

Most of the provisions of the 1957 Act express general principles of the modern **17.185** law of negligence. Children must be expected to be less careful than adults (section 2(3)(a)). A person on the premises in exercise of his calling can be expected to appreciate and guard against any special risks of his calling (section 2(3)(b)).[349] An occupier is not responsible for risks which the visitor has willingly accepted as his (section 2(5)). Warning a visitor of a danger may not be enough, unless the warning enables the visitor to be reasonably safe (section 2(4)(a)). Under section 2(4)(b) an occupier is not without more to be liable for a danger created by an independent contractor provided the occupier himself was not negligent. That is, the occupier's liability is not in such a case a simple vicarious liability.

(ii) Excluding liability

The exclusion of liability has caused difficulty. The duty is subject to section 2(1) **17.186** which allows the occupier to vary the duty 'so far as he is free to and does extend, restrict, modify or exclude his duty to any visitor or visitors by agreement

---

[345] *Maguire v Sefton MBC* [2006] EWCA Civ 316; [2006] 1 WLR 2550, CA.
[346] *Wheat v E Lacon & Co Ltd* [1966] AC 552, HL.
[347] *Dunster v Abbott* [1954] 1 WLR 58, CA.
[348] *McGeown v Northern Ireland Housing Executive* [1995] 1 AC 233, HL.
[349] *Roles v Nathan* [1963] 1 WLR 1117, CA.

or otherwise'. The phrase 'by agreement or otherwise' has been held by the majority of a divided Court of Appeal to enable an occupier to exclude liability for negligence by unilateral declaration.[350] This decision must now be read subject to the Unfair Contract Terms Act 1977 (as amended by the Occupiers' Liability Act 1984, section 2), which limits the power to exclude liability for breach of duties arising from the occupation of premises used for the business purposes of the occupier.[351] Liability for negligence causing death or personal injury on such premises cannot be excluded, liability for other loss or damage only if the exclusion is reasonable.

(iii) Trespassers and other uninvited entrants

17.187 The Occupiers' Liability Act 1984 replaces the common law on an occupier's responsibilities to persons who are not his visitors, either because they have entered as of right, or because they are trespassers. Until 1972, the law with regard to trespassers was harsh: an occupier was liable only for intentionally or recklessly harming a trespasser.[352] The rule became increasingly difficult to defend, particularly in the case of trespassing children, and was displaced by the House of Lords in *Herrington v British Railways Board*.[353]

17.188 The 1984 Act to a great extent adopts the *Herrington* decision. An occupier owes a duty to persons other than visitors if he is aware or has reasonable grounds to believe that the premises are dangerous, if he also knows or has reasonable grounds to believe that someone is or might be in the vicinity of the danger and if the risk is one against which in the circumstances he can reasonably be expected to offer some protection. But there will not be a duty unless there is an inherent danger in the premises themselves. An abandoned building will not be dangerous merely because it is alluring for children who may climb, and fall from, the walls or fire escapes.[354]

17.189 The duty under the 1984 Act, if there is one, is to take such care as is reasonable in all the circumstances of the case to see that the uninvited entrant does not suffer death or personal injury. The occupier must have actual knowledge of facts pointing to the danger to persons on the premises; it is not enough that he ought to have known.[355]

17.190 The 1984 Act contains provisions similar to the 1957 Act on warnings and assumption of risk, but says nothing about the effect of notices excluding liability.

---

[350] *White v Blackmore* [1972] 2 QB 651, CA.
[351] Unfair Contract Terms Act 1977, s 1(3); Occupiers' Liability Act 1984, s 2.
[352] *Robert Addie and Sons (Collieries) Ltd v Dumbreck* [1929] AC 358, HL.
[353] [1972] AC 877, HL.
[354] *Keown v Coventry Healthcare NHS Trust* [2006] EWCA Civ 39; [2006] 1 WLR 953, CA.
[355] *Herrington v British Railways Board* [1972] AC 877, 941, HL, *per* Lord Diplock.

It can be argued that the duty to uninvited persons is a minimum standard which cannot be excluded. The Act does not cover property damage and does not apply to persons using the highway.

The decision in *Tomlinson v Congleton BC*[356] was decided under the 1984 Act but shows that, like the 1957 Act, the 1984 Act also expresses general principles of the law of negligence. The local authority had converted an old gravel pit and the surrounding land into a lake and park which attracted many visitors. Families went there to picnic and paddle, but swimming was known to be dangerous. The local authority put up notices prohibiting it but knew that teenagers and others often ignored them. Tomlinson, intending to swim, walked into the water and then, standing knee-deep took a disastrous dive which broke his neck on a sandbank. Once he decided to swim he became a trespasser. His claim under the 1984 Act failed. The central reason, which would have been an answer to any action in negligence, was that, in the terms of s1(3) of the 1984 Act, it was not reasonable to expect the council to protect him from dangers manifestly inherent in his chosen activity. Even if there had been no notices the council would not have been liable. It was all the more unreasonable to expect protection given that effective measures to prevent swimming would have carried a high social cost, in that they would have reduced access and amenity for the thousands of visitors who used the site for the leisure activities for which it had been intended.[357]

17.191

(b) The Congenital Disabilities (Civil Liability) Act 1976

At the time the Congenital Disabilities (Civil Liability) Act 1976 was passed, there was no English authority on whether a child could sue the person responsible for causing him to be born disabled. It was widely thought that the courts would, following decisions in other jurisdictions, allow such an action at common law, and this view was subsequently confirmed by an action brought by children born before 1976.[358] Nevertheless the Law Commission recommended a statute to deal with the difficult policy issues involved.[359] The Act replaces the common law for claims by children born after the commencement date.

17.192

---

[356] [2003] UKHL 47; [2004] 1 AC 46, HL.

[357] A similar tragedy in *Donoghue v Folkestone Properties Ltd* [2003] EWCA Civ 231; [2003] QB 1008, CA was decided under s1(3)(b) of the 1984 Act. The claimant broke his neck when he hit a concealed pile in the defendant's harbour but he was diving at midnight in the middle of winter and, pursuant to that section, the claim was dismissed because there was no reason to suspect swimmers at that time.

[358] *Burton v Islington HA* [1993] QB 204, CA, discussed in I Kennedy and A Grubb, *Principles of Medical Law* (2nd edn, 2004). Cf P Cane, 'Injuries to Unborn Children' (1977) 51 Australian LJ 704.

[359] Law Commission, *Injuries to Unborn Children* (Law Com No 60, 1974, Cmnd 5709).

17.193 Under section 1 a right of action is given to any child born disabled as a result of an occurrence which affected the ability of his parents to have a normal child, or affected the mother during pregnancy or her or the child during birth. The child can sue the person responsible for the occurrence. If the person responsible was the child's mother, however, the child cannot sue her unless she caused the disability by driving a motor vehicle at a time when she knew or ought to have known that she was pregnant. The exception is obviously dictated by insurance considerations. It is not so easy to defend the discrimination between mothers and fathers. It has been recommended that the child should be able to sue either parent for activities for which insurance is compulsory, but neither parent otherwise.[360]

17.194 The Act was extended by the Human Fertilisation and Embryology Act 1990 to cover the case in which the child is born disabled because of negligence in infertility treatments, whether in implantation or in the storage of eggs or sperm. This right of action is subject to a most unusual limitation, namely that the child's right of action is conditional on there being a concurrent right of action by the parent: the defendant can only be liable if he was or would have been liable to the parent if the parent had suffered an injury and sued in due time.[361]

17.195 The special considerations raised by a claim by the child are shown in the defences to such an action. Although in theory the action is the child's, the child's claim may be affected by the contributory negligence of its parents, by a contract made by the parents or, in the case of an injury to the parents preceding the conception of the child, by the parents' knowledge of the risk of the child being born disabled, unless it was the father who knew the risk, and the mother did not.[362]

17.196 The Act has, apparently, not produced litigation, no doubt partly because of the difficulty of proving a connection between antenatal negligence and a congenital disability. Actions by parents for losses suffered by themselves due to the birth of a disabled or unwanted child are not affected by the Act, but are limited by other policy considerations.[363]

D. Negligence: Defences

17.197 The principal defences to a negligence action are contributory negligence and assumption of risk (traditionally embodied in a Latin tag: *volenti non fit injuria*,

---

[360] Report of the Royal Commission on Civil Liability and Compensation for Personal Injury (The Pearson Report), 1978, Cmnd 7054-1 paras 1471–2.

[361] Section 1A(2), criticized by M Brazier, *Medicine, Patients, and the Law* (3rd edn, 2003) 373–4.

[362] Section 1(4), (6), (7).

[363] *McFarlane v Tayside Health Board* [2000] 2 AC 59, HL; *Rees v Darlington Memorial Hospital NHS Trust* [2003] UKHL 52; [2004] 1 AC 309, HL. See discussion in para 17.44.

which means 'no wrong is done to one who consents'). A third defence, that the claimant should be barred from recovery because of his participation in illegal conduct, is sometimes accepted. Again reliance has in the past been placed on a Latin maxim: *ex turpi causa non oritur actio*, which means 'no action arises from a disgraceful cause'. This defence is controversial and its basis remains obscure.

(1) Contributory Negligence

At common law, the contributory negligence of the claimant was a complete **17.198** defence. Someone whose carelessness as to his own safety contributed to the damage otherwise caused by the defendant, was barred from recovery.[364] The manifest injustice of this rule, which took no account of the relative fault of the parties, was partly mitigated by the doctrine of last opportunity: that the party who had the last opportunity to avoid the accident and negligently failed to take it was treated as being solely responsible. Thus, where the claimant's donkey was killed when the defendant drove his cart into it, it was held that, despite the fact that the claimant had negligently allowed the animal to graze on the road, the defendant was liable because, but for his negligent driving, he could have avoided it.[365] In order further to mitigate the common law's basic position, the last opportunity doctrine was stretched to include cases in which the defendant did not in fact have the last opportunity to avoid the disaster but would have had if he had exercised due care.[366]

Both versions of the doctrine of last opportunity, actual and constructive, were **17.199** unsatisfactory. The common law rule was swept away by the Law Reform (Contributory Negligence) Act 1945. Following the precedent set by the Maritime Conventions Act 1911,[367] it was replaced by a regime which gave the courts a power to apportion responsibility for the damage between the parties. Section 1(1) of the 1945 Act provides:

> Where any person suffers damage as the result partly of his own fault and partly of the fault of any other person or persons, a claim in respect of that damage shall not be defeated by reason of the fault of the person suffering the damage, but the damages recoverable in respect thereof shall be reduced to such extent as the court thinks just and equitable having regard to the claimant's share in the responsibility for the damage.

---

[364] The foundational study remains Glanville Williams, *Joint Torts and Contributory Negligence* (1951).

[365] *Davies v Mann* (1842) 10 M & W 546, 152 ER 588.

[366] *British Columbia Electric Railway v Loach* [1916] 1 AC 719, PC. Analysis in Williams (n 364 above) 244–5.

[367] Itself 'to some extent declaratory of the Admiralty rule in this respect': *Admiralty Commissioners v SS Volute* [1922] 1 AC 129, 144, HL, *per* Viscount Birkenhead.

17.200 Since the abrogation of the common law rule, there has been no need for the last opportunity rule. Attempts to revive it as an aspect of the independent issue of causation were robustly resisted.[368] The operation of the 1945 Act can be discussed in terms of its constituent elements: fault, contribution, damage, and apportionment.

(a) Fault

17.201 The 1945 Act applies where a person suffers damage as the result partly of his own fault and partly of the fault of any other person or persons. 'Fault' is defined in section 4 to mean 'negligence, breach of statutory duty or other act or omission which gives rise to a liability in tort or would, apart from this Act, give rise to the defence of contributory negligence'. The first part of the definition clearly refers to the fault of the defendant.[369] It is not necessary to prove that the claimant's contributory fault was a tort; all that is necessary is that the claimant's damage was partly his own fault. It need not be shown that the claimant owed a duty to the defendant.[370]

17.202 'Fault' can include a deliberate act of self-injury by the claimant, since it would be absurd if damages were reduced for mere carelessness but not for intentional self-injury.[371] In this context contributory negligence is a description of the claimant's conduct, not his state of mind. Intentional wrongdoing by the defendant has a different result. If the defendant intended to deceive the claimant, he is not permitted to deny that his deceit was the sole effective cause of the damage. A person liable for deceit cannot plead contributory negligence.[372]

17.203 The criterion of contributory fault, or negligence, is an objective one. Children, however, are only expected to show the degree of care that could reasonably be expected of a child of that age.[373] It is probable that a similar test is applied to disabled persons, such as the blind.[374] There may be other relaxations of a strictly objective standard. Since it is part of an employer's duty to protect employees from the consequences of their own inattention, it is said that courts will be reluctant to find contributory negligence by the employee if the employer is in breach of a statutory duty to his employees. Similarly, courts are reluctant to

---

[368] *Davies v Swan Motor Co* [1949] 2 KB 291, 318 (Evershed LJ), 321 (Denning LJ), CA; cf *Jones v Livox Quarries Ltd* [1952] 2 QB 608, CA.

[369] Williams (n 364 above) 318.

[370] *Davies v Swan Motor Co Ltd* [1949] 2 KB 291, CA.

[371] *Reeves v Commissioner of Police of the Metropolis* [2000] 1 AC 360, HL.

[372] *Alliance & Leicester BS v Edgestop* [1993] 1 WLR 1462 confirmed by the House of Lords in *Standard Chartered Bank v Pakistan National Shipping Corp (No 2)* [2002] UKHL 43; [2003] 1 AC 959, HL.

[373] *Yachuk v Oliver Blais Co Ltd* [1949] AC 386, PC; *Mullin v Richards* [1998] 1 WLR 1304, CA.

[374] *Haley v London Electricity Board* [1965] AC 778, HL.

reduce the damages of someone injured in the act of rescue, but may do so if a professionally trained rescuer is careless as to his own safety.[375] If the defendant creates a dangerous emergency in which the claimant is forced to make an instant choice between 'alternative dangers', the claimant is not penalized for choosing the wrong one.[376]

(b) Contribution

Contributory negligence requires proof of causative effect. Just as the claimant must show that the defendant's negligence caused damage, so a defendant relying on contributory negligence must show that it was a partial cause of the claimant's damage. Hence, although it is negligent for a passenger in a car not to wear a seat belt, there will be no reduction of his damages for an accident caused by the driver unless there is evidence that wearing a seat belt would have reduced or prevented his injuries. **17.204**

It is a question of fact whether the negligence was causally relevant, but it is often more a matter of speculation than proof. In *Stapley v Gypsum Mines Ltd*,[377] Stapley and Dale, miners of equal status, were instructed not to work under an unsafe roof until they had repaired it. Finding that the repair would be difficult, by a joint decision they abandoned the task and went back to work. The roof collapsed and Stapley was killed. Stapley's negligence was clearly partly a cause of his death. The question which divided the House of Lords was whether Dale's agreement to abandon the repair had also contributed to the accident. The majority thought that, without Dale's agreement, Stapley would probably not have gone back to work. The minority pointed out that there was no evidence how far, if at all, Dale had influenced Stapley's decision. **17.205**

(c) Damage

The defence applies when the claimant's fault was partly the cause of his damage. In a typical case, negligence by both parties may have contributed to the accident, but this is not the test. Carelessness by the claimant in not wearing a crash helmet or a seat belt does not make an accident more likely, but may well make the injuries more serious if there is an accident, and thus contribute to the damage suffered by the claimant.[378] It is not clear how wide this category of contributory negligence, the failure to take safety measures at some time before commencing **17.206**

---

[375] *Harrison v British Railways Board* [1981] 3 All ER 679.

[376] *Jones v Boyce* (1816) 1 Stark 493, 171 ER 540: passenger leaped from coach in danger and broke his leg, though with hindsight it was clear that, had he not leaped, he would not have been injured.

[377] [1953] AC 663, HL.

[378] *O'Connell v Jackson* [1972] 1 QB 270, CA; *Froom v Butcher* [1976] QB 286, CA.

an activity, is. Seat belts and crash helmets are closely related to the activity which causes the injury. It is not obvious that a careless failure to take a prescribed drug on the morning of the accident, which has the effect of making the injuries sustained more serious, should be treated the same way.

(d) Apportionment

17.207   The Act provides that the claimant's damages 'shall be reduced to such extent as the court thinks just and equitable having regard to the claimant's share in the responsibility for the damage'.[379] It is not clear whether responsibility is to be assessed in terms of comparative blameworthiness or comparative causative significance. In so far as the question is discussed at all, it appears that the courts treat both approaches as relevant.[380] In any event a wide discretion is conferred to do whatever the court thinks is 'just and equitable'. Most apportionments are a matter of general impression, and not susceptible to much argument.

17.208   There is disagreement in Court of Appeal decisions on the question whether a finding of 100 per cent contributory negligence is possible.[381] The possibility of 100 per cent contributory negligence was not ruled out by the House of Lords in *Reeves v Commissioner of Police of the Metropolis*.[382] In that case the police had failed in their duty to take care to prevent a person in custody from committing suicide. It was decided in the end that the suicide was 50 per cent responsible for his own death.

17.209   In *Froom v Butcher*[383] the Court of Appeal, in order to avoid expensive enquiries in individual seat belt cases, said that, if the damage would have been prevented altogether by wearing a seat belt, the reduction for contributory negligence should be 25 per cent, but if the effect of a seat belt would have been to make the injuries less severe, the reduction should be 15 per cent. The wording of the Act suggests that the apportionment should be a matter for the judge in each case. Lord Denning, in giving this guidance, said that he thought that this tariff would be just and equitable in the great majority of cases.[384]

---

[379] Section 51(1).

[380] *Stapley v Gypsum Mines* [1953] AC 663, 682, HL, *per* Lord Reid.

[381] *Pitts v Hunt* [1991] 1 QB 24, 48, CA, *per* Beldam LJ. Compare Buxton LJ and contrast Morritt LJ in *Reeves v Commissioner of Police of the Metropolis* [1998] 2 All ER 381, CA.

[382] [2000] 1 AC 360, 372, HL.

[383] [1976] QB 286, CA.

[384] In *Gregory v Kelly* [1978] RTR 426 there was an aggravating factor, in that the driver who left his seat belt undone also knew the car was defective, so that 40% was deducted. In *Capps v Miller* [1989] 1 WLR 839, CA a motorcyclist who was wearing a crash helmet but had not fastened the chin-strap suffered a deduction of 10%.

In cases where the claimant is suing more than one defendant and is answered by **17.210** a plea of contributory negligence, it is important to keep distinct the exercises of apportioning responsibility under the 1945 Act and contribution proceedings between the defendants under the Civil Liability (Contribution) Act 1978. The question whether the claimant's damages are to be reduced for contributory negligence is decided as between the claimant on the one hand and the defendants jointly on the other, while contribution concerns only the defendants.[385]

(e) Contributory negligence and other torts

The Law Reform (Contributory Negligence) Act 1945, section 4 expressly makes **17.211** contributory negligence available as a defence to an action for breach of statutory duty. It is not a defence to an action for deceit.[386] The position where the defendant's liability is strict is less clear. The Animals Act 1971, section 10 and the Consumer Protection Act 1987, section 6(4) provide that contributory negligence is to be a defence. The Torts (Interference with Goods) Act 1977, section 11 excludes the defence in proceedings founded on conversion or intentional trespass to goods. It has been held by the New Zealand Court of Appeal that contributory negligence can be a defence to a claim based on breach of fiduciary duty.[387] However, that cannot be right.[388] It is of the essence of a fiduciary relationship that the beneficiary is relieved of the need to watch over his own affairs and monitor the fiduciary.

(2) Consent, Assumption of Risk

The Latin tag *volenti non fit injuria* (no wrong is done to one who consents) **17.212** embraces both the defence of consent to an act which would otherwise be a tort and the defence that the claimant agreed to assume the risk of injury. Consent is the appropriate formulation for intentional acts, assumption of risk better describes the operation of the *volenti* defence in a negligence action.

(a) The operation of the defence

Volenti non fit injuria, whether in the form of consent to intentional acts or **17.213** in the form of assumption of the risk of negligence, is an absolute defence. A person who has consented has not suffered a wrong and is not entitled to

---

[385] *Fitzgerald v Lane* [1989] AC 328, HL.

[386] *Alliance and Leicester BS v Edgestop* [1993] 1 WLR 1462; *Standard Chartered Bank v Pakistan National Shipping Corp (No 2)* [2002] UKHL 43; [2003] 1 AC 959, HL.

[387] *Day v Mead* [1987] 2 NZLR 443.

[388] R Meagher, D Heydon, M Leeming, *Meagher Gummow & Lehane's Equity Doctrines and Remedies* (4th edn, 2002) 2000–9. Cf Handley JA, writing extrajudicially, in PD Finn (ed), *Essays on Damages* (1992) 126–7.

any compensation. There is no apportionment. Consequently, although there may be a considerable overlap on the facts of a case between the defences of contributory negligence and *volenti*, the effect of the defences became markedly different in 1945.

17.214   Unsurprisingly, cases since 1945 have shown a reluctance to accept the *volenti* defence where apportionment for contributory negligence is available as an alternative. Although they may often overlap, there is an essential difference between the two defences: contributory negligence implies, however objectively, fault; consent and assumption of risk may not. It is not necessarily blameworthy to take risks; taking risks may be the object of the exercise. The desire to limit the scope of the defence has nevertheless led to fine distinctions in the cases and a substantial measure of statutory control.

(b) Acceptance of the risk

17.215   The requirements are that there must be both knowledge of the risk and free acceptance of it. The latter requirement has been particularly important in actions brought by employees against employers. The courts took the view that economic pressure to do dangerous work prevented the defence being used against an employee in all but the most exceptional cases.[389] The defence is always displaced where there is evidence of pressures, whether social, economic or merely force of habit.[390] Where, however, two workers combined together deliberately to short-circuit mandatory safety procedures, the House of Lords accepted, emphasizing the extreme nature of the facts, that each had accepted the risks inherent in the negligence of the other.[391]

17.216   The cases further distinguish between acceptance of the ordinary risks of an enterprise and acceptance of the risk that the enterprise will be carried out negligently; the former does not imply the latter.[392] Similarly in some cases a distinction is drawn between acceptance of the physical risk that one may be injured, and acceptance of the legal risk of not being compensated for the injury. Someone who gratuitously agrees to teach a neighbour to drive but makes specific enquiries about insurance cover is making it clear that he would expect to be compensated for injuries. The knowledge that injury might ensue did not amount to a relevant acceptance of the risk.[393]

---

[389] *Smith v Baker & Sons* [1891] AC 325, HL.
[390] *ICI v Shatwell* [1965] AC 656, 687–8, HL, *per* Lord Pearce.
[391] *ICI v Shatwell* [1965] AC 656, HL.
[392] *Slater v Clay Cross Co Ltd* [1956] 2 QB 264, CA.
[393] *Nettleship v Weston* [1971] 2 QB 691.

There is indeed some authority for the view that the defence only applies where   **17.217**
the facts show an agreement to waive any claim for negligence. In *Nettleship v
Weston*, for instance, Lord Denning MR went so far as to suggest that nothing
short of such agreement could be sufficient.[394]

The defence has been held inapplicable even where a prisoner found to be of   **17.218**
sound mind hanged himself, so that he himself chose to die. To have allowed the
defence would have rendered nugatory the duty on the police to take care to
prevent suicide by persons in custody. The defence therefore cannot be pleaded
where the voluntary act is precisely the one which the defendant is under a duty
to prevent.[395] The decision is explicable in terms of the well-known statistics on
the increased likelihood of suicide attempts by those suffering the stresses of
imprisonment. Duties to prevent others deliberately injuring themselves are
rare, but this is one of them.

It is generally accepted that assumption of risk cannot be pleaded against someone   **17.219**
injured whilst attempting to rescue a person in danger, whether the danger was
created by a third party or by the very person in danger.[396] This encouragement of
rescue attempts is also extended to members of public rescue services. A member
of a fire brigade injured in the course of fighting a fire can sue the householder
whose negligence started the fire.[397] Similarly, it is accepted that the intervention
of a rescuer is always to be regarded as reasonably foreseeable.

(c) Consent

Acceptance of risk is the appropriate language to cover all the cases of uninten-   **17.220**
tional contact, but where the contact is intentional the better substatement of
the defence is in terms of consent. The simplest example is participation in a
contact sport. Voluntary participation in rugby precludes an action for battery.[398]
It is different where the incident is completely outside the rules of the game,
as where one player commits a serious and dangerous foul on another.[399] Normal
physical contact in everyday life, jostling in a street or on a crowded bus, has
been regarded as protected by implied consent to such contact, but it may be that
there is simply a general exception from liability for all contact which is generally
acceptable in the ordinary course of everyday life.[400]

---

[394] ibid 701, CA. This position is approved by AJE Jaffey, '*Volenti non fit iniuria*' [1985] CLJ 87.
[395] *Reeves v Commissioner of Police of the Metropolis* [2000] 1 AC 360, HL.
[396] *Baker v TE Hopkins & Son Ltd* [1959] 1 WLR 966, CA; *Chadwick v British Railways Board*
[1967] 1 WLR 912; *Harrison v British Railways Board* [1981] 3 All ER 679.
[397] *Ogwo v Taylor* [1988] AC 431, HL.
[398] *Simms v Leigh RFC* [1969] 2 All ER 923.
[399] *Condon v Basi* [1985] 1 WLR 866, CA.
[400] *Re F (A Mental Patient: Sterilization)* [1990] 2 AC 1, 72–3, HL, *per* Lord Goff.

17.221 The most difficult questions about the operation of the defence of consent are those concerning consent to medical treatment.[401] A medical procedure involving physical contact is a battery if performed without the consent of the patient, except in special circumstances. An adult has an unquestioned right to refuse medical treatment, however irrationally, provided he understands the consequences of his decision.[402]

17.222 The first major difficulty is where the patient is unable to consent because, temporarily or permanently, he lacks capacity to do so. If an emergency arises during the course of an operation while the patient is unconscious, steps taken to deal with it may be justified by the argument of necessity, provided that no more is done than is reasonably required. If the patient is a child, parents may consent on his behalf or the child may be made a ward of court. If, due to mental disability, the incapacity is permanent, patients may be treated if it is in their best interests, to save life or to improve or prevent deterioration in their physical or mental health. Even the sterilization of a very seriously retarded adult patient can be justified under this head.[403]

17.223 The position of children is more complicated. A minor over the age of sixteen can consent to any medical treatment without parental consent.[404] *Gillick v West Norfolk & Wisbech AHA*[405] held that a child under sixteen can also give a valid consent provided that he is mature enough to understand the nature of the treatment.

17.224 It does not follow that children also have the right to refuse treatment. There is statutory provision that a child of sufficient understanding can refuse consent to medical and psychiatric investigations under the Children Act 1989, sections 38(6), 43(8), and 44(7). Outside these statutory provisions, several decisions have held that a child's refusal can be overridden by the consent of someone with parental responsibility.[406] If parents refuse their consent to medical treatment, the paramount consideration in deciding whether to override that refusal is the welfare of the child, but the reality may be that the welfare of the child is dependent on the co-operation of the parent.[407]

---

[401] Comprehensive discussion in I Kennedy and A Grubb, *Principles of Medical Law* (2nd edn, 2004) paras 3.01–4.223.

[402] *Re T (Adult: Refusal of Treatment)* [1993] Fam 95, CA; *Re B (Adult: Refusal of Treatment)* [2002] EWHC 429; [2002] 2 All ER 449.

[403] *Re F (A Mental Patient: Sterilization)* [1990] 2 AC 1, HL.

[404] Family Law Reform Act 1969, s 8.

[405] [1986] AC 112, HL.

[406] *Re R (Wardship: Consent to Treatment)* [1992] Fam 11, CA; *Re W (A Minor) (Medical Treatment)* [1993] Fam 64, CA.

[407] *Re T (A Minor) (Wardship: Medical Treatment)* [1997] 1 WLR 906, CA.

Consent must be freely given. Thus courts must be aware that apparent consent **17.225** to medical treatment by persons in prison may not be true consent. The reality of consent is a question of fact to be determined in the individual case.[408] If the patient is not told the nature and purpose of the operation, the consent will be ineffective and the operation a battery.[409] The doctor or surgeon has a duty of care to warn the patient of the risks of treatment. The extent of this obligation is controversial. The majority opinion in England, as laid down in *Sidaway v Royal Bethlem Hospital*,[410] is that it is to be judged in the same way as other claims of medical negligence, by asking whether the doctor followed a practice in warning of risks which would be accepted as proper by a competent body of professional opinion, subject to the overriding jurisdiction of the court to decide that disclosure of a particular risk was obviously necessary.

In the *Sidaway* case only Lord Scarman advocated the test, which has been adopted **17.226** elsewhere, of asking whether the risk was one which a prudent patient would wish to know, rather than one which doctors are accustomed to reveal.[411] In most cases there will not be a very big difference between the two approaches: most doctors will advise their patients of risks which a prudent patient would wish to know. But a doctor may withhold information which he believes would confuse or alarm a particular patient. The whole court in the *Sidaway* case agreed, however, that a patient's questions must be answered truthfully.

(d) Statutory invalidation of some consents

It frequently happens that protection from liability is sought through notices or **17.227** contractual terms which purport to secure the other's consent to acting at his own risk. A number of statutes have intervened to render some such consents or purported consents ineffective. The Consumer Protection Act 1987, section 7 which prevents the limitation or exclusion of the liability for defective products which is imposed by the Act by any contract term, notice or other provision, is typical.

The Road Traffic Act 1988, section 149, re-enacting earlier legislation, makes inef- **17.228** fective any antecedent agreement or understanding between the user of a vehicle and his passenger which purports to negative or restrict the user's liability to persons required by the Act to be covered by an insurance policy. Section 149(3) provides: 'The fact that a person so carried has willingly accepted as his the risk of negligence on the part of the user shall not be treated as negativing any such liability of the user.' After some initial hesitation, it is now settled that section 149(3)

---

[408] *Freeman v Home Office (No 2)* [1984] QB 524, CA.
[409] *Chatterton v Gerson* [1981] QB 432.
[410] [1985] AC 871, HL.
[411] ibid 886. Cf *Canterbury v Spence* 464 F 2d 772 (1972); *Rogers v Whittaker* (1992) 175 CLR 479, HCA.

covers implied assumption of risk as well as express agreements. So in *Pitts v Hunt*, it was held that the plea could not be raised even against a pillion passenger who had incited and encouraged a motor cyclist to drive dangerously while drunk, thus causing the accident in which the passenger was injured and the motor cyclist killed.[412] The passenger was, however, then barred from recovery by the defence of illegality, which will be discussed immediately below.

17.229   In situations where the Road Traffic Act 1988 does not apply, the courts unhesitatingly apply the defence of *volenti* to participants in drunken joyriding. *Morris v Murray* was an extreme case involving a flight in a light aircraft which ended in disaster.[413] The plane crashed, the claimant was injured, and the pilot was killed. The evidence was that the claimant and the pilot had been drinking heavily all afternoon. Nevertheless the claimant agreed to go flying with the pilot and helped him get the plane ready. The Court of Appeal held that the deceased's estate could not be liable because the claimant had accepted the risk.

17.230   The Unfair Contract Terms Act 1977 contains a general control of business liability. It restricts the effectiveness of attempts to restrict or exclude obligations arising in the course of a business or from the occupation of premises used for business purposes of the occupier.[414] Section 2 provides that in such contexts:

> A person cannot by reference to any contract term or to a notice given to persons generally or to particular persons exclude or restrict his liability for death or personal injury resulting from negligence.

17.231   In the case of other loss or damage, section 2(2) provides that a person cannot so exclude or restrict his liability for negligence except in so far as the term or notice satisfies the requirement of reasonableness. Further, under section 2(3) where a contract term or notice purports to exclude or restrict liability for negligence a person's agreement to or awareness of it is not of itself to be taken as indicating his voluntary acceptance of any risk.

17.232   The proper interpretation of section 2(3) is not certain. It may be that the distinction is between knowledge of or agreement to the term or notice, which of itself is not sufficient, and knowledge of and agreement to run the risk, which is. The requirement of full knowledge of and full consent to a risk should not be watered down by the blanket terms of a contract or notice.

---

[412] *Pitts v Hunt* [1991] 1 QB 24, CA.

[413] [1991] 2 QB 6, CA.

[414] Under s 14 'business' includes a profession and the activities of government departments and local and public authorities. See also s 1(3)(b), as amended by Occupiers Liability Act 1984, s 2.

(3) Illegality, Public Policy

The third general defence to a negligence action is the most obscure in both scope **17.233** and rationale. It is clear that in a number of cases a claimant's action may be defeated by his involvement in illegal or immoral conduct, either independently or in a joint illegal enterprise with the defendant. One burglar cannot hope to sue another for failing to take reasonable care in blowing open a safe. In *Clunis v Camden and Islington Health Authority*[415] the claimant was a mental patient who had been released from hospital. After his release he attacked and killed a man. He was convicted of manslaughter. He sued the health authority, alleging that its negligent care had brought his troubles upon him. The Court of Appeal threw the case out saying that he could not build a claim on homicide. Though all might agree on that proposition, the principle has proved difficult to enunciate.

(a) Theoretical and technical difficulties

If the claimant has committed a crime, he should pay the criminal penalty **17.234** appointed. To deprive him also of compensation for personal injuries is to use the law of tort to impose an extra punishment which may well be out of all proportion to the seriousness of the crime. Arguably, to bar the civil claim is to confuse the functions of the civil and the criminal law. Behind that theoretical problem there is the more technical one of drawing a line between the cases in which the criminality will and those in which it will not bring about a civil forfeiture.[416] The Law Commission has suggested, in a consultation paper, that the defence should be put on a statutory basis giving the courts a structured discretion.[417] In contrast, in *Vellino v Chief Constable of Greater Manchester*[418] Sedley LJ argued in his dissent for an apportionment solution based on the Law Reform (Contributory Negligence) Act 1945.

(b) Practical difficulties

The practical difficulties raised by the defence are serious ones. It is accepted that **17.235** not all illegal conduct will bar an action. Many parties in actions for personal injuries in a highway accident have at the time been committing a highway offence. Their right to compensation for their injuries is not questioned in any but the most extreme cases (as in the *Clunis* case above and in *Pitts v Hunt*, which is revisited immediately below). In actions for breach of statutory duty arising out of an injury at work, it has long been settled that the claimant worker's own breach of a

---

[415] [1998] QB 978, CA.
[416] The same difficulty confronts the law of restitution of unjust enrichment: paras 18.282–18.289.
[417] Law Commission, *The Illegality Defence in Tort* (Consultation Paper No 160, 2001).
[418] [2001] EWCA Civ 1249; [2002] 1 WLR 218, CA.

safety regulation will not bar the action, because the purpose of the regulation is to protect the worker.[419] The courts have been reluctant to identify the point along the scale of seriousness at which the claimant's illegal conduct bars the action.

17.236   Furthermore, the relationship between the illegality defence and the other defences has not been clarified. In *Pitts v Hunt*, it was decided that although the defence of assumption of risk was barred by the Road Traffic Act 1988, section 149(3), the defence of illegality was nonetheless available.[420] But in *National Coal Board v England*, it was held that the inclusion of breach of statutory duty in the definition of 'fault' in the Law Reform (Contributory Negligence) Act 1945 made it clear that contributory negligence was the appropriate defence where the claimant himself was in breach.[421]

(c) Justifications

17.237   A number of justifications for the defence have been put forward. One possible argument is that the need to deter criminal conduct justifies the use of tort to reinforce the criminal law. In formal terms this is unsatisfactory. Since in many cases both sides have been involved in the illegal conduct, the effect of the bar is that, while one side may be deterred, the other partner in the same criminal conduct is relieved of liability. The substance, of course, is likely to be that it is the defendant's insurance company which is relieved of liability, while the claimant's losses are met by social security and the National Health Service.

17.238   A second justification might be that the defence prevents the criminal claimant from profiting from his illegality. This is an accepted proposition in other areas of law and can sometimes be effective in a tort case. An action for personal injuries brought by a professional burglar would be unlikely to succeed in a claim for loss of future earnings.[422]

17.239   A more general argument is that the defence of illegality, though not generally appropriate in tort cases, is held in reserve for cases where it is necessary to uphold the dignity or integrity of the law. This was the position of the Supreme Court of Canada in *Hall v Hebert*. McLachlin J, delivering the majority judgment, said that the illegality bar should be used only in very limited circumstances. It is, she said, a weapon:

> . . .to preserve the integrity of the legal system, and is exercisable only where this concern is in issue. This concern is in issue where a damage award in a civil suit

---

[419] *National Coal Board v England* [1954] AC 403, HL; also *Progress & Properties v Craft* (1976) 135 CLR 651, HCA.

[420] Paras 17.228 and 17.242.

[421] [1954] AC 403, HL.

[422] *Burns v Edman* [1970] 2 QB 541.

would, in effect, allow a person to profit from illegal or wrongful conduct, or would permit an evasion or rebate of a penalty prescribed by the criminal law.[423]

This starts with integrity but it draws on other ideas too, such as the principle against profiting from wrongdoing and the need to support and not to undercut the criminal law. **17.240**

(d) The Australian approach

In a succession of cases,[424] the High Court of Australia developed a doctrine, based on common law principles, that illegality should bar an action where the illegal conduct was such as to make it inappropriate or impossible to formulate an appropriate standard of care. If a reasonable person would not engage in the activity in question, no reasonable standard can be set. If it is impossible to formulate a standard of care, there can be no duty of care. While this approach explains why one burglar cannot sue another for negligence in blowing up a safe, it is less satisfactory in activities, such as driving, in which there is a generally accepted standard of care but the question is whether that standard is to be applied to criminally engaged parties. And it could not explain the *Clunis* case introduced above, where it would not have been difficult to set a standard of health authority care of mental patients in the community. **17.241**

(e) The English cases

The English authorities are in a state of confusion. In *Pitts v Hunt*,[425] where the claimant had incited the defendant to heavy drinking and dangerous driving on the highway, a majority of the Court of Appeal purported to adopt the Australian approach. Beldam LJ, agreeing that the defence applied, preferred to ask whether the seriousness of the illegality was such that compensating the claimant would shock the public conscience. **17.242**

This 'public conscience' test was, however, disapproved by the House of Lords in *Tinsley v Milligan*, albeit in the different context of the assertion of property rights.[426] Noticing this disapproval, the Court of Appeal in *Clunis v Camden & Islington Health Authority*[427] held that the public conscience test was also inappropriate to distinguish between criminal activity which would bar recovery in tort **17.243**

---

[423] *Hall v Hebert* [1993] 2 SCR 159, 169; 101 DLR (4th) 129, 160 SCC.

[424] *Smith v Jenkins* (1970) 119 CLR 397, HCA; *Jackson v Harrison* (1978) 138 CLR 438, HCA; *Gala v Preston* (1991) 172 CLR 243, HCA. There is now a shadow cast upon these cases by the rejection of the Australian notion of 'proximity', which those cases had employed, as part of the test for duty of care. See *Joslyn v Berryman* (2003) 214 CLR 552, 564 [30], HCA.

[425] [1991] QB 24, CA.

[426] [1994] 1 AC 340, HL.

[427] [1998] QB 978; see also *Burns v Edman* [1970] 2 QB 541.

and activity which would not. Instead the Court of Appeal applied the test approved by the House of Lords for property matters. The rule, which, it is said, applies in all areas of law, is that the court will not lend its aid to a litigant who relies on his own illegal or immoral act in putting forward his case. Since the claim in this case was based on the claimant's conviction for manslaughter, which he alleged that proper treatment by the defendant would have prevented, his claim failed because it was necessarily based on his own illegal act.

17.244 By contrast, in *Revill v Newbery* the claimant was a burglar bringing an action against an occupier who had shot him.[428] On this occasion the Court of Appeal held that the claimant's action for personal injuries was not defeated by the fact that the claimant was a burglar attempting to enter the defendant's premises. It simply took the view that trespassers were entitled to some protection, and the defendant had exceeded the limits of legitimate self-defence.

17.245 It is equally difficult to reconcile the Court of Appeal's decisions on physical assault. In *Lane v Holloway*,[429] where gratuitous provocation provoked a disproportionate counterattack, Lord Denning took the view that illegal conduct by the claimant, though relevant to a claim for exemplary damages, should not affect his claim for compensatory damages. On the other hand, in *Murphy v Culhane*, an assault in the course of a fight raised the defences of illegality, *volenti non fit injuria* and 100 per cent contributory negligence, and the Court of Appeal seemed to think that the defence of illegality was available.[430] As things stand, therefore, the law here seems to offer not so much a principle as a safety valve.

E. Wrongs Actionable Concurrently with Negligence

17.246 English law has no objection to concurrent liability, whether between torts or equitable wrongs and some other category of cause of action such as contract[431] or between one wrong and another. We have already drawn attention to the fact that negligence cuts across nominate torts which derive their identity from the nature of the particular right which is infringed by their commission.[432] With every step the growth of negligence in the twentieth century increased the

---

[428] [1996] QB 567, CA.
[429] [1968] 1 QB 379, CA.
[430] [1977] QB 94, CA.
[431] *Henderson v Merrett Syndicates Ltd* [1995] 2 AC 145, HL.
[432] Paras 17.08–17.12.

frequency of this kind of concurrence.[433] The process still continues.[434] This section will look briefly at the principal torts with which negligence liability may co-exist.[435] In some cases the co-existence is peaceful; in others an infiltration of older rules by negligence is in progress.

The difference between co-existence and infiltration matters. Since the rights-based torts are not now protected by rules of priority and subsidiarity such as marked the early battles between established actions and the action on the case,[436] they can only survive so far as they continue to offer advantages over the innominate action for negligence. The advantage which most of them offer is that the claimant is relieved of the burden of proving fault. It follows that if the advance of negligence takes the form of infiltration—that is, the insertion in the nominate tort of a new requirement that negligence be proved—that infiltrated nominate tort must almost certainly sicken and die. For it thus loses the advantage which was the *raison d'être* of its survival. Weir thus says, of the relation between negligence and trespass to the person:

> The most obvious take-over of one tort by another took place in 1959 when Diplock, LJ decided at first instance that it no longer stated a cause of action to plead 'You shot me'—a classic allegation of trespass to the person—but that, in order to get into court one must add 'intentionally or negligently'.[437]

(1) Trespass

Trespass *vi et armis* (with force and arms) was once the dominant tort or family of torts. The requirement of 'force and arms' was satisfied by any contact with the claimant's body or goods and land in his possession. The claimant pleaded an attack dressed up as done with force and arms but only had to show that the defendant did the interfering act.[438] It is easy to understand the liability as having historically been strict, and it has frequently been so understood, but that is at best a formal truth. The reality was that a defendant would generally plead the general issue, affirming that he was not guilty of the trespass alleged. The real facts would come out before the jury, and the jury would not find for the claimant if

17.247

17.248

---

[433] Tony Weir, 'The Staggering March of Negligence' in P Cane and J Stapleton (eds), *The Law of Obligations: Essays in Celebration of John Fleming* (1998) 97, esp 102–18.

[434] *Spring v Guardian Assurance plc* [1995] 2 AC 296, HL (negligence cuts across defamation); *Cambridge Water Co Ltd v Eastern Leather plc* [1994] 2 AC 264, HL (negligence cuts across the liability in *Rylands v Fletcher* (1868) LR 3 HL 330): see paras 17.08–17.12.

[435] For breach of statutory duty, see para 17.182.

[436] JH Baker, *Introduction to English Legal History* (4th edn, 2002) 67, with 341, 394, 406, and 424.

[437] Tony Weir (n 433 above) 108. He adds that trespass to the person is clinging to its independent life: *Stubbings v Webb* [1993] AC 498, HL.

[438] JH Baker (n 436 above) 456–9.

the defendant had not been at fault. Nor was this the exercise of an illegitimate discretion for the law, when the old procedures allowed the judges to state it, held that there was no liability if the act happened 'utterly without the defendant's fault'.[439]

17.249 There was a significant departure from the substance of the earlier law when it was decided in relatively recent times that a claimant must allege and be prepared to prove either negligence or, in trespass, intention.[440] The important point is that proof of intention is understood simply as meaning proof that the interfering act was willed even if none of the consequences was desired. A person who digs on his land and strikes a cable which is hidden under the land is not liable for trespass because the 'act of interference' was not intended.[441] Liability is imposed, subject to defences, for the willed interfering act, however impossible it was for the defendant to discover, or avoid, the consequences. It seems that this must be the law for all kinds of trespass now.[442]

(a) Trespass to the person: battery

17.250 In cases of negligent contact leading to injury and damage there are now almost no advantages in suing in trespass instead of negligence, except perhaps its being actionable *per se* without proof of damage. In cases of intentional conduct actionability *per se* used to support, in an appropriately outrageous case, an award of exemplary damages.[443]

17.251 Of more general importance are cases of non-negligent contact. It remains the law that liability for an intentional trespass starts from an assumption of the prima facie unlawfulness of intentional contact, which the defendant has then to excuse or justify. This has enormous significance in relation to medical treatment. Every treatment involving direct contact with a patient's body, and necessarily, therefore, all surgery, is prima facie a battery—that is, a trespass with force and arms against the person.[444] Much of the law relating to medical practice thus turns on

---

[439] *Weaver v Ward* (1616), *Gibbons v Pepper* (1695). Both of these are now only to be read in JH Baker and SFC Milsom, *Sources of English Legal History: Private Law to 1750* (1986) 331–7, since the authors there use sources superior to the laconic printed reports. Cf D Ibbetson, *A Historical Introduction to the Law of Obligations* (1999) 156–8.

[440] *Fowler v Lanning* [1959] 1 QB 426; *Letang v Cooper* (1965) 1 QB 232, CA.

[441] *National Coal Board v JE Evans & Co (Cardiff) LD* [1951] 2 KB 861, CA.

[442] Even incursions into land: *League Against Cruel Sports v Scott* [1986] QB 240. For trespass or interference with title, see para 17.254.

[443] *Prince Albert v Strange* (1849) 2 De G & Sm 652, 690, 64 ER 293, 310, *per* Knight Bruce VC. Nowadays the same outcome can be reached in the form of compensatory damages for injury to feelings. It is no longer necessary to describe such awards as aggravated damages: *Richardson v Howie* [2004] EWCA Civ 1127, CA.

[444] The heterodox view expressed in *Wilson v Pringle* [1987] QB 237, CA that there must be a hostile contact was repudiated in *Re F (Mental Patient: Sterilization)* [1990] 2 AC 173, HL 563–4.

the definition of defences to that prima facie liability. Hence the case law focuses on the limits of consent and the extent to which necessity can be invoked in place of consent.[445]

(b) Trespass to the person: false imprisonment

False imprisonment is no more than a subform of trespass to the person. **17.252** 'Imprisonment' is a misnomer. False confinement would be nearer the mark. If, even for a short time, a person is confined on all sides, whether in a building or out of doors, the person who has brought about his confinement, or has instigated or induced it,[446] will have committed this tort. He will be liable unless he can point to a legal justification. It is not necessary for the claimant to have known at the time of his confinement that he was confined.[447] This form of trespass is an important bulwark in the defence of liberty, especially against agents of the state and courts which exceed their jurisdiction.[448] It shares this role with the tort of malicious prosecution.[449] Attempts to extend it to protect those already in prison from wrongful further confinement have not been successful, because a prisoner has 'no residual liberty'.[450] As a strict liability tort, the action exists even where a prison governor acts in good faith and in accordance with current case law which is subsequently overruled.[451]

False imprisonment is actionable *per se*, and negligence is not. Most false impris **17.253** onments involve an intention as to the consequence, in confining the claimant. But, as in other cases of trespass, it is enough that the interfering direct act is intended.

In that case a very seriously retarded woman was sterilized, and it was held that in the circumstances her best interests served the turn of consent. Full discussion in I Kennedy and A Grubb, *Principles of Medical Law* (2nd edn, 2004) 3.01–4.223.

[445] *Re F* (previous note) is now the leading case. Cf *Gillick v Wisbech and Norfolk AHA* [1986] AC 112 HL: children, consent of parents; *Marshall v Curry* [1933] 3 DLR 260 (SC of Nova Scotia): diseased testicle removed during hernia operation; *Murray v McMurchy* [1949] 2 DLR 442 (SC of B Columbia): sterilization during Caesarian.

[446] *Davidson v Chief Constable of North Wales* [1994] 2 All ER 597, CA. The case ultimately shows that merely to give information which leads to arrest and confinement does not amount to instigating and procuring the imprisonment.

[447] *Murray v Minister of Defence* [1988] 1 WLR 692, HL.

[448] *Houlden v Smith* (1850) 14 QB 841, 117 ER 323; *O'Connor v Isaacs* [1956] 2 QB 288, CA.

[449] Para 17.367. Cf discussion in *Davidson v Chief Constable of North Wales* [1994] 2 All ER 597, CA.

[450] *R v Deputy Governor of Parkurst Prison, ex p Hague* [1992] 1 AC 58, HL; cf FA Trindade, 'The Modern Tort of False Imprisonment', in N Mullany, *Torts in the Nineties* (1997) ch 8.

[451] *R v Governor of Brockhill Prison, ex p Evans (No 2)* [2001] AC 19, HL. However, if a court makes a mistake and issues a judgment for a sentence longer than was intended, the error has to be corrected by due process of law. If it is not corrected and the prisoner serves longer than he should have done, there is no false imprisonment on the part of the Governor: *Quinland v Governor of Swaleside Prison* [2002] EWCA Civ 174; [2003] QB 306.

In contrast, a negligent false imprisonment is actionable as negligence if it causes loss. For instance if I carelessly leave a building without keys and a high wind catches the door from my hand and blows the door shut, locking you inside.

(c) Trespass to land or goods

17.254 Trespass to land is committed by direct physical interference with another's possession of land without legal justification. The typical trespass is entering land without the consent (express or implied) of the possessor but other direct interferences with the possessor's rights are also trespasses. A visitor can become a trespasser if he exceeds the limits of his licence to enter, for example by disobeying a No Swimming notice.[452] Since possession of land includes possession of such airspace as is necessary for ordinary use and enjoyment, an advertising sign projecting over land can be a trespass,[453] but an aeroplane flying several hundred feet overhead is not.[454] The intrusion must be a voluntary act but it is no defence that the trespasser did not intend to trespass or thought the land belonged to him. There are, however, a number of recognized justifications, ranging from police powers to enter to legislation widening public access to the countryside.[455] Trespass to goods, direct interference with another's possession of goods, has been largely overshadowed in modern law by the tort of conversion, but is occasionally useful.[456]

(2) Nuisance

17.255 The tort of nuisance is divided into two strands, public nuisance and private nuisance.[457] Both private and public nuisance are frequently joined with claims in negligence.[458]

(a) Public nuisance

17.256 The word 'nuisance', which, like 'annoy', is connected with the Latin *nocumentum* (harm), is not inherently specialized. It can refer to any obnoxious conduct.

---

[452] *Tomlinson v Congleton BC* [2003] UKHL 47; [2004] 1 AC 46.

[453] *Kelsen v Imperial Tobacco Co* [1957] 2 QB 554.

[454] *Bernstein v Skyviews & General Ltd* [1978] QB 479, and Civil Aviation Act 1949.

[455] Countryside and Rights of Way Act 2000.

[456] *Penfolds Wines Pty Ltd v Elliott* (1946) 74 CLR 204, HCA. See also para 17.317 and 17.322.

[457] A comprehensive and reliable account of the fundamentals is RA Buckley, *The Law of Nuisance* (1981); see also AWB Simpson, 'Victorian Judges and the Problem of Social Cost: *Tipping v St Helens Smelting Company* (1865)' in his *Leading Cases in the Common Law* (1995) 163. The following two articles have received strong judicial approval: FH Newark, 'The Boundaries of Nuisance' (1949) 65 LQR 480; C Gearty, 'The Place of Private Nuisance in a Modern Law of Torts' [1989] CLJ 214.

[458] *Overseas Tankship (UK) Ltd v Miller Steamship Co Pty Ltd (The Wagon Mound) (No 2)* [1967] 1 AC 617, PC; *Bolton v Stone* [1951] AC 850, HL; *Goldman v Hargrave* [1967] 1 AC 645, HL. On the relation between nuisance and negligence, see paras 17.264–17.266.

Public nuisance is always stated with corresponding breadth as any interference with the rights of the public as such.[459] In practice the only recurrent case is obstructing or endangering the highway.[460] Public nuisance is a crime. It only becomes a tort when someone suffers 'special damage'—that is, when some individual is harmed to a degree quite different from the widespread annoyance to the general public.

(b) Private nuisance

Private nuisance is by contrast only a tort. It has become specialized as the arbiter **17.257** between competing uses of land. It is concerned with the relations between neighbours. The wider social interest in the control of land use falls mostly to public law, especially to the law relating to planning, public health, and the protection of the environment.

(i) The role of private nuisance

Private nuisance protects land and the enjoyment of land from interference **17.258** arising from unreasonable user of other land.[461] One neighbour's rights have to be balanced against another's. In *Bamford v Turnley*,[462] Pollock CB spoke of the 'compromises that belong to social life' and went on to observe that actionability must always turn on a somewhat vague standard of reasonableness in the circumstances. He emphasized the need for the law to be sensitive to context:[463]

> That may be a nuisance in Grosvenor Square which would be none in Smithfield Market, that may be a nuisance at midday which would not be so at midnight, that may be a nuisance which is permanent and continual which would be no nuisance if temporary or occasional.

The protected right is the use and value of private land or, more accurately, **17.259** the value of the use and enjoyment of private land.[464] Common examples of actionable nuisance are pollution from insistent noise, smells, smoke, and other fumes. In *Hunter v Canary Wharf Ltd*[465] the House of Lords decided that a huge

---

[459] *A-G v PYA Quarries Ltd* [1957] 2 QB 169, 190–1, CA, *per* Denning LJ.

[460] Including waterways: *Tate and Lyle Industries Ltd v GLC* [1983] 2 AC 509, HL; and bridges: *Wandsworth LBC v Railtrack plc* [2001] EWCA Civ 1236; [2002] QB 756, CA.

[461] *Hussain v Lancaster CC* [1999] 4 All ER 125, 144, CA. The defendant must be the creator of the nuisance, the occupier of the land from which it emanates, or the landlord. The landlord's liability is not vicarious but depends on his having adopted or continued the nuisance: *Lippiatt v South Gloucester CC* [1999] 4 All ER 149, CA, discussing the *Hussain* case above; see also *Southwark LBC v Mills* [2001] 1 AC 1, HL where, however, there was no nuisance for which the landlord council could be liable.

[462] 1860) 3 B & S 62, 122 ER 25.

[463] (1860) 3 B & S 62, 79, 122 ER 25, 31.

[464] *Hunter v Canary Wharf Ltd* [1997] AC 655, 688 (Lord Goff), 704–6 (Lord Hoffmann), HL.

[465] [1997] AC 655, HL.

skyscraper which had been built in the regeneration of the London docklands and which was otherwise a reasonable user of the land, did not become a nuisance when it turned out to interfere with its neighbours' television reception. The House of Lords was careful not to say that activities on land which interfered with television could never constitute a nuisance.

(ii) Unreasonable user

17.260 Private nuisance can take three forms: (i) causing an encroachment on neighbouring land, (ii) causing physical damage to neighbouring land, and (iii) unduly interfering with the use and enjoyment of neighbouring land.[466] The third of these forms is in practice dominant, and it is in relation to it, and not the first two, that the need arises for a balance to be struck, taking into account all the circumstances of time, place, level of activity, frequency, and so on. So, while, even as long ago as 1938, neighbours had to tolerate building operations in a busy London street such as Oxford Street, the weighing and balancing concluded that they did not have to put up with an insufferable quantity of dust and night shift working.[467] The nature of the locality will often be an important element in the balancing exercise.[468] A reasonable user in an industrial estate may well be quite unreasonable in a residential area.

17.261 The striking of this balance is essentially a question of fact. There are a number of guidelines. Thus, there is no protection for especially sensitive uses to which a claimant may have put his land.[469] And no ordinary everyday user of one's own property can ever amount to a nuisance.[470] It is no defence that the claimant came to the nuisance,[471] but the fact that the defendant and his activity were there first may affect the remedy;[472] nor is it a defence that the activity was carried on for the public benefit, although public interest may affect whether a claimant is awarded damages rather than an injunction;[473] statutory authority may also legitimate what would otherwise be an actionable nuisance, either expressly[474]

---

[466] A Dugdale and M Jones (eds), *Clerk and Lindsell on Torts* (19th edn, 2006) 20.06.

[467] *Andreae v Selfridge & Co* [1938] Ch 1, CA.

[468] *Halsey v Esso Petroleum Co Ltd* [1961] 1 WLR 683.

[469] *Bridlington Relay Ltd v Yorkshire Electricity Board* [1965] Ch 436.

[470] *Southwark LBC v Mills* [1999] 3 WLR 939, municipal flats with no soundproofing; sounds of all everyday activities, however annoying and inconvenient, could not amount to an actionable nuisance.

[471] *Sturges v Bridgman* (1879) 11 Ch D 852, CA.

[472] *Miller v Jackson* [1977] QB 966, CA; *Kennaway v Thompson* [1981] QB 88, CA.

[473] *Dennis v Ministry of Defence* [2003] EWHC 793, the public interest in training pilots for the Ministry of Defence was a factor in awarding damages and refusing to grant an injunction; *Blofeld v East Dorset District Council* [2006] EWHC 2378, insufficient public interest in motocross racing.

[474] *Allen v Gulf Oil Refining Ltd* [1981] AC 1001, HL: statutory authority to construct an oil refinery provided a defence in respect of such smells and fumes as were a necessary incident of refining oil. Cf *Tate and Lyle Industries Ltd v GLC* [1983] 2 AC 509, HL.

or by implication.[475] The fact that a development has planning permission does not in itself give any immunity,[476] but planning permission may be relevant in other ways, as in determining the character of the locality.[477] Finally, malice is relevant in determining the nature of a user of land as being unreasonable, for nobody should have to put up with malicious activities by neighbours. Hence a malicious interference with amenity will nearly always be unreasonable.[478]

(iii) Delimiting the sphere of nuisance

In *Hunter v Canary Wharf Ltd*[479] the House of Lords drew clearer lines around the **17.262** tort of nuisance, insisting on its role as protecting the enjoyment of land from misuse of other land. The clarification had two aspects. The first was a return to the strict rule that a claimant must be a person entitled to exclusive possession of the land. To allow a licensee or a family member to sue, as had happened,[480] was to overstep the boundary between protecting land and protecting personal interests.[481] Secondly, even a claimant entitled to exclusive possession must not under this head seek to recover for personal injuries, save in so far as they demonstrate an interference with the amenity of the land.[482] The decision in *Hunter* may have to be modified in light of the *Human Rights Act* 1998. In *McKenna v British Aluminium Ltd*[483] Neuberger J refused to strike out an action for nuisance by claimants that had no proprietary right. It is arguable that the *Human Rights Act* protects the homes and private lives of all citizens, not just as property owners. And in *Pemberton v Southwark LBC*[484] a 'tolerated trespasser' was held to have a sufficient interest to sue for nuisance.

Claims in respect of physical damage to the land itself, which have always been **17.263** within the tort of nuisance, may later be expelled. Professor Gearty has argued that interference with amenity, and in particular the availability of an injunction to bring that interference to an end, should be recognized as the only proper

---

[475] *Marcic v Thames Water Utilities Ltd* [2003] UKHL 66; [2004] 2 AC 42, HL. The House of Lords held that liability for common law nuisance would be inconsistent with the procedures for controlling the water industry under the *Water Industry Act* 1991.

[476] *Wheeler v JJ Saunders Ltd* [1996] Ch 19, CA.

[477] *Gillingham DC v Medway Dock Co* [1993] QB 343. See also *Hunter v Canary Wharf Ltd* [1997] AC 655, 710, HL, *per* Lord Hoffmann.

[478] *Hollywood Silver Fox Farm v Emmett* [1936] 2 KB 468, 476 offering an explanation of the difficult decision of *Bradford Corporation v Pickles* [1895] AC 587, HL, which might be taken as holding that there is no such thing in English law as a doctrine of malicious abuse of rights: see further para 17.357.

[479] [1997] AC 655, HL.

[480] *Khorasandjian v Bush* [1993] QB 727, CA.

[481] *Hunter v Canary Wharf Ltd* [1997] AC 655, 691–3, HL, *per* Lord Goff.

[482] ibid 696 (Lord Lloyd), 706 (Lord Hoffmann).

[483] [2002] Env LR 30.

[484] [2000] 1 WLR 1672.

business of nuisance.[485] The House of Lords was not unsympathetic to that analysis.[486]

(iv) The relationship between nuisance and negligence

17.264 Within the proper sphere of nuisance, the effect of the independent tort is to ensure recovery of a particular kind of economic loss, even in the absence of physical damage. The loss arises from the impairment of the enjoyment value of the land. It would be difficult, according to the general law of negligence, to formulate an action for negligently creating noise or evil smells. If the liability were, in addition, based on negligence, it might be possible to assert that the only function of the independent tort was to secure that exception to the general rule against the actionability of that kind of loss.[487] However, liability in nuisance is not based on negligence. Nor is it right to say that it is a strict liability. The truth is more complex.

17.265 Both torts employ the concept of reasonableness, though each with a different focus. The negligence inquiry is whether the defendant has taken reasonable care. In nuisance the question is whether the claimant has suffered an unreasonable interference with his property rights. But an affirmative answer to the latter question supposes unreasonableness on the part of the defendant and may indeed be influenced by carelessness or malice on his part.[488] It is also clear that in some cases the defendant will not be liable unless he has been negligent in the full sense. Thus, when the defendant is the occupier of the offending land and is being sued for a natural nuisance or for a nuisance created by some third party for whom he is not immediately responsible, he will only be liable if he has negligently allowed the nuisance to continue.[489] For instance, in *Delaware Mansions Ltd v Westminster City Council*[490] the House of Lords held that reasonable remedial expenditure could be recovered in respect of damage done by a continuing natural nuisance of which the defendant knew or ought to have known.[491] It was essential that the defendant had notice of the damage and a reasonable opportunity for

---

[485] C Gearty, 'The Place of Private Nuisance in a Modern Law of Torts' [1989] CLJ 214, 242.

[486] *Hunter v Canary Wharf Ltd* [1997] AC 655, 692, *per* Lord Goff.

[487] Paras 17.154–17.181.

[488] Cf para 17.261.

[489] *Sedleigh-Denfield v O'Callaghan* [1940] AC 880, HL; *Goldman v Hargrave* [1967] 1 AC 645, HL; *Leakey v National Trust* [1980] QB 485, CA.

[490] [2001] UKHL 55; [2002] 1 AC 321.

[491] Where the expenditure is carried out for the benefit of both parties the cost will be apportioned according to the benefits derived from the repair. So where a roof fell into disrepair the benefits of repair were judged to be equal to the owners of the floors below: *Abbahall Ltd v Smee* [2002] EWCA Civ 1831; [2003] 1 WLR 1472, CA.

abatement. Lord Cooke explained that the choice of label, nuisance or negligence, had no significance in this context.[492]

Even in other cases in which negligence is not necessary, there is much to be said for Lord Reid's view that nuisance always involves 'fault of some kind'.[493] This is not contradicted by the proposition that if the defendant is the creator of the nuisance, proof that he took reasonable care to prevent his activities causing a nuisance will not exonerate him if the interference is in fact unreasonable.[494] Although it may, therefore, be right to say that fault of a kind is always present in an actionable nuisance, this is not a case in which a requirement of negligence has simply been implanted.[495] Nuisance has not become a context-specific application of the tort of negligence.

17.266

(3) The Liability in Rylands v Fletcher

When a liability is named by reference only to a leading case, it is a sure sign of uncertainty as to its nature and provenance. In *Rylands v Fletcher*[496] the defendant employed a contractor to construct a reservoir on his land. As it was being filled for the first time, the dam burst and, through disused mine shafts, the water inundated an adjacent colliery. He was held liable without regard to fault. In the Court of Exchequer Chamber Blackburn J said:[497]

17.267

> We think the true rule of law is that the person who, for his own purposes, brings on his land and collects and keeps there anything likely to do mischief if it escapes, must keep it at his peril, and, if he does not do so, he is prima facie answerable for all the damage which is the natural consequence of its escape.

It is evident from the rest of his speech that Blackburn J thought that this strict liability for the escape of dangerous things causing damage to neighbouring land was already part of the law of nuisance. Its novelty and independence were later exaggerated. His formulation was approved on appeal, though in the House of Lords Lord Cairns LC added one restrictive requirement, that the dangerous activity must be a non-natural use of the land.[498] This was later interpreted

17.268

---

[492] ibid 333 [31].

[493] *The Wagon Mound (No 2)* [1967] 1 AC 617, 639, PC. He would express no opinion on *Wringe v Cohen* [1940] 1 KB 229, CA: landlord's liability independent of want of care.

[494] *Cambridge Water Co v Eastern Counties Leather plc* [1994] 2 AC 264, 300, HL, *per* Lord Goff.

[495] Co-existence, therefore, not infiltration: see para 17.247.

[496] (1868) LR 3 HL 330. AWB Simpson, 'Bursting Reservoirs and Victorian Tort Law' in his *Leading Cases in the Common Law* (1995) 194; GT Schwartz, '*Rylands v Fletcher*, Negligence and Strict Liability' in P Cane and J Stapleton (eds), *The Law of Obligations: Essays in Celebration of John Fleming* (1998) 209.

[497] (1866) LR 1 Ex 265, 279.

[498] (1868) LR 3 HL 330, 339.

instrumentally to narrow the strict liability. However, as we shall see immediately below, the House of Lords has now said that that kind of exaggerated artificiality should be abandoned.

(a) A general strict liability for dangerous things?

17.269 There was a question whether the prima facie strict liability was in respect of highly dangerous things generally or only in respect of highly dangerous escapes from land to land. An explosion in an armaments factory finally settled that question in the narrower sense. In *Read v Lyons*[499] the claimant was injured when a shell exploded. The House of Lords held that there was no strict liability except for escapes to other land.

(b) Reintegration into the general law

17.270 Cut down in this way, and in addition made subject to a number of defences, this strict liability barely justifies its independent existence. In Australia the High Court decided that it can be absorbed into negligence.[500] In England the approach was also to integrate *Rylands v Fletcher*, though back towards nuisance rather than negligence.

17.271 In *Cambridge Water Co v Eastern Counties Leather plc*[501] the defendants used a potent chemical in their tanning factory which, unknown to them and unforeseeably, slowly leaked into the claimant water company's borehole. The toxicity was such that the borehole had to be abandoned and a new one made in another place. Claims were made in negligence, nuisance, and *Rylands v Fletcher*.[502] In relation to the last of these, the House of Lords set out on a path which leads towards the reintegration of *Rylands v Fletcher* into the law of nuisance.[503]

17.272 In denying the claim, it was held that there could be no liability for an unforeseeable harm, for the rules of remoteness of damage should be the same as for nuisance. It was also said that the restrictive interpretation of the requirement of 'non-natural user' had become unnecessarily artificial and could be dispensed with in favour of a more generous understanding. Thus, the storage of large quantities

---

[499] [1947] AC 156, HL.
[500] *Burnie Port Authority v General Jones Pty Ltd* (1994) 179 CLR 520, HCA.
[501] [1994] 2 AC 264, HL.
[502] Such concurrent claims are common: *Halsey v Esso Petroleum Co Ltd* [1961] 1 WLR 683; *Weller v Foot and Mouth Disease Research Institute* [1966] 1 QB 569; *Rigby v Chief Constable of Northamptonshire* [1985] 1 WLR 1242.
[503] Much influenced by FH Newark, 'The Boundaries of Nuisance' (1949) 65 LQR 480, esp 487–8.

of chemicals on industrial premises would count as a non-natural user and there would be a strict liability for foreseeable harm in the event of an escape.[504]

In *Transco plc v Stockport Metropolitan Borough Council*,[505] an action was brought **17.273** to recover the costs of measures taken to protect a gas main from the escape of water from the water supply of a tower block. The House of Lords was invited to consider following the example of the High Court of Australia to absorb *Rylands v Fletcher* into negligence. This invitation was declined. Their Lordships decided, with varying degrees of enthusiasm, that strict liability still had a part to play, limited though it is by judicial interpretation and statutory regimes and, presumably by the requirement in nuisance of a proprietary right to land.[506] In following *Cambridge Water* and treating *Rylands v Fletcher* as a species of nuisance, three Lords explained that this excluded liability for personal injury. Lord Bingham and Lord Hoffmann also emphasized that the principle only applies where there is an exceptionally high risk of danger and mischief.[507] As for the test of cases excluded from the rule, Lord Bingham preferred 'ordinary user' over 'non-natural user'.[508] Use might well be quite out of the ordinary but not unreasonable.

To that extent *Rylands v Fletcher* may still have some life in it as a form of enterprise **17.274** liability in English law. However, Lord Macmillan's view, expressed in *Read v Lyons*, that personal injuries should never be recoverable under this head, was confirmed in *Transco*.[509]

(4) Liability for Animals

The law on liability for animals is multi-layered. It is possible to apply the general **17.275** law of negligence or nuisance. Thus, the smell of pigs can be an actionable nuisance.[510] And there can be liability in negligence for personal injuries caused by dogs on the run.[511] The applicability of these ordinary principles was formerly inhibited to some extent by the holding that there was no duty of care to keep animals from straying on to the highway.[512] Behind the general law, there is now a statutory regime derived directly from ancient common law.

---

[504] *Cambridge Water Co v Eastern Counties Leather plc* [1994] 2 AC 264, 309, HL, *per* Lord Goff.
[505] [2003] UKHL 61; [2004] 2 AC 1, HL.
[506] In *McKenna v British Aluminium Ltd* [2002] Env LR 30, Neuberger J held that a claimant in *Rylands v Fletcher* must, as in private nuisance generally, have a proprietary interest in land. But note para 17.262.
[507] [2003] UKHL 61; [2004] 2 AC 1, 10 [10] *per* Lord Bingham, 22 [49] *per* Lord Hoffmann, HL.
[508] ibid 11 [11].
[509] *Read v Lyons* [1947] AC 156, 170–1, HL confirmed [2003] UKHL 61; [2004] 2 AC 1, 10 [9] *per* Lord Bingham, 18 [35] *per* Lord Hoffmann, 22 [52] *per* Lord Hobhouse, HL.
[510] *Wheeler v JJ Saunders Ltd* [1996] Ch 19, CA.
[511] *Draper v Hodder* [1972] 2 QB 556, CA.
[512] *Searle v Wallbank* [1947] AC 341, HL.

(a) The common law

17.276 The common law early developed a special regime of strict liability,[513] resting in part on cattle trespass and in part on what was loosely known as the *scienter* rule.[514] The word *scienter* (knowingly) comes from the old pleadings which alleged that the defendant had 'knowingly kept' the dangerous animal.

17.277 For the purposes of the *scienter* liability, animals were divided into two categories, those wild by nature (*ferae naturae*) and those tame by nature (*mansuetae naturae*). In relation to tame species the owner would only be liable if the damage was due to a vicious abnormal propensity of which he actually knew. In relation to wild species people were taken to know of their savage propensities. So, for wild animals, liability was doubly strict. The distinction between the two categories had nothing to do with the individual animal. It was a classification of species. 'If a person wakes up in the middle of the night and finds an escaping tiger on top of his bed and suffers a heart attack, it would be nothing to the point that the intentions of the tiger were quite amiable.'[515]

(b) Statutory reform

17.278 In 1953 the Goddard Committee proposed that, with the exception of strict liability for cattle trespass, which was thought to be conveniently clear for farmers, the old law should be replaced by the general principles of negligence.[516] This simplification was rejected by the Law Commission in 1967.[517] The Commission's central argument was that this area was very suitable for strict liability, which gave a clear signal of the need to insure. The Commission's own proposal was an updating of the old common law categories. This was enacted as the Animals Act 1971.

17.279 An important change was the abolition, by section 8, of the *Searle v Wallbank* immunity in respect of animals straying on to the highway.[518] Other sections amended but left more or less intact the common law categories.

17.280 Rather than wild and tame, the Act categorizes species as dangerous or non-dangerous and creates special provisions for dogs and trespassing livestock. A dangerous species is one which is not usually domesticated in the British Isles

---

[513] For the old law, Glanville Williams, *Liability for Animals* (1939). And for the reformed regime, PM North, *The Modern Law of Animals* (1972).

[514] The name derives from a count which centrally alleged that the defendant *scienter retinuit* the animal.

[515] *Behrens v Bertram Mills Circus Ltd* [1957] 2 QB 1, 17–18, *per* Devlin J.

[516] Report of the Committee on the Law of Civil Liability for Damage done by Animals, 1953 Cmnd 8746.

[517] Law Commission, *Civil Liability for Animals* (Law Com No 13 1967).

[518] See n 512 above.

and which, when fully grown, is likely to cause severe damage. Liability for damage caused by such animals rests on the keeper or the head of the household of a keeper who is under 16.[519] Liability is strict, subject to defences. A similar liability attaches, under section 2(2) of the Act, to damage caused by a non-dangerous animal where the keeper knows of an abnormality which renders it likely to be dangerous and the damage is attributable to that known abnormality. Abnormality is used here as shorthand for the convoluted words of the section which refer to 'characteristics of the animal which are not normally found in animals of the same species or are not normally so found except at particular times or in particular circumstances.' In *Mirvahedy v Henley*[520] the House of Lords decided that the owners of a stampeding horse were liable to a driver who collided with the horse. With great difficulty the majority concluded that a horse which is frightened is a horse in particular circumstances and to bolt uncontrollably is a normal response in those circumstances. The minority considered that a horse in a field which is frightened by something is not 'in particular circumstances', reading 'particular' to mean 'special', as where a cow has a young calf with her.

The scheme of the Act is straightforward and continuous with the underlying history. Some of the drafting has caused trouble, so that litigation has been provoked in relation to the liability for non-dangerous species.[521]   **17.281**

(5) Product Liability

Donoghue v Stevenson[522] provided the basis for the modern law of liability in negligence for defective products. Lord Atkin stated the principle that a manufacturer owes a duty of care to the ultimate consumer.[523]   **17.282**

This principle has been construed broadly. Manufacturers include repairers.[524] And Lord Atkin's 'consumer' can be any foreseeable victim of physical injury, as for instance a pedestrian run over by a defective vehicle. Also, the pre-1932 category of things dangerous in themselves has become redundant, since the negligence standard can apply flexibly to all degrees of danger.[525]   **17.283**

---

[519] An animal may have more than one keeper. In such a case there is no reason why one keeper may not sue another: *Flack v Hudson* [2001] QB 698, CA.

[520] [2003] UKHL 16; [2003] 2 AC 491, HL.

[521] *Cummings v Grainger* [1977] QB 397, CA; *Curtis v Betts* [1990] 1 WLR 459, CA; *Wallace v Newton* [1982] 1 WLR 375.

[522] [1932] AC 562, HL.

[523] ibid 599.

[524] *Haseldine v CA Daw & Son Ltd* [1941] 2 KB 343, CA.

[525] *Griffiths v Arch Engineering Ltd* [1968] 3 All ER 217.

17.284 It is arguable that the principle is stated too narrowly in some respects. The possibility, or even the probability, of intermediate examination ought not to be a complete bar to liability now that the courts have the power to apportion responsibility for contributory negligence.[526] It is, however, still true that the manufacturer is not liable in tort for pure economic loss.[527] Nor is there any liability for failure to warn of a dangerous defect if in the event only economic loss materializes.[528]

17.285 Liability in negligence and liability in contract are supplemented by a strict liability regime for defective products.[529] This was enacted in Part 1 of the Consumer Protection Act 1987 to comply with European Community law in Directive (EEC) 85/374. By section 2(6) liability under the Act is cumulative with other remedies, and by section 7 it may not be excluded or limited. The same limitation periods apply as for personal injury cases but there is a long-stop of ten years from the date when the product was put into circulation, after which no action can be brought.[530] Difficult and unresolved questions can arise as to when a product is put into circulation, for example if this runs from the time it is provided to a subsidiary distributor.[531]

17.286 The aim of the Act was to impose strict liability for defective products which cause death or personal injury or damage to property which is intended for private use, occupation, or consumption, and so used.[532] A product is defective if its safety is not such as persons generally are entitled to expect.[533] The standard of safety that persons are generally entitled to expect has been discussed in several cases. In *A v National Blood Authority*,[534] where it was conceded that blood was a product for the purposes of the Act and that its preparation was an industrial process,[535] it was held that legitimate expectations were not limited by what was scientifically possible at the time, at least unless the public was warned as to dangers not discoverable. Thus the public was entitled to rely on blood being uninfected, even though there

---

[526] Law Reform (Contributory Negligence) Act 1945. See paras 17.198–17.200.

[527] *Murphy v Brentwood* [1991] 1 AC 398, HL; *Muirhead v Industrial Tank Specialities* [1986] QB 507, CA. See paras 17.159–17.170.

[528] *Hamble Fisheries Ltd v Gardner and Sons Ltd (The Rebecca Elaine)* [1999] 2 Lloyd's Rep 1, CA.

[529] J Stapleton, *Product Liability* (1994).

[530] *Limitation Act* 1980, s11A. The standard periods are 3 years from the damage, an alternative period from the date of the claimant's knowledge and a power to override the limitation period, subject to the long-stop.

[531] *O'Byrne v Sanofi Pasteur MSD Ltd* [2006] 1 WLR 1606, ECJ.

[532] Consumer Protection Act 1987, s 5.

[533] ibid s 3.

[534] [2001] 1 All ER 289.

[535] The correctness of this concession can be seen from Case C-203/99 *Veedfald v Arhus Amtskommune* [2001] ECR I-3569, *The Times*, 4 June 2001.

was no available test for Hepatitis C at that time.[536] In *Tesco Stores Ltd v Pollard*[537] the Court of Appeal held that what persons are generally entitled to expect need not be the same as a design standard, of which few people would be aware. In that case, a child resistant cap on dishwashing powder was harder to open than a screw top and as safe as persons were entitled to expect even though it did not conform to the British safety standard.

Those liable for damage caused by a defective product are the producer, includ- **17.287**
ing producers of component parts, a person who puts a brand name or trade name on a product, a person who imports the product into a member state from outside the member states, and a supplier who fails, on request, to identify the person who supplied the product to him.[538]

The defences to this strict liability are set out in section 4. The most controver- **17.288**
sial is the 'development risks' defence: 'that the state of scientific and technical knowledge at the relevant time was not such that a producer of products of the same description as the product in question might be expected to have discovered the defect if it has existed in his products while they were under his control'.[539] The defence is directed only to where there was actual or accessible knowledge of the risk. Whether it was possible to avoid the risk by taking reasonable care is irrelevant to a strict liability regime.[540] The effect of this defence is clearly to put the risk of harm from unsuspected side effects on the consumer rather than the producer. Criticisms have been made of the formulation of the defence in the 1987 Act, which appears more generous to producers than was required by the Directive.[541]

Much was expected of the introduction of strict liability for defective products. **17.289**
In the event it has produced very little litigation. The Act does not specify the damages awards available; it simply refers to liability 'for the damage'.[542] In 1993 it was held that exemplary damages were not available for this statutory wrong because of a purported principle that they were not available for any tort recognized after 1964.[543] That principle has since been overturned, leaving open the

---

[536] Cf *Richardson v LRC Products Ltd* [2000] Lloyd's Rep Med 280 (public awareness of unreliability of condoms) and *Abouzaid v Mothercare (UK) Ltd*, *The Times*, 20 February 2001, CA, criticized (2001) 151 NLJ 424 (eye lost through defective elastic strap, irrelevant that producer unaware of danger).

[537] [2006] EWCA Civ 393, CA.

[538] ibid s 2.

[539] ibid s 4(1)(e).

[540] *A v National Blood Authority* [2001] 3 All ER 289.

[541] Case C-300/95 *EC Commission v UK* [1997] ECR 1–2649.

[542] ibid s 2.

[543] *AB v South West Water Services Ltd* [1993] QB 507, CA.

possibility of exemplary damages under the Act.[544] However, exemplary damages are very unlikely to become prolific given the restraint exercised in their award in English law. Without the routine availability of exemplary damages there is little chance that strict product liability will be as important in Europe as it has been in the United States.

(6) Defamation

17.290 Until relatively recently defamation would not have been said to be a tort which overlapped with negligence and would have been treated in the section which is concerned with rights protected by strict liability.[545] However, the House of Lords has now allowed one incursion by negligence.[546] Although that incursion may yet be contained or even repulsed, it is on that basis that defamation is treated on this side of the line.

17.291 Defamation is notoriously the most technical of torts. Some degree of technicality is to be expected, not only because it protects a right which is immaterial, so that infringements are not delimited by physical facts,[547] but also because its protection of the right to reputation, and, to a degree,[548] self-esteem, is in constant conflict with the wider interest in freedom of speech. Artificiality is therefore inescapable.

17.292 Another factor militates in the same direction. Because of the importance of the interests at stake, and the difficulty not only of achieving the right balance but also of putting any conclusion for the claimant into money, defamation is almost the last outpost of the civil jury.[549] This means that there is much detailed regulation of the respective functions of the judge and the jury, as well as many niceties of pleading.

17.293 These factors explain but do not entirely justify the state of the law. Defamation has undoubtedly been a tort of great and often arbitrary complexity which for many years seemed highly resistant to reform. A number of important changes have now been made, and more are to be expected, particularly with the

---

[544] *Kuddus v Chief Constable of leicestershire Constabulary* [2001] UKHL 29; [2002] 2 AC 122, HL.

[545] From para 17.316. See P Mitchell, *The Making of the Modern Law of Defamation* (2005).

[546] Paras 17.11–17.12.

[547] Cf the discussion of pure economic loss from para 17.150.

[548] Through the award of 'aggravated damages': *Cassell & Co Ltd v Broome* [1972] AC 1027, HL. See paras 17.358–17.361.

[549] This may change: Defamation Act 1996, ss 8–10, providing for summary disposal of claims, whether by dismissal or the grant of summary relief.

implementation of the Human Rights Act 1998. In a few years time the picture may look very different.

(a) The defamatory statement

According to the traditional definitions, a defamatory statement is one which tends to bring the claimant into 'hatred, ridicule or contempt', or which tends to make right-thinking people 'shun or avoid him'. These traditional formulae are clearly too narrow for modern law, which interprets defamation increasingly broadly. Pluralism makes for additional difficulties, since it connotes the accept-ance of the existence of communities with different notions of 'right-thinking'. And times change. In 1934 the Court of Appeal held that it was defamatory to say of a Russian princess that she had been raped by the 'mad monk' Rasputin.[550] By 1996 it could be held actionable to say of an actor that he was 'hideously ugly'.[551] Such a case can clearly only be explained by a double evaluation, first of the subcommunity in which the statement is likely to take effect and then of the values of that community as themselves acceptable or unacceptable.[552]

17.294

A statement which is not defamatory on its face may nevertheless be defamatory by virtue of an innuendo. In such a case the claimant is generally obliged to plead and prove special facts which support the innuendo. A simple case involved the publication of a picture of 'X and his fiancée'. This was defamatory by innuendo because, to those who knew X's wife, the suggestion was that she cohabited with him without being married.[553]

17.295

(b) Libel and slander

The statement may be published in written or permanent form, in which case it will be a libel.[554] Otherwise, it will amount only to slander. Libel is actionable *per se*, without proof of actual damage. On the other hand, the same is true of the earliest forms of slander: imputations of criminal conduct, of unchastity in a woman, of certain contagious diseases, and of unfitness for any office, profession, calling, trade or business. Modern methods of communication have rendered the distinction between libel and slander pointless.[555]

17.296

---

[550] *Youssoupoff v Metro-Goldwyn-Mayer Pictures Ltd* [1934] 50 TLR 581, CA.

[551] *Berkoff v Burchill* [1996] 4 All ER 1008, CA.

[552] Failing at the second stage: *Sim v Stretch* [1936] 2 All ER 1237, HL; *Byrne v Deane* [1937] 1 KB 818, CA; cf *Blennerhasset v Novelty Sales Services Ltd* (1933) 175 Law Times Journal 393.

[553] *Cassidy v Daily Mirror Newspapers Ltd* [1929] 2 KB 331, CA. This kind of imputation could barely be regarded as defamatory these days.

[554] *Monson v Tussauds Ltd* [1894] 1 QB 671, CA: waxwork representation could be a libel.

[555] Broadcasting Act 1990, s 166; Theatres Act 1968, ss 4, 7. Its abolition was recommended as long ago as 1975: *Report of the Committee on Defamation 1975* (Cmnd 5909).

(c) Publication

17.297   The claimant must show that the defamatory statement was published to a third party. The first condition is that a third party must have received it. That is not sufficient in itself. It must at least have been foreseeable that the third party would receive it. For example, a defamatory statement in a letter to the claimant but sent to a business address, will be taken to have been published to his staff unless marked 'Private and Confidential', since the ordinary practice is for most letters to be opened other than by the addressee.[556] In *Hough v London Express Newspaper Ltd*[557] it was held that the publication of a defamatory statement need not be proved to have been made to a third party who did take the words to be defamatory, provided only that some people might have done. In that case the newspaper had described the claimant's wife in words which did not match her character and might have led people to believe that she was not in fact married to him. There was, however, no evidence that any person had actually taken the words in that sense.

(d) Strict liability

17.298   Though somewhat moderated by defences, liability is strict. The old allegation that the statement was published 'maliciously' has been emptied of meaning. This process has recently been documented anew, attention being drawn to the increasing tension with the protection of free speech.[558] It is not necessary to show that the defendant intended to injure the claimant, nor that the statement was intended to refer to the claimant, nor even, at common law, that the defendant could have known that it might be taken to be defamatory of the claimant. A fictional story of a character given the rare name 'Artemus Jones' was held to have defamed a barrister of that very name.[559] Moreover, it is not for the claimant to show that the statement was untrue.

17.299   Every repetition of a defamatory statement is a new publication and gives the claimant a separate action against each successive publisher, although statute now

---

[556] *Huth v Huth* [1915] 3 KB 32, CA.

[557] [1940] 2 KB 507, CA, not easily reconciled with *Sadgrove v Hole* [1901] 2 KB 1, CA.

[558] P Mitchell, 'Malice in Defamation' (1998) 114 LQR 639, rightly concluding, at 663–4, that tensions have been brought to the surface by the ruling in *Derbyshire CC v Times Newspapers Ltd* [1993] AC 534, HL that Article 10 of the European Convention of Human Rights, guaranteeing free speech, merely expresses the common law on the same matter. Without ruling out strict liability, the Court of Appeal in *Kerry O'Shea v MGN* [2001] EMLR 40, CA held that it would be a breach of Article 10 of the Convention to impose strict liability where a pornographic photograph caused some people to think that the claimant was the woman depicted.

[559] *E Hulton & Co v Jones* [1910] AC 20, HL; P Mitchell, 'Artemus Jones and the Press Club' (1999) 20 Jo Legal History 64; cf *Cassidy v Daily Mirror Newspapers Ltd* [1929] 2 KB 331, CA.

protects many of those who become unwittingly involved.[560] The person who made the original publication will himself also be answerable for the republications if republication was foreseeable.[561]

(e) Defences

It will be evident therefore that protection of free speech falls largely to the **17.300** defences, although in one important area the courts have taken a more positive stand and have eliminated the very possibility of actions for defamation.[562]

There are four common law defences, to some extent amended by statute, and **17.301** a number of statutory defences. The common law defences are justification (or truth), fair comment, absolute privilege, and qualified privilege. The defences of fair comment and qualified privilege are destroyed by proof of malice, which in this context has a substantive meaning, namely the abuse of free speech for an improper motive.

(i) Justification

Justification is an absolute defence.[563] Telling the truth can never be defamatory, **17.302** however unworthy the motive. The only exception relates to the provisions concerning reviving spent offences under the Rehabilitation of Offenders Act 1974. There is not yet a tort of protection of privacy in England but developments in the law relating to breach of confidence have now made it possible to say that the revelation of true but private facts can be actionable.[564]

(ii) Absolute privilege

In the same way, absolute privilege is absolute: malice makes no difference. **17.303** Statements absolutely privileged are those made in Parliament or in reports published by order of Parliament,[565] and those made in judicial proceedings and in accurate contemporaneous reports of judicial proceedings.[566] There are other narrow categories of absolute privilege, the precise limits of which are not perfectly clear, as for instance communications between high officials and their advisors and between lawyers and their clients.

---

560 Defamation Act 1996, s 1.
561 *Slipper v BBC* [1991] 1 QB 283, CA: newspaper reviews of a television programme; *McManus v Beckham* [2002] EWCA Civ 939; [2002] 1 WLR 2982, CA.
562 Para 17.310.
563 Defamation Act 1952, s 5; where there are several charges, substantial justification suffices.
564 See para 17.362–17.366.
565 Parliamentary Papers Act 1840; subject to waiver Defamation Act 1996, s 13.
566 Defamation Act 1996, s 15.

(iii) Qualified privilege

17.304 Qualified privilege is a defence in the absence of malice. The defence rests on both common law and statute, the statutory defence being additional to the common law.[567] The statutory defence applies to reports of notices and proceedings of public and semi-public bodies and general meetings of public companies. There is qualified privilege at common law wherever there is a duty to communicate information and an interest in receiving it. For the press the defence stops some way short of covering everything that the public might have some interest in hearing. It extends only to matters in respect of which there can be said to be a duty to report. A more private example is the writing of references, as for instance when a person applies for a new job. It is precisely at this point that the law of negligence has invaded the law of defamation, undermining the law which formerly seemed clear, that a referee could not be liable in the absence of malice proved by the claimant.[568]

17.305 It is clear that the law in this area is not in a satisfactory condition, not only because of this invasion, but because the concepts of duty and corresponding interest are inherently uncertain.[569] A particularly difficult question is whether there should be a general defence of qualified privilege in relation to all political information. The English answer has been that there should not. That is considered immediately below.[570] Another area of confusion has arisen because of the press privilege deriving from *Reynolds v Times Newspapers Ltd*,[571] considered below. In *Loutchansky v Times Newspapers (No 2)*[572] the newspaper had sought to expose a Russian businessman as a gangster and money launderer. It made no attempt to justify this allegation, preferring to plead qualified privilege. The Court of Appeal's judgment, delivered by Lord Phillips MR, held that the trial judge had been wrong to ask whether the newspaper had been under a duty to publish in the sense of being open to legitimate criticism if it had not done so. There certainly had to be cases in which publication would be privileged even though a decision not to publish would not have been open to criticism. The Court of Appeal sent this issue back for the judge to ask, bearing in mind the tensions between private and public interests, whether responsible journalists would have thought it right to publish. This test could not but pre-empt the issue of malice, in that responsible journalists would not publish on that motivation.

---

567 Defamation Act 1996, s 15, Sch 1.
568 Paras 17.11–17.12; *Spring v Guardian Assurance plc* [1995] 2 AC 296, HL.
569 The evolution of the defence is examined in P Mitchell, 'Duties, Interests, and Motives: Privileged Occasions in Defamation' (1998) 18 OJLS 381.
570 Para 17.311.
571 [2001] 2 AC 127, HL.
572 [2001] EWCA Civ 1805; [2002] QB 783, CA.

(iv) Fair comment on a matter of public interest

Fair comment on a matter of public interest is likewise a qualified defence. **17.306**
In *Reynolds v Times Newspapers Ltd*[573] it was recognized to be a bulwark of freedom of the press. The public interest is generously construed: the public has a legitimate interest in a wide range of subject matter.[574] Moreover, the comment need not in fact be 'fair' so long as it is honest. Lord Nicholls has suggested that the defence would better be called 'honest comment'.[575]

The broad interpretation of this defence is limited by its application only to **17.307**
comment, not to facts. In order to establish this defence the defendant must, subject to the Defamation Act 1952, section 6, show that the facts on which it commented were true facts. Section 6 refines that, requiring only that the expression of opinion be fair comment 'having regard to such of the facts alleged or referred to in the words complained of as are proved'. This is where the line is drawn between fair comment on a matter of public interest and qualified privilege. Where the latter defence is available, it will protect even a person who publishes facts which he cannot show to be true.

(v) Responsible reporting of issues of public interest

In *Reynolds v Times Newspapers Ltd*,[576] the House of Lords, and particularly **17.308**
Lord Nicholls, considered that a defence (which was inaccurately described as a privilege) should arise where a defendant could show that in the particular circumstances of an individual case there should be a defence for the publication of material which was in the public interest. The importance of the media, as watchdog and bloodhound, was fully recognized, and the courts were enjoined to incline in favour of free speech. This defence was applied in *Jameel v Wall Street Journal Europe Sprl*.[577] The Wall Street Journal published an article which suggested that there were reasonable grounds to suspect the involvement of the appellants in the witting or unwitting channelling of funds to terrorist organizations. A majority of the House of Lords held that the circumstances of publication met the conditions for this defence. The test to be applied is threefold. First, it must be in the public interest that the subject matter of the material be published. Second, making allowance for editorial judgement, the inclusion of the defamatory statement in the report must be justifiable; the more serious the allegation, the more important it is that it should make a real contribution to the public interest element in the article. Third, the steps taken to gather and publish the

---

[573] [2001] 2 AC 127, HL.
[574] *London Artists v Littler* [1969] 2 QB 375, CA.
[575] *Reynolds v Times Newspapers Ltd* [1999] 3 WLR 1010, 1015–16, HL.
[576] [2001] 2 AC 127, HL.
[577] [2006] UKHL 44; [2006] 3 WLR 642, HL.

information must be responsible and fair. In *Jameel* the first two requirements of this test were easily satisfied: the public interest in relation to financing of terrorist activities was plain and the inclusion of the names of large and respectable Saudi businesses was an important part of the story. The third element was satisfied having regard to the circumstances including the steps taken to verify the story, the opportunity given to the Jameel group to comment and the propriety of publication in the light of US diplomatic policy at the time.

(vi) Offer of amends

17.309   The most important statutory defence is the offer of amends. Under sections 2 to 4 of the Defamation Act 1996 an offer to publish a correction and an apology and to pay such compensation as may be agreed may bar any subsequent action for defamation, provided the defamer neither knew nor had reason to know that the statement was defamatory of the person in question.[578]

(f) Political speech and political institutions

17.310   Two decisions of the House of Lords have enlarged the freedom to comment on political matters. In *Derbyshire CC v Times Newspapers Ltd*,[579] *The Times* had published articles casting doubt on the propriety of the council's management of its pension funds. The House of Lords held that it would be directly contrary to the public interest if institutions of central or local government were to have the right to sue for defamation. It would impede the discovery of malpractices which ought to be revealed. This principle has since been extended to political parties.[580] Individual politicians are not thereby deprived of the right to sue.[581]

17.311   In *Reynolds v Times Newspapers Ltd*,[582] *The Times* newspaper was sued by the former Prime Minister of Ireland for articles alleging that he had misled the Irish Parliament, the Dáil. The newspaper argued that political information fell within the defence of qualified privilege as being invariably information which it was the duty of the media to publish and the interest of the public to know. The public for its part had a legitimate interest in demanding such information. This is a position taken in some major Commonwealth jurisdictions.[583] However, the House of Lords thought that a generic political defence of that kind would make an unnecessary sacrifice of the protection of reputation. It would be better to build up a case

---

[578] *Milne v Express Newspapers* [2004] EWCA Civ 664; [2005] 1 WLR 772, CA.
[579] [1993] AC 534, HL.
[580] *Goldsmith v Bhoyrul* [1998] QB 459.
[581] Cf *New York Times v Sullivan* 376 US 254, 84 S Ct 710 (1964), US Sup Ct.
[582] [2001] 2 AC 127, HL.
[583] FA Trindade, 'Defamatory Statements and Political Discussion' (2000) 116 LQR 185 and, in relation to the Court of Appeal's decision (1999) 115 LQR 175.

law profile of the circumstances in which a defence would arise for publication of political information. From this developed the defence of responsible reporting of issues of public interest discussed above.

(g) Damages

Exemplary and aggravated damages are discussed below.[584] Defamation not **17.312** infrequently gives rise to the latter and in one case to the former, namely where it is necessary to show that tort does not pay. It is only necessary to say here that there has been great concern about the inflated levels of awards, seemingly out of all proportion to the sums recovered for personal injury. This concern has resulted in a determination to exercise some control over the jury's freedom. Section 8 of the Courts and Legal Services Act 1990 allows the Court of Appeal to reduce excessive awards to a reasonable level.[585]

(h) Defamation and other torts

We have already seen the overlap between the tort of defamation, which pro- **17.313** tects the nominate right to reputation, and the general tort of negligence which is concerned with a general right not to suffer loss by the carelessness of another. We saw that the infiltration of negligence allows a claimant to prevent defences such as qualified privilege being raised.[586] Defamation also overlaps with another general tort which focuses upon the fault of the defendant rather than a particular right of the claimant, namely malicious falsehood. Defamation requires the publication of a defamatory statement. Malicious falsehood is designed to cover the case in which a lie told about someone does damage to his financial interests, without being defamatory. The original case was 'slander of title': it is not defamatory to say that a person has a bad title to his land, but it is a potent means of inflicting loss. Again, it is not defamatory to say that a person is no longer trading from such and such premises, but it can cost him business.[587]

The overlap arises because a false statement does not cease to be a malicious **17.314** falsehood merely because it is also defamatory. To say that a person is a thief is

---

[584] Paras 21.160–21.163 and 21.90.

[585] Invoked in *Rantzen v Mirror Group Newspapers Ltd* [1994] QB 670, CA. Other measures: *John v Mirror Group Newspapers Ltd* [1997] QB 586, CA. In *Tolstoy Miloslavsky v UK* Series A No 316, (1995) 20 EHRR 442 the European Court of Human Rights condemned the level of an award of £1.5m made against Count Tolstoy as in breach of Article 10 of the European Convention on Human Rights.

[586] See para 17.11. *Spring v Guardian Assurance plc* [1995] 2 AC 296, HL

[587] *Joyce v Motor Surveys Ltd* [1948] Ch 252.

defamatory, but to say it maliciously and so to harm his financial prospects is also malicious falsehood.[588]

17.315 Faced with a choice between the two torts the claimant will generally choose defamation. In the absence of privilege there is then no requirement to prove malice; the onus is on the defendant to prove that the allegations were true; and conditional fee arrangements are possible. On the other hand there is no legal aid for defamation cases, but for malicious falsehood there is. Such tactical choices are not frowned upon.[589]

F. Strict Liability: Interference with Property Rights

17.316 The law's protection of property rights has two aspects. There is first the protection of the claimant's right to the physical integrity of his assets. Here the law lays down what it will do about damage. Then there is the protection of the right to control the asset, where the law says what it will do when another person assumes control without consent, as for instance by finding, or taking, or buying from a non-owner.

17.317 When a chattel or land is damaged, redress is usually sought through the tort of negligence, although it may be sought in trespass, which was formerly the dominant wrong. Unlike negligence, trespass liability is strict although the act must be willed. This has already been considered.[590] The primary tort in relation to interference with chattels is now conversion, which focuses upon interferences with control. The first two subsections are concerned only with corporeal property. The third section deals briefly with incorporeals.

(1) Common Law

(a) No *vindicatio* at common law

17.318 In classical Roman law a claimant could go to court and make a direct assertion of his ownership of the asset in question: 'That cow, Buttercup, is mine!' That

---

[588] *Joyce v Sengupta* [1993] 1 WLR 337, CA. On the basis that some instrument is better than none, claimants whose real problem was harassment or invasion of privacy have chosen now defamation: *Tolley v JS Fry & Sons Ltd* [1931] AC 333, HL, now malicious falsehood: *Kaye v Robertson* [1991] 1 FSR 62, CA.

[589] But an ingenious attempt to switch from defamation to conspiracy in order to sidestep the defence of justification met with no sympathy in *Lonrho plc v Fayed (No 5)* [1993] 1 WLR 1489, CA.

[590] Paras 17.246–17.249, and 17.254.

assertion was called the *vindicatio*.[591] Such a claim has nothing to do with the law of torts or civil wrongs. It is a pure proprietary claim, in that it is nothing other than the assertion of the proprietary right. There is probably no system in which such a pure proprietary claim does all the work of protecting this right. But in some it stands in the front line.

In English law, on the common law side, if it comes to litigation, there is no *vindicatio*. Outside the court there is nothing to prevent the claimant saying, 'That cow, Buttercup, is mine!' The person in possession may concede and surrender Buttercup. Within imperfectly defined limits, the claimant can also have recourse to self-help to take back his asset.[592] However the common law simply does not recognize a demand in court which consists in the direct assertion of ownership. There is, in this sense, no pure proprietary remedy. In a recent dispute, which concerned ownership of money, Millett LJ said that the common law, while recognizing proprietary rights, had no proprietary remedies.[593] There is more than one meaning to be given to that statement, but one, which is certainly true, is that the common law has no *vindicatio*. **17.319**

The one exception to this might be said to be the action to recover land, formerly the action of ejectment. In the early days of the common law the writ of right and the writs of entry might have been said to be pure proprietary claims, with the additional and exceptional feature, unknown to the classical *vindicatio*, that judgment would be for the surrender of possession of the thing itself.[594] However, the real actions gave way to a special action of trespass with force and arms which was in turn in due course equipped with that characteristic which gave the real actions their name, the order to surrender the thing itself.[595] Statutory reforms, first as part of the abolition of the forms of action and then aimed to speed up the recovery of possession against squatters, have broken every meaningful link with the tort of trespass. The modern action to recover land is essentially a *vindicatio* which gives specific recovery. The claimant does not prove absolute entitlement but merely a better right to possession than the defendant. **17.320**

---

[591] WW Buckland, *A Textbook of Roman Law from Augustus to Justinian*, 3rd edn revised by P Stein (1963) 675; F Schulz, *Classical Roman Law* (1951) 368–72.

[592] Reasonable force, short of violence, may be used if no trespass to land is involved, and even some degree of trespass to land appears to be permitted, again without violence: S Gleeson, *Personal Property Law* (1997), 304; FH Lawson, *Remedies of English Law* (2nd edn, 1980) chs 1 and 2. Under the Consumer Credit Act 1974, owners within s 92 may not enter premises without a court order. Violent entry is a criminal offence under the Criminal Law Act 1977, s 6.

[593] See para 17.321.

[594] This is the root of 'real property'–property in respect of which a claim would yield the *res* (thing) itself. See paras 4.14–4.16.

[595] AWB Simpson, *The History of the Land Law* (2nd edn, 1986) 144–9; cf paras 4.18 and 4.41–4.42.

(b) Parasitic protection at common law

17.321   Although lacking direct protection through the simple assertion of property rights, the common law recognized two forms of claim in the law of obligations, one in the law of wrongs and the other in the law of unjust enrichment. The former says: 'You ought to pay me money because you have committed a wrong in that you have interfered with such and such a thing to which I had a better possessory right than you.' The latter says, 'You ought to pay me the value of such and such a thing to which I had a better right than you, by the receipt of which you have been enriched at my expense.' The law of unjust enrichment having been fragmented and concealed, the latter claim has rather rarely come out into the open. No more will be said of it here save to say that enrichment is concerned with an abstract measure of value and indirectly protects all assets, whilst a majority of the House of Lords has recently insisted that the torts involving interferences with property rights are confined to tangible things in which the claimant has a possessory right good against all the world.[596]

(i) Two wrongs under one statutory umbrella

17.322   The Torts (Interference with Goods) Act 1977 'abolished' the old action of detinue and created a loosely unified regime for all interferences with goods, including negligent damage which has already been dealt with.[597] For the protection of rights to possession and control of goods the Act left intact two wrongs. One is trespass with force and arms, in the form which used to be known as *de bonis asportatis* (concerning goods carried away). The tort of trespass to goods requires a direct and intentional interference with the claimant's possessory right to the chattel.[598] The other was conversion, which began life as one species of the originally supplementary actions called trespass on the case, or simply case. Although conversion is indisputably dominant it does not completely cover the field of trespass to chattels.[599] A car thief commits this form of trespass when he enters and drives off your car. But he also commits conversion.

---

[596]   *OBG v Allen* [2007] UKHL 21, [2007] 2 WLR 920. Lord Nicholls and Baroness Hale dissented on the basis that the distinction between tangibles and intangibles lacks any rhyme or reason although, oddly, both required proof of fault in an action for unlawful interference with (intangible) trade rights. Further discussion of unjust enrichment below at paras 18.11–18.21.

[597]   Torts (Interference with Goods) Act 1977, ss 1, 2.

[598]   A powerful, concurrent line of cases is historically opposed to the traditional requirement of 'directness': *McLaughlin v Pryor* (1842) 4 Man & G 48,59; 134 ER 21, 25; *Gregory v Piper* (1829) 9 B & C 591; 109 ER 220; *Manton v Brocklebank* [1923] 2 KB 212. We are grateful to Mr Simon Douglas for drawing our attention to these cases which are discussed in his ongoing doctoral work on tortious interferences with goods.

[599]   A car which is clamped is not damaged is probably not controlled and hence not converted, but the clamping can be a trespass: *Arthur v Anker* [1997] QB 564, CA, where however the clamper could rely on the defence of voluntary acceptance of the risk: *volenti non fit injuria*.

(ii) Conversion

17.323

The heart of the tort of conversion is an act of assertion of control, but it is an act denatured by the deletion of all traces of dishonesty or lesser degrees of fault. It is enough that the assertion of control is intended and without the consent of the defendant, who has the superior right to possession. In outline, the old action on the case for conversion used to recite, first, that the claimant was possessed of such and such a silver cup as of his own proper goods; secondly, that he casually lost the same and the defendant found it;[600] and thirdly that the defendant fraudulently converted the cup to his own use, to the claimant's damage.[601] At the heart of this heavily fictitious pleading was a notion of misappropriation. Conversion expanded from this action for misappropriation, to a central idea of control, covering much of the ground of detinue.[602] In 2002, Lord Nicholls said that it included any voluntary act, inconsistent with the rights of the owner, which excludes him from the use and enjoyment of the chattel.[603]

17.324

Strict liability.   Part of the reason why conversion expanded as a tort of strict liability might have been in order to allow it to do the work of the missing *vindicatio.* However, the tort of conversion went well beyond the Roman vindicatio, at least in its classical form, since the action was commonly brought even when the defendant no longer had possession.[604] The development of conversion was achieved in the manner characteristic of the law's development under the forms of action, by holding that the allegations of fraud could not be traversed, so that they became merely decorative: in its original scope involving misappropriations, the liability was established by the objective fact of the misappropriation, however innocent. Thus a cycle shop which sells my bicycle commits the tort, even if it has no reason whatever to think that the bicycle is not its own. And if one person grinds another's corn into flour without the other's consent, that too is a conversion.[605] As Cleasby B said in *Fowler v Hollins*, 'Persons deal with the property in

---

600 Because of this allegation of finding the action was often called 'trover' (cf the modern French '*trouver*'). The allegation of loss and finding was no more than a standard formal explanation of the arrival of the thing in the defendant's hands. The formal allegation could not be traversed. The real story would come out before the jury.

601 Examples in JH Baker and SFC Milsom, *Sources of English Legal History: Private Law to 1750* (1986) 531–9.

602 *Baldwin v Cole* (1705) 6 Mod 212, 212, 90 ER 1290, 1290 *per* Holt CJ.

603 *Kuwait Airways Corp v Iraqi Airways Co (Nos 4 and 5)* [2002] UKHL 19; [2002] 2 AC 883, [39] HL.

604 Ultimately the justification for the development of strict liability can only be the 'salutory rule for the protection of property rights': *Hollins v Fowler* (1871–2) LR 7 QB 616 (Ex) *per* Cleasy B.

605 *Hollins v Fowler* (1875) LR 7 HL 757, 768, *per* Blackburn J.

chattels or exercise acts of ownership over them at their peril.'[606] Both conversion and, in this function, trespass, are the same in this respect.

17.325 Assertion of control. Not only is liability strict but the expansion of conversion from misappropriation to an assertion of control means that the tort now includes any voluntary exercise of control over a thing which is inconsistent with the claimant's superior right to possession of it. Thus a carrier or warehouseman commits conversion if he delivers to the wrong person;[607] and an auctioneer converts when he sells for another;[608] and one who refuses to deliver up a thing to another with a better title is nowadays treated as converting the thing,[609] although such a refusal was formerly no more than evidence from which to infer a conversion;[610] and one who consumes or intentionally destroys a thing converts it, though mere damage is not a conversion;[611] and successive possessors who each act inconsistently with the claimant's right to possession can all be liable for conversion.[612] Storage is not in itself a conversion, since to store on the orders of the wrong person is not to deny the true owner's right to possession.[613] A careless act resulting in loss or destruction cannot be a conversion, for, even on an objective analysis, without a voluntary act there can be no assertion of rights inconsistent with those of the claimant.[614]

17.326 Claimant with a better right to possession. The proper claimant is a person with a better right to possession than the defendant, and this in turn means that the thing in question must be susceptible of possession,[615] which pure incorporeals are not. A finder can sue.[616] A finder has the general property in the goods, albeit by a very short possessory title. His very possession gives him a right to possess.

---

[606] (1872) LR 7 QB 616, 639.

[607] *Hiort v Bott* (1874) LR 9 Ex 86.

[608] *RH Willis & Son v British Car Auctions Ltd* [1978] 1 WLR 438, CA.

[609] *Howard E Perry & Co Ltd v British Railways Board* [1980] 1 WLR 1375.

[610] *Isaack v Clark* (1615) 2 Buls 306, 80 ER 1143, 1 Rolle 127, 81 ER 377; JH Baker and SFC Milsom, *Sources of English Legal History: Private Law to 1750* (1986) 541.

[611] *Simmons v Lillystone* (1853) 8 Exch 431, 255 ER 1417.

[612] *Kuwait Airways Corp v Iraqi Airways Co (No 3)* [2002] UKHL 19; [2002] 2 AC 883, HL.

[613] *Hollins v Fowler* (1875) LR 7 HL 757, 767, *per* Blackburn J. Applied in *Marcq v Christie, Manson & Woods Ltd* [2003] EWCA Civ 731; [2004] QB 286, CA: returning an unsold painting to the purported owner who had instructed the sale was not conversion although it would have been different if the painting had been delivered to a new purchaser.

[614] *The Arpad* [1934] P 189, 232, CA, *per* Maugham LJ. In breach with the nature of the tort, the Torts (Interference with Goods) Act 1977, s 2 imposes such a liability where the abolished action of detinue would have lain, where a bailee negligently allows destruction to happen in breach of his duties of care.

[615] Also, if it adds anything, the thing must be capable of possession as property, so that conversion cannot be brought in respect of a part of a human body, unless it has been transformed into a laboratory specimen: *Dobson v North Tyneside HA* [1997] 1 WLR 596, CA.

[616] *Armory v Delamirie* (1722) 1 Strange 505, 93 ER 664; see paras 4.414–4.415.

Similarly, a bailee in possession, whatever form that bailment takes, has a right to possess although the bailment gives him only a special property in the thing. The bailee who sues for conversion is under a duty to his bailor to account for that portion of the recovered damages which exceed his own loss.[617] Even a thief can sue. That there is almost no exception based on illegality on the part of the possessor is affirmed in a fine judgment of the Court of Appeal in *Costello v Chief Constable of Derbyshire Constabulary*.[618] Under section 19 of the *Police and Criminal Evidence Act* 1984 the police had seized from Costello a Ford Escort car. The temporary purpose of that seizure having been exhausted, they refused to return it on the ground that it had been stolen and Costello knew that. Although they were held to be correct in those beliefs they were compelled to return the car to him. The wrongful possessor had a right to possession which could only be defeated by statute. Statute apart, the only exception was that the court would not order the delivery up of something if it would be unlawful for him to receive it, as for instance prohibited drugs or a gun for which he held no licence.[619]

The importance of relative title was formerly emphasized by the rule that a defend- **17.327** ant could not plead a *jus tertii*—that is, he could not adduce evidence that a third party had a better title than the claimant—except in the case in which the claimant was relying solely on his own possession. This has been changed by section 8 of the Torts (Interference with Goods) Act 1977. In the *Costello* case the police were not in a position to resist Costello's claim by invoking this section because they could not identify the third party nor join him as a party to the action as the section requires.

Money orders. The tort of conversion gives rise to both loss-based and gain- **17.328** based rights.[620] This follows from the House of Lords' analysis of the meaning of the old language of 'waiver of tort' in *United Australia Ltd v Barclays Bank Ltd*.[621] Instead of the usual action for compensatory damages, an action for 'money had and received' could be brought for money obtained through the commission of a tort.[622] 'Waiver of tort' usually described that practice. The House of Lords held that, so far as concerned the tort of conversion, the proper analysis of that practice in a world no longer dominated by forms of action was that the tort gave rise to two secondary rights. The one cause of action gave the claimant a choice between a compensatory and a gain-based claim. It was not a case of switching from a cause

---

[617] *The Winkfield* [1902] P 42, CA.

[618] [2001] EWCA Civ 381; [2001] 1 WLR 1437, CA, following and further explaining *Webb v Chief Constable of Merseyside Police* [2000] 2 QB 427, CA.

[619] ibid 1451 [34].

[620] Paras 21.146–21.149.

[621] [1943] AC 1, HL.

[622] *Lamine v Dorrell* (1705) 2 Ld Raym 1216, 92 ER 303.

of action in tort to a cause of action in unjust enrichment and certainly did not connote any ratification or forgiveness of the tort.

17.329   Under section 3 of the Torts (Interference with Goods) Act 1977 the claimant's right to a money order is expressed as a right to damages. In view of the fact that the claimant has a choice between two measures of recovery, it has to be assumed that the word 'damages' includes both compensatory (loss-based) awards and gain-based awards.[623]

17.330   So far as compensatory damages are concerned, the Act allows recovery of the value of the chattel together with any consequential loss. There are three areas of difficulty. The first is the date for valuing the chattel. This will be important where the chattel has either depreciated or appreciated in value in the intervening period. So far as fluctuations of the market are concerned, the pre-1977 position seems to have been that in actions for conversion the relevant date was the date of the conversion, whereas in actions of detinue, the relevant date was that of the judgment. Although detinue is said to have been abolished, it is probably still necessary to identify in a claim whether, before 1977, the claim would have arisen in detinue or in conversion.[624] The second area of difficulty is in cases in which the value of the chattel is greater than the loss that has been suffered. There are cases pulling in both directions but the prevailing authority suggests that the award will not exceed the amount of the loss.[625] The third area of difficulty is causation of loss. Where there have been successive tortfeasors, such as successive converters, the application of the 'but for' test of causation leads to the conclusion than none but the first possessor is liable. We saw that the same difficulty arose in relation to successive events after a negligent act which are sufficient to cause the same loss. In *Kuwait Airways Corp v Iraqi Airways Co (Nos 4 and 5)*[626] during the invasion of Kuwait, the Iraqi Airforce took possession of several of the claimant's aircraft belonging to the claimants and flew them to Iraq. A law was passed incorporating the aircraft into the defendant's fleet and the defendants took possession and asserted control over the aircraft. The difficulty that the

---

[623] It is certain that the Act elsewhere uses 'damages' to include gain-based awards, even when the cause of action is unjust enrichment rather than a wrong: see the example give in s 6(2)(b). See also J Edelman *Gain-based Damages* (2002) 118.

[624] *BBMB Finance (Hong Kong) Ltd v Eda Holdings Ltd* [1990] 1 WLR 409, PC (date of conversion); *IBL Ltd v Coussens* [1991] 2 All ER 133, CA (date of judgment).

[625] [2002] UKHL 19; [2002] 2 AC 883, 1089 [63] HL, Lord Nicholls approving cases including *Hiort v London and North Western Railway Co* (1879) 4 Ex D 188, where no recovery was allowed when the claimant's goods were misdelivered but the claimant would equally have received no payment for his goods if, instead of misdelivering the goods, the railway company had delivered them in accordance with his instructions. See also *Borders (UK) Ltd v Commissioner of Police of the Metropolis* [2005] EWCA Civ 197, CA.

[626] [2002] UKHL 19; [2002] 2 AC 883, HL.

claimants faced was showing that their loss had been caused by the defendants. But for the defendants' possession, the Iraqi Airforce would still have deprived the claimants of their aircraft. In the leading speech in the House of Lords, Lord Nicholls explained that although it could not be said, by application of the but for test for causation, that each successive converter might not have caused an owner loss, the test for causation should focus only on whether the claimant would have suffered the loss in question had he retained the goods and not been deprived of them by the particular defendant.[627] The focus of the tort is the effect of the actions of the defendant on the claimant's property rights; acts of third parties are irrelevant.[628]

When damages are assessed so as to compensate the claimant for the whole value **17.331** of a claimant's right to goods, the payment of those damages extinguishes the claimant's right. The same applies to payments made on the same basis under settlements. The precise conditions under which this happens are spelled out in section 5 of the Act.

Specific delivery. Conversion formerly gave only a money award. The Act changed **17.332** that. In any action for interference with goods the claimant may choose instead to ask for an order for delivery up of the thing in question 'giving the defendant the alternative of paying damages by reference to the value of the goods, together in either alternative with payment of any consequential damages'.[629] In addition the court itself is entitled, in its discretion, to make an order for delivery up and payment of consequential damages without the option for payment of the value.[630]

Limitation. The operation of time limits here plays an important part in **17.333** the law's compromise between the sanctity of ownership and the security of transactions. Under the Limitation Act 1980 the basic time limit for actions of conversion is six years, and, exceptionally, the expiry of the period of limitation extinguishes the claimant's title.[631]

A thief commits conversion. Since the passing of the 1980 Act, time does not run **17.334** against a thief. Section 4(1) says, 'The right of any person from whom a chattel is stolen to bring an action in respect of the theft shall not be subject to the time limits under section 2 and 3(1) of this Act. . .'

---

627 ibid 1094-4 [78]–[86].

628 For example *Hiort v London and North Western Railway Co* (1879) 4 Ex D 188, see n 625 above.

629 Torts (Interference with Goods) Act 1977, s 3(2)(b), (3). Specific delivery orders are not available in the case of money: s 14(1).

630 ibid s 3(2)(a), (3). See *Pendragon plc v Walon Ltd* [2005] EWHC 1082.

631 Limitation Act 1980, ss 2 and 3.

17.335   A purchaser from the thief will also convert the goods. However, under section 4(2) of the Act, in respect of that conversion time will begin to run if the purchase is made in good faith, and after six years from that good faith conversion the title of the victim of the theft will be extinguished. In effect, the short proposition for stolen goods is that time runs from the first good faith conversion. Nevertheless the thief himself remains liable for his theftuous conversion. For section 4(1) of the Act, part of which is quoted above, concludes by saying that, where the victim's title is extinguished by the running of time from a good faith purchase, 'he may not bring an action in respect of a theft preceding the loss of his title, unless the theft in question preceded the conversion from which time began to run. . .'. Generally the theft does precede that good faith conversion, so that the effect of these last words is to preserve the action against the thief.

(2) Equity

(a) Exclusion from common law protections

17.336   An equitable owner has no access to the common law means discussed above. Nevertheless, we had recently to be reminded of this truth by the Court of Appeal. *In MCC Proceeds Inc v Lehman Bros International (Europe)*[632] American shares were held in trust for MCC Proceeds. The trustee, in breach of trust, mortgaged the shares as security for a loan. MCC's claim in equity encountered the objection that the defendants were bona fide purchasers for value without notice of the equitable right. In this case MCC tried to sue the defendant in conversion, to which there is in general no bona fide purchase defence. The claim failed on more than one ground, above all because MCC could not bring conversion, which is a common law action based on a right to immediate possession. Further, the common law does not recognize the equitable title of the beneficiary of a trust.[633]

17.337   There are just two qualifications. First, if a beneficiary under a trust is in possession he can bring an action for conversion, not *qua* equitable owner, but just in the same way as anyone who has a possessory title.[634] Secondly, a trustee almost always has the legal right and the legal means of protecting it. Unless the trustee has transferred that right himself,[635] or it has exceptionally passed against his will,[636] he can

---

[632] [1998] 4 All ER 675, CA.

[633] *MCC Proceeds Inv v Lehmann Bros International (Europe)* [1998] 4 All ER 675, 691, CA.

[634] *Healey v Healey* [1915] 1 KB 938. The extension of this case to an equitable owner with no possessory title in *International Factors Ltd v Rodriguez* [1979] QB 351, CA was illegitimate.

[635] As in *Re Montagu's Settlement Trusts* [1987] Ch 264.

[636] As in *Lipkin Gorman v Karpnale Ltd* [1991] 2 AC 548, HL, where, however, it was held that the trustees (for the account which had been raided was a client account), though they could not bring conversion could still bring the action for unjust enrichment. See further paras 18.47–18.49.

and must bring his common law action on the trust's behalf, and if he will not, he can be joined as co-defendant.

(b) The equitable *vindicatio*

By *'vindicatio'* is meant the direct assertion of a proprietary right. Unlike the com-   **17.338**
mon law, equity does know such a claim. A claimant can say, 'That Rolls Royce is mine!' What he actually asks for is a declaration that the defendant holds the Rolls Royce on trust for him. In *Macmillan Inc v Bishopsgate Investment Trust plc (No 3)*,[637] Macmillan's plea was essentially 'Please say, O Court, that all the financial institutions to which our trustee gave our Berlitz shares now hold those shares on trust for us, and please order them to hand them over.'

The *vindicatio* is abstract. 'That is mine!' is the assertion of a conclusion from   **17.339**
facts. Facts have to be adduced which in law substantiate the proposition. In the *Macmillan* case the relevant facts were all in place but encountered a defence. The disgraced tycoon, Maxwell, had procured a gratuitous transfer of Macmillan's shares in circumstances which made the transferee a resulting trustee, and then, very soon afterwards, he had caused the transferee to make an express declaration of trust in favour of Macmillan. Maxwell then transferred his shares to lending institutions as security for huge loans. Macmillan's difficulty was that its equitable ownership was vulnerable to destruction by bona fide purchase of the legal title.

(c) Parasitic protection in equity

There is further parasitic protection in equity through the obligation arising from   **17.340**
the knowing receipt of assets dissipated in breach of trust. This liability has a requirement of fault, variously put as dishonesty,[638] carelessness in the form of failing to make the inquiries which a reasonable person would have made in the circumstances,[639] and, more recently, an amorphous test of unconscionability.[640]

In many cases in which trust property gets into the wrong hands someone who has   **17.341**
assisted in the misdirection will incur a liability for 'dishonest assistance' and will have to make good the beneficiaries' loss, whether or not he received the property himself. 'Dishonest assistance' unequivocally requires proof of dishonesty on the part of the alleged accessory to the misdirection.[641]

---

[637] [1996] 1 WLR 387, CA. This was an earlier phase of the Maxwell episode already encountered in *MCC Proceeds Inc v Lehman Bros International (Europe)* [1998] 4 All ER 675, CA, (n 633 above). N Segal, 'Cross-border Security Enforcement: Restitution and Priorities' in FD Rose (ed), *Restitution and Banking Law* (1998) 99–120.

[638] *Re Montagu's Settlement Trusts* [1987] Ch 264.

[639] *Belmont Finance Corporation Ltd v Williams Furniture Ltd (No 2)* [1980] 1 All ER 393, CA.

[640] *Bank of Credit and Commerce International (Overseas) Ltd v Akindele* [2001] Ch 437, CA.

[641] See paras 17.381–17.384.

17.342 Extremely disruptive in this area has been the law's long history of failure to recognize the independence of the law of unjust enrichment. 'Knowing receipt' would very likely be subsumed within the wrong of dishonest participation/assistance in a breach of fiduciary duty if it were not constantly making up for the imperfect recognition of the unjust enrichment obligation in equity, as illustrated in *Ministry of Health v Simpson*.[642]

(3) Incorporeal Assets

17.343 Conversion and trespass focus on possession. And the Torts (Interference with Goods) Act 1977 not only makes no change in that but underlines the fact that its regime does not apply to incorporeal assets when in section 14(1) it defines goods as 'all chattels personal other than things in action and money'. For present purposes a 'thing in action', which contrasts with 'thing in possession' may be regarded as any valuable right which, failing voluntary compliance, depends for its realization on an action brought in court.

17.344 Documentary intangibles, such as cheques,[643] are in a special position. The paper, almost valueless in itself, is a corporeal chattel like any other. A benign interpretation allows that such paper is valued, not according to its own intrinsic value, but so as to include the value which it carries. 'Into this category fall rights embodied in bills of lading and other documents of title, negotiable instruments, negotiable certificates of deposit and bearer bonds and other bearer securities.'[644] In England this list does not include shares, unless they are bearer shares, which are nowadays rarely found.[645]

17.345 Among the most important incorporeal assets are intellectual property rights[646] and also confidential information, although confidential information is not protected solely as wealth but sometimes as a particular emanation of privacy. Of the intellectual property rights, only copyright is indirectly protected by the tort of conversion because the tort of conversion is concerned only with tangible things.[647] The ownership of reproduced copyrighted material vests in the holder of the copyright with the consequence that he can sue for conversion.[648] It is, however, broadly true that the regimes for redressing infringements of such

---

[642] [1951] AC 251, HL, affirming *Re Diplock* [1948] Ch 465, CA. See further para 18.50–18.51.
[643] *United Australia Ltd v Barclays Bank Ltd* [1941] AC 1, HL.
[644] Roy Goode, *Commercial Law* (3rd edn, 2004) 49.
[645] Contrast the American shares involved in *MCC Proceeds Inc v Lehman Bros International (Europe)* [1998] 4 All ER 675, CA.
[646] See Chapter 6 (intellectual property). For the torts of passing off and injurious falsehood, see paras 6.98–6.106.
[647] *OBG v Allen* [2007] UKHL 21, [2007] 2 WLR 920, HL. See para 17.321.
[648] *Caxton Publishing Co Ltd v Sutherland Publishing Co Ltd* [1939] AC 178, HL.

rights operate in much the same way as does the tort of conversion in relation to corporeal chattels. That is to say, the available remedial rights are commonly compensatory or disgorgement awards: they either make good the claimant's loss or strip out the infringer's profit. And these remedial rights are backed by injunctions to compel discontinuance of the infringement. Furthermore liability is strict, as it is in conversion. However, a difference has crept in, in that fault has sometimes been invoked both at common law and in statutes as relevant to the measure of compensation. This has not been approached in a principled manner, however, with the consequence that the presence and absence of fault has different consequences in relation to different infringements. These variations are considered below.[649]

G. Strict Liability: Breach of Fiduciary Duty

(1) Difficulty in Definition of a Fiduciary

Equity's wrong of strict liability is breach of fiduciary duty. Fiduciary is anglicized **17.346** Latin which conveys notions of honour, honesty, trust and faithfulness. The archetypal fiduciary is the trustee but there are other fiduciary relationships, such as a company director/company,[650] agent/principal[651] and solicitor/client,[652] which are characterized by these same notions of honour, honesty, trust and faith.[653] The expression 'trust' is generally used in the sense that 'one party is reasonably entitled to repose and does repose trust and confidence in the other.'[654] However, despite the etymology and constant reference to trust in fiduciary relationships, the concept is neither sufficient nor necessary for a fiduciary relationship. It is not sufficient because some relationships of trust have not traditionally been regarded as fiduciary: parent/child, teacher/student or doctor/patient.[655]

---

[649] From paras 21.150–21.151.

[650] *Regal (Hastings) Ltd v Gulliver* [1967] 2 AC 134, HL; *Ultraframe (UK) Ltd v Fielding* [2005] EWHC 1638.

[651] *Boston Deep Sea Fishing and Ice Co v Ansell* (1888) 39 Ch D 389, CA.

[652] *Hilton v Barker Booth Eastwood* [2005] UKHL 8, [2005] 1 WLR 567, HL.

[653] P Birks 'The Content of Fiduciary Obligation' (2002) 16 Trust Law Int 34, 36. In *Charitable Corporation v Sutton* (1742) 2 Atk 400, 26 ER 642, 9 Mod 349, 88 ER 500 Lord Hardwicke LC spoke of the duties owed by company directors as duties of 'trust'.

[654] *Estate Realties Ltd v Wignall* [1991] 3 NZLR 482, 492, NZCA; *Zhong v Wang* [2006] NZCA 242, [88], NZCA.

[655] In *Sidaway v Bethlem Royal Hospital* [1985] AC 871, 884, HL, Lord Scarman insisted that the doctor/patient relationship was not fiduciary. Canadian law insists that they are: *Norberg v Wynrib* (1992) 92 DLR (4th) 449; *McInerney v MacDonald* [1992] 2 SCR 138, SCC. Compare also *Hedley Byrne & Co Ltd v Heller & Partners Ltd* [1964] AC 465, 509, HL *per* Lord Hodson who asserted that parent/child was an accepted category of fiduciary relation.

It is also not sufficient because the presence of actual trust in a relationship does not create a fiduciary relationship; a purchaser and a vendor are not in a fiduciary relationship if the purchaser places actual trust and confidence in the vendor. On the other hand, the presence of actual trust is not a necessary condition because a bare trustee is still a fiduciary even though he has very little power to affect the interests of the beneficiary and even if the beneficiary has never met the trustee and has never placed any actual trust or confidence in him.

17.347 Another attempt at definition is the famous statement of Mason J in the High Court of Australia in *Hospital Products Ltd v United States Surgical Corporation*.[656] After referring to the concepts of trust and confidence, Mason J placed emphasis on a different characteristic:

> the fiduciary undertakes or agrees to act for or on behalf of or in the interests of another person in the exercise of a power or discretion which will affect the interests of that other person in a legal or practical sense.

Similarly, many cases refer to a hallmark of the fiduciary relation as 'vulnerability', in the sense of a high level of power that a fiduciary has to affect the interests of a beneficiary.[657] However, these concepts of power, discretion and vulnerability are too broad because many commercial relationships will involve one party with significant power to affect the interests of the other. Such commercial relationships are rarely fiduciary. A related definition of a fiduciary relationship focuses upon the requirement to serve exclusively the interests of a person or group of persons.[658] But this is circular: it defines the fiduciary relationship by reference to the duties which are imposed once a person is characterized as a fiduciary.

17.348 A third approach suggests that courts should reason by analogy from the core fiduciary case of a trustee to other similar trustee-like relationships of trust and confidence.[659] But this process of reasoning by analogy is fraught with difficulty: how can degrees of trust and confidence be measured? Where should a line be drawn? Can it really be said that analogies can be drawn between, for example, custodial trustees and non-custodial directors?[660] For the moment, it seems that the only safe course is to list those relationships which the courts have accepted to be fiduciary: trustee/beneficiary, director/company, solicitor/client, partner/

---

[656] (1984) 156 CLR 41, 68, HCA.

[657] *Hospital Products Ltd v United States Surgical Corporation* (1984) 156 CLR 41, 142, HCA, *per* Dawson J; *Frame v Smith* (1987) 42 DLR (4th) 81, 99, SCC *per* Wilson J.

[658] P Finn 'The Fiduciary Principle' in T Youdan (ed) *Equity, Fiduciaries and Trusts* (1989) 31.

[659] P Birks 'The Content of Fiduciary Obligation' (2002) 16 Trust Law Int 34.

[660] A point made in J Getzler 'Rumford Market and the Genesis of Fiduciary Obligations' in A Burrows and A Rodger (eds) *Mapping the Law: Essays in Honour of Peter Birks* (2006) ch 31.

partner and so on, whilst also remembering that a relationship may be fiduciary in relation to some of its incidents but not others.[661]

(2) Duties of Care Owed by Fiduciaries

We saw earlier in this chapter that in limited situations the common law regards **17.349** as wrongful the failure to act reasonably to protect the interests of another; a failure to take positive and reasonable action to protect another from harm.[662] Apart from contractual duties, situations of assumption of responsibility are the most obvious examples of situations in which such positive duties arise. Trustees and other fiduciaries are one class of persons who are subject to this duty of positive action. Their duty to protect the beneficiary from harm, such as by taking care in investment of trust assets is nothing but a requirement of positive action connoting a duty of care, with the consequence that the wrong committed by breach of that duty is not distinct from the tort of negligence.[663] But, in the case of fiduciaries, there is a further, higher, duty owed by the principal. The principal is also bound to abstain from any interest of his own which might tempt him to sacrifice the beneficiary's interests. This higher duty, to act in a disinterested way unless authorized otherwise, is the characteristic fiduciary obligation.

(3) The Fiduciary Duties of Loyalty

The fiduciary duty to act in a disinterested way unless authorized otherwise **17.350** has historically been expressed as two particular duties. The first is a duty on the fiduciary not to pursue, without authority, an interest which conflicts, or might conflict, with his duty to take positive and reasonable action to protect the interests of the principal. Second, he is under a duty not to profit from his fiduciary position without authorization. The two duties are closely related. Indeed, the first duty almost completely swallows the second because there will be few situations in which a fiduciary makes an unauthorized profit that do not arise from a conflict between his interests and the positive duty owed to his principal. But the second 'no-profit' duty still serves the important purpose of focussing upon situations in which there is a heightened degree of risk that the fiduciary will favour

---

[661] *New Zealand Netherlands Society 'Oranje' Inc v Kuys* [1973] 1 WLR 1126, 1130, PC.

[662] See paras 17.92–17.98.

[663] *Henderson v Merrett Syndicates Ltd* [1995] 2 AC 145, 205, HL, *per* Lord Browne-Wilkinson; *Bristol and West Building Society v Mothew* [1998] Ch 1, 16–18, CA, *per* Millett LJ; *Hilton v Barker Booth Eastwood* [2005] UKHL 8, [2005] 1 WLR 567, 575 [29], HL, *per* Lord Walker; P Birks 'The Content of Fiduciary Obligation' (2002) 16 Trust Law Int 34. This view is rejected by JD Heydon, 'Are the duties of company directors to exercise care and skill fiduciary?' and J Getzler 'Am I my Beneficiary's Keeper? Fusion and Loss-Based Fiduciary Remedies' in S Degeling and J Edelman (eds), *Equity in Commercial Law* (2005) chs 9 and 10.

his own interests.[664] It provides an easier evidential route for the protection of the interests of the beneficiary or principal than positive proof of the first no-conflict rule; this role of easing the proof of the claimant's case is consistent with the origins of the no-profit duty as an offshoot of the no-conflict duty.[665]

17.351 Unlike negligence, whether at common law or in equity, the most common remedy for a breach of a fiduciary duty is not compensation but either disgorgement of profits or an order that any asset acquired in breach of fiduciary duty is held on trust for the principal. The leading case is *Keech v Sanford*.[666] A lease of the profits of the Rumford Market had been devised to the defendant trustee to hold on trust for an infant. Towards the expiry of the term, the trustee asked to renew the lease for the infant but the lessor refused because he would not be able to protect his interest against an infant beneficiary. The trustee then renewed the lease for himself. King LC held that the trustee had breached his duty in taking the benefit of the lease: 'though I do not say that there is a fraud in this case, yet he should rather have let it run out, than to have had the lease to himself. . .the trustee is the only person of all mankind who might not have the lease'.[667] The lease was ordered to be assigned to the infant and the trustee was ordered to account for all the profit he had derived from the lease.

17.352 As we have seen, the trustee is the archetypal fiduciary but not the only one. A famous example of an order for disgorgement of unauthorized fiduciary profits in other relationships of trust and confidence is *Boardman v Phipps*.[668] The appellants were a solicitor to a trust and a beneficiary under the trust. They acquired information in the course of representing the trust which allowed them to make a considerable profit from the purchase of shares in a company in which the trust also owned shares. Although the trust could not have purchased the shares, and although the trust benefitted by the increased share price, the appellants were required to disgorge their profits to the beneficiaries. They were entitled to a

---

[664] M Conaglen 'The Nature and Function of Fiduciary Loyalty' (2005) 121 LQR 452, 467. The rule is 'based on the consideration that human nature being what it is, there is danger, in such circumstances, of the person holding a fiduciary position being sway by interest rather than duty': *Bray v Ford* [1896] AC 44, 51–2, HL *per* Lord Herschell. For a contrary view that the concern of these duties is with the motives, or deemed motives, of the principal see L Smith 'The Motive not the Deed' in J Getzler (ed) *Rationalizing Property, Equity and Trusts: Essays in Honour of Edward Burn* (2003).

[665] A McLean 'The Theoretical Basis of the Trustee's Duty of Loyalty' (1969) 7 Alberta L Rev 218, 219–227.

[666] (1726) Select Cas Temp King 61; 25 ER 223. Discussed in J Getzler 'Rumford Market and the Genesis of Fiduciary Obligations' in A Burrows and A Rodger (eds) *Mapping the Law: Essays in Honour of Peter Birks* (2006) ch 31.

[667] (1726) Select Cas Temp King 61, 62; 25 ER 223, 223.

[668] [1967] 2 AC 46, HL. See also *Regal (Hastings) Ltd v Gulliver* [1967] 2 AC 134, HL (liability of directors to disgorge profits made in breach of fiduciary duty).

deduction from the account of a liberal allowance for their work and skill, but despite their good faith were not excused from the breach of their fiduciary duty because they had not obtained fully informed consent for their actions from all the beneficiaries of the trust. One difficulty with the decision of the majority is their treatment of the beneficiary as owing fiduciary duties to the other beneficiaries in the same way as did the solicitor to the trust. But unlike the solicitor/client relation, the beneficiary/beneficiary relation does not share any of the usual attributes of a fiduciary relationship.[669] However, in the majority, Lord Cohen was content to observe that this point had not been taken in the courts below and, he thought, rightly so since it would have been a strange result if the solicitor were required to disgorge profits but the beneficiary, with whom he acted jointly, was not.[670]

It will be apparent from the discussion above that fiduciary duties, and the high level of loyalty that they require, are qualitatively different duties from the more standard duties of fiduciary and non-fiduciary alike including the ordinary duty to take care, as well as other duties which focus upon fault such as the fiduciary's duty not to act in bad faith.[671] However, the higher level duties of loyalty imposed on a fiduciary are closely related to these standard duties. As Birks has observed, the fiduciary duty cannot exist without the lower level duty of care because the fiduciary duty exists for the prophylactic purpose of ensuring that the fiduciary takes care in carrying out his duties.[672] Lord Nicholls has made a similar point, explaining that the most common remedy for breach of fiduciary duty—disgorgement of profits—has the function to 'reinforce the duty of fidelity owed by a trustee or fiduciary by requiring him to account for any profits he derives from his office or position. This ensures trustees and fiduciaries are financially disinterested in carrying out their duties.'[673]

17.353

A very difficult question is whether this degree of prophylactic protection is still required today. Over the last century there have been cries that the fiduciary obligation is too strict.[674] The great American trusts scholar John Langbein has

17.354

---

[669] *Featherstonhaugh v Fenwick* (1810) 17 Ves 298; *Kennedy v De Trafford* [1897] AC 180, 186–90, HL; *Re Biss* [1903] 2 Ch 40, CA.

[670] [1967] 2 AC 46, 104.

[671] *Klug v Klug* [1918] 2 Ch 67; *Tempest v Lord Camoys* (1882) 21 ChD 571. The duty upon a trustee not to act on the basis of irrelevant or inadequate considerations is better understood as a fiduciary *power* to avoid transactions rather than a duty. The exercise of the trustee's power effects restitution of an unjust enrichment obtained where the consent of the trustee is vitiated, usually by mistake: *Re Hastings Bass* [1975] Ch 75; *Sieff v Fox* [2005] EWHC 1312 (Ch); [2005] 3 All ER 693.

[672] P Birks 'The Content of Fiduciary Obligation' (2002) 16 Trust Law Int 34.

[673] *Attorney General v Blake* [2001] 1 AC 268, 280, HL.

[674] WG Hart 'The Development of the Rule in *Keech v Sandford*' (1905) 21 LQR 258; S Cretney 'The Rationale of Keech v. Sandford' (1969) 33 Conv (NS) 161.

now taken up this case for abolition of the no profit duty arguing that there are now many procedures by which a fiduciary can be monitored and that the no profit duty can work to prevent a fiduciary acting in the best interests of the principal.[675] Although it is unlikely that English law will adopt so drastic a solution, there is a developing view that the prophylactic principle does not require the full range of remedies against a fiduciary who infringes the 'no profit' or 'no conflict' duties. A decision of the Court of Appeal in 2003 suggested that the no profit rule was only a *duty* in cases involving dishonesty; if the fiduciary is honest then the rule is merely a disability.[676] In other words, although the whole range of remedies, including compensation for any losses suffered by the principal, are available against a dishonest fiduciary who makes profit or puts himself in a position of conflict,[677] an honest fiduciary who infringes these rules is only liable to disgorge unauthorized profits. However, more recently the Court of Appeal has treated the rule as a duty, the breach of which is wrongful and gives rise to compensation.[678]

H. Intentional Wrongs

17.355 Every civil wrong can be committed intentionally, but hitherto there has been no discussion of situations in which intent has to be proved in order to engender liability. 'Intention' is a slippery term used in the law of wrongs in different ways.[679] It is used in relation to the wrongs in this section to signify a desired harmful consequence. In contrast, we have seen that torts such as trespass, assault and battery are only intentional in the sense that the act of interference was willed. However, the definition of intention in relation to the wrongs in this section, as a desired harmful consequence, is not without difficulty. It is not enough that the defendant knows that his actions will cause the harmful consequence if they are not desired as an end or means to an end. Not is it enough that consequences are likely. Many of these cases involving intentional wrongs struggle with the question of the proof of this intention. An attractive solution was proposed by

---

[675] JH Langbein 'Questioning the Trust Law Duty of Loyalty: Sole Interest or Best Interest?' (2005) 114 Yale LJ 929; JH Langbein 'Mandatory Rules in the Law of Trusts' (2004) 98 NWU L Rev 1105. Cf J Getzler 'Rumford Market and the Genesis of Fiduciary Obligations' in A Burrows and A Rodger (eds) *Mapping the Law: Essays in Honour of Peter Birks* (2006) 577, 597–8 arguing that the weight of legal history and recent frauds in America suggest this call for abolition is premature.

[676] *Gwembe Valley Development Co Ltd v Koshy* [2003] EWCA Civ 1048; [2004] 1 BCLC 131, CA.

[677] *Broadhurst v Broadhurst* [2006] EWHC 2727, Edward Bartley Jones QC.

[678] *Wilson & Anor v Hurstanger Ltd* [2007] EWCA Civ 299, CA.

[679] Finnis, 'Intention in Tort Law', in Guest (ed) *Philosophical Foundations of Tort Law* (1995). See also *OBG v Allen* [2007] UKHL 21; [2007] 2 WLR 920, 940 [42]–[43], HL

Lord Millett. In his dissent in a recent decision concerning the tort of misfeasance in public office Lord Millett argued that intention could be proved either by evidence or by inference. Knowledge that conduct will harm the claimant is one way of establishing an inference.[680] The more uncertain the likelihood the more difficult it will be to draw the inference.

A difficulty with the bi-focal structure of the English law of civil wrongs is that it is unclear which intentional wrongs fall within the first group of wrongs, namely those concerned with infringement of rights, and which fall within the second group, namely those concerned with fault causing loss. In the first group, intentional wrongs are concerned with rights which are protected but only if the right is infringed intentionally. Strong examples are the non-economic rights which German law draws together under the word '*Persönlichkeit*' which is better translated by the non-existent 'personhood' rather than by the more obvious but misleading 'personality'. The quality of being a person, personhood, demands respect—respect for autonomy, privacy, and equal dignity. Infringements of these rights will be an important concern in the future, and not only because of the incorporation of the European Convention on Human Rights. Yet English law has barely begun to realize the extent to which it is equipped to deal with them.   **17.356**

In the second group, intentional wrongs are concerned with the fault of the defendant causing loss to the claimant. The intention, namely the desire for an illegitimate harmful consequence, is the required degree of fault. Although there is no general tort of intentionally causing loss to another, the tort of misfeasance in public office and the tort of simple conspiracy are strong candidates for classification in this group. In particular, the latter does not require a claimant to show any right which has been infringed—there usually will be no right because the harmful conduct is otherwise lawful—it is enough that the defendant intended the harmful consequences even though the defendant's conduct was lawful. Just as negligence overlaps with torts that protect particular rights, the tort of misfeasance in public office also overlaps with other torts which protect particular rights (such as the right to liberty).[681]   **17.357**

(1) Humiliation and Distress

It is well settled that mental injury is only actionable in the tort of negligence if it takes the form of a recognized psychiatric illness. It has been argued that if the   **17.358**

---

[680] *Three Rivers District Council v Governor and Company of the Bank of England (No 3)* [2003] 2 AC 1, 235, HL.

[681] *Karagozlu v Commissioner of Police of the Metropolis* [2006] EWCA Civ 1691; [2007] 2 All ER 1055, CA.

harm is caused intentionally, the scope of recovery should be wider, extending to anxiety, humiliation and distress.[682]

17.359 The recognition of a separate tort of intentionally causing emotional distress, while not excluded by the House of Lords, now seems unlikely. In *Wainwright v Home Office*,[683] Mrs Wainwright, on a visit to her son in prison, was subjected to an invasive strip search by prison officers looking for drugs. The search did not conform to established procedures. She suffered emotional distress but not psychiatric illness. One of her arguments was that the Home Office should be liable for this emotional distress. The argument failed because the prison officers had not intended to cause distress, but Lord Hoffmann reserved his position on whether intentionally causing distress actually is a tort, or whether it was desirable that it should be: 'in institutions and workplaces all over the country, people constantly do and say things with the intention of causing distress and humiliation to others. This shows lack of consideration and appalling manners but I am not sure that the right way to deal with it is always by litigation.'[684] Later decisions have refused recovery even where distress is intentionally inflicted by unlawful means.[685]

17.360 Where, however, a recognized tort has been committed intentionally, English law has always been willing to enhance the award of damages where the behaviour of the tortfeasor was outrageous, such as to indicate contempt for the victim, as a person of no account.[686] Such awards have in the past been described as 'aggravated damages', but are now more openly recognized as compensation for injury to feelings, including the indignity, mental suffering, humiliation or distress suffered by the victim.[687] The award makes good the infringement of the right to respect for persons as persons.

17.361 Some protection is also given by statutory remedies, civil and criminal, created by the Protection from Harassment Act 1997 for a course of conduct likely to cause harassment. The Act was designed to cover stalking and other forms of pestering[688] but the statutory language is broad.[689] Further development is likely to be under the aegis of the Human Rights Act 1998 or through development of

---

[682] P Glazebrook, '*Wilkinson v Downton*: A Centenary Postscript' (1997) 32 Irish Jurist 46, 48.

[683] [2003] UKHL 53; [2004] 2 AC 406.

[684] ibid [46] 426.

[685] *Mbasogo v Logo Ltd* [2006] EWCA Civ 1370, [96]–[100], CA.

[686] *Prince Albert v Strange* (1849) 2 De G & Sm 652, 690, 64 ER 293, 310, *per* Knight Bruce VC.

[687] *Richardson v Howie* [2004] EWCA Civ 1127, CA.

[688] Cf *Khorasandjian v Bush* [1993] QB 727, CA; *Burris v Azadani* [1995] 1 WLR 1372, CA. The Act protects individuals not corporate persons: *Daiichi UK Ltd v Stop Huntingdon Animal Cruelty* [2003] TLR 570.

[689] *Majrowski v Guys and St Thomas NHS Trust* [2006] UKHL 34; [2006] 3 WLR 12.

a tort of infringement of privacy.[690] When the *Wainwright* case went to the European Court of Human Rights, the Court held that the way in which the search was conducted was an infringement of the European Convention. Strict compliance with search procedures is required to 'protect the dignity of those being searched from being assailed any further than is necessary.'[691]

(2) Breach of Confidence and Infringement of Privacy[692]

The wrong of breach of confidence is another excellent example that shows torts **17.362** to be but a sub-category of the law of wrongdoing, which includes equitable wrongs. Breach of confidence historically arose at common law, it was nurtured and developed in the courts of equity and, with its modern expansion to cover the territory of privacy, has now been described by Lord Nicholls as a tort.[693]

Traditionally, the action for breach of confidence required the infringement of a **17.363** claimant's right to the confidentiality of information where the claimant was in a relationship with the defendant. This restrictive requirement of a prior relationship was doomed after the decision of the House of Lords in 1990 in *Attorney General v Guardian Newspapers (No 2)*.[694] The House of Lords held that a duty of confidence owed to the Crown was broken by the Sunday Times when it serialized parts of Peter Wright's book, *Spycatcher* which the Sunday Times knew to contain confidential State information although strictly there was no relationship between the Sunday Times and the Crown. It was also suggested in that case that the duty would arise even where the defendant accidentally came across an obviously confidential document.[695] In 2001, Sedley LJ took a further step and suggested that the wrong of breach of confidence had now given birth to a tort of infringement of privacy. In that case, *Douglas v Hello!*,[696] film stars were trying to stop unauthorized publication of their wedding pictures and Sedley LJ said that they had a 'right to privacy' which was 'grounded in the equitable doctrine of breach of confidence, which accords recognition to the fact that the law has to protect not only those whose trust has been abused but also those who find themselves subject to an unwanted intrusion into their personal lives'.[697] However, only two years later

---

[690] See paras 17.362–17.366.

[691] *Wainwright v United Kingdom* [2006] ECHR 807, [48], ECHR.

[692] The comprehensive and definitive study of this area is R Toulson and C Phipps *Confidentiality* (2nd edn, 2006), esp ch 7 'Confidentiality and Privacy'.

[693] *Campbell v MGN Ltd* [2004] UKHL 22; [2004] 2 AC 457, [14], HL.

[694] [1990] AC 109, HL.

[695] ibid 281. See also *Saltman Engineering Co Ltd v Campbell Engineering Co Ltd* [1948] 65 RPC 203, 215, CA.

[696] [2001] QB 967, CA.

[697] [2001] QB 967, 1001, CA.

cold water was poured on this development by the House of Lords in *Wainwright v Home Office* with the Lords denying that there was a tort of infringement of privacy, primarily because of difficulties of definition.[698]

17.364 Despite the forceful assertion that no right to privacy exists in English law, *Wainwright* did not have much effect of dampening the movement toward a tort of infringement of privacy. Instead, after the European Court of Justice decided that Mrs Wainwright's Convention rights had been infringed, a process of development began in which judges began to avoid simply having recourse to the vague language of privacy. Instead, an attempt began to bring precision to identifying the precise content of the right that is being protected. In *Campbell v MGN Ltd*[699] the defendant newspaper published an article about the attendance at Narcotics Anonymous by the supermodel, Naomi Campbell. The article was accompanied by an unflattering photo of her leaving the premises. A majority of the House of Lords held that this infringed her right to confidentiality of personal information. Lord Nicholls said that 'the essence of the tort is better encapsulated now as misuse of private information'.[700]

17.365 The decision of the House of Lords in *Campbell* was significantly affected by the *Human Rights Act* 1998 incorporating, in particular, Article 8 of the European Convention on Human Rights. Lords Nicholls and Hope and Baroness Hale were influenced by the European Convention, and in particular article 8. Lord Nicholls said that 'the time has come to recognize that the values enshrined in articles 8 and 10 are now part of the cause of action for breach of confidence'.[701] Article 8 of the Convention provides:

(1) Everyone has the right to respect for his private and family life, his home and his correspondence.

(2) There shall be no interference by a public authority with the exercise of this right except such as is in accordance with the law and is necessary in a democratic society in the interests of national security, public safety or the economic well-being of the country, for the prevention of disorder or crime, for the protection of health or morals, or for the protection of the rights or freedoms of others.

In *Von Hannover v Germany*[702] the European Court of Human Rights held that press photographs taken in public places of Princess Caroline of Hannover

---

[698] [2003] UKHL 53; [2004] 2 AC 406.

[699] [2004] UKHL 22; [2004] 2 AC 457, HL.

[700] *Campbell v MGN Ltd* [2004] UKHL 22; [2004] 2 AC 457, [17], HL. Although Lord Nicholls dissented in the result, finding that the information was not private.

[701] ibid [17].

[702] [2004] 40 EHRR 1, ECHR.

infringed her privacy and that the German courts had infringed her article 8 right to respect for her private and family life by denying her a remedy. The court said that article 8 required 'the adoption of measures designed to secure respect for private life even in the sphere of the relations of individuals between themselves'.[703] The European Court of Human Rights has also held that even acts done in public can be subject to a reasonable expectation of privacy.[704]

After *Campbell*, the central issue in actions for breach of a claimant's right to confidentiality of personal information will be determining what counts as personal information. The broad approach to this issue taken by the courts is developing a person's right to respect for private life consistently with the Convention. A public figure, like Naomi Campbell, was entitled to protection of personal information. The Prince of Wales had a right to the confidentiality of matters about which he wrote in his private journal, even when they related to issues upon which he spoke in public.[705] And in *Douglas v Hello! (No 3)*[706] the Court of Appeal held that *Hello!* magazine infringed the claimant film stars' right to personal information by publishing photographs of their gala wedding despite the fact that there had been considerable pre-event publicity in the tabloid press and despite the bride and groom's exclusive agreement giving a rival magazine rights to attend, take photographs and publish details about the wedding. In a separate appeal by *OK!*, a bare majority of the House of Lords held that this right to keep information private included even *OK!'s* commercial rights to the confidentiality of the information prior to publication.[707]

17.366

(3) Harassment by Legal Process

There are well-established torts which deal specifically with the use of the courts to harass another. Malicious prosecution is the most important. It is an important protection for the individual but one which is narrowly construed, for the obvious reason that it would otherwise unacceptably deter the bringing of prosecutions. The tort is committed when legal proceedings, nearly always criminal proceedings, fail, and the claimant, formerly defendant, can show that they were brought without reasonable cause and maliciously. These last words embody two requirements, which inevitably run together. Absence of reasonable and probable cause means absence of belief in the guilt or liability of the accused person or an honest

17.367

---

[703] [2004] 40 EHRR 1, [57], ECHR.
[704] *Peck v United Kingdom* [2003] EMLR 15, ECHR (suicide attempt caught on closed circuit television).
[705] *Associated Newspapers Ltd v Prince of Wales* [2006] EWCA Civ 1776, CA.
[706] [2005] EWCA Civ 595; [2006] QB 125, CA.
[707] Appeal conjoined in *OBG v Allen* [2007] UKHL 21; [2007] 2 WLR 920.

belief in guilt such that no ordinarily prudent person would have entertained on the basis of the facts as they were believed to be.[708] Malice means the presence of an ulterior motive beyond the desire to see the accused convicted, as for instance to continue a long-running dispute.[709] When, as often happens, a servant of the state is the defendant, this is a tort where exemplary damages are available.[710]

17.368 On a somewhat lower plane, the tort of abuse of legal process is committed when litigation is instituted in pursuit of an ulterior motive. The exact shape of this tort remains uncertain, and even its existence has been viewed with scepticism.[711] Nevertheless its existence is warranted by *Grainger v Hill*,[712] where the defendant was made liable for using arrest for debt as a means to force the claimant to give up the registration documents of his vessel, without which he could not sail.

(4) Intentionally Causing Economic Loss

17.369 The duty of care not to inflict pure economic loss negligently is closely restricted.[713] The same is true where economic loss is deliberately inflicted. There is no simple proposition to the effect that, if the claimant can prove intent to cause such loss, all those restrictions simply fade away. There usually has to be an additional element of wrongfulness. Subject to that qualification it is nevertheless true that the law does give more robust redress for intentionally inflicted economic loss.

17.370 In a competitive world individuals and corporations are constantly trying to do each other down. The leading case which underlines the obstacles to the simple proposition in the previous paragraph is *Allen v Flood*.[714] A trade union official told an employer that his men would not work alongside the claimants. In this way he brought it about that the employer got rid of the claimants, who then sued the official. The crucial fact was that all the workers in question were employed on a day-to-day basis. It followed that the official had not threatened a breach of contract, nor had he insisted that the employer break his contract with the claimants. The House of Lords held that a malicious motive could not render unlawful conduct which was in itself entirely lawful.

---

[708] *Glinski v McIver* [1962] AC 726, HL; cf *Gibbs v Rea* [1998] AC 786, PC.

[709] *Martin v Watson* [1996] 1 AC 74, HL.

[710] Paras 21.160–21.163. Public servants may also be liable for the tort of Misfeasance in a Public Office: see para 17.373.

[711] *Metall und Rohstoff AG v Donaldson, Lufkin, Jenrette Inc* [1990] 1 QB 391, CA.

[712] (1838) 4 Bing NC 212, 132 ER 769, applied in *Parton v Hill* (1864) 10 LT 415. The case is, however, susceptible of analysis in other ways, as for instance as an example of the tort of intimidation.

[713] See paras 17.150ff.

[714] [1898] AC 1, HL.

This decision has been regretted by some judges, Lord Devlin being one of them.[715] **17.371**
It nevertheless remains the foundation of the English law of intentionally inflicted pure economic loss. It means in effect that the element of unlawfulness which cannot usually be supplied by malice alone has to be satisfied by the recognition of a series of economic torts.

(a) Deceit, fraud and misfeasance in public office

Deceit is the most ancient of the economic torts. It is an obvious exception to any **17.372**
requirement of independent unlawfulness. Deceit is another wrong concurrently actionable both at common law and in equity.[716] In its modern incarnation it requires a false representation made by the defendant, intending that the claimant should act upon it. It is, however, still open to question whether deceit (which requires a representation) is not simply a species of the *genera* of acts done with fraudulent intention (described as *dolus* in Roman law). Other species of such a genus would include fraudulent acts such as bribery even though there is no representation made to the principal[717] and the tort of misfeasance in public office which involves a deliberate abuse of power by a public official causing loss to the defendant.[718] Like negligence, however, the general right not to suffer loss as a result of these fraudulent acts is restricted. In *Magill v Magill*[719] a husband brought a claim for losses as a result of fraudulent misrepresentations by his former wife that he was the father of their children. The High Court of Australia unanimously held that his former wife was not liable. Four judges explained that policy reasons required that the action for deceit stop outside the door of the family home.[720] Although, in a brief judgment, a first instance judge in England has reached the opposite conclusion[721] the reasoning of the High Court of Australia is compelling.

---

[715] *Rookes v Barnard* [1964] AC 1129, 1216, HL; P Devlin (Lord Devlin), *Samples of Law-Making* (1962), 10–13.

[716] *Peek v Gurney* (1873) LR 6 HL 377, 393, HL *per* Lord Chelmsford speaking of the action in equity: 'It is precisely analogous to the common law action for deceit. There can be no doubt that Equity exercises a concurrent jurisdiction in cases of this description, and the same principles applicable to them both must prevail both at Law and in Equity.'

[717] *Mahesan S/O Thambiah v Malaysian Government Officers Co-operative Housing Society* [1979] AC 374, 376, PC. Cf *Armitage v Nurse* [1998] Ch 241, 250, CA: 'the common law knows no generalised tort of fraud' *per* Millett LJ.

[718] The tort of misfeasance in public office: *Watkins v Secretary of State for the Home Office* [2006] UKHL 17; [2006] 2 AC 395, HL.

[719] [2006] HCA 51, HCA.

[720] [2006] HCA 51, [42] (Gleeson CJ), [88] (Gummow, Kirby and Crennan JJ), [140] (Hayne) cf [207] (Heydon J), HCA.

[721] *P v B (Paternity: Damages for Deceit)* [2001] 1 FLR 1041.

17.373 In cases of misfeasance by a public official which causes loss, the requisite element of intention is satisfied if the public official knows his act is illegal or is recklessly indifferent to its legality.[722] The same is true of deceit. The element of fraudulent intention requires that it be shown that the defendant knew that his statement was untrue, or had no belief in its truth, or was reckless as to whether it was true or false. This was the effect of the House of Lords' decision in *Derry v Peek*.[723] Mere negligence is not deceit. In the period after *Derry v Peek* it was thought that there was no liability in damages for negligent misstatements causing economic loss.[724] That changed in 1964 with *Hedley Byrne & Co Ltd v Heller & Partners Ltd*.[725] The two liabilities remain very different. In deceit, and presumably also for misfeasance in public office, in order to mark the law's disapproval of fraud, the defendant is liable for all losses flowing directly from the tort, whether they were foreseeable or not.[726] Further, the defence of contributory negligence is not available.[727]

(b) The economic torts

17.374 This label is used to describe a group of torts which are linked together by their subject matter, causing economic loss by interfering with the trade of others, and by their political history.[728] Many have been developed in cases involving trade union action. They stand, therefore, at the fringes of the laws controlling competition on the one hand and labour relations on the other. They also have a relationship with torts protecting intellectual property.[729] None of these wider implications can be explored in this outline. They are, however, the cause of much of the difficulty and uncertainty of the law in this area.

(i) Procuring breach of contract

17.375 The most straightforward of the economic torts is also one of the oldest. In *Lumley v Gye*[730] the claimant had a contract with an opera singer to sing in a series

---

[722] *Three Rivers District Council v Governor and Company of the Bank of England (No 3)* [2003] 2 AC 1, 193, HL.

[723] (1889) 14 App Cas 337, HL.

[724] *Candler v Crane Christmas & Co* [1951] 2 KB 164, CA. The equitable evasion in *Nocton v Ashburton* [1914] AC 932, HL remained discreetly in the shadows.

[725] [1964] AC 465, HL. See paras 17.171ff.

[726] *Doyle v Olby (Ironmongers) Ltd* [1969] 2 QB 158, CA; *Smith New Court Securities Ltd v Scrimgeour Vickers (Asset Management) Ltd* [1997] AC 254, HL. Further consideration of the measure of damages in *Clef Aquitaine SARL v Laporte Materials (Barrow) Ltd* [2000] 3 All ER 493, CA.

[727] *Alliance and Leicester BS v Edgestop Ltd* [1993] 1 WLR 1462; *Standard Chartered Bank v Pakistan National Shipping Co (No 2)* [2002] UKHL 43; [2003] 1 AC 959, HL.

[728] T Weir, *Economic Torts* (1997); P Cane, *Tort Law and Economic Interests* (2nd edn, 1996); H Carty, *An Analysis of the Economic Torts* (2001).

[729] See Chapter 6.

[730] (1852) 2 El & Bl 216, 118 ER 749. For an excellent historico-analytical study see S Waddams, 'Johanna Wagner and the Rival Opera Houses' (2001) 117 LQR 431.

of concerts. The defendant, knowing of this contract, persuaded her to break it by offering her more money to sing at his theatre. The court found for the claimant and the decision was subsequently approved in the House of Lords in *Allen v Flood*.[731] The tort can only be committed intentionally and the defendant must know, or at least be reckless as to the terms,[732] of the contract. There is a defence of justification in a few, not well-defined, circumstances.[733]

For a time the *Lumley v Gye* tort was extended from direct inducement of a breach   **17.376**
of contract to include indirect inducement,[734] and, much more controversially, to interference with the performance of a contract, even though no breach was caused.[735] The House of Lords has now affirmed that the distinction between direct and indirect inducement is unhelpful and that the tort is one of accessory liability so that without a breach of contract, interference with the performance of a contract cannot amount to the tort of inducing breach of contract.[736]

(ii) Intimidation

If it is tortious to persuade someone to break a contract, it may also be tortious to   **17.377**
threaten to break one. In *Rookes v Barnard*[737] the facts were very similar to those of *Allen v Flood*.[738] The one crucial difference was that the union had contracted not to engage in strike action. Hence the threat to withdraw labour was a threat of a breach of contract. The House of Lords held that this amounted to the tort of intimidation. In *Rookes v Barnard* the union's threat was that it would induce its members, a third party, to break their contracts with the claimant. It remains an open question whether the tort can be committed by a defendant threatening to break his own contract with the claimant.[739]

(iii) Causing loss by unlawful means

In *Merkur Island Shipping Corporation v Laughton*[740] Lord Diplock gave the bless-   **17.378**
ing of the House of Lords to this tort as the 'genus' tort of which he suggested that inducing breach of contract was a species. It might have been neat if this single unifying tort could have held together all these economic torts. However, there were at least two problems with Lord Diplock's reasoning. The first, identified by

---

731 [1898] AC 1, HL; para 17.370.
732 *Emerald Construction Co v Lowthian* [1966] 1 WLR 691, CA.
733 *Brimelow v Casson* [1924] 1 Ch 302; *Edwin Hill and Partners v First National Finance Corporation plc* [1989] 1 WLR 225.
734 *DC Thomson Ltd v Deakin* [1952] Ch 646, CA.
735 *Torquay Hotel Ltd v Cousins* [1969] 2 Ch 106, CA; cf Tony Weir, *Economic Torts* (1997) 37.
736 *OBG v Allen* [2007] UKHL 21; [2007] 2 WLR 920, 940–941 [44], HL.
737 [1964] AC 1129, HL.
738 [1898] AC 1, HL; para 17.370.
739 Described by Lord Hoffmann as raising 'different issues': *OBG v Allen* [2007] UKHL 21; [2007] 2 WLR 920, 945 [61], HL.
740 [1983] 2 AC 570, HL.

Lord Hoffmann in the leading speech in the House of Lords in *OBG v Allen*,[741] is that the tort of inducing breach of contract is a tort of accessory liability whereas the tort of causing loss by unlawful means is concerned with primary liability. He defined the latter as 'acts intended to cause loss to the claimant by interfering with the freedom of a third party in a way which is unlawful as against that third party and which is intended to cause loss to the claimant'.[742] A further obstacle exists to the genus tort in the form of the tort called conspiracy to injure.

(iv) Conspiracy

17.379 This tort can take two forms, depending on whether unlawful means are used. Unlawful means conspiracy is a relatively uncomplicated tort, the separate existence of which was confirmed by the House of Lords in *Lonrho plc v Fayed*.[743] By contrast, conspiracy to injure, which consists in a combination of two or more persons acting with the intention of harming the claimant, but not using unlawful means, is an anomaly. It is difficult now to explain why mere numbers should make unlawful what would otherwise be lawful. In *Lonrho plc v Shell Petroleum Ltd (No 2)*[744] Lord Diplock regretted the anomaly but thought it too well established to be discarded.[745] The tort is of little practical importance, because acts done with the predominant purpose of advancing the conspirators' own interests are justifiable.[746] Only a combination whose purpose is to harm the claimant is actionable. But a tort in which liability does depend on an unlawful purpose, rather than unlawful means, adds to the incoherence of this area of law.

17.380 The economic torts are full of difficulties. Almost every aspect of the rules which govern them has given rise to complicated litigation. What sort of intention is required?[747] What counts as an interference with trade?[748] What amounts to unlawful means?[749] However, as we saw in relation to 'intention', solutions have arisen to the intractable problems which underlie this area of the law.[750]

---

741 *OBG v Allen* [2007] UKHL 21; [2007] 2 WLR 920, 940–941 [44], HL.
742 ibid [51].
743 [1992] 1 AC 448, HL.
744 [1982] AC 173, HL.
745 ibid 189.
746 *Crofter Hand-Woven Harris Tweed Co Ltd v Veitch* [1942] AC 435, HL.
747 *Lonrho plc v Fayed* [1992] 1 AC 448, HL.
748 *RCA Corporation v Pollard* [1983] Ch 135, CA.
749 *Lonrho Ltd v Shell Petroleum Co Ltd (No 2)* [1982] AC 173, HL; *Michaels v Taylor Woodrow Developments Ltd* [2001] Ch 493.
750 *OBG v Allen* [2007] UKHL 21; [2007] 2 WLR 920, HL is now a step forward for clarity in this area, explaining 'unlawful' as any civil wrong and 'trade' as unnecessary.

(5) Dishonest Assistance in a Breach of Fiduciary Duty

Rarely, if ever, in discussion of wrongs that involve claims for economic loss do **17.381** academics or judges include the equivalent equitable wrongs. We have seen that the torts of deceit and negligence were historically actionable as wrongs in equity as well as at common law. An equitable wrong that lays fair claim to be treated alongside the economic torts, particularly the tort of inducing a breach of contract, is dishonest assistance in a breach of fiduciary duty. Lord Hoffmann has recently confirmed that this equitable wrong includes dishonest assistance in the breach of any fiduciary duty, not merely in a breach of trust.[751] The most difficult question considered by the courts so far is the meaning of 'dishonest'. A future issue that may arise is the meaning of breach of fiduciary duty in this context or whether dishonest assistance in a breach of any equitable duty should be sufficient. We have seen that a consensus is emerging that negligence by a fiduciary is not a breach of fiduciary duty. To adopt that approach here would reach the same conclusion as the common law does in refusing to recognize a 'free-standing' general tort of dishonest assistance in any tort.[752]

In 1995, Lord Nicholls gave the advice of the Privy Council in *Royal Brunei* **17.382** *Airlines v Tan*[753] in which the defendant managing director had misapplied money paid to it which was paid on trust for the airline. The managing director paid it into the company current account instead of the trust account into which he knew it was supposed to be paid. The Privy Council held that the test was one of dishonesty and in a commercial setting that simply means conduct which is 'commercially unacceptable'.[754] The managing director had acted dishonestly.

Subsequently, in the leading speech in the House of Lords in *Twinsectra Ltd v* **17.383** *Yardley*,[755] Lord Hutton said that dishonesty is 'a standard which combines an objective test and a subjective test. . .it must be established that the defendant's conduct was dishonest by ordinary standards of reasonable and honest people and

---

[751] *Barlow Clowes International Ltd v Eurotrust International Ltd* [2005] UKPC 37, [2006] 1 WLR 1476, 1483 [28], PC. In Australia the equitable wrong is described as knowing participation in a breach of fiduciary duty: *Consul Development Pty Ltd v DPC Estates Pty Ltd* (1975) 132 CLR 373 at 397, HCA; See also Lord Nicholls 'Knowing receipt: The need for a new landmark' in W Cornish et al *Restitution: Past Present and Future* (1998) 231, 244.

[752] *Credit Lyonnais Bank Nederland NV v Export Credits Guarantee Department* [2000] 1 AC 486, HL, where, at the least, it was held that the ECGD could not be vicariously liable for an employee where only the acts of assistance, not the tort assisted, were within the course of the employee's employment. However, the case shows that we are some distance from understanding 'assistance' at common law.

[753] [1995] 1 AC 378, PC.

[754] ibid quoting *Cowan de Groot Properties Ltd v Eagle Trust Plc* [1992] 4 All ER 700, 761 *per* Knox J.

[755] [2002] 2 AC 164, HL.

that he himself realised that by those standards his conduct was dishonest'.[756] Lord Hoffmann also said that dishonesty 'requires a dishonest state of mind, that is to say, consciousness that one is transgressing ordinary standards of honest behaviour.'[757] This seemed to be a combined objective/subjective test. It was heavily criticized both academically[758] and judicially.[759]

17.384 Matters were clarified in an appeal to the Privy Council from the Court of Appeal of the Isle of Man in *Barlow Clowes International Ltd v Eurotrust International Ltd.*[760] The case involved an enormous fraud by high-flying 1980's entrepreneurs who promised high returns from investment in gilt-edged securities to unsuspecting investors. A central question for the Privy Council was whether one of the directors of an off-shore company who had acted as intermediaries, had dishonestly assisted in the scheme to misappropriate the investors' funds. He had suspected that the funds received might have been derived from a fraud on the public but he decided not to make inquiries because of his subjective view that the client's instructions are all important. Lord Hoffmann argued that both his speech and Lord Hutton's speech in *Twinsectra* had been misunderstood. Neither he nor Lord Hutton meant to suggest that there was any subjective element to the test: the defendant need not have reflected at all on what were ordinary standards of honest behaviour and the decision in *Twinsectra* had not departed from the Privy Council's objective approach in *Tan*.[761] It was dishonest to act as intermediary whilst entertaining a clear suspicion that the money was held on trust or was being misappropriated by the directors.[762] The dust now appears to have settled in favour of this reinterpretation of *Twinsectra* and a objective test of dishonesty,[763] although a surprising recent decision of the Court of Appeal has held that a bank is not dishonest if it suspects a class of transaction as involving money laundering but does not suspect the particular transaction in question.[764]

---

[756] ibid [27].

[757] ibid [20].

[758] A Pedain 'Dishonest Assistance: Guilty Conduct or a Guilty Mind?'[2002] CLJ 524 at 525–526; C Rickett 'Quistclose trusts and dishonest assistance' [2002] RLR 112; Lord Walker 'Dishonesty and Unconscionable Conduct in Commercial Life—Some Reflections on Accessory Liability and Knowing Receipt' (2005) 27 Sydney Law Rev 187 at 197.

[759] *US International Marketing Ltd v National Bank of New Zealand Ltd* [2004] 1 NZLR 589, NZCA.

[760] [2005] UKPC 37, [2006] 1 WLR 1476, PC.

[761] ibid 1481 [15]–[16], [18].

[762] Difficult second-order questions still remain about how the line should be drawn between objective honesty and dishonesty: J Edelman 'The expansion of dishonest assistance in the Privy Council' (2006) 1 Journal of Equity 22.

[763] *Fresh 'N' Clean (Wales) Ltd (In Liq) v Miah* [2006] EWHC 903; *Abou Ramah v Abacha* [2006] EWCA Civ 1492, CA.

[764] *Abou Ramah v Abacha*, ibid.

I. Vicarious Liability

(1) Personal Liability and Vicarious Liability Distinguished

There are a number of situations in which one person is liable for the acts of another but in which the reason is that the person liable is himself contemplated as being in breach of duty. The claimant's cause of action is then the defendant's own wrong, and the defendant is personally, not vicariously, liable. Vicarious liability as understood in English law is liability imposed upon a person even although he has committed no wrong and simply because of his relationship to the person who has committed the wrong.[765] Vicarious liability therefore involves the attribution of the liability of the wrongdoer to the defendant, not attribution of the wrongdoer's act.[766] Provided the relationship of the defendant satisfies the requirements of vicarious liability, it does not matter if the wrong is a tort, equitable wrong or statutory wrong: 'the policy reasons underlying the common law principle are as much applicable to equitable wrongs and breaches of statutory obligations as they are to common law torts'.[767]

17.385

(a) Personal liability exemplified

There are a number of different ways in which one may incur a personal liability for the acts of another. It helps to keep them completely separate from vicarious liability.

17.386

(i) Personal duty of care

A corporation is personally liable for the authorized acts of its directors and employees because the corporation cannot act otherwise than by its directors and servants.[768] So too, a principal is personally liable for an agent acting with his authority: *qui facit per alium facit per se*. We have also seen that exceptional

17.387

---

[765] All of the acts comprising the wrongdoing must, however, be closely connected with the relationship between the wrongdoer(s) and the principal: *Credit Lyonnais Bank Nederland NV v ECGD* [2000] 1 AC 486, HL.

[766] *X (Minors) v Bedfordshire County Council* [1995] 2 AC 633, 739–40, HL; *Majrowski v Guys and St Thomas NHS Trust* [2006] UKHL 34; [2006] 3 WLR 125. Cf *Darling Island Stevedoring and Lighterage Co Ltd v Long* (1956) 97 CLR 36, 61 *per* Kitto J, 66 *per* Taylor J. Against the powerful tide of modern authority, the 'Master's Tort' theory—which sees 'vicarious liability' as based upon attribution of a servant's acts and therefore indistinguishable from personal liability—is favoured by R Stevens 'Vicarious liability and vicarious action' (2007) 123 LQR 30. See also G Williams 'Vicarious Liability: Tort of the Master or of the Servant?' (1956) 72 LQR 522.

[767] *Majrowski v Guys and St Thomas NHS Trust* [2006] UKHL 34; [2006] 3 WLR 125, 128 [10], HL.

[768] *Williams v Natural Life Health Foods Ltd* [1998] 1 WLR 830, HL.

circumstances may be such as to put the defendant under a common law duty of care in protecting the claimant from the acts of a third party.[769] In equity, too, a trustee is liable for negligent management, and negligent management includes negligent supervision of others more directly engaged in the trust affairs. A duty of care may also be broken by careless selection of an agent or other contractor (*culpa in eligendo*).[770]

(ii) Strict liability for careful provision

17.388 In isolated pockets there is the more extreme possibility that the defendant may be found to have been under a duty to ensure that care was taken of the claimant. That is to say, he may be under a strict liability in respect of the care provided through others. This is often somewhat confusingly referred to as a 'non-delegable duty of care'.

17.389 This terminology indicates that the person in question is deemed to be under a personal duty of care which, in the following sense, cannot be delegated, namely that, when he seeks to discharge it through others, the acts of those others are still his acts and their carelessness is his carelessness. This seems to be an unnecessarily complicated way of saying that such a person is strictly liable to ensure that care is exercised by others. The incidence of such a duty is of special importance wherever independent contractors are used, since there is no vicarious liability for an independent contractor.

17.390 Although this strict duty is sometimes not sufficiently differentiated from a duty of care in provision, supervision, and management,[771] there seems little doubt that Denning LJ intended to introduce it as a quite distinct basis for the liability of hospitals and health authorities.[772] However, in that field the exact status of this strict duty to ensure adequate care is still in doubt.[773] The increasing use of independently contracted staff, rather than employees, will bring the matter to a head. There are a number of other more or less secure examples: highway authorities and others employing contractors to work on the highways, although the courts

---

[769] *Stansbie v Troman* [1948] 2 KB 48, CA; *Home Office v Dorset Yacht Co* [1970] AC 1004, HL; para 17.77.

[770] *Aiken v Stewart Wrightson Members Agency Ltd* [1995] 1 WLR 1281. The liability for an agent imposed in *Gran Gelato v Richcliff (Group) Ltd* [1992] Ch 560 is, however, hard to explain; cf P Cane 'Negligent Solicitor Escapes Liability' (1992) 109 LQR 539.

[771] *Bull v Devon AHA* [1993] 4 Med LR 117, CA, discussed: I Kennedy (1993) 1 Med L Rev 384.

[772] *Cassidy v Ministry of Health* [1951] 2 KB 343, CA; *Roe v Minister of Health* [1954] 2 QB 66, CA.

[773] I Kennedy and A Grubb, *Principles of Medical Law* (2nd edn, 2004) 409–11.

have tended to narrow the ambit of their strict duty;[774] employers in relation to their employees, who are entitled to safe systems of work and equipment[775] and competent co-workers.[776]

(iii) Inducing or assisting

The third possibility is that in circumstances in which the criminal law would speak of accessory liability or liability in the second degree, a defendant may make himself liable for inducing, procuring or assisting the commission of a wrong. In the common law such a person is said to commit the tort in which he participates and may in some cases commit the tort of conspiracy;[777] we have also seen that in equity there is a distinct wrong of 'dishonest assistance in a breach of fiduciary duty'.[778]   **17.391**

(b) Vicarious liability properly so-called

Vicarious liability is a form of strict liability imposed without any suggestion that the person in question has been guilty of any breach of duty. The exposure to this kind of liability inheres in the position occupied by the person made liable and the relation which that position bears to that of the actual wrongdoer. As we shall see, the case of greatest importance is that of the employer. The employer is liable for the torts of his employee committed in the course of the employee's employment.   **17.392**

The vicariously liable employer is a joint tortfeasor with the employee. The victim can sue either or both, and in principle the employer's vicarious liability is secondary, so that, having paid the damages, the person liable, and by subrogation his insurer, has a right of recourse against the primary wrongdoer,[779] much as a surety has a right to reimbursement from the principal debtor.[780] In practice this right of recourse is little used; it lives in a limbo created by the certainty that, if it were, it would be abolished by Act of Parliament.[781]   **17.393**

---

[774] *Salsbury v Woodland* [1970] 1 QB 324, CA; *Rowe v Herman* [1997] 1 WLR 1390, CA. Especially in Australia: *Leichhardt Municipal Council v Montgomery* [2007] HCA 6, HCA.

[775] Employers' Liability (Defective Equipment) Act 1969; *Coltman v Bibby Tankers* [1988] AC 276, HL.

[776] *McDermid v Nash Dredging and Reclamation Co Ltd* [1987] AC 906, HL. Some confusion has been introduced by *Square D Ltd v Cook* [1992] Industrial Cases R 262, CA, which appears to have undermined the strictness of the duty.

[777] P Sales, 'The Tort of Conspiracy and Civil Secondary Liability' [1990] CLJ 491, esp 504.

[778] See paras 17.381–17.384.

[779] *Lister v Romford Ice and Cold Storage Co* [1957] AC 555, HL; *Morris v Ford Motor Co* [1973] QB 792, CA.

[780] Paras 18.216–18.220.

[781] In Canada La Forest J, in a minority judgment, argued that the courts should affirm that the employer's liability now displaced the liability of the employee altogether: *London Drugs Ltd v*

(2) Rationalia of Vicarious Liability

17.394 It is certain that, if there were no vicarious liability, there would be constant pressure on the edges of personal liability, as indeed there already is where vicarious liability is not available, for almost without exception tort victims prefer to sue the employer rather than the employee. The employer will have the longer purse and, even more importantly, is more likely to carry insurance. After all the employer can spread the risk by taking out insurance and treating the premiums as a cost of the business. The alternative would require individual employees to take out insurance themselves, but that would lead to all sorts of difficulties with uninsurable individuals. Avoiding those difficulties would almost certainly involve transferring the insurance burden back to employers.

17.395 Whether this practical reality discloses any thoroughly convincing case for the necessity of vicarious liability is open to question.[782] It must certainly be true that vicarious liability tends to encourage employers to take steps to ensure that their employees are properly trained to be aware of risks and so far as possible to avoid them. Economists have embroidered this simple fact so as to present vicarious liability as an engine of economic efficiency, tending to raise the costs of businesses which are inefficient.[783] Lord Nicholls has argued that the rationale for vicarious liability is a combination of all these matters.[784]

(3) Categories of Vicarious Liability

17.396 There is only one significant category of person subject to vicarious liability, namely employers. Their vicarious liability is then confined to the torts of employees committed in the course of their employment. The simplicity of this picture is disrupted in two ways. First, from time to time there have been attempts to extend the range of vicarious liability to other relationships loosely analogous to employment by reason of the control of one person over another. Secondly, there is great and increasing difficulty in distinguishing employment from other similar relationships.

Kuehne & Nagel [1992] 3 SCR 299, 97 DLR (4th) 261, SCC, discussed by J Fleming 'Employee's Tort in a Contractual Matrix: New Approaches in Canada' (1993) 13 OJLS 430. One way or another La Forest J's arguments are likely to prevail sooner or later. Meanwhile see *Merrett v Babb* [2001] QB 1174, CA (employee sued personally, employer having gone into liquidation).

[782] Full discussion in PS Atiyah, *Vicarious Liability* (1967) ch 2.

[783] This 'enterprise liability' rationale is presented in Canada as an argument that the party that gets the benefit should incur the burden: *Bazley v Curry* [1999] 2 SCR 534, SCC and *Jacobi v Griffiths* [1999] 2 SCR 470, SCC.

[784] *Majrowski v Guys and St Thomas NHS Trust* [2006] UKHL 34; [2006] 3 WLR 125, 128 [9], HL.

(a) Other relationships

Statute aside (eg Partnership Act 1890), enlargement of vicarious liability has not **17.397** gone far. Where it has been attempted it has been driven by the desire to give victims the benefit of insurance carried by the vicarious defendant. In *Launchbury v Morgans*[785] the defendant was Mrs Morgans whose car had been used by her husband to go out on the town with his friends. After a while, when drink had rendered him incompetent, one of his friends had taken over the driving and had crashed the car. The injured passengers sued Mrs Morgans on the basis that she was vicariously liable for the negligent driving of her car. This argument, having succeeded in the Court of Appeal, was heavily pruned in the House of Lords. But the House left intact the proposition that the vicarious liability would subsist in a case in which the car was being driven at the owner's request and for the owner's purposes.

This extension has had little or no impact, evidently because of changes in the law **17.398** and practice of car insurance. However, it stands as an invitation to extend the range of vicarious liability. In Ireland it seems that a householder is regarded as vicariously liable for the torts of those members of the family who help within the house, as in preparing and serving food and drink. The householder is their controller, as an employer controls employees.[786]

An example of the limits of enlargement of vicarious liability is a trustee who is **17.399** not vicariously liable for his co-trustee or for those whom he appoints as his agents in the management of the trust. If the trustee is to be liable for things that he has done, it will be because of his own breach of duty: 'The conduct of the [trustee] is to be judged by the standard applied in *Speight v Gaunt*,[787] namely, that a trustee is only bound to conduct the business of the trust in such a way as an ordinary prudent man would conduct a business of his own.'[788] In this way the trustee may incur a liability for having failed in supervising the agent or for having allowed unbusinesslike steps to be taken, but he will never be vicariously liable. That is to say, he will not be liable merely because of his position in relation to the actual delinquent.

(b) Employees

If the term 'employee' is used loosely it covers a variety of relationships. An employer **17.400** is only liable for those who come within the now outmoded term 'servant'.

---

[785] [1973] AC 127, HL.
[786] *Moynihan v Moynihan* [1975] IR 192, Sup Ct of Ireland.
[787] (1883) 9 App Cas 1, 13–15, 22–23, HL.
[788] *Re Lucking's Will Trusts* [1968] 1 WLR 866, 874, *per* Cross J, discussing Trustee Act 1925, ss 23 and 30(1).

The Romans distinguished between hire of services (*locatio conductio operarum*) and hiring out jobs to be done (*locatio conductio operis faciendi*). The servant of English law falls within the former: one whose service is hired, while the latter, one who takes on a job to be done, is an independent contractor. There is no vicarious liability for independent contractors. If an independent contractor commits a tort, the only way of reaching his 'employer' is to establish a personal liability, as discussed above.[789]

17.401 The line between employees and independent contractors has become increasingly difficult to draw, partly because of changing employment practices and partly because the word 'employee' (used in the sense of 'servant') has come under pressure by reason of its importance in many different contexts. Vicarious liability is one, but very different considerations creep in when the question is entitlement to benefits, compensation for unfair dismissal, or, very importantly, the selection of the appropriate tax regime.

17.402 It used to be thought that the key was control. If the worker was subject to close control in the manner in which he performed his task, he would be a servant but not if he enjoyed a measure of autonomy in achieving a given end. But the control test is controversial. The Court of Appeal recently held, in *Viasystems (Tyneside) Ltd v Thermal Transfer (Northern) Ltd*[790] that a fitter and his mate, provided by their employer, the third defendants, on a 'labour only' basis to the second defendant subcontractor was employed by both the second and third defendants. May LJ reasoned that both parties were employers because of the degree of control they both exerted over the fitter and fitter's mate but Rix LJ argued that both parties were employers because of the integration of the fitter and fitter's mate into each organization. An influential article by Professor Richard Kidner argues that the law will not be intelligible until it abandons hope of a single test of employment in all contexts and focuses in the present context on the function of vicarious liability as making businesses bear the risks inherent in their activity. He argues for a test based on a basket of factors weighed in the light of that overall goal.[791] A development along these lines seems inevitable.

17.403 Some brief examples will further illustrate the difficulties. In *Ready-Mixed Concrete v Minister of Pensions*[792] McKenna J had to decide whether for National Insurance purposes a lorry driver was an employee and held that he was not. He was

---

[789] E McKendrick, 'Vicarious Liability and Independent Contractors—A Re-examination' (1990) 53 MLR 770 argues for extension of that primary liability.

[790] [2005] EWCA Civ 1151; [2006] QB 510, CA. Distinguished on similar facts in *Hawley v Luminar Leisure* [2006] EWCA Civ 30, CA.

[791] R Kidner, 'Vicarious liability: for whom should the employer be liable?' (1995) 15 Legal Studies 47.

[792] [1968] 2 QB 497.

an independent contractor. The company had gone over to a new system using owner-drivers. The driver in question had switched to the new scheme, buying his own lorry on hire purchase. The driver's pattern of life did not change. His lorry was painted in the same livery, he wore the same uniform, and he took the same orders. On the other hand he was now paid piece rates, not a wage, and he had to meet the running expenses of his lorry. Furthermore—though this is not decisive[793]—his contract described him as an independent contractor. In the judgment of McKenna J the balance tipped against his being an employee. He was running his own business as a carrier.

In *O'Kelly v Trust House Forte plc*[794] casual waiters worked on a regular basis for **17.404** private functions, as needed. They were held not to be employees and therefore not entitled to compensation for unfair dismissal. There was no mutuality of obligation. That is, they were not bound to respond to the summons on any day. Similarly, in *Hall v Lorimer*[795] a 'vision mixer' working for a number of television companies and described as 'freelance' was held not to be an employee. There the issue was tax. By contrast, in *Lee Ting Sang v Chung Chi-Keung*[796] a skilled stonemason working as the need arose for different employers and remunerated on piece rates was held to be an employee in multiple employments and therefore entitled to compensation for personal injury as an employee.

As we have seen, the rationalia of vicarious liability are slippery. If one once accepts **17.405** its practical necessity in the modern world, that same necessity cannot easily be confined within the elusive technicalities of the 'master-servant' relationship. Much the same must be said of the restriction, as currently understood, to acts done by the servant in the course of his employment.

(4) The 'Course of Employment'

Difficult as it is to draw a clean line between employees *stricto sensu* and independ- **17.406** ent contractors, it is barely less awkward to find the boundary around those employee's torts for which the employer is vicariously liable and those for which he is not. The key concept has been the course of the employment. To attract vicarious liability the tort must be committed by the employee in the course of his employment. However, the formula has traditionally been easier to utter than to apply.

---

[793] *Ferguson v John Dawson & Partners Ltd* [1976] 1 WLR 1213, CA; on the other side of the line: *Massey v Crown Life Insurance Co* [1978] 1 WLR 676, CA.

[794] [1984] QB 90, CA.

[795] [1992] 1 WLR 939.

[796] [1990] 2 AC 374, PC.

(a) Misperformance of the employment contract

17.407 In one sense a tort can hardly ever be within the course of the employment. Unless authorized or ratified by the employer, every tort is at best a deviation from proper performance of the employment contract. Hence the line lies between misperformance of the contract and wrongs which can be said to have nothing relevantly to do with the contract. In *Century Insurance Co Ltd v Northern Ireland Road Transport Board*[797] a tanker driver delivering petrol to a garage began to smoke and thus caused an explosion. This has become the classic example of a misperformance in the course of employment. For a century the classic formulation was that of Sir John Salmond, who said that a wrongful act is deemed to be done by a 'servant' in the course of his employment if 'it is either (a) a wrongful act authorised by the master, or (b) a wrongful and unauthorised *mode* of doing some act authorised by the master'.[798]

17.408 But this test was notoriously difficult to apply. An example is *LCC v Cattermoles (Garages) Ltd*[799] in which a worker in a garage drove a vehicle out on to the highway and did damage. He had no driving licence and had been expressly forbidden to drive. Nevertheless, the Court of Appeal held the garage to be vicariously liable. It was admitted to be a borderline case. In *Rose v Plenty*[800] the Court of Appeal held employers liable where a milkman, in the teeth of contrary orders, had taken a thirteen-year-old helper on his rounds with him and had caused the boy an injury through bad driving. In *Kay v ITW Ltd*[801] the Court of Appeal came to the same conclusion where the defendant's driver did damage when driving another firm's lorry. Here the negligence was in the course of his employment only because he drove the other lorry in order to move it, so that his own truck could then get in.

17.409 Road accidents while driving to and from work were not in the course of employment, but where a job required driving a road accident would generally be within the course of that employment. In *Smith v Stages*[802] the employees had been sent out on an emergency repair mission. Having worked non-stop for twenty-four hours, they rushed home without taking a break. Negligent driving caused an accident. This was within the course of their employment. Similarly a coach driver

---

[797] [1942] AC 509, HL.

[798] Salmond, *Law of Torts* (1st edn, 1907) 83.

[799] [1953] 1 WLR 997, CA.

[800] [1976] 1 WLR 141, CA. Contrast *Twine v Bean's Express Ltd* (1946) 175 LT 131, CA; *Conway v George Wimpey & Co Ltd* [1951] 2 QB 266, CA.

[801] [1968] 1 QB 140, CA. Cf similar result in *Ilkiw v Samuels* [1963] 1 WLR 991, CA, where a driver allowed another to move his lorry for him without finding out whether the other was able to drive.

[802] [1989] AC 928, HL.

who, contrary to express instructions, allowed himself to be persuaded to take a long detour when bringing boys home from camp, was still within his course of employment when he crashed.[803]

(b) Wilful wrongs: fraud and violence

It used to be thought that an employer would never be liable for wilful wrongs **17.410** committed for the employee's own purposes. That seems to be the consequence of Sir John Salmond's test. But there were a number of cases where the employer was nevertheless held vicariously liable. When a bus conductor first grew abusive and then turned to violence against a passenger, it was held that this conduct, though on his bus, was outside the course of his employment.[804] On the other hand a dangerous prank involving deliberately pushing a motorized truck into a fellow employee was not outside the course of the driver's employment. His employers were therefore liable when the prank misfired and its victim was injured in earnest.[805]

(c) Reconciliation

Clarity in the definition of 'course of employment' has perhaps been enhanced **17.411** since the decision of the House of Lords to abolish the Salmond formulation in *Lister v Hesley Hall Ltd*.[806] The defendant in that case was a children's home which was held to be vicariously liable for the Warden's sexual abuse of two teenage boys. The Warden's conduct was in the course of his employment because his acts were sufficiently closely connected with the employment. The 'closely connected' test has since been applied in a number of other cases involving wilful tortious wrong-doing[807] and equitable wrongdoing[808] and there is little doubt that it will be applied in other cases of misperformance of an employment contract. Although legal clarity is enhanced, there remains the difficult factual question of when the wrong will be sufficiently 'closely connected' with the employment. All that can be said is that the question is an 'evaluative judgment'.[809]

---

803 *Hemphill Ltd v Williams* [1966] 2 Lloyd's Rep 101, HL. Applying Parke B in *Joel v Morrison* (1834) 6 Car & P 501, 503; 172 ER 1338, 1338–9.

804 *Keppel Bus Co Ltd v Ahmad* [1974] 1 WLR 1082, PC.

805 *Harrison v Michelin Tyre Co Ltd* [1985] 1 All ER 918.

806 [2001] UKHL 22; [2002] 1 AC 215, HL. Following the Canadian approach in *Bazley v Curry* [1999] 2 SCR 534, SCC and *Jacobi v Griffiths* [1999] 2 SCR 470, SCC and referring to P Cane, 'Vicarious Liability for Sexual Abuse' (2000) 116 LQR 21. The Australian courts have not followed this approach: *New South Wales v Lepore* (2003) 212 CLR 511, HCA and *Sweeney v Boylan Nominees Pty Ltd* [2006] HCA 18, HCA.

807 *Mattis v Pollock* [2003] EWCA Civ 887; [2003] 1 WLR 2158, CA; *Bernard v Attorney General of Jamaica* [2004] UKPC 47, PC.

808 *Dubai Aluminium Co Ltd v Salaam* [2002] UKHL 48; [2003] 2 AC 366, HL.

809 ibid 377–8 [25]–[26].

18

UNJUST ENRICHMENT

A. Introduction

(1) Unjust Enrichment and Restitution

18.01 The modern English law of unjust enrichment has been developed as the law of restitution. That nomenclature was determined by the decision of Goff and Jones[1] to follow the American Law Institute[2] in preferring response to event. Unjust enrichment at the expense of another is an event. A right to restitution is the law's response to that event. When one person is unjustly enriched at the expense of another, that other acquires a right to restitution of that enrichment— a right that that enrichment be given up to him.[3] Until recently, most English authors have abided by the choice of name made by Goff and Jones.[4]

18.02 The preference for 'restitution' turns out to be unsatisfactory. There are two reasons. First, the response-oriented name conceals the alignment of this subject with the cognate categories of contract and tort. Restitution suggests instead an alignment with categories of response, such as compensation, punishment, and prevention. Secondly, although many books on restitution are directed at unjust enrichment, it turns out to be incorrect to assume a one-to-one relationship between the two. Responses to unjust enrichment other than restitution are possible;[5] and a right to restitution may not arise from unjust enrichment. Thus, one person may agree to give back an enrichment to another. The promisee's consequent right to restitution arises from contract, not from unjust enrichment.[6]

Author's note. Most of this chapter was originally written by Peter Birks. He later came to take a different view of the law set out in parts D–G, in line with which he would have rewritten these parts, had his death in 2004 not made that impossible. His reasons are summarized at paras 18.40–18.43 and 18.115–18.117, where it is also explained why I believe such revision to be undesirable and unnecessary.

  [1] Robert Goff and Gareth Jones, *The Law of Restitution* (1966), now Lord Goff of Chieveley and Gareth Jones, *The Law of Restitution*, GH Jones (ed) (7th edn, 2007).

  [2] Law Institute (ALI), *Restatement of the Law, Restitution* (1937). The reporters were Austin Scott and Warren Seavey. Cf the hybrid title of the forthcoming third restatement, for which the reporter is Andrew Kull: *Restatement of the Law Third, Restitution and Unjust Enrichment*.

  [3] Compare section 1 of the *Restatement* (n 2).

  [4] P Birks, *Introduction to the Law of Restitution* (rev edn 1989); G McMeel, *The Modern Law of Restitution* (2000); P Jaffey, *The Nature and Scope of Restitution* (2000); A Burrows, *The Law of Restitution* (2nd edn, 2002); A Tettenborn, *The Law of Restitution* (3rd edn, 2002); G Virgo, *The Principles of the Law of Restitution* (2nd edn, 2006). Cf J Beatson, *The Use and Abuse of Unjust Enrichment* (1991); P Birks, *Unjust Enrichment* (2nd edn, 2005).

  [5] eg prophylactic remedies which prevent unjust enrichment: C Mitchell, *The Law of Contribution and Reimbursement* (2003) paras 2.33–2.44 (subrogation to subsisting rights) and paras 14.32–14.45 (declaratory orders and exonerative relief).

  [6] *Sebel Products Ltd v Customs and Excise Commissioners* [1949] Ch 409; *Nurdin & Peacock plc v DB Ramsden & Co Ltd* [1999] 1 WLR 1249, 1266–9; *Re Drake Insurance plc* [2001] 1 Lloyd's Rep IR 643. Contractual restitution displaces rights in unjust enrichment: *Pan Ocean Shipping Co Ltd v Creditcorp Ltd* [1994] 1 WLR 161, HL.

Again, the victim of an acquisitive wrong may acquire a right to restitution of the wrongdoer's gains. For example, if D has sold C's asset, D must give up the proceeds to C. D's conversion of the asset gives rise to more than one remedial right. Founding on the tort, C can claim either compensation of his own loss or restitution of D's gain. That restitutionary right arises from the wrong, not from unjust enrichment.[7] Again, if D is a spy who breaches a promise not to write unauthorized books, he must account for the profits of this breach of contract.[8] This is a paradigmatic example of restitution for a wrong and has nothing to do with unjust enrichment.

Rights arise by consent or independently of consent, and, when independently of consent, from wrongs, unjust enrichment, or miscellaneous other events. This same series can be rewritten: rights arise from wrongs or, in the absence of any wrong, from manifestations of consent, unjust enrichment, and miscellaneous other events. The two versions emphasize equally essential characteristics of unjust enrichment. The event so described is not a wrong, and it generates rights independently of consent. One who makes a mistaken payment obtains a right to restitution. The payee is enriched at the expense of the payer, and there is a reason why that enrichment ought to be given up, namely the mistake. But a mistaken payment is not a wrong. Nor, despite an inveterate temptation to explain it as resting on an implied contract, is the right to restitution attributable to any manifestation of the payee's consent. Restitution can be triggered by a wrong or a contract, but an unjust enrichment is never either. **18.03**

(2) Unjust Enrichment and Acquisitive Wrongs

A wider colloquial usage can blur the lines between the different categories of causative event and thus conceal the difference between restitution on the ground of unjust enrichment and restitution on other grounds, most commonly wrongs. A gain made through a wrong can quite naturally be described as an unjust enrichment, but the law of unjust enrichment has nothing to say about the responses to wrongs as such. Suppose D makes £100,000 by misusing confidential information obtained from C. Abuse of confidence is a wrong which does give rise to restitutionary as well as compensatory liability.[9] But that proposition belongs wholly to the law of wrongs, not the law of unjust enrichment. The question whether a wrong gives rise to punitive damages belongs to the law of wrongs. The question whether a wrong entitles a victim to a gain-based award is of the same order. **18.04**

---

[7] *United Australia Ltd v Barclays Bank Ltd* [1941] AC 1, HL.

[8] *A-G v Blake* [2001] 1 AC 268, HL.

[9] *Peter Pan Manufacturing Corporation v Corsets Silhouette Ltd* [1964] 1 WLR 96; cf in relation to a lifelong duty of confidence *A-G v Guardian Newspapers (No 2)* [1990] 1 AC 109, HL.

18.05   The law of unjust enrichment has nothing to say about the remedial rights arising from wrongs as such. The words 'as such' are crucial. A story which discloses a wrong may be susceptible of an alternative analysis as an unjust enrichment. If C is falsely imprisoned by D until he pays money for his release, C suffers a wrong— a trespass to his person. C can sue for that trespass as such, choosing between the compensatory and restitutionary remedial rights born of that wrong. But C can also lay aside the wrong and analyse the story instead as an unjust enrichment. Just as a mistaken payment is an impaired transfer of money, so also C has made an impaired transfer to D. The difference is that C's impairment is now not a mistake but rather an illegitimate pressure applied by D.

18.06   In this alternative analysis C at no point relies on the facts in their character as a wrong, whether to satisfy the phrase 'at the expense of' or to establish the injustice of D's retaining the enrichment. A claimant who invokes the language of unjust enrichment but does rely on a wrong in one or other of those roles will not be suing in unjust enrichment but in the law of wrongs. *Edwards v Lee's Administrator*[10] arose from the discovery of the Great Onyx Cave in Kentucky. Edwards stumbled on the entrance to this scenic cave on his land. He successfully promoted the cave as a tourist attraction. Lee then showed that one-third of the attractions extended under his land. Deep below the surface and inflicting no loss, every party of tourists committed trespass. The Kentucky Court of Appeals awarded Lee's estate one-third of Edwards' profits. If one looks behind the confusion of pre-*Restatement* language, it seems that the Court contemplated this as an account of the profits of the wrong as such, not as an unjust enrichment. As we shall see in the discussion of 'at the expense of', it is not yet clear whether English law would regard this as a case which was amenable to alternative analysis as an unjust enrichment. If 'at the expense of the claimant' is given the sense 'by committing a wrong against the claimant', these profits were made at Lee's expense. But a claimant who relies on that sense of 'at the expense of' is founding on a cause of action in the law of wrongs, not unjust enrichment.

18.07   To get within the law of unjust enrichment the claimant must use the subtractive sense of 'at the expense of'. That is, he must be able to show that the defendant was enriched from him. It is certain that Edwards obtained the use of the land from Lee. It is much less clear whether the money which Edwards received from the tourists can be said in a more subtle way to have been obtained from Lee. Their litigation over the Great Onyx Cave shows how the subtractive sense of 'at the expense of' guards the gate to alternative analysis.[11]

---

[10] 96 SW 2d 1028, 265 Ky 418 (Kentucky Court of Appeal, 1936).

[11] See para 18.28. For discussion of gain-based responses to wrongs *qua* wrongs, see paras 21.142–21.159; and also J Edelman, *Gain-Based Damages* (2002).

(3) Persistence of the Language of an Earlier Age

Before the American *Restatement* this area of the law was fragmented. The old **18.08** language of the various fragments is still encountered.[12] 'Quasi-contract', which was borrowed from Roman law, now makes only rare appearances, and the habit of hiding its matter under 'implied contract' has been repudiated.[13] However, vocabulary derived from the forms of action which were abolished in the nineteenth century has proved more durable. So long as the forms of action survived, in the courts of common law much of the work of unjust enrichment was done by the action for money had and received to the use of the plaintiff, a sub-form of *indebitatus assumpsit*. Some was done by its cousin in that family, the action for money paid to the use of the defendant. Claims in respect of work and goods fell to *assumpsit* for reasonable remuneration (*quantum meruit*) and reasonable value (*quantum valebat*).

The terminology of the parallel contribution of the Court of Chancery is hardly **18.09** less obscure, in particular subrogation and constructive and resulting trusts. Unlike the old language of the common law these for the moment still have real work to do and have to be mastered rather than displaced. It cannot be asserted that every instance of subrogation or constructive trust is a response to unjust enrichment, and the true nature of resulting trusts is controversial.[14] However, it is certain that trusts which arise by operation of law do frequently respond to unjust enrichment, and non-contractual subrogation probably always does so.

(4) Summary

Restitution is multi-causal. A right to restitution is not invariably triggered by **18.10** unjust enrichment. The principal aim of those who have written on restitution has nonetheless been to examine the law of unjust enrichment, albeit imperfectly differentiated from other restitution-yielding events, especially wrongful enrichment. The reversal of the semantic preference for response over event helps to overcome that handicap, without substantially changing the project which began with the *Restatement*. The fact that, by alternative analysis, some fact-situations can be presented as either an unjust enrichment or an acquisitive wrong in no way blurs the bright line between unjust enrichment and wrongs. Every lawyer knows that one set of facts may yield multiple causes of action. All these

---

[12] Further discussion: P Birks, *Unjust Enrichment* (2nd edn, 2005) 284–307.

[13] *Lipkin Gorman v Karpnale Ltd* [1991] 2 AC 548, HL; *Westdeutsche Landesbank Girozentrale v Islington LBC* [1996] AC 669, 710, HL; *Sempra Metals Ltd v IRC* [2007] UKHL 34; [2007] 3 WLR 354, [105]–[107] and [174]–[175]. Cf *Pavey & Matthews Pty Ltd v Paul* (1987) 162 CLR 221, 227 and 254–7, HCA; *Baltic Shipping Co v Dillon* (1993) 176 CLR 344, 356–7, HCA.

[14] See paras 18.129–18.131.

matters become easier to understand as archaic language gives way to rights-based terminology.

B. Enrichment

18.11 To establish a prima facie liability in unjust enrichment the claimant must show that the defendant was enriched, that this enrichment was received at the claimant's expense, and that the enrichment was unjust—that is, that it ought in law to be given up. We first deal with enrichment.

(1) One Law for all Enrichments Received

18.12 As a matter of history English law drew bright lines between different kinds of benefit received. Money received fell to the action for money had and received. The action for money paid to the use of the defendant dealt with benefits received from the claimant through a payment made by him to a third party, including debts paid off. Other actions dealt with other benefits. For example, *assumpsit* for *quantum meruit* dealt with services. Apart from the first, all these actions alleged that the benefit had been conferred 'at the special instance and request of the defendant'. An imposed liability could only be developed by cautiously identifying circumstances in which the allegation of a request could safely be deemed. In *Exall v Partridge*,[15] for example, the claimant had paid off the defendant's debt to his landlord following the lawful seizure of his carriage. He had taken his carriage to the defendant for repair and the landlord had then distrained for arrears of rent. On these facts the defendant's request could be 'implied'. In this way what now appears to be a clear example of liability for unjust enrichment was coaxed out of a form of action that was on its face unequivocally contractual.

18.13 Not everyone agrees that symmetry is attainable so as to have one law for all enrichments received, in whatever form.[16] However, such symmetry is logically inescapable. If there is no finding of enrichment, then the case falls outside the law of unjust enrichment and indeed beyond the range of the law of restitution.[17] In the miscellany of other causative events beyond contract, wrongs, and unjust

---

[15] (1799) 8 TR 308, 101 ER 1405.

[16] P Watts, 'Restitution: A Property Principle and A Services Principle' [1995] Restitution L Rev 30. This subdivision is imposed on a reanalysis of the law of restitution which is radically innovative, though it is reminiscent of the approach to which Viscount Stair sought to commit the Scots law: James Dalrymple, Viscount of Stair, *Institutions of the Law of Scotland*, DM Walker (ed) (tercentenary edn, 1981) 1.7 (Restitution) and 1.8 (Recompense).

[17] *Regalian plc v London Docklands Development Corporation* [1995] Ch 212.

enrichment, there may well be events which trigger entitlements to recompense for non-contractual services which cannot be regarded as enrichments.[18] Sir Jack Beatson has rightly insisted that the notion of enrichment must not be stretched in order to bring all such claims within the law of unjust enrichment.[19] But there is equally no need to exclude from the law of unjust enrichment those cases in which non-money benefits are clearly enriching.

(2) Money

Money is the very measure of enrichment. It is nearly always impossible to deny that a receipt of money is enriching. There is a question, however, as to the way in which the user value of money over time should be handled. Where a claimant pays money to a defendant who banks it in an account bearing compound interest, or would otherwise have borrowed an equivalent sum at compound interest, the benefit gained by the defendant includes the interest as well as the capital value of the money.

18.14

Nevertheless, in *Westdeutsche Landesbank Girozentrale v Islington LBC*,[20] the majority of the court held that in these circumstances compound interest is not payable unless the case falls within the scope of a special equitable jurisdiction, because otherwise the courts' power to award pre-judgment interest derives exclusively from their jurisdiction to award simple interest under the Supreme Court Act 1981, s 35A. As Lord Goff and Lord Woolf observed in their dissenting speeches, this was an unsatisfactory outcome as it left the courts unable to order restitution of the full benefit received by the defendant.[21]

18.15

In *Sempra Metals Ltd v IRC*,[22] the House of Lords revisited this issue and came to a different conclusion.[23] The claimant paid tax sooner than was legally required and, without disputing that the tax would eventually have become payable, sought to recover the user value of the money between the time of payment and the later time when payment should have been made, asserting that the measure of this benefit equated to a compound interest award. The claim succeeded, according to Lord Hope and Lord Nicholls because the claimant had a substantive claim in

18.16

---

[18] SJ Stoljar, 'Unjust Enrichment and Unjust Sacrifice' (1987) 50 MLR 603.
[19] J Beatson, *The Use and Abuse of Unjust Enrichment* (1991) ch 2.
[20] [1996] AC 669, HL.
[21] [1996] AC 669, 691 and 719–20, HL. See too Hobhouse J's comments at first instance: [1994] 4 All ER 890, 955.
[22] [2007] UKHL 34, [2007] 3 WLR 354.
[23] At [36] and [112] Lord Hope and Lord Nicholls stated that the *Westdeutsche* case could be distinguished because it concerned a claim to recover interest on money that had not been repaid before issue of the writ. However, Lord Walker more plausibly held at [183]–[184] that such a distinction would be anomalous and that *Westdeutsche* required overruling, a view also taken by Lord Mance at [240].

unjust enrichment at common law to recover the user value of the money,[24] and according to Lord Walker because the court should exercise an equitable discretion in the claimant's favour to award an equivalent sum.[25]

18.17 The amount awarded in the *Sempra* case represented a 'conventional' rate of interest which was lower than commercial rates to reflect the fact that the Government can borrow money more cheaply than commercial borrowers, eg by issuing Treasury Bills. Hence the case bears out the view, discussed immediately below, that defendants may rely on evidence of their personal characteristics to argue that non-money benefits are worth less to them than the market value.[26]

(3) Benefits in Kind

18.18 When benefits are received in kind the central problem is easy to understand. It turns on the subjectivity of value. While money is the very measure of enrichment, benefits in kind have different values to different people. Some people have their poodles permed, others abhor permed poodles. If C mistakenly pays D £100, D is unequivocally enriched. If C mistakenly perms D's poodle, D can object that it is impossible to affirm that he has been enriched without infringing his right to value benefits in kind according to his own priorities. There is a market, and a market price, but D must be free to dissociate himself from the demand that sets that price. English law accepts that D should generally have the freedom to make this choice, but it also holds that in some situations it is nonetheless appropriate to impose a monetary value on non-money benefits in D's hands.

(a) Where the defendant has a sufficient choice

18.19 A defendant who freely requests a benefit cannot complain of interference with his freedom of choice. So, in *Vedatech Corp v Crystal Decisions Ltd*[27] the defendant had to pay the market value of work requested from the claimant. A more controversial question is whether a market valuation should be imposed on a defendant who forgoes an opportunity to reject a benefit that has clearly not been offered gratis or at less than market value. On one view, this amounts to unconscientious

---

24 [2007] UKHL 34; [2007] 3 WLR 354, [26], [36], and [112]. At [149] and [153]. Lord Scott agreed that such claims can lie at common law but held that the claimant had failed to plead facts which established the defendant's enrichment.

25 [2007] UKHL 34; [2007] 3 WLR 354, [184]–[187]. At [231]–[240] Lord Mance agreed that the courts can make such discretionary awards in equity but he also thought that the claimant had failed to prove the defendant's enrichment.

26 [2007] UKHL 34; [2007] 3 WLR 354, [118]–[119] and [128].

27 [2002] EWHC 818. See too *William Lacey (Hounslow) Ltd v Davis* [1957] 1 WLR 932; *Pavey & Matthews Pty Ltd v Paul* (1987) 162 CLR 221, HCA.

conduct which precludes the defendant from making the argument based on respect for freedom of choice.[28] On another, imposition of market value would be unfair because the defendant's behaviour may simply reflect indifference to the benefit being rendered. On the latter view, it would be preferable to impose a market value only where the defendant's conduct clearly shows that he wants the benefit, but is unwilling to pay for it.[29] In *Cressman v Coys of Kensington (Sales) Ltd*[30] both tests were satisfied (and so the court did not need to choose between them). The defendant took steps to register in his name a car with a personalized number plate, knowing that the opportunity to do so had come to him through the claimant's mistake, and intending not to pay for the benefit he thereby acquired.

(b) Incontrovertible benefits

The law holds some benefits to be enriching whether or not the recipient chooses **18.20** to receive them. One example is the saving of an inevitable expense, such as the discharge of a debt,[31] or the receipt of necessary services, such as the services provided to a company by its managing director,[32] or sewerage services provided to a house-owner.[33] Another example arises where a benefit in kind has been realized: for example, where goods are mistakenly improved and subsequently sold.[34] In the *Coys* case, the Court of Appeal went further, and held that in cases where readily realizable benefits are in the hands of a defendant, the law should robustly order or assume a sale, whether or not the defendant actually plans to sell the relevant assets.[35]

(4) Summary

Enrichment does not stop at money. It includes value acquired in other forms. **18.21** The establishment of enrichment received other than in money has to allow for the subjectivity of value. However, a recipient will find it difficult to deny that he has been enriched when the non-money benefit is a necessary, when it has been

---

[28] P Birks, 'In Defence of Free Acceptance' in A Burrows (ed) *Essays on the Law of Restitution* (1991) 105.

[29] A Burrows, 'Free Acceptance and the Law of Restitution' (1988) 104 LQR 576; Burrows (n 4) 20–5.

[30] [2004] EWCA Civ 133; [2004] 1 WLR 2774, [26]–[32].

[31] *Exall v Partridge* (1799) 8 TR 308, 101 ER 1405; *Johnson v Royal Mail Steam Packet Co* (1867) LR 3 CP 38. The discharge of a debt is not always incontrovertibly enriching: *Boulton v Jones* (1857) 2 H & N 564, 157 ER 232; *Boscawen v Bajwa* [1996] 1 WLR 334, 340–1, CA.

[32] *Craven-Ellis v Canons Ltd* [1936] 2 KB 403, CA; cf *Proctor & Gamble Philippine Manufacturing Corporation v Peter Cremer GmbH (The Manila)* [1988] 3 All ER 843, 855.

[33] *Rowe v Vale of White Horse DC* [2003] EWHC 388; [2003] 1 Lloyd's Rep 418.

[34] *Greenwood v Bennett* [1973] QB 195, CA.

[35] *Coys* (n 30) [33]–[40].

chosen, and when its value has been realized or is readily realizable in money. If a non-money benefit is held not to be an enrichment, there will be no restitutionary liability of any kind, for restitutionary liabilities are definitively gain-based.

C. At the Expense of the Claimant

18.22 The claimant must show that the defendant was enriched 'from' him. If he relies on the 'wrong' sense—the defendant was enriched by committing a wrong against him—his action will arise in the law of wrongs, not in the law of unjust enrichment.[36] Provided that the subtractive sense of the phrase is satisfied, it does not matter whether the enrichment happens through a performance made by the claimant or without one, as where the defendant takes or finds.

(1) Corresponding Impoverishment

18.23 If you stow away on my aeroplane, intending to take a free ride, you gain a valuable benefit but I suffer no loss.[37] Should the law give me a claim in unjust enrichment? As long ago as 1776, in *Hambly v Trott*,[38] Lord Mansfield said that a claim for the value of such benefits would lie. Such a claim might be explained as restitution for a wrong but it is unlikely that Lord Mansfield was thinking along those lines. More recent cases can also be explained on the basis that a claimant in unjust enrichment need not show a loss corresponding to the defendant's gain. In *Kleinwort Benson Ltd v Birmingham CC*,[39] restitution was awarded although the claimant had eliminated its initial loss by passing it onto a third party; one reason given was that loss is irrelevant to claims in unjust enrichment, although other considerations also led the court to allow recovery.[40] In *Trustee of the Property of FC Jones & Son (a firm) v Jones*[41] the defendant used the claimant's money to speculate on the potato futures market and multiplied the amount received fivefold; she was not held to have committed a wrong, but she was ordered to pay over all that she had made. Collectively these authorities suggest that English law resembles German law, under which it matters only that a gain in the defendant's

---

[36] See para 18.04.

[37] Cf BGH NJW 609 (7.1.1971), translated by G Dannemann in B Markesinis, W Lorenz, and G Dannemann, *German Law of Obligations Vol I The Law Of Contracts and Restitution: A Comparative Introduction* (1997) 771.

[38] (1776) 1 Cowp 371, 375; 98 ER 1136, 1138. Cf *Sympson v Juxon* (1624) Cro Jac 699, 79 ER 607.

[39] [1996] 4 All ER 733, CA. See too *Mason v NSW* (1959) 102 CLR 108, 146, HCA, adopted in *Commissioner of State Revenue v Royal Insurance Australia Ltd* (1994) 182 CLR 51, HCA; *Roxborough v Rothmans of Pall Mall (Australia) Ltd* (2001) 208 CLR 516, HCA.

[40] See para 18.257.

[41] [1997] Ch 159, CA.

hands derived from the claimant, and it makes no difference whether the claimant suffered a corresponding loss.[42]

Against these authorities must be set *BP Exploration Co (Libya) Ltd v Hunt* **18.24**
(No 2),[43] which concerned a claim under the Law Reform (Frustrated Contracts) Act 1943. Under a joint venture with Hunt, BP undertook prospecting work in the Libyan desert which increased the value of Hunt's share of an oil concession from the Libyan government. The joint venture was frustrated when the concession was expropriated, and BP claimed that it was entitled to be paid a 'just sum' under section 1(3). Robert Goff J, who considered that the statute embodies principles of the law of unjust enrichment, held that the enhancement of Hunt's share was some $85 million. However he ordered Hunt to pay BP less than a quarter of this, a result that must be explained on the basis that this was the cost to BP of conferring the benefit. This suggests that English law resembles Canadian law, which insists that there must be not only a plus to the defendant but a corresponding minus to the claimant.[44] So too does Lord Scarman's statement in Parliament when introducing the bill that became the Civil Liability (Contribution) Act 1978,[45] that a claimant who settles with a creditor and then looks to a defendant for a contribution cannot 'recover a higher amount. . .than that which he has agreed to pay.'[46]

Should the English courts take the narrow Canadian or the wide German view? **18.25**
There are two reasons for thinking that the narrow view is preferable.[47] The first is that there is no normative justification for ordering a defendant to hand over a material gain which does not correspond to a claimant's material loss, in the absence of consent or wrongdoing. The law of unjust enrichment is concerned with reversing defective transfers, and in such a case there is no nexus of transfer between the parties. The second reason is that it wastes scarce judicial resources to divert a benefit from a defendant to a claimant when neither positively deserves it.[48]

---

[42] H-G Koppensteiner and EA Kramer, *Ungerechtfertigte Bereicherung* (2nd edn, 1988) 84, 85; HJ Wieling, *Bereicherungsrecht* (1993) 1–2.

[43] [1979] 1 WLR 783, aff'd [1981] 1 WLR 232, CA; [1983] 2 AC 352, HL.

[44] *Pettkus v Becker* [1980] 2 SCR 834, 848; *Pacific National Investments Ltd v City of Victoria* [2004] 3 SCR 575 [14] and [20]–[21]. It is uncertain where these and many other cases to the same effect have been left by *Kingstreet Investments Ltd v New Brunswick (Department of Finance)* 2007 SCC 1; [2007] 1 SCR 3, [44]–[47].

[45] 'The 1978 Act is an application of the principle that there should be restitutionary remedies for unjust enrichment': *Dubai Aluminium Co Ltd v Salaam* [2002] UKHL 48, [2003] 2 AC 366, [76].

[46] *Hansard*, HL (series 5) vol 395, col 251 (18 July 1978). Cf *Gnitrow Ltd v Cape plc* [2000] 3 All ER 763, 767, CA.

[47] M McInnes, 'At the Plaintiff's Expense: Quantifying Restitutionary Relief' [1998] CLJ 472, 476–7; LD Smith, 'Restitution: The Heart of Corrective Justice' (2001) 79 Texas LR 2115, 2147. Contrary to RB Grantham and CEF Rickett, 'Disgorgement for Unjust Enrichment' [2003] CLJ 159, it is not a further reason to adopt the narrow view that adoption of the wider view would render the law incoherent by merging the law of unjust enrichment with the law of restitution for wrongs; the effect of adopting the broader view would simply be to enlarge the incidence of alternative analysis.

[48] Where a claimant has passed on a loss to a third party who can himself recover from the claimant, it may still be desirable to let the claimant recover from the defendant, provided that he is legally

(2) Interceptive Subtraction

18.26   Various cases show that D can be enriched from C interceptively, where the asset which carries the value in question was destined for C, but has never been reduced to his ownership or possession. One example is the *Jones* case, considered above, where the yield of D's investments can only be said to have been obtained from C interceptively: D must be understood as intercepting wealth already attributed by the law to C by virtue of arising from the earning opportunities inherent in his ownership of the original sum. Other examples include[49] cases where D receives the profits of office due to C,[50] where D receives rent due to C,[51] and where land meant to be conveyed to C is mistakenly conveyed to D.[52]

18.27   Interceptive subtraction has dramatic consequences for alternative analysis between unjust enrichment and enrichment by wrongs. Such alternative analysis is possible when a claimant who has been the victim of an acquisitive wrong can present the facts as an unjust enrichment without placing any reliance on their characterization as a wrong. Some scholars think that gain-based claims for wrongs are always made in that way.[53] They think that restitution for wrongs as such is an illusion. That goes too far. But it is none the less true that if this broad interpretation of 'at the expense of' is adopted, then a great many of the cases which seem to exemplify restitution for wrongs as such can be understood, by alternative analysis, as cases of unjust enrichment.

18.28   The Kentucky case of the scenic cave provides an example. The owner of the entrance was made to account for the profits of trespassory tourism, to the extent that the cave extended under his neighbour's land.[54] It is clear that, so far as concerns the user of the land, the facts could have been reanalysed as an unjust enrichment—a valuable benefit taken from the neighbour without his consent. That analysis would have given the claimant a reasonable rental, that being the

---

bound to pass the benefit back up the line to the third party. Cf M Rush, *The Defence of Passing On* (2006) ch 10; and see paras 18.256 ff.

[49]   See too *Shamia v Joory* [1958] 1 QB 448 (where no property can have passed to the claimant); perhaps also *Ministry of Health v Simpson* [1951] AC 251, HL, notwithstanding LD Smith, 'Three-Party Restitution: A Critique of Birks's Theory of Interceptive Subtraction' (1991) 11 OJLS 481.

[50]   *Arris v Stukely* (1677) 2 Mod 260, 86 ER 1060; *Howard v Wood* (1679) 2 Lev 245, 83 ER 530. These need not be analysed as examples of wrongful enrichment.

[51]   *Official Custodian for Charities v Mackey (No 2)* [1985] 1 WLR 1308, 1314–5.

[52]   *Leuty v Hillas* (1858) 2 De G & J 110, 44 ER 929; *Craddock Bros v Hunt* [1923] 2 Ch 136, CA; both discussed in R Chambers *Resulting Trusts* (1997) 127.

[53]   J Beatson, 'The Nature of Waiver of Tort' in *The Use and Abuse of Unjust Enrichment* (1991) 206; D Friedmann, 'Restitution for Wrongs' in WR Cornish et al (eds), *Restitution, Past, Present, and Future* (1998) 87.

[54]   *Edwards v Lees Administrators* 96 SW 2d 1028, 265 Ky 418 (Kentucky Court of Appeals, 1936); cf *Olwell v Nissen and Nye Co* 26 Wash 2d 282, 173 P 2d 652 (Supreme Court of Washington, 1946).

value of the benefit taken. However, the *Jones* case suggests that the same reanalysis, independent of any wrong, must be possible in respect of the money paid by the tourists. If the yield from a successful investment of the claimant's money can be recovered as an unjust enrichment at his expense, the same must be true where the exploitation of the claimant's property consists in hiring it out. The two earning opportunities are of essentially the same kind and cannot be treated differently.

(3) Enrichment Immediately at the Expense of the Claimant

It has been suggested that the defendant must have been directly enriched at the expense of the claimant or, in other words, that there is a requirement of 'privity', a term uneasily inherited from implied contract days.[55] There is no absolute rule to that effect.[56] It is nevertheless helpful to start by asking when it can be said that the defendant is immediately enriched from the claimant. The question whether the claimant can leapfrog that immediate enrichee must be asked separately.

18.29

(a) Proprietary connections

In one situation the intervention of third parties makes no difference. If the defendant receives the claimant's property, it does not matter how many hands it has passed through. In *Lipkin Gorman v Karpnale Ltd*,[57] a partner in a firm of solicitors took money from the firm's client account and gambled it away at the defendant's casino. The House of Lords allowed the firm to recover from the casino, reasoning that if X takes C's money without C's consent and gives it to D, then, subject to defences, D becomes indebted to C in the sum received. This model also holds good where the claimant's interest in property is a power to avoid a voidable title. In *Banque Belge pour l'Etranger v Hambrouck*,[58] the bank paid money to a fraudster who had forged cheques; on the strength of its power to avoid his title the bank could recover from his mistress, to whom he gave some of the money.

18.30

(b) Contracts which confer benefits on non-parties

The fact that an enrichment has been conferred on D by C's own act is not conclusive of its having been received immediately at the C's expense. C may have been performing a contract made with a third party. In such circumstances the

18.31

---

[55] Burrows (n 4) 31–4; Virgo (n 4) 105–12.
[56] See paras 18.32–18.38.
[57] [1991] 2 AC 548, HL.
[58] [1921] 1 KB 321, CA. See too *Bainbrigge v Browne* (1881) 18 Ch D 188, 196–7; *Midland Bank plc v Perry* [1988] 1 FLR 161, 167.

ultimate recipient is immediately enriched only from that third party. Thus, if a garage does work on a crashed car, the car's owner is the ultimate beneficiary of the work. That benefit seems to come from the garage, but if the garage does the work under a contract with an insurance company, then the car's owner is immediately enriched at the insurance company's expense. The immediate enrichee of the garage's work is the insurance company.[59]

(4) Leapfrogging the Immediate Enrichee

18.32 Suppose that I mistakenly pay X £1000, and that my payment enables X to give you a different £500, something he would not otherwise have done. In one sense you have been enriched at my expense. But the connection between your gain and my loss is causal rather than proprietary, and so you are not my immediate enrichee. Suppose that X becomes insolvent. Can I leapfrog X and claim against you? It is significant that you are a donee. If you were a bona fide purchaser for value then you would have a defence in any event.[60] It is only worth asking whether leapfrogging claims are possible against remote recipients who cannot rely on this defence. What answer does the law give? It seems that in one common case leapfrogging is ruled out, but that otherwise the law does not forbid leapfrogging, leaving remote recipients to the protection of normal defences.

(a) Valid contracts

18.33 Suppose that D receives a benefit from, or because of, the performance of a contract between C and X, and that C, the party making the performance, has a valid contractual right to be paid for that performance by X. D is the immediate enrichee of X, and the remote enrichee of C. In this case C cannot leapfrog X, who procured the performance, and claim against D. One may never attack one's contractual counter-party's immediate enrichee because this would subvert the insolvency regime by allowing C to wriggle round the risk of X's insolvency inherent in the party's contract.

18.34 In *Uren v First National Home Finance Ltd,*[61] the claimants alleged that the defendant company had bought property from the receivers of two other companies in

---

59 *Brown and Davis v Galbraith* [1972] 1 WLR 997, CA; *Gray's Truck Centre Ltd v Olaf L Johnson Ltd* (CA, 25 January 1990). This model does not apply to the situation in *Barclays Bank plc v O'Brien* [1994] 1 AC 180, HL, and *Royal Bank of Scotland v Etridge (No 2)* [2001] UKHL 44; [2002] 2 AC 773, where C agrees with X to give security to D. Other possible distinctions aside, even if there is a contract between C and X that C shall confer a benefit on D (and X), that contract is, in the given situation, invalid. Hence D can be treated as the immediate enrichee.

60 See paras 18.248–18.255.

61 [2005] EWHC 2529.

the same group, after the claimants had advanced money to develop the property. The claimants alleged that the receiverships had been managed in bad faith, but Mann J held that even if this were true, so that the defence of bona fide purchase was unavailable, he would not permit the claimants 'to fashion a remedy based in unjust enrichment in order to overcome the inconveniences of the chain of contracts and incorporation that exist in this case and which have their own consequences'.[62]

(b) No valid contract

There is no compelling reason to deny leapfrogging where the claimant has **18.35** never entered a contract, or where he has entered a contract which is subsequently invalidated, for example because he has made a mistake. In such circumstances the policy objections to leapfrogging are not engaged, because the claimant has not voluntarily assumed the risk of his contractual counter-party's insolvency. German law permits claims where C gratuitously transfers a benefit to X, who transfers it to D with the result that any claims by C against X would be met by the defence of change of position.[63] At present it is impossible to say whether English law imposes that or some other restrictive requirement in addition to 'but for' causation, before allowing leapfrogging claims.

A series of subrogation cases bears out the view that English law allows leapfrog- **18.36** ging claims not only where C and X have never had a valid contract, but also where their contract is initially valid—provided that C acted under a causative mistake or the provision made for X's default is legally ineffective, *and* that there is no danger that the claim will contradict the valid contract under which he rendered his performance.[64] For example, in *Butler v Rice*[65] Mr Rice obtained a loan from Butler for the purpose of discharging a mortgage on property owned by Mrs Rice, by making fraudulent misrepresentations as to the ownership of the property. Mrs Rice did not participate in the transaction, and Butler never obtained the charge by which he expected his loan to be secured. Warrington J held that Butler was entitled to be subrogated to the charge over Mrs Rice's property which had been paid off with Butler's money.

---

[62] Ibid [28]. See too *Brown and Davis v Galbraith* [1972] 1 WLR 997, CA; *Pan Ocean Shipping Co Ltd v Creditcorp Ltd* [1994] 1 WLR 161, HL; *Lloyds Bank plc v Independent Insurance Co Ltd* [2000] 1 QB 110, CA; all discussed in P Birks *Unjust Enrichment* (2nd edn, 2005) 89–93.

[63] BGB §822.

[64] For detailed discussion, see C Mitchell and S W Watterson, *Subrogation: Law and Practice* (2007) paras 5.60–5.93.

[65] [1910] 2 Ch 277. See too *Chetwynd v Allen* [1899] 1 Ch 353; *Filby v Mortgage Express (No 2) Ltd* [2004] EWCA Civ 759 (where May LJ wrongly suggested that the loan contract was void, and not merely voidable).

18.37 In *Bannatyne v D&C MacIver* the London agents of the defendant firm borrowed money for them without authority. The claimant lenders mistakenly believed that they did have authority. The Court of Appeal upheld the claim against the firm to the extent that the money had been turned to their advantage. Romer LJ said:[66]

> Where money is borrowed on behalf of a principal by an agent, the lender believing that the agent has authority, though it turns out that his act has not been authorised, or ratified, or adopted by the principal, then, although the principal cannot be sued at law, yet in equity, to the extent to which the money borrowed has in fact been applied in paying legal debts and obligations of the principal, the lender is entitled to stand in the same position as if the money had originally been borrowed by the principal.

18.38 This is the same doctrine as underlies *B Liggett (Liverpool) Ltd v Barclays Bank Ltd*.[67] There a bank laid out money believing that it had the authority of a company which was its customer, when in fact it had only the authority of one director of the company. It was allowed to debit the company's account. The explanation of the case offered by majority of the Court of Appeal in *Re Cleadon Trust Ltd*,[68] was that the money was to be regarded as a mistaken advance to that one director applied by him to the discharge of the company's debts, which were indeed discharged because, though he had no authority to draw on the company's account, yet he did have authority to discharge the company's debts.[69]

(5) Summary

18.39 In the law of unjust enrichment 'at the expense of' cannot be used in the sense of 'by doing a wrong to'. The subtractive sense, which must be used, might be understood narrowly or broadly. English law has not yet committed itself to either understanding, but there are strong reasons of principle for favouring the narrower view. The notion of 'subtraction' from a claimant includes interceptive subtraction, which increases the potential range of unjust enrichment, as it enables many cases of restitution for wrongs to be alternatively explained as instances of unjust enrichment. Although most remote recipients will be protected by the defences of bona fide purchase and/or change of position, the defendant's enrichment need not be directly from the claimant, for it is possible to reach over first recipients to others who would not have received if they had not. A party who has conferred a benefit

---

[66] [1906] 1 KB 103, 109, CA. In *Reid v Rigby & Co* [1894] 2 QB 40 recovery was allowed at law, the facts being materially identical.
[67] [1928] 1 KB 48.
[68] [1939] Ch 286, CA.
[69] Ibid, 318 and 326.

on another in performance of a valid contract with a third party will, however, be confined to his rights against the third party.

D. Unjust or Unjustified?

The law has to say when an enrichment at another's expense is an unjust enrich-   **18.40**
ment. Civilian legal systems commonly approach this question by asking whether there is a legal ground for the transfer from claimant to defendant: if not, then the defendant's enrichment is unjustified and restitution will follow. English law approaches the task differently, by identifying specific 'unjust factors'. It is impossible to escape that ugly phrase. An unjust factor is a reason for restitution other than a contract or a wrong. In a payment by mistake the payment is the enrichment of the payee at the expense of the payer, and the mistake is the unjust factor.

In his last book,[70] Peter Birks argued that English law was sent in a new direction,   **18.41**
and committed to the civilian approach, by certain cases concerned with the recovery of payments under void but fully executed swap contracts.[71] He also contended that the 'no legal ground' approach is preferable to the 'unjust factors' approach, because it achieves a 'tighter unity' by grounding restitutionary recovery on a single principle, albeit one that does not express the reasons for restitution in accessible language. On this view, the law of unjust enrichment more closely resembles the law of contract than the law of torts.

These arguments rested on a tendentious reading of the case law. They ignored   **18.42**
alternative explanations of the swaps cases,[72] and glossed over some key authorities, in particular *Woolwich Equitable BS v IRC*, where Lord Goff declined to find for the claimant on the basis that there was no legal ground for the defendant's enrichment, because although English law 'might have developed so as to recognize a *condictio indebiti*—an action for the recovery of money on the ground that it was not due. . .it did not do so'.[73] Nor is there any reason to think that English law would work more efficiently, or produce fairer outcomes, if it adopted the 'no legal ground' approach. On the contrary, it seems likely that making such a

---

[70] P Birks *Unjust Enrichment* (2nd edn, 2005) ch 5.

[71] *Kleinwort Benson Ltd v Sandwell BC*, decided and reported with the first instance decision in *Westdeutsche Landesbank Girozentrale v Islington LBC* [1994] 4 All ER 890; and *Guinness Mahon plc v Kensington & Chelsea RLBC* [1999] QB 215, CA.

[72] In line with *Kleinwort Benson Ltd v Lincoln CC* [1999] 2 AC 349, HL, the same result could have been produced by allowing recovery on the ground of mistake of law. As discussed at paras 18.62–18.65, however, the mistake recognized in *Lincoln* was fictional. Hence, a surer ground for recovery may be found in failure of basis (see para 18.114) or in the policy considerations underlying the rule of law which rendered the parties' swaps contracts void (see paras 18.115–18.117).

[73] [1993] AC 70, 172. The *Woolwich* case is discussed further at paras 18.155–18.159.

change would produce confusion and uncertainty,[74] especially if the courts were to adopt Birks' 'limited reconciliation' of the two approaches by treating unjust factors as reasons why, higher up, there is no legal ground for the defendant's acquisition.[75]

18.43   The question whether English law takes a 'no legal ground' approach was answered in the negative in *Deutsche Morgan Grenfell plc v IRC*, where Lord Walker thought that this would 'represent a distinct departure from established doctrine',[76] and Lord Hoffmann held that:[77]

> at any rate for the moment,. . .unlike civilian systems, English law has no general principle that to retain money paid without any legal basis (such as debt, gift, compromise, etc) is unjust enrichment. . . In England, the claimant has to prove that the circumstances in which the payment was made come within one of the categories which the law recognizes as sufficient to make retention by the recipient unjust.

In line with these statements the following discussion will therefore proceed on the basis that claimants in unjust enrichment must demonstrate an unjust factor: a positive reason for restitution.

18.44   It has been said that the courts' jurisdiction to order restitution on the ground of unjust enrichment is subject 'to the binding authority of previous decisions', and that they do not have 'a discretionary power to order repayment whenever it seems. . .just and equitable to do so'.[78] It has also been said that claims in unjust enrichment must be pleaded by bringing them 'within or close to some established category or factual recovery situation'.[79] However *Woolwich Equitable BS v IRC*[80] shows that the courts are not limited to incremental development from existing categories of recovery, and may sometimes take a bolder approach.

---

[74] The structural differences between English law and German law, which takes a 'no legal ground' approach, are emphasized in T Krebs *Restitution at the Crossroads: A Comparative Study* (2001), but played down in A Burrows and Lord Rodger (eds), *Mapping the Law* (2006) 343–361 (Meier) and 363–377 (Dannemann).

[75] Birks (n 70) 116. Lord Walker 'saw attractions' in this idea in *Deutsche Morgan Grenfell plc v IRC* [2006] UKHL 49; [2007] 1 AC 558, [158]. But experience shows that the courts fare badly when asked to operate more than one test simultaneously: cf the CA's chaotic decision on negligence liability for pure economic loss in *Customs & Excise Commissioners v Barclays Bank plc* [2005] EWCA Civ 1555; [2005] 1 WLR 2082, only partially redeemed on appeal: [2006] UKHL 28; [2007] 1 AC 181.

[76] [2006] UKHL 49; [2007] 1 AC 558 [155].

[77] Ibid, [21]. See too *Sempra Metals Ltd v IRC* [2007] UKHL 34, [2007] 3 WLR 354, [23]–[25], where Lord Hope states it to be necessary to show an 'unjust factor'.

[78] *Kleinwort Benson Ltd v Birmingham CC* [1996] 4 All ER 733, 737 (Evans LJ).

[79] *Uren v First National Home Finance Ltd* [2005] EWHC 2529, [16]–[18] (Mann J).

[80] [1993] AC 70; see para 18.155. See especially Lord Goff's comments at 172, though contrast Lord Browne-Wilkinson's remarks at 197. Support for a bold approach can also be derived from *Westdeutsche Landesbank Girozentrale v Islington LBC* [1996] AC 669, 691 and 722, and *Kleinwort Benson v Lincoln CC* [1999] 1 AC 221, 372 and 393.

The unjust factors now known to English law divide into two classes. In one the **18.45**
reason for restitution reduces to the conclusion that the claimant did not mean to
part with the value in question. The varieties of that species are simply the different circumstances which prima facie support the assertion, 'I did not mean him to
have it.' The law then has to take its stance on each, allowing for any countervailing interest which competes with the claimant's interest in obtaining restitution.
The other class is residual—reasons for restitution which are not reducible to 'I
did not mean him to have it.'

E. Unjust: Deficient Intent

(1) No Intent

The strongest example of deficient intent is no intent at all. Sometimes wealth **18.46**
moves from C to D in circumstances in which C can say unequivocally that he had
no intent that D should receive it. C may be unaware of the haemorrhage, as
where D is a pickpocket and escapes with C's wallet. Or C may be aware but helpless, as where he sees D break into his car but is too far away to do anything about
it. Or C may be neither unaware nor helpless, as where he prefers to abstain from
violence and verbally, but in vain, prohibits D from taking the money. No intent
thus includes ignorance, helplessness, and flatly contrary intent.

(a) Common law

The common law allows an enrichment so obtained by D to be recovered by **18.47**
C, exactly as the amount of a mistaken payment can be recovered. In *Lipkin
Gorman v Karpnale Ltd*,[81] the very case in which the language of unjust enrichment first gained admittance to English law, a solicitor addicted to gambling took
hundreds of thousands of pounds from his firm's client account. He gambled
it away in the casino at the Playboy Club in Park Lane. The House of Lords held
that the club was under an obligation to repay the amount received, less its consequential payments out.[82] Although the proprietary relations were in fact more
complex, the model which their Lordships applied was that in which X finds C's
money and gives it to D. The club was in the same position as a donee from a
finder. It could not rely on its having given value in good faith, not because it had
not acted in good faith but because, gambling contracts being void even when

---

[81] (1991) 2 AC 548, HL, cf *Clarke v Shee and Johnson* (1774) 1 Cowp 197, 98 ER 1041; *Marsh
v Keating* (1834) 1 Bing NC 198, 131 ER 1094.
[82] See para 18.227.

lawful, there was no legal nexus between the money received and any value that might have been given.[83]

18.48 In many cases where C has no intent whatever that D shall receive, though not in the *Lipkin Gorman* case itself, property will not pass to D: C's original property right will persist in the money as it comes into the hand of the defendant. A very fundamental mistake will produce the same consequence.[84] If it were possible for C directly to assert that surviving proprietary right, and if he then chose to do so, his claim would not be based on unjust enrichment but on the event through which he acquired that property right. The common law knows no such claim, not even where the *res* in question remains identifiably in the defendant's hands.[85] An event of this kind therefore merely generates new rights in tort and unjust enrichment, between which the claimant must choose. If C chooses to sue in unjust enrichment, he will lose his property right,[86] just as he will if he sues in tort.[87]

18.49 It might reasonably be asked whether the restitutionary right seen in this situation is not parasitic upon the wrong of conversion. It would then be an example of restitution for that wrong rather than of unjust enrichment. It is not. In *Trustee of the Property of FC Jones & Son (a firm) v Jones*[88] the Court of Appeal allowed the trustee to recover not only money which had passed to the defendant without his knowledge but also the traceable product of its successful investment. At no point did the court suggest that it was necessary to show that the defendant had committed conversion. Moreover, in the *Lipkin Gorman* case it is clear that the club had never converted the firm's money.[89]

(b) Equity

18.50 All the cases above suppose a claimant entitled at law to the asset which passes from him absolutely without any intent on his part that it should. The liability is strict, subject to defences, just as in the case of mistaken payments. In equity

---

[83] See para 18.249.

[84] *Cundy v Lindsay* (1878) 3 App Cas 459; *Shogun Finance Ltd v Hudson* [2003] UKHL 62; [2004] 1 AC 919. Robert Goff J recognized the same possibility in relation to mistaken payments of money in *Barclays Bank Ltd v W & J Simms Son and Cooke (Southern) Ltd* [1980] QB 677, 689.

[85] Rare in money cases, but see *Moffatt v Kazana* [1968] 3 All ER 271 (money had and received for a biscuit tin full of banknotes which had been left behind when the owner moved house).

[86] Insufficiently emphasized in P Birks, 'Property and Unjust Enrichment: Categorical Truths' [1997] NZ L Rev 623, 654–6.

[87] Torts (Interference with Goods) Act 1977, s 5. In tort the relevant moment at which C's title is extinguished is when D pays the damages. An inference can be indirectly drawn from *United Australia Ltd v Barclays Bank Ltd* [1941] AC 1, HL that the same should be said of unjust enrichment. Although their Lordships contemplated only restitution for wrongs, this is presumably so.

[88] [1997] Ch 159, CA.

[89] [1991] 2 AC 548, 573, HL.

exactly the same results are reached where the claimant is entitled by way of succession to a deceased person and the deceased's personal representatives transfer to recipients who have no entitlement to receive.[90] However, if the equitable entitlement arises entirely *inter vivos*, as under an ordinary express trust, the recipient, though a donee, is said to incur no personal liability unless he was at fault. The cases are divided on the degree of fault which must be established against him, but although some insist on dishonesty,[91] the stronger authorities say that less will suffice.[92]

However, an occasional *inter vivos* case has accepted strict personal liability,[93] and subrogation has also been awarded without proof of fault to claimants whose money has been used without their knowledge or consent to pay off a charge on a defendant's property.[94] These cases must be right. Now that the defence of change of position has been recognized, the fault requirement is indefensible.[95] Equitable interests are indeed sometimes treated differently from legal interests,[96] but here there is not only asymmetry between law and equity but contradiction within equity. More importantly the requirement of fault is wrong in principle. Translated to mistaken payments it would result in an innocent mistaken payee's being allowed to retain an unintended enrichment even if he had not changed his position, so that his assets remained swollen. That is precisely the case in which strict liability produces the only acceptable outcome. What cannot be tolerated in

18.51

---

[90] *Ministry of Health v Simpson* [1951] AC 251, HL, affirming *Re Diplock* [1948] Ch 465, CA. Lionel Smith, 'Three-Party Restitution: A Critique of Birks's Theory of Interceptive Subtraction' (1991) 11 OJLS 481 points out that the claimants had no proprietary entitlement in the fund in the hands of the executors. It is not clear that the courts took that into account. They certainly accorded them not only personal restitutionary rights against the wrongly paid recipients but also proprietary restitutionary rights in the money received and its traceable proceeds. The latter would be difficult to explain if the claimants were contemplated as having no proprietary base.

[91] eg *Re Montagu's Settlement Trusts* [1987] Ch 264.

[92] *Belmont Finance Corp v Williams Furniture Ltd (No 2)* [1980] 1 All ER 399, 405, CA; *Houghton v Fayers* [2000] 1 BCLC 511, CA; *Bank of Credit and Commerce International (Overseas) Ltd v Akindele* [2001] Ch 437, CA (expressing this conclusion in the unhelpful language of 'unconscionability').

[93] eg *GL Baker Ltd v Medway Building & Supplies Ltd* [1958] 2 All ER 532; [1958] 3 All ER 540.

[94] *McCullough v Marsden* (1919) 45 DLR 645, Alberta CA (father); *Scotlife Homes (No 2) Ltd v Melinek* (1999) 78 P & CR 389, CA (wife); *Gertsch v Atsas* [1999] NSWSC 898 (legatee); *Primlake Ltd (in liq) v Matthews Associates* [2006] EWHC 1227, [2007] 1 BCLC 666 (Ch) (wife).

[95] The minority view has been greatly strengthened by Lord Nicholls, 'Knowing Receipt: The Need for a New Landmark' in WR Cornish et al (eds), *Restitution Past, Present and Future* (Oxford: Hart, 1998) 231, and Lord Walker, 'Dishonesty and Unconscionable Conduct in Commercial Life' (2005) 27 Sydney LR 187, 202. See also Lord Millett's obiter dicta in *Twinsectra Ltd v Yardley* [2002] UKHL 12; [2002] 2 AC 164, [105], and *Dubai Aluminium Co Ltd v Salaam* [2002] UKHL 48; [2003] 2 AC 366, [87].

[96] As stressed in LD Smith, 'Unjust Enrichment, Property, and the Structure of Trusts' (2000) 116 LQR 412, arguing against strict liability.

one who receives by mistake cannot be tolerated in one who receives without the claimant's knowledge or otherwise absolutely without his consent.[97]

(2) Impaired Intent

18.52 In this category the transferor forms an intent to transfer and executes that transfer but the decision-making process is impaired. The impairments commonly fall into one of the following categories: mistake, pressure, relational dependence, personal disadvantage, or transactional disadvantage.

(a) Two recurrent problems

18.53 Two problems which recur in the law's handling of these impairments merit some preliminary consideration. One relates to causation; the other to the role, if any, of superadded requirements, often of fault on the part of the enriched recipient. Both reflect tensions at the heart of the law of unjust enrichment—the constant anxiety that liberal restitution might unacceptably disturb the security of receipts and the need, in some cases, to inhibit the right to restitution in order to protect countervailing interests which have nothing to do with security of receipts.

(i) Causation

18.54 It is broadly true that the impairment must have caused the transfer. In some cases the issue is hidden by presumptions. When it is not, the requirement seems in general to be no more than that the impairing factor must have entered into the decision to transfer. It need not have been the decisive or determining cause.[98] A test of the latter kind is virtually impossible to apply, since most human decision-making proceeds on multiple variables.

18.55 In relation to spontaneous mistakes, the causal test asks for something more: in this case, it must be shown that the claimant would not have transferred the benefit but for his mistake.[99] We will see below that there has been a welcome liberalization of the test for identifying a restitution-yielding mistake, leaving it to the defence of change of position to protect the security of receipts. The stiffer

---

[97] Cf *Farah Constructions Pty Ltd v Say-Dee Pty Ltd* [2007] HCA 22; (2007) 81 ALJR 1107, [150] and [154]–[155], where the court failed to address the argument that strict liability in 'no intent' cases follows a fortiori from strict liability in 'deficient intent' cases.

[98] Misrepresentation: *Edgington v Fitzmaurice* (1885) 29 Ch D 459; duress: *Barton v Armstrong* [1976] AC 104, 119, 121, PC; cf *Alf Vaughan & Co Ltd (in administrative receivership) v Royscot Trust plc* [1999] 1 All ER (Comm) 856; non-disclosure: *Pan Atlantic Insurance Co Ltd v Pine Top Insurance Co Ltd* [1995] 1 AC 501, 538, HL.

[99] *Kleinwort Benson Ltd v Lincoln CC* [1999] 2 AC 349, 408, HL; *Dextra Bank & Trust Co Ltd v Bank of Jamaica* [2001] UKPC 50; [2002] 1 All ER (Comm) 193 [28]; *Deutsche Morgan Grenfell plc v IRC* [2006] UKHL 49; [2007] 1 AC 558, [59]–[60], [84], and [143].

causal test reflects the suspicion that the liberalization may have left more work to the defence of change of position than it can cope with.

(ii) Requirements of fault and other inhibitions of the right to restitution

Unless a very good reason exists to the contrary, every claim in unjust enrichment is vulnerable to the defence of change of position.[100] Subject to that and other defences, liability is strict. This means that, until he has changed his position, even the totally innocent recipient has no ground for suggesting that he should keep the enrichment. In general therefore fault only becomes relevant in deciding who should be disqualified from pleading change of position or another defence.   **18.56**

Where, however, the conclusion is that in relation to the particular unjust factor the defence does not sufficiently protect the interest in security of receipts, and where there are different countervailing interests in play which that defence cannot protect, the right to restitution can be restricted by imposing additional factual requirements.   **18.57**

We have seen that one possible restriction is a stiffer causal test. Another which lies to hand is a requirement that the transfer made by the claimant be manifestly disadvantageous or improvident. Yet another is to refuse restitution unless the defendant can be shown to have known of the impairment or, one step higher, to have knowingly exploited it. For example, dementia being chiefly an affliction of old age, the interest in maintaining the credit and dignity of the elderly conflicts with the interest in undoing transactions on that ground. A liberal regime of restitution on proof of dementia alone would drive all old people to obtaining medical certificates and written consents from their children before making any significant disposition. English law chooses to reconcile this conflict by restricting restitution for dementia to the relatively rare case in which the want of understanding was apparent to the other party at the time. It regards as insufficient a simple restriction of relief to cases of evident improvidence.[101]   **18.58**

Wherever a requirement of knowledge or knowing exploitation is imposed it is tempting to understand the relief given as based on the unconscientious behaviour of the recipient. However, it is safer not to create a separate category of that kind. Otherwise it is easily overlooked that another time, or another system, might reconcile the competing interests through a restrictive requirement having nothing to do with the knowledge or fault of the recipient.[102] The relief is given on the ground of the impairment. The competing interest requires a restriction. The chosen restriction happens to be a superadded requirement of knowledge.   **18.59**

---

100 See para 18.223, but note the discussion of special cases at paras 18.239–18.241.
101 *Hart v O'Connor* [1985] AC 1000, PC.
102 As New Zealand tried to do in *Archer v Cutler* [1980] 1 NZLR 386, NZCA.

There is no case in the law of unjust enrichment where restitution rests on unconscientious receipt absolutely independently of non-voluntariness on the part of the transferor.[103]

18.60 English law does not debar careless claimants from recovery.[104] Although momentarily counter-intuitive, strict liability is both correct and necessary against one who is still enriched at the claimant's expense. Carelessness on the part of a mistaken payer gives the recipient no better claim to keep what he was never intended to have, although the position is different where a payer consciously takes a risk that he might be wrong.[105]

(b) Five species of impairment

(i) Mistake

18.61 Recent years have seen a radical reinterpretation of the law in this area. *Kelly v Solari*[106] exemplifies the way things previously stood. Mr Solari died. He had insured his life. His widow, as his executrix, claimed under the policy and was paid. The insurer later discovered that the policy had lapsed before Mr Solari's death. Mr Solari had omitted to pay a premium. The policy had been marked 'lapsed'. The office overlooked this fact. The insurer recovered. At the time the crucial elements were that the claimant could show that he had been mistaken as to fact, not law, and that the mistake had given him the impression that he was under a legal liability. Neither is now required.

18.62 **Mistakes of law.** From the early nineteenth century onwards the English courts consistently denied restitution for mistake of law, but in *Kleinwort Benson Ltd v Lincoln CC*[107] the mistake of law bar was removed. The parties had entered an interest rate swap contract under which payments had been made for the full term of the contract in the belief that the contract was valid. Subsequently it was declared in an unconnected case, *Hazell v Hammersmith & Fulham BC,*[108]

---

[103] Contrary to P Birks, 'In Defence of Free Acceptance' in A Burrows (ed), *Essays in the Law of Restitution* (1991) 105. 'Unconscientiousness' here means blameworthiness at the time of the receipt, not to be confused with the inert conclusory form of 'unconscientiousness' encountered in the sentence 'It is unconscientious to retain a mistaken payment.' Here the reason why the payment has to be returned is that it was transferred by mistake, and what conscience dictates is that the recipient honour the strict liability so created.

[104] *Kelly v Solari* (1841) 9 M & W 54, 59; 152 ER 24, 26. See too *Banque Financière de la Cité v Parc (Battersea) Ltd* [1999] 1 AC 221, 227 and 235, HL; *Dextra Bank and Trust Co Ltd v Bank of Jamaica* [2001] UKPC 50; [2002] 1 All ER (Comm) 193, [45],

[105] ibid. See too *Deutsche Morgan Grenfell plc v IRC* [2006] UKHL 49; [2007] 1 AC 558, [26], clarifying *Kleinwort Benson Ltd v Lincoln CC* [1999] 2 AC 349, 410, HL, and *Brennan v Bolt Burdon (a firm)* [2004] EWCA 1017; [2005] QB 303, [21]–[22], [38]–[40].

[106] (1841) 9 M&W 54, 152 ER 24.

[107] [1999] 2 AC 349, HL.

[108] [1992] 2 AC 1, HL.

that statutory local authorities do not have the power to enter such contracts. The claimant bank therefore sought to recover its payments from the defendant local authority. To take advantage of the Limitation Act 1980, section 32(1)(c),[109] the bank framed its action as a claim in mistake, arguing that it had mistakenly believed the parties' contract to be valid when it had been void. Since any such mistake must have been a mistake of law, the bank had to argue for the removal of the bar against recovery on this ground.

It had previously been assumed that the bar was a necessary restriction on recovery for mistake, because mistakes of law would be very common and easily fabricated, also because of serious anxieties as to the possibility that interpretative development of the law would from time to time release clouds of restitutionary claims. However the House of Lords in the *Lincoln* case judged these fears to be unfounded. The court went very far. If impairment supposes wrong data fed into the decision-making process, their Lordships may even have allowed mistake entirely to escape that category. For here the only data which could falsify the belief by virtue of which the payment was made came into existence after it was made, in the form of the decision in *Hazell*. Their Lordships also accepted the notion of a retrospective mistake, holding that even where liability to make a payment has been established by judicial decision, parties who pay in line with this decision can recover on the ground of mistake if this decision is overruled.[110] **18.63**

Subsequent authorities confirm that both of these findings are problematic. In *Dextra Bank and Trust Co Ltd v Bank of Jamaica*,[111] the Privy Council emphasized the distinction between mistakes relating to presently verifiable facts (which give rise to a claim in unjust enrichment) and mispredictions concerning future events that cannot be verified (which do not). The court may have misapplied this principle to deny recovery on the facts, which were little different from *RE Jones Ltd v Waring & Gillow Ltd*,[112] where recovery was allowed. Nevertheless its clear statement that mispredictions do not generate rights in unjust enrichment undermines the *Lincoln* case, where the claimant's belief that the parties' contract was valid could not have been falsified other than by reference to a case decided subsequently. Hence there can have been no impairment but only an exercise of judgment that turned out to be incorrect. **18.64**

In *Deutsche Morgan Grenfell plc v IRC*,[113] money was paid as tax under a statutory regime, parts of which were later held by the European Court of Justice to have infringed the EC Treaty. The House of Lords held that the claimant could bring a **18.65**

---

[109] Discussed at paras 18.274–18.275.
[110] [1999] 2 AC 349, 378–80 (Lord Goff), and 400–1 (Lord Hoffmann), HL.
[111] [2001] UKPC 50, [2002] 1 All ER (Comm) 193.
[112] [1926] AC 670, HL.
[113] [2006] UKHL 49; [2007] 1 AC 558.

claim founded on mistake of law,[114] and retrospectively deemed the claimant to have made such a mistake in line with the *Lincoln* case.[115] As Park J recognized at first instance, however, retrospective mistakes of this kind cannot be said to have caused a claimant's payment on a 'but-for' basis unless others are also deemed to have made the same mistake.[116] Otherwise, when the causative effect of the claimant's mistake is tested by posing the counter-factual question, 'Would the claimant have paid if he had known the true state of the law?', a positive answer must be given, because the defendant would have met the claimant's failure to pay by successfully suing to enforce his legal rights. In other words, it does the claimant no good for the court to imagine that he alone knew the 'true' state of the law when he made his payment, for the defendant and the courts would only have let him withhold payment if they had known it too. This reinforces the view that retrospective mistakes of the kind recognized in *Lincoln* and *DMG* are fictional, and have nothing to do with the impairment of a claimant's actual thought processes.[117]

18.66 **Causative mistakes, and three exceptions.** In 1980 the great judgment of Robert Goff J in *Barclays Bank Ltd v W & J Simms Son and Cooke (Southern) Ltd*[118] showed that the requirement of a liability mistake produced arbitrary consequences and was not unequivocally supported in the cases. The bank had paid a stopped cheque, overlooking the stop. He held that the reason why it could recover from its immediate payee, a creditor of its customer, was not that it had contemplated itself as liable to its customer to make the payment to the creditor, but, more simply, because it had made a mistake which caused the payment.

18.67 The judgment in the *Simms* case acknowledged that the liberalization of the test required certain principled exceptions.[119] One was that claims must fall to the defence of change of position, something not fully achieved till a decade later.[120]

---

114 Overturning the CA's decision that the claimant could not rely on mistake because it could only rely on the ground of recovery recognized in *Woolwich Equitable BS v IRC* [1993] AC 70. This is discussed at paras 18.158–18.159.

115 [2006] UKHL 49; [2007] 1 AC 558, [23].

116 [2003] EWHC 1779, [2003] STC 1017 [25], holding that recovery could only be allowed by assuming that 'if the true state of the law had been understood, both DMG and the Revenue would have understood it'. This is only implicitly recognized in Lord Hoffmann's statement at [2006] UKHL 49; [2007] 1 AC 558, [32], that the claimant would 'undoubtedly' have taken steps to avoid paying, had it known that it was entitled to do so.

117 Like the claimant in *Lincoln*, the claimant in *DMG* framed its claim in mistake in order to take advantage of the Limitation Act 1980, s 32(1)(c) (see para 18.275).

118 [1980] QB 677.

119 Ibid, 695.

120 In *Lipkin Gorman v Karpnale Ltd* [1991] 2 AC 548, HL; see paras 18.222–18.241.

Next, there could be no recovery when a claimant did indeed have a wrong view of some matter but paid without regard to its truth or falsity, deliberately waiving inquiry. That is arguably not an exception, since such a finding, necessarily rare, will almost certainly indicate that the mistake did not cause the payment.

18.68 Robert Goff J's third exception is more difficult: had the bank's mistake left intact the customer's authority to pay, the bank could not have recovered. Thus, if its causative mistake had led it to suppose that the customer's account was in substantial credit when in fact it was not, it could not have recovered from its payee. This has since been confirmed by the Court of Appeal in *Lloyds Bank plc v Independent Insurance Co Ltd*.[121] Robert Goff J grounded this exception on a general proposition to the effect that a mistaken payer could not recover if he received good consideration for his payment. A bank, however mistaken, did receive good consideration if it paid with the customer's authority, since such a payment would secure the discharge for which it paid. Yet, since the result would almost certainly be the same if the payee were a donee from the customer, a safer explanation may be that, having dealt validly with the customer, the bank must bear the risk of his insolvency and must not seek to leapfrog the customer to reach the payee remotely enriched at his expense.[122]

18.69 The exception framed to exclude restitution for causative mistake where the payer has received good consideration still has a role if understood as a reaffirmation of the law's determination not to allow restitution of unjust enrichment to undermine or outflank the risks inherent in entering a valid contract.[123] Bargaining is a dangerous business, and the law takes the view that in general those who bargain take the risk of being mistaken. Thus a mistake will not generally destroy a contract unless it relates to an essential matter right outside the legitimate hopes and fears inherent in the bargain.[124]

18.70 Given that a merely causative mistake will not entitle a disappointed party to restitution unless it also destroys the contract, the general test for an operative mistake in all situations is that the mistake must be, first, causative and, secondly, such that relief will not disturb the risks inherent in any transaction between the

---

[121] [2000] 1 QB 110, CA.

[122] See paras 18.32–18.34.

[123] K Barker, 'Bona Fide Purchase as a Defence to Unjust Enrichment Claims' [1999] Restitution L Rev 75, 89.

[124] *Bell v Lever Brothers Ltd* [1932] AC 6, HL is the classic case of a 'but for' mistake leading to a claim for restitution of money received. Lever paid golden handshakes to executives whom it later found it could have dismissed out of hand. But contracts had been made to get rid of them quickly, and Lever in being denied restitution was quite rightly made to bear the risks inherent in those bargains.

parties. In a non-bargaining situation, such as a discharge or a gift, risks are rarely run, so that only the first limb seems to be in play.[125]

18.71 Difficult as it is to determine what risks are and are not inherent in any given bargain, two propositions are secure. First, the law does not require a party to bear the risk of mistakes induced by the misrepresentation of the other, however innocent.[126] Secondly, the law relieves a party of the risk of a mistake where and so far as the other is under a duty to disclose. Insurance is one such case, another is a contract between a fiduciary and the person relying on him.[127] Where there is a duty to disclose, non-disclosure, like misrepresentation, entitles the mistaken party to rescind and recover value transferred.[128]

(ii) Pressure

18.72 Pressure is sometimes litigated as duress and sometimes as undue influence. This bifurcation derives from the narrowness of the original common law concept of duress, which required threats to the body or to goods. This was supplemented from equity under a different name. Undue influence occurs where autonomy is impaired by either relational dependence or pressure.[129]

18.73 **Illegitimate pressure.** Pressures endemic in ordinary life do not impair autonomy. They define the obstacles through which free will has to pick its way. Decisions are only impaired when made under a pressure which is alien to society. The line is somewhat softer than that between lawful and unlawful.[130] Hence a payment made in response to an illegitimate pressure applied by another is recoverable. On the other side of the line, examples of legitimate pressures are a bona fide threat to sue[131] and a refusal to supply goods or credit in the absence of

---

[125] This is true even of voluntary deeds: *Re Butlin's Settlement Trusts* [1976] Ch 251; *Gibbon v Mitchell* [1990] 1 WLR 1304.

[126] *Redgrave v Hurd* (1881) 20 Ch D 1, CA; *Adam v Newbigging* (1888) 13 App Cas 308. A mistake induced by the misrepresentation of a third party is treated as spontaneous, unless the other has notice of the misrepresentation: *Barclays Bank plc v O'Brien* [1994] 1 AC 180, HL.

[127] Non-disclosure in insurance cases is an unjust factor, not a wrong which supports a claim for damages: *Banque Keyser Ullmann SA v Skandia Insurance Ltd* [1990] 1 QB 665, CA, affirmed on other grounds [1991] 2 AC 249, and reaffirmed *HIH Casualty and General Insurance Ltd v Chase Manhattan Bank* [2003] UKHL 6; [2003] 1 All ER (Comm) 349, [75].

[128] *Sybron Corporation v Rochem Ltd* [1984] Ch 112, where an executive taking a severance package had failed to disclose the wrongdoing and was held to have been bound to disclose, not his own, but colleagues' and subordinates' misdeeds.

[129] Examples of the latter are *Williams v Bayley* (1866) LR 1 HL 200; *Mutual Finance Co Ltd v Wetton and Sons Ltd* [1937] 2 KB 389; *Drew v Daniel* [2005] EWCA 507; [2005] 2 FCR 365. These are only historically separated from duress cases such as *Maskell v Horner* [1915] 3 KB 106 and *Barton v Armstrong* [1976] AC 104, PC.

[130] *Universe Tankships v ITWF (The Universe Sentinel)* [1983] AC 366, 385, HL; *Dimskal Shipping Co SA v ITWF (The Evia Luck)* [1992] 2 AC 152, 169, HL.

[131] *Marriot v Hampton* (1797) 7 TR 267, 101 ER 769; *Unwin v Leaper* (1840) 1 Man & Gr 747, 133 ER 533; *Goodall v Lowndes* (1844) 6 QB 464, 115 ER 173.

a contract to do so.[132] Pressure which is illegitimate does not become legitimate because the person applying it honestly thought he was entitled to do so. If I threaten to take or retain possession of your goods, it is no good my saying I mistakenly thought I had a right to do so.[133]

A well-known judgment of Oliver Wendell Holmes J not only underlines the **18.74** principle that pressure must be illegitimate but need not be unlawful, but also repudiates the notion that the effect of pressure is to be judged by an objective standard.[134] There a wife recovered money levied under a security extracted from her by threats to tell her husband of her son's alleged thefts.

The countervailing interest in renegotiation.   In cases in which the illegitimate   **18.75** pressure is a threat to break a contract, sometimes called 'economic duress', the law has run into trouble in resolving the tension between the sanctity of the binding contract and the general interest encouraging and upholding renegotiation to avoid a total collapse. If money obtained by a threat to break a contract were always recoverable there would be little room for renegotiation in any case in which the initiative came from the likely contract breaker.[135] Some cases in this context have therefore sought to restrict restitution by stiffening the causal test, requiring an overbearing of the will.[136] Since a test of that kind is almost impossible to apply, the countervailing interest may ultimately elicit an openly fault-based restriction.[137] A requirement of bad faith would put the claimant to the proof of opportunistic exploitation of his commercial vulnerability.[138]

---

[132]   *Smith v William Charlick* (1924) 34 CLR 38; more hesitant: *CTN Cash and Carry Ltd v Gallaher* [1994] 4 All ER 714, CA. Sometimes no more than lip service is paid to the difference between 'illegitimate' and 'unlawful': *Alf Vaughan & Co Ltd v Royscot Trust plc* [1999] 1 All ER (Comm) 856.

[133]   *Maskell v Horner* [1915] 3 KB 106; *Mason v NSW* (1959) 102 CLR 108.

[134]   *Silsbee v Webber* 171 Mass 378, 50 NE 555 (1898) Supreme Ct of Massachusetts; cf RJ Pothier (tr WD Evans), *Treatise on the Law of Obligations* (1806) vol 1, 18.

[135]   *Williams v Roffey Bros & Nicholls (Contractors) Ltd* [1991] 1 QB 1, CA, itself the rarer case in which the initiative in renegotiating the price comes from the client who would have to pay it, recognized the interest in renegotiation in its reinterpretation of the law on sufficiency of consideration.

[136]   *The Siboen and The Sibotre* [1976] 1 Lloyd's Rep 293, 335–6; *Pao On v Lau Yiu Long* [1980] AC 614, 636, PC. In *Huyton SA v Peter Cremer GmbH & Co* [1999] 1 Lloyd's Rep 620, Mance J said that a 'but-for' causal test was appropriate for cases of economic duress with the burden of proof on the party seeking to set the transaction aside. This too requires more than the 'a factor' test.

[137]   See paras 18.58–18.59.

[138]   Pointing that way: *B & S Contracts and Design Ltd v Victor Green Publications Ltd* [1984] ICR 419; *D & C Builders Ltd v Rees* (1966) 2 QB 617. The *Huyton* case (n 136) is to the contrary. *DSND Subsea Ltd v Petroleum Geo-Services ASA* [2000] BLR 530 suggests that a basket of factors must be taken into consideration when deciding whether withholding a contractual right amounts to illegitimate pressure.

(iii) Relational dependence

18.76 Within a particular relationship one party's autonomy may be compromised by extreme dependence on the other. He may then be unable to exercise independent judgment when asked to enter a transaction, with the result that a claim may lie to set the transaction aside on the ground of undue influence. In *Royal Bank of Scotland v Etridge (No 2)*[139] Lord Nicholls explained that two types of evidence might lead a court to conclude that a claimant lacked autonomy because he was unduly influenced by another person: evidence of pressure and evidence of relational dependence. He also described undue influence in terms which would make it an equitable wrong, speaking of it as an 'unacceptable' form of persuasion, and an 'improper' means of causing the claimant to act, which took in 'cases where a vulnerable person has been exploited'.[140] Since then the Privy Council has twice taken the same line.[141] However the undesirable effect of these decisions is to narrow the range of undue influence to pressure, bullying, and abuse. Undue influence has not historically been understood as a wrong, and the better approach, taken in a number of contrary cases in the Court of Appeal, is to treat undue influence as too much influence, impairing the autonomy of the weaker party.[142]

18.77 **Evidential presumptions.** A claimant who relies on evidence of relational dependence to make out a claim of undue influence can invoke the help of a presumption in cases where he has entered a transaction that is not 'readily explicable by the relationship of the parties'.[143] He will be presumed to lack autonomy where he is in a nominate relationship, such as solicitor/client, doctor/patient, priest/parishioner (or equivalent religious relationship), parent/child, and fiduciary/principal. Otherwise, he must prove that the continuing quality of the relationship was such that his autonomy was compromised generally or with regard to a particular class of transaction.[144] The relationship between spouses is not one in

---

[139] [2001] UKHL 44; [2002] 2 AC 773. See paras 8.204–8.209.

[140] Ibid, [7] and [11].

[141] *R v A-G for England and Wales* [2003] UKPC 22, [2003] EMLR 24; *National Commercial Bank (Jamaica) Ltd v Hew* [2003] UKPC 51.

[142] *Hammond v Osborn* [2002] EWCA 885; [2002] WTLR 1125 [14]; *Niersmans v Pesticcio* [2004] EWCA 372 [20]; *Goodchild v Bradbury* [2006] EWCA 1868; [2007] WTLR 463, [27]. All looking back to *Allcard v Skinner* (1887) 36 Ch D 145, CA, discussed in C Smith '*Allcard v Skinner*' in C Mitchell and P Mitchell (eds) *Landmark Cases in the Law of Restitution* (2006) 183.

[143] *Royal Bank of Scotland v Etridge (No 2)* [2001] UKHL 44; [2002] 2 AC 773, [21]. Lord Nicholls intended this terminology to replace the language of 'manifest disadvantage' deriving from Lord Scarman's speech in *National Westminster Bank v Morgan* [1985] AC 686, 703–7, which had come to be misunderstood. The key question is not whether the transaction leaves the party seeking relief any worse off, but whether his decision to enter the transaction is obviously attributable to the ordinary motives of an ordinary person.

[144] *Barclays Bank plc v O'Brien* [1994] AC 180, 189, HL. It was also said in *O'Brien* that once a want of autonomy was established a further presumption would be made, that this caused the

which the presumption automatically arises, but it is one in which it appears to be relatively easy to establish that in the particular case one habitually exercised undue influence over the other.[145] The presumptions are rebuttable by affirmative evidence that the transferor acted autonomously in making the transfer, as where he was emancipated from his dependence by independent advice.

(iv) Personal disadvantage

An open-ended list of handicaps. 'If the party is in a situation, in which he is **18.78** not a *free agent*, and is not *equal to protecting himself*, this Court will protect him.'[146] A transfer may be attributable to some personal handicap which permanently or temporarily compromises the transferor's capacity to manage his own affairs. Two well-established cases are easily identified, namely the immaturity of the young[147] and mental illness or decline.[148] Inebriation might be said to be a transient species of the latter.[149] However, relief which the Chancery sparingly extended to the 'ignorant and poor'[150] has in modern times been extended to include numerous shades of special personal vulnerability impairing the autonomy ascribed to the typical adult. If some examples from the Commonwealth are included, the list comprises relational inequality falling short of undue influence,[151] serious stress, as for instance in the midst of a divorce,[152] social and educational deprivation,[153] imperfect command of the language,[154] isolation from advisers usually relied upon,[155] and acute lovesickness.[156]

Restrictive requirements. In this area more than any other the courts proceed **18.79** cautiously and tend to insist on additional elements which restrict the incidence

---

party seeking relief to enter the relevant transaction. However it has since been held that this second presumption hardly merits the name, since the same conclusion would be expected to flow from the ordinary operation of the rules as to onus of proof: *Royal Bank of Scotland v Etridge (No 2)* [2001] UKHL 44; [2002] 2 AC 773, [14]–[18], [105]–[107], and [161].

145 In one particular context, namely the giving of domestic security for business borrowing, the pursuit of a protective policy has made this especially easy to establish: *Barclays Bank plc v O'Brien* [1994] AC 180, HL; *Royal Bank of Scotland v Etridge (No 2)* [2001] UKHL 44; [2002] 2 AC 773.

146 *Evans v Llewellin* (1787) 1 Cox 333, 340, 29 ER 1191, 1194 (Kenyon MR).

147 Under the Minors' Contracts Act 1987 a contract cannot be enforced against a minor but his right to recover value transferred is limited by, at least, a requirement of counter-restitution: *Valentini v Canali* (1889) 24 QBD 166; *Pearce v Brain* [1929] 2 KB 310.

148 *Hart v O'Connor* [1985] AC 1000, PC; *Williams v Williams* [2003] EWHC 742; cf *Ayres v Hazelgrove* (Russell J, 9 February 1984) and *Nichols v Jessup* [1986] 1 NZLR 159, NZCA.

149 *Matthews v Baxter* (1873) LR 8 Ex 132; *Blomley v Ryan* (1956) 99 CLR 362, HCA.

150 *Fry v Lane* (1888) 40 Ch D 312, 322.

151 *Crédit Lyonnais Bank Nederland NV v Burch* [1997] 1 All ER 144, CA.

152 *Creswell v Potter* [1978] 1 WLR 255; cf *Backhouse v Backhouse* [1978] 1 WLR 243.

153 *Fry v Lane* (1888) 40 Ch D 312; *Creswell v Potter* [1978] 1 WLR 255.

154 *Commercial Bank of Australia v Amadio* (1983) 151 CLR 447, HCA.

155 *Boustany v Pigott* [1993] EGCS 85, (1993) 42 West Indies R 175, PC.

156 *Louth v Diprose* (1992) 175 CLR 621, HCA.

of relief and limit it to facts which either justify an inference of actual exploitation of the weakness or, at least, show that the impairment has seriously prejudiced the vulnerable person. Such requirements might seem to justify treating all such cases as instances of unconscientious receipt or exploitation. The correct approach is, however, to take the handicaps one by one, to rest such relief as may be available firmly on the impairment which the handicap implies, and then to ask under what, if any, restrictions the cases indicate that relief can be allowed. Special countervailing interests aside,[157] some guidance is given by the proposition that the weaker or more common the impairment the more likely it is there will be no relief without evidence of blameworthy exploitation.

(v) Transactional disadvantage

18.80　The law has always identified some transactions as especially sensitive, in that parties, however autonomous in other contexts, cannot protect their own best interests through negotiation and contract. Either through statute or without statute it has taken measures to protect individuals who enter into such transactions by inter alia allowing them restitution of value transferred.

18.81　Credit and security have attracted this kind of intervention throughout the ages. Usury was long forbidden. The equity of redemption owes its origin to equity's intervention to protect mortgagors from the severe forfeiture entailed by the common law mortgage. Outside mortgages, relief is available when penalties are promised against non-performance or parties rashly agree to forfeit proprietary interests.[158] Nowadays a fiercely protective regime is developing in relation to all means of tapping the home and home life to fund business ventures.[159] Statutory protection for consumer credit is also in place.[160]

18.82　Other transactions catch people in desperate situations, where they have no room for manoeuvre. Market conditions have from time to time required would-be tenants to be protected from demands for premiums.[161] In insolvency those close to the debtor are protected from oppression by individual creditors seeking preferential treatment, but there the motivation is mixed and is clearly partly in the interest

---

[157] As for instance the dignity of the aged, para 18.58. By contrast minority attracts no such restrictive requirements.

[158] *Shiloh Spinners v Harding* [1973] AC 691, HL, considered in *On Demand plc v Gerson plc* [1999] 1 All ER (Comm) 512.

[159] The leading case is *Royal Bank of Scotland v Etridge (No 2)* [2001] UKHL 44; [2002] 2 AC 773, which effectively lays down a code of practice for lenders which is triggered whenever security for business borrowing is given by a person in a non-commercial relationship with the borrower. Only if they follow the code will lenders be insulated from undue influence and other vitiating factors arising between the borrower and the person giving security.

[160] Consumer Credit Act 1974, ss 140A-140D, inserted by the Consumer Credit Act 2006, ss 19–21 ('unfair relationships' between creditors and debtors).

[161] *Kiriri Cotton Co Ltd v Dewani* [1960] AC 192, PC.

of the other creditors.[162] The social conditions in which a woman needed protection from marriage broking have passed, but it is still formally the law that a woman who pays someone to procure a marriage is entitled to recover her payment.[163]

It is a matter for debate whether these instances of transactional disadvantage are **18.83** properly placed here as species of non-voluntariness or would be better considered below as examples of policy-motivated restitution, each dictated by its own species of protective policy. The argument for keeping them here is that the law intervenes because people who are otherwise autonomous lose their capacity for self-management when faced with transactions of this kind.

(3) Summary

Deficiently intended transfers include transfers which are not intended at all and **18.84** intended transfers in which the intention to transfer is impaired. The two subgroups touch in cases where the impairment is profound, as where the transferor acts under a very serious mistake or an extreme degree of pressure. In practice the commonest case of deficient intent, and in that sense the most important, is mistake, whether spontaneous or induced. In all cases the law is formed by the same forces. On the one hand the person under the impairment represents the interest in obtaining restitution. On the other hand opposing interests demand that the right to restitution be barred or restricted. The constant theme is therefore the search for a rational compromise based on a variety of restrictions which can be put on the right to restitution. The weaker and more endemic the impairment, the more such restrictions become necessary and the more they are likely to take the form of a requirement that the claimant show that he was knowingly exploited by the defendant.

F. Unjust: Qualified Intent

The model is provided by the great *Fibrosa* case.[164] Shortly before the outbreak of **18.85** the Second World War, a Polish company bought some machinery in England and paid for it in advance. With the German invasion of Poland, the contract was frustrated. The Polish company had received nothing for its money. The House of

---

[162] *Smith v Bromley* (1760) 2 Doug KB 696, 99 ER 441; *Smith v Cuff* (1817) 6 M&S 160, 105 ER 1203.

[163] *Hermann v Charlesworth* [1905] 2 KB 123.

[164] *Fibrosa Spolka Akcyjna v Fairbairn Lawson Combe Barbour* [1943] AC 32, HL.

Lords held that, suing through its officers in London, it had a right to restitution of the sum paid. The basis on which it had made its payment had failed.

18.86 Here the claimant does not rely on his having defectively intended the transfer. He points instead to its having been manifest *ab initio* that his intention to transfer was qualified. Such a qualification may be absolute but is usually conditional. An absolute qualification cannot be purged. As will be seen, absolute qualifications pose serious analytical problems.[165]

18.87 Where the qualification is conditional, the non-voluntary character of the transfer does not appear immediately from the qualification itself but from the fact that, as events turn out, the qualification is not purged. As Lord Wright put it in the *Fibrosa* case, when the basis of the transfer fails, the condition for the recipient's retaining the value fails too.[166] If the basis of the payment is the supply of machines, supply of the machines will purge the qualification; failure to supply renders the transfer non-voluntary.

(1) Conditional Qualifications: Terminology

18.88 Traditionally the common law has spoken of these transfers as 'made upon a consideration which happens to fail'[167] or simply of 'failure of consideration'.[168] This language carries the constant risk of being confused with, or tied to, the doctrine of consideration in the law of contract. The risk is exacerbated by the fact that in the English law of unjust enrichment the commonest failure of consideration is indeed the failure of contractual reciprocation. The *Fibrosa* model is such a case.

18.89 Lord Mansfield meant 'failure of consideration' to express in English the causative event which Roman law knew as *'causa data causa non secuta'*.[169] The Roman action of debt was called the *condictio*, and the *condictio causa data causa non secuta* was, half-translated, 'debt for things given upon a *causa*, that *causa* not following'. A central example was the giving of a dowry in contemplation of a marriage which

---

[165] Absolute qualifications are considered at paras 18.132 ff.

[166] *Fibrosa* (n 164) 65, HL.

[167] *Moses v Macferlan* (1760) 2 Burr 1005, 1013, 97 ER 676, 681.

[168] The *OED* shows that 'consideration' is first the act of thinking about or reflecting on something and then the matter so thought about or reflected upon, whence the reason or motive for action of some kind. The connection with the contractual doctrine is that, to make a promise binding, *quid pro quo* became the only kind of 'consideration' which could count.

[169] WD Evans (tr) *Pothier on Obligations*, vol II (London: Joseph Butterworth, 1806) 380 is unequivocal. Commenting on Lord Mansfield's words 'Or upon a consideration which happens to fail' he says 'The whole title in the digest *de Condictione Causa data, Causa, non secuta* [D.12.4], is an amplified view of this proposition.'

failed to happen.[170] The ground rule there was that the donor could bring the action of debt on the ground that the *causa* of his giving had not materialized. By '*causa*' the jurists meant 'reason' or 'basis'. If we abandon the attempt at literal translation, the *condictio causa data causa non secuta* becomes 'the action of debt where the ground of the indebtedness is that a transfer was made on a basis and that basis failed to hold good'.

Confusion between contract and unjust enrichment was largely responsible for the error which had to be corrected in the *Fibrosa* case.[171] The view had previously been taken that, if value had been transferred under a contract rendered binding within the terms of the doctrine of consideration, then, unless the contract was rescinded *ab initio*, it could never afterwards be said that there had been a failure of consideration.[172] The House of Lords said that was wrong. In general,[173] in the law of unjust enrichment the consideration for a pre-payment was not just the promise of the counter-performance but performance of that promise, and that consideration had failed.

18.90

In *Westdeutsche Landesbank Girozentrale v Islington LBC*[174] the same confusion resurfaced in an inverted form. Hobhouse J, faced with facts in which value had passed under a void interest rate swap contract, decided that, even where performance had been interrupted by the discovery of the contract's nullity, a claim in unjust enrichment for failure of consideration could not lie. Such a claim, in his view, could only be brought in respect of transfers made under an initially valid contract.[175] He therefore turned to an alternative unjust factor which he called 'absence of consideration'. In the higher courts 'absence of consideration' was not repudiated, but it was said that the claimant bank could have invoked failure of consideration as its ground for restitution.[176]

18.91

It is now indisputable that a restitutionary claim founded on failure of consideration is neither displaced where the transfer was made under an initially valid contract nor excluded where the transfer had no valid contractual matrix. But, in view of the history of error, a break has to be made with the old language. It will be much safer if the law of unjust enrichment leaves 'consideration' to the law of contract and speaks instead of failure of basis.

18.92

---

170 Ulpian, D.12.4.6.
171 [1943] AC 32, esp 52 (Lord Atkin), and 65 (Lord Wright), HL.
172 *Chandler v Webster* [1904] 1 KB 493, CA.
173 In some rare cases the basis for a transfer may still be the promise of counter-performance rather than the counter-performance itself: *Guinness Mahon v Kensington & Chelsea RLBC* [1999] QB 215, 226–7, CA, considering *Rover International Ltd v Cannon Film Sales Ltd* [1989] 1 WLR 912, 925, CA.
174 [1994] 4 All ER 890.
175 Ibid, 921–3.
176 [1994] 4 All ER 890, 960, CA (Dillon LJ); [1996] AC 669, 683 (Lord Goff).

18.93　For over two hundred years, until the latter part of the nineteenth century, English law gave the innocent party to a contract the right to 'rescind' the contract *ab initio* for breach by the other party, and required him to exercise this right before he could bring what would now be recognized as a claim in unjust enrichment to recover benefits conferred under the contract.[177] The rule that contracts can be 'retrospectively discharged' for breach no longer forms part of English law,[178] and as Lord Atkin held in the *Fibrosa* case, the right to recover money paid under a contract for a consideration that has subsequently failed does 'not depend on the contract being void ab initio'.[179] However, concerns remain that allowing a claim in unjust enrichment to recover benefits conferred under an initially valid contract would subvert the parties' contractual allocation of risk, suggesting that recovery should be permitted only to the extent that this would not contradict the terms of their bargain.[180]

18.94　A striking example of these principles is *Roxborough v Rothmans of Pall Mall (Australia) Ltd*,[181] where the High Court of Australia permitted the recovery of money paid under a contract which was neither rescinded nor terminated and which had been fully performed. The claimant retailers bought tobacco products at prices fixed to include payments of tax which both parties expected the defendant sellers to make to the NSW government, although the sellers did not promise to do so. The tax was then held to be unconstitutional and void, and the retailers were permitted to recover the tax element of the contract price. The court reasoned that the basis for this part of the payment was severable from the basis for the rest, that it had completely failed, and—significantly—that the parties had not bargained their way towards the amount of the tax element, but had proceeded on the basis that it had simply been fixed by statute.

(2) The Requirement of Total Failure

18.95　A restriction long placed on this cause of action was that the failure of consideration be total. The claimant would fail if he had received anything at all of what he

---

[177] *Dutch v Warren* (1720) 1 Stra 406, 93 ER 598, discussed in *Moses v Macferlan* (1760) 2 Burr 1005, 1010–1; 97 ER 676, 680; *Hochster v de la Tour* (1853) 2 E & B 678, 685; 118 ER 922, 924–5; and other cases cited in C Mitchell and C Mitchell 'Planché v Colburn' in C Mitchell and P Mitchell (eds) *Landmark Cases in the Law of Restitution* (2006) 65, 89–91.

[178] *Boston Deep Sea Fishing and Ice Co v Ansell* (1888) 39 Ch D 339, 365, CA; *Heyman v Darwins Ltd* [1942] AC 356, 399, HL; *Johnson v Agnew* [1980] AC 367, 393, HL.

[179] [1943] AC 32, 57.

[180] *Taylor v Motability Finance Ltd* [2004] EWHC 2619 [24]–[25] (Cooke J). See too G McMeel, 'Unjust Enrichment, Discharge for Breach, and the Primacy of Contract' in A Burrows and Lord Rodger (eds), *Mapping the Law* (2006) 223.

[181] (2001) 208 CLR 516, HCA.

paid for.[182] After years of manipulation,[183] the requirement of total failure seems now to have collapsed into the law relating to defences and, in most cases,[184] into the defence which makes counter-restitution a precondition of restitution.[185] In *Goss v Chilcott*[186] a loan had been made under a deed later rendered void by material alteration. The lenders claimed instead in unjust enrichment. The borrower objected that some money had been repaid. Lord Goff, giving the advice of the Privy Council, said that the claimant would not be barred merely because he had received something, so long as an allowance could satisfactorily be made for benefits he had received.[187] The series of cases on void interest swaps, exemplified by *Westdeutsche Landesbank Girozentrale v Islington LBC*,[188] all show, so far as they were decided on the ground of failure of consideration, that there is no need for a total failure. Under all these swaps each party had received from the other. When their nullity was discovered, the one who had to that point been winning had to make restitution, simply taking credit for the payments it had itself made.

In *Baltic Shipping Co v Dillon (The 'Mikhail Lermontov')*[189] the claimant sought **18.96** the return of the price paid for a luxury cruise which had come to an end when, eight days out, the liner sank off New Zealand. In rejecting her claim the High Court of Australia can easily be understood to have underlined and renewed the requirement of total failure. However, she needed to prove a total failure because she was insisting on a 100 per cent refund. She had already been given a rebate proportionate to the time lost.

(3) Three Types of Failure of Basis

The basis upon which a transfer is made may be (a) a contractual counter- **18.97** performance; (b) the coming about or continuation of some state of affairs; or

---

[182] *Hunt v Silk* (1804) 5 East 449, 102 ER 1142; *Whincup v Hughes* (1871) LR 6 CP 78 (contrast *Atwood v Maude* (1868) 3 Ch App 369); *Yeoman Credit v Apps* [1962] 2 QB 508, CA.

[183] As in *DO Ferguson & Associates v Sohl* (1992) 62 Building LR 95, CA in which the court said that there had been a total failure in respect of that part of a payment made to a builder for which the customer had not received money's worth.

[184] Some examples may possibly fall to be considered under change of position. *Stocznia Gdanska SA v Latvian Shipping Co* [1998] 1 WLR 574, HL might be such a case.

[185] Counter-restitution is dealt with below among defences, see paras 18.300–18.308.

[186] [1996] AC 788, PC. The need for this development was foreseen in E McKendrick, 'Total Failure of Consideration and Counter-Restitution: Two Issues or One?' in P Birks (ed), *Laundering and Tracing* (1995) 217; cf P Birks, 'Failure of Consideration' in FD Rose (ed), *Consensus ad Idem* (London, 1996) 179.

[187] [1996] AC 788, 798, PC; cf *Baltic Shipping Co v Dillon* (1993) 175 CLR 344, 353, HCA. Both accepted in *Ministry of Sound (Ireland) Ltd v World Online Ltd* [2003] EWHC 2178; [2003] 2 All ER (Comm) 823, [42] and [63]. However, caution is indicated: *Stocznia Gdanska SA v Latvian Shipping Co* [1998] 1 WLR 574.

[188] [1996] AC 669, HL.

[189] [1993] 176 CLR 344, HCA, noted K Barker [1993] LMCLQ 29.

(c) the application of the money or other matter transferred. There is an overlap between (a) and (c). Contractual obligations to apply the money or other matter transferred will be treated as belonging in (c).

(a) Failure of contractual counter-performance

18.98 Where value is transferred on the basis of a contractual counter-performance, failure to make the performance may then be due to (i) breach of contract by the enriched defendant; or (ii) breach by the claimant in unjust enrichment; or (iii) frustration of the contract; or (iv) discovery that the contract was void *ab initio*.

(i) Breach of contract by the enriched defendant

18.99 If the recipient of money paid in advance is in repudiatory breach of contract, the innocent party can terminate the contract and claim damages for the breach. In many cases it will be concurrently true, depending on the exercise of construction discussed below,[190] that the basis of his payment will have failed, so that he can also have recourse to the law of unjust enrichment to recover the payment.[191] The claim in unjust enrichment will clearly be preferable where the loss suffered is less than the sum paid.[192]

18.100 Even while the requirement of total failure remained in place, a series of cases held that a buyer who paid for goods and got them, but got no title, could use this claim. Since such a buyer from a non-owner is not obliged to make any allowance to the non-owner for the user, it follows that the buyer of a car, having used it for some months before being evicted by the true owner, can recover the full price.[193]

18.101 The influence of the forms of action, which required different pleadings for different benefits received, has obstructed the extension of the language of failure of consideration and failure of basis beyond cases of money received. In *Pavey and Matthews Pty Ltd v Paul*[194] builders who had worked under a contract which was unenforceable for want of writing successfully claimed the reasonable value

---

[190] See para 18.106.

[191] *Giles v Edwards* (1797) 7 TR 181, 101 ER 920; *Rugg v Minett* (1809) 11 East 210, 103 ER 985; *DO Ferguson & Associates v Sohl* (1992) 62 Building LR 95, CA.

[192] In the early American case of *Bush v Canfield* (1818) 2 Conn 485 a buyer had paid for flour to be delivered on a future date, by which day the market had collapsed. The seller surprisingly failed to deliver. The court allowed the buyer to recover his payment as damages for breach. Hosmer J, dissenting, rightly said that he could indeed have had restitution of the advance payment but not as damages for breach.

[193] *Rowland v Divall* [1923] 2 KB 500, CA; *Warman v Southern Counties Car Finance Co Ltd* [1949] 2 KB 576; *Butterworth v Kingsway Motors Ltd* [1954] 1 WLR 1286; *Barber v NWS Bank plc* [1996] 1 WLR 641, CA.

[194] (1987) 162 CLR 221, HCA.

of their work in unjust enrichment. The High Court of Australia found it difficult to identify the precise unjust factor. Had the builders been paid and not done the work, the client's action to recover the money would instantly have been characterized as a claim for failure of consideration. Nowadays it should be possible to see that the unjust factors familiar in money cases apply equally to enrichment transferred in other forms. The builders won because they had enriched Mrs Paul and because the basis on which they had done so had failed.

Claims of this kind by those who have conferred non-money benefits give rise **18.102** to serious problems of valuation. In some cases it is contentious whether the defendant has been enriched. Where the conclusion is that there has been no enrichment, the cause of action, if there is one, must be found elsewhere.[195] The question also arises whether the valuation should be permitted to escape the terminated contract altogether. In California *Boomer v Muir*[196] allowed contractors to recover more for a part performance than they would have obtained had they completed. They were building a dam. The other side repudiated the contract. The part performance, valued at market rates, was worth far more than they had agreed for the whole.[197]

In *Taylor v Motability Finance Ltd*, Cooke J considered that this decision would **18.103** not be followed in England because 'there can. . .be no justification. . .for recovery in excess of the contract limit'.[198] However it is arguable that the contract price should not serve as a ceiling on recovery because the allocation of price and risk is usually settled between the parties on the assumption that the contract will be entirely performed. A claimant might agree a contract price in the expectation of intangible benefits from entire performance such as further contracts or reputation. Hence there are reasons to prefer the contrary decision of the Privy Council in *Lodder v Slowey*.[199]

(ii) Breach by the claimant in unjust enrichment

Even a party whose own breach precipitated the termination of the contract **18.104** can be found to have transferred value on a basis which subsequently failed. He will be exposed to a claim for damages for his breach, but there is no reason why he should also be barred from his action in unjust enrichment. In this context the language of 'failure of consideration' has proved especially difficult to use.

---

[195] Cf C Mitchell and C Mitchell '*Planché v Colburn*' in C Mitchell and P Mitchell (eds) *Landmark Cases in the Law of Restitution* (2006) 65, 87–93.

[196] 24 P 2d 570 (1933), followed in *Renard Constructions (ME) Pty Ltd v Minister for Public Works* (1992) 26 NSWLR 234.

[197] Strongly criticized in GH Treitel, *Remedies for Breach of Contract: A Comparative Account* (1991) 104; cf A Skelton, *Restitution and Contract* (1998) 69–70, 75–85.

[198] [2004] EWHC 2619 [26].

[199] [1904] AC 442, PC.

When that phrase is not rigorously detached from contractual consideration, it seems singularly inappropriate in the mouth of a party in repudiatory breach. However, the results of the cases do confirm that a party in breach can claim restitution if the basis of his transfer has failed.

18.105 In *Dies v British and International Mining and Finance Co Ltd*[200] a buyer who had paid in advance for arms could no longer take delivery of them and recovered the prepayment. It has to be assumed that the defendant company had accepted the repudiation and terminated the contract, for there would be no question of restitution from a party anxious to hold to the contract and willing to perform it. In *Rover International Ltd v Cannon Film Sales Ltd*[201] two joint ventures had been directed to exploiting films owned by the defendants on the Italian cinema market and on television. The two joint venturers had done much work and paid large sums of money to the defendants when the latter terminated the contracts. The Court of Appeal held that the value of the work and the prepayments were recoverable.

18.106 Whether the claimant or the defendant is the party in breach, a sensitive exercise of construction always has to be conducted to determine what was the basis of the particular transfer and whether it failed. Even where the claimant seems not to have obtained what he wanted in return, the basis of the transfer may not have failed. For example, the basis of a payment will not have failed if it was intended to be a deposit to bind the payer to perform,[202] or to be payment for work actually done in the performance of the contract,[203] or to be recoverable only within a contractual regime for repayment.[204] In some such cases, where the basis has not failed, the disappointed claimant may yet have some slight hope of restitution under the courts' jurisdiction to relieve from penalties and forfeitures.[205]

18.107 Where the contract is for work to be done and the worker fails to complete the work, that same exercise has to decide whether it was contemplated that, as it progressed, every part of the work should, on the analogy of a deposit to bind, be regarded as security for completion. Where the contract specifies a single payment for the entire performance (an 'entire' contract), it will not be difficult to reach

---

[200] [1935] 1 KB 724.

[201] [1989] 1 WLR 912, CA.

[202] *Howe v Smith* (1884) 27 Ch D 89; *Monnickendam v Leanse* (1923) 39 TLR 445; *Mayson v Clouet* [1924] AC 980, PC.

[203] *Hyundai Heavy Industries Co Ltd v Papadopoulos* [1980] 1 WLR 1129, HL; *Stocznia Gdanska SA v Latvian Shipping Co* [1988] 1 WLR 574, HL.

[204] *Pan Ocean Shipping Corporation v Creditcorp Ltd (The Trident Beauty)* [1994] 1 WLR 161, HL.

[205] However the majority judgments in *Stockloser v Johnson* [1954] 1 QB 476, CA now have to be read in the restrictive light of *Shiloh Spinners Ltd v Harding* [1973] AC 691, HL and *Union Eagle Ltd v Golden Achievement Ltd* [1997] AC 514, HL; cf *On Demand Information plc v Michael Gerson (Finance) plc* [1999] 1 All ER (Comm) 512.

that conclusion.[206] The customer is not lightly to be deprived of his most effective means of ensuring completion of the work: no completion, no money. On the other hand the mere fact that a single price has been fixed cannot be conclusive.[207]

(iii) Frustration of the contract

The *Fibrosa* case,[208] overruling *Chandler v Webster*,[209] established that a party **18.108** who had paid in advance could recover his payment if the contract was frustrated before he had received anything of what he had paid for. With hindsight we can see that the law applicable to payments must from that moment have applied equally to transfers of other valuable benefits, subject only to the additional difficulty of establishing enrichment. However, that question was never put, for the law was almost immediately recast by the Law Reform (Frustrated Contracts) Act 1943.[210]

Subject to some exceptions,[211] a single section of the Act eliminated the insist- **18.109** ence on total failure, introduced a scheme of mutual restitution, and provided for certain allowances. Just as in the *Fibrosa* case Lord Wright invoked the law of unjust enrichment, so in *BP Exploration (Libya) Ltd v Hunt* Robert Goff J showed that the statute could be best understood as applying the principles of that area of law. Indeed he took the view that even the allowances which have just been mentioned should be regarded as reflecting a statutory acceptance of the defence of change of position.[212] The Court of Appeal, upholding his decision, emphasized that the Act had empowered the court to make discretionary adjustment between the parties, not necessarily tied to any one set of principles.[213]

Under section 1(2) money payable at the time of discharge ceases to be payable **18.110** and money paid is recoverable, subject to a discretionary allowance in respect of

---

[206] *Sumpter v Hedges* [1898] 1 QB 673; *Bolton v Mahadeva* [1972] 1 WLR 1009; cf *Cutter v Powell* (1795) 6 TR 320, 1001 ER 573.

[207] Law Commission, *Pecuniary Breach of Contract* (Law Com No 121, 1983) paras 2.28–2.60, discussed by Skelton (n 197) 96–100. In *Segnit v Cotton* (CA, 9 December 1999) a contract to do work on a marketing project in exchange for a share of profits was construed to have been entire because profits could not be calculated until the project was completed.

[208] *Fibrosa Spolka Akcyjna v Fairbairn Lawson Combe Barbour* [1943] AC 32, 65, HL; see para 18.85.

[209] [1904] 1 KB 493, CA.

[210] It is often said that the 1943 Act was enacted to correct the errors of the *Fibrosa* case, but it is more accurate to say that case and statute were successive stages in a single programme of law reform managed by Viscount Simon LC: P Mitchell '*Fibrosa Spolka Akcyjna v Fairbairn Lawson Combe Barbour*' in C Mitchell and P Mitchell (eds), *Landmark Cases in the Law of Restitution* (2006) 247.

[211] Contracting out, s 2(3); severable parts, s 2(4); charterparties other than time and demise charters and carriage by sea, s 2(5)(a); insurance, s 2(5)(b); some sales of goods, s 2(5)(c).

[212] [1979] 1 WLR 783, 799–800.

[213] [1981] 1 WLR 232, 238, CA, affirmed [1983] 2 AC 352, HL.

expenses incurred before the time of discharge in or for the performance of the contract. That the discretion allows results that the defence of change of position could not reach is shown by *Gamerco SA v ICM Fair Warning (Agency) Ltd*.[214] There the judge declined to make the allowance because the claimant, seeking restitution of payments made to the defendants, had incurred far greater wasted expenditure than had they.

18.111 Valuable benefits other than money are dealt with by section 1(3). The court is given a discretion to order the recipient to pay a just sum for any such benefit received. The discretion is constrained. The just sum must not be greater than the value to the recipient of the benefit received. And regard must be had to (a) expenses incurred by the recipient in or for performance of the contract and (b) the effect of the frustrating event on the benefit received.

18.112 The defendant in *BP Exploration (Libya) Ltd v Hunt* held an oil concession from the Libyan government over the Libyan desert. He entered a joint venture with BP. BP would explore the desert at its own expense and, in addition, make over to Hunt quantities of its own oil obtained from other fields. If an oil-field was found, BP would then reimburse itself 125 per cent of this input. Thereafter profits would be shared. A great oil-field was found, but, even before BP had reimbursed itself, the field was taken back into the Libyan government's hands. Compensation was later paid to Hunt. The joint venture having been frustrated by the confiscation, Robert Goff J held that on these facts he had to value the end product: what the BP work had produced for Hunt. The work had produced an enormous enhancement of the value of the concession but, having regard to the effect of the confiscation, that enhancement had left Hunt only the compensation money and such oil as had been made over to him.[215] However, the just sum to be awarded, within that maximum, was only about 45 per cent of the whole, because only that 45 per cent could be said to have been obtained at BP's expense, in the sense of having come from BP. Moreover, BP had already reimbursed itself in part before the confiscation.[216] In round numbers, therefore, having conferred a valuable benefit on Hunt approaching $100 million, BP had judgment for some $34 million.

18.113 That only a tiny number of cases have been fought suggests that the statutory regime of mutual restitution is understood and accepted. Where large values are at stake, doubts may yet have to be resolved in relation to non-money benefits. In particular it is not clear that Robert Goff J meant that the court must always value the end product as opposed to the value of the work itself. Also, while Robert Goff J thought that the effect of the frustrating event had to be considered when valuing

---

[214] [1995] 1 WLR 1226.
[215] [1979] 1 WLR 783, 802–4.
[216] ibid, 806.

the benefit received, the syntax of section 1(3) would allow it to bear on the just sum to be awarded. The approach of Robert Goff J, if applied in every case, would leave no room for any award at all where, as in *Appleby v Myers*,[217] fire destroyed the end product. Moments before the conflagration the defendant had indisputably received valuable machinery.

(iv) Discovery of the nullity of the contract

Performance interrupted. The results of the void swaps cases can now be explained in terms of mistake of law,[218] but most were not decided on that ground. When the nullity of the interest swaps made by local authorities was discovered, some of the contracts had been completed (closed swaps) and some were still running (interrupted swaps). Restitution under the interrupted swaps can be explained as resting on failure of basis. That is, the party reclaiming could say that its payments were all made on the basis that the swap would run on for the full period, which basis had failed.[219]   **18.114**

Performance completed. In relation to the closed swaps, the language of failure of consideration was also used by the judges in *Guinness Mahon & Co Ltd v Kensington and Chelsea Royal London BC*.[220] However, in that context it seemed to mean only that nullity itself was the unjust factor: when transfers were made under a void contract, restitution must follow automatically. If any phrase can do that work it is 'absence of consideration' or 'absence of basis'. There is no actual failure of basis when both sides have received exactly what they contracted for. Yet it can intelligibly be said that there was never a legal basis for the transfers factually so made.   **18.115**

Taxonomic disruption. The problem with this analysis is that nullity in itself, as 'absence of consideration', cannot fit into the English list of unjust factors. It is not a species of non-voluntariness. Operating independently of any examination of the dictates of the underlying policy, it could only be placed among policy-motivated unjust factors by presuming, fictitiously, that the policy underlying every nullity must dictate automatic restitution. It might be proposed to add it to the list as an independent third category of unjust factor. But a proposition to the effect that English law awards restitution where a transfer is made *sine causa* or *ohne rechtlichen Grund* (without legal ground) cannot be tacked on to the list of unjust factors. It must in the end displace them.   **18.116**

---

[217] (1867) LR 2 CP 651.
[218] See paras 18.62–18.63.
[219] Further discussion in P Birks and F Rose (eds), *Lessons of the Swaps Litigation* (2000) 9–18 (Birks) and 100–6 (McKendrick).
[220] [1999] QB 215, CA.

18.117 As discussed above, these considerations led Peter Birks to conclude that the *Guinness Mahon* case had committed English law to a civilian 'absence of basis' approach to determining when a defendant's enrichment is unjust.[221] However this view is not shared by the House of Lords,[222] and an alternative explanation of the *Guinness Mahon* case is that it was not the nullity of the parties' contract in itself but the policy behind the nullity which constituted the unjust factor. There are some passages in the judgments in the Court of Appeal which indicate that it was the policy of protecting the public that the court had in mind as requiring automatic restitution.[223] On this view all instances of nullity in which the policy underlying the nullity is judged to require restitution belong more properly in the category of policy-motivated unjust factors.

(b) Failure of basis: the coming about of some state of affairs

18.118 Here the recipient is not contemplated as under any obligation to bring about the state of affairs which is understood by both to be the basis of the transfer.[224] In *Chillingworth v Esche*[225] the claimant had paid a pre-contractual deposit 'subject to contract'. When no contract eventuated, the money was held to be recoverable. The court did not use the language of failure of consideration or failure of basis, but the ground should now be so understood. Construction of the phrase 'subject to contract' showed, at least in that context,[226] that the essential basis of the payment was the coming into existence of a binding contract.

18.119 Similarly, in *P v P*[227] money paid in contemplation of marriage was recoverable when no marriage ensued. In *Hussey v Palmer*[228] a mother-in-law recovered money which she had paid to her son-in-law on the basis that he would extend his house and she would then live there. When the relationship broke down and she had to find accommodation elsewhere, she recovered her money. Again this is not expressly ascribed to failure of consideration, but the best explanation is that the money was given and received on the basis that relations would be, and would

---

[221] See paras 18.40–18.43.

[222] *Deutsche Morgan Grenfell plc v IRC* [2006] UKHL 49; [2007] 1 AC 558, [21] and [155]; *Sempra Metals Ltd v IRC* [2007] UKHL 34; [2007] 3 WLR 354, [23].

[223] [1999] QB 215, 229 (Morritt LJ), 232 (Waller LJ), CA.

[224] It has been held that the parties must not have been at cross-purposes as to the basis: *Burgess v Rawnsley* [1975] Ch 429, CA. *Quaere* whether this should matter when on either view the basis has failed.

[225] [1924] 1 Ch 97, affirmed in *Gribbon v Lutton* [2001] EWCA 1956; [2002] QB 902 [64].

[226] That the exercise of construction must be context-specific is shown by *A-G of Hong Kong v Humphries Estate (Queen's Gardens) Ltd* [1987] AC 114, PC where value transferred at the pre-contractual phase was held to have been transferred entirely at the transferor's risk. See also *Regalian Properties plc v London Docklands Development Corporation* [1995] 1 WLR 212.

[227] [1916] 2 IR 400; cf *Re Ames' Settlement* [1946] Ch 217. A gift such as an engagement ring is now presumed to be absolute until the contrary is affirmatively proved by the claimant: Law Reform (Miscellaneous Provisions) Act 1970 s 3.

[228] [1972] 1 WLR 1286, CA.

continue to be, such as to allow her to live out her days in the son-in-law's house, and that basis failed. In *Muschinski v Dodds*[229] a woman recovered money which she had invested in a co-owned home on the basis that a personal and business relationship with the other co-owner would continue to subsist.

The facts have to be looked at carefully. Superficially similar cases may on close **18.120** examination fall on different sides of two crucial lines. It may turn out that the defendant was not enriched. Without enrichment the claim cannot be said to arise in unjust enrichment. Nor is the claimant in a position to ask for restitution. A difficult question then arises whether the claimant can make out any cause of action for compensation of his loss. That cause of action will have to be found either in wrongs or in the fourth, miscellaneous, class of causative event.[230] More sensitive still is the question whether the basis on which the value was transferred was that it should be at the risk of the transferor and hence that there was no failure when the outcome for which he hoped failed to materialize.[231]

In many commercial situations it is common for one party to incur considerable **18.121** costs in the quest for a contract. The construction industry is an obvious example. Builders and architects constantly invest sprats to catch mackerel. They and their clients know that they take the risk. So far as the potential client is concerned, any benefit that he receives is then transferred precisely on the basis that the builder risks getting nothing for it. However, a line can be crossed at which it becomes clear to both sides that the risk-taking is over and the benefits are no longer gratuitous. *William Lacey (Hounslow) Ltd v Davis*[232] was such a case. After tender the claimant builder was given to understand that his bid was preferred and he undertook further work in drawing up and amending plans for the development, confident that a contract would ensue. The client then suddenly sold on the site and project. Barry J upheld the builder's claim to the value of his work. Both sides had understood that it was done, not at the builder's risk, but on the basis that a contract would eventuate.

(c) Failure of basis: application

A transfer may be tied to a particular application. The recipient may then be **18.122** bound by contract to apply it. If the transferor intends that the recipient should

---

[229] (1985) 160 CLR 583, HCA.

[230] In *Sabemo Pty Ltd v North Sydney Municipal Council* [1977] 2 NSWLR 880 Shepherd J allowed a claim to 'restitution' in such a case, an illegitimate use of the word which obscured the fact that he was exploring a compensatory doctrine. Cf SJ Stoljar, 'Unjust Enrichment and Unjust Sacrifice' (1987) 50 MLR 603; E McKendrick, 'Work Done in Anticipation of a Contract which does not Materialise' in WR Cornish (ed), *Restitution, Past, Present, and Future* (1998) 163, 186.

[231] McKendrick (n 230) 163, 182–6. See also para 18.106.

[232] [1957] 1 WLR 932. On the same side of the line: *Countrywide Communications Ltd v ICL Pathway Ltd* (QBD 21 October 1999); *Vedatech Corp v Crystal Decisions Ltd* [2002] EWCA 818.

hold the money on trust for the particular application, the recipient will become a trustee, though the trust will fail immediately if there is no sufficient class of human beneficiaries. Either way, the transfer is made on a particular basis, namely that the value in question be applied in the specified manner. If that basis fails, the transferee who does not or cannot make the application will be unjustly enriched.

(i) Where the transferee is bound by contract

18.123 The transferor who obliges his transferee to apply value transferred in a particular manner will be able to prevent misapplications by injunction. When the contract is discharged before the application is complete, the basis of the transfer will have failed and the transferor will be entitled to restitution. In *Barclays Bank Ltd v Quistclose Investments Ltd*[233] the House of Lords went further, and held that a trust will be imposed on money advanced for a particular purpose in the event that the purpose becomes impossible of fulfilment, or is repudiated by the recipient. On this view of the law, this is then a case in which the law gives proprietary effect to the transferor's right to restitution. However, in *Twinsectra Ltd v Yardley*[234] the House of Lords subsequently explained '*Quistclose* trusts' in a way that left no role for the law of unjust enrichment. In their Lordships' view, the money is impressed with an express trust in the transferor's favour from the start, subject to a power vested in the recipient to apply the fund to the agreed purpose. The failure of the purpose then terminates the power. The transferor's proprietary interest does not arise from this failure, but was in place all along under the express trust.

18.124 It is not clear that a contract to lend money for a particular purpose will always be caught by the *Twinsectra* analysis. For example, where money is lent under a contract which places a positive obligation on the borrower to apply the money in a particular way, rather than a negative obligation not to use it for anything else, there is no obvious justification for downgrading the borrower's obligation to a power. In such cases, the court may prefer to say that the borrower owes a contractual obligation, and that failure of the purpose will lead to the imposition of a restitutionary trust for the lender, provided that an injunction would have been available to prevent the money being spent on other purposes.[235]

18.125 On some facts superficially similar to those of the latter kind, the appropriate construction may be that, in all or some events, the recipient was to take free of any fetter. That is to say, both the assets transferred and (which is a separate question)

---

[233] [1970] AC 567, HL.
[234] [2002] UKHL 12; [2002] 2 AC 164.
[235] W Swadling (ed), *The Quistclose Trust: Critical Essays* (2004), 77–120 (Chambers) and 121–143 (Birks).

their value were to become freely his. A construction of this kind may show either that the fetter was merely precatory, and as such illusory,[236] or indicate circumstances in which the contractual fetter was intended to be struck off.[237]

(ii) Where the transferee is bound by a trust

Where the tie to a particular application is construed as creating a trust, the trust will fail immediately if no beneficiary is named or no sufficiently certain class of such beneficiaries is identified. The basis of the transfer being that the transferee shall hold and apply the fund as a trustee, that basis then fails at once. If the trust is construed as having distributed some but not all of the equitable interest, the trust will fail as to that undistributed part.   **18.126**

In *Re Gillingham Bus Disaster Fund*[238] money was given by subscription to the   **18.127** mayors of the Medway Towns first to relieve the victims of the disaster and thereafter to other 'worthy causes'. The gift to 'worthy causes' was void as being a non-charitable purpose trust. The intended basis of the transfer to the trustees having to that extent failed, they held the surplus on resulting trust for the donors. Again in *Re Abbott Fund Trusts*[239] once it appeared that money had been given on trust only to maintain and care for two handicapped women during their lives, it followed that after their death the trustees held on resulting trusts for the donors. These are both cases in which the basis of the transfer failed as to part of the fund transferred.

In the *Vandervell* litigation it failed as to the whole fund. The problem arose   **18.128** from the mode in which millionaire Tony Vandervell had chosen to make a benefaction to the Royal College of Surgeons.[240] He intended to do it in a tax-efficient way by giving the College shares and then declaring a dividend on them. Once they had shed their dividend on the College, the shares were to be transferred to his family's trust company. To achieve that purpose, the transfer to the College was made subject to an option in favour of the trust company. The plan worked smoothly. The College received its money, and the trust company exercised its option.

---

[236] *Re Osoba* [1979] 1 WLR 247, CA; cf *Re Bowes* [1896] 1 Ch 507.

[237] Where a gift is construed as having been made to members of an association beneficially, tied to the association's purposes by the contract between the members themselves, then, when that contract goes, the property, even that part of it which was donated by outsiders, will generally be construed as the unfettered property of the surviving members: *Re St Andrew's Allotment Association Trusts* [1969] 1 WLR 229; *Re Bucks Constabulary Widows and Orphans' Fund Friendly Society (No 2)* [1979] 1 WLR 936; *Re Horley Town Football Club* [2006] EWHC 2386; [2006] WTLR 1817.

[238] [1959] Ch 62, CA affirming [1958] Ch 300. Cf *Air Jamaica Ltd v Charlton* [1999] 1 WLR 1399, PC, where the ultimate trust of a pension fund, intended to be triggered by the discontinuation of the fund failed for perpetuity.

[239] [1900] 2 Ch 326.

[240] *Vandervell v IRC* [1967] 2 AC 291, HL; *Re Vandervell's Trusts (No 2)* [1974] Ch 269, CA, reversing [1973] 3 WLR 744.

However, the Inland Revenue then successfully maintained that Vandervell had failed to escape his surtax liability on the benefaction: he had not divested himself of his entire interest in the shares, because the option was all along held on trust for him. The trustee company was not intended to receive the option (and thus the shares) for itself, but to hold them for beneficiaries. However Vandervell had never declared who the beneficiaries were to be. The basis of the transfer of the option to the trustee company thus failed, and a restitutionary trust arose in favour of Vandervell.

18.129 **A fictitious explanation.** In these cases in which there is a giving upon trust and that trust fails, the resulting trust has traditionally been ascribed to a presumption that the transferor intended that the transferee should, on the failure of the intended basis, hold for the benefit of transferor himself.[241] However, that is a fiction of the same order as the fiction of implied contract which used to be relied upon to explain why mistaken payments and other unjust enrichments should be given back. Just as there is no contract in these cases, so there is manifestly no intent to create a contingent resulting trust in the examples in which express trusts fail. As Harman J said in *Re Gillingham Bus Disaster Fund*[242] the real fact is that the transferors never contemplated the contingency in question. In the *Vandervell* saga a trust for himself was the very last thing that Tony Vandervell wanted. It contradicted his central purpose in structuring his benefaction as he did. Just as the law has escaped the implied contract theory of quasi-contract, so it cannot but accept the reality that 'the resulting trust arises by operation of law because the provider of the trust property did not intend to benefit the recipient'.[243]

18.130 **The first escape from fiction: proprietary arithmetic.** An attempt has been made to show that these cases illustrate the simple proposition that the transferor retains that which he has not succeeded in giving away: inevitably or 'automatically', the trustee holds for him that which he has not managed to dispose of.[244] However, that explanation will not work. Lord Browne-Wilkinson has shown that on such facts the transferor acquires, and does not retain, his equitable interest,

---

[241] Reasserted by Lord Browne-Wilkinson in *Westdeutsche Landesbank Girozentrale v Islington LBC* [1996] AC 669, 702, 708–9, HL drawing support from WJ Swadling, 'A New Role for Resulting Trusts' (1996) 16 LS 110. However Swadling relies on the 'automatic' explanation of these cases, which is rejected at para 18.130. His express trust interpretation is confined to the cases dealt with below as instances of absolute qualification.

[242] [1958] Ch 300, 310.

[243] R Chambers, *Resulting Trusts* (1997) 66. Cf *Air Jamaica Ltd v Charlton* [2000] 1 WLR 1399, 1412, PC; *Twinsectra Ltd v Yardley* [2002] UKHL 12; [2002] 2 AC 164, [91]; *Lavelle v Lavelle* [2004] EWCA Civ 223; [2004] 2 FCR 418, [13]–[14], CA; *Stack v Dowden* [2007] UKHL 17; [2007] 2 WLR 831, [60] and [114].

[244] Most clearly by Megarry J in *Re Vandervell's Trusts (No 2)* [1974] Ch 269, 289–97. Cf R Chambers, *Resulting Trusts* (1997) 51–5.

and that cases of this kind are essentially identical with cases where a resulting trust is imposed for the benefit of a transferor who has successfully transferred the whole beneficial interest in his property to a recipient and received nothing in exchange.[245]

The alternative explanation. Lord Browne-Wilkinson's dissent from the 'automatic' or 'arithmetic' explanation takes him back to the presumption and, thence, to the fiction of an intent to create the restitutionary trust. The better view, as Robert Chambers explains, is that where the defendant was intended to hold and apply the fund as a trustee, there is, when the trust fails, a prima facie failure of the basis of the transfer to him. The presumption which then comes into play is a presumption of non-beneficial intent. It presumes, in the absence of contrary evidence, that the claimant-settlor did not intend in that event that the benefit of the fund should accrue to the trustee himself. In this way the familiar features of the law are accounted for without recourse to fiction.

18.131

(4) Absolute Qualification

In all the cases considered so far the claimant's intent to part with the value in question is qualified but, provided the specified basis holds good, the qualification will be purged. There are some cases in which the qualification cannot be purged: the transferee shall never treat the thing as his own. So far as concerns the benefit normally inherent in ownership, such transfers are non-voluntary *ab initio*. The transferor manifests an intent that the transferee shall not benefit.[246] If this kind of transfer is construed as not even passing the property at law, the transaction will be construed as a deposit and the recipient will be a bailee. If the property does pass at law, the recipient will usually be an express trustee. I transfer to you a million shares on trust for me. That is an express trust. I transfer a million shares to you on terms that I am to remain the 'real' owner and you are to treat me as such. That is still an express trust. We know that a person can create a trust as Monsieur Jourdain talked prose, without knowing it.[247] A contract does not become an implied contract just because the word 'contract' is not used; a trust does not cease to be an express trust just because the word 'trust' is not used.

18.132

The new equitable interest carries the benefit of the shares away from the transferee and back to the settlor. The entitlement to the benefit arises and in the same

18.133

---

[245] *Westdeutsche Landesbank Girozentrale v Islington LBC* [1996] AC 669, 706, HL.

[246] Cf no intent (flatly contrary intent): paras 18.46 ff. Here there is an intent to transfer the thing but the intent is unconditionally qualified as to benefit.

[247] Monsieur Jourdain, a character in Molière's *Bourgeois Gentilhomme*, was invoked by Du Parq LJ in *Re Schebsman* [1944] Ch 83, 104, CA.

instant 'results', that is it 'jumps back' to the settlor.[248] A 'resulting' entitlement is a restitutionary entitlement. However, not every restitutionary entitlement arises from unjust enrichment: an unjust enrichment is an enrichment in respect of which there is a reason for restitution which is neither a wrong, nor a contract, nor some other manifestation of the consent of the person bound to make restitution. Here there is wealth acquired by one at the expense of another in the 'from' sense, and the interest arises because there is a very good reason why the recipient should surrender it. But the reason is an express trust: the settlor has intended, and the trustee has consented, that this wealth be held for another.

(a) Alternative analysis in unjust enrichment

18.134 However, this is a case in which an alternative analysis is possible. A transfer which is subject to an absolute qualification can also be understood as a strong form of non-voluntary transfer and, as such, as a case of unjust enrichment. Just as a loan which cannot be construed as a contract can be construed as an unjust enrichment,[249] so also in this context, when the facts are incompatible with there being an express trust, the alternative analysis in unjust enrichment shows through.

18.135 In *Hodgson v Marks*[250] a rogue called Evans, not a party to this action, won the confidence of Mrs Hodgson. He was a lodger in her house. Her nephew did not approve of him. Mrs Hodgson transferred the legal title to him, just to protect him from her nephew. As soon as he had the legal title, he sold the house to Marks over Mrs Hodgson's head. The competition was therefore between her and Marks. It was registered land, but she had at all times been in actual occupation. If she had any interest in the house, it would be an overriding interest, good against Marks. Did she have an interest? The Court of Appeal held that she did. Express trusts of land have to be declared in writing. There was no express trust. But she had shown, without the help of any presumption, that she did not intend him to have the beneficial interest. The Court held that the facts had turned Evans into a trustee for her. As Chambers says, 'Although the oral trust was ineffective, the absence of intention to make a gift gave rise to a resulting trust.'[251]

---

[248] The Latin verb '*salio, salire*' means 'leap' or 'jump', and the prefix '*re*' often indicates 'back'. Thus the compound '*resilio*' gives our word 'resile', and another compound '*resulto*' meaning 'jump back' gives us 'result' and 'resulting', which only lawyers still use in the 'jumping back' sense.

[249] *Goss v Chilcott* [1996] AC 788, PC; *Sinclair v Brougham* [1914] AC 98, HL as re-examined in *Westdeutsche Landesbank Girozentrale v Islington LBC* [1996] AC 669, 709–14, HL. Cf *Pavey and Matthews Pty Ltd v Paul* (1987) 162 CLR 221, HCA.

[250] [1971] Ch 892, CA.

[251] R Chambers, *Resulting Trusts* (Oxford: OUP, 1997) 139.

(b) Establishing non-beneficial intent by presumption

A non-beneficial intent of this kind is often established with the assistance of a **18.136** presumption. Except within certain close relationships, in which it is cancelled out by the counter-presumption of advancement, the presumption arises on facts which display the externalities of a gift. However, the analysis is not affected by the mode in which the non-beneficial intent is established, whether by evidence or by presumption.

In *Tinsley v Milligan*[252] two lesbian lovers involved themselves in a common form **18.137** of social security fraud. When they bought a house with money provided by both, one took the title so that the other could present herself as penniless. Later they fell out. The one with the legal title claimed to be beneficially entitled. However, the externalities indicated a gift by the latter to the former and, in the absence of a relationship of advancement, thus triggered the presumption of non-beneficial intent. There could be no express trust. Even if such a trust could have survived the objection of illegality, there was no writing. Express trusts of land have to be in writing. But again the non-beneficial intent was sufficient to turn the defendant into a trustee by operation of law.

Had the two women in this case been instead father and son, so that the son held **18.138** the paper title and the father had contributed some or all of the money, the counter-presumption of advancement would have applied. The father would then have had to show by evidence that he did not intend his son to take any benefit. As in *Hodgson v Marks* affirmative proof of that absolutely qualified intent would then suffice to raise the trust.[253] The presumption, when it arises, merely establishes the fact which would create the trust if it were proved. It is clear that, in many cases, the fact cannot be an express declaration of trust. A presumption of an intention to create a trust would achieve nothing in a situation in which an express declaration of trust would be of no effect.[254]

(c) Two possible unjust factors

There may be two ways of analysing the unjust enrichment in these cases. One **18.139** would make them examples of transfers on a basis which fails, as above. This has two stages: first, whether by presumption or by evidence, it is established that the transfer was made on the basis that the recipient would hold as a trustee (an express trust); next, that intended trust then fails for want of writing or for

---

[252] [1994] AC 340, HL.

[253] *Tribe v Tribe* [1995] 3 WLR 913, CA.

[254] Cf *Sinclair v Brougham* [1914] AC 398, 452, HL, where Lord Sumner was no doubt wrong to have recourse to the implied contract theory of unjust enrichment, but he was not then wrong to say that an implied contract could not be valid where express contract would be void.

some other reason, so that there is a failure of the basis of the transfer, exposing an unjust enrichment to which the law of trusts itself responds. That is a legalistic explanation, in the sense that only a lawyer could conclude that there was any failure of basis, since only a lawyer would construe the facts as an attempted transfer upon trust. The other is to say that the absolute qualification which consists in a flatly non-beneficial intent is an unjust factor in itself. The latter is the more natural explanation and is to be preferred.

G. Unjust: Policies Requiring Restitution

18.140 English law sometimes holds a defendant's enrichment at a claimant's expense to be unjust for reasons of policy, regardless of whether the claimant's intention to benefit the defendant was vitiated or qualified. We have already noticed that cases of transactional disadvantage might be treated as instances of policy-based restitution,[255] also that the vexed question of restitution under void contracts for 'absence of consideration' cannot easily be explained except as turning on either an actual assessment of the demands of the policy underlying the nullity or a presumption as to the demands of that policy.[256] Five other examples are considered here.

(1) Payments Pursuant to a Secondary Liability

18.141 It often happens that a claimant and a defendant are both legally liable to pay a third party in respect of the same debt or damage. The third party cannot accumulate recoveries by enforcing his rights against both of them, but to maximize his chances of recovery, the law allows him to recover in full from either. If his choice falls on the claimant, who must therefore pay him in full, then the claimant may be entitled to recover some or all of his payment from the defendant, on the ground that the defendant has been unjustly enriched at his expense.

18.142 The type of action brought in this class of case varies according to whether the claimant's payment has discharged the defendant's liability to the third party. If it has not, then the claimant will seek to take over the third party's subsisting right of action against the defendant by subrogation, and enforce this for his own benefit. If it has, then the claimant can bring a direct action for contribution or reimbursement in his own name against the defendant. If he has discharged securities over the defendant's property, then the court can also generate a new proprietary right in his favour which mirrors the third party's extinguished rights as holder of the securities: the claimant is treated, by a legal fiction, as though the

---

[255] See para 18.83.
[256] See para 18.117.

securities have not been discharged, but have instead been assigned to him. Confusingly, the latter remedy is also termed subrogation.[257]

In the language of the cases, the claimant will be entitled to these remedies where **18.143** the defendant was 'primarily' and the claimant only 'secondarily' liable for the defendant's share of their common obligation to the third party. To make out a cause of action, the claimant must establish several things.[258]

(a) Claimant and defendant both legally liable

The claimant must have paid the third party pursuant to an existing legal liability, **18.144** but his payment need not have been compelled by legal process: it is enough that he was legally compellable to pay.[259] It is not automatically fatal that the claimant's liability was voluntarily assumed, without any prior request from the defendant, rather than imposed by law; such voluntary assumption of liability is merely one factor which may bear on a court's decision whether to allow a claim.[260]

The defendant must also have owed a legal liability to the third party,[261] which **18.145** existed at the time of the claimant's payment.[262] It may even be enough that the defendant would inevitably have incurred a liability but for the claimant's payment. This was rejected in *Metropolitan Police District Receiver v Croydon Corp*,[263] where the claimant paid sick pay to its employee pursuant to a statutory duty, and then sought to recover this money from the tortfeasor responsible for injuring the employee. The Court of Appeal dismissed its claim: the tortfeasor had never incurred a liability to the employee to the extent that he had received sick pay, and the claimant's payments had therefore not enriched the tortfeasor. However, this reasoning has been criticized as 'over-technical' by the Law Commission.[264] It may also be contrasted with the reasoning in *AMP Workers' Compensation Services (NSW) Ltd v*

---

[257] See paras 18.216–18.219.

[258] For more detailed discussion, see C Mitchell, *The Law of Contribution and Reimbursement* (2003).

[259] *Stimpson v Smith* [1999] Ch 340, CA.

[260] Sureties: *Re a Debtor (No 627 of 1936)* [1937] 156, 166, CA. Co-sureties: *Deering v Earl of Winchelsea* (1787) 2 Bos & Pul 270, 126 ER 1276; *Smith v Wood* [1929] 1 Ch 14, 21, CA. Insurers: *Mason v Sainsbury* (1782) 3 Doug KB 61, 99 ER 538; *Caledonia North Sea Ltd v British Telecommunications plc* [2002] UKHL 4; [2002] 1 Lloyd's Rep 553. See too Mercantile Law Amendment Act 1856, s 5. These all cast doubt on statements to the contrary in *England v Marsden* (1866) LR 1 CP 529 and *Owen v Tate* [1976] 1 QB 402, CA.

[261] *Bonner v Tottenham & Edmonton Permanent Investment Building Society* [1899] 1 QB 161, CA; *Wessex Regional Health Authority v John Laing Construction Ltd* (1994) 39 Con LR 56.

[262] But cf *Legal & General Assurance Soc Ltd v Drake Insurance Co Ltd* [1992] QB 887, CA; *Eagle Star Insurance Co v Provincial Insurance plc* [1994] AC 130, PC; *O'Kane v Jones* [2003] EWHC 3470; [2004] 1 Lloyd's Rep 389, noted S Watterson [2005] LMCLQ 338.

[263] [1957] 2 QB 154, CA.

[264] Law Commission, *Damages for Personal Injury: Medical, Nursing and Other Expenses; Collateral Benefits* (Law Com No 262, 1999), para 12.30; cf paras 10.68–10.72, 12.7–12.10, and 12.28.

QBE Insurance Ltd.[265] There an injured party had a choice whether to sue one defendant or another or both. Both defendants carried liability insurance coverage. The injured party chose to sue one defendant only, whose insurer settled the claim. This insurer then sought a contribution from the other insurer, which refused to pay, arguing that it had never been under any legal liability because the injured party had never sued its insured. The New South Wales Court of Appeal ordered it to pay, reasoning that the claimant insurer's contribution right should not be defeated by the injured party's arbitrary exercise of choice.

(b) Third party may not accumulate recoveries

18.146 If the third party can accumulate recoveries, then the defendant will remain liable regardless of the claimant's payment, and the defendant cannot be enriched at the claimant's expense. When determining whether the third party may accumulate recoveries, the court must consider whether the liabilities owed by the claimant and defendant are assumed or imposed. Where they assumed their liabilities by agreement with the third party, the court must look to their respective agreements. For example, these explain why a creditor can accumulate recoveries from sureties who have guaranteed different debts, or different parts of the same debt, but not from sureties who have guaranteed the same debt subject to different limits which together exceed the total.[266] In contrast, where their liabilities are imposed by law, the court must ask whether it would be inconsistent with the policy which underpins the liability to allow the third party to accumulate recoveries. For example, the main purpose of imposing tort liability is to compensate tort victims for the harm which they suffer at the hands of tortfeasors; it is not to make them better off than they were before the tort was committed. So tort victims are forbidden to recover more than the amount of their losses by accumulating recoveries from concurrent tortfeasors.[267]

(c) Third party may recover in full from either claimant or defendant

18.147 This is almost always the case where a third party is forbidden to accumulate recoveries from claimant and defendant. English law does not generally adopt a system of proportionate liability, whereby the liability of claimant and defendant is limited to the amount of their proper share.[268] Instead, the third party can

---

[265] (2001) 53 NSWLR 35, NSWCA. And cf *McCarthy v McCarthy & Stone plc* [2006] EWHC 1851; [2006] 4 All ER 1127, affirmed [2007] EWCA Civ 664.

[266] *Ellis v Emmanuel* (1876) 1 Ex D 157, 162.

[267] *Clarke v Newsam* (1847) 1 Exch 131, 140; 154 ER 55, 59; *Dingle v Associated Newspapers Ltd* [1961] 2 QB 162, 188–9, CA (not considered on appeal: [1964] AC 371, HL).

[268] Law Commission, *Feasibility Investigation of Joint and Several Liability* (1996).

recover from either in full.[269] The unfairness which might be caused to a claimant who pays more than his proper share is redressed by giving him a claim in unjust enrichment against the defendant.

(d) Ultimate burden properly borne by defendant

As between the claimant and the defendant, some or all of the ultimate burden of paying the third party must rest on the defendant, so that it would be unjust if the defendant were relieved of this burden by the claimant. Several principles emerge from the authorities. First, where the relationship between the claimant and the defendant is affected by a contract that allocates responsibility for paying the third party, effect will generally be given to this contractual allocation.[270] Secondly, where there is no contractual allocation, the courts have adopted a default rule of equal apportionment.[271] Thirdly, this rule may be departed from, and a defendant may have to bear a larger share of the burden of paying the creditor, where: (i) his actions were a more potent cause of the creditor's loss than the claimant's actions;[272] (ii) his actions were more morally blameworthy than the claimant's actions;[273] and/or (iii) he gained a larger benefit than the claimant from the transactions which gave rise to their respective liabilities to the creditor.[274] Of these three factors, the last carries more weight than the other two.[275]

18.148

---

[269] For a rare exception see *Barker v Corus (UK) Ltd* [2006] UKHL 20; [2006] 2 AC 572, immediately reversed by legislation: Compensation Act 2006, s 3. See para 17.71.

[270] *Hutton v Eyre* (1815) 6 Taunt 289, 128 ER 1046; *Mawson v Cassidy* (CA 26 January 1995); *Morris v Breaveglen* (CA 9 May 1997).

[271] *Scholefield Goodman & Sons Ltd v Zyngier* [1986] AC 562, 575, HL; *Hampton v Minns* [2002] 1 WLR 1, [58].

[272] *Schott Kem Ltd v Bentley* [1991] 1 QB 61, CA; *Australian Breeders Co-operative Soc Ltd v Jones* (1997) 150 ALR 488, Fed Ct of Aus.

[273] *Betts v Gibbins* (1834) 2 Ad & El 57, 111 ER 22; *Baynard v Woolley* (1855) 20 Beav 583, 585–6; 52 ER 729, 730; *Jones v Wilkins* The Times 6 February 2001. In *Brian Warwicker Partnership plc v HOK International Ltd* [2005] EWCA Civ 962; (2005) 113 Con LR 112, this rule was extended to take in blameworthy behaviour unconnected with the defendant's liability to the third party, but it is hard to agree that this constitutes a good reason for increasing his liability to the claimant.

[274] *Butler v Butler* (1877) 7 Ch D 116, 121, CA; *Bonner v Tottenham & Edmonton Permanent Investment BS* [1899] 1 QB 161, 176, CA.

[275] *K v P* [1993] Ch 140, 149; *Dubai Aluminium Co Ltd v Salaam* [2002] UKHL 48; [2003] 2 AC 366; *Niru Battery Manufacturing Co v Milestone Trading Ltd (No 2)* [2004] EWCA Civ 487; [2004] 2 All ER (Comm) 289; *Cressman v Coys of Kensington (Sales) Ltd* [2004] EWCA Civ 47; [2004] 1 WLR 2774, [48]; *Charter plc v City Index Ltd* [2006] EWHC 2508; [2007] 1 WLR 26, [52]. The claimant must prove the defendant's benefit, and if he cannot then this factor will be ignored: *St Paul Travelers Insurance Co Ltd v Okporuah* [2006] EWHC 2107 [65].

(2) Benefits Conferred in an Emergency

18.149 Civil law systems provide for the reimbursement of a stranger who properly inter-venes in another person's affairs.[276] English courts have traditionally denied the existence of any such general principle, apparently fearful lest it 'breed overnight a nation of busy-bodies anxious to perform useless and meddlesome services for others and to try their luck with the courts'.[277]

(a) The traditional position

18.150 In *Nicholson v Chapman* Eyre CJ thought that a generalized right of recovery would encourage 'the wilful attempts of ill-designing people to turn. . .floats and vessels adrift, in order that they may be paid for finding them'.[278] In *Falcke v Scottish Imperial Insurance Co Ltd*, Bowen LJ stated that 'liabilities are not to be forced on people behind their backs', and that 'the general principle is, beyond all question, that work or labour done or money expended by one man to preserve or benefit the property of another do not according to English law create any lien upon the property saved or benefited, nor even, if standing alone, create any obligation to repay the expenditure'.[279] In *The Tojo Maru*, Lord Reid said that 'on land a person who interferes to save property is not in law entitled to any reward'.[280] In *The Goring*, in the Court of Appeal, Ralph Gibson LJ thought that the English courts' reluctance to acknowledge a generalized right of recovery 'has not rested. . .only on a lack of prior authority and the fear of innovation but can be supported by reasons',[281] while, in the same case in the House of Lords, Lord Brandon considered this view to be quite as 'forceful'[282] as Sir John Donaldson MR's dissenting opinion in the Court of Appeal, that salvage awards in respect of rescues undertaken on non-tidal waters should be allowed pursuant to a general policy of encouraging rescuers.[283]

---

[276] On *negotiorum gestio* (conduct of another's affairs): Civil Code of Quebec (SQ 1991, c 64), ch IV, s 1; Dutch Civil Code (1992) Book 6, Title 4, s 1, reproduced in English [1994] Restitution LR, 202–3; R Zimmermann, *The Law of Obligations* (1996) ch 14 and pp 875–8. To the extent that the doctrine comprehends the recovery of expenditure which has not enured to a defendant's benefit, it is not founded on unjust enrichment.

[277] EW Hope, 'Officiousness' (1930) 15 Cornell LQ 25, 36, regarding this outcome as unlikely; cf JP Dawson, 'Rewards for the Rescue of Human Life?' in KH Nadelmann et al (eds), *Twentieth Century Comparative and Conflicts Law: Legal Essays in Honour of HE Yntema* (1961) 142: 'official sources of American law have done their best to discourage good Samaritans'.

[278] (1793) 2 H Bl 254, 259, 126 ER 536, 539.

[279] (1886) 34 Ch D 234, CA.

[280] [1972] AC 242, 268, HL.

[281] [1987] QB 687, 708, CA.

[282] [1988] AC 831, 857, HL.

[283] [1987] QB 687, 706–7, CA.

(b) Exceptional cases

Notwithstanding this antipathy, in some cases recovery has been allowed. Success- **18.151**
ful claimants include: suppliers of necessaries to persons suffering from legal
incapacity;[284] acceptors for honour *supra* protest of bills of exchange;[285] private
individuals and local authorities who have discharged another person's duty to
bury the dead;[286] salvors (who do not always, although they do often, enter a
contract to render salvage services, and whose entitlement to a reward in the
former case is restitutionary to the extent that the amount of the reward is calculated by reference to the benefit conferred);[287] cargo owners whose property is
sacrificed to save other cargo and/or the vessel;[288] agents of necessity;[289] recovery
services who have removed vehicles from the public highway and stored them
at the request of the police;[290] doctors and hospitals who have provided medical
treatment to the victims of road traffic accidents;[291] voluntary carers of tort
victims (to the extent that they can share in the fruits of tort actions in which
damages has been awarded to reflect the cost of the care);[292] liquidators and
trustees who have done more work for their beneficiaries than is required of such

---

[284] *Williams v Wentworth* (1842) 5 Beav 325, 329, 49 ER 603, 605; *Re Rhodes* (1890) 44 Ch D
94, 105, CA; *West Ham Union v Pearson* (1890) 62 LT 638; *Re Clabbon* [1904] 2 Ch 465. See now
the Sale of Goods Act 1979, s 3(2).

[285] Bills of Exchange Act 1882, s 68(5), conferring a right of recovery via subrogation to the
position of the holder. Cf *Hawtayne v Bourne* (1841) 7 M & W 595, 599, 151 ER 905, 906. A direct
action may lie against a debtor whose debt has been discharged in an emergency: *Re a Debtor* [1937]
Ch 156, 166, CA; *Anson v Anson* [1953] 1 QB 636, 646; *Owen v Tate* [1976] 1 QB 402, 409–10
and 412, CA.

[286] *Besfich v Cogil* (1628) 1 Palm 559, 81 ER 1219; *Jenkins v Tucker* (1788) 1 H Bl 90, 126 ER 55;
Ambrose v Kerrison (1851) 10 CB 776, 138 ER 307; Public Health (Control of Disease) Act 1984,
s 46(5).

[287] For the factors which are material, see DW Steel and FD Rose, *Kennedy on Civil Salvage*
(5th edn, 1985) 458–9, approved in *The Bosworth (No 1)* [1959] 2 Lloyds Rep 511, 526 (Lord
Merriman P).

[288] FD Rose, 'General Average as Restitution' (1997) 113 LQR 569.

[289] *The Argos* (1873) LR 5 PC 134, 165 (Sir Montagu Smith); *Hingston v Vent* (1876) 1 QBD
367; *Tetley v British Trade Corp* (1922) 10 Lloyd's List LR 678.

[290] *White v Troups Transport* [1976] CLY 33, Stockton-on-Tees County Court; *Surrey Breakdown
Ltd v Knight* [1999] RTR 84, CA. See too Road Traffic Regulation Act 1984, ss 99–103.

[291] Road Traffic Act 1988, ss 158 and 159; Road Traffic (NHS Charges) Act 1999. The question
whether the NHS should have a general right to recoup the cost of care from tortfeasors is discussed
in Law Commission, *Damages for Personal Injury: Medical, Nursing and Other Expenses; Collateral
Benefits* (Law Com No 262, 1999), paras 3.19–3.43. Earlier times: *Simmons v Wilmott* (1800) 3 Esp
91, 170 ER 549; *Lamb v Bunce* (1815) 4 M & S 275, 105 ER 836; *Tomlinson v Bentall* (1826) 5 B
& C 738, 108 ER 274.

[292] It seems that this portion of the damages must be held on trust for the carer: *Hunt v Severs*
[1994] 2 AC 350, 358–63, HL; *H v S* [2002] EWCA Civ 792; [2003] QB 965, CA. But the
Government proposes to replace this trust with a personal liability: Department of Constitutional
Affairs *The Law on Damages* (CP 9/07, 2007) 48–50.

persons;[293] and bailees who have incurred expenses in preserving the bailor's property.[294]

(c) The possible emergence of a general doctrine

18.152 It remains to be seen whether the English courts will forge a general principle from these 'exceptions'. Certain limitations which are disclosed by the existing case law would be likely to attach to any such generalized right of action. First, the likelihood of imminent harm to the defendant's property or person must have been great.[295] Secondly, it must have been impracticable for the claimant to communicate with the defendant,[296] and recovery should not be allowed where intervention 'was contrary to the known wishes of the assisted person'.[297] However, in the latter case recovery might exceptionally be allowed if the defendant's rejection of the claimant's intervention was against the public interest.[298] Thirdly, the claimant must have been an appropriate person to act in the circumstances.[299] Fourthly, a claimant should be able to recover only in respect of expenses reasonably incurred in the circumstances.[300] Fifthly, it should be a bar to recovery that a claimant has acted for his own benefit and only incidentally conferred a benefit on the defendant in the course of doing so.[301]

18.153 As and when this issue falls to be considered, it will be necessary to distinguish three possible measures of recovery: reward, restitution of enrichment, and reimbursement of expenses. Since rewards are likely to remain confined to salvage, the choice will have to be made between restitution and reimbursement. The latter will take the right out of unjust enrichment and indeed out of the law of

---

[293] *Re Duke of Norfolk's ST* [1982] 1 Ch 61, CA; *Re Berkeley Applegate (Investment Consultants) Ltd* [1989] 1 Ch 32; *Foster v Spencer* [1996] 2 All ER 672; *Polly Peck International plc v Henry* [1999] 1 Butterworths Company Law Cases 407.

[294] *Great Northern Railway v Swaffield* (1874) 9 Ex 132; *Sachs v Miklos* [1948] 2 KB 23, 35–6, CA; *The Winson* [1982] AC 939, 958, HL; *Guildford BC v Hein* [2005] EWCA Civ 979, [33] and [80], CA.

[295] *The Bona* [1895] P 125, CA; *Sachs v Miklos* [1948] 2 KB 23, 36, CA; *Re F (Mental Patient: Sterilization)* [1990] 2 AC, 75, HL; *Surrey Breakdown Ltd v Knight* [1999] RTR 84, 88, CA.

[296] *Springer v Great Western Railway Co* [1921] 1 KB 257; *The Winson* [1982] AC 939, 961, HL.

[297] *Re F* (n 295) 75.

[298] As in *Great Northern Railway Co v Swaffield* (1874) LR 9 Exch 132; *Guildford BC v Hein* [2005] EWCA Civ 979. Cf BGB s 679, and other sources cited in R Zimmermann, *The Law of Obligations* (1996) 448, n 118.

[299] *Re Rhodes* (1890) 44 Ch D 94, 107, CA; *Macclesfield Corp v Great Central Railway Co* [1911] 2 KB 528, 541. Cf *Hardwicke v Hudson* [1999] 3 All ER 426, 435–6, CA.

[300] *Jenkins v Tucker* (1788) 1 H Bl 90, 126 ER 55 (burial costs recoverable if suited to deceased's station in life); *Re Rhodes* (1890) 44 Ch D 94, 105, CA (cost of necessaries supplied to an *incapax* recoverable if suited to her station in life); *White v Troups Transport* [1976] CLY 33 (only hire cost of smallest crane needed to remove lorry from highway can be recovered).

[301] Cf *Tanguay v Price* (1906) 37 SCR 657, Can SC.

restitution. The former, which will retain uninvited interventions within the law of unjust enrichment, will give a narrower ground of recovery.

(3) Payments to Public Authorities

(a) Statutory regimes

Various statutes provide for the recovery of money paid as tax that was not due. **18.154**
Most oust common law rights of recovery, expressly or by necessary implication.[302]
Hence, in practice 'the number of cases [concerning the recovery of undue payments to public authorities] where any principle of common law would need to be relied on is likely to be small',[303] and so is the number of cases where claimants will be allowed to rely on their common law rights in preference to those conferred by statute, for example because they wish to take advantage of a more favourable limitation period or right to interest.[304]

(b) Common law claims

In *Woolwich Equitable Building Society v IRC*[305] a building society paid money **18.155**
in response to a tax demand issued under regulations which were subsequently held to be *ultra vires* and void in judicial review proceedings.[306] The society had disputed the validity of the regulations from the outset, but had paid because it wished to avoid penalties and unfavourable publicity. Following the outcome of the judicial review proceedings, the Revenue returned the capital sum together with interest from the date of judgment, but stated that it did so *ex gratia*, and refused to pay interest from the date of receipt. To make good its claim to this interest, the society therefore had to show that it had been entitled as of right to the return of the money. As the law then stood, payments made in response to *ultra vires* public demands were recoverable only if made under illegitimate compulsion or mistake of fact. They could not be recovered simply because of their *ultra vires* nature. On the facts, the society had made no mistake, nor had it relevantly been subjected to illegitimate pressure. However, the House of Lords was persuaded that the dominant view was out of line with fundamental principle and had neglected authority which was not. Accordingly, the law

---

[302] See eg the Taxes Management Act 1970, s 33 (on which see *Deutsche Morgan Grenfell plc v IRC* [2006] UKHL 49; [2007] 1 AC 558, [19], HL, and *Monro v Revenue & Customs Commissioners* [2007] EWHC 114, [2007] BTC 325); the Inheritance Tax Act 1984, s 241; and the Value Added Tax Act 1994, s 80. See too M Chowdry and C Mitchell 'Tax Legislation as a Justifying Factor' [2005] RLR 1, 18–20.

[303] *Woolwich Equitable Building Society v IRC* [1993] AC 70, 200, HL (Lord Slynn).

[304] Cf *Commonwealth of Australia v SCI Operations Pty Ltd* (1998) 192 CLR 285, HCA.

[305] [1993] AC 70, HL.

[306] In *R v Inland Revenue Commissioners, ex p Woolwich BS* [1990] 1 WLR 1400, HL.

was reformulated,[307] and their Lordships then held that the society had been entitled to recover its money as of right from the moment of payment.

(i) The scope of the Woolwich principle

18.156 One policy justification for the *Woolwich* entitlement mentioned by Lord Goff[308] is that a general right to recover payments of tax levied without the authority of Parliament is needed to give full effect to the constitutional principle enshrined in the Bill of Rights 1689, art 4, that the Crown and its ministers may not impose direct or indirect taxes without Parliamentary sanction. Another, latent in their Lordships' speeches, is the related but wider public law principle of legality, that bodies invested with power by the state must respect the rule of law, and adhere to the limits of the jurisdictions conferred upon them. This would suggest that claims should lie not only against governmental bodies who have demanded tax but also against any other sort of public authority which has acted beyond its powers to demand duties, fees, and other levies,[309] and that the concept of a 'public authority' in this context should be given a wide connotation, to embrace not only governmental bodies, but also bodies such as privatized industries whose authority to charge is subject to and limited by public law principles.[310]

18.157 In *Boake Allen Ltd v HMRC*[311] the *Woolwich* principle was said in obiter dicta to apply only where money has been collected through the machinery of demand. If this approach prevails then it will preclude reliance on the *Woolwich* rule in many cases, since the collection of tax in the UK is heavily dependent on self-assessment mechanisms. However, it is hard to think that requiring proof of a tax demand is consistent with the *Woolwich* case, which was expressly fought and decided on the basis that the building society's payment had not been made in response to pressure exerted by the Revenue.

---

307 In accordance with the arguments made in WR Cornish, '"Colour of Office": Restitutionary Redress against Public Authority' (1987) 14 Jo of Malaysian and Comparative Law 41, and P Birks, 'Restitution from the Executive: A Tercentenary Footnote to the Bill of Rights' in PD Finn (ed), *Essays on Restitution* (1990) 164.

308 [1993] AC 70, 172, HL.

309 For example: charges to take extracts from a parish register (*Steele v Williams* (1853) Ex 625, 155 ER 1502); charges for the use of pier facilities (*Queens of the River SS Co v River Thames Conservators* (1889) 15 Times LR 474); stallage (cf *R v Birmingham CC, ex p Dredger* (1993) 91 LGR 532); charges for the provision of border control services (*Waikato Regional Airport Ltd v A-G of New Zealand* [2003] UKPC 50, [2004] 3 NZLR 1).

310 Cf *South of Scotland Electricity Board v British Oxygen Co Ltd* [1959] 1 WLR 587 (HL Sc). See too Law Commission, *Restitution: Mistakes of Law and Ultra Vires Public Authority Receipts and Payments* (Law Com No 227, 1994), paras 6.42–6.45; J Beatson, 'Restitution of Taxes, Levies and Other Imposts: Defining the Extent of the *Woolwich* Principle' (1993) 109 LQR 401, 417–8.

311 [2006] EWCA Civ 25; [2006] STC 606, [84], [89], and [140]–[147]; not considered on appeal: [2007] UKHL 25; [2007] 1 WLR 1386.

(ii) Relationship with mistake of law

In *Kleinwort Benson Ltd v Lincoln CC* Lord Goff observed that the abolition of the **18.158** mistake of law bar[312] had left English law with 'two separate and distinct regimes in respect of the repayment of money paid under a mistake of law', namely:[313]

> (1) cases concerned with repayment of taxes and other similar charges which, when exacted *ultra vires*, are recoverable as of right at common law on the principle in *Woolwich*, and otherwise are the subject of statutory regimes regulating recovery; and (2) other cases, which may broadly be described as concerned with repayment of money paid under private transactions, and which are governed by the common law.

In *Deutsche Morgan Grenfell plc v IRC*,[314] the defendant tax authority interpreted **18.159** these words to mean that a claimant who mistakenly pays money as tax, and who is not precluded from claiming at common law, may only rely on the *Woolwich* ground of recovery and may not base his claim on mistake of law. There is certainly something to be said for the view that claims to recover *ultra vires* payments to public authorities should be governed exclusively by public law principles, as these are best adapted to take account of the special relationship between the parties.[315] However little attempt seems to have been made to argue the point from first principles before the House of Lords, which rejected the defendant's reading of Lord Goff's words, and held that claimants can choose whether to rely on mistake of law or the *Woolwich* principle where both reasons for restitution are present on the facts of the case.

(4) Withdrawal from an Illegal Transaction

It often happens that claimants wish to recover benefits which they have conferred **18.160** on defendants pursuant to illegal transactions. The English courts have traditionally tended to identify the unjust factor in cases of this sort as one of the factors considered above, such as mistake[316] or duress[317] or failure of consideration,[318]

---

[312] See paras 18.62–18.63.

[313] [1999] 2 AC 349, 362, HL.

[314] [2006] UKHL 49; [2007] 1 AC 558.

[315] Precisely such considerations led the Supreme Court of Canada to hold in *Kingstreet Investments Ltd v New Brunswick (Department of Finance)* 2007 SCC 1, [2007] 1 SCR 3, that common law claims to recover *ultra vires* tax payments are governed by a unique set of special principles. The same reasoning might also lead one to conclude that the recovery of *ultra vires* disbursements by public authorities should also be governed by a special regime; at present these are recoverable via common law proceedings under the rule in *Auckland Harbour Board v R* [1924] AC 318, PC. Pressure to develop this principle may come from European Community law, under which state aid paid by member states to their citizens in breach of Community law must be repaid: A Jones, *Restitution and European Community Law* (2000), ch 5.

[316] As in eg *Oom v Bruce* (1810) 12 East 225, 104 ER 87.

[317] As in eg *Smith v Bromley* (1760) 2 Doug 696n, 99 ER 441.

[318] As in eg *Parkinson v College of Ambulance* [1923] 2 KB 1.

and to regard the illegality of the transaction as a matter which is relevant only to the question whether the defendant should have a defence to the claim.[319] They have relied on the maxim *in pari delicto potior est conditio defendentis* (where parties are involved in a wrong the defendant's position is the stronger) to hold that the loss should lie where it falls, and to deny recovery. For a long time, the claimant's only escape was to deny equal involvement in the illegality.[320]

(a) Two exceptional situations

(i) Proprietary claims

18.161 The first exception, difficult to defend, is the assertion of proprietary rights without positively relying on the illegality, that property in the defendant's hands should properly be regarded as belonging to him. This exception crystallized in *Tinsley v Milligan*,[321] in which a majority of the House of Lords held that a participant in an illegal scheme to defraud the Department of Social Security could assert a claim under a resulting trust to a share in a house which had been bought with her financial assistance, but which had been put into the other participant's name pursuant to the fraudulent scheme. Lord Browne-Wilkinson reasoned that because there was no special relationship giving rise to a presumption of advancement between the parties, the rules governing the imposition of resulting trusts merely required the claimant to lead evidence of her conferral of a benefit on the defendant, and of the fact that she had received nothing in exchange for this benefit—and they did not require her to rely on evidence of her own illegality before a resulting trust would be imposed. It followed that the court could simply ignore the existence of the parties' shared illegal purpose when imposing a resulting trust on the house in the claimant's favour.

18.162 *Tinsley v Milligan* has been widely criticized for its formalistic approach to the question when the parties' illegality should affect a claimant's right to recover, which produces arbitrary results by making the availability of a remedy turn on the nature of the right asserted and, within that, on an essentially irrelevant question, namely whether or not the parties were in a special relationship.[322]

---

[319] Illegality as a defence is considered below, from paras 18.282–18.289.

[320] As in eg *Holman v Johnson* (1775) 1 Cowp 341, 98 ER 1120.

[321] [1994] 1 AC 340, HL, applied in *Silverwood v Silverwood* (1997) 74 P & CR 453, CA, and *Lowson v Coombes* [1999] Ch 373, CA. Further discussion at paras 18.282ff.

[322] Law Commission, *Illegal Transactions: The Effect of Illegality on Contracts and Trusts* (Law Com No 154, 1999), paras 3.19–3.24; *Collier v Collier* [2002] EWCA Civ 1095; [2002] BPIR 1057, [105]–[106].

(ii) The policy in favour of withdrawal

The second exception, which is much older,[323] but which was recently reaffirmed   **18.163**
by the Court of Appeal in *Tribe v Tribe*,[324] is that recovery will be permitted where
a claimant has conferred a benefit on a defendant pursuant to an illegal transaction, but has withdrawn from the transaction before it has been carried through,
and hence within the *locus poenitentiae* (time for repentance). The facts of *Tribe v
Tribe* were not best suited to the application of this doctrine, since the claimant
was not so much aborting his illegal project as seeking help to carry through its
second stage. He had transferred shares to his son to hide them from creditors
(though none had in fact been defrauded). The time had come to resume full
ownership. At this point he had been betrayed by the son's insistence on treating
himself as their owner.

The Law Commission has taken the view that cases of this sort can be resolved   **18.164**
more coherently on the basis that the very ground for recovery is the general policy
of encouraging withdrawal from illegal transactions.[325] Though the English courts
have not clearly and expressly adopted this analysis, if they were to do so, it appears
that restitution would be barred once any part of the illegal transaction had been
carried out.[326] On the other hand, sincere repentance on the part of the claimant
would probably not be required.[327]

(5) Insolvency Policies

The Insolvency Act 1986, ss 239–41, retrospectively deem certain payments by   **18.165**
an insolvent company to its creditors prior to insolvency to constitute an enrichment unjustly gained by those creditors at the expense of the company's other
creditors, and accordingly empower the court to order restitution of such payments
to the liquidator. The policy goals of this statutory restitutionary regime are:
(i) fostering the collective insolvency process; (ii) enabling the equal distribution
of an insolvent's assets; (iii) deterring the dismemberment of companies on the
verge of insolvency.[328] The difficult question of when the innocent recipient of a

---

[323] See eg *Roberts v Roberts* (1818) Dan 143, 159 ER 862; *Groves v Groves* (1829) 3 Y & J 163,
148 ER 1136.

[324] [1996] Ch 107, CA.

[325] Law Com No 154 (n 322), paras 2.49–2.56.

[326] *Kearley v Thompson* (1890) 24 QBD 742, 747, CA doubting the more relaxed approach to
this question previously taken in *Taylor v Bowers* (1876) 1 QBD 291, CA.

[327] *Tribe v Tribe* [1996] Ch 107, 135, CA. But cf earlier cases requiring genuine repentance:
Parkinson v College of Ambulance Ltd [1925] 2 KB 1, 16 (Lush J); *Harry Parker Ltd v Mason* [1940]
2 KB 590; *Bigos v Boustead* [1951] 1 All ER 92.

[328] A Keay, 'The Recovery of Voidable Preferences: Aspects of Restoration' [2000] Company
Financial and Insolvency L Rev 1; S Degeling, 'Restitution for Vulnerable Transactions' in J Armour
(ed), *Vulnerable Transactions in Corporate Insolvency* (2003) 385.

voidable preference should be entitled to invoke a change of position defence has been considered in several Commonwealth cases construing similar statutory regimes, some of which specifically provide for such a defence in general terms.[329] In England it has also been held that this defence can be raised against a claim to recover benefits transferred under a transaction that is void by reason of the Insolvency Act 1986, section 127.[330]

H. Rights to Restitution

18.166   Unjust enrichment at the expense of another is an event, and the response to that event is a right to restitution. The right is sometimes personal (*in personam*) and sometimes proprietary (*in rem*).

(1) The Meaning of 'Restitution'

18.167   In ordinary speech 'restitution' can denote either the restoration of a person to some prior condition or the restoration of something to a person. The former sense can cover even the making good of a loss. The latter focuses on something obtained by the person who has to make restitution. Only the latter is in play here. It would avoid an obvious danger of confusion if the law could maintain a clean contrast between compensation and restitution by renouncing the other sense.[331]

(2) The Personal Right to Restitution Arising from Unjust Enrichment

18.168   The law of rights *in personam* is the law of obligations: C's right against the person of D, that D make some performance, correlates with D's obligation to make that performance. It follows that when we say that obligations arise from, among other events, unjust enrichment, we could as easily say that rights *in personam* so arise. Again, if we say that in English law unjust enrichment belongs largely but not exclusively in the law of obligations, we mean that the various species of that generic event usually, but not exclusively, generate rights *in personam*.

---

[329] T O'Sullivan, 'Defending a Liquidator's Claim for Repayment of a Voidable Transaction' (1997) 9 Otago L Rev 111; also *Re Ernst and Young Inc* (1997) 147 DLR (4th) 229, Alberta CA; *Countrywide Banking Corp Ltd v Dean* [1998] AC 338, PC; *Re Excel Freight Ltd (in liq)* (1999) 8 NZCLC 261,827, NZHC; *Cripps v Lakeview Farm Fresh Ltd (in rec)* [2006] 1 NZLR 238, NZHC.

[330] *Re Tain Construction Ltd* [2003] EWHC 1737; [2003] 1 WLR 2791.

[331] The Chancery courts have long used the term 'restitution' to denote a particular type of compensatory liability owed by defaulting trustees and fiduciaries: *Nocton v Lord Ashburton* [1914] AC 932, 952, HL; *Bartlett v Barclays Bank Trust Co Ltd (No 2)* [1980] Ch 515, 543, CA; *Swindle v Harrison* [1997] 4 All ER 705, 715–7, 726–7, 733, CA.

Almost every unjust enrichment gives rise to a personal restitutionary right.[332]   **18.169**
That is to say, the enriched defendant comes under an obligation to give up to the
claimant the enrichment received. The enrichment is measured at the moment of
its receipt, though the obligation to return it may be reduced or indeed extinguished by the operation of defences. Hence a right *in personam* is the standard
response, and enrichment received is the standard measure of that response.

This entitlement *in personam* to the value received is not an alternative held in   **18.170**
reserve for the case in which the specific asset can no longer be given up. The old
actions reveal this.[333] In the action for money had and received the claimant
declared that the defendant was indebted to him in such and such a sum, the *causa
debendi* being the receipt of that much money to the claimant's use. The claim was
not for the coins or notes received but in respect of the abstract debt thus created
in that sum. The same is true of related actions within the *assumpsit* family. It is
true, for example, of money paid to the use of the defendant, *quantum meruit*, and
quantum valebat. All these go directly for the money value of that which the
defendant received. This marks a major point of difference between the common
law approach and German law. In the latter the obligation is expressed as in the
first instance an obligation to surrender the specific asset received. The right to
the value arises only when it has become impossible to surrender (*herausgeben*)
the specific thing.[334]

In equity, free-standing obligations arising from unjust enrichment are likewise   **18.171**
obligations to pay value, not to transfer any specific thing.[335] Rights to specific
things, so far as they exist, are always proprietary. In equity that is a tautology,
since, wherever there is an obligation to transfer a specific thing, the maxim that
equity sees that as done which ought to be done will turn the recipient into a
trustee and thus raise a proprietary interest in the claimant.[336]

---

[332] Rescission of voidable transactions arguably constitutes an exception, but, in the light of (a)
the rise of pecuniary rescission as in *Mahoney v Purnell* [1996] 3 All ER 61 and (b) long-established
practice where the claimant has paid money rather than transferred a thing, it is difficult to deny the
initial personal obligation to repay the value obtained, so long as the defendant can be shown to have
been enriched.

[333] For the words of the action for money had and received, and of the other counts in *indebitatus
assumpsit*, see *Stephen on Pleading* (2nd edn, 1827) 312.

[334] BGB § 818 (2).

[335] *Ministry of Health v Simpson* [1951] AC 251, HL (*in personam* claim). 'Free-standing' indicates an obligation which is independent of any proprietary interest in the thing.

[336] In *A-G for Hong Kong v Reid* [1994] 1 AC 324, PC, which was a case of restitution for a
wrong, not a case of unjust enrichment, Lord Templeman thought that the corrupt prosecutor did
come under an obligation to transfer each bribe as it came in. The maxim then bit on that obligation
to make a specific transfer, turning him into a constructive trustee for his employer, who could thus
be said to have an equitable proprietary interest in the specific money received.

18.172 In most cases the only response in question is the personal right to restitution of enrichment received. In some contexts, above all in insolvency, it becomes necessary to ask whether the law responds to the unjust enrichment by raising a property right in the claimant.

(3) *Proprietary Restitutionary Rights Arising from Unjust Enrichment*

18.173 Whereas a personal right is a means to effecting restitution by the realization of an obligation incumbent on the enriched person, a proprietary right is a means of effecting restitution by the realization of a right in an asset held by the enriched person, whether the very asset which carried the enrichment to him or, more likely, an asset which is its traceable substitute. Personal rights, though diverse in content, are all of one kind in that they require a defendant to do something. Rights *in rem* (proprietary rights) by contrast cannot be considered without being sub-divided into different kinds.

18.174 A right *in rem* may be a power to alter the legal condition of a thing or a substantive interest in that thing; and, again, a right *in rem* which is a substantive interest may be a beneficial interest or a security interest. 'Substantive' underscores the contrast with a power. A power *in rem* is an interest in the thing, but it is an instrument for creating vested beneficial and security interests.

18.175 The most convenient strategy will be to ask first whether any species of proprietary interest is raised by any instance of unjust enrichment and only afterwards to ask what kind of proprietary right it might be.

(a) When will the claimant in unjust enrichment have a proprietary interest?

18.176 We have seen that an enrichment at the expense of the claimant will be unjust where the claimant had no intent to part with it, where his intent was impaired, where his intent was qualified, and where, independently of his intent, there is a policy reason requiring restitution. Each of these four will be considered in turn, but first must come three general propositions which apply throughout.

(i) *Three general doctrines*

18.177 **Substitution.**   If, immediately after the defendant's receipt, the claimant has a proprietary interest in the *res* received, he will later be able to claim a proprietary interest in any substitute for that original still traceably held by the recipient.

18.178 The recipient of money or other assets may later exchange them for other things. Money is likely to be exchanged almost immediately. Even putting it in the bank, or taking it out, entails a substitution, cash for personal claim, or vice versa. The chain of substitutions may be long or short. It may involve only clean substitutions but it is more likely to include mixed substitutions. A mixed substitution happens when someone acquires an asset with value derived from more than one source, as for instance £1,000 of his own and £2,000 received from another.

If each link in a chain of substitutions had to be proved by evidence, the chain would often break after the first or second exchange.[337] However, it is saved from so easily breaking by the artificial rules of tracing.[338] Tracing is no more than the process of identifying the application of value through one or more exchanges.[339] That process is neutral as to rights. When D receives Asset One from C, a tracing exercise which shows that Asset Ten in D's hands is its traceable substitute will only give C rights in Asset Ten if other facts establish C's entitlement.

18.179

The question whether C has proprietary rights in traced substitutes depends on his having had such rights in the asset at the head of the chain. The asset at the head of the chain is the asset received by D, contemplated at the moment after its receipt. It is there that C must establish his proprietary base. He may establish this proprietary base by the operation of the law of unjust enrichment as described below or by reference to doctrines which have nothing to do with the law of unjust enrichment. The efficacy of substitution in raising proprietary rights in the substitute depends on the establishment of a proprietary base at the first link of the chain, not on the nature of the facts relied on to establish that proprietary base. For example, D may have committed an acquisitive wrong which, exceptionally, turned him into a trustee for his victim.[340] Again it may be that D held as bailee, as where a solicitor was a depositee for safe-keeping of his client's bonds and sold them out.[341]

18.180

In such cases, just as much as in those in which the proprietary base itself arises directly from unjust enrichment, C's interest in the substitute arises from unjust enrichment.[342] Wherever one who holds an asset belonging to another uses that asset without the consent of that other to acquire wealth, that acquisition is obtained at the expense of the other, because the acquisitive opportunities inherent in property are attributed in law to its owner, and the acquisition is unjust by reason of the want of the owner's consent.[343] As for the proprietary nature of the response, that derives simply from the choice made by English law in favour of

18.181

---

337 *Trustee of FC Jones & Son (a firm) v Jones* [1997] Ch 159, CA is a rare counter-example, involving a series of clean substitutions.

338 Comprehensively treated by LD Smith, *The Law of Tracing* (1997).

339 *Boscawen v Bajwa* [1996] 1 WLR 328, 334, CA; *Foskett v McKeown* [2001] 1 AC 102, 127, HL; *Glencore International AG v Metro Trading International Ltd (No 2)* [2001] 1 Lloyd's Rep 284, [180].

340 *A-G of Hong Kong v Reid* [1994] 1 AC 324, PC. Reid received bribes which his employer traced to farms in New Zealand. He became a trustee of each bribe received (cf n 336). The government could then assert its beneficial interest in the traced substitutes.

341 *Re Hallett's Estate* (1879) 13 Ch D 696, CA.

342 So also Smith (n 338) 300–1.

343 See paras 18.26–18.29 and 18.46–18.49.

responding to every substitution by, inter alia, according to the claimant as nearly as possible the same rights in relation to the substitute as he enjoyed in the original at the moment when the original was received by the defendant. Many systems do not make that choice.

18.182   In *Foskett v McKeown*[344] the House of Lords held that proprietary rights to substitute assets are not generated by the law of unjust enrichment, but by the law of property. Their Lordships' analysis falsely opposes unjust enrichment (a source of rights) and property (a type of right). It implies that property rights never arise from unjust enrichment and conceals the event from which the proprietary right in the substitute arises. If I lose £5 and with it the finder buys a cake, my property in the cake cannot be regarded as arising from the same event as my property in the £5. Clearly something has happened which has made me owner of the cake. That event is non-consensual substitution. And non-consensual substitution cannot in general be classified as a manifestation of consent or a wrong. It must either be an unjust enrichment or an event in the miscellaneous fourth category of causative events.[345]

18.183   **Immediate knowledge.**   Several cases hold that a trust will be imposed on assets if they are transferred to a recipient who knows at the moment of receipt that the transferor is entitled to restitution. However the scope of this doctrine has been uncertain since the Court of Appeal sought to confine it to cases where the recipient has acted with a high degree of improbity.

18.184   In *Neste Oy v Lloyds Bank plc*[346] some ships' chandlers were in financial trouble. They were wont to receive payments in advance in respect of ships which they were to look after. One such payment arrived when they already knew that they would not be fulfilling the contract. That is, they knew the basis on which they received was going to fail. Bingham J held that they became trustees of that payment. In their insolvency that payment was therefore not a part of the fund available to creditors and, equally important, as they fell into insolvency it would have been proper, and not a voidable preference, for them to have returned it. The recipients knew at the moment of their receipt that the basis of the payment was going to fail.

18.185   In this case none of the five payments was tied to a particular application so as trigger a *Quistclose* trust.[347] Apart from the one payment caught by the immediate

---

[344]   [2001] 1 AC 102, HL.

[345]   Further discussion: P Birks, 'Property, Unjust Enrichment and Tracing' [2001] CLP 231; A Burrows, Proprietary Restitution: Unmaking Unjust Enrichment' (2001) 117 LQR 412; R Chambers 'Tracing and Unjust Enrichment' in J Neyers et al (eds), *Understanding Unjust Enrichment* (2004) 263.

[346]   [1983] 2 Lloyds Rep 658.

[347]   *Barclays Bank v Quistclose Investments Ltd* [1970] AC 567, HL; see para 18.123.

knowledge doctrine, the others all illustrate a situation in which there never will be a proprietary response. They were payments made for consideration which happened to fail but where the money was in the meantime freely at the disposal of the recipients.

The *Neste Oy* case was followed in *Re Farepak Food and Gifts Ltd (in admin)*.[348]   **18.186**
A company operated a Christmas savings scheme under which customers could spread their Christmas savings over a year. Small contributions could be made month by month so that enough had accumulated by the beginning of November to buy Christmas goods and vouchers. In October 2006 the directors decided to cease trading and instructed their agents to stop collecting payments, but money kept coming in for a while after the directors' decision. The administrators sought directions as to how they should distribute this money. None was impressed with a *Quistclose* trust because the company had never been obliged to segregate the customers' funds and apply them to the purchase of particular goods or vouchers. Nevertheless Mann J was willing to impose a trust on moneys in the company's hands 'insofar as it could be established that [these] were paid to Farepak by customers at a time when Farepak had decided that it had ceased trading'.[349]

Hodgson v Marks[350] is also amenable to a *Neste Oy* explanation, although in fact   **18.187**
the immediate knowledge doctrine was not invoked. An old lady conveyed her house to her lodger, Evans. He knew from the start that he was not meant to benefit. It was a contrivance, merely part of a scheme to make his position secure as against her nephew who wanted him out. Similarly, in *Tribe v Tribe*[351] the son knew from the start that as between him and his father the shares really still in substance were to belong to his father. They had only been transferred in order to keep them out of sight of any creditor in the event of the father's insolvency. The father's claim that the son was a trustee might have run into serious difficulties on the ground of illegality, but the Court of Appeal held that it did not. We will return to another explanation of these cases immediately below.[352]

In *National Bank of New Zealand v Waitaki International Processing (NI) Ltd*[353] the   **18.188**
bank persuaded itself that it owed Waitaki $500,000. It insisted on paying it over, in the teeth of warnings and protests. Waitaki knew that the bank had made a mistake. It knew that the money would have to go back. There was no word of trusteeship in the judgments, but the courts treated Waitaki exactly as though it were a trustee. It was found to have been honest, but, knowing that it was not

---

348   [2006] EWHC 3272; [2007] 2 BCLC 1. See too *Re Japan Leasing (Europe) plc* [1999] BPIR 911.
349   Ibid, [40].
350   [1971] Ch 892, CA.
351   [1996] Ch 107, CA.
352   See paras 18.197–18.202.
353   [1999] 2 NZLR 211, NZCA.

entitled, it was under a duty to look after the money and invest it on good security. It had not taken a good security and it was in principle liable to the extent that the security had been inadequate at the time of the investment. This is an application of the rule that would have applied to a trustee.

18.189 The *Neste Oy* principle was reviewed by the Court of Appeal in *Triffit Nurseries (a firm) v Salads Etcetera Ltd (in admin rec)*.[354] The claimants grew vegetables that were distributed by an agent company, which billed customers and remitted the proceeds to the claimants, deducting commission. The company was free to mix the sums collected with its own funds and use them for its own purposes, and did not hold them on an express trust for the claimants. The company went into administrative receivership at a time when there were amounts outstanding in respect of sales of the claimants' produce. The receivers collected the outstanding sums and the question arose whether this money should go to the claimants or the company's bank which held a charge over its book debts. Consistently with the foregoing cases one might have expected the court to impose a trust because the company could not conscionably have received the customers' money, knowing that it would not perform its contractual duty to account for an equivalent sum to the claimants. However the Court of Appeal held that this was an insufficient degree of improbity to convert the company into a trustee. It is hard to understand what distinguishes the recipients in *Neste Oy* and *Farepak* from the recipient in *Triffit Nurseries*. In the first two cases the relevant funds came from the claimants, while in the latter they came from third parties, but it is unclear why this should have made a difference.

18.190 Further uncertainty is also created by *Westdeutsche Landesbank Girozentrale v Islington LBC*.[355] The bank made payments to Islington under an interest rate swap which was interrupted when the contract turned out to have been void *ab initio*. In the courts below it was held, following *Sinclair v Brougham*,[356] that the bank had both a personal claim to restitution and a proprietary interest in the money paid over. The House of Lords said that was wrong. The bank had no proprietary interest. *Sinclair v Brougham*, which suggested the contrary, was overruled. The bank had not known at the start that the consideration would fail. Hence it was certainly not within the *Neste Oy* doctrine.[357] However, Lord Browne-Wilkinson enunciated a doctrine which would enlarge *Neste Oy*. He said that a recipient might be turned into a trustee if he acquired knowledge of the restitutionary

---

[354] [2000] 1 BCLC 761, CA.

[355] [1996] AC 669, HL.

[356] [1914] AC 398, HL.

[357] R Chambers, *Resulting Trusts* (1997) 158–63 reviews all the reasons why it might be said that Islington did not become a trustee for the bank and concludes, at 162, that the key fact was that the money was freely at the disposition of the recipient before the basis for the receipt failed, cf 144–7.

obligation at any time while proceeds remained traceable in his hands. This would cause proprietary interests to arise in many cases.³⁵⁸ It would have produced a different result in the *Westdeutsche* case itself if the defendants had held assets traceably derived from the original.

If Lord Browne-Wilkinson's doctrine is too generous, then the *Neste Oy* doctrine **18.191** must be limited to knowledge of non-entitlement concurrent with knowledge of the receipt, at the first opportunity to accept or reject. Just possibly it might be extended to cases in which the recipient acquires knowledge while he still has the specific *res* received as opposed to traceable substitutes.

Judicial discretion. In the *Westdeutsche* case Lord Browne-Wilkinson indicated **18.192** that a day might come when English courts would claim a discretion to turn defendants into trustees and to tailor the attendant proprietary interests to the circumstances of the case. This might be done, he thought, by introducing the 'remedial constructive trust'.³⁵⁹ That step has not been taken. The English Court of Appeal has since repudiated any such discretion. 'It is not that you need an Act of Parliament to prohibit a variation of property rights. You need one to permit it: see the Variation of Trusts Act 1958 and the Matrimonial Causes Act 1973.'³⁶⁰ In the unlikely event of the House of Lords later taking a different view, judicial discretion will have to take its place as the third general way in which a claimant in unjust enrichment can acquire a proprietary interest.

(ii) The four species of unjust enrichment

The paragraphs which follow deal with the effect of each of the four types of **18.193** unjust enrichment in engendering a proprietary response independently of the three general doctrines just discussed. Discussion of the kind of proprietary right engendered is so far as possible postponed to the next section.

No intent. Here the pre-existing proprietary right in general survives. That **18.194** surviving right cannot be said to arise from the unjust enrichment of the recipient. If C loses his money, the finder, D, takes subject to C's property in it. On these facts the law of unjust enrichment has nothing to say about the specific asset received, the note in the finder's hands. On the other hand it does put the recipient under an obligation to make restitution of the value.³⁶¹ The right

---

³⁵⁸ The doctrine was applied in *Commerzbank Aktiengesellschaft v IMB Morgan plc* [2004] EWHC 2771; [2005] 2 All ER (Comm) 564, [34]. See too *Papamichael v National Westminster Bank plc (No 2)* [2003] EWHC 341; [2003] 1 Lloyd's Rep 341, [221]–[231].

³⁵⁹ [1996] AC 669, 714–16, HL.

³⁶⁰ *Re Polly Peck (No 2)* [1998] 3 All ER 812, 831, CA (Nourse LJ). Compare *Fortex Group Ltd v MacIntosh* [1998] 3 NZLR 171, NZCA.

³⁶¹ *Holiday v Sigil* (1827) 2 Car & P 177, 172 ER 81; *Neate v Harding* (1851) 6 Ex 349, 155 ER 577; *Moffatt v Kazana* [1959] 2 QB 152; *Lipkin Gorman v Karpnale Ltd* [1991] 2 AC 548, HL.

in rem does not arise from unjust enrichment. The debt measured by the value received does.[362]

18.195   In some cases of 'no intent' this survival model cannot apply. Instead a new equitable proprietary interest arises from the unjust enrichment of the recipient. In the normal course a company has full legal ownership of its assets. If the directors, being fiduciaries, transfer assets without authority, then, unless that recipient has dealt with the company in good faith,[363] equity treats the recipient in the same way as a person who receives trust property from a trustee acting without the authority of the trust deed or the consent of his beneficiaries. In the latter case the recipient takes subject to the pre-existing equitable interest of the beneficiaries. The survival model applies. But in the former case there is no pre-existing equitable interest in the company. Equity therefore completes the analogy by raising a new interest in the assets received from the unauthorized fiduciary. Though it is tempting to attribute that new interest to a breach of fiduciary duty and hence to locate it in the law of wrongs, it is unnecessary to do so.[364]

18.196   **Impaired intent.**   Though not sufficient, intent is in general necessary to the passing of property.[365] Just as in absolutely involuntary transfers the property does not pass, so in some instances of severely impaired transfer the transferee takes subject to the transferor's pre-existing proprietary rights, as where the latter has laboured under a fundamental mistake.[366] However, the law generally gives the defectively intending transferor a more limited proprietary right as a means to restitution. Thus, subject to the appropriate fine-tuning, transfers made through mistake, misrepresentation, pressure, and relational or other disadvantage are all voidable. This implies at the very least that the transferor has a power *in rem*, a power to vest in himself that with which he has parted. We will return below to the question whether that is all that such a transferor obtains.[367]

18.197   **Qualified intent.**   The commonest qualified transfers do not generate proprietary rights. To determine which do and which do not, it is necessary to insist on the distinction between the abstract value received and the thing itself which

---

[362] For differences between common law and Chancery in this context, see paras 18.46–18.51.

[363] Companies Act 2006, s 40; for the case in which the board deals with a director or a person connected with a director, see Companies Act 2006, s 41.

[364] *Rolled Steel Products (Holdings) v British Steel Corporation* [1986] Ch 246, CA; *Precision Dippings Ltd v Precision Dippings Marketing Ltd* [1986] Ch 246, CA; *Criterion Properties Ltd v Stratford UK Properties Ltd* [2004] UKHL 28; [2004] 1 WLR 1846, [4].

[365] Thus, when the facts indicate a sale of specific goods, the Sale of Goods Act 1979, s 17(1), provides that property passes when it is intended to pass.

[366] *Cundy v Lindsay* (1878) 3 App Cas 459 (fundamental mistake of identity). In *Barclays Bank Ltd v WJ Simms Son and Cooke (Southern) Ltd* [1980] QB 677, 686 Robert Goff J expressly took account of the fact that in some restitutionary claims for mistake the property would not have passed.

[367] See paras 18.204ff.

carries that value to the defendant. *Ex hypothesi*, no qualified transfer can put the abstract value finally at the disposition of the transferee. However, the failure of the basis of the transfer will generate no proprietary interest unless an exercise of construction concludes that the qualification was such as also to ring-fence the thing received.[368] 'Thing' here includes money or, if no corporeal money actually passes, the fund or credit. As Robert Chambers says, there will be no proprietary interest if, before the basis fails, the recipient obtains the unrestricted use of the property.[369]

If money is construed to have been transferred solely for a particular purpose, **18.198** that construction easily carries with it the secondary conclusion that the money itself, or the credit, was never to be at the disposition of the recipient or, in short, that it was ring-fenced *ab initio*. In these circumstances, it may be that an express trust in favour of the transferor arises from the moment of receipt, subject to a power vested in the transferee to apply the money[370]—in which case there is no room for the law of unjust enrichment to operate. But in some situations where C transfers an asset to D on the basis that D will never treat himself as entitled to the benefit normally inherent in such a transfer, an express trust is excluded on the facts. Here, the law of unjust enrichment will turn the transferee into a trustee for the transferor.[371]

In *Hussey v Palmer*[372] an elderly lady advanced money for her son-in-law to extend **18.199** his house and provide her with accommodation. If he had not extended the house, it would have been easy to conclude that the money had been ring-fenced for that purpose. What actually happened was that the house was extended but the relationship broke down so that the mother-in-law had to find accommodation elsewhere. She wanted her money back and would have been content with a personal claim. The court insisted that she had a trust interest in the house. It makes perfect sense to say that the abstract value of the mother's money was not to be at her son-in-law's disposition if the accommodation limb of the arrangement broke down. There was a failure of consideration. But it is difficult to follow this line of reasoning to any conclusion that she had a proprietary interest in the house.

---

[368] *Westdeutsche Landesbank Girozentrale v Islington LBC* [1996] AC 669, 709–12, HL in overruling the proprietary aspect of *Sinclair v Brougham* [1914] AC 348, HL, classifies it as a case in which there was no ring-fencing. Cf *Re Goldcorp Exchange Ltd* [1995] 1 AC 74, PC and all the payments except the last in *Neste Oy v Lloyds Bank* [1983] 2 Lloyd's Rep 658 (see para 18.184).

[369] R Chambers, *Resulting Trusts* (1997) 148–51, 169. Note especially the passage from Harman J in *Re Nanwa Goldmines Ltd* [1955] 1 WLR 1080, 1083–4, cited by Chambers at 150.

[370] *Barclays Bank Ltd v Quistclose Investments Ltd* [1970] AC 567, HL, as interpreted in *Twinsectra Investments Ltd v Yardley* [2002] UKHL 12; [2002] 2 AC 164.

[371] *Tinsley v Milligan* [1994] 1 AC 340, HL.

[372] [1972] 1 WLR, 1286, CA. Similarly problematic is *Muschinski v Dodds* [1985] 160 CLR 583, HCA.

18.200 Many cases in which the failure of the intended basis of a transfer does turn the defendant into a trustee, and thus raises a proprietary interest in the transferor, could be decided on the *Neste Oy* basis, that the recipient knew from the moment of the receipt that he was not entitled to treat the asset as his own.[373] However, the proprietary response can be independently explained by the combination of the qualification and the construction of that qualification as requiring the segregation of the asset.

18.201 This independent explanation shows up particularly strongly in cases of absolute qualification whether the absolutely qualified intent is established by evidence or by presumption. In *Re Vinogradoff*[374] securities were transferred into the name of a four-year-old child, and the presumption of non-beneficial intent operated to turn the child into a trustee for the transferor. The *Neste Oy* doctrine could not run against a child.

18.202 Again in *Tinsley v Milligan*[375] one woman had contributed to the price of a house which went into the name of her lesbian partner. No question arose of her having to prove that the partner with the paper title knew *ab initio* that she was not intended to take the benefit of her contribution. On the particular facts, the claimant could take advantage of a presumption that she was not so intended. The *Neste Oy* doctrine could not work through presumptions. Yet the contributor's absolutely qualified intent, established by unrebutted presumption, was sufficient to raise a resulting trust.

18.203 **Policy-motivated unjust factors.** The three general propositions considered above can apply to policy-motivated unjust factors, but the special propositions relevant to the different kinds of non-voluntary transfer cannot. This might suggest that policy-motivated unjust factors should meet only a personal response. However, a surety is always entitled to a proprietary right via subrogation, where he has discharged a creditor's security.[376] Again, if an insured person receives money or some other valuable asset in diminution of a loss which the insurer has already made good, the insurer has, not only a personal claim to be repaid the over-indemnity, but also an equitable lien over that money or other asset so received.[377] It is not easy to detect the principle which determines that proprietary response. Similarly, arguments as to the proprietary consequences of payment of taxes not due are

---

373 See paras 18.183 ff.

374 [1935] WN 68.

375 [1994] AC 340, HL.

376 Mercantile Law Amendment Act 1856, s 5. The nature of the surety's (new) proprietary right is discussed at paras 18.216ff.

377 *Lord Napier and Ettrick v Hunter* [1993] AC 713, HL. The insurer's lien probably extends only to assets recovered from third parties, and not to any cause of action which the insured may have against them: *St Paul Travelers Insurance Co Ltd v Dargan* [2006] EWHC 3189, [2007] BPIR 117. (Ch).

unlikely to rest on any principled foundation.[378] In this sector the policy which dictates restitution must be expected also to determine the nature of the response.

(4) What Kind of Proprietary Right?

(a) Power or substantive interest?

Three models exist: the survival model, the power model, and the immediate interest model. The first supposes the survival of the pre-existing interest, itself not the creature of the recipient's unjust enrichment. In the second the claimant obtains a power to crystallize an interest in the thing received. The substantive interest will not arise till the power is exercised. In the third the law raises a new substantive interest as soon as the unjust enrichment happens.   **18.204**

(i) Traceable substitutes

D receives £10,000 from C, buys a painting with that money, and then exchanges the painting for a car. Even if the money came to D in circumstances in which C acquired, or retained, an immediate substantive interest in it, C would have only a power to crystallize a similar interest in first the painting, then the car. This power floats over the chain of substitutions. Only when C exercises the power by asserting his entitlement to the thing at the end of the chain does he acquire his substantive interest in that thing. The applicability of the power model here is controversial,[379] but the other model leads to very grave practical difficulties.[380]   **18.205**

(ii) The original asset received

Where the *Neste Oy* doctrine bites,[381] it produces an immediate trust and, necessarily, an immediate interest in the claimant. The *Neste Oy* doctrine apart, in cases of qualified intent there is either no proprietary response at all or, in those cases where the asset received is ring-fenced, the immediate interest model again applies. For example, if a fund is transferred upon trust and the trust fails,   **18.206**

---

[378] *Zaidan Group Ltd v City of London* [1990] 64 DLR (4th) 514, Ontario CA.

[379] In *Cave v Cave* (1880) 15 Ch D 639, a case of first impression, Fry J came down in favour of the immediate interest model, a view preferred by the leading treatise on tracing: LD Smith, *The Law of Tracing* (1997) 358–61. *Cave v Cave* was criticized in *Re Ffrench's Estate* (1887) 21 LR Ir 83 CA (IR) and is doubtfully compatible with *Re J Leslie (Engineers) Co Ltd* [1976] 1 WLR 292. The House of Lords indisputably applied the power model in *Lipkin Gorman v Karpnale Ltd* [1991] 2 AC 548, HL which concerned a legal interest: cf *Trustee of FC Jones & Son (a firm) v Jones* [1997] Ch 159, CA. It would be intolerable to encourage different analyses at law and in equity.

[380] Vividly illustrated on the facts of *Trustee of FC Jones & Son (a firm) v Jones* [1997] Ch 159, CA, discussed P Birks, 'On Taking Seriously the Difference between Tracing and Claiming' (1997) 11 Trust Law International 2.

[381] See paras 18.183ff.

there will be an immediate resulting trust;[382] and an absolute qualification likewise produces, without more, a resulting trust.[383]

18.207   In cases of impaired intent or no intent at all, the transfer is either voidable or void. If it is void, the recipient takes subject to the pre-existing proprietary right.[384] If the common law regards the transaction as voidable, as for fraudulent misrepresentation or duress, the power can be exercised at law without communication with the transferee, merely by manifesting in a suitably public manner the intention to rescind.[385] If the transaction is voidable only in equity, the transferor now appears to obtain a similar power to crystallize an equitable beneficial interest. Once that power is exercised, there will be a trust.[386] The beneficial owner in equity will then be in a position to demand the transfer of the legal title.

18.208   Some cases apply the immediate interest model to transfers voidable in equity. On this view the legal title passes voidably, in the sense that the court will order the transfer to be reversed but, from the moment of the transfer, the transferee already holds on trust for the transferor. No further act is required of the impaired transferee.[387] This model has never been repudiated. It has simply been departed from.

18.209   *Chase Manhattan Bank v Israel-British Bank*[388] is a lone modern survival of that line of cases, not obviously aware of its ancestry. The bank mistakenly made the same payment twice. It transferred $2m and then sent it again. The payee became insolvent. The personal claim, which undoubtedly lay, would have yielded little or nothing. A proprietary claim would give priority over unsecured creditors. Goulding J held that the effect of the mistake was immediately to turn the payee into a trustee of the second payment.

---

382   *Air Jamaica Ltd v Charlton* [1999] 1 WLR 1399, PC.

383   *Hodgson v Marks* [1971] Ch 892, CA.

384   Nullity does not necessarily prevent the property passing, but nullity from seriously impaired intent does: *Cundy v Lindsay* (1878) 3 App Cas 459, HL; *Shogun Finance Ltd v Hudson* [2003] UKHL 62; [2004] 1 AC 919.

385   *Car & Universal Finance Co Ltd v Caldwell* [1965] 1 QB 525.

386   *Lonrho plc v Fayed* [1992] 1 WLR 1, 11–12 (Millett J), followed in *Twinsectra Ltd v Yardley* [1999] Lloyd's Rep Banking 438, 461–2, CA; *Shalson v Russo* [2003] EWHC 1637; [2005] Ch 281, [121]–[127]. Very influential in this has been the judgment of Brennan J in *Daly v Sydney Stock Exchange* (1986) 160 CLR 371, HCA.

387   This model is strongly defended by Robert Chambers in his discussion of the emergence of 'mere equities': R Chambers, *Resulting Trusts* (1997) 171–81, relying on inter alia: *Stump v Gaby* (1852) 2 De GM & G 623, 42 ER 1015; *Gresley v Mousley* (1859) 4 De G & J 78, 45 ER 31; *Dickinson v Burrell* (1866) LR 1 Eq 377, CA; *Melbourne Banking Corp v Brougham* (1882) 7 App Cas 307, PC; *Blacklocks v JB Developments (Godalming) Ltd* [1982] Ch 183.

388   [1981] Ch 105, applied in *Bank Tejerat v Hong Kong and Shanghai Banking Corp* [1995] Lloyd's Rep 239; cf *R v Shadrokh-Cigari* [1988] Crim LR 465.

This case has more recently come under heavy pressure. Lord Browne-Wilkinson **18.210** has said that he could only reach the same result if he could find that the recipient bank knew that it was not entitled.[389] Lord Millett, writing extrajudicially, argues that an immediate trust can only be found where the payee is or receives through a fiduciary. For the rest he espouses wholeheartedly the power model of the proprietary reaction to unjust factors which are impairments of consent. The trust has to await the act of rescission: 'Pending rescission the transferee has the whole legal and beneficial interest in the property, but his beneficial interest is defeasible. . . It is not inappropriate to describe the transferee as holding the property on a constructive trust for the transferor, but only after rescission.'[390]

For impaired transfers, therefore, the power model is now in the ascendant. So **18.211** far as it turns simply on mistake, the *Chase Manhattan* case will have to be reinterpreted as having generated a power, not an immediate substantive interest. Only if the recipients could have been found to know *ab initio* that the money would have to be repaid will they, on this view, have been immediate trustees, under the *Neste Oy* doctrine.[391]

(b) Beneficial or security interest?

When the claimant's substantive interest accrues, whether immediately or by the **18.212** exercise of a power, it may be a beneficial interest or a lien securing the personal claim. The *Restatement of Restitution* appears to proceed on the unsafe assumption that a beneficial interest will always hit the defendant harder, for it makes that outcome depend on 'conscious wrongdoing'.[392] However, that approach creates a contradiction with the orthodox doctrine according to which equitable beneficial interests reflect the parties' contributions to an asset's acquisition. The premiss is anyhow unsound, for on some facts a lien will hit the defendant harder than a beneficial interest.[393]

The basic principle which governs this difficult question is that the claimant's **18.213** proprietary right should be as nearly as possible identical to that which he had at the beginning of the story. A supporting principle leaves it to the claimant to

---

[389] *Westdeutsche Landesbank Girozentrale v Islington LBC* [1996] AC 669, 715, HL. Cf *Barclays Bank plc v Box* [1998] Lloyd's Rep Banking 185, 200–201; *Bank of America v Arnell* [1999] Lloyds Rep Banking 399, 404; *Shalson v Russo* [2003] EWHC 1637; [2005] Ch 28, [108]–[127].

[390] 'Restitution and Constructive Trust' (1998) 114 LQR 399, 416.

[391] See paras 18.183ff.

[392] American Law Institute, *Restatement of Restitution* (1937) sections 202, 203, 210, 211. Some English cases offer oblique support in seeming to treat a charge as the normal proprietary response, though it is not clear that this is intentional: *Re Hallett's Estate* (1880) 13 Ch D 696; *El Ajou v Dollar Land Holdings plc* [1993] 3 All ER 717 (Millett J), reversed on a collateral point [1994] 2 All ER 685, CA.

[393] LD Smith, *The Law of Tracing* (OUP, 1997) 349.

choose between multiple rights which the law accords to him. English law now clearly gives effect to this principle and allows the claimant to choose between a beneficial interest proportionate to his contribution and a security interest for the amount of his contribution.[394] Naturally this principle of free choice can only operate where the law has not itself specified the nature of the interest which arises on the particular facts. In some areas it has done so, not always for a discernible reason. The House of Lords decided that money which diminishes a loss for which an insured person had already been indemnified is held subject to an equitable lien in favour of the insurer but does not turn the insured into a trustee so as to confer a beneficial interest on the insurer.[395] Where money is traced into improvements, it is also said that it generates at most a lien.[396] However, in such a situation there will be no claim at all unless the circumstances are such as to bar the argument from subjectivity of value.[397]

(c) Vulnerability to defences

18.214 As will be seen below,[398] the operation of the defences severely restricts the extent to which these proprietary rights can be realized. All rights arising from unjust enrichment, not excluding proprietary rights, are vulnerable to the defences described in the next section. The defence of change of position is open even to the immediate recipient. If the assets pass to a third party, the defence of bona fide purchase will destroy the claimant's right in all cases if the claimant has only a power or if money is in question. A substantive legal proprietary interest will otherwise be exigible against anyone, and a substantive equitable interest will be exigible against anyone but a bona fide purchaser of a legal interest. Assets which pass to a donee will be recoverable,[399] although nowadays such a donee will always be entitled to have any change of position taken into account.

18.215 Obiter dicta in the House of Lords suggest that, where a claimant purports to exercise a power to crystallize an interest in an asset which has passed to a third party, and the latter contests his right to do so, the onus is on the claimant to show

---

[394] *Foskett v McKeown* [2001] 1 AC 102, 130, HL.

[395] *Lord Napier and Ettrick v Hunter* [1993] AC 713, PC.

[396] *Foskett v McKeown* [2001] 1 AC 102, 109, HL. Cf *Re Esteem Settlement* 2002 JLR 53, 105–6, Jersey Royal Ct.

[397] *Re Diplock* [1948] Ch 465, 546–8. Contrast *Unity Joint Stock Mutual Banking Association v King* (1858) Beav 72, 44 ER 1192.

[398] See paras 18.224 ff.

[399] *Bridgeman v Green* (1757) 2 Ves Sen 627, 28 ER 379; *Huguenin v Baseley* (1807) 14 Ves Jun 275, 33 ER 526. In the latter case Lord Eldon LC said (at 289), invoking the former, 'I should regret that any doubt could be entertained that, whether it is not competent to a Court of equity to take away from third persons the benefits which they have derived from the fraud, imposition, or undue influence of others'.

that the third party was not a bona fide purchaser.[400] This must be regarded as controversial. A third party seeking to rely on change of position will certainly not be entitled to any such shift of the onus of proof.

(5) Subrogation

The word 'subrogation' means 'substitution'; it comes from the same Latin root as the more familiar word 'surrogate'. Thus the term envisages the substitution of one person for another for the purpose of exercising rights initially held by that other.[401] In some cases, this language accurately reflects the operation of the remedy: for example, where an insurer acquires its insured's subsisting rights against a third party responsible for causing an insured loss,[402] or where a tort victim acquires an insolvent insured tortfeasor's subsisting rights against the insurer, under the Third Parties (Rights Against Insurers) Act 1930.[403] In another class of case, however, this language is misleading.   **18.216**

When a claimant's money is used to discharge a creditor's rights against a defendant, the law may give him the right to be treated, by a legal fiction, as though the creditor's rights have been 'kept alive' and transferred to him so that he can enforce them for his own benefit.[404] The language of 'revival' and 'transfer' used in these cases is metaphorical. In fact the law of unjust enrichment generates new rights in the claimant's favour, whose content and characteristics resemble those of the creditor's extinguished rights, but are not identical with them.[405]   **18.217**

The imagery used in cases of this type has sometimes led the courts into error. They have worried unnecessarily about the mechanisms by which the creditor's extinguished rights might be revived and transferred, when no revival and transfer actually occur.[406] They have also forgotten that a claimant cannot be entitled to subrogation in this sort of case unless he also has a direct personal claim in unjust   **18.218**

---

[400] *Barclays Bank plc v Boulter* [1999] 4 All ER 513, 518–19, HL. The dicta go beyond the facts, on which it was rightly held that the party seeking relief bore the onus of proving that the other had notice of her disability.

[401] Civilians also know 'real subrogation', the substitution of one thing (*res*) for another, which is essentially what happens in English law with proprietary claims contingent on a successful tracing exercise.

[402] C Mitchell and S Watterson, *Subrogation: Law and Practice* (2007), ch 10.

[403] Ibid, ch 11.

[404] For the language of fictional revival see eg *Butler v Rice* [1910] Ch 277, 282; *Coptic Ltd v Bailey* [1972] Ch 446, 454; *UCB Group Ltd v Hedworth (No 2)* [2003] EWCA Civ 1717; [2003] 3 FCR 739, [146].

[405] *Banque Financière de la Cité SA v Parc (Battersea) Ltd* [1999] 1 AC 221, 236; *Cheltenham & Gloucester plc v Appleyard* [2004] EWCA Civ 291 [49]; *Filby v Mortgage Express (No 2) Ltd* [2004] EWCA 759 [63].

[406] *Re Diplock* [1948] Ch 465, 549, CA; corrected in *Boscawen v Bajwa* [1996] 1 WLR 328, 340, CA.

enrichment deriving from the fact that he has discharged the defendant's debt. Hence the fictional 'acquisition' of the creditor's rights is redundant unless these rights were secured.[407] The courts have sometimes failed to recognize this, or have chosen to ignore it, and have awarded a personal remedy in the form of a subrogation order while simultaneously denying the claimant a direct personal claim.[408] This is self-contradictory.

18.219   Unless the courts clearly recognize that the law of unjust enrichment generates new rights for claimants in this class of subrogation case, they will struggle to answer some of the difficult questions thrown up by the case law.[409] Examples are: whether the remedy should be awarded to a claimant who has paid only part of the defendant's debt;[410] whether a claimant who has paid off a mortgage debt can obtain an order for sale of the mortgaged property, after he has been repaid more than the amount of the mortgage debt;[411] whether interest awarded on a subrogation claim should be assessed on an independent basis,[412] or by reference to the interest that was previously payable on the defendant's extinguished debt;[413] and whether the priority status of a claimant's new proprietary right should mirror the priority status of the creditor's discharged security, or reflect the fact that the claimant has acquired a completely new equitable interest.[414]

18.220   The English courts have been slow to appreciate that the same rules should govern the acquisition of proprietary rights in subrogation cases as govern other proprietary responses to unjust enrichment. Thus, only obscure language conceals the

---

[407] A point which was apparently overlooked in *Filby v Mortgage Express (No 2) Ltd* [2004] EWCA Civ 759, where much time was spent discussing whether the claimant should have a subrogated claim, but it never seems to have been considered whether it might simply have a direct claim.

[408] *Marlow v Pitfeild* (1719) 1 P Wms 558, 24 ER 516; *Jenner v Morris* (1861) 3 De G F & J 45, 45 ER 795; *Baroness Wenlock v River Dee Co* (1888) 38 Ch D 534; *Re Walter's Deed of Guarantee* [1933] 1 Ch 321; *Niru Battery Manufacturing Co v Milestone Trading Ltd (No 2)* [2003] EWHC 1032; [2003] 2 All ER (Comm) 365, corrected on appeal: [2004] EWCA Civ 487; [2004] 2 All ER (Comm) 289.

[409] For discussion of which, see Mitchell and Watterson (n 402) chs 7, 8, and 9.

[410] *Gedye v Matson* (1858) 25 Beav 310, 53 ER 655; *ex p Brett* (1871) LR 6 Ch App 838, 841; *Chetwynd v Allen* [1899] 1 Ch 353; *McCullough v Elliott* (1922) 62 DLR 257 (Alberta CA); *Re T H Knitwear Ltd* [1988] 1 Ch 275, 287; *Banque Financière de la Cité v Parc (Battersea) Ltd* [1999] 1 AC 221, 236, HL; *Westpac Banking Corp v Adelaide Bank Ltd* [2005] NSWSC 517.

[411] *Halifax Mortgage Services Ltd v Muirhead* (1997) 76 P & CR 418, CA; *UCB Corporate Services Ltd v Williams* [2002] EWCA Civ 555; [2003] 1 P & CR 168, [70]–[75] and [101]–[103].

[412] As in eg *Thurstan v Nottingham Permanent Building Society* [1902] 1 Ch 1, CA, affirmed [1903] AC 6, HL; *Re Hill* (1974) 23 Fed LR 329, Fed Ct of Aus; *Congresbury Motors Ltd v Anglo-Belge Finance Co Ltd* [1970] Ch 294, affirmed [1971] Ch 81, CA; *Re Tramway Building & Construction Co Ltd* [1988] Ch 293; *Gertsch v Atsas* [1999] NSWSC 898 [99].

[413] As in eg *Western Trust & Savings Ltd v Rock* [1993] NPC 89, CA; *Castle Phillips Finance Ltd v Piddington* (1995) 70 P & CR 592, CA; *Filby v Mortgage Express (No 2) Ltd* [2004] EWCA Civ 759.

[414] The latter, according to *Cheltenham & Gloucester plc v Appleyard* [2004] EWCA Civ 291, [44], citing *Halifax plc v Omar* [2002] EWCA Civ 940. See also *National Westminster Bank plc v Mayfair Estates Property Investments Ltd* [2007] EWHC 287.

fact that, if a successful tracing exercise identifies, not shares or a yacht, but an extinguished security interest, the conditions which dictate the transfer of the shares or yacht will be the same conditions as will justify giving the claimant a new security that mirrors the extinguished charge. As the previously scattered fragments of the law of unjust enrichment become better integrated, common principles are more easily asserted. When contemplating whether to impose a trust or lien on the ground of unjust enrichment, the courts can usefully look across to subrogation cases where the remedy has been awarded on the ground of mistake, failure of consideration, or absence of consent.[415] They can also take note of the subrogation cases which hold that a claimant who lends money to a defendant may not acquire better rights than the ones he has bargained for,[416] and may not obtain a proprietary right at all where he has expressly agreed not to take security or has intended to make an unsecured loan.[417]

I. Defences

As the 'unjust factors' have been liberalized, defences have increasingly come to be seen as the better means of control and fine-tuning. They can be contemplated as falling into three families, according as they bear on enrichment, on 'at the expense of', or on 'unjust'.   **18.221**

(1) Enrichment-Related Defences

(a) Change of position

This defence is commonly put in very broad terms: if the defendant's circumstances alter to an extent which renders restitution inequitable, to that extent his obligation to make restitution shall be reduced. However, most examples actually seen are covered by a much narrower form of words: if, by the happening of an event which would not have happened but for the enrichment, the defendant's wealth is reduced, his obligation to make restitution is to that extent extinguished. In short the defence of change of position seems usually to be a defence of disenrichment. The safest tactic therefore seems to be to divide the defence in two.   **18.222**

---

[415] For discussion of which, see Mitchell and Watterson (n 402) chap 6.

[416] *Banque Financière de la Cité v Parc (Battersea) Ltd* [1999] AC 221, 235 and 236–7, HL; *Cheltenham & Gloucester plc v Appleyard* [2004] EWCA Civ 291, [41]; *Filby v Mortgage Express (No 2) Ltd* [2004] EWCA Civ 759 [62] and [63].

[417] *Boscawen v Bajwa* [1996] 1 WLR 328, 338, CA; *Halifax Mortgage Services Ltd v Muirhead* (1997) 76 P & CR 418, 426–7, CA; *Eagle Star plc v Karasiewicz* [2002] EWCA Civ 940 [19]; *Cheltenham & Gloucester plc v Appleyard* [2004] EWCA Civ 291, [38]; *Filby v Mortgage Express (No 2) Ltd* [2004] EWCA Civ 759, [39].

There is a defence of disenrichment and more rarely there is also a defence based on changes of position which do not reduce the defendant's enrichment. Non-disenriching changes of position will be considered among the unjust-related defences, below.[418]

(i) Rationale

18.223 The defence of disenrichment has a double rationale. First, it draws a line around the strict liability characteristic of the law of unjust enrichment. With the defence in place, that strict liability catches only those whose assets remain swollen. Secondly, the defence reconciles the interest in obtaining restitution of unjust enrichment with the competing interest in the security of receipts. There is a general interest in our being able freely to dispose of that wealth which appears to be at any one time at our disposition. Otherwise wealth would be sterilized in contingency funds and special insurance premiums, to guard against the danger of unsuspected restitutionary claims.

(ii) Proprietary claims

18.224 The defence of disenrichment bears more obviously and easily on the right *in personam* than the right *in rem*. Yet, exceptional exemptions apart, the defence must apply, and must be made to apply, to all entitlements arising from unjust enrichment. Otherwise there will be a new and unnecessary inducement to make proprietary claims, and bizarre results will be reached. If the House of Lords persists in its flawed doctrine of opposing unjust enrichment and property,[419] all proprietary claims will escape the defence, and a stampede towards proprietary claims will begin. That must not happen. It is the event, not the kind of right born of the event, that determines the available defences.

18.225 Suppose that D receives misdirected trust funds belonging to C worth £10,000, in circumstances in which D honestly believes himself entitled to the money. He invests it in shares. With the security of that investment behind him, and because of it, he decides that he can afford some frivolous expenditure. He treats himself to a short break, eats and drinks very well, and loses some cash at the casino. In this way he dissipates £5,000. All this money has come out of his current account. If C now sues him for £10,000, relying on his personal right to restitution, D's obligation to repay that sum will be reduced to £5,000. He has to that extent disenriched himself in good faith. But D is still traceably in possession of the proceeds of the £10,000. He has the shares in which he invested the mistaken money. If it were true that C's proprietary right to the shares was immune to the defence of change of position because it was not founded on unjust

---

[418] See paras 18.295–18.296.
[419] *Foskett v McKeown* [2001] 1 AC 102, HL. See para 18.182.

enrichment, there would be a new and powerful interest in establishing a proprietary claim. It clearly must not be immune. It is entirely a matter of chance whether the recipient funds his reliance extravagance from the mistaken money or from other resources. It would be very odd indeed if different rights arising from one event were vulnerable to quite different defences.

As for the implementation of the defence, if C's proprietary interest is a lien there   **18.226**
is no problem. The amount secured can be reduced. If it is a beneficial interest, the disenrichment is more difficult to allow for. The shares belong to C. However, although C can rightly claim that the shares are his, it is no less true that D has incurred expense which he would not have incurred but for the bona fide belief that they were his. There is no novelty in holding back an owner from asserting his ownership until he has paid the defendant's expenses. Roman law dealt with that problem within the wide-ranging *exceptio doli*, the defence based on 'fraud'. The mechanism in our law is to be found in the Chancery practice of putting a claimant on terms.[420] At common law, except in relation to land, the court does not have to order specific delivery,[421] and any money judgment can easily allow for D's disenrichment.

(iii) Relevant disenrichments

Where the defendant has changed his position by using up the enrichment, the   **18.227**
defence is, definitively, enrichment-related. It works because the defendant is allowed to set against the enrichment the disenrichment which would not have happened but for the enrichment. The example which Lord Goff used in the *Lipkin Gorman* case was a donation to charity which would not have been made but for the enrichment.[422] On the facts of that case, the casino was prima facie liable to make restitution to the solicitors of all the sums staked by the gambling partner. The gambler had occasionally won. When it paid him his winnings, the casino had reduced its wealth in a way in which it would not have done but for the receipt of the gambler's stake. Its liability was therefore reduced by the amount of his winnings.[423]

Lord Goff emphasized that a defendant may not have changed his position even   **18.228**
though he has spent the actual money received or no longer has the specific asset

---

[420] *Cooper v Phibbs* (1862) LR 2 HL 149; *Solle v Butcher* [1950] 1 KB 671, CA.

[421] Torts (Interference with Goods) Act 1977, s 5.

[422] *Lipkin Gorman v Karpnale Ltd* [1991] 2 AC, 548, 579, HL.

[423] A minor mystery is why the casino was permitted to aggregate all the winnings which it had paid out and to set the whole sum against all its takings in. On a strict view the firm would have recovered all the losing stakes in full while the casino would have been allowed to keep the few winning stakes.

which enriched him.[424] A recipient who spends the mistaken money on a meal which he would have bought anyhow has not disenriched himself. The abstract fund which is the totality of his wealth remains swollen. A recipient who spends the money on an asset which remains in his possession has not disenriched himself, either, save to the extent that the asset declines in value or (perhaps) would be disproportionately hard to sell.[425] Likewise a recipient who pays off a mortgage or a credit card debt generally pays what would have to have been paid anyhow.[426]

18.229 On the other hand an enrichee who allows his standard of living to drift up to match his new liquidity can rely on the defence, and the court will not strictly insist on proof that each and every item of expenditure was caused by the enrichment, particularly if he could not reasonably be expected to have kept a record of each transaction.[427] Again, an enrichee who discharges a mortgage and gives up salaried work in order to return to university is entitled to have taken into account the money that would have been earned but for the change of life induced by the enrichment.[428]

18.230 Must a defendant have made a positive decision to spend money in reliance on the enrichment, or is it enough that he loses money that he would not otherwise have had to lose? Dicta can be marshalled in support of the latter rule but the cases do not all go the same way.[429] In principle, the latter rule should be preferred, since it allows the defendant to escape liability where the enrichment is stolen or destroyed through his carelessness. The former rule would require everyone to take care of assets received from others, contrary to the philosophy underlying the change of position defence that recipients can be as careless as they like with assets that they

---

424 [1991] 2 AC, 548, 580, HL.

425 Compare *Lipkin Gorman v Karpnale Ltd* [1991] 2 AC, 548, 560, HL; *RBC Dominion Securities Inc v Dawson* (1994) 111 DLR (4th) 230, 239–40, Nfld CA; *Sullivan v Lee* (1994) 95 BCLR (2d) 195, 199, BCSC; *Corporate Management Services (Aust) Pty Ltd v Abi-Arraj* [2000] NSWSC 361, [23]–[24]; *Saunders & Co (a firm) v Hague* [2004] 2 NZLR 475, NZHC.

426 *RBC Dominion Securities v Dawson* (1994) 111 DLR (4th) 230, Nfld CA; *Scottish Equitable plc v Derby* [2000] 3 All ER 793; *Credit Suisse (Monaco) SA v Attar* [2004] EWHC 374 [98]. But cf *Boscawen v Bajwa* [1996] 1 WLR 32, 340–341, CA, explaining *Re Diplock* [1948] Ch 465, 549–50, CA.

427 *Philip Collins Ltd v Davis* [2000] 3 All ER 808, 829–30, affirmed *Scottish Equitable plc v Derby* [2001] EWCA Civ 369; [2001] 3 All ER 818, 827–8.

428 *Gertsch v Atsas* [1999] NSWSC 898 (Foster A-J).

429 *Scottish Equitable plc v Derby* [2001] EWCA Civ 369; [2001] 3 All ER 818, [30]–[31]; *Re Tain Construction Ltd* [2003] EWHC 1737; [2003] 1 WLR 2791, [49]; *Cressman v Coys of Kensington (Sales) Ltd* [2004] EWCA Civ 47; [2004] 1 WLR 2774, [41]; and cf *National Bank of New Zealand Ltd v Waitaki International Processing (NI) Ltd* [1999] 2 NZLR 211, 228–9, NZCA. To the contrary: *Streiner v Bank Leumi (UK) plc* QBD 31 October 1985; *Credit Suisse (Monaco) SA v Attar* [2004] EWHC 374, [98].

honestly believe to be their own. Only if a defendant knows that he is not entitled to an asset should he owe any duty in relation to its preservation.[430]

In *Dextra Bank and Trust Co v Bank of Jamaica*[431] the court held that there is no **18.231** reason to insist that the disenrichment must come after the enrichment, provided that the causal connection between the money received and the money paid out is clear, it makes no difference which comes first.[432] Dextra Bank sent the Bank of Jamaica a cheque for $3 million. Both were the victims of a fraud. The Bank of Jamaica thought that it was buying foreign currency. Dextra Bank thought that it was making a foreign currency loan. Even before it received Dextra Bank's cheque, the Bank of Jamaica reimbursed those whom it thought had paid Dextra Bank for the dollars. This payment gave it a complete defence to Dextra Bank's claim for the value of the cheque.

(iv) Disqualification

In the *Lipkin Gorman* case Lord Goff said that defendants may not rely on the **18.232** defence if they have acted in bad faith, or are wrongdoers.[433]

Bad faith. It is clear from *Dextra Bank* that bad faith does not include negli- **18.233** gence. There the Privy Council declined to engage in a process of apportioning blame between the parties, reasoning that in actions for the recovery of money paid under mistake, the carelessness of the claimant is irrelevant, and that it would seem intolerable to any defendant disqualified for negligence that the claimant's negligence should be left out of account.[434] Their Lordships also considered that the defence of change of position would become 'hopelessly unstable' if it were used to reflect relative fault, because the courts would then slide into an impressionistic and unpredictable exercise of discretion when deciding the extent to which the defence should apply.[435]

---

[430] Knowledge usually goes hand in hand with bad faith, but not always: *National Bank of New Zealand v Waitaki International Processing (NI) Ltd* [1999] 2 NZLR 211, NZCA, discussed at para 18.234.

[431] [2002] 1 All ER (Comm) 193, [35]–[39], PC, restricting Clarke J's previous finding to the contrary in *South Tyneside Metropolitan BC v Svenska International plc* [1995] 1 All ER 545 to its 'exceptional facts'. In that case there was arguably no reliance specifically on the relevant enrichment, which was the rolling difference between the payments made by each party: *Hinckley & Bosworth Borough Council v Shaw* (2000) LGR 9, 51.

[432] In *Commerzbank AG v Price-Jones* [2003] EWCA Civ 1663 the court said the same thing, but on the facts the defendant could not show any quantifiable disenrichment.

[433] *Lipkin Gorman v Karpnale Ltd* [1991] 2 AC 548, 580, HL.

[434] [2002] 1 All ER (Comm) 193, [45], PC. See too *National Bank of Egypt v Oman Housing Bank* [2002] EWHC 1760; [2003] 1 All ER 246, 251–2.

[435] ibid.

18.234   An exercise of this kind was undertaken by the New Zealand Court of Appeal in *National Bank of New Zealand v Waitaki International Processing (NI) Ltd*.[436] The claimant bank persuaded itself that it owed Waitaki $500,000 and insisted on paying it over, in the teeth of warnings and protests. Waitaki knew that the bank had made a mistake. It knew that the money would have to go back. It deposited it with a finance house to earn interest, taking a sound security. Later it agreed to vary the security. The new security proved inadequate. In due course all the money was lost. The court found that Waitaki had failed in its duty to the bank when the security was varied. The security which it took would have been suitable for up to two-thirds of the sum, from which it followed that Waitaki was independently liable for one-third of the loss. The court then went on to hold that the obstinately mistaken bank was more at fault than Waitaki and should therefore bear all but 10 per cent of the loss. On the same facts, it seems likely that an English court would allow a complete defence to the claim in unjust enrichment. But it would also allow an independent claim to recover 33 per cent of the loss on the basis that the defendant held the money on trust (having received it with knowledge of the claimant's mistake),[437] and then breached its duty as trustee to take reasonable care of the claimant's property.

18.235   At the other end of the fault spectrum, a defendant is clearly in bad faith if he acts either with self-conscious dishonesty of the type identified in *Twinsectra Ltd v Yardley*,[438] or with objective dishonesty of the kind identified in *Barlow Clowes International Ltd (in liq) v Eurotrust International Ltd*.[439] If an honest person would not act as the defendant acts, then he is not in good faith, and it makes no difference whether he is aware of this fact. A simple example is *Cressman v Coys of Kensington (Sales) Ltd*[440] where the court took no more than a few lines to refuse the defence to a defendant who had consciously sought to escape liability by transferring the benefit to his girlfriend.

18.236   A more difficult question is where the boundary between good and bad faith lies along the spectrum between negligence and dishonesty. In *Niru Battery Manufacturing Co v Milestone Trading Ltd* this was discussed by Moore-Bick J who declined to be prescriptive, but who considered that bad faith is 'capable of embracing a failure to act in a commercially acceptable way and sharp practice of a kind that falls short of outright dishonesty as well as dishonesty itself'.[441] Applying this test, he concluded that a bank could not rely on the defence where

---

[436]   [1999] 2 NZLR 211, NZCA.

[437]   *Westdeutsche Landesbank Girozentrale v Islington LBC* [1996] AC 669, HL; para 18.190.

[438]   [2002] UKHL 12; [2002] 2 AC 164.

[439]   [2005] UKPC 37, [2006] 1 WLR 1476.

[440]   [2004] EWCA Civ 47; [2004] 1 WLR 2774, [41].

[441]   [2002] EWHC 1425; [2002] 2 All ER (Comm) 705, [135]; endorsed in *Abou-Rahmah v Abacha* [2006] EWCA Civ 1492; [2007] 1 All ER (Comm) 827, where the court differed over the

it had released money to a customer that had been sent under a letter of credit in respect of a cargo which had not been shipped. The bank had known this, but had allowed itself to be persuaded by the customer that an alternative shipment would be arranged. On appeal this finding was upheld, but the court took a less satisfactory line, expressing the test for disqualification in the language of unconscionability.[442] This terminology offers no guidance, and no protection from a descent into relative fault that the Privy Council sought to prevent in *Dextra Bank*.

Wrongdoing. When Lord Goff said that wrongdoers could not rely on the change of position defence, he may have had it in mind to prevent defendants from relying on the defence in cases where a claim is made to recover the profits of wrongdoing—ie in cases which are not concerned with unjust enrichment, but with wrongs. However, his words have not subsequently been interpreted in this way, and in a number of cases the defence has been withheld from defendants in actions for unjust enrichment on the ground that they have committed criminal offences. In *Equiticorp Industries Group Ltd v R (No 47)*,[443] Smellie J held that the New Zealand government could not raise the defence in respect of payments which were made pursuant to a share purchase and buy-back scheme which infringed legislation prohibiting the purchase by a company of its own shares. In *Garland v Consumers' Gas Co Ltd*,[444] the Supreme Court of Canada held that a regulated gas utility could not raise the defence against a claim to recover money which it had collected from customers as 'late payment penalties', contrary to a law prohibiting the recovery of interest at a criminal rate. In *Barros Mattos Junior v General Securities & Finance Ltd*,[445] Laddie J held that the defendants could not raise the defence because although they had acted in good faith, they had converted US dollars which had been stolen from the claimant into Nigerian naira before paying the money away to third parties, contrary to a Nigerian law that requires foreign exchange dealings in Nigeria to be conducted through authorized intermediaries. **18.237**

The disparate nature of these cases suggests that the courts would do well to adopt a flexible attitude towards the question whether the gravity of a defendant's illegal actions should debar him from raising the change of position defence. Yet in *Barros*, Laddie J denied that the courts have any such discretion, and held that, subject to a *de minimis* threshold, they must always disallow the change of position defence in cases of illegality—even if this effectively means imposing **18.238**

---

question whether it is 'commercially acceptable' for a bank which suspects it customer of criminal enterprise to operate the account after reporting its suspicions to a regulatory agency.

442 [2003] EWCA Civ 1446; [2004] QB 985,[148]–[149], [162], 182]–[185] and [192].
443 [1998] 2 NZLR 481, 654 and 730, NZHC.
444 [2004] 1 SCR 629, [63]–[66], SCC.
445 [2004] EWHC 1188; [2005] 1 WLR 247.

an arbitrarily heavy penalty on a defendant for a comparatively minor breach of the law.[446] As a result, the defendants in *Barros* were left with an US$8 million liability because they changed the money into naira before paying it on to third parties, a liability they would not have incurred if they had simply paid over the money in US dollars. The harshness of this result suggests that Laddie J's approach is unduly rigid.

(v) Special cases

18.239 Although the change of position defence is normally available in response to claims in unjust enrichment, it seems that there are some special cases in which the defence is denied even to a careless defendant or is indeed excluded altogether. It appears, for example, that, where people, usually wives, are induced to give domestic security for business borrowing,[447] the protective policies operating in favour of the security-giver have the effect of denying the defence to the lender, usually a bank, which takes the security. The bank is not dishonest. It usually has only an attenuated constructive notice of impairment of the security-giver's decision. A lending bank inevitably changes its position by making the required advance or not calling in existing debts, but, if it could avail itself of the defence, the protection of the domestic security-giver would be utterly destroyed. Similar considerations also seem to underlie the rule that the change of position defence cannot be raised against a claim to recover benefits on the ground that the claimant lacked capacity to confer them.[448]

18.240 Again, it seems unlikely that a court would feel much enthusiasm for allowing a change of position defence to a public authority which has levied an *ultra vires* tax or charge, even though it has acted in good faith and has not consciously exceeded its powers. Public bodies are often apt to argue that fiscal chaos would follow any restitutionary award, but as William Cornish has observed, this argument 'seems to contain the imperative that, if governments are to exceed their taxing powers, this should be done on the grandest scale'.[449] In *Air Canada v British Columbia* the wish to avoid fiscal chaos led La Forest J to deny recovery,[450] but in her dissenting judgment Wilson J countered that:[451]

> if it is appropriate for the courts to adopt some kind of policy in order to protect the government against itself. . .it should be one which distributes the loss fairly across

---

[446] ibid, [22]–[30] and [42]–[43].

[447] The situation exemplified by *Barclays Bank plc v O'Brien* [1994] 1 AC 180, HL, and *Royal Bank of Scotland plc v Etridge (No 2)* [2001] UKHL 44; [2002] 2 AC 773.

[448] *Williams v Williams* [2003] EWHC 742.

[449] WR Cornish, ' "Colour of Office": Restitutionary Redress against Public Authority' [1987] J of Mal and Comp Law 41, 52.

[450] [1989] 1 SCR 1161, esp 1204–8, SCC.

[451] ibid, 1215; endorsed in *Woolwich Equitable BS v IRC* [1992] AC 70, 176, HL; *Kingstreet Investments Ltd v New Brunswick (Department of Finance)* 2007 SCC 1, [2007] 1 SCR 3, [28].

the public [and does not cause it to] fall on the totally innocent taxpayer whose only fault is that it paid what the legislature improperly said was due.

A better way to address the fiscal chaos problem is that adopted in *Re Eurig Estate*,[452] namely to defer any declaration that the state has acted beyond its powers pending the rearrangement of its financial affairs.

When value is transferred to a recipient on an agreed basis, he knows that he **18.241** may have to repay a like sum if the basis fails to materialize, suggesting that he cannot spend the money in good faith in reliance on a belief that the transferor's intention to benefit him was unqualified. So, if I pay you money to build a garage, and you spend it all on a holiday that you could not otherwise have afforded, the law will almost certainly not permit you to rely on this fact in the event that the garage is not built and I sue you to recover the money. Nonetheless it seems that payments to meet preparatory expenses will constitute expenditure on which you can rely. In *BP Exploration Co (Libya) Ltd v Hunt (No 2)*[453] Robert Goff J held that the statutory allowance for such expenses given by the Law Reform (Frustrated Contracts) Act 1943, section 1(2), should be seen as a statutory example of the change of position defence.

The paragraphs which follow consider two nominate defences—ministerial **18.242** receipt, and bona fide purchase from a third party—which certainly overlap with change of position *qua* disenrichment. They are considered here as applications of the disenrichment defence; so far as they can be said to have independent work of their own, they must be revisited as unjust-related defences.

(b) Ministerial receipt

This defence arises when an agent receives for a principal. It is handled differently **18.243** at law and in equity.

(i) At law

At common law, an agent recipient is a proper defendant, but he has a defence if **18.244** he has paid over to his principal without notice of the claim. In effect therefore the agent will be liable in two situations, namely (a) if he has not paid over to, or to the order of, the principal, and (b) if, though he has so paid over, he did so when he already had notice of the claimant's claim.[454] Since the agent recipient will often be a bank or lawyer or other professional, and the principal recipient may be much

---

452 [1998] 2 SCR 565, 586–7, SCC.
453 [1979] 1 WLR 783, 800.
454 *Kleinwort & Co v Dunlop* (1907) 97 LT 263, CA; *Admiralty Commissioners v National Provincial and Union Bank* (1922) 127 LT 452; *Gowers v Lloyds and National Provincial Bank* [1938] 1 All ER 766, CA; *Australia and NZ Banking Group Ltd v Westpac Banking Corporation* (1987) 164 CLR 662, HCA.

worse off, the right to sue the agent, however anomalous, is often very valuable. On the other hand, from the agent's point of view it is embarrassing, in that he can easily be placed in a dilemma, whether to pay his principal or the person who paid him.

18.245   The early editions of *Goff and Jones* show that, before the defence of change of position was secure and general, the argument that it should be so was based in part on the absurdity of confining it to agents. Attention was drawn to cases such as *Bayliss v Bishop of London*.[455] Under a statutory scheme the Bishop had administered the insolvency of the rector of a parish within his diocese. In taking in the revenues of the parish he had received certain payments which as it later turned out had been made by mistake. He had applied the entire fund in accordance with the requirements of the statutory scheme. He nevertheless had to make restitution. He could not be an agent because he had no principal. He could not take advantage of the agent's defence. In this way the agent's defence was made the bridgehead for the introduction of the defence of change of position.[456]

18.246   This being the history, it seems probable that ministerial receipt as understood at common law is nothing but a particular application of the disenrichment arm of change of position. If it makes sense to say that the agent was enriched in the first place, innocent payment over certainly disenriches him. It might be possible to open some clear water between the two defences, as by construing 'innocent' differently. But this would be inadvisable, and it would anyhow do no more than warn that the requirements of the defence of change of position may be susceptible of some modification in special contexts. So long as any doubt persists, the proper procedure will be to ask first what result the defence of change of position (disenrichment) will yield and thereafter to put a second question whether the defence of ministerial receipt could possibly lead to any other conclusion. It may be that the common law will revise its position more radically and decide, on the lines suggested in the modern equity cases, that the agent can after all only be sued when he commits a wrong. That position would accord better with the fundamental principles of the law of agency.

(ii) In equity

18.247   The rule of equity is that an action in unjust enrichment lies only against the principal and not against the agent.[457] The claimant must sue the principal. This does not touch the case in which the claimant can show that the agent has

---

[455] [1913] 1 Ch 127, CA.
[456] R Goff and G Jones, *The Law of Restitution* (1st edn, 1966) 482–5.
[457] *Agip (Africa) Ltd v Jackson* [1990] Ch 265, 291 (Millett J); affirmed [1991] Ch 547, CA; cf *Bank of NSW v Vale Corp (Management) Ltd* (NSWCA 21 October 1981); *Compagnie Commerciale Andre SA v Artibell Shipping Co Ltd* 2001 SC 653, 661–2.

committed some wrong against him. Civilian countries follow the same rule. The agent drops out.[458] This rule is unrelated to change of position, and amounts to the assertion that an agent is not enriched when he receives assets for which he must immediately account to his principal, and in respect of which the principal becomes immediately liable to the claimant. On this understanding of 'ministerial receipt', it makes no difference that the agent takes good title to the assets and uses them as his own.[459]

(c) Bona fide purchase from a third party

Unjust enrichments usually consist in simple transfers from C to D. Occasionally D has received from X, and C wants to say that, nevertheless, he must be regarded as having been enriched at his expense, albeit through X.[460] In cases of this configuration D will usually have a defence if he can show that he gave value to X in good faith and without notice of C's claim. **18.248**

(i) Giving value

In *Lipkin Gorman v Karpnale Ltd*[461] the House of Lords held that the firm could leapfrog its gambling partner, who was in prison, and sue the casino which had received from him at the firm's expense. The House also held that the casino could not plead bona fide purchase. The casino had received in good faith. It had also given value. But, because the contracts of licensed casinos with their customers are void, though not illegal, there was no legal nexus between what the casino gave and what it received from the gambler. This defines one important limitation on the defence. Even where it would otherwise be effective, it cannot work unless values pass under a valid contract between D, here the casino, and X, here the gambler. A factual exchange will not suffice. Had the gambler been addicted instead to straightforward luxury the result would have been different. If he had raided the client account so that he could stay at the Ritz and gorge himself on caviar and champagne, the Ritz would have been safe. It could have pleaded the defence of bona fide purchase. **18.249**

It is a question to what extent all the conditions of the long-established equitable defence of bona fide purchase for value without notice have to be satisfied **18.250**

---

[458] H Dörner, 'Change of Position and *Wegfall der Bereicherung*' in WJ Swadling (ed), *The Limits of Restitutionary Claims: A Comparative Analysis* (1997) 64, 65–6.

[459] JP Moore *Restitution from Banks* (unpublished DPhil dissertation, Oxford University, 2000) 213. Moore's analysis is summarized in C Mitchell, 'Assistance' in P Birks and A Pretto (eds), *Breach of Trust* (2002) 139, 184–7, and is preferable to the different view taken in R Stevens, 'Why Do Agents "Drop Out"?' [2005] LMCLQ 101, 109–118, and other writers cited by Stevens at 111, n 77.

[460] On leapfrogging, see paras 18.32–18.38.

[461] [1991] 2 AC 548, HL.

in this context. It has been accepted in this context that the value must be given in full, not merely promised.[462] Lord Goff accordingly observes, obiter, in the *Lipkin Gorman* case that a bank does not become a bona fide purchaser merely by receiving money in return for the promise of banking services but only by honouring its promise to pay out a like sum on demand.[463] Note, too, that the question whether full value has been given is assessed at the time when the defendant first has notice of the claim, rather than the time when he receives the relevant benefit.[464]

(ii) Disqualification: dishonesty and carelessness

18.251 The dishonest are clearly excluded from the defence of bona fide purchase. They cannot be said to give value in good faith.[465] However this defence has traditionally required not only good faith but also absence of notice of the adverse rights. In *Nelson v Larholt*[466] the defendant cashed cheques for a third party. The money which he received in return when he presented the cheques came from the estate of a deceased person which the third party was administering. After he had been replaced, the estate sought restitution. Denning J found that the defendant had honestly given value but had no defence because it was apparent on the face of the cheques that they were drawn on an estate account.

18.252 The question is what standard should apply. The Chancery doctrine, now in the Law of Property Act 1925, section 199, was evolved in relation to conveyancing. 'Without notice' meant 'without failing to make the inquiries that a reasonable person would make' and was made yet stricter by the assumption that the reasonable person always made the well-understood inquiries known to conveyancers. Outside the conveyancing context, the same strictness would bring commerce to a halt.[467] It is clear that this rigour does not apply to ordinary dealing where no fixed procedures are customary. Whether we say that a different standard applies or, letting the standard take the strain, that the reasonable man behaves very differently in different contexts, it is probable that 'without notice' now adds little if anything to the requirement of good faith. The reasonable person must not shut his eyes to obvious evidence of impropriety.[468]

---

462 *Story v Lord Windsor* (1743) 2 Atk, 630, 26 ER 776.

463 [1991] 2 AC 548, 577, HL.

464 *Sarkis v Watfa* [2006] EWHC 374.

465 Cf Sale of Goods Act 1979, s 61: 'A thing is deemed to be done in good faith within the meaning of this Act when it is in fact done honestly, whether it is done negligently or not.'

466 [1948] 1 KB 339.

467 '[I]f we were to extend the doctrine of constructive notice to commercial transactions we should be doing an infinite mischief and paralysing the trade of the country': *Manchester Trust v Furness* [1895] 2 QB 539, 545, CA (Lindley LJ).

468 *Eagle Trust v SBC Securities Ltd* [1993] 1 WLR 484, 505–6 (Vinelott J).

It was unequivocally laid down in *Re Nisbet and Potts' Contract*,[469] albeit still within **18.253** the conveyancing context, that the onus of proving every element of the defence lay on the defendant. Although the onus is easily shifted, contrary dicta cannot throw doubt on that proposition.[470]

(iii) Rationalia

There are two interpretations of this defence as it operates in the law of unjust **18.254** enrichment. In the one it is an unjust-related defence. We will meet it in that guise below.[471] In the other it is enrichment-related and no more than a particular application of the disenrichment limb of change of position. It is that version that justifies its treatment here in the group dominated by change of position.

In this version the reason why the defence defeats claims in unjust enrichment is **18.255** that, where there has been a valid exchange between the defendant and the third party from whom the defendant received, there is no way of denying that the values passing under it were equal. If the cost of a night's board and lodging at the Ritz is £5,000, the contract under which the customer gives that sum for those goods exchanges equal values. Hence the enrichment which the Ritz receives is exactly matched by its disenrichment. Even in a valid interest swap where at the end of ten years one might think there was an easily calculable difference between the winner's payments and the loser's payments, the values exchanged must be regarded as equal. The validity of the contract is crucial to the exercise of valuation. Take away the valid contract, and they become unequal. On this basis, the Ritz in our hypothetical case could equally plead disenrichment. X uses C's money to pay the Ritz; the Ritz can meet C's claim with a defence of bona fide purchase from X, meaning no more than that it was disenriched in the same measure as it was enriched.

(2) An Expense-Related Defence: Passing On

The phrase 'at the expense of' establishes the claimant's title to sue in respect of **18.256** the enrichment in question.[472] There is only one defence which bears on that phrase. It has not been recognized as a defence to common law claims in English law, but it has been recognized as a defence to various statutory claims to recover money paid as tax.[473] The defence of passing on asserts that the claimant has lost

---

[469] [1905] 1 Ch 391, 402.

[470] *Polly Peck International plc v Nadir (No 2)* [1992] 4 All ER 769, 781, CA (Scott LJ); *Barclays Bank plc v Boulter* [1999] 1 WLR 513, 518, HL.

[471] See paras 18.277–18.281.

[472] See paras 18.22 ff.

[473] eg Customs & Excise Management Act 1979, s 137A(3); Value Added Tax Act 1994, s 80(3); Finance Act 2001, s 32(2).

his title to sue because he has made good all the loss which the defendant's enrichment inflicted on him.

18.257   The defence of passing on arose in the swaps litigation from the practice of hedging. To cover payments out on interest swaps which later turned out to be void, some banks had entered valid back-to-back swaps in which the risks were exactly reversed. The hedge then ensured that every penny lost under the void swap would come back under the hedge. In *Kleinwort Benson Ltd v Birmingham CC*[474] a hedged party who lost and became a claimant in unjust enrichment found the defendant pointing to the hedge as evidence that the claimant had passed on the loss. This defence was rejected by the Court of Appeal for two reasons: first, because the payments received by the claimant under the hedge contract were not relevantly causally connected with the payments made by the claimant under the swaps contract;[475] and secondly, because a claimant in unjust enrichment need not show that the defendant's gain corresponds to a loss in the claimant's hands.[476]

18.258   The latter proposition has not been universally accepted by the courts, some of whom have held instead that a claimant's restitutionary entitlement should be capped at the amount of his loss, and there are reasons of principle for thinking that this narrower rule should be preferred.[477] Moreover, cases decided under the statutory regimes which allow the passing on defence demonstrate that other problems created by the defence are not insuperable: for example, the practical difficulty of measuring the success of steps taken by a claimant to pass on his loss to third parties.[478] The example of these regimes also suggests that if the courts ever revisit the availability of the passing on defence at common law, then they would do well to investigate the reason why the third party has borne the claimant's loss, since this may affect the question whether the claimant or the defendant has a better claim to the money. If a claimant mistakenly pays a defendant and then works harder at his business to generate extra sales to make up the deficit, then he will no longer be out of pocket, but he will still have a stronger claim than the defendant.[479] But if a claimant mistakenly pays a defendant on a third party's behalf, and the third party indemnifies him because he mistakenly thinks that he must, then neither claimant nor defendant deserves to keep the benefit which has been unjustly gained at the third party's expense. In the first case, the claim should

---

[474]   [1997] QB 380, CA.

[475]   ibid, 399 (Morritt LJ), discussed in M Rush, *The Defence of Passing On* (2006) 39.

[476]   ibid, 394–5 (Saville LJ).

[477]   See paras 18.23–18.25.

[478]   See eg *Marks & Spencer plc v C & E Commissioners (No 1)* [1999] 1 CMLR 1152; also Rush (n 475) 194–207. Cf FD Rose 'Passing On' in P Birks (ed), *Laundering and Tracing* (1995) 261, 284–5.

[479]   An example taken from Rush (n 475) 188.

be allowed; in the second, it should not be, unless the claimant is required to account for the fruits of his action to the third party.

These propositions can be illustrated by reference to the Value Added Tax Act 1994, section 80(3).[480] VAT is an indirect tax on consumers which is collected from suppliers and retailers who can choose whether to include a VAT element in the charges they make for their products or services. If a supplier does this, and it later transpires that the VAT was not due, then allowing him to recover his VAT payment would unjustly enrich him at the expense of his customers who effectively provided the money, unless secure mechanisms are in place to ensure that the repayment is passed back to them.[481] Otherwise, there is no reason why the supplier should recover the money, given that he has no better claim to it than Customs. On the other hand, if the supplier does not adjust his prices to include the VAT element, but instead absorbs the cost of paying output tax into his overheads, then allowing him to reclaim the payments would not unjustly enrich him at his customers' expense as they cannot have been the source of the money, and the defence does not apply.[482]

18.259

(3) Unjust-Related Defences

A defence belongs in this category if the defendant admits enrichment at the expense of the claimant but advances a reason for denying restitution which trumps the claimant's reason for obtaining restitution or, in other words, which overrides the claimant's unjust factor. Defences of this kind can be contemplated as falling into three sub-groups, according to the general nature of the reason for denying restitution which the defendant advances.

18.260

(a) Finality

The finality defences assert that, even supposing that the claimant did once have a right to restitution, the matter has been closed and cannot be reopened: *interest rei publicae ut sit finis litium* (it is in the public interest that there be an end

18.261

---

480 As explained in M Chowdry, 'Unjust Enrichment and Section 80(3) of the Value Added Tax Act 1994' [2004] BTR 620. Cf *Commissioner of State Revenue (Victoria) v Royal Insurance Australia) Ltd* (1994) 182 CLR 51, 78; *Roxborough v Rothmans of Pall Mall Australia Ltd* [2001] HCA 68; (2001) 208 CLR 516 [118]; and making the same point in a different context, *Niru Battery Manufacturing Co v Milestone Trading Ltd (No 1)* [2002] EWHC 1425, [2002] 2 All ER (Comm) 705, [145].

481 *Lamdec Ltd v C & E Commissioners* [1991] VATTR 296; *C & E Commissioners v McMaster Stores (Scotland) Ltd* 1996 SLT 935; *C & E Commissioners v National Westminster Bank plc* [2003] EWHC 1822; [2003] STC 1072. And note VATA 1994, s 80A.

482 *National Provincial BS v C & E Commissioners* [1996] V & DR 153; *Baines & Ernst Ltd v HMRC* [2006] EWCA Civ 1040; [2006] STC 1632, CA, stressing that the burden of proof is on HMRC to show that there has been no absorption.

to disputes). Since these are not peculiar to the law of unjust enrichment but derive from the general law, they are dealt with here only in outline.

(i) Res judicata

18.262   Payment made under a valid judgment cannot be recovered unless the judgment is set aside, even if the judgment was obtained by fraud.[483] Although he himself denied it, it is often said[484] that Lord Mansfield violated this principle in *Moses v Macferlan*.[485] There Macferlan had successfully sued Moses for a sum which he had promised not to claim. Moses in turn brought this action in the King's Bench to recover that sum, and he in turn succeeded. However, it is tolerably clear that Lord Mansfield regarded the case as what we would now call restitution for a wrong, the wrong being breach of contract. Viewed in that light, Lord Mansfield did not 'overhaul' the judgment of the lower court.[486]

18.263   When a judgment which has been paid is set aside, the right to restitution arises automatically and does not depend on the court's making an order for repayment.[487] In such a case the basis upon which the payment was made can be seen to have subsequently failed.[488]

(ii) Capitulation after initiation of legal proceedings

18.264   This defence is no more than an extension of the last. Even where there is no judgment to be set aside, payments made after litigation has begun cannot be recovered. In the words of Lord Halsbury, 'The principle of law is, not that money paid under a judgment, but that money paid under the pressure of legal process cannot be recovered.'[489] This strict rule is displaced in cases in which the party seeking to take advantage of it acted in bad faith, as for instance in snatching at a mistake made by the other.[490]

---

[483] *De Medina v Grove* (1846) 10 QB 152; *Huffer v Allen* (1867) LR 2 Ex 15. For an example of an appeal out of time where, but for the judgment, a claim could have been made for failure of basis, see *Barder v Caluori* [1988] AC 20, HL. Contrast *Dublin v The Ancient Guild of Brick and Stone Layers* [1996] 1 IR 468, where an arbitrator's award had not been set aside.

[484] *Phillips v Hunter* (1795) 2 HBl 402, 414, 126 ER 618, 624 (Eyre CJ); *Brisbane v Dacres* (1813) 5 Taunt 143, 160, 128 ER 641, 648 (Heath J).

[485] (1760) 2 Burr 1005, 97 ER 676.

[486] (1760) 2 Burr 1005, 1009–10, 97 ER 676, 678.

[487] *Commonwealth v McCormack* (1984) 155 CLR 273, HCA; cf DM Gordon, 'The Effect of Reversal of Judgment on Acts done between Pronouncement and Reversal' (1958) 74 LQR 517, 521–4.

[488] For discussion of this and other possible reasons for restitution in such cases, see B Macfarlane, 'The Recovery of Money Paid under Judgments Later Reversed' [2001] RLR 1.

[489] *Moore v Fulham Vestry* [1895] 1 QB 399, 401. There a summons had been taken out to compel the claimant, as a frontager, to make a statutory contribution to a road improvement. He paid and was refused restitution when he discovered subsequently that his holding was not within the contributing class. Cf *Hamlet v Richardson* (1833) 9 Bing 644, 131 ER 756.

[490] *Ward v Wallis* [1900] 1 QB 675.

(iii) Contract for finality

A contract for finality made before the initiation of legal proceedings may be called a compromise, a settlement, or a release.[491] Under whichever name, a party who has closed the matter in question for good consideration will not be able to reopen it so long as the contract remains in place. However, this bar is in two ways less absolute than that which is created by *res judicata* or capitulation. **18.265**

First, at least in respect of claims unknown to the parties at the time of the contract a fierce *contra proferentem* construction may deprive the defendant of the protection which he thought he had secured.[492] Secondly, the contract is vulnerable to vitiating factors like mistake, pressure, and undue influence. It has been suggested that, even if there is no contract, but only a payment in submission to an honest claim, the honest claim provides a defence.[493] If that were right, the exercise of construction would be much less important. But it cannot be right.[494] If it were, many mistaken payments would be irrecoverable. Even such a classic case as *Kelly v Solari*[495] would have to be decided differently, for nothing could be more certain than that the insurers there made their mistaken payment to the widow in response to an honest claim by her. **18.266**

(iv) Estoppel

Before the formal recognition that a change of position would operate as a defence to claims in unjust enrichment, some of its work was done by estoppel. This depended on establishing that the claimant had made a representation to the effect that payments might once and for all be relied on or had been finally checked and, further, that that representation had become binding by detrimental reliance.[496] *Avon County Council v Howlett*[497] confirmed that such an estoppel provided complete defence. The reliance need not have consumed the entirety of the enrichment received. **18.267**

It was predictable thereafter that, armed with change of position, which diminishes the liability *pro tanto*, the courts would lean against finding the facts necessary to support an estoppel. The Court of Appeal has twice shown itself unwilling to **18.268**

---

491 NH Andrews, 'Mistaken Settlements of Disputable Claims' [1989] LMCLQ 431.

492 *Bank of Credit International SA v Ali* [2002] 1 AC 251, HL.

493 Goff and Jones, 7th edn (n 1) 59–62.

494 S Arrowsmith, 'Mistake and the Role of "Submission to an Honest Claim"', in A Burrows (ed), *Essays in the Law of Restitution* (1991) 17.

495 (1841) 9 M&W 54, 152 ER 52.

496 *Skyring v Greenwood* (1825) 4 B & C 281, 107 ER 1064; *Holt v Markham* [1923] 1 KB 504, CA; *RE Jones Ltd v Waring & Gillow Ltd* [1926] AC 670, 692–4, HL.

497 [1983] 1 WLR 605, CA. A local authority had overpaid a teacher's sick pay and recovered nothing despite the teacher's putting in evidence reliance expenditure substantially less than the overpayments. It is, however, a question whether a mistaken representation in a non-bargaining context should be binding.

apply the logic of the *Avon* case to create a total defence regardless of the scale of the recipient's reliance. In each case the court invoked an exception to cover, and prevent, gross disproportion.[498] 'Gross' will soon mean 'any'. Under such a regime it will be impossible to effect a permanent, binding estoppel which will be stronger than the defence of change of position. Yet the two defences are different. Change of position is generally about disenrichment, while estoppel is about holding people to their undertakings. It is one thing to say that there was no representation, or that in the circumstances it was not reasonable to rely upon it, but it is quite another to find all the facts which support an estoppel and yet hold that the representation does not on this occasion bind. One might on the same basis brush aside a defence based on a contract for finality.

(v) Limitation and laches

18.269 The primary source for time limits is now the Limitation Act 1980. It contains nothing explicitly about unjust enrichment or restitution. In this it reflects the earlier cast of mind which hid this area of law under the corners of contract and trusts. Section 5 says: 'An action founded on simple contract shall not be brought after the expiration of six years from the date on which the cause of action accrued.' In *Westdeutsche Landesbank Girozentrale v Islington LBC* an elaborate exercise in statutory interpretation allowed Hobhouse J to conclude that section 5 applied to the claimants' application in unjust enrichment at common law in respect of money had and received to their use under the void swaps contract.[499]

18.270 The six-year period also applies to torts (section 6) and thus to many cases of restitution for wrongs, also to statutory dues (section 9). Claims to contribution under the Civil Liability (Contribution) Act 1978 have a two-year limit (section 10).

18.271 As the law of unjust enrichment was hidden partly under contract and partly under trusts, a question arises whether the six-year period applies on the trust side. Equity originally knew no rigid time limits. It would, however, bar claims for laches or on the ground of acquiescence. Acquiescence happens when a claimant, knowing his rights, stands by and allows them to be violated. Laches, pronounced 'laitches', denotes slackness or remissness. Laches will bar a claim where neglect to sue has prejudiced the defendant. There is no mechanical test. The judge has to decide whether the balance has swung against allowing the claim.[500]

---

[498] *Scottish Equitable plc v Derby* [2001] EWCA Civ 369; [2001] 3 All ER 818, [44]; *National Westminster Bank Plc v Somer International (UK) Ltd* [2001] EWCA Civ 970; [2002] QB 1286, [46]–[48] and [67].

[499] [1994] 4 All ER 890, 943. Cf *Maskell v Horner* [1915] 3 KB 106, where a stallholder paid market dues under duress of goods for some twelve years and recovered for six; *Re Diplock* [1948] Ch 465, 514, CA.

[500] *Nelson v Rye* [1996] 1 WLR 1378, 1392–5 (Laddie J).

Laches is nowadays a long-stop where no statutory period applies. However, the **18.272** courts can apply a statutory time-limit by analogy, and they are now more vigorous in doing so where equity is duplicating or imitating the common law. Thus in *Kleinwort Benson Ltd v South Tyneside MBC*, which was another case in the void interest-swaps series, Hobhouse J said, 'The six-year limit provided for in section 5 of the Limitation Act 1980 applies to an action for money had and received and by analogy to an equivalent equitable action.'[501] In *Paragon Finance plc v DB Thakerar & Co*[502] and *Coulthard v Disco Mix Club Ltd*[503] the courts said that a right to an account growing out of contract will not escape the six-year period simply because the accountant is in equity's eyes a fiduciary. In the latter case the manager and promoter of the claimant's music recording process, though a fiduciary, was held not to be accountable beyond the sixth year.

Section 21(3) directly applies a six-year limitation period to actions by beneficiar- **18.273** ies to recover trust property or in respect of breach of trust.[504] However, there are large exceptions within which there is no limitation period. Subsection (1) excludes actions by the beneficiary of a trust (a) in respect of fraud to which the trustee was privy and (b) against a trustee to recover trust property held by the trustee or previously converted to his use. Subsection (2) then says that an honest and reasonable trustee who is also a beneficiary shall not be liable after the normal limitation period for more than the excess over his proper share. Notwithstanding the drift of the cases mentioned immediately above, it seems unlikely that, where an unjust enrichment has the effect of turning the recipient into a trustee for the claimant, the claimant will be deprived of the benefit of section 21(1). It is not to be overlooked, however, that the equitable claim initially recognized in *Kleinwort Benson Ltd v South Tyneside MBC*[505] and in *Westdeutsche Landesbank Girozentrale v Islington LBC*,[506] to which the six-year period was applied by analogy, might well have been said to have fallen within section 21(1)(b).

---

[501] [1994] 4 All ER 972, 978; cf *Westdeutsche Landesbank Girozentrale v Islington LBC* [1994] 4 All ER 890, 943, where he described the same proposition as 'common ground between the parties'. It is not clear whether he meant to confine this to the assertion of a personal claim. He thought the claimant had acquired a proprietary right but the claim was a personal claim to restore the value.

[502] [1999] 1 All ER 400, CA, disapproving Laddie J in *Nelson v Rye* [1996] 1 WLR 1378, so far as he held that no statutory period applied to an account due from a musician's manager.

[503] [1999] 2 All ER 457.

[504] But claims to recover payments wrongfully made by the personal representatives out of a deceased person's estate are governed by section 22(a), considered in *Davies v Sharples* [2006] EWHC 362; [2006] WTLR 839.

[505] [1994] 4 All ER 972.

[506] [1994] 4 All ER 890.

18.274   Section 28 prevents time running against a person under a disability such as mental illness or minority, and section 32 provides that in cases of fraud, concealment, or mistake, the clock will not run until the claimant has discovered the true facts or could with reasonable diligence have done so.[507] The fraud or concealment may have been done by the defendant's predecessor in title, but in that case the extension of the limitation period will not be extended against a bona fide purchaser for value.[508]

18.275   It was to obtain the benefits of the extended limitation period under section 32(1)(c) that the claimants in both *Kleinwort Benson Ltd v Lincoln CC*[509] and *Deutsche Morgan Grenfell plc v IRC*[510] sought to ground their claims on mistake of law. Both cases were fought on the basis that the claimant could only take advantage of this provision if mistake was a necessary component of its cause of action. When the *Deutsche Morgan* case reached the House of Lords, however, the claimant amended its pleadings to argue for the first time that mistake did not need to be an essential element of its cause of action for the sub-section to apply, provided that a mistake could be discovered in the facts of the case.[511] In the event the court did not have to decide this point, but Lord Walker and Lord Hoffmann both favoured the claimant's contention.[512] However, Lord Scott preferred Pearson J's previous finding in *Phillips-Higgins v Harper*,[513] that the sub-section 'applies only where the mistake is an essential ingredient of the cause of action'.[514] The former reading should be preferred, as going to the substantive merits of the claimant's position rather than a pleading issue.

(b) Stultification

18.276   These defences assert that the law would be made ridiculous if the claim in unjust enrichment were allowed. It would be indefensibly conceding with the right hand something which it was endeavouring to prevent with the left.

---

[507] On reasonable diligence: *Peco Arts Inc v Hazlitt Gallery Ltd* [1983] 1 WLR 1315; also *Fea v Roberts* [2005] EWHC 2186; [2006] WTLR 255 (the clock does not start running before the accrual of the cause of action in the case of a carelessly mistaken payer).

[508] Section 32(2) and (3); *GL Baker Ltd v Medway Building and Supplies Ltd* [1958] 2 All ER 532 (Danckwerts J), [1958] 1 WLR 1216, CA: defendant was a donee from fraudster.

[509] [1999] 2 AC 349, HL, discussed at paras 18.62ff.

[510] [2006] UKHL 49; [2007] 1 AC 558, discussed at para 18.65. The Finance Act 2004, ss 320 and 321 now prevent claimants from relying on s 32(1)(c) where they have mistakenly paid money as tax after 8 September 2003.

[511] Prompted by J Edelman 'Limitation Periods and the Theory of Unjust Enrichment' (2005) 68 MLR 848.

[512] [2006] UKHL 49; [2007] 1 AC 558, [22] and [147].

[513] [1954] 1 QB 411, 419, considering the statutory precursor to s 32(1)(c), the Limitation Act 1929, s 26(c).

[514] [2006] UKHL 49; [2007] 1 AC 558, [91]–[92].

(i) Bona fide purchase (understood as protecting exceptions to nemo dat*)*

In the law of unjust enrichment this defence may often be explicable as a particu- **18.277**
lar application of the disenrichment limb of change of position.[515] A narrower
rationale explains it as preventing the stultification of the compromise which
the law of property makes between the sanctity of ownership and the security
of transactions.

In English law there are particular situations in which acquisition in good faith **18.278**
and for value will destroy prior interests. The most prominent examples are, at
law, that one who gives value for money in good faith becomes owner of that
money,[516] and, in equity, one who acquires the legal title for value in good faith
and without notice of adverse equitable interests takes clear of those adverse equitable interests.[517] Again, a legal right to rescind and revest will be destroyed if the
thing passes to a bona fide purchaser.[518] And in equity a right to rescind and revest
will be destroyed not only as against a bona fide purchaser of the legal estate but
even against the purchaser of an equitable interest.[519]

Wherever the general law gives a bona fide purchaser a good title, a personal claim **18.279**
in respect of the value received would stultify the law's protection of the security
of the bona fide purchaser's transaction. We discussed above the case in which X
takes C's money and spends it at the Ritz. The Ritz, giving value in good faith, gets
a good title to that money.[520] To allow C nonetheless to bring a personal claim in
unjust enrichment for the value of that money received would make nonsense of
the law of property's decision to sacrifice C to the security of transactions.

This explanation of bona fide purchase would not help D in a case in which X **18.280**
took a gold ring from C and sold it to D. Bona fide purchase does not generally
clear the title to a chattel at common law. D incurs a liability in conversion.
A personal claim in unjust enrichment by C against D would likewise encounter
no objection on the score of stultification. However, D could rely on the disenrichment version of the defence, or, perhaps more accurately, he could rely on
the defence of change of position so far as it applies to a bona fide purchase from
a third party.

---

[515] See paras 18.248ff.
[516] *Miller v Race* (1758) 1 Burr 452, 97 ER 398; *Clarke v Shee and Johnson* (1774) 1 Cowp 197,
98 ER 1041; D Fox, 'Bona Fide Purchase and the Currency of Money' [1996] CLJ 547.
[517] *Pilcher v Rawlins* (1872) LR 7 Ch App 259; *Re Nisbet and Pott's Contract* [1906] 1 Ch 386 (CA).
[518] Sale of Goods Act 1979, s 23.
[519] *Phillips v Phillips* (1862) 4 De G F & J 208, 215, HL (Lord Westbury); R Chambers, *Resulting
Trusts* (1997) 171.
[520] See para 18.255.

18.281   In *Royal Bank of Scotland plc v Etridge (No 2)*[521] the House of Lords drew a clear distinction between the defence of bona fide purchase and the absence of notice in the cases in which family homes have been made security for business borrowing. In these cases the reason why the lender has to be shown to have had some degree of knowledge of the undue influence or other vitiation is not that he would otherwise have the defence of bona fide purchase. The lender never claims to be a bona fide purchaser. It is an element of the cause of action of the party giving security, albeit in this context much watered down, that the lender must be shown to have known of the undue influence or misrepresentation which gives the security-giver a right to restitution. The competing interest in protecting the process of contracting from an inordinate need to make inquiries explains why it must be shown that the lender knew or ought to have known of the vitiating factor.[522]

(ii) Illegality

18.282   A party who has transferred value under an illegal contract may be able to make out a claim in unjust enrichment. The question then arises whether allowing that claim would make nonsense of the law's refusal to enforce the contract. If it would, the action in unjust enrichment will be barred. It is a separate question whether the claim in unjust enrichment is independently obstructed by grave turpitude.[523]

18.283   The law is nowadays more easily explained by stultification than by turpitude. The reason is that, even up to and including crimes of dishonesty, the courts no longer react to illegality with the decisive revulsion which they once were wont to show. No formal explanation of the results can conceal this truth in cases in which people bent on defrauding the social security system or deceiving their creditors have been allowed to recover.[524]

18.284   Any non-contractual action in respect of value which has passed under an illegal contract will prima facie be barred on the ground of stultification. C pays D money for an honour, and no honour is forthcoming.[525] There is a failure of consideration, but C will be defeated. It suffices to say, without entering into judgments on turpitude, that recovery of the money would stultify the invalidity of the contract. It would provide both a lever to compel performance and a safety net against the event of non-performance, reducing the risks of entering the illegal contract.

---

[521] [2001] UKHL 44; [2002] 2 AC 773.
[522] ibid, [38]–[43].
[523] See para 18.298.
[524] *Tinsley v Milligan* [1994] AC 340, HL; *Tribe v Tribe* [1996] Ch 107, CA.
[525] *Parkinson v College of Ambulance Ltd* [1925] 2 KB 1.

The lever argument and the safety net argument routinely indicate a prima facie **18.285** stultification, and this may be confirmed if it is found on closer inspection that the policy behind the illegality in question would indeed be stultified if the claimant were allowed any non-contractual recourse.[526] But stultification can also be negatived in two ways, by flat denial or by confession and avoidance.

It can be flatly denied where restitution would assist the underlying policy. **18.286** A prohibition on taking premiums for leases is likely to arise from a policy of protecting tenants from market forces. Restitution of illegal premiums positively helps. Once a court concludes that restitution would further the protective policy underlying the invalidity, there will be no question of stultification. Indeed the policy may itself constitute the unjust factor—the very reason why the enrichment must be returned.[527]

The prima facie stultification can be confessed and avoided in two ways. First, **18.287** those who can demonstrate their innocence of the illegality can be allowed to recover, because the innocent as a class will never be encouraged to enter illegal transactions on the faith of the lever and safety net. Hence, restitution can be allowed where a mistake concealed the illegality[528] or oppression compelled it.[529]

Secondly, the law will also not be stultified even where the guilty are allowed **18.288** to recover if it can be shown that the denial of restitution would entail some greater evil. Stultification is unexplained contradiction. The greater evil which is avoided provides the explanation. Thus, to allow an illegal immigrant to sue for the value of his work seems to stultify the refusal to enforce his contract, but to refuse the non-contractual action would leave the immigrant with no remedy at all and open the way to slave labour.[530] In such a case the law prefers the lesser evil.

Although the cases are said to turn on a special immunity of proprietary claims to **18.289** objections arising from illegality, a recurrent dilemma of this kind is faced whenever C transfers a temporary interest to D in circumstances in which the transaction between them is illegal. The dilemma consists in the fact that the lever and safety net arguments may be strong but refusal to allow recovery of the assets in

---

[526] As in *Wilson v First County Trust Ltd (No 2)* [2003] UKHL 40; [2004] 1 AC 816; cf *Dimond v Lovell* [2002] 1 AC 384, HL.

[527] *Kiriri Cotton Co Ltd v Dewani* [1960] AC 192, PC; *Singh v Kalubya* [1964] AC 142, PC; *Re Cavalier Insurance Co* [1989] 2 Lloyds Rep 430.

[528] *Oom v Bruce* (1810) 12 East 225, 104 ER 87; *Hughes v Liverpool Victoria Friendly Society* [1916] 2 KB 482. It is now an important question whether mistake of law will serve to establish innocence, though *Mohamed v Alaga & Co* [2000] 1 WLR 1815, CA suggests that it will.

[529] *Smith v Cuff* (1817) 6 M & S 160, 105 ER 1203.

[530] *Nizamuddowlah v Bengal Cabaret, Inc* 399 NYS 2d 854 (1977).

question will involve a disproportionate forfeiture of the reversionary interest.[531]
The non-contractual action in question in such cases may not arise in unjust
enrichment, but the same principle applies whatever its nature. In this group
properly belong all the cases on fraudulent concealment of assets. In substance
these invariably entail temporary transfers, although in form they often involve
out-and-out alienations.[532] The courts would never enforce the agreements which
underlie these fraudulent transfers, but the disproportionate forfeiture here provides the reason why it is not nonsense to override the lever and the safety net
arguments and allow recovery.

(iii) Other causes of contractual invalidity

18.290   Where there is no illegality, the safety net and lever arguments lose their weight.
The stultification question has to be asked, but it is generally found unnecessary
to bar the action in unjust enrichment. In *Pavey & Matthews Pty Ltd v Paul*[533] the
High Court of Australia had to ask itself whether allowing the claimant builders
their claim in unjust enrichment would subvert the policy of the New South
Wales Licensed Builders Act, which rendered the building contract unenforceable for want of writing. It decided that a claim in unjust enrichment would
not contradict that policy.[534] The same conclusion has been reached in relation to
formalities for the creation of express trusts.[535]

18.291   Contracts made by minors are unenforceable against the minor. The Minors'
Contracts Act 1987, section 3(1) says the court 'may, if it is just and equitable to
do so, require [the minor] to transfer to the [other] any property acquired by the
minor under the contract, or any property representing it'. The adult's common
law rights are not displaced by the statute. They probably allow a similar measure
of recovery, restricted to enrichment surviving in his hands.[536]

---

[531] *Bowmakers Ltd v Barnet Instruments Ltd* [1945] KB 65, CA. *Bigos v Bousted* [1951] 1 All ER
92 ought also to have been decided on this basis. Contrast *Taylor v Chester* (1869) LR 4 QB 309,
where the special property had not expired or been terminated.

[532] *Rowan v Dann* (1992) 64 P&CR 202, CA; *Tinsley v Milligan* [1994] 1 AC 340, HL; *Nelson
v Nelson* (1995) 184 CLR 338, HCA; *Tribe v Tribe* [1996] Ch 107, CA; *Lowson v Coombes* [1999]
Ch 373, CA.

[533] (1987) 162 CLR 221, HCA.

[534] For the long history: D Ibbetson, 'Implied Contracts and Restitution: History in the High
Court of Australia' (1988) 8 OJLS 312. Cf Lord Denning, '*Quantum Meruit* and the Statute of
Frauds' (1925) 41 LQR 79.

[535] *Hodgson v Marks* [1971] Ch 892, CA.

[536] The adult's right to restitution of the still surviving enrichment appears to have been tied to
'fraud' only in the loosest equitable sense of that term: *Clarke v Cobley* (1798) 2 Cox 173, 30 ER 80;
R Leslie Ltd v Sheill [1914] 2 KB 607; cf *Marlow v Pitfield* (1719) 1 PWms 558, 24 ER 516; *Lewis v
Alleyne* (1888) 4 TLR 650.

By contrast a minor has a good defence against claims to the amount received as opposed to the amount surviving.[537] However, that defence is probably not based on the danger of stultifying his protection from contractual liability. It is rather an assertion that the minor's protection is not focused solely on contracts but extends to all indebtedness: he must not be made to shoulder the burden of repayment, whatever the cause of indebtedness.[538]

18.292

The many cases on void interest swaps show that a body with limited capacity has no defence to a claim in respect of enrichment received under an *ultra vires* contract. The overruling of *Sinclair v Brougham*[539] in the *Westdeutsche* case[540] indicates, so far as *ultra vires* can be said to survive in private law, that their Lordships do not contemplate this as being peculiar to public authorities and, further, that they see no stultification even where, as in that case, the claim in unjust enrichment closely replicates the contractual action which is barred. *Sinclair v Brougham* involved *ultra vires* loans. The claim for failure of consideration, which their Lordships would now allow, would have yielded essentially the same performance.[541]

18.293

The reason why there is thought to be no stultification of the law's refusal to enforce the contract would seem to be that the courts take the protected party to be, not the *incapax* as in the case of the minor, but the public. They see the protection of the public as requiring not only the nullity of an *ultra vires* contract but also automatic restitution of any value passing under such a contract.[542]

18.294

(c) Other unjust-related defences

(i) Non-disenriching changes of position

We have already dealt with changes of position which disenrich.[543] Supervening hardships which were not induced by the enrichment, such as ill-health and marital breakdown, have been held irrelevant.[544] Little room is left for any kind of non-disenriching change of position, but examples can still arise.

18.295

---

[537] *Cowern v Nield* [1912] 2 KB 419; *R Leslie Ltd v Sheill* [1914] 2 KB 607; Goff and Jones, 7th edn (n 1) 642–4 say that *Cowern v Nield* should be overruled.

[538] *Bristow v Eastman* (1794) 1 Esp 172, 170 ER 317 shows he may nonetheless be liable for wrongs, provided that the wrong does not stultify his contractual protection: cf *R Leslie Ltd v Sheill* [1914] 2 KB 607.

[539] [1914] AC 398, HL.

[540] *Westdeutsche Landesbank Girozentrale v Islington LBC* [1996] AC 669, 714, 718, 738, HL.

[541] This has since been taken as justifying a similar approach to an illegal loan: see the treatment in *Mohamed v Alaga & Co* [1999] 3 All ER 699, CA; cf *Boissevain v Weil* [1950] AC 327, HL.

[542] *Guinness Mahon & Co Ltd v Kensington and Chelsea RLBC* [1999] QB 215, 229 (Morritt LJ), 233 (Waller LJ), CA.

[543] See paras 18.222ff.

[544] *Scottish Equitable plc v Derby* [2001] EWCA Civ 369; [2001] 3 All ER 818, 828.

18.296   In *Kinlan v Crimmin*,[545] the defendant was a shareholder and director of a company to which he sold his shares under an agreement which (unknown to the parties) was void for non-compliance with the Companies Act 1985, ss 164 and 159(3). Following the presumed sale he was excluded from participation in the business by the remaining shareholder who took a series of decisions in which the claimant did not participate, and which resulted in the company becoming insolvent. Although the company was prima facie entitled to recover its money on the ground of mistake of law, and even though the defendant might still have had the money or its traceable proceeds in his hands (a point that was not explored at trial), the claim was dismissed. The reason was that if the defendant had realized that the agreement was void, he would 'have wished to consider how his continuing interest in the company should be protected, either by his resuming his rights to protect himself as a quasi-partner in the business or by seeking reformulation of the agreement so as to ensure that it and the payments to him were valid.'[546]

(ii) Ministerial receipt (in the strong form recognized in equity)

18.297   Ministerial receipt (common law) may turn out to be nothing but change of position (disenrichment). However, ministerial receipt (equity) is quite different. It asserts that an agent ought never to be the defendant to an action in unjust enrichment because he is not relevantly enriched when he receives assets for which he must immediately account to his principal, and for the receipt of which the principal is immediately liable to the claimant.[547] This is best thought of as an assertion of the utility of the institution of agency and the need to preserve the notion that an agent is no more than an extension of the principal. It is sometimes said this is not a defence at all but merely a rule for identifying the proper parties.[548] That it is the latter does, perhaps, exclude its being the former too. In equity the defence is clearly based on the notion that when one person acts for another, the rights and duties are acquired only by that other. In other words, it is not based on disenrichment but on the fundamental idea of agency, that the agent is no more than an extension of his principal.

(iii) Turpitude

18.298   In most cases in which illegality is a defence to unjust enrichment, the reason is the need to avoid making nonsense of the law's refusal to enforce the contract. However, if C gave D money to procure a child for sexual abuse, and D did nothing, C's claim for failure of consideration would fail *in limine*. It would fail because

---

[545] [2006] EWHC 779, [2007] 2 BCLC 67.
[546] Ibid [60] (Philip Sales, sitting as a deputy High Court judge).
[547] Para 18.247.
[548] *Portman Building Society v Hamlyn Taylor Neck* [1998] 4 All ER 202, 207, CA.

no court would listen to such an odious claimant: *ex turpi causa non oritur actio* (from a disgraceful cause arises no action). It would not be necessary to ask whether, were it to allow the action in unjust enrichment, the law would stultify its own stance in relation to the contract. The evidence is that nowadays only really serious turpitude triggers this revulsion. The courts are less delicate than they once were. Claimants guilty of acquisitive dishonesty are not turned peremptorily away.[549]

(iv) Minority

Minors, as we saw, do have a defence to unjust enrichment claims, even when the claim does not replicate a contractual claim which could be made against them.[550] Some might regard that as explicable in terms of stultification of the protection extended to them in matters of contract. It seems better to affirm that minority is an independent defence to claims in the measure of enrichment received, on the ground that minors must be protected from indebtedness. On this basis a minor would have a defence to a claim for restitution of a mistaken payment, except in respect of surviving enrichment.

18.299

(v) Counter-restitution impossible

A claimant who seeks restitution of an unjust enrichment must make counter-restitution of benefits received from the defendant in exchange. If counter-restitution is impossible, the claim to restitution will be barred. Andrew Burrows has rightly said that, since the courts are nowadays content to see counter-restitution made in money, the case in which counter-restitution will be regarded as impossible may be vanishingly rare.[551] This defence overlaps with the disenrichment limb of change of position, in that value transferred to the claimant himself is capable of being treated as a relevant disenrichment. However, it cannot be fully explained in terms of disenrichment.

18.300

One proof that it is not merely a special manifestation of change of position is that even a defendant who has induced a claimant to transfer a benefit by a threat or a fraudulent misrepresentation is entitled to counter-restitution of benefits which he has conferred on the claimant.[552] He would be disqualified from pleading change of position. The disadvantage of the fraudster used to be that, while the

18.301

---

[549] *Tinsley v Milligan* [1994] AC 340, HL; *Tribe v Tribe* [1996] Ch 107, CA. In the light of these cases *Berg v Sadler and Moore* [1937] 2 KB 158 (money paid to obtain goods on false pretences) could not possibly be explained in terms of turpitude and probably cannot be explained at all.

[550] Para 18.292.

[551] AS Burrows, *The Law of Restitution* (2nd edn, 2002) 541.

[552] *Halpern v Halpern (No 2)* [2007] EWCA Civ 291; [2007] 2 Lloyd's Rep 56, [55]–[75], denying the existence of a special common law rule excluding the defence where a claimant has been induced to enter a transaction by duress.

innocent defendant was likely to be allowed to insist on counter-restitution *in specie*, the fraudster would have to put up with money in lieu.[553] This made 'counter-restitution impossible' readily available to the innocent as an absolute defence, while against a dishonest defendant it operated only as a pecuniary pre-condition of the restitution which the claimant sought. However, this difference has diminished in modern times.[554]

18.302 The Chancery was always more willing to enlist money as a means of flexibility in achieving counter-restitution,[555] and that approach has gradually spread to all cases. Recently, in a case of undue influence, this flexibility has been taken to extend to both restitution and counter-restitution through a money judgment for the difference in value between the two performances. In *Mahoney v Purnell*[556] an elderly man who had released his shareholding in a hotel company to his son-in-law in exchange for an annuity obtained a money judgment for the £200,000 difference in value between that which he gave and that which he received.

18.303 In marked contrast to its earlier position,[557] the common law has begun to take a similar position. In the string of cases on void interest swaps, it has set one performance off against the other and awarded restitution of the difference. Hobhouse J, who heard the early cases at first instance, proceeded on the basis that, as interest rates fluctuated and payments went back and forth, there was all along just a single rolling enrichment consisting in the difference between the value of the two performances.[558]

18.304 Under an interest swap each contracting party performs in money, one paying a fixed rate and the other a floating rate determined according to a formula. This means that setting off the value of one performance against another is merely a matter of arithmetic. The Privy Council subsequently accepted that wherever the mutual performances present no problems of valuation, the common law will always follow the same approach as that adopted by Hobhouse J.[559]

18.305 Even before the swaps cases, the courts had begun to find ways of escaping the old insistence on a perfect return, *in specie*, to the initial position. For example, in

---

[553] *Spence v Crawford* [1939] 3 All ER 271, HL.

[554] *O'Sullivan v Management Agency and Music Ltd* [1985] QB 428, CA was a milestone in this development.

[555] *Erlanger v New Sombrero Phosphate Co* (1878) 3 App Cas 1218, 1278–9, HL (Lord Blackburn). Compare the flexibility of *Atwood v Maude* (1868) 3 Ch App 369 with the unnecessary rigour of *Whincup v Hughes* (1871) LR 6 CP 78. *O'Sullivan v Management Agency and Music Ltd* [1985] QB 428, CA shows this flexibility in action: a pop star had to make counter-restitution in money for management and promotion services received over a long period.

[556] [1996] 3 All ER 61.

[557] *Hunt v Silk* (1804) 5 East 449, 102 ER 1142; *Freeman v Jeffries* (1869) LR 4 Ex 189.

[558] *Westdeutsche Landesbank Girozentrale v Islington LBC* [1994] 4 All ER 890, 941.

[559] *Goss v Chilcott* [1996] AC 788, 798, PC (Lord Goff).

DO Ferguson & Associates v Sohl[560] contractors had failed to finish the fitting out of a shop. Their repudiatory breach was accepted by the owner, who had already paid a large sum. The Court of Appeal accepted that the incomplete work which had been done by the defaulting builders could be valued and set against the amount he had paid. He therefore recovered the difference.

The rationale for the requirement of counter-restitution rests on the fact that, where there has been an exchange between claimant and defendant, it is inevitable that, if the claimant recovers his part the consideration for his own receipt must fail. Were he to recover without making counter-restitution the other would in the absence of exceptional circumstances have a claim against him on the ground of failure of consideration. Thus Sir Guenter Treitel, writing in relation to rescission for misrepresentation, says, 'The essential point is that the representee should not be unjustly enriched at the representor's expense.'[561] That is certainly right, but it does not explain why the defendant cannot be left to his own action. **18.306**

However, as German jurists have shown, the 'two claims theory (*Zweikondiktionentheorie*)' can produce bizarre results. One claimant may encounter an obstacle or bar which the other escapes, so that for very slight reasons the parties end up in very different situations, as for instance if one happens to be able to use the disenrichment defence and the other not. One escape from that danger is the old insistence that there be exact restitution and counter-restitution or no restitution at all, while the other, more flexible, lies in the 'difference theory (*Saldotheorie*)'. This proposes, exactly as Hobhouse J said in the swaps cases, that there is but one enrichment and one party enriched: the party who received the greater value is enriched by the difference between what he received and what he gave. '*Saldo*' means 'balance' or, here, 'difference'.[562] **18.307**

There are situations in which a claimant appears to be exempt from making counter-restitution, so that, having made restitution, the defendant is left to seek counter-restitution by an independent action, if one is available to him.[563] Though it is not clear that these are always those in which the defendant's claim is regarded as altogether barred, it is true that such exemptions seem chiefly to arise in respect of benefits which the defendant ought never to have traded. One who sells a car which is not his must make restitution of the price but cannot **18.308**

---

[560] (1992) 62 Building LR 95, CA.

[561] Sir Guenter Treitel, *The Law of Contract* (11th edn, 2004) 380.

[562] BS Markesinis, W Lorenz, G Dannemann, *The German Law of Obligations Vol I: The Law of Contracts and Restitution* (1997) 764–6; R Zimmermann and J du Plessis, 'Basic Features of the German Law of Unjustified Enrichment' [1994] Restitution Law Review 14, 41–2; D Reuter and M Martinek, *Ungerechtfertigte Bereicherung* (1978) 595–7; H-G Koppensteiner and EA Kramer, *Ungerechtfertigte Bereicherung* (2nd edn, 1988) 136–7.

[563] The German courts also sometimes move from the 'balance-theory' to the 'two-claims-theory': Markesinis et al (n 562) 765–6.

insist on counter-restitution of the months of use which the buyer enjoyed before the true owner came on the scene.[564] Again, in a case arising from serious malpractice during a take-over bid, a company recovered money paid to a director for special services in connection with the bid without making counter-restitution in respect of the services which it had indeed received. The ground of the company's recovery would seem to have been mistake, in that the money was paid in the belief that it was due under a contract when there was no contract. The services should have been offered by the director *qua* director, and he was in breach of fiduciary duty in taking a special payment for them. The House of Lords was clearly anxious not to spread a safety net below those who played fast and loose with fiduciary duties.[565]

---

[564] *Rowland v Divall* [1923] 2 KB 500.

[565] *Guinness plc v Saunders* [1990] 2 AC 663, HL, noted Birks [1990] LMCLQ 330. It is not easy to reconcile this with the liberal allowance for work and skill made against a fiduciary in breach of duty where the action was brought for that wrong as such: *Boardman v Phipps* [1967] 2 AC 46, HL. Compare *Nottingham University v Fishel* [2000] ICR 1462, 1499–1500; *Quarter Master UK Ltd (in liq) v Pyke* [2004] EWHC 1815 (Ch); [2005] 1 BCLC 245, [76]–[77]; *Murad v Al-Saraj* [2005] EWCA Civ 959; [2005] WTLR 1573, [88].

Part V

LITIGATION

19

INSOLVENCY

A. Introduction: Structure and Process

(a) Scope of chapter

Bankruptcy is concerned with the insolvency of individuals, and liquidation, or **19.01**
winding-up, with the insolvency of companies.[1] Both are collective procedures.
Bankruptcy and company liquidation have evolved separately with, at times,
bankruptcy law being applied by way of analogy to liquidation. Since the insolvency legislation of the mid-1980s, the two subjects have been treated in parallel
in a single statute, now the Insolvency Act 1986,[2] under which common rules, the
Insolvency Rules,[3] have been made.[4] So far as possible, they will be covered
together in this chapter.

---

[1] The subject of insolvent partnerships is left to specialist texts.

[2] References below to statutory sections are to the Insolvency Act 1986 unless otherwise stated.

[3] References below to rules are to the Insolvency Rules 1986, SI 1986/1925, as amended, unless
otherwise stated.

[4] By the Lord Chancellor with the concurrence of the Secretary of State pursuant to powers
under ss 411–12. See SI 1986/1925 (as amended).

19.02 Company administration is also dealt with in this chapter. It frequently, but not necessarily, precedes a winding-up. Sometimes administration leads into a voluntary arrangement between a company and its creditors. The various forms of corporate restructuring, however, remain outside the scope of this chapter. Although technically a collective procedure, administration may since the Enterprise Act 2002 also be invoked out of court by certain secured creditors in place of administrative receivership, confined since the 2002 Act to a limited number of cases.[5] Administrative receivership and the larger subject of receivership will also receive some coverage.

19.03 The focus of this chapter is on insolvency principles rather than the details of insolvency procedure. Since there is little scope for compromise in insolvency cases, principles of law are tested to their limits.

(b) Definition and effects of insolvency

19.04 Insolvency is a financial condition, as opposed to a legal status, that can lead to the winding-up of a company and to the bankruptcy of an individual. A company need not be insolvent when it is wound up; if it is not, any surplus assets after a company's creditors have been paid in full are then returned to its former members.[6] If a surplus is left when a bankrupt's creditors have been paid, it will be paid to the bankrupt himself.[7] Unlike companies that have been wound up, bankrupt individuals survive bankruptcy[8] and a discharged bankrupt may subsequently become bankrupt again, which creates a need for separate statutory provision.[9]

19.05 The Insolvency Act refers not to insolvency but to an inability to pay one's debts,[10] which is but one ground on which the court may order a company to be wound up.[11] The only ground on which a debtor's bankruptcy petition may be presented is the debtor's inability to pay his debts,[12] defined as either a failure for three months to respond to a creditor's statutory demand for payment or a failure to satisfy execution.[13] A creditor may present a bankruptcy petition only in respect

---

[5] Administrative receivers are a sub-category of receivers (sometimes referred to as receivers or managers).

[6] Section 107.

[7] Section 330(5).

[8] *Re Rae* [1995] BCC 102.

[9] See, eg, ss 334–5, Sch 11 para 16 and Insolvency Rules, rr 6.225–8.

[10] On which, see *Byblos Bank SAL v Al-Khudairy* (1986) 2 BCC 99, 549, CA. Genuinely disputed debts are excluded: see, eg, *Re Janeash Ltd* [1990] BCC 250.

[11] Section 122(1)(f).

[12] Section 272.

[13] Section 268(1). For the definition of the absence of a reasonable prospect to pay, see s 268(2).

of liquidated sums amounting to the statutory level,[14] and the debtor must either be unable to pay or have no reasonable prospect of making payment.[15]

The Act provides that a number of different events are each deemed to amount **19.06** to a company's inability to pay its debts for the purpose of compulsory winding-up: a statutory demand for a debt of at least £750 is not paid; an execution remains unsatisfied; and the company is unable to pay its debts as they fall due.[16] In this last case, inability is deemed also to include the case where a company's assets are less than its liabilities; hence, both cash flow and balance sheet insolvency are included in the definition of inability to pay. The first two cases reveal that compulsory winding-up can be used to control abusive debtor behaviour.

A company may be wound up voluntarily on a number of grounds, including **19.07** a special resolution that it be wound up and an extraordinary resolution that it is advisable that it be wound up as it cannot by reason of its liabilities continue in business.[17] In the case of a members' voluntary winding-up, the company's directors have to make a statutory declaration of solvency that the company will be able to pay its debts in full within a stipulated period not to exceed twelve months.[18] The prospect of the directors' personal liability for fraudulent and wrongful trading[19] serves as an inducement to set in train the winding-up of any company facing a hopeless future.

(c) The bankruptcy and liquidation process

(i) Bankruptcy

The estate of insolvent individuals is dealt with by the trustee-in-bankruptcy **19.08** and that of companies by the liquidator. Bankruptcy was modernized in the 1980s.[20] The bankruptcy process begins with the presentation of a petition by either the debtor, one or more creditors, or the supervisor of an individual voluntary arrangement.[21] Prior to the appointment of a trustee, and upon the making of a bankruptcy order, the official receiver administers the bankrupt's affairs[22] and, unless the debtor is himself the petitioner, will receive from the bankrupt a

---

[14] £750.

[15] Section 267.

[16] Section 123.

[17] Section 84.

[18] Section 89.

[19] Sections 213–14.

[20] For example, the act of bankruptcy and reputed ownership doctrines and the interim receivership procedure were abolished.

[21] Section 264 (which also deals with the criminal bankruptcy process). On the court's unfettered power to dismiss or adjourn a bankruptcy petition, see *Re Micklethwait* [2002] EWHC 1123; [2003] BPIR 101.

[22] Section 287. The provisions dealing with official receivers are to be found at ss 399ff.

statement of his affairs[23] and will investigate the conduct and affairs of the bankrupt.[24] The trustee, once appointed, will be subject to the supervision of a creditors' committee[25] and the control of the court.[26] The bankrupt has a duty to inform and co-operate with the trustee[27] and is also required to refrain from committing bankruptcy offences, such as the concealment of property and records and the fraudulent disposal of property.[28]

19.09   The bankrupt is normally discharged after a maximum period of one year from the making of the bankruptcy order.[29] The period is subject to the court's power to annul a bankruptcy order,[30] as it may do for example where the bankruptcy debts and expenses have been paid in full. With certain exceptions, discharge of a bankrupt releases him from all the bankruptcy debts.[31]

(ii) Winding-up

19.10   As stated above, there are two types of winding-up: compulsory and voluntary. Voluntary winding-up may be either a members' or a creditors' voluntary winding-up. Only the latter is truly an insolvency process. A members' voluntary winding-up can take place only if the directors make a statutory declaration of solvency.[32] There is also provision made for the conversion of a members' into a creditors' winding-up.[33]

19.11   A voluntary winding-up begins with a resolution to wind up which is then published.[34] The commencement of the winding-up is deemed to begin at the date the resolution is passed,[35] whereupon the company is to cease to carry on business except as required for its beneficial winding-up[36] and there are to be no more

---

[23] Section 288.

[24] Section 289.

[25] Section 301.

[26] Section 303.

[27] Section 333.

[28] Sections 350ff. In extreme cases, a bankrupt may be committed to prison for contempt of court.

[29] Section 279 as added by s 256 of the Enterprise Act 2002. The 2002 Act also contains a number of provisions that diminish post-bankruptcy restrictions on a bankrupt's activities and that reduce the number of bankruptcy offences (ss 257 and 265–88 and Schs 20–21, variously amending the Insolvency Act). Bankruptcy restrictions, which can last for up to 15 years, can be used to inhibit rogue directors from seeking sole trader status.

[30] Sections 279(4) and 282. The court has a broad discretion: *Harper v Buchler (No 2)* [2005] BPIR 577.

[31] Section 281. Discharge does not affect the rights of secured creditors (s 281(2)) and does not extend to debts arising out of 'fraud or fraudulent breach of trust' (s 281(3)).

[32] Sections 89–90.

[33] Section 96.

[34] Sections 84–5.

[35] Section 86.

[36] Section 87.

changes in the membership of the company.[37] In a creditors' voluntary winding-up, the company has to summon a meeting of its creditors, before whom the directors lay a statement of the company's affairs.[38] In the appointment of a liquidator the creditors have the decisive voice.[39] If a liquidation committee is formed, both creditors and company may appoint members.[40] The committee may sanction the continuing exercise by the directors of their powers, which otherwise cease on the appointment of the liquidator.[41]

A compulsory winding-up usually begins with a petition presented by the company, its directors, one or more creditors or one or more contributories.[42] In the meantime, proceedings pending against the company may be stayed or restrained[43] and there are further powers regarding the protection of the company's property after the commencement of a winding-up[44] and the control of proceedings against the company after the order has been made.[45] There may then follow an investigation of the company's affairs and an examination of its officers by the official receiver.[46] The court may appoint a provisional liquidator[47] before meetings are held by creditors and contributories separately for the appointment of a liquidator and for the (optional) appointment of a liquidation committee.[48] The liquidator's function is to get in, realize and distribute the company's property and to co-operate where necessary with the official receiver.[49] Upon the conclusion of the winding-up, the liquidator summons a final meeting of the creditors to receive his report and release him.[50] After its winding-up, the company is formally dissolved.[51]

19.12

There is no true corporate equivalent of the discharge of individuals from bankruptcy. Occasionally, however, a company that has been wound up and struck off the register will be restored to it upon application by the liquidator or other interested person.[52] One instance of this concerns insured defendants where in the last resort the injured claimant has direct rights of recovery against the insurer in

19.13

---

[37] Section 88.
[38] Sections 98–9.
[39] Section 100.
[40] Section 101.
[41] Section 103.
[42] Section 124.
[43] Section 126.
[44] Section 127, discussed at paras 19.70–19.81.
[45] Section 130(2).
[46] Sections 131–4.
[47] Section 135.
[48] Sections 139 and 141.
[49] Section 143.
[50] Section 146.
[51] Sections 201ff.
[52] Companies Act 2006, s 1029.

accordance with the statutory scheme.[53] Since a dissolved corporate defendant no longer has legal personality, its dissolution has to be nullified so that the claimant can go directly against the insurer.

(d) Voluntary arrangements

19.14 Voluntary arrangements are schemes for the composition of indebtedness that are an alternative to bankruptcy and liquidation[54] and that, by pre-empting the latter procedures, are designed to salvage a debtor in financial distress. As the law currently stands, corporate voluntary arrangements (CVAs) have proved to be less successful than individual voluntary arrangements (IVAs).

(i) CVAs

19.15 The rules concerning CVAs are to be found in Part I of the Insolvency Act. A CVA is a matter of contract for those party to it.[55] It need not entail a composition of claims[56] and it does not place an embargo on proceedings against the company.[57] Prior to liquidation and administration, only the directors of the company, and not the members or creditors, may propose an arrangement,[58] and thereafter only liquidators and administrators may do so. In the case of a directors' proposal, a nominee will be appointed to supervise the arrangement and may act in the character of 'trustee or otherwise'.[59] This nominee is obliged first to report to the court[60] before summoning separate meetings of the company's members and of all of its creditors.[61] Liquidators and administrators may proceed directly to the summoning of the meetings.[62] An agreed arrangement, which turns upon majority voting,[63] binds all of the company's members and its creditors with notice

---

[53] Third Parties (Rights Against Insurers) Act 1930.

[54] Hence they are taken before these procedures in the Insolvency Act and also do not require the company or individual to be insolvent as defined by the Act.

[55] *Johnson v Davies* [1998] EWCA Civ 483; [1999] Ch 117.

[56] See *Commissioners of Inland Revenue v Adam & Partners* [2001] 1 BCLC 222, CA.

[57] See *Alman v Approach Housing Ltd* [2001] 1 BCLC 530.

[58] Section 1(1), (3).

[59] Section 1(2). The conduct of the supervisor is open to review and the supervisor himself may apply for directions: s 7. Whether there is a trust over the CVA moneys is, like the range of assets included in the CVA, a matter of construction of the CVA: *Re Kudos Glass Ltd* [2001] 1 BCLC 390; *NT Gallagher & Son Ltd v Tomlinson* [2002] EWCA Civ 404; [2002] 1 WLR 2380.

[60] Members and unsecured creditors may challenge the arrangement in court where there has been unfair prejudice or material irregularity in the conduct of meetings: s 6.

[61] Sections 2–3. Creditors include those with contingent and unquantified claims: *Doorbar v Alltime Securities Ltd* [1996] 1 WLR 456, CA.

[62] Section 3(2).

[63] Rule 1.19 (three-quarters in value of debt owed to creditors present in person or by proxy and voting); r 1.20 (one-half in value of members present in person or by proxy and voting).

of the meeting.[64] Nevertheless, the concurrence of secured creditors[65] and of preference creditors is required if their rights are to be affected by the arrangement,[66] which reveals the limitations of the CVA process. The two meetings of members and creditors must approve the same arrangement.[67]

In the case of administration and liquidation, the prospects of an arrangement are **19.16** improved by the impediments placed on the taking of proceedings and (in the case of administration only) the enforcement of security against the company.[68] Since the Insolvency Act 2000, the directors may apply for an initial moratorium,[69] a feature previously applicable only to IVAs.

(ii) IVAs

The rules concerning IVAs,[70] which have proved to be popular with debtors **19.17** and to leave creditors with more than the bankruptcy process, are to be found in Part VIII of the Act.[71] They are *mutatis mutandis* the same as for CVAs. In those cases where an application is made for an interim order and is pending, there is a moratorium in the form of a stay of proceedings.[72] This is followed by the order itself whose effect is to prevent or discontinue bankruptcy petitions and to require the leave of the court for other proceedings, legal process and execution against the debtor or his property.[73] The debtor himself may apply for an interim order, as well as, in the case of an undischarged bankrupt, his trustee or the official receiver.[74] A nominee must be appointed to act as trustee or otherwise supervise the arrangement.[75] There follows the nominee's report, a summoning of a meeting of creditors if the report favours this and a decision of the meeting.[76]

---

[64] Section 5(2)(b).

[65] Who do not include landlords forfeiting a lease: *Razzaq v Pala* [1997] 1 WLR 1336 (which is consistent with *Re Park Air Services plc* [2000] 2 AC 172, HL).

[66] Section 4(3), (4).

[67] Section 5(1) (modifications to proposed scheme). For the power of the court to reconcile differences between the two meetings, see Insolvency Act (as amended by Sch 2 to the Insolvency Act 2000), s 4A.

[68] Discussed at paras 19.88–19.91.

[69] Clause 1 and Sch 1.

[70] Certain changes were introduced by Sch 3 to the Insolvency Act 2000 and, for post-bankruptcy IVAs, the Enterprise Act 2000 (s 264, amending the Insolvency Act, creating a fast-track procedure where the Official Receiver is the nominee).

[71] The procedure under the Deeds of Arrangement Act 1914 is different and mutually exclusive (s 260(3) of the 1986 Act) and, though still extant, barely used.

[72] Section 254.

[73] Section 252. The Insolvency Act 2000 extended this to include the levying of distress and re-entry by the landlord. For the assets subject to an IVA, see *Welburn v Dibb Lupton Broomhead* [2002] EWCA Civ 1601; [2003] BPIR 768.

[74] Section 253(3).

[75] Section 253(2).

[76] Sections 256–8.

(e) Other insolvency procedures for company debtors: receivership and administration

(i) Receivers

19.18 Receivership, and its sub-category, administrative receivership, are dealt with at length in the Insolvency Act. This receivership is provided for in the debentures evidencing the debt[77] and authorizes the creditor in stated circumstances, under the terms of an irrevocable power of attorney, to act in the name of the company by appointing a receiver whose function is to pay down the debt. The creditor is entitled to pursue self-interest when making the appointment.[78] Unlike most other legal systems, English law permits secured creditors to take steps to enforce their rights with minimal interference from company liquidators and trustees-in-bankruptcy. Despite its function in advancing the creditor's self-interest, receivership is widely credited as having saved many companies or salvable parts of the business. The receiver will be given broad powers of management but, in any case, the Act presumes in the case of administrative receivership such powers to be given in the debentures.[79] The receiver will act as the agent of the company[80] which the Act explicitly treats as being the case for administrative receivers prior to the liquidation of the company.[81] Those receivers appointed pursuant to a debenture secured by a charge or charges, including a floating charge, extending to at least substantially the whole of a company's property, pass the test of an administrative receiver under the Act.[82] They have special powers of contracting and of investigation[83] which takes them out of the realm of ordinary debt enforcement and justifies their prominent treatment in insolvency legislation. Since the Enterprise Act 2002, a power to appoint an administrative receiver can be created after the Act only in the case of designated transactions.[84]

(ii) Administrators

19.19 The Cork Report[85] drew attention to the corporate rescue attributes of receivership. It proposed, in cases where there was no debenture holder to appoint a

---

[77] The statutory power of a chargee or mortgagee to appoint a receiver under ss 101 and 109 of the Law of Property Act 1925 is very similar.

[78] *Shamji v Johnson Matthey* [1986] BCLC 278, CA.

[79] See s 42 and Sch 1.

[80] It is an unusual type of agency: *Gomba Holdings UK Ltd v Minories Finance Ltd* [1989] BCLC 115, 117, CA. Under s 109(2) of the Law of Property Act 1925, a receiver appointed thereunder is also the agent of the mortgagor or chargor.

[81] Section 44(1)(a).

[82] Section 29(2).

[83] Discussed at para 19.169.

[84] Section 249, adding ss 72B-G of the Insolvency Act (major capital market and financial market transactions, utility transactions and public-private finance transactions).

[85] *Report of the Review Committee on Insolvency Law and Practice* (Cmnd 8558, 1982).

receiver or manager, that a statutory power be granted to appoint an administrator able to achieve the same goal. This led to the enactment of Part II of the Insolvency Act. As someone appointed in default of an administrative receiver, the Act conferred on the administrator the same powers as those deemed to exist in the debentures giving rise to the appointment of an administrative receiver.[86] In addition, the administrator was given powers to interfere with the rights of secured creditors and of title-retaining creditors that are denied to administrative receivers.[87] Initially, administrators were appointed only by the court. Since the Enterprise Act,[88] they may now also be appointed out of court by the holder of a qualifying charge, which is or includes a floating charge and extends to the whole or substantially the whole of the company's property.[89] Administrators may also be appointed by the debtor company or its directors. In all cases, the administrator is an officer of the court.[90] The purpose of administration is either to rescue the company as a going concern, to achieve a better result for the creditors as a whole than liquidation or to realize property for distribution to secured or preference creditors.[91]

Administrators are appointed by the court if the company is unable to pay its **19.20** debts and if the court is satisfied that one or other purpose of administration will be served by the appointment.[92] They may be appointed by the holder of a qualifying charge if it provides for the appointment of an administrator (or an administrative receiver). The power of a company or its directors to appoint an administrator is essentially unrestricted,[93] except that the floating chargee is in the driving seat and can pre-empt an appointment by either of the other two means.[94] Administrators appointed out of court under a qualifying charge are required to exercise their functions in the interests of creditors as whole[95] and have certain responsibilities when carrying out their functions and reporting to creditors. Nevertheless, there is likely to be little practical difference in outcome between administrative receivership and an administration procured by the floating chargee.

---

86 Schs 1 and B1, para 60.
87 Discussed at paras 19.88–19.91.
88 See now Sch B1 of the Insolvency Act (as amended).
89 Schedule B1, para 14.
90 Schedule B1, para 5.
91 Schedule B1, para 3(1). For the use of administration to reorganize a business, see *Re British American Racing (Holdings) Ltd* [2004] EWHC 2947 (Ch); [2005] 2 BCLC 324. Administrators are empowered to distribute to secured and preferential creditors and, usually with the leave of the court, to other creditors: ibid paras 65–6; Insolvency Rules (as amended by Insolvency (Amendment) Rules 2003 (SI 2003/1730)), rr 2.68–71.
92 Schedule B1, para 11.
93 Schedule B1, para 22.
94 Schedule B1, para 7 (and the floating chargee's ability to move at speed).
95 Schedule B1, para 3.

(f) Legislative background and sources

19.21 For the most part, the statutory material on insolvency is to be found in the Insolvency Act (as amended) together with its accompanying Insolvency Rules. The 1986 Act was a consolidation measure following close on the heels of the Insolvency Act 1985, which in the areas of individual and corporate insolvency had repealed a wide range of statutory provisions and had also introduced a number of reforms to insolvency law. The distinguishing feature of the Acts of 1985 and 1986 was the way they brought corporate and individual insolvency under the same statutory roof. The former had previously been located in the Companies Acts and the latter in the Bankruptcy Acts. The main influence behind the Insolvency Acts of 1985 and 1986 was the Cork Report.[96] The Cork Committee had been given broad terms of reference extending to a review of the law and practice of insolvency, bankruptcy, liquidation and receivership, as well as the consideration of a comprehensive insolvency system. Its report, submitted after an interim report in 1979,[97] was followed quite rapidly by a green paper,[98] white paper[99] and Bill leading up to the 1985 Act.

19.22 Notwithstanding their shared statutory parentage, the individual and corporate insolvency regimes are by no means identical in their content. Parts I-VII of the 1986 Act deal with corporate insolvency, while Parts VIII-XI deal with individual insolvency and Parts XII-XIX are common to both regimes.

B. The Estate of the Insolvent and Its Distribution

(1) The Estate of the Insolvent in the Insolvency Process

(a) The content of the insolvent's estate

19.23 Insolvency officers distribute the estate of the insolvent among its creditors after the debtor's property has been realized. The property of bankrupt individuals first vests automatically in the trustee upon his appointment taking effect.[100] Before the changes of the 1980s, under the reputed ownership doctrine, it included '[a]ll goods. . .in the possession, order or disposition of the bankrupt, in his trade or business, by the consent of the true owner'.[101] Bankruptcy differs from

---

[96] Cmnd 8558 (1982).

[97] Cmnd 7968.

[98] Cmnd 7979.

[99] Cmnd 9175.

[100] Section 306. Nevertheless, as in the case of a winding-up, the property of the bankrupt will be impressed with a trust in favour of his creditors: *Ayerst v C&K (Construction) Ltd* [1976] AC 167, HL; *Re Yagerphone Ltd* [1935] Ch 392; *Re MC Bacon Ltd* [1991] Ch 127.

[101] Bankruptcy Act 1914, s 38(2)(c). The reputed ownership doctrine never applied to companies.

liquidation in that a portion of the property of the bankrupt is retained for his beneficial enjoyment and does not vest in the trustee.[102] There is provision in the case of compulsory (but not voluntary) liquidation for the liquidator to apply for a vesting order[103] but there is little practical need for this since the distribution of the estate can be accomplished through the powers conferred on the liquidator[104] after the liquidator has performed his statutory task of taking the property of the company into his custody.[105] The property of the company does not vest in an administrator, nor does it vest in an administrative receiver, both of whom enjoy broad powers in respect of the property.[106]

(i) The 'property' of the insolvent

Under section 436, the word 'property' embraces 'every description of property wherever situated and also obligations and every description of interest, whether present or future or vested or contingent, arising out of, or incidental to, property'.[107] It is hard to imagine a wider definition.[108] Indeed, an item need not have realizable value or be capable of being beneficially enjoyed by the creditors of the insolvent for it to be property.[109]

19.24

In the case of bankruptcy, the date for testing when an item is property is the date of appointment of the trustee when the vesting occurs. Items purely personal to the bankrupt at that time will not vest in the trustee. Thus the personal correspondence of the bankrupt, even if valuable, is excluded since the opposite conclusion would entail a 'gross invasion of privacy'.[110] Although an action for breach of contract for wrongful dismissal, occurring before the vesting date, will

19.25

---

[102] Namely, essential personal and vocational items (s 283) and personal rights of action: discussed at para 19.35. With regard to the bankrupt's home, see ss 283A and 313A of the Insolvency Act (as added by s 261 of the Enterprise Act 2002).

[103] Section 145.

[104] Sections 165 and 167, Sch 4. See *Smith v Bridgend County Borough Council* [2001] UKHL 58; [2002] 1 AC 336.

[105] Section 144. It is the function of trustees to 'get in' the bankrupt's estate (s 305(2)). Like a compulsory liquidator, the administrator takes into custody the company's property (Insolvency Act (as amended), Sch B1, para 67). No similar duty is laid down in the Act for voluntary liquidators: their functions will be set out in the terms of their appointment. An administrative receiver is empowered to 'take possession of, collect and get in' the company's property (Sch 1, para 1).

[106] Insolvency Act, Schs 1 and B1.

[107] That value may be indirectly realized. See *Re Rae* [1995] BCC 102 (fishing licences terminated on bankruptcy but the Ministry recognized bankrupt's 'entitlement' to apply for new licences).

[108] *Bristol Airport plc v Powdrill* [1990] Ch 744, 759, CA: *Re Rae* [1995] BCC 102, 113. Hence 'property' can include rights of pre-emption (*Dear v Reeves* [2001] EWCA Civ 277; [2002] Ch 1) and discretionary payments under a pension scheme (*Patel v Jones* [2001] EWCA Civ 779; [2001] BPIR 919).

[109] See *De Rothschild v Bell* [2000] QB 33, CA (continuation tenancy which could not be turned into money for the benefit of the bankrupt's creditors); *Morgan v Morris* [1998] BPIR 764 (vesting of moneys in an offshore trust).

[110] *Haig v Aitken* [2001] Ch 110, 118.

vest in the trustee,[111] the rights of a bankrupt under a continuing personal services contract will not. Nevertheless, if property rights of the bankrupt can be enjoyed only by him but entail expenditure that will affect the dividend available to his creditors, they are treated as property of the estate for the purpose of the trustee's disclaimer power.[112]

19.26 Property is defined widely in the insolvency process because, apart from gathering in an estate so that the maximum is available for distribution, its existence is a precondition for the exercise by an insolvency officer of the power of disclaimer. The exercise of this power[113] permits the removal from the estate of items that are worthless or even, because their burdens outweigh their benefits, possess negative value. Value, therefore, is not a precondition for the treatment of an item as property.[114] The meaning of property may depend upon its context,[115] but there is just one definition of property in the Insolvency Act and no justification for giving the word one interpretation when dealing with disclaimer, another when dealing with the gathering in and distribution of the estate and another when dealing with the enforcement of security over the property of a company in administration.[116]

19.27 Consequently, the definition of property is capable of including causes of action, in so far as their assignment does not infringe rules of public policy against champerty and maintenance.[117] It should include anything that can be held subject to the terms of a trust,[118] such as the benefit of a non-assignable contract.[119] Recently, in a case of disclaimer, property was held to include a waste management licence.[120] Under the relevant legislation, the statutory authority had a discretion to order the transfer of the licence and could revoke it; the holder could not transfer it. The licence was nevertheless held to be either property or an interest in property. A milk quota has also been held to be property. It was capable of

---

[111] *Bailey v Thurston & Co Ltd* [1903] 1 KB 137, CA. Any sums the bankrupt recovers in proceedings for a breach arising after the date of the trustee's appointment will be subject to the provisions on after-acquired property, discussed at paras 19.33–19.34. The approach in *Bailey v Thurston & Co Ltd* does not readily lend itself to corporate insolvency.

[112] *De Rothschild v Bell* [2000] QB 33, CA.

[113] Discussed at paras 19.41–19.49. An unprofitable contract can be disclaimed (ss 178(3)(a), 315(2)(a)); it should make no difference that the contract contains a no-assignment clause (see *De Rothschild v Bell* [2000] QB 33, CA).

[114] Whether in the actual sense (Is this in fact worth anything?) or in its potential sense (Is this capable of having value attributed to it?).

[115] *Nokes v Doncaster Amalgamated Collieries* [1940] AC 1014, 1051, HL.

[116] *Bristol Airport plc v Powdrill* [1990] Ch 744, CA (interest of lessee in aircraft).

[117] Discussed at paras 19.50–19.55.

[118] See *Swift v Dairywise Farms Ltd* [2000] 1 WLR 1177, affd [2001] EWCA Civ 145; [2003] 1 WLR 1606 (Note).

[119] See *King (Don) Productions Inc v Warren* [1998] 2 All ER 608, affd [2000] Ch 291, CA.

[120] *Re Celtic Extraction Ltd* [2001] Ch 475, CA.

forming the subject matter of a trust[121] so that its sale could be ordered on the application of a liquidator.[122] A milk quota is attached to a defined landholding. It can only be transferred with an interest in the land, such as a leasehold, but can thereafter be detached from the land to which it is appurtenant and attached to other land of the lessee. Consequently, the quota has the necessary attribute of transferability for it to be property, along with other necessary attributes of value and a framework of entitlement.

(ii) Beneficial property rights

The property available for distribution comprises only assets that are beneficially **19.28** owned by the insolvent. It does not extend to property held on trust,[123] or to property the subject of a reservation of title clause or of a security interest[124] by way of charge or mortgage. The insolvent's equity of redemption[125] is available for distribution but the insolvency officer may not interfere in the realization of the security, any more than he can interfere with the exercise of a lien, a right of retention or a right of stoppage of goods in transit.[126]

The immunity of trust property from distribution to the creditors of an insolvent **19.29** trustee is only apparently infringed in a case where the trustee, a bank that becomes insolvent, lawfully deposits trust money with itself so as to leave the trust with an unsecured claim in its insolvency.[127] The trust estate now comprises the personal debt claim against the trustee instead of the former trust money.

(iii) Trusts

Various forms of constructive and invented trusts are capable of affecting the size **19.30** of the insolvent's estate. First of all, the growth of restitutionary *in rem* claims, without regard to the effect of their creation on other creditors of the insolvent

---

121 *Swift v Dairywise Farms Ltd* [2000] 1 WLR 1177, affd [2001] EWCA Civ 145; [2003] 1 WLR 1606 (Note).

122 Under s 112.

123 Section 283(3)(a) (bankruptcy, but references in the Act to getting in and distributing company property impliedly recognize the rights of beneficiaries).

124 See s 283(5). Even if it has not been realized, the security also remains in existence after the discharge of the bankrupt: s 281(2).

125 Although a charge is merely an encumbrance and no property interest is conveyed to the chargee, it is common to say loosely that the chargor has, like the mortgagor, an equity of redemption in the property charged: see, eg, *Re Bank of Credit and Commerce International SA (No 8)* [1998] AC 214, HL.

126 Arising under the Sale of Goods Act 1979, ss 44–6. But note that a lien over a company's books, papers and records (excepting documents of title) is unenforceable against an administrator or liquidator: s 246(2),(3). For the power of the administrative receiver as office-holder to call for company papers and documents under s 234(2) when getting in its property, see *Re Aveling Barford Ltd* [1989] 1 WLR 360.

127 *Space Investments Ltd v Canadian Imperial Bank of Commerce Trust Co (Bahamas) Ltd* [1986] 1 WLR 1072, PC.

defendant, threatens to disrupt the system of rateable insolvency distribution. The so-called *Quistclose* trust, whether it takes the form of a trust attaching to money because of the terms on which it is paid[128] or of a trust declared by the payee upon the receipt of money,[129] has a particular impact in insolvency cases.[130] Other examples of equitable proprietary interests also exist, which prefer the claimant in the defendant's insolvency.[131] Nevertheless, there is a systemic reluctance to allow equitable proprietary interests to take root in the insolvency process.[132]

(iv) Clauses determining property interests

19.31 The estate of a bankrupt[133] may in effect be diminished by clauses in a will, assignment or similar instrument conferring a limited interest and determining that interest in the event of the holder's bankruptcy.[134] Such clauses are valid[135] provided there is no repugnancy between a clause of this nature and a clause in the same instrument that purports to assign property in absolute terms.[136] Nevertheless, a clause in an instrument is void if it divests an unlimited interest in the event of bankruptcy.[137] The distinction between inherently limited interests and unlimited interests divested upon bankruptcy is notoriously difficult to draw and to justify.[138]

---

[128] See for example *Barclays Bank Ltd v Quistclose Investments Ltd* [1970] AC 567, HL; *Re EVTR Ltd* [1987] BCLC 646, CA; *Re Chelsea Cloisters Ltd* (1980) 41 P&CR 98, CA; *Carreras Rothmans Ltd v Freeman Mathews Treasure Ltd* [1985] Ch 207; *Re Lewis's of Leicester Ltd* [1995] 1 BCLC 428; *Twinsectra Ltd v Yardley* [2002] UKHL 12; [2002] 2 AC 164 (Lord Millett). The imposition of restrictions on the use of money is not sufficient to establish the purpose that is necessary for the inference of a *Quistclose* trust: *Re Griffin Trading Co* [2000] BPIR 256.

[129] See *Re Kayford Ltd* [1975] 1 WLR 279.

[130] See M Bridge, 'The Quistclose Trust in a World of Secured Transactions' (1992) 12 OJLS 333.

[131] See for example *Chase Manhattan Bank SA v Israel-British Bank (London) Ltd* [1981] Ch 105; *Re Fleet Disposal Services Ltd* [1995] 1 BCLC 345; *Neste Oy v Lloyd's Bank plc* [1983] 2 Lloyd's Rep 658. See paras 18.183–18.191.

[132] See *Re Wait* [1927] 1 Ch 606, CA and *Re Goldcorp Exchange* [1995] 1 AC 74, PC. A similar conservatism is at work with regard to restitutionary claims in *Westdeutsche Landesbank Girozentrale v Islington London BC* [1996] AC 669, HL, *per* Lord Browne-Wilkinson, but the willingness to classify restitutionary claims as proprietary in the non-insolvency cases of *Lord Napier and Ettrick v Hunter* [1993] AC 713, HL and *A-G for Hong Kong v Reid* [1994] 1 AC 324, PC has implications for insolvency distribution. See paras 18.173ff.

[133] Or a company in liquidation.

[134] Direct payment clauses are discussed at paras 19.97–19.98.

[135] *Re Ashby* [1892] 1 QB 872.

[136] *Re Smith* [1916] 1 Ch 369.

[137] See *Money Markets International Stockbrokers Ltd v London Stock Exchange Ltd* [2002] 1 WLR 1150; *British Eagle International Airlines Ltd v Cie Nationale Air France* [1975] 1 WLR 758, HL. This subject is discussed in greater detail at para 19.95.

[138] According to Neuberger J in *Money Markets International Stockbrokers Ltd v London Stock Exchange Ltd* [2002] 1 WLR 1150, 1182: '[I]t is not possible to discern a coherent, or even an entirely coherent set of rules, to enable one to assess in any particular case whether. . .a provision falls foul of the principle' that a clause transferring property on an insolvency is void.

(v) Bankrupts, pensions, and after-acquired property

As stated above, not all of a bankrupt's assets vest in the trustee for distribution.[139] **19.32**
So that the bankrupt and his family will not be a burden on state provision, the
Insolvency Act excludes certain personal effects[140] as well as items used personally
by the bankrupt in his employment, business or vocation.[141] Nevertheless, as
stated above, the definition of property for the purpose of vesting in the trustee
is wide: this compensates for the advantage the bankrupt receives from being
forever released from personal payment obligations.[142] For example, although in
one case membership of a society was personal and could not be transferred, the
right to receive future royalty income from the society, to which the copyright
in certain musical works had been assigned, did vest in the trustee on his appointment, even though the amount of these future payments could not be ascertained at that date.[143]

Bankruptcy differs from corporate insolvency with respect to the continuing eco- **19.33**
nomic activities and life of the bankrupt between the date of commencement
of his bankruptcy and his discharge. The bankrupt will have earning power and
thus future assets falling in during the period of bankruptcy. Consequently, the
trustee may apply for an order requiring the bankrupt to pay over part of his
income for a designated period.[144] The position concerning the bankrupt's entitlement under a personal or an occupational pension plan is as follows. Prior to
1999, that entitlement, whether it took the form of the capital sum paid under
some schemes on taking retirement or the periodic income stream, though payable in the future was treated as a present asset that vested in the trustee at the
commencement of the bankruptcy.[145] Pension rights therefore automatically
vested and did not have to be the subject of a written claim by the trustee, a procedure which applies to after-acquired property.[146] Furthermore, moneys received

---

[139] Also excluded are certain types of tenancy (s 283(3A)) though the trustee may require them
by notice to be vested (s 308A).

[140] Section 283(2)(b): 'such clothing, bedding, furniture, household equipment and provisions
as are necessary for satisfying the basic domestic needs of the bankrupt and his family'.

[141] Section 283(2)(a): 'such tools, books, vehicles and other items of equipment as are necessary
to the bankrupt etc'. See also s 308 (trading down for cheaper substitutes).

[142] *Patel v Jones* [2001] EWCA Civ 779; [2001] BPIR 919; *Re Rae* [1995] BCC 102, 111.

[143] *Performing Right Society v Rowland* [1997] 3 All ER 336. But no vesting would occur in
respect of songs not yet written. Sums received by the bankrupt in respect of such songs would have
to be made the subject of an income payment order (s 310) if the trustee and the creditors were to
participate in them.

[144] Section 310 (discussed further below).

[145] *Patel v Jones* [1999] BPIR 509 (occupational plan); *Re Landau* [1998] Ch 223 (personal
plan); *Krasner v Dennison* [2001] Ch 76, CA. But the vesting was confined to pensionable service
occurring before the date of the trustee's appointment: *Patel v Jones* [2001] EWCA Civ 779; [2001]
BPIR 919.

[146] Section 307.

under such pensions did not fall within the income payments order system so that no order might be made in respect of them after discharge, and no order made before discharge could affect them unless the case fell within certain statutory exceptions.[147] The trustee could not apply for an income payments order in respect of a pension asset that had already vested in him.[148] Restrictions on the assignment of pension rights did not prevent those rights from vesting in the trustee under section 306.[149] Discretionary pension rights were a different matter which is why the income payment order could usefully be applied to income actually received by the bankrupt.[150] With the passing of the Welfare Reform and Pensions Act 1999, the rights of a bankrupt under an approved pension arrangement are excluded from his estate.[151] The same applies to unapproved pension arrangements where appropriate regulations are made.[152]

19.34   The release of the bankrupt from his due debts may also explain the trustee's power, exercised unilaterally and by notice, to claim for the estate after-acquired property falling in after the date of the trustee's appointment.[153] This power does not extend to the bankrupt's income[154] in respect of which, nevertheless, an income payment order may be made on the trustee's application so that the excess of the bankrupt's income vests in the trustee after provision has been made for the reasonable domestic needs of the bankrupt and his family.[155] This latter factor points to a broad interpretation being given to 'income' so that, especially where the bankrupt has little earning capacity, the word includes redundancy payments, money in lieu of notice and lump sum pension payments.[156]

---

147 Section 310(6); *Re Landau* [1998] Ch 223.

148 *Krasner v Dennison* [2001] Ch 76, CA (which reviews fully the position regarding pensions of different types).

149 *Re Landau* [1998] Ch 223; *Krasner v Dennison* [2001] Ch 76, CA.

150 *Krasner v Dennison* [2001] Ch 76, CA.

151 Section 11 of the 1999 Act.

152 Section 12 of the 1999 Act.

153 Insolvency Act, s 307. Under previous legislation, after-acquired property automatically vested in the trustee. After-acquired property includes financial loss claims vesting after bankruptcy in the bankrupt, even though these claims would have automatically vested in the trustee under s 306 had they been in existence at that time: *Mulkerrins v Pricewaterhouse Coopers* [2003] UKHL 41; [2003] 1 WLR 1937 (*res judicata* prevented any reopening of the district judge's ruling that an action for damages against financial advisers for being made bankrupt could not vest in the estate).

154 Section 307(5).

155 Section 310 (as amended by the Pensions Act 1995 so as not to entrench upon the guaranteed minimum pension and by s 259 of the Enterprise Act 2002). Such orders cannot be made after discharge and, if made before discharge, can affect income received after discharge for a limited time: s 310(6). A new income payments agreement was brought in by the Enterprise Act (s 260) to reduce the involvement of the court in non-contentious cases. It takes effect as a court order and is limited to three years and can operate after the bankrupt's discharge.

156 The trustee in *Patel v Jones* [2001] EWCA Civ 779; [2001] BPIR 919 conceded that statutory redundancy pay and pay in lieu of notice did not vest in him. Nevertheless, how can accruing pension rights arising from post-vesting employment not be after-acquired property under s 307? The system appears to depend upon the restraint of trustees.

(vi) Bankrupts and litigation

It was stated above that a cause of action for breach of contract vested in the **19.35**
trustee at the date of his appointment. Certain actions in tort are also capable of
vesting except in so far as 'damages are to be estimated by immediate reference to
pain felt by the bankrupt in respect of his body, mind, or character, and without
immediate reference to his rights of property'.[157] For that reason, a cause of action
in defamation will not vest,[158] though a judgment debt against the defendant
would undoubtedly vest; judgment rendered after the trustee's appointment
would give rise to after-acquired property to which the trustee could lay claim.[159]
In personal injury cases, the claimant may have a claim for pain and suffering as
well as a claim for loss of future earnings. The former type of claim is certainly
personal[160] but the latter is not. Yet there is only one cause of action[161] and, though
hybrid in nature, it vests in the trustee under section 306 of the Insolvency Act.[162]
Nevertheless, there is a separate property right in the bankrupt in the pain and
suffering claim, so that any damages recovered by the trustee respecting this claim
are to be held on constructive trust terms for the bankrupt.[163]

The effect of the bankrupt's property vesting in the trustee, coupled with the rule **19.36**
that upon the making of a bankruptcy order a creditor's claim must be submitted
to proof and cannot otherwise be asserted against the bankrupt or his property,[164]
means that he ceases to have an interest in either his assets or liabilities, apart from
any surplus that may become available.[165] Consequently, the bankrupt no longer
has a continuing interest in litigation in which he is the defendant and may not in
his own person appeal against a judgment,[166] except where the claimant is seeking

---

157 *Beckham v Drake* (1849) 2 HLC 579, 604, 9 ER 1213, HL. A cause of action for disablement
vests in the estate: *Cork v Rawlins* [2001] EWCA Civ 202; [2001] Ch 792.

158 *Wilson v United Counties Bank* [1920] AC 102, HL. See *Re Campbell* [1997] Ch 14, 21.
A cause of action for wrongful dismissal seeking reinstatement will not vest (*Grady v Prison Service*
[2003] EWCA Civ 527; [2003] 3 All ER 745), nor will a claim for discrimination or injury to feelings (*Khan v Trident Safeguards Ltd* [2004] EWCA Civ 624; [2004] ICR 1591).

159 Section 307.

160 Similarly, a claim under the criminal injuries compensation scheme: *Re a Bankrupt No 145/95*
The Times, 8 December 1995.

161 Despite the practice of itemizing damages awards instead of awarding a global sum, which
began with *Jefford v Gee* [1970] 2 QB 130, CA.

162 *Ord v Upton* [2000] Ch 352, CA (containing a full review of the authorities). See *Mulkerrins v
Pricewaterhouse Coopers* [2003] UKHL 41; [2003] 1 WLR 1937 where Lord Millett (generally
supported by Lords Bingham and Scott) saw some merit in the view that a cause of action against
financial advisers for being made bankrupt could not vest in the estate, since the object of damages
was to put the bankrupt in the position she occupied before the bankruptcy order was made.

163 ibid.

164 Section 285(3).

165 *Heath v Tang* [1993] 1 WLR 1421, 1422, CA.

166 ibid.

personal relief against the bankrupt, for example, by way of injunction.[167] This prevents 'the bankrupt's substance from being wasted in hopeless appeals and protects creditors from vexatious challenges to their claims'.[168] The rule is capable of causing hardship in those cases where the judgment against the bankrupt led to the bankruptcy order and the trustee lacks the means to conduct the appeal, whereas the bankrupt himself might qualify for legal aid.[169]

(b) Effect of insolvency on contracts

19.37   The state of insolvency or the commencement of a winding-up or bankruptcy[170] does not alone amount to a present or anticipatory breach of contract though there is nothing to prevent contracting parties from agreeing upon a right to withdraw from the contract in that event.[171] Similarly, the winding-up of one party does not automatically terminate the contract.[172] As the company's agent,[173] the liquidator has the power to transfer the company's property to a purchaser and to carry on its business so far as may be necessary for its beneficial winding-up.[174] This will include completing those contracts, presumably profitable ones, that he chooses not to disclaim or neglect to the point of breach. In this sense, the liquidator has an option to perform the contract.[175] The solvent co-contractant is protected by his entitlement to exercise any available lien or right of retention under a contract involving the sale of land or goods to the insolvent. If the liquidator elects to complete the contract, this must be done within a reasonable time.[176] Sometimes, the inaction of the liquidator will be treated as an offer of abandonment of the contract to the co-contractant who may accept that offer by declining to perform.[177] As against the liquidator, the co-contractant may apply to the court for

---

[167] *Dence v Mason* [1879] WN 177, CA.

[168] *Heath v Tang* [1993] 1 WLR 1421, 1427, CA.

[169] The court has however a discretion, on the application of the bankrupt (and creditors too) to modify decisions of the trustee: s 303(1).

[170] References to liquidation will also include bankruptcy unless otherwise indicated.

[171] *Shipton Anderson & Co (1927) Ltd v Micks Lambert & Co* [1936] 2 All ER 1032.

[172] *Griffiths v Perry* (1859) 1 E & E 680, 688, 120 ER 1065.

[173] *Re Silver Valley Mines* (1882) 21 Ch D 381, 386, CA; *Stewart v Engel* [2000] 2 BCLC 528. This is so for both voluntary and compulsory winding-up: *Re Anglo-Moravian Hungarian Junction Railway Co* (1875) 1 Ch D 130, 133, CA.

[174] Insolvency Act, Sch 4 paras 4 and 6. Since he is the company's agent, the liquidator will not in the absence of a contrary intention incur personal liability on any contract. A mere failure to disclaim personal liability will not render him liable: *Stead Hazel & Co v Cooper* [1933] 1 KB 840, 843, but a prudent liquidator will insist upon a disclaimer. Parties dealing with the liquidator look to the assets of the company for payment which counts as an expense of the liquidation: discussed at paras 19.101–19.103.

[175] Moneys arising from the performance of the contract by the liquidator will not be caught by a pre-insolvency assignment of book debts by the insolvent: *Wilmot v Alton* [1897] 1 QB 517; *Re Collins* [1925] Ch 557. In the case of bankruptcy, there is the further consideration that any property supplied or transferred under the contract will have vested in the trustee.

[176] *Ex p Stapleton* (1879) 10 Ch D 586, 590.

[177] *Morgan v Bain* (1874) LR 10 CP 15.

the exercise of its discretion to rescind the contract on such terms as it thinks just.[178] This jurisdiction would be most useful where the co-contractant lacks the security of a lien or mutually concurrent performance due from the insolvent, but it appears to be rarely exercised.

In one respect, a party's insolvency will vary contractual terms. This occurs where **19.38** goods are due to be supplied on credit terms to a buyer who becomes insolvent before delivery. Should the liquidator choose to proceed with performance, he will have to pay cash on delivery:[179] the seller should not be compelled to supply goods for an insolvency dividend. The amount paid out by the liquidator may be recovered as an expense of the liquidation.[180] The position here is consistent with the seller's right, notwithstanding a sale on credit terms, to recover the goods in transit in the event of the buyer's insolvency.[181]

Insolvency, though not amounting to a repudiation of the contract, may lead the **19.39** insolvent to commit a discharging breach by non-performance. The solvent co-contractant would then be free to terminate the contract.[182] The insolvency might also prevent the insolvent from performing certain future, perhaps contingent, acts, giving rise to a claim for damages, for which a proof would have to be made.[183]

The effect on contracts of a company going into administrative receivership or **19.40** administration is the same as for liquidation. Both administrative receiver and administrator are agents of the company.[184]

(c) Disclaimer of onerous property

(i) General

The right to disclaim onerous property is a long-standing feature of bankruptcy **19.41** law but was not introduced into company liquidations until the Companies Act 1929. Although there are separate statutory provisions in the 1986 Act, for winding-up[185] and for bankruptcy,[186] these provisions are essentially the same in their effect.[187]

---

178 Section 186.
179 *Ex p Chalmers* (1873) 8 Ch App 289; *Morgan v Bain* (1874) LR 10 CP 15.
180 Discussed at paras 19.101–19.103.
181 Sale of Goods Act 1979, ss 44–6.
182 *Powell v Marshall Parker & Co* [1899] 1 QB 710, CA; *Sale Continuation Ltd v Austin Taylor & Co* [1968] 2 QB 849, 860.
183 *Re Asphaltic Wood Pavement Co* (1885) 30 Ch D 216, CA.
184 Section 44(1)(a) and Sch B1, para (69). But a court-appointed receiver is not an agent of the company and consequently incurs personal liability since the company is not liable: *Burt Boulton & Hayward v Bull* [1895] 1 QB 276, CA.
185 Sections 178–82.
186 Sections 315–21.
187 References to the liquidator below should be read as referring also to the trustee-in-bankruptcy unless otherwise stated.

19.42   Onerous property is defined as any property that is unsaleable or not readily saleable or is such as to give rise to a liability to pay money or perform any other onerous act.[188] Onerous property will frequently but not necessarily detract from the value of the insolvent's estate. The need to distribute an estate expeditiously, for example, might make it appropriate for a liquidator to disclaim property that has a book value in excess of any costs to be incurred in maintaining it. Onerous property also includes unprofitable contracts,[189] where the statutory right to disclaim permits the liquidator unilaterally to terminate the contract. An alternative to disclaimer may be to permit the company to breach the contract thus giving the co-contractant a provable claim.

19.43   To effect a disclaimer, the liquidator files a notice of disclaimer in court and serves a copy of it on, as the case may be, any mortgagee or underlessee of leasehold property, co-contractants and any person he knows claims an interest in, or incurs a liability in respect of, disclaimed property.[190] The liquidator does not need the leave of the court and the property may be disclaimed despite his occupation of the property or exercise of ownership rights over it.[191] Disclaimer, nevertheless, will be disallowed if the liquidator has permitted a period of at least 28 days to expire without responding to an interested party's demand that he disclaim or not.[192] In addition, disclaimer of a contract will not be allowed where it would expropriate a co-contractant's proprietary interest in the subject matter of the contract.[193] An aggrieved party may also petition the court under its general discretionary power to reverse or modify decisions of the liquidator.[194] The court, however, will not sit in the liquidator's chair and will exercise this power only if the liquidator has acted perversely or in bad faith.[195]

19.44   It is not immediately obvious why a statutory power to disclaim is necessary. The mere fact, for example, of the company in liquidation having a leasehold interest in property would not make it equitable to treat the payment of rent as an expense of the winding-up[196] if the liquidator did not retain active possession.[197]

---

[188]   Section 178(3)(b).

[189]   Section 178(3)(a).

[190]   Rules 4.187(1), 4.188(2)–(4). See also r 4.189 (public interest).

[191]   Section 178(2).

[192]   Section 178(5).

[193]   *Re Bastable* [1901] 2 KB 518, CA (equitable interest of purchaser under contract to sell leasehold property), where however the trustee in bankruptcy could have reached the same result by disclaiming the lease itself (ibid 530 *per* Romer LJ).

[194]   Section 168(5).

[195]   *Re Hans Place Ltd* [1993] BCLC 768; cf *Re Katherine et Cie Ltd* [1932] 1 Ch 70, where the court's intervention was explained by its desire to preserve the liability of a surety, which survives today by other means. On the broad discretion given to a liquidator in managing an insolvent's estate, see s 168(4).

[196]   Expenses of the winding-up are discussed at paras 19.101–19.104.

[197]   *Re ABC Coupler and Engineering Co Ltd (No 3)* [1970] 1 WLR 702.

In the simple case of a contract being disclaimed, the statutory right to compensation of the co-contractant will be quantified in the same way as an action for damages[198] for breach of contract admitted to proof in the normal way. Nevertheless, disclaimer is important in bankruptcy, given that the assets of the bankrupt vest in the trustee,[199] since it relieves the trustee from personal liability.[200] In contract cases generally, disclaimer prevents the co-contractant from affirming the contract in the face of breach by the insolvent so as to leave open the possibility of maintaining a future claim for debt.[201] Most importantly, it facilitates the winding-up of the insolvent's affairs by a liquidator dealing with complex matters arising from property interests and long-term contracts. The liquidator is enabled to distribute the estate without fear of personal liability arising out of, for example, a failure to make provision for continuing rent due under a lease not yet (but which might in the future be) brought to an end by the landlord's re-entry or forfeiture of the lease.[202] Disclaimer also accords with the *pari passu* rule of distribution since it obviates the retention of disproportionate amounts to meet future liabilities.[203]

(ii) Disclaimer and leases

19.45 The treatment of leasehold property has posed difficulties when the rent payable under a lease or sublease is higher than the prevailing market rate. Problems can arise at various points in a chain of holdings. Suppose that A leases property to B. B may in turn assign the lease to C or sublet to C instead. The rent payable by B or the rent or subrent payable by C may be guaranteed by D. In the case of an assignment, B may remain liable to A for the payment of rent under the lease. The insolvent party may be B or it may be C.

19.46 If B becomes insolvent and C is an assignee of the lease, then C will be unaffected if B's liquidator disclaims any continuing liability in respect of performance by C of his covenants.[204] The position will be the same if there is a default by D, the guarantor of B's obligations. If C, however, is a subtenant, the position is as follows. The starting point is that the rights and obligations of third parties, counterparties and co-contractants are unaffected by the disclaimer except in so far as necessary for the purpose of releasing the company from its liabilities.[205]

---

[198] *Re Park Air Services plc* [2000] 2 AC 172, HL.
[199] Section 306; cf liquidation: *Re Hans Place Ltd* [1993] BCLC 768.
[200] Section 315(3)(b).
[201] *White & Carter (Councils) Ltd v McGregor* [1962] AC 413, HL (Sc).
[202] *Re Park Air Services plc* [2000] 2 AC 172, HL.
[203] *Re Celtic Extraction Ltd* [2001] Ch 475, 491, CA.
[204] Since the Landlord and Tenant (Covenants) Act 1995, the assignor is released from covenants that have to be complied with by the tenant.
[205] Section 178(4)(b); *Hindcastle Ltd v Barbara Attenborough Associates Ltd* [1997] AC 70, HL, *per* Lord Nicholls.

Upon disclaimer, persons suffering loss in consequence of it are given a statutory right to compensation as though they were creditors of the company.[206] In effect, they are post-insolvency creditors permitted retroactively to prove in the winding-up. In the case of sublet premises, a disclaimer of the lease by B's liquidator terminates C's rights against B. It also terminates B's interest in the property but not so as to affect C, who continues to hold his interest as if B's interest continued.[207] Matters might continue in an indefinite state if C takes the practical course of paying A the rent due under the lease, which C would be advised to do to prevent A from applying for a vesting order,[208] a course of action that C himself might also prudently take if he wishes to assume the lease.

19.47 If C becomes insolvent and C's liquidator disclaims, the position in the case of assignment is as follows. Where B remains primarily liable to pay the rent,[209] B is not released by C's disclaimer.[210] It was not easy to reconcile this position with the release of D where D had guaranteed payment of the rent by C,[211] a result that accorded with the general rule that the release of a debtor serves also to release a guarantor. The modern position regarding guarantors, that they remain liable notwithstanding the disclaimer of the assigned lease by C, is based upon a straightforward reading of the Insolvency Act that disclaimer affects parties other than the disclaiming party no more than 'is necessary for the purpose of releasing [the disclaiming party] from its liability. . .'.[212] If C's liquidator disclaims a sublease, then B will remain liable to pay rent due under the head lease in the normal way and the position of D, as guarantor of C's obligations, remains the same.

19.48 A further problem arising in the case of leasehold property concerns the claim of a landlord when the tenant's liquidator disclaims the lease. The landlord is entitled to claim for the discounted difference between the rent due under the lease and the rent that can be obtained in prevailing market conditions.[213] The landlord's

---

[206] Section 178(6).

[207] *Hindcastle Ltd v Barbara Attenborough Associates Ltd* [1997] AC 70, 89, HL, *per* Lord Nicholls. In the normal case of a forfeiture of a lease or re-entry, the subtenant would be at liberty to apply for relief which, if granted, would result in the grant of a new lease (Law of Property Act 1925, s 146(4)) or, less commonly, the substitution of the subtenant for the original tenant under the lease (Law of Property Act 1925, s 146(2)).

[208] Insolvency Act, s 181. A surety may seek a vesting order: *Re AE Realisations Ltd* [1987] 3 All ER 83.

[209] See however the Landlord and Tenant (Covenants) Act 1995.

[210] *Hill v East and West India Dock Co* (1884) 9 App Cas 448, HL; *Warnford Investments Ltd v Duckworth* [1979] Ch 127; *Hindcastle Ltd v Barbara Attenborough Associates Ltd* [1997] AC 70, HL.

[211] *Stacey v Hill* [1901] 1 KB 660, CA. For this reason, the result in *Warnford Investments Ltd v Duckworth* [1979] Ch 127 was unsuccessfully challenged in *Smith (WH) Ltd v Wyndham Estates Ltd* [1994] BCC 699.

[212] Section 178(4)(b). See also *Hindcastle Ltd v Barbara Attenborough Associates Ltd* [1997] AC 70, HL (overruling *Stacey v Hill* [1901] 1 KB 660, CA).

[213] *Re Hans Place Ltd* [1992] BCC 737; *Re Park Air Services plc* [2000] 2 AC 172, HL.

claim is not a debt claim for rent unpaid but rather a new claim arising upon the disclaimer and in the nature of damages.[214] Since damages principles apply, the landlord is treated as having to mitigate and also has to give credit for the discounted present value of future receipts.[215] The landlord may not therefore claim future rent on the assumption that he will not re-enter or forfeit the lease.

(iii) Disclaimer and waste management licences

In modern times, acute difficulties have also been presented by waste management licences. The principal question is one of statutory precedence. Environmental legislation provides that a waste management licence, which permits the licensee to carry out certain activities that would otherwise be criminal offences,[216] continues in force until the regulatory authority either revokes it or accepts its surrender.[217] How is this provision to be reconciled with the liquidator's unilateral power of disclaimer? Departing from earlier authority,[218] and rejecting arguments that the 'polluter pays' principle is paramount and that the disclaimer itself can under the environment legislation render criminal the disposal of waste no longer authorized by the terms of the licence, the Court of Appeal has held that the liquidator is entitled to disclaim the licence.[219] The 'polluter pays' principle does not require the unsecured creditors of the polluter to pay by forgoing their right to a *pari passu* distribution. The environmental legislation can be sensibly interpreted as dealing with the termination of licences by acts of the parties as opposed to 'external statutory force'.[220]

19.49

(d) Assignment of causes of action

(i) General

A primary goal of the insolvency process is to maximize the estate so as to give creditors as high a dividend as possible. Gathering in the estate, however, is time-consuming and expensive, especially where it involves litigation. An endemic problem facing liquidators in particular is that they are short of the funds needed to perform their statutory functions in this regard. In recent years, the spotlight has

19.50

---

[214] Under s 178(6); see *Hindcastle Ltd v Barbara Attenborough Associates Ltd* [1997] AC 70, HL. The landlord is not in the position of a creditor who has released security and has elected to put in a proof instead and r 11.13 has no application: *Re Park Air Services plc* [2000] 2 AC 172, HL.

[215] *Re Park Air Services plc* [2000] 2 AC 172, HL.

[216] It was treated as 'property' under s 436 in *Re Celtic Extraction Ltd* [2001] Ch 475, CA.

[217] Environmental Protection Act 1990, s 35(11).

[218] *Re Mineral Resources Ltd* [1999] 1 All ER 746.

[219] *Re Celtic Extraction Ltd* [2001] Ch 475. The effect of the disclaimer extends also to any fund set up to meet the company's obligations under the licence: *Environmental Agency v Hillridge Ltd* [2003] EWHC 3023 (Ch); [2004] 2 BCLC 358.

[220] *Re Celtic Extraction Ltd* (ibid).

been placed on attempts to deal with this problem of underfunding by assigning for value the company's causes of action. This practice is founded on the fact that companies and liquidators representing them are not eligible for legal aid whereas individuals are. This practice has long existed in the case of bankruptcy,[221] where trustees are also ineligible for legal aid, but it has only more recently come into prominence in the field of company liquidations. Such assignments may be set aside if made for inadequate consideration.[222]

19.51 A number of other issues are raised by this practice of assignment. The first is whether such assignments infringe public policy rendering void contracts for champerty and maintenance,[223] with the related issue whether an exception to this rule exists for insolvency. A second issue is, if such assignments are permissible, whether all causes of action available to the liquidator or the fruits of a recovery are capable of being assigned in this way. A third issue is whether such assignments abuse the system of legal aid.

(ii) Public policy

19.52 The definition of property of the company as including 'every thing in action. . .and every description of property. . .and also obligations' is more than wide enough to embrace causes of action as well as the fruits of recovery.[224] It is capable of including a cause of action in tort, provided that the cause of action is not so personal to the assignor as to be unassignable.[225] It includes also the net balance in favour of the insolvent reached after a set-off.[226] Since the liquidator has the statutory power to 'sell any of the company's property. . .with power to transfer. . .it to any person. . .',[227] assignments[228] are permitted that would otherwise amount to

---

[221] See *Kitson v Hardwick* (1872) LR 7 CP 473; *Seear v Lawson* (1880) 15 Ch D 426; *Ramsey v Hartley* [1977] 1 WLR 686, CA. The rules for assigning to bankrupts and to former officers of a company in liquidation are the same: *Freightex Ltd v International Express Co Ltd* [1980] CA Transcript 395 with the necessary difference that a cause of action can be assigned to the bankrupt himself: see *Kitson v Hardwick* (1872) LR 7 CP 473 ('any person').

[222] *Faryab v Smith* [2001] BPIR 246, CA.

[223] Maintenance is supporting litigation in which one has no interest and champerty is maintenance where the maintainer also takes a share of the proceeds of recovery: *Re Oasis Merchandising Services Ltd* [1998] Ch 170, CA.

[224] See *Re Oasis Merchandising Services Ltd* [1998] Ch 170, CA, disapproving the contrary view of Lightman J in *Grovewood Holdings plc v James Capel & Co Ltd* [1995] Ch 80, 86, concerning the fruits.

[225] *Empire Resolution Ltd v MPW Insurance Brokers Ltd* [1999] BPIR 486 (negligent misstatement), referring to case law dealing with causes of action vesting in the trustee in bankruptcy (discussed at paras 19.25 and 19.35).

[226] *Stein v Blake* [1996] AC 243, 258, HL.

[227] Insolvency Act, Sch 4 para 6. Similarly, the trustee has the power to 'sell any part of the property for the time being comprised in the bankrupt's estate' (Sch 5 para 9) and the administrator and administrative receiver have the power to 'sell or otherwise dispose of the property' (Sch 1 para 2).

[228] The word 'sell' is broad enough to capture assignments of a bare cause of action, although there has to be consideration, which may be the fictitious consideration that reposes in the form of a deed: *Ramsey v Hartley* [1977] 1 WLR 686, 694, CA.

unlawful champerty or maintenance.[229] The statute therefore trumps public policy. Even in the absence of such statutory legitimation, an assignment would not be void as against public policy if the assignee had a genuine commercial interest in the enforcement of another's claim.[230] This requirement was not fulfilled where the estate stood to gain nothing from the assignment because it had no interest in the recovered proceeds.[231]

(iii) Causes of action as property

With regard to the second issue, a close examination has to be made of what constitutes the property of the insolvent company.[232] The practical question is whether a liquidator may assign a cause of action against directors and other persons guilty of wrongful and fraudulent trading[233] as well as the right to challenge disposals of a company's property after the commencement of a winding-up[234] and unregistered charges granted by the company.[235] In order for the liquidator's assignment to shelter behind the statutory power to sell property belonging to the company,[236] the property in question must belong to the company at the commencement of the winding-up.[237] This distinction follows the scheme of the Insolvency Act and is consistent with the rule that recoveries by the liquidator in fraudulent trading actions, for example, are not attached by a charge granted by the company to a secured creditor.[238] Neither the cause of action nor its fruits are property of the company at the critical date, which is the commencement of the winding-up. Since, however, the company itself could have brought proceedings against directors for misfeasance,[239] the liquidator's power to sell the company's property applies here.[240]

19.53

---

229 *Guy v Churchill* (1889) 40 Ch D 481, 485 (bankruptcy); *Ramsey v Hartley* [1977] 1 WLR 686, 694, CA. This is why the assignments were attacked on other grounds in *Norglen Ltd v Reeds Rains Prudential Ltd* and *Circuit Systems Ltd v Zuken-Redac (UK) Ltd* [1999] 2 AC 1, HL (conjoined appeals).

230 *Trendtex Trading Corp v Credit Suisse* [1982] AC 679, HL. An assignment of the fruits of litigation, where the assignee does not influence the conduct of litigation, is just an assignment of future property and does not offend public policy: *Glegg v Bromley* [1912] 3 KB 474, CA.

231 *Turner v Schindler & Co* [1991] CA Transcript 665; *Circuit Systems Ltd v Zuken-Redac (UK) Ltd* [1997] 1 WLR 721, 733–34, CA, *per* Simon Brown LJ. This argument runs the risk of confusing what amounts to a void agreement with the question whether the assignment represents a proper exercise of the insolvency office holder's powers.

232 This issue is particularly appropriate to corporate insolvency.

233 Sections 213–4.

234 Section 127.

235 Companies Act 2006, s 860.

236 Insolvency Act, Sch 4 para 6. For trustees, see Sch 5 para 9.

237 *Re Oasis Merchandising Services Ltd* [1998] Ch 170, CA; *Re Ayala Holdings Ltd (No 2)* [1996] 1 BCLC 467.

238 *Re Yagerphone Ltd* [1935] Ch 392.

239 Section 212.

240 *Re Park Gate Waggon Works Co* (1881) 17 Ch D 234, CA; *Re Oasis Merchandising Services Ltd* [1998] Ch 170, CA.

19.54 Since any assignment of property that does not belong to the company at the date of the winding-up falls outside the liquidator's statutory power to sell, it has to be considered whether a liquidator[241] may nevertheless lawfully assign those causes of action and their fruits on other grounds. Now, the liquidator may not assign the causes of action themselves since only the liquidator is empowered to bring the proceedings.[242] There is no reason, however, why the fruits of recovery may not be assigned so long as the assignee does not interfere in the conduct of the proceedings so as to invalidate the assignment on the ground of maintenance.[243] Such interference would be offensive for the further reason that it could impede the liquidator in the exercise of his statutory functions by preventing him from applying to the court for directions in respect of any matter arising during the course of the winding-up.[244]

(iv) The legal aid system

19.55 The final issue concerns the matter of the legally aided claimant and the integrity of the legal aid system. It is clear that this is not a matter of insolvency law at all and therefore does not invalidate an assignment that otherwise complies with insolvency law principles.[245] Regulations dealing with legal aid are apt to deal with abuses in the system.

(e) Embargo on proceedings against the insolvent

(i) General

19.56 In the case of a compulsory winding-up, the leave of the court is required for an action or proceeding against the company or its property to be commenced or continued after the making of a winding-up order or the appointment of a provisional liquidator.[246] This follows on from another provision that, between the presentation of a winding-up petition and the making of a winding-up order, the company or any creditor or contributory may apply to the court for any further proceedings to be restrained or stayed.[247] In the case of both provisions, the action may be permitted or stayed, as the case may be, on such terms and conditions as the court thinks fit. The action or proceeding in question is commonly distress by

---

[241] The court in *Re Oasis Merchandising Services Ltd* [1998] Ch 170, CA, expressed considerable doubt about whether an administrator or administrative receiver could assign the fruits of a future action brought by the *liquidator*. This should not be possible if it diverts assets from the unsecured creditors of the company to the secured debenture holder.

[242] *Re Oasis Merchandising Services Ltd* [1998] Ch 170, CA.

[243] ibid.

[244] Section 168(3).

[245] *Norglen Ltd v Reeds Rains Prudential Ltd* [1999] 2 AC 1, HL.

[246] Section 130(2).

[247] Section 126.

a landlord[248] or by a creditor entitled to similar relief.[249] An ordinary creditor facing a bleak prospect of recovery will need little further discouragement to discontinue pending litigation and is unlikely to commence litigation once an insolvent winding-up supervenes. There are similar special provisions dealing with executions and attachments.[250]

The purpose of these various provisions[251] is to maintain the integrity of the company's estate so that it may be rateably distributed in the usual *pari passu* way, a process that is at odds with a judgment creditor's right to enforce a money judgment.[252] Upon the commencement of a winding-up, the individual process of debt collection gives way to a collective, solidary procedure in which creditors are treated as a class. Individual creditors of the company may not therefore act unilaterally to improve their position even if, as is the case with execution creditors, they have invested significant time and assets in the collection of what is owed to them and have been vigilant and energetic when other creditors may not have been. This result is consistent with the assets of a company in liquidation being held on the terms of a notional trust in favour of its creditors.[253]

19.57

(ii) Distress

Taking first the general provisions as they relate to actions and proceedings begun before the commencement of a winding-up, the discretion will be exercised so as to allow the distress, or other action or proceeding, to continue, unless special circumstances are shown rendering such continuance inequitable, since the general creditors have no intrinsic right to be preferred to the creditor taking action.[254] Once the winding-up has commenced, however, the general position is reversed and the landlord will not be allowed to distrain.[255] The burden of persuasion thereupon switches from the liquidator to the landlord, and the landlord would be compelled to show special reasons in the nature of fraud or unfair dealing if the

19.58

---

248 It is now settled beyond challenge that distress is a 'proceeding': *Re Herbert Barry Associates Ltd* [1977] 1 WLR 1437, HL; *Re Memco Engineering Ltd* [1986] Ch 86.

249 Other examples include an application for the appointment of a receiver: *Croshaw v Lyndhurst Ship Co* [1897] 2 Ch 154.

250 Sections 183–4. These apply to goods, land and debts.

251 The corresponding provisions for bankruptcy are ss 285 and 346–7. There are no such specific provisions for voluntary liquidation, but the same effect is reached under s 112, which permits a liquidator to apply to the court to exercise any powers that the court itself might exercise in a compulsory winding-up.

252 *Roberts Petroleum Ltd v Bernard Kenny Ltd* [1983] 2 AC 192, HL.

253 See *Ayerst v C&K (Construction) Ltd* [1976] AC 167, HL; *Re Yagerphone Ltd* [1935] Ch 392; *Re MC Bacon Ltd* [1991] Ch 127.

254 *Re Great Ship Co Ltd* (1862) 4 De GJ & S 63, 69, 46 ER 839; *Re Roundwood Colliery Ltd* [1897] 1 Ch 373, 381, CA.

255 *Thomas v Patent Lionite Co* (1881) 17 Ch D 250, CA, where a compulsory winding-up succeeded a voluntary winding-up, with the landlord distraining between the dates of commencement of each winding-up.

distress were to be allowed to continue.[256] In the exercise of its discretion, the court conducts a balancing exercise, considering the interests not of one particular class of creditor but of 'each' of them.[257] In an execution case involving a similar discretion, the court declined to draw a distinction between trade creditors and loan creditors on the ground that the latter were a less deserving class.[258]

(iii) Executions

19.59 In the case of executions against land or goods and attachments of debts, a creditor is not entitled to retain as against the liquidator the 'benefit of the execution' or attachment unless the execution or attachment has been completed before the commencement of the winding-up.[259] Whereas a former discretion was confined to trickery or dishonesty by the judgment debtor,[260] the court now has a broadly stated discretion to set aside the rights of the liquidator.[261] When exercised, the discretion can lead to a division of moneys between creditor and liquidator and may be invoked against impropriety and undue pressure by the debtor.[262] The conduct of the debtor leading up to judgment and up to the completion of execution are equally open to review.[263] The present statutory discretion, though not limited to an abuse of process by the debtor, will nevertheless be exercised with caution and only in special circumstances[264] since the execution creditor's gain is the loss, not of the debtor, but of the other creditors. It is possible that the discretion will be more liberally exercised in respect of the debtor's behaviour after judgment,[265] given the obvious judicial reluctance to interfere with the conduct of a defence in litigation. Delay on the part of an execution creditor and its

---

[256] *Venner's Electrical Cooking and Heating Appliances Ltd v Thorpe* [1915] 2 Ch 404, CA.

[257] *Re Great Ship Co Ltd* (1862) 4 De GJ & S 63, 69, 46 ER 839; *Re Roundwood Colliery Ltd* [1897] 1 Ch 373, 381, CA; *Venner's Electrical Cooking and Heating Appliances Ltd v Thorpe* [1915] 2 Ch 404, 407, CA.

[258] *Re Caribbean Products (Yam Importers) Ltd* [1966] Ch 331, 347–8, 351, CA, where the proposal was to divide the fruits of execution with other trade creditors to the exclusion of loan creditors who had anticipated becoming members of the company. The court was also reluctant to reward the execution creditor merely on the ground of his 'extra vigilance': ibid 347.

[259] Section 183 (compulsory and voluntary winding-up). The equivalent provision for bankruptcy is s 346(6). If the creditor has notice of the calling of a meeting at which a voluntary winding-up resolution is to be proposed, the date of such notice is substituted for the date of commencement of the winding-up: s 183(2)(a).

[260] *Armorduct Manufacturing Co Ltd v General Incandescent Co Ltd* [1911] 2 KB 143, CA.

[261] Section 183(2)(c).

[262] *Re Grosvenor Metal Co Ltd* [1950] 1 Ch 63.

[263] *Re Suidair International Airways Ltd* [1951] Ch 165, 172; *Landau v Purvis* (High Ct, 15 June 1999).

[264] *Re Buckingham International plc (No 2)* [1998] BCC 943, 962. A good example of such circumstances is present in *Landau v Purvis* (ibid).

[265] *Landau v Purvis* (High Ct, 15 June 1999), distinguishing *Re Buckingham International plc (No 2)* [1998] 2 BCLC 369.

advisers will be harmful to the prospects of the discretion being exercised.[266] It will not be enough for an execution creditor to show that it stayed its hand at the request of the debtor, for this would deny to other creditors the chance to show that they too had stayed their hand where the debtor had adopted a broad policy of stalling all of its creditors. Furthermore, the process of winding-up might have been accelerated anyway if the execution creditor had not stayed its hand.[267]

Completion of an execution against land occurs when it is seized, a receiver is **19.60** appointed or a charging order[268] is made against it.[269] The attachment of a debt is completed by the receipt of the 'debt' or rather its proceeds,[270] and an execution against goods when the goods are seized and sold[271] and the proceeds remitted to the creditor.[272] The position regarding goods is reinforced by a duty placed on the sheriff, as and when he has notice of the commencement of the winding-up,[273] to make over to the liquidator the goods as well as any money received or seized in part satisfaction of the judgment.[274] Further, a sheriff receiving moneys to avoid sale, or as a result of selling certain goods, must retain the moneys for 14 days. If within that time he is served with notice of a winding-up petition or of the calling of a meeting at which a winding-up resolution is to be proposed,[275] and there consequently follows a winding-up,[276] the sheriff must pay the moneys over to the liquidator.[277] This provision makes it very difficult for a major unsecured creditor to sue to judgment and complete an execution if the company's financial state is a parlous one. If the 14-day period elapses and moneys received in part execution have not been paid to the creditor, the liquidator is not entitled to them if

---

[266] *Landau v Purvis* (n 263 above).

[267] *Re Redman (Builders) Ltd* [1964] 1 WLR 541, 552.

[268] Under the Charging Orders Act 1979. The fact that the debtor is insolvent and will inevitably go into liquidation is no ground for refusing to make absolute a charging order *nisi*. There would have to be some additional significant factor present, such as a scheme of arrangement set on foot by the main body of creditors with a reasonable prospect of success: *Roberts Petroleum Ltd v Bernard Kenny Ltd* [1983] 2 AC 192, CA.

[269] Insolvency Act, s 183(3)(c).

[270] Section 183(3)(b).

[271] Section 183(3)(a) (or a (rare) charging order made under the Charging Orders Act 1979).

[272] *Bluston & Bramley Ltd v Leigh* [1950] 2 KB 548 (even though, prior to any divestment effected under s 183, the sheriff holds moneys received from the sale to the use of the judgment creditor).

[273] Section 184(1) (or of the appointment of a provisional liquidator).

[274] Section 184(2).

[275] As a provision divesting rights, this is to be construed against the liquidator: *Re Walton (TD) Ltd* [1966] 1 WLR 869 (notice adverting to the possibility of liquidation but making no mention of a winding-up resolution). But see *Bluston & Bramley Ltd v Leigh* [1950] 2 KB 548 (sufficient for notice to refer generally to the statutory provision and not its contents).

[276] For present purposes, a proposal for a voluntary winding-up resolution cannot be followed by a resolution for a compulsory winding-up: *Bluston & Bramley Ltd v Leigh* [1950] 2 KB 548.

[277] Section 184(3),(4). There is a first charge over the moneys for the costs of the execution. These provisions dealing with sheriffs are also subject to a broadly stated discretion in favour of the creditor: s 184(5).

execution remains uncompleted at the date of commencement of the winding-up. This is because the 'benefit of the execution'[278] means the charge created by the issue of execution and not any moneys paid over to avoid execution.[279]

19.61   This same view, that the benefit means the charge and not moneys received, underpinned the decision in one case[280] where a debtor paid certain sums directly to an execution creditor in order to avoid a sale. He failed to keep up the agreed schedule of payments. Execution was recommenced but was incomplete at the commencement of his bankruptcy. If the court had interpreted the benefit of the execution to mean moneys received, the debtor would, subject to any discretion and to any limitations defence, have had to pay over the sums he had received to the trustee no matter how long before the bankruptcy the moneys had been paid. The execution may not have been completed by the time of the commencement of the bankruptcy but the sums were paid outside the execution process altogether. Any other result would have discouraged forbearance by creditors where this is as much for the benefit of debtors as for creditors themselves.[281] A different view of the 'benefit of the. . .attachment' was, however, taken in another case[282] where a garnishee[283] paid only a part of the garnished debt before the commencement of a winding-up. In this conventional example of an incomplete attachment, the liquidator, subject to any discretion to the contrary, was entitled to recover moneys received by the debtor. The court also dismissed the creditor's argument that the absence of any statutory provision dealing with an action by the liquidator to recover money from the creditor indicated an intention that the creditor should retain moneys in hand. The same result should also apply to an incomplete execution against goods. Nevertheless, as seen above, these cases of incomplete execution and attachment are to be distinguished from cases where an incomplete payment is made outside the execution and attachment processes.

(iv) Administrators: general

19.62   In the case of administration, there is an equally compelling reason for constraining execution, attachments and related actions and proceedings by individual creditors. Indeed, the justification for restraint may be even more compelling given that administration may last longer than a winding-up, and that the administrator during that time carries on the company as a going concern while a liquidator

---

[278] Section 183(1).
[279] *Re Walkden Sheet Metal Co Ltd* [1960] Ch 170.
[280] *Re Andrew* [1937] 1 Ch 122, CA. See also *Re Samuels* [1935] Ch 341.
[281] *Re Andrew* [1937] 1 Ch 122, 133–4, CA, criticizing *Re Kern (PE and BE)* [1932] 1 Ch 555, 560.
[282] *Re Caribbean Products (Yam Importers) Ltd* [1966] Ch 331, CA.
[283] Here and in para 19.69, references to the former garnishee order should now be to a third party debt order and garnishor and garnishee should be adapted accordingly.

exercises limited powers of management. The administrator is not as such charged with *pari passu* distribution[284] since administration is an interim process and yields to a winding-up in those cases where the company cannot be saved. The administrator is charged with designated statutory purposes[285] and is supported by the Insolvency Act which prevents individual creditors from interfering with the attainment of those purposes. Hence, as soon as an administration application is made, there is a 'moratorium on other legal process' so that no 'legal proceedings, execution, distress. . .may be instituted or continued against the company'[286] without the leave of the court.[287] The same embargo continues upon the appointment of the administrator except that the administrator also may grant leave for the action or proceedings to continue.[288]

(v) Proceedings against a company in administration

In the case law, the difficulties have centred on the meaning of 'other legal process' **19.63** and related expressions, mention of which is made immediately after similar prohibitions on the passing of a resolution and the making of an order for a winding-up,[289] and on repossession under a title retention agreement and the enforcement of security.[290] The question is whether the list of actions and proceedings constitutes a genus so as to confine the generality of the words 'proceedings' and 'process'. The Inner House of the Court of Session has given support for the view that there is a genus exercising a limiting effect on the meaning of 'proceedings'.[291] These proceedings have to be in the nature of claims by creditors against the company. Hence, an application by a competitor airline to the Civil Aviation Authority for the revocation of the operating licence of the company in administration fell outside the prohibition.

This approach, however, is too narrow, given that the prohibition explicitly applies **19.64** earlier in the Schedule to winding-up petitions and resolutions. These are not proceedings 'against' the company. Consequently, the word 'other' in 'other legal process' is deprived of any significant meaning and there is no restrictive genus.

---

284 Powers are conferred by the Insolvency Act on the administrator for the running of the company: see *Bristol Airport plc v Powdrill* [1990] Ch 744, CA; *Smith v Bridgend County Borough Council* [2000] 1 BCLC 775, CA, revd on other grounds [2001] UKHL 58; [2002] 1 AC 336. Since the Enterprise Act 2002, however, the administrator has had some powers to make distributions: Insolvency Act, Sch B1, para 65.

285 Insolvency Act (as amended), Sch B1, para 3(1).

286 A statutory right of detention exercised under the Civil Aviation Act 1982, s 88(1), is not a right of distress for present purposes: *Bristol Airport plc v Powdrill* [1990] Ch 744, CA.

287 Insolvency Act (as amended), Sch B1, paras 43(6) and 44(5).

288 ibid. The exercise of the discretion to grant leave is discussed below.

289 Insolvency Act (as amended), Sch B1, para 42.

290 Insolvency Act (as amended), Sch B1, para 43(2), (3). The position of secured creditors and title retainers is dealt with below.

291 *Air Ecosse Ltd v Civil Aviation Authority* 1987 SC 285, 291–92, 294–95, 298–99, Inner House.

In accordance with this approach, the prohibition has been held applicable to industrial tribunal proceedings and specifically to an action by a dismissed employee for reinstatement,[292] to criminal proceedings under the Environmental Protection Act 1990,[293] and to proceedings in the Patent Court for the revocation of the company's patent.[294] This does not mean that the word 'proceedings' should be given an expansive interpretation: it should not, for example, extend to the acceptance of a repudiatory breach of contract by the company in administration.[295] The proceedings have to be legal or quasi-legal and do not include the exercise of a unilateral right of detention of an aircraft for unpaid airport charges.[296] The word 'proceedings' excludes an application to register a company charge out of time. The company itself is capable of making the application.[297]

19.65 There are no similar provisions interfering with actions or the exercise of rights against the company in the case of administrative receivership, which, since the Enterprise Act 2002, arises only in a limited number of cases. Unsecured creditors are free to sue the company to judgment and to seek execution but this is normally futile as it would simply precipitate the company into insolvency. It is a different matter if the creditor obtains a proprietary interest under a contract with the company, for receivership does not override this interest.[298] Furthermore, a creditor may be able to take action so as to prevent a non-proprietary claim against the company from arising. For example, a creditor may be entitled to injunctive relief restraining the administrative receiver from acting to bring about a breach of contract by the company where the receiver would not by so acting be preferring the interests of the debenture holder to those of the company.[299] Nevertheless, in the case of subsisting contracts, the receiver does not on his appointment incur personal liability so as to give the creditor a practical alternative to a hopeless

---

[292] *Carr v British International Helicopters Ltd* [1994] 2 BCLC 474 (EAT).

[293] *Re Rhondda Waste Disposal Ltd, sub nom Environment Agency v Clark* [2001] Ch 57, CA.

[294] *Biosource Technologies Inc v Axis Genetics Plc* [2000] 1 BCLC 286 (reviewing the authorities).

[295] *Bristol Airport plc v Powdrill* [1990] Ch 744, 766, CA, *per* Browne-Wilkinson VC. Also excluded is the service of a time of the essence notice (*Re Olympia & York Canary Wharf Ltd* [1993] BCLC 453).

[296] *Bristol Airport plc v Powdrill* [1990] Ch 744, CA, disagreeing on the width of 'proceedings' with the trial judge (Harman J) at [1990] BCC 130, 139 ('every sort of step against the company').

[297] *Re Barrow Borough Transport Ltd* [1989] Ch 227.

[298] *Freevale Ltd v Metrostore (Holdings) Ltd* [1984] Ch 199.

[299] *Ash and Newman Ltd v Creative Devices Research Ltd* [1991] BCLC 403. In the case of a court-appointed receiver, creditors may also be protected indirectly if the court declines to permit the receiver to repudiate contracts of the company on the ground that such action will damage the company's goodwill: *Re Newdigate Colliery Ltd* [1912] 1 Ch 468, CA. An insolvent company in receivership, however, may have no appreciable goodwill (but see *Airline Airspares Ltd v Handley Page Ltd* [1970] Ch 193 where damage to goodwill would seriously have affected the realization of net assets).

action against the company.[300] Landlords, however, are in a better position than ordinary unsecured creditors since if rent remains unpaid they may levy distress or re-enter the premises. The threat of this will often bring about an arrangement between the landlord and the administrative receiver for the payment of current and even accrued rent.

(vi) Execution, administration and administrative receivership

Under the Insolvency Act (as amended), the moratorium instituted in the event of an administration prevents an execution from being 'continued' without the consent of the administrator or the leave of the court.[301] Such leave or consent is unlikely to be given in those cases where an administrator is appointed out of court under a qualifying charge. In the great bulk of cases, administrative receivers have now been superseded by such administrators. The law on the completion of an execution for administrative receivership should therefore still be relevant for the purpose of determining when, for the purposes of administration, an execution has not yet been completed. The case law involving administrative receivers and other receivers has, for the purpose of priority against the debenture holder, centred on whether the execution or attachment was complete before the crystallization of a floating charge, which commonly occurs upon the appointment of a receiver. It is difficult to state the precise law in this area, which is bedevilled by the use of loose proprietary language and by statutory changes to the insolvency position that may to some extent spill over into receivership. A writ of *fieri facias* (or other writ of execution) binds the goods of the execution debtor as soon as the writ is delivered to the sheriff.[302] This means that the sheriff, on behalf of the execution creditor, has a right to seize the goods while they remain in his bailiwick; he does not as such have a proprietary interest in them.[303] The sheriff acquires a special or qualified property in the debtor's goods as from the date of actual seizure, which allows him to sue a third party tortfeasor in conversion.[304] Nevertheless, this property right is liable to be overridden by the fixed charge that is subsequently created upon the crystallization of a pre-existing floating charge, for the sheriff acquires his special property subject to existing equities.[305]

19.66

---

300 But an administrative receiver may incur personal liability on contracts of employment that he adopts and will also incur liability on contracts he enters into unless he disclaims personal liability: s 44(1)(b).

301 Schedule B1, para 43(6).

302 Supreme Court Act 1981, s 138(1).

303 *Ex p Williams* (1872) 7 Ch App 314, 316.

304 ibid 317–18.

305 *Re Standard Manufacturing Co* [1891] 1 Ch 627, 641, CA.

For this reason, the floating chargee takes precedence over the execution creditor when the charge crystallizes and the goods remain in the sheriff's hands.[306]

19.67 What the position is if the charge crystallizes before the proceeds of a sale by the sheriff are paid to the execution creditor is unclear.[307] The statutory provisions regarding incomplete executions in insolvency, where the liquidator in those circumstances would prevail over the execution creditor, appear to have modified the common law[308] and anyway do not extend to receivership. In favour of the view that the floating chargee should prevail in such a case is that it avoids an invidious distinction being drawn between insolvency and receivership. In the event of a winding-up, the secured debenture holder ranks ahead of unsecured creditors whose representative, the liquidator, would in the absence of the floating charge be entitled to demand the proceeds from the sheriff. It would be odd if the positions of floating charge and sheriff should be reversed just because a winding-up has not supervened. Nevertheless, it is unlikely that any court would require a garnishor to pay part of the proceeds of a debt to the floating chargee whose charge crystallizes before the debt has been paid in full. For the sake of consistency, an execution creditor should also prevail where goods are sold and the proceeds are still in the sheriff's hands at the time of crystallization.

19.68 Two further points need to be made. First, as long as the floating charge remains uncrystallized, the floating chargee may not selectively intervene in the affairs of the company so as to impede the payment of a judgment debt.[309] Secondly, the courts with a paucity of reasoning have, in the case of payments made to avoid a sale by the sheriff, approximated the position in winding-up and receivership. Just as such payments may not be recovered by an insolvency officer from an execution creditor,[310] so when payment of the entire sum due[311] or part of it[312] is made directly to the sheriff, receiving it as agent for the execution creditor, it may not be recovered by or on behalf of a floating chargee appointing a receiver before the sheriff accounts to the execution creditor.

19.69 Where the execution creditor attaches a debt through garnishee proceedings, the debt must actually be paid to the garnishor if the garnishor is to prevail against a

---

[306] *Re Standard Manufacturing Co* [1891] 1 Ch 627, CA; *Re Opera Ltd* [1891] 3 Ch 260, CA; *Taunton v Sheriff of Warwickshire* [1895] 2 Ch 319, CA.

[307] The point was left open by Lindley LJ in *Taunton v Sheriff of Warwickshire* [1895] 2 Ch 319, 322, CA, and in *Re Opera Ltd* [1891] 3 Ch 360, CA.

[308] See *ex p Williams* (1872) 7 Ch App 314.

[309] *Evans v Rival Granite Quarries Ltd* [1910] 2 KB 979, CA; *Robson v Smith* [1895] 2 Ch 118, CA.

[310] See discussion at paras 19.60 and 19.61.

[311] *Heaton and Dugard Ltd v Cutting Bros Ltd* [1925] 1 KB 655.

[312] *Robinson v Burnell's Vienna Bakery Co Ltd* [1904] 2 KB 624.

---

chargee whose floating charge has crystallized. The garnishee order, even when it becomes absolute, merely attaches the debt owed; it does not assign or transfer it to the garnishor. The debt remains owing to the company granting the charge that has now crystallized, and the effect of the order absolute is merely to empower the garnishor to give a good discharge of the debt to the garnishee upon payment being received.[313]

(f) Dispositions of the insolvent's property

(i) General

Upon the commencement of a compulsory winding-up, section 127 of the Insolvency Act provides that any disposition of the company's property is void unless the court otherwise orders.[314] The section treats in the same way transfers of shares and alterations in the status of the company and its members. The simple effect of the section is to avoid dispositions of the company's property. Its limitations are exposed where the company's property cannot be traced by common law or equitable means.[315] In the past, banks operating current accounts have been at some considerable risk of exposure to a claim for the recovery of moneys whose payment they could have prevented, since a disposition occurs in favour of the bank whenever the bank's indebtedness to the company account holder is diminished by the payment of cheques drawn on an account in credit.[316] More recently, the Court of Appeal has held that section 127 is not concerned with the bank's mandate to honour cheques and does not 'impinge on the legal validity of intermediate steps. . .which are merely part of the process by which dispositions of the company's property are made'. The section goes directly to the 'end result of the process of payment', namely, the payee's receipt of the proceeds of the collected cheque.[317]

19.70

---

[313] *Norton v Yates* [1906] 1 KB 112; *Cairney v Back* [1906] 2 KB 746; *Relwood Pty Ltd v Manning Homes Pty Ltd (No 2)* [1992] 2 Queensland R 197.

[314] A similar provision introduced in the 1980s applies in bankruptcy between the date the bankruptcy petition is presented and the date that the bankrupt's property vests in the trustee: s 284. The discretion is exercised in broadly the same way as the discretion under s 127: *Re Flint* [1993] Ch 319. Under the previous law, the title of the trustee to the bankrupt's assets related back to the commission of an act of bankruptcy, so that the preservation of the estate for *pari passu* distribution was achieved by other means.

[315] *Re Leslie (J) Engineers Co Ltd* [1976] 1 WLR 292. The difficulty of tracing payments *out of* a company's bank account has had the effect of challenges also being made in respect of payments *into* its account by the bank collecting cheques on behalf of the company payee: see para 19.79.

[316] *Re Gray's Inn Construction Co Ltd* [1980] 1 WLR 711, 716, CA.

[317] *Hollicourt (Contracts) Ltd v Bank of Ireland* [2001] Ch 555, 563, CA, reversing the court below at [2000] 1 WLR 895 and disapproving on this point *Re Gray's Inn Construction Co Ltd* [1980] 1 WLR 711, CA (where the relevant account was overdrawn).

19.71   The object of section 127 is to protect the estate of the insolvent[318] from improper dissipation[319] pending the appointment of a liquidator to take control and the eventual distribution of the estate in the usual way. A compulsory winding-up normally commences with the petition to wind up and not with the making of a winding-up order or the appointment of a provisional liquidator.[320] The date of commencement for a voluntary winding-up is the passing of the resolution,[321] whereupon the rules regarding the distribution of the estate come into effect[322] and the company ceases to carry on trading except for the purpose of a beneficial winding-up.[323] The directors' powers cease as soon as the liquidator is appointed.[324] In a voluntary winding-up, there is no backdating measure corresponding to section 127 that bars dispositions of property between the notice of a meeting at which a winding-up resolution is proposed and the passing of the resolution. The safety valve for creditors apprehensive about the directors' behaviour is to petition for the compulsory winding-up of the company instead. A further reason for the presence of backdating only in a compulsory winding-up is that transactions entered into by the company cannot be challenged as preferences or undervalue transactions if entered into after the date of the winding-up petition;[325] but in the case of a voluntary winding-up, they may be challenged if entered into at any time before the date of the winding-up resolution itself.[326]

19.72   Section 127 is a very wide provision. It extends to any disposition[327] of the company's property,[328] which for present purposes includes property the subject of a charge.[329] The company's hands are therefore completely tied. As from the commencement of the winding-up it is not at liberty to trade without the sanction of the court. Particular difficulties are posed with regard to the operation of the company's bank accounts,[330] which the bank will freeze only when it learns of a winding-up petition. All that stands between paralysis and continued trading is that the

---

[318] If the s 127 proceedings involve a company, it may not be insolvent. The expression 'insolvent' conveniently unites companies and individuals.

[319] *Re Wiltshire Iron Co* (1868) 3 Ch App 443, 446–7.

[320] Section 129(2).

[321] Section 86.

[322] Section 107.

[323] Section 87(1).

[324] Sections 91(2) and 103. Transfers of shares after the winding-up resolution are also avoided: s 88.

[325] Sections 129(2), 238(2), 239(2) and 240(3)(b).

[326] Sections 86, 238(2), 239(2) and 240(3)(b).

[327] Its companion provision, s 284, has been applied to reverse a court order vesting the matrimonial home in the wife of the bankrupt, counsel for the trustee not basing his submissions on the fact that the order was a consent order: *Re Flint* [1993] Ch 319.

[328] It therefore does not operate to strike down assumptions of liability or the consumption or exhaustion of the company's assets: *Coutts & Co v Stock* [2000] 1 WLR 906.

[329] *Mond v Hammond Suddards (No 1)* [1996] 2 BCLC 470.

[330] Discussed at para 19.79.

court's discretion to allow the disposition is stated in the section in the broadest terms and is, moreover, broadly exercised.[331] Furthermore, the court's sanction need not be sought in advance but can be given retrospectively, though prudence dictates a preliminary application, at least in the case of substantial or unusual transactions. Indeed, it may be desirable that an application be made even before the winding-up order is made by the court, which despite the language of section 127 is permissible, given that the section exists to protect creditors during the pendency of the petition.[332]

It is not always the case that the company is insolvent when a petition is presented **19.73** to wind it up. A compulsory winding-up may be the outcome of unresolvable deadlock in a closely held company. Furthermore, it is by no means inevitable that a petition will actually lead to the winding-up of the company. It may be possible to sell the company as a going concern. Consequently, it may be for the good of all parties interested in the assets of the company that it be permitted to trade on.[333]

(ii) The court's discretion

In exercising its discretion with regard to dispositions of the insolvent's property, **19.74** the court is principally guided by the *pari passu* principle.[334] This principle does not apply where, exceptionally, the disposition is challenged by a secured creditor, the outcome being that the recovered property is impressed with the security and is not distributed in favour of the unsecured creditors.[335] This may seem odd when a transaction entered into before the commencement of the winding-up cannot be challenged by the secured creditor as a preference or as an undervalue transaction, which grounds of challenge are available only to administrators and insolvency officers, with the fruits of recovery being held for all the creditors of the company.[336] Section 127 appears therefore to provide that secured creditor with something of a windfall. Assets of the company disposed of with that secured creditor's express or implied permission may as a result of a disposition being void fall back into a continuing security, whether of a fixed or floating kind.[337] The exercise by the court of its discretion to uphold the disposition would avoid such

---

331 *Re Wiltshire Iron Co* (1868) LR 3 Ch App 443; *Re Steane's (Bournemouth) Ltd* [1950] 1 All ER 21; *Re Levy (AI) Holdings Ltd* [1964] Ch 19.

332 *Re Levy (AI) Holdings Ltd* [1964] Ch 19; *Re Burton & Deakin Ltd* [1977] 1 WLR 390.

333 *Re Wiltshire Iron Co* (1868) LR 3 Ch App 443, 446.

334 *Re Gray's Inn Construction Co Ltd* [1980] 1 WLR 711, CA; *Denney v Hudson (J) & Co Ltd* [1992] BCLC 901, CA; *Re Leslie (J) Engineers Co Ltd* [1976] 1 WLR 292.

335 *Mond v Hammond Suddards (No 1)* [1996] 2 BCLC 470 (where a floating charge crystallized upon the appointment of receivers after the void disposition had taken place).

336 *Re Yagerphone Ltd* [1935] Ch 392.

337 See *Mond v Hammond Suddards (No 1)* [1996] 2 BCLC 470; cf *Campbell v Michael Mount PPB* (1996) 14 ACLC 218.

an anomaly. If the company has disposed of fixed charge assets without permission or of floating charge assets outside the ordinary course of business, the secured creditor may, subject to the rights of a *bona fide* purchaser of the legal estate, take proceedings to recover the assets. The court's discretion to uphold the disposition, it is submitted, ought not to be exercised in such a case.

19.75 The court's discretion under section 127 depends upon two principal variables: there is the effect of the disposition upon the company's business and its creditors, and there is also the state of mind and judgment of the parties to the disposition. There is no requirement that the disposition actually succeed in having a beneficial effect on the company[338] but it is highly probable that the approval of the court will retrospectively be given where the company has benefited from the disposition.[339] The court will sanction a disposition that is *apt* to benefit the company, a test that avoids a needlessly expensive and 'massive investigation' into the company's affairs.[340] It is not enough, however, that the disposition be shown merely to have no injurious effect.[341] Consequently, as the cases demonstrate, the court's discretion is widely exercised to ensure, not just the rateable distribution of the insolvent's estate, but also its maximization. The sale at arm's length of the company's property at the prevailing market rate will involve no issue of *pari passu* distribution; a sale at an undervalue would damage the estate and harm creditors.

19.76 Transactions that have given rise to dispositions approved under section 127 include payments arising from trade that are paid into a bank account to maintain an overdraft facility,[342] the speedy sale of property that commands an exceptionally good price,[343] the grant of security to a director injecting fresh capital into a company to help it pay its wages bill[344] and the payment of outstanding trade debts to a supplier whose goods are vital to the continuing trading prospects of the company.[345] Although, as stated above, the court's discretion under section 127 is mainly guided by the principle of *pari passu* distribution, the *object* of the section is the benefit of creditors that comes from preventing the dissipation of the estate. Hence, the discretion may exceptionally be exercised in favour of a creditor disponee whose debts are paid in full when other creditors receive no more than a dividend.[346] Creditors benefit more from a larger dividend and some measure of inequality than they do from equality and a smaller dividend.

---

[338] *Re Clifton Place Garage Ltd* [1970] Ch 477, CA.
[339] See *Re Park Ward and Co Ltd* [1926] Ch 828, 832.
[340] *Denney v Hudson (J) & Co Ltd* [1992] BCLC 901, 907–8, CA.
[341] *Re Webb Electrical Ltd* (1988) 4 BCC 230.
[342] *Re Construction (TW) Ltd* [1954] 1 WLR 540.
[343] *Re Gray's Inn Construction Co Ltd* [1980] 1 WLR 711, 717, CA.
[344] *Re Park Ward and Co Ltd* [1926] Ch 828.
[345] *Denney v Hudson (J) & Co Ltd* [1992] BCLC 901.
[346] ibid; *Re Gray's Inn Construction Co Ltd* [1980] 1 WLR 711, 718, CA.

The state of mind of the parties to the disposition, as well as the judgment of the **19.77** company's directors, is relevant to the court's discretion. A disposition of property may be caught by the legislation even though neither the insolvent nor the disponee was aware that a bankruptcy or winding-up petition had been presented. This makes a broad judicial discretion all the more necessary to avoid confounding reasonable expectations.[347] A creditor's ignorance of the presentation of a winding-up petition has been described as 'a very powerful factor' in the court's consideration, but it is not conclusive.[348] In particular, it cannot improve the position of a pre-existing creditor who receives a preferential payment[349] especially when, as seen above, the provisions dealing with preferences do not apply after the commencement of the winding-up.[350] Knowledge by the disponee of the existence of a winding-up petition is no bar to the court's approval of a disposition when the transaction under which the disposition took place was beneficial,[351] or perceived to be beneficial,[352] to the company. The court's approval of a disposition has been stated to depend on the existence of good faith[353] but this of itself is not enough. There must also be a judgment, reasonably entertained, that the disposition will be beneficial to the company.[354]

Section 127 does not list the persons eligible to seek approval for the disposition **19.78** but the usual applicant will be the company or the disponee. In one case, however, the successful applicant was a bank to which the disponee of land had granted a mortgage. Stressing the flexibility of the statutory discretion, the court upheld the transaction to a limited extent, namely, the extent of the bank's mortgage interest.[355] Section 127 also fails to list those who may challenge the disposition. As seen above, a secured creditor may invoke the provision. In one case of corporate deadlock, the court ruled that an individual shareholder had standing to bring the proceedings (though it gave no opinion as to whether a director could do the same).[356] No good reason existed in the case of dispositions to introduce an implied limitation on eligible applicants into section 127 that was not present for the

---

347 See *Re Steane's (Bournemouth) Ltd* [1950] 1 All ER 21.

348 *Re Leslie (J) Engineers Co Ltd* [1976] 1 WLR 292, 304.

349 ibid.

350 For present purposes, it is submitted that a court should take a broad view of what amounts to a preference and not the narrow view that has been taken under s 239: see discussion at paras 19.156–19.158.

351 *Re Park Ward and Co Ltd* [1926] Ch 828.

352 *Re Clifton Place Garage Ltd* [1970] Ch 477 (receiver misled by director of state of company's indebtedness).

353 See *Denney v Hudson (J) & Co Ltd* [1992] BCLC 901; *Re Gray's Inn Construction Co Ltd* [1980] 1 WLR 711, 718, CA.

354 *Re Clifton Place Garage Ltd* [1970] Ch 477. See also *Re Burton & Deakin Ltd* [1977] 1 WLR 390.

355 *Royal Bank of Scotland Plc v Bhardwaj* [2002] BCC 57.

356 *Re Argentum Reductions (UK) Ltd* [1975] 1 WLR 186.

other instances of its application. It was, however, one thing to say that a share-holder could bring proceedings but quite another to say that all proceedings were brought with equal weight, regardless of the applicant. In particular, while the burden of persuasion properly falls upon the applicant seeking to have a transaction upheld, where a shareholder challenges a transaction authorized by the company's managers it is the shareholder who will have to show compelling evidence that the transaction was likely to injure the company.[357]

(iii) Bank accounts

19.79 Finally, as stated above, the position of the company and its bankers has caused difficulties under section 127 with particular reference to defining what is the company's property and whether a disposition of it is taking place. The first difficulty arises when payments are made into a company's account. When a bank collects cheques on its customer's behalf and pays the proceeds into an overdrawn account, a disposition of the company's property has been said to be made since the effect of this payment in is *pro tanto* to diminish the customer's liability on the overdraft.[358] This view is not without its difficulties in that the effect of the bank's action is to exchange the customer's beneficial interest in the proceeds of the cheque for a reduction of the customer's indebtedness to the bank. The bank may be dealing away its corporate customer's property but it is replacing that property with an item of equal value. The customer's estate is not thus reduced yet the prospects of recovery of the customer's other creditors may be sensibly diminished. The object of section 127, which is to avoid the dissipation of the company's assets, at this point diverges from the principle of *pari passu* distribution, just as it does in a few other instances mentioned above. The Court of Appeal in *Re Gray's Inn Construction Co Ltd*[359] stated that the proper exercise of its discretion under section 127 was to freeze the company's account at the date of the petition, with subsequent dealings, when necessary for the conduct of the company's business, being carried out in a new account. This would avoid the preferential discharge of the company's overdraft with the bank.[360]

19.80 Where the customer's account is at all material times in credit, the payment of the proceeds of collected cheques into a bank account has been held not to be a disposition of the company's property.[361] Nevertheless, there has equally been a substitution of the company's property, namely the proceeds of the collection, for an increased indebtedness of the bank to the customer. In this instance,

---

[357] *Re Burton & Deakin Ltd* [1977] 1 WLR 390.
[358] *Re Gray's Inn Construction Co Ltd* [1980] 1 WLR 711, 715-16, CA. See also *Rose v AIB Group (UK) Plc* [2003] EWHC 1737 (Ch); [2003] 1 WLR 1791.
[359] [1980] 1 WLR 711, CA.
[360] ibid 719, CA.
[361] *Re Barn Crown Ltd* [1995] 1 WLR 147.

however, there has occurred no divergence of the *pari passu* principle and the preservation of the company's estate. Since a disposition is a proprietary transfer, it is present in both cases of accounts in credit and overdrawn accounts and is not negatived by the receipt of property in exchange.[362] The grounds for exercising the court's discretion under section 127 to uphold the disposition are stronger, however, where the account is in credit.

The second area of difficulty concerns payments out of the company's account. **19.81** According to dicta of the Court of Appeal in *Re Gray's Inn Construction Co Ltd*, all payments out of the company's account are dispositions of its property and not just any excess of payments out over payments in.[363] The same view that a disposition had occurred was rejected in a case where the account from which the payments were made was overdrawn.[364] The court held there had been no disposition but rather, as a result of the loan made by the bank when the overdraft was increased upon the payment out of the account, an increase in the company's liabilities. The dicta in *Re Gray's Inn Construction Co Ltd* were disapproved of in the case of an account in credit in *Hollicourt (Contracts) Ltd v Bank of Ireland*,[365] where as stated above the Court of Appeal focused on the end result of the payment, dismissing the relevance for the purpose of section 127 of intermediate steps taken by the bank pursuant to its mandate to honour cheques drawn on the account.

(2) Secured Creditors in the Insolvency Process

(a) Recognizing security

The assets available for distribution to unsecured creditors do not include assets **19.82** that are subject to a charge or other security granted by the insolvent[366] or that are still owned by a creditor seller supplying them under the terms of a valid reservation of title clause. Title reservation is more effective even than security, for the seller need not procure the registration of his reserved interest under the Companies Act 2006.[367] Moreover, title reservation defeats at source an earlier security, granted by the buyer and extending to future assets, whose description

---

362 Notwithstanding the reasoning in *Re Barn Crown Ltd* [1995] 1 WLR 147, 152–56, the customer is lending money to the bank when it causes its account to be credited with the proceeds of a cheque collected on its behalf by the bank, its agent.

363 [1980] 1 WLR 711, 719–20, CA.

364 *Coutts & Co v Stock* [2000] 1 WLR 906 (noting that the point had been conceded in *Re Gray's Inn Construction Co Ltd* [1980] 1 WLR 711, CA, that all payments out were dispositions of the company's property).

365 [2001] Ch 555, CA.

366 Except to the extent that the security can be overturned as a transaction concluded in the twilight period: see para 19.149.

367 Section 860.

covers the goods supplied by the seller, since that security only attaches to assets of the buyer.

19.83 The strength of the secured creditor's hand is further revealed by the rule that a security over future assets will attach to assets embraced by the security even if they fall into the estate of an insolvent during the bankruptcy or winding-up process. In that event, the assets fall in already encumbered and, to the extent of the encumbrance, are not subject to the trust in favour of unsecured creditors.[368] This is because an assignment by way of security over future assets confers 'an actual interest in the assignee as if the assignor had been possessed of the property at the date of the assignment'.[369] For the same reason, the payment of the proceeds of assets subject to a floating charge into an account with the creditor bank is not a disposition of the company's property for the purposes of section 127.[370]

19.84 Although assets caught by a security are not generally available for distribution, this does not mean that the secured creditor has first call on such assets. In the case of assets the subject of a charge that, as created, was a floating charge, preference creditors have priority in a winding-up ahead of the secured creditor.[371] Where an administrative receiver is appointed to enforce such a floating charge, the preference creditors' priority is expressed as a rule that, where other assets of the company are insufficient to pay the preference creditors,[372] a receiver is bound first to pay them before the secured creditor.[373] The same rule now applies to adminstrators too.[374] A similar rule prevents a secured creditor who enters into possession from paying himself off before the preference creditors.[375]

19.85 In those cases where registration of a security interest by way of charge or mortgage is required under the Companies Act 2006, but registration is not effected within 21 days of the creation of the charge, the charge will remain effective as between company and debenture holder[376] but will be void against liquidators and administrators.[377] In consequence, a secured creditor who has realized the

---

[368] On which, see paras 19.28 and 19.94ff.

[369] *Re Lind* [1915] 2 Ch 345, 355, CA, following *Tailby v Official Receiver* (1888) 13 App Cas 523, HL; *Re Margart Pty Ltd* [1985] BCLC 314, New South Wales; cf *Collyer v Isaacs* (1881) 19 Ch D 342, CA.

[370] *Re Margart Pty Ltd* [1985] BCLC 314 (NSW equivalent provision). Future assets clauses will not extend, however, to certain recoveries made by liquidators pursuant to proceedings taken under, for example, s 214 (wrongful trading): see para 19.167.

[371] Section 175(2)(b).

[372] Section 40(3).

[373] Section 40(2). This provision, together with s 175(2)(b) will be discussed in more detail at para 19.109.

[374] Insolvency Act (as amended), Sch B1, para 65(2).

[375] Companies Act 2006, s 754(2).

[376] See *Independent Automatic Sales Ltd v Knowles & Foster* [1962] 1 WLR 974.

[377] Companies Act 2006, s 874(1). It is also liable to be postponed in favour of a subsequent charge even where the chargee has actual notice of the earlier unregistered charge: *Re Monolithic Co* [1915] 1 Ch 643, CA.

security and no longer has it in his possession need not fear the later appointment of an administrator who cannot retrospectively claim the right to immediate possession needed to maintain an action in conversion against the creditor.[378] The commencement,[379] even the imminence,[380] of a winding-up may also be a ground for refusing to allow late registration outside the 21-day period under the statutory discretion.[381] In the case of individuals and partnerships, a narrower range of security bills of sale have to be registered under the Bills of Sale Acts 1878–91.[382]

The fact that a creditor is secured does not prevent that creditor from putting in a **19.86** proof where the security is insufficient to meet the claim. The Insolvency Rules provide that a creditor may prove for the balance after account has been taken of the security. The balance may be quantified by the secured creditor realizing the security.[383] It may also be quantified by means of valuing the security[384] (though surprisingly there is no provision in the Rules expressly allowing for a proof for the balance after valuation). The secured creditor himself may put a value on his security, which value may later be altered only with the leave of the insolvency officer or of the court.[385] If the insolvency officer is dissatisfied with the value placed on the security, he may require the security or any part of it to be offered for sale.[386] A secured creditor may be prompted to have the security revalued where, before it is realized, the insolvency officer gives notice of his intention to redeem the security at the value placed upon it by the secured creditor.[387] Finally, there will be rare cases where a secured creditor may wish to forgo the security and put in a proof instead.[388]

(b) Dealing with secured assets

(i) General

The onset of a winding-up or bankruptcy does not prevent the secured creditor **19.87** from taking practical steps to enforce the security since there is no moratorium

---

[378] *Smith v Bridgend County Borough Council* [2000] 1 BCLC 775, CA.

[379] *Re Mechanisations (Eaglescliffe) Ltd* [1966] Ch 20.

[380] *Re Ashpurton Estates* [1983] Ch 110, CA; *Re Braemar Investments Ltd* [1989] Ch 54.

[381] Under Companies Act 2006, s 873.

[382] The requirement of registration is extended by s 344 of the Insolvency Act from chattels in possession to book debts, more specifically to general assignments of book debts that are not assignments by way of charge.

[383] Rules 4.88(1) and 6.109(1). The secured creditor may call upon the liquidator or trustee to elect whether to exercise a power to redeem the security: rr 4.97(4) and 6.117(4).

[384] The value placed on the security will be overridden by the amount of a subsequent realization: rr 4.99 and 6.119.

[385] Rules 4.95(1) and 6.115(1). The leave of the court is necessary for revaluation if the secured creditor was the petitioner or has voted in respect of the unsecured balance of the debt: rr 4.95(2) and 6.115(2). On the effects of revaluing security, see r 11.9.

[386] Rules 4.98 and 6.118.

[387] Rules 4.97 and 6.117.

[388] Rules 4.88(2) and 6.109(2).

equivalent to the moratorium that takes place when the company goes into administration. The enforcement of security rights does not amount to actions or proceedings against the company requiring the leave of the court.[389] Nor does the termination of an administrative receiver's agency to act in the name of the company borrower, occurring when the company goes into liquidation,[390] prevent the receiver from enforcing the security in favour of the secured creditor who procured his appointment by the company.[391] In such a case, the liquidator of the company is in practical terms powerless to move in and distribute the estate if only because the contents of the estate cannot be defined until the receiver has carried out the responsibilities of the receivership. A novel attempt has been made by unsecured creditors to have the receiver ousted by the appointment of a provisional liquidator, on the ground that the receiver's imposition of harsh trading terms upon that creditor, in its capacity as a trading partner heavily dependent upon supplies from the company in receivership, amounted to blackmail. The court dismissed the application, holding that the receivers were entitled to exploit the company's only real asset, namely, its bargaining position against the creditor.[392] If, however, it should be necessary for a secured creditor to take legal proceedings to enforce his security, as might for example happen if a liquidator disputes the creditor's right to take possession, the creditor will need the leave of the court to take proceedings,[393] which should without undue difficulty be granted.[394]

(ii) Administration

19.88 Although the secured creditor is free to realize his security notwithstanding winding-up or bankruptcy, the position is different in the case of companies that are in administration. Once a petition for an administration order is presented, 'no step may be taken to enforce any security over the company's property'. Security has the conventional meaning of 'any mortgage, charge, lien or other security'.[395] It includes a solicitor's lien,[396] a carrier's lien[397] and a statutory right of

---

[389] Section 130(2). For the meaning of 'proceedings', see discussion in paras 19.63–19.64.

[390] Section 44(1)(a).

[391] *Sowman v Samuel (David) Trust* [1978] 1 WLR 22. The equivalent issue does not arise in administration because of the moratorium on insolvency proceedings: Insolvency Act (as amended), Sch B1, paras 40, 42.

[392] *Ford AG-Werke AG v TransTec Automotive (Campsie) Ltd* [2001] BCC 403.

[393] Sections 130(2) and 285(1).

[394] *Re Lloyd (David) & Co* (1877) 6 Ch D 339, CA.

[395] Section 248. The decision in *Re Park Air Services plc* [2000] 2 AC 172, HL, that security did not include a landlord's power of re-entry under a lease, was overtaken by the separate listing of re-entry as a step requiring the administrator's permission or the leave of the court: Insolvency Act (as amended), Sch B1, para 43(4).

[396] *Re Carter Commercial Developments Ltd* [2002] BCC 803.

[397] *Re Sabre International Products Ltd* [1991] BCLC 470.

detention akin to a lien conferred over aircraft in respect of unpaid airport charges.[398] Equally, upon the presentation of a petition, 'no step may be taken. . .to repossess goods in the company's possession under a hire-purchase agreement' except with the leave of the court.[399] Hire purchase is defined expansively in the Insolvency Act so as to include title-retention sales agreements, conditional sales and equipment leases lasting for at least three months.[400] If a receiver of part of the company's property is appointed before an administator, then that receiver is required to vacate office.[401] Formerly, the appointment of an administrator could be blocked by a floating chargee able to secure the appointment of an administrative receiver, but the replacement in the great bulk of cases of the administrative receiver by an administrator appointed out of court has dispensed with the need for such a provision.[402] In consequence, the moratorium on the enforcement of security and related rights will now serve mainly secured creditors with a qualifying floating charge at the expense of other creditors. This moratorium on creditors' rights does not expunge them. Consequently, if an administrator abusively withholds his consent to the enforcement of a security right, a creditor with a continuing right to immediate possession of goods has standing to sue in the tort of conversion.[403]

In *Re Atlantic Computer Systems plc*,[404] the court's discretion to grant leave to enforce a security received an authoritative exposition. The case concerned the lease and sub-lease of computer equipment, the lessee being in administration. The lessor unsuccessfully argued that the administrator was bound to pay rentals due under the head lease as expenses of the administration, in the same way that a liquidator would have to pay expenses of the winding-up. The amounts in question were significantly larger than the amount of sub-rentals paid under the various sub-leases since the latter had been entered into on disadvantageous terms and because, in some cases, sub-rentals had been withheld by the sub-lessees. Instead, the lessor was awarded the hollow victory of repossessing computer equipment adapted to the needs of the sub-lessees. The administrator was not entitled to retain the equipment in the cause of shoring up the lessee's client base, the lessee's only substantial asset. A balancing exercise[405] had to be conducted and the prejudice that the lessor would suffer as a result of the administrator retaining the equipment meant that the court exercised its discretion in favour of the lessor.

19.89

---

[398] *Bristol Airport plc v Powdrill* [1990] Ch 744, CA.

[399] Insolvency Act (as amended), Sch B1, para 43(3).

[400] Sections 10(4), 15(9) and 251 ('chattel leasing agreement', 'retention of title agreement').

[401] Insolvency Act (as amended), Sch B1, para 41(2).

[402] Former s 9(3)(a) of the Insolvency Act.

[403] *Barclays Mercantile Business Finance Ltd v Sibec Developments Ltd* [1992] 1 WLR 1253 (*semble*, both administrator and company might be liable).

[404] [1992] Ch 505, CA.

[405] See also *Re ARV Aviation Ltd* [1989] BCLC 664.

19.90 Besides the embargo on enforcing security without leave during an administration, secured creditors' rights are affected in other ways during the conduct of an administration. The administrator may deal with and dispose of property subject to a floating charge[406] without leave of the court,[407] but the chargee's priority is transferred to the proceeds.[408] Since, however, the administrator himself ranks ahead of the floating chargee (but not a fixed chargee) in respect of his remuneration and expenses,[409] and since sums payable in respect of debts or liabilities incurred by the administrator under contracts made, or contracts of employment adopted, during the conduct of the administration rank ahead of the administrator's personal claim,[410] the priority standing of a secured creditor with a floating charge is considerably diminished during administration.[411]

19.91 The administrator may also deal with and dispose of property subject to a fixed charge or hire purchase agreement with the leave of the court.[412] If the proceeds of disposal are less than the value of the property in the open market when sold by a willing vendor, then the administrator, in addition to paying over the actual proceeds, must also make good any deficiency out of company assets.[413]

(iii) Administrative receivership

19.92 Administrative receivership does not have the same capacity for interfering with the rights of secured creditors. Nevertheless, the administrative receiver may apply to the court under section 43 for permission to dispose of charged property where this 'would be likely to promote a more advantageous realization of the company's assets than would otherwise be effected'. This power would be appropriately exercised where the administrative receiver wants to dispose of a block of integrated assets or to hive down some or all of the assets of the company to another company. It is not needed if the secured creditor for whom he acts ranks ahead of any other secured creditor with an interest in the same assets. Typically, it will be needed where the floating charge, created by the debenture under which the administrative receiver was appointed, is subordinate in respect of one or more assets to a fixed charge or mortgage granted in favour of another creditor.

---

[406] Defined as such at the date of creation and ignoring subsequent crystallization: s 251. The floating chargee at risk here is not a floating chargee able itself to procure the appointment of an administrator in the first place.

[407] Insolvency Act (as amended), Sch B1, para 70(1).

[408] ibid para 70(2).

[409] ibid para 99(3).

[410] ibid para 99(4), (5).

[411] The above provisions of Sch B1 apply at the end of the period of administration: *Re A Company No 005174 of 1999* (High Ct, 20 August 1999). The implications of administration for the limitations rule are displayed in *Re Maxwell Fleet and Facilities Management Ltd (No 1)* [2001] 1 WLR 323.

[412] Insolvency Act (as amended), Sch B1, para 71.

[413] Insolvency Act (as amended), Sch B1, para 71(3).

This latter creditor has the first call on the proceeds of realization of the assets in question: section 43 does not alter priorities.

Unlike the case of administration, administrative receivership does not involve **19.93** the freezing of secured creditors' and title retainers' rights of enforcement. Nevertheless, in one decision,[414] the court ingeniously manufactured such a power in the interest of permitting the receivership to work. The title retainer sought an interlocutory injunction to prevent further dealings by the administrative receiver with the disputed goods, despite the latter's personal undertaking that the title retainer's rights would be respected by a later payment, but was denied it on the balance of convenience. The risk of non-payment of the title holder was too slight to justify an interlocutory injunction.

(3) Distributing the Insolvent's Assets

(a) The *pari passu* rule

(i) General

If insolvency law has one paramount principle, it is that the assets of the insolvent **19.94** are to be distributed *pari passu*, that is, rateably, amongst the creditors of the insolvent.[415] The influence of the rule is evident at various points in this chapter. For example, there are the rules dealing with fraudulent conveyances and vulnerable transactions.[416] Nevertheless, this fundamental principle is subject to statutory exceptions, such as the creation of preferential claims. Moreover, as a matter of economic reality, the *pari passu* rule does not succeed in preserving an appreciable estate for distribution. Creditors able to take security do so and, apart from the rules on unlawful preferences and late floating charges,[417] there is nothing to stop them from encumbering the assets of the future insolvent so that in the event of bankruptcy or winding-up there is nothing or very little left for distribution. Insolvency is the very event when the security will be enforced but security rights do not come into existence upon insolvency so as then to divest the insolvent of property rights.

It is this character of security that differentiates it from the forfeiture of property **19.95** rights upon insolvency,[418] which does offend the *pari passu* rule and therefore

---

[414] *Lipe Ltd v Leyland Daf Ltd* [1993] BCC 385.

[415] Sections 107 and 328(3); r 4.181. See G McCormack, *Proprietary Claims in Insolvency* (1997), ch 2; F Oditah, 'Assets and the Treatment of Claims in Insolvency' (1992) 108 LQR 459.

[416] Discussed at paras 19.147–19.161.

[417] Discussed at paras 19.162–19.164.

[418] To be distinguished from clauses in a proprietary transfer that *determine* interests upon an insolvency: discussed at para 19.35. The property rights must have value for this rule to be applied: *Money Markets International Stockbrokers Ltd v London Stock Exchange Ltd* [2002] 1 WLR 1150.

public policy. The prohibition has been put in the form of no one being entitled upon bankruptcy to bargain for an additional advantage.[419] So, if under a partnership deed one partner's share in a mining lease reverts to the other partner upon his bankruptcy, the clause providing for this is void.[420] Another example is the forfeiture of royalty payments owed to the owner by the licensee of a patent, against a debt owed by the owner to the licensee, in the event of the owner's bankruptcy.[421] Another void transaction occurs where the bankrupt qualifies or determines his own interest, as where he settles property on trust so that his life interest passes to the remainderman on his bankruptcy.[422] Again, in the case of a building lease where the builder's materials were to be forfeited to the landlord in the event of the builder's bankruptcy, the forfeiture clause was held to be void.[423] Nevertheless, if the clause empowers a forfeiture in the event of default, insolvency being merely one type of event that could trigger a default, *Re Garrud*[424] held that the transaction was valid. If this case is correct, the timing of the forfeiture and the presentation of a bankruptcy or winding-up petition would appear not to matter[425] and the *pari passu* rule could be excluded by skilful drafting.[426] In *Money Markets International Stockbrokers Ltd v London Stock Exchange Ltd*,[427] however, the court disapproved of this reasoning in *Re Garrud* on the ground that this was inconsistent with the decision of the House of Lords in *British Eagle International Airlines Ltd v Cie Nationale Air France*.[428]

(ii) The building industry

19.96   The *pari passu* rule has caused particular concern in the building industry where the tiered structure of separate contracts isolates the site owner (or employer) from the sub-contractor, the intervening contractor being bound to each of them separately. The site owner has a strong interest in the continuation of the building

---

[419] *Higinbotham v Holme* (1812) 19 Ves 88, 92, 34 ER 451, *per* Lord Eldon.
[420] *Whitmore v Mason* (1861) 2 J & H 204, 70 ER 1031.
[421] *Re Jeavons* (1873) 8 Ch App 643.
[422] *Re Brewer's Settlement* [1896] 2 Ch 503. See also *Fraser v Oystertec plc* [2004] EWHC 2225; [2004] BCC 233 (forfeiture of patent rights).
[423] *Re Harrison* (1880) 14 Ch D 19, CA.
[424] (1881) 16 Ch D 522, CA. See also *Re Waugh* (1876) 4 Ch D 524.
[425] *Re Garrud* (1881) 16 Ch D 522, CA. But cf *Re Walker* (1884) 26 Ch D 510, CA.
[426] In *Smith v Bridgend County Borough Council* [2001] UKHL 58; [2002] 1 AC 336 Lord Scott distinguished between a seizure of an insolvent contractor's machinery on account of the local authority's claim (not an unlawful forfeiture) from a seizure in satisfaction of the claim. A clause that imposes certain restrictions on, or even prohibits, assignment will not however prevent property from vesting in a trustee-in-bankruptcy, since a vesting in this way will not be treated as a prohibited assignment: *Re Landau* [1998] Ch 223; *Patel v Jones* [2001] EWCA Civ 779; [2001] BPIR 919 (regulations governing a pension scheme could have prevented a vesting in the trustee but were never made).
[427] [2002] 1 WLR 1150.
[428] [1975] 2 All ER 390, HL.

project notwithstanding the bankruptcy or winding-up of the contractor, and is at risk if the sub-contractor declines to continue because moneys due have not yet been paid by the contractor. There are various ways in which the position of the site owner might be protected: the contractor may be required, for example, to hold a portion of moneys received in trust for the sub-contractor. Another possibility is for the site owner to reserve the right to pay the sub-contractor directly in the event of the contractor's insolvency.

Direct payment clauses have been upheld in England where they have not referred specifically to insolvency.[429] New Zealand authority, taking its cue from a reaffirmation by the House of Lords of the *pari passu* rule,[430] has taken a different view.[431] An essential part of the New Zealand court's reasoning was that, upon liquidation, the insolvent company had a vested chose in action representing its right to be paid for work already done. The company was not permitted by contract to leave some of its creditors at a comparative disadvantage. This reasoning fails to appreciate the flawed quality of the company's right to be paid. If the site owner may elect in certain events to acquit its duty to pay by paying a sub-contractor directly, this seems to have little to do with any prohibition on the company against favouring, or even suffering to be favoured, one creditor at the expense of the others. The site owner's payment duty was shaped at the date of the contract, not that of the site owner's later insolvency.[432] One difficulty with this analysis, however, is that it leaves suspended the ownership of any debt owed until the contractor exercises its election, and in any case great care would have to be taken that there is a genuine election and not merely a duty to pay the contractor which is defeasible. **19.97**

In favour of the site owner is the fact that the moneys later paid could at that same date have been assigned by the contractor, whether absolutely or by way of security.[433] The site owner asserted its own interests in the bargaining process and had indeed a legitimate interest in the continuation of the building project that the payment of the sub-contractor would do much to safeguard. Any objection that direct payment rights are being used as a substitute for a provable damages claim is met by the response is that direct payment is no more objectionable than taking security over the assets of the contractor.[434] **19.98**

---

[429] *Re Wilkinson* [1905] 2 KB 713; *Re Tout and Finch Ltd* [1954] 1 WLR 178.

[430] In *British Eagle International Airlines Ltd v Cie Nationale Air France* [1975] 1 WLR 758, HL.

[431] *A-G v McMillan & Lockwood Ltd* [1991] 1 NZLR 53. See also the decision of the Northern Ireland court in *B Mullan & Sons (Contractors) Ltd v Ross* (NI High Ct, 7 December 1995).

[432] The liquidator takes the company's property subject to the same restrictions that lay upon it in the company's hands: *Glow Heating Ltd v Eastern Health Board* (1988) 6 ILT 237 (Ireland).

[433] *A-G v McMillan & Lockwood Ltd* [1991] 1 NZLR 53, 65 (Williamson J, dissenting).

[434] Concerns in the building industry about the effectiveness of direct payment clauses, however, resulted in the clause being dropped from the JCT 1980 form.

(iii) Settlement systems

19.99 The decision of the House of Lords in *British Eagle International Airlines Ltd v Cie Nationale Air France*[435] was given in very different circumstances. It concerned settlement arrangements amongst the various airline members of IATA. At the end of each settlement period, net debtor airlines paid over their net indebtedness to the settlement authority which in turn paid over these sums to net creditor airlines. In the present case, the airline in liquidation, British Eagle, was overall a net debtor but, as against Air France, was a net creditor. Could it avoid the settlement system and claim directly from Air France while leaving its creditors to put in a proof? The House of Lords held by a bare majority that the system of netting adopted in the present case, by diverting funds from Air France to British Eagle's airline creditors, preferred those creditors to British Eagle's other creditors.[436] The settlement process amounted to a mini-liquidation process carried out before the main liquidation of British Eagle. The airlines participating in the process were behaving as though they had charges over British Eagle's book debts, which was not the case.

19.100 Though concerned with airlines, this case demonstrated the vulnerability of settlement systems in the money markets. In particular, the insolvency of one member could not be isolated in the way that the settlement system promised, which gave rise to the threat of cascading insolvencies produced as one member brought down the next and so on. The threat was considered real enough for a system of mini-liquidation to be introduced by statute for designated money markets.[437]

(b) Expenses of the insolvency process

19.101 Various expenses are incurred in the conduct of a winding-up or bankruptcy that have to be paid before the balance of the insolvent's assets is distributed in the usual rateable way. The Insolvency Act and Insolvency Rules make provision for the priority treatment of the expenses of the winding-up incurred by the liquidator[438] and the expenses of the bankruptcy incurred by the trustee.[439] In putting the expenses claim ahead of preference creditors, these rules introduce complexities in the ranking of expenses, preference creditors, fixed chargees and floating charges. They also require a careful distinction to be drawn between

---

[435] [1975] 1 WLR 758, HL.

[436] See *North Atlantic Insurance Co Ltd v Nationwide General Insurance Co Ltd* [2004] EWCA Civ 423; [2004] 1 CLC 1131 (an arrangement among members of an underwriting pool about the proceeds of reinsurance could not affect the liquidator of a member from collecting that member's assets to distribute them to its creditors).

[437] Part VII of the Companies Act 1989.

[438] Section 175(2)(a); see also ss 107, 115 and 156, Sch 8 para 17 and rr 4.218–20 and 12.2.

[439] Section 328(2) and Sch 9 para 22 and rr 6.202, 6.224 and 12.2.

pre-liquidation expenses, provable in a winding-up, and expenses of the liquidation, which occupy a preferential position.[440]

Further difficulties arise because of the draftsman's varied terminology when refer-   **19.102**
ring to expenses.[441] Recoverable expenses[442] are specifically listed so as to include numerous items, such as the expenses of getting in the insolvent's assets; necessary disbursements[443] made by the official receiver or insolvency officer; the fees and remuneration of these persons; and the remuneration of those employed by a liquidator to perform services for the company. The costs of a liquidator's unsuccessful action taken to recover assets transferred at an undervalue or by means of an unlawful preference do not however rank as expenses of the liquidation.[444] Had the position been otherwise, the law as it then stood would have allowed the liquidator to charge the costs of the action against the bank whose floating charge had been unsuccessfully challenged in the action, leaving the successful bank litigant to bear both sets of costs. The statutory list of liquidation expenses is a definitive one. Language in the Insolvency Act appearing to create a general, open-ended category of liquidation expenses does not in fact have this effect, since the relevant provisions are concerned with priority amongst expenses claimants and not with the eligibility of expenses as expenses of the liquidation.[445] There is, nevertheless, an exception to the definitive listing of liquidation expenses in the Act. On just and equitable grounds, certain pre-liquidation expenses, such as the liability to pay rent under a continuing lease, are treated as if they were expenses of the liquidation.[446] The reason is that those for whose benefit the estate is being administered should bear the burden of debt incurred in the process.[447]

---

[440] *Re Toshoku Finance plc* [2002] UKHL 6; [2002] 1 WLR 671.

[441] Section 115 ('expenses properly incurred'); s 156 ('expenses incurred'); s 175(2) ('expenses of the winding-up'); r 4.218 ('expenses of the liquidation' with various sub-formulations, eg, 'expenses properly chargeable', 'necessary disbursements'). See *Mond v Hammond Suddards (No 2)* [2000] Ch 40, CA (the language in ss 115 and 156 being narrower than the language in s 175(2) and r 4.218).

[442] For allowable expenses of the administration, see Insolvency Rules (as amended by the Insolvency (Amendment) Rules 2003 (SI 2003/1730)), r 2.67.

[443] For example, tax liabilities: *Re Mesco Properties Ltd* [1980] 1 WLR 96, CA; *Re Toshoku Finance plc* [2002] UKHL 6; [2002] 1 WLR 671.

[444] *Re MC Bacon Ltd* [1991] Ch 127; *Mond v Hammond Suddards (No 2)* [2000] Ch 40, CA. In *Re MC Bacon Ltd*, Millett J added that any assets recovered in proceedings of the present kind, or under section 127 of the Insolvency Act, would not be the property of the company since they would be impressed with a trust in favour of the company's creditors and, anyway, would not be present assets of the company since they could only become so after successful defeasance proceedings.

[445] *Re MC Bacon Ltd* [1991] Ch 127; *Mond v Hammond Suddards (No 2)* [2000] Ch 40, CA. Different views were expressed in *Re Exchange (Travel Holdings) Ltd (No 3)* [1997] 2 BCLC 579, CA, and *Re Floor Fourteen Ltd* [1999] 2 BCLC 666 but these cannot now be considered good law.

[446] *Re Lundy Granite Co* (1871) 6 Ch App 462; *Re Toshoku Finance plc* [2002] UKHL 6; [2002] 1 WLR 671.

[447] *Re Atlantic Computer Systems plc* [1992] Ch 505, 522, CA.

19.103 Recoverable expenses are paid out in the order of priority laid down by the Insolvency Rules,[448] with the cost of getting in the assets at the head of the list, except that in the case of compulsory winding-up the court has a discretion to order payment in such order of priority as it thinks just if the company's assets are insufficient to meet its liabilities.[449]

(c) Priority: expenses, preferential creditors, unsecured creditors and members

19.104 Another critical difficulty is to determine whether expenses properly recoverable by the insolvency officer, and therefore ranking ahead of preference and other unsecured creditors, should be recoverable at the expense of secured creditors with a floating charge. The scheme of the Insolvency Act invites the assumption that, because expenses rank ahead of preference creditors,[450] who in turn rank ahead of secured creditors with a floating charge, it therefore follows that expenses rank ahead of floating chargees. The order of distribution in the case of insolvent companies would therefore be as follows: fixed chargees, expenses of the insolvency process, preference creditors, floating chargees, unsecured creditors and members. Subject to the special provision made for unsecured creditors by the Enterprise Act 2002, this ranking is confirmed by section 1282 of the Companies Act 2006, which overturned a House of Lords decision[451] that had altered the previous understanding of the law.

(i) Floating charges

19.105 Distribution takes place out of the assets of the company. It is particularly important to determine what those assets are in the case of preferential creditors and, since the Enterprise Act 2002, unsecured creditors participating in the special fund created by amendment to the Insolvency Act.[452] These assets do not include assets the subject of a fixed charge or mortgage[453] but they do include assets subject to a floating charge.[454] Nevertheless, before changes were made to insolvency legislation in the 1980s, it was held that preference creditors were not entitled to be

---

[448] Rules 4.218–20 and 6.224.

[449] Section 156. See *Re MC Bacon Ltd* [1991] Ch 127; *Re Toshoku Finance plc* [2002] UKHL 6; [2002] 1 WLR 671.

[450] Sections 115 and 175(2)(a).

[451] *Buchler v Talbot* [2004] UKHL 9; [2004] 2 AC 298.

[452] See Insolvency Act (as amended), s 176A, discussed at paras 19.112.

[453] The court has no inherent jurisdiction to interfere with the rights of secured creditors: *Re MC Bacon Ltd* [1991] Ch 127, 140. The company's equity of redemption in the assets would be subject to distribution in the normal way.

[454] *Re Barleycorn Enterprises Ltd* [1970] Ch 465, CA (in the light of legislative changes of 1888 and 1897 introducing the special category of preferential claims and ranking them ahead of floating chargees); *Re MC Bacon Ltd* [1991] Ch 127.

paid out of assets subject to a floating charge that had crystallized between the dates of the winding-up petition and order.[455] The assets at the relevant time had become the subject of a fixed charge. When the law was subsequently changed so that preference creditors were to be paid ahead of floating chargees, regardless of whether or when the charge had crystallized,[456] this gave rise to the modern problem of resolving the competing claims of liquidators, for the reimbursement of expenses of the liquidation, and of floating chargees. The position taken in *Re Barleycorn Enterprises Ltd*[457] was that, since floating charge assets were assets of the company, it followed that the order of distribution was, in respect of them, first, expenses of the liquidation, secondly, preferential debts, and thirdly, the claim of the floating chargee. In the so-called *Leyland Daf* litigation,[458] the same view was again initially taken but the House of Lords demonstrated in *Buchler v Talbot*[459] that the position was altogether different. There were two funds each bearing its own costs. The first fund consisted of the free assets of the company in liquidation, out of which the expenses of the liquidation were to be paid, ahead of any claim of the preferential creditors. The second fund, administered by a receiver (or administrator appointed out of court), would be charged with the expenses of the receivership or administration after the preferential creditors had been paid but before the floating chargee was paid.[460] The expenses of the liquidation would not be charged against this fund. *Buchler v Talbot* had hardly settled the law before it was overturned by section 1282 of the Companies Act 2006[461] as follows: '(1) The expenses of winding up in England and Wales, so far as the assets of the company available for payment of the general creditors of the company are insufficient to meet them, have priority over any claims to property comprised in or subject to any floating charge created by the company and shall be paid out of any property accordingly.' Sub-section (2) goes on to make it clear that expenses rank ahead of any claim of preferential creditors to those same assets, but not ahead of the claim of unsecured creditors to the fund created by section 176A of the Insolvency Act (as amended).

---

[455] *Re Christonette International Ltd* [1982] 1 WLR 1245, relying upon *Re Griffin Hotel Co Ltd* [1941] Ch 129.

[456] Sections 40 and 175, and Sch B1, para 65(2), of the Insolvency Act (as amended); s 754(2) of the Companies Act 2006.

[457] [1970] Ch 465, CA, followed in *Re Portbase (Clothing) Ltd* [1993] Ch 388.

[458] *Re Leyland Daf Ltd* [2001] 1 BCLC 419, affd *sub nom Buchler v Talbot* [2002] 1 BCLC 571, CA.

[459] [2004] UKHL 9; [2004] 2 AC 298.

[460] See Insolvency Act (as amended), ss 40(2), 45(3) and 175(2)(b), Sch B1, paras 65(2) and 99(3). Preferential creditors are expected to look first to the general fund before turning to the floating charge fund: ss 40(3) and 175(2)(b), Sch B1, para 65(2).

[461] Inserting s 176ZA into the Insolvency Act.

(ii) Preferential claims

19.106 In response to the recommendation of the Cork Committee,[462] the insolvency reforms of the 1980s drastically reduced the number of preferential claims. For example, local authorities' claims for unpaid rates lost their preferential status. When first enacted, the Insolvency Act listed six types of preference claim, but the number has now been reduced to three.[463] In the event of a bankruptcy or winding-up, preferential claims rank equally and therefore abate equally if there are insufficient assets to satisfy them all.[464] Since they are a closed list, there is no judicial discretion to create others, for example, by authorizing payments made to selected creditors under section 127.[465]

19.107 The three remaining preferential claims[466] are for all unpaid contributions to contributory pension schemes, remuneration up to £800 in amount[467] owed to employees in respect of the preceding four months, and ECSC coal and steel levies.[468] The time provisions are based on the 'relevant date', which is defined by reference to the particular circumstances of company and individual voluntary arrangements, voluntary and compulsory winding-up, winding-up preceded by an administration order and bankruptcy.[469] For example, the date for a voluntary winding-up is the passing of the resolution, for compulsory winding-up the date of the winding-up order or (where relevant) of the appointment of a provisional liquidator, and for bankruptcy the date of the order or (where relevant) of the appointment of an interim receiver.

19.108 A particular difficulty has arisen in defining preferential claims when a company is wound up after an administration. In the case of a compulsory winding-up, the claims are dated from the making of the administration order, while in the case of a voluntary winding-up the date is that of the winding-up resolution. Preferential claims will often be greater at the date of the order than at the date of the resolution, in which case preferential creditors will be reluctant to accede to a voluntary winding-up after administration, though this may be a less expensive and speedier option than compulsory winding-up and therefore beneficial to creditors as a whole. It is therefore sensible to proceed to a voluntary winding-up while safeguarding the interests of preferential creditors as at the date of the

---

[462] Cmnd 8558 (1982), ch 32.
[463] Enterprise Act 2002, s 251 (amending as necessary the Insolvency Act).
[464] Sections 175(2)(a) and 328(2).
[465] *Re Rafidain Bank (No 1)* [1992] BCLC 301.
[466] The three preferential claims abolished by the Enterprise Act 2002 were claims for PAYE tax deducted in the preceding twelve months, VAT and certain other taxes referable to the preceding six months, and social security contributions due in the preceding six months.
[467] Insolvency Proceedings (Monetary Limits) Order 1986, SI 1986/1996.
[468] Schedule 6.
[469] Section 387.

administration order. In one case,[470] regrettably, Lightman J was of the view that it was not possible, upon the administrator's application,[471] for the liquidator in the consequent voluntary winding-up to be directed to pay preferential creditors as at the date of the administration order instead of in accordance with the statutory scheme. Furthermore, a direction to the administrator to pay those preferential creditors could not be given[472] since it was not consonant with the purpose of the administration order in the present case, which was to secure the more advantageous realization, as opposed to distribution, of the company's assets. More recently, however, it has been held that the court may exercise its inherent jurisdiction over administrators to authorize them to make payments,[473] which appears to solve the problem.

(iii) Priority agreements

Preferential creditors are advanced not only in the event of bankruptcy or winding-up. Where a company is not in the course of being wound up, section 40 requires receivers,[474] out of the assets coming into their hands, to pay preferential creditors before payments are made to debenture holders[475] whose debentures are secured by a charge that as created was a floating charge.[476] The 'relevant date'[477] is the date of the appointment of the receiver.[478] So far as possible, the receiver should pay the preferential creditors out of assets available for the payment of general creditors.[479] The receiver is not bound to pay preferential creditors ahead of debenture holders with a floating charge where and to the extent that those debenture holders have a fixed charge over assets of the company.[480]

19.109

The interposition of preferential creditors between fixed and floating chargees has created a difficulty arising out of priority agreements where the fixed chargee surrenders priority to the floating chargee. For reasons stated, the fixed chargee ranks ahead of the preferential creditor who ranks ahead of the floating chargee who now, as a result of the priority agreement, ranks ahead of the fixed chargee, closing

19.110

---

[470] See *Re Powerstore (Trading) Ltd* [1997] 1 WLR 1280.

[471] Pursuant to s 18(3).

[472] Under s 14(3).

[473] *Re Mark One (Oxford Street) plc* [1999] 1 WLR 1445. See also *Re UCT (UK) Ltd* [2001] 1 WLR 436.

[474] And not merely administrative receivers. The position is the same for administrators: Insolvency Act (as amended), para 65(2).

[475] Who need not be the debenture holders at whose behest the receiver was appointed: *Re H & K Medway Ltd* [1997] 1 WLR 1422 (cf *Griffiths v Yorkshire Bank plc* [1994] 1 WLR 1427).

[476] See *Re Pearl Maintenance Services Ltd* [1995] 1 BCLC 449.

[477] For the purpose of identifying preferential debts.

[478] Section 387(4)(a).

[479] Section 40(3). Conceivably, a receiver enforcing a narrowly based floating charge might not have unencumbered assets coming into his hands.

[480] *Re Lewis Merthyr Consolidated Collieries Ltd* [1929] 1 Ch 498, CA.

the circle. Problems of circular priority need to be solved by breaking the circle at some point in a principled way. Since the rights of preferential creditors amount to a statutory expropriation of secured creditors, then the legislation should not be given an expansive interpretation. At first sight, the natural order of distribution is to rank the floating chargee first, by way of subrogation and to the extent of the fixed chargee's rights, followed by the preferential creditors, then by the floating chargee for the balance (if any) of its secured claim, and finally by the fixed chargee.[481]

19.111 Nevertheless, as sensible as the above approach is, it was not adopted in one case[482] where the priority agreement was construed as making the agreement creating the fixed charge subject to the agreement creating the floating charge. Since the legislation stated that the preferential creditors 'shall be paid' ahead of the floating chargee, this meant that the preferential creditors finished on top, thus receiving an undeserved windfall benefit as an accidental by-product of a priority agreement between parties who intended no such effect. If, instead of subsuming the fixed charge agreement under the floating charge agreement, there had been an assignment to the floating chargee of the fixed chargee's right to payment, the priority agreement would have been successful. The extraordinary promotion of preferential creditors can thus be avoided by competent drafting.

(iv) The special fund for unsecured creditors

19.112 The disadvantageous position of unsecured creditors in insolvency has attracted adverse judicial comment[483] and was responsible for the creation of preferential claims in the first place. A new section 176A of the Insolvency Act was added by the Enterprise Act 2002,[484] at the time when the ranks of preferential creditors were being reduced, to improve the position of unsecured creditors. Under section 176A, a prescribed part of the company's 'net property' is set aside to be applied by liquidators, administrators and receivers to unsecured claims. Net property includes assets the subject of a floating charge. The prescribed part of the company's property constituting the fund is not linked to the loss of the Crown's status as preferential creditor. Instead, given a minimum net property value of £10,000, 50 per cent of the first £50,000 is set aside for unsecured creditors, followed by 20 per cent of the remainder of the net property. The total amount constituting the fund, however, is capped at £600,000.[485]

---

[481] This was the uncontested order of distribution in *Re Woodroffes (Musical Instruments) Ltd* [1986] Ch 366.

[482] *Re Portbase Clothing Ltd* [1993] Ch 388.

[483] *Saloman v A Saloman & Co Ltd* [1897] AC 22, 53, HL (Lord Macnaghten); *Borden v Scottish Timber Products Ltd* [1981] Ch 25, 42 (Templeman LJ).

[484] Section 252.

[485] The Insolvency Act 1986 (Prescribed Part) Order 2003, SI 2003/2097.

(v) Final claimants

Last in the distribution list come unsecured creditors who have put in a proof of debt,[486] so far as they have not been paid in full out of the special fund, followed by members,[487] in the case of winding-up, and spouses,[488] in the case of bankruptcy. Furthermore, members may be liable as contributories[489] to contribute to the assets of the company in a winding-up,[490] for example, where their shares are not fully paid up. **19.113**

(d) Set-off (insolvency and receivership)

(i) General

An unsecured creditor who is also indebted to the insolvent is in a better position than an unsecured creditor who is not. The former may take advantage of set-off rights which, if the claim of the insolvent matches the claim of the creditor, permits the creditor to recover in full instead of receiving only the very limited dividend that would otherwise be paid. Set-off in fact operates as a form of security,[491] though it will often arise as a windfall benefit if insolvency supervenes at a time when the creditor happens to owe money to the insolvent. Indeed, it is more effective in that it can be exercised passively by the creditor and does not require any particular formalities or notice. **19.114**

Insolvency set-off[492] exists to work justice between creditor and insolvent. Unlike legal (or statutory) set-off, it is not a matter of accounting between two liquidated claims or debts in the cause of avoiding circuity of actions. Unlike equitable set-off, which is not confined to liquidated claims or debts, it is not a matter of one party's 'legal' title to a claim being undermined by the persuasive equity of the other party's closely connected cross-claim. Insolvency set-off applies to all claims and cross-claims, whether they are connected or not and whether they are liquidated or not. There are however certain limitations on the availability of insolvency set-off of which account has to be taken. **19.115**

Insolvency set-off is provided for in section 323 for bankruptcy and rule 4.90 for winding-up. Section 323 re-enacts, with only slight changes, section 31 of the Bankruptcy Act 1914. In the case of companies, set-off was first applied in **19.116**

---

[486] A debt can also include any liability, including liability in tort: Insolvency Rules (as amended by SI 2006/1272), r 13.12.

[487] Section 107.

[488] Section 329.

[489] Section 79.

[490] Section 74.

[491] *Stein v Blake* [1996] AC 243, 251, HL, *per* Lord Hoffmann.

[492] See generally R Derham, *Set-Off* (3rd edn, 2003); R Goode, *Principles of Corporate Insolvency Law* (3rd edn, 2005) ch 8.

winding-up as a result of the Judicature Act 1873,[493] the language of the bankruptcy section being extended by analogy to companies before language apt for companies was created in rule 4.90,[494] which is *mutatis mutandis* identical to section 323. Nevertheless, rule 4.90 is expressed so that it applies in solvent and insolvent windings-up alike; section 323 is obviously confined to bankruptcy.

(ii) Scope of set-off

19.117 According to rule 4.90, an account has to be taken of what is due from creditor to company and company to creditor where, before the company goes into liquidation, there have been 'mutual credits, mutual debts or other mutual dealings'. This results in the extinguishment of the two claims in favour of one net claim so that neither of the previous claims may thereafter be assigned.[495] A balance due to the company has to be paid to the liquidator; a balance in favour of the creditor is the subject of a proof. The cut-off date for amounts due from the company is the date when the creditor had notice that a meeting of creditors had been called or that a winding-up petition was pending, as the case may be.[496] Otherwise, an incentive would arise for debtors of the insolvent company to purchase claims against the company, which is impermissible.[497]

19.118 Mutuality is present even though the two claims are completely unrelated to each other.[498] Moreover, one claim may be a debt and the other for unliquidated damages.[499] At one time it was thought that a claim in tort could not be the subject of set-off in insolvency.[500] Subsequent case law justified this approach on the ground that a tort claim was not provable under the Bankruptcy Act 1914.[501] Since, under section 322, a tort claim is now provable, it follows that it may be the subject of a set-off, like any other provable claim consisting of a pecuniary demand.[502]

19.119 For the mutuality requirement to be met, the two claims must be commensurable. So, where money has been paid by the insolvent for a purpose that can no longer

---

[493] Section 10.

[494] Modified in significant respects by the Insolvency (Amendment) Rules 2005 (SI 2005/527), reg 23.

[495] *Stein v Blake* [1996] AC 243, HL.

[496] Rule 4.90(2), which as amended also cuts off claims arising during administration and claims acquired by assignment after the cut-off date. See *Re Eros Films Ltd* [1963] Ch 565; *Re Gray's Inn Construction Co Ltd* [1980] 1 WLR 711, CA.

[497] *Re Charge Card Services Ltd* [1987] Ch 150.

[498] *Re Daintrey* [1900] 1 QB 546, CA.

[499] *Mersey Steel and Iron Co v Naylor Benzon & Co* (1884) 9 App Cas 434, HL.

[500] *Re Mid-Kent Fruit Factory* [1896] 1 Ch 567; cf *Tilley v Bowman* [1910] 1 KB 745.

[501] *Re DH Curtis (Builders) Ltd* [1978] Ch 162.

[502] *Re Bank of Credit and Commerce International SA (No 8)* [1998] AC 214, HL; *Eberle's Hotels and Restaurant Co Ltd v Jonas (E) & Bros* (1887) 18 QBD 459, CA.

be accomplished, the insolvent's representative may recover the money without giving credit for a claim against the insolvent[503] since the dedication of money to a purpose takes it 'out of the course of accounts between the parties to be held. . .in suspense between them'.[504] Moneys held on the terms of a *Quistclose* trust will thus fall outside the bounds of commensurability. Indeed, since money is always paid for one purpose or other, it would be preferable to confine special purposes cases to the existence of such a trust or, at least, to cases where it would be a 'misappropriation' of the money to use it other than for the purpose for which it was paid.[505] Similarly, a claim asserted by one party as trustee for a third party is not commensurable with a cross-claim against the former party in his personal capacity.[506] A further restriction on set-off arises in respect of a contributory's claim against an insolvent limited liability company. As a contributor to the insolvency fund,[507] the contributory may not set off any claim he has against the company against his indebtedness as a contributory[508] unless the creditors of the company have been paid in full.[509] In limited circumstances, commensurability will be satisfied where one of the claims is not money-based but is for the return of goods that were subject to a direction to the recipient that they be sold.[510]

The case of bank insolvency has sharply pointed the features of mutuality where **19.120** directors of a corporate borrower have given security over personal deposits with the bank for moneys advanced by the bank to the company. The question is whether the bank may enforce payment by the company despite its indebtedness to the director. If the bank's indebtedness to the director were to be taken into account, the director would benefit in his personal capacity as shareholder of the company. On the face of it, there is no mutuality present for set-off since director and company are separate personalities and '[i]t is not the function of insolvency set-off to confer a benefit on a debtor of the insolvent who has not been a party to the mutual dealing',[511] the debtor in this case being the company and the dealing that between bank and director.

---

[503] *Re Pollitt* [1893] 1 QB 455, CA; *Re City Equitable Fire Insurance Co Ltd* [1930] 2 Ch 293, CA.

[504] *Re City Equitable Fire Insurance Co Ltd* [1930] 2 Ch 293, 312, CA.

[505] *National Westminster Bank Ltd v Halesowen Presswork and Assemblies Ltd* [1972] AC 785, 808, HL, *per* Lord Simon.

[506] *Re ILG Travel Ltd* [1995] 2 BCLC 128.

[507] See *Cherry v Boultbee* (1839) 4 My & Cr 442, 41 ER 171.

[508] *Re Overend Gurney* (1866) 1 Ch App 528.

[509] Section 149(3).

[510] *Rolls Razor Ltd v Cox* [1967] 1 QB 552, CA (confined to goods held by a salesman for sale as opposed to demonstration purposes).

[511] *Re Bank of Credit and Commerce International SA (No 8)* [1996] Ch 245, 257, CA, *per* Rose LJ.

(iii) Security and set-off

19.121 Nevertheless, the answer to this question turns upon whether the director has incurred personal liability on the loan by the bank to the company. Where the director undertakes liability to the bank as 'principal debtor', set-off will take effect automatically as between the director's claim against the bank and the bank's claim against the director.[512] Consequently, to the extent of the satisfaction of the debt to the bank arising out of the set-off, the bank's claim against the company is abated. If, however, the director charges his rights against the bank in favour of the bank[513] as security for the loan to the company, without undertaking a personal liability to the bank, there can be no set-off since there are no 'mutual credits, mutual debts or other mutual dealings' between the director and the bank.[514] Although insolvency set-off may not be excluded by agreement,[515] the parties are not prevented from defining their relationship in such a way as to place the director at financial risk without incurring personal liability. The intermediate case is that of the director who undertakes as surety secondary liability on the loan in such a way as not to become liable until a demand is made on him by the bank.[516] Set-off can be effected in respect of the bank's contingent claim against the director[517] but this holds little comfort for the director. The reason is that a solvent corporate borrower will be able to pay in full and the bank's liquidator will not call upon the director in such a case, or indeed in any case where the amount unrecovered from the company is less than the amount deposited by the director with the bank.

19.122 Another difficult aspect of set-off is provided by secured credit. The insolvency set-off rule applies in the case of 'any creditor. . .proving or claiming to prove for a debt' in the winding-up or bankruptcy.[518] A secured creditor not proving in the winding-up[519] should therefore be able to enforce the security unabated by the insolvent's cross-claim.[520] If, however, the secured claim is that of the insolvent and not of the creditor, or if a secured creditor proves in the insolvency, then the existence of security is no impediment to set-off.[521]

---

[512] *MS Fashions Ltd v Bank of Credit and Commerce International Ltd (No 2)* [1993] Ch 425, CA.

[513] It is now settled that a bank may take a charge over its own indebtedness to an account holder: *Re Bank of Credit and Commerce International SA (No 8)* [1998] AC 214, HL.

[514] *Re Bank of Credit and Commerce International SA (No 8)* [1998] AC 214, HL.

[515] See para 19.125.

[516] *Bradford Old Bank Ltd v Sutcliffe* [1918] 2 KB 833, CA.

[517] See *MS Fashions Ltd v Bank of Credit and Commerce International Ltd (No 2)* [1993] Ch 425, CA.

[518] Section 323(1); r 4.90(1).

[519] A secured creditor can petition for bankruptcy only if he waives the security or confines his petition to unsecured debt: see s 269. No similar provision exists for corporate insolvency.

[520] *Re Norman Holding Co Ltd* [1991] 1 WLR 10.

[521] *Ex p Barnett* (1874) 9 Ch App 293; *Hiley v People's Prudential Assurance Co Ltd* (1938) 60 Commonwealth LR 468, 498, Australian High Ct; *MS Fashions Ltd v Bank of Credit and Commerce International Ltd (No 2)* [1993] Ch 425, 446, CA; *Re ILG Travel Ltd* [1995] 2 BCC 128.

(iv) Contingent claims and set-off

Difficulties in applying set-off have arisen in the case of contingent claims. If **19.123** the contingent claim is that of the creditor, then it is usually a relatively simple matter of the insolvency officer putting a value on the claim in the same way that this is done in the case of any contingent claim outside set-off.[522] This position has now been explicitly confirmed by the Insolvency Rules.[523] Sometimes, however, the contingency affects not merely the quantum of a claim against the insolvent but the very possibility that a claim against the company will eventuate,[524] which before the change to the rules posed a problem in that the set-off rules refer to amounts that are 'due' between the parties. Where the contingent claim was that of a surety against the principal debtor, set-off had in the past been refused when no claim has yet been made against the surety by the creditor.[525] Later case law established, however, that set-off applied in the case of claims that were contingent and not merely claims whose exact quantum was determined by a contingent event. Hence, set-off was been permitted so that a factor might set off its contingent claim against the insolvent assignor to buy back receivables, if called upon to do so, against its indebtedness to that assignor under a retention fund.[526] The reference in the Insolvency Rules to the 'claim' being contingent confirms this later case law.

Where the contingent claim is that of the insolvent against the creditor, until recently **19.124** the position was as follows. No statutory machinery existed to effect a quantification of the claim since it 'would be unfair upon [the creditor] to have his liability to pay advanced merely because the trustee wants to wind up the bankrupt's estate'.[527] Nevertheless, quantification could sometimes be made with the benefit of hindsight in the light of events occurring after the making of the bankruptcy or winding-up order,[528] which is the date when the accounts have to be settled.[529] In other cases, where a company was finally wound up before the contingency

---

[522] Section 322(3); r 4.86(1). This is now explicitly permitted by r 4.90(4) (which has no bankruptcy counterpart). See *Re Asphaltic Wood Pavement Co* (1885) 30 Ch D 216, CA; *Baker v Lloyds Bank Ltd* [1920] 2 KB 322.

[523] Rule 4.90(4), (5) (as amended).

[524] See *Carreras Rothmans Ltd v Freeman Mathews Treasure Ltd* [1985] 1 Ch 207.

[525] *Re a Debtor (No 66 of 1955)* [1956] 1 WLR 1226, CA. See also *Re Fenton* [1931] 1 Ch 85, CA, *per* Lord Hanworth MR.

[526] *Re Charge Card Services Ltd* [1987] Ch 150. See also *Stein v Blake* [1996] AC 243, 252–3, HL.

[527] *Stein v Blake* [1996] AC 243, 253, HL.

[528] *Sovereign Life Assurance Co v Dodd* [1892] 2 QB 573, HL; *MS Fashions Ltd v Bank of Credit and Commerce International Ltd (No 2)* [1993] Ch 425, 432ff, CA, *per* Hoffmann LJ.

[529] *Re Daintrey* [1900] 1 QB 546, CA; *Re Charge Card Services Ltd* [1987] Ch 150, 177; *Re Dynamics Corp of America* [1976] 1 WLR 757, 762; *Stein v Blake* [1996] AC 243, HL. It will be the date of the resolution in the case of a voluntary liquidation: *Barclays Bank Ltd v TOSG Trust Fund Ltd* [1984] BCLC 1, 25, CA.

was ascertained, proceedings might be brought to restore the company to the register[530] for the purpose of bringing proceedings against the creditor. If this were to happen, the creditor would be entitled to set off his full claim, minus the dividend received, against the company's claim.[531] There would be little incentive to take this action if the dividend were only a modest one. In the case of companies, since 2005 the company's contingent claim against the creditor may be set off against the creditor's claim and that contingent claim can be quantified by the liquidator in the same way as the liquidator quantifies contingent claims against the company.[532] If subsequent events demonstrate that the claim against the creditor was overvalued, the creditor would have no recourse if the estate of the company had been distributed.

(v) Set-off mandatory

19.125 The final aspect of insolvency set-off concerns its mandatory character. It may not be excluded between the parties.[533] One reason is that the legislation requires that an account 'shall' be taken and the sums due 'shall' be set off against each other.[534] If the only reason for the legislation was to confer a benefit on the creditor of the insolvent, the legislation could be read as subject to contrary agreement on the ground that those for whose exclusive benefit a protective provision is introduced are entitled to surrender the benefit of that protection.[535] Nevertheless, the rule against contracting out of insolvency set-off, which does not apply to other types of set-off, has been justified on the somewhat unpersuasive ground that the set-off rules were introduced so that insolvents' estates 'are to be administered in a proper and orderly way' which 'is a matter in which the commercial community generally has an interest. . .'.[536] This has in the past been thought to pose problems for subordination agreements.[537]

(vi) Receivership and administration

19.126 Insolvency set-off is confined to the distribution of estates. It does not apply to receivership and has only recently been extended to administrators exercising their distribution powers.[538] For receivership, legal and equitable set-off have a

---

[530] Discussed at para 19.13.

[531] *MS Fashions Ltd v Bank of Credit and Commerce International Ltd (No 2)* [1993] Ch 425, 435, CA, *per* Hoffmann LJ.

[532] Rules 4.86(1), 4.90(4), (5).

[533] *National Westminster Bank Ltd v Halesowen Presswork and Assemblies Ltd* [1972] AC 785, HL.

[534] Section 323(2); r 4.90(2). The language of 'may' in the Bankruptcy Act 1849, s 171, became 'shall' in the Bankruptcy Act 1869, s 39.

[535] *National Westminster Bank Ltd v Halesowen Presswork and Assemblies Ltd* [1972] AC 785, HL.

[536] ibid 809 (Lord Simon). See also the analysis of this decision in *Re Maxwell Communications Corp* [1993] 1 WLR 1402.

[537] Discussed at paras 16.128–19.131.

[538] Insolvency Rules, r 2.85 (as added by SI 2003/1730 and amended by SI 2005/527).

part to play. In the case of receivership, particular problems have arisen in connection with the assignment of a borrower's assets in favour of the secured lender that takes place when a floating charge crystallizes. Like any other assignment, this takes effect subject to existing equities and defences at the time of notice of the assignment.[539] Consequently, those indebted to the borrower may not, upon receipt of notice of the appointment of a receiver, which is tantamount to notice of the assignment, acquire set-off rights by purchasing debts owed by the borrower to third parties.[540] This corresponds to the rule that notice of a winding-up or a bankruptcy petition is the cut-off date for the acquisition of new set-off rights against the insolvent.[541]

In the case of legal set-off, the claim in question must have accrued due, though it need not be payable, at the time when the cross-claim is assigned if it is to be set off against a demand for payment by the assignee.[542] Consequently, in one case[543] where A owed money to B for television sets the subject of a sale contract, and B in turn owed money to A for computer equipment supplied by A on hire-purchase terms, A could set off hire-purchase instalments that had fallen due at the time when A was notified of the appointment of a receiver of B. A could not, however, set off amounts subsequently due after accelerating future instalments, since A invoked its rights of acceleration only after notice of the assignment. Nor could A have fallen back on equitable set-off, the reason being that the sale and hire-purchase contracts were unrelated so that there was no sufficient connection between the amounts owed under both contracts for B's receiver to have to give credit to A for all sums owed under the hire-purchase contract. **19.127**

(e) Subordination agreements

The position of preferential creditors in the event of a priority agreement between a fixed chargee and a floating chargee was discussed above. The issue now is a different one and concerns an agreement or agreements by which one unsecured creditor subordinates itself to another in the event of the debtor's insolvency. Subordination arrangements of various kinds are valid, despite their apparent disturbance of the *pari passu* rule of distribution. Furthermore, they are not treated as running counter to the state's interest in the orderly distribution of insolvents' estates. **19.128**

---

539 Section 136 of the Law of Property Act 1925.

540 *Robbie (NW) & Co Ltd v Witney Warehouse Co Ltd* [1963] 1 WLR 1324, CA (trading in debts between associated companies).

541 Discussed at para 19.117.

542 *Watson v Mid-Wales Railway Co* (1867) LR 2 CP 593; *Re Pinto Leite and Nephews* [1929] 1 Ch 221.

543 *Business Computers Ltd v Anglo-African Leasing Ltd* [1977] 1 WLR 578.

19.129 Subordination agreements may take various forms. First of all, a creditor may under a turnover trust declare itself trustee, for the benefit of one or more named creditors, of any dividend distributed by the liquidator. The practical effect of this is to give the latter an added dividend but, since the trust attaches to money in the hands of the creditor after the estate has been distributed in the way sanctioned by the Insolvency Act, there is no reason to strike down this transaction any more than any other trust.[544] Turnover trusts have been stated not to be registrable charges granted by the subordinated creditor,[545] which sensibly diminishes insolvency risk associated with that creditor. A possibility similar to the turnover trust is the assignment by the subordinated creditor of the benefit of a future dividend.[546]

19.130 A different technique is contractual subordination which exists where, under the terms of the loan, creditor and debtor agree[547] that, in the event of the debtor's insolvency, the creditor will not receive a dividend until a favoured creditor or creditors have been paid in full. The debt owed to the subordinated creditor is therefore a type of flawed asset. In this case, a further distinction might be drawn between the simple surrender of a dividend, the effect of which would be to prefer *all* other creditors of the debtor, and the surrender of a dividend in favour of one or a limited number of other creditors. As regards the former, there is no reason in law why a creditor might not waive a debt owed by an insolvent or decline to submit a proof. On this reasoning, an agreement of this kind is lawful and does not infringe the *pari passu* rule. That rule prevents a creditor from bargaining for an advantage on the distribution of an insolvent's assets, which is not the case with a subordination agreement of this kind.[548] To strike down such a contractual subordination could have a prejudicial effect on the continued existence of companies that carry on with an infusion of funds from parent and associate companies that are prepared to accept subordination.[549]

19.131 A more questionable type of contractual subordination occurs where the subordination is expressed to benefit fewer than all of the remaining creditors. The favoured creditors themselves may not have contracted for the extra dividend, in the sense that they may not be parties to the subordination contract, but an

---

[544] *Re NIAA Corp Ltd* (1994) 12 Australian Corporations and Securities Reports 141, New South Wales.

[545] *Re SSSL Realisations (2002) Ltd* [2006] EWCA Civ 7; [2006] Ch 610.

[546] *Re Maxwell Communications Corp* [1993] 1 WLR 1402, 1416.

[547] The possibility of enforceable rights under this agreement on the part of the favoured creditor now arises in light of the Contract (Rights of Third Parties) Act 1999.

[548] *Re Maxwell Communications Corp* [1993] 1 WLR 1402. See also *Re British and Commonwealth Holding plc (No 3)* [1992] 1 WLR 672, where the subordinated holders of loan stock had no right to vote on a proposal for a scheme of arrangement at a meeting of unsecured creditors when the company's assets would be consumed in full by the claims of the favoured creditors.

[549] *Re Maxwell Communications Corp* [1993] 1 WLR 1402, 1416.

apparent stumbling block is the payment of differential dividends by a liquidator.[550] On the other hand, it is arguable that, if turnover trusts and assignments of the benefit of a dividend are permissible, then to strike down a subordination contract that produces the same effect would amount to the triumph of form over substance.[551] Apart from the subordinated creditor, no other creditor is any worse off as a result of the agreement.[552] This amounts to a forceful case in favour of this type of subordination contract,[553] yet there are plentiful examples of the triumph of form over substance in the pages of the law reports.

C. Powers and Liabilities of Insolvency Officers, Administrators and Administrative Receivers

(1) Dealing with the Estate

(a) Business, assets and creditors

(i) Powers of the liquidator

Schedule 4 to the Insolvency Act 1986 contains in Part I those powers of the liquidator that may be exercised with sanction, which will be the sanction of an extraordinary resolution for a members' voluntary winding-up and of the court or a liquidation committee for a creditors' voluntary winding-up. The remaining powers in Parts II and III of the Schedule may be exercised without sanction in a voluntary winding-up.[554] For a compulsory winding-up, the liquidator needs the sanction of the court or liquidation committee to exercise the powers in Parts I and II but needs no sanction to exercise the powers in Part III.[555] In the case of a creditors' voluntary winding-up, where the creditors have not yet met,[556] the sanction of the court is needed in all cases before the liquidator's powers may be exercised. This control is in place to counter the evil of 'centrebinding',[557] which consists of the members of a company appointing their own complaisant liquidator who acts to the disadvantage of creditors by stripping the company of its remaining assets before a deferred creditors' meeting is called.[558] There are other

19.132

---

[550] But see *Horne v Chester and Fine Property Developments Pty Ltd* [1987] VR 913.

[551] *Re Maxwell Communications Corp* [1993] 1 WLR 1402, 1416; *Re NIAA Corp Ltd* (1994) 12 ACSR 141, 156.

[552] *Re NIAA Corp Ltd* (1994) 12 ACSR 141.

[553] *Horne v Chester and Fine Property Developments Pty Ltd* [1987] VR 913.

[554] Section 165.

[555] Section 167.

[556] For the company's duty to call a meeting, see s 98.

[557] The name comes from *Re Centrebind Ltd* [1967] 1 WLR 377.

[558] At least as effective a control is the requirement that liquidators and other insolvency professionals be accredited insolvency practitioners: ss 388ff.

powers contained in the main body of the Act, relating to the settling of the list of contributories,[559] the making of calls,[560] the payment of debts[561] and the calling of meetings.[562] The liquidator may apply to the court for directions concerning matters arising in the course of the winding-up.[563] The court also exercises a continuing supervisory jurisdiction over his actions.[564]

19.133   The powers contained in Part I apply to actions concerning the assets of the company and the paying and composition of the company's debts. Part II deals with bringing or defending legal proceedings in the name of the company and carrying on the business of the company so far as necessary for its beneficial winding-up. Part III includes selling the company's property, putting in a proof in the name of the company in someone else's bankruptcy or winding-up, executing documents, becoming party to bills of exchange in the name of the company, granting security over the assets of the company, authorizing another agent to act on behalf of the company and doing anything else that is necessary for winding up the company and distributing its assets.

(ii) Powers of the trustee-in-bankruptcy

19.134   A similar structure of powers applies in the case of bankruptcy. There is a division between powers that may be exercised without sanction and powers that may be exercised with the sanction of the court or the creditors' committee.[565] Provided the court or the creditors' committee agrees, the trustee may employ the bankrupt to carry on his business or otherwise assist the trustee.[566] The trustee also has power to summon a general meeting of creditors.[567]

(iii) Powers of the administrator and the administrative receiver

19.135   The powers of an administrator and of an administrative receiver are both expansive and more or less identical,[568] except for the moratorium on enforcing rights and taking action.[569] The powers of an administrative receiver may be increased by agreement, which however is unlikely to exceed the administrator's power to do 'anything necessary and expedient for the management of the affairs, business

---

559   Section 165(4)(a) (voluntary winding-up).
560   Section 165(4)(b) (voluntary winding-up).
561   A duty: s 165(5) (voluntary winding-up).
562   Sections 165(4)(c) and 168(2).
563   Sections 112 and 168(3).
564   Sections 112 and 167(3).
565   Section 314. The powers are contained in Sch 5.
566   Section 314(2).
567   Section 314(7).
568   Schedule 1; s 42 and Sch B1, paras 59–60. The powers of a contractually-appointed receiver are purely a matter of contract.
569   Discussed at paras 19.87–19.91.

and property of the company'.[570] As befits the condition of the company, the powers in Schedule 1 go beyond conventional management. The prospect of insolvent liquidation bulks large, even though administrative receivers do not as such distribute assets[571] and perform the other functions of a liquidator. Administrators may, for example, present a petition for the winding-up of the company.[572] Both administrator and administrative receiver present proposals or report to a meeting of the company's creditors.[573] This meeting may establish a creditors' committee.[574] Administrators and administrative receivers[575] may apply to the court for directions.[576]

(b) Rights of those dealing with the insolvent

In managing the affairs of the insolvent, insolvency officers, administrators and administrative and other contractual receivers act as agents of the insolvent. The position at common law is that agents do not in normal circumstances incur personal liability on contracts they negotiate on behalf of their principal, providing that the principal is disclosed. Consequently, the co-contractants of an insolvent company or individual cannot assume that they can look to the financial integrity of an insolvency officer as an earnest of due performance by the insolvent. Their rights depend upon the particular insolvency regime in operation.

19.136

(i) Winding-up and bankruptcy

In the case of a winding-up, co-contractants are protected largely by the priority standing of their claims to be paid as expenses of the liquidation ranking ahead of preferential claims.[577] Sums owed to persons doing business with the company, and to landlords for rent arising out of the company's continuing occupation of premises,[578] are recoverable expenses even if the liquidator refuses to pay them. Moreover, as far as they are 'necessary disbursements' they rank ahead of the liquidator's own claim for remuneration.[579] It is no doubt open to co-contractants to require the liquidator to undertake personal liability on contracts concluded with the company in liquidation. Indeed the Insolvency Act expressly contemplates that utility suppliers of water, electricity, gas and telecommunications will require

19.137

---

[570] Schedule B1, para 59(1).
[571] The administrator may now distribute: Insolvency Act (as amended), Sch B1, para 65(1), (3).
[572] Sch 1 para 21.
[573] Section 48 and Sch B1, paras 49–54. But an administrator may make disposals in advance of the meeting: *Re Transbus International Ltd* [2004] EWHC 932 (Ch); [2004] 1 WLR 2654.
[574] Section 49 and Sch B1, para 57.
[575] In their general character as receivers or managers of the company's property.
[576] Section 35 and Sch B1, para 63.
[577] Section 175(2)(a).
[578] *Re ABC Coupler and Engineering Co Ltd (No 3)* [1970] 1 WLR 702.
[579] Rule 4.218(1)(m), (o); *Re Linda Marie Ltd* [1989] BCLC 46.

this of liquidators in the case of continuing supplies, though it prohibits demands for payment for past supplies as the condition for continuing to supply.[580]

19.138 The position in bankruptcy is very similar to that in winding-up. Section 324(1) requires the trustee when distributing dividends to retain such sums as are necessary for the expenses of the bankruptcy, and the priority order ranks 'necessary disbursements' ahead of the trustee's own claim for remuneration.[581]

(ii) Receivership: general

19.139 The standing of co-contractants during administration or administrative receivership is rather different. Taking first receivership, court-appointed receivers, who are not agents of the company, have always been personally responsible on contracts they conclude,[582] even if they make their status clear in documents addressed to the other contracting party. They are expected to look to the assets of the company for indemnification, though they may stipulate special terms excluding that liability with the other contracting party. Initially, the position was quite different with contractual receivers. Starting with legislation dating back fifty years,[583] those receivers are now personally liable on all contracts entered into by them in the performance of their functions, as well as on contracts of employment that they have adopted, in return for which they are indemnified from the assets of the company.[584] The indemnity has the practical effect of a security. The personal liability of administrators is organized on the same basis,[585] so that it is convenient to take them and contractual receivers together.

(iii) Receivers and contracts of employment

19.140 Besides liability for contracts concluded personally by the receiver,[586] the receiver is also liable for those contracts of employment that he 'adopts'. Case law developments in the 1990s were considered to pose such a grave threat to the rescue culture that emergency legislation had to be passed to alleviate the position of those receivers who were administrative receivers.

---

[580] Section 233 (s 372 for bankruptcy). The position under the section is the same for administrators, administrative receivers, provisional liquidators and the supervisors of voluntary arrangements.

[581] Rule 6.224(1)(m),(o).

[582] *Burt Boulton & Hayward v Bull* [1895] 1 QB 76, CA.

[583] For the development of the law, see Lord Browne-Wilkinson in *Powdrill v Watson* [1995] 2 AC 394, HL.

[584] Sections 37(1), (2) (receivers) and 44(1)(b) (administrative receivers).

[585] Schedule B1, para 99(4)–(6).

[586] The receiver is free to exclude liability as a matter of contract: ss 37(1)(a), 44(1)(b); *Re Ferranti International plc* [1994] BCC 658 (otherwise varied on appeal *sub nom Powdrill v Watson* [1995] 2 AC 394, HL).

The starting point is that the receiver has a period of grace: the adoption of a con- **19.141**
tract of employment does not occur because of anything done or omitted within
fourteen days of the receiver's appointment.[587] Overturning earlier authority
that a statement to employees that their contracts were not being adopted would
protect the receiver,[588] the House of Lords in *Powdrill v Watson* held that receivers
and administrators may by their actions adopt contracts of employment even
if they say that they are doing no such thing.[589]

Consequently, those employees kept on by receivers and administrators did **19.142**
better than those dismissed who had the rights only of preferential creditors.[590]
Nevertheless, *Powdrill v Watson* is authority that receivers should be bound only
in respect of liabilities 'incurred' during the receivership. This word, formerly
present in the case of administrators,[591] was read into the section dealing with
administrative receivers.[592] On the facts, the significance of 'incurred' was that it
protected administrator and administrative receiver from liability for employment
benefits accruing for periods of service before their appointment. The House of
Lords had thus gone some way to easing the particular predicament of administrative receivers who, unlike administrators,[593] are not discharged from liability
once their work is done.[594] As regards salary and pension benefits, however, administrative receivers still remained highly vulnerable since employees whose contracts were adopted carried forward from earlier service their entitlement to notice,
which could be very lengthy indeed in the case of a senior employee with many
years' service.

Before *Powdrill v Watson* was decided in the House of Lords, hastily enacted legis- **19.143**
lation[595] went further by limiting the employment liability of administrative
receivers to wages and pension contributions incurred during the period in which
they held office and in return for services rendered wholly or partly after the adoption of the contract of employment in question. The legislation was not made
retrospective and, for unexplained reasons, does not extend to contractually
appointed receivers.[596]

---

587 Sections 37(2) and 44(2).
588 *Re Specialised Mouldings* (High Ct, 1987).
589 [1995] 2 AC 394, HL.
590 The extent of whose claims are set out in ss 386–7 and Sch 6.
591 Section 19(4) (now repealed and replaced by Sch B1, para 99(3)).
592 The pre-1994 text of s 44.
593 Schedule B1, para 98(1).
594 Changes in the law occurring after they had accounting for all dealings with the assets of
the company posed a particular risk for them.
595 Insolvency Act 1994, adding s 44(2)(A)–(D) to the Insolvency Act.
596 Significant liabilities could still exist in their case from the running of a particular major
business, for example, a hotel.

(iv) Receivers, administrators and rates

19.144 Besides contracts of employment adopted by the receiver, and contracts entered into by the receiver, difficulties have arisen in connection with rates, which since the reforms of the 1980s are no longer preferential debts. Briefly, the question that arose in one case[597] was whether a receiver could refrain from selling a building in the expectation of the market rising, whilst not paying even the reduced rates due on an unoccupied building. A rating authority pursuing the company would merely precipitate a liquidation in which it would rank only as an unsecured creditor. The authority was not providing a service, like the supply of electricity, that would give it leverage against the receiver, so it asserted that the receiver had become personally liable to pay the rates under the relevant legislation as the person in possession of the building. The argument failed on the familiar ground that the receiver was only the agent of the company: it was the company itself that was in possession. The company's liability to pay rates was akin to its liability to perform pre-receivership contracts, for which the receiver would not be liable. The position of administrators should be no different.

(2) Bringing Proceedings

(a) Vulnerable transactions and fraudulent conveyances

(i) Distributable assets

19.145 It is only the assets of the insolvent at the time of the bankruptcy or winding-up order or resolution that are distributed. There is, however, a major exception that arises in the case of dispositions of the insolvent's assets occurring in the run up to bankruptcy or winding-up. In that period, certain transactions are vulnerable to challenge by insolvency officers[598] and administrators, but not by receivers. These challenges may be made under different heads, but their broad purpose, taken together, is to reinforce the *pari passu* rule by preserving the insolvent's assets for distribution and by preventing one creditor from being singled out for favourable treatment at the expense of the others. That said, the various heads suffer as a result of their heterogeneity and a certain incoherence of overall purpose. It is by no means certain that their broad purpose is served well by existing legislation.

19.146 In consequence of the purpose served by these heads of challenge and their confinement to insolvency officers and administrators, the moneys recovered are,

---

597 *Re Sobam BV* [1996] 1 BCLC 446.
598 The sanction of the court is needed for actions to be brought by liquidators and trustees: Insolvency Act, Sch 4, para (3A) (as added by s 253 of the Enterprise Act 2002) and Sch 5, para (2A) (as added by s 262 of the Enterprise Act).

correctly it is submitted, 'impressed. . .with a trust' for the benefit of the unsecured creditors, who are the eventual victims of the transactions in question. They are not assets of the company so as to be caught by a security given to one of its creditors.[599] Money paid under the impugned transactions ceases to be the property of the company. Consequently, there is no proprietary claim for its recovery. The conclusion that the unsecured creditors benefit from the liquidator's action means that an office-holder is not pointlessly bringing proceedings that can only benefit a secured creditor. On the other hand, so the argument runs, any inflation of the assets embraced by the security would have the kinetic effect of releasing other assets for the unsecured creditors, at least where the chargee is not undersecured.[600]

(ii) Undervalue transactions

The first head of challenge arises under section 238 and concerns transactions[601] **19.147** entered into at an undervalue.[602] This head, introduced for companies by the Insolvency Act 1985, was developed from earlier bankruptcy legislation.[603] An undervalue transaction exists either where the insolvent makes a gift,[604] or where the insolvent receives either no consideration[605] or a consideration that is worth 'significantly' less in money terms than the consideration provided in return.[606] The adequacy of consideration is calculated in terms of what a reasonably informed buyer would pay in an arm's length transaction.[607] These provisions are confined to transactions that deplete or reduce the value of the transferor's assets. On one view, an undervalue transaction was not concluded where a company granted a security to one of its existing creditors, a bank. Although this transaction 'adversely

---

[599] *Re Yagerphone Ltd* [1935] 1 Ch 352; *Re Oasis Merchandising Services Ltd* [1998] Ch 170, CA.

[600] On the proceeds of actions brought by the liquidator under ss 212–14, see the discussion in para 19.168.

[601] Section 436 defines 'transaction' as 'gift, agreement or arrangement', which is a broad definition: *Phillips v Brewin Dolphin Bell Lawrie Ltd* [1999] 1 WLR 2052, CA, affirmed on different grounds at [2001] UKHL 2; [2001] 1 WLR 143 where the word 'transaction' meant connected contracts in a complex business sale and permitted the value of the consideration to be drawn from a connected contract. Cf *National Westminster Bank plc v Jones* [2001] EWCA Civ 1541; [2002] 1 BCLC 55.

[602] For bankruptcy, the provision is s 339.

[603] Section 44 of the Bankruptcy Act 1914.

[604] *Re Barton Manufacturing Co Ltd* [1999] 1 BCLC 740.

[605] Consideration in favour of a third party would not suffice.

[606] Sections 238(4) and 339(3). The latter, bankruptcy provision also lists transactions in consideration of marriage. An example of undervalue would be the transfer by husband to wife of an interest in the matrimonial home that exceeds in value the mortgage commitments assumed by the wife: *Re Kumar* [1993] 1 WLR 224.

[607] *Phillips v Brewin Dolphin Bell Lawrie Ltd* [2001] UKHL 2; [2001] 1 WLR 143 at [30] (Lord Scott), HL, On the process of valuation, see *Agricultural Mortgage Corp plc v Woodward* [1995] 1 BCLC 1; *Jones v National Westminster Bank plc v Jones* [2001] EWCA Civ 1541; [2002] 1 BCLC 55; *Ramlort Ltd v Reid* [2004] EWCA Civ 800; [2005] 1 BCLC 331.

affect[ed] the rights of other creditors in insolvency', the only thing that the company lost as a result of the transaction was 'the right to apply the proceeds [of the charged assets] otherwise than in satisfaction of the secured debt',[608] which could not be valued in monetary terms. Nevertheless, the opposite view that section 238 does apply to the grant of security has been firmly and authoritatively expressed.[609]

19.148 For the transaction to be open to challenge, the insolvent must either be unable to pay its debts at that time or become so as a result of the transaction.[610] This financial state of affairs is presumed to exist where the other party is an associate of the bankrupt or connected to the company in winding-up.[611] Otherwise, the burden of proof will be on the administrator or liquidator.

19.149 The date of the transaction is relevant if it is to be challenged. In the case of companies, the transaction has to be entered into two years before the 'onset of insolvency',[612] which is the date of commencement of the winding-up[613] or, if the winding-up has been preceded by administration leading 'immediately' into the winding-up, the date the petition for an administration order was presented.[614] In the case of individuals, the period is five years.[615] Where the company going into liquidation has been in administration, care has to be taken that the winding-up follows directly on from the administration or else the passage of time during the administration will prevent the liquidator from challenging pre-administration transactions.[616]

19.150 In the case of companies, an order will not be made by the court if, despite the undervalue, the company carried out the transaction in good faith and for the purpose of carrying on its business, and if at the time of the transaction there were reasonable grounds for believing that the transaction would benefit

---

[608] *Re MC Bacon Ltd* [1991] Ch 127. See also *Re Lewis's of Leicester Ltd* [1995] 1 BCLC 428. On a sale of the secured asset, the value for undervalue purposes has been held to be the value of the asset minus the security: *Re Brabon* [2001] 1 BCLC 11.

[609] *Hill v Spread Trustee Co Ltd* [2006] EWCA Civ 542; [2007] 1 All ER 1106 at [93] (Arden LJ).

[610] Sections 240(2) and 341(2), (3). An apparent difference exists between bankruptcy and liquidation in that the bankruptcy provision is not confined to cash flow insolvency (inability to pay debts as they fall due) but extends also to balance sheet insolvency (assets exceeded by liabilities). Nevertheless, balance sheet insolvency is deemed elsewhere (s 123(2)) to amount to cash flow insolvency.

[611] Sections 240(2) and 341(2).

[612] Section 240(1)(a).

[613] Discussed in paras 19.11 and 19.12.

[614] In the case of administration, the transaction can occur at any time after the presentation of the administration petition and the making of an order: s 240(1)(c).

[615] Section 341(1)(a) (substituting the former period of ten years).

[616] For the procedure to overcome the various difficulties, see *Re Powerstore (Trading) Ltd* [1997] 1 WLR 1280; *Re Mark One (Oxford Street) plc* [1999] 1 WLR 1445; *Re Norditrack (UK)* [2000] 1 WLR 343.

the company.[617] The order made by the court is designed to restore the *status quo ante*, but the court has a discretion as to how this should be accomplished[618] and may indeed make no order at all[619] or an order on terms.[620]

(iii) Undervalue transactions and third parties

The order made may in certain cases affect the property of, or subject to liability, third parties who subsequently acquired assets from the other party to the under-value transaction.[621] The central idea is that *bona fide* third parties purchasing former company property should be put beyond the reach of a court order. Prior to the Insolvency (No 2) Act 1994, the position was that the broad sweep of the opening words of section 241(2),[622] allowing for the recovery of property and benefits from such third parties, was qualified by a defence available to those third parties. They had to show that they had acted in good faith, given value and had had no notice of the relevant circumstances. The relevant circumstances were the entry of the company into an undervalue transaction. The danger, which prompted the legislation, was that purchasers of unregistered land could be put upon notice when investigating a root of title over the preceding years, since they would dis-cover the price at which the land had previously been sold. This would disqualify them from claiming the above defence. **19.151**

The solution of the 1994 Act, producing the amended section 241, was to make notice a sub-category of good faith, and to expand notice of the relevant circum-stances so that it had to include notice of the relevant proceedings. Proceedings are defined to include winding-up, administration and administration leading into winding-up.[623] Section 241(2) makes the defence available to third parties acting in good faith and giving value. A third party with notice of the relevant circum-stances *and* the relevant proceedings is now presumed to have acted otherwise than in good faith.[624] This same presumption arises against persons connected or associated with the company or individual transferor even in the absence of such notice. In the case of the purchaser of unregistered land, notice of the relevant proceedings will thus not arise from searching title. The title that that purchaser acquires upon the conveyance ought therefore to be safe from the attentions of the administrator or insolvency officer. The third party defence of good faith purchase has thus become significantly easier to establish. **19.152**

---

617 Section 238(5). No equivalent provision exists for bankruptcy.
618 Sections 238(3) and 339(2).
619 *Re Paramount Airways Ltd* [1993] Ch 223, 239.
620 See, for example, *Weisgard v Pilkington* [1995] BCC 1108.
621 Sections 241(2) and 342(2).
622 For bankruptcy, s 342(2).
623 Section 241(3A), (3B), (3C).
624 Sections 241(2A) and 342(2A).

(iv) Fraudulent conveyances

19.153 The provisions dealing with undervalue transactions are similar in scope to section 423, which concerns fraudulent conveyances.[625] The transaction must be at an undervalue, which is defined in the same way as it is for undervalue transactions in bankruptcy in section 339,[626] and any order made by the court will be made on similar principles.[627] Furthermore, there has to be present an intended purpose of putting assets beyond the reach of present or future claimants or of otherwise prejudicing their interests, the burden of proof being on the person challenging the transaction though it can be inferred from the circumstances of the undervalue transaction.[628] This purpose need not be the only purpose[629] but it has to be a 'substantial' one.[630]

19.154 One example of a fraudulent conveyance is that of the lease of agricultural land by a farmer to his sons at an annual rent payable (unusually) in arrears, the effect of which was to place the sons in a 'ransom position' against the bank which had a charge over the land.[631] Consequently, the bank's interests had been prejudiced for the purpose of section 423. Moreover, it did not matter that, after the transaction, the bank still held security exceeding in value the debt owed. There was no realistic possibility of the bank being able to realize the freehold land and the debt was mounting from day to day. In another case,[632] the claimant financed the defendant's business by leasing coaches and aircraft to the defendant which in turn sub-leased them to end users. Fearing prospective litigation, the defendant transferred its business and assets, including the benefit of certain leases with the claimant, to an undercapitalized shell company. The shell company acquired the benefit of these leases for the same sum that the defendant had to pay under the various leasing agreements, but it paid for these benefits quarterly and in arrears. Furthermore, the shell company was paid by the defendant an

---

[625] Formerly, s 184 of the Law of Property Act 1925 and dating from the time of Elizabeth I. It has long been the practice to refer to such transactions as fraudulent conveyances, though there is no requirement of fraud in s 423 (see *Arbuthnot Leasing International Ltd v Havelet Leasing Ltd (No 1)* [1992] 1 WLR 455).

[626] Akin to the rules governing fraudulent conveyances are ss 342A to 342C (as amended by s 15 of the Welfare Reform and Pensions Act 1999), which give the court power to make such order as it thinks fit where a bankrupt has previously made excessive contributions to a pension scheme so as unfairly to prejudice his creditors. The individual's purpose in putting assets beyond the reach of his creditors is relevant in determining whether excessive contributions have been made. Amounts are excessive in the light of the individual's circumstances when the contributions were made.

[627] See *Arbuthnot Leasing International Ltd v Havelet Leasing Ltd (No 1)* [1992] 1 WLR 455.

[628] See *Barclays Bank plc v Eustice* [1995] 1 WLR 1238, CA.

[629] *Chohan v Saggar* [1992] BCC 306, 321, CA.

[630] *Royscot Spa Leasing Ltd v Lovett* [1995] BCC 502, CA (disapproving of 'dominant' in *Chohan v Saggar* [1992] BCC 306, CA); *Re Brabon* [2001] 1 BCLC 11.

[631] *Barclays Bank plc v Eustice* [1995] 1 WLR 1238, CA. See also *National Westminster Bank plc v Jones* [2001] EWCA Civ 1541; [2002] 1 BCLC 55.

[632] *Arbuthnot Leasing International Ltd v Havelet Leasing Ltd (No 1)* [1992] 1 WLR 455.

annual management fee of £1.5 million. The receipt of deferred payments in return for its income stream would itself have been enough to mark out the transfer as an undervalue transaction. Even legal advice to the effect that the transaction was a proper one did not preclude the existence of the purpose forbidden under section 423.

Certain differences exist between section 423 and section 238. The former provision is not subject to a qualifying period at all. Indeed, calculating the commencement of a limitation period, especially for a transaction transferring both present and future assets, is no easy matter.[633] Furthermore, a challenge to a transaction may be mounted, not just by insolvency officer and administrator, but by 'any victim',[634] who is treated as acting representatively on behalf of other victims too. The leave of the court is nevertheless required if a victim wishes to challenge a transaction entered into by a company in winding-up or administration.[635]   **19.155**

(v) Unlawful preferences

The provisions dealing with undervalue transactions[636] are also related to the provisions dealing with unlawful preferences. A number of sections of the Act apply to both, notably those dealing with the qualifying period, the order of the court and the protection given to good faith purchasers. The period of vulnerability, however, is in the case of unlawful preferences six months for both winding-up and bankruptcy except in the case of connected persons or associates where it is extended to two years.[637]   **19.156**

The preference itself exists where the insolvent 'does anything or suffers anything to be done which. . .has the effect of putting that person into a position which, in the event of the company going into an insolvent winding-up, will be better than the position he would have been in if that thing had not been done'. This will certainly include the giving of security, which does not constitute an undervalue transaction. An example of a preference was the payment of £2,000 to a 17-year-old management trainee (the son of the majority shareholder) a month before the company went into liquidation. It exceeded the amount that the trainee could have recovered in a breach of contract action.[638]   **19.157**

---

[633] See *Hill v Spread Trustee Co Ltd* [2006] EWCA Civ 542; [2007] 1 All ER 1106 (the period itself is twelve years).

[634] Anyone prejudiced by the transaction whether contemplated by the transferor or not: *Sands v Clitheroe* [2006] BPIR 1000.

[635] *National Bank of Kuwait plc v Menzies* [1994] 2 BCLC 306, CA. See the discussion above on proceedings against companies in administration and liquidation.

[636] Sections 239 and 340.

[637] Sections 240(1)(a), (b) and 341(1)(b), (c).

[638] *Re Clasper Group Services Ltd* [1989] BCLC 143.

19.158   A preference is not enough of itself for the transaction to be struck down. The person conferring the preference has to be 'influenced' by a 'desire' to bring about the preferential effect. The provisions in the Insolvency Act 1986 replaced earlier legislation striking down transactions in favour of certain creditors 'with a view of giving such creditor. . .a preference over the other creditors'. This was interpreted to require 'the dominant intention to prefer' the chosen creditor. The radical change in language in the current provisions means that authorities on the intention element in the old provision cannot be considered.[639] The preference need now only be influenced by the requisite desire and not dominated by it, and the intention to prefer must not merely have been intended but positively desired. The latter change seems to have made it almost impossible to prove an unlawful preference given that: 'Intention is objective, desire is subjective. A man can choose the lesser of two evils without desiring either.'[640] Where a company is pressed by a bank to give security,[641] or a store sets up a trading account on *Quistclose* terms in favour of concessionaires in order to keep them in the store in the run up to Christmas,[642] the necessary desire will not be present. Practical compulsion does not amount to desire.

19.159   In the case of preferences in favour of associates or connected persons, there exists a rebuttable presumption of a desire to prefer.[643] It is only in such cases that the legislation has real teeth, since the absence of desire may be nearly as hard to prove as its presence. In one case,[644] a publishing company granted a debenture to one of its directors who provided in return a borrowing facility to the company. The immediate purpose of the transaction was to reduce the bank overdraft to below its permissible ceiling of £60,000. The director was a guarantor of this overdraft. Payments of £20,000 were made directly into the company's account, thus benefiting the director who had a security for the sums advanced at the same time as he commensurately reduced his liability as guarantor. The presumption was rebutted because the company was actuated by proper commercial considerations, namely the need to obtain finance from someone other than the bank, while it kept going the publication of a 'valuable title' that it was seeking to sell.

(vi) Extortionate credit

19.160   A further head under which a transaction may be struck down at the behest of an insolvency officer or administrator is where the insolvent is a party to an

---

[639] *Re MC Bacon Ltd* [1991] Ch 127.
[640] ibid.
[641] *Re MC Bacon Ltd* [1991] Ch 127.
[642] *Re Lewis's of Leicester Ltd* [1995] 1 BCLC 428.
[643] Sections 239(6) and 340(5).
[644] *Re Fairway Magazines Ltd* [1993] BCLC 643.

extortionate credit transaction.[645] The relevant provisions in the Insolvency Act 1986 take their inspiration from provisions in the Consumer Credit Act 1974,[646] which repealed the old Moneylenders Acts 1900 to 1927, which struck down certain oppressive loans. They replace a provision that limited the rate of interest that could be applied for in bankruptcy and winding-up.

An extortionate credit transaction can be challenged in a three-year twilight period **19.161** preceding the commencement of bankruptcy, the making of an administration order or the company going into a winding-up. The terms have to be 'grossly exorbitant' or otherwise 'grossly contravene ordinary principles of fair dealing'. There is a presumption of extortion and the court has a discretion to set aside or vary the transaction.

(vii) Late floating charges

The final head of challenge arises under section 245 of the Insolvency Act 1986 **19.162** and concerns late floating charges granted by a company in the twelve months[647] preceding the onset of insolvency or at any time between the petition for an administration and the making of an administration order. Such charges are valid[648] only to the extent of the value of the money, goods or services supplied in consideration for the charge[649] 'at the same time as, or after, the creation of the charge'. The purpose of the section as to hold the ring embracing a company's unsecured creditors is thus manifest.

The formula concerning the timing of a charge departs slightly from earlier **19.163** legislation, which was interpreted flexibly to cover advances made before the granting of the charge and in contemplation of the grant of the charge,[650] which accommodated the advance of emergency funds.[651] The current, literalist position is that even a minimal time gap between the giving of value and the grant of the charge will be fatal,[652] though an informal charge granted at the time or before the value is given should not be invalidated by its subsequent reduction to writing.

---

[645] Sections 244 and 343.

[646] Sections 137–40, now repealed by the Consumer Credit Act 2006 (Sch 4), which modifies to a minor extent s 343(6).

[647] Two years for those connected with the company.

[648] Section 245 invalidates only the charge: see *Re Mace Builders (Glasgow) Ltd* [1985] BCLC 154.

[649] The phrase 'in consideration for' means 'as a result of', so that a bank's later factual forbearance from calling in a loan will suffice: *Re Yeovil Glove Co Ltd* [1965] Ch 148, CA.

[650] *Re Stanton (F and E) Ltd* [1929] 1 Ch 180. See also *Re Columbian Fireproofing Co* [1910] 2 Ch 120, CA.

[651] See *Re Fairway Magazines Ltd* [1993] BCLC 643.

[652] *Power v Sharp Instruments Ltd* (orse *Re Shoe Lace Ltd*) [1994] 1 BCLC 111, CA.

19.164 In calculating the value given for the charge, some difficulties have been presented where a portion of the value has found its way back to the secured creditor. Where there have been solid business reasons for the transaction, the courts have resisted invalidating the charge. Consequently, where moneys advanced to a company were used to pay off an unsecured debt owed to another creditor in which the secured creditor had an interest, the charge was upheld because the payment to that other creditor preserved goodwill and future supplies to the company.[653] No such judicial generosity will be shown if the company is merely a conduit through which the secured creditor repays himself money advanced to the company in return for the charge.[654] Finally, value granted later than the charge will be found in the case of a bank where the company maintains a current account so that, in accordance with the rule in *Clayton's Case*,[655] payments into the account discharge existing debts in order of seniority. If, for example, an overdraft limit of £20,000 before the charge remains £20,000 afterwards, the bank will nevertheless be able to rely upon the charge to the extent that any sum outstanding represents new debt coming into existence after the charge as a result of payments out of the account.[656] Payments into the account, which keep the overdraft down to the agreed limit, are offset against old debt. Eventually, the whole of the debt will represent advances made after the grant of the charge.

(b) Misfeasance and fraudulent and wrongful trading

(i) Misfeasance

19.165 A series of provisions in the Insolvency Act 1986 deals with misfeasance by directors and officers of a company and with wrongful and fraudulent trading in the run up to liquidation. Under section 212, a summary remedy for misfeasance lies in the course of winding up a company if there has been, on the part of directors and other persons taking part in the 'formation, promotion or management of the company',[657] conduct that amounts to the misapplication or retention of, or refusal to account for, the company's property or money, or to misfeasance[658] or a breach of any fiduciary or other duty owed to the company.[659] The breach of a duty owed to the company now extends under the current provision to a breach

---

653 *Re Ellis (Matthew) Ltd* [1933] Ch 458, CA.
654 *Re Destone Fabrics Ltd* [1941] 1 Ch 319, CA.
655 (1816) 1 Mer 572, 35 ER 781.
656 *Re Yeovil Glove Co Ltd* [1965] Ch 148, CA.
657 The section extends also to the conduct of liquidators, administrators and administrative receivers: see para 19.171.
658 Under the antecedent provision in companies legislation, misfeasance meant conduct in the nature of a breach of trust: *Coventry and Dixon's Case* (1880) 14 Ch D 660, CA.
659 A developing case law requires directors of an insolvent company to treat the interests of creditors as paramount: *Colin Gwyer and Associates Ltd v London Wharf (Limehouse) Ltd*, [2002] EWHC 2748 (Ch); [2003] 2 BCLC 153; *Miller v Bain* [2002] 1 BCLC 266.

of the duty of care in negligence[660] but otherwise the section merely creates a summary remedy without altering the law. The court may require restitution of the money or property and has a broad discretion to make a compensatory award.[661] The Insolvency Act 1986 also sets out a series of criminal offences arising out of fraud on the part of a company's officers in the period preceding a winding-up.[662]

(ii) Fraudulent trading

Like the misfeasance provision, the fraudulent and wrongful trading provisions **19.166** also deal with the emergence of prior wrongdoing in the course of winding up a company. Fraudulent trading, according to section 213, arises where the business of a company has been carried on with an intent to defraud creditors or for any other fraudulent purpose.[663] The test of fraud is a very difficult one to satisfy[664] and is not met just because the company's indebtedness arises at a time when it is known by its directors to be insolvent.[665] Only the liquidator can bring proceedings under the section.[666] In the unlikely event of those proceedings being successful, the court has a broad discretion to require defendants to make a contribution to the assets of the company.

(iii) Wrongful trading

The wrongful trading provision, section 214, was conceived by the Cork **19.167** Committee as an objective replacement for the subjective fraudulent trading provision[667] and in the event, while only supplementing the latter in the statute book, it renders it in practical terms redundant. Wrongful trading concerns conduct that the section never defines: the word trading appears only in the title of the section. It exists whenever a person does the prohibited thing (whatever it is)[668] at a time when that person was a director of a company[669] and should

---

[660] *Re D'Jan of London Ltd* [1994] 1 BCLC 561.

[661] Section 212(3).

[662] Sections 206ff.

[663] It is not enough that individual creditors were defrauded in the course of a business: *Morphitis v Bernasconi* [2003] EWCA Civ 289; [2003] Ch 552.

[664] But the knowledge of an employee can be attributed to an employer: *Bank of India v Morris* [2005] EWCA Civ 693; [2005] 2 BCLC 328.

[665] *Re Patrick and Lyon Ltd* [1933] Ch 786. Proceedings may be taken against anyone who knowingly is party to the carrying on of the business in a fraudulent manner: s 213(2). For the requirement of knowledge, see *Morris v Bank of America National Trust* [2000] 1 All ER 954, 963, CA.

[666] The sanction of the court is required for this and for wrongful trading actions: Insolvency Act, Sch 4, para (3A) (as added by s 253 of the Enterprise Act 2002).

[667] Cmnd 8558 (1982), paras 1775ff.

[668] Parliament rejected the Cork Committee's proposal that the conduct consist of incurring 'further debts or other liabilities': Cmnd 8558 (1982), para 1806.

[669] This includes shadow directors: ss 214(7) and 251.

have known that there was no reasonable prospect of the company avoiding the insolvent liquidation that subsequently occurred. Section 214 is laconic also to the point of not expressly requiring that the prohibited thing cause anyone loss,[670] except that an order shall not be made against the director if the court is satisfied that he took 'every step' to 'minimize' the 'potential loss' to the company's creditors.[671] The draftsmanship seems makeshift but its broad purpose is to wave the prospect of liability before directors in order to restrain them from trading on irresponsibly when they should be inviting the bank to send in a receiver or should be petitioning for administration or taking steps to wind up the company. The objective test of liability takes account of the director's general knowledge, skill and experience.[672] If liable, the director is required to contribute to the company's assets,[673] which points to a jurisdiction that is primarily compensatory rather than penal.[674]

(iv) Proceeds of actions

19.168   As in actions dealing with vulnerable transactions, the proceeds of wrongful and fraudulent trading actions are held for the general body of creditors.[675] The sections do speak of the orders made contributing, in the present tense, to the assets of the company, which are impressed with the statutory trust in favour of the general creditors. Furthermore, it has to be asked why a liquidator should wish to bring proceedings in actions that cannot be assigned to third parties, and which can only be brought by liquidators, if the proceeds are going to be scooped up by creditors with a charge over the future assets of the company. Nevertheless, in a misfeasance case,[676] it was held that the sum recovered could not be used to recoup the costs of the winding-up. In so far as the action leads to the recovery of property that ought not to have been alienated, there is good reason for it to be returned so that it falls within a secured creditor's charge, especially as misfeasance proceedings can be brought by any creditor and not just by a liquidator.

(c) Powers of investigation and examination

19.169   The liquidator has powers of investigation and examination to assist him in determining whether to challenge pre-liquidation transactions or to take proceedings against officers of the company. These powers assist also in gathering in the assets

---

670 According to *Marini Ltd v Dickenson* [2003] EWHC 334 (Ch); [2004] BCC 172 a net deficiency must exist in the company's estate between the time the directors realized liquidation was inevitable and the occurrence of liquidation.
671 Section 214(3).
672 Section 214(4).
673 Section 214(1).
674 *Re Produce Marketing Consortium Ltd* [1989] BCLC 520.
675 *Re Oasis Merchandising Services Ltd* [1998] Ch 170, CA; *Re MC Bacon Ltd* [1991] Ch 127.
676 *Re Anglo-Austrian Printing Co* [1895] 2 Ch 891, CA.

of the company. Under section 133, the compulsory liquidator may apply to the court for the public examination of former officers of the company and of receivers and administrators, as well as of those involved in the promotion, formation or management of the company.[677] A sufficient number of creditors or members may require an application to be made unless the court rules otherwise. A similar process of public examination applies to bankrupts.[678]

The Insolvency Act also contains duties on the part of identified individuals such as promoters, employees and officers of the company[679] to co-operate with office holders, namely the official receiver, the liquidator, the administrator and the administrative receiver, by supplying information and making themselves available.[680] This is backed up by a further provision for a judicial inquiry into a company's dealings calling for affidavits, books, papers and company records as well as for attendance by officers, promoters and persons suspected of having in their possession company property.[681] Books, papers and records will have to be surrendered even if the holder has a lien over them.[682] The inquiry must be necessary and must not oppress those who are summoned to appear.[683] Its purpose has been said to be to reconstitute the company's knowledge in the event of, for example, an ensuing winding-up[684] but the reason for it has also been put more broadly as the facilitation of the work of an office holder.[685] The inquiry should not take place where the decision to take proceedings against individuals has already been firmly taken[686] But it is permissible if the purpose is to gather evidence to determine if directors disqualification proceedings should be taken.[687] Nevertheless, persons summoned to appear are not protected by a privilege against self-incrimination[688] though this ruling should now be reconsidered in the light of the European Convention on Human Rights.[689]

19.170

---

[677] See *Re Richbell Strategic Holdings Ltd* [2000] 2 BCLC 794. For voluntary liquidation, see *Bishopsgate Investment Management Ltd v Maxwell Mirror Group Newspapers Ltd* [1993] Ch 1, CA.

[678] Section 290.

[679] Also administrators and administrative receivers.

[680] Section 235. The equivalent provisions for bankruptcy are ss 291(4) and 333.

[681] Section 236.

[682] Section 246. See *Akers v Lomas* [2002] 1 BCLC 655. For a demand made by an administrative receiver, see *Re Aveling Barford Ltd* [1989] 1 WLR 360.

[683] *Re British and Commonwealth Holdings plc (No 2)* [1993] AC 426, CA. The need for speed may outweigh the avoidance of oppressive conduct: *Shierson v Rastogi* [2002] EWCA Civ 1624; [2003] 1 WLR 586.

[684] See for example *Re Cloverbay Ltd (No 2)* [1991] Ch 90, CA.

[685] *Re British and Commonwealth Holdings plc (No 2)* [1993] AC 426, HL.

[686] *Re Cloverbay Ltd (No 2)* [1991] Ch 90, CA.

[687] *Re Pantmaenog Timber Co Ltd* [2003] UKHL 49; [2004] 1 AC 158.

[688] *Re Levitt (Jefferey S) Ltd* [1992] Ch 457.

[689] Article 6 (right to a fair trial). See *Saunders v United Kingdom* [1997] EHRR 313; *Shierson v Rastogi* [2002] EWCA Civ 1624; [2003] 1 WLR 586.

(3) The Conduct of Insolvency Officers, Administrators and Receivers

(a) Personal liability

19.171 The Insolvency Act provides for actions against liquidators who act in breach of certain duties. Section 212, the summary misfeasance provision,[690] applies also to liquidators.[691] The liquidator's misfeasance may consist of negligence in admitting to proof claims against the estate without making proper inquiry.[692] Proceedings may be launched by the official receiver, a creditor or a contributory.[693] Further control over the conduct of liquidators in office can be exercised by an application to the court to remove the liquidator 'on cause shown',[694] which is a broadly stated discretion that can be employed to deal with dilatory liquidators for the general advantage of those interested in the assets of the company.[695] Administrators and administrative receivers[696] are also open to misfeasance proceedings.[697] The leave of the court is required if proceedings are to be taken against liquidators and administrators after their release.[698] Administrators may be removed from office at any time by an order of the court.[699] The same applies to administrative receivers.[700] Liquidators, administrators and receivers are all exposed to public examination under section 133. Under section 235, liquidators, administrators and administrative receivers[701] are all under a duty to co-operate with the office-holder.

19.172 There is no statutory misfeasance provision for receivers but, when dealing with company assets, the question has arisen whether they may incur liability outside the Insolvency Act to the company and to others. A court-appointed receiver is under a duty to preserve the assets and goodwill of the company,[702] but there is no

---

690 Discussed in para 19.165.

691 The misfeasance provision for trustees-in-bankruptcy, who are liable on the same principles as liquidators, is s 304.

692 *Re Windsor Steam Coal Co* [1929] 1 Ch 151, CA; *Re Home and Colonial Insurance Co Ltd* [1930] 1 Ch 102 (a high standard of care and diligence is required).

693 Leave of the court is required in the case of a contributory: s 212(5).

694 Section 108(2).

695 *Re Keypak Homecare Ltd* [1987] BCLC 409558. The removal of trustees-in-bankruptcy is stated simply as occurring when the court so orders or a general meeting of the creditors so decides: s 298(1). Further provision is made for control of the trustee by the creditors' committee and by the court: ss 301 and 303.

696 But not other receivers except in so far as they have been involved in managing the company: s 212(1)(c).

697 In their case, the proceedings may be started by the liquidator. In the absence of a special relationship, an administrator owes no common law duty of care to creditors: *Kyrris v Oldham* [2003] EWCA Civ 1506; [2004] 1 BCLC 305.

698 Section 212(4).

699 Section 19(1).

700 Section 45(1).

701 But not other receivers.

702 *Re Newdigate Colliery Ltd* [1912] Ch 468, CA.

true corresponding and unqualified duty on contractual receivers.[703] The primary duty of the contractual receiver is owed to the debenture holder who procured his appointment and not to the company as such, which is not entitled to expect of him the performance of its own directors and managers.[704]

Yet there is a duty owed by the receiver. The starting point is the position of the **19.173** mortgagee who enforces a security directly without procuring the appointment of a receiver. That mortgagee is not a trustee of his power of sale for the mortgagor but may exercise it exclusively in his own interests without however fraudulently or recklessly sacrificing the interests of the mortgagor.[705] This is consistent with the rule that a debenture holder is not obliged to consult the interests of the company when deciding to send in a receiver.[706] Over the years, attempts have been made to introduce an element of due care into the performance by the receiver of his responsibilities. The fundamental issue that has arisen is whether a duty to take care, going beyond a duty to abstain from acting fraudulently, can sit with the receiver's right to place the interests of the debenture holder first. A secondary issue, whose late resolution has clouded the debate, has been the largely taxonomic one of determining whether the provenance of the receiver's duty lies in equity or in the tort of negligence.

In one important case, the Court of Appeal held that a mortgagee taking posses- **19.174** sion and exercising a power of sale owed a duty to the mortgagor to obtain a proper price.[707] The same approach was adopted in the case of a receiver when the matter arose collaterally as between the debenture holder and guarantor of the company's obligations.[708] Nevertheless, the Privy Council has trenchantly asserted that the law of tort has no part to play and that a receiver's duties lie only in equity,[709] stressing that the receiver's duty to others must not be allowed to conflict with the duty owed to the debenture holder.[710] In equity, the receiver must act in

---

[703] But see the attempt to move towards this position in *Astor Chemical Ltd v Synthetic Technology Ltd* [1990] BCC 97. The receiver's entitlement to act against the interests of the company's co-contractants is recognized in *Airlines Airspares Ltd v Handley Page Ltd* [1970] Ch 193 but he may be enjoined from disregarding contracts of the company to the extent that he is not preferring the interests of the debenture holder: *Ash and Newman Ltd v Creative Devices Research Ltd* [1991] BCLC 403.

[704] *Re B Johnson & Co* [1955] Ch 634, 661–2, CA.

[705] *Kennedy v de Trafford* [1896] 1 Ch 762, 772, CA.

[706] *Shamji v Johnson Matthey Bankers Ltd* [1991] BCLC 36, CA.

[707] *Cuckmere Brick Co Ltd v Mutual Finance Ltd* [1971] 1 Ch 949, CA. The creditor's freedom to choose the time to sell is not always easily reconciled with the duty to conduct a sale in a competent manner: see *Den Norske Bank ASA v Acemex Management Co Ltd* [2003] EWCA Civ 1559; [2004] 1 Lloyd's Rep 1.

[708] *Standard Chartered Bank v Walker* [1982] 1 WLR 1410, CA.

[709] *China and South Seas Bank v Tan* [1990] 1 AC 536, PC. See also *Silven Properties Ltd v Royal Bank of Scotland plc* [2003] EWCA Civ 1409; [2004] 1 WLR 997; *Raja v Austin Gray* [2002] EWCA Civ 1965; [2003] BPIR 725.

[710] *Downsview Nominees v First City Corporation Ltd* [1993] AC 295, PC.

good faith and refrain from wilful default. More recently, however, the equitable duty has been held to encompass an obligation on the part of a receiver to manage the affairs of a company with care when there is no conflict with the essential duty owed to the debenture holder.[711] Since the tort of negligence is sophisticated enough to tailor due care to the exigencies of the receiver's position, it hardly matters, as far as the company is concerned,[712] whether the duty is classified as equitable or tortious.

(b) Officers of the court and *ex p James*

19.175 Official receivers, compulsory liquidators, trustees-in-bankruptcy and administrators, all officers of the court,[713] are bound by a particular rule of ethical conduct to behave in a high-minded fashion and abstain from shabby conduct.[714] This is known as the rule in *ex p James*[715] which goes beyond any legal duties owed by the insolvent individual or company and concerns essentially the undue enrichment of the insolvent's estate.[716] There is no true proprietary claim against the officer and the estate,[717] but rather an application to the court to control the conduct of one of its own officers so as to nullify the effect of the enrichment.[718] Early cases concerned the officer's receipt of money paid over under a mistake of law.[719] The recoverability now of money paid in such circumstances[720] abridges the scope of the rule in *ex p James*, which however is not confined to mistake of law.[721] It is a matter of no small difficulty to estimate the reach of the rule, for 'questions of ethical propriety. . .will always be. . .the subject of honest difference among honest men'.[722] It does not, for example, prevent a trustee from bringing an action to recover the proceeds of collected cheques drawn by the bankrupt when paying gambling debts.[723]

---

[711] *Medforth v Blake* [2000] Ch 86, CA.

[712] Guarantors, for example, may well be a different matter.

[713] The rule therefore does not apply to voluntary liquidators (*Re TH Knitwear (Wholesale) Ltd* [1988] 1 Ch 275, CA) and contractual receivers (*Triffit Nurseries v Salads Etcetera Ltd* [2000] 1 BCLC 262). For its applicability to receivers, see *Wallace v Shoa Leasing (Singapore) PTE Ltd* [1999] BPIR 911. Insolvents receiving money for services they know they cannot provide may hold those moneys on constructive trust terms (*Neste Oy v Lloyds Bank plc* [1983] 2 Lloyd's Rep 658), which may be a more promising avenue in some cases than the rule in *ex p James*. See paras 18.183–18.191.

[714] Criticized as an 'anomalous' rule by Harman J in *Re Bateson (John) & Co* [1985] BCLC 259, 262.

[715] (1874) 9 Ch App 609.

[716] The rule appears to be confined to cases of enrichment: *Government of India v Taylor* [1955] AC 491, 513, HL; *Re Clark* [1975] 1 WLR 559, 563.

[717] *Re Tyler* [1907] 1 KB 865, 869, CA, explaining James LJ's reference to 'equity' in *ex p James*.

[718] *Re Clark* [1975] 1 WLR 559, 564 (and not to restore the claimant to the *status quo ante*).

[719] *Ex p James* (1874) 9 Ch App 609; *ex p Simmonds* (1885) 16 QBD 308, CA.

[720] *Kleinwort Benson Ltd v Lincoln City Council* [1999] 2 AC 349, HL.

[721] *Re Thellusson* [1919] 2 KB 735, CA; *Re Tyler* [1907] 1 KB 865, CA.

[722] *Re Wigzell* [1921] 2 KB 835, 845, CA.

[723] *Scranton's Trustee v Pearse* [1922] 2 Ch 87, CA.

20

PRIVATE INTERNATIONAL LAW

A. Introduction and Principles

(1) Conflict of Jurisdictions; Conflict of Laws

Private international law has three limbs. It determines when an English court has **20.01** jurisdiction to adjudicate where one or more of the parties, or some component of the analysis, is foreign: the conflict of jurisdictions. It determines the effect of a foreign judgment in the English legal order. And it determines whether an English court, hearing a case with some foreign element, will apply English or foreign law to the dispute: the conflict of laws. Its traditional source is the common law, and its historical focus was the development of choice of law rules. One textbook[1] has long exercised a dominating influence on the subject.

20.02 In recent years this emphasis has changed. Though there has been substantial legislation, much of it attributable to the harmonization of laws within Europe, the change of focus from conflict of laws to conflict of jurisdictions was first developed in the common law. The senior judiciary accepted that, as venue is often critical to the outcome of a case, more sophisticated and balanced jurisdictional rules were required, for once parties have fought on the issue of jurisdiction a case may well settle.

20.03 As to the conflict of laws, an English court applies English domestic law: common law, equity, and statute. It will not apply a foreign law to a question unless (1) choice of law rules provide that a foreign law is in principle applicable, (2) English legislation does not preclude its doing so, and (3) the party relying on foreign law pleads its applicability and proves its content to the satisfaction of the court.[2] No party is obliged to invoke foreign law, not even where an international convention stipulates that a particular law *shall* be applied. The judge has no power to investigate or apply foreign law *ex officio*, or on the basis that *curia novit jus* (the court knows the law, and therefore does not need to have it proved by the parties). In an English court, foreign law is a matter of fact to be pleaded and proved like any other fact. The proposition that foreign law is presumed to be the same as English law unless and until it is proved to be different is not now generally favoured.[3]

(2) The Methodology of Choice of Law

(a) Characterization of issues[4]

20.04 A choice of law rule is formulated by reference to connecting factors: capacity to marry is governed by the law of the domicile; liability in tort is governed by the *lex delicti*, and so on. This requires the facts to be accommodated within one or more legal categories to which a choice of law rule applies, by the characterization of the issue(s) presented by the dispute. The exercise is conducted within the conceptual structures of English domestic law, but bearing in mind that a flexible use of analogy may be needed to yield a rational answer. So a claim may be characterized

---

[1] LA Collins (ed) Dicey, Morris & Collins, *The Conflict of Laws* (14th edn, 2006); hereafter *Dicey*.

[2] See generally R Fentiman, *Foreign Law in English Courts* (1998).

[3] *Neilson v Overseas Projects Corp of Victoria Ltd* [2005] HCA 54, (2005) 223 CLR 331.

[4] *Dicey*, ch 2.

as contractual despite the absence of consideration for the promise;[5] a claim may be tortious even though there is nothing quite like it in English law;[6] an issue may still be one of capacity even though English law recognizes no such impediment.[7] New characterization categories may be developed. But where the question is whether to apply a rule contained in English legislation, a court may consider that the question is one of statutory construction, not one preceded by a question of characterization.[8]

(b) Renvoi[9]

Where foreign *law* is to be applied, this may mean the domestic law of the foreign **20.05** system, or the law, including the rules of the conflict of laws, which would be applied by a foreign judge were he hearing the case himself. Such reference to a third law[10] is a *renvoi*. Within the law of obligations an English[11] judge may look no further than the domestic rules of the chosen law,[12] and will disregard what a foreign judge might have done had he been hearing the case. But where status or the ownership of property is concerned, a court may accept the invitation, if the parties make it, to look beyond the domestic *lex causae* and to decide the case as the foreign judge would, by 'impersonating' him so far as the evidence of foreign law, and rules of procedure, permits it.[13]

(c) The operation of statutes and the Europeanization of private international law

A pervasive weakness in the conflict of laws lies in its handling of English statutes. **20.06** A court will only apply a foreign statutory rule if the foreign law is the *lex causae*. The reverse is not true: an English court may apply an English statute even though the rules for choice of law otherwise point to the application of a foreign law. All depends on the true construction of the statute, on whether Parliament has directed the judges to apply it without regard to, or despite, foreign elements in

---

[5] *Re Bonacina* [1912] 2 Ch 394.
[6] Private International Law (Miscellaneous Provisions) Act 1995, s 9.
[7] *Sottomayor v De Barros (No 1)* (1877) 3 PD 1, CA.
[8] *Raiffeisen Zentralbank Österreich AG v Five Star General Trading LLC* [2001] EWCA Civ 68; [2001] QB 825. See para 20.195.
[9] *Dicey*, ch 4. From the French 'to send'.
[10] Or back to the first law. It appears complicated if the chosen law refers back to English law, which would refer back to the foreign law, and so on. The possibility, which obsesses academic writers, has never arisen in a court, and is a paper tiger: see *Neilson v Overseas Projects Corp of Victoria Ltd* (n 3 above).
[11] The common law of Australia is different, at least in relation to torts: *Neilson v Overseas Projects Corp of Victoria Ltd* (n 3 above).
[12] Contracts (Applicable Law) Act 1990, Sch 1 art 15; Private International Law (Miscellaneous Provisions) Act 1995, s 9(5).
[13] O Kahn-Freund, *General Problems of Private International Law* (1976) 285.

the overall dispute.[14] Some, such as the Human Rights Act 1998, plainly override all contrary rules for choice of foreign law. Parliament, however, often legislates without making any clear statement of the international reach or 'legislative grasp' of its laws. The courts have to do the best they can.[15]

20.07   Though English legislation may sometimes be framed to fit within the scheme of the common law conflict of laws, applying only when the choice of law rules of the common law point to English law, no such assumption is applicable to legislation made by the European Union and effective under the European Communities Act 1972. European laws are made with an altogether different aim in mind; and it is wrong to read European legislative instructions as applicable only when the common law would point to the application of English law. European legislation defines its own sphere of operation, and is not designed to be passed through the filter of the common law.

(d) Connecting factors

20.08   Choice of law rules are usually expressed in terms of a connection between an individual, or an event, and a system of law. These 'connecting factors' are the building blocks for the choice of law, and they are almost all defined by English, and not by foreign, law. For example, if *X* is domiciled in France, this conclusion is unaffected by the possibility that French law might not agree.[16] If English law considers the law applicable to a contract to be Swiss, it is irrelevant that a Swiss court might have taken a different view.

20.09   The connection needs to be with a territory having *a* system of law, rather than with a larger political unit having many or none. For example, an individual may be domiciled in England, but not in the United Kingdom; in Florida, but not in the United States. But in cases where a foreign federal state is a single unit for certain legal purposes, the connection will depend on the context. So he may be domiciled in Australia (which is a single law district for the law of marriage) for the purposes of capacity to marry, but in Queensland for the purpose of making a will.

(i) Personal connecting factors

20.10   The basic personal connecting factor of the common law is domicile. Everyone has one; no-one can have more than one at the same time; and this law—the *lex domicilii*—has a prominent role in family and inheritance law. At a general level domicile may connote a person's permanent home, but the rules may ascribe a

---

14   For example, Unfair Contract Terms Act 1977, s 27.
15   See for example *Serco Ltd v Lawson* [2006] UKHL 3; [2006] ICR 250.
16   *Re Annesley* [1926] Ch 692.

domicile which is remote from the reality of the individual's life. There are three genera of the species. The domicile of origin is the domicile of one's father (or mother, when born out of wedlock or after the father's death). Though it is suppressed by the acquisition of a domicile of a different type, it is never eradicated. A domicile of choice is acquired by becoming resident in a particular country, intending to reside there permanently or indefinitely. So intention to reside in the United States, but not in a particular state, will not establish a domicile of choice in an American state;[17] an intention to remain for a fixed period, or until the occurrence of a certain event, such as retirement, does not suffice either.[18] It may be lost by abandonment (ceasing both to reside and to intend to reside), or displaced by acquiring a new domicile of choice. If abandonment is not contemporaneous with the acquisition of a new domicile of choice, the domicile of origin will reassert itself to prevent any domiciliary hiatus.[19] A child's domicile of dependency is that, from time to time, of the parent upon whom, until the age of sixteen or lawful younger marriage, the child is dependent. The domicile of dependency of married women was abolished in 1974.[20]

The rules of domicile can produce a capricious answer in a given case, especially **20.11** in Europe as political states and boundaries move and change.[21] But proposals for reform have been ignored. One particular consequence was that the common law conception of domicile was especially unsuitable to identify a court in which a person was liable to be sued in a civil or commercial action. For this reason the term 'domicile' in the Brussels I Regulation[22] is statutorily defined as separate and distinct from its common law homonym.[23]

'Habitual residence', or 'ordinary residence', which are more usually encountered **20.12** in laws deriving from international conventions, indicates a person's usual residence, but without the technical complications of the common law of domicile.

Nationality, as a connecting factor, is rare in the English conflict of laws. The **20.13** reasons are pragmatic but compelling. Nationality is ascribed by the law of the proposed state: no rule of English law can say whether someone is a French national. It is therefore immune to the judicial control applicable to other connecting factors. Moreover, dual nationality, or nationality in a federal or complex state such as the United States or the United Kingdom, would cause formidable

---

17 *Bell v Kennedy* (1868) LR 1 Sc & Div 307.
18 *IRC v Bullock* [1976] 1 WLR 1178, CA.
19 *Udny v Udny* (1869) LR 1 Sc & Div 441.
20 Domicile and Matrimonial Proceedings Act 1973, s 1.
21 *Re O'Keefe* [1940] Ch 124. Yugoslav domicile, for example, is a rather difficult connecting factor.
22 Council Regulation (EC) 44/2001, as to which see paras 20.33ff. The definition of domicile is in Civil Jurisdiction and Judgments Order 2001, SI 2001/3929, Sch 1.
23 See para 20.38.

difficulties. Nationality is rarely used in English law, but is commonly preferred in civilian systems.

(ii) Causal connecting factors

20.14 Expressions which describe a connection between an event and a law are also defined by reference to English law. They include the law of the court in which the trial is taking place (*lex fori*); the law applicable to a contract (*lex contractus*); the law of the place of the tort (*lex loci delicti*); the law of the place where a thing is (*lex situs*); the law of the place where a transaction took place (*lex loci actus*); the law of the place of celebration of marriage (*lex loci celebrationis*); the law of the place of incorporation (*lex incorporationis*); and in general the law applicable to the dispute (*lex causae*). No civilized person considers that these Latinate forms— elegant, economic, and hallowed by international usage—are improved by a verbose and clunking English paraphrase.

(e) The exclusive domain of the *lex fori*

20.15 Rules for choice of law will sometimes select the *lex fori* for the issue in question, but sometimes the *lex fori* supervenes to contradict the choice of law otherwise applicable. For convenience a partial summary of the role of the *lex fori* is now given: it examines three areas in which English law will simply apply the *lex fori* without regard to choice of law.

(i) Procedural matters[24]

20.16 Issues characterized as procedural are governed by English law. The question whether an intending litigant is competent to sue in an English court, the nature of the trial process, the admissibility of evidence, and so on, are governed by English law, albeit that this may be applied with a measure of flexibility. It does not follow that juristic persons unfamiliar to English law may not litigate: although the curator of a disappeared person has been denied *locus standi*,[25] a Hindu temple has been recognized as competent to sue.[26] Nor is there any rule which prevents the tendering of evidence acquired by means unknown to English law, so the product of oral discovery under US procedure is admissible at trial.[27] But the broad content of the trial process is governed by English law. And despite recent doubts, the assessment or quantification of damages is a matter of procedure, governed by English law, even when the substantive liability for a head of damages is governed by a foreign law.[28]

---

[24] *Dicey*, chs 7 and 8.
[25] *Kamouh v Associated Electrical Industries International Ltd* [1980] QB 199.
[26] *Bumper Development Corp v Commissioner of Police of the Metropolis* [1991] 1 WLR 1362, CA.
[27] *South Carolina Insurance Co v Assurantie Maatschappij 'De Zeven Provincien' NV* [1987] 1 AC 24.
[28] *Harding v Wealands* [2006] UKHL 32; [2006] 3 WLR 83.

An important sub-category of procedure is interim relief: this is ordered by an **20.17**
English court according to English law, and represents one of the main prizes at
stake when issues of jurisdiction are fought.[29] An English court cannot make
orders unknown to English procedural law. Specific limitations on the power of
the court may be imposed by international agreement or by the principles of
comity.[30] For example, an injunction freezing a defendant's assets worldwide,
which an English court may order, should not be made over assets within the
territorial jurisdiction of another EU Member State unless the English court is
seised of the substantive proceedings.[31] And an injunction ordering a person to
discontinue proceedings in a foreign court, explicable as an exercise of the power
to make procedural orders against someone subject to the jurisdiction, will be
made with restraint, to reflect the concurrent interest of the foreign court in the
matter.[32] But in all cases the relief is governed by English procedural law.

Until 1976 an English court lacked power to award damages in the foreign cur- **20.18**
rency in which the loss was sustained; it now may do so.[33] Until 1985, the limitation periods of English law applied to all actions brought in the English courts;
those of the *lex causae* were cumulatively applied if characterized as substantive,
but disregarded if characterized as procedural. Since the Foreign Limitation
Periods Act 1984 the limitation or prescription periods of the *lex causae* have
applied in place of those of English law, subject only to English public policy
where the application of the foreign period causes undue hardship; and only when
this happens will the English period be applied by default.[34]

(ii) Penal laws and revenue claims

An English court may not enforce a foreign penal law or a claim for foreign taxes.[35] **20.19**
So proceedings by a foreign state to enforce a bail bond,[36] or to collect taxes,[37] will
be struck out. In this context, 'penal' means 'criminal', and does not extend to
exemplary damages or indemnity costs.[38] The same principle is sometimes

---

[29] See generally LA Collins, *Essays in International Litigation and the Conflict of Laws* (1994) ch 1.
[30] *Motorola Credit Corp v Uzan* [2003] EWCA Civ 752; [2004] 1 WLR 113.
[31] Case C-391/95 *Van Uden Maritime BV v Deco-Line* [1998] ECR I-7091. As to the Brussels I
Regulation, see para 20.33 *et seq.*
[32] *Airbus Industrie GIE v Patel* [1999] 1 AC 119. No such order may be made if the foreign
proceedings are before the courts of an EU Member State: Case C-159/02 *Turner v Grovit* [2004]
ECR I-3565.
[33] *Miliangos v George Frank (Textiles) Ltd* [1976] AC 443; *Services Europe Atlantique Sud (SEAS) v
Stockholms Rederaktiebolag Svea of Stockholm (The Despina R)* [1979] AC 685.
[34] *Arab Monetary Fund v Hashim* [1996] 1 Lloyd's Rep 589, 599–600, CA.
[35] *Dicey*, Rule 3.
[36] *USA v Inkley* [1989] QB 255, CA.
[37] *Government of India v Taylor* [1955] AC 491.
[38] *SA Consortium General Textiles v Sun and Sand Agencies Ltd* [1978] QB 279, CA.

expressed as refusal to enforce a claim founded in a foreign sovereignty.[39] The prohibition extends to indirect enforcement, so an action to enforce a foreign judgment given against a defaulting taxpayer will be dismissed. But an application for the taking of evidence to assist a foreign revenue will not be refused:[40] there is no rule which requires the non-recognition of such laws unless they are so repellent that it would be contrary to public policy to accord them even that much effect.[41]

20.20 The line which separates indirect enforcement from recognition may be fine. A trader who sues on a foreign invoice which includes an element of sales tax should be entitled to judgment for the whole sum due; but part of the claim may be brought in his capacity as involuntary collector of taxes for the foreign state, and this looks much like indirect enforcement. On the other hand, if the foreign revenue has already demanded and received its payment from the claimant, or, conversely, will not be entitled to demand the payment until the trader receives the money, there will be no accrued and unsatisfied revenue claim at the date of the action,[42] and the principle will not be infringed if the trader succeeds on the whole of the claim.

20.21 To describe this as a rule where *lex fori* supervenes to prevent a claim may be misleading. One may better say that penal and revenue liabilities are governed by the *lex fori*. So a penal law may be 'enforceable' by the English law of extradition. A revenue law may be enforceable by recourse to the provisions of a treaty with the foreign state, given effect in England by domestic legislation. Seen in these terms the application of the *lex fori* is part of, and does not contradict, the rules for choice of law in the conflict of laws.

20.22 Some authority maintains that there is a third category, of 'other public laws'.[43] Laws analogous to penal and revenue laws (confiscation and nationalization, exchange control, laws regulating the security services, and so forth) should be dealt with similarly. Whether it is beneficial to call these 'other public laws' is doubtful.

(iii) Public policy

20.23 A rule of the *lex causae* will not be applied if repugnant to English public policy, or if the result of its application would be contrary to public policy. 'Public policy' in

---

[39] *Obiang Nguema v Logo Ltd* [2006] EWCA Civ 1370; [2007] 2 WLR 1062.

[40] *Re State of Norway's Application (Nos 1 and 2)* [1990] 1 AC 723.

[41] For example, *Kuwait Airways Corp v Iraqi Airways Co (Nos 4 and 5)* [2002] UKHL 19; [2002] 2 AC 883.

[42] Cf *Williams & Humbert Ltd v W & H Trade Marks (Jersey) Ltd* [1986] AC 368, 440–1; *QRS 1 Aps v Fransden* [1999] 3 All ER 289, CA.

[43] *A-G (UK) v Heinemann Publishers Australia Pty Ltd* (1988) 165 CLR 30.

this sense refers to the fundamental values of English law, and though this bears a restrictive meaning, it makes a distinctive contribution to the English conflict of laws. History offers some repellent illustrations. A law depriving a racial group of its property,[44] or invalidating inter-racial marriage, will, or should, be regarded as so offensive to public policy that it will be utterly ignored, no matter the context. So also a law which purported to dissolve a state and expropriate its property.[45] But a law giving a husband a unilateral right to divorce his wife while giving her no reciprocal right may be contrary to public policy when applied to a wife who is habitually resident in England,[46] yet be regarded differently when applied as between parties who have no connection with England. Much confusion is reduced when the two senses of public policy—the first absolute, the second contextual—are distinguished.

The common law does not apply the law or public policy of a country other than the *lex causae*. Article 7.1 of the Rome Convention offered the opportunity to do this in the context of contractual claims, but because it would have been an unprecedented novelty for English judges, and a disconcerting novelty for litigants, it was not enacted into English law.[47] But where a provision of the *lex causae* is also described within it as a rule of public policy, there is no reason whatever for an English court to decline to give it effect. **20.24**

(3) Scheme

The scheme of the remainder of this chapter is to look first at rules governing the jurisdiction of an English court, then at the treatment of foreign judgments, and then at choice of law for the various substantive areas of law. **20.25**

B. The Jurisdiction of English Courts

(1) Jurisdiction[48]

In general, a court must have jurisdiction over the subject matter of the claim, and over the defendant to it. **20.26**

So far as subject matter jurisdiction is concerned, there are few instances in which an English court lacks jurisdiction over the subject matter of a claim and **20.27**

---

[44] *Oppenheimer v Cattermole* [1976] AC 249.
[45] *Kuwait Airways Corp v Iraq Airways Co (Nos 4 and 5)* [2002] UKHL 19; [2002] 2 AC 883.
[46] Cf *Chaudhary v Chaudhary* [1985] Fam 19, CA.
[47] Convention on the Law Applicable to Contractual Relations (1980), enacted in England by Contracts (Applicable Law) Act 1990, ss 1, 2(2).
[48] *Dicey*, ch 11; A Briggs and P Rees, *Civil Jurisdiction and Judgments* (4th edn, 2005).

where no purported submission by the parties—which only establishes personal jurisdiction—can remedy the deficiency. There is no jurisdiction to adjudicate claims principally concerned with title to foreign land.[49] Authority also suggests that a court has no jurisdiction to adjudicate foreign patents or copyright, but the rule is less certain, and if such principle exists, its scope is contracting. And where the court has personal jurisdiction over the defendant by reason of the Brussels I Regulation it is doubtful whether these common law exclusions of jurisdiction may be invoked.[50]

20.28 The principles of state and diplomatic immunity restrict jurisdiction over claims brought against states[51] and diplomats; in relation to international organizations the instrument establishing the organization as a juridical person for the purposes of English law will usually define the extent of any immunity from the processes of the court.[52]

20.29 A court has personal jurisdiction over a defendant when process is served on him, and rules as to jurisdiction *in personam* are principally rules which delineate the right to serve process on the defendant.[53] The common law provides that any defendant present within the territorial jurisdiction of the court is liable to be served with process, but a defendant outside England is not so liable. But Civil Procedure Rules made under statutory authority permit a claimant to apply for permission to serve process on a defendant out of the jurisdiction: the instances in which this may be done are stated in rule 6.20.[54] For convenience these are together referred to as 'traditional' rules of jurisdiction, even though some are recent.

20.30 Since 1982 the adoption into English law of a series of European Conventions and Council Regulations, operating alongside the traditional rules, has radically altered the jurisdiction of English courts in civil and commercial matters.[55] A claimant must first consider whether these instruments confer jurisdiction on, or deny it to, an English court. If they do neither the traditional rules by which a court may have jurisdiction may be invoked.

20.31 Starting with civil or commercial disputes, this chapter treats these 'European' statutory rules as the heart of the subject, and the traditional rules as applying only

---

49 *British South Africa Co v Companhia de Moçambique* [1893] AC 602; cf Civil Jurisdiction and Judgments Act 1982, s 30.
50 *Pearce v Ove Arup Partnership Ltd* [2000] Ch 483, CA; cf *QRS 1 Aps v Fransden* [1999] 3 All ER 289, CA.
51 State Immunity Act 1978.
52 International Organizations Act 1968.
53 For the method of service see Civil Procedure Rules 1998 (CPR) Part 6.
54 Replacing Rules of the Supreme Court Ord 11, r 1(1).
55 Civil Jurisdiction and Judgments Act 1982 (the 1982 Act). Sch 1 (as amended) sets out the Brussels Convention; Sch 3C sets out the Lugano Convention. The Brussels I Regulation (44/2001/EC), 2001 OJ L12/1, is not separately enacted.

outside, and in the gaps left within, the domain of these instruments. It will be seen that the co-existence of these two systems of personal jurisdiction, each complex to begin with, leaves many complexities unresolved.

Jurisdiction in family matters, in the administration of estates, bankruptcy and **20.32** insolvency, and so on is examined in those sections of this chapter which deal with those as substantive topics. In summary, where the dispute raises a civil or commercial matter, the rules set out in this section will determine the jurisdiction of an English court.

(2) The Brussels and Lugano Rules

(a) The Conventions and the Regulation: scheme and domain

The Brussels Convention, as amended and reamended, regulates jurisdiction in **20.33** civil and commercial matters, serving as the basic jurisdictional statute of the member states of the European Union. Specified national courts were authorized to make references to the European Court of Justice (ECJ) for a preliminary ruling on the interpretation of the Convention.[56] Each Convention had an expert report as an essential aid to interpretation.[57] The Lugano Convention,[58] closely modelled on the Brussels Convention, operates in relation to Iceland, Norway, and Switzerland. Since 2004 the Brussels Convention was superseded[59] by a Regulation of the Council of Ministers: the 'Brussels I Regulation', the substance of which is little different from the Brussels Convention. Where these instruments confer jurisdiction on an English court, process may be served on the defendant as of right, whether inside, or (with the appropriate certification)[60] outside the jurisdiction.[61] References to the Brussels I Regulation may be taken to include the Brussels Convention and the Lugano Convention unless the contrary is stated.

Where the Brussels I Regulation confers international jurisdiction upon the courts **20.34** of a Member State, it indicates the courts of the United Kingdom rather than England, which is not a state. To respond to this, rules resembling those of the Regulation sub-allocate national jurisdiction to the courts of England and Wales, Scotland, or Northern Ireland.[62] These rules of United Kingdom law, which are

---

[56] 1982 Act, Sch 2. Reference was mandatory if a ruling was necessary and the court was one from which no appeal lay. With the Regulation, only final courts of appeal have power to make a reference.

[57] Jenard Report [1979] OJ C59/1; Schlosser Report ibid 71; Evrigenis Report [1986] OJ C298/1; Cruz Report [1989] OJ C189/35; 1982 Act, s 3(3).

[58] Jenard & Möller Report [1990] OJ C189/61.

[59] Denmark subscribed to the Regulation from July 1, 2007: 2006 OJ L 120/22.

[60] CPR 6.19; 6BPD, para 1.

[61] CPR 6.19.

[62] 1982 Act, Sch 4.

beneath the notice of the European Court of Justice,[63] apply where the Regulation gives jurisdiction to the courts of the United Kingdom, such as under Articles 2 (domicile), 9 and 12 (certain insurance claims), 16 (consumer contracts), 19 and 20 (employment contracts) and 22 (exclusive jurisdiction regardless of domicile). But where the Regulation confers jurisdiction directly upon a particular court, or upon the courts for a place, no sub-allocation of national jurisdiction is required.

20.35   Most definitional terms of the Brussels I Regulation bear 'autonomous' meanings, developed by the European Court of Justice, and quite distinct from the meanings of similar terms in English law. Moreover, as the basic principle is that a defendant shall be sued in the courts of the state where he is domiciled, a provision of the Regulation derogating from this will tend to receive a restrictive construction.[64] As the Regulation aims to make judgments obtained in one Member State freely enforceable in all others, rules which require non-recognition of judgments will be given a restrictive construction, and those which prevent parallel litigation will be construed amply.[65] Finally, as the courts of Member States have equal competence to interpret the Regulation, it is almost always inadmissible for the courts of one state to consider whether the courts of another erred in concluding that they had jurisdiction, and even more inadmissible to act on any such conclusion.[66]

(i) Civil and commercial matters

20.36   Where a claim falls within the domain of the Brussels I Regulation, the Regulation determines the jurisdiction of an English court. The practical hierarchy of these rules is reflected in the order in which they are examined below. 'Civil or commercial matters', explained in Article 1, may include claims made by public authorities, or by other public law entities, where the claims[67] advanced rely on rules of the general law as distinct from legal rights peculiar to public law. So a claim for the repayment or recovery of social assistance is civil or commercial if founded on the general law of restitution or subrogation, but not if it is founded on a special

---

[63] Case C-364/93 *Kleinwort Benson Ltd v City of Glasgow DC* [1995] ECR I-415. The extent to which decisions of the ECJ on the Convention are conclusive on the interpretation of Sch 4 was left unclear by *Kleinwort Benson Ltd v Glasgow City Council* [1999] 1 AC 153; cf *Agnew v Länsförsäkringsbolagens AB* [2001] 1 AC 223.

[64] The cases are innumerable.

[65] Case 144/86 *Gubisch Maschinenfabrik KG v Palumbo* [1987] ECR 4861.

[66] Case C-351/89 *Overseas Union Insurance Ltd v New Hampshire Insurance Co* [1991] ECR I-3317; Case C-159/02 *Turner v Grovit* [2004] ECR I-3565.

[67] Attention is paid to only the claim as distinct from any defence which may be raised: Case C-266/01 *Préservatrice Foncière TIARD v Netherlands* [2003] ECR I-4867.

statutory right given to the claimant as a matter of public law.[68] Even where a public body has power to require a trader to remove unfair terms from consumer contracts, the obligation enforced against him is civil or commercial.[69]

Article 1 excludes a claim which principally concerns customs, revenue or admin- **20.37** istrative matters, or status, marriage, matrimonial property or succession, or bankruptcy and insolvency, or social security, from the domain of the Regulation. Arbitration as a means of dispute resolution, and judicial measures to regulate it, lies outside the Regulation;[70] but the enforcement of judgments obtained in breach of an agreement to arbitrate is probably within it if the underlying subject matter was civil or commercial.[71] Proceedings to enforce a judgment from a non-Member State are not within the Regulation.[72] In all cases falling outside the domain of the Regulation, the jurisdiction of the English courts over the defendant is a matter for the traditional rules.

(ii) Domicile

Many of the rules of the Regulation turn upon whether the defendant is domi- **20.38** ciled in the United Kingdom or in another Member State. For an individual, domicile in the United Kingdom is determined by Civil Jurisdiction and Judgments Order 2001, Sch 1, rather than the common law. An individual is domiciled in the United Kingdom if resident in the United Kingdom, and this residence indicates a substantial connection with the United Kingdom: a fact which may be presumed from three months' residence.[73] Corresponding sub-rules determine whether an individual is domiciled in a part of the United Kingdom. For a company, domicile is generally[74] determined by a uniform defini-tion given in the Regulation itself: a company is domiciled where it has its statu-tory seat, or its central administration, or its principal place of business.[75] A trust is domiciled in England if English law is that with which the trust has its closest and most real connection.[76]

Whether an individual is domiciled in another Member State is stated by **20.39** Article 59 to be determined by the law of that state: whether he is domiciled in France is a matter for French law, and so on, so that an individual may have a

---

[68] Case C-271/00 *Gemeente Steenbergen v Baten* [2002] ECR I-10489; Case C-433/01 *Freistaat Bayern v Blijdenstein* [2004] ECR I-981.

[69] Case C-167/00 *VfK v Henkel* [2002] ECR I-8111.

[70] Case C-190/89 *Marc Rich & Co AG v Società Italiana Impianti PA* [1991] ECR I-3855.

[71] Case C-391/95 *Van Uden Maritime BV v Deco Line* [1998] ECR I-7091.

[72] Case C-129/92 *Owens Bank Ltd v Bracco* [1994] ECR I-117.

[73] 2001 Order, Sch 1 para 9.

[74] Though for the purposes of Art 22.2 of the Regulation (on which see para 20.42), the defini-tion of a company's seat is given by SI 2001/3929 Sch 1 para 10.

[75] Art 60.

[76] ibid s 45.

domicile in more than one Member State. Not so for a company: whether a corporation is domiciled in another Member State is determined by the definition given in Article 60 itself.

(b) Jurisdictional rules of the Brussels I Regulation

(i) Exclusive jurisdiction, regardless of domicile

20.40 Article 22 of the Regulation gives exclusive jurisdiction, regardless of domicile, to the courts of a Member State, in five areas. In the rare case where it confers exclusive jurisdiction on the courts of two Member States, Article 29 provides that only the first court seised has jurisdiction. Where Article 22 confers exclusive jurisdiction on a court, no other court has jurisdiction, not even if the parties agree to submit to it. In all cases the connection must lie with a Member State. If the land, patent, etc, is in a non-Member State the relevant question is whether a court with personal jurisdiction over the defendant may decline to exercise it.[77]

20.41 **Immoveables.** Article 22.1(a) covers proceedings which have as their principal object rights *in rem* in, or tenancies of, immoveable property in a Member State: exclusive jurisdiction vests in the state where the immoveable is; Article 6.4 permits a contractual action to be combined with the action *in rem*. Proceedings in which the tenancy is only part of the background to, or a minor part of, the overall dispute,[78] or claims which concern obligations enshrined in but not peculiar to tenancies,[79] are outside this provision; but disputing the existence of the tenancy does not disapply the Article.[80] Proceedings have as their object rights *in rem* where the claimant asserts that he is legal owner of the land, but not where he claims (for example, as contractual purchaser) to be entitled to become legal owner, or claims (for example, as beneficiary) to be equitable owner of the land under a trust, even though this is a right good against third parties.[81] Moreover, it is arguable that Article 22.1 is inapplicable where the relevant substantive law is not specifically land law or tenancy law.[82] Where the proceedings have as their object a private letting for six months or fewer, and landlord and tenant are domiciled in the same Member State, the courts of this state have concurrent exclusive jurisdiction under Article 22.1(b).[83]

---

77 See para 20.78.

78 Commonly so held in package or other holiday contracts: Case C-280/90 *Hacker v Euro-Relais* [1992] ECR I-1111; Case C-8/98 *Dansommer A/S v Götz* [2000] ECR I-393; Case C-73/04 *Klein v Rhodos Management Ltd* [2005] ECR I-8667.

79 Case 73/77 *Sanders v Van der Putte* [1977] ECR 2383 (business goodwill in shop lease). For the meaning of tenancy, see Case C-73/04 *Klein v Rhodos Management Ltd* [2005] ECR I-8667 (timeshare).

80 Case 158/87 *Scherrens v Maenhout* [1988] ECR 3791.

81 Case C-294/92 *Webb v Webb* [1994] ECR I-1717.

82 ibid.

83 On this point the Regulation, Brussels and Lugano Conventions slightly diverge.

Companies. Article 22.2 covers proceedings which have as their object the **20.42** validity of the constitution, the dissolution or winding-up, of companies, or the decisions of their organs: exclusive jurisdiction is vested in the Member State of the company's seat. Where the winding-up is simply a potential remedy such as for shareholder oppression[84] Article 22.2 is probably inapplicable.[85] Claims that an organ of the company acted without authority fall under Article 22.2, at least where this is the principal element of the claim; but allegations of misuse of authority do not.[86]

Registers. Article 22.3 gives exclusive jurisdiction to the Member State in which **20.43** a public register is kept if the proceedings have as their object the validity of an entry in that register. An action to rectify an entry on a land register on the basis of a pre-existing right will be covered.[87]

Patents, etc. Article 22.4 gives exclusive jurisdiction to the Member State in **20.44** which a patent or trade mark is registered or deposited where the proceedings have as their object the registration or validity of that right. Actions for infringement fall outside the Article,[88] but if invalidity is asserted as a defence, Article 22.4 applies to require validity to be determined in the Member State of registration. It is unclear whether raising this defence permits or requires the court seised with the infringement claim to cede jurisdiction to the court with exclusive jurisdiction to rule on the validity issue.[89]

Judgments. Article 22.5 gives exclusive jurisdiction to the Member State in **20.45** which a judgment from another Member State is being enforced if the proceedings are concerned with the enforcement. But there must be a judgment: proceedings which pave the way for enforcement of a prospective judgment are not included.[90]

(ii) Jurisdiction by appearance

Article 22 apart, a court before which the defendant enters an appearance has **20.46** jurisdiction: Article 24. A prior agreement on jurisdiction will be considered to have been waived by consent.[91] But appearance solely to contest the jurisdiction of the court[92] will not confer jurisdiction: the scheme of the Regulation encourages the defendant to appear without prejudice to argue about its

---

[84] Companies Act 2006, s 996.
[85] Cf Case C-294/92 *Webb v Webb* [1994] ECR I-1717.
[86] *Grupo Torras SA v Sheikh Fahad Mohammed al Sabah* [1996] 1 Lloyd's Rep 7, CA.
[87] *Re Hayward* [1997] Ch 45.
[88] Case 288/82 *Duijnstee v Goderbauer* [1983] ECR 3663.
[89] Case C-4/03 *GAT v LuK* [2006] ECR I-6509.
[90] Case C-261/90 *Reichert v Dresdner Bank (No 2)* [1992] ECR I-2149.
[91] Case 150/80 *Elefanten Schuh GmbH v Jacqmain* [1981] ECR 1671.
[92] CPR Part 11.

proper application. As long as the challenge is made at the first available opportunity he will not forfeit his jurisdictional defence if he is required to plead his substantive defence at the same time.[93]

(iii) Insurance, consumer, and employment contracts

20.47 In relation to disputes arising out of insurance contracts, certain consumer contracts, and contracts of individual employment, where the insurer, supplier or employer is domiciled (or was not, but made the contract from a local branch or agency which was itself domiciled) in a Member State, there may be such inequality between the parties that the insured, consumer, or employee needs special jurisdictional privileges. Articles 8–14 (insurance contracts), 15–17 (certain consumer contracts), and 18–21 (contracts of individual employment) contain complexes of rules in which the weaker party has the right to sue and be sued in 'his' courts,[94] the stronger party may sue only where the other is domiciled, and where jurisdiction agreements are generally binding only if entered into after the dispute arose, or if they widen the choice given to the weaker party. Where the defendant insurer, supplier, or employer is not domiciled in a Member State, Article 4 will apply.[95]

20.48 Insurance. The insurance contract provisions do not apply to reinsurance,[96] or to disputes between professional insurers,[97] where the parties can look after themselves. They do apply to direct actions by the injured party against the insurer. The insured may have a further choice to sue where the harmful event occurred (in liability insurance) or where the land is (property insurance).

20.49 Consumers. Consumer contracts are those which secure the needs of an individual in terms of private consumption.[98] They are further restricted to contracts for the sale of goods on instalment credit terms, or for a loan repayable by instalments to finance the purchase of goods, or those concluded with a person who pursues commercial or professional activities in the state of the consumer's domicile, or who directs his activities to such a state (most typically by advertising, or electronic means). Contracts for mixed purposes count as consumer contracts

---

[93] Case 27/81 *Rohr v Ossberger* [1981] ECR 2431.

[94] Domicile, in the case of insurance and consumer contracts; the place of work in employment contracts.

[95] See para 20.70.

[96] Case C-412/98 *Universal General Insurance Co v Groupe Josi Reinsurance Co SA* [2000] ECR I-5925.

[97] Case C-77/04 GIE *Réunion Européenne v Soc Zurich España* [2005] ECR I-4509.

[98] Case C-269/95 *Benincasa v Dentalkit Srl* [1997] ECR I-3767; see also Case C-99/96 *Mietz v Intership Yachting Sneek BV* [1999] ECR I-2277. On investment contracts entered into by private individuals, see Case C-89/91 *Shearson Lehmann Hutton v TVB* [1993] ECR I-139; Case C-318/93 *Brenner v Dean Witter Reynolds Inc* [1994] ECR I-4275.

only if the business element is negligible;[99] and if the rights of the consumer have been assigned to a non-consumer, the contract ceases to be a consumer contract.[100]

Employment. For contracts of individual employment,[101] the employee's **20.50** 'home' court, the jurisdictional advantage of which he is entitled to claim, is that of the Member State in which he habitually carries out his duties;[102] and where these are undertaken in more than one Member State, this will be understood to indicate the principal place, or place where the duties have their centre of gravity.[103]

(iv) Agreements on jurisdiction

Apart from the cases examined above, where their effect is restricted, agreements **20.51** on jurisdiction for the courts of a Member State are validated by Article 23. A compliant agreement binds the court chosen and those whose jurisdiction is excluded. Only if no party is domiciled in a Member State may the agreement be overridden if the nominated court has declined jurisdiction. There is otherwise no discretion to override a jurisdiction agreement, say on grounds of overall trial convenience.[104] An agreement nominating the courts of two Member States will be effective;[105] so also will one providing for non-exclusive jurisdiction.[106] Agreements for the courts of the United Kingdom are effective so far as the Regulation is concerned, but raise some practical difficulties. It probably prorogates the courts of any part of the United Kingdom unless it can be construed as being more precise than first appears.[107] An agreement for the courts of a non-Member State is outside Article 23, for the Regulation cannot bind such a court to accept jurisdiction: the relevant question is whether a court with jurisdiction under the Regulation may on this ground decline it.[108]

Formalities. To prevent ambush, Article 23 requires the agreement to be in **20.52** writing or evidenced in writing, or in a form which accords with the parties' established practice, or in a form which is well known to accord with international trade usage of which the parties were or should have been aware. So a printed term

---

[99] Case C-464/01 *Gruber v Bay Wa AG* [2005] ECR I-439.

[100] Case C-89/91 *Shearson Lehmann Hutton v TVB* [1993] ECR I-139.

[101] See *Benatti v WPP Holdings Italy* [2007] EWCA Civ 263; [2007] ILPr 403.

[102] Art 19.

[103] Case C-125/92 *Mulox IBC v Geels* [1993] ECR I-4075; Case C-383/95 *Rutten v Cross Medical Ltd* [1997] ECR I-57; Case C-37/00 *Weber v Universal Ogden Services Ltd* [2002] ECR I-2013.

[104] *Hough v P & O Containers Ltd* [1999] QB 834.

[105] Case 23/78 *Meeth v Glacetal Sàrl* [1978] ECR 2133 (but where each court had exclusive jurisdiction over the actions referred to it).

[106] As is now expressly confirmed by Art 23.

[107] Cf *Hellenic Steel Co v Svolmar Shipping Co (The Komninos S)* [1991] 1 Lloyd's Rep 370, CA.

[108] See para 20.78.

in standard conditions of business will be ineffective unless the parties have signed their agreement to it;[109] but a settled course of dealing will establish a binding form. The consent of a third party claiming to take the benefit of such an agreement, or succeeding to the obligations of the contract as a matter of law, need not be written if the formalities were originally satisfied.[110] Tension exists between the belief that strict insistence on the formality rules will prevent sharp practice, and awareness that it may, on occasion, license it. Though the European Court continues to insist on a strict application of the formalities,[111] it approved a more flexible approach in the context of international trade,[112] and when insistence on formal invalidity would manifest bad faith.[113] More creatively, a shareholder was held bound by a jurisdiction agreement contained in the company's constitution, on the ground that he knew or should have known of it, and assented to be bound by acquiring and retaining the shares.[114] The width of the reasoning in this case remains to be tested.

20.53 **Substance.** An agreement which complies with the formalities may not be impeached on the ground that it fails to comply with some provision of national law which would otherwise invalidate it.[115] Certainly, and sensibly, a submission that the entire contract is ineffective is irrelevant, for the jurisdiction agreement is regarded, as a matter of law and in accordance with the presumed intention of the parties, as severable from and independent of any contract containing it.[116] But where written 'consent' was procured by force or fraud, it must be open to a court to find that there was no 'agreement' to confer jurisdiction. The precise legal basis for this remains to be identified.

(v) General jurisdiction over defendants domiciled in the United Kingdom

20.54 If none of the foregoing confers jurisdiction, the rule in Article 2, that general jurisdiction exists where the defendant is domiciled, will apply. It is striking that

---

[109] Case 24/76 *Estasis Salotti v RUWA* [1976] ECR 1831; Case C-159/97 *Trasporti Castelletti Spedizioni Internazionali SpA v Hugo Trumpy SpA* [1999] ECR I-1597 (on an earlier version of Art 17).

[110] Case 71/83 *The Tilly Russ* [1984] ECR 2417; Case C-387/98 *Coreck Maritime GmbH v Handelsveem BV* [2000] ECR I-9337. Otherwise if the third party is said to be bound otherwise than by means of legal succession: Case C-112/03 *Soc financière et industrielle de Peloux v AXA Belgium* [2005] ECR I-3707.

[111] Case C-105/95 *MSG v Les Gravières Rhénanes SARL* [1997] ECR I-911.

[112] ibid.

[113] Case 221/84 *Berghöfer v ASA SA* [1985] ECR 2699.

[114] Case C-214/89 *Powell Duffryn plc v Petereit* [1992] ECR I-1745.

[115] Case 25/79 *Sanicentral GmbH v Collin* [1979] ECR 3423; Case 150/80 *Elefanten Schuh GmbH v Jacqmain* [1981] ECR 1671; Case C-159/97 *Trasporti Castelletti Spedizioni Internazionali SpA v Hugo Trumpy SpA* [1999] ECR I-1597.

[116] Case C-269/95 *Benincasa v Dentalkit Srl* [1997] ECR I-3767.

though this is the fundamental jurisdictional principle of the Regulation, its place in the hierarchy of rules is not prominent.

(vi) Special jurisdiction over defendants domiciled in another Member State

If none of the foregoing confers jurisdiction, Articles 5 and 6 permit 'special **20.55** jurisdiction' over defendants domiciled in another Member State. Article 5 acknowledges the sense of *forum conveniens*, but its application is not dependent on showing that the court being, in the instant case, a *forum conveniens*.[117] Article 5 may not be used as the anchor for claims over which the court would not otherwise have had jurisdiction: such general jurisdiction is conferred by Article 2, and this practical disincentive to invoke Article 5 is deliberate. Article 6 deals with multipartite litigation.

Matters relating to a contract.   Article 5.1 gives special jurisdiction to the courts **20.56** for the place of performance of the obligation in question. A matter does not relate to a contract unless it involves obligations freely entered into with another, but if it does it is not decisive that it would be regarded as non-contractual by national law.[118] So a claim to enforce the rules of an association,[119] or the obligations of a shareholder to a company,[120] is contractual even though a national law may disagree; a warranty claim by a sub-buyer against a manufacturer is excluded, even if contractual under national law.[121] Where the validity of the contract is disputed the rule still applies,[122] and this is so even if the claimant asserts that an alleged contract is ineffective.[123] But if it is common ground that the supposed contract was void *ab initio*,[124] or the complaint is that a contract was (wrongfully) not concluded, the matter does not relate to a contract.[125]

---

[117] Case C-228/92 *Custom Made Commercial Ltd v Stawa Metallbau GmbH* [1994] ECR I-2913.

[118] Case 34/82 *Peters v ZNAV* [1983] ECR 987.

[119] ibid.

[120] Case C-214/89 *Powell Duffryn plc v Petereit* [1992] ECR I-1745.

[121] Case C-26/91 *Jakob Handte GmbH v Traitements Mécano-chimiques des Surfaces* [1992] ECR I-3967.

[122] Case 38/81 *Effer SpA v Kantner* [1982] ECR 825.

[123] *Agnew v Länsförsäkringsbolagens AB* [2001] 1 AC 223; *Boss Group Ltd v Boss France SA* [1997] 1 WLR 351, CA.

[124] *Kleinwort Benson Ltd v Glasgow City Council* [1999] 1 AC 153 (on the intra-UK provisions of Sch 4 to the 1982 Act). The authority of this case is restricted by *Agnew* (ibid) to such rare cases.

[125] Case C-334/00 *Fonderie Officine Mecchaniche Tacconi SpA v HWS Maschinenfabrik GmbH* [2002] ECR I-7357.

20.57 The obligation in question means the performance obligation[126] (or the principal obligation if more than one)[127] upon which the claim is founded. However, in claims concerning contracts for the sale of goods, this is now[128] deemed to be where delivery was due; in contracts for the supply of services, the contractual place of supply. In any case where the place is not apparent, it is ascertained by recourse to the national law, including conflicts rules, of the court seised.[129] This approach has been criticized, but its respect for the autonomy of the parties, who may rely on the general rule contained in the law which governs their contract, is unassailable.

20.58 The obligation in question need not be one created by, or arising for performance under, the contract. It suffices that the obligation is associated with the contract.[130] So an obligation to present the risk to an insurer fairly, or not to lie to or coerce the opposite party, may be the obligation in question which locates special jurisdiction under Article 5.1.[131]

20.59 **Matters relating to tort.** Article 5.3 gives special jurisdiction to the courts for the place where the harmful event occurred or may occur. This identifies the place where the damage occurred or of the event giving rise to it: the claimant may elect between them.[132] Damage occurs where it first materializes, rather than where it is subsequently felt. So if property is taken, the damage occurs where the taking happens rather than where the financial records are kept;[133] where the negligent advice is received and acted on rather than where the adverse financial consequences of doing so are felt.[134] The relevant damage is that done to the immediate victim:[135] the killing of the deceased, rather than the shock or bereavement sustained by a relative. Moreover, in specifying and locating the damage and the event giving rise to it, an autonomous interpretation of the cause of action is taken.[136] For defamation, the event giving rise to the damage is the production of the newspaper rather than its sale to readers;[137] for negligent misrepresentation,

---

126 Case 14/76 *De Bloos Sprl v Bouyer SA* [1976] ECR 1497. It may be difficult to determine whether an obligation to pay a sum of money on the occurrence of a certain event is a performance, or a secondary, obligation.

127 Case 266/85 *Shenavai v Kreischer* [1987] ECR 239; Case C-420/97 *Leathertex Divisione Sintetici spa v Bodetex BVBA* [1999] ECR I-6747.

128 The sub-rule of the Regulation had no precursor in the Conventions.

129 Case 12/76 *Industrie Tessili Italiana Como v Dunlop AG* [1976] ECR 1473; Case C-440/97 *GIE Groupe Concorde v Master of Vessel 'Suhediwarno Panjan'* [1999] ECR I-6307.

130 Case C-27/02 *Engler v Janus Versand GmbH* [2005] ECR I-481.

131 *Agnew v Länsförsäkringsbolagens AB* [2001] 1 AC 223.

132 Case 21/76 *Handelskwekerij GJ Bier BV v Mines de Potasse d'Alsace* [1976] ECR 1875.

133 Case 364/93 *Marinari v Lloyds Bank plc* [1995] ECR I-2719.

134 *Domicrest Ltd v Swiss Bank Corp* [1999] QB 548.

135 Case C-220/88 *Dumez France SA v Hessische Landesbank* [1990] ECR I-49.

136 Case C-364/93 *Marinari v Lloyds Bank plc* [1995] ECR I-2719.

137 Case C-68/93 *Shevill v Presse Alliance SA* [1995] ECR I-415.

the making of the statement, not its reception:[138] in short, the relevant event is generally that which marks the beginning of the tort. Any uniformity which this may create will be ushered in by an age of uncertainty while it is decided whether, for example, the failure to test properly, or the marketing without adequate warning, is what gives rise to the damage in product liability cases.

A tort means any action which seeks to establish the liability of a defendant and which is not a matter relating to a contract within Article 5.1.[139] Despite the width of this formulation, it is probably limited to claims founded on recompense for wrongdoing, and does not extend to claims for pure restitution where it is alleged to be unjust to retain the enriching profit rather than unlawful to have inflicted the wrongful loss.[140] **20.60**

Branches and agencies.   Under Article 5.5, claims arising from the operations of a branch, agency, or other establishment may be brought where it is situated. A branch, as an entity, has to be sufficiently dependent, and sufficiently independent;[141] a useful criterion is whether it has power on its own account to make contracts which will bind its principal.[142] **20.61**

Civil claims in criminal proceedings.   Article 5.4 allows a court hearing a criminal claim to order damages or restitution to a claimant who has intervened as a 'civil party'. This has little practical relevance in England. **20.62**

Maintenance claims.   In relation to maintenance, Article 5.2 gives special jurisdiction to the maintenance creditor's place of domicile or habitual residence. The distinction between maintenance, and rights in property arising out of a matrimonial relationship (excluded from the domain of the Regulation by Article 1) is clear if the court states the purpose of the financial award, but less so if it does not.[143] **20.63**

Trusts.   Article 5.6 gives special jurisdiction over a settlor, trustee or beneficiary of a written or statutory trust, who is sued as such, to the place where the trust is domiciled. **20.64**

Salvage.   Article 5.7 gives special jurisdiction in salvage claims to the place where the ship was or could have been arrested to secure payment. **20.65**

---

138 *Domicrest Ltd v Swiss Bank Corporation* [1999] QB 548.
139 Case 189/87 *Kalfelis v Bankhaus SchröderMunchmeyer Hengst & Co* [1988] ECR 5565.
140 *Kleinwort Benson Ltd v Glasgow City Council* [1999] 1 AC 153, though note the contrary view of the Advocate-General in Case C-89/91 *Shearson Lehmann Hutton Inc v TVB* [1993] ECR I-139, 178.
141 Case 218/86 *SAR Schotte GmbH v Parfums Rothschild Sarl* [1987] ECR 4905.
142 Case C-89/91 *Shearson Lehmann Hutton v TVB* [1993] ECR I-139, 169.
143 Case C-220/95 *Van den Boogaard v Laumen* [1997] ECR I-1147.

20.66 **Connected claims.** The Regulation does not permit jurisdiction to be taken over another claim simply because the court has jurisdiction over one, and the two should be tried together to avoid the risk of irreconcilable judgments.[144] Article 6 makes partial amends, the better to co-ordinate the judicial function, but the limits upon its operation are restrictive, and it is undeniable that at this point the Regulation is unsatisfactory.

20.67 **Co-defendants.** Where a claim is brought against several defendants Article 6.1 allows them to be joined in the one action only if it is brought where one of them is domiciled and it is necessary to join the claims so as to avoid the risk of irreconcilable judgments resulting from separate proceedings:[145] there should be flexibility in the assessment of this condition.[146] But there is no analogous right to join co-defendants into proceedings in a court exercising special jurisdiction under Article 5, or jurisdiction by consent under Articles 23 or 24; and still less jurisdiction under Article 4.

20.68 **Third party claims.** Article 6.2 allows a claim against a third party for a contribution or indemnity, or in some other third party proceeding, to be brought in the court seised of the original action unless this was instituted with the sole object of establishing jurisdiction over the third party. The jurisdictional basis of the original action is irrelevant. The court may refuse joinder of the third party so long as this is not done for reasons which, in effect, contradict the general scheme of the Regulation.[147] But if there is a choice of court agreement between defendant and third party, Article 23 will preclude reliance on Article 6.2, no matter how inconvenient the overall result.[148]

20.69 **Counterclaims.** Article 6.3 allows a counterclaim to be brought in the court in which the original action is pending. The provision is limited to claims which arise out of the same relationship or other essential facts; it will not extend to a counterclaim against a party other than the original claimant.[149]

---

[144] The possibility is explicitly rejected by Case 189/87 *Kalfelis v Bankhaus Schröder Munchmeyer Hengst & Co* [1988] ECR 5565.

[145] ibid. Case C-103/05 *Reisch Montage AG v Kiesel Baumaschinen Handels GmbH* [2006] ECR I-6827 held it irrelevant that the claim against the local defendant was barred by a rule of national procedural law: *sed quaere.*

[146] But the contrary is suggested by Case C-51/97 *Réunion Européenne SA v Spliethoff's Bevrachtingskantoor BV* [1998] ECR I-6511; Case C-539/03 *Roche Nederland BV v Primus* [2006] ECR I-6535.

[147] Case C-365/88 *Kongress Agentur Hagen GmbH v Zeehaghe BV* [1990] ECR I-1845.

[148] *Hough v P & O Containers Ltd* [1999] QB 834.

[149] Cf *Jordan Grand Prix Ltd v Baltic Insurance Group* [1999] 2 AC 127, HL.

(vii) Defendants not domiciled in a Member State

If nothing else implicates him, the Regulation does not prescribe in detail when   **20.70**
jurisdiction may be taken over a defendant whose only connection is with a
non-Member State. Article 4 authorizes the claimant to invoke the traditional
jurisdictional rules of the court in which he wishes to sue: service by right on an
Australian defendant present in England, service out of the jurisdiction with permission on an American defendant under CPR Part 6, and so on. But as Article 4
operates within the overall Regulation scheme, and produces judgments enforceable under the Regulation, Articles 27 and 28, which regulate parallel litigation,
apply when jurisdiction is taken under it.[150] The extent to which a court may
decline jurisdiction under Article 4 is considered below.[151]

(viii) Removal of jurisdiction: lis pendens and related actions

The principle that judgments should be freely enforceable in other Member States   **20.71**
cannot countenance the concurrent litigation of disputes. Articles 27 and 28 provide the solution.

Lis pendens.   Where the same parties bring the same action before the courts of   **20.72**
two Member States, Article 27 requires the second to dismiss the action once the
court seised first has determined that it does have jurisdiction. The rule is simple
and chronological, taking no account of comparative appropriateness: all courts
with jurisdiction are equally appropriate, and all jurisdictional rules under the
Regulation, including Article 4, are equally proper. It forbids the second court to
rule that the first court erred in accepting jurisdiction, even where it was seised in
flagrant breach of a jurisdiction agreement for the second court:[152] all courts
are equally competent and bound to apply the Regulation,[153] and where the com-
petences are equal the first in time prevails. An exception may yet be admitted
where the second court has exclusive jurisdiction under Article 22.[154] Only if the
defendant in the first court contests its jurisdiction may the second court stay its
proceedings; but once the first court has confirmed its jurisdiction the second
court must dismiss the action. This can produce a tactical rush to commence
litigation and seise a party's preferred court; it may be catastrophic to threaten
the opposite party that proceedings will be commenced after a stated period.
'Seise first and write letters later' is the watchword.

---

[150] Case C-351/89 *Overseas Union Insurance Ltd v New Hampshire Insurance Co* [1991]
ECR I-3317.

[151] See para 20.78.

[152] Case C-116/02 *Erich Gasser GmbH v MISAT srl* [2003] ECR I-14693.

[153] *Overseas Union Insurance* (n 150 above).

[154] ibid.

20.73 Article 27 requires three 'identities': of parties (but procedural differences between the formulation of the claimants and defendants are not decisive, so an admiralty action *in rem* may involve the same parties as an action *in personam*);[155] of object (the two actions must have the same end in view); and of cause (they must be based on the same facts and rules of law).[156] So an action for damages for breach of contract shares identity with an action for a declaration that the contract was lawfully rescinded;[157] an action for damage to cargo is identical to one against the cargo-owner for a declaration of non-liability.[158] But a claim for damages for breach of warranty of quality is not identical with an action for the price of goods delivered.

20.74 Under the Conventions, the date on which a court became seised was that on which the matter became definitively pending before each court, and was identified by the procedural law of each court.[159] According to this, an English court was not seised until process was served on the particular defendant:[160] neither the issue of process, nor service on a co-defendant, nor obtaining interim relief from the court prior to service would do. Article 30 of the Regulation now applies a uniform rule: the date of issue in systems (like England) where issue precedes service, the date of service in those jurisdictions where a summons is served and then filed at court. This makes the question less difficult to answer, but it does not eliminate the race to commence proceedings.

20.75 **Related actions.** Article 28 may apply if the actions are related: that is, so closely connected that it is expedient to hear them together to avoid the risk of irreconcilable judgments resulting from separate proceedings. If this condition is fulfilled the second court may dismiss its action for consolidation with the proceedings pending in the first court, or it may stay its action to await the outcome in the first court. Article 22 therefore allows consolidation if the first court would have jurisdiction over the second action as well, but it does not create a new jurisdiction based on the bare fact of connexity. A preference for dismissal[161] is appropriate if the two actions involve different parties: binding all concerned into the one hearing is sensible. But if the same parties are litigating different causes of action it may be more efficient to stay the second action and apply rules of judgment recognition to limit the scope of the second action.

---

155 Case C-406/92 *The Tatry* [1994] ECR I-5439; in relation to insurers and insureds, Case C-351/96 *Drouot Assurances SA v CMI* [1998] ECR I-3075.

156 *The Tatry* (ibid).

157 Case 144/86 *Gubisch Maschinenfabrik KG v Palumbo* [1987] ECR 4861.

158 *The Tatry* (n 155 above).

159 Case 129/83 *Zelger v Salinitri (No 2)* [1984] ECR 2397.

160 *Dresser UK Ltd v Falcongate Freight Management Ltd* [1992] QB 502, CA.

161 *Sarrio SA v Kuwait Investment Authority* [1999] 1 AC 32.

(ix) Judicial discretion and Regulation jurisdiction

A remaining question is the extent to which an English court may supplement or **20.76** modify the jurisdictional scheme of the Regulation by rules on *forum conveniens*, anti-suit injunctions, and so forth. The fundamental problem is that judicial discretion, which permeates the common law on jurisdiction, is alien to civilian jurisdictions. Three issues must be examined.

Disputing jurisdiction.   When challenging jurisdiction *in limine*, a defendant **20.77** may deny that the court has the jurisdiction asserted by the claimant. The claimant must demonstrate a good arguable case that the ground on which he relies is satisfied on the facts.[162] However, this involves an exercise in judgment, not discretion.

Forum non conveniens.   If the court has jurisdiction under any of the rules of **20.78** the Regulation aside from Article 4, there is no power to stay proceedings on the ground of *forum non conveniens*, even in respect of a non-Member State, as the European Court considers a stay in such circumstances to be damaging to legal certainty and therefore intolerable.[163] Quite why the Regulation prevents a stay of English proceedings in favour of the courts of Jamaica is puzzling, for this appears to have little to do with the completion of the single market. But civilian hostility to the doctrine of *forum non conveniens* can seem almost pathological. However, if the connection to a non-Member State is that the proceedings concern title to land there, or the validity of patents granted under its law; or where there is a jurisdiction agreement for the courts of that non-Member State; or where there a *lis alibi pendens* in that non-Member State,[164] it is probable that a court may grant procedural relief according to common law principles. If this is because Articles 22, 23, 27 and 28 may be applied by analogy, the argument must not be pressed too far, as the relief which the court may order will be discretionary where the corresponding provision in the Regulation would have made it mandatory. Where jurisdiction is founded on Article 4, a court may consider *forum conveniens* in determining whether to grant or set aside permission to serve out, and also on an application to stay proceedings on grounds of *forum conveniens*, as *forum non conveniens* is indissociable from the rules of jurisdiction authorized for use by Article 4. It has even been held that this is permitted in favour of the courts of another Member State. As this implicates another Member State it is controversial, though the contrary answer would widen Article 4 jurisdiction still further, which would be hard to understand.[165]

---

162 *Canada Trust Co v Stolzenberg (No 2)* [2002] 1 AC 1.
163 Case C-281/02 *Owusu v Jackson* [2005] ECR I-1383.
164 Case 387/98 *Coreck Maritime GmbH v Handelsveem BV* [2000] ECR I-9337.
165 *Haji-Ioannou v Frangos* [1999] 2 Lloyd's Rep 337, CA.

20.79 **Anti-suit injunctions.** Given that a court seised second has no right to assess the jurisdiction of a court seised first, it follows that it has no right to order a party to discontinue his foreign action: this would involve ruling on the foreign court's jurisdiction and ordering relief on its lack. Despite the fact that the English courts were prepared to do this, especially in order to reinforce the rights created by a jurisdiction agreement,[166] and despite the English understanding that the injunction involves no assessment of the behaviour of the judge, but only of the individual who is invoking or who proposes to invoke the foreign court's jurisdiction, the European Court held that grant of anti-suit injunctions was wholly incompatible with the 'mutual trust' inherent in the Regulation scheme of jurisdiction.[167] It is therefore forbidden to grant them to prevent a respondent from bringing proceedings in a civil or commercial matter before the courts of another Member State. Where the injunction is sought in aid of an arbitration agreement by restraining civil or commercial proceedings brought before the courts of another Member State, it is unclear whether the prohibition applies.[168] Where an injunction to reinforce a jurisdiction agreement is forbidden, there is the possibility, as yet untested, of bringing proceedings for damages for breach of contract.

(x) Applications for provisional or protective measures

20.80 Where the claim falls within the domain of the Regulation, it is necessary to distinguish two cases in which provisional and protective measures may be applied for. If the court has jurisdiction on the merits the Regulation places no restriction upon the form of provisional relief which it may order.[169] If it does not, application may be made under Article 31, and the only jurisdictional requirements are those which national law places upon the applicant: there is no objection in this context to the use of exorbitant grounds of personal jurisdiction. But the Regulation imposes two further limitations: the measure must be one which is truly provisional, in that it is guaranteed to be reversible, not a final determination of rights, as well as protective; and its scope may not extend to assets within the territorial jurisdiction of another Member State.[170]

---

[166] *Continental Bank NA v Aeakos Compania Naviera SA* [1994] 1 WLR 588, CA.

[167] Case C-159/02 *Turner v Grovit* [2004] ECR I-3565.

[168] *Through Transport Mutual Insurance Association (Eurasia) Ltd v New India Assurance Association Co Ltd* [2004] EWCA Civ 1598; [2005] 1 Lloyd's Rep 67. The issue was referred to the European Court as Case C-185/07 *West Tankers Inc v Ras Riunione Adriatica di Securita Spa* [2007] UKHL 4; [2007] 1 Lloyds Rep 391.

[169] Case C-391/95 *Van Uden Maritime BV v Deco Line* [1998] ECR I-7091; Case C-99/66, *Mietz v Intership Yachting Sneek BV* [1999] ECR I-2277.

[170] Case C-220/95 *Van Uden Maritime BV v Deco-Line* [1998] ECR I-7091.

(3) *Common Law and Rules of Court*

(a) Domain of the traditional rules

If the dispute is not a civil or commercial matter, the traditional rules of English **20.81** law govern the jurisdiction of the court. Neither the Brussels I Regulation nor the Conventions will apply, and nor will the judgment qualify for recognition under these instruments.

It bears repeating that in a civil or commercial matter, where Article 4 of the **20.82** Regulation authorizes the rules of English law to apply, it is misleading to argue that the Regulation is inapplicable. The control of parallel litigation in the courts of Member States, and the recognition of judgments within them, will still be governed by the Regulation.[171] We proceed to examine the traditional approach to the jurisdiction of an English court.

(b) Jurisdiction based on service of process within England

(i) *Jurisdiction by service*

An individual who is present in England can be served with process as of right; **20.83** and this service establishes the jurisdiction of the court over him. The manner of service is prescribed by the Civil Procedure Rules and is examined in the chapter on civil procedure. Service on a partnership firm is also regulated by the CPR.[172] Service on a company or other corporation is examined below.[173]

(ii) *Objecting to the existence or exercise of jurisdiction*

A defendant who considers that the court lacks jurisdiction over him or over the **20.84** subject matter of the claim, or who contends that service was irregular, or on some other ground seeks to have service of process set aside, must first acknowledge service, and may then apply under CPR Part 11 to have the court declare that it has no jurisdiction. If he acknowledges service but does not apply, or takes a step in the action otherwise than under Part 11, he submits to the jurisdiction.

A defendant who cannot argue that the court lacks jurisdiction may apply under **20.85** CPR Part 11 to stay the proceedings[174] on the ground that the claimant should sue in the courts of another country instead. If the argument succeeds, the English action remains pending but in abeyance;[175] the claimant will be left to go to the

---

[171] See para 20.70.

[172] CPR 7 PD paras 5A and 5B.

[173] Para 20.242.

[174] Though an application for a stay is distinct from a jurisdictional challenge, CPR Part 11 makes it clear that both species of challenge must now be made within the one framework.

[175] For the view that the court may nevertheless dismiss the action, even though there is no objection to the jurisdiction, see *Haji-Ioannou v Frangos* [1999] 2 Lloyd's Rep 337, CA.

foreign court. A stay may be lifted if some unforeseen difficulty arises, or if an undertaking given by the defendant to the court is not performed. Two broad grounds exist for seeking a stay of proceedings commenced by service within the jurisdiction.

20.86 **Forum non conveniens.** If the defendant can show, clearly or distinctly, that there is another court which is more appropriate than England and available to the claimant, for the trial of the action, a stay will generally be ordered unless the claimant can establish that it would be unjust to require him to sue there.[176] The limbs of the test are distinct, with separate burdens of proof, but the overarching question is what the interests of justice require on the issue.

20.87 'Appropriateness' looks to the location of the events and the witnesses, the law which will be applied to decide the case, issues of trial convenience, the relative strengths of connection with England and with the alternative forum, and so on.[177] The fact that the claimant lacks the resources to sue in the foreign court does not make that court unavailable, though it may be relevant under the second limb,[178] as the interests of justice do not require a claimant to sue in a country in which he is unable to fund the litigation.[179]

20.88 If the natural forum is overseas, the claimant may seek to show that it is unjust to leave him to proceed in the foreign court. Arguments that damages will be lower, or civil procedure less favourable, will be generally unpersuasive so long as substantial justice will be done there, but if there is cogent evidence that he will not receive a fair trial it will be unjust to stay proceedings.[180] If he will lose in the foreign court, because the claim advanced in England will not be open to him in the foreign court, some authority holds that a stay will be refused, but such a partial approach, favouring claimant over defendant, is unprincipled.[181]

20.89 **Suing in England in breach of contract.** Alternatively, if there is a contractual agreement by which the claimant bound himself to sue in a foreign court a stay will be ordered unless strong reasons are shown not to do so.[182] The court must test

---

176 The leading cases are *Spiliada Maritime Corp v Cansulex Ltd* [1987] AC 460, and *Connelly v RTZ Corp plc* [1998] AC 854. Australia has adopted a more restrictive test: *Voth v Manildra Flour Mills Pty Ltd* (1990) 171 CLR 538 (Australia must be a clearly inappropriate forum).

177 The list of reported cases dealing with these points would be unworkably large; but the assessment is intended to be one for the judge at first instance with appeals being rare.

178 *Connelly v RTZ Corp plc* [1998] AC 854.

179 ibid; *Lubbe v Cape plc* [2000] 1 WLR 1545, HL. Human Rights Act 1998 would produce the same conclusion.

180 *Spiliada Maritime Corp v Cansulex Ltd* [1987] AC 460, 478.

181 The reasoning in the *Spiliada* case (ibid) and in *The Herceg Novi and the Ming Galaxy* [1998] 4 All ER 238, CA supports the proposition in the text. But cf *Banco Atlantico SA v British Bank of the Middle East* [1990] 2 Lloyd's Rep 504, CA.

182 *Donohue v Armco Inc* [2001] UKHL 64; [2002] 1 Lloyd's Rep 425.

the alleged agreement on jurisdiction for validity and effectiveness[183] by reference to its governing law (usually the law of the contract containing it),[184] and find that on its true construction the action being brought by the claimant amounts to a breach of contract.[185] Where it is, a stay of proceedings is the usual remedy, but is not inevitable. If England is the natural forum, and if there are further and powerful reasons why the claimant should be permitted to break this term of his contract, the action may be allowed to continue.[186] If there are third parties also affected by the dispute but who are not bound by the agreement, it may be very inconvenient for the litigation to take place in international fragments. A court has a public duty to secure the proper administration of justice which may not be served by allowing a private agreement on jurisdiction to prevail over a wider public interest.[187] If the action is allowed to proceed in England it is unclear what prevents the defendant counter-claiming for damages for any demonstrable loss flowing from the breach. Damages have been awarded for breach of contract in bringing proceedings before a foreign court which ordered their dismissal but did not award costs,[188] but it remains to be seen how far the principle will extend.

(c) Jurisdiction established by service outside England

(i) General

If the defendant is not in England to be served, process must be served on him **20.90** overseas in order to found the jurisdiction of the court. Since May 2000, the provisions have been those in CPR Part 6. The claimant applies, without notice, for permission to serve in accordance with CPR Part 6. He must identify the grounds on which the application is made and the paragraphs of Rule 6.20 relied on;[189] may not add new claims to supplement or amend those advanced when

---

[183] If the contract in which it is contained is impugned, the agreement on jurisdiction may still be regarded as valid: the principle of severance, established in the law of arbitration, applies here as a matter of common law or common sense. See *Fiona Trust & Holding Corp v Privalov* [2007] EWCA Civ 20; [2007] Bus LR 686 (a case on arbitration).

[184] *Hoerter v Hanover Telegraph Works* (1893) 10 TLR 103, CA.

[185] This is frequently expressed as requiring that the clause be 'exclusive', but it is possible to breach a non-exclusive jurisdiction clause (*Sabah Shipyard (Pakistan) Ltd v Pakistan* [2002] EWCA Civ 1643; [2003] 2 Lloyd's Rep 571). A clause governed by English law will tend to be construed as exclusive (*Sohio Supply Co v Gatoil (USA) Inc* [1989] 1 Lloyd's Rep 588, CA) and as encompassing as broad a range of claims as reasonably possible (*Harbour Assurance Co (UK) Ltd v Kansa General Insurance Co Ltd* [1993] QB 710, CA; *The Pioneer Container* [1994] 2 AC 324, PC; *Donohue v Armco Inc* [2002] 1 Lloyd's Rep 425, HL; *Fiona Trust & Holding Corp v Privalov* [2007] EWCA Civ 20; [2007] Bus LR 686).

[186] *The El Amria* [1981] 2 Lloyd's Rep 119, CA.

[187] *Bouygues Offshore SA v Caspian Shipping Co (Nos 1, 3, 4, 5)* [1998] 2 Lloyd's Rep 461, CA. *Donohue v Armco Inc* (n 185 above).

[188] *Union Discount Co v Zoller* [2001] EWCA Civ 1755; [2002] 1 WLR 1517.

[189] CPR 6.21(1)(a).

permission was sought;[190] and must be full and frank in making the application.[191] Once service has been made, the defendant is required to acknowledge it but may apply under CPR Part 11 for a declaration that the court has no jurisdiction. On the hearing of such application the claimant bears the burden of proof on those issues which determine whether the permission should have been granted in the first place.

20.91　The claimant is required to show that his claim or claims are within the letter and spirit[192] of one or more of the paragraphs of Rule 6.20. He must also show that England is the proper place in which to bring the claim;[193] and he must give written evidence of his belief that his claim has a reasonable prospect of success.[194] These elements are distinct and must be separately satisfied.

(ii) Jurisdiction to authorize service: the paragraphs of Rule 6.20

20.92　These identify the claims for which the court may grant permission to serve out. Uncertainty as to any fact required to bring the claim within the paragraph relied on requires the claimant to make out a good arguable case, rather than a balance of probability, that it is satisfied.[195] Each claim raised must fall within a paragraph; any which do not will be deleted.[196] The following list mentions only paragraphs of major importance. Those dealing with commercial causes of action are given first; then those also encountered in commercial litigation; and then the remainder.

20.93　**Contracts.**　Three paragraphs deal with contractual claims. Under paragraph 5, service out may be permitted where a claim is made in respect of a contract which was made within the jurisdiction, or was made through an agent trading or residing within the jurisdiction, or is governed by English law, or contains a term to the effect that the court shall have jurisdiction to determine any claim in respect of it. Under paragraph 6, service may be permitted when a claim is made in respect of a breach of contract committed within the jurisdiction. Paragraph 7 provides for service where a claim is made for a declaration that no contract exists where, if the contract were found to exist, it would have fallen within paragraph 5. If it is not admitted the contract must be proved according to rules of English private

---

190　*Parker v Schuller* (1901) 17 TLR 299, CA.

191　*Electric Furnace Co v Selas Corporation of America* [1987] RPC 23, CA; *The Hida Maru* [1981] 2 Lloyd's Rep 510, CA.

192　*The Hagen* [1908] P 189, CA; *Johnson v Taylor Bros* [1920] AC 144, 153; *Mercedes Benz AG v Leiduck* [1996] 1 AC 284, 289, PC.

193　CPR 6.21(2A).

194　CPR 6.21(1)(b).

195　*Seaconsar Far East Ltd v Bank Markazi Jomhouri Islami Iran* [1994] 1 AC 438.

196　For otherwise the scope of the paragraphs would be extended further: *Metall und Rohstoff AG v Donaldson Lufkin & Jenrette Inc* [1990] QB 391, CA.

international law,[197] but the place of its making is determined by reference to English domestic law.[198] Though the paragraphs are drawn widely, the contract must be one by which the claimant and defendant are alleged to be party or otherwise bound: it is insufficient that a contract *inter alios* forms the background to the claim.[199] For the purposes of paragraph 6, breach by a repudiatory act occurs where the act was done, breach by non-performance where the required act was to have been performed. It is supposed that paragraph 7 applies generally to claims which deny that a contractual duty is owed to the defendant, but which the defendant alleges is owed, and is not limited to cases in which it is claimed that no contract ever existed;[200] and that a claim for relief consequential upon holding that there is no contract is also within paragraph 7. Convenience suggests that it should.

Torts. Under paragraph 8, service out may be authorized where a claim is made **20.94** in tort where the damage was sustained within the jurisdiction, or where the damage sustained resulted from an act committed within the jurisdiction. The previous rule, which required that the claim be 'founded on a tort', had been held to require that there to be an actual tort, ascertained by reference to rules of English private international law.[201] Omission of the indefinite article makes it less certain that this is the correct interpretation of paragraph 8, and that there must be a tort, demonstrated (where it is not admitted) to the level of a good arguable case. If it remains correct, there must be a good arguable case that the defendant is liable, for without liability there is not a tort. If, by contrast, the paragraph only requires that the pleaded claim be formulated in the terminology of tort, or be characterized as tortious, there will be no need to show a good arguable case upon liability before service out may be authorized.[202]

Damage is sustained in England if some significant damage is sustained in England: **20.95** it need not be all, nor even most, of it.[203] It is unclear whether 'sustained' is intended to reflect the interpretation of where damage 'occurred' within Article 5.3 of the

---

[197] *Amin Rasheed Shipping Corp v Kuwait Insurance Co* [1984] AC 50; *Bank of Baroda v Vysya Bank Ltd* [1994] 2 Lloyd's Rep 87.

[198] *Chevron International Oil Co v A/S Sea Team* [1983] 2 Lloyd's Rep 356.

[199] *Finnish Marine Insurance Co v Protective National Insurance Co* [1990] 1 QB 1078 (originally or by assignment).

[200] A court will not grant leave to serve a claim for a negative declaration unless it is an appropriate case for the seeking of such relief: *Messier Dowty Ltd v Sabena SA* [2000] 1 Lloyd's Rep 427, CA.

[201] RSC Order 11, r 1(1)(f), as interpreted in *Metall und Rohstoff AG v Donaldson Lufkin & Jenrette Inc* [1990] QB 391, CA. For the rules of English private international law for torts, see Section E.

[202] Though the requirement of CPR 6.21(1)(b) will still need to be satisfied.

[203] *Metall und Rohstoff AG v Donaldson Lufkin & Jenrette Inc* [1990] QB 391, CA.

Brussels I Regulation;[204] in the case of purely economic losses, or damage to reputation, 'location' is artificial. An act is committed within the jurisdiction if the damage resulted from substantial and efficacious acts committed within the jurisdiction, even if other substantial acts were committed elsewhere.[205] Though it must be the act of the defendant, the act of one joint tortfeasor is the act of all.[206]

20.96 **Constructive trusteeship and restitution.** Paragraph 14 allows service to be authorized where a claim is made against the defendant as constructive trustee and his alleged liability arises out of acts committed within the jurisdiction. The former rule made it explicit that the acts committed within the jurisdiction were not required to be those of the defendant. Only some of the acts, not necessarily the receipt of the assets, need to take place within the jurisdiction.[207] Paragraph 15 allows service to be authorized where a claim is made for restitution where the defendant's alleged liability arises out of acts committed within the jurisdiction. This is a new provision, and it is uncertain whether the local acts relied on must be those of the defendant. On the footing that restitutionary claims are not necessarily based on wrongdoing by the defendant, but upon his relationship to acts done by the claimant, it is less likely that the acts of the defendant are those which must take place within the jurisdiction.

20.97 **Other claims.** Paragraph 1 applies if the defendant is domiciled within the jurisdiction.[208] Paragraph 2 applies if the claim is made for an injunction ordering the defendant to do or not to do something within the jurisdiction. The injunction must be a substantial element of the relief sought,[209] and must be an injunction in respect of substantive rights: an application for a freezing order, or other relief not predicated on the existence of substantive rights, is not within the paragraph, but is specifically provided for by paragraph 4 instead.[210] Paragraph 3 applies if the defendant is a necessary or proper party to a claim against someone who has been or will be served: this departs from the former rule which required service on the other party to have been made before permission could be sought to serve out.[211] Paragraph 9 applies if the proceedings seek the enforcement of any

---

204 *Batstone & Firminger Ltd v Nasima Enterprises (Nigeria) Ltd* [1996] CLC 1902 held that it was.
205 *Metall und Rohstoff* (n 203 above).
206 *Unilever plc v Gillette (UK) Ltd* [1989] RPC 583, CA.
207 *ISC Technologies Ltd v Guerin* [1992] 2 Lloyd's Rep 430; *Polly Peck International plc v Nadir* (CA, 17 March 1993) interpreting RSC Order 11, r 1(1)(t).
208 Within the meaning of the Civil Jurisdiction and Judgments Order 2001: CPR 6.18(g).
209 *Rosler v Hilbery* [1925] 1 Ch 250, CA.
210 *Mercedes Benz AG v Leiduck* [1996] 1 AC 284, PC.
211 *Kuwait Oil Tanker Co SAK v Bader* [1997] 2 All ER 855, CA; but for the power to cure errors of procedure, see CPR 3.10.

judgment or arbitral award.[212] And paragraph 17 applies when a party seeks an order that costs be awarded to or against a non-party to the proceedings.[213]

Property and trusts.   Claims concerning property in England fall under para-   **20.98** graph 10; claims to execute English trusts under paragraph 11; claims in the administration of the estate of an English domiciliary under paragraph 12; and probate actions under paragraph 13.

(iii) Discretion to authorize service

There are two distinct components to the discretion to authorize service.   **20.99** Rule 6.20(2A) re-enacts, in slightly modified language, the first requirement that England must be shown, clearly and distinctly, to be the most appropriate forum.[214] Those factors which are relevant when a stay is sought of English proceedings apply, *mutatis mutandis*. Secondly, service out cannot be authorized unless the claimant gives evidence that the claim has a reasonable prospect of success. If the defendant considers that the claim falls below this standard, he may challenge the obtaining of permission on the ground; and if he succeeds on this point the court will set aside the permission and the service of process.[215]

(d) Anti-suit injunctions

A court with personal jurisdiction over a respondent may restrain him by injunc-   **20.100** tion from bringing or continuing proceedings in a foreign court. This potent remedy gives the English court international clout to control wrongful recourse by a respondent to a foreign court. Well known to common law systems it is unknown in civilian systems. An injunction is not a direction to a foreign court, but to a respondent who has been made subject to the personal jurisdiction of the English court. But the foreign judge may not appreciate the subtlety of the distinction, and for this reason the principles of judicial comity police the exercise of the court's discretion.[216] However, where the foreign proceedings are brought in breach of a contract to sue only in England, an injunction to restrain the breach will be the usual remedy.[217]

There must first be personal jurisdiction over the respondent, who must be served   **20.101** with process in respect of the claim for an injunction. As an injunction is granted

---

[212] The judgment or award must have been given by the time permission is sought: *Mercedes Benz AG v Leiduck* [1996] 1 AC 284, PC.

[213] Supreme Court Act 1981, s 51.

[214] *Spiliada Maritime Corp v Cansulex Ltd* [1987] AC 460, interpreting RSC Order 11, r 4(2).

[215] Cf *Seaconsar Far East Ltd v Bank Markazi Jomhouri Islami Iran* [1994] 1 AC 438. It may be dangerous to make the argument by application under CPR 3.4(a) or CPR 24.2(a)(i), as these are not challenges to the jurisdiction of the court and will therefore risk being seen as submission.

[216] *Airbus Industrie GIE v Patel* [1999] 1 AC 119.

[217] *Donohue v Armco Inc* [2001] UKHL 64; [2002] 1 Lloyd's Rep 425.

as final relief in aid of legal or equitable rights, process must be served in accordance with the Regulation or the common law, as the case may be. No paragraph of CPR 6.20 provides specifically for applications for an anti-suit injunction, but there is nothing to prevent the permission being sought as relief under any available paragraph, such as for breach of a contract giving jurisdiction to the High Court.[218] Where the respondent is domiciled in another Member State, he may be brought before the English court only in accordance with the Regulation, but where the foreign proceedings objected to are before the courts of a non-Member State, the prohibition upon injunctions, contained in *Turner v Grovit*,[219] is inapplicable to the exercise of the court's discretion.

20.102 An injunction will generally not be ordered unless England is the natural forum for litigation of the dispute; but if it is, comity is not infringed by the intervention of the court.[220] Subject to this condition the applicant must in principle[221] show the respondent to be vexatious or oppressive in bringing the foreign action. The meaning of these terms is flexible, but if the action is brought in bad faith, or to harass, its bringer may be restrained. The absence of a real link between the acts complained of and the foreign court may indicate oppression; if it is otherwise unconscionable to bring the action it may be restrained.[222] According to Australian authority the foreign action is unobjectionable if it seeks relief not available from an Australian court,[223] but this is not the English view;[224] according to Canadian authority the application must be preceded by an application to the foreign court.[225] Though this has sometimes been said to be the general rule in England,[226] it is peculiarly offensive to grant the application after the foreign court has expressed its opposite view;[227] and reiteration of the requirement that England be the natural forum makes this an unnecessary condition in England.

20.103 The claim to an injunction may instead be founded on a contractual right not to be sued in the foreign court. Where England is the chosen court, there will be no difficulty:[228] an injunction in support of a legal right will be granted unless there

---

218 CPR 6.20(5)(d).

219 Case C-159/02, [2004] ECR I-3565, as to which, see para 20.79.

220 *Société Nationale Industrielle Aérospatiale v Lee Kui Jak* [1987] AC 871, PC; *Airbus Industrie GIE v Patel* [1999] 1 AC 119.

221 Not the only ground, but the one most widely utilized. For a wider expression of the principle, see *British Airways Board v Laker Airways Ltd* [1985] AC 58, 81.

222 *Midland Bank plc v Laker Airways Ltd* [1986] QB 689, CA.

223 *CSR Ltd v Cigna Insurance Australia Ltd* (1997) 189 CLR 345.

224 *Midland Bank plc v Laker Airways Ltd* [1986] QB 689, CA.

225 *Amchem Products Ltd v British Columbia (Workers' Compensation Board)* [1993] 1 SCR 897, (1993) 102 DLR (4th) 96.

226 *Barclays Bank plc v Homan* [1993] BCLC 680, 686–7 (*per* Hoffmann J), 703, CA.

227 *The Angelic Grace* [1995] 1 Lloyd's Rep 87, 95, CA.

228 *Continental Bank NA v Aeakos Compania Naviera SA* [1994] 1 WLR 588, CA; *The Angelic Grace* (ibid).

is good reason not to do so;[229] and if the court exercises its discretion against the specific enforcement of such a contractual promise, there is no reason to suppose that other remedies for breach are prohibited.

(e) Jurisdiction to obtain interim relief

Interim relief, which includes provisional and protective measures, may be ordered in support of actions in the English courts, or of civil or commercial claims in the courts in another Member State (Article 31 cases), or in support of other actions in those courts or elsewhere.[230] If the respondent is within the jurisdiction of the court he may be served with the application as of right: Article 31 makes it irrelevant that he may be domiciled in another Member State and so not otherwise subject to the jurisdiction of the English courts. If he is outside the jurisdiction, application for permission to serve the claim form out of the jurisdiction must be made under CPR 6.20(4); this is the case even in relation to applications falling within Article 31 of the Regulation. But in all cases, the fact that the court may not have jurisdiction to try the substantive case is a material factor in determining whether to grant the relief;[231] and it will also be relevant in deciding whether the court should grant permission to serve out, as CPR 6.21(2A) also applies to applications under CPR 6.20(4).   **20.104**

C. Recognition and Enforcement of Foreign Judgments

(1) General

The judgments of foreign courts have no direct effect in England, but may be given effect by the common law or statute in accordance with the schemes examined in the following paragraphs. An important distinction must be drawn at the outset. Recognition of a judgment means treating the claim which was adjudicated as finally determined, whether in favour of claimant or defendant. The matter is then held to be *res judicata*, and the losing party estopped from contradicting it.[232] This status depends on certain conditions, devised by English law, to specify the connection between the foreign court and the party said to be bound by it, and to define the nature of the judgment to which this status will be accorded. There may be *res judicata* in relation to entire causes of action ('cause of action estoppel') as well as on discrete issues which arose and were determined in   **20.105**

---

[229] *Donohue v Armco Inc* [2001] UKHL 64; [2002] 1 Lloyd's Rep 425.
[230] 1982 Act, s 25 (as amended).
[231] ibid s 25(2); *Motorola Credit Corp v Uzan* [2003] EWCA Civ 752; [2004] 1 WLR 1113.
[232] See G Spencer Bower, AK Turner and KR Handley, *The Doctrine of Res Judicata* (3rd edn, 1996).

the course of a trial ('issue estoppel').[233] If there is, as a matter of English law, a *res judicata*, a party bringing proceedings in England for a ruling which contradicts this foreign judgment may be met with the plea of estoppel by *res judicata*, and the action stopped in its tracks.

20.106 Recognition is frequently a defensive measure. But the victor may wish to go further, and enforce the judgment, for example, by collecting money which the foreign court ordered to be paid and which remains unpaid. To be enforced, a foreign judgment must first qualify for recognition. For enforcement the judgment must meet further limiting conditions. But once enforcement is ordered, the judgment may be executed as though it had been given by an English court.[234]

20.107 We first examine judgments in civil or commercial matters from the courts of EU Member States and from contracting states to the Brussels and Lugano Conventions[235] which, though the most recent, is also the most effective scheme for recognition and enforcement. We will then look at the procedure for recognition and enforcement of judgments at common law, which is restricted neither by geography nor by subject matter. Finally we will examine statutory registration schemes which were developed in order to simplify procedure for enforcement at common law, and which apply to specific courts in specified countries. The recognition of judgments in family law, the administration of estates, and insolvency, are dealt with within those substantive sections of this chapter.

(2) The Brussels and Lugano Scheme

(a) Recognition under the Regulation or Conventions

20.108 For a judgment to be recognized under the Brussels I Regulation or the Conventions, it must be from a court in a Member or Contracting State in a civil or commercial matter; impeachable neither for specified jurisdictional error; nor for specified procedural or substantive reasons; and not excluded from recognition by bilateral treaty. According to Article 33 of the Regulation recognition requires no form of action or procedure, though there is no objection to bringing proceedings if this would serve a purpose for the victor.[236]

---

233 *Carl Zeiss Stiftung v Rayner & Keeler Ltd (No 2)* [1967] 1 AC 853.

234 Either because it will be registered pursuant to statute which so provides, or because an English judgment on the obligation created by the foreign judgment is enforceable according to its terms.

235 The Brussels I Regulation is 44/2001/EC; the Conventions are set out in the Civil Jurisdiction and Judgments Act 1982, Sch 1 (Brussels) and Sch 3C (Lugano). In this Section, references to the Regulation may be taken to be references to the Conventions as well, unless the contrary is stated.

236 CPR 74.10.

(i) Judgments in civil or commercial matters

A judgment is an adjudication by a court in a Member State.[237] It excludes a 20.109
judgment from a non-Member State, even after it has been declared enforceable
in a Member State,[238] but it includes an interlocutory judgment, or one for costs;
and it includes judgments by consent.[239] A judgment for a periodical payment
imposed to penalize disobedience to a court order is included, though it may
be enforced only if the sum due has been finally quantified by the court which
ordered it.[240] Settlements approved by courts in the course of proceedings, and
authentic instruments (unknown to English law, these are documents authenticated by a public authority or a notary, and which may be enforceable without
prior legal proceedings)[241] are enforceable under Articles 57 and 58 under similar
conditions.[242]

The judgment must be in a civil or commercial matter.[243] The recognizing 20.110
court should decide for itself whether the judgment was given in a civil or commercial matter: it is not bound on this point by the conclusion of the adjudicating
court, not least because this court may not have needed to address and decide
the issue for itself.[244] It follows that a judgment must not be in a matter excluded
by Article 1 from the domain of the Regulation. Where a single judgment deals
with included and excluded matter it may be possible to sever it; where it is
not, the substantial presence of excluded matter in an indivisible judgment may
preclude recognition under the Regulation.[245] Where the judgment was obtained
in breach of an agreement to arbitrate it is arguable that recognition should be
withheld, as to do otherwise would oblige a court to contradict its law on arbitration, a matter lying outside the domain of the Regulation.[246] But if Article 1.4
simply means that the court lacked jurisdiction over the merits of a civil or commercial claim,[247] and as jurisdictional error furnishes no general basis for denying
recognition,[248] recognition of the offending judgment may be required though in

---

[237] Article 25.
[238] Case C-129/92 *Owens Bank Ltd v Bracco* [1994] ECR I-117.
[239] *Landhurst Leasing plc v Marcq* [1998] ILPr 822, CA.
[240] Article 49.
[241] Case C-260/97 *Unibank A/S v Christensen* [1999] ECR I-3715; [2000] 1 WLR 1060.
[242] For the differences, see Case C-414/92 *Solo Kleinmotoren GmbH v Boch* [1994] ECR
I-2237.
[243] See para 20.36.
[244] Case 29/76 *LTU GmbH & Co v Eurocontrol* [1976] ECR 1541; Case 145/86 *Hoffmann v
Krieg* [1988] ECR 645.
[245] Case C-220/95 *Van den Boogaard v Laumen* [1997] ECR I-1147; and see Article 48.
[246] Cf Case 145/86 *Hoffmann v Krieg* [1988] ECR 645.
[247] Case C-391/95 *Van Uden Maritime BV v Deco-Line* [1998] ECR I-7091.
[248] See para 20.112.

turn be withheld as conflicting with the public policy of enforcing agreements to arbitrate.[249]

(ii) Jurisdictional review

20.111 The adjudicating court may have erred by accepting jurisdiction when it should not have. Save in the exceptional cases mentioned below, this is irrelevant to the recognition of the judgment.[250] Superficially the reason is clear: the defendant should have made this argument to the adjudicating court, and having had one chance to make it once there is no reason to give him a second: indeed, there is every reason not to for it would greatly impede the enforcement of judgments. Though reasonable for European domiciliaries whose jurisdictional exposure is limited by the Regulation, this is unjust to those sued on the basis of Article 4, who may complain about the width of the jurisdictional rules asserted against them neither at trial nor at recognition. No European defendant is denied a hearing on the propriety of the jurisdictional rule invoked against him. That this was the calculated act of those who drafted the Brussels Convention,[251] and then copied into subsequent instruments, is disgraceful.[252]

20.112 Exceptions apply only where jurisdictional error violated the provisions on insurance contracts, consumer contracts, and exclusive jurisdiction regardless of domicile:[253] in these cases the jurisdictional rules enshrine policies which are so strong that they demand reinforcement by the recognizing court. Otherwise, the plea that the adjudicating court had no jurisdiction is inadmissible. The divergence from the approach of the common law at this point seems sharp,[254] but this is not altogether so. Under the Regulation the defendant may make a submission to the adjudicating court that it does not have jurisdiction according to what are *English* jurisdictional rules; outside the Regulation this argument cannot usefully be made to the foreign court, so arises first only at the point of recognition. The schemes therefore agree that *this* jurisdictional argument may be made once, at the earliest sensible point. They diverge in the identification of this point.

---

249 *Phillip Alexander Securities and Futures Ltd v Bamberger* [1997] ILPr 73.
250 Art 28.
251 Jenard was shameless: [1979] OJ C59/20.
252 By contrast, the guarantees of due process in the Fifth and Fourteenth Amendments to the Constitution of the United States extend to aliens: *Asahi Metal Industry Co v Superior Court of California* 480 US 102, 107 S Ct 1026 (1987).
253 Article 35, first paragraph. Breach of a jurisdiction clause is not included; nor is violation of the provisions on employment contracts.
254 Cf para 20.127.

(iii) Admissible grounds of objection

Article 34 lists four[255] defences to recognition. In principle they are given a restrictive construction, for judgments are intended to circulate freely around the Member States.[256] **20.113**

Public policy. If recognition would be contrary to public policy it will be denied: Article 34.1. The content of public policy is a matter for English law though operating within outer limits marked by the Regulation. An argument that the judgment was obtained by fraud will not prevent recognition if the state of origin has its own procedures for admitting such a plea.[257] But a judgment which failed to respect fundamental human rights,[258] or which was based on a law which in its application is manifestly contrary to English public policy may meet the standard of objection required: an example may be a law refusing to enforce a commercial arbitration agreement.[259] And recognition of a judgment obtained in defiance of an English injunction must be contrary to public policy.[260] **20.114**

Judgments in default of appearance. If judgment was given in default of appearance[261] and either the document instituting the proceedings was not served in accordance with the law of the adjudicating state, or was not served, according to the assessment of the recognizing state, in time to allow for the defence to be arranged,[262] recognition may be denied. But if the defendant failed to challenge the judgment when he discovered it had been entered, he loses his shield: Article 34.2. This newly-balanced[263] provision gives effect to the principle that the defendant must have had a right to be notified and heard, but also places some obligations on him once he is notified. Where orders obtained without notice to the respondent are denied recognition,[264] the question whether they lose this default character after an unsuccessful application to set them aside should depend upon whether the respondent was disadvantaged by the order having already been **20.115**

---

[255] The Conventions contain a fifth: that the judgment is irreconcilable the recognizing court's law on status. This does not appear in the Regulation, almost certainly because it is implicit in Article 1 in any event.

[256] It appears that they are not supposed to overlap, at least where Article 27.1 is concerned: Case C-78/95 *Hendrickman v Magenta Druck & Verlag GmbH* [1996] ECR I-4943.

[257] *Interdesco SA v Nullifire Ltd* [1992] 1 Lloyd's Rep 180.

[258] Case C-7/98 *Krombach v Bamberski* [2000] ECR I-1935.

[259] *Phillip Alexander Securities & Futures Ltd v Bamberger* [1997] ILPr 73, 103, CA.

[260] ibid 104, 115.

[261] It is not a precondition that the adjudicating court enter judgment on this ground: the essential question is whether the defendant was given a right to be represented or heard: Case C-78/95 *Hendrickman v Magenta Druck und Verlag GmbH* [1996] ECR I-4943.

[262] Case 228/81 *Pendy Plastic Products v Pluspunkt* [1982] ECR 2723; Case 49/84 *Debaecker and Plouvier v Bouwman* [1985] ECR 1779.

[263] The provision about failure to challenge the judgment had no precursor in the Conventions. See Case C-283/05 *ASML Netherlands BV v SEMIS* [2006] ECR I-12041.

[264] Case 125/79 *Denilauler v SNC Couchet Frères* [1980] ECR 1553.

made in proceedings in which he did not appear;[265] but courts in other Member States have shown no unwillingness to enforce English freezing injunctions confirmed after the respondent has had opportunity to apply to set them aside.

20.116 **Irreconcilability with English judgment.** If the judgment produces consequences which are incompatible with an English judgment, whether earlier or later than the foreign one, recognition will be denied: Article 34.3.[266] In principle Article 27, or the rules of *res judicata* if the English judgment came after the foreign judgment, should prevent this happening, but when it occurs a court is entitled to prefer its own judgment. A judgment that a contract was lawfully rescinded is irreconcilable with an order that damages be paid for its breach;[267] but a finding that A is liable to C for negligence may not be irreconcilable with a judgment that B was not so liable, or that A was not liable to D.[268]

20.117 **Irreconcilability with prior foreign judgment.** If a judgment was given in proceedings between the same parties and involving the same cause of action, which satisfied the criteria for recognition in the state of recognition, and which was handed down earlier in time, a later Member State judgment will not be recognized: Article 34.4.

(iv) Bilateral treaty requiring non-recognition

20.118 Article 59 of the Conventions allowed states to make bilateral treaties to provide for non-recognition of judgments from other contracting states, founded on Article 4 of the Convention and given against nationals or domiciliaries of the treaty state. The United Kingdom has such arrangements with Australia[269] and Canada.[270] They remain in force, but Article 70 of the Regulation means that no more bilateral treaties will be made.

(v) Effect of finding a judgment entitled to recognition

20.119 There is no other ground to impeach the judgment and deny it recognition. Article 35 precludes any further review of the jurisdiction of the foreign court, and explicitly provides that public policy may not be invoked to attack the jurisdiction of the adjudicating court; and Article 36 prohibits any review of the merits of the judgment. A court called on to recognize an order made under Article 31 must

---

265 Cf Case C-474/93 *Hengst Import BV v Campese* [1995] ECR I-2113.
266 Case 145/86 *Hoffmann v Krieg* [1988] ECR 645.
267 Case 144/86 *Gubisch Maschinenfabrik KG v Palumbo* [1987] ECR 4861.
268 Cf Case C-406/92 *The Tatry* [1994] ECR I-5439.
269 Reciprocal Enforcement of Foreign Judgments (Australia) Order 1994, SI 1994/1901, Sch, art 3.
270 Reciprocal Enforcement of Foreign Judgments (Canada) Order 1987, SI 1987/468, Sch, art IX.

ascertain that the order fell within the scope of Article 31, and may review the adjudication to that end.[271]

If an ordinary appeal is pending against the judgment in the state of origin Article 37 permits, though does not oblige, the recognizing court to stay proceedings in which the issue of recognition arises. **20.120**

Recognition of a judgment means giving it the effect it has under the law of the state in which it was given.[272] So a provisional order, which would not be taken as binding in subsequent proceedings in the adjudicating court, should be given neither greater nor lesser an effect in England. In certain cases a judgment may be regarded by the foreign law as impinging upon third parties to the action,[273] but whether this must be respected by an English court, which may consider that the third party has had insufficient opportunity to defend its interest, is unclear. **20.121**

(b) Enforcement under the Regulation

Any judgment entitled to recognition, and enforceable in the state in which it was given may, in principle, be enforced under Articles 38–56. In England, an application is made for an order that the judgment be registered in the High Court,[274] producing a certified copy of the judgment and proof that it is enforceable under the law of the state in which it was given.[275] When registered, the judgment has the same force and effect for the purposes of enforcement as if it were English. **20.122**

The documents are produced to a High Court Master,[276] without notice to the respondent. Departing from the corresponding provision in the Conventions, if the paperwork is in order Article 41 of the Regulation prevents the court finding that the judgment should not be registered. Registration is followed by notifying the respondent of the order in accordance with Article 42. **20.123**

Article 43 allows either party to appeal against the decision given on the first application; only in rare cases will the applicant need to, though. If the application was granted, the respondent has one month (if domiciled in the enforcing state) or two (if domiciled in another Member State), to appeal the order for registration. This marks the point in the procedure when the arguments touching recognition will be raised. Article 44 allows the order made on the hearing of the appeal to be appealed once, on a point of law. **20.124**

---

271 Case C-99/96 *Mietz v Intership Yachting Sneek BV* [1999] ECR I-2277.
272 Case C-145/86 *Hoffmann v Krieg* [1988] ECR 645.
273 Cf Schlosser [1979] OJ C59/71, 127–8.
274 Civil Jurisdiction and Judgments Order 2001, Sch 1, para 2.
275 Article 53 of the Regulation and CPR 74.4.
276 CPR 74.3.

20.125 Once an order for registration has been made Article 47 permits the court to grant protective measures against the property of the respondent. The court hearing an appeal, or further appeal, against registration appeal may order conditional enforcement on the provision of security against the subsequent setting aside of the order; if the original judgment is under appeal it may stay the hearing of the enforcement appeal: it is all a matter of balance.

(c) Accelerated enforcement: the European Enforcement Order

20.126 A judgment from the High Court in Leeds does not need to be scrutinized before being enforced in London; and the drive to reduce the Member States to a borderless legal area stretching from Lisbon to Latvia, led to the adoption of Regulation 805/2004/EC.[277] This permits a court in a Member State, hearing a claim within the material scope of the Regulation, to issue a 'European Enforcement Order' if it considers that the claim was uncontested and the rights of the defendant were not overridden. Faced with such an Order, the recognizing court is given practically no right to refuse recognition and enforcement. It is hard to believe that this can be acceptable to a court which has obligations under the European Convention on Human Rights, but it is hard not to suspect that this model for enforcement will shortly be extended to judgments in contested proceedings.

(3) *Recognition and Enforcement at Common Law*

20.127 The scheme of the common law is that if the foreign court was competent in English eyes to give a judgment by which the defendant was bound this may, and in the absence of a defence to the contention, will, be recognized as making the cause of action, or the issue, *res judicata*. It is sufficient to plead the *res judicata* effect of the foreign judgment, but if the judgment creditor wishes to enforce the judgment in offensive fashion he may bring an action at common law upon it. In this case the judgment must satisfy further criteria which determine its enforceability in the English courts.

(a) Recognition of judgments as *res judicata*

20.128 A judgment will be recognized at common law if it was a final judgment from a court which had international jurisdiction according to the English conflict of laws, and unless there is a defence to recognition. There is no requirement that it be from a superior court, but the decision of an arbitral tribunal or an administrative body is not sufficient. Only final orders are recognized, but an order on an

---

[277] [2004] OJL 143/15.

interlocutory matter may be recognized if it represents the final decision of the court on the point, such as an order dismissing an action on the ground that it was covered by a jurisdiction agreement for a specific court elsewhere.[278]

(i) *International jurisdiction*

A court has jurisdiction 'in the international sense' if the party against whom the judgment was given submitted to, or was present or resident within, the jurisdiction of the court when the proceedings were instituted. The grounds stated are exhaustive: English law does not admit jurisdictional competence on the basis that the foreign court exercised a jurisdiction which an English court would exercise itself,[279] though this step has been taken by the Supreme Court of Canada, which will recognize a judgment from a court which had a real and substantial connection with the dispute.[280] Though the law in England may be due for reconsideration, modern Canadian law makes real difficulty for a defendant who needs to know whether to defend in the foreign court. Any suggestion that the nationality of the defendant is sufficient[281] is discredited today.

20.129

Submission. If a person submits to the jurisdiction of a court it is not unjust for the judgment to bind him. So someone who submits is subject to the international jurisdiction of the foreign court.[282] A claimant or counter-claimant clearly submits to the jurisdiction, as does a defendant who makes a voluntary appearance. But if the latter appears for the purpose of contesting the jurisdiction of the court, or for seeking a stay in favour of another court or for arbitration, or to protect property threatened with seizure, the appearance is not, without more, a submission;[283] and if he is required, strictly or as a matter of good practice, to plead to the merits at the same time, or is compelled to submit to interim procedures to keep his jurisdictional challenge alive, the protection survives.[284] It is plausible that the challenge has to be to the international jurisdiction, rather than the local

20.130

---

[278] *The Sennar (No 2)* [1985] 1 WLR 490, HL; cf *Desert Sun Loan Corp v Hill* [1996] 2 All ER 847, CA.

[279] *Schibsby v Westenholz* (1870) LR 6 QB 155. The analogy is imperfect, for it takes no account of the fact that an English court would not have exercised the jurisdiction invoked unless it was also the natural forum for the claim.

[280] *Morguard Investments Ltd v De Savoye* [1990] 3 SCR 1077, (1991) 76 DLR (4th) 256; *Beals v Saldanha* [2003] 3 SCR 416, (2003) 234 DLR (4th) 1.

[281] *Emanuel v Symon* [1908] 1 KB 302, CA.

[282] On submission and additional claims, see *Murthy v Sivajothi* [1999] 1 WLR 467, CA.

[283] 1982 Act, s 33(1), effectively reversing the effect of *Henry v Geoprosco International* [1976] QB 726, CA.

[284] *Marc Rich & Co AG v Società Italiana Impianti PA (No 2)* [1992] 1 Lloyd's Rep 624, CA. If the foreign court does not characterize the defendant's participation as an appearance, an English court should not either: *Adams v Cape Industries plc* [1990] Ch 433, 461.

or internal jurisdiction of the court, as the existence or non-existence of internal jurisdiction is of no general relevance to the English law on recognition.[285]

20.131 Submission may also be made by contract. The dispute must fall within the four corners of the contractual provision, which must remain valid and enforceable at the date of the action.[286] It is said that an implied agreement to submit will not suffice, but the better view is that an implied agreement may be sufficient but will found only in the clearest of cases.[287]

20.132 **Presence or residence.** If the defendant was physically present within the jurisdiction of the foreign court when the proceedings were commenced he is subject to its international jurisdiction.[288] At one time the rule required residence, but it is now tolerably clear that either presence or residence will suffice.[289] It is arresting that this acknowledges a foreign jurisdictional competence wider than English law claims for itself: it is irrelevant that the foreign court was a *forum non conveniens* so that, if the roles were reversed, an English court might have stayed its proceedings. This divergence will not escape critical attention for ever, but it is at present the law.

20.133 Physical presence for an individual defendant is simple to ascertain. For a corporation it requires a fixed place of business maintained by it, from which its business is done.[290] A peripatetic representative is insufficient, even though the foreign court may regard it as sufficient for its own jurisdictional purposes, as is a local representative who merely acts as a conduit for those wishing to transact business with the defendant out of the jurisdiction.[291] But if the local representative may make contracts binding the defendant, it is probable that presence is established.[292] Though a company may therefore be present if another company is doing its business as well as its own, there is no broader English doctrine which allows all the members of an economic group to be regarded as present where any one is.[293]

---

285 *Pemberton v Hughes* [1899] 1 Ch 781. Whether a challenge to the existence of a power of attorney to accept service of process constitutes a challenge to the jurisdiction protected by s 33, arose in *Desert Sun Loan Corp v Hill* [1996] 2 All ER 847, CA.
286 *SA Consortium General Textiles v Sun and Sand Agencies Ltd* [1978] QB 279, CA.
287 *Vogel v RA Kohnstamm Ltd* [1973] 1 QB 133, not following *Blohn v Desser* [1962] 2 QB 116.
288 *Adams v Cape Industries plc* [1990] Ch 433, CA. If sued in a federal court he must be present within the federation; if in a state court, in the state: ibid 557.
289 *State Bank of India v Murjani Marketing Group Ltd* (CA, 27 March 1991).
290 *Adams v Cape Industries plc* [1990] Ch 433, CA.
291 Cf *Littauer Glove Corp v Millington (FW) (1920) Ltd* (1928) 44 TLR 746.
292 *Adams v Cape Industries plc* [1990] Ch 433, 531, CA.
293 ibid 532–9.

(ii) Defences to recognition

A judgment will be denied recognition as *res judicata*, and hence denied enforce- **20.134**
ment, if any of the defences established by English law is made out. The merits of
the judgment are not otherwise reviewable. The allegation that the foreign court
erred in its reasoning is no defence to the recognition of the judgment, neither is
it relevant that the foreign court manifestly went wrong in its attempt to apply
English law.[294] Were it otherwise, almost every judgment would be re-examinable
and the advantage of the rule would be lost.

Lack of internal jurisdiction.   It is not entirely clear whether this is an admissi- **20.135**
ble defence, for the authorities are old and inconclusive.[295] If the foreign judgment is a complete nullity, and not just voidable, under that law, it would be odd
if it were recognized in England, particularly if the defendant had been well
advised to ignore the proceedings.

Breach of arbitration or choice of court agreement.   If the foreign court took **20.136**
jurisdiction in breach of such an agreement its judgment will be refused recognition, even if it decided for itself that there was no breach. But if the other party
acquiesced or submitted to the jurisdiction the defence is waived.[296]

Fraud.   Though the merits of the judgment may not be re-examined, a different **20.137**
approach prevails if there is a credible allegation that it was procured by fraud.[297]
Fraud encompasses any duping of the foreign court, such as false pleading, fabrication of evidence, intimidation of witnesses. If, having particular regard to the
court of decision and the nature of its procedures, the allegation is credible, it will
be investigated,[298] even though it was specifically rejected by the foreign court.
The defendant need show no new discovery of evidence: he may even recycle the
evidence which failed to persuade the foreign court. The apparent suggestion that
the foreign court is less skilled than the English court at the detection of fraud
is delicate: if a new discovery of evidence is required to impeach an English
judgment for fraud,[299] should it be different for a foreign judgment?[300] But the
English[301] rule is soundly based. It is dangerous to require a defendant to make his

---

[294] *Godard v Gray* (1870) LR 6 QB 139.
[295] *Vanquelin v Bouard* (1863) 15 CBNS 341; *Pemberton v Hughes* [1899] 1 Ch 781.
[296] 1982 Act, s 32. And see *Marc Rich & Co AG v Società Italiana Impianti PA* [1992] 2 Lloyd's
Rep 624, CA.
[297] *Abouloff v Oppenheimer* (1882) 10 QBD 295, CA; *Vadala v Lawes* (1890) 25 QBD 310, CA;
Syal v Heyward [1948] 2 KB 443, CA; *Jet Holdings Inc v Patel* [1990] 1 QB 335, CA; *Owens Bank
Ltd v Bracco* [1992] 2 AC 443.
[298] *Jet Holdings Inc v Patel* [1990] 1 QB 335, CA.
[299] *Hunter v Chief Constable of the West Midlands* [1980] QB 283, CA.
[300] Cf *Keele v Findley* (1991) 21 NSWLR 444.
[301] The law of Canada is different (*Beals v Saldanha* [2003] 3 SCR 416, (2003) 234 DLR (4th) 1)
and objectionable for taking the side of the negligent against the fraudulent.

allegations in a court chosen only by the claimant. Moreover, finding fraud means only that the judgment may not be recognized in England. It does not purport to set it aside and prevent its enforcement elsewhere. It is less dramatic than setting aside an English judgment *in toto* and for all international purposes, and the justification for intervention may properly be rather more modest. However, if the allegation has already had an independent hearing in a court of the *defendant's* own choosing, it may thereafter be an abuse of the process of the English court to advance it all over again.[302] The abuse of process doctrine has the potential to negate much of the fraud defence, and the extent to which disquiet over the fraud rule will mean that it does remains to be seen.[303]

20.138 **Natural or substantial justice.** If the foreign court violated the rules of natural justice such as the right to be notified, represented, and heard; or if its procedure violated substantial justice such as by a non-judicial assessment of damages,[304] the judgment will be denied recognition. A distinct issue concerns the impact of the Human Rights Act 1998, which obliges English courts to give effect to the European Convention. Where a foreign court has given a judgment in circumstances which would have violated the Convention if replicated by a court in a contracting state, there is a powerful argument that an English court is precluded by statute from recognizing the judgment. But the House of Lords has taken a different view, which is most perplexing.[305]

20.139 **Public policy.** If recognition of the judgment would offend English public policy, it will not be recognized. Judgments based on laws repellent to human rights, for example, should be denied recognition; those obtained in defiance of an English injunction are treated likewise.[306]

20.140 *Res judicata.* If the judgment is inconsistent with an English judgment, or with an earlier foreign one which is entitled to recognition in England, it will not be recognized.[307]

(iii) Effect of recognition

20.141 If the party against whom the judgment was given was subject to the international jurisdiction of the foreign court, and no defence applies, the cause of action or the

---

302 *House of Spring Gardens Ltd v Waite* [1991] 1 QB 241, CA. There is no reason in principle why the findings against the judgment debtor in the second action should not give rise to an estoppel, but cf 1982 Act, s 33(1)(c).

303 *Owens Bank Ltd v Etoile Commerciale SA* [1995] 1 WLR 44, PC; *Desert Sun Loan Corp v Hill* [1996] 2 All ER 847, CA.

304 *Adams v Cape Industries plc* [1990] Ch 433, CA.

305 *Government of the USA v Montgomery (No 2)* [2004] UKHL 37; [2004] 1 WLR 2241, purporting to distinguish *Pellegrini v Italy* (2001) 35 EHRR 2 (ECtHR).

306 *Phillip Alexander Securities and Futures Ltd v Bamberger* [1997] ILPr 73, 104, 115, CA.

307 *Showlag v Mansour* [1995] 1 AC 431, PC.

issue will be regarded as against him as *res judicata* and immune from contradiction in later English proceedings.[308] If the party in whose favour it was given wishes to enforce it, he may bring an action to enforce the judgment, subject to the further limitations examined below. But if the party in whose favour it was given, *against* whom there is no *res judicata*, had been hoping for better, section 34 of the 1982 Act precludes him from suing for a second time on the same[309] underlying cause of action in the hope of a better result.[310]

(b) Action to enforce the judgment

As a matter of theory, a recognized foreign judgment creates an obligation which the judgment creditor may sue to enforce at common law. As the action is one for debt, only final judgments for fixed sums of money can be enforced. This means that foreign judgments ordering injunctions may not be enforced.[311] Even so, such a foreign judgment may be recognized as *res judicata*, and proceedings brought for an English injunction on the back of it. In this respect the difference between the enforcement of money judgments and the 'non-enforcement' of non-money judgments is slight. **20.142**

(i) Final judgments

A judgment can only be enforced if it is 'final and conclusive'. If it may be reviewed or revised by the court which gave it, it is not final,[312] though its being subject to appeal to a higher court is irrelevant. **20.143**

(ii) Money judgments

A debt claim must be based on a judgment for the payment of a fixed sum in money, so if the sum may yet be varied by the court which awarded it, it cannot be enforced. If the judgment was final as to liability but reviewable as to damages, or was a non-money order, the finding of liability may be recognized as *res judicata* if a second action is brought on the underlying cause of action. But there is no jurisdiction to enforce a foreign penal, revenue or analogous law; and if the action would have this effect it will be dismissed. So if a foreign taxing authority has obtained a judgment in its favour, enforcement of the judgment by action in England will fail.[313] Nor may an action be brought to recover any part of a foreign **20.144**

---

308 *Carl Zeiss Stiftung v Rayner & Keeler Ltd (No 2)* [1967] 1 AC 853.

309 Cf *Black v Yates* [1992] QB 526.

310 *Republic of India v India Steamship Co Ltd, (The Indian Grace)* [1993] AC 410; *Republic of India v India Steamship Co Ltd, (The Indian Grace) (No 2)* [1998] AC 878.

311 The Supreme Court of Canada has a different view: *Pro-Swing Ltd v Elta Golf Ltd* [2006] SCC 52; (2006) 273 DLR (4th) 663.

312 *Nouvion v Freeman* (1889) 15 App Cas 1.

313 *United States of America v Harden* [1963] SCR 366, (1963) 41 DLR (2d) 721, Can Sup Ct.

judgment for multiple damages, though it appears that judgments for exemplary damages do not generally offend the rule as long as the figure has not been calculated by multiplication of the sum fixed as compensation.[314]

(iii) Procedure

20.145 The claimant will plead the judgment debt as due and owing, and may apply under CPR 24.2 for summary judgment on the ground that the defendant has no real prospect of defending the claim. If the application succeeds judgment will be given forthwith; but if it is shown that the defendant has a real prospect of defending the claim the court will dismiss the application and the action will proceed in the usual way.

(4) Enforcement by Statutory Registration

20.146 Certain statutes provide a simplified procedure for enforcement of foreign judgments. They apply to specific courts in certain countries, and provide for an application to be made to register the judgment for enforcement. When registered, the judgment has the same effect as if given by an English court; and the judgment debtor may apply to have registration set aside. The statutory schemes mainly simplify the procedure; the substantive grounds on which registration may be obtained or set aside closely reflect the common law or the Conventions, as the case may be.

(a) Administration of Justice Act 1920

20.147 Part II of the 1920 Act applies to many colonial and commonwealth, territories: of the larger jurisdictions the Act applies to Malaysia, Singapore and New Zealand.[315] It applies to judgments from 'superior courts' which may be registered within twelve months of delivery.[316] The grounds of jurisdiction, and the defences to recognition, differ from those of the common law only in minor detail, but if the judgment is still subject to appeal it may not be registered.[317]

(b) Foreign Judgments (Reciprocal Enforcement) Act 1933

20.148 The Act has been applied to judgments from Australia, Canada,[318] Guernsey, Jersey, India, Isle of Man, Israel, Pakistan, Surinam, and Tonga, but applies only

---

[314] Protection of Trading Interests Act 1980, s 5.

[315] Reciprocal Enforcement of Judgments (Administration of Justice Act 1920, Part II) (Consolidation) Order 1984, SI 1984/129, as amended by SI 1985/1994, SI 1994/1901, SI 1997/2601. The entry for Hong Kong has been redundant since the cesser of sovereignty on 1 July 1997.

[316] Administration of Justice Act 1920, s 9.

[317] ibid s 9(2)(e).

[318] Québec is excluded.

to courts identified by name in the Order made in relation to the particular country; judgments from other courts may still be enforced by action at common law. The grounds of jurisdiction, and the defences to recognition,[319] differ from those of the common law only in minor detail; if the judgment is subject to appeal the application for registration may be stayed.[320]

(c) Civil Jurisdiction and Judgments Act 1982

Apart from providing the mechanism for the recognition and enforcement of judgments under the Brussels and Lugano Conventions, the 1982 Act provides for judgments from Scotland and Northern Ireland, and Gibraltar. Judgments from other parts of the United Kingdom, whether for money or otherwise, may be registered for enforcement subject to only minor restrictions.[321] Judgments from Gibraltar are recognized and enforced by reference to provisions which are materially identical to Articles 25–49 of the Brussels Convention.[322]   **20.149**

D. Contracts

(1) General[323]

Choice of law for contractual obligations is substantially governed by the 1980 Rome Convention, as enacted by the Contracts (Applicable Law) Act 1990.[324] The Rome Convention serves to harmonize contractual choice of law rules throughout the EU, and applies to contracts made after 1 April 1991.[325] It is sometimes claimed that it draws inspiration from the common law conflict of laws, but it would be unwise to place much weight on that allegation, or to interpret the Convention by the twilight of authorities on the common law. Moreover, the status of the Convention as an international text means that pressure for it to have a uniform interpretation[326] will inevitably draw it away from any common law ancestry which it may have had. The Giuliano and Lagarde Report[327]   **20.150**

---

[319] Foreign Judgments (Reciprocal Enforcement) Act 1933, s 4.
[320] ibid s 5.
[321] 1982 Act, s 18; Schs 6, 7.
[322] ibid s 39; Civil Jurisdiction and Judgments Act 1982 (Gibraltar) Order 1997, SI 1997/2602.
[323] See generally *Dicey*, ch 32; P Kaye, *The New Private International Law of Contract of the European Community* (1993); PM North (ed), *Contract Conflicts* (1982). On the interpretation of the Rome Convention, see the Report of Giuliano and Lagarde [1980] OJ C282/1.
[324] Hereafter the 1990 Act.
[325] Article 17; Contracts (Applicable Law) Act 1990 (Commencement No 1) Order 1991, SI 1991/707.
[326] Article 18.
[327] [1980] OJ C282/1.

is the authorized[328] aid to its interpretation. Work is underway to convert the Convention into a European Regulation having direct effect in all Member States.

20.151 Though matters excluded from the Convention continue to be governed by the common law,[329] these are very few and rather minor, and require mention of the rules of the common law only where they have a residual role.[330]

(2) *Choice of Law*

(a) Domain of the Rome Convention

20.152 The Rome Convention applies to contractual obligations, except for the cases specifically excluded by it. It applies in principle to all such cases litigated before an English court: it is irrelevant that no party has any connection with the European Union, or that the law which it makes applicable is that of a country not party to the Convention.[331] It is in force throughout the European Union, and it is to be construed with a view to securing uniformity of interpretation and application.[332] It follows that certain of its definitional terms will receive an independent or autonomous interpretation, and will not be read as though contained in domestic English legislation. The European Court of Justice has competence to give preliminary rulings on interpretation,[333] but at the time of writing no such reference has been made. The material scope of the Convention is defined inclusively and exclusively.

(b) Contractual obligations

20.153 'Contractual obligations' will encompass obligations regarded as contractual in English law; after the partial abolition of the doctrine of privity, consensual obligations enforceable by third parties will be included.[334] It is also arguable that other obligations, functionally close to contract, will be included within and governed by the Convention.[335] Gifts are included where these are seen as contractual: a curious proposition for an English lawyer.[336] Equitable obligations arising between contracting parties, such as the fiduciary obligations of an agent, will be

---

[328] 1990 Act, s 3(3).
[329] Save for insurance, excluded from the Convention by Article 1.3.
[330] The common law is set out in detail in Dicey & Morris, *The Conflict of Laws* (11th edn, 1987).
[331] Article 2.
[332] Article 18.
[333] Brussels Protocol: 1990 Act, Sch 3; Second Protocol: [1989] OJ L48/17.
[334] Contracts (Rights of Third Parties) Act 1999.
[335] Having regard to the likely autonomous definition of 'contractual obligations'.
[336] [1980] OJ C282/1, 10.

included; and certain obligations to exercise care in making representations, non-contractual only by reason of the absence of consideration, may also be 'contractual obligations'.[337] Cross-reference to the Brussels I Regulation[338] may mean that an 'obligation freely entered into in relation to another'[339] constitutes the point of departure in identifying a contractual obligation. Where contractual in this sense, the liability alleged to arise will be governed by the choice of law rules of the Rome Convention.

(c) Concurrent liability

In some cases—in the employment context,[340] and the provision of professional services,[341] for example—English common law permits a claim to be framed concurrently or electively in contract and in tort. It is uncertain whether this approach is consistent with the Convention, for the framing in tort of a claim which would otherwise fall within the four corners of the Convention means that a claim between contracting parties will be subjected to a law other than that specified by the Convention. Though the Court of Appeal declined to read the Rome Convention as abrogating this common law freedom,[342] if concurrent claims are found to be governed by the *lex contractus* in any event, the point will become moot.

20.154

(d) Excluded issues

The Convention eschews any claim to govern matters set out in Article 1.2. In large measure these were not seen as contractual issues as a matter of English private international law, so Article 1.2 mainly states a truism. It excludes the Convention from status and capacity of natural persons;[343] wills and succession and matrimonial property rights;[344] obligations arising from bills of exchange and promissory notes and other negotiable instruments where these arise from their negotiable character;[345] questions governed by the law of companies;[346] the power of an agent to bind a principal to a third party;[347] the constitution and internal

20.155

---

[337] Cf *Hedley Byrne & Co v Heller Bros* [1964] AC 465.
[338] Civil Jurisdiction and Judgments Act 1982, Sch 1, as amended.
[339] Case C-26/91 *Jakob Handte GmbH v Traitements Mécano-chimiques des Surfaces* [1992] ECR I-3967.
[340] Cf *Coupland v Arabian Gulf Oil Co* [1983] 1 WLR 1151, CA.
[341] *Henderson v Merrett Syndicates Ltd* [1995] 2 AC 145.
[342] *Base Metal Trading Ltd v Shamurin* [2004] EWCA Civ 1316; [2005] 1 WLR 1157.
[343] Article 1.2(a).
[344] Article 1.2(b).
[345] Article 1.2(c). Contracts under which these instruments are issued are not excluded: [1980] OJ C282/1, 10.
[346] Article 1.2(e).
[347] Article 1.2(f). But in so far as contractual, relations between principal and agent, and agent and third party, are not excluded: [1980] OJ C282/1, 13.

relationships of trusts;[348] evidence and procedure;[349] and from insurance where the risk is situated in the territory of the EEC (for which separate, and highly complex, system of regulation deals with choice of law).[350] For these matters, common law conflict of law rules will continue to apply. Article 1.2(d) also excludes agreements on arbitration and choice of court, contrary to the approach of English law that these are governed by the law of the larger contract in which they were contained.[351] As the Convention poses no obstacle to English private international law deciding, on its own authority, to subject jurisdiction and arbitration agreements to the law which applies to the rest of the contract, and this therefore remains the position in England.

(e) Capacity

20.156 Contractual capacity is governed by the common law conflict of laws, according to which an individual would be capable who had capacity either by the law of the country with which the contract was most closely connected, or by the law of his domicile.[352] Article 11 makes an inroad only where two individuals make a contract in the same country, and one later relies on an incapacity under some other law: this is forbidden unless the other was, or should have been, aware of it. For corporations, the existence and extent of contractual capacity is a matter for the *lex incorporationis*. But the effect in law of a contract made by a corporation without capacity to do so is a matter for the applicable law of the contract.

(f) The applicable law

(i) Choice of law expressed

20.157 Article 3 provides that a contract is governed by the law chosen by the parties provided the choice is expressed or demonstrable with reasonable certainty by the terms of the contract or the circumstances of the case. The parties may choose different laws for separate parts, and alter the applicable law at any time. Express choice is straightforward unless the choice is incoherent, such as the law of the United Kingdom, or is the law of something other than a country, such as the *lex mercatoria* or the teachings of some religious cult. 'Law' also means the domestic law of the country chosen: renvoi to another national law is excluded by Article 15. At common law, a choice of court or arbitration clause was presumed to point to the domestic law of the country of dispute resolution; there is no

---

348 Article 1.2(g).
349 Article 1.2(h).
350 Article 1.3. But the exclusion does not apply (so the Convention does apply) to reinsurance: Art 1.4.
351 See para 20.89. See also *Egon Oldendorff v Libera Corp* [1995] 2 Lloyd's Rep 64.
352 *Charron v Montreal Trust Co* (1958) 15 DLR (2d) 240, Ont CA.

reason why this presumption will not still work, at least before an English court; for though the Convention does not govern the validity of such agreements there is certainly no objection to taking account of them in determining the applicable law.[353]

(ii) *Absence of expressed choice*

Excepting consumer contracts, Article 4 provides that, if not expressly chosen, **20.158** the applicable law is that of the country with which the contract is most closely connected: the looked-for connection is to a country, not to a legal system. Presumptions[354] of questionable utility provide that this is the country of habitual residence (for a corporation, its central administration) of the party whose performance is characteristic of the contract, unless the contract is made in the course of that party's trade or profession, in which case it becomes the country of the principal place of business. For contracts concerning an immoveable it is the country where the immoveable is situated. The presumptions are generally inapplicable for contracts for the carriage of goods. It is debatable how far these presumptions improve the law. 'Characteristic performance' is usually taken as that performance for which the payment is made; but if a contract does not conform to the template of a simple cash sale the presumptions may be inapplicable. That said, the seller, supplier, insurer, or reinsurer, who undertakes performance for payment, will tend to be the characteristic performer. More controversially, in a distribution contract, the supplier, rather than the distributor, is the characteristic performer.[355] But if the characteristic performance cannot be determined, or if the contract appears to be more closely connected to another country, Article 4.5 provides that that the law of that country will apply instead.[356] So the presumption from Article 4.2 may be overridden, which weakens its impact; how far it does so is debatable. Some continental courts regard recourse to Article 4.5 as a very remote possibility; English courts simply say that it will be applied 'in a proper case', which formulation assists flexibility and commercial common sense.[357]

At common law it was occasionally said that a presumption of validity meant **20.159** that where the issues were finely balanced a contract should be governed by a law

---

[353] [1980] OJ C282/1, 12; see also *Egon Oldendorff v Libera Corp* [1995] 2 Lloyd's Rep 64; *Egon Oldendorff v Libera Corp (No 2)* [1996] 1 Lloyd's Rep 380.

[354] Articles 4.2–4.4.

[355] *Print Concept GmbH v GEW (EC) Ltd* [2001] EWCA Civ 352; [2002] CLC 382. The French courts agree: *Soc Ammann-Yanmar v Zwaans BVA*, Cass Civ I, 25.11.2003: Rev Crit 2004, 102.

[356] See generally *Bank of Baroda v Vysya Bank Ltd* [1994] 2 Lloyd's Rep 87.

[357] *Samcrete Egypt Engineers and Contractors SAE v Land Rover Exports Ltd* [2001] EWCA Civ 2019; [2002] CLC 533; *Ennstone Building Products Ltd v Stanger Ltd* [2002] EWCA Civ 916; [2002] 1 WLR 3059; *Iran Continental Shelf Oil Co v IRI International Corp* [2002] EWCA Civ 1024.

under which it would be valid.[358] The Rome Convention does not appear to accommodate this.

(iii) Consumer contracts

20.160 Article 5 modifies these rules in respect of certain consumer contracts. The Article applies where the contract is for sale or supply (or for credit for the purpose) to a person for a purpose outside his trade or profession;[359] and applies to a package holiday. It does not apply to a contract of carriage, or where the services are to be supplied wholly outside the country of the consumer's habitual residence. For a contract falling within Article 5, an express choice of law cannot deprive the consumer of the protection afforded him by mandatory rules of law of the country of his habitual residence if either (1) in that country the conclusion of the contract was preceded by a specific invitation addressed to him, or by advertising, and he had there taken all the necessary steps for conclusion of the contract, or (2) the supplier or his agent received the consumer's order in that country, or (3) the contract was for the sale of goods and the consumer travelled from that country to another and there placed his order, the journey having been arranged by the seller to induce the consumer to buy. In the absence of express choice a consumer contract is governed by the law of the country of the consumer's habitual residence.[360]

(iv) Individual employment contracts

20.161 For contracts of employment, Article 6 modifies the applicable law. If there is no express choice of law, the contract is governed by the law of the country where the employee habitually carried out his work[361] or, if there is no single such country, by the law of the country of the place of business which engaged him, unless (in either case) the contract appears to be more closely connected to another country.[362] An express choice operates subject to the mandatory protective laws of the country which would have applied in the absence of an express choice.

(v) General overriding of applicable law

20.162 In four instances the hegemony of the applicable law is further limited. The Convention identifies the first three as 'mandatory laws': a rather unhelpful expression whose meaning varies according to context. In these cases choice of

---

358 eg *Coast Lines Ltd v Hudig and Veder Chartering NV* [1972] 2 QB 34, 44, 48, CA.

359 It is not specified whether the supplier must be acting in the course of his trade or profession.

360 Article 5.4.

361 Where the duties of the employment are carried out in more than one country, see Case C-125/92 *Mulox IBC v Geels* [1993] ECR I-4075; Case C-383/95 *Rutten v Cross Medical Ltd* [1997] ECR I-515.

362 For cases in which the duties are carried on outside the jurisdiction of any state, see [1980] OJ C282/1, 26.

the applicable law is not set aside, but its operation is partially overridden. First, an express choice of law is still subject to laws of another country which may not be derogated from by contractual agreement (an English example would be the requirement of consideration), but only if all the relevant elements at the time of choice are connected with that country.[363] Secondly, laws of the forum which are mandatory and must be applied by a judge regardless of choice of law apply.[364] Examples might include provisions of the Unfair Contract Terms Act 1977 which prevent limitation or exclusion of liability without regard to choice of law,[365] the Carriage of Goods by Sea Act 1971, giving the force of law to the Hague-Visby Rules,[366] or of the Financial Services and Markets Act 2000[367] which invalidate an investment agreement made through an unauthorized person. Thirdly, the Convention[368] would have permitted the application of mandatory laws of a third country (neither applicable law, nor law of the forum) having a close connection with the contract: the provision was not enacted in England.[369] Fourthly, an applicable law will not apply where it would be manifestly contrary to public policy.[370]

(g) Domain of the applicable law

Subject to those points, the applicable law ascertained as above applies to the interpretation and performance of the contract; also to the consequences of breach and the extinction of obligations.[371] For formal validity, compliance with the applicable law is sufficient; otherwise compliance with the law of the place(s) where the parties were when they made the contract is also sufficient.[372] The effect is that, subject to the next paragraph, almost all points of construction, interpretation and discharge (by performance, frustration and breach) are within the domain of the applicable law as, in principle,[373] is the availability of remedies upon breach. The Convention does not demand that the consequences of nullity are governed by the applicable law, for the United Kingdom did not enact Article 10.1(e).[374]

20.163

---

[363] Article 3.3.
[364] Article 7.2.
[365] Unfair Contract Terms Act 1977, s 27(2).
[366] Cf *The Hollandia* [1983] 1 AC 565.
[367] ss 26, 27.
[368] Article 7.1; cf *The Torni* [1932] P 78, CA.
[369] 1990 Act, s 2(2).
[370] Article 16.
[371] Article 10.
[372] Article 9.
[373] Remedies not known to English law cannot be granted: Art 1.2(h). It is uncertain whether specific performance must be ordered in a case in which it would be available under the *lex contractus* but not, in these circumstances, under English domestic law.
[374] 1990 Act, s 2(2).

This issue is therefore dealt with under choice of law for restitutionary obligations.[375]

20.164 The position in relation to original or subsequent contractual invalidity is rather more complex. To begin with, an argument that there was no binding contract is resolved by reference to the law which would govern the contract were it assumed to be valid.[376] Accordingly, the failure of offer and acceptance, absence of consideration, or the effects of misrepresentation, mistake or duress, and other arguments alleged to lead to the invalidity of the contract will be assessed by the provisionally applicable law. But this is obviously unfair and irrational: if one party contends that there never was a binding contract it is unprincipled to evaluate his argument by assuming, even if only hypothetically, that he is wrong, and worse to use the applicable law generated by the very contract which he denies. Accordingly Article 8.2 allows the party who denies that he consented to rely on the law of his habitual residence[377] if it would be unreasonable to apply the applicable law to the question. But if he has dealt by reference to the foreign law before, or maybe simply because he was prepared to make an international contract, he may forfeit this protection.[378]

20.165 Illegality under the law of the place where the contract was to be performed is more complex. If the applicable law renders the contract unenforceable by reason of such illegality, that concludes the enquiry.[379] If it does not, it may still be unenforceable by action in an English court. The common law held that illegality in the place of performance rendered the contract unenforceable. But the exact status of the argument was acutely controversial: in almost every case where the issue arose the contract was governed by English law in any event, though the language of the judgments was more sweeping than this limitation might imply,[380] and it may be that the answer depends on the magnitude of the illegality, and on the awareness of the party prepared to commit it.[381] Recourse to Article 7.1 might have allowed an English court to apply the law of the place of performance, though this provision is not part of English law. However, the rule of the common law, whatever it was, may still operate in the gap left by the excision of Article 7.1 and be applied on the ground that to give effect to the applicable law would conflict with English public policy on the enforcement of contracts tainted by illegality.

---

375 See paras 20.182–20.185.
376 Article 8.1.
377 This form of legislative wording appears to restrict the privilege to individuals.
378 Cf *Egon Oldendorff v Libera Corp* [1995] 2 Lloyd's Rep 64.
379 Article 10.
380 *Ralli Bros v Compania Naviera Sota y Aznar* [1920] 2 KB 287, CA; *Foster v Driscoll* [1929] 1 KB 470, CA; *Regazzoni v KC Sethia (1944) Ltd* [1958] AC 301; *Lemenda Trading Co Ltd v African Middle East Petroleum Co Ltd* [1989] QB 728; *Euro-Diam Ltd v Bathurst* [1990] 1 QB 30.
381 *Royal Boskalis Westminster NV v Mountain* [1999] QB 674, CA.

E. Torts

(1) General[382]

There are two choice of law rules for torts. For torts which occurred before 1 May **20.166**
1996, and for all claims alleging defamation, malicious falsehood, and similar
complaints, the choice of rules of the common law are preserved by the Private
International Law (Miscellaneous Provisions) Act 1995.[383] For all other tort
claims the 1995 Act enshrines statutory rules which may become clearer with
the benefit of judicial and scholastic effort, but which begin surprisingly badly
drafted; and as they are defined by reference to the common law, these represent
the point of departure.

Tort claims will usually arise as civil or commercial matters, and jurisdiction over **20.167**
them will fall within the domain of the Brussels I Regulation.[384] For torts which
principally raise an issue of title to foreign land, or which involve adjudicating
on the validity of foreign intellectual property rights, the common law denied
jurisdiction.[385] Where a defendant is subject to the personal jurisdiction of the
English court under the Regulation, these common law limitations may be
inapplicable,[386] but the better argument is that a court may still decline to
adjudicate.[387]

(2) Choice of Law: Defamation (and Pre-1996 Torts)

Where the acts or omissions were committed before 1 May 1996, the rules of the **20.168**
common law apply.[388] These depend on where the tort was committed. If the elements of the claim are not concentrated in one place the initial question is 'where
in substance, and as a matter of English law, did the cause of action arise?'[389] For
example, if a dangerous pharmaceutical was sold and ingested in the one country,
that was where the cause of action arose, even if it was designed and manufactured
elsewhere.[390] If negligent advice was received and acted on in the one place, this

---

[382] See generally *Dicey*, ch 35.
[383] Hereafter 'the 1995 Act'. For the background to the 1995 Act, see Law Commission, *Private International Law: Choice of Law in Tort and Delict* (Law Com No 193, 1990); *Proceedings of the Special Public Bill Committee* (HL Paper (1995) No 36).
[384] See para 20.33 *et seq*.
[385] See para 20.27.
[386] ibid.
[387] See para 20.78.
[388] 1995 Act, s 13 (defamation), s 14(1).
[389] *Metall und Rohstoff AG v Donaldson Lufkin & Jenrette Inc* [1990] QB 391, CA.
[390] *Distillers Co Ltd v Thompson* [1971] AC 458, PC.

was where the cause of action arose, even though the information came from work done elsewhere or its economic consequences ramified elsewhere.[391] If a libellous statement was transmitted to a place where it was digested and the reputation of the victim injured, this was where the cause of action arose, even though the statement originated elsewhere.[392] Though occasionally rough and ready the test is hallowed by usage, and as long as it is remembered that it leaves a margin of appreciation to the judge, it is as workable as any 'place' rule could be.

20.169 The 1995 Act protects free speech by reference to English standards by preserving the common law choice of law rule for defamation, malicious falsehood, and torts (which will arise under foreign law) of a similar nature.[393] For these it is necessary to determine where the cause of action arose. But it is mostly the privilege of the claimant to define the facts and matters upon which he relies: if, as frequently happens, he sues only in respect of publication in England, England is where the cause of action arose.[394] If the complaint were extended to multi-national publication, it is probable that each substantial national publication must be taken, and the law chosen, separately, for as a matter of English law, and in fact, each publication is a separate and distinct tort, and this principle has been relied on in the context of the conflict of laws.[395]

(a) English torts

20.170 Where the cause of action arose in England, English domestic law applies, without any exception to reflect the fact that the facts may disclose an overwhelming connection with another country but none to England.[396] It follows that the rule for foreign torts, which may be summarized as of 'double actionability with exceptions', is inapplicable to them. A defendant seeking a stay of proceedings on the ground of *forum non conveniens* might have some chance of success, but the natural forum for an English tort is unlikely to be overseas.[397]

---

391 *Diamond v Bank of London and Montreal* [1979] QB 333, CA. For a different view in relation to negligent advice from an accountant see *Voth v Manildra Flour Mills Pty Ltd* (1990) 171 CLR 538, 568–9 (Aust HC).

392 *Bata v Bata* [1948] WN 366, CA; cf *Shevill v Presse Alliance SA* [1992] 2 WLR 1, CA, and as Case C-68/93 *Shevill v Presse Alliance SA* [1995] ECR I-415.

393 1995 Act, s 13.

394 *Schapira v Ahronson* [1998] ILPr 587, CA; *Berezovsky v Michaels* [2000] 1 WLR 1004, HL. The same principle has been applied to defamation by internet publication: *Dow Jones Inc v Gutnick* (2003) 210 CLR 575 (Aust HC).

395 See *Berezovsky v Michaels* (n 394 above).

396 *Metall und Rohstoff v Donaldson Lufkin & Jenrette Inc* [1990] QB 391, CA.

397 Cf *Berezovsky v Michaels* (n 394 above). Otherwise if the connection with England is so weak that the very bringing of proceedings is an abuse of the process of the court: *Dow Jones & Co Inc v Jameel* [2005] EWCA Civ 75; [2005] 1 QB 946.

(b) Overseas torts

Where the cause of action arose in a foreign country a claimant must show that **20.171**
the facts give rise to liability in tort as a matter of English domestic law, and also
give rise to civil liability under the *lex loci delicti*, the law of the place where the tort
occurred: a rule of 'double actionability'.[398] It follows that only claims for torts
known to English law will succeed. This rule serves to determine who is liable, to
allow defences, and to limit heads of damage recoverable, in accordance with
English tort law. Unless the claimant can show that he is entitled to recover under
both systems he stands to lose. So in a defamation claim, a defence of truth or
privilege or fair comment, made out under English law, will answer a claim even
though it would be irrelevant under the law of the place where the cause of action
arose; a defence under the foreign law, say of public interest unknown as such to
English law, will similarly prevail.

By way of exception, if the law of some other country is much more closely **20.172**
connected to an issue, or to the dispute, than is the *lex loci delicti*, reference to the
latter may be displaced. So where two English servicemen were involved in a
traffic accident in Malta, English law displaced Maltese law on the heads of recoverable damage;[399] where an English employment agency sent a labourer to work
and sustain injury on a German site, English law displaced German on the nature
of the duty of care owed by the agency.[400] In an appropriate case, the reference
to English law as *lex fori* may be displaced in favour of one having a much closer
connection than the *lex fori*.[401] The choice of law rule may be loosely described as
'double actionability with double flexibility'.

(3) Choice of Law: All Other Torts

Part III of the 1995 Act establishes the choice of law rule for all other torts. **20.173**
It applies to all issues which were, prior to 1 May 1996, governed by the common
law rule.[402] It is necessary to identify the material scope of the Act, and the law
which applies to cases falling within the Act.

(a) Statutory definition of 'tort'

The Act applies to torts without defining the term.[403] It cannot be restricted **20.174**
to causes of action regarded as torts under English domestic law, for this is half of

---

[398] *Boys v Chaplin* [1971] AC 356.
[399] ibid.
[400] *Johnson v Coventry Churchill International Ltd* [1992] 3 All ER 14.
[401] *Red Sea Insurance Co Ltd v Bouygues SA* [1995] 1 AC 190, PC.
[402] 1995 Act, s 10.
[403] ibid s 9.

the very rule which section 10 of the 1995 Act was passed to abolish, so it must extend to causes of action which are in a looser sense characterized as torts, which raises some difficulties. The best one can probably do is to define the scope of the rule as 'claims and issues which are sufficiently like torts as to justify being characterized as such'.

20.175 Three problems remain. First, section 10 states that the 1995 Act applies only to matters hitherto covered by the rule on double actionability. It would follow that the Act has no application to torts committed in England.[404] This may be unintended, but some muscular statutory construction will be needed to circumvent the plain language of the Act.[405] Secondly, it is unclear how the Act will apply to claims which may be regarded as tortious under some systems, but which fall into other legal categories as a matter of English private international law. Claims alleging breach of confidence or other breaches of equitable duty were not generally governed by the rule of double actionability,[406] neither were claims for contribution, nor other restitutionary claims, such as those against a defendant for knowing receipt of trust property or dishonest assistance of another's breach of trust.[407] If these are nevertheless torts under a potentially applicable foreign law, it is unclear whether their prior or potential non-tortious classification in English law renders the 1995 Act inapplicable. Thirdly, as will be seen, the Act[408] directs attention to the law of the place where the events giving rise to the tort occurred. This is unintelligible unless it has already been decided what law, and hence which law's definition of the elements which make up the tort, is applicable; yet this is what the test is meant to determine in the first place. A case involving English and Italian components may be seen as conversion under English law, and *injuria* in Italian law;[409] the two torts are constructed from distinct elements, and to apply the law of 'the' tort puts the cart before the horse. The practical solution may be to concentrate on the elements pleaded by the claimant as supporting his cause of action, at least unless this appears to be unduly self-serving.[410]

---

[404] ibid ss 10, 14(2); and see para 20.170.

[405] ibid s 9(6) is expressly subject to s 14(2), which itself takes the reader back to s 10; so it manifestly cannot overcome the limitation imposed by the enacting of ss 10 and 14(2).

[406] In so far as they were characterized as equitable or restitutionary obligations they had their own choice of law rule: and see para 20.183 *et seq*.

[407] Though *Arab Monetary Fund v Hashim (No 9)* [1994] TLR 502 used the rule of double actionability for a claim for dishonestly assisting a breach of trust, this was not on the basis that the claim was one in tort, meaning it is unaffected by the 1995 Act.

[408] 1995 Act, s 11.

[409] Cf Case C-364/93 *Marinari v Lloyds Bank plc* [1995] ECR I-2719.

[410] *Trafigura Beheer BV v Kookmin Bank Co* [2006] EWHC 1450 (Comm); [2006] 2 Lloyd's Rep 455.

(b) General rule

According to section 11 of the 1995 Act, if all the events constituting the tort **20.176** occur in one country, the law of that country applies to the claim. But if the events are less conveniently grouped, a claim in respect of death or personal injury (including disease, or impairment of physical or mental condition) is governed by the law of the place where the victim was when killed or injured;[411] a claim in respect of property damage by the law of the place where the property was when damaged;[412] and any other case by the law of the country in which the most significant element or elements of the events constituting the tort occurred.[413]

Personal injury covers psychiatric trauma or nervous shock; but a claim for **20.177** bereavement on death will be governed by the law of the place where the deceased was killed, not where the claimant was when bereaved. Where the damage manifests itself after and far away from the place of the original causative event, such as where asbestosis is diagnosed years after the inhalation of fibres, it appears that a claim for personal injury would initially be governed by the law of the place of inhalation, but a claim in respect of death by the law of the place where the victim died: and if this is unsatisfactory, the rule of displacement in section 12 of the 1995 Act should ameliorate the untidiness. Damage to property appears to exclude the loss of property, for example by theft or conversion. It does not appear to extend to cases of economic loss, though if a foreign law sees the tort as one of damage to the patrimony of the claimant the position is less clear. Infringement of intellectual property rights, though regarded as a tort, is not usually thought of as resulting in property damage, though it may be argued that this is exactly what an infringer does to the intellectual property of the claimant.

It is sometimes said that section 11 of the 1995 Act enacts a *lex loci delicti* rule.[414] **20.178** It certainly does not. Where all elements are grouped in the one place, any rational test will give the same answer which is no more a *lex loci delicti* rule than it is a place of damage rule, or a place of the act rule, or a proper law of the tort rule. But where the events are strewn about, it is neither necessary nor helpful to enquire about the place of the tort. The Law Commission, whose draft Bill provided the basis for the 1995 Act, explained that the *locus delicti* is too often fictitious or artificial to be useful.[415] The methodology preferred was to provide a simple, if arbitrary, rule; and to allow for exceptions whenever this was called for. It follows that old

---

[411] 1995 Act, s 11(2)(a).

[412] ibid s 11(2)(b).

[413] ibid s 11(2)(c). This involves making a 'value judgment': *Morin v Bonhams & Brooks Ltd* [2003] EWCA Civ 1802; [2004] 1 Lloyd's Rep 702.

[414] *Dicey*, 1544.

[415] Law Commission, *Private International Law: Choice of Law in Tort and Delict* (Law Com No 193, 1990), paras 3.6, 3.10.

authorities which seek to define the place of the tort are of no assistance to the general rule under the 1995 Act.

(c) Displacement of the general rule

20.179 Section 12 invites a comparison between the factors which connect the tort with the country whose law was ascertained by section 11, and the factors which connect it with another country. If it is substantially more appropriate to apply the law of the latter, the former is displaced in relation to the claim or any individual issue, as the case may be. So in the case of the two servicemen mentioned above[416] it would be substantially more appropriate to apply English law, and to disapply Maltese law, to the question of whether general damages should be recovered. And in the case of the contract labourer[417] it is substantially more appropriate to apply English law, and not to apply German law, to the question of whether the English agency owed liability for failing to provide a safe system of work. It has also been held, sensibly enough, that where the tort arises from a contractual relationship, it is likely to be governed by the *lex contractus*, even though this is deduced from connection to a *country*.[418]

(d) Exclusion of certain laws

20.180 Section 14 makes clear that the Act does not authorize the enforcement of foreign penal or revenue or other public laws, nor of any foreign law whose enforcement would conflict with public policy, nor of any foreign law which would prevent a matter of procedure being governed by English law; and it does not override the application of a rule of English law which is otherwise mandatory. As the assessment of damages is regarded as procedural, it is still done in accordance with English rules,[419] even where the cause of action is unknown to English law and one for which English law has no rules.

(e) Contractual defences to tort claims[420]

20.181 Where a defendant relies on a contractual promise that the claimant would not bring the action brought, distinctions must be drawn. Whether a contractual promise is admissible as a defence to a claim will be governed by the *lex delicti* as identified by the 1995 Act. After all, a defence of *volenti* is governed by this law, and *volenti* and a contractual promise not to sue are two species of the same genus. But whether a binding contractual promise was made, as distinct from whether it

---

[416] See para 20.172.
[417] ibid.
[418] *Trafigura Beheer BV v Kookmin Bank Co* (n 410 above).
[419] *Harding v Wealands* [2006] UKHL 32; [2006] 3 WLR 83.
[420] For the common law, see *Sayers v International Drilling Co NV* [1971] 1 WLR 1176, CA.

serves as a defence if intrinsically valid, is governed by the law applicable to the contract: the validity of a contract has its own distinct choice of law rule.[421] Take the case of an industrial injury. If the contract of employment contained an undertaking not to sue the employer but to participate in its insurance scheme and was governed by Saudi law, under which it was valid, the consequent question is whether the law which governs the tort admits such a valid promise as a defence. If it does not the contract will be disregarded. If it does, it will be given effect unless there is any rule of English law to the contrary which is of mandatory and overriding effect.

F. Other Obligations

(1) General

Obligations also exist outside contract and tort. Restitutionary obligations have **20.182** an independent juridical basis in the principle that unjust enrichment at the expense of another should be reversed. Equitable obligations spring from a distinct historical origin. Less clear is whether these two categories translate into private international law; whether, and if so, how, the conflict of laws gives separate treatment to claims which are, or are analogous to, those brought to enforce restitutionary and equitable obligations. The law is surprisingly under-developed. The analysis which follows is therefore put forward as one which makes the best use of the sparse material, and which attempts to propose a simple and practical framework for the development of the law. It is not the only view which may legitimately be held.

(2) Claims Founded on an Obligation to Reverse Unjust Enrichment[422]

(a) Within antecedent relationships

English private international law generally accepts that the right to reverse an **20.183** unjust enrichment is governed by the law with which the obligation has its closest and most real connection.[423] This formulation has been accepted as a statement

---

[421] See paras 22.150ff.

[422] See generally J Bird, 'Choice of Law' in FD Rose (ed) *Restitution and the Conflict of Laws* (1995).

[423] By analogy with contracts, transfers of intangibles, where the proper law is dominant. Analogy with tort would be more oriented towards the law of the place where the obligation to make restitution arose which, perhaps, supports the case for the law of the place where the enrichment occurred and (presumably) should have been reversed.

of general principle,[424] but putting flesh on its bones is the greater challenge. It is rational to draw a subordinate distinction. Within an antecedent relationship between claimant and defendant, the law governing the obligation to restore the benefit will be overshadowed, if not inevitably governed, by the law which applied to this prior relationship. So if the obligation arises upon the failure of a real or supposed contract, or from the commission of a tort, the law which governed the contract or the tort will have a strong claim also to govern the restitutionary obligation.[425] This is not because the restitutionary obligation is contractual or tortious, but because it arises in the context of a prior personal relationship, and because it is simply unreal to regard it as free-floating, independent of and uncoloured by its history. Moreover, consistency of result may be supported by such a choice of law rule where the laws governing history, claim and remedy dovetail with each other. So the proper law of the alleged obligation to repay sums paid under a 'void contract' will probably be that which governed the supposed contract, and if the parties' supposed contract expressed a governing law, this will probably govern the restitutionary obligation.[426] The proper law of the alleged obligation to account to one's employer for a bribe corruptly received from another should be the law governing the employment contract;[427] and the proper law of the obligation to account for profits made from committing a tort will probably be the law which governed the tort.[428]

(b) Where there is no antecedent relationship

20.184 Where there is no antecedent relationship between claimant and defendant the leading textbook authority proposes that the proper law of the obligation to make restitution is the law of the place where the enrichment occurred.[429] If in default of a better connected law there is some justification for the place of enrichment, which may provide a fixed point of sorts in a rootless set of facts, it should be no more than an easily rebuttable presumption. For example, in cases where there has been a passing of funds (or, more likely, of electronic data notionally representing funds) through many hands, accounts, and jurisdictions, there may be several places which could be regarded as that of 'the' enrichment, and none may be more

---

424 *Dicey*, Rule 230(1); *Arab Monetary Fund v Hashim* [1996] 1 Lloyd's Rep 589, CA; *Macmillan Inc v Bishopsgate Investment Trust plc (No 3)* [1996] 1 WLR 387, CA.

425 Cf *Baring Bros & Co v Cunninghame DC* [1997] CLC 108 (Ct of Session).

426 In *Dimskal Shipping Co SA v International Transport Workers' Federation (The Evia Luck)* [1992] 2 AC 152 a contract was avoided for duress by reference to its English proper law, and it was accepted without argument that restitution of money paid was governed by English law.

427 *Arab Monetary Fund v Hashim* [1996] 1 Lloyd's Rep 589, CA.

428 If the issue is characterized as one in tort under Private International Law (Miscellaneous Provisions) Act 1995 s 9(2), the statutory choice of law rule will apply.

429 *Dicey*, Rule 230(2)(c).

than artificial or casual.[430] In such a case a flexible proper law rule is inevitable, but if there is a clear location for the enrichment this law may apply to the restitutionary claim for want of a better choice. On the other hand, if there really is so little to point to a proper law, the argument for applying the *lex fori* is stronger than it usually is.

(c) Contribution claims

Where one party claims contribution from another on the ground that he has, by **20.185** paying a third party, discharged a liability owed by both, the claim for contribution may be seen as a restitutionary one.[431] In principle it should be governed by the choice of law scheme described above; but where the claim falls within the wording of the Civil Liability (Contribution) Act 1978 it has been held that the statutory rule applies without regard to choice of law.[432]

(3) Equitable Obligations

It is strongly arguable that the distinction between common law and equity is a **20.186** matter of domestic law, irrelevant to the conflict of laws, and that obligations analogous to those which are equitable in domestic law are to be regarded as tortious (breach of confidence, dishonest assistance of a breach of trust), or contractual (breach of an agent's fiduciary duty, not to act unconscionably in relation to contractual rights) or restitutionary (knowing receipt of trust property). On the other hand, this results in dissonance between domestic and private international law, and there is authority for the view that the equitable obligations of English domestic law are applicable as part of the *lex fori*, binding on anyone subject to the personal jurisdiction of the court.[433] On this view the role of a potentially connected foreign law is to contribute data to what English equity requires or imposes in a given case in order to decide whether relief should be granted. And if this is correct, the application of English equity does not depend upon the application of choice of law rules as such, but only upon jurisdiction and the

---

[430] Cf *Hong Kong and Shanghai Banking Corp Ltd v United Overseas Bank Ltd* [1992] Sing LR 495; *Thahir v Pertamina* [1994] 3 Sing LR 257 (CA).

[431] For example, Law Commission, *Private International Law: Choice of Law in Tort and Delict* (Law Com No 193, 1990) paras 3.47, 3.48.

[432] *Arab Monetary Fund v Hashim (No 9)* [1994] TLR 502. The judge admitted that in a case falling outside the statutory scheme, the proper law of the obligation to contribute would probably be applicable.

[433] *National Commercial Bank v Wimborne* (1978) 5 Butterworths Property Reports 11958, NSW; *United States Surgical Corporation v Hospital Products International Pty Ltd* [1982] 2 NSWLR 766, 797–8, affd [1983] 2 NSWLR 157, CA, revd on different grounds (1984) 156 CLR 41; *Paramasivam v Flynn* (1998–9) 160 ALR 203, 214–8, Aust Fed Ct; cf *Macmillan Inc v Bishopsgate Investment Trust plc (No 3)* [1995] 1 WLR 976, 989, affd without reference to this point [1996] 1 WLR 387, CA.

exercise of discretion.[434] If all equitable obligations were a manifestation of English public policy, this might be acceptable, but this would be an ambitious claim to make for the whole of equity.[435] It is therefore proposed that distinction drawn above for restitution should apply here as well. In cases of prior relationship between the parties, such as employment, any obligation, whether in the nature of equity, restitution or otherwise, is governed by the law governing the antecedent obligation. So an employee's duty to account for a bribe, or to account for profits made by breach of the employee's obligation of confidentiality,[436] is governed by the law of the employment relationship.[437] But in cases lacking such antecedent relationship English courts will apply English equity, though measuring the nature and extent of the equitable duty by reference to the content of any other law which has a close connection to the claim.[438] However, it is fair to say that the reasoning in the most recent cases does not directly support this, or any other, explanation of how choice of law works when claims are founded on equitable obligations which have an international element.[439]

G. Property

(1) Introduction

20.187 The law of property includes transactions *inter vivos* and dispositions on death. It is a large topic, which raises difficult questions about the relationship between jurisdiction and choice of law, and about the relationship between property and the law of obligations. As in most cases a court is asked to adjudicate title and make an order good and reliable against the world, and not just as between the parties to the action, a court will generally be entitled to apply foreign law in its *renvoi* sense, that is, as it would be applied by a judge sitting in the foreign country and hearing the case himself.[440]

---

[434] On this view also, it is hard to see how a foreign equity would be picked up for application.

[435] Cf S Lee, 'Restitution, Public Policy and the Conflict of Laws' (1998) 20 U Queensland LJ 1.

[436] Cf *A-G (UK) v Heinemann Publishers Australia Pty Ltd* (1987) 10 NSWLR 86, 192, NSW CA, affd without reference to this point (1988) 165 CLR 30, Aust HC. The conclusion of the High Court that the obligations on the employee could not be enforced in Australia by reason of a rule against the enforcement of a foreign public law presupposes that the duties, including equitable duties, owed by the employee arose under English law, and not under the *lex fori*.

[437] *Arab Monetary Fund v Hashim* [1996] 1 Lloyd's Rep 589, CA. *Kuwait Oil Tanker SAK v Al-Bader* [2002] 2 All ER (Comm) 271is generally, though not precisely, consistent with this view; *Base Metal Trading Ltd v Shamurin* [2004] EWCA Civ 1316; [2005] 1 WLR 1157 is consistent with this, in result if not precisely in reasoning.

[438] *Grupo Torras SA v Al Sabah* [2001 CLC 221, CA.

[439] *Kuwait Oil Tanker SAK v Al-Bader* [2002] 2 All ER (Comm) 271; *Grupo Torras SA v Al Sabah* [2001 CLC 221.

[440] See para 20.05.

Property divides into immoveables and moveables. The category of immoveables **20.188**
obviously includes land, but the common law also regarded intellectual property
rights as though they were immoveable[441] and until recently, when the old
certainty began to weaken,[442] applied the jurisdiction and choice of law rules
for immoveables to them. Moveables sub-divide into tangible and intangible
property. Whether a thing is an immoveable is determined by the law of the place
where it is, the *lex situs*.[443]

(2) Dealing with Property

(a) Immoveable property

At common law a court lacks jurisdiction to determine questions of title to foreign **20.189**
immoveable property and tort claims in which such an issue would arise.[444] The
law was amended to confer jurisdiction over tort claims where the issue of title is
not a principal one[445] but otherwise the jurisdictional rule prevails,[446] even where
the defendant is willing to submit. So questions of title to foreign immoveables
must be tried in the courts of the *situs*, and by parity of reasoning, foreign
judgments purporting to adjudicate title to English immoveables are unlikely to
be recognized.[447] Moreover, if the land is in an EU Member State, Article 22.1
denies jurisdiction where the proceedings have as their object rights *in rem* in, or
tenancies of, that land.[448]

However, if the claim may be formulated as one to enforce an obligation, **20.190**
albeit one binding the parties in relation to a foreign immoveable, there is no
jurisdictional impediment. The exception derives from *Penn v Baltimore*,[449] and
the principle is plain enough. If the claim is to enforce a contract, or an equitable
obligation, between the parties, the court does not lack jurisdiction even if the
obligation derives from a transaction relating to land.[450] So if the claim is that
the defendant has breached a contract for sale of land, or as bare trustee should
convey title to the claimant beneficiary, the court may enforce the obligation.

---

[441] *Potter v Broken Hill Pty Co Ltd* (1906) 3 CLR 459 (Aust HC).
[442] *Pearce v Ove Arup Ltd* [2000] Ch 403.
[443] *Dicey*, ch 22; *Re Hoyles* [1911] 1 Ch 179, 185.
[444] *British South Africa Co v Companhia de Moçambique* [1893] AC 602; *Hesperides Hotels Ltd v Aegean Turkish Holidays Ltd* [1979] AC 508.
[445] *Re Polly Peck International plc (in administration) (No 2)* [1998] 2 All ER 812, 828, CA.
[446] Civil Jurisdiction and Judgments Act 1982, s 30.
[447] Authority hardly exists. See *Duke v Andler* [1932] SCR 734, (1932) 4 DLR 529, Can Sup Ct.
[448] Para 20.41; and also *Griggs Group Ltd v Evans* [2005] Ch 153.
[449] (1750) 1 Ves Sen 444.
[450] Cf Case C-294/92 *Webb v Webb* [1994] ECR I-1717 (a case on what is now Art 22.1 of the Brussels I Regulation).

20.191 For choice of law, when the court has jurisdiction it determines title by applying the *lex situs* as this would be applied in a court at the *situs*, the justification for which is the alleged pointlessness of doing otherwise than a local judge would do. As justification this is hardly convincing, for the real question is whether the foreign judge would give effect to an English (to him, foreign) judgment, not whether he would have come to the same result himself. But it is hard to maintain a rational argument for the application of anything other than the *lex situs*.[451] Where the court enforces a contract or other obligation, it applies the proper law of that obligation, which may (but certainly need not) be the *lex situs*.

(b) Moveable property

(i) Tangible moveables

20.192 The category of tangible moveable property needs little explanation, though it includes negotiable instruments,[452] and to bearer shares, which are tangibles because transfer of the instrument serves to transfer all rights or property inherent in it. Disputes concerning title to tangible moveable property are governed by the *lex situs* at the date of the event in question.[453] So the question whether A obtained good title to a car he bought in Ruritania is governed by Ruritanian law; the question whether B loses title to his painting stolen from England and auctioned in Italy is governed by Italian law;[454] the question whether C reserved and retained title to materials after their use or on-sale by D is governed by the *lex situs* at the time of D's dealing with it;[455] the question whether E obtained title to property which he found is governed by the *lex situs* at the date of finding; and the question who owns the property of F and G which has become mixed is governed by the *lex situs* at the date of mixing.[456] Though in principle the law might trace the history of title from the beginning, the eventual question is usually the legal effect of the final transaction; and anterior questions are answered by looking through the eyes of the eventual *lex situs*, leaving the law of obligations to remedy wrongs committed along the way.

20.193 The rule allows for exceptions. If the goods are in transit and their *situs* unknown there is a case for applying instead the proper law of the transaction alleged to have affected title.[457] The fact that a disposition of goods is effected by document does not serve to by-pass the *lex situs* of the goods.

---

[451] *Bank of Africa v Cohen* [1909] 2 Ch 129, CA.

[452] Whether the thing is negotiable is determined by its *situs* at the time of its purported negotiation.

[453] *Cammell v Sewell* (1860) 5 H & N 728.

[454] *Winkworth v Christie, Manson & Woods Ltd* [1980] Ch 496.

[455] *Re Interview Ltd* [1975] IR 382; *Armour v Thyssen Edelstahlwerke AG* [1991] 2 AC 339.

[456] *Glencore International AG v Metro Trading Inc* [2001] 1 Lloyd's Rep 283.

[457] *Dicey*, Rule 124, Exception.

(ii) Intangible moveables

Intangible property raises issues of greater complexity. First, it is sometimes diffi- **20.194**
cult to see why intangibles are characterized as property as distinct from the contractual or analogous rights which they almost always are: the question of who is
entitled to an intangible will often be the same as asking who is now in privity with
the debtor or obliged party. This would suggest that the entire question is an
aspect of the law of contract, with a gloss supplied by laws regulating security and
insolvency, got up to look like something else. But secondly, not all intangibles are
contractual in nature, and the range of intangibles may be too broad for a single,
indiscriminate, choice of law rule to apply to them all.

Article 12 of the Rome Convention[458] provides, in relation to questions falling **20.195**
within its domain, that the mutual obligations of assignor and assignee are
governed by the law applicable to the contract between them, but that the law
governing the right assigned determines its assignability, the relationship between
assignee and debtor, the conditions for invoking the assignment against the debtor,
and the discharge of the debtor. In other words, issues involving the debtor are
governed by the proper law of the debt; issues between the creditors are governed
by the proper law of their relationship. It is useless to ask whether this is the answer
the common law would have given, because if the issue falls within the domain of
the Rome Convention in general and Article 12 in particular, Article 12 applies,
for any characterization of issues by the common law conflict of laws is overridden
by the Parliamentary instruction to apply Article 12 to all questions within its
scope.[459] Even if it were admissible, to ascribe a situs to intangible moveable
property is always artificial, and the advantages of a *lex situs* analysis are very hard
to see.

Shares. Transfers[460] of registered shares are governed by the *lex incorporationis* **20.196**
for the unassailable reason that any solution which diverges from that law is effectively unenforceable. In such cases, the general rule in Article 12 of the Rome
Convention is held to be inapplicable.[461]

Intellectual property. To the extent that the question is not governed by **20.197**
Convention or statute, and is not outside the jurisdiction of an English court,
patents, copyright and trade mark rights are governed by the law of the place of

---

[458] Contracts (Applicable Law) Act 1990, Sch 1.
[459] *Raiffeisen Zentralbank Österreich AG v Five Star Trading LLC* [2001] EWCA Civ 68; [2001]
QB 825.
[460] Assuming that shares are assigned, though the better analysis is surrender and re-issue, rather
than assignment by the original shareholder.
[461] *Macmillan Inc v Bishopsgate Investment Trust plc (No 3)* [1996] 1 WLR 378, CA.

the right (*lex protectionis*), which will determine whether and on what terms they are assignable.[462]

(c) Seizure and confiscation of property

20.198 Questions arising out of the seizure of property by governments require little more than an application of the *lex situs* rule set out above. If the property is within the territorial jurisdiction of the state, the *lex situs* rule produces the recognition of title acquired by reference to local law.[463] There is no question of an English court being called upon to 'enforce' the foreign law: once that law has, in the eye of the English conflict of laws, done what it set out to do there is nothing in it left to enforce.[464] Only if the law under which the seizure was made is utterly abhorrent to English standards will it be possible to deny recognition to the law and hence to the title acquired under it.[465] But there is no rule of English private international law which denies recognition unless compensation is paid.[466] By contrast, if the property was outside the territory of the seizing state, the *lex situs* rule will refer to this third country the question whether title was altered by such legislative or governmental act; if the property was in England, no change in title can occur by reference to a law which is, *ex hypothesi*, not the *lex situs*.[467]

20.199 It is sometimes suggested that the answer is more complicated if the property is removed from the territory of the state before it has been taken into the possession of the authorities. Where the *lex situs* requires this to be done as a precondition to the acquisition of title under it this is uncontroversial.[468] But there is no justification for imposing this as a requirement in cases where the *lex situs* makes no stipulation to this effect.[469] On the other hand, an action to recover the property will usually be characterized as a claim in tort, and a claim to recover the property or obtain other relief will be governed by the choice of law rules for torts. The issue of title may be a significant element within the tort analysis, but that it all it is.

---

[462] *Peer International Corp v Termidor Music Publishers Ltd* [2003] EWCA Civ 1156; [2004] 1 WLR 849.

[463] *Luther v Sagor* [1921] 3 KB 532, CA; *Princess Paley Olga v Weisz* [1929] 1 KB 718, CA.

[464] *Williams & Humbert v W & H Trade Marks (Jersey) Ltd* [1986] AC 368.

[465] *Oppenheimer v Cattermole* [1976] AC 276; *Kuwait Airways Corp v Iraqi Airways Co (Nos 4 and 5)* [2002] UKHL 19; [2002] 2 AC 883.

[466] *Williams & Humbert Ltd v W & H Trade Marks (Jersey) Ltd* [1986] AC 368.

[467] *Re Russian Bank for Foreign Trade* [1933] Ch 745.

[468] *A-G for New Zealand v Ortiz* [1984] AC 1, 41.

[469] For the suggestion, which may reflect the fact that the action for conversion focuses on the recovery of possession, and not the vindication of title, see *Brokaw v Seatrain UK Ltd* [1971] 2 QB 476, CA; *A-G for New Zealand v Ortiz* [1984] AC 1, 20, CA; affd on different grounds, ibid 41.

The rule applies to immoveable property, and to tangible property. In relation to **20.200** intangible property it plainly applies to shares situated where the company is incorporated.[470] It is less clear how it applies to simple contractual intangibles, but the *situs* of a debt is in general the place of residence of the debtor,[471] for it is there that he may be sued as a matter of right.

(d) Trusts[472]

The private international law of trusts is substantially contained in the Hague **20.201** Convention on the Recognition of Trusts, given force in England by the Recognition of Trusts Act 1987.[473] The Convention, however, has more to do with the identification of the governing law than with the recognition of foreign trusts. It defines a trust as the legal relationship, created *inter vivos* or on death, voluntarily and evidenced in writing, when the settlor places assets under the control of a trustee for the benefit of a beneficiary or for a specified purpose.[474] However, the 1987 Act extends this to include trusts of property arising under the law of any part of the United Kingdom, and to trusts created by judicial decision;[475] and applies it to trusts falling within its definition whatever the date of their creation.[476] Its application to implied, resulting and constructive trusts is therefore clear. The implied or constructive trust arising from the joint purchase of property will fall within the scope of the Act; but where a constructive trust is sought against or imposed upon a defendant found answerable in an equitable claim, the relevant choice of law rules are probably those in Section F of this chapter.

A trust is governed by the law chosen by the settlor; in default of demonstrable **20.202** choice it is governed by the law with which it is most closely connected.[477] In identifying the latter regard is to be had to the place of administration of the trust, the *situs* of the assets of the trust, the place of residence of the trustee, and the objects of the trust and the places where they are to be fulfilled. The governing law regulates the trust, its construction, effect, and administration;[478] but gives way to mandatory and conflicts rules of the *lex fori*, and to public policy.[479]

---

[470] *Williams & Humbert Ltd v W & H Trade Marks (Jersey) Ltd* [1986] AC 368.
[471] *Soc Eram Shipping Co Ltd v Hong Kong and Shanghai Banking Corp* [2003] UKHL 30; [2004] 1 AC 260 (applying this rule to third party debt orders).
[472] *Dicey*, ch 29.
[473] Hereafter the 1987 Act, Sch 1.
[474] Article 2.
[475] 1987 Act, s 1(2).
[476] Article 22.
[477] Articles 6, 7.
[478] Article 8.
[479] Article 18.

(e) Marriage and property rights[480]

20.203 The impact of marriage on property rights is part of a larger picture. Where a marriage terminates *inter vivos* many systems of law allow a court which dissolves or annuls it to make orders in relation to spousal property which override property rights created or existing prior to the marriage.[481] Where a marriage is terminated by death some systems have only rules of succession to apply, whereas under others the rules of a matrimonial property regime, often one of community of property, deal with the rights of the quick and the dead. But within these limitations it is expedient to examine the law of matrimonial property.

20.204 Where the parties make a matrimonial contract, the proper law of that contract governs its creation, validity, interpretation, and effect.[482] The proper law may be chosen but will otherwise be that with which the marriage has its closest and most real connection:[483] the earlier preference for the law of the husband's domicile has been indefensible at least since the abolition of the wife's dependent domicile in 1974. Capacity to make a marriage contract is governed by the individual's domicile at the date of marriage.[484] Principle would suggest that once a matrimonial contract has been made a change in matrimonial domicile cannot alter the rights created under it;[485] but there is nothing in principle to prevent the parties varying their contract by act and consent.

20.205 Where the parties do not make a matrimonial contract it was once thought that a distinct set of answers was applicable: that the law by reference to which they married (the matrimonial domicile) applied to determine the proprietary consequences of marriage,[486] but that this original regime did not necessarily survive a change of matrimonial domicile. The better view, however, is that the system which the parties opt into and which is imposed by the law of the matrimonial domicile, which may be a system of separation of property, and whether or not conceptualized as a tacit contract or default provision, continues to apply after a change in domicile for the same reasons as where there is an express contract.

---

480 *Dicey*, ch 28.
481 eg Matrimonial Causes Act 1973, s 24(1)(c).
482 *Re Fitzgerald* [1904] 1 Ch 573, CA.
483 *Duke of Marlborough v A-G* [1945] Ch 78, CA.
484 *Re Cooke's Trusts* (1887) 56 LT 737; *Cooper v Cooper* (1888) 13 App Cas 88.
485 *De Nicols v Curlier* [1900] AC 21.
486 *Re Egerton's Will Trusts* [1956] Ch 593.

(f) Death

(i) *Administration of estates*[487]

An order of the court is required to empower a person to deal with the assets of   **20.206**
a deceased, whether by proving a will to appoint a named and willing executor
or by obtaining a grant of letters of administration.[488] Though the court may
make a grant of representation of any deceased, it will be rarely that it does so
unless there is property of the deceased in England.[489] The making of a grant
confirms or vests, as the case may be, the property of the deceased in the grantee.
Where the deceased died domiciled in a foreign country, the court will usually
make a grant to the person who, under the law of the domicile, has been or is entitled to be appointed to administer the estate.[490] The representative may take all
steps to get in all property, wherever situated, of the deceased.[491] The substance of
the administration is governed by the law of the country under which the grant
of representation was made.[492] As a matter of English law, in the paying of
the deceased's debts foreign creditors and English creditors are treated alike;[493]
the admissibility and priority between claims is governed by English law as
lex fori.[494]

A foreign grant has, in principle, no effect in England; the person appointed must   **20.207**
obtain an English grant of representation, which contrasts with the fact that a for-
eign-appointed trustee in bankruptcy is recognized without further ado.[495]

(ii) *Succession to property*[496]

If a duly appointed representative is before it, an English court has jurisdiction to   **20.208**
determine a question of succession.[497] A foreign court has jurisdiction to determine succession to the property, wherever situated, of a deceased dying domiciled
in that country, and its decision will be recognized in England;[498] it also has jurisdiction to determine succession to all property within its territorial jurisdiction,
regardless of the domicile of the deceased.

---

[487] *Dicey*, ch 26.

[488] *New York Breweries Co v A-G* [1899] AC 62.

[489] Probate Registrar's Direction, 30 November 1932; *Aldrich v A-G* [1968] P 281.

[490] Supreme Court Act 1981, s 25(1).

[491] *Re Scott* [1916] 2 Ch 268, CA.

[492] *Re Kloebe* (1884) 28 Ch D 175; *Re Lorillard* [1922] 2 Ch 638, CA.

[493] *Re Kloebe* (ibid).

[494] *Re Kloebe* (n 492 above).

[495] *New York Breweries v A-G* [1899] AC 62.

[496] *Dicey*, ch 27.

[497] *Re Lorillard* [1922] 2 Ch 638, CA.

[498] *Re Trufort* (1887) 36 Ch D 600; *Ewing v Orr-Ewing* (1883) 9 App Cas 34; *Ewing v Orr-Ewing* (1885) 10 App Cas 5.

20.209 For testate succession, the capacity of a testator to make a will is governed by his domicile at the date of making the will,[499] and the capacity of a legatee to take is conferred by the law of either his own or of the testator's domicile.[500] Formal validity is satisfied if the will is formally valid according to the law of the place when and where it was executed, or the law of the place (at either the time of execution or death) where the deceased died domiciled or habitually resident, or of which he was a national.[501] The same laws govern the formal validity or the revocation of a will.[502] Wills of immoveables are formally valid if they conform to the *lex situs*.[503] Material validity is governed by the law of the testator's domicile at death,[504] except for immoveables, where essential validity is governed by the *lex situs*.[505] The interpretation of the will is governed by the law of the domicile at the date of its making.[506] The validity of an act of revocation is governed by the domicile of the testator at the date of revocation.[507]

20.210 Intestate succession is governed by the domiciliary law of the deceased at the date of death, except that succession to immoveables is governed by the *lex situs*.[508] The rule is one about succession, so does not extend to cases where a state assumes title to ownerless property as *bona vacantia* which is instead governed in all cases by the *lex situs*. When the application of the law of the domicile would vest the property of the deceased in the state, the process of characterization determines whether the right invoked by the state operates by way of succession; this is a question concerning the substance and mechanism of the legal rule, not merely an examination of its form.[509]

H. Family Law

(1) Introduction

20.211 Family law is the traditional stronghold of the law of the domicile, though not every issue is answered by recourse to it, and statutory reform has not left its hegemony untouched. In this context, the *law* usually indicates the law including its conflicts rules which would be applied by a judge hearing the case in his own

---

499 *In the Estate of Fuld (No 3)* [1968] P 675.
500 *Re Hellmann's Will* (1866) LR 2 Eq 363.
501 Wills Act 1963, s 1.
502 ibid s 2(1)(c).
503 ibid.
504 *Whicker v Hume* (1858) 7 HLC 124; *Re Groos* [1915] Ch 572; *Re Ross* [1930] 1 Ch 377.
505 *Nelson v Bridport* (1846) 8 Beav 547; *Freke v Carbery* (1873) LR 16 Eq 461.
506 *Ewing v Orr-Ewing* (1883) 9 App Cas 34.
507 *In bonis Reid* (1866) LR 1 P & D 74.
508 *Balfour v Scott* (1793) 6 Bro PC 550.
509 *Re Maldonado's Estate* [1954] P 233, CA.

court: the principle of renvoi permeates family law issues in which it is pleaded and proved.[510]

The plan of this section is to examine marriage, then matrimonial causes, financial **20.212** provision, and a final brief summary of the highly complex law of children.

(2) Adult Relationships

(a) Marriage

(i) Formal validity

The forms of a marriage ceremony are governed by the law of the place of cele- **20.213** bration, the *lex loci celebrationis*.[511] The need for a public, civil or religious ceremony,[512] for either party to be present in person,[513] or for parental or other third party consent to be given,[514] is governed by this law. A marriage formally invalid may be validated if compliant with the law to which a judge at the *locus celebrationis* would look if he were dealing with the issue.[515] But if it was impossible for the parties to comply with local forms (or if the place of celebration was under belligerent occupation),[516] it suffices for the marriage to satisfy the rudimentary requirements of the ancient common law: a marital declaration in the presence of witnesses with no need for a priest.[517] Statutory provision is made for members of HM Forces to marry while serving abroad, and for consular marriages.[518]

(ii) Essential validity

Several issues usually accommodated under the heading of essential validity. **20.214**

Capacity. Each party must have capacity to marry the other according to the **20.215** law of his or her ante-nuptial domicile.[519] Some authorities suggest that the law of the intended matrimonial home would be a more appropriate test for some issues of capacity, but none has so decided. The age of matrimonial capacity[520] and the degrees of prohibited relationship[521] fall within this rule, though the distinct issue

---

[510] See para 20.05.

[511] *Simonin v Mallac* (1860) 2 Sw & Tr 67, *Berthiaume v Dastous* [1930] AC 79, PC.

[512] *Taczanowska v Taczanowski* [1957] P 301, CA.

[513] *Apt v Apt* [1948] P 83, CA; *McCabe v McCabe* [1994] 1 FCR 257, CA.

[514] *Simonin v Mallac*; *Ogden v Ogden* [1908] P 46, CA.

[515] *Taczanowska v Taczanowski*, (n 512 above). In principle this law ought to be permitted to invalidate as well, but in practice this will be most unlikely.

[516] *Taczanowska v Taczanowski* (n 512 above); *Preston v Preston* [1963] P 411, CA.

[517] *Wolfenden v Wolfenden* [1946] P 61; *Penhas v Tan Soo Eng* [1953] AC 304, PC.

[518] Foreign Marriage Act 1892, ss 22 (as amended) and 1, respectively.

[519] *Brook v Brook* (1861) 9 HLC 193; *Sottomayor v De Barros (No 2)* (1879) 5 PD 94.

[520] Marriage Act 1949, s 2, applies to any marriage in England and requires each party to be 16 or above.

[521] *Brook v Brook* (n 519 above).

of the effect of a previous marriage dissolved or annulled by decree is examined below. Whether *lex loci celebrationis* also has a role is complex. If the marriage takes place in England it is probable that the parties must also satisfy the capacity requirements of local law;[522] if they marry overseas it is probable, though not certain, that they need not.[523] But if they marry in England, one party being domiciled in England, it suffices for the other to have capacity according to English domestic law.[524]

20.216 Consent and consummation. Each party must consent to marry the other, this being governed by the *lex domicilii*.[525] It is rational that physical impediments to marriage are referable to the law of the allegedly incapable party.[526]

20.217 Previous marriage. According to Family Law Act 1986, s 50, if a marriage has been dissolved or annulled by a decree accorded recognition by English law, subsequent remarriage is unaffected by the refusal of another system of law to recognize the decree.[527] So if a Maltese domiciliary is divorced by a decree recognized by English legislation but denied recognition under Maltese law, the remarriage may be valid even though his domiciliary law would regard him as still married. The reverse position, where a *lex domicilii* recognizes a decree which English legislation does not, is ungoverned by English authority, but if the *lex domicilii* regards an individual as capable of marriage it is hard to see why English law should contradict it.[528] However, where the recognition falls under the EU Regulation,[529] s 50 does not apply,[530] and it remains undecided whether a remarriage is adversely affected by another law's non-recognition of such a decree.

20.218 Polygamous marriage. A marriage is polygamous[531] if celebrated in polygamous form[532] and the husband's *lex domicilii* gives him capacity for polygamy.[533]

---

522 There is no authority to this effect, however.

523 *Breen v Breen* [1964] P 144 holds that there is such a requirement. If the law which gives the celebrant power to change the parties' status concludes that the celebrant has not married the parties, it has a powerful claim to be listened to, even though it will tend to increase the invalidity of marriages.

524 *Sottomayor v De Barros (No 2)* (1879) 5 PD 94; *Ogden v Ogden* (n 514 above) (alternative ratio).

525 *Szechter v Szechter* [1971] P 286, but cf *Vervaeke v Smith* [1983] 1 AC 145.

526 *Ponticelli v Ponticelli* [1958] P 204. Authority equally supports the *lex fori*, by presumed analogy with divorce.

527 Family Law Act 1986, s 50.

528 *Schwebel v Ungar* (1963) 42 DLR (2d) 622, Ont CA, supports the application of the *lex domicilii* over the non-recognition of the *lex fori*. This is hard to reconcile with the Family Law Act 1986, s 45.

529 Regulation 2201/2003/EC, as to which, see para 20.221.

530 European Communities (Matrimonial Jurisdiction and Judgments) Regulations 2001, SI 2001/310 (as amended by SI 2005/265), reg. 9.

531 Subject to the Private International Law (Miscellaneous Provisions) Act 1995, s 5, a marriage is polygamous if actually or potentially so.

532 *Lee v Lau* [1967] P 14.

533 *Hussain v Hussain* [1983] Fam 26, CA.

The first condition means that a marriage celebrated in England is inevitably monogamous; the second that a marriage celebrated overseas by an Englishman (though not woman) is not polygamous. While a woman domiciled in a polygamous country may contract a polygamous marriage, and an Englishwoman has no personal capacity for actual polygamy,[534] it has been held that her personal capacity to contract a polygamous marriage is actually governed by the law of her intended matrimonial home.[535]

Public policy. There is an opportunity for public policy to intervene at the point when a rule of the *lex causae*, even after making allowance for different cultural and social traditions, offends the English conception of marriage as a consensual monogamous union of a man and a woman of the age of discretion,[536] and as an institution which they are entitled to enter into without the impediment of capricious, discriminatory, or penal[537] restriction. Polygamy was accepted as marriage a century ago; and the marriage of uncle and niece has been held to be tolerable.[538] **20.219**

(b) Civil Partnerships

Marriage, for the purposes of the conflict of laws, does not include same-sex unions. Eligible[539] persons of the same sex may in England enter into civil partnerships. Eligible persons who enter into civil partnerships overseas, or who marry in those countries which permit persons of the same sex to marry, may have their union recognized as a civil partnership but not as a marriage.[540] It remains to be finally decided whether the statutory refusal to recognize as married persons who have contracted a marriage valid in the place of its celebration, is compatible with the European Convention on Human Rights. **20.220**

(c) Matrimonial causes

(i) Decrees from English courts

No broad principle underpins the jurisdiction of the English courts. The pragmatic aim of the law is to bring the divorce and annulment jurisdictions of the EU Member States into harmony. To achieve this, some complication was inevitable. **20.221**

---

[534] Private International Law (Miscellaneous Provisions) Act 1995, s 5, removes the incapacity of an English domiciliary to celebrate a potentially polygamous, but actually monogamous, marriage.

[535] *Radwan v Radwan (No 2)* [1973] Fam 35.

[536] *Mohamed v Knot* [1969] 1 QB 1.

[537] *Scott v A-G* (1886) 11 PD 128.

[538] *Cheni v Cheni* [1965] P 85.

[539] Civil Partnerships Act 2004 s 3 requires them to be 16 or older, not married or in a registered partnership, and not within the prohibited degrees.

[540] Civil Partnerships Act 2004, ss 212–215; Sch 20.

The jurisdiction of an English court to grant a decree of divorce, separation, or annulment is governed by Regulation 2201/2003,[541] and is stated[542] in terms of habitual residence or domicile. As to habitual residence in England,[543] it suffices that the spouses are habitually resident there, or were last habitually resident there, one of them still being so; or that the respondent is habitually resident there, or (if the parties make a joint application) that either party is; or if the applicant was resident for a year (or if domiciled in England, six months) immediately prior to the application. As to domicile, the court has jurisdiction if both parties are domiciled in England. If a spouse is habitually resident in a Member State, or is a national of a Member State other than the United Kingdom or Ireland, or is domiciled within the United Kingdom or Ireland, he or she may be sued only in the courts identified in Article 3. Where no Member State court has jurisdiction under Article 3, the 'residual jurisdiction' of the English courts is available if either party was domiciled in England on the date proceedings were instituted.[544] In situations of *lis pendens* the court seised first has jurisdiction.[545] It seems probable that if the English court has jurisdiction under Article 3 of the Regulation, it has no power to stay proceedings on the ground of *forum non conveniens*.[546]

20.222   As to choice of law, in proceedings for a divorce an English court[547] applies English domestic law. For nullity, the applicable law may be deduced from the grounds of invalidity examined in relation to the original validity of marriage. If the marriage is plainly a nullity, there is no need to obtain a decree to this effect, but where the alleged defect is in substance one unknown, neither precisely nor by analogy, to English law, no reported authority exists to confer the power to dissolve the marriage.[548]

(ii)   Decrees from EU Member States[549]

20.223   Decrees obtained in other Member States are now governed by Brussels II*bis* Regulation. The decree need not come from a court, as long as it emanates from the authority empowered to make such decrees.[550] Chapter III of the Regulation provides for recognition to be automatic unless on proceedings for a declaration

---

541 [2003] OJ L338/1, known as 'Brussels II*bis*.' It supersedes Regulation 1347/2000, which was known as 'Brussels II'.

542 Article 3 contains the principal grounds. Article 4 deals with counterclaims; Article 5 with the conversion of separation into divorce.

543 Article 66 makes England, rather than the United Kingdom, the relevant territory for the determination of connecting factors.

544 Art 7 of the Brussels II*bis* Regulation.

545 Article 19.

546 By the application of Case C-281/02 *Owusu v Jackson* [2005] ECR I-1383.

547 All English divorces must be obtained from a court: Family Law Act 1986, s 44.

548 Cf *Vervaeke v Smith* [1983] 1 AC 145.

549 Except Denmark, which opted out of the Regulation: Article 2.3.

550 Article 2.1.

of enforceability it is found that recognition is manifestly contrary to public policy, was given without the respondent having been served in time to arrange the
defence (the shield is lost if the respondent has unequivocally accepted the decree),
is irreconcilable with an English decision in proceedings between the same parties, or is irreconcilable with a foreign judgment which qualified for recognition:[551]
in other words, the rules closely and deliberately reflect Chapter III of the Brussels
I Regulation.[552] It is unsurprising that, therefore, neither the jurisdiction of the
court,[553] nor the substance,[554] may be reviewed. Whether the Brussels I regime
for civil and commercial judgments was fit for being extended to judgments on
personal status is debatable.

(iii)   *Effect of decrees from non-Member States*

Overseas decrees obtained outside the EU are recognized or not according to   **20.224**
whether they were obtained by means of proceedings (whether judicial or otherwise) or not:[555] a peculiarly pointless distinction. Problems arise with decrees
obtained by proceedings whose integral elements span two or more countries. It
has been held that if any significant element took place in England, the decree
cannot be seen as an overseas one, with the apparent conclusion that it is denied
recognition under either regime;[556] and the same reasoning may prevent its recognition if the elements took place in two overseas countries. Yet it would be absurd
to withhold recognition from an Australian judicial divorce simply because the
petition was served on the respondent in England, or to deny that a divorce
obtained from a judge in London was not obtained there because the petition had
to be served in France. The problem stems from the baffling assumption of the
legislator that all proceedings and decrees are confined within a single country;
and any attempt to make the statute connect with reality risks stumbling on this
piece of ineptitude.

A decree is obtained by proceedings if obtained by judicial or other proceed-   **20.225**
ings,[557] that is, with the involvement of an agency of or recognized by the state,
whose role is more than merely probative.[558] So a 'religious' divorce obtained
under the procedures of the (Pakistani) Muslim Family Law Ordinance 1961
would be obtained by proceedings,[559] so too, if less clearly, a Jewish religious

---

[551] Article 22.
[552] As to which, see para 20.108.
[553] Article 24.
[554] Article 26.
[555] ibid s 46.
[556] *Berkovits v Grinberg* [1995] Fam 142, effectively following *R v Secretary of State for the Home
Department, ex p Fatima* [1986] AC 527 (a case on the previous legislation).
[557] 1986 Act, s 54(1).
[558] *Chaudhary v Chaudhary* [1985] Fam 19, CA.
[559] *Quazi v Quazi* [1980] AC 744.

divorce by 'ghet';[560] but a Muslim 'talaq' divorce, simply effected by unilateral words of repudiation, will not.[561]

20.226 A decree obtained by means of proceedings must be obtained where either party was domiciled (either according to English law, or under the law of the place of obtaining),[562] or was habitually resident, or was a national; and it must be effective under that law to dissolve the marriage.[563] Where domicile or habitual residence are relied on this requires effectiveness in the relevant law district, such as Arizona; with nationality, it must be effective throughout the entire national territory such as the United States.[564] Recognition may be denied[565] on grounds of lack of notice or right to be heard, or if the matter is already *res judicata*. It may also be denied on grounds of public policy, and although the grounds upon which the decree was obtained are not stated as a ground of objection, in an extreme case they may be relevant.

20.227 If the decree is obtained without proceedings, it must be obtained where both parties were domiciled when it was obtained, or where one was domiciled, the country of domicile of the other party recognizing the decree. And it may not be recognized if either party had been habitually resident in the United Kingdom throughout the year prior to the obtaining.[566] The grounds of non-recognition include those applicable to decrees obtained by proceedings but recognition may also be denied if there is no official document certifying the effectiveness of the decree in the foreign country.[567]

(iv) Civil Partnerships

20.228 The jurisdiction of an English court to dissolve a civil partnership exists if both partners are habitually resident in England, or were last so resident and one still is, or the respondent is habitually resident, or the petitioner is and has been for a year (or six months if he is also domiciled in England) immediately prior to the institution of proceedings.[568] The grounds for dissolution and annulment closely follow English law on the dissolution and annulment of marriages.

---

560 *Berkovits v Grinberg* [1995] Fam 142.
561 *Chaudhary v Chaudhary* [1985] Fam 19, CA.
562 1986 Act, s 46(5).
563 ibid s 46(1); though not necessarily to reattribute marital capacity: s 50.
564 ibid s 49(3)(a).
565 ibid s 51.
566 ibid s 46(2).
567 ibid s 51(4). This requirement was read minimally in *Wicken v Wicken* [1999] Fam 224.
568 Civil Partnership (Jurisdiction and Recognition of Judgments) Regulations 2005, SI 2005/3334; the grounds for annulment are similar. There are further grounds of jurisdiction which will be of limited application. It is irrelevant whether the partnership was one registered in England or overseas.

Whether or not Brussels II*bis* applies to decrees dissolving or annulling a civil **20.229**
partnership, English law has taken it as the template for the rules for recognition
of decrees from Member States.[569] Much more surprising, perhaps is the fact that
recognition of decrees from non-Member States copies the law on dissolution and
annulment of marriages, including the making of separate provision for decrees
obtained by and not by proceedings.

(d) Financial Provision and Maintenance

(i) Orders from English courts

The rules are exceptionally complex. Until overtaken by European legislation, **20.230**
several bases of jurisdiction need to be distinguished. (1) English courts may order
financial provision on or before granting a decree of divorce, nullity or judicial
separation.[570] (2) Subject to the jurisdictional rules of the Brussels I Regulation
they may also make an order for financial provision after a foreign decree recognized in England if either party was domiciled in England when the divorce was
obtained or when applying for leave to proceed, or if either party was habitually
resident in England for the year preceding either of those dates, or if either has a
beneficial interest in a dwelling house (which was once a matrimonial home) at
the date of the application for leave to proceed.[571] (3) A court may order for financial provision on the ground of failure to provide reasonable maintenance if either
party is domiciled in England on the date of the application, or has been habitually resident for the year preceding that date, or if the respondent is present in
England on that date.[572] (4) A magistrates' court may make a maintenance order
if the respondent is resident in England,[573] or in a foreign country to which
the Maintenance Orders (Facilities for Enforcement) Act 1920 extends,[574] or is
resident in a country to which Part I of the Maintenance Orders (Reciprocal
Enforcement) Act 1972 extends,[575] or in accordance with Part II of the same
Act.[576] (5) English courts may vary an order if each of the parties is domiciled or
resident in England.[577] (6) English courts may make the orders in points (3), (4),
and (5) against anyone over whom personal jurisdiction is conferred by the rules

---

[569] Civil Partnership (Jurisdiction and Recognition of Judgments) Regulations 2005,
SI 2005/3334.
[570] Matrimonial Causes Act 1973, ss 22, 23 (as amended).
[571] Matrimonial and Family Proceedings Act 1984, ss 12, 15, 27.
[572] Matrimonial Causes Act 1973, s 27 (as amended).
[573] *Forsyth v Forsyth* [1948] P 125, CA.
[574] Domestic Proceedings and Magistrates' Courts Act 1978, s 30(3)(a).
[575] Maintenance Orders (Reciprocal Enforcement) Act 1972, s 3 (as amended).
[576] ibid ss 27A–28B.
[577] Matrimonial Causes Act 1973, s 35 (as amended).

of the Brussels I Regulation, or Brussels or Lugano Conventions. English law applies to substantive claims for financial provision.[578]

(ii) Orders from foreign courts

20.231 A foreign divorce, even if recognized in England, does not automatically terminate an English maintenance order.[579] A foreign maintenance order which is final and conclusive may be recognized and enforced in England at common law and under statute,[580] for it is a civil judgment *in personam*. The provisions for recognition are largely reciprocal with the grounds of jurisdiction exercised by English courts; those from EU Member States may be enforced under the Brussels I Regulation; the registration is made in the magistrates' court for the place where the respondent is domiciled for the purposes of this instrument.

(3) Children

(a) Guardianship and custody

20.232 The jurisdictional rules applicable in an English court are, in their detail, so complex that it is impossible to meet the twin aims of being concise and being accurate. But in outline, the English courts had (and to some extent still have) an inherent jurisdiction to make any order in respect of a child who is a British national, or was ordinarily resident or present in England. In relation to such children, that inherent jurisdiction was modified by statute, most recently in the Children Act 1989, to define jurisdiction to make guardianship, contact, residence and other orders. But two[581] EU Regulations override the jurisdictional scheme of the common law. Originally, this allowed a court with jurisdiction over a matrimonial cause to exercise 'ancillary' jurisdiction over a matter of parental responsibility. Now Brussels II*bis* deals with jurisdiction in matters of parental responsibility. General jurisdiction is given to the courts of the Member State of the child's habitual residence;[582] and where the child moves lawfully or is taken unlawfully to another Member State, and to varying extents, that general jurisdiction remains.[583] Jurisdiction also exists where a court is exercising matrimonial jurisdiction under Article 3 of Brussels II*bis* Regulation and an issue of parental responsibility is connected to the matrimonial proceedings.[584] There are two

---

[578] *Sealey v Callan* [1953] P 135, CA.

[579] *Macaulay v Macaulay* [1991] 1 WLR 179.

[580] Maintenance Orders Act 1950, Part II, Maintenance Orders (Facilities for Enforcement) Act 1920, Maintenance Orders (Reciprocal Enforcement) Act 1972, Civil Jurisdiction and Judgments Act 1982.

[581] Regulation 1347/2000/EC ('Brussels II'); Regulation 2201/2003/EC ('Brussels II*bis*').

[582] Article 8.

[583] Article 9 (lawful movement); Article 10 (abduction).

[584] Article 12.

default jurisdictional rules: if the habitual residence of the child cannot be established, presence will give jurisdiction;[585] and if no Member State has jurisdiction
under the Regulation, a court shall apply its own law on jurisdiction.[586]

A guardianship order made by a court of a country of which the child was a **20.233**
national or in which it was present will usually be recognized in England;[587] but
the power of the guardian will extend no further than the powers of a foreign
parent. A foreign custody order does not prevent an English court making such
order as it thinks fit in relation to the welfare of the child.[588] But where the
order has been made by a court of a Member State, its recognition is governed by
Chapter III of Brussels II*bis*. The basis of recognition, and the grounds admitted
for non-recognition, are very closely derived from the Brussels I Regulation.

(b) Abduction and removal[589]

The power to order the return of a child who has been abducted is a particular **20.234**
example of orders generally made in the interests of the welfare of the child.[590] But
the law is now largely contained in two international conventions: the Luxembourg
Convention on Recognition and Enforcement of Decisions Concerning Custody
of Children;[591] and the Hague Convention on the Civil Aspects of Child
Abduction[592] according to which the starting point is that a child, wrongfully
removed,[593] should be restored to custody in the country of its habitual residence,
whether or not a prior court order has been made. These Conventions prescribe
defences to the claim for restoration, such as acquiescence in the removal, but
English courts incline to read them restrictively. In relation to non-Convention
countries the courts will accord predominant weight to their assessment of the
welfare of the child, and do not immediately follow the principles of the
Convention.[594] The provisions of Brussels II*bis* add little to the rules established
by these Conventions.[595] The detail of the law is most appropriately examined in
Chapter 2 (Family Law).

---

585 Article 13.
586 Article 14.
587 *Re P (GE)(An Infant)* [1965] Ch 568, CA.
588 *McKee v McKee* [1951] AC 352, PC.
589 *Dicey*, ch 19.
590 *J v C* [1970] AC 688, PC; *Re H (Child Abduction: Rights of Custody)* [2000] 2 AC 291.
591 Child Abduction and Custody Act 1985, Sch 2.
592 ibid Sch 1.
593 *Re D (A Child) (Abduction: Rights of Custody)* [2006] UKHL 51; [2007] 1 AC 619.
594 *Re J (A Child) (Custody Rights: Jurisdiction)* [2005] UKHL 40; [2006] 1 AC 80.
595 Article 11.

(c) Adoption and legitimacy

20.235　The court has jurisdiction to make an adoption order if at least one of the applicants is domiciled, or has been for the past year habitually resident in, a part of the United Kingdom, and the child is unmarried and under the age of 19.[596] Foreign adoptions are dealt with in s 87 of the Adoption and Children Act 2002; it is examined in more detail in Chapter 2.

20.236　Legitimacy, now largely insignificant in English law, is not examined here.

I. Corporations and Bankruptcy

(1) Corporations

(a) Corporations and corporate status

(i) Creation and competence

20.237　A corporation is an artificial creation. The question whether, and with what powers, it was created is governed by the law under which it was created, the *lex incorporationis*. Likewise, the question who is empowered to act on its behalf is for the *lex incorporationis* (though the consequences in law of an act which an officer or organ was not entitled to do may also be referred to another law),[597] as is the liability of an individual for the acts of the corporation; and in principle, all issues having to do with the internal government and management of a corporation are referred to that law.[598]

(ii) Recognition of foreign corporations

20.238　English law recognizes the legal personality of corporations, and the dissolution of corporations, under the *lex incorporationis*. It extends this to entities created under the ordinances of a semi-state, like Taiwan, and a non-state, such as the *soi-disant* 'Turkish Republic of Northern Cyprus'.[599] Moreover, although English law does not recognize the legal personality of an international organization in the absence of domestic legislation to confer such status, where a foreign state has enacted such a law its result will be recognized in England.[600]

596　Adoption and Children Act 2002, ss 47–51.
597　*Janred Properties Ltd v ENIT* [1989] 2 All ER 444, CA.
598　*Risdon Iron and Locomotive Works v Furness* [1906] 1 KB 49, CA; *Bonanza Creek Gold Mining Co v R* [1916] 1 AC 566, PC; *Lazard Bros v Midland Bank* [1933] AC 289; *National Bank of Greece and Athens SA v Metliss* [1958] AC 509; *Carl Zeiss Stiftung v Rayner & Keeler Ltd (No 2)* [1967] 1 AC 853; *JH Rayner (Mincing Lane) Ltd v Department of Trade and Industry* [1990] 2 AC 418.
599　Foreign Corporations Act 1991, s 1.
600　*Arab Monetary Fund v Hashim (No 3)* [1991] 2 AC 114.

(iii) Dissolution and amalgamation

What a law creates it can also destroy, so the question whether a corporation has **20.239** been dissolved is a matter for its *lex incorporationis*.[601] A combination of the rules for creation and dissolution means that the amalgamation of corporations, the recognition of the new corporation, and whether it succeeds to the rights and liabilities of the dissolved corporation, are in principle for the *lex incorporationis*,[602] though the question whether this discharges the liabilities of the old corporation is a distinct question, governed by the law applicable to those obligations.[603] But the court may conclude that the process is not a true succession or amalgamation notwithstanding the language used by the foreign legislator.[604]

(iv) Domicile of corporations

A corporation is domiciled at the place of its incorporation,[605] though for certain **20.240** purposes, mainly jurisdictional, the law may consider it to have a seat at the place where its central management and control are exercised.[606]

(v) Contracts made by corporations

A corporation which had capacity to enter into the contract causes no particular **20.241** problem; where it did not, the contract is ultra vires. Even so, the corporation may in a proper case be estopped by its own conduct from relying on its own incapacity.[607] Where the corporation had capacity but it is alleged that the person purporting to act on its behalf lacked personal authority, the effect of the contract so made is a matter for the law applicable to that contract.[608] If a corporation has been dissolved and amalgamated with another the question whether dissolution terminates the contract as a source of obligation is a matter for the law of the contract. So if the amalgamation provides for the vesting of all liabilities in the new corporation it cannot discharge those liabilities, then or later, unless it is also the law applicable to them.[609]

---

[601] *Lazard Bros v Midland Bank* [1933] AC 289; *Russian and English Bank v Baring Bros* [1932] 1 Ch 435 (if there is a branch in England it cannot sue after the corporation has been dissolved, and should be wound up).

[602] *National Bank of Greece and Athens SA v Metliss* [1958] AC 509; if the two corporations are incorporated in different countries the *lex incorporationis* of each must rationally recognize the amalgamation. See also *Adams v National Bank of Greece and Athens SA* [1961] AC 255 for cases where there may not be a full succession to the rights and liabilities of the former companies.

[603] *Adams v National Bank of Greece and Athens SA* [1961] AC 225.

[604] *The Kommunar (No 2)* [1997] 1 Lloyd's Rep 8.

[605] *Gasque v Inland Revenue Commissioners* [1940] KB 80.

[606] See para 20.38.

[607] *Janred Properties Ltd v ENIT* [1989] 2 All ER 444, CA.

[608] *Chatenay v Brazilian Submarine Telegraph Co* [1891] 1 QB 279; *Maspons v Mildred* (1882) 9 QBD 530, CA; *Ruby SS Corporation v Commercial Union Assurance Co Ltd* (1933) 150 LT 38, CA.

[609] *Adams v National Bank of Greece and Athens SA* [1961] AC 255.

(b) Jurisdiction over corporations

20.242 A corporation is amenable to the jurisdiction of an English court when process can be served on it in accordance with law; but service is more complex than with individual defendants. Service on a company is principally governed by legislation,[610] which distinguishes between companies incorporated in the United Kingdom, and overseas companies. In addition to statutory service under the Companies Acts a company may be served in accordance with CPR Part 6.[611]

(i) United Kingdom companies

20.243 English companies may be served at the registered office[612] (if in liquidation, upon the liquidator and not without the leave of the court[613]); a company registered in Scotland with a place of business in England may be served at its principal place of business in England.[614]

(ii) Overseas companies[615]

20.244 An 'overseas company' is one incorporated outside the United Kingdom.[616] It is[617] required to register certain particulars with the Registrar of Companies, which include provisions for the service of process,[618] and the individuals authorized to accept service of process.[619] But if these particulars are not supplied, or those nominated refuse to accept service, service may be made at any place of business established by the company in the United Kingdom.[620] In this context a place of business connotes somewhere fixed and definite and from which the business of the company (usually the making of contracts) is carried on: if there is such a place of business, jurisdictional competence is not limited to the activities of the place of business.[621]

---

610 Companies Act 2006.

611 CPR 6.2(2); *Saab v Saudi American Bank* [1999] 4 All ER 321, CA; *Sea Assets Ltd v PT Garuda International* [2000] 4 All ER 371.

612 Companies Act 2006, s 1139. In addition, personal service may be made on a director or secretary (s 1140), or by leaving process with a person holding a senior position: CPR 6.4(4).

613 Insolvency Act 1986, s 130. If in administration, not without the consent of the administrators or the leave of the court: ibid s 11(3)(d).

614 Companies Act 2006, s 1139(4).

615 Service under CPR Part 6 is permitted on overseas companies as an alternative to statutory service: CPR 6.2(2).

616 Companies Act 2006, s 1044.

617 ibid s 1046(2). For companies incorporated in Gibraltar the requirement is permissive, not mandatory.

618 ibid s 1046.

619 ibid s 1056.

620 ibid s 1139(2)(b).

621 *Okura & Co Ltd v Forsbacka Jernverks AB* [1914] 1 KB 715; cf *Adams v Cape Industries plc* [1990] Ch 433, CA.

(iii) Companies with seat in Member States

Where the company is domiciled in an EU Member State,[622] Article 22.2 gives **20.245** exclusive jurisdiction to the courts of the seat of the corporation in proceedings having as their object the validity of the constitution, the nullity or dissolution of companies or decisions of their organs.[623]

(iv) Other corporations

Corporations falling outside the Companies Acts may be served by leaving it with **20.246** a person holding a senior position within the corporation.[624]

(c) Winding-up[625]

According to the Brussels I Regulation, the English court may not wind up a **20.247** solvent company if its seat is only in another EU Member State.[626] Subject to that reservation, the traditional approach of English law is that the court may wind up a company registered in England,[627] and may wind up an unregistered company having a sufficient connection with England if it is insolvent and it is not otherwise inappropriate.[628] 'Sufficient connection' exists if persons in England could benefit from a winding-up order and there is enough connection with England to justify making the order.[629] Indeed, an insolvent company which has been dissolved under the *lex incorporationis* may be revived for the purpose of its being wound up.[630] On making the order, the assets of the company are subjected to a trust for the benefit of those interested in the winding-up. The liquidator must get in all the assets to which the company appears to be entitled, and is obliged to use them to discharge English and foreign liabilities. If there is also a foreign liquidation he is obliged to seek to secure equal treatment for all claimants, not just for English creditors.[631] Many of the provisions of the Insolvency Act 1986 dealing with orders which may be made in the course of liquidation are silent as to their international scope, but they will probably be interpreted as requiring a sufficient connection with England.[632]

---

[622] Or a contracting state to the Brussels or Lugano Conventions.
[623] See para 20.42.
[624] CPR 6.4(4); for the definition of 'senior position', see CPR PD 6, para 6.2(2).
[625] See generally, I Fletcher, *Insolvency in Private International Law* (2nd edn, 2005).
[626] Article 22.2. Article 16.2 of the Brussels and Lugano Conventions are to the same effect.
[627] Insolvency Act 1986, s 117.
[628] ibid ss 220, 221; *Re A Company (No 00359 of 1987)* [1988] Ch 210; *Re Paramount Airways Ltd* [1993] Ch 223, CA.
[629] *Re A Company (No 00359 of 1987)* [1988] Ch 210; *Re A Company (No 003102 of 1991), ex p Nyckeln Finance Co Ltd* [1991] BCLC 539.
[630] Insolvency Act 1986, s 225.
[631] *Re Bank of Credit and Commerce International SA* [1992] BCLC 570.
[632] *Re Paramount Airways Ltd* [1993] Ch 223, CA; cf *Re Seagull Manufacturing Co Ltd (No 2)* [1994] Ch 91 (notice under Company Directors Disqualification Act 1986).

20.248 However, if the centre of a debtor's main interests is in an EU Member State,[633] jurisdiction to open collective insolvency proceedings, whether in relation to an individual or a corporate entity, is governed by the EU Insolvency Regulation.[634] Main proceedings may be opened in that Member State only, but secondary or territorial proceedings may be opened in other Member State if the debtor has an establishment there.[635]

20.249 No matter the basis on which jurisdiction is taken, choice of law is the *lex fori* except where the court is given statutory power to apply the insolvency law of another country.[636]

20.250 At common law, a liquidator appointed under the *lex incorporationis* will be recognized,[637] but there appears to be no authority on the recognition of a liquidator appointed under the law of a third country. Under the Insolvency Regulation,[638] an order from a court in a Member State opening insolvency proceedings must be given the same effect as it has under the law of the country in which it was made. The status of a liquidator appointed in those proceedings will also be recognized.

20.251 The courts of the United Kingdom have a statutory obligation to assist each other in a winding-up;[639] in relation to countries outside the United Kingdom the Secretary of State may designate states whose courts (but not liquidators acting on their own authority)[640] may request co-operation from an English court;[641] the court will assist unless there is some good reason for not doing so.[642] In recent years, however, the strong public interest in increasing the coordination of judicial activity in corporate insolvency has been acknowledged. Some courts have accepted that there is a broader power to respond to requests for assistance from courts in other jurisdictions which are supervising various forms of corporate reconstruction.[643] The legal basis for this is not altogether clear but it is plain that

---

633 Excluding Denmark. The relevant time is the lodging of the request: Case C-1/04 *Staubitz-Schreiber* [2006] ECR I-701.

634 Reg 1346/2000/EC, [2000] OJ L160/1.

635 Article 3. See Case C-341/04 *Eurofoods IFSC Ltd* [2006] Ch 508, ECJ.

636 Insolvency Act 1986, s 426(10).

637 *Bank of Ethiopia v National Bank of Egypt and Ligouri* [1937] Ch 513.

638 Under Chapter II of the Regulation.

639 Insolvency Act 1986, s 426(4).

640 *Re Bank of Credit and Commerce International SA (No 9)* [1994] 3 All ER 764.

641 Insolvency Act 1986, s 426(4),(11); Co-operation of Insolvency Courts (Designation of Relevant Countries and Territories) Order 1986, SI 1986/2123. And see *Re HIH Casualty & General Ltd* [2006] EWCA Civ 732; [2007] BusLR 250.

642 *Hughes v Hannover Ruckversicherungs AG* [1997] 1 BCLC 497, CA.

643 *Cambridge Gas Transport Corp v Official Committee of Unsecured Creditors of Navigator Holdings plc* [2006] UKPC 26; [2007] 1 AC 508. It is not possible to override substantive provisions of law even when the principal administration is overseas: *Re BCCI SA* [1997] Ch 213.

the giving of assistance is not now restricted to requests made within the statutory scheme.

Further, a Model Law on Cross-Border Insolvency was adopted at the 30th session of the UNCITRAL, given force in England by regulations made under the Insolvency Act 2000.[644] It has the broad effect of allowing and requiring an English court to improve the cooperation and efficiency of cross-border insolvencies. **20.252**

(2) Bankruptcy[645]

(a) English bankruptcy

(i) Jurisdiction

As a matter of common law and statute, the English courts have jurisdiction to declare bankrupt any debtor who is domiciled or present in England on the day of presentation of the petion.[646] They also have jurisdiction if he was ordinarily resident, or had a place of residence, or carried on business (or was a member of a partnership firm which carried on business) in England at any time within the three years prior to the presentation.[647] A debtor who has subjected himself to a voluntary arrangement submits to the jurisdiction by doing so.[648] In deciding whether to exercise their discretion to make the order the courts will consider the location of assets, any foreign bankruptcy, and other issues of general convenience.[649] The bankrupt may be examined by order of the court, but the private examination of any other person is probably limited to those who are present within the jurisdiction to be served with the summons.[650] But the Insolvency Regulation applies to individual bankruptcy as it applies to corporate insolvency, and the jurisdictional limitations imposed by that instrument apply to bankruptcies.[651] **20.253**

(ii) Choice of law

An English court applies English law to the bankruptcy.[652] The making of the order operates as a statutory assignment of all the debtor's property, wherever situated, to his trustee;[653] the bankrupt may be ordered to assist the trustee in **20.254**

---

[644] Cross Border Insolvency Regulations 2006, SI 2006/1030.
[645] See I Fletcher, *Insolvency in Private International Law* (2nd edn, 2005).
[646] Insolvency Act 1986, s 265.
[647] ibid.
[648] ibid s 264.
[649] *Re Behrends* (1865) 12 LT 149; *Re Robinson, ex p Robinson* (1883) 22 Ch D 816, CA.
[650] Cf *Re Seagull Manufacturing Co Ltd* [1993] Ch 345, CA.
[651] Para 20.248.
[652] *Re Kloebe* (1884) 28 Ch D 175; *Re Doetsch* [1896] 2 Ch 836.
[653] Insolvency Act 1986, ss 283, 306, 436.

recovering property outside the control of the court. A creditor subject to the personal jurisdiction of the court may be restrained from taking proceedings overseas, in order to safeguard the principle of equal division.[654] Foreign debts must be proved under the law under which they arise, but the court will use its own rules to secure, as best it may, equality between creditors of the same class.[655] The power of the court to set aside an antecedent transaction is not subject to express limitation, but the defendant against whom reversal of the transaction is sought must be (or by service out with leave of the court, be made) subject to the jurisdiction of the court, and the test is whether it is just and convenient in all the circumstances of the case to make the order.[656]

(iii) Discharge

20.255 An English discharge operates in relation to all the debts provable in the bankruptcy, irrespective of the law which governed the debt;[657] and a discharge under the law which governed the debt will be effective in England.[658]

(b) Foreign bankruptcy

20.256 As a matter of common law, a foreign bankruptcy will be recognized if the debtor was domiciled[659] in or submitted[660] to, the jurisdiction of the court; and the bankruptcy will vest English moveables (but not land) in the assignee if this is the effect it has under the foreign law.[661] The result may be that the debtor no longer has property in England, and this will tell strongly against making an English order. A discharge from a foreign bankruptcy is effective in England only if it is effective under the law which governed the debt.[662] A court may not question the bankruptcy jurisdiction of a Scottish or Northern Irish court; and the effect of such an order extends to all property in England, not excluding land.[663] But the duty to recognize orders made under the Insolvency Regulation applies to bankruptcies as it applies to corporate insolvencies.

---

654 *Barclays Bank plc v Homan* [1993] BCLC 680, CA.
655 *Re Scheibler* (1874) 9 Ch App 722.
656 *Re Paramount Airways Ltd* [1993] Ch 223, CA.
657 Insolvency Act 1986, s 281.
658 *Gibbs and Sons v Soc Industrielle et Commerciale des Métaux* (1890) 25 QBD 399, CA.
659 *Re Hayward* [1897] 1 Ch 905.
660 *Re Anderson* [1911] 1 KB 896.
661 *Re Craig* (1916) 86 LJCh 62.
662 *Gibbs and Sons v Soc Industrielle et Commerciale des Métaux* (1890) 25 QBD 399, CA.
663 Insolvency Act 1986, s 426.

21

JUDICIAL REMEDIES

A. A General Survey

(1) Introduction

The concept of a remedy has rarely been subjected to rigorous analysis.[1] Views **21.01** may differ as to precisely what one is talking about. In this chapter, a remedy is used to denote the relief (whether an order or a pronouncement) that a person can seek from a court. The focus is therefore entirely on judicial remedies and not on what are sometimes termed 'self-help' remedies (which are available without coming to court). There is a wide range of judicial remedies. It is helpful to distinguish between those available pre-trial, those available at trial, and those available post-trial. Although we shall briefly mention the first and the last,[2] our concern in this chapter will essentially be with judicial remedies available at trial.

---

[1] Recent notable exceptions include P Birks, 'Rights, Wrongs, and Remedies' (2000) 20 OJLS 1; and R Zakrzewski, *Remedies Reclassified* (2005).

[2] See paras 12.03–12.05.

21.02 Within the law of obligations (and leaving aside specialist areas such as family law)[3] a judicial remedy granted at trial can be said to be a response to a cause of action. For example, contractual remedies respond to a breach of contract; tort remedies respond to a tort; restitutionary remedies respond to an unjust enrichment. It follows that judicial remedies at trial cannot be fully understood in isolation from—and an exposition must to some extent be structured by—the relevant cause of action. An alternative way of expressing this is to say that there is a division—albeit one where the two sides of the division are closely connected—between issues going to liability (for example, has the defendant committed a breach of contract or tort against the claimant or has the defendant been unjustly enriched at the claimant's expense?) and issues going to remedies (for example, what will the courts award or grant to redress a breach of contract or tort or to reverse an unjust enrichment?).

(2) Pre-trial and Post-trial Judicial Remedies

21.03 These are further examined in Chapter 22. Only the barest of outlines is therefore called for here.

21.04 Pre-trial judicial remedies can be helpfully categorized into remedies designed to assist a litigant's preparation for trial; and remedies designed to protect a claimant's rights against pre-trial delay. The former includes, for example, orders for disclosure,[4] orders for further information,[5] and search orders (*Anton Piller* orders).[6] The latter includes interim injunctions,[7] freezing injunctions (*Mareva* injunctions),[8] and interim payments.[9] In many cases, the time factor and circumstances are such that by giving a claimant an interim injunction, which protects its rights against delay pre-trial, or by refusing that remedy, the need for a trial is avoided. That is, the decision regarding the pre-trial remedy in practice resolves the dispute. This is one of the reasons why the House of Lords' approach to interim injunctions in the leading case of *American Cyanamid Co v Ethicon Ltd*[10] has been criticized. In that case, their Lordships laid down that the courts should

---

3 For judicial remedies in respect of family law (eg divorce decrees, decrees of nullity of marriage, separation orders and adoption orders) see Chapter 2. Other examples of judicial remedies in specialist areas—and not covered in this chapter—include the appointment of an administrative receiver or a liquidator and the winding-up of a company (see Chapter 19); and the dissolution of a partnership.

4 See paras 22.53–22.60.
5 CPR Part 18.
6 See paras 22.28–22.29.
7 See paras 22.35–22.37.
8 See paras 22.20–22.27.
9 See para 22.34.
10 [1975] AC 396. See paras 22.36–22.37.

decide whether or not an interim injunction should be granted on the basis of what is more convenient pending trial. The merits of the claim should not be looked at except as a last resort where it is otherwise unclear where the balance of convenience lies. The objection to this is that, where the decision on the inter-locutory application will effectively decide the dispute, the courts cannot fairly decide the interlocutory application without taking a view on the merits of the claim.[11]

Post-trial judicial remedies are concerned with the enforcement or execution of the remedies ordered at trial. For some non-monetary remedies, such as injunctions and specific performance, enforcement is by proceedings for contempt of court, with the ultimate sanction being imprisonment;[12] whereas for monetary remedies, such as damages and the award of an agreed sum, there are several post-trial judicial remedies concerned to enforce payment, examples being a warrant of execution,[13] an attachment of earnings third party debt,[14] a third party debt order,[15] a charging order,[16] or a post-trial freezing injunction (*Mareva* injunction).[17] **21.05**

(3) Judicial Remedies Available at Trial

(a) General

In examining judicial remedies available at trial, a number of distinctions can be drawn. One can contrast orders (that is, coercive remedies) such as damages, specific performance, injunctions, the award of money had and received, the award of an agreed sum, or delivery up of goods; with pronouncements (that is, non-coercive remedies) such as declarations, rescission, rectification, constructive and resulting trusts, and liens.[18] One can further contrast monetary remedies (that is, awards of money) such as an account of profits, damages, and the award of an agreed sum; with non-monetary remedies (for example, injunctions). Another distinction is between specific remedies, which order the defendant to comply with his primary duty or to 'undo' breach of a primary duty (for example, injunctions, specific performance, the award of an agreed sum) and substitutionary **21.06**

---

[11] This objection has been recognized and the *American Cyanamid* test rejected or modified or reinterpreted in, eg, *Cayne v Global Natural Resources plc* [1984] 1 All ER 225, CA; *Cambridge Nutrition Ltd v BBC* [1990] 3 All ER 523, CA; *Series 5 Software v Clarke* [1996] 1 All ER 853.

[12] See paras 22.130–22.131.

[13] See paras 22.126–22.127.

[14] CCR Ord 27 in Sch 2, CPR.

[15] See para 22.128.

[16] See para 22.129.

[17] See paras 22.20–22.27.

[18] With the exception of declarations, pronouncements by a court alter the legal rights of the parties: FH Lawson, *Remedies of English Law* (2nd edn, 1980) ch 17 refers to such pronouncements as 'constitutive remedies'.

remedies, which order the defendant to pay a 'substitute sum' for having failed to comply with a primary duty (for example, damages). Some remedies are personal remedies, which are not tied to particular property in the defendant's possession and hence do not give priority to the claimant on the defendant's insolvency (for example, damages, the award of an agreed sum, the award of money had and received, and an account of profits); while others are proprietary remedies, which are concerned to return property owned by the claimant or to confer proprietary rights on the claimant over property in the defendant's possession, and which do give priority to the claimant on the defendant's insolvency (for example, delivery up of goods, recovery of land, some constructive and resulting trusts and, in some situations, rescission). Then there is the historical division, reflecting the organization of the courts before the Judicature Acts 1873–1875, between common law remedies (for example, damages and the award of an agreed sum) and equitable remedies (for example, an account of profits, specific performance and injunctions). Common law remedies are those awarded pre-1875 by the common law courts. Equitable remedies are those awarded pre-1875 by the Court of Chancery. Table 21.1 shows the main judicial remedies available at trial categorized according to the major remedial distinctions referred to in this paragraph.

21.07 Some of these major distinctions can be further subdivided. For example, monetary remedies are sometimes subdivided—and for some rules of law must be subdivided[19]—into (unliquidated) damages, on the one hand, and debts or liquidated claims on the other. The latter include, for example, the award of an agreed sum, the award of money had and received, and a *quantum meruit*.[20]

21.08 Some of the above distinctions, while commonly made, do not appear particularly significant or illuminating. Moreover, in contrast to remedies for wrongs, there is relatively little to say (see paras 21.09–21.13) in relation to remedies for the cause of action of unjust enrichment that has not already been said in discussing that cause of action.[21] The treatment of judicial remedies in this chapter therefore concentrates on remedies for civil wrongs, whether the wrong be a breach of contract, a tort or an equitable wrong.[22] A primary aim is to expose and analyse the purposes pursued by remedies for wrongs. *Broadly speaking, the purposes are as follows: (1) compensation; (2) restitution and punishment; (3) compelling performance or preventing (or compelling the undoing of) a wrong; and (4) declaring rights. These purposes form the structure for the bulk*

---

19 See eg Limitation Act 1980, s 29(5) (acknowledgement or part payment).
20 *Amantilla Ltd v Telefusion plc* (1987) 9 Con LR 139.
21 See Chapter 18.
22 Equitable wrongs can be regarded as comprising breach of fiduciary duty (including breach of trust), breach of confidence, assisting or procuring a breach of fiduciary duty, and breach of a duty arising under the doctrine of proprietary estoppel.

Table 21.1 Main judicial remedies available at trial categorized by principal remedial distinctions

Remedy	Coercive/non-coercive	Monetary/non-monetary	Specific/substitutionary	Personal/proprietary	Common law/equitable
Damages	Coercive	Monetary	Substitutionary	Personal	Normally common law but can be equitable
Equitable compensation	Coercive	Monetary	Substitutionary	Personal	Equitable
Award of an agreed sum	Coercive	Monetary	Specific	Personal	Common law
Specific performance	Coercive	Non-monetary	Specific	Normally personal	Equitable
Injunction	Coercive	Non-monetary	Specific	Normally personal	Equitable
Delivery up of goods	Coercive	Non-monetary	Specific	Proprietary	Statutory (equitable roots)
Delivery up for destruction	Coercive	Non-monetary	Specific	Proprietary	Equitable
Recovery of land	Coercive	Non-monetary	Specific	Proprietary	Common law
Award of money had and received	Coercive	Monetary	Normally specific	Personal	Common law
Award of money paid to claimant's use	Coercive	Monetary	Specific	Personal	Common law
Quantum meruit/quantum valebat	Coercive	Monetary	Specific	Personal	Common law
Account of money received/account of profits	Coercive	Monetary	Normally substitutionary	Personal	Equitable
Declaration	Non-coercive	Non-monetary	–	–	Statutory (equitable roots)
Rescission	Non-coercive	Non-monetary	–	Both	Normally equitable but can be common law
Rectification	Non-coercive	Non-monetary	–	Both	Equitable
Constructive/resulting trusts	Non-coercive	Non-monetary	–	Proprietary	Equitable
Liens	Non-coercive	Non-monetary	–	Proprietary	Equitable

Table 21.2 Purposes of main judicial remedies available at trial for wrongs

Purpose	Remedy
Compensation	Compensatory damages. Equitable compensation.
Restitution	Restitutionary damages. Account of profits. Award of money had and received. Constructive trust.
Punishment	Punitive damages.
Compelling performance (of positive obligations)	Specific performance. Award of an agreed sum. Mandatory enforcing injunction.
Preventing a wrong	Prohibitory injunction. Delivery up for destruction or destruction on oath.
Compelling the undoing of a wrong	Mandatory restorative injunction. Delivery up of goods.
Declaring rights	Declaration. Nominal damages.

of this chapter. Table 21.2 shows the purposes of the main judicial remedies available at trial for wrongs.

(b) Restitutionary remedies to reverse unjust enrichment

21.09   As will have been apparent from Chapter 18, there is a range of judicial remedies which seek to reverse an unjust enrichment. They include both common law remedies (for example, the award of money had and received, the award of money paid to the claimant's use, and a *quantum meruit*) and equitable remedies (for example, an account of money received or a resulting trust); coercive remedies (for example, an award of money had and received) and non-coercive remedies (for example, rescission, a resulting trust, and a lien); monetary remedies (for example, an award of money had and received) and non-monetary remedies (for example, rescission of an executed contract which revests goods or land in the claimant); personal remedies (for example, the award of money had and received, a *quantum meruit* and an account of money received) and proprietary remedies (for example, a resulting trust and a lien).

21.10   Some of the restitutionary remedies overlap and could be rationalized and reduced. In particular, the award of money had and received and its equitable equivalent—an account of money received—perform precisely the same role and it appears that history alone explains their dual existence. Similarly, within the realm of personal common law remedies, it is not clear that one needs the separate remedies of an award of money had and received, the award of money paid to the claimant's use, a *quantum meruit*, and a *quantum valebat*. Admittedly each of these remedies has come to be associated with particular factual situations. For example, the award of money had and received is the standard remedy for restitution of money paid by the claimant to the defendant under mistake or duress or for a consideration that has failed;[23] the award of money paid to the claimant's use is the conventional remedy for compulsory discharge of another's debt;[24] and a *quantum meruit* and a *quantum valebat* effect restitution of the value of services and goods respectively.[25] The law would be simplified and, arguably, improved if one swept away these different remedies and talked instead of a single personal remedy of 'restitution of value received'.

The remedy of rescission of a contract (or deed of gift) is one of the most difficult **21.11** remedies to analyse. Rescission (or as one can otherwise term it 'setting aside' a contract) is a remedy available where a party has entered into a voidable contract under, for example, duress[26] or undue influence;[27] or as a result of a misrepresentation or non-disclosure.[28] It wipes away a contract ab initio. It is both a self-help and a judicial remedy. It is normally subject to four bars: lapse of time, affirmation, third party rights and *restitutio in integrum* being impossible.[29] While one can regard it as always being a contractual remedy in the sense that it wipes away and allows escapes from a contract, it is also a restitutionary remedy reversing unjust enrichment where a contract has been wholly or partly executed and where the effect of the rescission is therefore to restore benefits to the contracting parties. The rescission may effect personal restitution (for example, by entitling the payor to the repayment of a purchase price);[30] but it is also commonly a proprietary restitutionary remedy in that it revests the proprietary rights to goods or land transferred under the contract.[31] Rescission is, therefore, difficult to analyse

---

[23] See paras 18.08, 18.61–18.75 and 18.85ff.

[24] See paras 18.08 and 18.141ff.

[25] See paras 18.08.

[26] See paras 18.203, 18.72–18.75 and 18.207.

[27] See paras 8.204–8.206 and 18.76–18.79.

[28] See paras 8.159–8.201.

[29] See paras 8.180–8.187. Furthermore, where rescission is thought too harsh a remedy against the *misrepresentor* (eg where the misrepresentation was wholly innocent and relatively trivial), damages can be awarded for a non-fraudulent misrepresentation in lieu of rescission under s 2(2) of the Misrepresentation Act 1967: see *William Sindell plc v Cambridgeshire CC* [1994] 1 WLR 1016, CA; *Govt of Zanzibar v British Aerospace (Lancaster House) Ltd* [2000] 1 WLR 2333 (laying down that, if rescission is barred, so are damages under s 2(2)).

[30] eg *Redgrave v Hurd* (1881) 20 Ch D 1. Rescission sometimes carries with it the award of a restitutionary indemnity indemnifying the claimant against expenses incurred that the defendant would otherwise have had to incur: see, eg, *Newbigging v Adam* (1886) 34 Ch D 582; *Whittington v Seale-Hayne* (1900) 82 LT 49. For rescission plus equitable compensation to the claimant, see *Mahoney v Purnell* [1996] 3 All ER 61, para 21.130.

[31] eg *Erlanger v New Sombrero Phosphate Co* (1878) 3 App Cas 1218, HL. This case shows that, where property is revested in the claimant, the claimant may have to give counter-restitution, through an equitable account of profits, for benefits derived from use of the property. More problematic is the extent to which, if at all, a claimant should be required to give the other party an equitable allowance for a deterioration in the property returned by the claimant: see the *Erlanger* case, (1878) 3 App Cas 1218, 1278–9.

because it may involve contract and unjust enrichment, personal and proprietary restitution, and restitution of payments and restitution for benefits in kind.

21.12   An unresolved, yet fundamental, question is the extent to which, if at all, restitutionary remedies reversing unjust enrichment are, or should be, proprietary rather than merely personal.[32] A personal restitutionary remedy reverses an unjust enrichment received by the defendant irrespective of whether he or she still retains particular property. It does not afford priority on the defendant's insolvency. In contrast, a proprietary restitutionary remedy affords priority on the defendant's insolvency and is dependent on the defendant's retention of particular property.

21.13   If one puts to one side pure proprietary remedies, which are concerned to enable an owner to recover property which he continues to own, such as the remedy of ejectment from land or delivery up of goods,[33] and concentrates instead on the creation of new proprietary rights in response to unjust enrichment, the following may be regarded as examples of restitutionary proprietary rights.[34]

(1)   Equitable proprietary rights created following equitable tracing.[35] Although it may be tempting to regard those equitable rights as responding to the defendant retaining property that previously belonged in equity to the claimant (so that these are pure proprietary remedies), they are better viewed as restitutionary proprietary rights. They involve the creation of new proprietary rights over property which does not already belong to the claimant but is rather a substitution of property previously owned in equity by the claimant. So if one is entitled to trace from one's pig to a horse to a car one cannot say, without invoking fiction or a leap in reasoning, that one has proprietary rights in the car merely because one owned the pig that is now represented by the car. The most convincing analysis is that one's ownership of the pig, which has been substituted by the car, entitles one to claim new ownership of the car because the owner of the car is unjustly enriched at one's expense. The tracing rules are being invoked to show that the subtraction of one's pig has become the defendant's enrichment in the form of the car so that the car has been gained at the claimant's expense. It should be stressed, however, that this unjust enrichment analysis of rights after tracing was rejected by the House

---

32   See paras 18.173–18.203. For the same question in respect of restitution for wrongs, see para 21.155.

33   See para 17.332, and paras 21.223–21.225.

34   See A Burrows, *The Law of Restitution* (2nd edn, 2002) 64–75; P Birks, *Unjust Enrichment* (2nd edn, 2005) ch 8.

35   eg *Re Hallett's Estate* (1880) 13 Ch D 696, CA; *Re Oatway* [1903] 2 Ch 356; *Re Diplock* [1948] Ch 465, CA; *Barlow Clowes International Ltd v Vaughan* [1992] 4 All ER 22, CA; *Bishopsgate Investment Management Ltd v Homan* [1995] Ch 211, CA; *Foskett v McKeown* [2001] 1 AC 102, HL. See paras 18.177–18.182, and 18.205.

of Lords in *Foskett v McKeown*[36] which thought that the pre-existing proprietary rights were a sufficient explanation of the proprietary rights in the traced substitute.

(2) Some examples of subrogation: that is, situations where the claimant is entitled to take over the third party's proprietary, rather than merely personal, rights against the defendant.[37]

(3) Equitable liens over land for the value of improvements mistakenly made to it.[38]

(4) Rescission of an executed contract which revests the proprietary rights to goods or land transferred under the contract.[39]

(5) Some resulting (or constructive) trusts.[40] But the role of resulting (and constructive) trusts in reversing unjust enrichment is a matter of continuing controversy. On one view, the equitable proprietary interest held to exist prior to tracing in *Chase Manhattan Bank v Israel-British Bank (London) Ltd*[41] is a valid example of proprietary restitution being granted in respect of payments made under a mistake of fact.[42] But in *Westdeutsche Landesbank Girozentrale v Islington London BC*[43] the House of Lords, in laying down that payments made under a void 'interest rate swap' transaction were not held by the payee on a resulting trust for the payor, rejected the reasoning (although, possibly, not the result) in the *Chase Manhattan* case.

B. Compensation

Compensation means the award of a sum of money which, so far as money can **21.14** be so, is equivalent to the claimant's loss. The loss may be pecuniary (that is, a loss of wealth) where the equivalence to the claimant's loss can be precise; or non-pecuniary (for example, pain and suffering and loss of amenity, loss of reputation, and mental distress generally) where the sum to be awarded as compensation cannot be precisely equivalent to the loss and where the only way to ensure consistency of awards is through conventionally accepted tariffs of value.

---

[36] [2001] 1 AC 102, HL.

[37] eg Mercantile Law Amendment Act 1856, s 5; *Nottingham Permanent Benefit Building Society v Thurstan* [1903] AC 6; *Butler v Rice* [1910] 2 Ch 277; *Lord Napier & Ettrick v Hunter* [1993] AC 713, HL; *Boscawen v Bajwa* [1996] 1 WLR 328, CA. See paras 18.216–18.220.

[38] eg *Cooper v Phibbs* (1867) LR 2 HL 149.

[39] eg *Car and Universal Finance Co Ltd v Caldwell* [1965] 1 QB 525, CA.

[40] See paras 4.309–4.316, and 18.173–18.203.

[41] [1981] Ch 105.

[42] See P Birks, *Unjust Enrichment* (2nd edn, 2005) ch 8; R Chambers, *Resulting Trusts* (1997).

[43] [1996] AC 669, HL.

21.15 Compensation is generally achieved for the common law civil wrongs comprising torts and breach of contract through the remedy of compensatory damages (that is, damages designed to compensate). For equitable wrongs[44] the equivalent remedy is equitable compensation. For all civil wrongs, there is also the notion of equitable damages, which are awarded in addition to, or in substitution for, specific performance or an injunction under section 50 of the Supreme Court Act 1981.[45] Equitable damages are normally concerned to compensate the claimant. The rules applicable to compensatory damages, equitable compensation and equitable (compensatory) damages are not in all respects identical, so that it is still necessary to distinguish them, even though they are concerned with the common function of compensation. This is an unfortunate consequence of the historical divide between common law and equity.

21.16 This section primarily examines (common law) compensatory damages, which are available for torts and breach of contract.[46] It examines more briefly equitable compensation[47] and equitable (compensatory) damages.[48]

(1) Compensatory Damages: Breach of Contract

(a) The compensatory aim

(i) Protection of the expectation interest

21.17 The general aim of damages for breach of contract is to put the claimant into as good a position as if the contract had been performed. The classic authority for this is *Robinson v Harman* where Parke B said, 'The rule of common law is that where a party sustains a loss by reason of a breach of contract he is, so far as money can do it, to be placed in the same situation, with respect to damages as if the contract had been performed.'[49] This central aim is often referred to as the protection of the claimant's expectation interest.[50]

---

[44] See n 22 above.

[45] Formerly this power was contained in the Chancery Amendment Act 1858 (Lord Cairns's Act), s 2.

[46] See paras 21.17–21.129. For (compensatory) damages under s 8 of the Human Rights Act 1998 see *R (on the application of Greenfield) v Secretary of State for the Home Department* [2005] UKHL 14; [2005] 1 WLR 673 (laying down that such damages are sui generis and should not be equated to damages for domestic torts). See also *English Public Law* paras 19.42–19.53.

[47] See paras 21.130–21.134.

[48] See paras 21.135–21.139.

[49] (1848) 1 Exch 850, 855. The date for assessing damages is normally the date of the breach of contract but this is not an inflexible rule and will be departed from if, on facts known at trial and taking into account the duty to mitigate, that would not effect true compensation: *Johnson v Agnew* [1980] AC 367, HL; *Golden Strait Corp v Nippon Yusen Kubishika Kaisha, The Golden Victory* [2007] UKHL 12; [2007] 2 WLR 691.

[50] The term was coined by L Fuller and WR Perdue, 'The Reliance Interest in Contract Damages' (1936–37) 46 Yale LJ 52. It is also sometimes referred to as the 'performance interest'.

Theoretically an alternative aim of compensation for a breach of contract would **21.18** be to put the claimant into as good a position as if no contract had been made. This would be to protect the claimant's reliance interest.[51] But while a claimant can opt to frame the claim in this way, the courts regard this as subservient to the expectation interest, so that the claimant cannot escape from a proven bad bargain by claiming the reliance interest.[52] The advantage to a claimant of framing the claim in this alternative way is, therefore, that it throws onto the defendant the burden of proving that the claim for reliance loss exceeds the claimant's expectation interest; or, put another way, the claimant has the benefit of a rebuttable presumption that it would, at the very least, have made gains to cover its proven reliance expenses (which can include pre-contractual expenses).

(ii) Difference in value or cost of cure

In compensating the claimant for a breach of contract, the courts often face a **21.19** choice between awarding the difference in value or the cost of cure. The former directly awards the claimant the financial advantage it has lost by being deprived, partially or wholly, of the benefit to which it was contractually entitled. The cost of cure, on the other hand, seeks to award the claimant the additional financial sacrifice it would have to incur to put itself into as good a position as if it had received the benefit to which it was contractually entitled. In many situations the difference in value is in practice the only possible measure because no replacement benefit is available at any cost: for example, the party in breach may alone be capable of performing the contract or the delay may have made the performance impossible. But where both are possible measures, which will be awarded?

The answer turns on a range of factors, including the reasonableness of the **21.20** claimant's conduct in response to the breach and, most importantly, whether the claimant has cured or genuinely intends to cure. To illustrate this, let us take an example of a building contract where a builder, in breach of contract, refuses to carry out work or carries it out defectively.[53] Is the owner entitled to the difference

---

[51] ibid.

[52] *C and P Haulage v Middleton* [1983] 1 WLR 1461, CA; *CCC Films (London) v Impact Quadrant Films Ltd* [1985] QB 16. See also *Anglia Television Ltd v Reed* [1972] 1 QB 60, CA; *Commonwealth of Australia v Amann Aviation Pty Ltd* (1991) 66 ALJR 123, High Court of Australia.

[53] See also, eg, contracts for the sale of goods where general measures are set out in the Sale of Goods Act 1979 and are tied to what it is reasonable for the claimant to do. For a seller's breach in failing to deliver goods, Sale of Goods Act 1979, s 51(3) lays down that the generally appropriate measure is market price at time fixed for delivery minus contract price. This refers to the market buying price (for buying substitute goods) and is a cost of cure measure. For the ignoring of the resale price in this context, see *William Bros Ltd v Agius Ltd* [1914] AC 510, HL. Where a seller is in breach in delivering defective goods, the Sale of Goods Act 1979, s 53(3), lays down that the generally appropriate measure is the market price that the goods would have had if the contracted-for quality minus the market price of the goods delivered. This refers to the market selling price and is a difference in value measure. For the ignoring of resale prices in this context, see *Slater v Hoyle*

in value of the property (that is, the value that his property would have had if the work had been properly completed minus its present value) or is he instead entitled to the cost of cure (that is, the cost of repairing any defects and having any remaining work completed)? Two cases repay examination.

21.21 In *Radford v De Froberville*,[54] the claimant had sold a plot of land to the defendant on condition that the defendant erected a wall on the plot so as to divide it from the claimant's land. The defendant had failed to build the wall. One question was whether the claimant was entitled to damages assessed according to the cost of cure (that is, the cost of building a wall on his land) which at the time of trial would have cost £3,400; or according to the difference in the land's value with and without the wall, which was almost nil. Oliver J, applying *Tito v Waddell (No 2)*,[55] held that the claimant was entitled to the cost of cure. He said, 'In the instant case, I am entirely satisfied that the plaintiff genuinely wants this work done, and that he intends to expend any damages awarded on carrying it out'.[56]

21.22 In the leading case of *Ruxley Electronics and Construction Ltd v Forsyth*,[57] the claimant contracted to have a swimming pool built with the depth at the deep end of 7ft 6ins. When built the pool was in fact only 6ft 9ins at the deep end. Nevertheless, it was still perfectly safe for swimming and diving so that the difference in resale value of the property was not affected by the admitted breach of contract. To increase the depth of the pool to the agreed depth would cost £21,460 (nearly a third of the total price of the pool). Overturning the Court of Appeal, the House of Lords refused to award the claimant the cost of cure of £21,560; that would be unreasonable, because of the contrast with the nil difference in value. Moreover, the first instance judge had found that the claimant had no intention to use the damages to rebuild the pool. But rather than awarding the claimant no damages at all for the breach the House of Lords upheld the first instance judge's award of damages of £2,500 for loss of amenity.

21.23 We can therefore see from these decisions that the courts may award damages measured by a cost of cure that is higher than the difference in value but will not do so where the claimant has not cured and does not intend to cure; and, although

---

and Smith [1920] 2 KB 11, CA, although doubt was cast on this in *Bence Graphics Int Ltd v Fasson UK Ltd* [1998] QB 87, CA. For breach by a buyer in refusing to accept goods, the Sale of Goods Act 1979, s 50(3) lays down that the general measure is the contract price minus the market price at the date of breach. This refers to the market selling price and is a difference in value measure. For the ignoring of a resale price here, see *Campbell Mostyn (Provisions) Ltd v Barnett Trading Co* [1954] 1 Lloyd's Rep 65. For an exception to s 50(3), see *Thompson Ltd v Robinson (Gunmakers) Ltd* [1955] Ch 177. See generally paras 10.59, 10.63–10.66.

54 [1977] 1 WLR 1262.
55 [1977] Ch 106.
56 ibid 1284.
57 [1996] AC 344.

this is more controversial (and seems unsatisfactory given that the claimant contracted for performance) a cost of cure measure may possibly be denied, even though the claimant has cured or intends to cure, if to do so would be unreasonable (ie economically wasteful) because of a disparity with the difference in value.

(iii) Loss of a chance

What happens when all that the claimant can establish is that he has lost the **21.24** chance to make a gain? The leading case in relation to contract damages is *Chaplin v Hicks*.[58] The claimant entered a beauty competition organized by the defendant. Fifty of the entrants were to be selected for interview and, from those, twelve were to be offered theoretical engagements. The claimant was selected as one of the fifty for interview but, through the defendant's breach of contract, she was not informed in time. It was held by the Court of Appeal that, while the claimant was not entitled to damages on the basis that she would have won an engagement, nevertheless she was entitled to damages for the lost chance of winning an engagement. That is, she was entitled to damages scaled down proportionately in accordance with what the chances of gain were thought to be.

It is important to clarify that the approach of awarding damages according to the **21.25** chances of gain is appropriate only where the uncertainty relates to hypothetical or future events, rather than a past fact.[59] In *Chaplin v Hicks*, the uncertainty was over whether those conducting the interview would have chosen the claimant for a theatrical engagement if she had been interviewed.[60] But where the uncertainty is in relation to past fact (or, it would seem, the hypothetical conduct of the claimant) the courts apply an all-or-nothing 'balance of probabilities' test. If the claimant cannot meet that standard of proof, the claim for that head of loss fails entirely; whereas if he can meet that standard of proof, he is entitled to full damages on the basis that that past fact was definitely true.

(b) Limiting principles

There are a number of principles which limit compensatory damages for breach **21.26** of contract and mean that the claimant is not put fully into as good a position as if the contract had been performed. Most of these principles, albeit sometimes

---

[58] [1911] 2 KB 786, CA. A leading case in relation to tort damages is *Davies v Taylor* [1974] AC 207, HL. See also *Allied Maples Group Ltd v Simmons & Simmons* [1995] 1 WLR 1602, CA (action in contract and tort for solicitor's negligence).

[59] See paras 21.75–21.78.

[60] It is normally assumed that the interviewing panel was a third party. However, close scrutiny of the facts reveals that the rules had been changed so that the sole decision-maker was the defendant himself. Normally a minimum obligation rather than a 'chances' approach is applied to hypothetical conduct of the defendant: see 21.60–21.63.

with differences, apply also to compensatory damages for torts (for example, the duty to mitigate).[61]

(i) Remoteness

21.27 A principal restriction is that a defendant will not be liable for loss suffered by the claimant that is too remote from the breach of contract. In policy terms, the remoteness restriction is based on the view that it is unfair to a defendant, and imposes too great a burden, to hold him responsible for losses however unusual and however far removed from the breach of contract. It has also been regarded as having an economic efficiency rationale in encouraging the disclosure of information regarding unusual potential losses, so that the defendant, with full knowledge of the risk involved, can plan and act rationally.

21.28 **The trilogy of leading cases.** The test for remoteness in contract has been laid down in three leading cases. The first is perhaps the best-known of all English contract cases, *Hadley v Baxendale*.[62] The claimant's mill was brought to a standstill by a broken crank-shaft. The claimant engaged the defendant's carrier to take it to Greenwich as a pattern for a new one, but in breach of contract the defendant delayed delivery. The claimant sought damages for loss of profit arising from the fact that the mill was stopped for longer than it would have been if there had been no delay. The court held that the loss of profit was too remote and that therefore the carriers were not liable for it.

21.29 The test for remoteness was regarded as comprising two rules by Alderson B. He said:

> Where two parties have made a contract which one of them has broken, the damages which the other party ought to receive in respect of such breach of contract, should be such as may fairly and reasonably be considered, either arising naturally, ie according to the usual course of things from such breach of contract itself, or such as may reasonably be supposed to have been in the contemplation of both parties, at the time they made the contract as the probable result of the breach of it.[63]

21.30 On the facts neither of these two rules was satisfied. The loss was not the natural consequence of the delay because it was felt that in the vast majority of cases the absence of a shaft would not cause a stoppage at a mill as usually a mill-owner would have another shaft in reserve or be able to get one. Nor was the loss in the contemplation of both parties because the special circumstance that the mill could not restart until the shaft came back was not known to the defendant.

---

[61] See paras 21.79–21.91.
[62] (1854) 9 Exch 341.
[63] ibid 354.

In the second case of the trilogy, *Victoria Laundry (Windsor) Ltd v Newman* **21.31**
Industries Ltd,[64] the claimants decided to extend their laundry business and
contracted to buy a boiler from the defendants. The defendants knew that the
claimants wanted the boiler for immediate use in their business, but in breach of
contract delivered the boiler five months late. The claimants sought damages for
the ordinary loss of profit that would have resulted from using the boiler during
those months, including damages for the exceptional loss of profits that they
would have been able to gain from contracts with the Ministry of Supply. The
Court of Appeal held that, applying *Hadley v Baxendale*, damages should be
awarded for the ordinary loss of profits but not for the exceptional loss of profits.
The exceptional profits were too remote because they did not arise naturally and
were not in the contemplation of the parties at the time of contracting because the
defendants knew nothing about the Ministry of Supply contracts. Asquith LJ
took the view that the two rules of *Hadley v Baxendale* could be reformulated as
comprising a single rule, centring on reasonable contemplation or, as he preferred,
reasonable foreseeability. That is, if in applying the second rule in *Hadley v
Baxendale*, one includes as important what the defendant should have reasonably
contemplated or foreseen if he had thought about the breach at the time of contracting, it swallows up the first rule; for something arising naturally is something that should have been reasonably contemplated by the defendant if he had
thought about the breach.

In *Koufos v Czarnikow Ltd, The Heron II*[65] a ship was chartered to carry sugar **21.32**
from Constanza to Basrah. At the time of contracting the claimant charterer
intended to sell the sugar as soon as it reached Basrah. The defendant shipowner
did not actually know this but did know that there was a market for sugar at
Basrah. In breach of contract the shipowner reached Basrah nine days late. During
those nine days the market price of sugar at Basrah fell and the claimant sought
damages for the profit lost by reason of that fall. The House of Lords held that he
should recover such damages because the loss of profit was not too remote.
Concentration in the case was focused on what degree of likelihood of the loss
occurring was required to have been reasonably contemplatable by the defendant
at the time of the contract and, in particular, was it the same degree of likelihood
of loss occurring that was required to be reasonably foreseeable under the tort
test of remoteness laid down in *The Wagon Mound*?[66] The Law Lords agreed that
a higher likelihood of the loss occurring was required in contract than in tort,
so that losses may be too remote in contract that are not too remote in tort.
Unfortunately, there was no clear consensus as to how the degree of likelihood

---

64 [1949] 2 KB 528, CA.
65 [1969] 1 AC 350, HL.
66 [1961] AC 388, PC. See paras 17.82–17.83.

required in contract should be expressed. Perhaps the clearest way of expressing the essence of the reasoning is that, while a slight possibility of the loss occurring is required in tort, a serious possibility of the loss occurring is required in contract. Taking this interpretation the full contract test applied in *Heron II* can be expressed as follows: a loss is too remote if the defendant did not contemplate, or could not reasonably have contemplated, that loss as a serious possibility, if he had thought or did think about the breach at the time the contract was made.[67]

21.33 **Complications shown in some subsequent cases.** On the face of it, the above trilogy of cases has established a straightforward remoteness test in contract. Difficulties arise, however, when one takes into account cases that have regarded it as necessary or relevant to deal in greater detail with the 'fit' between the remoteness tests in tort and contract. The most notorious is *Parsons v Uttley Ingham & Co Ltd*.[68] The question at issue was whether the supplier of a defective pig hopper was liable in contract for the loss of 254 pigs that had died from a rare intestinal decease after eating nuts that had gone mouldy in the hopper. The Court of Appeal decided that the loss of the pigs was not too remote, but the judges found this difficult to reconcile with the traditional *Hadley v Baxendale* approach. The majority, Scarman and Orr LJJ, said that the crucial question was whether the type of loss, not the extent or precise nature of the loss, was reasonably contemplatable; and that as illness of pigs and death of pigs were both the same type of loss, and the former was reasonably contemplatable, the death of the 254 pigs was not too remote. The majority judges also went out of their way to try to equate the remoteness tests in contract and tort. Scarman LJ said, '. . . The law must be such that in a factual situation where all have the same actual or imputed knowledge. . .the amount of damages recoverable does not depend on whether, as a matter of legal classification, the plaintiff's cause of action is breach of contract or tort.'[69]

21.34 In *Brown v KMR Services Ltd*,[70] one of the questions, in claims by Lloyd's names against their members' agents for breach of contract (and the tort of negligence), was whether the loss was too remote. The defendants' argument was that the magnitude of the financial disasters that had struck, and the consequent scale of the loss, was unforeseeable and uncontemplatable. The Court of Appeal held that the loss was not too remote because it was the type and not the extent of the loss that needed to be foreseen or contemplated: here the relevant type of loss was

---

[67] *Jackson v Royal Bank of Scotland plc* [2005] UKHL 3; [2005] 1 WLR 377 provides an excellent recent illustration of the application of the contract remoteness test. It was stressed that the relevant date in applying the test is when the contract was made not the date of breach.

[68] [1978] QB 791, CA.

[69] ibid 807.

[70] [1995] 4 All ER 598, CA.

underwriting loss and that was clearly foreseeable. *Parsons v Uttley Ingham* was cited with approval.

In the light of the *Brown* case, it seems clear that the majority in *Parsons v Uttley* **21.35** *Ingham* did correctly state the law and that, as in tort, the remoteness test in contract focuses on the type of loss in question and not the specific loss that occurred. The difficult issue now is not whether the emphasis on the type of loss is appropriate, but how types of loss should be divided up.

If, as the *Parsons* and the *Brown* cases indicate, the courts are taking a broad view **21.36** of types of loss, it may well be that the distinction drawn in the *Victoria Laundry* case, between recoverable loss of ordinary profits and irrecoverable loss of exceptional profits, can no longer stand (albeit that the *Victoria Laundry* case was distinguished in the *Brown* case). And in applying the contract remoteness test it appears that, in so far as the specific loss suffered was not reasonably contemplatable, the crucial question is whether there is any broader category of loss, that was reasonably contemplatable, which it is appropriate to regard as encompassing the actual loss suffered.

Two additional points on remoteness in contract. First, the test of remoteness **21.37** does not take into account the amount of the contractual consideration to be received by the defendant. In other words, the fact that the claimant's losses are out of all proportion to what the defendant was to receive under the contract is irrelevant. For example, in *Hadley v Baxendale*[71] itself, the fact that the claimant's loss of profits from delay was out of all proportion to the price to be paid to the defendant for carrying the mill-shaft was irrelevant. It is true that in a few cases, particularly concerning carriers, the courts have applied a different, more restrictive, test of whether the defendant has accepted liability for the unusual risk as a term of the contract.[72] This approach has some attraction, but it has clearly been rejected, both impliedly by the approval of *Hadley v Baxendale* in *The Heron II*,[73] and also explicitly by the Court of Appeal in *GKN Centrax Gears Ltd v Matbro Ltd*.[74] Secondly, where the claimant's actual loss of profits is too remote, and irrecoverable, it is still entitled to a lesser sum of damages measured by the loss of profit that would have been non-remote.[75]

---

[71] (1854) 9 Exch 341.
[72] See eg *British Columbia and Vancouver Island Spa, Lumber and Saw Mill Co Ltd v Nettleship* (1868) LR 3 CP 499; *Horne v Midland Railway Co* (1873) LR 8 CP 131.
[73] [1969] 1 AC 350, HL.
[74] [1976] 2 Lloyd's Rep 555, CA.
[75] *Cory v Thomas Iron Works Co* (1868) LQR 3 QB 181.

(ii) Intervening cause

21.38   The limiting principle of 'intervening cause' has been discussed far less in the context of breach of contract than in respect of torts.[76] But the idea is the same. Although the defendant's breach of contract has been a cause of the claimant's loss, the claimant should not be able to recover damages for that loss where another intervening cause has been so much more responsible for the loss that it can be regarded as having broken the chain of causation between the breach and the loss.

21.39   The intervening cause may be a natural event, the conduct of a third party, or the conduct of the claimant. There is no clear test to which one can turn to decide whether any of these intervening causes is regarded as breaking the chain of causation. But one can say that it will be rare for a natural event to break the chain of causation; that, in the context of intervention by a third party, the courts will tend to ask themselves whether or not the defendant had a duty to prevent the third party's intervention;[77] and, in the context of the claimant's own conduct, it will be important to ascertain how unreasonable the conduct has been. The last point is illustrated by *Quinn v Burch Bros (Builders) Ltd*.[78] The defendants in breach of contract failed to supply a step-ladder to the claimant. The claimant was injured when he fell from an unfooted trestle which he had made use of instead. The Court of Appeal held that the defendants were not liable for the claimant's injuries because their breach of contract did not cause them: the claimant's own unreasonable acts broke the chain of causation.

21.40   The concept of intervening cause has figured prominently in cases in which it has been held that an auditor's breach of contract in negligently auditing the claimant company's accounts was not the effective cause of the company's trading losses and insolvency. In other words, market forces and the company's own decisions have been treated as intervening causes thereby cutting back the liability of auditors for (contractual or tortious) negligence.[79]

(iii) The duty to mitigate

21.41   The idea behind the duty to mitigate is that a claimant should not sit back and do nothing to minimize loss flowing from a breach of contract but should rather use its resources to do what is reasonable to put itself into as good a position as if the contract had been performed. On the other hand, it should not unreasonably incur expense subsequent to the breach. The policy is one of encouraging the

---

[76]   For intervening cause in respect of torts, see paras 17.76–17.78.
[77]   *Stansbie v Troman* [1948] 2 KB 48, CA; cf *Weld-Blundell v Stephens* [1920] AC 956, HL.
[78]   [1966] 2 QB 370, CA. See also *Lambert v Lewis* [1982] AC 225, HL.
[79]   See eg *Galoo v Bright Grahame Murray* [1994] 1 WLR 1360.

claimant, once a breach has occurred, to be to a reasonable extent self-reliant or efficient, rather than pinning all loss on the defendant.

The main rule encompassed by the duty to mitigate is that a claimant must take **21.42** all reasonable steps to minimize its loss so that it cannot recover for any loss which it could reasonably have avoided but has failed to avoid.[80] Clearly whether a step should reasonably have been taken to minimize loss depends on the particular facts in question. Nevertheless, some indication can be given of the sort of factors that have been considered important in past contract cases in deciding this.

(1) Where the claimant has been wrongfully dismissed, he need not accept an offer of re-employment from his former employer if, for example, the new work would involve a reduction of status; and/or employment elsewhere would be more likely to be permanent; and/or the claimant has no confidence in his employers because of their past treatment of him.[81]

(2) In relation to a contract of sale, if the defendant makes an offer of alternative performance, it will generally be unreasonable for the claimant to turn it down if acceptance would reduce its loss.[82]

(3) The claimant need not take action which would put its commercial reputation or good public relations at risk.[83]

(4) The claimant need not take steps which would involve it in complicated litigation.[84]

(5) The claimant need not take steps which it cannot financially afford; that is, impecuniosity is an excuse for failure to mitigate.[85]

It is a corollary of the above main rule of the duty to mitigate that, where the **21.43** claimant does take reasonable steps in an attempt to minimize its loss, it can recover for loss incurred in so doing even though the resulting loss is in the event greater than it would have been had the mitigating steps not been taken.[86]

---

[80] The classic expression of this rule is by Viscount Haldane LC in *British Westinghouse Electric and Manufacturing Co Ltd v Underground Electric Rlys Co of London Ltd* [1912] AC 673, 689, HL.

[81] *Yetton v Eastwoods Froy Ltd* [1967] 1 WLR 104; *Brace v Calder* [1895] 2 QB 253, CA.

[82] *Payzu Ltd v Saunders* [1919] 2 KB 581, CA; *Strutt v Whitnell* [1975] 1 WLR 870, CA.

[83] *James Finlay & Co Ltd v Kwik Hoo Tong* [1929] 1 KB 400, CA; *London and South of England Building Society v Stone* [1983] 1 WLR 1242, CA.

[84] *Pilkington v Wood* [1953] Ch 770. Cf *Walker v Medlicott* [1999] 1 All ER 685, CA.

[85] *Clippens Oil Co Ltd v Edinburgh and District Water Trustees* [1907] AC 291, 303, HL (Sc); *Lagden v O'Connor* [2003] UKHL 64; [2004] 1 AC 1067.

[86] *Banco de Portugal v Waterlow & Sons Ltd* [1932] AC 452, HL; *Bacon v Cooper (Metals) Ltd* [1982] 1 All ER 397. In the first of these cases, Lord MacMillan also stressed, at 506, that the courts will not treat too favourably an argument by a defendant that the claimant has been unreasonable because it could have taken less expensive steps than it has taken to mitigate its loss: see also *London and South of England Building Society v Stone* [1983] 1 WLR 1242, CA.

(iv) Contributory negligence

21.44 If applicable as a defence, contributory negligence (which means that the claimant has been at fault for his own loss) leads to a reduction of damages. This is in contrast, for example, to the duty to mitigate and intervening cause, which are all or nothing restrictions.[87] The contributory negligence defence is enshrined in the Law Reform (Contributory Negligence) Act 1945 and, while the defence applies to nearly all torts and, in particular, to the most important tort of negligence, the courts have taken the view that, subject to where there is concurrent liability with tort, it does not apply to breach of contract.

21.45 In *Forsikringsaktieselskapet Vesta v Butcher*[88] it was said that contract cases should be divided, for the purposes of construing section 4 of the 1945 Act, into three categories. A category 1 case is where the defendant has been in breach of a strict contractual duty. A category 2 case is where the defendant has been in breach of a contractual duty of care. A category 3 case is where the defendant has been in breach of a contractual duty of care and is also liable in the tort of negligence.

21.46 According to *Vesta v Butcher* (where, strictly speaking, the discussion was obiter dicta) and *UCB Bank plc v Hepherd Winstanley & Pugh*[89] it is in a category 3 case only that section 4 of the 1945 Act allows contributory negligence to be a defence to breach of contract. While the Court of Appeal in *Barclays Bank Ltd v Fairclough Building Ltd*[90] accepted that contributory negligence is applicable in a category 3 case, the main point of that decision was that it is not applicable in a category 1 case.

21.47 This state of affairs is most unsatisfactory. It stems from the fact that the definition of fault in the 1945 Act is geared towards tort and not contract. While it is true that, since the House of Lords' acceptance of concurrent liability in *Henderson v Merrett Syndicates Ltd*,[91] there is little prospect of a case falling within category 2 but outside category 3,[92] there is much to be said in principle for contributory negligence applying to all three categories.[93]

---

[87] ie if one focuses on particular loss, a failure in the duty to mitigate that loss means that no damages will be awarded for it. In contrast, contributory negligence in relation to a loss means that damages are reduced, not eliminated, for that loss.

[88] [1989] AC 852, CA, affirmed on a different point [1989] AC 880, HL.

[89] [1999] Lloyd's Rep PN 963, CA.

[90] [1994] 3 WLR 1057.

[91] [1995] 2 AC 145, HL.

[92] For an unusual example, see *Raflatac Ltd v Eade* [1999] 1 Lloyd's Rep 506 (Colman J said that it was a category 2 case, and hence contributory negligence was inapplicable, where the head-contractor was under a contractual duty (of care) to procure work by a sub-contractor but did not owe a duty of care in relation to the sub-contractor's performance).

[93] But the Law Commission in *Contributory Negligence as a Defence in Contract* (Law Com No 219, 1993) recommended merely extending contributory negligence to category 2.

(v) Mental distress

Traditionally, the House of Lords' decision in *Addis v Gramophone Co Ltd* [94] was **21.48**
regarded as barring damages for mental distress in an action for breach of contract.
In that case, no damages were awarded for the harsh and humiliating manner of
the claimant's wrongful dismissal. But this restrictive approach was departed from
by a series of cases in the 1970s; and the situations in which one can recover damages for mental distress for breach of contract have stabilized in recent years. It is
now clear that they are recoverable in two categories but two categories only. [95]

The first, and most important, is where the predominant, or an important, object **21.49**
of the contract from the claimant's point of view was to obtain mental satisfaction
whether enjoyment or relief from distress. The ruined holiday cases such as *Jarvis v
Swan's Tours Ltd* [96] and *Jackson v Horizon Holidays Ltd* [97] most obviously fall within
this. So does *Heywood v Wellers* [98] where the defendant solicitors, in breach of
their contractual duty of care, failed to gain an injunction to stop molestation
of the claimant by her former boyfriend. Also within this category is the House of
Lords' decision in *Ruxley Electronics & Construction Ltd v Forsyth*, [99] in which the
damages of £2,500 for loss of amenity is best rationalized as flowing from the fact
that the claimant's primary object in specifying the particular depth for the swimming pool was mental satisfaction.

In *Farley v Skinner* [100] the House of Lords examined the width of this first category **21.50**
and decided that it extended to where *an important object* of the contract was
mental satisfaction or freedom from distress even though that was not the very,
or predominant, object. The claimant was considering buying a house 15 miles
from Gatwick Airport and engaged the defendant as his surveyor. He specifically
asked him to investigate whether the property was affected by aircraft noise
and the surveyor reported that it was unlikely that the property would suffer
greatly from such noise. In fact aircraft noise substantially affected the property.

---

94 [1909] AC 488, HL. In *Johnson v Unisys Ltd* [2001] UKHL 49; [2002] 2 AC 732 it was held
that, whatever the normal position at common law, there is a special reason to deny damages for
mental distress (and psychiatric illness and loss of reputation) *for wrongful dismissal* because of the
need to avoid undermining the statutory cap on compensation for unfair dismissal. For the drawing
of the line between wrongful dismissal and a breach of the employment contract that is sufficiently
distinct from wrongful dismissal as to fall outside the *Unisys* bar to damages, see *Eastwood v Magnox
Electric plc* [2004] UKHL 35; [2004] 3 WLR 322.
95 For examples of cases falling outside the two categories and therefore denying mental distress
damages, see *Bliss v South East Thames Regional Health Authority* [1985] IRLR 308, CA; *Hayes v James
& Charles Dodd* [1990] 2 All ER 815, CA; *Johnson v Gore Wood & Co* [2002] 2 AC 1, HL.
96 [1973] QB 233, CA. See also *Diesen v Samson* 1971 SLT 49.
97 [1975] 1 WLR 1468, CA.
98 [1976] QB 446, CA.
99 [1996] AC 344, HL. See para 21.22.
100 [2001] UKHL 49; [2002] 2 AC 732.

Having decided not to sell, the claimant sued the surveyor in the tort of negligence and for breach of contract. It was held that although the claimant had suffered no financial loss, he was entitled to mental distress damages of £10,000 because an important object of the contract with the surveyor, albeit not its very object, was peace of mind in relation to the aircraft noise.[101]

21.51   The second category is where the claimant's mental distress is directly consequent on physical inconvenience caused by the defendant's breach of contract. Hence in *Perry v Sidney Phillips & Son*[102] and *Watts v Morrow*[103] mental distress damages for the distress and inconvenience of living in poor accommodation, purchased as a result of negligent surveys, were awarded against surveyors for breach of contract. In *Farley v Skinner* it was decided that the award of mental distress damages could be justified as falling within this second category as well as the first: aircraft noise causes physical inconvenience because that phrase should be interpreted in a wide sense to include matter detrimentally affecting sight, hearing or smell.

(vi) Loss of reputation

21.52   Until recently, *Addis v Gramophone Co Ltd*[104] was also the leading authority denying contractual damages for loss of reputation. The House of Lords held that, in the claimant's action for wrongful dismissal, he should be confined to damages for his direct pecuniary loss, such as loss of salary, and should not be compensated for any loss of his reputation or for the fact that the dismissal might make it more difficult for him to obtain another job.

21.53   Yet in many cases outside the context of wrongful dismissal, damages for loss of reputation have been awarded in respect of the pecuniary loss flowing from a loss of reputation. The distinction between the irrecoverable non-pecuniary loss constituted by the loss of reputation itself and the recoverable pecuniary loss consequent on the loss of reputation was particularly clearly applied in *Aeriel Advertising Co v Batchelors Peas Ltd*.[105] There the defendants had contracted with

---

[101] For a case falling within the first category, as expanded by *Farley v Skinner*, see *Hamilton Jones v David & Snape* [2003] EWHC 3147 (Ch); [2004] 1 All ER 657 (solicitor's breach of contract and tortious negligence leading to a mother's loss of custody of her children).

[102] [1982] 1 WLR 1297, CA.

[103] [1991] 1 WLR 1421, CA. For discussion of the quantum of damages for discomfort and inconvenience consequent on a landlord's breach of repairing obligations, see *Shine v English Churches Housing Group* [2004] EWCA Civ 434; *Earle v Charalambous* [2006] EWCA Civ 1090.

[104] [1909] AC 488, HL. See also, eg, *O'Laoire v Jackel International Ltd (No 2)* [1991] ICR 718, CA.

[105] [1938] 2 All ER 788. See also, eg, *Rolin v Steward* (1854) 14 CB 595 (refusal to honour cheque causing damage to credit and reputation); *Wilson v United Counties Bank Ltd* [1920] AC 102, HL (breach of contract in proper vision leading to claimant's bankruptcy); *Marbé v George Edwardes (Daly's Theatre) Ltd* [1928] 1 KB 269, CA; *Herbert Clayton v Oliver* [1930] AC 209, HL;

the claimants to advertise their peas by trailers from a plane. In breach of contract the claimants flew the plane with the advertising trailers over a city centre during minutes of silence in armistice services. The public was horrified and the defendants' sales dropped. Atkinson J held that, while they were not entitled to damages for loss of reputation itself, they were entitled to damages for loss of sales following on that loss of reputation.

It is clear therefore that, outside the context of wrongful dismissal, the courts **21.54** have been prepared to award contractual damages compensating pecuniary loss (but not non-pecuniary loss) flowing from loss of reputation. The general position can therefore be regarded as that so clearly expressed by Hallett J in *Foaminol Laboratories v British Artid Plastic Ltd*:[106] '. . .If pecuniary loss be established, the mere fact that the pecuniary loss is brought about by the loss of reputation caused by a breach of contract is not sufficient to preclude the plaintiffs from recovering in respect of that pecuniary loss.'

That that is a correct statement of the law was authoritatively established in **21.55** *Malik v Bank of Credit and Commerce International SA*.[107] Former employees of the corrupt bank, BCCI, claimed damages from the bank for loss of reputation: that is, they sought compensation for their handicap in the labour market flowing from the dishonesty stigma that attached to employees of BCCI. It was laid down that damages were recoverable for the pecuniary loss of reputation flowing from the employer's breach of the implied term not to undermine the employee's trust and confidence.[108] Lord Nicholls specifically cited with approval Hallett J's statement in *Foaminol*.

(vii) The only obligation broken is to pay money

As laid down in *London, Chatham and Dover Railway Company v South Eastern* **21.56** *Railway*,[109] where the only obligation broken is to pay money, no damages can be awarded and the sole remedy is for the unpaid sum in an action for the award

---

Tolnay v Criterion Films Productions Ltd [1936] 2 All ER 1625; *Joseph v National Magazine* Co [1959] Ch 14 (all an actor's or author's loss of publicity); *Anglo-Continental Holidays Ltd v Typaldos Lines (London) Ltd* [1967] 2 Lloyd's Rep 61, CA; *GKN Centrax Gears Ltd v Matbro Ltd* [1976] 2 Lloyd's Rep 555, CA (supplying of defective goods and services damaging claimant's reputation with customers).

[106] [1941] 2 All ER 393, 400.
[107] [1998] AC 20, HL.
[108] The *Addis* case was departed from. But as laid down in *Johnson v Unisys Ltd* [2001] UKHL 13; [2003] 1 AC 518, the need to avoid undermining the cap on compensation for unfair dismissal is a special reason to maintain the bar on damages for loss of reputation for wrongful dismissal: see n 94 above.
[109] [1893] AC 429, HL.

of the agreed sum. The main practical consequence of this rule[110] is that no damages can be awarded for the general loss of the use of money (that is, damages cannot be awarded for loss of interest).

21.57   Where the claimant can show a special loss caused by the defendant's failure to pay a sum of money, damages are recoverable. In *Wadsworth v Lydall* [111] the defendant failed to pay all of an agreed sum so that the claimant had to take out a mortgage in order to finance a contract for the purchase of land and also incurred legal costs. He was awarded damages for interest charges paid on the mortgage and for his legal costs. The Court of Appeal distinguished the *London, Chatham and Dover Railway* case on the ground that, while it prevents general damages for failure to pay a sum of money, it does not prevent special damages.

21.58   Moreover, interest is recoverable by statute. By section 35A of the Supreme Court Act 1981, a court has a discretion to award simple interest on an agreed sum from the date of the cause of action until the date of the judgment or payment. And, although section 35A does not apply where the agreed sum was paid in advance of proceedings to recover it, the Late Payment of Commercial Debts (Interest) Act 1998 gives a creditor an automatic right to simple interest after 30 days on an unpaid commercial debt.[112]

21.59   Recently in *Sempra Metals Ltd v Commissioners of Inland Revenue* [113] the House of Lords has effectively buried the rule in the *London, Chatham and Dover Railway* case by accepting that damages can be awarded for a proved general loss of interest (including compound interest) subject to normal limiting principles, such as remoteness and the duty to mitigate.

(viii)   No damages beyond the defendant's minimum contractual obligation

21.60   Where a contract entitles the defendant to perform in alternative ways or, as it is sometimes expressed, the defendant has a discretion as to the contractual benefits to be conferred on the claimant, damages have traditionally been assessed on the basis that the defendant would have performed in the way most favourable to itself. As Diplock LJ said in *Laverack v Woods of Colchester Ltd*, 'The first task of the assessor of damages is to estimate as best he can what the plaintiff would

---

110   This rule has never been regarded as affecting the claimant's right to terminate the contract and to recover damages for the defendant's repudiatory breach, presumably because a repudiatory breach always goes beyond being the breach of an obligation to pay money (eg a seller of goods can sue the buyer for non-acceptance).

111   [1981] 1 WLR 598, CA.

112   The Act applies to contracts for the supply of goods or services (other than excluded contracts) where the purchaser and supplier are each acting in the course of business. The rate of interest has been fixed at the base rate plus 8%. By s 5 the interest may be remitted, wholly or in part, because of the creditor's conduct.

113   [2007] UKHL 34.

have gained. . .if the defendant had fulfilled his legal obligation and had done no more'.[114]

So, for example, if in a contract for the carriage of goods by sea the cargo-owner has the right to choose between a number of different ports for the cargo to be unloaded, damages for his failure to provide the cargo to the carrier will be based on the assumption that he would have chosen the most distant port for unloading.[115] In a contract for the sale of goods, where the seller has an option as to the exact quantity to be delivered, damages for non-delivery are based on the assumption that he would have delivered the smallest quantity.[116] And in the *Laverack* case itself no damages were awarded in relation to bonuses under a service contract that still had two years eight months to run because it was at the employer's discretion whether such payments should be made.

21.61

Two qualifications should be borne in mind. The first is that where, on the construction of the contract, it was the parties' intention that the defendant's discretion should be exercised reasonably, damages will be assessed on the basis of the defendant's minimum reasonable performance.[117] A second qualification is that, while a particular performance may be the least burdensome to the defendant when judged solely according to the contract, this may not be the basis upon which damages are assessed because the courts judge the defendant's least burdensome performance by taking all other potential losses into account. So in the *Laverack* case Diplock LJ said that, '. . .one must not assume that he [the defendant] will cut off his nose to spite his face and so [act] as to reduce his legal obligation to the plaintiff by incurring greater loss in other respects'.[118]

21.62

It would seem that the rationale for giving no damages beyond the defendant's minimum contractual obligation is that that is all that the claimant is legally entitled to. Had the contract been on foot, the claimant could not have complained if the defendant had merely performed its bare contractual obligation. But it is not clear that this is the correct approach in contrast to an assessment of how the defendant was likely to have performed (which may or may not coincide with its minimum legal obligation). The latter approach was adopted, and *Laverack* distinguished, by the Court of Appeal in *Horkulak v Cantor Fitzgerald International*.[119] In assessing damages for a wrongful dismissal, the claimant

21.63

---

114 [1967] 1 QB 278, 294.

115 *Kaye Steam Navigation Co v W & R Barnett* (1932) 48 TLR 440. See also, eg, *Kurt A Becher GmbH v Roplak Enterprises SA (The World Navigator)* [1991] 2 Lloyd's Rep 23, CA.

116 *Re Thornett & Fehr and Yuills Ltd* [1921] 1 KB 219.

117 *Abrahams v Herbert Reiach Ltd* [1922] 1 KB 477, CA; *Paula Lee Ltd v Robert Zehil & Co Ltd* [1983] 2 All ER 390.

118 [1967] 1 QB 278, 295.

119 [2004] EWCA Civ 1287; [2005] ICR 402. See also *Lion Nathan Ltd v C-C Bottlers Ltd* [1996] 1 WLR 1438, PC (although there the reasoning was ultimately that there was no discretion).

employee was held entitled to the bonus that the defendant company would have paid rather than the minimum that the company acting reasonably and in good faith could have paid.

(c) Additional issues

(i) Compensating advantages

21.64 An issue that has received relatively little attention in relation to claims for breach of contract, as opposed to claims in tort for personal injury and death,[120] is the extent to which benefits accruing to the claimant as a result of the breach of contract are to be taken into account in assessing damages.

21.65 In general, it would seem that where the benefit arises from what the claimant has done in response to the breach (that is, it arises out of an act of mitigation even though there was no duty to act), that benefit will be taken into account in assessing damages. A leading case is *British Westinghouse v Underground Electric Railways Company of London Ltd*.[121] The defendants in breach of contract supplied to the claimants turbines which were defective. The claimants subsequently replaced them with other turbines. The replacement turbines turned out to be more efficient and profitable than the old turbines would have been if non-defective. The House of Lords held that the greater efficiency of the replacements should be taken into account as mitigating the defendants' loss.

21.66 But indirect compensating advantages will not be taken into account. This is shown by *Lavarack v Woods of Colchester Ltd*.[122] The claimant was wrongfully dismissed from his employment with the defendants and so freed from the provision in his contract with them that he should not, without their written consent, be engaged or interested in any other business. After his dismissal the claimant took employment with a company called Martindale at a lower salary than he had earned with the defendants, acquired half the shares in Martindale and bought shares in a company called Ventilation. The value of both the Martindale and Ventilation shares increased. The Court of Appeal held that, while his new salary and the profit from the Martindale shares should be deducted in assessing his damages for wrongful dismissal, the profits from the Ventilation shares should not be. The latter were too indirect to be taken into account.

---

120 See paras 21.106–21.107 and 21.125.

121 [1912] AC 673, HL.

122 [1967] 1 QB 278, CA. For other examples of the non-deduction of compensating advantages in assessing contractual damages, see *Hussey v Eels* [1990] 2 QB 227, CA; *Gardner v Marsh & Parsons* [1997] 1 WLR 489, CA; *Needler Financial Services Ltd v Taber* [2002] 3 All ER 501; *Primavera v Allied Dunbar Assurance plc* [2002] EWCA Civ 1327; [2003] PNLR 12.

It can be seen from this that 'directness' puts a limit on the extent to which com- **21.67**
pensating advantages are deducted. It operates in an analogous, but reverse, way
to 'remoteness' and 'intervening cause'. They counter the compensatory principle
by limiting the claimant's damages; whereas directness here counters compensation, as strictly applied, by allowing the claimant to recover more than his loss.

It must be stressed that to be relevant as a compensating advantage the benefit **21.68**
that the claimant has subsequently gained must have accrued from the breach.
That is, it must have been factually caused by the breach. If the claimant would
have made the gain even if there had been no breach, it will not be taken into
account in assessing damages.[123]

(ii) Damages in a contract for the benefit of a third party

What is the measure of damages if the promisee chooses to sue on a contract made **21.69**
for another's benefit? Applying the normal expectation principle, the claimant is
entitled to be put into as good a position as it would have been if the contract had
been performed; that is, the relevant loss is the claimant's not the third party's.
However, this does not mean that the promisee is necessarily restricted to nominal
damages.[124] One would expect that in some contracts made for a third party's
benefit, the defendant's failure to benefit the third party would also constitute a
substantial pecuniary loss to the promisee. This may be, for example, because the
promisee required the defendant to pay the third party in order to pay off a debt
owed by the promisee to the third party. Or the promisee may have stood to gain
from the use to be made by the third party of the promised benefits. Moreover,
by analogy to the cases allowing a cost of cure in excess of a difference in value,[125]
the claimant should be entitled to substantial damages (measured by the cost
of cure) where it has subsequently conferred the benefit on the third party or
intends to do so.

Moreover, there have been a number of important cases on construction contracts **21.70**
in which, contrary to the general rule, it has been held that a promisee can recover
the third party's loss rather than its own loss. In *Darlington BC v Wiltshier Northern
Ltd*[126] the principle applied by the Court of Appeal was in effect as follows:
wherever the breach of a contract for work on property causes loss to a third
party, who is an owner of that property, and it was known or contemplated by

---

[123] *Thompson Ltd v Robinson (Gunmakers) Ltd* [1955] Ch 177 can be regarded as an illustration
of this. As supply exceeded demand, the subsequent sale of a car was not a compensating advantage
to the vendor and the purchaser had to pay damages for the vendor's loss of profit on the sale between
them.

[124] See eg *Woodar Investment Development Ltd v Wimpey Construction UK Ltd* [1980] 1 WLR
277, HL.

[125] See paras 21.19–21.23.

[126] [1995] 1 WLR 68, CA.

the contracting parties that the third party was, or would become, owner of the property and the third party has no direct right to sue for breach of contract, the promisee, who has the right to sue, can recover substantial damages compensating the third party's loss.[127]

21.71   In *Alfred McAlpine Construction Ltd v Panatown Ltd*[128] the House of Lords, by a majority, dismissed a promisee's claim for substantial damages emphasizing that the above exceptional principle does not apply where, as in the case at hand, the third party has a direct contractual right to sue the promisor.

(2) *Compensatory Damages: Torts*

21.72   In relation to torts, as opposed to breach of contract, it is not straightforward to distinguish matters going to liability from matters going to damages. A breach of contract is actionable without proof of loss or damage so that the liability question is simply one of whether the defendant has committed a breach of contract. The same can be said of torts actionable per se, such as trespass and libel. In contrast, the most important tort, the tort of negligence, along with, for example, the tort of nuisance is actionable only on proof of damage; and for such torts the line between liability and quantum is less easy to draw and has to be drawn in a different place than for wrongs actionable per se. In particular, for torts actionable only on proof of damage, remoteness of damage and intervening cause will normally be matters going to liability (that is, to the question whether the tort has been committed) rather than to damages. For this reason, remoteness and causation have been dealt with in the general examination of the law of tort above and will only be briefly mentioned again here.

(a) The compensatory aim and limiting principles

(i) *The compensatory aim*

21.73   The general aim of damages for a tort is to put the claimant into as good a position as he would have been in if no tort had been committed. Lord Blackburn's statement in *Livingstone v Rawyards Coal Co*,[129] a case concerning trespass to goods, is the most cited authority on this. He said that the measure of damages was: '. . .that sum of money which will put the party who has been injured, or has

---

127   This is an extension to the approach of the House of Lords in *Linden Gardens Trust Ltd v Lenesta Sludge Disposals Ltd* [1994] 1 AC 85 which in itself had applied to real property the exceptional principle applicable to a changed ownership of goods established in *Dunlop v Lambert* (1839) 6 CL & F 600 and *The Albazero* [1977] AC 774.

128   [2001] 1 AC 518, HL. For contrasting views of this controversial decision, see B Coote, 'The Performance Interest, *Panatown*, and the Problem of Loss' (2000) 117 LQR 81; A Burrows, 'No Damages for a Third Party's Loss' (2001) OUCLJ 107.

129   (1880) 5 App Cas 25, 39.

suffered, in the same position as he would have been in if he had not sustained the wrong for which he is now getting his compensation or reparation'.

This aim applies even in relation to the tort of deceit or negligent misrepresentation: **21.74** so the claimant is entitled to be put into as good a position as if no representation had been made but is not entitled to be put into as good a position as if the statement had been true.[130] Given that the compensatory aim differs as between a claim for misrepresentation and a claim for breach of contract, it is essential to distinguish between mere representations, where the sole action is for tortious misrepresentation, and warranties, where the claimant can sue for breach of contract; or, to put it another way, between statements inducing the making of a contract and the terms of the contract.

In seeking to put the claimant into as good a position as if no tort had been **21.75** committed, the courts inevitably encounter the question of how to deal with uncertainties (for example, whether a consequential loss will or will not be suffered in the future). Where the uncertainty relates to future events, the courts will award damages in proportion to their assessment of the chances provided those chances are not so small as to be dismissed as 'entirely speculative'.[131] In contrast, where the uncertainty relates to a past fact (or, it would seem, the hypothetical conduct of the claimant), the courts decide the issue on the balance of probabilities. In *Mallett v McMonagle*[132] Lord Diplock summarized the law as follows:

> In determining what did happen in the past a court decides on the balance of probabilities. Anything that is more probable than not it treats as certain. But in assessing damages which depend upon its view as to what will happen in the future or would have happened in the future if something had not happened in the past, the court must make an estimate as to what are the chances that a particular thing will or would

---

[130] *Smith New Court Securities Ltd v Scrimgeour Vickers (Asset Management) Ltd* [1997] AC 254, HL (deceit). See also *Doyle v Olby (Ironmongers) Ltd)* [1969] 2 QB 158, CA (deceit); *East v Maurer* [1991] 1 WLR 461, CA (deceit); *Esso Petroleum Co Ltd v Mardon* [1976] QB 801, CA (negligent misrepresentation); *Cemp Properties (UK) Ltd v Dentsply Research & Development Corpn* [1991] 2 EGLR 197, 201, CA (Misrepresentation Act 1967, s 2(1)); *Royscot Trust Ltd v Rogerson* [1991] 2 QB 297, 304–5, CA (Misrepresentation Act 1967, s 2(1)). Much needless confusion has been caused by *South Australia Asset Management Corpn v York Mantague Ltd* [1997] AC 191, HL ('SAAMCO') which concerned contractual and tortious claims for negligent property valuations. The reasoning appears to cut across long-established principles of compensation, legal causation and remoteness and, although courts have felt obliged to apply it generally in contract and tort cases on negligent misrepresentation and negligent failure to provide information, it is best viewed as a specific policy decision that valuers should not normally be held liable for falls in the property market. For examples of the difficulties in applying it, see, eg, *Platform Homes Loans Ltd v Oyston Shipways Ltd* [2000] 2 AC 190, HL; *Aneco Reinsurance Underwriting Ltd v Johnson & Higgins Ltd* [2001] UKHL 51; [2001] 2 All ER (Comm) 929. For detailed criticism of the reasoning in *SAAMCO* see A Burrows, *Remedies for Torts and Breach of Contract* (3rd edn, 2004) 109–122.

[131] See eg *Davies v Taylor* [1974] AC 207, HL.

[132] [1970] AC 166, 176. See also *Brown v Ministry of Defence* [2006] EWCA Civ 546; [2006] PIQR Q9.

have happened and reflect those chances, whether they are more or less than even, in the amount of damages which it awards.

21.76 A leading case is *Hotson v East Berkshire Area Health Authority*.[133] The claimant injured his hip in a fall and later developed a permanent hip disability. He brought an action for negligence against the defendant claiming that, if his injury had been properly diagnosed at the start, his permanent disability would have been avoided. The trial judge found that, even if the defendant had treated the claimant properly, there was still a 75 per cent chance that his disability would have developed. Nevertheless, he awarded the claimant damages (of 25 per cent of the full damages) for being deprived by the defendant's negligence of the 25 per cent chance of avoiding the disability. But that award was overturned by the House of Lords. Their Lordships stressed that what was in question was a matter of past fact to which the all or nothing balance of probabilities standard of proof applied. Applying that test, their Lordships concluded that the claim failed because the claimant had not established that the negligence of the defendant had caused his hip disability.

21.77 This area of the law was reviewed in the difficult case of *Gregg v Scott*[134] where it would appear that the uncertainty could not be clearly isolated as one of past fact as opposed to the hypothetical or future medical condition of the claimant. A doctor negligently diagnosed a lump under the claimant's left arm as benign when it was in fact cancerous. This led to a delay of nine months in the claimant receiving proper treatment. It was found that, on the balance of probabilities, the claimant would not have been 'cured' of cancer (with 'cure' meaning surviving for more than ten years) even if there had been no delay. It was also found that the delay had reduced the claimant's chances of cure from 42 per cent to 25 per cent. The majority of the House of Lords (Lord Hoffmann, Lord Phillips and Baroness Hale) refused to award the claimant damages for the reduction in the chances of cure. The case has left at least two troubling uncertainties. The first is that no clear justification was given as to why a loss of the chance approach is thought appropriate—as many past cases have established that it is[135]—for professional negligence cases causing pure economic loss but not for medical negligence. The second is that the precise status of Stuart-Smith LJ's influential judgment in *Allied Maples Group Ltd v Simmons & Simmons* is left unclear. Stuart-Smith LJ had there attempted to rationalize the law on hypothetical events by laying down that a loss of the chance approach was appropriate where the uncertainty was as to the

---

[133] [1987] AC 750, HL.

[134] [2005] UKHL 2, [2005] 2 WLR 268.

[135] eg *Kitchen v Royal Air Force Association* [1948] 1 WLR 563; *Allied Maples Group Ltd v Simmons & Simmons* [1995] 1 WLR 1602, CA; *Sharif v Garrett & Co* [2001] EWCA Civ 1269; [2002] 1 WLR 3118.

hypothetical conduct of third parties, but not the hypothetical conduct of the claimant who could be expected to prove, on the balance of probabilities, one way or the other, what he would have done had there been no breach of duty by the defendant.

A further complication has been added by *Barker v Corus (UK) Plc*.[136] The relevant **21.78** damage in question (in applying the exception to causation recognized in *Fairchild v Glenhaven Funeral Services Ltd*)[137] was treated as the material increase of risk of contracting mesothelioma (ie the loss of the chance of avoiding the disease). But it was stressed that this applied only because there was a single causal agent (asbestos) and the outcome was known ie the relevant disease had been contracted. Their Lordships did not see themselves as opening the door to the recovery of damages simply because a defendant had negligently materially increased the risk of a claimant suffering a particular disease or injury.

(ii) Limiting principles

Remoteness. As we have seen above,[138] the leading case is *Overseas Tankship* **21.79** *(UK) Ltd v Morts Dock & Engineering Co Ltd (The Wagon Mound)*[139] which established that a loss is too remote if it was not reasonably foreseeable at the time of the breach of duty. Subsequent cases show that it is a slight possibility (ie a low degree of likelihood) of the loss occurring that needs to be reasonably foreseeable;[140] and that it is the type of loss suffered, and not the specific loss suffered, that needs to have been reasonably foreseeable.[141] Although at one time it was thought that the tort remoteness test was significantly different from the contract test, the emphasis in recent contract cases on it being the type of loss, rather than the specific loss, that needs to be reasonably contemplated has brought the two closer together.[142] But there still appears to be a higher degree of likelihood required under the contract 'reasonable contemplation' test than under the tort 'reasonable foreseeability' test.

The Wagon Mound lays down the remoteness test for most, but not all, torts. **21.80** An exception is the tort of deceit where the remoteness test is wider and, as authoritatively laid down in *Smith New Court Securities Ltd v Scrimgeour Vickers*

---

136 [2005] UKHL 20; [2006] 2 WLR 1027. For mesothelioma, the effect of the decision was reversed by the Compensation Act 2006, s 3. See generally paras 17.69–17.73.

137 [2002] UKHL 20; [2003] 1 AC 32.

138 See para 21.32, and see also paras 17.82–17.83.

139 [1961] AC 388, PC.

140 *Overseas Tankship (UK) v Miller SS Co Pty Ltd (The Wagon Mound)(No 2)* [1967] 1 AC 617, PC.

141 *Hughes v Lord Advocate* [1963] AC 837, HL.

142 See paras 21.33–21.36.

(Asset Management) Ltd [143] is one of 'direct consequence' irrespective of whether the loss is reasonably foreseeable.

21.81 **Intervening cause.** The operation of intervening causation in relation to tort has been considered above. [144] Suffice it to say here that there is no clear test for deciding whether or not a natural event, the conduct of a third party, or the conduct of the claimant breaks the chain of causation.

21.82 **The duty to mitigate.** The duty to mitigate applies in much the same way to damages for torts as it does to damages for breach of contract. As we have seen in relation to breach of contract, [145] a claimant must take all reasonable steps to minimize the loss to him so that he cannot recover for any loss which he could so have avoided but has failed to avoid. Whether a step should reasonably have been taken depends on the particular facts in question. Some of the factors which have been considered important in past tort cases are as follows:

(1) An injured claimant acts unreasonably if he refuses an operation contrary to firm medical advice. [146] But the claimant need not submit himself to a surgical operation involving substantial risk or where the outcome is uncertain. [147]

(2) It will generally be unreasonable for the claimant to refuse offers of help which would have prevented further property damage. [148]

(3) The claimant need not take action which will put its good public relations at risk. [149]

(4) The claimant need not take steps which it cannot financially afford. [150]

21.83 It follows from the main rule of the duty to mitigate that, where the claimant does take reasonable steps in an attempt to minimize loss, it can recover for loss incurred in so doing even though the resulting loss is in the event greater than it would have been had the mitigating steps not been taken. [151] As has been noted in relation to the duty to mitigate in relation to breach of contract, the courts

---

143 [1997] AC 254, HL. This confirmed *Doyle v Olby (Ironmongers) Ltd* [1969] 2 QB 158, CA. In *Royscot Trust Ltd v Rogerson* [1991] 2 QB 297, CA, it was held that the wider remoteness test for deceit also applied to damages under s 2(1) of the Misrepresentation Act 1967. In the *Smith New Court* case it was left open whether the *Royscot* case was correctly decided on this point: [1997] AC 254, 267, 283.

144 See paras 17.76–17.78.

145 See para 21.42.

146 *McAuley v London Transport Executive* [1957] 2 Lloyd's Rep 500, CA.

147 *Geest plc v Lansiquot* [2002] UKPC 48; [2002] 1 WLR 3111.

148 *Anderson v Hoen (The Flying Fish)* (1865) 3 Moo PCCNS 77, PC.

149 *London and South of England Building Society v Stone* [1983] 1 WLR 1242, CA (where the action against the defendant valuer was brought in both contract and tort).

150 *Clippens Oil Co Ltd v Edinburgh & District Water Trustees* [1907] AC 291, 303, HL; *Lagden v O'Connor* [2003] UKHL 64, [2004] 1 AC 1067.

151 *Esso Petroleum Co Ltd v Marden* [1976] QB 801.

will lean in favour of the claimant in deciding whether or not expenses were reasonably incurred.[152]

Contributory negligence. In contrast to claims for breach of contract, it is **21.84** clear that contributory negligence applies to most torts and, in particular, to the tort of negligence. The defence applies where the defendant can establish three elements. First, the claimant must have been at fault or negligent towards himself. To illustrate this by reference to cases of personal injury or death, the claimant is most obviously negligent towards himself if he negligently causes an accident involving himself,[153] or puts himself in an inherently dangerous position,[154] or renders an inherently non-dangerous position dangerous by failing to take safety precautions.[155] Secondly, the claimant's negligence must have been a factual cause of his loss. Thirdly, the claimant's negligence must have exposed him to the particular risk of the type of injury suffered.[156]

Once it has been decided that contributory negligence applies to the case in **21.85** hand, the court must decide the extent of the reduction in damages by reason of that contributory negligence. Section 1(1) of the Law Reform (Contributory Negligence) Act 1945 lays down that the damages '. . .shall be reduced to such extent as the court thinks just and equitable having regard to the claimant's share in the responsibility for the damage'. How exactly the courts apply these words is difficult to clarify; but what can be said, as stressed by Denning LJ in *Davies v Swan Motor Co (Swansea) Ltd*,[157] is that the courts consider both the causal potency and the comparative blameworthiness of the parties' conduct.

In *Froom v Butcher*[158] Lord Denning, recognizing the difficulty of deciding to **21.86** what extent to reduce damages and in his desire to avoid prolonging cases, suggested standard figures for reducing damages where the claimant has been contributorily negligent by not wearing a seat-belt. If the damage would have been prevented altogether a reduction of 25 per cent should be made and if it would have been considerably less severe a reduction of 15 per cent should be made.

In deciding on the appropriate reduction, one must keep contributory negligence **21.87** distinct from the issue of contribution between tortfeasors. In the leading case

---

[152] *London and South of England Building Society v Stone* [1983] 3 All ER 105, 121. See also para 21.43.

[153] For example where two motorists negligently collide.

[154] See for example *Jones v Livox Quarries Ltd* [1952] 2 QB 608, CA; *Owens v Brimmell* [1977] QB 859; *Gregory v Kelly* [1978] RTR 426.

[155] See for example *Froom v Butcher* [1976] QB 286, CA (failing to wear a seat-belt); *O'Connell v Jackson* [1972] 1 QB 27, CA (failing to wear a crash helmet on a motor-bike).

[156] *Jones v Livox Quarries Ltd* [1952] 2 QB 608.

[157] [1949] 2 KB 291, 326.

[158] [1976] QB 286, cf *Capps v Miller* [1989] 1 WLR 839, CA (not fastening a chin-strap on a helmet led to a 10% reduction for contributory negligence).

of *Fitzgerald v Lane*[159] the claimant was hit by two cars one after the other on a pelican crossing. The claimant and each of the drivers was found to have been equally to blame for the claimant's injuries. It was held by the House of Lords that the appropriate reduction for contributory negligence should have been 50 per cent and not 33.3 per cent. What has to be contrasted is the claimant's conduct on the one hand with the totality of the tortious conduct of the defendants on the other.

21.88 It was held by the House of Lords in *Standard Chartered Bank v Pakistan National Shipping Corp (No 2)*[160] that contributory negligence does not apply to the tort of deceit and probably not to other intentional torts, such as intentional trespass to the person.[161] In addition, the Torts (Interference with Goods) Act 1977, section 11,[162] specifically lays down that contributory negligence is not a defence to conversion or intentional trespass to goods.

21.89 **Damages for mental distress and loss of reputation.** In contrast to damages for breach of contract, restrictions on the type of damages recoverable in tort tend to be issues going to liability rather than to quantum. For example, there is generally no liability in the tort of negligence for the infliction of mere mental distress which falls short of a recognizable psychiatric illness.[163] However, once liability has been established (that is, once the tort has been made out) damages for mental distress are commonly recoverable. So, for example, a person who has been physically injured by the defendant's negligence can recover damages for pain and suffering. And damages for loss of reputation are, of course, recoverable for the tort of defamation, the very essence of which is to protect a person's reputation.[164]

---

159 [1989] AC 328, HL.

160 [2002] UKHL 43; [2003] 1 AC 959.

161 The reasoning in the *Standard Chartered Bank* case indicates that Lord Denning's suggestion that contributory negligence might apply to reduce damages for trespass to the person should be rejected although at [45] Lord Rodger expressly said that he was leaving that open. See also *Corporacion Nacional del Cobre de Chile v Sogemin Metals Ltd* [1997] 1 WLR 1396 in which contributory negligence was held to be inapplicable in a bribe case founded on various dishonestly-committed torts (including deceit, conspiracy, and inducing breach of contract) and the equitable wrong of assisting a breach of fiduciary duty.

162 This must be read subject to the Banking Act 1979, s 47.

163 *Alcock v Chief Constable of South Yorkshire Police* [1992] 1 AC 310, 401, 409–10, 416, HL. As recognized in eg *Perry v Sidney Phillips & Son* [1982] 1 WLR 1297 and *Hamilton Jones v David & Snape* [2003] EWHC 3147 (Ch); [2004] 1 All ER 657 an exception is where there is concurrent liability in tort and contract: mental distress damages are recoverable in the tort action if they are, or would be, recoverable for breach of contract because falling within one of the two categories (see paras 21.48–51) where such damages are recoverable.

164 In *John v MGN Ltd* [1997] QB 586, CA, it was held that, in defamation cases, the scale of awards for non-pecuniary loss in personal injury cases (see para 21.105) could be drawn to the attention of juries and that the level of an appropriate award could be indicated by the judge. For guidelines on the level of compensatory (and punitive) damages for false imprisonment and malicious prosecution actions against the police, see *Thompson v Commissioner of Police for the Metropolis* [1998] QB 498, CA.

Damages for mental distress are also often recoverable under the head of 'aggra- **21.90** vated damages'.[165] In *Rookes v Barnard* [166] aggravated damages were stressed to be compensatory—albeit compensating for mental distress—and not punitive. But the confusion between the two lingers on. This is not surprising since aggravated damages have traditionally only been awarded where the defendant's behaviour has been particularly reprehensible.[167] All confusion would be avoided by abandoning the label of 'aggravated damages' and by referring only to 'damages for mental distress' or 'damages for injured feelings'.[168]

Although damages for mental distress or loss of reputation are widely recoverable **21.91** for torts, there are exceptional torts for which only pecuniary loss—and not mental distress or loss of reputation—is recoverable. The clearest illustration is lawful means conspiracy.[169]

(b) Damages for personal injury

In practice, the commonest and most important area in which tort damages **21.92** have to be assessed is for personal injury, caused usually by the tort of negligence or breach of statutory duty.[170] The area of damages for personal injury has developed its own scheme of rules and principles, which we will now set out in some detail. But it must be remembered that this scheme is in line with the general principles set out above: in particular, the guiding aim is to compensate the claimant by putting him into as good a position as if the personal injury had not occurred.

---

165 eg for the torts of trespass to the person, malicious prosecution, and defamation. See, eg, *Walter v Alltools Ltd* (1944) 61 TLR 39, CA (false imprisonment); *Savile v Roberts* (1698) 1 Ld Raym 374 (malicious prosecution); *McCarey v Associated Newspapers Ltd* [1965] 2 QB 86, CA (libel).

166 [1964] AC 1129, HL. See also paras 21.160–21.163.

167 If follows that a court may combine aggravated damages with (ordinary) mental distress damages: see eg *Appleton v Garrett* [1996] PIQR P1; *Vento v Chief Constable of West Yorkshire Police (No 2)* [2002] EWCA Civ 1871; [2003] IRLR 102. For judicial criticism of this combination (because one is simply dealing with the one type of damages, namely mental distress damages) see *McConnell v Police Authority of Northern Ireland* [1997] IRLR 625, 629; *Gbaja-Biamila v DHL International (UK) Ltd* [2000] ICR 730 at [32].

168 This has been recommended by the Law Commission in its report on *Aggravated, Exemplary and Restitutionary Damages* (Law Com No 247, 1997), para 2.42. See also *Richardson v Howie* [2004] EWCA Civ 1127; [2005] PIQR Q3, where it was said, in an trespass to person case, that a court should not characterize as aggravated damages an award of damages for injury to feelings except possibly in a wholly exceptional case.

169 *Lonrho plc v Fayed (No 5)* [1994] 1 All ER 188, CA.

170 Although rare, a claim for personal injury and death can be founded on a breach of contract: see eg *Summers v Salford Corporation* [1943] AC 283, HL; *Matthews v Kuwait Bechtel Corporation* [1959] 2 QB 57, CA. If so, the same basic principles apply in respect of the assessment of damages for the personal injury and death as where the claim is brought in tort.

(i) Damages for pecuniary loss

21.93 **The different types of recoverable pecuniary loss.** The claimant is entitled to recover his loss of net earnings.[171] He can also recover all medical, nursing and hospital expenses which have been, or will be, reasonably incurred.[172] It follows that if the claimant does not, or will not, incur those expenses because he makes use of, or is likely to make use of, the NHS, he cannot recover what he would have been paid had he had private treatment.[173] So as not to overcompensate, ordinary living expenses saved are deducted from the cost of staying in a private hospital or home;[174] and by section 5 of the Administration of Justice Act 1982 any saving to the claimant, which is or will be attributable to his maintenance by the NHS, is to be set-off against his loss of earnings.[175] By section 2(4) of the Law Reform (Personal Injuries) Act 1948 the possibility that the claimant could have avoided expenses by using the facilities of the NHS is to be disregarded.

21.94 There is still a valid claim for nursing expenses even though they have been rendered gratuitously by a third party. In *Donnelly v Joyce*[176] this was rationalized as compensating the claimant's loss. But in *Hunt v Severs*[177] the House of Lords decided that it was unrealistic to regard the claimant as suffering any pecuniary loss. Rather it was the gratuitous carer who suffered the loss. The claimant was entitled to recover damages in respect of the gratuitous care but should hold them on trust for the carer. It followed, and this was the actual decision in the case, that where the nursing services were gratuitously rendered by the tortfeasor, no damages for that gratuitous care should be awarded. To award such damages would be circular; the defendant would be paying them only for the claimant to hold them on trust for the defendant.

---

[171] One deducts the tax (*British Transport Commission v Gourley* [1956] AC 185, HL) and national insurance contributions (*Cooper v Firth Brown Ltd* [1963] 1 WLR 418) that the claimant would have paid out of the gross earnings. The claimant may additionally (or alternatively) be awarded loss of earnings for being 'handicapped in the labour market': *Smith v Manchester Corpn* [1974] 17 KIR 1.

[172] See, eg, *Sowden v Lodge* [2004] EWCA Civ 1370; [2005] 1 All ER 581.

[173] *Cunningham v Harrison* [1973] QB 942, CA; *Lim Poh Choo v Camden and Islington Area Health Authority* [1980] AC 174, HL; *Woodrup v Nicol* [1993] PIQR Q104 CA. The same applies to social services provided free by a local authority: *Eagle v Chambers* [2004] EWCA Civ 1033; [2004] 1 WLR 3081.

[174] *Shearman v Folland* [1950] 2 KB 43, CA; *Lim Poh Choo v Camden and Islington Area Health Authority* [1980] AC 174, HL.

[175] The same approach was applied in *O'Brien v Independent Assessor* [2007] UKHL 10; [2007] 2 WLR 544 in the different context of the statutory compensation scheme for those whose convictions have been quashed for a miscarriage of justice: the saved cost of food, clothing and accommodation while in prison was held to be deductible from the compensation for loss of earnings.

[176] [1974] QB 454, CA.

[177] [1994] 2 AC 350, HL.

A claimant can also recover for loss of housekeeping capacity. In *Daly v General* **21.95**
Steam Navigation Co Ltd,[178] it was held that, while loss of housekeeping capacity
could be compensated for the future, even though a third party would gratuitously carry out the duties, it was only recoverable for the past either where the
claimant actually had employed someone or where a third party had given up
earnings so as to help gratuitously with the housekeeping. Otherwise the Court
of Appeal thought that the past loss of housekeeping capacity should be regarded
as a non-pecuniary loss, which was recoverable at least where the claimant had
struggled on with the housekeeping despite injury.

The claimant can also recover the cost of buying, fitting out and moving to special **21.96**
accommodation. But the capital cost of a new house, as opposed to the cost of the
capital, is not awarded since the claimant still has that capital in the form of the
house. In the leading case of *Roberts v Johnstone*[179] it was laid down that the claimant can recover 2 per cent per annum of the capital cost of the purchase as the cost
of the capital. More recently, in *Wells v Wells*[180] the House of Lords decided that
the appropriate interest rate is that on index-linked government stock (ILGS) and
for the time being that rate was regarded as being 3 per cent.[181]

Most other expenses and pecuniary losses consequent on the injury are recover- **21.97**
able, provided they are not too remote or do not infringe the duty to mitigate.
An exception is losses consequent on a divorce caused by the personal injury.[182]

Calculating damages for pecuniary loss. The calculation of damages for **21.98**
pre-trial pecuniary loss is relatively straightforward. It is essentially merely a question of adding together the expenses that the claimant has incurred; or multiply-
ing the claimant's pre-injury monthly earnings by the number of months during
which the claimant could not work. The latter calculation clearly depends upon
the assumption that, but for the injury, the claimant would have continued to
earn at the same rate. If this assumption is not justified (for example, because the
claimant would have been promoted and had higher earnings) an adjustment
must be made.

The calculation of damages for future pecuniary loss is more complex. Elements **21.99**
of uncertainty inevitably enter into the calculation, such as the claimant's life
expectancy, and what would have happened to the claimant had he not been
injured. The standard method of assessment (the so-called 'multiplier' method) is

---

178 [1979] 1 Lloyd's Rep 257, CA.
179 [1989] QB 878, CA.
180 [1999] 1 AC 345, HL.
181 The figure applied should now be 2.5 per cent as that is the discount rate fixed by the Lord
Chancellor: see para 21.100.
182 *Pritchard v JH Cobden Ltd* [1988] Fam 22, CA.

to multiply the assessed net annual loss by a multiplier.[183] The starting point for the multiplier is the number of years during which the loss is likely to endure and thus, typically, the remaining period that the claimant would have worked. This figure is then reduced to take account not only of the element of uncertainty (for example, would the claimant in any event have been unemployed or sick) but, more importantly for the fact that the claimant receives a lump sum which he can invest. The basis of the award is that the total sum will be exhausted at the end of the period contemplated and that during the period the claimant will draw upon both the income derived from the investment of the sum awarded and the capital.

21.100   The courts conventionally used multipliers based on a discount of about 4.5 per cent. But in *Wells v Wells*,[184] the House of Lords held that this was incorrect and that the claimant was entitled to be treated as risk-averse. It was therefore appropriate that the (relatively low) rate of interest on ILGS should be taken as the appropriate discount rate for calculating multipliers. At the time of the decision, the ILGS rate was 3 per cent (net of tax) and this was therefore laid down as the appropriate basis for multipliers for the time being. This meant that significantly higher multipliers would be used than where the discount rate was 4.5 per cent. Exercising his powers under section 1(1) of the Damages Act 1996, the Lord Chancellor has since set a discount rate of 2.5 per cent.[185] Although by section 1(2) of the Damages Act 1996, a court may apply a different rate from that set if it is 'more appropriate in the case in question', the Court of Appeal has shown no willingness to depart from the 2.5 per cent rate.[186]

21.101   One should also note that, despite earlier judicial reluctance to take account of actuarial evidence, it was laid down in *Wells v Wells* that it is appropriate in working out the correct multiplier to make use of the Ogden actuarial tables.[187]

21.102   As the calculation is now being based on ILGS, this neatly takes account of future inflation.[188] It also follows that the costs of investment advice are irrecoverable: the assumed ILGS investment is straightforward and does not require the sort

---

[183] Sometimes, especially where fixing a multiplicand is difficult, the courts will estimate future pecuniary loss by roughly assessing a general global figure: see, eg, *Joyce v Yeomans* [1981] 1 WLR 549, CA.

[184] [1999] 1 AC 345, HL.

[185] Damages (Personal Injury) Order 2001, SI 2001/2301.

[186] *Warriner v Warriner* [2002] EWCA Civ 81, [2002] 1 WLR 1703; *Cooke v United Bristol Health Care* [2003] EWCA Civ 1370, [2004] 1 WLR 251.

[187] *Actuarial Tables for Use in Personal Injury and Fatal Accident Cases* (6th edn, 2007). These are produced by a working party of lawyers and actuaries. The first chairman was the late Sir Michael Ogden QC.

[188] Prior to reliance on ILGS, the courts ruled that no adjustment should be made for future inflation: *Cookson v Knowles* [1979] AC 556, HL: *Lim Poh Choo v Camden and Islington Area Health Authority* [1980] AC 174, HL.

of advice that investing in gilts and equities would do.[189] The standard multipliers assume that standard rate tax will be paid on the investment income but, according to *Hodgson v Trapp*,[190] no further uplift of the multiplier is normally appropriate to account for any higher rate tax that the claimant has to pay.

Where the injury has reduced the claimant's life expectancy, the multiplier is **21.103** calculated according to his life expectancy prior to the injury, with a deduction for the living expenses which he would have incurred during the 'lost years' that he will no longer live through. That damages can be recovered for the 'lost years' was laid down in *Pickett v British Rail Engineering Ltd.*[191] The living expenses deducted are what the claimant spent on maintaining himself at the standard of living appropriate to his case and includes a pro-rata amount of his family expenditure on, for example, housing, heating and lighting.

(ii) Damages for non-pecuniary loss

In addition to the claimant's pecuniary losses which, at least in theory, can be **21.104** mathematically assessed, the claimant is entitled to damages for his non-pecuniary loss. That is, he is entitled to damages for the pain and suffering and loss of amenity[192] consequent on the injury. The amount of damages is awarded in accordance with a tariff system whereby the courts are guided by awards made in past cases for similar personal injuries. This system has traditionally depended on the publication (in, for example, Kemp and Kemp, *The Quantum of Damages*) of judicial awards listed under the different types of personal injury (such as deafness, loss of thumb, loss of leg, quadriplegia) with brief details of the claimant's circumstances. The tariff or bracket of damages for that injury will provide the basic range of award in the instant case; but it will be adjusted flexibly by the judge to take account of the claimant's particular circumstances. For example, the injury may have been accompanied by a great deal of pain in one case but not so in another. There may also be particular deprivations brought about by the injury. For example, the claimant who has lost a hand may have been a pianist. The loss of amenity aspect of the award is assessed objectively in the sense that it is made irrespective of the claimant's own appreciation of his condition; in contrast, pain and suffering is subjectively assessed so that if the claimant is not capable of experiencing the pain or suffering no damages should be awarded for them.[193]

---

[189] *Page v Plymouth Hospital NHS Trust* [2004] EWHC 1154; [2004] 3 All ER 367; *Eagle v Chambers* [2004] EWCA Civ 1033; [2004] 1 WLR 3081.
[190] [1989] AC 807, HL.
[191] [1980] AC 136, HL.
[192] ie loss of enjoyment of life.
[193] *Wise v Kaye* [1962] 1 QB 638, CA; *West v Shepherd* [1964] AC 326, HL; *Lim Poh Choo v Camden and Islington Area HA* [1980] AC 174, HL.

21.105 In an attempt to produce greater consistency of awards, and in generally seeking to make the judicial tariff of values more accessible, the Judicial Studies Board in 1992 produced *Guidelines for the Assessment of General Damages in Personal Injury Cases*. The eighth edition of the *Guidelines* was published in 2006. They set out, in easily understood form, the range of awards for various injuries. At at June 2006, the range runs from less than £100 for minor cuts and bruises through to about £235,000 for the most serious injuries.[194] The courts have laid down that past awards must be uplifted for inflation by taking into account changes in the retail prices index since the past award was made.[195]

(iii) Compensating advantages

21.106 What happens where, as a result of the injury, the victim receives benefits from other sources (often referred to as collateral benefits)? For example, he may receive sick pay or charitable payments or payments from a personal accident insurance policy or social security benefits. Adherence to the compensatory principle would suggest that, provided the benefit is not too indirectly related to the injury, it should be deducted. But it is clear that English law does not rigidly apply the compensatory principle in this regard. Rather some collateral benefits are deducted and others are not. In particular, while sick pay is deducted,[196] the proceeds of an accident insurance policy,[197] sums received under a disability pension,[198] and charitable payments[199] are not deducted.

21.107 In respect of social security benefits the law is now largely contained in the Social Security (Recovery of Benefits) Act 1997.[200] This basically lays down that social security benefits paid, as a result of the injury, or likely to be so paid, for a maximum period of five years from the accident[201] are to be deducted but that the state (through the Compensation Recovery Unit) is entitled to recoup the

---

194 In *Heil v Rankin* [2001] QB 272, CA, awards for more serious injuries were increased because they had fallen behind what was considered fair, just and reasonable.

195 *Wright v British Railways Board* [1983] 2 AC 773, HL; *Heil v Rankin* [2001] QB 272, CA.

196 *Hussain v New Taplow Paper Mills Ltd* [1988] AC 514, HL.

197 *Bradburn v Great Western Railway Co* (1874) LR 10 Exch 1.

198 *Parry v Cleaver* [1970] AC 1, HL; *Smoker v London Fire and Civil Defence Authority* [1991] 2 AC 502, HL.

199 *Redpath v Belfast and County Down Rly* [1947] NI 167. But the policy of not discouraging benevolence means that gratuitous payments made by the tortfeasor will be deducted: *Gaca v Pirelli General plc* [2004] EWCA Civ; [2004] 1 WLR 2683.

200 The common law position, which applies to state benefits not covered by the 1997 Act, is that state benefits should be deducted: *Hodgson v Trapp* [1989] AC 807, H; *Clenshaw v Tanner* [2002] EWCA Civ 1848.

201 Benefits after the five years are to be ignored: see ss 3 and 17 of the 1997 Act.

amount of the benefits paid from the tortfeasor. However, there is to be no deduction from damages awarded for non-pecuniary loss.[202]

(iv) Interest

Simple interest on damages for personal injury and death (exceeding £200) must be awarded (unless there are special reasons for it not to be).[203] It was laid down in *Jefford v Gee*[204] that, for the purposes of interest, personal injury awards must be itemized into non-pecuniary loss, pre-trial pecuniary loss, and future pecuniary loss. As regards non-pecuniary loss, interest on damages is awarded at the rate of 2 per cent[205] from the date of service of the writ to the date of trial.[206] Interest on pre-trial pecuniary loss awards is normally payable from the date of the accident until trial on the full sum awarded and the normal rate is half the average rate on the special account over that period.[207] No interest is payable on damages for future pecuniary loss.[208]

21.108

(v) Provisional damages

By section 32A of the Supreme Court Act 1981, and the accompanying rules of court, the courts have power to award provisional damages in actions 'for damages for personal injuries in which there is proved or admitted to be a chance that at some definite or indefinite time in the future the injured person will, as a result of the act or omission which gave rise to the cause of action, develop some serious disease or suffer some serious deterioration in his physical or mental condition'. In such a case the court is able to assess the damages on the assumption that the injured person will not develop the disease or suffer deterioration but can then award further damages at a future date if the risk should in fact materialize. However, the power can only be used if the claimant has pleaded a claim for provisional damages. The order for an award of provisional damages must specify

21.109

---

[202] By s 8 of, and Sch 2 to, the 1997 Act, recoupment shall only be against compensation for loss of earnings, cost of care and loss of mobility, and then only 'like for like'. The tortfeasor is therefore being held liable for the pure economic loss caused to the state by the tort. See analogously the right of hospital authorities to charge the costs of treatment to tortfeasors under the Health and Social Care (Community Health and Standards) Act 2003, Part 3.

[203] Supreme Court Act 1981, s 35A(2); County Courts Act 1984, s 69(2).

[204] [1970] 2 QB 130.

[205] After *Wells v Wells* [1999] 1 AC 345, HL, one might have thought that the appropriate rate should be the ILGS rate. But this argument was rejected in *Lawrence v Chief Constable of Staffordshire* [2000] PIQR Q349, CA.

[206] *Wright v British Railways Board* [1983] 2 AC 773.

[207] *Jefford v Gee* [1970] 2 QB 130, CA; *Cookson v Knowles* [1979] AC 556, HL. Half-rate on the full sum is a rough-and-ready substitute for calculating the full average rate on each loss from when it occurred until trial. In exceptional cases, a more precise calculation is appropriate: see, eg, *Dexter v Courtaulds Ltd* [1984] 1 WLR 372, CA. The special account (sometimes referred to as the special investment account) is an investment account used for court funds.

[208] *Jefford v Gee* [1970] 2 QB 130, CA.

the disease or type of deterioration in respect of which an application may be made at a future date and will normally specify the period within which such application may be made, although the period may be extended on an application by the claimant. Only one application for further damages may be made in respect of each disease or type of deterioration specified in the order for the award of provisional damages.

21.110 The introduction of provisional damages marked an important theoretical break with the once-and-for-all lump sum system. However, they represented only a small departure from the traditional approach and are different from (reviewable) periodical payments. In practice, most claimants do not claim provisional damages. That is, they choose to forgo the possibility of higher damages in the long term, by taking what at trial is a higher award under the traditional once-and-for-all approach.

(vi) (Reviewable) periodical payments

21.111 On April 1, 2005 a fundamental departure from lump sums was introduced by the Courts Act 2003, sections 100–101 (amending the Damages Act 1996), the Damages (Variation of Periodical Payments) Order 2005[209] and accompanying Civil Procedure Rules.[210] In the case of damages for future pecuniary loss in respect of personal injury or death, the courts are empowered (and are required to consider whether) to make an order that the damages are to take the form of periodical payments.[211] Moreover, the periodical payments order may be made variable so that it can be reviewed by the courts.[212] These provisions, therefore, give the courts, for the first time, the power to order (reviewable) periodical payments. It is clear that a particularly influential 'political' factor behind the introduction of the new regime was that, in respect of litigation against the National Health Service, periodical payments are more attractive to the NHS (at least in the short term) than having to find large capital sums.[213] However, before such an order can be made, a court has to be satisfied that the continuity of payment is reasonably secure.[214] Other than in respect of public sector defendants, this will essentially be so where the defendant's insurer purchases an annuity.[215]

---

[209] SI 2005/841.

[210] CPR, r 41.4–41.10.

[211] Damages Act 1996, s 2(1), as substituted by the Courts Act 2003, s 100.

[212] Damages Act 1996, s 2B, as substituted by the Courts Act 2003, s 100; and Damages (Variation of Periodical Payments) Order 2005.

[213] The Explanatory Notes to the Act make this clear.

[214] Damages Act 1996, s 2(3).

[215] The new system therefore builds on and absorbs the 'structured settlement' which was introduced in the 1980s as a consequence of the acceptance by the Inland Revenue that, if the defendant's insurer purchased an annuity for the claimant, payments received were tax free. But structured settlements could not be imposed by the courts.

Protection for claimants in the event of an insurer's insolvency or a public body's non-existence is provided by the Damages Act 1996, sections 4 and 6, as amended by the Courts Act 2003, section 101. By section 2(8) periodical payments are to be updated by reference to the retail prices index although this can be modified under section 2(9). It has been decided that section 2(9) allows a different index than the RPI to be applied.[216] The reviewability provisions closely match those on 'provisional damages'. The original court can make a variable order but only to deal with the development of some serious disease or the suffering of some serious deterioration or significant improvement in the claimant's condition. Moreover, only one application to vary a variable order can be made in respect of each specified disease or type of deterioration or improvement.

(vii) Claims by the deceased's estate

The Law Reform (Miscellaneous Provisions) Act 1934, section 1(1) provides **21.112** that, on the death of any person, causes of action vested in him, subject to certain exceptions,[217] survive for the benefit of his estate.[218] The most important consequence of this is that the deceased's action for personal injury survives for the benefit of his estate.

Thus the deceased's personal representatives will be awarded damages for all **21.113** the deceased's recoverable loss, both non-pecuniary[219] and pecuniary,[220] but only until the time of the death, applying the normal principle that all events known about at trial are taken into account.

In one respect, however, the principles governing compensatory damages for **21.114** the deceased's estate differ from those governing the injured claimant's damages. By section 4(2) of the Administration of Justice Act 1982, amending section 1(2) of the Law Reform (Miscellaneous Provisions) Act 1934, no damages may be awarded for lost income in respect of any period after the death of the injured person; that is, the claim for loss of earnings in the 'lost years'[221] does not survive for the benefit of the estate.

---

[216] *Flora v Wakom (Heathrow) Ltd* [2006] EWCA Civ 1103; [2007] 1 WLR 482; *Thompstone v Tameside and Glossop Acute Services NHS Trust* [2006] EWHC 2833 (QB) (the Annual Survey of Hours and Earnings ('ASHE' 6115) was used for updating future care costs).

[217] ie actions for defamation, bereavement damages, and exemplary damages.

[218] By section 1(2)(c) of the 1934 Act, where the defendant was responsible for the death, damages may be awarded to the estate for funeral expenses incurred: plainly this is distinct from the survival of the deceased's cause of action.

[219] See *Rose v Ford* [1937] AC 826, HL; *Andrews v Freeborough* [1967] 1 QB 1, CA; *Murray v Shuter* [1976] QB 972, CA.

[220] *Murray v Shuter* [1976] QB 972 (deceased's loss of earnings); *Rose v Ford* [1937] AC 826 (deceased's medical expenses).

[221] See para 21.103.

(c) Damages for death: Fatal Accidents Act 1976

21.115 At common law no action could be brought for loss suffered through the killing of another. This was altered by the Fatal Accidents Act 1846. The governing statute is now the Fatal Accidents Act 1976. This gives a statutory action '. . .if death is caused by any wrongful act, neglect or default. . .'.[222]

(i) Actionability by injured person

21.116 By section 1(1) of the 1976 Act, an action can only succeed if the wrongful act, neglect or default which caused the death 'is such as would (if death had not ensued) have entitled the person injured to maintain an action and recover damages in respect thereof'. Therefore if the deceased was killed entirely through his own fault, or if the defendant had validly excluded all liability to the deceased, or if the deceased's action had become time-barred before his death, or if the deceased had settled his claim or obtained judgment against the defendant, the dependants will have no action.

21.117 By section 5 of the 1976 Act, where the deceased was contributorily negligent in relation to his death, and hence his damages would have been reduced by a certain amount under the Law Reform (Contributory) Negligence Act 1945, the damages recoverable by the dependants under the 1976 Act are to be reduced to a proportionate extent.[223]

(ii) Loss of dependency

21.118 Damages are primarily awarded under the 1976 Act to dependants for the loss of their expected non-business pecuniary benefits consequent on the death. This most obviously covers loss of support from the deceased's earnings. It also covers loss of 'services'; for example, a husband will be awarded damages in respect of his wife's housekeeping in the home;[224] children will be compensated for the loss of their mother's daily care and work on their behalf;[225] and a wife and children will be compensated for the loss of a husband's and father's services as a handyman around the house.[226]

21.119 As laid down in section 1(2), the action under the 1976 Act is for the benefit of the dependants of the deceased (subject to a narrower restriction on who can be

---

[222] Normally such statutory actions are founded on a tort by the defendant. But the basis may be breach of contract: *Grein v Imperial Airways Ltd* [1937] 1 KB 50.

[223] In accordance with normal principle, under the Law Reform (Contributory Negligence) Act 1945, a dependant's contributory negligence in relation to the death will reduce that dependant's damages for pecuniary loss: see *Mulholland v McCrea* [1961] NI 135.

[224] *Berry v Humm & Co* [1915] 1 KB 627.

[225] *Hay v Hughes* [1975] QB 790, CA; *Spittle v Bunney* [1988] 1 WLR 847; *Stanley v Saddique* [1992] QB 1, CA.

[226] *Clay v Pooler* [1982] 3 All ER 570.

awarded bereavement damages).[227] The meaning of 'dependant' is laid down in a list (the present list being an extension of previous lists). By section 1(3) the list now comprises the spouse or former spouse of the deceased, including a person whose marriage has been annulled or declared void; a civil partner or former civil partner of the deceased; any person who was living as the husband or wife or civil partner of the deceased in the same household immediately before the date of the death and has been so living for at least two years before the death; any parent or ascendant of the deceased; any person who was treated by the deceased as his parent; any child or other descendant of the deceased; any person who has been treated by the deceased as a child of the family in relation to any marriage or civil partnership of the deceased; and any person who is, or is the issue of, a brother, sister, uncle or aunt of the deceased. A relationship by marriage or civil partnership is treated as a relationship by consanguinity, a relationship of the half-blood as a relationship of the whole blood and the stepchild of any person as his child. An illegitimate person is to be treated as a child of his mother and reputed father.

21.120 Although the list of dependants is now a wide one, it is still capable of causing hardship, which calls into question the need for a restriction beyond financial dependency. For example, a financially dependent friend and companion of the deceased remains excluded.

21.121 As with damages for future pecuniary loss consequent on a personal injury, damages for loss of a pecuniary benefit under the 1976 Act are calculated using a multiplier method. However, in the context of fatal accident claims, in contrast to personal injury claims, the multiplier is used to assess all the pecuniary loss from the date of death and not merely the post-trial pecuniary loss. In *Cookson v Knowles*[228] the House of Lords laid down that the dependant's pecuniary loss prior to trial should be assessed separately from that after the trial. This is essentially because the former is less speculative and because no interest is to be paid on the future loss but is payable on the pre-trial loss. In *Graham v Dodds*[229] it was clarified that that itemization does not entail that the multiplier method should be abandoned for pre-trial loss. Rather the multiplier should continue to be calculated from the date of death, rather than from the date of trial, on the basis that, in contrast to a personal injury case, there can be no certainty even that the deceased would have survived until trial. So if, for example, the multiplier is 14, and 4 years have elapsed between death and trial, the pre-trial loss will be calculated using a multiplier of 4 and the post-trial loss will be calculated using a multiplier of 10. But a separate pre-trial and post-trial multiplicand is generally appropriate to take account of facts known at trial (for example, the rate of wages for the job that

---

[227] See para 21.128.
[228] [1979] AC 556, HL.
[229] [1983] 1 WLR 808, HL.

the deceased had). The multiplicands will be the pre-trial and post-trial annual pecuniary loss to the dependant calculated by, for example, deducting from the deceased's notional annual net earnings his living expenses; and living expenses here means expenses for the deceased's own purposes exclusively.[230] There will then be an adjustment to take account, for example, of the prospects of promotion that the deceased had.

21.122 It is strongly arguable that it would be more accurate to calculate multipliers for post-trial pecuniary loss from the date of death with pre-trial loss being calculated in much the same straightforward way as in personal injury cases (with the qualification that there would need to be a general discount for the uncertainty as to whether the deceased would have lived to trial). The difficulties of the present approach are illustrated by *Corbett v Barking, Havering & Brentwood HA*,[231] where there had been a long delay between death and trial (11½ years). Controversially, the Court of Appeal (Ralph Gibson LJ dissenting) held that it did not contradict *Graham v Dodds* to increase the normal multiplier, calculated from the date of the death, to take into account the known fact that the child dependant had survived to the age of 11½. In *White v ESAB Group (UK) Ltd*[232] Nelson J, in the light of the views of the Law Commission and the Ogden Working Party, would have preferred to calculate the multiplier from the date of trial, but held himself precluded from doing so by *Cookson v Knowles* and *Graham v Dodds*. In his view, those decisions had not been expressly or impliedly overruled by *Wells v Wells*. The decision in the *Corbett* case was held not to be applicable since, in contrast to that case, there were, in this case, no unusual significant facts that had arisen between the date of death and the trial. In *H v S*[233] the Court of Appeal approved Nelson J's refusal to depart from the traditional 'date of death' approach.

21.123 The starting point for the multiplier is the estimated number of years (taking into account, for example, the deceased's and dependant's life expectancies) from the date of death that the dependant would have received the pecuniary benefits. The starting figure is then discounted by 2.5 per cent because the dependant receives a capital sum now, which he can invest, rather than periodical payments over the years. There may then be a small adjustment for the contingencies of life other than mortality (such as the deceased's possible unemployment). The basis of the award is that the total sum will be exhausted at the end of the period contemplated and that during the period the dependant will draw upon both the income derived from the investment of the sum awarded and the capital itself.

---

[230] Contrast the living expenses deducted in calculating the injured person's 'lost years' damages: see para 21.103.
[231] [1991] 2 QB 408.
[232] [2002] PIQR Q6.
[233] [2002] EWCA Civ 792; [2003] QB 965, at [36].

In calculating the dependant's loss of pecuniary benefit the court must make **21.124** its best estimate of the future. However, by section 3(3) of the Fatal Accidents Act 1976, in assessing a widow's claim in respect of her husband's death, 'there shall not be taken into account the remarriage of the widow or her prospects of remarriage'. Parliament introduced this provision primarily to put a stop to the degrading judicial 'guessing game' of assessing a widow's prospects of remarriage. But this is at the expense of not deducting what is a direct compensating advantage and the effect can be that, for example, a widow who marries a very wealthy husband, even prior to trial, is still entitled to damages in respect of her dependency on her former husband. It should also be noted that section 3(3) applies only to a widow's claim and therefore a mother's remarriage or prospects of remarriage must still be taken into account in assessing a child's claim. Similarly, where the claim is brought by a cohabitee her marriage or prospects of marriage are to be taken into account. Also outside the scope of section 3(3) is a widower's remarriage or prospects of remarriage which therefore are relevant in assessing damages.

By section 4 of the 1976 Act, 'in assessing damages in respect of a person's **21.125** death in an action under this Act, the benefits which have accrued or will or may accrue to any person from his estate or otherwise as a result of his death shall be disregarded'. So, for example, charitable payments, payments under a life assurance policy, a widow's pension, and social security benefits are not to be deducted in assessing damages under the 1976 Act. The width of section 4 is a cause of uncertainty[234] although, as regards gratuitous care provided to the dependant consequent on the death, the law has been made more rational by the application to a Fatal Accidents Act case in *H v S*[235] of the approach in *Hunt v Severs*[236] (the leading personal injury case on gratuitous services). Infant children, following the death of their mother, were receiving care from their father, who was not the tortfeasor and had not previously provided them with any care or support. Although under section 4 of the Fatal Accidents Act 1976 the value of such gratuitous services was not to be deducted, the damages in respect of the lost services of the deceased mother were to be held on trust for the gratuitous carer (the father).

It should be emphasized that the 1976 Act is concerned only to compensate **21.126** dependants for non-business pecuniary benefits consequent on the death. Benefits flowing from the business relationship between the dependant and the deceased

---

[234] See eg the contrast between the decisions in *Stanley v Saddique* [1992] QB 1, CA; and *Hayden v Hayden* [1992] 1 WLR 986, CA. See also *R v Criminal Injuries Compensation Board, ex p K* [1999] 2 WLR 948.

[235] [2002] EWCA Civ 792; [2003] QB 965.

[236] [1994] 2 AC 350, HL: see para 21.94.

are irrecoverable. For example, *in Burgess v Florence Nightingale Hospital For Gentlewomen*[237] it was held that a husband could not recover damages for his loss of income as a dancer resulting from the death of his dancing partner wife.

21.127 Although not a loss of pecuniary benefit, but rather an expense necessary as a consequence of the death, section 3(5) of the 1976 Act lays down that funeral expenses incurred by dependants in respect of the deceased are recoverable.

(iii) Bereavement damages

21.128 By section 1A of the 1976 Act damages are to be awarded for the mental distress (that is the sorrow, grief and loss of enjoyment) consequent on the death. Called 'damages for bereavement', a fixed sum, at present £10,000,[238] can be claimed for the benefit of the spouse of the deceased or, where the deceased was a minor who was never married or a civil partner, the parents of the deceased (or, if the child was illegitimate, his mother). By section 1A(4) if both parents claim bereavement damages, the fixed sum is to be divided equally between them.

(iv) Relationship between actions under the Law Reform (Miscellaneous Provisions) Act 1934 and the Fatal Accidents Act 1976

21.129 Where the defendant's wrong has caused a death, an action may be brought under both the Law Reform (Miscellaneous Provisions) Act 1934 and the Fatal Accidents Act 1976. Where the death is not instantaneous, the survival action enables recovery, on behalf of the estate, of damages for the deceased's pre-death losses both pecuniary and non-pecuniary, while the Fatal Accidents Act action enables dependants to recover for their loss of dependency and a spouse or parent to recover damages for bereavement. Funeral expenses may be recovered in either action (although clearly they will not be awarded twice over). On the other hand, where the death is instantaneous, and there has been no property damage, no damages can now be recovered under the 1934 Act, other than where the estate has incurred the funeral expenses.[239]

(3) Equitable Compensation

21.130 Although, until recently, there has been surprisingly little examination of it, a major remedy for equitable wrongs—of which the prime example is breach of

---

[237] [1955] 1 QB 349.

[238] The Lord Chancellor's power to alter the amount, so far exercised twice, is conferred by section 1A(5) of the 1976 Act.

[239] Formerly a claim for loss of earnings in the 'lost years' survived for the benefit of the estate, but this is no longer so: see para 21.114.

fiduciary duty—is equitable compensation.[240] This is a monetary personal remedy the purpose of which is to compensate the claimant. Although sometimes referred to as 'accounting for loss' (or, very misleadingly, 'restitution') this contrasts with 'accounting for profits' which is the other main monetary remedy for equitable wrongs.[241] Accounting for profits is concerned to effect restitution, whereas equitable compensation is concerned to effect compensation.[242] Equitable compensation therefore equates to (common law) compensatory damages; and a topical question is the extent to which, if at all, the principles governing equitable compensation differ from those applicable to (common law) compensatory damages.[243]

The courts have recently recognized that, in general terms, there is little difference   **21.131** between equitable compensation and compensatory damages. In particular, the House of Lords in *Target Holdings Ltd v Redfern*[244] rejected the argument that a breach of trust required loss to the trust to be restored even though that loss would have been suffered even if there had been no breach of duty.[245] In other words, it was accepted that equitable compensation will not be awarded unless loss has

---

[240] eg *Re Dawson* [1966] 2 NSWR 211; *Bartlett v Barclays Bank Trust Co (No 2)* [1980] Ch 515; *Target Holdings Ltd v Redfern* [1996] AC 421, HL; *Bristol & West Building Society v Mothew* [1998] Ch 1, CA; *Swindle v Harrison* [1997] 4 All ER 705, CA; I Davidson, 'The Equitable Remedy of Compensation' (1982) 13 Melbourne UL Rev 349. For equitable compensation for dishonestly assisting a breach of fiduciary duty, see *Twinsectra v Yardley* [2002] UKHL 12; [2002] 2 AC 164; *Barlow Clowes International Ltd v Eurotrust International* Ltd [2005] UKPC 37; [2006] 1 WLR 1476. Monetary compensation, best viewed as the remedy of equitable compensation, has been awarded under the doctrine of proprietary estoppel: *Dodsworth v Dodsworth* (1973) 228 EG 1115 (the compensation was 'secured' by giving the claimant possession of the land until payment by the defendant); *Baker & Baker v Baker* (1993) 25 Housing LR 408, CA; *Gillett v Holt* [2001] Ch 210, CA; *Jennings v Rice* [2002] EWCA Civ 159; [2003] 1 P & CR 8; cf *Hussey v Palmer* [1972] 1 WLR 1286. There appears to be no English case in which equitable compensation has been awarded for breach of confidence. It was suggested in *Mahoney v Purnell* [1996] 3 All ER 61 that rescission plus equitable compensation could be awarded for undue influence. But undue influence is not a wrong and the better view is that it triggers rescission and restitution not compensation: see P Birks, 'Unjust Factors and Wrongs: Pecuniary Rescission for Undue Influence' [1997] Restitution Law Review 72.

[241] See paras 21.153–21.155.

[242] See para 21.160 for consideration of whether equitable compensation can ever be awarded to punish the equitable wrongdoer.

[243] Equitable damages—awarded in substitution for an injunction or specific performance—can be awarded for equitable wrongs just as they can for common law wrongs: see paras 21.135–21.139.

[244] [1996] AC 421, HL.

[245] See also *Gwembe Valley Development Co Ltd v Koshy* [2003] EWCA Civ 1048; [2004] 1 BCLC 131 at [142]–[160] (no loss caused by breach of fiduciary duty by director and therefore no equitable compensation could be awarded). For criticism of this approach, on the ground that the trustee's liability was to account for the course of his trusteeship and that the account remedy is analogous to an action in debt which should not be equated to compensation, see P Millett, 'Equity's Place in the Law of Commerce' (1998) 114 LQR 214, 224–7; S Elliott and C Mitchell, 'Remedies for Dishonest Assistance' (2004) 67 MLR 16, 23–36; C Mitchell, 'Equitable Rights and Wrongs' (2006) 59 CLP 267.

been factually caused (applying a 'but for' test) by the breach of duty. On the other hand, Lord Browne-Wilkinson, giving the leading speech, said that the common law rules of remoteness of damage and legal causation do not apply to equitable compensation.[246] But it is not obvious that this is correct, particularly given the flexibility of the common law rules relating to legal causation and remoteness. So, for example, Lord Browne-Wilkinson seemed to have it in mind that a contrast with the common law position was shown where the immediate cause of the loss was the dishonesty or failure of a third party. In that situation, the trustee would still be liable to compensate the trust estate if loss was factually caused by the breach of duty. However, the same might be true at common law in respect of the tort of negligence if the purpose of the duty of care was to guard against the very risk of third party intervention that has occurred. Moreover, it is clear that at common law the test of remoteness is wider (and does not require the loss to have been reasonably foreseen) in respect of the tort of deceit than in respect of the tort of negligent misrepresentation.[247] And it has long been open to question whether the normal foreseeability test of remoteness applies to torts of strict liability.

21.132 In *Bristol & West Building Society v Mothew*[248] Millett LJ argued that one could assimilate equitable compensation and damages in respect of breach of an equitable duty of skill and care. He said:

> Although the remedy which equity makes available for breach of the equitable duty of skill and care is equitable compensation rather than damages, this is merely the product of history and in this context is in my opinion a distinction without a difference. Equitable compensation for breach of the duty of skill and care resembles common law damages in that it is awarded by way of compensation to the plaintiff for his loss. There is no reason in principle why the common law rules of causation, remoteness of damage and measure of damages should not be applied by analogy in such a case.[249]

21.133 On the other hand, Millett LJ, more controversially, went on to say that the same assimilation could not be made in respect of other types of breach of fiduciary duty. 'This leaves those duties which are special to fiduciaries and attract those remedies which are peculiar to the equitable jurisdiction and are primarily restitutionary or restorative rather than compensatory.'[250]

---

[246] See also *Swindle v Harrison* [1997] 4 All ER 705 (*per* Mummery LJ).

[247] See para 21.80. For the drawing of an analogy between the remoteness rules for deceit and the remoteness rules for equitable compensation using, in relation to the latter, a general concept of equitable fraud, see *Canson Enterprises Ltd v Boughton* [1991] 3 SCR 534; cf *Swindle v Harrison* [1997] 4 All ER 705 (*per* Evans LJ).

[248] [1998] Ch 1, CA.

[249] [1998] Ch 1, 17. See also *Bank of New Zealand v New Zealand Guardian Trust Co Ltd* [1999] 1 NZLR 664.

[250] [1998] Ch 1, 18.

Apart from the controversy over the applicability of causation and remoteness to **21.134** equitable compensation, there is some doubt whether contributory negligence applies where equitable compensation is being claimed.[251] But again, even if often not applicable, this is not necessarily different from the position at common law where contributory negligence is not a defence to the tort of deceit or, it would seem, other intentional torts.[252]

(4) Equitable (Compensatory) Damages

By section 50 of the Supreme Court Act 1981, where the High Court 'has juris- **21.135** diction to entertain an application for an injunction or specific performance, it may award damages in addition to, or in substitution for, an injunction or specific performance'. This power was formerly contained in section 2 of the Chancery Amendment Act 1858 (Lord Cairns's Act).

As regards additional damages, the power is self-explanatory. But, for the purpose **21.136** of 'damages in substitution for an injunction or specific performance', there has been some difficulty in deciding what is meant by the court having 'jurisdiction to entertain an application for an injunction or specific performance'. The tradi- tional approach has been to decide whether the particular reason for denying spe- cific performance or the injunction is jurisdictional or discretionary and only if it is the latter can damages in substitution be awarded.[253] A simpler and preferable approach, and one which could equally well justify past decisions, is to ask whether the claimant had an arguable case for specific performance or an injunction at the time the claim was brought; if so, equitable damages in substitution can be awarded. It should also be noted that, as laid down in *Horsler v Zorro*,[254] section 50 does not allow the award of equitable damages in substitution in the unusual case where the claimant would have been granted specific performance or an injunction had he claimed it but he has made no such claim because what he wants is damages in substitution.

Why should a claimant want equitable damages rather than normal common law **21.137** damages? After all, section 49 of the Supreme Court Act 1981 allows the claimant to combine a claim for common law damages with an action for specific perform- ance or an injunction. Moreover, it was clearly laid down in *Johnson v Agnew*[255]

---

[251] See *Day v Mead* [1987] 2 NZLR 443. Cf *Pilmer v The Duke Group Ltd* (2001) 75 AJLR 1067, High Court of Australia.

[252] See para 21.88. In *Corporacion Nacional del Cobre de Chile v Sogemin Metals Ltd* [1997] 1 WLR 1396 contributory negligence was held to be inapplicable to various dishonestly committed wrongs, whether common law or equitable: see n 161.

[253] *Price v Strange* [1978] Ch 337.

[254] [1975] Ch 302.

[255] [1980] AC 367, HL.

that the assessment of equitable damages is no different from that for normal common law damages. The normal measure of equitable damages will therefore be compensatory and they will be assessed in the same way as common law compensatory damages.

21.138 But there is one major advantage of equitable damages. This is that they may be awarded even though there is no cause of action at common law and hence no possible award of common law damages. In particular this means that damages can be awarded in addition to, or in substitution for, a '*quia timet*' injunction, which is an injunction to prevent a threatened wrong where no wrong has yet been committed.[256] For example, in *Leeds Industrial Co-operative Society Ltd v Slack*[257] damages were held recoverable in substitution for a quia timet injunction to prevent the defendant constructing buildings which, when complete, would have obstructed the claimant's ancient lights but as yet were causing no obstruction. Similarly, in respect of continuing torts or a continuing breach of contract equitable damages in substitution for an ordinary (ie not a *quia timet*) injunction are more advantageous than common law damages in compensating for an antici-pated rather than just an accrued cause of action.[258] Common law damages, in contrast, compensate only for loss (whether past or prospective) caused by a tort or breach of contract that has already been committed.

21.139 Three other illustrations may be given of the application of this major advantage offered by equitable damages. First, a third party can be awarded damages in addi-tion to or in substitution for an injunction, available under the principle laid down in *Tulk v Moxhay*[259] for the breach of a restrictive covenant concerning land, although he would have no cause of action at common law because of the doctrine of privity of contract. Secondly, equitable damages can be awarded for an antici-patory breach of contract that has not been accepted because specific performance can be awarded for such a breach even though there is no cause of action at com-mon law.[260] Thirdly, while common law damages cannot yet be awarded for breach of confidence, because that is still regarded as an equitable wrong and not a tort,[261] equitable damages can be:[262] presumably the same also applies in respect of other equitable wrongs, such as breach of fiduciary duty.

---

256 See para 21.199.

257 [1924] AC 851, HL.

258 See eg *Bracewell v Appleby* [1975] Ch 408 and *Jaggard v Sawyer* [1995] 1 WLR 269, CA (damages in substitution for an injunction to prevent the defendant continuing to trespass over the claimant's land).

259 (1848) 18 LJ Ch 83.

260 *Oakacre Ltd v Claire Cleaners (Holdings) Ltd* [1982] Ch 197.

261 *Douglas v Hello! Ltd (No 3)* [2005] EWCA Civ 595; [2006] QB 125 at [96]. Cf *Ash v McKennitt* [2006] EWCA Civ 1714 at [8].

262 *Saltman Engineering Co Ltd v Campbell Engineering Ltd* (1948) 65 Reports of Patents Cases 203, CA; *Seager v Copydex Ltd* [1967] 1 WLR 923, CA. In *Campbell v MGN Ltd* [2004] UKHL 22,

C. Restitution and Punishment

This section examines exceptional monetary remedies for wrongs that are con- **21.140**
cerned not to compensate the innocent party but to strip away gains made by the
wrongdoer (restitution)[263] or to punish the wrongdoer (punishment). Restitution
for common law wrongs, stripping away gains made by the wrongdoer, has only
been judicially recognized relatively recently and remains controversial; and, since
Rookes v Barnard[264] in 1964, punishment of the wrongdoer, through 'exemplary'
or 'punitive' damages, has been treated as an unusual and peripheral remedy in
English civil law.

But to accept that restitution and punishment are less central responses to a **21.141**
wrong than compensation should not lead one to pretend that they do not exist.
One must therefore view with scepticism attempts that are commonly made to
analyse all awards of 'restitutionary damages' as if they were really awards of
'compensatory damages'.[265] On the contrary, one can argue that, to ensure proper
protection of victims, the law should recognize as wide a range of remedial
responses to civil wrongs as possible. It is also important to realize that, through
the remedy of an 'account of profits', restitution for equitable wrongs, such as
breach of fiduciary duty and breach of confidence, has long been awarded without
being questioned. On the contrary, it is the remedy of equitable compensation
that has been undeveloped for equitable wrongs.[266] The contrast with the controversy generated by the notion of restitution for common law wrongs is a stark
one. It is yet another example of the unacceptable inconsistency between common law and equity.

(1) Restitution for Wrongs

The most obvious reason why a claimant may seek restitution for a wrong, **21.142**
rather than compensation, is in order to recover a higher award. This is so where
the gain the defendant has made by the wrong exceeds loss caused to the claimant

---

[2004] 2 AC 457, the House of Lords upheld an award for breach of confidence of £2,500 damages
for mental distress plus £1000 aggravated damages without making any comment as to the jurisdictional basis of those damages.

263 This is sometimes referred to as 'disgorgement'.
264 [1970] AC 652, HL.
265 A well-known example is the article by R Sharpe and S M Waddams, 'Damages for Lost
Opportunity to Bargain' (1982) 2 OJLS 290.
266 See para 21.130.

by the wrong.[267] It is also conceivable that bars (for example, limitation periods) to compensation may apply differently than to restitution.[268]

21.143 Historically a number of differently labelled remedies have performed the role of stripping away gains made by a civil wrongdoer: for example, the award of money had and received (especially in the so-called 'waiver of tort' cases), an account of profits, and 'restitutionary damages' (where the damages are assessed according to the gains made by the wrongdoer rather than the loss to the claimant). The Law Commission has recommended that, as there is no rational reason for having these different personal restitutionary remedies, rather than a single remedy, it would be appropriate, in the context of restitution for wrongs, for judges and practitioners to abandon the labels 'action for money had and received' and 'account of profits' in favour of the single term 'restitutionary damages'.[269]

21.144 Although it is arguable that, in principle, there is no justification for this, a claimant cannot be awarded both a restitutionary remedy (for example, an account of profits or the award of money had and received) and compensatory damages for a wrong.[270] Restitutionary and compensatory remedies are regarded as 'alternative and inconsistent' and cannot be combined: the claimant must elect between them, albeit that the election need not be made until judgment and even then it can be changed if the judgment is unsatisfied.[271]

---

[267] This is most clearly illustrated by cases awarding restitution of bribes: eg *Reading v A-G* [1951] AC 507; *A-G for Hong Kong v Reid* [1994] 1 AC 324, PC. See para 21.155.

[268] See *Chesworth v Farrar* [1967] 1 QB 407. But the Limitation Act 1980 is largely drafted in terms of causes of action not remedies. Unless one takes the view that restitution for wrongs rests on a different cause of action than compensation for wrongs, the six-year time limit applicable, eg, to 'an action founded on tort' (s 2 of the 1980 Act) should apply to restitution for torts as well as compensation for torts. By s 23 of the 1980 Act, an action for an account of profits 'shall not be brought after the expiration of any time limit under this Act which is applicable to the claim which is the basis of the duty to account', which appears to mean that, if the basis is tort, tort limitation periods should apply. The limitation periods for breach of trust are laid down in s 21 of the 1980 Act. There are no limitation periods explicitly laid down in the 1980 Act for other equitable wrongs, although for breach of fiduciary duty a six-year period is applied by analogy under s 36(1) of the 1980 Act (*Paragon Finance plc v DB Thakerar & Co* [1999] 1 All ER 400, CA) and for breach of confidence the equitable doctrine of laches will apply.

[269] *Aggravated, Exemplary and Restitutionary Damages* (Law Com No 247) (1997) paras 3.82–3.84. (For a similar argument in respect of restitution for the cause of action of unjust enrichment, see para 21.10.) J Edelman, *Gain-Based Damages* (2002) prefers, as a general label, 'gain-based damages' with a subdivision between 'disgorgement damages' and 'restitutionary damages'.

[270] *Neilson v Betts* (1871) LR 5 HL 1, HL; *De Vitre v Betts* (1873) LR 6 HL 319, HL; *Colbeam Palmer Ltd v Stock Affiliates Pty Ltd* (1968) 122 CLR 25, HC; *Mahesan v Malaysia Government Officers' Co-op Housing Society Ltd* [1979] AC 374; *Island Records Ltd v Tring International plc* [1996] 1 WLR 1256; *Tang Min Sit v Capacious Investments Ltd* [1996] AC 514, PC. See also s 61(2), Patents Act 1977. For analysis of the 'election' requirement, see A Burrows, *Remedies for Torts and Breach of Contract* (3rd edn, 2004) 14–16, 388–390.

[271] *United Australia Ltd v Barclays Bank Ltd* [1941] AC 1, HL.

It is convenient to examine the present law on restitution for wrongs in three **21.145** parts: restitution of enrichments gained by a tort: restitution of enrichments gained by an equitable wrong; and restitution of enrichments gained by a breach of contract.

(a) Enrichments gained by a tort

One first needs to explain what is meant by 'waiver of tort'. This is a confusing **21.146** concept and it carries more than one meaning. It is normally used to refer to a situation in which a claimant seeks a restitutionary remedy for a tort (ie the cause of action is the tort) rather than compensatory damages. For example, in the leading case of *United Australia Ltd v Barclays Bank Ltd*,[272] the claimant brought an action for money had and received by conversion of a cheque. This was a claim for restitution of the gains made by the tort of conversion and the claimant was described as 'waiving the tort'. Yet this did not mean that the claimant was excusing the tort, so that, when that claim was abandoned prior to judgment, the claimant was nevertheless entitled to bring an action claiming compensatory damages for conversion of the cheque by another party. There are two other meanings of the phrase 'waiver of tort'. One refers to a principle of agency law whereby the victim of a tort can choose to give up his right to sue for a tort by treating the tortfeasor as having been authorized to act as the claimant's agent and then relying on the standard remedies against an agent to recover the profits made. In this situation, the tort is truly extinguished.[273] The other meaning refers to where the claimant chooses to ignore the tort and instead rests his claim to restitution on the cause of action of unjust enrichment; for example, a claimant, who has been induced to transfer money to the defendant by the defendant's fraudulent misrepresentation, may ignore the tort of deceit and seek restitution of the payment from the defendant on the basis that it was made by mistake. In this section we are essentially concerned with 'waiver of tort' in its first, and usual, sense. That is, we are concerned with restitution *for* a tort.

In examining restitution for torts, it is helpful to divide between proprietary **21.147** torts, excluding the protection of intellectual property; intellectual property torts; and other torts.

(i) *Proprietary torts other than those protecting intellectual property*

The restitutionary remedy of an award of money had and received has long **21.148** been granted for proprietary torts, such as conversion,[274] trespass to goods,[275] and

---

[272] [1941] AC 1.

[273] For a rare example of this, see *Verschures Creameries Ltd v Hull & Netherlands SS Co Ltd* [1921] 2 KB 608.

[274] *Lamine v Dorrell* (1705) 2 Ld Raym 1216; *Chesworth v Farrar* [1967] 1 QB 207.

[275] *Oughton v Seppings* (1830) 1 B & Ad 241.

trespass to land.[276] Moreover, damages which are arguably best analysed as restitutionary being concerned to strip away some or all of the defendant's gains (although commonly analysed as compensating for loss of an opportunity to bargain or to prevent the wrong) have been awarded for trespass to goods,[277] trespass to land[278] and nuisance.[279] In assessing damages, the courts have often found it helpful to think of a hypothetical bargain that the parties might reasonably have struck for a 'purchase' of the right. Important to the restitutionary analysis is that in deciding on that hypothetical price the courts have generally taken a fair percentage of the wrongdoer's anticipated profits; and that it has been irrelevant that the claimant would not have been willing to sell the right.

21.149 A significant feature of restitution for proprietary torts is that it is not a precondition that the defendant was acting dishonestly or in bad faith or cynically. While it may be said that the proprietary torts normally require intentional conduct (for example, the tort of conversion normally requires that the defendant intended to deal with the goods in question), it is no defence to the tort, including a restitutionary remedy for the tort, that the defendant honestly and reasonably believed that the property was his rather than the claimant's. So if the defendant commits the tort of conversion by selling the claimant's goods, the claimant is entitled to restitution of the sale profits in an action for money had and received even though the defendant honestly believed them to be his own. Similarly if the defendant commits the tort of trespass to goods by using another's goods, it would seem that the owner is entitled to damages assessed according to a reasonable hiring charge, even though the defendant honestly believed them to be his own.

(ii) Intellectual property torts

21.150 These are civil wrongs which are either statutory torts (for example infringement of a patent, infringement of copyright, infringement of design right) or common law torts (for example, passing off). The reason why it is convenient to treat them separately from other proprietary torts is that restitution for these torts, through

---

276 *Powell v Rees* (1837) 7 Ad & El 426.

277 *Strand Electric and Engineering Co Ltd v Brisford Entertainments Ltd* [1952] 2 QB 246, 254–255 (per Denning LJ; cf Somervell and Romer LJJ, who analysed the award as compensatory).

278 *Penarth Dock Engineering Co Ltd v Pounds* [1963] 1 Lloyd's Rep 359; *Bracewell v Appleby* [1975] Ch 408; *Ministry of Defence v Ashman* (1993) 66 P & CR 195, CA; *Jaggard v Sawyer* [1995] 1 WLR 269, CA; *Severn Trent Water Ltd v Barnes* [2004] EWCA Civ 570.

279 *Carr-Saunders v Dick McNeill Associates Ltd* [1986] 1 WLR 122; *Tamares (Vincent Square) Ltd v Fairpoint Properties (Vincent Square) Ltd* [2007] EWHC 212. Cf *Stoke-on-Trent City Council v W & J Wass Ltd* [1988] 1 WLR 1406, CA (nominal damages only for the deliberate commission of the tort of nuisance by operating a market within a distance infringing the claimant's proprietary market right).

the equitable remedy of an account of profits, is very well-established. This reflects the fact that these torts started life as equitable wrongs.

So an account of profits may be ordered for passing off [280] or infringement of trade **21.151** mark,[281] although it appears that dishonesty is here a pre-condition of an account of profits,[282] albeit not of a claim for damages.[283] It is explicitly laid down in statute that an account of profits may be ordered for infringement of a patent,[284] infringement of copyright,[285] infringement of design right,[286] and infringement of performer's property right.[287] Statutory provisions further lay down that negligence is required to trigger an account of profits for patent infringement,[288] whereas for infringement of copyright,[289] primary infringement of a design right,[290] and infringement of a performer's property right,[291] an account of profits may be ordered on a strict liability basis: that is, it is not a defence that the defendant did not know, and had no reason to believe, that copyright or design right or performer's right existed in the work to which the action relates. As we have seen above, a strict liability approach to restitutionary remedies for the tort is applied in respect of other proprietary torts;[292] although, as noted at the start of this paragraph, it clashes with what appears to be the approach in respect of passing off and infringement of trade mark.

(iii) Non-proprietary torts

When one moves to non-proprietary torts, it is much more difficult to find **21.152** examples of cases illustrating the award of restitution for a tort. In particular, 'waiver of tort' cases that are sometimes cited as illustrations[293] turn out on closer inspection to be better (or, at least, equally well) interpreted as cases on restitution for the cause of action of unjust enrichment: that is, 'waiver of tort' is being used

---

[280] *Lever v Goodwin* (1887) 36 Ch D, CA; *My Kinda Town Ltd v Soll* [1982] FSR 147, reversed on liability [1983] RPC 407, CA.

[281] *Edelsten v Edelsten* (1863) 1 De GJ & Sm 185; *Slazenger & Sons v Spalding & Bros* [1910] 1 Ch 257; *Colbeam Palmer Ltd v Stock Affiliates Pty Ltd* (1968) 122 CLR 25, HC; cf Trade Marks Act 1994, s 14(2).

[282] See especially the decision of Windeyer J in the High Court of Australia in *Colbeam Palmer Ltd v Stock Affiliates Pty Ltd* (1968) 122 CLR 25.

[283] *Gillette UK Ltd v Edenwest Ltd* [1994] RPC 279.

[284] Patents Act 1977, s 61(1)(d).

[285] Copyright, Designs and Patents Act 1988, s 96(2). See *Potton Ltd v Yorkclose Ltd* [1990] FSR 11.

[286] Copyright, Designs and Patents Act 1988, s 229(2).

[287] ibid s 191I(2).

[288] Patents Act 1977, s 62(1) The same approach applies to damages.

[289] Copyrights, Designs and Patents Act 1988, s 97(1). A different approach applies to damages.

[290] ibid s 233(1). A different approach applies to damages.

[291] ibid s 191J(1). A different approach applies to damages.

[292] See para 21.149.

[293] eg *Hill v Perrott* (1810) 3 Taunt 274 (deceit); *Universe Tankships of Monrovia v International Transport Workers Federation (The Universe Sentinel)* [1983] 1 AC 366, HL (duress).

in the third sense set out above.[294] It is also significant that in *Halifax Building Society v Thomas*[295] the Court of Appeal denied a claimant a restitutionary claim to the gains made by the tort of deceit, albeit in a situation where the defendant was the subject of a criminal conviction and confiscation order which was sufficient to reverse the gains he had made from civil fraud and to punish him for that fraud. Yet, as we shall see below,[296] Lord Devlin's second category of punitive damages is concerned to punish those who cynically commit torts with a view to making profits. If the courts are prepared to award punitive damages against the cynical profit-seeking tortfeasor, they must be willing to go to the less extreme lengths of awarding restitution against such a tortfeasor. This is particularly obvious when one realizes that a restitutionary remedy need not strip away all the gains made by the tortfeasor; rather the remedy can be tailored to remove a fair proportion of the gains, taking into account, for example, the skill and effort expended by the defendant.[297]

(b) Enrichments gained by an equitable wrong

21.153   It is a surprising fact, which reflects the unfortunate influence still exerted by the common law/equity divide, that when one turns one's attention from torts to equitable wrongs, such as breach of fiduciary duty and breach of confidence, the availability of restitution, through the remedy of an account of profits, is well-established. The account of profits is, therefore, standardly awarded to ensure that a fiduciary does not make secret unauthorized profits out of his position,[298] and to ensure the disgorgement to principals of bribes made to their fiduciaries.[299] The account of profits may be awarded even if (as shown in the secret profit cases) the fiduciary was not acting dishonestly or in bad faith. Similarly, it is well-established that an account of profits can be awarded for breach of confidence. For example, in the leading case of *Attorney-General v Guardian Newspapers Ltd (No 2)*[300] the Sunday Times was held liable to an account of profits, for breach of confidence to the Crown, in publishing extracts of Peter Wright's book, *Spycatcher*, at an early stage before the information had reached the public domain.

---

[294] See para 21.146.

[295] [1996] Ch 217, CA.

[296] See para 21.161.

[297] See eg *Boardman v Phipps* [1967] 2 AC 46, HL (breach of fiduciary duty); *Redwood Music Ltd v Chappell & Co Ltd* [1981] RPC 109, 132 (copyright infringement); cf *Guinness plc v Saunders* [1990] 2 AC 663 HL.

[298] eg *Regal (Hastings) Ltd v Gulliver* [1942] 1 All ER 378, HL; *Boardman v Phipps* [1967] 2 AC 46, HL; *Murad v Al-Saraj* [2005] EWCA Civ 959.

[299] eg *Reading v A-G* [1951] AC 507, HL.

[300] [1990] 1 AC 109, HL. See also, eg, *Peter Pan Manufacturing Corpn v Corsets Silhouette Ltd* [1964] 1 WLR 96.

In the context of breach of confidence, it may be that the courts will award dam-   **21.154**
ages, whether restitutionary or compensatory, rather than an account of profits, if
the breach of confidence was committed without dishonesty. This is one explanation for *Seager v Copydex Ltd* [301] in which the defendants had manufactured a
carpet grip, honestly and unconsciously making use of confidential information
given to them by the claimant. The Court of Appeal ordered damages to be
assessed apparently on a restitutionary basis. [302]

Restitution for breach of fiduciary duty and breach of confidence is so well-   **21.155**
established that the area of debate focuses, not on whether restitution rather than
compensation should be awarded, but rather on whether restitution should be
effected by merely a personal remedy (account of profits) or by a proprietary
remedy (constructive trust). Despite *Lister v Stubbs*, [303] which denied that a proprietary remedy should be awarded in respect of a bribe and sought to maintain a
clear divide between obligation and ownership, the law appears now to recognize
that a proprietary restitutionary remedy through a constructive trust is appropriate for all instances of (at least dishonest) breach of a fiduciary duty and breach
of confidence. If so, this further widens the gulf between restitution for equitable
wrongs and for common law wrongs (where proprietary restitution has never
been granted). Particularly important was the Privy Council's decision in *Attorney-
General for Hong Kong v Reid* [304] in which it was decided that, contrary to *Lister v
Stubbs*, a bribe was held on constructive trust. This had the result that the claimant
was entitled to land bought with the bribe.

(c) Enrichments gained by a breach of contract

Until recently, restitution could not be awarded for a breach of contract.   **21.156**
Admittedly, it has long been the law that restitutionary remedies, such as the
recovery of money had and received where there has been a total failure of
consideration [305] or a *quantum meruit*, [306] can be claimed by an innocent party once
it has validly terminated a contract for breach. But they are remedies for
the cause of action of unjust enrichment; they are not remedies for the cause of

---

[301] [1967] 1 WLR 923, CA. See also *Seager v Copydex Ltd (No 2)* [1969] 1 WLR 809, CA.
[302] Another explanation is that the court awarded damages, rather than an account of profits
because, as a matter of factual causation, the contribution of the confidential information to the
profits made was relatively minor.
[303] [1890] 45 Ch D 1, PC.
[304] [1994] 1 AC 324, PC. This was applied, and *Lister v Stubbs* distinguished, in *Daraydon
Holdings Ltd v Solland International* Ltd [2004] EWHC 622 (Ch); [2005] Ch 119. See also *LAC
Minerals Ltd v International Corona Resources Ltd* (1989) 61 DLR (4th) 14, SC (breach of confidence). See generally paras 4.294–4.305, 4.307–4.308.
[305] eg *Giles v Edwards* (1797) 7 Term Rep 181; *Rowland v Divall* [1923] 2 KB 500, CA.
[306] eg *De Bernardy v Harding* (1853) 8 Exch 822.

action of breach of contract.[307] So, for example, in *Surrey County Council v Bredero Homes Ltd*[308] the Court of Appeal declined to award restitutionary damages for a breach of contract where the defendants, to whom the claimant had sold land for a housing estate, had built more houses on the site than they had covenanted to build, thereby making a greater profit. Nominal damages were awarded on the ground that the claimant had suffered no loss. Restitutionary damages were held to be inappropriate because this was an action for ordinary common law damages for breach of contract: it involved neither a tort nor an infringement of proprietary rights nor equitable damages.

21.157 The reference to proprietary rights and equitable damages reflects the fact that in *Wrotham Park Estate Co Ltd v Parkside Homes Ltd*[309] Brightman J, using a 'hypothetical bargain' approach, did award damages that are arguably best rationalized as restitutionary[310] for breach of restrictive covenants preventing the building of houses that were enforceable in equity by the claimants.

21.158 However, this traditional approach to restitution for breach of contract was shattered by the House of Lords in *Attorney-General v Blake*.[311] It was there recognized that, in exceptional cases, an account of profits can be ordered for a breach of contract. Such an order was made to deprive George Blake, the spy, of profits made or to be made from a book that he had written in breach of his undertaking to the Crown. Lord Nicholls, giving the leading speech, said that exceptionally an account of profits is appropriate where other contractual remedies are inadequate. 'A useful general guide. . .is whether the plaintiff had a legitimate interest in preventing the defendant's profit-making activity. . .'[312]

21.159 Although *Blake* has only been directly applied in one subsequent case to order an account of profits for breach of contract,[313] it has been influential in encouraging courts to assess contractual damages, albeit exceptionally, on the hypothetical bargain approach favoured in the *Wrotham Park* case. Those damages are, arguably, best analysed as restitutionary. For example, in *Experience Hendrix LLC v PPX Enterprises Inc*[314] the defendant record company, in breach of a contractual

---

307 See paras 18.98–18.103.

308 [1993] 1 WLR 1361, CA.

309 [1974] 1 WLR 798.

310 This is not only because of Brightman J's general reasoning but because he made clear that the claimants would not have accepted that sum for relaxing the covenant. See Steyn LJ in *Surrey CC v Bredero Homes Ltd* [1993] 1 WLR 1361. But the Court of Appeal in *Jaggard v Sawyer* [1995] 1 WLR 269 has said that the damages in the *Wrotham Park* case were compensatory and not restitutionary.

311 [2001] 1 AC 268, HL.

312 ibid at 285.

313 *Esso Petroleum Co Ltd v Niad Ltd* [2001] 1 All ER (D) 324 (Nov).

314 [2003] EWCA Civ 323, [2003] 1 All ER (Comm) 830. See also *Lane v O'Brien Homes Ltd* [2004] EWHC 303 (QB) and *WWF World Wide Fund for Nature v World Wrestling Federation Entertainment Inc* [2007] EWCA Civ 286 in both of which *Wrotham Park* damages were

settlement with Jimi Hendrix, used certain master tapes that should have been delivered up to Jimi Hendrix. Although *Blake* was distinguished—in the sense that an account of profits, stripping the defendant of all its gains made from the breach of contract, was not awarded—*Wrotham Park*, as endorsed by *Blake* was applied in holding that the claimant was entitled to damages based not on compensating loss but on what was a reasonable sum to pay taking into account the gains made by the defendant from its use of the forbidden tapes. Although the Court of Appeal was not required to assess that reasonable sum, it thought that one-third of the defendant's royalties on the retail selling price of records made from the forbidden tapes would probably be an appropriate reasonable sum.

(2) Punishment

A remedy concerned to punish a defendant for a civil wrong is rare in English **21.160** law. The exception is 'punitive' (or 'exemplary') damages which, as laid down in *Rookes v Barnard*[315] and *Kuddus v Chief Constable of Leicestershire*[316] can be awarded in certain limited categories for some torts but not, as yet, for breach of contract.[317] As regards equitable compensation or equitable damages, while there has recently been increased discussion of this issue,[318] there is no authority in England for punishment being an aim.[319] In other words, punishment has not been authoritatively recognized as an aim of remedies for equitable wrongs, such as breach of fiduciary duty and breach of confidence. This is perhaps surprising given the standard willingness of the courts to award restitution, through an account of profits, for equitable wrongs.

The House of Lords in *Rookes v Barnard* laid down that punitive damages can be **21.161** awarded in only three categories of case. First, where there has been oppressive, arbitrary or unconstitutional wrongdoing by a servant of government;[320] secondly,

---

conceptualized as compensatory not restitutionary. The force of the latter is undermined by the CA's view that even an account of profits is a compensatory and not a gains-based award.

[315] [1964] AC 1129, HL. For a wide-ranging review of the law on exemplary damages, see *Aggravated, Exemplary and Restitutionary Damages* (Law Com No 247, 1997).

[316] [2001] UKHL 29; [2002] 2 AC 122.

[317] *Addis v Gramophone Company Ltd* [1909] AC 488, HL; *Perera v Vandiyar* [1953] 1 WLR 672, CA; *Newcastle-upon-Tyne CC v Allan* [2005] ICR 1170, EAT. For an interesting example of punitive damages being awarded for breach of contract by the Supreme Court of Canada, see *Whiten v Pilot Insurance Co* (2002) 209 DLR (4th) 257.

[318] Triggered particularly by *Acquaculture Corp v New Zealand Green Mussel Co Ltd* [1990] 3 NZLR 299, NZCA; *Harris v Digital Pulse Pty Ltd* (2003) 56 NSWLR 298, NSWCA.

[319] Lindsay J in *Douglas v Hello! Ltd (No 3)* [2003] EWHC 786; [2003] 3 All ER 996 at [273] assumed, without deciding, that 'exemplary damages (or equity's equivalent)' are available for breach of confidence.

[320] eg *Huckle v Money* (1763) 2 Wils 205; *Wilks v Wood* (1763) Lofft 1; *White v Metropolitan police Commissioner* The Times, 24 April 1982; *Holden v Chief Constable of Lancashire* [1987]

where the defendant has committed a wrong cynically calculating that it will be profitable so to do;[321] and, thirdly, where expressly authorized by statute.[322] The Court of Appeal in *AB v South West Water Services Ltd* [323] added a second restriction, namely that punitive damages could only be awarded if they were awarded for that particular wrong pre-1964 (that is, before *Rookes v Barnard* was decided). However, this 'cause of action' test was removed by the House of Lords in *Kuddus v Chief Constable of Leicestershire*. On the facts of the case this meant that, if the other requirements for the award of punitive damages were satisfied, punitive damages could be awarded for the tort of misfeasance in public office. It was noted that the need to search through old authorities to find a pre-1964 award of punitive damages was unfortunate, especially since aggravated and punitive damages have only been clearly distinguished since *Rookes v Barnard* itself, and it may well be difficult to determine the characterization of an award of damages in an older case. The removal of the cause of action test in *Kuddus* means that, apart from infringement of a Convention right under the Human Rights Act 1998 (where the wording of the Act[324] and the jurisprudence of the European Court of Human Rights indicate that no exemplary damages can be awarded), punitive damages can be awarded for any tort provided the facts fall within the *Rookes v Barnard* categories.

21.162   Even if a claimant can show that the defendant's wrong falls within one of the three categories punitive damages may still not be awarded for a number of reasons. For example, they will not be awarded unless a court is satisfied that the sum which it seeks to award as compensation is inadequate to punish the defendant for his outrageous conduct, to deter him and others from engaging in similar conduct, and to mark the court's disapproval of such conduct. This is the so-called 'if, but only if' test.[325] Punitive damages will also not be awarded where a defendant

---

QB 380; *Treadaway v Chief Constable of West Midlands* The Times, 25 October 1994; *Thompson v Commissioner of Police for the Metropolis* [1998] QB 498, CA.

321 *Bell v Midland Rly Co* [1861] 10 CBNS 287; *Broome v Cassell* [1972] AC 1027, HL; *Drane v Evangelou* [1978] 1 WLR 455, CA; *Guppys (Bridport) Ltd v Brookling and James* (1983) 14 HLR 1, CA; *McMillan v Singh* [1984] HLR 120, CA; *Design Progression v Thurloe Properties Ltd* [2004] EWHC 324 (Ch); [2004] 10 EG 184 (CS) (breach of statutory duty under Landlord and Tenant Act 1988, s 1(3)); *Borders (UK) Ltd v Commissioner of Police of the Metropolis* [2005] EWHC Civ 197.

322 The only clear example is the Reserve and Auxiliary Forces (Protection of Civil Interests) Act 1951, s 13 (2). Perhaps the Copyright, Designs and Patents Act 1988 s 97(2) does so but in *Redrow Homes Ltd v Bett Brothers plc* [1999] 1 AC 197 HL (Sc), Lord Clyde said that 'additional damages' under s 97(2) were more probably aggravated rather than punitive damages.

323 [1993] QB 507, CA.

324 s 8(3) of the Human Rights Act 1998 refers to the award being necessary to afford 'just satisfaction' to the claimant which appears to be a reference to compensation alone. See *Anufrijeva v London Borough of Southwark* [2003] EWCA Civ 1406; [2004] QB 1124.

325 *Rookes v Barnard* [1964] AC 1129, 1228, HL; *Broome v Cassell* [1972] AC 1027, 1062, 1089, 1096, 1104, 1118, 1121–2, 1134, HL.

has already been punished by the criminal law in respect of the facts upon which the claimant now founds his tortious action; a person should not be punished twice for the same offence.[326] Punitive damages may also be denied where the claimant has provoked the wrongful action by his own conduct.[327]

21.163 If it has been decided that punitive damages are to be awarded, there are a number of factors which the courts have considered relevant in assessing those damages. Punitive awards should be moderate.[328] The means of the defendant and all mitigating circumstances should be taken into account.[329] Where there are joint defendants punitive damages must not exceed the lowest sum that any of the defendants ought to pay.[330] And where there are multiple claimants the total amount of punitive damages considered fair for the defendant to pay should first be decided on and then divided among the claimants.[331]

D. Compelling Performance or Preventing (or Compelling the Undoing of) a Wrong

21.164 In this section, we examine what may be termed 'specific' remedies for wrongs. In general, these are orders requiring a defendant to comply with his primary duty not to commit a wrong. Where the duty in question is a positive one (as, for example, with most contractual duties) the remedies (for example, specific performance or the award of an agreed sum) order the defendant to perform his positive duty. In other words, the remedies seek to compel performance.[332] Where the duty in question is a negative one (as, for example, with most duties imposed by tort) the remedies (for example, a prohibitory injunction) order the defendant not to act in such a way as to commit, or to continue to commit, a wrong. In other words, the remedies seek to prevent a wrong. Also covered in this section are remedies

---

[326] *Archer v Brown* [1985] QB 401, CA.

[327] *Holden v Chief Constable of Lancashire* [1987] QB 380, CA.

[328] *Rookes v Barnard* [1964] AC 1129, HL; *John v MGN Ltd* [1997] QB 586, CA; *Thompson v MPC* [1998] QB 498, CA. In the *Thompson* case, the Court of Appeal laid down guideline figures for juries on quantum (including punitive damages) in false imprisonment and malicious prosecution actions against the police.

[329] *Rookes v Barnard* [1964] AC 1129.

[330] *Broome v Cassell* [1972] AC 1027, HL.

[331] *Riches v News Group Newspapers* [1986] QB 256, CA.

[332] A further judicial remedy concerned to 'enforce' a defendant's positive duties (but which goes one step beyond ordering the defendant to do something) is the court's appointment of a receiver and manager. Apart from the specialist area of insolvency (see Chapter 19), the High Court has long had an equitable jurisdiction to appoint a receiver and this is now embodied in the Supreme Court Act 1981, s 37(1). For examples of such an order (which may be interim or final), being made in response to a wrong, see *Riches v Owen* (1868) 3 Ch App 820; *Leney & Sons Ltd v Callingham and Thompson* [1908] 1 KB 79, CA; *Hart v Emelkirk Ltd* [1983] 1 WLR 1289.

(for example, a mandatory restorative injunction or delivery up of goods) which seek to stop the continuing effects of a wrong by compelling a defendant to 'undo' the wrong.

21.165 It should be noted that specific remedies for wrongs, with the exception of the award of an agreed sum, are equitable rather than common law remedies. As equitable remedies, they are discretionary rather than being available as of right. But it would be a mistake to imagine that this means that the law on equitable specific remedies is not clear and certain. In truth, all that is meant is that, in contrast to common law remedies, there are numerous, albeit clearly established, bars to the equitable remedies.

21.166 A central underlying question is the extent to which a claimant can choose a specific remedy rather than compensation. On the face of it, one might expect the claimant to have a free choice. After all, the specific remedies more directly protect the claimant's right not to be the victim of a wrong than does compensation. But while in relation to negative duties, the prohibitory injunction is freely available—and can be regarded as the primary remedy as against compensatory damages—the same cannot be said of the enforcement of positive duties through specific performance and mandatory injunctions. They are secondary remedies to compensatory damages in the sense that they will not be awarded unless damages are inadequate. Whether this approach is rationally justified, as opposed to being a product of the historical divide between common law and equity, is a matter which we shall discuss below.

(1) Award of an Agreed Sum

21.167 This contractual remedy can be regarded as a hybrid, being like damages in that it is a common law and monetary remedy, but like specific performance in that its function is to compel performance of a positive contractual duty. It plainly protects the claimant's expectation interest.[333]

(a) Award of an agreed price

21.168 The most important agreed sum is an agreed 'price', whether for, for example, goods, services, real property, or a loan of money. Indeed an action for the price (that is, the standard action for a debt owed) is the commonest claim brought for breach of contract.

21.169 For a claimant to be entitled to this remedy, the defendant must plainly be in breach of a valid contractual obligation to pay the agreed price. The contract must not, therefore, be void or unenforceable, and must not have been rescinded; nor

---

[333] See para 21.17.

must the obligation to pay be one that has been wiped away by termination of the contract for frustration or breach. Also the sum must be due. An agreed price is only regarded as due, in the absence of any express provision as to advance payment, where the claimant has completed or substantially completed what it is being paid for: for example, a seller of goods is generally not entitled to the agreed price until property in the goods has passed to the buyer, as laid down in section 49(1) of the Sale of Goods Act 1979; and a builder is generally not entitled to the agreed price until he has completed or substantially completed the stage of the building to which the payment relates.[334]

An issue of great controversy is whether an action for the agreed price may fail where the defendant has clearly repudiated the contract but the claimant, instead of accepting the repudiation and suing for damages, has kept the contract open. **21.170**

There are two major contradictory approaches to this issue. First, one might say that the claimant has an unfettered option to hold the contract open and recover the agreed price; that is, that the duty to mitigate does not apply to an action for the agreed price and that it is no bar that damages are adequate. The alternative view is that the claimant may not be entitled to hold a contract open and recover the agreed price; the duty to mitigate does apply to an action for the agreed price and, where damages are adequate to compensate a claimant for his loss, it is contrary to that duty for the claimant to carry on with his unwanted performance and claim the agreed price: rather, he should accept the repudiation, claim damages and make substitute contracts. **21.171**

The leading case is *White and Carter (Councils) Ltd v McGregor*.[335] The claimants supplied to local authorities litter bins on which they let advertising space. The defendants contracted to pay for the display of adverts, but later that day they repudiated the contract. The claimants refused to accept the repudiation and went ahead and displayed the adverts for the three year period of the contract. They then claimed the agreed price. The House of Lords held, by a 3–2 majority, that they were entitled to the agreed price. Two of the majority (Lords Hodson and Tucker) adopted the first of the two views set out in para 21.171. The third, Lord Reid, while basically taking that view, suggested a possible qualification. He said, '[I]t may well be that, if it can be shown that a person has no legitimate interest, financial or otherwise, in performing the contract, rather than claiming damages, he ought not be allowed to saddle the other party with an additional burden with no benefit to himself.'[336] Lords Morton and Keith, dissenting, took the second of the two views set out above. **21.172**

---

[334] *Hoenig v Isaacs* [1952] 2 All ER 176, CA.
[335] [1962] AC 413, HL.
[336] ibid 431.

21.173   In some subsequent cases, courts have shown a reluctance to follow the *White and Carter* case. It has been distinguished on one of two main grounds. The first is that, as Lord Reid himself observed, the *White and Carter* case can only apply where the claimant is able to carry on with his performance without the defendant's co-operation. Some judges have distinguished the *White and Carter* case by giving a wide interpretation to this restriction.[337] Secondly, Lord Reid's qualification of the claimant having 'no legitimate interest' in performing the contract or, as other judges have termed it, of the claimant acting 'wholly unreasonably',[338] has been given a wide interpretation, thereby enabling a different decision to be reached, where damages are adequate, than in the *White and Carter* case.[339]

21.174   It should be realized that the approach in the *White and Carter* case contrasts with the traditional approach to the remedy of specific performance in that, as we shall see below,[340] if damages are adequate, specific performance will not be granted.

(b) Award of agreed sums other than the price

21.175   Awards of agreed sums other than the price may be payable on breach or payable on an event other than breach. The former comprise 'liquidated damages and penalties'. They raise different questions from the agreed price in that they constitute the parties' own fixing of damages for breach of contract. Specific enforcement of a liquidated damages clause does not therefore require a defendant to comply with his primary duty to perform the contract;[341] rather the liquidated damages clause is itself a response to breach of that primary duty. The question at issue is whether the parties' own assessment of damages through that clause should oust the assessment of damages by a court.

21.176   The short answer is that the courts will award the agreed sum if it is liquidated damages. But if it is a penalty, the promise to pay is invalid and the courts will

---

[337]   See for example *Hounslow London Borough v Twickenham Garden Developments Ltd* [1971] Ch 233; *Attica Sea Carriers v Ferrostaal (The Puerto Buitrago)* [1976] 1 Lloyd's Rep 250, 256, CA.

[338]   See *Gator Shipping Corp v Trans-Asiatic Oil Ltd SA (The Odenfeld)* [1978] 2 Lloyd's Rep 357 (*per* Kerr J). Cf *Ocean Marine Navigation Ltd v Koch Carbon Inc, The Dynamic* [2003] EWHC 1936 (Comm); [2003] 2 Lloyd's Rep 693 at [22]–[23] (*per* Simon J). In *The Odenfeld* and in *Reichman v Beveridge* [2006] EWCA Civ 1659 Lord Reid's qualification was held not to be made out so that, applying *White and Carter*, the agreed sums claimed were awarded.

[339]   See for example *Clea Shipping Corporation v Bulk Oil International Ltd (The Alaskan Trader)* [1984] 1 All ER 129 (*per* Lloyd J).

[340]   See paras 21.184–21.186.

[341]   Cf paras 21.06 and 21.164. Strictly speaking, therefore, the award of liquidated damages falls outside the main scope of this section. Nevertheless, it has been thought most convenient to deal with it here rather than in the section on compensation. Note also that, strictly speaking, the questions raised on liquidated damages concern the validity of the defendant's promise rather than the judicial remedy itself.

instead award normal (unliquidated) damages. Liquidated damages are a sum which represents a genuine pre-estimate of the loss caused by the breach, that is, of what is needed to put the claimant into as good a position as if the contract had been performed. A penalty, on the other hand, is a sum which is greater than such a genuine pre-estimate. It is inserted to punish the other party in the event of breach and to pressurize him into carrying out his contractual obligation. The distinction was emphasized in Lord Dunedin's seminal speech in *Dunlop Pneumatic Tyre Ltd v New Garage and Motor Co Ltd*.[342] In that case £5 was made payable for every tyre which the defendants bought from the claimant that was then sold or offered by the defendants in breach of their agreement not, for example, to sell the tyres to the public below list price. The House of Lords held that this sum was liquidated damages. Although there were several ways in which tyres could be sold or offered in breach of the agreement, the loss likely to result for any such breach was difficult to assess and £5 represented a genuine attempt to do so.

More recently in *Phillips Hong Kong Ltd v A-G of Hong Kong*[343] Lord Woolf, **21.177** giving the opinion of the Privy Council in upholding as liquidated damages a clause in a road construction contract, considered that the courts should not be too zealous to knock down clauses as penal. It was stressed that a clause can be a genuine pre-estimate of loss even though hypothetical situations could be presented in which the claimant's actual loss would be substantially lower. To hold otherwise would be to render it very difficult to draw up valid liquidated damages clauses in complex commercial contracts. Moreover, it was thought acceptable to take account of the fact that, as matters had turned out, the actual loss was not much greater than the agreed damages. Although the issue must be judged as at the date the contract was made, what actually happened can provide valuable evidence as to what could reasonably have been expected to be the loss at the time the contract was made.

Controversial issues on agreed damages under the present law include; first, **21.178** whether the loss that needs to be genuinely pre-estimated includes loss that is legally irrecoverable (for example, because recovery of the loss would be contrary to the claimant's duty to mitigate);[344] secondly, what happens where the agreed damages clause is a penalty but the claimant's loss turns out to be greater than

---

[342] [1915] AC 79, HL. See also, eg, *Bridge v Campbell Discount Co Ltd* [1962] AC 600, HL (penalty); *Wadham Stringer Finance Ltd v Meaney* [1981] 1 WLR 39 (liquidated damages); *Lordsvale Finance plc v Bank of Zambia* [1996] QB 752, 762; *Murray v Leisureplay plc* [2005] EWCA Civ 963; [2005] IRLR 946 (liquidated damages). In *Jobson v Johnson* [1989] 1 WLR 1026, CA, the law on penalty clauses was extended to a clause to transfer shares rather than to pay money.

[343] (1993) 61 Building LR 41, PC.

[344] See eg *Robophone Facilities Ltd v Blank* [1966] 1 WLR 1428, CA (Diplock LJ considered that liquidated damages could properly include loss that was irrecoverable because too remote).

that penalty;[345] and thirdly, whether a liquidated damages clause is valid if it seeks to underestimate and hence limit the claimant's damages.[346]

21.179 Agreed sums, other than the price, payable on an event other than breach have traditionally been treated in the same way as an agreed price. This means that once the event has occurred the sum can be recovered without any type of liquidated damages/penalty analysis.[347]

(2) Specific Performance

21.180 Specific performance is an equitable remedy which seeks specific enforcement of a defendant's positive contractual duty. It plainly protects the claimant's expectation interest.[348] Prohibitory injunctions also enforce contractual duties but differ in that the duties in question are negative. If what is in form a prohibitory injunction, in substance orders specific performance, or if the courts consider that in practice the injunction amounts to specific performance,[349] it is governed by specific performance principles and is dealt with in this section.

21.181 Strictly speaking, it is not an essential prerequisite of specific performance that the defendant is in breach of contract.[350] Rather an action for specific performance is based on the mere existence of the contract, coupled with circumstances which make it 'equitable' to grant a decree. But, in practice, it is a breach of contract, actual or threatened, that renders it 'equitable' to grant specific performance.

21.182 Specific performance, being an equitable remedy, may be granted 'on terms'. The most common example occurs where the vendor of land seeks specific performance against the purchaser and there is some non-substantial defect in the property; specific performance will be ordered 'with compensation', that is, subject to the vendor paying compensation to the purchaser to cover the defect.[351]

21.183 In contrast to damages, specific performance is not available for every breach of contract. Indeed, as in this section, specific performance is best approached

---

345 See eg *Wall v Rederiaktiebolaget Luggude* [1915] 3 KB 66 (penalty clause inapplicable even though lower than claimant's actual loss).

346 See eg *Cellulose Acetate Silk Co v Widnes Foundry Ltd* [1933] AC 20, HL (valid liquidated damages even though seeking to underestimate, rather than pre-estimate, the claimant's loss).

347 *Alder v Moore* [1961] 2 QB 57, CA; *Export Credit Guarantee Department v Universal Oil Products Co* [1983] 1 WLR 399, 402, HL.

348 See para 21.17.

349 But see para 21.206.

350 *Hasham v Zenab* [1960] AC 316, PC; *Zucker v Tyndall Holdings plc* [1992] 1 WLR 1127, CA.

351 *Re Fawcett and Holmes' Contract* (1889) 42 Ch D 150, CA; *Shepherd v Croft* [1911] 1 Ch 521. For other examples of specific performance on terms see *Baskcomb v Beckwith* (1869) LR 8 Eq 100; *Price v Strange* [1978] Ch 337, CA; *Harvela Investments Ltd v Royal Trust Co of Canada Ltd* [1986] AC 207, HL.

negatively, that is by examining the numerous restrictions on its availability. Positively, it then follows that if the remedy is not barred by such restrictions, a claimant who applies for it will succeed.

(a) The primary restriction—adequacy of damages

Specific performance will not be ordered unless damages are inadequate. It is this **21.184** that fundamentally distinguishes the approach to specific performance of the common law, from that of the civil law, which has no such hurdle. There are two main reasons why the courts may consider damages to be inadequate.

The first and most important reason is if money cannot buy a substitute for the **21.185** promised performance: that is, the non-availability of a substitute. Most discussion of this has been in relation to contracts of sale, where the issue has generally been expressed as being one of the 'uniqueness' of the subject-matter. So contracts for the sale of land have traditionally been specifically enforceable on the ground that each piece of land is unique and cannot be replaced in the market.[352] Similarly, contracts for the sale of physically unique goods, like works of art, ornaments and ships, have been specifically enforced.[353] In some decisions, but not all, it has also been accepted that specific performance can be ordered for the sale of commercially unique goods.[354] Goods can be said to be commercially unique (a term coined by Professor Treitel)[355] where, although the goods may not be physically unique, buying substitutes will be so difficult or cause such delay that the claimant's business will be seriously disrupted.

A second main reason why damages may be considered inadequate is because of **21.186** the injustice that an award of nominal damages will cause where a contract has been made for a third party's benefit. The classic illustration is *Beswick v Beswick*.[356] A coal merchant transferred his business to his nephew, who in return promised that, after his uncle's death, he would pay £5 per week to his widow. The uncle died and his widow brought an action for specific performance of the nephew's promise, suing both personally and as administratrix. The House of Lords, upholding the doctrine of privity, held that while the widow could not maintain a successful action suing personally, she could as administratrix succeed in an action for specific performance because damages were inadequate. This meant that the nephew was ordered to pay the £5 a week to the widow in her personal capacity as promised. But why were the damages considered to be inadequate?

---

[352] *Sudbrook Trading Estate Ltd v Eggleton* [1983] 1 AC 444, 478, HL.
[353] *Falcke v Gray* (1859) 4 Drew 651; *Behnke v Bede Shipping Co Ltd* [1927] 1 KB 649.
[354] Contrast, eg, *Sky Petroleum Ltd v VIP Petroleum Ltd* [1974] 1 WLR 576 with *Société des Industries Métallurgiques SA v Bronx Engineering Co Ltd* [1975] 1 Lloyd's Rep 465, CA.
[355] 'Specific Performance in the Sale of Goods' (1966) JBL 211.
[356] [1968] AC 58, HL.

The reasoning was as follows: if a party sues on a contract made for the benefit of a third party the damages, which are assessed according to his own loss, are often nominal; where this produces injustice, as in this case where the nephew had got the business and would end up paying almost nothing for it, nominal damages should be regarded as inadequate, thereby permitting specific performance to be granted to enforce the defendant's promise. It is noteworthy that all their Lordships, and in particular Lord Reid, explained the relationship between damages and specific performance not simply in terms of the inadequacy of damages but rather in terms of the appropriateness or justice of granting specific performance. One can interpret their Lordships as wishing to effect a radical change in the relationship between damages and specific performance. But even if this interpretation is correct, it has not been followed through in subsequent cases which have largely continued to talk, and think, in terms of whether damages are adequate or not.

(b) The constant supervision objection

21.187   Traditionally, specific performance has not been ordered where this would require constant supervision. What this means is that specific performance will be denied of a contractual obligation that demands continuous acts, on the ground that this would involve constant supervision by the courts: that is, too much judicial time and effort will be spent in seeking compliance with the order.

21.188   A leading authority is *Ryan v Mutual Tontine Westminster Chambers Association*.[357] The lease of a service flat to the claimant lessee included an obligation on the part of the defendant lessor to provide a resident porter who would be 'constantly in attendance'. The lessor in fact appointed as resident porter someone who was absent every weekday for several hours. The claimant brought an action for specific performance of that obligation. The Court of Appeal held that specific performance should be refused because this would involve constant supervision by the courts.

21.189   However, in more recent times—and until the decision of the House of Lords in *Co-operative Insurance Society Ltd v Argyll Stores (Holdings) Ltd*[358]—there has been a movement against accepting constant supervision as a bar to specific performance. For example, in *Tito v Waddell (No 2)*[359] Megarry V-C was faced with the question whether specific performance should be ordered of a contractual obligation to replant land that had been mined. While ultimately refusing specific performance Megarry V-C thought that it was no longer a valid objection that the order involved constant supervision by the court. Instead he thought that,

---

[357] [1893] 1 Ch 116, CA.
[358] [1998] AC 1, HL.
[359] [1977] Ch 106.

'The real question is whether there is a sufficient definition of what has to be done in order to comply with the order of the court.'[360] Other older cases support the idea that it is the uncertainty of the obligation, rather than constant supervision, that constitutes the bar to specific performance.[361]

In *Co-operative Insurance Society Ltd v Argyll Stores (Holdings) Ltd* [362] the House of **21.190**
Lords controversially reaffirmed the constant supervision objection in overturning the Court of Appeal's order for specific performance of a covenant in a 35-year lease to keep premises open for retail trade during usual hours of business. Lord Hoffmann, giving the leading speech, said that there had been some misunderstanding about what is meant by continued superintendence. 'It is the possibility of the court having to give an indefinite series of rulings in order to ensure the execution of the order which has been regarded as undesirable.'[363] He added that it was oppressive (and, moreover, put the claimant in an undesirably strong position) to have to run a business under the threat of proceedings for contempt. His Lordship distinguished between orders to carry on activities and orders to achieve results (regarding, for example, building contracts as falling within the latter category), arguing that the possibility of repeated applications for rulings on compliance with the order which arises in the former type of case does not exist to anything like the same extent in relation to the latter type of case. His Lordship further thought that, in the case at hand, the order could not be drawn up with sufficient precision to avoid arguments over whether it was being complied with. With respect, Lord Hoffmann's reasoning is unconvincing. In particular, it is hard to see why the order could not be drawn up with sufficient precision; and nor is it clear why the constant supervision objection should be thought valid in respect of orders to carry on activities but not orders to achieve results. This is not to say that the decision in this case was wrong. To force a defendant to carry on with a business that is losing money may well fall foul of the severe hardship bar or a separate specific bar. But this should have been addressed separately rather than being confused with the constant supervision objection.

---

[360] ibid 322.

[361] eg *Wolverhampton Corpn v Emmons* [1901] 1 KB 515, CA. See also, subsequent to *Co-operative Insurance Society Ltd v Argyll Stores (Holdings) Ltd* [1998] AC 1, *Rainbow Estates Ltd v Tokenhold Ltd* [1999] Ch 64 (specific performance can exceptionally be ordered of a tenant's repairing covenant: Lawrence Collins QC said, at 73, '[T]he problems of defining the work and the need for supervision can be overcome by ensuring that there is sufficient definition of what has to be done in order to comply with the order of the court').

[362] [1998] AC 1, HL. For an interesting contrast with the law in Scotland, see *Co-operative Insurance Society Ltd v Halfords Ltd (No 2)* 1999 SLT 685, OH.

[363] [1998] AC 1, 12.

(c) Contracts for personal service

21.191 It is traditionally a well-established rule that the courts will not award specific performance of a contract for personal service, of which the prime example is the contract of employment.[364] One reason for this bar is that such a contract creates a relationship of mutual confidence and respect and where that has broken down, it cannot be satisfactorily rebuilt by a court order: on the contrary, to force the relationship to continue is only likely to lead to friction between the parties. Another reason is that where services are of an artistic kind, like opera-singing, it would not be possible to judge whether an order of specific performance against the employee was being properly complied with.[365] Perhaps the most fundamental objection to specific performance of a contract for personal service from the employee's point of view is that specific performance would result in involuntary servitude. Thus in *De Francesco v Barnum*[366] Fry LJ said that the courts were afraid of turning 'contracts of service into contracts of slavery'.[367] From the employer's side the analogous rationale, seemingly implicitly accepted by the courts, is that as he has to organize and pay for the work the employer should have the prerogative to decide who remains employed by him.

21.192 As regards an employee being ordered to carry out a contract of service, the bar still applies in full force, being enshrined in the Trade Union and Labour Relations (Consolidation) Act 1992, section 236. However, on the other side of the relationship, there has been some movement in the cases so that the bar is less absolute than it once was. For example, in *Hill v CA Parsons & Co Ltd*[368] the Court of Appeal confirmed the grant of an interim injunction which amounted to temporary specific performance of a contractual obligation to employ the claimant. The defendant employers had a closed shop agreement with a trade union and gave the claimant one month to join that union. When he failed to do so, he was given one month's notice of termination of employment. The court held that the defendants were in breach of contract by giving only one month's notice. The majority of the Court of Appeal (Lord Denning and Sachs LJ) held that the interim injunction sought should be granted even though this amounted to temporary specific performance of a contract for personal service. In a particularly influential judgment, Sachs LJ stressed that there was no breakdown in mutual confidence between employer and employee. Again in *Powell v Brent London BC*[369] the claimant was appointed principal benefits officer for the defendant local authority.

---

[364] eg *De Francesco v Barnum* (1890) 45 Ch D 430; *Johnson v Shrewsbury and Birmingham Rly Co* (1853) 3 De GM & G 914.

[365] See *Giles & Co Ltd v Morris* [1972] 1 WLR 307, 318.

[366] (1890) 45 Ch D 430.

[367] ibid 438.

[368] [1972] Ch 305, CA.

[369] [1988] ICR 176, CA.

A few days after starting work, she was told that her appointment was invalid because there might have been a breach of the defendant's equal opportunity code of practice in employing her. She sought an interim injunction requiring the defendant to treat her as if she were properly employed as principal benefits officer and, even though that would amount to temporary specific performance, the Court of Appeal granted it. Ralph Gibson LJ, giving the leading judgment, relied on *Hill v Parsons*, especially Sachs LJ's judgment, to justify a departure from the general bar to specific performance. He said that specific performance would be ordered where it was clear that, first, there was sufficient confidence on the part of the employer in the employee's ability and other necessary attributes for it to be reasonable to make the order; and, secondly, it was otherwise just to make the order.[370]

It should be noted that there are two other aspects of the law in relation to an **21.193** employee's rights which, while not directly infringing the rule against specific performance, do modify its ambit. First, office-holders (ie those in public employment) have always been able to gain a measure of specific protection of their positions through the application of public law principles.[371] Secondly, there is the statutory regime of unfair dismissal, embodied in the Employment Protection (Consolidation) Act 1978 which, while not protecting employees by any equivalent to specific performance, may make it expensive for employers to dismiss unfairly their employees.[372]

(d) Want of mutuality

Fry in his book on specific performance, first published in 1858,[373] stated a rule of **21.194** mutuality to the effect that a court will not in general order specific performance against the defendant unless, from the time the contract was made, he could have got specific performance against the claimant had the claimant been in breach. In the leading modern case on mutuality, *Price v Strange*,[374] the Court of Appeal rejected Fry's rule. The defendant was the head-lessee of some flats in a house. She orally agreed to grant the claimant a new under-lease of his flat in return for his promise to carry out certain repairs to the house. The claimant did half of the repairs but the defendant refused to allow him to complete them, had them done

---

[370] [1988] ICR 176, 194.

[371] See eg *Vine v National Dock Labour Board* [1957] AC 488, HL; *Malloch v Aberdeen Corp* [1971] 1 WLR 1578, HL; *R v East Berkshire Health Authority, ex p Walsh* [1985] QB 152, CA.

[372] Although, by ss 68–71 of the Employment Protection (Consolidation) Act 1978, reinstatement or re-engagement, rather than compensation, can be ordered of an employee who has been unfairly dismissed, non-compliance does not constitute contempt and is instead dealt with by an award of extra compensation.

[373] *Fry on Specific Performance* (6th edn, 1921) 219.

[374] [1978] Ch 337, CA.

at her own expense, and refused to grant him the under-lease. The claimant brought an action for specific performance of the promise to grant the new under-lease. Specific performance was granted by the Court of Appeal subject to the claimant compensating the defendant for the expense she had incurred in having the remaining repair work done. The defendant had argued that, in accordance with Fry's rule, specific performance should not be granted because, from the time the contract was made, she could not have obtained specific performance against the claimant because his obligation to repair was not specifically enforceable. But Fry's rule was held to be wrong and as, on these facts, there could be no risk of the claimant not performing (the work had already been completed) specific performance was granted.

21.195 It was, however, left unclear what the correct rule of mutuality is. Perhaps most helpful was Buckley LJ's formulation of the true rule as follows: 'The court will not compel a defendant to perform his obligations specifically if it cannot at the same time ensure that any unperformed obligations of the plaintiff will be perfectly performed, unless, perhaps, damages will be an adequate remedy to the defendant for any default on the plaintiff's part'.[375]

(e) Other bars

21.196 In addition to the four main bars that we have so far looked at, there are other bars to specific performance. For example, specific performance will not be ordered if the terms of the contract do not allow a sufficiently certain order to be made.[376] There will be no specific performance of a contract made by deed or supported merely by nominal consideration (ie 'equity will not assist a volunteer').[377] Specific performance will be denied where the contract has been unfairly obtained.[378] Specific performance will not be ordered where performance is physically impossible or where this would require the defendant to do something he is not lawfully competent to do.[379] Specific performance will be refused where it would cause severe hardship to the defendant.[380] Specific performance will not be awarded where the claimant's conduct has been generally inequitable (embodied, for example, in the maxims 'he who comes to equity must come with clean hands' or 'he who seeks equity must do equity').[381] And specific performance will be

---

[375] ibid 367–8.
[376] *Joseph v National Magazine Co* [1959] Ch 14. See also paras 21.189–21.190.
[377] *Cannon v Hartley* [1949] Ch 213.
[378] *Walters v Morgan* (1861) 3 De GF & J 718.
[379] *Ferguson v Wilson* (1866) 2 Ch App 77; *Warmington v Miller* [1973] QB 877, CA.
[380] *Patel v Ali* [1984] Ch 283.
[381] *Lamare v Dickson* (1873) LR 6 HL 414; *Chappell v Times Newspapers Ltd* [1975] 1 WLR 482, CA.

denied because of delay (ie laches) by the claimant in applying for specific performance.[382]

(f) The trend in favour of specific performance

Having examined the various bars to specific performance, it can be seen that the **21.197** general picture, despite *Co-operative Insurance Society Ltd v Argyll Stores (Holdings) Ltd*,[383] is one of a trend in favour of specific performance. In relation to several of the bars there have been modern cases favouring specific performance. It appears, therefore, that a claimant will now find it easier than ever before to obtain this remedy. In this sense, English law has moved closer to the approach taken in civil law jurisdictions. However, the essential difference remains—and it is a significant difference—that a claimant in English law has to overcome the substantial hurdle of first showing that damages are inadequate before he will be entitled to specific performance. There is no such initial hurdle in civil law jurisdictions, such as France, Germany and Scotland.[384]

(3) Injunctions

An injunction is an equitable remedy. The special principles governing interim **21.198** (that is, pre-trial) injunctions will be examined in the last chapter.[385] We are here, therefore, solely concerned with final injunctions (that is, injunctions granted at the trial of the action or at another hearing in which final judgment is given).[386] Injunctions are of two main types: prohibitory and mandatory. Prohibitory injunctions seek to prevent the commission or continuation of a wrong by enforcing negative duties. Mandatory injunctions, which are less common, require the defendant to do something: they enforce positive primary duties (other than for breach of contract where the appropriate remedy is specific performance) or, in the form of a mandatory 'restorative' injunction, they require the defendant to 'undo' a wrong.

Both prohibitory and mandatory injunctions may be awarded '*quia timet*' where **21.199** no wrong has yet been committed but is merely threatened. Although there is no reason why a *quia timet* injunction cannot be ordered to restrain the commission of any wrong,[387] the commonest examples concern the tort of nuisance.

---

[382] *Milward v Earl of Thanet* (1801) 5 Ves 720n; *Lazard Bros & Co Ltd v Fairfield Properties Co (Mayfair) Ltd* (1977) 121 Sol Jo 793.
[383] [1998] AC 1, HL. See para 21.190.
[384] See *Co-operative Insurance Society Ltd v Halfords Ltd (No 2)* 1999 SLT 685, OH.
[385] See Chapter 22.
[386] eg summary judgment.
[387] But in relation to breach of contract, if one regards an anticipatory breach as a breach, even though unaccepted, it will never be appropriate to describe an injunction as being awarded '*quia timet*'.

In addition to the normal principles governing prohibitory and mandatory injunctions, a claimant seeking a *quia timet* injunction must show that the tort is highly probable to occur and to occur imminently.[388]

(a) Prohibitory injunctions

(i) Breach of contract

21.200 The prohibitory injunction is the appropriate remedy for restraining the breach of a negative contractual duty. It therefore belongs on the reverse side of the coin from specific performance which enforces a positive contractual duty. However, in contrast to specific performance, and presumably because the law considers it less of an infringement of individual liberty to be ordered not to do something than to be ordered to do something, a prohibitory injunction is much easier to obtain than specific performance. In particular, while there is technically an adequacy of damages bar, it is very easily overcome. In other words, damages are in this context hardly ever considered adequate and one can rightly regard the prohibitory injunction as the primary remedy as against compensatory damages.[389]

21.201 To say that the prohibitory injunction is the primary remedy does not of course mean that it will never be refused. Two main grounds for refusal are that the claimant has acted inequitably[390] or that he has acquiesced in the wrong.[391] But indisputably the most discussed ground for refusal is that to grant the prohibitory injunction would amount to indirect specific performance of a contractual promise for which specific performance would not be directly ordered under the principles we have looked at earlier. This will now be examined in relation to express negative promises in contracts for personal service, which is the main area where the problem has arisen.[392]

21.202 The classic case is *Lumley v Wagner*.[393] Johanna Wagner undertook that for three months she would sing at Mr Lumley's theatre (Her Majesty's Theatre) in Drury Lane on two nights a week and not use her talents at any other theatre without Mr Lumley's written consent. She then agreed to sing for Mr Guy at Covent Garden for more money. Lord St Leonards LC granted an injunction restraining her from singing except for Mr Lumley, and considered that this did not amount

---

388 eg *Redland Bricks v Morris* [1970] AC 652, HL; *Hooper v Rogers* [1975] Ch 43, CA.

389 *Doherty v Allman* (1878) 3 App Cas 709, 720, HL.

390 eg *Telegraph Despatch and Intelligence Co v McLean* (1873) 8 Ch App 658.

391 eg *Shaw v Applegate* [1977] 1 WLR 970, CA.

392 For examples of the same issue in relation to contracts for the sale of goods, see *Metropolitan Electric Supply Co Ltd v Ginder* [1901] 2 Ch 799; *Decro-Wall International SA v Practitioners in Marketing Ltd* [1971] 2 WLR 361, CA; *Evans Marshall v Bertola SA* [1973] 1 WLR 349, CA.

393 (1852) 21 LJ Ch 898.

to indirect specific performance of her obligation to sing for Mr Lumley, which he recognized could not be granted.

This approach was followed and explained further in *Warner Bros Pictures Inc v **21.203** Nelson*,[394] where the film actress Bette Davis had agreed that she would render her exclusive services as an actress to the claimants for a certain period and would not during that time render any similar services to any other person. In breach of that contract she entered into an agreement to appear for another film company. The claimants were granted an injunction restraining her for three years from appearing for any other film company. Branson J reasoned that this did not amount to indirectly ordering specific performance of her contract with the claimants: for, while the defendant was being ordered not to work as a film actress for anyone else, she was left free to work elsewhere in any other capacity.

A different approach was taken in *Page One Records v Britton*.[395] 'The Troggs' **21.204** pop group employed the claimant as their sole agent and manager for five years, and agreed not to make records for anyone else during that time. In breach of that contract they then entered into an agreement to be managed by someone else. The claimant sought an interim injunction to restrain this breach. Stamp J refused to grant it because he thought that it would amount to indirect specific performance of the Troggs' personal obligations. Although to grant the injunction would still leave the Troggs free to take up any other employment, they were wanting to continue as a pop group; and, therefore, preventing them taking on any other manager would 'as a practical matter' compel them to carry on engaging the claimant as manager.

The latter approach was preferred to that taken in *Warner Bros v Nelson*, on **21.205** grounds of 'realism and practicality', by the Court of Appeal in *Warren v Mendy*.[396] This concerned a dispute over the management of the boxer Nigel Benn. The case differed from the usual restrictive covenant case in that the injunction being sought by the claimant was not against Benn for breach of contract but against another manager in a tort action for inducing breach of Benn's contract with the claimant. But the Court of Appeal felt that, as the claimant would seek an injunction against anyone who arranged to manage Benn, the same principle should be applied as if the injunction had been sought against Benn for breach of contract. The injunction was refused on the ground that to grant it would constitute indirect specific performance of Benn's contract to be exclusively managed by the claimant for the three-year contract period. While disapproving the approach in *Warner Bros v Nelson*, the Court of Appeal thought *Lumley v Wagner* was a correct

---

[394] [1937] 1 KB 209.
[395] [1968] 1 WLR 157.
[396] [1989] 1 WLR 853, CA.

decision because of the short contract period involved, which did not make it unrealistic to see the injunction as distinct from specific performance.

21.206 In *LauritzenCool AB v Lady Navigation Inc*[397] the Court of Appeal, in upholding the grant of an injunction to restrain a shipowner from breaking a time charter by employing the ship with any other charterer, distinguished *Warren v Mendy* on the grounds that the personal service element involved in a time charter is far less significant than in a close working relationship between, eg, a boxing manager and a boxer. That is no doubt correct but it is far from clear that it justified the grant of the injunction in this case given that it was accepted that specific performance could not be ordered. A controversial distinction was drawn between a prohibitory injunction that juristically would amount to specific performance (eg an injunction restraining the defendant from taking any step which would prevent performance of the contract) and one that *as a practical matter* would amount to specific performance. Specific performance principles were thought applicable to the former but not the latter.

(ii) Torts

21.207 While a prohibitory injunction can be granted in respect of any tort that can be continued or repeated—prohibitory injunctions have been granted, for example, to prevent trespass to the person,[398] inducing breach of contract,[399] defamation,[400] infringement of copyright,[401] infringement of patent,[402] and passing off[403]—it has mainly been sought, particularly at the final rather than the interlocutory stage, to restrain torts protecting the claimant's real property rights, namely nuisance and trespass to land.

21.208 In relation to these two torts—and there is no reason to suppose that different principles apply to other torts—it is clear that the prohibitory injunction rather than compensatory damages (which will usually be equitable damages awarded under section 50 of the Supreme Court Act 1981)[404] is the primary remedy.

---

397 [2005] EWCA Civ 579; [2005] 1 WLR 3686.

398 *Egan v Egan* [1975] Ch 218 (interim injunction).

399 *Emerald Construction Co Ltd v Lowthian* [1966] 1 WLR 691, CA (interim injunction). The availability of the prohibitory injunction contrasts here with the reluctance to grant specific performance of positive obligations in the main contract.

400 *Saxby v Easterbrook* (1878) 3 CPD 339; *Bonnard v Perryman* [1891] 2 Ch 269, CA (interim injunction). The desire to protect free speech means that the courts are reluctant to grant an interim injunction to restrain defamation: *Herbage v Pressdram Ltd* [1984] 1 WLR 1160, CA; Human Rights Act 1998, s 12(3).

401 *Performing Right Society Ltd v Mitchell & Booker Ltd* [1924] 1 KB 762.

402 *Coflexip SA v Stolt Comex Seaway MS Ltd* [2001] 1 All ER 952 (note), CA.

403 *Erven Warnink v J Townend & Sons (Hull) Ltd* [1979] AC 731, HL; *British Telecommunications plc v One In A Million Ltd* [1991] 1 WLR 903.

404 See paras 21.135–21.139.

The leading case illustrating this is *Shelfer v City of London Electric Lighting Co.*[405] An electric housing station had been built next to a pub and the vibration and noise caused by the operation of the machine generating the electricity constituted an actionable nuisance to the lessee of the pub. The Court of Appeal granted the injunction and said that damages should only be awarded in substitution for an injunction: 'If the injury to the plaintiff's legal rights is small. And is one which is capable of being estimated in money. And is one which could be adequately compensated by a small money payment. And the case is one in which it would be oppressive to the defendant to grant an injunction.'[406] This statement has been applied many times since, a good example being in *Kennaway v Thompson*,[407] where the Court of Appeal awarded a prohibitory injunction to limit power-boat racing, the noise from which was causing the claimant a nuisance.

Naturally, this does not mean that damages will never be awarded instead of a **21.209** prohibitory injunction. For example, the claimant's inequitable conduct may bar him from the injunction. There is conflict in the authorities as to whether a prohibitory injunction will be refused where the interference with the claimant's rights is trivial. On the one hand, there are cases such as *Behrens v Richards*[408] where, having decided that the defendants, local inhabitants, were trespassing on the claimant's land by crossing it to reach a beach, Buckley J refused a prohibitory injunction because the trespass was causing no real harm to the claimant. Nominal damages were considered sufficient. On the other hand, the Court of Appeal in *Patel v W H Smith (Eziot) Ltd*[409] preferred the view that an injunction can be granted irrespective of the harm suffered and *Behrens v Richards* was put to one side as an exceptional case.

But while the courts rarely refuse a prohibitory injunction to restrain a continuing **21.210** tort, they do often suspend or restrict its operation, and it is through this power that some account is taken of the defendant's hardship or the public interest. So, for example, in *Pride of Derby and Derbyshire Angling Association Ltd v British Celanese Ltd*[410] an injunction restraining the defendants polluting a river with untreated sewage was suspended for two years. And the injunction granted in

---

[405] [1895] 1 Ch 287, CA. For a recent illustration see *Regan v Paul Properties DPF (No 1) Ltd* [2006] EWCA Civ 1319; [2006] 3 WLR 1131 where an injunction was granted to stop the construction of a building that would infringe the claimant's right to light. (The principles applied were those for prohibitory injunctions albeit that the court referred to the injunction as mandatory.)

[406] ibid 322–3.

[407] [1981] QB 88, CA.

[408] [1905] 2 Ch 614. See also, eg, *Llandudno UDC v Woods* [1899] 2 Ch 705; *Armstrong v Sheppard & Short Ltd* [1959] 2 QB 384, CA.

[409] [1987] 1 WLR 853, CA. See also *Anchor Brewhouse Developments Ltd v Berkley House Docklands Ltd* [1987] 2 EGLR 173.

[410] [1953] Ch 149.

Kennaway v Thompson[411] is notable for its particularly detailed specifications of what was and was not permitted: for example, rather than being an unrestricted injunction, it was laid down how many days a week power-boat racing was to be allowed, when international events were to be allowed, and when club events were to be allowed.

21.211   Moreover, there have been cases that cannot be reconciled with the traditional approach affording the prohibitory injunction such primacy. The best-known example is the Court of Appeal's refusal to award an injunction against a cricket club in *Miller v Jackson*.[412]

(iii) Equitable wrongs

21.212   A prohibitory injunction can be granted to restrain the continuation or repetition of any equitable wrong. There are numerous illustrations of injunctions being granted to restrain a breach of trust. For example, injunctions have been awarded to prevent a trustee in breach of trust, from completing a detrimental contract for the sale of trust property;[413] or to restrain a proposed distribution of trust property contrary to the terms of the trust;[414] or to restrain a sale of trust property where the vendor was not complying with statutory requirements for the sale.[415] Prohibitory injunctions have also been commonly granted to restrain a breach of confidence;[416] or to prevent a defendant acting contrary to a claimant's rights acquired under the doctrine of proprietary estoppel.[417]

21.213   The same principles apply here as in relation to prohibitory injunctions restraining a tort (or breach of contract). In particular, the prohibitory injunction rather than equitable compensation (or equitable damages awarded in substitution for the injunction) is the primary remedy.

---

411 [1981] 1 QB 88, CA. Cf *Tetley v Chitty* [1986] 1 All ER 663.

412 [1977] QB 966, CA. See also, eg, *Bracewell v Appleby* [1975] Ch 408. In *Dennis v Ministry of Defence* [2003] EWHC 793 (QB) a declaration (treated as equivalent to an injunction) was refused to restrain a private nuisance constituted by the noise from RAF Wittering where fighter pilots are trained. But the public interest invoked was particularly strong because it concerned the defence of the realm and, for that reason, one should perhaps not see the decision as departing from traditional principles.

413 *Dance v Goldingham* (1873) LR 8 Ch App 902.

414 *Fox v Fox* (1870) LR 11 Eq 142.

415 *Wheelwright v Walker* (1883) 23 Ch D 752.

416 See, eg, *Peter Pan Manufacturing Corp v Corsets Silhouette Ltd* [1964] 1 WLR 96; *Duchess of Argyll v Duke of Argyll* [1967] Ch 302; *X v Y* [1988] 2 All ER 648. Where free speech is in issue, the courts may be reluctant to grant interim injunctions to restrain breach of confidence: see *Woodward v Hutchins* [1977] 1 WLR 760, CA; *Lion Laboratories Ltd v Evans* [1984] 3 WLR 539, CA; *Cream Holdings Ltd v Banerjee* [2003] EWCA Civ 103; [2003] Ch 650; Human Rights Act 1998, s 12(3).

417 *Ward v Kirkland* [1967] Ch 194 (injunction restraining the defendant interfering with the passage of water through drains); *Lim Ten Huan v Ang Swee Chuan* [1992] 1 WLR 113, PC (on a counterclaim, defendant granted an injunction, conditional on payment by defendant to claimant, restraining the claimant from entering land).

(b) Mandatory injunctions

(i) Breach of contract

At first sight, one might expect that the mandatory injunction would be the appropriate remedy to enforce a positive contractual promise. But, leaving aside interim injunctions, this role is entirely taken over by the remedy of specific performance.[418] This leaves for consideration here the mandatory restorative injunction, which is the appropriate remedy for undoing what the defendant has done in breach of a negative contractual promise.

21.214

A leading case is *Shepherd Homes Ltd v Sandham*[419] where what was being sought was an interim mandatory injunction to remove a fence that the claimant alleged had been erected in breach of a restrictive covenant. Ultimately the injunction was refused, Megarry J stressing that the courts are particularly reluctant to grant interim mandatory injunctions and would not do so here, where it was unclear whether a mandatory injunction would be granted at trial, and where the claimant had delayed in bringing his application. In discussing the relevant principles Megarry J said that a mandatory injunction was not as easy to obtain as a prohibitory injunction. That is, damages (in substitution) are generally regarded as sufficient and are the primary remedy. Megarry J preferred not to try to particularize all the grounds upon which a mandatory injunction might be refused but he said that they at least included '. . .the triviality of the damage to the plaintiff and the existence of a disproportion between the detriment that the injunction would inflict on the defendant, and the benefit that it would confer on the plaintiff'.[420]

21.215

Of course this does not mean that a mandatory injunction will never be granted to remove the effects of the breach of a negative promise. A good example is *Charrington v Simons & Co Ltd*[421] where the Court of Appeal granted a mandatory injunction ordering the defendant to remove a tarmac farm road, the height of which contravened a restrictive covenant with the claimant.

21.216

(ii) Torts

Given the rarity of positive tort obligations, mandatory injunctions for torts are almost invariably mandatory restorative injunctions concerned to undo the tort.[422] The classic discussion of the general principle governing mandatory injunctions

21.217

---

[418] See paras 21.180–21.197.

[419] [1971] Ch 340.

[420] ibid 351. See also, eg, *Sharp v Harrison* [1922] 1 Ch 502; *Wrotham Park Estate Co Ltd v Parkside Homes Ltd* [1974] 1 WLR 798, CA.

[421] [1971] 1 WLR 598, CA. See also, eg, *Wakeham v Wood* (1982) 43 P & CR 40, CA.

[422] Although conceivably a mandatory injunction could be granted to enforce a positive tort obligation, there is no obvious example of its having been granted.

is Lord Upjohn's speech in *Redland Bricks v Morris*.[423] The injunction being sought was for steps to be taken by the defendants to restore support to the claimant's land. The House of Lords discharged the mandatory injunction that had been granted because it left as too uncertain what the defendants were required to do. Therefore uncertainty is a bar to mandatory injunctions as it is to specific performance and prohibitory injunctions.[424] But Lord Upjohn clearly accepted that the mandatory injunction is not granted as readily as a prohibitory injunction. He said, 'The grant of a mandatory injunction is, of course, entirely discretionary, and unlike a negative injunction can never be "as of course".'[425]

21.218 So it is the case that, while the injunction may be the better remedy for the claimant, damages (in substitution) are generally regarded as sufficient and are the primary remedy. It follows that no mandatory injunction will generally be granted where the tortious interference is merely trivial.[426] Furthermore, in contrast to a prohibitory injunction, the hardship to the defendant is a bar to a mandatory restorative injunction. In *Redland Bricks v Morris*[427] Lord Upjohn indicated that hardship can here be a very wide restriction since, even in contrast to specific performance, the test can be a relative one; that is, so long as the defendant has acted reasonably, albeit wrongly, the courts can weigh the burden to him against the benefit to the claimant. Applying this to the facts, it was held that a mandatory injunction ordering the defendant to carry out the restoration work, while probably overcoming the uncertainty objection so long as set out in detail, would impose an excessive burden on the defendant who had acted reasonably. Such work might cost £35,000 while the value of the claimant's land affected by the slip was only about £1,500.

21.219 On the other hand, Lord Upjohn made clear that no sympathy will be shown for a defendant who has tried 'to steal a march' on the claimant, or has otherwise acted 'wantonly and quite unreasonably'.[428]

21.220 It should also be noted that, while constant supervision has traditionally been a bar to mandatory injunctions,[429] recent developments in relation to specific performance[430] suggest that it may no longer be so regarded.

---

423 [1970] AC 652, HL.
424 See also eg *Kennard v Cory Bros Co Ltd* [1922] 1 Ch 265, 274; [1922] 2 Ch 1, 13, CA.
425 [1970] AC 652, 665.
426 *Isenberg v East India House Estate Co Ltd* (1863) 3 De GJ Sm 263; *Colls v Home and Colonial Stores Ltd* [1904] AC 179, HL; cf *Kelsen v Imperial Tobacco Co* [1957] 2 QB 334.
427 [1970] AC 652, HL.
428 [1970] AC 652, 666. See also *Daniel v Ferguson* [1891] 2 Ch 27; *Colls v Home and Colonial Stores Ltd* [1904] AC 179, HL; *Pugh v Howells* (1984) 48 P & CR 298, CA.
429 See *Powell Duffryn Steam Coal Co v Taff Vale Rly Co* (1874) Ch App 331; *Kennard v Cory Bros & Co Ltd* [1922] 2 Ch 1, CA.
430 See paras 21.187–21.190.

(iii) Equitable wrongs

A mandatory injunction is the appropriate remedy to enforce a trustee's positive **21.221**
fiduciary duties.[431] Such an injunction has also been granted ordering a defendant
to convey the fee simple[432] or grant a lease[433] to a claimant under the doctrine of
proprietary estoppel. In principle, a mandatory restorative injunction can be
granted in respect of an equitable wrong but no illustration of this in the case law
has been found.

(4) Delivery Up of Goods; Delivery Up for Destruction or Destruction on Oath

Delivery up of goods is a remedy which, like the mandatory restorative injunction, **21.222**
compels a defendant to 'undo' a wrong. Delivery up for destruction or destruction
on oath may, at first sight, be thought to have the same purpose: but in general a
claimant is concerned not with the mere continued existence of infringing material but with the harmful use of that material so that the primary function of the
remedy is best viewed as being to prevent acts infringing the claimant's rights.

(a) Delivery up of goods

This is the appropriate remedy for the claimant to recover his goods where the **21.223**
defendant is tortiously 'interfering' with them (whether by the tort of conversion
or trespass to goods).[434] The power to order delivery up is enshrined in section 3
of the Torts (Interference with Goods) Act 1977. By the remedy the defendant
is ordered to deliver the goods to, or to allow them to be taken by, the claimant.

There is no reason to think that the 1977 Act has affected the principles govern- **21.224**
ing when delivery up will be ordered. The primary principle, deriving from the
remedy's roots in equity, is that delivery up will not be ordered if damages are
adequate. The same approach to adequacy has traditionally been adopted as for
specific performance of a contract for the sale of goods and specific performance
and delivery up are regarded as directly analogous remedies. It can therefore be

---

[431] *Fletcher v Fletcher* (1844) 4 Hare 67 (trustees ordered to pay beneficiaries what was owing to
them under a trust). Analogously, but going one step further, the court has jurisdiction to appoint
a receiver to ensure that the duties owed by a fiduciary are performed: Supreme Court Act 1981,
s 37(1); *Middleton v Modswell* (1806) 13 Ves 266.
[432] *Pascoe v Turner* [1979] 1 WLR 431, CA (note that it was ordered that, in default of conveyance by the defendant, the conveyance should be settled by the defendant's solicitors); *Voyce v Voyce*
(1991) 62 P & CR 290, CA.
[433] *Griffiths v Williams* (1978) 248 EG 947, CA.
[434] An analogous remedy, for breach of confidence, is delivery up of material containing confidential information belonging to the claimant: *Alpteron Rubber Co v Manning* (1917) 86 LJ Ch 377;
Industrial Furnaces Ltd v Reaves [1970] RPC 605.

said that delivery up will not be ordered for most goods on the ground that damages will enable substitutes to be bought in the market.[435] But delivery up will be ordered of physically unique goods[436] or 'commercially unique' goods.[437] Even where damages are inadequate, delivery up may still be refused. For example, given its equitable roots, the court may deny the remedy, while granting damages, because of the claimant's conduct, such as his acquiescence or 'unclean hands'. Like specific performance and injunctions, delivery up may also be ordered on terms, for example that the claimant compensates the defendant for improvements made to the goods.[438]

(b) The action for the recovery of land—a contrast to delivery up of goods

21.225 The common law action for the recovery of land (formerly known as the action for ejectment) enables a claimant to recover possession of his land by ordering the defendant to give up possession. But it is not as such a remedy for the tort of trespass. So, for example, unlike a claim for that tort, the action for the recovery of land is necessarily available to an owner who is out of possession; and the limitation period is twelve years rather than six.[439] It follows that, in contrast to delivery up of goods, the action for the recovery of land has retained its identity as a remedy solely within the law of property without becoming dependent on wrongdoing by the defendant.

(c) Delivery up for destruction or destruction on oath

21.226 Where there has been a wrongful interference with intellectual property rights (whether by infringement of copyright,[440] patent,[441] trademark,[442] or design[443]) or a breach of confidence[444] the courts have an inherent jurisdiction to order the

---

435 *William Whitley Ltd v Hilt* [1918] 2 KB 808, 819; *Cohen v Roche* [1927] 1 KB 169.

436 *Pusey v Pusey* (1684) 1 Vern 273 (the Pusey horn); *Somerset (Duke) v Cookson* (1735) 3 P Wms 390 (antique altarpiece); *Fells v Read* (1796) 3 Ves 70 (ornaments); *Lowther v Lowther* (1806) 13 Ves 95 (a painting); *Earl of Macclesfield v Davies* (1814) 3 Ves & B 16 (heirlooms).

437 *North v Great Northern Rly Co* (1860) 2 Giff 64. For 'commercial uniqueness' see para 21.185. See also *Howard Perry & Co v British Rly Board* [1980] 1 WLR 1375 where interim delivery up under s 4 of the 1977 Act was ordered in respect of 500 tons of steel.

438 As expressly laid down in s 3(7) of the 1977 Act.

439 Limitation Act 1980, s 15(1).

440 *Mergenthaler Linotype Co v Intertype Co Ltd* (1926) 43 RPC 381.

441 *Paton Calvert & Co Ltd v Rosedale Associated Manufacturers Ltd* [1966] RPC 61.

442 *Slazenger & Sons v Feltham & Co* (1889) 6 RPC 531.

443 *Rosedale Associated Manufacturers Ltd v Airfix Products Ltd* [1956] RPC 360.

444 *Prince Albert v Strange* (1849) 2 De G & Son 704; *Peter Pan Manufacturing Corpn v Corsets Silhouette Ltd* [1963] 3 All ER 402; *Ansell Rubber Co Pty Ltd v Allied Rubber Industries Pty Ltd* [1972] RPC 811.

defendant to deliver up for destruction, to the claimant or the court, or himself to destroy on oath, articles made in infringement of the claimant's rights (or even in some cases the means of making those articles).[445] The remedy goes one step beyond, and protects the claimant more effectively than, a prohibitory injunction; and it appears that there is no power to order destruction where a prohibitory injunction has not been granted.[446] Of course just because an injunction has been granted does not mean that the courts will exercise their power to order destruction. If the claimant's rights can be effectively protected by ordering something less than destruction, this will be preferred.[447] It is important to stress that this remedy is granted even though the claimant does not own the articles ordered to be destroyed.

Although this remedy is clearly ideally suited for the wrongful infringement of intellectual property rights, there are other torts for which one would have thought it would be equally appropriate.[448] The explanation for its non-availability beyond the intellectual property torts (and breach of confidence), although hardly a justification, is presumably that the intellectual property torts have their roots in equity and delivery up for destruction is an equitable remedy. **21.227**

E. Declaring Rights

While all remedies impliedly declare what the parties' rights are, a declaration is a remedy, generally regarded as statutory albeit with equitable roots, by which a court pronounces on, without altering, the rights (or even the remedies) of the parties.[449] Available in relation to any kind of legal right, a declaration can quickly and easily and without invoking any coercion, aid the resolution of a dispute or prevent one from arising. **21.228**

---

[445] By ss 99 and 230 of the Copyright, Designs and Patents Act 1988 (and see analogously ss 195 and 204 as regards a person's performer's or recording rights and s 16 of the Trade Marks Act 1994 as regards infringement of trade mark), the courts have a specific statutory power to order delivery up of infringing copies or articles, or anything designed or adapted for making infringing copies or articles. Moreover, while the courts may require the material delivered up to be destroyed they can also simply order it to be forfeited, for example, to the copyright or design right owner. Delivery up and forfeiture may be regarded as occupying a mid-position between delivery up of (one's goods) and delivery up for destruction.

[446] *Mergenthaler Linotype Co v Intertype Co Ltd* [1926] 43 RPC 381, 382.

[447] eg in *Slazenger & Sons v Feltham & Co* (1889) 6 RPC 531 the defendant was ordered merely to erase the claimant's trademark from tennis racquets, rather than being ordered to destroy all racquets bearing the trademark.

[448] An obvious example is libel: a claimant who has obtained an injunction would be even better protected by the destruction (or erasing) of libellous material.

[449] Declarations are to be contrasted with remedies by which a court pronounces on, and alters, the legal rights of the parties: see para 21.06, n 18.

21.229   Early last century it was thought that the discretion to grant a declaration should be exercised with extreme caution.[450] There is no such reluctance in modern times so that a declaration is readily granted. It has also now been accepted that, while an unusual remedy, a negative declaration (that the claimant is under no liability) can be granted where it would serve a useful purpose.[451] This of course does not mean that a declaration will never be refused. The claimant must have a real interest in the matter and must not be merely an interfering busybody. Nor will a declaration be granted where no dispute or infringement of legal rights has yet taken place and the chances of that occurring are regarded as too hypothetical.[452] Moreover, there must be a dispute between the parties.[453] Given its equitable roots, it would also appear, although there is little authority on this, that equitable defences, such as laches, acquiescence and 'unclean hands', bar a declaration.

21.230   As a remedy for a civil wrong a declaration is generally concerned to pronounce authoritatively that the defendant's conduct did or does amount to a wrong. For example in *Harrison v Duke of Rutland*[454] the defendant, on a counterclaim, was granted a declaration that the claimant was trespassing when he rode his bicycle along the defendant's road as a means of interfering with the defendant's grouse shooting.

21.231   Two further points are noteworthy. First, in some cases the courts have found it useful to be able to grant a declaration, while refusing or suspending the more drastic remedy of an injunction.[455] Secondly, the courts now have power to award an interim declaration.[456]

21.232   An award of nominal damages can also be regarded as having the purpose of declaring rights. Nominal damages are awarded in respect of wrongs that are actionable without proof of damage. Where the court is satisfied that the claimant has not suffered any damage, the claimant is still entitled to damages for the defendant's wrong (for example the defendant's breach of contract or tort actionable per se). Nominal damages comprise a trivial sum of money, usually about £2–£10. Nominal damages are therefore not compensatory and must be distinguished from a small sum of compensatory damages. Given that the remedy

---

[450] *Faber v Gosworth UDC* (1903) 88 LT 539, 550.
[451] *Messier-Dowty Ltd v Sabena SA (No 2)* [2000] 1 WLR 2040, 2050 (*per* Lord Woolf MR).
[452] *Mellstrom v Garner* [1970] 1 WLR 603, CA.
[453] *Meadows Indemnity Co Ltd v Insurance Corporation of Ireland Ltd* [1989] 2 Lloyd's Rep 218.
[454] [1893] 1 QB 142, CA.
[455] *Llandudno UDC v Woods* [1899] 2 Ch 705; *Stollmeyer v Trinidad Lake Petroleum Co* [1918] AC 485, PC. See para 21.210.
[456] CPR r 25.1(1)(b).

of a declaration is specifically designed to declare rights, it would appear that nominal damages are superfluous and could happily be abolished. Certainly there are no longer any practical consequences turning on whether an award of nominal damages has been made or not (for example, a claimant awarded nominal damages is no longer necessarily to be regarded as a successful claimant for the purpose of costs).[457]

---

[457] *Anglo-Cyprian Trade Agencies v Paphos Wine Industries Ltd* [1951] 1 All ER 873.

22

CIVIL PROCEDURE

A. Introduction

(1) Civil Procedure Rules 1998 (CPR)[1]

22.01 The CPR, a 'new procedural code', took effect on 26 April 1999.[2] Earlier, Lord Woolf in his reports had identified various aims:

(1) to speed up civil justice;

(2) to render civil procedure more accessible to ordinary people;

(3) to promote swift settlement;

(4) to simplify the language of civil procedure;

(5) to make litigation more efficient; and

(6) to make litigation less costly.

Aims (5) and (6) were to be promoted by avoiding excessive and disproportionate resort to procedural devices.[3] Of these, (1), (2), (3), and (5) have improved. But the success of (4) is severely open to question, certainly when one considers the complexity of the CPR system of rules and practice directions. As for reducing the cost of litigation, aim number (6), this has been shown to be 'the Achilles heel' of the CPR system (see further 22.108).

22.02 Until the enactment of the CPR, English procedure was based on the 'adversarial principle' or 'principle of party control' which permitted the parties and their lawyers to control pre-trial development of the litigation. Since the CPR, however, the parties have much less scope to control such development. Instead the

---

[1] Detailed account: Neil Andrews, *English Civil Procedure* (2003) ch 2.

[2] So described in CPR 1.1(1).

[3] Lord Woolf, *Access to Justice, Interim Report* (1995) and *Access to Justice, Final Report* (1996); responses to these reports: S Flanders 'Case Management: Failure in America? Success in England and Wales?' (1998) 17 CJQ 308; M Zander, 'The Government's Plans on Civil Justice' (1998) 61 MLR 383–389 and 'The Woolf Report: Forwards or Backwards for the New Lord Chancellor?' (1997) 16 CJQ 208; AAS Zuckerman and R Cranston (eds) *Reform of Civil Procedure: Essays on 'Access to Justice'* (1995); AAS Zuckerman, 'The Woolf Report on Access to Justice' (1997) 2 ZZP Int 31.

courts now have extensive 'case management' powers and duties.[4] A related change is that the parties can no longer relax the rules or directions governing the progress and timetabling of the action.[5] Furthermore, the parties and their lawyers 'are required to help the court to further 'the Overriding Objective' in CPR Part 1.[6]

(2) Sources of English Civil Procedure[7]

(a) Civil Procedure Rules and Practice Directions

The CPR is by far the largest source of procedural rules. Until April 1999 there **22.03** were two sets of rules, the Rules of the Supreme Court (RSC) dealing with matters in the High Court and Court of Appeal, and the County Court Rules (CCR) with county court litigation.[8] But since 26 April 1999 a unified set of rules applies to both the High Court and county courts, as well as the Court of Appeal.[9] These rules have been drafted by the Rule Committee, which replaced the former separate rules committees responsible for the RSC and CCR.[10] The Heads of Divisions of the High Court have power to issue practice directions governing matters of procedure.[11]

(b) Judicial decisions

This source of procedural law concerns the case law of the High Court and higher **22.04** appellate courts.[12] Judges in these courts apply the procedural rules authoritatively and develop new principles or doctrines. Many decisions have provided guidance or commentary upon the CPR.[13] The creativity of these courts must be admired.[14] European case law is also important, notably the Strasbourg court's

---

4 CPR 1.4(2) 3.1; on the new system from the perspective of the traditional adversarial principle, Neil Andrews, 'A New Civil Procedural Code for England: Party-Control "Going, Going, Gone"'(2000) 19 CJQ 19; Neil Andrews, English Civil Procedure (2003) 13.12 to 13.41; 14.04 to 14.45; 15.65 to 15.72.

5 CPR 3.8(3); cf non-mandatory time provisions, CPR 2.11, eg, the period for service of claim form: *Thomas v The Home Office* [2006] EWCA Civ 1355; [2007] 1 WLR 230; noted J Sorabi [2007] CJQ 168.

6 CPR 1.3; eg, *Hertsmere Primary Care Trust v Rabindra-Anandh* [2005] EWHC 320; [2005] CP Rep 41; and the court's 'active' case-management responsibility includes 'encouraging the parties to co-operate with each other in the conduct of the proceedings': CPR 1.4(2)(a).

7 Detailed account: Neil Andrews, *English Civil Procedure* (2003) 1.01 to 1.38.

8 On the history of the RSC, M Dockray (1997) 113 LQR 120, notably nn 32–33.

9 CPR 2.1 defines the scope of the new rules.

10 Civil Procedure Act 1997, ss 2–4; its full title is 'the Civil Procedure Rule Committee'.

11 Civil Procedure Act 1997, s 5.

12 Sir Jack Jacob, *The Fabric of English Justice* (1987) 57 ff.

13 eg, *Biguzzi v Rank Leisure plc* [1999] 1 WLR 1926, CA (range of court's disciplinary powers); *Daniels v Walker* [2000] 1 WLR 1382 CA (discussion of single, joint experts).

14 On eight fundamental judicial innovations, Neil Andrews, 'Development in English Civil Procedure' (1997) 2 ZZPInt 7.

jurisprudence concerning Article 6(1) of the European Convention on Human Rights.[15] Article 6(1) creates the following guarantees: access to justice (a right which has been implied by the European Court of Human Rights);[16] 'a fair hearing', which includes various rights[17] (to be present at an adversarial hearing, to equality of arms, to fair presentation of the evidence, to cross examine, to a reasoned judgment);[18] 'a public hearing'; 'a hearing within a reasonable time';[19] and 'a hearing before an independent and impartial tribunal established by law'.

(c) Other sources

22.05   The main procedural guides are: the Chancery Guide (2005), the Admiralty and Commercial Courts Guide (2006) (see further 22.48), and the Queen's Bench Division Guide (2000).[20] Authoritative literature can have 'persuasive' force.[21]

B. Stages in the Course of a Civil Action

(1) Pre-Action Stage

22.06   The CPR system introduced an important set of 'pre-action protocols'. These form a framework of responsibilities for prospective parties and their legal representatives. The protocols are intended to enable each side to know the strengths and weaknesses of his opponent's case. For example, a person who alleges that he

---

[15] On the case law of the European Court of Human Rights (Strasbourg) concerning Article 6(1) of the European Convention on Human Rights (1953) (Cmd 8969) and Sch 1 to the Human Rights Act 1998: L Mulcahy, *Human Rights and Civil Practice* (2001) chaps 10–12; R Clayton and H Tomlinson, *The Law of Human Rights* (2000) 2 vols; and 2001 supplement; S Grocz, J Beatson and P Duffy, *Human Rights: the 1998 Act and the European Convention* (2000); A Lester and D Pannick, *Human Rights Law and Practice* (1999); A Le Sueur, 'Access to Justice in the United Kingdom' [2000] EHRLR 457; for a review of Art 6(1) *Brown v Stott* [2000] UKPC D3; [2003] 1 AC 681, PC, especially Lords Bingham and Steyn; the other European court is the European Court of Justice (Luxembourg), especially applying the Jurisdiction Regulation: (EC) No 44/2001 of 22 December 2000 on 'jurisdiction and the recognition and enforcement of judgments in civil and commercial matters': [2001] OJ L 12/1.

[16] *Golder v UK* (1975) 1 EHRR 524, ECtHR, at [35].

[17] R Clayton and H Tomlinson, *The Law of Human Rights* (2000) 11.201; JM Jacob, *Civil Justice in the Age of Human Rights* (2007).

[18] On the duty to give reasons, *English v Emery Reimbold & Strick Ltd* [2002] EWCA Civ 605; [2002] 1 WLR 2409, CA; Neil Andrews, *English Civil Procedure* (2003), at 5.39 to 5.68.

[19] Proceedings which lasted nearly 10 years, from complaint to prospective defendant to conclusion of final appeal; violation of Art 6(1): *Blake v UK* (68890/01) [2006] ECHR 805.

[20] These Guides are accessible at <www.dca.gov.uk/civil/procrules_fin/menus/rules.htm>.

[21] eg *Arlidge, Eady and Smith on Contempt* (3rd edn, 2005); *Cross and Tapper on Evidence* (10th edn, 2004); *Dicey, Morris and Collins on the Conflict of Laws* (14th edn, 2006); Spencer Bower, Turner and Handley, *Res Judicata* (3rd edn, 1996).

was the victim of medical negligence can gain access to hospital or medical records under this system of pre-action protocols. The 'Practice Direction on Protocols' states:[22] 'In all cases not covered by any approved protocol, the court will expect the parties. . .to act reasonably in exchanging information and documents relevant to the claim and generally in trying to avoid the necessity for the start of proceedings.' An pre-action admission of liability can be withdrawn when the defence is pleaded, provided this change of position will neither involve an abuse of process nor 'obstruct the just disposal of the case'.[23] The latter problem might arise, for example, if evidence has been lost or destroyed as a result of the earlier admission. Other aspects of pre-action disclosure are considered at 22.54. But here it should be noted that it can be an offence for a prospective defendant, sensing that litigation is imminent, to destroy documents, delete e-mails, or take other steps to eliminate potential evidence. Morritt V-C in *Douglas v Hello! Ltd* (2003)[24] approved Australian guidance, that: 'the criterion. . .is whether that [pre-action] destruction or disposal amounts to an attempt to pervert the course of justice. . .'.[25] The Australian court left open the possibility that such destruction might also involve criminal contempt of court.[26] It is also hoped that settlement will be promoted by efficient exchange of information.[27] For the moment (at April 2007), specific protocols applied to the following topics: 'Construction and Engineering Disputes', 'Defamation', 'Personal Injury Claims', 'Resolution of Clinical Disputes', 'Professional Negligence', 'Judicial Review', 'Disease and Illness Claims', 'Housing Disrepair Cases', and 'Possession Claims based on Rent Arrears'.[28] The Civil Justice Council is considering whether a consolidated pre-action protocol might be attractive.

If a dispute does proceed to formal civil proceedings, the court can make an **22.07** appropriate costs order to indicate disapproval of a person's failure to comply with a protocol. Thus the court can modify the normal costs order (see 22.107), with the result that the victorious party will not receive his costs, or at least these will be reduced.[29] This aspect of pre-action protocols applies to all categories of

---

[22] 'Practice Direction on Protocols', 4.1.

[23] *Walley v Stoke-on-Trent CC* [2006] EWCA Civ 1137; [2007] 1 WLR 352 at [34], [35] (note Brooke LJ's plea for reform at [45]); considering *Sowerby v Charlton* [2005] EWCA Civ 1610; [2006] 1 WLR 568.

[24] *Douglas v Hello! Ltd* [2003] EWHC 55 (Ch) at [86]; [2003] 1 All ER 1087 (brief note).

[25] *British American Tobacco Australia Services Ltd v Cowell & McCabe* [2002] VSCA 197, esp at [173] to [175] (Supreme Court of Victoria, Australia).

[26] ibid, at [173].

[27] For comments on pre-action protocols, *Carlson v Townsend* [2001] EWCA Civ 511; [2001] 3 All ER 663, CA; *Ford v GKR Construction Ltd* [2000] 1 WLR 802, 807, CA.

[28] A new version of the 'Construction and Building Disputes' protocol was issued in April 2007: see <www.dca.gov.uk/civil/procrules_fin/index.htm>.

[29] CPR 44.3(5)(a); PD (Protocols) 2.3.

civil litigation.[30] But it would go against the whole spirit of the pre-action protocol system to issue a costs sanction against a party who has conscientiously abandoned issues during the pre-action action phase.[31]

(2) Commencement, Service, and Pleadings

22.08 In the ordinary case, an action begins by the claimant issuing a claim form. The case is later allocated to the appropriate 'track': small claims litigation, fast-track litigation, or multi-track. In addition, multi-track litigation must be further allocated to a county court or the High Court, and within the latter court to the appropriate division (the three divisions are Queen's Bench, Chancery, and Family) and even to a specific constituent 'court', for example, the Commercial Court (see further 22.48) or Technology and Construction Court, which are parts of the Queen's Bench Division. If the case is to be defended, both the claimant and defendant must produce a sworn 'statement of case' (formerly known as 'pleadings') setting out the main aspects of the claim or defence. There is no need to include in a 'statement of case' any detailed evidence or details of legal argument. The claimant should also specify the relief he is seeking.

(3) Evidence Gathering and the Exchange of Information

22.09 Under the common law system, the parties present for the court's consideration rival versions of the evidence relevant to the controversy or issue. The CPR system has not altered the court's essentially 'responsive' role with respect to evidence, although the judge must control proceedings in the interests of efficiency and prevent them becoming unduly prolonged or complicated (see 22.46, 22.71 and 22.101). Thus the decision to call particular factual witnesses and to use particular documents lies with each party. The court does not compel a party to produce particular witnesses or documents. Each party must normally produce a witness statement in respect of each factual witness, including the party's own intended factual evidence. No witness can be heard unless such a statement has been made and exchanged before trial. The judge will be expected to have read the witness statements before trial. At trial this evidence can be supplemented by oral examination. Disclosure of Documents[32] and Expert Evidence are considered in detail at Sections F (22.53 ff) and H (22.71 ff); and the topic of privileges at Section G (22.61 ff). As for evidence at pre-trial hearings, in respect of 'accelerated and

---

[30] *Ford v GKR Construction Ltd* [2000] 1 WLR 1397, 1403, CA.

[31] *McGlinn v Waltham Contractors Ltd* [2005] EWHC 1419 (TCC); [2005] 3 All ER 1126, at [14].

[32] Detailed account: Neil Andrews, *English Civil Procedure* (2003) ch 26.

interim relief' (see Section D, at 22.20), witness evidence is received in the form of sworn statements.

(4) Trial, Appeal, and Enforcement

Adjudication at trial is nearly always by a single judge, without a jury.[33] The proc- **22.10**
esses of trial and appeal are examined at Section J (at 22.96 ff). Enforcement is considered at Section M (at 22.125).

C. Commencement of Proceedings

(1) Issue of Process

The main form of commencement is by claim form.[34] An alternative 'Part 8 **22.11**
procedure' is used where the claimant seeks 'the court's decision on a question which is unlikely to involve a substantial dispute of fact'.[35] No claim can be commenced in the High Court unless the sum in issue is for more than £15,000 or, in the case of damages for personal injuries, more than £50,000.[36] Allocation of business to the High Court and county court is determined by reference to the claim's 'value', 'complexity' and public importance.[37] The claimant can choose whether to include in the claim form the particulars of claim or to serve these later.[38] Accompanying the particulars of claim, the claimant must serve forms enabling the defendant to defend the claim, or to admit the claim, and to acknowledge service.[39] The time of commencement of civil proceedings is when the court enters the date on the claim form.[40] The same date governs the *lis alibi pendens* rules under the Brussels jurisdictional regime.[41] As for the topics of 'Group

---

[33] Jury trial in civil actions is confined to the torts of defamation, malicious prosecution, and false imprisonment: Neil Andrews, *English Civil Procedure* (2003) 34–06 ff.

[34] CPR 7.2; PD (7) 3, 4.

[35] CPR 8.1(6).

[36] Respectively, PD (7) 2.1, 2.2; for transfers between these courts, CPR Part 30.

[37] PD (7) 2.4.

[38] CPR 7.4.

[39] CPR 7.8(1).

[40] CPR 7.2(2); for limitation purposes, the date can be earlier: when the claim form was received in the court office: PD (7) 5.1; thus in *Barnes v St Helens MBC* [2006] EWCA Civ 1372; [2007] 1 WLR 879 (noted J Sorabi [2007] CJQ 166) it was held that a claim was 'brought' when a claimant's request for the issue of a claim form was delivered to the correct court office during its opening hours on the day before the expiry of the limitation period, even though the claim was not issued by the court office until four days later, by which date it was out of time.

[41] (EC) No 44/2001 of 22 December 2000 on 'jurisdiction and the recognition and enforcement of judgments in civil and commercial matters': [2001] OJ L 12/1.

Litigation Orders' and representative proceedings, for reasons of space, the reader is referred to other sources.[42]

(2) Service of Process

22.12 Service of the claim form must normally be made within four months from the date of issue.[43] Where the claim form is to be served outside the jurisdiction, the period is six months.[44] The parties can agree in writing an extension.[45] The claimant can seek an extension of this period for service either before the period for service has elapsed[46] or after.[47] In the former situation, the courts have glossed a bare discretion by deciding that a 'very good reason' is enough, but not a 'weak' reason, such as sheer forgetfulness.[48] But if the four month period has already elapsed at the time the application for an extension is made, the rules prescribe the following restrictive criteria: 'the court has been unable to serve the claim form or the court has been unable to serve the claim form and, in either case, the claimant has acted promptly in making the application'.[49] There has been elaborate judicial discussion of discretionary powers of extension.[50] The court will serve the claim form (provided the defendant's address for service is specified in the claim form)[51] unless the claimant tells it that he wishes to do so, or there is rule, practice direction, or order releasing the court from itself serving the process.[52]

---

[42] Apart from the reference at n 654 below, the reader should consult: Neil Andrews, *English Civil Procedure* (2003); R Mulheron *The Class Action in Common Law Legal Systems: A Comparative Perspective* (2004) (reviewed, S Gibbons (2006) 122 LQR 336); 'Some Difficulties with a Group Litigation Order-and Why a Class Action is Superior' (2005) CJQ 40; Mulheron (forthcoming article) 2007 MLR; J Seymour, 'Justice and the Representative Parties Rule: An Overriding Interest?' (2006) LS 668; C Hodges 'The Europeanisation of Civil Justice: Trends and Issues' (2007) CJQ 96, which includes reference to the DTI's consultation on an 'UK Representative Actions mechanism': <www.dti.gov.uk/consultations/page30259.html>.

[43] CPR 7.5(2).

[44] CPR 7.5 (3); *Habib Bank Ltd v Central Bank of Sudan* [2006] EWHC 1767 (Comm); [2007] 1 WLR 470 (validity of service abroad); distinguished, *Olafsson v Gissurarson* [2006] EWHC 3162 (QB); [2007] 1 All ER 88 (invalid service in Iceland could not be cured under CPR 3.10).

[45] *Thomas v The Home Office* [2006] EWCA Civ 1355; [2007] 1 WLR 230, considering CPR 2.11; noted J Sorabi [2007] CJQ 168.

[46] CPR 7.6(2).

[47] *Thomas v The Home Office* [2006] EWCA Civ 1355; [2007] 1 WLR 230.

[48] *Hashtroodi v Hancock* [2004] EWCA Civ 652; [2004] 1 WLR 3206, [19], [20].

[49] CPR 7.6(3).

[50] *Collier v Williams* [2006] EWCA Civ 20; [2006] 1 WLR 1945 examining, in particular, *Hashtroodi v Hancock* [2004] EWCA Civ 652; [2004] 1 WLR 3206; and case law cited below at n 65.

[51] CPR 6.13.

[52] CPR 6.3.

The modes of service, whether by the court or by the claimant, are: in accordance **22.13** with a prior contract;[53] personal service[54] upon the defendant (whether an individual, company or partnership);[55] first class post[56] (the place for valid service by this method is specified in the rules;[57] when service is made by the court, postal service is the normal method);[58] leaving the claim form at an address (which can include the relevant office of the defendant's solicitor) specified in advance for these purposes by the defendant;[59] leaving the claim form at the defendant's (in the case of an individual, business proprietor, or firm) 'usual or last known residence'[60] or other place specified in the rules;[61] through a document exchange (unless prohibited in advance by the intended defendant);[62] by fax or other electronic means (both these modes are in fact circumscribed);[63] the court can order service by some alternative method;[64] or the court can even dispense with service.[65] The rules specify the 'deemed day of service' in these various situations.[66]

(3) Pleadings

The matters in dispute are to be ascertained from the 'statement of case'.[67] This **22.14** phrase embraces the claim form, particulars of claim (if separate from the claim form), the defence, a possible reply to defence, as well as 'further information'[68]

---

[53] CPR 6.15.

[54] CPR 6.2(1)(a).

[55] CPR 6.4(3)(4)(5).

[56] CPR 6.2(1)(b).

[57] CPR 6.5(6).

[58] PD (6) 8.1.

[59] CPR 6.5(1)-(4).

[60] CPR 6.5(6); *Collier v Williams* [2006] EWCA Civ 20; [2006] 1 WLR 1945 at [63] ff (and rejecting view that C's reasonable belief that D resided in a particular place is enough if in fact D never resided there).

[61] CPR 6.5(6).

[62] CPR 6.2(1)(d); PD (6) 2.

[63] CPR 6.2(1)(e); PD (6) 3 (restrictive both for faxes and e-mail); *Kuenyehia v International Hospitals Group Ltd* [2006] EWCA Civ 21; [2006] CP Rep 34.

[64] CPR 6.8.

[65] CPR 6.9; however, the courts will not use CPR 6.9 to relieve liberally against ineffective, defective, or late service: see the statement of principle by Neuberger LJ, in the *Kuenyehia* case, [2006] EWCA Civ 21; [2006] CP Rep 34 at [26], considering a farrago of cases, especially *Godwin v Swindon BC* [2001] EWCA Civ 1478; [2002] 1 WLR 997, CA, *Anderton v Clwyd CC* [2002] EWCA Civ 933; [2002] 1 WLR 3174 and *Cranfield v Bridegrove* [2003] EWCA Civ 656; [2003] 1 WLR 2441, CA.

[66] CPR 6.7; *Akram v Adam* [2004] EWCA Civ 1601; [2005] 1 WLR 2762, at [42] and [43] (service effective under this deeming regime even if notice was never received).

[67] For this wide definition, CPR 2.3(1).

[68] CPR 18.1.

(formerly 'further and better particulars') and a counterclaim or third party proceeding. The claim form must contain a concise statement of the nature of the claim and specify the remedy sought.[69] But the court can grant a remedy even if it is unspecified in the claim form.[70] The particulars of claim must include 'a concise statement of the facts on which the claimant relies' and include any claim for interest.[71] The claimant is not required to adduce at this early stage details of his intended evidence. The defendant can respond in any of three ways: (i) by stating which allegations in the particular of claim he denies or (ii) requires to be proved or (iii) which allegations he admits.[72] The defendant will be 'taken to admit' a particular allegation if the defence contains no response to it, whether direct or indirect.[73] A party can include in a statement of claim 'any point of law on which his claim or defence. . .is based', and 'the name of any witness he proposes to call', and 'a copy of any document which he considers is necessary to his claim or defence. . .(including any expert's report to be filed in accordance with [CPR] Part 35)'. 'Statements of case' must be verified by a statement of truth.[74] A dishonest statement can lead to contempt proceedings.[75] Special rules govern amendment of statements of case.[76]

(4) Limitation of Actions[77]

22.15 In general, expiry of a limitation period does not extinguish the claimant's right. And so a limitation defence must be pleaded in the defendant's statement of case.[78] If the defence is not raised, the action is sound.[79] However, the contrary principle of automatic extinction applies in a few exceptional contexts,[80] notably

---

[69] CPR 16.2(1); PD (16), 12 to 14 for matters which must be included in defences.

[70] CPR 16.2(5).

[71] CPR 16.4.

[72] CPR 16.5(1).

[73] CPR 16.5(5).

[74] CPR 22.1(1)(a).

[75] PD (22) 3.1.

[76] Limitation Act 1980, s 35; CPR 17.4; *Charles Church Developments v Stent Foundations Ltd* [2006] EWHC 3158; [2007] 1 WLR 1203; *O'Byrne v Aventis Pasteur MSD Ltd* [2006] EWHC 2562 (QB); [2007] 1 WLR 757; *BP plc v AON Ltd* [2005] EWHC 2554 (Comm); [2006] 1 Lloyd's Rep 549 at [46] to [63]; *Martin v Kaisary* [2005] EWCA Civ 594; [2005] CP Rep 35; *Goode v Martin* [2001] EWCA Civ 1899; [2002] 1 All ER 620, CA; Neil Andrews, *English Civil Procedure* (2003) 10.78 ff; *Zuckerman on Civil Procedure* (2006) 6.36 ff.

[77] Andrews, ibid, ch 12 and *Zuckerman*, ibid, 24.4 ff; A McGee, *Limitation Periods* (2006); Law Commission's discussion, *Limitation of Actions* (Law Com No 270, HC 23, 2001; and L Com CP No 151, 1998); on which, Neil Andrews [1998] CLJ 588; R James (2003) 22 CJQ 41.

[78] PD (16) 13.1.

[79] *Ketteman v Hansel Properties* [1987] AC 189, 219, HL.

[80] L Com CP No 151, 1998, para 9.4, noting certain international conventions, eg, *Payabi v Armstel Shipping Corpn* [1992] QB 907 (the Hague Rules); claims made under the Consumer Protection Act 1987; the tort of conversion, Limitation Act 1980, s 3(2); recovery of land, 1980

a foreign limitation period.[81] Claims for injunctive relief or specific performance are subject to the equitable bars of 'laches' and acquiescence, and the statutory periods of limitation do not apply.[82]

A person under a disability, including a minor, has three years from the date the disability ceases (or he reaches 18, in the case of a minor).[83] There are also special limitation provisions where the action is based on the defendant's fraud, or facts relevant to the claim have been deliberately concealed by the defendant,[84] or the action is for relief from the consequences of mistake.[85] The main limitation periods will now be set out. **22.16**

Defamation and malicious falsehood claims are subject to a one year rule.[86] For personal injury and fatal accident claims, the period is three years from the date of damage or (later) date when the claimant acquired 'knowledge' of the wrong.[87] There is a discretionary power to lift the statutory bar in the case of actions for personal injury or fatal accidents.[88] Until legislation amends the law, a non-extendable six year period governs assault claims, including instances of alleged sexual abuse.[89] Claims in tort for 'latent damage', other than claims for personal injury or fatal accidents, are subject either to a six year period, reckoned from the date at which the cause of action accrued, or a three year period running from the 'starting date' (when the claimant acquired knowledge of the claim and of his capacity to bring it).[90] The latent damage rules apply only to **22.17**

Act, s 17; see also discussion in *Financial Services Compensation Scheme Ltd v Larnell (Insurances) Ltd* [2005] EWCA Civ 1408; [2006] QB 808 at [40] ff.

[81] Foreign Limitation Periods Act 1984; eg, *Gotha City v Sotheby's The Times* 8 October, 1998.

[82] *P & O Nedlloyd BV v Arab Metals Co* [2006] EWCA Civ 1717; for literature and other authorities, see Neil Andrews, *English Civil Procedure* (2003) 12.81 ff; L Com CP No 151, 1998, paras 9.12 to 9.22; L Com No 270, HC 23, 2001, paras 2.97 to 2.99.

[83] Limitation Act 1980, s 28; L Com CP No 151, 1998, paras 8.2–8.10; noting *Headford v Bristol & District Health Authority* [1995] PIQR P180, CA (proceedings commenced 1992 concerning hospital incident in 1964; claimant permanently brain-damaged at birth).

[84] 1980 Act, s 32; *Cave v Robinson, Jarvis and Rolf* [2002] UKHL 18; [2003] 1 AC 368, HL (T Prime (2002) 21 CJQ 357) considered in *Williams v Fanshaw Porter & Hazelhurst* [2004] EWCA Civ 157; [2004] 1 WLR 3185.

[85] 1980 Act, s 32; *Kleinwort Benson Ltd v Lincoln CC* [1999] 2 AC 349, HL.

[86] 1980 Act, ss 4A, 32A.

[87] 1980 Act, ss 11, 12 to 14; L Com CP No 151 (1998) paras 3.38 ff; *Adams v Bracknell Forest Borough Council* [2004] UKHL 29; [2005] 1 AC 76; R Moules (2005) CJQ 37.

[88] 1980 Act, s 33; *Adams v Bracknell Forest Borough Council* [2004] UKHL 29; [2005] 1 AC 76; R Moules (2005) CJQ 37; *KR v Bryn Alyn Community (Holdings) Ltd* [2003] EWCA Civ 85; [2003] QB 1441; *Horton v Sadler* [2006] UKHL 27; [2006] 2 WLR 1346: reversing *Walkley v Precision Forgings Ltd* [1979] 1 WLR 606, HL.

[89] 1980 Act, s 2; *A v Hoare* [2006] EWCA Civ 395; [2006] 1 WLR 2320, applying *Stubbings v Webb* [1993] AC 498, HL.

[90] 1980 Act, s 14A, added by Latent Damage Act 1986; *Haward v Fawcetts (a firm)* [2006] UKHL 9; [2006] 1 WLR 682; J O'Sullivan, 'Limitation, Latent Damage and Solicitors' Negligence' (2004) 20 Journal of Professional Negligence 218.

negligence pleaded in tort (and not in contract).[91] A 'long-stop' provision bars a latent damage claim once fifteen years have elapsed since the act of alleged negligence.[92]

22.18 Subject to the preceding special tort provisions (see preceding paragraph), other tort actions (for damages) or contractual claims (for damages or debt) are subject to a six year rule.[93] The Court of Appeal has held that the remedy of specific performance for breach of contract is not subject to the six year rule.[94] Instead, this equitable remedy is subject to the doctrines of laches and acquiescence (see 22.15).[95] As for damages or debt claims in respect of deeds (or 'covenants'), the period is twelve years.[96] The interplay of contractual and tort claims must be noted. As Lord Nicholls observed, 'in cases of breach of contract the cause of action arises at the date of the breach of contract' but 'in cases in tort the cause of action arises, not when the culpable conduct occurs, but when the plaintiff first sustains damage'.[97] The House of Lords, in a tort claim concerning negligent accounting, held that a contingent liability does not constitute 'damage', and that the relevant date is when damage actually materializes.[98] Where there are overlapping rights in contract and tort, that is, a 'concurrence' of claims, a claimant can sue both in contract and tort.[99] The Contracts (Rights of Third Parties) Act 1999 applies the six year rule and twelve year rule, respectively, to third party claims upon simple contract and contracts founded upon deeds.[100] A two-year period applies to statutory contribution claims.[101] There is no general provision governing actions for restitution, but the statutory limitation rules have been applied in a piece-meal way to many such claims.[102]

22.19 Finally, there are special provisions concerning actions for the recovery of land, or concerning mortgages or for non-fraudulent breaches of trust.[103]

---

[91] *Iron Trade Mutual Insurance Co Ltd v JK Buckenham Ltd* [1990] 1 All ER 808; affmd *Société Générale de Réeassurance v Eras (International) Ltd* (note) [1992] 2 All ER 82, CA.

[92] 1980 Act, s 14B.

[93] 1980 Act, ss 2, 5, respectively.

[94] *P & O Nedlloyd BV v Arab Metals Co* [2006] EWCA Civ 1717 at [52].

[95] ibid, at [55] ff.

[96] 1980 Act, s 8.

[97] *Nykredit Mortgage Bank plc v Edward Erdman Group Ltd (No 2)* [1997] 1 WLR 1627, 1630, HL.

[98] *Law Society v Sephton & Co (a firm)* [2006] UKHL 22; [2006] 2 AC 543.

[99] *Henderson v Merrett Syndicates Ltd* [1995] 2 AC 145, 184–194, HL.

[100] Contracts (Rights of Third Parties) Act 1999, s 7(3).

[101] Limitation Act 1980, s 10 (claims under the Civil Liability (Contribution) Act 1978); *Aer Lingus v Gildacroft Ltd* [2006] EWCA Civ 4; [2006] 1 WLR 1173 (date runs from time that primary liability is quantified).

[102] L Com No 270, HC 23, 2001, paras 2.48 to 2.51.

[103] 1980 Act, ss 15–17 (recovery of land); s 20 (mortgages); see also s 16.

D. Accelerated and Interim Relief [104]

(1) Preservation of Assets: Freezing Injunctions [105]

These were formerly known as '*Mareva* injunctions'.[106] CPR Part 25 contains the **22.20**
standard forms.[107] The injunction operates at first 'without notice' (*ex parte*), usually before the main proceedings have commenced. Surprise is its essence. Most
freezing injunctions are awarded by the High Court rather than the county
courts.[108] A freezing injunction preserves assets from dissipation pending final
execution against the defendant. This is an *in personam* order which compels a
defendant to refrain from dealing with his assets, normally bank accounts. It also
imposes a collateral restraint upon non-parties, such as the defendant's bank. It
does not give the applicant any proprietary interest in the defendant's assets.[109]
Assets above the protected sum will remain 'unfrozen'. The defendant is permitted
to satisfy his ordinary domestic or business expenses, and to pay for legal advice
when resisting the order.[110] An ancillary disclosure order will normally compel the
respondent to disclose details of his assets in England (or, where appropriate, elsewhere),[111] whether or not the assets are in his own name, and whether or not solely
owned.[112] A non-party can also be compelled to provide certain information if he
has assisted, albeit innocently, another's wrongdoing.[113]

---

[104] On the material examined in this section, see Neil Andrews, *English Civil Procedure* (2003)
ch 17 to 21, and 37, section A; *Zuckerman on Civil Procedure* (2006) ch 8, 9; IS Goldrein (ed),
Commercial Litigation: Pre-emptive Remedies (2005) chs 1–6.

[105] The leading work is S Gee, *Commercial Injunctions* (2004); see also Neil Andrews, *English Civil
Procedure* (2003) ch 17; *Zuckerman on Civil Procedure* (2006) 9.139 ff; IS Goldrein (ed), *Commercial
Litigation: Pre-emptive Remedies* (International Edition, 2005) ch 2; for references, Neil Andrews,
op cit, 17.01 at n 7 and Neil Andrews, 'Provisional and Protective Measures: Towards an Uniform
Provisional Order' (2001) VI Uniform L Rev (Rev dr unif) 931, at n 4 ('blue-print' for an international
code or practice relating to freezing relief, preservation of evidence, and asset disclosure orders); on
arbitration, A Redfern, 'Interim Measures' in LW Newman and RD Hill (eds) *The Leading Arbitrators'
Guide to International Arbitration* (2004) 217–43; M Mustill and S Boyd, *Commercial Arbitration*
(2001, Companion Volume) at 314–6, 323–4.

[106] CPR 25.1(1)(f) renames the injunction.

[107] PD (25): accessible at <www.dca.gov.uk/civil/procrules_fin/menus/rules.htm>.

[108] PD (25): Masters or District judges can only make such orders in special cases.

[109] *Cretanor Maritime Co Ltd v Irish Marine Maritime Ltd* [1978] 3 All ER 164, CA; *Capital
Cameras Ltd v Harold Lines Ltd* [1991] 1 WLR 54; *Flightline v Edwards* [2003] EWCA Civ 63;
[2003] 1 WLR 1200, CA.

[110] PD (25); *United Mizrahi Bank v Doherty Ltd* [1998] 1 WLR 435.

[111] *Derby & Co Ltd v Weldon (No 1)* [1990] Ch 48, CA; *Derby & Co Ltd v Weldon (Nos 3 & 4)*
[1990] Ch 65, 86, 94–5, CA; *Bank of Crete SA v Koskotas* [1991] 2 Lloyd's Rep 587, CA; LA Collins
(1989) 105 LQR 262, 286 ff; C McLachlan 'The Jurisdictional Limits of Disclosure Orders:
Transnational Fraud Litigation' (1998) ICLQ 3.

[112] PD (25); *AJ Bekhor & Co Ltd v Bilton* [1981] 1 QB 923, CA; *A v C (Note)* [1981] 1 QB 956,
Goff J; *Bankers Trust Co v Shapira* [1980] 1 WLR 1274, CA.

[113] On the 'mere witness' rule, *Norwich Pharmacal Co v Customs and Excise* [1974] AC 133, HL,
Bankers Trust Co v Shapira [1980] 1 WLR 1274, CA, *Arab Monetary Fund v Hashim (No 5)* [1992]

22.21 The following criteria govern the decision whether to grant this type of injunction.[114] First, the applicant must show a good arguable case that he is entitled to damages or some other underlying relief.[115] The House of Lords in 2007 held that a freezing injunction had been invalidly awarded when the applicant had made no attempt at all to indicate the nature of its substantive claim.[116] Secondly, the court must also be satisfied that the underlying cause of action has 'accrued', that is, a breach of duty or a debt obligation has arisen.[117] Thirdly, there must also be a real risk that the respondent's assets will be removed or dissipated unless the injunction is granted,[118] indeed clear and strong evidence of this risk must be shown.[119] 'Dissipation' includes any act of alienation or charging of property[120] but not innocent transactions made in the ordinary course of business.[121] Non-business dealings need not be unconscionable: it is enough that the applicant's eventual judgment will go unsatisfied unless a freezing injunction is granted.[122] Fourthly, the court must be satisfied that the applicant will be unable to receive satisfaction of the claim unless he receives an injunction.[123] The court will

---

2 All ER 911, Hoffmann J; on the whole topic, Neil Andrews, *English Civil Procedure* (2003) 26.102 to 26.128.

[114] *Flightwise Travel Service Ltd v Gill* [2003] EWHC 3082 (Ch); *The Times* 5 December 2003, Neuberger J at [18] to end, contains a good re-statement of various forms of protection aimed at ensuring that freezing relief is applied fairly.

[115] *Ninemia Maritime Corpn v Trave* [1983] 2 Lloyd's Rep 600, Mustill J (approved [1983] 1 WLR 1412, CA); on different perceptions of an applicant's claim by successive Commercial Court judges, *Laemthong International Lines Co Ltd v ARTIS* [2004] EWHC 2226 (Comm); [2005] 1 Lloyd's Rep 100; [2004] 2 All ER (Comm) 797, Colman J.

[116] *Fourie v Le Roux* [2007] UKHL 1; [2007] 1 WLR 320 (noted D Capper (2007) CJQ 181); the speeches emphasize the draconian nature of this jurisdiction and the need to maintain appropriate safeguards; Lord Hope at [6] and [7] referred to Scottish authorities which consider possible conflict with European human rights law (Article 1 of the First Protocol to the European Convention on Human Rights) unless such safeguards are maintained, citing *Karl Construction Ltd v Palisade Properties plc* 2002 SC 270; *Advocate General for Scotland v Taylor* 2003 SLT 1340.

[117] *Veracruz Transportation Inc v VC Shipping Co Inc ('The Veracruz')* [1992] 1 Lloyd's Rep 353, CA, noted LA Collins (1992) 108 LQR 175–81; *Zucker v Tyndall Holdings plc* [1992] 1 WLR 1127, CA, noted R Harrison (1992) New LJ 1511–2; *Dicey, Morris and Collins on the Conflict of Laws* (14th edn, 2006) 8–009 (also 8–022 ff) criticize the *Veracruz* case, noting Lord Nicholls's doubts in the *Mercedes Benz* case [1996] AC 284, 312, PC and *Patterson v BTR Engineering (Australia) Ltd* (1989) 18 NSWLR 319, NSWCA; W Kennett, *The Enforcement of Judgments in Europe* (2000) 161, n 97, notes that the English approach has not been adopted in Austria, Germany, and Belgium.

[118] *Refco Inc v Eastern Trading Co* [1999] 1 Lloyd's Rep 159, 171, CA, (no such risk on the facts).

[119] *Laemthong International Lines Co Ltd v ARTIS* [2004] EWHC 2226 (Comm); [2005] 1 Lloyd's Rep 100; [2004] 2 All ER (Comm) 797, Colman J at [60], citing *Thane Investments Ltd v Tomlinson* [2003] EWCA Civ 1271.

[120] Dispositions, pledges, charges: *CBS UK Ltd v Lambert* [1983] Ch 37, 42, CA; *Z Ltd v A-Z* [1982] 1 QB 558, 571, CA, citing phrase 'otherwise dealing with' in Supreme Court Act 1981, s 37(3).

[121] PD (25).

[122] *Ketchum International plc v Group Public Relations Holdings Ltd* [1997] 1 WLR 4, 13, CA; *Commissioner of Customs & Excise v Anchor Foods Ltd* [1999] 1 WLR 1139 (if proposed transaction is *bona fide*, the discretion to grant injunction should be exercised very circumspectly); this factor was not satisfied in *Re Q's Estate* [1999] 1 All ER (Comm) 499.

[123] *Etablissements Esefka International Anstalt v Central Bank of Nigeria* [1979] 1 Lloyd's Rep 445.

take into account whether the applicant already has adequate security against such a risk.[124] Finally, 'the court [must be] satisfied that any damage which the respondent may suffer through having to comply with the order is compensatable under the cross-undertaking or that the risk of uncompensatable loss is clearly outweighed by the risk of injustice to the applicant if the order is not made'.[125]

An applicant[126] and his lawyer(s) must make full and frank disclosure.[127] Failure **22.22** to make full disclosure will normally cause the injunction to be summarily set aside, unless the failure was innocent and either made no difference[128] or the importance of providing freezing relief, especially to combat fraud, outweighs this aspect of procedural fairness.[129]

The injunction's standard provisions[130] require the applicant, inter alia, (i) to **22.23** indemnify the respondent if the injunction is wrongly granted; the applicant should provide a guarantee to support this;[131] (ii) to pay the reasonable costs or any loss suffered by non-parties when complying with the order, whether or not the injunction is properly granted; and (iii) to return to court for a 'with notice' review.[132]

A respondent will be in contempt of court if he breaches an injunction (generally **22.24** on contempt, see 22.130).[133] He might then be fined, imprisoned or, in the

---

124 *Refco Inc v Eastern Trading Co* [1999] 1 Lloyd's Rep 159, 171, CA.

125 *Re First Express Ltd The Times* 8 October, 1991, Hoffmann J.

126 PD (25); leading cases are: *Brink's Mat Ltd v Elcombe* [1988] 1 WLR 1350, CA; *Lloyds Bowmaker Ltd v Britannia Arrow Holdings plc* [1988] 1 WLR 1337, CA; *Behbehani v Salem* [1989] 1 WLR 723, CA; and (an important survey) *Memory Corporation plc v Sidhu (No 2)* [2000] 1 WLR 1443, 1453–6, CA; *Re S (A Child) (Family Division: Without Notice Orders)* [2001] 1 WLR 211, 219, 222–3; *Knauf UK GmbH v British Gypsum Ltd* [2001] EWCA Civ 1570; [2002] 1 WLR 907, CA.

127 *Memory Corporation plc v Sidhu (No 2)* [2000] 1 WLR 1443, 1455, CA.

128 *Brink's Mat Ltd v Elcombe* [1988] 1 WLR 1350, 1358, CA; *Lloyds Bowmaker Ltd v Britannia Arrow Holdings plc* [1988] 1 WLR 1337, 1347, CA (these two statements were cited in *Memory Corporation plc v Sidhu (No 2)* [2000] 1 WLR 1443, 1454 CA); *Behbehani v Salem* [1989] 1 WLR 723, CA; *Gulf Interstate Oil Corpn LLC v Ant Trade & Transport Ltd of Malta ('The Giovanna')* [1999] 1 Lloyd's Rep 867; in *Laemthong International Lines Co Ltd v ARTIS* [2004] EWHC 2226 (Comm); [2005] 1 Lloyd's Rep 100; [2004] 2 All ER (Comm) 797, Colman J at [64] held that failure to reveal a comment made by another judge in an earlier and unsuccessful 'without notice' application did not satisfy this 'decisive influence' test.

129 *Marc Rich & Co Holdings GmbH v Krasner* (CA, unreported, 17 January, 1999).

130 PD (25).

131 ibid.

132 Such protection of non-parties is not standard practice for all types of injunctions: *Smithkline Beecham plc v Apotex Europe Ltd* [2006] EWCA Civ 658; [2007] Ch 71 at [23] ff.

133 *Motorola Credit Corpn v Uzan (No 2)* [2003] EWCA Civ 752; [2004] 1 WLR 113, CA [45]–[58], [148]–[156]; *Federal Bank of the Middle East Ltd v Hadkinson* [2000] 2 All ER 395, 411, CA; information disclosed under a disclosure order, including in response to cross-examination, ancillary to a freezing order can be used for contempt purposes, *Dadourian Group International Inc v Simms* [2006] EWCA Civ 1745; [2007] 2 All ER 329.

case of a company, suffer sequestration of assets. Gross or prolonged negligence suffices.[134]

22.25 The impact of these injunctions on non-parties must now be noted. It is common to notify the respondent's bank(s) of the injunction even before he receives notice. A non-party is obliged not to act inconsistently with the terms of the injunction.[135] Thus a non-party bank must refrain from honouring its client's cheques and instructions, except where such dealings are permitted by the order.[136] A non-party will be in contempt if it deliberately or 'knowingly' acts, or omits to act, with the result that the injunction is undermined, or if it aids and abets the respondent's breach of the order.[137] However, the non-party's only duty is towards the court. In *Customs & Excise Commissioners v Barclays Bank plc* (2006) the House of Lords (reversing the Court of Appeal)[138] held that a non-party owes no common law duty of care to the recipient of freezing relief.[139]

22.26 Freezing injunctions can apply to assets located outside England and Wales.[140] Indeed 'worldwide' freezing injunctions are common.[141] The accompanying 'worldwide' disclosure order is, however, of greater tactical importance than the freezing injunction.[142] This is because the latter is merely a 'holding operation' to give the claimant time to apply to the relevant foreign court(s) for appropriate supplementary or substantive relief.[143] To prevent oppressive proceedings, an

---

134 *Z Bank v D1* [1994] 1 Lloyd's Rep 656, Colman J; Steyn LJ in *Guildford BC v Valler The Times* 15 October, 1993, CA (dictum); on the duty to respond to an order for information, *Bird v Hadkinson The Times* 4 March, 1999, Neuberger J (respondent to answer accurately after exercising reasonable care).

135 PD (25).

136 *Z Ltd v A* [1982] QB 558, CA.

137 PD (25); *Z Ltd v A* [1982] QB 558, 567, CA; *Re Supply of Ready Mixed Concrete (No 2)* [1995] 1 AC 456, HL; and *A-G v Newspaper Publishing plc* [1997] 3 All ER 159, 169, CA.

138 In its decision, now reversed by the House of Lords, the Court of Appeal held that the contempt regime is inadequate for two reasons: first, contempt in this context requires proof of knowing non-compliance by the non-party Bank, as distinct from mere negligence; secondly, the sanction for contempt is punishment administered by the court, rather than an order to compensate the injured party.

139 [2006] UKHL 28; [2007] 1 AC 181 (reversing [2004] EWCA Civ 1555; [2005] 1 WLR 2082).

140 C McLachlan, 'Extraterritorial Court Orders Affecting Bank Deposits' in Meessen (ed), *Extraterritorial Jurisdiction in Theory and Practice* (1996).

141 PD (25); *Babanaft Co SA v Bassatne* [1990] Ch 13, CA; *Republic of Haiti v Duvalier* [1990] QB 202, CA; *Derby & Co v Weldon (No 1)* [1990] Ch 48, CA; *Derby & Co Ltd v Weldon (Nos 3 & 4)* [1990] Ch 65, CA; LA Collins, 'The Territorial Reach of *Mareva* Injunctions' (1989) 105 LQR 262–99; LA Collins, chs VIII and IX, in *Essays in International Litigation* (1993); *Dicey, Morris and Collins on the Conflict of Laws* (14th edn, 2006) 8–011 ff; D Capper, 'Worldwide *Mareva* Injunctions' (1991) 54 MLR 329–48; A Malek and C Lewis 'Worldwide Injunctions—The Position of International Banks' [1990] LMCLQ 88; Rogers [1991] LMCLQ 231; the English Court can grant worldwide relief in the context of post-judgment relief under the Jurisdiction Regulation, *Banco Nacional De Comercio Exterior SNC v Empresa De Telecomunicationes De Cuba SA* [2006] EWHC 19 (Comm).

142 *Crédit Suisse Fides Trust SA v Cuoghi* [1998] QB 818, 827–8, CA.

143 *Babanaft International Co SA v Bassatne* [1990]Ch 13, 41, CA.

applicant cannot make a related application for enforcement of a worldwide English freezing order in a foreign jurisdiction without first obtaining the English court's permission.[144] The Court of Appeal in *Dadourian Group International Inc v Simms* (2006) enumerated eight principles in this regard.[145] Further protection in this 'extra-territorial' context is provided by the '*Babanaft*'[146] and '*Baltic*' provisos.[147]

The English High Court can grant freezing injunctions and connected orders for **22.27** disclosure of assets in support of substantive civil proceedings throughout the world.[148] This supportive English jurisdiction applies whether or not the relevant foreign jurisdiction is party to the Brussels or Lugano jurisdictional regimes.[149] The Court of Appeal has provided guidance on this.[150]

(2) Preservation of Evidence: Civil Search Orders[151]

First established by the Court of Appeal in *Anton Piller v Manufacturing Processes* **22.28** (1976),[152] these orders have been placed on a statutory basis.[153] CPR Part 25

---

144 PD (25).

145 [2006] EWCA Civ 399; [2006] 1 WLR 2499, at [25] with commentary on each at [26] ff; noted T Rutherford (2006) NLJ 837 and F Meisel [2007] CJQ 176.

146 PD (25); this protection originated in *Babanaft Co SA v Bassatne* [1990] Ch 13, CA.

147 PD (25); this protection originated in *Baltic Shipping v Translink Shipping Ltd* [1995] 1 Lloyd's Rep 673.

148 *Dicey, Morris and Collins on the Conflict of Laws* (14th edn, 2006) 8–024; G Maher and BJ Rodger, 'Provisional and Protective Remedies: The British Experience of the Brussels Convention' (1999) 48 ICLQ 302; see also Andrews and Johnson two footnotes below.

149 Civil Jurisdiction and Judgments Act 1982 s 25; Civil Jurisdiction and Judgments Act 1982 (Interim Relief) Order 1997 (SI 1997, No 302) (the 1982 Act, s 25, gives effect to the United Kingdom's obligation to effectuate Article 24 of the 1968 Brussels Convention (now Article 31 of the Brussels I Regulation); from 1 April, 1997, the English High Court's jurisdiction to grant interim relief under the 1982 Act was extended to include non-Convention and non-Member States; and to apply to civil proceedings outside the rather restricted scope of Article 1 of the Brussels Convention and its successor, the Jurisdiction Regulation: (EC) No 44/2001 of 22 December 2000 on 'jurisdiction and the recognition and enforcement of judgments in civil and commercial matters': [2001] OJ L 12/1.

150 *Motorola Credit Corpn v Uzan (No 2)* [2003] EWCA Civ 752; [2004] 1 WLR 113, CA at [115]; the earlier case law is analysed in Neil Andrews, *English Civil Procedure* (2003) 17.74 ff and by A Johnson in M Andenas, Neil Andrews, R Nazzini, *The Future of Transnational Civil Litigation* (reprinted, British Institute of International and Comparative Law, 2006) ch 11; the English Court can grant worldwide relief in the context of post-judgment relief under the Jurisdiction Regulation (see preceding note), *Banco Nacional De Comercio Exterior SNC v Empresa De Telecomunicationes De Cuba SA* [2006] EWHC 19 (Comm).

151 Re-named as such, CPR 25.1(1)(h); the standard order is prescribed by PD (25); S Gee, *Commercial Injunctions* (2004); Neil Andrews, *English Civil Procedure* (2003) ch 17; *Zuckerman on Civil Procedure* (2006) 14.175 ff; IS Goldrein (ed), *Commercial Litigation: Pre-emptive Remedies* (International Edition, 2005) ch 3.

152 [1976] Ch 55, CA.

153 Civil Procedure Act 1997, s 7, following 'Anton Piller Orders: A Consultation Paper' ('the Staughton Committee') Lord Chancellor's Department, November 1992; M Dockray & K Reece Thomas, (1998) 17 CJQ 272; Supreme Court Act 1981, s 72 (privilege against self-incrimination).

provides the standard form.[154] These orders are useful in tackling breaches of intellectual property rights and confidentiality. They are granted 'without notice' and enable the applicant to inspect premises and seize vital evidence before it is lost or destroyed. A respondent commits a contempt of court if he fails to admit the applicant.[155] A search order can be granted before or after the main proceedings have commenced, or even after judgment.[156] Only the High Court can issue such an order.[157]

22.29   The applicant must have a very strong prima facie case on the substance of the main complaint.[158] There must be a very serious risk of damage to the applicant's interests unless this special order is granted.[159] Furthermore, the court must be satisfied both that the respondent possesses relevant material and that he will destroy this material unless subjected to a surprise search.[160] Finally, 'the harm likely to be caused by the execution of the. . .order to the respondent and his business affairs must not be excessive or out of proportion to the legitimate object of the order'.[161] The standard order also contains numerous provisions aimed at controlling the process of executing these orders, especially seizure of material.[162] There should be an independent and supervisory solicitor present to ensure fairplay and prevent oppression.[163] He must not be an employee or member of the applicant's firm of solicitors and should be suitably experienced.[164] The respondent need not disclose material protected by legal professional privilege (on which see 22.63 ff). As for the privilege against self-incrimination, statutory provisions override this privilege in the context of criminal fraud or in respect of intellectual property claims.[165]

---

[154] PD (25).

[155] ibid.

[156] On this last situation, *Distributori Automatici Italia SpA v Holford General Trading Co Ltd* [1985] 1 WLR 1066.

[157] Civil Procedure Act 1997, s 7(8).

[158] *Anton Piller KG v Manufacturing Processes Ltd* [1976] Ch 55, 62, CA.

[159] ibid.

[160] ibid, at 59–60, *per* Lord Denning: 'grave danger that vital evidence will be destroyed'.

[161] Criterion proposed by the report into 'Anton Piller Orders', (Consultation Paper, Lord Chancellor's Department, 1992) para 2.8, following *Columbia Picture Industries v Robinson* [1987] 1 Ch 38, 76, and *Lock International plc v Beswick* [1989] 1 WLR 1268, 1281.

[162] ibid; for earlier comment, *Columbia Picture* case [1987] Ch 38.

[163] PD (25); eg, *IBM v Prima Data International Ltd* [1994] 1 WLR 719, 724–5.

[164] PD (25); for instance where the supervisory solicitor lacked sufficient experience, *Gadget Shop Ltd v Bug.Com Ltd* [2001] CP 13; *The Times* 28 June 2000, noted L Mulcahy, *Human Rights and Civil Practice* (2001) 10.62.

[165] Neil Andrews, *English Civil Procedure* (2003) 29.24 to 29.28 and (on possible reform) 29.56 ff; B Thanki (ed), *The Law of Privilege* (2006) ch 8 and *Zuckerman on Civil Procedure* (2006) ch 17; see now Fraud Act 2006, s 13, considered in *Kensington International Ltd v Republic of the Congo* [2007] EWHC 1632; see further n 329 below.

(3) Security for Costs[166]

A defendant can seek an order for security for costs against a claimant. Such an **22.30** order might be aimed at meeting one of three problems: that the claimant lacks sufficient funds; or he is a shifty litigant manifestly disposed to avoid liability for costs; or the foreign jurisdiction where he resides does not provide a dependable or straightforward system for enforcing an English costs order. A security for costs order is discretionary.[167] The rules specify various 'gateways', any one of which the defendant must ordinarily[168] establish. The latter must then further convince the court that it is proper to exercise its discretion (on the latter, see text below) by awarding security.[169] The three main gateways are: (i) 'the claimant is resident out of the English and Welsh jurisdiction but not resident in a Member State of the European Union or a Lugano Convention Contracting State'; or (ii) 'the claimant is a company or other body (whether incorporated inside or outside Great Britain) and there is reason to believe that it will be unable to pay the defendant's costs if ordered to do so'; or (iii) 'the claimant has taken steps in relation to his assets that would make it difficult to enforce an order for costs against him'.[170]

The case law has identified the following (non-exhaustive) factors which the court **22.31** should consider when deciding whether to award security for costs:[171] (i) the action is a sham or is made in good faith; (ii) the claimant has a reasonably good prospect of success in the case; (iii) there is an admission by the defendant in the statement of case or elsewhere that the money is due or the claim is otherwise sound; (iv) there is a substantial payment into court or offer to settle; (v) the application is being used by the defendant to stifle an honest and sound claim; (vi) the claimant's lack of funds has been caused, or aggravated, by the defendant's failure to pay; (vii) the application for security for costs has been made late.

A claimant who is an individual and resident in the United Kingdom, or in a **22.32** Member State of the European Union, or Lugano Convention Contracting State,

---

[166] Neil Andrews, *English Civil Procedure* (2003) ch 37; MJ Cook *Cook on Costs 2006* (2006) ch 13; P Hurst *Civil Costs* (3rd edn, 2004) ch 15; *Zuckerman on Civil Procedure* (2006) 9.182 ff; IS Goldrein (ed), *Commercial Litigation: Pre-emptive Remedies* (2005) ch 4; *Dicey, Morris and Collins on the Conflict of Laws* (14th edn, 2006), 8–092 ff.

[167] CPR 25.13(1) states: 'The court may make an order for security for costs...if (a) it is satisfied, having regard to all the circumstances of the case, that it is just to make such an order.'

[168] In *Olatawura v Abiloye* [2002] EWCA Civ 998; [2003] 1 WLR 275, the court recognized a power to make an order for a security payment by an individual claimant resident outside the jurisdiction, and having modest financial means; this power subsists independently of the general regime concerning security for costs contained in CPR Part 25, Section II.

[169] CPR 25.13(2).

[170] *Harris v Wallis* (Ch D, 15 March 2006, All England Reporter) on the phrase 'taken steps in relation to his assets that would make it difficult to enforce an order for costs against him'; no need to show improper motivation by claimant.

[171] *Sir Lindsay Parkinson v Triplan Ltd* [1973] QB 609 at 626–7, CA, *per* Lord Denning MR.

cannot be made to provide such security simply on the basis of his financial inability to pay costs. To do so would bar his access to justice. By contrast, an impecunious corporate claimant enjoys no such favourable treatment.

22.33 Most non-UK residents are likely to be non-UK citizens. And so the foreign residence ground, cited at 22.30, has the potential to infringe Article 14 of the European Convention on Human Rights. This prohibits direct or indirect discrimination by reference to (among other things) 'national or social origin. . .or other status'.[172] In the *Nasser* case (2002) the Court of Appeal rejected 'any inflexible presumption that any person not resident in a Brussels or Lugano state should provide security for costs'.[173] Instead, security must be based on 'objectively justified grounds relating to obstacles to or the burden of enforcement in the context of the particular foreign claimant or country concerned', such as 'costs or delay, in enforcing an English judgment. . .'.[174]

(4) Interim Payments[175]

22.34 An interim payment order enables the claimant to obtain advance payment, often well before trial, of a 'reasonable proportion' of the claim. An order is possible if the defendant has admitted liability or the court 'is satisfied' that, if the case went to trial, the claimant would obtain judgment for a 'substantial' monetary award against the defendant, other than costs. After receiving such an award, the claimant cannot discontinue the proceedings unless the defendant consents in writing or the court gives permission.[176] Interim payments are not disclosed to the court at trial until all questions concerning liability have been considered.[177]

(5) Interim Injunctions[178]

22.35 The court has jurisdiction to issue interim injunctions where the relief sought at trial is a final injunction.[179] Recipients of interim injunctions are normally bound

---

172 *Nasser v United Bank of Kuwait* [2001] EWCA Civ 556; [2002] 1 All ER 401, CA; for a review of this context, *Al-Koronky v Time-Life Entertainment Group Ltd* [2006] EWCA Civ 1123; [2006] CP Rep 47, at [24].

173 *Nasser* case ibid.

174 ibid.

175 CPR 25.6 to 25.9; and PD (25) 'Interim Payments'; Neil Andrews, *English Civil Procedure* (2003) 18–04 ff; *Zuckerman on Civil Procedure* (2006) 9–205 ff; IS Goldrein (ed), *Commercial Litigation: Pre-emptive Remedies* (2005) 590 ff.

176 CPR 38.2(2)(b).

177 CPR 25.9.

178 Neil Andrews, *English Civil Procedure* (2003) 18–41 ff; S Gee, *Commercial Injunctions* (2004) ch 2; IS Goldrein (ed), *Commercial Litigation: Pre-emptive Remedies* (2005) pp 1 ff; *Zuckerman on Civil Procedure* (2006) 9–5 ff; S Gee [2006] LMCLQ 181.

179 Supreme Court Act 1981, s 37.

by a 'cross-undertaking' (an implied promise to the court for the benefit of the other litigant) to indemnify the respondent if the interim order is subsequently held, for whatever reason, to have been wrongly granted.[180] The Court of Appeal has rejected the proposition that, outside the context of freezing injunctions, non-parties are entitled to claim under the cross-undertaking.[181]

The House of Lords in *American Cyanamid Ltd v Ethicon Ltd* (1974) established **22.36** the general principle for the award of such interim injunctions: that the court must not attempt to consider the 'merits', that is, provisional evaluation of the substantive claim and defence.[182] Instead the court must assess the litigants' competing interests in, respectively, gaining interim restraint of the defendant's alleged misconduct, and preserving freedom from that restraint. The court must strive to balance the hardship to the applicant caused by refusal of relief against the hardship to the other party if he is temporarily bound by an injunction. Consideration of the case's factual merits is justified only if the court discovers no real difference in weight between the parties' respective potential hardships.

The 1974 decision remains controversial. Later case law has established various **22.37** situations where efficiency and fairness demand pre-trial examination of the 'merits' (as explained above). Of these situations, the three most important are:[183] first, transparent cases where the factual merits of the application are 'plain and uncontroversial' or the application is plainly hopeless; secondly, the matter is so urgent that the decision on the interim application will be likely to dispose of the whole litigation; thirdly, the case concerns the respondent's freedom of expression: 'No such relief is to be granted so as to restrain publication before trial unless the court is satisfied that the applicant is likely to establish that publication should not be allowed.'[184]

(6) Preliminary Issues[185]

The court can be asked to pronounce in final form on a preliminary issue, such as **22.38** a point of general law, or interpretation of a document, before the factual issues have been investigated. A 'preliminary' decision is final. Often the point singled

---

[180] *F Hoffmann—La Roche & Co AG v Secretary of State for Trade & Industry* [1975] AC 295, 360–1, HL; *American Cyanamid Co v Ethicon Ltd* [1975] AC 396, 407–9, HL; *Cheltenham & Gloucester Building Society v Ricketts* [1993] 1 WLR 1545, CA; *Goldman Sachs International v Philip Lyons The Times* 28 February, 1995, CA; *Barratt Manchester Ltd v Bolton MBC* [1998] 1 WLR 1003, CA; *Customs & Excise Commissioners v Anchor Foods Ltd* [1999] 1 WLR 1139.

[181] *Smithkline Beecham plc v Apotex Europe Ltd* [2006] EWCA Civ 658; [2007] Ch 71 at [23] ff.

[182] [1975] AC 396, HL.

[183] Neil Andrews, *English Civil Procedure* (2003) 18.53 to 18.65.

[184] Human Rights Act 1998, s 12(3); *Cream Holdings Inc v Banerjee* [2004] UKHL 44; [2005] 1 AC 253.

[185] Neil Andrews, *English Civil Procedure* (2003) 9.33, 9.34, 34.17.

out for accelerated treatment is a 'crux' on which the entire fate of the litigation might depend: points concerning limitation of actions ('prescription');[186] consensual time bars;[187] exclusion clauses;[188] disputable duties of care.[189]

(7) Summary Judgment[190]

22.39   This streamlined procedure allows claimants or defendants to gain final judgment if they can show that their opponent's claim or defence lacks a 'real prospect' of success. The court receives only written evidence.[191] This procedure can be used to test both the legal and factual merits of a claim or defence.[192] The court can itself initiate a summary judgment hearing. The governing rule states:[193]

> The court may give summary judgment against a claimant or defendant. . .if (a) it considers that (i) that claimant has no real prospect of succeeding on the claim or issue; or (ii) that defendant has no real prospect of successfully defending the claim or issue and (b) there is no other reason why the case or issue should be disposed of at a trial.

In *Swain v Hillman* (2001), Lord Woolf said that the words 'no real prospect' denote that the claim or defence must have a 'realistic' rather than a 'fanciful' chance of success.[194] He added that the function of summary judgment would be distorted if summary judgment hearings were allowed to become 'mini-trials'. Instead, issues involving detailed factual investigation require the case to progress through disclosure under CPR 31 and preparation of witness statements, perhaps culminating in cross-examination at trial.[195]

22.40   The court can (i) give judgment for the applicant, whether this is the claimant or the defendant, and whether on the whole of the claim or merely on a particular issue;[196]

---

[186]   ibid, at 9.33 n 39; *Haward v Fawcetts* [2006] UKHL 9; [2006] 1 WLR 682, HL (Limitation of Actions Act 1980, s 14A).

[187]   *Senate Electrical Wholesalers Ltd v Alacatel Submarine Networks Ltd* [1999] 2 Lloyd's Rep 243, CA; noted (1998) 17. CJQ 355; *Laminates Acquisition Co v BTR Australia* [2003] EWHC 2540 (Comm).

[188]   *Cremdean Properties v Nash* (1977) 244 EG 547, CA.

[189]   eg *Customs & Excise v Barclays Bank plc* [2006] UKHL 28: [2007] 1 AC 181; *Deep Vein Thrombosis and Air Travel Group Litigation* [2005] UKHL 72; [2006] 1 AC 495.

[190]   Neil Andrews, *English Civil Procedure* (2003) ch 20; IS Goldrein (ed), *Commercial Litigation: Pre-emptive Remedies* (2005) ch 6; *Zuckerman on Civil Procedure* (2006) 8–39 ff.

[191]   CPR 24.5.

[192]   PD (24) 1.2, 1.3.

[193]   CPR 24.2.

[194]   [2001] 1 All ER 91, 92, CA; obfuscatory references to this test in PD (24) were deleted, as explained in the *Swain* case, ibid, at 93.

[195]   For judicial emphasis of this point under the pre-CPR rules, Neil Andrews, *Principles of Civil Procedure* (1994) 9–024 to 9–026.

[196]   CPR 24.1 and 24.2; PD (24) 5.1(1),(2).

or strike out or dismiss the claim or defence, or part of it;[197] or (ii) dismiss the application for summary judgment;[198] or (iii) grant a conditional order where 'it appears to the court that a claim or defence may succeed but improbable that it will do so'.[199] The possible conditions are: a payment into court or some other 'specified step'.[200] The interaction between summary judgment, counterclaims and the defence of set-off is examined elsewhere.[201]

(8) Striking Out Claims or Defences[202]

A defective claim or defence can be 'struck out' without a trial, often at a very early   **22.41**
stage of the proceedings. Striking out can be exercised whether or not a party makes an application to the court.[203] The court can strike out a pleading (now known as a 'statement of case', whether it is a claim, defence, reply, or counterclaim, or any part of one) on any of these grounds:[204]

(a) the statement of case discloses no reasonable grounds for bringing or defending the claim; or

(b) the statement of case is an abuse of the court's process or is otherwise likely to obstruct the just disposal of the proceedings; or

(c) failure to comply with a rule, practice direction or court order.[205]

Ground (a) overlaps with the court's jurisdiction to award summary judgment under CPR Part 24. Both the striking out and summary judgment processes enable the court to eliminate bad or tenuous claims or defences. Both are subject to the evidential constraint that the court can only receive oral evidence at trial.

---

[197] PD (24) 5.1(2) which should be construed in the light of CPR 24.1 and 24.2 where 'claim' is clearly used compendiously to embrace both an active claim and a possible defence to that active claim.

[198] PD (24) 5.1(3); in the case of applications under the old 'Order 14', this result was known as 'granting the defendant unconditional leave to defend'.

[199] PD (24) 4; consistent with *Yorke Motors Ltd v Edwards* [1982] 1 WLR 444, HL; Neil Andrews, *Principles of Civil Procedure* (1994) 9–028, on the background to the *Yorke* case; for case law on imposition of conditions under CPR Part 24, see *Halsbury's Laws of England* (4th edn, 2001) 'Practice and Procedure', vol 37, [921] at n 10.

[200] Note to CPR 24.6; PD (24) 5.2.

[201] CPR 16.6; Neil Andrews, *English Civil Procedure* (2003) 11–07 ff; esp at 11.20; *Zuckerman on Civil Procedure* (2006) 3–50 to 3–57; SR Derham, *Set-off* (3rd edn, 2003); see also R Zimmermann, *Comparative Foundations of a European Law of Set-off and Prescription* (2002).

[202] Andrews, ibid, ch 21; *Zuckerman* (2006) 8–30 ff.

[203] Similarly, the court at its own initiative can order a summary judgment hearing to examine whether a claim or defence should be dismissed because it has 'no real prospect of succeeding': see CPR 24.5(3).

[204] CPR 3.4(2).

[205] CPR 3.4(2)(a)(b)(c); for case law on striking out, see *Halsbury's Laws of England* (4th edn, 2001) 'Practice and Procedure', vol 37, [917] at nn 5,6,7.

The Court of Appeal in *S v Gloucestershire CC* (2000)[206] affirmed settled principle[207] that striking out on the factual or legal merits (see rule 3.4(2)(a) cited above) is justified only in 'the clearest case'[208] based only on consideration of written evidence.[209] The upshot is that summary judgment permits closer scrutiny than striking out.[210] The House of Lords in *Three Rivers DC v Bank of England (No 3)* (2001) also noted the potentially concurrent application of striking out and summary judgment procedures.[211] Unfortunately, a majority of the House of Lords fatefully allowed this case to proceed to trial. The claimant eventually discontinued it, before judgment, on 'day 256' of the trial.[212] This very lengthy trial demonstrates that appeal courts should be slow to upset a striking out decision, even if the case is 'complicated' and involves 'extensive documentation'. English law should also consider a focused pre-trial *oral* hearing to probe weak claims which might otherwise proceed to lengthy trial.

22.42 In 1998 the European Court of Human Rights at first castigated the English courts for employing striking out to dismiss *legally* unfounded claims, but the same European court in 2001 acknowledged that such a pre-trial *legal* filter is compatible with the human right to a 'fair hearing'. And so an English court must only strike out if it has considered pertinent differences between factual situations.[213]

(9) Default Judgment[214]

22.43 Judgment by default is an important means of accelerating the legal process. The claimant can obtain 'judgment without trial where a defendant (a) has failed to file an acknowledgment of service; or (b) has failed to file a defence'[215] in respect of a claim for 'a specified amount of money',[216] or 'an amount of money to be decided by the court',[217] or delivery of goods where the claim form gives the

---

[206] *S v Gloucestershire CC* [2000] 3 All ER 346, 370–3, CA.
[207] Authorities collected at Neil Andrews, *Principles of Civil Procedure* (1994) 10–23.
[208] *S v Gloucestershire CC* (n 206 above) at 373.
[209] ibid, at 372–3.
[210] ibid, at 373.
[211] [2001] UKHL 16; [2001] 2 All ER 513, HL, notably at [90] ff, and [134] ff.
[212] *Three Rivers DC v Bank of England* [2006] EWHC 816 (Comm) (12 April 2006) Tomlinson J at [1].
[213] *Z v UK* (2002) 34 EHRR 97; (2001) BHRC 384, ECtHR, not following *Osman v UK* (1999) 29 EHRR 245; (1998) BHRC 293; for comment Neil Andrews, *English Civil Procedure* (2003) 7–64 ff; ACL Davies (2001) 117 LQR 521 and other literature cited Andrews, op cit, p 167 nn 114 ff.
[214] Neil Andrews, *English Civil Procedure* (2003) ch 19; IS Goldrein (ed), *Commercial Litigation: Pre-emptive Remedies* (2005) ch 5; *Zuckerman on Civil Procedure* (2006) 8–3 ff.
[215] CPR 12.1 and 12.3; see also CPR 10.2 and CPR 15.3.
[216] Formerly known as 'liquidated claims'.
[217] Formerly known as 'unliquidated claims'.

defendant the alternative of paying their value.[218] In these situations, the claimant can normally apply for judgment by administrative process without troubling a judge.[219] If the claimant seeks some other remedy, default judgment must be sought by specific application to the court.[220] Certain classes of claim are not subject to default judgment.[221]

The court can set aside or vary a regular judgment if 'the defendant has a real prospect of successfully defending the claim' or 'there is some other good reason' why judgment should be set aside or varied.[222] When the default judgment was obtained on the question of liability, the power to set aside exists whether or not the defendant also failed to contest quantification of liability.[223] When deciding whether to set aside the judgment, the court will consider whether the defence has objective merits and why the defendant failed to acknowledge service or file a defence.[224] The substantive defence 'must carry some degree of conviction'; if so, 'judges should be very wary of trying issues of fact' without trial.[225] If the defence is rejected on the merits at this stage, the decision establishes a 'final and binding judgment' which can only be re-considered on appeal.[226] As a condition of setting aside a regular default judgment, the defendant might be required to provide security for the claimant's costs,[227] or to make a payment into court.[228]   **22.44**

Setting aside proceeds summarily in the following situations: (i) judgment was procedurally premature (it preceded expiry of the time for acknowledging service or filing a defence,[229] or an application for summary judgment was still pending);[230] or (ii) the defendant had fully discharged the claim (including costs);[231] or (iii) the defendant had admitted liability in full and requested more   **22.45**

---

[218] CPR 12.4(1)(a)-(c).

[219] The main exceptions (where judgment must be sought by application to the court) are: claims for costs (other than fixed costs) or service was made out of the jurisdiction without leave under the Civil Jurisdiction and Judgments Act 1982, claims against the Crown, tort claims by a spouse against another, claims against children and patients: CPR 12.9, 12.10, 12.11 for full details.

[220] CPR 12.4(2) 12.10, 12.11.

[221] CPR 12.2; PD (12) 1.2.

[222] CPR 13.3.

[223] *Strachan v The Gleaner Co Ltd* [2005] UKPC 33; [2005] 1 WLR 3204, PC.

[224] The leading pre-CPR (but still illuminating) decision is *Alpine Bulk Transport Co Inc v Saudi Eagle Shipping Co Inc ('The Saudi Eagle')* [1986] 2 Lloyd's Rep 221, CA; considered in *Shocked v Goldschmidt* [1998] 1 All ER 372, 376, CA (non-appearance at trial).

[225] *Day v RAC Motoring Services Ltd* [1999] 1 WLR 2150, 2157, CA.

[226] *Clapp v Enron* [2005] EWCA Civ 1511 at [36] ff, citing *Odyssey (London) Ltd v OIC Run-off* [2001] Lloyd's Rep (Insurance) 1, CA.

[227] *Burchmore v Hills* (1935) 79 LJ 30.

[228] *City Construction Contracts (London) Ltd v Adam The Times* 4 January, 1988, CA.

[229] CPR 13.2, 12.3(1)(2).

[230] CPR 13.2, 12.3(3).

[231] CPR 13.2(c) 12.3(3)(b).

time to pay.[232] Finally, if the defendant satisfies the court that he was unaware of the relevant claim form, the court will 'normally' set aside the default judgment 'unless it is pointless to do so'.[233] There is a cognate power to set aside a judgment where the relevant party fails to attend trial and his claim or defence is struck out.[234] In this situation the court will 'almost always' set aside a judgment if the defendant did not receive notice of the claim form.[235]

E. Case Management[236]

(1) Case Management in General

22.46 As examined in the next paragraph, the courts possess extensive 'case management' powers. In his reports of 1995–96[237] Lord Woolf adopted this technique as the mainstay for actions on the 'multi-track', thus including all High Court litigation.[238] The court must now ensure that matters are properly focused, procedural indiscipline checked, expense reduced, progress accelerated, and that just outcomes are facilitated or awarded. Case management has three main functions:[239] to encourage the parties to pursue mediation, where this is practicable;[240] secondly, to prevent the case from progressing too slowly and inefficiently; finally, to ensure that judicial resources are allocated proportionately, as required by 'the Overriding Objective' in CPR Part 1. This requires the court and parties to consider the

---

[232] CPR 13.2, 12.3(3)(c) 14.4, 14.7.

[233] *Godwin v Swindon BC* [2001] EWCA Civ 1478; [2002] 1 WLR 997, CA at [49], considering CPR 13.3(1)(b); *Akram v Adam* [2004] EWCA Civ 1601; [2005] 1 WLR 2762, CA at [42], [43] (service technically effective under the deemed service regime even if notice was never received).

[234] CPR 39.3(5); which requires, among other things, proof of a 'good reason' for non-attendance at trial; *Estate Acquisition and Development Ltd v Wiltshire* [2006] EWCA Civ 533; [2006] CP Rep 32; for the general common law principles governing this context, *Gaydamak v UBS Bahamas Ltd & Anor (Bahamas)* [2006] UKPC 8; [2006] 1 WLR 1097.

[235] *Nelson v Clearsprings (Management) Ltd* [2006] EWCA Civ 1854; [2007] CP Rep 2, at [56]; [2007] 2 All ER 407.

[236] On the new system from the perspective of the traditional adversarial principle, Neil Andrews, 'A New Civil Procedural Code for England: Party-Control "Going, Going, Gone"' (2000) 19 CJQ 19–38; Neil Andrews, English Civil Procedure (2003) 13.12 to 13.41; 14.04 to 14.45; 15.65 to 15.72.

[237] Lord Woolf's two reports are: *Access to Justice: Interim Report* (1995) and *Access to Justice: Final Report* (1996): for comment, A Zuckerman and R Cranston, *The Reform of Civil Procedure: Essays on 'Access to Justice'* (1995); see also R Cranston, *How Law Works* (2006) ch 5.

[238] eg, Neil Andrews, *English Civil Procedure* (2003) chs 13, 14, 15; *Zuckerman on Civil Procedure* (2006) at 1.74 ff, ch 10, 11.53 ff.

[239] On case management and settlement, S Roberts 'Settlement as Civil Justice' (2000) 63 MLR 739, 745–7.

[240] See 22.94 and 22.95.

competing demands of other litigants who wish to gain access to judges, the court's 'scarce resources'.[241]

The CPR lists various managerial responsibilities. These are not intended to be **22.47** exhaustive statements of the court's new active role.[242] Judges, especially at first instance, have the following managerial responsibilities: *co-operation and settlement*: encouraging co-operation between the parties;[243] helping parties to settle all or part of the case;[244] encouraging alternative dispute resolution;[245] if necessary, staying the action to enable such extra-curial negotiations or discussions to be pursued (see further 22.94 below);[246] *determining relevance and priorities*: helping to identify the issues in the case;[247] deciding the order in which the issues are to be resolved;[248] deciding which issues need a full trial and which can be dealt with summarily;[249] *making summary decisions*: deciding whether to initiate a summary hearing (under CPR Part 24);[250] or whether the claim or defence can be struck out as having no prospect of success;[251] or whether to dispose of a case on a preliminary issue;[252] excluding issues from consideration;[253] *maintaining impetus*: fixing timetables and controlling in other ways the progress of the case;[254] giving directions which will bring the case to trial as quickly and efficiently as possible;[255] *regulating expenditure*: deciding whether a proposed step in the action is cost-effective,[256] taking into account the size of the claim ('proportionality').[257] Lord Woolf commented on these powers: '. . .judges have to be trusted to exercise the wide discretions which they have fairly and justly. . .[Appeal courts] should not interfere unless judges can be shown to have exercised their powers in some way which contravenes the relevant principles'.[258] A party must obtain permission to appeal

---

[241] eg Neil Andrews, *English Civil Procedure* (2003) chs 13, 14, 15; *Zuckerman on Civil Procedure* (2006) at 1.74 ff, ch 10, 11.53 ff.

[242] CPR 1.4(2); CPR 3.1(2); CPR Parts 26, 28, 29.

[243] CPR 1.4(2)(a).

[244] CPR 1.4(2)(f).

[245] CPR 1.4(2)(e).

[246] CPR 3.1(2)(f).

[247] CPR 1.4(2)(a).

[248] CPR 1.4(2)(d); 3.1(2)(j).

[249] CPR 1.4(2)(c).

[250] PD (26) 5.1, 5.2.

[251] CPR 3.4(2).

[252] CPR 3.1(2)(l).

[253] CPR 3.1(2)(k).

[254] CPR 1.4(2)(g).

[255] CPR 1.4(2)(l).

[256] eg, the suggestion that video-conferencing be used for short appeals: *Black v Pastouna* [2005] EWCA Civ 1389; [2006] CP Rep 11, *per* Brooke LJ.

[257] CPR 1.4(2)(h) and 1.1(2)(c).

[258] *Biguzzi v Rank Leisure plc* [1999] 1 WLR 1926, 1934 F, CA, *per* Lord Woolf MR.

from a case management decision, but this will be difficult to obtain.[259] Appellate courts are prepared to show considerable deference to judges' case management decisions, unless they are incorrect in principle.[260]

(2) Case Management in the Commercial Court[261]

22.48 The Commercial Court is part of the Queen's Bench Division within the High Court.[262] It has its own detailed procedural code: 'The Admiralty and Commercial Courts Guide'[263] Its judges hear all pre-trial applications, including case management hearings.[264] This contrasts with the general pattern in the Queen's Bench Division where full High Court judges ('puisne judges') are generally involved in civil litigation only at trial and Masters hear many pre-trial matters.[265]

22.49 There are two important pre-trial hearings, the 'case management conference' (CMCs) and the 'pre-hearing review'. The following documents must be prepared for a CMC: (i) an agreed case memorandum,[266] that is, a 'short and uncontroversial description' of 'what the case is about'; (ii) a 'list of issues' which should comprise: 'important. . .issues of fact and issues of law' and 'what is common ground between the parties. . .';[267] (iii) two 'case management information sheets'[268] setting out the parties' respective proposals regarding documentary disclosure, preliminary issues, factual and expert witnesses (names or at least their fields of

---

[259] PD (52) 4.4, 4.5: 'Case management decisions include decisions made under rule 3.1(2) [containing a long list of procedural powers] and decisions about disclosure, filing of witness statements, or experts reports, directions about the timetable of the claim, adding a party to a claim, and security for costs.' In this context, a decision concerning permission to appeal requires consideration whether 'the issue is of sufficient significance to justify the costs of an appeal', 'the procedural consequences of an appeal (eg loss of trial date) outweigh the significance of the case management decision', and whether 'it would be more convenient to determine the issue at or after trial'.

[260] *Thomson v O'Connor* [2005] EWCA Civ 1533 at [17] to [19], *per* Brooke LJ; *Three Rivers DC v Bank of England* [20005] EWCA Civ 889; [2005] CP Rep 46, at [55] see also the authorities cited in Neil Andrews, *English Civil Procedure* (2003) 13.61 to 13.68, 38.49; *Zuckerman on Civil Procedure* (2006) 23.193 ff.

[261] A Colman, *Commercial Court* (5th edn, 2000) ch 5.

[262] Supreme Court Act 1981, s 6(1)(2).

[263] *The Admiralty and Commercial Courts Guide* (7th edn, 2006); Colman, *Commercial Court* (5th edn, 2000) 19–20; R Cranston, 'Complex Litigation: the Commercial Court' (2007) 26 CJQ 190.

[264] Colman, *Commercial Court* (5th edn, 2000) 6–7.

[265] 'Puisne' is the adjective used to describe High Court judges who are knighted or decorated as 'Dame'.

[266] *The Guide* (n 263 above) D5; Colman (n 263 above) 64–5; for an example, Colman 83.

[267] *The Guide* (n 263 above) D6; Colman (n 263 above) 65–6, and for an example, 84.

[268] *The Guide* (n 263 above) D8.5 and appendix 6; see also PD (58) 10.7; Colman (n 263 above) 66.

expertise), and estimate of readiness for, and length of, trial;[269] (iv) a draft order (agreed by the parties) for consideration by the judge and a statement signed by each advocate explaining plans for ADR or why the dispute is not suitable for that technique;[270] (v) the claimant must also prepare a case management bundle.[271] A CMC is generally oral.[272] Clients need not attend, unless the court orders. Each party should send a solicitor and at least one advocate.[273] The judge will discuss with the advocates the issues raised in the case, and fix the pre-trial timetable,[274] including a 'progress monitoring date'.[275] The judge might make an 'ADR order'[276] and 'stay' the proceedings (see 22.94 and 22.95). Finally, the judge will consider 'the possibility of the trial of preliminary issues' which might shorten the action (see 22.38). After this conference, the parties must arrange with the clerk to the court a fixed date for trial.

22.50 The purpose of the pre-trial review is to ensure that trial proceeds efficiently and fairly:[277] 'The judge may set a timetable for the trial and give such other directions for the conduct of the trial as he considers appropriate.'[278] Each party must later confirm that he has satisfied these directions and is ready for trial.[279]

(3) Sanctions and Procedural Discipline

22.51 The main sanctions for breach of a procedural requirement are: costs orders;[280] stay of the proceedings;[281] and striking out part or all of the claim or defence.[282] Breach of a judicial order or injunction can involve contempt of court (see 22.130), for example a freezing injunction.[283]

---

[269] Various questions are posed in the case management information sheet (see Appendix 6 to the Guide, para 15).

[270] *The Guide*, D8.3(e).

[271] *The Guide* (n 263 above) D7; Colman (n 263 above) 67.

[272] *The Guide* (n 263 above) D8.3; Colman (n 263 above) 69–70.

[273] *The Guide* (n 263 above) D8.2; Colman (n 263 above) 69–70.

[274] *The Guide* (n 263 above) D8.10, D8.11.

[275] ibid, D12.

[276] For details of the Commercial Court's special version of this 'order', see Appendix 7 of the Guide.

[277] *The Guide* (n 263 above) D18.

[278] ibid, D18.4.

[279] *The Guide*, D14, states: 'Not later than three weeks before the date fixed for trial each party must send to the Listing Office (with a copy to all other parties) a completed check-list confirming final details for trial (a "pre-trial checklist") in the form set out in Appendix 13 [to the Guide].'

[280] CPR 3.8(2).

[281] CPR 3.1(2)(f).

[282] CPR 3.4(2)(c).

[283] eg, *Daltel Europe Ltd v Makki* [2006] EWCA Civ 94; [2006] 1 WLR 2704.

22.52 Zuckerman has contended that the courts have not been consistent and tough enough in exercising their powers of case management.[284] In particular, he contends that they have shown undue clemency towards procedural default. In his view, the courts are wrong to relieve parties and their lawyers from failure to comply efficiently with the procedural framework and specific orders administered during case management. Against this it might be suggested that it is important to apply the principle of 'procedural equity'.[285] 'Procedural non-compliance' cannot be treated as uniformly reprehensible. Examples of procedural default vary greatly in their intrinsic importance. They also cause, or have the potential to cause, different degrees of 'collateral' impact, that is, disturbing the 'case flow' of other litigation in the same 'list' of actions. For example, the courts have sensibly refrained from making draconian orders where parties have slightly delayed in making disclosure of expert reports or witness statements, provided this delay can be acceptably explained.[286] Furthermore, litigants in person require special consideration.[287]

F. Disclosure[288]

22.53 Disclosure between adversaries (prospective or present parties), in its various forms, serves three main functions: it can achieve equality of access to information; and facilitate settlement of disputes; finally, it avoids so-called 'trial by ambush', that is, the situation when a party is unable to respond properly to a surprise revelation at the final hearing.

---

[284] AAS Zuckerman in M Andenas, Neil Andrews, R Nazzini (eds) *The Future of Transnational Commercial Litigation: English Responses to the ALI/UNIDROIT Draft Principles and Rules of Transnational Civil Procedure* (British Institute of Comparative and International Law, London; reprinted 2006) ch 12; and in N Trocker and V Varano (eds) *The Reforms of Civil Procedure in Comparative Perspective* (2005) 143ff, and *Zuckerman on Civil Procedure* (2nd edn, 2006) ch 10, esp at 10.139 and 10.164ff; D Piggott, 'Relief from Sanctions and the Overriding Objective' (2005) CJQ 103–29.

[285] Neil Andrews, *English Civil Procedure* (2003) 6.66ff; recent examples, *Keen Phillips (a Firm) v Field* [2006] EWCA Civ 1524; [2007] 1 WLR 686 at [18]; *Estate Acquisition and Development Ltd v Wiltshire* [2006] EWCA Civ 533; [2006] CP Rep 32; *Horton v Sadler* [2006] UKHL 27; [2006] 2 WLR 1346; *Baldock v Webster* [2004] EWCA Civ 1869; [2006] QB 315; but there are limits, eg, *Olafsson v Gissurarson* [2006] EWHC 3162 (QB); [2007] 1 All ER 88 (invalid service in Iceland could not be cured under CPR 3.10).

[286] *Meredith v Colleys Vacation Services* Ltd [2001] EWCA Civ 1456; [2002] CP 10; *RC Residuals Ltd v Linton Fuel Oils Ltd* [2002] EWCA Civ 11; [2002] 1 WLR 2782; N Madge in L Blom-Cooper (ed), *Experts in Civil Courts* (2006) 4.34 ff; cf, in a slightly different context, *Calden v Nunn* [2003] EWCA Civ 200 (where the trial window would be missed and the application for permission to adduce the report of a party-appointed expert was unacceptably late); and for refusal to make a disproportionate order in respect of late disclosure of a witness report, *Halabi v Fieldmore Holdings Ltd* (Ch D 11 May 2006, All England Reporter).

[287] *Hougie v Hewitt* (Ch D Lawtel 27 September 2006) (relief from striking out for breach of an 'unless order'; litigant in person's default mitigated by depression).

[288] Neil Andrews, *English Civil Procedure* (2003) ch 26; P Matthews and H Malek, *Disclosure* (3rd edn, 2007).

(1) Pre-Action Orders

The rules empower the court to make a pre-action documentary disclosure   **22.54**
order against any type of prospective defendant.[289] However, in *Black v Sumitomo
Corporation* (2002) the Court of Appeal refused to open the door to roving and
'deep-sea fishing' expeditions in commercial contexts.[290] Specific rules provide that
property, for example factory equipment, can be preserved for inspection.[291] It is
an offence for a prospective defendant to destroy documents, or other evidence,
in order to spoil his opponent's chances of winning the relevant case.[292] The reader
is referred to 22.28 for discussion of civil search orders to prevent a prospective
defendant from destroying vital evidence.

(2) Disclosure Against Non-Parties

'*Norwich Pharmacal* orders',[293] a non-statutory form of relief, can be granted to   **22.55**
compel a person (not necessarily a prospective defendant) to disclose documents
or non-documentary information if he was 'involved', whether culpably or innocently, in an alleged civil wrong. Such an order is normally made before the main
proceedings and to discover the following: the main wrongdoer's identity; or the
location, nature and value of the prospective defendant's assets; or whether the
applicant has fallen victim of a civil wrong, such as defamation, committed behind
his back; or to identify and discipline a dishonest or defaulting employee within
the applicant's organization.[294] After commencement of proceedings, the court
has a statutory power to order disclosure of documents against a non-party in
any type of case.[295] The rule states that an applicant must satisfy the court that
the document is 'likely' to be supportive in those proceedings, but this has

---

[289] CPR 31.16 (3).

[290] [2002] 1 WLR 1562, CA; Neil Andrews, *English Civil Procedure* (2003) 26.70.

[291] Supreme Court Act 1981, s 33, providing for a court order regarding '*the inspection, photo-
graphing, preservation, custody and detention of property which appears to the court to be property which
may become the subject-matter of subsequent proceedings. . .or as to which any question may arise in such
proceedings*'.

[292] *Douglas v Hello!* [2003] EWHC 55 (Ch); [2003] 1 All ER 1087 (brief note), Morritt V-C; see
22.06 for detail.

[293] In *Ashworth Hospital Authority v MGN Ltd* [2002] UKHL 29; [2002] 1 WLR 2033, HL,
Lord Woolf CJ re-stated the principles governing this jurisdiction, which was resuscitated in
Norwich Pharmacal v Customs & Excise Commrs [1974] AC 133, HL; and see next note; the power
is exercisable in support of foreign proceedings, *Equatorial Guinea v Bank of Scotland International
(Guernsey)* [2006] UKPC 7 at [5]; but the jurisdiction is one of last resort, *Mitsui & Co Ltd v Nexen
Petroleum UK Ltd* [2005] EWHC 625 (Ch); [2005] 3 All ER 511, [18] ff, esp [24] [28] [37] [39];
for the sequel to the *Ashworth* case, *Mersey Care NHS Trust v Ackroyd* [2006] EWHC 107 (QB); *The
Times* 9 February, 2006.

[294] Neil Andrews, *English Civil Procedure* (2003) 26–102 ff on these various categories.

[295] CPR 31.17; this rule concerns only documents: see CPR 31.17(3)(4).

been interpreted to require only something weightier than a mere 'fanciful chance'.[296]

(3) Disclosure of Documents During the Main Proceedings

22.56 In accordance with automatic or case management directions, each party must prepare a list of documents on which he will rely, or which might assist the other party.[297] A party is obliged both to provide a list of documents ('disclosure') and to allow inspection of these by the other side.[298] Such information only becomes evidence if it is 'adduced' by one party for the purpose of a trial or other 'hearing' (on evidence at trial, see 22.98 ff). The CPR defines a 'document' as 'anything in which information of any description is recorded'.[299] That definition does not catch information held in a human memory, nor does it catch non-documentary 'things', such as the claimant's body, physical chattels, or immovable property.[300] Special provision exists for disclosure of electronic information.[301]

22.57 'Standard disclosure' concerns documents which satisfy one of the following criteria:[302] documents on which a party will rely; or which adversely affect his case; or adversely affect the opponent's case; or support the opponent's case; or any other documents of which disclosure is required under a practice direction.[303] The obligation to make disclosure applies to 'documents' (defined above), whether or not currently available and whether created before or during the relevant litigation.[304] These documents must either fall within the scope of standard disclosure (as discussed above), or they must have been referred to in that party's statement of case (see 22.14). A party's duty to make 'disclosure' embraces documents which 'are or have been in [the relevant party's] control'; and 'control' refers to material which 'is or was in his physical possession', or other material to which he has or has had a 'right to possession' or 'a right to inspect or take copies'.[305] However, there is no obligation to produce for inspection (as distinct from listing

---

[296] *Three Rivers DC v Bank of England (No 4)* [2002] EWCA Civ 1182; [2003] 1 WLR 210 CA at [32], [33].

[297] CPR Part 31.

[298] CPR 31.10(2) and 31.15, subject to certain qualifications added at CPR 31.3(2).

[299] CPR 31.4.

[300] eg, Civil Evidence Act 1968, s 14.

[301] PD (31) 2A.1.

[302] CPR 31.6.

[303] The court can order narrower disclosure in special situations: CPR 31.5(1),(2).

[304] On the continuing duty to make disclosure until the end of the relevant proceedings, CPR 31.11.

[305] CPR 31.8; *Three Rivers DC v Bank of England (No 4)* [2002] EWCA Civ 1182; [2003] 1 WLR 210, CA, at [46] to [51] (application to obtain disclosure held by non-party, HM Treasury, at the National Archive, Kew; held that the defendant Bank of England had no possession of these documents; nor any right to possess them; nor any right to inspect them).

during the first stage of discovery) material which is subject to any of the following privileges (generally, see 22.61 ff):[306] legal advice or litigation privilege (together known as 'legal professional privilege', on which see 22.63 ff);[307] public interest immunity;[308] the privilege against self-incrimination;[309] the privilege relating to 'without prejudice' negotiations;[310] or 'mediation privilege'.[311] In applications for judicial review, disclosure of documents is not automatic. It is also more circumscribed than in ordinary civil proceedings. However, the House of Lords has recognized the need for a slightly more liberal approach to this context.[312]

The duty to make disclosure extends to non-privileged confidential material.[313] **22.58** However, when deciding whether to order disclosure and inspection of confidential material, the courts will consider these questions:[314] is the information available to the other side from some other convenient source;[315] might sensitive material be blanked out;[316] might the class of recipients be restricted?[317]

The 'implied undertaking' ensures that the recipient can use the information only **22.59** in the present proceedings and he must not reveal it to any non-party.[318] The CPR provides: 'a party to whom a document has been disclosed may use the document only for the purpose of the proceedings in which it is disclosed,[319] except (a) where the document has been read to or by the court, or referred to, at a hearing which has been held in public; or (b) the court gives permission;[320] or (c) the party who disclosed the document and the person to whom the document belongs agree'.[321]

---

306 CPR 31.3(1)(b).

307 Neil Andrews, *English Civil Procedure* (2003) ch 27; on recent judicial discussion, Neil Andrews (2005) CJQ 185–93; C Tapper (2005) 121 LQR 181–5; J Seymour [2005] CLJ 54–6; C Passmore (2006) NLJ 668–9.

308 Neil Andrews, *English Civil Procedure* (2003) ch 30.

309 ibid, ch 29; and for other references see n 328 below.

310 ibid, at 25.01 to 25.44; see also 22.91.

311 ibid, at 25.45 to end; see also 22.91.

312 *Tweed v Parades Commission for Northern Ireland* [2006] UKHL 53; [2007] 2 All ER 273.

313 *Wallace Smith Trust Co v Deloitte Haskins & Sells* [1997] 1 WLR 257, CA.

314 eg, when deciding whether to order specific disclosure under CPR 31.12.

315 See *Wallace Smith* case [1997] 1 WLR 257, CA.

316 *GE Capital etc v Bankers Trust Co* [1995] 1 WLR 172, CA.

317 Neil Andrews, *Principles of Civil Procedure* (1994) 11–056.

318 SMC Gibbons, 'Subsequent use of documents obtained through disclosure in civil proceedings. . .' (2001) 20 CJQ 303; *Omar v Omar* [1995] 1 WLR 1428; *Watkins v AJ Wright (Electrical) Ltd* [1996] 3 All ER 31; *Miller v Scorey* [1996] 1 WLR 1122.

319 Cf, before CPR 'collateral' use included certain uses in same action: *Milano Assicurazioni SpA v Walbrook Insurance Co Ltd* [1994] 1 WLR 977; and *Omar v Omar* [1995] 1 WLR 1428; respectively, proposed amendments to writ or statement of claim.

320 *SmithKline Beecham Biologicals SA v Connaught Laboratories Inc* [1999] 4 All ER 498, CA.

321 CPR 31.22; even in situation (a) however, the court can make a special order restricting or prohibiting use of a document: CPR 31.22(2).

22.60 A person will be in contempt of court if he presents a deliberately false statement contained in a statement of case, witness statement, disclosure declaration (under CPR Part 31), or in an expert's report (see 22.130 on contempt). The court can also dismiss a claim or defence if there has been deliberate destruction or falsification of evidence. For example, in *Arrow Nominees Inc v Blackledge* (2001), where a litigant had falsified documents, the Court of Appeal concluded that the litigant's behaviour had destroyed all credibility in his evidence.[322] The court can also draw adverse inferences against a party who has failed to comply with the disclosure rules in CPR Part 31.[323] Such a 'soft sanction' is more generally recognized in other legal systems as a response to procedural disobedience.[324] It is also an offence for a prospective defendant to destroy documents, or other evidence, in order to spoil his opponent's chances of winning the relevant case.[325]

G. Legal Advice and Litigation Privileges

(1) Privileges in General

22.61 'Evidential privileges' in English law confer immunity upon the privilege holder (which can be a person, company or organization) against compulsion to supply information under legal obligation. The potential compulsion can arise in two main[326] contexts: as an order for a witness to give evidence at a civil or criminal trial; or, secondly, during the pre-trial process of information gathering (known in English civil proceedings as 'disclosure', on which see 22.53 ff).[327] The privileges recognized in English law are:[328] confidential discussion between lawyer and

---

[322] [2000] 2 BCLC 167; [2001] BCC 591, CA; Chadwick LJ said: 'it is no part of the court's function to proceed to trial if to do so would give rise to a substantial risk of injustice', and Ward LJ said: 'Striking out is not a disproportionate remedy for such an abuse... Deception of this scale and magnitude will result in a party's forfeiting his right to continue to be heard.'

[323] eg the first instance decision in *Infabrics v Jaytext* [1985] FSR 75 (affmd [1987] FSR 529, CA) decided under the old rules, but still relevant.

[324] *ALI/UNIDROIT: Principles of Transnational Civil Procedure* (2006), Principles 17.3, 21.3, acknowledge this 'soft sanction'.

[325] *Douglas v Hello! Ltd* [2003] EWHC 55 (Ch); [2003] 1 All ER 1087, Morritt V-C; see further 22.06.

[326] Sometimes the privilege is asserted outside the context of the formal legal process: eg, *R (on the Application of Morgan Grenfell & Co Ltd) v Special Commissioners of Income Tax* [2002] UKHL 21; [2003] 1 AC 563 (legal advice privilege available against a tax inspector's demand for documents); B Thanki (ed), *The Law of Privilege* (2006) 1–05.

[327] Predominantly covered by CPR Part 31; Neil Andrews, *English Civil Procedure* (2003) ch 26; C Hollander, *Documentary Evidence* (9th edn, 2006) chs 7 to 10; *Zuckerman on Civil Procedure* (2nd edn, 2006) ch 14.

[328] Neil Andrews, *English Civil Procedure* (2003) chs 25, 27 to 30; *Cross and Tapper on Evidence* (10th edn, 2004) chs 9, 10; C Hollander, *Documentary Evidence* (9th edn, 2006) chs 11 to 20; *Phipson on Evidence* (16th edn, 2005) chs 23 to 26; B Thanki (ed), *The Law of Privilege* (2006) (the most

client ('legal advice privilege'); documents created for the dominant purpose of use in pending or contemplated criminal or civil proceedings (including arbitration proceedings) ('litigation privilege'); settlement negotiations explicitly or implicitly conducted on a secret basis ('without prejudice communications privilege'; on which see 22.91); mediation or conciliation negotiations conducted on a confidential basis ('mediation privilege'; on which see 22.91); the privilege against self-incrimination;[329] and 'public interest immunity',[330] that is protection against use in civil proceedings of information protected in the public interest, for example, high-level state secrets or information supplied to identify criminal wrongdoers.

(2) Privilege and 'Confidentiality'

Non-confidential information cannot be privileged. If information ceases to be **22.62** confidential, privilege will also lapse. As a matter of 'substantive law', confidential information can be protected by the equitable remedies of injunction,[331] and by pecuniary remedies.[332] But not all confidential information is privileged. For example, confidential discussion between a person and a priest or religious advisor, or between a patient and doctor, and across the whole gamut of professional relationships,[333] is undoubtedly subject to general equitable protection, through injunctions and

---

powerful analysis of this topic); C Passmore, *Privilege* (1998); *Zuckerman on Civil Procedure* (2nd edn, 2006) chs 15–18; see also, J Auburn, *Legal Professional Privilege: Law and Theory* (2000).

[329] Defined by Civil Evidence Act 1968, s 14, as follows: 'The right of a person in any legal proceedings other than criminal proceedings to refuse to answer any question or produce any document or thing if to do so would tend to expose that person [or his or her spouse] to proceedings for an offence or for the recovery of a penalty [under UK law].' A majority in *C plc v P* [2007] EWCA Civ 493, at [26] to [38], and [74], held that there is no privilege in things or documents existing prior to the relevant order; see also *Cross & Tapper on Evidence* (10th edn, 2004) 445 ff; IH Dennis, *The Law of Evidence*, (2nd edn, 2002) ch 5; C Hollander, *Documentary Evidence* (9th edn, 2006) ch 17 (reproducing, also by C Hollander, *Phipson on Evidence* (16th edn, 2005) 24–40 ff); B Thanki (ed), *The Law of Privilege* (2006) ch 8; *Zuckerman on Civil Procedure* (2nd edn, 2006) ch 17; see also 'The Privilege against Self-incrimination in Civil Proceedings' (Consultation Paper, Lord Chancellor's Dept, 1992); I Dennis, 'Instrumental Protection, Human Right or Fundamental Necessity? Re-assessing the Privilege against Self-incrimination' [1995] 54 CLJ 342.

[330] Neil Andrews, *English Civil Procedure* (2003) ch 30.

[331] eg, abundant case law concerning protection of 'client information' by injunctions: *Marks and Spencer Group plc v Freshfields Bruckhaus Deringer* [2004] EWCA Civ 741; *Koch Shipping Inc v Richards Butler* [2002] EWCA Civ 1280; *GUS Consulting GmbH v Leboeuf Lamb, Greene & McCrae* [2006] EWCA Civ 683; [2006] CP Rep 40; *Bolkiah v KPMG* [1999] 2 AC 222, HL; the topic is considered in C Hollander and S Salzedo, *Conflicts of Interest and Chinese Walls* (2nd edn, 2005); for US and comparative discussion: G Hazard and A Dondi, *Legal Ethics* (2004) ch 5, 'Loyalty', and ch 6, 'Confidentiality'.

[332] On the remedies of damages and 'account' in this context, *Douglas v Hello! Ltd (No 3)* [2005] EWCA Civ 595; [2006] QB 12.

[333] R Pattenden, *The Law of Professional–Client Confidentiality: Regulating the Disclosure of Confidential Personal Information* (2003).

even damages. But the holder of those types of confidentiality cannot invoke privilege if ordered by the court to give evidence or produce documents relating to this information. In short, privilege is confidentiality admitted to a higher level of legal protection; not all confidential relations are raised to that level.

(3) Legal Advice Privilege

22.63 This is undoubtedly the most important head of evidential privilege. In the United States it is known as 'attorney-client' privilege. The leading English decision is *Three Rivers DC v Governor and Company of the Bank of England (No 6)* (2004).[334] There the House of Lords held that legal advice privilege is not confined to confidential consultation between a lawyer and his client concerning the latter's legal rights and obligations. For example, it can include so-called 'presentational' advice to a client on how to formulate submissions to an inquiry into alleged wrongdoing or commercial default. As for the meaning of 'lawyer', the reader should note that, at the time of writing, there are important proposals before Parliament concerning the re-organization of legal practices.[335]

22.64 In *Three Rivers (No 6)* Baroness Hale noted that the whole House wished to 'endorse the approach', formulated by Taylor LJ in the *Balabel* case, that 'legal advice is not confined to telling the client the law; it must include advice as to what should prudently and sensibly be done in the relevant context'.[336] She added:[337] 'We want people to obey the law, enter into valid and effective transactions, settle their affairs responsibly when they separate or divorce, make wills which will withstand the challenge of the disappointed, and present their best case before all kinds of court, tribunal and inquiry in an honest and responsible manner.' According to the House of Lords, legal advice privilege must arise from a 'relevant legal context', including 'presentational' advice for participation in an Inquiry.[338] However, legal advice privilege does not extend to a lawyer's assistance in a general commercial capacity if this assistance or advice could be provided equally well by a non-lawyer (the 'mere man of business' limitation).[339]

---

334 [2004] UKHL 48; [2005] 1 AC 610; noted Neil Andrews (2005) CJQ 185; S Partington and J Ward [2005] JBL 231; J Seymour [2005] CLJ 54; C Tapper (2005) 121 LQR 181.

335 For comment on the 'Legal Services Bill', (for reference to this Bill, see end of this note) K Underwood, 'The Legal Services Bill-Death by Regulation?' (2007) 26 CJQ 124; clause 182 of the Bill refers to legal professional privilege; the text of the Bill, which is being debated in Parliament in mid 2007, is available at: <www.publications.parliament.uk/pa/pabills/200607/legal_services.htm>.

336 [2004] UKHL 48; [2005] 1 AC 610, at [62], referring to Taylor LJ's statement in *Balabel v Air India* [1988] Ch 317, 330, CA.

337 [2004] UKHL 48; [2005] 1 AC 610, at [62].

338 ibid at [120].

339 ibid, at [38]; for detail on this problematic topic, B Thanki (ed), *The Law of Privilege* (2006) 2–115 ff.

The lawyer-client relationship is easy to identify when the client is an individual. **22.65**
But the matter is problematic if the client is a company or organization. This topic
is presently governed by the Court of Appeal's decision in *Three Rivers (No 5)*[340]
which the House of Lords in the *Three Rivers (No 6)* case chose not to examine.
The present law can be formulated as follows: when an event involving or affecting a company (or other organization) is being investigated or considered, English
law does not extend legal advice privilege to confidential communications between
the lawyer and all the various members and echelons within that client company
or other organization; and this is so, even though this legal discussion is designed
to gather the facts surrounding the relevant event. The Court of Appeal held that
the 'client' should be defined narrowly to comprise only a small segment of the
company or organization. Legal consultation beyond that 'core' 'client' group of
officials or employees will not attract legal advice privilege. Admittedly, legal consultation beyond this 'core' 'client' group might be privileged on the basis of 'litigation' privilege (on which see 22.67). However, litigation privilege is confined to
confidential communications in relation to 'adversarial' proceedings, as distinct
from an Inquiry.[341]

The US Supreme Court in *Upjohn Co v United States* (1981) adopted a broader **22.66**
approach than the English Court of Appeal's to the question of a 'corporate
client'.[342] That American case involved a confidential 'internal trawl' conducted
by in-house counsel for information from a company's employees. The US
Supreme Court held that attorney-client privilege attaches to documents and
communications which enable lawyers (in-house counsel in the *Upjohn* case) to
give confidential legal advice to the company's leading officials. The internal
inquiry in this case involved allegations of wrongdoing. The case is conveniently
analysed by Thanki.[343] The House of Lords in *Three Rivers (No 6)* chose not to
decide whether they regarded the *Upjohn* decision as offering an attractive
approach. English commentators are divided. Hollander (writing both in his own

---

[340] *Three Rivers DC v Governor and Company of the Bank of England (No 5)* [2003] EWCA Civ
474; [2003] QB 1556; *Zuckerman on Civil Procedure* (2nd edn, 2006) 15.37 ff; *Three Rivers (No 5)*
was applied in *National Westminster Bank v Rabobank Nederland* [2006] EWHC 218 (Comm).
[341] *Re L* [1997] AC 16, HL.
[342] 449 US 383 (1981); cf the US material collected at *Zuckerman on Civil Procedure* (2nd edn,
2006) 15.43 ff, at nn 70 to 82, also noting J Sexton 'A Post-*Upjohn* consideration of Corporate-
Client privilege' (1982) 57 NYULR 442; on the danger of corporate 'cloaking', B Thanki (ed),
The Law of Privilege (2006) 2.28 n 73, noting Australian discussion, most recently in *Esso v Federal
Commissioner of Taxation* (1999) 201 CLR 49 (considering *Grant v Downs* (1976) 135 CLR 674);
Thanki (n 339 above) at 2–39, notes the non-binding view of Lord Scott in argument in *Three
Rivers (No 6)* that the (entire) company is normally the client.
[343] B Thanki (ed), *The Law of Privilege* (2006) 2.41 ff, noting at 2.45 Burger CJ's test at 449 US
383, 402–3 (1981).

book and in *Phipson on Evidence*)[344] and the editors of Thanki's *Law of Privilege*[345] support a wide approach to corporate legal advice privilege; Zuckerman[346] is firmly against; and Tapper[347] is equivocal. Perhaps the arguments just tip in favour of maintaining the current and restrictive English law, even though this presents difficulty for companies engaged in internal fact-finding.

(4) Litigation Privilege[348]

22.67 This privilege shields a party's (or lawyer's) attempt to prepare a case for litigation conducted *inter partes*. Each party's (or prospective party's, see next paragraph) private investigation into the case's facts and background can be conducted in the knowledge that an opponent cannot discover either the target or fruit of the other party's forensic investigation. There is no general duty, therefore, to reveal 'bad points' discovered during this process (for an exceptional positive duty to disclose 'bad points' in the context of 'without notice' applications, see 22.22). However, a litigant or lawyer must not positively mislead the court.

22.68 The elements of 'litigation privilege' are:

(1) it concerns confidential[349] communication (including the creation of documentary material) between third parties and either the client or lawyer;

(2) the communication must have occurred, or this material must have been created, for the dominant purpose[350] of use in pending or anticipated proceedings; if not already commenced, the relevant proceedings must be in reasonable prospect;[351]

---

[344] C Hollander, *Documentary Evidence* (9th edn, 2006) 13.12; *Phipson on Evidence* (16th edn, 2005) 23.58 to 23.61 (highly critical of *Three Rivers DC (No 5)* [2003] QB 1556, CA; [2003] EWCA Civ 474).

[345] B Thanki (ed), *The Law of Privilege* (2006) 2.168 (Thanki QC had been counsel for the Bank of England).

[346] *Zuckerman on Civil Procedure* (2nd edn, 2006) 15.37 to 15.51.

[347] C Tapper's case note (2005) 121 LQR 181, 182 is equivocal on this point, but the tenor of his note is hostile to expansion of legal advice privilege.

[348] For details, Neil Andrews, *English Civil Procedure* (2003) 27–21 ff; C Hollander, *Documentary Evidence* (9th edn, 2006) ch 14; B Thanki (ed), *The Law of Privilege* (2006) ch 3; *Zuckerman on Civil Procedure* (2nd edn, 2006) ch 15.

[349] An unsolicited communication with a potential witness would be privileged even if the witness has not indicated that he intends to respect confidence: *ISTIL Group Inc v Zahoor* [2003] 2 All ER 252; [2003] EWHC 165 (Ch) at [63] *per* Lawrence Collins; B Thanki (ed), *The Law of Privilege* (2006) 3.35.

[350] On the 'dominant purpose' test, B Thanki (ed), *The Law of Privilege* (2006) 3–73 ff.

[351] A 'real prospect' rather than a 'mere possibility': *USA v Philip Morris Inc (No 1)* [2004] EWCA Civ 330; [2004] 1 CLC 811; Brooke LJ at [66] to [69] explained that Moore-Bick J's 'real likelihood' test at first instance, [2003] EWHC 3028 (Comm) at [46], was perhaps not an improvement on the traditional formulation of a 'real prospect'; that the level of likelihood did not have to

(3) the proceedings can be criminal or civil, foreign or domestic, and involve courts, tribunals or arbitration;

(4) the proceedings must be adversarial in nature, as distinct from an inquisitorial procedure.[352] Element (4) needs to be revisited by the courts.[353] It appears to prevent this head of privilege attaching to communications with third parties relating to any type of 'Inquiries'.[354] Such communication can only be protected under the aegis of 'legal advice privilege' (on which see 22.63 to 22.66). However, legal advice privilege only applies to direct communications between client and lawyer.

What is the relationship between legal advice and litigation privileges? Legal **22.69** advice privilege applies to lawyer-client consultation, whether or not the relevant advice concerns litigation: whereas litigation privilege is concerned with communications between the privilege holder (the 'party') and a third party or the privilege holder's lawyer and a third party. Litigation privilege, therefore, unlike legal advice privilege, concerns confidential discussion or investigation outside the lawyer/client relationship.[355] It is submitted that the better view is that there is no overlap between these privileges.[356] A communication or document should be analysed as privileged under one head rather the other, and not as privileged under both.[357]

Finally, it should be noted that litigation privilege has become controversial. This **22.70** is because it is in tension with the modern ethos of co-operation between litigants,

---

be 50 per cent or higher; and that a 'mere possibility' of proceedings was insufficient; B Thanki (ed), *The Law of Privilege* (2006) 3.47 ff.

[352] *Re L* [1997] AC 16, HL.

[353] B Thanki (ed), *The Law of Privilege* (2006) 3.57 to 3.65.

[354] In the *Three Rivers* litigation, counsel for the Bank had conceded that the Bingham Inquiry was not an 'adversarial' procedure and that 'litigation privilege' could not, therefore, apply (on the basis of *Re L* [1997] AC 16, HL); with respect, it might be contended that the special context of that case—child protection proceedings—should be taken to restrict the ambit of that decision; however, that concession appears to have been later supported by Lord Scott in the *Three Rivers* appeal [2004] UKHL 48; [2005] 1 AC 610, at [10]; however, Lord Rodger, ibid, at [53] suggested that the 'adversarial' and 'inquisitorial' distinction might require further examination (also noting that Lord Nicholls, a dissentient in *Re L*, ibid at 31 G to 32 L, had cautioned against a rigid distinction); see also the critical comments in *Zuckerman on Civil Procedure* (2nd edn, 2006) 15.110 ff.

[355] Several Law Lords in *Three Rivers (No 6)* [2004] UKHL 48; [2005] 1 AC 610 acknowledged this distinction between legal advice and litigation privilege: see Lord Scott at [10], Lord Rodger at [50] and [51], and Lord Carswell at [65] and [72]; Lord Rodger at [51] noted that Lord Edmund-Davies in *Waugh v BR Board* [1980] AC 521, 541–2, HL, had said that this distinction had not always been borne in mind, and that lawyers had sometimes loosely spoken of a global 'legal professional privilege' doctrine; in *Waugh's* case it was also made clear that litigation privilege is subject to a 'dominant purpose' test; the House of Lords in the *Three Rivers* case assumed that a 'dominant purpose' test also applies to legal advice privilege; on this last issue, B Thanki (ed), *The Law of Privilege* (2006) 2–169 ff.

[356] Thanki (ed), ibid, 1–08, 3–08 to 3–09.

[357] Cf the contention that there is overlap: *Zuckerman on Civil Procedure* (2nd edn, 2006) 15.17.

and of the expectation that litigants will place their 'cards on the table' (face up). More generally, there are judicial dicta hostile to litigation privilege.[358] Arguably there is a *via media* between outright abolition of litigation privilege and maintaining the present law without modification. Thus Zuckerman has attractively suggested that evidence given at civil trial should be open to 'probing' beyond the limits currently set.[359]

H. Experts[360]

(1) Nature of Expert Opinion

22.71 Expert evidence can concern questions of opinion on a range of matters.[361] The leading textbook distinguishes four categories.[362] The CPR was intended to curb the excesses of the party-appointed 'battle of experts'. The foremost problem is that expert witnesses hired by a litigant can lose objectivity and tailor their report to suit that party's case, indeed 'on occasion becoming more partisan than the parties'.[363] Other aims of the CPR regime are to control the number of experts to ensure 'proportionality'[364] and to promote 'equality of arms' between rich and poor parties. The primary rule is that no expert evidence can be presented in a case

---

358 For judicial statements on this issue, B Thanki (ed), *The Law of Privilege* (2006) 3.110 to 3.129.

359 *Zuckerman on Civil Procedure* (2nd edn, 2006) 15.73.

360 Neil Andrews, *English Civil Procedure* (2003) ch 32; L Blom-Cooper (ed), *Experts in Civil Courts* (2006); S Burn, *Successful Use of Expert Witnesses in Civil Disputes* (2005); *Cross and Tapper on Evidence* (10th edn, 2004) pp 568 ff; IR Freckleton, *The Trial of the Expert* (1987); T Hodgkinson and M James, *Expert Evidence: Law and Practice* (2nd edn, 2006) (the leading English discussion); C Hollander, *Documentary Evidence* (9th edn, 2006) ch 24; M Iller, *Civil Evidence: the Essential Guide* (2006) ch 12; *Phipson on Evidence* (16th edn, 2005) ch 33; *Zuckerman on Civil Procedure* (2nd edn, 2006) ch 20; A Edis, 'Privilege and Immunity: Problems of Expert Evidence' (2007) 26 CJQ 40, and DM Dwyer 'The Duties of Expert Witnesses of Fact and Opinion' (2003) 7 E & P 264; Dwyer 'The Effective Management of Bias in Civil Expert Evidence' (2007) 26 CJQ 57; Law Reform Committee's 17th Report 'Evidence of Opinion and Expert Evidence' (Cmnd 4489, 1970); Lord Woolf, *Access to Justice, Interim Report* (1995) and *Access to Justice, Final Report* (1996).

361 For discussion of this range, see Law Reform Committee's 17th Report, 'Evidence of Opinion and Expert Evidence' (Cmnd 4489, 1970) 1 ff; JA Jolowicz, *On Civil Procedure* (2000) 224–5; PL Murray and R Stürner, *German Civil Justice* (2004) 280–2.

362 T Hodgkinson and M James, *Expert Evidence: Law and Practice* (2nd edn, 2006) 1–012, 2–006: 'opinion on facts adduced before the court', 'to explain technical subjects or technical words', 'evidence of fact only observable, comprehensible, or open to description by experts', 'admissible hearsay of a specialist nature' (observing that sometimes an expert can refer to facts as a necessary preliminary to his expert evidence).

363 Sir Thomas Bingham MR in a pre-CPR case concerning appointment of a court expert under the old RSC Ord 40, in *Abbey National Mortgages plc v Key Surveyors Ltd* [1996] 1 WLR 1534, 1542, CA; on the question of party-appointed experts' partiality and the question of 'transparency', A Edis 'Privilege and Immunity: Problems of Expert Evidence' (2007) 26 CJQ 40 and DM Dwyer 'The Effective Management of Bias in Civil Expert Evidence' (2007) 26 CJQ 57.

364 CPR 35.1 states: 'Expert evidence shall be restricted to that which is reasonably required to resolve the proceedings'.

governed by the CPR unless the court has granted permission.[365] This control is a facet of the court's case management powers (on which, generally, see 22.47).

Under the CPR, there are three ways in which the court, which is not itself com-   **22.72** posed of experts, can receive expert opinion: assessors (a minor category in England; see 22.73); 'single, joint experts' (22.74), and party-appointed experts (22.76).[366] The middle category is important in most cases in the county court system, whereas party-appointed experts remain predominant in high-value litigation in the High Court. Indeed, Lord Woolf in his 1996 report said that 'in large and strongly contested cases the full adversarial system, including oral cross-examination of opposing experts, is the best way of producing a result. That will apply particularly to issues on which there are tenable rival schools of thought, or where the boundaries of knowledge are being extended.'[367]

(2) Assessors[368]

In England the assessor's task is to advise the judge on disputed matters of fact.   **22.73** Assessors are mainly used in cases concerning maritime collisions, patent litigation, and some appeals concerning costs. By contrast, in civilian systems, court-appointed experts are used much more extensively.[369] English assessors' advice must be disclosed to the parties.[370]

(3) Single, Joint Expert System

In relatively straightforward claims, or peripheral matters in large litigation,[371]   **22.74** the expert will be a 'single, joint expert', appointed to act for both parties.[372]

---

[365] CPR 35.4(1) to (3).

[366] The decision-making members of the relevant tribunal might themselves be 'expert': cf the constitution of Coroners Courts, medical appeal tribunals, etc. This specialization is not available amongst the ordinary judiciary.

[367] Lord Woolf, *Access to Justice: Final Report* (1996) ch 13, at [19].

[368] CPR 35.15; PD (35) 7.1 to 7.4; T Bingham, *The Business of Judging* (2000) 19–24; Neil Andrews, *English Civil Procedure* (2003) 32–76 to 32–77; L Blom-Cooper (ed), *Experts in Civil Courts* (2006) ch 8; DM Dwyer, 'The Future of Assessors under the CPR' (2006) 25 CJQ 219; T Hodgkinson and M James, *Expert Evidence: Law and Practice* (2nd edn, 2006) ch 5.

[369] JA Jolowicz, *On Civil Procedure* (2000) ch 12; L Cadiet et E Jeuland, *Droit Judiciare Privé* (4th edn, Litec, Paris, 2004) 454 ff; PL Murray and R Stürner, *German Civil Justice* (2004) 280 ff.

[370] *Owners of the Ship Bow Spring etc* [2004] EWCA Civ 1007; [2005] 1 WLR 144, CA.

[371] Sometimes proportionality will justify use of a single, joint expert on a relatively short issue which forms only a part of a more substantial litigation; eg, the quantification of liability in an action for professional negligence against a defendant accountant might be the subject of a single, joint expert's report, but the (prior) question of liability might be the subject of party-appointed experts: I am grateful to Master John Leslie, Queen's Bench Division, for this observation.

[372] L Blom-Cooper (ed), *Experts in Civil Courts* (2006) ch 5; T Hodgkinson and M James, *Expert Evidence: Law and Practice* (2nd edn, 2006) ch 5; as CPR 35.7 mentions, this presupposes that more than one party wishes to adduce expert evidence on a particular issue.

However, in low value cases, it might be disproportionate to give permission even for this type of expert evidence.[373] Where permission for use of a single, joint expert is granted, the parties should try to agree on the relevant individual, failing which the court can select him from lists supplied or agreed by the parties.[374] The parties share the cost of the expert.[375] Each party has an opportunity to instruct the expert and to ask written questions. Such an expert should not communicate, meet or discuss the case or his evidence with one party, independently of the others.[376] His report must summarize any range of opinion on the relevant issue and give reasons for preferring the opinion given.[377] Although, in the interests of economy,[378] the courts at first expressed a strong disinclination to hear oral evidence from such an expert, the Court of Appeal has since confirmed that a court can give permission for a single, joint expert to be cross-examined.[379]

22.75 Use of single, joint experts carries the risk of inaccuracy.[380] Although the single, joint expert's opinion is likely to be adopted in most cases, the court can reject the evidence, if it appears unsound. In *Armstrong v First York Ltd* (2005) the Court of Appeal held that a court is not bound to adopt an expert's opinion even if it directly contradicts the factual evidence given by one party: 'we do not have trial by expert in this country; we have trial by judge'.[381] Furthermore, occasionally, the courts are prepared to permit a party to rely upon evidence of another expert instructed by him if a single, joint expert's report is unacceptable to that party. But, to pre-

---

373 *Casey v Cartwright* [2006] EWCA Civ 1280; [2007] CP Rep 3; [2007] 2 All ER 78 (guidance on use of such experts in whiplash claims).

374 I am also grateful to Master John Leslie for the following insight into this practice: 'If the parties cannot agree on a single, joint expert, I direct that they are to exchange the CVs of three (or some other number) experts, each party listing them in their order of preference; that they are then to send in written reasons as to why they do not accept the opposing parties' proposed experts and why they say that their own are to be preferred and justifying their order of preference.'

375 A cheaper single, joint expert might be appointed, if the more expensive expert's fees are disproportionate to the case's value: *Kranidotes v Paschali* [2001] EWCA Civ 357; [2001] CP Rep 81; T Hodgkinson and M James, *Expert Evidence: Law and Practice* (2nd edn, 2006) 4–018.

376 *Peet v Mid-Kent Care Healthcare Trust* [2001] EWCA Civ 1703; [2002] 1 WLR 210 at [24]: CJC's Protocol at 17.12.

377 PD (35) 2.2(6).

378 *Daniels v Walker* [2000] 1 WLR 1382, 1388 A, CA (cross-examination of a single, joint evidence is a possibility); similarly, *Peet* case [2001] EWCA Civ 1703; [2002] 1 WLR 210, at [28], *per* Lord Woolf CJ.

379 *R v R* [2002] EWCA Civ 409 at [14] to [18]; L Blom-Cooper (ed), *Experts in Civil Courts* (2006) 5.37 to 5.39 noting also remarks in *Popel v National Westminster Bank plc* [2002] EWCA Civ 42; [2002] CPLR 370, at [28], [29] and *Austen v Oxfordshire CC* [2002] All D 97 (CA); 17 April 2002 (in the unusual circumstances of this case, cross-examination was allowed).

380 DM Dwyer 'The Effective Management of Bias in Civil Expert Evidence' (2007) 26 CJQ 57, 78.

381 Brooke LJ in *Armstrong v First York Ltd* [2005] EWCA Civ 277; [2005] 1 WLR 2751, at [28], approving comment in *Liddell v Middleton* [1996] PIQR P36.

vent the system of single, joint witnesses from unravelling, the leading authority, *Daniels v Walker* (2000), requires, first, that the relevant party must show reasons which are 'not fanciful' for supplementing the report; secondly, that the proposed use of a party-appointed experts will not result in disproportionate costs.[382]

(4) Party-Appointed Experts

In large claims, each party will receive permission to appoint his own expert or experts. This will be expressed either in relation to 'the expert named' or 'the field identified'.[383] If permission exists to call a 'named' expert, that party must obtain the court's further permission to substitute another expert.[384] But such further permission will be conditional on that party's disclosing the first expert's report.[385] 'Transparency' can then be achieved. However, this condition cannot be imposed if permission has been expressed in terms of a 'field' of expertise.[386] In that situation, there is no check upon so-called 'expert shopping'. **22.76**

The expert's report must supply his qualifications.[387] He should not have any close connection with the appointing party or persons involved in the case. Some decisions have permitted expert evidence to be received from a party's employee, although this lack of independence will reduce the weight of his evidence.[388] It is **22.77**

---

[382] [2000] 1 WLR 1382 CA; Neil Andrews, *English Civil Procedure* (2003) 32.68 to 32.74; in *Cosgrove v Pattison* [2001] CP Rep 68; *The Times* 13 February 2001, Neuberger J suggested eight factors: (i) nature of the dispute; (ii) number of issues requiring expertise; (iii) reasons for requiring second expert; (iv) amount and number of issues at stake; (v) possible impact of second expert on conduct of trial; (vi) possible delay caused; (vii) special features; (viii) overall justice to the parties; on this last aspect, resting on 'the Overriding Objective' in CPR Part 1, *Stallwood v David* [2006] EWHC 2600 (QB); [2007] 1 All ER 206 at [32].

[383] CPR 35.4(2); generally on 'court management' of experts, L Blom-Cooper (ed), *Experts in Civil Courts* (2006) ch 4; in *Morgan Chase Bank v Springwell Navigation Corporation* [2006] EWHC 2755 (Comm) Aikens J noted at [30] to [32] that expert evidence will not be admissible from a lawyer on construction of commercial contracts (subject to English law); this is a question of law for the court; unless the parties have used technical expressions outside the expertise of the judge (eg *Kingscroft Insurance Co Ltd v Nissan Fire & Marine Insurance Co Ltd (No 2)* [1999] Lloyd's Insurance and Reinsurance Reports page 603 at 622, Moore-Bick J).

[384] *Vasiliou v Hajigeorgiou* [2005] EWCA Civ 236; [2005] 1 WLR 2195, CA (applying *Beck v Ministry of Defence* [2003] EWCA Civ 1043; [2005] 1 WLR 2206 (note), even though in the *Beck* case the relevant order had not mentioned an expert by name).

[385] *Vasiliou* case (applying *Beck* case) ibid.

[386] *Vasiliou* case, ibid considering CPR 35.4(2)(a); for example, in a recent High Court case involving very severe brain injury, assessment of the claimant's mental capacity to conduct the litigation without Court of Protection direction was assessed by six experts: two neurologists, two neuro-psychologists, two neuro-psychiatrists; I am grateful to Master John Leslie, Queen's Bench Division, for this illustration.

[387] PD (35) 2.2(1) for the latter requirement.

[388] *Field v Leeds CC* [2000] 1 EGLR 54 CA; *R (Factortame Ltd) v Secretary of State for the Environment, Transport and the Regions (No 8)* [2003] QB 381, CA; [2002] EWCA Civ 932 at [70]; Neil Andrews, *English Civil Procedure* (2003) 32.43 to 32.45 noting the following case law;

improper to pay an expert witness on a conditional or contingency fee basis.[389] All experts in civil proceedings owe a duty to the court 'to help the court on the matters within his expertise'.[390] This duty overrides any obligation owed by the expert to the instructing party.[391]

22.78 A litigant, or prospective litigant, enjoys 'litigation privilege' in confidential communications between him (or his lawyer) and a prospective expert (see 22.67 to 22.70 on this head of privilege).[392] The CPR has, however, removed litigation privilege in the 'instructions', written or oral, provided by the litigant to an expert.[393] Such loss of privilege occurs only when 'the party decides that the particular report on which he wishes to rely should be disclosed'.[394]

22.79 Expert evidence must be given in a written report, unless the court directs otherwise.[395] The rules prescribe the form of the report.[396] The expert must provide: 'details of any literature or other material which the expert has relied on in making the report';[397] he must 'summarise the range of opinion and give reasons for his own opinion';[398] 'if the expert is not able to give his opinion without qualification, [he must] state the qualification'.[399] 'The expert's report must state the *substance of all material instructions*, whether written or oral, on the basis of which the report was written.'[400] 'Instructions' include 'material supplied by the instructing

---

T Hodgkinson and M James, *Expert Evidence: Law and Practice* (2nd edn, 2006) 1–030 and DM Dwyer 'The Effective Management of Bias in Civil Expert Evidence' (2007) 26 CJQ 57).

[389] *R (Factortame Ltd) v Secretary of State for the Environment, Transport and the Regions (No 8)* [2003] QB 381, CA; [2002] EWCA Civ 932 at [54] [57] [87] [90] [91], Lord Phillips MR; but an expert not acting as witness can validly agree a percentage return for litigation support: *Mansell v Robinson* (QBD 31 January 2007, All England Reporter).

[390] CPR 35.3(1); *The Ikarian Reefer* [1993] 2 Lloyds Rep 68, at 81–82, Cresswell J; T Hodgkinson and M James, *Expert Evidence: Law and Practice* (2nd edn, 2006) 7–005 (14 point enumeration of the elements of this duty); on the expert's duty to the court, L Blom-Cooper (ed), *Experts in Civil Courts* (2006) ch 11.

[391] Or duty owed to 'the instructing parties', in the case of a single, joint witness under CPR 35.7(2); or 'any obligation' owed by the expert to the person 'by whom [the expert] is paid'); see CPR 35.3.

[392] eg, *Carlson v Townsend* [2001] EWCA Civ 511; [2001] 1 WLR 2415, CA; *Jackson v Marley Davenport Ltd* [2004] EWCA Civ 1225; [2004] 1 WLR 2926, CA, at [13] [14] [22], cited *Vasiliou v Hajigeorgiou* [2005] EWCA Civ 236; [2005] 1 WLR 2195, CA at [28].

[393] CPR 35.10(4).

[394] *Jackson* (n 392 above) at [22], Peter Gibson LJ; see also A Edis 'Privilege and Immunity: Problems of Expert Evidence' (2007) 26 CJQ 40–56.

[395] CPR 35.5; generally on expert reports, L Blom-Cooper (ed), *Experts in Civil Courts* (2006) ch 6.

[396] CPR 35.10 and PD (35) 2.2, (see also CJC's Protocol, at 13).

[397] PD (35) 2.2(2).

[398] ibid, at 2.2(6).

[399] ibid, at 2.2(8).

[400] CPR 35.10(3).

party to the expert as the basis on which the expert is being asked to advise'.[401] But a summary will do: 'The only obligation on the expert is to set out "material instructions".'[402] These do not include material lying behind a written summary presented to the expert and containing 'assumed facts'.[403] The expert's report must 'contain a statement that the expert understands his duty to the court, and has complied with that duty'.[404] Because his report can cover both matters of fact and, of course, opinion, the rules prescribe a special 'Statement of Truth': 'I confirm that insofar as the facts stated in my report are within my own knowledge I have made clear which they are and that I believe them to be true, and that the opinions I have expressed represent my true and complete professional opinion.'[405] As for amendment at the instructing party's behest, the Civil Justice Council's Protocol states: 'experts should not be asked to, and should not, amend, expand, or alter any parts of reports in a manner which distorts their true opinion, but may be invited to amend or expand reports to ensure accuracy, internal consistency, completeness and relevance to the issues and clarity'.[406]

The court's order can be for simultaneous or sequential disclosure of reports by the opposing parties.[407] Without pre-trial disclosure of the expert's report, a party 'may not use the report at the trial or call the expert to give evidence orally unless the court gives permission.'[408] Disclosure is confined to 'the expert's intended evidence'. It does not extend to 'earlier and privileged drafts of what might or might not become the expert's evidence', unless the final report is 'on its face' a 'partial or incomplete document'.[409] Parties can pose written questions for the attention of the other side's expert witness or the single, joint witness.[410] Answers become part of the main report.[411] **22.80**

---

[401] *Lucas v Barking, Havering and Redbridge Hospitals NHS Trust* [2003] EWCA Civ 1102; [2004] 1 WLR 220, CA, at [34].

[402] ibid, Waller LJ at [36].

[403] *Morris v Bank of India* (unreported, 15 Nov 2001, Chancery), Hart J; on which Neil Andrews, *English Civil Procedure* (2003) 32.51 to 31.56; and comments in *Lucas v Barking, Havering and Redbridge Hospitals NHS Trust* [2003] EWCA Civ 1102; [2004] 1 WLR 220, CA at [8].

[404] CPR 35.10(2).

[405] PD (35) 2.4; PD (35) 2.5 notes that making a false statement involves contempt of court: see 22–130 below.

[406] CJC's Protocol, 15.2.

[407] Normally simultaneous; but fairness and clarity might sometimes justify sequential disclosure: T Hodgkinson and M James, *Expert Evidence: Law and Practice* (2nd edn, 2006) 4–020.

[408] CPR 35.13.

[409] *Jackson v Marley Davenport Ltd* [2004] 1 WLR 2926, CA, [14] and [18]; Longmore LJ commented at [18]: '. . .it would in my view be a retrogression and not an advance in our law if earlier reports of experts, upon which they did not intend to rely, had to be routinely disclosed before they could give evidence.'

[410] See PD (35) 5.1 to 5.3.

[411] CPR 35.6(3).

(5) Discussions Between Experts

22.81   The court can direct that there should be a 'discussion' between experts, followed by a 'joint statement':[412] 'the court may direct that following a discussion between the experts they must prepare a statement for the court showing: (a) those issues on which they agree; and (b) those issues on which they disagree and a summary of their reasons for disagreeing'.[413] Such discussions can engender settlement, reduce the adversarial sting of the contest, narrow the scope of the dispute, and produce ideas for further streamlining the dispute. The Civil Justice Council's Protocol states:[414] 'The parties' lawyers may only be present at discussions between experts if all the parties agree or the court so directs; and if they do attend, they should not normally intervene except to answer questions put to them by the experts or to advise about the law.' Such a meeting is not contrary to the guarantee in Article 6(1) of the European Convention on Human Rights of a fair trial and process.[415] Baroness Hale (as she now is) has suggested that it would be good practice to agree that a legally qualified chairman, independent of the parties, might preside during expert discussions involving matters of sensitivity.[416]

22.82   Experts' discussions are privileged.[417] But the joint statement is not privileged and in fact becomes available to the court in the proceedings (CPR 35.12(3) '. . .must prepare a statement for the court. . .').[418] This statement is not formally binding on the parties, but in practice they will find it difficult to sidestep. The Court of Appeal in *Stanton v Callaghan* (2000) held that an expert is immune from liability in negligence when agreeing a joint statement. Therefore, the instructing party cannot sue him, alleging negligence or fraud.[419] What if one party wishes to substitute a new expert, following this process? In *Stallwood v David* (2006) Teare J held that permission for a substitute should be refused unless: the expert plainly acted beyond his expertise; or was incompetent for this task; or (as in the present

---

[412] CPR 35.12; L Blom-Cooper (ed), *Experts in Civil Courts* (2006) ch 7.

[413] CPR 35.12(3).

[414] CJC's Protocol, 18.8; R Clements in L Blom-Cooper (ed), *Experts in Civil Courts* (2006) 7.12 ff and T Hodgkinson and M James, *Expert Evidence: Law and Practice* (2nd edn, 2006) 4–024; a lawyer's presence might be useful in saving the expert the embarrassment, and avoiding the injustice to a party, in the expert misapplying the law (eg the civil standard of proof: *Temple v S Manchester HA* [2002] EWCA Civ 1406); besides next note, see A Whitfield QC's review of arguments for and against legal presence at these discussion in 'Clinical Risk' 2000 vol 6, 149; accessible at <www.clinical-disputes-forum.org.uk/files/projectfiles/project3-app1.doc>.

[415] *Hubbard v Lambeth, Southwark and Lewisham AHA* [2001] EWCA Civ 1455; *The Times*, 8 October 2001, Hale LJ at [17], Tuckey LJ.

[416] *Hubbard* case, ibid, at [29].

[417] CPR 35.12(4).

[418] *Aird v Prime Meridian Ltd* [2006] EWCA Civ 1866 at [3].

[419] [2000] 1 QB 75, CA; the expert discussion in that case preceded the CPR and was not at the court's direction; nevertheless, the court's reasoning would seem to apply to CPR 35.12 discussions.

case) the application is reheard on appeal and it appears that the first hearing was vitiated by unsympathetic comments based on the judge's own personal experience (in the present case, the first instance judge's autobiographical remarks on his stoical resistance to prolonged back-pain).[420] The *Stanton* and *Stallwood* cases establish important constraints. Without them, the salutary system of experts' discussions would soon unravel.

(6) Witness Immunity

This doctrine can be conveniently discussed in connection with expert witnesses, **22.83** although it also protects factual witnesses. Lord Hoffmann in *Arthur JS Hall v Simons* (2002) said:[421] '. . .a witness is absolutely immune from liability for anything which he says in court. . . .[He] cannot be sued for libel, malicious falsehood, or conspiring to give false evidence. . . The policy of this rule is to encourage persons who take part in court proceedings to express themselves freely.' In *Darker v Chief Constable of the West Midlands Police* (2001) the House of Lords distinguished (i) the false presentation of evidence in court, whether deliberately or not (if deliberate the crime of perjury arises), and (ii) out-of-court steps taken to produce false evidence, such as fabrication of evidence and conduct aimed at 'setting up' an accused; or destroying evidence.[422] Matters falling within (ii) do not attract witness immunity. Therefore, a lie told in the witness box, although attracting criminal liability for perjury, will not also expose the witness to civil liability, for example in tort.

In *Stanton v Callaghan* (2000) Chadwick LJ said:[423] '[witness] immunity does not **22.84** extend to protect an expert who has been retained to advise as to the merits of a party's claim in litigation from a suit by the party by whom he has been retained in respect of that advice, notwithstanding that it was in contemplation at the time when the advice was given that the expert would be a witness at the trial if that litigation were to proceed'.[424] But this has been doubted.[425] A more attractive approach, it is submitted, is whether the expert advice was given with a view to

---

[420] [2006] EWHC 2600 (QB); [2007] 1 All ER 206; noted A Zuckerman (2007) 26 CJQ 159.

[421] [2000] UKHL 38; [2002] 1 AC 615, 697, HL; A Edis, 'Privilege and Immunity: Problems of Expert Evidence' (2007) 26 CJQ 40.

[422] [2001] 1 AC 435; similarly, *L (A Child) v Reading BC* [2001] EWCA Civ 346; [2001] 1 WLR 1575, 1593, CA.

[423] [2000] 1 QB 75, CA.

[424] Considering *Palmer v Durnford Ford* [1992] QB 483 and *Landall v Dennis Faulkner & Alsop* [1994] 5 Med LR 268.

[425] *Karling v Purdue* [2004] Scot CS 221 (29 September 2004) (Outer House, Court of Session) at [38].

possible use in pending or reasonably contemplated litigation: this should be an objective inquiry.[426]

22.85 In *Phillips v Symes (Costs No 2)* (2005) Peter Smith J held that a party-appointed expert can be ordered to pay costs wasted by his reckless or grossly negligent advice.[427] The judge rejected the suggestion that the spectre of wasted costs liability might deter experts from giving evidence. And so witness immunity was held not to preclude such a wasted costs order.[428] This seems persuasive, for several reasons: experts are nearly always remunerated; the present jurisdiction requires proof of 'gross dereliction of duty or recklessness'; the aggrieved party's primary recourse for financial compensation is against the litigant who hired the expert ('the hiring party') who is alleged to have been guilty of gross dereliction of his duty.[429] On the facts of the *Phillips* case, this was not possible because the hiring party was bankrupt.

22.86 The Court of Appeal in *Meadow v General Medical Council* (2006) held that an expert (whether giving evidence in a criminal or civil case) can be disciplined by his professional body if he has given evidence in a thoroughly unsatisfactory way.[430] Witness immunity does not protect an expert from such disciplinary proceedings. Sir Anthony Clarke MR said:[431] 'the threat of [professional disciplinary] proceeding...helps to deter those who might be tempted to give partisan evidence and not to discharge their obligation to assist the court by giving conscientious and objective evidence' and it 'helps to preserve the integrity of the trial process and public confidence both in the trial process and in the standards of the professions from which expert witnesses come'.

---

[426] On witness immunity with respect to experts' pre-hearing involvement, Scottish decision in *Karling v Purdue* ibid, at [65].

[427] [2004] EWHC 2330 (Ch); [2005] 1 WLR 2043; noted Neil Andrews [2005] CLJ 566.

[428] On witness immunity, *Arthur JS Hall v Simons* [2000] UKHL 38; [2002] 1 AC 615, HL; *Taylor v Director of the Serious Fraud Office* [1999] 2 AC 177; *Stanton v Callaghan* [2000] 1 QB 75, CA; *Darker v Chief Constable of the West Midlands Police* [2000] UKHL 44; [2001] 1 AC 435, HL, *L v Reading BC* [2001] EWCA Civ 346; [2001] 1 WLR 1575, CA, *Raiss v Palmano* [2001] PNLR 540, Eady J; *X v Bedfordshire CC* [1995] 2 AC 633, 754–5, HL; Neil Andrews, *English Civil Procedure* (2003) 31.50, 31.51 and 32.83 to 32.94; and see the discussion in the next paragraph of the *Meadow* case.

[429] eg *Re Colt Telecom Group plc* [2002] EWHC 2815 (Ch), at [80] and [110], where Jacob J ordered indemnity costs against a party who selected an expert whose report was seriously defective.

[430] [2006] EWCA Civ 1390; [2007] 2 WLR 286 reversing on the immunity point Collins J in [2006] EWHC 146 (Admin); on the general question of remedies against the defaulting expert, L Blom-Cooper (ed), Experts in Civil Courts (2006) ch 9 and DM Dwyer, 'The Effective Management of Bias in Civil Expert Evidence' (2007) 26 CJQ 57.

[431] [2006] EWCA Civ 1390; [2007] 2 WLR 286, at [46]; the other members agreed, [106] and [249].

I. Settlement and Mediation

(1) Importance of Settlement[432]

Trial seldom happens.[433] The great majority of actions are settled, or withdrawn, or **22.87**
terminated by judgment without trial (striking out, summary or default judgments,
on which see Section D at 22.39 ff). Furthermore, since the CPR was introduced
in 1999, there has been a general decline of circa nine per cent in civil litigation
(see the figures cited in the footnote below).[434] High Court litigation has ceased to
be the main response to a problematic business or civil dispute, even if it involves
a significant sum.[435] London solicitors report difficulty in 'selling' High Court litigation to their clients.[436] Often mediation and arbitration are favoured alternatives.

---

[432] Neil Andrews, *English Civil Procedure* (2003), chs 23–25; H Genn 'Understanding Civil
Justice' (1997) 48 CLP 155, 177ff; S Roberts 'Settlement as Civil Justice' (2000) 63 MLR
739–47 (and earlier 'Alternative Dispute Resolution and Civil Justice. . .' (1993) 56 MLR 452; 'The
Paths of Negotiation' (1996) 49 CLP 97–109); S Roberts and M Palmer, *Dispute Processes* (2005);
M Galanter and M Cahill 'Most Cases Settle: Judicial Promotion and Regulation of Settlements'
(1994) 46 Stanford L Rev 1329 (on the US practice); a highly detailed practitioner manual is
D Foskett, *The Law and Practice of Compromise* (6th edn, 2005); for a much shorter account, Foskett,
Settlement under the Civil Procedure Rules (1999).

[433] For example, Sir Leonard Hoffmann 'Changing Perspectives on Civil Litigation' (1993) 56
MLR 297, noting the increasing resort to pre-trial summary procedures, pre-action disclosure,
witness statements, and provisional and protective relief; since 1998, to this list must be added,
'pre-action protocols', expansion of pre-action disclosure orders, the CPR's imposition of case-
management, and judicial stays and costs orders to promote mediation.

[434] *Judicial Statistics*, annual reports, for the years 1999 and 2005: (available online: <www.dca.
gov.uk/dept/depstrat.htm>). These record the following: County Court claims commenced in 1999,
2,000,337 (source 1999 report, p 39) and in 2005, *1,870,374* claims (source 2005 report, p 46; of
these 2005 claims, 48 per cent were for less than £500); Chancery Division claims (High Court)
commenced in 1999, *37, 281* (source 1999 report, p 21) and *34,125* in 2005 (source 2005 report,
p 27); Queen's Bench Division (High Court) claims commenced in 1999, *72,161* (source 1999
report, p 27) and in 2006, *15,317* (source 2005 report, p 37); Commercial Court (High Court)
claims commenced 1999, *1205* (source 1999 report, p 35) and *981* in 2005 (source 2005 report,
p 41); Technology and Construction Court (High Court) claims commenced in 1999, *483* (source
1999 report, p 35) and *340* in 2005 (source 2005 report, p 50); 'Civil Court Fees' (Court Service,
September 2002) at paras 3.7ff (between 1998 and 2001 there was a 22.5 per cent reduction
in the number of county court claims and, during the same period, a 76 per cent fall in High
Court claims); on the withering of the US civil trial, see Oscar Chase, *The Rise of ADR in Cultural
Context, in Law, Culture, and Ritual: Disputing Systems in Cross-Cultural Context* (2005) ch 6 and
D Spencer and M Brogan, *Mediation: Law and Practice* (2006) 490ff; and for a similar decline in
NSW, Australia, Spencer et al, ibid, 486ff.

[435] The creation of a Supreme Court under the Constitutional Reform Act 2005 will strengthen
the tendency for the highest echelon of judges to devote a high percentage of their time to public law,
human rights, and constitutional matters, rather than private law and commercial disputes; media
attention to these high-profile cases will distract attention from the important business of providing adjudication of matters relevant to commerce: I am grateful to Professor Shetreet, Hebrew
University, Jerusalem, for observations on this topic: seminar University of Cambridge, 2006.

[436] Informal comment to the author.

22.88   For many years, influential English judges have extolled the benefits of settlement.[437] In particular, Lord Woolf said in 1995: 'the philosophy of litigation should be primarily to encourage early settlement of disputes'.[438] According to this view, it is better to conclude a settlement, even one based on imperfect knowledge and perhaps slightly skewed by economic or other factors, rather than submit to the long and ultimately public process of hearing witnesses, experts, and presenting submissions of law.[439] Furthermore, the Practice Direction on '[Pre-Action] Protocols' emphasizes the duty of prospective parties and their legal advisors to consider ADR:[440] 'The courts increasingly take the view that litigation should be a last resort, and that claims should not be issued prematurely when a settlement might still be achieved. Therefore, the parties should consider whether some form of ADR might be more suitable than litigation.' The CPR emphasizes that, where appropriate, the court must try to help the parties to settle the case,[441] and encourage them to pursue out-of-court ADR.[442] The Law Society for England and Wales in 2005 issued a 'practice advice' recommending that solicitors should routinely consider whether their clients' disputes are suitable for ADR.[443] The European Commission has proposed a directive on the topic.[444] Similar trends have occurred elsewhere, notably in the USA[445] and in Australia.[446]

---

[437] Quotations collected in Neil Andrews, *English Civil Procedure* (2003) 9.25.

[438] *Access to Justice: Interim Report* (HMSO, 1995) ch 7, para 7(a).

[439] On disparities and uncertainties in the settlement process, H Genn 'Understanding Civil Justice' (1997) 50 CLP 155, 178ff; H Genn, *Hard Bargaining: Out of Court Settlement in Personal Injury Actions* (1987) (reviewed Neil Andrews [1989] CLJ 506, 507, describing this book as 'a powerful antidote to complacency').

[440] Practice Direction—'Protocols', para 4.7; see also text of the Pre-Action 'Protocol for Construction and Engineering Disputes' (April 2007) 5.4 for emphasis on ADR as an alternative to litigation in that context.

[441] CPR 1.4(2)(f).

[442] CPR 1.4(2)(e).

[443] Law Society Gazette (2005) (16 June) 38; S Roberts 'Settlement as Civil Justice' (2000) 63 MLR 739, 741 and 'Alternative Dispute Resolution and Civil Justice. . .' (1993) 56 MLR 452, 460, traces enthusiasm for ADR, within the mainstream of civil litigation, to Sir Roy Beldam's 'Report of the Committee on Alternative Dispute Resolution' (Bar Council, October 1991).

[444] COM (2004) 718 final, Brussels dated 22.10.2004 (draft directive on 'certain aspects of mediation in civil and commercial matters'): <www.eur-lex.europa.eu/LexUriServ/site/en/com/2004/com2004_0718en01.pdf>; for the European Code of Conduct for Mediators: <ec.europa.eu/civiljustice/adr/adr_ec_code_conduct_en.pdf>

[445] On the USA, D Spencer and M Brogan, *Mediation: Law and Practice* (2006) 25ff; DR Hensler 'Out Courts, Ourselves: How the ADR Movement is Reshaping our Legal System' (2003) 108 Penn State L Rev 165; Oscar Chase 'ADR and the Culture of Litigation: the Example of the United States of America' in L Cadiet, T Gray and E Jeuland (eds) *Médiation et Arbitrage* (2005) 135–151; and in O Chase, *The Rise of ADR in Cultural Context, in Law, Culture, and Ritual: Disputing Systems in Cross-Cultural Context* (2005) ch 6; O Fiss and J Resnik, *Adjudication and Its Alternatives* (2003); Judith Resnik 'Many Doors? Closing Doors? Alternative Dispute Resolution and Adjudication' (1995) 10 Ohio State Journal on Dispute Resolution 211; Steve Subrin 'A Traditionalist Looks at Mediation' (2003) 3 Nevada LJ 196.

[446] D Spencer and M Brogan, *Mediation: Law and Practice* (2006) 30ff.

A settlement agreement need not be in writing. The Court of Appeal has upheld **22.89** a settlement reached by telephone between the parties' solicitors.[447] A settlement agreement can be clothed as a consent order and become enforceable.[448] First, a monetary settlement can be enforced as a debt claim. Secondly, settlements (of money or other types of claim) agreed after commencement of formal proceedings can be entered as a 'consent order'.[449] One form of consent order preserves confidentiality in the terms of the settlement (a so-called 'Tomlin Order').[450]

(2) Mediation Agreements[451]

Commercial agreements often include a mediation clause.[452] In *Cable & Wireless* **22.90** *v IBM United Kingdom Ltd* (2002), a technology support contract contained a dispute resolution clause, a so-called 'tiered' dispute resolution clause.[453] The clause in the present case stated that, if settlement negotiations failed, mediation would be obligatory; only thereafter was court litigation permitted. In fact, after negotiations failed, one party by-passed mediation and brought a claim before the English High Court. Colman J held that it was a breach of the dispute resolution clause to take this short-cut to litigation. To remedy this, he placed a 'stay' upon the High Court proceedings.

(3) Privileges Protecting Mediation and Settlement Negotiations[454]

Mediator's standard terms of engagement often render mediation proceedings **22.91** confidential.[455] But, independently of such confidentiality clauses, the English

---

[447] *Littlefair, Williamson, & Beardall v Vinamul* [2006] EWCA Civ 31 at [34] (no need for oral agreement to be confirmed in writing); cf *Brown v Rice and Patel* (Ch D 14 March 2007, Stuart Isaacs QC); held that agreement following mediation, on these facts, see at [52], required written form.

[448] K Mackie, D Miles, W Marsh, T Allen, *The ADR Practice Guide* (2000) 12.2.

[449] D Foskett, *The Law and Practice of Compromise* (6th edn, 2005) 9.09ff.

[450] K Mackie, et al (n 448 above) Appendix F, at 351, for model 'Tomlin order' agreements; D Foskett, ibid, 9.21ff, and 10.31.

[451] D Joseph, *Jurisdiction and Arbitration Agreements and their Enforcement* (2005) at Part III; K Mackie, D Miles, W Marsh, T Allen (n 448 above) ch 6; see also the web-site of 'CEDR': Centre for Effective Dispute Resolution at: <www.cedr.co.uk/library/documents/contract_clauses.pdf>; D Spencer and M Brogan, *Mediation: Law and Practice* (2006) ch 12 for Australian material.

[452] eg K Mackie, D Miles, W Marsh, T Allen (n 448 above) 31 (last para) and 102.

[453] *Cable & Wireless plc v IBM UK* [2002] EWHC 2059 (Comm); [2002] 2 All ER (Comm) 1041, Colman J; extra-judicial comment in A Colman 'ADR: An Irreversible Tide?' (2003) 19 Arbitration International 303.

[454] K Mackie, D Miles, W Marsh, T Allen, *The ADR Practice Guide* (2000) ch 5.

[455] *Instance v Denny Bros Printing* [2000] FSR 869; *The Times* 28 February 2000, Lloyd J; D Spencer and M Brogan, *Mediation: Law and Practice* (2006) 342 for Australian material.

courts respect the implicit confidentiality of the mediation process.[456] Indeed a new head of privilege has arguably emerged, namely 'mediation privilege'.[457] Sir Thomas Bingham MR in 1993 had attractively explained its rationale: '...parties [to mediation] will not make admissions or conciliatory gestures, or dilute their claims, or venture out of their entrenched positions unless they can be confident that their concessions and admissions cannot be used as weapons against them if conciliation [or mediation] fails and full-blooded litigation follows'.[458] It is possible that mediation privilege will ultimately establish itself as a distinct head of privilege, separate from 'without prejudice' communications, with its own set of 'exceptions'.[459] But these categories of privilege are presently elided in some judgments[460] and the separate status of mediation privilege has been formally but unconvincingly denied at first instance.[461] At any rate, these two privileges can operate concurrently with respect to different aspects of the parties' communications. As Jacob LJ observed, 'just because there is a mediator' there is 'no reason for the parties not to talk to each other [viz not in his presence] if that is found to be helpful at some point in the process'.[462]

(4) Settlement Offers and Costs Incentives to Compromise

22.92 CPR Part 36 allows a claimant or defendant to make a settlement offer.[463] Prospective parties can also make settlement offers.[464] A new rule (April 2007)

---

[456] *Re D (Minors)* [1993] Fam 231, CA.

[457] *Cross and Tapper on Evidence* (10th edn, 2004) 501–2; Neil Andrews, *English Civil Procedure* (2003) 25.45 to 25.48 and B Thanki (ed), *The Law of Privilege* (2006) 7.24, 7.38 to 7.39; P Matthews & H Malek, *Disclosure* (2nd edn, 2000) 9–118 to 9–120; see also D Spencer and M Brogan, *Mediation: Law and Practice* (2006) ch 9, noting, esp at 329, Australian legislation on this topic; cf allegation of threats made during mediation, *Hall v Pertemps Group Ltd The Times* 23 December 2005, Lewison J; *Brown v Rice and Patel* (Ch D 14 March 2007, Stuart Isaacs QC), held that privilege does not prevent court determining whether settlement has been reached; agreement on these facts requiring written form.

[458] *Re D (Minors)* [1993] Fam 231, 236, CA.

[459] The emerging notion of 'abuse of a privileged occasion' (Neil Andrews, *English Civil Procedure* (2003) ch 25, esp 25.33, 25.43; B Thanki (ed), *The Law of Privilege* (2006) 7–26 to 7–29) is illustrated by *Brunel University v Vaseghi* [2006] UKEAT 0307_06_1610 (16 October 2006) (employee alleging victimization by employer in connexion with racial discrimination complaint against latter; EAT at [24] concluding that settlement privilege should yield because employee's claim would be unfairly hampered).

[460] *Aird v Prime Meridian Ltd* [2006] EWCA Civ 1866 at [5] *per* May LJ.

[461] *Brown v Rice and Patel* (Ch D 14 March 2007, Stuart Isaacs QC) at [19], [20]; although the point was not material to the eventual decision, see [20].

[462] Jacob LJ in *Reed Executive plc v Reed Business Information Ltd* [2004] EWCA Civ 887; [2004] 1 WLR 3026, at [30] (whose judgment does seem to contemplate distinct heads of privilege, despite Isaac QC's contrary judgment in *Brown v Rice and Patel* (Ch D 14 March 2007) at [19], [20]).

[463] CPR Part 36 was amended in April 2007 (discussion based on the pre-April 2007 rules: D Foskett, *The Law and Practice of Compromise* (6th edn, 2005) chs 14 to 26; Neil Andrews, *English Civil Procedure* (2003) ch 24; *Zuckerman on Civil Procedure* (2006) ch 25).

[464] CPR 36.3(2) (April 2007 rules).

allows defendants to make a settlement offer rather than having to make a payment into court.[465] The offer will be open to acceptance by the other party (offeree) within a specified period (normally 21 days).[466] If the offeree decides not to accept the offer, he will take the following 'costs risks'.[467] Where a claimant rejects a settlement offer, but fails at trial to beat the amount offered, he must pay the defendant's costs incurred after the date when the offer might have been validly accepted. The defendant is only liable for the claimant's costs incurred before that date.[468] If the defendant is the party who rejects a settlement offer, and the claimant later obtains significantly superior redress at trial (or summary judgment),[469] the defendant-offeree must pay an aggravated measure of costs ('indemnity' costs) rather than the ordinary measure of costs ('standard' costs) (on this distinction, see 22.113). In this situation, the court can also order a high level of interest on those costs. These are the usual costs rules affecting rejected settlement offers, but the court retains a discretion. Thus where a claimant only narrowly 'beats' a settlement offer, the court might wish to register disapproval of the claimant's unjustified strategy in raising hopeless points. For example, in *Jackson v Ministry of Defence* (2006), the claimant had been injured while participating in military training.[470] The claim was for roughly £1 million. A large component of this was for alleged permanent disability. But the defendant's settlement offer was for £150,000. At trial, the claimant obtained damages of only £155,000, narrowly exceeding the amount of the rejected settlement offer. But the claimant failed to establish permanent disability, his main head of claim. The trial judge reduced the claimant's costs by 25 per cent, and the Court of Appeal suggested that the reduction might have been greater.

(5) Judicial Influence upon Settlement

In general, English courts do not engage actively in suggesting specific terms of settlement to the parties.[471] Instead they prefer to procure settlement indirectly by **22.93**

---

[465] CPR Part 36.4, effective April 2007; cases precipitating this change were: *Crouch v King's Healthcare NHS Trust* [2005] 1 WLR 2105, CA; [2004] EWCA Civ 1332; *Stokes Pension Fund v Western Power Distribution plc* [2005] EWCA Civ 854; [2005] 1 WLR 3595.

[466] Acceptance by the claimant of the offer entitles him to standard basis costs: CPR 36.10(3); *Lahey v Pirelli Tyres Ltd* [2007] EWCA Civ 91; [2007] 1 WLR 998 (offeree entitled to all such costs, as assessed on that basis; considering parallel pre-April 2007 rule).

[467] CPR 36.14 (April 2007 rules).

[468] If the claimant's rejection of settlement offer is especially unreasonable, because the claim had *become* hopeless, indemnity costs order might be ordered: *EQ Projects v Alavi* [2006] EWHC 29 at [38]; *a fortiori* claims known *from outset* to be doomed: *Waites Construction Limited v HGP Greentree Alchurch Evans Limited* [2005] EWHC 2174 (TCC).

[469] *Petrotrade Inc v Texaco Ltd* [2002] 1 WLR 947, CA (2000, note).

[470] [2006] EWCA Civ 46.

[471] S Roberts 'Settlement as Civil Justice' (2000) 63 MLR 739, 741, contrasting US practices, M Galanter 'The Emergence of the Judge as Mediator in Civil Cases' (1986) 69 Judicature 257 and

suggesting mediation, where appropriate, supporting this suggestion by use of 'stays' and 'costs sanctions', as will be explained in the ensuing paragraphs. But there are two qualifications. First, the court must approve proposed settlements affecting the interests of children (those under 18) and 'patients', that is a person 'incapable of managing and administering his property and affairs by reason of mental disorder within the meaning of the Mental Health Act 1983'.[472] The question whether a person over the age of 17 is mentally incapable to this degree can itself require extensive inquiry.[473] The court does not propose terms of settlement, but exercises supervision.[474] Secondly, another form of judicial intervention into the process of settlement is 'early neutral evaluation' in the Commercial Court ('ENE'). This involves non-binding evaluation of the case's merits by a judge. The ENE judge must not also be involved in that action's case management or eventual trial. Both parties must assent to 'ENE'.[475]

22.94 The English court can direct that the proceedings be stayed for a month or longer[476] to allow the parties to pursue ADR or other settlement negotiations.[477] A party can seek a stay, or the judge can propose it for discussion. A 'stay' does not dismiss an action but merely holds it in abeyance. It can be resumed if this becomes appropriate. The Commercial Court can make a so-called 'ADR order', even without a stay.[478]

22.95 There has been much development of the topic of costs sanctions in this context. A party might decide to reject a suggestion by the court or opponent that a dispute be referred to mediation. The court can apply either of the following costs sanctions if this refusal to co-operate is adjudged to have been unreasonable: (i) denial of costs in favour of a victorious party;[479] or (ii) an order of aggravated

---

M Galanter and M Cahill 'Most Cases Settle: Judicial Promotion and Regulation of Settlements' (1994) 46 Stanford L Rev 1329; see also, for more detail, S Roberts, 'Alternative Dispute Resolution and Civil Justice. . .' (1993) 56 MLR 452, 458 ff, 469–70; see also D Spencer and M Brogan, *Mediation: Law and Practice* (2006) 388–407 for Australian discussion.

[472] CPR 21.10, adopting old RSC Ord 80 procedure.

[473] eg, in a High Court case involving very severe brain injury, assessment of the claimant's mental capacity to conduct the litigation without Court of Protection direction was assessed by six experts: two neurologists, two neuro-psychologists, two neuro-psychiatrists; I am grateful to Master John Leslie, Queen's Bench Division, for this illustration; see also *Bailey v Warren* [2006] EWCA Civ 51; [2006] CP Rep 26 on this test.

[474] D Foskett, *The Law and Practice of Compromise* (6th edn, 2005) ch 35.

[475] 'The Admiralty and Commercial Courts Guide' at section G2.

[476] CPR 26.4(3).

[477] CPR 3.1(2)(f); CPR 26.4(1)(2).

[478] K Mackie, D Miles, W Marsh, T Allen, *The ADR Practice Guide* (2000) 7.6.2.

[479] P Hurst, *Civil Costs* (3rd edn, 2004) pp 14–16; MJ Cook, *Cook on Costs 2006* (2006) 113–6; *Hurst v Leeming* [2002] EWHC 1051 (Ch); [2003] 1 Lloyd's Rep 379 (reasonable

costs (known as 'indemnity costs', as distinct from 'standard' costs, on this distinction, see 22.113).[480] In situation (i), the losing party bears the burden of proving unreasonableness on the part of the ultimately victorious party. Failure to accede to a judicial suggestion is, it seems, necessarily unreasonable. Where the opponent had suggested mediation, the question of the rejecting party's alleged 'unreasonableness' is assessed according to the Court of Appeal's (non-exhaustive) criteria in *Halsey v Milton Keynes General NHA Trust* (2004):[481] 'the nature of the dispute; the merits of the case; the extent to which other settlement methods have been attempted; whether the costs of the ADR would be disproportionately high; whether any delay in setting up and attending the ADR would be prejudicial; whether the ADR had a reasonable prospect of success'.

J. Trial, Evidence, and Appeal

(1) Trial

Trials are heard by a judge sitting alone, nearly always without a jury.[482] The judge will have read a 'trial bundle' in preparation for the hearing. This will comprise:[483] the claim form and statements of case; a case summary; witness statements 'to be relied on as evidence' and witness summaries; hearsay evidence notices; plans, photographs etc;[484] medical reports and responses to them, and other expert reports and responses; any order giving directions as to the conduct of the trial. In large actions, a core bundle must also be prepared.[485]

22.96

---

refusal to mediate; mediation had no reasonable prospect of success); *Société Internationale de Télécommunications Aéronautiques SC v Wyatt Co (UK) Ltd* [2002] EWHC 2401 (Ch); (2003) 147 Sol Jo LB 27; *Dunnett v Rail Track plc* [2002] EWCA Civ 303; [2002] 1 WLR 2434, CA, at [13] ff.

[480] *Virani Ltd v Manuel Revert y Cia SA* [2003] EWCA Civ 1651; [2004] 2 Lloyd's Rep 14; on the difference between standard basis and indemnity costs, P Hurst, *Civil Costs* (3rd edn, 2004) 4–20; MJ Cook, *Cook on Costs 2006* (2006) 120ff, Neil Andrews, *English Civil Procedure* (2003) 36.21ff; *Three Rivers DC v The Governor & Company of the Bank of England* [2006] EWHC 816 (Comm) *per* Tomlinson J at [14].

[481] [2004] EWCA Civ 576; [2004] 1 WLR 3002, at [16] ff; for a strong application of this costs regime, *P4 Ltd v Unite Integrated Solutions plc* [2006] EWHC 2924 (TCC), Ramsey J; a defendant's refusal to negotiate a settlement, if it believes the case is strong, should not be castigated: *Daniels v Commissioner for Police for the Metropolis* [2005] EWCA Civ 1312; [2006] CP Rep 9, at [30] to [32].

[482] Jury trial is confined to serious criminal cases (for example, murder, rape, armed robbery) and civil actions for defamation or misconduct by the police (the torts of defamation, malicious prosecution, and false imprisonment): Neil Andrews, *English Civil Procedure* (2003) 34–06ff.

[483] PD (39) 3.2.

[484] The notice requirement is strict: CPR 33.6(3).

[485] PD (39) 3.6.

22.97 Normally trial (and appeal)[486] must be in public.[487] To protect a person's safety,[488] the court can order that the identity of a party or of a witness must not be disclosed.[489] The courts are prepared to allow a party to give evidence by video-link, normally from abroad.[490] The trial proceeds as follows:

(1) counsel's opening speech (although this can be dispensed with);[491]

(2) examination-in-chief of claimant's witnesses (although this will not be oral where, as usual, the witness statement is received as a substitute for oral testimony);[492]

(3) cross-examination of claimant's witnesses by defendant's counsel;

(4) re-examination of witnesses;

(4A) at this stage there is an exceptional possibility that the court will give judgment in favour of the defendant on the basis that he has 'no case to answer';[493]

(5) examination-in-chief of defendant's witnesses (although this will not be oral where, as usual, the witness statement is received as a substitute for oral testimony);[494]

(6) cross-examination of the same by claimant's counsel;

(7) re-examination of same;

(8) defendant counsel's final speech;

(9) claimant counsel's final speech (the reason this is the last party intervention at trial is that the claimant bears the burden of proof, and so deserves to have the last say);

---

486 *Three Rivers DC v Bank of England* [2005] EWCA Civ 933; [2005] CP Rep 47.

487 CPR 39.2(1); CPR 39.2(3) and PD (39) 1.5 set out exceptions; the primary source is Supreme Court Act 1981, s 67; J Jaconelli, *Open Justice* (2002).

488 But witness' medical condition not sufficient reason in *Three Rivers DC v Bank of England* [2005] EWCA Civ 933; [2005] CP Rep 47.

489 CPR 39.2(4); PD (39) 1.4A emphasizes the need to consider the requirement of publicity enshrined in Art 6(1) of the European Convention on Human Rights (incorporated into English law, Human Rights Act 1998, Sch 1).

490 *Polanski v Condé Nast Publications Ltd* [2005] UKHL 10; [2005] 1 WLR 637; *McGlinn v Waltham Contractors Ltd.* [2006] EWHC 2322 (TCC); in neither case was the relevant absentee's reason for not coming to England held to bar use of video-linking (respectively, avoidance of extradition to the USA, and avoidance of tax liability within the UK).

491 Fast-track: PD (28) 8.2; multi-track: PD (29) 10.2; detailed account: Neil Andrews, *English Civil Procedure* (2003) 31.21 to 31.24.

492 CPR 32.5(2).

493 In *Graham v Chorley Borough Council* [2006] EWCA Civ 92; [2006] CP Rep 24, at [29] ff, Brooke LJ explained (noting *Benham Ltd v Kythira Investments Ltd* [2003] EWCA Civ 1794 at [32], [36]) that a 'no case to answer' judgment for the defendant without hearing the defendant's evidence is highly perilous (eg in the *Graham* case, the judge's decision in favour of the claimant was set aside and a re-trial ordered); cross-examination of the defendants' witnesses might have strengthened the claimant's exiguous case; before reaching 'the no case to answer' decision, the judge must give appropriate weight to the fact that the defendant elected not to call his own witnesses (drawing 'adverse inferences').

494 CPR 32.5(2).

(10) judgment;[495]

(11) order for costs, including in appropriate cases a summary assessment of costs (on which see 22.112).[496]

(2) Evidence at Trial

Factual witness testimony is the main source of evidence at trial.[497] Witnesses **22.98** can be compelled to attend a trial (or other hearing) by the issue of a 'witness summons'.[498] The witness must be offered compensation for his travel to and from court, and for loss of time.[499] The procedure for receipt of witness evidence is as follows. A proposed witness's testimony (his so-called 'evidence-in-chief') must be prepared in written form, signed and then served on the other parties.[500] This 'witness statement' must be supported by a statement of truth by the witness or his legal representative (the same applies to an expert's report).[501] It is an act of contempt of court to make, or to cause to be made, a dishonest and false statement and then to purport to verify this by a statement of truth.[502] Normally a witness statement will be received as evidence and so dispense with the need for the witness to give oral evidence on behalf of the party who has called him (so-called 'examination-in-chief').[503] This is because it would be inefficient to require him to repeat what he has already recorded in writing. However, the court can allow the witness orally to amplify his statement and to introduce matters which have subsequently arisen.[504]

At the trial, the witness will give evidence on oath. The crime of perjury is com- **22.99** mitted if false evidence is deliberately given by a witness at trial. Conviction can result in imprisonment or fines. The witness will answer questions posed by that opponent's lawyer (barrister or other advocate). This process of intense questioning is known as 'cross-examination'. During this oral process, the court does not

---

[495] Or direction to the jury; on judgments, CPR 40 and PD (40); on the court's discretion whether to complete judgment once it has begun to deliver it (or to deliver it initially in draft form) *Prudential Assurance Co v McBains* [2000] 1 WLR 2000, CA; on the court's power to re-open a case before perfecting a judgment, *Stewart v Engel* [2000] 1 WLR 2268, CA.

[496] CPR 44.3, 44.7(a).

[497] Neil Andrews, *English Civil Procedure* (2003) 31.41 to 31.51.

[498] This phrase replaces the terms *subpoena ad testificandum* (order to attend to give oral evidence) and *subpoena duces tecum* (order to attend with relevant documents or other items): CPR 34.2.

[499] CPR 34.7; PD (34) 3, referring to provisions applicable also to compensation for loss of time in criminal proceedings.

[500] CPR 32.10.

[501] CPR 22.1(1)(c) 22.3.

[502] CPR 32.14.

[503] CPR 32.5(2).

[504] CPR 32.5(3)(4).

itself conduct the examination of witnesses. Instead the judge is expected to listen to the parties' presentation of evidence. However, the judge might intervene to seek clarification, especially to assist a litigant in person (a party who is unassisted by a lawyer). It is a breach of procedure for the judge persistently to interrupt: this would be to 'arrogate to himself a quasi-inquisitorial role', something which is 'entirely at odds with the adversarial system'.[505]

22.100 The next most important source of evidence is 'documentary evidence', which covers paper-based or electronically recorded information. 'Real evidence' refers to 'things', such as the physical objects or site relevant to the case, or body samples. As for 'expert evidence', this has been examined at 22.71.

22.101 The court at trial has powers of 'evidential veto' in the following respects: 'the issues on which it requires evidence'; 'the nature of the evidence which it requires'; 'the way in which evidence is to be placed before the court';[506] excluding admissible evidence; limiting cross-examination;[507] restricting the number of witnesses (both lay and expert) used by each party;[508] restricting the time devoted to examining witnesses. This battery of powers must be exercised with caution.[509] Preliminary questions of law or fact can be separated from other matters, in the interest of economy.[510] Appeals are unlikely to succeed against such orders for the marshalling of the issues.[511]

22.102 There has been a spring-cleaning of civil evidence over the last few decades. The civil jury's virtual disappearance in modern English practice has stimulated this.[512] Various 'exclusionary rules', designed to protect the civil jury against 'potentially unreliable' material, have been removed or profoundly modified. This series of developments is consistent with a global trend towards 'free evaluation' of

---

[505] *Southwark LBC v Maamefowaa Kofiadu* [2006] EWCA Civ 281 at [148].

[506] CPR 32.1(1); *GKR Karate (UK) Ltd v Yorkshire Post Newspapers Ltd* [2000] 2 All ER 931, CA.

[507] CPR 32.1(2)(3); *Grobbelaar v Sun Newspapers Ltd The Times* 12 August, 1999, CA (prolix defence in libel action); *Three Rivers DC v Bank of England* [2005] EWCA Civ 889; [2005] CP Rep 46 (upholding the Commercial Court judge's humane restriction in long-running trial).

[508] Fast-track: CPR 28.3(1) and PD (28) 8.4; CPR 32.1 (all tracks).

[509] A Colman (with V Lyon and P Hopkins) *The Practice and Procedure of the Commercial Court* (5th edn, 2000) 218–9, especially curtailment of the power to cross-examine the other party's witnesses.

[510] CPR 3.1(2)(j)(l); for the pre-CPR emergence of this aspect of trial management, *Ashmore v Corporation of Lloyd's* [1992] 1 WLR 446, HL; *Thermawear Ltd v Linton The Times* 20 October, 1995, CA.

[511] *Ward v Guinness Mahon plc* [1996] 1 WLR 894, CA, *Grupo Torras Sa v Al Sabah (No 2) The Times* 17 April, 1997, CA.

[512] On the historical influence of trial by judge and jury, Neil Andrews, *English Civil Procedure* (2003) 34–06 ff; the jury no longer sits in English civil trials except in actions for defamation, or in claims of false imprisonment or malicious prosecution; see ibid for details.

evidence, a concept endorsed by the American Law Institute/UNIDROIT's *Principles of Transnational Civil Procedure*.[513] These changes will now be listed.

The 'hearsay rule' is used to provide a barrier to admitting relevant evidence. This rule concerned: second-hand or remoter reports of oral statements ('the defendant told me that his wife had said, "let's concoct a claim against these people"'); and documents composed out-of-court. Here there has been a fundamental change. Statute now allows a party to use out-of-court oral statements, and documents, as evidence: 'In civil proceedings evidence shall not be excluded on the ground that it is hearsay', that is, 'a statement made otherwise than by a person giving oral evidence'.[514] The court is required to assess the 'weight' to be attached to the hearsay evidence, according to various factors, including: 'whether it would have been reasonable and practicable for the party by whom the [hearsay] evidence was adduced to have produced the maker of the original statement as a witness' and 'whether any person involved had any motive to conceal or misrepresent matters'; and 'whether the original statement was an edited account, or was made in collaboration with another'.[515]

22.103

Two other evidential rules have been radically transformed. First, the so-called best evidence rule has been abandoned. A person is no longer obliged to produce the original version of a document. He can instead tender a copy. However, he must provide a satisfactory explanation for his inability to produce the original.[516] Further, 'similar fact' evidence is now admissible in civil cases: the court can legitimately take into account the fact that very similar events have occurred if this casts doubt upon a party's case and supports the other party's version of the dispute.[517]

22.104

What if evidence has been improperly obtained? If evidence (which is not privileged material) has been obtained unlawfully, unfairly, or in violation of a party's rights, the court will 'balance' the heinousness of the way it was collected against its relevance and weight if admitted into evidence. There are no hard-and-fast

22.105

---

[513] Rule 25 in *ALI/UNIDROIT: Principles of Transnational Civil Procedure* (2006) pp 137ff.

[514] Civil Evidence Act 1995, s 1.

[515] ibid, s 4; Lord Nicholls in *Polanski v Condé Nast Publications Ltd* [2005] UKHL 10; [2005] 1 WLR 637, at [36] said: 'The principle underlying the Civil Evidence Act 1995 is that in general the preferable course is to admit hearsay evidence, and let the court attach to the evidence whatever weight may be appropriate, rather than exclude it altogether. This applies to jury trial [in civil cases] as well as trials by judge alone. . . .' S Salako, 'The Hearsay Rule and the Civil Evidence Act 1995: Where are we now?' (2000) 19 CJQ 371.

[516] In *Springsteen v Masquerade Music Ltd* [2001] EWCA Civ 513; [2001] Entertainment and Media LR 654, CA, Jonathan Parker LJ explained: 'the time has now come when it can be said with confidence that the best evidence rule, long on its deathbed, has finally expired. In every case where a party seeks to adduce secondary evidence of the contents of a document, it is a matter for the court to decide, in the light of all the circumstances of the case, what (if any) weight to attach to that evidence.'

[517] *O'Brien v Chief Constable of South Wales Police* [2005] UKHL 26; [2005] 2 AC 534.

rules here, as *Jones v University of Warwick* (2003) illustrates.[518] In this case, the claimant alleged that she had suffered a serious disabling injury to her hand. The defendant did not accept this. Its investigator gained access to the claimant's home, posing as a market researcher, and took secret video evidence of the claimant's use of her injured hand in her home.[519] Lord Woolf CJ in the Court of Appeal held that, on balance, the evidence should be admitted. In the court's view, the manner of its collection had not been especially 'outrageous'.

(3) Appeals[520]

22.106 Nearly all appeals require permission (formerly known as 'leave').[521] Permission must be requested from the appeal court (if it has not been obtained from the lower court) within such period as directed by the lower court or within fourteen days after the date of the relevant lower court's decision.[522] The parties cannot agree to extend this limit.[523] In general, an appeal proceeds to the next level of civil judge (district judge to circuit judge, Master to High Court judge, circuit judge to High Court judge, High Court judge to Court of Appeal).[524] The appeal court will rarely receive oral evidence. Nor will it normally consider fresh evidence which was available to be presented to the lower court.[525] But the appeal court can 'draw any inference of fact which it considers justified on the evidence'.[526] The

---

518 [2003] EWCA Civ 151; [2003] 1 WLR 954, CA.

519 This involved a tort (trespass) and an invasion of privacy (as recognized by Article 8 of the European Convention on Human Rights).

520 Detailed account: Neil Andrews, *English Civil Procedure* (2003) ch 38; CPR Part 52 was examined in *Tanfern Ltd v Cameron-MacDonald* [2000] 1 WLR 1311, 1314–21, CA; on the system requiring 'permission' in nearly all cases, IR Scott (1999) 18 CJQ 91–98; for background, *Review of the Court of Appeal (Civil Division)* (report to Lord Chancellor, September 1997; the 'Bowman Report'); for US comparison, PS Atiyah and R Summers, *Form and Substance in Anglo-American Law* (1987) ch 10; for reflections on the private and public functions of civil appeals, especially in the highest chamber, reports by JA Jolowicz, P-H Lindblom, S Goldstein in P Yessiou-Faltsi (ed), *The Role of the Supreme Courts at the National and International Level* (Thessaloniki, Greece, 1998); for comparative perspectives on appeals, JA Jolowicz, *On Civil Procedure* (2000) chs 14 to 16.

521 CPR 52.3(1): except decisions affecting a person's liberty.

522 CPR 52.4(2); appeals out of time will only exceptionally be permitted: *Smith v Brough* [2005] EWCA 261; [2006] CP Rep 17.

523 CPR 52.6(1) (2).

524 PD (52).

525 CPR 52.11(2); *Riyad Bank v Ahli United Bank (UK) plc* [2005] EWCA Civ 1419 at [26] ff (noting that the '*Ladd v Marshall*' (1954) principles were re-adopted in *Hamilton v Al Fayed The Times* 13 October, 2000, CA: those principles are: (1) that the evidence could not have been obtained with reasonable diligence for use at the trial; (2) the evidence would probably have an important influence on the result of the case, though it need not be decisive; (3) the evidence must be credible though it need not be incontrovertible; and in the *Riyad* case at [28] it was added that 'the Court of Appeal should be particularly cautious where what is intended is to put in, in effect, further cross-examination of a witness, including an expert, where that expert or witness has been cross-examined at a trial'.

526 CPR 52.11(4).

court will allow an appeal when the lower court's decision was 'wrong' or 'unjust because of a serious procedural or other irregularity in the proceedings in the lower court'.[527] It has been suggested that video-conferencing be used for short appeals.[528]

K. Costs[529]

(1) The Cost-Shifting Rule

The main rule in England is that a victorious party ('the receiving party') should be paid his (recoverable) costs by the opponent ('the paying party').[530] This basic 'costs-shifting' rule is a species of strict liability: regardless of reasonableness or motive, the losing party has either brought or defended a case on grounds judicially determined to be unsound; and so that losing party should indemnify the other whose contrary position has been vindicated. The rule also acts as a disincentive against bringing or defending claims: any litigant is aware of the risk of a huge costs liability (his own and his opponent's costs) if he has the misfortune to lose the case.

22.107

The sum to be paid as costs can be very large, both absolutely and in relation to the value of the substantive claim.[531] There is widespread dissatisfaction with the expensiveness of civil proceedings in England and Wales. This is one of the reasons for recent expansion of mediation. The largest element in a party's expenditure upon costs is the expense of hiring a lawyer, or perhaps a team of lawyers. Solicitors are normally paid 'by the hour', although nowadays they are required to give an estimate of their likely fee to the client at the beginning of the litigation.[532]

22.108

---

[527] CPR 52.11(3).

[528] *Black v Pastouna* [2005] EWCA Civ 1389; [2006] CP Rep 11, *per* Brooke LJ.

[529] Specialist works: MJ Cook *Cook on Costs: 2006* (2006); P Hurst Civil Costs (3rd edn, 2004); costs generally, Neil Andrews, English Civil Procedure (2003) chs 35–37; A Zuckerman Civil Procedure (2nd edn, 2006) ch 26; for a recent survey, P Hurst '. . .Costs including conditional fees in England and Wales' (2005) 10 ZZP 39 ff; for a wide-ranging set of recommendations on access to justice and funding, Civil Justice Council's 'Improved Access to Justice–Funding Options and Proportionate costs' (August 2005) pp 148: <www.civiljusticecouncil.gov.uk/files/Improved_Access_to_Justice.pdf>.

[530] CPR 44.3(2) states the following 'general' rule: that the unsuccessful party will be ordered to pay the costs of the successful party; but the court may make a different order; for discussion in the context of discontinuance by a claimant, *Wylde v Culver* [2006] EWHC 1313 (Ch); [2006] 1 WLR 2674.

[531] eg, *Daniels v Commissioner for Police for the Metropolis* [2005] EWCA Civ 1312; [2006] CP Rep 9, at [32], [35].

[532] *Garbutt v Edwards* [2005] EWCA Civ 1206; [2006] 1 WLR 2907; Zuckerman in 'Lord Woolf's Access to Justice. . .' (1996) 59 MLR 773 has argued that the only way of reducing the expense of English civil litigation is to introduce a general system of fixed fees which reflect a claim's value, as in Germany, on which, he notes D Leipold, 'Limiting Costs for Better Access to Justice—the German Experience' in AAS Zuckerman and R Cranston (eds) *The Reform of Civil Procedure: Essays*

Barristers receive an agreed fee for appearing at court, which can be supplemented by further fees if the case lasts for longer than expected.

(2) Protective Costs Orders and Costs Capping

22.109 In special cases, so far confined to 'public interest' litigation, the courts exercise a discretion to protect a claimant or a defendant[533] against potential liability for costs. The leading case establishes these criteria:[534] the issues raised are of general public importance; the public interest requires that those issues be resolved; the applicant has no private interest in the matter;[535] the order is fair when account is taken of the parties' respective resources and the amount of costs likely to be incurred; finally, without the order, the claim will probably be discontinued.

22.110 The courts can impose an *ex ante* 'cap' on costs liability, at least in the context of defamation actions brought under conditional fee agreements without 'after-the-event' legal expenses insurance (on such fee arrangements, see 22.116).[536] So far the courts have been reluctant to expand this 'costs capping' jurisdiction beyond that special context,[537] and have preferred to control excessive costs by use of case management powers and *ex post facto* costs decisions.[538]

(3) The Court's Discretionary Adjustment of Costs

22.111 The court's costs decisions are discretionary in various respects: whether to order one party to pay the other's costs; the amount of those costs; for what period costs are to be paid; when costs are to be paid; and questions of interest upon these payments.[539] Lord Woolf MR, in an attempt to temper the rigidity of

---

on 'Access to Justice' (1995); on fixed costs, A Cannon 'Designing Cost Policies to Provide Sufficient Access to Lower Courts' (2002) 21 CJQ 198, 219. However, possible counter-arguments to wholesale adoption of fixed costs are (i) inflexible bureaucratic influence upon the civil justice system; (ii) unrealistic depression of lawyers' rates; (iii) weakening legal recruitment and retention; (iv) those who can pay more will stay pay more, because this is merely a cap on recoverable costs.

533 *R (Ministry of Defence) v Wiltshire and Swindon Coroner* [2005] EWHC 889 (Admin); [2006] 1 WLR 134, Collins J at [34] ff.

534 *R (Corner House Research) v Secretary of State for Trade and Industry* [2005] EWCA Civ 192; [2005] 1 WLR 2600; *R (Burkett) v Hammersmith LBC* [2004] EWCA Civ 1342; *R (England) v Tower Hamlets LBC* [2006] EWCA Civ 1742.

535 Cf *Weir v Secretary of State for Transport* [2005] EWHC 24 (Ch) (claimant making private claim as well as other disinterested claims).

536 *King v Telegraph Group Ltd* [2004] EWCA Civ 613; [2005] 1 WLR 2282, CA, esp at [101].

537 *Knight v Beyond Properties Pty Ltd* [2006] EWHC 1242 (Ch); [2007] 1 WLR 625, where Mann J cautiously acknowledged a wider jurisdiction but declared that it would be exercised only in very extreme cases; see also *Willis v Nicholson* [2007] EWCA Civ 199 at [24].

538 *Knight v Beyond Properties Pty Ltd*, ibid.

539 CPR 44.3(1); P Hurst '. . .Costs including conditional fees in England and Wales' (2005) 10 ZZP 39, 40.

the 'winner takes all' approach (see 22.107), said in *AEI Rediffusion Music Ltd v Phonographic Performance Ltd* (1999): 'too robust an application of the "follow the event principle" encourages litigants to increase the costs of litigation'; and he suggested 'if you recover all your costs as long as you win, you are encouraged to leave no stone unturned in your effort to do so'.[540] The courts apply the following criteria when determining whether costs were unreasonably incurred or unreasonable in amount (the following is a paraphrase):[541] the parties' conduct before and during the proceedings, including efforts made to resolve the dispute; the amount or value of the case, its importance of the matter to the parties, and its complexity, difficulty, or novelty; the skill, effort, specialized knowledge and responsibility involved; time spent on the case; and the circumstances in which the work was done.

22.112 Costs decisions are made by the trial judge or by the court hearing the pre-trial matter or appeal. In some situations, the only court proceedings concern costs.[542] Assessment of costs can be: by summary assessment (on the spot and often rough-and-ready costs determinations);[543] by detailed assessment (before costs judges);[544] in accordance with fixed costs rules (in specific situations);[545] or in accordance with the parties' agreement.[546]

(4) Indemnity and Standard Basis Costs[547]

22.113 The normal award is for 'standard costs'. But in some contexts, especially where the paying party's procedural conduct has been reprehensible, costs liability is

---

540 [1999] 1 WLR 1507, 1522–3, CA.

541 CPR 44.5(3); for rejection of an exorbitant costs claim, *Henry Boot Construction Ltd v Alstom Combined Cycles Ltd* [2005] EWCA Civ 814; [2005] 1 WLR 3850, CA, at [87] to [90] (costs claim was 'breathtaking'); for an example of the court reducing a party's costs award because of his failure to establish more than one fifth of the damages claimed, *Jackson v Ministry of Defence* [2006] EWCA Civ 46 (examined 22–92 above); similarly, award of only a percentage of costs claimed, to reflect merely partial success on the points raised, *Kew v Bettamix Ltd* [2006] EWCA Civ 1535; *The Times* 4 December 2006.

542 CPR 44.12A ('costs-only proceedings'); applicable where 'the parties to a dispute have reached an agreement on all issues (including which party is to pay the costs) which is made or confirmed in writing; but they have failed to agree the amount of those costs; and no [substantive] proceedings have been started.'

543 CPR 44.7.

544 ibid; and CPR Part 47.

545 CPR Part 45.

546 CPR 48.3.

547 The word 'indemnity' is used in the context of costs in three different senses: (i) in contrast with 'standard basis costs' (see next note); (ii) to denote the basic costs-shifting rule (see 22–107); (iii) to denote the traditional principle, that a receiving party is entitled to legal fees only if that payment arises under a legally enforceable agreement between him and his lawyer (considered in *Garbutt v Edwards* [2005] EWCA Civ 1206; [2006] 1 WLR 2907); (iii) is now qualified by the need to accommodate conditional fee agreements, on which, CPR 43.2(3).

assessed in a manner more generous to the 'receiving party', namely on the 'indemnity' basis. 'Indemnity costs' expose the paying party to liability for nearly all costs incurred by the other in the relevant litigation. 'Standard costs' are calculated more stingily towards the receiving party,[548] because the costs claimed by that party must be proportionate overall. By contrast, 'proportionality' does not regulate 'indemnity costs'. The Court of Appeal has prescribed the following approach to assessment of 'standard costs': 'If the costs as a whole are not disproportionate. . .then all that is normally required is that each item should have been reasonably incurred and the costs for that item should be reasonable'; and it added, 'If on the other hand the costs as a whole appear disproportionate then the court will want to be satisfied that the work in relation to each item was necessary and, if necessary, that the cost of the item was reasonable.'[549] Examples of awards of indemnity costs are: a defendant's unjustified refusal to accept a Part 36 settlement offer (see discussion at see 22.92); hopeless litigation;[550] reliance on a seriously defective report from one's own expert.[551]

(5) 'Wasted Costs' Orders Against Lawyers

22.114 A lawyer might be ordered to pay costs as a result of his improper conduct of the case, or be prevented from recovering costs because of such misconduct. 'Wasted costs' are made in respect of 'costs incurred by a party (a) as a result of any improper, unreasonable or negligent act or omission on the part of any legal or other representative or any employee of such a representative; or (b) which, in the light of any such act or omission occurring after they were incurred, the court

---

548 *Virani Ltd v Manuel Revert y Cia SA* [2003] EWCA Civ 1651; [2004] 2 Lloyd's Rep 14; on the difference between standard basis and indemnity costs, see P Hurst, *Civil Costs* (3rd edn, 2004) 4–20; MJ Cook, *Cook on Costs 2006* (2006) 120ff, Neil Andrews, *English Civil Procedure* (2003) 36.21ff; Hurst states: 'On the standard basis the court will only allow costs which are proportionate to the matters in issue and will resolve any doubt which it may have as to whether the costs were reasonably incurred or reasonable and proportionate in amount in favour of the paying party' (noting CPR 44.4(10(2)); and he comments, 'Where costs are to be assessed on the indemnity basis the court will resolve any doubt which it may have as to whether costs were reasonably incurred, or were reasonable in amount, in favour of the receiving party. There is no requirement for the costs to be proportionate on the indemnity basis' (noting CPR 44.4(3)); see also *Three Rivers DC v The Governor & Company of the Bank of England* [2006] EWHC 816 (Comm) *per* Tomlinson J at [14]; see also *Fourie v Le Roux* [2007] UKHL 1; [2007] 1 WLR 320 at [8] to [11]; [38] to [40], [46], [49].

549 *Home Office v Lownds* [2002] EWCA Civ 365; [2002] 1 WLR 2450 at [31], *per* Lord Woolf CJ.

550 *EQ Projects v Alavi* [2006] EWHC 29 (TCC) at [38]; *Waites Construction Limited v HGP Greentree Alchurch Evans Limited* [2005] EWHC 2174 (TCC); *Three Rivers DC v Bank of England* [2006] EWHC 816 (Comm).

551 *Re Colt Telecom Group plc* [2002] EWHC 2815 (Ch) at [80] and [110], *per* Jacob J.

considers it is unreasonable to expect that party to pay.'[552] A court can make a wasted costs order against a solicitor or barrister not just in respect of a hearing, but in respect of out-of-court drafting of statements of case or other documents immediately relevant to the exercise of a right of audience.[553] But judges must be wary of making wasted costs orders where the relevant lawyer's client is unwilling to waive legal advice privilege.[554] The courts will try to prevent wasted costs proceedings becoming a protracted form of 'satellite litigation'.[555]

(6) Costs Orders Against Non-Parties

The court can order a non-party to pay costs.[556] The first category of non-party to be mentioned is generally immune from costs liability, but the other two categories are not. In category (1), costs orders will not normally be made against 'pure' funders who are acting for reasons of friendship, natural affection, or political allegiance. Thus in *Hamilton v Al Fayed (No 2)* (2002) the Court of Appeal refused to make an order for costs against altruistic non-party funders, who were friends and political supporters of a former Member of Parliament.[557] But this general limitation is open to review in the House of Lords.[558] In category (2), a non-party 'commercial' funder might be liable for costs, up to the amount of his contribution to the case.[559] Of this category, the Court of Appeal in the *Arkin* case (2005) explained: 'if the funding is provided on a contingency basis of recovery, the funder will require, as the price of the funding, a greater share of the recovery should the claim succeed' but this is preferable to denying defendants a 'right to recover any costs from a professional funder whose intervention has permitted the continuation of a claim which has ultimately proved to be without merit'.[560] Category (3) is wide (covering a 'myriad forms'):[561] costs can be awarded if the non-party has a specific interest in the outcome of the litigation and has taken steps to influence its conduct, or he is the

22.115

---

[552] Supreme Court Act 1981, s 51(6)(7)(13), inserted by Courts and Legal Services Act 1990, s 4.

[553] *Medcalf v Mardell (No 2)* [2002] UKHL 72; [2003] 1 AC 120 (substantially endorsing *Ridehalgh v Horsefield* [1994] Ch 205, CA); in *Gray v Going Places Leisure Travel Ltd* [2005] EWCA Civ 189 at [11] to [15] guidance was given on the timing of wasted costs applications and hearings; *Regent Leisuretime Ltd v Skerett* [2006] EWCA Civ 1032; [2006] CP Rep 42 illustrates the high threshold for making such an order.

[554] *Medcalf* case, ibid.

[555] ibid.

[556] Supreme Court Act 1981, s 53(1)(3); *Aiden Shipping Ltd v Interbulk Ltd* [1986] AC 965, HL.

[557] [2002] EWCA Civ 665; [2003] QB 1175.

[558] See the doubts of Hale LJ in the *Hamilton* case at [73], [86], [87]; and the comment in *Arkin v Borchard Lines* Ltd [2005] EWCA Civ 655; [2005] 1 WLR 3055, at [44].

[559] *Arkin*, ibid, at [40]: a non-party 'commercial funder' of litigation brought by A was found liable to pay the victorious party B's costs to the extent that the non-party provided finance in that litigation; funding agreement was not champertous.

[560] ibid, at [41]; see also [42] and [43].

[561] *Goodwood Recoveries Ltd v Breen* [2005] EWCA Civ 414; [2006] 1 WLR 2723 at [74].

real party interested in the case's outcome, or he has behaved in some other way that makes it just and reasonable to make an order.[562]

(7) Conditional Fee Agreements [563]

22.116 As explained at 22.117, conditional fee agreements (CFAs) have received legislative approval. But the Common Law (expressed in earlier judicial decisions) remains opposed to lawyers having a financial stake in the outcome of their clients' litigation or arbitration. This traditional objection is based on two related factors, potential harm to the lawyer-client relationship and to the legal process. First, such a financial interest might warp a lawyer's objectivity, causing him to give a client advice which is not impartial. Secondly, such financial inducements might even seduce lawyers into perverting the process of justice, for example, by tailoring the evidence of witnesses, presenting only half-truths to the court, or by other examples of trickery and bad faith.[564] The three forms of potential financial interest are: success fees payable to the victorious party's lawyer; secondly, the normal fee might be reduced[565] or waived[566] (the 'speculative fee' system); thirdly, the USA 'contingency fee system',[567] that is the successful claimant's lawyer might recover a percentage of the value of any eventual judgment (or settlement) won by his client. The American type of contingency fee arrangement remains unlawful

---

562 *Dymocks Franchise Systems (NSW) Pty Ltd v Todd* [2004] UKPC 39; [2004] 1 WLR 2807, at [25], *per* Lord Brown; *Goodwood* case [2005] EWCA Civ 414; [2006] 1 WLR 2723 (director or shareholder controlling litigation; no need for dishonesty or bad faith; causal test); *Barndeal Ltd v London Borough of Richmond Upon Thames* [2005] EWHC 1377 (QB); *CIBC Mellon Trust Co v Stolzenberg* [2005] EWCA Civ 628; [2005] CP Rep 45 at [25]; and see *Arkin* case (n 558 above).

563 MJ Cook *Cook on Costs: 2006* (2006) ch 42; M Harvey, *Guide to Conditional Fee Agreements* (2nd edn, 2006); Neil Andrews, *English Civil Procedure* (2003) ch 35.

564 A Walters (2000) 116 LQR 371, 372; on maintenance and champerty, *R (Factortame Ltd) v Secretary of State for the Environment, Transport and the Regions (No 8)* [2002] EWCA Civ 932; [2003] QB 381, at [31]to [44]; earlier, *Thai Trading Co v Taylor* [1998] QB 781, 785–8, CA, cited in *Awwad v Geraghty & Co* [2001] QB 570, 578, CA.

565 eg *Aratra Potato Co Ltd v Taylor Joynson Garrett* [1995] 4 All ER 695, Garland J (20 per cent reduction in fee if claim lost; agreement unlawful at common law because 'champertous', viz lawyer having stake in outcome of action; such a fee arrangement is now lawful under Courts and Legal Services Act 1990, s 58(2)(a), as substituted by Access to Justice Act 1999, s 27(1)).

566 eg *Thai Trading Co v Taylor* [1998] QB 781, CA (noted Neil Andrews [1998] CLJ 469); for comment, 'The Ethics of Conditional Fee Arrangements' (Society for Advanced Legal Studies, 2001) 2.9.2.

567 A Cannon 'Designing Cost Policies to Provide Sufficient Access to Lower Courts' (2002) 21 CJQ 198, at 226; M Zander 'Where are We Heading with the Funding of Civil Litigation' (2003) 22 CJQ 23; Zander 'Will the Revolution in the Funding of Civil Litigation in England Eventually Lead to Contingency Fees?' (2003) 52 DePaul LR 259; 'The Ethics of Conditional Fee Arrangements' (Society for Advanced Legal Studies, 2001); for discussion of the US perspective, T Rowe, 'Shift Happens: Pressure on Foreign Attorney-Fee Paradigms from Class Actions' (2003) 13 Duke J Comp & Int L 125; JG Fleming, *The Contingent Fee and its Effect on American Tort Law* (1988); Michael Horowitz, 'Making Ethics Real, Making Ethics Work: A Proposal for Contingency Fee Reform' (1995) 44 Emory LJ 173.

in English law.[568] But the first two forms are now lawful in England if, as will now be explained, the lawyer complies with the statutory scheme.[569]

22.117 Since 1998, statute has made conditional fee agreements (CFAs) available in all civil litigation or arbitration, other than certain family law matters.[570] Because of the position at Common Law (see the preceding paragraph), a CFA must comply with this statutory regime to be enforceable. A CFA is defined as an agreement concerning advocacy or litigation services and providing for the client's 'fees and expenses, or any part of them, to be payable only in specified circumstances'.[571] The agreement usually specifies that the lawyer can receive a 'success fee', as well as his ordinary fee;[572] the success element is a 'percentage increase';[573] it cannot exceed 100 per cent of the normal fee.[574] The defeated opponent is liable to pay both the success fee and any insurance premium paid by the victorious party to protect him against costs liability in the event of defeat (normally called 'after-the-event' insurance, 'ATE').[575] There has been extensive litigation concerning appropriate levels of both success fees[576] and insurance premiums.[577] Specific rules govern reasonable success fees in claims concerning road traffic accidents and employers' liability.[578]

22.118 In 2005 Parliament revoked complicated regulations prescribing formalities for valid CFAs.[579] Failure to satisfy such formalities, originally intended as consumer protection for parties contemplating CFAs, had been seized upon by defendants'

---

[568] *Callery v Gray* [2001] EWCA Civ 1117; [2001] 1 WLR 2112, 2115, at [6], CA.

[569] 1990 Act, ss 58 and 58A (as amended).

[570] Main provisions: Courts and Legal Services Act 1990, ss 58, 58A (substituted by Access to Justice Act 1999, s 27); Supreme Court Act 1981, s 51(2) (as amended by Access to Justice Act 1981, s 31); Conditional Fee Agreements Order 1998 (SI 1998, No 1860); Conditional Fee Agreements (Revocation) Regulations 2005 (SI 2005/2305); CPR 43.2(1)(a) (l) (m) (o) 44.3A, 44.3B, 44.5, 44.15, 44.16, 48.9; PD (48) 55.

[571] Courts and Legal Services Act 1990, s 58(1) (as substituted by Access to Justice Act 1999, s 27); for the limits of 'advocacy or litigation services', *Gaynor v Central West London Buses Ltd* [2006] EWCA Civ 1120; [2007] 1 WLR 1045.

[572] CPR 48.9(2).

[573] ibid.

[574] Conditional Fee Agreements Order 1998 (SI 1998, No 1860), Art 4.

[575] Access to Justice Act 1999, s 29.

[576] *Callery v Gray (Nos 1 and 2)* [2002] UKHL 28; [2002] 1 WLR 2000, HL; *Halloran v Delaney* [2002] EWCA Civ 1258; [2003] 1 WLR 28 CA; *Claims Direct Test Cases* [2003] EWCA Civ 136; [2003] 4 All ER 508, CA; *Atack v Lee* [2005] EWCA Civ 1712; [2005] 1 WLR 2643.

[577] *Callery v Gray* [2001] EWCA Civ 1117; [2001] 1 WLR 2112, CA, at [54]; *Callery v Gray (Nos 1 and 2)* [2002] 1 WLR 2000, HL; *Sarwar v Alam* [2001] EWCA Civ 1401; [2002] 1 WLR 125, CA (relationship between 'before-the-event' and 'after-the-event' legal expenses insurance cover); *Rogers v Merthyr Tydfil County BC* [2006] EWCA Civ 1134; [2007] 1 WLR 808 (validity of staged ATE premium).

[578] CPR 45.15 to 45.22 (pre-trial conclusion of case: 12.5 per cent success fee for road traffic accident claims; 25 per cent if a claim against employer for personal injury): *Nizami v Butt* [2006] EWHC 159 (QB); [2006] 1 WLR 3307.

[579] Conditional Fee Agreements (Revocation) Regulations 2005 (SI 2005/2305): revoking, notably, Conditional Fee Agreements Regulations 2000 (SI 2000/692).

insurers seeking to escape costs liability for success fees and insurance premiums. This type of challenge had generated an intense 'costs-war'.[580] Since 2005, however, it is enough that 'the solicitor should explain the circumstances in which the client may be liable for their own costs and for the other party's costs; the client's right to assessment of costs, wherever the solicitor intends to seek payment of any or all of their costs from the client; and any interest the solicitor may have in recommending a particular policy or other funding'.[581]

22.119   Zander has contended that England should go further and adopt the US system of contingency fees (USCFs), for these reasons:[582] USCFs are simpler than English CFAs to explain to clients; the percentage of the attorney's USCF remuneration is necessarily 'proportionate' to the value of the client's damages; USCFs provide an incentive for the attorney to maximize damages recovery; USCFs are less likely to spawn satellite litigation (but this is only because in the USA there is no basic costs-shifting rule); finally, under the American arrangement, there is no incentive for an attorney to run up hourly costs, unlike the position in England under CFAs. This last point is arguably Zander's best challenge to the English system of CFAs. The English practice of billing by the hour enables CFA-sponsoring law firms, unrestrained by the need to justify a costs bill to their own clients, to generate quite disproportionate amounts of costs. *Ex post facto* costs assessments are an expensive and uncertain check upon such CFA fee 'churning'. Furthermore, the courts might not become aware of the size of the problem, because cases are often settled without a costs challenge by the defendant (see discussion of *ex ante* 'costs capping' at 22.110). However, arguments are not all one way. Zander must concede that the US contingency fee is paid from the plaintiff's damages. Moreover, this generous remuneration can lead to very large damages awards by judges and juries in the US. Furthermore, within the United Kingdom, there is widespread anxiety that to import USCFs would stimulate aggressively 'entrepreneurial' activity by prospective claimants' lawyers.

---

[580] On this war, *The Accident Group Test Cases* [2003] 4 All ER 590 CA, at [226]; battles include *Garbutt v Edwards* [2005] EWCA Civ 1206; [2006] 1 WLR 2907; *Garrett v Halton BC* [2006] EWCA Civ 1017; [2007] 1 WLR 554; *Nizami v Butt* [2006] EWHC 159 (QB); [2006] 1 WLR 3307.

[581] The Solicitors' Practice (Client Care) Amendment Rule (2005) amending the Law Society's 'Solicitors' Costs Information and Client Care Code' (1999); receiving party's lawyer's failure to give receiving party a costs estimate does not relieve paying party of liability for costs, *Garbutt* case, ibid.

[582] M Zander 'Where are We Heading with the Funding of Civil Litigation?' (2003) 22 CJQ 23; M Zander 'Will the Revolution in the Funding of Civil Litigation in England Eventually Lead to Contingency Fees?' (2003) DePaul LR 39.

L. Res Judicata and the Principle of Finality

(1) Cause of Action and Issue Estoppels

The doctrine of *res judicata* bars successive litigation of the same claim or issues   **22.120**
between the same parties.[583] It concerns 'claim or issue preclusion'.[584] The under-
pinning maxims are: *nemo debet bis vexari pro una et eadem causa* and *interest res
publicae ut finis litium sit* ('no one should be disturbed twice in the same matter'
and 'it is in the public interest that law suits should have an end'). Estoppel by *res
judicata* has three elements: (i) decisions or aspects of decision in civil matters
(whether this be a final decision,[585] or a relevant type of consent order)[586] made by
(ii) a competent civil court or tribunal[587] (including courts recognized under
English rules of private international law[588] and arbitration proceedings)[589] can
bind (iii) the parties (and their privies[590] or successors).[591] Next one must consider
the distinction between 'cause of action' and 'issue estoppel', the two species of
estoppel by *res judicata*.

'Cause of action estoppel' arises where the cause of action[592] in the later proceed-   **22.121**
ings is the same as that adjudicated in the earlier action and the pieces of litigation

---

[583] The leading work is Spencer Bower, Turner and Handley, *The Doctrine of Res Judicata* (3rd edn, 1996).

[584] This terminology, current in the USA and in Canada, has been adopted in *ALI/UNIDROIT's Principles of Transnational Civil Procedure* (2006) Principles 28.2, 28.3.

[585] Including a final decision of an interim application: *R v Governor of Brixton Prison, ex p Osman* [1991] 1 WLR 281; *Possfund v Diamond* [1996] 2 All ER 774, 779, citing *Chanel Ltd v FW Woolworth & Co Ltd* [1981] 1 WLR 485, 492–3, CA; for an example of a non-final decision, *Buehler AG v Chronos Richardson Ltd* [1998] 2 All ER 960, CA.

[586] eg *Palmer v Durnford Ford* [1992] 1 QB 483; *Green v Vickers Defence Systems Ltd* [2002] EWCA Civ 904; *The Times* 1 July 2002, CA; *Gairy v Att-Gen of Grenada* [2001] UKPC 30; [2002] 1 AC 167, PC, at [27] *per* Lord Bingham: 'a consent order may found a plea of res judicata even though the court has not been asked to investigate and pronounce on the point at issues'.

[587] *Green v Hampshire CC* [1979] ICR 861; *Crown Estate Commrs v Dorset CC* [1990] Ch 297.

[588] P Rogerson, 'Issue Estoppel and Abuse of Process in Foreign Judgments' (1998) CJQ 91 (reviewing this and other case law).

[589] *Ron Jones (Burton-on-Trent) Ltd v JS Hall* (unreported, 3 August 1999).

[590] *McIlkenny v Chief Constable of the West Midlands* [1980] 1 QB 283, CA; *House of Spring Gardens Ltd v Waite* [1991] 1 QB 241, CA; *Black v Yates* [1992] 1 QB 526, 545–9; Spencer Bower, Turner and Handley, *The Doctrine of Res Judicata* (3rd edn, 1996) [231], [232].

[591] eg, *Green v Vickers Defence Systems Ltd* [2002] EWCA Civ 904; *The Times* 1 July 2002, CA (consent order between victim of asbestosis and employer; held that terms of settlement included admission of liability for causation; victim's estate and dependants able to take advantage of this admission in the consent order).

[592] 'Cause of action' denotes the set of material facts supporting a recognized legal ground of claim *Cooke v Gill* (1873) LR 8 CP 107; *Brunsden v Humphrey* (1884) 14 QBD 141, CA; *Letang v Cooper* [1965] 1 QB 232, 243, CA; *Republic of India v India Steamship Co Ltd* [1993] AC 410, 419,

were identical both with regard to the parties (or their privies and successors in title) and subject matter.[593] This form of estoppel is an absolute bar to re-litigation of points decided in the earlier proceedings, unless fraud or collusion can be established to impugn that decision.[594]

22.122 'Issue estoppel' concerns adjudication of issues forming a necessary element in a cause of action (including foreign adjudication).[595] This estoppel applies if one of the parties to that decision seeks to re-open that issue in later proceedings between the same parties involving a different cause of action to which the same issue is relevant.[596] Unlike cause of action estoppel, issue estoppel can be relaxed in either of these situations: (i) there has been a retrospective change in the law which renders the point covered by issue estoppel 'plainly' wrong;[597] or (ii) new evidence has emerged which 'entirely changes the aspect of the case', provided that, showing 'reasonable diligence', the relevant party could not have discovered this evidence at the time of the earlier litigation.[598]

(2) *The Rule in* Henderson v Henderson *(1843)*[599]

22.123 In 2002 this long-standing rule was re-stated as follows: '. . .parties who are involved in litigation are expected to put before the court all the issues relevant

---

HL; *Walkin v South Manchester Health Authority* [1995] 1 WLR 1543, 1547, CA; *Brown v KMR Services Ltd* [1995] 4 All ER 598, 640, CA; *Paragon Finance v DB Thakerar & Co* [1999] 1 All ER 400, 405–6, CA.

593 *Arnold v National Westminster Bank plc* [1991] 2 AC 93, HL; noted Neil Andrews [1991] CLJ 419; for an example, where the causes of action were different, see *Buehler AG v Chronos Richardson Ltd* [1998] 2 All ER 960, CA.

594 *Arnold* case ibid 104.

595 *Carl Zeiss Stiftung v Rayner & Keeler Ltd (No 2)* [1967] 1 AC 853, HL; *Carl Zeiss Stiftung v Rayner & Keeler Ltd (No 3)* [1970] Ch 506; *The Sennar (No 2)* [1985] 1 WLR 490, 499, HL; see Dicey, Morris, and Collins, *The Conflict of Laws* (14th edn, 2006) 14–110 ff; P Rogerson, 'Issue Estoppel and Abuse of Process in Foreign Judgments' (1998) CJQ 91.

596 *Arnold v National Westminster Bank plc* [1991] 2 AC 93, 105, HL; *Thoday v Thoday* [1964] P 181, 198, CA; *The Sennar (No 2)* [1985] 1 WLR 490, 499, HL; *Republic of India v India Steamship Co Ltd ('The Indian Grace')* [1993] AC 410, 419, HL.

597 *Arnold* case, [1991] 2 AC 93, 112, HL (and see *Arnold* case [1990] Ch 573, 598, 600, CA; not disturbed on final appeal); *S v S (Ancillary Relief: Consent Order)* [2002] EWHC 223 Fam; [2003] Fam 1, at [30] ff.

598 *Phosphate Sewage Co v Molleson* (1879) 4 App Cas 801, 814, HL; the *Phosphate* case test applies to the abuse of process doctrine: *Hunter v Chief Constable of West Midlands* [1982] AC 529, 545, HL and *Smith v Linskills* [1996] 1 WLR 763, 771, CA.

599 *Henderson v Henderson* (1843) 3 Hare 100, 115, Wigram V-C; the leading modern examination is *Johnson v Gore Wood & Co* [2000] UKHL 65; [2002] 2 AC 1, HL; considered *De Crittenden v Estate of Bayliss (Deceased)* [2005] EWCA Civ 547 at [22] to [26] (earlier contract action; second action to plead a tracing action sufficiently closely tied to facts of first action; abuse of process); for radical comment, G Watt, 'The Danger and Deceit of the Rule in *Henderson v Henderson*: A new approach to successive civil actions arising from the same factual matter' (2000) 19 CJQ 287 and KR Handley 'A Closer Look at *Henderson v Henderson*' (2002) 118 LQR 397.

to that litigation. If they do not, they will not normally be permitted to have a second bite at the cherry.'[600] The rule applies not only when the first action was concluded by judgment but also when it was compromised out-of-court.[601] Unlike *res judicata*, the *Henderson* principle does not concern adjudicated matters, but non-adjudicated matters. Those matters only escaped decision because they were not raised, when they might have been, in earlier civil proceedings. This principle can be regarded as an adjunct to *res judicata*, linked by the unifying principle of finality. But it should not be confused as an aspect of *res judicata*. The House of Lords in *Johnson v Gore Wood & Co* (2002) said that the *Henderson* doctrine should not be applied too zealously or mechanically.[602] Lord Millett suggested that this doctrine creates no presumption: 'the burden should always rest with the defendant [in the second action] to establish that it is oppressive or an abuse of process for him to be subjected to the second action'.[603] Perhaps litigation might be an abuse of process even when the parties in the second action are not the same as those in the first action.[604]

(3) Other Aspects of Finality

Six further rules or doctrines deserve mention. First, a claimant cannot obtain **22.124** damages in successive actions in respect of the same cause of action: damages resulting from one and the same cause of action must be assessed and recovered once and for all.[605] Secondly, affiliation proceedings[606] and civil litigation concerning the welfare of children, such as care and custody proceedings,[607] do not give rise to *res judicata*: finality yields to higher public interests in accurate determinations of paternity and in the need to promote the children's welfare. Thirdly, statute now bars attempts to re-litigate in England certain

---

[600] *Taylor v Lawrence* [2002] EWCA Civ 90; [2003] QB 528 at [6], Lord Woolf.

[601] *Johnson* case [2000] UKHL 65; [2002] 2 AC 1, 32–3, 59, HL.

[602] [2002] 2 AC 1, 22, 59, HL; *Gairy v Att-Gen of Grenada* [2001] UKPC 30; [2002] 1 AC 167, PC, at [26], [27].

[603] *Johnson* case (n 601 above) 59–60, HL.

[604] As suggested in *Johnson* case (n 601 above) at 60; and see *Bradford & Bingley Building Society v Seddon* [1999] 1 WLR 1482, 1491–2, CA.

[605] *Brunsden v Humphrey* (1884) 14 QBD 141, 147, CA; LA Collins (1992) 108 LQR 393, 394 (case note); *Republic of India v India Steamship Co Ltd ('The Indian Grace')* [1993] AC 410, 420–1, HL; *Rowner v Allen & Sons* (1936) 41 Com Cas 90; *Jaggard v Sawyer* [1995] 1 WLR 269, 284, CA; *Deeny v Gooda Walker Ltd* [1995] 1 WLR 1206, 1214 (offering postponement of assessment of damages); Spencer Bower, Turner and Handley, *The Doctrine of Res Judicata* (3rd edn, 1996) ch 21; but on the need for caution in applying this rule, *Barrow v Bankside Agency Ltd* [1996] 1 WLR 257, 269, CA; *Cachia v Faluyi* [2001] 1 WLR 1966, CA, at [18] to [20].

[606] *Hager v Osborne* [1992] Fam 94, following nineteenth century authority.

[607] *Re B (A Minor) The Times* 18 January 2000, CA, noting *Re B (Minors: Care Proceedings: Issue Estoppel)* [1997] Fam 117.

foreign judgments.[608] But this bar can be displaced by agreement, estoppel by convention, or acquiescence.[609] Fourthly, the Court of Appeal in *Taylor v Lawrence* (2002) held that, in very exceptional situations, it can review, and if necessary rescind or modify, one of its own ostensibly final decisions.[610] The CPR has now codified this practice for appeals decided by the High Court or Court of Appeal.[611] Fifthly, the court will be very reluctant to give permission for an appeal out of time (on the need for such permission, see 22.106).[612] Finally, a court can strike out as an abuse of process an unjustified collateral attack by civil action upon a criminal *conviction*.[613] 'Such re-litigation would. . .bring the administration of justice into disrepute.'[614]

M. Enforcement[615]

22.125 The Tribunals, Courts and Enforcement Act 2007 (Parts 3 to 5) has modified the law of enforcement as follows. First, it introduces a new regime for 'taking control of goods' which replaces the system of 'seizure of goods'.[616] Secondly, it creates new methods of obtaining information concerning a debtor's assets

---

608 Civil Jurisdiction and Judgments Act 1982, s 34; *Black v Yates* [1992] 1 QB 526; on the necessity for this provision, *Republic of India v India Steamship Co Ltd ('The Indian Endurance No 1')* [1993] AC 410, 417, HL; for the sequel, *Republic of India v India Steamship Co Ltd ('The Indian Endurance No 2')* [1998] AC 878, HL.

609 *The Indian Endurance No 2* [1998] AC 878, HL.

610 [2002] EWCA Civ 90; [2003] QB 528, CA; on which see IR Scott (2000) 21 CJQ 194; this decision has been examined in various cases, notably, *In Re Uddin* [2005] EWCA Civ 52; [2005] 1 WLR 2398, CA; see also *R v Bow Street Metropolitan Stipendiary Magistrate, ex p Pinochet Ugarte (No 2)* [2000] 1 AC 119, HL.

611 CPR 52.17.

612 *Smith v Brough* [2005] EWCA 261; [2006] CP Rep 17; and see 22–106 above.

613 The leading case is: *Hunter v Chief Constable of West Midlands Police* [1982] AC 529, HL (affirming CA sub nom *McIlkenny v Chief Constable of West Midlands Police Force* [1980] QB 283); for a luminous re-statement, *Smith v Linskills* [1996] 1 WLR 763, CA (Sir Thomas Bingham MR); the *Hunter* case was applied in *Somasunaram v M Julius Melchior & Co* [1988] 1 WLR 1394, CA, noted JA Jolowicz [1989] CLJ 196; the *Hunter* decision was distinguished in *Acton v Graham Pearce & Co* [1997] 3 All ER 904, 925 (earlier criminal conviction later set aside by CA, Criminal Division); the *Hunter* case was also distinguished in *Walpole v Partridge & Wilson* [1994] QB 106, CA (collateral attack doctrine inapplicable where possible appeal from criminal conviction not pursued, as a result of a lawyer's negligence); nor does the *Hunter* rule against collateral challenge apply when a civil *defendant* seeks to contradict his criminal conviction, *J v Oyston* [1999] 1 WLR 694 (considering Civil Evidence Act 1968, s 11(2)(a)); nor does it apply where proceedings for disqualification of a company director follow a regulatory investigation: *Re Barings (No 2)* [1999] 1 All ER 311, 335–6, 340, CA; see also Spencer Bower, Turner and Handley, *Res Judicata* (3rd edn, 1996) at [447].

614 *Arthur JS Hall & Co v Simons* [2000] UKHL 38; [2002] 1 AC 615, 685, HL.

615 C Sandbrook, *Enforcement of a Judgment* (2006).

616 Tribunals, Courts and Enforcement Act 2007, sections 62 to 70, Schs 12 and 13.

and indebtedness.[617] Thirdly, it 'introduces a package of measures to help those who are willing and able to pay off their debts over time and a new personal insolvency procedure for some people who have fallen into debt but have no foreseeable way out of it' (see the various categories of protection in Part 5 of the Act).[618]

It remains an axiom of this procedural area that judgment creditors are free to **22.126** choose from the portfolio of available enforcement methods.[619] Money judgments can be enforced by: a writ of *fieri facias* or warrant of execution;[620] (these are re-named 'writs of control' and 'warrants of control' by the Tribunals, Courts and Enforcement Act ('TCE Act'), see further 22.127);[621] a third party debt order (see 22.128);[622] a charging order (against land; see 22.129); a stop order (against securities or funds in court); a stop notice (against securities);[623] or by appointment of a receiver;[624] some types of pecuniary enforcement are available only in county courts, namely attachment of earnings orders[625] and 'administration orders'.[626] (Part 5 of the TCE Act introduces various categories of protection for debtors). Enforcement of non-money judgments is unaffected by the new legislation. Such judgments can be enforced as follows: *goods*: by warrants of specific delivery or delivery (in county courts)[627] and writs of specific delivery or of delivery (in the High Court);[628] *land*: by warrants of possession (in county courts);[629] and writs of possession (in the High Court);[630] *injunctions and other orders*: by committal

---

[617] ibid, ss 95–105.

[618] The following background materials are available at <www.dca.gov.uk/legist/tribenforce. htm>: 'Effective Enforcement: improved methods of recovery for civil court debt and commercial rent and a single regulatory regime for warrant enforcement agents', White Paper, LC Dept (Cm 5744, 2003); 'A Choice of Paths: better options to manage over-indebtedness and multiple debt', Consultation Paper, DCA (CP23/04, 2004); 'Relief for the Indebted: an Alternative to Bankruptcy', Consultation Paper, Insolvency Service (2005).

[619] CPR 70.2(2).

[620] RSC Ord 46 & 47 and CCR Ord 26, in Schs 1 & 2, CPR.

[621] Tribunals, Courts and Enforcement Act 2007, ss 62–70, Schs 12 and 13.

[622] CPR Part 72.

[623] CPR Part 73.

[624] See RSC Orders 30 and 51, in Sch 1, CPR, which apply both in the High Court and county courts.

[625] CCR Ord 27, in Sch 2, CPR.

[626] County Courts Act 1984, s 112; such an order prevents named creditors from petitioning for bankruptcy against the judgment debtor, and makes provision for payment of creditors by instalments; the order can last for three years.

[627] CCR Ord 26, r 16 in Sch 2, CPR.

[628] RSC Ord 45, r 4 in Sch 1, CPR.

[629] CCR Ord 26, r 17 in Sch 2, CPR; or by summary proceedings for the recovery of land against trespassers, CCR Ord 24 (see Sch 2, CPR) and CPR Part 55.

[630] RSC Ord 45, r 3 in Sch 1, CPR.

proceedings (see 22.130, 22.131).[631] The CPR enables judgment creditors to apply for an order compelling a judgment debtor (or in the case of a company, one of its officers) to attend the court and to supply information concerning the debtor's means and financial commitments[632] (the TCE Act creates new methods of obtaining information concerning debtor's assets and indebtedness: sections 95 to 105). The main methods of enforcement will now be explained.

22.127 Seizure of goods (re-named 'taking control of goods' by the Tribunals, Courts and Enforcement Act) is the most common form of enforcement. The traditional operation of this method of enforcement has been (i) to seize or physically secure the debtor's goods and (ii) to sell them at public auction, or threaten to sell them, (iii) in order to realize a sum which will satisfy the judgment debt. Elements (ii) and (iii) will not be affected by the TCE Act. But that Act introduces a new regime governing element (i). These are the main features of this new system.[633] High Court (under-)sheriffs and county court bailiffs are re-named 'enforcement agents'. The High Court writ of *fieri facias* is renamed a 'writ of control' and county court warrants of execution become 'warrants of control'. Property in all the debtor's goods (defined to cover all 'property of any description, other than land') will become 'bound' by the writ or warrant once that document is received by the enforcement agent. However, innocent third party purchasers can obtain good title to such goods if they acquired the debtor's goods 'in good faith', 'for valuable consideration', and 'without notice'. Enforcement officers can gain physical 'control' of goods. 'Control' involves physically 'securing' them (including removing them) or entering into a 'controlled goods agreement' with the debtor. Before gaining 'control', the enforcement agent must give the debtor 'notice'. Enforcement agents can use reasonable force to enter premises, including domestic premises. Force, however, is not to be exercised against a person. 'Exempt goods' will be defined by regulations.

22.128 'Third party debt orders',[634] previously known as 'garnishee orders', enable a judgment creditor to divert or intercept money payable to the judgment debtor, for example money held to his order in a bank or building society.[635] In one case this process was used to obtain an order for a non-party bank to pay costs incurred in

---

631 RSC Ord 45 & 52; CCR Ord 25, 29 in Schs 1 & 2, CPR.
632 CPR Part 71; PD (71).
633 Tribunals, Courts and Enforcement Act 2007, ss 62–70, Schs 12–13.
634 CPR Part 72; PD (72).
635 CPR 72.1(2): provided the bank or building society 'lawfully accepts deposits in the United Kingdom'; banks and building societies can become subject to obligations to reveal details of all accounts which the judgment debtor holds with them: CPR 72.6; for money in court standing to the credit of the judgment debtor, CPR 72.10; on the threshold level of proof that a bank etc account exists, *Alawiye v Mahmood* [2006] EWHC 277 (Ch); [2007] 1 WLR 79.

proceedings against an unincorporated association.[636] The procedure concerns 'any amount of any debt due or accruing due to the judgment debtor from the third party'.[637] The procedure involves the making of an interim[638] and a final order.[639] The process is not exercisable against debts 'situated' outside England and Wales,[640] even if the foreign jurisdiction is within the Brussels or Lugano jurisdictional system.[641] The relevant non-party must also be 'within the [English] jurisdiction'.[642]

Charging orders[643] can be made in respect of a money judgment, including one **22.129** expressed in terms of a foreign currency.[644] CPR Part 73 governs charging orders against the judgment debtor's *land or interest in land*; or 'stop orders' preventing various dealings in respect of *securities* or *funds in court*; or 'stop notices' preventing various dealings in respect of *securities*.[645] A judgment debtor's interest in jointly held real property can be charged.[646] A charging order can also be applied against the proceeds of sale of land held under a trust for sale.[647] In all these situations, the procedure involves an interim and a final order. The criteria for making a final charging order include:[648] '(a) the personal circumstances of the debtor and (b) whether any other creditor would be likely to be unduly prejudiced by the making of the Order'. No final order will be made if the judgment debtor becomes insolvent after the interim order. To make a final order would in that situation cut

---

[636] *Huntingdon Life Sciences Group plc v Stop Huntingdon Animal Cruelty* [2005] EWHC 2233 (QB).

[637] CPR 72.2(1)(a).

[638] *Alawiye v Mahmood* [2006] EWHC 277 (Ch); [2007] 1 WLR 79.

[639] CPR 72.2(2).

[640] *Kuwait Oil Tanker Company SAK 7 Ors v UBS AG* [2003] UKHL 31; [2004] 1 AC 300 (third party debt-a bank account in defendant's name—'situated' in Switzerland; English judgment debt; third party bank having branch in London); *Société Eram Shipping Company Ltd v Hong Kong and Shanghai Banking Corporation Ltd* [2003] UKHL 30; [2004] 1 AC 260 (third party debt–also a bank account- 'situated' in Hong Kong; French judgment debt, recognized in England; third party bank having branch in London); reasoning criticized by P Rogerson [2003] CLJ 576.

[641] As in the *Kuwait* case [2003] UKHL; [2004] 1 AC 300; see n 149 above for references to the Brussels and Lugano jurisdictional systems.

[642] CPR 72.1(1).

[643] CPR Part 73; PD (73); Charging Orders Act 1979.

[644] *Carnegie v Giessen* [2005] EWCA Civ 191; [2005] 1 WLR 2510, CA (English judgment payable in US dollars; valid charging order).

[645] Charging Orders Act 1979, s 2(2)(a) to (c) respectively; CPR 73, Sections I to III; notable decisions on trusts, subrogation and restitution law in this context are *Boscawen v Bajwa* [1996] 1 WLR 328, CA; *Banque Financiere de la Cité v Parc (Battersea) Ltd* [1999]1 AC 221, HL; for the types of disposition prevented by stop orders, see CPR 73.13 (funds in court) and 73.14 (securities); for the types of dealing prevented by stop notices, see CPR 73.18 (securities).

[646] Charging Orders Act 1979, s 2(1)(b)(iii).

[647] *National Westminster Bank Ltd v Stockman* [1981] 1 WLR 67.

[648] Charging Orders Act 1979, s 1(5).

across the insolvency scheme of distribution.[649] Final orders against interests in land should be registered.[650]

22.130 Finally, it is necessary to supply coercive machinery to support injunctions (including specific performance).[651] A person will be guilty of contempt of court if he breaches an injunction addressed to him, including an order for disclosure of assets within a freezing injunction,[652] or if he fails to honour an undertaking made to the court.[653] The representative mechanism can be used for effective injunctive relief against a disruptive unincorporated association ('protest groups').[654] In these various situations, it is not necessary that the non-compliance was deliberate or calculated:[655] it normally suffices that the act or omission is not accidental.[656] An order directed at a company is breached if one of its employees acts inconsistently with it, even if the company expressly prohibited such conduct, provided the employee acted within the course of his employment.[657] A party who disobeys an injunction will be guilty of contempt even if he later persuades the court to set aside the relevant order or injunction.[658] A non-party who receives notice of an

---

649 *Roberts Petroleum Ltd v Bernard Kenny* [1983] AC 192, HL.

650 On registration's effect, *Clark v Chief Land Registrar* [1994] Ch 370, CA.

651 RSC Ord 45 & 52; CCR Ord 25, 29: appended to CPR; *Arlidge, Eady and Smith on Contempt* (3rd edn, 2005).

652 *Raja v Van Hoogstraten* [2004] EWCA Civ 968; [2004] 4 All ER 793.

653 eg, the implied undertaking applicable to information disclosed under compulsory disclosure powers, CPR 31.22; instances of contempt in that context are *Miller v Scorey* [1996] 3 All ER 18 and *Watkins v AJ Wright (Electrical) Ltd* [1996] 3 All ER 31; or the various undertakings imposed pursuant to freezing injunctions or search orders; for emphatic affirmation that breach of an undertaking is as serious as breach of an injunction, *Cobra Golf Inc v Rata* [1998] Ch 109, 128, 163, *per* Rimer J, citing authority; on the court's discretion to release a party from an undertaking, *Di Placito v Slater* [2003] EWCA Civ 1863; [2004] 1 WLR 1605, [27] ff.

654 *Oxford University v Webb* [2006] EWHC 2490 (QB) Irwin J applying CPR 19.6, and considering, at [56] ff, *M Michael's (Furrier's) Limited v Askew* (CA, unreported, 23 June 1983) and other authorities.

655 *Miller v Scorey* [1996] 3 All ER 18; *Watkins v AJ Wright (Electrical) Ltd* [1996] 3 All ER 31 (both concerning breaches of the implied undertaking protecting information disclosed during discovery under CPR 31.22).

656 *Heatons Transport (St Helens) Ltd v Transport and General Workers Union* [1973] AC 15, 109, HL; applied in *Z Bank v D1* [1974] 1 Lloyd's Rep 656, Colman J; *Director General of Fair Trading v Pioneer Concrete Ltd* [1995] 1 AC 456, 478, HL; in *Bird v Hadkinson The Times* 4 March, 1999, Neuberger J refused to follow the test of deliberate breach adopted in *Irtelli v Squatriti* [1993] QB 83, CA.

657 *Re Supply of Ready Mixed Concrete (No 2)* [1995] 1 AC 456, HL; the question of corporate criminal liability was considered by the Court of Appeal (Criminal Division) in a leading decision in *Attorney-General's Reference (No 2) of 1999* [2000] QB 796, CA, which considered: *Meridian Global Funds Management Asia Ltd v Securities Commission* [1995] 2 AC 500; *R v British Steel plc* [1995] 1 WLR 1356; *In Re Supply of Ready-Mixed Concrete (No 2)* [1995] 1 AC 456, HL; *R v Associated Octel Ltd* [1996] 1 WLR 1543; *R v Gateway Foodmarkets Ltd* [1997] ICR 382.

658 *Motorola Credit Corporation v Uzan (No 2)* [2003] EWCA Civ 752; [2004] 1 WLR 113, at [148] to [156] (considered in *Raja v Van Hoogstraten* [2004] EWCA Civ 968; [2004] 4 All ER 793);

injunction is guilty of contempt if he aids or abets breach of that injunction, or acts independently to undermine it.[659]

A contemnor can be committed for contempt of court.[660] Civil contempt is **22.131** classified as a quasi-criminal wrong. The standard of proof is 'beyond reasonable doubt' rather than the lower civil standard of proof 'on the balance of probabilities'.[661] Hearsay evidence is admissible.[662] A person found guilty of contempt can be imprisoned for up to two years[663] or fined. When deciding whether to punish, the court will consider whether the contemnor has been guilty of deliberate or negligent conduct or omission.[664] The court will also consider whether the contemnor has 'contumaciously' flouted the law.[665] The court will cease to punish a contemnor if it becomes evident that he will not accept the court's authority and he has already received adequate punishment,[666] or because the contemnor has 'purged' his contempt and, therefore, further punishment is unnecessary.[667] Inadvertent breach of an injunction will not normally justify punishment.[668] The court might instead make a disciplinary costs order;[669] or strike out the contemnor's claim or

---

Isaacs v Robertson [1985] AC 97, PC; *Bhimji v Chatwani* [1991] 1 WLR 989; *Wardle Fabrics Ltd v Myristis (G) Ltd* [1984] FSR 263.

[659] *Seaward v Paterson* [1897] 1 Ch 545; *Elliott v Klinger* [1967] 1 WLR 1165; *Z Ltd v A-Z and AA-LL* [1982] QB 558, CA (containing a good survey of the principles); *Attorney-General v Times Newspapers Ltd* [1992] AC 191, HL; *Att-Gen v Punch Ltd* [2002] UKHL 50; [2003] 1 AC 1046.

[660] RSC Ord 52, Sch 1, CPR; CCR Ord 29, Sch 2, CPR; on the need for due process to protect contemnors, *Raja v Van Hoogstraten* [2004] EWCA Civ 968; [2004] 4 All ER 793, conclusion at [106]; *Newman v Modern Bookbinders Ltd* [2000] 1 WLR 2559, CA; for discussion of the court's willingness to commit a contemnor, despite technical procedural defects, see *Bell v Tuohy* [2002] EWCA Civ 423; [2002] 3 All ER 975, CA, at [31] to [59], examining *Nicholls v Nicholls* [1997] 1 WLR 314, 326, CA; and for problems of overlapping criminal and civil proceedings, *Lomas v Parle* [2003] EWCA Civ 1804; [2004] 1 WLR 1642.

[661] *Z Bank v D1* [1974] 1 Lloyd's Rep 656, 660, Colman J.

[662] *Daltel Europe Ltd v Makki* [2006] EWCA Civ 94; [2006] 1 WLR 2704.

[663] *Harris v Harris* [2001] EWCA Civ 1645; [2002] Fam 253, CA, at [12] to [14], noting Contempt of Court Act 1981, s 14(1), restricting the period to a maximum of two years' imprisonment; also noting the statutory duty to release a contemnor who has served half of a term of less than 12 months: Criminal Justice Act 1991, s 45(3).

[664] *Guildford BC v Valler The Times* 15 October 1993, CA.

[665] *Bhimji v Chatwani* [1991] 1 WLR 989; good illustrations are *X v Y* [1988] 2 All ER 648, 666 and *Watkins v AJ Wright (Electrical) Ltd* [1996] 3 All ER 31; on the question when a litigant's defiance in open court of a judicial or court order will justify imprisonment for contempt, *Bell v Tuohy* [2002] EWCA Civ 423; [2002] 3 All ER 975, CA, [60] to [66].

[666] *Re Barrell Enterprises* [1973] 1 WLR 19, CA; RSC Ord 52, r 8, Sch 1, CPR.

[667] The court's flexibility is not without limit: *Harris v Harris* [2001] EWCA Civ 1645; [2002] Fam 253, CA (court lacks power to permit release of contemnor from prison on condition that he does not commit fresh contempt).

[668] eg, *Adam Phones Ltd v Gideon Goldschmidt* (unreported, 9 July 1999) (innocent failure to comply with a court order for delivery up of materials).

[669] *Miller v Scorey* [1996] 3 All ER 18; *Watkins v AJ Wright (Electrical) Ltd* [1996] 3 All ER 31.

defence; or bar him from bringing an appeal,[670] although in these last two respects caution is now required.[671] In the case of both individuals[672] and companies, the court can order 'sequestration' of their assets.[673] This involves 'sequestrators' (officers of the court) seizing the contemnor's property, including land,[674] and eventually selling it.[675]

---

[670] *Raja v Van Hoogstraten* [2004] EWCA Civ 968; [2004] 4 All ER 793 at [81] to [83], [112]; and see the authorities (not all of which were cited in the *Raja* case), noted at Neil Andrews, *English Civil Procedure* (2003) 39.63.

[671] *Motorola Credit Corporation v Uzan (No 2)* [2003] EWCA Civ 752; [2004] 1 WLR 113, at [81] to [83]; *Days Healthcare UK Ltd v Pihsiang MM Co Ltd* [2006] EWHC 1444 (Comm); [2007] CP Rep 1.

[672] *Raja v Van Hoogstraten* [2004] EWCA Civ 968; [2004] 4 All ER 793 at [71] ff; although the court has such jurisdiction against individuals who are contemnors, the order was procedurally defective on the facts, see [105].

[673] Sch 1, CPR, at RSC Ord 45, rr 3 (1)(c) 4(2)(c) 5(1)(b)(i)(ii); RSC Ord 46, r 5; on the court's inherent power, *Webster v Southwark LBC* [1983] QB 698.

[674] *Mir v Mir* [1992] Fam 79.

[675] On sequestrators' potential liability for negligence, *IRC v Hoogstraten* [1985] QB 1077, CA.

INDEX